CT and MR Imaging of the Whole Body

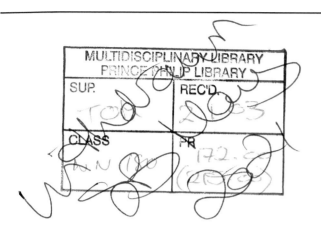

Volume One
Fourth Edition

John R. Haaga, MD, FACR
Chairman and Medical Director
Department of Radiology
University Hospitals of Cleveland
Cleveland, Ohio

Charles F. Lanzieri, MD, FACR
Professor of Radiology and Neurosurgery
Department of Radiology
University Hospitals of Cleveland/Case Western
    Reserve University
Cleveland, Ohio

Robert C. Gilkeson, MD
Section Head, Thoracic Radiology
Department of Radiology
Case Western Reserve University
Cleveland, Ohio

Part I
Edited by Jeffrey L. Duerk, PhD
Director, Physics Radiology
Department of Radiology
University Hospitals of Cleveland/Case Western
    Reserve University
Cleveland, Ohio

Part IV
Edited by Jeffrey L. Sunshine, MD, PhD
Assistant Professor of Radiology
Case Western Reserve University
Cleveland, Ohio

Mosby
An Affiliate of Elsevier Science

11830 Westline Industrial Drive
St. Louis, Missouri 63146

Library of Congress Cataloging-in-Publication Data

Computed tomography and magnetic resonance imaging of the whole body/[edited by] John R. Haaga,
Charles F. Lanzieri—4th ed.
    p. cm.
  Includes bibliographical references and index.
  ISBN 0-323-01133-0
  1. Tomography. 2. Magnetic resonance imaging. I. Haaga, John R. (John Robert).
II. Lanzieri, Charles F.

RC78.7.T6 C6425 2002
616.07′54—dc21   2001042808

Acquisitions Editor: Janice Gaillard
Developmental Editor: Rebecca Gruliow
Project Manager: Norman Stellander
Design Coordinator: Gene Harris

MC/MVY

Printed in the United States of America.

Last digit is the print number: 9 8 7 6 5 4 3 2 1

D E D I C A T I O N

This book is dedicated to Elizabeth E. Haaga, daughter of John and Ellen Haaga, who was born on August 19, 1972, and died December 9, 1985. Beth had a disseminated neuroblastoma, which was diagnosed in 1984. She was treated with a bone marrow transplant and died from graft versus host disease and infection. As her parents, we loved her dearly and cherish the memory of her early years when she was well. After the onset of her illness, we came to know that her gentle and loving nature was accompanied by a remarkably strong character. She endured her pain and suffering without bitterness and never sought to hurt those who loved her. Indeed, most incredulously, she tried to lessen our emotional pain even while enduring her physical discomforts. Many authors have marveled at the qualities of children, and although Beth's short life and premature death have left us saddened beyond comprehension, her remarkable courage and sweetness have given us a lasting pride and respect. We remember her lovingly.

Contributors

James J. Abrahams, MD
Associate Professor (Diagnostic Radiology and Surgery) and
Director of Medical Studies, (Diagnostic Radiology), Section of
Neuroradiology, Yale University School of Medicine, New
Haven; Attending Physician, Yale–New Haven Medical Center,
New Haven; West Haven Veterans Administration Hospital,
West Haven, Connecticut
The Orbit

Jamshid Ahmadi, MD
Professor of Radiology, Neurology and Neurological Surgery,
University of Southern California Keck School of Medicine and
Los Angeles County–University of Southern California Medical
Center, Los Angeles, California
Cerebral Infections and Inflammation

Kimberly E. Applegate, MD, MS
Associate Professor of Radiology, Department of Radiology,
Indiana University School of Medicine and Riley Hospital for
Children, Indianapolis, Indiana
Pediatric Spleen

Mark A. Augustyn, MD
Neuroradiology Fellow, University of Pennsylvania School of
Medicine, Philadelphia, Pennsylvania
Temporal Bone

Errol M. Bellon, MD
Professor of Radiology, Case Western Reserve University
School of Medicine; Chairman, Department of Radiology,
MetroHealth Medical Center, Cleveland, Ohio
Magnetic Resonance Physics: An Introduction

Javier Beltran, MD
Clinical Professor of Radiology, New York University School of
Medicine, New York; Chairman, Department of Radiology,
Maimonides Medical Center, Brooklyn, New York
The Knee

Ellen C. Benya, MD
Associate Adjunct Clinical Professor of Radiology, University of
Florida College of Medicine; Attending Physician, Department
of Radiology, Shands Hospital at the University of Florida,
Gainesville, Florida
Hepatobiliary System

Sheila C. Berlin, MD
Assistant Professor of Radiology, Case Western Reserve
University School of Medicine; Staff, Division of Pediatric
Radiology, University Hospital of Cleveland, Cleveland, Ohio
Heart and Great Vessels

Daniel T. Boll, MD
Resident, University Hospitals of Ulm, Ulm, Germany
*Liver: Normal Anatomy, Imaging Techniques, and Diffuse
Diseases*

Lawrence M. Boxt, MD
Professor of Clinical Radiology, Albert Einstein College of
Medicine; Chief of Cardiovascular Imaging, Beth Israel Medical
Center, New York, New York
Magnetic Resonance Imaging of the Heart

Hans-Juergen Brambs, MD
Full Professor, Medical School, University of Ulm; Chairman,
University Hospitals of Ulm, Ulm, Germany
*Liver: Normal Anatomy, Imaging Techniques, and Diffuse
Diseases*

Lynn S. Broderick, MD
Associate Professor, University of Wisconsin—Madison,
Madison, Wisconsin
Computed Tomography of the Heart and Pericardium

Kenneth A. Buckwalter, MD
Associate Professor of Radiology, Indiana University School of
Medicine, Indianapolis, Indiana
Multislice Helical Computed Tomography: Clinical Applications

Donald W. Chakeres, MD
Professor of Radiology, Head of Neuroradiology, and Director
of MRI Research, The Ohio State University College of
Medicine and Public Health, Columbus, Ohio
Temporal Bone

Ja-Kwei Chang, MD
Professor of Radiology, State University of New York Upstate
Medical University; Director, Division of Neuroradiology,
Department of Radiology, University Hospital, Syracuse, New
York
Intracranial Neoplasms

Wui K. Chong, MBBS, FRCR
Assistant Professor of Radiology, Virginia Commonwealth
University School of Medicine, Richmond, Virginia; Medical
College of Pennsylvania, Philadelphia, Pennsylvania; Vanderbilt
University School of Medicine, Nashville, Tennessee
Thyroid and Parathyroid Glands

Richard H. Cohan, MD
Professor, University of Michigan School of Medicine and
University of Michigan Hospital, Ann Arbor, Michigan
The Retroperitoneum

Hugh D. Curtin, MD
Professor and Chief of Radiology, Harvard Medical School and
Massachusetts Eye and Ear Infirmary, Boston, Massachusetts
The Larynx

Murray K. Dalinka, MD
Professor of Radiology and Chief, Musculoskeletal Radiology,
University of Pennsylvania School of Medicine and Hospital of
the University of Pennsylvania, Philadelphia, Pennsylvania
The Shoulder

Mony J. de Leon, MD
Professor of Psychiatry and Radiology, and Director of the
Neuroimaging Research Laboratory, New York University
School of Medicine, New York, New York
Neurodegenerative Disorders

Pedro J. Diaz, PhD
Assistant Professor, Departments of Radiology and Biomedical
Engineering, Case Western Reserve University School of
Medicine and MetroHealth Medical Center, Cleveland, Ohio
Magnetic Resonance Physics: An Introduction

Huy M. Do, MD
Assistant Professor of Radiology and Neurosurgery, Stanford
University Medical Center, Stanford, California
Image-Guided Spinal Interventions

Vikram Dogra, MD
Assistant Professor of Radiology, Case Western Reserve
University School of Medicine; Section Head, Genitourinary
Radiology, and Head, Director of Ultrasound, University
Hospitals of Cleveland, Cleveland, Ohio
The Kidney

Lane F. Donnelly, MD
Professor of Radiology and Pediatrics, University of Cincinnati
College of Medicine; Associate Director, Department of
Radiology, Children's Hospital Medical Center, Cincinnati, Ohio
Chest

Jeffrey L. Duerk, PhD
Professor Departments of Radiology and Biomedical
Engineering and Director, Physics Radiology, Department of
Radiology, University Hospitals of Cleveland/Case Western
Reserve University School of Medicine, Cleveland, Ohio
Magnetic Resonance Physics: An Introduction

James D. Eastwood, MD
Assistant Professor, Department of Radiology, Division of
Neuroradiology, Duke University School of Medicine, Durham,
North Carolina
Stroke

John C. Egelhoff, DO
Professor of Radiology and Pediatrics, University of Cincinnati
College of Medicine; Staff Neuroradiologist, Children's Hospital
Medical Center, Cincinnati, Ohio
Pediatric Head and Neck Imaging

Jeremy J. Erasmus, MD
Associate Professor of Radiology, Diagnostic Radiology, The
University of Texas M.D. Anderson Cancer Center, Houston,
Texas
Primary Pulmonary Neoplasms; The Mediastinum

Jon Mark Fergenson, MD
Neuroradiology Fellow, Yale–New Haven Medical Center, New
Haven; West Haven Veterans Administration Hospital, West
Haven, Connecticut
The Orbit

Thorsten R. Fleiter, MD
Associate Professor of Radiology, University of Ulm Medical
School; Staff Radiologist, University Hospitals of Ulm, Ulm,
Germany
*Liver: Normal Anatomy, Imaging Techniques, and Diffuse
Diseases; Multislice Helical Computed Tomography: Clinical
Applications*

Donald P. Frush, MD
Associate Professor, Department of Radiology, Duke University
School of Medicine and Medical Center, Durham, North
Carolina
*Computed Tomography and Magnetic Resonance Imaging in the
Pediatric Patient: Special Considerations*

Melanie B. Fukui, MD
Formerly, Associate Professor of Radiology, University of
Pittsburgh School of Medicine; Director of Neuroradiology,
Allegheny General Hospital, Pittsburgh, Pennsylvania
Meningeal Processes

Amilcare Gentili, MD
Assistant Professor, Musculoskeletal Section, University of
California, Los Angeles, Department of Radiological Sciences,
Los Angeles, California
Musculoskeletal Tumor

Ajax E. George, MD
Professor of Radiology, New York University School of
Medicine, New York, New York
Neurodegenerative Disorders

Robert C. Gilkeson, MD
Section Head, Chest Radiology, and Assistant Professor of
Radiology, University Hospitals of Cleveland and Case Western
Reserve University, Cleveland, Ohio
*Computed Tomography and Magnetic Resonance Imaging of the
Thoracic Aorta*

John L. Go, MD
Assistant Professor of Radiology and Otolaryngology, University
of Southern California Keck School of Medicine, Los Angeles,
California
Cerebral Infections and Inflammation

Ashok K. Gupta, MD
Clinical Associate, Duke University, Durham, North Carolina
The Retroperitoneum

Hyun Kwon Ha, MD
Associate Professor, University of Ulsan College of Medicine;
Staff Radiologist, Abdominal Radiology, Department of
Radiology, Asan Medical Center, Seoul, Korea
The Gastrointestinal Tract

E. Mark Haacke, PhD
Director, The MRI Institute for Biomedical Research, Detroit,
Michigan; Professor and Director of MRI Center of Radiology,
Wayne State University; Adjunct Professor of Physics, Case
Western Reserve University, Cleveland, Ohio
*Magnetic Resonance Angiography: Fundamentals and
Techniques*

John R. Haaga, MD
Chairman and Medical Director, Department of Radiology, University Hospitals of Cleveland, Cleveland, Ohio
The Gallbladder and Biliary Tract; The Pancreas; Peritoneum and Mesentery; Image-Guided Micro Procedures: CT and MRI Interventional Procedures

Tamara Miner Haygood, PhD, MD
Radiologist, Fayette Memorial Hospital, LaGrange, Texas
The Shoulder

Thomas E. Herbener, MD
Assistant Professor, Department of Radiology, University of Ohio, Cleveland, Ohio
The Gallbladder and Biliary Tract

Leo Hochhauser, MD
Associate Professor of Radiology, State University of New York, Upstate Medical University, Syracuse, New York
Central Nervous System Trauma

Roy A. Holliday, MD
Department of Radiology, New York University School of Medicine, New York, New York
Cervical Adenopathy and Neck Masses

Andrei I. Holodny, MD
Associate Professor of Radiology, Memorial Sloane-Kettering Cancer Center, New York, New York
Neurodegenerative Disorders

David S. Jacobs, MD
Director of Neuroradiology and MRI, Hillcrest Hospital, Cleveland Clinic Health System, Mayfield Heights, Ohio
Degenerative Diseases of the Spine

Sassan Karimi, MD
Assistant Professor of Radiology, Memorial Sloane-Kettering Cancer Center, New York, New York
Neurodegenerative Disorders

Stephen A. Kieffer, MD
Professor of Radiology, University of Minnesota Medical School; Attending Neuroradiologist, Fairview-University Medical Center, Minneapolis, Minnesota
Intracranial Neoplasms

Jeong Kon Kim, MD
Fellow, University of Ulsan College of Medicine, Abdominal Radiology, Department of Radiology, Asan Medical Center, Seoul, Korea
The Gastrointestinal Tract

Paul Kim, MD
Assistant Professor of Clinical Radiology, University of Southern California Keck School of Medicine, Los Angeles, California
Cerebral Infections and Inflammation

J. Bruce Kneeland, MD
Professor, University of Pennsylvania School of Medicine, Philadelphia, Pennsylvania
The Shoulder

Barbara L. Knisely, MD
Assistant Professor of Diagnostic Radiology, University of Wisconsin Medical School, Hospital, and Clinics, Madison, Wisconsin
Pleura and Chest Wall

Scott Kolodny, MD
Assistant Professor of Radiology, Case Western Reserve University, Cleveland, Ohio
The Spinal Cord; Computed Tomography and Magnetic Resonance Imaging of the Thoracic Aorta

Kenyon K. Kopecky, MD
Professor of Radiology, Indiana University School of Medicine, Indianapolis, Indiana
Multislice Helical Computed Tomography: Clinical Applications

Janet E. Kuhlman, MD, MS
Professor of Radiology, University of Wisconsin Medical School, Hospital and Clinics, Madison, Wisconsin
Non-neoplastic Parenchymal Lung Disease

Lester Kwock, PhD
Professor of Radiology, University of North Carolina at Chapel Hill School of Medicine, Chapel Hill, North Carolina
Brain Magnetic Resonance Spectroscopy

Barton Lane, MD, FACR
Professor of Neuroradiology and Neurosurgery, Stanford University Medical School and Medical Center, Stanford; Chief of Radiology, Palo Alto Veterans Administration Medical Center, Palo Alto, California
Leukoencephalopathies and Demyelinating Disease; Image-Guided Spinal Interventions

Charles F. Lanzieri, MD, FACR
Professor of Radiology and Neurosurgury, Department of Radiology, University Hospitals of Cleveland/Case Western Reserve University School of Medicine, Cleveland, Ohio
The Sinonasal Cavity; Magnetic Resonance Imaging of Infections of the Spine

Theodore C. Larson III, MD
Associate Professor of Radiology and Radiological Sciences and Associate Professor of Otolaryngology, Vanderbilt University School of Medicine; Director of Head and Neck Radiology and Director of Interventional Neuroradiology, Vanderbilt University Medical Center, Nashville, Tennessee
Cerebral Aneurysms and Vascular Malformations; Thyroid and Parathyroid Glands

Errol Levine, MW, PhD, FACR, FRCR
Professor and Head, Sections of Computed Body Tomography, Magnetic Resonance Imaging, and Uroradiology, Department of Diagnostic Radiology, University of Kansas Medical Center, Kansas City, Kansas
The Kidney

Jonathan S. Lewin, MD
Professor of Radiology, Oncology, and Neurological Surgery, Case Western Reserve University School of Medicine; Vice Chairman, Research and Academic Affairs, and Director of Magnetic Resonance Imaging, University Hospitals of Cleveland, Cleveland, Ohio
Nasopharynx and Oropharynx

Weili Lin, PhD
Associate Professor, University of North Carolina at Chapel Hill School of Medicine, Chapel Hill, North Carolina
Magnetic Resonance Angiography: Fundamentals and Techniques

Neal Mandell, MD
Visiting Professor, Yale University School of Medicine, New Haven; Chairman, Department of Radiology, Charlotte Hungerford Hospital, Torrington, Connecticut
The Orbit

William H. Martin, MD
Assistant Professor of Radiology and Medicine, Vanderbilt University School of Medicine and Veterans Administration Medical Center, Nashville, Tennessee
Thyroid and Parathyroid Glands

H. Page McAdams, MD
Associate Professor, Department of Radiology, Duke University Medical Center; Staff Radiologist, Duke University Hospital, Durham, North Carolina
Primary Pulmonary Neoplasms; The Mediastinum

Jeffrey D. McTavish, MD
Instructor in Radiology, Harvard Medical School; Director of Body MRI, Brigham & Women's Hospital, Boston, Massachusetts
Hepatic Mass Lesions

Carolyn Cidis Meltzer, MD
Associate Professor of Radiology and Psychiatry, University of Pittsburgh School of Medicine; Medical Director, Positron Emission Tomography Facility, University of Pittsburgh Medical Center, Pittsburgh, Pennsylvania
Meningeal Processes

Elmar M. Merkle, MD
Associate Professor of Radiology, Medical School, Case Western Reserve University; Director of Body MR Imaging, Department of Radiology, University Hospitals of Cleveland, Cleveland, Ohio
Liver: Normal Anatomy, Imaging Techniques, and Diffuse Diseases

Floro Miraldi, MD, PhD
President, Neo-pet, LLC, Cleveland Heights, Ohio
Imaging Principles in Computed Tomography

Mark D. Murphey, MD
Chief, Musculoskeletal Radiology, Department of Radiologic Pathology, Armed Forces Institute of Pathology, Washington, D.C.; Associate Professor, Uniformed Services University of the Health Sciences, Departments of Radiology and Nuclear Medicine, Bethesda; Clinical Professor, University of Maryland School of Medicine, Department of Radiology, Baltimore, Maryland
The Hip

M. Hossain Naheedy, MD
Associate Professor of Radiology, Case Western Reserve University School of Medicine; Director, Radiology, at Louis Stokes Cleveland Veterans Affairs Medical Center, Cleveland, Ohio
Normal Computed Tomography and Magnetic Resonance Imaging Anatomy of the Brain and the Spine

Dean A. Nakamoto, MD
Assistant Professor, Department of Radiology, Case Western Reserve University School of Medicine and University Hospitals of Cleveland, Cleveland, Ohio
The Spleen

Sherif Gamal Nour, MD
MRI Research Associate, School of Medicine, Case Western Reserve University; Research Fellow of Interventional MRI, Department of Radiology, University Hospitals of Cleveland/ Case Western Reserve University, Cleveland, Ohio; Assistant Lecturer of Diagnostic Radiology, Department of Diagnostic Radiology, Cairo University Hospitals, Cairo, Egypt
Nasopharynx and Oropharynx

Raymond P. Onders, MD
Assistant Professor, Department of Surgery, University Hospitals at Cleveland and Case Western Reserve University School of Medicine, Cleveland, Ohio
The Spleen

Eric K. Outwater, MD
Professor of Radiology, University of Arizona School of Medicine; Attending Physician, University Medical Center, Veterans Hospital, and Kino Community Hospital, Tucson, Arizona
Magnetic Resonance Imaging of the Pelvis

Kathleen Gallagher Oxner, MD
Radiologist, Greenville Radiology, Greenville, South Carolina
The Shoulder

Cheryl A. Petersilge, MD
Assistant Clinical Professor of Radiology and Orthopedic Surgery, Case Western Reserve University School of Medicine; Director, Musculoskeletal and Emergency Radiology, Hillcrest Hospital, Cleveland, Ohio
The Hip

Jay J. Pillai, MD
Associate Professor of Radiology, Medical College of Georgia School of Medicine; Staff Attending Neuroradiologist, Medical College of Georgia Hospital and Clinics, Angusta, Georgia
Brain Magnetic Resonance Spectroscopy

Donna M. Plecha, MD
Assistant Professor of Radiology, Case Western Reserve University School of Medicine and University Hospitals of Cleveland, Cleveland, Ohio
Extramedullary Spinal Tumors

Deborah L. Reede, MD
Long Island College of Medicine, Brooklyn, New York
Cervical Adenopathy and Neck Masses

Pablo R. Ros, MD, MPH
Professor of Radiology, Harvard Medical School; Executive Vice Chair, Department of Radiology, Brigham & Women's Hospital, Boston, Massachusetts
Hepatic Mass Lesions

Santiago E. Rossi, MD
Jefe de Trabajos Practicos, Universidad de Buenos Aires and Universidad de Ciencias Biomedicas Rene Tavaloro; Hospital Universitario de Clinicas Jose de San Martin; Director, Centro de Diagnostico Dr. Enrique Rossi, Buenos Aires, Argentina
Primary Pulmonary Neoplasms

Anna Rozenshtein, MD
Assistant Professor of Clinical Radiology, College of Physicians and Surgeons of Columbia University; Director of Thoracic Radiology, St. Luke's–Roosevelt Hospital Center, New York, New York
Magnetic Resonance Imaging of the Heart

Jonas Rydberg, MD
Associate Professor of Radiology, Indiana University School of Medicine, Indianapolis, Indiana
Multislice Helical Computed Tomography: Clinical Applications

Ken L. Schreibman, PhD MD
Associate Professor of Radiology, University of Wisconsin School of Medicine, Madison, Wisconsin
The Foot and Ankle

Hervey D. Segall, MD
Professor of Radiology, University of Southern California Keck School of Medicine and Los Angeles County–University of Southern California Medical Center, Los Angeles, California
Cerebral Infections and Inflammation

Steven Shankman, MD
Vice-Chairman, Department of Radiology and Resident Program Director, Maimonides Medical Center, Brooklyn, New York
The Knee

Patrick F. Sheedy II, MD
Professor, Department of Radiology, Mayo Medical School; Department of Radiology, Mayo Clinic and Mayo Foundation; Department of Radiology, Saint Marys Hospital and Rochester Methodist Hospital, Rochester, Minnesota
The Adrenal Glands

Marilyn J. Siegel, MD
Professor of Radiology, Mallinckrodt Institute of Radiology, Washington University School of Medicine, St. Louis, Missouri
Pediatric and Adolescent Pelvis

Michael S. Sims
President and CEO, UltraGuide, Inc., Cleveland, Ohio
Imaging Principles in Computed Tomography

Carlos J. Sivit, MD
Professor of Radiology and Pediatrics, Case Western Reserve University; Director of Pediatric Radiology, Rainbow Babies and Childrens Hospital, Cleveland, Ohio
Pancreas; Gastrointestinal Tract, Peritoneal Cavity, and Mesentery

Michelle M. Smith, MD
Department of Radiology, Froedtert Hospital, Milwaukee, Wisconsin
Thyroid and Parathyroid Glands

John A. Spencer, MA, MD, MRCP, FRCR
Consultant Radiologist, St. James's University Hospital, Leeds, United Kingdom, and Röntgen Professor of the Royal College of Radiologists
Computed Tomography of the Pelvis

Charles E. Spritzer, MD
Professor, Department of Radiology, Duke University, School of Medicine and Medical Center; Staff Radiologist, Duke University Hospital, Durham, North Carolina
The Mediastinum

Peter J. Strouse, MD
Assistant Professor, Section of Pediatric Radiology, Department of Radiology, University of Michigan Medical School; Attending Physician, C. S. Mott Children's Hospital, Ann Arbor, Michigan
Musculoskeletal System

Jeffrey L. Sunshine, MD, PhD
Assistant Professor of Radiology, Case Western Reserve University, Cleveland, Ohio
The Spinal Cord

Sarah E. Swift, MR, MRCP, FRCR
Consultant Radiologist, St. James's University Hospital, Leeds, United Kingdom
Computed Tomography of the Pelvis

Robert D. Tarver, MD
Professor, Department of Radiology, Indiana University School of Medicine, Indianapolis, Indiana
The Mediastinum

John J. Wasenko, MD
Associate Professor of Radiology and Director of Magnetic Resonance Imaging, State University of New York Upstate Medical University, Syracuse, New York
Central Nervous System Trauma

Timothy J. Welch, MD
Associate Professor, Mayo Medical School; Consultant, Mayo Clinic, Rochester, Minnesota
The Adrenal Glands

Ernest J. Wiesen, BSEE
Formerly, Assistant Professor, Department of Radiology, Case Western Reserve University School of Medicine; Radiologic Physicist, Department of Radiology, MetroHealth Medical Center, Cleveland, Ohio
Imaging Principles in Computed Tomography

Wade H. Wong, MD
Professor of Radiology, University of California, San Diego, California
Image-Guided Spinal Interventions

Chi-Shing Zee, MD
Professor of Radiology and Neurosurgery and Director of
Neuroradiology, University of Southern California Keck School
of Medicine, Los Angeles, California
Cerebral Infections and Inflammation

J. Michael Zerin, MD
Professor of Radiology, Wayne State University School of
Medicine; Director of Ultrasound Imaging, Department of
Pediatric Imaging, Children's Hospital of Michigan, Detroit,
Michigan
Kidneys and Adrenal Glands

Preface

The progress in computed imaging over the past 25 years has been remarkable, to say the very least. These new modalities have revolutionized the delivery of health care around the world and improved the lives of innumerable citizens of the planet. The astonishing development of technology has truly spread worldwide so that even people in the remotest country or island have the benefit of imaging (albeit the highest technology still is present in the developed countries). A graphic demonstration of this spread of technology and medical knowledge can be appreciated by noting the new trend to have international interpretation of night-time studies around the world. Medicine now chases the sun in its use of computerized imaging and beams the images between countries so that night-hawk reading services help rationalize radiology care by making the best use of manpower around the world.

The impact of computed tomography (CT) and magnetic resonance imaging (MRI) on medicine can be further appreciated by noting a recent survey of physicians' views on the importance of 30 medical innovations. Fuchs and Sox published an article, titled "Physicians' Views of the Relative Importance of Thirty Medical Innovations in Health Affairs," in September/October 2001. In their survey of 225 leading internists in the United States, the replies showed that 75% of respondees believed CT and MRI were the most significant innovation, followed by ACE inhibitors, angioplasties, statins, and mammography.

The acceptance and wide application have come at a philosophical and pragmatic price and risk to the profession of radiology. While government planners and HMOs have tried to stem the tide of imaging progress, the science and technology have moved ahead with unstoppable momentum. The result of the attempts of these organizations to prevent the application of these new modalities was an ill-conceived movement to limit the training of radiologists during the era of primary-care physician promotion.

By attempting to prevent the use of imaging in health care, they interfered with the natural market forces of manpower supply and demand. The result is the current manpower shortage at a time when the need for imaging grows on a daily basis. The shortage has impaired training programs because faculty required to train radiologists have been enticed into more lucrative positions in the marketplace.

It is quite evident that the role of imaging will continue to grow and provide a positive impact on the health of all citizens. Its future is ensured by the new emphasis by the National Institutes of Health (NIH) on molecular imaging and also the image-guided microsurgery procedures performed with CT and MRI. We are quite proud to note that a radiologist, Elias Zerhouni, MD, has been appointed as current director of the NIH. Furthermore, we are proud that Dr. Zerhouni was a section editor in the third edition of this text.

Figure 1

It is exciting to reflect back on other high technology developments that have occurred, such as aviation (Fig. 1). If one looks at the progress made in aviation since the first flight of the Wright flyer and contrast it with the Space Shuttle, there was an increase in speed of approximately 600 times (42 mph compared to 25,000 mph) in a 100-year period. With CT scanning (Fig. 2), there has been an increase in scan time of almost 1200 times in a 25-year period (7 minutes per single scan compared to 300 msec on current multislice devices).

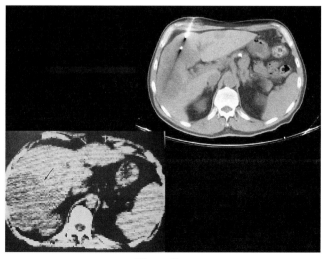

Figure 2

We are pleased to note the wide application of the new image-guided microsurgical procedures (the term *interventional radiology* is not specific enough or a unique descriptor). Progress in this area will continue and further improve the delivery of health care. Indeed, at the time of publication of this edition, we are even working on methodology using CT procedures to treat mediastinal collections of anthrax-laden lymph nodes in patients with inhalational anthrax. Data are very preliminary, but it seems that the heat from radiofrequency can be used to kill the vegetative forms of anthrax, and other strategies can be used to stimulate spores to germinate and become susceptible to local instillation of polymer-containing antibiotics.

We are especially grateful to all of our colleagues who have contributed to this edition because of the many difficulties they have overcome. Historically, it has always been difficult for authors to find time to contribute high-quality work. During this current period of faculty shortage at university centers, the commitment and dedication to our project required even more effort by our contributors.

We are delighted with the content of this fourth edition and believe it provides the most up-to-date information on MRI and CT. Information about the new, fast-sequence MRI and multislice scanners is provided. We are confident that the readers of this book will be intellectually rewarded.

Preface to First Edition

Since the introduction of computed tomography (CT) in 1974, there has been a remarkable revolution in the medical treatment of patients. The clinical use of CT has had a broad positive impact on patient management. Literally thousands of patients have been saved or their quality of life improved as a result of the expeditious and accurate diagnosis provided by CT. This improvement in diagnosis and management has occurred in all medical subspecialties, including neurological, pulmonary, cardiac, gastrointestinal, genitourinary, and neuromuscular medicine. Aside from the imaging advantages provided, the role of CT in planning and performing interventional procedures is now recognized. It is the most accurate method for guiding procedures to obtain cytological, histological, or bacteriological specimens and for performing a variety of therapeutic procedures.

The evolution and refinement of CT equipment have been as remarkable as the development of patient diagnosis. When we wrote our first book on CT, the scanning unit used was a 2-minute translate-rotate system. At the time of our second book the 18-second translate-rotate scanning unit was in general use. Currently standard units in radiological practice are third and fourth generation scanners with scan times of less than 5 seconds. All modern systems are more reliable than the earlier generations of equipment. The contrast and spatial resolution of these systems are in the range of 0.5% and less than 1 mm, respectively. The sophistication of the computer programs that aid in the diagnosis is also remarkable. There are now programs for three-dimensional reconstructions, quantitation of blood flow, determination of organ volume, longitudinal scans (Scoutview, Deltaview, Synerview, and Topogram), and even triangulation programs for performing percutaneous biopsy procedures.

CT units are now being installed in virtually every hospital of more than 200 beds throughout the United States. Most radiologists using these units are generalists who scan all portions of the anatomy. Because of the dissemination of this equipment and its use in general diagnosis, there exists a significant need for a general and complete textbook to cover all aspects of CT scanning. Our book is intended to partially supplement the knowledge of this group of physicians. We have attempted to completely and succinctly cover all portions of CT scanning to provide a complete general reference text. In planning the book, we chose to include the contributions of a large number of talented academicians with expertise different from and more complete than our own in their selected areas. By including contributors from outside our own department, we have been able to produce an in-depth textbook that combines the academic strengths of numerous individuals and departments.

The book is divided into chapters according to the organ systems, except for some special chapters on abscesses and interventional procedures. In each of the chapters the authors have organized the material into broad categories, such as congenital, benign, or neoplastic disease. Each author has tried to cover the major disease processes in each of the general categories in which CT diagnosis is applicable. Specific technical details, including the method of scanning, contrast material, collimation, and slice thickness, are covered in each chapter. The interventional chapter extensively covers the various biopsy and therapeutic procedures in all the organ systems. Finally, the last chapter presents an up-to-the-minute coverage of current and recent developments in the CT literature and also provides extensive information about nuclear magnetic resonance (NMR) imaging. At this time we have had moderate experience with the NMR superconducting magnetic device produced by the Technicare Corporation and have formulated some initial opinions as to its role relative to CT and other imaging modalities. A concise discussion of the physics of NMR and a current clinical status report of the new modality are provided.

We would like to thank all those people who have worked so diligently and faithfully for the preparation of this book. First, we are very grateful to our many contributors. For photography work, we are deeply indebted to Mr. Joseph P. Molter. For secretarial and organizational skills, we are indebted especially to Mrs. Mary Ann Reid and Mrs. Rayna Lipscomb. The editorial skills of Ms. B. Hami were invaluable in preparing the manuscript. Our extremely competent technical staff included Mr. Joseph Agee, Ms. Ginger Haddad, Mrs. E. Martinelle, Mr. Mark Clampett, Mrs. Mary Kralik, and numerous others.

Finally, we are, of course, very appreciative of the support, patience, and encouragement of our wonderful families. In the Haaga family this includes Ellen, Elizabeth, Matthew, and Timothy, who provided the positive motivation and support for this book. Warm gratitude for unswerving support is also due to Rose, Sue, Lisa, Chris, Katie, Mary, and John Alfidi.

John R. Haaga
Ralph J. Alfidi

Contents

Part IX   Special Considerations

Part I

Principles of Computed Tomography and Magnetic Resonance Imaging

Edited by
Jeffrey L. Duerk

1

Imaging Principles in Computed Tomography

Floro Miraldi, Michael S. Sims,
Ernest J. Wiesen

A computed tomography (CT) image is a display of the anatomy of a thin slice of the body developed from multiple x-ray absorption measurements made around the body's periphery. Unlike conventional tomography, in which the image of a thin section is created by blurring out the information from unwanted regions, the CT image is constructed mathematically using data arising only from the section of interest. Generating such an image is confined to cross-sections of the anatomy that are oriented essentially perpendicular to the axial dimension of the body (Fig. 1–1). Reconstruction of the final image can be accomplished in any plane, but conventionally it is performed in the transaxial plane.

In its most basic form, the fundamental principles of CT are the same as those for radiography and tomography. Each approach directs a source of ionizing radiation through an object to recreate an image of the original object based on the x-ray absorption of the object. The basic equation used is the same for each,

$$I = I_0 e^{-\mu x} \tag{1}$$

where

I_0 is the incident intensity of an x-ray beam on the surface of an object of thickness, x
I is the transmitted intensity
e is Euler's constant (2.718)
μ is the linear attenuation coefficient (Fig. 1–2)[7, 19]

Attenuation is dependent on (1) the atomic number and density of the material through which the x-rays pass and (2) the energy spectrum of the incident x-ray beam.[19] With conventional radiography and tomography, the differential absorption of x-rays passing through an object is recorded on film, a qualitative measurement that cannot accurately reflect subtle differences in object contrast. On the other hand, differential absorption for CT is recorded by special detectors, which are quantitative and can measure subtle changes in x-ray attenuation. Radiography's most major shortfall is the superimposition of the structures on film, which has been only partially overcome by conventional tomography.

The earliest CT was designed by Godfrey Hounsfield to overcome the visual representation challenges in radiography and tomography by collimating the x-ray beam and transmitting x-rays only through small cross-sections of an object. The idea revolutionized the practice of radiology and helped win Hounsfield a share of the Nobel Prize. More recent CT developments since the mid-1980s have advanced CT from a radiology tool limited to anatomic representations to a tool capable of demonstrating physiologic and pathogenic information.

This chapter presents the physics of CT image production in qualitative terms to familiarize the practicing radiologist with the basic principles of CT. Equipment and factors that affect CT image quality are discussed, and an introduction to emerging applications using CT is provided.

Basic Principles

The fundamental concept of CT is that the internal structure of an object can be reconstructed from multiple projections of the object (Fig. 1–3). The object in Fig. 1–3A is composed of a number of equal blocks from which the central four have been removed to represent an internal structure. For the sake of simplicity, assume that an x-ray beam is passed through each row and column of blocks and the transmitted radiation is measured. Since each block is the same, the measured attenuation is proportional to the number of blocks encountered in each row or column.

The numbers shown at the right and beneath the object represent the relative measured attenuation (i.e., the number of blocks in each row or column). These attenuation measurements are then added (Fig. 1–3B) to produce a numeric representation of the object (Fig. 1–3C). Although this array of numbers contains all the information of the process, it is difficult to interpret; thus, the array is converted into picture form by assigning a gray scale to the numbers. Large numbers are represented by light shades of gray, and small numbers are represented by dark shades of gray. The result is the image shown in Figure 1–3D. The resultant image can then be manipulated to highlight certain areas. For example, if the gray scale is narrowed to include only black and white, a perfect reproduction of the object is obtained by assigning black to all numbers equal to four or less and white to all numbers greater than four.

In Figure 1–3E, an imperfect representation is obtained because the gray scale is chosen so that values of six and lower are black and values above six are white. In CT, the method of obtaining the array of numbers is more complex

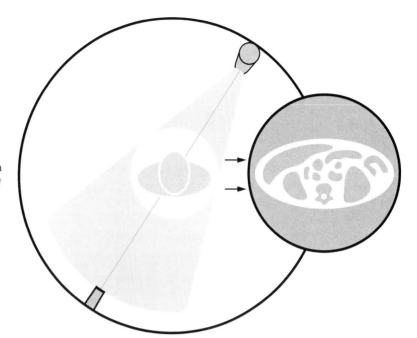

Figure 1–1. A CT image represents anatomy of a transaxial slice of the body obtained from many transaxial attenuation measurements.

and the number of projections obtained is much greater; however, the principle is the same.

The example of Figure 1–3 also provides a basis for a number of definitions of CT terms. Each of the blocks in Figure 1–3A represents a small attenuating volume of material and is referred to as a *voxel*. The numbers at the side and bottom of Figure 1–3A represent single attenuation measurements and are called *ray projections*, or *ray sums*. The array of numbers in Figure 1–3C is a *matrix*, and the individual numbers are elements of that matrix.

Each of the blocks of gray that are used for the construction of the images in Figure 1–3D–F is a picture element *(pixel)*. The process of choosing the number of gray shades for a display is referred to as "selecting a window." The width of the window (Fig. 1–3E and F) is narrow because it only contains two shades of gray (black and white) compared with the wider window in Figure 1–3D, which contains three shades of gray. The number at which the

window setting is centered is called the *window level*. In Figure 1–3E, the level is set at four; in Figure 1–3F, it is set at six.

To present attenuation data (either I or μ) at every point throughout the body would be ideal in an x-ray examination. The degree to which this is attained depends on the manner in which the measured intensities, I and I_0, are registered or manipulated. In conventional radiography, the transmitted intensity (I) is seen as the darkening of a film. Because x-ray exposure of the film blackens it, the image of a dense object is lighter on the film than the image of a less dense material. In a typical radiographic film of the chest, for example, the image is light where many x-rays are absorbed or scattered (large μ), such as in bone, and dark where many x-rays are transmitted because of low absorption (small μ), such as in the regions of the lung parenchyma.

Two different areas of such a chest film may show the same darkening and therefore demonstrate equal total attenuation of the beam in the two positions. However, the attenuation profile through the body may be quite different. This is diagrammatically shown in Figure 1–4, with one beam passing through a region of relatively uniform density and the other beam passing through a region of nonuniform densities.

In conventional radiography, therefore, the different shades of gray seen on the film represent the differences in the transmission of an x-ray beam as it passes through the body. CT, however, approaches the ideal by presenting the average attenuation of each small volume element that comprises the body slice. Thus, CT unscrambles the attenuation information of the x-ray beam and presents it quantitatively with accuracy far greater than that accomplished by conventional techniques. This is equivalent to providing the individual values μ_1, μ_2, and μ_3 of Figure 1–4 rather than the total value described for conventional radiography.

All CT systems use a similar three-step process to generate a CT image: (1) scan, or data acquisition, (2)

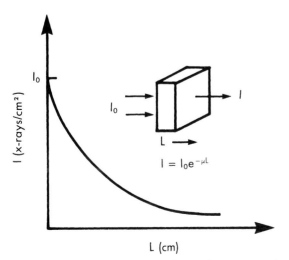

Figure 1–2. Exponential behavior of x-ray beam attenuation.

$$I = I_0 e^{-\mu L}$$

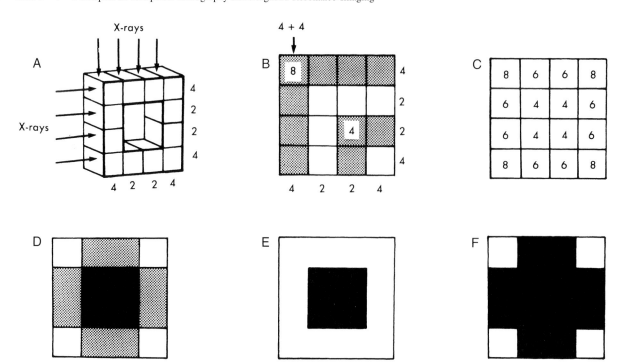

Figure 1–3. Principle of image reconstruction. (From Christensen EE, Curry TS III, Dowdey JE: An Introduction to the Physics of Diametric Radiology, 2nd ed. Philadelphia, Lea & Febiger, 1978.)

reconstruction, and (3) display; each process is considered separately throughout this chapter. In the most basic form, the flow of all CT systems includes the conversion of an x-ray source consisting of a collection of rays (*projection* or *view*). A single ray is considered the portion of the x-ray beam that falls onto one detector.

Data Acquisition

The scanning process begins with data acquisition. CT scanning is the systematic collection of projection data. Data collection encompasses all of the geometric properties of the x-ray beam and the relationship of the x-ray tube to the detector, including all of the beam-shaping devices and conversion of transmitted x-rays to digital signals for use by the reconstruction system. Since Hounsfield's invention, CT scanning geometry has evolved considerably. Before

we address the evolution of CT data acquisition and CT scanning geometry, it is valuable to review the basic components of every CT data acquisition system.

Components of a Data Acquisition System

Scan Frame

Early CT scanners (in the 1980s) deployed rotating frames and recoiling system cables. This design was limited to step-and-shoot scan methods and considerably limited scanner rotation times. Current systems employ slip rings, electromechanical devices that transmit electrical energy across a rotating surface. Slip rings permit the scan frame to rotate continuously, enabling spiral or helical CT scanning and eliminating the need to rewind system cables.

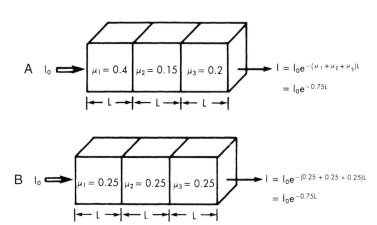

Figure 1–4. Total attenuation of equal amount in two different cases. *A*, Nonuniform attenuation coefficients. *B*, Uniform medium.

X-ray Generators

Most CT scanners today use high-frequency generators to produce x-ray quanta required for today's demanding CT protocols. Typical operating frequencies range from 5 to 50 kHz. Generator power can range from as low as 15 kilowatts (kW) to as high as 60 kW, and recent developments are likely to support ranges as high as 70 to 80 kW. In any case, most generators support a wide range of exposure techniques from 80 to 140 kilovolts (kV) and 30 to 500 milliamperes (mA). The generators are located on rotating scan frames within the CT gantry to accommodate new spiral scanning requirements.

X-ray Tubes

Early-generation CT technology used fixed-anode, oil-cooled x-ray tubes with fairly limited capability. Today's x-ray tubes include rotating anodes with unique cooling methods designed to enhance a system's ability to cover large areas of anatomy at diagnostic levels of x-ray output. Tube ratings typical in CT scanners today vary from 2 million heat units (2 MHU) of storage capability, with 300 thousand heat units (kHU)/minute cooling, up to 7 MHU of anode heat storage capability and cooling rates as fast as 1 million heat units (MHU)/minute. Future enhancements will not preclude tubes with greater than 10 MHU capacity and continuous output power capability of 60 kW. Both x-ray generator and x-ray tube developments are expected to open up the door for true volumetric CT applications with large area detectors designed to cover entire sections of patient anatomy within one revolution of the CT scanner's rotating frame.

X-ray Beam Filtration System

It is assumed that CT employs a monochromatic beam. The opposite is true; radiation from CT x-ray tubes is polychromatic. To compensate for this fact, the x-ray beam is shaped by *compensation filters*. The filters serve two purposes:

1. They remove the long-wavelength x-rays, which do not contribute to the CT image but do contribute to patient dose as these so-called soft rays are absorbed by the patient.
2. They serve to minimize the effects of beam hardening and provide a more uniform beam, as seen from the perspective of the detector.

Different filters are used for half-field (head) scanning and full-field (body) scanning. Additional corrections for beam hardening are made during the CT reconstruction process with software.

Data Acquisition Systems

Data acquisitions systems are the heart of a CT scanner. They include (1) the detector system, (2) analog-to-digital conversion, and (3) some data preprocessing for use by the scanners reconstruction system. The major functions are as follows[34]:

- To convert x-ray flux to electric current
- To convert electric current to voltage
- To convert analog voltage to digital form
- To subtract background offset signal
- To provide logarithmic conversion of data
- To transmit data to the preprocessing system

Early data acquisition systems employed xenon (gas ionization detectors). These detectors directly convert x-ray energy to electrical energy but are inefficient. Most modern systems include the use of solid-state detectors. Two primary crystal materials are in use today, cadmium tungstate and gadolinium oxysulfide. The crystals convert the x-rays to light proportional to the quantity of photons striking the crystal. The light is converted to current and hence a voltage across a resistance and then to digital data for use by the reconstruction system.

The conversion of analog signals to digital data (A to D conversion) by the data acquisition system creates a *quantization error*. Sampling speed of the A to D converter and the number of digital output combinations available determine quantization error. This quantization error, along with electronic noise in the amplifier, generally characterizes the performance of the data acquisition system. The system's ability to measure low-level signals accurately over a wide dynamic range largely contributes to CT's overall image quality capabilities per a given x-ray flux.

Evolution of Data Acquisition Systems and CT System Geometry

First-Generation System

First-generation CT data acquisition was based on parallel-beam geometry with a translate-rotate principle of the tube/detector combination. The x-ray beam was collimated to dimensions of roughly 2×13 mm. The 13-mm dimension corresponded to the slice thickness (voxel length). Small detectors monitored the intensity of the beam before entering the body to yield the value of the incident intensity (I_0). After passing through the body, the beam was detected by a scintillation crystal, collimated to receive, primarily, those photons that were not scattered or absorbed. The amount of transmitted intensity (I) was then recorded and stored in the computer memory.

The x-ray tube and detector system were moved continuously across the patient, making 160 multiple measurements during the translation. At the end of each translation, the x-ray tube and detector system were rotated 1 degree and the translation repeated. The translate-rotate process was repeated for 180 translations, yielding 28,800 (160×180) measurements. The 160 measurements made during one complete translation are called a *profile* or *view*.

From a clinical standpoint, the first-generation machine had the major disadvantage of long scanning times. Image quality severely suffered from the effects of patient motion, since 5 minutes was required to gather the 28,800 ray sums. This disadvantage limited use to body parts such as the head, which can be made immobile.

Second-Generation System

Second-generation data acquisition and scanner geometry included fan-beam reconstruction with a linear detector array. The x-ray beam was converted to a fan shape with a

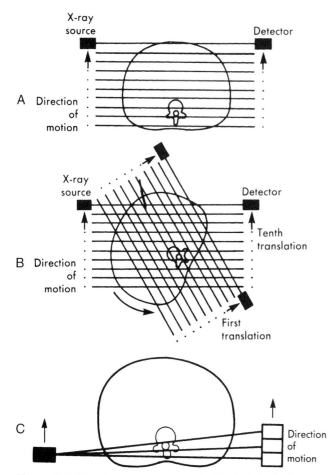

Figure 1–5. Translate-rotate scanner. *A*, Original single-detector system, single translation. *B*, Two separate translations. *C*, Second-generation system with fan beam source and multiple detectors.

diverging angle of between 3 and 10 degrees (Fig. 1–5). Multiple x-ray detectors were then placed adjacent to each other to intercept this beam. Because more x-ray detectors were used with this system, the number of angular rotations could be decreased and an adequate number of views obtained in much shorter intervals. With second-generation data acquisition, scanners could obtain a scan in periods as short as 18 seconds. From Figure 1–5, it is obvious that each detector obtains a different view during a translation because the rays from the x-ray tube to the detectors are not parallel.

The next few developments in CT involved a widening of the fan beam so that it encompasses the object entirely.

Third-Generation System

Third-generation data acquisition and scanner geometry use wide-angle fan beam geometry (50 to 55 degrees); an arc of detectors and an x-ray tube rotate continuously around the patient for 360 degrees. As the x-ray tube and detector arc are rotated, projection data (or data samples) are obtained, and for every fixed point of the tube and detector, a view is created (Fig. 1–6).

As Figure 1–6 demonstrates, the detectors are fixed

radially and do not view the scan area uniformly. Only the center detectors in the array "see" the pixels at the center of the *field of view* (FOV). However, this fixed relationship allows the detectors to be highly collimated, which greatly reduces scatter radiation; as discussed later, this also reduces "image noise" (mottle, or grainy background) and improves image quality.

As a result of the fixed position of the tube/detector combination the associated detectors and electronics system must be stable, uniform, and capable of tracking over a wide dynamic range. Noncompensation for errors as small as a few thousandths of 1% can cause visible (ring) artifacts (see Fig. 1–39). In addition, spatial resolution, a key image quality parameter of CT (see later), can be limited by the data sampling. In this geometric relationship, the number of detectors in the arc or array determines data sampling; that is, spatial resolution depends on how closely spaced the rays are in each view.

The typical number of detectors ranges from about 600 to more than 900. These numbers result in a limiting spatial resolution of approximately 5 to 10 line pairs per centimeter (lp/cm), depending on the reconstruction matrix size and scan FOV. Sampling theory (Nyquist) requires that to visualize a particular frequency, the sampling frequency must be at least twice that value. In practice, even higher sampling rates are desirable. Axial resolution of greater than 5 to 10 lp/cm (0.5 to 1.0 mm) may be limiting for specific clinical applications.

To overcome this challenge, manufacturers have introduced various methods. One method of increasing sampling (and spatial resolution) is to offset the detector array relative to the center of rotation by a quarter-ray or eighth-ray. This permits data collected during the second half of a 360-degree rotation to be interleaved with that of the first half, effectively doubling the sampling and resolution. Unfortunately, patient motion can minimize this effect. In addition, this method is restricted with spiral CT scanning (see later) to certain modes in which 360 degrees of data is available for interleaving.

Another more effective method of increasing data sampling is to scan or oscillate the x-ray tube focal spot a few millimeters during a scan (Fig. 1–6*B*) in order to achieve interleaved data samples. The position of the focal spot is accurately controlled and synchronized with rotational speed and position of the rotating frame.

Spatial resolution also requires adequate view sampling to prevent "aliasing" artifacts. Views in this case are limited by the electronic measurement capability of the scanner, which is typically not the gating factor for maximum resolution. These factors vary for every CT manufacturer, which can dramatically affect the overall performance of a scanner.

Fourth-Generation System

Fourth-generation data acquisition and scanner geometry (Fig. 1–7) also use a wide-angle rotating fan beam (50 to 55 degrees); in this case, though, the tube rotates within a 360-degree arc of stationary detectors. Instead of the focal spot as the focus of views, as in a third-generation system, views are seen from the perspective of the detector. With

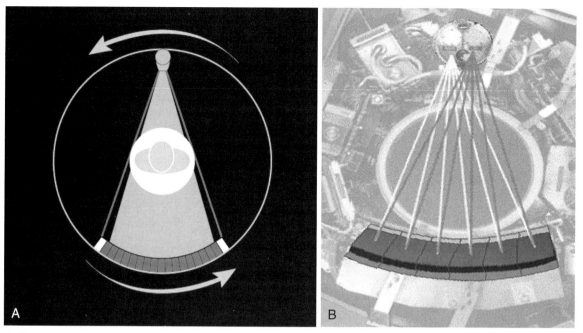

Figure 1–6. *A,* Third-generation rotate-only scanner geometry showing fixed relationship of x-ray tube and detectors. *B,* Dynamic focal spot technology (Marconi Medical Systems) effectively doubles the data sampling rate.

this approach, data samples are obtained over the width of the fan angle and several data samples are acquired per detector. The output of each detector constitutes a view. Therefore, views are limited to the number of detectors in the 360-degree arc.

In this geometric configuration, data sampling is limited by the system electronics, not by the number of detectors. The collection of equivalent, closely spaced ray sums using

this geometry permits a very high spatial resolution (>20 lp/cm) (Fig. 1–8),[28] although it forces a wider collimation of the detector, which in turn can cause an increase in detection of scattered radiation. Several techniques are employed to minimize the effect of scattered radiation. Most important, natural rejection of scatter is minimized with appropriate distance between the patient and detectors.

With fourth-generation geometry, small, closely spaced

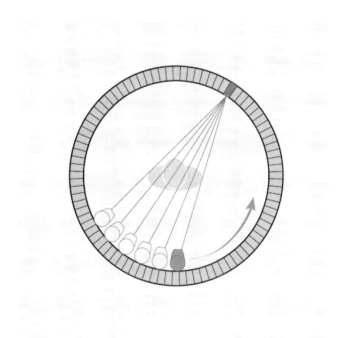

Figure 1–7. Fourth-generation scanner geometry, Model PQ6000 (Marconi Medical Systems). Views are seen from the perspective of the detector.

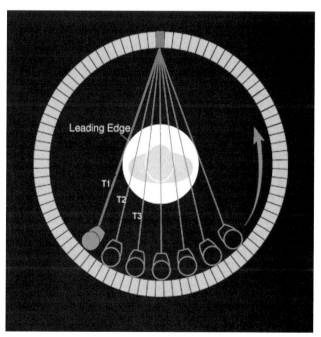

Figure 1–8. Overlapped measurements. Leading edge of the x-ray beam is shown at three different times (T1, T2, and T3), representing small, closely spaced data samples during a scan.

data samples require many individual measurements, which can affect reconstruction time. To overcome this challenge, views are averaged to reduce this effect. Most systems have many more detectors and views available to exceed the limiting resolution of the system.

There are unique advantages and disadvantages to today's CT geometry beyond spatial resolution, including (1) detected quantum efficiency, (2) noise, and (3) contrast resolution. The performance of each system depends largely on the manufacturer and not the scanning geometry used.

Spiral/Helical Computed Tomography

Until the late 1980s, CT scanners, regardless of system geometry (third or fourth generation), acquired data in discrete slices of patient anatomy in a method commonly called *axial scanning*. In axial (cross-sectional) CT, each revolution of the x-ray tube around the patient produced a single data set *(slice).* During data collection, the patient table is motionless. To create an additional slice, the table is indexed a given amount and the x-ray tube is once again rotated around the patient. Each rotation or slice produces a single image. The advent of slip ring technology and new data reconstruction techniques provided a gateway to the data acquisition currently in use namely, (1) spiral/helical CT and (2) multislice spiral or multidetector/multirow CT data acquisition systems.

In spiral/helical CT, the patient table translates through the gantry while the x-ray tube (fourth generation) or the x-ray tube/detector combinations (third generation) rotate continuously around the patient, creating a volume of data. This permits new options in reconstruction. For example, once a volume of data is collected, an image can be reconstructed at any point along the effective path traced by the x-ray tube. At this point, it may be helpful to define the terms associated with spiral scanning (Table 1–1):

Acquisition is the entire volume of data collected during a continuous spiral scan.
Revolutions refer to the number of 360-degree rotations of the x-ray tube during a single acquisition.
Pitch is the distance the couch travels during one 360-degree revolution of the x-ray tube.

Table 1–1. Spiral Scanning Terms in Computed Tomography

Acquisition (spiral)	The process by which a single, continuous volume of computed tomography data are acquired without a pause
Revolution	One per each 360-degree rotation of the x-ray tube around the patient or object of interest
Pitch	The distance the couch or patient travels through the gantry during one 360-degree beam rotation
Pitch factor	A unitless parameter in which pitch can be designated. This is defined as the pitch (mm) divided by the collimated slice thickness (mm)
Interpolation	A mathematical technique used to estimate the value of a function from values on either side of it

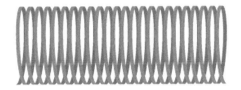

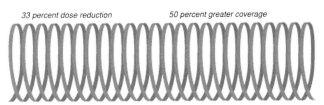

Figure 1–9. Extending the pitch factor from 1:1 to 1.5:1 increases volume coverage by 50% and decreases patient dose by 33%.

Pitch factor is the pitch divided by the collimated slice thickness, or effective width of the beam at the isocenter of the gantry. The term "pitch" has become synonymous with "pitch factor."
Interpolation is a reconstruction method (most accurately described as "deconvolution") that permits the realignment of spiral/helical scan data for reconstruction of an axial (cross-sectional) slice.

Spiral CT has many advantages over conventional or axial CT, including[30]:

- The ability to minimize motion artifacts
- Decreased incidence of misregistration between consecutive axial slices
- Reduced patient dose
- Improved spatial resolution in the z-axis
- Enhanced multiplanar (MPR) or three-dimensional (3D) renderings

The ability to minimize motion artifacts in spiral CT is due to the faster scan times associated with every examination (versus step-and-shoot axial scanning) and the ability for many spiral CT examinations to be completed in a single patient breath-hold.

The faster scan times associated with spiral CT also permit accurate slice-to-slice registration and eliminate misregistration associated with inconsistent breath-holds related to conventional axial scanning. Reconstructions can be overlapped or ideally positioned for accurate visualization of small lesions.

Spiral scanners achieve reduced patient dose by extending the pitch factor for a given study. For example, consider a typical thorax, abdomen, or pelvis examination. Typical slice widths range from 5 to 10 mm. With spiral CT, the same examination can be completed with a given slice thickness as conventional CT with 50% greater table speed using a pitch of 1.5; this results in a 33% reduction in patient dose (Fig. 1–9). The nominal downside to this approach is a slight broadening of the slice sensitivity profile (effective axial slice thickness) based on the type of spiral reconstruction chosen. The slice thickness formula is given as[32]

$$\sigma = \frac{D^2}{12} + \frac{T^2}{24} \qquad (2)$$

where

D is detector collimation
T is table speed
σ is the standard deviation (SD) of the slice sensitivity profile

See "Reconstruction" for further details.

With continuous collection of data, as just described, spiral CT enables a reduction in image-to-image separation, thus improving spatial resolution in the z-axis. Although conventional CT might overcome this challenge by overlapping consecutive axial slices, this would increase the patient radiation dose and would lengthen scan times to cover a given region of patient anatomy.

Multiplanar and 3D renderings are enhanced as a result of the ability of spiral CT to reconstruct overlapped planar and axial slices from a continuous volume of data. The optimal number is two to three transverse slices per detector collimation[32] and is given as the formula

$$n = \frac{3}{\pi\sqrt{\dfrac{1}{12} + \dfrac{p^2}{24}}} \qquad (3)$$

where

n is the slice number per collimation
p is pitch (table speed over collimation)

Spiral CT data acquisition systems must be capable of collecting large volumes of data at extremely fast data rates. Data sampling for most systems is in the range of 3 kHz and can provide up to nearly 2400 projections or views per rotation of the gantry. Data rates for many new systems exceed 200 megabits/second. This extremely fast sampling capability enables high spatial resolution and enhanced z-axis sampling of patient anatomy.

The increased speed of data acquisition systems and a number of other technologic developments paved the way for data acquisition at subsecond rotation speeds of the rotating frame. Subsecond spiral data acquisition permits temporal resolution on the order of 250 to 480 msec, depending on the manufacturer. Temporal resolution of this magnitude enables more examinations to be accomplished within a single breath-hold and dramatically improves the anatomy that can be covered in a single scan. This improves clinical applications such as CT angiography, which requires precise timing of a bolus injection and rapid acquisition during the arterial phase. Subsecond data acquisition also can improve the z-axis resolution (slice thickness) for a given study by covering the same amount of anatomy in the same time with thinner slices, However, spiral CT is not without limitations and many examinations might benefit from an even more dramatic increase in data acquisition rates.

Multislice Spiral CT

The latest development in data acquisition—multislice spiral CT—overcomes the limits of spiral CT. All multislice spiral CT systems today use third-generation geometry (rotate only) with the added dimension of multiple arcs of detectors. The first deployment of this technology included a dual-arc detector (Fig. 1–10).[38] In this configuration, two parallel arcs of detectors are used to simultaneously acquire data during a single revolution of the scan frame, dividing the total x-ray beam into two equal beams described by the detector aperture of each row of detectors. Considering small gaps between rows, which can be ignored from the perspective of data acquisition, the total x-ray beam collimation now becomes the sum of detector row collimations (Fig. 1–11) and is described as

$$d(mm) = \frac{D(mm)}{2} \qquad (4)$$

where

d is the detector row collimation
D is the x-ray beam collimation
2 is the number of detector rows

This can be extended to include n rows of detectors.

Four-Slice Design

Since the introduction of dual-detector technology in the early 1990s, other manufacturers have introduced four-slice configurations. Two four-slice design approaches are described.

Equal-Width Detector

As with the dual-beam array, detectors of equal widths are stacked back to back in the z-axis (Fig. 1–12). In the case of one manufacturer, 16 rows of 1.25-mm detectors (effective width at isocenter) are aligned in the z-axis. To achieve different slice widths, the detectors are electronically coupled at the beginning of each scan according to the requested slice width. The total z-axis dimension of the detector covers 20 mm. This approach limits the minimal z-axis resolution to the nominal width (at isocenter) of the individual detectors. Figure 1–13 demonstrates the use of multiple detector combinations per requested slice width.

Variable-Width Detector

A second approach (Fig. 1–14) combines fewer detectors of variable widths and a postpatient collimator to define slice widths. This approach is more geometrically efficient because there is less unusable space in the z-axis (Fig. 1–15A). This combination also permits slice widths as small as 0.5 mm, enabling isotropic imaging (submillimeter voxel dimensions are equal in all planes) (Fig. 1–15B).

In either case, the clinical benefits of multislice CT can best be described by comparing clinical protocols versus single-ring spiral CT. For a given protocol, multislice CT is more efficient by the number of detector rings used. Consider a typical single-slice spiral CT protocol of 40 seconds, at 1 second per revolution (scan time), with a slice thickness of 5 mm, using 200 mA, with 200 mm of

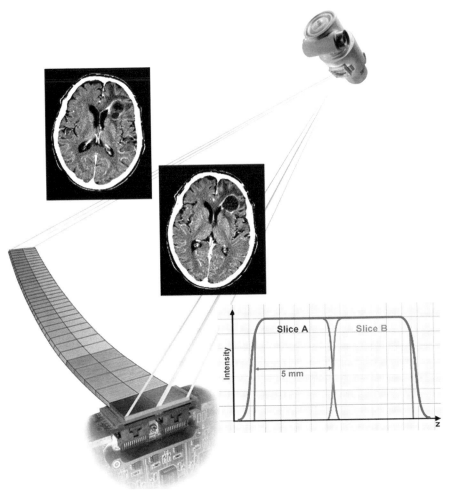

Figure 1–10. The first multislice detector system (Marconi Medical Systems dual-arc detector). Two detectors are aligned consecutively in the z-axis, creating a 2D detector matrix/array and two images per gantry revolution. (Courtesy of J. S. Arenson.)

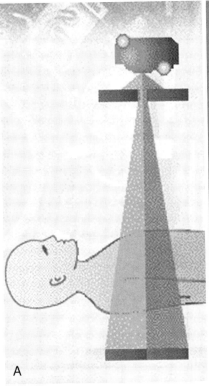

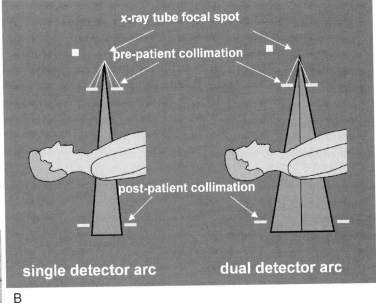

Figure 1–11. *A*, Z-axis perspective of dual slice detector array. *B*, Total x-ray beam (source collimation) is the sum of consecutive detector row collimations in the z-axis (in this case, two).

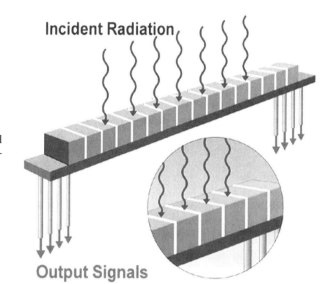

Figure 1–12. Multislice spiral CT Matrix detector (GE Medical Systems) with 16 rows of equal width (1.25 mm at isocenter) detector elements.

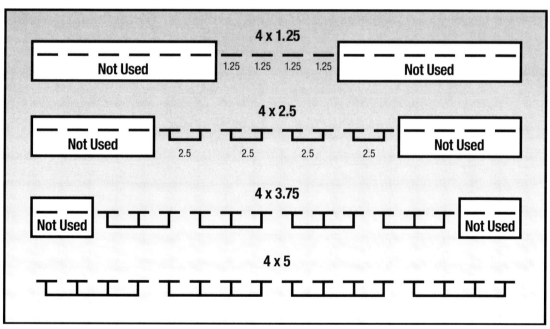

Figure 1–13. Matrix detector. Electronic combination of individual elements produces slice collimation configurations of 4 × 1.25 mm, 4 × 2.5 mm, 4 × 3.75 mm, and 4 × 5 mm.

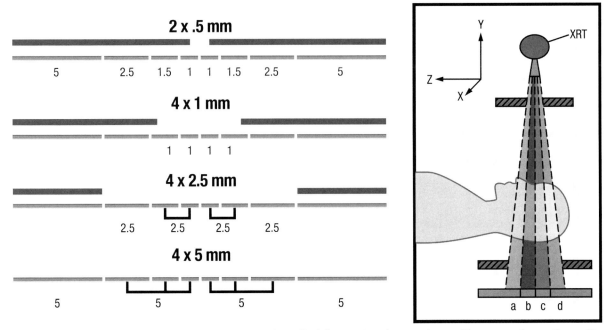

Figure 1–14. Asymmetrix variable detector array (Marconi Medical Systems) and postpatient collimator produces slice collimation configurations of 2 × 0.5 mm, 4 × 1 mm, 4 × 2.5 mm, and 4 × 5 mm.

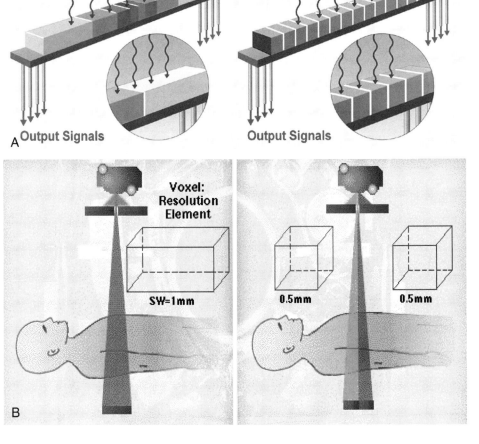

Figure 1–15. *A,* Comparison of z-axis geometric efficiency of multislice CT detectors. At wide collimations, variable detector array is more efficient. *B,* A 2- × 0.5-mm slice width with ultrahigh in-plane resolution produces isotropic imaging; voxel width is equal in all dimensions.

total anatomic coverage. Using a multislice data acquisition system with n rings, the same protocol can be modified to:

1. Enhance z-axis resolution by a factor of n. The slice thickness is divided by n rings with the same total anatomic coverage, scan time, and milliampere-seconds (mAs).
2. Enhance the speed of anatomic coverage by n. The 40-second continuous spiral run is divided by n, with the same nominal slice thickness, scan coverage, and mAs.
3. Enhance the anatomic coverage of the examination by n; 200 mm of coverage is multiplied by n using the same nominal slice thickness, scan time, and mAs.
4. Increase effective milliamperage by n. By dividing the pitch by n rings, the 200 mAs is effectively increased by a factor of n, maintaining the same nominal slice thickness, scan time, and coverage.

As described earlier, pitch or pitch factor is the distance in millimeters the couch is moved during one revolution of the gantry. Pitch is determined by dividing the movement of the table through the gantry during one 360-degree rotation by the x-ray beam collimation at the source (prepatient collimator). By segmenting the usable x-ray beam into n segments, multislice CT complicates the equation. There are two commonly used definitions (Fig. 1–16):

1. Pitch is defined using the model described earlier; however, a prefix added to the pitch indicates the number of detector rings used (e.g., single, one ring; dual, two rings; quad, four rings). A pitch of quad-1 would refer to a scan in which the table moves the distance of the source (prepatient) collimation during one revolution of the gantry. For a given protocol, a pitch 1 scan delivers the same patient dose and fundamentally produces the same image quality in a single-slice, dual-slice, or quad-slice scanner.
2. Pitch is defined as the result of dividing the movement of the table through the gantry by the effective slice width at the isocenter of a single detector (or n rings × effective slice thickness of an individual slice). Thus, a pitch of 4 is equivalent to a quad-pitch 1 (see first definition).

An accepted convention will emerge, but at first glance it appears that the second definition is confusing and offers less information. For example, from definition 2, a pitch 2 could refer to single-pitch 2, dual-pitch 1, or quad-pitch 0.5.

As of this writing, several manufacturers have introduced four-slice models, but future configurations of 8, 16, 32, 64, and perhaps even flat panel detectors of several hundred square millimeters are on the horizon.

In each case, multislice CT complicates fan-beam reconstruction techniques by adding a divergence of the fan beam along the longitudinal axis (z-axis), creating a cone shape (cone beam) (Fig. 1–17). This new technique, *cone-beam reconstruction*, is considered later (see "Reconstruction").

Electron Beam Computed Tomography

A modification of the fourth-generation concept of data acquisition involves moving the x-ray beam electronically instead of mechanically. This scanning method reduces the scan time to approximately 0.02 second per slice and, with a small delay for consecutive slices, up to 17 slices per second.

An electron beam is accelerated along the axis of rotation of the CT scanner and is electronically deflected to any one of four fixed tungsten x-ray targets. Each target is an arc of tungsten of 210 degrees with a radius of 90 cm. The electron beam is deflected through the 210-degree arc of the target, creating the scan.

Opposite the target are two sets of stationary detectors with arcs of 216 degrees. One detector arc has 432 detectors; the other, a higher-resolution ring, has 864 detectors. Each individual detector consists of a cadmium tungstate crystal matched with a silicon photodiode and a preamplifier. Adjacent detectors of the high-resolution ring can be summed to match the other ring for dynamic imaging, or can be used singly, for high-resolution imaging.

During dynamic scanning, two slices can be acquired simultaneously. Scanning takes place over 180 degrees instead of the 360 degrees of most conventional scanners. An image can be reconstructed with 180 degrees of data.

Once the signals are generated, the remainder of the scanner is fairly conventional in design. This system design has many image quality shortfalls for routine imaging, but its superior temporal resolution has led the way for CT into the realm of cardiac imaging.[24]

Figure 1–16. Naming conventions for pitch. *A,* Single-ring spiral CT definition in which pitch equals table speed/source collimation. *B,* Alternative definitions for multislice spiral CT, with definition 1 representing table speed/source collimation as quad-pitch 1 and definition 2 representing table speed divided by the single-slice collimation (detector collimation) as pitch 4. Both are accepted.

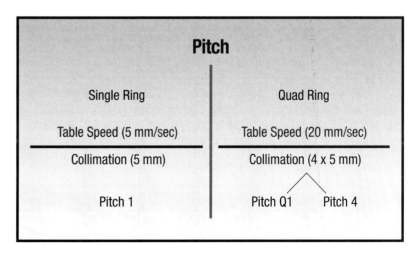

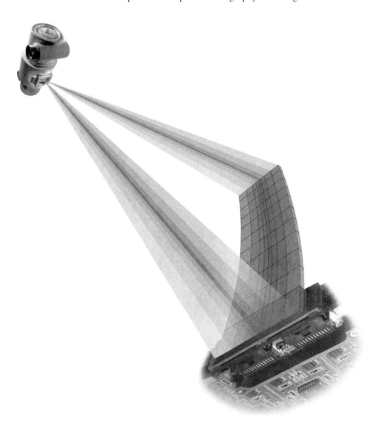

Figure 1–17. The x-ray fan beam is divergent in the z-axis, creating a cone beam.

Reconstruction

Reconstruction includes all of the system components necessary to perform the mathematical computations that are required to convert the digital data (representing the log of attenuation coefficients) provided by the data acquisition system. The reconstruction system delivers CT data to the display system in a manner that is suitable for viewing on a viewing monitor. Regardless of the scanner type, the result of a scan is a large number of individual ray sums. The reconstruction of the image from these measurements is, in principle, the same for every CT scanner.

The fundamental equation describing the behavior of the measurements is given in Equation 5, and a few simple manipulations of this relationship should help one to understand CT image reconstruction.

Figure 1–18 shows a number of thin slabs with an initial x-ray intensity (I_0) impinging on the first slab. The exit intensity from the first slab (I_1) becomes the entrance intensity for the second slab, and its exit intensity (I_2) is the entrance intensity for the third slab, and so forth. We can then write

$$I_1 = I_0 e^{-\mu_1 L_1}$$

$$I_2 = I_1 e^{-\mu_2 L_2} = (I_0 e^{-\mu_1 L_1}) e^{-\mu_2 L_2} \quad (5)$$

$$I_n = I_{n-1} e^{-\mu_n L_n}$$

The equation for the emergent beam after passing through n slabs can then be deduced as

$$I = I_0 (e^{-\mu_1 L_1})(e^{-\mu_2 L_2}) \ldots (e^{-\mu_n L_n}) \quad (6)$$

$$= I_0 e^{-\mu_1 L_1 + \mu_2 L_2 + \ldots \mu_n L_n}$$

For simplicity, the subscript n on I_n has been dropped. Therefore, the total attenuation is equivalent to the simple equation

$$I = I_0 e^{-\mu L} \quad (7)$$

where

$$\mu L = \mu_1 L_1 + \mu_2 L_2 + \ldots \mu_n L_n \quad (8)$$

When $L_1 = L_2 = L_3 = \ldots = L_n$ (i.e., all the slabs have equal thickness), Equation 8 can be written as

$$\mu L = (\mu_1 + \mu_2 + \ldots \mu_n)L \quad (9)$$

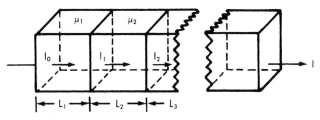

Figure 1–18. Illustration of Equation 6 (see text).

If we now take the natural logarithm (ln) of both sides of Equation 7 and rearrange it, the result is

$$\mu = (\mu_1 + \mu_2 + \dots \mu_n) = \frac{1}{L}\ln\frac{I_0}{I} \qquad (10)$$

Equation 10 shows that, if the incident intensity I_0, transmitted intensity I, and segment length L are known, the sum of the attenuation coefficients along the path of the x-ray beam can be calculated.

Because there are n unknowns (one of each segment), each value of the attenuation coefficient cannot be determined from a single equation. Algebraic theory requires that there be n independent equations to obtain solutions for the n unknown values of μ. To get n independent equations, a number of views must be taken; it is then possible to gather sufficient data for the multiple equations.

A comparison with conventional radiography shows that because only one measurement is made in radiography, only the average value of μ or the sum of the μLs can be obtained. Thus, the information on the film is less detailed than the information on a CT image.

Reconstruction Process

For each ray projection measurement made during a CT scan, Equation 10 is generated and the complete set of such equations must then be solved to obtain the individual values of μ for each matrix element. Because thousands of ray projections are obtained for a scan, thousands of equations must be solved simultaneously and the need for high-speed computers is obvious.

Note that L is not related to the slice thickness (voxel length) and is chosen for the reconstruction process by selecting a matrix size. Provided that sufficient ray projections have been made, the image can be reconstructed in any matrix size, which is paramount to choosing any value of L. The voxel length is set by the collimation of the scanner when a slice thickness is selected. *A picture element (pixel), therefore, represents the attenuation coefficient (μ) of a volume element with length determined by the slice thickness chosen during the data acquisition and cross-sectional area that has a side dimension (L) chosen at the time of reconstruction.*

Many methods have been devised to solve the set of equations generated in a scan; however, most manufacturers have settled on the filtered back-projection method because it allows short computation time with relatively accurate solutions.[2, 4, 5, 8, 9] It also allows processing of each ray sum immediately after it is obtained while the data acquisition continues for other ray sums. This permits the final image to be available for viewing almost immediately after completion of the scanning process. It is important to understand the basic concepts underlying reconstruction procedures, since their manner of application affects the quality of the final image.

The back-projection method is an attempt to approximate the solution by projection of a uniform value of attenuation over the path of the ray such that the calculated attenuation over the path is proportional to the measured

attenuation. These values are then stored in the computer for the matrix elements involved, and the process is repeated for each ray sum of the scan. Each matrix element thus receives a contribution from each ray that passes through it. For those voxels through which the beam passes obliquely, a correction is made to the contribution (Fig. 1–19). The final image obtained is rather blurred as a result of the assumption that the beam attenuation occurs uniformly over the entire path of the ray.

The process is exemplified in Figure 1–20, which demonstrates the result of applying this procedure to a uniform field with a circular object of high-density embedded in it. In the example, only a few rays are used.

Two observations should be made: (1) the procedure generates a star pattern, and (2) it tends to approximate the image better as more views are obtained.

No matter how many views are used, however, the blurring effect is never completely eliminated. Thus, a second mathematical maneuver called a *convolution operation*, or *filtering*, is used.[5, 13] The purpose of the filtering process is to modify the ray sum data such that the back-projections consist of both positive and negative values. In the example of Figure 1–21, the profile of the back-projected density is modified to look like the one in *B* rather than that in *A*. The result is the cancellation of some of the back-projected densities of other ray sums and removal of the unsharpness.

The filtering procedure involves a mathematical operation on the ray sum with a "filter function" or convolution "kernel." The filter function is a complex one that depends on many parameters, including x-ray tube geometry and

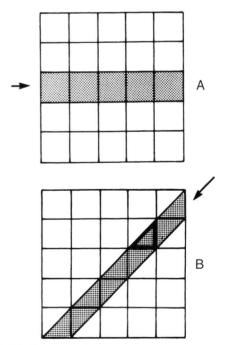

Figure 1–19. Ray projections. *A,* The projection includes only voxels parallel to the matrix representation, and entire voxels are covered. *B,* The projection is oblique to the matrix. A weighting factor must be included for the back-projections to avoid giving these pixels undue influence.

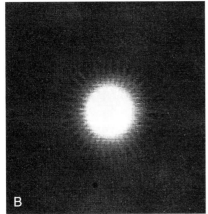

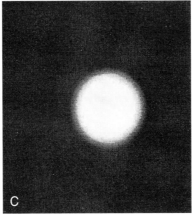

Figure 1–20. Reconstruction by back-projection of a high-density object in diffuse media. Back-projection with 18 views *(A)*, 36 views *(B)*, and 72 views *(C)*. Notice improvement of the image but persistence of star patterns with an increasing number of views. (Courtesy of Michael Mennett, Technicare Corporation, and George Kambic, Marconi Medical Systems.)

detectors. It can take on a number of forms, depending on the desired result.[3, 10] For example, one form of the filter function might enhance edges and thus sharpen the image, whereas another would blur edges for more gradual density changes. The edge-sharpening filter enhances spatial resolution but simultaneously decreases density resolution.

Thus, the choice of filter or kernel affects image quality, and the radiologist should be able to choose the best filter for a particular study. Some manufacturers automatically select the filters for particular procedures instead of requiring the radiologist to choose. Figure 1–22 illustrates the difference in applying various filter functions to the same data.

Image Reconstruction for Spiral CT

As described earlier, spiral scan data are acquired as the patient is moved continuously through the scan field by the table. If the data over a 360-degree rotation of the scan frame were reconstructed as in conventional (axial) CT, motion artifacts attributable to the movement of the table or patient would be visible.[30]

To minimize these artifacts and to reconstruct a planar image anywhere throughout the volume of collected data, some data must be synthesized or interpolated. The simplest form of interpolation is *linear*. Prior to reconstruction, projection data are weighted to produce individual sections of data at select locations. Spiral interpolators apply

weighting factors to segments of the spiral data to estimate the data that would have been measured if an axial scan had occurred at a particular location.

Two common spiral linear interpolators are shown in Figure 1–23. A 360-degree interpolator uses two sets of spiral projections 360 degrees apart. This method assumes that projection data 360 degrees apart would be the exactly the same without patient motion. A 180-degree interpolator assumes that two measurements along the same path but in opposite directions would be the same without patient motion or other errors.

Generally, the more scan data that are used to reconstruct each image, the less noise, the wider the slice profile, and the longer the temporal resolution of the resulting image. Ultimately, the requested slice thickness, pitch, and spiral interpolator used for reconstruction affect the resulting z-axis resolution of spiral scan data.

As mentioned earlier, multislice CT complicates the fan-beam reconstruction techniques used by conventional and spiral CT by adding a divergence of the fan beam along the longitudinal axis (z-axis), creating a cone shape (cone beam) (see Fig. 1–17).

If the number of rows of detectors is limited to a small number (e.g., four rows), the cone-beam divergence is very small relative to the resolution of the detector element. This greatly simplifies the reconstruction of multislice data follows; just as in single-ring spiral reconstruction, only the alignment of projection rays as they cross the z-axis needs to be considered in the interpolation process. In

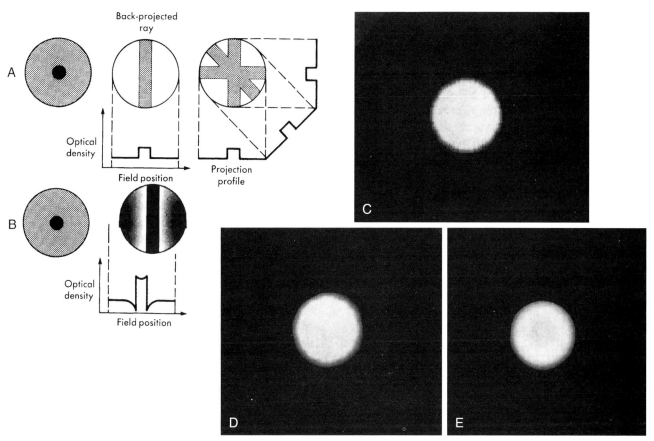

Figure 1–21. Effect of filtering in the back-projection method. *A,* Technique without filtering. *B,* Technique with filtering. The back-projected ray now has an area of decreased intensity directly adjacent to it, as shown by the profile of the back-projected ray optical density. When many projections are used, the negative aspects of the back-projections tend to smooth the image. *C–E,* Effects of performing the filtration function on the images of Figure 1–20 with 18, 36, and 72 views, respectively.

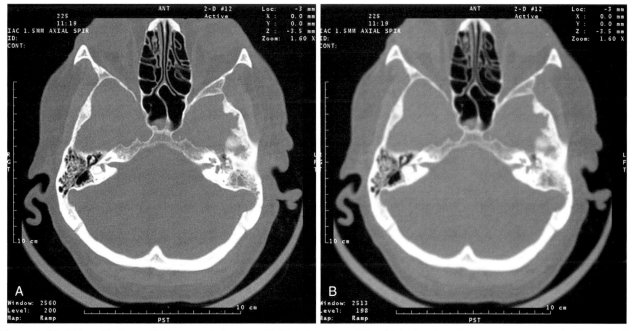

Figure 1–22. Filter effects on CT images. *A,* Image with high-frequency filter. Note the sharp image appearance and enhanced edge detail. *B,* Image with low-frequency (smoothing) filter. Note the blurry effects and decreased image sharpness. This filter increases density resolution at the expense of spatial resolution. (*A* and *B,* Courtesy of Marconi Medical Systems.)

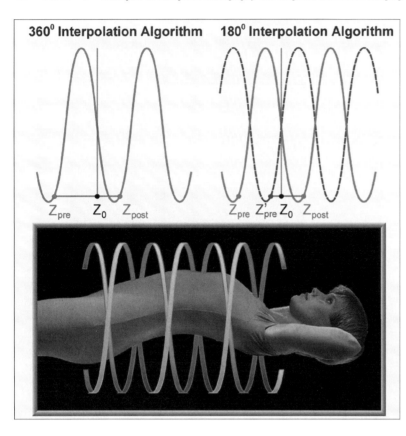

Figure 1–23. Algorithms showing 360- and 180-degree linear spiral interpolation. The 360-degree interpolator weights spiral data over two revolutions of the gantry, and the 180-degree interpolator weights spiral data over one revolution of the gantry.

the case of multislice interpolation, projection rays—either from neighboring detector rows or from rays 180 degrees apart (or more)—may be included in the interpolation.[37]

One interpolation method (spatially invariant) is described as follows:

1. For a scan with a quad-pitch factor of 0.625, up to four rays in the neighborhood of the target slice position are weighted by an interpolation function (designed to extend over the width of two detectors), synthesizing projections for the reconstructed slice.
2. For quad-pitch factors less than 1, this weighting function consistently generates slices with an effective slice width that is 30% broader than the width of one detector.
3. For quad-pitch factors greater than 1, reconstructions are generated from projections synthesized by interpolating only two neighboring projections, again resulting in an effective slice width 30% broader than the width of one detector.

This approach to multislice reconstruction maintains a more uniform resolution for different pitch factors, allowing the user to simply choose smaller pitches for higher effective milliamperage and lower spiral artifacts and larger pitches for maximum patient coverage.

Other multislice reconstruction techniques are available where the interleaving of data is best suited at optimal pitches only.[37] For example, using a linear interpolator at quad-pitch 1.5 (or pitch 6) creates slice-profile broadening of nearly 30%, whereas a quad-pitch of 0.75 (or pitch 3) creates little broadening.[37] Quad-pitches of 0.5 (2), 1 (4), 1.5 (6) and 2 (8) compare in z-axis sampling to single-ring spiral scanning with a pitch of 2.

Display

Image display includes all of the system components necessary to convert the digital data provided by the reconstruction system to electrical signals used by the CT display monitor (cathode ray tube) or flat panel (liquid crystal display), enabling a graphic display of individual CT numbers representing attenuation values of individual sections of anatomy. In addition, the display system includes the ability to display patient information, scan protocol, and reconstruction parameters, and it provides the user many graphic aids to assist in the interpretation of clinical images.

CT Number Scale

After a CT scanner reconstructs an image, the relative pixel values represent the relative linear attenuation coefficients because the process of reconstruction is not conducive to the calculation of the absolute values of the attenuation coefficients. However, it is valuable to quantify the pixel value so that the physician can compare the composition of one tissue with that of another. A CT numbering system that relates a CT number to the linear attenuation coefficients of x rays has been devised and is given by

$$\text{CT number} = \frac{K(\mu - \mu_w)}{\mu_w} \qquad (11)$$

where

μ_w equals the attenuation coefficient of water
μ is the attenuation coefficient of the pixel in question

Although the original EMI CT scanner (Electronics Music Industries, Ltd.) used a value of K = 500, the value of K now used on all CT scanners is 1000. In honor of Godfrey Hounsfield, the inventor of CT scanning,[14] a CT unit is called a *Hounsfield unit* (HU). When HUs are used, air has a value of −1000; water, 0; and dense bone, +1000.

In theory, it is immaterial which value of K is used to construct a CT number scale as long as it can accommodate the accuracy of the scanner. For example, if the density resolution of the scanner is ±0.5%, the relative accuracy for density resolution is 1 part in 200 and a scale of 200 (K = 200) or greater is needed to depict the density resolution accurately. Using a value of K = 1000 expands the scale even more, representing a resolution of 1 part in 2000, or ±0.1%. Magnifying the scale does not improve the accuracy of a scanner; for example, an accuracy of ±0.5% translates to ±2.5 CT numbers with a scale of 500 and to +5 CT numbers with a scale of 1000.

As a general rule, the human eye cannot appreciate contrast differences of less than about 10%, whereas CT scanners can easily demonstrate differences of less than 1%. Thus, the small density-resolution difference measured by the CT scanner must be exaggerated to permit viewing. This is accomplished by enabling the user to select a small range of gray levels from the entire CT number scale and to reset the black and white limits.

For example, the CT numbers of liver tissues lie approximately in the range of 40 to 90 HU on a Hounsfield scale of 1000. If a portion of the scale with a CT number equal to 40 HU or lower is set at black and a CT number equal to 90 HU or greater is set at white, the scale of visualization is 50 HU and the entire range of liver tissues covers a contrast range of 100%. Now a density change of 10 HU on the original scale, which represents a true 1% contrast change, is converted to a 20% (10/50) contrast change on the adjusted range. This provides a large increase in visual contrast.

The range of CT numbers selected for gray scale ampli-

fication is called the *window width* and can generally be selected in scanners from 1 to full scale. (At the setting of 1, all pixels are either black or white.) The position describing the center of the scale is called the *window level*. Figure 1–24 shows a liver scan with different window settings. In this example, one can see the importance of the interactive display and the choice of settings by noting that in wide windows liver metastases are not well visualized.

Other display features and graphic aids assist the user in the interpretation of clinical images beyond window width and level control. For example, users have the ability to select a region of interest (ROI). Magnification of the image within the region of interest for better viewing is called *zoom reconstruction*. Some systems merely expand the image in the region of interest by expanding the pixel size on the viewing screen. This does not improve the accuracy of the scan but does allow possible visualization of some smaller structures because of better optical perception. Other systems increase image size but reconstruct the image with a smaller pixel size. This maneuver not only improves visualization of structures, because of optical reasons, but also increases spatial resolution if the pixel size is not smaller than the inherent resolution of the data (Fig. 1–25) (see "Matrix Size").

The region of interest is also used to acquire more information about pixel statistics, such as values of CT numbers in individual pixels, the average value in a number of pixels, or the number of pixels in a particular circumscribed region.

Several other display features are common to most device manufacturers, including the ability to pan and zoom images, scroll images, or view images in a cine mode. Image orientation can be inverted left to right or up and down. User-defined scales, straight or curved, may be placed anywhere on images. Finally, alphanumeric annotations may be placed anywhere on the displayed image to be filmed at a later time.

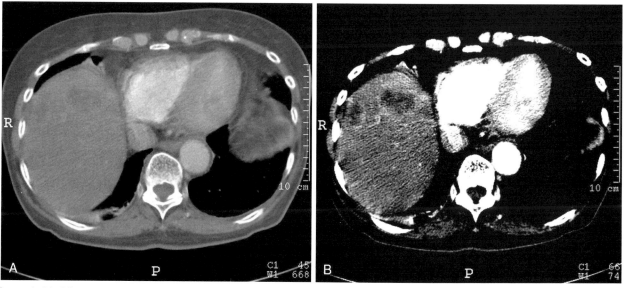

Figure 1–24. Liver scan. *A,* Wide window setting; some lesions are blurred and not visible. *B,* A more appropriate window setting enhances the presence of lesions. (MX8000 multislice CT images courtesy of Dr. John Haaga.)

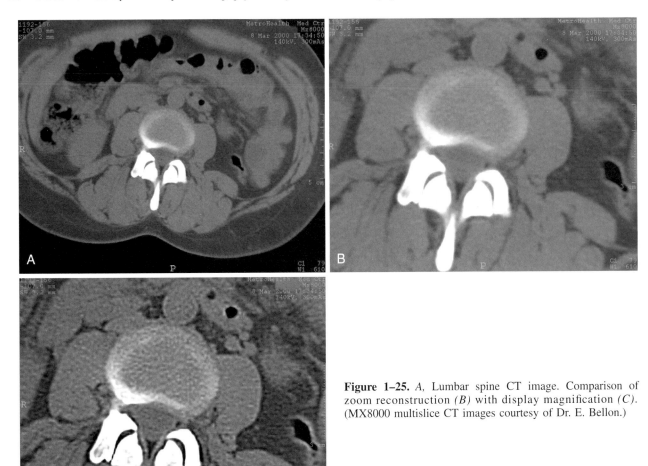

Figure 1–25. *A*, Lumbar spine CT image. Comparison of zoom reconstruction *(B)* with display magnification *(C)*. (MX8000 multislice CT images courtesy of Dr. E. Bellon.)

Advanced Display

Multiplanar Reformatting

Because a conventional CT study consists of several contiguous axial images perpendicular to the long axis of the body (see Fig. 1–1), coronal or sagittal images are not possible except when the gantry is tilted or the body is positioned to show the image in the desired plane. This limitation of CT can be overcome by image manipulation commonly referred to as *multiplanar reformatting* (MPR).

In this process, image data are taken from several axial slices and are reformatted to form images. In this viewing mode, the user defines the number of imaging planes, their position, orientation, thickness, and spacing, and the reformatted image is displayed in sagittal, coronal, or oblique planes. In the x-y plane direction, the pixel of the reformatted image has the same length as the axial image; in the z-direction, however, the pixel length is the same as the slice thickness. Since in most scans the pixel length is considerably smaller than the slice thickness, the reformatted scan can have an unusual appearance (Fig. 1–26). The resolution is quite good in one direction but very poor in another. This problem can be improved by scanning at a small-slice thickness and, as described earlier, the image is best enhanced with the use of spiral/multislice CT scan-

ning, in which longitudinal resolution permits a slice thickness resembling minimal pixel length in the x-y plane. Scanning in this mode is commonly referred to as *isotropic imaging*. Isotropic voxels permit increased visualization of anatomy of complex shapes that do not run linearly along the z-axis (patient axis).

Multiplanar Reconstruction Viewing Mode for Interventional Procedure Guidance

With the use of spiral CT data, an interactive viewing mode consisting of axial and MPR views, as just described, can be employed in conjunction with an articulated arm to create a planning tool for image-guided CT interventional procedures. The arm is mounted on the CT gantry and is calibrated to the CT scanner's coordinate system, including integrated movement of the patient table. As an interventionist moves the arm's needle guide along the patient's skin, axial and MPR images are displayed, representing the needle guide position, trajectory, and depth of a virtual needle path in correlation with the interventional field. Correlation between actual needle placement and the virtual needle path in this method is within a radius of 2 mm (Fig. 1–27A and B).

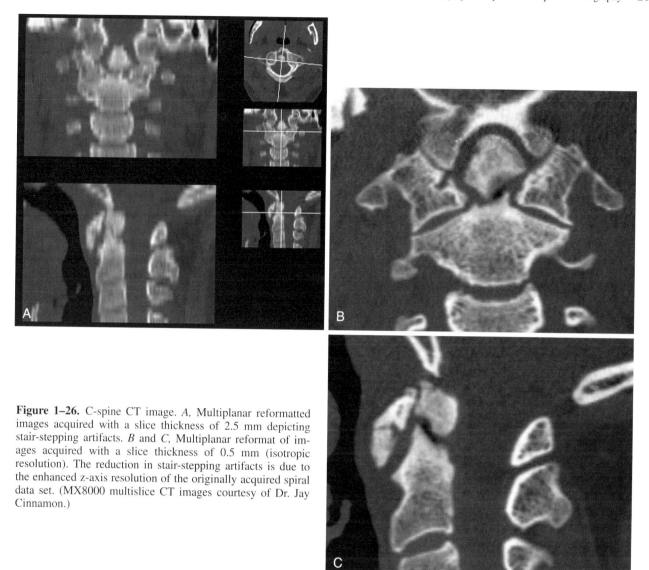

Figure 1–26. C-spine CT image. *A*, Multiplanar reformatted images acquired with a slice thickness of 2.5 mm depicting stair-stepping artifacts. *B* and *C*, Multiplanar reformat of images acquired with a slice thickness of 0.5 mm (isotropic resolution). The reduction in stair-stepping artifacts is due to the enhanced z-axis resolution of the originally acquired spiral data set. (MX8000 multislice CT images courtesy of Dr. Jay Cinnamon.)

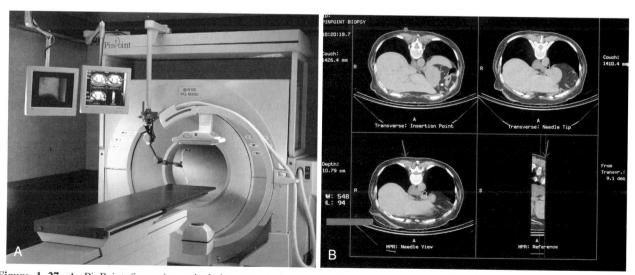

Figure 1–27. *A*, PinPoint five-point articulating arm and needle guide demonstrating relationship of arm to gantry. *B*, PinPoint multiplanar reconstruction (MPR) views used to visualize a virtual needle path to plan interventional procedures.

Data from successive slices can also be reformatted to generate other viewing modes. Three-dimensional *shaded surface, volume rendering,* and *maximum intensity projection* (MIP) are a few examples. Each of these rendering techniques is described in detail.

Figure 1–28A illustrates a small segment of eight voxels representing a large volume data set for demonstration purposes. Each of the eight voxels is shown with their values displayed. A *viewpoint* is defined from where imaginary rays are projected. To simplify the example, we can assume that each ray intersects two voxels, one behind the other.

Three-Dimensional Shaded Surface

For a surface rendition, the user selects a threshold range (Fig. 1–28B). This allows the user to select only the tissue (e.g., bone) to be rendered. The voxels with Hounsfield values within the threshold range are set to the "on" state, whereas the rest of the voxels are set to the "off" state. Depending on the number of bits used for display, "on" and "off" voxels are assigned appropriate values. For an 8-bit display, "on" would be 256 and "off" would be 0.

The second step is to project rays through the entire volume. As the rays pass through the data, they stop when they identify the first "on" voxel. For that particular ray, this first "on" voxel is part of the surface; the other voxels are ignored. This is done for all the rays, and all the "on" voxels are used to create the surface. For our example, the "on" voxels that are part of the surface would be yellow in Figure 1–29C. As the name suggests, only a surface is displayed in this method; there are no details within the surface. Shading the voxels enhances the effect, so that the volume image appears to be illuminated by light sources. Multiple light sources can be used, but a single light source is used in most medical applications.

Three-Dimensional Depth-Based Shading

One type of shading technique is called *depth-based shading.* With this method, those voxels that are closer to the viewer are illuminated at a greater intensity than those that are farther back. As described earlier, it is also possible for the operator to select a range of CT numbers to display. If an operator were interested in a 3D view of the skull, he or she would select the range of CT numbers of the skull. The computer would then assemble those selected voxels

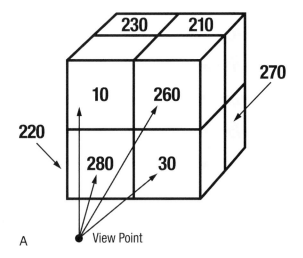

A

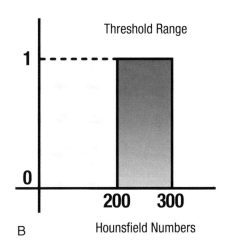

B

Figure 1–28. *A,* Sample of eight-voxel data set with displayed CT number values. *B,* User-defined threshold of CT number values for tissue definition. *C, Shaded* voxels represent defined tissue surface (shaded-surface display). (Courtesy of Shalabh Chandra, Marconi Medical Systems.)

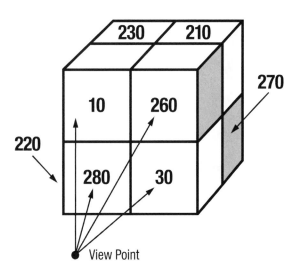

C Gray voxels contribute to the 3D shaded surface

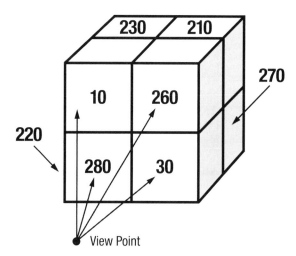

Figure 1–29. Sample of eight-voxel data set with representative opacity values assigned to various CT number ranges. (Courtesy of Shalabh Chandra, Marconi Medical Systems.)

Opacity values for the voxels is given by:

$HU < 50. \ \alpha = 0.0: 50 <= HU < 200. \ \alpha = 0.2: 200 <= HU. \ \alpha = 0.5$

into a 3D image. The result is a reconstructed 3D image of the skull with the soft tissue removed.

As with sagittal and coronal images, the quality of the image is improved by interpolating the data between slices to form a smooth, continuous image. When various 3D views are selected sequentially in time, the 3D image can appear to rotate. These images pose the same challenges as do sagittal and coronal images. The vertical resolution is the same as the slice thickness and not nearly as good as it is in other directions. Thus, spiral/multislice CT dramatically improves 3D viewing because of the inherent ability to cover the same anatomy as a conventional CT scanner at much thinner slice thicknesses and with over-lapped image reconstructions.

Volume Rendering

Another possible viewing mode is *compositing/volume rendering* (VR). VR is an advanced rendering technique that displays an entire volume set with control of the opacity or translucency of selected tissue types. In this case, each voxel has an associated intensity in addition to an associated opacity value. Figure 1–29 shows the same 8-voxel block as Figure 1–28A, with each voxel having an opacity value associated with it. The user can define the opacity values for various HUs. Once the opacity values are assigned, the second step is to pass rays through the volume, accumulating values along the way. The formula for accumulating the values is given as

$$\text{final value} = I_1 \times \alpha_1 + I_2 \times \alpha_2 + \ldots + I_n \times \alpha_n \quad (12)$$

where

$\alpha_{1+} \ldots + \alpha_n \leq 1.0$

I_n is the intensity of the voxel n

α_n is the opacity associated with the voxel n

n is the number of voxels added before the opacity values sum up to 1.0, or it is the total number of voxels along that ray for that data set

Using this formula along with the voxel intensity and opacity values shown in the example, one can calculate the final image. Figure 1–30 demonstrates the results.

The obvious advantage of VR over 3D shaded-surface rendering is that it provides volume information. By using transparency, the operator can visualize information beyond the surface. For example, VR is the preferred viewing mode for stent evaluation because stents can be made transparent to view the lumen of vessels. Other clinical examples include the ability to make plaque transparent for more accurate diagnosis of vessel stenosis.

Maximum Intensity Projection

Using *maximum* or *minimum intensity projection* (MIP) for visualization permits easy viewing of vascular structures or air-filled cavities. Compared with 3D or volume-rendering techniques, MIP is a relatively simple method. Unlike 3D shaded-surface and VR displays, no preprocessing is required. The rays are cast throughout the volume, and depending on whether it is maximum or minimum intensity projection, maximum or minimum values along the rays are used in the final image display. On the basis of the 8-voxel example described earlier, Figure 1–31A and B shows the final pixel values for maximum and minimum intensity projections.

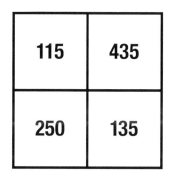

Volume Rendered, 4-D Angio, Composited

Figure 1–30. Image results for volume-rendered image of Figure 1–29.

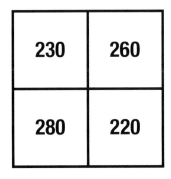

MIP - Maximum Intensity Projection
A

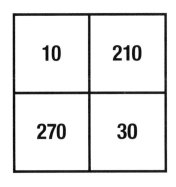

MIP - Minimum Intensity Projection
B

Figure 1–31. *A,* Maximum intensity projection of a sample voxel in which only maximum values are displayed. *B,* Minimum intensity projection in which only minimum values are displayed.

MIP is a preferred method for many CT angiography applications, since visualization of contrast-filled vasculature is fast and easy. Maximum intensity projection enables easy viewing of an entire vessel in one image. This is true because voxels representing the contrast-filled vessels are most likely to be the ones with the highest values along the ray (assuming no bone along the ray). Along the same lines, minimum intensity projection can be used to demonstrate air-filled cavities.

Image Quality

Several quantitative measurements are used to define a CT system's image quality:

- Spatial resolution
- Contrast resolution
- Noise
- Slice sensitivity profile
- Temporal resolution
- Dose

Spatial Resolution

Spatial resolution is measured by the ability of a CT system to distinguish two small high-contrast objects located very close to each other under noise-free conditions. Optimal spatial resolution is required for evaluating high-contrast areas of anatomy, such as the inner ear, orbits, sinuses, and bone in general because of their complicated shapes.

Spatial resolution can be specified by spatial frequencies, which indicate how efficiently the CT scanner represents different frequencies. *Modulation transfer function* (MTF) describes this property. A 2D *Fourier transform* of the point spread function, taken with a very thin wire, provides MTF values. These concepts will be described shortly.

Consider the image of a point source that can be obtained by placing a thin wire on end in water or plastic and then scanning across the wire. Ideally, the resulting image should be a uniform background with a bright dot denoting the position of the wire. In fact, the image does demonstrate the bright dot but with a fading periphery rather than an absolutely sharp edge.

A profile across the image (i.e., a plot of the picture density along a line passing through the point source center) produces a bell-shaped distribution, called the *point response distribution.* The height of this curve represents the maximum value of the density, and the width represents the uncertainty in the measurement of the exact boundaries of the wire.

Full width at half-maximum (FWHM) is the width of the curve at the point where the attenuation values are 50% of the peak value (Fig. 1–32). The smaller the FWHM, the better the resolution. One can appreciate this fact by noting that a large FWHM reflects a larger fading periphery, which means a poorer reproduction of the actual object.

Another method of examining spatial resolution is to consider line images. This is similar to examining point images; however, the scan would be done parallel to a wire in a medium rather than across the axis. If a series of lines of different spacing or of different sizes were used, the ability to distinguish separate lines in an image would measure the spatial resolution.

With very fine lines, a measure of the resolution can be stated in terms of the number of lines that are still discernible, packed together in a given distance. Thus, one would speak of the number of lines per centimeter that could be visualized in the image. Describing the spatial resolution in terms of lines per centimeter is said to describe the resolution in the frequency domain. The frequency, in this case, is the parameter, lines per centimeter. A profile across the line image yields the *line response curve,* which is similar to the *point response curve.* Again, one can speak of FWHM, and the analysis is similar to that done with the point source. Obviously, the two response curves are related.

Performing a mathematical operation, the Fourier transform, on these response curves yields the MTF.[7, 19] The physical interpretation of the MTF is that it displays the relative fidelity of the image compared with the actual object.

Another description of MTF is shown in Figure 1–33. The rectangular profile represents the density profile of an object composed of dense lines. The density profile of the reconstructed image is shown as rectangles with rounded corners.

As the lines become closer together, the region between lines fills in because of the overlap of the response functions. The ratio of the height of the rectangles to the height

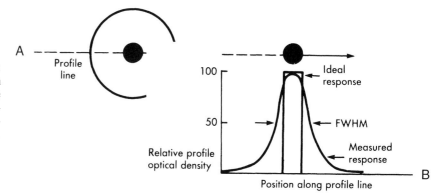

Figure 1–32. Definition of full width at half-maximum (FWHM). *A,* Solid body in uniform media. *B,* Profile across the image demonstrates the fading periphery of the image of the body. The rectangular curve represents the ideal response with sharp edges.

of the valley between lines becomes smaller as the lines become closer in the reconstructed image but, obviously, is fixed in the object. This change, or decrease, in ratio is seen as a decrease in contrast and is a manifestation of the decreasing ability of the system to resolve small objects (or small separation of objects). The MTF is basically the value of this ratio in the image divided by the value of the ratio in the object. As the frequency increases (i.e., more lines per centimeter), the ability of the system to reproduce the lines and valleys accurately is decreased and the fidelity also therefore decreases.

With widely separated lines, the MTF is 1—the maximum value; as the frequency increases, the MTF drops. Thus, the higher the MTF at a given frequency, the better the fidelity (i.e., the better the resolution).

In systems with large values of MTF at high frequencies, edges are more clearly defined; such systems produce images that appear sharp. If high frequencies are exaggerated relative to low frequencies, the result is an edge enhancement. Techniques for such high-frequency enhancement are often used to advantage in radiology, and this is the main purpose of xeroradiographic methods or

subtraction methods. In Figure 1–34, curve A denotes a system with an MTF better than that shown by curve B; in this case, system A would have better resolution than system B.

The spatial resolution (composite MTF) is affected by many design parameters. The most important are as follows:

- Choice of filter used in reconstruction
- Opening size of detector aperture
- Number of projection profiles obtained
- Matrix (or pixel) size
- Focal spot size of the x-ray tube
- Relative object-to-background contrast (density)

The last two parameters in this listing are presented after the topic "Contrast/Density Resolution and Image Noise" (see later). Samples (rays and view or number of detectors), and not other parameters, gate the composite MTF for most third-generation systems. Focal spot size or detector aperture size typically gates the composite MTF of fourth-generation systems.

Filter Effects on Resolution

As discussed earlier, the major role of the convolution filter is to remove the image blurring created by the back-

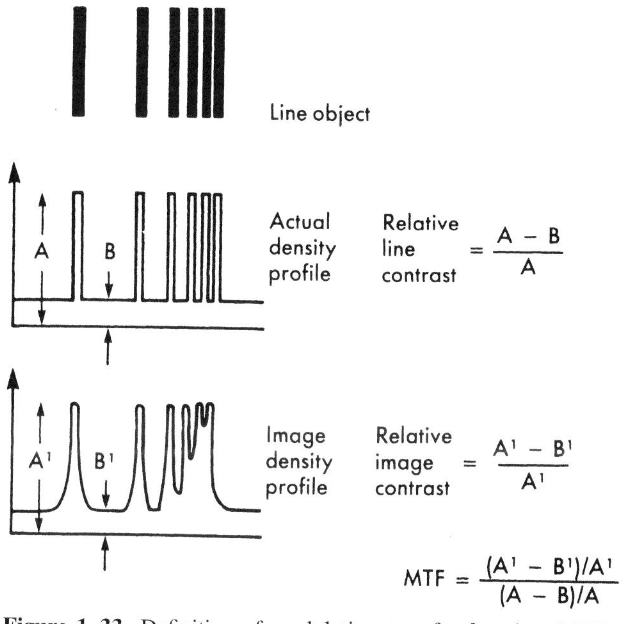

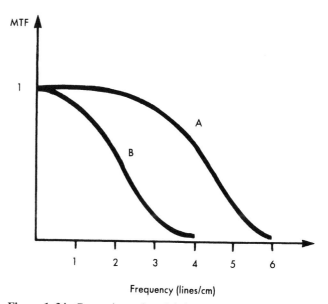

Figure 1–33. Definition of modulation transfer function (MTF). As the line frequency increases, the relative image contrast decreases, which is reflected in the fall of the MTF.

Figure 1–34. Comparison of modulation transfer function (MTF) of two theoretical systems. The system represented by *A* demonstrates a better spatial resolution than that of *B.*

projection process. Various filters control the amount of image blurring created by accentuating high-frequency components found in the data. For a crisp image, the high spatial frequencies are accentuated, and this has the effect of sharpening the edges and improving resolution. If the high spatial frequencies are not accentuated, the image of the object appears more blurred.

A tradeoff is that image noise increases and the density resolution diminishes with accentuation of high spatial frequencies. One pays for a crisp picture with a decrease in density resolution. Similarly, by increasing density resolution, one pays by loss of some spatial resolution and image crispness.

Opening Size of Detector Aperture

The detector aperture MTF curve is dependent on the magnification factor of the system (focal spot to detector distance/focal spot to object distance) and the physical size of the detector.

Consider the rotate-only scanner (Fig. 1–35). As the system rotates, the ray projection for a particular detector acts as the cord of the circle rotating about the center at a distance, R. The aperture opening for a particular detector, therefore, is associated with a particular data ring about the center. It is clear from the diagram that as the aperture size increases or decreases, the width of the data ring increases or decreases correspondingly. The width of this data ring characterizes the attenuation profile and is crucial to the spatial resolution. For example, if the object being viewed is smaller than the width of the data ring, it will be difficult to resolve because it occupies only a fraction of the space seen by the detector.

Typical detector apertures of CT systems today range from less than 1 mm to 1.5 mm, with center-to-center detector spacing of approximately 1 mm.

Number of Projection Profiles

As stated previously, to obtain a solution for the image reconstruction, Equation 10 must be obtained for each

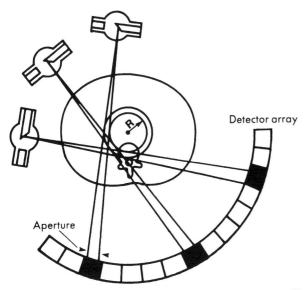

Figure 1–35. Single-ring, third-generation detector aperture. The thickness of the ring depends on the aperture opening.

value of λ needed. Therefore, if one wishes to reconstruct an image with a matrix of n columns by n rows, then n^2 measurements or ray sums must be obtained. With the large number of detectors used in present machines, this criterion is easily met. Although this criterion is necessary, it is not sufficient to guarantee the requisite resolution, and the question of optimum number of angular measurements or views must be answered.

Review Figure 1–35, and note that the resolution depends not only on the thickness of the data ring but also on the arc length of the data ring section between radiation measurements. Theoretically, this optimum number depends on required resolution and object size.[18, 26] To obtain resolution of 1 mm with small or average-sized bodies, 300 to 400 views may suffice; for larger bodies, 700 to 800 views may be needed. All current instruments of both the stationary detector type and rotate-only type have the capability of meeting these requirements. In many machines, these needs are exceeded significantly, allowing spatial resolution down to the range of 0.25 mm.

Matrix Size

It is rather obvious that the spatial resolution can be no better than the size represented by the pixel length. In reality pixel size should be 1½ to 2 times smaller than the desired resolution. Unless a matrix element exactly coincides with an object, the object representation will be averaged over two or more pixels and thus may not be visualized. It must be realized that the pixel size refers to the FOV (or body), not the viewing screen or film. For example, in a field size of 50 cm in diameter, a matrix size of 512 × 512 would indicate that each pixel represents a 0.98 × 0.98 mm area in the FOV:

$$\text{pixel size (mm)} = \frac{\text{FOV (500 mm)}}{\text{matrix (512)}} \qquad (13)$$

Typical matrix sizes available in scanners today are 512 × 512 and 1024 × 1024. Most CT scanner display systems include zoom factors. If a zoom factor is used, the formula for pixel size must be modified to reflect the decreased FOV as follows:

$$\text{pixel size} = \frac{\text{scan FOV}}{\text{matrix} \times \text{zoom}} \qquad (14)$$

The imaging goal is to match the pixel size with the inherent resolution of the CT system and scan protocol/filter selection for each examination. As discussed earlier, spatial resolution is measured in line pairs per centimeter. To convert this to millimeters, use the following formula:

$$\text{spatial resolution (mm)} = \frac{10}{2} \times \frac{\text{lp}}{\text{cm}} \qquad (15)$$

To illustrate the concept, consider a high-resolution study with a protocol and reconstruction filter designed to achieve a spatial resolution of 20 lp/cm and an FOV of 250 mm. Converting 20 lp/cm to spatial resolution in millimeters using the preceding formula results in 0.25 mm spatial resolution.

In the figure: Detector array, Aperture, R

To achieve a pixel size of 0.25 mm without zooming, the reconstructed FOV requires a matrix of 1024 × 1024 (250 mm/0.25 = 1000). To use a matrix of less than 1024 × 1024 would suggest a visual loss of spatial detail. The data are available but cannot be viewed.

Spiral and Multislice Spiral CT Effects on Spatial Resolution

Factors that affect in-plane spatial resolution for spiral and multislice spiral CT are the same as for conventional CT, although spatial resolution greater than 10 lp/cm (see third-generation CT earlier) is limited to axial modes of scanning or to manufacturers who employ special x-ray tube focal spot techniques to increase the data sampling rate during spiral scanning.

Unlike *in-plane* resolution, reconstruction in this chapter refers to a potential loss of z-dimension *(through-plane)* spatial resolution (for a given slice width) during spiral or multislice spiral CT. The loss of resolution, as measured at the FWHM of the slice sensitivity profile, is dependent on the spiral interpolation algorithm used during reconstruction and, in some cases, the pitch factor used. This phenomenon is less relevant for multislice spiral CT. This is evidenced by the fundamental clinical benefit of multislice spiral CT in covering more anatomy with thinner slices (better z-axis spatial resolution) compared with the benefits of conventional spiral CT.

The issue of degraded slice sensitivity profiles based on interpolating techniques in this case is fairly moot. For example, a best-case, single breath-hold examination, completed with the use of single-ring spiral CT at a given dose and level of image quality, may require a slice thickness of 5 mm. This same examination can be completed in less time with a slice thickness of 2.5 mm using multislice spiral CT.

Whether the slice sensitivity profile at FWHM broadens to 2.8 mm or to 3.2 mm becomes irrelevant. However, radiologists should become familiar with the typical slice broadening associated with different protocols on the CT scanner in use at their practice. Some manufacturers report the actual slice thickness, whereas others report only the requested slice thickness. It is important for radiologists to know the difference because the slice sensitivity profile indicates the CT scanner's ability to image objects within a given slice thickness. If the actual slice thickness is larger than expected, partial-volume averaging may affect the axial image quality. In addition, MPR reconstruction may be moderately affected.

Contrast/Density Resolution and Image Noise

The second major factor affecting the ability of a scanner to accurately describe anatomy is contrast, or density resolution, or the ability to differentiate the attenuation coefficients of adjacent areas of tissue. Because most soft tissues have densities that are very nearly the same, usually the differentiation of variations of a few percent or less are considered. In the computation of any single pixel value,

there is error in the form of statistical variation; it is this variation that limits the ultimate contrast resolution. This variation (called image noise) is manifested as a grainy background, or mottle. The parameter used to evaluate this variation is the standard deviation (SD, or σ), and the usual procedure for evaluating a system is to obtain a scan of a uniform substance, such as water, and to compute the SD by the following formula:

$$SD = \sigma = \sqrt{\frac{\sum_{i=1}^{n}(CT_i - \overline{CT})^2}{n-1}} \qquad (16)$$

$$\overline{CT} = \frac{1}{n}(CT_1 + CT_2 + \ldots + CT_n) \qquad (17)$$

where

n is the number of pixels used in the evaluation
$\overline{CT}$ is the average pixel value for n pixels
CT_i represents individual pixel values

The meaning of the SD is that rescanning of the same water bath and a recalculation of the same pixel CT numbers would yield values in a range equal to the previously calculated value ± SD in approximately two out of three instances. The SD, therefore, describes the uncertainty in a measurement and is commonly expressed in terms of percentages. This percentage is obtained by dividing the computed SD in CT units by the range of the scale.

For example, SD equal to 5 HU on a Hounsfield scale of +1000 would translate to 5 HU/1000 HU = 0.005, or 0.5%. The interpretation is that two adjacent pixels are not significantly different if their CT numbers vary by 5 HU or less.

Since noise is the ultimate limitation in the accuracy of the density resolution, parameters that affect or induce noise need to be understood. The most important parameters are (1) photon flux, (2) x-ray scatter, (3) computation-induced error, (4) filter frequency response, and (5) voxel size. The effect of filters was discussed previously.

In any ray measurement, the statistical variation associated with that measurement is directly proportional to the number of photons detected. If I is the number of detected photons, the SD is given by the square root of I, and the relative noise in a ray measurement is given by

$$\frac{\sqrt{I}}{I}$$

which reduces to

$$\frac{1}{\sqrt{I}}$$

Because the variation in a ray measurement is propagated into every pixel computation, which involves the ray, the relative image noise is affected inversely as the square root of the detected photon flux. Large photon fluxes, or increases in milliamperes, as controlled by the radiologist, can reduce relative noise; unfortunately, they also increase radiation dose levels. Therefore, limits on CT image noise reduction are imposed by practical limitations of increased dose to patients. The radiologist has an obligation to accept the highest noise image (lowest dose protocol) that is possible consistent with a definitive diagnosis.

The photon intensity that is detected, not the intensity impingement on the patient, must be taken into consideration, as mentioned previously. The efficiency of the detector, impinging photon flux, size of the patient, and presence of high-attenuation materials affect the detected intensity and, in turn, the uncertainty in the measurement. The image of a large patient thus has a more mottled appearance than the image of a small patient for the same tube output. Similarly, the presence of a high-contrast object, such as bone or a prosthesis, causes increased noise by reducing the transmitted photon flux.

Another aspect of noise is x-ray scatter. Because image-energy discrimination cannot be used in systems with the continuous energy spectrum obtained from an x-ray tube, no detector in particular can discriminate between a primary photon directly from the source and a scattered photon arising from an area not in the line of the ray projection. In the energy range used in scanners, many photons are scattered through small angles. The effect is to alter the recorded values in adjacent detectors. This produces a decrease in differences between adjacent measurements with a concomitant decrease in contrast resolution. The sharp interfaces between tissues also are diminished by this phenomenon, causing a reduction in spatial resolution.

The amount of scattering that is detected is controlled by collimation of the detectors. Smaller apertures reduce scattering and therefore reduce the noise component due to scattered photons. The measured intensity is also affected by the voxel length (i.e., slice thickness). If the slice thickness is reduced by 50%, the detector collimator size must be reduced accordingly, which in turn reduces the intensity by the same amount. To retain the same accuracy, one must restore the detected photon intensity, which means doubling the dose.

Similarly, decreasing pixel size increases the relative inaccuracy unless the photon flux is raised. If the pixel side

length is reduced by half, the voxel volume represented by the pixel is reduced by a factor of 4. The SD of the resulting calculated CT number, shown earlier to vary as the square root, would double. The image would become more mottled in appearance, and the contrast resolution would deteriorate. To restore the uncertainty to its previous value, one would need to increase the radiation dose by a factor of 4.

These relationships between the factors of slice thickness (h), pixel size (L), SD (σ), and radiation dose (D) are shown[6] as

$$\sigma = \frac{C}{[DhL^2]^{1/2}} \qquad (18)$$

where C is a constant.

This relationship also emphasizes that low contrast/density resolution (as reflected through the SD) is related to spatial resolution (as reflected through aperture opening or pixel size), and these two factors of image quality cannot be treated completely separately. Spatial resolution is usually stated for objects of high contrast. In CT scanning, attenuation coefficient differences of approximately 12% or greater are considered high contrast. As contrast differences decrease, spatial resolution also decreases. Figure 1–36 demonstrates the resolution obtained by viewing similar line phantoms but with various contrast differences.[1]

For a given dose level, regardless of the size of the object, a minimum density resolution exists, and, regardless of dose or contrast, there is a minimum size that can be resolved. Changing the dose level alters the minimum density resolution but not the spatial resolution limits[11] (Fig. 1–37).

Spiral and Multislice Spiral CT Effects on Contrast Resolution and Image Noise

The same variables that affect image noise and contrast resolution for conventional CT—slice thickness, kilovolt-

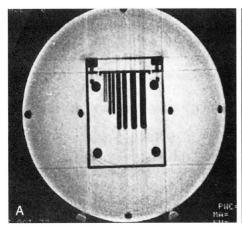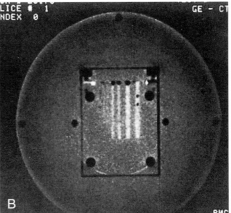

Figure 1–36. Line phantom. *A,* High-contrast line pairs; note the clarity. The diameter of the pairs and center-to-center distances are 5, 3, 2, and 1 mm. *B,* The same phantom with low contrast difference between the lines and the surrounding media. Notice the relatively poor spatial resolution, compared with *A,* and the inability to visualize the finer lines. This demonstrates the relationship between contrast and spatial resolution. (From Bellon EM, Miraldi FD, Wiesen EJ: Performance of evaluation of computed tomography scanners using a phantom model. Am J Roentgenol 132:345–352, 1979. Copyright American Roentgen Ray Society, 1979.)

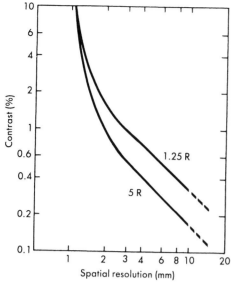

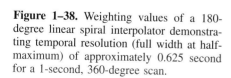

Figure 1–37. Interplay of spatial resolution, density resolution, and radiation dose. As the dose level increases, contrast resolution improves. High-contrast resolution is fixed and cannot be improved by the dose level. For a given dose level, objects with sizes and contrast that lie above the curve can be resolved; those below the curve cannot be resolved. (From CT/T Continuum: Evaluation Criteria. Milwaukee, General Electric Medical Systems, 1980.)

age, milliamperage, patient size, voxel size, and convolution filter—affect spiral and multislice spiral CT, with the added variables of table speed (pitch) and spiral interpolation algorithm. For a given pitch, using more scan data to reconstruct an image (with linear interpolation) reduces noise and enhances contrast resolution at the expense of z-axis spatial resolution.[20, 29]

Temporal resolution refers to the ability of a CT scanner to capture objects that change shape or position over time and depends primarily on the gantry rotation speed and the reconstruction method used. For conventional CT using a full 360 degrees of scan data, temporal resolution is equivalent to scan time per rotation. A 1-second scan has a 1-second temporal resolution.

For spiral or multislice spiral CT, temporal resolution is dependent on the gantry rotation speed and the spiral interpolating algorithm used during reconstruction. Figure 1–38 depicts a 180-degree linear interpolator that demonstrates the relative spiral weighting values applied to projection data at the center of an axial slice. The central 180 degrees of data, including the fan angle (~50 to 55 degrees) are acquired in approximately 0.625 second for a gantry rotating at a speed of one revolution per second. The temporal resolution (FWHM) for a 360-degree linear interpolator, which uses 720 degrees of scan data, is approximately 1.25 seconds, or double that of the 180-degree interpolator.

A recent advancement that permits the reconstruction of projection data at prescribed intervals coincident with a patient's heart rate (electrocardiographic waveform) permits reconstruction techniques that can reduce effective temporal resolution to approximately 100 msec or less for data acquired using 0.5-second gantry rotation speeds. As described in Chapter 63, temporal resolution of this magnitude permits entirely new applications for CT such as cardiac and functional CT imaging.

Patient Radiation Dose

The amount of irradiation a patient receives during a CT examination is a function of many parameters. The dose can vary considerably from scanner to scanner and from image to image, depending on what is required by the radiologist (see preceding discussion). There are many methods of measuring and characterizing radiation delivered by CT.

Most methods use a standard cylindrical dosimetry phantom, with the dosimeters placed on the surface of and inside the phantom.[1, 22, 25] Measurements made on this type of phantom should not be considered a precise measurement of patient dose. True patient dose is not very well simulated by a perfectly cylindrical plastic phantom because of such factors as positioning errors, variations in patient shape, and uncertain x-ray attenuation. However, these methods are useful in demonstrating how dose varies as a function of operating conditions and between scanners.

Figure 1–38. Weighting values of a 180-degree linear spiral interpolator demonstrating temporal resolution (full width at half-maximum) of approximately 0.625 second for a 1-second, 360-degree scan.

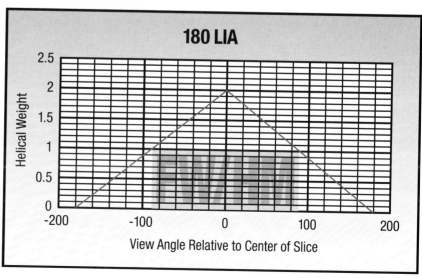

Most methods involve measuring the surface and internal doses for single slices and multiple, contiguous slices. There is a nonuniformity of absorbed dose distribution from different CT scanners because of various scanning conditions, system geometries, x-ray beam collimations, and filtration systems that make single-number dose descriptions, such as peak and average doses, inadequate.

Another concept suggested by Bureau of Radiological Health personnel to overcome some of these problems is the *computed tomography dose index* (CTDI).[25] To obtain the CTDI, a pencil-shaped ion chamber is inserted in a hole drilled in a plastic phantom. One single-slice measurement is taken. Because the ion chamber is long in relation to slice thickness, the ion chamber measures primary radiation as well as all scatter radiation. A single number that represents the average dose for a single scan is obtained. Holes may be placed at any depth along the axis of the phantom to measure the dose at any depth.

The *multiple scan average dose* (MSAD) represents the average dose delivered to a patient for a series of axial scans. This dose can be calculated by multiplying the ratio of the slice width to table index by the CTDI.

Values of skin dose can vary from a few tenths of 1 rad to high values above 15 rad and are controlled by the technique set by the operator. Depending on the x-ray beam primary energy, the amount of filtering in the beam, and the number of slices scanned, the patient internal dose may approach the skin dose for multiple slices.[25] Organs located outside the scanned volume will receive a dose because of scattered radiation from that volume and some leakage radiation from the x-ray tube housing. At distances of more than 1 cm from the scanned volume, the internal dose is relatively low.[22]

From the previous sections and as related by Equation 18, the inclination is to improve image quality by increasing the dose. Obviously, the radiologist must exercise prudence to obtain the necessary clinical information at the lowest possible radiation levels. Several published studies[16, 21, 27] have demonstrated that results of adequate clinical examinations can frequently be obtained with a great reduction in dose and with picture aesthetics as the only significant difference.

As described earlier, both spiral CT and multislice spiral CT generate axial/planar slices from a volume of data collected while the patient is continuously moved through the x-ray beam. As such, controlling the speed of table movement (pitch) can affect the average patient dose for the total examination.

As an example, consider a protocol with a slice width of 5 mm and a pitch of 5 mm, or pitch factor of 1:1. Extending the pitch factor from 1:1 to 2:1 by increasing the pitch to 10 mm effectively reduces the average patient dose in this examination by 50%. Conversely, reducing the pitch factor from 1:1 to 0.5:1 by slowing the pitch from 5 mm to 2.5 mm effectively increases the average dose by a factor of 2.

Multislice spiral CT complicates this equation somewhat, and z-axis dose efficiency must be considered. In this case, z-axis dose efficiency is defined as the ratio of the FWHM of the sensitivity profile to the FWHM of the radiation profile expressed as a percentage. For multislice systems, the FWHM of the sensitivity profile is the sum of the individual slices produced by that radiation profile. The z-axis efficiency of multislice CTs varies by manufacturer but can be expected to approach 100% at slice thicknesses between 5 and 10 mm, gradually falling off in efficiency to approximately 75% at slice thicknesses of 1mm. This falloff in efficiency is due to the penumbra-to-umbra ratio of the x-ray beam and is unique to multislice spiral CT. This is true because both the penumbra and umbra are detected with single-ring spiral CT systems but not true for today's multislice CT systems.

System geometry, x-ray tube focal spot length, and other collimation factors affect this ratio. In general, the wider the collimated beam, the smaller the penumbra-to-umbra ratio and, therefore, the lower the effect on z-axis efficiency. Manufacturers continue to develop new methods to improve z-axis efficiency with multislice spiral CT, and improvements are probable in the near term.

One final note: As the z-axis width of detectors increases from today's quad-slice systems to 8, 16, 32, 48 slices and beyond, z-axis efficiency will improve.

Image Artifacts and Their Causes

There are many causes of artifacts on an image, and it is important for the radiologist to recognize all types so that they can be eliminated or minimized.

Streak and Ring Artifacts

Streak and ring artifacts are usually the result of difficulty with the detector (Fig. 1–39*A* and *B*). With third-generation scanners, ring artifacts are seen if the x-ray detector is not properly calibrated.

In Figure 1–36, each detector is associated with a data ring. A malfunction of any one detector incorrectly back-projects along the data ring to produce the ring artifact. If a detector is not matched or is not intercalibrated accurately, the back-projection for each data ring would be slightly different, causing multiple rings. Poor alignment of tube and detector causes misplacement of calculated values, since measured values are occurring in lines different from those assumed by the reconstruction algorithm. The result can be blurring edges if the misalignment is slight or ring or streak artifact if the misalignment is great. Detectors in the center of the detector arc are most sensitive.

Fourth-generation scanners are more sensitive to streak artifacts due to failure of a detector. However, because of the large number of views available, data for the failed detector can be synthesized through interpolation.

Metal and Bone Artifacts

The presence of objects having an exceptionally high or low attenuation can create artifacts by forcing the detector to operate in a nonlinear response region. Because this incorrect response occurs at specific directions of the beam through the object, incomplete cancellation of the back-projected rays during reconstruction occurs and yields streaking artifacts. Metallic pins, for example, can give rise to streaks, as can gas (Fig. 1–40).

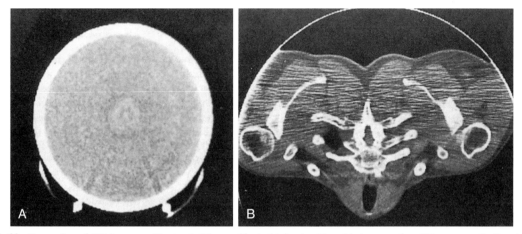

Figure 1–39. Examples of CT image artifacts. *A,* Ring artifact obtained with a third-generation CT scanner. *B,* Streak artifacts.

The range of x-ray intensity values to which the scanner can accurately respond linearly is called the *dynamic range*. The larger the dynamic range, the less prone the instrument is to creating such artifacts. In most new scanners, the dynamic range is a factor of 1 million to 1, which greatly reduces the metallic artifact problem.[12]

Beam-Hardening Artifacts

Beam-hardening artifacts result from the preferential absorption of low-energy photons from the beam. In the range of kilovoltage used in CT scanners, a prominent mode of interaction is the photoelectric process, and in this region the low-energy photons are preferentially absorbed. Thus, as a beam traverses the body, the average beam photon energy is progressively increased. Accordingly, toward the end of the x-ray path, the attenuation is less than at the beginning because the attenuation coefficient is smaller with higher energy. The reconstruction program, however, assumes a monochromatic beam and attributes any change in beam intensity to a change in tissue composition rather than to the result of a shift in average photon

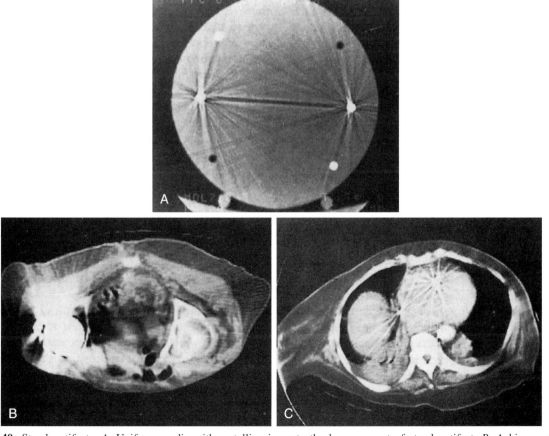

Figure 1–40. Streak artifacts. *A,* Uniform media with metallic pin; note the large amount of streak artifact. *B,* A hip prosthesis. *C,* Starburst streaks from clips in the pulsating heart of conventional (single-ring) CT scanner.

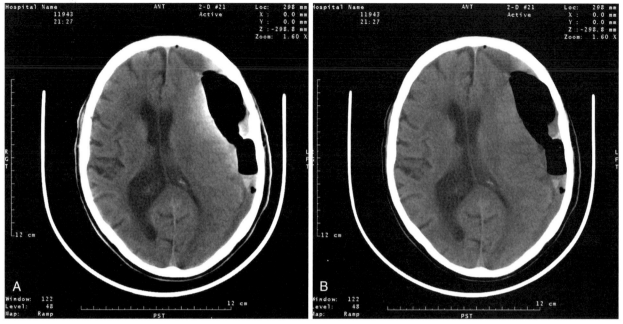

Figure 1–41. Beam-hardening artifacts. *A,* Postoperative CT image of the brain in an adult. *B,* Comparison of reductions in beam-hardening artifacts with use of iterative reconstruction technique. A corrected image using UltraImage reconstruction technique. (Courtesy of Marconi Medical Systems.)

energy. The assigned attenuation coefficients are thus in error, and the densities seen on the image are in error. The effect is most pronounced in regions of large attenuation, such as bone.

The artifact is seen as a shadow beneath the ribs, for example, or increased shadows in the mediastinum or skull (Fig. 1–41*A* and *B*). This effect occurs throughout the image, but qualitatively it is not usually perceived except where there is a great deal of hardening (e.g., in the vicinity of bone). This effect can be compensated for by use of a correction method that consists of forward-projecting only the "bone" portion of an image and by determining the required correction via a polynomial.[36]

Partial-Volume Artifacts

When tissues of widely varying absorption properties occupy the same voxel, the beam attenuation is proportional to the average value of the attenuation coefficient of the voxel. A volume average is computed for such voxels, leading to the partial-volume error. A common site of such an effect is the lung-diaphragm interface, where an increased density may be attributed to the lung base when, in reality, it does not exist (Fig. 1–42). A partial-volume artifact can be subtle and gradual, requiring care in interpretation. Another common partial-volume artifact is observed in scans of the head in the posterior fossa region.[31]

Motion Artifacts

A motion-induced artifact is usually streak or starburst in appearance and occurs where there are high-density or low-density interfaces (e.g., gas in the bowel) (Fig. 1–43). This occurs because movement during the measurement process causes structures to be in different positions when

different views are taken so the back-projections are not added correctly. Artifacts can also appear as "double imaging," with the same outline shown twice.

Stair-Stepping Artifacts

Stair-stepping artifacts (see earlier) occur when in one direction the pixel of the reformatted image has the same length as the axial image but in the other direction the pixel length is the same as the slice thickness. Because pixel length in most scans is considerably smaller than slice thickness, the reformatted scan has an unusual appearance (see Fig. 1–26).

Spiral Pitch Artifacts

Pitch artifacts appear primarily because larger pitch factors are used to attain maximum coverage. Spiral artifacts exhibit similar stepping as axial scans in reformatted images, except that the steps appear as a spiral groove (Fig. 1–44).

Multislice pitch artifacts (again for large pitch factors) have a unique appearance in axial scans; a star pattern is seen off of sharp edges, where the number of spokes in the star is directly related to the number of multislice detector rows (Fig. 1–45).[35, 37] This is because each row contributes only a portion of its projection data to the multislice reconstruction.

Cone-Beam Artifacts

As the number of rows in a multislice scanner increases, the divergence of the cone beam along the z-axis becomes significant relative to the detector width. For a small num-

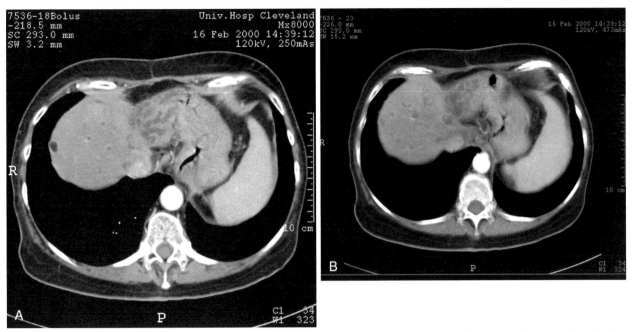

Figure 1–42. Liver scan representing enhanced lesion detection and reduced partial-volume artifacts in *A* (2.5-mm slice thickness) versus *B* (10-mm slice thickness). (Multislice CT image courtesy of Dr. John Haaga.)

ber of rows, this effect is small and noticeable only for sharp objects distant from the scan center. For scanners with eight or more rows, the cone-beam effect becomes more significant, requiring the reconstruction process to account for the divergence effect (Fig. 1–46).

Summary

The tradeoff between spatial resolution (x-y), contrast resolution, and patient dose has been optimized for CT since the early 1980s. To obtain more low-contrast resolution for a given spatial resolution, the patient dose must increase. To obtain more contrast resolution while maintaining patient dose, spatial resolution must decrease. In short, before the late 1980s, the fundamental laws of physics prevented significant improvements in 2D CT imaging without increasing patient dose. The advent of spiral and multislice spiral CT has not changed these limiting factors; however, by permitting radical improvements in z-axis spatial resolution, multislice CT enhances CT imaging of submillimeter anatomic and pathologic structures. Subsecond scanning techniques with rapid-volume coverage are enabling new functional imaging methods using CT. Finally, rapid developments of computer technology are enabling radiologists to take advantage of new 3D and 4D imaging methods, moving CT from a 2D anatomy-only tool to a 3D tool that can provide functional as well as anatomic information.

Many more clinical applications are on the horizon; this is just the beginning of a very promising future for CT as perhaps the most cost-effective, value-driven diagnostic imaging tool. Examples of many of the new CT clinical applications are described in the upcoming chapter on multislice spiral CT and are represented throughout this book.

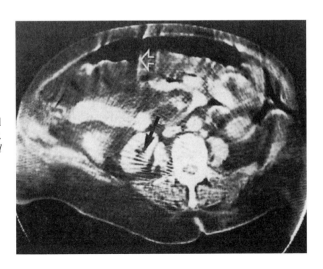

Figure 1–43. Streak artifact (*open arrow*) caused by motion of bowel gas in a slow abdominal scan of a conventional single-ring CT scanner. Machine-caused streaks are also seen. Streak artifact shown with *solid arrow* represents a wobbly rotor in the x-ray tube.

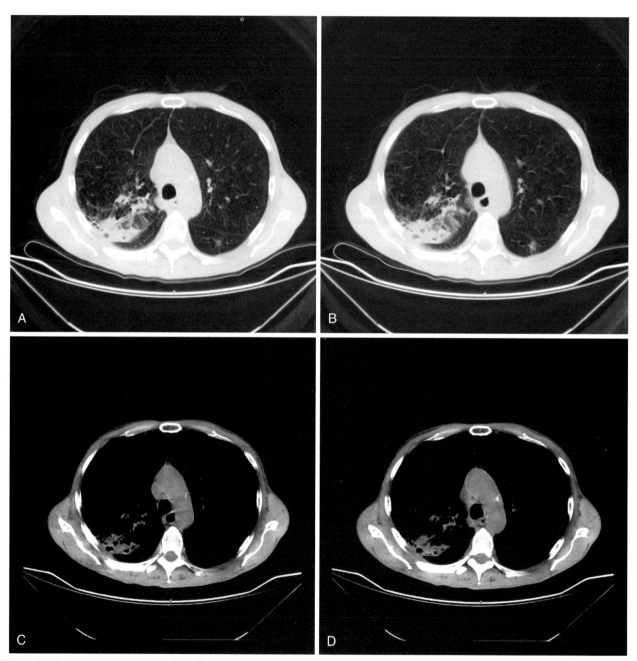

Figure 1–44. Lung scan demonstrating effects of extending spiral pitch with single-ring spiral CT. High spatial and z-axis resolution at pitch 1 *(A)* and pitch 2 *(B)*. *C*, Same scan as *B* but windowed to demonstrate spiral pitch artifacts. *D*, Same scan as *A*, but windowed to demonstrate pitch artifacts. Note the increased spiral pitch artifacts at pitch 2 *(C)* versus those at pitch 1 *(D)*.

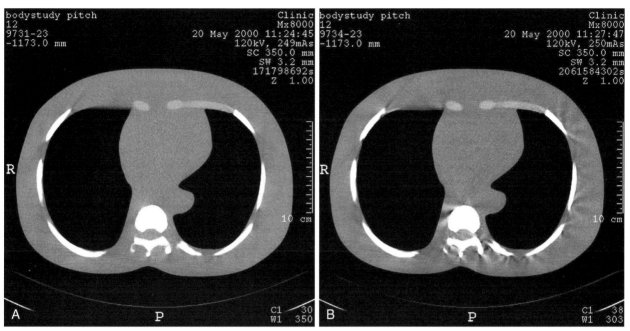

Figure 1–45. Phantom study demonstrating reduced appearance of multislice spiral CT pitch artifacts at quad-pitch 0.675 *(A)* versus quad-pitch 1.25 *(B)*. (Simulations courtesy of D. J. Heuscher and M. Vembar, Marconi Medical Systems.)

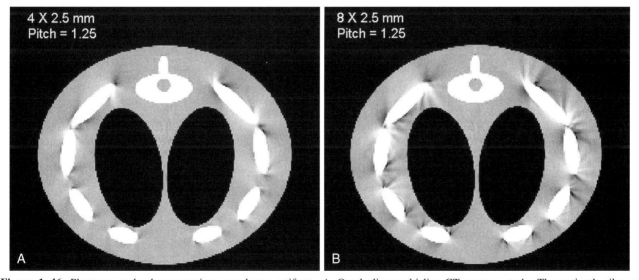

Figure 1–46. Phantom study demonstrating cone-beam artifacts. *A,* Quad slice multislice CT scanner study. The patient's ribs are positioned at a severe angle along the z-axis to demonstrate cone-beam artifact at quad-pitch 1.25. *B,* Enhanced contribution of multislice CT cone-beam artifacts caused by divergence of the x-ray beam in the z-axis when the number of detector rings used to acquire a CT image is increased from four to eight. (Simulations courtesy of D. J. Heuscher, M. Vembar, and C. Vrettos, Marconi Medical Systems.)

Acknowledgment

We thank Shalabh Chandra, M.S., Chris Vretos, M.S., and Dominic Heuscher, Ph.D., for their contributions to this chapter.

References

1. Bellon EM, Miraldi FD, Wiesen EJ: Performance evaluation of computed tomography scanners using a phantom model. Am J Roentgenol 132:345–352, 1979.
2. Brasewell RN: Strip integration in radioastronomy. Aust J Phys 9: 198–217, 1956.
3. Brasewell RN, Riddle AC: Inversion of fan-beam scans in radioastronomy. Astrophys J 150:427–434, 1967.
4. Brasewell RN, Wernealse SJ: Image reconstruction over a finite field of view. J Opt Soc Am 65:1342–1346, 1975.
5. Brooks RA, DiChiro G: Theory of image reconstruction in computed tomography. Radiology 117:561–572, 1975.
6. Brooks RA, DiChiro G: Statistical limitations in x-ray reconstructive tomography. Med Phys 3:237–240, 1976.
7. Christensen EE, Curry TS III, Dowdey JE: An Introduction to the Physics of Diagnostic Radiology, 2nd ed. Philadelphia, Lea & Febiger, 1978.
8. Cormack AM: Representation of a function by its line integrals with some radiological applications. J Appl Phys 34:2722–2727, 1963.
9. Cormack AM: Representation of a function by its line integrals with some radiological applications: II. J Appl Phys 35:2908–2913, 1964.
10. Coulam C: The Physical Basis of Medical Imaging. New York, Appleton-Century-Crofts, 1981.
11. CT/T Continuum: Evaluation Criteria. Milwaukee, General Electric Medical Systems, 1980.
12. CT9800 Computed Tomographic Systems. Milwaukee, General Electric Medical Systems, 1982.
13. Gordon R, Herman GT: Three dimensional reconstruction from projections: A review of algorithms. Int Rev Cytol 38:111–151, 1974.
14. Haaga JR, Reich NE: Computed tomography of abdominal abnormalities. St. Louis, CV Mosby, 1978.
15. Haaga JR, Alfidi RJ, MacIntyre WJ, et al: CT longitudinal scan. Am J Roentgenol 127:1059–1060, 1976.
16. Haaga JR, Miraldi F, MacIntyre W, et al: Effect of mAs variation upon computed tomography image quality as evaluated by in vivo and in vitro studies. Radiology 138:449–454, 1981.
17. Hounsfield GN: Computerized transverse axial scanning (tomography): I. Description of system. Br J Radiol 46:1016–1022, 1973.
18. Huesman RH: The effects of a finite number of projection angles and finite lateral sampling of projections on the propagation of statistical error in transverse section reconstruction. Phys Med Biol 22:511–521, 1977.
19. Johns HE, Cunningham JR: The Physics of Radiology, 3rd ed. Springfield, Ill, Charles C Thomas, 1969.
20. Kalender WA, Polacin A: Physical performance characteristics of spiral CT scanning. Med Phys 18:910–915, 1991.
21. Marmolya G, Wiesen E, et al: Paranasal sinuses: Low-dose CT. Radiology 181:689–691, 1991.
22. McCullough EC, Payne JT: Patient dosage in computed tomography radiology. Radiology 129:457–463, 1978.
23. Price J: Nuclear Radiation Detection. New York, McGraw-Hill, 1958.
24. Rumberger JA, Sheedly PE, Stanson AW: Ultrafast (cine) CT: advantages and limitations in cardiovascular assessment. Intern Med Specialist 9:1–8, 1988.
25. Shape TB, Gagne RM, Johnson GC: A method of describing the dose delivered by transmission x-ray computed tomography. Med Phys 8: 488–495, 1982.
26. Synder DL, Cox JR Jr: An overview of reconstructive tomography and limitations imposed by a finite number of projections. In Ter-Pogossian M, Phelps ME, Brownell GL (eds): Reconstruction Tomography in Diagnostic Radiology and Nuclear Medicine. Baltimore, University Park Press, 1977.
27. Wiesen E, Crass JR, Bellon EM, et al: Improvement in CT pelvimetry. Radiology 178:259–262, 1991.
28. Reynolds MD, Heuscher DJ, Vembar M: Evaluation of spiral CT on a fourth generation system. Eur J Radiol 5:102–109, 1995.
29. Heuscher DJ, Vembar M: Reduced partial volume artifacts using spiral computed tomography and an integrating interpolator. Med Phys 26:276–286, 1999.
30. *Theory of Spiral CT.* Marconi Medical Systems, 1994.
31. Glover GH, Pelc NJ: Nonlinear partial volume artifacts in x-ray computed tomography. Med Phys 7:238–248, 1980.
32. Wang G, Vannier M: Optimal pitch in spiral computed tomography. Med Phys 24:1635–1639, 1997.
33. Siebert JA, Barnes GT, Gould RG (eds): Specification, Acceptance Testing and Quality Control of Diagnostic X-ray Imaging Equipment. Woodbury, NY, American Association of Physicists in Medicine and the American Institute of Physics, 1994.
34. Vrettos C: Data Acquisition Systems in CT. Marconi Medical Systems, 1991.
35. McCullough C, Zinc F: Performance evaluation of a multislice CT system. Med Phys 26:2223–2230, 1999.
36. Newton TH, Potts DG: Radiology of the Skull and Brain: Technical Aspects of Computed Tomography, St. Louis, Mosby, 1971.
37. Hui H: Multislice helical CT: Scan and reconstruction. Med Phys 26: 5–19, 1999.
38. Arenson JS, Levinson R, Freundlich D: Dual slice scanner. U.S. Patent No. 5 228 069, 1993.

2

Magnetic Resonance Physics: An Introduction

Errol M. Bellon, Pedro J. Diaz,
Jeffrey L. Duerk

The magnetic resonance imaging (MRI) study, as seen on a computer screen or on hard-copy film, is a translation, into visual format, of numerical values residing in a computer memory. The N × M numerical values that make up the image are referred to as *pixels* (picture elements). These values are generated from MRI signals acquired during scanning in a computational process known as *Fourier transform*. Thus, MRI represents a form of computed imaging, with the numerical value of the pixel represented on the screen as a level of gray using a digital-to-analog conversion process.

The intensity of the displayed pixel is proportional to its numerical value and reflects the cumulative strength of the radiofrequency (RF) signal received from a corresponding volume element *(voxel)* within the slice of tissue examined. This RF signal is dependent on these factors:

- Strength of the magnetic field
- Size and location of the RF detector (antenna, coil, surface coil)
- Relaxation parameters (T1 and T2) of the tissue
- Amount of mobile protons in the tissue (its proton density)
- Parameters of the MRI acquisition

In an MRI experiment, or scan, the patient is placed in the external magnetic field of the MRI magnet. The magnetic dipole moment of hydrogen nuclei in the body, which are normally oriented randomly in the weak magnetic field of the earth, are affected by this much stronger external field and undergo a net alignment parallel to the field. For example, a 1.5 Tesla (T) MRI system has a magnetic field approximately 30,000 times stronger than that of the earth in most of the United States. At this field strength, only about 2 to 4 in every 2 million protons from the patient contributes to the MRI signal; all others are canceled by protons pointing in the opposite direction.

Individually, the proton magnetic moments precess about the static field, but they can be evaluated collectively such that the net magnetization is initially pointed along the static field. When subjected to brief periods of RF energy, the hydrogen nuclei in the patient's tissues absorb the RF energy and alter their orientation. In this new alignment, the net magnetization can be shown to precess about the static field. The absorbed RF energy and subsequent precession and realignment of the nuclei allow them to function as miniature RF transmitters as they return to their previous parallel alignment. Their RF signal is measured (received) by means of an external RF antenna *(coil)*.

Repetitive systematic variations in the strength of a second magnetic field (generated by gradient coils inside the magnet) during the time the nuclei are stimulated by the external RF signal makes it possible to selectively excite individual areas of the body. Recording and subsequent processing of these spatially localized data result in the clinical MRI scan.

A detailed discussion of the underlying physics of MRI is beyond the scope of this chapter. Hence, an overview of the concepts and most common technologies that are part of the process of MRI generation is presented in this chapter.

Nuclear Spin, Magnetism, and Magnets

Atomic nuclei have a property called *nuclear spin*. Nuclei, which possess an odd number of individual neutrons, protons, or both, have a net spinning charge. For the hydrogen nucleus, which consists of a solitary proton, its single moving electrical charge creates a tiny magnetic field. This magnetic field is analogous to that generated by current flowing in a wire loop, and it behaves like a small bar magnet (or magnetic *dipole)* oriented along the spin axis of the nucleus (Fig. 2–1). These magnetic dipoles, in the absence of external influences, are oriented randomly and, as such, have zero net magnetization (Fig. 2–2). In the presence of an external field, the laws governing the rotation of this spinning nucleus are analogous to those governing a spinning top. The spinning top, because of its mass and moment of inertia, precesses about the earth's gravitational field. The nucleus, because of its magnetic dipole field, precesses about the external magnetic field (Fig. 2–3).

When a hydrogen proton is placed within a magnetic field, the dipole aligns itself with the field in one of two ways: either in the direction of the field *(parallel)* or opposite to the field *(antiparallel)*. These orientations correspond to lower-energy and higher-energy states of the

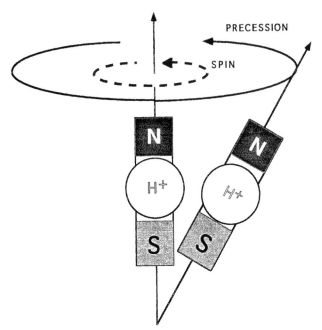

Figure 2–1. Representation of magnetic properties of the proton. The equivalent bar magnet arises as a result of nuclear spin about the axis *(dotted line).* The introduction of an external magnetic field (B_0) causes the bar magnet to precess about its axis *(solid line).*

frequency is specific for each nuclear species and is related to the field strength by the following formula:

$$f_{Larmor} = \gamma B_0$$

where

f_{Larmor} = the Larmor or resonance frequency
B_0 = the applied magnetic field strength
γ = the gyromagnetic ratio

The resonance frequency at 1.5 T is 64 MHz and at 1.0 T is 42.6 MHz. Hence, γ is 42.6 MHz/T for protons. Other nuclei have different gyromagnetic ratios. A shift of the net magnetization from the parallel to antiparallel state can be achieved by supplying energy to the spins in the form of an RF field at the Larmor frequency. When the applied RF field is removed, the magnetic dipoles return to their equilibrium state by releasing the previously applied RF energy. The release of this energy is also at the Larmor frequency. Prior to their return to alignment parallel to the static magnetic field, the magnetic dipoles precess about the field at the Larmor frequency, thereby creating a time varying magnetic field, much like that produced by a spinning bar magnet.

Perturbation of the net magnetization by applying an RF field at the resonance frequency and the measurement of its precession about the static field and its return to equilibrium is the underlying principle behind the MRI equipment.

dipole, respectively. By analogy, consider the task of aligning a spinning top that can be secured only at its tip, with the gravitational field of the earth. In one case, if one is very careful, the top is pointed up even though gravity is trying to pull the top over. If the top is secured at its tip, it is more likely that the top would hang down, along the gravitational field. Clearly, the top that is aligned with the gravitational field is in a lower-energy state and hence is more probable to occur in exactly the same way that the proton aligned with the magnetic field is in a lower-energy state and hence more likely to occur. The magnetic dipole of the proton is thus oriented anywhere around the surface of either one of two cones (prescribed by the precessing dipole), depending on whether the nucleus is in a parallel or antiparallel state.

Normally, a slight net excess of dipoles align in the lower-energy (parallel) direction in contrast to the higher-energy (antiparallel) direction. The excess is referred to as the *net magnetization.* This excess generates the signal measured in the MRI experiment.

Net magnetization increases with field strength, as does the difference in energy level between the parallel and antiparallel states. For these reasons, MRI signal strength increases in proportion to the external magnetic field. Thus, magnets with higher field strength are needed to increase the strength of the emitted signal. In clinical imaging, only one or two protons out of each million are in the parallel state versus the antiparallel state. Thus, only a small portion of the total pool of nuclei participate in the generation of the MRI signal.

The precession frequency of a magnetic dipole in an external field depends on the strength of the field. This

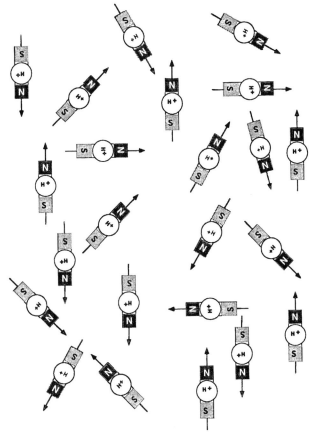

Figure 2–2. In the absence of an external magnetic field, magnetic dipoles are randomly oriented, resulting in a zero net magnetic field.

B_O

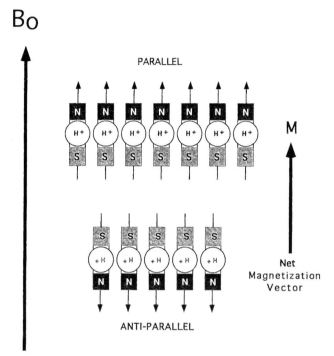

PARALLEL

M

Net
Magnetization
Vector

ANTI-PARALLEL

Figure 2–3. The introduction of an external magnetic field (B_0) forces the magnetic dipoles to align in one of two states: parallel (low energy) or antiparallel (high energy). A small excess in the parallel direction results in a nonzero net magnetic field (M).

Principles of Magnetic Resonance

Consider a simple analogy for the (resonance) phenomenon that underlies the MRI experiment. Resonance is manifested by enhanced and relatively abrupt absorption of energy occurring at a particular frequency.

For example, water contained in a glass goblet begins to vibrate or resonate and emits a sound if a tuning fork of the correct frequency is struck and placed near it. Imagine a goblet that contains an appropriate volume of water (e.g., 100 mL) to "ring" at pitch A. Now imagine an oscillating tuning fork, also oscillating at this frequency, placed nearby. Even though the tuning fork is not placed in contact with the goblet, the vibration of the nearby air molecules causes the goblet to also begin to vibrate because the tuning fork and the goblet have the same resonant frequency. We can observe the vibration of the water by seeing movement of the surface, heard as the sound corresponding to pitch A, or detected as a signal by an oscilloscope. The oscilloscope displays an image of what is heard in graphic form. The number of oscillations per second is a measure of the frequency of the goblet vibration, and the amplitude of the oscillation is a measure of its loudness.

If 100 goblets are placed on 10 shelves within a cabinet with opaque walls and each goblet contains 100 mL of water, as in the previous example, the peak amplitude of the signal displayed on the oscilloscope will correspond to their total loudness and will thus be a function of the entire number of goblets in the cabinet. Increasing or reducing the amount of water in the goblet modifies the resonant frequency (Fig. 2–4). However, the resonance phenomenon

(i.e., vibration of the goblet) occurs only if the resonant frequency of the tuning fork matches that of the goblet.

In clinical MRI, the atomic nuclei are analogous to the goblets. The amount of water in the goblet corresponds to the strength of the external magnetic field. The tuning fork is analogous to the RF pulse. Thus, an MRI resonance, and thus the voltage, can be detected in a receiver if the frequency of the RF pulse matches the resonant frequency of the nuclei at that magnetic field strength.

The frequencies of interest in MRI are much higher than those used in our analogy and are usually expressed in megahertz (MHz) or millions of cycles per second (Hz). For example, hydrogen nuclei in a 1.0 T magnetic field resonates at a frequency of 42.6 MHz. Other MRI-sensitive nuclei have different resonant frequencies, just as differently shaped goblets, when filled with the same volume of water, also have different resonant frequencies. With the appropriate equipment, it is possible to measure signals from these other nuclei in vivo.

The initial stimulus in clinical MRI is provided by a burst or pulse of RF energy at the appropriate frequency, comparable to the effect of the tuning fork at a given tone. The nuclei resonate at that same frequency, and the amplitude of their emitted signal after removal of the stimulus reflects the number of nuclei contributing to the signal. Again, the electromagnetic oscillation induced in the receiver or detector is matched (i.e., it is tuned) to the frequency of the resonating nuclei in the same way that a radio is tuned to a specific frequency to detect a specific station.

To continue our analogy, imagine that every position, right to left, within the cabinet vibrated at a different frequency following the initial resonance phenomenon that caused it to start vibrating. Those goblets on the rightmost corner are at the highest frequency; those at the left side

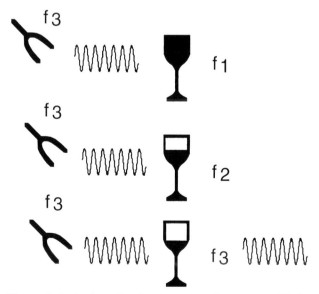

Figure 2–4. Analogy for the resonance phenomenon. Tuning forks with specific frequency (f_3) are placed in proximity to goblets with different water levels and resonance properties. Only the goblet whose resonance frequency matches frequency of the tuning forks absorbs and subsequently emits energy.

are at the lowest frequency. The sound, heard as a whole, is the sum of the component sounds emitted by each goblet at each position.

A mathematical technique, the Fourier transformation, is then employed to sort each component's amplitude and frequency. In this way, positional information regarding the location of the goblets is available because of the one-to-one relationship between spatial location and frequency of the sounds present. The number of goblets at each position is determined from the amplitude of the sound at each frequency. Thus, the positions of the goblets and number of goblets at each position can be determined even though the goblets are located in a cabinet with opaque walls and so cannot be observed directly.

The same phenomenon is used in MRI when a magnetic field gradient is applied following the resonant excitation of the RF pulse in order to establish a one-to-one mapping between position and precessional frequency. The magnetization's voltage is Fourier transformed to tell us at which locations (i.e., frequencies) protons are present and how many are at each location.

Radiofrequency and the MRI Experiment

For convenience, the direction of the external applied magnetic field (B_0) is along the z-axis. The transverse plane is perpendicular to the main field and contains the x-axis and the y-axis. The small net excess of dipoles aligned in the lower-energy parallel position are represented by a net magnetization vector (M) located along the z-axis in the direction of the field.

Application of the RF pulse causes each proton's magnetic moment aligned along the z-axis to rotate away from it, thereby causing the net magnetization vector to also rotate away from the z-axis. The amount of rotation is referred to as the *flip angle*. The greater the strength and duration (i.e., the greater the energy delivered by the RF pulse, the greater the flip angle). The flip angle is user-selectable, with the choice determined by the particular imaging sequence.

For spin-echo imaging, one would use a 90-degree RF pulse, which by definition is a pulse of sufficient strength to rotate M so that it is flipped from the z-axis to an orientation entirely in the transverse plane. This transverse component of M is entirely responsible for the MRI signal. Within this plane, M precesses around the z-axis at the Larmor frequency, returning to its equilibrium state by releasing energy to its environment in a process called *relaxation*. A receiving antenna or coil can be used to detect the time varying magnetization during precession. The resulting signal is referred to as a *free induction decay* (FID) (Fig. 2–5).

Relaxation

The maximum longitudinal magnetization along the z-axis is known as the *equilibrium magnetization*; for a given field strength and temperature, it is directly proportional to the proton density (ρ). The return of nuclear magnetization

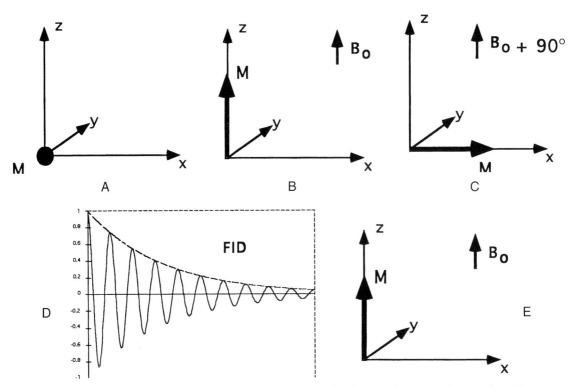

Figure 2–5. Diagrammatic representation of a basic MRI experiment. *A,* In the absence of an external magnetic field, net magnetization (M) is zero. *B,* Net magnetization is created by the application of an external static magnetic field (B_0). *C,* The application of energy, in the form of a 90-degree radiofrequency (RF) pulse, "tips" the magnetization vector onto the x-y plane. *D,* The precessing magnetization decays exponentially back to equilibrium ($+z$). The amplitude of the x-y component of the magnetization versus time (free induction decay [FID]) is shown. *E,* The system is back at equilibrium.

(M) after an RF pulse to its low-energy or equilibrium position along the z-axis is the result of interactions between the nuclei and the local electrochemical environment, its surrounding nuclei, and the strength of the B_0 field. The return of the magnetization to its equilibrium alignment and equilibrium value follows an exponential function of time. Because different tissues create different physical and electrochemical environments, their relaxation occurs at different rates, and their exponential recoveries are described by their relaxation times, T1. Hence, different tissues have different T1s.

As noted earlier, once the magnetization M is tipped into the transverse plane, an FID (induced voltage from the magnetization free of the RF pulse) is obtained. Careful examination of the FID reveals that its amplitude decreases exponentially with time. Hence, the transverse magnetization can be shown to also relax, and a parameter, T2, is used to describe the rate of this exponential loss of signal in the transverse plane. Different tissues have different T2s, just as they differ in T1 and proton density. Therefore, the strength of the MRI signal at any time during its induction is dependent on three parameters—proton density, T1, and T2; these parameters are responsible for the contrast in MRI images.

T1 Relaxation

Any input of RF power that tips the magnetization vector, M, away from the z-axis reduces its intensity along the z-axis to some value between the maximum and the negative of the maximum. Following cessation of the RF pulse, the nuclei return toward their equilibrium magnetization, M rotates from the x-y plane to the z-axis and M returns to the initial magnetization at some finite time later. The process of returning toward the equilibrium magnetization constitutes T1 relaxation, or *longitudinal relaxation.*

When a 90-degree RF pulse rotates M into the x-y or transverse plane, the entire vector is located in that plane, and its value along the z-axis is zero. The value slowly returns from zero to its initial strength, according to a simple exponential time constant such that its value after one T1 interval is 63% of the maximum value and reaches 99% at 5T1 (Fig. 2–6A). The process is caused by release of energy into the surrounding tissue (i.e., into the molecular environment or lattice around the proton). Hence T1 relaxation is also referred to as *spin-lattice relaxation.*

The return of longitudinal magnetization with time can be plotted as a curve, which has an exponential shape toward an upper limit. Thus, the difference between the curve's initial and final height is always a fixed proportion of the displacement from the maximum value, and the length of time taken to move from any point on the curve to one that is 63% closer to equilibrium is identified as the *time constant* (T1) for that curve. The Bloch equations summarize these observations and describe the regaining of *longitudinal magnetization* after an RF pulse.

Among the factors that influence the T1 value of a tissue are:

1. The particular chemical substance and its physical state.
2. Field strength (T1 increases with field strength, therefore recovery is slower).

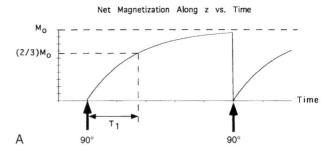

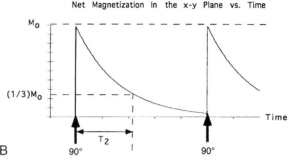

Figure 2–6. *A,* Exponential recovery of z magnetization after 90-degree pulse. The rate of recovery is dependent on T1. *B,* Exponential decay of x-y magnetization after 90-degree pulse. The rate of recovery is dependent on T2.

3. Temperature (longer T1 with increased temperature in biological samples).
4. The liquid surrounding the protons.
5. The mobility of the proton; for example, protons in bone are much less mobile than those in water.

In imaging, RF pulses can be specifically designed to maximize or minimize image contrast dependence on T1 differences. The finite length of T1 limits how rapidly the RF pulses can be repeated and still yield a measurable MRI signal; that is, sufficient time must exist for longitudinal magnetization to regrow between pulses. Varying the strength and repetition time of RF pulses allows one to maximize or minimize the contrast between tissues with different T1 properties. With short *repetition times* (TRs), differences in magnetization are largely dependent on T1 differences, whereas the dependence at long TRs (hence following long recovery times) is due primarily to differences in proton density only.

T2 Relaxation

Immediately following a 90-degree RF pulse, the individual magnetic moments are all located in the transverse plane; more important, however, they are *coherent* (pointing in the same direction at nearly the same frequency). In other words, all protons have the same rotating phase.

Because the FID is the sum of voltages from many protons at each spatial location, the protons must precess at the same frequency and with the same alignment so that their magnetizations work together. As time goes on, following the RF excitation pulse the individual magnetic moments begin to become spread out in the transverse plane, much like cars of different speed on a race track. One cause of the different speeds is due to small local variations in the static magnetic field resulting from random interactions from the magnetic moments of nearby protons. It is this spreading out that causes the vector sum to decrease. With time, therefore, the individual spins exchange energy between themselves until eventually they become completely incoherent, or *dephased*. Thus, T2 relaxation is also referred to as *spin-spin relaxation*.

The signal totally disappears when all phase coherence is lost. A curve that plots the disappearance of the signal with time shows an exponential decay toward zero, and the time taken for the signal to lose 63% of its initial intensity represents its time constant and is the T2 value for that substance, or *transverse relaxation* (Fig. 2–6*B*). T2 limits the time during which the signal is available after an RF pulse and thus limits the period of observability of the signal. This relaxation effect is also described by the Bloch equations. Thus, the dephasing resulting from interaction between adjacent spins is referred to as *T2 relaxation*.

Dephasing also occurs from local imperfections in the magnetic field and in thermal noise. All sources of dephasing—spin-spin and local inhomogeneities—are included in the single term *T2**, pronounced "tee-two-star." Fortunately, different tissues have different T2s. In clinical applications, T2 relaxation is exploited to produce image contrast.

T1 and T2 relaxations occur simultaneously, although T2 relaxation is a much more rapid process. T1 relaxation is field-dependent and increases with field strength; T2 relaxation is less dependent on field strength because it depends mainly on molecular interactions that occur at a much lower rate than the resonance frequency. Hence, imaging protocols developed at one field strength will exhibit differences in image signal-to-noise (SNR) ratio and image contrast if they are attempted at other field strengths owing to differences in T1 relaxation rates at different fields.

The phenomenon of signal decay and recovery in MRI may be summarized as follows. The T1 and T2 values for a substance are its time constants for acquiring or reacquiring its equilibrium state. The longitudinal magnetization of a substance (i.e., its ability to produce a signal) grows along the T1 curve after any disturbance in the equilibrium magnetization. A 90-degree RF pulse rotates all the longitudinal magnetization into the transverse plane, where T2 dephasing can also be observed. Basic differences in signal recovery as a result of different T1 and T2 values in the body tissues create differences in the magnetization vector of these tissues (Figs. 2–7 and 2–8).

The time constant for the substance to lose irrecoverably its transverse magnetization represents its T2 value. The loss of transverse magnetization cannot be slower than the gain in longitudinal magnetization and, in fact, can happen more rapidly, especially when there is loss of phase coherence.

The Imaging Process

The steps involved in the production of an MRI study may be summarized as follows:

1. A powerful, uniform, external magnetic field is employed to align a small but measurable fraction of the

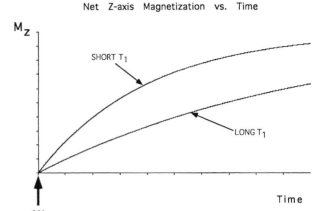

Figure 2–7. Exponential recovery of z magnetization after 90-degree pulse for two substances. The difference between the two curves determines contrast.

normally randomly oriented water proton's nuclear magnetic dipoles contained in the tissue being examined. Some of the randomly oriented nuclei lose energy to the lattice via T1 relaxation, causing a net magnetization to develop.

2. Next, this alignment (or magnetization) is perturbed or disrupted by introduction of external RF energy at an appropriate frequency so as to induce resonance. Spatial localization is obtained through application of a spatially dependent magnetic field (*gradient*) during the same time that RF energy is introduced into the tissue. The gradient field selectively modulates the resonant frequency of the patient in accordance to the Larmor equation (Fig. 2–9).

3. The nuclei return toward their initial alignment and precess about the static magnetic field. The magnetization along the static field grows while the precessing signal (and hence precessing magnetization) decreases through various relaxation processes. While the magnetization is precessing, the time varying magnetization induces a voltage in a receiver coil.

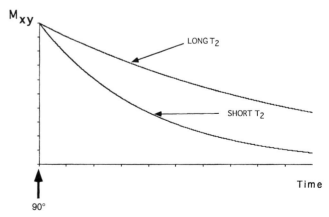

Figure 2–8. Exponential decay of x-y magnetization after 90-degree pulse for two substances. The difference between the two curves determines contrast.

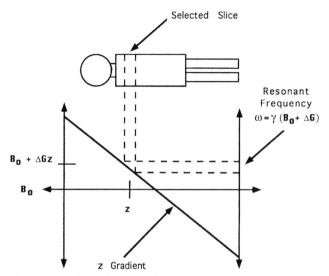

Selected Slice

Resonant
Frequency
$\omega = \gamma \, (\mathbf{B_0} + \Delta \mathbf{G})$

$\mathbf{B_0} + \Delta \mathbf{G}z$

$\mathbf{B_0}$

z

z Gradient

Figure 2–9. A z-axis slice selection using gradient field. Value of the net field (B_0 + gradient) at any given z value determines the resonant frequency. Radiofrequency excitation at a given frequency excites only a specific location.

4. After an appropriate period following initial RF deposition, the emitted signals are measured or read out during application of additional magnetic field gradients (typically measured in milliTesla per meter [mT/m]).

5. A mathematical process called *Fourier transformation* is used to convert the frequency information contained in the signal from each location in the imaged plane to corresponding intensity levels, which are then displayed as shades of gray in a matrix arrangement of, for example, 256×256 pixels.

6. Protons in the various tissues in the imaged slice realign with the magnetic field at (via T1) or decay in the transverse plane (via T2) at different rates, so that at any given moment there is a difference in signal strength between various tissues. This difference in signal strength from region to region constitutes the basis of tissue contrast and forms the substrate for interpretation of the image.

Radiofrequency Pulses

The RF energy used to perturb the protons as they align in the external magnetic field is delivered as a burst of input energy referred to as the *RF pulse*. The pulse consists of a signal at a fixed frequency, duration, and amplitude. The duration is typically a few milliseconds, and the amplitude, or power, is usually given in kilowatts. The strength of the applied RF field is on the order of microTesla (millionths of Tesla).

As the RF pulse tip angle is increased, the strength of the observed signal (i.e., the net portion of the equilibrium magnetization oriented along the x-y plane) reaches a maximum, after which further increases in the input power produce progressively less signal each time. This continues up to a point at which a pulse with a duration twice that of the one producing the maximum signal produces no signal at all.

The smallest power of the RF pulse input that produces a maximum response in the evoked signal is called the *90-degree pulse* (or a *π/2 pulse*). This pulse tips the transverse magnetization to the x-y plane.

A pulse with twice that strength that produces no evoked signal is called the *180-degree pulse* (or a *π pulse*). This pulse tips the transverse magnetization antiparallel to equilibrium (the $-z$ direction). If the magnetization is already in the transverse plane, the 180 degree RF pulse will cause the magnetization to "pancake flip" over.

The RF transmitter is turned off or inactivated when one wishes to detect the MRI signal (on the order of nanoTesla or billionths of Tesla) so that the much stronger RF pulse does not mask the small MR signal. In the typical MRI study, several hundred signals are collected, so that the study usually consists of a series of events with the following order: RF pulse, read after some time (echo time [TE]), wait for some longitudinal recovery to occur (repetition time [TR]); RF pulse, read, wait. . . .

Each series is a repetition of the one preceding it in the order and timing of the RF pulses used. The particular combination is referred to as the *RF pulse sequence*. Several pulse sequences are discussed later.

Magnets and Field Gradients

The variation of any physical quantity with distance is referred to as a *gradient*. For example, in a harp, the strings nearer the performer are shorter than those farther away. Each string is spaced at a uniform distance from the one preceding it. In the water goblet example, positional information can be derived by knowing the frequency of a signal. In MRI studies, field gradients are employed to make the MRI signal contain spatial information. The gradient magnetic field spatially alters the resonant frequency of the imaging volume in accordance to the Larmor equation (see Fig. 2–9).

A typical variation in applied field strength-static magnetic field (B_0) + gradient magnetic field-across the imaging volume is approximately 100 gauss (G) (0.01 T). Thus, for a 1.0 T magnet, the magnetic field superimposed on the main magnetic field for spatial encoding spreads the proton resonance frequency out over a range that spans 0.4 MHz or less. Recording the frequencies over this entire range and spatially decoding using the Fourier transform achieve precise localization of their source.

The gradient field is superimposed on the main magnetic field through employment of gradient coils: three orthogonal sets of coils, one each for the x-axis, the y-axis, and the z-axis. The gradients produced by these coils are spatially linear and produce a difference in field strength such that the difference between any two planes in the imaged volume is directly proportional to the distance between those planes. The nuclei at the weak end of the field resonate at a lower frequency, and those at the stronger end resonate at a slightly higher frequency. Because resonant frequency is directly proportional to field strength, imposing a linear field gradient on a magnetic field makes the resonant frequency of the nucleus vary linearly across the volume. By having an orthogonal arrangement of gradient coils, one can achieve linear gradients in any desired direction and thus can create a series of parallel planes with linearly decreasing field strength.

The amplitude and direction of the gradient are thus user-selectable. Each gradient coil is connected to an amplifier that supplies current to create the field variation. The amplifier can be turned on and off and applied at different strengths so that the gradients also become time-dependent. Because the coils are independent and used to define orthogonal scan planes, it is possible to acquire oblique scan planes electronically without physical reorientation of the patient or the hardware, simply by providing appropriate gradient waveforms to combinations of the gradient coils.

Gradients, Field of View, and Resolution

As noted earlier, each gradient coil is connected to an independent amplifier and the amount of current that the amplifier provides produces a proportionate alteration in the strength of the gradient field. It can be shown that:

1. For a fixed RF pulse, the minimum slice thickness is directly proportional to the maximum gradient strength.
2. For a fixed signal sampling time and image matrix size, the minimum field of view (FOV)—and, hence, minimum resolution—is directly proportional to the maximum gradient strength.
3. The minimum TE and minimum TR of a sequence depend on the time it takes for the gradient waveform to go from zero amplitude to its final value. The parameter that describes the MRI system's rate of change of the gradient field is the *slew rate*, given in mT/m per msec. Typical values for a common system today are near 50 mT/m per msec; typical gradient strengths for a whole body system are on the order of 25 mT/m per msec.
4. The sensitivity of the gradient coils in producing the desired field is related to the amount of field produced per unit of current. This sensitivity is related to the size of the coils, whether they are self-shielded and the spatial arrangement of the conductors that make up the coil.

These relationships establish a number of interesting possibilities. For example, the FOV along the phase encoding direction is governed by the size of the change in gradient pulse from one TR to the next. Because this is independent of the read gradient sampling, the FOV in the phase encode and read gradient can be specified independently, as can the resolution along the two axes.

Imagine that the torso is being imaged. In most people, the width of the torso (left to right [L-R]) is greater than its height. Hence, a 400-cm FOV may be required along the R-L read direction; only 300 mm is required along the anterior-posterior (A-P) phase-encode direction by acquiring a 400 × 300 mm FOV image (i.e., rectangular FOV). The phase-encoding resolution is equal to FOV/Ny, where Ny is the number of phase encoding steps. Hence, Ny can be reduced if the FOV is reduced from 400 to 300 mm, thus saving acquisition time. The only sacrifice is a small loss in the image's SNR ratio, since the SNR is proportional to $\sqrt{Ny}$ at constant resolution. Additionally, it is possible to alter the number of phase-encoding steps so as

to alter the resolution such that it differs along the read and phase directions.

The gradient coils are essentially large inductors. Thus, to have the system go from zero gradient strength to the desired spatial magnetic field gradient, current must be applied to the gradient coils. The rate of change of the gradient field, or slew rate, is related to the rate of change of current. In electric circuits, the voltage across an inductor (gradient coil) is related to the inductance of the coil and the rate of change of the current (hence the slew rate of the gradient field). Thus, gradient amplifiers must produce hundreds of amps of current throughout the acquisition and at hundreds of volts during the ramping of the gradient. In very rapid sequences, such as in *echo-planar imaging*, which can achieve a complete acquisition in approximately 100 msec, the MRI gradient subsystem may be asked to produce up to 0.25 MW of power along each of the gradient axis, yet the total energy delivered may be only a few thousand kilojoules.

In many discussions of MRI pulse sequences, the various gradient lobes required are drawn as instantaneous changes in the amplitude of the gradient. In reality, however, the slew rate of the imaging system prevents this. Hence, in actual MRI pulse sequences, the gradient lobes ramp-up from some value to that required for achieving the specified field of view or slice selection thickness. Figure 2–10A shows the difference between real and symbolic pulse sequence gradient lobes.

Pulse Sequences

MRI pulse sequences in clinical use can be grouped into three basic classes:

- Spin-echo sequences
- Inversion recovery sequences
- Gradient-echo sequences

Many techniques have been developed using these basic sequences, thus covering a broad range of mechanisms for generating contrast between tissues.

Spin-Echo Sequences

A 90-degree pulse is applied to tip the spins into the x-y plane. As previously described, the rotating bulk magnetization vector M generates a signal (the FID). The initial strength of the FID diminishes because of loss of coherence between the precessing protons in the tissue of interest. This loss of coherence arises from spin-spin relaxation (T2) and local field inhomogeneities (T2* effects), which cause the protons to rapidly spin out of phase with each other.

In spin-echo sequences, the FID is not of interest and is ignored. A second 180-degree RF pulse is applied a short time after the 90-degree pulse. The time between these two pulses is usually referred to as tau (τ). This second 180-degree pulse rephases the portion of the protons that had lost coherence because of time-independent, static magnetic field homogeneities. The signal arising from this rephasing peaks at a time, τ, after the 180-degree pulse and is called a *spin echo*. The time between the application of the initial 90-degree pulse and the peak of the spin echo is referred to as the *echo time*, or TE (Fig. 2–10B). It

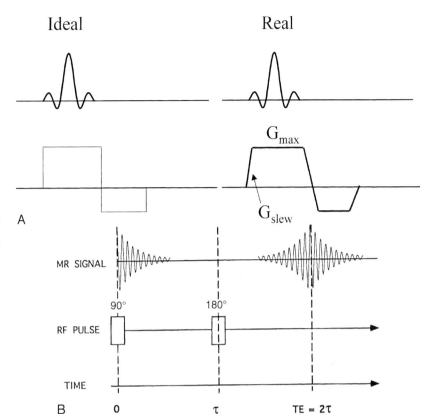

Figure 2–10. *A,* The difference between ideal and real gradient waveforms is a result of the finite slew rate of the MRI systems. Each gradient waveform takes a finite, rather than an infinitesimal, time to reach the final gradient strength. *B,* Timing diagram for spin-echo pulse sequence. TE, echo time.

essentially is equal to the time from generating the transverse magnetization until the center of the signal acquisition (see earlier).

Repeated with a long interval between the excitation pulses, the 90-τ/180-τ sequence produces an image whose strength is dependent on the proton density and the T2 of the tissue alone (T2-weighted). If the TE is short such that little dephasing occurs and with a short interval between repeated acquisitions, the image will be primarily dependent on variations in T1 between tissues (T1-weighted). Long TRs corresponding to full recovery of the magnetization (and hence limited variation due to T1 differences) and short TE corresponding to little signal loss from T2 decay, provide an image that is primarily dependent only on proton-density differences between tissues. Examples of T1, proton density, and T2-weighted images of a normal brain are shown in Figure 2–11*A–C.*

Fast (Turbo) Spin-Echo Sequences

In a conventional spin-echo pulse sequence, the 180-degree pulse allows the magnetization dephasing from field inhomogeneities to be recovered and to thus generate an echo of the initial transverse magnetization. The total imaging time is given as TR * NSA * Ny, where NSA is the number of signal repetitions that are averaged together and Ny is the number of phase-encoding steps performed.

The spatial resolution along the phase-encoding axis is given by FOV/Ny. If additional 180-degree pulses were applied, additional echoes would be obtained after the first one. These additional echoes can be combined in a few different ways. For example, if additional phase encoding is performed prior to each echo, each collected signal

acquires a different one of the Ny encodings. The total imaging time is reduced because multiple phase encodings are performed after each 90-degree pulse. That is, the number of echoes (echo train length [ETL]) is acquired for each TR; echo train length is the number of echoes per TR. The total imaging time under these conditions is TR * NSA * Ny/ETL and, hence, represents a reduction in the imaging time when compared to a conventional spin-echo acquisition. These acquisitions have become known as "turbo spin-echo," or fast spin-echo scans.

A different way to use the multiple echoes is to perform no phase encoding for each echo and to collect each echo as one view for an image at a new TE. In this way, multiple images are obtained over TR * NSA * Ny, each acquired at a different TE. This technique has been widely used to acquire a short TE and a long TE acquisition at a long TR so that both proton-density weighting and T2-weighted scans are acquired in the imaging time.

Inversion Recovery Sequences

Various modifications of this standard spin-echo technique have been developed to provide enhanced contrast for many tissue and disease types. One example is the *inversion recovery* (IR) *technique.* In this sequence, a 180-degree inversion pulse is applied some time before *inversion time* (TI), the standard 90- to 180-degree spin-echo sequence previously described. The 180-degree inversion pulse flips the equilibrium magnetization vector M so that it is antiparallel to the field.

Following this pulse, the spins begin to revert to equilibrium by transferring energy to the surrounding medium (or lattice). The z-axis component of the magnetization shrinks

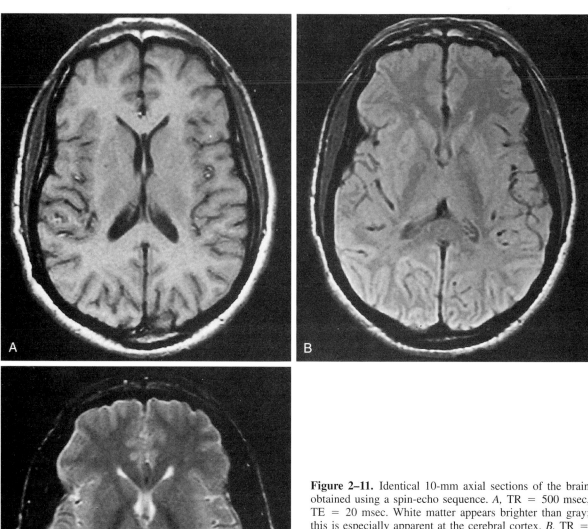

Figure 2–11. Identical 10-mm axial sections of the brain obtained using a spin-echo sequence. *A,* TR = 500 msec, TE = 20 msec. White matter appears brighter than gray; this is especially apparent at the cerebral cortex. *B,* TR = 2000 msec, TE = 20 msec. Gray and white matter are nearly isointense. *C,* TR = 2000 msec, TE = 100 msec. Gray matter is brighter than white matter (contrast reversal from sequence used for *A*).

from the antiparallel direction to zero, after which it regrows into the equilibrium (aligned) direction exponentially with the constant T1. Measurement of the magnetization M at some time TI after the initial 180-degree pulse via the 90- to 180-degree excitation of the partially recovered longitudinal magnetization and detection of the created transverse magnetization provides a measure of the T1 recovery of the tissue. Simple alteration of TI values allows for the selection of different T1 contrast points.

STIR Imaging

The time that it takes the longitudinal magnetization to reach zero is $\ln(2) * T1 \sim 0.7 * T1$. This technique to

eliminate the signal from one tissue in an image has been used in two different applications. Fat, which has a T1 of approximately 240 msec at 1.5 T, can be eliminated from the image by using a TI of approximately 170 msec. Known as *short tau inversion recovery* (STIR), these acquisitions have been widely used in musculoskeletal and body MRI.

Figure 2–12*A* shows an example of a T1-weighted acquisition of the lower leg via a conventional spin-echo acquisition and an inversion recovery sequence with spin-echo read out in which the signal from fat is removed. Note the difference in contrast in the marrow, the site of the actual disease, once the fatty component is removed

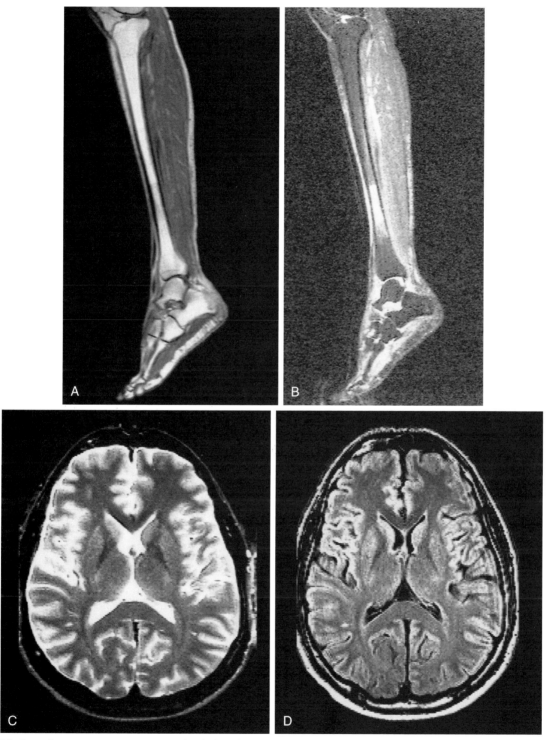

Figure 2–12. Inversion recovery sequences can be designed to generate transverse magnetization when the longitudinal magnetization has relaxed to zero following an initial inversion. *A,* Conventional T1-weighted spin echo. *B,* Conventional T1-weighted short tau inversion recovery (STIR) in which the signal from fat is removed. Note the appearance of a significant signal in the marrow once the fatty component is removed. *C,* Conventional T2-weighted spin echo. Note the high signal amplitude in the ventricles. *D,* Fluid-attenuating inversion recovery (FLAIR) acquisition in which the basic contrast between tissues in the parenchyma is unchanged from the original T2-weighted spin echo, except for the loss of the cerebrospinal fluid (CSF) signal.

via the STIR acquisition designed to eliminate the fat component (Fig. 2–12*B*).

FLAIR Imaging

The second application for signal suppression is in brain imaging, in which T2-weighted acquisitions have found great application in providing enhanced signal for pathologic processes due to edema and increased T2s in these tissues. Unfortunately, the T2 of cerebrospinal fluid (CSF) is also long, making identification of pathology in the parenchyma adjacent to the ventricles difficult as a result of high-intensity signal from both the pathology and the CSF in immediate contact.

Fluid-attenuating inversion recovery (FLAIR) methods have been developed in which the TI is approximately 2000 msec or so (the T1 of CSF is 2000 to 4000 msec) so that the CSF signal is eliminated at the time of the 90-degree pulse for the long TE spin-echo pulse sequence. Figure 2–12*C* and *D* provides a comparison of a conventional T2-weighted spin echo and a FLAIR acquisition at the same location. Adjacent to the ventricles, the high-signal amplitude of the CSF is removed and would permit visualization of "bright" signal, if present, in the brain parenchyma.

Gradient-Echo Acquisitions

Gradient-echo sequences replace the 180-degree refocusing RF pulse of the spin-echo sequence with a fast reversal of the magnetic field gradient (Fig. 2–13). The initial portion of the refocusing gradient places the protons along the applied gradient in different strength magnetic fields, causing differences in the precessional frequency and hence dephasing of the magnetization. The second portion of the gradient reverses the dephasing of the protons by rapidly reversing the gradient direction, forcing the nuclei back in phase and generating an echo.

The 90-degree RF pulse used in the initiation of the spin echo is replaced by a different (and variable) strength RF pulse. Depending on the strength of the pulse, the magnetization vector is rotated toward the x-y plane. The

amount of rotation resulting from this pulse is called the *flip angle*.

Fast (Spoiled) Gradient-Echo Acquisitions

In normal spin-echo and IR pulse sequences, it can be safely assumed that the transverse magnetization has decayed to zero prior to the application of the next RF pulse at the end of TR. This is not necessarily true in gradient-echo acquisitions in which the TR may be very short. This has led to two types of gradient echo acquisitions: (1) those that *utilize* the residual transverse magnetization available at the end of TR and (2) those that *spoil* it. These two types of sequences have very different contrast characteristics as a function of the pulse sequence parameters.

The variation of the flip angle is an important factor in creating contrast differences and shortening imaging time. In spoiled acquisitions (e.g., FLASH, spoiled GRASS), the degree of "T2-weightedness" of the signal varies roughly with the flip angle. The smaller the flip angle, the more the gradient-echo image looks "T2-like," since the influence of spin-lattice relaxation differences is minimized. Short times between pulse repetitions are made possible also by the use of small flip angles, because longitudinal magnetization has been altered only slightly with small tip angles, sufficient time to recover and return to equilibrium.

An additional twist to the gradient-echo techniques can be achieved by using a spoiler gradient or random-phase RF pulse to eliminate the transverse component of the "steady-state" magnetization. This method results in T1-weighted images (at flip angles of 30 degrees or more). Another common name for these sequences is T1-FAST.

Short TE times are usually used in gradient-echo sequences to minimize the effect of static field inhomogeneities within the volume of interest. Unlike the spin-echo sequence, the gradient echo does not compensate for the effect of time-independent magnetic field homogeneities; hence, gradient-echo images are essentially T2*-weighted images.

Table 2–1 describes various scan sequences and their appearance for different tissues.

Unspoiled Fast Gradient-Echo Sequences

In our previous discussion, and in the presentation of contrast versus sequence parameter given in Table 2–1, it is assumed that the time between excitations is sufficiently long that transverse magnetization is sufficiently decayed (TR > T2). If this is not the case, steady-state effects must be taken into account because their effect on contrast can be significant. For these short TR cases, the RF pulse alters the residual transverse magnetization as well as the partially recovered longitudinal magnetization. A steady state of unrecovered magnetization is maintained by the fast repetition. This different (from fully recovered) initial magnetization can be manipulated to provide additional contrast possibilities. Depending on the manufacturer, these sequences go by the names FAST, GRASS, or FISP. The longitudinal component of the magnetization is dependent on the steady-state magnetization which is, in turn, dependent on the amount of T2 decay between pulses.

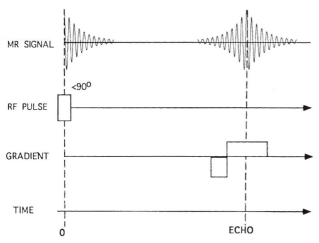

Figure 2–13. Timing diagram for gradient-echo pulse sequence.

Table 2–1. Tissue Characteristics for Various Scan Sequences

Sequence	Parameter	Parameter	Contrast Type (Weighting)	CSF	Gray Matter	White Matter	Fat	Muscle	Disk
Spin echo	Long TR	Short TE	Spin density	Gray	Isointense	Gray-black	Bright	Isointense	Bright gray
Spin echo	Short TR	Short TE	T1	Dark	Gray	Bright gray	Bright	Isointense	Isointense
Spin echo	Long TR	Long TE	T2	Bright	Gray	Black	Gray-black	Gray-black	Bright
Inversion recovery		Long TE	T2	Bright	Gray	Black	Gray-black	Gray-black	Bright
Inversion recovery	Short T1	Short TE	T1	Dark	Gray	Bright gray	Bright	Isointense	Isointense
Gradient echo	Flip angle <20°	Long TE	T2	Bright	Gray	Dark	Gray-black	Isointense	Isointense
Gradient echo	Flip angle >45°	Short TE	T1	Dark	Gray	Bright gray	Bright	Gray-black	Bright

CSF, cerebrospinal fluid; TE, echo time; TR, repetition time.

Three-Dimensional Gradient-Echo Acquisitions

In most conventional acquisitions, the imaged volume results from signal from distinct planes excited by the selective RF pulses applied in the presence of a magnetic field gradient. At soon as the signal from one slice is collected, excitation of the next spatial location can occur. In this way, the acquisition of slice information is interleaved in time within the TR. The acquisition time largely appears independent of the number of slices acquired.

In rapid gradient-echo acquisitions, TR is very short (i.e., on the order of tens of msec versus hundreds or thousands of msec or less), thereby leaving little time for slice interleaving when multiple slices are needed. A different mechanism is used to obtain information over the image volume. In three-dimensional (3D) gradient echo acquisitions, instead of information being acquired from distinct planes, signal is obtained from the entire imaging volume for each acquisition. Frequency encoding and phase encoding are performed along the image planes as in a typical acquisition, yet an additional phase encoding is also applied along the slice select direction. Excitation is performed over a slab instead of a slice, and the phase encoding along the slice select direction subdivides the signal in this direction just as it does in conventional MRI. Thus, in 3D acquisitions, image resolution along the slab-select direction is not dependent on the slice select RF pulse bandwidth and the gradient strength but, instead, on the slab thickness and the phase-encoding gradient process, just as the phase-encoding process determines the image resolution along the phase-encoding axis in a two-dimensional (2D) image.

A 2D and a 3D pulse sequence is shown in Figure 2–14. Because phase encodings are performed along multiple axes, the total acquisition time becomes TR * Ny * NSA * Nz. Typical values for Ny in any acquisition are 128 to 512, whereas Nz for a 3D acquisition may vary from 4 to 256. Although the acquisition time in 3D acquisitions seems to be Nz times longer in a 3D gradient-echo than a spin-echo acquisition, the TRs in these sequences are typical only a few milliseconds in duration in comparison to the hundreds or thousands in spin-echo methods. The advantages of a 3D acquisition are the high spatial resolution along the slab select direction and the wide range of contrasts available from spoiled or unspoiled gradient-echo sequences.

Review and Integration

Any MRI study directly shows received signal amplitude as a function of position. For a given pixel, amplitude depends on the (1) T1, T2, and proton density of the substance being imaged; (2) motion, such as flow; (3) system noise, and (4) pulse sequence used.

Most components of the body contain approximately similar quantities of hydrogen and, therefore, have similar equilibrium magnetization. Air spaces are an exception. The MRI signal elicited in solids disappears extremely rapidly (often within microseconds) and can take hours or days to reestablish equilibrium magnetization. Thus, solids have a long T1 and a short T2. The solid tissues encountered in clinical practice are cortical bone, tooth enamel, and dentin. Conversely, in liquids potential signal can be

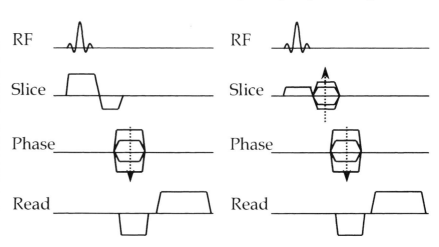

Figure 2–14. A 2D gradient-echo sequence consists of a radiofrequency (RF) slice selection and phase encoding along a separate axis. The read gradient is used for encoding along the third image axis. The RF pulse excites a thin slice of tissue, and signal only comes from that slice. In a 3D sequence, a weaker gradient pulse is used to excite a slab of tissue. The slab is then subdivided by a phase encoding, also performed along the slice direction in a manner comparable to dividing the field of view with the phase-encoding gradients in a normal sequence. A 3D Fourier transform reconstruction is used.

regained almost as quickly as actual signal is lost; that is, T2 approaches T1 and the value for both is on the order of milliseconds to seconds.

The remaining body components are tissues that are neither entirely solid nor liquid. They have a higher viscosity than liquids and less crystalline structure than solids. Making a liquid more viscous would shorten its T1. The T2 cannot be longer than T1, and thus viscous liquids have short and roughly equal T1 and T2. If the viscosity increases further, the substance becomes more like a solid, and T1 is longer than its T2. In clinical imaging most tissues have a T1 between 200 msec (fat) and 3 or 4 seconds (CSF). The T2 values lie between 30 msec (muscle) to about 2 or 3 seconds (CSF). Cortical bone and teeth are exceptions in both cases and are not typically seen in images because of low proton density and relaxation times that hinder signal detection and generation.

For a given field strength and a constant temperature, the strength of a substance's equilibrium magnetization is directly proportional to its proton density (p). In imaging objects that are not chemically uniform, such as the brain, in which all tissues have essentially the same proton density and therefore the same equilibrium magnetization, one can exploit the difference in T1 values. Plotting the curve of longitudinal magnetization versus time, all curves start at zero value following the 90-degree pulse and recover longitudinal magnetization along their own T1. After a long waiting period the magnetization will be near maximum for each; each pixel value will also be near its maximum, and the pixels will be uniformly bright over the whole image, provided that T2 differences are minimized via short TEs.

If one shortens the waiting period to an intermediate point, the signal strength will be moderately reduced; however, the signal from areas with long T1 will be more diminished than from areas with short T1. Thus, the image will reflect differences in T1 values, so that the shorter the T1 of a substance, the brighter it will appear on the image.

Finally, if the waiting period is very short, the pulses will be too close to each other to allow any significant recovery of longitudinal magnetization during the waiting period, so that signal strength is weak and the SNR ratio will be low. Thus, for T1 weighting in SE sequences, the TR should be low—but not so low as to allow an insufficient time for magnetization T1 recovery between pulses.

The difference in signal strength, as reflected by the separation between the curves of the various tissues in the previous example, constitutes the contrast in the image (see Figs. 2–7 and 2–8). Reference to the figures allows selection of an appropriate waiting time after the 90-degree pulse, at which one can obtain maximum separation between the curves and thus obtain maximum contrast between tissues in the MR image.

Because of differences in tissue composition (e.g., differences in proton density), in some circumstances the curves referred to previously do not follow the same contour but, instead, cross each other (Fig. 2–15). At such crossover points, there is no difference in perceived signal intensity, and thus the image will not show any contrast

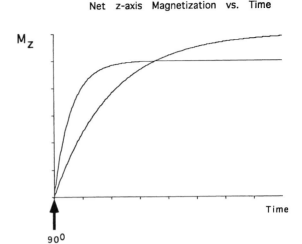

Figure 2–15. Recovery of z-axis magnetization for two substances with different proton density and T1. Note the crossover of signal difference, which results in contrast reversal.

between the two tissues. Gray matter and white matter in brain are examples of this crossover phenomenon, as a function of TR. Gray matter has a longer T1 and a higher proton density than whiter matter. Thus, white matter exhibits rapid recovery of longitudinal magnetization (because of its short T1) and appears brighter than gray matter. At a slightly longer pulse delay, the gray matter and the white matter become indistinguishable; at even longer recovery times, the gray matter achieves higher equilibrium magnetization and appears brighter than white matter in the image (see Fig. 2–11A–C).

For almost any two substances, an RF pulse sequence and TR can be selected to completely obscure any visible distinction between the two substances; however, imaging parameters that provide maximum contrast between tissues can also be found. However, maximum contrast is rarely obtained because other considerations (e.g., imaging time, slice coverage) cause compromises in one of the pulse sequence parameters so that "adequate versus optimal" contrast is obtained. In addition, the contrast observed on one side of the crossover point produces a different kind of contrast than on the other side. In similar fashion, a family of curves results as one plots transverse magnetization against time. The height of each curve is at peak amplitude initially and decays exponentially.

In spin-echo sequences, the longer the delay between the 90-degree and the 180-degree pulses, the more T2 relaxation will have occurred and the less signal there will be to recover. The signal from substances with short T2 values falls off more than from those with long T2 values (see Fig. 2–7). Eventually, all signal disappears except for the signal from substances with long T2 values. Thus, in a T2-weighted image, only substances with long T2 values remain visible. Tissues with long T2 values produce more signal than signals with short T2 values.

3

Magnetic Resonance Angiography: Fundamentals and Techniques

E. Mark Haacke, Weili Lin

Magnetic resonance angiography (MRA) has become commonplace in the last few years.[1, 23, 49] The improvements in pulse sequence design, hardware design, and postprocessing methods make it possible to acquire data in a short period with excellent vascular visualization in a variety of clinical applications. This chapter introduces the concepts behind MRA, the techniques used to obtain MRA studies, and its clinical applications.

Fundamentals of Imaging

Gradient Echoes

The ability to collect an image with magnetic resonance is the result of the dependence of the frequency on the local field. This relationship is governed through the Larmor equation:

$$\omega = \gamma B_0 \tag{1}$$

where

ω = the angular frequency known as the Larmor frequency
γ = the gyromagnetic ratio ($2\pi \times 42.6$ MHz/T)
B_0 = the static magnetic field

For example, for a field strength of 1.5 Tesla (T), the Larmor frequency is equal to 64 MHz.

This frequency dependence is used to spatially discriminate information by applying a gradient field (G) throughout the region of interest in one or more directions. Now the frequency response is spatially dependent (Fig. 3–1):

$$\omega(x) = \gamma B(x) \tag{2}$$
$$= \gamma(B_0 + G \times x)$$

If the signal is measured during the application of the gradient and subsequently Fourier transformed, the spectral amplitudes (the signal as a function of frequency) are obtained. This sampled signal is referred to as the *free induction decay* (FID) (Fig. 3–2).

The signal can also be obtained by using a bipolar gradient structure to create an echo (Fig. 3–3). However, the bipolar gradient structure is able to give only one side of the frequency spectrum (either positive or negative frequency components), which, in theory (as in the FID case) is sufficient to reconstruct an image by taking advantage of the *hermitian symmetry* (see "Partial Fourier Imaging" later on) of the Fourier transform. In practice, it is not enough to reconstruct an image by using only one side of the frequency spectrum because of signal distortion caused by local field inhomogeneities. Therefore, the second lobe of this gradient structure is lengthened by a factor of two, so that both the positive and negative frequency spectra can be obtained. Using all the data gives a more robust image when the echo is not properly centered or when local gradients are present as a result of field inhomogeneities. Further, it also gives a $\sqrt{2}$ improvement in the signal-to-noise ratio (SNR).

Phase

Relative to the echo time, for a constant gradient, the phase as a function of time is determined from

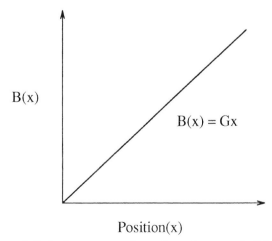

Figure 3–1. In the presence of a gradient, the magnetic field has a linear dependence on position. The horizontal axis represents the position, and the vertical axis represents the magnetic field.

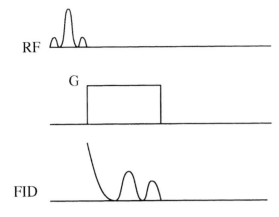

RF

G

FID

Figure 3–2. When a radiofrequency (RF) pulse is applied followed by a single-lobed gradient (G), a free induction decay (FID) of spins is formed. The time constant of the FID depends on the T2 of the material.

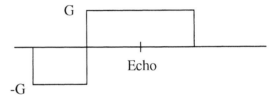

G

-G

Echo

Figure 3–3. When a radiofrequency pulse is applied, followed by bipolar gradient structure, an echo is formed. At the echo the stationary tissue has accumulated a net phase of zero.

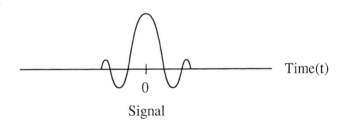

Time(t)

0

Signal

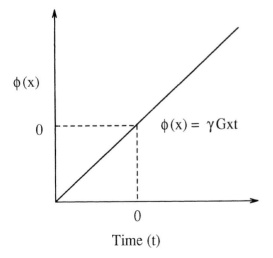

$\phi(x)$

0

$\phi(x) = \gamma Gxt$

0

Time (t)

Figure 3–4. Phase behavior for stationary spins. Phase is a function of time, gradient strength, and location of spins. As shown, at t = 0 an echo is formed and the phase of stationary spins is zero. Here we assume x is nonzero.

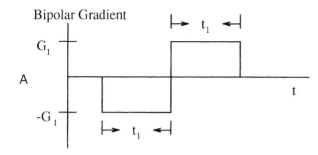

Bipolar Gradient

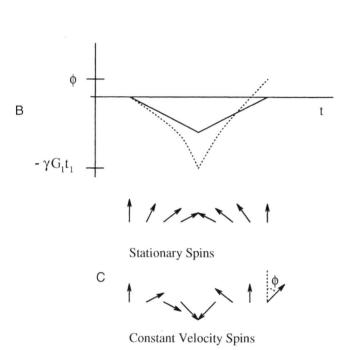

Stationary Spins

Constant Velocity Spins

Figure 3–5. *A*, Pictorial representation of the phase for stationary and constant velocity spins as a function of time when a bipolar gradient structure is used. *B* and *C*, Graphical and vector representations of the phase, respectively. The *solid line* is for stationary spins, and the *dotted line* is for constant velocity spins. φ indicates the phase shift of constant moving spins at the echo.

$$\phi(t) = \omega t = \gamma Gxt \quad (3a)$$

As shown in Figure 3–4, the phase is a function of time and gradient strength. Since $G_1 = G$, $G_2 = -G$ and $t_1 = t_2$, equation 3a can be rewritten as

$$\phi(t) = \gamma x(G_1t_1 + G_2t_2) = 0 \quad (3b)$$

Therefore, the accumulated phase at the echo is always zero for these bipolar gradient structures (Fig. 3–5).

For stationary spins, the phase is generally determined from

$$\phi(t) = \gamma x \int G(t)dt \quad (4)$$

Figure 3–5*B* shows a linear growth in phase during the dephase portion of the gradient and a linear decrease in phase after the gradient is reversed for stationary tissues. No change in phase occurs when there is no gradient on.

The velocity phase behavior is quadratic and overshoots the zero phase mark at the echo.

T2* Dephasing

In the presence of a local field inhomogeneity, the effective decay of the signal is quickened, and T2* is modified as

$$R2* = R2_0 + \gamma\Delta B \quad (5)$$

where $R2* = 1/T2*$ and $R2_0 = 1/T2_0$ where $T2_0$ is the T2 value when no field inhomogeneities (ΔB) are present. This can be qualitatively understood, since the spins "see" different fields and become out of phase. If the time of the echo is calculated locally, it is discovered that it has shifted away from the center. The farther the echo shifts, the less signal remains in the sampling window (Fig. 3–6).

Chemical Shift

The presence of local field variations causes a shift in the frequency for different molecules. Lipids, for example, precess at a frequency (Δf), 3.35 parts per million (ppm)

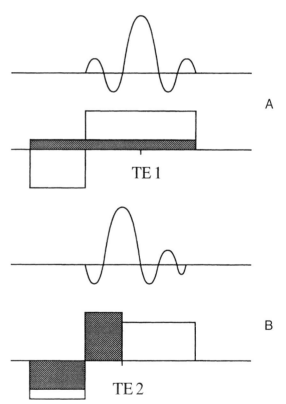

Figure 3–6. Local field inhomogeneities introduce a shift of the location of the echo. *A*, A two-lobed gradient structure is shown with an echo at the center of the second lobe (TE1); therefore, the signal is symmetrical. The gray indicates the area under the gradient from local field inhomogeneities. *B*, The location of the echo is shifted to the left (TE2) compared with *A*, and the signal becomes asymmetrical. If the shift is large enough, it will cause significant signal loss.

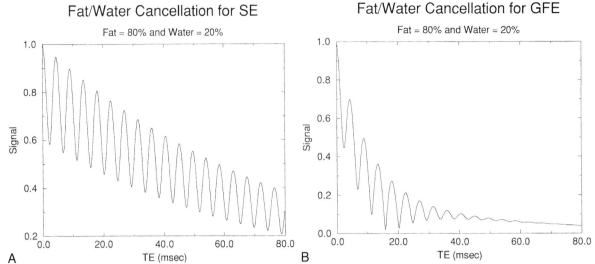

Figure 3–7. When a voxel contains water (20%) and lipid (80%) components, the signal intensity of the voxel is a function of echo time (TE). As shown in the plot, the signal intensity is modulated by a sinusoidal function with a period of 224 Hz (3.35 parts per million at 1.5 T). The spin-echo behavior is shown in *A*, and gradient field echo (GFE) behavior is shown in *B*. A T1 of 950 msec, T2 of 100 msec, and T2* of 50 msec (gray matter) are used as water relaxation parameters and T1/T2/T2* = 250/80/10 msec (fat) are used as lipid relaxation parameters. The signal behavior for a fat and water voxel is further modulated by an exponential decay (T2*). The frequency of modulation appears to be doubled at the lower values of TE because fat overwhelms the water and creates a negative signal, which is then made positive by taking the magnitude of the image. SE, spin echo.

lower than that for water. They therefore have a different phase development as a function of time and at the echo will not necessarily be in phase with water. When a voxel contains fat and water components, the signal intensity of this voxel depends on the echo time (TE) used (Fig. 3–7). At 1.5 T, for a voxel containing 50% each of water and fat, the signal intensity of this voxel will be one unit when TE = 4.5 msec (since fat and water are in phase so that the total signal is the sum of both components) and zero when TE = 6.7 msec (since fat and water are out of phase, and signal intensity is the absolute difference between these two components). To see this, note that the phase difference between the two is $\gamma\Delta BTE$, which is 2π at 4.5 msec and 3π at 6.7 msec. Consequently, the opposed phase nature can be used to suppress fat signal.[27, 60]

Resolution

The data are sampled in the read direction over n points. If the field of view (FOV) is defined as L, the resolution in the image will be (at best) L/n, or

$$\Delta x = L/n \qquad (6)$$

For example, if the carotid vessel is being imaged, its lumen is 10 mm before the bifurcation and the magnetic resonance imaging (MRI) resolution is 1 mm, the smallest percentage of stenosis that can be measured is 100/10%. To detect a high percentage of stenosis, the resolution of images must be improved.

Clearly, high-resolution imaging plays an important role in MRA.[25, 37–39, 56] First, it can be used to reduce flow-related artifacts through the reduction of the intravoxel dephasing.[25, 37, 56] Second, it is able to improve the visibility

of the vascular system[37, 38] (Fig. 3–8). This is especially true for the peripheral vascular system and stenotic regions. Third, the partial volume artifacts can be reduced, and hence vascular contrast is improved (Fig. 3–9). However, there are two major disadvantages associated with high-resolution imaging methods. The SNR will be reduced because of the smaller voxel size, and the minimum repetition time (TR) will be increased because the number of sampling points is increased. Therefore, when the SNR is poor, more acquisitions may be needed to compensate for the SNR lost.

Contrast

The main strength underlying the success of MRI studies is the soft tissue contrast. *Contrast* is defined as the signal difference between two tissues. *Relative contrast* is the signal difference normalized to the signal of one of the two signals. The contrast is the result of the tissue properties ρ, T1, and T2. Blood flow adds another variable to the calculation of contrast. Consider a simple imaging experiment with a very short TE and a long TR relative to the T1 values of all tissues. In this case, contrast is determined solely by spin density (Fig. 3–10). As TR is shortened to on the order of the T1 of a tissue, the image becomes T1-weighted (Fig. 3–11). For gradient-echo sequences, the TR can be shortened much below T1 and the radiofrequency (RF) pulse reduced to an angle well under 90 degrees. For no transverse magnetization before any RF pulse and after equilibrium has been reached, the signal as a function of flip angle (θ) can be expressed as

$$s(\theta) = \frac{\rho \sin\theta (1 - E1)}{1 - E1 \cos\theta} \qquad (7)$$

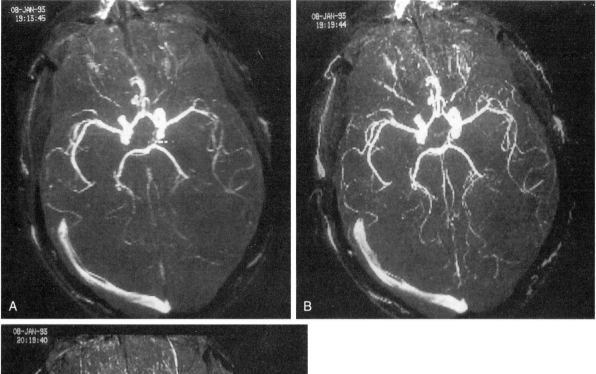

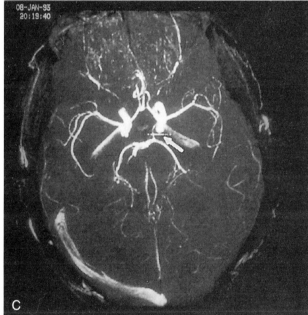

Figure 3–8. Comparison of vascular visibility when different matrix sizes are used. The field of view was kept constant for this comparison. The matrix sizes used were 128 × 256 *(A)*, 256 × 256 *(B)*, and 512 × 256 *(C)*, respectively. When the in-plane resolution is improved, more peripheral vessels can be seen in the images. However, the signal-to-noise ratio is reduced accordingly. The 512 image has little stair-step artifact, although it does suffer a *DC* bright line artifact in the center of the image *(arrow)*.

where ρ is the effective spin density and $E1 = \exp(-TR/T1)$.

The response as a function of flip angle shows why an intermediate flip angle between 0 and 90 degrees gives the best signal. The peak signal occurs when $\cos \theta = E1$; this is referred to as the *Ernst angle* (Fig. 3–12).

Two-Dimensional and Three-Dimensional Imaging

Two-dimensional (2D) and three-dimensional (3D) images can be obtained by adding a phase-encoding gradient table in each remaining direction to be imaged. The resolution in each phase-encoding direction is the FOV divided by the number of phase-encoding steps, as

$$\Delta y = L_y/n_y \tag{8}$$

for the in-plane phase encoding or

$$\Delta z = L_z/n_z \tag{9}$$

for the through-plane phase encoding (also referred to as *partition encoding*). In general, the 3D imaging method is preferable when a thinner slice is desired and flow velocity is high enough so that the flow saturation problem is not significant. Moreover, 3D imaging methods have a better SNR and are less sensitive to field inhomogeneities than

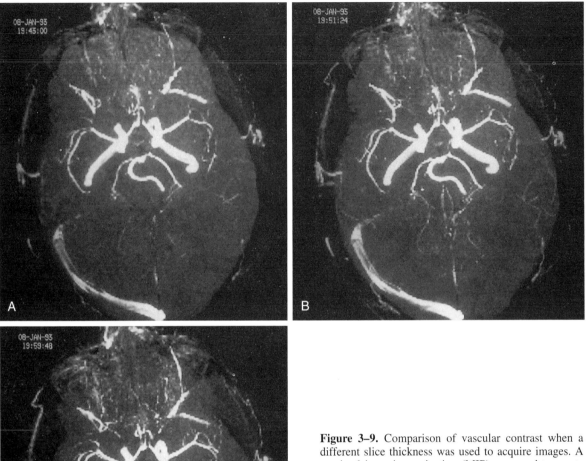

Figure 3–9. Comparison of vascular contrast when a different slice thickness was used to acquire images. A maximal intensity projection (MIP) was used to create axial projection images. The coverage of all three MIPs was kept the same, but with a slice thickness of 2 mm *(A)*, 1.5 mm *(B)*, and 1 mm *(C)*. Since the thinner slice was used, the vascular contrast was improved because of the reduction of partial volume effects.

2D imaging methods. This is easily understood from two perspectives. First, the smaller the voxel size, the less dephasing is across a pixel, since the phase error (e.g., that caused by field inhomogeneity $\phi = \gamma\Delta BTE$) is invariant spatially as the imaging parameters are changed. If there is a 2π phase variation across a voxel, this would cause complete signal loss for a uniform distribution of spins (Fig. 3–13A). However, for twice the resolution, the phase variation is cut in half, being 0 to pi in the first, smaller voxel and π to 2π in the second voxel (Fig. 3–13B). The conventional sequence diagrams for both 2D and 3D acquisition methods are shown in Figure 3–14. The phase encoding in the slice select direction is often referred to as the *partition encoding*, a term we will use here. The field-echo time (FE) refers to the time from the beginning of the gradient structure to the echo along the read direction.

The echo time refers to the time from the center of the RF pulse to the echo.

Fundamentals of Flow Effects
Effects of Motion on the Phase

The previous discussion of phase needs to be modified when a spin moves. As an example, consider just the simple case of constant velocity moving spins:

$$x(t) = x_0 + vt \qquad (10)$$

where x_0, v, and t represent the initial position of the spins, constant velocity, and time, respectively.

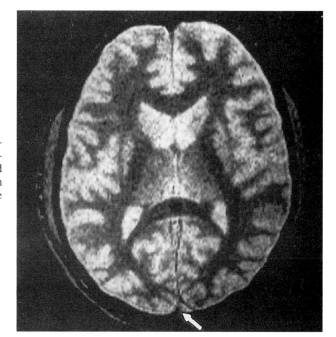

Figure 3–10. Spin-density image of the head acquired with a 5-degree flip angle (Figure 3–11 provides imaging parameters). Because blood vessels sit in gray matter (GM) and GM and blood have the same spin density, it is not possible to distinguish between the two. The sagittal sinus *(arrow)* is saturated and isointense with GM.

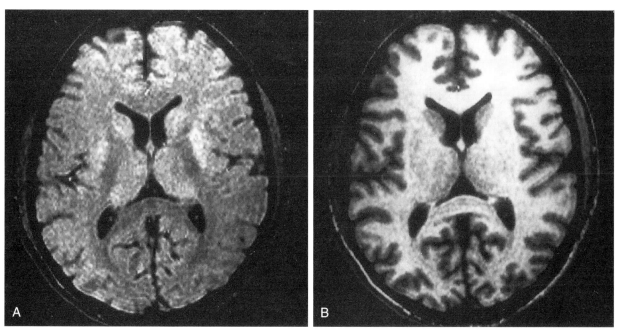

Figure 3–11. T1-weighted image of the head for *(A)* 15 degrees and *(B)* 30 degrees. Since the T1 of blood is longer than that of gray matter, it appears darker if it is saturated but may appear isointense if some inflow effect remains. Imaging parameters: TR = 40 msec, TE = 8 msec; 64 partitions, 2-mm slice thickness; matrix size, 256 × 256.

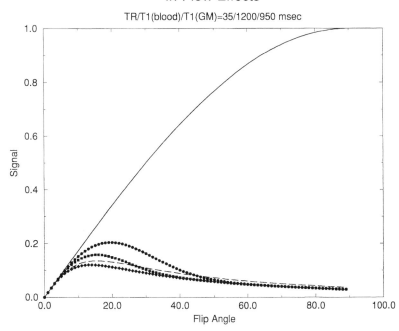

In-Flow Effects

TR/T1(blood)/T1(GM)=35/1200/950 msec

Figure 3–12. Signal intensity as a function of flip angle (see Equation 7 in text). A TR of 35 msec is used with T1 of blood equal to 1200 msec and gray matter (GM) equal to 950 msec. The *solid line* indicates the ideal case that blood experiences only one (N = 1) radiofrequency (RF) pulse. In contrast, when blood experiences more RF pulses, as when N = 5 *(line of circles)*, N = 10 *(line of squares)*, or N = 20 *(line of diamonds)*, the signal of blood is reduced. The signal behavior of GM is also plotted *(long dashed line)*. As shown, the blood may become isointense with GM at 15 degrees when N is greater than 10 and less than 20.

Figure 3–13. *A*, Pictorial representation of intravoxel dephasing. When a larger pixel is used, the integration of spins from 0 to 2π will give a zero signal (0). In contrast, when the resolution is reduced by a factor of 2, the integration of spins will be from 0 to π for the first pixel and π to 2π for the second pixel *(B)* and little signal loss occurs (see Table 3–1).

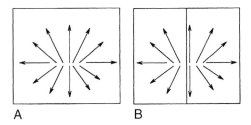

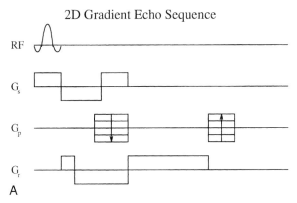

Figure 3–14. Sequence diagrams of both 2D *(A)* and 3D *(B)* sequences. The only difference between these two sequences is in the slice select direction. For the 3D sequence, an extra phase table *(dashed line)* is added to encode information along the slice select direction.

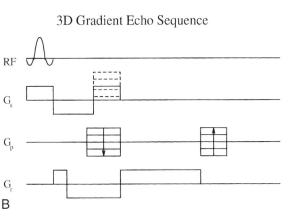

The phase during sampling is found from the expression

$$\phi(t) = \gamma \int G(t)x(t)dt \qquad (11)$$

For a simple bipolar pulse as shown in Figure 3–5, the phase at the echo is

$$\phi(t) = \gamma v G(t)t_1^2 \qquad (12)$$

This simple dependence of the phase on velocity is the fundamental behavior from which many MRA concepts can be understood.

Dephasing

For plug flow, all spins move in the same direction at the same speed independent of the location of the spins with respect to the vessel wall. When all the spins within a voxel are added together, they add coherently and the final signal has the same phase. In contrast, for laminar flow, the velocity of spins is dependent on the location with respect to the vessel wall (Fig. 3–15). The spins at the center of the vessel have the highest speed, and those at the edge of the vessel have the lowest. Consequently, a velocity distribution inside a given voxel causes a different phase shift for each isochromat of spins inside the voxel. The total signal in one voxel is obtained from an integration of the local signal across the entire voxel.

When the total phase shift across a voxel is uniformly distributed from 0 to 2π, there will be complete signal dropout. This phenomenon is known as *flow dephasing* or *flow void*. It usually can be seen in stenotic regions or tortuous vessels when insufficient motion compensation is used. For example, in the regions of the carotid bulb and poststenosis, a secondary flow or vortex flow is normally seen. This flow pattern also introduces signal loss (Fig. 3–16).

Table 3–1 shows the relationship between the degree of dephasing and the remaining signal.

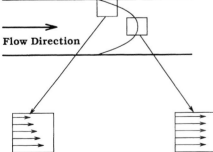

Figure 3–15. Laminar flow pattern inside a blood vessel. Because flow velocity is location-dependent, the spins have a nonuniform distribution compared with that of plug flow. As shown, the voxel close to the center of the vessel has more uniform spin distribution compared with that at the edge of the vessel. This nonuniform spread in velocity can lead to spin dephasing.

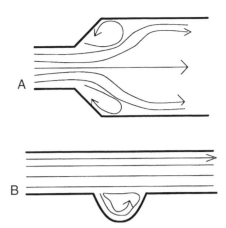

Figure 3–16. *A*, The same concept as in Figure 3–15 also holds for poststenosis regions, where secondary flow develops inside an aneurysm or beyond an aneurysm. *B*, In the region of the carotid bulb, a secondary flow pattern is normally seen because of the pressure gradient change. This causes flow dephasing as well as saturation and results in signal void in this part of the blood vessel.

Compensating Moving Spins

To eliminate or reduce the problems associated with spin dephasing, a short echo time can be used.[32, 39, 54] Alternatively, a velocity compensation gradient structure can be used.[24, 34, 44] It is possible to keep both stationary and moving spins in phase at the echo. This is accomplished by adding a third gradient lobe to the original gradient structures so that the total area still adds to zero, and the stationary spins are therefore still rephased, while the first moment of the phase is also zero for any speed. Expressed mathematically, the following conditions are applied:

$$\gamma x \int G(t)dt = 0 \qquad (13)$$

and

$$\gamma v \int G(t)t\,dt = 0 \qquad (14)$$

To compensate constant acceleration spins, four lobes are required to give three degrees of freedom so that stationary spins, constant velocity spins, and acceleration spins can all have a zero phase at the echo. The tradeoff by using a four-lobed gradient structure is that the echo time will be increased. This can cause some spin dephasing problems when higher-order motion effects are present, such as in secondary or disturbed flow, or for tortuous flow, such as in the carotid syphon.

Table 3–1. Relationship Between Degree of Dephasing and Remaining Signal

$\Delta\phi$	S/S_0
2π	0
$3\pi/2$	$2\sqrt{2}/3\pi$
π	$2/\pi$
$\pi/2$	$2\sqrt{2}/\pi$

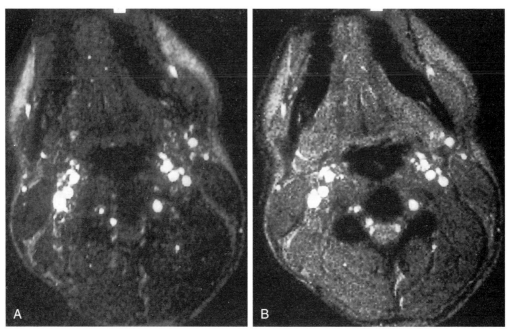

Figure 3–17. *A,* Image of the neck acquired by a 2D sequence with a flip angle of 90 degrees. Because of the pulsatility of blood flow, ghosting artifacts are seen along the phase-encoding direction (y-axis). *B,* When the flip angle was decreased to 20 degrees with the same sequence, the signal intensity of the "ghosts" was decreased.

Higher-Order Terms

Even with velocity compensation, higher-order motion effects can still be seen in tortuous or stenotic flow. For the same bipolar gradient structure, acceleration compensation varies as FE^3 or as FE^2 if constant velocity spins are compensated.

Ghosting Artifacts

Ghosting artifacts are commonly seen in MRI studies. Two reasons can account for this type of artifact. First, uncompensated (or pulsatility of) moving blood causes the duplication of the blood vessels along the phase-encoding direction. The locations of the ghosting depend on the cardiac cycle and TR. This phenomenon is usually seen in peripheral MRA studies (i.e., of the legs) because of the high degree of pulsatility. When a large flip angle is used, the signal intensity of the ghosting artifacts will be significant (Fig. 3–17).

On the other hand, physiologic motion such as eye or cerebrospinal fluid (CSF) movement can also cause ghosting along the phase-encoding direction. To avoid having "ghosts" obscure other structures, the frequency and phase-encoding directions are usually swapped before any data acquisition so that the direction of ghosting becomes horizontal instead of vertical.

Inflow

Given that all spins are now rephasing at TE, any velocity profile can be imaged. The main effect of obtaining a blood signal comes from the fact that inflowing blood has experienced fewer RF pulses and has more signal than tissue with similar T1 values, which experience many

RF pulses and is essentially saturated (Fig. 3–18). This phenomenon is well known as flow enhancement or an inflow effect. The MRA imaging method based on this concept is called time-of-flight (TOF) MRA to differentiate it from the phase-contrast (PC) method (see later), which uses the phase shift introduced by moving spins.

Saturation

The inflow effect makes it possible to obtain good contrast between vessels and stationary tissue because the stationary tissue experiences more RF pulses and eventu-

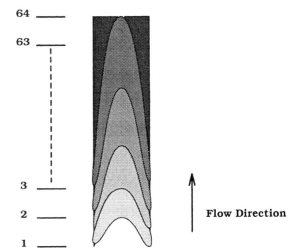

Figure 3–18. For through-plane flow with a laminar flow profile, blood will have higher signal at the entry region *(slice 1)* when compared with the region where blood flows deep into the slab. Numbers represent slice numbers.

ally the magnetization becomes saturated. Consequently, when the velocity of blood in a vessel is slow, both background tissue and blood magnetization are saturated; hence blood vessels become isointense to the stationary tissue. This is usually the case in the head because gray matter (GM) and blood have similar spin densities and T1 values. In addition, this problem is seen more in 3D TOF imaging methods, since a larger imaging volume is normally acquired.[26, 41]

Saturation Pulses

It is also possible to apply another RF pulse just before the usually low flip angle pulse to saturate the signal from stationary tissue and see fresh blood flow into this saturated band. Flow that takes place between the saturation pulse and the echo time can be seen as bright in the saturated band. This band can also be applied parallel to the usual 3D slice select direction, but offset from it, to saturate spins coming from one side of the slab to be imaged. An example is shown in Figure 3–19, in which a saturation pulse was used to saturate the venous blood magnetization and only the arteries were seen in the image (Fig. 3–19*B*).

Phase Contrast

One way to eliminate the problems associated with flow saturation is to obtain flow information by collecting two images, each of which is not perfectly compensated in one direction so that a phase shift exists at the echo along the uncompensated direction, which is different for the two sequences.[14, 15] This is the primary difference between PC methods and TOF MRA. Subtracting one image from the next eliminates the background. This can be done with the complex data or the phase images themselves. The sequence diagram of an interleaved PC method is shown in

Figure 3–20. This method has the advantage that when saturation is a problem (as it is for slow flow), the background is easily removed. The resulting phase images contain values only from $-\pi$ to π as long as the peak velocity is such that $|\phi(v)| < \pi$. The velocity at which $|\phi(v)| = \pi$ is referred to as the *velocity-encoding value* (VENC).

Unfortunately, several disadvantages are associated with PC methods, which require at least four separated scans to extract flow in all three directions yet given the very short TR values that can be used, rapid acquisition of data is still possible. Because subtraction is used to remove the background signal and extract flow information from four scans, patient motion must be avoided. Eddy currents also affect the phase behavior in the images. Moreover, this method requires a choice of the maximum velocity so that aliasing will not occur in the phase images. One way to overcome the problem of the correct choice for the VENC is to use a multiple VENC in one sequence so that a wide range of velocity information can be obtained.

Finally, this method, like TOF methods, is apt to suffer from spin dephasing because of the rapid flow. A shorter TE is necessary for PC methods as well. The TOF and PC methods are likely to complement each other in the future.

Projection Images

The use of 2D TOF over thick slices is often referred to as projection imaging because of the projection of information over the slice thickness. In these methods, excellent background suppression is required. Interleaved 2D PC is the method of choice when rapid imaging is required.

Sequence Parameters

As mentioned earlier, 2D and 3D imaging methods have different advantages and disadvantages and are suitable for

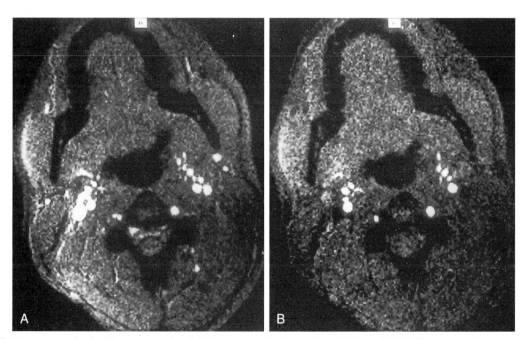

Figure 3–19. Images acquired with a conventional 2D sequence in the region of the neck. *A*, When saturation was not used, both arteries and veins were seen in the image. *B*, In contrast, when a saturation pulse was placed above the image slice, the veins were saturated and only arteries were seen in the image.

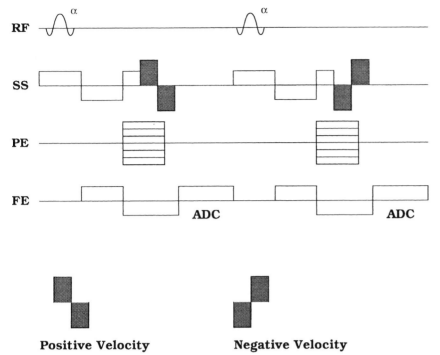

Positive Velocity Encode

Negative Velocity Encode

Figure 3–20. Sequence diagram for an interleaved phase contrast acquisition method. A flow-encoding gradient (bipolar gradient) shown in gray was placed along the slice select direction. As shown, the sign of this flow-encoding gradient was reversed for the second part of the data acquisition when compared with the first part. Because an interleaved data acquisition method was used, the effective TR was increased by a factor of 2. Slice select (SS), phase-encoding (PE), frequency-encoding (FE) directions; and analog-to-digital converter (ADC). RF, radiofrequency.

different applications. Consequently, the imaging parameters for 2D and 3D imaging methods are different to optimize vascular contrast.

Two-Dimensional Imaging

In general, 2D imaging is used to image slow flow because this method is less sensitive to flow saturation. Moreover, 2D imaging is also suitable for dynamic studies because of its short data acquisition time. Unfortunately, 2D imaging is highly sensitive to local field inhomogeneities. It is also more difficult to achieve high resolution along the slice select direction compared with 3D imaging.

Three-Dimensional Imaging

In contrast to 2D imaging, 3D acquisition is used to cover a large region of interest and to achieve high resolution along the slice select direction. Moreover, the SNR is normally higher than in 2D imaging because more points are acquired along the slice select direction. However, 3D TOF suffers from flow saturation effects when a large volume is covered or when slow flow is present. As discussed previously, 3D PC is less affected. General advantages of 2D versus 3D imaging are shown in Table 3–2.

Technical Developments in MRA Sequences

Saving Time

Once a good MRA scan has been collected, one can look at methods to speed up its acquisition. This will invariably mean a loss of SNR, given that resolution remains the same.

Rectangular Field of View

A simple trick is to reduce the number of phase-encoding steps while decreasing the FOV in the phase-encoding direction. For example, reducing the number of steps from 256 to 128 and reducing the FOV from 256 to 128 mm maintain the resolution, cut the imaging time in half, but reduce the SNR by a factor of $\sqrt{2}$. For imaging a child's head, this is possible; for adults, however, the reduction is usually to 192 steps—still giving a considerable savings in time of 25%. When nonintegral ratios between the original FOV and the reduced FOV are used, a careful interpolation algorithm must be employed to retain the correct aspect ratio of images. Figure 3–21 shows a comparison with (Fig. 3–21*A*) and without (Fig. 3–21*B*) the use of rectangular FOV.

Partial Fourier Imaging

Use in the Phase-Encoding Direction. There is a special symmetry property of the Fourier transform for a real object that makes it possible to design a data collection

Table 3–2. Comparison of Two-Dimensional (2D) and Three-Dimensional (3D) Imaging

2D		3D	
Advantages	*Disadvantages*	*Advantages*	*Disadvantages*
Faster	Thicker slice	Thinner slices	Slower
Better inflow	More T2* loss	Less T2* loss	Blood saturation
High CNR	Low SNR	High SNR	Low CNR

CNR, contrast-to-noise ratio; SNR, signal-to-noise ratio.

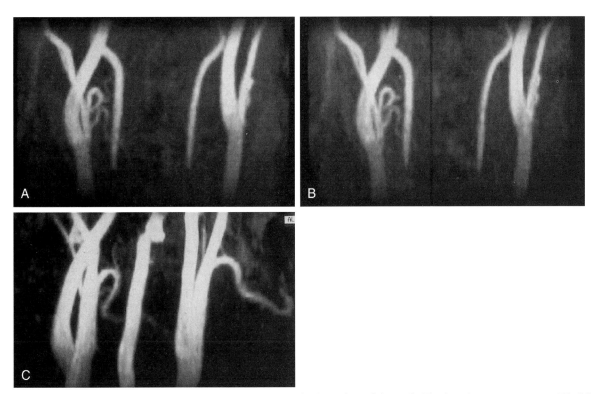

Figure 3–21. *A*, Image acquired with a conventional 3D sequence in the region of the neck. The imaging parameters are TR, 35 msec; TE, 8 msec; flip angle, 15 degrees; and matrix size, 256 × 256. The total data acquisition time is about 10 minutes. *B*, The same imaging parameters are used, except that the matrix is reduced to 160 × 256 and the rectangular field of view (FOV) is used to acquire the image. Although the signal-to-noise ratio (SNR) is reduced accordingly, the total data acquisition time is reduced to 7 minutes. *C*, At this stage, data in the neck are often collected with a 256 × 512 acquisition. Although this image was not obtained using a reduced FOV, the SNR is sufficient that it would be possible to do so if the carotid bifurcation were the region of interest.

method that in theory saves a factor of 2 in data collection time. This property, known as *hermitian symmetry*, relates the negative data to the positive data so that only the positive data, for example, need be collected and the negative data will be recreated from it. The expression is simply

$$s(-k) = s \times (k) \qquad (15)$$

where

k represents the phase-encoding value
s(k) is the signal

In practice, more than half the data is collected and special algorithms are used to reconstruct the data (Fig. 3–22). Once again, a factor of nearly $\sqrt{2}$ is lost in SNR.[25] A comparison is shown in Figure 3–23 to demonstrate the partial Fourier reconstruction method.

Use in the Read Direction. This trick can also be used to reduce the echo time by putting the echo off center with respect to the data sampling window[25] (Fig. 3–24). This reduced echo time allows better suppression of the dephasing of moving spins from higher-order motion. For example, a 25% asymmetrical echo with 256 sampling points indicates 64 points before the echo and 192 points collected after the echo. Mathematically it represents a symmetrical echo multiplied by a rectangular pulse in the time domain, and it translates to a convolution of the ideal image with a complex filter function. This reduces the sharpness of the

reconstructed image. Therefore, the half-Fourier reconstruction is necessary to eliminate this artifact. Figure 3–25 shows sequence diagrams of the TE = 5.1 msec sequence (even shorter echo times are available today).

To achieve high resolution, longer echo times may have to be used because of the limitation of the maximum gradient strength in the system. Consequently, the longer echo time would increase the flow-related artifact since the higher-order motion-dephasing effects increased. Alternatively, an off-center echo can be used such as 6.25%, 12.5%, or 25%, and the echo time decreases accordingly.

Overcoming Saturation Effects

Two solutions can be used to reduce the saturation problems associated with 3D TOF imaging methods: (1) increase the blood signal, and/or (2) reduce the background tissue signal so that the contrast between blood vessels and background tissue can be improved. Alternatively, postprocessing methods can be used to remove unwanted tissue structures (see "Processing and Image Display").

Increasing Signal from Blood

Central k-Space Reordering. In certain sequences, there is a wait time (TW) between application of the partition and phase-encoding loops. In this case, central reordering collects the largest signal at the lowest values

A

Phase

Encoding

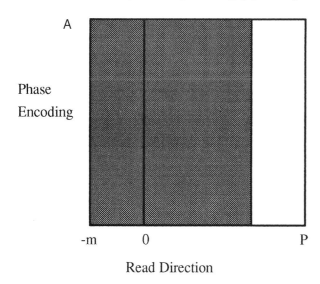

-m   0   P

Read Direction

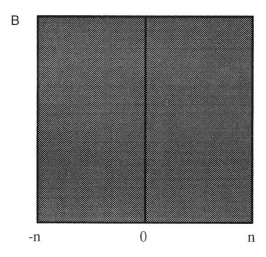

B

-n   0   n

Figure 3–22. Pictorial representation of k-space coverage. Instead of collecting the entire k-space, only three fourths of the k-space was acquired along the read direction. A partial Fourier reconstruction was used to recover the lost information without blurring the image. The shaded portion represents the data used for the partial Fourier reconstruction, and the entire figure represents the data collected from the imager *(A)*. *B*, After reconstruction, data space is symmetrically covered. The data are collected with m points before the echo and P points after the echo, with m + P − 1 = 2n.

of the k-space or at the low spatial frequency values (Fig. 3–26). This enhances the signal not only from the fast blood but also from any blood that has this TW to regrow. In addition, when a T1 reduction contrast agent such as gadolinium–diethylenetriaminepentaacetic acid (Gd-DTPA) is administered, the centric reordered k-space scheme can be used to further improve the vascular contrast, since the half-life of Gd-DTPA is short and Gd-DTPA is most effective immediately after the injection of contrast agents.

Variable Flip Angle as a Function of Radiofrequency Pulse Number. Signal can also be enhanced by not applying a constant RF pulse angle every time. A constant RF pulse usually leads to saturation of the signal (it always does for stationary tissue if the angle is greater than the Ernst angle). If the flip angle is varied to give constant transverse magnetization each time the RF pulse is applied, the signal can be enhanced (even specifically at low k-space if desired).

Contrast Agents. One of the main difficulties associated with 3D TOF MRA studies is the saturation of slow flow. To reduce the saturation problem, a thinner 3D slab can be used so that more fresh blood can flow into the imaging volume.[6, 7, 45] However, this method requires several overlapping thin slabs to cover the region of interest, and

cooperation of the patient is required. Alternatively, a contrast agent, Gd-DTPA, may be used to shorten the T1 over reasonably long periods[8, 11, 38] (its half-life in the blood is about 12 minutes). For example, when a high dose of Gd-DTPA is used, the T1 of blood may be reduced by a factor of 4 and the contrast between blood and stationary tissue will be substantially increased (Fig. 3–27). An example of preadministration and postadministration Gd-DTPA is shown in Figure 3–28. As expected, after injection (Fig. 3–28B), more small vessels are seen as compared with Figure 3–28A. It can also be used to see T2* effects during the first minute of its application, after which its concentration is so low that T2* effects disappear.

Multiple Thin-Slab Acquisition. Multiple thin-slab acquisition methods can also be used to reduce spin saturation problems because spins experience fewer RF pulses compared with single thick-slab acquisition methods (Fig. 3–29). Consequently, the region of coverage is reduced accordingly. To cover a large region of interest, several thin slabs with 25% to 50% overlap can be used. Better-quality images in the regions of overlap and in the rest of the images can then be combined using maximum intensity projection (MIP) processing to generate the projection images (see later).

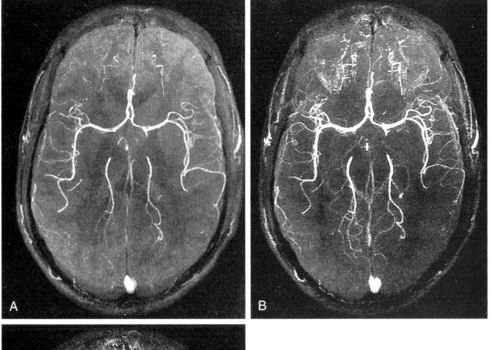

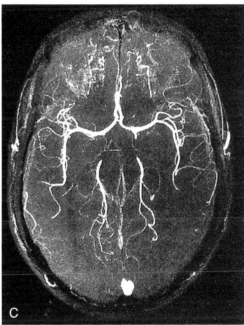

Figure 3–23. *A*, Image collected with 64 points before the echo and 192 points after. It is zero filled in-plane to 512 and then reconstructed with a 2D fast Fourier transform to create a 512 × 512 image. *B*, The image was reconstructed using 64 points before and 192 points after the echo with the partial Fourier reconstruction method to create an equivalent 384 points along the read direction and zero filled to make 512 × 512 images. *C*, The image was collected with 64 points before the echo and 448 points after, with 512 phase-encoding steps to create 512 × 512 images. Note the improved resolution and loss of signal-to-noise ratio compared with *B*. Even the 512 × 512 acquisition with the conventional reconstruction does not lose the same vessel sharpness. (Courtesy of Ramesh Venkatesan, B. S., Case Western Reserve University, Cleveland, Ohio.)

Improving Background Tissue Suppression

Too high a signal from background obscures the blood vessels. By reducing background signal, the vessels become more visible.

Spatially Variable Flip Angle or TONE Pulses. One method of keeping the signal uniform in response across the FOV in the slice select direction (for blood flow perpendicular to the imaging plane—that is, in the slice select direction) is to vary the flip angle spatially (Fig. 3–30). Using small flip angles and increasing to large flip angles keep inflowing blood fairly uniform as it passes through the volume.[35] The principle is the same as that previously described, but it is accomplished by appropriately redesigning the RF pulse to accomplish the desired shape of the RF response. This is most often useful in neck studies (Fig. 3–31).

Magnetization Transfer Saturation. Bound macromolecules have very short T2 values (<1 msec), whereas more mobile protons have much longer values (50 to 100 msec). Through a cross-relaxation mechanism, the latter exchange with the former and are dephased as a result of the local field environment. By exciting a pulse at an off-resonance value of roughly 2 kHz, those water-like tissues with a long T1 are saturated and do not contribute to the signal.[13, 62] Gray matter is affected less than white matter, but the effect is still large enough that up to a 40% drop in brain parenchyma signal has been seen.[63] This makes the vessels much easier to visualize because the partial-volume artifact is reduced. In practice, a frequency offset saturation pulse can be applied to suppress background tissue with negligible effect on the moving blood by an optimal choice of offset frequency and bandwidth of the saturation pulse.[16, 48]

SYMMETRIC ECHO

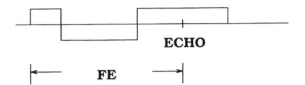

ECHO

FE

ASYMMETRIC ECHO

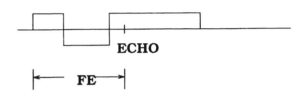

ECHO

FE

Figure 3–24. Pictorial representation of a symmetrical and an asymmetrical echo along the frequency-encoding direction. In this manner, the frequency encoding (FE) can be reduced substantially. Here the FE is defined as the duration from the beginning of the gradient to the echo.

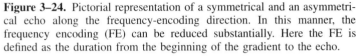

Figure 3–25. Sequence diagram of TE = 5.1 msec, which has an asymmetrical echo of 12.5% of the entire sampling window. The sequence is velocity compensated along the frequency-encoding and slice select directions. The slice select direction is also phase-encoded, and this encoding is usually referred to as "partition" encoding to distinguish it from "in-plane phase" encoding. (Courtesy Dee Wu, Ph.D., Case Western Reserve University, Cleveland, Ohio.)

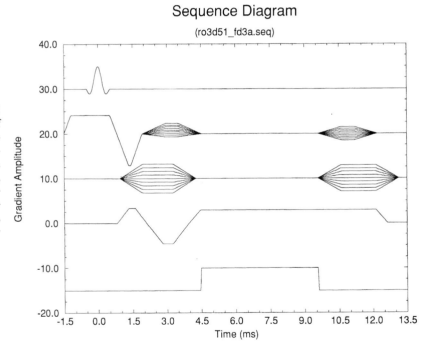

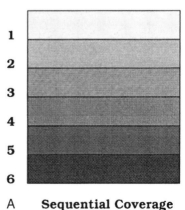

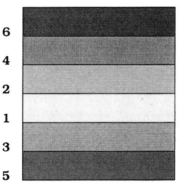

A   **Sequential Coverage**   B   **Centric Coverage**

Figure 3–26. Two different methods are used to cover the k-space: sequential *(A)* and centric *(B)*. For the sequential order, either the positive or negative high-frequency components are collected first and then the lower-frequency components. The gray-scale levels indicate the time during which the data are collected. The darker the color, the later the data are collected. For centric ordering, the low-frequency components are collected before the high-frequency components.

In-Flow Effects

TR/T1(blood)/T1(GM)=35/300/950 msec

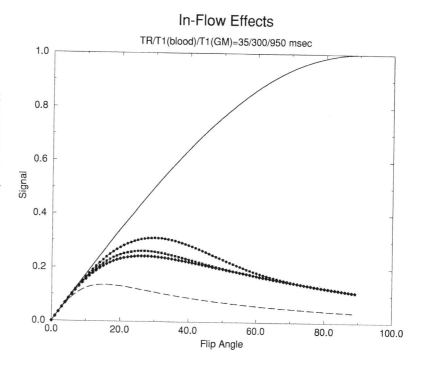

Figure 3–27. When a T1 reduction contrast agent is used, such as gadolinium-DTPA, the T1 of the blood will be reduced dramatically immediately after the injection. Here a T1 of 300 msec is used to create this plot. This plot is analogous to that in Figure 3–12. The *solid line* indicates that the blood experiences only one radiofrequency (RF) pulse (N = 1); the *line of circles* plots data for N = 5; the *line of squares*, for N = 10; and the *line of diamonds*, for N = 20, and the *dashed line* represents gray matter (GM). Even when blood experiences 20 RF pulses, the contrast between blood vessel and GM remains high.

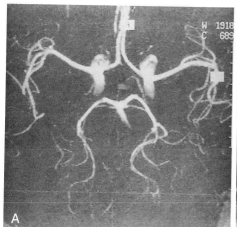
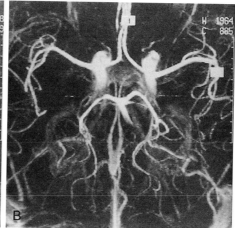

Figure 3–28. Comparison without *(A)* and with *(B)* the injection of gadolinium (Gd)-DTPA. When Gd-DTPA is used, more small vessels are seen than without injection. However, more enhanced veins are also seen in the image, which tends to obscure vessels in the maximum intensity projection images. The imaging parameters were TR = 35 msec, TE = 8 msec, 64 partitions, slab thickness 70 mm, and matrix size 256 × 512 (phase by read).

Figure 3–29. Lateral view of intracranial vessels. Images were acquired with a TE of 6.5 msec and 64 slices per slab. Two slabs with 50% overlap were combined to create the maximum intensity projection images. A large region of interest was covered without the problem of spin saturation.

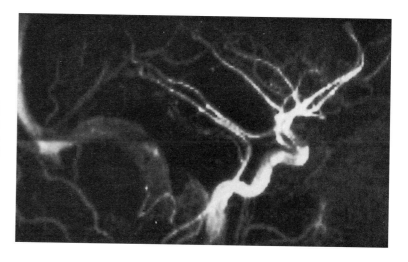

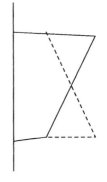

Slice Select

RF Profile

Figure 3–30. A pictorial representation of the flip angle along the slice select direction as it is varied spatially. The slope of this TONE pulse can be chosen according to the flow velocity to optimize response along the slice select direction. If the arterial flow *(dashed line)* is up, the solid line would be used to optimize arterial blood signal uniformity. RF, radiofrequency.

This contrast enhancement is especially helpful for visualizing slow flow in the regions of peripheral vessels as well as aneurysms[39] (Fig. 3–32).

Several problems are associated with this method:

1. The power deposited may be high.
2. The saturation pulse may also saturate the moving spins because of the local field change.
3. This saturation will have no effect on the fatty tissue; hence, fatty tissue will appear relatively bright compared with the background.

To overcome the problem associated with the specific absorption rate (SAR) limit, a double side band saturation pulse can be applied to achieve the same effect as that of a single side band but with half of the SAR. Moreover, a temporal variable saturation pulse can be applied so that a large saturation pulse is applied when the low spatial frequency components are collected to suppress most of the background tissue. However, a smaller saturation pulse can then be applied for the high-frequency portion. In this way, the total SAR can be reduced and yet have the same effect as that of a constant saturation pulse.[58] On the other hand, a frequency-selective fat saturation pulse can be used to suppress the unwanted fat signal[39] (see Fig. 3–32).

Fat Saturation. As mentioned earlier, fat and water have different resonant frequencies. When a frequency-selective, small bandwidth saturation pulse centered on the fat resonant frequency is used, it should be possible to suppress fat signal without affecting the water signal.[12,31] Because of the nonuniform static field, it is difficult to obtain uniform fat suppression throughout the entire imaging volume. Moreover, the choice of offset frequency and bandwidth of the fat saturation pulse requires fine-tuning so that the best combination of the parameters can be obtained.

A sequence diagram is shown in Figure 3–33. A frequency-selective fat saturation RF pulse is applied outside of the normal 3D encoding direction so that the fat saturation is applied only once every 3D encoding loop. Because the fat signal will be at a minimum immediately after the application of the fat saturation pulse, a centric reordering along the slice select direction is used so that the low-frequency component will be collected while the fat signal is at a minimum[39] (Fig. 3–32C).

Alternate Imaging Schemes

TOF bright blood imaging is not the only way to collect angiographic information. Bright blood techniques and PC techniques have been discussed; here we consider three other possible methods.

Black Blood

There are at least six ways to get blood to appear dark in an MRA study:

1. If the blood is not motion compensated and flow is fast enough, the signal within a voxel with a gradient large enough to create a 2π phase change across the voxel will vanish.

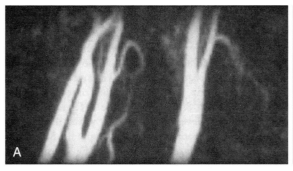
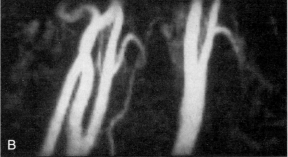

Figure 3–31. Conventional 3D MRA study with a constant radiofrequency pulse *(A)* versus a caudal to cranial increase in flip angle spatially *(B)*. Note the more uniform response along the slice selection direction when the latter, TONE, pulse is used.

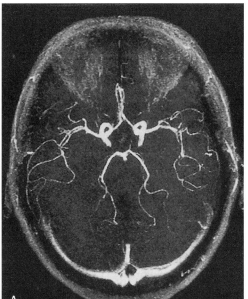

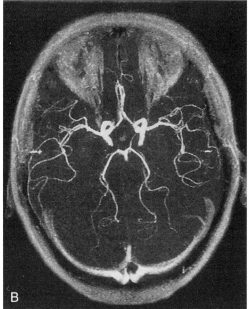

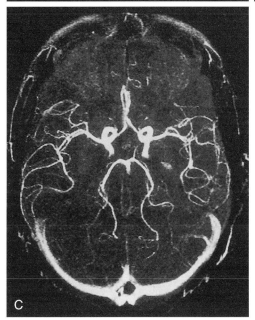

Figure 3–32. Comparison without *(A)* and with *(B)* the use of magnetization transfer saturation (MTS) pulse. The MTS pulse used here has an offset frequency at 1.5 kHz and a bandwidth of 250 Hz. The total duration time of this pulse was about 8 msec. When the MTS pulse is used, more small vessels are seen. However, the fat also becomes apparently brighter because the MTS pulse has no effect on the fatty tissue. *C*, When a frequency-selective fat saturation pulse is used outside the 3D loop, the fat signal is suppressed substantially. (From Lin W, Tkach JA, Haacke EM, et al: Intracranial MR angiography: Application of magnetization transfer contrast and fat saturation to short gradient-echo, velocity-compensated sequences. Radiology 186: 753–761, 1993.)

2. Saturation can be used to suppress the signal from the blood before it enters the imaging volume.
3. A π pulse can be used to invert the spins from blood and the signal acquired at the null point of blood (Fig. 3–34).
4. A flow-sensitive fast-imaging method can be used.
5. The old-fashioned signal void can be created by letting blood flow out of a slice between a π/2 pulse and a π pulse of a spin-echo acquisition.
6. A T2* contrast agent can be used to dephase the signal from blood.

The primary advantage of using black blood acquisition methods is to reduce the problems associated with higher-order motion artifacts (spin dephasing)[17,18] since all the blood vessels will appear dark. However, this method requires special postprocessing methods so that blood vessels can be separated from other low signal intensity structures such as sinuses.

Steady-State Free Precession Bright Blood

Steady-state free precession imaging can also play a role in bright blood MRA studies. For tissue with small T1/T2 ratios and large flip angle, short TR scans can give high SNR. Blood has a T1/T2 ratio of about 6, which is small enough that at a large flip angle it will have significantly brighter signal than that of the surrounding muscle or brain parenchyma.[49]

Spin-Density Approach

Fast imaging can also be used to highlight spin-density differences.[49] Blood has an effective spin density (i.e., spin density weighted by T2*) higher than all of muscle, fat, or brain parenchyma. Therefore, using a low flip angle (much less than the Ernst angle) can bring about excellent contrast even if the blood is not flowing (i.e., this would be good for obstructed flow studies).

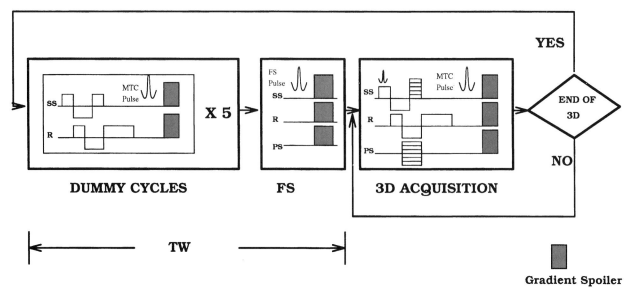

Gradient Spoiler

Figure 3–33. Sequence diagram showing the use of magnetization transfer saturation (MTS) and fat saturation (FS) pulses. The fat saturation pulse is applied outside the 3D loop so that it will be applied only once for one step of the 3D encoding procedure (including slice select [SS], read [R], and phase-encoding [PE] gradient timings). To acquire the data when the fat signal is at a minimum, a centric reordering scheme is used along the SS direction so that the low-frequency components are collected before the high-frequency components. There is a delay time (TW) between the end of one 3D encoding and the next phase-encoding step to apply the MTC and FS pulses and adjust contrast as desired. (From Lin W, Tkach JA, Haacke EM, et al: Intracranial MR angiography: Application of magnetization transfer contrast and fat saturation to short gradient-echo, velocity-compensated sequences. Radiology 186:753–761, 1993.)

Flow Quantification

PC methods can be used in a cine format to generate information on the flow rates throughout the cardiac cycle in just a few minutes. A variety of methods exist to do this, including a one-dimensional (1D) method called real-time acquisition and velocity evaluation (RACE), a 2D cine phase method, and a 1D or 2D projective Fourier

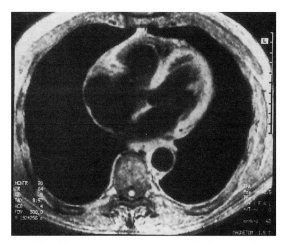

Figure 3–34. By applying an extra nonselective π pulse before collecting the data, followed by a selective π pulse to reinvert the spins in the volume to be imaged, a delay time of T1 is used to null inflowing blood while leaving stationary tissue bright. This is demonstrated in the heart from a single partition (1 of 16 collected) of 2.5-mm thickness. Note the bright wall of the aorta and myocardium. (Courtesy of Debiao Li, Ph.D., Washington University, St. Louis.)

phase method. The latter has been used to measure wave speeds.

RACE

Collecting just velocity information in one direction allows for the acquisition to be on the order of a tenth of one heartbeat. This is accomplished by projecting along the usual phase-encoding direction to examine phase changes at that position in the read direction.[43] The sequence diagram is shown in Figure 3–35. Usually a 2D plane is excited, but the method is best applied when a cylinder is excited and no partial voluming is present to degrade the signal.[28, 42]

One example of RACE is shown in Figure 3–36 in the region of the aorta. The problem associated with this method comes with the nature of the projection image. When two vessels are located in the same row (column) along the projection direction, the flow velocity information is projected into the same pixel, obscuring the velocity information. However, this method can provide very high temporal resolution (equal to TR) and can be used to monitor the dynamic change of flow velocity.

Fourier Phase

Another projection method to obtain flow velocity information is called the *Fourier phase method*.[29, 57] The sequence structure of this method is identical to a 2D sequence (Fig. 3–37). However, instead of putting the phase-encoding gradients along the phase-encoding direction, the encoding gradients are put into, for example, the slice select direction to encode flow velocity along the slice select direction. Therefore, for a Fourier phase image, one

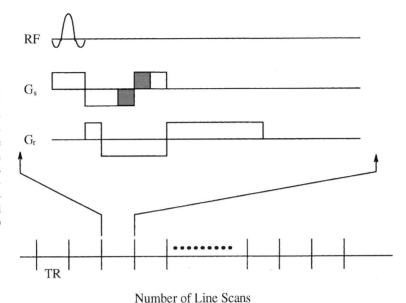

Figure 3–35. Sequence diagram for real-time acquisition and velocity evaluation (RACE). Basically this sequence is identical to a conventional 2D sequence, except that there is no phase-encoding gradient so that all the information in the image plane will collapse into one line. The temporal resolution is equivalent to TR. The shaded portion represents the velocity-encoding gradients. Velocity-compensated gradients are used along the frequency-encoding direction. (G_s and G_r represent slice select and (radio)frequency-encoding directions, respectively.) RF, radiofrequency.

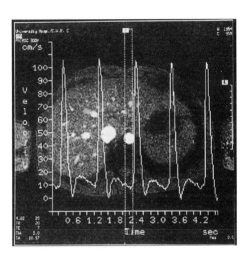

Figure 3–36. Example of a real-time acquisition and velocity evaluation (RACE) image. The velocity was measured in the region of the descending aorta. As shown, the peak velocity is about 110 cm/second, and five cardiac cycles were measured. (From Haacke EM, Smith AS, Lin W, et al: Velocity quantification in magnetic resonance imaging. Top Magn Reson Imaging 3:34–49, 1991.)

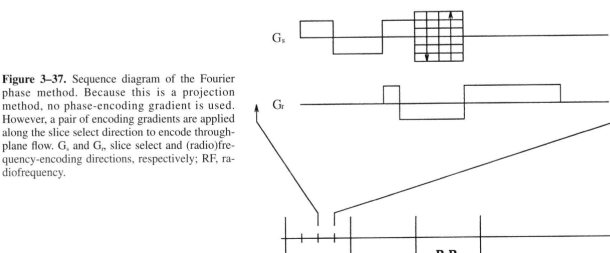

Figure 3–37. Sequence diagram of the Fourier phase method. Because this is a projection method, no phase-encoding gradient is used. However, a pair of encoding gradients are applied along the slice select direction to encode through-plane flow. G_s and G_r, slice select and (radio)frequency-encoding directions, respectively; RF, radiofrequency.

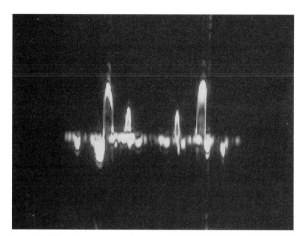

Figure 3–38. Example of the Fourier phase method. This image was obtained during diastole so that the common carotid arteries on both sides show high flow velocity (the signal extends far away from the DC line). Two vertebral arteries show slower velocity compared with the common carotid arteries. Moreover, the jugular vein shows slower negative flow.

axis represents spatial position and the other represents velocity. Unlike the preceding method, no conversion from phase to velocity is needed and the effects are clear from the image. Cardiac gating is used to collect velocity information during the cardiac cycle. Figure 3–38 illustrates an example application of this approach in the neck.

Again, this is a projection method, and overlapping vessels affect its accuracy. This problem may be completely eliminated when an echo planar method is used. Moreover, the inconsistent heart rate creates ghosting, which may obscure the measurement of the velocity. Aliasing has to be avoided by appropriate choice of the encoding gradient strength to meet the Nyquist criterion. The SNR may be too low for fast flow to be seen because of spin dephasing. For measuring slow flow, high signal from stationary tissue at the direct current (DC) line may obscure the flow information.

Two-Dimensional Cine

When cardiac gating is used along with short TR, a set of 2D images can be collected in a given cardiac cycle. For example, if the heart rate is T, the number of slices (phases) that can be imaged is T/TR. By interleaving a velocity-sensitive gradient structure with its negative structure and subtracting the former image from the latter image, a cine set of images with velocity in one direction is obtained.[5, 20, 46, 47, 59]

The number of phases that can be acquired is limited by the TR and heart rate. To improve the temporal resolution, it may be better to have a delay time after the R wave to ensure that the peak velocity during systole will be sampled.

Disadvantages associated with this method include:

1. Inconsistent heart rate affects the accuracy of the velocity measurement.
2. Eddy current effects can cause distortion of phase information and hence velocities.
3. Spin dephasing can occur from higher-order motion artifacts.

4. Aliasing may occur caused by the poor choice of maximum velocity—which is the common problem usually seen with the PC method.

Bolus Tracking

One method is to use excitation of the blood followed by a parallel multislice read to find the blood that had an increasing signal.[19, 33] Knowing the distance traveled by the blood and the time between the excitation pulse and data acquisition, it is possible to calculate the velocity of the flow. Alternatively, presaturation pulses can be applied to the normal gradient-echo sequences (2D or 3D) to saturate tissue in a fixed region but to otherwise leave the image unaffected. The dark band created by the presaturation pulse can be used as a region to view inflowing spins that enter it between the saturation pulse and data acquisition. Again, if the distance the blood travels inside the dark band and the duration between presaturation pulses and data acquisition is known, the flow velocity can be calculated (Fig. 3–39).

Several disadvantages are associated with bolus tracking methods. Motion during the sampling gradients causes distortion of the signal and, hence, of the images. Blood T2 relaxation time may affect detectability when the TE is long. Spin dephasing caused by higher-order motion artifacts may interfere with the measurement of the distance traveled by the blood. This method is also limited by the T1 relaxation of blood (which affects the appearance of the saturation band) as well as the flow profile and RF pulse profiles, which may not saturate the blood well when the profile itself is poorly defined.

Evaluating Microcirculation via Functional Images

During the past few years a great deal of interest has been generated in functional imaging in MRI.[3, 4, 21, 22] This

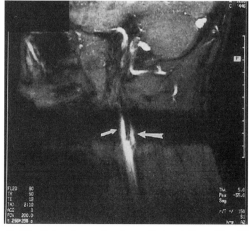

Figure 3–39. Saturation pulse is applied axially with a 2D sagittal acquisition to create a dark band in the maximum intensity projection image so that the distance that blood travels from the bottom of the dark band can be used as a means to calculate flow velocity. Note the more rapid flow in the internal carotid artery *(small arrow)* compared with that in the external carotid artery *(large arrow)*.

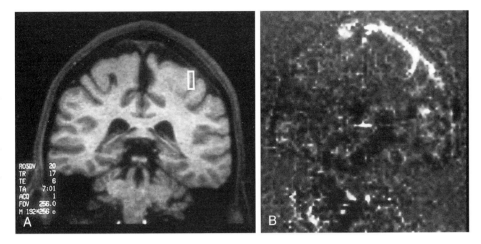

Figure 3–40. Functional imaging is possible even at 1.5 T when a long echo time (TE) sequence is used. *A*, One slice from a 3D T1-weighted scan is used to locate the central sulcus. *B*, A subtraction of poststimulation minus prestimulation by moving the right hand shows the region of the motor cortex on the left side. The motor cortex sits in the gray matter adjacent to the sulcus anteriorly.

is based on the fact that T2* is reduced when deoxyhemoglobin is present in the blood. For activation states such as motor or visual cortex stimulation, blood flow increases but the percentage of deoxyhemoglobin remains the same. Hence, T2* dephasing is not as severe and the signal increases. The subtraction of two images before and after stimulation then gives an image displaying that portion of the brain where the microcirculation increases.

An example of a 3D image used to localize the central sulcus for motor cortex studies is shown in Figure 3–40*A*. The subtraction of an image collected before moving the right-hand fingers from that collected when the right-hand fingers were moving in a sequential finger-touching mode is shown in Figure 3–40*B*. The bright region sits on the gray matter of the central sulcus. The exciting part of this research direction is that these images can be acquired with excellent resolution, and each image only takes seconds.

Processing and Image Display

To create a conventional angiography–type image from which the primary diagnosis is generally made, some special postprocessing methods and display techniques can be used. This is especially true today, thanks to the improvements in computer power; many methods are becoming more accessible because there is little waiting for the processed images to be reviewed. Having rapid image display makes it possible to modify acquisition strategy. In most of the cases, these methods can further improve the accuracy of the images for better diagnosis. These methods can be divided into two main categories: display techniques and image-processing methods.

Display Techniques

Maximum Intensity Projection

The maximum intensity projection (MIP) approach is a method to display 3D vascular data onto a 2D projection. The idea is simple; the maximum value along any ray is used as the 2D intensity value for that pixel through which the ray intersects the plane orthogonal to the viewing direction. Consequently, it can be used to create a projection at any desired angle by rotating the viewing direction (Fig. 3–41). A cine display method can then be used to generate a movie-like display of vascular information in which the vascular structures can be viewed from all angles.

Since the concept of this method is simple and does not require intensive computation, and the results can be obtained in less than a minute, it has been widely used as a regular protocol for MRA studies. However, some

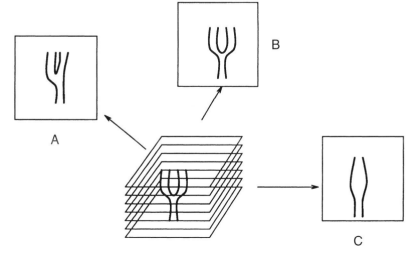

Figure 3–41. Pictorial representation demonstrating the maximum intensity projection algorithm. *A*, Oblique view. *B*, Posteroanterior view. *C*, Lateral view.

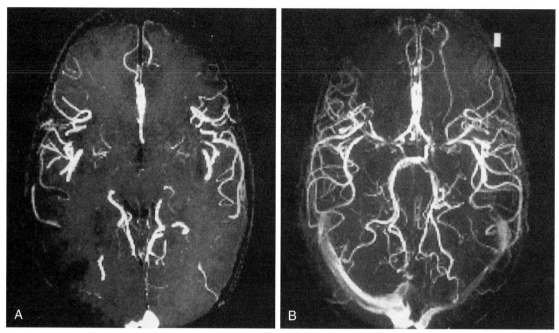

Figure 3–42. Comparison of local maximum intensity projection (MIP) and full MIP. Since the MIP algorithm tends to reduce CNR, some of the small vessels may be lost in the processing of MIP. *A*, A local MIP is one way to solve this problem, since only a few slices are used to perform MIP. However, the global vascular information is lost compared with full MIP *(B)*. (From Lin W, Haacke EM, Masaryk TJ, et al: Automated local maximum-intensity projection with three-dimensional vessel tracking. J Magn Reson Imaging 2:519–526, 1992.)

disadvantages are associated with this method.[2, 9] If MIP is done over the entire 3D space, a great deal of noise is picked up and contrast is lost between vessels and background tissue (Fig. 3–42). Also, when fat is too bright (or signal from other tissues overwhelms the blood signal), the MIP image will lose the vessels.

Summation Methods

When all intensities are summed over a vessel, the background noise is suppressed and intersections of vessels are clearly displayed as bright. One disadvantage is that background signal can become too high and overwhelm the blood signal. One way around this problem is to sum only when the signal is above some threshold or to sum over the vessel-tracked images (see next).

Optical and Shading Methods

A computer graphic method, surface rendering, can also be applied to create the surface of blood vessels so that a shading method according to a light source can then be used to generate a visual 3D perspective image. This complements the depth information loss in the MIP images. However, to do so, the vascular information must be extracted from other nonvascular structures. Some of the vascular segmentation methods are discussed next.

Processing Methods

Single Slice and Multiplanar Reconstruction

Each slice from a set of MRA images contains blood vessel information. Whenever images are postprocessed for display, it is possible that information is lost. The best

images to look at from a 3D data set are the original unprocessed images. A simple processing method that can prove highly useful is reformatting the data along any plane through the volume; this is referred to as *multiplanar reconstruction* (MPR). Some interpolation of the image data is required, but it is usually a good technique if the 3D data are collected isotropically. The best results are obtained when the data are "sync" interpolated (i.e., the Fourier data are zero-filled to a larger matrix size and then transformed) until they are as close to isotropic as possible.[60]

Vessel Tracking

The basic concepts of the vessel-tracking method are based on the assumptions that all vessels are connected with each other and that blood vessels have a reasonable uniform signal distribution.[9, 10, 30, 36, 53, 55] Accordingly, we can extract vascular structures from other background tissue. This makes it possible to segment out the vessels so that they can be displayed independently of the background. After vessel-tracking processing, only the points that are classified as blood vessels will keep their original signal intensity and other points will be assigned a zero intensity. In this manner, the vascular information is extracted from other nonvascular structures.

This method is able to overcome the difficulties associated with MIP. Since only the points that contain vessel information are used to create the MIP images, the contrast is 100% and fatty structures or other bright tissues will not obscure vascular structures. Moreover, the processed images are ready for use in a surface-rendering program. The difficulties of this method are that it may not be able to accurately extract vascular information when the SNR or CNR is low. Further, the nonperfect RF profiles and nonuniform receiver coils will affect the uniformity of vessel signal distribution. To overcome this problem, vessel tracking can be coupled with a traveling MIP (TMIP) method[55] to remove the signal variation at the edge of the vessel. This method is analogous to the vessel-tracking method. One of the difficulties of vessel tracking is to choose the optimum thresholds. TMIP serves as an alternate method that is less sensitive to the choice of thresholds or at least makes it possible to eliminate boxy artifacts and see where vessel tracking failed.

Superposition Methods

The ability to collect high-resolution 3D images makes it possible for accurate surgical information to be obtained from vessel-tracked images. Today, 1- to 2-mm^3 3D information obtained using MRI is standard (Fig. 3–43). Some applications even allow data for the larger vessels to be simultaneously acquired with a 3D T1-weighted study (Fig. 3–43). With the use of vessel tracking and 3D shading, both the vascular information and background tissue can then be superimposed onto each other.

Clinical Applications

The focus of this chapter so far has been on techniques, with the examples being in the head and neck. The major use for MRA has been in intracranial and carotid studies for evaluating stenosis (Fig. 3–44), aneurysms (Fig. 3–45), arteriovenous malformation (AVM) (Fig. 3–46), sickle cell disease (Fig. 3–47), and other vessel abnormalities (Fig. 3–48). The multislab 3D method can also be applied to the aortic arch with some success (Fig. 3–49).

In the chest wall, respiratory motion has long been the bane of MRI studies. Nevertheless, 3D MRA methods can be useful in both the lungs (Fig. 3–50) and heart (Fig. 3–51). In the latter case, both fat saturation and magnetization transfer contrast (MTC) are required for optimal visualization of the blood pool. In the abdomen, 2D TOF with breath-holding is most often used (Fig. 3–52). Still, 3D has found some application in the renal arteries (Fig. 3–53).

Peripheral vessels are often the most difficult to visualize because obstruction leads to slow flow and techniques based on moving blood are less likely to succeed. Two-dimensional TOF often works best in these cases, as illustrated in the upper legs of two patients (Figs. 3–54 and 3–55). The use of Gd-DTPA may prove most useful in the legs; a single high-resolution 3D coronal scan covering both legs can be accomplished in only 10 to 20 minutes. Tissue properties themselves can be used to discriminate blood from surrounding vessels in peripheral studies.

Dynamic Contrast-Enhanced MRA

As already mentioned, the use of T1-reducing contrast agents is an excellent means by which to enhance the blood signal. The previous discussion focused on a steady-state approach that required several minutes to acquire the data. For very-high-resolution studies, data acquisition might take up to 10 minutes for a 3D volume acquisition approach with a 512×512 matrix. The main disadvantage of steady-state imaging postcontrast injection is that arteries and veins are equally bright.

Dynamic contrast-enhanced imaging refers to acquiring the data rapidly immediately following injection of the contrast agent.[50, 52] The novel aspect of this method is that for roughly the first 30 seconds after injection, the contrast agent remains predominantly in the arteries.[40] Hence, this early time period is called the *arterial phase*, the best time for collecting data to avoid signal from the veins. If data are collected for longer than 30 seconds, the signal from the veins continues to increase. One way to avoid a problem from this increase in venous signal is to relegate it to the edges of k-space so that it only contributes to the high-spatial-frequency components. This can be accomplished by using a doubly centric (either square spiral or elliptical[61]) ordered k-space coverage (i.e., all data collected in the arterial phase are for the central part of k-space). After 30 seconds, the outer parts of k-space are collected from the inntermost parts at early times to the outermost parts at later times.

There are two drawbacks to this approach:

1. It is possible to miss the full effect of the arterial phase; this situation sometimes leads to an infiltration of venous signal.
2. In 30 seconds, only a limited amount of k-space can be covered in 3D; this situation leads to a low-resolution scan. Current gradient strengths have helped reduce TR and TE to 5 and 2 msec, respectively, which are helpful.

For a 200-mm FOV and 200 phase-encoding steps, only 30 slices can be collected in 30 seconds. To cover a reasonably thick slab thus requires a slice thickness of 2 to 3 mm. This makes reformatting into a rotating view of the vessels inappropriate. Also, a 30-second breath-hold is already rather long.

Despite these drawbacks, this approach is becoming the method of choice for abdominal MRA, in which speed is a priority because of respiratory and cardiac motion. For imaging of the heart and the coronary arteries in particular, data are collected for only 128 msec during the cardiac cycle. For FOV = 128 mm, TR = 4 msec, 64 phase-encoding steps, and 16 slices, only 32 seconds is needed to collect images with a resolution of $1 \times 2 \times 2$ mm. This is not great resolution but does result in some very informative images of the proximal coronary vessels.

To demonstrate these principles, we show results of dynamic scans in the neck and aortic arch (Fig. 3–56), pulmonary system (Fig. 3–57), heart (Fig. 3–58), and peripheral vasculature (Fig. 3–59). For the pulmonary system, a later scan also reveals the entry of venous signal at this time. In the leg, for example, a very-high-resolution, steady-state image demonstrates the potential of increased resolution even though the data are acquired both during and after the arterial phase.

Venographic Imaging and Cerebral Blood Volume

The major focus of this chapter, and of the medical community for the past 100 years, has been on the side of

Text continued on page 81

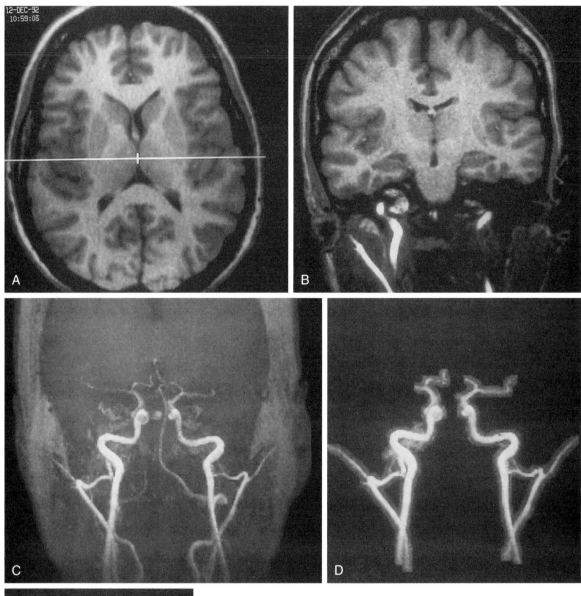

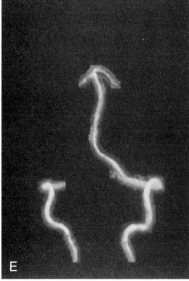

Figure 3–43. When a large 3D volume is collected, it is possible to display the images in various orientations, for example, transverse *(A)* and coronal *(B)*. *B*, The image was obtained by cutting through the 3D volume along the line shown. *C*, The maximum intensity projection of the entire volume obscures information shown in the multiplanar reconstruction image *(B)* or in the maximum intensity projections taken about the vessel-tracked images of the internal carotid artery (ICA) *(D)* or the vertebral and basilar arteries *(E)*.

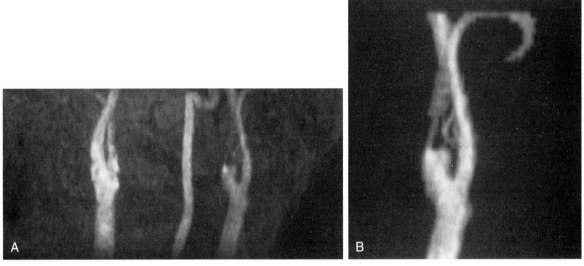

Figure 3–44. *A,* High-resolution carotid stenosis shown after taking the maximal intensity projection (MIP) of a 3D MRA study. *B,* The vessel-tracked image (similar to a local MIP) shows just the stenotic region without interference from overlapping structures. The resolution in-plane and through-plane is roughly $0.45 \times 0.9 \times 1.1$ mm^3.

Figure 3–45. Patient study shows intracranial aneurysms. The individual images were acquired by the TE = 8 msec and TE = 5.1 msec sequences, respectively. Both sequences have a magnetization transfer contrast (MTC) pulse to suppress background tissue. Moreover, the TE = 5.1 sequence was used in the sequence structure showing in Figure 3–33. *A* and *B,* Three intracranial aneurysms are seen in both cases *(small arrows).* However, improved aneurysm visualization and lumen definition are obtained when the TE = 5.1 msec sequence was used *(B).* For example, the smaller aneurysm at the M2 section of the right major coronary artery (MCA) *(A)* shows flow-related dephasing and is relatively smaller as compared with that shown in *B.* In this example, the difference in sequence performance is especially striking since small aneurysms tend to have highly complex and fast flow. Moreover, *B* also shows better lumen definition and continuity at the right anterior cerebral artery (ACA) *(unfilled arrow)* compared with *A* (TE = 8 msec, *open arrow*). The digital subtraction angiography (DSA) image was available to compare with these two studies. It is evident from the comparison of *A* to *C* that the TE = 5.1 msec images and MIPs show the best correlation with the DSA image. (From Lin W, Tkach JA, Haacke EM, et al: Intracranial MR angiography: Application of magnetization transfer contrast and fat saturation to short gradient-echo, velocity-compensated sequences. Radiology 186:753–761, 1993.)

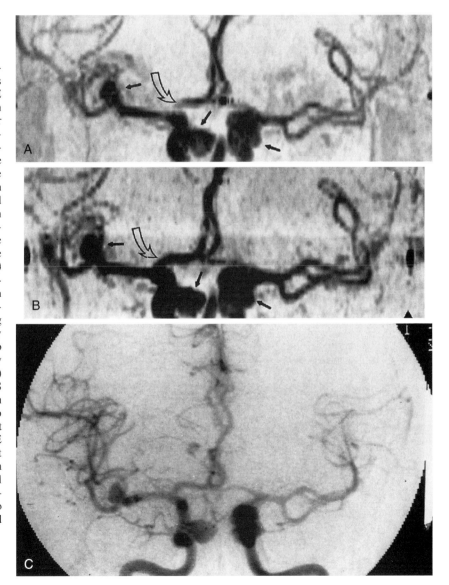

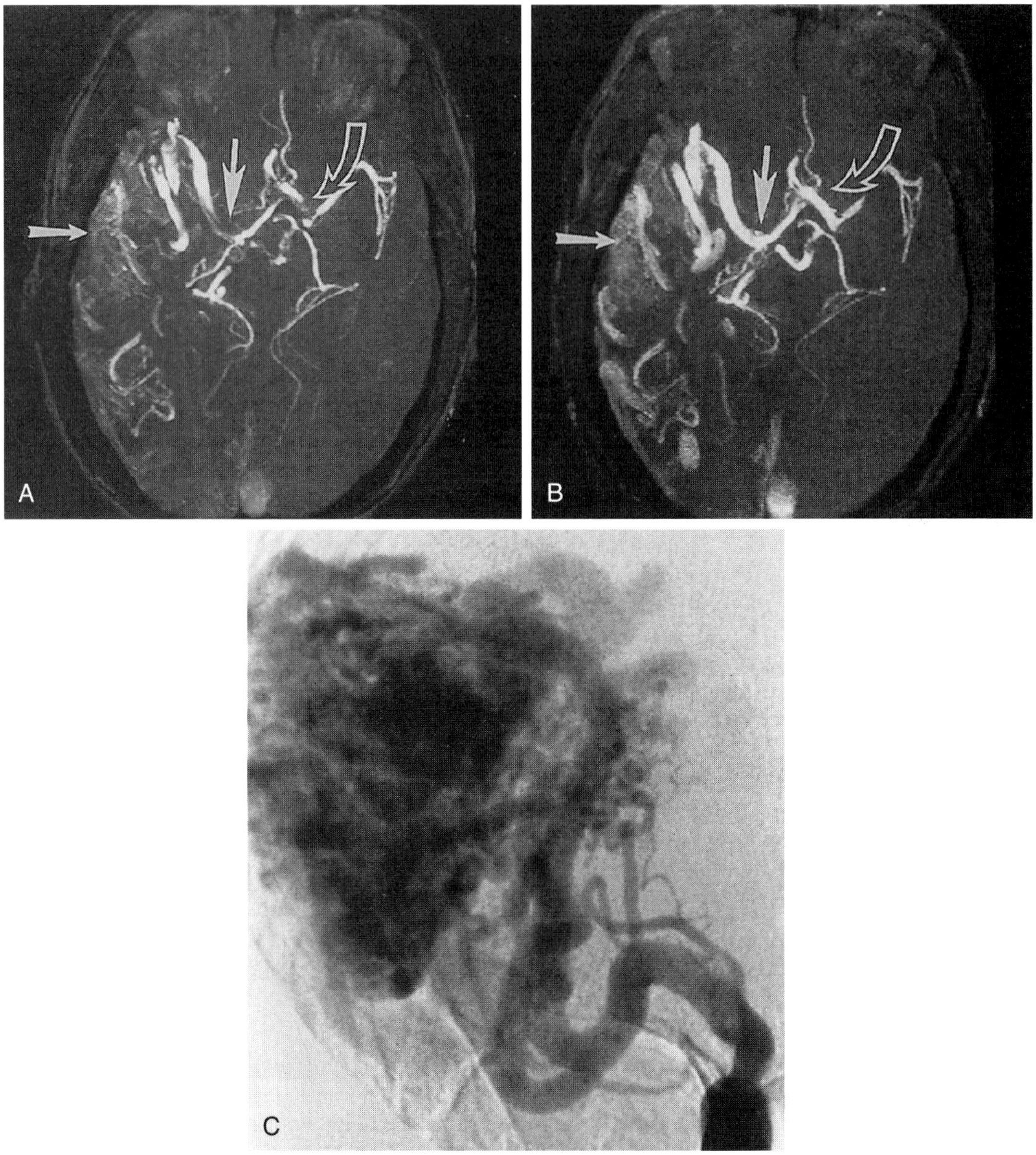

Figure 3–46. Patient study shows a large arteriovenous malformation (AVM) on the right side of brain *(small arrows)*. Maximum intensity projection images are shown to compare the lumen definition in the region of rapid flow. *A,* The TE = 8 msec sequence shows signal dropout at the right middle cerebral artery *(large solid arrow)* and left anterior cerebral artery *(unfilled arrow)* from the flow-related dephasing. However, when the TE = 5.1 msec sequence is used *(B),* no signal dropout occurs in these regions and superior lumen definition is obtained *(large solid arrow, open arrow)*. In both cases, the AVM is clearly seen. *C,* The results were compared with digital subtraction angiography (DSA). Good correlations between TE = 5.1 msec sequence and DSA were obtained. Specifically, in the regions where the TE = 8 msec sequence showed flow dephasing, there was no evidence of vessel narrowing in the TE = 5.1 msec sequence. Again, both sequences had a magnetization transfer contrast (MTC) pulse to suppress background tissue, and the TE 5.1 sequence used the sequence structure shown in Figure 3–33. (From Lin W, Tkach JA, Haacke EM, et al: Intracranial MR angiography: Application of magnetization transfer contrast and fat saturation to short gradient-echo, velocity-compensated sequences. Radiology 186:753–761, 1993.)

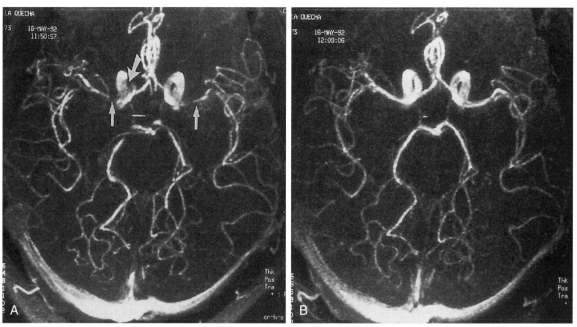

Figure 3–47. A 19-year-old female with sickle cell disease. The resulting vessel lumen definition obtained from both the TE = 8 msec and TE = 5.1 msec sequences is shown in *A* and *B*, respectively. At both the right and left MCAs *(small arrows)* and the right internal carotid artery *(large arrow)*, the TE = 8 msec sequence shows signal dropout, which suggests a possible high-grade stenosis. In contrast, the TE = 5.1 msec sequence shows high signal intensity and good lumen definition in the same regions *(large and small arrows)*. Again, both sequences have an MTC pulse to suppress background tissue, and the TE = 5.1 sequence used the sequence structure shown in Figure 3–33. (From Lin W, Tkach JA, Haacke EM, et al: Intracranial MR angiography: Application of magnetization transfer contrast and fat saturation to short gradient-echo, velocity-compensated sequences. Radiology 186:753–761, 1993.)

Figure 3–48. Base of skull MRA study. Axial collapse image from 3D phase-contrast MRA TR/TE, 22/9, flip angle 30 degrees, all-direction flow encoding, velocity encoding (VENC) = 30 cm/second. The approximate acquisition time was 15 minutes. Each slice is 1.5 mm thick. Note the loop in the posterior inferior cerebellar artery *(open arrow)* arising from the vertebral artery. (Courtesy of Fred Steinberg, M.D., Magnetic Resonance Institute of Boca Raton, Fla.)

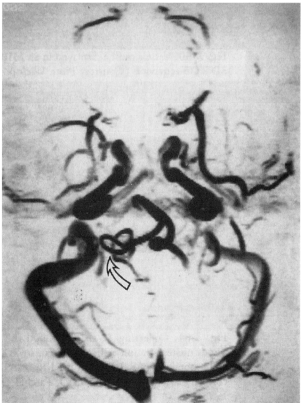

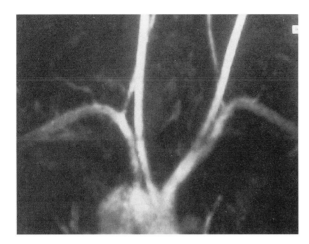

Figure 3–49. Two-slab acquisition of the aorta arch with 3D time-of-flight acquisition method. (From Lewin JS, Laub G, Hausmann R: Three-dimensional time-of-flight MR angiography: Applications in the abdomen and thorax. Radiology 179:261–264, 1991.)

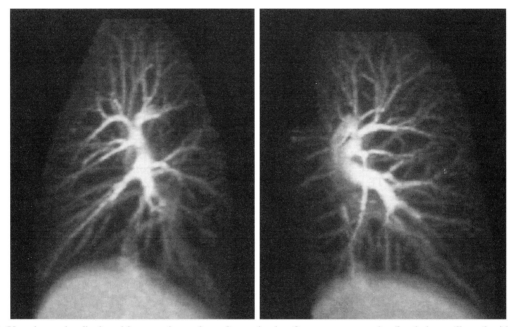

Figure 3–50. Vessels can be displayed in a maximum intensity projection format at any angle after being collected with a 3D time-of-flight sequence. (Courtesy of Piotr Wieloposki, Ph.D., Deaconess Hospital, Boston.)

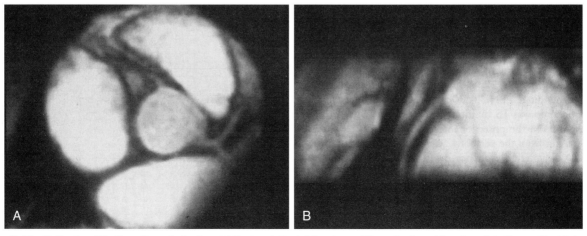

Figure 3–51. Collecting 32 slices through the heart (all at end-diastole) using a 3D method avoids misregistration artifact inherent in 2D imaging and allows a high-quality multiplanar reconstruction image to be obtained *(A).* It is then used to search for an appropriate plane to visualize the right coronary artery *(B).* (From Li D, Paschal CB, Haacke EM, et al: Coronary arteries: Three-dimensional MR imaging with fat saturation and magnetization transfer contrast. Radiology 187:401–406, 1993.)

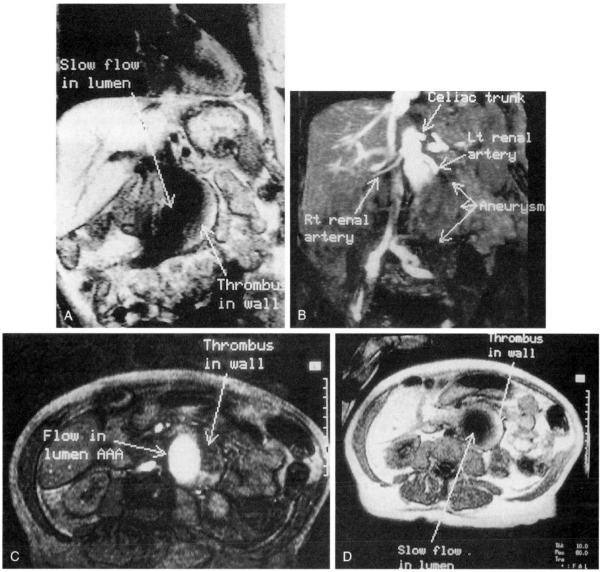

Figure 3–52. Infrarenal abdominal aortic aneurysm (AAA). *A,* Coronal black blood TurboFLASH image shows blood within the lumen (labeled) and thrombus in the wall (labeled). *B,* Coronal projection angiogram gated to systole shows both renal arteries above the aneurysm and shows poor flow enhancement downstream resulting from in-plane saturation. *C,* The same sequence in the axial plane yields good flow contrast between the lumen and thrombus in the wall, and these correlate well on the axial black blood image *(D).* (Courtesy of Paul Finn, M.D., Northwestern University, Chicago.)

arterial imaging. Although the impetus for this method is well founded on the need to understand the delivery of oxygen-bearing blood to the tissue and to visualize the arteries themselves to discover diseased vessels, the venous blood carries with it the information about tissue function. One can consider the arterial blood as reflecting *input* function and the venous blood as reflecting *output* function. If oxygen saturation in the veins could be measured, it would serve as a means to quantify the cerebral metabolic uptake of oxygen by the brain tissue.

Today, major veins in the brain can be visualized after use of a contrast agent or with a 2D TOF approach. Still, smaller veins are difficult to see with conventional methods, because the background parenchymal signal also increases thanks to its local blood volume content after the

injection of a contrast agent. By using the blood oxygenation level–dependent (BOLD) effect, however, we can design a 3D sequence to highlight the veins as dark structures while leaving the arteries with as much or more signal than the background tissue.[51] We choose an echo time in which the phase of the veins becomes opposed to that of the surrounding tissue for vessels parallel to the main magnetic field. This occurs at roughly 40 to 50 msec at 1.5 T.

Now consider a two-compartment model in which λ is the venous signal fraction of blood in that voxel. If the normalized signal at any given echo time is $1 - \lambda$ for the parenchyma and λ for the veins, then when $\varphi = \pi$, the summed signal of both components is $1 - 2\lambda$ and the veins will look darker than the surrounding tissue. The

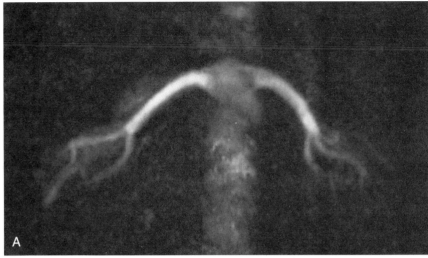

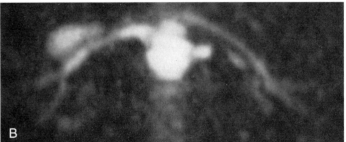

Figure 3–53. Images were obtained using a 3D phase contrast technique, which included 32 slices with 2-mm-thick partitions, a 128×256 matrix, and 24-cm field of view, TR = 34 msec, and TE = 9 msec. The velocity-encoding (VENC) value was equal to 40 cm/second and two averages were used. Three-directional velocity encoding was used and resulted in an 18-minute data acquisition time. *A*, A normal pair of renal arteries. *B*, Stenosis of the right renal artery. (Courtesy of Thomas M. Grist, University of Wisconsin.)

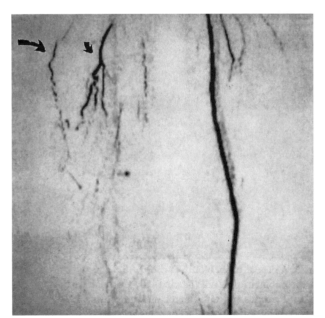

Figure 3–54. Occluded right superficial femoral artery. Coronal cine phase contrast MRA study: TR/TE, 24/11, 30 degrees, superior inferior flow encoding, velocity-encoding (VENC) value = 60 cm/second, 40 cm-field of view. The approximate acquisition time was 2 minutes 20 seconds. This image used a projection-dephasing gradient so that the slice thickness was infinite. Note the collateral flow in the right profunda femoral artery *(small arrow)* and the deep muscular branch collateral *(larger arrow).* (Courtesy of Fred Steinberg, M.D., Magnetic Resonance Institute of Boca Raton, Fla.)

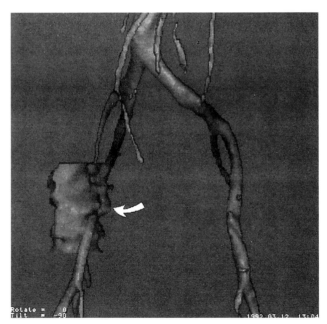

Figure 3–55. Encasement of the right iliac vein by metastatic lymph node. Coronal projection of 2D time-of-flight MRA study with arterial presaturation. This color-encoded image shows the mass *(white arrow)* encasing the iliac vein in this patient with right leg swelling. (Courtesy of Fred Steinberg, M.D., Magnetic Resonance Institute of Boca Raton, Fla.)

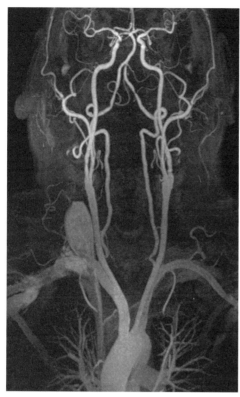

Figure 3–56. Dynamic contrast-enhanced image of the neck and aortic arch acquired in 18 seconds. (Courtesy of Paul Finn, M.D., Northwestern University, Chicago.)

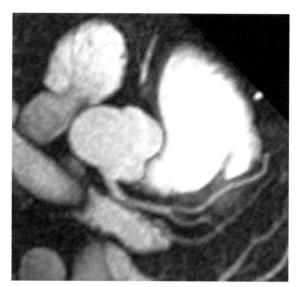

Figure 3–58. Contrast-enhanced image of the left coronary artery system, including the left main coronary artery, a portion of the circumflex artery, and the left anterior descending artery and its first branching into secondary vessels. Other portions of the heart and pulmonary system are also visible in the image. These data were collected in a breath-hold after the injection of a T1-reducing contrast agent. (Courtesy of Debiao Li, Ph.D., Washington University, St. Louis.)

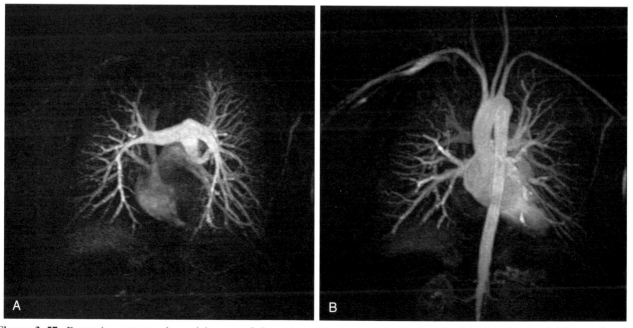

Figure 3–57. Dynamic contrast-enhanced images of the pulmonary system immediately after injection *(top)* and 10 seconds after injection *(bottom)*. Each scan is acquired in a short breath-hold. (Courtesy of Paul Finn, M.D., Northwestern University, Chicago.)

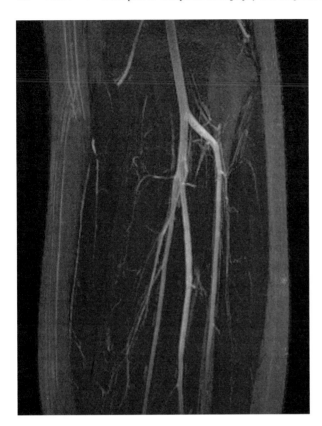

Figure 3–59. Contrast-enhanced image of the peripheral vessels. This data set has a resolution of 0.5 mm × 0.5 mm × 0.7 mm and took roughly 10 minutes to collect. Because the collection was conducted with central reordering, the veins do not show up as bright (except for their edges).

larger λ is, the stronger the cancellation. A series of these images is viewed using a minimum intensity projection to show the connectivity of the venous vessels.

An example of this method along with a contrast-enhanced image for comparison is shown in Figure 3–60. Figure 3–60*A* represents a minimum intensity projection over five 2-mm slices from this venographic technique. Figure 3–60*B* represents a maximum intensity projection over the same region from a T1-weighted data set acquired after injection of contrast material.

Future Directions

MRA has come a long way since the mid-1980s. Much of its progress is due to the ingenuity of the many investigators who have contributed to this field. A great deal is also owed to the developments of better gradients and the ability to image significantly faster than before. But the real progress comes with the combination of the hardware and the methodology with the new high-relaxivity contrast agents. This advance opens the door to continued new

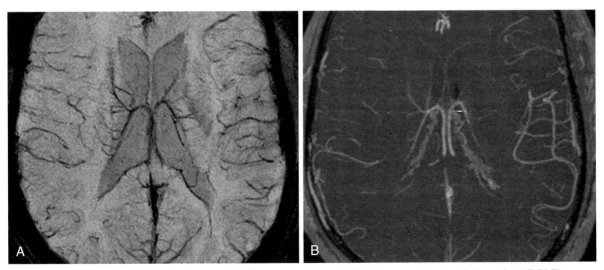

Figure 3–60. *A*, Minimum intensity projection over five 2-mm slices from the blood oxygenation level–dependent (BOLD) venographic technique. *B*, Maximum intensity projection over the same region from a T1-weighted data set acquired after contrast injection.

developments in the field, faster acquisition of data, better resolution, and availability of more functional information. From measuring flow to visualizing coronary arteries, MRI is making it possible to create the "vascular-visible" human (see www.mrimaging.com).

References

1. Anderson CM, Edelman RR, Turski PA: Clinical Magnetic Resonance Angiography. New York, Raven Press, 1993.
2. Anderson CM, Saloner D, Tsuruda JS, et al: Artifacts in maximum-intensity-projection display of MR angiograms. AJR Am J Roentgenol 154:623–629, 1990.
3. Belliveau JW, Kennedy DN, McKinstry RC, et al: Functional mapping of the human visual cortex by magnetic resonance imaging. Science 254:716–719, 1991.
4. Belliveau JW, Rosen BR, Kantor HL, et al: Functional cerebral imaging by susceptibility contrast NMR. Magn Reson Med 14:538–546, 1990.
5. Bendel P, Buonocore E, Bockisch A, et al: Blood flow in the carotid arteries: Quantification by using phase-sensitive MR imaging. AJR Am J Roentgenol 152:1307–1310, 1989.
6. Blatter DD, Parker DL, Ahn SS, et al: Cerebral MR angiography with multiple overlapping thin slab acquisition. Part II. Early clinical experience. Radiology 183:379–389, 1992.
7. Blatter DD, Parker DL, Robinson R: Cerebral MR angiography with multiple overlapping thin slab acquisition. Part I. Quantitative analysis of vessel visibility. Radiology 179:805–811, 1991.
8. Chakeres DW, Schmalbrock P, Brogan M, et al: Normal venous anatomy of the brain: demonstration with gadopentetate dimeglumine in enhanced 3D MR angiography. AJR Am J Roentgenol 156:161–172, 1991.
9. Cline HZ, Dumoulin CL, Lorensen WE, et al: Volume rendering and connectivity algorithm for MR angiography. Magn Reson Med 18:384–394, 1991.
10. Cline HZ, Lorensen WE, Kikinis R, et al: Three-dimensional segmentation of MR images of the head using probability and connectivity. J Comput Assist Tomogr 14:1037–1045, 1990.
11. Creasy JL, Price RR, Presbrey T, et al: Gadolinium-enhanced MR angiography. Radiology 175:280–283, 1990.
12. Dixon WT: Simple proton spectroscopic imaging. Radiology 153:189–194, 1984.
13. Dixon WT: Use of magnetization transfer contrast in gradient-recalled echo images. Radiology 179:15–16, 1991.
14. Dumoulin CL, Souza SP, Walker MF, et al: Three dimensional phase contrast angiography. Magn Reson Med 9:139–149, 1989.
15. Dumoulin CL, Souza SP, Walker MF, et al: Time-resolved magnetic resonance angiography. Magn Reson Med 6:275–286, 1988.
16. Edelman RR, Ahn SS, Chien D, et al: Improved time-of-flight MR angiography of the brain with magnetization transfer contrast. Radiology 184:395–399, 1992.
17. Edelman RR, Chien D, Kim D: Fast selective black blood imaging. Radiology 181:655–660, 1991.
18. Edelman RR, Mattle HP, Wallner B, et al: Extracranial carotid arteries: evaluation with "black blood" MR angiography. Radiology 177:45–50, 1990.
19. Feinberg DA, Crooks LE, Hoenninger J, et al: Pulsatile blood velocity in human arteries displayed by magnetic resonance imaging. Radiology 153:177–180, 1984.
20. Feinberg DA, Crooks LE, Sheldon P, et al: Magnetic resonance imaging the velocity vector components of fluid flow. Magn Reson Med 2:555–566, 1985.
21. Frahm J, Bruhn H, Merboldt K-D, et al: Dynamic MR imaging of human brain oxygenation during rest and photic stimulation. J Magn Reson Imaging 2:501–505, 1992.
22. Frahm J, Merboldt K-D, Hanicke W: Functional MRI of human brain activation at high spatial resolution. Magn Reson Med 29:139–144, 1992.
23. Haacke EM, Brown RW, Thompson MR, Venkatesan R. Magnetic Resonance Imaging: Physical Principles and Sequence Design. New York, John Wiley & Sons, 1999.
24. Haacke EM, Lenz GW: Improving MR image quality in the presence of motion by using rephasing gradients. AJR Am J Roentgenol 148:1251–1258, 1987.
25. Haacke EM, Lindskog E, Lin W: Partial-Fourier imaging: a fast, iterative, POCS technique capable of local phase recovery. J Magn Reson 126–145, 1991.
26. Haacke EM, Masaryk TJ, Wielopolski PA, et al: Optimalizing blood vessel contrast in fast 3D MRI. Magn Reson Med 14:102–121, 1990.
27. Haacke EM, Patrick JL, Lenz GW, et al: The separation of water and lipid components in the presence of field inhomogeneities. Rev Magn Reson Med 1:123–154, 1986.
28. Hardy CJ, Pearlman JD, Moore J, et al: Continuous cardiography with a half-echo MR M-mode method. In SMRM 10th Annual Meeting, Book of Abstracts, vol 1. New York, 1990, p 280.
29. Henning J, Mueri M, Brunner P, et al: Quantitative flow measurement with the fast Fourier flow technique. Radiology 166:237–240, 1988.
30. Hu X, Alperin N, Levin DN, et al: Visualization of MR angiographic data with segmentation and volume-rendering techniques. J Magn Reson Imaging 1:539–546, 1991.
31. Keller PJ, Hunter WW, Schmalbrock P: Multislice fat-water imaging with chemical shift selective presaturation. Radiology 164:539–541, 1987.
32. Krug B, Kugel H, Friedmann G, et al: MR imaging of poststenotic flow phenomena: experimental studies. J Magn Reson Imaging 1:585–591, 1991.
33. Kwait D, Elnav S, Elad D: A magnetic resonance imaging method of flow by successive excitation of moving slice. Med Phys 17:258–263, 1990.
34. Laub GW, Kaiser WA: MR angiography with gradient motion refocusing. J Comput Assist Tomogr 12:377–382, 1988.
35. Laub GW, Purdy DE: Variable-tip-angle slab selection for improved three-dimensional MR angiography. In SMRI 10th Annual Meeting, Book of Abstracts, 1992, Chicago, p 167.
36. Lin W, Haacke EM, Masaryk TJ, et al: Automated local maximum-intensity projection with three-dimensional vessel tracking. J Magn Reson Imaging 2:519–526, 1992.
37. Lin W, Haacke EM, Smith AS: Lumen definition in MR angiography. J Magn Reson Imaging 1:327–336, 1991.
38. Lin W, Haacke EM, Smith AS, et al: High resolution magnetic resonance angiography using gadopentetate dimeglumine with adaptive vessel tracking: preliminary results in studying the intracranial circulation. J Magn Reson Imaging 2:277–284, 1992.
39. Lin W, Tkach JA, Haacke EM, et al: Intracranial MR angiography: Application of magnetization transfer contrast and fat saturation to short gradient-echo, velocity-compensated sequences. Radiology 186:753–761, 1993.
40. Maki JH, Prince MR, Londy FJ, Chenevert TL: The effects of time varying intravascular signal intensity and k-space acquisition order on three-dimensional MR angiography image quality. J Magn Reson Imaging 6:642–651, 1996.
41. Masaryk TJ, Modic MT, Ross JS, et al: Intracranial circulation: Preliminary clinical results with three-dimensional (volume) MR angiography. Radiology 171:793–799, 1989.
42. Matsuda T, Shimizu K, Sakurai T, et al: Spin-echo M-mode NMR imaging. Magn Reson Med 27:238–246, 1992.
43. Mueller E, Laub G, Grauman R, et al: RACE—real time acquisition and evaluation of pulsatile blood flow on a whole body MRI unit. In SMRM 7th Annual Meeting, Book of Abstracts. San Francisco, 1988, p 729.
44. Nishimura DG, Macovski A, Pauly JM: Magnetic resonance angiography. IEEE Trans Med Imaging MI-5:140–151, 1986.
45. Parker DL, Yuan C, Blatter DD: MRA angiography by multiple thin slab 3D acquisition. Magn Reson Med 17:434–451, 1991.
46. Pelc NJ, Shimakawa A, Glover GH: Phase contrast cine MRI. In SMRM 8th Annual Meeting, Book of Abstracts, Amsterdam, The Netherlands, 1989.
47. Pettigrew RI, Dannels W, Galloway JR, et al: Quantitative phase-flow MR imaging by using standard comparison with in vivo flowmeter measurement. AJR Am J Roentgenol 148:411–414, 1987.
48. Pike GB, Hu BS, Glover GH, et al: Magnetization transfer time-of-flight magnetic resonance angiography. Magn Reson Med 25:372–379, 1992.
49. Potchen EJ, Haacke EM, Siebert JE, Gottschalk A (eds): Magnetic Resonance Angiography: Concepts and Applications, St. Louis, CV Mosby, 1993.
50. Prince MR, Yucel EK, Kaufman JA, et al: Dynamic gadolinium-enhanced 3D abdominal MR arteriography. J Magn Reson Imaging 3:877–881, 1993.
51. Reichenbach JR, Venkatesan R, Schillinger D, et al: Small vessels in

the human brain: MR venography with deoxyhemoglobin as an intrinsic contrast agent. Radiology 204:272–277, 1997.

52. Revel D, Loubeyre P, Delignette A, et al: Contrast-enhanced magnetic resonance tomoangiography: A new imaging technique for studying thoracic great vessels. Magn Reson Imaging 11:1101–1105, 1993.

53. Saloner D, Hanson WA, Tsuruda JS, et al: Application of a connected-voxel algorithm to MR angiographic data. J Magn Reson Imaging 1: 423–430, 1991.

54. Schmalbrock P, Yuan C, Chakeres DW, et al: Volume MR angiography: Methods to achieve very short echo times. Radiology 175: 861–865, 1990.

55. Smith AS, Haacke EM, Lin W, et al: Carotid MR angiography: Technique for improved maximal intensity projection resolution and decreased cost. In 76th Scientific Assembly and Annual Meeting of the Radiological Society of North America, Oak Brook, Ill, Book of Abstracts, 1990, p 89.

56. Smith AS, Lin W, Haacke EM, et al: Cerebrovascular high resolution MR angiography—techniques application. In Book of Abstracts, vol 2, Tenth Annual Meeting in SMRM, 1991, p 938.

57. Thomsen C, Stahlbert F, Stubgarrd M, et al: Fourier analysis of cerebrospinal fluid flow velocities: MR imaging study. Radiology 177:659–665, 1990.

58. Tkach JA, Lin W, Masaryk TJ, et al: The use of spatial and/or temporal modulation of the excitation flip angle to reduce blood saturation in 3D TOF MRA of the ICV's. In SMRI 11th Annual Meeting, Book of Abstracts, 1992, p 3124.

59. Underwood SR, Firmin DN, Klipstein RH, et al: Magnetic velocity mapping: Clinical application of a new technique. Br Heart J 57: 404–412, 1987.

60. Venkatesan R, Haacke EM: Role of high resolution in magnetic resonance (MR) imaging: Applications to MR angiography, intracranial T1-weighted imaging, and image interpolation. Int J Imaging Systems Technol 8:529–543, 1997.

61. Wehrli FW, Perkins TG, Shimakawa A, et al: Chemical shift–induced amplitude modulations in images obtained with gradient refocusing. Magn Reson Imaging 5:157–158, 1987.

62. Wilman AH, Riederer SJ, King BF, et al: Fluorscopically triggered contrast-enhanced 3D MR angiography with elliptical centric view order: Application to the renal arteries. Radiology 205:137–146, 1997.

63. Wolff SD, Balaban RS: Magnetization transfer contrast (MTC) and tissue water proton relaxation in vivo. Magn Reson Med 10:135–144, 1989.

64. Wolff SD, Eng J, Balaban RS: Magnetization transfer contrast: Method for improving contrast in gradient-recalled echo images. Radiology 179:133–137, 1991.

Part
II

Brain and Meninges

Edited by
Charles Lanzieri

4

Normal Computed Tomography and Magnetic Resonance Imaging Anatomy of the Brain and the Spine

M. Hossain Naheedy

CT and MRI Anatomy of the Brain

In this section of the chapter, a brief review of the gross surface anatomy precedes the explanation of computed tomography (CT) and magnetic resonance imaging (MRI) techniques and is followed by a discussion of sectional anatomy in multiplanar axes, as seen in these two modalities.

Overview of Surface Anatomy[10, 21, 33, 34]

Dura and Dural Structures

The brain substance is covered by cerebrospinal fluid (CSF) to allow the brain to float in the intracranial cavity of the calvarium. The brain is separated from the calvarium by pia mater, arachnoid membrane, and dura mater. The pia mater follows all the gyri and is separated from the arachnoid membrane by CSF. The outer layer of the dura is attached to the periosteum of the bony calvarium. The dura is separated from the arachnoid membrane by potential subdural space. The dural sinuses are venous structures made between the dural reflections and their opposing edges, thereby forming the superior and inferior sagittal, transverse, sigmoid, cavernous, and straight sinuses. These sinuses drain to the jugular venous system.

Ventricles

There are four ventricles within the brain that contain choroid plexus–producing CSF.

Lateral Ventricles

Traditionally, the left lateral ventricle is labeled first, followed next by the right lateral ventricle. The two lateral ventricles join to the third ventricle via the midline foramen of Monro (Fig. 4–1). The lateral ventricles are open C-shaped cavities extending from front to back within deep brain tissue. They are covered by a layer of ependymal cells, forming inner walls.

The anterior extensions into the frontal lobes are called *frontal horns*. The frontal horns are separated from each other midline by the septum pellucidum. Sometimes a cavity exists between the two layers of septum, which produces the cavum septi pellucidi, most commonly seen in early infancy. Posterior extension of this cavity between the two lateral ventricles produces the cavum vergae, which unites with the subarachnoid spaces behind the pineal region. The frontal horns are outlined laterally by the head of the caudate nuclei.

Anteriorly, the frontal horns are bound by the genu of the corpus callosum. The body of the lateral ventricles extends posteriorly over the corpus callosum and is outlined by the body of the caudate nuclei. The posterior extension of the body of the lateral ventricles forms the occipital horns.

Medially, the occipital horns are bound by the splenium of the corpus callosum, causing the peculiar shape of the occipital horns. The temporal horns are the extension of the lateral ventricles into the temporal lobes. The place where the temporal and occipital horns and the body of the lateral ventricles meet is called the *atrium* and is the most expanded part of the lateral ventricles. The main portion of the choroid plexus is located in the atrium, with some portions extending into the temporal and occipital horns.

Third Ventricle

The third ventricle is a midline structure situated between the two thalami. Anteriorly, the floor of the third ventricle is formed by the tuber cinereum; posteriorly, it is bounded by the cerebral peduncles. The roof of the third ventricle is formed by the velum interpositum. Occasionally, a cavity exists between these two layers of velum, forming the cavum velum interpositum, which is readily visible in coronal and sagittal MRI studies.

Fourth Ventricle

The fourth ventricle is located in the posterior fossa between the pons and cerebellum. The fourth ventricle is

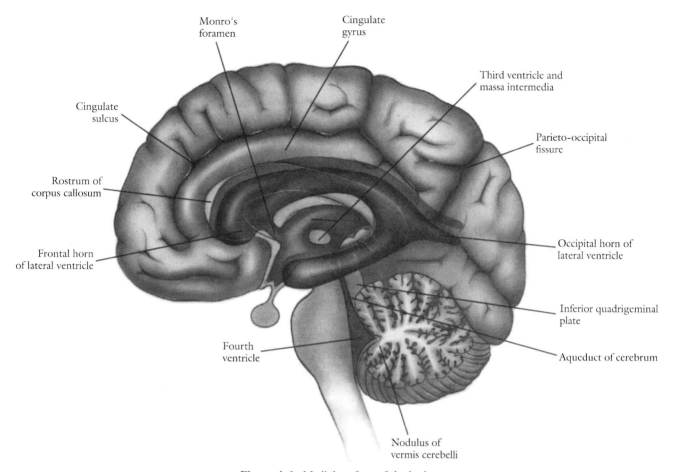

Figure 4–1. Medial surface of the brain.

connected to the third ventricle via the cerebral aqueduct. CSF, which is excreted by the choroid, flows from the lateral ventricles to the third ventricle and from there to the fourth ventricle, exiting the ventricles (via the foramen of Magendie in midline and the foramen of Luschka on either side of the fourth ventricle) to drain into the cisterna magna.

Cerebral Hemispheres[10, 15]

The two cerebral hemispheres are separated by interhemispheric fissures and falx cerebri. The deep fissures separate the lobes, and the sulci separate the adjacent gyri. On the lateral surface of the brain, the sylvian fissure begins anteriorly and inferiorly, separating the frontal lobe as it extends posteriorly and superiorly.

The rolandic fissure (central fissure) starts from the superior midhemisphere and extends anteriorly and inferiorly to separate the frontal lobe from the parietal lobe, ending at the junction of the anterior and middle thirds of the sylvian fissure over the lateral surface of the brain. There is no anatomic landmark to separate the occipital lobe from the parietal lobe. Three sulci over the lateral surface of the frontal lobe divide it into superior, middle, and inferior frontal gyri. Two small sulci divide the lower frontal lobe into the orbital, opercular, and triangular gyri.

Two transverse sulci divide the temporal lobe into superior, middle, and inferior temporal gyri. Heschl's gyrus is located anterolateral over the upper superior temporal gyrus and inferior to the sylvian fissure. The postcentral sulcus separates the postcentral gyrus from the remainder of the parietal lobe. The precentral sulcus separates the precentral gyrus from the remainder of the frontal lobe. The transverse sulcus divides the parietal lobe into superior and inferior parietal gyri.

On the medial aspect, the two hemispheres are connected by the corpus callosum. The callosal fissure separates the corpus callosum from the cingulate gyrus, and it is separated from the frontal lobe by the cingulate sulcus. On the medial aspect, the frontal lobe has several sulci separating the orbitofrontal, frontal polar, anterior inferior frontal, middle internal frontal, and posterior interior frontal gyri (Fig. 4–2). In the parietal bone, the marginal sulcus separates the paracentral lobule from the superior parietal lobe. On the medial aspect, the occipital lobe is separated from the parietal lobe by the parieto-occipital sulcus. The hippocampal gyrus is located between the medial aspect of the temporal lobe and the lateral aspect of the midbrain. The hippocampal gyrus is separated from the parahippocampal gyrus by the hippocampal sulcus. These two gyri unite to form the uncus of the temporal lobe.

Hemispheric White Matter

The axons of the neurons from the cerebral cortex and basal ganglia form the white matter. Some white matter

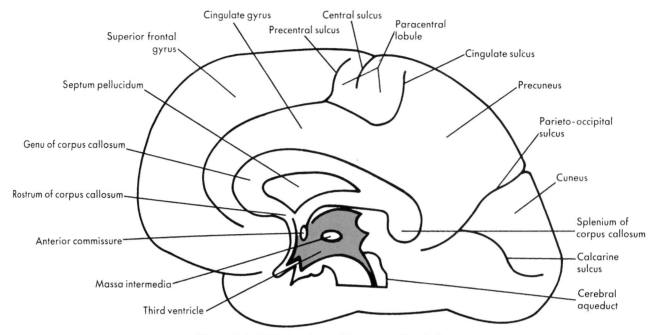

Figure 4–2. Medial surface of the cerebral hemisphere.

fibers connect the adjacent lobes, and some connect the two hemispheres.

The interhemispheric commissures are the following:

1. Anterior commissure, connecting the temporal lobes.
2. Posterior commissure, connecting the rostral midbrain nuclei, located behind the third ventricle.
3. Corpus callosum, a large commissure connecting the two hemispheres: it is located over the lateral ventricles and extends anteroposteriorly from the fornices, genu, body, and splenium.

The intrahemispheric commissures are the following:

1. Visual radiations, connecting the lateral geniculate bodies to the occipital lobes.
2. Superior longitudinal fasciculus, connecting the occipital lobes to the parietal and frontal lobes.
3. Arcuate fasciculus, connecting the temporal lobe to the superior longitudinal fasciculus.
4. Cingulate fibers, connecting the cingulate gyrus to the middle temporal gyrus.
5. Fornix, connecting the hippocampus to the ipsilateral mammillary body.

Posterior Fossa (Fig. 4–3)

The posterior fossa contains the cerebellum, brain stem, pons, and medulla, and it is outlined by the clivus, petrous, and occipital bones. The superior boundary of the posterior fossa is the tentorium cerebelli, which opens into the tentorial notch, permitting the connection of the infratentorial structures to the supratentorial structures. The posterior fossa is divided into two compartments by the fourth ventricle. Anteriorly, the brain stem occupies about one third of the posterior fossa; posteriorly, the cerebellum occupies the posterior two thirds.

The brain stem has three anatomically recognizable components: (1) midbrain, (2) pons, and (3) medulla.

The *midbrain* consists of cerebral peduncles anteriorly and colliculi posteriorly. The cerebral peduncles are separated from each other by the interpeduncular fossa, a CSF-filled space that merges with the suprasellar cistern. The basilar artery lies in this fossa. In the dorsal aspect of the cerebral peduncles are four nubbins of colliculi, outlined by the quadrigeminal cistern. This cistern extends laterally and anteriorly to merge with the perimesencephalic cistern. Superiorly, this space is limited by the tentorium and the great vein of Galen. Anteriorly, this space is connected to the velum interpositum over the top of the third ventricle. This space as well as the interpeduncular fossa should almost always be visible on axial CT or MRI scans. Any asymmetry of the quadrigeminal plate cistern is indicative of a mass effect.

The *pons* is characterized by anterior bulging, which is caused by the middle cerebellar peduncles and the pontocerebellar connections. Laterally, the pons rests against the medial posterior aspect of the petrous bone. There is a CSF-filled space between the lateral aspect of the pons and the anterior aspect of the cerebellum (floccular lobules), called the *cerebellopontine angle* (CPA). The seventh and eighth cranial nerves cross this space to enter the internal auditory meatus. In the most caudal aspect, the ninth and tenth cranial nerves cross this space; superiorly, the fifth nerve crosses it.

The *medulla* is the most caudal portion of the brain stem and connects to the cervical cord at the level of the foramen magnum. The medulla is separated from the pons by the transverse sulcus. The pyramids and other longitudinal tracts cause minimum anterior bulging in the long axis on the ventral surface of the medulla, making its appearance different from the pons. The inferior cerebellar peduncle makes the superior protrusion on the lateral aspect of the medulla.

The two cerebellar hemispheres are joined by the midline structure of the vermis. Transverse fissures and sulci

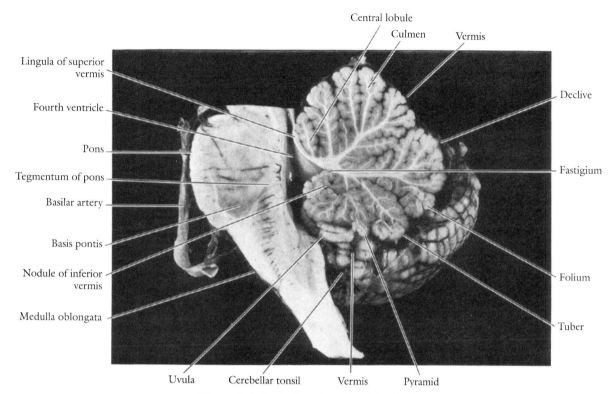

Figure 4–3. Sagittal section of the hind brain.

(cerebellar folia) separate the laminae. The anterosuperior fissure (primary fissure) divides the cerebellum into anterior and posterior lobes. The posterior lobe is divided by another major fissure (the posterolateral fissure) in the flocculonodular and nodular lobules.

Vascular Supply[1, 10, 14, 21]

The brain derives its vascular supply (Fig. 4–4) via two carotid and two vertebral arteries. The internal carotid artery, after giving off the ophthalmic branch and posterior communicating and anterior choroidal arteries in the supraclinoid portion, divides into the anterior and middle cerebral arteries. The anterior cerebral artery supplies blood mainly to the frontal lobe medially and mediolaterally, with some supply to the parasagittal parietal lobe. The lenticulostriate arteries, arising from the horizontal portion of the anterior cerebral artery, supply the medial basal ganglia and part of the internal capsule. The anterior choroidal branch of the internal carotid artery supplies the remaining portion of the internal capsule as well as the choroid plexus. The lenticulostriate arteries, arising from the horizontal portion of the middle cerebral artery, supply the lateral basal ganglia. At this juncture, the middle cerebral artery branches in the anterior inferior sylvian fissure into two or three branches that supply the temporal and parietal lobes. The posterior cerebral arteries, terminal branches of the basilar artery, supply the occipital lobes. The thalamoperforate arteries, arising from the posterior communicating artery and the most proximal portion of the posterior cerebral arteries, supply the thalami. The posterior temporal branch of the posterior cerebral artery supplies the posterior temporal lobe.

On axial CT scans, one can readily delineate the vascular territory by drawing a line along the anterior and posterior course of the lateral border of the lateral ventricles (see Fig. 4–4). The area between the anterior portion of the interhemispheric fissure and a line along the anterior lateral wall of the lateral ventricle is the anterior cerebral territory. The area between the posterior portion of the interhemispheric fissure and a line along the posterior lateral wall of the lateral ventricle is the posterior cerebral territory. The area between the lines along the lateral ventricle wall is the middle cerebral territory.

In high-convexity slices above the ventricular levels, almost all parasagittal areas of the frontal and parietal lobes are supplied by branches of the anterior cerebral artery, with the small portion in the posterior medial area supplied by the branches of the posterior cerebral artery. The ill-defined anterior area between the anterior cerebral artery and the middle cerebral artery is called the *anterior watershed region*. The posterior watershed area lies between the territory of the middle cerebral and posterior cerebral arteries. These two areas are more susceptible to hypotensive infarctions than other areas of the brain are.

In the posterior fossa, the inferior vermis, inferior cerebellar hemispheres, and choroid plexus of the fourth ventricle are supplied by the posterior inferior cerebellar artery and its branches, which arise from the vertebral artery before or at about the level of the foramen magnum. The area of the CPA and the anterior inferior cerebellar hemispheres are supplied by the branches of the anterior inferior cerebellar artery, which is a branch of the basilar artery. The perforator branches of the basilar artery supply the pons. The superior cerebellar arteries, arising from the

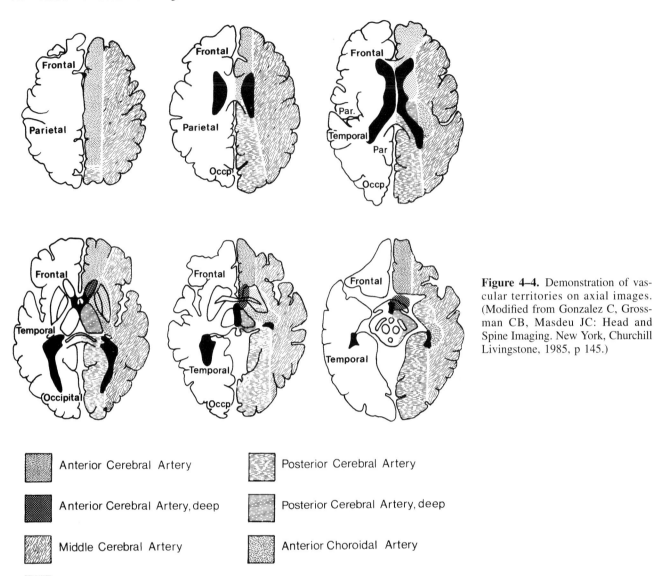

Figure 4–4. Demonstration of vascular territories on axial images. (Modified from Gonzalez C, Grossman CB, Masdeu JC: Head and Spine Imaging. New York, Churchill Livingstone, 1985, p 145.)

Anterior Cerebral Artery

Anterior Cerebral Artery, deep

Middle Cerebral Artery

Middle Cerebral Artery, deep

Posterior Cerebral Artery

Posterior Cerebral Artery, deep

Anterior Choroidal Artery

basilar artery, supply the superior portion of the cerebellar hemispheres.

CT Technique[11, 22, 36]

Routine head CT is performed in an axial axis with a 15- to 20-degree angulation of the gantry to the canthomeatal line. This angulation decreases radiation to the eyes. There has been a tendency, on CT scans, to reduce this angle parallel to the canthomeatal line to match the MRI slices. The latter technique is preferred in axial imaging of the orbits and the sellar region. Slice thickness varies among different scanners and can be adjusted according to the area of interest. In routine studies, slices 8 to 10 mm thick are used. In evaluation of the orbits, the pituitary gland, the suprasellar and parasellar regions, and the CPA, thinner slices—1.5 to 3 mm thick—are needed. In these situations, coronal CT scans are also essential. Using the bony algorithm is highly important to review the bony

detail in evaluating trauma patients with facial bone and petrous bone diseases.

Contrast Studies

Except in acute trauma, excluding bleed in acute stroke, hydrocephalus, and follow-up of trauma patients, the use of intravenous (IV) contrast medium is routine. At least 100 mL, preferably 150 mL, of a 60% iodinated contrast agent should be given for optimal study results. In evaluating arteriovenous malformation, neoplastic disease (either primary or metastatic), the pituitary gland, or the sellar region, a contrast agent is essential unless renal disease or a history of sensitivity to contrast medium contradicts this usage.

In postcontrast studies, the following structures enhance physiologically without any break in the blood-brain barrier:

1. The pituitary gland and its stalk, which enhance homo-

geneously. Heterogeneity is an indication of pathologic processes.

2. Dural structures, including the interhemispheric falx, falx cerebelli, tentorium along the cavernous sinus, the tentorial notch.
3. Arterial structures in the suprasellar region, including the circle of Willis and proximal portions of the anterior, middle, and posterior cerebral arteries. The deep venous structures, such as the internal cerebral vein, vein of Galen, and dural sinuses, do show enhancement.
4. The choroid plexus within the lateral, third, and fourth ventricles. Care should be given not to confuse the nodular enhancement in the fourth ventricle, or a comma-shaped enhancement within the temporal horns connecting to the rest of the plexus in the atrium, with the enhancing mass.

Intrathecal use of contrast medium has become nearly obsolete in the evaluation of intracranial disease. This technique was commonly used for the evaluation of CPA masses, sellar region masses, and empty-sella syndrome.

MRI Technique

Routine MRI studies of the brain are performed in axial, coronal, and, sometimes, in sagittal axes in varying thickness from 5 to 10 mm. T1 images have a shorter repetition time (TR) of less than 1000 msec and a short echo time (TE) of less than 30 msec. The T2-weighted images have a long TR of more than 1500 msec. The first echo of T2 images with shorter TE is called *proton density*, or balanced T1 and T2 images. The second echo of T2 images with a longer TR of over 60 msec represents real T2 images. Studies have shown that most pathologic processes cause an increase in the water content of the brain. Therefore, T2 images are highly sensitive in detecting brain pathology.

Routinely, T1 and T2 axial and T2 coronal studies are performed. The T2 images contain a first echo with short TR and a second echo of long TR. In the evaluation of sellar and posterior fossa regions, sagittal and coronal images of 2 to 4 mm thick are needed. Specific techniques are needed to diagnose various pathologic processes; these are mentioned in related chapters.

The CSF has a long T1, which demonstrates low signal intensity in T1 images, but becomes slightly higher in intensity in the first echo T2 images. In real T2 (long TE and very long TR) images, the CSF has very high signal intensity. The basal ganglia, dentate nuclei of the cerebellum, and red nuclei of the midbrain have low signal intensities in T2 images because of their mineral content.[6] The gray matter has a slightly higher signal intensity in relation to white matter in almost all spin-echo images. The very high signal intensity of fat in T1 images can be appreciated within the diploic space and is outlined by the low signal intensity of cortical bone. Vascular structures show signal void in all regular T1, T2, and proton-density images because of the moving protons of circulating blood. Flowing CSF can have the same effect, demonstrating signal void in the cerebral aqueduct.[29] The appearance of the vessels can be changed if the special technique of magnetic resonance angiography (MRA) is applied.

So far, gadolinium compounds are the only contrast medium approved by the Food and Drug Administration that may be used intravenously. The regular dose is about 0.1 mmol/kg of body weight, and the agent must be injected at a slow rate. The same structures that enhance with IV use of contrast medium on CT scans enhance similarly on MRI scans.

Sectional Anatomy

Normal Axial CT and MRI Anatomy[10, 11, 21, 22]

CT scans are reviewed from the caudal to cephalic levels; the scans are obtained at a 15- to 20-degree angulation to the canthomeatal line. MRI scans are generally obtained parallel to this line. These scans are divided into posterior fossa cuts of 5-mm increments and supratentorial cuts of 8-mm increments.

Posterior Fossa Cuts

Four slices from the foramen magnum to the suprasellar region are now reviewed.

Above the Foramen Magnum Level (Fig. 4–5)

The cerebellar tonsils can be seen lateral to the medulla. Most of the structures in the anterior and middle fossa are components of the base of the skull and the orbits. In the middle fossa, the foramen ovale and spinosum can be visualized if a wide window setting is used. They transmit the third branch of the fifth cranial nerve and the middle meningeal artery, respectively. The inferior portion of the cisterna magna outlines the posterior aspect of the cerebellar hemispheres.

Level of the Fourth Ventricle (Fig. 4–6)

The lower pons is seen in front of the fourth ventricle, connecting to the cerebellar hemispheres by the middle cerebellar peduncles. The pons is outlined by the anterior and lateral mesencephalic cisterns containing CSF. On MRI examinations, the seventh and eighth cranial nerves can be seen at this level. Posteriorly, the fourth ventricle is outlined by the nodulous in the midline and cerebellar hemispheres laterally. The choroid plexus within the fourth ventricle, which may enhance, can simulate a true nodule and should not be mistaken as the true parenchymal nodule.

Above the Fourth Ventricular Level (Fig. 4–7A–C)

The superior cerebellar surface is seen with separation of the two hemispheres by the superior vermis. With contrast studies, the transverse sinuses can be seen joining together in the torcula. In the middle fossa, the temporal lobes are separated from the frontal lobe by the sylvian fissure. The temporal horn, seen as a comma-shaped structure in the middle of the temporal lobe, is easily visualized in patients older than 50 years of age. Sometimes enhancement of both the choroid plexus within the temporal horn, extending to the atrium and the tentorium medially, can mimic an enhancing nodule in this region. The medial aspect of the temporal lobes bounds the suprasellar cistern and contains the internal carotid artery, the optic chiasm, the infundibulum, the mammillary bodies, and the top of the basilar artery (Fig. 4–7D–F). In the anterior fossa, the

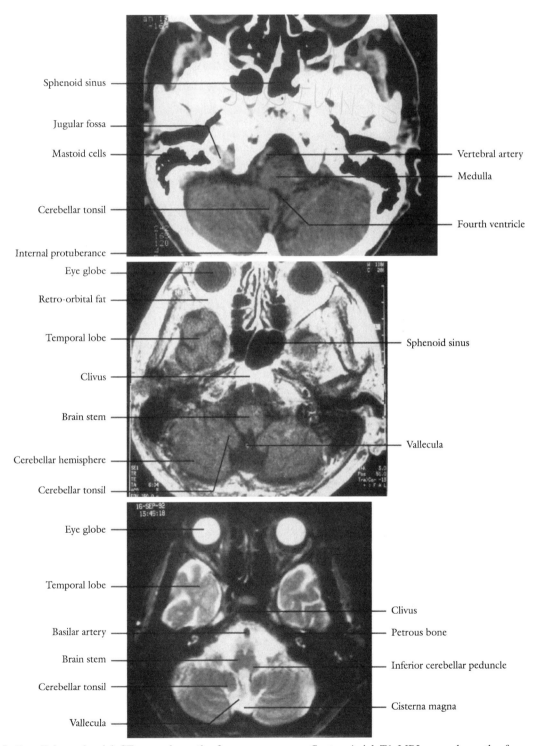

Sphenoid sinus

Jugular fossa

Mastoid cells

Cerebellar tonsil

Internal protuberance

Vertebral artery

Medulla

Fourth ventricle

Eye globe

Retro-orbital fat

Temporal lobe

Clivus

Brain stem

Cerebellar hemisphere

Cerebellar tonsil

Sphenoid sinus

Vallecula

Eye globe

Temporal lobe

Basilar artery

Brain stem

Cerebellar tonsil

Vallecula

Clivus

Petrous bone

Inferior cerebellar peduncle

Cisterna magna

Figure 4–5. *Top*, Enhanced axial CT scan above the foramen magnum. *Center*, Axial T1 MRI scan above the foramen magnum. *Bottom*, Axial T2 MRI scan above the foramen magnum.

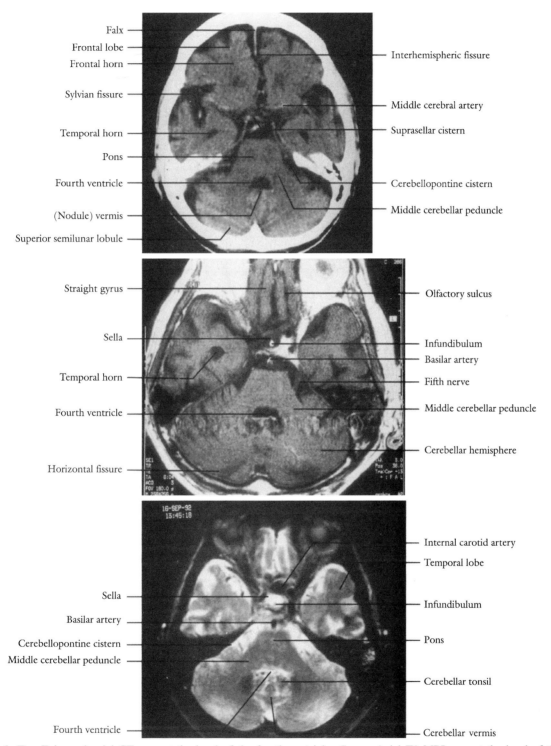

Figure 4–6. *Top*, Enhanced axial CT scan at the level of the fourth ventricle. *Center*, Axial T1 MRI scan at the level of the fourth ventricle. *Bottom*, Axial T2 MRI scan at the level of the fourth ventricle.

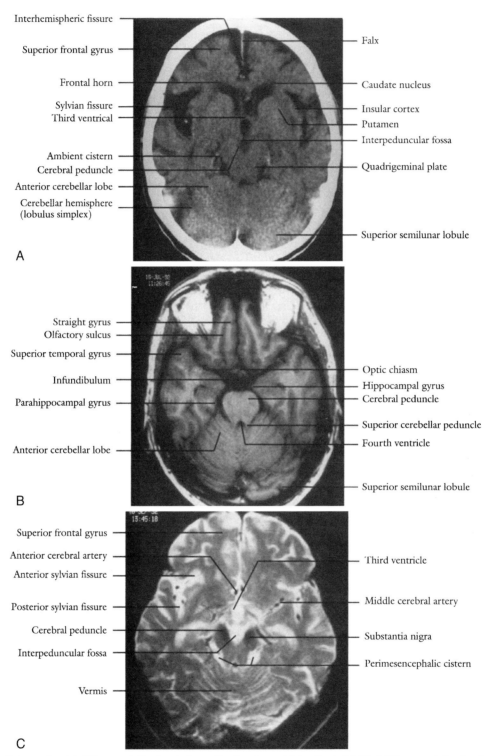

Interhemispheric fissure

Superior frontal gyrus

Frontal horn

Sylvian fissure
Third ventrical

Ambient cistern
Cerebral peduncle
Anterior cerebellar lobe
Cerebellar hemisphere
(lobulus simplex)

Falx

Caudate nucleus

Insular cortex
Putamen
Interpeduncular fossa

Quadrigeminal plate

Superior semilunar lobule

A

Straight gyrus
Olfactory sulcus
Superior temporal gyrus

Infundibulum

Parahippocampal gyrus

Anterior cerebellar lobe

Optic chiasm
Hippocampal gyrus
Cerebral peduncle

Superior cerebellar peduncle

Fourth ventricle

Superior semilunar lobule

B

Superior frontal gyrus
Anterior cerebral artery
Anterior sylvian fissure

Posterior sylvian fissure

Cerebral peduncle

Interpeduncular fossa

Vermis

Third ventricle

Middle cerebral artery

Substantia nigra

Perimesencephalic cistern

C

Figure 4–7. *A,* Enhanced axial CT scan at the level above the fourth ventricle. *B,* Axial T1 MRI scan at the level above the fourth ventricle. *C,* Axial T2 MRI scan at the level above the fourth ventricle.

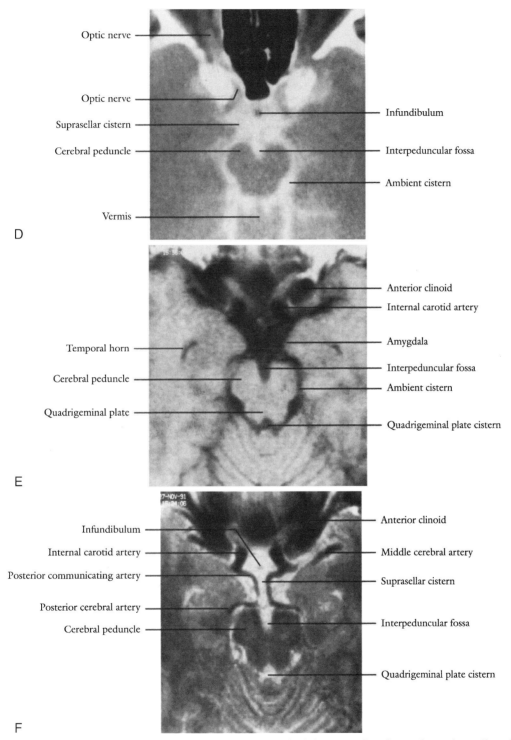

Figure 4–7 *Continued. D*, Intrathecal enhanced axial CT scan at the level of the suprasellar cistern shows the outline of the midbrain by contrast with defects of the infundibulum and optic nerves. *E*, Axial T1 MRI scan of the suprasellar cistern. *F*, Axial proton-density MRI scan through the suprasellar cistern.

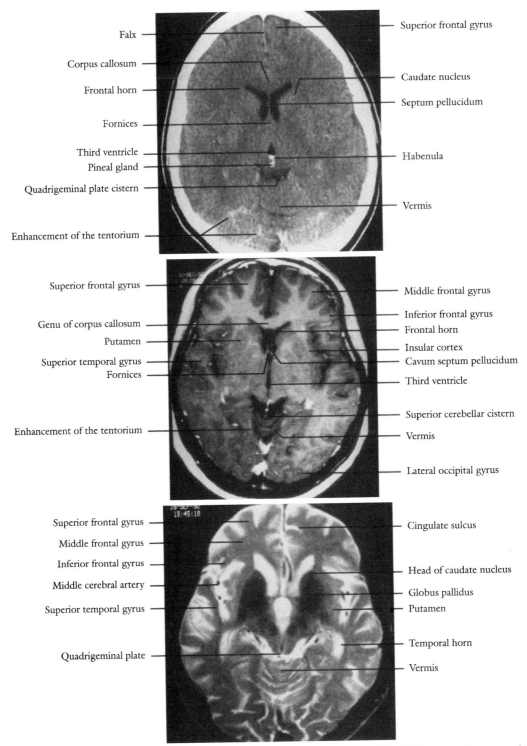

Falx

Corpus callosum

Frontal horn

Fornices

Third ventricle

Pineal gland

Quadrigeminal plate cistern

Enhancement of the tentorium

Superior frontal gyrus

Caudate nucleus

Septum pellucidum

Habenula

Vermis

Superior frontal gyrus

Genu of corpus callosum

Putamen

Superior temporal gyrus

Fornices

Enhancement of the tentorium

Middle frontal gyrus

Inferior frontal gyrus

Frontal horn

Insular cortex

Cavum septum pellucidum

Third ventricle

Superior cerebellar cistern

Vermis

Lateral occipital gyrus

Superior frontal gyrus

Middle frontal gyrus

Inferior frontal gyrus

Middle cerebral artery

Superior temporal gyrus

Quadrigeminal plate

Cingulate sulcus

Head of caudate nucleus

Globus pallidus

Putamen

Temporal horn

Vermis

Figure 4–8. *Top,* Axial enhanced CT scan at the level of the tentorium. *Center,* Axial T1 MRI scan at the level of the tentorium. *Bottom,* Axial T2 MRI scan at the level of the tentorium.

most inferior part of the frontal lobe can be seen separated by the interhemispheric fissure.

Tentorial Level (Fig. 4–8)

The V-shaped enhancement of the tentorial notch outlines the superior vermis and junction of the pons to the midbrain. In axial scans, it is sometimes difficult to separate an infratentorial lesion from a supratentorial lesion because of partial averaging. If the lesion is lateral to

the tentorial notch, it is probably supratentorial. In such circumstances MRI plays an important role in localizing these lesions in the sagittal or coronal axis.

Supratentorial Cuts

Third Ventricular Level (Fig. 4–9)

The most inferior aspects of the frontal lobes can be seen with part of the posterior inferior interhemispheric

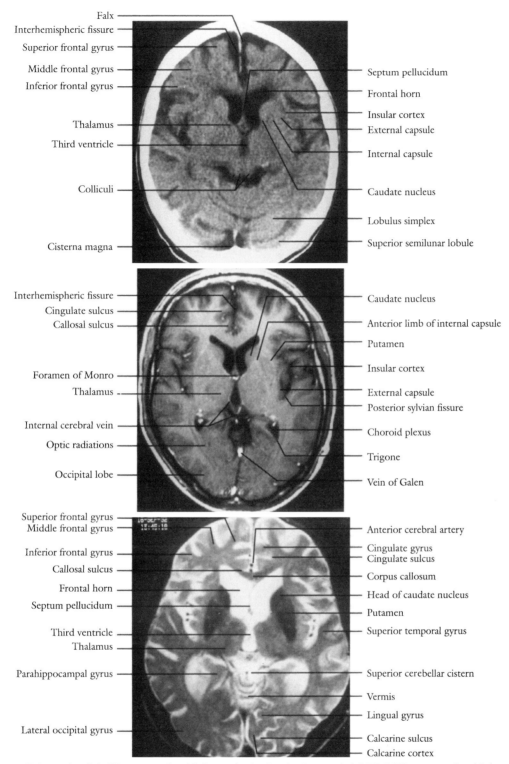

Figure 4–9. *Top,* Enhanced axial CT scan at the third ventricular level. *Center,* Axial T1 MRI scan at the third ventricular level. *Bottom,* Axial T2 MRI scan at the third ventricular level.

fissure medial to them. The third ventricle (a midline structure) is seen as a slitlike cavity. Generally, its transverse diameter should not exceed 5 mm. Superficially, the sylvian fissures can be seen extending medially to separate the frontal lobe from the temporal lobe. Medial to the medial aspect of the sylvian fissure, the insular cortex, external capsule, putamen, and globus pallidus are visualized. Be-

hind the third ventricle, part of the upper brain stem, including the quadrigeminal plates and cistern, can be seen.

Low Ventricular Level (Fig. 4–10)

The superior portion of the frontal horns is seen outlined by the head of the caudate nuclei. Anteriorly, the frontal

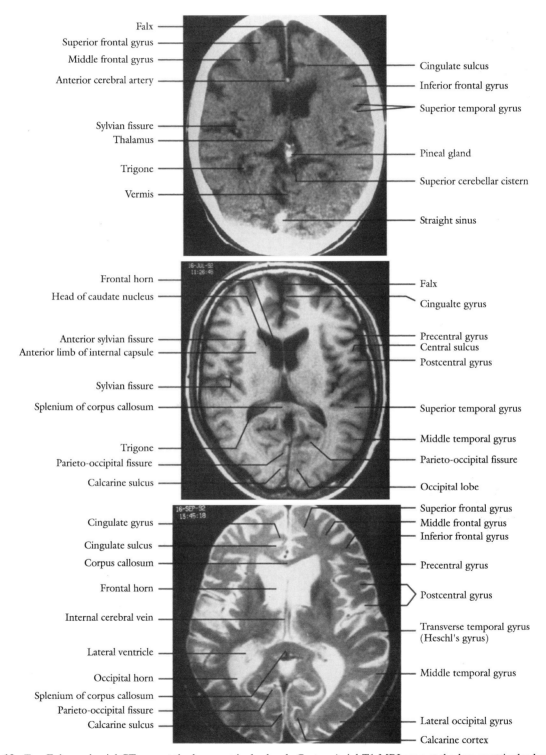

Figure 4–10. *Top,* Enhanced axial CT scan at the low ventricular level. *Center,* Axial T1 MRI scan at the low ventricular level, slightly above the CT scan level. *Bottom,* Axial T2 MRI scan at the low ventricular level, slightly above the CT scan level.

horns are shaped by indentation of the genu of the corpus callosum. The cingulate sulcus is seen separating the corpus callosum from the cingulate gyrus. With IV contrast injection, the junction of the internal cerebral vein and thalamostrite veins can be seen in the region of the foramen of Monro. Pineal gland calcification is located behind the third ventricle. Occasionally, some calcification of the habenula occurs anterior to the pineal gland calcification.

Behind the pineal gland, the great vein of Galen may show slightly increased attenuation value in precontrast studies as a result of circulating blood. With contrast injection, the vein and its junction to the straight sinus can be easily identified. The pineal gland and the vein of Galen are in the large subarachnoid space formed by the juncture of the supracerebellar cistern, the cephalic portion of the quadrigeminal cistern, and the interpositum cistern. Within the lateral ventricle, the most commonly calcified choroid plexus can be identified. On contrast studies, the anterior portion of the choroid plexus, which may not be calcified, demonstrates enhancement. The posterior horns of the lateral ventricles, including the atrium, are seen at this level.

Midventricular Level (Fig. 4–11)

The superior extension of the sylvian fissure and the superior temporal gyrus are seen. The central sulcus, slightly anterior to the sylvian fissure, separates the temporal lobe from the parietal lobe. The most superior aspect of the frontal horns is outlined anteriorly by the anterior portion of the corpus callosum, and the most superior aspect of the caudate nuclei binds them laterally. The posterior medial aspect of the occipital horns is seen bound by the white matter fibers of the splenium of the corpus callosum. The posterior portion of the cingulate sulcus, separating the cingulate gyrus from occipital lobe, can be seen connecting to the posterior interhemispheric fissure.

Above the Ventricular Level (Fig. 4–12)

The scans mainly include the frontal, the parietal, and a small portion of the occipital lobes. Because it is deep, the central sulcus can be identified in the midportion of the scan. Precentral and postcentral sulci outline motor and sensory cortices. The interhemispheric fissure can be seen in its entire length with the falx between. Generally, the falx has a higher attenuation value because of its fibrous texture and because of the presence of calcification.

Sectional Anatomy: Review of Coronal Scans

Coronal CT scanning has never equaled high-quality MRI because of significant motion artifacts and linear artifacts from dental fillings. Next, four slices are analyzed.

Frontal Horn Level (Fig. 4–13)

The frontal horns, outlined by the head of the caudate nuclei and corpus callosum, are visualized, separated by a thin layer of septum pellucidum. The sylvian fissure is seen superficially, with its superior and inferior branches separating the temporal lobe from the frontal lobe and insula.

Third Ventricular Level (Fig. 4–14)

The optic chiasm superior to the infundibulum of the pituitary gland can be identified. The suprasellar cistern outlining the optic chiasm and the superior aspect of the pituitary gland shows the CSF intensity. Some extension of this space into the interior of the pituitary fossa is now considered a normal finding rather than a manifestation of the empty-sella syndrome. In the parasellar region, the cavernous sinus is outlined by the low-intensity area of the dura, which contains the third, fourth, fifth, and sixth cranial nerves. The signal void of the internal carotid arteries within the cavernous sinus can be identified on T1 images.

Midventricular Level (Fig. 4–15)

The body of the lateral ventricles, containing portions of the choroid plexus, is seen. The precentral and postcentral sulci, the central sulcus, and the sylvian fissure are visualized, demonstrating the CSF signal in all MR images. Heschl's gyrus and the temporal lobe gyri can be easily identified. The cerebral aqueduct and midbrain structures are also visualized.

Occipital Horn Level (Fig. 4–16)

The splenium of the corpus callosum can be seen outlining the medial aspects of the occipital lobes. In the infratentorium, the cerebellar hemispheres, the fourth ventricle, the supracerebellar cistern, and the inferior, middle, and superior cerebellar peduncles are all clearly visualized on MRI studies.

Sectional Anatomy: Review of Sagittal Scans

Midsagittal Level (Fig. 4–17)

MRI has revolutionized the field by its capability to obtain sagittal and coronal images without special positioning of the patient. Therefore, patients are more comfortable, and the images are less susceptible to motion artifacts, which can arise from special positioning. Sagittal images are essential in the evaluation of sellar and parasellar lesions, posterior fossa lesions, and intraventricular lesions as well as the vascular anatomy. Sagittal images are also essential in three-dimensional (3D) visualization of intracranial lesions. At this level, the following structures can be identified:

- Venous structures—superior and inferior sagittal sinuses, the vein of Galen, and the straight sinus
- Ventricular system—third and fourth ventricles, including clear visualization of the sylvian aqueduct
- Subarachnoid spaces—suprasellar, perimesencephalic, quadrigeminal, interpeduncular supracerebellar cisterns; the cisterna magna; the central sulcus; precentral and postcentral sulci; the parieto-occipital fissure; the cingulate sulcus; and other sulci separating the frontal and parietal gyri
- Gray matter—cerebral cortices of the frontal, parietal, and occipital lobes and a comma-shaped cingulate gyrus over the corpus callosum and thalamus
- White matter—a comma-shaped corpus callosum over the lateral ventricle, the optic chiasm and optic nerves, and the pons

Text continued on page 109

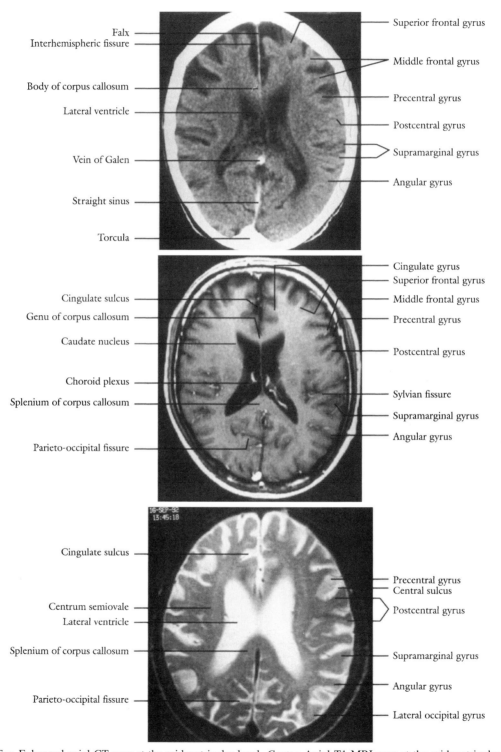

Falx
Interhemispheric fissure

Body of corpus callosum

Lateral ventricle

Vein of Galen

Straight sinus

Torcula

Superior frontal gyrus

Middle frontal gyrus

Precentral gyrus

Postcentral gyrus

Supramarginal gyrus

Angular gyrus

Cingulate sulcus
Genu of corpus callosum

Caudate nucleus

Choroid plexus
Splenium of corpus callosum

Parieto-occipital fissure

Cingulate gyrus
Superior frontal gyrus
Middle frontal gyrus
Precentral gyrus

Postcentral gyrus

Sylvian fissure
Supramarginal gyrus
Angular gyrus

Cingulate sulcus

Centrum semiovale
Lateral ventricle

Splenium of corpus callosum

Parieto-occipital fissure

Precentral gyrus
Central sulcus
Postcentral gyrus

Supramarginal gyrus

Angular gyrus

Lateral occipital gyrus

Figure 4–11. *Top*, Enhanced axial CT scan at the midventricular level. *Center*, Axial T1 MRI scan at the midventricular level. *Bottom*, Axial T2 MRI scan at the midventricular level.

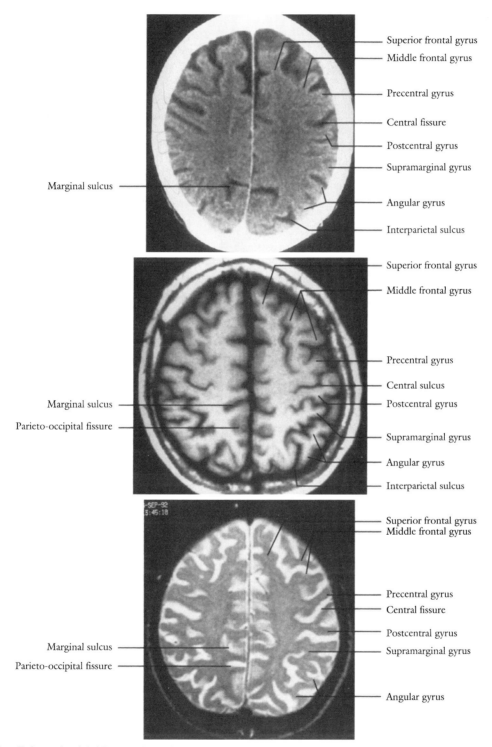

Figure 4–12. *Top,* Enhanced axial CT scan above the ventricular level. *Center,* Axial T1 MRI scan above the ventricular level. *Bottom,* Axial T2 MRI scan above the ventricular level.

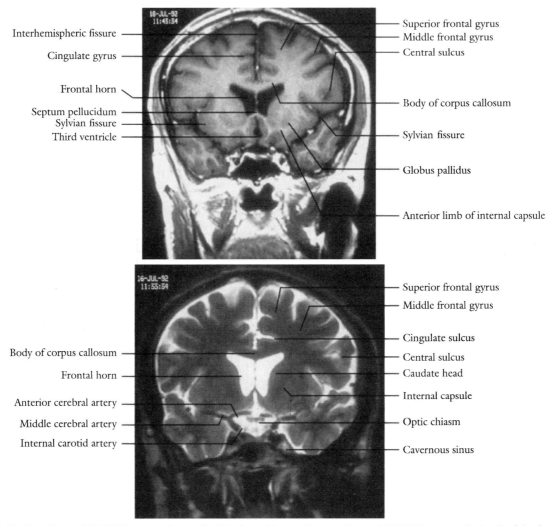

Figure 4–13. *Top*, Coronal T1 MRI scan at the level of the frontal horns. *Bottom*, Coronal T2 MRI scan at the level of the frontal horns.

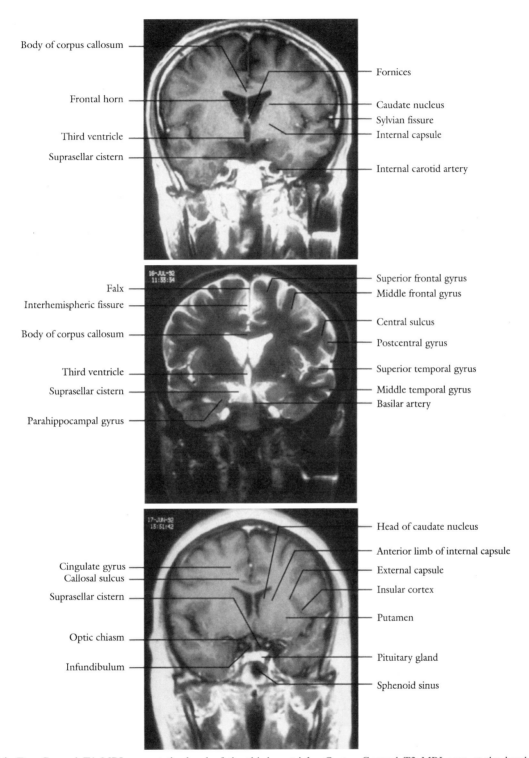

Figure 4–14. *Top*, Coronal T1 MRI scan at the level of the third ventricle. *Center*, Coronal T2 MRI scan at the level of the third ventricle. *Bottom*, Coronal T1 MRI scan through the suprasellar level.

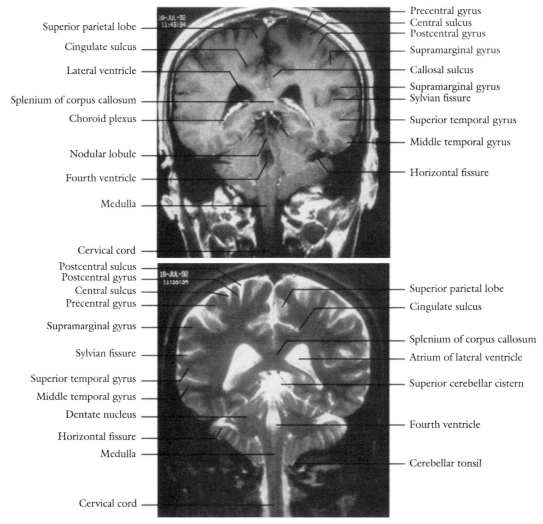

Superior parietal lobe
Cingulate sulcus
Lateral ventricle
Splenium of corpus callosum
Choroid plexus
Nodular lobule
Fourth ventricle
Medulla
Cervical cord

Precentral gyrus
Central sulcus
Postcentral gyrus
Supramarginal gyrus
Callosal sulcus
Supramarginal gyrus
Sylvian fissure
Superior temporal gyrus
Middle temporal gyrus
Horizontal fissure

Postcentral sulcus
Postcentral gyrus
Central sulcus
Precentral gyrus
Supramarginal gyrus
Sylvian fissure
Superior temporal gyrus
Middle temporal gyrus
Dentate nucleus
Horizontal fissure
Medulla
Cervical cord

Superior parietal lobe
Cingulate sulcus
Splenium of corpus callosum
Atrium of lateral ventricle
Superior cerebellar cistern
Fourth ventricle
Cerebellar tonsil

Figure 4–15. *Top*, Coronal T1 MRI scan at the mid-to-posterior ventricular level. *Bottom*, Coronal T2 MRI scan at the mid-to-posterior ventricular level.

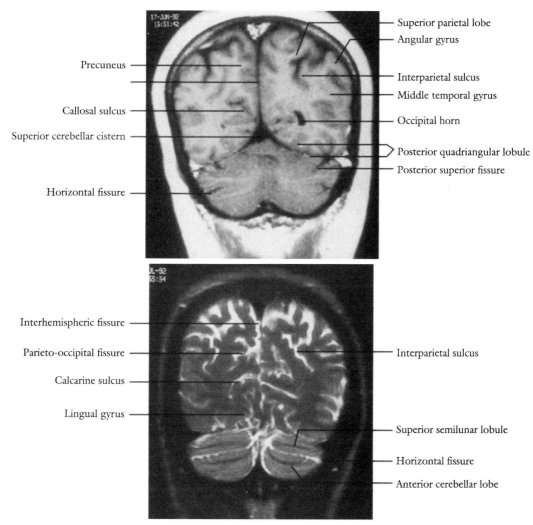

Precuneus

Callosal sulcus

Superior cerebellar cistern

Horizontal fissure

Superior parietal lobe

Angular gyrus

Interparietal sulcus

Middle temporal gyrus

Occipital horn

Posterior quadriangular lobule

Posterior superior fissure

Interhemispheric fissure

Parieto-occipital fissure

Calcarine sulcus

Lingual gyrus

Interparietal sulcus

Superior semilunar lobule

Horizontal fissure

Anterior cerebellar lobe

Figure 4–16. *Top*, Coronal T1 MRI scan slightly posterior to the occipital horns. *Bottom*, Coronal T2 MRI scan slightly posterior to the occipital horns.

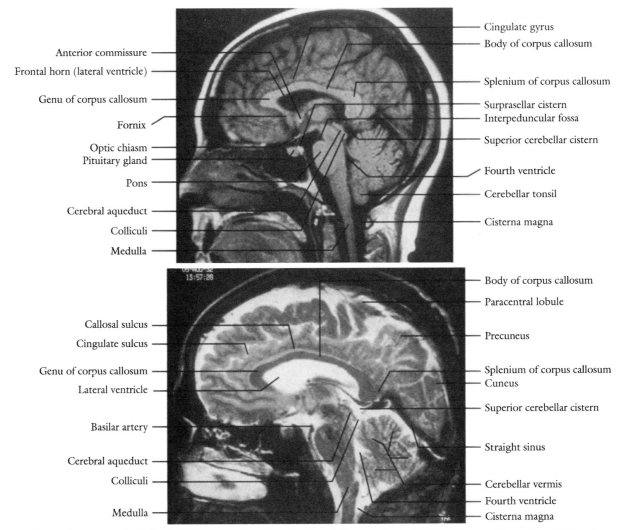

Figure 4–17. *Top*, Sagittal T1 MRI scan at the midsagittal level. *Bottom*, Sagittal T2 MRI scan at the midsagittal level.

• Other structures—the pituitary gland, the clivus, the sphenoid sinus, the frontal sinus, the cerebellar cortex and white matter, the medulla, and the cerebellar tonsils

Parasagittal Level through the Lateral Ventricular Body (Fig. 4–18)

The following structures can be identified: the central sulcus as well as the precentral and postcentral sulci; the superior frontal gyrus; the body of the caudate nucleus; the cingulate sulcus and the gyrus; the putamen; the dentate nuclei; the cerebellar peduncles; and the parieto-occipital fissure.

Lateral Orbital Level (Cortical Level) (Fig. 4–19)

The following structures can be identified: the central, precentral, and postcentral sulci; the supramarginal gyrus; the angular gyrus; the lateral occipital gyrus; the horizontal fissure of the cerebellum; the superior and inferior semilunar lobules; the middle and inferior frontal gyri; the sylvian fissure; and the superior, inferior, and middle temporal lobe gyri.

Normal Calcifications

The following calcifications seen on CT and MRI of the brain are considered to be normal.

Choroid Plexus[23, 33]

Calcification occurs mainly in the glomus located within the atrium of the lateral ventricles. Calcification of the choroid plexus in the third or fourth ventricle is rare. Within the lateral ventricles, calcification is rare under the age of 3 years. With age, the incidence increases, reaching 75% by the fifth decade.

Basal Ganglia[4]

Before the age of 9 years, calcification within the basal ganglia is uncommon but becomes frequent after age 40 years. This calcification is usually minimal. If the degree of the calcification is massive and associated with dentate nuclei calcification, the possibility of Fahr's disease should be ruled out.

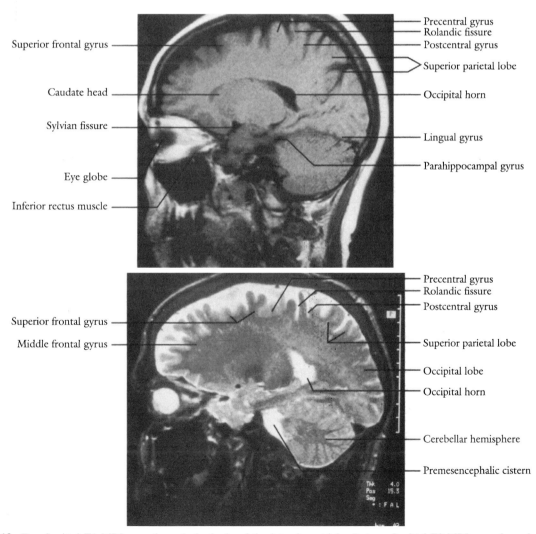

Figure 4–18. *Top*, Sagittal T1 MRI scan through the body of the lateral ventricle. *Bottom*, Sagittal T2 MRI scan through the body of the lateral ventricle.

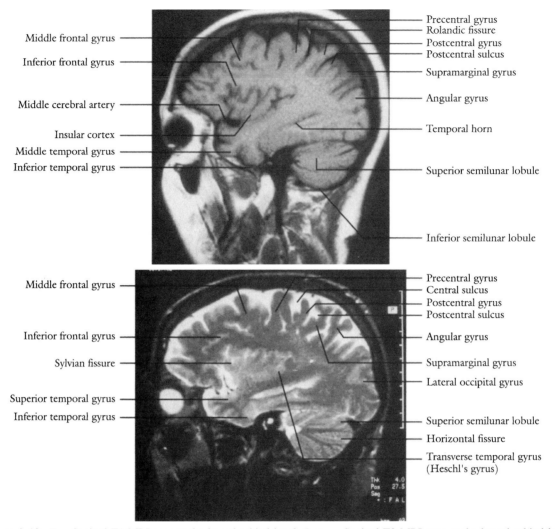

Middle frontal gyrus — Precentral gyrus — Rolandic fissure — Postcentral gyrus — Postcentral sulcus — Supramarginal gyrus — Inferior frontal gyrus — Angular gyrus — Middle cerebral artery — Temporal horn — Insular cortex — Middle temporal gyrus — Inferior temporal gyrus — Superior semilunar lobule — Inferior semilunar lobule

Middle frontal gyrus — Precentral gyrus — Central sulcus — Postcentral gyrus — Postcentral sulcus — Inferior frontal gyrus — Angular gyrus — Sylvian fissure — Supramarginal gyrus — Lateral occipital gyrus — Superior temporal gyrus — Inferior temporal gyrus — Superior semilunar lobule — Horizontal fissure — Transverse temporal gyrus (Heschl's gyrus)

Figure 4–19. *Top*, Sagittal T1 MRI scan at the lateral orbital level. *Bottom*, Sagittal T2 MRI scan at the lateral orbital level.

Pineal Gland and Habenula[23, 37]

After the age of 30 years, 15% of CT scans show habenula calcification.[10] However, pineal gland calcification is common, occurring in more than 83% of the patients older than age 30 years. If calcification of the pineal gland is larger than 12 mm × 12 mm × 12 mm, the possibility of a pineal gland region tumor should be considered.

Falx Calcification

Calcification of the falx is commonly seen in the posterior interhemispheric fissure in adults. If increased attenuation of the falx extends to the medial sulci, the possibility of subarachnoid bleeding should be excluded.

CT and MRI Anatomy of the Spine

Prior to a review of the normal anatomy, the techniques used in performing CT scans and MRI studies are discussed.

CT Technique[19, 35]

CT scanning of the spine is generally done in the axial axis in 3- to 5-mm increments. In the cervical spine, thin cuts of 1.5-mm increments are necessary to evaluate disk disease. A stacking method can be used without angling the gantry (Fig. 4–20). This method has the advantage of visualizing the entire scanned area in one column without interruption to reconstruct the images in a different orientation for further evaluation. Another method involves angling the gantry and the x-ray beam perpendicular to the disk and scanning from midbody of one vertebra to midbody of the next vertebra. At each level, scans require different angulation and thus not all of the slices can be reconstructed together.

Targeting to zoom to the spine area increases the detail and resolution of the scans. Images should be filmed at two different settings, one with a narrow window for evaluation of the soft tissue shadows and disk and the other with a wide window setting for evaluation of bony structures (Figs. 4–21 and 4–22). This is very important in postintrathecal contrast studies.

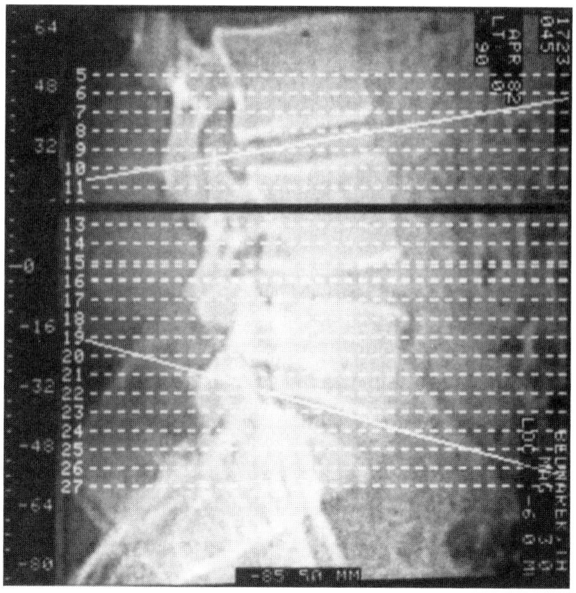

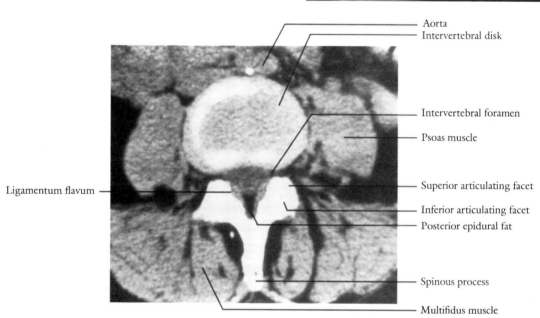

Figure 4–20. Lateral view of the lumbar spine by a scanogram showing stacking method of the axial CT scanning technique. Lines demonstrate the exact level of each side. A single angled cut can be obtained through each intervertebral disk at a perpendicular angle.

Aorta
Intervertebral disk

Intervertebral foramen

Psoas muscle

Superior articulating facet

Inferior articulating facet

Posterior epidural fat

Ligamentum flavum

Spinous process

Multifidus muscle

Figure 4–21. Axial CT scan through the intervertebral disk in the midlumbar region. Minimal averaging of the cortex causes increased attenuation value at the periphery. At these regular window and level settings, the facet joints cannot be readily seen. The fat in the epidural space is seen within the intervertebral foramen and posterior to the thecal sac.

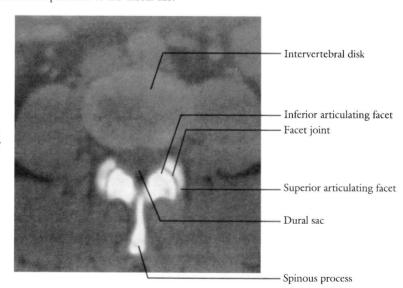

Figure 4–22. Axial CT scan through intervertebral disk. Wide window setting allows visualization of low attenuation of the facet joint between the facets.

Intervertebral disk

Inferior articulating facet
Facet joint

Superior articulating facet

Dural sac

Spinous process

Generally, IV contrast is not necessary unless the vascularity of a spinal lesion is to be evaluated. Prior to the advent of MRI, IV contrast was used for evaluation of both cervical disk herniation and postoperative spine in an attempt to visualize the epidural venous plexus.[27]

MRI Technique[2, 18]

MRI of the spine is routinely done in the axial and sagittal axes, rarely in the coronal axis. Our routine includes T1 and fast spin-echo images in the sagittal plane and T1 images in the axial plane in the lumbar region. In cervical spine studies, axial gradient echo is added to this menu (see Fig. 4–27). If clinically infectious diseases of the spine or intra-axial lesions are suspected, T2 axial and sagittal studies are also needed. The slice thickness is routinely 4 to 5 mm; however, it should be tailored to fit the clinical presentation. The use of IV gadolinium DTPA or DOTA is limited to evaluation of infectious disease, nonepidural neoplasms, or postoperative spine studies.[5, 27]

Normal Anatomy*

The vertebral column comprises 32 or 33 vertebrae: 7 in the cervical, 12 in the thoracic, 5 in the lumbar, 5 in the sacral, and 3 or 4 segments in the coccygeal area.

The review of CT and MRI anatomy is divided into *osseous* and *soft tissue* structures.

Osseous Structures

Vertebral Bodies (Figs. 4–23 to 4–25)

In the cervical region (Fig. 4–24), the transverse diameter is wider than the anteroposterior diameter. The uncovertebral joint is between the uncinate process and a small depression in the inferior aspect of the vertebral body above it. The vertebral bodies become wider between the C3 and C7 levels.

In the thoracic area, the transverse and anterioposterior diameters are the same (Fig. 4–25). The vertebral bodies are cone-shaped in the axial plane. In the lumbar region, the vertebral bodies become wider in the transverse diameter. They are generally larger than at the thoracic level. In the midportion of the posterior cortex, the basivertebral vein enters into the vertebral body, bifurcating into branches and making a Y-shaped defect in the axial images.

On CT studies, dense cortical bone has very high attenuation value with less attenuation in the center because of cancellous bone. On axial scans, if a slice averages through the end plate and disk space, the central part of the vertebral body will have decreased density, mimicking a destructive process (Fig. 4–23C).

Vertebral bodies are isointense on T1 images (Figs. 4–25, 4–26B, and 4–27B), with a decrease in signal intensity on gradient echo images. The cortex with dense bone has a low signal intensity on T1 images. On T2 images, the signal intensity of vertebral bodies decreases.

*See References 2, 5, 7–9, 12, 13, 16–18, 25, 28, 31, and 32.

Pedicles

Pedicles extend from the vertebral bodies posteriorly to reach the articular pillars. They are very short in the cervical area and increase in length cephalocaudally. In the thoracic area, the pedicles are located in the upper half of the vertebral bodies, resulting in a higher location of the intervertebral foramina in relation to disk spaces. In the lumbar region, the pedicles are larger in the superior aspect than in the inferior aspect. On axial scans, the pedicles are seen outlining the lateral borders of the spinal canal, forming a full circle of bone. In the scans above or below the pedicles, the lateral borders of the canal are interrupted by the intervertebral foramina.

Laminae (Fig. 4–26; see Fig. 4–23)

The two laminae at each level extend posteriorly and medially to meet in midline and fuse into the spinous process. The superior fusion is slightly more anterior than the inferior fusion. In the thoracic area, the laminae are broader and shorter, with some overlap. In the lumbar region, the laminae do not overlap. A larger space is found between adjacent laminae in the upper lumbar spine than in the lower lumbar spine.

Spinous Processes (see Figs. 4–23 and 4–26)

The spinous processes start from the junction of two laminae and extend posteriorly and downward. In midcervical areas, they have a bifid appearance. In the thoracic region, they are slender and longer. In the lumbar area, they are larger and taller with rectangular shape on a lateral view.

Transverse Processes (Fig. 4–27; see Fig. 4–23)

In the cervical area, the transverse processes have an anterior and posterior component that meet laterally in a horizontal plane to form the transverse foramina. These foramina permit the passage of the vertebral arteries from the C7 to the C2 level (Fig. 4–27).

In the thoracic region, the transverse processes are close to the heads, necks, and tubercles of the corresponding ribs. In the lumbar area, the transverse processes extend laterally and posteriorly. The transverse processes of L1 and L5 are thicker and shorter.

Articulating Pillars

The articulating pillar is created by the superior and inferior facets.

Intervertebral Foramina (see Figs. 4–23 and 4–27)

The foramina are bounded medially by the posterior vertebral body and the intervertebral disk space, superiorly by the inferior margin of the upper vertebral pedicle, and inferiorly by the superior pillars. The intervertebral foramina contain corresponding spinal nerve, veins, fat, arteries, and connective tissue. At the thoracic level, the foramina are at the lower half of the vertebral bodies. The neck of the rib participates in creating the boundaries of the foramen anterolaterally.

In the lumbar region, the foramina are larger and longer.

Text continued on page 116

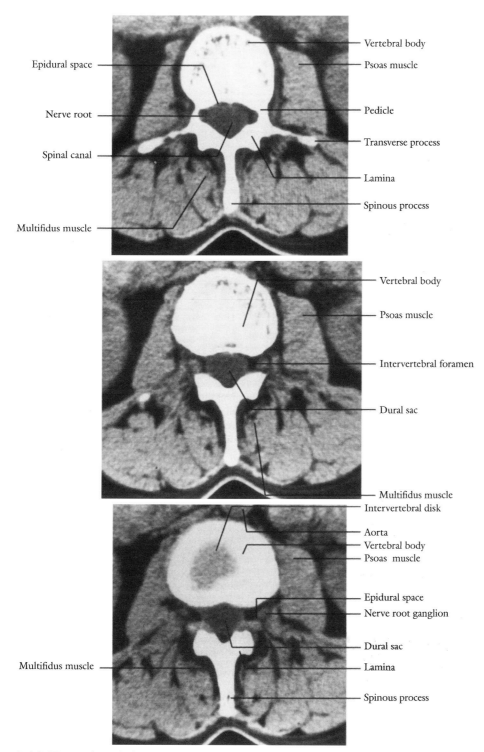

Figure 4–23. *Top,* Axial CT scan through the upper half of the vertebral body demonstrating the full circle of bony canal made by the vertebral body, pedicles, laminae, and the spinous process. *Center,* Axial CT scan through the intervertebral foramen in the midlumbar region. Low attenuation of fat and the slightly increased attenuation of ligamentum flavum help to determine the border of the thecal sac. *Bottom,* Axial CT scan through the midvertebral body in the lumbar region. The ganglion is seen in the most proximal portion of the intervertebral foramen (canal) surrounded by fat.

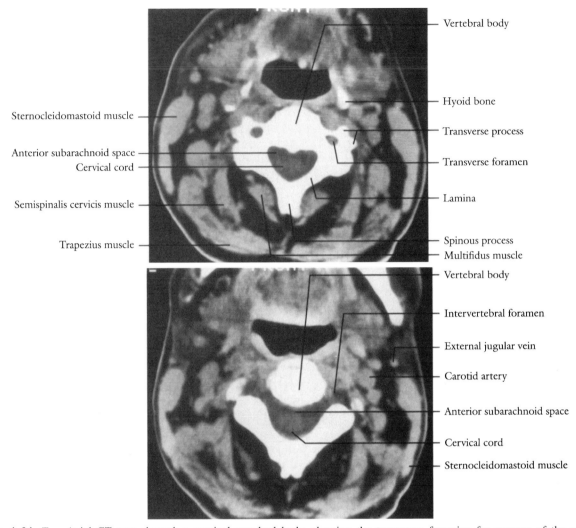

Sternocleidomastoid muscle —

Anterior subarachnoid space —
Cervical cord —

Semispinalis cervicis muscle —

Trapezius muscle —

— Vertebral body

— Hyoid bone

— Transverse process

— Transverse foramen

— Lamina

— Spinous process
— Multifidus muscle

— Vertebral body

— Intervertebral foramen

— External jugular vein

— Carotid artery

— Anterior subarachnoid space

— Cervical cord

— Sternocleidomastoid muscle

Figure 4–24. *Top*, Axial CT scan through a cervical vertebral body, showing the transverse foramina for passage of the vertebral arteries. *Bottom*, Axial CT scan through the intervertebral foramen in the midcervical region. The large amount of cerebrospinal fluid in front and back of the cervical cord helps to delineate the cervical cord and the roots.

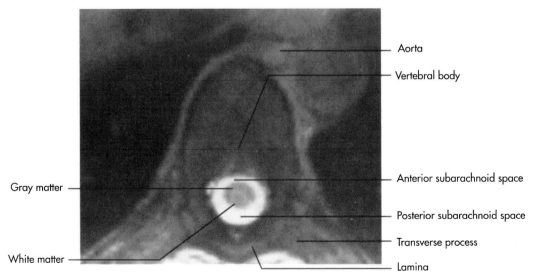

Gray matter —

White matter —

— Aorta

— Vertebral body

— Anterior subarachnoid space

— Posterior subarachnoid space

— Transverse process

— Lamina

Figure 4–25. Axial T2 MRI at the midthoracic level. The thoracic cord has a more rounded appearance. Note the larger subarachnoid space posteriorly with high signal intensity in this T2 study.

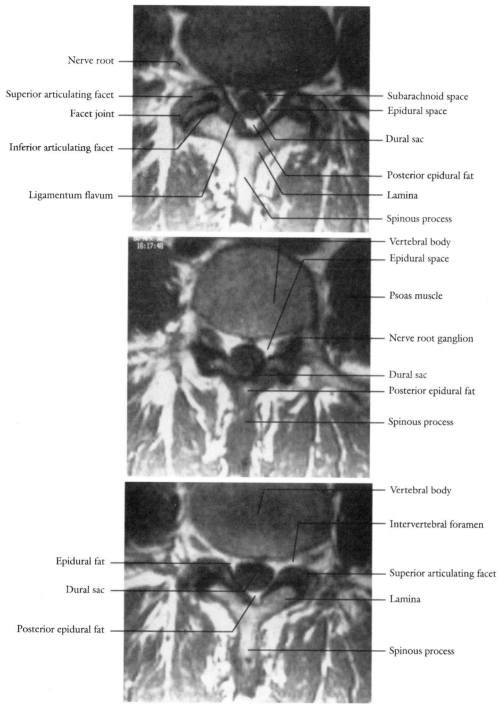

Nerve root

Superior articulating facet

Facet joint

Inferior articulating facet

Ligamentum flavum

Subarachnoid space

Epidural space

Dural sac

Posterior epidural fat

Lamina

Spinous process

Vertebral body

Epidural space

Psoas muscle

Nerve root ganglion

Dural sac

Posterior epidural fat

Spinous process

Vertebral body

Intervertebral foramen

Superior articulating facet

Lamina

Spinous process

Epidural fat

Dural sac

Posterior epidural fat

Figure 4–26. *Top*, Axial T1 MRI through the facet joints. The ligamentum flavum, medial to the lamina, is seen bordering the posterior lateral aspect of the canal. The thecal sac is separated from the ligament by fat. *Center*, Axial T1 MRI scan through midportion of the vertebral body in the lumbar region. Fat with high signal intensity is seen anterior to the thecal sac and within the intervertebral foramen. The nerve root ganglion is seen inside the foramen. Dense cortical bone has lower signal intensity relative to the rest of the vertebral body. *Bottom*, Axial T1 MRI of fat in the epidural space helps to outline the thecal sac. Ligamentum flavum, which has a low-signal-intensity border, outlines the canal posterolaterally.

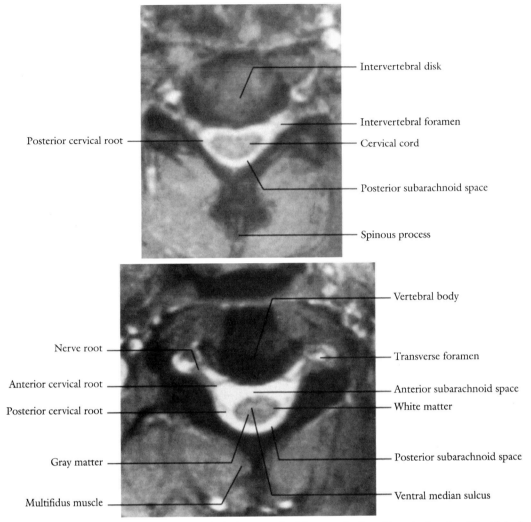

Posterior cervical root

Intervertebral disk

Intervertebral foramen

Cervical cord

Posterior subarachnoid space

Spinous process

Nerve root

Anterior cervical root

Posterior cervical root

Gray matter

Multifidus muscle

Vertebral body

Transverse foramen

Anterior subarachnoid space

White matter

Posterior subarachnoid space

Ventral median sulcus

Figure 4–27. *Top,* Axial gradient-echo MRI scan through the intervertebral foramen in the midcervical region. The high-signal-intensity cerebrospinal fluid outlines the cervical cord and the roots (similar to the appearance on intrathecal contrast-enhanced CT scan). Any protrusion into the foramen by degenerative joint disease or disk herniation can be appreciated in this imaging. *Bottom,* Axial gradient-echo MRI scan in the midcervical region, just caudal to the top image, showing the distal end of the intervertebral foramen (canal). The transverse foramina are seen allowing passage of vertebral arteries.

They have a canal-like appearance and are oriented anteriorly and laterally.

On MRI studies, the high signal intensity of the fat on the T1 within the epidural space and the foramina outlines the isointense nerve root, covered by the low signal intensity of CSF (see Fig. 4–26B, C). On gradient-echo images, the CSF becomes high in signal intensity, outlining the diminished signal intensity of the spinal nerve root and cord (Fig. 4–28B).

On CT scans, the water attenuation value of the nerve root and ganglion are seen within the intervertebral foramina, with some low attenuation of the fat in the epidural space (see Fig. 4–23B, C). The entire length of the foramen, which is actually a canal, can be seen by following the scans from cephalic to caudal levels.

Spinal Canal[8, 35]

The canal measures about 27 mm at the C1 level and 21 mm in the lower cervical area in the sagittal midline plane. The lowest normal diameters of the canal are 12 mm in the lower cervical area and 15 to 16 mm at C1–C2.[32]

In the thoracic area, the spinal canal is completely outlined by bones in the upper half, with some discontinuity of the bone in the lower half to form the facet joints. The canal is rounded and is fairly constant in size and contour, with a triangular appearance in the lower region. In the lumbar area, the canal has a round to oval shape in the upper lumbar region and a triangular shape caudally. In the lower lumbar region, the laminae bow inward with some indentation toward the canal.

On T1 sagittal images, the canal can easily be measured in the anteroposterior diameter (Figs. 4–28 to 4–30). Anteriorly, the canal is outlined by a low signal from the posterior cortex and the posterior longitudinal ligament. The spinal cord, which is isointense on T1 images, is outlined by the low signal intensity of CSF (Figs. 4–28 and 4–29). On gradient images, the intensity of the cord and that of CSF are similar, making it very difficult to measure the spinal cord.

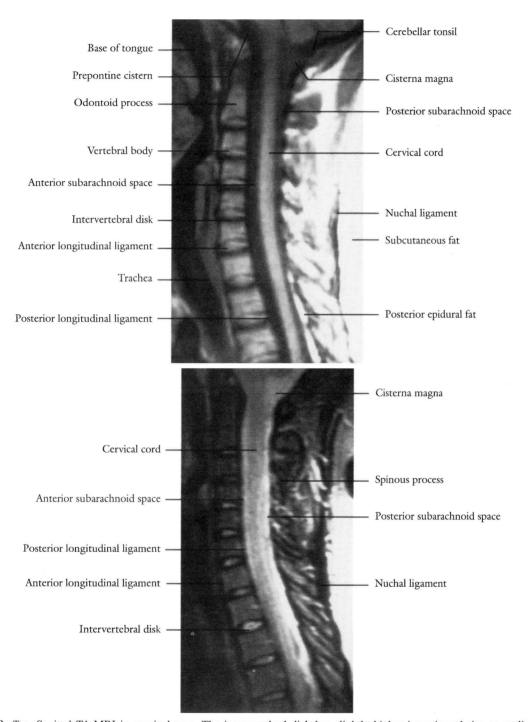

Base of tongue

Prepontine cistern

Odontoid process

Vertebral body

Anterior subarachnoid space

Intervertebral disk

Anterior longitudinal ligament

Trachea

Posterior longitudinal ligament

Cerebellar tonsil

Cisterna magna

Posterior subarachnoid space

Cervical cord

Nuchal ligament

Subcutaneous fat

Posterior epidural fat

Cervical cord

Anterior subarachnoid space

Posterior longitudinal ligament

Anterior longitudinal ligament

Intervertebral disk

Cisterna magna

Spinous process

Posterior subarachnoid space

Nuchal ligament

Figure 4–28. *Top,* Sagittal T1 MRI in cervical area. The intervertebral disk has slightly higher intensity relative to outlining cortical bone and the ligaments. The subarachnoid space is larger from C1 to C3 posteriorly, whereas it becomes larger in the midcervical and lower cervical areas anteriorly. *Bottom,* Sagittal gradient-echo study of cervical spine showing increased signal intensity of cerebrospinal fluid similar to that in a T2 study. The healthy intervertebral disk has higher signal intensity as a result of its water content. The anterior and posterior longitudinal ligaments can readily be seen outlining the spinal canal.

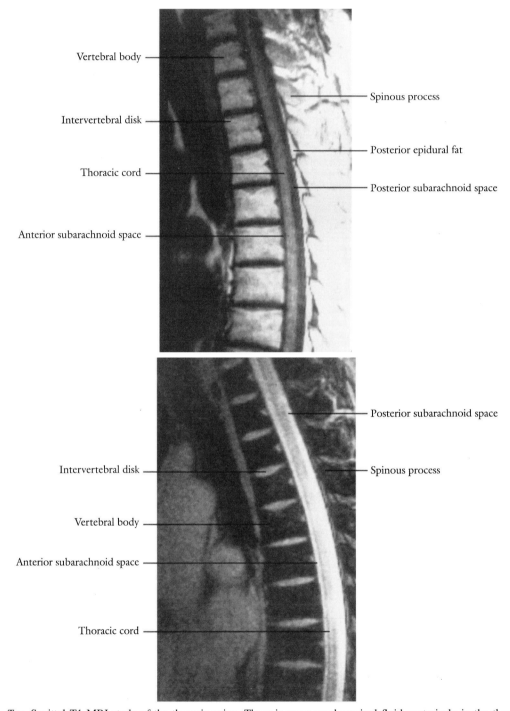

Vertebral body

Intervertebral disk

Thoracic cord

Anterior subarachnoid space

Spinous process

Posterior epidural fat

Posterior subarachnoid space

Posterior subarachnoid space

Intervertebral disk

Spinous process

Vertebral body

Anterior subarachnoid space

Thoracic cord

Figure 4–29. *Top,* Sagittal T1 MRI study of the thoracic spine. There is more cerebrospinal fluid posteriorly in the thoracic area. The spinal cord can be measured more accurately with this technique than with gradient-echo or T2 studies. *Bottom,* Sagittal T2 MRI of the thoracic spine. In this image, the border to the thoracic cord is not as clear as in the top image. The high signal intensity indicates a healthy disk.

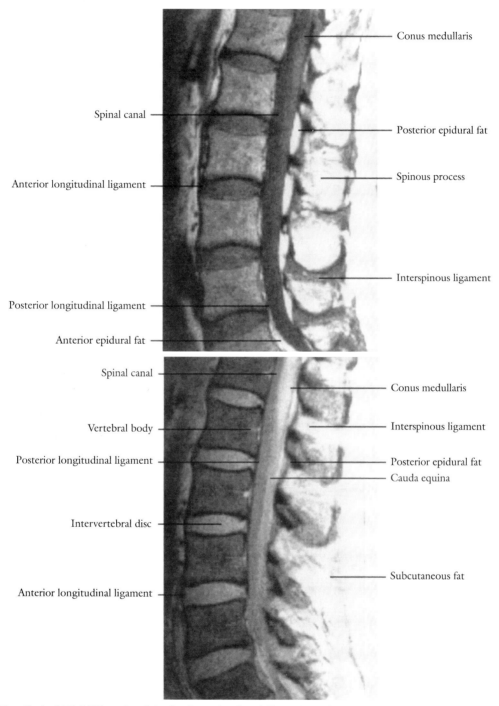

Spinal canal

Anterior longitudinal ligament

Posterior longitudinal ligament

Anterior epidural fat

Conus medullaris

Posterior epidural fat

Spinous process

Interspinous ligament

Spinal canal

Vertebral body

Posterior longitudinal ligament

Intervertebral disc

Anterior longitudinal ligament

Conus medullaris

Interspinous ligament

Posterior epidural fat
Cauda equina

Subcutaneous fat

Figure 4–30. *Top,* Sagittal T1 MRI study of the lumbar spine in midline. The epidural fat behind the thecal sac and in front of the distal lumbar area shows high signal intensity. The intervertebral disk space has slightly lower intensity relative to the vertebral body. *Bottom,* Sagittal gradient-echo MRI study of the lumbar area in midline. The cerebrospinal fluid has slightly increased signal intensity. The anterior and posterior longitudinal ligaments are seen outlining the vertebral bodies and intervertebral disk spaces. The interspinous ligaments connect the two adjacent spinous processes.

On T2 images, the CSF has high signal intensity, thereby outlining the decreased intensity of the cord. Care should be taken that the cord measurements on T2 images may be less than their actual size because of partial-averaging volume of the CSF and the cord. On CT scans, the canal border can be identified by the bony margins of the spinous processes, laminae, and posterior aspects of the venous processes (see Figs. 4–22 and 4–23). The cord in the cervical region can be seen without intrathecal contrast (see Fig. 4–24). In the lumbar and thoracic areas, however, intrathecal contrast is needed to evaluate the spinal cord and intracanal abnormalities. The fat within the epidural space and the intervertebral foramina help to outline the disease processes affecting the margins of the spinal canal.

Soft Tissues, Joints, and Ligaments

Intervertebral Disk

The disk spaces separate the two adjacent vertebral bodies. No disk space exists between C1 and C2. The disk comprises the central portion of the nucleus pulposus and the peripheral segment of the annulus fibrosus. The nucleus pulposus is softer with greater water content. The annulus fibrosus comprises hard fibrous tissue surrounding the nucleus. Because of the curvature of the disk spaces in the cervical area, angulation of the gantry to cut through the disk is not always possible unless slices 1.5 mm thick are taken. In the cervical region, the disks are thinner compared to those of the thoracic and lumbar regions. The disks have an attenuation value of 50 to 110 Hounsfield units. The thoracic disks are thinner but larger in the cross-sectional area. In the thoracic area, ligaments connect the crest of the head of the ribs to corresponding disk spaces.

The lumbar disks are thicker and larger. The height of a lumbar disk varies from 8 to 12 mm. The posterior margins are concave or flat except at the level of L5–S1, and these can be convex, bulging into the canal centrally. On T1 images, a disk will have low intensity (Figs. 4–26A and 4–27A), with increased intensity on gradient-echo images (Fig. 4–30); see Figs. 4–28 and 4–29) and T2 images.

Especially on T2 images, the disk should have high signal intensity (see Fig. 4–29B). Decreased signal intensity on T2 images is indicative of a decrease in water content, a manifestation of disk degeneration. On sagittal images, anterior and posterior disk margins appear outlined by the anterior and posterior longitudinal ligaments (see Fig. 4–30). Discontinuity of the ligament may suggest a tear resulting from a herniated disk.

On CT scans, the water attenuation of a disk is similar to that of muscle (see Fig. 4–22). The disk border should not extend beyond the posterior aspect of the adjacent vertebral bodies, except at the L5–S1 level, where the disk bulges in midline (Fig. 4–31). With degeneration, a disk will bulge diffusely, extending beyond the border of the vertebral body. Evidence of gas (air density) within a disk suggests the vacuum phenomenon or is a manifestation of an infectious process that requires further investigation. On CT scans, disks and ligaments cannot be distinguished because of their similar attenuation values.

Uncovertebral Joints[3]

In the cervical area, these joints are between the uncinate process and the adjacent vertebral body. With degenerative joint diseases and narrowing of the disk spaces, the joint space also becomes narrowed.

Facet Joints (Fig. 4–32; see also Fig. 4–26)

These are joints between the superior articulating facet of the lower vertebra and the inferior facet of the upper vertebra. They are oriented halfway in the sagittal and axial axes. The superior articulation facet of the lower vertebra is always anterior to the inferior articulating facet of the upper vertebra. The facet joints are oriented almost in the coronal plane in the thoracic region. The articular surfaces are flat, with some convex shape to the nonarticulating parts. Joint spaces are found between the heads of the ribs and the vertebral bodies as well as between the ribs and the transverse processes.

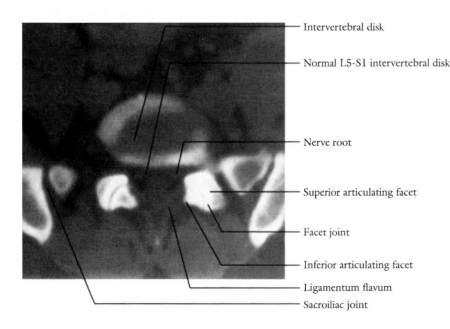

Intervertebral disk

Normal L5-S1 intervertebral disk

Nerve root

Superior articulating facet

Facet joint

Inferior articulating facet

Ligamentum flavum

Sacroiliac joint

Figure 4–31. Axial CT scan through the intervertebral disk space of L5–S1, demonstrating the flat, slightly concave border of the disk posteriorly, a normal finding. The posterior aspect of the disk spaces is concave in remainder of spinal column.

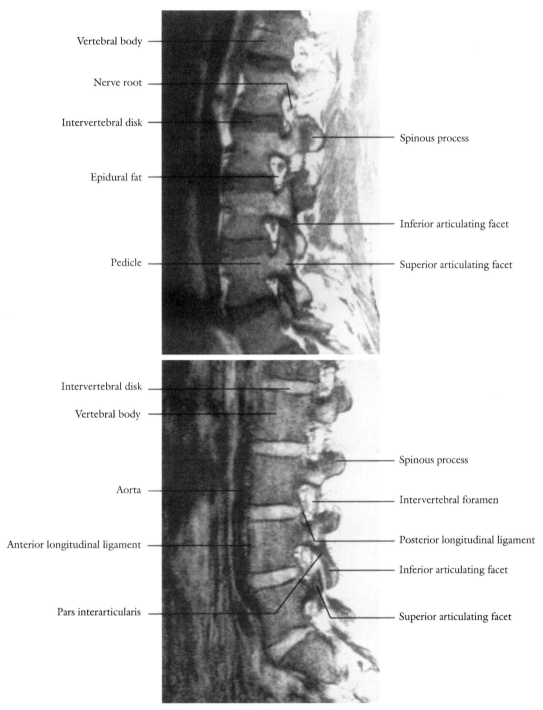

Figure 4–32. *Top*, Sagittal T1 MRI scan in the lumbar spine. The boundary of the intervertebral foramen (pedicle, posterior inferior portion of the vertebral body, intervertebral disk, anterior superior aspect of superior articulating facet) can readily be identified in this para-midline sagittal plane. *Bottom*, Sagittal MRI study of lumbar area in para-midline plane. The very low signal intensity of the cortical bone helps to visualize the upper and lower border of the intervertebral disk. The foramina and the facet joints are clearly visualized on this image. Defects within the pars interarticularis and foraminal narrowing can be appreciated in this axis.

The facet joints are oriented in a parasagittal plane in the upper lumbar area with an oblique orientation in the lower lumbar area. The joint spaces are 2 to 4 mm³. The synovium extends into the canal to attach to the ligamentum flavum that covers the anterior end of the joint space. Sagittal MRI studies are useful for evaluation of the facet joints and their orientation (see Fig. 4–32).

Spondylolysis defects can easily be identified on these images. In addition, the fluid within the joint space, which has signal intensity similar to that of water, can be seen outlined by the very low signal of the dense cortical bone of the facets and the isointense ligamentum flavum. Narrowing of the facet joints and spurring can easily be detected on axial CT scans or MRI studies. With CT scans, the dense cortex of the articulating facet is separated by the low attenuation value of the facet joint space (Fig. 4–22).

Ligaments

Anterior Longitudinal Ligament (see Figs. 4–28 to 4–30). This ligament starts from the axis as the anterior atlantoaxial ligament and extends to the sacral segments, connecting the anterior aspects of the vertebral bodies and disk spaces (see Fig. 4–30). On CT scans, the ligament cannot be separated from the bony structures and the disk space. Thickening of the ligament results in a narrowing of the canal in the sagittal diameter.

Posterior Longitudinal Ligament. This ligament begins on the posterior surface of the axis and extends to the sacrum to connect the posterior aspects of the vertebral bodies and disk spaces (see Fig. 4–30).

Interspinous Ligament (see Fig. 4–30). This ligament connects the spinous processes. It has a slightly higher attenuation value, making it recognizable on CT scans.

Nuchal Ligament. This ligament connects the base of the occipital bone to the spinous processes of C1 to C7 (see Fig. 4–28B).

Ligamentum Flavum. This ligament has both stretchability and retractability functions, and it is attached to the laminae. It does have a higher attenuation value that can

be identified on CT scans. It measures 3 to 5 mm in thickness and extends to the level of the first sacral segment (see Fig. 4–21). The ligamentum flavum and interspinous ligaments can easily be seen on T1 MRI images (Fig. 4–26A). Their hypertrophy results in narrowing of the canal, posteriorly and laterally.

Epidural Space (see Figs. 4–23, 4–26, and 4–30). This space contains fat, vessels, and neural elements. In the cervical area, the anterior space is thinner and less visible on CT scans. The internal vertebral veins have no valves, thereby facilitating the spread of infectious processes and metastasis. The anterior and posterior epidural spaces can be visualized by IV injection of contrast medium for evaluation of extradural diseases. The basivertebral vein penetrates the vertebral body to join the internal plexus. The external vertebral plexus lying outside of the vertebral bodies is linked to the internal plexus by veins passing through the ligamentum flavum and the neural foramina.[20]

The epidural space has more fat posteriorly in the thoracic region,[13] with a minimal amount anteriorly (see Fig. 4–29A). The venous structures of the epidural space are similar in the cervical and thoracic areas except for a possible link between the anterior and posterior vertebral plexus with the intercostal veins and the azygous system.[30] The epidural space is larger in the lower lumbar area. This is helpful in outlining the disk border. Obliteration of fat in the epidural space is an indication of an epidural process.

Dura Mater, Intradural Space, and Spinal Cord. The dura mater is a hard membrane that forms a sleeve around the subarachnoid space to cover the cord and intracanal component of the nerve roots. It extends beyond the canal to cover the root within the foramina and fuses with the perineurium of the spinal nerves to close the extension of the subarachnoid space (see Fig. 4–27). The cervical cord is wider in the ventral surface and is indented by the anterior median fissure (see Fig. 4–27). The posterior median fissure is shallow.[31] The cervical cord is larger from C3 to C6 as identified on myelography. Because of the larger subarachnoid space in the cervical area, the cord can easily be seen on plain CT scans without intrathecal contrast (see Fig. 4–24). With intrathecal contrast, visualization

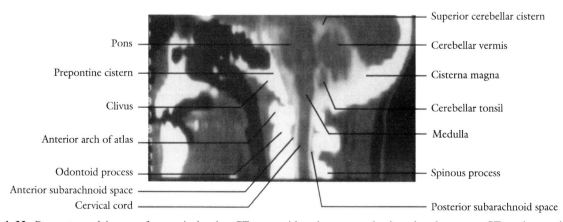

Figure 4–33. Reconstructed image of a cervical spine CT scan with enhancement by intrathecal contrast CT at the craniocervical junction. The upper cervical cord, medulla, pons, cerebellar tonsils, and vermis are surrounded by contrast material.

of the cervical cord and roots can be enhanced significantly (Fig. 4–33).

Eight pairs of cervical spine nerves exist. The first cervical spine nerve passes posterior to the atlanto-occipital joint. The remaining nerves pass through the intervertebral foramina. The number of nerve roots in the cervical region corresponds to the lower vertebral count number (e.g., the root passing through the C5–6 foramen is the C6 that lies medial to the pedicle of C5). In the thoracic area, the cord has a more rounded appearance[26, 30] (see Fig. 4–25). The cord becomes larger from T9 to T12,[32] terminating in conus with rapid tapering in its diameter.

In the upper thoracic region, the location of pathology is about two vertebrae higher than the corresponding clinical level. The discrepancy increases to three segments in the lower thorax. The spinal nerves are difficult to visualize on plain CT scans. The dura terminates at the level of S2 and fuses with the filum terminale to terminate at the coccyx. The lumbar canal contains the conus, cauda equina, and the filum terminale. The conus medullaris ends at the L1–2 disk space (see Fig. 4–30), becoming the filum terminale. In the lumbar area, the spinal nerves can be seen on plain CT scans, exiting medial to the corresponding pedicles (see Figs. 4–23A and 4–31).

References

1. Berman SA, Hayman LA, Hinck VC: Correlation of CT cerebral vascular territories with function: 1. Anterior cerebral artery. AJNR Am J Neuroradiol 1:259–263, 1980.
2. Berry I, Sigal R, Lebas J, et al: Magnetic resonance imaging: principles, technique and imaging protocols. In Manelfe C (ed): Imaging of the Spine and Spinal Cord. New York, Raven Press, 1992, pp 157–194.
3. Carrera GF, Haughton VM, Syvertsen A: Computed tomography of the lumbar facet joints. Radiology 134:145–148, 1980.
4. Cohen CR, Duchesneau PM, Weinstein MA: Calcification of the basal ganglia as visualized by computed tomography. Radiology 134:97–99, 1980.
5. Donovan Post JM, Sze G, Quencer RM: Gadolinium-enhanced MR in spinal infection. J Comput Assist Tomogr 14:721–729, 1990.
6. Drayer BP, Burger P, Dawrin R, et al: MRI of brain iron. AJNR Am J Neuroradiol 7:373–380, 1986.
7. Dryer PB, Rosenbaum AE, Reigel DB: Metrizamide computed tomography cisternography: Pediatric application. Radiology 124:349–357, 1977.
8. Dryer PB, Rosenbaum AE, Higman HB: Cerebrospinal fluid imaging using serial metrizamide CT cisternography. Neuroradiology 13:7–17, 1977.
9. Epstein BS: The Spine: A Radiological Text and Atlas. Philadelphia, Lea & Febiger, 1976.
10. Goss C (ed): Gray's Anatomy, 29th ed. Philadelphia, Lea & Febiger, 1973.
11. Hanaway J, Scott W, Strother C: Atlas of the Human Brain and the Orbit for Computed Tomography. St. Louis, Warren Green, 1977.
12. Haughton VM, Syvertsen A, Williams AL: Soft tissue anatomy within the spinal canal as seen on computed tomography. Radiology 134:649–655, 1980.
13. Haughton VM, Williams AL: CT anatomy of the spine. CRC Diagn Imaging 15:173–192, 1981.
14. Hayman LA, Berman SA, Hinck VC: Correlation of CT cerebral vascular territories with function: Posterior cerebral artery. AJNR Am J Neuroradiol 2:219–225, 1981.
15. Kido DK, LeMay M, Levinson AW, et al: Computed tomographic localization of the precentral gyrus. Radiology 135:373–377, 1980.
16. Kido DK, O'Reilly GVA, Naheedy MH: Radiological perspective on idiopathic low back pain. In White AA, Gordon SL (eds): Symposium on Idiopathic Low Back Pain. St. Louis, CV Mosby, 1982, pp 178–194.
17. Kjos BO, Norman D: Strategies for efficient imaging of the lumbar spine. In Brantzawaski M, Norman D (eds): Magnetic Resonance Imaging of the Central Nervous System. New York, Raven Press, 1987, pp 279–287.
18. Labischong P, et al: Normal anatomy of the spine, spinal cord, and nerve roots. In Manelfe E (ed): Imaging of the Spine and Spinal Cord. New York, Raven Press, 1992, pp 1–91.
19. LaMasters DL, et al: Computed tomography of the spine and spinal cord. In Newton TH, Potts DG (eds): Modern Neuroradiology, vol 1. San Anselmo, Clavadel Press, 1983, pp 53–113.
20. Lewit K, Sereght T: Lumbar epiduragraphy with special regard to the anatomy of the lumbar spine. Neuroradiology 8:233–240, 1975.
21. Masdeu JC, Grossman BC (eds): Head and Spine Imaging. New York, John Wiley & Sons, 1985.
22. Matsui T, Hirano A: An Atlas of the Human Brain for Computed Tomography. New York, Igaku-Shoin, 1978.
23. McPherson P, Matheson MS: Comparison of calcification of pineal, habenular commissure, and choroid plexus on plain films and computed tomography. Neuroradiology 18:67–72, 1979.
24. Modic MT: Calcification of the choroid plexus visualized by computed tomography. Radiology 135:369–372, 1980.
25. Naidich TP, Moran CJ, Pudlowski RM, et al: Advances in diagnosis: Cranial and spinal computed tomography. Med Clin North Am 63:849–895, 1979.
26. Resjo IM, Harwood-Nash DC, Fitz CR: Normal cord in infants examined with computed tomographic metrizamide myelography. Radiology 130:691–696, 1979.
27. Ross JS, Modic MT, Masaryk TJ, et al: Assessment of extradural degenerative disease with Gd-DTPA-enhanced MR imaging: Correlation with surgical and pathologic findings. AJNR Am J Neuroradiol 10:1243–1249, 1989.
28. Russell EJ, D'Angelo CM, Zimmerman RD, et al: Cervical disc herniation: CT demonstration after contrast enhancement. Radiology 152:703–712, 1984.
29. Sherman JL, Citrin CM: MR demonstration of normal CSF flow. AJNR Am J Neuroradiol 7:3–6, 1986.
30. Taylor AJ, Haughton VM, Doust BD: CT imaging of the thoracic spinal cord without intrathecal contrast medium. J Comput Assist Tomogr 4:223–224, 1980.
31. Theron J, Moret J: Spinal Phlebography: Lumbar and Cervical Techniques. New York, Springer-Verlag, 1978.
32. Thijssen HO, Rombouts JJ, Walder HA: Morphology of the cervical spinal cord on computed myelography. Neuroradiology 18:57–62, 1979.
33. Truex RC, Carpenter MB: Human Neuroanatomy, 6th ed. Baltimore, Williams & Wilkins, 1969.
34. Williams PL, Warwick R: Functional Neuroanatomy of Man. Philadelphia, WB Saunders, 1975.
35. Wolpert SM: Appropriate window settings for CT anatomic measurements. Radiology 132:775, 1979.
36. Zatz LM: Basic principle of computed tomography scanning. In Newton TH, Potts DG (eds): Radiology of the Skull and Brain: Technical Aspects of Computed Tomography, vol. 5. St. Louis, CV Mosby, 1981, pp 3853–3876.
37. Zimmerman RA, Bilaniuk LT: Age-related incidence of pineal calcification detected by computed tomography. Radiology 142:659–662, 1982.

5

Intracranial Neoplasms

Stephen A. Kieffer, Ja-Kwei Chang

Primary neoplasms of the central nervous system (CNS) represent nearly 10% of all tumors reported in large autopsy series.[286] The American Cancer Society estimates that nearly 17,000 primary intracranial neoplasms were newly diagnosed in the United States in 1999.[182] The brain and meninges are also common sites of secondary tumor implantation; hematogenous metastases likely account for more intracranial tumors than primary brain neoplasms.[203, 264]

Approximately 10% of primary brain tumors occur in children. Brain tumors, the most common solid neoplasms of childhood, are second in frequency only to the leukemias among childhood malignancies.[25, 352] Although the incidence of intracranial neoplasms and the proportion of higher grade (more malignant) tumors are both considerably lower in children than in adults, primary brain tumors are nevertheless the leading cause of cancer related deaths in children younger than 15 years.[245]

In 1993, the World Health Organization (WHO) issued a major revision of its classification system for tumors of the brain and CNS.[163, 303] This system is based on the presumed cell of origin and assigns a numerical grade estimating the biologic potential of the particular neoplasm.[303] The revised classification has been widely accepted around the world. A further revision issued in 2000 serves as the basis for the organization of this chapter (Table 5-1).[164]

Approximately 40% of intracranial neoplasms are of neuroepithelial origin, including astrocytomas, glioblastomas, oligodendrogliomas, ependymomas, medulloblastomas, and less common variants and combinations of these cell types.[342] Meningiomas (15% to 18%), pituitary adenomas (7% to 8%), and schwannomas (6%) also occur relatively frequently within the cranial vault.[342]

The presenting symptoms in most patients with intracranial neoplasms are often nonspecific, initially mild, or both. Headache, reported by about 50% of patients with brain tumors, is the most common initial complaint.[85, 264] The headache is frequently described as diffuse and more severe in the morning and often dissipates in a few hours even without treatment.[85] When unilateral, it can accurately indicate the hemisphere involved by tumor.[108] Episodes of confusion or change in behavior also commonly bring the patient to the physician. Unfortunately, headache and personality change are often attributed to other causes.[263] Manifestations of focal cerebral dysfunction (e.g., unilateral weakness, aphasia) are less common presenting complaints, but a careful history often reveals the prior occurrence of less specific symptoms.

It is the progressive nature of the symptoms that eventually leads to consideration of brain tumor as a diagnostic possibility, but this is often late in the course of the tumor. An exception to this more typical pattern—insidious onset and slow progression with resultant late diagnosis of intracranial neoplasm—is the abrupt onset of seizures, which are typically focal but may become generalized and lead to loss of consciousness.[85] Seizure is the presenting complaint in 15% to 95% of patients with brain tumors, occurring more frequently in low grade gliomas and meningiomas than in higher grade gliomas and lymphomas.[85]

Intracranial neoplasms produce symptoms by three mechanisms[331]: (1) infiltration and destruction of normal tissues (e.g., by a glioblastoma), (2) localized cortical irritation or depression (e.g., by a convexity meningioma), or (3) expansion within the rigid and unyielding cranial vault. Edema of the white matter adjacent to the tumor is often extensive and may account for much of the patient's symptomatology and neurologic deficit,[106, 286] an impression that is verified by the striking improvement, both clinical and on imaging, exhibited by many patients after systemic administration of corticosteroids.[75]

An increase in intracranial pressure above the normal level of 180 mm H_2O commonly accompanies an expanding intracranial mass. Headache, nausea, vomiting, and sixth cranial nerve palsy may reflect increased intracranial pressure.[85] Prolonged or significantly elevated intracranial pressure manifests clinically as loss of attentiveness, apathy, and drowsiness.[328] These signs of depressed cerebral function are most likely caused by diminished cerebral blood flow secondary to distention of the intracranial contents. This distention also produces traction on the overlying meninges, probably accounting for the headache, nausea, and vomiting that occur with chronic intracranial hypertension.

Diagnostic Imaging

The goals of diagnostic imaging in the patient with suspected intracranial tumor include *detection* of the presence of a neoplasm, *localization* of the extent of the tumor (including definition of involvement of key structures and assessment of the presence and severity of secondary changes, e.g., edema, herniation, hemorrhage), and *characterization* of the nature of the process.

Imaging (usually magnetic resonance imaging [MRI]) is also extensively utilized in treatment planning before surgery or radiation to define the gross tumor margins and to permit selection of the safest approach to the lesion.[276]

Table 5–1. Classification of Tumors of the Nervous System

Gliomas
Astrocytomas
   Circumscribed astrocytomas
      Juvenile pilocytic astrocytoma
      Pleomorphic xanthoastrocytoma
      Subependymal giant cell astrocytoma
   Diffuse astrocytomas
      Low grade astrocytoma
         Optic pathway glioma
         Brainstem glioma
      Anaplastic astrocytoma
      Glioblastoma multiforme
      Gliomatosis cerebri
      Gliosarcoma
Oligodendrogliomas
   Low grade oligodendroglioma
   Anaplastic oligodendroglioma
Ependymomas
   Ependymoma
   Subependymoma
Choroid plexus tumors
   Choroid plexus papilloma
   Choroid plexus carcinoma
Nonglial Tumors
Neuronal and mixed neuronal/glial tumors
   Ganglioglioma
   Gangliocytoma
   Dysplastic gangliocytoma of the cerebellum (Lhermitte-Duclos)
   Desmoplastic infantile ganglioglioma
   Dysembryoplastic neuroepithelial tumor
   Central neurocytoma
Pineal parenchymal tumors
   Pineoblastoma
   Pineocytoma
Embryonal tumors
   Medulloblastoma
   Supratentorial primitive neuroectodermal tumor

Tumors of the Cranial Nerves
   Schwannoma
   Neurofibroma
   Malignant peripheral nerve sheath tumors
Tumors of the Meninges
   Meningioma
   Hemangiopericytoma
   Mesenchymal nonmeningothelial tumors
   Melanocytic tumor
   Hemangioblastoma
Tumors of the Hematopoietic System
   Primary CNS lymphoma
   Secondary CNS lymphoma
   Histiocytic lesions
   Granulocytic sarcoma (chloroma)
Germ Cell Tumors
   Germinoma
   Teratoma
   Other germ cell tumors
Tumors of the Sellar Region
   Pituitary adenoma
      Microadenoma
      Macroadenoma
   Craniopharyngioma
   Rathke cleft cyst
   Tumors of the neurohypophysis
   Chordoma
Metastatic Tumors
   Metastases to the brain
   Metastases to the skull and intracranial dura
   Leptomeningeal metastasis (leptomeningeal carcinomatosis)

Based on the World Health Organization (WHO) Classification (2000 Revision). This classification has been adapted and modified from Kleihues P, Cavenee WK (eds): Pathology and Genetics of Tumours of the Nervous System. Lyon, International Agency for Research on Cancer, 2000.

Functional MRI is increasingly employed preoperatively to determine the location of functionally eloquent cortex, which can then be avoided during an operative approach.[185] Interactive computerized neuronavigational devices utilize these data (1) to allow administration of very high doses of precisely focused radiation to small (up to 3 cm) intracranial tumors while sparing the adjacent normal brain[260, 325] and (2) to accurately register the previously acquired image data set onto intraoperative space, thus enabling precise intraoperative localization of surgical instrumentation relative to tumor margins, key vascular structures, and other critical anatomy.[202, 325] A relatively new and highly promising application is image guided surgery, in which the entire surgical resection is guided by direct real time MRI in the operating room environment.[337]

Followup assessment of intracranial neoplasms utilizes CT and MRI and related techniques extensively, including MR spectroscopy and MR perfusion weighted imaging, to monitor post-treatment complications and to detect the presence of residual or recurrent tumor.[231, 276]

Computed Tomography

Before the introduction of computed tomography (CT) in the early 1970s, confirmation of the presence or absence of brain tumor involved the use of invasive diagnostic procedures (e.g., cerebral angiography or pneumoencephalography) that required hospitalization and carried some morbidity and risk. Clinicians were often reluctant to submit patients with uncertain history and findings to such risks.

The advent of CT significantly altered the method and timing of diagnostic evaluation of the patient with suspected brain tumor.[13, 14] CT evaluation of the brain is relatively noninvasive and is therefore easily and rapidly accomplished. In the mid-1970s, CT emerged as the primary diagnostic screening modality for the *detection* of intracranial disease. Areas of structural abnormality (e.g., tumors) appeared on CT as regions of altered tissue radiographic density.[15] Accuracy of *localization* with CT exceeded the accuracy that could be achieved by cerebral angiography or other invasive diagnostic procedures. Another important advantage of CT was the demonstration of *no* disease in the symptomatic patient who did not have a neoplasm or other structural abnormality, thus affording reassurance to the patient and physician and avoiding costly hospitalization and more invasive or more hazardous diagnostic procedures.[13, 355] Conversely, CT occasionally revealed abnormalities (including tumors) that were not suspected clinically in patients with relatively nonspecific complaints.[14, 346]

Magnetic Resonance Imaging (MRI)

Since its introduction as a clinically practicable diagnostic modality in the early 1980s, MRI has rapidly earned recognition as the optimal screening technique for the detection of most intracranial neoplasms.[10, 11, 37, 172, 275] Compared with CT, MRI using spin echo, gradient echo, and combination spin and gradient echo pulsing sequences before and after intravenous (IV) administration of paramagnetic contrast agents provides inherently greater contrast resolution between structural abnormalities and adjacent brain parenchyma and has proved to be even more sensitive in the detection of focal lesions of the brain.[158, 172, 275] Early experience suggested that 3% to 30% more focal intracranial lesions could be identified on MRI than on CT.[37, 100]

Lesions and tissues with increased water content appear even more conspicuous on T2-weighted MR images than on CT images obtained after IV infusion of contrast agents.[36] Delineation by MRI of normal and abnormal soft tissue anatomy in the posterior cranial fossa, near the base of the skull, and in other areas of the brain that lie adjacent to dense bone is considerably better than with CT because of MRI's lack of the beam hardening artifacts secondary to absorption of x-rays in bone seen on CT.[39] Accuracy of lesion localization on MRI is enhanced by its direct multiplanar capability, which permits acquisition of images in the coronal and sagittal planes in addition to the axial plane conventionally used in CT. MRI offers superior contrast resolution, including greater sensitivity for the detection of subacute and chronic hemorrhage in association with tumors and other structural lesions of the brain.[9, 276] The ability with MRI (using conventional anatomic imaging protocols as well as MR angiography sequences that display blood flow) to visualize vessels supplying and draining structural lesions in the brain adds yet another important dimension of information that can contribute to the diagnostic assessment.

Even with current state of the art equipment utilizing very high magnetic fields and rapidly switching gradient coils, MR nevertheless suffers two disadvantages in comparison with CT in the assessment of intracranial structural abnormalities: (1) MRI requires significantly longer image acquisition times, and (2) abnormalities involving cortical bone, intratumoral calcification, and hyperacute hemorrhage are more clearly and accurately assessed with CT. Newer multi-slice helical or spiral CT scanners are capable of providing highly collimated submillimeter thickness sectional images in extremely short acquisition times, and thus areas of hyperostosis or bone destruction, intratumoral calcifications, and early intratumoral or peritumoral hemorrhage are more completely defined with greater certainty on CT than on MRI.[36, 275] The much faster acquisition capability of current CT units strongly favors their use in patients who are critically ill or medically unstable. Also, in patients with magnetically controlled cardiac pacemakers and other internal paramagnetic metallic devices, the risk of the MRI magnet interacting with such devices may preclude the use of MRI.[297]

Given both the higher cost and more restricted availability of MR equipment to date as well as continuing improvements in CT equipment and scanning techniques that permit shorter examination times with improved spatial and contrast resolution, it is not surprising that CT remains a major imaging technique for the followup of intracranial mass lesions. In current clinical practice, initial diagnosis and localization of brain lesions are most often accomplished with MRI, but the imaging modality of convenience for followup studies is often CT.

Diagnostic Uncertainties

Resolution of soft tissue anatomy underlying thick dense bony structures remains a significant problem with CT. Small hyperdense lesions at the periphery of the brain may be overlooked on CT because they may "blend" with the adjacent bone unless relatively high center and window width settings are employed.[287]

Small lesions with a diameter less than or approximating the thickness of the CT or MR "slice" may not be accurately depicted, because the density or signal intensity reflects averaging of the lesion and the adjacent tissues included in the slice volume.[91] Unless very thin slices are employed, small tumors may thus be obscured.

Localization of a peripherally situated neoplasm as either within (intraaxial) or outside (extraaxial) the brain may be difficult on CT. The presence of inward "buckling" of the adjacent gray-white matter junction indicates that the tumor is extracerebral (see Fig. 5–36A); when this sign is demonstrated, it appears to be reliable and valid, but it was identified on CT in only 40% of one large group of superficially situated meningiomas.[113] In contradistinction, peripherally located intraaxial tumors tend to spread and widen the adjacent white matter, displacing the gray-white junction outwardly.[16, 276] Other factors that may aid in establishing on CT that a lesion is extraaxial are the demonstration of adjacent bone destruction or hyperostosis (see Fig. 5–36), widening of the surface subarachnoid spaces adjacent to the margins of the lesion, and continuity of the tumor with the falx or tentorium.[218, 276]

CT in the modified coronal projection and MRI in the true coronal projection have proved to be of considerable help in the evaluation of questionable areas at the periphery of the brain, where the previously described problems of volume averaging and lesion detection or localization occur.[210] Coronal MR images are also valuable in establishing whether a tumor is supratentorial or infratentorial, because the tentorium is oriented nearly horizontally, and imaging in the coronal plane allows precise determination of the relationship of adjacent mass lesions to this structure.[276] Multiplanar MRI also increases the diagnostic precision with which paraventricular masses can be differentiated from intraventricular masses. Paraventricular tumors characteristically displace the choroid plexus and compress the lateral ventricles, whereas intraventricular masses cause local ventricular expansion and generally conform to the shape of the ventricle.[173]

Contrast Enhancement

IV administration of iodinated contrast medium causes a transient increase in the attenuation coefficient of normal gray matter and accentuates the difference in radiographic density on CT images between white matter and gray matter in the normal brain.[112] Similarly, IV administration of paramagnetic contrast agent (e.g., gadolinium chelates) transiently induces shortening of both the T1 and T2 relaxation times of normal gray matter and accentuates the difference in MR signal intensity between normal cerebral gray matter and white matter.[1] Most intracranial neoplasms also exhibit "contrast enhancement" in all or part. The presence, extent, and pattern of tumor contrast enhancement has proved to be of significant value in improving the detection, localization, and characterization of intracranial neoplasms by CT[16, 53] and MRI.[100]

Although the passage of *intravascular* contrast agent through brain parenchyma causes brief transient enhancement of the normal cerebral cortex,[1, 112] leakage of contrast material into the *extravascular* extracellular space accounts for the more pronounced and somewhat longer lasting contrast enhancement seen in many tumors and other structural abnormalities of the brain on both CT[51, 53] and MRI.[1] The mechanisms involved in contrast enhancement of intracranial neoplasms on CT and MRI and in the uptake of radionuclide by such tumors appear to be identical.[10, 53, 103, 112]

In normal brain, tight intercellular junctions between capillary endothelial cells create a "blood-brain barrier" that prevents escape of radionuclide or contrast agent from the intravascular space. In gliomas, electron microscopic studies have demonstrated that the endothelial junctions are frequently patent and that the level of junctional patency is proportional to the degree of tumor malignancy.[198] It therefore seems reasonable to postulate that the intensity of contrast enhancement in gliomas and other intracranial tumors reflects the degree of blood-brain barrier breakdown.[51, 53, 236, 289] Experimental data support this hypothesis by demonstrating that the peak intensity of tumor contrast enhancement in malignant gliomas occurs 20 to 60 minutes later than the peak serum concentration of contrast agent.[236, 293] Furthermore, glucocorticoids, which are known to diminish defects in the blood-brain barrier, also significantly reduce the extent of contrast enhancement in primary and secondary brain tumors.[75, 86, 134]

Factors involved in maximizing contrast enhancement of intracranial neoplasms on CT or MRI include the quantity of injected contrast agent and the timing of the images. Conventional protocols for IV administration of contrast media for CT use 28 to 42 grams of iodine (100 to 150 mL of 60% iodine concentration injected as a bolus or 200 to 300 mL of 30% iodine concentration delivered as an infusion). Doubling of the dose of contrast material has been reported to significantly increase the incidence, extent, and intensity of contrast enhancement in both gliomas and metastases on CT images obtained 60 to 90 minutes after injection,[137, 294, 299] without permanent alteration of serum creatinine levels.[136] Not only are more lesions identified with this delayed double dose technique but also hypodense centers within "ring" lesions have been observed to gradually opacify.[236, 294] Because of the potential for permanent renal damage with such high doses of iodinated contrast agents and because the serum creatinine concentration does not assay all aspects of renal function, use of this double dose technique should be restricted to situations in which the clinical suspicion of one or more focal lesions is high

and results of previous studies have been equivocal or negative.

The standard dose of paramagnetic contrast agent (typically a chelate of gadolinium) administered intravenously for MRI is 0.1 millimoles per kilogram of body weight.[100] In a comparative study, the sensitivity of contrast enhanced MRI using conventional single dose technique for the detection of cerebral metastases exceeded that of contrast enhanced CT, even with double dose of contrast material and delayed imaging.[82]

The diagnostic efficacy of a double dose of gadolinium (0.2 mmol/kg) has been open to question, and few centers currently use it. A triple dose (0.3 mmol/kg) has also been advocated, with some evidence that its use demonstrates more lesions in the brain.[135, 359]

Contrast enhancement on MRI is usually assessed on T1-weighted images obtained with fat saturation. However, enhancement is also demonstrated on T2-weighted images obtained with fluid attenuated inversion recovery (FLAIR); this latter technique has proved to be advantageous in the evaluation of peripherally located superficial lesions of the brain and in meningeal disease.[211]

Application of a strong radiofrequency pulse that is slightly offset from the resonance frequency of water protons before initiation of the standard T1-weighted spin-echo pulsing sequence produces saturation of protons in macromolecules, which is then transferred to the free water protons, thus diminishing their signal intensity. Because this maneuver does not affect the T1 shortening caused by IV administration of gadolinium, the intensity and conspicuity of resultant contrast enhancement are increased.[105] This phenomenon is known as *magnetization transfer* (MT), and its application in brain tumor MRI has been judged as equivalent to the improvement gained with administration of high doses of gadolinium.[1] However, because of greater suppression of white matter signal, magnetization transfer alters tissue contrast relationships such that certain structures (basal ganglia, pulvinar, substantia nigra) become more conspicuous on noncontrast MT images, whereas other structures that normally enhance (choroid plexus, cerebral veins and dural venous sinuses, body of caudate nucleus, pituitary gland) do so more conspicuously on MT images acquired after contrast administration.[1] The reader must therefore exercise caution in interpreting areas of apparent contrast enhancement as possibly signifying disease.

Newer Diagnostic Techniques

Accumulated experience together with continuing improvements in contrast discrimination and spatial resolution have permitted highly accurate correlation between CT and MRI appearance and histologic grading of supratentorial gliomas.[10, 51, 84, 191, 276] However, noninvasive differentiation between high grade glioma with a cystic or necrotic center, solitary metastatic carcinoma with central necrosis, resolving hematoma, resolving infarction, atypical masslike presentation of a tumefactive multiple sclerosis plaque, and cerebral abscess on the basis of CT or MRI findings remains a difficult task.[5, 38, 348] Also, precise and accurate separation of infiltrating high grade glioma from surrounding edema is not currently attainable with either conventional MRI or CT, even after IV administration of contrast medium.[45, 95] Differentiation between recurrent tumor and radiation necrosis is another major diagnostic problem in the management of the patient with malignant glioma who has already undergone surgical resection with postoperative radiation therapy.[89] Newer diagnostic techniques based on magnetic resonance are addressing these problems (see later).[23, 183]

Magnetic Resonance Spectroscopy (MRS)

In magnetic resonance spectroscopy (MRS), the resonance signal that is utilized to generate an image in MRI is instead used to generate a frequency spectrum reflecting the components that make up that image.[179] In normal brain tissue, these components reflect both the water content of the brain and the metabolism of the normal neurons and glial cells. If the signal from water is suppressed, the frequency spectrum (expressed in parts per million [ppm]) reflects the cellular metabolism of the brain in the voxel or section of tissue being interrogated.

The highest peak amplitude in the normal brain frequency spectrum is that of N-acetyl aspartate (NAA), which occurs at a frequency of 2.0 ppm. NAA is a specific marker of neuronal density and viability. The next highest peak in the normal brain spectrum is that of creatine (Cr), at 3.03 ppm; creatine is involved in energy dependent processes of cellular metabolism in many different types of cells. The third highest peak of the normal brain spectrum is that of choline (Cho), which is involved in and reflects the metabolism of cellular membrane turnover; its frequency peak is 3.2 ppm. In normal brain, the ratio of the height of the choline peak to that of the creatine peak (Cho/Cr) is less than 1.0.

Another important metabolite peak occurs at approximately 1.32 ppm and reflects both lipids and lactate. Lactate is not a normal constituent of brain metabolism; its presence indicates that the normal cellular oxidative metabolism has been altered and that glycolysis is taking place via anaerobic pathways. An elevated lactate peak is seen in the presence of cellular necrosis and reflects lesions that have outgrown their blood supply—for example, the central portions of abscesses, malignant gliomas, lymphomas, and carcinomatous metastases. Lipids resonate at a similar frequency and are also found in highly malignant tumors.[60]

When the interrogating voxel is placed on the peripheral contrast enhancing rim of a rounded intracerebral mass with central hypointensity on T1-weighted MRI, the MR spectroscopic pattern demonstrating elevation of the choline peak with depression of the NAA and creatine peaks is typical for both primary and secondary malignant tumors of the brain and does not aid in their differentiation (see Fig. 5–14B).[60, 262] MRS of the central hypointense region of such a mass demonstrates elevated lactate and lipid signals, which indicate only the presence of necrosis and do not provide differential information. However, the choline peak in peripheral viable tissue is not elevated in inflammatory processes such as fungal, parasitic, and bacterial abscesses, possibly representing an important differential finding.[131, 262]

It is clearly established that in malignant gliomas, infiltrating tumor cells are present well beyond the contrast enhancing tumor margins seen on CT scans and MR images.[45, 49] However, in metastasis, the peritumoral region contains no infiltrating tumor cells.[49] Studies involving MR spectroscopic interrogation of the peritumoral region in patients with solitary brain tumors have documented elevated choline levels with reversal of the normal Cho/Cr ratio in the peritumoral region in patients who have infiltrating high grade gliomas but not in patients who have metastases.[23, 183] This finding on MRS may enable the discrimination between malignant glioma and metastasis and suggests that the peritumoral hyperintensity on T2-weighted images and the peritumoral hypointensity on T1-weighted images seen in association with malignant gliomas may reflect not only vasogenic edema (see later) but also tumor infiltration, whereas the lack of reversal of the Cho/Cr ratio in the peritumoral tissue surrounding metastases suggests that the similar MRI appearance of this tissue is likely due to edema or gliosis.[183]

Perfusion-Weighted MRI

Another difference between patients with malignant glioma and those with metastasis has been noted on dynamic contrast enhanced perfusion-weighted MRI utilizing a first pass image acquisition protocol after bolus IV administration of gadolinium.[183] One study has demonstrated a significant increase in relative cerebral volume (rCBV) in the peritumoral region in patients with malignant gliomas, and a diminished rCBV in the peritumoral region in patients with metastases.[183] Increased peritumoral perfusion in patients with malignant gliomas is presumed to be due to tumor infiltration into the peritumoral region with associated loss of blood-brain barrier integrity. Diminished peritumoral perfusion in the tissue surrounding a metastasis may reflect an intact blood-brain barrier with the vasogenic edema causing local compression of the microcirculation.[183]

Positron Emission Tomography

Studies of cerebral oxygen metabolism using the positron-emitting isotope fluorine-18 (^{18}F) tagged to fluorodeoxyglucose (FDG), an analogue of glucose, have established that most malignant brain tumors have increased glucose uptake and metabolism compared with normal brain parenchyma,[88] that the level of ^{18}FDG uptake correlates well with histologic grade in cerebral gliomas,[88] and that ^{18}FDG positron emission tomography (PET) is a good predictor of prognosis in these tumors.[17]

Differentiation between recurrent tumor and radiation necrosis remains a major unsolved problem in the management of patients with malignant gliomas.[89] Both processes can present the heterogeneous appearance of a growing infiltrative mass with irregularly marginated contrast enhancement on CT and MRI. Early work suggested that necrotic tissue failed to take up the radioactivity and appeared hypometabolic and that actively growing tumor demonstrated strong hypermetabolic uptake.[89] This finding was verified on a subsequent study demonstrating high sensitivity and specificity for ^{18}FDG PET.[161] However, other studies have questioned the accuracy and specificity, and therefore the utility, of [18]FDG PET for this indication.[275]

Complications of Brain Tumors
Brain Edema

Edema or swelling of the brain is a common accompaniment of many brain tumors and other structural abnormalities of the brain. When sufficiently severe, edema may be responsible for both focal and generalized signs of brain dysfunction.[106, 286] Edema is not a single pathologic response to a variety of insults but rather occurs in at least three different forms,[162] vasogenic (secondary to tumor, inflammation, hemorrhage, extensive infarction, or contusion), cytotoxic (in response to hypoxia, early infarction, or water intoxication), and interstitial (resulting from acute obstruction to the flow or absorption of cerebrospinal fluid [CSF]).

Vasogenic edema is the form of brain swelling most typically associated with intracranial neoplasms. It is caused by a breakdown in the blood-brain barrier with seepage of a plasma filtrate containing plasma proteins through patent junctions between capillary endothelial cells.[106] Gray matter is relatively resistant to the development of edema, and the extracellular plasma filtrate mainly accumulates in the white matter, extending along the major white matter fiber tracts. The subcortical arcuate (U) fibers between adjacent gyri offer greater resistance to the spread of edema than the long white matter tracts and are therefore involved relatively later and in more severe cases.

The severity of edema associated with various brain tumors varies widely, even between lesions of identical histology. In general, white matter swelling is greatest in association with carcinomatous metastases, and it is not unusual for a small metastasis to provoke a disproportionately large amount of edema.[286, 364] In order of declining severity, edema is associated with metastases, glioblastomas, meningiomas, and low grade gliomas, but exceptions to this order are common.[219] Rarely, a low grade glioma may be surrounded by extensive edema, whereas occasional metastases or meningiomas may have little associated white matter swelling.

On CT, vasogenic edema appears as widening and diminished density of the major white matter tracts with finger-like extensions into the arcuate fibers in each gyrus.[94, 219] The overlying cortical gray matter is compressed and thinned by the expanded pseudopods of edematous white matter (see Figs. 5–12 and 5–17).

On noncontrast enhanced MRI, the high water content in the edematous peritumoral white matter causes prolonged T1 and T2 relaxation in the involved white matter; these findings manifest as an increase in signal intensity on T2-weighted images and as a less conspicuous decrease in signal intensity on T1-weighted images (see Figs. 5–1A, 5–13, 5–20B).[175] It is often difficult to delineate the boundary between tumor and edema on these nonenhanced images; IV administration of paramagnetic contrast agent permits gross demarcation on T1-weighted (see Fig. 5–20C) and FLAIR images in many tumors (e.g., metastases) but not in malignant gliomas, as noted previously.[45, 95]

Systemic administration of glucocorticoids minimizes the blood-brain barrier defect inherent in most higher grade brain tumors, with resultant reduction in fluid and protein extravasation. Diminution in peritumoral white matter swelling as well as in the volume and intensity of tumor contrast enhancement is often evident on followup imaging studies within a few days after institution of steroid therapy.[75, 134]

Interstitial edema secondary to obstruction of CSF pathways appears on CT as poorly circumscribed periventricular hypodensity[94] and on T2-weighted MRI as bandlike periventricular hyperintensity of varying thickness and margination.[175, 374] These findings are often symmetrical and are most evident surrounding the anterosuperior margins of the dilated frontal horns of the lateral ventricles (see Fig. 5–2D) and the posterior margins of the occipital horns.[175] Fluid accumulates in the periventricular white matter as a result of transependymal seepage of ventricular fluid across microscopic breaks in the ependymal lining of the ventricles. Systemic glucocorticoids do not affect this type of edema, but surgical insertion of a shunt catheter above the level of obstruction usually results in prompt decompression of the ventricles and disappearance of the periventricular hypodensity/hyperintensity.[94]

Herniations

An expanding mass within the rigid cranial vault, whether due to tumor, edema, or a combination of both processes, compresses and distorts the adjacent normal brain, producing internal herniation of the brain under the relatively rigid falx or through the tentorial incisura.

Laterally placed masses in the cerebral hemispheres, particularly those located in the superior temporal, midfrontal, or frontoparietal regions, displace the deep central structures (basal ganglia, thalamus, third ventricle, lateral ventricles, septum pellucidum) medially.[280] The ipsilateral cingulate gyrus is compressed and displaced across the midline under the free edge of the falx (*subfalcial herniation*). Medially located high frontoparietal (parasagittal) masses depress and also displace the cingulate gyrus contralaterally but without significantly affecting the deep central structures. Subfalcial herniation is most clearly depicted on coronal CT scans and MR images, which also demonstrate depression and contralateral displacement of the corpus callosum and the underlying body of the ipsilateral ventricle (Fig. 5–1). The septum pellucidum and third ventricle are bowed away from the side of the mass. On axial CT scans and MR images, the ipsilateral ventricle appears compressed and displaced contralaterally.

Tumors of the temporal lobe and middle cranial fossa displace the uncus and parahippocampal gyrus on the medial aspect of the temporal lobe toward the midline, with resultant encroachment on the lateral aspect of the suprasellar and ambient (circummesencephalic) cisterns and the tentorial incisura (*descending transtentorial herniation*) (see Figs. 5–7 and 5–18A).[280, 286, 331] The ipsilateral margin of the midbrain is compressed, displaced contralaterally, and rotated by the impinging temporal lobe. Noncontrast MRI, contrast enhanced CT, or both may demonstrate medial displacement of the posterior communicating and posterior cerebral arteries, narrowing of the contralateral crural

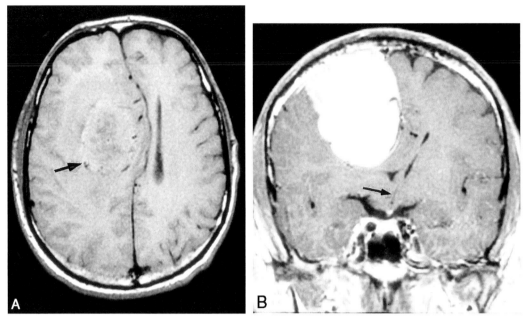

Figure 5–1. Right high frontal convexity meningioma causing subfascial herniation. *A,* Axial T1-weighted noncontrast MR image at the level of the cingulate gyri. The right cingulate gyrus is displaced to the left of the midline under the free edge of the falx cerebri by a large lobulated rounded heterogeneous hypo- and isointense parasagittal mass *(arrow).* Note that the mass is surrounded by focal signal voids representing enlarged vessels on the surface of this extraaxial tumor. A wide band of slight hypointensity surrounding the mass represents vasogenic edema of the peritumoral white and gray matter. *B,* Coronal T1-weighted postintravenous gadolinium image through the level of the mid third ventricle demonstrates marked downward and medial displacement of the right side of the corpus callosum and the frontal horn of the right lateral ventricle. The third ventricle *(arrow)* is bent and displaced across the midline by this large homogeneously contrast enhancing dural based tumor.

and circummesencephalic cisterns, and widening of their ipsilateral counterparts behind the impinging temporal lobe.[312] Late secondary signs include hemorrhages in the compressed midbrain and unilateral or bilateral medial occipital infarctions (due to occlusion of one or both posterior cerebral arteries).[286, 312] Large centrally located cerebral masses for which the primary vector of force is directly downward may cause bilateral transtentorial herniation.

Ascending transtentorial herniation with upward displacement of the superior cerebellar vermis through the posterior aspect of the tentorial incisura is caused by expanding masses in the superior portion of the posterior compartment of the posterior cranial fossa, including the upper half of the cerebellum.[286] As the superior cerebellar vermis is forced anteriorly and superiorly into the incisura, it protrudes into and compresses the superior cerebellar cistern from below and flattens the normal posterior convexity of the quadrigeminal cistern from behind.[239] Increasing severity of herniation leads to reversal of that convexity and eventually to obliteration of the quadrigeminal and superior cerebellar cisterns (Fig. 5–2*A* and *B*) with flattening of the posterior margin of the third ventricle.

Tumors of the lower half of the cerebellum and other masses in the inferior portion of the posterior compartment of the posterior fossa may produce downward displacement of the cerebellar tonsils through the foramen magnum *(tonsillar herniation).*[286] This situation can be visualized directly on T1-weighted MRI in the sagittal plane (see Fig. 5–2*A* and *C*) and can be suggested on axial CT or MRI if the cisterna magna and upper cervical posterior subarach-

noid spaces are encroached on and partially or completely obliterated by soft tissue density.

Hemorrhage

Hemorrhage is not a common accompaniment of most intracranial neoplasms at initial presentation. In a series of 973 intracranial tumors, CT demonstrated acute intratumoral bleeding in 28 patients (3%) at the time of initial diagnosis and in 7 additional patients (0.7%) who experienced clinical deterioration during their subsequent course.[369] In Cushing and Eisenhardt's[78] meticulously reported experience, hemorrhage was found in association with intracranial gliomas in 31 of 832 cases (3.7%). Acute hemorrhage was demonstrated on CT in 6 of a series of 131 meningiomas (4.6%).[287]

Intratumoral bleeding is more common in certain tumors, notably metastases from choriocarcinoma, melanoma (see Fig. 5–62), carcinomas of the lung and thyroid, and renal cell carcinoma,[12, 205] as well as in neuroblastoma, lymphoma, and medulloblastoma.[362] In metastatic melanoma and choriocarcinoma, the typically hyperdense appearance of the metastatic nodules on CT has been attributed to the presence of acute hemorrhage or hemosiderin within the tumor.[116]

Because many of the breakdown products of blood have paramagnetic properties, MRI provides a unique and highly sensitive method for detection of subacute or chronic intracranial bleeding.[12, 122] Hemorrhage associated with intracranial tumors may occur centrally within a necrotic tumor cavity (in glioblastoma [see Fig. 5–12] and some metastases) or peripherally around the tumor (seen in other metastases and meningiomas). Signal intensity (MR) or density (CT) is typically more heterogeneous in tumor bleeds than in benign intracranial hemorrhage.[9, 12] On occasion, hemorrhage may completely mask the presence of the underlying neoplasm, but images obtained after injection of contrast medium may demonstrate enhancement of tumor along a margin of the hematoma or in other locations within the brain.[10, 369] Hemorrhage into a pituitary adenoma is a common cause of "pituitary apoplexy" and may obliterate not only the entire tumor but also the normal pituitary (see Figs. 5–55 and 5–56).[267, 316] Intracranial hemorrhage not related to underlying tumor may occur in patients receiving systemic chemotherapy for acute leukemia who demonstrate bone marrow depression with low levels of circulating platelets.[246]

Resolution and organization of acute intratumoral and peritumoral hematomas are often somewhat delayed in comparison with those of other intracranial hematomas.[9, 10] In fact, high signal intensity on T1- and T2-weighted MR images in an area of parenchymal hemorrhage that persists beyond the expected time of hematoma resolution should raise the possibility that the hemorrhage has occurred within tumor tissue.[10] It is probable that atypical hypodense regions on CT within some meningiomas and pituitary adenomas represent foci of necrosis or cystic change secondary to old hemorrhage.[267, 287]

Gliomas

Gliomas represent 40% to 45% of all intracranial tumors.[286, 344] They include all primary brain tumors of astrocytic, oligodendroglial, or ependymal origin—astrocytomas, oligodendrogliomas, and ependymomas as well as choroid plexus papillomas and carcinomas.

Astrocytomas

Astrocytomas (tumors derived from astrocytes) are the most common of all primary intracranial neoplasms.[303] They account for approximately 60% of all primary tumors of the brain.[61] In the 1993 revision of the WHO classification of brain neoplasms, astrocytomas were subdivided into four histologic grades.[163] This histologic grading system has demonstrated a high positive correlation with the biologic potential and behavior of tumors. Tumors of lower histologic grades (I and II) demonstrate few mitoses, little cellular structural variation (pleomorphism), and no vascular proliferation or necrosis. Tumors in grades III (anaplastic astrocytoma) and IV (glioblastoma multiforme) are characterized by more frequent mitoses, higher degrees of cellular dedifferentiation, and increasing angioneogenesis at the tumor periphery and by necrosis within the more central portion of the tumor.

Astrocytomas are characterized on both gross dissection and diagnostic imaging into two groups, circumscribed and diffuse. Generally speaking, the diffuse astrocytomas are more common, tend to occur more in adulthood, and are more infiltrative or aggressive with spread along the white matter tracts.[61]

Circumscribed Astrocytomas

Three histologic types of astrocytoma are assigned to the circumscribed group. They are the juvenile pilocytic astrocytoma (JPA), the pleomorphic xanthoastrocytoma (PXA), and the subependymal giant cell astrocytoma (SCGA).[47, 303] All three types occur mainly in children and have a less aggressive biologic potential than the diffuse astrocytomas.

Juvenile Pilocytic Astrocytoma. The most common type of circumscribed astrocytoma, JPA represents 2% to 6% of all primary brain tumors.[303] It most commonly (60% of cases) occurs in the cerebellum (hemispheres more often than vermis) in children (Figs. 5–2 and 5–3), with a peak age distribution between 5 and 15 years. JPA is also frequently found, however, in the intracranial optic nerves and chiasm and the adjacent hypothalami (Fig. 5–4), usually in slightly younger children (2 to 3 years) and often in association with neurofibromatosis type I (NF1, also known as von Recklinghausen's disease).[6, 47, 303]

JPA is the classic well circumscribed brain neoplasm, but it lacks a true tumor capsule. It grows mainly by expansion rather than by infiltration. It is widely considered to be a benign (biologically stable) neoplasm and is classified as histologic grade I.[47] It may be densely cellular or more loosely arranged with intervening microcysts, and both patterns may coexist in different portions of the same tumor. Mitoses are rare in this lesion, and necrosis is not seen. Most often, the tumor represents a mural nodule in the wall of a well circumscribed cyst. The origin and nature of the cyst are not well understood, but the cyst fluid is proteinaceous and is probably secreted from coiled capillaries found in the midst of the nodular tumor. With the exception of the mural tumor nodule, the wall of the cyst consists of compacted normal brain or nonneoplastic gliotic tissue.[47] Intratumoral calcification is occasionally identified (5% to 25% of cases), but hemorrhage into or adjacent to the tumor is rare.[303]

The clinical presentation of children with JPA depends on the tumor site. The cerebellar tumors typically manifest with headache, nausea, and vomiting because of hydrocephalus secondary to obstruction of the fourth ventricle.[56] Weakness and loss of equilibrium are not uncommon. The optic tumors typically cause difficulties with vision, but signs of hydrocephalus may appear if the tumor has extended into the hypothalamus and is obstructing the third ventricle.[6]

On CT, the typical JPA appears as a smoothly marginated, hypodense cystlike mass with a well defined, less hypodense tumor nodule on one wall (see Fig. 5–3A). The nodule may contain one or more areas of dense calcification. The cyst fluid is less hypodense than the CSF (15–25 Hounsfield units [HU]) because of the high protein concentration.[226] Typically, after IV administration of a contrast agent, dense homogeneous contrast enhancement of the tumor nodule, but not of the other walls of the cyst, is seen (see Fig. 5–3B, C).[190, 200, 226] More extensive enhancement of the cyst walls suggests a more aggressive (higher histologic grade) tumor.[56]

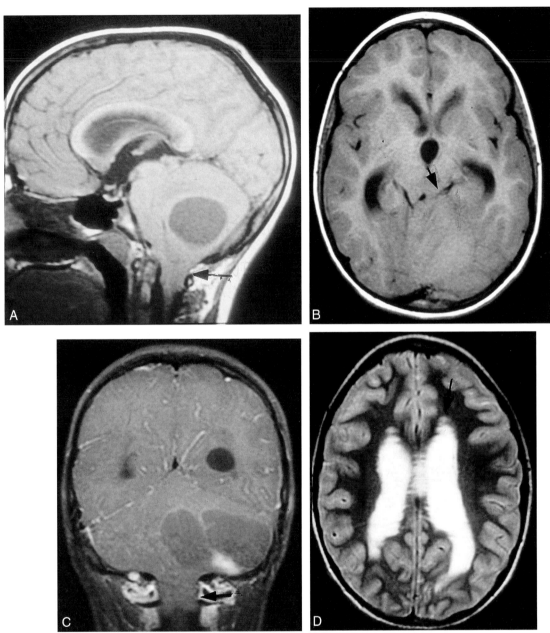

Figure 5–2. Juvenile pilocytic astrocytoma of the cerebellum causing interstitial edema and upward transtentorial herniation and tonsillar herniation. *A,* Left parasagittal T1-weighted MR image without intravenous contrast. A large sharply marginated cyst in the left cerebellar hemisphere causes downward herniation of the cerebellar tonsils into the upper cervical spinal canal *(arrow).* The cystic mass compresses the fourth ventricle and pons from behind and displaces the superior vermis upward through the tentorial notch, obliterating the superior cerebellar and quadrigeminal cisterns and elevating and displacing forward the floor and posterior wall of the third ventricle. *B,* Axial T1-weighted noncontrast image at the level of the quadrigeminal cistern demonstrates forward displacement and compression of the quadrigeminal plate and cistern on the left *(arrow)* by the upwardly herniating superior cerebellar vermis and hemisphere. Note enlargement of the aqueduct, third ventricle, and temporal horns of the lateral ventricles secondary to obstruction of the fourth ventricle. *C,* Coronal T1-weighted image at the level of the posterior aspect of the foramen magnum following intravenous administration of gadolinium. Both cerebellar tonsils have herniated downward through the foramen magnum *(arrow).* Note homogeneous contrast enhancement of a solid tumor nodule in the floor of the left cerebellar hemisphere cystic mass. *D,* Axial T2-weighted image at the level of the superior aspect of the lateral ventricles. The ventricles are markedly distended, and cerebrospinal fluid has dissected across the ependymal margins of the ventricles into the adjacent periventricular white matter anteriorly *(arrow)* and in the corpus callosum.

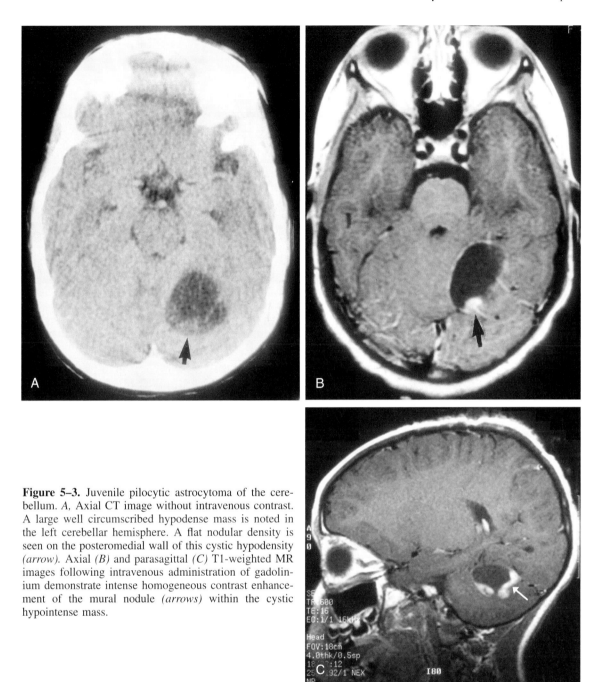

Figure 5–3. Juvenile pilocytic astrocytoma of the cerebellum. *A,* Axial CT image without intravenous contrast. A large well circumscribed hypodense mass is noted in the left cerebellar hemisphere. A flat nodular density is seen on the posteromedial wall of this cystic hypodensity *(arrow).* Axial *(B)* and parasagittal *(C)* T1-weighted MR images following intravenous administration of gadolinium demonstrate intense homogeneous contrast enhancement of the mural nodule *(arrows)* within the cystic hypointense mass.

On MRI, the mural nodule appears homogeneously hyperintense to gray matter on T2-weighted images and hypointense to isointense on T1-weighted images.[190, 200, 226] Intratumoral calcification may cause a more heterogeneous appearance. The associated cyst is even more hyperintense on T2-weighted images and even more hypointense on T1-weighted images (see Fig. 5–2A). Edema of the adjacent white matter is usually minimal. Homogeneous contrast enhancement of the tumor nodule is characteristic (see Figs. 5–2C and 5–3B and C), although a calcific focus, if present, does not demonstrate enhancement.

The clinical prognosis of JPA is guardedly optimistic. The cerebellar tumor nodule can often be totally excised,

and 5- and 10-year survival rates exceeding 75% are commonly reported.[47, 56] The location and extent of the optic-chiasmatic-hypothalamic tumors typically preclude total excision, but irradiation and chemotherapy often achieve long-term tumor control.[47, 368]

Pleomorphic Xanthoastrocytoma. PXA was newly designated in the 1993 WHO revised classification.[163, 303] The number of cases documented in the literature is still small. PXA is presumed to arise from subpial astrocytes near the surface of the cerebral hemispheres.[70, 159] Rare tumors have also been described in the posterior cranial fossa and in the spinal cord. The gross morphology resem-

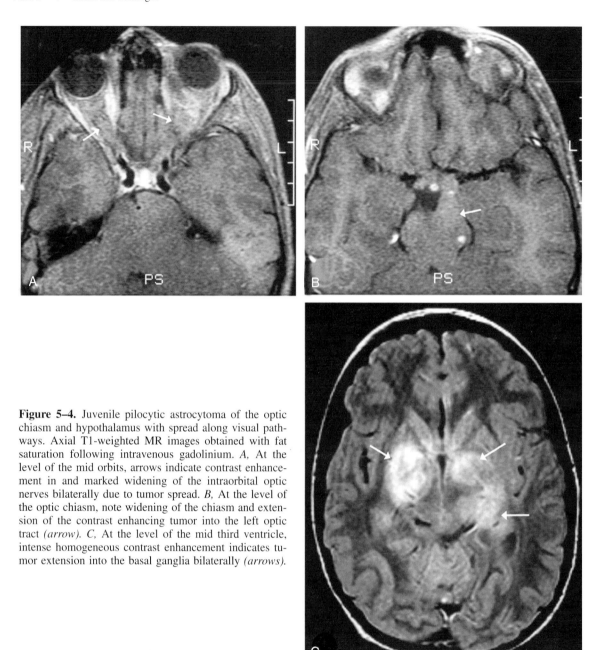

Figure 5–4. Juvenile pilocytic astrocytoma of the optic chiasm and hypothalamus with spread along visual pathways. Axial T1-weighted MR images obtained with fat saturation following intravenous gadolinium. *A,* At the level of the mid orbits, arrows indicate contrast enhancement in and marked widening of the intraorbital optic nerves bilaterally due to tumor spread. *B,* At the level of the optic chiasm, note widening of the chiasm and extension of the contrast enhancing tumor into the left optic tract *(arrow). C,* At the level of the mid third ventricle, intense homogeneous contrast enhancement indicates tumor extension into the basal ganglia bilaterally *(arrows).*

bles the nodule and cyst appearance of the pilocytic astrocytoma. The nodule is often based on the pial surface of the brain.

On CT and on MRI, the appearance is similar to that of the pilocytic astrocytoma: well circumscribed, hypodense to isodense on CT, hypointense on T1-weighted and hyperintense on T2-weighted MR images, often with cystic component (Fig 5–5A). However, the location is supratentorial (order of descending frequency: temporal, frontal, parietal) and superficial with little or no mass effect.[195, 333] Although the tumor presents a circumscribed appearance, it usually grows slowly and may infiltrate the overlying pia, even causing focal thickening of the meninges (dural tail). Intense homogeneous contrast enhancement of the tumor nodule is the rule (Fig. 5–5B, C).

Histologically, as the name implies, the tumor nodule is pleomorphic, but cells with a foamy myxoid cytoplasm are common.[70] PXA is usually classified as grade II, but later dedifferentiation into higher grade neoplasm may occur.[70, 159] The clinical presentation most commonly consists of seizures that may be intractable. Most reported cases have been in adolescents or young adults; the median age at diagnosis is 14 years.[303]

Subependymal Giant Cell Astrocytoma. This low-grade (WHO grade I) astrocytic tumor occurs almost exclusively in patients with tuberous sclerosis in their late teens or 20s.[298] It is estimated that 10% to 15% of patients with tuberous sclerosis develop this grade I neoplasm.[301, 303] These tumors arise from subependymal nodules located on

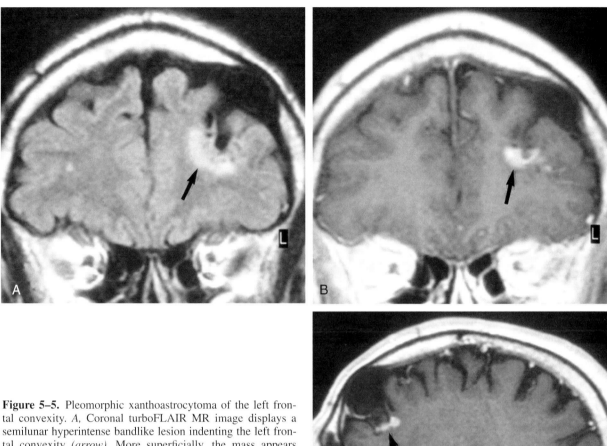

Figure 5–5. Pleomorphic xanthoastrocytoma of the left frontal convexity. *A,* Coronal turboFLAIR MR image displays a semilunar hyperintense bandlike lesion indenting the left frontal convexity *(arrow).* More superficially, the mass appears hypointense and mushrooms outward, eroding the calvarium and bulging into the overlying scalp. T1-weighted coronal *(B)* and parasagittal *(C)* images following intravenous gadolinium demonstrate contrast enhancement of the mural nodule *(arrows).* The findings suggest a superficial cystic tumor with mural nodule of long standing.

the lateral wall of the lateral ventricle overlying the head of the caudate nucleus.[298, 349] By convention, subependymal nodules that are more than 1 cm in diameter or that become symptomatic are considered giant cell astrocytomas.[349] The tumor does not invade into the underlying caudate head but rather grows outward into the ventricular lumen near the foramen of Monro, which may be obstructed either unilaterally or bilaterally. Despite this tendency for intraventricular growth, the overlying ependyma remains intact, and dissemination via the CSF is rare.[303] Intratumoral calcification is common and may be heavy.

Histologically, the tumor is seen to contain large multinucleated giant cells of uncertain origin.[25, 349] On cytochemical analysis, some of these cells display GFAP (glial fibrillary acidic protein) reactivity, a feature consistent with an astrocytic origin, whereas others contain neuron-specific enolase, a finding consistent with neuronal origin.[25]

Subependymal giant cell astrocytomas present a charac-teristic appearance on CT.[200, 226, 303] They appear as large, hypodense, polypoid, sharply marginated intraventricular masses at the level of the foramen of Monro (Fig. 5–6A). The tumor may be heavily calcified and may obstruct the foramen unilaterally or bilaterally, causing gross enlargement of one or both lateral ventricles. Other manifestations of tuberous sclerosis are usually evident, including cortical tubers and subependymal hamartomatous nodules.[226] On MRI, subependymal giant cell astrocytoma appears as a heterogenous, sharply demarcated intraventricular mass that is mildly hyperintense on T2-weighted images and hypointense or isointense on T1-weighted images. It is located within the frontal horn of the left ventricle without evidence for deep invasion or spread within the basal ganglia.[200, 303] On both CT and MRI, intense but heterogeneous contrast enhancement is often demonstrated (Fig. 5–6B). The heterogeneous signal on MRI both with and without contrast enhancement reflects the presence of dense

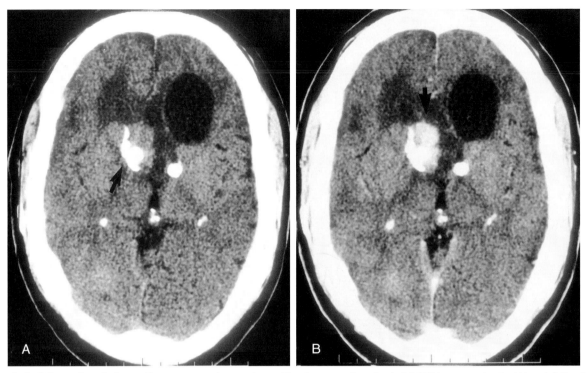

Figure 5–6. Subependymal giant cell astrocytoma in a patient with tuberous sclerosis. Axial CT images prior to *(A)* and following *(B)* intravenous administration of iodinated contrast medium. A partially calcified *(arrow* in *A)* multilobulated mass arising on the medial surface of the head of the right caudate nucleus fills and obscures the frontal horn of the right lateral ventricle. On the left, a calcified tuber (not neoplastic) obstructs the foramen of Monro; the dilated left frontal horn is compressed and displaced by a cyst, which is likely secondary to previous ventriculostomy complication. The noncalcified portion of the right frontal intraventricular tumor demonstrates homogeneous contrast enhancement *(arrow* in *B).*

calcification in these tumors. Differentiation of this tumor from the subependymal hamartomatous nodules that are so ubiquitous in patients with tuberous sclerosis is sometimes problematic, but the factors usually considered are the characteristic tumor location, its larger size, and the presence of contrast enhancement (not seen in the nontumorous nodules).[200, 303]

Diffuse Astrocytomas

Poorly marginated diffuse astrocytomas demonstrate much more aggressive infiltrative behavior than circumscribed astrocytomas. Progression from lower histologic grade (astrocytoma, WHO grade II) to higher grades (anaplastic astrocytoma, WHO grade III; glioblastoma multiforme, WHO grade IV) is common.[286, 303]

Low Grade Astrocytoma. Low grade (WHO grade II) supratentorial astrocytomas are hypercellular tumors that demonstrate few mitoses and moderate pleomorphism but no vascular proliferation or necrosis.[61, 165] On immunohistochemistry studies, they demonstrate strong affinity for GFAP.[165] These tumors, often simply labeled astrocytomas without any modifier, constitute 10% of all intracranial tumors and 15% to 20% of all gliomas.[191, 303, 342, 345] They arise in white matter and grow by infiltration, predominantly along white matter tracts, extending between and separating anatomic landmarks. The involved area of the brain eventually appears larger than its contralateral counterpart. Cerebral astrocytomas are usually solid masses

that, because of their infiltrative characteristics, are poorly circumscribed and blend imperceptibly with the adjacent cerebral parenchyma. Small and large cysts are occasionally found within these tumors,[286] but hemorrhage is rare.

Low grade astrocytomas arise mainly in the frontal, parietal, and temporal lobes (Fig. 5–7). They typically provoke little or no edema in the surrounding tissues. Because such a tumor begins in the white matter without affecting the more eloquent cortical centers, symptoms are usually vague and nonlocalizing until the lesion gains sufficient size, extends into eloquent cortex, or undergoes dedifferentiation into a grade III or IV tumor.[304] The peak age range for occurrence of low grade astrocytoma is the third through fifth decades of life.

Some diffuse (initially low grade) astrocytomas occur in childhood, notably involving the optic nerves and chiasm, optic tracts, and visual pathways as well as the hypothalamus and thalamus. More than half of the optic pathway gliomas of early childhood involve the optic chiasm and hypothalamus, and 40% of these are diffuse fibrillary astrocytomas.[4] In contradistinction to the young children with neurofibromatosis type I in whom more circumscribed pilocytic astrocytomas of the visual pathways develop,[6] the more solid and diffuse astrocytomas arise in a similar age group (peak age 2 to 3 years) but without any identifiable genetic predilection.[61] However, the diffuse fibrillary tumors share with their adult counterparts a more aggressive biologic progression and thus merit a more aggressive course of management.[4]

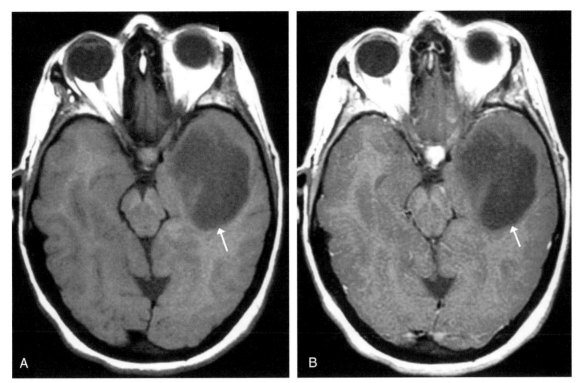

Figure 5–7. Low grade astrocytoma of the temporal lobe. Axial T1-weighted MR images prior to *(A)* and following *(B)* intravenous administration of gadolinium. A mostly ill defined homogeneously hypointense mass expands the left anterior temporal lobe *(arrow)*. There is no contrast enhancement and no surrounding edema. Note medial displacement of the medial margin (uncus and parahippocampal gyrus) of the left temporal lobe indicating early transtentorial herniation with compression of the left ambient cistern and the anterolateral aspect of the left cerebral peduncle.

Another relatively common location of diffuse low grade astrocytoma in childhood is in the brain stem. Brain stem gliomas constitute 10% to 20% of all pediatric brain tumors.[200] The peak age of occurrence is 5 to 10 years. These tumors arise mainly in the pons but commonly involve the midbrain and medulla.[366] Despite their proximity to the aqueduct and fourth ventricle, considerable tumor growth may take place without causing obstruction of the ventricular system. Cranial nerve deficits, long tract signs, and ataxia are the most common presenting findings.[200, 206, 366] Although these tumors are often regarded as low grade lesions, histologic heterogeneity with intermixed areas of higher grade neoplastic change is common.[3] Approximately 60% demonstrate foci of glioblastomatous change with central necrosis.[286] Five year survival rates range from 15% to 30%.[200]

On CT scans, low grade diffuse cerebral astrocytomas appear most commonly as poorly marginated areas of decreased attenuation involving the white matter of one or more lobes of the brain with mild to moderate mass effect.[53, 191, 208, 275, 303] A more heterogeneous appearance with patchy areas of normal or slightly higher tissue density intermixed with hypodensity is seen in a small number of cases. Contrast enhancement is usually absent, reflecting a lack of tumor vascularity, blood-brain barrier breakdown, or both.[303]

Because low grade astrocytomas are predominantly hypodense (15 to 30 HU) and usually do not exhibit contrast enhancement, it is often not possible to differentiate the

margin of the tumor from the adjacent white matter with CT. However, because the blood-brain barrier is intact, extensive peritumoral edema is unusual in low grade astrocytomas.[5, 191, 303] Grossly identifiable areas of intratumoral hemorrhage or necrosis are also not seen on CT or MRI studies in these lesions. Calcification is identified in 20% of these tumors, and cysts are occasionally demonstrated.[275] The presence of hemorrhage, necrosis, edema, and/or contrast enhancement suggests progression to a higher tumor grade.

Optic chiasm–hypothalamic diffuse astrocytomas appear on CT as rounded or lobulated thickening of the optic chiasm that appears homogeneously hypodense; the tumor may encase the arteries of the circle of Willis and invade the floor of the third ventricle, causing obstructive hydrocephalus.[4, 165, 303] Necrosis and hemorrhage are uncommon; the demonstration of contrast enhancement in these solid tumors suggests a transition to a higher tumor grade.

Brain stem gliomas typically appear on CT as ill defined diffuse heterogeneously hypodense and isodense expansions of the pons and medulla with dorsal displacement of the floor of the fourth ventricle and aqueduct and ventral encroachment upon the pontine cistern (Fig. 5–8*A*, *B*).[3, 28, 303, 366] Despite the impression of the tumor on the aqueduct and the floor of the fourth ventricle, hydrocephalus is a relatively late finding. Approximately 50% of brain stem gliomas exhibit some contrast enhancement on CT and MRI after IV administration of contrast medium (Fig. 5–8*C*). Enhancement is usually patchy and heterogeneous.[28, 197]

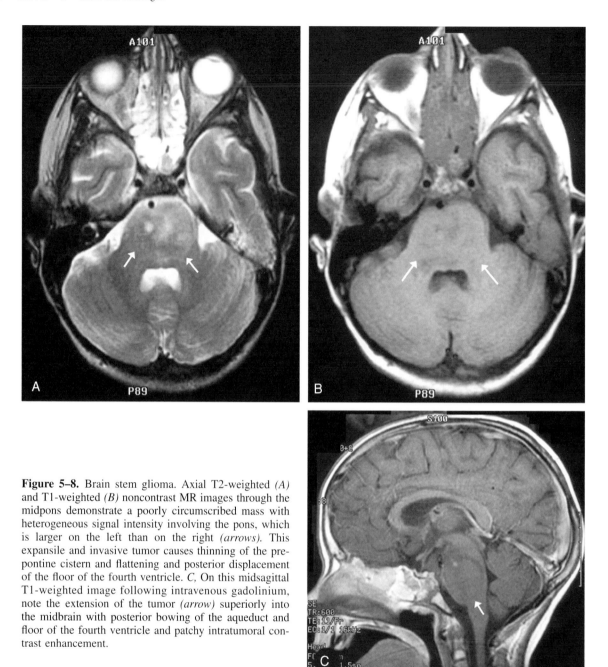

Figure 5–8. Brain stem glioma. Axial T2-weighted *(A)* and T1-weighted *(B)* noncontrast MR images through the midpons demonstrate a poorly circumscribed mass with heterogeneous signal intensity involving the pons, which is larger on the left than on the right *(arrows)*. This expansile and invasive tumor causes thinning of the prepontine cistern and flattening and posterior displacement of the floor of the fourth ventricle. *C,* On this midsagittal T1-weighted image following intravenous gadolinium, note the extension of the tumor *(arrow)* superiorly into the midbrain with posterior bowing of the aqueduct and floor of the fourth ventricle and patchy intratumoral contrast enhancement.

On MR images, diffuse low grade astrocytomas appear relatively homogeneous and demonstrate varying degrees of prolonged T1 and T2 relaxation. They therefore appear homogeneously hypointense on T1-weighted images and hyperintense on T2-weighted images in comparison with normal brain (see Figs. 5–7A and 5–8A, B).[10, 95, 275] Because of the inherently higher contrast resolution of MRI, astrocytomas are often better demarcated from adjacent normal white matter on MRI than on CT, reflecting their higher water content. Nevertheless, as on CT, the apparent margins of the lesion on the MRI (with or without contrast enhancement) do not closely correlate with histopathologic evidence of tumor extent.[95, 175] As on CT, contrast enhance-

ment on MRI is absent in diffuse low grade cerebral astrocytomas (Fig. 5–7B); the demonstration of contrast enhancement should raise the strong suspicion of a higher tumor grade.[51, 100, 125, 275, 303]

The differential imaging diagnosis of low grade diffuse astrocytoma on CT and MRI is ubiquitous. Principal considerations are cerebral infarction, cerebritis, and higher grade gliomas (e.g., anaplastic astrocytoma). Infarctions generally (but not always) have less mass effect, tend to involve adjacent cortical gray matter more extensively, and are often more sharply delineated from the adjacent cerebral parenchyma.[219] Inflammatory processes and higher grade gliomas are often associated with blood-brain barrier breakdown and exhibit contrast enhancement and surrounding edema.[275]

The prognosis in low grade astrocytoma is guarded. Most of these tumors in young adults progress to a higher grade.[213] Median survival has been reported as 5 to 8 years.[213, 275]

Anaplastic Astrocytoma. As the name implies, anaplastic astrocytomas (WHO grade III) exhibit considerable variation in cellular morphology, with high cellularity, frequent mitoses, and foci of vascular proliferation, findings that are not present in low grade (grade II) astrocytomas.[303] However, no necrosis is present in anaplastic astrocytomas, on either gross inspection or microscopic evaluation.[275] These tumors tend to occur in a slightly older age group (peak age mid-40s) than the grade II lesions and, in many cases (some estimates are as high as 75%), represent a progressive dedifferentiation of a previously low grade tumor.[247]

Reflecting the increased histologic variation, the imaging findings are also less homogeneous than in the lower grade tumors (Fig. 5–9A). On T2-weighted MRI, anaplastic astrocytomas are most often heterogeneously hyperintense and are associated with a greater degree of vasogenic edema and overall mass effect. Contrast enhancement on both CT and T1-weighted MRI is common (Fig. 5–9B); compared with glioblastoma (grade IV), the enhancement pattern is not ringlike but, rather, more patchy.

Current estimates indicate that anaplastic astrocytomas represent about 25% of all primary gliomas of the brain.[240] Median survival for patients with anaplastic astrocytoma is 2 to 3 years. Most tumors progress relatively rapidly to frank glioblastoma with intratumoral necrosis.

Glioblastoma Multiforme. Glioblastoma multiforme (WHO grade IV) is the most common primary tumor of the CNS, accounting for more than half of all intracranial gliomas.[342] It is biologically the most aggressive of the gliomas, with rapid progression of clinical signs and symptoms and a mean survival time in the range of 12 months. Like all other astrocytomas, glioblastoma characteristically involves the cerebral white matter, but this highly malignant process readily infiltrates and destroys the gray matter with loss of gray-white differentiation.[286] As their name implies, these highly malignant tumors have a variegated histologic appearance, with interspersed areas of hypercellularity, cellular pleomorphism, endothelial proliferation, and intratumoral necrosis.[49]

It is probable that most glioblastomas arise by anaplastic change within preexisting low grade cerebral astrocytomas, although some likely occur de novo.[286] Although most commonly focal and singular in their presentation, glioblas-

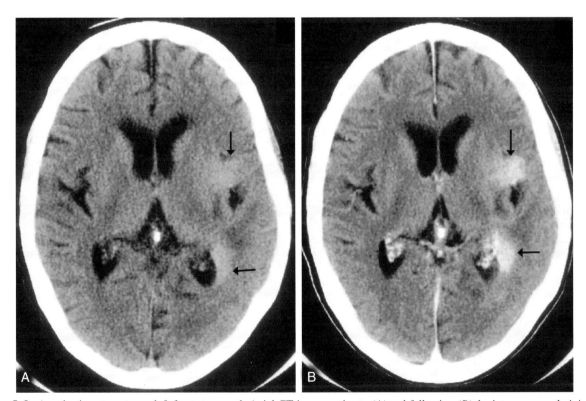

Figure 5–9. Anaplastic astrocytoma, left frontotemporal. Axial CT images prior to *(A)* and following *(B)* the intravenous administration of iodinated contrast medium. On the noncontrast image *(A)*, patchy areas of hyperdensity *(arrows)* are noted on both sides of the left sylvian fissure, involving the medial (insular) and lateral (temporal) aspects. There is mild mass effect on the lateral margin of the atrium of the left lateral ventricle by the posterior extension of this tumor *(posterior arrow)*. Note the ill defined diffuse hypodensity extending between and surrounding the hyperdense regions; this likely represents a mixture of infiltrating tumor cells and reactive edema. *B,* On the postcontrast image, there is diffuse contrast enhancement of the previously hyperdense regions *(arrows)*. Note that the enhancement reaches the ependymal surface of the left atrium. There is no evidence of intratumoral necrosis.

tomas may be multifocal or multicentric in origin.[20] The peak age of incidence of glioblastoma is during the fifth and sixth decades of life, some 10 to 20 years later than the peak age for astrocytoma. However, glioblastoma is not rare in younger adults or even in children; of all glioblastomas, approximately 3% occur in childhood, mainly in the brain stem and cerebellum. Studies indicate that the incidence of malignant gliomas is increasing significantly in the elderly.[80]

On gross inspection, glioblastomas appear more or less spherical when confined to one lobe of a cerebral hemisphere. However, these rapidly growing neoplasms invariably infiltrate into adjacent lobes, the corpus callosum ("butterfly gliomas"), and the contralateral hemisphere. Tumors that have extended widely tend to have more irregular configurations with lobulated margins. Infiltration of the ependyma of the lateral and third ventricles and penetration of the cerebral cortex with invasion of the overlying meninges occur commonly and may lead to seeding through the CSF pathways.[214, 286] Vascular endothelial proliferation with formation of large sinusoidal channels (angioneogenesis) is a typical finding in glioblastomas, and intratumoral hemorrhage is not rare.[366] The central portions of these tumors frequently undergo ischemic coagulative necrosis, leaving only a peripheral rim of viable tumor of variable thickness.[286] Cysts of varying size representing the residua of central necrosis may be found within the more solid portions of many glioblastomas.

The gross pathologic findings previously described are accurately portrayed on CT and MRI. Although smaller tumors are generally rounded, more extensive lesions have irregular configurations indicating their spread along white matter pathways and penetration into and through cerebral cortex. These tumors typically appear on CT as heterogeneous masses with irregular borders of normal or slightly increased density intermixed with or surrounding cystlike areas of diminished attenuation (see Fig. 5–12).[191]

Findings on MRI parallel those on CT. Because of the greater inherent sensitivity of MRI for the detection of subacute and chronic hemorrhage and for the demonstration of tumor hypervascularity (curvilinear and racemose signal voids), the overall appearance of the lesion is even more heterogeneous on MRI than on CT.[175] Areas of intratumoral necrosis, which tend to dominate the appearance of the most aggressive of these tumors, appear notably hyperintense on T2-weighted images except where interrupted by more solid masses of cellular debris (Fig. 5–10A). Compared with this central necrotic hyperintensity, the surrounding rim of viable and growing tumor appears significantly less hyperintense (owing to its hypercellularity), with unsharp margins, and may blend with or be indistinguishable from the peritumoral edema.

Virtually all glioblastomas are associated with vasogenic edema in the surrounding peritumoral white matter, usually graded as moderate or severe (Figs. 5–11A and 5–13A).[5, 191] The origin of this edema is uncertain; it may reflect production of a vascular permeability factor by the tumor cells.[10] Grossly evident mildly hyperdense or hyperintense

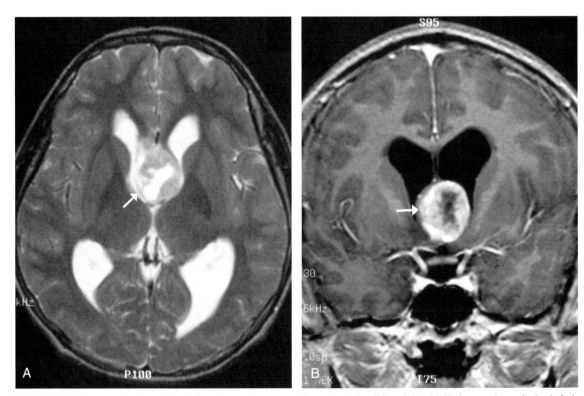

Figure 5–10. Glioblastoma multiforme involving the septum pellucidum. *A,* Axial T2-weighted MR image through the inferior aspect of the frontal horns of the lateral ventricles. An ovoid heterogeneously hyperintense mass *(arrow)* arising from the inferior aspect of the septum pellucidum indents and partially occludes the frontal horns bilaterally. Note the irregularly marginated intratumoral marked hyperintensity suggesting central necrosis. *B,* Following intravenous administration of gadolinium, a coronal T1-weighted image demonstrates intense contrast enhancement *(arrow)* of the thick peripheral rind with nonenhancement of the central cavity.

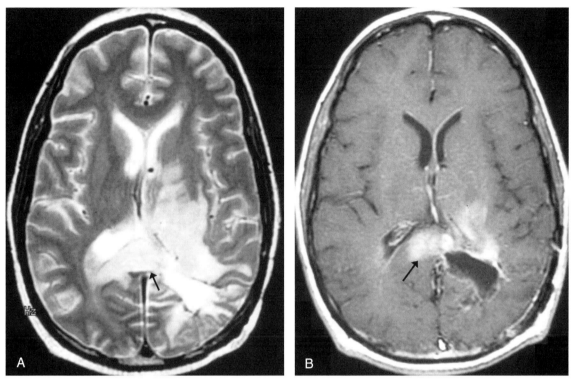

Figure 5–11. Left deep frontoparietal glioblastoma with extension through corpus callosum. *A,* Axial T2-weighted MR image through the level of the upper third ventricle. A large area of diffuse hyperintensity involves the left posterior thalamus and basal ganglia and extends posteriorly to involve the subcortical white matter in the left parietooccipital convexity. It is not possible on this image to either define the tumor margins or to separate gross tumor from surrounding edema. The third ventricle and the flow voids of the two parallel internal cerebral veins are bowed to the right of the midline secondary to the left sided deep mass effect. Note that this hyperintensity also extends into and widens the splenium of the corpus callosum *(arrow),* crossing the midline into the contralateral hemisphere and creating a ''butterfly glioma'' pattern. *B,* Axial T1-weighted image following intravenous gadolinium demonstrates patchy heterogeneous contrast enhancement within the splenium *(arrow)* and surrounding the dilated and posteriorly displaced atrium of the left lateral ventricle; the tumor has blocked the posterior portion of the ventricle, and the marginal contrast enhancement of the atrium suggests subependymal tumor spread.

tumor margins are typically unsharp, but they stand out in contrast to the surrounding hypodense or hypointense edematous white matter on CT and on T1-weighted MRI, respectively, after IV administration of a contrast agent.[38, 51, 95, 111]

Hemorrhage within the tumor is common in these aggressive tumors with extensive angioneogenesis. The appearance of hemorrhage in glioblastoma on both CT and MRI differs from that seen in nonneoplastic intracerebral hemorrhage, in that the former is more heterogeneous because of the surrounding and intermixed tumor and necrotic debris (Fig. 5–12).[215] Also, evolution of intratumoral hemorrhage usually proceeds more slowly compared with hypertensive, posttraumatic, or other nonneoplastic types of parenchymal hematomas.[9]

Contrast enhancement of viable tumor, including the peripheral rim and the intratumoral solid portions, is nearly universal in glioblastomas (Figs. 5–10*B,* 5–11*B,* and 5–13*B*).[5, 51, 52, 191, 208] The opacifying tumor ring is typically irregular and of varying thickness. The intensity of the enhancement is often significant and correlates with the level of cellular anaplasia,[51] but it does not accurately reflect the extent of microscopic tumor infiltration.[44, 95] Careful imaging–histopathologic correlation studies have

conclusively established the presence of viable tumor cells well beyond the margin of contrast enhancement, and the zone of apparent edema in the surrounding white matter must be understood as including foci of microscopic tumor infiltration.[45, 46, 95]

Differentiation by CT or MR among glioblastoma (or other grade IV gliomas), carcinomatous metastasis, and lymphoma is often difficult. All three processes may appear as irregularly rounded, contrast enhancing, ringlike masses with walls of varying thickness. In all, the viable tumor rim is typically irregular and nonuniform in thickness, and histologic examination is usually required for definitive diagnosis. Primary CNS lymphoma is typically more central in location and homogeneously solid (see Fig. 5–45), but central necrosis, infiltration into the corpus callosum and other major white matter pathways, and tumor extension into the meninges and along the ependyma (all common late manifestations in glioblastoma) are not rare occurrences with lymphoma. Occasionally, a large area of active demyelination with inflammation and edema secondary to previously undiagnosed multiple sclerosis may also simulate a glioblastoma on CT or MRI.[35]

When images demonstrate multiple nodular or ringlike masses, multicentric glioblastoma must be included in the

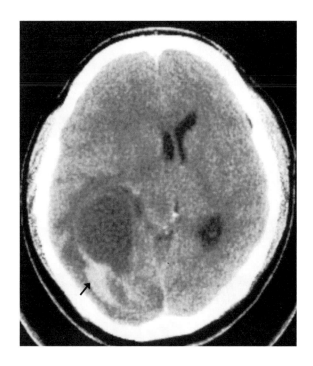

Figure 5–12. Intratumoral hemorrhage into large right posterior fronto-parietal glioblastoma. Axial CT image without intravenous contrast. A large well demarcated hypodense cystic cavity in the deep right fronto-parietal white matter is surrounded by poorly defined hypodensity. On the posterior margin of this cavity, there is a sharply defined scythelike hyperdense collection *(arrow)* representing intratumoral hemorrhage. Note the considerable mass effect secondary to diffuse edema in the right frontal lobe with shift of the lateral and third ventricles and the septum pellucidum to the left of the midline. The atrium of the left lateral ventricle is compressed and displaced anteromedially by this cavitated tumor.

differential diagnosis (see Fig. 5–13),[160, 271] along with metastases and pyogenic cerebral abscesses.[268] The peripheral rim of an abscess is typically (but not always) thinner and more uniform than that of a glioblastoma or a metastasis.[50, 348] MRS has been suggested as a method for differentiating abscess from glioblastoma or metastasis with central necrosis; the chemical shift spectrum in the center of the lesion reflects high lactate signal in both necrotic tumor and abscess. Sampling of the peripheral rim and adjacent edematous white matter, however, typically demonstrates depressed NAA and elevated choline levels in the case of tumor (Fig. 5–14*B*), compared with normal choline and NAA levels in the abscess margin.[131] Our experience to date with MR spectroscopy has supported this differentia-

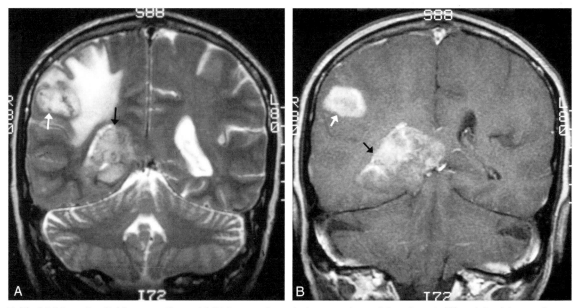

Figure 5–13. Multicentric glioblastoma. Coronal MR images through the posterior atrial region. *A,* T2-weighted image demonstrates a hyperintense rounded mass in and deep to the high right frontoparietal convexity *(upward pointing white arrow)* and a second similar mass in the inferomedial right temporooccipital cortex and white matter *(downward pointing black arrow)*. Between these masses is a large area of greater hyperintensity, likely representing edema with probable microscopic tumor infiltration, which effaces the overlying convexity cortex and severely compresses and obscures the atrium of the right lateral ventricle. *B,* On a T1-weighted image following intravenous gadolinium administration, both lesions demonstrate inhomogeneous contrast enhancement. The inferomedial tumor has invaded the splenium of the corpus callosum, extending across the midline into the left hemisphere. Note also extension of this tumor inferiorly, protruding into the tentorial notch and impinging on the right side of the superior cerebellar vermis.

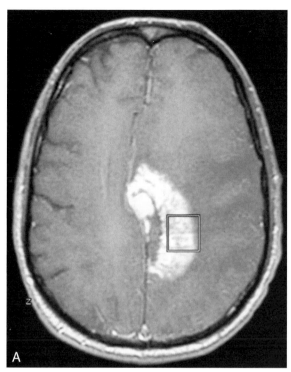

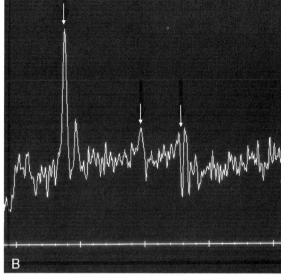

Figure 5–14. Glioblastoma with MR spectroscopic correlation. *A,* Axial T1-weighted postgadolinium MR image demonstrates an irregularly marginated contrast enhancing left posterior frontal parasagittal tumor involving the white and gray matter of the left cingulate gyrus with associated subfalcine herniation. The square outline overlying the midportion of the enhancing mass indicates the voxel selected for spectroscopic interrogation. *B,* Graphic display of proton spectroscopic interrogation of the tissue included within the voxel outlined on *A* demonstrates markedly reduced concentration of n-acetyl aspartate (NAA) *(middle arrow)* with slight elevation of lactate peak *(right arrow)* and marked elevation of choline *(left arrow)*. The elevation in lactate reflects tissue necrosis, while the markedly elevated choline peak indicates increased cell membrane turnover. These findings support the diagnosis of a malignant glioma.

tion. However, needle biopsy under imaging guidance remains the most definitive method for establishing the diagnosis and instituting definitive treatment.[220]

A commonly encountered clinical problem is the need to differentiate radiation necrosis from recurrent glioblastoma in a patient who has undergone surgical resection and a complete course of radiation therapy and now, several months after the radiation therapy, demonstrates a change in neurologic status. If the followup imaging study demonstrates increases in the size of the apparent tumor mass and the extent of contrast enhancement, differentiation of recurrent tumor from radiation necrosis on the basis of CT or MRI is not possible. In such circumstances, [18]FDG PET studies of brain glucose metabolism have shown the level of glucose utilization to be a valid measure of tumor growth,[89] although one study has challenged these results.[276] MRS may be able to provide similar prognostic information (Fig. 5–15), but clinical experience to date is limited.[183]

Gliomatosis Cerebri. A comparatively uncommon pattern of glial neoplasia, gliomatosis cerebri is characterized by widespread diffuse neoplastic infiltration in multiple lobes and both cerebral hemispheres. The extent of infiltration is disproportionate with the other histopathologic features, such as the level of anaplasia and the relative lack of destruction of normal tissues. Despite the extent of tumor infiltration, neural connections are preserved, and

the clinical signs and symptoms are relatively mild. Nevertheless, the clinical course is relentlessly progressive over periods varying from weeks to years.

The process tends to extend along the white matter tracts but also involves the adjacent gray matter with loss of clear gray-white distinction. Grossly, the involved parenchyma is both expanded and distorted by the tumor infiltration. Microscopically, the tumor cells infiltrate between myelinated fibers without destroying them, much like in a low grade astrocytoma, but there is greater cellular atypia and mitotic frequency, and foci of necrosis are occasionally seen.

Diagnostic imaging studies demonstrate the extensive and scattered areas of parenchymal involvement with multiple ill defined areas of hyperintensity on T2-weighted MR images and subtle hypodensity on CT scans (Fig. 5–16A).[309] Focal expansion and distortion are seen as areas of diffuse effacement of sulci and compression and displacement of the adjacent ventricles and cisterns. The incidence and level of contrast enhancement are often less than the extent of apparent tumor infiltration (Fig. 5–16B), because enhancement relates closely to the degree of cellular dedifferentiation.[10] Clinically, the principal differential diagnosis is with multiple sclerosis, but the imaging pattern of multiple widespread areas of expansion and distortion as well as the relatively rapid and consistent progressive clinical course favor a diagnosis of neoplasm.

Gliosarcoma. A rare tumor, gliosarcoma consists of

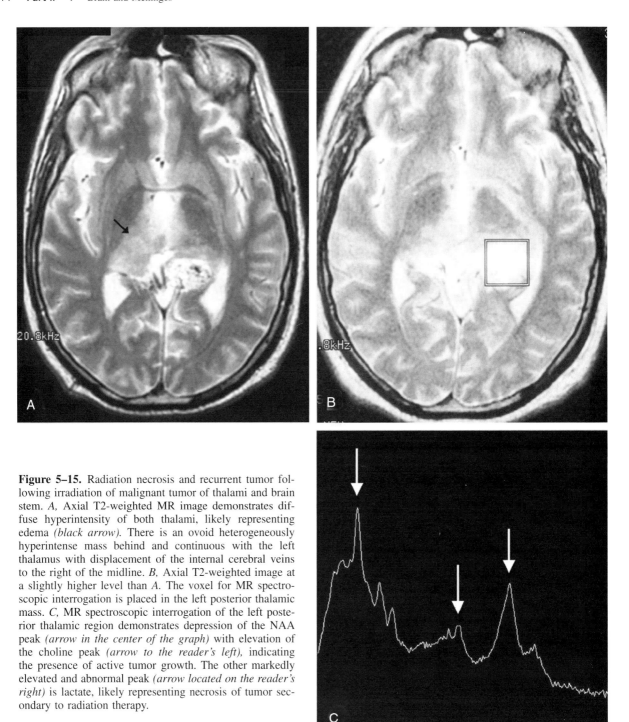

Figure 5–15. Radiation necrosis and recurrent tumor following irradiation of malignant tumor of thalami and brain stem. *A,* Axial T2-weighted MR image demonstrates diffuse hyperintensity of both thalami, likely representing edema *(black arrow).* There is an ovoid heterogeneously hyperintense mass behind and continuous with the left thalamus with displacement of the internal cerebral veins to the right of the midline. *B,* Axial T2-weighted image at a slightly higher level than *A.* The voxel for MR spectroscopic interrogation is placed in the left posterior thalamic mass. *C,* MR spectroscopic interrogation of the left posterior thalamic region demonstrates depression of the NAA peak *(arrow in the center of the graph)* with elevation of the choline peak *(arrow to the reader's left),* indicating the presence of active tumor growth. The other markedly elevated and abnormal peak *(arrow located on the reader's right)* is lactate, likely representing necrosis of tumor secondary to radiation therapy.

both glial and mesenchymal elements. Most reported patients have been between 50 and 70 years old. The origin of the mesenchymal element remains uncertain and controversial; it presumably arises from spontaneous neoplastic transformation of vascular elements within the glial neoplasm, but prior radiation therapy has been implicated in a few case reports. The mesenchymal element is usually a fibrosarcoma, but other sarcomas have been reported. Immunohistochemistry studies demonstrate both GFAP reactivity, confirming the astrocytic nature of the glial component, and positive staining for collagen and reticulin, confirming the mesenchymal component.[70]

The glial component of these mixed tumors is typically glioblastoma, and gross pathology as well as both CT and MRI demonstrate the variegated pattern of that tumor with areas of central necrosis and peripheral infiltration both along white matter tracts and into adjacent gray matter (Fig. 5–17). Invasion into and involvement of the overlying meninges are often noted (Fig. 5–17B); invasion into bone and extracranial soft tissue likely reflects the sarcomatous

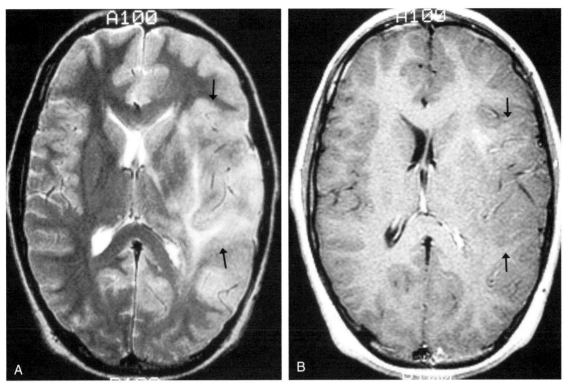

Figure 5–16. Gliomatosis cerebri in the left cerebral hemisphere. *A,* On this axial T2-weighted MR image, there is evidence of diffuse enlargement of the left frontal, temporal, and parietal lobes with extensive but ill defined hyperintensity involving the temporoparietal convexity cortex and adjacent white matter *(arrows).* *B,* Axial T1-weighted image following intravenous gadolinium demonstrates widely separated patchy areas of faint contrast enhancement *(arrows),* which represent scattered foci of malignant gliomatous infiltration.

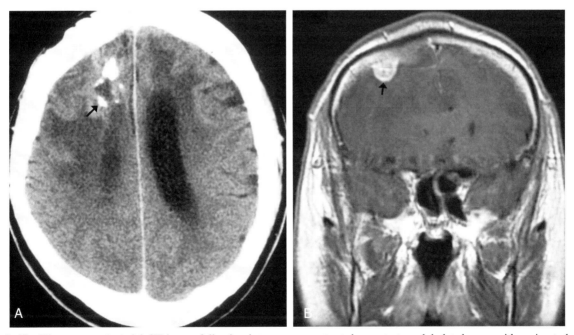

Figure 5–17. Gliosarcoma. *A,* Axial CT image following intravenous contrast demonstrates a lobulated mass with variegated contrast enhancement in the high right frontal convexity with multiple intratumoral calcifications *(arrow)* surrounding an area of central hypodensity that likely represents necrosis. The contrast enhancement crosses the midline into the high left frontal convexity. Extensive white matter hypodensity, likely representing edema, involves the surrounding frontal lobe white matter bilaterally. *B,* Coronal T1-weighted MR image post intravenous gadolinium confirms the presence of a lobulated high right frontal convexity contrast enhancing tumor and also clearly demonstrates the extensive spread of this tumor along the inner table of the skull bilaterally with bandlike meningeal thickening over the convexities of both cerebral hemispheres.

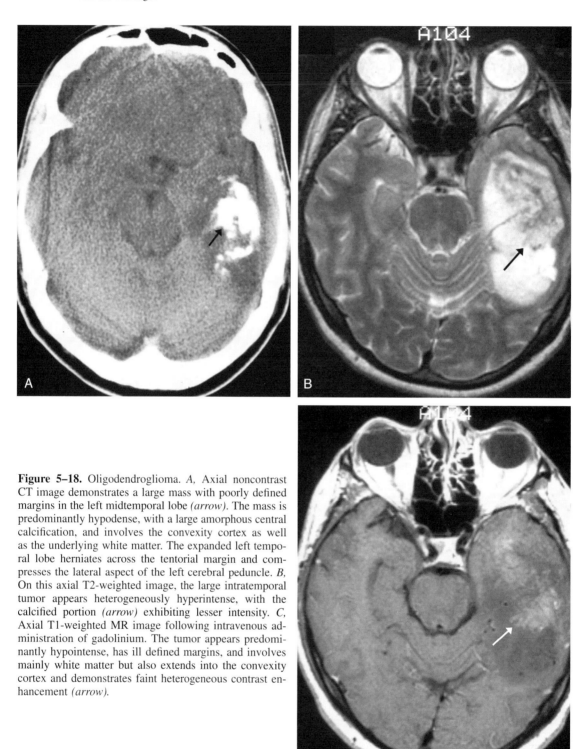

Figure 5–18. Oligodendroglioma. *A,* Axial noncontrast CT image demonstrates a large mass with poorly defined margins in the left midtemporal lobe *(arrow).* The mass is predominantly hypodense, with a large amorphous central calcification, and involves the convexity cortex as well as the underlying white matter. The expanded left temporal lobe herniates across the tentorial margin and compresses the lateral aspect of the left cerebral peduncle. *B,* On this axial T2-weighted image, the large intratemporal tumor appears heterogeneously hyperintense, with the calcified portion *(arrow)* exhibiting lesser intensity. *C,* Axial T1-weighted MR image following intravenous administration of gadolinium. The tumor appears predominantly hypointense, has ill defined margins, and involves mainly white matter but also extends into the convexity cortex and demonstrates faint heterogeneous contrast enhancement *(arrow).*

element within the tumor, and systemic metastasis (a rare occurrence in glioblastoma) is well described for gliosarcoma.[48, 70, 187]

Oligodendrogliomas

Oligodendrogliomas (tumors derived from oligodendrocytes) represent 15% to 20% of intracranial gliomas and 5% to 10% of all intracranial neoplasms.[71, 376] The diagnosis is made much more commonly now than in the past, reflecting a reevaluation of the histologic and immunochemical criteria that define the distinction between oligodendroglioma and astrocytoma.[70, 71] These tumors occur principally in the supratentorial white matter. Like low grade astrocytomas, they tend to infiltrate along white matter tracts in a nondestructive manner. However, more commonly than astrocytomas, oligodendrogliomas may also invade the adjacent cortex, and involvement of deep structures is also common.[286] Eighty-five percent occur in the cerebral hemispheres, more than half in the frontal lobes.[81, 191, 296]

The peak age of incidence of oligodendrogliomas is in the fourth and fifth decades of life; these tumors are much less common in childhood or adolescence.[70, 273] The initial clinical presentation is most often a seizure.[274] Tumor growth is generally slower than in astrocytomas of similar grade, but a more biologically aggressive category is now recognized in the revised WHO classification as anaplastic oligodendroglioma.[70, 71, 168, 274] Cytogenetic studies have noted loss of the 1p and 19q chromosomes in approximately half of patients with anaplastic oligodendroglioma; on imaging studies, patients with loss of 1p have demonstrated a significant association with positive response to multiagent nitrosourea-based chemotherapy.[54]

Oligodendrogliomas are typically densely cellular and solid, contain multiple irregular masses of dystrophic calcification, and grow very slowly. They can attain considerable size before they produce symptoms.[70] Areas of cystic degeneration are found in 20% of cases, mainly in the larger tumors.[189] Intratumoral hemorrhage is also a frequent finding.[189]

Foci of astrocytoma are frequently found in association with oligodendroglioma, and when these are prominent, the tumor is termed a *mixed glioma*.[365] When there is a clear preponderance of neoplastic oligodendrocytes (75% to 90%), the tumor is classified as an oligodendroglioma.[303]

On CT, oligodendrogliomas most often appear as masses of heterogeneous density (predominantly hypodense) in the frontal lobe with irregular and poorly defined margins involving the more superficial white matter and frequently infiltrating into the overlying cortex and obscuring the gray-white interface. The characteristic feature in the great majority of cases is the presence of large irregular calcifications, sometimes described as ribbonlike or gyriform in character, within the tumor (Fig. 5–18A).[341] The frequency of intratumoral calcification in oligodendrogliomas (70% to 90%) is the highest of any cerebral neoplasm,[341] but overall, intratumoral calcification is most common in astrocytomas (frequency, 25%) because of the much greater prevalence of that lesion.[168] Intratumoral cyst formation is common (20%),[189] but frank intratumoral necrosis is unusual and indicates a poor prognosis.[42] Contrast enhancement is noted in approximately two thirds of oligodendrogliomas (Fig. 5–18C), but the degree of enhancement is variable and appears to correlate with higher histologic grade and lower survival.[303, 341]

On MRI, oligodendrogliomas appear heterogeneous on both T1- and T2-weighted spin-echo images because of the presence of intratumoral cysts and calcifications.[145] On T1-weighted images, the tumors appear predominantly hypointense to gray matter, and on T2-weighted images, they are most often hyperintense, with small intratumoral cysts and focal calcifications and hemorrhages contributing to the overall heterogeneity (Fig. 5–18B).[168, 189] Peritumoral edema is noted in about a third of cases, but erosion of the overlying calvaria may be identified on both CT and MRI when the lesion is peripheral; this finding indicates the long-standing course commonly associated with oligodendrogliomas.[189]

Ependymoma

The ependyma lining the floor of the fourth ventricle is the most common site of origin of intracranial ependymomas (65%). Nevertheless, approximately 30% occur above the tentorium, arising from the walls of the lateral or third ventricles or from ependymal cell rests in the cerebral white matter adjacent to the lateral ventricles.[226, 286, 303, 315] Infratentorial ependymomas occur predominantly in children between the ages of 1 and 6 years; supratentorial ependymomas occur mainly in the second through the fourth decades of life.[7, 110, 315]

Posterior fossa ependymomas compose approximately 10% to 15% of all primary CNS neoplasms of childhood and approximately 5% to 10% of all intracranial neoplasms.[141, 286, 341] They are the fourth most common posterior fossa tumor of childhood,[18, 22] exceeded only by medulloblastoma, juvenile pilocytic astrocytoma, and brain stem glioma.[228] Ependymomas are usually slow growing tumors of moderate malignancy (WHO grade II), but the prognosis is guarded because of their notable tendency to recur locally and to disseminate via the subarachnoid spaces. The incidence of seed metastases via the CSF is approximately 10% overall but is considerably higher in the infratentorial tumors of early childhood; tumor seeding into the subarachnoid spaces is found initially or on followup studies in approximately a third of fourth ventricle ependymomas.[101, 226, 286]

Supratentorial ependymomas are commonly paraventricular, located most frequently within cerebral parenchyma near the atrium of the lateral ventricle or the foramen of Monro and presumably arising from ependymal cell rests.[226] Infratentorial ependymomas are lobulated, well circumscribed, exophytic masses that expand within the cavity of the fourth ventricle rather than infiltrate into the surrounding parenchyma. They often extend in a tonguelike fashion through the lateral recesses into the lateral medullary and cerebellopontine angle cisterns (15%) or through the foramen of Magendie into the vallecula (10%).[18, 226, 286, 303] Tumor growth within the fourth ventricle eventually leads to occlusion of the ventricle with resultant obstructive hydrocephalus.

These tumors are highly cellular, with uniform cells that tend to form characteristic perivascular pseudorosettes.[25] Although they do not invade through the ventricular walls, they are firmly attached to the ventricular floor, and complete resection of the tumor base is frequently not possible. The rate of local tumor recurrence after surgical resection is 90% to 95% within 3 years, and the 5 year survival is currently 45% to 70%.[138, 141, 228, 273, 304] Furthermore, about 25% of ependymomas exhibit features of anaplasia with a high mitotic rate, cellular pleomorphism, and intratumoral necrosis; these are considered WHO grade III.[25, 70]

Intratumoral calcification and cyst formation are common in ependymomas (20% to 50% of reported cases).[7, 226, 315, 361] Peritumoral edema is a prominent and frequent finding in association with both cerebellar and cerebral ependymomas.

On noncontrast CT, ependymomas appear as hypodense or isodense, heterogeneous, midline, rounded masses within the fourth ventricle that partially or completely obliterate it.[200, 226, 303, 315, 361] The tumor is typically well defined by a prominent hypodense halo of peritumoral edema. Aggregates of calcification, usually small and round but sometimes quite large, are found in up to half of these lesions, and focal lucencies resulting from cyst formation are nearly as common.[200] In supratentorial tumors, the cysts are both larger and more frequent (up to 80%) than in the fourth ventricle ependymomas (see Fig. 5–20A).[7] Intratumoral hemorrhage is relatively less common, with reported frequency of 20% or less.[200] After IV administration of contrast agent, the solid portions and cyst walls of the tumor mass exhibit moderate but variable and heterogeneous enhancement.[7, 110, 200, 315, 361]

The MRI appearance of ependymomas is heterogeneous, reflecting mixed signals from intratumoral calcification, cysts, and hemorrhage. Usually, these tumors are isointense to hypointense relative to white matter on T1-weighted

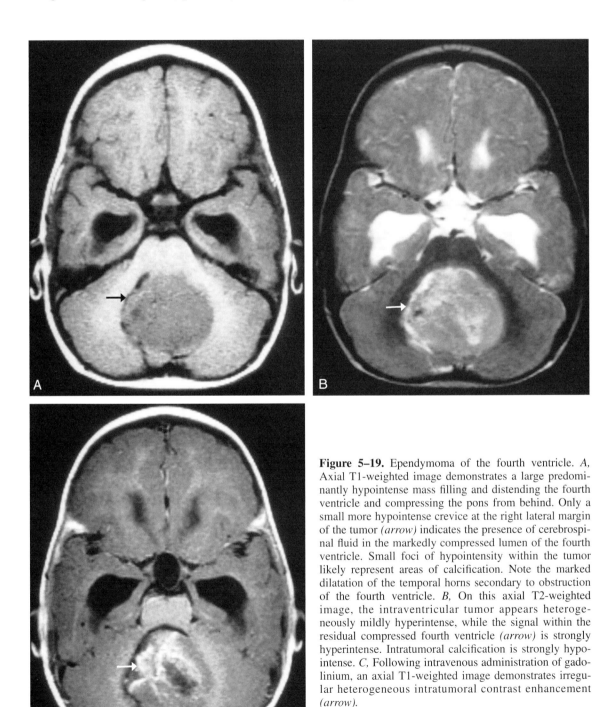

Figure 5–19. Ependymoma of the fourth ventricle. *A,* Axial T1-weighted image demonstrates a large predominantly hypointense mass filling and distending the fourth ventricle and compressing the pons from behind. Only a small more hypointense crevice at the right lateral margin of the tumor *(arrow)* indicates the presence of cerebrospinal fluid in the markedly compressed lumen of the fourth ventricle. Small foci of hypointensity within the tumor likely represent areas of calcification. Note the marked dilatation of the temporal horns secondary to obstruction of the fourth ventricle. *B,* On this axial T2-weighted image, the intraventricular tumor appears heterogeneously mildly hyperintense, while the signal within the residual compressed fourth ventricle *(arrow)* is strongly hyperintense. Intratumoral calcification is strongly hypointense. *C,* Following intravenous administration of gadolinium, an axial T1-weighted image demonstrates irregular heterogeneous intratumoral contrast enhancement *(arrow).*

images and isointense to hyperintense to white matter on T2-weighted images (Figs. 5–19A, B, and 5–20B).[110, 200, 311] As on CT, contrast enhancement is the rule for MRI, but it is variable in degree and typically not uniform (Figs. 5–19C and 5–20C). Although the MRI features of ependymoma are nonspecific,[18, 128, 311] the multiplanar capabilities of this modality offer unique visualization of infratentorial tumor

extent within the cranial vault and the region of the cervicocranial junction.[10]

On both CT and MRI as well as in the clinical setting, the presentation of ependymoma of the fourth ventricle may closely resemble that of medulloblastoma and of JPA. The incidence and extent of intratumoral calcification, heterogeneity of density or signal intensity, and propensity for

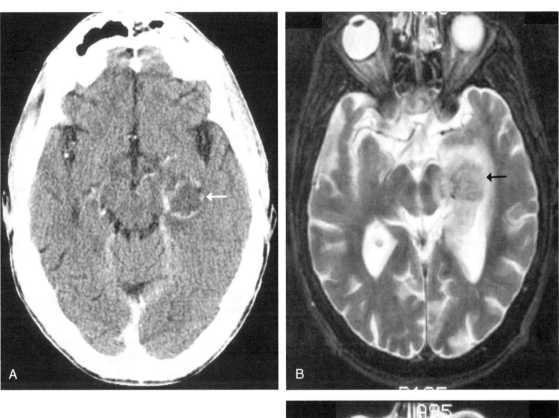

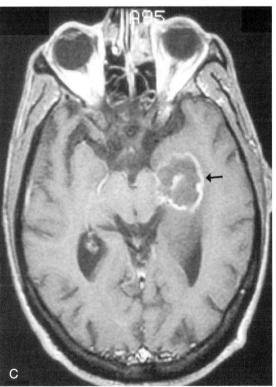

Figure 5–20. Supratentorial ependymoma. *A,* Axial CT image post intravenous contrast demonstrates a cystic appearing hypodense mass with irregular rimlike contrast enhancement *(arrow)* in the medial aspect of the left temporal lobe. *B,* On this axial T2-weighted MR image, the tumor *(arrow)* exhibits mixed signal intensity; it is predominantly isointense with gray matter and hypointense to cerebrospinal fluid. A tiny ovoid hypointensity in its posteromedial surface likely represents calcification. There is extensive surrounding edema in the temporal lobe and in the lateral aspect of the left cerebral peduncle. *C,* Axial T1-weighted postgadolinium image demonstrates irregular rimlike and central contrast enhancement *(arrow)* with medial extension into the lateral margin of the midbrain.

tumor extension into the fourth ventricular recesses are greater in ependymomas than in medulloblastomas or astrocytomas. In general, medulloblastomas appear more dense on CT with a lower frequency of intratumoral calcification, and they exhibit more homogeneous contrast enhancement than ependymomas. Definitive differentiation in a given case on the basis of CT or MRI findings may not, however, be possible.[200] Astrocytomas tend to occur in slightly older patients and are much less frequently centered in the midline.

Subependymoma

A rare variant of ependymoma that actually consists of both highly differentiated ependymal cells and astrocytes, subependymoma is classified as a benign (WHO grade I) glial neoplasm. It is considered to arise from beneath the ventricular lining and projects into the ventricular cavity as a sharply outlined intraventricular mass but does not extend deeply from its base into the adjacent brain parenchyma (Fig. 5–21). Subependymomas are typically solid and homogeneous, although larger tumors may contain calcifications, microcystic changes, and evidence of intratumoral hemorrhage.[10]

Subependymomas occur mainly in the fourth ventricle in older adults; they are often asymptomatic and found incidentally at autopsy.[10] Those that become symptomatic (causing obstructive hydrocephalus) occur mostly in the lateral ventricle in relation to the septum pellucidum and foramen of Monro and much less commonly in the region of the aqueduct.

On CT and MRI, symptomatic lesions in the lateral ventricles usually arise from the septum pellucidum and appear homogeneous in density and signal intensity. On T2-weighted MRI, the tumor appears homogeneously hyperintense to adjacent brain. There is little or no tumoral enhancement after IV administration of contrast medium (Fig. 5–19C). However, larger tumors may exhibit internal heterogeneity of density and signal owing to intratumoral calcification and hemorrhage.[110, 311]

The differential diagnosis includes central neurocytoma, ependymoma, and subependymal giant cell astrocytoma. Patient age, the nature of the symptoms, the presence of associated disease, tumor size, the presence and extent of calcification, cystic change, evidence of hemorrhage, and contrast enhancement are the key factors in making the differentiation.

Choroid Plexus Papilloma and Carcinoma

Papillomas arising in the choroid plexus are benign intraventricular neoplasms that locally expand the involved ventricle and cause hydrocephalus, which may be secondary to ventricular obstruction, overproduction of CSF, or impairment of CSF absorption. Choroid plexus papillomas represent less than 1% of all brain tumors but are more common in young children (3% of all pediatric brain tumors), particularly in the neonatal period; 85% occur in the first 5 years of life, and these tumors represent 40% of all brain tumors in the first 60 days of life.[200, 270, 303]

The atria of the lateral ventricles and the fourth ventricle are the most common sites of involvement. An age disparity exists with regard to tumor location, the lateral ventricle tumors occurring mainly in young children and the fourth ventricle papillomas appearing more commonly in adults.[11, 286] It is not uncommon for the fourth ventricle tumors to extend through the lateral recesses and protrade into the cerebellopontine angle cisterns.[253]

Histologically, choroid plexus papillomas consist of well differentiated proliferation of both the surface epithelium of the choroid plexus and the underlying vascular connective tissue core and are usually classified as WHO grade I.[70, 286] They grow slowly and are noninvasive, tending to expand within the confines of the ventricle or its outlet foramina.[70, 253, 303] Occasionally, however, the epithelium may exhibit malignant change, and in such cases, the tumors are classified as carcinomas; they may extend into the adjacent brain parenchyma.[221] The prognosis in these malignant choroid plexus tumors depends on the completeness of surgical resection, but overall, the 5 year survival ranges from 26% to 40%.[254]

Because of the friability and high vascularity of choroid plexus papillomas, intratumoral and intraventricular hemorrhage are common.[70, 201, 304]

On CT, choroid plexus papillomas appear as large, rounded or lobulated, isodense or hyperdense intraventricular masses that engulf and separate the normal choroid plexus calcifications and exhibit intense homogeneous contrast enhancement.[166, 221, 370] Small hypodense, nonenhancing foci are occasionally identified within these tumors.[166, 370]

On MRI, choroid plexus papillomas are usually isointense or hypointense with respect to brain on T1-weighted images and heterogeneously hyperintense relative to brain on T2-weighted images (Fig. 5–22A, B);[65, 200] the heterogeneity of signal intensity within the tumor mass may be due to areas of vascularity, calcification, or previous hemorrhage (Fig. 5–22A). As noted previously, the tumor typically expands the ventricle locally at the site of origin and may obstruct ventricular drainage, causing dilatation (entrapment) of the more proximal portion of the affected ventricle.[11] On both CT and MRI, these tumors usually demonstrate intense contrast enhancement (Fig. 5–22C), which may be homogeneous or heterogeneous, depending on the tumor contents.

The differential diagnosis of choroid plexus papilloma on imaging studies usually includes ependymoma in older children and adults and meningioma in adults. The lobulated tumor margins, the lack of invasion of brain parenchyma despite the large tumor size, and the heterogeneous signal pattern within the tumor all aid in distinguishing this lesion.

Nonglial Tumors
Neuronal and Mixed Neuronal and Glial Tumors

In this group of tumors of neuroepithelial origin, neuronal and glial differentiation are present in varying degrees. The 1993 revised WHO classification of tumors of the CNS includes the following recognized entities:

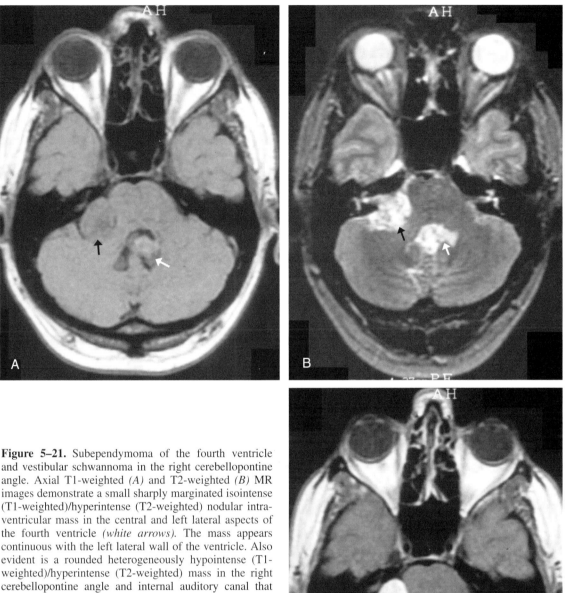

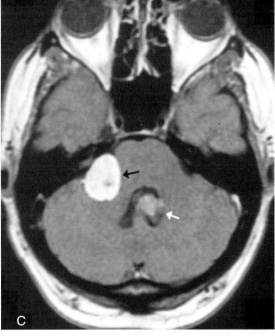

Figure 5–21. Subependymoma of the fourth ventricle and vestibular schwannoma in the right cerebellopontine angle. Axial T1-weighted *(A)* and T2-weighted *(B)* MR images demonstrate a small sharply marginated isointense (T1-weighted)/hyperintense (T2-weighted) nodular intraventricular mass in the central and left lateral aspects of the fourth ventricle *(white arrows)*. The mass appears continuous with the left lateral wall of the ventricle. Also evident is a rounded heterogeneously hypointense (T1-weighted)/hyperintense (T2-weighted) mass in the right cerebellopontine angle and internal auditory canal that indents the lateral aspect of the pons and middle cerebellar peduncle and the anterior margin of the right cerebellar hemisphere *(black arrows). C,* Axial T1-weighted image post intravenous gadolinium administration demonstrates nearly homogeneous contrast enhancement of both lesions; the uptake of contrast in the intraventricular nodule is more subtle than in the cerebellopontine angle lesion.

ganglioglioma, gangliocytoma, dysplastic gangliocytoma of the cerebellum (Lhermitte-Duclos disease), desmoplastic infantile ganglioglioma, dysembryoplastic neuroepithelial tumor, and central neurocytoma.[163, 303]

Ganglioglioma and Gangliocytoma

Gangliogliomas are uncommon low grade tumors consisting of a mixture of neoplastic astrocytes and dysplastic neurons. Slow growing neoplasms with well differentiated ganglion cells and a low grade astrocytomatous stroma,[286] these tumors are considered WHO grade I or II.[70, 168] Gangliocytomas (also known as ganglioneuromas) are relatively less common and contain only neuronal elements; they are classified as WHO grade I.[200] Together, these tumors account for 1.3% of all primary brain tumors.[168]

Gangliogliomas and gangliocytomas occur in young

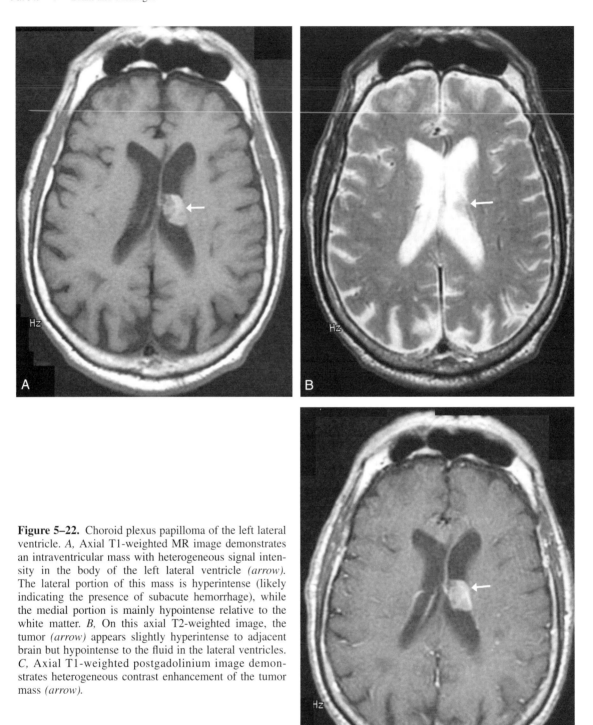

Figure 5–22. Choroid plexus papilloma of the left lateral ventricle. *A,* Axial T1-weighted MR image demonstrates an intraventricular mass with heterogeneous signal intensity in the body of the left lateral ventricle *(arrow).* The lateral portion of this mass is hyperintense (likely indicating the presence of subacute hemorrhage), while the medial portion is mainly hypointense relative to the white matter. *B,* On this axial T2-weighted image, the tumor *(arrow)* appears slightly hyperintense to adjacent brain but hypointense to the fluid in the lateral ventricles. *C,* Axial T1-weighted postgadolinium image demonstrates heterogeneous contrast enhancement of the tumor mass *(arrow).*

people (peak incidence in the second decade of life) and constitute approximately 3% to 4% of primary brain tumors in children.[155, 226] They are found most commonly in the temporal lobes but may occur anywhere in the cerebral hemispheres.[229, 363] The clinical presentation is usually with seizures of long duration, and gangliogliomas are considered the most common cause of chronic temporal lobe epilepsy.[229] These tumors are usually well circumscribed solid masses but may include one or more cysts.[59, 70] Gross total resection of a tumor is the treatment of choice. Overall, gangliogliomas and gangliocytomas have a 92% 3 year survival.[155] In approximately 10% of cases, however, the tumor is more aggressive; in these cases, the malignant element is always glial.[70]

Diagnostic imaging findings are relatively nonspecific and are similar to those in other low grade intracerebral neoplasms.[168, 200] Noncontrast CT scans demonstrate relatively well circumscribed hypodense (occasionally isodense with adjacent brain) lesions typically located in the periphery of the hemisphere with little associated mass effect or surrounding vasogenic edema. Foci of calcification are identified in a third to 40% of cases and cysts in half of cases.[155, 226, 363, 371] Calcification is less common in the noncystic tumors.[168] Rarely, a peripherally located indolent tumor may erode the inner table of the overlying skull.[226] Hemorrhage is rare in these tumors.[226] Contrast enhancement is observed in about 50% of cases and may be homogeneous or heterogeneous, depending on the presence and size of cystic and calcific changes.[59, 155, 363]

On MRI, these tumors (like many other intracerebral neoplasms) are usually heterogeneous in appearance, predominantly hypointense to gray matter on T1-weighted images and hyperintense on T2-weighted images (Fig. 5–23A).[59, 155, 323, 364, 368] Mild to moderate contrast enhancement of the solid noncystic portion of the tumor is found in the majority of cases on both CT and MRI (Fig. 5–23B).[59]

The findings on CT and MRI in these ganglion cell tumors are not characteristic; oligodendroglioma is a common differential consideration. However, in a young patient with a protracted history of seizures and a relatively well circumscribed cystic tumor containing calcification in the periphery of the temporal lobe with little or no associated mass effect, ganglioglioma should be strongly considered.[59, 155, 275, 314, 363]

Dysplastic Gangliocytoma of the Cerebellum

A rare lesion, dysplastic gangliocytoma of the cerebellum (Lhermitte-Duclos disease) is considered a complex hamartoma or malformation and is classified as WHO grade I.[350] Dysplastic gangliocytoma may exist as an isolated entity or as part of Cowden's disease, a rare syndrome with multiple mucosal hamartomas.[178, 350] The clinical presentation is usually ataxia and signs of increased intracranial pressure in a young adult. A large dysplastic mass occupies most or all of the cerebellar hemisphere with thickening of the granular and molecular layers of the overlying cerebellar cortex (Fig. 5–24A). The enlarged mass causes displacement and compression of the fourth ventricle. On MRI, the mass is poorly demarcated, hypointense on T1-weighted images and hyperintense on T2-weighted images, and the thickened folia present a distorted striate pattern (Fig. 5–24B).[307] Contrast enhancement of either the tumor or the thickened cerebellar folia is unusual (Fig. 5–24C).[177]

Desmoplastic Infantile Ganglioglioma

Desmoplastic infantile ganglioglioma (DIG) is an unusual lesion that occurs in young infants. It consists of immature neurons and astrocytes together with extensive fibrocollagenous (desmoplastic) thickening and cyst formation. The solid desmoplastic portion is often located adja-

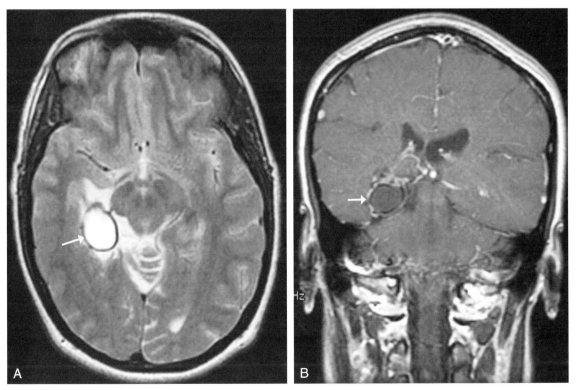

Figure 5–23. Ganglioglioma of the right temporal lobe. *A,* Axial T2-weighted MR image demonstrates a well circumscribed cystic mass *(arrow)* with a hypointense rim (secondary to calcification) in the region of the right parahippocampal gyrus and surrounding hyperintensity (due to edema). There is associated mass effect with effacement of the sulci of the right temporooccipital convexity, but there is no evidence of tentorial herniation. *B,* On this postgadolinium T1-weighted coronal image, peripheral rimlike contrast enhancement *(arrow)* outlines the margins of this cystic tumor, which is located immediately above the right leaf of the tentorium. The contents of the cyst are slightly hyperintense relative to cerebrospinal fluid, reflecting a higher protein content.

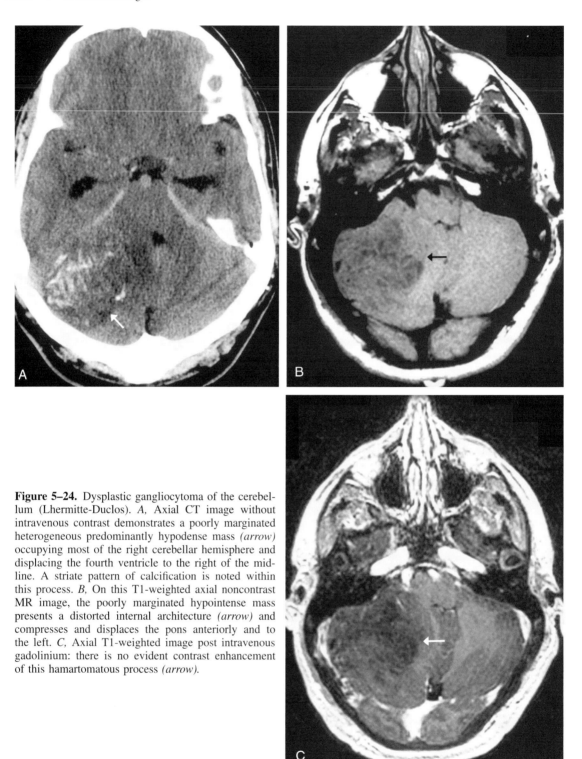

Figure 5–24. Dysplastic gangliocytoma of the cerebellum (Lhermitte-Duclos). *A,* Axial CT image without intravenous contrast demonstrates a poorly marginated heterogeneous predominantly hypodense mass *(arrow)* occupying most of the right cerebellar hemisphere and displacing the fourth ventricle to the right of the midline. A striate pattern of calcification is noted within this process. *B,* On this T1-weighted axial noncontrast MR image, the poorly marginated hypointense mass presents a distorted internal architecture *(arrow)* and compresses and displaces the pons anteriorly and to the left. *C,* Axial T1-weighted image post intravenous gadolinium: there is no evident contrast enhancement of this hamartomatous process *(arrow).*

cent to the meninges. Despite its variegated appearance, this tumor is classified as WHO grade I and has a favorable long term prognosis after complete excision.[155]

DIGs are large and superficial hemispheric tumors that occur mainly in the frontal and parietal lobes and present a markedly heterogeneous appearance on both gross inspection and MRI (Fig. 5–25).[155, 209, 326] The solid portions of this tumor are hypointense relative to normal brain on T2-weighted images and frequently demonstrate intense contrast enhancement.[155, 326] DIG differs from the usual ganglioglioma in that it presents in infancy, is predominantly frontoparietal in location, and has dense desmoplasia.[200] On MRI, the intermixed collagenous and multicystic pattern of this lesion most resembles that of a primitive neuroectodermal tumor (PNET), which carries a much less favorable prognosis; however, PNET is also

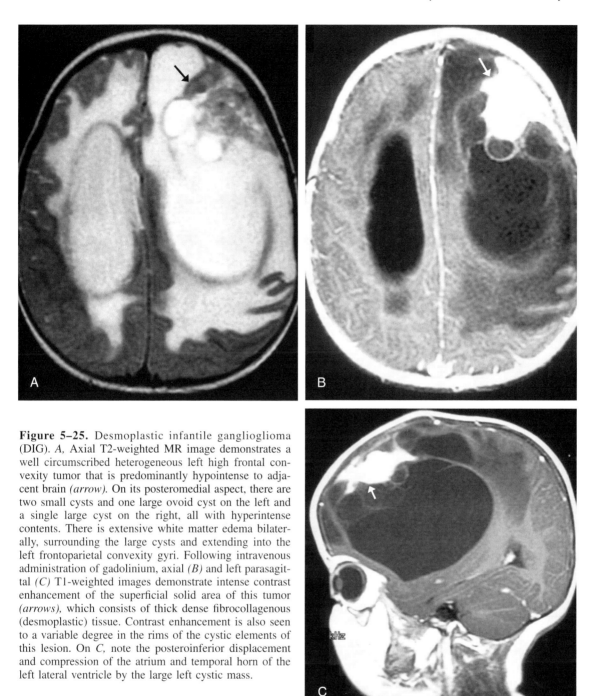

Figure 5–25. Desmoplastic infantile ganglioglioma (DIG). *A,* Axial T2-weighted MR image demonstrates a well circumscribed heterogeneous left high frontal convexity tumor that is predominantly hypointense to adjacent brain *(arrow).* On its posteromedial aspect, there are two small cysts and one large ovoid cyst on the left and a single large cyst on the right, all with hyperintense contents. There is extensive white matter edema bilaterally, surrounding the large cysts and extending into the left frontoparietal convexity gyri. Following intravenous administration of gadolinium, axial *(B)* and left parasagittal *(C)* T1-weighted images demonstrate intense contrast enhancement of the superficial solid area of this tumor *(arrows),* which consists of thick dense fibrocollagenous (desmoplastic) tissue. Contrast enhancement is also seen to a variable degree in the rims of the cystic elements of this lesion. On *C,* note the posteroinferior displacement and compression of the atrium and temporal horn of the left lateral ventricle by the large left cystic mass.

characterized by the common presence of intratumoral calcification, hemorrhage, and necrosis, findings that are uncommon in DIG.[200]

Dysembryoplastic Neuroepithelial Tumor

Dysembryoplastic neuroepithelial tumors (DNETs) are uncommon benign intracortical tumors that characteristically occur in young patients (<20 years) above the tentorium, mainly in the temporal lobe (60% to 80%) or frontal lobe.[79, 80, 168, 169, 303] They can be multifocal and rarely arise in the deep cortical structures. The patients typically present with intractable partial seizures. Partial or complete

excision is the treatment of choice, and no recurrences have been reported.[80] The tumor is termed "dysembryoplastic" because of its multinodularity, with areas of cortical dysplasia at the margins between the tumor nodules and the adjacent brain.[79, 80]

DNETs are lesions of long standing that most frequently involve the convexity cortex and often protrude beyond the adjacent cortical margin, eroding the overlying inner table of the calvarium.[168, 169, 303] The imaging findings, except for the superficial cortical location, are similar to those of other low grade glial tumors (astrocytoma, oligodendroglioma). On CT, DNET typically appears as a well circumscribed hypodense superficial mass, occasionally with intratumoral calcification, or cystic change, or both.[168, 242, 303] MRI demonstrates a mass centered in the convexity cortex and bulging externally that is hypointense to adjacent brain on T1-weighted images (Fig. 5–26B) and hyperintense on T2-weighted images (Fig. 5–26A) with no surrounding edema.[168, 169, 303] The protruding external margin may present a "soap bubble" appearance, reflecting internal cystic change.[178] Contrast enhancement is seen in only a minority of these lesions (Fig. 5–26C).[169, 178, 242]

Central Neurocytoma

A relatively rare, benign, slow growing (WHO grade II) intraventricular tumor, central neurocytoma has now been recognized as a separate entity.[70, 303] It occurs almost exclusively in the anterior portion of the lateral ventricle, arising from the superolateral ventricular wall and extending medially adjacent to the septum pellucidum and the foramen of Monro; extension through the foramen into the third ventricle is unusual. No such tumors have been

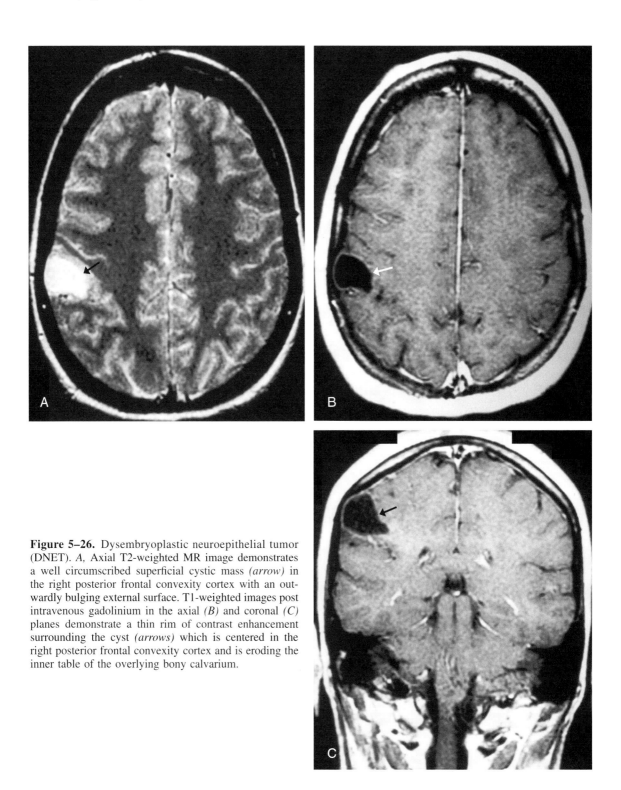

Figure 5–26. Dysembryoplastic neuroepithelial tumor (DNET). *A,* Axial T2-weighted MR image demonstrates a well circumscribed superficial cystic mass *(arrow)* in the right posterior frontal convexity cortex with an outwardly bulging external surface. T1-weighted images post intravenous gadolinium in the axial *(B)* and coronal *(C)* planes demonstrate a thin rim of contrast enhancement surrounding the cyst *(arrows)* which is centered in the right posterior frontal convexity cortex and is eroding the inner table of the overlying bony calvarium.

reported arising in the third or fourth ventricles, and only a few hemispheric lesions have been found.[241] Central neurocytomas are tumors of young adults and are rare in children and the elderly. Patients typically present clinically with headache and signs of increased intracranial pressure secondary to ventricular obstruction.[70, 241] Partial or complete surgical excision is the treatment of choice, and no deaths from tumor growth or recurrence have been reported.[356]

Histologically, central neurocytoma is identical to oligodendroglioma. It is characterized by nests of small well differentiated cells separated by thin fibrovascular septa.[10, 356] Intratumoral calcification and multiple small cysts are common findings, but hemorrhage (either intratumoral or intraventricular) is unusual. It is only with electron microscopy and immunohistochemistry that its neuronal origin can be determined.[70]

CT scans demonstrate a sharply marginated, inhomogeneous, isodense to slightly hyperdense intraventricular mass with a broad-based attachment to the wall of the frontal horn or anterior body of the lateral ventricle and abutting the septum pellucidum. Calcifications, either coarse or globular, and multiple small intratumoral hypodense cysts are found in 50% or more of central neurocytomas. Mild to moderate contrast enhancement of the isodense to hyperdense regions is common.[33, 119, 356]

The findings on MRI are similar. The tumor demon-strates a heterogeneous pattern with intermixed foci of isointensity (compared with adjacent gray matter) and hypointensity (due to calcifications and cysts) on T1-weighted images and isointensity to hyperintensity on T2-weighted images (Fig. 5–27A). Inhomogeneous mild contrast enhancement is common (Fig. 5–27B).[33, 119, 356]

The differential diagnosis is that of a well circumscribed intraventricular mass at or near the foramen of Monro and includes ependymoma and subependymoma. The absence of both deep extension into adjacent brain parenchyma and intratumoral hemorrhage as well as the relatively young age of the patient favors the diagnosis of central neurocytoma.[10, 241]

Pineal Parenchymal Tumors

Tumors arising within the parenchyma of the pineal gland constitute less than 1% of all primary brain tumors in adults.[70] However, pineal tumors represent nearly 10% of all pediatric brain tumors.[200] The most common tumors to involve the pineal gland are the germ cell tumors, which constitute 50% to 70% of pineal region tumors and are discussed elsewhere in this chapter.

Pineal parenchymal tumors represent only 15% to 30% of pineal region neoplasms.[305, 360] They include a range from primitive undifferentiated (pineoblastoma) through

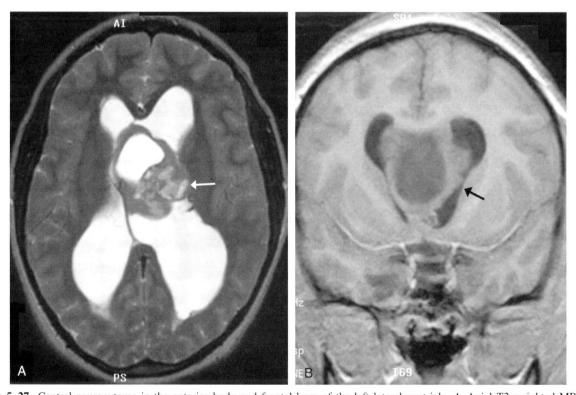

Figure 5–27. Central neurocytoma in the anterior body and frontal horn of the left lateral ventricle. *A,* Axial T2-weighted MR image demonstrates a large multilobulated heterogeneous but predominantly isointense (with gray matter) intraventricular mass arising from the lateral wall of the left lateral ventricle *(arrow)* with multiple small hyperintense foci and one large intratumoral hyperintense cyst. The tumor expands the left lateral ventricle. Enlargement of both lateral ventricles is likely secondary to obstruction of the foramen of Monro by this mass. *B,* Coronal T1-weighted spoiled gradient echo image following intravenous gadolinium: the plane of section passes through the anterior portion of the tumor. The more solid portion of this tumor demonstrates faint contrast enhancement. Note the extension of the tumor inferiorly and medially at a level just anterior to the foramen of Monro.

transitional forms to moderately mature and well differentiated (pineocytoma).[200, 292]

Pineoblastoma

Pineoblastomas are pediatric tumors with a peak incidence in the first two decades of life and rarity after age 30. These malignant, highly cellular, undifferentiated small cell tumors are histologically and histochemically identical with other primitive neuroectodermal tumors and exhibit similar biologic behavior. They are locally invasive and may spread into the third ventricle, the thalami, and the quadrigeminal plate. Pineoblastomas frequently contain areas of hemorrhage and necrosis, and intratumoral calcification is common.[10, 292] Presenting symptoms include precocious puberty (possibly related to destruction of normal pineal tissue with loss of melatonin secretion),[25] Parinaud's syndrome and other cranial nerve deficits, and obstructive

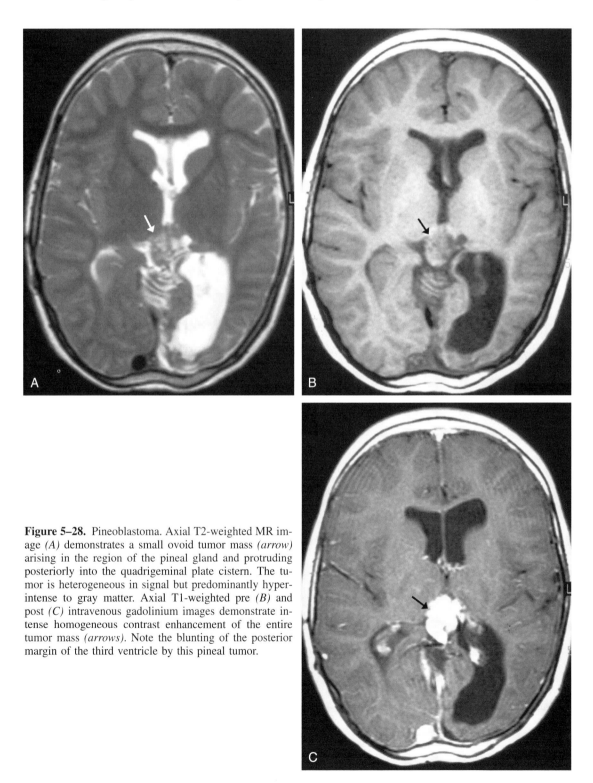

Figure 5–28. Pineoblastoma. Axial T2-weighted MR image *(A)* demonstrates a small ovoid tumor mass *(arrow)* arising in the region of the pineal gland and protruding posteriorly into the quadrigeminal plate cistern. The tumor is heterogeneous in signal but predominantly hyperintense to gray matter. Axial T1-weighted pre *(B)* and post *(C)* intravenous gadolinium images demonstrate intense homogeneous contrast enhancement of the entire tumor mass *(arrows)*. Note the blunting of the posterior margin of the third ventricle by this pineal tumor.

hydrocephalus. Dissemination via the CSF with leptomeningeal and ependymal metastases occurs in 10% of cases and may be found at the time of initial diagnosis. The 5-year survival rate is 58%.[292]

On CT, pineoblastomas appear hyperdense with irregular intratumoral calcification, infiltration into neighboring structures, and mass effect upon the posterior aspect of the third ventricle and the tectum of the midbrain. They demonstrate dense contrast enhancement. On MRI, pineoblastomas appear heterogeneous in signal, predominantly hypointense to gray matter on T1-weighted images and isointense with gray matter on T2-weighted images, with interspersed foci of hypointensity secondary to intratumoral necrosis and calcification (Fig. 5–28A, B).[10, 305, 332, 360] As on CT, contrast enhancement of the solid portion of the tumor is the rule (Fig. 5–28C). The chief differential consideration is germinoma, which may look identical on CT and MRI.

A rare occurrence that is nevertheless important for recognition and management is the association of bilateral retinoblastomas with pineoblastoma, often termed *trilateral retinoblastoma*. This condition, an inherited disorder occurring in very young children (<2 years), is found in 3% of patients with bilateral retinoblastomas.[269]

Pineocytoma

Pineocytomas are tumors of adults with a mean age of presentation of 36 years. Compared with pineoblastomas, these lesions are less densely cellular with well differentiated cells that have more cytoplasm arranged in lobules in an architecture similar to that of the normal pineal gland.[25, 292] They tend to follow a slower and more benign clinical course, but transitional tumors intermediate in cellularity and mitotic activity also exist.[70, 292] Intratumoral calcification is present in more than 50%. Subarachnoid seeding is not seen in the more benign neoplasms. The 5 year survival for pineocytomas is 67%.[292]

On CT, the typical appearance is of a rounded, well circumscribed, homogeneously hyperdense, lobulated expansile mass with intratumoral calcification situated at and often obstructing the posterior margin of the third ventricle (Fig. 5–29A).[200, 269] There is no evidence of invasion of neighboring structures. Multiplanar MRI demonstrates a rounded or ovoid mass compressing the posterior margin of the third ventricle and the superior aspect of the quadrigeminal plate. The mass is homogeneously hypointense to isointense on T1-weighted images and hyperintense relative to gray matter on T2-weighted images.[200, 305, 332, 360] The signal characteristics reflect the higher water content of these more mature tumors compared with pineoblastomas.[10] Contrast enhancement of all or a major portion of a pineocytoma is the rule on both CT (Fig. 5–29B) and MRI.

Embryonal Tumors

The terminology regarding primitive or embryonal tumors of neuroepithelial origin has been a source of controversy for nearly two decades. Gradually, however, a con-

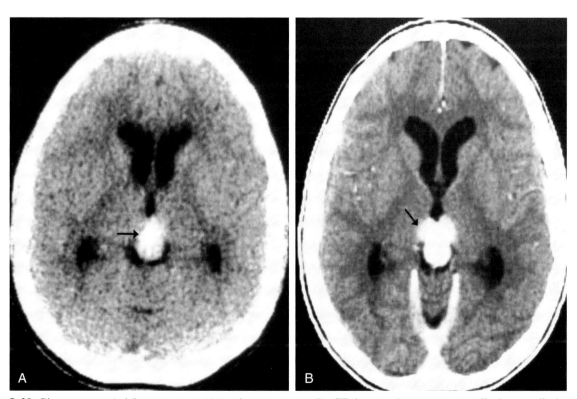

Figure 5–29. Pineocytoma. Axial noncontrast *(A)* and postcontrast *(B)* CT images demonstrate a well circumscribed markedly hyperdense mass in the midline *(arrow in A)* in the pineal region with bilateral lobulated intense contrast enhancement impinging on the medial aspects of both thalami *(arrow in B)*. The tumor is partially obstructing the posterior aspect of the third ventricle, accounting for the enlarged lateral and anterior third ventricles.

sensus appears to be emerging concomitant with advances in applied molecular biology.[25] Primitive neuroectodermal tumors (PNETs) of the CNS appear to be one group of a larger category of embryonal tumors that occur throughout the body (e.g., neuroblastomas of the adrenal and sympathetic ganglia).[25, 281] These are the second most common intracranial tumors of childhood, representing approximately 15% to 20% of all childhood brain tumors and exceeded in frequency only by the astrocytomas.[25] They have a common histology, consisting of densely packed undifferentiated round cells with a high nuclear-to-cytoplasmic ratio and high mitotic activity but follow divergent patterns of differentiation.[281]

The classic PNET is the medulloblastoma of the cerebellar vermis, which constitutes 85% of this group of tumors.[25] The remaining 15%, almost all supratentorial, include pineoblastomas (see earlier), ependymoblastomas, and medulloepitheliomas. The histogenesis of PNETs is undetermined, but one hypothesis is that they arise from immature pluripotential precursor cells in the subependymal layers of the developing ventricular system and in the external granular layer of the cerebellum.[25, 281]

Medulloblastoma

An invasive and highly malignant tumor (WHO grade IV), medulloblastoma is the second most common primary brain tumor of childhood and the most common pediatric posterior fossa neoplasm.[115, 168] Although medulloblastomas may occur at any age, 75% present clinically before age 15 years. There are two distinct age peaks, at 4 to 8 years and 15 to 35 years.[168] In children, medulloblastomas are primarily tumors of the cerebellar vermis (Fig. 5–30), but in adults, they tend to be located more laterally in the cerebellar hemispheres (Fig. 5–30).[48, 167, 281, 286, 372] The typical clinical presentation consists of signs of obstructive hydrocephalus, cerebellar dysfunction, or both—headache, nausea, vomiting, and ataxia.[168]

These aggressive tumors grow rapidly, with extension from the vermis into the fourth ventricle, and spread inferiorly into its recesses and outlet foramina and superiorly into the aqueduct.[303, 335] More than 90% present clinically with hydrocephalus.[200] They have a strong tendency to seed via the CSF, and approximately 40% demonstrate subarachnoid or retrograde ependymal metastases at the time of initial diagnosis.[96, 176] They are highly radiosensitive, and the standard treatment approach is gross total resection plus chemotherapy and total craniospinal axis irradiation.[176] Ten year survival rates are in the range of 50% to 70%, but the prognosis is poorer in children younger than 3 years.[34, 92, 200] Recurrence after the initial treatment regimen is about equally distributed between local regrowth at the primary tumor site and distant metastasis.[34] Systemic metastasis, a highly unusual occurrence with most CNS primary neoplasms, is identified in approximately 5% of patients, mainly to bone.[168]

Compared with other highly aggressive brain tumors, medulloblastomas appear relatively discrete and solid with convex margins on gross inspection but may contain foci of necrosis and hemorrhage.[25, 200] Microscopically, the tumor cells tend to be arranged in pseudorosettes, and areas of vascular proliferation, cellular pleomorphism, and calci-

fication are occasionally identified. Electron microscopy and immunostaining usually confirm neuronal differentiation.[25] Approximately 15% of medulloblastomas contain a significant amount of collagen and reticulin and may demonstrate a nodular pattern; designated desmoplastic medulloblastomas, these tumors are relatively more common in the cerebellar hemispheres in adolescents and young adults.[25, 193]

On noncontrast CT scans, medulloblastomas appear as rounded or oblong, mainly homogeneous, isodense to slightly hyperdense masses centrally located in the inferior vermis and cavity of the fourth ventricle (Fig. 5–30A).[19, 226, 320, 372] Differentiation of medulloblastoma from diffuse solid cerebellar astrocytoma is most reliably made on noncontrast CT.[372] The solid hyperdense appearance of medulloblastoma reflects the dense cellular nature of this tumor, whereas astrocytomas are typically rather uniformly hypodense.[109, 112] Obstruction of the fourth ventricle, inferior aqueduct, or both with resulting enlargement of the third and lateral ventricles is commonly seen on CT at the time of clinical presentation. Punctate or nodular intratumoral calcifications are identified in 10% to 20% of cases.[167, 168, 335, 362] Hypodense intratumoral foci of necrosis and cysts are found in up to 50% of medulloblastomas (see Fig. 5–30A).[226, 320, 362] Many medulloblastomas are surrounded by a thick, poorly marginated, hypodense halo representing extensive peritumoral edema. The imaging findings in young adults are similar, except for the more lateral (hemispheric) location of the tumor.[372]

After IV administration of contrast medium, moderate to intense homogeneous enhancement of the solid tumor mass is the rule in medulloblastomas,[19, 167, 335, 372] although approximately 10% do not demonstrate contrast enhancement on CT.[226] Areas of tumor seeding in the posterior fossa cisterns or in the third or lateral ventricles exhibit similar homogeneous contrast enhancement in a nodular or sheetlike configuration.[320, 372]

The appearance of medulloblastomas is less specific on MRI than on CT. The tumors are mildly hypointense to isointense relative to the adjacent cerebellar vermis on T1-weighted images and isointense to slightly hyperintense on T2-weighted images (Figs. 5–30B, C and 5–31A). Isointensity (or even hypointensity) of the tumor matrix on T2-weighted images are likely due to the hypercellularity and high nuclear-to-cytoplasmic ratio of this tumor.[22, 83, 128, 197] However, heterogeneity of signal intensity is often seen on the T2-weighted images (Figs. 5–30C and 5–31B) secondary to intratumoral cysts, necrosis, vascular flow voids, and hemorrhage.[168, 200, 335] Contrast enhancement of the solid portions of the tumor, seen in more than 90% of patients, is typically intense and homogeneous (Fig. 5–31B) but may be irregular and patchy (Fig. 5–30D).[168, 173, 278, 335] MRI with gadolinium enhancement is very sensitive for the detection of tumor spread and metastatic seeding in the cranial and spinal subarachnoid spaces.[173, 278, 303, 335]

Supratentorial Primitive Neuroectodermal Tumor

Fifteen percent of all PNETs of the CNS occur above the tentorium.[25] However, they represent less than 1% of all pediatric brain tumors. Like their infratentorial counter-

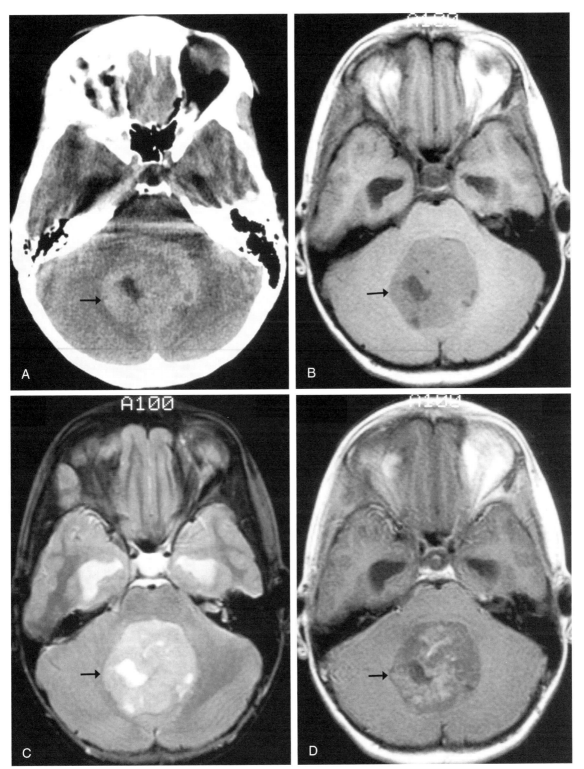

Figure 5–30. Medulloblastoma of the cerebellar vermis in an 11-year-old child. *A,* Axial noncontrast CT image demonstrates a large lobulated hyperdense round tumor *(arrow)* with an internal hypodense cavity to the right of the midline that compresses the fourth ventricle from behind. An ill defined faintly hypodense band surrounding the hyperdense mass represents white matter edema. The intratumoral area of marked hypodensity to the right of the midline likely represents necrosis. A smaller focus of lesser hypodensity on the left posterolateral tumor margin suggests an intratumoral cyst. These findings are confirmed on noncontrast axial T1-weighted *(B)* and T2-weighted *(C)* MR images; the solid portion of the tumor appears mildly hypointense on T1-weighting and mildly hyperintense on T2-weighting *(arrows)*. Following intravenous gadolinium, an axial T1-weighted image *(D)* demonstrates irregular patchy contrast enhancement of the solid areas of the tumor *(arrow)*.

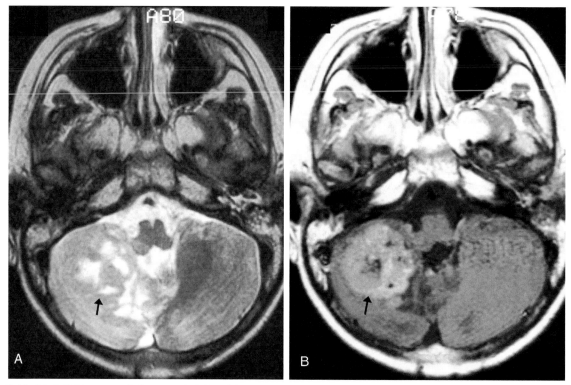

Figure 5–31. Medulloblastoma of the anteroinferior right cerebellar hemisphere in a 26-year-old patient. *A,* Axial T2-weighted MR image demonstrates a poorly circumscribed mass with a heterogeneous signal pattern in the anteroinferior portion of the right cerebellar hemisphere. Irregular areas of pronounced hyperintensity *(arrow)* are interspersed in a mildly hyperintense background that likely represents surrounding edema. The tumor extends medially into the inferior vermis. *B,* After intravenous administration of gadolinium, the tumor demonstrates homogeneous contrast enhancement with well circumscribed margins *(arrow).* Punctate intratumoral hypointensities represent enlarged vascular channels and/or focal calcifications.

parts, they occur mainly in the very young (65% of patients <5 years, 85% <10 years).[62] Patients may present clinically with seizures or with symptoms and signs of increased intracranial pressure. The distribution of these aggressive tumors within the cerebral hemispheres is, in diminishing order of frequency, frontal, parietal, temporal, and occipital.[200] Approximately one third are pineoblastomas; the remainder are central neuroblastomas,[62, 83] ependymoblastomas,[92] ganglioneuroblastomas, medulloepitheliomas, and other rare immature round cell tumors.[281]

On CT scans, supratentorial PNETs appear heterogeneous and well circumscribed. The heterogeneity reflects cystic or necrotic changes and intratumoral hemorrhage.[201] The solid elements are hyperdense because of their high cellularity and demonstrate contrast enhancement. Coarse calcifications are described in 50% to 70%, a much higher proportion than in cerebellar medulloblastomas.[200, 281] Supratentorial PNETs share with their infratentorial counterparts a strong propensity for spread via CSF.[83]

MRI also demonstrates heterogeneity of signal intensity on both T1-weighted and T2-weighted images (Fig. 5–32). They are often large tumors with relatively lesser degrees of surrounding edema.[83, 92] The differential diagnosis includes other large well circumscribed supratentorial tumors, such as ependymomas and oligodendrogliomas.[200] As on CT, the solid portions of the tumor demonstrate strong contrast enhancement, a feature that may aid in the differentiation.

Tumors of the Cranial Nerves

Approximately one third of all intracranial masses are nonglial primary neoplasms of the CNS, almost all of which are extraaxial in origin and location.[302] The most common of these are schwannomas of the cranial nerves and meningiomas.

Within the brain and spinal cord, the nerve fiber tracts are surrounded by oligodendrocytes. However, as the cranial nerves emerge from the brain, there is a transition zone beyond which the oligodendrocytes do not extend but are instead replaced by Schwann cells (also called neurilemmal cells), which surround and ensheath the extraaxial portions of the cranial nerves, the spinal nerve roots and nerves, and the peripheral nerves. Within the cranial vault, tumors arising from these nerves nearly all represent schwannomas.

The other major primary tumor of the cranial nerves is neurofibroma. Neurofibromas differ from schwannomas not only in site of origin but also in histology and natural history.[48, 354] Malignant degeneration is essentially unknown in schwannomas, but both malignant degeneration of neurofibromas and primary malignant peripheral nerve sheath tumors are recognized but uncommon occurrences.[339, 354]

Schwannoma

Schwannoma is a benign (WHO grade I) encapsulated tumor that arises from the Schwann cells of the nerve

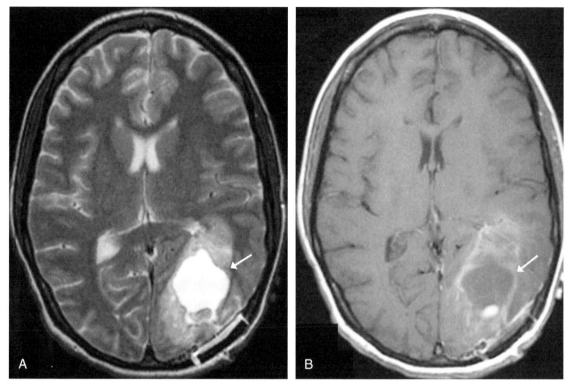

Figure 5–32. Primitive neuroectodermal tumor in the left parietooccipital region (postcraniotomy). *A,* Axial T2-weighted MR image demonstrates an ovoid heterogeneously hyperintense mass in the left parietooccipital white matter with extension into the overlying convexity cortex and a single large intratumoral sharply marginated central collection of marked hyperintensity, likely representing a combination of necrosis, surgical resection cavity, and/or cyst formation *(arrow).* The mass compresses and displaces the atrium of the left lateral ventricle from behind. *B,* Following intravenous gadolinium, an axial T1-weighted image demonstrates irregular contrast enhancement within the tumor interstices without enhancement of the central cavity *(arrow).*

sheaths of cranial and spinal nerves.[354] It is estimated to account for between 5% and 10% of primary intracranial neoplasms and for nearly 30% of intraspinal tumors.[57, 302]

Intracranial schwannomas occur in all age groups, but the peak incidence is in the fourth through the seventh decades of life.[57, 302, 354] There is a distinct sex predilection with a female-to-male ratio of 2:1, although no such predilection exists in regard to spinal schwannomas.[57, 302]

By far the most common site of intracranial involvement is the superior vestibular division of the eighth cranial nerve.[207, 302] Trigeminal nerve schwannomas are much less common, with facial, trochlear, and abducens nerve tumors only rarely reported.[241] Only the first (olfactory) and second (optic) cranial nerves lack Schwann cell sheaths and are therefore not potential sites of origin. The clinical presentation varies according to the site of origin. Vestibular schwannoma (also called acoustic neuroma or neurinoma) typically presents with symptoms of a mass in the cerebellopontine angle, including tinnitus, sensorineural hearing loss, and facial paresthesias.[241, 302, 354] Despite the tumor's origin from the vestibular nerve, symptoms and signs of vestibular dysfunction do not become manifest until relatively late. These tumors have a distinct propensity to involve the sensory nerve roots, and motor symptoms are uncommon.[354]

Multiplicity of intracranial schwannomas strongly suggests the presence of neurofibromatosis 2 (NF2), a congenital inherited disorder associated with a mutation on the long arm of chromosome 22.[223] The occurrence of bilateral acoustic schwannomas (see Fig. 5–34) is pathognomonic of this disorder, which has also been termed MISME (multiple inherited schwannomas, meningiomas, and ependymomas).[304] In fact, labeling this disorder neurofibromatosis is a misnomer, because neurofibromas are not a part of its constellation of abnormalities. Patients with this disorder typically present clinically in the second and third decades of life, much earlier than those with the sporadic intracranial schwannoma.[302]

On gross inspection, schwannomas appear as focal, well circumscribed, globular or ovoid masses that do not infiltrate the nerve but rather arise and grow eccentrically, displacing the uninvolved portion of the cranial nerve of origin to the side.[48, 241, 302] As the tumor grows and matures, it may undergo cystic degeneration or develop patchy areas of lipid accumulation.[48, 354] Vestibular schwannomas typically enlarge within the cerebellopontine angle cistern and may displace and compress the adjacent pons, medulla, and fourth ventricle. They can attain considerable size before becoming clinically evident. Obstruction of the ipsilateral cerebellopontine angle cistern may occur, with formation of one or more extratumoral arachnoid cysts.[241, 306] Trigeminal schwannomas tend to occur more commonly in the parasellar region of the middle cranial fossa than in the posterior fossa, although approximately 25% extend through the tentorial notch, involving both fossae.[241]

Microscopic evaluation of a schwannoma typically demonstrates a well encapsulated tumor containing collections of spindle-shaped Schwann cells in both compact cellular (Antoni A) and less cellular, more loosely textured (Antoni B) arrangements.[48, 354] Histologic variations are commonly encountered in larger tumors, including intratumoral clusters of lipid-laden cells, confluent microcysts and larger cysts, and dilated vascular sinusoids surrounded by foci of hemorrhage.[354]

The diagnosis of vestibular schwannoma on CT rests on the demonstration of a well circumscribed, globular or ovoid, hypodense to isodense (with respect to the adjacent pons and cerebellum) extraaxial mass in the cerebellopontine angle cistern with its base on the posterior aspect of the petrous temporal bone in the region of the internal auditory meatus. Images displayed in a bone window may demonstrate fusiform widening of the internal auditory canal with erosion of its bony margins. However, soft tissue detail within the cisternal portion of the tumor is often obscured by beam hardening artifacts caused by the adjacent dense cortical bone and pneumatized air cells of the petrous pyramid. Tumors up to about 1 cm in diameter typically demonstrate homogeneous density and homogeneously strong contrast enhancement, but larger tumors often demonstrate heterogeneity of both density and contrast enhancement because of the presence of intratumoral cystic degeneration, xanthomatous change, or intermixed areas of hypercellularity and hypocellularity.[66, 241, 302]

On MRI, smaller tumors can be more reliably detected, especially within the internal auditory canal, because of the lack of bone induced artifact and the multidimensional capability of this modality. The transition zone between the central (oligodendroglial) and peripheral (Schwann cell) portions of the eighth (vestibulocochlear) nerve, the presumed site of origin of schwannomas of this nerve, occurs within the canal. Tumors less than 5 mm in diameter can be reliably identified on thin section T1-weighted MRI, appearing as homogeneously mildly hypointense or isointense (to adjacent brain) ovoid or tubular intracanalicular masses with intense homogeneous contrast enhancement (Fig. 5–33).[222, 241, 275, 302, 306] On T2-weighted pulsing sequences, small vestibular schwannomas appear mildly to markedly hyperintense and may be obscured by the similarity in signal intensity to that of the surrounding CSF.[11]

As these tumors enlarge, the intratumoral degenerative changes previously described cause increasing heterogeneity of signal within the main tumor mass in the cerebellopontine angle cistern.[241, 302] On axial images, the tumor often has a commalike shape with a globular cisternal mass medially and a short tapered fusiform extension laterally into the internal auditory canal. Contrast enhancement is seen in nearly all schwannomas and may be homogeneous (two thirds of cases) or heterogeneous (see Figs. 5–21, 5–33, and 5–34).[241, 302, 306] Larger tumors compress and displace the adjacent anterolateral margin of the cerebellar hemisphere posteromedially, displace, compress, and rotate the pons and medulla, and narrow the fourth ventricle, elongating it in the anteroposterior direction (Figs. 5–21 and 5–34). Peritumoral vasogenic edema is frequently observed, and (as noted previously) associated arachnoid cysts are visualized in 5% to 10% of cases.[222]

Vestibular schwannomas represent 80% to 85% of cerebellopontine angle masses.[275, 306] The major differential di-

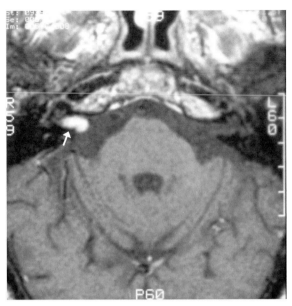

Figure 5–33. Vestibular schwannoma. Axial T1-weighted image of the posterior fossa and skull base following intravenous administration of gadolinium. A small intensely enhancing intracanalicular ovoid mass protrudes slightly medially into the cerebellopontine angle cistern on the right *(arrow)*.

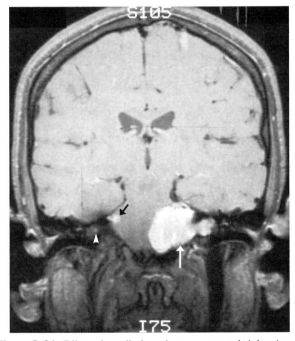

Figure 5–34. Bilateral vestibular schwannomas and right trigeminal schwannoma in a patient with neurofibromatosis type 2. Coronal postgadolinium T1-weighted MR image demonstrates three intensely contrast enhancing lesions in the posterior cranial fossa. The large left sided lobulated vestibular schwannoma fills the left cerebellopontine angle cistern *(white arrow)*, compresses, indents and displaces the left lateral margin of the pons inward, and extends laterally into the widened left internal auditory canal. A tiny punctate focus of contrast enhancement in the right petrous temporal region *(white arrowhead)* represents a small intracanalicular vestibular schwannoma. A third focus of contrast enhancement abuts and indents the right lateral margin of the pons *(black arrow)*; this is a trigeminal (fifth cranial nerve) schwannoma.

agnostic considerations include meningioma and epidermoid tumor.[241, 275, 306] Meningioma involving the dura of the posterior margin of the petrous temporal bone can project posteriorly into the cerebellopontine angle and simulate a vestibular schwannoma (Fig. 5–35). Such lesions represent about 10% of cerebellopontine angle masses.[306] Although meningiomas are typically more dense on CT, these two neoplasms may have identical signal intensity characteristics on MRI. Intense homogeneous or slightly heterogeneous contrast enhancement is another shared characteristic (Fig. 5–35B).[275] However, meningiomas are usually situated eccentric to the internal auditory canal and form a more obtuse angle with the petrous ridge than schwannomas.[181] Extension of meningioma into the internal auditory canal is uncommon but not unknown,[275] and rarely, schwannoma may simulate the appearance of a dural tail on contrast enhanced images.[252]

Epidermoid may resemble vestibular schwannoma on noncontrast CT but typically appears more lobulated and more hypodense and tends to insinuate more extensively into the subarachnoid spaces adjacent to the pons without causing major compression of the pons and fourth ventricle. On both CT and MRI, epidermoid does not demonstrate contrast enhancement. On MRI, larger epidermoids appear more homogeneous than schwannomas of similar size and may mimic CSF in intensity, with high T2 signal and low T1 signal.[11, 275, 306, 322]

Neurofibroma

Neurofibromas are well demarcated infiltrative intraneural or diffusely infiltrative extraneural benign tumors that consist of a mixture of neoplastic Schwann cells, perineurial cells, and fibroblasts in a collagenous and mucoid matrix.[241, 354] They are histologically benign and considered WHO grade I. With only extremely rare exception, neurofibromas do not arise within the intracranial portions of the cranial nerves.[241, 354] However, they can arise peripherally and extend retrogradely into the cranial vault, notably in the facial nerve (CN VII) and the ophthalmic division of the trigeminal nerve (CN V$_1$).[241]

The tumors exhibiting this retrograde intracranial extension are usually plexiform neurofibromas, which involve multiple nerve fascicles or trunks with fusiform multinodular enlargement often described as ropelike. On noncontrast CT, they appear isodense with adjacent muscle, and on MRI they are isointense with adjacent muscle on T1-weighted images and hyperintense on T2-weighted images.[241] Contrast enhancement is variable, with areas of moderate to strong enhancement after IV administration of gadolinium.

Multiple neurofibromas are typically associated with NF1 (also known as von Recklinghausen disease), an autosomal dominant congenital disorder associated with a gene defect on the long arm of chromosome 17.[339] Approximately 50% of patients report no family history and are presumed to represent new spontaneous germline mutations.[241, 339] In addition to multiple neurofibromas of the spinal and peripheral nerves, NF1 also includes optic nerve and chiasm gliomas, foci of "hamartomatous" change of uncertain etiology in the region of the basal ganglia and in the optic tracts and radiations, cerebral peduncles, and brain stem, astrocytomas of the spinal cord, multiple café au lait spots, axillary and inguinal freckling, malignant

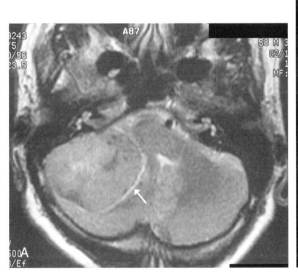 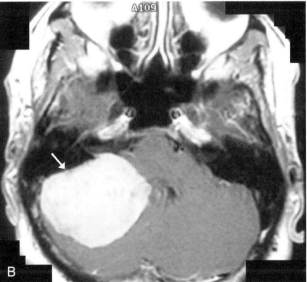

Figure 5–35. Meningioma arising from the posterior aspect of the left temporal bone. *A,* Axial T2-weighted MR image demonstrates a large rounded extraaxial tumor mass in the right side of the posterior fossa with its base on the posterior dura of the left temporal bone. The mass is slightly hyperintense relative to gray matter and compresses and displaces the right cerebellar hemisphere posteriorly and medially. A narrow cleft of cerebrospinal fluid *(arrow)* separates the medial margin of the tumor from the adjacent compressed cerebellum and pons. Note that the internal auditory canals bilaterally are filled with cerebrospinal fluid. *B,* Following intravenous administration of gadolinium, an axial T1-weighted image demonstrates intense homogeneous contrast enhancement of this large dural-based tumor *(arrow).*

peripheral nerve sheath tumors, iris hamartomas, and dysplastic osseous lesions (sphenoid wing dysplasia, pencil-like thinning of the long bones).[223, 321, 339] Patients with NF1 usually present clinically very early in life, whereas those with sporadic solitary neurofibroma involving a cranial nerve may present in later youth and adult life.

On noncontrast CT, plexiform neurofibroma appears as a poorly circumscribed irregular widening of the involved root, which is isodense with adjacent muscles. Erosion of adjacent bone with widening of bony foramina may be evident. MRI demonstrates the widened nerve, which is isointense with adjacent muscle on T1-weighted images and hyperintense on T2-weighted images. Contrast enhancement after IV administration of gadolinium is the rule, varying from moderate to intense.[25, 241]

Malignant Peripheral Nerve Sheath Tumors

Malignant peripheral nerve sheath tumors are rare tumors that appear to arise de novo in the cranial nerves, the fifth cranial nerve being more frequently involved than any other.[354] Elsewhere in the body, almost two thirds of reported cases of malignant peripheral nerve sheath tumors have arisen from preexisting neurofibromas, often plexiform and in the setting of NF1.[354] Approximately 50% occur in association with NF1. The incidence of malignant progression in patients with plexiform neurofibroma is approximately 5%. Imaging findings include irregularity and loss of clear tumor margins together with inhomogeneous contrast enhancement. Evidence of diffuse invasion of the skull base may also be present.[241]

Tumors of the Meninges

A wide variety of primary tumors can arise from and develop within the meninges.[199] By far the most common is meningioma. Another important meningeal tumor, until 1993 considered a variant of meningioma, is the hemangiopericytoma. Additionally, nonmeningothelial mesenchymal tumors, both benign (lipoma, chondroma, benign fibrous histiocytoma) and malignant (chondrosarcoma, osteosarcoma), can originate in the meninges. Also, tumors of melanocytic origin can rarely arise within the intracranial meninges. Finally, although the histogenesis is uncertain, neuropathologists usually assign hemangioblastomas to this category.

Meningioma

Meningiomas are solid, well circumscribed, highly cellular, slow growing tumors that are usually benign histologically (WHO grade I). These spherical and sometimes lobulated tumors are composed of neoplastic meningothelial cells originating from the arachnoid layer of the meninges with a broad attachment to the adjacent dura. Most commonly, they project inward from the dura, indenting and compressing the underlying brain, causing neurologic symptoms and signs through compression of the adjacent cortex.

Meningiomas are the most common primary extracerebral tumors of the CNS, accounting for approximately 20% of primary brain tumors.[184, 199] They occur mainly in middle and old age, with a peak incidence in the fifth through seventh decades of life[277]; these tumors can, however, be found in all age groups. Meningiomas exhibit a strong sex predilection, occurring preponderantly in females, with a female-to-male ratio of at least 2:1.[302] However, meningiomas associated with hereditary tumor syndromes, such as NF2, generally occur in younger patients and do not demonstrate a female predilection.[199]

Common sites of origin are the frontal and parietal convexities and the parasagittal region, often in close association with the falx cerebri (about 50%), as well as the sphenoid wings, olfactory grooves, sylvian fissures, and parasellar regions (about 35%).[120, 199] Less than 10% arise below the level of the tentorium, mainly from the clivus, the leaves and free edge of the tentorium, and the petrous pyramid.[282] Multiple meningiomas are reported in 6% to 9% of cases,[286] occurring both as a component of NF2[223] and, less commonly, sporadically.

Although most meningiomas are slow growing and well encapsulated globular masses, variations in shape and histology are not unusual. Invasion of the dura and encasement or invasion of the nearby dural venous sinuses are common.[199] Tumors arising in relation to the sphenoid wing are frequently flat (en plaque) and tend to invade through both layers of the cranial dura into the adjacent bone, provoking a notable bony reaction with thickening and sclerosis (meningioma bone).[120, 277] Such bony changes are a source of considerable controversy; many clinical neuroscientists regard bony sclerosis and thickening as highly indicative of tumor infiltration into the haversian canals of the calvaria,[199] whereas others state that such hyperostosis can also occur without histologic evidence of bone infiltration by tumor.[277] Meningiomas arising adjacent to the cribriform plate and planum sphenoidale and those occurring over the high cerebral convexities are more typically rounded and invaginate the underlying brain; however, they also show a propensity for stimulating adjacent bony thickening and sclerosis (Fig. 5–36).[120]

Several different histologic types of meningioma have been described.[31, 199, 257, 286] A small but significant minority (4% to 8%) of meningiomas are identified as atypical on the basis of increased mitotic activity and high nuclear-to-cytoplasmic ratio. The most aggressive exhibit the histologic features of frank malignancy (anaplastic and malignant meningiomas) and may invade the adjacent cerebral parenchyma.[199] Atypical and anaplastic meningiomas occur more frequently in the high cerebral convexities and the falx. Most meningiomas are homogeneously solid tumors, but foci of necrosis and scarring (probably secondary to ischemia), microcystic change or areas of heavy lipid storage (lipomatous/lipoblastic meningiomas) (see Fig. 5–38) can be identified in approximately 5% to 15% of excised tumors.[99, 204, 287]

Approximately three quarters of meningiomas appear on noncontrast CT as sharply circumscribed, rounded and sometimes lobulated, homogeneous masses of slightly increased density (40 to 50 HU) compared with adjacent brain.[5, 40, 233] The hyperdensity is related to the dense cellularity of these tumors and does not reflect psammomatous

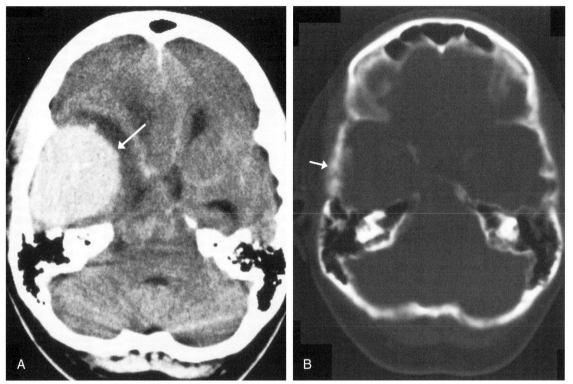

Figure 5–36. Sphenoid wing meningioma with underlying hyperostosis ("meningioma bone"). *A,* Axial postcontrast CT image demonstrates intense homogeneous contrast enhancement of a large round extracerebral tumor with its base on the right greater sphenoid wing *(arrow).* On its inner aspect, the tumor is surrounded by a thick band of hypodensity representing edema of the adjacent cerebral cortex and white matter. There is a marked shift of the midline vessels to the left. *B,* On an axial CT image displayed in a bone window setting, the underlying greater sphenoid wing and squamous portion of the temporal bone demonstrate heterogeneous bony thickening *(arrow).*

change within the tumor. Meningioma typically has a broad base on a dural surface. The invaginating mass displaces and compresses the underlying brain and causes flattening of the adjacent cerebral cortex (Fig. 5–36A). Inward buckling of the white matter can be identified in about 40% of meningiomas.[113] A hypodense rim (representing trapped CSF) may be insinuated between the invaginating mass and the invaginated cerebral parenchyma; cystic changes in the arachnoid may also be identified adjacent to the tumor margins.[287] About 10% of meningiomas appear isodense with the adjacent brain on noncontrast CT,[233] and an occasional tumor contains areas of hypodensity that correlate pathologically with foci of ischemic scar, microcysts, or lipoblastic change.[40, 99, 204, 287]

Vasogenic edema of the adjacent cerebral white matter is identified in 50% to 75% of meningiomas.[5, 302] The mechanism responsible for the occurrence of peritumoral intracerebral edema is uncertain, and there is no correlation between tumor size and extent of edema.[233] Significant edema is found more commonly in patients with lateral convexity tumors than in those with tumors in other sites.[233] The occurrence of intracerebral edema appears to correlate with a poorer prognosis, a correlation that may be related to reduced resectability.[302] Hyperostosis and thickening of adjacent bone in sphenoid wing, skull base, and high convexity meningiomas, as described previously, can be clearly delineated on CT if high center and wide window settings are employed (Fig. 5–36B).

After IV administration of contrast medium, a meningioma typically displays a striking homogeneous enhancement (increase of 40 to 50 HU or more) (see Fig. 5–36A).[5, 302] Even the occasional isodense meningiomas exhibit this intense opacification. However, meningiomas that are predominantly microcystic may not enhance strongly or uniformly.[199] In 5% to 15% of cases, focal areas of nonenhancement can be identified within the tumor mass.[233, 287] These areas have been correlated pathologically with regions of necrosis, old hemorrhage, scarring, cystic degeneration, and lipoblastic change[287]; they usually do not interfere with the accuracy of diagnosis. Occasionally, however, the heterogeneity of contrast enhancement may be sufficient to raise the question of glioblastoma.[5, 233, 287]

Parasagittal meningiomas of sufficient size may compress (Fig. 5–37A, B) or invade the adjacent superior sagittal sinus; interruption of the sinus can be identified on coronal postcontrast CT or noncontrast MR images and is an important preoperative finding for which the radiologist must search. Indistinct irregular tumor margins, a mushroomlike extension of opacified tumor well away from the main ovoid tumor mass, and prominent venous drainage centrally from the tumor are CT and MRI signs that may suggest an aggressive anaplastic or malignant meningioma invading the brain.[234, 295]

In a multiinstitutional prospective study, the sensitivity of contrast enhanced CT for detection of an intracranial mass in patients with meningioma was 96%.[233] Ten percent

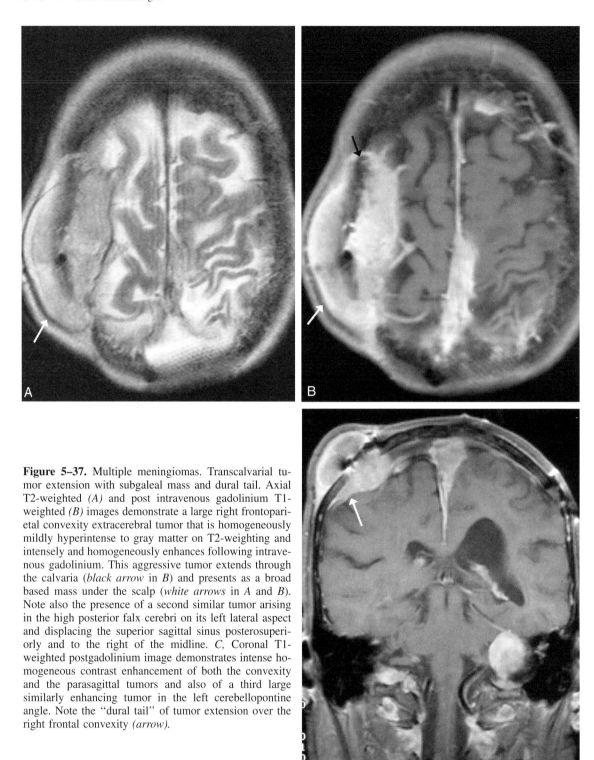

Figure 5–37. Multiple meningiomas. Transcalvarial tumor extension with subgaleal mass and dural tail. Axial T2-weighted *(A)* and post intravenous gadolinium T1-weighted *(B)* images demonstrate a large right frontoparietal convexity extracerebral tumor that is homogeneously mildly hyperintense to gray matter on T2-weighting and intensely and homogeneously enhances following intravenous gadolinium. This aggressive tumor extends through the calvaria *(black arrow* in *B)* and presents as a broad based mass under the scalp *(white arrows* in *A* and *B).* Note also the presence of a second similar tumor arising in the high posterior falx cerebri on its left lateral aspect and displacing the superior sagittal sinus posterosuperiorly and to the right of the midline. *C,* Coronal T1-weighted postgadolinium image demonstrates intense homogeneous contrast enhancement of both the convexity and the parasagittal tumors and also of a third large similarly enhancing tumor in the left cerebellopontine angle. Note the "dural tail" of tumor extension over the right frontal convexity *(arrow).*

of the masses were not detected on the noncontrast scans. The differential diagnosis of a hyperdense or isodense peripherally situated extracerebral mass with homogeneous contrast enhancement includes metastatic malignancy (particularly, carcinoma of the lung and melanoma),[116, 268] acute leukemia,[347] systemic lymphoma,[11] and (at the skull base) schwannoma of a cranial nerve.[286] Criteria for differentiation are lesion location and configuration, definition of margins, and presence or absence of associated bony changes (erosion or hyperostosis).

On noncontrast MRI, the majority of meningiomas present a homogeneous appearance similar to that seen on CT. Tumor signal intensity on T1-weighted images tends to approximate that of the adjacent cerebral cortex in about

50% of cases and to be hypointense to cortex in 50%. On T2-weighted images, about 50% are mildly hyperintense relative to adjacent gray matter (see Fig. 5–37A) and 50% are isointense with the cortex (see Fig. 5–35A).[11, 99] On T2-weighted images, comparison of signal intensity of tumor with that of cortex may have histologic correlation; in one reported series, hyperintensity correlated strongly with either syncytial or angioblastic types of meningioma,

whereas fibroblastic and transitional meningiomas failed to demonstrate hyperintensity.[99] A minority of meningiomas appear heterogeneous on both T1- and T2-weighted images because of the presence of intratumoral lipoblastic or cystic changes (Figs. 5–1A and 5–38A, B), calcifications, or prominent vessels.[11, 100]

MRI enables more accurate localization and evaluation of these extracerebral tumors than CT. This superiority is

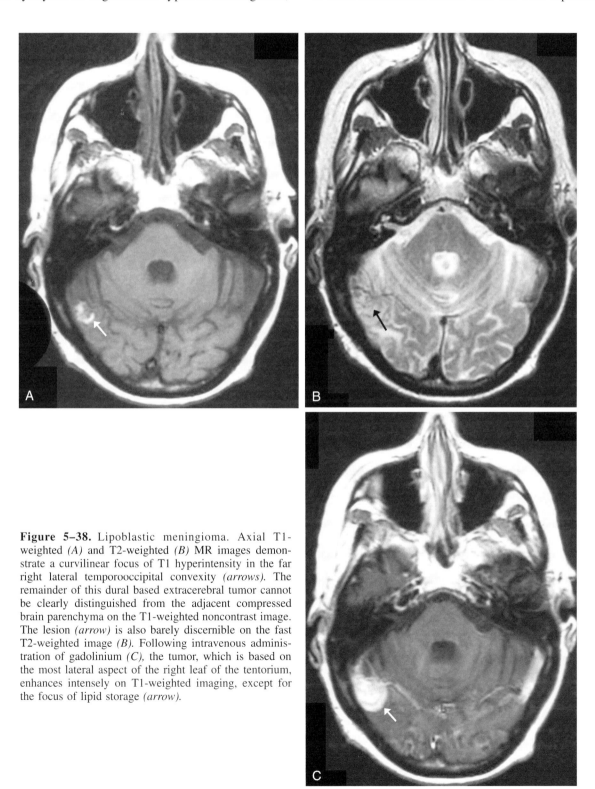

Figure 5–38. Lipoblastic meningioma. Axial T1-weighted *(A)* and T2-weighted *(B)* MR images demonstrate a curvilinear focus of T1 hyperintensity in the far right lateral temporooccipital convexity *(arrows)*. The remainder of this dural based extracerebral tumor cannot be clearly distinguished from the adjacent compressed brain parenchyma on the T1-weighted noncontrast image. The lesion *(arrow)* is also barely discernible on the fast T2-weighted image *(B)*. Following intravenous administration of gadolinium *(C)*, the tumor, which is based on the most lateral aspect of the right leaf of the tentorium, enhances intensely on T1-weighted imaging, except for the focus of lipid storage *(arrow)*.

due not only to the visualization of the mass in all three dimensions and the lack of beam hardening artifact at the base of the brain with MR. In approximately two thirds of cases, the interface between the inner margin of the extracerebral tumor mass and the invaginated or displaced cortex can be recognized on MRI from the presence of a cleft of CSF (see Fig. 5–35A) or the interposition of vascular flow voids of the displaced arteries and veins on the pial surface of the brain (see Fig. 5–1A).[11] Also, invasion of adjacent brain by meningiomas arising from the tentorium, the falx, and the dura of the lateral wall of the cavernous sinus can be recognized as a breech in the hypointense dural rim at the tumor margin.[11] Finally, arterial encasement and partial dural venous sinus invasion are more readily and accurately depicted by the contrast between the flow void and the tumor tissue.[11]

As on CT, meningiomas usually demonstrate rapid and pronounced contrast enhancement after IV administration of paramagnetic contrast agent, and the strong, often striking, homogeneous contrast enhancement seen in most meningiomas enables their accurate detection and localization (Figs. 5–1B, 5–35B, 5–37B, C, 5–38C, and 5–39B).[11, 158, 275]

A thickened tapered extension of contrast enhancing dura is commonly identified at the margins of the tumor (Fig. 5–35C). This *dural tail* may indicate the presence of tumor infiltration[121] or may be due to dural reaction.[225] Because a major prognostic factor in the recurrence of meningiomas after surgery is the extent of tumor resec-

tion,[199] careful assessment must be made of preoperative postcontrast MR images for the presence of a dural tail.

The arachnoid contributes embryologically to the formation of the choroid plexuses, so intraventricular meningiomas may arise within the choroid plexus of the lateral ventricle and locally expand the ventricle to conform to the size and shape of the tumor (Fig. 5–39).[221, 300, 302] These tumors share the imaging characteristics of extracerebral meningiomas as previously described. The normally compact choroid glomus calcifications may be fragmented and spread by the expanding tumor mass.[300] Differentiation from choroid plexus papilloma is based on (1) patient age (papillomas of the lateral ventricles occur mainly in infants and very young children), (2) tumor surface characteristics (papillomas tend to have a nodular irregular margin, whereas meningiomas tend to be smoothly rounded), and (3) size and shape of the cerebral ventricles (papillomas are often associated with diffuse enlargement of all ventricles, whereas meningiomas cause only focal enlargement).[11]

Hemangiopericytoma

Hemangiopericytoma is now recognized in the WHO classification of tumors of the CNS as a distinct entity separate from meningioma.[147] This dural based tumor was formerly considered an "angioblastic" meningioma be-

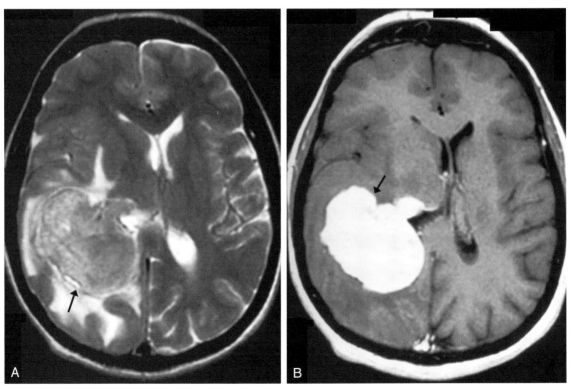

Figure 5–39. Intraventricular meningioma. *A*, A large round mildly hyperintense (to gray matter) tumor fills and distends the atrium of the right lateral ventricle *(arrow)* on this axial T2-weighted MR image. Note the dilatation of the anterior right temporal horn proximal to the obstruction caused by this mass. Edema of the surrounding white matter contributes to the right sided mass effect, which causes compression of the right frontal horn and marked shift of the septum pellucidum to the left of the midline. *B*, An axial T1-weighted postgadolinium image demonstrates intense homogeneous contrast enhancement of this large multilobulated intraventricular meningioma *(arrow)*.

cause of its hypervascularity. However, despite many gross pathologic, histopathologic, and imaging similarities to meningioma, the aggressive clinical behavior of hemangiopericytomas differs considerably from the majority of meningiomas, and it is now possible to distinguish the two entities immunohistochemically.[147] The cell of origin is the pericyte, a perivascular cell of mesenchymal origin, and the intracranial tumors are identical histologically to their counterparts in the somatic soft tissues.[147]

Like meningiomas, hemangiopericytomas are dural based, extraaxial rounded masses, well circumscribed and highly cellular. They are often more lobulated in contour than the typical meningioma and are more commonly located in the occipital region near the confluence of the dural venous sinuses, to which they are often attached.[148] They are comparatively rare, with a ratio of 1 hemangiopericytoma to 40 or 50 meningiomas.[129, 148] They tend to occur in younger patients, typically in their 40s, and the sex distribution (male-to-female ratio = 1.4:1) differs markedly from that of meningiomas.[147]

Histologically, hemangiopericytomas appear highly cellular with moderate nuclear atypia and prominent mitotic activity comparable to that of anaplastic meningiomas.[147] They are richly vascular tumors with arterial supply from both the meningeal and cerebral arteries, and numerous large and branching vascular channels ("staghorn sinusoids") with perivascular fibrosis are a prominent microscopic finding.[147] Invasion and destruction of overlying bone is not unusual, but these tumors do not provoke a hyperostotic ("meningioma bone") response. Infiltration of underlying brain parenchyma can also occur. Hemangiopericytomas exhibit a marked tendency to recur locally despite apparently complete surgical excision and postoperative irradiation of the former tumor bed; in one large series, the 15 year recurrence rate was 85%.[129] They also tend to metastasize beyond the cranial cavity; in the same large series,[129] 60% of tumors had metastasized after 15 years, mainly to bone, lung, and liver.

The findings on diagnostic imaging tend to mimic those of meningiomas. These sharply circumscribed extraaxial masses appear hyperdense on noncontrast CT and are generally homogeneous and hypointense to white matter and isointense with gray matter on T1-weighted noncontrast MRI (Fig. 5–40A). On T2-weighted images, hemangiopericytomas typically are slightly hyperintense and more heterogeneous in appearance (Fig. 5–40B). As noted previously, hemangiopericytomas often appear more lobulated and exhibit a higher incidence and degree of heterogeneity of attenuation (CT) and signal intensity (MRI) than meningiomas owing to the presence of multiple flow voids.[302] Contrast enhancement of hemangiopericytomas is usually intense and homogeneous (Fig. 5–40C). Points of differentiation from meningioma include a greater frequency of internal heterogeneity and external lobulation, a tendency toward a more narrow base of dural attachment, and absence of tumor calcification and hyperostosis of adjacent bone.[53]

Mesenchymal Nonmeningothelial Tumors

A diverse group of relatively rare tumors, mesenchymal nonmeningothelial tumors may arise within the cranial vault, either in the skull base, the calvaria and sutures, the meninges, or (most rarely) within the cerebral parenchyma. They may be of primitive mesenchymal origin but have not differentiated along the meningothelial line. Rather, these unusual lesions exhibit fibrous, fibrohistiocytic, adipose, myoid, endothelial, chondroid, or osseous differentiation and cannot be distinguished histologically from their more common counterparts in the somatic soft tissues.[251]

These tumors vary widely in location, histology, pathologic grade, and clinical behavior. Some (e.g., lipomas and hemangiomas) are benign (WHO grade I) and mainly asymptomatic, and some (e.g., osteosarcomas and rhabdomyosarcomas) are highly malignant (WHO grade IV) and highly invasive. Tumors arising in the meninges are more common than those originating within cerebral parenchyma. Although most of these lesions occur supratentorially in adults, many rhabdomyosarcomas occur below the tentorium in young children. Lipomas typically occur in or near the midline and are associated with malformations of the corpus callosum, whereas chondrosarcomas arise most commonly in the skull base off the midline (e.g., the petroclival suture).

Lipomas are not true neoplasms but instead likely represent congenital malformations.[356] They enlarge only with somatic growth. Intracranial lipomas are usually subarachnoid in location and occur most commonly in the pericallosal sulcus. Other sites are the chiasmatic, circummesencephalic, interpeduncular, and quadrigeminal cisterns and, in the posterior fossa, the cerebellopontine angle cistern.[11] More than 50% of pericallosal lipomas are associated with partial agenesis or dysgenesis of the adjacent corpus callosum, with the rostrum, genu, and anterior portion of the body more commonly affected than the posterior body or splenium.[356]

Two types of pericallosal lipomas are recognized. The tubonodular lipomas are large and rounded, are located anteriorly, and have a high incidence of associated corpus callosal dysgenesis as well as anomalies of the frontal lobes.[239] The curvilinear type tend to be more posteriorly situated, appear long and thin, curve around the splenium, and are associated with a normal or only slightly dysgenetic corpus callosum (Fig. 5–41).[238] These lesions are tightly adherent to the adjacent brain, and lipoma in the cerebellopontine angle cistern may envelop and compress the seventh and eighth cranial nerves where they pass through the cistern.[67]

Lipomas are typically asymptomatic and discovered only incidentally when the head is imaged for other reasons. Even on plain skull radiographs, the tubonodular masses are recognized from their well demarcated homogeneous lucency in the midline anteriorly, often associated with marginal curvilinear calcification bilaterally (see Fig. 5–41). On CT scans, the smoothly demarcated mass appears more hypodense than CSF (−50 to −100 HU) and is often marginated laterally by nodular or curvilinear calcification (see Fig. 5–41). On MRI, lipomas appear mainly homogeneously hyperintense on both T1-weighted and fast spin-echo T2-weighted images, but areas of low signal, secondary to the marginal calcification, are commonly noted peripherally.[114] Central flow voids, representing pericallosal arteries coursing through the substance of the tumor, are prominent within the tumor mass.

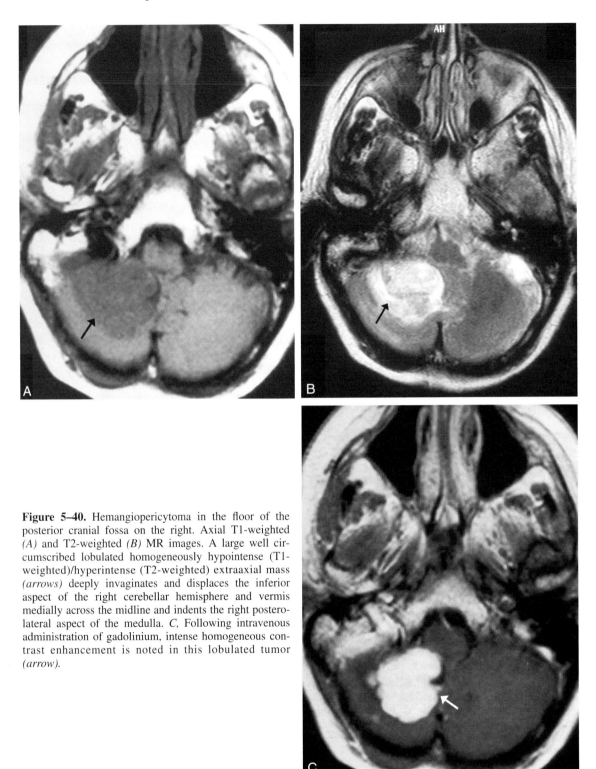

Figure 5–40. Hemangiopericytoma in the floor of the posterior cranial fossa on the right. Axial T1-weighted *(A)* and T2-weighted *(B)* MR images. A large well circumscribed lobulated homogeneously hypointense (T1-weighted)/hyperintense (T2-weighted) extraaxial mass *(arrows)* deeply invaginates and displaces the inferior aspect of the right cerebellar hemisphere and vermis medially across the midline and indents the right posterolateral aspect of the medulla. *C,* Following intravenous administration of gadolinium, intense homogeneous contrast enhancement is noted in this lobulated tumor *(arrow).*

Osteocartilaginous tumors occasionally arise within dural structures such as the falx. The CNS is the most common site of occurrence of extraosseous *chondrosarcoma*.[251] This mesenchymally derived malignancy occurs more frequently in the skull base, notably in the region of the intrasphenoid synchondrosis or the adjacent petroclival suture, and it may invade the overlying brain (Fig. 5–42). Whether arising from dura or from skull base structures, chondrosarcomas manifest as soft tissue masses with focal bone destruction. Intratumoral calcifications, identified in about half of tumors, contribute to a heterogeneous appearance on MRI, with intratumoral nodules which appear hypointense to isointense with adjacent brain on T1-weighted images and hyperintense to brain on T2-weighted images.[216] Intense contrast enhancement of the soft tissue mass is the rule (Fig. 5–42*B*).

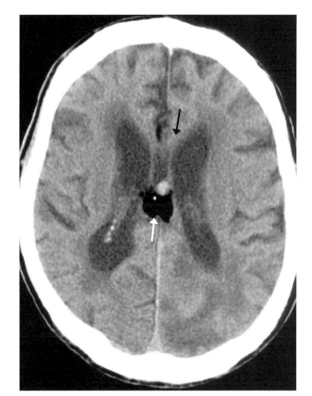

Figure 5–41. Pericallosal lipoma and partial agenesis of the corpus callosum. Axial noncontrast CT image demonstrates widely separated and parallel bodies of the lateral ventricles with an intervening elevated and dilated third ventricle *(black arrow);* these findings are consistent with partial agenesis of the anterior portion of the corpus callosum. In the midline more posteriorly, a markedly hypodense rhomboid-shaped curvilinear lipoma *(white arrow)* with two internal foci of calcification separates the lateral ventricles.

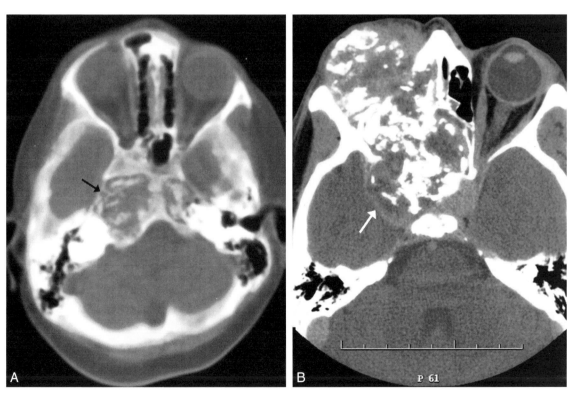

Figure 5–42. Chondrosarcomas of the skull base. *A,* Axial noncontrast CT image displayed in a bone window demonstrates bilateral irregularly marginated areas of bone destruction in the region of the intrasphenoid synchondrosis with multiple intratumoral hyperdensities respresenting foci of calcification and/or bony sequestra. The bony destruction involves the right lateral margin of the clivus *(arrow)* and the right petrous apex. *B,* In another patient, an axial CT image following intravenous contrast displayed in a soft tissue window demonstrates more extensive bone destruction involving the entire body of the sphenoid bone, the right ethmoid sinus, and the right orbit with foci of intratumoral calcification and/or bony sequestra. The soft tissue components of this tumor demonstrate heterogeneous contrast enhancement *(arrow)* with multiple ill defined areas of nonenhancement.

Other mesenchymal malignancies may also rarely originate within the cranial vault but more commonly arise in extracranial structures and secondarily invade the skull and brain, notably the *embryonal rhabdomyosarcoma*.[237, 251] This is the most common soft tissue sarcoma in children, and the head and neck are the most common site of occurrence, especially the orbit and the nasopharynx as well as the middle ear.[237] The tumor is almost uniformly fatal within 2 years of presentation, despite intensive chemotherapy and radiotherapy.[251] An extremely aggressive neoplasm, embryonal rhabdomyosarcoma commonly invades through the skull base into the adjacent brain. Evidence of invasion of the anterior skull base, the cavernous sinuses, or both is identified on MRI in 35% of embryonal rhabdomyosarcomas originating in the nasopharynx.[180]

Perineural and meningeal spread of tumor is also common in this tumor.[238] Imaging studies demonstrate large soft tissue masses with evidence of aggressive bone destruction. On MRI, these lesions appear isointense with muscle on T1-weighted images and hyperintense to brain and muscle on T2-weighted images, findings that are nonspecific and similar to those seen in nasopharyngeal carcinoma, myeloma, and neuroblastoma.[180, 237] Embryonal rhabdomyosarcomas exhibit contrast enhancement, which varies in both extent and intensity.

Melanocytic Tumors

A wide spectrum of tumors of melanocytic origin, varying from benign and diffuse (melanocytosis) to benign and well circumscribed (melanocytoma) to malignant (primary malignant melanoma), can originate within the meninges and the CNS.[151] They are thought to arise from leptomeningeal melanocytes derived from the neural crest. These tumors are all uncommon lesions, but the benign forms are less rare than the primary malignancies.

Melanocytomas of the meninges, which represent less than 0.1% of all brain tumors, present as solitary solid, round or flat extraaxial masses occurring mainly near the foramen magnum or in the region of Meckel's cave. Histologically, they demonstrate monomorphic cells with variable melanin content in their cytoplasm and a low mitotic rate.[151] Immunohistochemical studies show most tumors reacting to antimelanosomal antibody.[151] Presenting symptoms are those related to local compression of the underlying brain or obstruction of CSF flow. They can be found in patients of all age groups, with a peak incidence in the fifth decade of life.[151] Females are affected more commonly than males, with a reported 2:1 ratio.[227] On MRI, melanocytomas of the meninges appear as well-circumscribed extraaxial masses that are isointense to hyperintense, depending on the quantity of melanin in the tumor cells on T1-weighted images and hypointense to gray matter on T2-weighted images. Like the majority of meningeal tumors, they exhibit homogeneous contrast enhancement.[196, 338]

Hemangioblastoma

Hemangioblastomas are benign (WHO grade I) vascular neoplasms of uncertain origin that consist of abundant endothelial pericytes forming a rich capillary network intermixed with vacuolated (lipid-containing) stromal cells.[32] Although relatively uncommon overall (1% to 2.5% of all primary CNS tumors), hemangioblastoma is the most common primary intraaxial posterior fossa tumor in adults.[168, 186, 286] The great majority (80% to 85%) of CNS hemangioblastomas occur in the cerebellum, 2% to 3% in the medulla, and only 1% to 1.5% above the tentorium.[142, 286] The remainder (10% to 15%) arise within the spinal cord.[142]

Seventy-five percent to 85% of hemangioblastomas are sporadic in occurrence and solitary. They typically present clinically in young adults with peak incidence in the third to fifth decades of life and are rare in children. The natural history is that of a slow growing mass in the cerebellum that is frequently associated with a cyst. Approximately 60% of these tumors are cystic at the time of clinical presentation.[142] Symptoms are usually related to obstruction of CSF flow in the fourth ventricle by the solid tumor or the associated cyst.[32] Hemorrhage is uncommon in hemangioblastoma despite the prominent vascularity, and necrosis is rare. The advent of microsurgical excision techniques has significantly improved the prognosis in patients with sporadically occurring hemangioblastomas; mortality is low, and permanent neurologic deficits are rare.[32]

On gross inspection, hemangioblastomas are well demarcated, highly vascularized, small (5 to 10 mm), rounded solid lesions located peripherally within the cerebellum, brain stem, or spinal cord, usually abutting a pial surface (Fig. 5–43).[32, 104] The most striking lesions are those associated with well circumscribed cysts in which the solid tumor is a mural nodule.[286] Like the cyst associated with juvenile pilocytic astrocytoma of the cerebellum with a mural nodule, the cyst associated with a hemangioblastoma is essentially extratumoral, lacking any tumor tissue in its margin except for the eccentrically located solid nodule.[286] The cyst wall is composed of compressed brain parenchyma or reactive gliosis.[142]

Approximately 25% of hemangioblastomas are associated with von Hippel–Lindau disease, a phakomatosis that is inherited as an autosomal dominant trait caused by a germline mutation of a suppressor gene on the 3p chromosome.[32] Lindau[194] originally described this disease complex in 1926; it is characterized by the development of capillary hemangioblastomas in the CNS in association with identical tumors in the retina (originally described by von Hippel[340] in 1906); clear cell renal carcinomas, pheochromocytomas, and pancreatic, renal, and hepatic cysts are also frequently found in patients with the disease.

Multiplicity of hemangioblastomas of the cerebellum, brain stem, and spinal cord is common (10% to 40% of cases) in patients with von Hippel–Lindau disease,[104] and multiple tumors are found almost exclusively in patients with the disease (Fig. 5–44).[32, 232] Patients with von Hippel–Lindau disease become symptomatic at an earlier age (mean age at diagnosis, 29 years) than those with solitary sporadically occurring tumors.[32] Despite improved surgical techniques, the most common cause of death in patients with von Hippel–Lindau disease is hemangioblastoma.[157]

Noncontrast CT scans usually demonstrate a large, sharply marginated, hypodense, cystic cerebellar hemi-

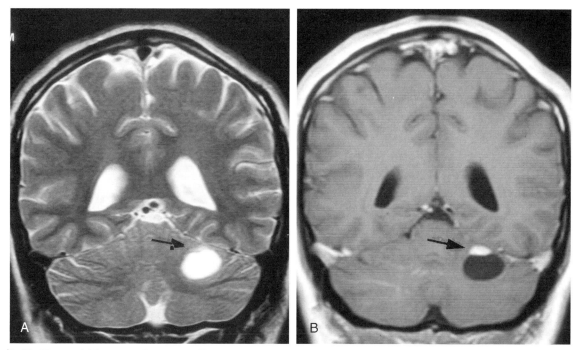

Figure 5–43. Hemangioblastoma of the cerebellum. *A,* A coronal T2-weighted MR image demonstrates a sharply marginated ovoid hyperintense mass in the superior aspect of the left cerebellar hemisphere. On the superior margin of this cystic mass, a flat nodule that is isointense to adjacent gray matter is identified *(arrow). B,* Following intravenous administration of gadolinium, a coronal T1-weighted image demonstrates intense homogeneous contrast enhancement of the mural nodule *(arrow),* which is located on the superior surface of the cerebellum. The adjacent cyst is hypointense, and its margins do not demonstrate contrast enhancement.

spheric mass with a slightly more dense rounded mural nodule. There is typically little or no peritumoral edema, and the solid lesion or mural nodule may not be distinguishable from surrounding normal cerebellar parenchyma, particularly if the lesion is located inferiorly within the posterior fossa, where it may be masked by dense adjacent bone and beam hardening artifact.[157] Calcifications have not been detected in these tumors.[168] After IV administration of a contrast agent, the solid tumor or mural nodule enhances homogeneously and intensely adjacent to a pial surface.[241] Because of the intense vascularity of even the smallest solid tumor nodules, angiography may be more sensitive than CT or MRI in the detection of hemangioblastoma.

On MRI, the cysts typically are sharply and smoothly marginated and homogeneously hypointense relative to adjacent brain parenchyma on T1-weighted images and hyperintense on T2-weighted images (Fig. 5–43A).[142, 241] The solid tumors and mural nodules are usually inhomogeneous in signal pattern but predominantly isointense with normal gray matter on T1-weighted images and slightly hyperintense on T2-weighted images. Areas of increased signal within the nodule or the cyst on T1-weighted images are occasionally noted secondary to hemorrhage.[142, 168, 186] Serpentine signal voids due to enlarged vessels supplying and draining the tumor may be identified at the periphery of the mass or nodule, a finding that should strongly suggest the diagnosis in the appropriate clinical setting.[186, 241] As with CT, contrast enhancement of the solid tumor or mural nodule on T1-weighted MRI is characteristically homogeneous and intense (see Figs. 5–43B and 5–44).[10, 142, 241]

Tumors of the Hematopoietic System

During the last two decades of the 20th century, tumors and tumor-like conditions of the hematopoietic system involving the CNS increased in both frequency and clinical and societal significance. Most notable in this regard was a greater than 10-fold increase in incidence of primary CNS non-Hodgkin's lymphoma in the United States.[217] The vast majority of these tumors are malignant B-cell lymphomas, which carry a poor prognosis.[249] Their site of origin is unknown, because the normal brain lacks lymphatics and lymphoid tissue. The rise in incidence of these tumors has been associated with the human immunodeficiency virus (HIV) epidemic; up to 10% of patients in the terminal stages of acquired immunodeficiency syndrome (AIDS) experience an Epstein-Barr virus–associated B-cell malignant cerebral lymphoma.[249] The concomitantly growing number of non–HIV-positive immunocompromised patients who have primary cerebral lymphoma, notably those undergoing long term immunosuppressive therapy after allograft organ transplantation, has also contributed to the higher incidence of primary CNS lymphoma.[10, 143, 254, 286]

Lymphomas arising systemically may involve the brain and meninges secondarily. They include T-cell lymphoma, plasmacytoma, angiotropic lymphoma, and Hodgkin's disease. In current practice, secondary involvement of the CNS by systemic lymphoma is much less common than the primary intracranial malignant B-cell variety.[217]

A heterogeneous group of tumors and tumor-like pro-

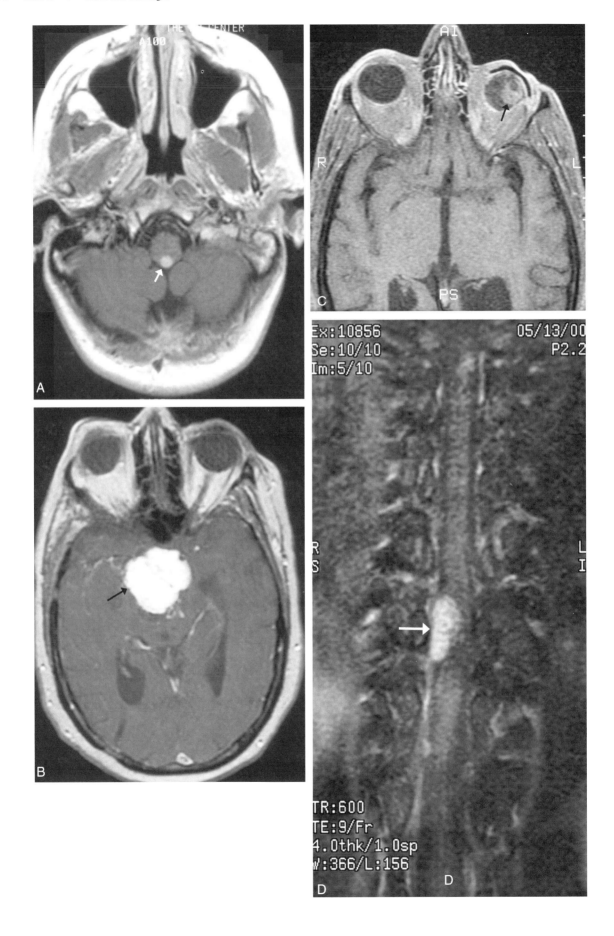

cesses of histiocytic origin rarely involve the brain, notably Langerhans cell histiocytosis.[250] Although the leukemias in their advanced stages may involve the meninges, leading to detection of malignant cells on CSF cytology, radiologically detectable dural based or intracerebral masses are rare.[248]

Primary Central Nervous System Lymphoma

Primary malignant lymphomas of the CNS are extranodal tumors arising in the CNS in patients with no obvious lymphoma outside the nervous system at the time of initial diagnosis.[217] Historically, this entity constituted about 1% of all primary tumors of the CNS; by the early 1990s, however, this proportion had increased to 6.6%,[217] mainly as a consequence of the AIDS epidemic. The incidence of this neoplasm in the AIDS population (4.7 per 1000 person-years) is approximately 3600 times that in the general population.[73] Approximately 10% of patients with AIDS experience primary CNS lymphoma, mainly during the late stages of their illness.[55] In transplant recipients who are immunosuppressed, the incidence of primary CNS lymphoma exceeds 20%.[255]

Primary CNS lymphoma affects all ages, but the peak incidence in immunocompetent individuals is in the sixth and seventh decades. In patients who have AIDS or have received organ transplants and are receiving immunosuppressive therapy, the median age of onset is in the late 30s. This tumor shows a definite sex predilection, with a 3:2 male-to-female ratio in immunocompetent patients and a 9:1 ratio in patients with AIDS.[217] The presenting symptoms and signs are nonspecific; focal neurologic deficits are most common, but seizures, signs of increased intracranial pressure, neuropsychological symptoms, and visual disturbances are also frequent.[217] Primary CNS lymphoma carries a guarded prognosis in immunocompetent patients and a poor prognosis in immunocompromised and immunosuppressed patients. In immunocompetent patients, the initial response rate to radiotherapy, chemotherapy, or both is 85%, but the survival rate is 40% to 70% at 2 years and 25% to 45% at 5 years; in patients with AIDS, the median survival after multimodal therapy is 13.5 months.[217]

On gross inspection, primary CNS lymphoma presents as one or more (usually multiple) firm or friable, centrally located, deep seated masses with variable demarcation from adjacent cerebral parenchyma. The tumors are often located in close proximity to the ventricles and may infiltrate through and along the ependymal ventricular walls (Fig. 5–45).[70] The corpus callosum and the basal ganglia are common sites of involvement. Intratumoral hemorrhage and necrosis are uncommon, and peritumoral edema is usually mild in immunocompetent patients, but in immunocompromised patients, lesion growth is more rapid, hemorrhage and necrosis are much more common, and edema of the surrounding white matter is often extensive.[70, 217] Involvement of the leptomeninges is a common but late finding.

Histologically, 98% of primary CNS lymphomas are high grade B-cell tumors that characteristically demonstrate an angiocentric infiltration pattern, in which collars of small neoplastic lymphocytes surround and infiltrate the walls of the small penetrating vessels of the brain and the perivascular (Virchow-Robin) extensions of the subarachnoid space.[70, 217] From these perivascular foci, tumor cells invade the adjacent neural parenchyma and coalesce, forming diffuse masses. In AIDS-associated cases, the diffuse masses tend to be multifocal with intervening areas of necrosis.[70, 217]

CT shows that the tumor masses involve the deep gray matter structures, the periventricular white matter, and the corpus callosum; they appear homogeneously isodense to moderately hyperdense (reflecting dense packing of small tumor cells with a high nuclear-to-cytoplasmic ratio), have relatively ill defined margins, and demonstrate diffuse strong homogeneous contrast enhancement (see Fig. 5–45).[10, 149, 241, 310] Peritumoral edema is less extensive than that seen in association with primary gliomas and metastases of similar size.[10] Central necrosis with peripheral ring-like contrast enhancement is uncommon in immunocompetent patients but is noted more frequently and involves wider areas with larger lesions in immunocompromised patients.[10, 149, 241] Extension along the ventricular walls with ependymal contrast enhancement (Fig. 5–45C) and leptomeningeal tumor spread, with hyperdensity in and contrast enhancement of the cisterns and sulci, are common late findings.[143]

On MRI, the deeply seated tumor nodules exhibit a variable signal intensity pattern. Most often, the tumors are homogeneously isointense with gray matter on both T1- and T2-weighted images, findings that are similar to those for other small cell hypercellular tumors.[10, 241, 279] However, some lesions may exhibit marked T2 hyperintensity. Almost all primary CNS lymphomas demonstrate intense contrast enhancement after IV administration of gadolin-

Figure 5–44. Multiple hemangioblastomas in a patient with von Hippel–Lindau disease. *A,* Axial T1-weighted MR image following intravenous administration of gadolinium demonstrates a sharply defined round homogeneously contrast enhancing nodule on the dorsal aspect of the lower medulla *(arrow).* Note the absence of a surrounding cyst. *B,* Axial T1-weighted postgadolinium image at the level of the suprasellar cistern. A large lobulated homogeneously intensely contrasting hypothalamic tumor protrudes inferiorly, filling and distending the suprasellar cistern *(arrow)* and insinuating into the interpeduncular cistern with spreading apart of the cerebral peduncles. Intratumoral hypointense linear and round foci likely represent flow voids within the rich tumor vasculature. This is a most unusual location for a hemangioblastoma. Also, the comparatively large size of this mass without an associated cyst is unusual. *C,* Axial T1-weighted postgadolinium image of the orbits and anterior brain obtained with fat saturation. A relatively large contrast enhancing nodule is identified within the lateral aspect of the left globe *(arrow);* a partially intranodular cyst is visualized anteriorly. *D,* Coronal T1-weighted postgadolinium image of the thoracic spine demonstrates an elongated nodular homogeneously enhancing tumor located eccentrically within the lower thoracic spinal cord on the right and protruding into and widening the right lateral subarachnoid space *(arrow);* the differential diagnosis of this lesion would include meningioma, schwannoma, and leptomeningeal metastasis.

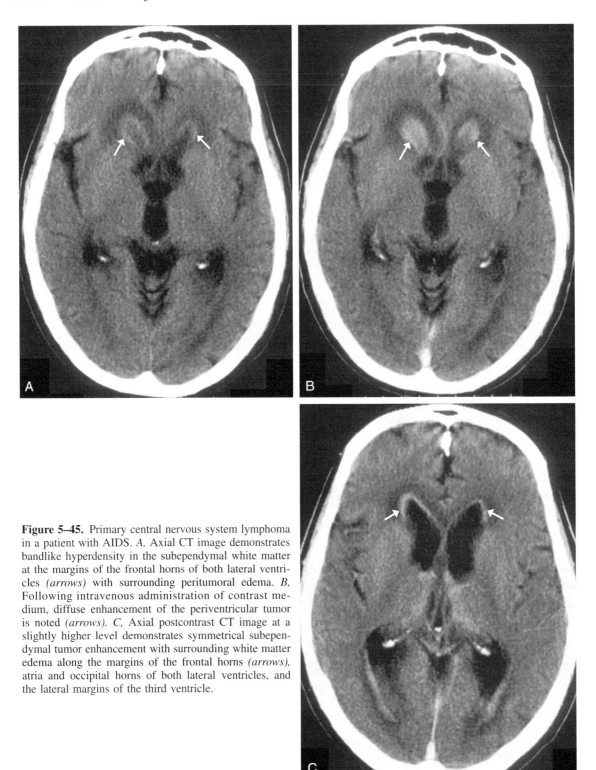

Figure 5–45. Primary central nervous system lymphoma in a patient with AIDS. *A,* Axial CT image demonstrates bandlike hyperdensity in the subependymal white matter at the margins of the frontal horns of both lateral ventricles *(arrows)* with surrounding peritumoral edema. *B,* Following intravenous administration of contrast medium, diffuse enhancement of the periventricular tumor is noted *(arrows). C,* Axial postcontrast CT image at a slightly higher level demonstrates symmetrical subependymal tumor enhancement with surrounding white matter edema along the margins of the frontal horns *(arrows),* atria and occipital horns of both lateral ventricles, and the lateral margins of the third ventricle.

ium. In immunocompromised patients, this enhancement is often ringlike (reflecting central necrosis) and associated with extensive peritumoral edema, and the clinical and radiologic presentation can simulate that of toxoplasmosis, a common occurrence in patients with AIDS.[90] The differential diagnosis favors toxoplasmosis if there is associated hemorrhage, whereas the presence of subependymal extension with contrast enhancement of the ventricular walls favors lymphoma.[10] In such circumstances, a short trial of anti-*Toxoplasma* therapy followed by evaluation of the clinical and imaging response may be sufficient to avoid invasive biopsy.

Leptomeningeal seeding occurs in up to 60% of patients with primary CNS lymphoma, generally late in the course of the disease. Although malignant cells may be readily detected on CSF cytology, detection of subarachnoid tumor spread on imaging studies has been problematic. Imaging verification of leptomeningeal neoplasm, which is visible as parallel linear streaklike contrast enhancement, may be more easily and reliably detected on T1-weighted postgadolinium MRI than on contrast enhanced CT.[143, 318]

An unusual form of presentation of primary CNS lymphoma simulates diffuse white matter disease, with patchy and diffuse infiltration of deep white matter as well as deep gray matter. Poorly marginated areas of T2 hyperintensity are seen scattered through the deep cerebral white and gray matter and in the pons. The pattern is similar to that of gliomatosis cerebri. This entity has been termed *lymphomatosis cerebri*.[241]

In an immunocompetent patient, the differential diagnosis of solitary or multiple deep seated tumors that are relatively homogeneous, appear isointense with gray matter on MRI and hyperdense on CT, and demonstrate dense contrast enhancement with mild surrounding edema would include, in addition to primary CNS lymphoma, high grade glioma (e.g., anaplastic astrocytoma), sarcoid, and intraventricular meningioma.

Secondary CNS Lymphoma

Approximately one third of patients with systemic lymphoma demonstrate secondary brain or spinal involvement.[21] The majority of secondary CNS lymphomas are T-cell lymphomas with a propensity to first involve the leptomeninges surrounding the brain and then extend into cerebral parenchyma along the Virchow-Robin spaces in the periphery of the cerebral hemispheres. Both focal and diffuse thickening of the arachnoid occurs, and infiltration also extends into the overlying dura. As in the primary CNS lymphomas, multicentricity is common, but the masses are predominantly peripherally rather than deeply situated. Thick plaques of tumor on the brain surface that are isointense with the adjacent brain on T1- and T2-weighted images and demonstrate homogeneous contrast enhancement (Fig. 5–46) may simulate the appearance of meningioma; in general, the tumor masses of lymphoma are more numerous and more extensive than those of meningioma and often extend into the subarachnoid space and underlying brain parenchyma.[10]

Histiocytic Lesions

Histiocytic lesions represent a heterogeneous group of tumors and tumor-like masses of the brain of unknown etiology that are composed of histiocytes (macrophages) and are often but not always associated with histologically identical extracranial lesions.[250] The most common of these disorders is *Langerhans cell histiocytosis (LCH),* a disease that usually occurs in children and causes solitary (eosinophilic granuloma) or multifocal (Hand-Schüller-Christian) osteolytic lesions of the skull base and membranous skull.[126] In the multifocal form, there is often irregularly marginated bone destruction in the region of the sella turcica with associated thickening of the pituitary stalk and hypothalamus. The lesions, whether in brain or in bone, appear to be granulomatous infiltrates composed mainly of Langerhans cell histiocytes in an admixture of lymphocytes, macrophages, plasma cells, and eosinophils.[250] Very rarely, multiple foci of demyelination and gliosis with minimal or no granular parenchymal infiltrates may be found within the cerebral or cerebellar white matter in patients with cranial and extracranial LCH; these appear as small poorly marginated areas of hypodensity on CT scans and of hyperintensity on T2-weighted MR images (Fig. 5–47).[259]

Leukemia

Granulocytic sarcoma (formerly known as *chloroma*) is a focal collection of leukemic cells that form a solid mass projecting inward from the meninges or within the brain parenchyma contiguous with the ventricular wall ependyma in patients with systemic leukemia, typically acute or chronic myelogenous leukemia.[117, 127, 241] In approximately one third of cases, the tumor may actually precede the development of the systemic disease.[117] On CT, the lesion appears hyperdense or isodense relative to brain parenchyma with unsharp margins. On MRI, it demonstrates heterogeneous isointensity or hypointensity relative to gray matter on T1-weighted images and isointensity to hyperintensity on T2-weighted images. Homogeneous contrast enhancement of the tumor is the rule (Fig. 5–48).[117, 127, 248]

Germ Cell Tumors

Tumors arising from primordial germ cells represent only 0.3% to 0.5% of all primary intracranial neoplasms, although in Asia the figure is 2%.[284] Germ cell tumors represent about 3% of primary pediatric intracranial neoplasms, except in Asia, where the proportion has been reported as 10% to 15%.[212] These tumors are the intracranial morphologic homologues of germinal neoplasms arising in the gonads and in other sites. They present mainly in children and adolescents, with an age peak of 10 to 12 years.[284] Approximately 90% arise in patients younger than 20 years with a strong (2:1) male predilection.

Intracranial germ cell tumors occur mainly in or near the midline in the vicinity of the third ventricle. The most common sites of occurrence are the pineal region (65%) and the suprasellar region (30%).[154] Nearly two thirds (65%) of intracranial germ cell neoplasms are germinomas, the intracranial morphologic equivalent of the testicular seminoma, whereas 16% represent teratomas, 6% are endodermal sinus (yolk sac) tumors or embryonal cell carcinomas, 4% are choriocarcinomas, and the remaining 9% are mixed tumors incorporating elements of two or more germ cell types.[250] These lesions may be multifocal with involvement of both the pineal and suprasellar regions.

The clinical presentation depends on the location of the tumor mass.[284] Patients with pineal region tumors typically present with complaints of headache, because the tumor compresses and obstructs the aqueduct, causing a noncommunicating hydrocephalus. Compression on or invasion of the quadrigeminal plate causes a Parinaud syndrome, with paralysis of upward gaze and convergence. Tumors in the floor of the third ventricle or the suprasellar region typi-

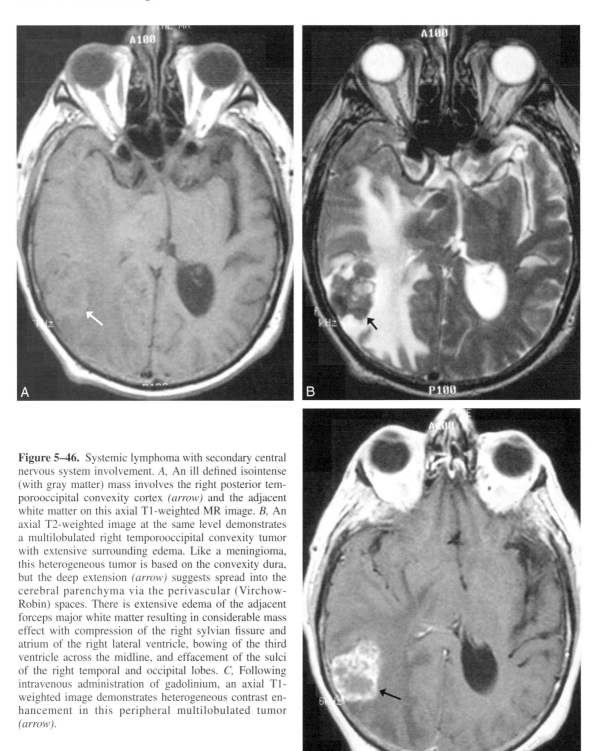

Figure 5–46. Systemic lymphoma with secondary central nervous system involvement. *A,* An ill defined isointense (with gray matter) mass involves the right posterior temporooccipital convexity cortex *(arrow)* and the adjacent white matter on this axial T1-weighted MR image. *B,* An axial T2-weighted image at the same level demonstrates a multilobulated right temporooccipital convexity tumor with extensive surrounding edema. Like a meningioma, this heterogeneous tumor is based on the convexity dura, but the deep extension *(arrow)* suggests spread into the cerebral parenchyma via the perivascular (Virchow-Robin) spaces. There is extensive edema of the adjacent forceps major white matter resulting in considerable mass effect with compression of the right sylvian fissure and atrium of the right lateral ventricle, bowing of the third ventricle across the midline, and effacement of the sulci of the right temporal and occipital lobes. *C,* Following intravenous administration of gadolinium, an axial T1-weighted image demonstrates heterogeneous contrast enhancement in this peripheral multilobulated tumor *(arrow).*

cally impinge upon the optic chiasm (causing visual field defects) or the hypothalamic-pituitary pathways (causing diabetes insipidus, growth retardation, or precocious puberty).

Examination of the serum and CSF for the presence of certain oncoproteins elaborated by germ cell tumors often provides valuable differential diagnostic information and is also useful in monitoring the course of treatment.[284] Elevation of placental alkaline phosphatase (PLAP) in these fluids favors the diagnosis of germinoma, whereas a rise in concentration of alpha-fetoprotein (AFP) suggests the presence of yolk sac endoderm, as in an endodermal sinus (yolk sac) tumor or an immature teratoma. Human chorionic gonadotropin (β-HCG) is elaborated by syncytial tro-

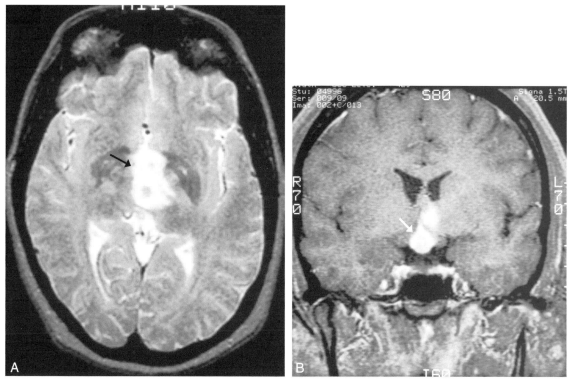

Figure 5–47. Langerhans cell histiocytosis of the hypothalamus and pituitary stalk. *A*, Axial T2-weighted MR image displays a large ill defined area of hyperintensity (likely representing edema) in the region of the hypothalamus *(arrow)*. Within this hyperintensity can be seen two smaller isointense (with gray matter) foci. *B*, Coronal T1-weighted postgadolinium image demonstrates homogeneous contrast enhancement of the two foci; the larger lesion *(arrow)* extends into and widens the pituitary stalk.

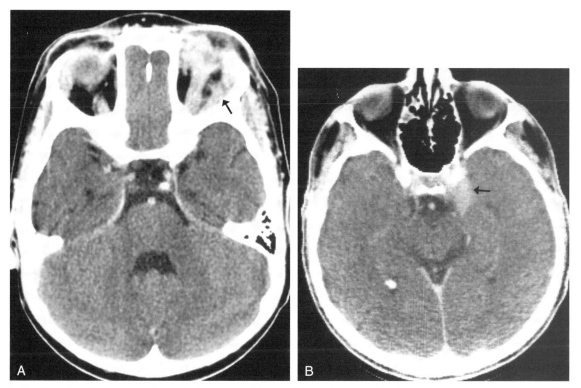

Figure 5–48. Granulocytic sarcoma (formerly known as chloroma) involving the left orbit and cavernous sinus. *A* and *B*, Axial CT images following intravenous contrast administration. In *A*, a sharply outlined irregular contrast enhancing mass is seen in the the lateral aspect of the left orbit *(arrow)*. The mass slightly displaces the superior aspect of the left globe and the composite density of the levator palpebrae superioris and superior rectus muscles medially. At a slightly lower level *(B)*, the tumor extends into and diffusely widens the left cavernous sinus *(arrow)*.

phoblasts, and elevation of this marker points to the presence of choriocarcinoma.

There is a higher risk of intracranial and mediastinal germ cell tumors in patients with Klinefelter syndrome, a complex chromosomal disorder with a 47XXY karyotype. The most common cause of hypogonadism in young males, Klinefelter syndrome is characterized by testicular atrophy, gynecomastia, and lack of secondary sex characteristics.[152, 284] Affected individuals are also at greater risk for development of breast carcinoma. Histopathologic examination of tumor tissue is essential for treatment planning and prognosis.[102, 284] Although germinomas and teratomas often occur as pure tumor types, the nongerminomatous neoplasms are often of mixed cellular composition, and immunohistochemical studies performed on excised tissue to detect and localize the oncoproteins expressed by these tumors (mentioned in the preceding paragraph) are valuable for their characterization.

Germinoma

Germinomas are usually solid tumors that may contain cystic foci. The most common germ cell tumor is a pure germinoma, composed of sheets or lobules of uniform cells with large nuclei and clear cytoplasm that exhibit immunohistochemical labeling for PLAP on their cell membrane surfaces.[284] Mitoses are common, but intratumoral hemorrhage and necrosis are uncommon. These tumors are not encapsulated, and they tend to grow by invasion of neighboring structures. In the pineal region, they surround and engulf the pineal calcifications and may

invade the adjacent thalami and quadrigeminal plates.[109, 305] In the suprasellar region, these tumors appear as rounded or lobulated masses in the floor of the third ventricle, compressing and invading the optic chiasm and surrounding the pituitary stalk[19]; they may also extend superiorly, infiltrating the walls of the third ventricle. Seeding of tumor cells may occur into the CSF with both ependymal and subarachnoid spread of tumor.

More than 90% of pineal region germinomas occur in males, whereas for tumors in the suprasellar region, the sex distribution is approximately equal.[19, 360]

Pure germinomas are highly radiosensitive, and 5 year survival rates of 65% to 95% are reported.[284] Adjuvant chemotherapy may permit reduction in radiation dosage with comparable survival rates. Extent of disease at the time of diagnosis is an important prognostic factor.[152]

On both CT and MRI, germinomas in the pineal and suprasellar regions appear as well circumscribed and mostly homogeneous rounded or lobulated masses.[19, 109, 305, 360] Their hypercellularity explains their notable hyperdensity on CT (Fig. 5–49A) and their isointensity to gray matter and hypointensity relative to CSF on T2-weighted MR images (Fig. 5–50A, B). Intratumoral cysts are occasionally found and are easily distinguished from the surrounding solid tumor. Intratumoral hemorrhage and necrosis are rare occurrences. CT visualization of intratumoral calcification in a cluster likely signifies engulfment or displacement of the normal calcified pineal gland; widely dispersed calcifications favor a diagnosis of a primary pineal cell neoplasm.[284] The solid parts of these tumors exhibit uniform contrast enhancement, and spread of tumor from the pineal region into the quadrigeminal plate or

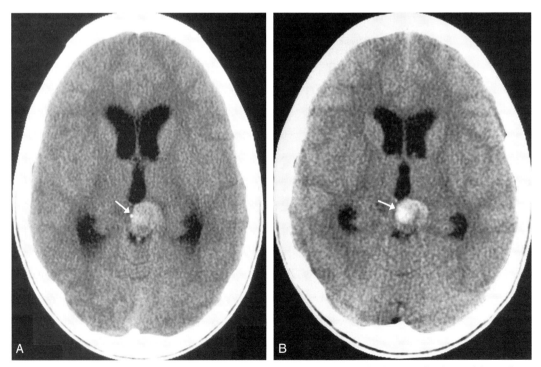

Figure 5–49. Germinoma of the pineal region. *A,* Axial CT image demonstrates a well circumscribed round hyperdense mass in the pineal region extending slightly to the left and indenting the posteromedial aspect of the left thalamus *(arrow)* with a thin hypodense rim (likely representing edema) at the interface with the left thalamus. *B,* Following intravenous contrast administration, the mass demonstrates diffuse contrast enhancement *(arrow)*.

thalami or from the floor of the third ventricle into the optic chiasm and pituitary stalk can be clearly delineated on either CT or MRI images after IV administration of contrast medium (Figs. 5–49*B* and 5–50*C*).[19, 241] Differentiation of suprasellar germinoma from JPA on either CT or MRI may be difficult, but clinical differences in age and presenting symptoms usually permit accurate characterization.[19]

Teratoma

Teratomas are the second most common germ cell tumors. They originate from multipotential germ cells that recapitulate normal somatic development by developing elements of the three embryonic germ layers—ectoderm, endoderm, and mesoderm.[284] They are subdivided pathologically into mature and immature teratomas. *Mature teratomas* are composed entirely of fully differentiated tissue elements that may be arranged in patterns simulating those of normal organogenesis and originating from ectoderm (skin, brain, choroid), mesoderm (bone, tooth, cartilage, fat, muscle), and endoderm (intestine, respiratory).[284] *Immature teratomas* occur more commonly,[200] demonstrate greater hypercellularity and mitotic activity, and are composed of incompletely differentiated tissue elements resembling fetal tissues (e.g., the developing neural tube).[284] An occasional teratoma contains a malignant component, such as rhabdomyosarcoma, undifferentiated sarcoma, squamous cell carcinoma, or adenocarcinoma.[284]

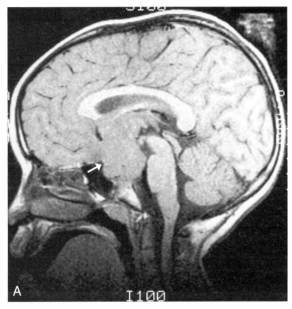

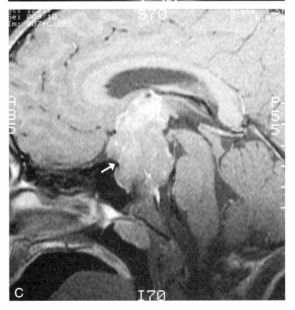

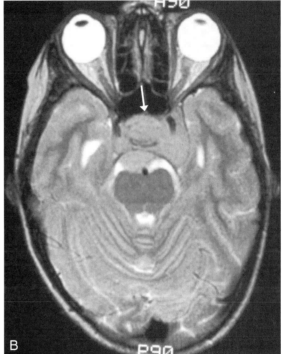

Figure 5–50. Germinoma of the suprasellar region. *A,* Sagittal T1-weighted MR image demonstrates a bulky lobulated ill defined isointense (with gray matter) tumor that nearly completely fills the third ventricle and extends downward into the sella *(arrow)* and posteriorly into the prepontine cistern. The belly of the pons is flattened and displaced posteriorly by this extensive tumor. *B,* Axial T2-weighted image through the level of the sella. The homogeneously isointense intrasellar tumor *(arrow)* extends bilaterally to encase the adjacent internal carotid arteries and posteriorly into the prepontine cistern, abutting the ventral surface of the pons on the right. *C,* Following intravenous administration of gadolinium, a sagittal T1-weighted image demonstrates patchy contrast enhancement of this extensive tumor *(arrow).*

Teratomas occur almost exclusively in males in the pineal, parapineal, and suprasellar regions. The clinical presentation for these lesions is earlier than for germinomas, usually during the first decade of life.[10, 144, 200] On gross inspection, teratomas are typically well defined lobulated masses containing multiple structures, including mucus-filled cysts, nodules of cartilage and bone, and, rarely, teeth and hair.[284] In the pineal region, these tumors are not usually invasive.[19] For mature teratomas that can be completely excised, the 5-year survival rate is 80% to 90%.[200]

On both CT and MRI, teratomas are characterized by their striking heterogeneity in density and signal.[10, 19, 109, 241, 305, 360] Intratumoral cysts with well-defined margins and variable density or signal of contents (watery, proteinaceous, lipid) are intermixed with calcifications or ossifications and areas of variegated soft tissue appearance, including hemorrhage. Dilatation of the lateral and third ventricles may indicate compression of the cerebral aqueduct by the tumor mass. Contrast enhancement is variable and, when patchy or ringlike, raises the possibility of malignant degeneration (Fig. 5–51).[19] Invasion of neighboring structures can best be assessed on postcontrast images.

Other Germ Cell Tumors

Endodermal sinus (yolk sac) tumor is characterized by the accumulation of a myxoid matrix within a meshwork of primitive epithelial cells. *Embryonal carcinoma* is composed of large primitive cells that form abortive papillae and may attempt to replicate the structure of the early embryo. *Choriocarcinoma* consists of very large multinucleated trophoblastic cells that attempt to simulate placental tissue and include ectatic vascular channels that are prone to hemorrhage. Elements of these tumors may be found in germinomas or teratomas, and such tumors are then classified as mixed germ cell tumors.[102, 284] Approximately 10% of germ cell tumors contain more than one cell type.[19, 102]

All of these neoplasms, including the mixed germ cell tumors, have a high mitotic rate and a worse prognosis than pure germinomas or teratomas.[152, 212, 284] These lesions exhibit a strong propensity for seeding via the CSF, for hematogenous metastasis to lung and bone, and even for spread of tumor via a ventriculoperitoneal shunt catheter into the peritoneal cavity.

Differentiation of these lesions on CT or MRI studies from pure germinoma or teratoma depends on demonstration of a pineal region or suprasellar region mass with areas of intratumoral necrosis and hemorrhage. Hemorrhage is particularly common in choriocarcinoma, reflecting the vascular stroma of that tumor. However, these findings are nonspecific, and individual tumor type is best established with immunohistochemical evaluation of excised tumor tissue.[19, 241, 284, 305]

Tumors of the Sellar Region

Tumors of the pituitary gland and adjacent structures reflect the variety of tissues involved in the formation of these structures. Intrasellar, suprasellar, and parasellar tumors affect the CNS by expansion, with resultant compression of cranial nerves and the base of the brain, or by interference with the hypothalamic-neurohypophyseal pathway. Alternatively, certain neoplasms, mainly intrasellar, may become clinically manifest because of endocrine hyperfunction.

The most common neoplasms in this region are pituitary adenomas and craniopharyngiomas, both of which are considered to arise from derivatives of Rathke's pouch, the embryonic infolding of endoderm that extends superiorly from the stomodeum and gives rise in early fetal development to the adenohypophysis (anterior lobe of the pituitary gland). The anterior lobe constitutes 75% of the volume of the pituitary gland.[237] The posterior lobe of the pituitary gland is of neuroectodermal origin, extending inferiorly from the hypothalamus through the pituitary stalk (infundibulum). Neoplasms arising in the posterior pituitary are extremely rare.

Less common masses in the sellar region, all of nonhypophyseal origin, are chordomas, meningiomas, gliomas of the optic pathways, germinomas, teratomas, and metastases.

Pituitary Adenoma

Adenomas of the anterior pituitary are relatively common benign neoplasms, representing 10% to 15% of all intracranial tumors.[171] They are mainly tumors of adulthood, with less than 3% occurring in individuals younger than 18 years.[237] Pituitary adenomas vary greatly in size, but the vast majority are less than 10 mm in diameter and are designated by convention as *microadenomas*. In a series of 1000 unselected autopsy specimens, 3.1% of pituitary glands contained microadenomas, all from individuals older than 40 years.[237]

Microadenoma

Microadenomas are typically well demarcated lesions. Although they lack a definite capsule, they can be distinguished on gross inspection from the normal pituitary gland because they have a pseudocapsule of compressed pituitary tissue.[201] Approximately 75% of pituitary adenomas are hormonally active; compared with nonfunctional (endocrinologically inactive) adenomas, hormonally active adenomas usually present earlier in their course of evolution when they are much smaller, with symptoms and signs of endocrine hyperfunction.[201] They are generally classified on the basis of the hormone produced—for example, lactotroph (prolactin), somatotroph (growth hormone), corticotroph (ACTH), thyrotroph (TSH), and gonadotroph (FSH).[171] Cells that secrete prolactin and growth hormone and the tumors arising from them tend to be located in the lateral portions of the gland, whereas cells that secrete ACTH, TSH, and FSH and the tumors arising from them tend to be located centrally.[171, 201, 237]

Approximately 50% of hormonally active adenomas are prolactinomas.[201] They arise mainly in women (female-to-male ratio, 4–5:1), who typically present in young adulthood with amenorrhea, galactorrhea, and infertility.[237] Loss of libido and impotence are the most common presenting symptoms in males. The symptoms and signs are less

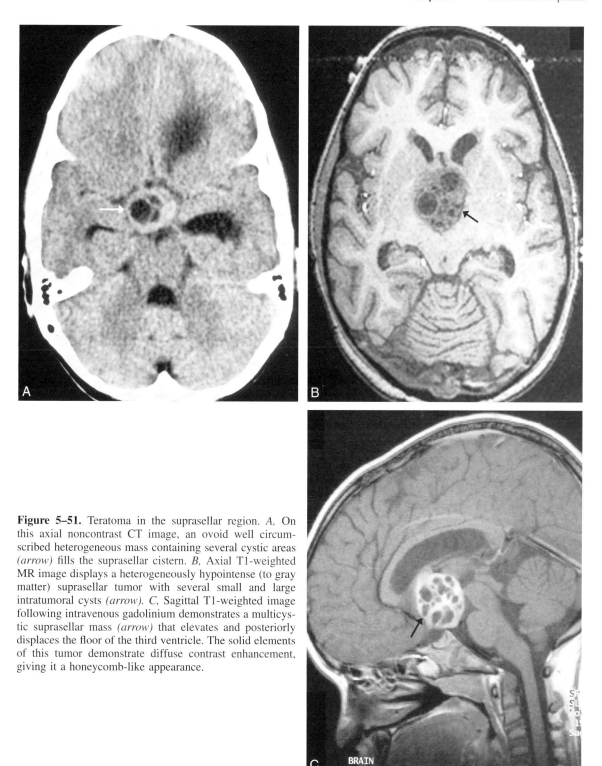

Figure 5–51. Teratoma in the suprasellar region. *A,* On this axial noncontrast CT image, an ovoid well circumscribed heterogeneous mass containing several cystic areas *(arrow)* fills the suprasellar cistern. *B,* Axial T1-weighted MR image displays a heterogeneously hypointense (to gray matter) suprasellar tumor with several small and large intratumoral cysts *(arrow)*. *C,* Sagittal T1-weighted image following intravenous gadolinium demonstrates a multicystic suprasellar mass *(arrow)* that elevates and posteriorly displaces the floor of the third ventricle. The solid elements of this tumor demonstrate diffuse contrast enhancement, giving it a honeycomb-like appearance.

pronounced in postmenopausal women and in men, in whom the tumors may manifest clinically only when they have become large enough to compress the visual pathways or cause pituitary hypofunction.[201] The great majority of prolactin-secreting tumors lie in the lateral aspect of the anterior pituitary.

Elevation of the serum prolactin concentration above the normal upper limit of 20 ng/mL raises the level of

suspicion for the presence of prolactinoma, but elevated serum prolactin values can also be associated with ingestion of certain drugs (notably the phenothiazines and the tricyclic antidepressants), the presence of a suprasellar mass compressing the hypothalamus or pituitary stalk, and primary hypothyroidism.[201] Although markedly elevated serum prolactin values (>150 ng/mL) are almost always due to the presence of a prolactinoma, many patients with this tumor present with prolactin values between 20 and 150 ng/mL; in this group, diagnostic imaging often provides evidence allowing differentiation of prolactinoma from nonneoplastic causes of hyperprolactinemia.

Somatotrophic and corticotrophic tumors each account for approximately 15% of microadenomas.[98] The former cause gigantism in children and acromegaly in adults and are usually located laterally within the pituitary gland. The latter are located centrally, cause Cushing's disease, and are typically very small. The great majority (75%) of patients presenting with Cushing's disease are female. Thyrotrophic and gonadotrophic tumors are relatively rare. About 10% of microadenomas secrete more than one hormone, most commonly prolactin and growth hormone.[171]

Approximately 25% of pituitary adenomas are nonfunctional, that is, they do not cause nor are they directly associated with endocrine hyperfunction.[98] These tumors are detected accidentally as microadenomas when patients undergo diagnostic imaging for other clinical indications, are discovered incidentally at autopsy, or present clinically at a later stage as macroadenomas when they are large enough to compress the pituitary stalk, the optic chiasm, the cranial nerves in the cavernous sinus or suprasellar cistern, or the base of the brain.[98, 201]

On CT and MRI, the pituitary gland is best visualized in the coronal plane. Because of the lack of bone artifact and the greater intrinsic soft tissue contrast on MRI, this modality has largely supplanted CT for the initial detection and localization of pituitary microadenoma. Approximately 80% to 85% of these tumors demonstrate focal subtle

hypointensity on T1-weighted images and focal mild hyperintensity on T2-weighted images. However, the differential signal intensity between the tumor and surrounding normal pituitary tissue is often very slight (Fig. 5–52A), thus explaining the 15% to 20% false-negative rate for MRI evaluation.[174]

Intratumoral calcification occurs only rarely in pituitary adenomas and even more rarely in the microadenomas.[237] Intratumoral necrosis, cyst formation, and hemorrhage are also infrequent occurrences that are much more likely to be found in the larger tumors. These changes typically cause heterogeneity of the density or signal pattern within the lesion.

The use of thin section T1-weighted images obtained after IV bolus administration of gadolinium improves the sensitivity and specificity of MRI for the detection and localization of pituitary microadenomas.[235] The normal pituitary gland lacks a blood-brain barrier and thus opacifies rapidly and homogeneously after IV administration of contrast medium. The uptake of contrast agent by microadenomas is slower than that of the gland, and this difference provides greater conspicuity of the relatively hypointense tumor over the first 1 to 2 minutes after injection (Fig. 5–52B). Rapid sequence coronal single slice T1-weighted imaging of the sella immediately after IV bolus administration of gadolinium with images obtained consecutively at 10 second intervals provides a "dynamic" demonstration of the difference in contrast uptake between tumor and normal pituitary (Fig. 5–53).[201] A similar result can be obtained on CT with the use of thin-section coronal scans

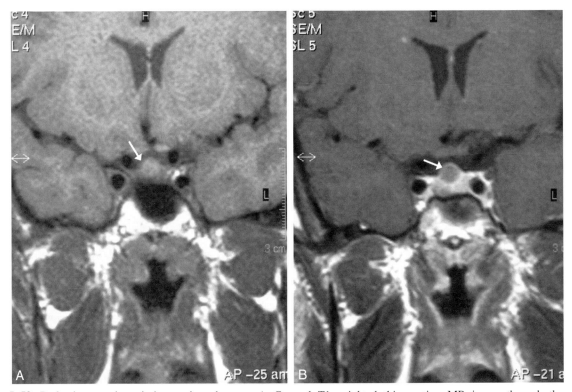

Figure 5–52. Prolactin secreting pituitary microadenoma. *A,* Coronal T1-weighted thin section MR image through the midsella demonstrates a round isointense mass arising from the right side of the pituitary gland and projecting upward into the suprasellar cistern *(arrow). B,* Coronal T1-weighted image obtained shortly following intravenous gadolinium administration. Normal pituitary tissue demonstrates homogeneous contrast enhancement, while the round mass shows little or no enhancement.

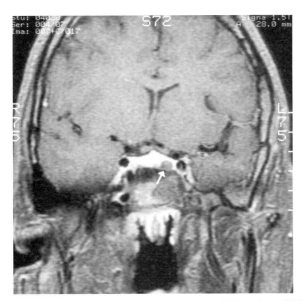

Figure 5–53. Pituitary microadenoma. Coronal T1-weighted MR image obtained during a dynamic scanning sequence following bolus intravenous administration of gadolinium. A 5 mm in diameter ovoid hypointense lesion in the left inferior aspect of the pituitary gland *(arrow)* fails to take up the contrast medium as rapidly as the surrounding normal pituitary tissue.

obtained after IV bolus administration of iodinated contrast medium; on early rapid sequence serial images, the microadenoma appears hypodense relative to the homogeneously contrast enhancing normal pituitary tissue. This difference in contrast enhancement effect fades after several minutes, and later or delayed images may mask the presence of the tumor or rarely may demonstrate reversal of the image contrast pattern, with the adenoma enhancing more strongly than the surrounding tissue.[201]

Laterally placed microadenomas may cause either unilateral upwardly convex bulging of the overlying superior margin of the pituitary gland into the suprasellar cistern or downward protrusion of the inferior margin into the floor of the sella, or both. Also, the pituitary stalk may be displaced contralaterally by the expanding microadenoma. However, these findings are inconstant, depending on the size of the tumor and the location of its epicenter; when present, they may raise the level of confidence in the diagnosis of microadenoma, but their absence does not detract from the significance of an intrasellar hypodense or hypointense mass. Also, pituitary stalk deviation can be seen in individuals without symptoms, signs, or imaging evidence of intrasellar or suprasellar tumor.[2]

The differential diagnosis of pituitary microadenoma on MRI or CT is limited. Pituitary adenomas may contain cells that are undergoing mitosis or may demonstrate dural invasion without being classified as malignant. The diagnosis of primary pituitary carcinoma is made only rarely and then usually in the circumstance of distant metastasis.[330] Most malignancies occurring within the gland are metastases from primary carcinomas of the breast, lung, kidney, and gastrointestinal tract,[156, 330] although metastases account for only about 1% of intrasellar and parasellar tumors.[237] Often multiple and tiny, metastases are demonstrated only on postcontrast high resolution images.

Nonneoplastic inflammatory entities that may involve the anterior lobe of the pituitary gland include lymphocytic hypophysitis and sarcoidosis. Lymphocytic hypophysitis is a rare disorder, likely autoimmune, that occurs mainly in young women during late pregnancy or postpartum. It is characterized by diffuse lymphocytic infiltration of the anterior pituitary. On imaging studies, the pituitary gland appears diffusely enlarged and demonstrates contrast enhancement.[192] Sarcoidosis, another autoimmune disorder, affects the CNS in about 5% of cases, notably involving the meninges and parenchymal structures at the base of the brain. On imaging studies, multiple foci of ill-defined contrast enhancement are seen within and enveloping the surfaces of the hypothalamus, optic chiasm, and pituitary stalk (Fig. 5–54).[72]

Intrapituitary focal abnormalities are commonly identified on MRI of asymptomatic volunteers[130] and as incidental findings in large autopsy series.[171] These include not only microadenomas but also Rathke's cleft cysts (see Fig. 5–59) (see later) and other benign cysts of uncertain origin. The incidence of such cysts on autopsy series varies from 5.8% to 8.3% of individuals older than 30 years.[171] In one double-blinded series of asymptomatic adult volunteers, MRI demonstrated intrapituitary focal hypointensities on T1-weighted imaging that were consistent with microadenoma or benign pituitary cyst in 15% of subjects.[130] Another possible explanation proposed for these "incidentalomas" is magnetic susceptibility induction of signal distortion in the floor of the sella near the junction with

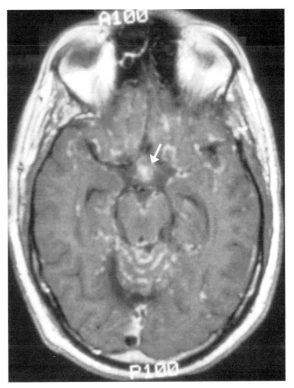

Figure 5–54. Sarcoidosis involving the base of the brain. Axial postgadolinium T1-weighted MR image demonstrates patchy diffuse contrast enhancement of the leptomeninges enveloping the base of the brain. A large focus *(arrow)* involves the pituitary stalk.

the sphenoid sinus.[201] Most of these lesions, apparent or real, are very small (<3 mm) and, in the absence of correlating clinical symptoms or signs, can be followed with periodic monitoring on an annual or biannual basis.[201]

Macroadenoma

When an adenoma of the pituitary gland reaches or exceeds 10 mm in diameter, it is designated by convention a *macroadenoma*. The great majority of such lesions are endocrinologically nonfunctional, although immunohistochemical and electron microscopic studies now suggest that these "null cell" tumors may be elaborating proteins that are involved in the formation or control of hormones.[329] The tumors often become clinically evident in middle age, when they reach sufficient size to compress the optic chiasm, causing a disturbance in vision, typically an asymmetric bitemporal hemianopsia. Detailed clinical and laboratory evaluation may reveal evidence of hypopituitarism due to compression of the normal pituitary gland or stalk, but this is rarely a presenting symptom.[330]

Macroadenomas originate as intrasellar masses that slowly expand in all directions, notably upward out of the sella, protruding into the suprasellar cistern and eventually elevating and compressing the optic chiasm, the hypothalamus, and the floor of the third ventricle (Fig. 5–55B, C). They also spread laterally and can invade across dura into the cavernous sinus and partially or completely encase the internal carotid artery.[201] Slow tumor growth in the inferior direction leads to thinning and erosion of the floor of the sella with protrusion into the underlying sphenoid sinus. On plain films and CT images this chronic slow enlargement causes expansion of the sellar cavity with thinning of the bony cortex of the dorsum, floor, and anterior wall of the sella.

Histologically, pituitary adenomas consist of small oval or polyhedral cells in a sheetlike monomorphous array, which contrasts markedly with the pleomorphic acinar pattern of the normal anterior pituitary gland.[329] Cellular pleomorphism and even occasional mitoses may be seen in pituitary adenomas but do not indicate aggressive biologic behavior.[97] Calcification in these tumors is rare (in the range of 1%)[237] but may be more common in prolactin-secreting tumors.[97]

Intratumoral necrosis, cystic change, and hemorrhage all occur more frequently in macroadenomas than in microadenomas.[201] Hemorrhage is present in 20% to 30% of macroadenomas; it may be associated with pituitary apoplexy, an

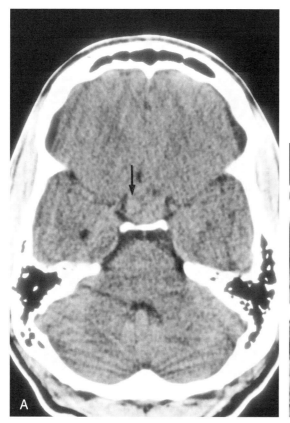
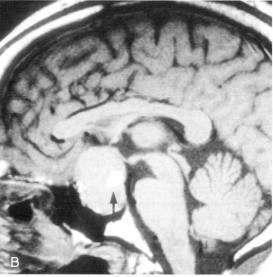

Figure 5–55. Pituitary macroadenoma with intratumoral hemorrhage and cystic changes. *A,* Axial noncontrast CT image demonstrates a soft tissue mass filling the suprasellar cistern. The tumor is mainly isodense with adjacent brain, but a faintly hyperdense focus at the right lateral margin *(arrow)* suggests recent hemorrhage. On a sagittal T1-weighted MR image *(B),* the tumor is seen to enlarge the sella and extend into the suprasellar cistern, elevating and slightly posteriorly displacing the optic chiasm and the anterior floor of the third ventricle. It is mainly homogeneously isointense with adjacent brain, but contains several hyperintense foci (the largest is located in the posterior portion of the tumor and is indicated by an *arrow*) which likely represent subacute hemorrhage.

Illustration continued on opposite page

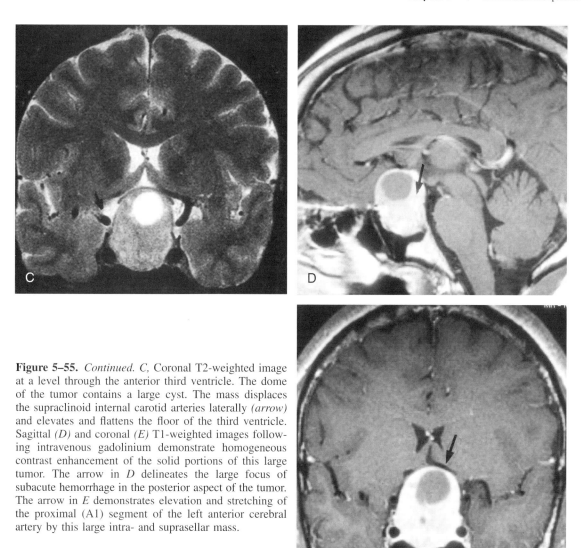

Figure 5–55. *Continued. C,* Coronal T2-weighted image at a level through the anterior third ventricle. The dome of the tumor contains a large cyst. The mass displaces the supraclinoid internal carotid arteries laterally *(arrow)* and elevates and flattens the floor of the third ventricle. Sagittal *(D)* and coronal *(E)* T1-weighted images following intravenous gadolinium demonstrate homogeneous contrast enhancement of the solid portions of this large tumor. The arrow in *D* delineates the large focus of subacute hemorrhage in the posterior aspect of the tumor. The arrow in *E* demonstrates elevation and stretching of the proximal (A1) segment of the left anterior cerebral artery by this large intra- and suprasellar mass.

acute clinical event characterized by sudden onset of severe headache, visual loss, and hypotension. More often, however, intratumoral hemorrhage is subclinical and discovered incidentally on MRI (Figs. 5–55B and 5–56A).[201, 243] Hemorrhage occurs even more commonly in patients with prolactinomas who are being treated with bromcriptine.[357]

On CT, macroadenomas often appear as large, homogeneously isodense, rounded midline masses arising out of the sella and insinuating upward to elevate and compress the optic chiasm and overlying third ventricle (Fig. 5–55A).[237] On occasion, a tumor may grow so large as to invaginate the floor and walls of the third ventricle and obstruct the foramen of Monro. Areas of intratumoral necrosis or cystic degeneration appear as hypodensities within the tumor mass, whereas acute or subacute hemorrhage causes focal intratumoral hyperdensity.

Because MRI offers multiplanar imaging capabilities and is not degraded by beam hardening artifacts due to adjacent bone, it is the preferred modality for visualizing the pituitary gland. Pituitary macroadenomas appear hypo-

intense relative to gray matter on T1-weighted images and hyperintense on T2-weighted images (Figs. 5–55B, C and 5–56A).[237] The T2 hyperintensity appears to correlate with softening of the tumor observed at the time of surgical removal and may reflect intratumoral necrosis.[201, 308] Normal pituitary tissue is usually severely compressed downward into the sellar floor by these bulky tumors and cannot be recognized.[201]

After IV administration of a contrast agent, delayed moderate contrast enhancement of the solid portions of the tumor mass appears on both CT and MRI (Figs. 5–55D, E and 5–56B).[174, 201, 235, 237] A major advantage of MRI is the ability to demonstrate the location and status of the internal carotid arteries relative to the tumor. Lateral tumor extension into the cavernous sinus may displace the carotid flow void laterally (Figs. 5–55C and 5–56). Further tumor extension may surround the flow void, indicating the presence of vessel encasement.[68] In contradistinction to meningioma, such encasement by macroadenoma rarely causes arterial constriction or occlusion.

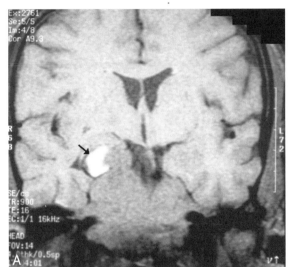
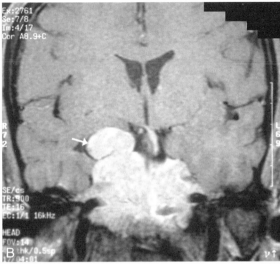

Figure 5–56. Pituitary macroadenoma with intratumoral hemorrhage. *A,* Coronal T1-weighted MR image demonstrates a very large multilobulated well circumscribed homogeneously hypointense tumor widening the sella and extending superiorly and bilaterally, more to the right than to the left. The most superolateral extension of this mass contains a large focal hyperintensity representing late subacute hemorrhage *(arrow).* The pituitary stalk is deviated to the left of the midline by the predominantly right sided tumor. Note that the supraclinoid internal carotid arteries on both sides are compressed and displaced far laterally, as are the medial aspects of both temporal lobes. *B,* Following intravenous administration of gadolinium, an axial T1-weighted image demonstrates diffuse homogeneous contrast enhancement of this multilobulated tumor *(arrow).*

Craniopharyngioma

Craniopharyngiomas are benign, partly cystic, epithelial tumors that occur almost exclusively in the sellar region and are presumed to arise from remnants of Rathke's pouch epithelium.[150] They represent 1.2% to 4.6% of all intracranial tumors but are more common in children, in whom they represent 5% to 10% of intracranial neoplasms.[43] They are most frequently suprasellar in location with an intrasellar component; less commonly (about 20% of cases), they may be entirely suprasellar, and approximately 5% are purely intrasellar.[133, 150]

These tumors have a bimodal age distribution that largely corresponds to two clinicopathologic forms, adamantinomatous and papillary.[150] Approximately two thirds of cases of craniopharyngioma occur in the first two decades of life, mainly between ages 5 and 14 years; the great majority of these are of the adamantinomatous variety.[150, 202, 369] The second age peak is in middle age (40 to 50 years); almost all papillary craniopharyngiomas occur in this group.[76, 150] Craniopharyngioma has no sex predilection.

Craniopharyngiomas are slow growing tumors that extend superiorly and often insinuate into the third ventricle. They may also expand anteriorly under the frontal lobes (30%), posteriorly into the interpeduncular cistern with impingement on and posterior displacement of the ventral margins of the midbrain and upper pons (20%), and laterally into the medial aspect of the middle cranial fossa (20%).[133, 150] The adamantinomatous tumors provoke an intense gliosis in the adjacent brain and become firmly adherent to adjacent brain and vessels. On gross inspection, they have a multilobulated inner aspect with nodules of solid tissue separated by cysts of varying size.[150] The cystic component is usually predominant in the adamantinoma-

tous tumors and much less prominent in the papillary variety.[201] The papillary tumors often involve the third ventricle.[150]

Calcification is present in the solid portions of nearly 90% of adamantinomatous craniopharyngiomas but is much less common in the papillary tumors.[201, 291, 369] The cyst contents have a "machine oil" color and consistency and frequently contain suspended debris with a high cholesterol content.[150] Microscopically, the adamantinomatous tumors consist of broad strands and cords of stratified squamous epithelium with nodules of keratin and dystrophic calcification.[150] In the papillary tumors, sheets of squamous epithelium form papillae with a fibrovascular stroma, but keratin, cholesterol deposits, and calcification are typically lacking.[76, 150]

Like pituitary macroadenomas, these slow growing tumors present clinically most commonly with visual disturbances secondary to compression of the optic chiasm, nerves, or tracts.[150, 201, 369] Endocrine deficiencies are slightly less frequent. Compression of the neurohypophysis leads to diabetes insipidus in up to 15% of children and up to 30% of adults.[150] Symptoms and signs of increased intracranial pressure (headache, nausea, vomiting, papilledema) secondary to third ventricular obstruction are also common presenting findings that may lead to cognitive impairment and personality changes.[150, 201]

On CT, these tumors typically appear as heterogeneously hypodense suprasellar masses with nodular solid areas intermixed with cystic areas of varying size. The cyst contents are more dense than CSF. More than 80% of craniopharyngiomas in children (usually of the adamantinomatous variety) demonstrate nodular and curvilinear calcifications in the solid nodules and in the cyst walls (Fig. 5–57A).[133, 238, 369] Papillary craniopharyngiomas in adults appear more solid and rarely demonstrate calcification.[76]

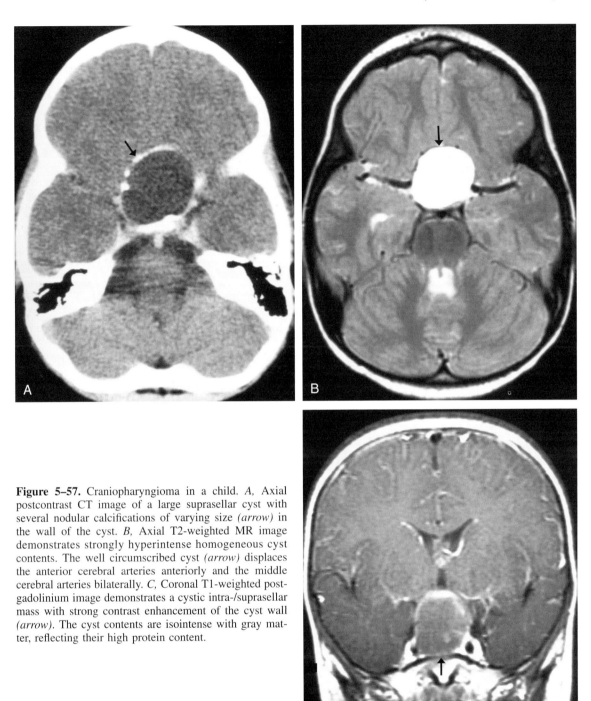

Figure 5–57. Craniopharyngioma in a child. *A,* Axial postcontrast CT image of a large suprasellar cyst with several nodular calcifications of varying size *(arrow)* in the wall of the cyst. *B,* Axial T2-weighted MR image demonstrates strongly hyperintense homogeneous cyst contents. The well circumscribed cyst *(arrow)* displaces the anterior cerebral arteries anteriorly and the middle cerebral arteries bilaterally. *C,* Coronal T1-weighted post-gadolinium image demonstrates a cystic intra-/suprasellar mass with strong contrast enhancement of the cyst wall *(arrow)*. The cyst contents are isointense with gray matter, reflecting their high protein content.

Cysts are found in approximately 50% of papillary tumors versus about 90% of adamantinomatous neoplasms.[291] In contrast to pituitary adenomas, slow growing craniopharyngiomas do not usually enlarge the sella but rather gradually erode the posterior clinoid processes and the upper portion of the dorsum sellae.

The adamantinomatous suprasellar tumors appear as heterogeneous masses of variable intensity on T1-weighted MR images.[201] Areas containing calcification usually appear more hypointense. The cystic components are well margined and vary in signal but are commonly hyperintense relative to gray matter, reflecting high concentration of protein in the cyst contents (Figs. 5–57*C* and 5–58*B, C*).[291] On T2-weighted images, the solid areas vary from hypointense to mildly hyperintense as compared with gray matter, whereas the cysts present a more internally uniform, hyperintense appearance (Figs. 5–57*B* and 5–58*A*).[201] The papillary tumors have a more uniform and homogeneous appearance.[201, 237, 291]

On both CT and MRI, after IV administration of contrast agents, enhancement of the noncalcified solid components of the adamantinomatous tumors and of the solid papillary tumors is typically intense and uniform (Figs. 5–57*C* and 5–58*B, C*).[76, 133, 203, 237, 291, 369]

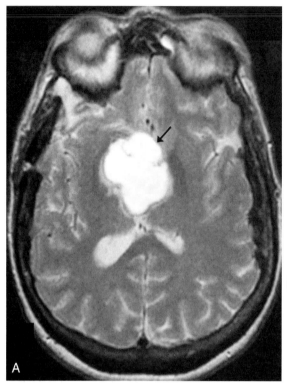

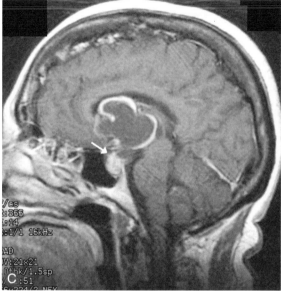

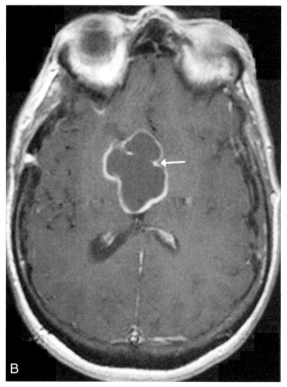

Figure 5–58. Craniopharyngioma in an adult. *A,* Axial T2-weighted MR image demonstrates a multilobulated multicystic hyperintense midline tumor *(arrow)* with irregular margins that has insinuated itself between the basal ganglia of the two cerebral hemispheres. The tumor extends more to the right than to the left of the midline, and the right globus pallidus is compressed and displaced laterally. The cyst contents are more hyperintense than the solid tumor rim in this papillary tumor. Axial *(B)* and right parasagittal *(C)* T1-weighted images following intravenous gadolinium demonstrate contrast enhancement of the solid tumor rim *(arrow).* The cyst contents are hyperintense relative to cerebrospinal fluid, reflecting their high protein content. On the sagittal image, note that this cystic tumor extends into and nearly obliterates the third ventricle with its superior margin projecting into the floor of the right lateral ventricle; posteroinferiorly, the tumor projects into the interpeduncular cistern and displaces the midbrain posteriorly.

Both adamantinomatous and papillary craniopharyngiomas are managed surgically. Ten-year recurrence free survival rates vary from 64% to 96%.[76, 150] The extent of surgical resection is the most important factor in predicting recurrence; because of the intense gliotic reaction provoked by the tumor as it impinges on adjacent brain and the adhesion of large tumors to vascular structures in the suprasellar region, incomplete surgical resection remains a significant problem, especially in tumors larger than 5 cm in diameter.[150]

Rathke Cleft Cyst

Both Rathke cleft cysts and craniopharyngiomas are considered to arise from embryonic rests of Rathke's pouch.[290] In normal embryonic development, Rathke's pouch regresses by the sixth week of gestation into a narrow cleft. Persistence and enlargement of that cleft is believed to be the cause of Rathke cleft cysts, which are lined by cuboidal or columnar epithelium and are usually located in the pars intermedia between the anterior lobe (adenohypophysis) and posterior lobe (neurohypophysis) of the pituitary gland.[97]

Rathke cleft cysts are typically small (2 to 10 mm), thin-walled, smoothly marginated intrapituitary cysts with mucinous contents.[97] Less commonly, the contents may be serous.[74] They are usually asymptomatic and found incidentally on MRI or at autopsy. In an unselected series of 1000 cases, incidental Rathke cleft cysts were found in 11.3%.[327] Nearly 90% occur in the center of the pituitary gland.[327] Larger cysts may be both intrasellar and suprasellar and may become symptomatic if they compress the pituitary gland, pituitary stalk, or optic chiasm, but such compression is unusual. They are found in patients in all age groups but are usually identified in adults. A 2:1 to 3:1 female predominance has been reported,[285] but this figure may reflect selection bias, because more women than men undergo pituitary imaging, mainly for menstrual problems, hyperprolactinemia, and infertility.

On CT, 75% of Rathke cleft cysts appear as round, well-marginated, hypodense intrapituitary lesions.[285] The density of the cyst likely reflects the concentration of mucoprotein in the cyst contents. Calcification is not found in these cysts.[201, 237] On MRI also, they appear discrete and sharply marginated. On T1-weighted images, approximately two thirds of Rathke cleft cysts appear hyperintense and one third hypointense relative to gray matter (Fig. 5–59B)[285]; this variance is also likely related to the protein content of the cyst fluid. On T2-weighted MR images, approximately 50% exhibit moderate to strong hyperintensity relative to gray matter (Fig. 5–59A), another 25% appear isointense, and a like number are hypointense.[285] After IV administration of contrast agent, Rathke cleft cyst does not enhance on either CT or MRI, although the surrounding compressed pituitary tissue may exhibit rimlike enhancement.[238]

Tumors of the Neurohypophysis

Neoplasms arising in the posterior lobe of the pituitary gland or the pituitary stalk are very uncommon.

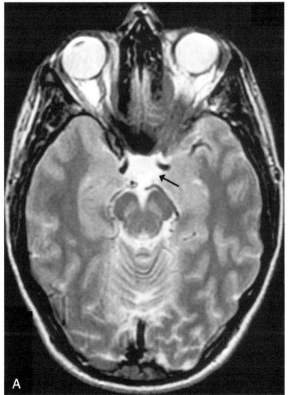
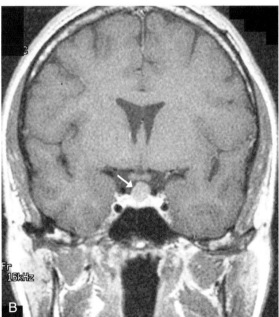

Figure 5–59. Rathke cleft cyst. Axial T2-weighted *(A)* and coronal postgadolinium T1-weighted *(B)* images demonstrate a small smoothly marginated cystic mass *(arrows)* within and projecting above the pituitary gland. The cyst appears slightly hyperintense relative to gray matter on both T1-weighting *(B)* and T2-weighting *(A)*. There is no contrast enhancement of its contents or margins.

Granular cell tumor of the neurohypophysis (also known as choristoma or pituicytoma) is a rarely occurring, benign, slow growing intrasellar or suprasellar mass that originates within the posterior pituitary or the pituitary stalk and presents as a well defined rounded mass composed of densely packed nests of large cells with a granular cytoplasm.[343] These tumors, considered to be of neural crest or glial origin, exhibit intense immunoreactivity for the S-100 tumor marker.[124] Like many intrasellar and suprasellar neoplasms, granular cell tumors usually develop insidiously and present with hormonal and visual disturbances secondary to compression of normal pituitary and optic pathway structures. On imaging studies, they appear as well circumscribed round masses within the posterior pituitary or on the posterior aspect of the pituitary stalk. The tumors are isodense with brain on CT and isointense with gray matter on T1- and T2-weighted MR images.[69, 201, 237] The posterior pituitary "bright spot" on T1-weighted images is effaced or absent.[343] Granular cell tumors are described as richly vascular and demonstrate strong contrast enhancement.[238, 343]

Langerhans cell histiocytosis involves the sellar region as a component of the Hand-Schüller-Christian syndrome; granulomas may be found in the pituitary stalk, hypothalamus, or both in association with destruction of the bony margins of the sella (see above). Imaging studies may demonstrate thickening and contrast enhancement of these structures (see Fig. 5–47).[334]

Chordoma

Chordomas are histologically benign neoplasms derived from remnants of the embryonic notochord. Despite their benign histology, they are locally invasive and destructive, behaving clinically like low grade malignancies.[132] These tumors arise in or near the midline and occur most commonly at the proximal (clivus-basisphenoid) and distal (sacrum) ends of the notochord. Approximately 40% of chordomas arise in the basisphenoid region.[70] They are uncommon tumors, representing less than 0.2% of all intracranial neoplasms.[132] Chordomas can present clinically in any age group, but their peak incidence is in patients between 20 and 50 years, and less than 5% are identified in children.[70, 132]

Chordomas arising in the upper clivus expand slowly and inexorably in all directions, infiltrating and eroding the surrounding bone. Posterior extension leads to the presence of a bulky lobulated mass in the prepontine cistern, compressing and displacing (but not invading) the pons and midbrain posteriorly. Anterior extension may manifest as a nasopharyngeal mass.[77, 201] Upward growth causes destruction of the walls of the sella with extension of tumor into and above the sella. Tumor infiltration into the cavernous sinuses with encasement of arteries and nerves is common. Sequestra of intratumoral necrotic bone and calcification and foci of intratumoral hemorrhage are common findings.[77, 132, 201] Histologically, chordoma consists of clusters of large vacuolated physaliferous (Greek for "bubble-bearing") cells interspersed with abundant extracellular mucinous material and separated into lobules by fibrous septa.[70, 132]

The clinical presentation of this slowly expanding neoplasm is insidious and depends on its precise location. The majority of patients present with head or neck pain and cranial nerve deficits.[132] The most common presenting complaint is diplopia, noted in 60% to 90% of cases.[107] Upward extension of chordoma causes visual disturbances and hypopituitarism, whereas posterior extension leads to extraocular nerve palsies.[201] Hearing loss and dysphagia are relatively common presenting findings that correlate with downward and anterior spread of tumor.

CT of clival chordoma demonstrates irregularly marginated erosion and destruction of the bony clivus with heterogeneous attenuation of the associated intraosseous and extraosseous lobulated soft tissue mass.[132] The heterogeneity is due to the presence of hyperdense intratumoral bony sequestra and calcifications intermixed with areas of hypodensity and hyperdensity secondary to cystlike mucinous collections as well as intratumoral hemorrhage.[77] On T1-weighted MR images, the infiltrating tumor appears isointense with gray matter in 75% of patients and mildly hypointense in the remaining 25% (Fig. 5–60A, C). In either case, the tumor presents a striking contrast to the diffusely hyperintense T1 signal of the adjacent normal marrow fat of the clivus.[201, 319] On T2-weighted images, chordoma demonstrates moderate heterogeneity of signal with areas of hyperintensity intermixed with linear strands of hypointensity (Fig. 5–60B).[201, 216, 319] After IV administration of contrast material, varying and heterogeneous contrast enhancement is seen within the tumor mass on both CT and MRI (Fig. 5–60C).[93]

Differentiation of chordoma from *chondrosarcoma*, both on imaging and gross and microscopic examination, may be very difficult.[77, 132] There is considerable overlap of both imaging and histological appearances between these two tumors. Tumor location may be of limited help in this differentiation; chordoma arises in or near the midline, whereas the majority of chondrosarcomas of the skull base tend to arise laterally in or near the petroclival junction. However, chondrosarcomas often spread medially into the clivus and posteriorly into the cerebellopontine angle, extending into the ipsilateral cavernous sinus and encasing the arteries of the circle of Willis in a manner similar to chordoma.[93] Immunohistochemical studies also aid in this differentiation; chordoma is of neural crest origin and stains positively for epithelial membrane antigen (EMA) and cytokeratin, but chondrosarcoma, being of mesodermal origin, does not take up these markers.[283]

Other neoplasms occurring in or metastasizing to the sellar region, including meningiomas, gliomas of the optic pathways, epidermoid tumors, germ cell tumors, and carcinomatous metastases, are considered elsewhere in this chapter.

Metastatic Tumors

Hematogenous metastases from extracranial primary malignant neoplasms may involve the skull, the dura, the leptomeninges, or the brain parenchyma. In adults, metastasis to the brain is most common.

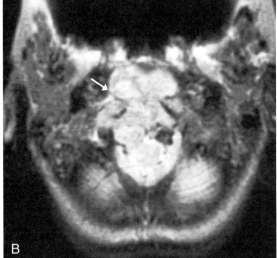

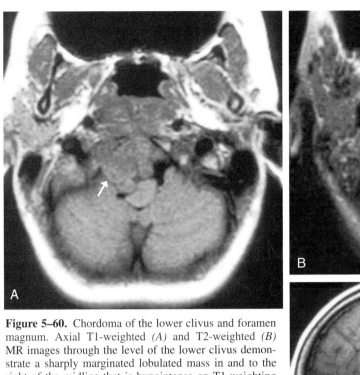

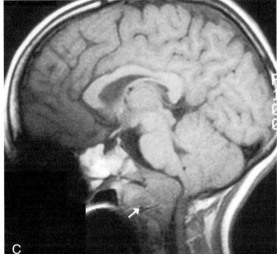

Figure 5–60. Chordoma of the lower clivus and foramen magnum. Axial T1-weighted *(A)* and T2-weighted *(B)* MR images through the level of the lower clivus demonstrate a sharply marginated lobulated mass in and to the right of the midline that is hypointense on T1-weighting and hyperintense on T2-weighting and has destroyed the lower clivus, infiltrating anteriorly into the longus colli muscles *(arrow in B)* and extending posteriorly into the premedullary cistern *(arrow in A)*, displacing the medulla posteriorly and indenting its right ventrolateral margin. In *(B)*, note that the tumor has encased the vertebral arteries bilaterally. *C*, Sagittal T1-weighted postgadolinium image demonstrates faint homogeneous contrast enhancement of this extensive tumor that presents anteriorly as a submucosal nasopharyngeal mass *(arrow)* and projects posteriorly to compress the medulla and upper cervical spinal cord against the posterior margin of the foramen magnum.

Metastases to the Brain

More than 30% of intracranial tumors detected in a multi-institutional prospective CT study were metastatic malignancies.[16] Autopsy studies have demonstrated the presence of intracranial metastasis in approximately 25% of patients with cancer.[266] The incidence of intracranial metastasis is rising because of (1) the wider availability and greater refinement of cross-sectional diagnostic imaging and (2) continuing improvements in other diagnostic and treatment modalities with resultant prolonged survival of patients with systemic tumors.[230, 263]

The most common sources of intracranial metastasis, in order of decreasing frequency, are carcinomas of the lung and breast, malignant melanoma, and carcinomas of the kidney and gastrointestinal tract.[10, 230, 268, 286] Certain primary malignancies, particularly bronchogenic carcinoma,[52, 321, 324] carcinoma of the breast,[231, 322] choriocarcinoma,[286] and melanoma,[41, 116] have a notable propensity to metastasize to the brain. Between 30% and 65% of patients with carcinoma of the lung exhibit cerebral metastases at autopsy, many of which were not clinically evident during life.[154, 286, 321, 353]

The most common cause of death in patients with melanoma is metastasis to the brain; autopsy studies reveal cerebral metastases in up to 90% of patients with melanoma.[41]

Cerebral metastases occur most frequently at the junction of cortex and underlying white matter,[268] a finding likely related to obstruction by circulating tumor cell emboli of the penetrating arteries, which abruptly narrow as they enter the subcortical white matter.[87, 230, 286] Eighty percent of brain metastases are located in the arterial distribution zones of the cerebral hemispheres, with 3% in the basal ganglia and 15% in the cerebellum.[230] A notable departure from this pattern occurs in the case of mucinous adenocarcinomas of gastrointestinal origin; although these tumors represent only 5% of intracranial metastases, approximately 50% occur in the posterior fossa, mainly in the cerebellum.[87] Metastasis to the cerebellum occurs mainly at the junction of the superior and inferior cerebellar artery distributions.[230]

Differentiation between solitary and multiple cerebral metastases has a major impact on the further management of the patient. The relative ratio of solitary-to-multifocal cerebral metastases in autopsy series has been reported as approximately 50:50.[230] However, experience with advances in diagnostic imaging, particularly with contrast enhanced MRI, suggests that about 70% of patients with cerebral metastasis demonstrate more than one lesion.[10, 153, 238]

On gross inspection, small metastases are usually discrete, spherical, well circumscribed tumors (Fig. 5–61).[230] However, microscopic examination often reveals tumor cell infiltration into the adjacent surrounding normal tissue with angioneogenesis, perivascular invasion, and reactive gliosis.[230, 286] Histologically, metastases typically recapitulate the pattern of the tumor of origin.[153] These are markedly malignant neoplasms with high rates of mitotic activity.[153] Edema of the adjacent white matter is often disproportionately extensive in comparison with the small size of the tumor and may spread along white matter fiber tracts for a considerable distance.[10, 230, 286, 321] As the tumor implant grows, it penetrates and distorts the surrounding gray and white matter. Further growth is typically associated with central necrosis like that seen in glioblastoma, leaving recognizable tumor tissue only at the periphery and around the blood vessels.[230] Intratumoral hemorrhage is found in about 20% of cerebral metastases, notably in melanomas (Fig. 5–62), choriocarcinomas, and carcinomas of the lung, kidney, and thyroid.[10, 205]

Although metastases to the CNS can occur in all age groups, more than 75% are found in older patients. The age-specific incidence rises steeply after age 45 years.[27, 256] Approximately 30% of patients with cerebral metastases are asymptomatic at the time of initial diagnosis—that is, the tumors are discovered incidentally during evaluation for other causes (e.g., head trauma) or are found on screening imaging surveys of patients who have primary tumors with a known high incidence of hematogenous seeding to the brain.[27] When symptoms occur, they are usually of insidious onset and slow progression and relate either to increased intracranial pressure or to localized mass effect; they include headache (in approximately 50%), nausea and vomiting, mental status or behavioral change, progressive neurologic deficit, and seizures. These symptoms do not differ from those caused by primary gliomas in the same area.[27]

Mean survival time after pathologic confirmation of the diagnosis of cerebral metastasis is 1 to 3 months.[30] Despite advances in surgery, irradiation, and chemotherapy, the prognosis for patients with cerebral metastases from extracranial primary malignant neoplasms has only minimally improved, with survival in the range of 3 to 6 months.[58] When only a solitary parenchymal lesion of the brain can be identified and the extent of the disease in other organs is not progressing, surgical excision of the cerebral metastasis correlates with improvement in both quality and length of life.[313]

The appearance of hematogenous cerebral metastasis on noncontrast CT scans corresponds closely to the gross pathologic changes already described. Small tumors appear as rounded homogeneously isodense or, less commonly, slightly hyperdense nodules relative to adjacent normal brain.[5, 10, 52, 153, 268] The isodense lesions merge imperceptibly with the adjacent cortex and may be detected only when they distort the inner margin of the cortex. The hyperdense nodules typically represent small round cell tumors or other tumors with high nuclear-to-cytoplasmic ratios.[153] However, most metastases from melanoma and choriocarcinoma as well as some metastases from carcinomas of the thyroid and kidney appear hyperdense because of hemorrhage within the tumor (Fig. 5–62A). Some small lesions and virtually all large metastases have undergone central necrosis by the time they are detected and appear as ringlike masses with central lucency and a peripheral isodense or slightly hyperdense rim of irregular thickness.[268] As already noted, edema (hypodensity) of the surrounding white matter is usually extensive and produces considerable mass effect (see Fig. 5–62). Calcification is rarely found in association with intracerebral metastases because of their rapid growth; however, it may occasionally be found in metastases originating from carcinoma of the breast or gastrointestinal tract.[87]

Contrast enhancement is virtually universal in these tumors. Less than 4% of the metastases in a multiinstitutional prospective CT study did not demonstrate contrast enhancement of the viable peripheral tumor rim (in lesions with central necrosis) or of the entire tumor (in small solid lesions of homogeneous density).[268] The enhancement is typically intense and fairly uniform within viable portions of the neoplasm, enabling clear separation of small tumor foci that are isodense on precontrast CT images from surrounding edema. The use of a double dose of iodinated contrast agent in combination with delayed image acquisi-

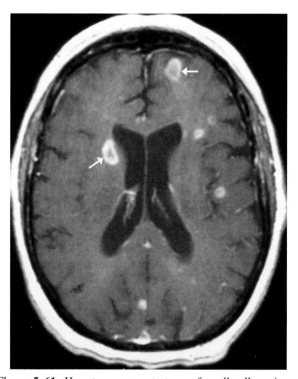

Figure 5–61. Hematogenous metastases of small cell carcinoma of the lung to the brain. Axial T1-weighted postgadolinium image demonstrates multiple contrast enhancing ring and ovoid lesions of varying size *(arrows)* at the junction of gray and white matter in both cerebral hemispheres. Although numerous, these tumors are relatively small and have not yet provoked grossly evident surrounding white matter edema.

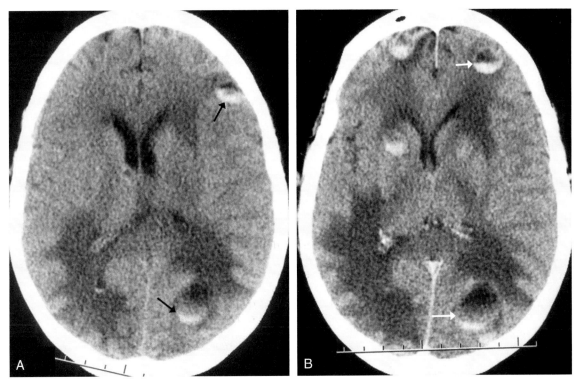

Figure 5–62. Hematogenous metastases of melanoma to the brain with intratumoral hemorrhage. *A,* An axial noncontrast CT image demonstrates at least four foci of varying size located at gray/white junctions in both cerebral hemispheres. All four lesions contain blood/fluid levels *(arrows)* indicating the presence of intratumoral hemorrhage. The lesions in the frontoparietal regions bilaterally and the left deep frontal area have provoked considerable surrounding edema. *B,* An axial CT image at an adjacent level following intravenous contrast injection demonstrates faint ringlike contrast enhancement of the margins of several of these tumors *(arrows).*

tion increases the conspicuity of small tumor foci that might otherwise be overlooked and further improves both the sensitivity and the specificity of the examination.[82, 294]

Definitive preoperative differentiation of metastasis from glioblastoma with CT is often not possible in an individual case, even though larger metastases generally retain a spherical or ovoid outline and extensive glioblastomas most commonly have much more irregular lobulated configurations and exhibit greater heterogeneity of density on contrast enhanced images. Definitive differentiation of multiple metastases from multiple pyogenic cerebral abscesses also is not usually possible with CT; although virtually all abscesses demonstrate uniformity and smoothness of contrast enhancing wall thickness, so may many small metastases. Extensive surrounding edema is also characteristic of both processes.

As noted previously, CT with contrast injection has been used for the preoperative screening evaluation of patients with carcinoma of the lung,[53] malignant melanoma,[116] and choriocarcinoma who have no cerebral symptoms or neurologic deficit. In one study of individuals without clinical evidence of brain involvement, cerebral metastases were found on CT in 40% of patients with adenocarcinoma of the lung and 11% of patients with oat cell carcinoma of the lung[324]; in another study, 11% of patients with melanoma were found on CT to have metastatic intracranial lesions.[116] Demonstration of unsuspected cerebral metastases in such patients may eliminate unnecessary surgery and permit earlier institution of more appropriate forms of treatment.

On evaluation with MRI, most intracerebral metastatic lesions have prolonged relaxation times (diminished signal on T1-weighted images and increased signal on T2-weighted images compared with normal brain).[10] As with CT, differentiation of the lesion or lesions from surrounding white matter edema is often problematic on noncontrast images. Additionally, signal intensity of the tumor can be highly variable, depending on the tumor constituents; the signal characteristics in a given metastasis depend on the cellularity of the lesion, the extent of intratumoral necrosis, the presence and age of hemorrhage, the presence and extent of calcification, and the severity of surrounding edema.[8–10, 153] Melanoma has a somewhat characteristic appearance if there has not been previous hemorrhage; the lesion is hyperintense on T1-weighted images and isointense with brain on T2-weighted images, most likely because of the free radical content of the melanin.[8, 9] Metastases from mucinous adenocarcinomas of gastrointestinal origin often appear hypointense on T2-weighted images because of the high protein content of the mucin.[10] If intratumoral hemorrhage has occurred, the signal pattern is determined by the nature of the blood degradation products, i.e., the age of the hemorrhage.[9, 123]

Contrast enhanced MRI has proven even more sensitive than contrast enhanced CT for detection of intracranial metastatic disease.[8, 140, 288] Multiplanar T1-weighted MR images obtained after IV administration of gadolinium, usually in a dose of 0.1 mmol per kg of body weight, are currently the most sensitive method for evaluation of intracranial metastatic disease.[10, 238] As on CT, contrast enhancement on MRI allows the reader to distinguish the gross margins of the metastasis from the surrounding edema (see Fig. 5–61), a differentiation not often permitted on precontrast T1- or T2-weighted MR images.

Several investigators have suggested that higher doses of gadolinium (0.2 to 0.3 mmol/kg) further improve the sensitivity of this examination for the detection of additional lesions, although (unlike CT) delayed MR images do not increase the contrast between the tumor and the surrounding brain.[135, 359] In patients with known extracranial primary malignancy in whom standard dose contrast enhanced MRI of the brain appears to demonstrate a solitary parenchymal enhancing metastasis, it would seem appropriate and cost effective to repeat the postcontrast images with a higher dose of gadolinium, so as to more conclusively exclude the possibility of more metastases before surgical resection of the apparent solitary lesion is undertaken.

Metastases to the Skull and Intracranial Dura

Metastasis to the cranial vault or the base of the skull is associated with intracranial metastasis in 5% to 10% of cases.[139, 286] Hematogenous metastasis to the calvarial diploë often leads to destruction of the internal and external tables and extension of tumor into the adjacent epidural space. In one autopsy series of patients with primary extracranial malignancy and intracranial metastasis, 18% demonstrated dural involvement (including epidural or subdural neoplasm) as the only site of intracranial metastasis.[11, 266] Occasionally, dural metastasis may occur without an associated calvarial lesion, either as a nodular plaquelike focus or as a more extensive diffuse thickening of the dura.[82, 230] Epidural or dural metastasis is most often secondary to carcinoma of the breast, lymphoma, carcinoma of the prostate, and neuroblastoma.[266] Other common sources are carcinomas of the lung and kidney.[11] Although the dura is usually an effective barrier to further deep invasion, spread of tumor in the epidural space with nodular or bandlike soft tissue thickening is common. Symptoms usually relate to compression of the underlying brain parenchyma.[11]

Irregularly marginated focal osseous destruction of the bony calvaria or the skull base caused by metastasis to the diploë or marrow can be best defined on noncontrast CT scans obtained through the use of a bone targeting algorithm with wide window and high center settings.[238] Destruction of the inner table of the skull allows extension of tumor into the intracranial epidural space, which can be demonstrated on CT scans obtained after IV administration of iodinated contrast medium with the use of a soft tissue algorithm and appropriate ("subdural window") soft tissue window and center settings. These tumors typically demonstrate intense contrast enhancement, but recognition of the enhancing biconvex epidural tumor mass can be masked by the adjacent bone unless relatively wide window and high center settings are employed.

In current practice, early detection of small metastases in the diploë or in the dura can best be accomplished by utilizing T1-weighted MR images both before and after IV administration of gadolinium.[11] Small foci of intradiploic

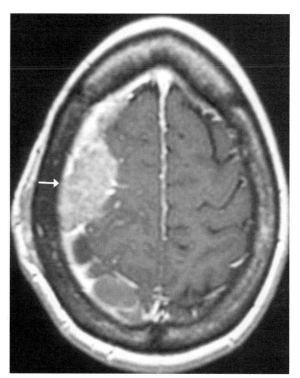

Figure 5–63. Diffuse pachymeningeal and calvarial metastasis from carcinoma of the breast. Axial T1-weighted postgadolinium MR image demonstrates diffuse nodular and bandlike contrast enhanced thickening of the dura over the high right frontoparietal convexity. The process extends into the falx and across the midline into the high left frontal convexity dura. Several ovoid and plaquelike masses in the right frontoparietal convexity represent outcroppings of dural metastasis *(arrow)* and compress the underlying frontal and parietal lobes with resultant effacement of the sulci. Note the loss of normal fatty marrow signal in the diploë of the overlying right parietal bone, indicating the presence of calvarial tumor involvement. Immediately posterior and lateral to the arrow is a focal plaque of tumor extension into the subgaleal space, with elevation of the overlying subcutaneous fat of the scalp.

metastasis appear hypointense on noncontrast T1-weighted images and differ sharply from the adjacent hyperintense fatty marrow in the diploic space (Fig. 5–63). Postgadolinium T1-weighted images obtained with fat suppression typically demonstrate intense contrast enhancement of tumor in the epidural space or dura, which appears as nodular or curvilinear, bandlike thickening (see Fig 5–63); the underlying cerebral cortex is displaced inward, and (unlike leptomeningeal metastasis) the enhancing tumor does not extend into the cerebral sulci.[317] The findings may simulate those of meningioma, but epidural or dural metastasis typically appears hyperintense to adjacent cerebral cortex on T2-weighted images, whereas meningioma is nearly isointense with cortex on this pulsing sequence.[11, 238, 317]

Leptomeningeal Metastasis (Leptomeningeal Carcinomatosis)

Hematogenous metastasis from primary extracranial malignant tumors may occur directly to the meninges, but leptomeningeal carcinomatosis may also result from parenchymal neoplasm that breaches either the ependymal lining of the ventricles or the pia overlying the cortex, with seeding of tumor cells into the CSF and subsequent spread by implantation on meningeal surfaces.[170, 286] These metastases tend to occur most commonly in the basal cisterns and in areas of relative CSF stasis.[317] The malignant infiltrate induces a reactive inflammatory response of the leptomeninges, and communicating hydrocephalus may develop as a result of obstruction of the basal cisterns or the pacchionian granulations.[11, 286] Sources include most primary parenchymal neoplasms of the brain, even relatively low grade gliomas,[64] as well as carcinomas of the breast, lung, and gastrointestinal tract, melanoma, lymphoma, and leukemias, notably acute lymphatic leukemia.[230, 286, 317] Of the secondary causes, carcinomas of the breast and lung are most common; in as many as 50% of patients with small cell carcinoma of the lung, leptomeningeal metastasis may be found at autopsy.[317]

Leptomeningeal metastasis is nearly always symptomatic, and the simultaneous presentation of signs and symptoms in widely scattered areas of the CNS is typical.[344] Headache is the most common initial complaint, occurring in 50% of patients, and weakness is found on clinical examination in 80%.[344] Cranial nerve palsies are presenting complaints in 40% of patients, and lethargy and confusion are found in 20%.[344] Although on occasion, the diagnosis of leptomeningeal metastasis may be established before the primary tumor becomes symptomatic, the interval between primary diagnosis of neoplasm and diagnosis of leptomeningeal involvement is typically between 6 months and 3 years; at this stage, most patients also have evidence of metastatic disease outside the CNS.[317] The diagnosis is usually established by lumbar puncture and microscopic examination of the CSF; abnormal cytologic results are obtained in approximately 50% of patients on the initial analysis and in 95% after six lumbar punctures.[344] Supporting findings include elevation of CSF pressure above 160 mm Hg, increase in protein concentration above 20 gm/L, and elevated white blood cell count (usually lymphocytes), all of which are found in at least one half of patients.[224]

Although CT has proved highly sensitive for the detection of cerebral parenchymal metastases, leptomeningeal metastasis has been demonstrated on contrast enhanced CT images in less than a third of patients with cytologic evidence of CSF seeding.[16, 116, 188] The sensitivity of MRI without and with paramagnetic contrast enhancement for detection of leptomeningeal metastasis appears to be approximately twice that of CT.[118, 317, 318, 358] MRI findings strongly suggestive of leptomeningeal metastasis include (1) nodular or plaquelike thick curvilinear hyperintensity of the involved subarachnoid cisterns and spaces on FLAIR images and (2) homogeneous contrast enhancement on postcontrast T1-weighted images that diffusely involves one or more subarachnoid cisterns, coats the surfaces of the adjacent brain parenchyma, and extends into the sulci (Fig. 5–64).[11, 118, 317, 358] The leptomeningeal tumor may also invade the underlying brain parenchyma and infiltrate the perivascular spaces surrounding the penetrating vessels.[317] The greater sensitivity of MRI for detecting leptomeningeal tumor spread has established this technique as the diagnos-

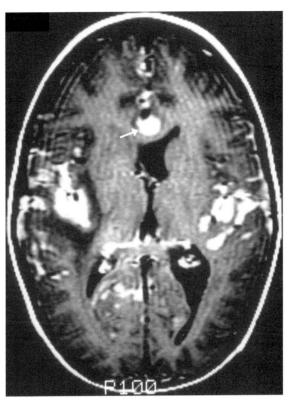

Figure 5–64. Leptomeningeal metastasis/carcinomatosis from carcinoma of the breast. Axial T1-weighted postgadolinium MR image. Numerous and diffuse nodular foci of leptomeningeal thickening with intense contrast enhancement are seen in the sylvian fissures, over the convexity surfaces, and in the convexity and parasagittal sulci bilaterally. A large nodule fills the pericallosal sulcus anteriorly *(arrow)*. There is associated mass effect in the right frontotemporal region with resultant compression of the frontal horn of the right lateral ventricle and slight displacement of the third ventricle to the left of the midline.

tic modality of choice for the evaluation of possible leptomeningeal carcinomatosis.[11]

The differential diagnosis of leptomeningeal contrast enhancement includes bacterial and fungal meningitis, sarcoid (see Fig. 5–54), and postoperative inflammatory changes in the meninges.[11, 118, 258, 317] On the basis of imaging alone, definitive differentiation of tumor from inflammation or infection is not possible. Local or diffuse meningeal contrast enhancement at the site of previous craniotomy or at the site of insertion of a ventriculostomy shunt catheter reflects an inflammatory response of the traumatized dura and leptomeninges with eventual fibrosis.[146] Nodularity of the contrast enhancing tissue may favor neoplastic over inflammatory processes, but by no means is this true in all cases.[146, 258, 317]

References

1. Abdullah ND, Mathews VP: Contrast issues in brain tumor imaging. Neuroimaging Clin North Am 9:733–749, 1999.
2. Ahmadi H, Larsson EM, Jinkins JR: Normal pituitary gland: Coronal MR imaging of infundibular tilt. Radiology 177:389–392, 1990.
3. Albright AL, Guthkelch AN, Packer RJ, et al: Prognostic factors in pediatric brain-stem gliomas. J Neurosurg 65:751–755, 1986.
4. Alshail E, Rutka JT, Becker LE, et al: Optic chiasmatic-hypothalamic glioma. Brain Pathol 7:799–806, 1997.

5. Amundsen P, Dugstad G, Syvertsen AH: The reliability of computer tomography for the diagnosis and differential diagnosis of meningiomas, gliomas, and brain metastases. Acta Neurochirurg 41:177–190, 1978.

6. Aoki S, Barkovich AJ, Nishimura K, et al: Neurofibromatosis types I and II: Cranial MR findings. Radiology 172:527–534, 1989.

7. Armington WG, Osborne AG, Cubberly DA, et al: Supratentorial ependymoma: CT appearance. Radiology 157:367–372, 1985.

8. Atlas SW: Adult supratentorial tumors. Semin Roentgenol 25:130–154, 1990.

9. Atlas SW, Grossman RI, Gomori JM, et al: Hemorrhagic intracranial malignant neoplasms: Spin-echo MRI. Radiology 164:71–77, 1987.

10. Atlas SW, Lavi E, Fisher PG: Intraaxial brain tumors. In Atlas SW (ed): Magnetic Resonance Imaging of the Brain and Spine, 3rd ed. Philadelphia, Lippincott Williams & Wilkins, 2002, pp 565–693.

11. Atlas SW, Lavi E, Goldberg HI: Extraaxial brain tumors. In Atlas SW (ed): Magnetic Resonance Imaging of the Brain and Spine, 3rd ed. Philadelphia, Lippincott Williams & Wilkins, 2002, pp 695–772.

12. Atlas SW, Thulborn KR: Intracranial hemorrhage. In Atlas SW (ed): Magnetic Resonance Imaging of the Brain and Spine, 3rd ed. Philadelphia, Lippincott Williams & Wilkins, 2002, pp 773–832.

13. Baker HL Jr: The impact of computed tomography on neuroradiologic practice. Radiology 116:637–640, 1975.

14. Baker HL Jr, Campbell JK, Houser OW, et al: Computer assisted tomography of the head: An early evaluation. Mayo Clin Proc 49:17–27, 1974.

15. Baker HL Jr, Campbell JK, Houser OW, et al: Early experience with the EMI scanner for the study of the brain. Radiology 116:327–333, 1975.

16. Baker HL Jr, Houser OW, Campbell JK: National Cancer Institute study: Evaluation of computed tomography in the diagnosis of intracranial neoplasms. I: Overall results. Radiology 136:91–96, 1980.

17. Barker FG 2nd, Chang SM, Valk PE, et al: 18-Fluorodeoxyglucose uptake and survival of patients with suspected recurrent malignant glioma. Cancer 79:115–126, 1997.

18. Barkovich AJ: Brain tumors of childhood. In Pediatric Neuroimaging, 2nd ed. New York, Raven Press, 1995, pp 321–437.

19. Barkovich AJ: Germ cell tumors. In Pediatric Neuroimaging, 2nd ed. New York, Raven Press, 1995, pp 397–403.

20. Barnard R, Geddes J: The incidence of multifocal cerebral gliomas: A histologic study of large hemispheric sections. Cancer 60:1519–1531, 1987.

21. Barnard RO, Scott T: Patterns of proliferation in cerebral lymphoreticular tumors. Acta Neuropathol (Suppl vi):125–130, 1975.

22. Barnes PD, Kupsky WJ, Strand RD: Cranial and intracranial tumors. In Wolpert SM, Barnes PD (eds): MRI in Pediatric Neuroradiology. St. Louis, Mosby-Year Book, 1992, pp 204–298.

23. Bartscher IM, Skageberg G, Geijer B, et al: Proton MR spectroscopy and preoperative diagnostic accuracy: An evaluation of intracranial mass lesions characterized by stereotaxic biopsy findings. AJNR Am J Neuroradiol 21:84–93, 2000.

24. Batzdorf U, Malamud N: The problem of multicentric gliomas. J Neurosurg 20:122–136, 1963.

25. Becker LE: Pathology of pediatric brain tumors. Neuroimaging Clin North Am 9:671–690, 1999.

26. Beges C, Revel MP, Gaston A, et al: Trigeminal neuromas: Assessment of MRI and CT. Neuroradiol 34:179–183, 1992.

27. Bentson JR, Steckel RJ, Kagan AR: Diagnostic imaging in clinical cancer management: Brain metastases. Invest Radiol 23:335–341, 1988.

28. Bilaniuk LT, Zimmerman RA, Littman P, et al: Computed tomography of brain stem gliomas in children. Radiology 134:89–95, 1980.

29. Bilaniuk LT: Adult infratentorial tumors. Semin Roentgenol 25:155–173, 1990.

30. Bindal RK, Sawaya R, Leavens ME, et al: Surgical treatment of multiple brain metastases. J Neurosurg 79:210–216, 1993.

31. Black PM: Brain tumors. N Engl J Med 324:1471–1476, 1555–1564, 1991.

32. Bohling P, Plate KH, Haltio MJ, et al: Von Hippel-Lindau disease and capillary hemangioblastoma. In Kleihues P, Cavenee WK (eds): Pathology and Genetics of Tumours of the Nervous System. Lyon, International Agency for Research on Cancer, 2000, pp 223–226.

33. Bolen JW Jr, Lipper MH, Caccamo D: Intraventricular central neurocytoma: CT and MR findings. J Comput Assist Tomogr 13:495–497, 1989.

34. Bouffet E, Doz F, Demaille MC, et al: Improving survival in recurrent medulloblastoma: Earlier detection, better treatment or still an impasse? Br J Cancer 77:1321–1326, 1998.

35. Brant-Zawadzki M: Multiple sclerosis and its imitators. In Huckman MS (ed): Neuroradiology Categorical Course Syllabus. Detroit, American Roentgen Ray Society, 1992, pp 229–232.

36. Brant-Zawadzki M, Badami JP, Mills CM, et al: Primary intracranial tumour imaging: A comparison of magnetic resonance and CT. Radiology 150:435–440, 1984.

37. Brant-Zawadzki M, Norman D, Newton TH, et al: Magnetic resonance of the brain: The optimal screening technique. Radiology 152:71–77, 1984.

38. Braun IF, Chambers E, Leeds NE, et al: The value of unenhanced scans in differentiating lesions producing ring enhancement. Am J Neuroradiol 3:643–647, 1982.

39. Brooks RA, DiChiro G: Beam hardening in x-ray reconstructive tomography. Phys Med Biol 21:390–398, 1976.

40. Buetow MP, Buetow PC, Smirniotopoulos JG: Typical, atypical and misleading features in meningioma. Radiographics 11:1087–1106, 1991.

41. Bullard DE, Cox EB, Seigler HF: Central nervous system metastases in malignant melanoma. Neurosurgery 8:26–30, 1981.

42. Bullard DE, Rawlings CE III, Phillips B, et al: Oligodendroglioma: An analysis of the value of radiation therapy. Cancer 60:2179–2188, 1987.

43. Bunin GR, Surawicz TS, Witman PA, et al: The descriptive epidemiology of craniopharyngioma. J Neurosurg 89:547–551, 1998.

44. Burger PC, Dubois PJ, Schold C Jr, et al: Computerized tomographic and pathologic studies of the untreated, quiescent, and recurrent glioblastoma multiforme. J Neurosurg 58:159–169, 1983.

45. Burger PC, Heinz ER, Shibata T, et al: Topographic anatomy and CT correlations in the untreated glioblastoma multiforme. J Neurosurg 68:698–704, 1988.

46. Burger PC, Scheithauer BW: Tumors of neuroglia and choroid plexus epithelium. In Tumors of the Central Nervous System. Washington, DC, Armed Forces Institute of Pathology, 1994, pp 25–161.

47. Burger PC, Scheithauer BW, Paulus W, et al: Pilocytic astrocytoma. In Kleihues P, Cavenee WK (eds): Pathology and Genetics of Tumours of the Nervous System. Lyon, International Agency for Research on Cancer, 2000, pp 45–51.

48. Burger PC, Scheithauer BW, Vogel FS: Brain tumors. In Surgical Pathology of the Nervous System and Its Coverings, 3rd ed. New York, Churchill Livingstone, 1991, pp 193–437.

49. Burger PC, Vogel FS, Green SB, et al: Glioblastoma multiforme and anaplastic astrocytoma: Pathologic criteria and prognostic implications. Cancer 56:1106–1111, 1985.

50. Burrows EH, Leeds NE: Neuroradiology. New York, Churchill Livingstone, 1981, pp 252–253.

51. Butler AR, Horii SC, Kricheff II, et al: Computed tomography in astrocytomas: A statistical analysis of the parameters of malignancy and the positive contrast-enhanced CT scan. Radiology 129:433–439, 1978.

52. Butler AR, Leo JS, Lin JP, et al: The value of routine cranial computed tomography in neurologically intact patients with primary carcinoma of the lung. Radiology 131:399–401, 1979.

53. Butler AR, Passalaqua AM, Berenstein A, et al: Contrast enhanced CT scan and radionuclide brain scan in supratentorial gliomas. Am J Roentgenol 132:607–611, 1979.

54. Cairncross JG, Ueki K, Zlatescu MC, et al: Specific genetic predictors of chemotherapeutic response and survival in patients with anaplastic oligodendrogliomas. J Natl Cancer Inst 90:1473–1479, 1998.

55. Camilleri-Broet S, Davi F, Feuillard J, et al: AIDS-related primary brain lymphomas: Histopathologic and immunohistochemical study of 51 cases. The French study group for HIV-associated tumors. Hum Pathol 28:367–374, 1997.

56. Campbell JW, Pollack IF: Cerebellar astrocytomas in children. J Neurooncol 28:223–231, 1996.

57. Casadei GP, Komori T, Scheithauer BW, et al: Intracranial parenchymal schwannoma: A clinicopathological and neuroimaging study of nine cases. J Neurosurg 79:217–222, 1993.

58. Cascio TL: Neurologic complications of systemic cancer. Med Clin North Am 77:265–279, 1993.

59. Castillo M, Davis PC, Takei Y, et al: Intracranial ganglioglioma: MR, CT, and clinical findings in 18 patients. Am J Roentgenol 154:607–612, 1990.

60. Castillo M, Kwock L: Proton MR spectroscopy of common brain tumors. Neuroimaging Clin North Am 8:733–752, 1998.

61. Cavenee WK, Furnari FB, Nagane M, et al: Diffusely infiltrating astrocytomas. In Kleihues P, Cavenee WK (eds): Pathology and Genetics of Tumours of the Nervous System. Lyon, International Agency for Research on Cancer, 2000, pp 10–21.

62. Chambers EF, Turski PA, Sobel D, et al: Radiologic characteristics of primary cerebral neuroblastomas. Radiology 139:101–104, 1981.

63. Chiechi MV, Smirniotopoulos JG, Mana H: Intracranial hemangiopericytomas: MR and CT features. AJNR Am J Neuroradiol 17: 1365–1371, 1996.

64. Civitello LA, Packer RJ, Rorke LB, et al: Leptomeningeal dissemination of low-grade gliomas in childhood. Neurology 38:562–566, 1988.

65. Coates TL, Hinshaw DB Jr, Peckman N, et al: Pediatric choroid plexus neoplasms: MR, CT, and pathologic correlation. Radiology 173:81–88, 1989.

66. Cohen LM, Schwartz AM, Rockoff SD: Benign schwannomas: Pathologic basis for CT inhomogeneities. Am J Roentgenol 147: 141–143, 1986.

67. Cohen TI, Powers SK, Williams DW III: MR appearance of intracanalicular eighth nerve lipoma. AJNR Am J Neuroradiol 13:1188–1190, 1992.

68. Coltier J, Destrieux C, Brunereau L, et al: Cavernous sinus invasion by pituitary adenoma: MR imaging. Radiology 215:463–469, 2000.

69. Cone L, Srinivasan M, Romanul FCA: Granular cell tumor (choristoma) of the neurohypophysis: Two cases and a review of the literature. AJNR Am J Neuroradiol 11:403–406, 1990.

70. Coons SW, Ashby LS: Pathology of intracranial neoplasms. Neuroimaging Clin North Am 9:615–649, 1999.

71. Coons SW, Johnson PC, Scheithauer BW, et al: Improving diagnostic accuracy and interobserver concordance in the classification and grading of primary gliomas. Cancer 79:1381–1393, 1997.

72. Cooper SD, Brady MB, Williams JP, et al: Neurosarcoidosis: Evaluation using CT and MRI. J Comput Assist Tomogr 12:96–99, 1988.

73. Cote TR, Manns A, Hardy CR, et al: Epidemiology of brain lymphoma among people with or without acquired immunodeficiency syndrome. AIDS/Cancer Study Group. J Natl Cancer Inst 88:675–679, 1996.

74. Crenshaw WB, Chew FS: Rathke's cleft cyst. Am J Roentgenol 158:1312, 1993.

75. Crocker EF, Zimmerman, RA, Phelps ME, et al: The effect of steroids on the extravascular distribution of radiographic contrast material and technetium pertechnetate in brain tumors as determined by computed tomography. Radiology 119:471–474, 1976.

76. Crotty TB, Scheithauer BW, Young WF Jr, et al: Papillary craniopharyngiomas: A clinicopathological study of 48 cases. J Neurosurg 83:206–214, 1995.

77. Curtin HD: The skull base. In Atlas SW (ed): Magnetic Resonance Imaging of the Brain and Spine, 3rd ed. Philadelphia, Lippincott Williams & Wilkins, 2002, pp 1283–1362.

78. Cushing H, Eisenhardt L: Meningiomas: Their Classification, Regional Behavior, Life History, and Surgical End Results. Springfield, Ill, Charles C Thomas, 1938.

79. Daumas-Duport C: Dysembryoplastic neuroepithelial tumors. Brain Pathol 3:283–295, 1993.

80. Daumas-Duport C, Pietsch T, Lantos PL: Dysembryoplastic neuroepithelial tumour. In Kleihues P, Cavenee WK (eds): Pathology and Genetics of Tumours of the Nervous System. Lyon, International Agency for Research on Cancer, 2000, pp 103–106.

81. Daumas-Duport C, Tucker ML, Kolles H, et al: Oligodendrogliomas. Part II: A new grading system based on morphological and imaging criteria. J Neurooncol 34:61–78, 1997.

82. Davis PC, Hudgins PA, Peterman SB, Hoffman JC Jr: Diagnosis of cerebral metastases: Double-dose delayed CT vs contrast-enhanced MR imaging. AJNR Am J Neuroradiol 12:293–300, 1991.

83. Davis PC, Wichman RD, Takei Y, et al: Primary cerebral neuroblastoma: CT and MR findings in 12 cases. AJNR Am J Neuroradiol 11:115–120, 1990.

84. Dean BL, Drayer B, Bird CR, et al: Gliomas: Classification from MR imaging. Radiology 174:411–415, 1990.

85. DeAngelis LM: Brain tumors. N Engl J Med 344:114–123, 2001.

86. Deck MDF, Messina AV, Sackett JF: Computerized transaxial tomography in metastatic disease of the brain. Radiology 119:115–120, 1976.

87. Delattre JY, Krol G, Thaler HT, et al: Distribution of brain metastases. Arch Neurol 45:741–744, 1988.

88. Di Chiro G, De La Paz RL, Brooks RA, et al: Glucose utilization of cerebral gliomas measured by [18F] fluorodeoxyglucose and positron emission tomography. Neurology 32:1323–1329, 1982.

89. Di Chiro G, Oldfield E, Wright DC, et al: Cerebral necrosis after radiotherapy and/or intraarterial chemotherapy for brain tumors: PET and neuropathologic studies. Am J Roentgenol 150:189–197, 1988.

90. Dina T: Primary central nervous system lymphoma versus toxoplasmosis in AIDS. Radiology 179:823–828, 1991.

91. Dohrmann GJ, Geehr RB, Robinson F: Small hemorrhages vs. small calcifications in brain tumors: Difficulty in differentiation by CT. Surg Neurol 10:309–312, 1978.

92. Dorsay TA, Rovira MJ, Ho VB, et al: Ependymoblastoma: MR presentation. Pediatr Radiol 25:433–435, 1995.

93. Doucet V, Peretti-Viton P, Figarella-Branger D, et al: MRI of intracranial chordomas: Extent of tumour and contrast enhancement: Criteria for differential diagnosis. Neuroradiology 39:571–576, 1997.

94. Drayer BP, Rosenbaum AE: Brain edema defined by cranial computed tomography. J Comput Assist Tomogr 3:317–328, 1979.

95. Earnest F IV, Kelly PJ, Scheithauer BW, et al: Cerebral astrocytomas: Histopathological correlation of MR and CT contrast enhancement with stereotactic biopsy. Radiology 166:823–827, 1988.

96. Edwards MSB, Hudgins RJ: Medulloblastomas and PNET of the posterior fossa. In McLaurin RL, Schut L, Venes JL, Epstein F (eds): Pediatric Neurosurgery, ed 2. Philadelphia, WB Saunders, 1989, pp 346–356.

97. Ellison D, Love S, Chimelli L, et al: Rathke cleft cyst. In Neuropathology: A Reference Text of CNS Pathology. St. Louis, Mosby, 1998, pp 44.1–44.11.

98. Elster AD: Modern imaging of the pituitary. Radiology 187:1–14, 1993.

99. Elster AD, Challa VR, Gilbert TH, et al: Meningiomas: MR and histopathologic features. Radiology 170:857–862, 1989.

100. Elster AD, Moody DM, Ball MR, et al: Is Gd-DTPA required for routine cranial MRI? Radiology 173:231–238, 1989.

101. Enzmann DR, Norman D, Levin V, et al: Computed tomography in the follow-up of medulloblastomas and ependymomas. Radiology 128:57–63, 1978.

102. Felix I, Becker LE: Intracranial germ cell tumors in children: An immunohistochemical and electron microscopic study. Pediatr Neurosci 16:156–162, 1990–1991.

103. Felix R, Schorner W, Laniado M, et al: Brain tumors: MR imaging with gadolinium-DTPA. Radiology 156:681–688, 1985.

104. Filling-Katz MR, Choye PL, Oldfield E, et al: Central nervous system involvement in von Hippel-Lindau disease. Neurology 41: 41–46, 1991.

105. Finelli DA, Hurst GC, Gullapali RP, et al: Improved contrast of enhancing brain lesions on postgadolinium T1-weighted spin-echo images with use of magnetization transfer. Radiology 190:553–559, 1994.

106. Fishman RA: Brain edema. N Engl J Med 293:706–711, 1975.

107. Forsyth PA, Cascino TL, Shaw EG, et al: Intracranial chordomas: A clinicopathological and prognostic study of 51 cases. J Neurosurg 78:741–747, 1993.

108. Forsyth PA, Posner JB: Headaches in patients with brain tumors: A study of 111 patients. Neurology 43:1678–1683, 1993.

109. Fujimaki T, Matsutani M, Funada N, et al: CT and MRI features of intracranial germ cell tumors. J Neurooncol 19:217–226, 1994.

110. Furie DM, Provenzale JM: Supratentorial ependymomas and subependymomas: CT and MR appearances. J Comput Assist Tomogr 19:518–526, 1995.

111. Gado M, Huete I, Mikhael M: Computerized tomography of infratentorial tumors. Semin Roentgenol 12:109–120, 1977.

112. Gado MH, Phelps MB, Coleman RE: An extravascular component of contrast enhancement in cranial computed tomography. I: The tissue-blood ratio of contrast enhancement. Radiology 117:589–593, 1975.

113. George AE, Russell EJ, Kricheff II: White matter buckling: CT sign of extraaxial intracranial mass. Am J Neuroradiol 1:425–430, 1980.

114. Georgy BA, Hesselink JR, Jernigan TL: MR imaging of the corpus callosum. Am J Roentgenol 160:949–955, 1993.

115. Giangaspero F, Bigner SH, Kleihues P, et al: Medulloblastoma. In Kleihues P, Cavenee WK (eds): Pathology and Genetics of Tumours

of the Nervous System. Lyon, International Agency for Research on Cancer, 2000, pp 129–137.

116. Ginaldi S, Wallace S, Shalen P, et al: Cranial computed tomography of malignant melanoma. Am J Neuroradiol 1:531–535, 1980.

117. Ginsberg LE, Leeds NE: Neuroradiology of leukemia. Am J Roentgenol 165:525–534, 1995.

118. Ginsberg LE: Contrast enhancement in meningeal and extra-axial disease. Neuroimaging Clin North Am 4:133–152, 1994.

119. Goergen SK, Gonzales MF, McLean CA: Intraventricular neurocytoma: Radiologic features and review of the literature. Radiology 182:787–792, 1992.

120. Gold LHA, Kieffer SA, Peterson HO: Intracranial meningiomas: A retrospective analysis of the diagnostic value of plain skull films. Neurology 19:873–878, 1969.

121. Goldsher D, Litt AW, Pinto RS, et al: Dural tail associated with meningiomas on Gd-DTPA enhanced MR images: Characteristics, differential diagnostic value, and possible implications for treatment. Radiology 176:447–450, 1990.

122. Gomori JM, Grossman RI, Goldberg HI, et al: Intracranial hematomas: Imaging by high field MR. Radiology 157:83–93, 1985.

123. Gomori JM, Grossman RI: Mechanisms responsible for the MR appearance and evolution of intracranial hemorrhage. Radiographics 8:427–440, 1988.

124. Gonzales MF: Classification and pathogenesis of brain tumors. In Kaye AH, Laws ER Jr (eds): Brain Tumors: An Encyclopedic Approach. London, Churchill Livingstone, 2001, pp 29–49.

125. Graif M, Bydder GM, Steiner RE, et al: Contrast-enhanced MR imaging of malignant brain tumors. Am J Neuroradiol 6:855–862, 1985.

126. Grois N, Broadbent V, Favara BE, et al: Report of the Histiocyte Society workshop on central nervous system (CNS) disease in Langerhans cell histiocytosis (LCH). Med Pediatr Oncol 29:73–78, 1997.

127. Guermazi A, Feger C, Rousselot P, et al: Granulocytic sarcoma (chloroma): Imaging findings in adults and children. Am J Roentgenol 178:319–325, 2002.

128. Gusnard DA: Cerebellar neoplasms in children. Semin Roentgenol 25:263–278, 1990.

129. Guthrie BL, Ebersold MJ, Scheithauer BW, et al: Meningeal hemangiopericytoma: Histopathological features, treatment and long-term follow-up of 44 cases. Neurosurgery 25:514–522, 1989.

130. Hall WA, Lucciano MG, Doppman JL, et al: A prospective double-blind study of high resolution MRI in normal human subjects: Occult pituitary adenomas in the general population. J Neurosurg 92:342A, 1990.

131. Hansman Whiteman ML, Bowen BC, Donovan Post MJ, Bell MD: Intracranial infection. In Atlas SW (ed): Magnetic Resonance Imaging of the Brain and Spine, 3rd ed. Philadelphia, Lippincott Williams & Wilkins, 2002, pp 1099–1175.

132. Harsh GR IV: Chordomas and chondrosarcomas of the skull base. In Kaye AH, Laws ER Jr (eds): Brain Tumors: An Encyclopedic Approach, 2nd ed. London, Churchill Livingstone, 2001, pp 857–868.

133. Harwood-Nash DC: Neuroimaging of childhood craniopharyngioma. Pediatr Neurosurg 21(Suppl 1):2–10, 1990.

134. Hatam A, Bergstrom M, Yu Z-Y, et al: Effect of dexamethasone treatment on volume and contrast enhancement of intracranial neoplasms. J Comput Assist Tomogr 7:295–300, 1983.

135. Haustein J, Laniado M, Niendorf H-P, et al: Triple-dose versus standard-dose gadopentetate meglumine: A randomized study in 199 patients. Radiology 186:855–860, 1993.

136. Hayman LA, Evans RA, Fahr LM, et al: Renal consequences of rapid high dose contrast CT. Am J Neuroradiol 1:9–11, 1980.

137. Hayman LA, Evans RA, Hinck VC: Delayed high iodine dose contrast computed tomography: Cranial neoplasms. Radiology 136:677–684, 1980.

138. Healey EA, Barnes PD, Kupsky WJ, et al: The prognostic significance of postoperative residual tumor in ependymoma. Neurosurgery 28:666–672, 1991.

139. Healy JF, Marshall WH, Brahme FJ, et al: CT of intracranial metastases with skull and scalp involvement. Am J Neuroradiol 2:335–338, 1981.

140. Healy ME, Hesselink JR, Press GA, et al: Increased detection of intracranial metastases with intravenous Gd-DTPA. Radiology 165:619–624, 1987.

141. Hendrick EB, Raffel C: Tumors of the fourth ventricle: Ependymomas, choroid plexus papillomas and dermoid cysts. In McLaurin RL, Schut L, Venes JL, Epstein F (eds): Pediatric Neurosurgery, ed 2. Philadelphia, WB Saunders, 1989, pp 366–372.

142. Ho VB, Smirniotopoulos JG, Murphy FM, et al: Radiologic-pathologic correlation: Hemangioblastoma. AJNR Am J Neuroradiol 13:1343–1352, 1992.

143. Hochberg FH, Miller CD: Primary central nervous system lymphoma. J Neurosurg 68:835–853, 1988.

144. Hoffman HJ, Otsubo H, Hendrick EB, et al: Intracranial germ-cell tumors in children. J Neurosurg 74:545–551, 1991.

145. Holland BA, Kucharcyzk W, Brant-Zawadzki M, et al: MR imaging of calcified intracranial lesions. Radiology 157:353–356, 1985.

146. Hudgins PA, Davis PC, Hoffman JC: Gadopentetate dimeglumine-enhanced MR imaging in children following surgery for brain tumor: Spectrum of meningeal findings. AJNR Am J Neuroradiol 12:301–307, 1991.

147. Jaaskelainen J, Louis DN, Paulus W, et al: Haemangiopericytoma. In Kleihues P, Cavenee WK (eds): Pathology and Genetics of Tumours of the Nervous System. Lyon, International Agency for Research on Cancer, 2000, pp 190–192.

148. Jaaskelainen J, Servo A, Haltia M, et al: Meningeal haemangiopericytoma. In Schmidek H (ed): Meningiomas and Their Surgical Treatment. Orlando, WB Saunders, 1991, pp 73–82.

149. Jack CR, O'Neill BP, Banks PM, Reese DF: Central nervous system lymphoma: Histologic types and CT appearance. Radiology 167:211–215, 1988.

150. Janzer RC, Burger PC, Giangaspero F, Paulus W: Craniopharyngioma. In: Kleihues P, Cavenee WK (eds): Pathology and Genetics of Tumours of the Nervous System. Lyon, International Agency for Research on Cancer, 2000, pp 244–246.

151. Jellinger K, Chou P, Paulus W: Melanocytic lesions. In Kleihues P, Cavenee WK (eds): Pathology and Genetics of Tumours of the Nervous System. Lyon, International Agency for Research on Cancer, 2000, pp 193–195.

152. Jennings MT, Gelman R, Hochberg F: Intracranial germ-cell tumors: Natural history and pathogenesis. J Neurosurg 68:155–167, 1985.

153. Johnson BA: Central nervous system metastases. In Drayer BP, Enzmann DR, Smirniotopoulos JG, Lukin RR (eds): Core Curriculum Course in Neuroradiology. Part II: Neoplasms and Infectious Diseases. Oak Brook, Ill, American Society of Neuroradiology, 1996, pp 23–31.

154. Johnson DH, Windham WW, Allen JH, et al: Limited value of CT brain scans in the staging of small cell cancer. Am J Neuroradiol 3:649–652, 1982.

155. Johnson JH, Hariharan S, Berman J, et al: Clinical outcome of pediatric gangliogliomas: Ninety-nine cases over 20 years. Pediatr Neurosurg 27:203–207, 1997.

156. Juneau P, Schoene WC, Black P: Malignant tumors in the pituitary gland. Arch Neurol 49:555–558, 1992.

157. Karsdorp N, Elderson A, Wittebol P, et al: Von Hippel-Lindau disease: New strategies in early detection and treatment. Am J Med 97:158–168, 1994.

158. Kelly WM, Brant-Zawadzki M: Magnetic resonance imaging and computed tomography of supratentorial tumors. In Taveras JM, Ferrucci JT (eds): Radiology—Diagnosis, Imaging, Intervention, vol 3. Philadelphia, JB Lippincott, 1986, pp 1–21.

159. Kepes JJ, Louis DN, Giannini C, Paulus W: Pleomorphic xanthoastrocytoma. In Kleihues P, Cavenee WK (eds): Pathology and Genetics of Tumours of the Nervous System. Lyon, International Agency for Research on Cancer, 2000, pp 52–54.

160. Kieffer SA, Salibi N, Kim RC, et al: Multifocal glioblastoma: Diagnostic implications. Radiology 143:709–710, 1982.

161. Kim EE, Chung SK, Haynie TP, et al: Differentiation of residual or recurrent tumors from post-treatment changes with F-18 FDG PET. Radiographics 12:269–279, 1992.

162. Klatzo I: Neuropathological aspects of brain edema. J Neuropathol Exp Neurol 26:1–14, 1967.

163. Kleihues P, Burger PC, Scheithauer BW: Histological classification of CNS tumours. In Sobin LH (ed): Histologic Typing of Tumours of the Central Nervous System, 2nd ed. Berlin, Springer-Verlag, 1993, pp 1–105.

164. Kleihues P, Cavenee WK (eds): Pathology and Genetics of Tumours of the Nervous System. Lyon, International Agency for Research on Cancer, 2000.

165. Kleihues P, Davis RL, Ohgaki H, et al: Diffuse astrocytoma. In: Kleihues P, Cavenee WK (eds): Pathology and Genetics of Tumours of the Nervous System. Lyon, International Agency for Research on Cancer, 2000, pp 22–26.

166. Klibanski A, Zervas NT: Diagnosis and management of hormone-secreting pituitary adenomas. N Engl J Med 324:822–831, 1991.

167. Koci TM, Chiang F, Mehringer CM, et al: Adult cerebellar medulloblastoma: Imaging features with emphasis on MR findings. AJNR Am J Neuroradiol 13:1319–1325, 1992.

168. Koeller KK: Central nervous system neoplasms: Intraaxial. In Smirniotopoulos JG (ed): Categorical Course in Diagnostic Radiology: Neuroradiology, 2000 Syllabus. Oak Brook, Ill, Radiological Society of North America, 2000, pp 105–121.

169. Koeller KK, Dillon WP: Dysembryoplastic neuroepithelial tumors: MR appearance. AJNR Am J Neuroradiol 13:1319–1325, 1992.

170. Kokoris CP: Leptomeningeal carcinomatosis: How does cancer reach the pia-arachnoid? Cancer 51:154–160, 1983.

171. Kovacs K, Horvath E, Asa SL: Classification and pathology of pituitary tumors. In Wilkins RH, Rengachary SS (eds): Neurosurgery. New York, McGraw-Hill, 1985, pp 834–842.

172. Kramer ED, Rafto S, Packer RJ, et al: Comparison of myelography with computed tomography follow-up vs. gadolinium magnetic resonance imaging for subarachnoid metastatic disease of children. Neurology 41:46–50, 1991.

173. Kricheff II: Strategies for the evaluation of supratentorial brain neoplasms. In Huckman MS (ed): Neuroradiology Categorical Course Syllabus. Detroit, American Roentgen Ray Society, 1992, pp 9–12.

174. Kucharczyk W, Davis DO, Kelly WM, et al: Pituitary adenoma: High resolution MRI at 1.5T. Radiology 161:761–765, 1986.

175. Kucharczyk W, Kelly WM, Chuang SH, et al: The brain. In Kucharczyk W (ed): MRI: Central Nervous System. Philadelphia, JB Lippincott, 1990, pp 1.1–1.78.

176. Kuhl J: Modern treatment strategies in medulloblastoma. Child Nerv Syst 14:2–5, 1998.

177. Kulkantrakorn K, Awwad EE, Levy B, et al: MRI in Lhermitte-Duclos disease. Neurology 48:725–731, 1997.

178. Kuroiwa T, Bergey GK, Rothman MI, et al: Radiologic appearance of the dysembryoplastic neuroepithelial tumor. Radiology 197:233–238, 1995.

179. Kwock L: Localized MR spectroscopy: Basic principles. Neuroimaging Clin North Am 8:733–752, 1998.

180. Laine FJ, Nadel L, Braun IF: CT and MR imaging of the central skull base. Radiographics 10:797–821, 1990.

181. Lalwani AK, Jacklen RK: Preoperative differentiation between meningioma of the cerebellopontine angle and acoustic neuroma using MRI. Otolaryngol Head Neck Surg 109:88–95, 1993.

182. Landis SH, Murray T, Bolder S, Wingo PA: Cancer statistics, 1999. CA Cancer J Clin 49:8–31, 1999.

183. Law M, Cha S, Knopp EA, et al: High-grade gliomas and solitary metastases: Differentiation by using perfusion and proton spectroscopic MR imaging. Radiology 222:715–721, 2002.

184. Laws ER, Thapar K: Brain tumors. CA Cancer J Clin 43:263–271, 1993.

185. Lee CC, Ward HA, Sharbrough FW, et al: Assessment of functional MR imaging in neurosurgical planning. AJNR Am J Neuroradiol 20:1511–1519, 1999.

186. Lee SR, Sanders J, Mark AJ, et al: Posterior fossa hemangioblastomas: MR imaging. Radiology 171:463–468, 1989.

187. Lee Y-Y, Castillo M, Nauert C, et al: Computed tomography of gliosarcoma. Am J Neuroradiol 6:527–531, 1985.

188. Lee Y-Y, Glass JP, Geoffrey A, et al: Cranial computed tomographic abnormalities in leptomeningeal metastasis. Am J Neuroradiol 5:559–563, 1984.

189. Lee Y-Y, van Tassel P: Intracranial oligodendrogliomas: Imaging findings in 35 untreated cases. AJNR Am J Neuroradiol 10:119–127, 1989.

190. Lee Y-Y, van Tassel PV, Bruner JM, et al: Juvenile pilocytic astrocytomas: CT and MR characteristics. AJNR Am J Neuroradiol 10:363–370, 1989.

191. Leeds NE, Elkin CM, Zimmerman RD: Gliomas of the brain. Semin Roentgenol 19:27–43, 1984.

192. Levine SN, Benzel EC, Fowler MR, et al: Lymphocytic hypophysitis: Clinical, radiological, and magnetic resonance imaging characteristics. Neurosurgery 22:987–941, 1988.

193. Levy RA, Bliavas M, Muraszko K, et al: Desmoplastic medulloblastoma: MR findings. AJNR Am J Neuroradiol 18:1364–1366, 1997.

194. Lindau R: Studien uber kleinhirncysten: Bau, pathogenese und bezeihungen zur angiomatosis retinae. Arch Pathol Microbiol Scand Suppl 1, 1926.

195. Lipper MH, Eberhard DA, Phillips CD, et al: Pleomorphic xanthoastrocytoma, a distinctive astroglial tumor: Neuroradiologic and pathologic features. AJNR Am J Neuroradiol 14:1397–1404, 1993.

196. Litofsky NS, Zee C-S, Breeze RE, et al: Meningeal melanocytoma: Diagnostic criteria for a rare lesion. Neurosurgery 31:945–948, 1992.

197. Lizak PF, Woodruff WW: Posterior fossa neoplasms: Multiplanar imaging. Semin Ultrasound CT MR 13:182–206, 1992.

198. Long DM: Capillary ultrastructure and the blood-brain barrier in human malignant brain tumors. J Neurosurg 32:127–144, 1970.

199. Louis DN, Scheithauer BW, Budka H, et al: Meningiomas. In Kleihues P, Cavenee WK (eds): Pathology and Genetics of Tumours of the Nervous System. Lyon, International Agency for Research on Cancer, 2000, pp 176–184.

200. Luh GY, Bird CR: Imaging of brain tumors in the pediatric population. Neuroimaging Clin North Am 9:691–716, 1999.

201. Lum C, Kucharczyk W, Montanera WJ, Becker LE: The sella turcica and parasellar region. In Atlas SW (ed): Magnetic Resonance Imaging of the Brain and Spine, 3rd ed. Philadelphia, Lippincott Williams & Wilkins, 2002, pp 1283–1362.

202. Macinunas RJ, Berger MS, Copeland B, et al: A technique for interactive image-guided neurosurgical intervention in primary brain tumors. Neurosurg Clin North Am 7:245–266, 1996.

203. Mahaley MS Jr, Mettlin C, Natarajan N, et al: National survey of patterns of care for brain-tumor patients. J Neurosurg 71:826–836, 1989.

204. Maiuri F, Iaconetta G, de Divitis O, et al: Intracranial meningiomas: Correlations between MR imaging and histology. Eur J Radiol 31:69–75, 1999.

205. Mandybur TI: Intracranial hemorrhage caused by metastatic tumors. Neurology 27:650–655, 1977.

206. Mantravardi RVP, Phatak R, Bellur S, et al: Brainstem glioma: An autopsy study of 25 cases. Cancer 49:1294–1296, 1982.

207. Mark AS: Contrast-enhanced magnetic resonance imaging of the temporal bone. Neuroimaging Clin North Am 4:117–131, 1994.

208. Marks JE, Gado M: Serial computed tomography of primary brain tumors following surgery, irradiation, and chemotherapy. Radiology 125:119–125, 1977.

209. Martin DS, Levy B, Awwad EE, et al: Desmoplastic infantile ganglioglioma: CT and MR features. AJNR Am J Neuroradiol 12:1195–1197, 1991.

210. Mass S, Norman D, Newton TH: Coronal computed tomography: Indications and accuracy. Am J Roentgenol 131:875–879, 1978.

211. Mathews VP, Caldemeyer KS, Lowe MJ, et al: Gadolinium enhanced fast FLAIR imaging of the brain. Radiology 211:257–263, 1999.

212. Matsutani M, Sano K, Takakura K, et al: Primary intracranial germ cell tumors: A clinical analysis of 153 histologically verified cases. J Neurosurg 86:446–455, 1997.

213. McCormack BM, Miller DC, Budzilovich GN, et al: Treatment and survival of low-grade astrocytoma in adults: 1977–1988. Neurosurgery 31:636–642, 1992.

214. McGeachie RE, Gold LHA, Latchaw RE: Periventricular spread of tumor demonstrated by computed tomography. Radiology 125:407–410, 1977.

215. Meyer JR, Gorey MT: Differential diagnosis of nontraumatic intracranial hemorrhage. Neuroimaging Clin North Am 8:263–293, 1998.

216. Meyers SP, Hirsch WL Jr, Curtin HD, et al: Chondrosarcomas of the skull base: MR imaging features. Radiology 184:103–108, 1992.

217. Miller DC, Hochberg FH, Harris NL, et al: Pathology with clinical correlations of primary central nervous system non-Hodgkin's lymphoma: The Massachusetts General Hospital experience 1958–1989. Cancer 74:1383–1397, 1994.

218. Miller EM, Newton TH: Extra-axial posterior fossa lesions simulating intra-axial lesions on computed tomography. Radiology 127:675–679, 1978.

219. Monajati A, Heggeness L: Patterns of edema in tumors vs. infarcts: Visualization of white matter pathways. Am J Neuroradiol 3:251–255, 1982.

220. Moran CJ, Naidich TP, Gado MH, et al: Central nervous system lesions biopsied or treated by CT-guided needle placement. Radiology 131:681–686, 1979.

221. Morrison G, Sobel DF, Kelley WM, et al: Intraventricular mass lesions. Radiology 153:435–442, 1984.
222. Mulkens TH, Parizel PM, Martin J-J, et al: Acoustic schwannoma: MR findings in 84 tumors. AJR Am J Roentgenol 160:395–398, 1993.
223. Mulvihill JJ, Parry DM, Sherman JL, et al: NIH conference: Neurofibromatosis 1 (Recklinghausen disease) and neurofibromatosis 2 (bilateral acoustic neurofibromatosis)—an update. Ann Intern Med 113:39–52, 1990.
224. Murray JJ, Greco FA, Wolff SN, Hainsworth JD: Neoplastic meningitis: Marked variations of cerebrospinal fluid composition in the absence of extradural block. Am J Med 75:289–294, 1983.
225. Nagele T, Petersen D, Klose U, et al: The "dural tail" adjacent to meningiomas studied by dynamic contrast-enhanced MRI: A comparison with histopathology. Neuroradiology 36:303–307, 1994.
226. Naidich TP, Zimmerman RA: Primary brain tumors in children. Semin Roentgenol 19:100–114, 1984.
227. Naul LG, Hise JH, Bauserman SC, et al: CT and MR of meningeal melanocytoma. AJNR Am J Neuroradiol 12:315–316, 1991.
228. Nazar GB, Hoffman HJ, Becker LE, et al: Infratentorial ependymoma in childhood: Prognostic factors and treatment. J Neurosurg 72:408, 1990.
229. Nelson JS, Bruner JM, Wiestler OD, et al: Ganglioglioma and gangliocytoma. In Kleihues P, Cavenee WK (eds): Pathology and Genetics of Tumours of the Nervous System. Lyon, International Agency for Research on Cancer, 2000, pp 96–102.
230. Nelson JS, von Deimling A, Petersen I, Janzer RC: Metastatic tumours of the CNS. In Kleihues P, Cavenee WK (eds): Pathology and Genetics of Tumours of the Nervous System. Lyon, International Agency for Research on Cancer, 2000, pp 249–253.
231. Nelson SJ: Imaging of brain tumors after therapy. Neuroimaging Clin North Am 9:801–819, 1999.
232. Neumann HPH, Eggert HR, Scheremat R, et al: Central nervous system lesions in von Hippel-Lindau syndrome. J Neurol Neurosurg Psychiatry 55:898–901, 1992.
233. New PFJ, Aronow S, Hesselink JR: National Cancer Institute study: Evaluation of computed tomography in the diagnosis of intracranial neoplasms. IV: Meningiomas. Radiology 136:665–675, 1980.
234. New PFJ, Hesselink JR, O'Carroll CP, et al: Malignant meningiomas: CT and histologic criteria, including a new CT sign. Am J Neuroradiol 3:267–276, 1982.
235. Newton DR, Dillon WP, Norman D, et al: Gd-DTPA-enhanced MR imaging of pituitary adenomas. AJNR Am J Neuroradiol 10:949–954, 1989.
236. Norman D, Stevens EA, Wing D, et al: Quantitative aspects of contrast enhancement in cranial computed tomography. Radiology 129:683–688, 1978.
237. Osborn AG, Rauschning W: Brain tumors and tumorlike masses: Classification and differential diagnosis. In Osborn AG (ed): Diagnostic Neuroradiology. St. Louis, Mosby, 1994, pp 401–528.
238. Osborn AG: Miscellaneous tumors, cysts, and metastases. In Osborne AG (ed): Diagnostic Neuroradiology. St. Louis, Mosby, 1994, pp 626–670.
239. Osborn AG, Heaston DK, Wing SD: Diagnosis of ascending transtentorial herniation by cranial CT. Am J Roentgenol 130:755–760, 1978.
240. Osborn AG: Astrocytomas and other glial neoplasms. In Osborne AG (ed): Diagnostic Neuroradiology. St. Louis, Mosby, 1994, pp 529–578.
241. Osborn AG: Meningiomas and other nonglial neoplasms. In Osborne AG (ed): Diagnostic Neuroradiology. St. Louis, Mosby, 1994, pp 579–625.
242. Ostertun B, Wolf HK, Campos MG, et al: Dysembryoplastic neuroepithelial tumors: MR and CT evaluation. AJNR Am J Neuroradiol 17:419–430, 1996.
243. Ostrov SG, Quencer RM, Hoffman JC, et al: Hemorrhage within pituitary adenomas: How often associated with pituitary apoplexy syndrome? AJNR Am J Neuroradiol 10:503–510, 1989.
244. Packer RJ: Childhood medulloblastoma: Progress and future challenges. Brain Dev 21:75–81, 1999.
245. Packer RJ: Childhood tumors. Curr Opin Pediatr 9:551–557, 1997.
246. Pagani JJ, Libshitz HI, Wallace S, et al: Central nervous system leukemia and lymphoma: Computed tomographic manifestations. Am J Neuroradiol 2:397–403, 1981.
247. Parisi JE, Scheithauer BW: Glial tumors. In Nelson JS, Parisi JE, Scheithauer BW (eds): Principles and Practice of Neuropathology. St. Louis, Mosby, 1993, pp 123–183.
248. Parker K, Hardjasudarma M, McLellan RL, et al: MR features of an intracerebellar chloroma. AJNR Am J Neuroradiol 17: 1592–1594, 1996.
249. Paulus W, Jellinger K, Morgello S, Deckert-Schluter M: Malignant lymphomas. In Kleihues P, Cavenee WK (eds): Pathology and Genetics of Tumours of the Nervous System. Lyon, International Agency for Research on Cancer, 2000, pp 198–203.
250. Paulus W, Kepes JJ, Jellinger K: Histiocytic tumors. In Kleihues P, Cavenee WK (eds): Pathology and Genetics of Tumours of the Nervous System. Lyon, International Agency for Research on Cancer, 2000, pp 204–206.
251. Paulus W, Scheithauer BW: Mesenchymal, non-meningothelial tumours. In Kleihues P, Cavenee WK (eds): Pathology and Genetics of Tumours of the Nervous System. Lyon, International Agency for Research on Cancer, 2000, pp 185–189.
252. Paz-Fumagalli R, Daniels DL, Millen SJ, et al: Dural "tail" associated with an acoustic schwannoma in MR imaging with gadopentetate dimeglumine. AJNR Am J Neuroradiol 12:1206, 1991.
253. Pencalet P, Sainte-Rose C, Lelauch-Tubiana A, et al: Papillomas and carcinomas of the choroid plexus in children. J Neurosurg 88: 521–528, 1998.
254. Penn I: Development of cancer as a complication of clinical transplantation. Transplant Proc 9:1121–1127, 1977.
255. Penn I, Porat G: Central nervous system lymphomas in organ allograft recipients. Transplantation 59:240–244, 1995.
256. Percy AK, Elveback LR, Okazaki H, Kurland LT: Neoplasms of the central nervous system: Epidemiologic considerations. Neurology 22:40–48, 1972.
257. Perry A, Stafford SL, Scheithauer BW, et al: Meningioma grading: An analysis of histologic parameters. Am J Surg Pathol 21:1455–1465, 1997.
258. Phillips ME, Ryals TJ, Kambhu SA, Yuh WTC: Neoplastic vs inflammatory meningeal enhancement with Gd-DTPA. J Comp Assist Tomogr 14:536–541, 1990.
259. Poe LB, Dubowy RL, Hochhauser L, et al: Demyelinating and gliotic cerebellar lesions in Langerhans cell histiocytosis. AJNR Am J Neuroradiol 15:1921–1928, 1994.
260. Pollock BE, Lunsford LD, Kondziolka D, et al: Outcome analysis of acoustic neuroma management: A comparison of microsurgery and stereotactic radiosurgery. Neurosurgery 36:215–224, 1995.
261. Poon T, Matoso I, Tchertkoff V, et al: CT features of primary cerebral lymphoma in AIDS and non-AIDS patients. J Comp Assist Tomogr 13:6–9, 1989.
262. Poptani H, Gupta RK, Roy R, et al: Characterization of intracranial mass lesions with in vivo proton MR spectroscopy. AJNR Am J Neuroradiol 16:1593–1603, 1995.
263. Posner JB: Brain tumors. CA Cancer J Clin 43:261–262, 1993.
264. Posner JB: Neurologic Complications of Cancer. Philadelphia, FA Davis, 1995.
265. Posner JB: Neurological complications of systemic cancer. Med Clin North Am 63:783–800, 1979.
266. Posner JB, Chernik NL: Intracranial metastases from systemic cancer. Adv Neurol 19:579–592, 1978.
267. Post MJD, David NJ, Glaser JS, et al: Pituitary apoplexy: Diagnosis by computed tomography. Radiology 134:665–670, 1980.
268. Potts DG, Abbott GF, von Sneidern JV: National Cancer Institute study: Evaluation of computed tomography in the diagnosis of intracranial neoplasms. III: Metastatic tumors. Radiology 136:657–664, 1980.
269. Provenzale JM, Weber AL, Klinworth GK, et al: Radiologic-pathologic correlation: Bilateral retinoblastoma with coexistent pineoblastoma (trilateral retinoblastoma). AJNR Am J Neuroradiol 16:157–165, 1995.
270. Radkowski MA, Naidich TP, Tamita T, et al: Neonatal brain tumors: CT and MR findings. J Comput Assist Tomogr 12:10–20, 1988.
271. Rao KCVG, Levine H, Itani A, et al: CT findings in multicentric glioblastoma: Diagnostic-pathologic correlation. J Comput Tomogr 4:187–192, 1980.
272. Rawlings CE, Giangaspero F, Burger PL, et al: Ependymomas: A clinicopathologic study. Surg Neurol 29:271–281, 1988.
273. Razack N, Baumgartner J, Bruner J: Pediatric oligodendrogliomas. Pediatr Neurosurg 28:121–129, 1998.
274. Reifenberger G, Kros JM, Burger PC, et al: Oligodendroglioma. In Kleihues P, Cavenee WK (eds): Pathology and Genetics of Tumours of the Central Nervous System. Lyon, International Agency for Research on Cancer, 2000, pp 56–61.

275. Ricci PE: Imaging of adult brain tumors. Neuroimaging Clin North Am 9:651–669, 1999.

276. Ricci PE, Karis JP, Heiserman JE, et al: Differentiating recurrent tumor from radiation necrosis: Time for reevaluation of positron emission tomography? AJNR Am J Neuroradiol 19:407–413, 1998.

277. Rohringer M, Sutherland G, Louis D, et al: Incidence and clinico-pathological features of meningioma. J Neurosurg 71:665–672, 1989.

278. Rollins N, Mendelsohn D, Mulne A, et al: Recurrent medulloblastoma: Frequency of tumor enhancement on Gd-DTPA MR imaging. AJNR Am J Neuroradiol 11:583–587, 1990.

279. Roman-Goldstein SM, Goldman DL, Howieson J, et al: MR in primary CNS lymphoma in immunologically normal patients. AJNR Am J Neuroradiol 13:1207–1213, 1992.

280. Ropper AH: Lateral displacement of the brain and level of consciousness in patients with an acute hemispheral mass. N Engl J Med 314:953–958, 1986.

281. Rorke LB, Trojanowski JQ, Lee VMY, et al: Primitive neuroectodermal tumors of the central nervous system. Brain Pathol 7:765, 1997.

282. Rosenbaum AE, Rosenbloom SB: Meningiomas revisited. Semin Roentgenol 19:8–26, 1984.

283. Rosenberg AE, Nielsen GP, Keel SB, et al: Chondrosarcoma of the base of the skull: A clinicopathological study of 200 cases with emphasis on its distinction from chordoma. Am J Surg Pathol 23:1370–1378, 1999.

284. Rosenblum MK, Matsutani M, Van Meir EG: CNS germ cell tumors. In Kleihues P, Cavenee WK (eds): Pathology and Genetics of Tumours of the Nervous System. Lyon, International Agency for Research on Cancer, 2000, pp 207–214.

285. Ross DA, Norman D, Wilson CB: Radiologic characteristics and results of surgical management of Rathke's cysts in 48 patients. Neurosurgery 30:173–179, 1992.

286. Russell DS, Rubinstein LJ: Pathology of tumours of the nervous system, ed 5. Baltimore, Williams & Wilkins, 1989.

287. Russell EJ, George AE, Kricheff II, et al: Atypical computed tomographic features of intracranial meningioma: Radiological-pathological correlation in a series of 131 consecutive cases. Radiology 135:673–682, 1980.

288. Russell EJ, Geremia GK, Johnson CE, et al: Multiple cerebral metastases: Detectability with Gd-DTPA-enhanced MR imaging. Radiology 165:609–617, 1987.

289. Sage MR: Blood-brain barrier: Phenomenon of increasing importance to the imaging clinician. Am J Neuroradiol 3:127–138, 1982.

290. Samii M, Tatagiba M: Craniopharyngioma. In Kaye AH, Laws ER Jr (eds): Brain Tumors: An Encyclopedic Approach, 2nd ed. London, Churchill Livingstone, 2001, pp 945–964.

291. Sartoretti-Schefer S, Wichmann W, Aguzzi A, Valavanis A: MR differentiation of adamantinomatous and squamous-papillary craniopharyngiomas. AJNR Am J Neuroradiol 18:77–87, 1997.

292. Schild SE, Scheithauer BW, Schomberg PJ, et al: Pineal parenchymal tumors. Cancer 72:870–880, 1993.

293. Schorner W, Laniedo M, Niendorf HP, et al: Time-dependent changes in image contrast in brain tumors after gadolinium-DTPA. Am J Neuroradiol 7:1013–1020, 1986.

294. Shalen PR, Hayman LA, Wallace S, et al: Protocol for delayed contrast enhancement in computed tomography of cerebral neoplasia. Radiology 139:397–402, 1981.

295. Shapir J, Coblentz C, Melanson D, et al: New CT finding in aggressive meningioma. Am J Neuroradiol 6:101–102, 1985.

296. Shaw EG, Scheithauer BW, O'Fallon JR, et al: Oligodendrogliomas: The Mayo Clinic experience. J Neurosurg 76:428–434, 1992.

297. Shellock FG (ed): Magnetic Resonance Procedures: Health Effects and Safety. Boca Raton, Fla, CRC Press, 2001.

298. Shepherd CW, Scheithauer BW, Gomez MR, et al: Subependymal giant cell astrocytoma. Neurosurgery 28:864–868, 1991.

299. Sighvatsson V, Ericson K, Tomasson H: Optimising contrast-enhanced cranial CT for detection of brain metastases. Acta Radiol 39:718–722, 1998.

300. Silver AJ, Ganti SR, Hilal SK: Computed tomography of tumors involving the atria of the lateral ventricles. Radiology 145:71–78, 1982.

301. Sinson G, Sutton LN, Yachnis AT, et al: Subependymal giant cell tumor in children. Pediatr Neurosurg 20:233–239, 1994.

302. Smirniotopoulos JG: Extraaxial masses of the central nervous system. In Smirniotopoulos JG (ed): Categorical Course in Diagnostic Radiology: Neuroradiology. Oak Brook, Ill, Radiological Society of North America, 2000, pp 123–132.

303. Smirniotopoulos JG: The new WHO classification of brain tumors. Neuroimaging Clin North Am 9:595–613, 1999.

304. Smirniotopoulos JG, Murphy FM: The phakomatoses. AJNR Am J Neuroradiol 13:725–746, 1992.

305. Smirniotopoulos JG, Rushing EJ, Mena H: Pineal region masses: Differential diagnosis. Radiographics 12:577–596, 1992.

306. Smirniotopoulos JG, Yue NC, Rushing EJ: Cerebellopontine angle masses: Radiologic-pathologic correlation. Radiographics 13:1131–1147, 1993.

307. Smith RR, Grossman RI, Goldberg HI, et al: MR imaging of Lhermitte-Duclos disease: A case report. AJNR Am J Neuroradiol 10:187–189, 1989.

308. Snow RB, Johnson CE, Morgello S, et al: Is magnetic resonance imaging useful in guiding the operative approach to large pituitary tumors? Neurosurgery 26:801–803, 1990.

309. Spagnoli MV, Grossman RI, Packer RJ, et al: Magnetic resonance imaging determination of gliomatosis cerebri. Neuroradiology 29:15–18, 1987.

310. Spillane JA, Kendall BE, Moseley IF: Cerebral lymphoma: Clinical radiological correlation. J Neurol Neurosurg Psychiatry 45:199–208, 1982.

311. Spoto GP, Press GA, Hesselink JR, et al: Intracranial ependymoma and subependymoma: MR manifestations. AJNR Am J Neuroradiol 11:83–91, 1990.

312. Stovring J: Descending tentorial herniation: Findings on computed tomography. Neuroradiology 14:101–105, 1977.

313. Sundaresan N, Galicich JH: Surgical treatment of brain metastases: Clinical and computerized tomography evaluation of the results of treatment. Cancer 55:1382–1388, 1985.

314. Sutton LS, Packer RJ, Rorke LB, et al: Cerebral gangliogliomas during childhood. Neurosurgery 13:124–128, 1983.

315. Swartz JD, Zimmerman RA, Bilaniuk LT: Computed tomography of intracranial ependymomas. Radiology 143:97–101, 1982.

316. Symon L, Mohanty S: Hemorrhage in pituitary tumors. Acta Neurochir 65:41–49, 1982.

317. Sze G: Meningeal carcinomatosis. In Drayer BP, Enzmann DR, Smirniotopoulos JG, Luken RR (eds): Core Curriculum Course in Neuroradiology. Part II: Neoplasms and Infectious Disease. Oak Brook, Ill, American Society of Neuroradiology, 1996, pp 145–150.

318. Sze G, Soletsky S, Bronen R, et al: MR imaging of the cranial meninges with emphasis on contrast enhancement and meningeal carcinomatosis. AJNR Am J Neuroradiol 10:965–975, 1989.

319. Sze G, Uichanco LS, Brant-Zawadski MN, et al: Chordomas: MRI. Radiology 166:187–191, 1988.

320. Tadmor R, Harwood-Nash DCF, Savoiardo M, et al: Brain tumors in the first two years of life: CT diagnosis. Am J Neuroradiol 1:411–417, 1980.

321. Tally PW, Laws ER, Scheithauer BW: Metastases of central nervous system neoplasms. J Neurosurg 68:811–816, 1988.

322. Tampieri D, Melanson D, Ethier R: MR imaging of epidermoid cysts. AJNR Am J Neuroradiol 10:351–356, 1989.

323. Tampieri D, Moumdjian R, Melanson D, et al: Intracerebral gangliogliomas in patients with partial complex seizures: CT and MR imaging findings. AJNR Am J Neuroradiol 12:749–755, 1991.

324. Tarver RD, Richmond BD, Klatte EC: Cerebral metastases from lung carcinoma: Neurological and CT correlation. Radiology 153:689–692, 1984.

325. Tatter SB: Neurosurgical management of brain tumors. Neuroimaging Clin North Am 9:779–799, 1999.

326. Tenreiro-Picon OR, Kamath SV, Knorr JR, et al: Desmoplastic infantile ganglioglioma: CT and MRI features. Pediatr Radiol 25:540–543, 1995.

327. Teramoto A, Hirakawa K, Sanno N, et al: Incidental pituitary lesions in 1000 unselected autopsy specimens. Radiology 193:161–164, 1994.

328. Tew JM Jr, Feibal JH, Sawaya R: Brain tumors: Clinical aspects. Semin Roentgenol 19:115–128, 1984.

329. Thapar K, Kovacs K: Tumors of the sellar region. In Bigner DD, McLendon RE, Bruner JM (eds): Russell and Rubinstein's Pathology of Tumors of the Nervous System. Baltimore, Williams & Wilkins, 1998, pp 561–677.

330. Thapar K, Laws ER Jr: Pituitary tumors. In Kaye AH, Laws ER Jr (eds): Brain Tumors: An Encyclopedic Approach, 2nd ed. London, Churchill Livingstone, 2001, pp 803–853.

331. Thomas LM: Acute increased intracranial pressure and the pathophysiology of mass lesions. In Youmans JR (ed): Neurological Surgery. Philadelphia, WB Saunders, 1973.

332. Tien RD, Barkovich AJ, Edwards MSB: MR imaging of pineal tumors. AJNR Am J Neuroradiol 11:557–565, 1990.

333. Tien RD, Cardenas CA, Rajagopalan S: Pleomorphic xanthoastrocytoma of the brain: MR findings in six patients. Am J Roentgenol 159:1287–1290, 1992.

334. Tien RD, Newton TH, McDermott MW, et al: Thickened pituitary stalk on MR images in patients with diabetes insipidus and Langerhans' cell histiocytosis. AJNR Am J Neuroradiol 11:703–708, 1990.

335. Tortori-Donati P, Fondelli MP, Rossi A, et al: Medulloblastoma in children: CT and MRI findings. Neuroradiology 38:352–359, 1996.

336. Truwit CL, Barkovich AJ: Pathogenesis of intracranial lipomas: An MR study in 42 patients. AJNR Am J Neuroradiol 11:665–674, 1990.

337. Tummala RP, Chu R, Liu H, et al: Optimizing brain tumor resection: High-field interventional MR imaging. Neuroimaging Clin North Am 11:673–683, 2001.

338. Uematsu Y, Yukawa S, Yokoto H, et al: Meningeal melanocytoma: Magnetic resonance imaging characteristics and pathological features: Case report. J Neurosurg 76:705–709, 1992.

339. Von Deiming A, Foster R, Krone W: Neurofibromatosis type 1. In Kleihues P, Cavenee WK (eds): Pathology and Genetics of Tumours of the Nervous System. Lyon, International Agency for Research on Cancer, 2000, pp 216–218.

340. Von Hippel E: Uber eine sehr selbene Erkrankung der Netzhaub. Graefe's Arch 59:83–86, 1904.

341. Vonofakos D, Marcu H, Hacker H: Oligodendrogliomas: CT patterns with emphasis on features indicating malignancy. J Comput Assist Tomogr 3:783–788, 1979.

342. Walker MD: Malignant Brain Tumors. New York, American Cancer Society, 1975.

343. Warzok RW, Vogelgesang S, Faiden W, Shuangshoti S: Granular cell tumour of the neurohypophysis. In Kleihues P, Cavenee WK (eds): Pathology and Genetics of Tumours of the Nervous System. Lyon, International Agency for Research on Cancer, 2000, pp 247–248.

344. Wasserstrom WR, Glass JP, Posner JB: Diagnosis and treatment of leptomeningeal metastases from solid tumors: Experience with 90 patients. Cancer 49:759–772, 1982.

345. Weir B, Grace M: The relative significance of factors affecting postoperative survival in astrocytomas, grades one and two. Can J Neurol Sci 3:47–50, 1976.

346. Weisberg LA: Incidental focal intracranial computed tomographic findings. J Neurol Neurosurg Psychiatry 45:715–718, 1982.

347. Wendling LR, Cromwell LD, Latchaw RE: Computed tomography of intracerebral leukemic masses. Am J Roentgenol 132:217–220, 1979.

348. Whelan MA, Hilal SK: Computed tomography as a guide in the diagnosis and follow-up of brain abscesses. Radiology 135:663–671, 1980.

349. Wiestler OD, Lopes BS, Green AJ, Vinters HV: Tuberous sclerosis complex and subependymal giant cell astrocytoma. In Kleihues P, Cavenee WK (eds): Pathology and Genetics of Tumours of the Nervous System. Lyon, International Agency for Research on Cancer, 2000, pp 227–229.

350. Wiestler OD, Padberg GW, Steck PA: Cowden disease and dysplastic gangliocytoma of the cerebellum/Lhermitte-Duclos disease. In Kleihues P, Cavenee WK (eds): Pathology and Genetics of Tumours of the Nervous System. Lyon, International Agency for Research on Cancer, 2000, pp 235–237.

351. Wiestler OD, Schiffer D, Coons SW, et al: Ependymoma. In Kleihues P, Cavenee WK (eds): Pathology and Genetics of Tumours

of the Nervous System. Lyon, International Agency for Research on Cancer, 2000, pp 72–76.

352. Wilson CB: Current concepts in cancer: Brain tumors. N Engl J Med 300:1469–1471, 1979.

353. Winstanley DP: Fruitless resection. Thorax 23:327, 1968.

354. Woodruff JM, Kourea HP, Louis DN, et al: Tumours of cranial and peripheral nerves. In Kleihues P, Cavenee WK (eds): Pathology and Genetics of Tumours of the Nervous System. Lyon, International Agency for Research on Cancer, 2000, pp 163–174.

355. Wortzman G, Holgate RC, Morgan PP: Cranial computed tomography: An evaluation of cost effectiveness. Radiology 117:75–77, 1975.

356. Yasargil M, von Ammon K, von Deimling A, et al: Central neurocytoma: Histopathological variants and therapeutic approaches. J Neurosurg 76:32–37, 1992.

357. Yousem DM, Arrington JA, Zinreich SJ, et al: Pituitary adenomas: Possible role of bromocriptine in intratumoral hemorrhage. Radiology 170:239–243, 1989.

358. Yousem DM, Patrone PM, Grossman RI: Leptomeningeal metastases: MR evaluation. J Comput Assist Tomogr 14:255–261, 1990.

359. Yuh WT, Fisher DJ, Runge VM, et al: Phase III multicenter trial of high-dose gadoteridol in MR evaluation of brain metastases. AJNR Am J Neuroradiol 15:1037–1051, 1994.

360. Zee CS, Segall H, Apuzzo M, et al: MR imaging of pineal region neoplasms. J Comput Assist Tomogr 15:56–63, 1991.

361. Zee CS, Segall HD, Ahmadi J, et al: Computed tomography of posterior fossa ependymomas in childhood. Surg Neurol 20:221–226, 1983.

362. Zee CS, Segall HD, Miller C, et al: Less common CT features of medulloblastoma. Radiology 144:97–102, 1982.

363. Zentner J, Wolf HK, Ostertun B, et al: Gangliogliomas: clinical, radiological, and histopathological findings in 51 patients. J Neurol Neurosurg Psychiatry 57:1497–1502, 1994.

364. Zhang M, Olsson Y: Hematogenous metastases of the human brain: Characteristics of peritumoral brain changes—a review. J Neurooncol 35:81–89, 1997.

365. Zimmerman HM: The pathology of brain tumors. Semin Roentgenol 19:129–138, 1984.

366. Zimmerman RA: Neuroimaging of primary brainstem gliomas: Diagnosis and course. Pediatr Neurosurg 25:45–53, 1996.

367. Zimmerman RA: Pediatric supratentorial tumors. Semin Roentgenol 25:225–248, 1990.

368. Zimmerman RA: Supratentorial pediatric brain tumors, In Drayer BP, Enzmann DR, Smirniotopoulos JG, Lukin RR (eds): Core Curriculum Course in Neuroradiology. Part II: Neoplasms and Infectious Diseases. Oak Brook, Ill, American Society of Neuroradiology, 1996, pp 103–111.

369. Zimmerman RA, Bilaniuk LT: Computed tomography of acute intratumoral hemorrhage. Radiology 135:355–359, 1980.

370. Zimmerman RA, Bilaniuk LT: Computed tomography of choroid plexus lesions. J Comput Tomogr 3:93–102, 1979.

371. Zimmerman RA, Bilaniuk LT: Computed tomography of intracerebral gangliogliomas. J Comput Tomogr 3:24–30, 1979.

372. Zimmerman RA, Bilaniuk LT, Pahlajani H: Spectrum of medulloblastomas as demonstrated by computed tomography. Radiology 126:137–141, 1978.

373. Zimmerman RA, Bilaniuk LT, Dolinskas C: Cranial computed tomography of epidermoid and congenital fatty tumors of maldevelopmental origin. J Comput Tomogr 3:40–50, 1979.

374. Zimmerman RD, Fleming CA, Lee BCP, et al: Periventricular hyperintensity as seen by magnetic resonance: Prevalence and significance. Am J Neuroradiol 7:13–20, 1986.

375. Zulch KJ: Tumors of neuroepithelial tissue. In Brain Tumors: Their Biology and Pathology, 3rd ed. Berlin, Springer-Verlag, 1986, pp 210–343.

6

Cerebral Infections and Inflammation

Chi-Shing Zee, John L. Go, Paul Kim, Hervey D. Segall, Jamshid Ahmadi

Since the advent of computed tomography (CT) scanning and magnetic resonance imaging (MRI), a significant decrease has occurred in the morbidity and mortality of patients with intracranial infections.[123] Although conventional cerebral angiography may be required in selected circumstances to confirm suspected vasculitis or mycotic aneurysm, CT and MRI studies are generally the modalities of choice in the evaluation of intracranial infection. CT and MRI, with stereotactic devices, have permitted biopsy of the intracranial focus of infection to identify the pathogen and subsequent drainage of abscesses through needle aspiration.[148] Recent advances in technology have allowed us to utilize additional imaging modalities in the evaluation of intracranial infection, such as positron emission tomography (PET), single photon emission computed tomography (SPECT), diffusion imaging, and magnetic resonance proton spectroscopy (MRS).

Two main sources of intracranial infection exist:

1. *Hematogenous*, in which infectious agents are carried to the meninges, corticomedullary junction, and choroid plexus by way of the bloodstream from a remote focus such as a lung infection; for instance, children with cyanotic heart disease have a high incidence of intracranial infection because of a right-to-left shunt. Retrograde venous spread can also occur via anastomotic connections between superficial veins of the face and scalp and cortical veins.

2. *Direct extension*, resulting from otitis media, mastoiditis, sinusitis, and open wounds from the trauma. In addition, certain viral infections can occur by spreading along the nerve in retrograde fashion.

Certain external factors appear to enhance the risk of intracranial infections (e.g., diabetes mellitus, alcoholism, malignancy, agammaglobulinemia, radiation or chemotherapy, steroid therapy). Patients with acquired immunodeficiency syndrome (AIDS) now account for a significant number of cases of intracranial infection, but the disease spectrum in these individuals is different. Various infectious processes involve the central nervous system (CNS). Pyogenic infection is discussed in detail in this chapter with categorization according to the anatomic site of involvement. Other infectious processes are also discussed, including viral infections, granulomatous disease, spirochete infections, fungal diseases, and parasitic diseases.

Meningitis

Meningitis is an inflammation of the dura, leptomeninges (the pia mater and the arachnoid membrane), and the adjacent subarachnoid space.[72] The diagnosis is usually made clinically. The role of neuroimaging is to exclude complications of meningitis (e.g., abscess, ventriculitis, empyema) that may call for different treatment. With appropriate window settings, CT scans may provide information regarding diseases of the paranasal sinuses or mastoids, which may be a source of intracranial infection. MRI studies are extremely sensitive in detecting diseases in the paranasal sinuses and the mastoids, especially on T2-weighted images.

In older people, *Streptococcus pneumoniae* and *Listeria monocytogenes* are often the causative agents. In young adults and older children, purulent meningitis is caused mainly by *Neisseria meningitidis*. In young children and infants, the cause may be *Haemophilus influenzae, S. pneumoniae,* and *N. meningitidis.* In infants younger than 1 month of age, causes include *Streptococcus agalactiae* (group B) and *Escherichia coli.*[36]

The initial pathologic responses of the dura and leptomeninges to infection include vascular congestion, edema, and minute hemorrhages. CT and MRI findings may be normal early in the disease process[21, 170] and remain normal with prompt and adequate treatment.

Once infection progresses, unenhanced CT scans frequently show obliteration of the basal cisterns. This probably results from a combination of hypervascularity in the acutely inflamed leptomeninges and exudate in the subarachnoid space. Diffuse cerebral swelling may be seen. Contrast-enhanced CT scans may show enhancement in the basal cisterns and sylvian fissure, regardless of the causative organism.

Routine MRI scans show obliteration of the basal cisterns on T1-weighted images. Contrast-enhanced MRI studies may show basal cisternal and sylvian enhancement as well as enhancement deep within the cortical sulci. Enhancement can be seen along the tentorium, falx, and the convexities—which can be better appreciated with MRI because of its greater contrast resolution[20, 112, 138] (Fig. 6–1).

Early complications of meningitis include abscess, subdural empyema, ventriculitis, and infarction. Late complications include subdural effusion, encephalomalacia, hydrocephalus, and atrophy.[21, 129]

On contrast-enhanced CT scans, the differential diagnosis includes meningeal carcinomatosis and subacute stage of subarachnoid hemorrhage. The clinical histories, however, are entirely different in these disease entities. The MRI differential diagnosis includes only meningeal carcinomatosis, since subacute subarachnoid hemorrhage shows

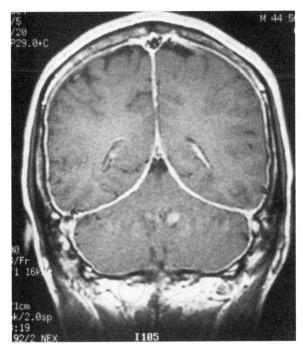

Figure 6–1. Meningitis. Gadolinium-enhanced MRI study shows enhancement along the tentorium, falx, and convexities.

distinct hyperintensity on T1-weighted images before injection of contrast material.

Contrast-enhanced MRI has been shown to be more sensitive than contrast-enhanced CT in detection of meningitis and its complications in experimental studies.[93] The radiology literature reports that abnormal contrast enhancement on intravenous (IV) gadolinium-enhanced MRI is seen in only 55% to 70% of patients with the clinical diagnosis of meningitis. The fluid attenuation inversion-recovery (FLAIR) technique is very sensitive and relatively specific in the diagnosis of intracranial subarachnoid space disease and meningeal disease.[135]

Subdural Effusion

Subdural effusions are believed to be caused by irritation of the dura by the infectious agents or its by-products or by inflammation of subdural veins with loss of fluid and albumin into the subdural space.[17] *H. influenzae* is a common pathogen associated with subdural effusion.[12] On neuroimaging, these effusions have a similar appearance to cerebrospinal fluid (CSF) and are frequently seen in the frontal region.[138] On contrast-enhanced imaging studies, there is no evidence of abnormal enhancement seen in the adjacent brain parenchyma. The subdural effusion usually resolves spontaneously without any treatment unless there is superimposed infection.

Subdural Empyema

Subdural empyema accounts for about 13% to 20% of all cases of intracranial infection. Subdural empyema is a collection of pus between the dura and the leptomeninges,

which often occurs as a complication of meningitis, paranasal sinusitis, otitis media, osteomyelitis, or a penetrating wound of the skull.[73, 125]

Frontal sinusitis is the most common cause of subdural empyema. Infective organisms probably enter the subdural space in a retrograde fashion through a dural sinus or through bridging veins.[125] Occasionally, a subdural effusion induced by meningitis may become infected. Subdural empyemas, even when small, usually cause focal neurologic deficits in addition to acute febrile illness. Subdural empyema is considered a neurosurgical emergency because of its progressive clinical course. Despite recent improvement in surgical technique and antibiotics, mortality remains high (25% to 40%).[125]

Complications of subdural empyema include venous thrombosis and infarction. On a CT scan, subdural empyema appears as a hypodense or isodense crescentic or lenticular area adjacent to the inner table of the skull.[83, 99] On a contrast-enhanced CT scan, enhancement of the medial rim may be seen. Empyemas are better visualized with MRI than with CT. Empyemas show slightly higher intensity, compared with CSF, on both T1-weighted and T2-weighted images, which can help to differentiate them from sterile subdural effusion. The higher signal intensity is caused by the increased protein content of the empyema. On T2-weighted images, adjacent cerebritis or infarction may present as high-signal-intensity areas with irregular margins[138] (Fig. 6–2*A*). Enhancement of the medial rim is invariably seen (Fig. 6–2*B* and *C*); enhancement of the lateral rim adjacent to bony calvarium may sometimes be visible. Subdural empyemas may also be parafalcine,[54] and they may occur over the tentorium. Occasionally, enhancement of the subjacent cerebral cortex may be seen in a gyriform pattern in contrast-enhanced CT or MRI scans, suggesting the presence of concomitant cerebritis or infarction.

Epidural Empyema

Epidural empyema, a collection of pus between the dura and calvaria, occurs as a complication of otitis media, mastoiditis, sinusitis, or osteomyelitis of the skull.[59] Generally, infection in these patients is not as toxic as that in patients with subdural empyema. In addition to the presence of an extracerebral collection, imaging studies may show displacement of the falx and dural sinuses away from the inner table of the skull, which is an important and useful sign indicating the epidural location of a collection.[78]

A hypointense rim, representing inflamed dura, is seen on T2-weighted MR images in an epidural, but not a subdural, empyema.[151] Contrast-enhanced CT or MRI scans show a reasonably well-demarcated rim of enhancement representing inflamed dura. Because the dura usually acts as a barrier to organisms, the cerebral cortex beneath an epidural empyema is generally normal, and no enhancement in the underlying brain is seen.

Ten percent of epidural empyemas may be associated with subdural empyema (Fig. 6–3). An unenhanced CT scan shows a lentiform hypodense or isodense collection. MRI shows a slightly higher-signal-intensity collection, compared with CSF, on both T1-weighted and T2-weighted images because of the increased protein content of the pus.

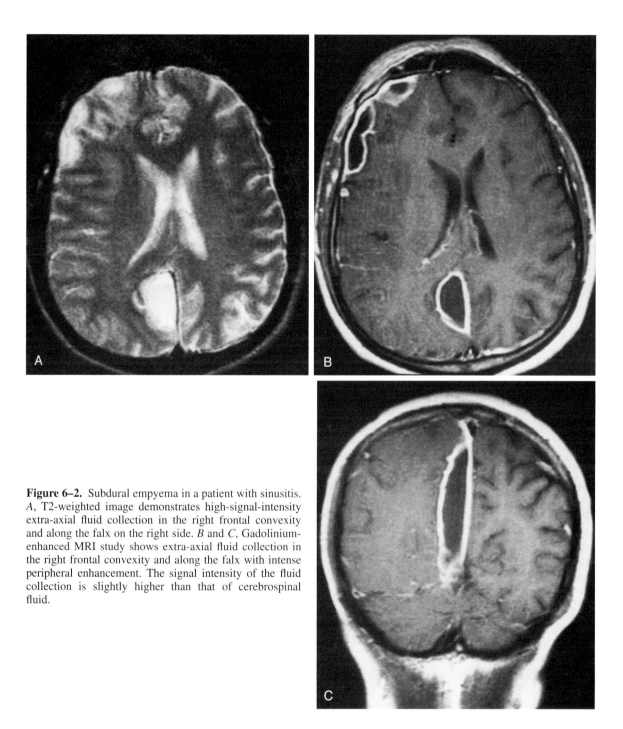

Figure 6–2. Subdural empyema in a patient with sinusitis. *A*, T2-weighted image demonstrates high-signal-intensity extra-axial fluid collection in the right frontal convexity and along the falx on the right side. *B* and *C*, Gadolinium-enhanced MRI study shows extra-axial fluid collection in the right frontal convexity and along the falx with intense peripheral enhancement. The signal intensity of the fluid collection is slightly higher than that of cerebrospinal fluid.

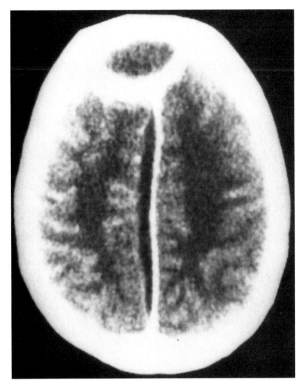

Figure 6–3. Frontal epidural empyema and interhemispheric fissure subdural empyema. Lentiform low-density collection is seen in the frontal region with displacement of the sagittal sinus away from the inner table of skull. An interhemispheric subdural collection is also seen.

Encephalitis

Encephalitis refers to diffuse inflammation of the brain with a parenchymal infiltration of inflammatory cells, usually caused by a virus. The brain damage caused by acute infective encephalitis is due to a combination of intracellular viral growth and the host's inflammatory response.

The most common viral agents are herpes simplex virus type 1 (HSV-1) and type 2 (HSV-2). Other causes include herpes zoster, arbovirus, and enteroviruses. Viral encephalitis in immunosuppressed patients can result from the human immunodeficiency virus (HIV), cytomegalovirus (CMV), and papovavirus. Other nonviral agents of encephalitis in immunosuppressed patients include *Toxoplasma*, *Aspergillus*, and *L. monocytogenes*.

Herpes Simplex Encephalitis

Herpes Simplex Type 1 Encephalitis

HSV-1 most commonly affects adults, whereas HSV-2 affects neonates. HSV-1 is the cause of 95% of all cases of herpetic encephalitis and is the most common cause of sporadic encephalitis. HSV-1 encephalitis is a fulminating, necrotizing meningoencephalitis that characteristically involves the temporal lobes and frontal lobes.

In the adult form, unenhanced CT scans show hypodense areas with mass effect in both temporal lobes and frontal lobes; these changes are less likely to be observed in parietal lobes. The findings are often asymmetrical.[27, 84] Sparing of the lenticular nucleus is said to be characteristic,[173] although such sparing may be observed in patients with infarction or glioma. An unenhanced CT scan infrequently shows hemorrhage in the low-density area early in the disease process, even though petechial hemorrhage is a frequent finding pathologically.

Contrast enhancement is a later finding in the disease process. Many published reports have documented uptake of technetium Tc 99m pertechnetate in various parts of the brain but most commonly in the temporal lobes. However, the scans become positive only at 2 days after the onset of clinical symptoms.[44, 50, 58] There are published reports that hexamethyl-propyleneamineoxime (HM-PAO)–SPECT is capable of detecting increased activity early on in the disease process.[44]

Enhanced CT scans show streaky, linear enhancement in the region of the sylvian fissure and the island of Reil[97] (Fig. 6–4). Unfortunately, CT studies, even high-resolution ones, show minimal changes, or results may be normal in the first 5 days despite the presence of obvious clinical symptoms. CT scans must be studied carefully to detect subtle changes that support the clinical diagnosis and to allow the institution of early antiviral therapy.

MRI studies show hypointensity on T1-weighted images and hyperintensity on T2-weighted images (Fig. 6–5). The temporal lobes and insular cortex are the areas of early involvement. The frontal lobe and the cingulate gyrus are involved later.[61] The contrast enhancement pattern of MRI is similar to that of CT. MRI is more sensitive than CT for early findings, especially when FLAIR imaging is used.[3] End-stage disease consists of encephalomalacia and atrophy in the previously involved areas; later, calcification may develop in these areas.

Definitive diagnosis is made either with positive fluorescein antibody staining or with a culture of the virus from a brain biopsy. Mortality is high, up to 70%. Successful treatment depends on early diagnosis and early institution of therapy before the onset of coma.[158]

Herpes Simplex Type 2 Encephalitis

HSV-2 encephalitis may be acquired through the placenta or during delivery.[41, 126] During the first trimester, HSV-2 encephalitis infection may have significant teratogenic effects on the fetal nervous system, including microphthalmia, encephalomalacia, and retinal dysplasia as well as mental and developmental retardation.[102, 136, 139]

Initial CT abnormalities include low density in the white matter diffusely, not just in the temporal lobes, and finger-like areas of increased cortical density on unenhanced scans 2 to 30 days after presentation. A gyriform pattern of enhancement may be seen later.

MRI shows hypointensity in the white matter on T1-weighted images and hyperintensity on T2-weighted images. The enhancing pattern in MRI studies is similar to that on contrast-enhanced CT scans.

End-stage HSV-2 encephalitis may be characterized by cystic encephalomalacic change and cortical calcification.[62] Periventricular calcification and parenchymal calcification

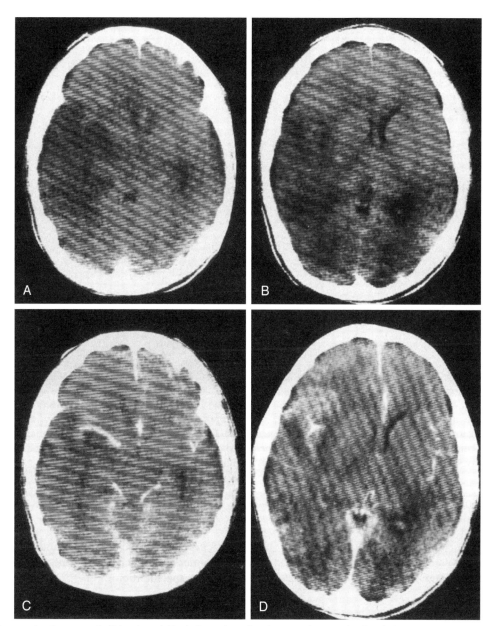

Figure 6–4. Herpes simplex encephalitis. *A* and *B*, A large low-density area is seen in the right temporal lobe with sparing of the lenticular nucleus. Significant mass effect has occurred with compression of the right lateral ventricle. *C* and *D*, Postcontrast scans show streaky linear enhancement in the region of the sylvian fissure.

are better seen on unenhanced CT scans than in MRI studies.[34] Mortality and morbidity rates are high.[158]

Herpes Zoster Encephalitis

Herpes zoster encephalitis is thought to be secondary to reactivation of a latent viral infection of earlier chickenpox. It is more commonly seen in immunosuppressed patients.[33, 65] CNS involvement is frequently seen in patients with skin lesions.

CT scans show multiple low-density lesions in the deep white matter. Hemorrhage may be seen as areas of poorly defined high density within the low density. MRI studies show hyperintensity in the deep white matter on T2-weighted images.

Herpes zoster virus has been implicated in the cause of granulomatous angiitis.[85, 125] Small cerebral arteries are typically involved, although large vessels may also be affected (Fig. 6–6). Cerebral infarction or aneurysm formation may be seen.

Arbovirus Encephalitis

Human infection caused by arbovirus is transmitted from birds through ticks and mosquitoes. There are more than 250 types of arbovirus, including eastern and western equine encephalitis, St. Louis encephalitis, Japanese encephalitis, and so on. CT and MRI may show abnormalities intracranially without the propensity to involve any specific region.[128, 132]

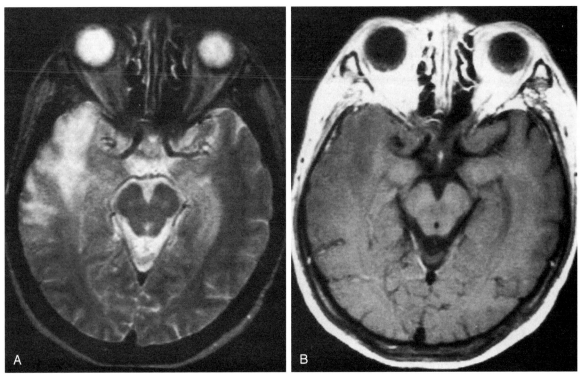

Figure 6–5. Herpes simplex encephalitis. *A,* T2-weighted image shows high signal intensity involving the gray and white matter of the right temporal lobe. Note the effacement of the adjacent cortical sulci, indicating the presence of mass effect. *B,* Gadolinium-enhanced image demonstrates no definite contrast enhancement in the early stage of disease. Low signal intensity with mass effect in right temporal lobe is obvious.

Acute Disseminated Encephalomyelitis

Acute disseminated encephalomyelitis is caused by an immune response to a preceding viral infection or vaccination. Patients usually present with neurologic signs and symptoms 5 days to 2 weeks later. Both humoral and cell-mediated immunity are implicated as the cause of pathologic changes. Vasculitis is thought to be caused by

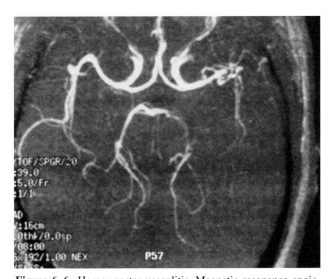

Figure 6–6. Herpes zoster vasculitis. Magnetic resonance angiogram demonstrates narrowing of the left middle cerebral artery branches as well as the proximal left posterior cerebral artery. There is a small infarct in the left middle cerebral artery territory.

complement activation as a result of antigen-antibody complexes. A hypersensitivity reaction to a myelin protein is thought to cause demyelination. Perivenous demyelination is the hallmark of the disease.

The disease primarily involves white matter, but change may also be apparent in gray matter and brain stem. CT may show low density in the periventricular white matter, and MRI may show hyperintensity in the white matter on T2-weighted images.[67, 75, 89, 104] Some of the lesions may exhibit contrast enhancement following IV injection of gadolinium.

The differential diagnosis include multiple sclerosis, vasculitis, and embolic infarction. In later stages of the disease, encephalomalacia, ventriculomegaly, and atrophy may be seen.

Other Encephalitides

Creutzfeldt-Jakob Disease

Creutzfeldt-Jakob disease is a human spongiform encephalopathy that results from an infection by a "slow virus." The mode of transmission has been traced to inoculations by injections of human growth hormone, transplantation of corneas, and implantation of cerebral electrodes.[118] In addition, butchers and meat handlers are at greater risk of contracting the disease. A new variant of Creutzfeldt-Jakob disease is due to bovine spongiform encephalopathy (so-called mad cow disease).

The infective prion is a proteinaceous particle that contains little or no nucleic acid. The disease occurs in adults in their late 50s. However, the new variant of the disease can affect all age groups. Dementia with rapid progression to stupor is seen clinically. CT and MRI studies are useful to document the rapid progression of atrophy.[78, 147] Cortical gray matter involvement without cerebral atrophy may represent an early phase of the disease.[45] Hyperintensity may be seen in cortical gray matter on T2-weighted images or FLAIR images, and on diffusion-weighted images, which may reflect areas of gliosis and microvacuolization pathologically.[6, 28, 44]

Subacute Sclerosing Panencephalitis

Subacute sclerosing panencephalitis is caused by the measles virus. Elevated levels of a neutralizing antibody to the virus can be detected in the blood and CSF. The disorder is usually seen in children and young adults. CT scans may show low-density changes in subcortical white matter as well as in basal ganglia. MRI studies show hyperintensity in the periventricular white matter and basal ganglia on T2-weighted images.[146] Atrophy is a late-stage finding.

Reye's Syndrome

Reye's syndrome is a disease of unknown etiology in children. It usually follows a viral infection such as type A or B influenza and varicella. Exogenous toxins, such as salicylates, and intrinsic metabolic defects have been implicated as being other factors associated with the disease.

Gross pathologic specimens demonstrate diffusely swollen brain. CT scans show diffuse low density of the supratentorial structures, a finding consistent with diffuse cerebral edema.[124]

Rasmussen's Encephalitis

Rasmussen's encephalitis is a childhood disease. The child presents with severe epilepsy and progressive neurologic deficits.[143] Seizures are usually of the partial motor seizure type and tend to be intractable. The intractable nature of the seizure may make hemispherectomy necessary if medical therapy is ineffective.

Early in the disease process, CT and MRI findings may be normal. MRI may reveal hyperintensity in the white matter and putamen on T2-weighted images.[143] PET imaging using fluorodeoxyglucose-18 (FDG-18) may show decreased hemispheric activity.

Encephalitis in Immunocompromised Patients

Human Immunodeficiency Virus Encephalitis

HIV is a neurotropic virus, which typically causes a subacute form of encephalitis. CT scans may show low density in the periventricular white matter. MRI may show hyperintensity in the periventricular white matter on T2-weighted and FLAIR images.[114] Normal neuroimaging studies do not exclude HIV encephalitis.

Progressive Multifocal Leukoencephalopathy

Progressive multifocal leukoencephalopathy is caused by papovavirus. It is uncertain whether it represents a reactivation of a latent infection. Pathologically, the major target cell is the oligodendrocyte. Because this cell is responsible for myelin maintenance, its destruction leads to demyelination.

CT scans characteristically show low density in the parietal and occipital white matter. Frontal involvement is seen later on. Early involvement may assume an asymmetrical pattern, but the changes in later disease are highly symmetrical and diffuse. Contrast enhancement is usually absent but may occur.[155] The presence of contrast enhancement may actually suggest the relative presence of host immunity and thus indicates a better prognosis.

MRI shows hypointensity in the white matter on T1-weighted images and hyperintensity on T2-weighted images (Fig. 6–7). MRI is more sensitive than CT in detecting abnormalities.[56]

Cytomegalovirus Encephalitis

In immunocompromised patients, CMV may cause meningoencephalitis or subacute encephalitis.[106] CMV can produce demyelination and necrosis within the white matter.

CT scans show low density in the white matter, which may or may not enhance with contrast agents. MRI shows high signal intensity in the white matter on T2-weighted images and is more sensitive than CT in detecting leukoencephalitis.[92]

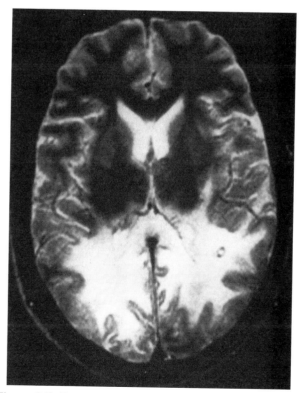

Figure 6–7. Progressive multifocal leukoencephalopathy. T2-weighted image shows high signal intensity in the parieto-occipital white matter bilaterally.

Neonatal cytomegalic inclusion disease is a severe disseminated necrotizing encephalitis with a tendency to involve the periventricular tissue. Unenhanced CT scans show periventricular calcification with ventricular dilatation[4] (Fig. 6–8).

Cerebritis and Abscess

Pathologically, there are four stages in the evolution of cerebral abscess as demonstrated by experimental studies by Enzmann and colleagues[38]:

1. *Acute cerebritis* (the first 4 to 5 days). The organism grows in the parenchyma. Acute inflammatory cells, particularly polymorphonuclear leukocytes, migrate into the parenchyma to ingest or destroy bacteria. Opening of the blood-brain barrier produces edema. Microscopic hemorrhage may be seen during the acute cerebritis stage but is unusual later.
2. *Late cerebritis* (at 7 to 10 days). The small areas of necrosis coalesce into one large focus filled with necrotic debris. Granulation tissue forms at its margin, containing macrophages. Edema and small foci of cerebritis are seen surrounding this area. These small foci later form satellite lesions adjacent to the large abscess.
3. *Early abscess* (at 10 to 14 days). Formation of a collagenous capsule by fibroblasts is seen. The central necrotic area is liquefied. Surrounding edema persists.
4. *Mature abscess* (>14 days). A decrease in surrounding edema is seen. A gliotic reaction develops at the outer margin of the abscess capsule. The wall of the mature abscess consists of three layers: (1) an inner inflammatory layer of granulation tissue containing macrophages,

(2) a middle collagenous layer, and (3) an outer gliotic layer.[172]

Acute cerebritis is not often identified on neuroimaging studies because symptoms do not usually develop until later.[139] Initially, acute cerebritis usually manifests in white matter with vascular congestion and edema, so that ill-defined areas of low density and mass effect in the white matter are noted on unenhanced CT scans.[21, 101] On MRI studies, edema is seen as hypointensity on T1-weighted images and hyperintensity on T2-weighted images. MRI is superior to CT in detecting cerebral edema and subtle mass effect.[57, 128]

In early cerebritis, mild central nodular enhancement may be seen on contrast-enhanced CT or MRI scans (Fig. 6–9). In the late cerebritis stage, experimental studies of the evolution of brain abscess following inoculation of organisms have demonstrated brain enhancement on CT scans.[38] On MRI studies, the enhancing pattern is similar to that with CT. A relatively thick, slightly irregular, ringlike enhancement is seen interposed between the peripheral edema and central necrosis (Fig. 6–10).

As the lesion matures, the ringlike enhancement becomes thinner and smoother. The most distinctive feature of abscess on imaging is the presence of a smooth, thin capsule with a moderate amount of cerebral edema.[57] It is located at the corticomedullary junction and usually extends into the white matter. The abscess cavity has necrosis and liquefaction within its center. Unenhanced CT scans show a low-density area with mass effect and compression of the ventricular system. Between the central low-density area (representing the cavity) and the surrounding low-density edematous zone, a ring of higher density may be seen.[70, 137, 153] Visualization of spontaneous gas within the

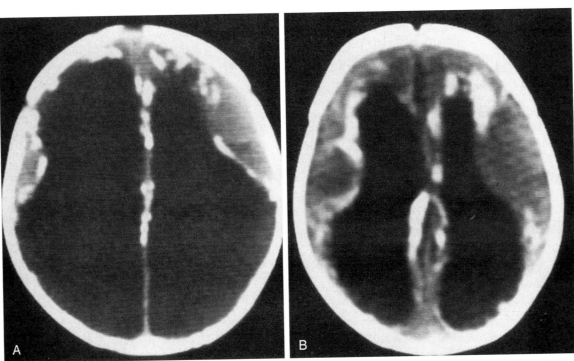

Figure 6–8. *A* and *B*, Cytomegalic inclusion disease. Unenhanced CT scan in a newborn shows periventricular calcification and ventricular dilatation.

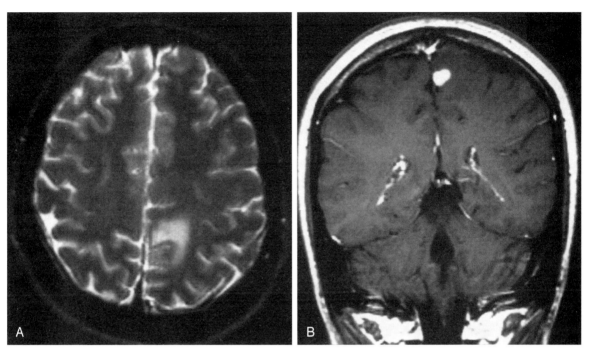

Figure 6–9. Early cerebritis. *A*, T2-weighted image demonstrates a low-signal-intensity focus with surrounding high-signal-intensity edema. *B*, Gadolinium-enhanced MRI study shows nodular enhancement with surrounding edema.

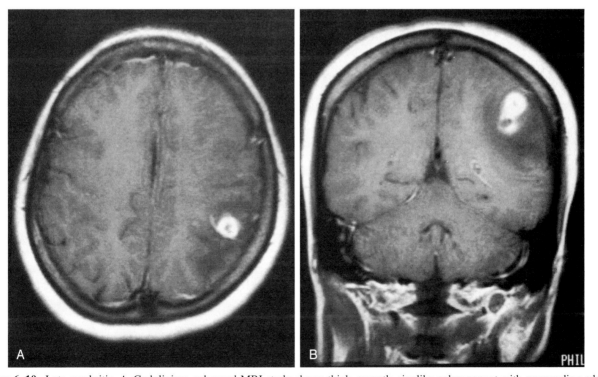

Figure 6–10. Late cerebritis. *A*, Gadolinium-enhanced MRI study shows thick, smooth, ringlike enhancement with surrounding edema. *B*, Gadolinium-enhanced MRI study (coronal view) shows a second, small, adjacent ringlike enhancement.

abscess cavity indicates the presence of gas-forming organisms[99, 101] (Fig. 6–11). Contrast-enhanced CT scans show ringlike enhancement, which is usually thin and uniform in thickness. Occasionally, thick irregular ring enhancement may be seen—especially following partial treatment—and may mimic neoplasm.

The CT features of abscess vary, depending on the function of the host reaction to infection and different stages in the evolution of the abscess.[97, 172] On MRI scans, the capsule is better visualized as compared with CT. The capsule is isointense to hyperintense to gray matter on T1-weighted images and hypointense on T2-weighted images. The hypointensity on the abscess capsule is consistently seen with abscess and may be useful in characterizing the lesion[57] (Fig. 6–12A). However, other lesions, such as metastasis, glioma, and cysticercosis, may show a similar hypointense ring on T2-weighted images. The capsule enhances with IV administration of contrast material on CT or MRI studies.

The presence of satellite lesions is a unique feature of cerebral abscess (Fig. 6–12B). Firmness of the capsule wall depends on how long the lesion has been present. Usually, more than 2 weeks is required to form a firm capsule. Clinical improvement with medical therapy has been correlated with a decrease in both the degree of ring enhancement and the amount of surrounding edema (Fig. 6–13).[71, 121]

A serious fulminating complication is rupture of the abscess into an adjacent ventricle. Abscesses tend to rupture medially into the ventricular system because the medial wall is thinner than the lateral wall.[153] This is related to the white matter having less vascular supply than gray matter. A more intense perivascular response is seen at the site of gray matter.[137]

The differential CT diagnosis of cerebral abscess includes primary or metastatic neoplasm, subacute infection, and resolving hematoma. The enhancing ring of an abscess is usually thinner and more uniform than that found in the neoplasm. Granulomatous abscesses tend to have a thicker ring than pyogenic abscesses and have less surrounding edema. Infarcts often show gyral enhancement, occasionally mimicking ring enhancement. Resolving hematoma may have a dense center with ringlike enhancement and much less surrounding edema.

The MRI differential diagnosis of abscess is similar to the CT diagnosis except for hematomas, which can be recognized by their characteristic MRI signal intensity patterns, depending on the age of the hematomas.

Various authors have given different explanations of capsular hypointensity.[68, 139, 171] The most plausible hypothesis seemed to suggest that macrophages within the granulation layer of the abscess capsule are the cause of the hypointensity. Macrophages kill bacteria with respiratory burst, during which molecular oxygen is converted into atomic oxygen, which then generates a series of short-lived highly reactive oxygen free radicals that interact with the bacteria. Because these free radicals are intracellular, they may be capable of producing similar susceptibility effects as intracellular methemoglobin or deoxyhemoglobin with resultant T2 shortening.[68, 139, 171]

The features of abscess tend to differ in immunocompromised patients receiving steroids. In such patients, edema may be minimal and the abscess capsule may be thick and irregular. Hypointensity of the capsule seen on T2-weighted images may not be obvious. Extraparenchymal spread into the ventricles and meningitis are more common.

The differential diagnosis of brain abscesses is quite

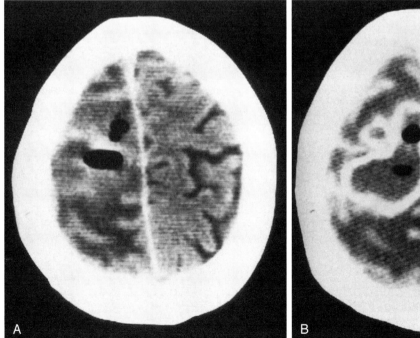
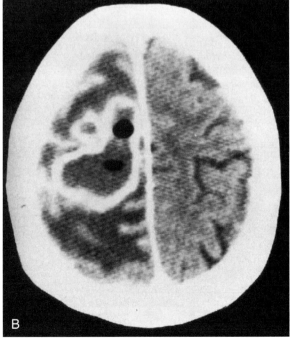

Figure 6–11. Abscess caused by gas-forming organism. *A*, Gas is seen with a surrounding low-density area on noncontrast CT scan. *B*, Contrast CT scan shows irregular, ringlike enhancement; gas is visible within the cavity. The causative organism was *Escherichia coli*.

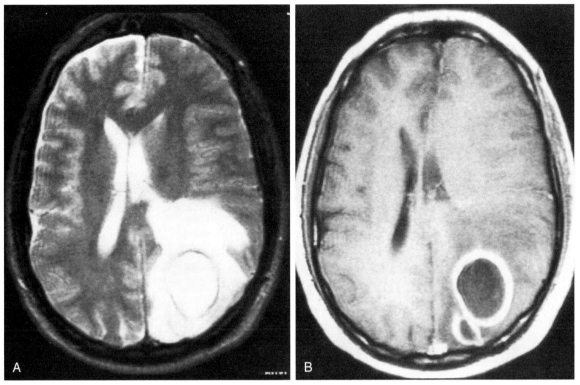

Figure 6–12. Mature abscess. *A*, T2-weighted image shows a mature abscess with hypointense rim, central cavity, and adjacent surrounding edema. A small satellite lesion is also seen. *B*, Gadolinium-enhanced MRI study demonstrates smooth, ringlike enhancement corresponding to the hypointense rim seen on T2-weighted images.

extensive and includes necrotic primary brain tumor, cystic metastatic tumor, infarction, resolving hematoma, cysticercosis, and thrombosed aneurysm. Thallium 201 SPECT or PET may be useful in differentiating an abscess from a necrotic tumor. Preferential uptake of thallium is seen in tumor, especially high-grade tumor, but not in abscess.[44] Tumor has higher glucose utilization than that of abscess, as shown on FDG PET imaging.

Recently, much work has been done with advanced imaging techniques such as diffusion-weighted imaging and proton MRS. The central portion of an abscess cavity tends to show depression of apparent diffusion coefficient, thus increased signal intensity on diffusion-weighted images (Fig. 6–14), whereas tumor necrosis exhibits an increase in apparent diffusion coefficient.

A significant number of studies of proton MRS have been performed in differential diagnosis of abscess and necrotic brain tumors. It is well documented that abscess cavities contain amino acids, succinate, and acetate, which are not seen in the necrotic center of the tumor.[30] Furthermore, MRS may be useful as the follow-up examination in evaluation of the response to therapy.[31]

Mycotic Aneurysm

Intracranial septic emboli may lead to the formation of mycotic aneurysms, usually seen in patients with a history of IV drug abuse, cyanotic heart disease, and subacute bacterial endocarditis. Mycotic aneurysms probably result from infarction of the arterial wall secondary to infected

emboli. Mycotic aneurysms may be solitary or multiple, and they usually involve middle cerebral artery branches. The relative frequency of middle cerebral artery branch involvement is probably explained by the likelihood of emboli being carried into this territory.

Rupture of a mycotic aneurysm may produce an intracerebral or subdural hematoma[134] (Fig. 6–15). An unruptured mycotic aneurysm may occasionally be detected by contrast-enhanced CT or MRI studies.[2] Associated infarction or small areas of cerebritis or abscess formation may be seen on imaging. Follow-up imaging studies can be useful when mycotic aneurysms are being treated medically with antibiotics. A single mycotic aneurysm may warrant surgical extirpation.

Ependymitis

Ventriculitis, or ependymitis, is an inflammation of the ependymal lining of the ventricular system. Spread of infection to the ventricles may result from rupture of a periventricular abscess or from retrograde spread of infection from the basal cisterns by way of the fourth ventricle. Hydrocephalus may result from intraventricular adhesions and septation caused by organization of intraventricular exudate and debris, resulting in blockage of the interventricular foramina.[129, 166] A trapped fourth ventricle may result from obstruction of its outlets and the aqueduct because of ependymitis.[169]

The noncontrast CT scan may be normal or may show only slightly increased density in the region of the affected

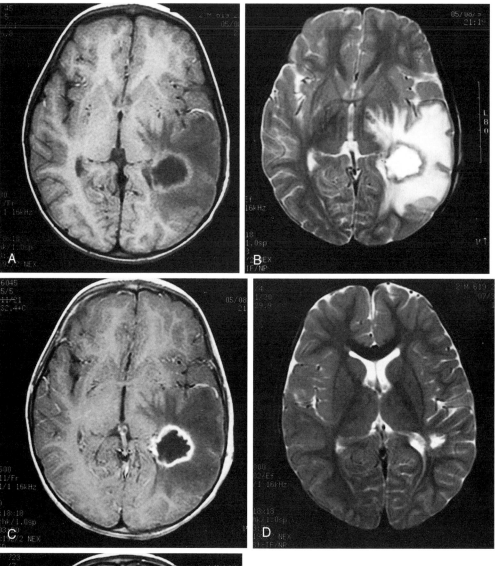

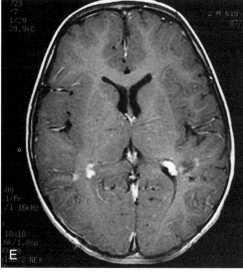

Figure 6–13. Abscess treated conservatively with antibiotics. *A*, T1-weighted image shows a low-signal-intensity mass with an isointense ringlike rim and surrounding edema in the left posterior temporal lobe. *B*, T2-weighted image shows a high-signal-intensity mass with low-signal-intensity rim and marked surrounding edema. *C*, Gadolinium-enhanced image demonstrates avid ringlike enhancement of the ringlike rim with a central cavity and surrounding edema. *D*, Follow-up T2-weighted image obtained 8 weeks later reveals a significant decrease in the size of the abscess and surrounding edema. *E*, Follow-up gadolinium-enhanced image demonstrates minimal residual enhancement.

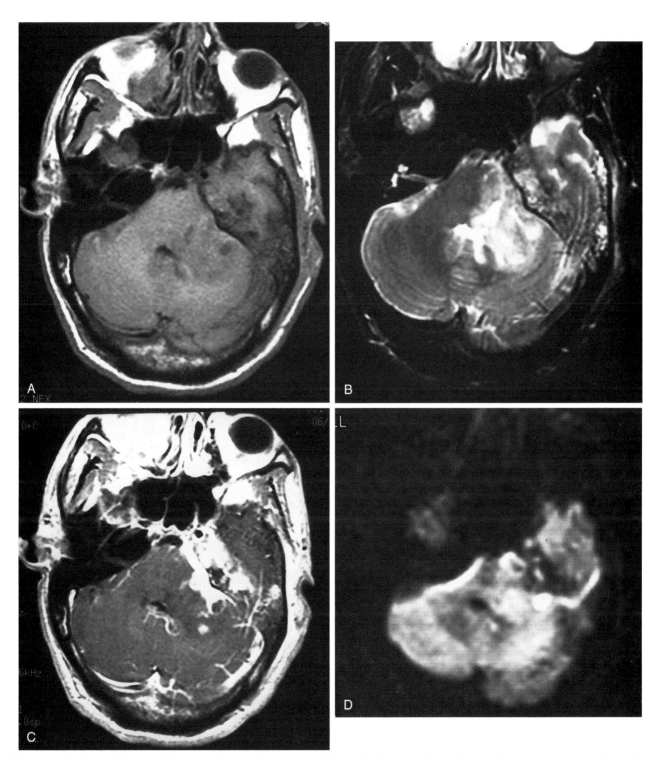

Figure 6–14. Mastoiditis, cerebritis, and abscess formation. *A*, T1-weighted image shows abnormal low signal intensity in the left temporal lobe, left brachium pontis, and left mastoid. *B*, T2-weighted image shows heterogeneous high signal intensity involving the left temporal lobe, left brachium pontis, and left mastoid. *C*, Gadolinium-enhanced image demonstrates abnormal enhancement involving the left temporal lobe, left brachium pontis, and left mastoid. Note the presence of a small ringlike enhancement in the posterior aspect of the brachium pontis. *D*, Diffusion-weighted image reveals a focal area of increased signal intensity, corresponding to the ringlike enhancement. This is consistent with restricted diffusion in an abscess.

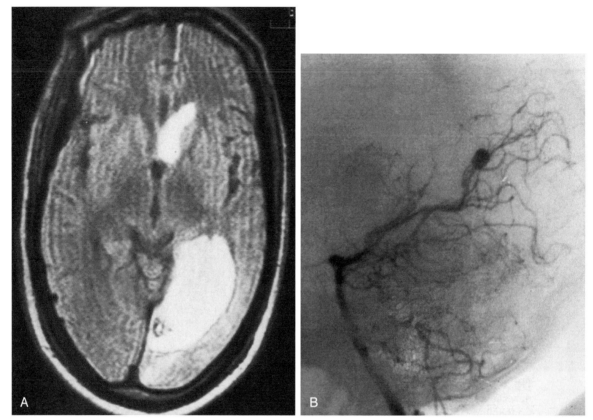

Figure 6–15. Mycotic aneurysm. *A*, Proton-density–weighted image shows high-signal-intensity hemorrhage in the left occipital lobe as well as in the ventricle. A small, ringlike, low-signal-intensity area is seen within the hemorrhage. *B*, A mycotic aneurysm was found on cerebral angiogram, corresponding to the small, ringlike, low-signal-intensity area seen on the MRI study.

ependyma.[101, 170] MRI studies may show marginal ventricular abnormality or only slightly increased signal intensity in the region of affected ependyma on proton-density–weighted images. The fluid within the ventricles may show slightly increased intensity, indicating the presence of cells and inflammatory debris as well as increased protein concentration in the CSF.

Contrast-enhanced CT or MRI studies show uniform, thin ependymal enhancement (Fig. 6–16).

The differential diagnosis on CT and MRI studies includes ependymal seeding of intracranial neoplasm. The ependymal enhancement may be irregular or nodular if it is secondary to seeding of neoplasm. Obviously, the clinical history may be helpful in arriving at the correct diagnosis.

Granulomatous Infection
Tuberculosis

Tuberculosis meningitis results from the hematogenous spread of bacilli from a primary lesion in the chest or genitourinary tract or from direct extension from an intracerebral focus. Primarily, very young and very old persons are affected, with the highest incidence in the first 3 years of life.[111] More recently, an increased incidence of tuberculosis has been seen in immunocompromised patients. In the patient with tuberculous meningitis, the exudate, which is commonly seen in the basal cisterns, tends to be thick and adhesive. Communicating hydrocephalus may result from obstruction at the level of the basal cisterns. Vascular involvement of the arteries at the base of the brain or sylvian fissures may result from vasculitis and surrounding meningeal inflammation.

On noncontrast CT or MRI studies, the basal cisterns and sylvian fissures may be partially or completely obscured by the presence of purulent exudate and inflammatory tissue, which appears to have a density or signal intensity similar to that of the adjacent brain on CT scans or T1-weighted MRI studies, respectively.

On contrast-enhanced CT or MRI studies, the involved cisterns show intense enhancement[5, 16, 138, 154] (Fig. 6–17). MRI studies are more sensitive than CT scans for detection of tuberculous meningitis.[14] Ischemic infarcts, meningeal enhancement, and ventriculitis are better shown by MRI than by CT. Gadolinium injection is essential in evaluation of patients with intracranial tuberculosis. Calcification in the basal cisterns has been demonstrated a few years after the onset of disease and is better shown with CT scans.[87] Cerebral infarction may result from arterial or venous involvement. Middle cerebral artery territory is a common location[9] (Fig. 6–18).

Arriving at a definitive diagnosis of tuberculoma may be difficult because 52% of patients with intracranial tuberculomas have no extracranial disease.[94] Tuberculomas may be found in any portion of the intracranial compartment. Histologically, tuberculomas consist of a central zone of caseous material surrounded by reactive epithelial cells, Langhans' giant cells, polymorphonuclear cells, plasma cells, and lymphocytes.[154]

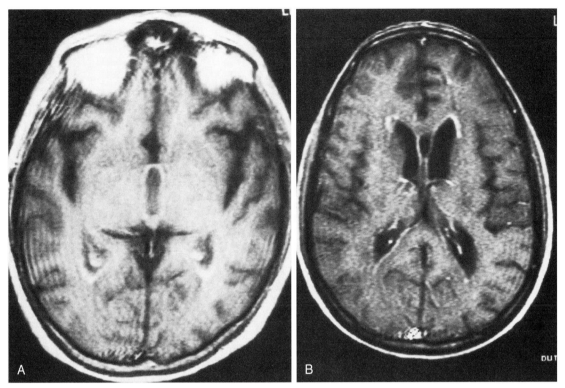

Figure 6–16. Ependymitis. *A* and *B*, Gadolinium-enhanced MRI study shows thin, smooth ependymal enhancement in an AIDS patient with cytomegalovirus ependymitis.

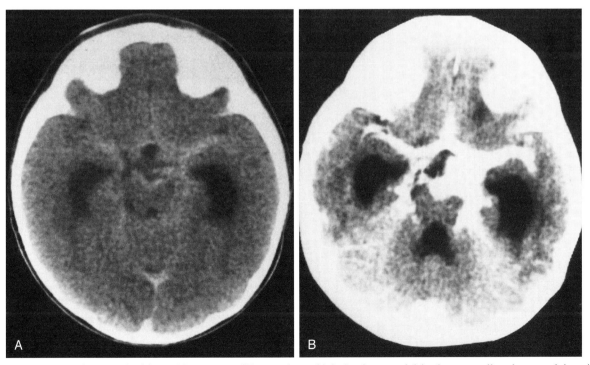

Figure 6–17. Tuberculous meningitis. *A*, Noncontrast CT scan shows high-density material in the suprasellar cistern, sylvian cistern, and perimesencephalic cistern. Dilation of both temporal horns is seen. *B*, Contrast CT scan shows diffuse intense enhancement in the involved cisterns.

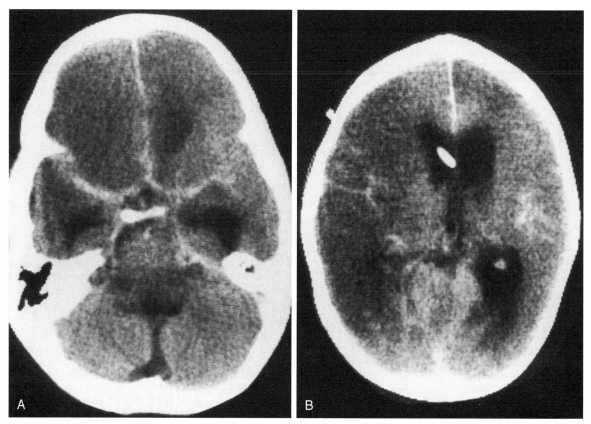

Figure 6–18. Cerebral infarction as a complication of tuberculous meningitis. *A,* Large low-density area is seen in the right temporal frontoparietal region in the right middle cerebral artery distribution, consistent with an infarct. *B,* Enhancement is seen in the sylvian fissures and along the tentorial margin, consistent with meningitis.

On unenhanced CT scans, tuberculomas may be isodense, hyperdense, or of mixed density. On contrast-enhanced CT scans, tuberculomas may present a pattern of ringlike enhancement[152] or, less likely, areas of nodular enhancement (Fig. 6–19) or irregular nonhomogeneous enhancement.[21, 109, 116] A central nidus of calcification with surrounding ringlike enhancement, known as the *target sign,* suggests tuberculoma.[152]

Gadolinium-enhanced MRI studies show enhancing patterns similar to those on contrast-enhanced CT scans[20, 29] (Fig. 6–20). Unenhanced MRI studies show mixed, predominantly low-signal-intensity lesion with a central zone of high signal intensity and surrounding high-signal-intensity edema on T2-weighted images or FLAIR images. A central high-signal-intensity zone on T2-weighted or FLAIR images corresponds to caseating necrosis. The low signal intensity of the capsule may be related to a layer of collagenous fibrosis with high protein concentration and low water content and a layer of outer inflammatory cells.[130]

On MRS, tuberculomas show only lipid resonance, with specific components of serine and phenolic lipids.[130] Follow-up CT or MRI studies are useful in monitoring the response to medical treatment.

Parenchymal infection of tuberculosis may occur with or without meningitis. Tuberculosis cerebritis or abscess may have an appearance on neuroimaging studies similar to that of pyogenic bacterial infection. Tuberculous abscess is rare and is characterized by a central area of liquefaction

with pus (Fig. 6–21). These abscesses should not be confused with tuberculomas with central caseation and liquefaction mimicking pus.[52, 156]

Continued growth of tuberculoma with unresponsiveness to therapy, despite adequate medical treatment, is a known phenomenon called *paradoxical expansion.* Various immunologic mechanisms have been advanced as explanations, including defective local tissue immune response and poor penetration of drugs.[130]

Sarcoidosis

The intracranial compartment is involved in 15% of patients with known sarcoidosis.[24, 120, 133, 150] On rare occasions, CNS involvement may be the sole manifestation of sarcoidosis.[13, 53] Sarcoid is more prevalent in the 3rd and 4th decades of life. It may present as leptomeningitis or intracerebral granulomas. A third form of sarcoidosis, meningoencephalitis, is rarely seen.[96] Granulomatous meningitis often involves the basal cisterns in the region of the optic chiasm and hypothalamic-pituitary axis. Hydrocephalus may occur as a result of obstruction at the aqueduct, fourth ventricle, or leptomeninges.[80, 90]

Contrast-enhanced MRI is the imaging modality of choice for evaluation of meningeal sarcoidosis. Solitary or multiple lesions involving the meninges may be seen, and occasionally they may present as a large extra-axial mass (Fig. 6–22). The lesions are hypointense to isointense to

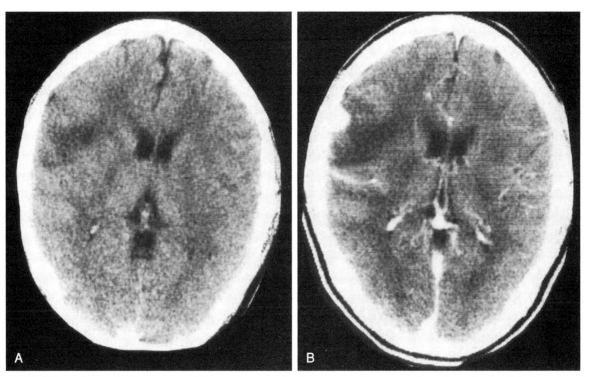

Figure 6–19. Tuberculoma. *A,* Noncontrast CT scan shows an isodense area with surrounding edema in the right frontal region. *B,* Contrast CT scan demonstrates nodular homogeneous enhancement.

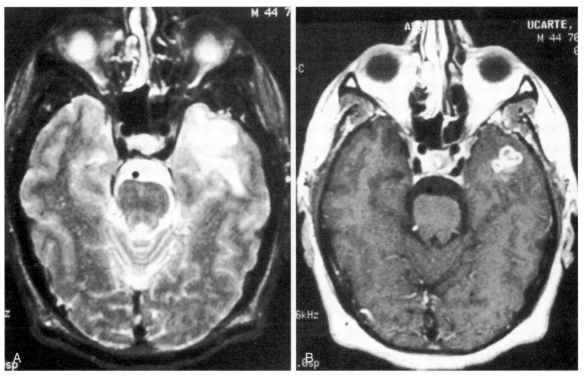

Figure 6–20. Tuberculoma. *A,* T2-weighted image shows an area of high signal intensity in the left temporal lobe. *B,* Gadolinium-enhanced MRI study demonstrates multiring enhancement with surrounding edema.

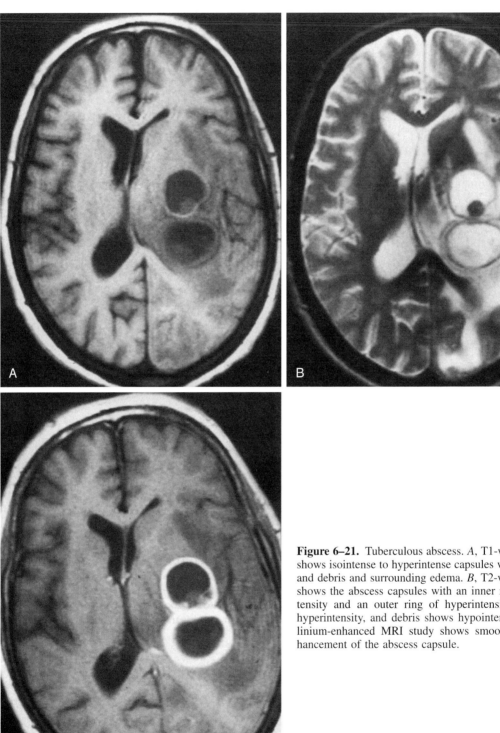

Figure 6–21. Tuberculous abscess. *A*, T1-weighted image shows isointense to hyperintense capsules with central pus and debris and surrounding edema. *B*, T2-weighted image shows the abscess capsules with an inner ring of hypointensity and an outer ring of hyperintensity; pus shows hyperintensity, and debris shows hypointensity. *C*, Gadolinium-enhanced MRI study shows smooth ringlike enhancement of the abscess capsule.

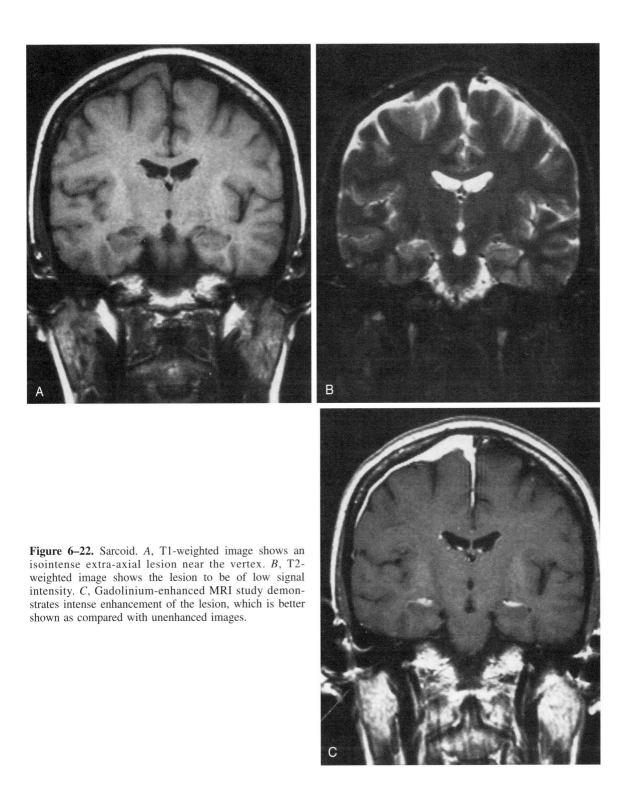

Figure 6–22. Sarcoid. *A*, T1-weighted image shows an isointense extra-axial lesion near the vertex. *B*, T2-weighted image shows the lesion to be of low signal intensity. *C*, Gadolinium-enhanced MRI study demonstrates intense enhancement of the lesion, which is better shown as compared with unenhanced images.

brain on T1-weighted images and are of variable but frequently low signal intensity on T2-weighted images. Homogeneous enhancement is seen with contrast-enhanced MRI as with contrast-enhanced CT.

The differential diagnosis may include meningiomas, metastatic disease, and lymphoma. Diffuse meningeal disease is more common than focal disease in sarcoidosis. Leptomeningeal enhancement involving the basal cisterns can be seen on contrast-enhanced MRI studies (Fig. 6–23).[131] However, a normal contrast-enhanced MRI study does not exclude the possibility of meningeal sarcoidosis.

The differential diagnosis of basal leptomeningeal enhancement may include bacterial, tuberculous, fungal, or cysticercal meningitis and meningeal seeding from metastasis, lymphoma, or leukemia. The noncaseating granulomas may be single or multiple, sometimes mimicking primary or metastatic neoplasm.[53, 127, 133]

On unenhanced CT scans, the granulomatous lesion shows hyperdense or isodense areas with minimum surrounding edema. Contrast-enhanced CT scans reveal homogeneous enhancement of these lesions.[74] Improvement with a decrease in size and number of lesions may be observed following steroid treatment. The intracranial granulomas may be single or multiple in the cortical or subcortical region.

On MRI studies, the lesions show heterogeneous and hyperintense signal pattern on T2-weighted images. Contrast-enhanced MRI studies show homogeneous enhancement.[60, 131] The differential diagnosis may include primary or metastatic neoplasms. Occasionally, meningeal disease

extends into the deep cortical tissue and may mimic a parenchymal lesion. Diffuse periventricular white matter high-signal-intensity lesions on T2-weighted images are among the most common findings in neurosarcoidosis. The areas of involvement may show enhancement following IV injection of gadolinium. These lesions are probably secondary to involvement of the small arteries in the white matter.[60, 76, 131]

In the rare form of meningoencephalitis, contrast-enhanced CT scans may show linear and nodular meningeal enhancement extending into the parenchyma through the Virchow-Robin spaces.[96] Hypodense lesions in the white matter have been described and are probably secondary to involvement of the small arteries in the white matter.[76]

SPIROCHETE INFECTION

Lyme Disease

Lyme disease is caused by the spirochete *Borrelia burgdorferi* and is transmitted by deer ticks.[107] *Borrelia* is a neurotrophic bacterium that can produce acute neurologic symptoms or can remain dormant for many years.

Like syphilis, Lyme disease presents clinically in stages. The characteristic finding in the *early* stage is the skin rash known as erythema chronicum migrans seen at the site of tick bite.[79] Flulike symptoms and arthralgia associated with regional lymphadenopathy are also seen in the early stage. A disseminated form of early Lyme disease can occur in

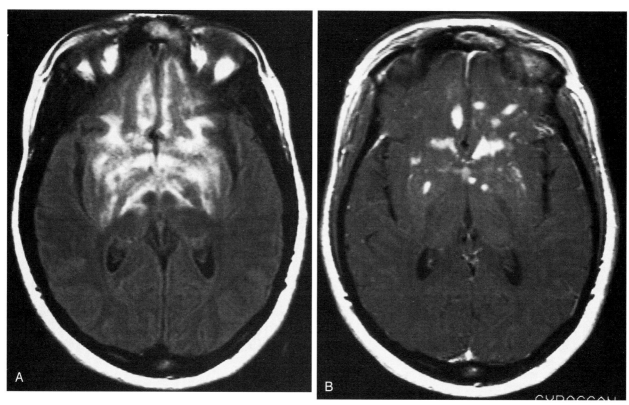

Figure 6–23. Sarcoidosis. *A,* Fluid-attenuating inversion recovery (FLAIR) image shows diffuse, irregular, abnormal high signal intensity extending from the subarachnoid space into the brain parenchyma of frontal lobes and basal ganglia. *B,* Gadolinium-enhanced image demonstrates patchy contrast enhancement involving the frontal lobes and basal ganglia.

which the organs primarily involved are skin, joints, heart, and nervous system.

Late symptoms occur in approximately 10% of untreated patients. Signs and symptoms of chronic neurologic damage include headache, memory impairment, papilledema, irritability, facial palsy, and peripheral neuropathies.

In many patients, neuroimaging studies may be normal. MRI findings, when present, include multiple bilateral periventricular, subcortical white matter, basal ganglia, and brain stem hyperintense lesions seen on T2-weighted or FLAIR images. The lesions are said to resemble multiple sclerosis plaques.[46, 119] Peripheral enhancement of these lesions may be seen. In some patients, diffuse meningeal enhancement is seen, indicating the presence of an encephalopathic process.

Syphilis

Syphilis is usually a sexually transmitted disease caused by *Treponema pallidum*, and CNS involvement occurs in the tertiary stage. Patients with AIDS usually show CNS involvement earlier, within 3 to 18 months. Acute syphilitic meningitis is a common manifestation in HIV-positive patients who are infected by *T. pallidum*.

Neurosyphilis can be divided into (1) meningovascular syphilis and (2) syphilitic gumma.

Meningovascular Syphilis

Pathologically, meningovascular syphilis is manifested by widespread thickening of the meninges, with lymphocytic infiltration involving the meninges and around the small vessels.[108] CT shows multiple low-density areas involving both gray and white matter.[48] Contrast-enhanced CT scans show linear, nonhomogeneous enhancement.

MRI is superior to CT scans in demonstrating additional foci of abnormality.[64] Contrast-enhanced MRI studies may demonstrate meningeal enhancement in addition to a gyriform pattern of enhancement.

Syphilitic Gumma

Gummas consist of masses of granulation tissue and are rare. They originate in the meninges and blood vessels and spread into the brain parenchyma.

On CT scans, gummas are well-delineated masses with ringlike or nodular enhancement. On MRI scans, gumma shows a high-signal-intensity ring on T1-weighted images and low signal intensity with surrounding high-signal-intensity edema on T2-weighted images. On contrast-enhanced MRI, gumma shows nodular or ringlike enhancement. Cerebral atrophy may develop in patients with neurosyphilis.[51]

Fungal Disease

Fungal infection may involve intracranial blood vessels, leptomeninges, and brain parenchyma. Intracranial infection is frequently secondary to pulmonary disease. Prior to the era of immunosuppressive therapy in organ transplant patients and the increase in HIV infection, fungal infection

of the CNS was rare. Other conditions that predispose patients to fungal infection include diabetes, pregnancy, and malignancy.

Depending on the genera, fungi may exist as single cells (yeast) or in a branched appearance (hyphal form). The yeast and hyphal forms may coalesce and form mycelia. The fungi of yeast forms tend to spread hematogenously to the meningeal microcirculation, with resultant leptomeningitis attributable to their smaller size; the larger hyphal form more commonly involves the brain parenchyma, with resultant cerebritis or encephalitis.

The genera that are present predominantly as yeast forms include *Blastomyces, Candida, Coccidioides, Cryptococcus, Histoplasma, Paracoccidioides,* and *Torulopsis.* Hyphal forms include *Aspergillus, Mucor* and other agents of mucormycosis, and *Pseudoallescheria.*[49]

CNS fungal infection displays neuroimaging features similar to those seen with tuberculosis. It is known that CT scanning underestimates the extent of the disease in patients with widespread fungal infection, and MRI probably better represents the extent of the disease. CT or MRI findings are not specific for various types of fungal infection.

Aspergillosis

Aspergillus fumigatus infection is seen predominantly in immunocompromised patients.[26] CNS aspergillosis is more commonly caused by hematogenous spread of pulmonary disease and less commonly caused by direct extension of disease in the nasal cavity and paranasal sinuses. Pathologically, diffuse vascular invasion with thrombosis of cerebral vessels occurs.[161] Necrotizing arteritis of small vascular channels is also seen.

CT scans show low-density areas with little or no contrast enhancement and mass effect, representing areas of infarction.[40, 55] At times, hemorrhagic infarction may be seen. Cerebritis or abscess formation may also be seen secondary to hematogenous spread of the disease. CT scans show a slightly hyperdense, ringlike lesion with central low density and surrounding edema. Some contrast enhancement may be seen.[77] Focal areas of hemorrhage within the lesion may be seen.[148]

MRI studies demonstrate a peripheral ring of low signal intensity with an isointense (to gray matter) center and high signal surrounding edema on T2-weighted images. The ring of low signal intensity corresponds to a dense population of *Aspergillus* hyphal elements and small areas of hemorrhage histologically.

Coccidioidomycosis

Coccidioidomycosis is caused by the airborne fungus *Coccidioides immitis.* This fungus is endemic in the southwestern United States as well as in portions of Mexico and central South America.

Pathologically, coccidioidomycosis is characterized by thickened, congested leptomeninges and multiple granulomas in the basal cisterns. Meningitis is most intense at the base of the brain. Hydrocephalus is seen as a result of granulomatous meningitis.[10] Meningeal involvement is the most common manifestation of CNS disease, occurring in up to 50% of the patients with disseminated systemic disease. Males are affected five to seven times more commonly than females. Adult nonwhites often have acute, rapidly fatal meningitis, whereas children and adult whites usually have subacute or chronic meningitis.

Unenhanced CT or MRI studies show isodense or isointense granulomatous tissue filling the basal cisterns. Contrast-enhanced CT or MRI studies show extensive basal cisternal or convexity enhancement (Fig. 6–24). Parenchymal granulomas occur infrequently; ringlike enhancement with minimum surrounding edema may be seen on contrast-enhanced CT or MR studies[35, 40, 98] (Fig. 6–25).

A lytic lesion involving the calvarium may be seen without parenchymal disease. Hydrocephalus may be secondary to meningitis or ependymitis. Small-vessel arteritis occurs in 40% of patients with meningitis, resulting in cerebral ischemia or infarction.[49]

Cryptococcosis

Cryptococcosis is a systemic infection that is worldwide in distribution. Despite the high prevalence of cryptococci in the environment, cryptococcal infection is uncommon but commonly occurs in immunocompromised patients. A selective impaired lymphocyte response to cryptococci in otherwise healthy patients has been demonstrated.[111] Cryptococcosis is the most common fungal infection in patients with AIDS.

CNS infection is usually secondary to pulmonary infection. Cryptococcosis is the most frequent clinically encountered CNS fungal infection. CNS cryptococcosis may present as meningitis, meningoencephalitis, or cryptococcal mass. Meningitis is the most common presentation. Hydrocephalus is seen as a result of the meningitis. Meningeal infection may extend from the basal cistern via dilated Virchow-Robin spaces into the basal ganglia and thalami.[144] Visual symptoms are common in patients with cryptococcal meningitis.

Two mechanisms have been implicated in patients with visual loss and optic atrophy: (1) increased intracranial compression with resultant damage to the optic nerve, and (2) direct cryptococcal involvement of the optic nerve.[103, 140]

Contrast-enhanced CT or MR studies may show meningeal enhancement involving the basal cisterns, sylvian fissure, and cortical sulci; nodular or ringlike enhancement may be seen[25] (Fig. 6–26). Dilated Virchow-Robin spaces may be seen on CT scanning or MR imaging, which is highly suggestive of cryptococcosis.[144]

On contrast-enhanced MR images, enhancement within the Virchow-Robin space may be seen (Figs. 6–27 and 6–28) . However, similar findings may be seen in coccidioidomycosis and candidiasis. Optic atrophy is better demonstrated by MRI than by CT.

Mucormycosis

Mucormycosis occurs in immunocompromised patients, most often in patients with poorly controlled diabetes. There are two forms of CNS mucormycosis:

1. The common form is rhinocerebral infection, with or without intracranial extension, with a predilection for patients with diabetes.[43]
2. The rare form is focal intracerebral infection in the absence of sinus disease. It is most often encountered in IV drug users. Anatomically, there is a predilection for the basal ganglia.[141]

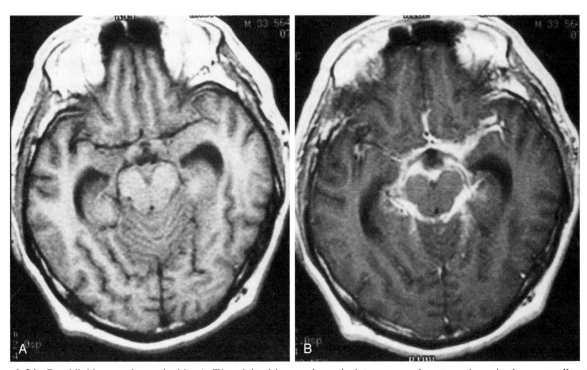

Figure 6–24. Coccidioidomycosis meningitis. *A,* T1-weighted image shows isointense granulomatous tissue in the suprasellar cistern. *B,* Gadolinium-enhanced image demonstrates intense enhancement in the basal cisterns.

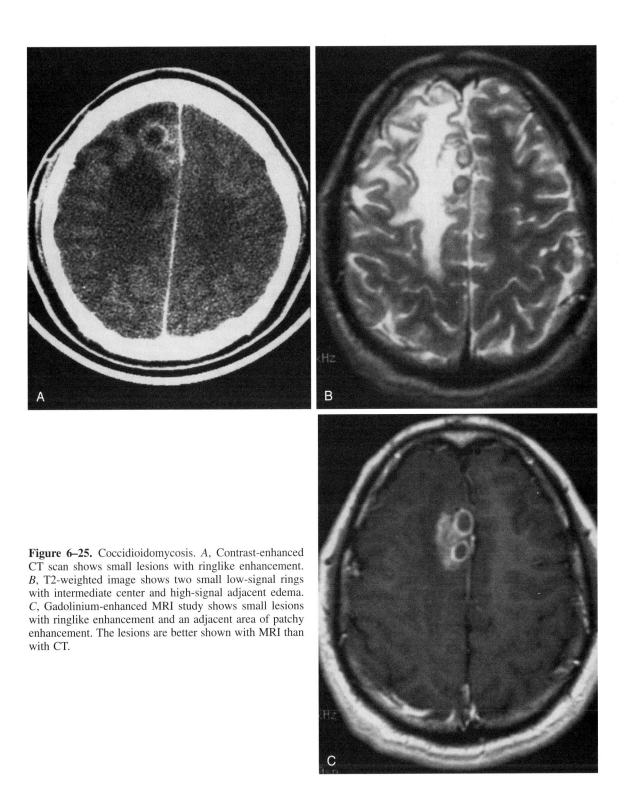

Figure 6–25. Coccidioidomycosis. *A,* Contrast-enhanced CT scan shows small lesions with ringlike enhancement. *B,* T2-weighted image shows two small low-signal rings with intermediate center and high-signal adjacent edema. *C,* Gadolinium-enhanced MRI study shows small lesions with ringlike enhancement and an adjacent area of patchy enhancement. The lesions are better shown with MRI than with CT.

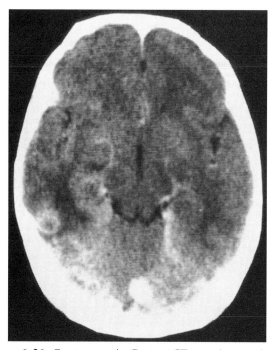

Figure 6–26. Cryptococcosis. Contrast CT scan shows a ringlike enhancement in the right posterior temporal lobe with surrounding edema.

Rhinocerebral mucormycosis spreads from the nasal cavity and paranasal sinuses by means of perivascular perineural channels through the cribriform plate into the frontal lobe and through the orbital apex into the cavernous sinus.[82] Pathologically, there is a predilection for the vasculature, particularly the arteries. It proliferates along the internal elastic lamina of the arterial walls, and hyphae may penetrate through the endothelium into the lumen, causing thrombosis with resultant infarction.

In the appropriate clinical setting, extensive paranasal sinus disease, with or without intracranial or nasopharyngeal extension, on CT or MRI studies should suggest mucormycosis. Extension of mucormycosis through bony partitions may occur without radiologic evidence of bone destruction.[47] Unenhanced CT scans may show low-density areas intracranially.

Contrast-enhanced CT scans may show ringlike enhancement with little surrounding edema. On MRI studies, sinus disease may exhibit near signal void (similar to air) on T2-weighted sequences, indistinguishable from normal aerated sinuses, which some suggest is the result of a high concentration of iron and manganese within the fungal mass.[141]

Primary intracerebral mucormycosis may reveal low density on unenhanced CT scans. Patchy, irregular enhancement is seen on contrast-enhanced CT scans. Focal

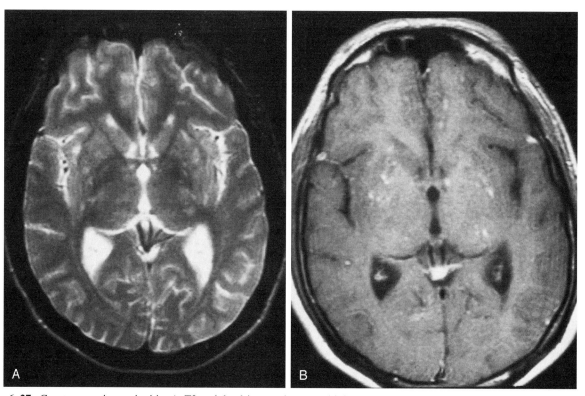

Figure 6–27. Cryptococcosis meningitis. *A*, T2-weighted image shows multiple small high-signal-intensity areas in the basal ganglia, consistent with a dilated Virchow-Robin space. *B*, Gadolinium-enhanced MRI study demonstrates small nodular enhancement, corresponding to the high signal intensity seen on T2-weighted images.

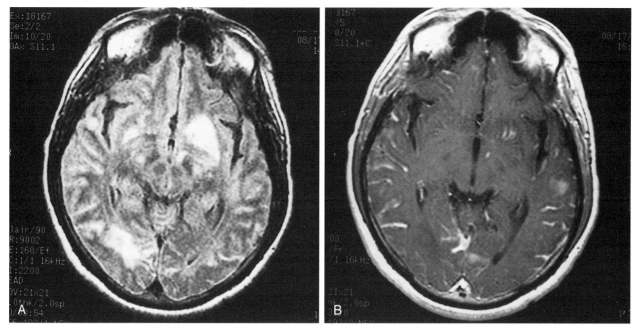

Figure 6–28. Cryptococcosis meningitis. *A,* Fluid-attenuating inversion recovery (FLAIR) image shows multiple high-signal areas in the basal ganglia as well as in the cortical sulci and subcortical white matter. *B,* Gadolinium-enhanced image demonstrates curvilinear abnormal enhancement in the basal ganglia and cortical sulci.

areas of hemorrhage may be seen within the lesion. With MRI, low signal intensity is seen on T1-weighted images, and areas of high signal intensity, mixed with very low signal intensity (near signal void), are seen on T2-weighted images. Patchy enhancement may be seen on contrast-enhanced MR images[128] (Fig. 6–29).

Candidiasis

Candida albicans is part of the normal flora in the gastrointestinal (GI) tract and mucocutaneous regions. *Candida* is also present in the vagina of healthy nonpregnant females and, more frequently, in pregnant females. *C. albicans* is the most common cause of human fungal infection[8] and represents 75% of the fungal infections in patients with neoplasm. Candidiasis occurs in immunocompromised patients. Systemic candidiasis is an opportunistic mycosis, with the GI tract being the usual portal of entry. Any organ may be involved in systemic candidiasis including kidney, GI tract, brain, and respiratory system. CNS involvement occurs as a result of hematogenous spread or direct invasion from the oral cavity or orbit. There is a higher incidence of renal and cardiac candidiasis in patients with intracranial disease. Approximately 80% of patients with myocardial or valvular involvement have had cerebral candidiasis. Candidiasis may present as meningitis, granuloma, or microabscess.

Unenhanced CT scans usually show low-density areas. Contrast-enhanced CT scans may show little or no enhancement or irregular, ringlike enhancement.[18, 37, 142] Mycotic aneurysms associated with candidiasis have been reported.[86] Calcification in healed lesions has also been reported.[66]

Nocardiosis

Nocardiosis is an uncommon bacterial disease that has traditionally been included in medical mycology. *Nocardia asteroides* is usually the causative organism. *Nocardia* is found in the soil worldwide. Nocardiosis occurs mostly in immunocompromised patients, patients with diabetes, and those with collagen-vascular disease or preexisting pulmonary disease. The organism is airborne, and the primary focus of infection is usually pulmonary. CNS involvement is usually secondary to hematogenous spread of pulmonary disease, and occurs in about 25% of patients.[157] The most common manifestation is abscess formation, which may be multiple. Pathologically, polymorphonuclear cells are primarily responsible for the inflammatory response. Granuloma formation is rare.

Unenhanced CT scans show low-density areas. MRI studies show low-signal-intensity areas on T1-weighted images and high-signal-intensity areas on T2-weighted images. Contrast-enhanced CT scanning or MRI shows ring-like enhancement, which may be multiple or multiloculated.[37]

Parasitic Disease
Cysticercosis

Cysticercosis is one of the most common parasitic diseases involving the brain. It is caused by ingesting the ova of the pork tapeworm *(Taenia solium),* usually on unwashed, fecally contaminated vegetables or water. The human being serves as the intermediate host of the pork tapeworm, and the main intermediate host of *T. solium* is the pig. By ingesting poorly cooked pork infected with cysticercosis, the human becomes the definitive host for *T.*

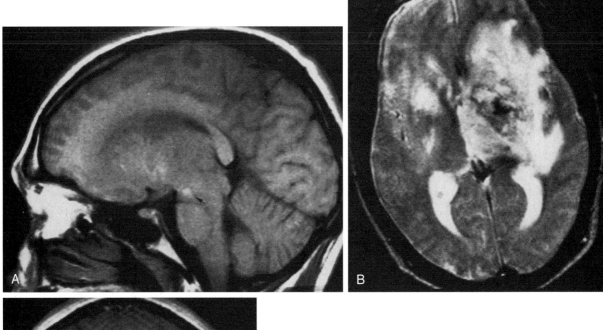

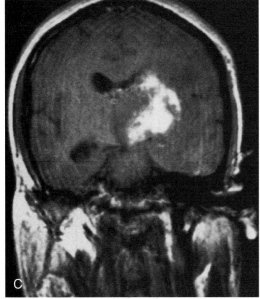

Figure 6–29. Mucormycosis. *A,* T1-weighted sagittal image demonstrates mass effect in the region of the left basal ganglia and thalamus extending into the midbrain with some poorly defined high signal intensity, suggesting hemorrhage *(arrow). B,* T2-weighted axial image shows a lesion of mixed high and low signal intensity in the left basal ganglia and thalamus with surrounding high-signal-intensity edema. Abnormal high signal intensity is also seen in the right basal ganglia. *C,* Gadolinium-enhanced coronal image demonstrates an enhancing lesion in the left basal ganglia and thalamus, producing compression and shift of the third ventricle. (From Terk MR, Underwood DJ, Zee CS, et al: MR imaging in rhinocerebral and intracranial mucormycosis with CT and pathologic correlation. Magn Reson Imaging 10:81–87, 1992.)

solium. Humans infected with *T. solium* tapeworm excrete eggs of the tapeworm in the fecal material, which then contaminates water and vegetables in areas with poor hygiene. Of course, it is easy for a person with tapeworm in the intestine to become infected with cysticercosis through the anus-finger-mouth route. The disease has been reported to be endemic in parts of Latin America, Eastern Europe, Asia, and Africa. A recent increase in incidence has been noted in the southern and southwestern United States because of immigration.

The intracranial compartment is involved in 60% to 90% of patients with cysticercosis. The location of involvement can be meningobasal, parenchymal, intraventricular, or a combination of these sites.[95] Parenchymal cysticercosis has a varied appearance on neuroimaging. Following arrival in the brain parenchyma, the precysticercosis embryo transforms into an encysted larva that contains liquid and is covered by a thin membrane. Initially, this cysticercosis

embryo is a living organism, exhibiting morphologic features to signify that it is viable. Similarly, certain morphologic alterations may indicate that the parasite is dead.

Pathologists have identified a series of alterations occurring within and surrounding the larva from its earliest viable stage to its final stage. Escobar,[42] in providing an interesting account of the disease, has identified four stages that the parasite undergoes within the brain parenchyma.

In the *vesicular stage,* the tiny (4 to 5 mm) live spherical larva appears as a whitish nodule invaginated into a small cyst containing transparent fluid. The cyst has a thin, friable, translucent whitish capsule. The larva can still be found in the colloidal vesicular stage, but it already shows signs of hyalin degeneration and early mineralization. In this stage, the fluid becomes turbid or jelly-like. The capsule steadily thickens with each succeeding phase, so that its walls are noticeably thicker and collagenous by the time the cyst has reached the granular nodule stage. The cyst

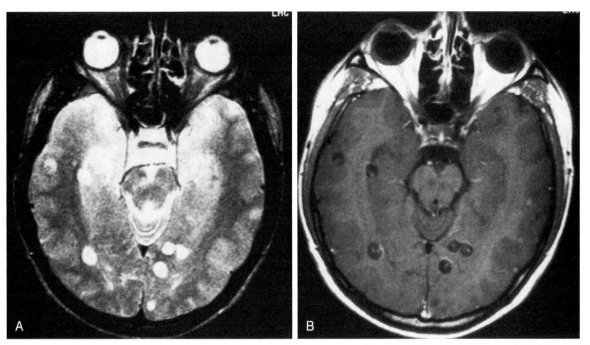

Figure 6–30. Parenchymal cysticercosis. *A,* T2-weighted image shows multiple high-signal-intensity lesions. *B,* Gadolinium-enhanced image shows multiple low-signal-intensity lesions with an eccentric isointense scolex. A few of the cysts show partial enhancement of the cyst wall.

reduces its size, and its content changes into coarse granules that are mineralized with calcium salts.

In the *nodular calcified stage,* this granular material appears completely mineralized, with the lesion having shrunk to one half or one quarter of the size of the original live cysticercosis embryo.

On the basis of the preceding data, it seems likely that a cysticercal lesion in the vesicular stage would be identified as such on imaging studies. The cyst fluid would be isodense to CSF on CT and isointense to CSF on MRI studies. The scolex is isodense to brain parenchyma on CT and hyperintense on MRI studies (Fig. 6–30).

With aging, the parenchymal cysts evolve into the *colloidal vesicular stage.* The cyst wall may show enhancement on contrast-enhanced CT or MRI studies (Fig. 6–31). The cyst fluid may show increased density with CT and intensity with MRI. The scolex begins to degenerate and shrink.

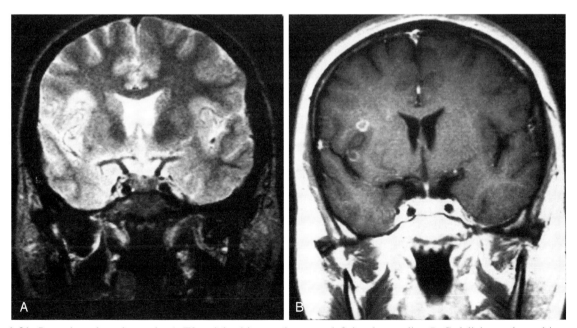

Figure 6–31. Parenchymal cysticercosis. *A,* T2-weighted image shows no definite abnormality. *B,* Gadolinium-enhanced image shows two ringlike enhancing lesions in the right insular cortex.

In the *granular nodular stage*, calcification may be identified within the scolex and along the cyst wall on CT scans. A nodular type of enhancement may be seen on contrast-enhanced CT or MRI. Calcification is much better demonstrated on CT than on MRI.

In the nodular calcified stage, calcification may be seen within the dead larva (Fig. 6–32). Surrounding edema is seen in the colloidal vesicular and granular nodular stages.[15, 164, 166] Note that evolution of cysticercosis is a dynamic process, and cysts do not change from one stage to another in an abrupt fashion. It is possible to observe cysts in transition from one stage to another.[163]

Intraventricular cysticercosis is potentially lethal; in our series, 6 of 46 patients with intraventricular cysticercosis cysts died of acute obstructive hydrocephalus shortly after hospital admission.[168] The need for early diagnosis of intraventricular cysticercosis cysts cannot be overemphasized. The cysts can be identified by CSF density or signal intensity. Cyst fluid surrounded by a thin wall is a high-density or high-signal-intensity scolex seen on CT or MRI scans (Figs. 6–33 and 6–34). Depending on the stage of the cyst, enhancement of the cyst wall may be identified on the contrast-enhanced CT or MRI study. A thick, ringlike enhancement associated with intraventricular cysticercosis cysts has been correlated with the finding of granular ependymitis in surgical patients (Fig. 6–35). Cysticercosis cysts may migrate within the ventricular system (Fig. 6–36). If time has elapsed since the initial diagnosis, reconfirmation of the location of the intraventricular cysticercosis cyst is advisable before surgery. Metrizamide entrance into an intraventricular cysticercosis cyst has been described.[167]

Cysticercosis cysts are seen in the basal cisterns and sylvian fissure. If large enough, these cysts may expand and distort the basal cisterns. MRI studies are more sensitive than CT scans in demonstrating cisternal cysts, which tend to agglomerate in a racemose form, and the body or scolex of the parasite is usually not recognizable (Fig. 6–37). It is interesting to consider why cysticercosis cysts present as a racemose form in the basal cisterns. Trelles and coworkers[145] suggested that disordered perforation of the cyst wall is associated with disappearance of the scolex. Martinez[91] held that the racemose cysts are an arrested form in the development of the cyst, the scolex never being formed. Adhesive arachnoiditis develops as a local inflammatory meningeal reaction in the basal cisterns. Contrast-enhanced MRI may show basal meningeal enhancement (Fig. 6–38). Communicating hydrocephalus may also develop as a result of basal arachnoiditis. The inflammatory reaction may involve the adjacent blood vessels and cranial nerves. The walls of the arteries are invaded by inflammatory cells, leading to vasculitis, which can lead to cerebral infarction or mycotic aneurysm formation.[151] Spinal cysticercosis cysts can be secondary to intracranial cisternal cysts.[164]

Echinococcosis

Hydatid disease, or echinococcosis, is the larval stage of *Echinococcus granulosus*. The definitive host of *E. granulosus* is the dog, and the intermediate hosts are sheep, cattle, and camels. Human infection occurs by accidental ingestion of contaminated dog feces containing ova of a dog tapeworm. The disease is endemic in many sheep-raising and cattle-raising countries in the world.[22] Hydatid disease frequently involves the liver and lung. CNS involvement is rare.[28] Hydatid cysts of the brain are usually large and spherical, and they may be solitary or multiple.

Extradural cysts have been reported.[106] On unenhanced CT or MRI studies, they appear as large intraparenchymal cystic lesions with sharp margins (Fig. 6–39). Cyst fluid is of CSF density or signal intensity. The lack of surrounding edema is an important feature that serves to differentiate this lesion from cerebral abscess.[1] Contrast enhancement may be seen partially or completely involving the wall. Calcification of the wall may also be seen (Fig. 6–40). Recurrent disease following surgery may present with intense enhancement of the cyst wall and surrounding edema (Fig. 6–41).

Paragonimiasis

Paragonimiasis is the result of infestation by *Paragonimus westermani* in freshwater crabs and crayfish. It is endemic in East and Southeast Asia, West Africa, and Latin America.[63] The lungs are the most common site of infestation. Cerebral infection occurs in approximately 1% of patients with pulmonary paragonimiasis.[19]

Plain films show characteristic "soap bubble" intracranial calcifications. CT scans show multiple, densely calcified areas with various nodular shapes around and within the lateral ventricles and high over the cerebral convexities.[160]

Toxoplasmosis

Toxoplasmosis is caused by infestation with the parasite *Toxoplasma gondii*, a protozoan. The adult form usually

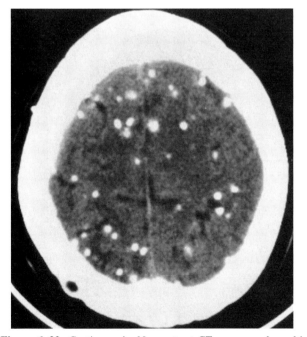

Figure 6–32. Cysticercosis. Noncontrast CT scan reveals multiple intracranial calcifications, consistent with dead larvae.

Text continued on page 240

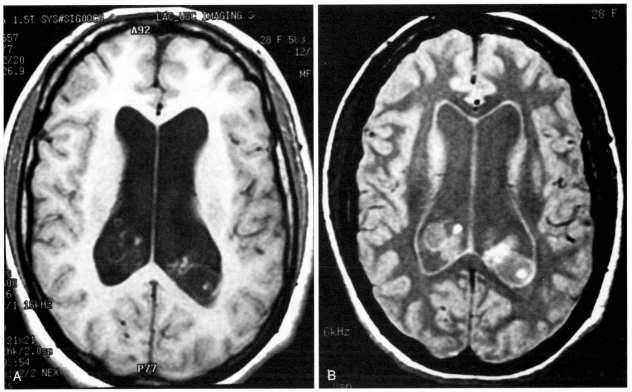

Figure 6–33. Intraventricular cysticercosis. *A*, T1-weighted image shows multiple cysts in the dependent portions of the lateral ventricles. *B*, The proton-density–weighted image shows the presence of scolices in some of the cysts better than the T1-weighted image does.

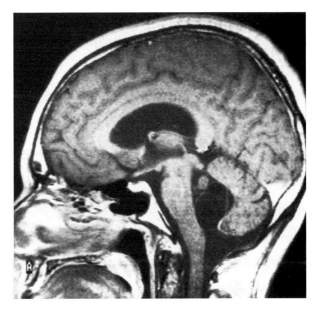

Figure 6–34. Intraventricular cysticercosis. A thin-walled cyst is seen expanding the fourth ventricle. An isointense, eccentrically located scolex is seen.

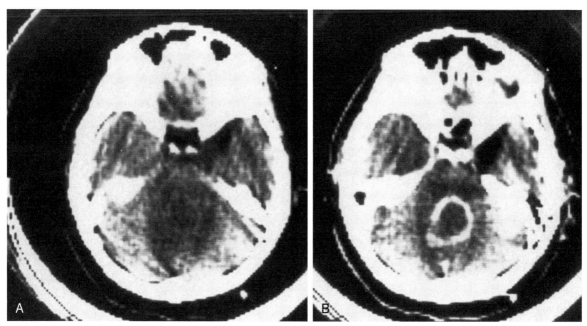

Figure 6–35. Enhancing intraventricular cysticercosis cyst. *A,* Noncontrast CT scan shows a low-density area in the region of the fourth ventricle. The fourth ventricle is obliterated. *B,* Contrast CT scan demonstrates a ringlike enhancement. (From Zee C, et al: Unusual neuroradiological feature of intracranial cysticercosis. Radiology 137:397–407, 1980.)

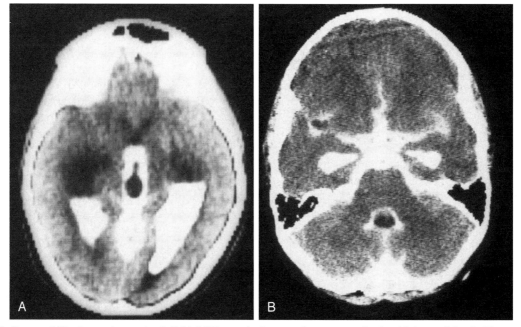

Figure 6–36. Cyst mobility in cysticercosis. *A,* Initial CT ventriculogram shows a cyst in the third ventricle. *B,* The cyst moved into the fourth ventricle on the metrizamide CT ventriculogram performed on the morning of surgery. (From Zee C, et al: Intraventricular cysticercal cysts: Further neuroradiologic observations and neurosurgical implications. AJNR Am J Neuroradiol 5:727–730, 1984. Copyright American Society of Neuroradiology, 1984.)

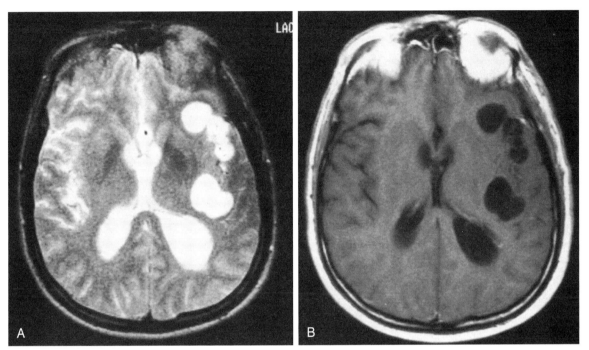

Figure 6–37. Cisternal cysts and intraventricular cyst. *A*, T2-weighted image shows multiple cisternal cysts in the region of the left sylvian fissure. *B*, Gadolinium-enhanced image shows multiple cisternal cysts in the region of the left sylvian fissure. No enhancement of these cysts is seen in this case. Incidentally, a cyst is seen in the atrium of the left lateral ventricle.

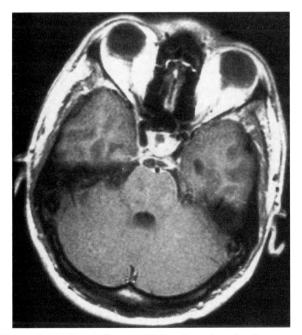

Figure 6–38. Cisternal cyst with basal meningeal enhancement. Gadolinium-enhanced MRI study shows ovoid ringlike enhancement in the pontine cistern and enhancement at the left ambient cistern.

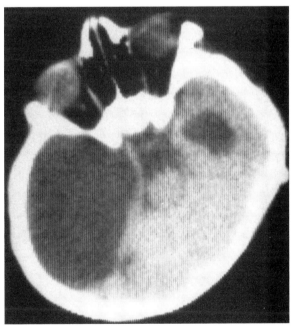

Figure 6–39. Echinococcosis. Large echinococcal cyst is seen in the right temporal lobe in this child. The left temporal horn is dilated. (Courtesy of Dr. Lawrence O'Connor.)

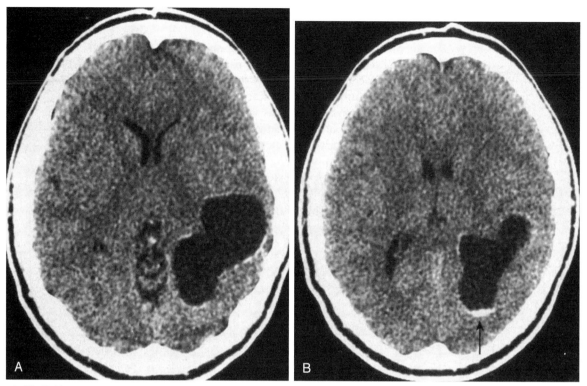

Figure 6–40. Echinococcosis. *A* and *B*, Contrast-enhanced CT scans show a large lobulated cyst with marginal calcification *(arrow* in *B)* and minimum cyst wall enhancement.

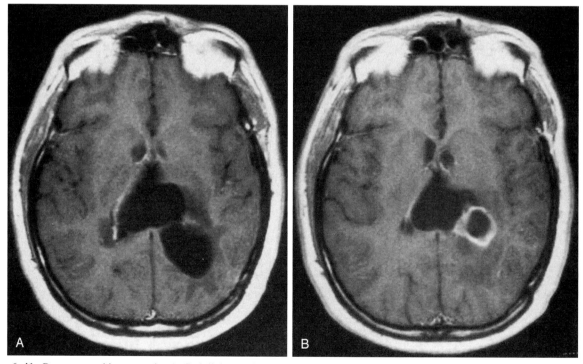

Figure 6–41. Recurrent echinococcosis. *A*, Gadolinium-enhanced MRI study shows recurrent cysts. No contrast enhancement is seen at this stage. *B*, Gadolinium-enhanced MRI study obtained a year later shows a decrease in the size of these cysts and contrast enhancement of one of the cysts.

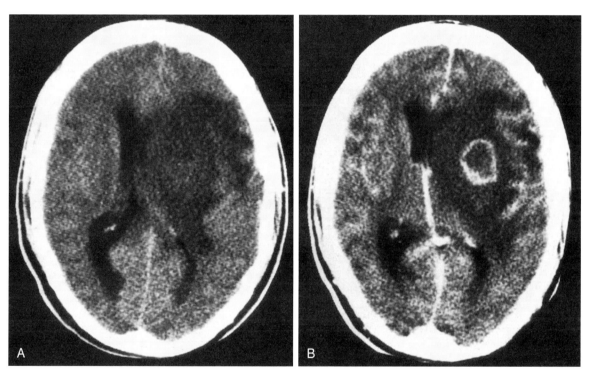

Figure 6–42. Toxoplasmosis. *A*, Noncontrast CT scan shows a large low-density area in the left frontoparietal region and left basal ganglion, with significant mass effect in a patient with acquired immunodeficiency syndrome. *B*, Contrast CT scan demonstrates a ringlike enhancing lesion.

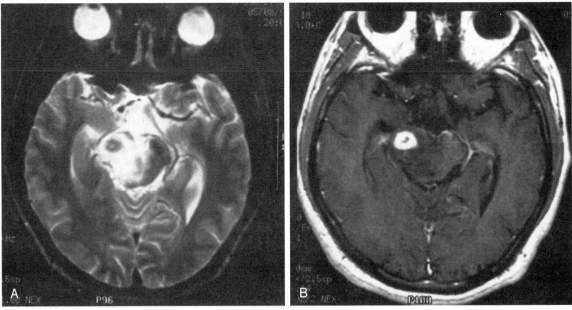

Figure 6–43. Toxoplasmosis. *A*, T2-weighted image shows a low-signal-intensity lesion in the right cerebral peduncle with surrounding edema. *B*, Gadolinium-enhanced MRI study shows a ringlike enhancing lesion in the right side of the midbrain.

occurs in immunocompromised patients or in patients with AIDS. Toxoplasmosis may appear as meningoencephalitis or as granulomas. In patients with AIDS, *Toxoplasma* encephalitis is the most common opportunistic infection. The granulomas may be situated at the corticomedullary junction or in the periventricular areas.

Noncontrast CT scans show multiple low-density areas. Contrast CT scans may show no enhancement, nodular enhancement, or ringlike enhancement (Fig. 6–42). MRI studies are more sensitive in detecting the *Toxoplasma* lesions than contrast-enhanced CT scans.[165] They exhibit hypointensity on T1-weighted images and variable intensity on T2-weighted images. Gadolinium-enhanced MRI studies show enhancing patterns similar to those seen on contrast-enhanced CT scans (Fig. 6–43).[114]

The differential diagnosis includes lymphoma and progressive multifocal leukoencephalopathy.[81] When treated, healed *Toxoplasma* lesions become calcified. These calci-

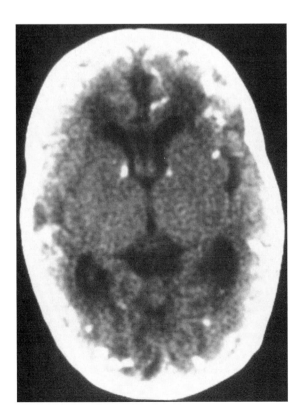

Figure 6–44. Neonatal toxoplasmosis. Noncontrast CT scan shows hydrocephalus and scattered intracranial calcifications, with a few seen in the periventricular region.

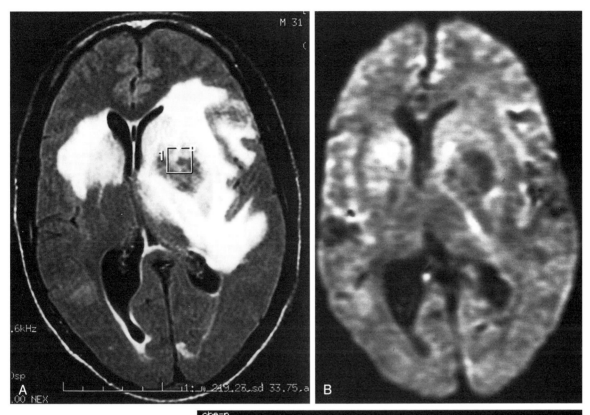

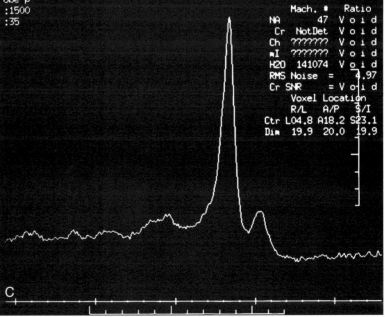

Figure 6–45. Toxoplasmosis. *A,* Fluid-attenuating inversion recovery (FLAIR) image shows an irregular mixed-signal-intensity lesion in the left basal ganglia with marked surrounding edema. *B,* Diffusion-weighted image shows the lesion to be of low signal intensity, indicating no evidence of restricted diffusion. *C,* MR proton spectroscopy shows high lipid/lactate at 0.9 to 1.5 ppm and no choline at 3.2 ppm, excluding the diagnosis of lymphoma in a patient with acquired immunodeficiency syndrome.

fications are revealed more effectively by CT than by MRI. In newborns with toxoplasmosis, noncontrast CT scans may show hydrocephalus and scattered calcifications in the parenchyma as well as in the periventricular region (Fig. 6–44). These findings may be seen in cytomegalic inclusion disease, herpes encephalitis, and congenital rubella involving newborns. With cytomegalic inclusion disease, however, calcifications are seen predominantly in the periventricular region.

Various noninvasive methods have been used to differentiate toxoplasmosis and lymphoma in AIDS patients, including SPECT, PET, and MRS. On PET imaging using FDG-18, increased tracer activity is seen in lymphoma as a result of hypermetabolic activity, but it is not seen in toxoplasmosis. On SPECT imaging, thallium 201 uptake also reflects hypermetabolism. On MRS, increased lipid and lactate peaks with a decrease in other metabolites are characteristic for toxoplasmosis (Fig. 6–45). Lymphoma shows a large increase in choline peak with only a mild increase in lipid and lactate peaks. The increased choline peak in lymphoma is believed to be due to increased cell membrane turnover and high cellularity of the lymphoma.[117]

References

1. Abbassioun K, Rahmat H, Ameli NO, et al: Computerized tomography in hydatid cyst of the brain. J Neurosurg 49:408–411, 1978.
2. Ahmadi J, Segall HD, Zee CS: Computed tomography in childhood intracranial infections. Semin Neurol 2:166–188, 1982.
3. Albertyn LE: Magnetic resonance imaging in herpes simplex encephalitis. Australas Radiol 34:117–121, 1990.
4. Anders BJ, Lauer BA, Foley LC: Computerized tomography to define CNS involvement in congenital cytomegalovirus infection. Am J Dis Child 134:795–797, 1980.
5. Arimitsu T, Jabbari B, Buckler RE, et al: Computed tomography in a verified case of tuberculosis meningitis. Neurology 29:384–386, 1979.
6. Bahn MM, Parchi P: Abnormal diffusion weighted magnetic resonance images in Creutzfeldt-Jakob disease. Arch Neurol 56:577–583,1999.
7. Bentson JR, Wilson GH, Helmer E: CT in intracranial cysticercosis. J Comput Assist Tomogr 1:464–471, 1977.
8. Black JT: Cerebral candidiasis: Case report of brain abscess secondary to Candida albicans and review of literature. J Neurol Neurosurg Psychiatry 33:864–870, 1970.
9. Bonafe A, Mnelfe C, Gomez MC, et al: Tuberculous meningitis: Contribution of computerized tomography to its diagnosis and prognosis. J Neuroradiol 12:302, 1985.
10. Bouza E, Dreyer JS, Hewitt WL, et al: Coccidioidal meningitis: An analysis of thirty-one cases and review of the literature. Medicine 60:139–172, 1981.
11. Brooks ML, Wang A, Black P, et al: Subdural mass lesion secondary to sarcoid granuloma MR and CT findings and differential diagnosis. Comput Med Imaging Graph 13:199, 1989.
12. Cabral DA, Flodmark O, Farrell K, et al: Prospective study of computed tomography in acute bacterial meningitis. J Pediatr 111:201–205,1987.
13. Cahill DW, Salchuman M: Neurosarcoidosis—a review of the rare manifestation. Surg Neurol 15:204–211, 1981.
14. Caparros-Lefebvre D, Salomez JL, Petit H: Multiple intracranial tuberculomas: Magnetic resonance imaging and ofloxacin efficacy. Ann Med Interne (Paris) 140:699, 1989.
15. Carbajal JR, Palacio E, Azar-Kia B, et al: Radiology of cysticercosis of the CNS, including CT. Radiology 125:127–131, 1977.
16. Casselman ES, et al: CT of tuberculous meningitis in infants and children. J Comput Assist Tomogr 4:211–216, 1980.
17. Centeno RS, Winter J, Bentson JR, et al: CT evaluation of Haemo-

18. philus influenzae meningitis with clinical and pathologic correlation. Comput Radiol 7:243–249, 1983.
18. Chaabane M, Krifa H, Ladeb MF, et al: Cerebral candidiasis: Computed tomography appearance. Pediatr Radiol 19:436, 1989.
19. Chang KH, Cho SY, Hesselink JR, et al: Parasitic diseases of the central nervous system. Neuroimaging Clin North Am 1:159–178, 1991.
20. Chang KH, Han MH, Roh JK, et al: Gd-DTPA-enhanced imaging of brain in patients with meningitis: Comparison with CT. AJNR Am J Neuroradiol 11:69–76, 1990.
21. Claveria LE, Du Boulay GH, Moseley IF: Intracranial infections: Investigations by C.A.T. Neuroradiology 12:59–71, 1976.
22. Coates R, von Sinner W, Rahm B: MR imaging of an intracerebral hydatid cyst. AJNR Am J Neuroradiol 11:1249–1250, 1990.
23. Cockrill HH, et al: CT in leptomeningeal infections. Am J Roentgenol 130:511–515, 1978.
24. Colover J: Sarcoidosis with involvement of the nervous system. Brain 71:451–475, 1948.
25. Cornell SA, Jacoby CG: The varied computed tomographic appearance of intracranial cryptococcosis. Radiology 143:703–707, 1982.
26. Danziger A, Price H: Computed axial tomography in intracranial aspergillosis—a report of two cases. S Afr Med J 54:706–708, 1978.
27. Davis JM, Darris KR, Kleinman GM, et al: CT of herpes simplex encephalitis with clinicopathological correlation. Radiology 129:409–417, 1978.
28. Demaerel P, Heiner L, Robberecht W, et al: Diffusion weighted MRI in sporadic Creutzfeldt-Jakob disease. Neurology 52:205–208, 1999.
29. Demaerel P, Wilms G, Marchal G: MRI findings in tuberculous meningo-encephalitis. Fortschr Rontgenstr 152:384–387, 1990.
30. Desprechins B, Stadnik T, Koerts G, et al: Use of diffusion weighted MR imaging in differential diagnosis between intracerebral necrotic tumors and cerebral abscesses. AJNR Am J Neuroradiol 20:1252–1257, 1999.
31. Dev R, Gupta RK, Poptani H, et al: Role of in vivo proton magnetic resonance spectroscopy in the diagnosis and management of brain abscess. Neurosurgery 42:37–42, 1998.
32. Dew HR: Hydatid disease of the brain. Surg Gynecol Obstet 59:312–319, 1934.
33. Dolin R, Reichman RC, Mazur MH, et al: Herpes zoster varicella infections in immunosuppressed patients. Ann Intern Med 89:375–388, 1978.
34. Dublin AB, Merten DF: CT in the evaluation of herpes simplex encephalitis. Radiology 125:133–134, 1977.
35. Dublin AB, Phillips HE: CT of disseminated cerebral coccidioidomycosis. Radiology 135:361–368, 1980.
36. Durack DT, Perfect JR: Acute bacterial meningitis. In Wilkins RH, Rengachary SS (eds): Neurosurgery. New York, McGraw-Hill, 1985.
37. Enzmann DR, Brant-Zawadzki M, Britt RH: Computed tomography of central nervous system infections in immunosuppressed patients. AJNR Am J Neuroradiol 1:2349–243, 1980.
38. Enzmann DR, Britt RH, Yeager AS: Experimental brain abscess evolution: Computed tomographic and neuropathologic correlation. Radiology 133:113–122, 1979.
39. Enzmann DR, Chang Y, Augustyn G: MR findings in neonatal herpes simplex encephalitis type 2. J Comput Assist Tomogr 14:453–457, 1990.
40. Enzmann DR, Norman D, Mani J, et al: CT of granulomatous basal arachnoiditis. Radiology 120:341–344, 1976.
41. Enzmann DR, Ranson B, Norman D, et al: CT of herpes simplex encephalitis. Radiology 129:419–425, 1978.
42. Escobar A: The pathology of neurocysticercosis. In Palacios E, Rodriguez-Carbajal J, Taveras J (eds): Cysticercosis of the Central Nervous System. Springfield, Ill, Charles C Thomas, 1983, pp 27–54.
43. Estrem SA, Tully R, Davis WE: Rhinocerebral mucormycosis: Computed tomographic imaging of cavernous sinus thrombosis. Ann Otol Rhinol Laryngol 99:160–161, 1990.
44. Falcone S, Donovan Post MJ: Encephalitis, cerebritis, and brain abscess. Neuroimaging Clin North Am 10:333–353, 2000.
45. Falcone S, Quencer RM, Bowen B, et al: Creutzfeldt-Jakob disease: Focal symmetrical cortical involvement demonstrated by MR imaging. AJNR Am J Neuroradiol 13:403–406, 1992.
46. Fernandez RE, Rothberg M, Ferencz G, et al: Lyme disease of the CNS: MR imaging findings in 14 cases. AJNR Am J Neuroradiol 11:479–481, 1990.

47. Gamba JL, et al: Craniofacial mucormycosis: Assessment with CT. Radiology 160:207–212, 1986.

48. Ganti SR, et al: Computed tomography of cerebral syphilis. J Comput Assist Tomogr 5:345–347, 1981.

49. Go JL, Kim PE, Ahmadi J, et al: Fungal infections of the central nervous system. Neuroimaging Clin North Am 10:409–425, 2000.

50. Go RT, Yousef MM, Jacoby CG: The role of radionuclide brain imaging and computed tomography in the early diagnosis of herpes simplex encephalitis. J Comput Tomogr 3:286–296, 1979.

51. Godt P, et al: The value of computed tomography in cerebral syphilis. Neuroradiology 18:197–200, 1979.

52. Gonzalez PRM, Herro CV, Joachim GF, et al: Tuberculous brain abscess: Case report. J Neurosurg 52:419, 1980.

53. Griggs RC, Manesberry WR, Condemi JJ: Cerebral mass due to sarcoidosis: Regression during corticosteroid therapy. Neurology 23:981–989, 1973.

54. Grinnell VS, et al: Diagnosis of interhemispheric subdural empyema by CT. J Comput Assist Tomogr 1:99–105, 1977.

55. Grossman RI, Davis KR, Taveras JM, et al: Computed tomography of intracranial aspergillosis. J Comput Assist Tomogr 5:646–650, 1981.

56. Guilleux MH, Steiner RE, Young IR: MR imaging in PML. AJNR Am J Neuroradiol 7:11033–11035, 1986.

57. Haimes AB, Zimmerman RD, Morgello S, et al: MR imaging of brain abscesses. AJNR Am J Neuroradiol 10:279, 1989.

58. Halpern SE, Smith CW Jr, Ficken V: ^{99m}Tc brain scanning in herpes virus type I encephalitis. J Nucl Med 11:548–550, 1970.

59. Handel SF, Klein WC, Kim YU: Intracranial epidural abscess. Radiology 111:117–120, 1974.

60. Hayes WS, Sherman JL, Stern BJ, et al: MR and CT evaluation of intracranial sarcoidosis. AJR Am J Roentgenol 149:1043, 1987.

61. Healton EB, Zito G, Chauhan P, et al: Intracranial subdural sarcoid granuloma. J Neurosurg 56:728, 1982.

62. Herman TE, et al: CT of neonatal herpes encephalitis. AJNR Am J Neuroradiol 6:773–775, 1985.

63. Higashi K, Aoki H, Tatebayashi K, et al: Cerebral paragonimiasis. J Neurosurg 34:515–527, 1971.

64. Holland BA, Perret LV, Mills CM: Meningovascular syphilis: CT and MR findings. Radiology 158:439–442, 1986.

65. Horten B, Price RW, Jimenez D: Multifocal varicella zoster virus: Local encephalitis temporally remote from herpes zoster. Ann Neurol 9:251–266, 1981.

66. Ikeda K, Yamashita J, Fujisawa H, et al: Cerebral granuloma and meningitis caused by *Candida albicans*: Useful monitoring of mannan antigen in cerebrospinal fluid. Neurosurgery 26:860–863, 1990.

67. Johnsen SD, Sidell AD, Bird CR: Subtle encephalitis in children: A variant of acute disseminated encephalomyelitis. J Child Neurol 4:214–217, 1989.

68. Johnston RB: Oxygen metabolism and the microbicidal activity of macrophages. Fed Proc 37:2759, 1978.

69. Jordan J, Enzmann DR: Encephalitis. Neuroimaging Clin North Am 1:17–38, 1991.

70. Joubert MD, Stephanov S: CT and surgical treatment in intracranial suppuration. J Neurosurg 47:73–78, 1977.

71. Kamin M, Biddle D: Conservative management of focal intracerebral infection suppuration. J Neurosurg 47:73–78, 1977.

72. Kanamalla US, Ibarra RA, Jinkins R: Imaging of cranial meningitis and ventriculitis. Neuroimaging Clin North Am 10:309–331, 2000.

73. Kaufman DM, Leeds NE: CT in the diagnosis of intracranial abscesses. Neurology 27:1069–1073, 1977.

74. Kendall BE, Tateler GLV: Radiological findings in neurosarcoidosis. Br J Radiol 51:81–92, 1978.

75. Kesselring J, Miller DH, Robb SA, et al: Acute disseminated encephalomyelitis: MRI findings and the distinction from multiple sclerosis. Brain 113:291–302, 1990.

76. Ketonen L, et al: Hypodense white matter lesions in computed tomography of neurosarcoidosis. J Comput Assist Tomogr 10:181–183, 1986.

77. Klein HJ, Richter HI, Schachenmayr W: Intracerebral *Aspergillus* abscess: Case report. Neurosurgery 13:306–309, 1983.

78. Kovanen J, Erkinguntti T, Iivaananninen M, et al: Cerebral MR and CT imaging of Creutzfeldt-Jakob disease. J Comput Assist Tomogr 9:125–128, 1983.

79. Kornbluth CM, Dastian S: Imaging of rickettsial, spirochetal, and parasitic infections. Neuroimaging Clin North Am 10:375–390, 2000.

80. Kumpe DA, et al: Intracranial neurosarcoidosis. J Comput Assist Tomogr 3:324–330, 1979.

81. Kupfer MC, Zee CS, Colletti PM, et al: MRI evaluation of AIDS-related encephalopathy: toxoplasmosis vs. lymphoma. Magn Reson Imaging 8:51–57, 1990.

82. Lazo A, Wilner HI, Metes JJ: Craniofacial mucormycosis: Computed tomographic and angiographic findings in two cases. Radiology 139:623–629, 1981.

83. Lee SH: Infectious diseases. In Lee SH, Rao KCVG (eds): Cranial Computed Tomography. New York, McGraw-Hill, 1983.

84. Leo JS, Weiner RL, Lin JP, et al: Computed tomography in herpes simplex encephalitis. Surg Neurol 10:313–317, 1978.

85. Linnemann CC Jr, Alvira MN: Pathogenesis of varicella zoster angiitis in the CNS. Arch Neurol 37:239–240, 1980.

86. Lipton SA, Hickey WF, Morris JH, et al: Candidal infection in the central nervous system. Am J Med 76:101–108, 1984.

87. Lorber J: Intracranial calcification following tuberculous meningitis in children. Acta Radiol 50:204–210, 1958.

88. Lott T, et al: Evaluation of brain and epidural abscess by CT. Radiology 122:371, 1977.

89. Lukes SA, Norman D: CT findings in acute disseminated encephalomyelitis. Ann Neurol 13:567–572, 1983.

90. Lukin RR, Chambers AA, Soleimanpour M: Outlet obstruction of the fourth ventricle in sarcoidosis. Neuroradiology 10:65–68, 1975.

91. Martinez A: Anatomia patologica dela cisticercosis cerebral. Neurochirurgie 19:191–201, 1961.

92. Masdeu JC, Small CB, Weiss L, et al: Multifocal cytomegalovirus encephalitis in AIDS. Ann Neurol 23:97–99, 1988.

93. Mathews VP, Kuharik MA, Edwards MK: Gd-DTPA enhanced MR imaging of experimental bacterial meningitis: Evaluation and comparison with CT. AJNR Am J Neuroradiol 9:1045–1050, 1988.

94. Mayers MM, Kaufmann DF, Miller MM: Recent cases of intracranial tuberculomas. Neurology 28:256–260, 1978.

95. McCormick GF, Giannotta S, Zee CS, et al: Carotid occlusion in cysticercosis. Neurology 33:1078–1080, 1983.

96. Mirfakhraee M, et al: Virchow-Robin space: A path of spread in neurosarcoidosis. Radiology 158:715–720, 1986.

97. Nahser HC, et al: Development of brain abscesses—CT compared with morphological studies. Adv Neurosurg 9:32–35, 1981.

98. Nakazawa G, Lulu RE, Koo AH: Intracerebellar coccidioidal granuloma. AJNR 4:1243–1244, 1983.

99. New PFJ, Davis KR: The role of CT scanning in diagnosis of infections of the central nervous system. In Remington J, Swartz M (eds): Current Clinical Topics in Infectious Diseases, New York, McGraw-Hill, 1980.

100. New PFJ, Davis KR, Ballantine HT: Computed tomography in cerebral abscess. Radiology 121:641–646, 1976.

101. Nielsen H, Gyldenstadt C: CT in the diagnosis of cerebral abscess. Neuroradiology 12:207–217, 1977.

102. Noorbehesht B, Enzmann DR, Sullendar W, et al: Neonatal herpes simplex encephalitis: Correlation of clinical and CT findings. Radiology 162:813–819, 1987.

103. Ofner E, Butler WT: Ophthalmologic complications of cryptococcal meningitis. J Clin Neuro Ophthalmol 7:45–48, 1987.

104. Okuno T, Fuseya Y, Ito M, et al: Reversible multiple hypodense areas in the white matter diagnosed as acute disseminated encephalomyelitis. Case report. J Comput Assist Tomogr 5:119–121, 1981.

105. Osenbach RK, Blumenkopf B, Ramirez H, et al: Meningeal neurosarcoidosis mimicking convexity en-plaque meningioma. Surg Neurol 26:387, 1986.

106. Ozgen T, Erbengi A, Bertan V, et al: The use of computerized tomography in the diagnosis of cerebral hydatid cysts. J Neurosurg 50:339–342, 1979.

107. Pachner AR, Duray P, Steere AC: Central nervous system manifestations of Lyme disease. Arch Neurol 46:790–795, 1989.

108. Parker JC Jr, Dyer MC: Neurologic infections due to bacteria, fungi, and parasites. In Doris RL, Robertson DM (eds): Textbook of Neuropathology. Baltimore, Williams & Wilkins, 1985, pp 632–703.

109. Pearfield RC, Shawdon HH: Five cases of intracranial tuberculoma followed by serial CT. J Neurol Neurosurg Psychiatry 42:373–379, 1979.

110. Perfect JR, Kurack DT, Gallis HA: Cryptococcemia. Medicine 62:98–109, 1993.

111. Pfuetz KH, Radner DB (eds): Clinical Tuberculosis: Essentials of Diagnosis and Treatment. Springfield, Ill, Charles C Thomas, 1966.

112. Philips ME, Ryals YJ, Kambhu SA, et al: Neoplastic vs. inflamma-

tory meningeal enhancement with Gd-DTPA. J Comput Assist Tomogr 14:536–541, 1990.

113. Post MJD, Kursunoglu SJ, Hensley GT, et al: Cranial CT in acquired
immunodeficiency syndrome: Spectrum of diseases and optimal contrast enhancement technique. AJNR Am J Neuroradiol 6:743–754,
1985.

114. Post MJD, Tate LG, Wuencer RM, et al: CT, MR, and pathology
in HIV encephalitis and meningitis. AJR Am J Roentgenol 151:
373–380, 1988.

115. Post MJD, et al: Cytomegalic inclusion virus encephalitis in patients
with AIDS: CT, clinical and pathologic correlation. AJNR Am J
Neuroradiol 7:275–280, 1986.

116. Price HI, Danziger A: CT in cranial tuberculosis. Am J Roentgenol
130:769–771, 1978.

117. Provenzale JM, Jinkins RJ: Brain and spine imaging findings in
AIDS patients. Radiol Clin North Am 35:1997.

118. Prusiner SB: Prions and neurodegenerative diseases. N Engl J Med
317:1571–1581, 1987.

119. Rafto SE, Milton WJ, Galetta SL, et al: Biopsy confirmed CNS
Lyme disease at 1.5 T. AJNR Am J Neuroradiol 11:482–484,
1990.

120. Ricker W, Clark M: Sarcoidosis: A clinicopathologic review of 300
cases, including 22 autopsies. Am J Clin Pathol 19:725–749, 1949.

121. Robertheram EB, Kessler LA: Use of computerized tomography
in non-surgical management of brain abscess. Arch Neurol 36:
25–26, 1979.

122. Rodriguez-Carbajal J, Salgado P, Gutierrez-Alvarado R: The acute
encephalitic phase of neurocysticercosis: Computed tomographic
manifestations. AJNR Am J Neuroradiol 4:51–55, 1983.

123. Rosenbaum ML, Hoff JT, Norman D, et al: Decreased mortality
from brain abscesses since the advent of computerized tomography.
J Neurosurg 49:658, 1978.

124. Russet EJ, Zimmerman RD, Leeds NE: Reye's syndrome: CT documentation of disordered intracerebral structure. J Comput Assist
Tomogr 3:217–220, 1979.

125. Sadhu VK, Handel SF, Pinto RS, et al: Neuroradiologic diagnosis
of subdural empyema and CT limitations. AJNR Am J Neuroradiol
1:39–44, 1980.

126. Sage MR, et al: Rapid development of cerebral atrophy due to
perinatal herpes simplex encephalitis. J Comput Assist Tomogr 7:
763–766, 1981.

127. Saltzman GF: Roentgenologic changes in cerebral sarcoidosis. Acta
Radiol (Diagn) (Stockh) 50:235–241, 1958.

128. Schroth G, Kretzschmar K, Gawehn J, et al: Advantage of MRI in
the diagnosis of cerebral infections. Neuroradiology 29:120–126,
1987.

129. Schultz P, Leeds NE: Intraventricular septations complicating neonatal meningitis. J Neurosurg 38:620–626, 1973.

130. Shah R: Tuberculosis. Neuroimaging Clin North Am 10:355–374,
2000.

131. Sherman JL, Stern BJ: Sarcoidosis of the CNS: Comparison of
unenhanced and enhanced MR images. AJNR Am J Neuroradiol 11:
915, 1990.

132. Shoji H, Murakami T, Murai I, et al: A follow-up study by CT
and MRI in 3 cases of Japanese encephalitis. Neuroradiology 32:
215–219, 1990.

133. Silverstein A, Feuer MM, Siltzbach LE: Neurologic sarcoidosis:
Study of 18 cases. Arch Neurol 12:1–11, 1965.

134. Simmons KC, Sage MR, Reilly PL: CT of intracerebral hemorrhage
due to mycotic aneurysms—case report. Neuroradiology 19:215–
217, 1980.

135. Singer MB, Atlas SW, Drayer BP: Subarachnoid space disease:
Diagnosis with fluid-attenuated inversion recovery MR imaging and
comparison with gadolinium-enhanced spin echo MR imaging—blinded reader study. Radiology 208:417–422, 1998.

136. South MA, et al: Congenital malformation of the CNS associated
with genital type (type 2) herpes virus. Pediatr 75:13–18, 1969.

137. Stevens EA, Norman D, Kramer RA: CT brain scanning in intraparenchymal pyogenic abscesses. Am J Roentgenol 130:111–114, 1978.

138. Sze G, Soloetsky S, Bronen R, et al: MR imaging of the cranial
meninges with emphasis on contrast enhancement and meningeal
carcinomatosis. AJNR Am J Neuroradiol 10:965–975, 1989.

139. Sze G, Zimmerman RD: The magnetic resonance imaging of infections and inflammatory diseases. Radiol Clin North Am 26:839–
859, 1988.

140. Tan CT: Intracranial hypertension causing visual failure in *Cryptococcus* meningitis. J Neurol Neurosurg Psychiatry 51:944–946,
1988.

141. Terk MR, Underwood DJ, Zee CS, et al: MR imaging in rhinocerebral and intracranial mucormycosis with CT and pathologic correlation. Magn Reson Imaging 10:81–87, 1992.

142. Thron A, Wietholter H: Cerebral candidiasis: CT studies in a case
of brain abscess and granuloma due to *Candida albicans*. Neuroradiology 23:223–225, 1982.

143. Tien RD, Ashdown BC, Lewis DV, et al: Rasmussen's encephalitis:
Neuroimaging findings in four patients. AJR Am J Roentgenol 158:
1329–1332,1992.

144. Tien RD, Chu PK, Hesselink JR, et al: Intracranial cryptococcosis
in immunocompromised patients: CT and MR findings in 29 cases.
AJNR Am J Neuroradiol 12:283–289, 1991.

145. Trelles JO, Rocca E, Pavens R: Estudios sobre neurocisticercosis:
Sobre la fina estructura de la membrana vesicula quistica y racem-
osa-deducciones pathologicas. Rev Neurol Psiquist 15:1–35,
1952.

146. Tsuchiya K, Yamauchi T, Furui S, et al: MR imaging versus CT in
subacute sclerosing panencephalitis. AJNR Am J Neuroradiol 9:
943–946, 1988.

147. Uchino A, Yoshinaga M, Shiokawa O, et al: Serial MR imaging in
Creutzfeldt-Jakob disease. Neuroradiology 33:364–367, 1991.

148. Visudhiphan P, et al: Cerebral aspergillosis: Report of 3 cases. J
Neurosurg 39:472–476, 1973.

149. Walker RJ, El Gammal T, Allen MB Jr: Cranial arteritis associated
with herpes zoster: Case report with angiographic findings. Radiology 107:109–110, 1973.

150. Weiderholt WC, Siekert RG: Neurological manifestations of sarcoidosis. Neurology 15:1147–1154, 1965.

151. Weingarten K, Zimmerman RD, Becker RD, et al: Subdural and
epidural empyemas: MR imaging. AJNR Am J Neuroradiol 10:
81–87, 1989.

152. Welchman JM: CT of intracranial tuberculomata. Clin Radiol 30:
567–573, 1979.

153. Whelan MA, Hilal SK: Computed tomography as a guide in the
diagnosis and follow-up of brain abscesses. Radiology 135:663–
671, 1980.

154. Whelan MA, Stern J: Intracranial tuberculoma. Radiology 138:
75–81, 1981.

155. Whiteman MLH, Post MJ, Berger J, et al: PML in 45 HIV positive
patients: Neuroimaging with pathologic correlation. Presented at the
77th Scientific Assembly and Annual Meeting of the Radiological
Society of North America, November 1991.

156. Whitener DR: Tuberculous brain abscess: Report of a case and
review of the literature. Arch Neurol 35:148, 1978.

157. Wood M, Anderson M (eds): Neurological Infections. Philadelphia,
WB Saunders, 1988.

158. Whitley RJ: Herpes simplex virus infections of the central nervous
system in children. Semin Neurol 2:87–96, 1982.

159. Whitley RJ, Soong SJ, Dolin R, et al: Adenine arabinoside therapy
of biopsy-proven herpes simplex encephalitis. N Engl J Med 297:
289–294, 1977.

160. Yoshida M, Moritaka K, Kuga S, et al: CT findings of cerebral
paragonimiasis in the chronic state. J Comput Assist Tomogr 6:
195–196, 1982.

161. Young RC, Bennett JE, Vogel CL, et al: Aspergillosis: The spectrum
of the disease in 98 patients. Medicine 49:147–173, 1970.

162. Zee CS, Apuzzo MJ, Segall HD: Neuroradiology for imaging-di-
rected stereotactic biopsy. In Chandrasoma PT, Apuzzo MJ (eds):
Stereotactic Brain Biopsy. New York, Igaku-Shoin, 1992.

163. Zee CS, Go JL, Kim P, et al: Imaging of neurocysticercosis. Neuroimaging Clin North Am 10: 391–407, 2000.

164. Zee CS, Segall HD, Boswell W, et al: MR imaging of neurocysticercosis. J Comput Assist Tomogr 12:927–934, 1988.

165. Zee CS, Segall RD, Roger C, et al: MR imaging of cerebral toxoplasmosis: Correlation of computed tomography and pathology. J
Comput Assist Tomogr 9:797–799, 1985.

166. Zee CS, Segall HD, Ahmadi J, et al: Unusual neuroradiological
feature of intracranial cysticercosis. Radiology 137:397–407,
1980.

167. Zee CS, Segall HD, Ahmadi J, et al: Entrance of metrizamide into
an intraventricular cysticercosis cyst. AJNR Am J Neuroradiol 2:
189–191, 1981.

168. Zee CS, Segall HD, Ahmadi J, et al: Intraventricular cysticercal cysts: Further neuroradiologic observations and neurosurgical implications. AJNR Am J Neuroradiol 5:727–730, 1984.

169. Zimmerman RA, Bilaniuk LT, Gallo E: CT of the trapped fourth ventricle. Am J Roentgenol 130:503–506, 1978.

170. Zimmerman RA, Patel S, Bilaniuk LT: Demonstration of purulent bacterial intracranial infections by computed tomography. Am J Roentgenol 127:155–165, 1976.

171. Zimmerman RD, Weingarten K: Neuroimaging of cerebral abscess. Neuroimaging Clin North Am 1:1–16, 1991.

172. Zimmerman RA, Bilaniuk LT, Shipkin PM, et al: Evolution of cerebral abscess: Correlation of clinical features with computed tomography. Neurology 27:14–19, 1977.

173. Zimmerman RD, Russell EJ, Leeds NE, et al: CT in the early diagnosis of herpes simplex encephalitis. AJNR Am J Neuroradiol 134:61–66, 1980.

7

Stroke

James D. Eastwood

Worldwide, stroke is the second leading cause of death,[54] and it is the leading cause of permanent disability.[7] Stroke is also among the most common indications for diagnostic imaging of the brain.

The term *stroke* is most accurately used to describe a clinical event that consists of the sudden onset of neurologic symptoms, and use of the term implies that symptoms are caused by cerebrovascular disease (i.e., a "cerebrovascular accident"). *Cerebral infarction,* by contrast, is a term that describes a lethal tissue-level ischemic event that may or may not cause symptoms. Cerebral infarction accounts for approximately 85% of all strokes.[4] *Primary* cerebral hemorrhages (e.g., subarachnoid hemorrhage and intraparenchymal hemorrhage) account for most of the remainder.

A number of practical topics are related to clinical imaging of ischemic stroke, and physicians who interpret imaging studies of the brain should be familiar with them. These practical topics form the basis of this chapter.

Etiology of Ischemic Stroke

Ischemic stroke is most often caused by obstruction of cerebral arteries or cerebral veins, although stroke due to obstruction of cerebral *arteries* is substantially more common than stroke due to obstruction of cerebral *veins*. It is useful to consider strokes that are caused by obstruction of *large* cerebral arteries separately from those that are caused by obstruction of *small* cerebral arteries, because the locations and extents of brain tissue involved by these two types of stroke are different. Similarly, the locations and extents of stroke that are caused by obstruction of cerebral veins are generally different than the locations and extents of stroke that are caused by obstruction of cerebral arteries.

In certain situations, cerebral infarction occurring without obstruction of cerebral arteries or veins may also occur, for example, cerebral infarction that is associated with a toxic or an anoxic insult or stroke caused by slow flow, such that seen in patients who experience sustained arterial hypotension. In this chapter, nonocclusive strokes are considered separately from strokes caused by vascular occlusion.

Risk Factors for Stroke

A number of medical conditions are associated with atherosclerotic disease and stroke. Hypertension, smoking, obesity, hyperlipidemia, diabetes mellitus, and homocystinemia are all examples of such conditions that are risk factors for atherosclerosis and stroke.[14, 43]

Atherosclerosis of the carotid artery is one of the most important conditions that predisposes to stroke.[6] Indeed, it has been implicated as the etiologic mechanism in approximately one third or more cases of ischemic stroke.[57] Many types of cardiac disease (e.g., valvular and ischemic heart disease, dysrhythmia, and right-to-left intracardiac shunting of blood) predispose to embolic stroke.[76] Atrial fibrillation, in particular, causes a substantial number of cardiogenic strokes.[23] Aortic arch atherosclerotic disease is also significantly associated with stroke, presumably as a result of associated thrombotic emboli.[27]

Many other conditions are often associated with stroke. For example, patients with conditions that predispose to hypercoagulable states, such as those patients with increased levels of factor V Leiden or antiphospholipid antibodies, are at increased risk.[29, 62] Cerebral ischemia and stroke due to vasospasm are the most important causes of morbidity and mortality in patients with subarachnoid hemorrhage. In addition, about 15% of children with sickle cell disease are afflicted by cerebral infarction.[5] Stroke may also afflict those with other vasculopathic conditions, such as fibromuscular dysplasia and the vasculopathy associated with neurofibromatosis type 1.

Pathophysiology in Ischemic Stroke

Knowledge of some of the pathophysiologic changes that occur in acute stroke can be helpful to understanding the imaging findings present in patients with acute stroke. Likewise, some of the histopathologic findings that are seen in the first days and weeks after stroke are relevant to an understanding of the imaging findings seen in these patients. A brief discussion of the most essential elements is provided.

Cytotoxic Edema

One concept that is helpful to understanding the changes that are seen in stroke is the development of *cytotoxic edema* associated with ischemia. When regional cerebral blood flow (CBF) falls below about 15 to 18 mL/100 g per minute, electrical activity within human neurons ceases.[2, 21] With further decreases in CBF (i.e., below about 8 mL/100 g per minute), the associated decrease in availability of oxygen and glucose results in decreased production of adenosine triphosphate (ATP).[38] With the loss of ATP production, Na^+/K^+ ATPase, an enzyme that is important to cell homeostasis, fails. This event permits the unbalanced influx of extracellular calcium and sodium and, secondarily, the influx of extracellular water into cells. This increased intracellular water is termed cytotoxic edema. The formation of cytotoxic edema is postulated to be the cause of most of the computed tomography (CT) and magnetic resonance imaging (MRI) findings seen in acute ischemic stroke.

Effects of Cytotoxic Edema on CT and MRI Studies

Because water is lower in density than normal brain tissue, one effect of edema on the appearance of the brain on CT images is a decreased density of brain tissues. This decrease has two primary (albeit related) effects on the appearance of the brain on CT scans (Fig. 7–1):

1. A diminished difference in density that normally exists between gray and white matter. This decrease in contrast may be seen in cortical regions and also at the base of the brain.
2. An overall decreased density in a region of the brain.

Water is also associated with longer T1 and T2 relaxation times than those for normal brain tissue. Therefore, one effect of cytotoxic edema on MRI scans is to increase the T1 and T2 relaxation times of involved tissues. Although regions of the brain that are involved with ischemic stroke may be depicted as areas of relative T1 and T2 prolongation, the changes on a T1-weighted image are not usually seen as early as the changes on T2-weighted images. In the acute stroke patient, the earliest findings on conventional MRI scans are regions of increased signal intensity on long repetition time (TR) images.

Cytotoxic edema can also influence the appearance of brain tissues on imaging studies by creating regional *mass effect*. In acute stroke cases involving the cortex of the brain, stroke-related edema is commonly associated with swelling of the cortical gyri. Gyral swelling is typically identified on imaging studies by the observation that the sulci between the gyri are effaced (i.e., narrowed). Regional sulcal effacement is, therefore, a sign that can be used to detect the changes of acute stroke (see Fig. 7–1).

Mass effect that is associated with acute stroke usually peaks at about 72 hours after the initial ischemic insult, with a gradual decrease in mass effect beginning after that time. When the extent of cerebral infarction is great, the possibility exists that mass effect from brain edema will result in *brain herniation*. Brain herniation represents an important complication of stroke because compression of brain tissues and vascular structures against nonmobile cranial structures (e.g., falx, tentorium, skull base) can result in new neurologic deficits and may exacerbate ischemia and elevate intracranial pressure. Brain herniation can also result in obstruction of cerebral ventricles (i.e., *ventricular trapping*), a problem that also increases intracranial pressure.

When stroke-related edema is extensive and life-threatening, it is sometimes called *malignant brain edema*.[64] The use of the word *malignant* to describe brain edema associated with stroke should not be confused with the type of brain edema associated with brain neoplasms (i.e., *vasogenic* edema). Life-threatening brain edema that is associated with stroke occurs most commonly in patients with extensive ischemia in the territory of a middle cerebral artery (MCA). Patients with cardiac embolus, internal ca-

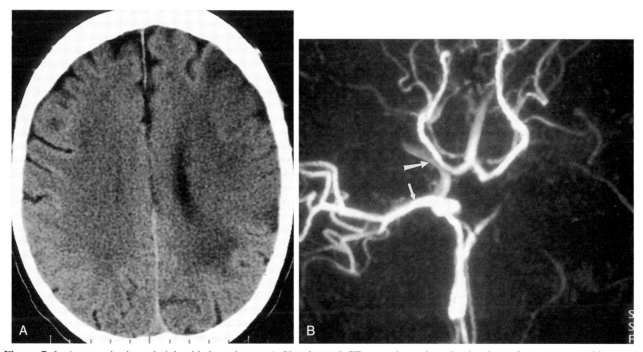

Figure 7–1. Acute aphasia and right-sided weakness. *A,* Unenhanced CT scan shows low density, loss of gray matter–white matter contrast, and effacement of sulci within the territory of the left middle cerebral artery. *B,* Maximum intensity projection image (anterior displayed at the bottom of the image) from intracranial 3D time-of-flight MRA shows no signal within the left middle cerebral artery or the left internal carotid artery. The normal appearance of the right internal carotid artery *(arrow)* and the middle cerebral artery *(small arrow)* is well visualized by comparison.

rotid artery (ICA) occlusion, and ICA dissection appear to be at highest risk for development of life-threatening brain edema from stroke.[9] When necessary, control of intracranial pressure may initially be attempted with the use of cerebrospinal fluid (CSF) diversion (e.g., with ventriculostomy catheters). In some cases, severe stroke-related edema may be managed by ipsilateral decompressive craniectomy to reduce intracranial pressure.[18]

In addition to the effects on brain CT density, MRI relaxation rates, and local mass effect, the formation of cytotoxic edema may also be related to the changes that are seen on DW magnetic resonance images in acute stroke patients. Such changes may be mediated by an increase in intracellular water with or without a secondary effect on extracellular water diffusion.[75, 77] DW changes in acute stroke are detailed later (see "Time Course of Diffusion-Weighted Images in Stroke").

T2 Fogging in Late Subacute Infarction

In some patients, during the 3rd week following a stroke, the typical hyperintense signal that is associated with ischemic stroke may regress. In some cases, signal intensity that appears normal may be seen transiently during this period. Such a decrease in signal intensity on a T2-weighted image (T2WI) is called "fogging." The causes of fogging are not clear, but it has been proposed that a decrease in edema, accompanied by increased macrophage activity, may be responsible.[1, 68] In such cases, parenchymal enhancement on T1-weighted images is typically seen after injection of gadolinium contrast material.

Chronic Stroke

After about 4 weeks, brain tissue that has undergone infarction has completed most of the pathologic changes related to reparation and resorption. Glial scar and areas of cystic necrosis typically have replaced neural tissue. If the volume of infarcted tissue was substantial, there may be evidence of volume loss, such as enlargement of adjacent sulci, cisterns, and ventricles. CT density is typically low, and MRI signal intensities reflect prolonged T1 and T2.

In some cases, areas of gyral increased density and increased signal on T1-weighted images may appear to reflect mineralization (i.e., calcification) within areas of cortical necrosis.[8] Gyral signal changes may be the most easily identified imaging feature associated with remote infarction, or signal changes associated with chronic stroke may be minimal, with regional volume loss representing the most readily detected evidence of prior ischemia.

Hemorrhage Associated with Cerebral Infarction

Hemorrhage that is associated with ischemic stroke may be symptomatic or asymptomatic. Cerebral hemorrhage that occurs secondary to ischemia is often called a *hemorrhagic infarction* or a *hemorrhagic transformation*. By

comparison, cerebral hemorrhage that is the result of a process other than ischemia (e.g., cerebral hematoma or subarachnoid hemorrhage) can, like ischemic stroke, be associated with abrupt onset of neurologic symptoms. When this occurs, a primary cerebral hemorrhage is sometimes called a *hemorrhagic stroke*.

Because these two types of cerebral hemorrhage that are associated with stroke symptoms have different causes and are often treated differently, the imaging specialist should exercise care when using these terms. Furthermore, the diagnostic investigations undergone by patients with primary hemorrhages of the brain (e.g., MRI, cerebral angiography) are often substantially different from the diagnostic investigations undergone by patients with infarction (e.g., echocardiography, carotid ultrasonography). Because distinguishing primary cerebral hemorrhage from cerebral hemorrhage secondary to ischemic stroke can be of clinical importance, care should be taken to communicate (to the extent possible) whether the primary event appears to be hemorrhage or ischemia.

Evidence that ischemic cerebral hemorrhage is secondary to ischemic stroke is the absence of such hemorrhage on the initial imaging study obtained after the onset of symptoms (Figs. 7–2 and 7–3). Imaging findings suggestive of an ischemic cause of stroke (e.g., dense artery or parenchymal abnormality within a vascular territory) on the initial scan are also helpful. It is typically during the subacute, or reparative, phase (beginning after about 24 hours following the onset of initial symptoms) that hemorrhage may be seen in association with ischemic stroke. By contrast, primary cerebral hemorrhage is typically seen on imaging studies that are obtained at the time of initial symptoms. Primary hemorrhages are discussed in Chapter 16.

Two main forms of hemorrhage may be seen on imaging studies after an ischemic stroke: (1) *petechial* and (2) *space-occupying.*

Petechial hemorrhages are not associated with new mass effect and are often limited to the cortical gray matter. They are thought to be caused by red blood cell diapedesis through small breaches that occur in the endothelium following a stroke (Fig. 7–4).

When greater disruption of blood vessels occurs, space-occupying hemorrhages may occur (see Fig. 7–3). Although the exact cause of these hemorrhages (i.e., hematomas) that occur secondary to ischemic stroke is not certain, it is thought that reperfusion of ischemic tissue, such as may be seen after lysis of a proximal embolus, may be responsible. The use of anticoagulant therapy may also be a risk factor for symptomatic, space-occupying hemorrhage following stroke.

Hemorrhage is also common in stroke caused by venous obstruction. However, the pattern of such hemorrhages often differs from the pattern associated with stroke due to arterial obstruction. In stroke due to venous obstruction, associated hemorrhage is more commonly found in subcortical locations (Fig. 7–5).

On CT scans, the appearance of hemorrhage caused by ischemic stroke is that of increased density. On MRI scans, the appearance of hemorrhage due to ischemic stroke varies with time, but petechial hemorrhages due to ischemic stroke are usually detected as areas of hyperintense signal

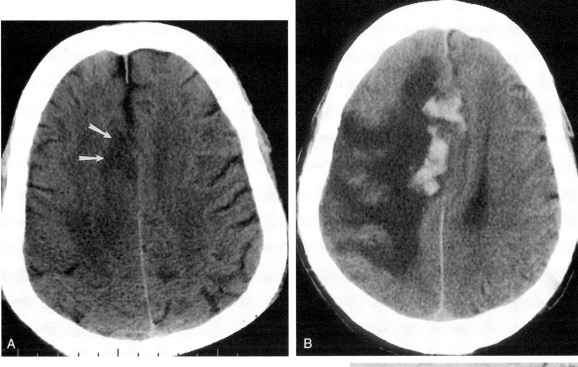

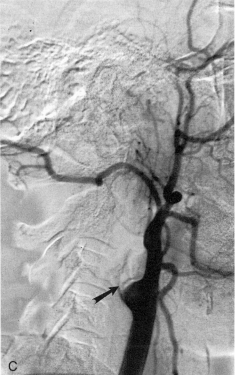

Figure 7–2. Hemorrhagic infarction. *A,* Unenhanced axial CT shows low density in the right anterior cerebral artery territory *(arrows). B,* Three days later, low density has extended into the middle cerebral artery territory (MCA), and the anterior cerebral artery territory infarct shows evidence of new hemorrhage. *C,* Lateral catheter angiogram shows occlusion of the right internal carotid artery proximally with a small patent stump *(arrow).*

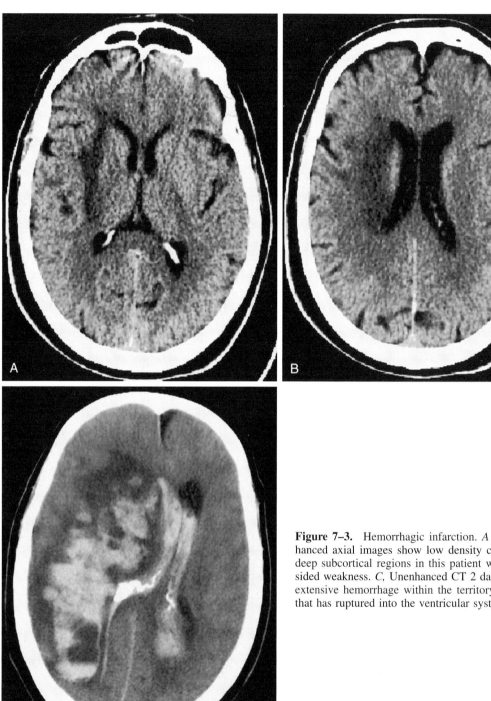

Figure 7–3. Hemorrhagic infarction. *A* and *B*, Unenhanced axial images show low density confined to the deep subcortical regions in this patient with acute left-sided weakness. *C*, Unenhanced CT 2 days later shows extensive hemorrhage within the territory of infarction that has ruptured into the ventricular system.

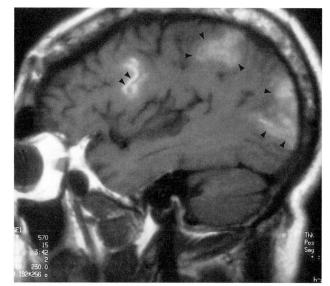

Figure 7–4. Multiple hemorrhagic infarctions. T1-weighted sagittal image shows several areas of gyral high signal *(arrowheads)* compatible with petechial hemorrhage.

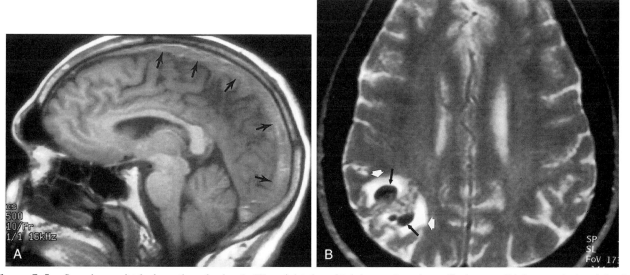

Figure 7–5. Superior sagittal sinus thrombosis. *A,* T1-weighted sagittal image (unenhanced) shows mild increased signal in the superior sagittal sinus *(arrows). B,* T2-weighted axial image shows subcortical decreased signal *(black arrows)* surrounded by increased signal edema *(small arrows).* The subcortical location of hemorrhage is characteristic of venous infarction.

on T1-weighted images (see Fig. 7–4), whereas acute hematomas are often depicted as regions of low signal intensity on T2-weighted images (see Fig. 7–5).

Time Course of Contrast Enhancement in Ischemic Stroke

Changes in brain enhancement can be associated with ischemia and infarction. One of the earliest changes in enhancement that can be seen on MRI scans in patients with acute stroke is increased enhancement in the cortical vessels and meninges overlying an ischemic region of the brain (Fig. 7–6). This can be seen in the first hours after onset of symptoms. The precise cause of this increased intravascular enhancement associated with ischemic stroke is not known, but one possibility is delayed wash-out of contrast material due to slow flow. Another possibility is autoregulatory vasodilation. These possible mechanisms would be expected to increase the enhancement seen in vessels by increasing the concentration of contrast material and the size of blood vessels, respectively.

Parenchymal enhancement associated with ischemic stroke, by comparison, is most commonly seen in the subacute time frame and, using standard techniques (i.e., 0.1 mmol/kg gadolinium contrast material and no magnetization transfer pulse), is seen to some degree in most patients by 7 days following an ischemic stroke (Fig. 7–7). Studies have shown that enhancement of the parenchyma can be demonstrated in the acute setting with the use of magnetization transfer (MT) techniques or with high-dose gadolinium injections.[45] The added clinical value of MT in stroke remains to be determined.

When mass effect and parenchymal enhancement are present in a case of subacute infarction, one must occasionally differentiate infarction from brain neoplasm, such as primary cerebral glioma. Often, simply observing that a given lesion conforms to the expected territory of supply of a cerebral artery (e.g., MCA) can be helpful (see Fig. 7–7). Additionally, apparent diffusion coefficient (ADC) analysis of diffusion-weighted (DW) MR images may also provide evidence of restricted diffusion in a region of enhancement. In such cases, the diagnosis of infarction should be favored. After 5 to 7 days, however, infarction is typically associated with normal to increased ADC values. If clinical suspicion of infarction is high, another MRI scan in 2 to 4 weeks can document decreasing enhancement and mass effect.

Alternatively, magnetic resonance spectroscopy (MRS) can be used to document low *N*-acetyl-aspartate (NAA) peak and increased lactate peak that would be expected in a region of cerebral infarction.[13, 20] The MRS findings in neoplasms are discussed in Chapter 11. Biopsy should only rarely be necessary to distinguish infarction from tumor. Enhancement due to infarction decreases after 4 to 6 weeks.

CT Versus MRI in the Setting of Acute Stroke

MRI is more sensitive than CT in the setting of acute stroke.[65] This advantage has increased with the recent clinical availability of DW MRI. DW MR images have the highest sensitivity and specificity for acute cerebral infarction of any imaging tool presently available.[36] Nonetheless, CT remains the first imaging test performed at many institutions, even when MRI is subsequently performed. CT is the only imaging test performed in the setting of acute stroke at other institutions. The reasons for this appear to be the high sensitivity of CT for detecting hemorrhage and its greater availability at many institutions.

Small-Artery Stroke

Occlusion of the small end-arteries that penetrate the brain results in focal, deeply located areas of infarction. Such infarctions can be multiple and can occur in the absence of significant disease involving the large arteries. Areas of infarction in the territories of small arteries are frequently called *lacunar* infarctions (Fig. 7–8). It is often assumed that patient histories of hypertension and diabetes mellitus are associated with lacunar infarction more frequently than with other stroke subtypes. However, this concept has recently been challenged.[58] Locations that are commonly involved with small-artery stroke are as follows:

- Basal ganglia and internal capsule (lenticulostriate arteries)
- Thalamus (thalamoperforate arteries)
- Deep hemispheric white matter (deep cortical perforators)
- Brain stem (pontine perforators and other small brain stem perforating arteries)

Occasionally, a large perivascular space (Virchow-Robin space) may mimic the appearance of a small-artery infarction.[25] However, perivascular spaces are most prominent near the surfaces of the brain and have imaging features typical of CSF. A proton-density–weighted image and/or a fluid-attenuated inversion recovery (FLAIR) image can be used to separate infarction (bright) from CSF (dark) (Fig. 7–9).

The imaging specialist can often differentiate infarction in the territory of pontine perforating arteries from other lesions that involve the pons by noting that infarctions in the territories of the paramedian arteries typically have medial margins that approach, but do not cross, the plane of midline (Fig. 7–10). Findings of ischemia that are due to disease involving the small perforating arteries are not limited to lacunar infarctions. Regions of T1 and T2 prolongation (or CT hypodensity) that are larger and less well defined than regions of lacunar infarction may be seen in many elderly patients as well as in patients with a history of hypertension or diabetes. These regions are commonly symmetrical and involve the white matter of the central pons (see Fig. 7–8).

Large-Artery Stroke

Occlusions of large cerebral arteries generally result in regions of ischemic involvement that differ substantially in extent than those produced by occlusion of small cerebral arteries. Nonetheless, it is useful to note that ischemic stroke in the territory of a large cerebral artery may result

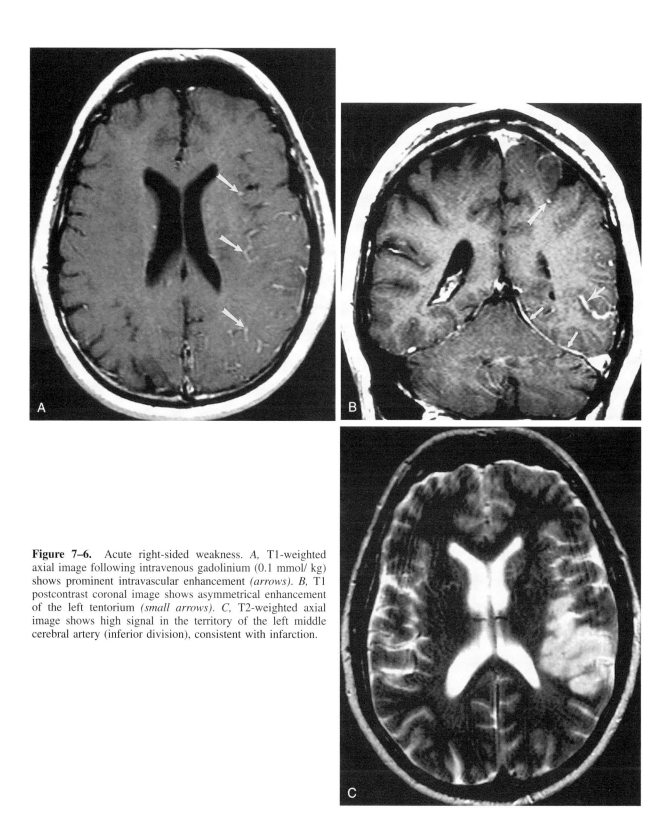

Figure 7–6. Acute right-sided weakness. *A,* T1-weighted axial image following intravenous gadolinium (0.1 mmol/ kg) shows prominent intravascular enhancement *(arrows). B,* T1 postcontrast coronal image shows asymmetrical enhancement of the left tentorium *(small arrows). C,* T2-weighted axial image shows high signal in the territory of the left middle cerebral artery (inferior division), consistent with infarction.

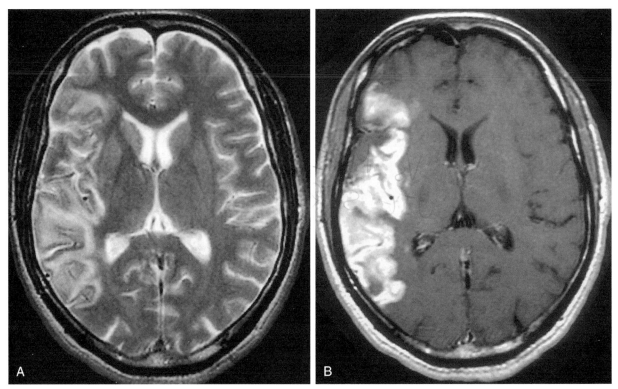

Figure 7–7. Enhancing infarction (1 week after symptom onset). *A*, T2-weighted axial image shows increased signal within the cortical territories of the right middle cerebral artery. *B*, T1-weighted axial image following intravenous gadolinium (0.1 mmol/kg) reveals gyral and subcortical enhancement. An enhancing infarct can often be differentiated from tumor by clinical information (e.g., acute onset of symptoms) and extent that conforms to the territory of a cerebral vessel.

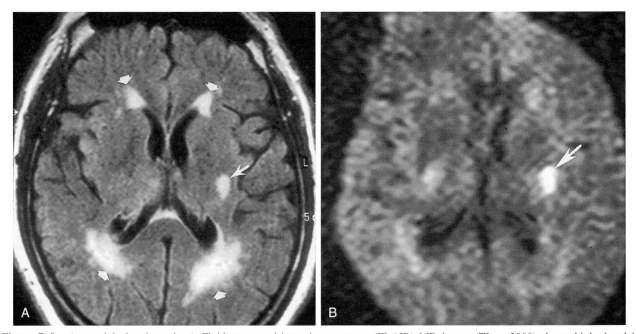

Figure 7–8. Acute right hemiparesis. *A*, Fluid-attenuated inversion recovery (FLAIR) MR image (TI = 2000) shows high signal in the periventricular regions *(small arrows)* and posterior limb of the left internal capsule *(arrow)*. *B*, Axial diffusion-weighted image (b = 980) shows increased signal only in the left internal capsule, consistent with acute stroke *(arrow)*. Other areas that were hyperintense on the FLAIR image presumably represent older ischemic changes.

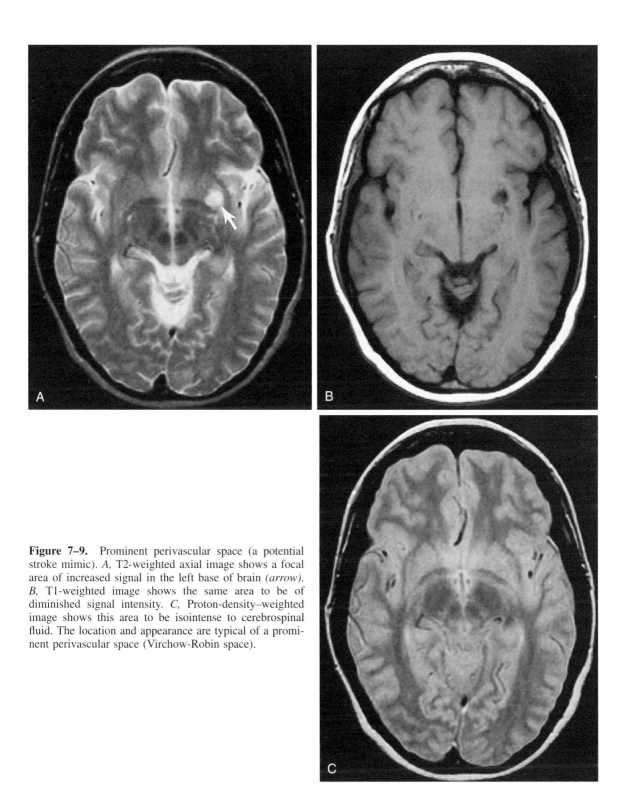

Figure 7–9. Prominent perivascular space (a potential stroke mimic). *A,* T2-weighted axial image shows a focal area of increased signal in the left base of brain *(arrow).* *B,* T1-weighted image shows the same area to be of diminished signal intensity. *C,* Proton-density–weighted image shows this area to be isointense to cerebrospinal fluid. The location and appearance are typical of a prominent perivascular space (Virchow-Robin space).

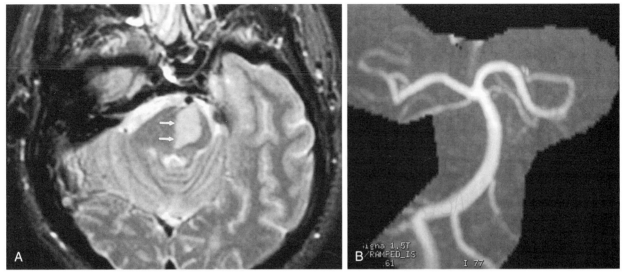

Figure 7–10. Acute pontine perforator infarct. *A,* T2-weighted axial image shows increased signal within the central pons. The medial border of this infarct does not cross the plane of the midline. This tendency to respect the midline is typical of paramedian branch infarction. *B,* Three-dimensional time-of-flight MRA shows no narrowing of the basilar artery in this patient with small-vessel infarction.

in infarctions in the territories of multiple small arteries that receive their supply from the large artery in question. A common example of this phenomenon is the extensive basal ganglia infarctions that may occur in proximal MCA occlusion as a result of loss of supply to the lenticulostriate arteries. Occasionally, the territories of supply of the lenticulostriate arteries may be the only regions that undergo infarction in MCA stroke (Fig. 7–11).

On imaging studies, one feature that can help to differentiate large-artery from small-artery stroke is involvement of cortical gray matter. With large-artery stroke, the earliest changes that are apparent on T2 and proton-density–

weighted images typically are seen in the cortex. As time passes, subcortical hyperintensity becomes more evident and is usually well visualized at 24 hours.

One exception to the rule that cortical findings precede subcortical findings in large-vessel stroke, however, may occur when subcortical low signal intensity accompanies acute cortical hyperintense changes.[22] In an animal ischemia model, reversible decreases in T2 relaxation may precede changes on DW scans.[15] An example of subcortical hypointensity associated with a region of presumed ischemia is shown in Figure 7–12.

On occasion, a large-vessel occlusion can result in deep

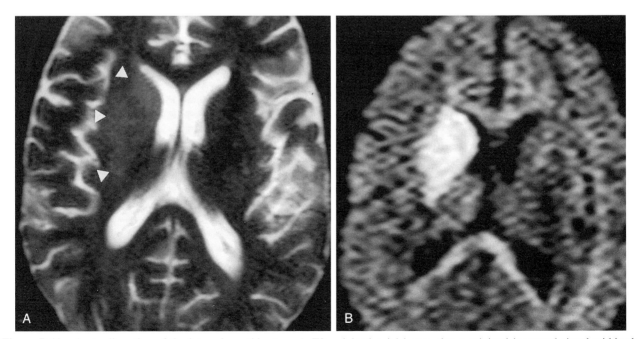

Figure 7–11. Acute dissection of the internal carotid artery. *A,* T2-weighted axial image shows minimal increased signal within the right basal ganglia (triangles). *B,* Diffusion-weighted (b = 970), echo-planar image shows hyperintensity within the same region that is substantially more conspicuous. Diffusion-weighted images have greater sensitivity for acute infarction.

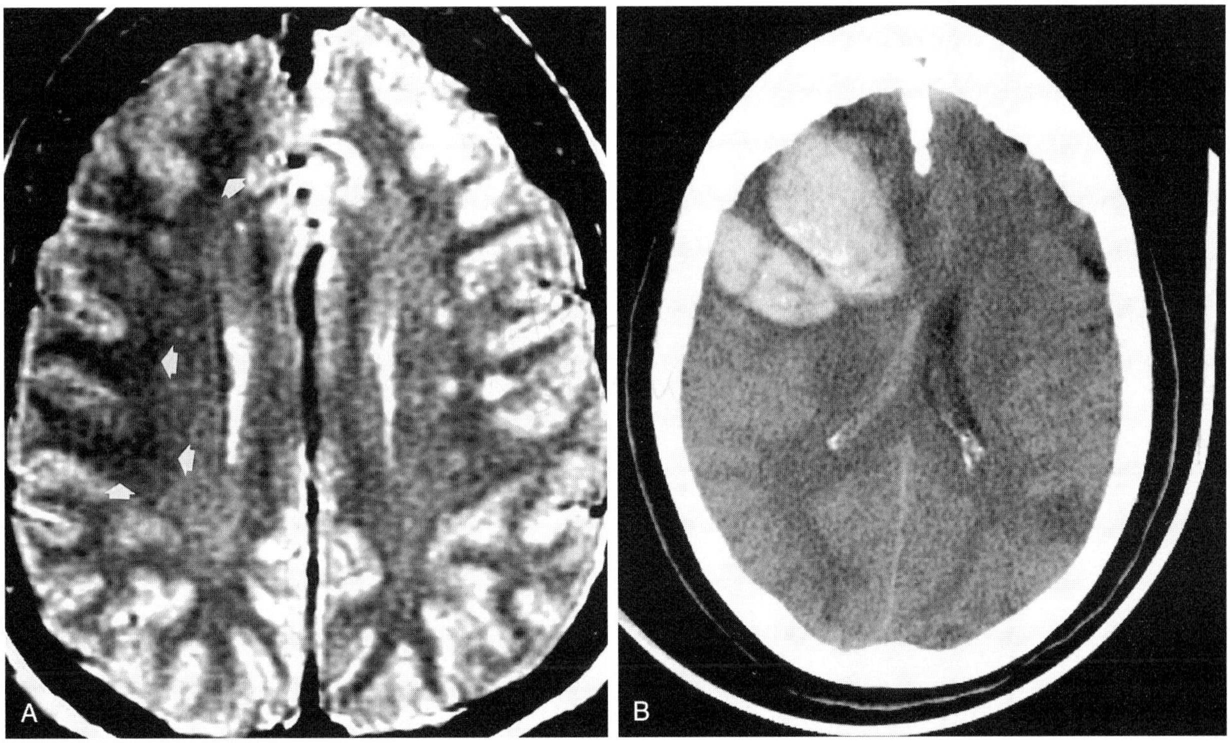

Figure 7–12. Acute left-sided weakness. *A,* T2-weighted axial image shows extensive subcortical low signal in the right frontal lobe *(arrows). B,* Unenhanced CT 36 hours later shows development of right frontal hematoma. Hypointense changes on T2-weighted images appear to have preceded hemorrhagic infarction.

subcortical white matter infarction with relative sparing of the cortex. This is presumably a hemodynamic phenomenon caused by a low rate of flow that is not sufficient to supply the territories of the deep perforating arteries (see Fig. 7–3). The terms *internal watershed stroke* and *deep watershed stroke* apply to this pattern of infarction. In such cases, it is the extent of abnormality that helps to distinguish regional subcortical ischemia from other lesions.

Stroke Caused by Internal Carotid Artery Disease

It is thought that diseases resulting in narrowing of the lumen of the ICA can lead to stroke by two likely interrelated mechanisms:

1. *Hemodynamic compromise by obstruction of flow.* Hemodynamic compromise of brain tissues may be minimal when adequate collateral flow is present. Because gradual occlusion of the ICA (e.g., because of atherosclerosis or fibromuscular disease) often allows time for adequate collateral development, gradual occlusion is often clinically better tolerated by patients than sudden occlusion (e.g., acute arterial dissection). Furthermore, in some cases gradual carotid occlusion does not result in neurologic symptoms or brain infarction.
2. *Thrombotic emboli.* In arteries that are irregular or very narrowed, emboli that involve vessels such as the MCA and the anterior cerebral artery (ACA) may be produced.[78] This concept is supported by diminished stroke rates in patients with carotid artery disease treated with

antiplatelet agents, such as aspirin, as compared with the rates in control patients.[17]

The most important disease of carotid arteries that can lead to stroke is atherosclerosis of the ICA (Fig. 7–13). Stenosis due to atherosclerotic plaque most commonly occurs at the level of the carotid bulb. By contrast, stenosis of the carotid artery by fibromuscular dysplasia is more likely to occur distal to the bulb, above the level of the C3 vertebral body.[70] Type II fibromuscular dysplasia is associated with a characteristic appearance on conventional catheter angiograms consisting of alternating narrowing and dilation, the appearance of which has been likened to a "string of beads."

Acute dissection of the extracranial cerebral vessels is another relatively common cause of stroke that often occurs following trauma, though some cases occur spontaneously in patients with hypertension or in patients with various arteriopathies (e.g., fibromuscular dysplasia, Ehlers-Danlos syndrome). Patients with dissection of the ICA frequently present with ipsilateral cerebral or retinal symptoms.

Alternatively, patients with carotid dissection may present with ipsilateral Horner's syndrome, consisting classically of ptosis, meiosis, and anhidrosis of the affected eye. Horner's syndrome due to dissection is thought to be related to disruption of the postganglionic sympathetic plexus that is associated with the cervical carotid artery.

Characteristic locations for cervical arterial dissection include the distal cervical ICA and the cervical loop of the vertebral artery (at the C1 and C2 levels), although other locations may be involved. Vertebral artery injuries, including dissection, may occur in association with cervical spine

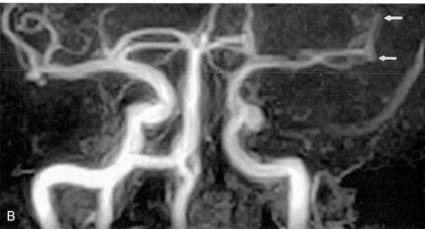

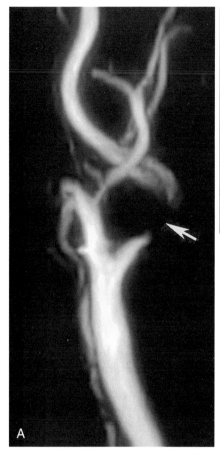

Figure 7–13.   Atherosclerotic stenosis of the internal carotid artery. *A,* Maximum intensity projection image from 2D time-of-flight MRA shows focal loss of signal ("flow gap") in the proximal left internal carotid artery *(arrow),* suggestive of flow-limiting stenosis. *B,* Maximum intensity projection image from intracranial 3D time-of-flight MRA shows diminished signal in the left M2 branches *(small arrows).* The diminished signal is thought to be a result of slow flow and resultant spin saturation.

trauma.[79] Fractures involving the transverse foramina raise concern for associated vertebral artery injury, including dissection.[81]

MRI scans and CT angiograms obtained in patients with extracranial dissection may reveal tapered or irregular narrowing of the affected vessel, with or without evidence of an intimal flap on magnetic resonance angiography (MRA) source images (Figs. 7–14 and 7–15). T1-weighted axial MRI may also reveal hyperintense thrombus within the false lumen of the artery. In cases of suspected dissection, evidence of pseudoaneurysm complicating dissection should be sought. Any evidence of focal outpouching should be confirmed angiographically.

Diseases of the ICA that predispose to embolus formation may result in embolic occlusion of any of the intracranial arteries that receive all or most of their supply from the ICA. Stroke in the territories of the ophthalmic artery, ACA, and MCA are commonly associated with ICA disease.

The anterior choroidal artery also arises from the ICA. It originates at the posterior aspect of the distal ICA, usually just beyond the junction of the ICA with the posterior communicating (PCom) artery. The territory of the anterior choroidal artery includes several regions that can give rise to focal neurologic symptoms, and occlusion of this artery may produce infarction in the optic tract, cerebral peduncle, and posterior limb of the internal capsule. The anterior choroidal artery is not usually seen directly on MRI or CT scans; instead, it is identified angiographically.

Middle Cerebral Artery Stroke

Stroke in the territory of the MCA is associated with the greatest degree of morbidity and mortality and is among the most common types of ischemic stroke. For the purposes of hyperacute stroke management, a thorough understanding of acute MCA stroke imaging is needed for optimal patient care.

In general, the most important initial goal of acute stroke imaging is to exclude hemorrhage as the cause of new neurologic symptoms. Acute primary intracerebral hematoma and subarachnoid hemorrhage are conditions that represent absolute contraindications to thrombolytic and anticoagulation (e.g., heparin) therapies.

Once hemorrhage has been excluded (typically by CT imaging), the next goals are (1) to help confirm the clinical diagnosis of stroke and (2) to determine the extent of irreversible ischemia. When extensive, irreversible ischemia is associated with a poor prognosis and an increased rate of hemorrhage related to thrombolysis.

Confirming the diagnosis of stroke, by observing the earliest imaging signs associated with stroke and excluding other possible causes of symptoms, can be of value in choosing optimal therapy and minimizing complications.[16]

Middle Cerebral Artery Territory

Knowledge of the usual territory of supply of the MCA is essential to understanding the changes seen in acute MCA stroke. The territory of supply of the MCA artery

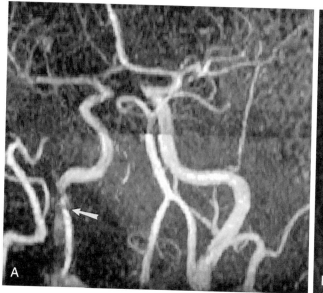
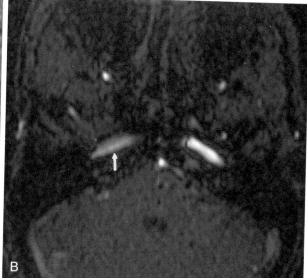
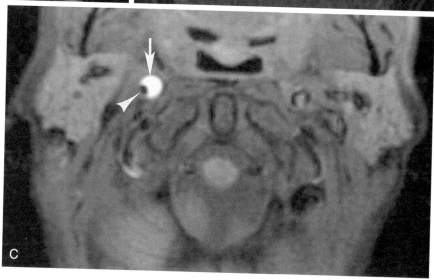

Figure 7–14. Acute dissection of the internal carotid artery. *A,* Maximum intensity projection image from 3D time-of-flight MRA shows a focal area of irregularity in the distal portion of the cervical segment of the right internal carotid artery *(arrow). B,* Axial "source" image from the same sequence shows diminished signal in the petrous segment of the right internal carotid artery *(small arrow). C,* Unenhanced axial T1-weighted image obtained through the upper neck with fat saturation shows crescentic hyperintense signal representing thrombus *(arrow).* A small, flow-related signal void represents the residual lumen at this point *(arrowhead).*

can be considered to consist of a cortical territory and subcortical territory (i.e., that territory supplied by lenticulostriate perforator arteries). The cortical territory of supply of the MCA is reciprocal with that of the posterior cerebral artery (PCA) and the ACA.

The cortical territory of the MCA can be understood to be composed of two main parts: (1) a more anterior part that supplies the frontal lobe and (2) a more posterior part that supplies the parietal and temporal surfaces of the brain.

In common clinical use, the territory of the MCA that is more anterior is said to be supplied by the *superior division* of the MCA; the territory of the MCA that is more posterior is said to be supplied by the *inferior division* of the MCA. This separation of the MCA into two major divisions is based on the proximal branching of the MCA into (usually) two dominant segments. For practical purposes, it is useful to recognize that one main MCA division may become occluded (e.g., by embolus), whereas the other main division remains patent and that the imaging findings of ischemia may reflect this separation.

Substantial variation in territory of supply may occur among patients. Nonetheless, the cortical extent of the MCA territory may, for practical purposes, be approximated as the insula, the anterior and lateral portions of the temporal lobe, the frontal and parietal opercula, and most of the frontal and parietal convexities. At the level of the ventricles, the MCA territory is approximately delimited by imaginary lines that connect the frontal horns and atria with the cortical surfaces of the frontal and occipitotemporal lobes, respectively. Furthermore, these imaginary lines approximate the hemodynamic watershed zones that lie between the major vascular territories. The concept of a hemodynamic watershed has been proposed to be the basis of a specific type of stroke associated with low flow. So-called watershed strokes are discussed later.

In addition to the cortical branches of the MCA, numerous small perforating arteries originate from the proximal (horizontal) segment of the MCA (the M1 segment). These small arteries are collectively known as the lenticulostriate arteries. Their territories of supply include the basal ganglia, the internal capsule, and portions of the overlying cerebral white matter.

Infarction in the territory of a single lenticulostriate artery results in a lacunar infarct, an event that commonly

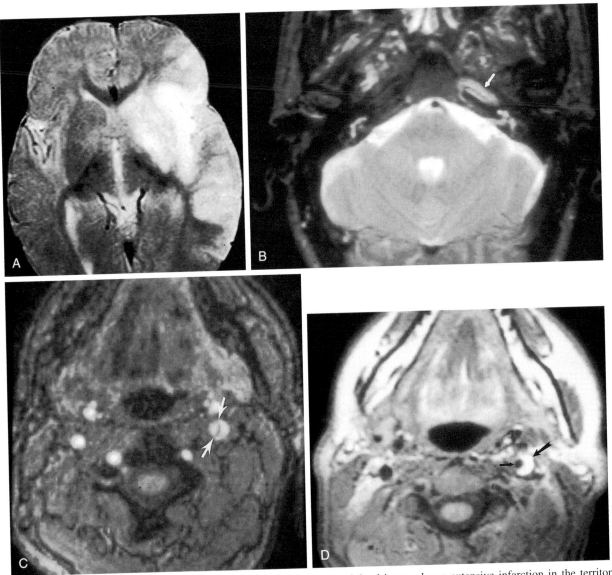

Figure 7–15. Acute left internal carotid artery dissection. *A,* Axial T2-weighted image shows extensive infarction in the territory of the left middle cerebral artery. *B,* Axial T2-weighted image through the left of the temporal bone shows abnormal increased signal within the petrous segment of the internal carotid artery *(small arrow). C,* Axial "source" image from 3D time-of-flight MRA shows the presence of a low-signal intimal flap *(arrows)* within the upper cervical internal carotid artery. *D,* Unenhanced axial T1-weighted image through the same level reveals a crescentic area of high signal representing thrombus *(arrows).* A small focus of flow-related signal void represents the remaining portion of the lumen.

occurs independently of MCA stroke. Nonetheless, occlusion of the M1 artery typically results in infarction in the territories of multiple lenticulostriate arteries (i.e., striato-capsular infarction). Infarction in the basal ganglia due to MCA occlusion can occur with or without infarction in the territories of the cortical MCA branches (see Fig. 7–11). When occlusion of the MCA occurs distal to the M1 segment (and thus distal to the origins of the lenticulostriate arteries), infarction in the cortical territory of the MCA may occur without infarction of the basal ganglia.

Imaging Findings in Acute Middle Cerebral Artery Stroke

The most important early CT evidence of irreversible brain tissue damage after a hyperacute stroke is hypoden-

sity.[44] Early CT hypodensity, when extent is greater than or equal to one third of the expected MCA territory, is associated with unfavorable risk of symptomatic hemorrhage following thrombolytic therapy.[16]

It is often assumed that changes seen on DW MR scans after a hyperacute stroke reflect irreversible ischemia (i.e., infarction). Although this assumption may be valid in many cases, recent evidence suggests that with human stroke at least some early changes that are depicted on DW images may be reversed following thrombolytic therapy.[30] With additional study, criteria may be developed that would allow irreversible ischemia to be reliably distinguished from reversible ischemia, perhaps with the use of DW imaging or DW imaging in combination with another modality, such as perfusion imaging. Because such criteria have not yet been developed and accepted, the following discussion focuses on the role of early CT imaging in the diagnosis and management of acute MCA stroke.

A number of early CT signs of MCA ischemia have been reported and may be used to confirm clinically suspected stroke of the MCA. One helpful CT sign, when present, is hyperdensity within the MCA.[59] This finding, in the setting of clinical signs of stroke in the territory of the dense vessel, signifies thrombus within the lumen of the artery (Fig. 7–16). However, a unilateral dense MCA should always be correlated with patient symptoms, since the specificity of this finding alone is not high.[63]

An important pitfall to avoid is comparing the density of a cerebral artery (e.g., the MCA) with adjacent brain tissue rather than with other vascular structures. The density of the MCA should be compared with that of other vascular structures of similar size, such as the opposite MCA, the ICA, the basilar artery, the large veins, and the dural venous sinuses. Although the hyperdense MCA sign can sometimes assist in the diagnosis of stroke, identification of a hyperdense MCA has some prognostic value and may predict increased morbidity, mortality, and increased risk of life-threatening brain edema.[39]

Two other helpful early CT signs of acute MCA stroke are obscuration of the lentiform nucleus and loss of the insular ribbon.[72, 73] These signs are, presumably, the result of ischemia in the territory of the lenticulostriate arteries arising from the M1 segment. The confirmation of these findings, therefore, suggests the presence of proximal occlusion of the MCA. Normally, the insula may be distinguished from the adjacent external capsule by their differing densities. In early MCA stroke, the contrast between these structures may be lost, presumably as a result of early cytotoxic edema (Fig. 7–17). Decreased density of the basal ganglia, also assumed to be caused by cytotoxic edema, results in obscuration of the lentiform nucleus (see Fig. 7–16).

Although observation of the hyperdense MCA sign, obscuration of the lentiform nucleus, and loss of the insular ribbon signs can help confirm the diagnosis of proximal MCA occlusion, careful examination of the cortical territory of the MCA is also important. Hypodensity, loss of gray matter to white matter contrast, and sulcal effacement should all be sought in the cortical territories. Manual adjustment of the display window and level settings may assist in detecting regions of hypodensity related to early stroke.[42]

Additional Findings in Chronic Middle Cerebral Artery Stroke

In the chronic stage, infarction in the territory of the MCA (and, to a lesser degree, elsewhere along the corticospinal pathways) may affect the appearance of the brain elsewhere. A common example is wallerian degeneration. When the corticospinal fibers are interrupted, as often happens in MCA stroke, the corticospinal fibers inferior to the lesion may undergo degeneration. The appearance of wallerian degeneration consists of volume loss and increased signal on T2-weighted images (Fig. 7–18).

Another example of change in the appearance of regions

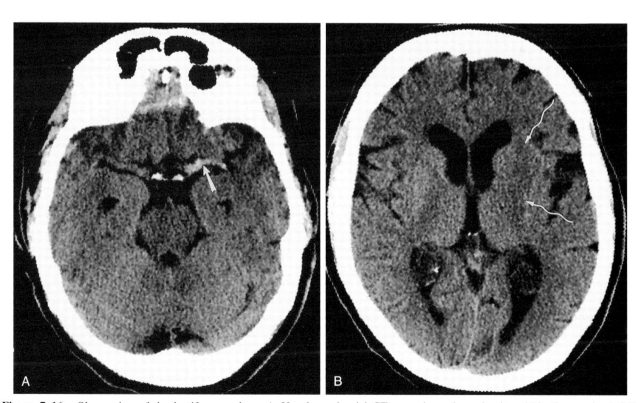

Figure 7–16. Obscuration of the lentiform nucleus. *A,* Unenhanced axial CT scan shows hyperdensity within the proximal (M1) segment of the middle cerebral artery *(arrow). B,* There is decreased density with loss of definition within the left basal ganglia *(wavy arrow).* Obscuration of the lentiform nucleus and hyperdense middle cerebral artery is one of the earliest signs of stroke on an unenhanced CT scan.

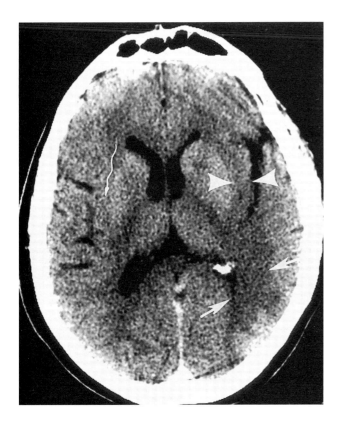

Figure 7–17. Loss of the insular ribbon. Unenhanced axial CT scan in a patient with acute right hemiparesis. There is decreased density with loss of distinction of the insular gray matter from the underlying external capsule *(large arrowheads).* Diminished density is also present in the posterior left temporal lobe *(arrows).* The right insular ribbon appears normal *(wavy arrow).*

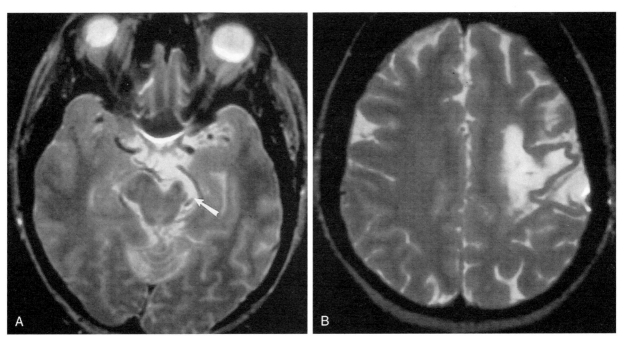

Figure 7–18. Wallerian degeneration. *A,* Axial T2-weighted MR image shows the left cerebral peduncle to be of decreased size and increased signal intensity *(arrow). B,* T2-weighted image located more superiorly shows evidence of old middle cerebral artery territory infarction. Axonal degeneration is thought to produce the remote subcortical changes.

of the brain outside the territory of ischemia is known as *crossed cerebellar diaschisis*. In general, these changes are seen mainly on hemodynamic (i.e., perfusion) or metabolic studies. In patients with a cerebral injury, diaschisis may be considered to be functional impairment at an anatomic location that is remote from the area that sustained the injury. Diaschisis is thought to occur because of a loss of afferent input to the remote (noninjured) site. In the case of cerebral hemisphere injury, the opposite cerebellar hemisphere may show evidence of decreased blood flow,[56] decreased blood volume,[82] and decreased metabolism.[69] In the case of crossed cerebellar diaschisis, it is thought that the fibers that are interrupted are those within the corticopontocerebellar tract.

Anterior Cerebral Artery Stroke

The territory of the ACA is typically the anterior medial surface of the hemisphere and a small but variable amount of the frontal convexity and inferior frontal lobe (Fig. 7–19). Infarction in the territory of the ACA may occur in isolation (e.g., because of embolus or vasospasm following aneurysm rupture) or in combination with infarction in the territory of the ipsilateral MCA. This latter situation occurs most often with ICA occlusion when the anterior communicating artery (ACoA) is small or absent. Infarction in the territory of Heubner's artery may accompany ACA infarction because the origin of this vessel arises from the ACA in the vicinity of the ACoA. Heubner's artery is a

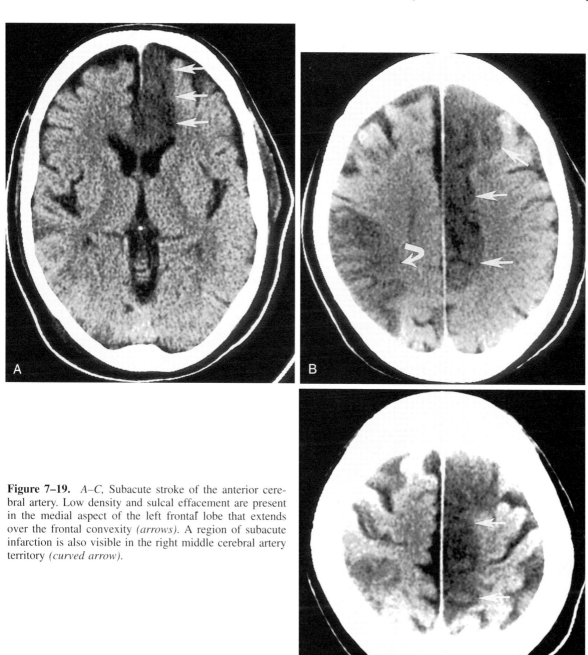

Figure 7–19. *A–C,* Subacute stroke of the anterior cerebral artery. Low density and sulcal effacement are present in the medial aspect of the left frontal lobe that extends over the frontal convexity *(arrows).* A region of subacute infarction is also visible in the right middle cerebral artery territory *(curved arrow).*

small perforating artery that usually supplies the head of the caudate nucleus and the anterior limb of the internal capsule.

Posterior Cerebral Artery Stroke

The cortical territory of the PCA includes the occipital lobes, the medial and inferior temporal lobes, and the posterior and medial portions of the parietal lobes (Figs. 7–20 and 7–21). The thalamoperforate arteries are small end-arteries that arise from the proximal PCA and the

PCom artery. A consequence of this relationship is that infarction in the territory of the PCA may be associated with lacunar infarctions of the thalamus[9] (Fig. 7–22). Other small perforating arteries from the proximal PCA supply the cerebral peduncles and upper midbrain.

The PCA usually arises from the basilar artery. Because of this, disease in the vertebral and basilar arteries may result in infarction in the territory of the PCA. However, a common variant of the PCA is an origin from the ICA. In such a case, the vessel is described as having a *fetal origin.* This common variant is associated with severe hypoplasia or absence of the P1 segment (i.e., the segment of the PCA

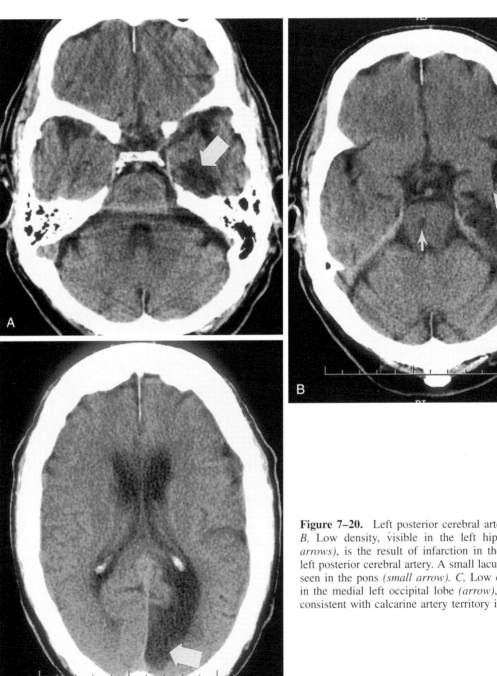

Figure 7–20. Left posterior cerebral artery stroke. *A* and *B*, Low density, visible in the left hippocampus *(large arrows)*, is the result of infarction in the territory of the left posterior cerebral artery. A small lacunar infarct is also seen in the pons *(small arrow)*. *C*, Low density is present in the medial left occipital lobe *(arrow)*, a finding that is consistent with calcarine artery territory infarction.

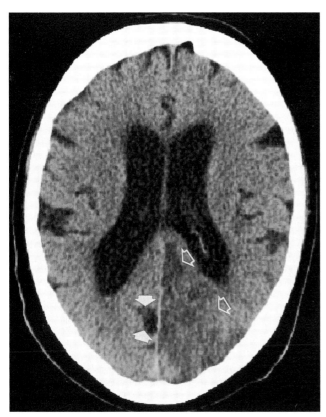

Figure 7–21. Infarct of the posterior cerebral artery (parietal-occipital branch). There is a wedge-shaped area of decreased attenuation in the medial portions of the parietal and occipital lobes *(open arrows)*. The parietal-occipital sulcus contains the parietal occipital branch of the posterior cerebral artery. The normal location and appearance of the right parietal occipital sulcus are shown *(small solid arrows)*.

between the basilar artery and the PCom artery). In patients with this variant, anterior circulation (i.e., carotid) disease can sometimes result in PCA infarction.

Posterior Fossa Stroke

The basilar artery is the sole source of blood supply to the brain stem. Occlusion of the basilar artery is poorly tolerated and can result in rapid progression of ischemic neurologic deficits and infarction (Fig. 7–23). Sometimes collateral supply to the distal basilar artery territory may be present in cases of occlusion of the proximal segment of the basilar artery via retrograde flow from one or both PCAs.

Basilar artery thrombosis can be detected on CT scans by the appearance of hyperdense clot within this artery and variable ischemic hypodensity in the brain stem, cerebellum, thalami, and PCA territory. Careful clinical correlation is recommended when the diagnosis of basilar artery thrombosis is suggested on the basis of unenhanced CT findings, since the appearance of basilar artery thrombosis in some older patients may be mimicked by increased arterial density related to atherosclerotic calcification.

The diagnosis of basilar artery thrombosis may be confirmed with CT angiography or MR angiography, or, more

commonly, with conventional catheter angiography. Basilar artery thrombosis may produce complete or incomplete occlusion of the basilar artery with variable visualization of intraluminal thrombus.

Three arteries provide most of the blood supply to the cerebellum. The posterior inferior cerebellar arteries (PICAs) arise from the intracranial portions of the vertebral arteries. The PICAs supply the posterior-lateral aspects of the medulla, the cerebellar tonsils, and the inferior and posterior surfaces of the cerebellar hemispheres. Occlusion of the proximal PICA can cause infarction of the lateral medulla and tonsil, whereas a more distal occlusion results in infarction mainly along the inferior cerebellar hemisphere (Figs. 7–24 and 7–25).

The anterior inferior cerebellar arteries (AICAs) are usually small vessels that provide reciprocal supply of the cerebellum along with the PICAs. The AICAs are occasionally duplicated and may arise together from a common trunk with the PICA. The AICA gives rise to the artery of the internal auditory canal. Therefore, in addition to causing inferior cerebellar infarction, occlusion of the AICA can result in sensorineural hearing loss, nausea, vertigo, and facial paralysis.

The superior cerebellar arteries (SCAs) arise from the distal basilar artery and supply the superior portions of the cerebellar hemispheres. They often appear duplicated (or triplicated) on angiograms. Infarction of the SCA territory may involve a variable amount of the superior portion of the hemisphere (Fig. 7–26).

The pontine perforator arteries include about 15 to 20 small paired vessels that arise from either side of the basilar artery. Infarction in the paramedian branches of these arteries may result in a centrally located area of abnormal low density or increased signal on long TR images. Infarctions in the territory of paramedian branches of the pontine perforator arteries typically do not cross the plane of midline This feature can be helpful in the differential diagnosis of deep pontine lesions (see Fig. 7–10). The anterolateral surface of the pons is supplied by the short circumferential branches of the pontine arteries.

An unusual arterial variant whose territory should be recognized is the artery of Percheron.[41] This small artery usually arises from the terminal portion of the basilar artery, then bifurcates to produce two small median thalamoperforate arteries that supply small portions of the medial aspects of both thalami (Fig. 7–27). Knowledge of the territory of supply of this artery, along with the MR appearance of a given lesion, can encourage the imaging specialist to suggest the vascular nature of a lesion in this location.

Infarction Caused by Venous Occlusion

Occlusion of cerebral venous structures may lead to increased intracranial pressure and nonfocal neurologic symptoms, such as headache and seizure, without resulting cerebral infarction. Occlusion of venous structures may also lead to focal cerebral infarction associated with focal or nonfocal neurologic symptoms. Since local cerebral perfusion pressure is related to the difference between local

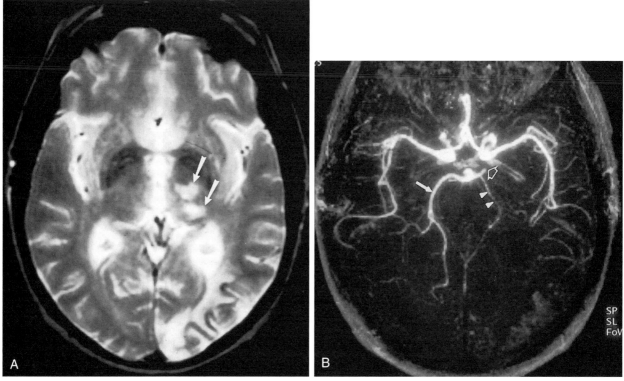

Figure 7–22. Left posterior cerebral artery (PCA) stroke. *A*, T2-weighted axial image shows increased signal in the left occipital lobe. Focal areas of increased signal are also seen in the left thalamus *(arrows)*. Infarction of the thalamus may accompany PCA stroke as a result of occlusion of thalamoperforate arteries originating from the proximal PCA. *B*, Maximum intensity projection image (viewed from beneath) from 3D time-of-flight MRA. The left PCA is occluded proximally *(open arrow)*. The right PCA has a normal appearance *(arrow)*. The left superior cerebellar artery is visible *(arrowheads)*.

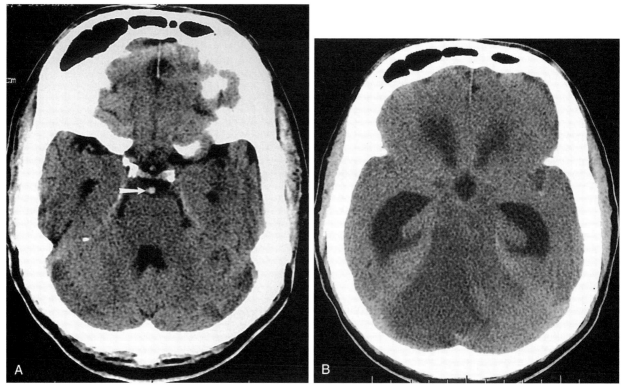

Figure 7–23. Basilar artery thrombosis. *A*, Unenhanced axial CT image shows increased density within the basilar artery *(arrow)*. *B*, Unenhanced axial CT the following day shows extensive cerebellar hypodensity and hydrocephalus due to fourth ventricular and aqueductal compression.

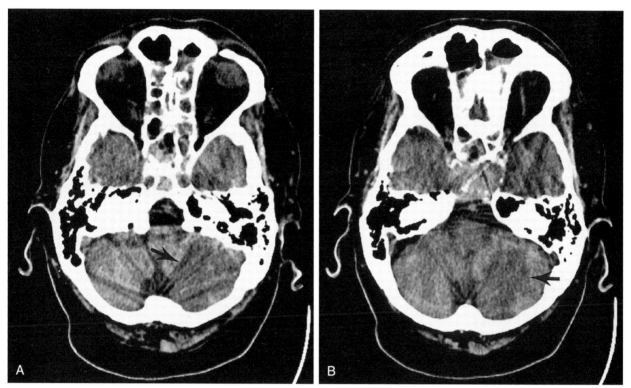

Figure 7–24. Stroke of the posterior inferior cerebellar artery. *A* and *B,* Unenhanced CT scan shows well-defined hypodensity in the distal territory of this artery *(arrows).*

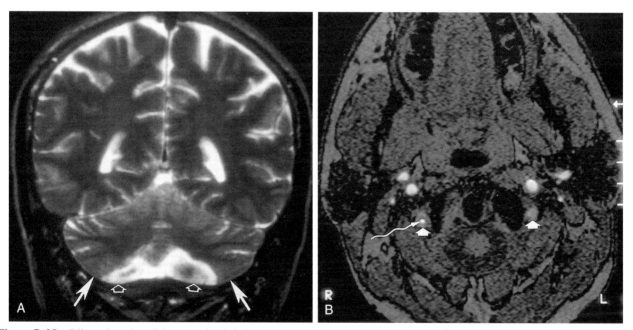

Figure 7–25. Bilateral stroke of the posterior inferior cerebellar artery (PICA). *A,* T2-weighted coronal MR image shows high signal in the territories of this artery bilaterally *(open arrows).* The territories of the anterior inferior cerebellar arteries are spared *(arrows).* *B,* Axial source image from a 2D time-of-flight MRA study shows diminished signal within both vertebral arteries *(short arrows).* A small channel of flow is present in the right vertebral artery *(long wavy arrow).* The findings are those of bilateral vertebral artery thrombosis.

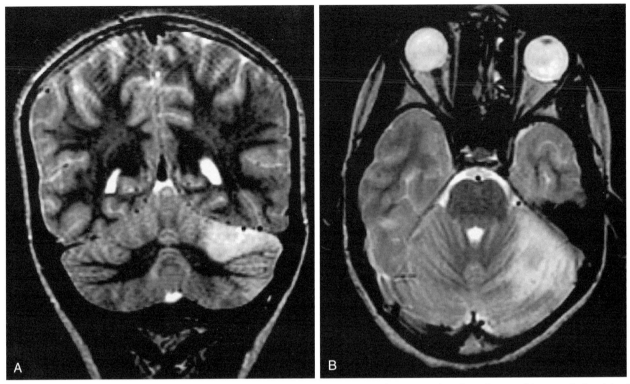

Figure 7–26. Ataxia in an 8-year-old girl. *A,* Coronal T2-weighted MR image shows a wedge-shaped area of increased signal in the superior left cerebellar hemisphere. *B,* Axial T2-weighted image confirms abnormality in the territory of the superior cerebellar artery. Biopsy showed evidence of evolving infarction.

arterial and venous pressures, the probable mechanism of ischemia in venous infarction is a regional decrease in perfusion pressure that is due to regional elevation of venous pressures.

In most cases, the cause is thrombosis of one or more veins or dural venous sinuses. Cerebral vein and dural sinus thrombosis are often associated with certain predisposing conditions such as dehydration, infection, polycythemia, and sickle cell disease. The presence of a hypercoagulable state also appears to be an important risk factor.[11, 61] Intracranial venous thrombosis may also occur in the peripartum period[37] and may be seen in nonpregnant women taking oral contraceptive medications.

Compared with the location and extent of strokes resulting from arterial occlusion, the location and extent of strokes due to venous occlusion are much more variable. Nonetheless, location and extent of ischemia reflect, to some degree, the location and extent of venous occlusion. For example, when venous occlusion is limited to a cortical vein, findings of infarction may be unilateral and limited in extent to the region of the occluded vein. When venous thrombosis is more extensive, such as when extensive thrombus is present within a major dural sinus structure (e.g., the superior sagittal sinus), the findings of brain ischemia may be bilateral and more extensive. Hemorrhage is frequently associated with venous infarction, although the precise reasons are not known. Furthermore, the hemorrhages that are seen in ischemia as a result of venous occlusion are commonly subcortical in location.[28]

The imaging signs that are often most helpful for diagnosis of venous occlusion are those that indicate the presence of thrombus within a venous structure. On CT scans, the presence of hyperdense material within a venous channel and lack of appropriate central enhancement with contrast material are the most important signs (Fig. 7–28). MR images may show increased T1 signal within venous structures occluded by thrombus (see Fig. 7–5). Lack of appropriate flow-related signal void within the venous structure on T2-weighted images and lack of enhancement within the venous structure following injection of gadolinium-containing contrast agents are also typical (Fig. 7–29). Flow-sensitive sequences, such as time-of-flight and phase-contrast MR venograms, can be used to document the presence and extent of venous occlusion.[3]

A number of pitfalls must be recognized when one is evaluating an MRI scan (including MR venogram studies) for the presence of venous thrombus.[3] First, thrombus that is hyperintense on T1-weighted images may be mistaken for flow on time-of-flight images. The imaging specialist can minimize this pitfall by carefully inspecting the unenhanced T1- and T2-weighted images for evidence of clot and by using phase-contrast MR venography alone or in combination with time-of-flight methods. Phase-contrast methods are affected not by the relaxation properties (e.g., T1) of the imaged tissues; they are influenced only by the net displacement (i.e., flow) of spins.

Interpretation of MR scans performed for the evaluation of the dural venous sinuses can also be affected by the fact that flowing blood can appear hyperintense on T1-weighted images, potentially mimicking hyperintense signal due to thrombus. Flowing blood is typically brightest near the edges of the imaged volume, an artifact that can be helpful

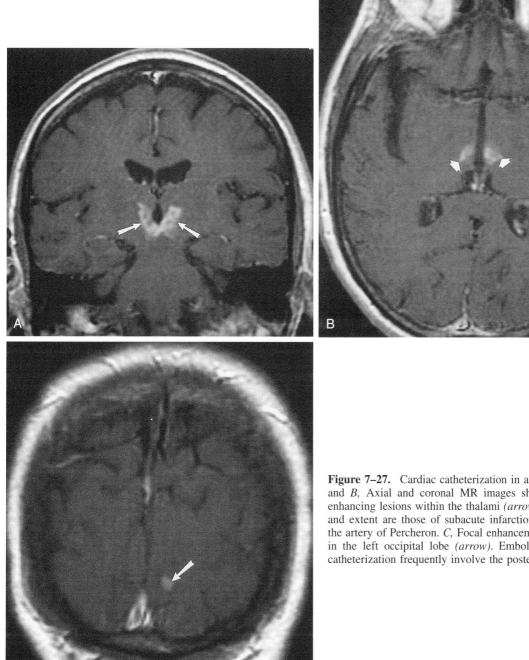

Figure 7–27. Cardiac catheterization in a 70-year-old man. *A* and *B*, Axial and coronal MR images show paired bilateral enhancing lesions within the thalami *(arrows)*. The appearance and extent are those of subacute infarction in the territory of the artery of Percheron. *C*, Focal enhancement is also apparent in the left occipital lobe *(arrow)*. Embolic complications of catheterization frequently involve the posterior circulation.

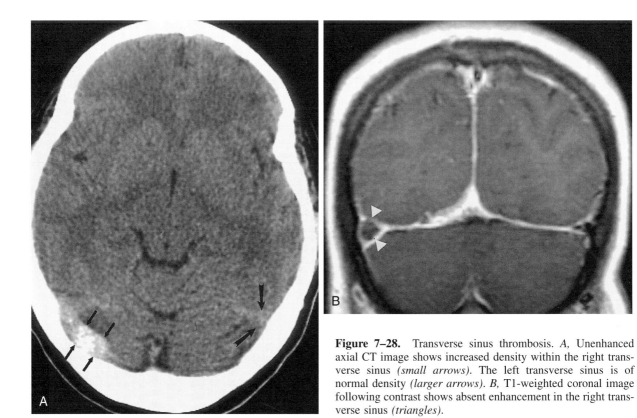

Figure 7–28.   Transverse sinus thrombosis. *A,* Unenhanced axial CT image shows increased density within the right transverse sinus *(small arrows).* The left transverse sinus is of normal density *(larger arrows). B,* T1-weighted coronal image following contrast shows absent enhancement in the right transverse sinus *(triangles).*

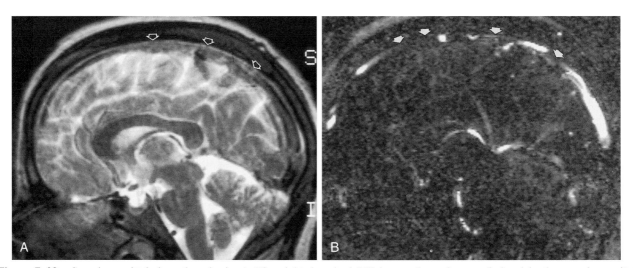

Figure 7–29.   Superior sagittal sinus thrombosis. *A,* T2-weighted sagittal MR image shows increased signal in the superior sagittal sinus *(open arrows). B,* Partition image from a phase-contrast MR venogram study (VENC = 5 cm/second) shows regions of absent flow within the superior sagittal sinus *(small arrows).*

in analysis of the findings in a given case. Inspection of the T2-weighted image can also be helpful because absence of signal on long echo-time (TE) images usually suggests that flow is present.

Many patients have congenital absence or hypoplasia of one transverse venous sinus (most often the left), which can mimic occlusion of the sinus on MR venogram studies. In addition, flow gaps within one or both transverse sinuses may be a normal finding in about 30% of patients and should not be mistaken for clot.[3] In addition, small papillary arachnoid villi may project into the lumina of dural sinuses and thus may appear as small filling defects that can mimic clot on MR venogram studies. These villi typically appear hyperintense on T2-weighted images, allowing them to be distinguished, in some cases, from thrombus.

Thrombosis of the deep cerebral veins produces a devastating clinical course and characteristic appearance on imaging studies.[35] Thrombosis of the internal cerebral veins, the vein of Galen, and the straight sinus may also be accompanied by occlusion of the basal veins (of Rosenthal). Infarction of the thalami, midbrain, and basal ganglia may occur, often associated with hemorrhage (Fig. 7–30).

CT venography is a relatively new but promising modality that provides an alternative to MR venography for the evaluation of the cerebral venous system.[77] This study is performed with the use of helical acquisition with thin collimation and rapid, continuous infusion of iodinated contrast material. Available commercial postprocessing software can provide surface-shaded renderings and projection-type images of the cerebral venous system. The most important clinical application of this modality is for the investigation of the cerebral venous system for occlusion (Fig. 7–31).

Nonocclusive Stroke and Other Problems

Purely hemodynamic stroke can occur in patients without sources of emboli and with episodic hypotension.[6] In such cases, the extent of abnormality on imaging studies depends on the degree and duration of systemic hypotension. When hypotension has been relatively mild in degree or short in duration, ischemic changes may be seen in the territories of the watershed zones between major vascular territories or in the deep watershed zones that correspond to the deep cerebral white matter.[51] A parasagittal location, a chainlike pattern, and a deep location all suggest infarction caused by low flow (Fig. 7–32).

Cerebral infarction may also occur in patients who have suffered toxic or anoxic insult. Hypoxemia, carbon monoxide poisoning, and hypoglycemia all have the potential to result in selective or global infarction. Metabolic enzyme and mitochondrial defects can also lead to ischemia and infarction (Fig. 7–33). Selective involvement of the basal ganglia may be seen in many of the processes described. In particular, carbon monoxide poisoning is associated with selective infarction of the globus pallidus, whereas Leigh's disease, a mitochondrial enzyme abnormality, most commonly affects the striatum.[74] Hypoglycemia can cause a pattern of diffuse ischemia that predominantly affects the parietal and occipital regions.[53]

Hypoxic-ischemic encephalopathy (HIE) can result in a diffuse or focal infarction in young children and infants (Fig. 7–34). Especially vulnerable are the deep periatrial white matter regions, areas that form part of the deep watershed in infants. On postnatal MRI or CT scans, end-stage periventricular leukomalacia (PVL) is depicted as the symmetrical pattern of periatrial white matter abnormality and volume loss (Fig. 7–35). A number of causes other than hypoxia or ischemia can produce PVL, including infectious and metabolic abnormalities.

Other commonly encountered stroke mechanisms include vasospasm and vasculitis. Following aneurysm rupture, vasospasm of the intracranial arteries is the cause of a substantial part of the morbidity and mortality caused by subarachnoid hemorrhage. Typically, CT or MRI signs of infarction are seen in the territory of arterial insufficiency (Fig. 7–36).

Vasculitis of the cerebral arteries may be primary or secondary to a systemic problem, such as systemic vasculitis or lupus erythematosus. Patients with lupus erythematosus have a particularly high incidence of secondary CNS vasculitis. On CT and MRI studies, the presence of multiple areas of ischemia suggests vasculitis, especially when a substantial number of small cortical and subcortical lesions are present (Fig. 7–37). CT and MRA can depict vasculitic changes in the medium-sized vessels of the circle of Willis; however, visualization of the small cortical arteries is limited with these techniques. Catheter angiography is considered to be the imaging test with the highest degree of sensitivity and specificity for CNS vasculitis.

Cortical laminar necrosis is a histologic, pathologic term that also can be used to describe a particular type of postischemic pattern of injury on CT and MR images. Ischemic injury, occasionally, can be limited to one or more cell layers of the cortex without involvement of the remaining layers. When this occurs, mineralization may develop within the affected layers, producing a gyriform pattern of increased density or signal intensity (on T1-weighted images) (Fig. 7–38).

Diffusion-Weighted Imaging in Acute Stroke

DW images are MR images that are created by applying a pair of magnetic gradient pulses that sensitize the sequence to motion. By applying very large gradients and allowing sufficient time to pass between gradient lobes (pulses), one can sensitize the scan to microscopic motions that are occurring within the imaging voxel.[48]

The amount of diffusion weighting of a DW image is determined by the magnitude of the applied gradients, how long they are switched on, and the time between the two lobes. The magnitude of diffusion weighting is connoted by the "b" value of the image. Typical "b" values (in seconds per square millimeter) for imaging stroke are on the order of 400 to 1000 seconds/mm^2. By comparing a diffusion-sensitized image (or images) to a similar scan without diffusion-sensitizing gradients (i.e., the "b zero" image), one can compute the amount of diffusion that appears to have occurred.[40] If this is done on a pixel-by-

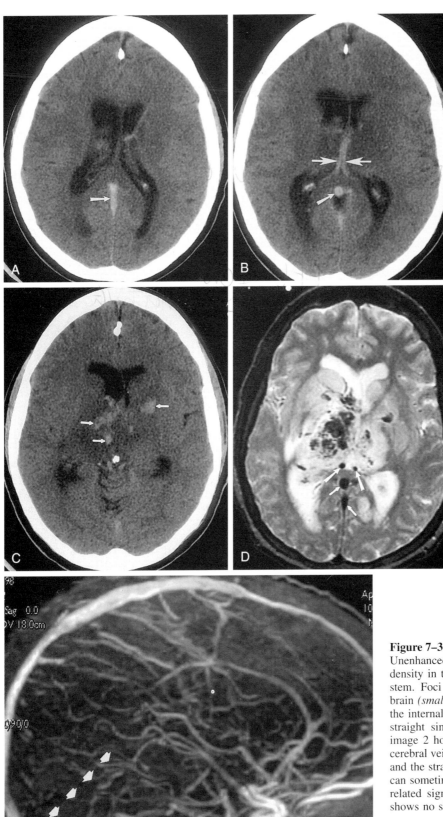

Figure 7–30.   Deep cerebral venous thrombosis. *A–C,* Unenhanced axial CT images show extensive low density in the basal ganglia, thalami, and upper brain stem. Foci of hemorrhage are also seen within the brain *(small arrows)*. Increased density is seen within the internal cerebral veins, the vein of Galen, and the straight sinus *(larger arrows)*. *D,* T2-weighted MR image 2 hours later shows low signal in the internal cerebral veins *(larger arrows)* and in the vein of Galen and the straight sinus *(small arrows)*. Acute thrombus can sometimes appear as low signal, mimicking flow-related signal void. *E,* Time-of-flight MR venogram shows no signal in the straight sinus *(small arrows)*.

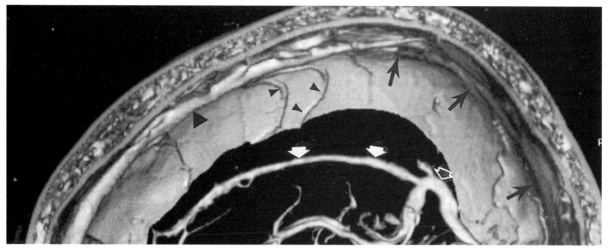

Figure 7–31. Superior sagittal sinus thrombosis. Surface-rendered CT venogram study shows absent opacification in the posterior portion of the superior sagittal sinus *(black arrows)*. The anterior portion of the superior sagittal sinus is patent *(triangle)*. Small cortical veins are depicted *(arrowheads)*. The inferior sagittal sinus *(small arrows)* and the vein of Galen are also seen *(open arrow)*.

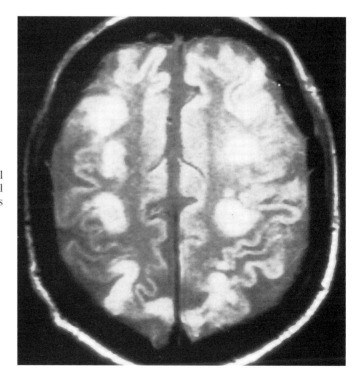

Figure 7–32. Watershed stroke. Intermediate-weighted axial image in a child shows bilateral, symmetrical parasagittal increased signal. The "chainlike" appearance depicted here is often seen with hemodynamic stroke.

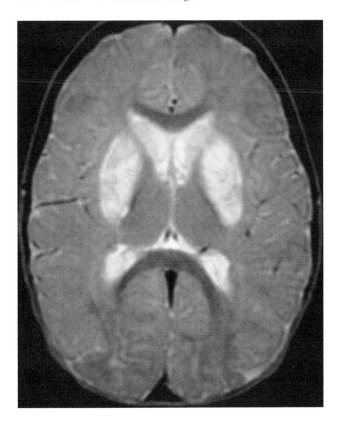

Figure 7–33. Leigh's disease in an 18-month-old child. T2-weighted axial image shows increased signal in the basal ganglia bilaterally. Some toxic and anoxic injuries can produce a similar pattern of ischemic injury.

pixel basis, the result is a computed map of apparent diffusion known as an "ADC map."

DW images are highly sensitive to the diffusion restriction that occurs in acute stroke.[24] Regions of acute cerebral ischemia are typically hyperintense on DW images and result in diminished ADC values of up to 40%. In experimental stroke models, hyperintensity on DW images can be seen before changes on T2-weighted images are visible.[49]

It is often assumed that hyperintense signal on DW images represents irreversible ischemia. However, studies of experimental stroke and some reports in humans suggest that some changes in diffusion depicted on imaging studies represent potentially reversible ischemia.[30, 57]

Artifacts on Diffusion-Weighted Images

Acute stroke is characterized by high signal intensity on DW images (Fig. 7–39); however, there are other causes of high signal intensity on these images. Knowing these other causes can be helpful in assessing the likelihood that a given patient has evidence of cerebral ischemia.

One commonly seen artifact that can mimic the appearance of acute stroke is known as *T2 shine-through.* Because DW scans also typically have substantial spin density and T2 weighting, areas of T2 prolongation may result in carryover of hyperintense signal to the DW image. Careful comparison with a reference image (i.e., the "b zero" image) or another type of T2-weighted image can be helpful in recognizing this artifact.

Another artifact that can mimic the appearance of acute stroke on DW images is hyperintensity due to white matter diffusion anisotropy. If one reviews DW images that have been sensitized to diffusion in only one direction (e.g., the phase-encoding direction), the white matter tracts that run orthogonal to the direction of sensitization appear relatively bright. This artifact can be recognized with experience, although comparison with DW images obtained with the diffusion-sensitizing gradients applied in other directions can also be helpful. One can eliminate this artifact completely by reviewing only images that have isotropic weighting (i.e., DW images that have been combined so that weighting is applied in all three cardinal directions). Such images are also called *trace-weighted* or, simply, *trace* images. Both expressions refer to the diagonal numerical terms that are part of a 3×3 (nine-element) tensor matrix of data that expresses the diffusion properties of an object.[80]

Another artifactual cause of hyperintense signal on DW scans is related to magnetic susceptibility artifacts. Most DW scans are made using *echo-planar imaging* techniques. These very rapid MRI methods are commonly used for DW images because DW scans are highly sensitive to patient motion.

One potential problem with echo-planar images is that they are very sensitive to susceptibility artifacts at soft tissue/bone and soft tissue/air interfaces. Foreign bodies (e.g., shunt catheters) may also produce susceptibility artifacts on DW echo-planar images. Susceptibility artifacts are usually easy to recognize because:

1. They occur in locations (e.g., calvarium and skull base) that are prone to such artifacts.
2. They are often flame-shaped.
3. When severe, they can cause regional anatomic distortion in addition to causing increased signal intensity.

Text continued on page 279

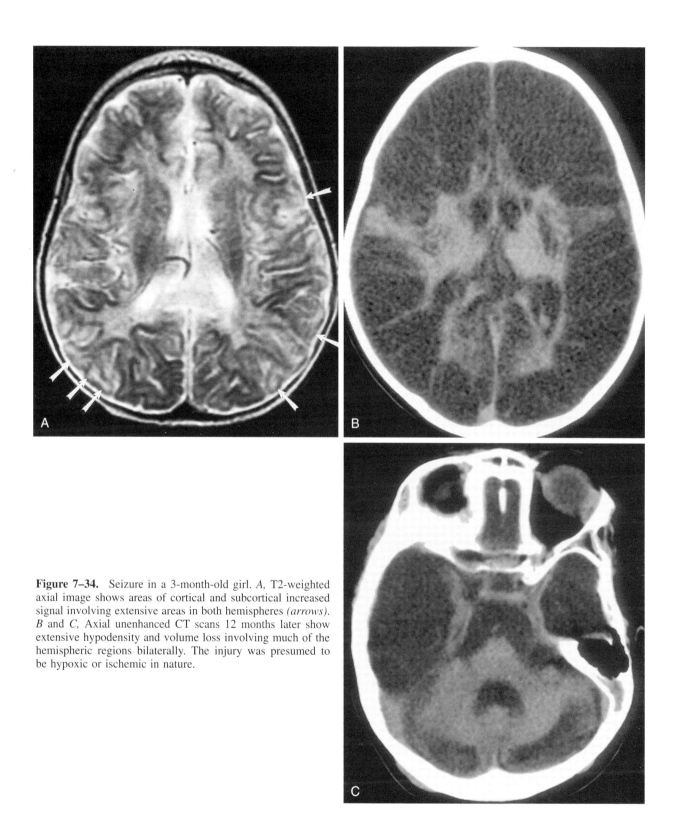

Figure 7–34. Seizure in a 3-month-old girl. *A,* T2-weighted axial image shows areas of cortical and subcortical increased signal involving extensive areas in both hemispheres *(arrows).* *B* and *C,* Axial unenhanced CT scans 12 months later show extensive hypodensity and volume loss involving much of the hemispheric regions bilaterally. The injury was presumed to be hypoxic or ischemic in nature.

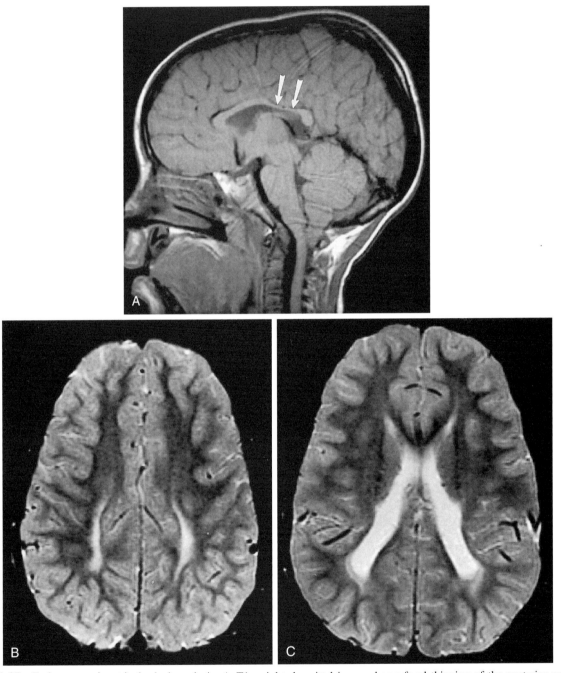

Figure 7–35.   End-stage periventricular leukomalacia. *A,* T1-weighted sagittal image shows focal thinning of the posterior portion of the body of the corpus callosum *(arrows). B* and *C,* T2-weighted axial images show dilation of the atria of the lateral ventricles and increased signal in the deep periventricular white matter. There are a number of causes of periventricular leukomalacia, one of which is hypoxic-ischemic encephalopathy.

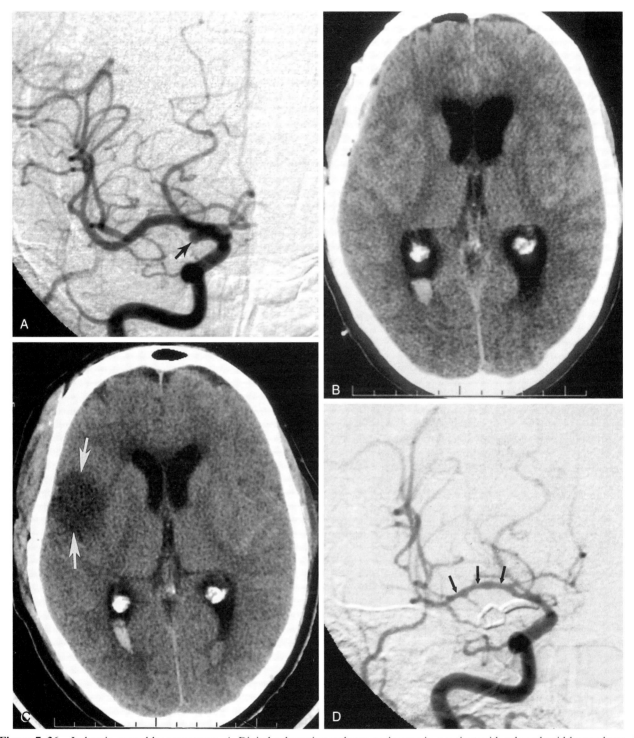

Figure 7–36. Ischemia caused by vasospasm. *A,* Digital subtraction catheter angiogram in a patient with subarachnoid hemorrhage. A ruptured posterior communicating artery–internal carotid artery junction aneurysm is seen *(arrow)*. *B,* Unenhanced axial CT image immediately following ligation of the aneurysm shows postoperative changes but no evidence of infarction. *C,* Unenhanced CT 3 days later, after the onset of left-sided weakness, shows new focal hypodensity *(arrows)*. *D,* A subsequent angiogram shows significant vasospasm in the right M1 segment *(small arrows)*.

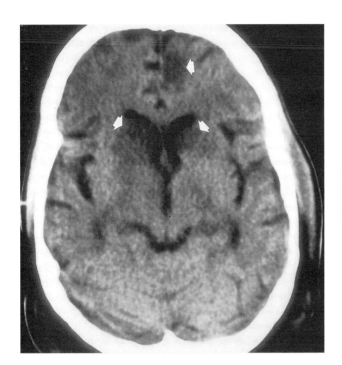

Figure 7–37. Vasculitis. Unenhanced axial CT image shows abnormal low density in the basal ganglia bilaterally and in the left frontal lobe *(arrows)*. Multiple areas of cortical and subcortical infarction may be seen in patients with vasculitis.

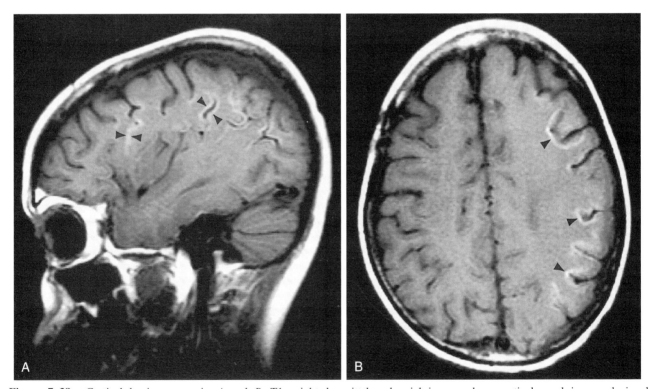

Figure 7–38. Cortical laminar necrosis. *A* and *B*, T1-weighted sagittal and axial images show cortical gyral increased signal *(arrowheads)* without substantial volume loss. The extent matches the expected left cortical middle cerebral artery territory. The signal changes are thought to represent mineralization within tissue damaged by ischemia.

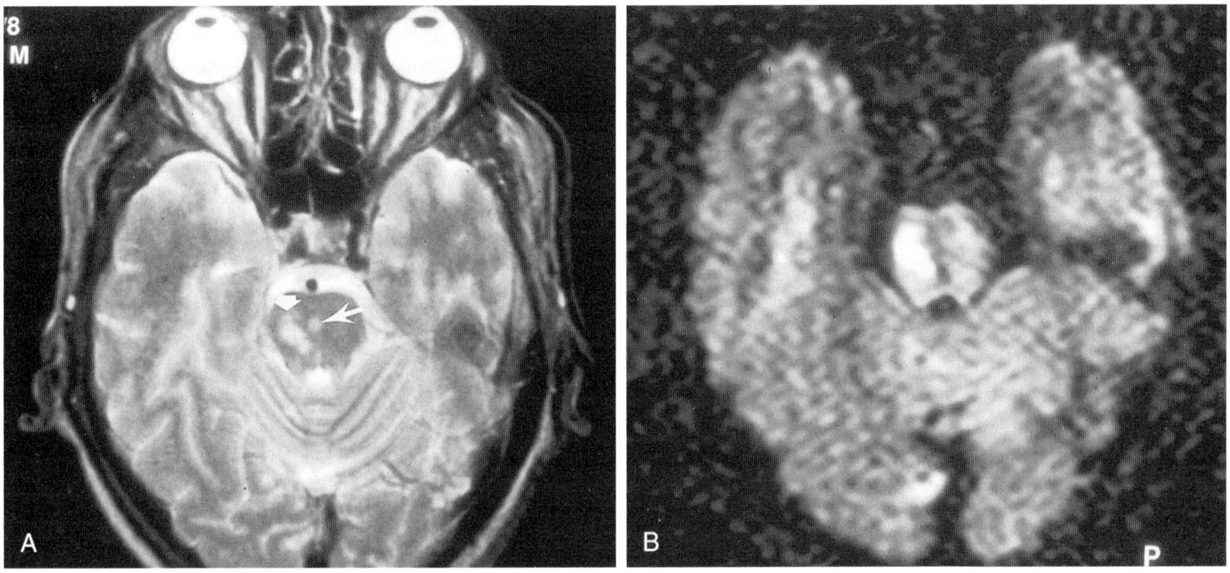

Figure 7–39. The patient is a 59-year-old man with acute stroke. *A,* T2-weighted axial image shows increased signal focally within the central *(arrow)* and lateral *(small arrow)* portions of the pons. *B,* Axial diffusion-weighted image shows hyperintense signal within the lateral abnormality, suggesting that only this area represents acute infarct. The smaller, central hyperintensity, presumably, represents a more remote ischemic lesion.

Finally, some conditions other than stroke can be associated with diffusion restriction, for example, cerebral abscess.[31] Cerebral trauma resulting in diffuse axonal injury can also result in foci of hyperintensity on DW scans.[42a]

Time Course of Diffusion-Weighted Images in Stroke

The very earliest change that can be seen on DW images after an acute stroke is minimal hyperintensity. As mentioned, some early hyperintense changes on DW images may be reversible, both in human stroke patients and in animal subjects. Such findings suggest that separate thresholds of ischemia may exist for early diffusion changes and irreversible cell damage.

ADC values vary with the age of ischemic stroke,[60] a fact that can influence the analysis of clinical cases. In the first hours after the onset of ischemia, ADC values decrease rapidly, often to 30% or more below normal. ADC values lower than about 60×10^{-4} mm²/second are usually seen in ischemia, and values below 50×10^{-4} mm²/second are often seen. After about 24 hours, ADC values begin to increase again, approaching normal values at about 5 to 7 days. This tendency for ADC values to increase and return to the normal range after the initial decrease that occurs in acute cerebral infarction is termed *pseudonormalization.* After about 2 weeks, ADC values are typically increased within the territory of infarction.

One can often distinguish acute stroke from other diagnoses that are associated with T2 prolongation by measuring diminished brain ADC values within the lesion (i.e., many disease processes are associated with *increased* ADC values). Because ADC values increase with the age of a given infarction, one cannot reliably use ADC measurements to distinguish subacute and chronic infarction from other diagnoses.

Despite these changes in ADC values that occur after a stroke, cerebral infarction on DW images often remains hyperintense throughout most of the time course of stroke. The reason that the appearance of stroke remains hyperintense on DW images throughout its time course is presumably related to T2 shine-through. That is, the fact that the region of infarction is bright on T2-weighted images influences the appearance of the stroke on DW images (which typically have substantial T2 weighting).

In addition to standard DW images and ADC maps, a third type of diffusion image can be created that combines some of the advantages of each. If one divides the DW image by the "b zero" reference image, one can create a calculated image known as the *ratio image,* or *exponential image.*[47] Such an image is similar to standard DW scans, in that areas of acute ischemia appear hyperintense. Unlike standard DW images, however, so-called exponential images do not have any T2 weighting and thus do not show the effects of T2 shine-through (Fig. 7–40).

Cerebral Perfusion Imaging
Hemodynamic Pathophysiology in Cerebral Ischemia

The cerebral perfusion parameters CBF and cerebral blood volume (CBV) are related by the central volume principle, which is expressed as the relation

$$CBF = \frac{CBV}{MTT}$$

where MTT is the mean transit time of a nondiffusible tracer in a volume of brain tissue.[34]

The pathophysiology of ischemia can be considered in four stages, based on autoregulatory physiology:

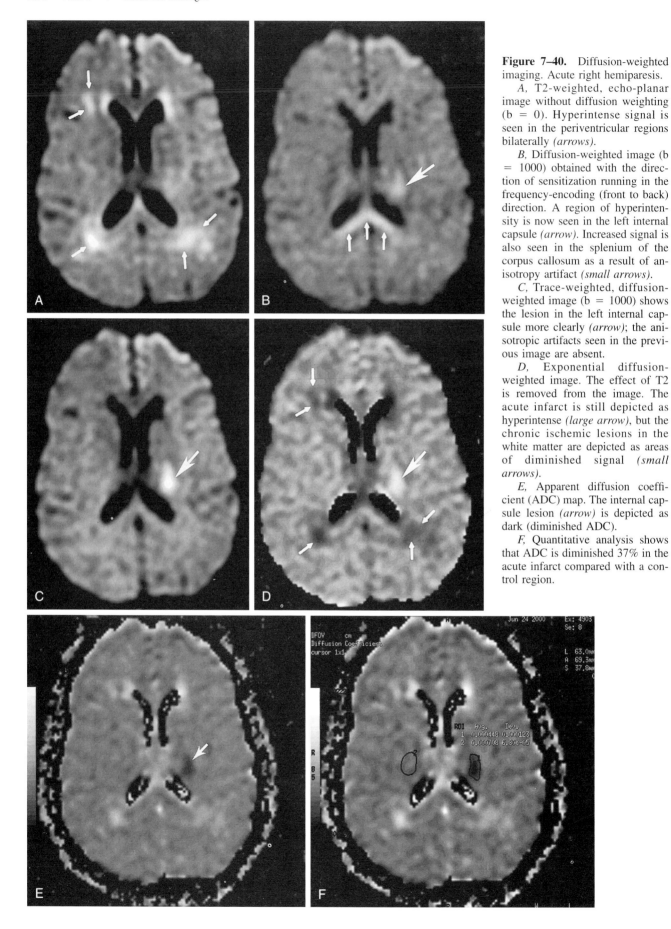

Figure 7–40. Diffusion-weighted imaging. Acute right hemiparesis.

A, T2-weighted, echo-planar image without diffusion weighting (b = 0). Hyperintense signal is seen in the periventricular regions bilaterally *(arrows).*

B, Diffusion-weighted image (b = 1000) obtained with the direction of sensitization running in the frequency-encoding (front to back) direction. A region of hyperintensity is now seen in the left internal capsule *(arrow).* Increased signal is also seen in the splenium of the corpus callosum as a result of anisotropy artifact *(small arrows).*

C, Trace-weighted, diffusion-weighted image (b = 1000) shows the lesion in the left internal capsule more clearly *(arrow);* the anisotropic artifacts seen in the previous image are absent.

D, Exponential diffusion-weighted image. The effect of T2 is removed from the image. The acute infarct is still depicted as hyperintense *(large arrow),* but the chronic ischemic lesions in the white matter are depicted as areas of diminished signal *(small arrows).*

E, Apparent diffusion coefficient (ADC) map. The internal capsule lesion *(arrow)* is depicted as dark (diminished ADC).

F, Quantitative analysis shows that ADC is diminished 37% in the acute infarct compared with a control region.

- *First stage,* normal hemodynamics.
- *Second stage,* characterized by an initial decrease in perfusion pressure. Initially, autoregulatory vasodilation preserves CBF, at the same time increasing CBV. MTT is also typically increased.
- *Third stage,* characterized by greater decrease in perfusion pressure and by an initial decrease in CBF value. CBV typically remains increased.
- *Fourth stage,* characterized by further decrease in perfusion pressure and decreases in both CBF and CBV. This stage is associated with tissue ischemia and hemodynamic failure.

Perfusion Imaging in Stroke

An important goal of hemodynamic stroke imaging is the depiction of tissue at risk for infarction that might be saved though intervention. In the setting of acute stroke, if the location and extent of viable tissue at risk for infarction were known, such knowledge could help clinicians to weigh the risks associated with stroke therapies. Viable tissue that is at risk for infarction is commonly called the *ischemic penumbra,* or the tissue outside the (nonviable) core of infarction that is nonetheless underperfused. It is postulated that the ischemic penumbra differs from viable tissue that is not at risk by the (decreased) amount of blood flow that it receives.

A number of methods of imaging cerebral perfusion are available. Imaging with radioisotopes is possible with single-photon emission computed tomography (SPECT) and positron emission tomography (PET). It is also possible to image CBF with CT using inhaled stable xenon.[10] This method is capable of depicting extent of hemodynamic abnormality in stroke.[71] Although xenon CT remains an attractive tool for the assessment of CBF, this method has not yet achieved widespread clinical use. One possible reason may be the requirement for specialized equipment to administer and ventilate the gas.

It is now possible to obtain dynamic, contrast-enhanced perfusion scans using either CT or MR scanners[32, 66] (Figs. 7–41 and 7–42). Generally, a volume of contrast material is injected rapidly into an arm vein by an automatic (power) injector, and the bolus of contrast material is tracked by the scanner through a slice or slab of brain tissue that is repeatedly scanned over the course of about 45 to 60 seconds. For best results, temporal resolution of 2 seconds or faster is needed.

It has been proposed that MR perfusion imaging may complement DW imaging in depicting the region of penumbra.[26] The premise is that DW imaging is thought to depict the region of core infarction, whereas the region of perfusion abnormality represents both the core and the penumbra. The difference between the extent of the diffusion abnormality and the extent of perfusion abnormality is thus thought to represent penumbra.

An alternate approach for determining the extent of penumbra is to use perfusion maps alone to distinguish the core of infarction from the penumbra, usually with the use of perfusion parameter value thresholds. The most commonly used perfusion parameter is the mean CBF value. Earlier work with xenon CT in stroke patients has

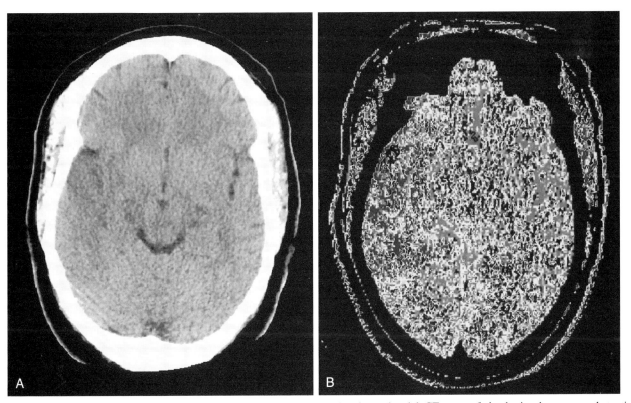

Figure 7–41. Acute stroke of the right middle cerebral artery. *A,* Unenhanced axial CT scan of the brain shows no substantial abnormalities. *B,* Mean transit time (MTT) map from dynamic CT perfusion scan depicts a well-defined region of MTT prolongation. The extent and degree of regional hemodynamic abnormalities can be determined by perfusion imaging techniques.

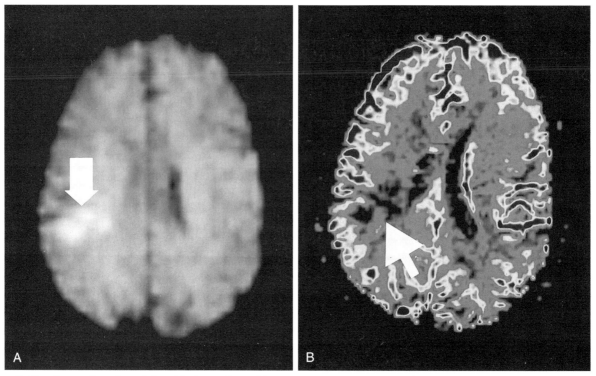

Figure 7–42. Acute dissection of the right internal carotid artery. *A,* Trace-weighted, diffusion-weighted image (b = 1000) shows cortically based region of hyperintense signal consistent with acute middle cerebral artery territory infarction *(arrow). B,* Negative enhancement integral image (relative cerebral blood volume) from gadolinium-enhanced dynamic sequence. The extent of a region of *(arrow)* diminished perfusion is identical to the diffusion-weighted image abnormality *(arrow).* This represents a "matched" perfusion and diffusion defect.

described thresholds for infarct core (CBF values < 7 mL/ 100 g per minute) and penumbra (CBF values between 7 and 20 mL/100 g per minute).[18]

The perfusion parameter CBV may provide additional information about tissue viability that CBF alone cannot provide. Studies using MRI with SPECT and xenon CT with dynamic CT have shown that for tissues associated with moderately low CBF values, CBV value can help to predict tissue viability.[50] These studies suggest that moderately decreased CBF values and increased CBV values may carry a better prognosis than that for tissues in which both CBF and CBV values are diminished.

References

1. Asato R, Okumura R, Konishi J: "Fogging effect" in MR of cerebral infarct. J Comput Assist Tomogr 15:160–162, 1991.
2. Astrup J, Siesjo B, Symon L: Thresholds in cerebral ischemia—the ischemic penumbra. Stroke 12:723–725, 1981.
3. Ayanzen RH, Bird CR, Keller PJ, et al: Cerebral MR venography: Normal anatomy and potential diagnostic pitfalls. AJNR Am J Neuroradiol 21:74–78, 2000
4. Bamford J, Sandercock P, Dennis M, et al: A prospective study of acute cerebrovascular disease in the community: The Oxfordshire Community Stroke Project, 1981–1986: Part 2. Incidence, case fatality rates, and overall outcome at one year of cerebral infarction, primary intracerebral and subarachnoid hemorrhage. J Neurol Neurosurg Psychiatry 53:16–22, 1990.
5. Bernaudin F, Verlhac S, Freard F, et al: Multicenter prospective study of children with sickle cell disease: Radiographic and psychometric correlation. J Child Neurol 15:333–343, 2000.
6. Bladin CF, Chambers BR: Frequency and pathogenesis of hemodynamic stroke. Stroke 25:2179–282, 1994.
7. Bonita R: Epidemiology of stroke. Lancet 339:343–344, 1992.
8. Boyko OB, Burger PC, Shelbourne JD, Ingram P: Non-heme mechanisms for T1 shortening: Pathologic, CT, and MR elucidation. AJNR Am J Neuroradiol 13:1439–1445, 1992.
9. Brandt T, Steinke W, Thie A, et al: Posterior cerebral artery territory infarcts: Clinical features, infarct topography, causes, and outcome. Cerebrovasc Dis 10:170–182, 2000.
10. Caille JM, Constant P, Renou AM, Billerey J: Prognostic value of rCBF measurements and CT in focal cerebral ischemia. Neuroradiology 16:238–241, 1978.
11. Dulli DA, Luzzio CC, Williams EC, Schutta HS: Cerebral venous thrombosis and activated protein C resistance. Stroke 27:1731–1733, 1996.
12. Fisher M: Occlusion of the internal carotid artery. Arch Neurol Psychiatry 65:346–377, 1951.
13. Ford CC, Griffey RH, Matwiyoff NA, Rosenberg GA: Multivoxel ¹H-MRS of stroke. Neurology 42:1408–1412, 1992.
14. Gerhard GT, Duell PB: Homocysteine and atherosclerosis. Curr Opin Lipidol 10:417–428, 1999.
15. Grohn OH, Lukkarinen JA, Oja JM, et al: Noninvasive detection of cerebral hypoperfusion and reversible ischemia from reductions in the magnetic resonance imaging relaxation time, T2. J Cereb Blood Flow Metab 18:911–920, 1998.
16. Hacke W, Kaste M, Fieschi C, et al: Intravenous thrombolysis with recombinant tissue plasminogen activator for acute hemispheric stroke: The European Cooperative Acute Stroke Study. JAMA 274: 1017–1025, 1995.
17. Hankey GJ, Sudlow CL, Dunbabin DW: Thienopyridines or aspirin to prevent stroke and other serious vascular events in patients at high risk of vascular disease? A systematic review of the evidence from randomized trials. Stroke 31:1779–1784, 2000.
18. Hatazawa J, Shimosegawa E, Toyoshima H, et al: Cerebral blood volume in acute brain infarction: A combined study with dynamic susceptibility contrast MRI and ⁹⁹ᵐTc-HMPAO-SPECT. Stroke 30: 800–806, 1999.
19. Heinsius T, Bogousslavsky J, Van Melle G: Large infarcts in the middle cerebral artery territory: Etiology and outcome patterns. Neurology 50:341–350, 1998.

20. Henriksen O, Gideon P, Sperling B, et al: Cerebral lactate production and blood flow in acute stroke. J Magn Reson Imaging 2:511–517, 1992.

21. Hossmann KA: Viability thresholds and the penumbra of focal ischemia. Ann Neurol 36:557–565, 1994.

22. Ida M, Mizunuma K, Hata Y, Tada S: Subcortical low intensity in early cortical ischemia. AJNR Am J Neuroradiol 15:1387–1393, 1994.

23. Johnson WD, Ganjoo AK, Stone CD, et al: The left atrial appendage: Our most lethal human attachment! Surgical implications. Eur J Cardiothorac Surg 17:718–722, 2000.

24. Jones SC, Perez-Trepichio AD, Xue M, et al: Magnetic resonance diffusion-weighted imaging: Sensitivity and apparent diffusion constant in stroke. Acta Neurochir Suppl (Wien) 60:207–210, 1994.

25. Jungreis CA, Kanal E, Hirsch WL, et al: Normal perivascular spaces mimicking lacunar infarction: MR imaging. Radiology 169:101–104, 1988.

26. Kaufmann AM, Firlik AD, Fukui MB, et al: Ischemic core and penumbra in human stroke. Stroke 30:93–99, 1999.

27. Kazui S, Levi CR, Jones EF, et al: Risk factors for lacunar stroke: A case-control transesophageal echocardiographic study. Neurology 54: 1385–1387, 2000.

28. Keiper MD, Ng SE, Atlas SW, Grossman RI: Subcortical hemorrhage: Marker for radiographically occult cerebral vein thrombosis on CT. J Comput Assist Tomogr 19:527–531, 1995.

29. Kenet G, Sadetzki S, Murad H, et al: Factor V Leiden and antiphospholipid antibodies are significant risk factors for ischemic stroke in children. Stroke 31:1283–1288, 2000.

30. Kidwell CS, Saver JL, Mattiello J, et al: Thrombolytic reversal of acute human cerebral ischemic injury shown by diffusion/perfusion magnetic resonance imaging. Ann Neurol 47:462–469, 2000.

31. Kim YJ, Chang KH, Song IC, et al: Brain abscess and necrotic or cystic brain tumor: Discrimination with signal intensity on diffusion-weighted MR imaging. AJR Am J Roentgenol 171:1487–1490, 1998.

32. Koenig M, Klotz E, Luka B, et al: Perfusion CT of the brain: Diagnostic approach for early detection of ischemic stroke. Radiology 209:85–93, 1998.

33. Koh MS, Goh KY, Tung MY, Chan C: Is decompressive craniectomy for acute cerebral infarction of any benefit? Surg Neurol 53:225–230, 2000.

34. Kohlmeyer K, Graser C: Comparative studies of computed tomography and measurements of regional cerebral blood flow in stroke patients. Neuroradiology 16:233–237, 1978.

35. Lafitte F, Boukobza M, Guichard JP, et al: Deep cerebral venous thrombosis: Imaging in eight cases. Neuroradiology 41:410–418, 1999.

36. Lansberg MG, Albers GW, Beaulieu C, Marks MP: Comparison of diffusion-weighted MRI and CT in acute stroke. Neurology 54: 1557–1561, 2000.

37. Lanska DJ, Kryscio RJ: Risk factors for peripartum and postpartum stroke and intracranial venous thrombosis. Stroke 31:1274–82, 2000.

38. Lassen NA, Astrup J: Ischemic penumbra. In Wood JH (ed): Cerebral Blood Flow: Physiologic and Clinical Aspects. New York, McGraw-Hill, 1987, 1994.

39. Launes J, Ketonen L: Dense middle cerebral artery sign: An indicator of poor outcome in middle cerebral artery area infarction. J Neurol Neurosurg Psychiatry 50:1550–1552, 1987.

40. Le Bihan D, Breton E, Lallemand D, et al: Separation of diffusion and perfusion in intravoxel incoherent motion MR imaging. Radiology 168:497–505, 1988.

41. Lepore FE, Gulli V, Miller DC: Neuro-ophthalmological findings with neuropathological correlation in bilateral thalamic-mesencephalic infarction. J Clin Neuroophthalmol 5:224–228, 1985.

42. Lev MH, Farkas J, Gemmete JJ, et al: Acute stroke: Improved nonenhanced CT detection—benefits of soft-copy interpretation by using variable window width and center level settings. Radiology 213:150–155, 1999.

42a. Liu AY, Maldjian JA, Bagley LJ, et al: Traumatic brain injury: Diffusion-weighted MR imaging findings. AJNR Am J Neuroradiol 20:1636–1641, 1999.

43. MacWalter RS: Secondary prevention of stroke. Thromb Haemost 82(Suppl):95–103, 1999.

44. Marks MP, Holmgren EB, Fox AJ, et al: Evaluation of early computed tomographic findings in acute ischemic stroke. Stroke 30:389–392, 1999.

45. Mathews VP, King JC, Elster AD, Hamilton CA: Cerebral infarction: Effects of dose and magnetization transfer saturation at gadolinium-enhanced MR imaging. Radiology 190:547–552, 1994.

46. Mattle HP, Wentz KU, Edelman RR, et al: Cerebral venography with MR. Radiology 178:453–458, 1991.

47. Meier P, Zierler KL: On the theory of the indicator-dilution method for measurement of blood flow and volume. J Appl Physiol 6: 731–744, 1954.

48. Merboldt KD, Bruhn H, Frahm J, et al: MRI of "diffusion" in the human brain: New results using a modified CE-FAST sequence. Magn Reson Med 9:423–429, 1989.

49. Mosely ME, Kucharczyk J, Mintorovitich J, et al: Diffusion-weighted MRI of acute stroke: Correlation with T2-weighted and magnetic susceptibility-enhanced MRI in cats. AJNM Am J Neuroradiol 11: 423–429, 1990.

50. Muizelaar JP, Fatouros PP, Schroder ML: A new method for quantitative regional cerebral blood volume measurements using computed tomography. Stroke 28:1998–2005, 1997.

51. Mull M, Schwarz M, Thron A: Cerebral hemispheric low-flow infarcts in arterial occlusive disease: Lesion patterns and angiomorphological conditions. Stroke 28:118–123, 1997.

52. Muller TB, Haraldseth O, Jones RA, et al: Combined perfusion and diffusion-weighted magnetic resonance imaging in a rat model of reversible middle cerebral artery occlusion. Stroke 26:451–457, 1995.

53. Murakami Y, Yamashita Y, Matsuishi T, et al: Cranial MRI of neurologically impaired children suffering from neonatal hypoglycaemia. Pediatr Radiol 29:23–72, 1999.

54. Murray CJ, Lopez AD: Mortality by cause for eight regions of the world: Global Burden of Disease Study. Lancet 349:1269–1276, 1997.

55. Norris DG, Niendorf T, Leibfritz D: Healthy and infarcted brain tissues studied at short diffusion times: The origins of apparent restriction and the reduction in apparent diffusion coefficient. NMR Biomed 7:304–310, 1994.

56. Pantano P, Lenzi GL, Guidetti B, et al: Crossed cerebellar diaschisis in patients with cerebral ischemia assessed by SPECT and ^{123}I-HIPDM. Eur Neurol 27:142–148, 1987.

57. Pessin MS, Duncan GW, Mohr JP, Poskanzer DC: Clinical and angiographic features of carotid transient ischemic attacks. N Engl J Med 296:358–362, 1977.

58. Petty GW, Brown RD, Whisnant JP, et al: Ischemic stroke subtypes: A population-based study of incidence and risk factors. Stroke 30: 2513–2516, 1999.

59. Pressman BD, Tourje EJ, Thompson JR: An early CT sign of ischemic infarction: Increased density in a cerebral artery. AJR Am J Roentgenol 149:583–586, 1987.

60. Provenzale JM, Engelter ST, Petrella JR, et al: Use of MR exponential diffusion-weighted images to eradicate T2 "shine-through" effect. AJR Am J Roentgenol 172:537–539, 1999.

61. Provenzale JM, Loganbill HA: Dural sinus thrombosis and venous infarction associated with antiphospholipid antibodies: MR findings. J Comput Assist Tomogr 18:719–723, 1994.

62. Rademacher J, Sohngen D, Specker C, et al: Cerebral microembolism, a disease marker for ischemic cerebrovascular events in the antiphospholipid syndrome of systemic lupus erythematosus? Acta Neurol Scand 99:356–361, 1999.

63. Rauch RA, Bazan C 3d, Larsson EM, Jinkins JR: Hyperdense middle cerebral arteries identified on CT as a false sign of vascular occlusion. AJNR Am J Neuroradiol 14:669–673, 1993.

64. Rudolf J, Grond M, Stenzel C, et al: Incidence of space-occupying brain edema following systemic thrombolysis of acute supratentorial ischemia. Cerebrovasc Dis 8:166–171, 1998.

65. Salgado ED, Weinstein M, Furlan AJ, et al: Proton magnetic resonance imaging in ischemic cerebrovascular disease. Ann Neurol 20: 502–507, 1986.

66. Schlaug G, Benfield A, Baird AE, et al: The ischemic penumbra: Operationally defined by diffusion and perfusion MRI. Neurology 53: 1528–1537, 1999.

67. Schlaug G, Siewert B, Benfield A, et al: Time course of the apparent diffusion coefficient (ADC) abnormality in human stroke. Neurology 49:113–119, 1997.

68. Scuotto A, Cappabianca S, Melone MB, Puoti G: MRI "fogging" in cerebellar ischemia: Case report. Neuroradiology 39:785–787, 1997.

69. Shamoto H, Chugani HT: Glucose metabolism in the human cerebellum: An analysis of crossed cerebellar diaschisis in children with unilateral cerebral injury. J Child Neurol 12:407–414, 1997.

70. So EL, Toole JF, Dalal P, Moody DM: Cephalic fibromuscular dysplasia in 32 patients: Clinical findings and radiologic features. Arch Neurol 38:619–622, 1981.
71. Sorensen AG, Copen WA, Ostergaard L, et al: Hyperacute stroke: Simultaneous measurement of relative cerebral blood volume, relative cerebral blood flow, and mean tissue transit time. Radiology 210: 519–527, 1999.
72. Tomura N, Uemura K, Inugami A, et al: Early CT finding in cerebral infarction: Obscuration of the lentiform nucleus. Radiology 168: 463–467, 1988.
73. Truwit CL, Barkovich AJ, Gean-Marton A, et al: Loss of the insular ribbon: Another early CT sign of acute middle cerebral artery infarction. Radiology 176:801–806, 1990.
74. Valanne L, Ketonen L, Majander A, et al: Neuroradiologic findings in children with mitochondrial disorders. AJNR Am J Neuroradiol 19:369–377, 1998.
75. van Gelderen P, de Vleeschouwer MH, DesPres D, et al: CT: Water diffusion and acute stroke. Magn Reson Med 31:154–163, 1994.
76. Wein TH, Bornstein NM: Stroke prevention: Cardiac and carotid-related stroke. Neurol Clin 18:321–341, 2000.
77. Wetzel SG, Kirsch E, Stock KW, et al: Cerebral veins: Comparative study of CT venography with intraarterial digital subtraction angiography. AJNR Am J Neuroradiol 20:249–255, 1999.
78. Wijman CA, Babikian VL, Winter MR, Pochay VE: Distribution of cerebral microembolism in the anterior and middle cerebral arteries. Acta Neurol Scand 101:122–127, 2000.
79. Willis BK, Greiner F, Orrison WW, Benzel EC: The incidence of vertebral artery injury after midcervical spine fracture or subluxation. Neurosurgery 34:435–441, 1994.
80. Wong EC, Cox RW, Song AW: Optimized isotropic diffusion weighting. Magn Reson Med 1995 34:139–143, 1995.
81. Woodring JH, Lee C, Duncan V: Transverse process fractures of the cervical vertebrae: Are they insignificant? J Trauma 34:797–802, 1993.
82. Yamauchi H, Fukuyama H, Nagahama Y, et al: Decrease in regional cerebral blood volume and hematocrit in crossed cerebellar diaschisis. Stroke 30:1429–1431, 1999.

8

Cerebral Aneurysms and Vascular Malformations

Theodore C. Larson III

Cerebral Aneurysms

Incidence and Natural History

Cerebral aneurysms are found in approximately 0.5 to 5% of the population.[130a, 139, 193, 242, 255, 261, 262, 326, 339a] Women have a variably greater incidence of cerebral aneurysms compared with men, and aneurysm development increases with advancing age.[15, 139, 242, 297, 326] Some families demonstrate a genetic predisposition to develop cerebral aneurysms.[43, 214, 305] The risk of new aneurysm development is approximately 2% per year.[139] Subarachnoid hemorrhage, the most common presenting symptom of a cerebral aneurysm, is the second most common cause of subarachnoid hemorrhage, after trauma.[261] Eighty percent to 90% of nontraumatic subarachnoid hemorrhages are due to a ruptured cerebral aneurysm, a far more common cause than an arteriovenous malformation, which accounts for 15% of subarachnoid hemorrhages.[301] Other, less common presenting signs and symptoms, which are due to mass effect or neighboring inflammation, aneurysm thrombosis, or aneurysm-generated emboli, are cranial nerve palsy, headache, seizure, and transient or permanent neurologic dysfunction.[242] These nonhemorrhagic symptoms can be seen with aneurysms of any size but occur more commonly with posterior circulation or internal carotid aneurysms.[242]

The annual incidence of rupture of an asymptomatic cerebral aneurysm has been estimated at approximately 0.5% to 2%, or roughly 10 cases per 100,000 population.[135, 139, 255, 273, 326] Symptomatic intact aneurysms have a higher rate of bleeding—4% or more per year. Some studies have suggested that for aneurysms less than 1 cm in diameter, the incidence of annual rupture is less than 0.1%.[315a, 326] Other reports, however, have documented that the majority of ruptured aneurysms are less than 9 to 10 mm in diameter,[130a, 141, 255] and that even small (2 to 3 mm) aneurysms may cause subarachnoid hemorrhage.[10a, 273, 288, 340] The presence of a daughter sac probably raises the likelihood of rupture.[273, 326] Younger patients may have a greater propensity for aneurysmal hemorrhage, especially if they have multiple aneurysms.[139]

A ruptured cerebral aneurysm carries significant morbidity and mortality, the 30-day mortality traditionally being stated as 40% to 60%.[139, 141, 255, 262] Untreated patients with ruptured cerebral aneurysms have a rebleeding rate of 10% to 50% in the first 2 weeks to 6 months. The rebleeding rate is highest in the first day, with a 50% mortality[5, 40a, 135, 141, 231a, 236a, 297]; thereafter, the bleeding rate is approximately 3% per year.[135, 139] Initial aneurysm size is not a prognostic factor influencing rebleeding in the acute period.[141] Approximately 14% to 23% of survivors of rupture of a cerebral aneurysm are left with significant morbidity[255, 267]; in 13% to 32% of cases, the morbidity is the direct result of delayed vasospasm-caused ischemia.[193, 231a, 236a, 267] Twenty-one percent of patients who enter the hospital for treatment of subarachnoid hemorrhage eventually die.[267] Surgical clipping of acutely ruptured aneurysms results in improved functional outcome compared with delayed intervention.[218] These data also argue for elective treatment of an unruptured aneurysm.

Unruptured cerebral aneurysms are most often asymptomatic but can cause local mass effect and headache. Focal mass effect can compress adjacent cranial nerves or brain parenchyma, a typical example being third nerve palsy due to a posterior communicating aneurysm. Other diseases can cause neurologic deficits similar to those due to aneurysms, however. For example, third nerve palsy could be caused by diabetes or microvascular disease instead of a posterior communicating aneurysm. When magnetic resonance imaging (MRI) and MR angiography (MRA) fail to diagnose the cause of the patient's third nerve palsy, catheter cerebral angiography may be required to exclude a cerebral aneurysm, because the morbidity and mortality associated with cerebral aneurysms are so significant. When catheter cerebral angiography does not demonstrate an aneurysm in a patient with no history of subarachnoid hemorrhage, the patient can be assumed to have small-vessel cerebrovascular disease. Sometimes the angiogram supports this diagnosis by showing other areas of atherosclerotic disease.

Types of Aneurysms, Etiology, and Pathology

Aneurysms may be divided into different classifications according to morphology, size, location, or etiology. Most cerebral aneurysms are acquired lesions and are saccular or fusiform. Older medical reports proposed that saccular or berry cerebral aneurysms were due to an embryologic abnormality of the walls of cerebral vessels.[221] Stehbens[293] and others have refuted this theory. Most cerebral aneurysms develop from hemodynamic stresses,[143a, 262, 293] which typically occur at vessel bifurcations or terminations, or along the outer curvature of looping vessels.[143a, 197, 244, 273, 293] The aneurysm's location is a continuation of the primary flow direction in the parent vessel, especially if the parent vessel is tortuous.[244] Rupture and thrombosis of cerebral aneurysms are also believed to be due to hemodynamic forces.[97, 293] Supporting this theory of an underlying etiology is the higher incidence of cerebral aneurysms in patients with intracranial vascular anomalies, including fenestrations and congenital or iatrogenic vascular variants of the circle of Willis (e.g., persistent trigeminal artery, unilateral absence of the A1 segment of an anterior cerebral artery, azygous proximal anterior cerebral artery, and occlusion or absence of an internal carotid artery).[205, 236, 264, 272] Primary causes of aneurysms are as follows: (1) atherosclerosis, (2) hypertension, (3) smoking, (4) abuse of cocaine, methamphetamine, ephedrine, heroin, and other drugs with resultant arteritis or hypertension,[132, 139, 206, 230] (5) vascular malformations (approximately 6% to 10% incidence of aneurysm, both proximal flow–related and nidal[11, 44, 60, 90, 148, 186, 204]), (6) specific vascular diseases, such as fibromuscular dysplasia (20% to 50% incidence of aneurysm[113, 272]), spontaneous cervical carotid or vertebral artery dissection (more commonly seen in women[272]), Takayasu's arteritis,[111] polycystic kidney disease (10% incidence of aneurysm), and neurofibromatosis,[117] and (7) the connective tissue disorders, such as Marfan's syndrome and Ehlers-Danlos syndrome (in which aneurysms of the carotid siphon to supraclinoid segment are more common).[272] The walls of saccular cerebral aneurysms contain intima and adventitia but the media and internal elastic membrane are thinned or absent.[49, 50]

A number of patients with cerebral aneurysms demonstrate collagen type III abnormalities.[272] Most cerebral aneurysms arise from the circle of Willis and middle cerebral artery bifurcations. Ninety percent involve the anterior circulation, and 10% the posterior circulation.[11, 221] The most common sites are the anterior communicating artery at its junction with the adjacent anterior cerebral artery (30% to 35%), the posterior communicating artery at its union with the internal carotid artery (30% to 35%), the middle cerebral artery bifurcation (20% to 25%), the basilar terminus (5%), the carotid terminus (5%), and the origin of the ophthalmic artery (5%).[227] Less commonly, aneurysms occur along the course of the anterior cerebral arteries, particularly at the origin of the callosomarginal artery, the middle cerebral arteries, posterior cerebral arteries, superior cerebellar arteries, anterior inferior cerebellar arteries, and posterior inferior cerebellar arteries.[15, 115, 130a, 244, 259]

In 15% to 30% of patients, multiple aneurysms are found, more often in women than in men by a 5:1 ratio,[139, 141, 297, 297a, 307a, 316] and most frequently involving the middle cerebral artery.[340] Of the patients with multiple cerebral aneurysms, 75% have two, 15% have three, and 10% have four or more.[297] When one of multiple aneurysms ruptures and causes subarachnoid hemorrhage, it is most often the largest[340] although this is not always the case. For instance, Nehls and colleagues[209] have reported the propensity for anterior communicating aneurysms to rupture when several are present simultaneously. Vasculopathies, such as fibromuscular dysplasia and connective tissue disorders, as well as syndromes such as polycystic kidney disease are associated with a higher incidence of multiple cerebral aneurysms. Bilateral symmetrical aneurysms are called *mirror*

aneurysms, and they most often involve the internal carotid arteries or the middle cerebral artery bifurcations.[297]

Other causes of cerebral aneurysms, identified in less than 5% of patients, are (1) penetrating and nonpenetrating trauma, (2) dissection (post-traumatic or otherwise), (3) inflammation or mycosis due either to septic emboli causing destruction of the endothelium or to spread of infection to the vasa vasorum with subsequent vessel wall destruction and focal dilatation, and (4) neoplasm; rarely, cerebral aneurysms may be congenital.[5, 139, 161, 170, 212] Except for congenital aneurysms, aneurysms with these uncommon causes often develop in unusual locations that are distal to the circle of Willis.

Trauma typically results in a pseudoaneurysm rather than a true aneurysm, because no normal vascular components constitute the sac within a hematoma that communicates with the injured vessel. Post-traumatic pseudoaneurysms occur in locations not common for other cerebral aneurysms, including the proximal internal carotid artery, particularly at the skull base[280]; the meningeal vessels, which often are associated with overlying skull fractures and epidural hematomas[311]; the posterior cerebral or anterior cerebral arteries, caused by tentorial or falcine impaction, respectively[170, 205, 212, 280]; and in extracranial vessels within the scalp, such as the superficial temporal artery and the occipital artery.[281] Penetrating, high-velocity trauma, such as from gunshot wounds, is more likely to produce a traumatic aneurysm if the entrance site is in the temporal or peritemporal region, if fragments cross the midline, and if the pseudoaneurysm is surrounded by hematoma. The surrounding anterior and middle cerebral arteries are most often involved.[9] Initially, traumatic pseudoaneurysms may not be visualized, but then they rapidly enlarge.[205, 280] Fifty percent of untreated, post-traumatic aneurysms bleed, with an almost uniformly fatal outcome.[9, 205]

Uncommon neoplastic aneurysms are also pseudoaneurysms, resulting from primary or metastatic tumor invasion of a vessel or metastatic emboli to the vessel lumen or its vasa vasorum.[92, 116a] Pituitary adenomas are associated with a higher incidence of cerebral aneurysms, acromegaly-producing adenomas theorized to sometimes produce diffuse cerebrovascular ectasia and unilateral or bilateral cavernous carotid aneurysms due to growth hormone secretion.[11, 327]

Dissection of the internal carotid artery or more commonly the vertebral artery can be spontaneous, post-traumatic, or secondary to disease of the vessel wall such as fibromuscular dysplasia.[200a] A pseudoaneurysm accompanies up to a third of internal carotid dissections and 7% of vertebral artery dissections.[5, 289] Dissecting pseudoaneurysms may manifest as ischemic symptoms due to emboli or small arterial branch occlusion in addition to subarachnoid hemorrhage.[5] Dissecting pseudoaneurysms more commonly present as subarachnoid hemorrhage when occurring in the posterior circulation.[85a] Rebleed rates are particularly high with accompanying significant mortality.[200a]

Fusiform aneurysms are vascular ectasias due to advanced focal atherosclerotic disease that has degraded the vessel's media.[5, 293] The vertebrobasilar system is more commonly affected than the anterior circulation. The involved vessel is frequently elongated and tortuous, so that in effect, the native vessel is replaced by aneurysmal dilatation with no neck. Although fusiform aneurysms may rupture, thrombosis due to blood stagnation may be the mode of presentation. Local mass effect, ischemia due to penetrating vessel occlusion, and cranial nerve palsies are other pathologic sequelae.[5, 302]

An infundibulum represents the residua of a developmental vessel that has undergone incomplete regression. It most commonly involves the junction of the internal carotid artery and posterior communicating artery, and less commonly the origin of the anterior choroidal artery from the internal carotid artery. Infundibula are usually 3 mm or less in diameter. They can be difficult to differentiate from cerebral aneurysms unless the characteristic origination of the emerging vessel from the dome of the infundibulum is identified.

Imaging Evaluation of Cerebral Aneurysms

Imaging objectives for the identification of a cerebral aneurysm are (1) visualization of subarachnoid hemorrhage, (2) confirmation of the size, location, and morphology of the cerebral aneurysm, (3) evaluation of the adjacent cerebral vasculature, including evidence of spasm, atherosclerosis, displacement, and incorporation into the aneurysm's wall, and (4) demonstration of any accompanying adjacent brain pathology.

The typical patient with a ruptured cerebral aneurysm is a woman between 40 and 60 years old who presents with "the worst headache of my life," with or without a neurologic deficit. Clinical assessment of the patient classifies into Hunt and Hess grades I through V (Table 8–1).[124a] CT scan of the head identifies subarachnoid hemorrhage, and the patient undergoes catheter angiography, which is timed to precede surgical treatment with either craniotomy or endovascular coiling. In patients in whom CT scan shows no hemorrhage, lumbar puncture should be performed. Patients with a positive lumbar puncture result then undergo catheter cerebral angiography, unless the lumbar tap was traumatic. In some situations, MRI and MRA may be performed to evaluate the subarachnoid hemorrhage and to identify a cerebral aneurysm, for example, when the suspicion for a cerebral aneurysm is low or the patient is a poor candidate for cerebral angiography or aneurysm intervention (i.e., is elderly or severely injured). MRI and MRA may also be employed as screening tests in populations known to have a higher incidence of cerebral aneurysms (see preceding discussion) or for monitoring known, untreated aneurysms. Although the permanent neurologic risk

of catheter cerebral angiography is low—approximately 0.8% in the usual patient population with ruptured cerebral aneurysms—one should always keep in mind the morbidity of stroke when deciding whether a particular patient should undergo the procedure.

Computed Tomography

The most important role for CT in the patient with a cerebral aneurysm is in the identification of acute subarachnoid hemorrhage, which is demonstrated as increased density within a cisternal space (Fig. 8–1). The location of the subarachnoid hemorrhage may help determine the location of the underlying cerebral aneurysm.[1, 5, 259, 277, 297] For example, blood in the sylvian fissure most likely has arisen from a middle cerebral aneurysm, and blood in the fourth ventricle is a common sign of rupture of a posterior inferior cerebellar artery aneurysm.[259] Some subarachnoid hemorrhage patterns are not diagnostic of aneurysm location, and none is foolproof.

The CT demonstration of subarachnoid hemorrhage progressively decreases until it disappears by approximately 3 weeks,[107, 259] depending on the initial amount of subarachnoid hemorrhage. In 5% to 10% of CT scans, subarachnoid hemorrhage is not identifiable. For this reason, any patient in whom acute subarachnoid hemorrhage is suspected but CT scanning does not demonstrate intracranial blood should undergo lumbar puncture.

A small amount of aneurysmal subarachnoid hemorrhage adjacent to the brain stem may be mistaken for perimesencephalic (prepontine and interpeduncular) hemorrhage, a finding believed to be due to the rupture of small perimesencephalic veins[139a, 248] and usually resulting in a good outcome, unlike an aneurysm rupture.

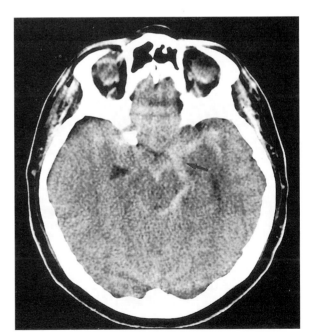

Fig. 8–1. CT demonstrating subarachnoid hemorrhage (*arrow*) from aneurysm rupture.

TABLE 8–1. Hunt and Hess Grading Scale for Subarachnoid Hemorrhage

Grade I	Asymptomatic or minimal headache
Grade II	Moderate to severe headache, nuchal rigidity, oculomotor palsy, normal level of consciousness
Grade III	Confusion, drowsiness, mild focal neurologic deficit
Grade IV	Stupor or hemiparesis
Grade V	Comatose or moribund with decerebrate posturing

CT is also excellent for identifying intraventricular hemorrhage (seen in 13% to 28% of cases[259]), parenchymal hematoma (20% to 30%), and the occasional subdural hematoma, findings that often help localize the underlying aneurysm.

CT examination is secondarily important to identify cerebral aneurysms, typically 5 mm or larger in diameter. The rate of identification of cerebral aneurysms by thin-section, high-resolution, contrast-enhanced CT scanning has been reported to be at least 67% for aneurysms 3 to 5 mm in diameter and to approach 100% for larger aneurysms.[271, 274] Focal, slightly dense areas of luminal blood in typical locations where aneurysms arise,[342] focal globular or elongated areas of contrast enhancement,[210] variable calcification involving the aneurysm's walls, and clot within larger aneurysms characterize cerebral aneurysms.[108] Large aneurysms have a transverse dome diameter of 1.0 to 2.4 cm, and giant aneurysms are 2.5 cm or more in diameter. Large and giant cerebral aneurysms are typically more easily identifiable because of their conspicuous size but also often from the presence of internal clot and peripheral wall calcifications, especially in giant aneurysms (Fig. 8–2). Giant aneurysms are most commonly identified in middle-aged women, are typically located in the extradural

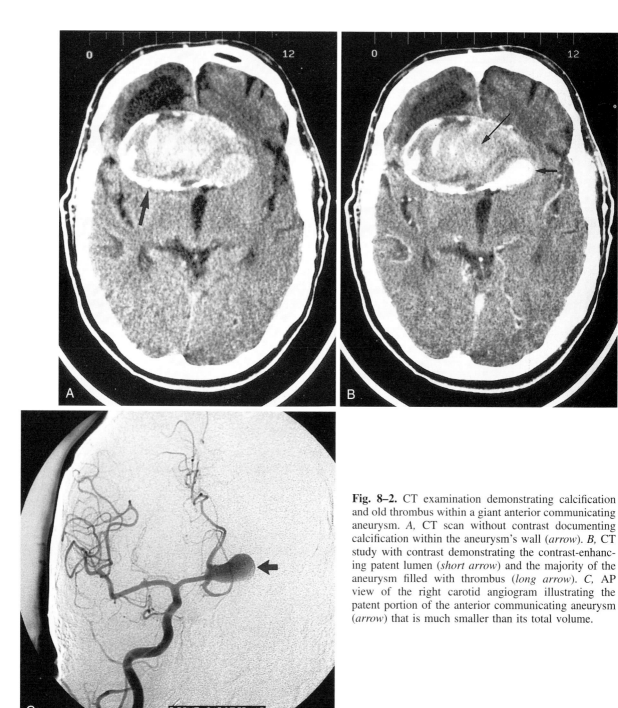

Fig. 8–2. CT examination demonstrating calcification and old thrombus within a giant anterior communicating aneurysm. *A,* CT scan without contrast documenting calcification within the aneurysm's wall (*arrow*). *B,* CT study with contrast demonstrating the contrast-enhancing patent lumen (*short arrow*) and the majority of the aneurysm filled with thrombus (*long arrow*). *C,* AP view of the right carotid angiogram illustrating the patent portion of the anterior communicating aneurysm (*arrow*) that is much smaller than its total volume.

carotid artery, the middle cerebral artery bifurcation, or the basilar summit, and usually manifest with a mass effect but can present as subarachnoid hemorrhage.[48, 69, 141] Any large aneurysm can have a mass effect on adjacent brain or cranial nerves. CT is excellent for identifying skull base erosion due to large or giant aneurysms, especially if thin sections (3 mm or less) are obtained.

Brain parenchymal hemorrhage, which may be associated with any of the cerebral aneurysms, is thought to occur from acute or chronic rupture of the cerebral aneurysm into adjacent brain substance after the blood passes through overlying pia. Both parenchymal and subarachnoid hemorrhages often obscure an underlying ruptured cerebral aneurysm.

MRI

The identification of acute subarachnoid hemorrhage by routine MRI has been notoriously poor,[19, 217] although there are reports that claim otherwise.[136] The following two reasons have been postulated for the lack of visualization of acute subarachnoid hemorrhage on MRI[104] (1) normal P_{O_2} (partial pressure of oxygen) in CSF inhibits the development of deoxyhemoglobin and (2) lysis of red blood cells in subarachnoid CSF prevents heterogenous magnetic susceptibility. However, with the employment of pulse sequences including intermediate-weighted spin-echo with TE (echo time) values of 22 to 45 msec, T1 weighting, FLAIR (fluid-attenuated inversion recovery) imaging, and gradient-echo imaging, acute subarachnoid hemorrhage can frequently be identified. Other imaging problems can obscure precise identification of subarachnoid hemorrhage on MRI, including CSF and vascular pulsation artifact and magnetic susceptibility artifact along the skull base. Significant experience is therefore required to correctly identify acute subarachnoid hemorrhage on MRI. Subarachnoid hemorrhage older than 12 to 24 hours can routinely be identified on MR images, often helping pinpoint the underlying ruptured cerebral aneurysm by a collection of blood.

Thin-section MRI examination can often identify cerebral aneurysms more than 3 mm in diameter.[197] The identification may be easier if the aneurysm is unruptured. It may be difficult, however, to differentiate normal vascular tortuous anatomy or bone such as the anterior clinoid process from a cerebral aneurysm. When large enough, cerebral aneurysms can be positively identified on MRI as flow artifacts or characteristic findings with the use of different pulse sequences. Phase-encoding artifact due to flow-producing signal mismapped in the phase-encoding direction is optimally seen on the short TE, long TR, spin-echo pulse sequence, which may be the best sequence for positive identification of aneurysms (Fig. 8–3). Other flow effects, such as a swirling appearance inside the aneurysm due to spin dephasing, rephasing, and turbulence, even-echo or gradient rephasing, diastolic pseudogating, slow flow, variable intraluminal flow rates, entry slice enhancement, and signal void due to rapidly flowing blood on all pulse sequences except those using short TE, short TR, relatively large flip angle gradient echo scans that are typically employed for time-of-flight (TOF) MRA studies, are often also helpful to identify cerebral aneurysms.[12, 39, 252a, 321]

Contrast enhancement of the aneurysm highlights its central lumen and can exaggerate the aforementioned artifacts, particularly the phase mismapping effects. For instance, these clues can often reliably diagnose cavernous carotid segment aneurysms and differentiate them from pituitary masses. A partially thrombosed aneurysm contains peripheral layers of clot of different ages, usually with the oldest clot located most peripherally.[13, 108, 302] MRI may identify intramural thrombus in dissecting aneurysms, aiding in their distinction from fusiform aneurysms.[5] The signal intensities of intraluminal clot correspond to the expected age of hemorrhage on MRI according to the magnetic field strength employed.[13, 108] Fibrosis and cellular infiltration can accompany the clot.

Completely thrombosed aneurysms or aneurysms with extremely slow flow can rarely mimic tumors, including sellar and parasellar masses. Catheter cerebral angiography should be undertaken in these problematic cases, to prevent "surprises" during craniotomy and potentially catastrophic hemorrhage during trans-sphenoidal or other operations.

The brain parenchymal changes adjacent to cerebral aneurysms may be absent unless the aneurysm is large enough to cause edema and localized mass effect. MRI is superior for evaluating the relationship of the aneurysm with adjacent brain structures because of the inherent soft tissue contrast limitations to and posterior fossa beam-hardening artifact seen with CT. If the aneurysm has ruptured, an adjacent intraparenchymal or subarachnoid clot may be identified. This finding is especially useful for determining which aneurysm has ruptured in a patient with multiple aneurysms, especially when clinical localizing signs are not helpful.[107, 297] The imaging location of the clot can subsequently guide treatment.[107] Chronic changes include gliosis and deposition of hemosiderin or ferritin; the latter two substances represent hemorrhagic breakdown products, which are best demonstrated on long TE, long TR, T2-weighted spin-echo or T2* gradient-echo MRI sequences. Superficial siderosis represents intracellular (most often macrophage) and extracellular hemosiderin or ferritin coating the leptomeninges, cranial nerves, and superficial central nervous system parenchyma.[95] The siderosis is secondary to any cause of subarachnoid hemorrhage, usually repetitive, but can also occur on the ventricular ependymal surfaces.[95] Focal or generalized neurologic deficits correspond to the location and extent of central nervous system involvement.[95]

MRI is superior to CT for the localization of cerebral aneurysms, their relationship with adjacent structures, and associated changes in neighboring brain tissue.

MRA and CT Angiography

MRA has made tremendous strides in the identification of cerebral aneurysms. Between 55% and 86% of cerebral aneurysms may be identified with routinely available MRA.[17, 128a, 240, 256, 275] Sensitivity of MRA for detection of aneurysms can be increased when MRA is combined with MRI,[256, 275] thereby overcoming the inherent difficulties of imaging slow flow, turbulent flow, or intraluminal clot with MRA. Because almost all aneurysms larger than 3 mm

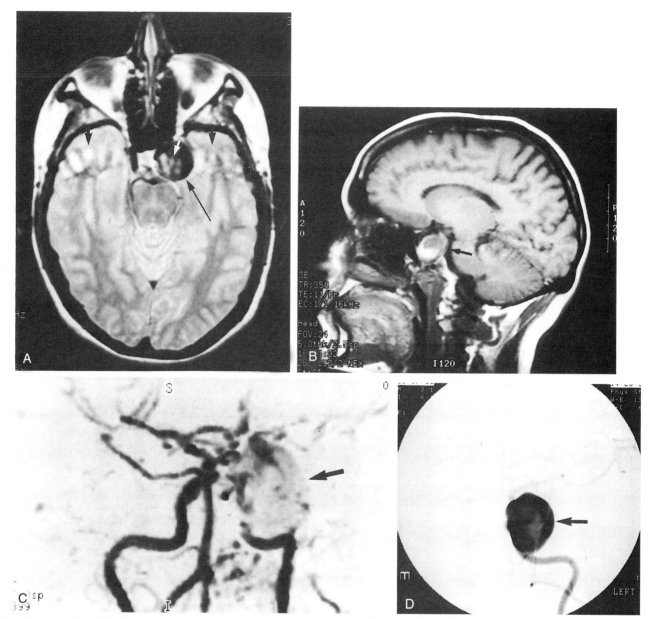

Fig. 8–3. MRI and MRA examination demonstrating flow effects associated with a giant left cavernous carotid aneurysm. *A*, Axial short TE, long TR MR image demonstrating the aneurysm (*long arrow*) with internal and external phase encoding artifact (*short arrows*) due to mismapped flow. *B*, Sagittal T1-weighted image falsely gives the appearance of thrombus within the aneurysm (*arrow*) due to slow flow. *C*, Three-dimensional time-of-flight MRA poorly outlines the aneurysm (*arrow*) because of internal slow flow. *D*, AP view of left carotid angiogram confirms giant left cavernous carotid aneurysm (*arrow*). (Case courtesy of Daryl Harp, MD.)

can be visualized,[149] MRA can function as a screening examination.[45, 240]

The most commonly employed sequence is TOF three-dimensional (3D) MRA, which typically provides submillimeter in-plane resolution. A variant of this is MOTSA (multiple overlapping thin-slab acquisition),[33, 34, 232] which attempts to combine the advantages of 3D with two-dimensional (2D) MRA. MOTSA is especially helpful when the slow flow in an aneurysm located distally within the imaging slab is not imaged on a 3D TOF study because of flow saturation. The T1 shortening effect of subacute subarachnoid blood or intraluminal or perianeurysmal clot can obscure an aneurysm or mimic flowing blood on a TOF imaging sequence.[126]

An alternative pulse sequence is phase-contrast (PC) MRA, which has excellent background, susceptibility artifact, and stagnant blood suppression and may help image in-plane flow and slow flow, two causes of flow saturation degradation of TOF MRA.[73, 127] It can be combined with cardiac gating using electrocardiogram leads or peripheral photoplethysmography to create cine PC MRA, a technique that has been used to document a greater pulsatility change in aneurysm size with ruptured than with unruptured aneurysms.[302] PC MRA has poorer spatial resolution, depends on a prescribed velocity encoding gradient with the potential for aliasing, can be altered by complex flow, and requires longer imaging and processing times than TOF MRA.[127] Although PC MRA may identify fewer aneurysms than TOF MRA,[137] the slow flow within fusiform aneurysms is often better imaged with PC MRA. A patent double lumen in a dissecting aneurysm would also be best imaged with PC MRA.

MRA combined with MRI can often demonstrate internal flow patterns within large and giant cerebral aneurysms; faster flow is located more peripherally, and stagnant flow more centrally.[97, 102, 298] Vascular loops may be confused with cerebral aneurysms on MRA. Gadolinium-based intravenous contrast agents are not typically employed in the identification of cerebral aneurysms but can be helpful to highlight aneurysms that are small, are in atypical locations, or have slow or stagnant flow or to document the residual patent lumen in an incompletely thrombosed aneurysm.[252a] The use of contrast enhancement with MRI or MRA increases flow-dependent artifact and can obscure cerebral aneurysms because of enhancement of dural sinuses, intracranial veins, and extracranial structures,[59] unless a PC MRA technique is utilized.[127] In large or giant, partially or completely thrombosed aneurysms, the aneurysmal wall may show enhancement.

Special MRI techniques may help in the positive identification of cerebral aneurysms; they include magnetization transfer pulses,[75, 146] progressive increases in radiofrequency pulse flip angles, and multiple postprocessing algorithms.[21, 123, 169] It is important that both the 3D reconstructed MRA images and the source, 2D planar images are scrutinized, so that small aneurysms and aneurysms with slow flow are not missed. Standard maximum intensity projection (MIP) images have some artifact-derived limitations.[3] Targeted MIPs select a region of interest and help exclude confounding extraneous vessels and other structures.[127] Review of the source images also best demonstrates the neck of the aneurysm and its relationship to the parent vessel. Vessel loops and magnetic susceptibility artifact from air-filled sinuses or bone at the skull base may obscure aneurysms.

CT angiography (CTA) is a relatively new development that can well demonstrate the morphology and location of cerebral aneurysms. Thin-section spiral CT slices are acquired during rapid intravenous infusion of a contrast agent. The axial images and the reconstructed 3D images, created with MIP and other processing methods, reproduce the proximal cerebral vasculature for analysis.[207, 216, 217] Both the source images and the reconstructed images should be reviewed.[345] The exclusion of adjacent skull base bone and the contrast enhancement of nonarterial structures can be problematic.[274]

3D CTA has a reported sensitivity of 67% to 90% for identifying cerebral aneurysms.[274, 345] Aneurysms less than 5 mm in diameter may be missed.[345] CTA has some benefits over MRA for evaluation of calcified atherosclerotic disease of adjacent vessels and, in some instances, for visualization of the aneurysm neck or dome and their relationship to osseous skull base structures such as the anterior clinoid process. 3D rotational views of both CT angiograms and MR angiograms help elucidate the precise anatomic relationships of cerebral aneurysms with adjacent vessels. Software reconstruction enhancements can provide endoscopic views of the dome and neck of an aneurysm.[188a]

Catheter cerebral angiography remains the standard for evaluation of cerebral aneurysms. Catheter-based angiography has better spacial resolution than MRA or CTA, but it evaluates only the intraluminal portion of the aneurysm that contains flowing blood. The inability of catheter cerebral angiography to demonstrate aneurysmal clot can lead to underestimation of the size of the aneurysm. This deficiency of catheter cerebral angiography is significant in comparison with MRI, which can demonstrate not only clot but also its age as well as the relationship of the aneurysm with adjacent brain structures. Cerebral angiography has the benefit, however, of better demonstrating cerebral vasospasm, the aspects of the aneurysm's morphology, such as dome irregularity or lobulation, which are possible predictors of hemorrhage, and a focal tit or dimple indicating the site of recent aneurysmal hemorrhage.[340] Aneurysms evaluated soon after rupture often are smaller than when intact, because of clot compression and spasm of either the aneurysm or adjacent artery, but they subsequently enlarge if surgery is delayed.[141, 209, 273, 326]

Cerebral Aneurysm Evaluation after Surgery

Controversy has arisen regarding the use of MRI to evaluate patients who have undergone cerebral aneurysm clipping. Most cerebral aneurysm clips are currently MRI compatible[281a] but create local ferromagnetic artifact on MRI that obscures precise evaluation of the neck of the clipped aneurysm (Fig. 8–4).[103] Issues have been raised regarding clip-to-clip variability, distortion of the aneurysm clip during surgical application, manufacturer liability, warnings from the U.S. Food and Drug Administration regarding rotational and translational aneurysm clip motion in a magnetic field, and the necessity of institutional assurance that all aneurysm clips are MR compatible.[139b] Because of these issues, many facilities have denied MRI to patients with cerebral aneurysm clips, even though an MRI permits better evaluation of brain parenchyma than CT. In fact, fatal cerebral hemorrhage attributed to the MR's magnetic field has been reported in a patient in whom a stainless steel, MRI-incompatible aneurysm clip had been placed on a middle cerebral artery aneurysm.[146]

Gugliemi detachable platinum coils, which are used to treat cerebral aneurysms endovascularly, are MRI compatible.[67a, 281a] However, localized artifact caused by the platinum coils on either MRI or CT often do not permit precise evaluation of the aneurysm.[66a, 96a, 313] Less metallic artifact is present in both the endovascularly treated and surgically clipped aneurysm patient than CT.[136] Catheter angiography remains the only method to determine whether the aneurysm has been completely clipped or coiled.

Cerebral Vascular Malformations

Cerebral vascular malformations can be divided into four primary types[38, 194, 258]:

- Arteriovenous malformation (AVM)
- Cavernous angioma
- Capillary telangiectasia
- Venous angioma

These types of vascular malformations can also be mixed—incorporating elements of two or more types.[23, 74, 98, 219, 246, 247, 305] The four classic types of cerebral vascular

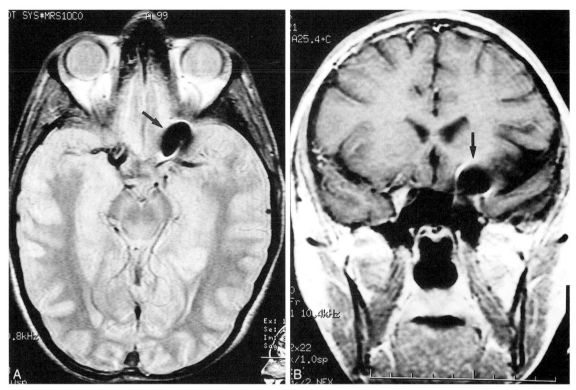

Fig. 8–4. Ferromagnetic artifact produced by cerebral aneurysm clip on MRI. Short TE, long TR (*A*) and coronal post-contrast T1-weighted (*B*) images demonstrating an ophthalmic aneurysm clip (*arrows*).

malformations are based on their congenital origin and do not include acquired arteriovenous cerebral fistulas, which are dural in location, or acquired or congenital direct arteriovenous fistulas. The term *occult cerebral vascular malformations* has been used to describe cavernous angiomas, capillary telangiectasias, and thrombosed AVMs because they could not be visualized with catheter cerebral angiography. Because all of these lesions, except some capillary telangiectasias, can be demonstrated on MRI, they are no longer truly "occult," and the term therefore has little current relevance.

The overall incidence of vascular malformations of all types in the general population is estimated to be 2%.

Arteriovenous Malformations

Incidence and Pathology

Approximately 0.1% of the general population harbor a cerebral AVM, the most common symptomatic cerebral vascular malformation.[235] AVMs are most commonly identified in women in the second to fourth decades.[332] Roughly 30% to 55% of patients present with intracranial hemorrhage,[2, 43, 58, 223, 237] a heralding event that is also most common in children with cerebral AVMs. Seventy percent of patients with intracranial hemorrhage due to AVMs present prior to age 40.[20a, 43, 94] Intracranial hemorrhage is most commonly intraparenchymal but may be intraventricular or subarachnoid. Nontraumatic subarachnoid and intraventricular hemorrhages are more commonly due to rupture of cerebral aneurysms. Spontaneous thrombosis of a draining vein and rupture of a nidal aneurysm are believed to be the most common causes of AVM hemorrhage. Exclusive central venous drainage and a periventricular or intraven-

tricular location have been reported as other characteristics indicating a propensity for AVM hemorrhage. Peripheral venous drainage or mixed peripheral and central venous drainage, along with angiomatous change, dilated arterial collaterals that pass through brain to supply the AVM, have been correlated with a decreased incidence of AVM hemorrhage.[185, 186] AVMs 3 cm or less in diameter have been reported to bleed more frequently and to produce larger hematomas than larger AVMs.[135, 238] The rate of hemorrhage of a cerebral AVM is estimated to be 2% to 3.5% per year and to increase with advancing age; this figure is higher than the yearly rupture rate for cerebral aneurysms.[20a, 43, 58, 99, 116, 223, 294] Mortality of 10% to 30% is associated with each instance of hemorrhage, for an overall annual mortality rate of less than 1%. The risk of permanent neurologic deficit is 20% to 30% with each AVM hemorrhage,[20a, 43, 94] resulting in an annual incidence of approximately 1%. The risk of rebleeding after a first hemorrhage is approximately 6% in the first year[99] and subsequently decreases to an annual rate of 3%.[43, 235, 303, 309]

The second most common clinical presentation of cerebral AVMs is seizures, which are reported in 22% to 60% of cases.[99, 196, 235, 237, 322] Seizures manifest more commonly in patients who are younger than 30 years and with AVMs that are large or diffuse. Large AVMs are also more commonly identified with progressive neurologic deficit. The overall risk of a seizure disorder in a patient with an AVM is 18%, and the risk of a neurologic deficit is 25% to 30%.[4, 43, 58] There is an approximately 1 in 4 risk that a patient will become intellectually disabled because of a brain AVM, without or with previous hemorrhage.

Brain AVMs cause nonhemorrhagic symptoms because of (1) blood flow steal from adjacent normal territories and

(2) regional venous hypertension due to the engorged, high-flow, draining veins of the AVM. Clinical sequelae are seizures, neurologic deficit, and headache. Acute neurologic deficits, however, are most commonly associated with intracranial hemorrhage due to an AVM. Occasionally, brain AVMs can result in mass effect or hydrocephalus due either to vascular compression of CSF pathways or communicating hydrocephalus secondary to previous hemorrhage. Headache is identified in more than 50% of patients with brain AVMs.[341] Thirty percent of patients report a bruit, which is due to transmission of blood pulsations from the AVM.[43] Calvarial auscultation of a cranial bruit is unusual, however. Occasionally, an AVM may cause either hemifacial spasm or cranial nerve neuralgia or palsy if the AVM in whole or in part is located in the basilar cisterns[341] or if subarachnoid hemorrhage has occurred previously.

More than 80% of cerebral AVMs are located supratentorially, and the remainder within the posterior fossa. AVMs may be multiple in up to 2% of patients,[263] often as part of Rendu-Osler-Weber disease,[2] an autosomal dominant inherited condition in which mucosal, skin, gastrointestinal, and cerebral hereditary hemorrhagic telangiectasias, brain cavernous angiomas, and pulmonary AVMs are also found (Fig. 8–5), and in the Wyburn-Mason syndrome (also termed mesencephalo-occulofacial angiomatosis), which is signified by the presence of cutaneous nevi and retinal angiomas together with brain AVMs.[201, 336] AVMs may also be located extracranially or intracranial AVMs may be associated with additional extracranial AVMs.

Pathologically, the cerebral AVM represents a direct communication between arteries and veins without intervening capillaries,[10a, 140, 221] the communicating vascular channels being larger than capillaries yet arbitrarily smaller than fistulas. Fistulas often reside within the AVM nidus, however. The nidus represents the central compact tangle of low-resistance vessels constituting the junction of the feeding arteries and draining veins. The nidus does not contain normal brain parenchyma, although the enlarged feeding arteries and draining veins can traverse normal tissue.[49] Large, diffuse AVMs may contain normal neurons and white matter, however.[54a] Brain AVMs may be located in the subarachnoid space, intraparenchymally, or intraventricularly or may transgress several spaces, including the cranial vault. The AVM nidus volume together with characteristics such as the presence of fistulas, the chronicity of the lesion (the age of the patient), and the rate of flow through the AVM determine the size and tortuosity of feeding arteries and draining veins.

AVMs may be supplied by any of the cerebral vessels, including meningeal contributors in 15% to 50% of cases.[198] Approximately 10% of AVMs have an arterial feeder, nidus, or remote arterial aneurysm,[186, 232, 339] the flow-related aneurysms most often located on feeding vessels.[60, 148, 199, 232] Some of these flow-related aneurysms are pseudoaneurysms.[234] The aneurysms contribute to the incidence of hemorrhage from AVMs.[339] Varices can develop in draining veins and can become quite large. Areas of stenosis, thrombosis, or occlusion can occur in supplying arteries or exiting veins. The findings of vascular stenoses and aneurysm formation are attributed to local hemodynamic stresses.[234]

Histologic examination of cerebral AVMs demonstrate thickened walls of both variably enlarged feeding arteries and draining veins, the walls demonstrating smooth muscle hyperplasia, fibroblast infiltration, and increased connective tissue. Arteries are differentiated from veins on the basis

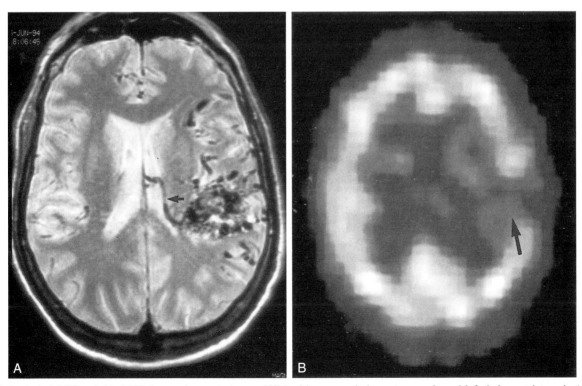

Fig. 8–5. *A,* Axial T2-weighted MR image demonstrates an AVM with venous drainage to an enlarged left thalamostriate vein (*arrow*). *B,* Axial Ceretec SPECT brain scan demonstrating diminished cerebral perfusion within the AVM (*arrow*).

TABLE 8–2. Cerebral AVM Grade

	Assigned Points
Nidus size	
Small (<3 cm)	1
Medium (3–6 cm)	2
Large (>6 cm)	3
Adjacent brain eloquence	
Noneloquent	0
Eloquent	1
Venous Drainage	
Superficial only	0
Deep	1
Total number of points = Grade I–V	

of the presence of elastic lamina and muscular layers within arteries. Adjacent brain parenchyma may exhibit atrophy, gliosis, and demyelinization[49, 220, 222] due to ischemic steal by the AVM,[52] compressive mass effect, venous hypertension, and prior hemorrhage. If previous hemorrhage has occurred, ferritin and hemosiderin staining of brain will be demonstrated. Calcification may be identified within component vessel walls as well as in adjacent brain parenchyma because of chronic venous hypertension or hemorrhage. Overlying leptomeninges may be thickened by venous engorgement or as a result of previous hemorrhage, which is also denoted by hemosiderin or ferritin staining.[50a]

The most commonly used AVM grading system was proposed by Spetzler and Martin.[291] This system assigns a numerical grade to the AVM on the basis of the size of the nidus, the location of the nidus in relationship to eloquent functional brain, and the venous drainage (superficial or deep) (Table 8–2). The intent of such a grading system is to predict therapeutic risk and outcome, and its application is fairly simple; the details of many AVMs are not completely explained by this classification system, however.

The therapy of brain AVMs is based on one of the following four options: conservative observation, surgical resection, radiosurgery, and endovascular embolization. The various treatment options may be combined. Complete surgical resection has been reported in approximately 80% of brain AVMs, with morbidity and mortality rates reaching approximately 10% regardless of AVM grade.[116] Radiosurgery is typically employed for brain AVMs that are 3 cm or less in diameter, but it can be used for an AVMs whose nidus is larger. Radiosurgery has obliterated AVMs at 3-year follow-up in more than 80% of reported series. The procedure has a complication rate of less than 3%, adverse events being most often due to radiation necrosis.[79, 174, 175, 294, 295] Embolization is often performed to reduce the flow and size of brain AVMs prior to surgical resection or radiosurgery, but in a few instances, complete cure can be achieved with embolization alone.[30]

CT and MRI

CT imaging of brain AVMs demonstrates a focal collection of isointense to slightly hyperintense vessels on unenhanced scans but may be completely unremarkable without the administration of a contrast agent. Acute hemorrhage is well documented when present.[23] Occasionally, mass

effect, surrounding edema, calcification (25% to 30% of cases), or adjacent brain atrophy may be identified.[153] Intravenous contrast enhancement is essential for identifying the typical "bag of worms" appearance of a brain AVM as well as its enlarged supplying arteries and draining veins.

MRI examination is, for the most part, superior to CT for identifying and evaluating cerebral AVMs. MRI not only outlines the nidus and permits evaluation of its size but also identifies supplying arteries and draining veins. A cluster of vessels of variable signal intensities, depending upon the imaging sequences used, characterize the AVM nidus. Flow-dependent phenomena such as dephasing, rephasing, slow flow, entry slice enhancement, and phase encoding mismapping may all be demonstrated (Fig. 8–6).[39] Most often, the nidus vessels demonstrate signal void on spin-echo pulse sequences and bright signal intensity on gradient-echo sequences, findings that are also typical within enlarged feeding arteries and draining veins. Adjacent brain parenchyma can be well evaluated for edema or gliosis, which has bright signal intensity on T2-weighted spin-echo studies (Fig. 8–7).[50a, 287] MRI is crucial for localizing the AVM in relationship to eloquent cortex or deeper gray matter structures and significant white matter fiber tracts as well as demonstrating any mass effect. MRI well demonstrates the expected evolutionary appearance of acute, subacute, and chronic hemorrhage. Chronic hemorrhage with resultant ferritin- or hemosiderin-stained brain, including superficial or ependymal hemosiderosis,[50a, 95, 287] is displayed as areas of parenchymal decreased signal intensity on T2-weighted spin-echo and T2*-weighted gradient-echo sequences.[52] Gadolinium-based contrast agents are of limited if any utility in the MRI evaluation of cerebral AVMs because of inconsistent enhancement and the production of excessive flow artifact. Functional MRI utilizes cortical blood flow changes based on deoxyhemoglobin levels to create activation maps, which may be used to evaluate brain function adjacent to an AVM before therapeutic interventions are undertaken.[122, 178] In some instances, the tested neurologic function is expressed in an unexpected cerebral region secondary to neural plasticity, a consequence of the congenital nature of the AVM and the development of alternative neural circuits.[178]

MRA and CTA can help in the evaluation of cerebral AVMs, but these studies may be nonrevealing for AVMs that are small or have slow flow. CTA and MRA of the circle of Willis as well as the territory containing the nidus must be performed so that all critical features of the AVM are imaged. Evaluation of the source planar images acquired during MRA may reveal a small AVM as bright vessels differentiated from intravascular or extravascular clot, which may obscure an AVM on conventional MRI and the reconstructed 3D MRA. Both TOF and PC methods can be used in MRA examinations.[188] MOTSA and PC MRA are better suited to diagnose AVMs with slow flow.[33, 188] MRA is notorious for incompletely visualizing AVMs because of variable flow effects and related artifact. Aneurysms are frequently unidentifiable. Both MRA and CTA have difficulty discriminating the AVM's supplying arteries from draining veins. The precise angioarchitecture of cerebral AVMs is best demonstrated with traditional catheter angiography, which can identify flow-related and nidal aneurysms, the rate of AVM flow, characteristic early

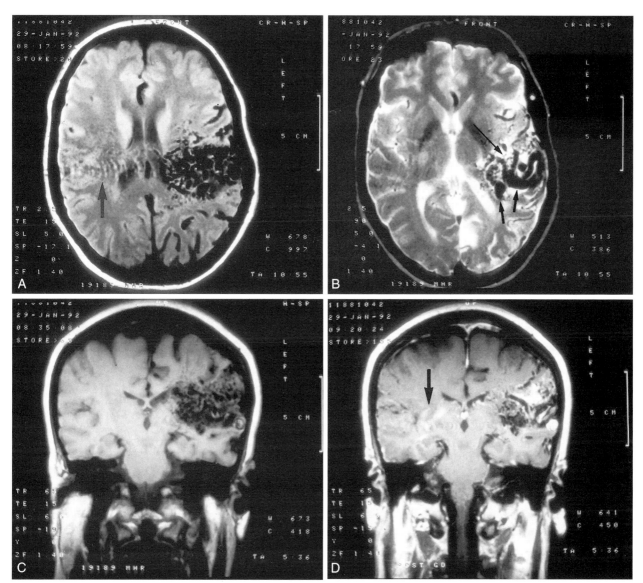

Fig. 8–6. *A,* Short TE, long TR axial MR image illustrating a cerebral AVM extending from cortex to ventricle. The AVM nidus is of decreased signal intensity due to rapid flow, which produces phase encoding artifact (*arrow*). *B,* Axial T2-weighted MR image demonstrates some of the AVM's draining veins (*short arrows*) and less uniform decreased signal intensity in smaller nidus vessels, some of which have increased signal intensity (*long arrow*). *C,* Coronal T1-weighted MR image illustrates the triangular shape of the AVM. *D,* Coronal T1-weighted contrast-enhanced image illustrates variable contrast enhancement of the AVM's nidus due to differential flow rates, faster flow producing less enhancement. Note the phase encoding artifact (*arrow*).

filling veins, all of the contributing arteries and draining veins, and arterial and, particularly, venous stenoses.

The differential diagnosis of cerebral AVMs is limited. Incompletely or totally thrombosed AVMs can appear similar to other masses, including vascular neoplasms such as hemangioblastoma. When a thrombosed AVM has an accompanying intraparenchymal hematoma, differentiating it from a hemorrhagic metastasis, a high-grade glioma, or a nonmalignant cause of hemorrhage, such as hypertension or amyloid angiopathy, can be difficult.

Occasionally, moyamoya can mimic basilar cistern or basal ganglia AVMs. An unusual occurrence in North America, moyamoya is more commonly identified in Japan. It may manifest as intraparenchymal (60%), intraventricular (40%), or, rarely, subarachnoid hemorrhage,[300, 344] transient or permanent ischemic stroke, or seizures and is seen in both children and adults. The most typical age at presentation in adults is in the fourth decade. Moyamoya is characterized by progressive obliteration of large proximal anterior circulation vessels with the development of small "puff of smoke" arterial collaterals. Causes of findings similar to those of moyamoya include neurofibromatosis, sickle cell disease, prior radiation therapy, and Down syndrome. The MRI appearance of moyamoya is notable for the numerous small vessels seen within the inferior brain substance, which represent the collaterals for severely narrowed or occluded distal internal carotid or proximal anterior or middle cerebral arteries.[86, 112] Hemorrhage or infarction may also be demonstrated.

MRI examination is also well suited to evaluate cerebral

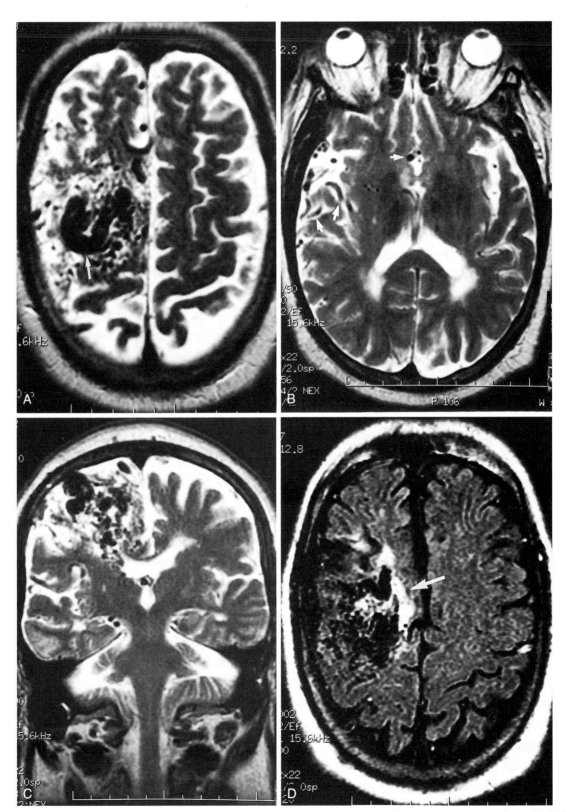

Fig. 8–7. Brain AVM with bordering reactive astrocytosis (gliosis). *A,* T2-weighted axial MR study demonstrating a high flow right frontoparietal AVM. Draining vein (*arrow*). *B,* More inferior T2-weighted axial section reveals enlarged right MCA and ACA branches (*arrows*) supplying the AVM. *C,* Coronal T2-weighted image illustrating the AVM's extent from cortex to ventricle. *D,* FLAIR image highlighting reactive astrocytosis (gliosis) bordering the AVM, seen as bright signal intensity (*arrow*).

AVMs after therapy, particularly radiosurgery or embolization,[145, 287] to demonstrate decreased size and reduced flow.[174, 182, 183] The use of a contrast agent is helpful for identifying any residual AVM nidus; however, contrast enhancement may also be secondary to postoperative gliosis, radiation necrosis, or infarction. Hemorrhage may sometimes occur as a component of radiation necrosis, which may develop as soon as 3 months after radiation therapy. Perinidal edema after radiosurgery, seen as increased signal intensity on T2-weighted spin-echo MR images, is expected and does not necessarily indicate impending radiation necrosis.

Cavernous Angioma

Cavernous angiomas account for approximately 10% to 15% of all cerebral vascular malformations,[229] and are found in approximately 0.4% of the general population.[234] They are the second most common type of symptomatic vascular malformation. Cavernous angiomas typically present as focal parenchymal intracranial hemorrhages between the third and fifth decades of life. Those found in the brain occur equally in males and females. The most common location is in the cerebral hemispheres, with only 10% identified in deep gray matter or white matter tracts. Approximately 25% are found infratentorially, in equal numbers within the brain stem and cerebellum. The pons is the most common location in the brain stem. Unusual cases may arise from the leptomeninges,[276, 285] dura, ependyma, choroid plexus, or cranial nerves, or extradurally. In 30% to 50% of cases, cavernous angiomas are multiple. Spinal cord cavernous angiomas may be isolated or may be associated with cerebral cavernous angiomas.[37] A genetic predisposition manifests when cavernous angiomas are found in 10% to 15% of family members in addition to the index case.[31, 57, 245] When a familial tendency exists, the propensity for multiple cavernous angiomas rises to 80%.[346] Multiple cavernous angiomas can be seen in Rendu-Osler-Weber disease.

The clinical presentation of cavernous angiomas typically consists of seizure activity or of acute or progressive neurologic deficit due to cerebral hemorrhage,[247] but in one study, only 61% of patients were symptomatic.[49, 55, 250, 346] Seizures, the most common symptom, occur in approximately 50% of patients. Seizures are believed to be secondary to mass effect from the cavernous angioma and adjacent brain parenchymal hemosiderin or ferritin and gliosis. Symptomatic hemorrhage manifesting as headache, seizures, or acute neurologic deficit most often occurs in the second and third decades of life and has an incidence of approximately 0.5% to 1% per year.[28, 61, 250] Subclinical hemorrhage is not uncommon, and clinically significant hemorrhage occurs in only 10% to 13% of cases.[49] Hemorrhage from a cavernous angioma uncommonly extends into the ventricular system or the subarachnoid space. It is unclear whether cavernous angiomas, once having bled, have a propensity for subsequent hemorrhage. Cavernous angiomas may initially be tiny and grossly unrecognizable, then suddenly enlarge because of new hemorrhage and thrombosis. They often change over time in size, shape, and character because of intermittent and recurrent hemorrhage and thrombosis, recannulization, vascular ingrowth,

and granulation tissue.[37, 284] When an angioma is large enough, mass effect can produce cranial nerve palsies and focal neurologic deficits. Cranial radiation therapy may cause thrombosis and hemorrhage to develop in preexistent, unrealized cavernous angiomas, making them appear as new findings on serial MRI studies.

On pathologic examination, cavernous angiomas are well circumscribed and have a mulberry configuration. The lesions are not encapsulated but contain a compact or sometimes racemose network of multiple endothelium-lined, sinusoidal, nonuniform vascular channels containing thrombosed blood of varying ages.[49, 220] Compartment walls are irregularly thickened with collagen, hyalin, and scattered calcium deposition and contain no muscularis or elastic lamina layers. No interposed brain tissue is identified within the cavernous angioma. Adjacent brain may be calcified, laden with hemosiderin or ferritin, atrophic, and gliotic. Cavernous angiomas are typically parenchymal lesions sometimes marginating a pial or ependymal surface. Capillary telangiectasias may coexist with or may be mixed with the cavernous angioma.[23, 210] Venous angiomas may also coexist.[98, 247, 305]

CT and MRI

CT scans of cavernous angiomas typically demonstrate an isodense to hyperdense focal area within the brain parenchyma that may or may not contain calcification (Fig. 8–8). They may or may not enhance after intravenous administration of an iodinated contrast agent.[269] Mass effect

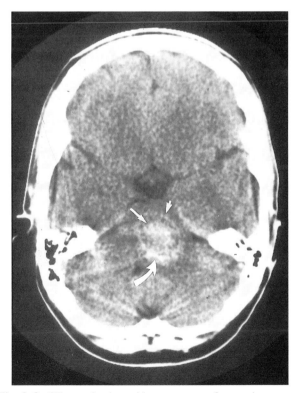

Fig. 8–8. CT examination without contrast of a pontine cavernous angioma demonstrating focal calcification (*curved arrow*) and peripheral (*short arrow*) and central (*long arrow*) hemorrhagic degradation products.

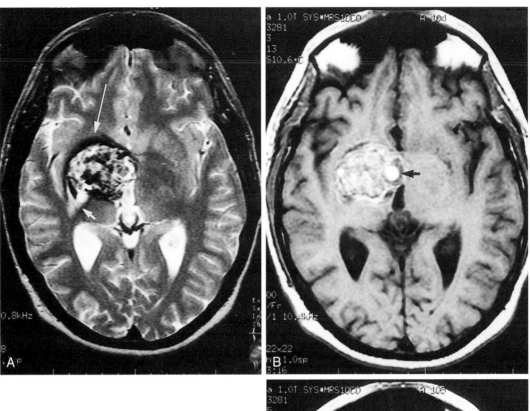

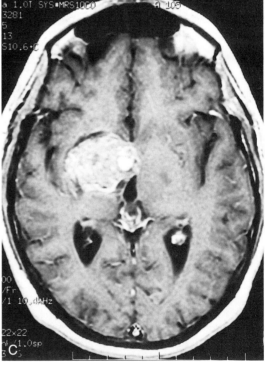

Fig. 8–9. MRI examination of a cavernous angioma demonstrating typical variegated appearance containing hemorrhage of varying ages. *A,* T2-weighted image of a right subinsular/lenticular nucleus/thalamic/internal capsule cavernous angioma. Note the peripheral hemosiderin/ferritin (*long arrow*) and edema located at the site of recent hemorrhage (*short arrow*). *B,* T1-weighted image without contrast. Note the subacute hemorrhage (*arrow*). *C,* T1-weighted image with contrast. Note the lack of appreciable contrast enhancement. (Case courtesy of David Watts, MD.)

and edema associated with the cavernous angioma may be present, depending on its size.[152]

MRI is superior to CT for the identification of cavernous angiomas.[245] It typically demonstrates a mass characterized as popcorn in appearance owing to the varying ages of internal hemorrhages.[96] The margin of the cavernous angioma is of decreased signal intensity on T2*-weighted gradient-echo and T2-weighted spin-echo images if chronic hemorrhage is present.[96] This finding is due to the magnetic susceptibility–caused phase incoherence created by the he-

mosiderin and ferritin residua from previous hemorrhage (Fig. 8–9).[37] The signal intensity of the rim of the cavernous angioma is also decreased because of fibrin and collagen deposition. T2*-weighted gradient-echo scans, which are best for the identification of hemosiderin and ferritin, should always be performed in the evaluation for intracranial hemorrhage. In some cases, the T2* gradient-echo study reveals multiple cavernous angiomas when the T2-weighted spin-echo study illustrates only a solitary lesion. Hemosiderin and ferritin may cause a dark flaring appearance extending into the adjacent brain parenchyma because macrophages and astrocytes remove blood breakdown products, including hemosiderin and ferritin, along white matter fibers.[49] Owing to MRI's exquisite sensitivity for blood degradation products, cavernous angiomas may be incidentally discovered as asymptomatic lesions.[245] Gadolinium-based contrast agents typically produce some enhancement of the cavernous angioma.

Unusual extra-axial cavernous angiomas may have a typical or atypical MRI appearance. Extra-axial cavernous angiomas may resemble meningiomas with homogeneous, intense contrast enhancement but bright signal intensity on T2-weighted spin-echo images.[142, 150, 171]

Catheter cerebral angiography is indicated only to exclude a true arteriovenous malformation as the cause of intracranial hemorrhage when the diagnosis of cavernous angioma using MRI is uncertain. Catheter angiography displays cavernous angiomas as avascular masses, occasionally demonstrating very late capillary staining without arteriovenous shunting.[269] When present, an associated venous angioma may be demonstrated.

Therapy for cavernous angiomas consists of medical treatment for seizure control, surgical excision when the lesion is accessible and clinically indicated, and radiosurgery.

The differential diagnosis of cavernous angiomas includes previous hypertensive hemorrhage, treated toxoplasmosis, previous radiation therapy, amyloid angiopathy, and disseminated intravascular coagulopathy. The demonstration of a lesion containing hemorrhages of multiple ages, a complete peripheral hemosiderin/ferritin ring with flaring into neighboring brain, and the lack of surrounding edema help differentiate cavernous angioma from hemorrhagic metastasis; in some instances, however, particularly with melanoma, only follow-up MRI examinations documenting typical hemorrhage evolution confirm the diagnosis of cavernous angioma.

Capillary Telangiectasia

Capillary telangiectasias are small, usually clinically silent lesions that most commonly occur in the pons or cerebellum but can occur in other locations in the brain parenchyma. They are the second most common cerebral vascular malformation, after venous angiomas, and are usually multiple.[222] The histology of capillary telangiectasias is characterized by dilated, thin-walled capillaries. Unlike cavernous angiomas, normal brain parenchyma is identified within the capillary telangiectasia.[49, 220] Adjacent brain is most often normal but may contain gliosis or hemosiderin/ferritin from previous hemorrhage.[49] Capillary telangiectasias are believed to bleed rarely, however.

Other types of cerebral vascular malformations can be found together with capillary telangiectasias, especially cavernous angiomas.[247] Cerebral capillary telangiectasias can be found in Rendu-Osler-Weber disease, also known as hereditary hemorrhagic telangiectasias, along with telangiectasias in other visceral, mucosal, and cutaneous sites plus pulmonary and cerebral true AVMs. Approximately 28% of patients with Rendu-Osler-Weber disease have cerebral AVMs, with cerebral capillary telangiectasias being less common.[2, 167] Cerebellar capillary telangiectasias may also be a component of the ataxia-telangiectasia syndrome.

CT and MRI

Capillary telangiectasias are most often not identified on unenhanced MRI studies using all available pulse sequences. Rare capillary telangiectasias that have hemorrhaged demonstrate expected MR findings of blood. Most often the hemorrhage is minor and remote, best demonstrated on T2*-weighted gradient-echo studies. Enhancement with gadolinium-based contrast agents demonstrates a lacy network of vessels constituting the capillary telangiectasia (Fig. 8–10). A coexisting cavernous angioma may

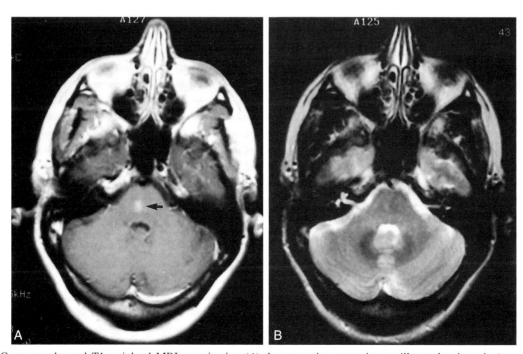

Fig. 8–10. Contrast-enhanced T1-weighted MRI examination (*A*) demonstrating a pontine capillary telangiectasia (*arrow*) that is not well visualized on the T2-weighted study (*B*).

obscure identification of the capillary telangiectasia.[23] CT usually demonstrates no abnormality.

Venous Angiomas

Venous angiomas are the most common cerebral vascular malformation, accounting for almost two thirds of the total and having an incidence in the general population of approximately 2%.[156, 222, 266, 312] This vascular malformation represents a developmental variant of normal venous drainage,[156] composed entirely of venous elements, and some writers prefer to call them "developmental venous anomalies," dropping the term "angioma."[156] The association of venous angiomas with neuronal migration anomalies and the absence of normal venous drainage from regional brain containing the venous angioma emphasizes their embryologic origin (Fig. 8–11).[156, 312] Typically solitary and located in any part of the brain parenchyma, although most often in the frontal lobe, then the cerebellum,[229, 318] venous angiomas range in size from small to large enough to drain an entire hemisphere.[312] Multiple venous angiomas are not rare, particularly when they occur bilaterally in the cerebellum,[312] and their multiplicity has been described in the blue rubber bleb nevus syndrome.

Venous angiomas are characterized by a medusa head of enlarged medullary veins draining to a collector vein, which continues to either the superficial or subependymal cerebral venous drainage system or a combination of these.[98, 312, 318, 329] Venous angiomas are occasionally found intraventricularly. An unusual case of a venous angioma draining to the foramen of Monro and resulting in obstructive hydrocephalus has been reported.[312, 318] The brain parenchyma through which the venous angioma passes is typically normal and shows no evidence of previous bleeding.

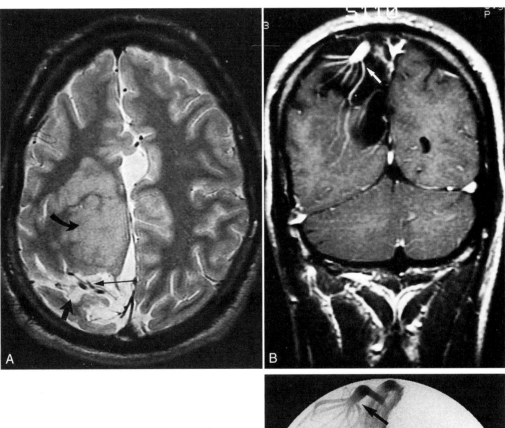

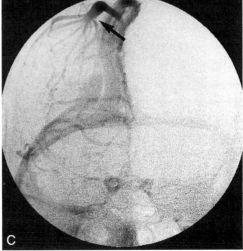

Fig. 8–11. Venous angioma associated with a neuronal migration anomaly. *A,* T2-weighted MR image demonstrates a right parietal schizencephalic cleft (*short arrow*) containing a venous angioma (*long arrow*). Bordering cortical dysplasia (*curved arrow*) *B,* Coronal post-contrast T1-weighted MR image illustrating the venous angioma (*arrow*) within the schizencephaly. *C,* AP view of right carotid cerebral angiogram confirming the venous angioma (*arrow*). (Case courtesy of David Watts, MD.)

Some writers believe that venous angiomas may rarely cause venous infarction with or without hemorrhage, or hemorrhage alone, more often subarachnoid than parenchymal[155, 160, 314, 318, 337, 339] the hemorrhage is possibly due to acquired venous outflow restriction by stenosis or thrombosis[68, 156] secondary to hemodynamic stresses. A venous varix or ectatic component is rarely seen and is explained by similar obstructive mechanisms or hemodynamic forces.[156] The higher incidence of associated contiguous cavernous angiomas in as many as one third of cases,[98, 229] however, is often used to explain any clinically significant hemorrhage being derived from the cavernous angiomas (Fig. 8–12).[23, 170, 192, 247, 312] Rarely, seizures, focal neurologic deficit, cerebellar signs, tinnitus, and headache have been

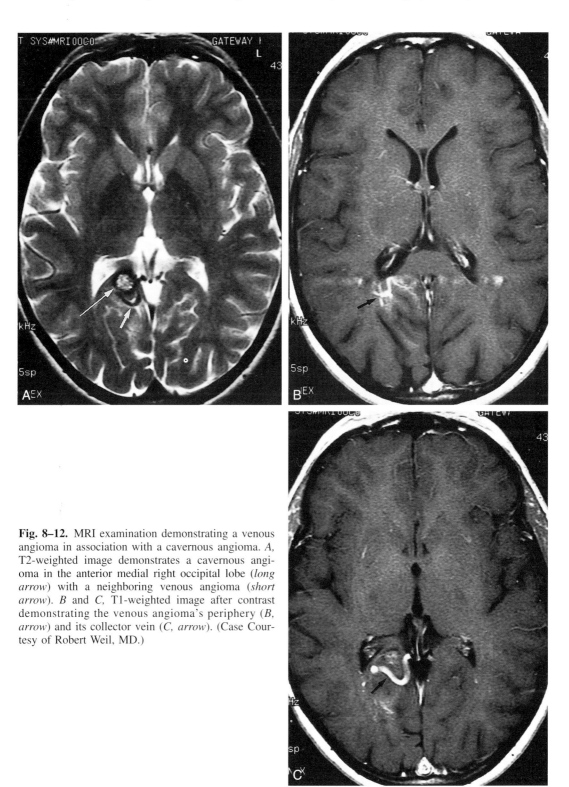

Fig. 8–12. MRI examination demonstrating a venous angioma in association with a cavernous angioma. *A,* T2-weighted image demonstrates a cavernous angioma in the anterior medial right occipital lobe (*long arrow*) with a neighboring venous angioma (*short arrow*). *B* and *C,* T1-weighted image after contrast demonstrating the venous angioma's periphery (*B, arrow*) and its collector vein (*C, arrow*). (Case Courtesy of Robert Weil, MD.)

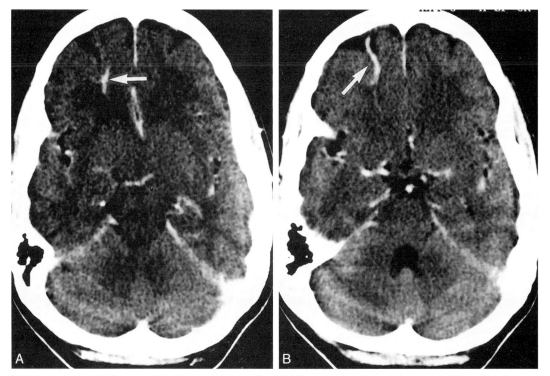

Fig. 8–13. Contrast-enhanced CT examination demonstrating a frontal lobe venous angioma (*A, arrow*). Note the collector vein (*arrow*) illustrated in *B*.

ascribed to venous angiomas,[32, 156, 229, 314, 318, 337, 339] depending on their location, but these clinical presentations are controversial.

CT scanning of a venous angioma demonstrates a contrast-enhancing vascular structure with a thistle-shaped collection of veins coursing to a single dominant draining vein (Fig. 8–13).[312, 318] Calcification of these lesions is unusual, and without calcification, they are typically not identified on unenhanced CT scans. A large venous angioma, however, may be demonstrated by CT as a slightly dense solitary vessel or collection of vessels.[318]

MRI best demonstrates venous angiomas and has revealed their true incidence in the general population. A venous angioma appears as a cluster of small vessels with signal void if flow within them is rapid or dephased; or the vessels may produce increased signal intensity due to slow flow, entry slice phenomenon, even-echo rephasing, or when gradient-moment nulling techniques are utilized. Spatial misregistration artifact occurs in venous angiomas when gradient-moment nulling techniques are used on T2-weighted spin-echo images.[154] T2*-weighted gradient-echo techniques or TOF or PC MRA can demonstrate venous angiomas as a bright grouping of veins if the flow is fast enough or if MRA techniques crafted to take advantage of slow flow, such as thin-slice, 2D TOF, oriented perpendicular to venous inflow are employed (Fig. 8–14).[229]

MRA is typically not necessary to image venous angiomas, however. The rate of blood flow within the venous angioma usually depends on its overall size and determines its signal intensity on MRI[337] together with its orientation to the plane of acquisition. Contrast-enhanced T1-weighted spin-echo or gradient-echo MRI sequences best demonstrate venous angiomas and their relationship to adjacent brain parenchyma.[229, 337, 339] Contrast-enhanced CT or MRI may reveal a focal parenchymal stain around the venous angioma's caput medusa. Frequently, venous angiomas are imaged on MRI as incidental findings because most are clinically silent. They also can be overlooked on MRI scans if small and similar to normal venous drainage.

Venous angiomas should be differentiated from aberrant venous drainage on the basis of the classic findings of a cluster of enlarged medullary veins continuing into a larger collector vein in venous angiomas, anomalous veins lacking more than one or two visualized upstream small veins. The MRI appearance of venous angiomas is so characteristic that catheter cerebral angiography should not be performed in their evaluation. It should be noted that small venous angiomas can be overlooked on catheter cerebral angiography, being thought another example of variant venous drainage, although characteristically they appear later and persist longer than normal veins.[229]

Sinus Pericranii

Sinus pericranii is a soft, compressible venous malformation that by definition lies adjacent to the skull and communicates with the intracranial dural sinuses, most often by enlarged emissary veins.[35, 260] Its etiology is most likely congenital, although it has been reported to occur spontaneously or after trauma.[35, 260] Sinus pericranii may be associated with other vascular malformations, such as cavernous angiomas and venous angiomas, or may be seen as a component of the blue rubber bleb nevus syndrome.[35, 260]

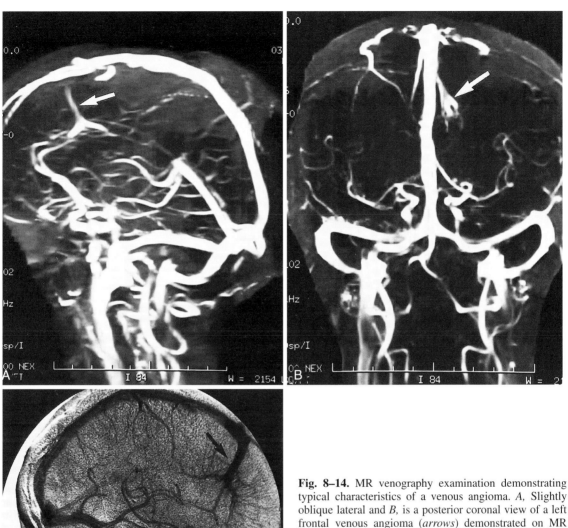

Fig. 8–14. MR venography examination demonstrating typical characteristics of a venous angioma. *A,* Slightly oblique lateral and *B,* is a posterior coronal view of a left frontal venous angioma (*arrows*) demonstrated on MR venography. Lateral view of venous phase during carotid angiography confirms the venous angioma (*arrow*).

Sinus pericranii most commonly occurs in the frontal scalp near the midline.[35, 260] An asymptomatic cosmetic scalp lump is found typically in a patient younger than 30 years. The lesion is twice as common in men as in women and is remarkable for its enlargement with Valsalva maneuvers.[260]

On imaging, sinus pericranii has been described as a vascular soft tissue scalp mass that is slightly hyperdense on unenhanced CT, demonstrates flow on MRI, and enhances strongly with use of a contrast agent on both CT and MRI.[35, 260] CT best identifies associated osteolytic changes from the vascular mass and its associated diploic veins.[35, 260]

Arteriovenous Fistulas
Terminology

Arteriovenous fistulas (AVFs) are usually acquired[53] but may be congenital in some instances. Congenital fistulas most often represent an anomaly of cerebral vascular development and are part of a spectrum of cerebral vascular disorders. Single or multiple arterial venous connections or a true AVM nidus with one or more associated arterial venous fistulae illustrates the variety of pathologic presentations (Fig. 8–15). AVFs may be located intracranially or extracranially within the scalp or facial structures. The arterial venous shunting with increased venous pressure

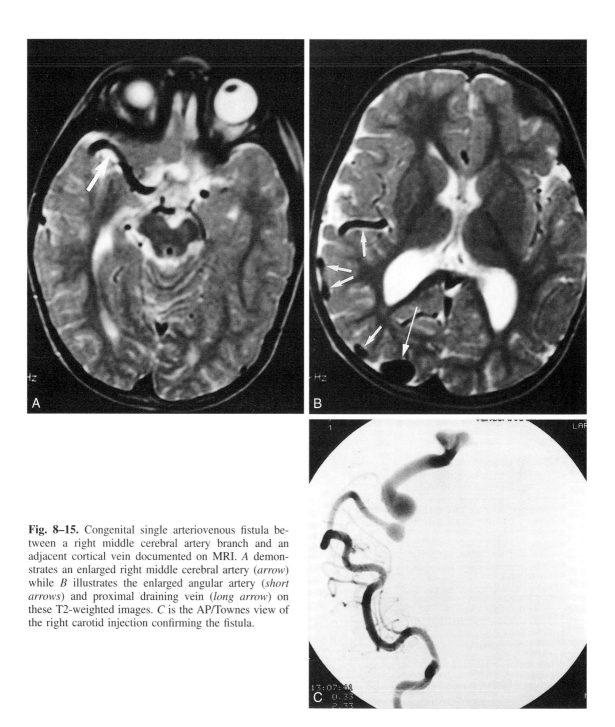

Fig. 8–15. Congenital single arteriovenous fistula between a right middle cerebral artery branch and an adjacent cortical vein documented on MRI. *A* demonstrates an enlarged right middle cerebral artery (*arrow*) while *B* illustrates the enlarged angular artery (*short arrows*) and proximal draining vein (*long arrow*) on these T2-weighted images. *C* is the AP/Townes view of the right carotid injection confirming the fistula.

and flow within any of the AVFs can result in variably sized varices that, when large enough, can produce mass effect such as brain parenchymal or cranial nerve compression or obstructive hydrocephalus.[65, 120, 121, 157, 179, 319, 320]

Most dural arterial venous fistulae are spontaneous and are believed to be acquired after thrombosis of the draining dural sinus with the subsequent development of multiple fistulous shunts to the involved sinus.[121, 133] Chronic venous hypertension without dural sinus thrombosis has also been postulated.[307] Other causes of dural AVFs are trauma, surgery, infection, systemic hypertension, and hypercoagulable

states, including pregnancy, contraception pills, and dehydration.[27, 120, 121, 179] Another type of acquired AVF is best illustrated by the post-traumatic direct carotid cavernous fistula.

Dural AVFs are characterized pathologically by abnormal, direct communications between normal sinus wall arteries and veins.[211] Hemodynamic stresses lead to pathologic disorganization and thickening (less commonly, thinning) of the walls of supplying arteries, draining cortical and medullary veins, and the dural sinus wall at the site of the fistula as well as thrombosis, stenosis, and occlusion of the involved vascular elements, most commonly the dural sinus itself and least commonly the feeding arteries.[121, 179, 211] Angiogenesis factors are probably involved in the propagation of dural AVFs.[179]

Dural AVFs represent approximately 10% to 15% of intracranial vascular malformations[45, 120, 190, 320] and are more common in women than men.[320] Most often, the dural AVF involves a single sinus, sometimes with involvement of contiguous sinuses. Multiple disparate dural AVFs are rare[45] and are typically in close proximity,[179] even the bilateral dural carotid cavernous fistulas possibly related by the interconnecting circular sinus and clival veins.

Dural AVFs may spontaneously obliterate[15, 179]; however, closure of such a lesion may be associated with intracranial hemorrhage.[157] Approximately 15% of patients present with intraparenchymal, subarachnoid, or subdural hemorrhage, listed in decreasing order of frequency.[45, 120, 157] Significant in the production of intracranial hemorrhage is reversal of flow within the involved dural sinus into variably dilated cortical veins, which results in venous rupture or venous hypertension in the involved cerebral territory.[120, 157, 238] The risk of hemorrhage from a dural AVF is 1.8% per year, with a 20% mortality for each hemorrhage.[45] Risk factors for producing hemorrhage include AVF location in the anterior cranial fossa (ethmoidal), superior petrosal sinus, or deep veins, leptomeningeal venous drainage, draining vein stenosis, and a venous varix.[45, 110, 179, 190, 320]

Dural AVFs have been categorized on the basis of their venous drainage pattern (Table 8–3).[55a] Over time, dural AVFs may change and so be assigned to a different type.[179] Symptomatology and risk of hemorrhage roughly correspond to more abnormal venous drainage.[179]

Dural AVFs may also cause seizures or neurologic deficits owing to venous hypertension-caused hemorrhage or ischemia/infarction or, less commonly, to arterial steal.[45, 121, 157, 304, 315, 320] Pulsatile tinnitus and headache, the most common complaints,[45, 320] may be mild enough and of such chronicity that the patient does not seek medical attention until other symptoms develop, such as cranial nerve palsies due to arterial steal or abnormal venous drainage and congestion.[157] Dural AVFs most often become symptomatic in patients between 40 and 60 years of age.[225]

Communicating hydrocephalus may be the result of the dural AVF producing dural sinus hypertension, dural sinus thrombosis, or prior subarachnoid hemorrhage.[157] Increased intracranial pressure without communicating hydrocephalus

may be due to cerebral venous congestion, increased cerebral blood volume, elevated intrasinus pressure, and impaired cerebral venous drainage.[121, 320]

Arterial supply to dural AVFs is from meningeal branches of the external carotid artery (e.g., the middle meningeal, ascending pharyngeal, and occipital arteries), the internal carotid artery (e.g., the tentorial artery of the meningohypophyseal trunk), and the vertebral artery (e.g., the posterior meningeal artery).[45, 226] Pial arteries derived from the carotid or vertebrobasilar system can also supply dural arteriovenous fistulae.

In one third to two thirds of cases, dural AVFs involve the sigmoid and transverse sinuses.[45, 49] The cavernous sinus is the second most common location, accounting for 12% to 20% of AVFs and being most common in middle-aged women.[45, 65] The symptoms of cavernous sinus dural AVFs include palsies of cranial nerves III, IV, and VI, which produce diplopia, proptosis, conjunctival engorgement, retro-orbital or cranial nerve V pain, increased intraocular pressure and secondary glaucoma; all of these are due to the abnormal venous hypertension within the cavernous sinus and retrograde venous drainage into the involved orbit.[120, 147, 306] More ominous consequences are papilledema, choroidal or retinal detachment, central retinal vein thrombosis, and diminished visual acuity.[179] Other sites of dural AVF are the tentorium and its incisura, the superior and inferior petrosal sinuses, the occipital and marginal sinuses, the superior and inferior sagittal sinuses, the straight sinus, the vein of Galen, and the anterior and middle cranial fossae.[65, 190] Adjacent cortical veins may also incorporate AVFs within their walls.[179]

Unenhanced CT scans of dural AVFs are normal unless intracranial hemorrhage, edema or infarction from venous hypertension, or thrombosis of a dural sinus or draining vein is identified. Contrast-enhanced scans may occasionally demonstrate enlarged cortical or medullary veins or stenotic or enlarged dural sinuses (Fig. 8–16). These findings are noted in up to half of patients with dural carotid cavernous fistulas, with expansion of the involved cavernous sinus and increased size of the draining superior ophthalmic vein.

MRI demonstration of cerebral AVFs depends on the type of fistula encountered. With congenital direct AVF, MRI demonstrates an enlarged supplying artery that communicates directly within an enlarged draining vein (see Fig. 8–15). In a post-traumatic direct carotid cavernous fistula, MRI shows enlargement of the cavernous sinus containing diminished signal intensity due to excessive blood flow within the sinus, and dilated superior and inferior ophthalmic veins as well as other smaller orbital veins with accompanying orbital proptosis and extraocular muscle enlargement. Dural carotid cavernous fistulas often show similar but less dramatic findings.[147] Either type of carotid cavernous fistula may produce bilateral cavernous sinus and orbital findings on MRI because of intersinus midline venous communications. The MRI findings with dural AVFs are more subtle if the more easily appreciated findings of intracranial hemorrhage, edema, or infarction are not present.

MRI and MRA are notorious for missing uncomplicated dural AVF unless the venous drainage into enlarged cortical or medullary veins is demonstrated.[65] In such instances,

---

TABLE 8–3. Classification of Dural AVFs

Type I
Antegrade drainage into sinus

Type II

II a	Antegrade and retrograde drainage into sinus
II b	Antegrade drainage into sinus and retrograde drainage into cortical veins
II a & b	Antegrade drainage into sinus and retrograde drainage into sinus and cortical veins

Type III
Retrograde drainage into cortical veins

Type IV
Retrograde drainage into cortical veins with venous ectasia

Type V
Drainage into spinal veins

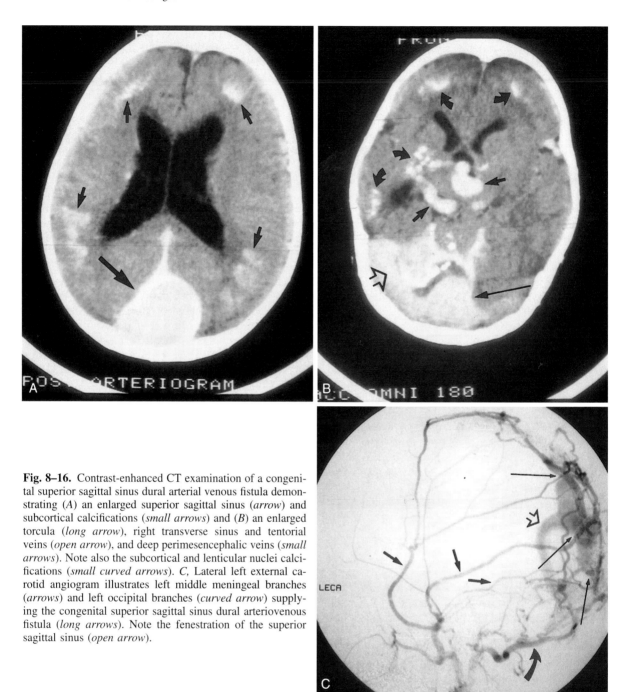

Fig. 8–16. Contrast-enhanced CT examination of a congenital superior sagittal sinus dural arterial venous fistula demonstrating (*A*) an enlarged superior sagittal sinus (*arrow*) and subcortical calcifications (*small arrows*) and (*B*) an enlarged torcula (*long arrow*), right transverse sinus and tentorial veins (*open arrow*), and deep perimesencephalic veins (*small arrows*). Note also the subcortical and lenticular nuclei calcifications (*small curved arrows*). *C,* Lateral left external carotid angiogram illustrates left middle meningeal branches (*arrows*) and left occipital branches (*curved arrow*) supplying the congenital superior sagittal sinus dural arteriovenous fistula (*long arrows*). Note the fenestration of the superior sagittal sinus (*open arrow*).

venous varices may also be identified. Although MRI can be used to document an occluded or stenosed dural sinus or vein,[268] the evaluation can be problematic because of typically encountered variable venous signal intensity, caused by flowing blood within dural sinuses on various spin-echo pulse sequences, and the changing appearance of clot depending on its age. Other difficulties with MRI are the small caliber of the feeding arteries in dural arteriovenous malformations and the focal or diffuse rather that masslike site of the abnormal dural shunts, which are often

located next to flowing blood and near cortical bone making their distinction difficult. MR venography can be used to define patent, occluded, or stenotic dural sinuses.

Catheter cerebral angiography is always necessary for full evaluation of the angioarchitecture of cerebral AVFs.

Vein of Galen Malformations

The vein of Galen malformation is a congenital anomaly in which AVFs supply the embryologic precursor to the vein of Galen. Some writers have divided vein of Galen malformations into two types, choroidal and mural. The choroidal type (Type I), which is more common, consists of one or more anterior and posterior choroidal, distal pericallosal, thalamoperforating, and sometimes superior cerebellar arteries directed to the dorsal vein of the prosencephalon, which continues into the median prosencephalic vein. With this type, the posterior choroidal vessels are typically the dominant supply. The mural type (Type II) of malformation consists of collicular and posterior choroidal arteries supplying the wall of the median prosencephalic vein, although additional arteries, such as the thalamoperforators, may also be contributors. These features distinguish the vein of Galen malformation from congenital parenchymal AVMs, acquired dural AVFs, and vein of Galen or straight sinus stenoses, which feature a dilated vein of Galen. The primitive median prosencephalic vein, the precursor of the vein of Galen, is usually abnormally dilated in vein of Galen malformations. Normal deep veins drain not into the median prosencephalic vein but through

alternate routes, because the true vein of Galen is absent. The persistent median prosencephalic vein drains to a falcine sinus rather than the straight sinus, and the straight sinus is often absent. Venous outflow restriction is common in the vein of Galen malformation and contributes to further dilatation of the median prosencephalic vein, also commonly referred to as a dilated vein of Galen. Other venous anomalies are often associated with the vein of Galen malformation, including absence of or hypoplastic sigmoid or jugular sinuses, duplicated sinuses, and persistent marginal or occipital sinuses.[89] Venous-to-arterial shunting through a patent foramen ovale or persistent ductus arteriosus may coexist.[59a, 176, 191a]

The venous drainage of the enlarged median prosencephalic vein or vein of Galen typically demonstrates a dilated venous varix continuing into an accessory or inferior falcine sinus. If the venous outflow stenosis is severe enough, some Vein of Galen malformations have been documented to proceed to thrombosis which may lead to spontaneous cure but also can result in acute hydrocepha-

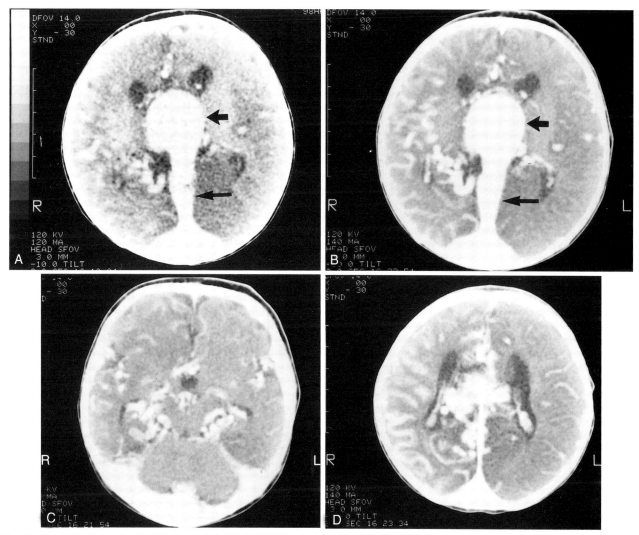

Fig. 8–17. CT examination of a vein of Galen malformation before (*A*) and after (*B*) contrast. *B, C, D,* Note the enlarged primitive median prosencephalic vein (*short arrow*) continuing to the falcine sinus (*long arrow*). Both structure are dense without contrast in an infant. *C* and *D* illustrate numerous enlarged arteries supplying this choroidal type of vein of Galen malformation.

lus, intracranial hemorrhage, or central venous hypertension.

The extent of high-flow shunting and the amount of venous outflow restriction in a vein of Galen malformation determine the age of the patient at presentation. Patients with high-flow multiple fistulas and no venous outflow stenosis (usually type I) are often identified at birth with high-output congestive heart failure, intracranial bruit, macrocephaly, and hydrocephalus. If the vein of Galen shunt is severe enough, the infants can demonstrate metabolic lactic acidosis due to multiorgan hypoperfusion and quickly progress to death. Patients who have decreased flow through the a vein of Galen malformation, typically those with high-grade venous outflow restriction (usually type II), may present later in childhood, even as adults. In such patients, cardiomegaly may be asymptomatic, and developmental delay and ocular symptoms are more common. Seizures, enlarging head circumference, intracranial hemorrhage that may be parenchymal, subarachnoid, or intraventricular, focal neurologic deficit, pulsatile tinnitus, and cranial bruit can be seen in any patient with a vein of Galen malformation, although hemorrhage is rare and is usually seen only with venous drainage thrombosis.

CT and MRI

CT scans clearly demonstrate the enlarged primitive median prosencephalic vein, which appears as a mass in the tentorial incisura of slightly increased density on unenhanced scans and markedly enhances with use of an iodin-ated contrast agent (Fig. 8–17). Intravenous contrast administration also may demonstrate the feeding arteries as well as the disproportionate outflow restriction, which is often characterized by diffuse or focal narrowing of the falcine sinus or, less commonly, of the straight sinus. Unenhanced CT scanning is valuable for identifying brain parenchymal calcifications located in the hemispheric venous watershed zones owing to chronic deep venous hypertension.

MRI provides a 3D display of the vein of Galen malformation, documenting the dilated primitive median prosencephalic vein, the falcine sinus, and the abnormal arterial supply (Fig. 8–18). Flow-related artifacts are related to the size of and rate of flow through the vein of Galen malformation. MRA can also display the malformation.

MRI, CT, and ultrasonography can demonstrate brain parenchymal encephalomalacia, atrophy, hemorrhage, thrombosis, and ischemic changes. Each modality's efficacy depends on the patient's age at presentation and the corresponding degree of brain myelination or, in the case of ultrasonography, the size of the skull fontanels. Each imaging technique also accurately depicts hydrocephalus. The enlargement of the ventricular system is due to venous hypertension and impedance of CSF resorption (communicating hydrocephalus) or, less commonly, to obstruction of the aqueduct of Sylvius by the enlarged vein of Galen (obstructive hydrocephalus). In utero, hydrocephalus may produce cerebral developmental dysplasia.

Transcranial ultrasound examination in the fetus or neonate is often used to provide the initial diagnosis of vein of Galen malformations. Catheter cerebral angiography is

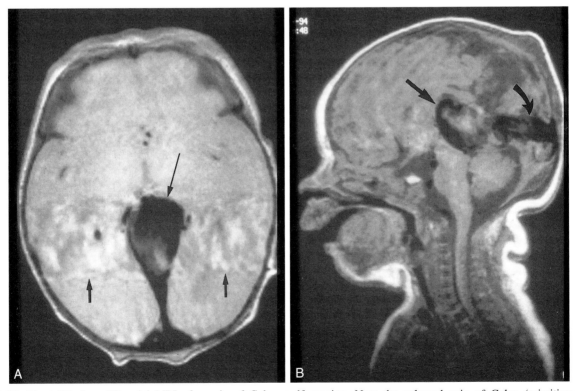

Fig. 8–18. Short TE, long TR axial MRI of a vein of Galen malformation. Note the enlarged vein of Galen (primitive median prosencephalic vein) (*long arrow*) producing flow artifact (*short arrows*). B, Sagittal T1-weighted MRI illustrates the vein of Galen malformation including the enlarged vein of Galen (primitive median prosencephalic vein) (*straight arrow*) and a low falcine vein (*curved arrow*). (Case courtesy of Michelle Smith, MD.)

necessary to define the angioarchitecture of the malformations and to correctly categorize it.

Vein of Galen malformations are typically treated with endovascular or combined operative transtorcular and endovascular methods.

References

1. Aalmaani WS, Richardson AE: Multiple intracranial aneurysms: Identifying the ruptured lesion. Surg Neurol 9:303–305, 1978.
2. Aesch B, Lioret E, de Toffol B, Jan M: Multiple cerebral angiomas and Rendu-Osler-Weber disease: Case report. Neurosurgery 29:599–602, 1991.
3. Anderson CM, Saloner D, Tsuruda JS, et al: Artifacts in maximum intensity projection display of MR angiograms. AJR Am J Roentgenol 154:623–629, 1990.
4. Anderson EB, Petersen J, Mortensen EL, Udesen H: Conservatively treated patients with cerebral arteriovenous malformation: Mental and physical outcome. J Neurol Neurosurg Psychiatry 51:1208–1212, 1988.
5. Andoh T, Shirakami S, Nakashima T, et al: Clinical analysis of a series of vertebral aneurysm cases. Neurosurgery 31:987–993, 1992.
6. Anson J, Cromwell RM: Craniocervical arterial dissection. Neurosurgery 29:89–96, 1991.
7. Anzalone N, Triulzi F, Scotti G: Acute subarachnoid hemorrhage: 3D time-of-flight MR angiography versus intra-arterial digital angiography. Neuroradiology 37:257–261, 1995.
8. Aoki S, Sasaki Y, Machida T, et al: Cerebral aneurysms: Detection and delineation using 3-D-CT angiography. AJNR Am J Neuroradiol 13:1115–1120, 1992.
9. Arabi B: Traumatic aneurysms of brain due to high velocity missile head wounds. Neurosurgery 22:1056–1063, 1988.
10. Armstrong DC: Presented at the 29th Annual Scientific Meeting of the American Society of Neuroradiology, Washington, DC, May 1991.
11. Atkinson JLD, Sundt TM Jr, Houser OW, et al: Angiographic frequency of anterior circulation intracranial aneurysms. J Neurosurg 70:551–555, 1989.
12. Atlas SW, Fram EK, Mark AS, Grossman RI: Vascular intracranial lesions: Applications of fast scanning. Radiology 169:455–461, 1988.
13. Atlas SW, Grossman RI, Goldberg HI, et al: Partially thrombosed giant intracranial aneurysms: Correlation of MR and pathologic findings. Radiology 162:111–114, 1987.
14. Atlas SW, Grossman RI, Gomori JM, et al: Hemorrhagic intracranial malignant neoplasms: Spin-echo MR imaging. Radiology 164:71–77, 1987.
15. Atlas SW, Listerud J, Chung W, Flamm E: Intracranial aneurysms: Depiction on MR angiograms with a multi-feature extraction postprocessing algorithm. Radiology 192:129–139, 1994.
16. Atlas SW: Intracranial vascular malformations and aneurysms: Current imaging applications. Radiol Clin North Am 26:821–837, 1988.
17. Atlas SW: MR angiography in neurological disease: State of the art. Radiology 193:1–16, 1994.
18. Atlas SW: Imaging vascular intracranial disease: Current status. Curr Opin Radiol 2:18–25, 1990.
19. Atlas SW: MR imaging is highly sensitive to acute subarachnoid hemorrhage . . . not! Radiology 186:319, 1993.
20. Atlas S (ed): Intracranial Vascular Malformations and Aneurysms: Magnetic Resonance Imaging of the Brain and Spine, 2nd ed. Philadelphia, Lippincott-Raven, 1996.
20a. Auger RG, Wiebers DO: Management of unruptured intracranial arteriovenous malformations: A decision analysis. Neurosurgery 30:561–569, 1992.
21. Augustyn G, Scott J, Olson E, et al: Cerebral venous angiomas: MR imaging. Radiology 156:391–395, 1985.
22. Awad I, Little J: Dural arteriovenous malformations. In Barrow D (ed): Intracranial Vascular Malformations. Park Ridge, Ill, AANS, 1990, pp 219–226.
23. Awad I, Robinson J, Mohanty S, Estes M: Mixed vascular malformations of the brain: Clinical and pathogenetic considerations. Neurosurgery 33:179–188, 1993.
24. Axel L: Blood flow effects in magnetic resonance imaging. AJR Am J Roentgenol 143:1157–1166, 1984.

25. Baenziger O, Martin E, Willi V, et al: Prenatal brain atrophy due to a giant vein of Galen malformation. Neuroradiology 35:105–106, 1993.
26. Barker CS: Peripheral cerebral aneurysm associated with a glioma. Neuroradiology 34:30–32, 1992.
27. Barnwell SL, Halbach VV, Dowd CF, et al: Multiple dural arteriovenous fistulas of the cranium and spine. AJNR Am J Neuroradiol 12:441–445, 1991.
28. Barrow D, Krisht A: Cavernous malformations and hemorrhage. In Awad I, Barrow D (eds): Cavernous Malformations. Park Ridge, Ill, AANS, 1993, pp 65–80.
29. Belliveau J, Kennedy D, McKinstry R, et al: Functional mapping of the human visual cortex by magnetic resonance imaging. Science 254:716–719, 1991.
30. Berenstein A, Lasjaunias P: Surgical Neuroangiography. New York, Springer-Verlag, 1992.
31. Bicknell J, Carlow T, Kornfield M, et al: Familial cavernous angiomas. Arch Neurol 35:746–749, 1978.
32. Blackmore CC, Mamourian AC: Compression from venous angioma: MR findings. AJNR Am J Neuroradiol 17:458–460, 1996.
33. Blatter DD, Parker DL, Ahn SS, et al: Cerebral MR angiography with multiple overlapping thin slab acquisition. Part II: Early clinical experience. Radiology 183:379–389, 1992.
34. Blatter DD, Parker DL, Robison RO: Cerebral MR angiography with multiple overlapping thin slab acquisition. Part I: Quantitative analysis of vessel visibility. Radiology 179:805–811, 1991.
35. Bollar A, Allut AG, Prieto A, et al: Sinus pericranii: radiological and etiopathological considerations. J Neurosurg 77:469–472, 1992.
36. Bosmans H, Marchal G, Van Hecke P, Vanhoenacker P: MRA review. Clin Imaging 16:152–167, 1992.
37. Bourgouin PM, Tampieri D, Johnston W, et al: Multiple occult vascular malformations of the brain and spinal cord: MRI diagnosis. Neuroradiology 34:110–111, 1992.
38. Burger P, Scheithauer B, Bernd, Vogel FS: Surgical Pathology of the Nervous System and Its Covering, 3rd ed. New York, Churchill Livingstone, 1991.
39. Bradley WG, Waluch V: Blood flow: Magnetic resonance imaging. Radiology 154:443–450, 1985.
40. Bradley WG, Widoff BE, Yan K, et al: Comparison of routine and gadodiamide-enhanced 3D time-of-flight MR angiography in the brain. RSNA Book of Abstracts 122, 1992.
40a. Brott T, Mandybur TI: Case-control study of clinical outcomes after aneurysmal subarachnoid hemorrhage. Neurosurgery 19:891–895, 1986.
41. Brown BM, Soldevilla F: MR angiography and surgery for unruptured familial intracranial aneurysms in persons with a family history of cerebral aneurysms. AJR Am J Roentgenol 173:133–138, 1999.
42. Brown E, Prager J, Lee H-Y, Ramsey RG: CNS complications of cocaine abuse: Prevalence, pathophysiology, and neuroradiology. AJR Am J Roentgenol 159:137–147, 1992.
43. Brown RD Jr, Wiebers DO, Forbes G, et al: The natural history of unruptured intracranial arteriovenous malformations. J Neurosurg 68:352–357, 1988.
44. Brown RD, Wiebers DO, Forbes GS: Unruptured intracranial aneurysms and arteriovenous malformations: Frequency of intracranial hemorrhage and relationship of lesions. J Neurosurg 73:859–863, 1990.
45. Brown RD Jr, Wiebers DO, Nichols DA: Intracranial dural arteriovenous fistulae: Angiographic predictors of intracranial hemorrhage and clinical outcome in nonsurgical patients. J Neurosurg 81:531–538, 1994.
46. Brunereau L, Cottier JP, Sonier CB, Medioni B, et al: Prospective evaluation of time-of-flight MR angiography in the follow-up of intracranial saccular aneurysms treated with Guglielmi detachable coils. J Comput Assist Tomogr 23:216–223, 1999.
47. Brust JCM, Richtor RW: Stroke associated with cocaine abuse? NY State J Med 77:1473–1475, 1989.
48. Bull J: Massive aneurysms at the base of the brain. Brain 92:535–570, 1969.
49. Burger PC, Schuthauer BW: Vascular tumors and tumor-like lesions. In Tumors of the Central Nervous System. Washington, DC, Armed Forces Institute of Pathology, 1994, pp 287–299.
50. Burger PC, Schuthaver BW, Vogel FS: Surgical Pathology of the Nervous System and its Coverings, 3rd ed. New York, Churchill Livingstone, 1991, pp 439, 443.

50a. Burger PC, Schuthauer BW, Vogel FS: Surgical Pathology of the Nervous System and Its Coverings, 3rd ed. New York, Churchill Livingstone, 1991.

51. Camarata PJ, Latchaw RE Jr, Rüffenacht DA, Heros RC: Intracranial aneurysms. Invest Radiol 28:373–382, 1993.

52. Chappell PM, Steinberg GK, Marks MP: Clinically documented hemorrhage in cerebral arteriovenous malformations: MR characteristics. Radiology 183:719–724, 1992.

53. Chaudhary MY, Sachdev VP, Cho SH, et al: Dural arteriovenous malformations of the major venous sinuses: An acquired lesion. AJNR Am J Neuroradiol 3:13–19, 1982.

54. Chen JC, Tsuruda JS, Halbach VV: Suspected dural arteriovenous fistula: Results with screening MR angiography in seven patients. Radiology 183:265–271, 1992.

54a. Chin LS, Raffel C, Gonzales-Gomez, et al: Diffuse arteriovenous malformations: A clinical, radiological, and pathological description. Neurosurgery 31:863–868, 1992.

55. Churchyard A, Khangure M, Grainger K: Cerebral cavernous angioma: A potentially benign condition? Successful treatment in 16 cases, J Neurol Neurosurg Psychiatry 55:1040–1045, 1992.

55a. Cognard C, Gobin YP, Picrot L, et al: Cerebral dural arteriovenous fistulas: Clinical and angiographic correlation with a revised classification of venous drainage. Radiology 194:671–680, 1995.

56. Cohen HCM, Tucker WS, Humphreys RP, et al: Angiographically cryptic histologically verified cerebrovascular malformations. Neurosurgery 10:704–714, 1982.

57. Cosgrove R, Bertrand G, Fontaine S, et al: Cavernous angiomas of the spinal cord. J Neurosurg 68:31–36, 1988.

58. Crawford PM, West CR, Chadwick DW, Shaw MDM: Arteriovenous malformations of the brain: Natural history in unoperated patients. J Neurol Neurosurg Psychiatry 49:1–10, 1986.

59. Creasy J, Price RR, Presbrey T, et al: Gadolinium-enhanced MR angiography. Radiology 175:280–283, 1990.

60. Cunha e Sa MJ, Stein BM, Solomon RA, McCormick PC: The treatment of associated intracranial aneurysms and arteriovenous malformation. J Neurosurg 77:853–859, 1992.

61. Curling O, Kelly D: The natural history of intracranial cavernous and venous malformations. Persp Neurol Surg 1:19–39, 1990.

62. Curling OP, Kelly DL, Elster AD, Craven TE: An analysis of the natural history of cavernous hemangiomas. J Neurosurg 75:702–708, 1991.

63. Davis JM, Zimmerman RA: Injury of the cortical and vertebral arteries. Neuroradiology 25:55–69, 1983.

64. Davis WL, Warnock SH, Harnsberger HR, et al: Intracranial MRA: single volume vs. multiple thin slab 3D time-of-flight acquisition. J Comput Assist Tomogr 17:15–21, 1993.

65. De Marco JK, Dillon WP, Halback VV, Tsuruda JS: Dural arteriovenous fistulas: Evaluation with MR imaging. Radiology 175:193–199, 1990.

66. DeMarco JK, Dillon WP, Halback VV, Tsuruda JS: Dural arteriovenous fistulas: Evaluation with MR imaging. Radiology 175:193–199, 1990.

67. deTilly, LN, Willinsky R, Ter Brugge K, et al: Cerebral arteriovenous malformation causing epistaxis. AJNR Am J Neuroradiol 13:333–334, 1992.

68. Dillon WP: Venous angiomas. Presented at the 29th Annual Meeting of the American Society of Neuroradiology, Washington, DC, June 9–14, 1991.

69. Drake CG: Giant intracranial aneurysms: Experience with surgical treatment in 174 patients. Clin Neurol 26:12–95, 1979.

70. Dross P, Raji MR, Dastur KJ: Cerebral varix associated with a venous angioma. ANJR Am J Neuroradiol 8:373–374, 1987.

71. Dumoulin CL, Hart HR: Magnetic resonance angiography. Radiology 161:717–720, 1986.

72. Dumoulin CL, Souza SP, Hart HR: Rapid scan magnetic resonance angiography. Magn Reson Imaging 5:238–245, 1987.

73. Dumoulin CL, Souza SP, Walker MF, et al: Three-dimensional phase contrast angiography. Magn Reson Med 9:139–149, 1989.

74. Ebeling JD, Tranmer BI, Davis KA, et al: Thrombosed arteriovenous malformations: A type of occult vascular malformation. Neurosurgery 23:605–610, 1988.

75. Edelman RR, Ahn SS, Chien D, et al: Improved time-of-flight MR angiography of the brain with magnetization transfer contrast. Radiology 184:395–399, 1992.

76. Eng J, Ceckler TL, Balaban RS: Quantitative 1H magnetization transfer imaging in vivo. Magn Reson Med 17:304–314, 1991.

77. Enomoto H, Goto H: Spinal epidural cavernous angioma. Neuroradiology 33:462–465, 1991.

78. Evans AJ, Blinder RA, Herfkens RJ, et al: Effects of turbulence on signal intensity in gradient echo images. Invest Radiol 23:512–518, 1988.

79. Fabrikant J, Levy R, Steinberg G, et al: Charged particle radiosurgery for intracranial vascular malformations. Neurosurg Clin North Am 3:99–139, 1992.

80. Farres MT, Ferraz-Leite H, Schindler E, Muhlbauer J: Spontaneous subarachnoid hemorrhage with negative angiography: CT findings. J Comput Assist Tomogr 16:534–537, 1992.

81. Firmin DN, Nayler GL, Underwood SR, et al: MR angiography, flow velocity, and acceleration measurements combined using a field even-echo rephasing (FEER) sequence. Chicago, 127, 1986.

82. Fogelholm R: Subarachnoid hemorrhage in middle Finland: Incidence, early prognosis and indication for neurosurgical treatment. Stroke 12:296–301, 1981.

83. Fox PT, Raichle ME, Mintun MA, Dence C: Nonoxidative glucose consumption during focal physiologic neural activity. Science 241:462–464, 1988.

84. Fox PT, Raichle ME: Focal physiological uncoupling of cerebral blood flow and oxidative metabolism during somatosensory stimulation in human subjects. Proc Natl Acad Sci U S A 83:1140–1144, 1986.

85. Fram EK, Dimick R, Hedlund LW, et al: Parameters determining the signal of flowing fluid in gradient refocused MR imaging: Flow velocity, TR and flip angle (abstract). Abstracts of the Fifth Annual Meeting, SMRM, 84–85, 1986.

85a. Friedman AH, Drake CG: Subarachnoid hemorrhage from intracranial dissecting aneurysm. J Neurosurg 60:325–334, 1984.

86. Fujisawa I, Asato R, Nishimura K, et al: Moyamoya disease: MR imaging. Radiology 164:103–105, 1987.

87. Fujiwara T, Mino S, Nagao S, Ohmoto T: Metastatic choriocarcinoma with neoplastic aneurysms cured by aneurysm resection and chemotherapy: Case report. J Neurosurg 76:148–151, 1992.

88. Fukusumi A, Okudera T, Huang YP, et al: Neuroradiological analysis of medullary venous malformations in the cerebellar hemisphere. Neuroradiology 33:359, 1991.

89. Garcia-Monaco R, Lasjaunias P, Berenstein A: Therapeutic management of vein of Galen aneurysmal malformations in interventional neuroradiology. In Vinvela F, Halback VV, Dion JE (eds): Endovascular Therapy of the Central Nervous System. New York, Raven Press, 1992.

90. Garcia-Monaco R, Rodesch G, Alvarez H, et al: Pseudoaneurysms within ruptured intracranial arteriovenous malformations: Diagnosis and early endovascular management. AJNR Am J Neuroradiol 14:315–321, 1993.

91. Gerosa MA, Cappellotto P, Licata C, et al: Cerebral arteriovenous malformations in children (56 cases). Childs Brain 8:356–371, 1981.

92. Giannakapoulos G, Nair S, Snider C, Amenta DS: Implications for the pathogenesis of aneurysm formation: Metastasis choriocarcinoma with spontaneous splenic rupture. Surg Neurol 38:236–240, 1992.

93. Goldwyn D, Cardenas C, Murtagh F, et al: MRI of cervical extradural cavernous hemangioma. Neuroradiology 34:68–69, 1992.

94. Golfinos JG, Wascher TM, Zabramski JM, Spetzler RF: The management of unruptured intracranial vascular malformations. BNI Q 8:2–11, 1992.

95. Gomori JM, Grossman RI, Bilaniuk LT, et al: High-field MR imaging of superficial siderosis of the central nervous system. J Comput Assist Tomogr 9:972–975, 1985.

96. Gomori JM, Grossman RI, Goldberg HI, et al: Occult cerebral vascular malformations: High-field MR imaging. Radiology 158:707–713, 1986.

97. Gonzales CF, Cho YI, Ortega HV, Moret J: Intracranial aneurysms: Flow analysis of their origin and progression. AJNR Am J Neuroradiol 13:181–1888, 1992.

98. Goulao A, Alvarez H, Monaco RG, et al: Venous anomalies and abnormalities of the posterior fossa. Neuroradiology 31:476–482, 1990.

99. Graf CJ, Perret GE, Torner JC: Bleeding from cerebral arteriovenous malformations as part of their natural history. J Neurosurg 58:331–337, 1990.

100. Graves VB, Duff TA: Intracranial arteriovenous malformations: Current imaging and treatment. Invest Radiol 25:952–960, 1990.

101. Graves YB, Duff TA: Intracranial arteriovenous malformations: Current imaging and treatment. Invest Radiol 25:952, 1990.

102. Graves VB, Strother CM, Partington CR, Rappi A: Flow dynamics of lateral carotid artery aneurysms and their effect on coils and balloons: An experimental study in dogs. AJNR Am J Neuroradiol 13:189–196, 1992.

103. Grieve JP, Stacey R, Moore E, et al: Artefact of MRA following aneurysm clipping: An in vitro study and prospective comparison with conventional angiography. Neuroradiology 41:680–686, 1999.

104. Grossman RI, Kemp SS, Yu IC, et al: The importance of oxygenation in the appearance of acute subarachnoid hemorrhage on high-field magnetic resonance imaging. Acta Radiol (Suppl) 369:56–58, 1986.

105. Guo W-Y, Lindquist M, Lindquist C, et al: Sterotaxic angiography in gamma knife radiosurgery of intracranial arteriovenous malformations. AJNR Am J Neuroradiol 13:1107–1114, 1992.

106. Haase A, Frahm J, Matthaei D, et al: Rapid NMR imaging using low flip-angle pulses. J Magnet Reson 67:258–266, 1986.

107. Hackney DB, Lesnick JE, Zimmerman RA, et al: MR identification of bleeding site in subarachnoid hemorrhage with multiple intracranial aneurysms. J Comput Assist Tomogr 10:878–880, 1986.

108. Hahn FJ, Chg E, McComb R, Leibrock L: Peripheral signal void ring in giant vertebral aneurysm: MR and pathology findings. J Comp Asst Tomogr 10:1036–1038, 1986.

109. Halback VV, Barkovich AJ: Anomalies of cerebral vasculature. In Barkovich AJ (ed): Pediatric Neuroimaging, 2nd ed. New York, Raven Press, 1995.

110. Halback VV, Higashida RT, Heishima GB, et al: Transvenous embolization of dural fistulas involving the transverse and sigmoid sinuses. AJNR Am J Neuroradiol 10:385–392, 1989.

111. Hargraves RW, Spetzler RF: Takayasu's arteritis: Case report. BNI Q 7:20–23, 1991.

112. Hasuo K, Tamura S, Kudo S, et al: Moyamoya disease: The use of digital subtraction angiography in its diagnosis. Radiology 157:107–111, 1985.

113. Healton EB: Fibromuscular dysplasia. In Barnett HJM (ed): Stroke, vol 2. New York, Churchill Livingstone, 1986, pp 831–843.

114. Heiserman JE, Drayer BP, Fram EK, Keller PJ: MR angiography of cervical fibromuscular dysplasia. AJNR Am J Neuroradiol 13:1454–1457, 1992.

115. Herneshiemi J, Tapaninaho A, Vapalahti M, et al: Saccular aneurysms of the distal anterior cerebral artery and its branches. Neurosurgery 31:994–999, 1992.

116. Heros RC, Korosue K: Arteriovenous malformations of the brain. Curr Opin Neurol Neurosurg 3:63–67, 1990.

117. Hoffmann KR, Hosten N, Liebig T, et al: Giant aneurysm of the vertebral artery in neurofibromatosis type 1: Report of a case and review of the literature. Neuroradiology 40: 245–248, 1998.

118. Holtas S, Olsson M, Romner B, et al: Comparison of MR imaging and CT in patients with intracranial aneurysm clips. AJNR Am J Neuroradiol 9:891–897, 1988.

119. Hormann E, Becker T, Romberg-Hahnloser R, et al: Cranial MRI and CT in patients with left atrial myzoma. Neuroradiol 34:57–61, 1992.

120. Houser O, Baker HJ, Rhoton AJ, et al: Intracranial dural arteriovenous malformations. Radiology 163:55–64, 1972.

121. Houser O, Campbell J, Campbell R, Sundt T: Arteriovenous malformation affecting the transverse dural venous sinus: An acquired lesion. Mayo Clin Proc 54:651–661, 1979.

122. Howard RS, Maldjian J, Alsop D, et al: Functional MRI in the assessment of cerebral gliomas and AVMs prior to surgical or endovascular therapy (abstract). SMR Annual Meeting Book of Abstracts, San Francisco, 1994.

123. Hu X, Alperin N, Levin DN, et al: Visualization of MR angiographic data with segmentation and volume-rendering techniques. J Magn Reson Imaging 1:539–546, 1991.

124. Huk WJ: Vascular malformations. In Huk WJ, Gademann G, Friedmann G (eds): MRI of the Central Nervous System. Berlin, Springer-Verlag, 1990, pp 325–346.

124a. Hunt WE, Hess RM: Surgical risks as related to time of intervention in the repair of intracranial aneurysms. J Neurosurg 28:14–20, 1968.

125. Hurst RW, Kagetser NJ, Berenstein A: Angiographic findings in two cases of aneurysmal malformation of vein of Galen prior to spontaneous thrombosis: Therapeutic implications. AJNR Am J Neuroradiol 13:1446–1450, 1992.

126. Huston J III, Ehman RL: Comparison of time-of-flight and phase-contrast MR neuroangiographic techniques. Radio-Graphics 13:5–19, 1993.

127. Huston J III, Rufenacht DA, Ehman RL, Wiebers DO: Intracranial aneurysms and vascular malformations: Comparison of time-of-flight and phase-contrast MR angiography. Radiology 181:721–730, 1991.

128. Huston J III, Nichols DA, Leutrer PH, et al: Blinded prospective evaluation of sensitivity of MR angiography to known intracranial aneurysms: Importance of aneurysm size. AJNR Am J Neuroradiol 15:1607–1614, 1994.

129. Iizuka Y, Lasjaunias P, Garcia-Monaco R, et al: Multiple cerebral arteriovenous malformations in children (15 patients). Neuroradiology 33:538, 1991.

130. Ikawa F, Sumida M, Uozumi T, et al: Comparison of three-dimensional phase-contrast magnetic resonance angiography with three-dimensional time-of-flight magnetic resonance angiography in cerebral aneurysms. Surg Neurol 42:287–292, 1994.

131. Iwata K, Misu N, Terada K, et al: Screening for unruptured asymptomatic intracranial aneurysms in patients undergoing coronary angiography. J Neurosurg 75:52–55, 1991.

132. Jacobs IG, Roszler MH, Kelly JK, et al: Cocaine abuse: Neurovascular complications. Radiology 170:223–227, 1989.

133. Jacobs J: Angiography in intracranial hemorrhage. Neuroimaging Clin North Am 2:89–106, 1992.

134. Jafar JJ, Davis AJ, Berenstein A, et al: The effect of embolization with N-butyl cyanoacrylate prior to surgical resection of cerebral arteriovenous malformations. J Neurosurg 78:60–69, 1993.

135. Jane JA, Kassell NF, Torner JC, Winn HR: The natural history of aneurysms and arteriovenous malformations. J Neurosurg 62:321–323, 1985.

136. Jenkins A, Hadley DM, Teasdale GM, et al: Magnetic resonance imaging of acute subarachnoid hemorrhage. J Neurosurg 68:731–736, 1988.

137. Jinkins JR, Dadsetan MR, Sener RN, et al: Value of acute-phase angiography in the detection of vascular injuries caused by gunshot wounds to the head: Analysis of 12 cases. AJNR Am J Neuroradiol 169:365–368,1992.

138. Johnston IH, Whittle IR, Besser M, et al: Vein of Galen malformation: Diagnosis and management. Neurosurgery 20:747–758, 1987.

139. Juvela S, Porras M, Heiskanen O: Natural history of unruptured intracranial aneurysms: A long-term follow-up study. J Neurosurg 79:174–182, 1993.

140. Kaplan HA, et al: Vascular malformations of the brain: An anatomical study. J Neurosurg 27:630, 1961.

141. Kassel NJ, Torner JC: Size of intracranial aneurysms. Neurosurgery 12:291–297, 1983.

142. Katayama Y, Tsubokawa T, Miyasaki S, et al: Magnetic resonance imaging of cavernous sinus cavernous hemangioma. Neuroradiology 33:118–122, 1991.

143. Kaufman SL, White RI Jr, Harrington DP, et al: Protean manifestations of mycotic aneurysms. Am J Roentgenol 131:1019–1025, 1978.

144. Kim J, Kucharczyk W, Henkelman R: Cavernous hemangiomas: Dipolar susceptibility artifacts at MR imaging. Radiology 187:735–741, 1993.

145. Kjellberg RN, Hanamura T, Davis KR, et al: Bragg-peak proton beam therapy for arteriovenous malformations of the brain. N Engl J Med 309:269–274, 1983.

146. Klucznik R, Carrier D, Pyka R, Haid R: Placement of a ferromagnetic intracerebral aneurysm clip in a magnetic field with a fatal outcome. Radiology 187:612–614, 1993.

147. Komiyama M, Fu Y, Yagura H, et al: MR imaging of dural AV fistulas at the cavernous sinus. J Comp Asst Tomogr 14:397–401, 1990.

148. Kondziolka D, Nixon BJ, Lasjaunias P, et al: Cerebral arteriovenous malformations with associated arterial aneurysms: Hemodynamic and therapeutic considerations. Can J Neurol Sci 15:130–134, 1988.

149. Korogi, Y, Takahashi M, Mabuchi N, et al: Intracranial aneurysms: Diagnostic accuracy of the three dimensional, Fourter transform, time-of-flight MR angiography. Radiology 193: 181–186, 1994.

150. Krief O, Sichez JP, Chedid G, et al: Extraaxial cavernous hemangioma with hemorrhage. AJNR Am J Neuroradiol 12:988–990, 1990.

151. Krysl J, de Tilly LN, Armstrong D: Pseudoaneurysm of the internal carotid artery: Comparison of deep neck space infection. AJNR Am J Neuroradiol 14:696–698, 1993.

152. Kucharczyk W, Lemme-Pleghos L, Uske A, et al: Intracranial vascular malformations: MR and CT imaging. Radiology 156:383–389, 1985.

153. Kumar AJ, Vinuela F, Fox AJ, Rosenbaum AE: Unruptured intracranial arteriovenous malformations do cause mass effect. AJNR Am J Neuroradiol 6:29–32, 1985.

154. Larson TC III, Kelly WM, Ehman RL, Wehrili FW: Spatial misregistration of vascular flow during MR imaging of the CNS: Cause and clinical significance. AJNR Am J Neuroradiol 11:1041–1048, 1990.

155. Lasjaunias P, Berenstein A: Functional Vascular Anatomy of Brain, Spinal Cord, and Spine. New York, Springer-Verlag, 1990.

156. Lasjaunias P, Burrows P, Planet C: Developmental venous anomalies (DVA): The so-called venous angioma. Neurosurg Rev 9:233–244, 1986.

157. Lasjaunias P, Chue M, TerBrugge K: Neurological manifestations of intracranial dural arteriovenous malformations. J Neurosurg 64:724–730, 1986.

158. Lasjaunias P, Garcia-Monaco R, Rodesch G, TerBrugge K: Deep venous drainage in great cerebral vein (vein of Galen) absence and malformations. Neuroradiology 33:234–238, 1991.

159. Lasjaunias P, TerBrugge K, Ibor LL, et al: The role of dural anomalies in vein of Galen aneurysms: Report of six cases and review of the literature. AJNR Am J Neuroradiol 8:185–192, 1987.

160. Latchaw RE, Truwit CL, Heros RC: Venous angioma, cavernous angioma, and hemorrhage. AJNR Am J Neuroradiol 15:1255–1257, 1994.

161. Lawrence-Friedl D, Bauer KM: Bilateral cortical blindness: An unusual presentation of bacterial endocarditis. Ann Emerg Med 21:1502–1504, 1992.

162. Lazar EB, Russell EJ, Cohen BA, et al: Contrast-enhanced MR of cerebral arteritis: Intravascular enhancement related to flow stasis within areas of focal arterial ectasia. AJNR Am J Neuroradiol 13:271–276, 1992.

163. Lazinski D, Willinsky RA, TerBrugge K, Montanera W: Dissecting aneurysms of the posterior cerebral artery: Angioarchitecture and a review of the literature. Neuroradiology 42:128–133, 2000.

164. Leavine SR, Brust JCM, Futrell N, et al: A comparative study of the cerebrovascular complication of cocaine: Alkaloidal versus hydrochloride—a review. Neuroradiology 41:1173–1177, 1991.

165. Lee KS, Liu SS, Spetzler RF, Rekate HL: Intracranial mycotic aneurysms in an infant: Report of a case. Neurosurgery 26:129–133, 1990.

166. Lewin JS, Laub G: Intracranial MR angiography: Direct comparison of three time-of-flight techniques. AJNR Am J Neuroradiol 12:1133–1139, 1991.

167. Licata C, Pasqualin A, Freschini A, et al: Management of associated primary cerebral neoplasms and vascular malformations. 1: Intracranial aneurysms. Acta Neurochir (Wien) 82:28–38, 1986.

168. Lichtenfeld PJ, Rubin DB, Feldman RS: Subarachnoid hemorrhage precipitated by cocaine snorting. Arch Neurol 41:223–224, 1984.

169. Lin W, Haacke EM, Smith AS, Clampitt ME: Gadolinium-tracking: Preliminary results in the intracranial circulation. Magn Reson Imaging 2:277–284, 1992.

170. Lindquist C, Guo W-Y, Karlsson B, Steiner L: Radiosurgery for venous angiomas. J Neurosurg 78:531–536, 1993.

171. Linsky ME, Sekhar LN: Cavernous sinus hemangioma: A series, a review, and an hypothesis. Neurosurgery 3:101–108, 1992.

172. Luessenhop A, Gennarelli T: Anatomical grading of supratentorial arteriovenous malformations for determining operability. Neurosurgery 1:30–35, 1977.

173. Luessenhop A, Rosa L: Cerebral arteriovenous malformations. J Neurosurgery 60:14–22, 1984.

174. Lunsford L, Flickinger J, Coffey R: Stereotactic gamma knife radiosurgery: Initial North American experience in 207 patients. Arch Neurol 7:169–175, 1990.

175. Lunsford L, Kondziolka D, Bissonette D, et al: Stereotactic radiosurgery of brain vascular malformations. Neurosurg Clin North Am 3:79–98, 1992.

176. Lylyk P, March AD, Kohan GA, Vinuela F: Alternative therapeutic approaches in intravascular embolization of vein of Galen vascular malformations. In Vinvela F, Halback VV, Dion JE (eds): Endovascular Therapy of the Central Nervous System. New York, Raven Press, 1992.

177. Mabuchi S, Kamiyama H, Abe H: Distal aneurysms of the superior cerebellar artery and posterior inferior cerebellar artery feeding an associated arteriovenous malformation: Case report. Neurosurgery 30:284–287, 1992.

178. Maldjian J, Howard R, Alsop DA, et al: Functional MRI in AVMs prior to surgical or endovascular therapy (abstract). In Book of Abstracts, Annual Meeting of the Radiological Society of North America, 1994.

179. Malek AM, Halbach VV, Dowd CF, Higashida RT: Diagnosis and treatment of dural arteriovenous fistulas. Neuroimaging Clin North Am 8:445–468, 1998.

180. Malik GM, Morgan JK, Boulos RS, Ausman JI: Venous angiomas: An underestimated cause of intracranial hemorrhage. Surg Neurol 30:350–358, 1988.

181. Mann CI, Dietrick RB, Schrader MT, et al: Posttraumatic carotid artery dissection in children: Evaluation with MR imaging. AJR Am J Roentgenol 160:134–136, 1993.

182. Marks MP, DeLapaz RL, Fabrikant JI, et al: Intracranial vascular malformations: Imaging of charged-particle radiosurgery. Part I: Results of therapy. Radiology 168:447–455, 1988.

183. Marks MP, DeLapaz RL, Fabrikant JI, et al: Intracranial vascular malformations: Imaging of charged-particle radiosurgery. Part II: Complications. Radiology 168:457–462, 1988.

184. Marks MP, Lane B, Steinberg G, Chang P: Vascular characteristics of intracerebral arteriovenous malformations in patients with clinical steal. AJNR Am J Neuroradiol 12:489–496, 1991.

185. Marks MP, Lane B, Steinberg GK, Chang PJ: Hemorrhage in intracerebral arteriovenous malformations: Angiographic determinants. Radiology 176:807–813, 1990.

186. Marks MP, Lane B, Steinberg GK, Snipes GJ: Intracranial aneurysms in cerebral arteriovenous malformations: Evaluation and endovascular treatment. Radiology 183:355–360, 1992.

187. Marks MP, Lane B, Steinberg GK, Chang PJ: Hemorrhage in intracerebral aneurysms and arteriovenous malformations: Frequency of intracranial hemorrhage and relationship of lesions. J Neurosurg 73:859–863, 1990.

188. Marks MP, Pelc MJ, Ross MR, Enzmann DR: Determination of cerebral blood flow with a phase-contrast cine MR imaging technique: Evaluation of normal subjects and patients with arteriovenous malformation. Radiology 182:467–476, 1992.

189. Martelli A, Scotti G, Harwood-Nash DC, et al: Aneurysm of the vein of Galen in children: CT and angiographic correlations. Neuroradiology 20:123–133, 1980.

190. Martin N, King W, Wilson C, et al: Management of dural arteriovenous malformations of the anterior cranial fossa. J Neurosurg 72:692–697, 1990.

191. Masaryk TJ, Ross JS, Modic MT, et al: Carotid bifurcation: MR imaging: Work in progress. Radiology 166:461–466, 1988.

192. McCormick P, Michelson W. Management of cavernous and venous malformations. In Barrow D (ed): Intracranial Vascular Malformations. Park Ridge, Ill, AANS, 1990, pp 197–217.

193. McCormick PW, McCormick J, Zimmerman R, et al: The pathophysiology of acute subarachnoid hemorrhage. BNI Q 7:18–26, 1991.

194. McCormick WF: The pathology of vascular ("arteriovenous") malformations. J Neurosurg 24:807–816, 1966.

195. McCormick WF, Acosta-Rua GJ: The size of intracranial saccular aneurysms: An autopsy study. J Neurosurg 33:422–427, 1970.

196. Mendalow A, Erfurth A, Grossary K, et al: Do cerebral arteriovenous malformations increase in size? J Neurol Neurosurg Psychiatry 50:980–987, 1987.

197. Meyer FB, Huston J III, Reiderer SS: Pulsatile increases in aneurysm size determined by cine phase-contrast MR angiography. Neurosurgery 78:879–883, 1993.

198. Miyachi S, Negoro M, Harda T, Sugita K: Contribution of meningeal arteries to cerebral arteriovenous malformations. Neuroradiology 35:205–209, 1993.

199. Miyasaka K, Wolpert SM, Prager RJ: The association of cerebral aneurysms, infundibula and intracranial arteriovenous malformations. Stroke 13:196–203, 1982.

200. Miyasaka Y, Yada K, Ohwada T, et al: Pathophysiologic assessment of stagnating arteries after removal of arteriovenous malformations. AJNR Am J Neuroradiol 14:15–18, 1993.

200a. Mizutani T, Aruga T, Kirino T, et al: Recurrent subarachnoid hemorrhage from untreated ruptured vertebrobasilar dissecting aneurysms. J Neurosurg 36:905–913, 1995.

201. Mizutani T, Tanaka H, Aruza T: Multiple arteriovenous malforma-

tions located in the cerebellum, posterior fossa, spinal cord, dura, and scalp with associated port wine stain and supratentorial venous anomaly. Neurosurgery 31:137–141, 1992.

202. Mohr J, Kistler J, Zambranski J, et al: Intracranial aneurysms. In Barnett H, Mohr J, Stein B, Yatsu F (eds): Stroke: Pathophysiology, Diagnosis, and Management. New York, Churchill Livingstone, 1986, pp 643–677.

203. Mokri B: Traumatic and spontaneous extracranial internal carotid artery dissection. J Neurol 237:356–361, 1990.

204. Monaco RG, Alvarez H, Goulao A, et al: Posterior fossa arteriovenous malformations: Angioarchitecture in relation to their hemorrhagic episodes. Neuroradiology 31:471–475, 1990.

205. Nakstad P, Nornes H, Hauge HN: Traumatic aneurysms of the pericallosal arteries. Neuroradiology 28:335–338, 1986.

206. Nalls G, Disher A, Darybagi J, et al: Subcortical cerebral hemorrhages associated with cocaine abuse: CT and MR findings. J Comp Asst Tomor 13:1–5, 1989.

207. Napel S, Marks MP, Rubin GP, et al: CT angiography with spiral CT and maximum intensity projection. Radiology 185:607–610, 1992.

208. Nayler GL, Firmin GL, Longmore DB: Blood flow imaging by cine magnetic resonance. J Comput Assist Tomogr 10:715, 1986.

209. Nehls DG, Flom RA, Carter LP, Spetzler RF: Multiple intracranial aneurysms: Determining the site of rupture. J Neurosurg 63:342–348, 1985.

210. Newell DW, LeRoux PD, Dacey RG Jr, et al: CT infusion scanning for the detection of cerebral aneurysms. J Neurosurg 71:175–179, 1989.

211. Nishijima M, Takaku A, Endo S, et al: Etiological evaluation of dural arteriovenous malformations of the lateral and sigmoid sinuses based on histopathological examinations. J Neurosurg 76:600–606, 1992.

212. Nov AA, Cromwell LD: Traumatic pericallosal artery aneurysm. J Neuroradiol 11:3–8, 1984.

213. Nussel F, Wegmuller H, Huber P: Comparison of magnetic resonance angiography, magnetic resonance imaging, and conventional angiography in cerebral arteriovenous malformations. Neuroradiology 33:56–61, 1991.

214. Obuchowski NA, Modic MT, Magdinec M: Current implications for the efficacy of noninvasive screening for occult intracranial aneurysms in patients with a family history of aneurysms. J Neurosurg 83:42–49, 1995.

215. O'Neill M, Hope T, Thompson G: Giant intracranial aneurysms: Diagnosis with special reference to computerized tomography. Clin Radiol 31:27–39, 1980.

216. Ogawa S, Lee TM, Kay AR, Tank DW: Brain magnetic resonance imaging with contrast dependent on blood oxygenation. Proc Natl Acad Sci U S A 87:9868–9872, 1990.

217. Ogawa T, Inugami A, Shimosegawa E, et al: Subarachnoid hemorrhage: Evaluation with MR imaging. Radiology 186:345, 1993.

218. Ohman J, Heiskanen O: Timing of operation for ruptured supratentorial aneurysms: A prospective randomized study. J Neurosurg 70:55–60, 1989.

219. Okazaki H, Scheithauer B: Atlas of Neuropathology. New York, Gower Medical, 1988.

220. Okazaki H: Fundamentals of Neuropathology. New York, Igaku-Shoin, 1983.

221. Okazaki H: Malformative vascular lesions. In Fundamentals of Neuropathology, 2nd ed. New York, Igaku-Schoin, 1989, pp 70–74.

222. Okazaki H: Cerebrovascular disease. In Fundamentals of Neuropathology, 2nd ed. New York, Igaku-Shoin, 1989, pp 27–94.

223. Ondra S, Troupp H, George E, Schwab K: The natural history of symptomatic arteriovenous malformations of the brain. J Neurosurg 73:387–391, 1990.

224. Osborn AG: Intracranial aneurysms. In Handbook of Neuroradiology. St. Louis, Mosby-Year Book, 1991, pp 79–84.

225. Osborn AG: Intracranial vascular malformations. In Introduction to Cerebral Angiography. St. Louis, Mosby-Year Book, 1991, pp 85–91.

226. Osborn AG: Introduction to Cerebral Angiography. Harper and Row, 1980, pp 49–86.

227. Osborn A: Intracranial aneurysms. In Diagnostic Neuroradiology, St. Louis, Mosby-Year Book, 1994.

228. Osborn A: Intracranial vascular malformations. In Diagnostic Neuroradiology. St. Louis, Mosby-Year Book, 1994.

229. Osterton B, Solymosi L: Magnetic resonance angiography of cerebral developmental anomalies: Its role in differential diagnosis. Neuroradiology 35:97–104, 1993.

230. Oyesiku N, Colohan ART, Barow DL, Reisner A: Cocaine-induced aneurysmal rupture: An emergent negative factor in the natural history of intracranial aneurysms? Neurosurgery 32:518–526, 1993.

231. Parent AD, Harkey HL, Touchstone DA, et al: Lateral cervical spine dislocation and vertebral artery injury. Neurosurgery 31:501–509, 1992.

232. Parker DL, Yuan C, Blatter DD: MR angiography by multiple thin slab 3D acquisition. Magn Reson Med 17:434–451, 1991.

233. Pellitieri L, Carlsson C, Grevsten S, et al: Surgical versus conservative treatment of intracranial arteriovenous malformations: A study in surgical decision making. Acta Neurochir (Wien) 29(Suppl):1–86, 1979.

234. Perata HJ, Tomsick TA, Tew JM Jr: Feeding artery pedicle aneurysms: Association with parenchymal hemorrhage and arteriovenous malformation in the brain. J Neurosurg 80:631–634, 1994.

235. Perret G, Nishioka H: Arteriovenous malformations: An analysis of 545 cases for craniocerebral arteriovenous malformations and fistulae reported to the cooperative study. J Neurosurg 25:467–490, 1966.

236. Picard L, Roy D, Bracard S, et al: Aneurysm associated with a fenestrated basilar artery: Report of two cases treated by endovascular detachable balloon embolization. AJNR Am J Neuroradiol 14:591–594, 1993.

237. Piepgras DG, Sundt TM Jr, Ragoowansi AT, Stevens L: Seizure outcome in patients with surgically treated cerebral arteriovenous malformations. J Neurosurg 78:5–11, 1993.

238. Pierot L, Chiras J, Meder J-F, et al: Dural arteriovenous fistulas of the posterior fossa draining into subarachnoid veins. AJNR Am J Neuroradiol 13:315–323, 1992.

239. Prayer L, Wimberger D, Kramer J, et al: MRI—a noninvasive tool for evaluating therapeutic embolization of cerebral arteriovenous malformations. Eur Radiol 1:51–57, 1991.

240. Raaymakers TW, Buys PC, Verbeeten B Jr, et al: MR angiography as a screening tool for intracranial aneurysms: Feasibility, test characteristics and interobserver agreement. AJR Am J Roentgenol 173:1469–1475, 1999.

241. Rao KCVG, Chiantella NM, Arora S, Gellad F: Intracranial venous aneurysms: Vein of Galen and other similar vascular anomalies. J Comp Tomogr 7:345–350, 1983.

242. Raps EC, Rogers JD, Galeta SL, et al: The clinical spectrum of unruptured intracranial aneurysms. Arch Neurol 50:265–268, 1993.

243. Raybaud CA, Strother CM, Hald JK: Aneurysms of the vein of Galen: Embryonic considerations and anatomical features relating to the pathogenesis of the malformations. Neuroradiology 31:109–128, 1989.

244. Rhoton A: Anatomy of saccular aneurysms. Surg Neurol 14:59–66, 1980.

245. Rigamonti D, Hadley MN, Drayer BP, et al: Cerebral cavernous malformations: Incidence and familial occurrence. N Engl J Med 319:343–347, 1988.

246. Rigamonti D, Johnson PC, Spetzler RF, et al: Cavernous malformations and capillary telangiectasia: A spectrum within a single pathological entity. Neurosurgery 28:60–64, 1991.

247. Rigamonti D, Spetzler D: The association of venous and cavernous malformations: Report of form cases and discussions of the pathophysiological, diagnostic and therapeutic implications. Acta Neurochir (Wien) 92:100–105, 1988.

248. Rinkel GJE, Wijdicks EFM, Vermeulen M, et al: Nonaneurysmal perimesencephalic subarachnoid hemorrhage: CT and MR patterns that differ from aneurysmal rupture. AJNR Am J Neuroradiol 12:829–834, 1991.

249. Rinkel GJE, Wijdicks EFM, Hasan D, et al: Outcome in patients with subarachnoid haemorrhage and negative angiography according to pattern of haemorrhage on computed tomography. Lancet 338:964–968, 1991.

250. Robinson J, Awad I, Little J: Natural history of the cavernous angioma. J Neurosurg 75:709–714, 1991.

251. Robinson JR Jr, Awad IA, Magdinec M, Paranandi L: Factors predisposing to clinical disability in patients with cavernous malformations of the brain. Neurosurgery 32:730–736, 1993.

252. Rodesch G, Lasjaunias P: Physiopathology and semeiology of dural arteriovenous shunts. Riv di Neuroradiol 5:11–21, 1992.

253. Ronleainem A, Puranen MI, Hernesniemi JA, et al: Intracranial aneurysms: MR angiographic screening in 400 asymptomatic individuals with increased familial risk. Radiology 195: 35–40, 1995.

254. Rosenorn J, Eskesen V, Madsen F, Schmidt K: Importance of cerebral pan-angiography for detection of multiple aneurysms in patients with aneurysmal subarachnoid haemorrhage. Acta Neurol Scand 87: 215–218, 1993.

255. Rosenorn J, Eskesen V, Schmidt K: Unruptured intracranial aneurysms: An assessment of the annual risk of rupture based on epidemiological and clinical data. Br J Neurosurg 2:369–378, 1988.

256. Ross JS, Masaryk TJ, Modic MT, et al: Intracranial aneurysms: Evaluation by MR angiography. AJNR Am J Neuroradiol 11:449–456, 1990.

257. Ruggieri PM: Presented at the 78th Annual Scientific Assembly of the Radiological Society of North America, Chicago, Nov 29–Dec 4, 1992.

258. Russell DS, Rubinstein LJ: Pathology of Tumors of the Nervous System, 5th ed. Baltimore, Williams & Wilkins, 1989.

259. Sadato N, Numaguchi T, Rigamonti D, et al: Bleeding patterns in ruptured posterior fossa aneurysms: a CT study. J Comp Asst Tomogr 15:612–617, 1991.

260. Sadler LR, Tarr RW, Jungreis CA, Sekhar L: Sinus pericranii: CT and MR findings. J Comp Asst Tomogr 14:124–127, 1990.

261. Sahs AL, Perret GE, Locksley HB, et al: Intracranial Aneurysms and Subarachnoid Hemorrhage: A Cooperative Study. Philadelphia, JB Lippincott, 1969.

262. Sakaki T, Tominaga M, Miyamoto K, et al: Clinical studies of de novo aneurysms. Neurosurgery 32:512–517, 1993.

263. Salcman M, Scholtz H, Numaguchi Y: Multiple intracerebral arteriovenous malformations: Report of three cases and review of the literature. Surg Neurol 38:121–128, 1992.

264. Sanders WP, Sorek PA, Mehta BA: Fenestration of intracranial arteries with special attention to associated aneurysms and other anomalies. AJNR Am J Neuroradiol 14:675–680, 1993.

265. San-Galli F, Leman C, Kein P, et al: Cerebral arterial fenestrations associated with intracranial saccular aneurysms. Neurosurgery 30: 279–283, 1992.

266. Sarwar M, McCormick W: Intracerebral venous angioma: Case report and review. Arch Neurol 35:323–325, 1978.

267. Saveland H, Hillman J, Brandt L, et al: Overall outcome in aneurysmal subarachnoid hemorrhage. J Neurosurg 76:729–734, 1992.

268. Savino PJ, Grossman RI, Schatz NJ, et al: High-field magnetic resonance imaging in the diagnosis of cavernous sinus thrombosis. Arch Neurol 43:1081–1082, 1986.

269. Savoiardo M, Strada L, Passerini A: Intracranial cavernous hemangioma: Neuroradiologic review of 36 operated cases. AJNR Am J Neuroradiol 4:945–950, 1983.

270. Scazzeri F, Prosetti D, Nenci R, et al: Angioma venoso. Riv di Neuroradiol 4:201–208, 1991.

271. Schievink WI, Limburg M, Dreissen J Jr, et al: Screening for unruptured familiar aneurysms: Subarachnoid hemorrhage 2 years after angiography negative for aneurysms. Neurosurg 29:434–438, 1991.

272. Schievink WI, Mokri B, Piepgras DG: Angiographic frequency of saccular intracranial aneurysms in patients with spontaneous cervical arterial dissection. J Neurosurg 76:62–66, 1992.

273. Schievink WI, Piepgras DG, Wirth FP: Rupture of previously documented small asymptomatic saccular intracranial aneurysms. J Neurosurg 76:1019–1024. 1992.

274. Schmid UD, Steiger HJ, Huber P: Accuracy of high resolution computed tomography in direct diagnosis of cerebral aneurysms. Neuroradiology 29:152–159, 1987.

275. Schuierer G, Huk WJ, Laub G: Magnetic resonance angiography of intracranial aneurysms. Neuroradiology 35:50–54, 1992.

276. Scott RM, Barnes P, Kupsky W, Adelman LS: Cavernous angiomas of the central nervous system in children. J Neurosurg 76:38–46, 1992.

277. Scotti G, Ethier R, Melancon D, et al: Computed tomography in the evaluation of intracranial aneurysms and subarachnoid hemorrhage. Radiology 123:85–90, 1977.

278. Seidenwurm D, Berenstein A, Hyman A, Kowalsla H: Vein of Galen malformation: Correlation of clinical presentation, arteriography, and MR imaging. AJNR Am J Neuroradiol 12:347–345, 1991.

279. Seidenwurm D, Berenstein A: Vein of Galen malformation: Clinical relevance of angiographic classification, and utility of MRI in treatment planning. Neuroradiology 33(Suppl): 153–155, 1991.

280. Senegor M: Traumatic pericallosal aneurysm in a patient with no major trauma. J Neurosurg 75:475–477, 1991.

281. Sharma A, Tyagi G, Sahai A, Baijal SS: Traumatic aneurysm of superficial temporal artery: CT demonstration. Neuroradiol 33:510–512, 1991.

282. Sherry RG, Walker ML, Olds MV: Sinus pericranii and venous angioma in the blue-rubber bleb nevus syndrome. AJNR Am J Neuroradiol 5:832–834, 1984.

283. Shi YQ, Chen XC: A proposed scheme for grading intracranial arteriovenous malformations. J Neurosurg 65:484–489, 1986.

284. Sigal R, Krief O, Houtteville JP, et al: Occult cerebrovascular malformations: Follow-up with MR imaging. Radiology 176:815–819, 1990.

285. Simard JM, Garcia-Bengochea F, Ballinger WEJ, et al: Cavernous angioma: A review of 126 collected and 12 new clinical cases. Neurosurgery 18:162–172, 1986.

286. Sisti MD, Kader A, Stein BM: Microsurgery for 67 intracranial arteriovenous malformations less than 3 cm in diameter. J Neurosurg 79:653–660, 1993.

287. Smith HJ, Strother CM, Kikuchi Y, et al: MR imaging in the management of supratentorial intracranial AVMs. AJNR Am J Neuroradiol 9:225–235, 1988.

288. Solomon RA, Fink ME, Pile-Spellman J: Surgical management of unruptured intracranial aneurysms. J Neurosurg 80:440–446, 1994.

289. Sorek PA, Silbergleit R: Multiple asymptomatic cervical cephalic aneurysms. AJNR Am J Neuroradiol 14:31–33, 1993.

290. Spetzler RF, Hargraves RW, McCormick PW, et al: Relationship of perfusion pressure and size to risk of hemorrhage from arteriovenous malformation. J Neurosurg 76:918–923, 1992.

291. Spetzler RF, Martin NA: A proposed scheme for grading intracranial arteriovenous malformations. J Neurosurg 65:476–483, 1986.

292. Spetzler RF, Wilson CB, Weinstein P, et al: Normal perfusion pressure breakthrough theory. Clin Neurosurg 25:651–672, 1978.

293. Stehbens WE: Etiology of intracranial berry aneurysms. J Neurosurg 70:823–831, 1989.

294. Steiner L, Lindquist C, Adler JR, et al: Clinical outcome of radiosurgery for cerebral arteriovenous malformations. J Neurosurg 77:1–8, 1992.

295. Steiner L: Radiosurgery in cerebral arteriovenous malformations. In Flamm E (ed): Cerebrovascular Surgery. New York, Springer-Verlag, 1986.

296. Steinmeier R, Schramm J, Muller H, Fahlbush R: Evaluation of prognostic factors in cerebral arteriovenous malformations. Neurosurgery 24:193–200, 1989.

297. Stone JL, Crowell RM, Gandhi YN, Jafar JJ: Multiple intracranial aneurysms: Magnetic resonance imaging for determination of the site of rupture. Neurosurgery 23:97–100, 1988.

298. Strother CM, Graves VB, Rappe A: Aneurysm hemodynamics: An experimental study. AJNR Am J Neuroradiol 13: 1089–1095, 1992.

299. Sugita K, Kobayashi S, Takemae T, et al: Giant aneurysm of the vertebral artery. J Neurosurg 68:960–966, 1988.

300. Suzuki J, Kodama N: Moyamoya disease: A review. Stroke 14: 104–109, 1983.

301. Suzuki S, Kayama T, Sakurai Y, et al: Subarachnoid hemorrhage of unknown origin. Neurosurg 21:310–313, 1987.

302. Symon L: Surgical experiences with giant intracranial aneurysms. Acta Neurochir (Wien) 118:53–58, 1992.

303. Szabo M, Crosby G, Sundaram P, et al: Hypertension does not cause spontaneous hemorrhage of intracranial arteriovenous malformations. Anesthesiology 70:761–763, 1989.

304. Takahashi S, Tomura N, Watarai J, Mizoi K, Manabe H: Dural arteriovenous fistula of the cavernous sinus with venous congestion of the brain stem: report of two cases, AJNR Am J Neuroradiol 20: 886–888, 1999.

305. Takamiya Y, Takayama H, Kobayashi K, et al: Familial occurrence of multiple vascular malformations of the brain. Neurol Med Chir (Tokyo) 24:271–277, 1984.

306. Taniguchi RM, Goree JA, Odom GL: Spontaneous carotid cavernous shunts presenting diagnostic problems. J Neurosurg 35:384–391, 1971.

307. Terada T, Higashida R, Halbach VV, et al: Development of acquired arteriovenous fistulas in rats due to venous hypertension. J Neurosurg 80:884–889, 1994.

308. Tien RD, Wilkins RH: MRA delineation of the vertebrovascular system in patients with hemifacial spasm and trigeminal neuralgia. AJNR Am J Neuroradiol 14:34–36, 1993.

309. Toffol GJ, Gruener G, Naheedy MH: Early-filling cerebral veins. J Am Osteopath Assoc 88:1007–1009, 1988.

310. Tomlinson FH, Howser OW, Scheithauer BW, et al: Cavernous angioma: Angiographically occult vascular malformations: A correlative MR imaging and histological study. J Neurosurg 78:328, 1993.

311. Toro VE, Fravel JF, Weidman TA: Posttraumatic pseudoaneurysm of the posterior meningeal artery associated with intraventricular hemorrhage. AJNR Am J Neuroradiol 14:264–266, 1993.

312. Truwit CL: Venous angioma of the brain: History, significance and imaging findings. AJR Am J Roentgenol 159:1299–1307, 1992.

313. Tsuruda J, Saloner D, Norman D: Artifacts associated with MR neuroangiography. AJNR Am J Neuroradiol 13:1411–1422, 1992.

314. Uchino A, Imador H, Ohno M: Magnetic resonance imaging of intracranial venous angioma. Clin Imaging 14:309–314, 1990.

315. Uchino A, Kato A, Kuroda S et al: Pontine venous congestion caused by dural carotid-cavernous fistula: Report of two cases. Eur Radiol 7:405–408, 1997.

315a. Unruptured intracranial aneurysms—Risk of rupture and risks of surgical intervention. N Engl J Med 339:1725–1733, 1998.

316. Vajda J: Multiple intracranial aneurysms: A high-risk condition. Acta Neurochir (Wien) 118:59–75, 1992.

317. Valavanis A, Schubiger O, Wichmann W: Classification of brain arteriovenous malformation nidus by magnetic resonance imaging. Acta Radiol Suppl 369:86–89, 1986.

318. Valavanis A, Wellauer J, Yasargil MG: The radiological diagnosis of cerebral venous angioma: Cerebral angiography and computed tomography. Neuroradiology 24:193–199, 1983.

319. Vinuela F, Drake CG, Fox AJ, Pelz DM: Giant intracranial varices secondary to high-flow arteriovenous fistulae. J Neurosurg 66:198–203, 1987.

320. Vinuela F, Fox AJ, Pelz DM, Drake CG: Unusual clinical manifestations of dural arteriovenous malformations. J Neurosurg 64:554–558, 1986.

321. von Schulthess GK, Higgins CB: Blood flow imaging with MR: Spin-phase phenomena. Radiology 157:687–695, 1985.

322. Waltimo O: The relationship of size, density and localization of intracranial arteriovenous malformations to the type of the initial symptom. J Neurol Sci 19:13–19, 1973.

323. Wascher TM, Golfinos J, Zabramski JM, Spetzler RF: Management of unruptured intracranial aneurysms. BNI Q 8:2–7, 1992.

324. Wedeen VJ, Rosen BR, Chesler D, Brady TH: MR velocity imaging by phase display. J Comput Assist Tomogr 9:530–536, 1985.

325. Wehrli FW, Shimakawa A, Gullberg GT, MacFall JR: Time-of-flight MR flow imaging: Selective saturation recovery with gradient refocusing. Radiology 160:781–785, 1986.

326. Weibers DO, Whisnant JP, Sundt T, et al: The significance of unruptured intracranial aneurysms. J Neurosurg 66:23–29, 1987.

327. Weir B: Pituitary tumors and aneurysms: Case report and review of the literature. Neurosurgery 30:585–591, 1992.

328. Weir BKA: Intracranial aneurysms. Curr Opin Neurol Neurosurg 3:55–62, 1990.

329. Wendling LR, Moore JS Jr, Kieffer SA, et al: Intracerebral venous angioma. Radiology 119:141–147, 1976.

330. Westra SJ, Curran JG, Duckwiler GR, et al: Pediatric intracranial vascular malformations: Evaluation of treatment results with color doppler US. Radiology 186:775–783, 1993.

331. Wiebers DO, Torner JC, Meissner I: Impact of unruptured intracranial aneurysms on public health in the United States. Stroke 23:1416–1419, 1992.

332. Wilkins RH, Rengachary SS: Vascular malformations. In Neurosurgery. New York, McGraw-Hill, 1985, pp 1448–1473.

333. Willinsky R, TerBrugge K, Montanera W, et al: Microarteriovenous malformations of the brain: Superselective angiography in diagnosis and treatment. AJNR Am J Neuroradiol 13:325–330, 1992.

334. Willinsky R, TerBrugge K, Montanera W, et al: Venous congestion: an MR finding in dural arteriovenous malformations with cortical venous drainage. AJNR Am J Neuroradiol 15:1501–1507, 1994.

335. Willinsky RA, Fitzgerald M, TerBrugge K, et al: Delayed angiography in the investigation of intracranial intracerebral hematomas caused by small arteriovenous malformations. Neuroradiology 35:307–311, 1993.

336. Willinsky RA, Lasjaunias P, TerBrugge K, Burrows WP: Multiple cerebral arteriovenous malformations (AVMs): Review of our experience from 203 patients with cerebral vascular lesions. Neuroradiology 32:207–210, 1990.

337. Wilms G, Demaerel P, Marchi G, et al: Gadolinium-enhanced MR imaging of cerebral venous angiomas with emphasis on their drainage. J Comput Assist Tomogr 15:199–206, 1991.

338. Wilms G, Goffin J, VanDriessche J, Demaerel P: Posterior fossa venous anomaly and ipsilateral acoustic neuroma: Two cases. Neuroradiology 34:337–339, 1992.

339. Wilms G, Marchal G, Vas Hecke P, et al: Cerebral venous angioma: MR imaging at 1.5 tesla. Neuroradiology 32:81–85, 1990.

340. Wood EH: Angiographic identification of the ruptured lesion in patients with multiple cerebral aneurysms. J Neurosurg 21:182–198, 1964.

341. Woodard E, Barrow D: Clinical presentation of intracranial arteriovenous malformations. In Barrow D (ed): Intracranial Vascular Malformations. Park Ridge, Ill, AANS, 1990, pp 53–61.

342. Yamamoto Y, Asari S, Sunami N et al: Computed angiotomography of unruptured cerebral aneurysms. J Comp Assist Tomogr 10:21–27, 1986.

343. Yapor WY, Gutierrez FA: Cocaine-induced intratumoral hemorrhage: Case report and review of the literature. Neurosurgery 30:288–291, 1992.

344. Yonakawa Y, Handa J, Okuno T: Moyamoya disease: Diagnosis, treatment, and recent achievement. In Barnett HJ, Stein BM, Mohr JP, Yatsu FM (eds): Stroke: Pathophysiology, Diagnosis, and Management, 2nd ed. New York, Churchill Livingstone, 1985, pp 805–831.

345. Young N, Dorsch NW, Kingston RJ: Pitfalls in the use of spiral CT for identification of intracranial aneurysms. Neuroradiology 41:93–99, 1999.

346. Zambramski JM, Wascher TM, Spetzler RF, et al: The natural history of familial cavernous malformations: Results of an ongoing study. J Neurosurg 80:422–432, 1994.

9

Central Nervous System Trauma

John J. Wasenko
Leo Hochhauser

The neuroradiology of trauma has undergone dramatic changes since the advent of computed tomography (CT) and more recently with the establishment of magnetic resonance imaging (MRI) as a diagnostic imaging tool. With the ubiquitous availability of CT in the 1970s, the diagnosis and management of head trauma have changed significantly. Elaborate neurologic testing to appropriately localize a space-occupying lesion such as an intracerebral hemorrhage is no longer of paramount importance, because CT precisely defines the nature and location of the lesion, thus facilitating rapid implementation of treatment. Since the early days of CT scanning, when the contents of the skull were imaged noninvasively for the first time, CT has been the primary modality for evaluating patients with acute head injuries.[1, 52] The ability of CT scans to rapidly demonstrate a surgically correctable lesion, fracture, and subarachnoid hemorrhage (SAH) makes it the modality of choice in the evaluation of acute head injury. CT scans delineate acute hemorrhage from brain edema and allow one to determine whether a hematoma is intracerebral or extracerebral. Modern high-resolution CT scanning, with the direct display of axial anatomy, has replaced angiography as the prevalent method of demonstrating the indirect sign of intracerebral, epidural, or subdural hematomas (SDHs). Although the extent and multiplicity of lesions can be well evaluated by CT scans, MRI, with its greater sensitivity, frequently shows additional areas of contusion and shear injury.

MRI is playing an increasingly important role in the evaluation of head trauma. It has proved more sensitive than CT in the detection of diffuse axonal (shear) injury, nonhemorrhagic contusions, and SDHs and is equivalent to CT in the depiction of hemorrhagic contusions.[37–39, 50, 136] The development of MRI-compatible life-support equipment, such as nonferromagnetic ventilators, allows the severely injured, comatose patient to be evaluated with MRI. The use of adequate sedation minimizes patient discomfort and motion, which may severely degrade image quality. Disadvantages of MRI that preclude its use in the evaluation of acute head injury include long scan time and the inability to detect fractures, SAH, and hyperacute hemorrhage. MRI is the modality of choice in the subacute and chronic stages of head injury because it is more sensitive than CT in the detection of both hemorrhagic and nonhemorrhagic lesions.

Technique
Computed Tomography

Ten-millimeter scans without interslice gap are made at an angle of 15 to 20 degrees to the canthomeatal line and parallel to the skull base. To reduce beam-hardening artifacts and increase the conspicuity of small lesions, the posterior fossa may be studied with 5-mm slices from the Cl arch, through the level of the posterior clinoids, followed by 10-mm slices from the sella through the vertex. From the array of image-processing algorithms, the one specially designed for soft tissue densities or a combination of soft tissues and bone is best suited for making a diagnosis and establishing appropriate management in the acute trauma situation. Algorithms for high spatial resolution imaging are necessary for trauma to regions with great density differences such as the face (air–soft tissue and air–bone interfaces), the skull base and the temporal bone, and occasionally, the cranial vault.

We frequently use the intermediate algorithm ("Detail," GE; "High," Siemens; "Soft," Picker) because it provides good resolution for soft tissues, gives excellent resolution for edema and hemorrhage, and defines fractures well without blooming artifact from bone (which often occurs with the soft tissue algorithms). Therefore, this algorithm is particularly well suited to image associated facial injuries in which density differences range from air to bone densities. Specific algorithms for bone densities are well suited to examine fracture sites of the facial bones, skull base, and cranial vault.

Hard copies are printed in the following three different window settings to allow for routine viewing of three different areas of interest: (1) the soft tissues of the brain for infarct or hemorrhage, (2) the extracerebral spaces to detect hematomas adjacent to the dense bone of the skull vault and skull base, and (3) the bones for the detection of fractures. Intravenous contrast agent usually not required. If, however, there is unexplainable mass effect or the study is normal but the patient is comatose or lethargic or presents with a focal neurologic deficit, the administration of intravenous contrast material may become necessary. Often, MRI, with its inherent greater sensitivity, may be required for these patients. Small SDHs are difficult to visualize with CT, whereas they pose no difficulty with MRI. Isodense SDHs can usually be visualized with current third- and fourth-generation CT imaging equipment. Intravenous contrast agents may facilitate their detection by increasing the density of the cortical vessels, thus creating a density interface between blood and the diffusely enhancing cortex or cortical vessels, which are displaced from the inner table of the skull.

Axial CT scans performed with current high image resolution scanners provide exquisite image detail and are usually sufficient in the emergency situation. Imaging in the coronal plane is frequently better for the evaluation of fractures of the skull base but may not be feasible because of the patient's condition. Coronal reconstructions are adequate only when thin slices (≤3 mm) are used, but they usually lack the rich detail of direct coronal scans.

Magnetic Resonance Imaging

Conventional T1- and T2-weighted spin-echo (SE) images are used in the evaluation of head trauma. Proton-density and T2-weighted sequences are sensitive in the detection of nonhemorrhagic lesions such as contusions and diffuse axonal (shear) injury, because of the sensitivity of these sequences to the presence of extracellular free water. The T2-weighted sequences are also sensitive in the detection of acute and chronic hemorrhage, especially at high field strength (1.5 T).[44] The use of T1-weighted sequences readily allows the detection of subacute hemorrhagic lesions. Acute hemorrhagic lesions are poorly seen on T1-weighted images because they are isointense or slightly hypointense. Conventional SE sequences may be supplemented with T2* gradient-recalled echo (GRE) sequences, which are highly sensitive in the detection of small acute and chronic hemorrhagic lesions.[3, 28] Fast spin-echo (FSE) sequences may be used in place of conventional SE sequences, resulting in much faster scan time, which is an important consideration in critically injured patients. FSE sequences offer similar lesion conspicuity in the visualization of nonhemorrhagic lesions.[58] Magnetic susceptibility effects are less evident on FSE images, and as a result, hemorrhagic lesions are not as hypointense as with SE sequences. Although the hemorrhagic lesions are not as hypointense on FSE images, they are still evident and almost equivalent to that noted on SE images.[57] The multiplanar imaging capability and superior contrast resolution of MRI are advantages over CT in that they allow the accurate localization and characterization of intracranial injuries.[39] Sagittal T1-weighted and axial T2-weighted sequences supplemented with a T2* GRE sequence enable the detection and localization of both nonhemorrhagic and hemorrhagic lesions.

Image parameters for T1-weighted images (TR = 500 msec, TE = 20 msec, 2 excitations), for proton-density images (TR = 2000 msec, TE = 30 msec, 1 excitation), and for T2-weighted images (TR = 2000 msec, TE = 80 msec, 1 excitation) achieve a high enough signal-to-noise ratio to allow the detection of small lesions. T2* GRE image parameters (TR = 500 to 700 msec, TE = 20 to 25 msec, flip angle 15 to 20 degrees) provide sufficient sensitivity to magnetic susceptibility effects. FSE proton-density (TR = 2500 msec, TE = 17 msec, 1 excitation), echo train 4 sequences and T2-weighted (TR = 3500 msec, TE = 102 msec, 1 excitation), echo train 8 sequences, acquired separately, may be used in place of conventional SE sequences with a decrease in scan time.

Images with higher signal-to-noise ratio, contrast, and spatial resolution values may also be obtained in a comparable scan time with the use of more excitations. A 5-mm slice thickness with a 2.5-mm gap and a 256 × 192 matrix provides adequate signal-to-noise ratio and spatial resolution.

Fractures

Demonstration of a fracture on skull radiographs indicates that a significant force has been applied to the bony vault. However, the lack of visualization of a fracture does not exclude significant injury to the underlying brain. CT evaluation of the skull and brain has therefore superceded the primary evaluation with skull films. In the emergency room assessment of a trauma victim, the primary concern is the diagnosis of injury to the brain and life-threatening post-traumatic changes of intracranial hemorrhage and vascular spasm. Fractures may involve the skull vault, the skull base, or both.

Linear Fracture

Linear fractures that run parallel in the axial plane are easily missed on CT scans, and are usually negligible if no associated brain injury is demonstrated (Fig. 9–1).

Depressed Fracture

A fragment is considered depressed when its outer table is displaced below the level of the inner table of the skull (Fig. 9–2). Although skull films are frequently diagnostic,

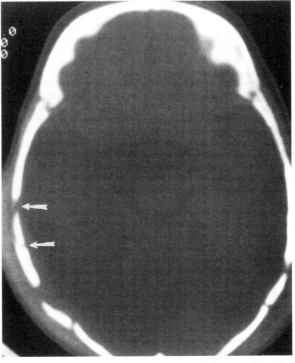

Figure 9–1. Axial CT scan with bone window setting shows nondepressed fractures of the right temporal bone (*arrows*).

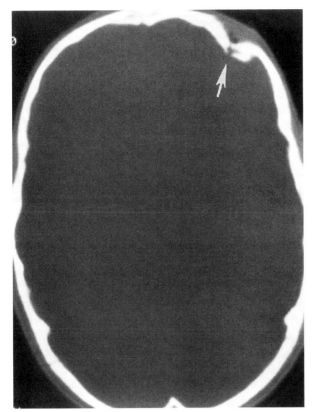

Figure 9–2. Depressed fracture with fragment of the left frontal bone (*arrow*).

the depression can usually be identified during CT on the preliminary computer generated scout image of the skull. Depressed fractures near the vertex or the skull base require direct coronal imaging or reconstructions in a plane parallel to the vector of impact. Delineation of a depressed fracture is important because it may be the cause for an underlying dural tear, extracerebral hematoma, or brain contusion. Although compound depressed fractures frequently require surgical treatment, the majority of such injuries are managed conservatively. The goals of treatment are the prevention of infection and post-traumatic epilepsy and the amelioration of neurologic deficits.[125] Depressed fractures adjacent to venous sinuses are usually left in place because of the danger of uncontrollable hemorrhage when fragments are removed.

Basilar Skull Fracture

If a basilar skull fracture is clinically suspected, high spatial resolution CT scans with a thickness of 3 mm or less are required to delineate a fracture of the chondrocranium. Alternatively, CT scans may suggest a basilar skull fracture before it becomes clinically evident. An air-fluid level in the paranasal sinuses or the mastoid in cells should be viewed as secondary to a basilar skull fracture until proven otherwise.

Frontal Sinus Fracture

It is important to visualize fractures of the posterior wall of the frontal sinus because they frequently require surgical

closure of the disrupted dura to prevent cerebrospinal (CSF) leakage and infection. Some surgeons treat only the severely comminuted fracture or when there is overt CSF leakage or pneumocephalus, and "simple" comminuted fractures are treated conservatively.[125] Fractures of the cribriform plate are commonly associated with anosmia.

Pneumocephalus

Air locules in the extracerebral spaces usually indicate traumatic air entry resulting from fracture of a paranasal sinus or mastoid air cells abutting the dura (Fig. 9–3). When associated with a dural tear, they may be complicated by CSF leakage, empyema, meningitis, or brain abscess. Most post-traumatic CSF leaks cease spontaneously, and the responsible fractures may never be visualized.[123]

Growing Fracture

Enlarging skull fractures have been described in 0.75% of skull fractures in children. Most cases are associated with a history of significant trauma, such as experiencing a motor vehicle accident, being struck by a train, or falling out of a window, that causes a skull fracture and contusion of the underlying brain. Growing fractures commonly occur in the growing skull, although occasional reports of such lesions in adults are on record.[71] The ongoing normal growth of the child's brain is considered an aggravating factor.[126] Children with growing fractures present weeks to

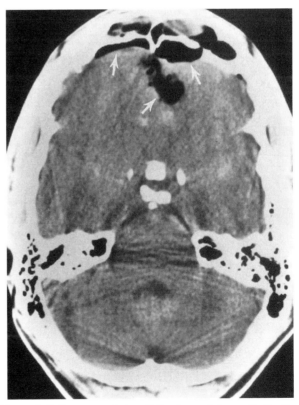

Figure 9–3. Pneumocephalus. Collections of air overlie the frontal lobes and extend along the anterior interhemispheric fissure (*arrows*).

years after injury with a pulsatile mass or rarely with a depressed calvarial defect.[75] Kingsley and coworkers reported 10 cases in children seen over 10 years.[64] The lesions seem to occur when a skull fracture in childhood is accompanied by a dural tear or rent, with focal protrusion of the arachnoid membrane into the fracture gap. The unabating CSF pulsations transmitted to the entrapped arachnoid protrusion result in the remodeling of bone of the growing skull at the fracture site, causing enlargement of the fracture line (Fig. 9–4). The frequently underlying porencephaly or encephalomalacia appears to be the result of an associated contusion from the initial trauma rather than the pathogenetic factor in the enlargement of the fracture. The term "leptomeningeal cyst" is obsolete.[54, 71]

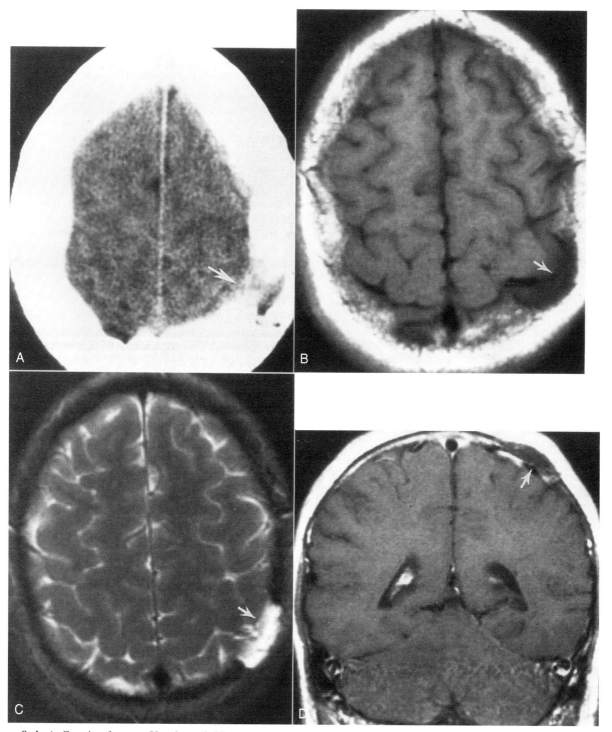

Figure 9–4. *A,* Growing fracture. Unenhanced CT can shows a defect in the left parietal bone (*arrow*). *B* and *C,* Axial T1-weighted (500/15) and T2-weighted (2500/80) MR images reveal mass isointense with CSF (*arrows*). *D,* Coronal enhanced T1-weighted (500/15) image shows no enhancement of lesion (*arrow*).

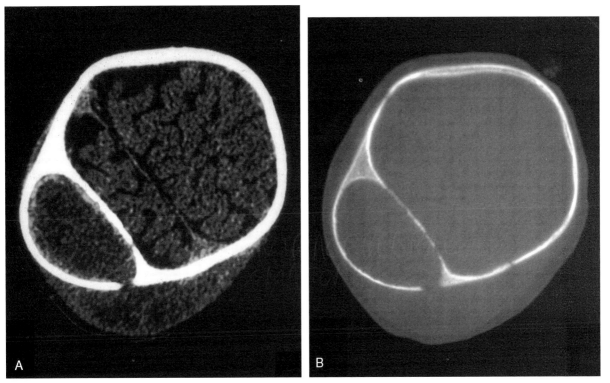

Figure 9–5. *A* and *B,* Cephalhematoma. CT scans with soft tissue and bone windows show partially ossified cephalhematoma overlying the right parietal bone. Note remodeling of the underlying parietal bone. Soft tissue swelling is present, overlying and posterior to the cephalhematoma.

Cephalhematoma may occur as a result of a difficult labor and delivery. A shell of cortical bone forms around the periphery of a subperiosteal hematoma, which may result in deformity of the calvarium (Fig. 9–5).

Intracerebral Hematoma

Intracerebral hematomas are differentiated from hemorrhagic contusions in that the former are homogeneously hyperdense, sharply marginated, and surrounded by a rim of decreased density (Fig. 9–6).[66] Considerable mass effect may be present, depending on the size of the lesion. The most common sites of involvement are the frontal and temporal lobes.[66, 132] Other rare sites of involvement are the basal ganglia and posterior fossa.[60, 119] Hematomas may be bilateral or multiple and are frequently associated with other lesions, such as SAH and SDHs.[26, 66, 132] Not infrequently there is associated rupture of the hematoma into the ventricular system.[132]

Intracerebral hematomas occur most commonly at the time of injury; however, they may be delayed, with most appearing within 48 hours following head injury.[73] Rarely an intracerebral hematoma appears several weeks after the episode of trauma. Possible etiologies of a delayed intracerebral hematoma include focal loss of autoregulation in an area of brain contusion and surgical evacuation of a lesion such as an SDH with relief of a tamponade effect and subsequent hemorrhage into the area of traumatized brain.[73]

Intracerebral hematomas demonstrate a typical pattern of evolution as blood products are gradually broken down

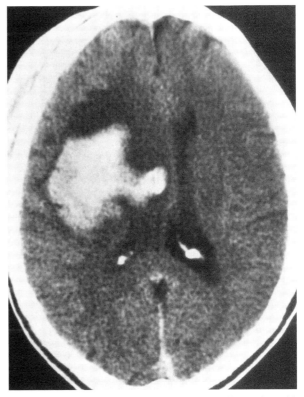

Figure 9–6. Intracerebral hematoma. Large, well-marginated hematoma in the right parietal lobe with rupture into the ventricular system.

and resorbed.[82] Initially the intracerebral hematoma is hyperdense from clotted blood with surrounding edema and mass effect. Enhancement may be evident within or around the hematoma with the administration of intravenous contrast material.[120] The hematoma gradually becomes isodense with brain parenchyma over several weeks to a month.[23, 82] Mass effect persists after the hematoma has become isodense because the decrease in mass effect does not occur simultaneously with decrease in the density of the hematoma.[23, 82] At this time, the hematoma exhibits ringlike enhancement from the surrounding capillary proliferation.[120] Decreased density eventually appears over 1 to several months. Encephalomalacia is evident as low density with adjacent sulcal enlargement and ventricular dilatation.

The MRI appearance of intracerebral hematoma has been described at low and high field strengths.[21, 25, 44, 110, 137] The following description of the evolution of intracerebral hematomas is at a field strength of 1.5 T.[44, 45] *Acute hematomas* are less than 1 week old, *subacute hematomas* are more than 1 week and less than 4 weeks old, and *chronic hematomas* are more than 1 month old. Acute hematomas are isointense or slightly hypointense on T1-weighted images and very hypointense on T2-weighted images. The extreme hypointensity is caused by preferential T2 proton relaxation enhancement (PRT2PRE) of intracellular deoxyhemoglobin, which is dependent on the square root of the magnetic field strength and the interecho interval. The PRT2PRE phenomenon is caused by the dephasing of water protons in areas of local magnetic field inhomogeneity. As the echo time lengthens, signal loss increases as water protons experience the local field inhomogeneity for a longer period. Acute hemorrhage is therefore slightly hypointense on a proton-density–weighted image and very hypointense on a T2-weighted image.

Subacute hematomas have a variable appearance at high field strength.[45] The hematoma in the subacute state is composed of methemoglobin, a paramagnetic material. Paramagnetic materials produce T1 and T2 shortening, which theoretically results in hyperintensity on T1-weighted images and hypointensity on T2-weighted images. The concentration of methemoglobin, however, determines the signal intensity present on any image sequence. Concentrated (undiluted) intracellular methemoglobin acts as a true paramagnetic material and appears hyperintense on T1-weighted images and very hypointense on T2-weighted images. Undiluted extracellular methemoglobin is hyperintense on T1-weighted images and slightly hypointense on T2-weighted images. Dilute extracellular methemoglobin is hyperintense on both T1- and T2-weighted images (Fig. 9–7). The mechanism of relaxation for methemoglobin is proton-electron dipole-dipole relaxation enhancement (PEDDRE). The hyperintense signal is present initially at the periphery of the hematoma and gradually progresses toward the center of the hematoma. Chronic hematomas are isointense to slightly hypointense on T1-weighted images and very hypointense on T2-weighted images because of the presence of hemosiderin. The signal intensity of the chronic hematoma is similar to that of acute hematoma because of a similar mechanism of relaxation—PRT2PRE.

GRE acquisition imaging is highly sensitive to the detection of acute and chronic hemorrhage,[3, 28, 103, 122] because

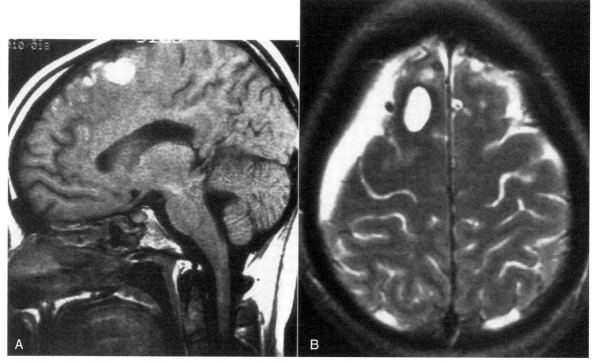

Figure 9–7. *A* and *B,* Right frontal lobe subacute intracerebral hematoma is hyperintense on sagittal T1-weighted (500/15) and axial T2-weighted (2500/80) MR images. The hyperintensity reflects the presence of dilute intracellular methemoglobin. Note the right convexity subacute subdural hematoma.

of the sensitivity of GRE sequences to the magnetic susceptibility effects of acute and chronic hemorrhage.[28] Hemorrhagic lesions are more evident, and more are detected with GRE than with conventional SE sequences.[31] The conspicuity of hemorrhagic lesions on SE sequences is superior at 1.5 T than at 0.5 T. The addition of a GRE sequence at lower field strength provides depiction of a hemorrhagic lesion equal to that obtained at higher field strength.[103]

The development of FSE sequences results in decreased scan time and motion artifact. Lesion conspicuity with FSE sequences is similar to that obtained with SE sequences.[58] FSE sequences are, however, less sensitive in the detection of hemorrhage because they are not as sensitive to magnetic susceptibility effects as conventional SE sequences.[80] Despite the relative lack of sensitivity of FSE sequences to the presence of hemorrhage, they are comparable to SE sequences in hemorrhage detection.[57] The addition of a GRE sequence allows the detection of small foci of hemorrhage that may not be visualized on FSE images.

Epidural Hematoma

Epidural hematomas are characteristically biconvex or lentiform (Fig. 9–8).[25] Uncommonly, epidural hematomas may be bilenticular, crescentic, or irregular.[19] The shape is determined by the dura, which is firmly adherent to the inner table of the skull. A blow to the calvarium results in damage to the underlying vessel, with subsequent displacement of the dura away from the inner table of the skull. The vessel may be damaged, even without fracture of the adjacent bone, as is commonly seen in children. Fracture of the adjacent bone is, however, common.[128] The most

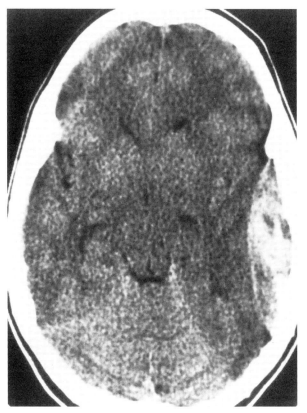

Figure 9–9. Heterogeneous left temporal convexity epidural hematoma exhibits considerable mass effect. Heterogeneous areas represent unclotted blood.

common location for epidural hematomas is over the temporal lobe, followed by the parietal, frontal, and occipital lobes with the posterior fossa the least common location.[19] Damage to the middle meningeal artery is responsible for most epidural hematomas; however, they may occur as a result of laceration of diploic veins or dural sinuses.[128]

Epidural hematomas may be classified as acute, subacute, and chronic. An acute epidural hematoma is heterogeneous in attenuation, containing areas of hyperdense blood and isodense serum (Fig. 9–9). Subacute epidural hematoma is homogeneously hyperdense in attenuation, consisting of solid blood clot (Fig. 9–10). Heterogeneous or decreased attenuation, as well as an enhancing membrane, are characteristics of chronic epidural hematoma, as a result of degradation of blood products.[128] Peripheral enhancement representing dura and membrane formation between the epidural hematoma and adjacent brain parenchyma may be seen in chronic epidural hematomas with the use of intravenous contrast.[90] Delayed epidural hematoma is most commonly from slow venous bleeding from rupture of a dural sinus (Fig. 9–11).[54, 90, 110] Other causes of delayed epidural hematoma are pseudoaneurysm rupture of an epidural vessel and arteriovenous fistula.[84] In some instances, when minimal neurologic signs and symptoms are present, epidural hematoma may undergo spontaneous resolution, which is visualized on serial CT scanning.[124] Some hematomas expand 1 to 2 weeks after injury and then gradually resolve. This expansion correlates with an increase in or persistence of symptoms.[92] The imaging

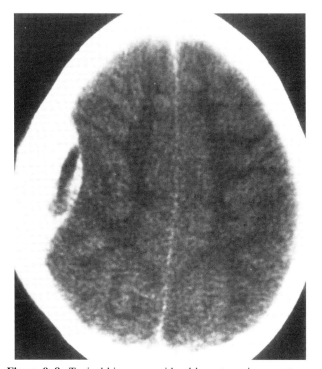

Figure 9–8. Typical biconvex epidural hematoma is present over the right parietal lobe.

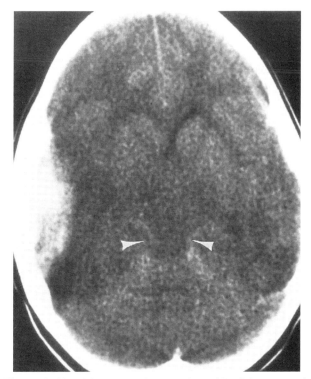

Figure 9–10. Right temporal convexity epidural hematoma is largely homogeneous in density, indicating the presence of clotted blood. Note the effacement of the basal cisterns (*arrowheads*).

criteria in determining whether an epidural hematoma may be treated conservatively are (1) a diameter of less than 1.5 cm and (2) a minimal midline shift of less than 2 mm. The patient must be neurologically intact without focal deficit.[48,104] Parenchymal abnormalities are not present as frequently with epidural hematomas as with acute SDHs. Surgical evacuation of the hematoma results in marked clinical improvement. Little or no residual hematoma is evident on postoperative scans.[24]

Posterior fossa epidural hematomas are rare; however, delay in detection may result in fatal brain stem injury.[119] Many posterior fossa epidural hematomas are not readily visualized on CT because of beam-hardening artifact. The use of contrast material facilitates the detection by demonstrating displacement of the dural sinuses, the torcular herophili, or both as well as displacement of the dura away from the calvarium.[119]

MRI studies allow the distinction between epidural hematomas and SDHs, which may not be possible with CT scans when a hematoma is small or is not typically biconvex. In epidural hematomas, the dura is seen as a curvilinear band of decreased signal intensity between the hematoma and brain parenchyma (Figs. 9–12 and 9–13).[39] Venous epidural hematomas may be differentiated from arterial hematomas on the basis of the former's proximity to a dural sinus and displacement of the involved sinus away from the inner table of the skull.[36,84] The majority of posterior fossa epidural hematomas are of venous origin and may not be well visualized with CT scans because of beam-hardening artifact from adjacent bone structure.[128]

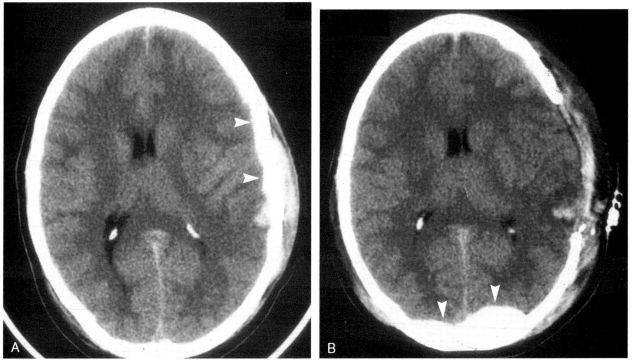

Figure 9–11. Delayed epidural hematoma. *A,* Acute subdural hematoma is present over the left parietal convexity (*arrowheads*). Note the small hemorrhagic contusion in the left parietal lobe. *B,* The patient has undergone craniectomy and drainage of the subdural hematoma. Note the new posterior parieto-occipital epidural hematoma (*arrowheads*).

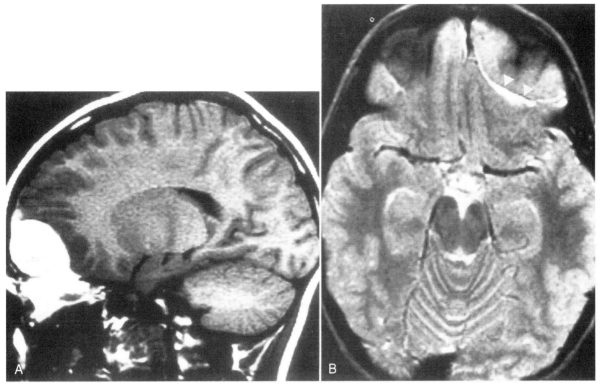

Figure 9–12. *A* and *B,* Sagittal T1-weighted (500/15) and axial T2-weighted (2500/80) MR images show large subacute epidural hematoma overlying the left frontal lobe. Note the displacement of the hypointense dura away from the inner table of the calvarium (*arrowheads*).

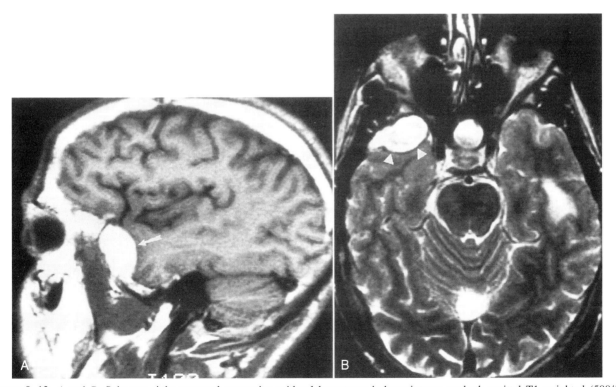

Figure 9–13. *A* and *B,* Subacute right temporal convexity epidural hematoma is hyperintense on both sagittal T1-weighted (500/15) (*arrow*) and axial fast spin-echo T2-weighted (4000/108) MR images (*arrowheads*). The band of hypointensity corresponds to the displaced dura (*arrowheads*). Retention cyst is present in the sphenoid sinus.

The lack of artifact from bone on MRI studies readily enables the detection of a small epidural hematoma.

Subdural Hematoma

SDHs are most commonly caused by shear forces that result in the tearing of the bridging veins present in the subdural space.[35] Laceration of cortical arteries and parenchymal contusions are other causes of SDHs.[105] Rarely, an SDH may be caused by rupture of an aneurysm or arteriovenous malformation.[96] Unlike an epidural hematoma, which is focal, an SDH is diffuse and may overlie an entire cerebral hemisphere. The potential subdural space offers little or no resistance to the expansion of the hematoma within the subdural space.

Underlying brain injury, such as hemorrhagic contusion and edema, are frequently seen with acute SDH.[26,132] These injuries are seen more commonly with SDH than with epidural hematoma.[24] The degree of mass effect seen with SDH is often out of proportion to the size of the hematoma. This mass effect is from the presence of hemorrhagic contusions and edema rather than the SDH.[24,132]

The typical appearance of an acute SDH is a hyperdense crescent-shaped collection with a convex lateral border and concave medial border overlying the cerebral convexity (Fig. 9–14).[26,132] Occasionally the hematoma may be biconcave, simulating the appearance of an epidural hematoma.[12] This biconcavity can be seen particularly when the hematoma is large.[34] The majority of acute SDHs are hyperdense because of the attenuating properties of the hemoglobin molecule. In one report, SDHs were found to be hyperdense in all patients with a history of acute injury.[102] An acute SDH may be isodense with brain parenchyma in patients with anemia as a result of a reduced concentration of hemoglobin.[113] The typical acute SDH gradually approaches the density of brain parenchyma and appears isodense with brain over an interval of 1 to 5 weeks.[26] This change occurs from the breakdown and absorption of blood products.

The classic homogeneous, hyperdense appearance of acute SDH is not always present. The hematoma may appear mixed rather than homogeneous in attenuation.[95] It may have one of three patterns: marginal hypodensity, central irregular areas of hypodensity, or laminar areas of hypodensity (Figs. 9–15 and 9–16). The low density may be secondary to unclotted blood or possibly CSF resulting from arachnoid tears. The mixed SDH is usually larger and has more mass effect than the classic hyperdense SDH.

SDHs located adjacent to the tentorium may simulate an intra-axial lesion. Several features serve to distinguish the subdural location of the lesion. Supratentorial SDHs located adjacent to the tentorium have a well-defined medial margin corresponding to the edge of the tentorium. A sheetlike area of increased density that slopes laterally is present, and the trigone of the lateral ventricle is rotated anteriorly and superiorly.[69] When the hematoma is located below the tentorium, the lesion has a sharp lateral margin corresponding to the tentorium and increased density that slopes medially (Fig. 9–17).

Interhemispheric SDHs occur in the posterosuperior aspect of the interhemispheric fissure (Fig. 9–18).[135] Anterior extension of the lesion occurs less commonly. This lesion may be differentiated from a normal or calcified falx and SAH. SDH in the interhemispheric location has a character-

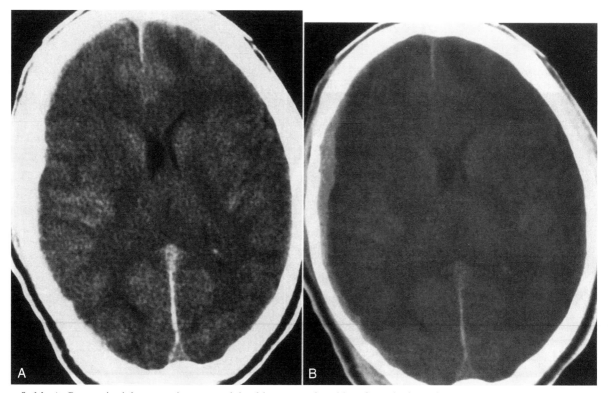

Figure 9–14. *A,* Crescentic right convexity acute subdural hematoma is evident from the irregular contour on the brain window setting. *B,* The subdural hematoma is better demonstrated with an intermediate window setting.

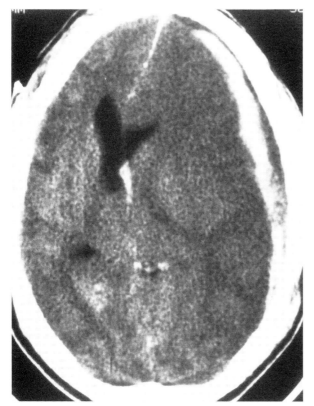

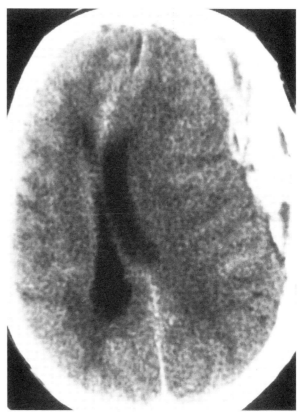

Figure 9–15. Acute left convexity subdural hematoma has marginal hypodensity, representing unclotted blood or cerebrospinal fluid.

Figure 9–16. Irregular areas of hypodensity indicate that unclotted blood or cerebrospinal fluid is present in this acute left convexity subdural hematoma.

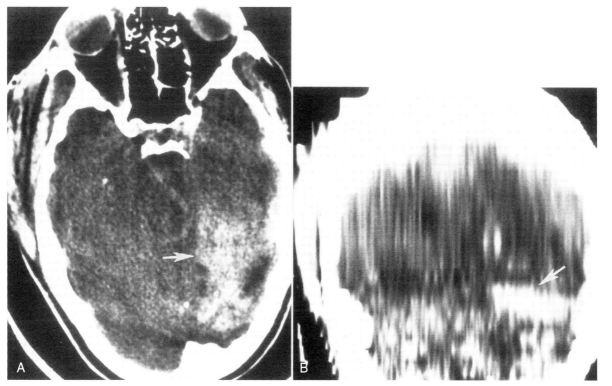

Figure 9–17. *A,* It is difficult to localize this ill-defined subdural hematoma *(arrow). B,* Coronal reconstruction localizes the hematoma to the infratentorial space by its smooth-appearing superior border *(arrow).*

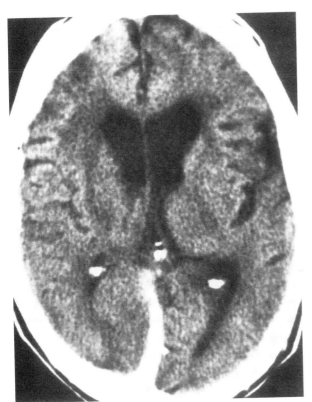

Figure 9–18. Interhemispheric subdural hematoma. The flat medial border of this acute hematoma localizes it to the subdural space above the tentorium.

istic crescentic shape with a flat medial border that abuts the falx and a convex lateral border that abuts the brain. The hematoma is located posterior and superior to the splenium of the corpus callosum. When anterior extension is present, the hyperdensity extends inferiorly in the subdural space to the termination of the falx, which is superior to the genu of the corpus callosum. It can be differentiated from SAH that occurs in the anterior interhemispheric fissure, which has a zigzag configuration conforming to the cortical sulci. In children, increased density along the falx represents SAH because falx calcification rarely occurs in this age group.[22] The SAH extends from the calvarium inferiorly to the rostrum of the corpus callosum, differentiating it from an SDH. Posterior fossa SDHs are rare lesions.[119] Distinction between SDHs and epidural hematomas may be accomplished with the use of intravenous contrast agents that allow differentiation between the two lesions.[119]

Postoperatively, residual SDH may be seen from failure to find the origin of bleeding and difficulty in removing blood clot adherent to the arachnoid (Fig. 9–19).[31] Small SDHs are not surgically evacuated and are managed by observation. These lesions are gradually resorbed over time as fibrinolysis and absorption of blood clot occurs.[5]

The majority of SDHs differ in attenuation from adjacent brain, being either hyperdense or hypodense relative to brain, and are readily diagnosed with CT scanning. Isodense SDHs—with attenuation values near or equal to those of brain parenchyma—may be difficult to diagnose. As blood products become degraded, a hyperdense SDH

gradually decreases in attenuation, becoming isodense with brain. Occasionally, rebleeding into a chronic SDH results in an isodense lesion.[26] Acute isodense SDH may rarely be seen, occurring in patients with anemia.[113] Other possible causes of isodense SDH are dilution with CSF secondary to arachnoidal tear and local or disseminated coagulopathy.[8, 61]

Effacement of the cortical sulci over the cerebral convexity and mass effect on the ventricular system or midline shift indicate the presence of an isodense SDH (Fig. 9–20).[2] Mass effect on the ventricular system may be negligible or absent when bilateral collections are present.[34] Delayed contrast-enhanced CT scans performed 4 to 6 hours after injection of the contrast agent reveal enhancement of the subdural collection.[2, 82] Contrast-enhanced CT scans may also demonstrate enhancement of cortical veins that are displaced medially from the inner table of the calvarium; however, this enhancement is not seen in all cases.[63] The use of rapid high-dose contrast enhancement allows the more accurate detection of an isodense SDH.[49] The majority of patients with an isodense SDH may have three or four of the following signs: posterior displacement of the ipsilateral anterior horn of the lateral ventricle, compression of the ipsilateral posterior and temporal horns, anterior displacement of the ipsilateral posterior and temporal horns, anterior displacement of the ipsilateral glomus calcification, and widening of the contralateral ventricle.[85] In a patient with a history of head trauma, the presence of small compressed ventricles with the absence of cortical sulci should raise the possibility of bilateral isodense SDH.[63] High-resolution CT scans allow the differentiation of gray matter from white matter. The presence of an extra-axial mass displaces the gray-white matter interface medially, producing buckling of the central white matter.[40] Buckling of the white matter is virtually diagnostic of an extra-axial mass (see Fig. 9–20).

Chronic SDHs are most commonly caused by trauma; however, the traumatic episode is frequently so minor that it is forgotten or ignored.[16, 59] The chronic SDH is caused by a torn bridging vein in the subdural space through which venous blood slowly flows.[24] In one series, no acute SDH evolved into a chronic SDH.[24]

Chronic SDHs are most commonly hypodense on CT scans (Fig. 9–21).[66] The are typically crescentic, however, they may be biconcave or lentiform as a result of fluid absorption into the hematoma.[34] Another possible cause is the formation of adhesions. A capsule composed of a capillary-rich membrane develops and surrounds the SDH.[59] This capillary-rich membrane is responsible for repeated episodes of rebleeding and subsequent increase in size of the hematoma. As the hematoma enlarges, the patient becomes symptomatic, showing signs of increased intracranial pressure, hemiparesis, or intellectual and personality change.[16] Repeated episodes of rebleeding may result in a mixed-density collection containing areas of hypodense, isodense, and increased attenuation (Fig. 9–22). A chronic SDH may appear hyperdense from acute hemorrhage, simulating an acute process.[26, 102] Fluid-fluid levels may be seen as blood products settle in the dependent aspect of the subdural collection, which becomes hyperdense relative to the superior aspect. Enhancement of the SDH may be seen on delayed CT scans obtained 3 and 6

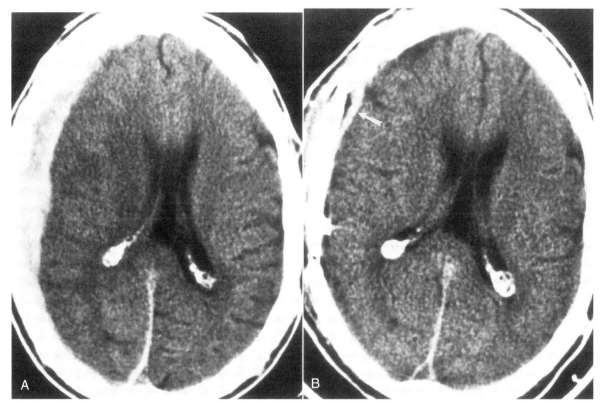

Figure 9–19. *A,* Acute subdural hematoma is present over the right cerebral convexity with extension into the interhemispheric fissure posteriorly. *B,* Postoperative scan reveals small residual hematoma *(arrow).*

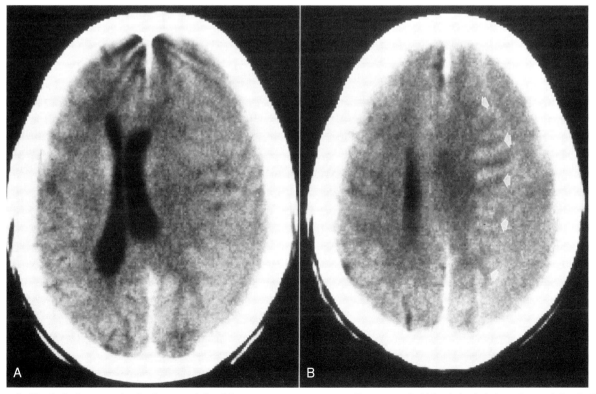

Figure 9–20. *A,* Left convexity isodense: subdural hematoma causes mass effect on and shift of the left lateral ventricle. *B,* White matter buckling *(arrows)* indicates the presence of the extra-axial subdural collection.

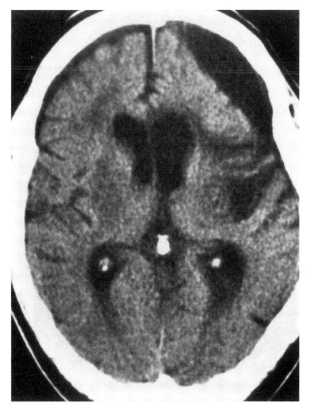

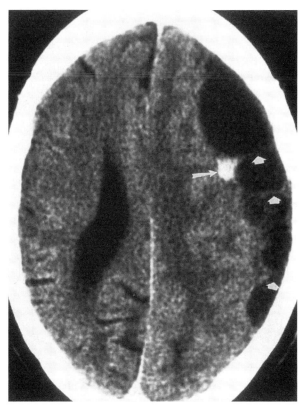

Figure 9–21. Bilateral frontal convexity chronic subdural hematomas are present. Note the slight shift of the septum pellucidum to the right.

Figure 9–22. Large chronic subdural hematoma overlies the left cerebral convexity. The hyperdense area represents recurrent hemorrhage *(long arrow)*. Note the septations within the hematoma *(small arrows)*.

hours after intravenous administration of contrast material.[59]

A subdural hygroma is a hypodense extracerebral collection equal in density to CSF (Fig. 9–23). The lesions are crescentic and may be bilateral. It is not possible to distinguish a subdural hygroma from a chronic SDH with CT scanning, because the two lesions are identical in appearance. At surgery, clear fluid and lack of a membrane allow the diagnosis of a subdural hygroma.[51,102]

The MRI appearance of SDH has been well documented.[33, 86,111] In the acute phase (<1 week old), an SDH is isointense or slightly hypointense relative to gray matter on T1-weighted images and very hypointense on T2-weighted images. Early subacute hematomas (>1 one week and <2 weeks old) are characterized by a rim of hyperintensity surrounding a center of hypointensity on T1- and T2-weighted images. In the late subacute hematoma (>2 weeks and <1 month old), the lesion is hyperintense on both T1- and T2-weighted images (Fig. 9–24). Chronic SDH (>1 month old) are isointense relative to gray matter on T1-weighted images and hyperintense on T2-weighted images (Fig. 9–25). Usually no hypointensity is evident in chronic SDHs on T2-weighted images, most likely because of the lack of a blood-brain barrier and resorption of hemosiderin from the collection. Occasionally hemosiderin may be seen in thickened membranes and areas of rehemorrhage. Fluid-fluid levels of different signal intensity suggest rebleeding. It is possible to distinguish a chronic subdural hygroma from a chronic SDH because the hygroma is of CSF signal intensity on all pulse sequences (Fig. 9–26).[33]

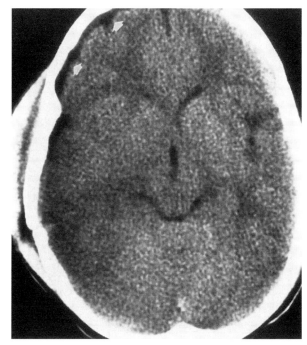

Figure 9–23. Cerebrospinal fluid–density collection representing a cerebrospinal fluid hygroma is present over the right frontal convexity *(arrows)*. The initial CT scan 3 days earlier showed no subdural collection.

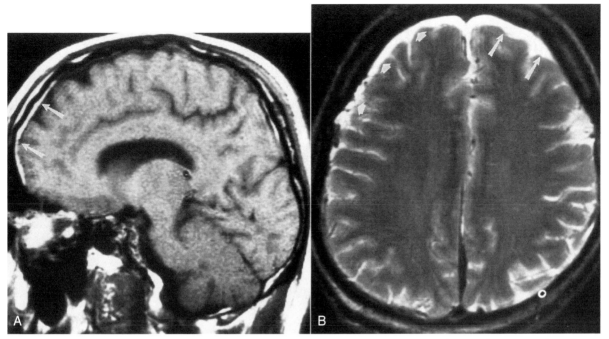

Figure 9–24. *A* and *B*, Sagittal T1-weighted (500/15) and axial T2-weighted (2500/80) MR images demonstrate hyperintense left frontal convexity subacute subdural hemorrhage. Right frontal convexity subacute hematoma is seen on the axial T2-weighted image *(small arrows).*

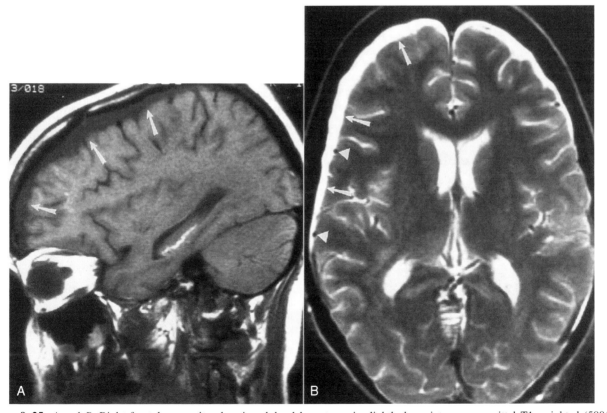

Figure 9–25. *A* and *B*, Right frontal convexity chronic subdural hematoma is slightly hyperintense on sagittal T1-weighted (500/15) and isointense on axial T2-weighted (2500/80) MR images relative to cerebrospinal fluid *(arrows).* Note displacement of the subdural veins away from inner table of the calvarium *(arrowheads).* A small left frontal convexity subdural hemorrhage is present.

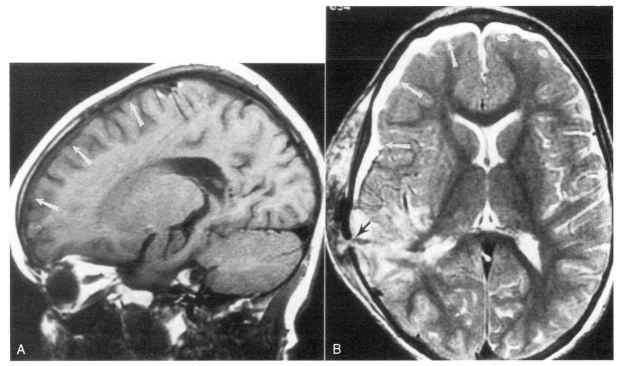

Figure 9–26. *A* and *B,* Same case as shown in Figure 6–23. Sagittal T1-weighted (500/15) and axial fast spin-echo/T2-weighted (3500/108) MR images show cerebrospinal fluid hygroma over right frontotemporoparietal convexity *(arrows).* The small left frontal convexity hygroma not evident on the CT scan is well visualized on the MRI study *(small arrows).* Note the right temporal lobe contusion and herniation of the temporal lobe through the temporal bone fracture *(black arrow).*

It is not always possible to distinguish a subdural hygroma from atrophy because the findings of mass effect and sulcal effacement associated with subdural hygroma may be subtle. Visualization of cortical veins adjacent to displaced cortex is indicative of subdural hygroma. A diagnosis of atrophy is made when cortical veins are seen traversing a widened subarachnoid space.[79]

Subarachnoid Hematoma

SAH is frequently present in the acutely injured patient. It is often associated with other lesions, such as intracerebral hematoma. SAH is caused by damage to blood vessels on the pia-arachnoid. Intraparenchymal hematoma with rupture into the ventricular system may gain access to the subarachnoid space via the foramina of Mangendie and Luschka. On CT scans, hyperdensity representing acute hemorrhage is visualized in the sulci overlying the cerebral convexities, within the sylvian fissures, basal cisterns, and interhemispheric fissure (Fig. 9–27). Hemorrhage is rapidly cleared from the subarachnoid space. The majority of CT scans performed within 1 week appear normal.[66]

CT is the modality of choice in the evaluation of SAH because of the hyperdensity of clotted blood. It is difficult to visualize with MRI studies because the high oxygen concentration in CSF prevents the degradation of oxyhemoglobin to deoxyhemoglobin.[10, 21, 39] This process has been described in detail in both clinical and experimental situations.[10, 17] SAH may be seen on MRI studies only when large volumes of clot are present.[39] Acute SAH is isointense

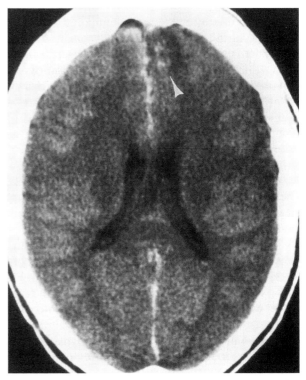

Figure 9–27. Subarachnoid hematoma is present along the interhemispheric fissure. Blood in the sulci is responsible for the zigzag appearance of the interhemispheric hemorrhage. Hemorrhagic contusion is present adjacent to the falx in the left frontal lobe *(arrowhead).*

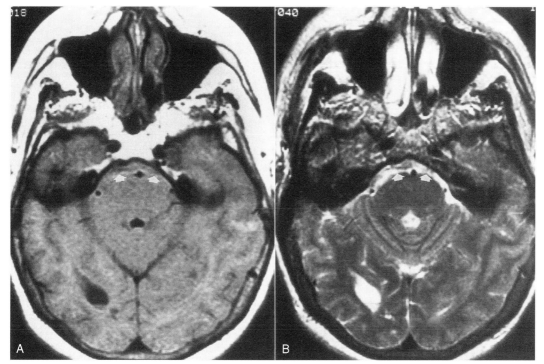

Figure 9–28. *A,* Acute subarachnoid hemorrhage in pontine cistern is isointense on axial T1-weighted (500/15) MR image (*arrows*). *B,* Hypointense hemorrhage is poorly seen on axial fast spin-echo T2-weighted (3900/108) image (*arrows*) because it is masked by hyperintense cerebrospinal fluid.

on T1-weighted images and hypointense on T2-weighted images with respect to brain (Fig. 9–28). Toward the end of the first week, the SAH exhibits T1 shortening and appears hyperintense on T1-weighted images.[10] Subacute SAH does not evolve like intraparenchymal hematoma, which as stated previously becomes isointense or slightly hypointense on T1-weighted images and very hypointense on T2-weighted images in the chronic stage. This may be from the high oxygen concentration of CSF, which may prevent the further degradation of methemoglobin to hemosiderin, or from CSF pulsation, which may aid in clot dissolution and resorption. The residual of SAH may be evident as hypointensity in the leptomeninges because of hemosiderin deposition present in macrophages.[43] This reflects the preferential T2 shortening that occurs as water protons precess through a local heterogeneous magnetic field and lose signal intensity. The effect is more evident at high field strength.[44] A T2* GRE sequence with a short flip angle and relatively long TE has been utilized in the improved detection of intraparenchymal hemorrhage.[28, 122] The improved ability of these sequences to detect hemorrhage stems from their sensitivity to inhomogeneities in the magnetic field that are produced by paramagnetic blood products. The use of GRE sequences may allow improved detection of acute SAH. Fast fluid-attenuated inversion recovery (FLAIR) sequences have proved to be sensitive in the detection of SAH. It is, however, nonspecific as leptomeningeal carcinomatosis and meningitis can have a similar appearance.[109a]

Contusion

Contusions are the most commonly encountered lesions due to head trauma.[26, 66, 130] The lesions are characterized pathologically as areas of hemorrhage, necrosis, and edema. The mechanism of contusion production is complex and depends on many factors, with lesions occurring at the site of impact as well as at sites remote from impact; they are referred to as coup and contrecoup lesions, respectively. A *coup* lesion is produced by transient inbending of the calvarium with resultant compression of the underlying brain. Fracture of the calvarium is not always present. The *contrecoup* lesion is produced when the calvarium decelerates but the brain continues in motion and strikes the irregular inner surface of the calvarium.[46]

Contusions appear as areas of heterogeneous increased density mixed with or surrounded by areas of decreased or normal density (Figs. 9–29 to 9–31).[26, 66, 130, 132] Mass effect may or may not be present, depending on the size of the lesion. The frontal lobe convexity and the lateral temporal areas are the most common sites for coup injury.[130] Contrecoup injuries typically involve the inferior surface of the frontal and temporal lobes.[130]

Hemorrhagic contusions have a typical pattern of evolution that occurs over several months.[130] The initial area of heterogeneous increased density progresses to an area of decreased density within 1 week. At 2 weeks, the contusion is not visualized because it is isodense with brain parenchyma. Enhancement occurs during the acute and subacute stages.[120, 130] Focal encephalomalacia becomes evident by 1 month after injury. Contusions may be isodense if they consist of equal amounts of hemorrhage and edema. The use of intravenous contrast material allows the detection of these isodense lesions as contrast material accumulates in areas of blood-brain barrier breakdown.[117, 120]

In the posterior fossa, contusions may be difficult to detect because of beam-hardening artifact from adjacent

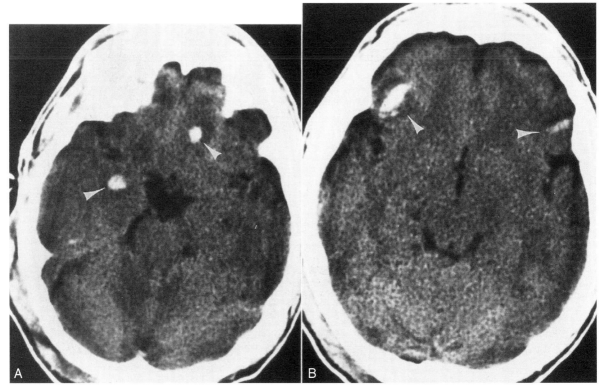

Figure 9–29. *A,* Hemorrhagic contusions with surrounding edema are evident in the inferior left frontal and anterior right temporal lobe (*arrowheads*). *B,* CT scan at higher level reveals additional cortical hemorrhagic contusions in the frontal lobe (*arrowheads*).

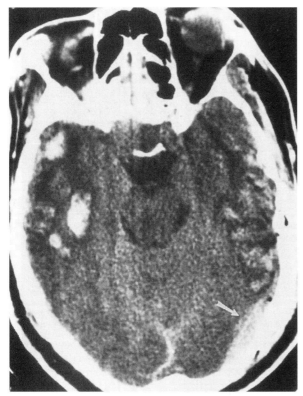

Figure 9–30. Axial CT scan demonstrates multiple hemorrhagic contusions in the temporal lobes. Note the small left occipital lobe convexity subdural hematoma (*arrow*).

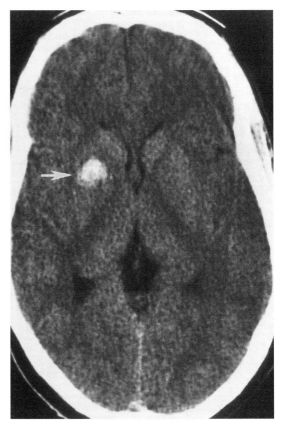

Figure 9–31. Deep gray matter contusion. Hemorrhagic contusion involves the right lentiform nucleus (*arrow*).

bony structure (Fig. 9–32). In some instances, no lesion can be identified, and the presence of indirect signs such as effacement of the pontine, cerebellopontine angle, and perimesencephalic cisterns must be used to suggest the presence of brain stem injury.[118] Isodense contusions not visualized on unenhanced CT scans will become evident with the use of intravenous contrast material.[118] Brain stem injuries may be primary, occurring at the time of injury, or secondary, occurring at a later time from downward transtentorial herniation or direct compression by other lesions.[118] Hemorrhagic lesions in the rostral midbrain may also occur at the time of injury (Fig. 9–33).[83] Injury to the brain stem carries a grave prognosis and is associated with a high mortality.[119]

MRI studies are equivalent to CT scans in the detection of hemorrhagic cortical contusions but are more sensitive in the detection of nonhemorrhagic contusions.[39,136] In some cases, acute hemorrhagic contusions visible on CT scans may not be visualized with MRI.[50] As the hemorrhagic contusion evolves, it becomes isodense and finally hypodense on CT scans and is poorly seen. It is in the subacute and chronic stages that MRI studies are more sensitive than CT in the detection of contusions.[50] MRI studies also allow the contusions to be better characterized.[62] Contusions tend to be multiple and to involve the cortex with sparing of the underlying white matter. A hemorrhagic component is evident in many lesions.[37]

Acute hemorrhagic contusions are isointense or slightly hypointense in signal on T1-weighted images and very hypointense on T2-weighted images (Fig. 9–34). This feature reflects the preferential T2 shortening of intracellular deoxyhemoglobin. Subacute lesions are hyperintense on

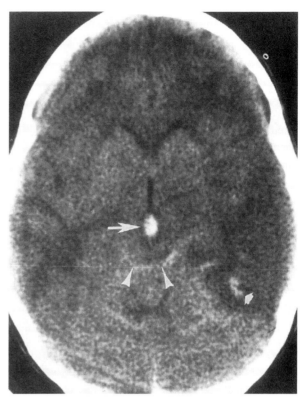

Figure 9–33. Acute hemorrhagic contusion is demonstrated in the rostral midbrain (*arrow*). Note the effacement of the quadrigeminal cistern (*arrowheads*) and the left temporal lobe contusion (*small arrow*).

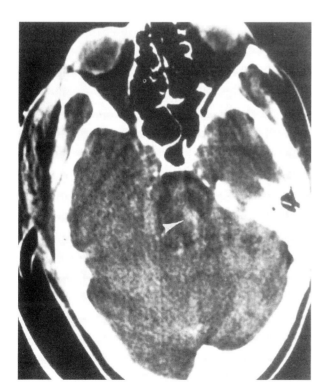

Figure 9–32. Pontine contusion. Hemorrhagic contusion is seen in the left posterolateral pons (*arrowhead*).

T1- and T2-weighted images because of the effect of extracellular methemoglobin (Fig. 9–35).[44] Hypointensity from hemosiderin and encephalomalacia are evident in chronic lesions. The discrepancy between CT and MRI in the detection of nonhemorrhagic contusions is due to the superior spatial resolution of MRI and its sensitivity in the detection of changes in water content in damaged tissue. The use of supplemental T2* GRE sequences should allow the detection of small hemorrhagic contusions that are visualized on CT scans but not with conventional SE MRI studies (Fig. 9–36).

In the posterior fossa, contusions typically occur along the posterolateral aspect of the midbrain and lateral aspect of the cerebral peduncle.[38] They are primary injuries occurring at the time of injury. Secondary injuries occur later in the ventral, ventrolateral, and paramedian aspects of the brain stem.[38] MRI studies are more sensitive than CT scans in the detection of contusions in the posterior fossa because of the lack of artifact from the adjacent bone. Indirect signs of brain stem injury, which may be the only abnormalities present on the CT scan, are well demonstrated in addition to intrinsic lesions.[38,50] Secondary foci of hemorrhage, located in the midline of the rostral midbrain, occur from tearing of penetrating arteries that supply the brain stem.[38] Although a high percentage of patients with brain stem contusions and normal CT findings have a good clinical outcome, 20% with normal CT scans do poorly because of undetected lesions or secondary complications.[74] MRI stud-

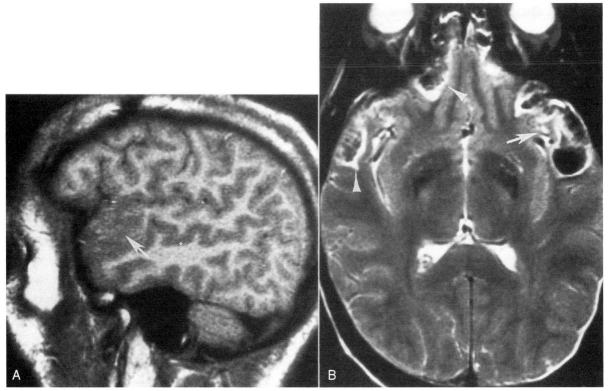

Figure 9–34. *A*, Acute left temporal lobe hemorrhagic contusion is isointense with gray matter on sagital T1-weighted (500/15) MR image (*arrow*). *B*, Hemorrhagic contusion is hypointense on axial T2-weighted (2500/80) image (*arrow*). Note additional hemorrhagic contusions in the right frontal and temporal lobes (*arrowheads*).

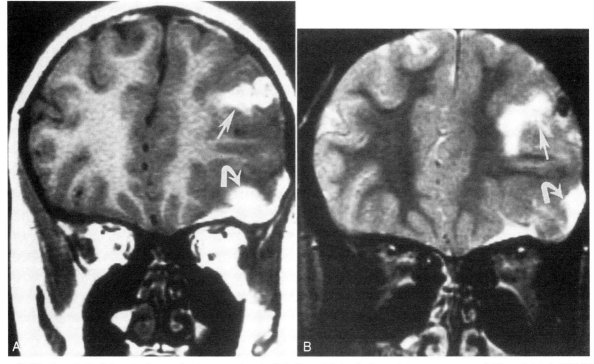

Figure 9–35. *A* and *B*, Subacute hemorrhagic contusion in left frontal lobe is hyperintense on coronal T1-weighted (500/15) and largely hyperintense on coronal T2-weighted (2500/80) MR images, indicating the presence of methemoglobin (*arrows*). In addition, there is a small left frontal, convexity subacute subdural hematoma (*curved arrows*).

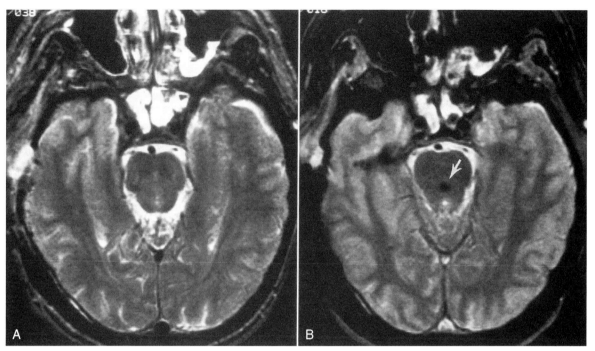

Figure 9–36. *A,* Axial T2-weighted (2600/80) MR image shows no abnormality in a comatose patient. *B,* Axial T2* gradient-recalled echo (600/17), 20-degree flip-angle image reveals a small acute hemorrhagic contusion in the pons (*arrow*).

ies are more accurate in the assessment of subacute and chronic injuries and may provide a more reliable correlation with clinical findings to better predict clinical outcome.

Diffuse Axonal (Shear) Injury

Diffuse axonal (shear) injury is frequently encountered in patients with head trauma.[39] Shearing injuries to the white matter were first described in the CT literature in 1978[129] and have been described extensively in the neuropathological literature in the past. A study by Strich and Oxon[115] in 1961 described these injuries as axonal tears with or without microscopically visible hematoma. They reported on five patients who sustained head injury, died of brain swelling, and were found at autopsy to have white matter degeneration. Midbrain damage in patients with closed head injury has been frequently described at autopsy. In another study, 80% of patients dying of injuries resulting from head trauma had midbrain lesions at autopsy that were not visualized by CT scans.[98] Although blunt head trauma has been associated with a significant number of hemorrhagic foci in the corpus callosum at autopsy,[72] the outcome of corpus callosum hematoma is not invariably dismal, because many patients with such lesions diagnosed by CT scans have been shown to survive.

Coma, decerebrate posturing, vegetative state, and no increase in intracranial pressure are present in many patients with diffuse axonal injury.[129] This injury is caused by rotational forces that produce shear strain, resulting in tissue damage. Shear strain is maximum at the junction of tissues with different densities such as the gray-white junction.[37] The presence of diffuse axonal injury is of great prognostic significance because the lesions are often associated with a poor outcome.[129]

CT findings in diffuse axonal injury include diffuse cerebral swelling, corpus callosal hemorrhage, and SAH. Hemorrhage may also be present in the area of the third ventricle and hemispheric white matter.[132] Although CT scans do not reveal the actual axonal lesion demonstrated with histology, they do show the associated edema and hemorrhage (Fig. 9–37).[128]

MRI studies are more sensitive than CT scans in the detection of diffuse axonal injury. Lesions are readily demonstrated by MRI in patients in whom the CT scan shows no abnormality.[37–39,136] The injuries are demonstrated with CT only when greater than 1.5 cm or when present in the corona radiata or internal capsule.[39]

Diffuse axonal injury lesions are usually multiple, range from 0.5 to 1.5 cm, and are typically oval or elliptical. The lesions are most commonly located in the subcortical white matter of the frontal and temporal lobes, splenium of the corpus callosum, corona radiata, and internal capsule (Figs. 9–38 and 9–39). The parieto-occipital lobes and cerebellum are less commonly involved.[37] In the brain stem, the lesions are located in the dorsolateral aspect of the midbrain and upper pons (Fig. 9–40). More than 80% of the lesions are nonhemorrhagic, being most evident as foci of hyperintensity on T2-weighted images.[38]

Brain Swelling and Edema

Brain swelling and edema occur commonly in patients with head trauma. Brain swelling is observed more commonly in children than in adults.[131] Minor episodes of trauma may result in brain swelling. Patients may experience a lucid interval after the episode of trauma, followed by the sudden onset of headache, nausea, vomiting, and

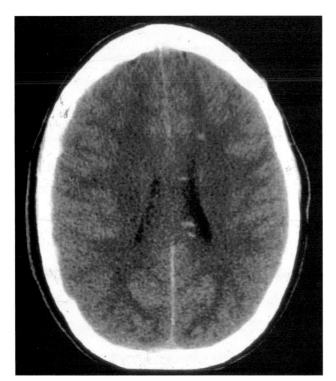

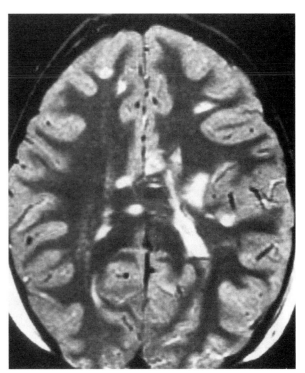

Figure 9–37. Diffuse axonal injury. CT scan demonstrates small hemorrhagic diffuse axonal injuries in the deep white matter and corpus callosum.

Figure 9–38. Diffuse axonal injury. Axial T2-weighted (2500/80) MR image demonstrates typical locations of diffuse axonal injury: subcortical white matter, corpus callosum, and corona radiata.

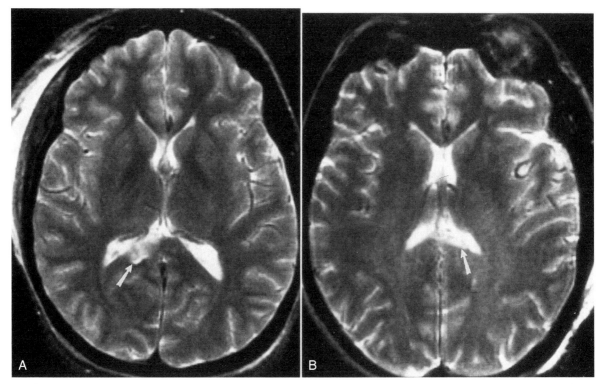

Figure 9–39. *A* and *B*, Diffuse axonal injury in two different patients. Hyperintense lesions are present in the splenium of the corpus callosum on axial T2-weighted (2500/80) MR images (*arrows*).

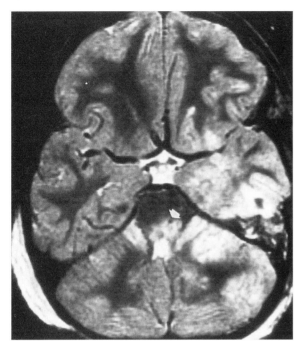

Figure 9–40. Axial T2-weighted (2500/80) MR image shows areas of diffuse axonal injury in the pons, middle cerebellar peduncles, and left-cerebellar hemisphere. The pontine lesion contains a focus of acute hemorrhage (*small arrow*). Hemorrhagic contusion is present in the left temporal lobe.

loss of consciousness.[131] SAH and contusions are often seen in association with this type of abnormality.[14, 55]

Brain swelling is evident in the majority of patients with head trauma, occurring at the time of injury or several hours afterwards.[55] CT findings consist of compression of the lateral and third ventricles and perimesencephalic cistern (Figs. 9–41 and 9–42). There is an associated increase in density of the white matter from transient hyperemia.[131] It is thought that loss of autoregulation results in an increase in cerebral blood flow and blood volume. This increase in blood flow forces CSF out of the ventricles and subarachnoid space, resulting in the compressed appearance. Serial CT scans show the gradual resolution of brain swelling over a period of 3 to 5 days.[55] The initial white matter hyperdensity gradually returns to normal as the swelling subsides. In more than one third of cases in children, extracerebral collections and sulcal and ventricular enlargement are seen to develop on follow-up CT scans.[131]

Cerebral edema may be cytotoxic, interstitial, or vasogenic in origin. In the immediate post-traumatic interval, cerebral edema is vasogenic, reflecting breakdown of the blood-brain barrier with leakage of intravascular contents into and around areas of damaged tissue. Edema is evident as decreased density within and surrounding areas of contusion and intraparenchymal hematoma.[26, 66, 82] Edema may occur as an isolated finding, appearing as an area of decreased density.[66] Cerebral edema typically appears 24 hours after injury, then increases and becomes maximum at 3 to 5 days and then gradually resolves.

Brain swelling and edema are evident with MRI stud-

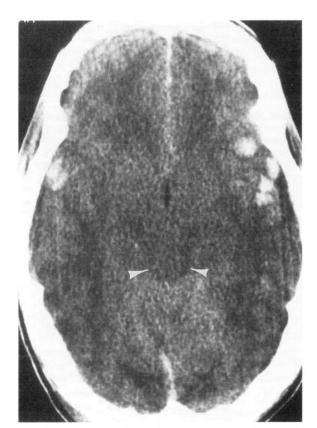

Figure 9–41. Brain swelling. Effacement of the perimesencephalic cistern indicates brain swelling (*arrowheads*). Note the bilateral temporal lobe contusions.

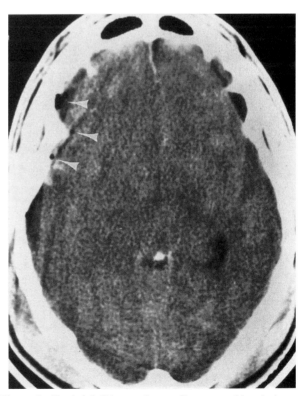

Figure 9–42. Axial CT scan shows effacement of basal cisterns, and third ventricle representing brain swelling. Note pneumocephalus overlying the right frontotemporal convexity (*arrowheads*).

ies.[37, 50, 62, 136] The exquisite sensitivity of MRI to the presence of extracellular free water enables the detection and visualization of small regions of edema, particularly on T2-weighted images.

Penetrating Injury

Gunshot wounds are a common cause of penetrating head injury. CT scans allow one to rapidly locate the position of a missile and determine the extent of intracranial injury.[4, 109] The missile, its track and fragments, as well as skull fracture and displaced intraparenchymal bone fragments are readily identified (Fig. 9–43). Hematoma along the missile track, intraventricular hemorrhage and SAH, diffuse edema, and pneumocephalus, both extracerebral and intracerebral, are frequently seen on CT scans.[109] Laceration of a major blood vessel may result in massive intraparenchymal hemorrhage, which is an indication for early surgical intervention.[109] Injuries beyond the missile track may sometimes be seen if the missile is of a large-caliber or high-velocity type.[4] Prognosis is best when damage is limited to a single lobe, worse with unilateral multilobe injury, and poorest with bilateral hemispheric injury.[88] Damage to vital structures such as the diencephalon and mesencephalon is also associated with a poor prognosis.[109] Complications of penetration injuries include CSF leak, osteomyelitis, abscess, and seizures.[88] Repeat CT scans may reveal the development of encephalomalacia along the missile track and intraparenchymal cystic areas

of CSF density.[4] The presence of metal projectiles is a relative contraindication to an MRI study because projectiles containing steel are deflected when placed in a magnetic field. Nonferromagnetic missiles are a contraindication to MRI when they contain ferromagnetic contaminants.[112] Any metal distorts the local magnetic field, the magnitude of which depends on the degree of ferromagnetism of the metal alloy. In addition to undergoing deflection, stainless steel or alloys with ferromagnetic contaminants distort the local magnetic field to a greater degree than titanium compounds and, if in the region of interest, severely degrade image quality.

Vascular Injury

Injury to the carotid or vertebral arteries may be produced by blunt force, penetrating injury, strangulation, and hyperextension.[41] Dissection, laceration, thrombosis, and pseudoaneurysm or arteriovenous fistula formation may occur.[20] The site of injury depends on the nature of the forces on the vessels and the occurrence of nearby skull fractures.[87] Arterial injury may be diagnosed with CT scanning; however, angiography remains the modality that best defines the site of arterial injury.

An intimal tear in the arterial wall may result in dissection and thrombus formation.[87] Although one third of patients are symptomatic at the time of injury, the majority experience a lucent interval varying from hours to days before the onset of symptoms.[87] Symptoms are variable and

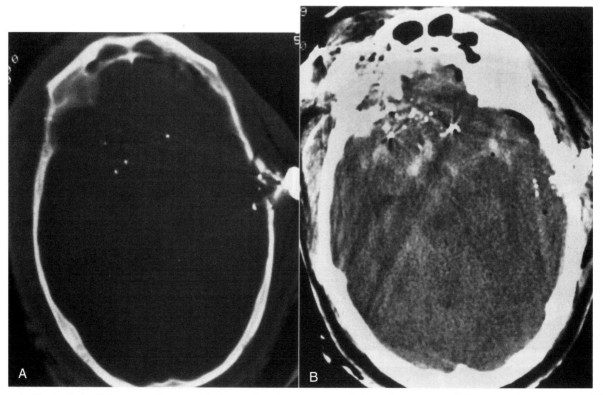

Figure 9–43. *A,* Axial CT scans with bone window setting demonstrates missile adjacent to the left temporal bone, temporal bone fracture, and missile-fragments in brain parenchyma. *B,* Brain window setting reveals multiple hemorrhagic-foci in the frontal and temporal lobes, effacement of the basal cisterns, and pneumocephalus.

include headache, Horner's syndrome, transient ischemic attacks, and completed stroke.

The diagnosis of arterial dissection may also be accomplished with MRI studies.[42] Abnormal signal intensity representing hemorrhage is seen in a thickened arterial wall on all pulse sequences. The signal intensity depends on the age of the hematoma. The hematoma is usually contained by a thin rim of hypointensity that represents the adventitia.

In addition, the arterial lumen appears narrow. Arteries normally appear hypointense or demonstrate flow void phenomena on MRI.[9] In arterial dissection, the slow flow distal to the area of dissection produces hyperintense signal within the vessel lumen. However, the hyperintense signal is not specific for dissection and may be the result of slow flow from stenosis caused by atherosclerotic disease. The hyperintensity of slow arterial flow must be differentiated

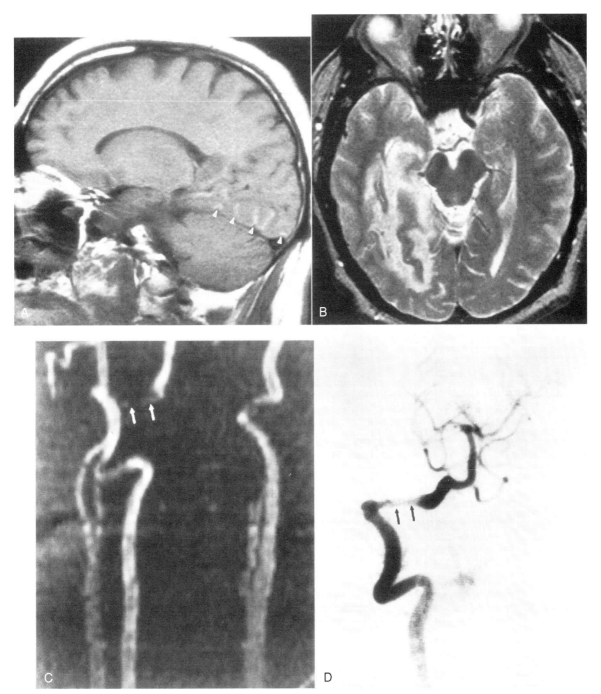

Figure 9–44. *A,* Arterial dissection. Sagittal T1-weighted (500/15) MR image shows cortical ribbon of hyperintensity representing subacute hemorrhage in the right temporal lobe (*arrowheads*). *B,* Hyperintense signal is evident on axial T2-weighted (2500/80) image. Findings are consistent with acute infarction. *C,* Two-dimensional time-of-flight MR angiography study demonstrates irregular narrowing of the right vertebral artery consistent with dissection (*arrows*). *D,* Intraarterial digital subtraction angiogram of the right vertebral artery confirms the dissection (*arrows*).

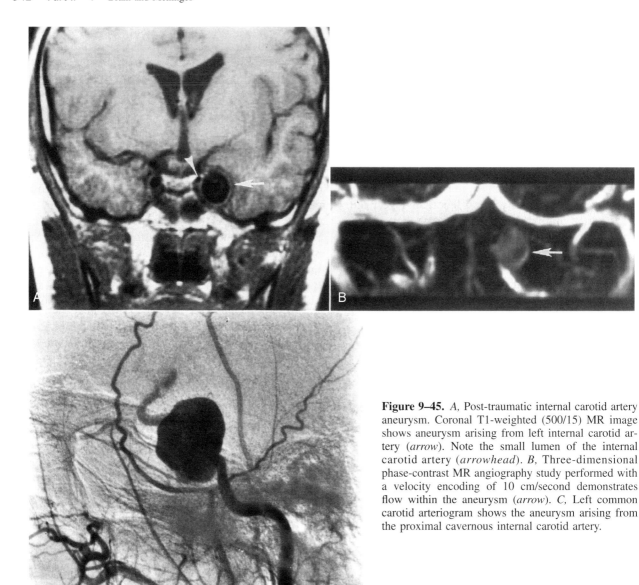

Figure 9–45. *A,* Post-traumatic internal carotid artery aneurysm. Coronal T1-weighted (500/15) MR image shows aneurysm arising from left internal carotid artery (*arrow*). Note the small lumen of the internal carotid artery (*arrowhead*). *B,* Three-dimensional phase-contrast MR angiography study performed with a velocity encoding of 10 cm/second demonstrates flow within the aneurysm (*arrow*). *C,* Left common carotid arteriogram shows the aneurysm arising from the proximal cavernous internal carotid artery.

from arterial thrombosis, which appears as isointense signal within the vessel lumen. Arterial thrombus is composed of fibrin and platelets, rather than hemoglobin containing red blood cells, and as a result is isointense in signal intensity. This is in contradistinction to the signal intensity of intraparenchymal hematoma or venous thrombus in various stages of evolution.[67] Magnetic resonance angiography (MRA) can demonstrate the concentric luminal narrowing and irregularity of carotid dissection and may eliminate the need for conventional angiography (Fig. 9–44).

Disruption of the three layers of the arterial wall—intima, media, and adventitia—may result in pseudoaneurysm formation.[87] Symptoms are variable, include headache, tinnitus, and vertigo, and may appear years after injury.[20] Although CT and MRI studies are capable of demonstrating a pseudoaneurysm, angiography is required to accurately depict the lesion. The MRI appearance of a pseudoaneurysm is variable, depending on the size and presence of thrombus. Areas of signal void, representing

residual lumen, and areas of mixed signal intensity, representing thrombus of variable age, may be seen. An advantage of MRI is that it demonstrates the true size of the aneurysm, including the patent lumen as well as intraluminal thrombus, whereas conventional angiography demonstrates only the patent lumen (Fig. 9–45).

MRA has the capability to demonstrate both small and large aneurysms. Aneurysms as small as 3 mm may be visualized with current imaging techniques.[1a] The three-dimensional time-of-flight technique is sensitive to the detection of small aneurysms, whereas the phase-contrast technique is better able to depict large aneurysms.[53,99]

Laceration of the intracavernous carotid artery with rupture into the cavernous sinus results in traumatic carotid cavernous fistula.[89] Symptoms and signs include orbital bruit, proptosis, conjunctival redness and swelling, blurred vision, pain, and pulsatile exophthalmos. CT and MRI studies demonstrate proptosis, enlargement of the rectus muscles, superior ophthalmic vein, and cavernous sinus

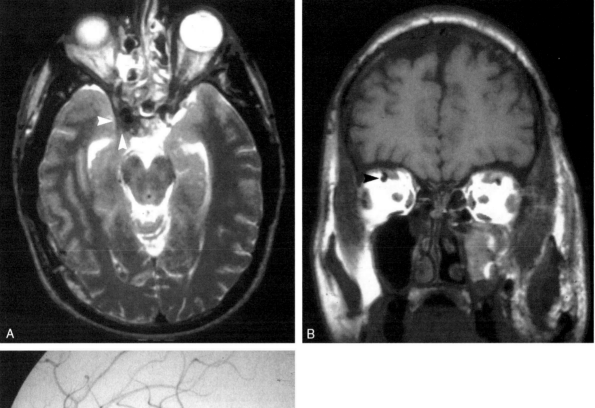

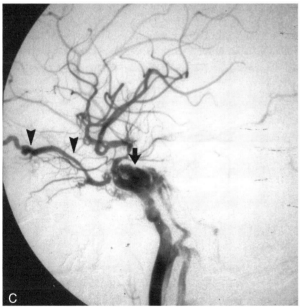

Figure 9–46. *A,* Carotid cavernous fistula. Axial T2-weighted image (TR = 2500 msec, TE = 80 msec). Increased flow void is present in the region of the cavernous right internal carotid artery (*arrowheads*). *B,* Coronal T1-weighted image (TR = 500 msec, TE = 15 msec) reveals dilatation of the right superior ophthalmic vein (*arrowhead*). *C,* Lateral projection of right internal carotid artery arteriogram demonstrates opacification of the right cavernous sinus (*arrow*) with drainage into the right superior ophthalmic vein (*arrowheads*).

(Fig. 9–46). MRI shows flow void within the enlarged superior ophthalmic vein and cavernous sinus. Angiography is, however, necessary to visualize the site of the fistula. Phase-contrast MRA studies show promise in the detection of the fistulous communication.[121]

Child Abuse

Child abuse is a major cause of morbidity and mortality. Most victims of child abuse are younger than 2 years, with the majority younger than 1 year; however, older children up to adolescence may also be victims.[18,134] The abused child may present with a variety of symptoms, including breathing difficulty, irritability, lethargy, poor feeding, and seizures.[27] The clinical outcome depends on the severity of the injuries sustained. Minor disabilities may be present, such as visual disturbance, extremity weakness, and seizures.[18] Children with severe impairment, such as mental retardation, or those existing in a vegetative state require institutional placement. It is important to recognize the CT findings encountered in child abuse; these findings may be the only signs of abuse because commonly there is no external evidence of injury.[13] Clinical features may not allow the differentiation of the abused child from the child injured in an accident.

The mechanism of injury in child abuse was previously thought to be caused by shaking—the so-called shaken baby syndrome. Shaking alone, however, does not generate the force required to produce head injury.[26] Rather, most victims of child abuse have evidence of blunt trauma to the head, and it is the force of the blunt impact that is responsible for the observed head injuries.[27] The child is likely first shaken and subsequently thrown, and the head strikes an object—the so-called shaken impact syndrome.[13]

The most common CT finding seen in child abuse on early-generation CT scanners was an acute interhemispheric SDH located in the parieto-occipital area (Fig. 9–47). The SDH is secondary to tearing of the bridging cerebral veins at their attachment to the falx. Infarction or cerebral swelling in the parieto-occipital lobes was a frequent associated abnormality.[133,134] The most common finding observed on later-generation CT scanners is SAH.[18] Other findings frequently seen include cerebral edema, intraparenchymal hemorrhage, SDH, infarction, and skull fracture. It may sometimes be difficult to differentiate interhemispheric SDH from SAH, and in some instances, they may coexist.[18] In children who are victims of strangulation, large infarctions and SDHs may be present, usually involving the supratentorial brain.[16] Skull radiographs should be obtained in victims of child abuse because fractures may not be evident on CT scans. Radiographic features of skull fractures may allow the differentiation of the abused child from the child injured in an accident.[81] These features are multiple, bilateral fractures that cross suture lines. Focal or diffuse atrophy with sulcal and ventricular enlargement is evident on repeat CT scans in all patients; infarction is evident in some patients.[18,134]

Although CT scans are performed in acutely injured patients to exclude a surgical lesion, MRI studies should be used when the clinical symptoms do not correlate with the CT findings. MRI is also more useful in the evaluation of subacute and chronic head injury because the technique is more sensitive than CT scans in the detection of small SDH, cortical contusion, and diffuse axonal injury. The advantage of MRI lies in the ability to determine the age of subdural blood on the basis of signal intensity. The presence of SDHs in various stages of evolution, signifying a difference in age, may be an indicator of child abuse.[100]

Complications of Central Nervous System Trauma

Hydrocephalus

Hydrocephalus is a possible complication of head injury. Diffuse brain injury or obstruction of CSF pathways results in enlargement of the ventricular system. In the former, as diffuse edema resolves, there is a gradual enlargement of the ventricular system, which retains a normal configuration.[26] Noncommunicating hydrocephalus may be evident initially or shortly after injury, with intraventricular hemorrhage impeding the outflow of CSF at the level of obstruction.[26] Communicating hydrocephalus is the result of decreased absorption of CSF at the level of the arachnoid villi over the cerebral convexities. This may be observed as a gradual enlargement of the ventricular system on serial CT scan.[66] Enlargement of the ventricular system occurs in the majority of patients within 2 weeks of injury, however, it may rarely develop over several months to 1 year after injury.[65] The clinical outcome in patients who experience

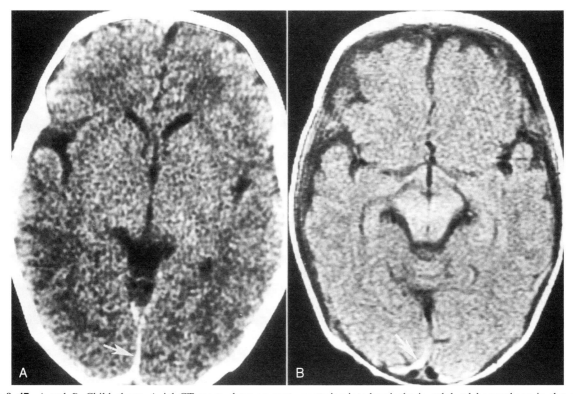

Figure 9–47. *A* and *B,* Child abuse. Axial CT scans show an acute posterior interhemispheric subdural hemorrhage in the occipital area (*arrows*).

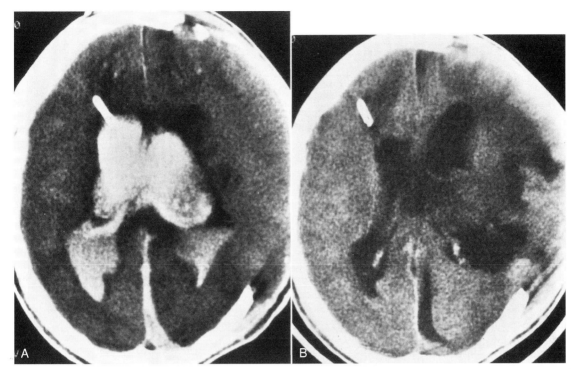

Figure 9–48. *A,* Hydrocephalus. Axial CT scan shows ventricular enlargement with massive intraventricular hemorrhage. A shunt tube is present in the right lateral ventricle. Posterior interhemispheric subdural hematoma and frontal lobe contusions are present. *B,* Ten days later, the intraventricular hemorrhage has resolved, and the ventricles have decreased in size but remain enlarged.

hydrocephalus is much worse than in those who do not, with the majority sustaining moderate to severe disability.[65]

The CT appearance of communicating hydrocephalus consists of dilatation of the ventricular system and effacement of the cortical sulci (Fig. 9–48). In the acute stage, decreased density representing transependymal fluid shift is present in the periventricular white matter. The transependymal fluid shift is visible as a thin rim of hyperintensity in the periventricular white matter on proton-density and T2-weighted MR images. Other findings that may be observed are dilatation of the anterior third ventricle, inferior displacement of the hypothalamus, depression of the posterior fornix, and elevation of the corpus callosum—which are seen on sagittal T1-weighted images.[29]

The CSF flow void sign is from the turbulent flow of CSF and indicates the presence of flow in the aqueduct of Sylvius and third and fourth ventricle.[106] Absence of the flow void sign in the aqueduct in the presence of hydrocephalus is an indication of obstruction or stenosis at the level of the aqueduct.[107] Intraventricular hemorrhage within the aqueduct results in absence of the flow void sign. The flow void sign is present in normal individuals as well as in patients with normal-pressure hydrocephalus, acute communicating hydrocephalus, and atrophy.[11] Although the flow void sign is present in all of these conditions, it is most evident in normal-pressure hydrocephalus and is not as evident in atrophy and acute communicating hydrocephalus.[31] However, it cannot be used to differentiate acute communicating hydrocephalus from atrophy.[108]

Atrophy

Areas of porencephaly may result from head trauma at the site of intracerebral hematoma or infarction. Porencephaly is a cystic defect that may or may not communicate with the ventricular system. In the communicating type, the defect communicates with the ventricular system or is separated from it by only a thin layer of tissue. In closed porencephaly, the cyst does not communicate with the ventricular system. The CT appearance is that of a well-defined area of CSF density with no contrast enhancement.[94] Shift of the midline structures and the ventricular system is usually toward and rarely away from the defect. MRI studies demonstrate the porencephalic defect to be of CSF signal intensity on all pulse sequences.

Infarction

Infarction may be a sequela of head trauma secondary to vasospasm, vascular occlusion, or direct vessel damage.[66] In the acute stage, decreased density or isodense cerebral swelling with mass effect and midline shift may be seen on CT scans (Fig. 9–49).[18,134] The use of intravenous contrast material demonstrates luxury perfusion around areas of infarction.[18] Focal encephalomalacia or porencephaly with ventricular and sulcal dilatation are seen in the chronic stage.[66] MRI is more sensitive than CT in the detection of infarction. Brain swelling is seen on T1-weighted images within several hours after the onset of symptoms, before any signal change is evident on T2-weighted images.[127] Hyperintense signal may be evident between 8 and 24 hours on T2-weighted images, whereas the CT scan may be normal up to 2 days after the onset of symptoms. Intravascular and meningeal enhancement may be present within the first several days after administration of gadopentetate dimeglumine.[30,127]

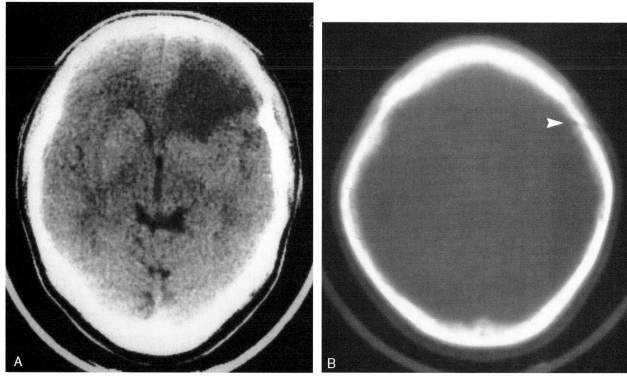

Figure 9–49. *A,* Infarction secondary to assault with a hammer. Unenhanced CT scan shows acute left frontal lobe infarction in the distribution of the left anterior cerebral artery. *B,* CT scan with bone window reveals nondepressed fracture of the left frontal bone (*arrowhead*).

Post-traumatic Leak

A CSF leak indicates abnormal communication between the intracranial and extracranial environments. It most commonly occurs after penetrating injury or fracture along the skull base and usually involves the cribriform plate or the temporal bone. CSF leak indicates communication with the paranasal sinuses and, less likely, the mastoid air cells or the middle ear cavity. The clinical significance ranges from entirely benign, because it is frequently self-limited, to infection and brain abscess if it is associated with persistent extracerebral communication.[97]

The most common sites of fractures and CSF leaks are in the sphenoethmoid region of the anterior cranial fossa. Leakage may occur through the nose, mouth, or the middle ear and depends on the location of the fracture. Precise detection of the sites of leakage is difficult. An air-fluid level in the sphenoid sinus suggests a fracture of the cribriform plate, although a CSF leak from anywhere between the frontal sinus and sphenoid bone may result in retrograde flow of CSF into the sphenoid ostium.[116] Most CSF leaks are related to high-velocity trauma.[68, 70, 97]

The demonstration of a post-traumatic leakage site requires thin-section, high-spatial resolution[68, 70, 97] direct coronal scans. Such scans may demonstrate a bony dehiscence of the skull base near a sinus or an air cell and, thus, localize the level of air entry. A cisternogram may be of help if there is an active leak at the time of the study but is otherwise not necessary, particularly when high-spatial-resolution, direct coronal scanning is performed (Fig. 9–50).[77]

Infection

Infection of the central nervous system may uncommonly occur as a complication of trauma associated with fracture. Direct extension of microorganisms through a

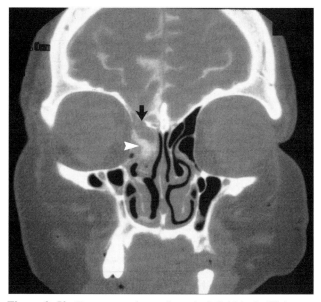

Figure 9–50. Post-traumatic cerebrospinal fluid leak. High-resolution direct coronal CT cisternogram demonstrates leakage of contrast material in the right ethmoid sinus (*arrowhead*) and the fracture site in the right cribriform plate (*arrow*).

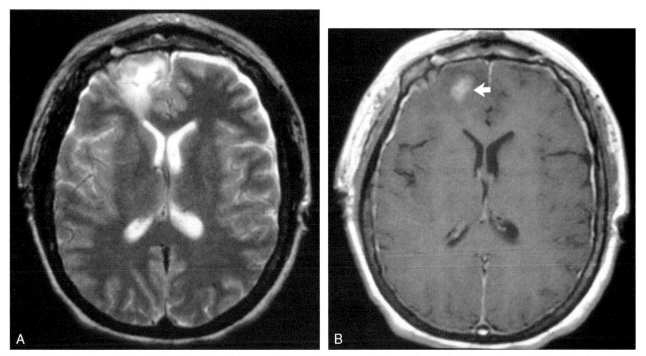

Figure 9–51. *A,* Cerebritis. Axial T2-weighted image (TR = 2500 msec, TE = 80 msec) shows edema in the right frontal lobe. Small, bilateral, convexity subdural hematomas are present. *B,* Contrast-enhanced T1-weighted image (TR = 500 msec, TE = 15 msec) reveals focus of nodular enhancement (*arrow*).

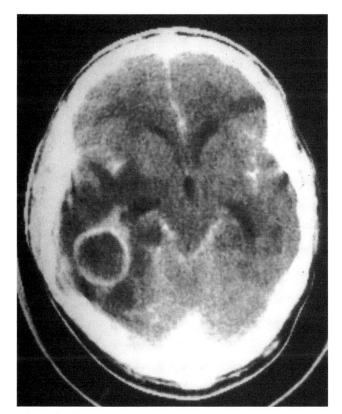

Figure 9–52. Abscess secondary to right temporal bone fracture. Contrast-enhanced CT scan shows ring enhancing abscess caused by *Staphylococcus* in the right temporal lobe.

fracture site may result in meningitis, cerebritis, abscess, or, less commonly, subdural or epidural empyema. The initial CT scan is often normal with meningitis. A second CT scan may demonstrate hydrocephalus, effacement of the basal cisterns secondary to inflammatory exudate, and enhancement of the basal cisterns and meninges with intravenous contrast material.[15] Contrast-enhanced MRI is more sensitive than contrast-enhanced CT in detecting meningeal enhancement.[78] Cerebritis is more readily demonstrated with MRI than with CT.[47,101] Hyperintense edema is evident on T2-weighted images, whereas nodular enhancement can be seen on contrast-enhanced T1-weighted images (Fig. 9–51). Contrast-enhanced CT and MRI depict intraparenchymal abscess as a ring enhancing mass with surrounding edema (Fig. 9–52).

Tension Pneumocephalus

Air may enter the cranial cavity through a fistulous connection in sufficient amounts to cause mass effect.[7, 32,91] Its mechanism is poorly understood. This is a rare complication usually caused by trauma or surgery to the skull base, it has also been described after infection with gas-forming organisms or congenital defects of the skull base.[76]

References

1. Ambrose J: Computerized transverse axial scanning (tomography). Part 2: Clinical application. *Br J Radiol* 46:1023–1047, 1973.
1a. Adams WM, Laitt RD, Jackson A: The role of MR angiography in the pretreatment assessment of intracranial aneurysms: A comparative study. *AJNR Am J Neuroradiol* 21:1618–1628, 2000.
2. Amendola MA, Ostrum BJ: Diagnosis of isodense subdural hematomas by computed tomography. *AJR* 129:693–697, 1977.

3. Atlas SW, Mark AS, Grossman RI, et al: Intracranial hemorrhage: gradient-echo MR imaging at 1.5 T. *Radiology* 168:803–807, 1988.
4. Bakay L: The value of CT scan in gunshot injuries of the brain. *Acta Neurochir (Wien)* 71:189–204, 1984.
5. Bergstrom AS, Ericson K, Levander B, et al: Computed tomography of cranial subdural and epidural hematomas: Variation of attenuation related to time and clinical events such as rebleeding. *J Comput Assist Tomogr* 1:449–455, 1977.
6. Bird CR, McMahan JR, Gilles FH, et al: Strangulation in child abuse: CT diagnosis. *Radiology* 163:373–375, 1987.
7. Black PM, Davis JM, Kjellberg RN, Davis KR: Tension pneumocephalus of the cranial subdural space: A case report. *Neurosurgery* 5:368–370, 1979.
8. Boyko OB, Cooper DF, Grossman CB. Contrast-enhanced CT of acute isodense subdural hematoma. *AJNR Am J Neuroradiol* 12:341–343, 1991.
9. Bradley WG Jr: Carmen lecture: Flow phenomena in MR imaging. *AJR* 150:983–994, 1988.
10. Bradley WG Jr, Schmidt PG: Effect of methemoglobin formation on the MR appearance of subarachnoid hemorrhagic. *Radiology* 156:99–103, 1985.
11. Bradley WG Jr, Kortman KE, Burgoyne B: Flowing cerebrospinal fluid in normal and hydrocephalic states: Appearance on MR images. *Radiology* 159:611–616, 1986.
12. Braun J, Borovich B, Guilburd JN, et al: Acute subdural hematoma mimicking epidural hematoma on CT. *AJNR Am J Neuroradiol* 8:171–173, 1987.
13. Bruce DA, Zimmerman RA: Shaken impact syndrome. *Pediatr Ann* 18:482–494, 1989.
14. Bruce DA, Alavi A, Bilanluk L, et al: Diffuse cerebral swelling following head injuries in children: The syndrome of "malignant brain edema." *J Neurosurg* 54:170–178, 1981.
15. Cabral DA, Flodmark O, Farrell K, et al: Prospective study of computed tomography in acute bacterial meningitis. J Pediatr 111:201–205, 1987.
16. Cameron M: Chronic subdural haematoma: A review of 114 cases. *J Neurol Neurosurg Psychiatry* 41:834–839, 1978.
17. Chakeres DW, Bryan RN. Acute subarachnoid hemorrhage: In vitro comparison of magnetic resonance and computed tomography. *AJNR Am J Neuroradial* 7:223–228, 1986.
18. Cohen RA, Kaufman RA, Myers PA, et al: Cranial computed tomography in the abused-child with head injury. *AJNR Am J Neuroradiol* 6:883–888, 1985.
19. Cordobes F, Lobato RD, Rivas JJ, et al: Observations on 82 patients with extradural hematoma. Comparison of results before and after the advent of computerized tomography. *J Neurosurg* 54:179–186, 1981.
20. Davis JM, Zimmerman RA: Injury of the carotid and vertebral arteries. *Neuroradiology* 25:55–69, 1983.
21. DeLa Paz RL, New PF, Buonanno FS, et al: NMR imaging of intracranial hemorrhage. *J Comput Assist Tomogr* 8:599–607, 1984.
22. Dolinskas CA, Zimmerman RA, Bilaniuk LT: A sign of subarachnoid bleeding on cranial computed tomograms of pediatric head trauma patients. *Radiology* 126:409–411, 1978.
23. Dolinskas CA, Bilaniuk LT, Zimmerman RA, et al: Computed tomography of intracerebral hematomas. I. Transmission CT observations on hematoma resolution. *AJR* 129:681–688, 1977.
24. Dolinskas CA, Zimmerman RA, Bilaniuk LT, Gennarelli TA: Computed tomography of post-traumatic extracerebral hematomas: Comparison to pathophysiology and responses to therapy. *J Trauma* 19:163–169, 1979.
25. Dooms GC, Ustse A, Brant-Zawadski M, et al: Spin-echo MR imaging of intracranial hemorrhage. *Neuroradiology* 28:132–138, 1986.
26. Dublin B, French BN, Rennick JM: Computed tomography in head trauma. *Radiology* 122:365–369, 1977.
27. Duhaime AC, Gennarelli TA, Thibault LE, et al: The shaken baby syndrome: A clinical pathological, and biomechanical study. *J Neurosurg* 66:409–415, 1987.
28. Edelman RR, Johnson K, Burton R, et al: MR of hemorrhage: A new approach. *AJNR Am J Neuroradiol* 7:751–756, 1986.
29. El Gammal T, Allen MB Jr, Brooks BS, Mark EK: MR evaluation of hydrocephalus. *AJR* 149:807–813, 1987.
30. Elster AD, Moody DM: Early cerebral infarction: Gadopentetate dimeglumine enhancement. *Radiology* 177:627–632, 1990.
31. Fell DA, Fitzgerald S, Moiel RH, Caram P: Acute subdural hematoma. Review of 144 cases. *J Neurosurg* 42:37–42, 1975.
32. Findler G, Hoffman HJ, Munro IR: Tension pneumocephalus complicating craniofacial surgery in a shunted hydrocephalic patient: case report. *Neurosurgery* 7:525–528, 1980.
33. Fobben ES, Grossman RI, Atlas SW, et al: MR characteristics of subdural hematomas and hygromas at 1.5 T. *AJNR Am J Neuroradiol* 10:687–693, 1989.
34. Forbes GS, et al: Computed tomography in die evaluation of subdural hematomas. *Radiology* 126:143–148, 1978.
35. Gennarelli TA, Thibault LE: Biomechanics of acute subdural hematoma. *J Trauma* 22:680–685, 1982.
36. Gentry LR: Head trauma. In Atlas SW (ed): *Magnetic Resonance Imaging of the Brain and Spine.* New York, Raven Press, 1991.
37. Gentry LR, Godersky JC, Thompson BH: MR imaging of head trauma: Review of the distribution and radiopathologic features of traumatic lesions. *AJNR Am J Neuroradiol* 9:101–110, 1988.
38. Gentry LR, Godersky JC, Thompson BH: Traumatic brain stem injury: MR imaging. *Radiology* 171:177–187, 1989.
39. Gentry LR, Godensky JC, Thompson B: Prospective comparative study of intermediate-field MR and CT in the evaluation of closed head trauma. *AJNR Am J Neuroradiol* 9:91–100, 1988.
40. George AE, Russell EJ, Kricherf IL: White matter buckling. CT sign of extraaxial intracranial mass. *AJR* 135:1031–1036, 1980.
41. Glickman MG: Angiography in head trauma. In Newton TH, Potts DG (eds): *Radiology of the Skull and Brain.* St. Louis, CV Mosby, 1974.
42. Goldberg HI, Grossman RI, Gomori JM, et al: Cervical internal carotid artery dissecting hemorrhage: Diagnosis using MR. *Radiology* 158:157–161, 1986.
43. Gomori JM, Grossman RI, Bilanluk LT, et al: High-field MR imaging of superficial siderosis of the central nervous system. *J Comput Assist Tomogr* 9:972–975, 1985.
44. Gomori JM, Grossman RI, Goldberg HI, et al: Intracranial hematomas: Imaging by high-field MR. *Radiology* 157:87–93, 1985.
45. Gomori JM, Grossman RI, Hackney DB, et al: Variable appearances of subacute intracranial hematomas on high-field spin-echo MR. *AJR* 150:171–178, 1988.
46. Gurdjian ES, Gurdjian ES. Cerebral contusions: Re-evaluation of the mechanism of their development. *J Trauma* 16:35–51, 1976.
47. Haimes AB, Zimmerman RD, Morgello S, et al: MR imaging of brain abscesses. AJNR Am J Neuroradiol 10:279–291, 1989.
48. Hamilton M, Wallace C: Nonoperative management of acute epidural hematoma diagnosed by CT: the neuroradiologist's role *AJNR* 13:853–859, 1992.
49. Hayman LA, Evans RA, Hinck VC: Rapid high dose contrast computed tomography of isodense subdural hematoma and cerebral swelling. *Radiology* 131:381–383, 1979.
50. Hesselink JR, Dowd CF, Healy ME, et al: MR imaging of brain contusions: a comparative study with CT. *AJNR Am J Neuroradiol* 9:269–278, 1988.
51. Hoff J, Bates E, Bames B, et al: Traumatic subdural hygroma. *J Trauma* 13:870–876, 1973.
52. Hounsfield GN: Computerized transverse axial scanning (tomography). Part I: Description of system. *Br J Radiol* 46:1016–1022, 1973.
53. Huston J III, Rufenacht DA, Ehman RL, Wiebers DO: Intracranial aneurysms and vascular malformations: Comparison of time-of-flight and phase-contrast MR angiography. *Radiology* 181:721–730, 1991.
54. Ito H, Miwa T, Onodra Y: Growing skull fracture of childhood. *Child's Brain* 3:116–126, 1977.
55. Ito U, Tomita H, Yamazaki SH, et al: Brain swelling and brain oedema in acute head injury. *Acta Neurochir (Wien)* 79:120–124, 1986.
56. Iwakuma T, Brunngraher CV: Chronic extradural hematoma: A study of 21 cases. *J Neurosurg* 38:488–493, 1973.
57. Jones KM, et al: Brain hemorrhage: Evaluation with fast spin-echo and conventional dual spin-echo images. *Radiology* 182:53–58, 1992.
58. Jones KM, Multkern RV, Schwartz RB, et al: Fast spin-echo MR imaging of the brain and spine: Current concepts. *AJR* 158:1313–1320, 1992.
59. Karasawa H, Tomira S, Suzuki S: Chronic subdural hematoma: Time-density curve and iodine concentration in enhanced CT. *Neuroradiology* 29:36–39, 1987.

60. Katz DI, Alexander MP, Seliger GM, Bellas DN: Traumatic basal ganglia hemorrhage: Clinicopathologic features and outcome. *Neurology* 39:897–904, 1989.

61. Kaufman HH, Singer JM, Sadhu VK, et al: Isodense acute subdural hematoma. *J Comput Assist Tomogr* 4:557–559, 1980.

62. Kelly AB, Zimmerman RD, Snow RB, et al: Head trauma: Comparison of MR and CT—experience in 100 patients. *AJNR Am J Neuroradiol* 9:699–708, 1988.

63. Kim KS, Hemmati M, Weinberg PE: Computed tomography in isodense subdural hematoma. *Radiology* 128:71–74, 1978.

64. Kingsley D, Till K, Hoare R: Growing fractures of the skull. *J Neurol Neurosurg Psychiatry* 41:312–318, 1978.

65. Kishore PRS, Lipper MH, Miller JD, et al: Post-traumatic hydrocephalus in patients with severe head injury. *Neuroradiology* 16:261–265, 1978.

66. Kon AH, LaRoque RL: Evaluation of head trauma by computed tomography. *Radiology* 123:345–350, 1977.

67. Lane JL, Flanders AE, Doan HT, Bell RD: Assessment of carotid artery parency on routine spin-echo MR imaging of the brain. *AJNR Am J Neuroradiol* 12:819–826, 1991.

68. Lantz EJ, Forbes GS, Brown ML, Laws ER Jr: Radiology of cerebrospinal fluid rhinnorhea. *AJR* 135:1023–1030, 1980.

69. Lau LSW, Pike JW: The computed tomographic findings of peritentorial subdural hemorrhage. *Radiology* 146:699–701, 1983.

70. Leech PJ, Patterson A: Conservative and operative management for cerebrospinal fluid leakage after closed head injury. *Lancet* 1:1013–1016, 1973.

71. Lende RA: Enlarging skull fractures of childhood. *Neuroradiology* 7:119–124, 1974.

72. Lindenberg R, Fischer RS, Durlacher SH, et al: Lesions of the corpus callosum following blunt mechanical trauma to the head. *Am J Pathol* 31:287–317, 1955.

73. Lipper MH, Kishore PRS, Girevendulis AK, et al: Delayed intracranial hematoma in patients with severe head injury. *Radiology* 133:645–649, 1979.

74. Lipper MH, Kishore PRS, Enas GG, et al: Computed tomography in the prediction of outcome in head injury. *AJNR Am J Neuroradiol* 6:7–10, 1985.

75. Luerssen TG: Heart injuries in children. *Neurosurg Clin North Am* 2:399–410, 1991.

76. Lunsford LD, Maroon JC, Sheptak PE, Albin MS, et al: Subdural tension pneumacephalus. *J Neurosurg* 50:525–527, 1979.

77. Manelfe C, Cellerier P, Sobel D, et al: Cerebrospinal fluid rhinorrhea: evaluation with metrizamide cisternography. *AJR Am J Roentgenol* 138:471–476, 1982.

78. Mathews VP, Kuharik MA, Edwards MK: Gd-DTPA enhanced MR imaging of experimental bacterial meningitis: Evaluation and comparison with CT. *AJNR Am J Neuroradiol* 9:1045–1050, 1988.

79. McCluney KW, Yeakley JW, Fenstermacher MJ, et al: Subdural hygromas versus atrophy on MR brain scans: "The cortical vein sign." *AJNR Am J Neuroradiol* 13:1335–1339, 1992.

80. Melki PS, Mulkern RV, Panych LP, Jolesz FA: Comparing the FAISE method with conventional dual-echo sequences. *JMRI* 1:319–326, 1991.

81. Meservy CJ, Tabin R, McLaurin RL, et al: Radiographic characteristics of skull fractures resulting from child abuse. *AJR* 149:173–175, 1987.

82. Messina AV, Chernik NL: Computed tomography: the "resolving" intracerebral hemorrhage. *Radiology* 118:609–613, 1975.

83. Meyer CA, Mirvis SE, Wolf AL, et al: Acute traumatic midbrain hemorrhage: Experimental and clinical observations with CT. *Radiology* 179:813–818, 1991.

84. Milo R, Razon N, Schiffer J: Delayed epidural hematoma: A review. *Acta Neurochir (Wien)* 84:13–23, 1987.

85. Moller A, Ericson K: Computed tomography of isoattenuating subdural hematomas. *Radiology* 130:149–152, 1979.

86. Moon KL Jr, Brant-Zawadzki M, Pitts LH, Mills CM: Nuclear magnetic resonance imaging of CT-isodense subdural hematomas. *AJNR Am J Neuroradiol* 5:319–322, 1984.

87. Morgan MK, Besser M, Johnston I, Chaseling R: Intracranial carotid artery injury in closed head trauma. *J Neurosurg* 66:192–197, 1987.

88. Nagib MG, Rockswold GL, Sherman RS, Lagaard MW: Civilian gunshot wounds to the brain: Prognosis and management. *Neurosurgery* 18:533–536, 1986.

89. Newton TH, Troost BT: Arteriovenous malformations and fistulae.

In Newton TH, Potts DG (eds): *Radiology of the Skull and Brain.* St. Louis, CV Mosby, 1974.

90. Omar MM, Binet EF: Peripheral contrast enhancement in chronic epidural hematomas. *J Comput Assist Tomogr* 2:332–335, 1978.

91. Osborn AG, Daines JH, Wing SD, Anderson RE: Intracranial air on computerized tomography. *J Neurosurg* 48:355–359, 1978.

92. Pang D, Horton JA, Herron JM, et al: Nonsurgical management of extradural hematomas in children. *J Neurosurg* 59:958–971, 1983.

93. Pozzati F, Tognetti F, Cavallo M, Acciarri N: Extradural hematomas of the posterior cranial fossa: Observations on a series of 32 consecutive cases treated after the introduction of computed tomography scanning. *Surg Neurol* 32:300–303, 1989.

94. Ramsey RG, Huckman MS: Computed tomography of porencephaly and other cerebrospinal fluid–containing lesions. *Radiology* 123:73–77, 1977.

95. Reed D, Robertson WD, Graeb DA, et al: Acute subdural hematomas: Atypical CT findings. *AJNR Am J Neuroradiol* 7:417–421, 1986.

96. Rengachary SS, Szymanski DC: Subdural hematomas of arterial origin. *Neurosurgery* 8:166–171, 1981.

97. Robinson J, Donald PJ: Management of associated cranial lesions. In Pitts L, Wagner FC (eds): *Craniospinal Trauma.* New York, Thieme Medical, 1989.

98. Rosenblum WI, Greenberg RP, Seelig JM, Becker DP: Midbrain lesions: Frequent and significant prognostic feature in closed head injury. *Neurosurgery* 9:613–620, 1981.

99. Ross JS, Masaryk TJ, Modic MT, et al: Intracranial aneurysms: Evaluation by MR angiography. *AJNR Am J Neuroradiol* 11:449–456, 1990.

100. Sato Y, Yuh WC, Smith WL, et al: Head injury in child abuse: Evaluation with MR imaging. *Radiology* 173:653–657, 1989.

101. Schroth G, Kretzschmar K, Gawehn J, et al: Advantage of magnetic resonance imaging in the diagnosis of cerebral infections. Neuroradiology 29:120–126, 1987.

102. Scotti G, Terbrugge K, Melancon D, Belanger G: Evaluation of the age of subdural hematomas by computerized tomography. *J Neurosurg* 47:311–315, 1977.

103. Seidenwurm D, Meng TK, Kowalski H, et al: Intracranial hemorrhagic lesions: Evaluation with spin-echo and gradient-refocused MR imaging at 0.5 and 1.5 T. *Radiology* 172:189–194, 1989.

104. Servadei F, Faccani G, Roccella P, et al: Asymptomatic extradural haematomas: Results of a multicenter study of 158 cases in minor head injury. *Acta Neurochir (Wien)* 96:39–45, 1989.

105. Shenkin HA: Acute subdural hematoma: Review of 39 consecutive cases with high incidence of cortical artery rupture. *J Neurosurg* 57:254–257, 1982.

106. Sherman JL, Citrin CM: Magnetic resonance demonstration of normal CSF flow. *AJNR Am J Neuroradiol* 7:3–6, 1986.

107. Sherman JL, Citrin CM, Bowen BJ, Gangarosa RE: MR demonstration of altered cerebrospinal fluid flow by obstructive lesions. *AJNR Am J Neuroradiol* 7:571–579, 1986.

108. Sherman JL, Citrin CM, Gangarosa RE, Bowen BJ: The MR appearance of CSP flow in patients with ventriculomegaly. *AJR Am J Roentgenol* 148:193–199, 1987.

109. Shoung HM, Sichez JP, Pertuiset B: The early prognosis of craniocerebral gunshot wounds in civilian practice as an aid to the choice of treatment. *Acta Neurochir (Wien)* 74:27–30, 1985.

109a. Singer MB, Atlas SW, Drayer BP: Subarachnoid space disease: Diagnosis with fluid-attenuated inversion-recovery MR imaging and comparison with gadolinium-enhanced spin-echo MR imaging—blinded reader study. *Radiology* 208:417–422, 1998.

110. Sipponen JT, Sepponen RE, Sivula A: Nuclear magnetic resonance (NMR) imaging of intracerebral hemorrhage in the acute and resolving phases. *J Comput Assist Tomogr* 7:954–959, 1983.

111. Sipponen JT, Sepponen RE, Sivula A: Chronic subdural hematoma: Demonstration by magnetic resonance. *Radiology* 150:79–85, 1984.

112. Smith AS, Hurst GC, Duerk JL, Diaz PJ: MR of ballistic materials: imaging artifacts and potential hazards. *AJNR Am J Neuroradiol* 32:567–572, 1991.

113. Smith WP Jr, Batnitzky S, Rengachary SS: Acute isodense subdural hematomas: a problem in anemic patients. *AJNR Am J Neuroradiol* 2:37–40, 1981.

114. Sparacio RR, Khatib R, Chiu J, Cook AW: Chronic epidural hematoma. *J Trauma* 12:435–439, 1972.

115. Strich SJ, Oxon DM: Shearing of nerve fibres as a cause of brain

damage due to head injury: A pathological study of twenty cases. *Lancet* 2:443–448, 1961.

116. Tamakawa Y, Hanafee WN: Cerebrospinal fluid rhinorrhea: The significance of an air-fluid level in the sphenoid sinus. *Radiology* 135:101–103, 1980.

117. Tsai FY, Huprich JE: Further experience with contrast-enhanced CT in head trauma. *Neuroradiology* 16:314–317, 1978.

118. Tsai FY, Teal JS, Quinn MF, et al: CT of brainstem injury. *AJNR Am J Neuroradiol* 1:23–29, 1980.

119. Tsai FY, Teal JS, Itabashi HH, et al: Computed tomography of posterior fossa trauma. *J Comput Assist Tomogr* 4:291–305, 1980.

120. Tsai FY, Huprich JE, Gardner FC, et al: Diagnostic and prognostic implications of computed tomography of head trauma. *J Comput Assist Tomogr* 2:323–331, 1978.

121. Turski PA, Korosec F: Technical features and emerging clinical applications of phase-contrast magnetic resonance angiography. *Neuroimaging Clin North Am* 2:785–800, 1992.

122. Unger EC, Cohen MS, Brown TR: Gradient-echo imaging of hemorrhage at 1.5 Tesla. *Magn Reson Imaging* 7:163–172, 1989.

123. Van den Heever CM, Van der Merwe DJ: Management of depressed skull fractures: Selective conservative management of nonmissle injuries. *J Neurosurg* 71:186–190, 1989.

124. Weaver D, Pobereskin L, Jane JA: Spontaneous resolution of epidural hematomas: Report of two cases. *J Neurosurg* 54:248–251, 1981.

125. Wilberger J, Chen DA: The skull and meninges. *Neurosurg Clin North Am* 2:341–350, 1991.

126. Winston KR, Beatty RM, Fischer EG: Consequences of dural defects acquired in infancy. *J Neurosurg* 59:839–846, 1983.

127. Yuh WTC, Crain MR, Loes DJ, et al: MR imaging of cerebral ischemia: Findings in the first 24 hours. *AJNR Am J Neuroradiol* 12:621–629, 1991.

128. Zimmerman RA, Bilaniuk LT: Computed tomographic staging of traumatic epidural bleeding. *Radiology* 144:809–812, 1982.

129. Zimmerman RA, Bilaniuk LT, Gennarelli T: Computed tomography of shearing injuries of the cerebral white matter. *Radiology* 127:393–396, 1978.

130. Zimmerman RA, Bilaniuk LT, Dolinska C, et al: Computed tomography of acute intracerebral hemorrhagic contusion. *Comp Ax Tomogr* 1:271–279, 1977.

131. Zimmerman RA, Bilaniuk LT, Bruce D, et al: Computed tomography of pediatric head trauma: Acute general cerebral swelling. *Radiology* 126:403–408, 1978.

132. Zimmerman RA, Bilaniuk LT, Gennarelli T, et al: Cranial computed tomography in diagnosis and management of acute head trauma. *AJR* 131:27–34, 1978.

133. Zimmerman RA, Bilaniuk LT, Bruce D, et al: Interhemispheric acute subdural hematoma: A computed tomographic manifestation of child abuse by shaking. *Neuroradiology* 16:39–40, 1978.

134. Zimmerman RA, Bilaniuk LT, Bruce D, et al: Computed tomography of craniocerebral injury in the abused child. *Radiology* 130:687–690, 1979.

135. Zimmerman RA, Russell EJ, Yurberg E, Leeds NE, et al: Falx and interhemispheric fissure on axial CT. II: Recognition and differentiation of interhemispheric subarachnoid and subdural hemorrhage. *AJNR Am J Neuroradiol* 3:635–642, 1982.

136. Zimmerman RA, Bilaniuk LT, Hackney DB, et al: Head injury: Early results of comparing CT and high-field MR. *AJNR* 7:757–764, 1986.

137. Zimmerman RD, Heier LA, Snow RB, et al: Acute intracranial hemorrhage: Intensity changes on sequential MR scans at .5T. *AJR* 150:651–661, 1988.

10

Neurodegenerative Disorders

Andrei I. Holodny, Ajax E. George,
Mony J. de Leon, Sassan Karimi

Advances in magnetic resonance imaging (MRI) have significantly improved the assessment of neurodegenerative disorders, including the dementias, hydrocephalus, and movement disorders. Often it is difficult to differentiate clinically between various neurodegenerative disorders and even between pathologic processes and the normal aging process. In recent years, specific and sensitive radiologic criteria have been developed to accurately establish the correct diagnosis in these disorders. MRI, with its ability to image the structure and function of the living brain, has become an invaluable tool. The value of understanding the MRI appearance of neurodegenerative disorders will increase as the population ages and as new therapies for these disorders are developed.

Normal Aging

The brain changes that occur as part of normal aging include ventricular and sulcal dilatation due to cerebral atrophy (Fig. 10–1).[21, 26, 27, 46, 67, 75, 88, 102, 111] Despite these structural changes, cerebral metabolism, as measured by positron emission tomography (PET) with the glucose analogues fluorine deoxyglucose (18-FDG) and carbon deoxyglucose (^{11}C-2DG) does not decline with age.[24, 25] The severity of normally occurring brain atrophy is variable, ranging from minimal to moderately severe. Sulcal dilatation is a prominent feature of the aging process, even in the absence of ventricular enlargement. Some subjects over 60 years of age show no ventricular enlargement and demonstrate only mild or no sulcal dilatation. These subjects may be more appropriately considered "supernormals" because of the minimal structural changes that are present despite their age.

On average, ventricular volume increases approximately twofold between young (ages 20 to 30) and elderly (ages 60 to 80) normal subjects. The ventricular volume remains relatively stable up to age 60 years, after which time there is an accelerated increase in size. MRI quantification studies of this type have confirmed the findings reported in the literature on computed tomography (CT) showing that in young normal subjects sulcal volume is approximately equal to that of the ventricular system. In normal subjects over age 60, sulcal volume is greater than that of ventricular volume.[102] MRI-based measurements have shown that in normal healthy volunteers the volumes of the hippocampus, amygdala, and temporal horn remain stable until age 60, with progressive volume loss seen with more advanced age.[86]

Dementia

Dementia can be caused by myriad pathologic processes: (1) *anatomic* (e.g., tumor, subdural hematoma, or normal-pressure hydrocephalus), (2) *physiologic* (electrolyte imbalance), or (3) *psychiatric* (depression). It is often difficult to establish the cause by clinical examination alone. During radiologic assessment, it is imperative to rule out the presence of treatable causes of dementia. The advent of new pharmacologic agents and neurosurgical techniques has increased the number of dementias, which are at least potentially treatable, making the accurate radiologic assessment even more important.

Alzheimer's Disease

Alzheimer's disease (AD)[6, 7] has been recognized as one of the most significant health problems of the 20th century.[73] AD is estimated to afflict 10% of people over 65 years of age and 50% of individuals over age 85 years.[37] It is the most common dementing disorder of the elderly.[119] According to the *Diagnostic and Statistical Manual of Mental Disorders* (*DSM-IV*)[29] patients with AD present with "a multifaceted loss of intellectual abilities, such as memory, judgment, abstract thought, and other higher cortical functions, and changes in personality and behavior." However, these clinical findings are not specific for AD and often are seen with other causes of dementia.

In up to 40% of cases, genetic factors have been implicated in the etiology of AD. Three genes, when mutated, have been identified to cause AD. Some cases of AD are inherited as autosomal dominant trait. In addition, sporadic cases have been identified and account for up to 20% of cases of AD.[22]

A number of pharmacologic trials have been undertaken to improve or stem the advancement of the clinical symptoms of AD. Some have been encouraging. Cholinergic enhancement achieved by pharmacotherapy improves cognitive and noncognitive abilities in a number of patients.[42]

With the introduction of CT in the 1970s, investigators tried to correlate the degree of cerebral atrophy to the degree of dementia in patients with AD. Several early CT studies reported ventricular and sulcal enlargement in association with AD.[21, 26, 27, 46, 75, 79, 80, 111, 114] These atrophic changes, therefore, accentuate those of normal aging. However, there was a large overlap between patients with AD and normal age-matched controls. Some patients with severe cortical atrophy had normal cognition, whereas some patients with severe dementia had minimal cortical atrophy.

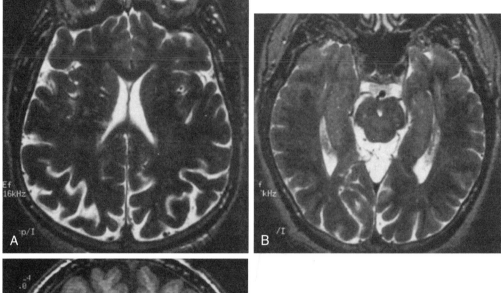

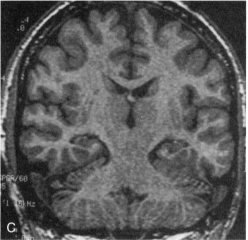

Figure 10–1. *A,* T2-weighted transverse axial image at the level of the bodies of the lateral ventricles in a normal, elderly male volunteer. *B,* Negative angle (infraorbital-meatal plane) cut at the level of the temporal horns. *C,* Coronal T1-weighted gradient-echo image at the level of the hippocampus. There is mild cortical atrophy. The lateral ventricles are not appreciably enlarged. The temporal lobes show minimal, if any, atrophy. Prominent perivascular (Virchow-Robin) spaces emanate from the lateral ventricles *(A),* representing a normal variant. Faint peritrigonal T2 hyperintensities in *A* indicate minimal microvascular disease.

Neuropathologic evidence has shown severe focal cell loss and neurofibrillary tangle formation of the subiculum and entorhinal cortex in AD.[88] The focal pattern of pathology in this region apparently isolates the hippocampal formation from much of its output and input, thereby contributing to the memory disorder characteristic of AD patients. The pathologic changes include senile plaques, neurofibrillary tangles, and granulovacuolar degeneration with progressive neuronal loss and atrophy of the hippocampal formation.[10, 64, 74, 121] There are also neural transmitter deficits and a severe loss in the density of synaptic terminals.[57] In view of the involvement of this region, AD has been characterized as a hippocampal dementia.[10]

In view of this neuropathologic evidence, imaging studies, including our own,[21, 26, 27, 46, 75, 76, 79, 80, 111, 114] have focused on specific evaluation of the temporal lobes. These studies strongly suggest that AD may be diagnosed in life by MRI or CT. Thus, the role of neuroimaging and the diagnosis of this process, which has long been based on the method of exclusion, is now changing.

The transverse fissure of Bichat separates the telencephalon from the diencephalon. A medial part separates the thalamus from the fornix and corpus callosum, and a lateral part is situated between the thalamus and the parahippocampal gyrus. Medially the transverse fissure communicates with the perimesencephalic cistern[60] (Figs. 10–2 and 10–3).

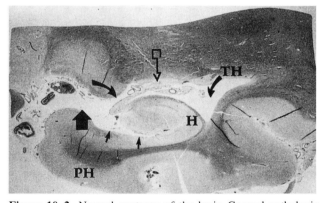

Figure 10–2. Normal anatomy of the brain Coronal pathologic section through the medial temporal lobe, including the hippocampus (H). The perihippocampal fissures, including the transverse fissure of Bichat *(large arrow),* the hippocampal fissure *(small arrows),* and the choroidal fissure *(curved arrows)* are seen. The transverse fissure of Bichat communicates with the perimesencephalic cistern *(lower left).* The choroid plexus and the fimbria *(arrow with square)* form a physical barrier between the temporal horn (TH) and the choroidal fissure. PH, parahippocampal gyrus. (From Holodny AI, George AE, Golomb J, et al: The perihippocampal fissures: Normal anatomy and disease states. Radiographics 18:653–665, 1998.)

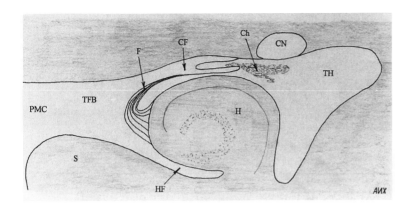

Figure 10–3. Normal brain anatomy. Coronal diagram shows the medial temporal lobe structures, including the perihippocampal fissures. The medial aspect is to the left and the lateral aspect is to the right. The perihippocampal fissures are visible but are not dilated. The choroid plexus (Ch) and the fimbria (F) form a physical barrier between the temporal horn (TH) and the choroidal fissure (CF). CN, caudate nucleus; H, hippocampus; HF, hippocampal fissure; PMC, perimesencephalic cistern; S, subiculum; TFB, transverse fissure of Bichat. (From Holodny AI, George AE, Golomb J, et al: The perihippocampal fissures: Normal anatomy and disease states. Radiographics 18:653–665, 1998.)

Figure 10–4. Anatomic changes in a patient with Alzheimer's disease. Coronal diagram shows the medial temporal lobe structures, including the perihippocampal fissures. Compared to the normal individual in Figure 10–3, there is volume loss of the hippocampus and corresponding dilatation of the perihippocampal fissures. The choroid plexus (Ch) and the fimbria (F) form a physical barrier between the temporal horn (TH) and the choroidal fissure (CF). CN, caudate nucleus; H, hippocampus; HF, hippocampal fissure; PMC, perimesencephalic cistern; S, subiculum; TFB transverse fissure of Bichat. (From Holodny AI, George AE, Golomb J, et al: The perihippocampal fissures: Normal anatomy and disease states. Radiographics 18:653–665, 1998.)

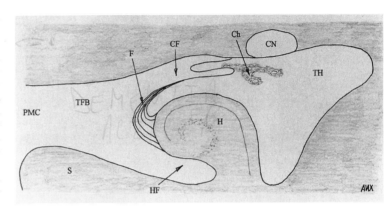

Temporal lobe changes are highly sensitive markers of AD.[27, 46, 61] The use of either CT or MRI negative-angle, thin-section cuts that parallel the temporal lobes or coronal thin-section MRI scans perpendicular to the axial plane maximizes the demonstration of temporal lobe pathology. Almost all patients with AD show at least a moderate degree of hippocampal atrophy as well as atrophy of the parahippocampal gyrus, dentate gyrus, and subiculum. These atrophic changes lead to enlargement of the transverse fissure of Bichat and the hippocampal and choroidal extensions as well as dilatation of the temporal horn (Fig. 10–4). Although high-resolution coronal images display this anatomy optimally, even mild hippocampal atrophy and the resultant dilatation of the perihippocampal fissures can be seen on standard MRI and CT images[27] (see Figs. 10–5 and 10–6).

The longitudinal study of normal subjects and patients with AD for structural brain changes shows a greatly increased rate of change in the AD patients as compared with normal subjects.[26, 41] We found that 90% of patients with AD showed progressive atrophy of the temporal lobes when they were longitudinally studied over a 3-year period[26] (see Fig. 10–12). More important is that the presence of medial temporal lobe atrophy in normal individuals[49] may represent a significant risk factor for the subsequent development of AD.[27]

In addition, it appears that an atrophic hippocampus not only is a radiologic marker for the presence of AD but also may actually serve as a predictor for the future development of this disorder. In a landmark study by de Leon and coworkers,[27] 86 older adult patients who were either normal

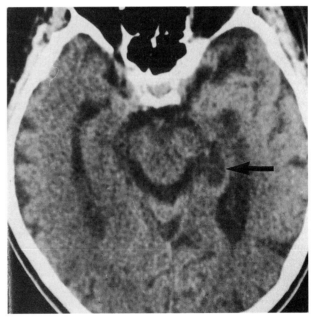

Figure 10–5. Clinical Alzheimer's disease. Reverse-angle CT scan (angled parallel to the hippocampus) demonstrates an area of decreased density in the medial aspect of the temporal lobe (*arrow*). The density of this area approaches that of cerebrospinal fluid. This corresponds to dilatation of the perihippocampal fissures and is an accurate indicator of hippocampal atrophy. (From Holodny AI, George AE, Golomb J, et al: The perihippocampal fissures: Normal anatomy and disease states. Radiographics 18: 653–665, 1998.)

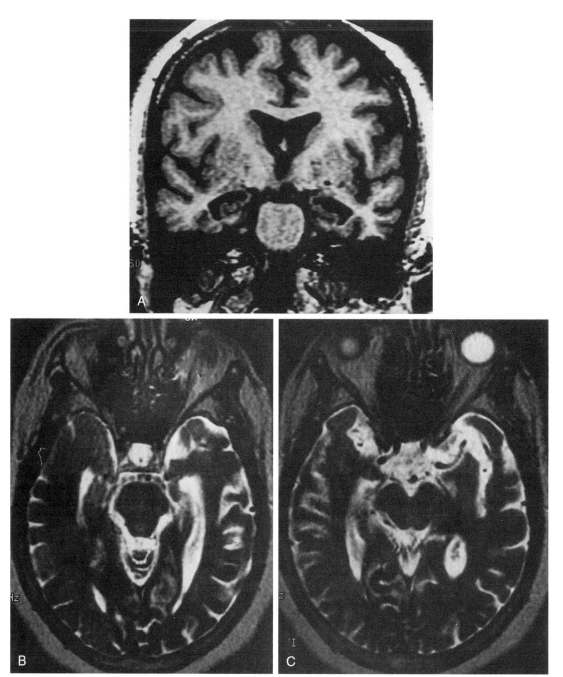

Figure 10–6. Presumed Alzheimer's disease in a 60-year-old woman. *A,* Coronal T1-weighted MR image demonstrates severe atrophy of the hippocampus and dilatation of the perihippocampal fissures. *B* and *C,* Reverse-angle axial T2-weighted images in the same patient. These images demonstrate the importance of evaluating for prominence of the perihippocampal fissures and hippocampal atrophy in the correct plane. *B* is inferior to *C.* In *B,* the left medial temporal lobe demonstrates prominent perihippocampal fissures (the area of increased signal intensity between the temporal horn and the pons). The right medial temporal lobe on image B fails to demonstrate this area of increased signal intensity. This is because the patient is slightly tilted and one is actually scanning through the area of the parahippocampal gyrus (see Fig. 10–1), not the atrophic hippocampus. An analogous situation exists in *C.* The dilated perihippocampal fissures are seen on the right. The scanning plane on the left side is directed superior to the perihippocampal fissures and therefore does not demonstrate the area of increased signal intensity associated with dilated perihippocampal fissures. (From Holodny AI, George AE, Golomb J, et al: The perihippocampal fissures: Normal anatomy and disease states. Radiographics 18: 653–665, 1998.)

or who had minimal cognitive impairment were monitored for four years. Dilatation of the perihippocampal fissures at the time of entry into the study was a predictor of future deterioration and development of AD, with a sensitivity of 91% and a specificity of 89%.

Hydrocephalus

Classification

Hydrocephalus, from the Greek *hydro* (water) and *cephalus* (brain) is an abnormal accumulation of intracranial fluid (i.e., water on the brain) resulting from a structural or functional block to the normal flow of cerebrospinal fluid (CSF). The ventricles may become significantly enlarged.

The diagnosis of hydrocephalus in patients under age 60 years is usually straightforward. In patients over age 60, however, often confounding superimposed changes of atrophy are caused by normal aging and possible coexisting AD.[48] Hydrocephalus is initially associated with increased intracranial pressure, but it may later reach a state of equilibrium known as *arrested*, or *normal-pressure*, *hydrocephalus*.

When the block to the flow of CSF occurs along the ventricular system, the condition is known as *obstructive hydrocephalus*. Since all hydrocephalus is obstructive, the term *intraventricular obstructive hydrocephalus* has been proposed as a more accurate description for this type of obstruction. If the block to CSF is distal to the ventricular system, either at the base of the skull or as distal as the level of the pacchionian granulations, the hydrocephalus is described as *communicating* (i.e., the ventricular system communicates with the extraventricular subarachnoid space). A more accurate term for this condition would therefore be *extraventricular obstructive hydrocephalus*. The term *hydrocephalus ex vacuo* is sometimes used to refer to cerebral atrophy; this term is best avoided, however, because of its confusing implications.

The terms *communicating hydrocephalus* and *noncommunicating* (or *obstructive*) *hydrocephalus* have prevailed since the early days of neuroradiologic diagnosis. Dandy and Blackfan[23] introduced a color dye (phenolsulfonphthalein) by ventricular catheter into the hydrocephalic ventricular system. If the color dye could be extracted by lumbar spinal tap within 2 to 3 minutes, the hydrocephalus was then described as "communicating." If the dye did not appear on spinal tap or was greatly delayed, the hydrocephalus was considered obstructive, or "noncommunicating."

The CT and MRI features of communicating hydrocephalus are as follows:

1. *Early dilatation and rounding of the temporal horns.* These features may be the earliest manifestation of ventricular obstruction and may be seen before obvious enlargement of the bodies of the lateral ventricles. In contradistinction, temporal horn dilatation as a manifestation of temporal lobe atrophy occurs later in the progression of a degenerative brain disease and is invariably associated with the presence of enlargement of the perihippocampal fissures (the transverse fissure of Bichat, and the choroidal and hippocampal fissures). The cisternal spaces and their extensions (the perihippocampal fissures) do not communicate with the temporal lobe; therefore, the dilatation of the temporal horn caused by obstructive hydrocephalus may actually displace the hippocampus medially and cause compression of the perihippocampal fissures[59] (Figs. 10–7 and 10–8).

2. *Rounding and enlargement of the frontal horns.* Figure 10–8 shows the MRI scan of a 47-year-old woman with hydrocephalus. The scan shows severe lateral and third ventricular dilatation. The frontal horns are ballooned, and the angle formed by their medial walls (the septal angle) is acute. In atrophy, the frontal horns are typically enlarged but not ballooned. The septal angle is often obtuse.

3. *Enlargement and ballooning of the third ventricle.* In atrophy, the third ventricle tends to enlarge by increasing the distance between its walls, which tend to remain parallel to each other. Ballooning and rounding of the third ventricle are characteristic of hydrocephalus. In the sagittal projection, the roof of the third ventricle may be flattened by the often huge lateral ventricular bodies.

4. *Severe dilatation of the bodies of the lateral ventricles and increased height of the ventricles.* The degree of dilatation of the lateral ventricles in hydrocephalus is typically notably greater than that occurring secondary to atrophy. The corpus callosum is thinned and bowed, forming an arch. Interpeduncular height may be decreased.[35] Typically, a patient with severe ventricular

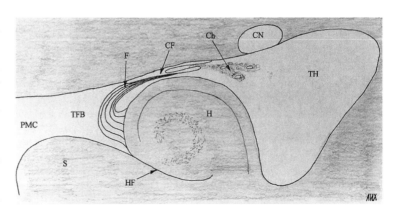

Figure 10–7. Anatomic changes in hydrocephalus. Coronal diagram shows the structures of the medial temporal lobe, including the perihippocampal fissures. Compared to the normal individual in Figure 10–3, there is dilation of the temporal horn of the lateral ventricle. The hippocampus is displaced medially, and the perihippocampal fissures are compressed. The choroid plexus (Ch) and the fimbria (F) form a physical barrier between the temporal horn (TH) and the choroidal fissure (CF). CN, caudate nucleus; H, hippocampus; HF, hippocampal fissure; PMC, perimesencephalic cistern; S, subiculum; TFB, transverse fissure of Bichat. (From Holodny AI, George AE, Golomb J, de Leon MJ, Kalnin AJ: The perihippocampal fissures: Normal anatomy and disease states. Radiographics 18:653–665, 1998.)

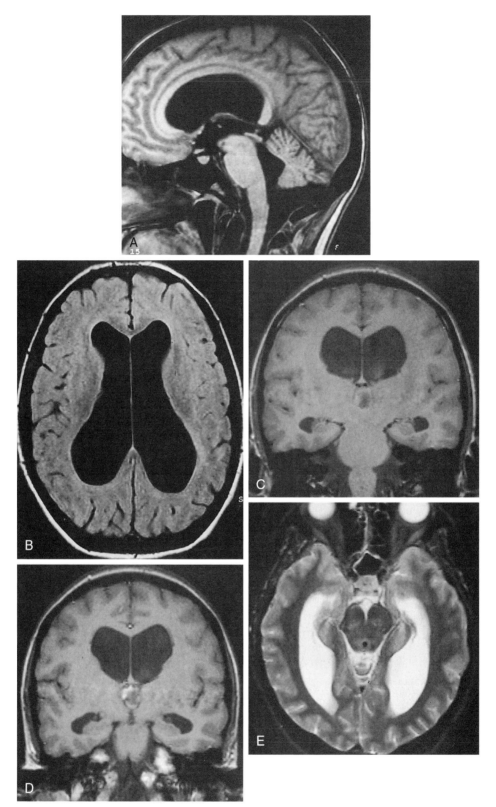

Figure 10–8. Hydrocephalus in a 47-year-old patient. *A,* Sagittal T1-weighted image demonstrates dilatation of the lateral, third, and fourth ventricles. There is bowing of the corpus callosum. *B,* Axial fluid-attenuated inversion recovery (FLAIR) image demonstrates marked dilatation of the ventricles out of proportion to the sulci. *C* and *D,* Coronal T1-weighted images demonstrate marked dilatation of the lateral ventricles, including the temporal horns. There is no hippocampal atrophy. *E,* Hydrocephalus is confirmed on this axial T2-weighted image. (From Holodny AI, George AE, Golomb J: Neurodegenerative disorders. In Edelman R, Hesselink JR (eds): Clinical Magnetic Resonance Imaging, 2nd ed. Philadelphia, WB Saunders, 1996.)

dilatation caused by hydrocephalus may show a minimal cognitive deficit. In contrast, a patient with comparably severe ventricular dilatation caused by atrophy usually shows profound cognitive impairment. Note the relatively modest ventricular enlargement in patients with severe dementia. A motoric deficit, especially gait impairment, is a characteristic feature of hydrocephalus. The motoric deficit may be severe to the point that patients may be wheelchair-bound or bed-bound. Ventricular shunting in these patients may have dramatic results, with significant improvement in gait and motor function.

5. *Enlargement of the fourth ventricle.* This finding presupposes that the hydrocephalus is communicating. In chronic obstructive hydrocephalus, however, the fourth ventricle may also enlarge secondarily from incisural obstruction created by the enlarged ventricles, dilated temporal horns, and swollen temporal lobes, which tend to herniate into the incisural notch. When present, dilatation of the fourth ventricle can be helpful in establishing the diagnosis of hydrocephalus. However, fourth-ventricular enlargement may be absent or minimal despite the presence of definite hydrocephalus.

6. *Sulcal effacement.* When present, sulcal effacement is usually diagnostic of hydrocephalus in the elderly age group because cortical atrophy is almost invariably present as part of the normal aging process. Hydrocephalus, however, may coexist with large sulci and, in particular, with large sylvian fissures. This occurs when the block is at the level of the high convexity or the pacchionian granulations. Consequently, the sulci and fissures dilate because of the damming of fluid proximal to the block. In effect, the sulci and fissures dilate in the same way as the ventricular system because of the distal obstruction. In such patients, ventricular shunting may lead to collapse of the sylvian fissures, the sulci, and other convexity CSF collections.[60]

7. *Periventricular edema.* This finding is seen especially in the periventricular white matter of the frontal horns in acute and subacute phases of hydrocephalus. In older people, however, it is usually not possible to distinguish between periventricular T2 changes resulting from microvascular parenchymal disease (see later) and the periventricular edema of hydrocephalus. In fact, hydrocephalus may lead to chronic microvascular changes, as shown in animal hydrocephalus models.[59] It was initially thought that MRI might help identify ventricular enlargement due to hydrocephalus by the presence of a periventricular high-signal halo on T2-weighted images. Because periventricular high-signal changes as a result of microvascular disease are also seen, the finding is therefore nonspecific and not helpful.[97] Furthermore, in chronic stages of hydrocephalus, periventricular edema resolves and is not visualized by either CT or MRI.

Obstructive Hydrocephalus

The sites where the ventricular system is normally narrow (i.e., the foramina) are particularly vulnerable to obstruction. Causes of intraventricular obstruction at the level of the foramen of Monro include (1) colloid cyst of the third ventricle, (2) ependymoma, (3) teratoma, (4) congenital atresia, and (5) involvement by adjacent glioma.

The posterior third ventricle may be obstructed by pinealomas and aneurysms of the vein of Galen. Aqueductal obstruction can also occur in association with aqueductal stenosis, periaqueductal gliomas, arteriovenous malformations, and cysts of the quadrigeminal region.

Communicating Hydrocephalus

Communicating hydrocephalus may result from previous infection such as meningitis or may be secondary to previous hemorrhage caused by trauma, surgery, or rupture of an aneurysm with subarachnoid hemorrhage. It is also seen in association with Arnold-Chiari malformation and in the presence of subarachnoid seeding of tumor (meningiocarcinomatosis). A functional hydrocephalus in the presence of elevated CSF protein is seen in association with spinal cord tumors, typically ependymomas. Overproduction of CSF caused by choroid plexus papilloma or carcinoma may also result in hydrocephalus.

Normal-Pressure Hydrocephalus

An idiopathic form of communicating hydrocephalus, usually seen in older adults and known as normal-pressure hydrocephalus (NPH), was described originally by Adams and Hakim and their colleagues.[3, 56] These authors reported a clinical triad of gait impairment characterized as magnetic gait, dementia, and urinary incontinence. Symptoms can be relieved by ventricular shunting, with the most dramatic improvement usually seen in gait. The typical patient with NPH who is likely to respond to a shunt exhibits a mild cognitive impairment along with a significant gait disturbance.

Differentiating NPH from cerebral atrophy can be extremely difficult. Initial enthusiasm for the concept of NPH as a treatable cause of dementia and gait impairment resulted in shunt procedures in patients who either failed to respond or showed an initial improvement but subsequently continued to deteriorate. Because of these discouraging results, the number of shunt procedures for NPH in the elderly has significantly decreased. The failure of patients to respond to the shunt procedure probably resulted from erroneous diagnosis of hydrocephalus in patients who were suffering from degenerative brain disease such as cerebral atrophy associated with AD. This has led to more stringent criteria to identify potential shunt candidates. These criteria include (1) radioisotope cisternography,[84] (2) continuous intracranial pressure recordings,[98] (3) spinal effusion,[90] and (4) CT cisternography with intrathecal iodinated contrast material.[36] Despite these criteria, a reliable study predicting shunt outcome has not been established.

In terms of MRI, two approaches can be used to differentiate NPH from cerebral atrophy: the anatomic approach and the functional approach. Anatomically, in patients with AD, volume loss of the hippocampus develops and resultant dilatation of the perihippocampal fissures ensues (see Fig. 10–4). Patients with NPH have dilation of the temporal horn (Fig. 10–7).[61] Although the hippocampus and the

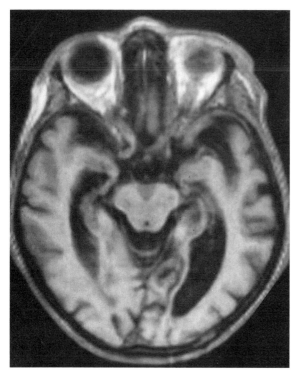

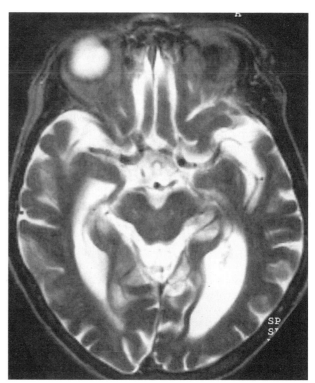

Figure 10–9. Clinical Alzheimer's disease in a woman. Reverse-angle axial T1-weighted MR image (Global Deterioration Scale = 5). There is decreased signal intensity between the temporal horns and the perimesencephalic cistern. This represents dilatation of the perihippocampal fissures (PHFs) and atrophy of the structures of the medial temporal lobe, including the hippocampus. The size of the PHFs was assessed as moderately dilated. Compare with Figures 10–11 and 10–12. (From Holodny AI, Waxman R, George AE, et al: MR differential diagnosis of normal-pressure hydrocephalus and Alzheimer disease: Significance of the perihippocampal fissures. AJNR Am J Neuroradiol 19:813–819, 1998.)

Figure 10–10. Alzheimer's disease in a 73-year-old patient. Axial T2-weighted images angled parallel to the hippocampi demonstrate marked atrophy of the hippocampus and marked dilatation of the perihippocampal fissures. By comparison, the ventricles and cortical sulci are only mildly dilated. Compare with Figures 10–11 and 10–12. (From Holodny AI, Waxman R, George AE, et al: MR differential diagnosis of normal-pressure hydrocephalus and Alzheimer disease: Significance of the perihippocampal fissures. AJNR Am J Neuroradiol 19:813–819, 1998.)

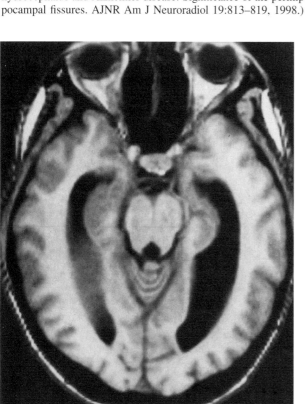

Figure 10–11. Reverse-angle axial T1-weighted MR image of normal-pressure hydrocephalus in a 72-year-old man who improved after the placement of a ventriculoperitoneal shunt. There is no abnormally decreased signal intensity of the structures of the medial temporal lobes; therefore, there is no dilatation of the perihippocampal fissures or atrophy of the structures of the medial temporal lobe, including the hippocampus. The size of the perihippocampal fissures was graded as normal. This is in contrast to the patients from the group with Alzheimer's disease in Figures 10–9 and 10–10. There is dilatation of the temporal horns to a degree similar to patients from the Alzheimer group. (From Holodny AI, Waxman R, George AE, et al: MR differential diagnosis of normal-pressure hydrocephalus and Alzheimer disease: Significance of the perihippocampal fissures. AJNR Am J Neuroradiol 19:813–819, 1998.)

perihippocampal fissures are best seen in the coronal plane on MRI, it is important to stress that the anatomic changes occurring in NPH and AD can be appreciated to a large degree on axial MRI and CT (Figs. 10–9 to 10–12).[59]

Occasionally, patients with NPH present with dilated sylvian fissures and rarely with focally dilated cortical sulci.[60] In a number of cases of shunt-proven NPH, there was actually paradoxical decrease in the size of the dilated cortical fissures and sulci that paralleled the decrease in the size of the lateral ventricles following successful shunting. Therefore, sulcal dilatation (especially when focal) should not be taken to imply cortical atrophy, and the maxim that hydrocephalus is defined as ventricles dilated out of proportion to the sulci does not always apply (Figs. 10–13 and 10–14).

Because AD is rather prevalent in the elderly, it can occasionally coexist with NPH. Earlier literature suggested that patients with dementia due to AD are not candidates for intraventricular shunting. However, more recent work suggests that for patients with accurately diagnosed NPH, concomitant AD does not strongly influence the clinical response to shunt placement.[50]

Another MRI approach to the diagnosis of NPH is the quantification of CSF flow in the aqueduct. Work by Bradley and coworkers[14] has demonstrated that in patients with shunt-proven NPH, the CSF stroke volume and CSF velocity in the aqueduct are both increased. However, the presence or absence of a flow void in the aqueduct does not appear to be an accurate predictor of shunt response.[14]

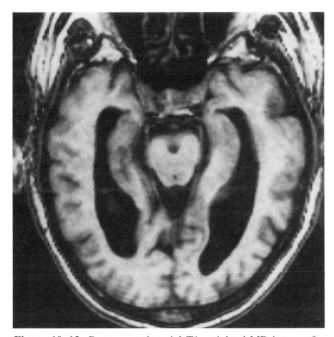

Figure 10–12. Reverse-angle axial T1-weighted MR image of a patient with normal-pressure hydrocephalus. There is a mild degree of decreased signal intensity of the structures of the medial temporal lobes. Therefore, the size of the perihippocampal fissures was graded as mildly dilated. Compare with Figures 10–9 and 10–10. (From Holodny AI, Waxman R, George AE, et al: MR differential diagnosis of normal-pressure hydrocephalus and Alzheimer disease: Significance of the perihippocampal fissures. AJNR Am J Neuroradiol 19:813–819, 1998.)

In summary, using the combination of radiologic and clinical criteria in conjunction with the results of measurements of cerebral blood flow and cerebral metabolism, we may more reliably and with greater accuracy identify patients with hydrocephalus who are likely to respond to shunt. Functional MRI techniques now becoming available may noninvasively provide similar functional information as that derived from PET and single photon emission computed tomography (SPECT). As a result of these advances, interest has been renewed in the surgical management of patients with hydrocephalus.

Pick's Disease

Pick's disease, another cause of dementia in adults, was first described in 1892.[97] The onset of dementia is often in the presenile age group, and a familial occurrence has been reported.[54] Pick's disease is much less prevalent than AD. The clinical presentation in most patients is suggestive of frontal lobe damage. There is an insidious deterioration in intellectual capacity and difficulty in concentration and memory. There is a slow but steady progression to marked dementia, which is usually more rapidly progressive than with AD.

On pathologic examination, there is atrophy of the brain, particularly of the frontal lobes and the anterior aspects of the temporal lobes. The parietal and occipital lobes are usually spared. Histologically, there is an intense loss and misalignment of neurons as well as subcortical gliosis in the affected areas of the brain. Many of the remaining neurons are small and contain characteristic intracytoplasmic, argentophilic inclusion bodies (Pick's bodies), which are well seen with Bielschowsky silver stain and antibody immunostaining.[2]

Prior to the advent of cross-sectional imaging, Pick's disease could be definitively diagnosed only at autopsy; however, the introduction of CT and MRI has allowed for the accurate diagnosis of Pick's disease in vivo and to differentiate it from other neurodegenerative disorders.[40] Radiographically, Pick's disease parallels the findings seen on pathologic studies, and marked atrophy of the anterior temporal and frontal lobes are characteristics. The sulci of these lobes become so atrophic that they have been described as icicle-like. There is usually a sparing of the posterior aspect of the superior frontal gyrus and the brain posterior to it.[33]

Leukoencephalopathy of Aging, Multi-Infarct Dementia, and Binswanger's Disease

MRI is exquisitely sensitive to the detection of white matter disease. As in the atrophic changes described in the first part of this chapter, understanding the MRI characteristics and the underlying pathophysiology can allow one to arrive at the accurate diagnosis. Since this chapter focuses on neurodegenerative diseases, it covers only the limited number of white matter diseases that apply to this category.

Long repetition time (TR) (T2, proton-density) and fluid-attenuating inversion recovery [FLAIR] hyperintensities are common in the elderly.[45] These white matter lesions

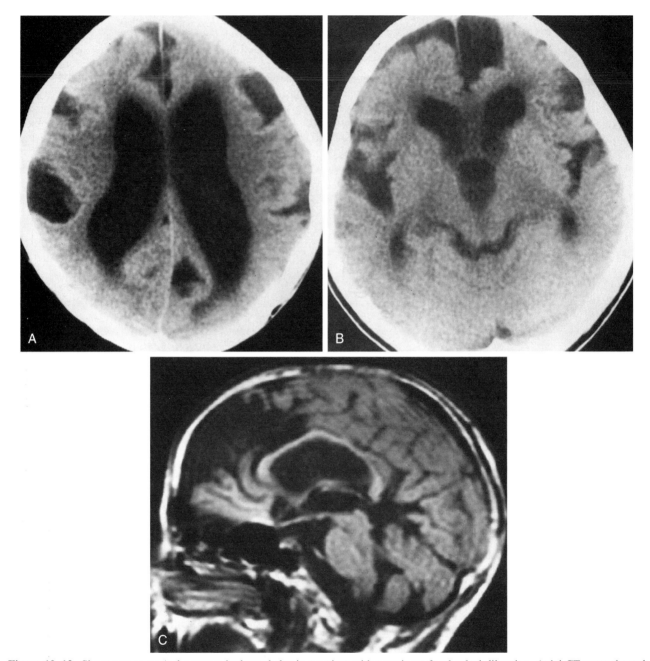

Figure 10–13. Shunt-proven normal-pressure hydrocephalus in a patient with prominent focal sulcal dilatation. Axial CT scans through the bodies of the lateral ventricles *(A)* and third ventricle *(B)* and midsagittal MR image *(C)* demonstrate marked dilatation of the lateral ventricles. The temporal horns are moderately enlarged. The third ventricle is severely dilated and rounded. There is marked dilatation of the following sulci: the sylvian fissures bilaterally, the central sulci bilaterally, the anterior aspect of the interhemispheric fissure, the left parieto-occipital fissure and the left calcarine fissure. In addition, there is marked focal dilatation of the cingulate sulcus on the right, the precentral sulcus on the left, and the frontal sulci bilaterally. There is also dilatation of the suprasellar and quadrigeminal plate cisterns. The remaining sulci are compressed. There is no evidence of dilatation of the choroidal and parahippocampal fissures, hippocampal atrophy, or cerebellar or brain stem abnormalities. (From Holodny AI, George AE, de Leon MJ, et al: Focal dilatation and paradoxical collapse of cortical fissures and sulci in patients with normal-pressure hydrocephalus. J Neurosurg 89:742–747, 1998.)

are typically patchy or punctate and involve the peritrigonal region preferentially. The second most common area involves the white matter adjacent to the frontal horns. Brain stem lesions are less common. Typically, this process spares the arcuate fibers and the corpus callosum. Variously termed *leukoencephalopathy, leukoaraiosis,*[16, 55] *deep white matter ischemia,* or *white matter hyperintensities of aging,* the lesions are strongly related to age and have increasing prevalence in individuals over age 60 years.[44] It is also seen earlier and to a greater degree in patients with microvascular diseases, such as diabetes and hypertension. White matter is more susceptible than gray matter to chronic ischemic changes because it is supplied by long, small-caliber vessels, which are affected these diseases.

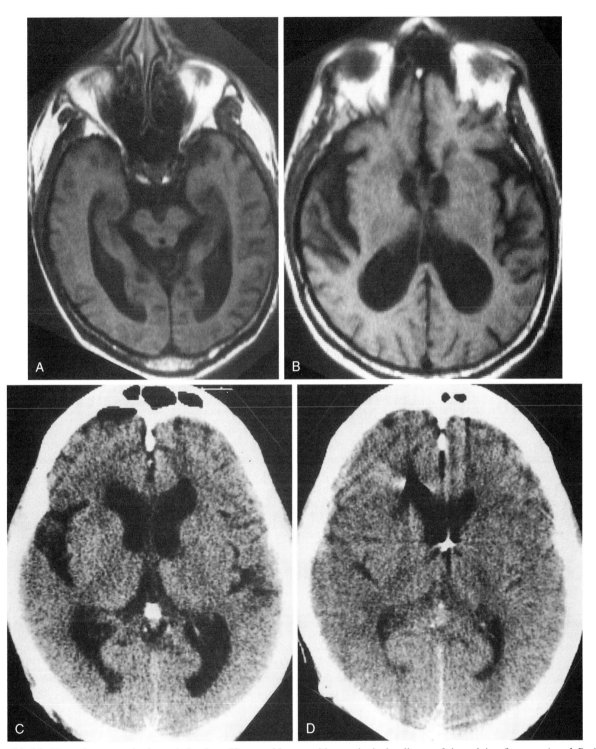

Figure 10–14. Normal-pressure hydrocephalus in a 68-year-old man with paradoxical collapse of the sylvian fissures. *A* and *B*, Axial T1-weighted images demonstrate enlarged lateral ventricles, including the temporal horns as well as moderately distended sylvian fissures. Several months after successful shunting, the patient returned with recurrent symptoms. *C*, A CT scan demonstrated evidence of shunt failure with distention of the lateral ventricles. Sylvian fissure dilatation was also present. *D*, Following shunt revision, a CT scan demonstrated a decrease in the size of the lateral ventricles as well as a decrease in the size of the sylvian fissures. (From Holodny AI, George AE, de Leon MJ, et al: Focal dilatation and paradoxical collapse of cortical fissures and sulci in patients with normal-pressure hydrocephalus. J Neurosurg 89:742–747, 1998.)

Leukoencephalopathy cannot be considered a benign entity.[16] We and others have found that these brain changes are related to gait disturbances and increased incidence of falls in the elderly,[83] deficits of fine motor coordination,[77] and an increased frequency in cerebral infarcts.[44, 45, 69, 122] The increased incidence of falls is particularly of concern in older people.[83] The microvascular lesions themselves are not associated with dementia; however, the cognitive deficit associated with preexisting AD or other dementing disorders may be potentiated by the presence of the white matter lesion.[44]

Autopsy work, including our own, has shown changes of the hypertensive type in the white matter associated with hyalinosis of arterioles and rarefaction of the white matter.[19, 44, 52, 82, 100] In addition, mild gliosis, increased interstitial fluid, and "myelin pallor" are seen. Frank infarction occurs in more advanced cases and can be seen as well-defined areas of decreased signal intensity on the T1-weighted images. The T1 characteristics allows one to differentiated leukoencephalopathy from frank infarction.

Multiple-infarct dementia (MID) is the second most common cause of dementia in the elderly representing 10% to 20% of cases in patients over 65 years old.[121] Clinically, these patients present with a sudden onset of dementia, day-to-day fluctuation, and spontaneous improvement early in the disease. These patients present radiographically with focally dilated fissures and multiple areas of focal cortical volume loss. Multiple subcortical infarcts and infarcts involving certain strategic structures (e.g., parts of the thalamus, caudate, or genu of the internal capsule) can also result in dementia.[81]

In 1894, Binswanger[6] described a slowly progressive disease characterized by loss of memory and intellectual impairment associated with recurring neurologic deficits. Binswanger was apparently describing a type of multi-infarct dementia with severe hypertensive type microvascular changes, multiple subcortical infarcts, and dementia. The presence of periventricular T2 hyperintensities on MRI scans should not prompt a diagnosis of *Binswanger's disease* or multi-infarct dementia unless evidence clearly shows that infarcts are also present and that dementia is clinically present. Multiple infarcts, whether cortical or subcortical and especially when bilateral, may be associated with dementia. One should also keep in mind that even numerous subcortical infarcts may lead to only mild dementia. Because periventricular white matter hyperintensities are widely prevalent, especially in the elderly, the terms *multi-infarct dementia* and *Binswanger's disease* should not be used to describe these radiologic findings.[95]

Creutzfeldt-Jakob Disease

Creutzfeldt-Jakob disease (CJD) is a rare cause of rapidly progressive dementia and is one of several associated neurodegenerative illnesses whose pathogenesis is related to a small, nonviral, 30- to 35-kD proteinaceous infectious particle known as a *prion*. The loci of pathology involve the cerebral and cerebellar cortices as well as the basal ganglia, where neuronal loss, reactive astrocytosis and the formation of cytoplasmic vacuoles within the glia and neurons give the tissue a characteristic spongiform appear-

ance on light microscopy. All of these changes occur in the absence of an inflammatory response.

The clinical syndrome is typically one of rapid cognitive decline, often with psychosis and delirium. Motor abnormalities of cerebellar dysfunction can appear, and almost all patients evidence pronounced myoclonus prior to the final phase of deepening unresponsiveness and coma. The time course of the disease from presentation until death is usually less than 1 year.

In the very early stages of the disease, CT and even MRI findings may be normal.[125] Early changes are symmetrical increased signal intensity in the basal ganglia[11, 30, 85, 118] and occasionally in the white matter.[131] Occasionally, the changes in the basal ganglia occur before the typical clinical and neurophysiologic signs of CJD develop.[101] In three patients, cortical diffusion-weighted imaging abnormalities were reported to occur before the onset of abnormal signal in the basal ganglia on routine sequences.

The year 1986 heralded the appearance of a new form of CJD—bovine spongiform encephalitis (BSE), or "mad cow disease." This new variant (nvCJD) was first detected in humans in 1996. The possibility of direct transmission of BSE from cows to humans has raised serious concerns, especially in Europe.[127] nvCJD tends to affect a younger population, with a median age at death of 29 years.[129] The earliest MRI findings are abnormal signal intensity on the long TR-weighted images of the pulvinar.[129, 132]

During the late stages of the disease, significant atrophy develops and progresses rapidly.[125] Symmetrical increased T2 signal abnormality with mass effect in the occipital cortex, predominantly in a gray matter distribution, has been reported.[38] A study using magnetic resonance spectroscopy (MRS) detected a decrease in *N*-acetylaspartate (NAA) and other metabolites in late CJD.[53]

Huntington's Disease

Huntington's disease (HD) is a degenerative neurologic disease that is inherited in an autosomal dominant fashion with complete penetrance. It is determined by a gene localized to the short arm of chromosome 4. Patients usually become symptomatic before age 50 and tend to present with abnormalities of affect and personality. Within time, dementia becomes evident, accompanied by gradual disintegration of motor control and the emergence of choreoathetoid movements. Occasionally, rigidity rather than chorea is the most salient motor abnormality (Westphal variant).

Neuropathologically, the most conspicuous finding in patients with HD is atrophy of the basal ganglia, generally proceeding medial to lateral and dorsal to ventral.[58, 99, 126] Degenerative changes can also affect the frontal and temporal cortices. The degenerative process is accompanied by diminished neurotransmitter concentrations of acetylcholine and gamma-aminobutyric acid (GABA). In early cases, neuronal loss is generally first appreciated in the head of the caudate.[126] This has been confirmed by a number of MRI studies showing atrophy of the basal ganglia in patients with HD, which is most prominent in the head of the caudate, appearing as focal enlargement of frontal horns on imaging. The atrophy of these structures worsens as the disease progresses.[9] MRS studies indicate a decrease in

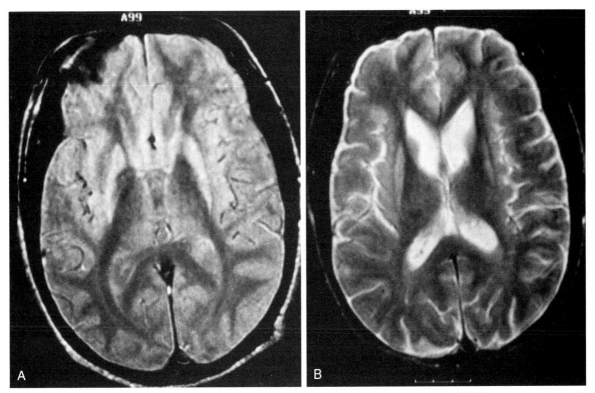

Figure 10–15. Huntington's disease in a 33-year-old man. Axial proton-density (*A*) and T2-weighted (*B*) images demonstrate abnormal signal intensity in the putamen and caudate nuclei. (From Sclar G, Kennedy CA, Hill JM: Cerebellar degeneration associated with HIV infection [letter]. Neurology 54:1012–1013, 2000.)

NAA and creatine in the basal ganglia of 60% in symptomatic patients and a decrease of 30% in presymptomatic gene carriers.[114]

A number of investigators have reported that in addition to atrophic changes, patients with HD present with areas of abnormal T2 signal hyperintensity in the basal ganglia (Fig. 10–15). Two groups have reported that such changes are present in all patients with the rigid form of HD but only occasionally in the classic hyperkinetic form.[93, 107]

More advanced cases of HD present with atrophy of other parts of the central nervous system, including the olives, pons, and cerebellum[108]; the thalamus, mesial temporal lobe and white matter tracts[70]; and the cerebral cortex.[115] Cortical atrophy, as seen on the MRI scan, has been shown to correlate well with specific neuropsychological deficits.[115]

Parkinson's Disease

Parkinson's disease (PD) affects approximately 1% of the population over 50 years of age and is perhaps the most common neurologic explanation of progressive motor impairment among older adults. Onset of symptoms is typically seen between 40 and 70 years of age. The disease is caused by an acceleration of the normal age-dependent depletion of dopamine synthesizing pigmented cells within the pars compacta of the substantia nigra. The loss of dopaminergic input to the striatum caused by this cell loss produces a characteristic syndrome, of which the most salient features are progressive bradykinesis, rigidity,

masked facies, hypophonia, festinating gait with stooped posture, and a coarse resting tremor. Dementia may occur in up to 30% of patients, which may reflect the concomitant presence of AD. In addition to the substantia nigra, patients at autopsy reveal a loss of pigmented cells within the locus ceruleus and the dorsal motor nucleus of the vagus. These regions exhibit reactive astrocytosis, and some of the remaining neurons contain eosinophilic cytoplasmic inclusions called Lewy bodies.

Radiographs show a significant narrowing of the pars compacta of the substantia nigra, best visualized on T2-weighted sequences. Multiple studies have demonstrated very little overlap between patients with PD and normal age-matched controls.[15, 34] Early PD has been reported to show a loss of signal in a lateral to medial gradient of the pars compacta, thereby indicating the potential for detecting presymptomatic disease.[63] The diagnostic role of MRI in patients with suspected PD is to exclude other neurodegenerative syndromes with a clinical presentation similar to that of PD.[17, 110]

With the advent of deep brain stimulator (DBS) implants, which have been successful in treatment of medically refractory tremor, MRI plays an important role in targeting the nucleus ventralis intermedius (Vim) of the thalamus during the stereotactic implantation of the device.[5]

Multiple-System Atrophy

In contrast to PD, in which extrapyramidal clinical manifestations result from a loss of dopaminergic input to the striatum, other diseases produce progressive motor dysfunction by means of primary degenerative processes that simultaneously affect groups of several subcortical anatomic structures. This group of disorders has been referred to by the clinical term *Parkinson's plus syndrome* or by the anatomic term *multiple-system atrophy* (MSA). Various forms of MSA can present with a clinical picture similar to that of PD. These two disorders can be especially difficult to differentiate clinically early on in the presentation.

Neurologically, MSA is suspected when patients presumed to have PD do not respond to L-dopa therapy. Anatomically, the patient's disease is due to the involutional change undergone by various combinations of striatal, cerebellar, pontine, brain stem, and spinal cord nuclei. With the growing ability of MRI to show detailed anatomy, a number of recent investigators have demonstrated the atrophic and signal abnormality changes in patients with the various forms of MSA, which allows differentiation from PD.

One neuropathologic pattern of MSA is termed *striatonigral degeneration* (SND). In patients with this condition, a PD-like syndrome results from a progressive atrophy and neuronal depletion of the putamen and caudate, accompanied by cell loss within the zona compacta of the substantia nigra without Lewy body deposition. Radiographically, patients with SND also exhibit thinning of the pars compacta of the substantia nigra, a presentation similar to that seen in PD.[8, 116] This is expected from the histopathology of the disease. However, SND also exhibits a number of specific findings that allows one to differentiate it from PD radiographically.

The most prominent distinguishing feature of SND is the presence of hypointensities in the putamen,[78, 92, 117, 120, 123] thought to be due to increased iron deposition.[28, 103] Focal atrophy in the quadrigeminal plate[104] and putamen[92] has also been reported. These findings are not seen in PD. When MSA patients present with hemiparkinsonism, MRI findings have consistently demonstrated abnormalities, including (1) T2 hypointensity of the posterior lateral putamen and (2) atrophy of the putamen, caudate nucleus, and pars compacta of the substantia nigra on the contralateral side.[71, 78]

Another form of MSA is olivopontocerebellar atrophy (OPCA) in which degeneration involves the pontine nuclei, transverse pontine fibers, middle cerebellar peduncles, cerebellar cortex, and inferior olives. Clinically, the syndrome results in progressive ataxia and bulbar dysfunction. OPCA is typically a disorder of adult onset and can be both familial (usually autosomal dominant) as well as sporadic.

Radiographically, patients present with atrophy of the transverse fibers of the pons, cerebellum,[87, 120] and middle cerebellar peduncles[106] (Fig. 10–16). There is a mild decrease in the width of the pars compacta of the substantia nigra.[9] The T2 hypointensity seen in SND is not seen in OPCA.[123] These radiographic findings are in concert with the histopathology. They appear to be specific for the disease and should be identified before the diagnosis of OPCA is made.

Other cases have been identified in which the anatomic loci of degenerative change are even more widespread and involve brain stem motor nuclei, corticospinal pathways, and such spinal cord structures as the dorsal columns, anterior horns, and spinocerebellar tracts. OPCA can occur independently or in tandem with SND.

Many patients with MSA undergo cell loss within the autonomic intermediolateral nuclei of the spinal cord, producing symptoms of orthostatic hypotension, anhidrosis, incontinence, and sexual dysfunction in addition to the those of MSA. This is known as *Shy-Drager syndrome* (SDS). MRI findings reflect the atrophic changes and T2 abnormalities seen in MSA.[96, 105]

Progressive Supranuclear Palsy

Progressive supranuclear palsy (PSP) is a neurodegenerative disorder without known familial predilection that affects middle-aged and older adults. The pathologic changes involve neuronal loss and astrocytosis within the globus pallidus, dentate nucleus, and several diencephalic structures, including the subthalamic nucleus, periaqueductal gray matter, and pretectal regions. Single-stranded neurofibrillary pathology is a distinctive histopathologic feature of this condition. The clinical presentation is characterized by pseudobulbar signs, supranuclear oculomotor disturbances, axial dystonia, gait dysfunction, and dementia.

Radiographically, patients with PSP present with atrophy of the pretectum, dorsal pons, tectum and midbrain.[4] In addition, decreased T2 relaxation times have been reported in the superior colliculi, globus pallidus, and putamen, which are more pronounced than in patients with MSA.[33] These radiographic findings are confirmed by the histopathology of the disease and are useful in distinguishing PSP from clinically similar entities such as PD.[33, 109]

Friedreich's Ataxia

Friedreich's ataxia (FA) is a progressive spinocerebellar degeneration transmitted both by autosomal dominant and recessive modes of inheritance that affect both children and young adults. Spinal cord degeneration involves the dorsal columns, lateral corticospinal tracts, Clarke's column, and spinocerebellar tracts. Degeneration also occurs within the dorsal root ganglia, dentate nucleus, cerebellar vermis, and inferior olive. Children typically present with ataxia and are often incapable of walking by 5 years of age. Later, bilateral Babinski signs with areflexia, tremor, slurred speech, and nystagmus appear. Other associated abnormalities include pes cavus deformity, kyphoscoliosis, and cardiomyopathy.

Radiographic findings include FA spinal cord atrophy, which is often severe[128] and which is seen even in early cases.[89] Moderate cerebellar or bulbar atrophy is occasionally seen.[128] In advanced cases, atrophy of the cerebellar vermis and medulla has been reported (Fig. 10–17).[94]

Amyotrophic Lateral Sclerosis

Amyotrophic lateral sclerosis (ALS), is the most common form of a broader class of motor system diseases characterized by primary degeneration of the motor neurons within the brain, brain stem, and spinal cord. Patients

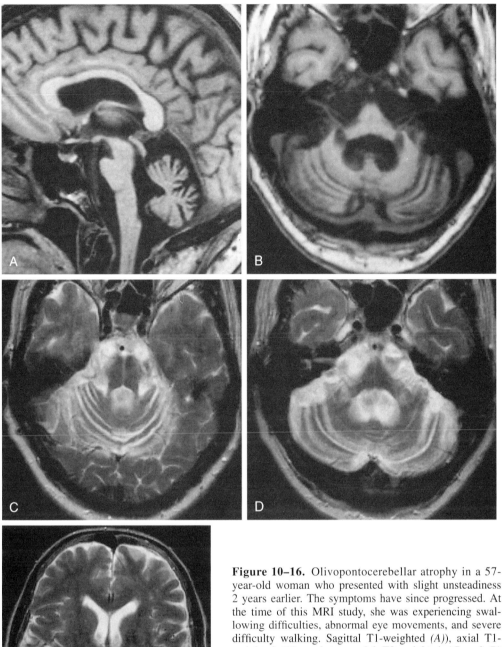

Figure 10–16. Olivopontocerebellar atrophy in a 57-year-old woman who presented with slight unsteadiness 2 years earlier. The symptoms have since progressed. At the time of this MRI study, she was experiencing swallowing difficulties, abnormal eye movements, and severe difficulty walking. Sagittal T1-weighted *(A)*, axial T1-weighted *(B)*, and two axial T2-weighted *(C* and *D)* images demonstrate atrophy of the transverse fibers of the pons, the cerebellum, the middle cerebellar peduncles, and the inferior olives. *E,* Axial T2-weighted image through the lateral ventricles fails to demonstrate atrophy or hydrocephalus. (From Holodny AI, George AE, Golomb J: Neurodegenerative disorders. In Edelman R, Hesselink JR [eds]: Clinical Magnetic Resonance Imaging, 2nd ed. Philadelphia, WB Saunders, 1996.)

typically present with progressive muscle weakness and limb and truncal atrophy combined with signs of spacticity. Mean age at the time of diagnosis is 55 years, and the incidence of new cases is 1 per 100,000 population.[18] Familial transmission is seen in 10% of the cases as both autosomal dominant and recessive traits and sporadic in the remaining 90% of the cases.[112] Prognostically, about 50% of patients die within 3 years and 90% die within 6 years following onset of symptoms.

In ALS, both anterior horn neurons in the spinal cord

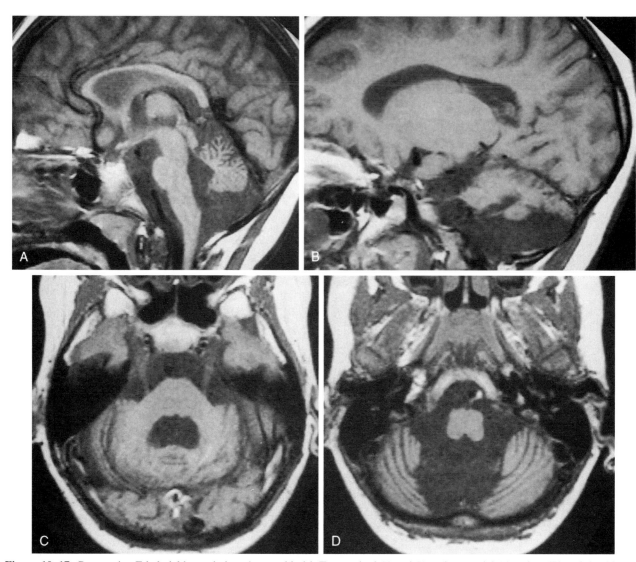

Figure 10–17. Progressive Friedreich's ataxia in a 4-year-old girl. Two sagittal (*A* and *B*) and two axial (*C* and *D*) T1-weighted images demonstrate severe atrophy of the cerebellum. (From Holodny AI, George AE, Golomb J: Neurodegenerative disorders. In Edelman R, Hesselink JR [eds]: Clinical Magnetic Resonance Imaging, 2nd ed. Philadelphia, WB Saunders, 1996.)

as well as pyramidal Betz cells within the primary motor cortex (precentral gyrus) undergo progressive involutional change. Histopathologic features include astrocytosis, lipofuscin deposition, and, occasionally, the accumulation of intracytoplasmic inclusion bodies. Secondary degeneration of the descending corticospinal fibers occurs with variable demyelination and lipid-filled macrophage buildup. Corticospinal tract involvement is most evident within the lateral and anterior columns of the lower spinal cord but can also affect the cerebral white matter of the internal capsule, corona radiata, and centrum semiovale.

MRI reveals abnormal signal intensity along the motor pathways. In the precentral gyrus (i.e., the location of the perikarya of the motor neurons, which are affected by ALS), T2 hypointensity is thought to represent increased deposition of iron.[91, 130] In the subcortical white matter tracts, patients with ALS typically demonstrate abnormal hyperintensity on long TR images (T2, proton-density, and FLAIR). These areas of signal abnormality extend from the motor cortex to the centrum semiovale, the corona radiata, the posterior third quarter of the internal capsule, and the pons.[1, 51, 65, 66, 124] Radiologic-pathologic studies have shown that these signal abnormalities represent degeneration of the corticospinal tract and myelin pallor.[65] These signal abnormalities are distinctly different from normally appearing areas of hypointensity on T1 and hyperintensity on T2, which represent normal fibers of the corticospinal tract traversing the internal capsule. Similar areas of T2 hyperintensity have been identified in the corticospinal tracts in the spinal cord.[39]

MRI shows an increase in the mean choline and myoinositol and a decrease in glutamine and *N*-acetyl in the precentral gyrus.[13] Magnetization transfer measurements have also been reported to be sensitive in the early identification of ALS.[71]

References

1. Abe K, Yorifuji S, Nishikawa Y: Reduced isotope uptake restricted to the motor area in patients with amyotrophic lateral sclerosis. Neuroradiology 35:410–411, 1993.

2. Adams JH, Duchen LW: Greenfield's Neuropathology. New York, Oxford University Press, 1992.

3. Adams RD, Fisher CM, Hakim S: Symptomatic occult hydrocephalus with "normal" cerebrospinal fluid pressure: A treatable syndrome. N Engl J Med 273:117–126, 1965.

4. Aiba I, Hashizume Y, Yoshida M, et al: Relationship between brainstem MRI and pathological findings in progressive supranuclear palsy—study in autopsy cases. J Neurol Sci 152:210–217, 1997.

5. Alterman RL, Reiter GT, Shils J, et al: Targeting for thalamic deep brain stimulator implantation without computer guidance: Assessment of targeting accuracy. Stereotact Funct Neurosurg 72:150–153, 1999.

6. Alzheimer A: Über eine eigenartige Erkrankung der Hirnrinde. Allg Z Psychiatr Psych Med 64:146, 1907.

7. Alzheimer A: Über eine eigenartige Erkrankung der Hirnrinde. Zentralb gesamte Neurologie Psychiatrie, 18:177–179, 1907.

8. Aotsuka A, Shinotoh H, Hirayama K, et al: Magnetic resonance imaging in multiple system atrophy. Rinsho Shinkeigaku 32(8): 815–821, 1992.

9. Aylward EH, Li Q, Stine OC, et al: Longitudinal change in basal ganglia volume in patients with Huntington's disease. Neurology 48:394–399, 1997.

10. Ball MJ, Fishman M, Hachinski V, et al: A new definition of Alzheimer's disease: A hippocampal dementia. Lancet 1:14–16, 1985.

11. Barboriak DP, Provenzale JM, Boyko OB: MR diagnosis of Creutzfeldt-Jakob disease: Significance of high signal intensity in the basal ganglia. AJR Am J Roentgenol 162:137–140, 1994.

12. Baron SA, Jacobs L, Kinkel W: Changes in size of normal lateral ventricles during aging determined by computerized tomography. Neurology 26:1011–1013, 1976.

13. Bowen BC, Pattany PM, Bradley BG, et al: MR imaging and localized proton spectroscopy of the precentral gyrus in amyotrophic lateral sclerosis. AJNR Am J Neuroradiol 21:647–658, 2000.

14. Bradley WG, Scalzo D, Queralt J, et al: Normal-pressure hydrocephalus: Evaluation with cerebrospinal fluid flow measurements at MR imaging. Radiology 198:523–529, 1996

15. Braffman BH, Grossman RI, Goldberg HI, et al: MR imaging of Parkinson's disease with spin-echo and gradient-echo sequences. AJR Am J Roentgenol 152:159–195, 1989.

16. Briley DP, Haroon S, Sergent SM, Thomas S: Does leukoaraiosis predict morbidity and mortality? Neurology 54:90–94, 2000.

17. Brooks DJ: Morphological and functional imaging studies on the diagnosis and progression of Parkinson's disease. J Neurol 247 (suppl 2):II11–II18, 2000.

18. Brown RH: Amyotrophic lateral sclerosis: Insights from genetics. Arch Neurol 54:1246–1250, 1997.

19. Burger PC, Burch JG, Kunze U: Subcortical arteriosclerotic encephalopathy (Binswanger's disease): A vascular etiology of dementia. Stroke 7:626–631, 1976.

20. Cala LA, Thickbroom GW, Black JL, et al: Brain density and cerebrospinal fluid space size: CT of normal volunteers. Am J Neuroradiol 2:41–47, 1981.

21. Convit A, de Leon MJ, Golomb J, et al: Hippocampal atrophy in early Alzheimer's disease: Anatomic specificity and validation. Psychiatr Q 64:371–387, 1993.

22. Cruts M, Van Broeckhoven C: Molecular genetics of Alzheimer's disease. Ann Med 30:560–565, 1998.

23. Dandy WE, Blackfan DK: An experimental and clinical study on internal hydrocephalus. JAMA 61:2216, 1913.

24. de Leon MJ, George AE, Ferris SH, et al: Positron emission tomography and computed tomography assessments of the aging human brain. J Comput Assist Tomogr 8:88–94, 1984.

25. de Leon MJ, George AE, Tomanelli J, et al: Positron emission tomography studies of normal aging: A replication of PET III and 18-FDG using PET VI and 11C-2DG. Neurobiol Aging 8: 319–323, 1987.

26. de Leon MJ, George AE, Reisberg B, et al: Alzheimer's disease: Longitudinal CT studies of ventricular change. AJNR Am J Neuroradiol 10:371–376, 1989.

27. de Leon MJ, Golomb J, George AE, et al: The radiologic prediction of Alzheimer disease: The atrophic hippocampal formation. AJNR Am J Neuroradiol 14:897–906, 1993.

28. De Volder AG, Francart J, Laterre C, et al: Decreased glucose utilization in the striatum and frontal lobe in probable striatonigral degeneration. Ann Neurol 26:239–247, 1989.

29. Diagnostic and Statistical Manual of Mental Disorders, 4th ed. Washington, DC, American Psychiatric Association, 1994.

30. Di Rocco A, Molinari S, Stollman AL, et al: MRI abnormalities in Creutzfeldt-Jakob disease. Neuroradiology 35:584–585, 1993.

31. Drayer BP, Olanow W, Burger P, et al: Parkinson plus syndrome: Diagnosis using high field MR imaging of brain iron. Radiology 159:493–498, 1986.

32. Drayer BP: Imaging of the aging brain: I. Normal findings. Radiology 166:785–796, 1988.

33. Drayer BP: Imaging of the aging brain: II. Pathological conditions. Radiology 166:797–806, 1988.

34. Duguid JR, De La Paz R, DeGroot J: Magnetic resonance imaging of the midbrain in Parkinson's disease. Ann Neurol 20:744–747, 1986.

35. El Gammal T, Allen MB Jr, Brooks BS, et al: Evaluation of hydrocephalus. AJNR Am J Neuroradiol 8:591–597, 1987.

36. Enzmann DR, Norman D, Price NC, Newton TH: Metrizamide and radionuclide cisternography in communicating hydrocephalus. Radiology 13:681–686, 1979.

37. Evans DA, Funkenstein HH, Albert MS, et al: Prevalence of Alzheimer's disease in a community population of older persons: Higher than previously reported. JAMA 262:2551–2556, 1990.

38. Falcone S, Quencer RM, Bowen B, et al: Creutzfeldt-Jakob disease: Focal symmetrical cortical involvement demonstrated by MR imaging. AJNR Am J Neuroradiol 13:403–406, 1992.

39. Freidman DP, Tartaglino LM: Amyotrophic lateral sclerosis: Hyperintensity of the corticospinal tracts on MR images of the spinal cord. AJR Am J Roentgenol 160:604–606, 1993.

40. Fukui J, Kertesz A: Volumetric study of lobar atrophy in Pick's complex and Alzheimer's disease. J Neurol Sci 174:111–121, 2000.

41. Gado M, Patel J, Hughes CP, et al: Brain atrophy in dementia judged by CT scan ranking. Am J Neuroradiol 4:499–500, 1983.

42. Gauthier S: Do we have a treatment for Alzheimer's disease? Yes. Arch Neurol 56:738–739, 1999.

43. George AE, de Leon MJ: Computed tomography and positron emission tomography in aging and dementia. In Latchaw RE (ed): MR and CT Imaging of the Head, Neck, and Spine, 2nd ed. Chicago, Year Book Medical Publishers, 1991, pp 413–442.

44. George AE, de Leon MJ, Gentes CJ, et al: Leukoencephalopathy in normal and pathologic aging: Part 1. CT of brain lucencies. Am J Neuroradiol 7:567–570, 1986.

45. George AE, de Leon MJ, Kalnin A, et al: Leukoencephalopathy in normal and pathologic aging: Part 2. MRI of brain lucencies. Am J Neuroradiol 7:567–570, 1986.

46. George AE, de Leon MJ, Stylopoulos LA, et al: CT diagnostic features of Alzheimer disease: Importance of the choroidal/hippocampal fissure complex. AJNR Am J Neuroradiol 11:101–107, 1990.

47. Glydenstead C, Kosteljanetz M: Measurements of the normal ventricular system with computed tomography. Neuroradiology 10:205–215, 1976.

48. Golomb J, de Leon MJ, George AE, et al: Hippocampal atrophy correlates with severe cognitive impairment in elderly patients with suspected normal pressure hydrocephalus. J Neurol Neurosurg Psychiatry 57:590–593, 1993.

49. Golomb J, de Leon MJ, Kluger A, et al: Hippocampal atrophy in normal aging: An association with recent memory impairment. Arch Neurol 50:967–976, 1993.

50. Golomb J, Wisoff J, Miller DC, et al: Alzheimer's disease comorbidity in normal pressure hydrocephalus: Prevalence and shunt response. J Neurol Neurosurg Psychiatry 68:778–781, 2000.

51. Goodin DS, Rowley HA, Olney RK: Magnetic resonance imaging in amyotrophic lateral sclerosis. Ann Neurol 23:418–420, 1988.

52. Goto K, Ishii N, Fukasawa H: Diffuse white matter disease in the geriatric population: A clinical neuropathological and CT study. Radiology 141:687–695, 1981.

53. Graham GD, Petroff OA, Blamire AM, et al: Proton magnetic resonance spectroscopy in Creutzfeldt-Jakob disease. Neurology 43: 2065–2068, 1993.

54. Groen JJ, Hekster RE: Computed tomography of Pick's disease: Findings in a family affected in three consecutive generations. J Comput Assist Tomogr 6:907–911, 1982.

55. Hachinski VC, Potter P, Merskeu H: Leuko-araiosis. Arch Neurol 44:21–23, 1987.

56. Hakim S, Adams RD: The special clinical problem of symptomatic hydrocephalus with normal cerebrospinal fluid pressure. J Neurol Sci 2:307–327, 1965.

57. Hamos JE, DeGennaro LJ, Drachman DA: Synaptic loss in Alzheimer's disease and other dementias. Neurology 39:355–361, 1989.

58. Harris GJ, Pearlson GD, Peyser CE, et al: Putamen volume reduction on magnetic resonance imaging exceeds caudate changes in mild Huntington's disease. Ann Neurol 31:69–75, 1992.

59. Holodny AI, George AE, Golomb J, et al: The perihippocampal fissures: Normal anatomy and disease states. Radiographics 18:653–665, 1998.

60. Holodny AI, George AE, de Leon MJ, et al: Focal dilatation and paradoxical collapse of cortical fissures and sulci in patients with normal-pressure hydrocephalus. J Neurosurg 89:742–747, 1998.

61. Holodny AI, Waxman R, George AE, et al: MR differential diagnosis of normal-pressure hydrocephalus and Alzheimer disease: Significance of the perihippocampal fissures. AJNR Am J Neuroradiol 19:813–819, 1998.

62. Hughes CP, Gado M: Computed tomography and aging of the brain. Radiology 139:391–396, 1981.

63. Hutchinson M, Raff U: Structural changes of the substantia nigra in Parkinson's disease as revealed by MR imaging. AJNR Am J Neuroradiol 21:697–701, 2000.

64. Hyman BT, Van Horsen GW, Damasio AR, Barnes CL: Alzheimer's disease: Some specific pathology isolates the hippocampal formation. Science 22:1168–1170, 1984.

65. Ishikawa K, Nagura H, Yokota T, Yamanouchi H: Signal loss in the motor cortex on magnetic resonance images in amyotrophic lateral sclerosis. Ann Neurol 33:218–222, 1993

66. Iwasaki Y, Kinoshita M, Ikeda K, et al: MRI in patients with amyotrophic lateral sclerosis: Correlation with clinical features. Int J Neurosci 59:253–258, 1991.

67. Jack CR Jr, Peterson RC, O'Brien PC, Tangalos EG: MR based hippocampal volumetry in the diagnosis of Alzheimer's disease. Neurology 42:183–188, 1992.

68. Jacoby RJ, Levy R, Dawson JM: Computed tomography in the elderly: I. The normal population. Br J Psychiatry 136:249, 1980.

69. Janota I: Dementia, deep white matter damage and hypertension: "Binswanger's disease." Psychol Med 11:39–48, 1981.

70. Jernigan TL, Salmon DP, Butters N, Hesselink JR: Cerebral structure on MRI: Part II. Specific changes in Alzheimer's and Huntington's diseases. Biol Psychiatry 29:68–81, 1991.

71. Kato T, Kume A, Ito K, et al: Asymmetrical FDG-PET amd MRI findings of striatonigral system in multiple system atrophy with hemiparkinsonism. Radiat Med 10:87–93, 1992.

72. Kato Y, Matsumura K, Kinosada Y, et al: Detection of pyramidal tract lesions in amyotrophic lateral sclerosis with magnetization transfer measurements. AJNR Am J Neuroradiol 18:1541–1547, 1997.

73. Katzman R: Alzheimer's disease. N Engl J Med 314:964–973, 1986.

74. Kemper T: Neuroanatomical and neuropathological changes in normal aging and in dementia. In Albert ML (ed): Clinical Neurology of Aging. New York, Oxford University Press, 1984, pp 9–52.

75. Kesslak JP, Nalcioglu O, Cotman CW: Quantification of magnetic resonance scans for hippocampal and parahippocampal atrophy in Alzheimer's disease. Neurology 41:51–54, 1991.

76. Kido DK, Caine ED, LeMay M, et al: Temporal lobe atrophy in patients with Alzheimer disease: A CT study. AJNR Am J Neuroradiol 10:551–555, 1989.

77. Kluger A, Gianutsos J, de Leon MJ, et al: Significance of age-related white matter lesions. Stroke 19:1054–1055, 1988.

78. Kume A, Shiratori M, Takahashi A, et al: Hemi-parkinsonism in multiple system atrophy: A PET and MRI study. J Neurol Neurosurg Psychiatry 52:1221–1227, 1989.

79. LeMay M: CT changes in dementing diseases: A review. Am J Neuroradiol 7:841–853, 1986.

80. LeMay M, Stafford JL, Sandor T, Albert M, et al: Statistical assessment of perceptual CT scan ratings in patients with Alzheimer type dementia. J Comput Assist Tomogr 10:802–809, 1986.

81. Loeb C, Meyer JC: Vascular dementia. J Neurol Sci 143:31–40, 1996.

82. Lotz PR, Ballinger WE Jr, Quisiling RG: Subcortical arteriosclerotic encephalopathy: CT spectrum and pathologic correlation. Am J Neuroradiol 7:817–822, 1986.

83. Masdeu J, Lantos G, Wolfson L: Periventricular white matter lesions correlate with falls in the elderly. Acta Radiol Suppl 369:392, 1986.

84. McCullough DC, Harbert JC, Di Chiro G, Ommaya AK: Prognostic criteria for cerebrospinal shunting from isotope cisternography in communicating hydrocephalus. Neurology 20:594–598, 1970.

85. Milton WJ, Atkas SW, Lavi E, Mollman JE: Magnetic resonance imaging of Creutzfeldt-Jakob disease. Ann Neurol 29:438–440, 1991.

86. Mu Q, Xie J, Wen Z, et al: A quantitative study of the hippocampal formation, the amygdala and the temporal horn of the lateral ventricle in healthy subjects 40 to 90 years of age. AJNR Am J Neuroradiol 20:207–211, 1999.

87. Mukai E, Makino N, Fujishiro K: Magnetic resonance imaging of parkinsonism. Rinsho Shinkeigaku 29:720–725, 1989.

88. Narkiewicz O, de Leon MJ, Convit A, et al: Dilatation of the lateral part of the transverse fissure of the brain in Alzheimer's disease. Acta Neurobiol Exp 53:457–465, 1993.

89. Nicolau A, Diard F, Fontan D, et al: Magnetic resonance imaging in spinocerebellar degenerative diseases. Pediatrie 42:359–365, 1987.

90. Nosaka Y: Hydrocephalus associated with subarachnoid hemorrhage: Clinical study of computed tomography, radioisotope cisternography and constant infusion test. Acta Med Okayama 35:45–60, 1981.

91. Oba H, Araki T, Ohtomo K, et al: Amyotrophic lateral sclerosis: T2 shortening in motor cortex at MR imaging. Radiology 189:843–846, 1993.

92. O'Brien C, Sung JH, McGeachie RE, Lee MC: Striatonigral degeneration: Clinical, MRI and pathological correlation. Neurology 40:710–711, 1990.

93. Oliva D, Carella F, Savoiardo M, et al: Clinical and magnetic resonance features of the classical and akinetic-rigid variants of Huntington's disease. Arch Neurol 50:17–19, 1993.

94. Ormerud IE, Harding AE, Miller DH, et al: Neuropsychological deficits accompanying striatonigral degeneration. J Clin Exp Neuropsychol 13:773–788, 1991.

95. Pantoni L, Garcia JH: The significance of cerebral white matter abnormalities 110 years after Binswanger's report: A review. Stroke 26:1293–1301, 1996.

96. Pastakia B, Polinsky R, Di Chiro G, et al: Multiple system atrophy (Shy-Drager syndrome): MR imaging. Radiology 159:499–502, 1986.

97. Pick A: Ueber die Benziehungen der senile n Hirnat ophiel zur Aphasie. Prager Med Wochenschr 17:165, 1892.

98. Pickard JD: Adult communicating hydrocephalus. Br J Hosp Med 27:35–40, 1982.

99. Roos RAC, Pruyt JFM, de Vries J, Bots GTA: Neuronal distribution in the putamen in Huntington's disease. J Neurol Neurosurg Psychiatry 48:422–425, 1985.

100. Rosenberg GA, Kornfeld M, Stouring J, Bicknell JM: Subcortical arteriosclerotic encephalopathy (Binswanger): Computerized tomography. Neurology 29:1102–1106, 1979.

101. Rother J, Schwartz A, Harle M, et al: Magnetic resonance imaging follow-up in Creutzfeldt-Jakob disease. J Neurol 239:404–406, 1992.

102. Rusinek H, de Leon MJ, George AE, et al: Alzheimer disease: Measuring loss of cerebral gray matter with MR imaging. Radiology 78:109–114, 1991.

103. Rutledge JN, Hilal SK, Silver AJ, et al: Study of movement disorders and brain iron by MR. AJNR Am J Neuroradiol 8:397–411, 1987.

104. Sanchez-Pernaute R, Garcia-Segura JM, del Barrio Alba A, et al: Clinical correlation of striatal 1H MRS changes in Huntington's disease. Neurology 53:806–812, 1999.

105. Savoiardo M, Strada L, Girotti F, et al: MR imaging in progressive supranuclear palsy and Shy-Drager syndrome. J Comput Assist Tomogr 13:555–560, 1989.

106. Savoiardo M, Strada L, Girotti F, et al: Olivopontocerebellar atrophy: MR diagnosis and relationship to multisystem atrophy. Radiology 174:693–696, 1990.

107. Savoiardo M, Strada L, Oliva D, et al: Abnormal MRI signal in the rigid form of Huntington's disease. J Neurol Neurosurg Psychiatry 54:888–891, 1991.

108. Sax DS, Bird ED, Gusella JF, Myers RH: Phenotypic variation in 2 Huntington's disease families with linkage to chromosome 4. Neurology 39:1332–1336, 1989.

109. Schrag A, Good CD, Miszkiel K, et al: Differentiation of atypical parkinsonian syndromes with routine MRI. Neurology 54:697–702, 2000.

110. Schultz JB, Skalej M, Wedekind D, et al: Magnetic resonance imaging-based volumetry differentiates idiopathic Parkinson's syndrome from multiple system atrophy and progressive supranuclear palsy. Ann Neurol 45:65–74, 1999.

111. Seab JP, Jagust WS, Wong SFS, et al: Quantitative NMR measurements of hippocampal atrophy in Alzheimer's disease. Magn Reson 8:200–228, 1988.

112. Siddique T, Nijhawan D, Hentati I: Familial amyotrophic lateral sclerosis. J Neural Trans Suppl 49:219–233, 1997.

113. Soininen R, Puranen M, Riekkinen PJ: Computed tomography findings in senile dementia and normal aging. J Neurol Neurosurg Psychiatry 45:50–54, 1982.

114. Squire LR, Amaral DG, Press GA: Magnetic resonance imaging of the hippocampal formation and mammillary nuclei distinguish medial temporal lobe and diencephalic amnesia. J Neurosci 10:3106–3117, 1990.

115. Starkstein SE, Brandt J, Bylsma F, et al: Neuropsychological correlates of brain atrophy in Huntington's disease: A magnetic resonance imaging study. Neuroradiology 34:487–489, 1992.

116. Stern MB, Braffman BH, Skolnick BE, et al: Magnetic resonance imaging in Parkinson's disease and parkinsonian syndromes. Neurology 39:1524–1526, 1989.

117. Sullivan EV, De La Paz R, Zipursky RB, Pfefferbaum A: Neuropsychological deficits accompanying striatonigral degeneration. J Clin Exp Neuropsychol 13:773–778, 1991.

118. Tartaro A, Fulgente T, Delli Pizzi C, et al: MRI alterations as an early finding in Creutzfeldt-Jakob disease. Eur J Radiol 17:155–158, 1993.

119. Terry RD: Senile dementia of the Alzheimer type. Ann Neurol 14:497–506, 1983.

120. Testa D, Savoiardo M, Fetoni V, et al: Multiple system atrophy. Clinical and MR observations on 42 cases. Ital J Neurol Sci 14:211–216, 1993.

121. Tomlinson BE, Corsellis JAN: Ageing and dementias. In Adams JH, Corsellis JAN (eds): Greenfield's Neuropathology, 4th ed. New York, LW Duchen Wiley, 1984, pp 951–1025.

122. Tomonaga M, Hiroski Y, Tohgi H: Clinicopathologic study of progressive subcortical vascular encephalopathy (Binswanger type) in the elderly. J Am Geriatr Soc 30:524–529, 1982.

123. Tsuchiya K: High-field MR findings of multiple system atrophy. Nippon Igaku Hoshasen Gakkai Zasshi 50:772–779, 1990.

124. Udaka F, Sawada H, Seriu N, et al: MRI and SPECT findings in amyotrophic lateral sclerosis. Neuroradiology 34:389–393, 1992.

125. Urchino A, Yoshinaga M, Shiokawa O, et al: Serial MR imaging in Creutzfeldt-Jakob disease. Neuroradiology 33:364–367, 1991.

126. Vonsattel JP, Meyers RH, Stevers TJ: Neuropathologic classification of Huntington's disease. J Neuropathol Exp Neurol 44:559–577, 1985.

127. Weber T, Otto M, Bodemer M, Zerr I: Diagnosis of Creutzfeldt-Jakob disease and related human spongiform encephalopathies. Biomed Pharmacother 51:381–387, 1997.

128. Wessel K, Schroth G, Diener HC, et al: Significance of MRI-confirmed atrophy of the cranial spinal cord in Friedreich's ataxia. Eur Arch Psychiatry Neurol Sci 238:225–230, 1989.

129. Will RG, Zeidler M, Stewart GE, et al: Diagnosis of new variant Creutzfeldt-Jakob disease. Ann Neurol 47:575–582, 2000.

130. Yagashita A, Nakano I, Oda M, Hirano A: Location of the corticospinal tract in the internal capsule at MR imaging. Radiology 191:455–460, 1994.

131. Yamamoto K, Morimatsu M: Increased signal in the basal ganglia and white mater on magnetic resonance imaging in Creutzfeldt-Jakob disease. Ann Neurol 32:114, 1992.

132. Zeidler M, Sellar RJ, Collie DA, et al: The pulvinar sign on magnetic resonance imaging in variant Creutzfeldt-Jakob disease. Lancet 355:1412–1418, 2000.

11

Brain Magnetic Resonance Spectroscopy

Jay J. Pillai, Lester Kwock

A Brief History

Magnetic resonance spectroscopy (MRS) is a means of noninvasive physiologic imaging of the brain that measures relative levels of various tissue metabolites. Absolute quantitation of these metabolites is also possible, although in standard clinical practice ratios are commonly used to describe relative concentrations of these metabolites. MRS enables evaluation of metabolic derangements that are specific to certain central nervous system (CNS) diseases or categories of disease. Thus, MRS may aid in the diagnosis of various CNS diseases when standard structural magnetic resonance imaging (MRI) findings may be nonspecific. MRS may also be used to monitor therapy and to provide prognostic information in certain conditions. This chapter presents the basic principles of MRS, followed by a discussion of basic clinical applications.

The discovery of the phenomenon of nuclear magnetic resonance (NMR) can be traced to Purcell and coworkers and Bloch and coauthors in 1946, who found that magnetic dipoles of atomic nuclei resonated when placed in an external magnetic field and demonstrated nuclear induction (induction of an electromotive force in a surrounding recording coil).[20, 116, 185] MRS, in the 1970s, involved phosphorus (^{31}P) spectroscopy in animals, including evaluation of red blood cells and rat leg muscle tissue.[101, 116, 161] Human applications became possible in the early 1980s, when larger-bore magnets became available; applications in the extremities were followed by applications in the CNS.[116] The first human brain applications involved ^{31}P spectroscopy in infants.[32, 99, 116, 197] Bottomley and Radda and their coauthors then described applications of in vivo ^{31}P spectroscopy in the adult brain, followed in 1985 by the earliest in vivo brain hydrogen (^{1}H) spectroscopic studies.[22, 23, 116, 186]

With the advent of technical advances that allowed for improved spatial localization and water suppression, MRS has rapidly progressed in clinical utility and acceptance in the late 1980s to near its current status. Today MRS—in particular, ^{1}H MRS—has become a valuable physiologic imaging tool with wide clinical applicability.

Technical Considerations
Basic Principles

What is the difference between MRS and MRI? The answer to this most frequently asked question is that basically there is no difference, because both techniques are governed by the same physical principles of magnetism. MRS and MRI differ only in the manner in which the data are processed and presented. With MRI, the data collected are analyzed in the time domain (free induction decay [FID] signal) to obtain information about the nuclear relaxation time (namely, T1 and T2), which is processed to generate an anatomic image. In MRS, time domain information is converted to frequency domain information via Fourier transformation of the FID time domain signal.

What is the frequency domain, and why do the protons of water resonate at a different frequency (H_2O, 4.7 parts per million at pH = 7.4) from that of the protons located in other metabolites, such as the following?

1. The *N*-acetyl methyl group of *N*-acetylaspartate ($CH_3C{=}ONH{-}R$; 2.0 ppm).
2. The *N*-methyl groups of choline (($CH_3)_3N{-}$); 3.2 ppm).
3. The *N*-methyl group of creatine ($CH_3{-}NH{-}R$).

As presented in a number of reviews, NMR is based on the principle that some nuclei have associated magnetic spin properties that allow them to behave like small magnets.[123, 206, 213] In the presence of an externally applied magnetic field, the magnetic nuclei interact with that field and distribute themselves to different energy levels. With protons having a magnetic spin number of 1/2, the nuclei distribute themselves into two energy states. Conceptually, these energy states correspond to the proton nuclear spins, either aligned in the direction of (low-energy spin state) or against the applied magnetic field (high-energy spin state).

If energy is applied to the system in the form of a radiofrequency (RF) pulse that exactly matches the energy between both states, a condition of *resonance* occurs. That is, nuclei in the lower-energy state can absorb this energy and are promoted to the higher-energy state. The Larmor frequency equation describes this phenomenon:

$$\Delta E = h\omega_0 = h/2\pi\gamma B_0$$

where

ω_0 is the Larmor precessional frequency (cycles/second [Hz])
h is Planck's constant
γ is the gyromagnetic ratio for that nucleus (MHz/Tesla [T])
B_0 is the applied magnetic field (T)

This equation states that the resonance frequency of a

magnetic nucleus (the RF needed to excite a given nucleus to the higher spin state) is directly proportional to the magnetic field environment it experiences. Chemical elements having different atomic numbers such as hydrogen (^{1}H) and phosphorus (^{31}P) resonate at different Larmor RFs because of the differences in the magnetic properties in the nucleus of these atoms; that is, at 1.5 T the Larmor RF for ^{1}H is 63.86 MHz; for ^{31}P it is 25.85 MHz.

This difference in the Larmor RF has been used to identify magnetic nuclei having different atomic numbers. Even for a given magnetic nucleus having the same atomic number, however, chemical compounds containing this nucleus can have slightly different Larmor RFs. The reason for this is due to the electrons (negatively charged subatomic particles) that surround the nucleus of the atom. The circulating electrons form an "electron cloud" that surrounds the nucleus. Like protons and neutrons in the nucleus of the atom, electrons have magnetic spin properties. Thus, when exposed to an externally applied magnetic field, electrons precess and produce a small magnetic field, B*, around the nucleus. These local magnetic fields generated by the electrons (normally in the range of parts per million of B_0) can add or subtract from the applied magnetic field, B_0. Consequently, the nucleus of the atom experiences a slightly different magnetic field from B_0. This field is defined as $B_{effective}$ and is equal to (B_0 − B*).

Because of this small change in the local magnetic field, the nucleus of the atom resonates at a shifted Larmor RF; i.e.,

$$\Delta E = h2/\pi \, (B_0 - B^*) = h(\omega_0 - \omega^*)$$

This phenomenon is called the chemical shift and is the basis of MRS.

Single-Volume versus Multivolume MRS Techniques

Single-Volume Proton Magnetic Resonance Spectroscopy

At present, two single-volume proton localization techniques are employed in clinical MRS studies[24]:

- Stimulated echo acquisition mode (STEAM)
- Point-resolved spectroscopy (PRESS)

Both methods are highly effective, each with its advantages and disadvantages.

Advantages of STEAM

STEAM enables observation of proton metabolites that have short T2 relaxation processes, such as *myo*-inositol (MI), glutamate (Glu), and glutamine (Gln), because echo times (TEs) less than 20 msec can be used; with PRESS, they cannot. STEAM also affords more effective suppression of the water resonance signal because water suppression *chemical shift–selective* (CHESS) pulses can be placed not only at the preparation phase of the volume localization pulse sequence but also within the localization sequence (at the TM phase of the STEAM sequence) without penalty to the TE being used. This is a major advantage, especially when short TEs (<20 msec) are used. At short TEs, the

signal intensity of the water resonance can be severalfold greater than at higher TEs; thus, higher or more water suppression pulses must be used to attenuate the water signal.

In PRESS, the water suppression CHESS pulses can be placed only at the beginning of the localization pulse sequence.

Disadvantages of STEAM

There are two major disadvantages of STEAM:

1. There is a theoretical factor-of-2 loss in signal intensity.
2. STEAM is much more susceptible to motion, multiple quantum effects (i.e., homonuclear coupling), and diffusion processes that lead to difficulties in phasing and baseline corrections in the spectrum.[162]

The twofold signal loss in signal intensity in the STEAM sequence is due to the imperfect refocusing of the spin magnetization when the second 90-degree pulse is applied, which rotates only half the spins of interest into the longitudinal axis; this part of the magnetization eventually generates the stimulated echo. The other half of the spin magnetization that remains in the transverse axis is dephased by the TM spoiling gradient and does not lead to any rephased magnetization at the time of acquisition.

Advantage of PRESS

The major advantage of the PRESS sequence is the theoretical twofold gain in signal intensity compared to the STEAM sequence. PRESS is also much less sensitive to patient motion, homonuclear coupling effects, and eddy current effects.[162]

Multivolume Magnetic Resonance Spectroscopy

Multivolume MRS is normally called either *chemical shift imaging* (CSI) or *spectroscopic imaging* (SI) because the signal intensity, peak resonance areas, or ratios of peak areas or signal intensities of the metabolites can be converted to an image format and overlaid onto anatomic magnetic resonance (MR) images, thus showing a qualitative or quantitative distribution of the metabolite within the brain area examined.[179] Utilizing the CSI/SI multivolume technique, one can obtain spectroscopic information from multiple adjacent volumes over a large region of interest in a single measurement. Volume elements as small as 1 mL can be examined in reasonable acquisition times, namely, 6 to 12 minutes.[26, 74, 250]

The MRS pulse and gradient sequences used to obtain the localized multivolume spectroscopic data are similar to MRI sequences except that no readout gradient is applied during the data collection.[132] Either PRESS or STEAM pulse sequences are used for volume selective pulse sequences for the CSI/SI multivolume technique, which defines a large slice. Spatial localization is achieved by phase encoding in one dimension (1D CSI/SI), two dimensions (2D CSI/SI), or three dimensions (3D CSI/SI):

The 1D CSI/SI generates a column of *n* volume elements within the defined slice (*n* = number if phase-encoding steps in a defined phase-encoding direction).

The 2D CSI/SI generates $n_1 \times n_2$ adjacent volume elements within a defined slice plane.

The 3D CSI/SI generates multiple defined adjacent slice planes with $n_1 \times n_2 \times n_3$ spectroscopic volume elements or voxels.

Practical Considerations in Spatially Localized Magnetic Resonance Spectroscopy

Suppression of Water Peak in Localized Proton Magnetic Resonance Spectroscopy

The concentration of protons of water is 110 molar, whereas the concentrations of tissue proton metabolites are typically in the millimolar concentration range. This difference in concentration between water protons and tissue metabolites leads to a large dynamic concentration range effect on the observed signal intensity in the MR spectrum.

If the water peak is not suppressed or attenuated, the spectrum is dominated by the water resonance and no other resonances can be observed. This is due to the fact that when the analogue-to-digital conversion of the time domain signal occurs within the receiver of the spectrometer, the intensity of the peaks are scaled relative to the most intense signal found in the frequency domain. Thus, because of the large difference in the concentrations between water and tissue metabolites, if the water signal is not selectively suppressed or attenuated, only the water signal will be observed.

Additionally, a water suppression pulse sequence that only partially suppresses the water signal can lead to residual eddy current effects that can severely distort the phase of the signals and baseline of the spectrum. These distortions may not be corrected for by the postprocessing procedures used to correct for the phase of the signals and the baseline of the spectrum and thus will render the spectrum uninterpretable.

One usually accomplishes suppression of the water peak by using a frequency-selective pulse, centered over the resonance frequency of the water protons, and increasing the amplitude of this pulse until maximal attenuation of the water peak is achieved via a peak saturation process. The water-selective frequency pulse is applied before the beginning of the volume localization pulse sequence.[132]

Field Homogeneity

The magnetic field homogeneity of the volume being analyzed should be as uniform as possible. In most cases, the water shim should be less than 0.2 ppm ($\sim$12 Hz at 1.5 T), as judged by measuring the width of the water signal at half-peak height.

Inhomogeneities in the magnetic field of the volume lead to slightly different Larmor frequencies for proton nuclei from the same molecule in different parts of the volume. This leads to observation of broader peak signals because the signal observed is an average of the peak signal at different Larmor frequencies throughout the volume. This line broadening is undesirable because it not only reduces the signal to noise ratio but also can make it more difficult to distinguish between two closely neighboring resonance peaks. This can lead to errors in determining peak areas or signal intensities used for quantification of metabolite levels.

Choice of Echo Time

In MRI, the contrast observed in the anatomic images is dependent on the TE and the time between repetition times (TRs) used. If a short TE and a long TR are used, the image contrast becomes more dependent upon the total number of spins or density of protons in each pixel. If a long TE and TR are used, the contrast in each pixel forming the image is more dependent on the T2 or spin-spin relaxation time of the proton nuclei.

Similarly, in MRS, changing the TE changes the type of information obtained as well as the appearance of the frequency domain spectrum. *The choice of TE or TEs to be used should be decided by the clinical question being asked.*

For instance, if a patient is thought to have Alzheimer's disease, MRS should be performed using a short TE ($<$30 msec), because the *myo*-inositol/creatine (MI/Cr) ratio would be significantly elevated in this patient.[217] MI can be observed with only short TEs.

To determine whether a hypoxic event is occurring, a TE = 135 msec should be used because the major question is whether lactate (Lac) is present. At a TE of 135 msec, an inverted doublet should be observed in the spectrum centered at 1.3 ppm, which suggests the presence of Lac.[244]

Finally, to determine whether the lesion is a tumor, a TE of 270 msec should be used because we are interested in examining differences in the *N*-acetylaspartate/creatine (NAA/Cr) and choline/creatine (Cho/Cr) ratios. At this long TE, differences between NAA, Cho, and Cr signal intensities are maximized because of the differences in the concentration of these metabolites and T1 relaxation times in tumor versus normal tissue.[183]

Clinical Applications of Proton Magnetic Resonance Spectroscopy

Important Metabolites

Several important metabolites are evaluated in long TE (135 to 288 msec) proton MR spectra (Fig. 11–1):

- *N*-acetylaspartate (NAA)
- Choline (Cho)
- Creatine/phosphocreatine (Cr)
- Lactate (Lac)

When short TEs (20 to 30 msec) are used, a greater number of metabolites can be identified in the MR spectra; in addition to NAA, Cho, Cr, and Lac, the following may be identified[18, 35, 102, 163, 182, 193, 200, 251]:

- Glx (glutamate [Glu])
- Glutamine (Gln)
- Gamma-amino butyric acid (GABA)
- MI
- Alanine (Ala)
- Glucose (Gc)

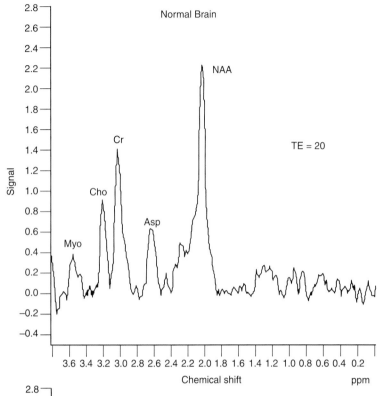

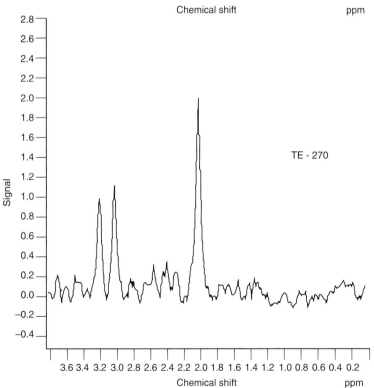

Figure 11–1. Normal adult brain, proton MR spectra. Example of normal single-voxel spectra obtained with echo time (TE) values of 20 and 270. Asp, aspartate; Cho, choline; Cr, creatine; Myo, *myo*-inositol; NAA, *N*-acetylaspartate.

- Lipids and proteins
- Scyllo-inositol/taurine (scyMI/Tau)

Although it may appear advantageous to obtain spectra routinely at only short TEs to distinguish among different clinical entities, some disadvantages of short TE studies exist. For example, short TE spectra display greater baseline distortion, and estimating peak areas calls for more sophisticated processing software algorithms.[169] Methods of absolute measurement of peak areas have been developed and are rapidly gaining acceptance,; however, most proton MR spectra today are described in terms of metabolite ratios, with creatine often used as the reference standard.[14]

NAA

NAA accounts for the majority of the NAA resonance at 2.01 ppm; this peak is the most prominent one in normal adult brain proton MRS and is used as a reference for determination of chemical shift.[12, 125, 126] The NAA peak also contains contributions from other *N*-acetyl groups, such as *N*-acetylaspartylglutamate (NAAG), glycoproteins, and amino acid residues in peptides.[12, 125, 126] NAA is second only to Glu as the most abundant free amino acid in the normal adult brain.[144] The function of this amino acid is not fully understood despite its early discovery in 1956 by Tallan.[229, 230]

From animal studies, NAA is believed to be involved in coenzyme A (CoA) interactions and in lipogenesis within the brain.[8, 16, 29, 60] Specifically, such studies suggest that NAA is synthesized in the mitochondria from aspartate and acetyl CoA and transported into the cytosol, where it is converted by aspartoacylase into aspartate and acetate.[16, 40, 60] Although NAA is widely regarded as a nonspecific neuronal marker, it has also been detected in immature oligodendrocytes and astrocyte progenitor cells.[200, 243]

Normal absolute concentrations of NAA in the adult brain are generally in the range of 8 to 9 mmol/kg, although regional and age-related variations in NAA concentration have been noted by Kreis and others.[127, 153, 182] In normal adults, NAA concentrations in cortical gray matter are higher than those in white matter; in infants, the concentrations in gray and white matter are similar (highly active lipid synthesis in immature white matter accounts for this difference from the adult pattern).[29, 157] NAA concentrations are decreased in many brain disorders, resulting in neuronal and/or axonal loss, such as in neurodegenerative diseases, stroke, brain tumors, epilepsy, and multiple sclerosis, but are increased in Canavan's disease.[21]

Creatine

The main Cr peak is present at 3.03 ppm and demonstrates major contributions from methyl protons of creatine and phosphocreatine as well as minor contributions from GABA, lysine, and glutathione.[125, 126] A second, usually smaller Cr peak is seen at 3.94 ppm. Cr is probably involved in maintenance of energy-dependent systems in brain cells by serving as a reserve for high-energy phosphates in muscle cells and neurons and as a buffer in cellular adenosine triphosphate/diphosphate (ATP-ADP) reservoirs.[38, 40, 127, 155] Thus, this Cr peak is an indirect indicator of brain intracellular energy stores.

The Cr peak is often used as an internal reference standard for characterizing other metabolite signal intensities, because it tends to be relatively constant in each tissue type in normal brain; however, this is not always true in abnormal brain tissue, particularly in areas of necrosis.[139] Cr concentrations in the brain are relatively high, with progressive increases noted from white matter to gray matter to cerebellum.[182, 200] Kreis and coworkers noted a mean absolute Cr concentration in normal adult brains of 7.49 ± 0.12 mmol/kg on the basis of a sample of 10 normal subjects,[127, 202] whereas Michaelis and colleagues reported a similar value of 5.3 mmol/kg.[115, 153] Cr values tend to be abnormally reduced in all brain tumors, particularly malignant ones.[36]

Choline

The Cho resonance is present at 3.2 ppm and is attributable to trimethylammonium residues of free choline as well as phosphocholine, phosphatidylcholine, and glycerophosphocholine. This peak reflects cell membrane synthesis and degradation.[21] Thus, all processes resulting in hypercellularity (e.g., primary brain neoplasms or gliosis) or myelin breakdown (demyelinating diseases) lead to locally increased Cho concentration, whereas hypomyelinating diseases result in decreased Cho levels.[21, 36] Kreis and coworkers have described a mean absolute Cho concentration in normal adult brain tissue of 1.32 ± 0.07 mmol/kg.[127, 202] Michaelis and others have reported a similar value of 1.6 mmol/kg.[115, 153]

Myo-inositol

MI produces two peaks, noted at 3.56 ppm and 4.06 ppm. MI is the major component of the peak at 3.56 ppm, although contributions from MI-monophosphate and glycine are also present.[193] MI is believed to be a glial marker because it is present primarily in glial cells and is absent in neurons.[25]

A role in osmotic regulation of the brain has been attributed to MI.[200] In addition, MI may represent both a storage pool for membrane phosphoinositides involved in synaptic transmission and a precursor of glucuronic acid, which is involved in cellular detoxification.[35, 38, 104, 128] A derivative, MI-1,4,5-triphosphate, may act as a second messenger of intracellular calcium-mobilizing hormones.[38, 43]

The mean absolute concentration of MI in normal brain tissue obtained in the Kreis series was 6.56 ± 0.43 mmol/kg.[127, 198] MI concentrations are abnormally increased in patients with demyelinating diseases and in those with Alzheimer's disease.[38, 153]

Lactate

Lac resonance is identified as a doublet (splitting into two distinct resonant peaks separated by 0.2 ppm, produced by magnetic field interactions among adjacent protons (referred to as J-coupling) centered at 1.32 ppm. A second Lac peak is present at 4.1 ppm but tends to be inconspicuous on spectra obtained with water suppression owing to its proximity to the water peak.[38] Because Lac levels in normal brain tissue are absent or extremely low (<0.5 mmol/L), they are essentially undetectable on normal spectra.[200] The presence of a visible Lac peak constitutes a nonspecific indicator of cellular anaerobic glycolysis, which may be seen with brain neoplasms, infarcts, hypoxia, metabolic disorders, or seizures.[200] Lac may also accumulate within cysts or foci of necrosis.[38, 200]

Changing the TE using a PRESS sequence enables confirmation of the presence of an abnormal Lac doublet and differentiation from lipid peaks; at TE = 272 msec, the Lac doublet projects above baseline; at TE = 136 msec, the doublet is inverted below the baseline.[38] In encephalopathic neonates, however, a doublet very similar to Lac may be seen at 1.15 ppm, which corresponds to propan-1,2-diol and which may be easily mistaken for Lac; propan-1,2-diol is a solvent commonly used for administration of anticonvulsant medications to neonates.[14]

Glutamate, Glutamine, and GABA

The Glx peaks are a complex set of resonances noted between 2.1 and 2.5 ppm and consist of Glu, Gln, and GABA components. Glutamate is an excitatory neurotransmitter involved in neuronal mitochondrial metabolism and is the most abundant amino acid in the human brain.[38, 40, 247] Glutamine is involved in both cellular detoxification and regulation of neurotransmitter activities.[38, 153] GABA is a product of Glu and serves as an inhibitory neurotransmitter.[200] Abnormalities in this peak complex have been noted in schizophrenia and epilepsy.[40]

Alanine

The Ala resonance is present between 1.3 and 1.5 ppm and is easily overshadowed by the Lac resonance when also present. Ala is a nonessential amino acid with no known specific function.[38, 200] However, its elevation is frequently noted in meningiomas.[35]

Fats and Proteins

Lipids produce multiple resonances, the most important of which are noted at 0.8 to 0.9 and 1.2 to 1.3 ppm because of methyl and methylene protons, respectively.[38, 110, 181, 200] Membrane lipids are not usually identified unless very short TEs are employed, since they have very short relaxation times.[38] Although artifactual accentuation of these peaks may be seen with voxel contamination by adjacent subcutaneous fat, it may also be noted in high-grade gliomas, meningiomas, demyelination, necrotic foci, and inborn errors of metabolism.[200]

Scyllo-inositol

Scyllo-inositol is a nonmetabolized isomer of MI that may inhibit the incorporation of MI into phospholipids. It demonstrates a single peak at 3.35 ppm.[14] Most authorities in the field believe that this peak results from scyllo-inositol rather than from taurine (Tau), as had been thought in the past.[14]

Normal Brain Development During Childhood

Although most neurons are formed during intrauterine life, proliferation of dendrites, astroglia, and oligodendroglia continues after birth.[212] In particular, the processes of myelination and neuronal and dendritic development are associated with changes in various brain metabolites during infancy and early childhood, which are demonstrated by MRS.[107, 118, 127, 245]

NAA is present in very low concentrations in the newborn brain, compared to those in the adult brain, but levels rapidly increase during the first 2 to 3 years of life and may even double according to one study.[107] Preterm infants were noted to have lower brain NAA levels than full-term infants.[200]

MI forms the most prominent peak in the newborn MR spectrum, whereas Cho dominates the spectrum of older infants.[21] The reason for the prominence of these two components of the infant spectrum is presumed to be the presence of active myelination.[212] In fact, MRS may enable earlier detection of white matter myelination abnormalities in infants than is possible with conventional MRI sequences because changes in the Cho and NAA peaks occur before white matter signal abnormalites on standard imaging sequences.[212]

Although NAA and Cr levels increase during the first few weeks of life, Cho and MI levels decrease.[21] In fact, the MI peak declines rapidly in the first 3 to 4 months and decreases to adult levels by approximately 1 year of age.[200] Cr levels rise to adolescent levels by 4 months of age, presumably as a result of increasing energy demands of the developing brain.[187, 237] The spectral pattern stabilizes during early adulthood, and NAA levels then begin to decrease with advancing age.[21]

The Cr/Cho ratio increases in gray matter during the first 2 years of life, whereas the ratio remains nearly constant in white matter.[14] The scyllo-inositol peak is also highest in newborns and decreases over time.[96, 104, 152]

Lac peaks are normally seen in preterm and small-for-gestational-age infants.[14, 200] However, in appropriate-for-gestational-age term infants, it is abnormal to find higher than trace amounts of Lac, particularly following the first few hours of life; such abnormal amounts of Lac signify brain injury.[14] In preterm infants, the levels of Lac decrease progressively until the age of 40 postconceptional weeks.[14, 136, 176]

Significant regional heterogeneity in spectral patterns has been noted in both the developing brain and in mature brains.[4, 83, 255] In the developing brain, proton MR spectra demonstrate that different parts of the brain mature at different rates and at different times and that the more metabolically mature areas demonstrate lower MI and higher NAA levels than those in less mature regions of brain; specifically, the basal ganglia, perirolandic cortex, and visual cortex mature before areas such as the prefrontal cortex and temporal cortex.[14, 108, 140]

Tedeschi and colleagues[232] have noted significant regional variations in metabolite ratios in young adults; NAA/Cho and NAA/Cr ratios varied by more than a factor of 2 for different brain regions with particularly high levels of Cho and Cr and low levels of NAA found in the cerebellar vermis.[255] In addition, Ando and coworkers noted that NAA/Cho ratios in the frontal region were lower than those in the parietal lobe at birth with subsequent increase during the first 6 months of life.[4]

Grachev and Apkarian have demonstrated metabolic

heterogeneity in normal brain tissue that appears to be age-dependent and gender-dependent as well as specific for brain region.[83] For example, in their series they noted that the total metabolite concentrations were highest in the prefrontal regions in all subjects studied and that higher metabolite concentrations were present in the orbital frontal cortex and sensorimotor cortex in the 25- to 31-year age group than in the 19- to 20-year age group.[83] Furthermore, they observed that women demonstrated higher metabolite concentrations in these two areas than men did.[83]

Brain Tumors

To date, a wide variety of brain tumors have been studied with MRS, and the numerous studies published in this area have demonstrated certain consistent patterns of metabolic abnormalities in both glial and nonglial tumors.* Proton MRS allows reliable differentiation of tumor margins from adjacent brain parenchymal edema, which is not possible with conventional gadolinium-enhanced MRI.[36] In fact, conventional MRI underestimates or overestimates tumor size in approximately 40% of cases.[172]

Although it is possible to clearly distinguish glial neoplasms from normal brain tissue by MRS, controversy exists regarding the reliability of MRS in distinguishing among different histologic grades of astrocytomas and other brain tumors.[38, 129, 168, 215] For example, Shimizu and associates[215] demonstrated that through semiquantitation of MRS peak intensities as a ratio to that of an external reference, it was possible to predict tumor malignancy; higher-grade brain tumors were associated with higher Cho/reference and lower NAA/reference values in their series.[220]

In another series involving children, linear discriminant analysis and proton MRS demonstrated an 83% success rate in establishing the correct diagnosis of histologic grade of brain tumors.[253] In their series of 27 patients with biopsy-confirmed brain tumors, Meyerand and colleagues[150] showed that the combination of Lac/water and choline/water ratios obtained from regions of contrast-enhancing brain tumor (with normalization of each metabolite peak area to the area of the unsuppressed water peak) permitted differentiation of low-grade astrocytomas from anaplastic astrocytomas and glioblastoma multiforme (GBM). In a multicenter study involving 86 cases of glial tumors, however, Negendank and coauthors showed that each type and grade of tumor was a metabolically heterogeneous group with significant overlap in spectral NAA/Cr and Cho/Cr ratios with tumors in other categories; all tumors demonstrated abnormally decreased NAA/Cr and increased Cho/Cr ratios with respect to normal brain parenchyma.[168]

Burtscher and colleagues have described a series of 26 intracranial tumors in which MRS allowed differentiation of infiltrative processes from circumscribed lesions but did not allow differentiation of different types of lesions within each category.[30]

Astrocytomas typically demonstrate reduced NAA levels, moderately reduced Cr levels, and elevated Cho levels compared to normal brain parenchyma[27] (Figs. 11–2 to 11–4). These absolute reductions result in abnormally low

NAA/Cr ratios and elevated Cho/Cr ratios.[200] In fact, the NAA level in astrocytomas is reduced to 40% to 70% of that of normal brain parenchyma.[148] Furthermore, Cho has been reported to be substantially elevated in the more malignant astrocytomas, and this elevation may reflect increased cellularity and cell membrane synthesis.[148, 245] There is evidence to suggest that the elevation of Cho is proportional to the degree of tumor malignancy.[36] However, highly malignant primary brain tumors with extensive necrosis may actually demonstrate decreased levels of Cho. Elevated Cho levels are seen more consistently in anaplastic astrocytomas, which do not demonstrate histologic evidence of necrosis, than in GBM, and ependymomas display higher Cho/Cr ratios than those noted for astrocytomas in general.[36, 253]

Lac levels may be elevated in some astrocytomas as well. However, a higher incidence of Lac in more aggressive or higher-grade astrocytomas is controversial because Lac may also be present in benign pilocytic astrocytomas.[74, 111, 168, 172, 242] It is thought that Lac may be present across the entire spectrum of grades of astrocytomas because Lac may arise not only from hypoxia developing within the tumor itself as a result of disruption of normal vascular networks but also from necrosis or cysts within the tumor.[36, 38, 215] In fact, Lac levels may be elevated in all cysts regardless of etiology.[36]

The presence of Lac has been attributed to (1) the extent of anaerobic glycolysis, (2) the efficiency of electron transport, and (3) the rate of washout from tumor tissue.[111, 138, 200] In highly vascular tumors, Lac may be rapidly removed from the tumor as a result of increased blood flow; even in high-grade vascular tumors, therefore, Lac may not be present in the MR spectra.[36]

The value of Lac identification following radiation therapy or surgery is controversial, but the Lac concentration may be proportional to tumor size.[36, 236] Lac has been reported following radiation therapy and surgery, including stereotactic biopsy, although postsurgical porencephaly may lead to artifactual increases in Lac levels, since cerebrospinal fluid (CSF) is known to be rich in Lac.[36, 74, 141]

The presence of elevated lipid levels has also been used to differentiate low-grade from high-grade neoplasms.[138, 168, 172, 181, 242] Some studies suggest that mobile lipids tend to be present in higher-grade neoplasms, with highest levels noted in GBM; however, although high levels of mobile lipids may be specific for anaplastic astrocytoma or GBM, their absence in MR spectra does not exclude the possibility of such high histologic grades.[168] Lipids may originate from tumor cells within high-grade astrocytomas, macrophages along the tumor periphery, or areas of necrosis.[36] Lipids may be present as a result of microscopic cellular necrosis, which may not be apparent on conventional MR images.[36]

It must be understood that in adults the biologic behavior of low-grade astrocytomas with identical histologic grades is heterogeneous, with more than half of low-grade tumors eventually recurring as or evolving into more aggressive tumors.[164] Some investigators believe that differences in MR spectral ratios of various metabolites, like differences in glucose metabolism in positron emission tomography (PET), may be of prognostic significance even if they are not of diagnostic value in such cases of low-

---

*See References 36, 38, 63, 111, 168, 172, 180, 183, 200, 215, 221, 225, 241, 242, and 252.

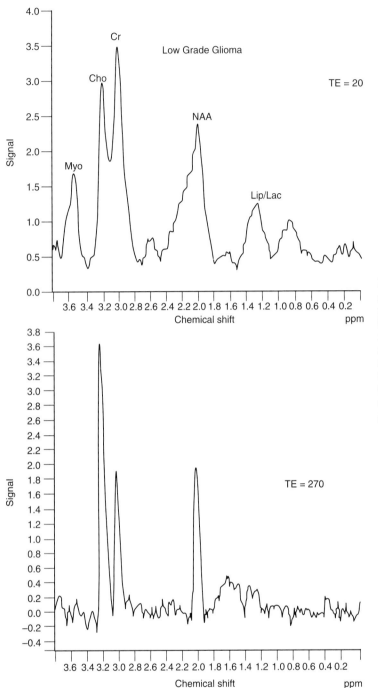

Figure 11–2. Low-grade glioma. A representative single-volume proton MR spectrum of a histologically proven low-grade glioma was examined using a STEAM (stimulated echo acquisition mode) sequence for the TE = 20 msec spectrum and a PRESS (point-resolved spectroscopy) sequence for the TE = 270 msec spectrum. The TR used was 1500 msec in both the TE = 20 and the TE = 270-msec studies. Note the intensity of the *myo*-inositol (3.56 ppm) and choline (3.2 ppm) resonances at a TE = 20 msec in the low-grade lesions compared to the higher-grade lesions.

grade neoplasms.[98, 117, 168, 173] In addition, proton MRS may be used to monitor responses of astrocytomas to therapy[38, 245] (Figs. 11–5 to 11–7). Proton MRS may allow detection of tumor recurrence before abnormalities can be identified on conventional MRI.[38]

Meningiomas have also been studied extensively with proton MRS, and they display certain characteristic features on MR spectra. Marked elevation of Cho levels up to 300 times that of normal brain parenchyma has been reported, particularly in recurrent meningiomas.[36, 38, 129] The Cho/Cr ratio has been reported to be higher in malignant meningiomas than in benign meningiomas.[36, 172]

Theoretically, NAA is not present in meningiomas, which arise from arachnoid structures and not from within the CNS; however, in clinical experience it is not uncommon to detect NAA in these extra-axial tumors, particularly in atypical and malignant varieties.[27, 36, 38, 79] The reason for the presence of NAA in these tumors may be contamination of the voxel by adjacent normal brain parenchyma, use of large voxels, or inadequate voxel placement.[36] In addition, mobile lipids have been reported in meningiomas, and this may be due to fatty degeneration or contamination of the MRS voxel from subcutaneous tissues or fat at the skull base.[27, 36, 172] Furthermore, the presence of alanine, although not invariably present, is considered to be characteristic of meningiomas.[27, 36, 38, 172]

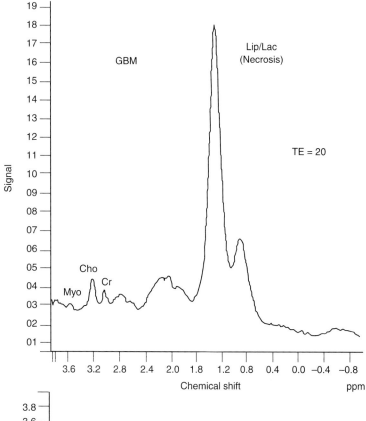

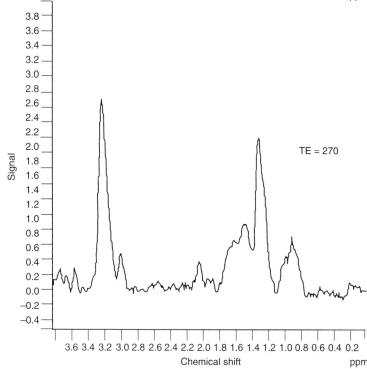

Figure 11–3. Glioblastoma multiforme (GBM). Representative single-volume proton MR spectra of a histologically proven GBM using a STEAM sequence for the TE = 20 msec spectrum and a PRESS sequence for the TE = 270 msec spectrum and a TR = 1500 msec for both studies. Note the large lipid/lactate (Lip/Lac) peak between 0.4 and 1.8 ppm, which probably represents the necrotic core of the tumor, and the lower *myo*-inositol resonance, compared with the lower-grade brain tumors and the elevated choline peak intensity relative to creatine peak intensity for the GBMs.

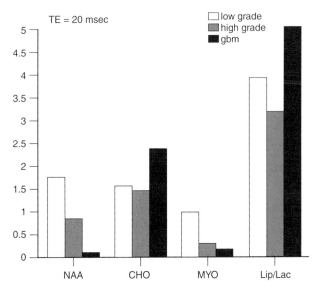

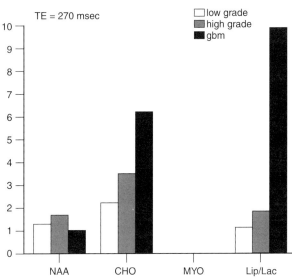

Figure 11–4. Table of relative brain metabolite levels in brain tumors. The bar graph represents the average of the relative levels of *N*-acetylaspartate (NAA), choline (CHO), *myo*-inositol (MYO), and lipase/lactate (Lip/Lac) found in 10 histologically proven cases of low-grade glioma, high-grade glioma, and glioma multiforme. The relative values were determined by dividing the peak resonance area of each metabolite found in the tumor volume by the peak resonance area of Cr found in the tumor volume examined. Ratios were determined on single-volume MRS studies conducted at both a TE = 20 and a TE = 270 msec with a TR = 1500 msec.

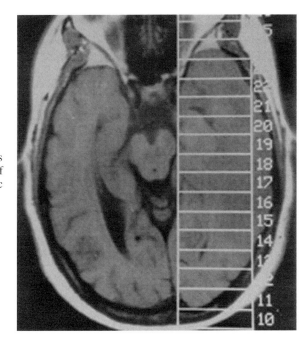

Figure 11–5. Chemical shift imaging Planscan of tumor region. MRI is used to plan the multivolume 1D proton spectroscopic imaging study of a 49-year-old man with a histologically proven high-grade anaplastic astrocytoma located in the left temporal lobe.

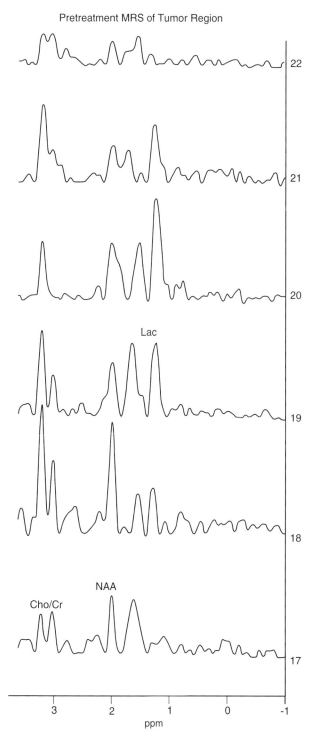

Pretreatment MRS of Tumor Region

Figure 11–6. Chemical shift imaging pretreatment of tumor. Multivolume one-dimensional spectroscopic image (1D SI) of high-grade anaplastic astrocytoma located in the left frontotemporal lobe before treatment with a chemotherapy (BCNU) regimen. The patient did not respond to a complete course of radiation therapy and two courses of intra-arterial cisplatin. Volume elements are $1 \times 2 \times 3$ cm in size, and studies were performed using a 1D PRESS sequence, with TE = 272 msec and TR = 1600 msec. Note the presence of elevated choline resonances (3.2 ppm) in volumes 18 to 21.

Lac levels may be elevated in some meningiomas.[27, 38] However, Castillo and colleagues have reported that in their experience meningiomas may be indistinguishable from astrocytomas on the basis of their proton MR spectra and only rarely display an identifiable alanine peak.[38] Although characteristic conventional MRI features usually allow confident diagnosis of these tumors (which are the most common adult extra-axial neoplasms), proton MRS is very helpful in atypical cases.

Metastases are another class of intracranial neoplasms that have been studied with proton MRS. Although they usually do not pose much of a diagnostic challenge when they are multiple, based on conventional MRI, metastases can be problematic when they are solitary because it may be difficult to distinguish them from primary brain neoplasms.[36] Unfortunately, the proton MR spectra of intracranial metastases are often nonspecific and indistinguishable from those of primary brain tumors; using long TE PRESS technique, they display low NAA levels, low Cr levels, and elevated Cho levels.[35, 36, 38, 129, 172]

Although in theory NAA should not be present in metastases because of their lack of neural or glial components, it

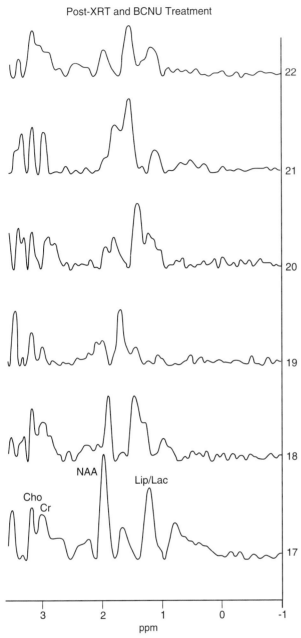

Post-XRT and BCNU Treatment

Figure 11–7. Chemical shift imaging of tumor after treatment. Multivolume one-dimensional spectroscopic image (1D SI) of high-grade anaplastic astrocytoma 3 months after completion of BCNU chemotherapy rounds. Note the marked decreases in choline resonances at 3.2 ppm in volumes 18 to 21. The patient was alive 5 years after treatment of his brain tumor.

frequently is present in proton MR spectra, presumably secondary to voxel contamination with adjacent brain parenchyma or due to the presence of *N*-acetylated metabolites on their cell membranes.[36] One study indicated that although no statistically significant difference existed between peak areas of Cho, Cr, and NAA in spectra of metastases and those of high-grade astrocytomas, a trend toward higher Cho/Cr and Cho/NAA ratios in astrocytomas did exist, and lipid and Lac peaks were more common in intracranial metastatic lesions[36] (Figs. 11–8 and 11–9). Another study

suggested that lipid peaks were often present in metastases, particularly those from breast carcinoma.[38, 220]

Kinoshita and colleagues suggested that glycine levels may be used to distinguish metastatic tumors from glial tumors or neuroectodermal tumors; glycine levels were noted to be markedly elevated in GBMs, high-grade astrocytomas, an ependymoma, and a medulloblastoma, whereas they were low in metastatic tumors.[115, 121]

One study has evaluated the MR spectrum of acoustic schwannomas, and absence of Cr, marked reduction in NAA, and increased lipids were noted.[27, 36] Other MRS studies have attempted to distinguish astrocytomas from ependymomas and primitive neuroectodermal tumors (PNETs); these studies have demonstrated reduced NAA/Cho and elevated Lac/Cho ratios in astrocytomas and ependymomas in comparison with PNETs.[200, 225, 226, 241, 252]

One report described MRS findings in gliomatosis cerebri; these cases all demonstrated elevated Cho/Cr and Cho/NAA levels as well as varying degrees of decreased NAA/Cr ratios.[15] This study demonstrated a maximum Cho/NAA ratio of 1:3 in low-grade lesions, compared with 2.5 for anaplastic tumors; in addition, Lac peaks were noted in grade III and IV lesions.[15]

MRS may be able not only to facilitate diagnosis and accurate classification of de novo brain tumors but also to allow differentiation of recurrent tumor and tumor progression from radiation necrosis, post-treatment effects, or edema.[21, 36, 38, 200] Thus, MRS may be useful in evaluating the response to therapy in patients with brain tumors. Radiation necrosis occurs from approximately 6 to 24 months after completion of therapy, is seen more commonly with high-grade astrocytomas, and may be indistinguishable from recurrent tumor by conventional gadolinium-enhanced MRI.[38] Elevated Lac levels are seen in proton MR spectra of patients who have received 40 Gy or more of radiation to the brain, even when the conventional MRI study does not yet demonstrate any structural abnormality within the resection bed.[38]

One study involving 25 patients with cerebral astrocytomas who received a combination of radiation and chemotherapy demonstrated increased Cho/NAA and Cho/Cr ratios as well as the presence of Lac, in cases of recurrent tumor, compared to markedly decreased levels of NAA, Cho, and Cr and the presence of a broad intense peak between 0 and 2.0 ppm in cases of radiation necrosis.[38, 67] This broad peak, between 0 and 2.0 ppm, consists of free fatty acids, Lac, and amino acids.[38, 67] However, because most therapy-induced tissue damage occurs in combination with areas of viable tumor, single-voxel techniques are not optimal for evaluation of these patients; 3D MR spectroscopic imaging (MRSI) is preferable for distinguishing among areas of residual or recurrent tumor, radiation necrosis, and viable normal brain tissue.[36] Sensitivity and specificity of proton MRS for the detection of residual/recurrent tumor in radiated patients in one series were 71% and 100%, respectively, and serial MRS in the same series allowed differentiation of necrosis and tumor progression; progressive decreases in Cho levels and mild increases in NAA levels correlated well with therapy success.[36, 231]

Other groups have reported similar success in distinguishing radiation necrosis from recurrent tumor with proton MRS, although a few have reported contradictory re-

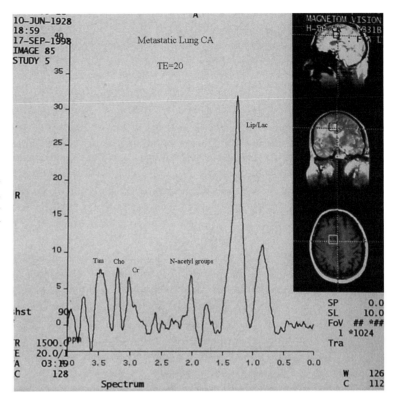

Figure 11–8. Metastatic lung carcinoma (CA). A single-volume brain proton MR spectrum was obtained using a TE = 20 msec in a 70-year-old patient presumed to have metastatic lung carcinoma. The definitive diagnosis was primary lung carcinoma.

sults; the reasons for differences in results may include the fact that Cho levels may be elevated in early radiation-induced lesions because of demyelination and reactive astrocytosis.[44, 49, 56, 74, 113, 200] In addition, Bizzi and coworkers reported that MRS is useful in the surveillance of lymphoma following treatment.[19, 36] Furthermore, Tedeschi and coauthors demonstrated that interval changes in Cho levels during long-term (3.5 years) follow-up with MRS allow differentiation of stable from progressive varieties of glioma.[21, 235] A recent study by Henry and associates suggested

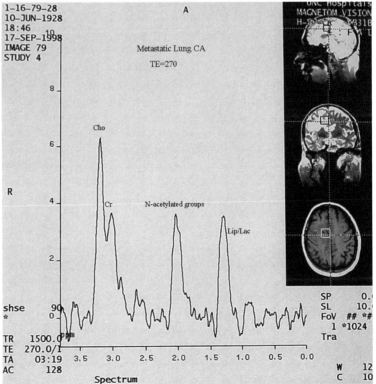

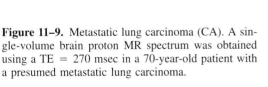

Figure 11–9. Metastatic lung carcinoma (CA). A single-volume brain proton MR spectrum was obtained using a TE = 270 msec in a 70-year-old patient with a presumed metastatic lung carcinoma.

that MRS and MR perfusion imaging (relative cerebral blood volume mapping) may be complementary modalities that, when combined, may be able to noninvasively differentiate tumor from necrosis, post-treatment effects, or edema in patients with treated gliomas better than either modality alone.[94]

Another application of proton MRS is the differentiation of gliomas from hamartomas, particularly in the setting of phakomatoses such as neurofibromatosis, type I.[200] NAA/Cho, NAA/Cr, and Cr/Cho ratios in hamartomas are closer to those of normal brain tissue than to those of gliomas; specifically, studies have demonstrated Cho/Cr ratios greater than 2.0 in gliomas, between 1.3 and 2.0 in hamartomas, and less than 1.3 in normal brain tissue.[33, 81, 200]

Therefore, a multitude of applications of proton MRS exist in the field of brain tumor diagnosis and management, and MRS is clearly playing an increasingly valuable clinical role that complements the roles of conventional structural MRI and other physiologic imaging modalities such as PET.

Epilepsy

Proton MRS has a major clinical application in the localization of subtle epileptogenic foci that are not evident on conventional structural MRI sequences as well as in the prognostication and planning of epilepsy surgery. Specifically, single-voxel MRS may confirm a structurally abnormal epileptogenic focus, whereas MRSI may detect foci that appear normal on conventional structural MR images but demonstrate definite metabolic abnormalities, such as those associated with very subtle malformations of cortical development.[54, 169] In fact, one study suggested that the sensitivity of MRS for the detection of subtle neuronal

dysfunction was greater than that of PET.[2, 200] The advent of viable surgical approaches to the management of epilepsy, as well as the potential for future less invasive treatment modalities such as Gamma knife radiosurgery, has made precise localization of seizure foci critical.[169]

Most of the applications of MRS in epilepsy have been involved with temporal lobe epilepsy (TLE), the most common type of partial epilepsy, and many cases have been refractory to medical therapy.[21] The most common lesion associated with TLE is mesial temporal sclerosis (also called hippocampal sclerosis), noted in approximately 65% of cases of TLE.[9, 21, 54] Although in classic cases of mesial temporal sclerosis (MTS) the involved hippocampus is easily identified by a combination of volume loss and signal hyperintensity on T2-weighted and fluid-attenuated inversion recovery (FLAIR) sequences, 20% of patients with TLE have normal structural MRI scans and the findings in children generally tend to be more subtle than those in adults.[169, 200] NAA, NAA/Cho, NAA/Cr, and NAA/(Cho + Cr) all are decreased in atrophic hippocampi, as well as in nonatrophic hippocampi with abnormal electroencephalographic (EEG) findings, according to the results from the series by Ende and coworkers[21, 68] (Figs. 11–10 and 11–11).

In addition, even when seizure onset and structural MRI abnormalities are clearly unilateral, MRS has shown that bilateral temporal lobe abnormalities are present; bilateral metabolic abnormalities are found in approximately 40% to 50% of TLE cases, and in such cases these abnormalities appear to be more diffuse than the corresponding structural abnormalities would suggest.[53, 54, 58, 68, 95, 170]

Kuzniecky and colleagues also argued that the lack of correlation between structural hippocampal volume loss and proton MRSI metabolic abnormalities reflects the presence of distinct pathophysiologic processes that are coexistent in cases of MTS.[131] Gadian's investigators, examining

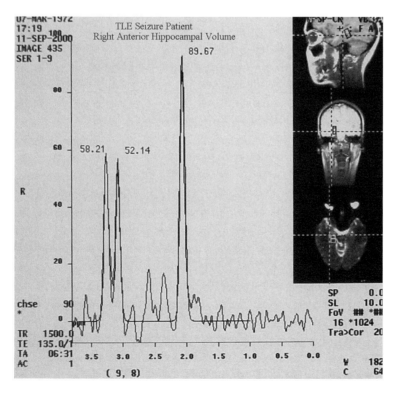

Figure 11–10. Study of temporal lobe epilepsy (TLE), right anterior hippocampal volume. Oblique spectroscopic imaging (SI) study of the hippocampus of a 28-year-old patient with TLE. This volume represents the peak resonance area of the metabolites of the normal right hippocampus. A TE = 135 msec and a TR = 1500 msec were used. The SI study used an angled SI region of interest of 25 degrees, which was parallel to and covered both the left and right hippocampal regions. Each volume element was 1 × 1 × 1.5 cm in dimensions.

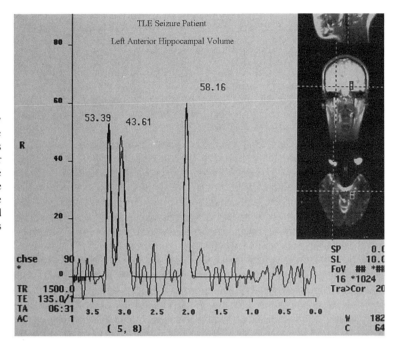

Figure 11–11. Study of temporal lobe epilepsy (TLE), left anterior hippocampal volume. Oblique spectroscopic imaging (SI) study of the hippocampus of a 28-year-old patient with TLE. This left anterior SI volume of the hippocampus was found to have an approximately 40% decrease in N-acetylaspartate (NAA) peak resonance area compared to the volume examined on the contralateral right hippocampus and coincided with the electroencephalographic findings indicating a left temporal lobe seizure focus.

a mixed group of patients with partial seizures, mostly with TLE, reported a 9% decrease in the NAA content of the epileptogenic temporal lobe, with an increase of 14% and 17%, respectively, in the levels of Cr and Cho.[75, 120]

Additional multivoxel MRS studies have shown not only reduced NAA levels in the diseased hippocampus but also the presence of Lac peaks in the spectra of epileptogenic foci when studied within 6 hours of seizure activity.[41, 50, 170, 200, 223] The postictal Lac peak has been described as having potential lateralizing value, since only one side demonstrates a peak in Lac, even in patients with bilateral disease.[50, 223]

Cendes and associates noted that correct lateralization of the seizure focus in patients with TLE was possible in 83% of cases in their large series with MR volumetry and 86% with MRSI.[42, 120] Ende and coauthors found that the NAA/(Cho + Cr) ratio was the most sensitive measure for lateralization compared with ictal EEG[68, 120]; they also noted that in unilateral TLE, the reduced levels of NAA in the hippocampus contralateral to the atrophic one predicted poor clinical outcome following surgical resection of the epileptic focus.[21, 68] Thus, MRS may provide important prognostic as well as diagnostic information.

MRS has also shown promise in the evaluation of patients with extratemporal epilepsy, including those with neocortical epilepsy. This class includes the second largest group of patients with complex partial seizures refractory to medical therapy—those with frontal lobe epilepsy.[1]

Garcia and coworkers[76] reported that, in a series of eight patients with frontal lobe epilepsy, the mean NAA/Cr ratio in the epileptogenic frontal lobe was decreased by 27%, compared with that of the contralateral frontal lobe, with decreases of at least 5% in each individual.[1] In addition, in patients with structural MR evidence of malformations of cortical development (MCD) or neuronal migration disorders (NMD), MRS provides insight into both the pathophysiology and true spatial extent of the disease processes.

Li and coworkers[137] showed that the maximal NAA/Cr ratio decrease, indicative of metabolic dysfunction, localized to the structural malformation noted on conventional MRI in 23 cases of MCD (including focal cortical dysplasia, heterotopia, polymicrogyria, and tuberous sclerosis); however, less impressive decreases also extended to normal-appearing areas of brain tissue adjacent to the structural lesion.

Simone and colleagues,[222] in their series of 15 patients with NMD, noted abnormally decreased NAA/Cr and Cho/Cr ratios in these lesions when compared with gray and white matter of neurologic controls; they also noted abnormally decreased Cho/Cr ratios in the normal-appearing brain contralateral to the identified NMD, when compared with gray and white matter of neurologic controls. The absence of correlation between the NAA/Cr decrease, EEG abnormalities, and NMD lateralization suggested that the metabolic abnormality may be related more to the underlying structural and functional alterations within the focus of NMD than to actual epileptic activity in the lesions, and that the Cho/Cr ratio decreases may reflect more extensive diffuse hypomyelination than what the structural MRI had suggested.[222]

Alzheimer's Disease

Alzheimer's disease is the most common form of dementia in older adults and represents approximately 40% to 60% of all such dementias.[21, 38] The disease is characterized by decreased cortical acetylcholine, neuronal loss, amyloid deposits, and neurofibrillary tangles. Diagnosis, which may be difficult, is based primarily on clinical criteria, and imaging has been used primarily for excluding other possible causes of dementia, such as intracranial mass lesions and subcortical vascular disease. Nevertheless, structural MRI can confirm clinical findings in Alzheimer's disease by demonstrating preferential atrophy of the hippocampi and temporoparietal cortices. MRS, however, may enable earlier diagnosis of this disease.

The proton MR spectrum in Alzheimer's disease demonstrates an abnormally elevated MI/Cr ratio and an abnormally decreased NAA/Cr ratio.[156, 158, 159, 197, 217] This combination of spectroscopic findings distinguishes Alzheimer's disease from normal conditions in the elderly, whereas the elevated MI/Cr ratio distinguishes Alzheimer's disease from other dementias, with the possible exception of Pick's disease.[197]

Reduced levels of NAA are noted in the frontoparietal regions and temporal lobes, including the hippocampi.[21, 209, 234] In Pick's disease, however, decreased NAA levels and elevated MI levels are noted in the frontal lobes, and no such similar metabolic abnormalities are present in these brain regions in those with Alzheimer's disease; thus, the differentiation between Alzheimer's disease and Pick's disease was made correctly on the basis of proton MRS findings in 92% of cases in one series.[21, 69] However, many confounding metabolic disorders can also result in abnormal MI/Cr ratios: renal failure, diabetes mellitus, chronic hypoxic encephalopathy, and hypernatremia can all result in elevated MI concentrations, whereas hepatic encephalopathy and hyponatremia can result in decreased MI concentrations.[124–126, 135, 154, 197, 249]

Degenerative and Metabolic Brain Disorders

Various brain metabolic disorders, including primary leukodystrophies and mitochondrial disorders, have been studied with proton MRS. Although the MR spectral findings, conventional imaging findings, and clinical symptoms of most of these degenerative brain disorders (many of which present in childhood) are nonspecific, MRS can sometimes be useful in distinguishing the various clinical entities.

Wang and Zimmerman[255] have divided brain metabolic disorders into five general categories:

1. Disorders of lipid metabolism.
2. Disorders of carbohydrate metabolism and respiratory chain.
3. Disorders of amino acid metabolism and the urea cycle,
4. Primary white matter disorders.
5. Miscellaneous metabolic disorder not fitting into the previously described categories.

Furthermore, peroxisomal and mitochondrial disorders may be considered to be subcategories of these five categories.[255]

Disorders of lipid metabolism include the following[255]:

1. Abnormalities of long-chain fatty acid metabolism (peroxisomal diseases), such as Zellweger's syndrome (in which peroxisomes are deficient or absent).
2. Rhizomelic chondrodysplasia punctata (in which several peroxisomal enzymes are absent).
3. Adrenoleukodystrophy (in which a single peroxisomal enzyme is deficient).

Adrenoleukodystrophy is unique, in that among hereditary leukodystrophies it is the only one associated with an increased Cho signal at times other than during the early stage of acute demyelination.[21] In childhood adrenoleuko-

dystrophy, decreased NAA/Cr and increased Cho/Cr ratios are present in addition to elevated Lac, Glu, Gln, and MI peaks.[38, 240] The decline in the NAA/Cr ratio in X-linked adrenoleukodystrophy both parallels disease progression and can predate emergence of white matter hyperintensities on conventional T2-weighted MRI scans.[51, 214]

Disorders of carbohydrate metabolism include diabetes mellitus and galactosemia. In diabetes mellitus, MR spectra reveal elevated glucose signal and an acetone peak at 2.2 ppm owing to hyperglycemia and ketogenesis.[194] In addition, it is suggested that the extent of brain injury in severe diabetic ketoacidosis may be evaluated with MRS because elevated Lac levels have been noted in individuals eventually dying of cerebral herniation and cardiac arrest.[255] Furthermore, in galactosemia, a condition in which one of various inborn errors of metabolism prevents normal conversion of galactose to glucose, neonates demonstrate elevated brain galactitol peaks in proton MR spectra at 3.67 and 3.74 ppm at the time of symptom onset; this corresponds to elevated levels of galactitol in brain autopsy specimens in fatal cases.[254, 257]

Disorders of the respiratory chain include mitochondrial disorders such as mitochondrial myopathy, encephalopathy, lactic acidosis, and strokes (MELAS) and myoclonic epilepsy with ragged red fibers (MERRF), Kearns-Sayre syndrome, and pyruvate dehydrogenase deficiency (PDD). MRS may provide useful information regarding the extent of metabolic derangement, severity of disease, and response to therapy.[64, 92, 119, 255] All of these diseases are characterized by brain Lac accumulation secondary to impaired mitochondrial oxidative phosphorylation.[255] Figure 11–12 illustrates an example of a MELAS spectrum.

MRSI is the preferred approach of evaluating distributions of cerebral metabolites in these disorders, since the distribution of Lac in the brain may vary significantly across different anatomic regions and since metabolic abnormalities may be present even when no corresponding conventional brain MRI abnormalities are present.[34, 146] The most striking Lac elevations are noted in regions of brain displaying the most marked structural abnormalities on conventional MR studies. The peaks have been noted in the parieto-occipital gray and white matter in MELAS; occipital cortex in MERRF; brain stem, basal ganglia, and occipital cortex in Leigh's syndrome; and cortical gray matter in Kearns-Sayre syndrome.[200] All of these syndromes are also associated with decreased NAA/Cr ratios, presumably related to neuronal loss or dysfunction.[89, 146] However, PDD has been associated more marked reductions in NAA/Cr ratios in addition to elevated Lac levels and decreased Cho/Cr ratios; in fact, Zimmerman and Wang have noted one case in which NAA was completely absent from the spectrum.[214, 255, 262]

Disorders of amino acid metabolism include entities such as phenylketonuria (PKU), the most prevalent of this class of disorders, and maple syrup urine disease (MSUD).

PKU results from a deficiency of the hepatic enzyme phenylalanine hydroxylase and demonstrates an autosomal recessive mode of inheritance.[210] In patients with PKU, the proton MR spectrum is remarkable only for an abnormal elevation of the phenylalanine signal at 7.3 ppm, which is a finding that is specific for this disease.[255]

In patients with MSUD, long TE proton MR spectra

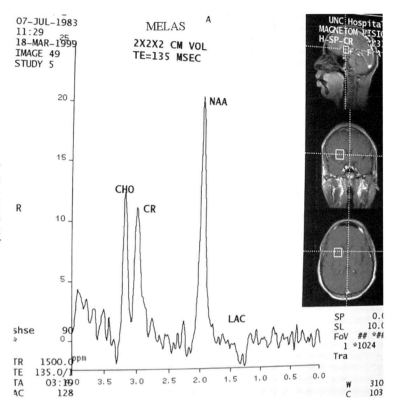

07-JUL-1983
11:29
18-MAR-1999
IMAGE 49
STUDY 5

MELAS   A
2X2X2 CM VOL
TE=135 MSEC

Figure 11–12. Mitochondrial encephalomyelopathy–lactic acidosis–and stroke-like symptoms syndrome (MELAS) in a 16-year-old patient. Single-volume proton MRS study (2 × 2 × 2 cm) over the basal ganglia. A TE of 135 msec was used to determine the presence of an inverted peak at 1.3 ppm. Both the left and right basal ganglia area showed the presence of an inverted lactate peak, centered at 1.3 ppm.

reveal a peak at 0.9 to 1.0 ppm in addition to a reversible decrease in the NAA/Cr ratio during acute metabolic decompensation.[71, 253, 255] Abnormal accumulation of valine, leucine, and isoleucine occurs in the CSF, blood, and tissues as a consequence of defective oxidative decarboxylation.[65, 255]

Ornithine transcarbamylase deficiency is the most common disorder of the urea cycle and is inherited in an X-linked dominant fashion. In patients with this condition, hyperammonemia and intracerebral glutamine accumulation lead to cerebral edema, neuronal loss, and white matter gliosis.[122, 255] Reported MR spectral abnormalities include elevated glutamine levels in a case of hyperammonemia and decreased MI with a normal glutamine level in one patient with a normal serum ammonia level.[52, 194]

The primary white matter disorders include Canavan's disease, Alexander's disease, and Pelizaeus-Merzbacher disease, among others. In patients with Canavan's disease, which is the only primary white matter disorder with truly specific findings on MRS, markedly increased NAA levels have been noted, probably secondary to impaired NAA breakdown related to a deficiency in the enzyme aspartoacyclase[21, 38, 89, 143] (Fig. 11–13). Canavan's disease is the only metabolic disorder that is associated with an elevated NAA level.[253, 255, 259] Other findings in Canavan's disease include elevated MI levels and decreased Cho and Cr peaks; the decreased Cho is probably due to failure of myelination, whereas a decreased Cr level may reflect spongy degeneration.[255]

In patients with Alexander's disease, decreased NAA levels and elevated Lac levels are observed, most prominently in the frontal lobe; the structural white matter abnormality extends from the frontal lobes posteriorly.[89, 255]

Pelizaeus-Merzbacher disease may be characterized by normal spectra or slight decreases in NAA in the basal ganglia in the early stages and by more prominent NAA decreases and Cho increases in advanced disease.[89, 133, 228]

Several as-yet unclassified primary white matter diseases have also been reported. For example, van der Knaap and coauthors[248] have reported a new leukoencephalopathy in nine children manifested by severe white matter degeneration with elevated Lac and Glu and virtual disappearance of most other metabolites in MR spectra.[255] In addition, the studies of Tedeschi and associates[21, 233] have described a new white matter syndrome resulting from a metabolic defect producing hypomyelination and secondary axonal dysfunction characterized by a prominent decrease in NAA, Cho, and Cr levels and an increase in Lac.

In general, childhood demyelinating disorders and neuronal degenerative disorders typically demonstrate decreased NAA/Cr ratios, with the degree of decrease corresponding to the extent of white matter disease and degree of cortical atrophy, respectively, depicted on conventional MR images.[38, 246] Decreased NAA levels and elevated Lac levels are noted in Schilder's and Cockayne's diseases in addition to the disorders described earlier.[38, 89]

Still other metabolic disorders are characterized by specific pathologic changes in proton MR spectra. For example, abnormal lipid peaks are seen in Niemann-Pick disease type C (a lysosomal disorder), low Cr levels are present in guanidinoacetate methyltransferase deficiency, and elevated Gly levels are present in nonketotic hyperglycinemia.[199] Furthermore, in adult hepatic encephalopathy, increased levels of Glu and decreased levels of MI and Cho in proton MR spectra have been described; the Glu elevation is thought to be secondary to hyperammonemia.[196, 255] MRS

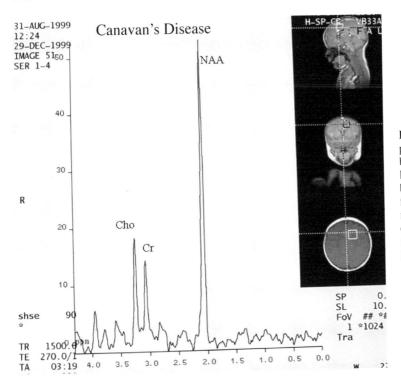

Figure 11–13. Canavan's disease. A single-volume proton, TE = 270 msec MRS study of a 4-month-old baby with a diagnosis of Canavan's disease. Note the level of *N*-acetylaspartate (NAA), which was found to be three times higher than that found in the normal frontal lobe of age-matched infants using TE = 20 msec STEAM proton MR spectrum of Canavan's disease. (See Wang ZJ, Zimmerman RA: Proton MR spectroscopy of pediatric brain metabolic disorders. Neuroimaging Clin North Am 8:781–807, 1998.)

may even be able to detect subclinical encephalopathy, since the reduction in MI level may occur even in patients with hepatic disease without neurologic symptoms.[38, 126, 195] The specificity of these abnormalities may be useful in both diagnosis and monitoring of therapeutic efficacy in these conditions.

Stroke

Stroke is another clinical condition in which MRS has been applied. Although the utility of MRS in the acute stroke setting may be less than that of diffusion and perfusion MRI, or even noncontrast CT, since a critical need for rapid imaging exists in the hyperacute and acute setting for decision making regarding need for thrombolysis, MRS may be very useful in the chronic phase and for monitoring recovery from stroke.[169, 175]

The first detectable change in the MR spectrum that occurs following the onset of cerebral ischemia is the appearance of the Lac doublet.[189] The Lac peak has been noted within minutes of induction of ischemia in animal models, and its level tends to rise over the first few hours after onset.[3, 160, 165, 189] A blood flow threshold of 20 mL/100 g of brain tissue per minute has been described in animal models for the appearance of Lac, but whether a similar threshold exists for humans is not certain.[57]

Studies in humans have also noted the presence of Lac during the first few days following symptom onset, correlated with ischemia and resultant edema[169, 256] (Fig. 11–14). Not only does MRS demonstrate spectral changes before comparable changes in signal intensity of ischemic tissue on conventional T2-weighted MR images occur, but also the extent of cerebral tissue displaying metabolic abnormalities exceeds the extent of signal hyperintensity on the T2-weighted images.[10, 80, 160, 165, 189] In addition, the con-

centration of Lac in ischemic tissue is not homogeneous; rather, the center of the infarct tends to demonstrate higher concentrations than the infarct periphery.[77] Concentrations of Lac during the evolution of an infarct also demonstrate temporal as well as spatial variability.[84, 189] Although the presence of Lac signifies ischemia, it does not necessarily signify actual irreversible infarction.[10, 17, 80, 189]

A later and more specific spectral change signifying actual cerebral infarction that occurs during the evolution of a clinical stroke is a reduced NAA concentration.[189] Several studies have demonstrated both a reduction in NAA and appearance of Lac in human stroke.[10, 86, 207, 256] The reduced NAA level is thought to be related to actual neuronal damage (neuronal cell death or replacement by non–NAA-containing cells, such as glial cells, which occurs in a delayed fashion relative to the changes seen in Lac levels) and is correlated highly with clinical outcome.[165, 166, 169, 189]

Pereira and coworkers studied a series of 31 patients with new middle cerebral artery distribution infarcts within the first 72 hours following clinical onset of stroke symptoms with proton MRS and T2-weighted structural MRI. The authors noted that the combination of infarct volume and NAA concentration could accurately predict clinical outcome.[178]

Decreases in NAA levels can often be identified in initial MR spectra; in fact, one study using an animal model demonstrated NAA reduction within 30 to 60 minutes following induction of cerebral infarction.[96, 174, 189] Regional variability in NAA concentrations is noted, just as with Lac, and the areas demonstrating the greatest elevation of Lac within an infarct also demonstrate the most marked NAA depression.[10, 70, 84, 189]

Changes in Cho and Cr concentrations during acute infarction are more variable than changes involving Lac and NAA. Many studies have reported decreases in Cr levels.[28, 70, 72, 77, 85, 207] Nevertheless, a few studies docu-

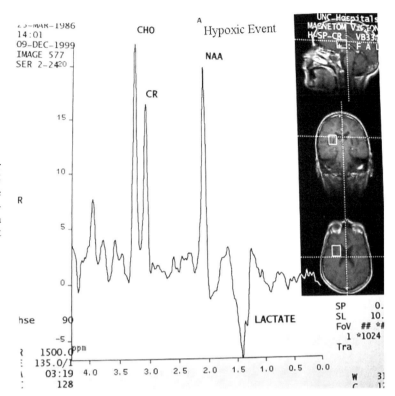

Figure 11-14. Hypoxic event/mitochondrial disorder in a 13-year-old patient. A single-volume, TE = 135 msec PRESS proton MRS study showed the presence of an inverted lactate peak in the basal ganglia. Lactate was found in both the left and right basal ganglia areas and also in various areas of the left and right frontal lobes.

mented no consistent change in Cr levels,[72, 77, 84, 207] and two studies have even noted increased levels of Cr.[10, 80]

Variability in Cho levels has been equally problematic. Elevated Cho levels have been reported in acute infarction, and this elevation may be related to ischemic demyelination.[10, 80, 189] However, this finding is not consistent, since several studies have noted decreased[28, 84] or unchanged[72, 77, 207] Cho levels.

In the subacute stage, Lac levels decrease progressively from the peak levels that are present in the acute stage with an approximately 36% reduction in Lac levels noted per week.[85] Lac may disappear or persist in low levels in the chronic stage; it may also disappear in the subacute stage and recur in the chronic stage.[10, 78, 84, 85, 100, 204] The reasons for the persistence of Lac peaks into the subacute and chronic phases are not entirely clear.[189]

In the chronic stage, NAA, Cr, and Cho levels all decrease.[189, 207] Specifically, the NAA level decreases in an irreversible fashion at an average rate of approximately 29% per week.[10, 70, 77, 85, 100] The rate of decrease of Cr and Cho is less than that of NAA, although these levels also decrease in the subacute and chronic phases.[66, 70, 77, 189] The smaller relative decrease of Cho and Cr is probably related to both the relatively decreased vulnerability of glial cells to ischemia compared to neurons and the reactive gliosis that occurs as a result of ischemic brain injury.[85, 189]

Hypoxic-Ischemic Injury

MRS has been used to evaluate brain damage due to perinatal asphyxia, or hypoxic-ischemic injury (HIE).[11, 87, 90, 208] HIE is the main cause of developmental injury that leads to cerebral palsy. In many cases, the most severe damage (selective neuronal necrosis) involves the occipital gray matter and is manifested as a reduction in NAA and Cr levels and a proportional increase in Cho levels.[208] This suggests that significant astrocyte survival may be present in these cases of neuronal necrosis secondary to HIE.[208]

In particularly severe cases, a Lac peak may also be present, with the Lac peak appearing during the first 24 hours and persisting for at least 48 hours.[177] This finding often precedes the reduction in the NAA/Cr ratio and the increase in the Cho/Cr ratio, both of which have been noted on MRS studies performed 1 to 2 weeks after the initial insult.[214] The severity of the MRS changes appears to be well correlated with the severity of the initial insult and the clinical outcome; persistent NAA and Cho peak abnormalities and the presence of Lac are associated with poor prognosis.[13, 90, 97, 208, 218] Specifically, the presence of Lac in the acute phase has been associated with poor neurocognitive status at 1 year of age.[13] Barkovich and coauthors[13] have demonstrated that Lac/Cho ratios in the basal nuclei had particularly highly statistically significant associations with clinical outcome.

The distribution of Lac elevation in the brain also correlates well with the severity of the injury; in severe asphyxia, the basal ganglia demonstrate greater Lac elevation than the arterial watershed regions; in mild to moderate asphyxia, the watershed regions demonstrate greater Lac elevation.[14] Penrice and colleagues have shown that Lac/NAA ratios in the thalami, in particular, correlate highly with degree of severity of asphyxia; the ratios in normal infants were less than 0.3, the ratios in infants with asphyxia were greater than 0.4, and the ratios in severely affected infants were greater than 0.5.[14, 176]

Finally, Pu and others have shown that cases of moderate to severe HIE display detectable brain glutamate/glutamine (Glx) peaks on proton MR spectra.[184] Elevated Glx/(Cr + PCr) ratios in these cases correlated positively with the Sarnat stage of HIE on both initial and follow-up MRS studies.[184]

Cerebral Infections

Most of the applications of proton MRS in evaluation of intracranial infections have involved the study of acquired immunodeficiency syndrome (AIDS) and AIDS-related conditions. Nevertheless, evaluation of cerebral abscesses with MRS has been documented.

Cerebral abscesses can be differentiated from necrotic brain neoplasms by MRS. Grand and coworkers, in their series of 34 cystic intracranial lesions, showed that at a TE of 136 msec, the detection of an amino acid resonance at 0.9 ppm in bacterial abscesses allows differentiation from necrotic neoplasms, which do not demonstrate this spectral peak.[88] MR spectra of brain abscesses demonstrate absent or low Cho and Cr levels and a relatively decreased level of NAA as well as the possible presence of substantial amounts of Lac.[38, 188] MR spectra of abscesses may show other peaks at 0.97, 1.24, 1.36, 1.50, 1.89, 2.02, and 2.14 ppm, and the exact significance of these additional peaks is not known.[38]

Various studies have shown resonances from acetate, succinate, and some amino acids (peaks not seen in brain neoplasms), in addition to Lac, Ala, and lipid peaks (which may also be seen with certain brain tumors).[39] Similar findings have been reported by Castillo and colleagues and others in cases of toxoplasmosis and cysticercosis[38, 39] (Figs. 11–15 and 11–16).

The few reports in the literature regarding MR spectra of other infectious processes include studies of intracranial tuberculomas, Creutzfeldt-Jakob disease, and herpes simplex encephalitis.[39] Prominent lipid resonances have been noted in intracranial tuberculomas, with particularly important peaks at the 1.3 and 0.9 ppm, corresponding to the methylene and terminal methyl groups of fatty acids, respectively.[39] Abnormally decreased NAA levels in both white matter and gray matter, as well as abnormally increased levels of MI in the white matter, have been noted in Creutzfeldt-Jakob disease, whereas reductions in the NAA/Cho and NAA/Cr ratios and the presence of Lac peaks have been noted in herpes encephalitis[39] (Figs. 11–17 and 11–18).

Acquired Immunodeficiency Syndrome

Various studies of applications of MRS to the evaluation of metabolic disturbances related to HIV infection have been recently performed; these studies have demonstrated reduced NAA concentrations in HIV-positive patients,[45–48, 112, 155, 203, 227, 239] including those who are asymptomatic[151] or who display normal structural MRI findings.[239] Increases in Cho and progressive decreases in NAA levels have been noted with disease progression[45–48, 112, 155, 169, 203, 227, 239]

Increased levels of glutamine and MI have been noted in the late stages of HIV dementia.[46] One study reported a decrease of both NAA and Cr along with increases in Cho and MI both in structural brain lesions and in normal-appearing areas of brain (on conventional MRI) in patients with AIDS.[21, 149] It is not clear whether the metabolic abnormalities in AIDS are due directly to the virus or whether they represent secondary effects related to opportunistic infection or AIDS-related neoplasms.[21] Nevertheless, it appears that MRS may be able to detect subclinical metabolic abnormalities prior to clinical and brain struc-

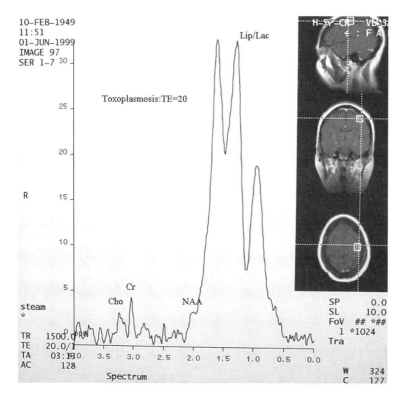

Figure 11–15. Toxoplasmosis. This was a single-volume STEAM MRS study (TE = 20 msec) of a 50-year-old patient with human immunodeficiency virus (HIV) infection with proven toxoplasmosis. Note the large decrease in metabolites and the presence of a large lipid or cellular breakdown peak between 0.5 and 1.8 ppm.

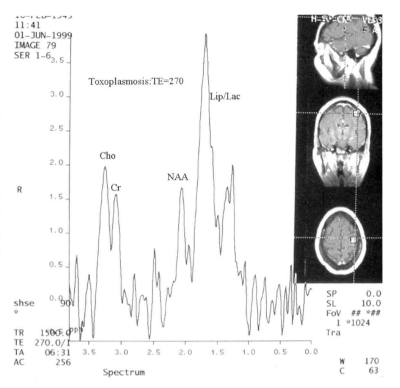

Figure 11–16. Proven toxoplasmosis in a 50-year-old patient with human immunodeficiency virus (HIV) infection. The MRS study used a TE = 270 msec PRESS. Again, note the decreased levels of brain metabolites and the presence of lipids and cellular breakdown peaks. Note the relationship between the choline and creatine peak in toxoplasmosis versus viral encephalitis. Normally, these peak ratios (TE = 270 msec, between 1.2 and 1.4) in patients with toxoplasmosis are much less than those observed in the active viral inflammatory processes. (Normally, choline-to-creatine peak area ratios using a TE = 270 msec are greater than 1.5 in viral inflammatory processes.)

tural manifestations of the disease.[199] The diffuse cortical atrophic changes and white matter hyperintensities noted on T2-weighted images are late findings in the AIDS dementia complex.

MRS may be particularly useful in the evaluation of infants of HIV-infected mothers; it may be able to demonstrate abnormalities in the infant brain as early as 10 days after birth, whereas seroconversion is difficult to determine during the first 6 months and conventional brain MR images may be normal.[38, 55]

MRS may also prove to be a useful means of monitoring both disease progression and treatment effects in patients with AIDS.[48, 169, 203] Specifically, it has been suggested that monitoring of the efficacy of antiretroviral therapy—and even prediction of a patient's response to therapy—may be performed with MRS.[199, 258]

Multiple Sclerosis

Multiple sclerosis (MS) is a disease that is manifested primarily as multifocal demyelination, although significant axonal injury and wallerian degeneration are usually present as well.[7, 109, 145, 169, 199] In fact, the axonal loss, rather than

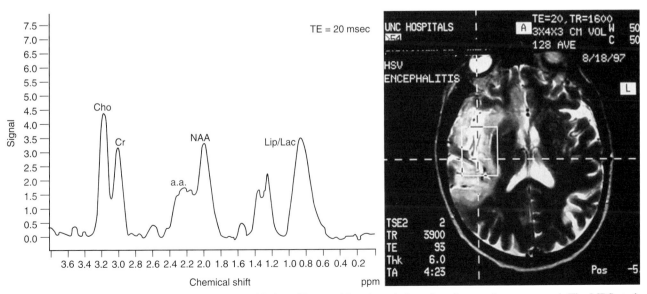

Figure 11–17. Herpes simplex viral (HSV) encephalitis in a 55-year-old patient. A 3 × 4 × 3 cm volume was used. The MRS study used a STEAM TE = 20 msec sequence. a.a., amino acids.

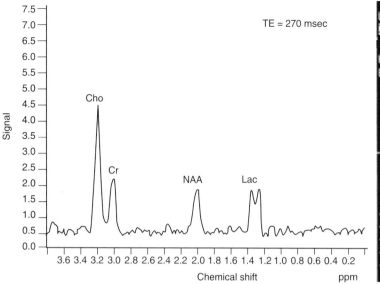

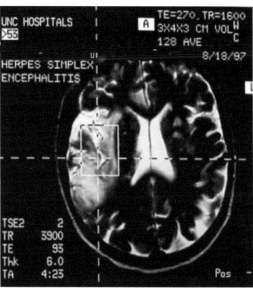

Figure 11–18. Active case of herpes simplex viral (HSV) encephalitis in a 55-year-old patient. This was a PRESS MRS study (TE = 270 msec).

the demyelination, may be responsible for the neurologic impairment seen in patients with MS.[147, 199]

Active demyelinating plaques generally demonstrate enhancement on gadolinium-enhanced MR scans in addition to displaying hyperintensity on T2-weighted and FLAIR conventional MR sequences.[38] Substantial reductions in NAA concentration are noted in acute (active) MS lesions, and these reductions correlate highly with clinical neurologic impairment; partial recovery of NAA levels is also not uncommon, and these changes are also reflected in clinical improvement.[199] Whether the partial recovery of NAA levels is due to reduction of edema or to actual recovery of neuronal function is not clear.[33, 199]

In the acute phase, marked increases in Cho concentration, moderate increases in Lac, and increases in mobile lipid peaks and "marker peaks" in the range of 2.0 to 2.6 ppm may be present.[7, 21, 91] The increase in Cho levels is due to release of phosphocholine and glycerophosphocholine during active demyelination.[21] The mobile lipid peaks are products of myelin breakdown, and the "marker peaks" are of uncertain etiology but appear to be typical of demyelinating conditions in general.[21, 38] One study even suggested that lipid concentration increases may precede signal hyperintensity development on T2-weighted conventional MR sequences.[167, 199]

The presence of Lac may be related to local inflamma-

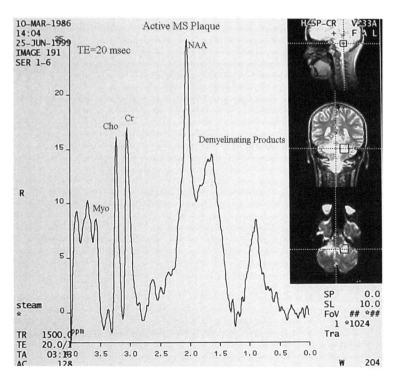

Figure 11–19. Active multiple sclerosis (MS) plaque. A single-volume proton STEAM MR study used a TE of 20 msec and a TR of 1500 msec in a patient with MS. The 2 × 2 × 2 cm volume was centered over the gadolinium-enhancing lesion located in the left cerebellum. Note the level of *myo*-inositol and other sugars (3.5 to 3.8 ppm) in the active plaque volume compared to the level in a non–gadolinium-enhancing inactive MS lesion.

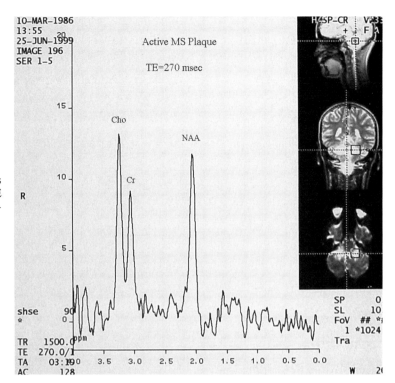

Figure 11–20. Active multiple sclerosis (MS). This was a single-volume proton PRESS MRS study (TE = 270 msec) of a patient with a gadolinium-enhancing MS lesion.

tory infiltrates associated with the demyelinating plaques and their effects on local cerebral vasculature.[7, 199]

A transient but significant decrease in Cr levels in the hyperacute stage may revert to normal in the subacute and chronic stages.[199]

Increases in MI concentrations may be seen on short TE spectra; MI is usually detected when the demyelinating process is severe[21, 61, 199] (Figs. 11–19 and 11–20).

Reduction of NAA/Cr ratios has been noted not only in structural lesions (visible demyelinating plaques) but even in white matter, which appears normal by conventional T2-weighted MRI; thus, these MRS findings suggest that conventional MR sequences may underestimate the true extent of brain tissue involvement by MS.[21, 62, 73, 196] Although much of the reduction has been attributed to decreases in absolute concentrations of NAA, controversy exists regarding possible increases in Cr levels as well.[62, 169, 192] Actually, the metabolite changes noted in MRS may be better correlated with actual clinical status than the number or volume of hyperintense structural brain lesions on conventional T2-weighted sequences.[5, 210, 238] In fact, the reduction in NAA in the normal-appearing white matter correlates best with the degree of clinical disability.[199] Furthermore, preliminary data suggest that MRS may be used to monitor responses to therapy in patients with MS.[169, 209] Gonen and colleagues[82] have suggested that measurement of whole brain NAA concentration may serve as an effective and reproducible measure of disease load in MS and may be used to measure disease progression.

In the chronic phase of MS, axonal loss and mild cortical atrophy may occur. Although acute plaques demonstrate edema and demyelination, chronic plaques demonstrate gliosis and mild associated neuronal loss.[21]

Incomplete recovery of axonal damage leads to irreversible clinical disabilities. NAA levels are decreased in both the structural lesions identified on conventional MR sequences and in surrounding normal-appearing white matter in the chronic phase, and this NAA decrease corresponds to the axonal and mild neuronal loss.[199] In addition, the fact that NAA levels may be normal in the acute phase of MS suggests that the axons in these cerebral regions have not yet sustained permanent damage, whereas in the chronic phase, when axonal loss has occurred, NAA levels are decreased.[38] Free mobile lipids and "marker peaks" may also be seen in MR spectra in the chronic phase in MS.[38]

Because MRS provides valuable insight into the various stages of the evolution of MS plaques and the physiologic and metabolic changes associated with this evolution, in the near future it may also provide a reliable means of effectively monitoring responses to new therapeutic interventions. A recent study has already explored serial spectroscopic changes in active MS plaques during pharmacologic intervention.[142] These interventions may be designed to target particular stages in the development and maturation of these plaques and thus may prevent progression of the disease.

Other Applications of Proton Magnetic Resonance Spectroscopy in the Central Nervous System

Other CNS applications of proton MRS include the study of psychiatric diseases, upper motor neuron disease (e.g., amyotrophic lateral sclerosis [ALS]), Huntington's disease, and parkinsonian syndromes, among other clinical entities.

In patients with schizophrenia, the most consistent findings include decreased NAA levels in the temporal lobes.[116]

In bipolar affective disorder, elevated Cho, NAA, and MI levels in the basal ganglia as well as elevated levels of glutamate (Glu) in the parietal lobes have been described.[37, 212]

Children with attention deficit hyperactivity disorder (ADHD) demonstrate abnormally elevated NAA/Cr, Glu/Cr, and Cho/Cr ratios in the frontal lobes when compared with age-matched controls.[37]

In patients with ALS, the NAA/Cr ratio is significantly decreased in the motor and premotor cortices, and similar decreases are present in the brain stem.[21, 59]

In Huntington's disease, a reduced NAA/Cho ratio is present in both the basal ganglia and the cerebral cortex, and Lac elevations in these areas may also be present.[114, 199]

MRS evaluation of the parkinsonian syndromes has revealed typical absence of metabolic abnormalities in the basal ganglia in idiopathic Parkinson's disease, as opposed to reductions in the basal ganglia NAA/Cr and NAA/Cho ratios in other parkinsonian syndromes such as progressive supranuclear palsy and corticobasal degeneration.[199]

Certainly, the range of applications of proton MRS in the diagnosis and therapeutic monitoring of CNS disease will continue to grow as clinicians become more aware of the tremendous clinical potential of this imaging technique.

Phosphorus Magnetic Resonance Spectroscopy

Although much work has been performed to date utilizing ^{31}P MRS, applications to the CNS have constituted only a small fraction of this work; applications involving muscle tissue, liver, heart, and even other organs have been studied. Since a thorough discussion of phosphorus MRS is beyond the scope of this chapter and since the overall clinical utility of this modality is much lower than that of proton MRS because of a decreased signal-to-noise ratio and poorer spatial resolution, only a brief introduction to its applications to the study of the brain is provided.

The seven major metabolite peaks that can be detected in phosphorus MR spectra of the brain include the following[116]:

- Three peaks of ATP, seen at approximately -7.8, -16.3, and -2.7 ppm (known as alpha, beta, and gamma ATP peaks, respectively)
- Phosphocreatine (PCr) peak, seen at 0 ppm
- Phosphodiester (PDE) compounds peak, seen at 2.6 ppm
- Inorganic phosphate (Pi) peak, seen at 4.9 ppm
- Phosphomonoester (PME) compounds peak, seen at 6.5 ppm

All of these are markers of energy utilization and transfer within the cells, and levels of these compounds are affected by intracellular energy balance. PCr serves as a high-energy phosphate storage compound in brain and muscle tissue, whereas PME and PDE compounds are found in membrane phospholipids and are involved in cell membrane synthesis and degradation. Elevations in PME compounds have been noted in cases of rapid cell membrane synthesis, such as in tumors and in normal developing infant brain (levels of PDE compounds are low in infants). Levels of PME compounds decrease whereas PDE compounds increase from birth to approximately 3 years of age, when these levels stabilize.

The chemical shift of the Pi peak relative to the PCr peak has been used to determine intracellular pH, since it is pH-dependent. Multiple studies have shown that the pH of normal brain varies from 6.95 to 7.03.[6, 31, 93, 103, 106, 115, 224] Little variation in pH between gray and white matter is noted, and brain tumors consistently demonstrate elevations in pH relative to normal brain tissue.[31, 115]

Several studies have shown that tumor differentiation based on tissue pH is not possible.[6, 31, 93, 224] Findings regarding alteration of the concentrations of the metabolites PCr and Pi in gliomas have been inconsistent and inconclusive.[115] However, PDE is decreased in all gliomas relative to normal brain tissue, and its levels are higher in patients with GBM than in those with lower-grade tumors.[6, 103] In addition, markedly elevated PME levels have been described in GBM.[6, 31, 93, 171, 211] In addition, both the PME:ATP and PDE:ATP ratios tend to be elevated in glial tumors, particularly in GBM.[31, 115, 201] Higher-grade tumors also demonstrate relatively elevated PME peaks and relatively decreased PDE peaks, which probably signify increased cell turnover.[115]

Studies utilizing ^{31}P MRS in patients with epilepsy have shown ictal increases in Pi and Lac and decreases in PCr and pH in TLE.[120, 216, 260] Postictally, pH is noted to increase with development of alkalosis prior to Lac normalization.[120, 219] Interictal increased pH in the temporal lobe ipsilateral to the seizure onset has been noted in adults with TLE.[223] In addition, ipsilaterally increased Pi and decreased PME without significant differences in other metabolites have been noted in TLE.[105, 134, 223] In neonates, Younkin and coworkers have noted a 50% decrease in the PCr/Pi ratio in the seizure region with reestablishment of normal ratio postictally.[261] Studies of frontal lobe epilepsy have shown elevated pH and decreased PME in the affected frontal lobe.[130]

Additional applications of ^{31}P MRS have been described, particularly in pediatric neuroradiology. These and additional applications of phosphorus MRS, undoubtedly, will continue to evolve in the near future in light of the unique metabolic information that can be provided by this physiologic MR modality.

Other Nuclei and Functional Magnetic Resonance Spectroscopy

Spectroscopy using nuclei other than ^{1}H and ^{31}P has been performed for the study of CNS disease. The nuclei that have been used for this purpose include carbon 13 (^{13}C), sodium 23 (^{23}Na), and fluorine 19 (^{19}F). However, since none of these nuclei has been used widely for clinical applications, they are not discussed in this chapter.

Another exciting research application of MRS is functional MRS, which enables evaluation of temporal changes in metabolite concentrations during visual and auditory stimulation or performance of language tasks.[195] A special fast spectroscopic imaging technique, called proton echoplanar spectroscopic imaging (PEPSI), has been used by Richards and colleagues to study language activation during performance of a silent verb generation task.[190] Increases in Lac and Cr have been noted in the left temporal lobe during this language task, and transient elevation of Lac has also been noted during visual and auditory stimulation in the respective sensory cortices.[190, 195] Functional MRS is a promising new method for studying brain activation that may complement other techniques, such as functional MRI, magnetoencephalography, and PET, which are currently in widespread use for the study of transient physiologic changes in the brain.

References

1. Achten E: Aspects of proton MR spectroscopy in the seizure patient. Neuroimaging Clin North Am 8:849–862, 1998.
2. Achten E, Santens P, Boon P, et al: Single-voxel proton MR spectroscopy and positron emission tomography for lateralization of refractory temporal lobe epilepsy. AJNR Am J Neuroradiol 19: 1–8, 1998.
3. Allen K, Busza AL, Crockard HA, et al: Acute cerebral ischaemia: Concurrent changes in cerebral blood flow, energy metabolites, pH, and lactate measured with hydrogen clearance and ^{31}P and ^{1}H nuclear magnetic resonance spectroscopy: III. Changes following ischaemia. J Cereb Blood Flow Metab 8:816–821, 1988.
4. Ando K, Ishikura R, Morikawa T, et al: Regional differences of in vivo proton MR spectroscopy in developing human brain. Nippon Igaku Hoshasen Gakkai Zasshi 60:199–204, 2000.
5. Arnold DL, Matthews PM, Francis GS, Antel JP: Proton magnetic resonance spectroscopy of human brain in vivo in the evaluation of multiple sclerosis: Assessment of the load of the disease. Magn Reson Med 14:154–159, 1990.
6. Arnold DL, Emrich JF, Shoubridge EA, et al: Characterization of astrocytomas, meningiomas, and pituitary adenomas by phosphorus magnetic resonance spectroscopy. J Neurosurg 74:447–453, 1991.
7. Arnold DL, Matthews PM, Francis GS, et al: Proton magnetic resonance spectroscopic imaging for metabolic characterization of demyelinating plaques. Ann Neurol 31:235–241, 1992.
8. Austin SJ, Connelly A, Gadian DG, et al: Localized ^{1}H NMR spectroscopy on Canavan's disease: A report of two cases. Magn Reson Med 19:439–445, 1991.
9. Babb TL, Brown WJ: Pathological findings in epilepsy. In Engel J Jr (ed): Surgical Treatment of the Epilepsies. New York, Raven Press, 1987, pp 511–540.
10. Barker PB, Gillard JH, van Ziji PCM, et al: Acute stroke: Evaluation with serial proton MR spectroscopic imaging. Radiology 192:723–732, 1994.
11. Barkovich AJ, Westmark K, et al: Perinatal asphyxia: MR findings in the first 10 days. AJNR Am J Neuroradiol 16:427–438, 1995.
12. Barkovich AJ: Pediatric Neuroimaging, 2nd ed. Philadelphia, Lippincott-Raven, 1996, pp 47–52.
13. Barkovich AJ, Baranski K, Vigneron D, et al: Proton MR spectroscopy for the evaluation of brain injury in asphyxiated term neonates. AJNR Am J Neuroradiol 20:1399–1405, 1999.
14. Barkovich AJ: Pediatric Neuroimaging, 3rd ed. Philadelphia, Lippincott Williams & Wilkins, 2000, pp 55–59, 168, 199–202.
15. Bendszus M, Warmuth-Metz M, Klein R, et al: MR spectroscopy in gliomatosis cerebri. AJNR Am J Neuroradiol 21:375–380, 2000.
16. Benuck M, D'Adamo JAF: Acetyl transport mechanisms: Metabolism on N-acetyl-L-aspartic acid in the non-nervous tissues of the rat. Biochem Biophys Acta 152:611–618, 1968.
17. Berkelbach van der Sprenkel JW, Luyten PR, et al: Cerebral lactate detected by regional proton magnetic resonance spectroscopy in a patient with cerebral infarction. Stroke 19:1556–1560, 1988.
18. Birken DL, Oldendorf WH: N-acetyl-L-aspartic acid: A literature review of a compound prominent in ^{1}H-NMR spectroscopic studies of brain. Neurosci Biobehav Rev 13:23–31, 1989.
19. Bizzi A, Movsas B, Tedeschi G, et al: Response of non-Hodgkin lymphoma to radiation therapy: Early and long-term assessment with H-1 spectroscopic imaging. Radiology 194:271–276, 1995.
20. Bloch F, Hansen WW, Packard ME: Nuclear induction. Phys Rev 69:127, 1946.
21. Bonavita S, Di Salle F, Tedeschi G: Proton MRS in neurological disorders. Eur J Radiol 30:125–131, 1999.
22. Bottomley PA, Hart HR, Edelstein WA, et al: Anatomy and metabolism of the normal human brain studied by magnetic resonance at 1.5 Tesla. Radiology 150:441–446, 1984.
23. Bottomley PA, Edelstein WA, Foster TH, Adams WA: In vivo solvent-suppressed localized hydrogen nuclear magnetic resonance (NMR): A new window to metabolism? Proc Natl Acad Sci U S A 82:2148–2152, 1985.
24. Bottomley PA: Spatial localization in NMR spectroscopy in vivo. Ann N Y Acad Sci 508:376–385, 1987.
25. Brand A, Richter-Landsberg C, Leibfritz D: Multinuclear NMR studies on the energy metabolism of glial and neuronal cells. Dev Neurosci 15:289–98, 1993.
26. Brown TR, Kincaid BM, Ugurbil K: Chemical shift imaging in 3 dimensions. Proc Natl Acad Sci U S A 79:3523–3526, 1982.
27. Bruhn H, Frahm J, Gyngell ML, et al: Noninvasive differentiation of tumors with use of localized H-1 MR spectroscopy in vivo: Initial experience in patients with cerebral tumors. Radiology 172: 541–548, 1989.
28. Bruhn H, Frahm J, Gyngell ML, et al: Cerebral metabolism in man after acute stroke: New observations using localized proton NMR spectroscopy. Magn Reson Med 9:126–131, 1989.
29. Burri R, Steffen C, Herschkowitz N: N-acetyl-L-aspartate is a major source of acetyl groups for lipid synthesis during rat brain development. Dev Neurosci 13:403,1991.
30. Burtscher IM, Skagerberg G, Geijer B, et al: Proton MR spectroscopy and preoperative diagnostic accuracy: An evaluation of intracranial mass lesions characterized by stereotactic biopsy findings. AJNR Am J Neuroradiol 21:84–93, 2000.
31. Cadoux-Hudson TA, Blackledge MJ, Rajagopalan B, et al: Human primary brain tumor metabolism in vivo: A phosphorus magnetic resonance spectroscopy study. Br J Cancer 60:430–436, 1989.
32. Cady EB, Costello AM, Dawson MJ: Noninvasive investigation of cerebral metabolism in newborn infants by phosphorus nuclear magnetic resonance spectroscopy. Lancet i:1059–1063, 1983.
33. Castillo M, Green C, Kwock L, et al: Proton MR spectroscopy in patients with neurofibromatosis type I: Evaluation of hamartomas and clinical correlation. AJNR Am J Neuroradiol 16:141–147, 1995.
34. Castillo M, Kwock L, Green C: MELAS syndrome: Imaging and proton MR spectroscopic findings. AJNR Am J Neuroradiol 16: 233–239, 1995.
35. Castillo M, Kwock L, Mukherji SK: Clinical applications of proton MR spectroscopy. AJNR Am J Neuroradiol 17:1–15, 1996.
36. Castillo M, Kwock L: Proton MR Spectroscopy of common brain tumors. Neuroimaging Clin North Am 8:733–752, 1998.
37. Castillo M, Kwock L, Courvoisie HE, et al: Proton MR spectroscopy in psychiatric and neurodevelopmental childhood disorders: Early experience. Neuroimaging Clin North Am 8:901–912, 1998.
38. Castillo M, Kwock L, Scatliff J, Mukherji SK: Proton MR spectroscopy in neoplastic and non-neoplastic brain disorders. Magn Res Imaging Clin North Am 6:1–20, 1998.
39. Cecil KM, Lenkinski RE: Proton MR spectroscopy in inflammatory and infectious brain disorders. Neuroimaging Clin North Am 8: 863–880, 1998.
40. Cecil KM: Technical Aspects of Performing and Interpreting Proton MR spectroscopy (syllabus, Advanced Imaging Symposium: Preparing the neuroradiologist for the new millennium, pp 29–36). Paper presented at Annual Meeting of the American Society of Neuroradiology, April 2000, Atlanta.
41. Cendes F, Andermann F, Preul MC, et al: Lateralization of temporal lobe epilepsy based on regional metabolic abnormalities in proton magnetic resonance spectroscopic images. Ann Neurol 35:211–216, 1994.
42. Cendes F, Caramano Z, Andermann F, et al: Proton magnetic resonance spectroscopic imaging and magnetic resonance imaging volumetry in the lateralization of temporal lobe epilepsy: A series of 100 patients. Ann Neurol 42:737–746, 1997.
43. Ceodan S, Parrilla R, Santoro J, et al: H-1 NMR detection of cerebral myo-inositol. FEBS Lett 187:167–172, 1985.
44. Chan Y-l, Yeung DKW, Leung S-F, et al: Proton magnetic resonance spectroscopy of late delayed radiation-induced injury of the brain. J Magn Reson Imaging 10:130–137, 1999.
45. Chang L: In vivo magnetic resonance spectroscopy in HIV and HIV-related brain diseases. Rev Neurosci 6:365–378, 1995.
46. Chang L, Ernst T: MR spectroscopy and diffusion-weighted MR imaging in focal brain lesions in AIDS. Neuroimaging Clin North Am 7:409–426, 1997.

47. Chang L, Ernst T, Tornatore C, et al: Metabolite abnormalities in progressive multifocal leukoencephalopathy by proton magnetic resonance spectroscopy. Neurology 48:836–845, 1997.
48. Chang L, Ernst T, Leonido-Yee M, et al: Cerebral metabolite abnormalities correlate with clinical severity of HIV-1 cognitive motor complex. Neurology 52:100–108, 1999.
49. Chiang CS, McBride WH, Withers HR: Radiation-induced astrocytic and microglial responses in mouse brain. Radiother Oncol 29:60–68, 1998.
50. Comair YG, Ng T, Xue M, et al: Early post-ictal lactate detection in temporal lobe epilepsy for localization of seizure focus: A chemical shift imaging study (abstract). In Book of Abstracts. San Francisco, Society of Magnetic Resonance in Medicine, 1994, p 401.
51. Confort-Gouny S, Vion-Dury J, Chabrol B, et al: Localized proton magnetic resonance spectroscopy in X-linked adrenoleukodystrophy. Neuroradiology 37:568–575, 1995.
52. Connelly A, Cross J, Gadian D, et al: Magnetic resonance spectroscopy shows increased brain glutamine in ornithine carbamoyl transferase deficiency. Pediatr Res 33:77–81, 1993.
53. Connelly A, Jackson GD, Duncan JS, Gadian DG: Proton MRS in temporal lobe epilepsy. Neurology 44:1411–1417, 1994.
54. Connelly A, Paesschen WV, Porter DA, et al: Proton magnetic resonance spectroscopy in MRI-negative temporal lobe epilepsy. Neurology 51:61–66, 1998.
55. Cortey A, Jarvik JG, Lenkinski RE, et al: Proton MR spectroscopy of brain abnormalities in neonates born to HIV-positive mothers. AJNR Am J Neuroradiol 15:1853–1859, 1994.
56. Cousins JP, Seymour PA, Weaver S, et al: Clinical differentials of CNS tumors and radiation necrosis using single voxel H1-MRS correlated with pathology. Proceedings of the 5th Annual Scientific Meeting of the International Society for Magnetic Resonance in Medicine, 1997, Vancouver, p 1126.
57. Crockard HL, Gadian DG, Frackowiak SJ, et al: Acute cerebral ischaemia: Concurrent changes in cerebral blood flow, energy metabolites, pH, and lactate measured with hydrogen clearance and ^{31}P and ^1H nuclear magnetic resonance spectroscopy: II. Changes during ischaemia. J Cereb Blood Flow Metab 7:394–402, 1987.
58. Cross JH, Connelly A, Jackson GD, et al: Proton magnetic resonance spectroscopy in children with temporal lobe epilepsy. Ann Neurol 39:107–113, 1996.
59. Cwik VA, Hanstock CC, Allen PS, et al: Estimation of brainstem neuronal loss in amyotrophic lateral sclerosis with in vivo proton magnetic resonance spectroscopy. Neurology 50:72–77, 1998.
60. D'Adamo AF, Jr, Smith JC, Woiler C: The occurrence of N-acetyl-aspartate amidohydrolase (aminoacylase II) in the developing rat. J Neurochem 20:1275–1278, 1973.
61. Davie CA, Hawkins CP, Barker GJ, et al: Serial proton magnetic resonance spectroscopy in acute multiple sclerosis lesions: Part 1. Brain 117:49–58, 1994.
62. Davie CA, Barker GJ, Webb S, et al: Persistent functional deficit in multiple sclerosis and autosomal dominant cerebellar ataxia is associated with axon loss: Part 6. Brain 118:1583–1592, 1995.
63. Demaerel P, Johannik K, van Heche P, et al: Localized H-1 NMR spectroscopy in fifty cases of newly diagnosed intracranial tumors. J Comput Assist Tomogr 15:67–76, 1991.
64. De Stefano N, Matthews P, Ford B, et al: Short-term dichloroacetate treatment improves indices of cerebral metabolism in patients with mitochondrial disorders. Neurology 45:1193–1198, 1995.
65. Diezel P, Martin K: Die Ahornsirupkrankheit mit familarem Befall. Virchows Arch Pathol Anat 337:425–445, 1964.
66. Duijn JH, Matson GB, Maudsley AA, et al: Human brain infarction: Proton MR spectroscopy. Radiology 183:711–718, 1992.
67. Ende J, Scatliff JH, Powers S, et al: Spectral proton and P-31 MR spectroscopy patterns of treated human brain tumors. Paper presented at the Annual Meeting of the Society of Magnetic Resonance in Medicine, 1992.
68. Ende G, Laxer K, Knowlton R, et al: Temporal lobe epilepsy: Bilateral hippocampal metabolite changes revealed at proton MR spectroscopic imaging. Radiology 202:809–817, 1997.
69. Ernst T, Chang L, Melchor R, et al: Frontotemporal dementia and early Alzheimer disease: Differentiation with frontal lobe H-1 MR spectroscopy. Radiology 203:829–836, 1997.
70. Felber SR, Aichner FT, Sauter R, et al: Combined magnetic resonance imaging and proton magnetic resonance spectroscopy of patients with acute stroke. Stroke 23:1106–1110, 1992.
71. Felber SR, Sperl W, Chemelli A, et al: Maple syrup urine disease: Metabolic decompensation monitored by proton magnetic resonance imaging and spectroscopy. Ann Neurol 33:396–401, 1993.
72. Fenstermacher MJ, Narayana PD: Serial proton magnetic resonance spectroscopy of ischemic brain injury in humans. Radiology 25:1034–1039, 1990.
73. Fu L, Matthews PM, De Stefano N, et al: Imaging axonal damage of normal appearing white matter in multiple sclerosis. Brain 121:103–113, 1998.
74. Fulham MJ, Bizzi A, Dietz MJ, et al: Mapping of brain tumor metabolites with proton spectroscopic imaging: Clinical relevance. Radiology 185:675–686, 1992.
75. Gadian DF, Connelly A, Duncan JS, et al: ^1H magnetic resonance spectroscopy in the investigation of intractable epilepsy. Acta Neurol Scand Suppl 152:116–121, 1994.
76. Garcia PA, Laxer KD, van der Grond J, et al: Proton magnetic resonance spectroscopic imaging in patients with frontal lobe epilepsy. Ann Neurol 37:279–281, 1995.
77. Gideon P, Henriksen O, Sperling B, et al: Early time course of N-acetylaspartate, creatine, and phosphocreatine, and compounds containing choline in the brain after acute stroke: A proton magnetic resonance spectroscopy study. Stroke 23:1566–1572, 1992.
78. Gideon P, Sperling B, Arlien-Soborg P, et al: Long-term follow-up of cerebral infarction patients with proton magnetic resonance spectroscopy. Stroke 25:967–973, 1994.
79. Gill SS, Thomas DGT, Van Bruggen N, et al: Proton MR spectroscopy of intracranial tumors: In vivo and in vitro studies. J Comput Assist Tomogr 14:497–504, 1990.
80. Gillard JH, Barker PB, van Zijl PCM, et al: Proton MR spectroscopy in acute middle cerebral artery stroke. AJNR Am J Neuroradiol 17:873–886, 1996.
81. Gonen O, Wang ZJ, Viswanathan AK, et al: Three-dimensional multivoxel proton MR spectroscopy of the brain in children with neurofibromatosis type I. AJNR Am J Neuroradiol 20:1333–1341, 1999.
82. Gonen O, Catalaa I, Babb JS, et al: Total brain N-acetylaspartate: A new measure of disease load in MS. Neurology 54:15–19, 2000.
83. Grachev ID, Apkarian AV: Chemical heterogeneity of the living human brain: A proton MR spectroscopy study on the effects of sex, age, and brain region. Neuroimage 11(5 Part 1):554–563, 2000.
84. Graham GD, Blamire AM, Howseman AM, et al: Proton magnetic resonance spectroscopy of cerebral lactate and other metabolites in stroke patients. Stroke 23:333–340, 1992.
85. Graham GD, Blamire AM, Rothman DL, et al: Early temporal variation of cerebral metabolites after human stroke. Stroke 24:1891–1896, 1993.
86. Graham GD, Kalvach P, Blamire AM, et al: Clinical correlates of proton magnetic resonance spectroscopy findings after acute cerebral infarction. Stroke 26:225–229, 1995.
87. Graham SH, Meyerhoff DJ, Bayne L, et al: Magnetic resonance spectroscopy of N-acetylaspartate in hypoxic-ischemic encephalopathy. Ann Neurol 35:490–494, 1994.
88. Grand S, Passaro G, Ziegler A, et al: Necrotic tumor versus brain abscess: Importance of amino acids detected at ^1H MR spectroscopy—initial results. Radiology 213:785–793, 1999.
89. Grodd W, Krageloh-Mann W, Klose U, et al: Metabolic and destructive brain disorders in children: Findings with localized proton MR spectroscopy. Radiology 181:173–181, 1991.
90. Groenendaal F, Veenhoven RH, et al: Cerebral lactate and N-acetyl-aspartate/choline ratios in asphyxiated full-term neonates demonstrated in vivo using proton magnetic resonance spectroscopy. Pediatr Res 35:148–151, 1994.
91. Grossmann RI, Lenkinski RE, Ramer KN, et al: MR proton spectroscopy in multiple sclerosis. AJNR Am J Neuroradiol 13:1535–1543, 1992.
92. Harada M, Tanouchi M, Arai K, et al: Therapeutic efficacy of a case of pyruvate dehydrogenase complex deficiency monitored by localized proton magnetic resonance spectroscopy. Magn Reson Imaging 14:129–133, 1996.
93. Heindel W, Bunke J, Glathe S, et al: Combined ^1H-MR imaging and localized ^{31}P-spectroscopy of intracranial tumors in 43 patients. J Comput Assist Tomogr 12:907–916, 1988.
94. Henry RG, Vigneron DB, Fischbein NJ, et al: Comparison of relative cerebral blood volume and proton spectroscopy in patients with treated gliomas. AJNR Am J Neuroradiol 21:357–366, 2000.

95. Hetherington H, Kuzniecky R, Pan J, et al: Proton nuclear magnetic resonance spectroscopic imaging of human temporal lobe epilepsy at 4.1 T. Ann Neurol 38:396–404, 1995.

96. Hida K: In vivo ^{1}H and ^{31}P NMR spectroscopy of the developing rat brain. Hokkaido J Med Sci 67:272–281, 1992.

97. Holshouser BA, Ashwal S, Luh GY, et al: Proton MR spectroscopy after acute nervous system injury: Outcome prediction in neonates, infants, and children. Radiology 202:487–496, 1997.

98. Holzer T, Herholz K, Jeske J, et al: FDG-PET as a prognostic indicator in radiochemotherapy of glioblastoma. J Comput Assist Tomogr 17:681–687, 1993.

99. Hope PL, Costello AM, Cady EB, et al: Cerebral energy metabolism studied with phosphorus NMR spectroscopy in normal and birth-asphyxiated infants. Lancet ii:366–370, 1984.

100. Houkin K, Kamada K, Kamiyama H, et al: Longitudinal changes in proton magnetic resonance spectroscopy in cerebral infarction. Stroke 24:1316–1321, 1993.

101. Hoult DI, Busby SJW, Gadian DG, et al: Observation of tissue metabolites using phosphorus nuclear magnetic resonance. Nature 252:285–287, 1974.

102. Howe FA, Maxwell RJ, Saunders DE, et al: Proton spectroscopy in vivo. Magn Reson Q 9:31–59, 1993.

103. Hubesch B, Sappey-Marinier D, Roth K, et al: P-31 MR spectroscopy of normal human brain and brain tumors. Radiology 174:401–409, 1990.

104. Hueppi PS, Posse S, Lazeyras F, et al: Developmental changes in 1H spectroscopy in human brain. In Lafeber HN (ed): Fetal and Neonatal Physiological Measurements. New York, Elsevier, 1991, pp 33–41.

105. Hugg JW, Laxer KD, Matson GB, et al: Lateralization of human focal epilepsy by ^{31}P magnetic resonance spectroscopic imaging. Neurology 42:2011–2018, 1992.

106. Hugg JW, Matson GB, Twieg DB, et al: Phosphorus-31 MR spectroscopic imaging (MRSI) of normal and pathological human brains. Magn Reson Imaging 10:227–243, 1992.

107. Huppi P, Posse S, et al: Magnetic resonance in preterm and term newborns: H spectroscopy in developing human brain. Pediatr Res 30:574–578, 1991.

108. Huppi PS, Fusch C, Boesch C, et al: Regional metabolic assessment of human brain during development by proton magnetic resonance spectroscopy in vivo and by high-performance liquid chromatography/gas chromatography in autopsy tissue. Pediatr Res 37:145–150, 1995.

109. Husted CA, Goodin DS, Hugg JW, et al: Biochemical alterations in multiple sclerosis lesions and normal-appearing white matter detected by in vivo ^{31}P and ^{1}H spectroscopic imaging. Ann Neurol 36:157–165, 1994.

110. Hwang J-H, Graham GD, Behar KL, et al: Short echo time proton magnetic resonance spectroscopic imaging of macromolecule and metabolite signal intensities in the human. Magn Reson Med 35:633–639, 1996.

111. Hwang J-H, Egnaczyk GF, Ballard E, et al: Proton MR spectroscopic characteristics of pediatric pilocytic astrocytomas. AJNR Am J Neuroradiol 19:535–540, 1998.

112. Jarvik JG, Lenkinski RE, Saykin AJ, et al: Proton spectroscopy in asymptomatic HIV-infected adults: Initial results in a prospective cohort study. J Acquir Immune Defic Syndr Hum Retrovirol 13:247–253, 1996.

113. Jaysundar R, Bakshi A, Singh VP, et al: Diagnostic potential of proton MRS in differentiating between tumor recurrence and radiation necrosis? Paper presented at the Fifth Annual Scientific Meeting of the International Society for Magnetic Resonance in Medicine, 1997, Vancouver, BC, p 1142.

114. Jenkins BG, Koroshetz WJ, Beal MF, Rosen BR: Evidence for impairment of energy metabolism in vivo in Huntington's disease using localized ^{1}H NMR spectroscopy. Neurology 43:2689–2695, 1993.

115. Kaibara T, Tyson RL, Sutherland GR: Human cerebral neoplasms studied using MR spectroscopy: A review. Biochem Cell Biol 76:477–486, 1998.

116. Kegeles LS, Humaran TJ, Mann JJ: In vivo neurochemistry of the brain in schizophrenia as revealed by magnetic resonance spectroscopy. Biol Psychiatry 44:382–398, 1998.

117. Kim CK, Alavi JB, Alavi A, et al: New grading system of cerebral gliomas using positron emission tomography with F-18 fluorodeoxyglucose. J Neurooncol 10:85–91, 1991.

118. Kimura H, Fujii Y, Matsuda T, et al: Metabolic alterations in the neonate and infant brain during development: Evaluation with proton MR spectroscopy. Radiology 194:483–489, 1995.

119. Kimura S, Ohtuki N, Nezu A, et al: Clinical and radiologic improvements in mitochondrial encephalomyelopathy following sodium dichloroacetate therapy. Brain Dev 19:535–540, 1997.

120. King D, Baltuch GH: Magnetic resonance imaging and temporal lobe epilepsy. Acta Neurol Scand 98:217–223, 1998.

121. Kinoshita Y, Kajiwara H, Yokota A, Koga Y: Proton magnetic resonance spectroscopy of brain tumors: An in vitro study. Neurosurgery 35:606–614, 1994.

122. Kornfeld M, Woodfin B, Papile L, et al: Neuropathology of ornithine carbamyl transferase deficiency. Acta Neuropathol 65:261–264, 1985.

123. Koutcher JA, Burt CT: Principles of nuclear magnetic resonance. J Nucl Med 25:101–111, 1984.

124. Kreis R, Farrow NA, Ross BD: Localized ^{1}H NMR spectroscopy in patients with chronic hepatic encephalopathy: Analysis of changes in cerebral glutamine, choline and inositols. NMR Biomed 4:109–116, 1991.

125. Kreis R, Ross BD: Cerebral metabolic disturbances in patients with subacute and chronic diabetes mellitus: Detection with proton MR spectroscopy. Radiology 184:123–130, 1992.

126. Kreis R, Ross BD, Farrow NA, Ackerman Z: Metabolic disorders of the brain in chronic hepatic encephalopathy detected with H-1 MR spectroscopy. Radiology 182:19–27, 1992.

127. Kreis R, Ernst T, Ross BD: Development of the human brain: In vivo quantification of metabolite and water content with proton magnetic spectroscopy. Magn Reson Med 30:424–437, 1993.

128. Kreis R, Ernst T, Ross BD: Absolute quantitation of water and metabolites in the human brain: II. Metabolite concentrations. J Magn Reson 102:9–15, 1993.

129. Kugel H, Heindel W, Ernestus RI, et al: Human brain tumors: Spectral patterns detected with localized H-1 MR spectroscopy. Radiology 183:701–709, 1992.

130. Kuzniecky R, Elgavish GA, Hetherington HP, et al: In vivo ^{31}P nuclear magnetic resonance spectroscopy of human temporal lobe epilepsy. Neurology 42:1586–1590, 1992.

131. Kuzniecky R, Hugg JW, Hetherington H, et al: Relative utility of ^{1}H spectroscopic imaging and hippocampal volumetry in the lateralization of mesial temporal lobe epilepsy. Neurology 51:66–71, 1998.

132. Kwock L: Localized MR spectroscopy. Neuroimaging Clin North Am 8:713–731, 1998.

133. Lam WWM, Wang ZJ, Zhao H, et al: ^{1}H MR spectroscopy of the basal ganglia in childhood: A semiquantitative analysis. Neuroradiology 40:315–232, 1998.

134. Laxer KD, Hubesch B, Sappey-Marinier D, Weiner MW: Increased pH and inorganic phosphate in temporal seizure foci demonstrated by ^{31}P MRS. Epilepsia 33:618–623, 1993.

135. Lee JH, Arcinue E, Ross BD: Organic osmolytes in the brain of an infant with hypernatremia. N Engl J Med 331:439–442, 1994.

136. Leth H, Toft PB, Pryds O, et al: Brain lactate in preterm and growth-retarded neonates. Acta Pediatr 84:495–499, 1995.

137. Li LM, Cendes F, Bastos AC, et al: Neuronal metabolic dysfunction in patients with cortical developmental malformations: A proton magnetic resonance spectroscopic imaging study. Neurology 50:755–759, 1998.

138. Lichter T, Dohrman GJ, Gets GS: Respiratory deficiency and increased glycolysis in benign human tumors. Surg Forum 35:486–488, 1994.

139. Lowry OH, Berger SJ, Chi M-Y, et al: Diversity of metabolic patterns in human brain tumors: I. High energy phosphate compounds and basic composition. J Neurochem 29:959–977, 1977.

140. Lu D, Pavlakis SG, Frank Y, et al: Proton MR spectroscopy of the basal ganglia in healthy children and children with AIDS. Radiology 199:423–428, 1996.

141. Luyten PR, Marien AJH, Heindel W, et al: Metabolic imaging of patients with intracranial tumors: H-1 MR spectroscopic imaging and PET. Radiology 176:791–799, 1990.

142. Mader I, Roser W, Kappos L, et al: Serial proton MR spectroscopy of contrast-enhancing multiple sclerosis plaques: Absolute metabolic values over 2 years during a clinical pharmacological study. AJNR Am J Neuroradiol 21:1220–1227, 2000.

143. Marks HG, Caro PA, Wang Z, et al: Use of computed tomography,

magnetic resonance imaging, and localized ^{1}H magnetic resonance spectroscopy in Canavan's disease: A case report. Ann Neurol 30: 106–110, 1991.

144. Matalon R, Michals K, Sevesta D, et al: Asparto-acylase deficiency and N-acetylaspartic aciduria in patients with Canavan's disease. Am J Med Genet 20:463–471, 1988.

145. Matthews PM, Francis G, Antel J, Arnold DL: Proton magnetic resonance spectroscopy for metabolic characterization of plaques in multiple sclerosis Neurology 41:1251–1256, 1991 (correction in Neurology 41:1828, 1991).

146. Matthews PM, Andermann F, Silver K, et al: Proton MR spectroscopic characterization of differences in regional brain metabolic abnormalities in mitochondrial encephalomyopathies. Neurology 43: 2484–2490, 1993.

147. Matthews PM, De Stefano N, Narayanan S, et al: Putting magnetic resonance spectroscopy studies in context: Axonal damage and disability in multiple sclerosis. Semin Neurol 18:327–336, 1998.

148. Maudsley AA, Twieg DB, Sappey-Marinier D, et al: Spin echo ^{31}P spectroscopic imaging in the human brain. Magn Reson Med 14: 415–422, 1990.

149. Menon DK, Baudouin CJ, Tomlinson D, et al: Proton MR spectroscopy and imaging of the brain in AIDS: Evidence of neuronal loss in regions that appear normal with imaging. J Comput Assist Tomogr 14:882–885, 1990.

150. Meyerand ME, Pipas JM, Mamourian A, et al: Classification of biopsy-confirmed brain tumors using single-voxel MR spectroscopy. AJNR Am J Neuroradiol 20:117–123, 1999.

151. Meyerhoff DJ, Bloomer C, Cardenas V, et al: Elevated subcortical choline metabolites in cognitively and clinically asymptomatic HIV + patients. Neurology 52:995–1003, 1999.

152. Michaelis T, Helms KD, Merboldt W, et al: First observation of scyllo-inositol in proton NMR spectra of human brain in vitro and in vivo. Paper presented at Annual Meeting of the Society of Magnetic Resonance in Medicine, Berlin, 1992.

153. Michaelis T, Merboldt KD, Bruhn H, et al: Absolute concentrations of metabolites in the adult human brain in vivo: Quantification of localized proton MR spectra. Radiology 187:219–227, 1993.

154. Michaelis T, Videen J, Linsey MS, et al: Cerebral abnormalities in end stage renal disease. Paper presented at the Second Annual Meeting of the Society of Magnetic Resonance in Medicine, 1994, San Francisco, p 306.

155. Miller B: A review of chemical issues in ^{1}H NMR spectroscopy: N-acetyl-aspartate, creatine and choline. NMR Biomed 4:47–52, 1991.

156. Miller BL, Moats R, Shonk T, et al: Alzheimer disease: Depiction of increased cerebral myo-inositol with proton MR spectroscopy. Radiology 187:433–437, 1993.

157. Miyake M, Kakimoto Y: Developmental changes of N-acetyl-L-aspartic acid, N-acetyl-L-aspartylglutamic acid, and beta-citryl-L-glutamic acid in different brain regions and spinal cords of rat and guinea pig. J Neurochem 37:1064–1067, 1981.

158. Moats RA, Ernst T, Kreis R, et al: Well-localized standardized, quantitized short TE ^{1}H MRS permits new diagnostic accuracy in patients with Alzheimer disease. TAMU Newsletter 413:13–14, 1993.

159. Moats RA, Ernst T, Shonk TK, et al: Abnormal cerebral metabolite concentrations in patients with probable Alzheimer disease. Magn Reson Med 32:110–115, 1994.

160. Monsein LH, Mathews VP, Barker PB, et al: Irreversible regional ischemia: Serial MR imaging and proton MR spectroscopy in a non-human primate model. AJNR Am J Neuroradiol 14:963–970, 1993.

161. Moon RB, Richards JH: Determination of intracellular pH by ^{31}P magnetic resonance. J Biol Chem 248:7276–7278, 1973.

162. Moonen CTW, van Zijl PCM, Frank JA, et al: Comparisons of single shot localization methods (STEAM and PRESS) for in vivo proton NMR spectroscopy. NMR Biomed 2:201–208, 1989.

163. Moore GJ: Proton magnetic resonance spectroscopy in pediatric neuroradiology. Pediatr Radiol 28:805–814, 1998.

164. Morantz RA: The management of the patient with low-grade cerebral astrocytomas. In Morantz, RA, Walsh JW (eds): Brain Tumors: A Comprehensive Text. New York, Marcel Dekker, 1994, pp 387–415.

165. Moseley ME, Cohen Y, Mintorovitch J, et al: Early detection of regional ischemia in cats: Comparison of diffusion- and T2-weighted MRI and spectroscopy. Magn Reson Med 14:330–346, 1990.

166. Nagatomo Y, Wick M, Prielmeier F, et al: Dynamic monitoring of

cerebral metabolites during and after transient global ischemia in rats by quantitative proton NMR spectroscopy in vivo. NMR Biomed 8: 265–270, 1995.

167. Narayana PA, Doyle TJ, Lai D, Wolinsky JS: Serial proton magnetic resonance spectroscopic imaging, contrast-enhanced magnetic resonance imaging, and quantitative lesion volumetry in multiple sclerosis. Ann Neurol 43:56–71, 1998.

168. Negendank WG, Sauter R, Brown TR, et al: Proton magnetic resonance spectroscopy in patients with glial tumors: A multicenter study. J Neurosurg 84:449–458, 1996.

169. Nelson SJ: MR Spectroscopy in adults: Current and future applications (syllabus, Advanced Imaging Symposium: Preparing the neuroradiologist for the new millennium, pp 37–43). Presented at the American Society of Neuroradiology Annual Meeting, April 2000, Atlanta.

170. Ng TC, Comair YG, Xue M, et al: Temporal lobe epilepsy: Presurgical localisation with proton chemical shift imaging. Radiology 193: 465–472, 1994.

171. Oberhaensli RD, Hilton-Jones D, Bore PJ, et al: Biochemical investigation of human tumors in vivo with phosphorus-31 magnetic resonance spectroscopy. Lancet 2(8497):8–11, 1986.

172. Ott D, Hennig J, Ernst T: Human brain tumors: Assessment with in vivo proton MR spectroscopy. Radiology 186:745–752, 1993.

173. Patronas NJ, Di Chiro G, Kufta C, et al: Prediction of survival in glioma patients by means of positron emission tomography. J Neurosurg 62:816–822, 1985.

174. Peeling J, Wong D, Sutherland GR: Nuclear magnetic resonance study of regional metabolism after forebrain ischemia in rats. Stroke 20:633–640, 1989.

175. Pendlebury ST, Blamire AM, Lee MA, et al: Axonal injury in the internal capsule correlates with motor impairment after stroke. Stroke 30:956–962, 1999.

176. Penrice J, Cady EB, Lorek A, et al: Proton magnetic resonance spectroscopy of the brain in normal preterm and term infants and early changes after perinatal hypoxia-ischemia. Pediatr Res 40:6–14, 1996.

177. Penrice J, Lorek A, Cady EB, et al: Proton magnetic resonance spectroscopy of the brain during acute hypoxia-ischemia and delayed cerebral energy failure in the newborn piglet. Pediatr Res 41:795–802, 1997.

178. Pereira AC, Saunders DE, Doyle VL, et al: Measurement of initial N-acetyl aspartate concentration by magnetic resonance spectroscopy and initial infarct volume by MRI predicts outcome of patients with middle cerebral artery territory infarction. Stroke 30:1577–1582, 1999.

179. Pfefferbaum A, Adalsteinsson E, Spielman D, et al: In vivo spectroscopic quantification of the N-acetyl moiety, creatine, and choline from large volumes of brain gray and white matter: Effects of normal aging. Magn Res Med 41:276–284, 1999.

180. Poptani H, Gupta RK, Roy R, et al: Characterization of intracranial mass lesions with in vivo proton MR spectroscopy. AJNR Am J Neuroradiol 16:1593–1603, 1995.

181. Posse S, Schuknecht B, Smith ME, et al: Short echo time proton MR spectroscopic imaging. J Comput Assist Tomogr 17:1–14, 1994.

182. Pouwels PJW, Frahm J: Regional metabolite concentrations in human brain determined by quantitative localized proton MRS. Magn Reson Med 39:53–60, 1998.

183. Preul MC, Caramanos Z, Collins DL, et al: Accurate, noninvasive diagnosis of human tumors by using proton magnetic resonance spectroscopy. Nature Med 2:323–325, 1996.

184. Pu Y, Li QF, Zeng CM, et al: Increased detectability of alpha brain glutamate/glutamine in neonatal hypoxic-ischemic encephalopathy. AJNR Am J Neuroradiol 21:203–212, 2000.

185. Purcell EM, Torrey HC, Pound RV: Resonance absorption by nuclear magnetic moments in a solid. Phys Rev 69:37–38, 1946.

186. Radda GK, Bore PJ, Rajagopalan B: Clinical aspects of ^{31}P NMR spectroscopy. Br Med Bull 40:155–159, 1984.

187. Rakic P, Bourgeois JP, Eckenhoff MF et al: Concurrent overproduction of synapses in diverse regions of the primate cerebral cortex. Science 232:232–235, 1986.

188. Remy C, Grand S, Lai ES, et al: ^{1}H MRS of human brain abscesses in vivo and in vitro. Magn Reson Med 34:508–514, 1995.

189. Ricci PE: Proton MR spectroscopy in ischemic stroke and other vascular disorders. Neuroimaging Clin North Am 8:881–900, 1998.

190. Richards TL, Dager SR, Panagiotides HS, et al: Functional MR

spectroscopy during language activation: A preliminary study using proton echo-planar spectroscopic imaging (PEPSI). Int J Neuroradiol 3:490, 1997.

191. Richards TL, Dager SR, Posse S: Functional MR spectroscopy of the brain. Neuroimaging Clin North Am 8:823–834, 1998.

192. Rooney WD, Goodkin DE, Schuff N, et al: H MRS of normal appearing white matter in multiple sclerosis. Mult Scler 3:231–237, 1997.

193. Ross BD: Biochemical considerations in ^{1}H spectroscopy. Glutamate and glutamine: Myo-inositol and related metabolites. NMR Biomed 4:59–63, 1991.

194. Ross B, Kreis R, Ernst T: Clinical tool for the 90s: Magnetic resonance spectroscopy and metabolite imaging. Eur J Radiol 14:128–140, 1992.

195. Ross BD, Jacobson S, Villamil F, et al: Subclinical hepatic encephalopathy: Proton MR spectroscopic abnormalities. Radiology 193:457–463, 1994.

196. Ross B, Danielsen E, Bluml S: Proton magnetic resonance spectroscopy: The new gold standard for diagnosis of clinical and subclinical hepatic encephalopathy? Dig Dis 14(suppl 1):30–39, 1996.

197. Ross BD, Bluml S, Cowan R, et al: In vivo MR spectroscopy of human dementia. Neuroimaging Clin North Am 8:809–822, 1998.

198. Ross BD: A biochemistry primer for neuroradiologists (syllabus, Advanced Imaging Symposium: Preparing the neuroradiologist for the new millennium, pp 13–27). Paper presented at the Annual Meeting of the American Society of Neuroradiology, April 2000, Atlanta.

199. Rudkin TM, Arnold DL: Proton magnetic resonance spectroscopy for the diagnosis and management of cerebral disorders. Arch Neurol 56:919–926, 1999.

200. Ruggieri PM: Practical MR spectroscopy in pediatric neuroradiology (syllabus, Advanced Imaging Symposium: Preparing the neuroradiologist for the new millennium, pp 45–53). Paper presented at the Annual Meeting of the American Society of Neuroradiology, April 2000, Atlanta.

201. Rutter A, Hugenholtz H, Saunders JK, Smith IC: One-dimensional phosphorus-31 chemical shift imaging of human brain tumors. Invest Radiol 30:359–366, 1995.

202. Salibi N, Brown MA: Clinical MR Spectroscopy. New York, Wiley-Liss, 1998.

203. Salvan AM, Vion-Dury J, Confort-Gouny S, et al: Brain proton magnetic resonance spectroscopy in HIV-related encephalopathy: Identification of evolving metabolic patterns in relation to dementia and therapy. AIDS Res Hum Retroviruses 13:1055–1066, 1997.

204. Sappey-Marinier D, Calabrese G, Hetherington HP, et al: Proton magnetic resonance spectroscopy of the human brain: Applications to normal white matter, chronic infarction, and MRI white matter signal hyperintensities. Magn Reson Med 26:313–327, 1992.

205. Sarchielli P, Presciutti O, Tarducci R, et al: H-MRS in patients with multiple sclerosis undergoing treatment with interferon β-1a: Results of a preliminary study. J Neurol Neurosurg Psychiatry 64:204–212, 1998.

206. Sarchielli P, Presciutti O, Pelliccioli GP, et al: Absolute quantification of brain metabolites by proton magnetic resonance spectroscopy in normal-appearing white matter of multiple sclerosis patients. Brain 121:513–521, 1999.

207. Saunders DE, Howe FA, Van Den Boogaart: Continuing ischemic damage after acute middle cerebral artery infarction in humans demonstrated by short-echo proton spectroscopy. Stroke 26:1007–1013, 1995.

208. Scarabino T, Popolizio T, Bertolino A, Salvolini U: Proton magnetic resonance spectroscopy of the brain in pediatric patients. Eur J Radiol 30:142–153, 1999.

209. Schuff N, Amend D, Ezekiel BA, et al: Changes of hippocampal N-acetyl aspartate and volume in Alzheimer's disease: A proton MR spectroscopic imaging and MRI study. Neurology 49:1513–1521, 1997.

210. Scriver C, Kaufman S, Woo S: The hyperphenylalaninemias. In Scriver CR, Beaudet AL, Sly WS, et al (eds): The Metabolic Basis of Inherited Disease. New York, McGraw-Hill, 1989, pp 495–546.

211. Segebarth CM, Baleriaux DF, de Beer R, et al: ^{1}H image-guided localized ^{31}P MR spectroscopy of human brain: Quantitative analysis of ^{31}P MR spectra measured on volunteers and on intracranial tumor patients. Magn Reson Med 11:349–366, 1989.

212. Sharma R, Venkatasubramanian PN, Barany M, et al: Proton MRS of the brain in schizophrenia and affective disorders. Schizophr Res 8:43–49, 1992.

213. Shaw D: The fundamental principles of nuclear magnetic resonance. In Wehrli FW, Shaw D, Kneeland JB (eds): Biomedical Magnetic Resonance Imaging. New York, VCH Publishers, 1988, pp 1–45.

214. Shevell MI, Ashwal S, Novotny E: Proton magnetic resonance spectroscopy: Clinical applications in children with nervous system diseases. Semin Pediatr Neurol 6:68–77, 1999.

215. Shimizu H, Kumabe T, Tominaga T, et al: Noninvasive evaluation of malignancy of brain tumors with proton MR spectroscopy. AJNR Am J Neuroradiol 17:737–747, 1996.

216. Shnall MD, Yoshizaki K, Chance B, Leigh JS: Triple nuclear NMR studies of cerebral metabolism during generalized seizure. Magn Reson Med 6:15–23, 1988.

217. Shonk TK, Moats RA, Gifford P, et al: Probable Alzheimer disease: Diagnosis with proton MR spectroscopy. Radiology 195:65–72, 1995.

218. Shu SK, Ashwal S, Holshouser BA, et al: Prognostic value of ^{1}H MRS in perinatal CNS insults. Pediatr Neurol 17:309–318, 1997.

219. Siesjo BK, von Hanwehr R, Nergelius G, et al: Extra- and intracellular pH in the brain during seizures and in the recovery period following arrest of seizure activity. J Cereb Blood Flow Metab 5:47–57, 1985.

220. Sijens PE, van Dijk P, Oudkerk M: Correlation between choline level and Gd-DTPA enhancement in patients with brain metastases of mammary carcinoma. Magn Reson Med 32:549–555, 1994.

221. Sijens PE, Knopp MV, Brunetti A, et al: H-1 spectroscopy in patients with metastatic brain tumors: A multicenter study. Magn Reson Med 33:818–826, 1995.

222. Simone IL, Federico F, Tortorella C, et al: Metabolic changes in neuronal migration disorders: Evaluation by combined MRI and proton MR spectroscopy. Epilepsia 40:872–879, 1999.

223. Sitoh Y, Tien RD: Neuroimaging in epilepsy. J Magn Reson Imaging 8:277–288, 1998.

224. Sutton LN, Lenkinski RE, Cohen BH, et al: Localized ^{31}P magnetic resonance spectroscopy of large pediatric brain tumors. J Neurosurg 72:65–70, 1990.

225. Sutton LN, Wang Z, Gusnard D, et al: Proton magnetic resonance spectroscopy of pediatric brain tumors. Neurosurgery 31:195–202, 1992.

226. Sutton LN, Wehrli SL, Gennareli L, et al: High-resolution ^{1}H-magnetic resonance spectroscopy of pediatric posterior fossa tumors in vitro. J Neurosurg 81:443–448, 1994.

227. Swindells S, McConnell JR, McComb RD, Gendelman HE: Utility of cerebral proton magnetic resonance spectroscopy in differential diagnosis of HIV-related dementia. J Neurovirol 1:268–274, 1995.

228. Takanashi J-I, Sugita K, Osaka H, et al: Proton MR spectroscopy in Pelizaeus-Merzbacher disease. AJNR Am J Neuroradiol 18:533–535, 1997.

229. Tallan HH: Studies on the distribution of N-acetyl-L-aspartic acid in brain. J Biol Chem 224:41–45, 1956.

230. Tallan HH, Moore S, Stein WH: N-acetyl-L-aspartic acid in brain. J Biol Chem 219:257–264, 1956.

231. Taylor JS, Langston JW, Reddick WE, et al: Clinical value of proton magnetic resonance spectroscopy for differentiating recurrent or residual brain tumor from delayed cerebral necrosis. Int J Radiat Oncol Biol Phys 36:1251–1261, 1996.

232. Tedeschi G, Bertolino A, Righini A, et al: Brain regional distribution pattern of metabolite signal intensities in young adults by proton magnetic resonance spectroscopic imaging. Neurology 45:1384–1391, 1995.

233. Tedeschi G, Schiffmann R, Barton NW, et al: Proton magnetic resonance spectroscopic imaging in childhood ataxia with diffuse white matter hypomyelination. Neurology 45:1526–1532, 1995.

234. Tedeschi G, Bertolino A, Lundbom N, et al: Cortical and subcortical chemical pathology in Alzheimer's disease as assessed by multislice proton magnetic resonance spectroscopic imaging. Neurology 47:696–704, 1996.

235. Tedeschi G, Lundbom N, Raman R, et al: Increase of choline signal coincides with malignant degeneration of cerebral gliomas: A serial proton magnetic resonance spectroscopic imaging study. J Neurosurg 87:516–524, 1997.

236. Tien RD, Lai PH, Smith JS, et al: Single-voxel proton brain spectroscopy exam (PROBE/SV) in patients with primary brain tumors. AJR Am J Roentgenol 167:201–209, 1996.

237. Toft PB, Leth H, Lou HC, et al: Metabolite concentrations in the developing brain estimated with proton MR spectroscopy. J Magn Reson Med 4:674–680, 1994.

238. Tourbah A, Stievenart JL, Gout O, et al: Localized proton magnetic resonance spectroscopy in relapsing remitting versus secondary progressive multiple sclerosis. Neurology 53:1091–1097, 1999.

239. Tracey I, Lane J, Chang I, et al: ¹H magnetic resonance spectroscopy reveals neuronal injury in a simian immune deficiency virus macaque model. J Acquir Immune Defic Syndr Hum Retrovirol 15:21–27, 1997.

240. Tzika AA, Ball WS, Vigneron DB, et al: Childhood adrenoleukodystrophy: Assessment with proton MR spectroscopy. Radiology 189:467–480, 1993.

241. Tzika AA, Vigneron DB, Dunn RS, et al: Intracranial tumors in children: Small single-voxel proton MR spectroscopy using short- and long-echo sequences. Neuroradiology 38:254–263, 1996.

242. Tzika AA, Vajapeyam S, Barnes PD: Multivoxel proton MR spectroscopy and hemodynamic MR imaging of childhood brain tumors: Preliminary observations. AJNR Am J Neuroradiol 18:203–218, 1997.

243. Urenjak J, Williams SR, Gadian DG, et al: Specific expression of *N*-acetylaspartate in neurons, oligodendrocyte-type 2 astrocyte progenitors, and immature oligodendrocytes in vitro. J Neurochem 59:55–61, 1992.

244. van der Grond J, van Everdingen KJ, Eikelboom BC, et al: Assessment of borderzone ischemia with a combined MR imaging–MR angiography–MR spectroscopy protocol. J Magn Reson Imaging 9:1–9, 1999.

245. van der Knaap MS, vanderGrond J, van Rijen PC, et al: Age-dependent changes in localized proton and phosphorus MR spectroscopy of the brain. Radiology 176:509–515, 1990.

246. van der Knaap MS, van der Grond J, Luyten PR, et al: H-1 and P-31 magnetic resonance spectroscopy of the brain in degenerative cerebral disorders. Ann Neurol 31:202–211, 1993.

247. van der Knaap MS, Valk J: Uses of MR in inborn errors of metabolism. In Kucharczyk J, Mosely M, Barkovich AJ (eds): Magnetic Resonance Neuroimaging. Boca Raton, Fla, CRC Press, 1994, pp 245–318.

248. van der Knaap MS, Barth P, Gabreels F, et al: A new leukoencephalopathy with vanishing white matter. Neurology 48:845–855, 1997.

249. Videen JS, Michaelis T, Pinto P, et al: Human cerebral osmolytes during chronic hyponatremia: A proton magnetic resonance spectroscopy study. J Clin Invest 95:788–793, 1995.

250. Vigneron DB, Nelson SJ, Kurhanewicz J: Proton chemical shift imaging of cancer. In Higgins CB, Hricak H, Helms CA (eds): Magnetic Resonance of the Body. Philadelphia, Lippincott-Raven, 1997, pp 205–220.

251. Vion-Dury J, Meyerhoff DJ, Cozzone PJ, et al: What might be the impact on neurology of the analysis of brain metabolism by in vivo magnetic resonance spectroscopy? J Neurol 241:354–371, 1994.

252. Wang Z, Sutton LN, Cnaan A, et al: Proton MR spectroscopy of pediatric cerebellar tumors. AJNR Am J Neuroradiol 16:1821–1833, 1995.

253. Wang Z, Zimmerman RA, Sauter R: Proton MR spectroscopy of the brain: Clinically useful information obtained in assessing CNS diseases in children. AJR Am J Roentgenol 167:191–199, 1996.

254. Wang ZJ, Berry GT, Dreha SF, et al: In vivo proton brain MRS of galactosemia. Paper presented at the Sixth Annual Meeting of the International Society of Magnetic Resonance in Medicine, 1998, Sydney, Australia, p 538.

255. Wang ZJ, Zimmerman RA: Proton MR spectroscopy of pediatric brain metabolic disorders. Neuroimaging Clin North Am 8:781–807, 1998.

256. Wardlaw JM, Marshall I, Wild J, et al: Studies of acute ischemic stroke with proton magnetic resonance spectroscopy: Relation between time from onset, neurological deficit, metabolite abnormalities in the infarct, blood flow, and clinical outcome. Stroke 29:1618–1624, 1998.

257. Wells W, Pittman T, Wells H, et al: The isolation and identification of galactitol from the brains of galactosemia patients. J Biol Chem 240:1002–1004, 1965.

258. Wilkinson ID, Lunn S, Miszkiel KA, et al: Proton MRS and quantitative MRI assessment of the short term neurological response to antiretroviral therapy in AIDS. J Neurol Neurosurg Psychiatry 63:477–482, 1997.

259. Wittsack H, Kugel H, Roth B, et al: Quantitative measurements with localized ¹H MR spectroscopy in children with Canavan's disease. J Magn Reson Imaging 6:889–893, 1996.

260. Yaksh TL, Anderson RE: In vivo studies on intracellular pH, focal flow, and vessel diameter in the cat cerebral cortex: Effects of altered CO_2 and electrical stimulation. J Cereb Blood Flow Metab 7:332–341, 1987.

261. Younkin DP, Delivoria PM, Maris J, et al: Cerebral metabolic effects of neonatal seizures measured with in vivo ³¹P NMR spectroscopy. Ann Neurol 20:513–519, 1986.

262. Zimmerman RA, Wang Z: Proton spectroscopy of the pediatric brain. Riv Neuroradiol 5(suppl 1):5–8, 1992.

12

Meningeal Processes

Melanie B. Fukui, Carolyn Cidis Meltzer

Anatomy and Embryology
Meninges

The meninges, which form the coverings of the brain and spinal cord, develop from the meninx primitiva.[68] The neural tube is surrounded by this dense cellular layer, the meninx primitiva, shortly after the neural tube closes.[122] As early as 32 days and as late as 44 of gestation, the primitive meninx begins to cavitate to form the cerebral cisterns by gradually decreasing its cellular component and enlarging its intercellular space.[122] The periphery of the meninx primitiva, however, develops more dense cellularity to become the primitive dura mater.[122]

The earliest subarachnoid space (SAS) is that ventral to the brain stem.[122] As this space expands, the prepontomedullary cisterns and anterior spinal SAS are formed.[122, 155] At approximately 41 days, the space is extended to create perimesencephalic and dorsal mesencephalic cisterns.[121, 122, 155] The primitive meninx is composed of totipotential mesenchymal cells of neural crest origin.[68] The remnants of incomplete differentiation of these pluripotential cells may be seen as deposits of fat, or lipomas, in and around the basal cisterns, corpus callosum, and cavernous sinuses.[155] The order of regression of the primitive meninx is reflected in the distribution of lipomas, as described by Salvi.[155] Thus, intracranial lipomas are thought most appropriately to represent developmental, rather than neoplastic, pathology of the meninges.[155]

This network of concentric membranes consists of the pachymeninx (dura mater) and the leptomeninges (arachnoid and pia mater) (Fig. 12–1). The dura mater is the most superficial membrane, a thick, tough structure composed of dense connective tissue.[21] The dura is composed of 2 layers: (1) an outer periosteal layer, which is highly vascularized, serves as the true periosteum of the inner table of the calvaria, and is not of meningeal origin,[142] and (2) an inner meningeal layer, derived from the meninx. The cranial dural layers split to form the venous sinuses.

The term *dura* (from Latin, *durus*, meaning "hard") is an apt descriptor of the structure that maintains the position of the cerebral hemispheres and posterior fossa structure by its reflections, such as the falx cerebri and tentorium cerebelli. The arachnoid and pia mater constitute the leptomeninges (from Greek, *lepto* and *meninx*, meaning slender membrane). The delicate arachnoid is adjacent to the inner surface of the dura and is thinner over the convexities than at the base of the brain. The pia mater is a fine membrane that extends into the depths of the sulci.

Extra-axial Spaces

The meninges delimit the extra-axial compartments of the central nervous system (CNS). The epidural space is created when the dura is separated from the calvaria. Although the subdural space (between the dura and arachnoid membranes) has conventionally been characterized as a potential space containing minimal fluid, cells of the arachnoid actually form an intimate network with those of the meningeal dural layer.[46] Electron microscopy has provided evidence that cells belonging to the inner dural layer may be found on *both* sides of this space when collections form in the subdural space.[46, 64] The subdural space, therefore, is formed by cleavage through the inner layer of the dura rather than by a true separation of dura and arachnoid and, as such, probably exists only in pathologic states.[64]

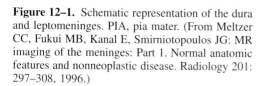

Figure 12–1. Schematic representation of the dura and leptomeninges. PIA, pia mater. (From Meltzer CC, Fukui MB, Kanal E, Smirniotopoulos JG: MR imaging of the meninges: Part 1. Normal anatomic features and nonneoplastic disease. Radiology 201: 297–308, 1996.)

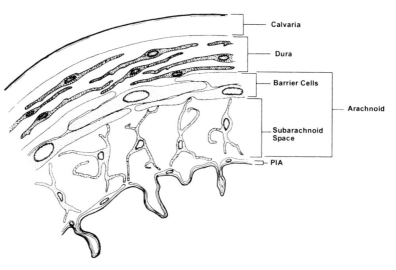

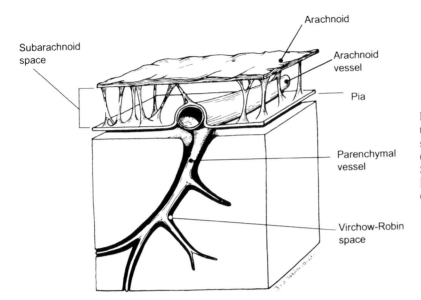

Figure 12–2. Diagram illustrating the anatomy of the perivascular (Virchow-Robin) space with respect to the pia mater and the subarachnoid space. (Modified from Fukui MB, Meltzer CC, Kanal E, Smirniotopoulos JG: MR imaging of the meninges: Part 2. Neoplastic disease. Radiology 201:605–612, 1996.)

The SAS (between the arachnoid and pia mater) contains cerebrospinal fluid (CSF) that flows throughout the CNS and drains into the venous sinuses through the valves of the arachnoid granulations.[142] The pia and the arachnoid are joined by fine connective tissue and cellular septa that traverse the SAS.[19] Near the base of the brain, though, the pia and arachnoid widely separate to accommodate the basal cisterns. Perivascular, or Virchow-Robin, spaces were originally thought to be potential pathways connecting the CSF and deep brain structures by virtue of continuity with the SAS.[41] More recent studies, however, have concluded that perivascular spaces are within the subpial space, separated from the SAS by pia mater[3] (Fig. 12–2).

Extra-axial Collections

Fluid collections in the epidural space assume a localized biconvex configuration as a result of the strong force needed to detach the firmly adherent dura from the inner table of the calvaria. The outer dural layer is most tightly adherent at sutures; classic teaching therefore holds that epidural collections do not cross suture lines.[60] Uncommon exceptions to this rule do occur, however. After administration of paramagnetic contrast medium, the dura adjacent an epidural hematoma (EDH) has a curvilinear, enhancing appearance. An inflammatory reaction, with formation of granulation tissue on the outer surface of the dura, may produce increased thickness and intensity of enhancement in the dura immediately subjacent to an EDH, as demonstrated in Figure 12–3.[67]

Greater tissue contrast and multiplanar imaging capability contribute to the superior sensitivity of magnetic resonance imaging (MRI) compared with computed tomography (CT) in detecting small subdural fluid collections.[85] MRI is especially useful in cases of subacute subdural hematoma (SDH), which may appear isodense to cortex on CT. Subdural hygromas result from leakage of CSF into the subdural space, probably after a tear in the arachnoid. MRI can distinguish subdural hematoma from subdural hygroma by improved detection of blood products, which are absent in a hygroma, but it cannot distinguish simple

from infected subdural fluid, however, since peripheral dural enhancement may be seen in both infected and noninfected subdural collections (Fig. 12–4). A diffusely enhancing, infected subdural collection may mimic an en plaque meningioma.[102]

Imaging
Imaging Modalities

MRI is substantially more sensitive than CT for visualizing both normal and abnormal meninges[37, 55, 70, 104, 152, 154]

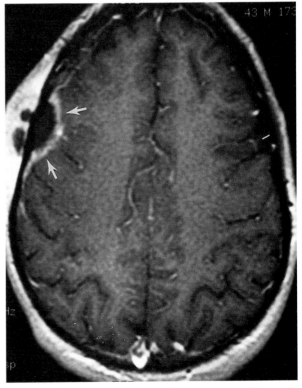

Figure 12–3. Epidural abscess. Enhanced axial T1-weighted image shows a lentiform epidural collection of pus with dural enhancement *(arrows)* that could mimic an epidural hematoma.

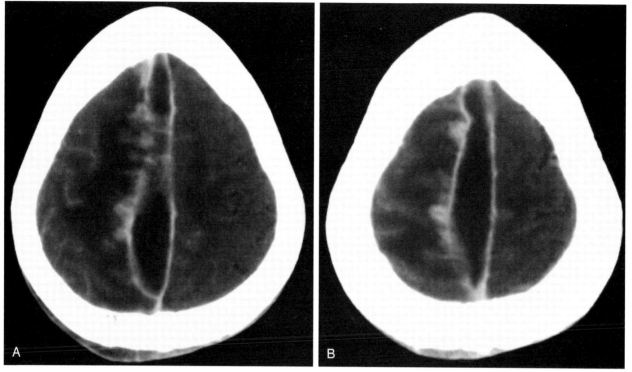

Figure 12–4. Subdural empyema. *A* and *B,* Enhanced axial CT images at the level of the falx cerebri show dural enhancement surrounding a subdural empyema.

(Fig. 12–5). Beam-hardening and other artifacts adjacent the calvaria may be partly responsible for the diminished detection of meningeal enhancement with CT. Experimental evidence suggests, in addition, that more intense enhancement results in areas of blood-brain barrier disruption with gadolinium-DTPA–enhanced MRI than with CT performed after iodinated contrast.[92, 136]

It has been suggested that MRI may be equally sensitive or even superior to CT in detecting subarachnoid hemorrhage (SAH) in the subacute and chronic phases and when a fluid-attenuated inversion recovery (FLAIR) pulse sequence is used.[115, 117] Other evidence suggests that FLAIR sequences may result in false-negative interpretations in the setting of SAH.[167]

Normal Meninges on Magnetic Resonance Imaging

The normal meninges may demonstrate short segments of thin, low signal intensity on standard spin-echo sequences.[43] Intravenous (IV) administration of gadolinium-DTPA results in enhancement of the normal cranial dura, which lacks a blood-brain barrier, in an interrupted pattern of short linear

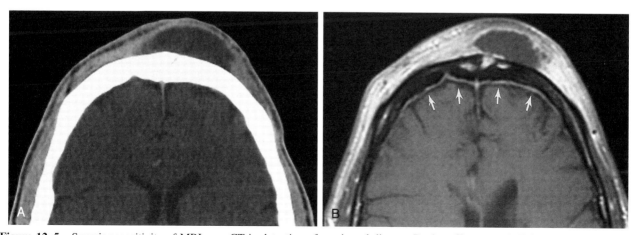

Figure 12–5. Superior sensitivity of MRI over CT in detection of meningeal disease: Pott's puffy tumor. *A,* Enhanced axial CT image at the level of an extracranial subperiosteal collection of pus. *B,* Enhanced axial MR image obtained after administration of gadolinium at the same level shows enhancement of the subjacent dura/arachnoid *(arrows).* Detection of this meningeal enhancement prompted a change of antibiotics to improve cerebrospinal fluid drug penetration.

segments that is typically most prominent parasagittally[27, 152] (Figs. 12–6 and 12–7). Field strength may influence the conspicuity of "normal" meningeal enhancement as well as the detection of pathologic enhancement. Earlier literature reported a distinct lack of enhancement of normal meningeal structures with relatively low-field-strength MRI.[20] The greater signal-to-noise levels achieved at relatively higher field strengths potentiate increased detection of meningeal enhancement (see Fig. 12–6).

Cohen and colleagues[27] reported that when meningeal enhancement was present on more than three contiguous 1.5 Tesla (T) spin-echo MR images, it was highly correlated with significant intracranial abnormality. Thick, long, or intensely enhancing segments, as well as nodular meningeal enhancement, are particularly suspect. The normal falx and dura may occasionally enhance in a thin uniform pattern.[86] The typical lack of normal meningeal enhancement observed in MRI of the spine may reflect the absence of the vascular outer dural layer that is found in the cranial pachymeninx.

Technique

The selection of MRI has a significant impact upon the conspicuity of normal meningeal enhancement and sensitivity in detecting meningeal disease (see Figs. 12–6 and 12–7). Numerous factors influence the appearance of the meninges on MR images, including (1) the presence and amount of MR contrast agent administered, (2) the type of pulse sequence performed, and (3) the exact pulse sequence parameters.

For partial saturation (spin echo or gradient echo), short echo time (TE) sequences, crucial imaging parameters include the repetition time (TR) and excitation flip angle. The shorter the TR, the greater the degree of saturation of magnetization (i.e., decreased signal intensity) from all imaged tissues. As a result, contrast-enhancing tissue will be more conspicuous against the more saturated (i.e., hypointense) background tissues on a typical short TR, large flip angle gradient-echo study than on a spin-echo study. Therefore, the normal meninges usually exhibit diffuse enhancement on such ultrashort TR, large flip angle gradient-echo imaging sequences[43] (see Fig. 12–7). Imaging plane also affects visualization of meningeal enhancement; the coronal plane is preferred to axial MRI data for evaluating meningeal enhancement over the cerebral convexity.

Similarly, factors that either increase the signal from the meninges or decrease signal from background tissues enhance the contrast-to-noise ratio (CNR) and, therefore, the conspicuity of the enhancing meninges. Double-dosing and triple-dosing of paramagnetic contrast agents have demonstrated improved detection of parenchymal lesions with MRI,[69] and there is evidence to support a similar dose effect for enhanced MRI of meningeal disease.[82, 83, 137] More recently, cases of leptomeningeal metastases that had been diagnosed by MRI and high-dose (0.3 mmol/kg) gadolinium have been reported that were not visualized with standard dose (0.1 mmol/kg) technique (Fig. 12–8).[59, 83] Also, the use of fat saturation or magnetization transfer

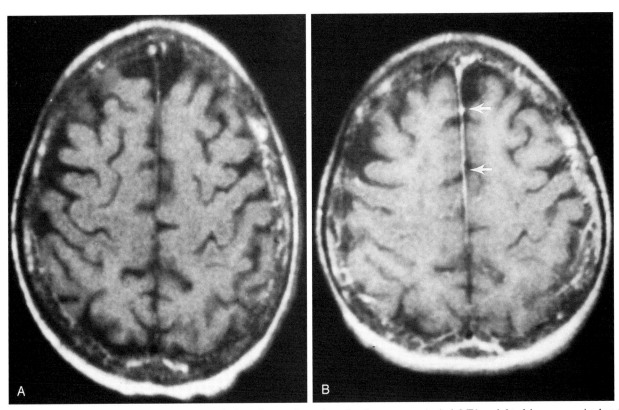

Figure 12–6.   Effects of field strength on conspicuity of normal meningeal enhancement. *A,* Axial T1-weighted image acquired at 0.5 T immediately after injection of 0.1 mmol/kg gadolinium. *B,* Axial T1-weighted image acquired at 1.5 T, one day later, in the same patient, immediately after injection of the same dose of gadolinium shows more prominent enhancement of the falx *(arrows)* than in *A.* (From Meltzer CC, Fukui MB, Kanal E, Smirniotopoulos JG: MR imaging of the meninges: Part 1. Normal anatomic features and nonneoplastic disease. Radiology 201:297–308, 1996.)

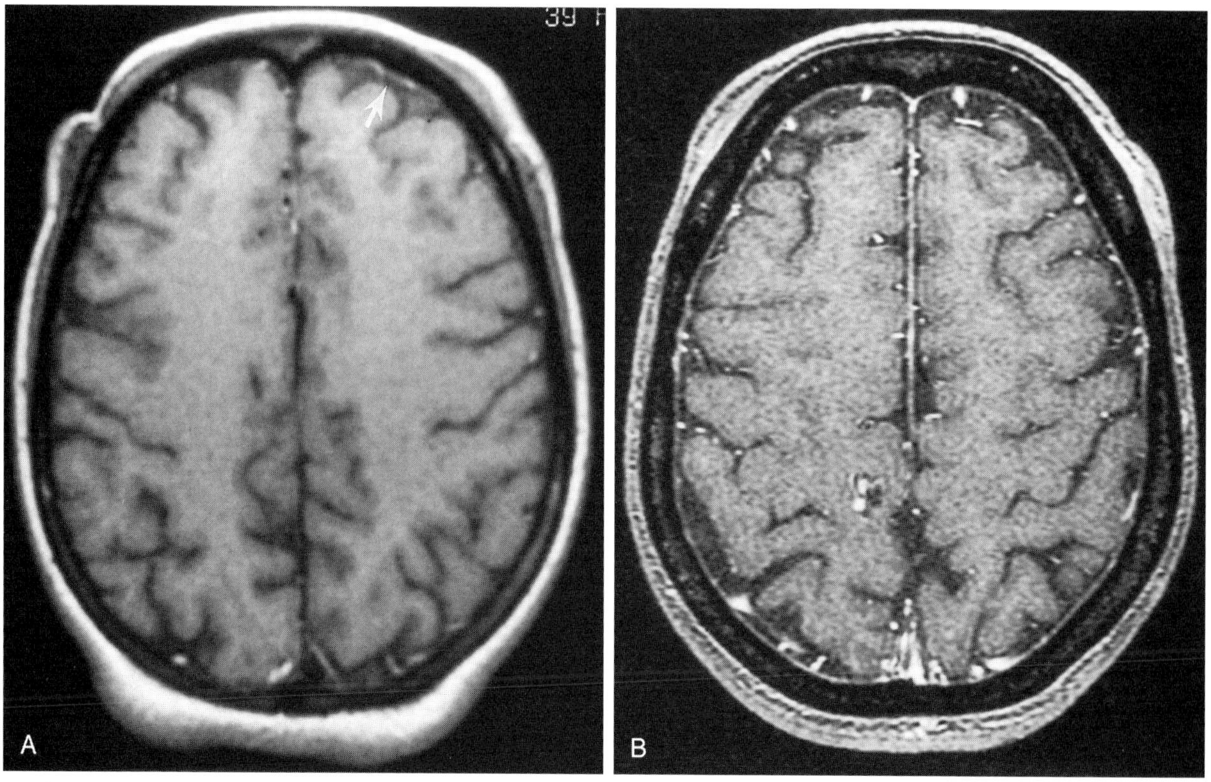

Figure 12–7. Effects of and pulse sequence on conspicuity of normal meningeal enhancement. *A,* Axial T1-weighted spin-echo image in another patient shows faint, short segment meningeal enhancement *(arrow)*. *B,* Axial, spoiled-gradient, recalled-echo image in the same patient shows thin, continuous enhancement in a dura/arachnoid pattern. (From Meltzer CC, Fukui MB, Kanal E, Smirniotopoulos JG: MR imaging of the meninges: Part 1. Normal anatomic features and nonneoplastic disease. Radiology 201:297–308, 1996.)

options increases the CNR by decreasing the signal from the background tissues.[38, 137]

The optimal imaging protocol for detection of meningeal disease is based on (1) sensitivity, (2) technique, (3) role, (4) cardinal signs, and (5) principal patterns (Table 12–1).

Sensitivity of Magnetic Resonance Imaging

In the past, unenhanced spin-echo MRI was insensitive in detecting meningeal disease.[104] The advent of the FLAIR sequence has greatly improved the sensitivity of MRI performed in the absence of gadolinium to detect meningeal and SAS abnormalities.[145, 167] Singer and coworkers evaluated the use of FLAIR MRI in 62 patients (21 with proven SAS or meningeal disease) and 41 control patients.[145] The sensitivity, specificity, and accuracy of FLAIR for SAS disease were 85%, 93%, and 90%, respectively.[145] Although

Table 12–1. Protocol for Magnetic Resonance Imaging Performed at 1.5 Tesla

Axial FLAIR image
Axial T1-weighted image
Axial and coronal T1-weighted image after administration of a double or a triple dose of gadolinium with a fat-saturation pulse or magnetization transfer

FLAIR, fluid-attenuated inversion recovery.

all six cases of acute SAH were interpreted as abnormal on FLAIR images in the Singer series, this was a source of false-negative interpretation in the series by Williams and associates.[145, 167]

Poor detection of SAH has been attributed to the relatively high oxygen tension in the SAS, which does not permit evolution to deoxyhemoglobin[62] and to the diluting effect of CSF. In 24 patients who underwent both FLAIR and gadolinium-enhanced T1-weighted MRI, FLAIR imaging (sensitivity, specificity, and accuracy, 86%, 91%, and 89%, respectively) was superior to gadolinium-enhanced T1-weighted imaging (43%, 88%, and 74%).[145]

Williams and coauthors[167] prospectively evaluated 376 consecutive cases performed with FLAIR imaging and showed that FLAIR may result in false-negative diagnoses of meningeal or SAS disease in cases of infectious meningitis, carcinomatosis, and SAH.[167] In this series, a false-positive diagnosis of meningeal or SAS pathology was made in the presence of normal and hyperintense cortex, susceptibility artifact, prominent pial vessels, concatenated saturation pulse, or flow artifact.[167] Neoplastic or inflammatory processes involving the SAS are best evaluated with paramagnetic contrast agents for visualization of enhancement of the accompanying meningeal involvement (Fig. 12–9).

Role of Imaging

Before and after gadolinium administration, MRI plays an important role in the diagnosis of meningeal neoplasm

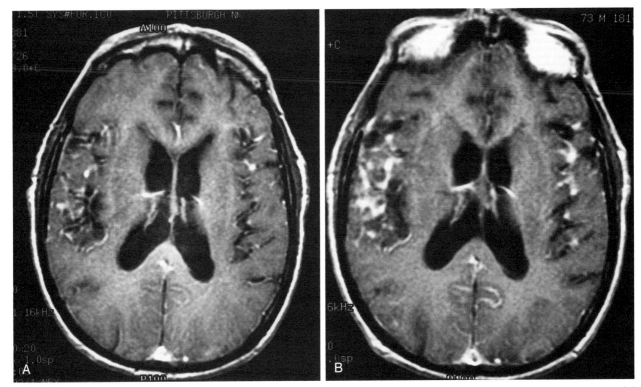

Figure 12–8. Effect of contrast dose on meningeal enhancement. Axial T1-weighted images obtained after administration of 0.1 mmol/kg *(A)* and 0.2 mmol/kg *(B)* doses of gadolinium show increased enhancement in a pia/subarachnoid space pattern at the higher dose in this patient with carcinomatosis of the meninges from gastric carcinoma.

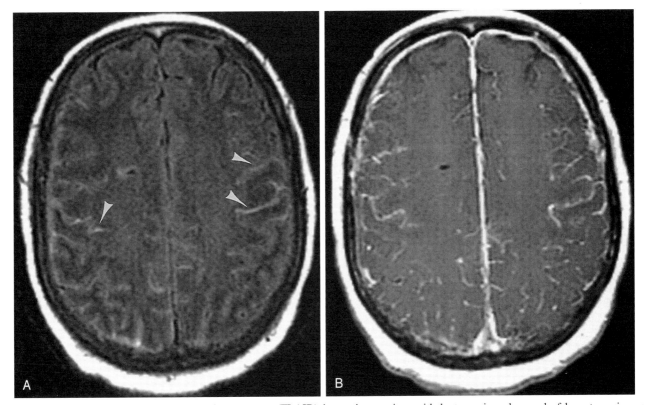

Figure 12–9. Axial fluid-attenuated inversion recovery (FLAIR) image in a patient with leptomeningeal spread of breast carcinoma *(A)* shows signal abnormality in a pia/subarachnoid space pattern *(arrowheads)* that enhances on the T1-weighted image after administration of gadolinium *(B)*.

in the asymptomatic patient when CSF cytologic examination results are equivocal, or when lumbar puncture is contraindicated.[23, 47, 52, 152] Imaging, however, does not replace CSF examination in diagnosis of meningeal neoplasm.

The limited sensitivity of CSF cytologic examination continues to be a significant obstacle and reinforces the complementary role of imaging.[53] The percentage of positive spinal CSF cytology in cases of primary CNS tumors with histologically confirmed meningeal involvement varies from 12% to 63% and is increased in symptomatic patients.[6, 56, 89, 112] With meningeal metastases from non-CNS neoplasms, CSF cytology was positive in between 45% and 80% of cases with higher yields after multiple spinal taps.[118, 161] The modest sensitivity of CSF cytology has fueled the search for CSF tumor markers to detect dissemination of neoplasm. Like CSF cytology, tumor detection with CSF markers is also restricted by suboptimal sensitivity and specificity.[114, 157]

The sensitivity of MRI in detecting meningeal neoplasm was originally reported to be lower than that of CSF cytology, with high false-negative rates: 30 to 33% for MRI and 58% for CT.[24, 173] The early studies, however, may have unwittingly introduced a selection bias by using positive cytology as an inclusion criterion.[24, 173] Later series comparing CT myelography with MRI showed an increased detection rate of CSF metastases with MRI (65% to 72%) compared with CT myelography (45% to 47%) and with cytology (29%).[70, 91]

A more recent Memorial Sloan-Kettering Cancer Center study[47] showed that when the patient cohort was not restricted to patients with positive cytologic findings, the rate of detection of meningeal carcinomatosis was increased. This study examined 137 patients with signs and symptoms of meningeal disease.[47] CT and MRI were assessed for signs of meningeal or SAS neoplasm, including hydrocephalus, enhancement of the dura, leptomeninges, and cranial nerves.[47] Leptomeningeal metastases were identified in 77 of 137 patients.[47] The diagnosis of leptomeningeal metastases was based on the clinical and imaging findings *alone*, in 31% of those cases.[47] Abnormal imaging findings were reported much more frequently in cases of solid tumor primaries (90%) than in hematologic neoplasms (55%).[47] A caveat in using MRI for the diagnosis of leptomeningeal tumor involvement, then, is that MRI is less sensitive in detecting involvement of the meninges resulting from hematologic malignancies in contrast to detecting solid tumors.[24, 47, 173]

When the distinction between meningeal neoplasm and inflammatory meningeal disease cannot be established by CSF and clinical data, MRI can support the diagnosis of neoplasm and guide meningeal biopsy.[80, 96] Although infectious meningitides are often uncovered by CSF analysis, MRI may be used to target meningeal biopsies when needed.

Cheng and coworkers[26] reported an improved yield from meningeal biopsy specimens in cases of chronic meningitis when tissue specimens were obtained from enhancing regions identified on MRI (Fig. 12–10). MRI has an advantage over CSF examination in its ability to characterize bulky neoplastic disease that may be more responsive to radiation therapy.[23] Because CSF cytologic examination

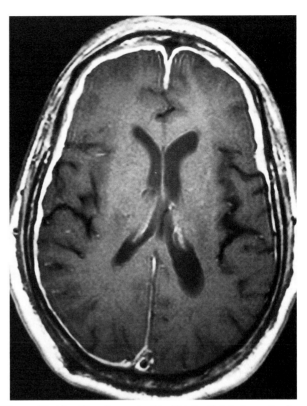

Figure 12–10. Chronic meningitis. Thick, slightly irregular dura/arachnoid enhancement on axial T1-weighted imaging proved to be idiopathic hypertrophic pachymeningitis on biopsy.

produces a higher false-negative rate in focal (rather than diffuse) disease,[13, 53] imaging may be of particular value in detecting focal spread of neoplasm to the meninges or SAS. MRI also has the potential to allow noninvasive monitoring of treatment response, although it is conceivable that the imaging abnormalities may persist beyond the eradication of neoplastic cells in the CSF.[169] In a series of patients with coccidioidal meningitis, diminution of meningeal enhancement was seen in treated patients with improving CSF profiles.[171] Therefore, MRI also may be useful as a means of monitoring a response to therapy in fungal meningeal disease.[171]

Imaging is a useful adjunct for the diagnosis of neoplastic meningeal disease in the appropriate clinical setting along with CSF examination to exclude infectious or noninfectious processes of the meninges.[47]

Finally, imaging may allow the clinician to assess outcome, since diffuse leptomeningeal involvement confers a poor prognosis.[14]

Cardinal Signs

The main imaging findings that have been associated with meningeal pathology are as follows[30, 40, 47, 78, 91, 132, 151, 152, 173]:

- Hydrocephalus (Fig. 12–11)
- Dura and arachnoid enhancement or signal abnormality (see Fig. 12–10)
- Pia and SAS enhancement or signal abnormality (see Fig. 12–11)

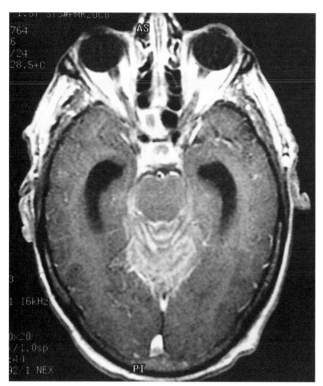

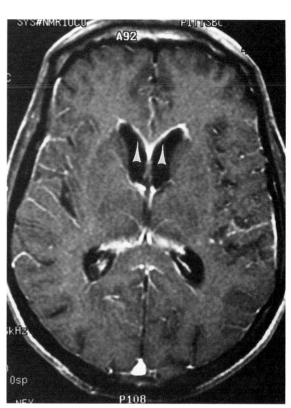

Figure 12–11. Hydrocephalus and pia/subarachnoid space abnormality. Enlargement of the temporal horns of the lateral ventricles and a pia/subarachnoid enhancement pattern over the cerebellum indicates meningeal spread of lung carcinoma.

Figure 12–12. Ependymal enhancement. Thin, linear enhancement of ependyma *(arrowheads)* on T1-weighted imaging in addition to pia/subarachnoid enhancement is present in this patient with disseminated small-cell lung carcinoma.

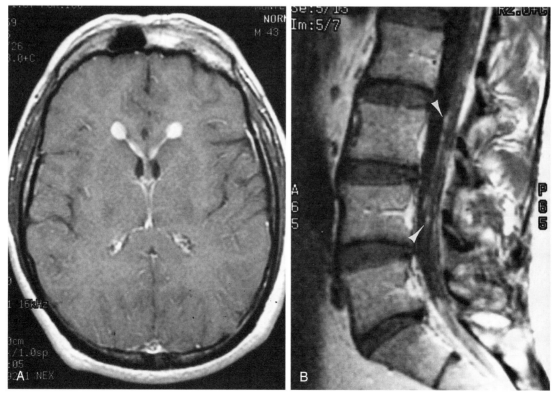

Figure 12–13. Focal, nodular ependymal enhancement. *A,* Nodular enhancement of the ependyma of the frontal horns was the probable entry point for subarachnoid spread of melanoma. *B,* Sagittal T1-weighted image of the lumbar spine shows nodular, enhancing drop metastases to the cauda equina *(arrowheads).*

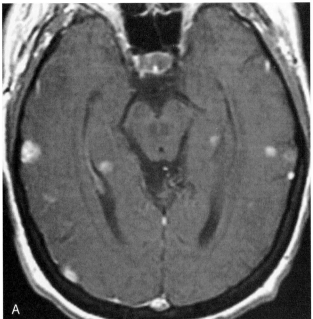

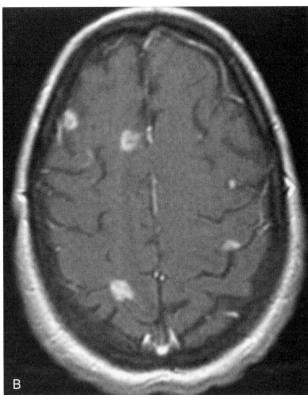

Figure 12–14. Diffuse, nodular pia/subarachnoid space enhancement. *A* and *B,* Multiple pial-based enhancing nodules are present in this patient with disseminated lung carcinoma.

- Subependymal enhancement or signal abnormality (Fig. 12–12)

Hydrocephalus may or may not be associated with enhancement of the meninges or ependyma. In this setting, hydrocephalus alone implies a resorptive block to CSF flow. Hydrocephalus may occur in the setting of SAH, infectious or noninfectious meningitis, and, of course, neoplasm. In the patient with neoplastic meningeal disease, hydrocephalus is more likely when leptomeningeal invasion or SAS has occurred rather than when neoplasm is limited to the dura.[162]

Enhancement of the meninges may occur in the spine or brain. Meningeal or subependymal enhancement may be focal (Fig. 12–13) or diffuse (see Fig. 12–12) and may have either a smooth or nodular contour (Fig. 12–14; see Fig. 12–13). Diffuse leptomeningeal involvement is a harbinger of a worse prognosis than focal disease.[14] Although a nodular pattern of enhancement may suggest neoplasm, it is not specific, since non-neoplastic entities such as sarcoidosis may also produce nodular thickening of the meninges (Fig. 12–15B). Infiltration of the leptomeninges overlying the convexities or in the basal cisterns may result in sulcal or cisternal obliteration on a non-contrast T1-weighted image (Fig. 12–16) or a FLAIR sequence (see Fig. 12–9). Minimal shortening of T1 and T2 relaxation times in the cisternal CSF ("dirty CSF sign") may be seen on unenhanced MR images[16] (see Fig. 12–16). In rare instances, subarachnoid tumor or inflammatory exudates may result in distention of the SAS (Fig. 12–17).

Imaging Patterns

Two distinct patterns of meningeal enhancement or signal abnormality may be observed with MRI. The *dura/arachnoid* pattern follows the inner contour of the calvaria (Fig. 12–18), whereas the *pia mater/SAS* abnormality extends into the depths of the sulci (Fig. 12–19). Enhancement or signal abnormality surrounding the brain stem is always of the pia mater/SAS type, since the arachnoid is clearly separated from the pia mater by the intervening basal cisterns in this region. Although pia mater/SAS enhancement does occur more commonly in the setting of meningitis than with tumor involvement, both inflammatory and neoplastic processes may demonstrate either pattern.[87, 128] A diffuse appearance favors an inflammatory etiologic mechanism, whereas nodular meningeal enhancement suggests a neoplasm (Tables 12–2 to 12–6).

Table 12–2. Differential Diagnosis: Focal Dura/ Arachnoid Pattern

Infectious

Adjacent petrous apicitis/sinusitis/mastoiditis
Adjacent abscess or cerebritis
Fungal infection (*Aspergillus*)

Noninfectious Inflammatory

Reactive
   Calvarial metastasis
   Subdural or epidural hematoma
   Acute infarction
   Iatrogenic
      Catheter or craniotomy
Sarcoidosis

Neoplastic

Meningioma
Breast carcinoma
Prostate carcinoma
Lymphoma
Post-transplant lymphoproliferative disorder (PTLD)

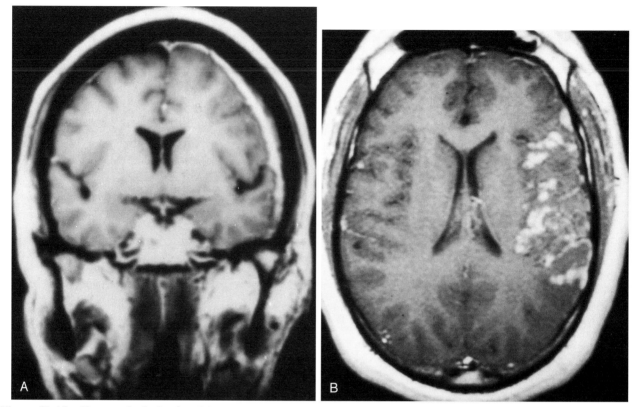

Figure 12–15. Non-neoplastic focal nodular and linear meningeal enhancement. *A,* Focal, linear enhancement in a dura/arachnoid pattern in sarcoidosis. (From Meltzer CC, Fukui MB, Kanal E, Smirniotopoulos JG: MR imaging of the meninges: Part 1. Normal anatomic features and nonneoplastic disease. Radiology 201:297–308, 1996.) *B,* Focal, nodular enhancement in a pia/subarachnoid pattern mimics neoplasm in another case of sarcoidosis. (Courtesy of Robert L. Williams, M.D., University of Pittsburgh Medical Center, Pittsburgh, Pa.)

Dura/Arachnoid Pattern

Because the dura and arachnoid are closely approximated, the distribution of meningeal enhancement does not reliably distinguish purely pachymeningeal (dural) from leptomeningeal (arachnoidal and pial) involvement. As a

Table 12–3. Differential Diagnosis: Diffuse Dura/ Arachnoid Pattern

Infectious

Bacterial (unusual)

Noninfectious Inflammatory

Reactive
  Diffuse calvarial metastases
  Extensive subdural hematoma
  Iatrogenic
    Response to catheter or craniotomy
  Low intracranial pressure states
    Cerebrospinal fluid leak
    After lumbar puncture (unusual)
    Spontaneous intracranial hypotension (rare)
  Hypertrophic cranial pachymeningitis (rare)
  Wegener's granulomatosis (rare)
  Multiple sclerosis (rare)

Neoplastic

Breast carcinoma
Prostate carcinoma

result, the dura/arachnoid pattern of enhancement does not imply that the leptomeninges or the SAS is spared. This fact has practical importance because some authors report a lower incidence of positive CSF cytologic findings with the dural pattern, in contrast to the pial pattern, implying a lack of subarachnoid space neoplasm.[123]

A surprisingly moderate rate (55%) of positive CSF cytologic results was reported in a subset of 11 patients with a dura/arachnoid enhancement pattern on MRI.[47] The presence of malignant cells in the CSF of patients in this subgroup implies neoplastic involvement of the arachnoid and SAS. This confirms the limitation of MRI in distinguishing abnormal enhancement of the dura from that of the arachnoid.[47] When restricted to the dura, however, meningeal carcinomatosis often results in negative CSF cytology; in this setting, MRI can play an important role in disease detection.

The dural tail sign, once considered specific for meningioma, may be observed in a wide variety of other extra-axial lesions, including schwannoma (Fig. 12–20), dural metastases (Fig. 12–21), lymphoma, tuberculoma, and sarcoidosis.[106] Occasionally, a dural tail may be seen in association with intra-axial mass lesions, such as gliomas or non-CNS metastases.[106] Although this imaging feature has been useful in suggesting the diagnosis of meningioma, its lack of specificity may occasionally cause misleading interpretation of MR images.[106] Similar signal, shape, and enhance-

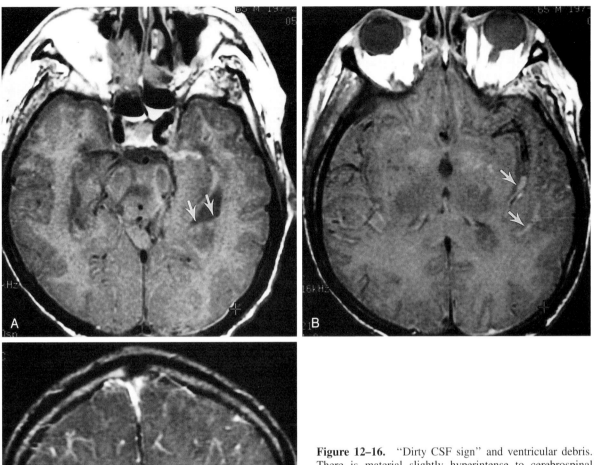

Figure 12–16. "Dirty CSF sign" and ventricular debris. There is material slightly hyperintense to cerebrospinal fluid producing an irregular debris/fluid level in the ventricles *(A)* *(arrows)* and present in the subarachnoid space *(B)* *(arrows)* on a T1-weighted image in a patient with gram-negative meningitis. After gadolinium administration *(C),* there is extensive pia/subarachnoid space enhancement on the coronal image.

ment characteristics found with several of these lesions may further confound the distinction between meningiomas and other entities.[106]

Pia Mater/Subarachnoid Space Pattern

Similarly, the pia mater/SAS pattern of enhancement may reflect neoplasm within the SAS, tumor infiltration of the pia mater, or both.[173] The pia mater/SAS pattern is more common in patients with infectious meningitis than in those with a neoplasm,[87, 128] although the pia mater/SAS distribution is not at all specific for inflammation.

A higher rate of positive CSF cytologic findings has

been reported in conjunction with the pia mater/SAS pattern than with the dura/arachnoid pattern of enhancement in cases of neoplasm.[123] This may reflect the anatomy of the blood-brain barrier with respect to the meninges.[87] The dura lacks a blood-brain barrier, since its capillary endothelium has a discontinuous cell layer, whereas the outer layer of the arachnoid has capillaries with a continuous cell layer and tight junctions.[139, 140] Bloodborne neoplastic cells, therefore, may gain access to the dura more easily than to the SAS.[87] A pia mater/SAS pattern may reflect SAS enhancement, pial enhancement, or both.[45] Gadolinium may leak through capillary tight junctions that have been disrupted by neoplastic invasion of the meninges[45] and directly enter the CSF.

Table 12–4. Differential Diagnosis: Focal Pia Mater/Subarachnoid Space Pattern

Infectious	**Neoplastic**
Bacterial meningitis	Primary CNS
Tuberculous meningitis (basal)	Glioblastoma multiforme
Fungal (*Aspergillus, Cryptococcus, Coccidioides*)	Astrocytoma
Viral (herpes)	Primitive neuroectodermal tumor
Adjacent abscess or cerebritis	Medulloblastoma
Spirochetal (neurosyphilis)	Germinoma
	Ependymoma
Noninfectious Inflammatory	Secondary neoplasm
Reactive	Melanoma
Sarcoid	Breast carcinoma
Subarachnoid hemorrhage	Lung carcinoma
Multiple sclerosis (rare)	False-positive on FLAIR image
	Normal, hyperintense cortex (especially at convexities)
Vascular	Susceptibility artifact
Pial vascular malformation (e.g., Sturge-Weber syndrome)	Prominent pial vessels
Subarachnoid hemorrhage	Flow artifact (especially in basal cisterns)
Superficial siderosis	
Granulomatous angiitis	
Hamartomatous	
Meningioangiomatosis	

CNS, central nervous system; FLAIR, fluid-attenuated inversion recovery.

Non-neoplastic Meningeal Disease
Infectious Meningitis
Bacterial Meningitis

Bacterial meningitis results either from hematogenous spread of infection or, occasionally, from direct extension from a paranasal sinus or mastoid source.[88] The mechanism of entry of bacteria from the intravascular space into the CSF is not well understood.

Animal studies have suggested that bacterial cell wall elements provoke an inflammatory response that brings about opening of tight intercellular junctions in the arachnoidal capillary bed.[87] This breakdown in the leptomeningeal blood-brain barrier allows the bacteria to gain access to the SAS. Early congestion and hyperemia of the lepto-

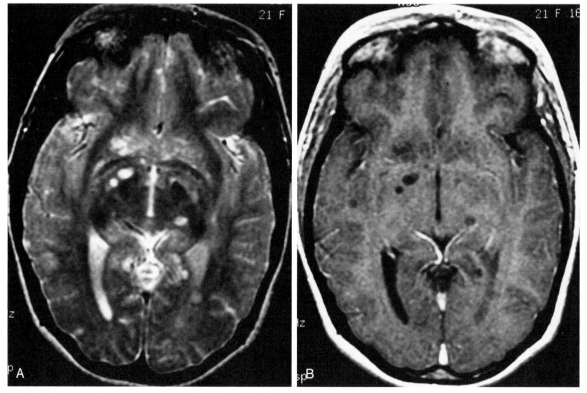

Figure 12–17.   Perivascular space pattern. Axial T2-weighted image *(A)* and enhanced T1-weighted image *(B)* show distention of the perivascular spaces at the base of the brain by the gelatinous, nonenhancing pseudocysts of cryptococcosis.

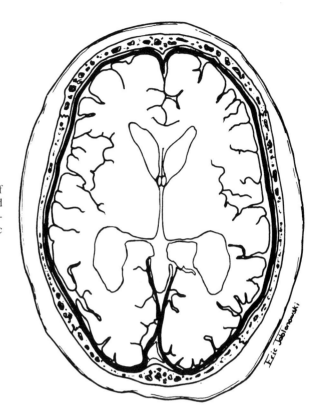

Figure 12–18. Diagram illustrating the dura/arachnoid pattern of meningeal abnormality that follows the inner table of the skull and the dural reflections. (From Meltzer CC, Fukui MB, Kanal E, Smirniotopoulos JG: MR imaging of the meninges: Part 1. Normal anatomic features and nonneoplastic disease. Radiology 201:297–308, 1996.)

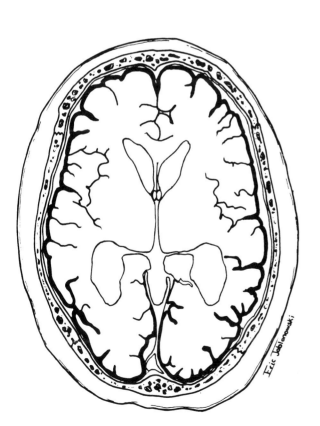

Figure 12–19. Diagram illustrating the pia/subarachnoid space pattern of meningeal abnormality that invaginates into sulci. (From Meltzer CC, Fukui MB, Kanal E, Smirniotopoulos JG: MR imaging of the meninges: Part 1. Normal anatomic features and nonneoplastic disease. Radiology 201:297–308, 1996.)

Table 12–5. Differential Diagnosis: Perivascular Space Pattern

Infectious	Neoplastic
Enhancing	Carcinomatosis
Tuberculosis	Breast carcinoma
Nonenhancing	Lung carcinoma
Cryptococcosis	

meninges are succeeded by mixed inflammatory cell infiltration with exudate in the subarachnoid space, especially over the cerebral convexity (see Fig. 12–16).

A link between meningeal enhancement and the degree of inflammatory cell infiltration of the leptomeninges has been proposed by Mathews and coworkers.[104] The lack of gadolinium enhancement in some areas of minimal inflammation suggests a threshold effect, whereby a critical degree of inflammatory reaction is required before meningeal enhancement may be observed.[104] MRI is superior to CT in the evaluation of complications of meningitis, including subdural empyemas, dural venous thrombosis, secondary ischemia, and parenchymal lesions.[25] Septic thrombosis of the superior sagittal sinus, although uncommon since the advent of antibiotics, may complicate bacterial meningitis[147] (Fig. 12–22).

When thrombosis is suspected, MRI is the imaging modality of choice for confirming the presence of throm-

Table 12–6. Differential Diagnosis: Diffuse Pia Mater/Subarachnoid Space Pattern

Infectious

Bacterial
Spirochetal
   Neurosyphilis
   Lyme disease
Viral ("aseptic") meningitis
   CMV
   Varicella-zoster (spinal in AIDS)

Noninfectious Inflammatory

Reactive
   Irritative ("aseptic") meningitis
      Response to foreign material:
         Contrast agents
         Chemical (e.g., ruptured dermoid)
         Subarachnoid hemorrhage

Vascular

Subarachnoid hemorrhage

Neoplastic

Primary CNS
   AIDS lymphoma
   Glioblastoma multiforme
   Astrocytoma
   Primitive neuroectodermal tumor
   Primary leptomeningeal gliomatosis (very rare)
Secondary neoplasm
   Melanoma
   Breast carcinoma
   Lung carcinoma
False-positive result on FLAIR image
   Concatenated saturation pulse

AIDS, acquired immunodeficiency syndrome; CMV, cytomegalovirus; CNS, central nervous system; FLAIR, fluid-attenuated inversion recovery.

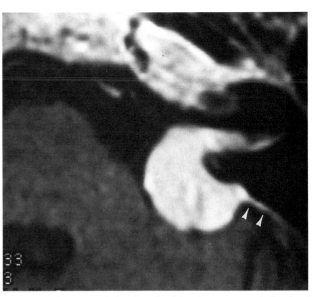

Figure 12–20. Focal dura/arachnoid enhancement. A dural tail *(arrowheads)* adjacent a left acoustic schwannoma illustrates the nonspecificity of this sign as an indicator of meningioma on an enhanced axial T1-weighted image.

bus. Absent flow may be detected as lack of a normal flow void in the sagittal sinus on short TR images and optimally demonstrated by magnetic resonance angiography (MRA) using two-dimensional (2D) phase-contrast techniques.[81] Conversely, localized meningeal enhancement may also be seen overlying an adjacent parenchymal infectious process, such as a brain abscess or encephalitis. Bacterial meningitis may result in ventriculitis, especially in the setting of gram-negative and iatrogenic infections.[48] An early finding in ventriculitis may be that of irregular debris in the dependent portions of the ventricles[48] (see Fig. 12–16). Infectious meningeal processes may occasionally spread across the pial barrier to cause cerebritis.

Mycobacterial Meningitis

CNS tuberculosis is increasing in frequency, partly as a result of its proclivity to occur with human immunodeficiency virus (HIV) infection. Tuberculous meningitis commonly occurs as a result of disseminated pulmonary infection, usually along with parenchymal brain involvement, although it rarely may be seen as the sole manifestation of the disease.[107] In contrast to bacterial meningitis, tuberculous infection is associated with a more insidious onset, fewer changes in the CSF profile, and higher rates of mortality and complications, such as infarction. Although tuberculosis tends to involve the basal meninges, tuberculomas may occur within the brain parenchyma or subarachnoid, subdural, or epidural spaces[16, 129] (Fig. 12–23). In one series, meningeal enhancement was observed in 36% of HIV-infected patients with CNS tuberculosis evaluated with MRI.[165]

MRI of tuberculous meningitis demonstrates meningeal enhancement, most often in the basal cisterns, reflecting the known predilection of tuberculosis for the base of the brain. Calcification of the basal meninges may also be seen and is more easily appreciated with CT than with MRI.

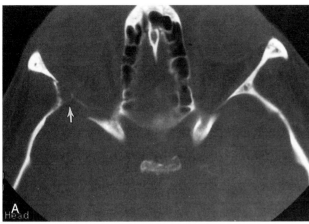
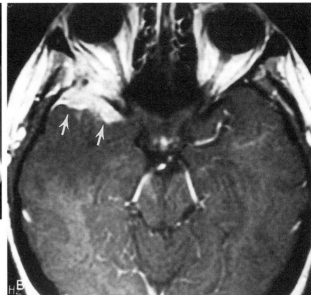

Figure 12–21. Focal dura/arachnoid mass. CT scan *(A)* shows metastatic breast carcinoma to the calvaria *(arrow)* extending to the dura on an enhanced axial T1-weighted image *(B) (arrows)*.

Focal or diffuse dura/arachnoid enhancement may be observed on contrast-enhanced MRI scans of the spine in cases of suspected active tuberculous meningitis.[93] Thickening, inflammation, and fibrosis of the leptomeninges are commonly seen at histopathologic examination.

Meningitis may also be caused by a virus or fungus, a fact that is of particular importance in immunocompromised patients. In patients with acquired immunodeficiency syndrome (AIDS), a polyradiculomyelitis may develop, in rare circumstances, as a result of cytomegalovirus (CMV) or varicella-zoster virus infection.[51] Diffuse enhancement of the cauda equina on MRI should alert the clinician to exclude these causes in AIDS patients.[164]

Fungal Meningitis

Fungal meningitis usually results from hematogenous dissemination of disease and is also often seen in immuno-suppressed hosts. Fungal meningitides, such as those caused by *Aspergillus*, *Cryptococcus*, and *Coccidioides*, may be demonstrated by contrast-enhanced MRI.[105, 110, 171]

Aspergillosis is an important cause of morbidity and mortality in organ transplant recipients and may be associated with focal, thick dura/arachnoid enhancement that resolves with treatment.[110]

Cryptococcus frequently infects patients with AIDS, but meningeal enhancement is seen only occasionally in cryptococcal meningitis, probably because of the blunted host response.[105, 141] Meningeal enhancement was observed in only one in five autopsy-proven cases of AIDS-related cryptococcosis studied with gadolinium-enhanced MRI.[105] Cryptococcal infection tends to spread from the basal cisterns via perivascular spaces to the basal ganglia, brainstem, internal capsule, and thalamus.[163] This produces a characteristic appearance on MRI scans of nonenhancing,

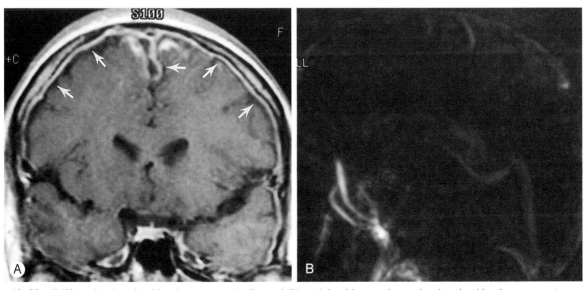

Figure 12–22. Diffuse dura/arachnoid enhancement. *A,* Coronal T1-weighted image shows dura/arachnoid enhancement *(arrows)* in a patient with meningitis and subsequent superior sagittal sinus thrombosis. *B,* There is an absence of flow in the superior sagittal sinus on a sagittal phase-contrast MR angiogram.

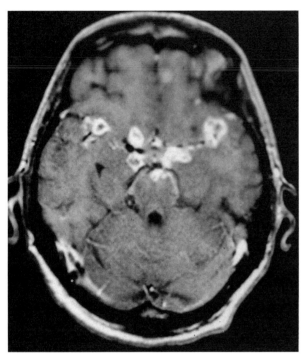

Figure 12–23. Multiple ring-enhancing tuberculomas are distributed throughout the perivascular spaces and basal pial surfaces on an axial T1-weighted image after administration of gadolinium.

dilated perivascular spaces, caused by infestation with the gelatinous pseudocysts of cryptococcal material (see Fig. 12–17).

In contrast to the pattern seen with *Cryptococcus*, Wrobel and colleagues[171] reported MRI enhancement of the meninges in 7 of 11 patients with coccidioidal meningitis. Enhancement was most prominent in the basilar cisterns, the sylvian and interhemispheric fissures, and the upper cervical SAS. Spirochetal infections may exhibit both localized and diffuse meningeal enhancement.[18] Similarly, smooth, diffuse pia/SAS enhancement of the brain stem and the entire spinal cord has been reported in Lyme disease, even in the absence of MRI evidence of parenchymal disease.[33]

Aseptic Meningitis

Meningitis is designated "aseptic" when CSF cultures are sterile. Aseptic meningitis may have a variety of causes, including viral infection and irritation after introduction of foreign substances into the CSF (e.g., blood, chemical agents, or contrast materials), or it may be seen against the backdrop of connective tissue disorders.[107] MRI may demonstrate meningeal enhancement or subarachnoid signal abnormality (Fig. 12–24). In cases of suspected aseptic meningitis, performing MRI after administration paramagnetic contrast medium may help prevent delays in diagnosis.[42]

Noninfectious Inflammatory Meningitis

Noninfectious granulomatous disease can also involve the meninges. Approximately 5% of patients with sarcoido-

sis have neurologic manifestations; of those, the most common sign is that of cranial nerve palsies.[150] Gadolinium-enhanced MRI is the study of choice to document meningeal involvement and may show either the pia mater/SAS or the dura/arachnoid[143, 144, 174] (see Fig. 12–15). Striking thickening of the meninges may also be demonstrated. Sarcoid was present in 31% of 37 patients with chronic meningitis of unknown etiology examined with enhanced MRI and meningeal biopsy and, as such, was the most frequent cause of chronic meningitis in that series.[26]

Meningeal abnormality may also occur in Wegener's granulomatosis[131] (Fig. 12–25). Thickened, nodular meninges on both enhanced CT and MR images in a patient with Wegener's granulomatosis were reported by Tishler and colleagues.[153] The imaging features reflect the histopathologic findings of dural and brain biopsies that revealed granulomatous infiltration of the dura and development of fibrosis and granulomas of the pia mater and arachnoid.

Hypertrophic cranial pachymeningitis is a rare type of diffuse granulomatous inflammation that produces thickening, chronic inflammation, and fibrosis of the dura.[101, 103] Common presenting symptoms include headache, cranial nerve palsies, and ataxia. Diffuse dural enhancement (on enhanced T1-weighted images) or hypointense and thickened dura (on T2-weighted images) may be demonstrated on MRI (see Fig. 12–10). Diagnosis requires confirmation with dural biopsy. The disease may progress despite corticosteroid therapy.

In rare instances, meningeal enhancement has been reported to accompany demyelinating disease. We are aware of two reports of meningeal enhancement on MRI in cases of multiple sclerosis (MS). One case displayed a diffuse dura/arachnoid pattern; the other showed focal pial enhancement.[9, 32] Serial MRI of MS plaques suggests that parenchymal lesion enhancement is related to the inflammatory process associated with active demyelination.[9] Analogously, meningeal enhancement in MS may result from extension of perivascular lymphoplasmacytic infiltration into the leptomeninges, found in 41% of autopsy cases.[63] A similar inflammatory etiology was proposed by Fulbright and coauthors[49] in describing enhancement of multiple cranial nerves in Guillain-Barré syndrome, a disorder characterized by peripheral demyelination.

Iatrogenic Meningeal Enhancement

Benign meningeal enhancement on MRI may result from mechanical disruption of the meninges from a variety of causes. Localized or diffuse dural enhancement may occur after craniotomy and may persist indefinitely[20, 37] (Fig. 12–26). It may be difficult to distinguish normal reactive postoperative enhancement from meningeal tumor involvement following craniotomy for tumor resection. Postoperative meningeal enhancement usually regresses over time, often resolving between 1 and 2 years after craniotomy.[37] In addition, the distribution of enhancement may support a benign etiologic mechanism.

In contrast to the typically basilar pattern of neoplastic meningitis, postoperative enhancement occurs more often over the convexities.[20] The morphology of enhancement may also provide clues as to the cause. A nodular dural

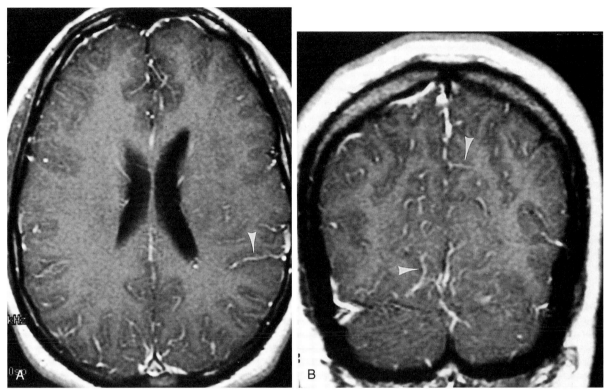

Figure 12–24. Aseptic meningitis. *A* and *B,* Thin, linear pia/subarachnoid space enhancement *(arrowheads)* is seen in a patient with headache and no organism growth on cerebrospinal fluid culture on axial and coronal enhanced T1-weighted images.

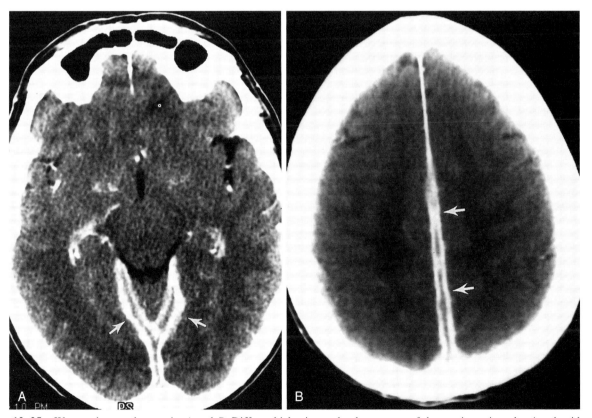

Figure 12–25. Wegener's granulomatosis. *A* and *B,* Diffuse thickening and enhancement of the meninges in a dura/arachnoid pattern *(arrows)* are present in a patient with biopsy-proven Wegener granulomatosis on a contrast-enhanced CT scan.

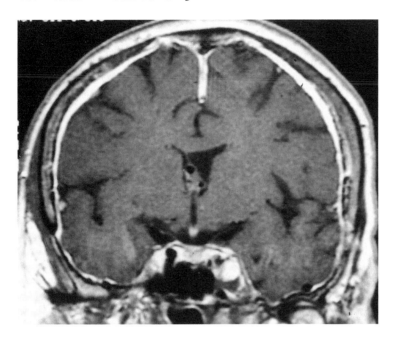

Figure 12–26. Postoperative meningeal enhancement. Coronal T1-weighted image shows diffuse, linear enhancement in a patient who had undergone previous craniotomy for meningioma.

enhancement pattern or thick pia mater/SAS enhancement suggests recurrent tumor.[75] Placement of a ventricular catheter may also result in diffuse or localized dural enhancement. In rare instances, dura/arachnoid enhancement may result from uncomplicated lumbar puncture.[108] Dural enhancement after lumbar puncture occurs more commonly, however, when intracranial hypotension results, suggesting a CSF leak.[15]

Vascular Disease

Occasionally, an acute cerebral infarction may demonstrate adjacent meningeal enhancement (Fig. 12–27). This "meningeal enhancement sign" occurs between day 2 and day 6 after infarction. It is seen with large supratentorial infarcts and usually has a dura/arachnoid configuration.[36, 39] Although the cause of meningeal enhancement in cerebral infarction is not established, possible contributing factors include reactive hyperemia and local inflammation following meningeal irritation.[36]

Hemorrhage into the SAS also irritates the leptomeninges, causing inflammation of the pia mater and arachnoid.[66] In severe cases, fibrosis may ensue and, eventually, may obliterate the SAS. Superficial siderosis is a rare condition resulting from deposition of hemosiderin in the leptomeninges and surface of the brain following recurrent SAH and is a cause of hearing loss.[22, 76, 79] The leptomeninges are thickened and pigmented on pathologic examination. A characteristic hypointense rim is observed along the brain surface on T2-weighted images[17, 22] (Fig. 12–28). This hypointense border of hemosiderin deposits in superficial siderosis becomes exaggerated, and thus more readily detected, on gradient-echo MRI as a result of augmented magnetic susceptibility effects.[79] The thickened meninges may also enhance with gadolinium. Vasculitis rarely involves the meninges. Preferential involvement of small leptomeningeal vessels in granulomatous angiitis may result in meningeal enhancement.[113]

MRI is the modality of choice for evaluation of Sturge-Weber syndrome, a phakomatosis characterized by deranged vasculature of the face, brain, and meninges.[146] Poor venous drainage and chronic ischemic damage to the underlying cortex develop as a result of the leptomeningeal vascular malformation that originates in the subarachnoid space. MRI of the brain shows superficial gyriform enhancement. This enhancement likely results from slow flow within the leptomeningeal vascular malformation with or without enhancement of ischemic[11, 160] (Fig. 12–29).

Meningioangiomatosis is a rare hamartomatous disorder of the leptomeninges, distinguished by meningovascular proliferation and leptomeningeal calcification.[2, 65, 126] A cortical mass with meningeal extension and heterogeneous signal intensity on T2-weighted images and demonstrating contrast enhancement on MRI has been reported (Fig. 12–30).[126, 166] Halper and coworkers[65] have theorized that meningioangiomatosis is caused by a proliferation of both meningothelial cells and leptomeningeal vessels within perivascular spaces as they penetrate the cortex.

A combined pia mater/SAS and dura/arachnoid pattern of enhancement has been rarely reported in association with migraine headaches.[29, 97] This unusual finding is attributed to hyperperfusion, documented on single photon emission computerized tomography (SPECT) or transcranial Doppler imaging.[29, 97]

Toxic Meningeal Enhancement

Chemical meningitis may arise following rupture of dermoid or epidermoid cyst. This inflammation is likely provoked by the irritating effect of cholesterin crystals and keratin material discharged into the CSF.[31, 98] In such cases, the diagnosis of ruptured dermoid is usually verified by demonstration of droplets of high signal lipid material dispersed throughout the SAS on unenhanced T1W MR images.

Meningeal irritation resulting in contrast enhancement

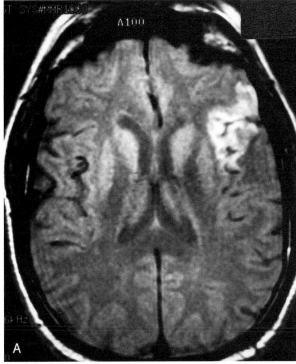

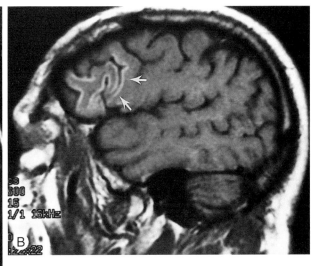

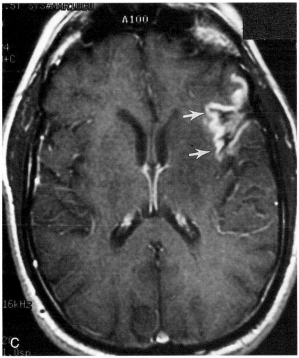

Figure 12–27. Meningeal enhancement after infarction. *A*, Axial proton-density–weighted image shows the left frontal infarct. *B*, Sagittal T1-weighted image shows bright signal in the cortex of the left temporal infarct *(arrows)*. *C*, There is gyriform enhancement on the axial T1-weighted image that is probably a combination of cortical and pial enhancement *(arrows)*.

on MRI has also been reported in the setting of adverse drug reactions. Eustace and Buff[42] reported a case of ibuprofen-induced meningitis depicted by meningeal enhancement on MRI. Meningeal enhancement persisted on repeated MRI scans 1 week later despite resolution of symptoms within 12 hours of drug cessation.

Spontaneous Intracranial Hypotension

Like the low intracranial pressure headache after complicated lumbar puncture, spontaneous intracranial hypotension is identified by a postural headache that resolves after placement of an epidural blood patch.[135] A CSF pressure of less than 60 mm of water in the absence of previous lumbar puncture establishes the diagnosis.

MRI has shown striking, thick, diffuse dural/arachnoid enhancement.[44, 74] Subdural fluid collections may occur in conjunction with this low-pressure state.[135] An unsuspected, spontaneous CSF leak may be the inciting factor (Fig. 12–31), and thus recognition of this combination of imaging and clinical findings should prompt a search for the source of leak. Identification of this treatable cause of

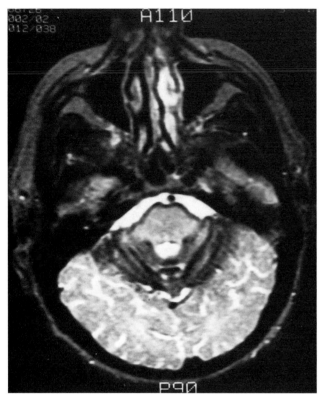

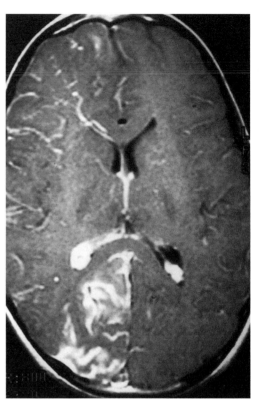

Figure 12–28. Siderosis. The dark signal from hemosiderin outlines the pial surface of the cerebellum in this patient with superficial siderosis in an axial T2-weighted image.

Figure 12–29. Sturge-Weber syndrome. Gyriform enhancement defines the pial vascular malformation and adjacent ischemic occipital cortex on an axial T1-weighted image.

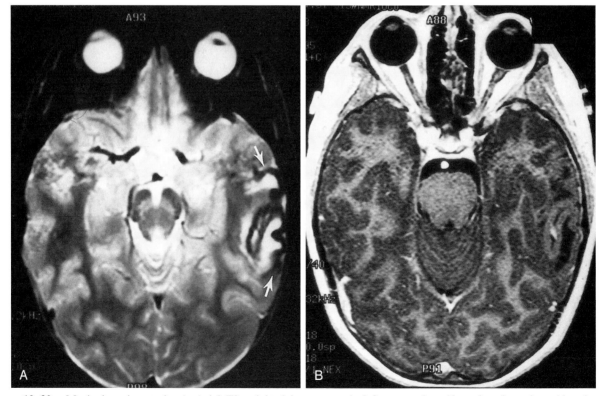

Figure 12–30. Meningioangiomatosis. *A,* Axial T2-weighted image reveals left temporal gyriform hypointensity with subcortical hyperintensity *(arrows)* that may represent the meningovascular proliferation. *B,* This axial spoiled GRASS image does not reveal enhancement. GRASS, gradient-recalled acquisition in a steady state.

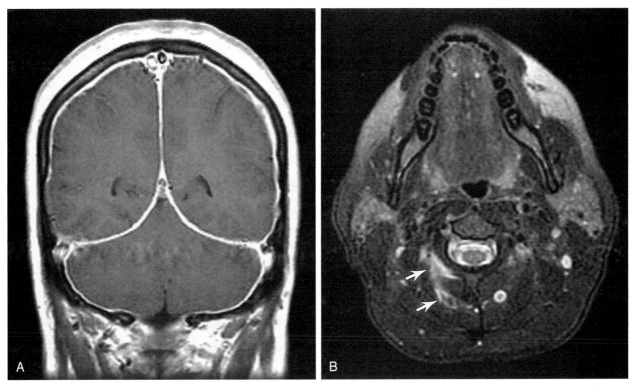

Figure 12–31. Intracranial hypotension. Coronal T1-weighted image demonstrates diffuse dura/arachnoid enhancement in this patient who presented with severe headaches and whose CSF pressure was low on lumbar puncture. The axial T2-weighted image shows fluid, presumed to be cerebrospinal fluid in the soft tissues of the upper neck *(arrows)*. The patient recovered after surgery despite the fact that, although myelography revealed a leak, the exact site could not be found at operation.

meningeal abnormality in association with the germane clinical features may prevent diagnostic delay and unnecessary meningeal biopsy.

Neoplastic Meningeal Disease

Primary Involvement

Primary dural neoplasms are rare. Neoplasms arising from the dura are mesenchymal in origin because the dura is composed of fibrous tissue.[138] Primary dural tumors bridge the entire range of benign (fibromas) to intermediate (fibromatosis) to malignant (sarcomas).[134] An assortment of dural sarcomas has been reported, including chondrosarcoma, fibrosarcoma, and malignant fibrous histiocytoma.[5, 95, 100] Previous radiation therapy for another disease has been connected with some sarcomas.[5]

The most common primary tumor arising from the leptomeninges is meningioma (Figs. 12–32 and 12–33).[138] Meningiomas originate from meningothelial cells of the arachnoid.[138] A hormonal influence has been implicated in the pathogenesis of meningiomas because they are more common in women than in men, occur more often in patients with breast cancer, and may become symptomatic during pregnancy.[12, 77, 138] Radiation therapy has also been implicated as a causative factor in meningioma,[50, 149] especially in patients treated for tinea capitis or vascular nevi in childhood. Fifty percent of meningiomas are isointense with gray matter on T1-weighted and T2-weighted im-

aging; the remaining half vary in signal intensity.[148] Heterogeneous signal intensity on MRI may result from calcification, vascular, or cystic components.[148]

Additional primary leptomeningeal neoplasms, such as glioma (Fig. 12–34),[34, 73, 96, 125] melanoma,[4] melanocytoma

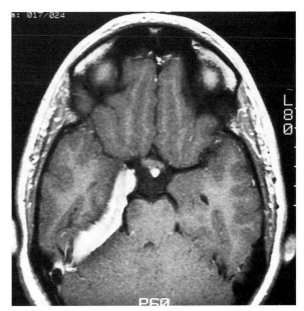

Figure 12–32. Focal, linear dura/arachnoid enhancement characterizes this right tentorial en plaque meningioma.

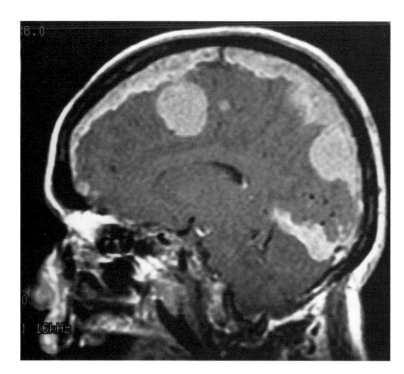

Figure 12–33. Meningiomatosis in neurofibromatosis, type 2 (NF 2). Meningiomatosis (multiple meningiomas) was found in this patient with diffuse, nodular dura and arachnoid enhancement.

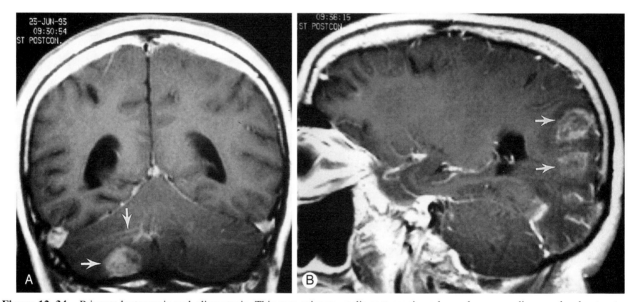

Figure 12–34. Primary leptomeningeal gliomatosis. This rare primary malignant meningeal neoplasm was diagnosed only at autopsy. There is both linear and nodular enhancement in a pia/subarachnoid space pattern *(arrows)* on a coronal image *(A)* and a sagittal enhanced T1-weighted image *(B)*. (Courtesy of Bernhard C. Sander, M.D., and Tibor Mitrovics, M.D., Freie Universitatsklinikum Rudolf Virchow, Berlin, Germany.)

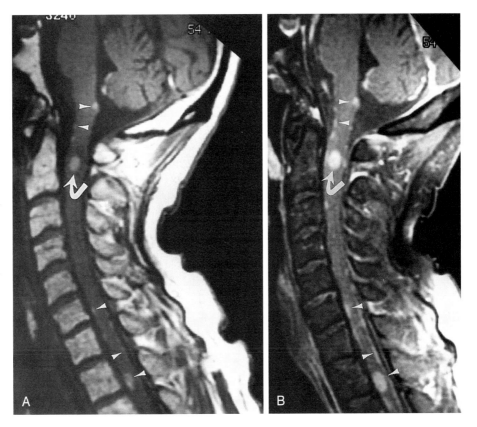

Figure 12–35. Primary leptomeningeal melanocytosis. Sagittal T1-weighted images obtained before *(A)* and after *(B)* administration of gadolinium show multiple, tiny nodular foci of hyperintensity *(arrowheads)* along the pial surface of the cervical spinal cord with enhancement in this case of primary leptomeningeal melanocytosis. There is also an intramedullary lesion *(curved arrow)*.

(Fig. 12–35),[111] sarcoma,[127, 138] and lymphoma,[94] are very rare. Primary leptomeningeal gliomas probably originate from heterotopic rests of glial tissue within the meninges and SAS.[28, 170]

Secondary Involvement

Breast carcinoma (CA), lymphoma, leukemia, lung CA, malignant melanoma, gastrointestinal CA, and genitourinary CA are the most common neoplasms to progress to meningeal dissemination.[71, 118, 161] Primary CNS neoplasms, such as medulloblastoma and primitive neuroectodermal tumor (PNET), pineoblastoma (Fig. 12–36), ependymoma, germ cell tumor (Fig. 12–37), astrocytoma (Fig. 12–38), and glioblastoma (Fig. 12–39), also have a propensity for meningeal spread.[6, 7, 119, 120, 124] Most tumors tend to produce focal involvement in a dura/arachnoid or pia/SAS distribution. Exceptions to this are very aggressive tumors, such as lung and breast CA, that may result in diffuse meningeal neoplasm.

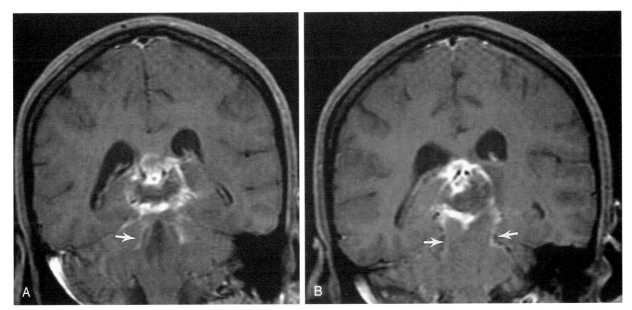

Figure 12–36. Subarachnoid spread of pineoblastoma. *A* and *B*, Coronal enhanced T1-weighted images show the pineal region mass with pia/subarachnoid space enhancement *(arrows)* in this patient with cerebrospinal fluid dissemination of pineoblastoma.

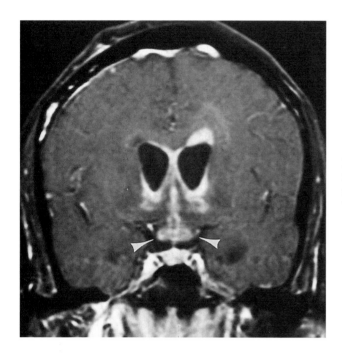

Figure 12–37. Disseminated germ cell tumor. This pineal region neoplasm demonstrates ependymal and subarachnoid spread involving the optic chiasm *(arrowheads)* on an enhanced coronal T1-weighted image.

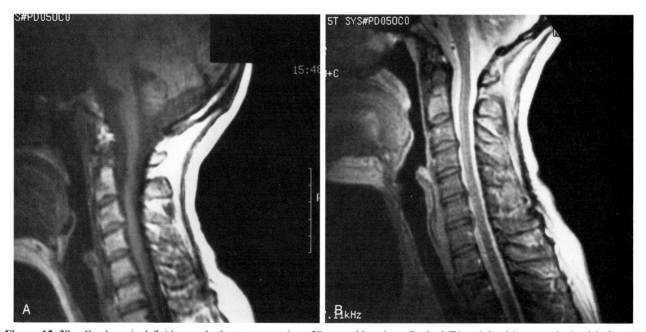

Figure 12–38. Cerebrospinal fluid spread of astrocytoma in a 30-year-old patient. Sagittal T1-weighted images obtained before *(A)* and after *(B)* gadolinium administration show such extensive enhancement of the subarachnoid space that the enhanced T1-weighted image mimics a T2-weighted sequence. The patient had been treated for astrocytoma 3 years earlier.

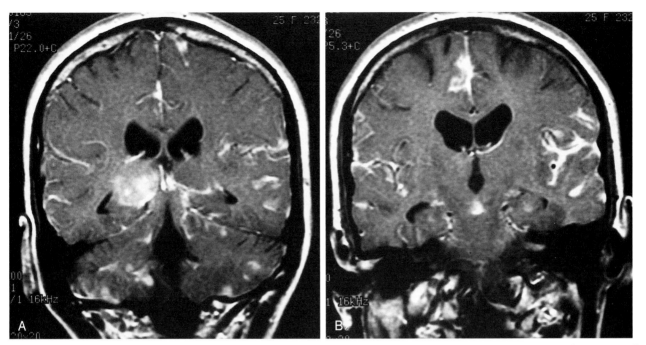

Figure 12–39. Cerebrospinal fluid spread of glioblastoma multiforme after biopsy in a 40-year-old patient. Six weeks after stereotactic biopsy, an enhanced coronal T1-weighted image shows the primary right thalamic glioblastoma and extensive, thick dissemination of neoplasm in a pia/subarachnoid space pattern.

Risk Factors for Leptomeningeal Dissemination of Neoplasm

The risk factors for leptomeningeal dissemination differ somewhat for primary CNS and non-CNS neoplasms but are largely related to tumor dedifferentiation and proximity to CSF spaces.

Characteristics of primary CNS neoplasms that correlate highly with a tendency to CSF spread are (1) poor glial fibrillary acidic protein (GFAP) staining, indicating poor differentiation of neoplasm,[119] and (2) close proximity to CSF spaces.[57, 158] Patient risk factors for leptomeningeal dissemination of primary CNS neoplasm include extended survival[7] and previous operation (see Fig. 12–39).[6, 8]

In cases of non-CNS neoplasm, prolonged survival[116, 118, 172] and the presence of other metastatic foci[14, 116, 156] increase the probability of meningeal dissemination. Dispersion of non-CNS neoplastic cells is likely a multistep process, according to the analysis of the pathways of metastases performed by Viadana and colleagues.[159] This "cascade" phenomenon postulates that spread of the primary tumor occurs to at least one intermediate organ, from which it may disseminate widely.[159] The observation that vertebral body (especially in breast CA),[14, 156] bone marrow, and liver metastases (especially in lung CA)[116] are commonly present in cases of meningeal carcinomatosis lends credence to this predisposition of tumors to first spread to an intervening organ before disseminating widely. The breast, lung, and stomach, in addition to melanoma, are primary sites of solid tumors that tend to metastasize to the leptomeninges.[71, 72, 118, 161] Hematologic neoplasms such as leukemia and lymphoma are also inclined to CSF spread.[72]

Mechanisms of Meningeal Neoplastic Dissemination

Dura

The two major mechanisms of spread of neoplasm to the dura are (1) hematogenous dissemination and (2) direct extension.

Hematogenous Spread

One pathway for neoplasm to reach the dura is as a sequela of bone metastases; this route is common in patients with breast CA. Vertebral bone metastases disseminate hematogenously through Batson's plexus and then to the intracranial dural venous sinuses[156] (Fig. 12–40). For example, dural metastases are as likely as parenchymal brain metastases in cases of disseminated breast CA, reflecting the high incidence of vertebral involvement.[156]

Direct Extension

A second route is dural infiltration, with neoplasm extending directly from vertebral or calvarial lesions[1] (Fig. 12–41).

Leptomeninges

The major mechanisms of seeding into the CSF and leptomeninges are also hematogenous spread and direct extension, but these may take a variety of forms.

Hematogenous Spread

There are three main modes by which neoplasm is spread hematogenously to the leptomeninges and CSF.

Figure 12–40. Diagram of the route of hematogenous spread to dura via Batson plexus. (From Fukui MB, Meltzer CC, Kanal E, Smirniotopoulos JG: MR imaging of the meninges: Part 2. Neoplastic disease. Radiology 201:605–612, 1996.)

First, the choroid plexus may become seeded hematogenously that results in tumor deposits that are then sloughed into the CSF.[35, 58, 71, 72] This pathway is presumably more common than is clinically evident. The frequency of choroid metastases is likely to be underestimated on MRI because the normal choroid plexus is irregular in contour. Metastases occur frequently when the choroid plexus is

sectioned at pathologic examination; however, the choroid plexus may not be examined routinely.[109, 118]

The second hematogenous route is via parenchymal blood vessels in the Virchow-Robin (perivascular spaces) to the pia mater and then into the SAS[54, 72] (see Fig. 12–2). This mechanism of seeding of the leptomeninges and SAS may result in tumor spread either *to* or *from* the SAS.[54, 72, 109]

Third, neoplasm may interrupt the thin walls of microscopic vessels in the arachnoid to enter the SAS[130] (see Fig. 12–2). This pathway of spread occurs more commonly in leukemia and lymphoma than in solid tumors.[130]

Direct Extension

Direct extension, the other major means by which neoplasm gains access to the leptomeninges, can also take one of three forms.

First, parenchymal neoplasm close to CSF borders, such as cortical or subependymal tumor, may shed cells into the CSF[35, 168] (see Fig. 12–13). Non-CNS neoplasms may induce a fibrous reaction that tends to prevent CSF spread; thus, this pathway may be more common among tumors of CNS origin.[71, 118]

Second, an overlying dural neoplasm may invade the leptomeninges directly.[61, 71, 72]

Third, spinal epidural neoplasm can spread contiguously along nerve roots or their lymphatics.[10, 14, 35, 90, 118, 156] This route of spread is somewhat controversial; some authors assert that the frequency of leptomeningeal carcinomatosis would be greater if this were an important pathway, considering the common occurrence of vertebral metastases.[71]

Complications of Meningeal Neoplasms

Once the CSF has been seeded, neoplasm has the potential to disseminate widely from a focus in the leptomeninges, throughout the arachnoid and pia mater, through the perivascular (Virchow-Robin) spaces, or along the sleeves of cranial nerves and spinal nerve roots.[58] Extension into the perivascular spaces or partial obstruction of the vessel lumen by tumor cells can result in ischemic complications

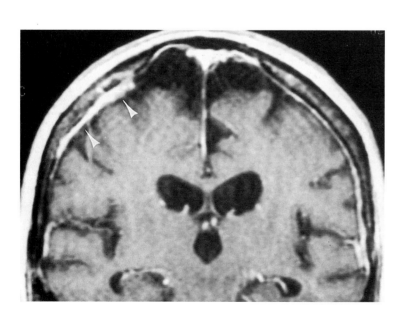

Figure 12–41. Focal, direct extension of breast carcinoma calvarial metastasis to dura. Coronal enhanced T1-weighted image shows focal dural thickening *(arrowheads)* and enhancement deep to a calvarial focus of breast carcinoma (see also Fig. 12–21).

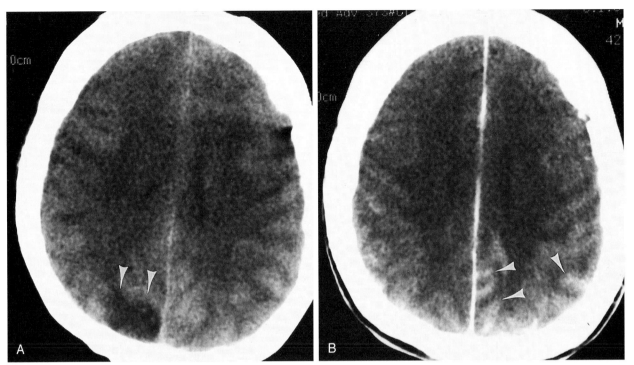

Figure 12–42. Carcinomatous encephalitis. *A,* Axial CT of the head obtained before contrast medium shows hypoattenuation in the posterior parietal lobe *(arrowheads)* in a 42-year-old patient who presented with a 4-month history of seizures. *B,* After contrast administration, pial enhancement is minimal *(arrowheads).* The patient was initially thought to have subarachnoid hemorrhage, but autopsy showed extensive adenocarcinoma in the perivascular spaces and meninges, with multiple ischemic foci in the brain and a primary focus in the lung.

of leptomeningeal carcinomatosis (Fig. 12–42).[118, 161] The term "carcinomatous encephalitis" refers to the rare occurrence of diffuse perivascular (Virchow-Robin space) infiltration resulting in ischemia.[71, 99] Neoplasm adjacent to the meninges or a small site of meningeal tumor involvement may also provoke a diffuse fibrous response of the meninges.[118] Since both the meningeal reaction to neoplasm and the neoplasm itself usually enhance on MRI, this finding is not specific.

Summary

A wide spectrum of non-neoplastic and neoplastic conditions may affect the meninges. MRI with FLAIR sequences or enhanced T1-weighted images is an effective modality for characterizing meningeal pathology. The cardinal MRI findings in meningeal disease are hydrocephalus and smooth or nodular enhancement or signal abnormality of the dura/arachnoid, the pia mater/SAS, and the ependyma of the brain or spine.

Two major patterns of disease are identified: (1) a dura/arachnoid pattern, which follows along the inner table of the calvarium, and (2) a pia mater/SAS pattern, which extends into the sulcal spaces. Nodular disease, in particular, may suggest neoplasm. Meningeal neoplasm may be clinically silent, and false-negative results on CSF cytologic study are common.[6, 8, 13, 118] The addition of MRI to the clinical data and CSF examination may increase the detection of meningeal involvement and may allow tumor staging.

Understanding the routes of neoplastic spread to the meninges permits identification of imaging features of the primary tumor that predispose to CSF dissemination, such as proximity to the SAS or ventricles. Although there is considerable overlap in the MR appearance of meningeal involvement in various diseases, the pattern and distribution of enhancement may provide guidance for diagnosis, management, and treatment monitoring of disorders affecting the meninges. Correlation of imaging findings with clinical and CSF data is essential to ensure that treatable disease is not overlooked.

References

1. Ahmadi J, Hinton D: Dural invasion by craniofacial and calvarial neoplasms: MR imaging and histopathologic evaluation. Radiology 188:747–749, 1993.
2. Aizpuru R, Quencer R, Norenberg M, et al: Meningioangiomatosis: Clinical, radiologic, and histopathologic correlation. Radiology 179:819–821, 1991.
3. Alcolado R, Weller R, Parrish E, Garrod D: The cranial arachnoid and pia mater in man: Anatomical and ultrastructural observations. Neuropathol Appl Neurobiol 14:1–17, 1988.
4. Allcutt D, Michowitz S, Weitzman S, et al: Primary leptomeningeal melanoma: An unusually aggressive tumor in childhood. Neurosurgery 32:721–729, 1993.
5. Anonymous: Case records of the Massachusetts General Hospital: Weekly clinicopathological exercises. Case 26–1988. A 40-year-old man with a persistent dural abnormality after treatment for an astrocytoma. N Engl J Med 318:1742–1750, 1988.
6. Arita N, Taneda M, Hayakawa T: Leptomeningeal dissemination of malignant gliomas, incidence, diagnosis and outcome. Acta Neurochir 126:84–92, 1994.
7. Awad I, Bay J, Rogers L: Leptomeningeal metastasis from supratentorial malignant gliomas. Neurosurg 19:247–251, 1986.

8. Balhuizen J, Bots G, Schaberg A, Bosman F: Value of cerebrospinal fluid cytology for the diagnosis of malignancies in the central nervous system. J Neurosurg 48:747–753, 1978.

9. Barkhof F, Valk J, Hommes O, Scheltens P: Meningeal Gd-DTPA enhancement in multiple sclerosis. AJNR Am J Neuroradiol 13:397–400, 1992.

10. Batson O: The function of the vertebral veins and their role in the spread of metastases. Ann Surg 112:138–149, 1940.

11. Benedikt R, Brown D, Walker R, et al: Sturge-Weber syndrome: Cranial MR imaging with Gd-DTPA. AJNR Am J Neuroradiol 14:409–415, 1993.

12. Bickerstaff E, Small J, Guest I: The relapsing course of certain meningiomas in relation to pregnancy and menstruation. J Neurol Neurosurg Psychiatry 21:89–91, 1958.

13. Bigner S, Johnston W: The cytopathology of cerebrospinal fluid: II. Metastatic cancer, meningeal carcinomatosis and primary central nervous system neoplasms. Acta Cytol 25:461–479, 1981.

14. Boogerd W, Hart A, van der Sande J, Engelsman E: Meningeal carcinomatosis in breast cancer: Prognostic factors and influence of treatment. Cancer 67:1685–1695, 1991.

15. Bourekas E, Wildenhain P, Lewin J, et al: The dural tail sign revisited. AJNR Am J Neuroradiol 16:1514–1516, 1995.

16. Bowen B, Donovan Post M: Intracranial infection. In Atlas S (ed): Magnetic Resonance Imaging of the Brain and Spine. New York, Raven Press, 1991, pp 501–538.

17. Bracchi M, Savoiardo M, Triulzi F, et al: Superficial siderosis of the CNS: MR diagnosis and clinical findings. AJNR Am J Neuroradiol 14:227–236, 1993.

18. Brightbill T, Ihmeidan I, Donovan Post M, et al: Neurosyphilis in HIV-positive and HIV-negative patients: Neuroimaging findings. AJNR Am J Neuroradiol 16:703–711, 1995.

19. Brodal P: The Central Nervous System. New York, Oxford University Press, 1992, p 464.

20. Burke J, Podrasky A, Bradley W: Meninges: Benign postoperative enhancement on MR images. Radiology 174:99–102, 1990.

21. Carpenter MB: Meninges and cerebrospinal fluid. In Wilkins W (ed): Core Text of Neuroanatomy, 2nd ed. Baltimore, Williams & Wilkins, 1978, pp 1–14.

22. Castelli M, Husband A: Superficial siderosis of the central nervous system: An underestimated cause of hearing loss. J Laryngol Otol 111:60–62, 1997.

23. Chamberlain M: Current concepts in leptomeningeal metastasis. Curr Opin Oncol 4:533–539, 1992.

24. Chamberlain M, Sandy A, Press G: Leptomeningeal metastasis: A comparison of gadolinium-enhanced MR and contrast-enhanced CT of the brain. Neurology 40:435–438, 1990.

25. Chang K, Han M, Roh J, et al: Gd-DTPA-enhanced MR imaging of the brain in patients with meningitis: Comparison with CT. AJNR Am J Neuroradiol 11:69–76, 1990.

26. Cheng T, O'Neill B, Scheithauer B, Piepgras D: Chronic meningitis: The role of meningeal or cortical biopsy. Neurosurgery 34:590–596, 1994.

27. Cohen J, Quint D, Eldevik O: Patterns of normal meningeal enhancement on 1.5-T MR imaging. American Roentgen Ray Society Proceedings Book, 1995, p 127.

28. Cooper I, Craig M, Kernohan J: Tumors of the spinal cord: Primary extramedullary gliomas. Surg Gynecol Obstet 92:183–190, 1951.

29. Crawford J, Konkol R: Familial hemiplegic migraine with crossed cerebellar diaschisis and unilateral meningeal enhancement. Headache 37:590–593, 1997.

30. Davis P, Friedman N, Fry S, Malko J, et al: Leptomeningeal metastasis: MR imaging. Radiology 163:449–454, 1987.

31. De Klerk D, Spence J: Chemical meningitis with intracranial tumours. S Afr Med J 48:131–135, 1974.

32. Demaerel P, Robberecht W, Casteels I, et al: Focal leptomeningeal MR enhancement along the chiasm as a presenting sign of multiple sclerosis. J Comput Assist Tomogr 19:297–298, 1995.

33. Demaerel P, Wilms G, Van Lierde S, et al: Lyme disease in childhood presenting as primary leptomeningeal enhancement without parenchymal findings of MR. AJNR Am J Neuroradiol 15:302–304, 1994.

34. Dietrich P-Y, Aapro M, Pizzolato G: Primary diffuse leptomeningeal gliomatosis (PDLG): A neoplastic cause of chronic meningitis. J Neurooncol 15:275–283, 1993.

35. Dinsdale H, Taghavy A: Carcinomatosis of the meninges. Can Med Assoc J 90:505–512, 1964.

36. Elster A: Magnetic resonance contrast enhancement in cerebral infarction. Neuroimaging Clin North Am 4:89–100, 1994.

37. Elster A, DiPersio D: Cranial postoperative site: Assessment with contrast-enhanced MR imaging. Radiology 174:93–98, 1990.

38. Elster A, Mathews V, King J, Hamilton C: Improved detection of gadolinium enhancement using magnetization transfer imaging. Neuroimaging Clin North Am 4:185–399, 1994.

39. Elster A, Moody D: Early cerebral infarction: Gadopentetate dimeglumine enhancement. Radiology 177:627–632, 1990.

40. Enzmann D, Krikorian J, Yorke C, Hayward R: Computed tomography in leptomeningeal spread of tumor. J Comput Assist Tomogr 2:448–455, 1978.

41. Esiri M, Gay D: Immunological and neuropathological significance of the Virchow-Robin space. J Neurol Sci 100:3–8, 1990.

42. Eustace S, Buff B: Magnetic resonance imaging in drug-induced meningitis. Can Assoc Radiol J 45:463–465, 1994.

43. Farn J, Mirowitz S: MR imaging of the normal meninges: Comparison of contrast-enhancement patterns on 3D gradient-echo and spin-echo images. AJR Am J Roentgenol 162:131–135, 1994.

44. Fishman R, Dillon W: Dural enhancement and cerebral displacement secondary to intracranial hypotension. Neurology 43:609–611, 1993.

45. Frank J, Girton M, Dwyer A, et al: Meningeal carcinomatosis in the VX2 rabbit tumor model: Detection with Gd-DPTA–enhanced MR imaging. Radiology 167:825–829, 1988.

46. Frederickson R: The subdural space interpreted as a cellular layer of meninges. Anat Rec 230:38–51, 1991.

47. Freilich R, Krol G, DeAngelis L: Neuroimaging and cerebrospinal fluid cytology in the diagnosis of leptomeningeal metastasis. Ann Neurol 38:51–57, 1995.

48. Fukui M, Williams R, Mudigonda S: CT and MR imaging signs of pyogenic ventriculitis. Paper presented at Proceedings of the American Society of Neuroradiology (ASNR), 1999, San Diego.

49. Fulbright R, Erdum E, Sze G, Byrne T: Cranial nerve enhancement in the Guillain-Barré syndrome. AJNR Am J Neuroradiol 16:923–925, 1995.

50. Giaquinto S, Massi G, Ricolfi A, Vitali S: On six cases of radiation meningiomas from the same community. Ital J Neurol Sci 5:173–175, 1984.

51. Gilden D, Beinlich B, Rubenstien E, et al: Varicella-zoster virus myelitis: An expanding spectrum. Neurology 44:1818–1823, 1994.

52. Ginsberg L, Leeds N: Neuroradiology of leukemia. AJR Am J Roentgenol 165:525–534, 1995.

53. Glass J, Melamed M, Chernik N, Posner J: Malignant cells in cerebrospinal fluid (CSF): The meaning of a positive CSF cytology. Neurology 29:1369–1375, 1979.

54. Globus J, Meltzer T: Metastatic tumors of the brain. Arch Neurol Psychiatry 48:163–226, 1942.

55. Goldsher D, Litt A, Pinto R, et al: Dural "tail" associated with meningiomas on Gd-DTPA–enhanced MR images: Characteristics, differential diagnostic value, and possible implications for treatment. Radiology 176:447–450, 1990.

56. Gondos B, King E: Cerebrospinal fluid cytology: Diagnostic accuracy and comparison of different techniques. Acta Cytol 20:542–547, 1976.

57. Grabb P, Albright A, Pang D: Dissemination of supratentorial malignant gliomas via the cerebrospinal fluid in children. Neurosurgery 30:64–71, 1992.

58. Grain G, Karroo J: Diffuse leptomeningeal carcinomatosis: Clinical and pathologic characteristics. Neurology 5:706–722, 1955.

59. Gray L, Macula J, Provenzale J, et al: High dose MR contrast agent for the diagnosis of leptomeningeal disease (abstract). Radiology 197(P):410, 1995.

60. Greenberg R, Lane E, Cinnamon J, et al: The cranial meninges: Anatomic considerations. Semin Ultrasound CT MRI 15:454–465, 1994.

61. Griffin J, Thompson R, Mitchinson M, et al: Lymphomatous leptomeningitis. Am J Med 51:200–208, 1971.

62. Grossman R, Kemp S, Yu I, et al: The importance of oxygenation in the appearance of acute subarachnoid hemorrhage on high-field magnetic resonance imaging. Acta Radiol (Suppl) 369:56–58, 1986.

63. Guseo A, Jellinger K: The significance of perivascular infiltrations in multiple sclerosis. J Neurol 211:51–60, 1975.

64. Haines D: On the question of a subdural space. Anat Rec 230:3–21, 1991.

65. Halper J, Scheithauer B, Okazaki H, Laws E: Meningioangio-

matosis: A report of six cases with special reference to the occurrence of neurofibrillary tangles. J Neuropathol Exp Neurol 45:426–446, 1986.

66. Hammes E: Reaction of the meninges to blood. Arch Neurol Psychiatry 52:505–514, 1944.

67. Hardman J: Cerebrospinal trauma. In Davis R, Robertson D (eds): Textbook of Neuropathology, 2nd ed. Baltimore, Williams & Wilkins, 1991, pp 962–1002.

68. Harvey S, Burr H: The development of the meninges. Arch Neurol Psychiatry 15:545–567, 1926.

69. Haustein J, Laniado M, Niendorf H-P, et al: Triple-dose versus standard-dose gadopentetate dimeglumine: A randomized study in 199 patients. Radiology 186:855–860, 1993.

70. Heinz R, Wiener D, Friedman H, Tien R: Detection of cerebrospinal fluid metastasis: CT myelography or MR? AJNR Am J Neuroradiol 16:1147–1151, 1995.

71. Henson R, Urich H: Carcinomatous meningitis. In Henson R, Urich H (eds): Cancer and the Nervous System. Boston, Blackwell Scientific, 1982, pp 101–119.

72. Henson R, Urich H: Diffuse infiltration by lymphoma and leukemia. In Henson R, Urich H (eds): Cancer and the Central Nervous System. Boston, Blackwell Scientific, 1982, pp 227–267.

73. Ho K-L, Hoschner J, Wolfe D: Primary leptomeningeal gliomatosis: Symptoms suggestive of meningitis. Arch Neurol 38:662–666, 1981.

74. Hochman M, Naidich T, Kobetz S, Fernandez-Maitin A: Spontaneous intracranial hypotension with pachymeningeal enhancement on MRI. Neurology 42:1628–1630, 1992.

75. Hudgins P, Davis P, Hoffman J Jr: Gadopentetate dimeglumine–enhanced MR imaging in children following surgery for brain tumor: Spectrum of meningeal findings. AJNR Am J Neuroradiol 12:301–307, 1991.

76. Hughes J, Oppenheimer D: Superficial siderosis of the central nervous system. Acta Neuropathol (Berl) 13:56–74, 1969.

77. Jacobs D, McFarlane M, Holmes F: Female patients with meningioma of the sphenoid ridge and additional primary neoplasms of the breast and genital tract. Cancer 60:3080–3082, 1987.

78. Jaeckle K, Krol G, Posner J: Evolution of computed tomographic abnormalities in leptomeningeal metastases. Ann Neurol 17:85–89, 1985.

79. Janss A, Galetta S, Freese A, et al: Superficial siderosis of the central nervous system: Magnetic resonance imaging and pathological correlation. J Neurosurg 79:756–760, 1993.

80. Jennings M, Slatkin N, D'Angelo M, et al: Neoplastic meningitis as the presentation of occult primitive neuroectodermal tumors. J Child Neurol 8:306–312, 1993.

81. Johnson B, Fram E: Cerebral venous occlusive disease: Pathophysiology, clinical manifestations, and imaging. Neuroimaging Clin North Am 2:769–783, 1992.

82. Kallmes D, Gray L, Brown M, Glass J: Triple dose gadolinium in the diagnosis of leptomeningeal metastases. American Society of Neuroradiology (ASNR) Proceedings Book, 1994, p 208.

83. Kallmes D, Gray L, Glass J: High-dose gadolinium-enhanced MRI for diagnosis of meningeal metastasis. Neuroradiology 40:23–26, 1998.

84. Katz D, Taubenberger J, Raine C, et al: Gadolinium-enhancing lesions on magnetic resonance imaging: Neuropathologic findings (abstract). Ann Neurol 28:P92, 1990.

85. Kelly A, Zimmerman R: Head trauma: Comparison of MR and CT: Experience in 100 patients. AJNR Am J Neuroradiol 9:699–708, 1988.

86. Kilgore D, Breger R, Daniels D, et al: Cranial tissues: Normal MR appearance after intravenous injection of Gd-DTPA. Radiology 160:757–761, 1986.

87. Kioumehr F, Dadsetan M, Feldman N, et al: Postcontrast MRI of the cranial meninges: Leptomeningitis versus pachymeningitis. J Comput Assist Tomogr 19:713–720, 1995.

88. Kirkpatrick J: Neurologic infections due to bacteria, fungi, and parasites. In Davis R, Robertson D (eds): Textbook of Neuropathology, 2nd ed. Baltimore, Williams & Wilkins, 1991, pp 719–803.

89. Kline T: Cytological examination of the cerebrospinal fluid. Cancer 15:591–597, 1962.

90. Kokkoris C: Leptomeningeal carcinomatosis: How does cancer reach the pia-arachnoid? Cancer 51:154–160, 1983.

91. Kramer E, Rafto S, Packer R, Zimmerman R: Comparison of myelography with CT follow-up versus gadolinium MRI for subarachnoid metastatic disease in children. Neurology 41:46–50, 1991.

92. Krol G, Sze G, Malkin M, Walker R: MR of cranial and spinal meningeal carcinomatosis: Comparison with CT and myelography. AJR Am J Roentgenol 151:583–588, 1988.

93. Kumar A, Montanera W, Willinsky R, et al: Case report: MR features of tuberculous arachnoiditis. J Comput Assist Tomogr 17:127–130, 1993.

94. Lachance D, O'Neill B, Macdonald D, et al: Primary leptomeningeal lymphoma: Report of 9 cases, diagnosis with immunocytochemical analysis, and review of literature. Neurology 41:95–100, 1991.

95. Lee Y-Y, Van Tassel P, Raymond A: Intracranial dural chondrosarcoma. AJNR Am J Neuroradiol 9:1189–1193, 1988.

96. Leproux F, Melanson D, Mercier C, et al: Leptomeningeal gliomatosis: MR findings. J Comput Assist Tomogr 17:317–320, 1993.

97. Lindner A, Reiners K, Toyka K: Meningeal hyperperfusion visualized by MRI in a patient with visual hallucinations and migraine. Headache 36:53–57, 1996.

98. Lunardi P, Missori P, Rizzo A, Gagliardi F: Chemical meningitis in ruptured intracranial dermoid: Case report and review of the literature. Surg Neurol 32:449–452, 1989.

99. Madow L, Alpers B: Encephalitic form of metastatic carcinoma. Arch Neurol Psychiatry 65:161–173, 1951.

100. Malat J, Virapongse C, Palestro C, Richman A: Primary intraspinal fibrosarcoma. Neurosurgery 19:434–436, 1986.

101. Mamelak A, Kelly W, Davis R, Rosenblum M: Idiopathic hypertrophic cranial pachymeningitis: Report of three cases. J Neurosurg 79:270–276, 1993.

102. Mark A: Nondegenerative, non-neoplastic diseases of the spine and spinal cord. In Atlas S (ed): Magnetic Resonance Imaging of the Brain and Spine. New York, Raven Press, 1991, pp 967–1011.

103. Martin N, Masson C, Henin D, et al: Hypertrophic cranial pachymeningitis: Assessment with CT and MR imaging. AJNR Am J Neuroradiol 10:477–484, 1989.

104. Mathews V, Kuharik M, Edwards M, et al: Gd-DTPA–enhanced MR imaging of experimental bacterial meningitis: Evaluation and comparison with CT. AJR Am J Roentgenol 152:131–136, 1989.

105. Mathews VP, Alo PL, Glass JD, et al: AIDS-related CNS *Cryptococcus*: Radiologic-pathologic correlation. AJNR Am J Neuroradiol 13:1477–1486, 1992.

106. Meltzer C, Smirniotopoulos J, Fukui M: The dural tail. Int J Neuroradiol 4:33–40, 1998.

107. Miller J, Jubelt B: Bacterial infections. In Rowland L (ed): Merritt's Textbook of Neurology, 8th ed. Philadelphia, Lea & Febiger, 1989, pp 63–96.

108. Mittl R, Yousem D: Frequency of unexplained meningeal enhancement in the brain after lumbar puncture. AJNR Am J Neuroradiol 15:633–638, 1994.

109. Moberg A, Reis G: Carcinosis meningeum. Acta Med Scand 170:747–755, 1961.

110. Murai H, Kira J, Kobayashi T, et al: Hypertrophic cranial pachymeningitis due to *Aspergillus flavus*. Clin Neurol Neurosurg 94:247–250, 1992.

111. Naul L, Hise J, Bauserman S, Todd F: CT and MR of meningeal melanocytoma. AJNR Am J Neuroradiol 12:315–316, 1991.

112. Naylor B: The cytologic diagnosis of cerebrospinal fluid. Acta Cytol 8:141–148, 1964.

113. Negishi C, Sze G: Vasculitis presenting as primary leptomeningeal enhancement with minimal parenchymal findings. AJNR Am J Neuroradiol 14:26–28, 1993.

114. Newton H, Fleisher M, Schwartz M, Malkin M: Glucose phosphate isomerase as a CSF marker for leptomeningeal metastasis. Neurology 41:395–398, 1991.

115. Noguchi K, Ogawa T, Inugami A, et al: MR of acute subarachnoid hemorrhage: A preliminary report of fluid-attenuated inversion-recovery pulse sequences. AJNR Am J Neuroradiol 15:1940–1943, 1994.

116. Nugent J, Bunn P, Matthews M, et al: CNS metastases in small cell bronchogenic carcinoma. Cancer 44:1885–1893, 1979.

117. Ogawa T, Inugami A, Fujita H, et al: MR diagnosis of subacute and chronic subarachnoid hemorrhage: Comparison with CT. AJR Am J Roentgenol 165:1257–1262, 1995.

118. Olson M, Chernik N, Posner J: Infiltration of the leptomeninges by systemic cancer. Arch Neurol 30:122–137, 1974.

119. Onda K, Tanaka R, Takahashi H, et al: Cerebral glioblastoma with cerebrospinal fluid dissemination: A clinicopathological study of 14 cases examined by complete autopsy. Neurosurgery 25:533–540, 1989.

120. Onda K, Tanaka R, Takahashi H, et al: Symptomatic cerebrospinal fluid dissemination of cerebral glioblastoma. Neuroradiology 32: 146–150, 1990.

121. O'Rahilly R, Muller F: The meninges in human development. J Neuropathol Exp Neurol 45:588–608, 1986.

122. Osaka K, Handa H, Matsumoto S, Yasuda M: Development of the cerebrospinal fluid pathway in the normal and abnormal human embryos. Childs Brain 6:26–38, 1980.

123. Paako E, Patronas N, Schellinger D: Meningeal Gd-DTPA enhancement in patients with malignancies. J Comput Assist Tomogr 14: 542–546, 1990.

124. Packer R, Siegel K, Sutton L, et al: Leptomeningeal dissemination of primary central nervous system tumors of childhood. Ann Neurol 18:217–221, 1985.

125. Park J, Van den Noort S, Kim R, et al: Primary diffuse leptomeningeal gliomatosis with signs of increased intracranial pressure and progressive meningeal enhancement on MRI. J Neuroimaging 6: 250–254, 1996.

126. Partington C, Graves V, Hegstrand L: Meningioangiomatosis. Am J Neuroradiol 12:549–552, 1991.

127. Pfluger T, Weil S, Weis S, et al: MRI of primary meningeal sarcomas in two children: Differential diagnostic considerations. Neuroradiology 39:225–228, 1997.

128. Phillips M, Ryals T, Kambhu S, Yuh W: Neoplastic vs. inflammatory meningeal enhancement with Gd-DTPA. J Comput Assist Tomogr 14:536–541, 1990.

129. Praharaj S, Sharma M, Prasad K, et al: Unilateral meningeal thickening: A rare presentation of tuberculous meningitis. Clin Neurol Neurosurg 99:60–62, 1997.

130. Price R, Johnson W: The central nervous system in childhood leukemia: I. The arachnoid. Cancer 31:520–533, 1973.

131. Provenzale J, Allen N: MR findings in Wegener's granulomatosis. American Society of Neuroradiology (ASNR) Proceedings Book, 1995, p 130.

132. Pui M, Langston J, Arai Y: Gd-DTPA enhancement of CSF in meningeal carcinomatosis. J Comput Assist Tomogr 17:940–944, 1993.

133. Quagliarello V, Scheld W: Bacterial meningitis: Pathogenesis, pathophysiology, and progress. N Engl J Med 327:864–872, 1992.

134. Quest D, Salcman M: Fibromatosis presenting as a cranial mass lesion. J Neurosurg 44:237–240, 1976.

135. Rando T, Fishman R: Spontaneous intracranial hypotension: Report of two cases and review of the literature. Neurology 42:481–487, 1992.

136. Runge V, Clanton J, Price A, et al: Evaluation of contrast-enhanced MR imaging in a brain-abscess model. AJNR Am J Neuroradiol 6: 139–147, 1985.

137. Runge V, Wells J, Williams N, et al: Detectability of early brain meningitis on MR images with pathologic correlation (abstract). Radiology 197P: 480, 1995.

138. Russell D, Rubinstein L: Pathology of Tumours of the Nervous System, 5th ed. London, Edward Arnold, 1989, p 1012.

139. Sage M: Blood-brain barrier: Phenomenon of increasing importance to the imaging clinician. AJNR Am J Neuroradiol 3:127–138, 1982.

140. Sage M, Wilson A: The blood-brain barrier: An important concept in neuroimaging. AJNR Am J Neuroradiol 15:601–622, 1994.

141. Sakamoto S, Kitagaki H, Ishii K, et al: Gadolinium enhancement of the cerebrospinal fluid in a patient with meningeal fibrosis and cryptococcal infection. Neuroradiology 39:504–505, 1997.

142. Sarnat H, Netsky M: Evolution of the Nervous System, 2nd ed. New York, Oxford University Press, 1981, p 504.

143. Seltzer S, Mark A, Atlas S: CNS sarcoidosis: Evaluation with contrast-enhanced MR imaging. AJNR Am J Neuroradiol 12:1227–1233, 1991.

144. Sherman J, Stern B: Sarcoidosis of the CNS: Comparison of unenhanced and enhanced MR images. AJNR Am J Neuroradiol 11: 915–923, 1990.

145. Singer M, Atlas S, Drayer B: Subarachnoid space disease: Diagnosis with fluid-attenuated inversion-recovery MR imaging and comparison with gadolinium-enhanced spin-echo MR imaging—blinded reader study. Radiology 208:417–422, 1998.

146. Smirniotopoulos J, Murphy F: The phakomatoses. AJNR Am J Neuroradiol 13:725–746, 1992.

147. Southwick F, Richardson E, Swartz M: Septic thrombosis of the dural venous sinuses. Medicine 65:82–106, 1986.

148. Spagnoli M, Goldberg H, Grossman R, et al: Intracranial meningiomas: High-field MR imaging. Radiology 161:369–375, 1986.

149. Spallone A, Gagliardi F, Vagnozzi R: Intracranial meningiomas related to external cranial radiation. Surg Neurol 12:153–159, 1979.

150. Stern B, Krunholz A, Johns C, et al: Sarcoidosis and its neurological manifestations. Arch Neurol 42:909–917, 1985.

151. Sze G: Diseases of the intracranial meninges: MR imaging features. AJR Am J Roentgenol 160:727–733, 1993.

152. Sze G, Soletsky S, Bronen R, Krol G: MR imaging of the cranial meninges with emphasis on contrast enhancement and meningeal carcinomatosis. AJNR Am J Neuroradiol 10:965–975, 1989.

153. Tishler S, Williamson T, Mirra S, et al: Wegener granulomatosis with meningeal involvement. AJNR Am J Neuroradiol 14:1248–1252, 1993.

154. Tokumaru A, O'uchi T, Tsuneyoshi E, et al: Prominent meningeal enhancement adjacent to meningioma on Gd-DTPA–enhanced MR images: Histopathologic correlation. Radiology 175:431–433, 1990.

155. Truwit C, Barkovich A: Pathogenesis of intracranial lipoma: An MR study in 42 patients. AJR Am J Roentgenol 155:855–864, 1990.

156. Tsukada Y, Fouad A, Pickren J, Lane W: Central nervous system metastasis from breast carcinoma: Autopsy study. Cancer 52:2349–2354, 1993.

157. Twijnstra A, Van Zanten A, Nooyen W, et al: Cerebrospinal fluid beta$_2$-microglobulin: A study in controls and patients with metastatic and non-metastatic neurological disease. Eur J Cancer Clin Oncol 22:387–391, 1986.

158. Vertosick F, Selker R: Brainstem and spinal metastases of supratentorial glioblastoma multiforme: A clinical series. Neurosurgery 27: 516–522, 1990.

159. Viadana E, Bross I, Pickren JW: Cascade spread of blood-borne metastases in solid and nonsolid cancers of humans. In Weiss L, Gilbert HA (eds): Pulmonary Metastasis. Boston, GK Hall, 1978, pp 142–167.

160. Vogl T, Stemmler J, Bergman C, et al: MR and MR angiography of Sturge-Weber syndrome. AJNR Am J Neuroradiol 14:417–425, 1993.

161. Wasserstrom W, Glass J, Posner J: Diagnosis and treatment of leptomeningeal metastases from solid tumors: Experience with 90 patients. Cancer 49:759–772, 1982.

162. Watanabe M, Tanaka R, Takeda N: Correlation of MRI and clinical features in meningeal carcinomatosis. Neuroradiology 35:512–515, 1993.

163. Wehn S, Heinz E, Burger P, Boyko O: Dilated Virchow-Robin spaces in cryptococcal meningitis associated with AIDS: CT and MR findings. J Comput Assist Tomogr 13:756–762, 1989.

164. Whiteman M, Dandapani B, Shebert R, Donovan Post M: MRI of AIDS-related polyradiculomyelitis. J Comput Assist Tomogr 18: 7–11, 1994.

165. Whiteman M, Espinoza L, Post M, et al: Central nervous system tuberculosis in HIV-infected patients: Clinical and radiographic findings. AJNR Am J Neuroradiol 16:1319–1327, 1995.

166. Wiebe S, Munoz D, Smith S, Lee D: Meningioangiomatosis: A comprehensive analysis of clinical and laboratory features. Brain 122:709–726, 1999.

167. Williams R, Fukui M, Tishkoff N, et al: MR imaging of the subarachnoid space utilizing FLAIR: Pathology and pitfalls. Radiology 213:552, 1999.

168. Willis R: Pathology of Tumours, 4th ed. New York, Appleton-Century-Crofts, 1967, p 1019.

169. Witham T, Fukui M, Meltzer C, et al: Survival using intrathecal thiotriethylenephosphoramide (thio-TEPA) for the treatment of ependymal or leptomeningeal gliomatosis in patients with high grade gliomas. Cancer 86:1347–1353, 1999.

170. Wolbach S: Congenital rhabdomyoma of the heart: Report of a case associated with multiple nests of neuroglial tissue in the meninges of the spinal cord. J Med Res 16:495–519, 1907.

171. Wrobel C, Meyer S, Johnson R, Hesselink J: MR findings in acute and chronic coccidioidomycosis meningitis. AJNR Am J Neuroradiol 13:1241–1245, 1992.

172. Yap H-Y, Yap B-S, Tashima C, et al: Meningeal carcinomatosis in breast cancer. Cancer 42:283–286, 1978.

173. Yousem D, Patrone P, Grossman R: Leptomeningeal metastases: MR evaluation. J Comput Assist Tomogr 14:255–261, 1990.

174. Zouaoui A, Maillard J-C, Dormont D, et al: MRI in neurosarcoidosis. J Neuroradiol 19:271–284, 1992.

13

Leukoencephalopathies and Demyelinating Disease

Barton Lane

The cerebral (and cerebellar) white matter may be affected by various disease processes. With its ability to detect these alterations in white matter, neuroimaging contributes to the diagnosis and management of these disorders.

It is useful to briefly consider the underlying mechanisms that account for the changes seen on magnetic resonance (MR) images and computed tomography (CT) scans in white matter disease. Demyelinating disorders result in increased water content of the white matter because myelin (rich in solids) is lost, leaving behind more hydrated material. This water is found in extracellular fluid; astrocytes; and, possibly, inflammatory cells. The magnitude of the change depends on the severity of the disease. The abnormally increased water content causes reduced attenuation on CT scans and prolongation of T1 and T2 values on MR scans. In the late stages of demyelination, extreme shrinkage of the affected white matter, accompanied by gross cerebral atrophy, may result.[6]

Cerebral edema, trauma, ischemic lesions, and infection are among the causes of abnormal white matter, as visualized by CT and magnetic resonance imaging (MRI), and may therefore be included in the differential diagnosis of primary myelin disorders. Further, secondary myelin (wallerian) degeneration[84] occurs when axons are severed or destroyed. This chapter emphasizes primary diseases of white matter or those disorders in which the white matter is the primary focus of the pathologic process.

The classification of white matter disease may seem confusing and arbitrary; it can be undertaken on biochemical, etiologic, clinical, pathologic, or radiologic bases. Some diseases cross nosologic lines; an example is progressive multifocal leukoencephalopathy (PML), in which myelin is destroyed as a result of viral infection, which is in turn secondary to immune compromise. The classification in this chapter is based on that of Waxman.[95]

Normal White Matter

CT Appearance

Normal cerebral white matter in the adult has an x-ray attenuation coefficient 0.5% to 0.8% less than normal gray matter of the cerebral cortex. Average values of 35 to 40 Hounsfield units (HU) for adult human gray matter and 29 to 33 HU for white matter have been derived from clinical studies. These figures agree with in vitro studies performed on human and primate brains. This small attenuation difference (5 to 7 HU) is detectable on CT as a relative lucency of white matter, as compared with gray matter.

The cause of the lower attenuation in white matter is its myelin content. Myelin accounts for the whitish appearance, the high lipid content, and the relatively low water content of white matter when compared with gray matter (72% versus 82%).[9, 10] Although white matter is less vascular than gray matter, the low blood content of white matter accounts for only a small fraction of the attenuation difference. Contrast infusion increases the differences in density only slightly. This difference is probably caused by the higher cerebral blood volume in gray versus white matter.

White matter in the infant differs significantly from that in the adult. It is known that complex biochemical and morphologic changes occur in the white matter in utero and throughout the first years of life. Extensive myelination occurs in the first few months after birth and is virtually complete by the end of the second year. Some slower myelination continues throughout childhood and adolescence. Thereafter, the white matter is relatively stable during adulthood.

Immature myelin, compared with the adult form, has a much greater water content. As myelination proceeds in the brain, the white matter loses water and gains lipids and proteolipids until, in the adult, white matter has three times as much lipid as does gray matter. CT density measurements show an average linear increase in brain density from term to 20 weeks, after which the density increases only slightly.[63]

This high water content of immature myelin has a predictable effect, as seen on CT scans. The white matter in premature and normal full-term infants shows greater lucency (i.e., lesser attenuation) than in adults (Figs. 13–1 and 13–2). This finding must not be mistaken for a pathologic process.[22, 49, 66] (The thinner neonatal calvaria may also contribute to better gray-white discrimination, since there is less beam-hardening and a better signal-to-noise ratio.)

When the patient is about 6 months of age, the difference in gray-white matter is similar to that in the adult. From ages 2 to 17 years, the normal white matter density values are identical to those of adults.

Constant identifiable changes in white matter in aging human brains have been described. After middle age, the total amount of certain myelin lipids decreases and the

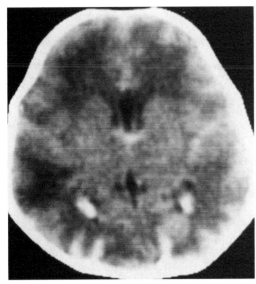

Figure 13–1. Immature myelination in a premature infant. CT scan, obtained at 1 month of age, demonstrates the typical lucency of incompletely myelinated white matter in premature infants. The internal capsules that myelinate first are not visible.

MRI Appearance

On the basis of the neuropathologic differences in the water and lipid content of white matter versus gray matter (as just explained), MRI can be used to exploit these differences in imaging the brain.

T1 and T2 relaxation values in normal white matter are shorter than in gray matter. Thus, on T1-weighted images, white matter is relatively brighter in signal intensity; on T2-weighted images, white matter is less intense, or darker. In general, MRI is superior to CT in delineating differences in white and gray matter, the various gray matter nuclei, and white matter tracts. MRI is more sensitive than CT in demonstrating accurately the extent and distribution of histologically verified central nervous system (CNS) disease, and for that reason MRI should be the imaging procedure of choice in suspected white matter abnormalities. Still, familiarity with the CT findings is important because some patients may undergo CT as the initial imaging procedure or may, for whatever reason, be unable to undergo MRI.

Assessment of myelination patterns in the newborn and in the developing brain by MRI has been well addressed by several MRI investigators.[2, 5, 20, 34] Myelination of the brain occurs in a more or less orderly fashion, proceeding caudal to rostral, and with more primitive structures myelinating before "newer" ones. Timetables for myelination of specific structures have been published and are useful in assessment of pediatric brain MR images. Generally, nonmyelinated tissue is *hypointense* (darker) on T1-weighted sequences but *hyperintense* (brighter) on T2-weighted sequences; as structures myelinate, they become hyperintense (bright) on T1-weighted sequences but hypointense (dark) on T2-weighted sequences (Figs. 13–3 and 13–4).

cerebral hemispheres show increased water content. These changes appear as decreased attenuation of the cerebral white matter in CT scans of older patients.[9] This generalized decrease in white matter density has been correlated with dementia and other clinical symptomatology[83]; however, the imaging specialist must be cautious when interpreting CT scans in the very aged (as well as the very young) because the observed white matter differences may be a part of the maturation or aging process.

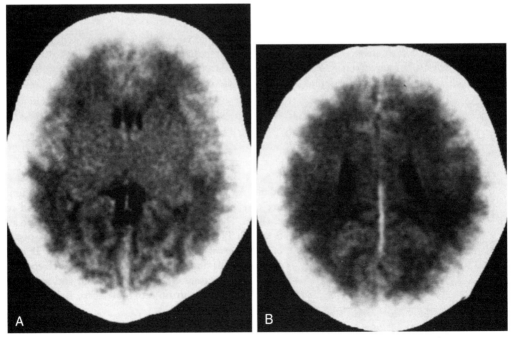

Figure 13–2. CT scans of myelin in a normal neonate. The immature myelin with its high water content imparts a generalized lucency to the central white matter. Note especially the discrete border with overlying cortical tissue. The internal capsule, however, having more mature myelination, is not visualized separately.

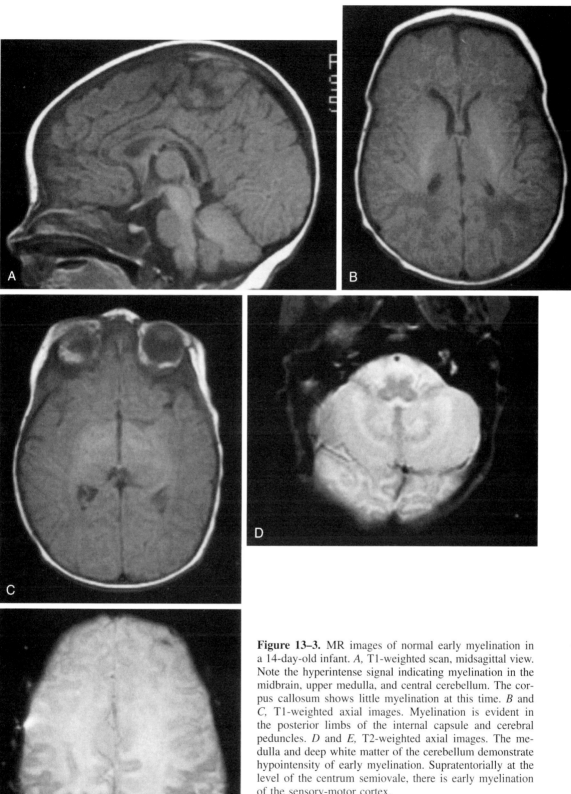

Figure 13–3. MR images of normal early myelination in a 14-day-old infant. *A,* T1-weighted scan, midsagittal view. Note the hyperintense signal indicating myelination in the midbrain, upper medulla, and central cerebellum. The corpus callosum shows little myelination at this time. *B* and *C,* T1-weighted axial images. Myelination is evident in the posterior limbs of the internal capsule and cerebral peduncles. *D* and *E,* T2-weighted axial images. The medulla and deep white matter of the cerebellum demonstrate hypointensity of early myelination. Supratentorially at the level of the centrum semiovale, there is early myelination of the sensory-motor cortex.

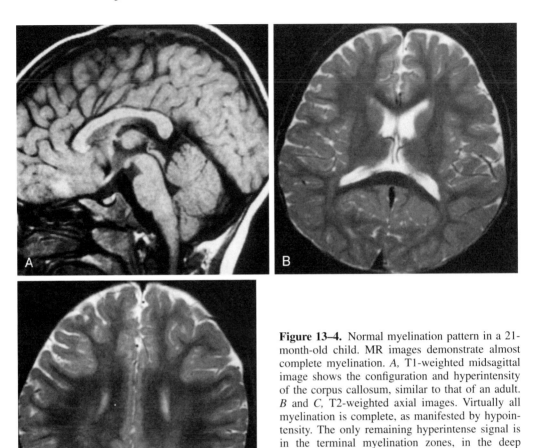

Figure 13–4. Normal myelination pattern in a 21-month-old child. MR images demonstrate almost complete myelination. *A,* T1-weighted midsagittal image shows the configuration and hyperintensity of the corpus callosum, similar to that of an adult. *B* and *C,* T2-weighted axial images. Virtually all myelination is complete, as manifested by hypointensity. The only remaining hyperintense signal is in the terminal myelination zones, in the deep periventricular white matter of the parieto-occipital region.

Diffusion-weighted imaging (DWI) and diffusion tensor techniques are MRI methods that further characterize brain tissue, especially white matter. Diffusion-weighted imaging, although used mostly for imaging of stroke, has been applied to many demyelinating and metabolic brain diseases, including Krabbe's disease and multiple sclerosis (MS).[31, 78]

Viral and Postviral Demyelination

Among the diseases that may directly involve the white matter are those in which hypersensitivity and immunity play a predominant role. In such cases, the cerebral hypersensitivity reaction causes the observed clinical and pathologic state, whether the initial offending antigen is a virus, foreign protein, or autoantigen. *Acute disseminated encephalomyelitis* (ADEM), or *immune-mediated encephalomyelitis* (IME), affects white matter to a greater or lesser degree and may be identified by CT or MRI. In patients with this condition, the viral agent cannot be detected in the CNS.

Conversely, there are patients with diminished immunity in whom a virus, which normally cannot gain a foothold in the CNS, propagates there unchecked and results in demyelination; such a disease is PML. Some virus-associated demyelinating conditions are described next.

Acute Disseminated Encephalomyelitis

ADEM has been associated with varicella zoster infections and measles as well as with rubella, influenza, and possibly infectious mononucleosis. The postvaccinal types result from inoculation for rabies, yellow fever, or influenza or from other brain-derived vaccines.[77] In some subacute forms of ADEM, the onset is slower and the course of the disease is prolonged. Corticosteroid medication may be beneficial in these conditions.[71]

The distribution of the encephalomyelitis is predominantly in the white matter, characterized pathologically by lymphocytic and mononuclear perivenous inflammation. The demyelination may be local or diffusely confluent, and variable degrees of edema may be present.

Although low-attenuation lesions in the white matter have been described on CT scans,[50] MRI is much more

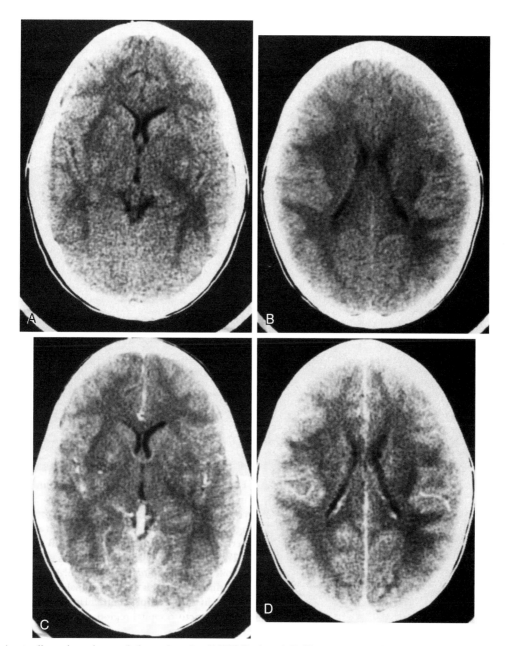

Figure 13–5. Acute disseminated encephalomyelopathy (ADEM). *A* and *B,* Non–contrast-enhanced CT scans demonstrate multifocal white matter lucencies, most visible in the basal ganglia bilaterally as well as in the parieto-occipital white matter. *C* and *D,* There is no contrast enhancement. The multiplicity of lesions is typical.

sensitive and is the imaging method of choice in demonstrating the lesions of ADEM (Figs. 13–5 and 13–6). T2-weighted MR images are the most sensitive, with asymmetrical white matter foci of hyperintensity. The size and number of lesions are variable. Even gray matter may be involved.

Enhancement with gadolinium may be prominent, either as punctate foci or, less commonly, as ringlike lesions.[12] Corresponding lesions may be also be seen in the spinal cord and less commonly in the optic nerves. An important differential diagnostic consideration is MS, but fortunately the time course of the two diseases differs.[41] MS is relapsing-remitting, whereas ADEM is a monophasic illness.

Another important diagnostic consideration is vasculitis, which may mimic the lesions of ADEM. ADEM usually resolves, and the prognosis for recovery is good.

Progressive Multifocal Leukoencephalopathy

A compromised immune system may predispose to viral replication in the brain, resulting in leukoencephalopathy.

PML is a rare, subacute demyelinating disease caused by replication of polyoma virus in the brain of an individual with immunosuppression, first reported with malignant

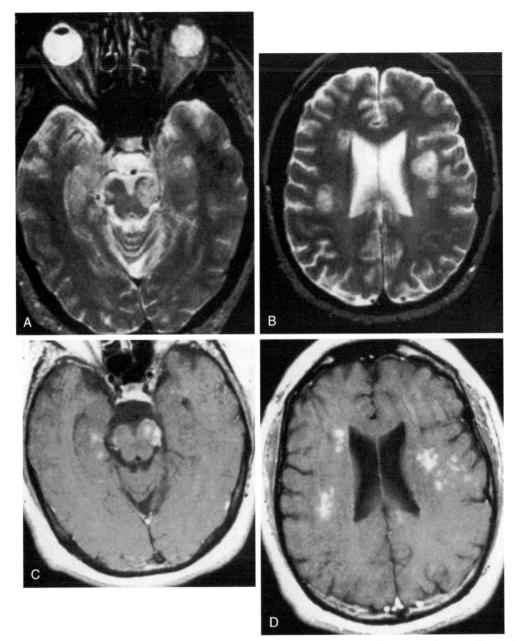

Figure 13–6. Acute disseminated encephalomyelopathy (ADEM) in a 52-year-old man with memory loss, apathy, and inflammatory cells in the cerebrospinal fluid. *A* and *B,* Cranial MR T2-weighted axial images show multiple, hyperintense lesions involving the right medial temporal lobe, both cerebral peduncles, and the mesencephalic deep white matter. *C* and *D,* Gadolinium contrast-enhanced, T1-weighted MR images at the same levels show patchy multinodular contrast enhancement within the lesions.

lymphoproliferative disease.[65, 92] PML has been associated with acquired immunodeficiency syndrome (AIDS) and is now the most frequently encountered predisposing disease.[47]

PML has a characteristic radiographic appearance on CT and MRI scans (Figs. 13–7 to 13–12).[53, 97] Subcortical foci of demyelination are seen with scalloped lateral borders following the outline of the intact overlying cortex. With CT, the lesions show decreased attenuation; with MRI, they are correspondingly intense on proton-density and T2-weighted images. In my experience, there is a predilection for the parieto-occipital region. The corpus callosum, the internal and external capsules, and the poste-

rior fossa structures are less commonly involved. The disease is progressive, and early minimal lesions can be followed temporally by CT and MRI as they become larger and coalesce.

Mass effect is usually absent on both pathologic and radiologic examinations and radiographically. In rare cases, the lesions are edematous and swollen, making the imaging diagnosis more problematic. Contrast enhancement, which helps to distinguish this disease from toxoplasmosis and other opportunist infections and acute MS, is not usually present. In later stages of the disease, shrinkage of the affected white matter may cause ipsilateral atrophic changes.

Figure 13–7. Progressive multifocal leukoencephalopathy (PML) in a 63-year-old man with worsening right hemiparesis and a lung nodule. On the basis of this CT scan, a left frontal brain biopsy, which was diagnostic of PML, was performed. A large, low-density lesion occupies the entire left centrum semiovale. Other, lower sections showed the lesion extending down into the internal capsule; a second, much smaller lesion was also visible in the right parietal white matter. The clearly defined borders of the lesion, the absence of contrast enhancement, and the lack of mass effect, despite the lesion's considerable extent, are typical of PML.

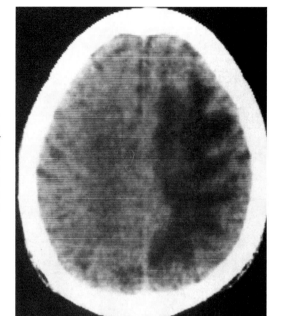

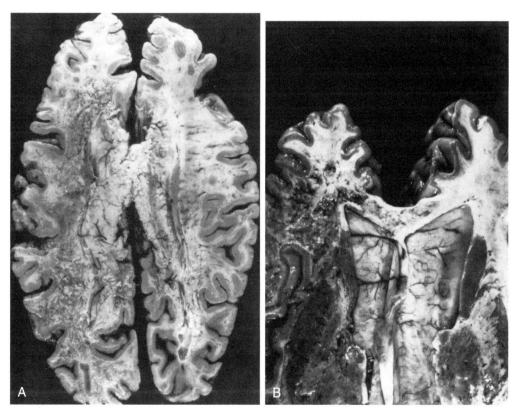

Figure 13–8. Progressive multifocal leukoencephalopathy (PML), typical pathologic specimen. The patient is a 51-year-old woman with a 7-month history of personality changes, blindness, dementia, and eventual coma. *A* and *B,* Horizontal brain sections obtained at autopsy. Almost the entire right hemispheric white matter has been replaced by a granular necrotic process. A similar process has begun in the left hemisphere. *B,* Close-up view of unfixed right frontal lobe. The typical lesion of PML has destroyed the central white matter and extends across the corpus callosum. Note the spared cortical mantle.

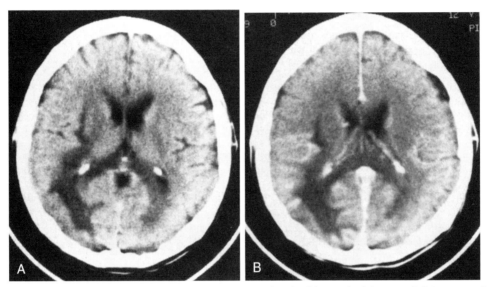

Figure 13–9. Progressive multifocal leukoencephalopathy (PML) associated with acquired immunodeficiency syndrome (AIDS). *A,* This non–contrast-enhanced CT scan, in this patient with rapidly progressive neurologic disease, shows a well-defined area of lucency in the right parieto-occipital white matter extending forward into the external capsule and medially into the splenium of the corpus callosum. Lesser involvement in the opposite occipital lobe is also present. *B,* Postcontrast image at the same level shows nonspecific enhancement of the overlying cortex but none within the white matter lesions. The diagnosis of PML was confirmed by biopsy.

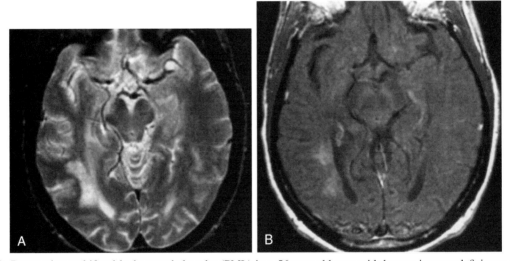

Figure 13–10. Progressive multifocal leukoencephalopathy (PML) in a 56-year-old man with human immunodeficiency virus infection and hemiparesis. *A,* Cranial T2-weighted axial MR image shows a confluent hyperintense white matter lesion adjacent laterally to the right occipital horn. Note the sparing of the overlying gray matter cortex. *B,* Magnetization transfer (MT) postgadolinium-enhanced MR axial image. Note the minimal contrast enhancement, which was not seen on CT or standard T1-weighted MR images.

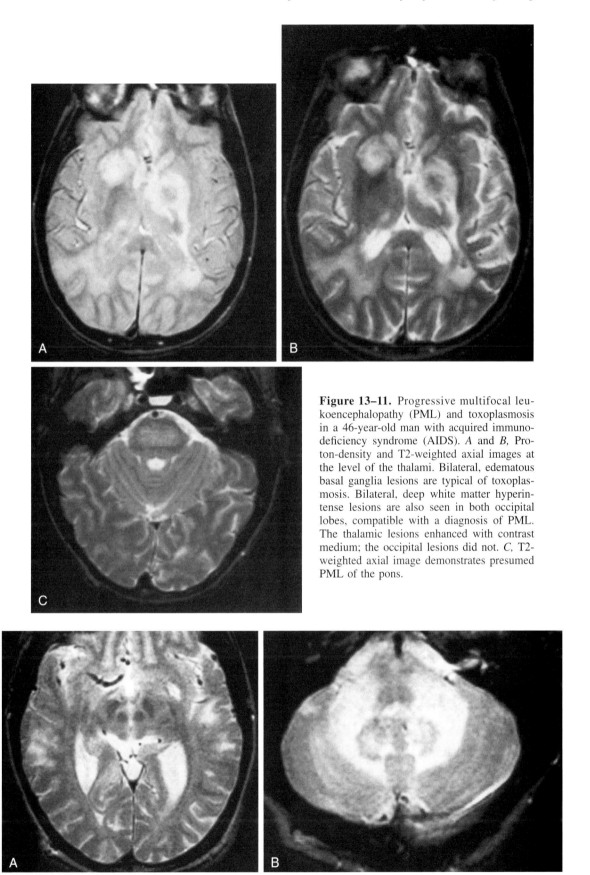

Figure 13–11. Progressive multifocal leukoencephalopathy (PML) and toxoplasmosis in a 46-year-old man with acquired immunodeficiency syndrome (AIDS). *A* and *B,* Proton-density and T2-weighted axial images at the level of the thalami. Bilateral, edematous basal ganglia lesions are typical of toxoplasmosis. Bilateral, deep white matter hyperintense lesions are also seen in both occipital lobes, compatible with a diagnosis of PML. The thalamic lesions enhanced with contrast medium; the occipital lesions did not. *C,* T2-weighted axial image demonstrates presumed PML of the pons.

Figure 13–12. Progressive multifocal leukoencephalopathy (PML) in a 44-year-old man with chronic lymphocytic leukemia. Cranial T2-weighted axial MR images. *A,* At the level of the midbrain, there are bilateral temporal white matter lesions, with complete sparing of the overlying cortex. *B,* Symmetrical, hyperintense cerebellar white matter lesions are seen in the brachium pontis and corpus medullaris. The diagnosis of PML was confirmed by biopsy.

In the appropriate clinical setting, MRI or CT can be of value in confirming the clinical suspicion of PML when radiographic findings are typical. Equally valuable is the exclusion of underlying tumor or abscess.

AIDS-Related Leukoencephalitis

It is now known that the human immunodeficiency virus (HIV) is not only lymphotrophic but also neurotropic. It replicates in multinucleated giant cells within the CNS, resulting eventually in demyelination. This demyelination is characterized by negligible edema and a lack of inflammation. Neuroimaging of HIV encephalitis, whether by CT or MRI, tends to lag behind the pathologic involvement. Generalized atrophy is the most common abnormality that is nonspecific. With more severe involvement, CT discloses symmetrical white matter hypodensity, usually seen bifrontally. There is no contrast enhancement or mass effect.

With MRI, there is greater sensitivity, with diffuse increase in signal on T2-weighted and proton-density images (Fig. 13–13). Patchy white matter lesions may become confluent and extensive; this may cause diagnostic confusion with PML, also commonly associated with AIDS.[60, 70] Patients with PML are usually much more symptomatic, with more rapid deterioration.

Toxic and Traumatic Encephalomyelopathies

Many toxic and traumatic processes may selectively damage or destroy the myelinated portions of the brain. Among the agents implicated are (1) gamma radiation, (2) various chemotherapeutic agents, (3) heavy metals, (4) chemical toxins, and (5) specific surgical lesions. The demyelination may result from two more agents acting in concert, such as methotrexate therapy combined with cranial irradiation.

Radiation-Induced Demyelination

Radiation to the brain may cause *radiation necrosis* (radionecrosis) or *diffuse leukoencephalopathy.* These two types differ in their clinical course and in their pathologic and radiographic appearance.

Radiation Necrosis

Radiation necrosis is characterized by coagulative destruction of the white matter, accompanied by fibrinoid necrosis of the capillary blood vessels. The lesion is the result of high-dose focal radiation therapy to the brain, usually appearing after a latent period of 4 months to several years. Characteristically, radionecrosis appears on CT scan as abnormal low-density white matter with mass effect and may have a higher density central core that enhances (Fig. 13–14).

MRI is more sensitive and specific than CT and shows prominent white matter edema on T2-weighted and proton-density images. A core of enhancing mass may be present, and the differential diagnosis from recurrent tumor may be difficult. Often the distinction can be made only by positron emission tomography (PET) or by magnetic resonance spectroscopy (MRS) to distinguish the metabolically active tumor from the inactive radiation necrosis. Stereotactic biopsy may be necessary in selected cases.

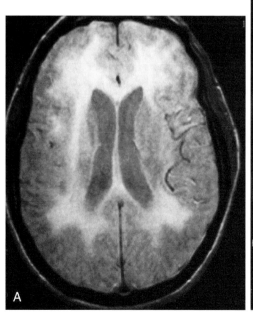
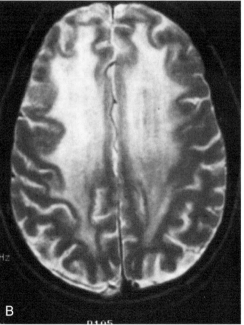

Figure 13–13. Human immunodeficiency virus encephalitis in a 39-year-old patient with acquired immunodeficiency syndrome (AIDS) and rapidly worsening dementia. *A* and *B,* Proton-density and T2-weighted axial MR images show widespread diffuse hyperintensity of the deep cerebral white matter. Not shown is similar involvement of the pons and mesencephalon.

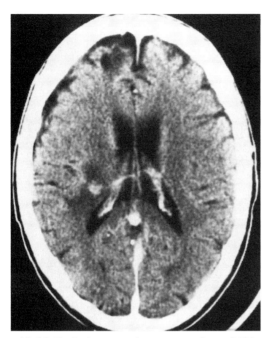

Figure 13–14. Radiation necrosis, contrast-enhanced CT scan. A small, enhancing focus within the right posterior corona radiata is surrounded by white matter lucency. (The right frontal pole encephalomalacia resulted from a previous biopsy establishing the diagnosis of intracranial lymphoma.) The differential diagnosis of the contrast-enhancing lesion includes infection or recurrent tumor. At autopsy, radiation necrosis was found without lymphoma or abscess.

Diffuse Radiation-Induced Leukoencephalopathy

Diffuse radiation-induced leukoencephalopathy is more common than radiation necrosis.[74, 87] This diffuse leukoencephalopathy may involve all visible cerebral white matter when whole brain irradiation has been given, or it may correspond closely to irradiated volumes after treatment for a solitary brain tumor.

CT scans show diffuse, low-density white matter without contrast enhancement and no mass effect. The surrounding cortical gray matter ribbon is preserved. Correspondingly, MRI shows abnormal signal intensity in the white matter on T2-weighted and proton-density images (Fig. 13–15). The lesions may start as small foci, which then coalesce to become symmetrical. Some of the most symmetrical white matter involvement in any disease category is seen in diffuse radiation-induced leukoencephalopathy.

Patients may have dementia or may have focal neurologic findings, but MRI is so sensitive that the lesions may be discovered incidentally during follow-up examinations of relatively asymptomatic individuals. In some patients, the changes are stable; in others, they may progress. Changes are more severe with advancing age and an increasing radiation dose.

Disseminated Necrotizing Leukoencephalopathy

Disseminated necrotizing leukoencephalopathy (DNL), or *subacute leukoencephalopathy*, closely related to radia-

tion necrosis, is an iatrogenic complication of intensive chemotherapy directed to CNS malignancy.[27] Responsible agents appear to be combined whole brain irradiation with chemotherapy, most commonly methotrexate.

DNL has been associated with multiagent chemotherapy without irradiation in such conditions as adult leukemia and bone marrow transplantation for breast cancer.[91] On pathologic examination, the lesions consist of discrete multifocal necrosis disseminated randomly in the white matter and becoming confluent and extensive in extreme cases.

CT and MRI findings are similar to those seen with postradiation encephalopathy (Fig. 13–16). In milder forms, CT and MRI show diffuse symmetrical white matter lesions similar to those seen with radiation alone.[62, 74] Again, as in radiation-induced injury, the most severe cases lead to swelling with ventricular compression and midline shift and to contrast enhancement.

Mineralizing Microangiopathy

Another sequela of radiation treatment and chemotherapy results in intracerebral calcifications, commonly located in the subcortical zones and basal ganglia, and, less commonly, in the cortex. These findings are usually associated with generalized atrophy and diffuse white matter disease, seen as lucency on CT scans and hyperintensity on MR images. This is one entity in which CT scanning may be more diagnostic, since MRI is relatively insensitive to the calcifications unless gradient techniques are used (Figs. 13–17 and 13–18).

Marchiafava-Bignami Disease

Marchiafava-Bignami disease (MBD), originally described in Italian alcoholic patients, is characterized by toxic demyelination of the corpus callosum and, frequently, by extension to the centrum semiovale.

Pathologically, the myelin loss may be striking and may be accompanied by axonal degeneration. Acute deterioration is common, but survival with little permanent deficit is possible. Both CT and MRI show prominent involvement of the corpus callosum, resulting in lucency on CT scans and hyperintensity on T2-weighted and proton-density MR images (Fig. 13–19). MRI is superior to CT in demonstrating the extracallosal sites of involvement.[16, 25, 75, 100]

Hypoxic-Ischemic Leukoencephalopathies

The white matter of the brain is susceptible to hypoxic-ischemic events and may be involved even when the insult is systemic and generalized. Thus, a leukoencephalopathy can be the end result of long-standing hypertension or a single hypotensive episode (e.g., perinatal hypoxia).[8, 11] These and other related disorders are considered in the following sections.

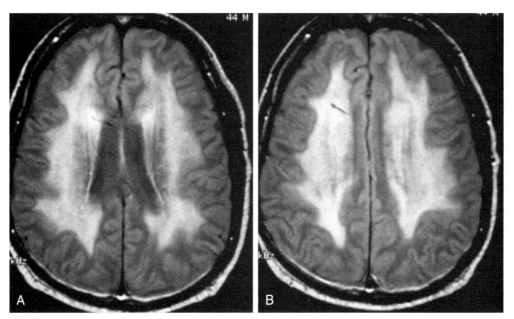

Figure 13–15. Leukoencephalopathy secondary to radiation and intraventricular methotrexate chemotherapy. *A* and *B*, Proton-density axial cranial MR image. There is extensive diffuse, confluent white matter hyperintensity.

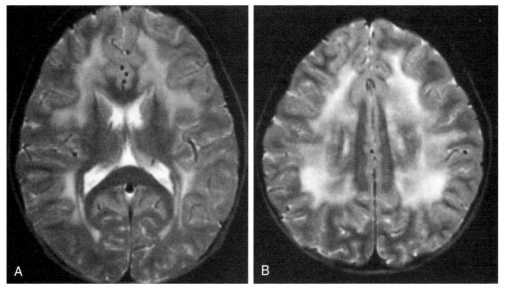

Figure 13–16. Leukoencephalopathy secondary to multiagent chemotherapy for acute lymphocytic leukemia without radiotherapy. *A* and *B*, T2-weighted axial cranial MR images show diffuse, mild hyperintensity in the deep white matter bilaterally. Despite the MR appearance, this patient had minimal neurologic signs and was doing well in school.

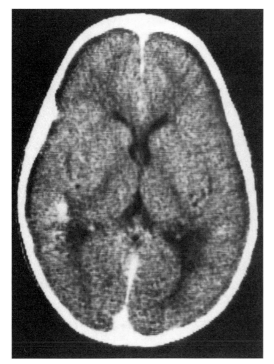

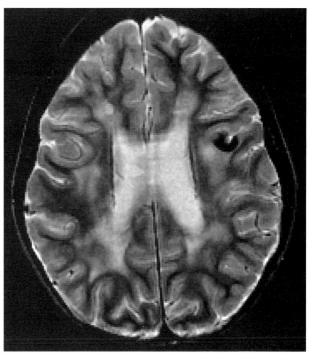

Figure 13–17. CT scan shows calcification with leukoencephalopathy (mineralizing microangiopathy). The patient is a 7-year-old girl who, 1 year previously, had received 55 Gy to the posterior fossa for a cerebellar astrocytoma. At the time of the scan, she was asymptomatic. The heavily calcified focus in the right parietotemporal region is typically situated at the interface between the cortex and white matter; the latter is abnormally lucent just medial to the calcification. Similar subtle changes are mirrored in the opposite hemisphere.

Figure 13–18. Diffuse necrotizing leukoencephalopathy (DNL) in a 20-year-old man with acute lymphoblastic leukemia several years after intrathecal methotrexate therapy and craniospinal irradiation. This T2-weighted axial MR image demonstrates widespread demyelination; there also is a focus of T2-weighted hypointensity in the left frontal deep cortex, indicating dystrophic calcification (mineralizing microangiopathy).

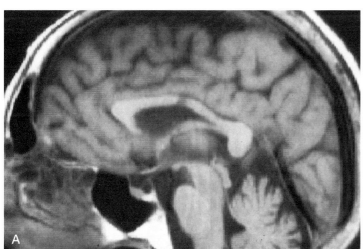

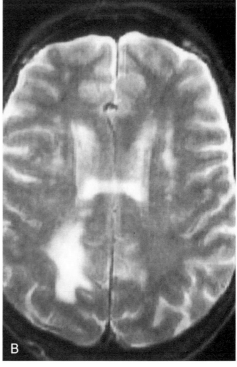

Figure 13–19. Marchiafava-Bignami disease. MRI demonstrates callosal and extracallosal demyelination. *A,* T1-weighted sagittal image of through-and-through demyelination focus in body of corpus callosum. *B,* T2-weighted axial scan with hyperintensities in corpus callosum as well as bilateral cerebral white matter.

Global Hypoperfusion Syndromes

Prolonged hypoxia with accompanying systemic hypotension and acidosis can cause selective injury to cerebral white matter. Common etiologic factors include drug overdose, cardiac and respiratory arrest, anesthesia accidents, profound hypoglycemia, strangulation, postoperative shock, carbon monoxide poisoning, status epilepticus, and vasospasm from a ruptured aneurysm.[14] Selective cerebral edema, elevated venous pressure, and structural peculiarities in the microvascularity of white matter have been proposed as causes for the apparently greater vulnerability of myelinated brain to hypoxic insults.

The damage to white matter ranges from myelinopathy to patchy or confluent frank necrosis. The severity of the lesion seems to correlate with the degree of systemic metabolic acidosis and systolic hypotension associated with the hypoxia.[42]

Lesions in cerebral cortex and basal ganglia are often observed in contiguity with the leukoencephalopathy. These changes are especially prominent in arterial boundary watershed zones, which may make differentiation from infarction difficult (Fig. 13–20). The gray matter, however, may be unaffected in the presence of severe white matter damage. Sparing of gray matter is particularly likely in so-called delayed hypoxic encephalopathy, observed in some patients who survive the initial insult and then develop subsequent neurologic signs.

The imaging appearance of global hypoperfusion states is therefore variable.[42] Symmetrical hypodensity of the white matter and lentiform nuclei has been reported in CT scans of patients after anoxia or cardiac arrest. Diffusion-weighted MRI can be of value in characterizing global cerebral anoxia and hypoxic-ischemic brain injury in neonates.[1, 98]

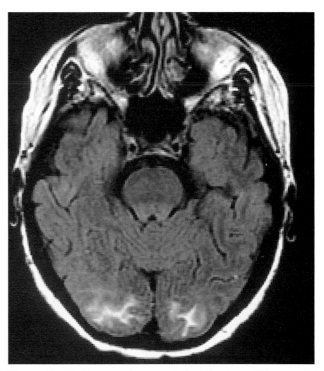

Figure 13–21. Hypertensive encephalopathy (reversible posterior leukoencephalopathy syndrome). T2-weighted axial MR scan shows symmetrical hyperintensity of occipital lobe white matter. The patient, a 52-year-old woman, experienced visual changes and acutely elevated blood pressure.

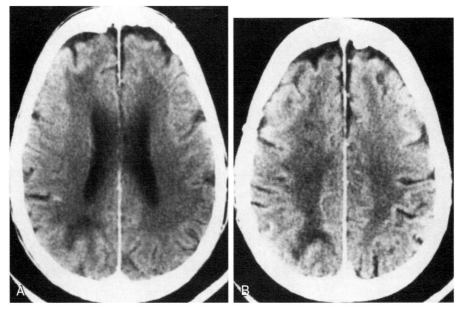

Figure 13–20. Deep watershed infarction mimicking primary leukoencephalopathy. Two CT images demonstrate right-sided white matter lesions, most prominent in the frontal and occipital region but confluent in the corona radiata. This represents ischemic leukoencephalopathy, secondary to acute deep watershed infarction. The CT scan had been normal 1 week previously at the onset of symptoms.

The following topics consider the CT and MRI findings in ischemia-related leukoencephalopathies. Primary gray matter (cortex and basal ganglia) lesions and syndromes are beyond the scope of this chapter and are not included. Even though some overlap exists with toxic encephalopathies, the major causative factor in the examples discussed here is vascular pathology.

Hypertensive Encephalopathy

An encephalopathy may develop in hypertensive patients with a rapidly rising blood pressure. This encephalopathy is caused by vascular alterations, which in turn lead to widespread cerebral edema, parenchymal microinfarcts, and even petechial hemorrhages. CT scans of patients with clinical hypertensive encephalopathy show extensive, symmetrical, well-defined hypodensity in the centrum semiovale, internal and external capsules, and periventricular white matter.[45, 69, 96] MR images are even more revealing, with T2-weighted and proton-density sequences more sensitive for the edema (Figs. 13–21 and 13–22).

Eclampsia

A specialized type of hypertensive disorder occurs in pregnancy, usually in the last trimester. Neurologic complications may include seizures, focal neurologic deficits, and even decreased level of consciousness. Most commonly, the posterior hemispheres are involved, often in a symmetrical fashion. On CT scans, the white matter shows symmetrical decreased density[26]; on MR images, long repetition time (TR) images show hyperintensity in the deep white matter of the occipital lobes.[7, 24] In other cases, scattered subcortical white matter lesions may also appear, and even basal ganglia involvement has been reported. Fortunately, with aggressive clinical treatment, most patients recover (Figs. 13–23 and 13–24).

A similar mechanism may explain the *reversible posterior leukoencephalopathy syndrome*, which affects some

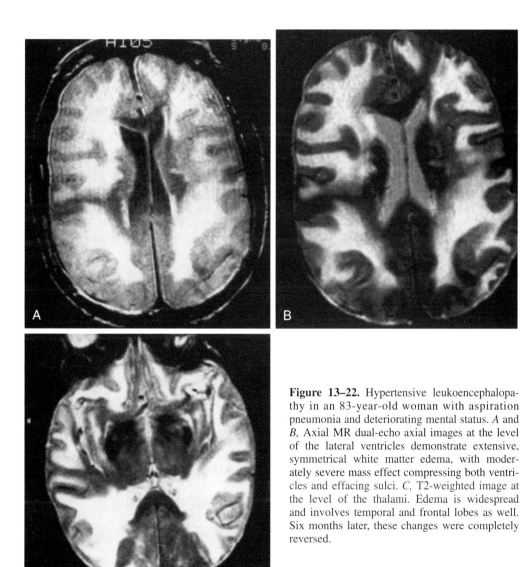

Figure 13–22. Hypertensive leukoencephalopathy in an 83-year-old woman with aspiration pneumonia and deteriorating mental status. *A* and *B,* Axial MR dual-echo axial images at the level of the lateral ventricles demonstrate extensive, symmetrical white matter edema, with moderately severe mass effect compressing both ventricles and effacing sulci. *C,* T2-weighted image at the level of the thalami. Edema is widespread and involves temporal and frontal lobes as well. Six months later, these changes were completely reversed.

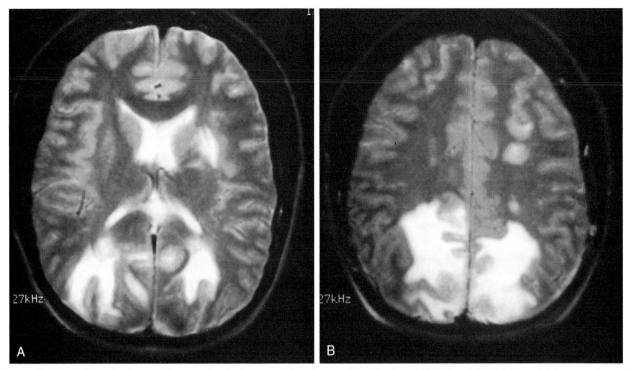

Figure 13–23. Eclampsia (reversible posterior leukoencephalopathy syndrome). *A* and *B*, T2-weighted MR axial images show the predominantly occipital white matter swelling. Cortical and left basal ganglia involvement are present.

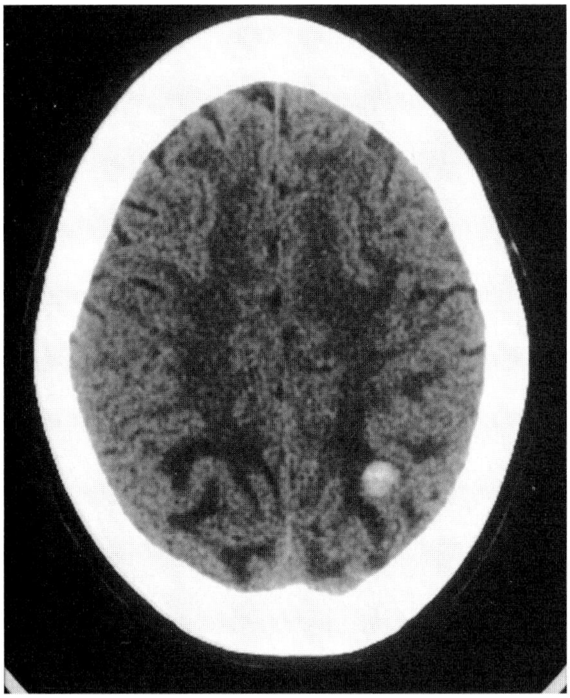

Figure 13–24. HELLP syndrome (hemolysis, elevated liver enzymes, low platelets), a severe form of eclampsia. Axial CT scan demonstrates bilateral occipital vasogenic edema and a small subcortical hemorrhage.

patients treated with cyclosporine or combination chemotherapy.[13, 36]

Binswanger's Disease

Binswanger's disease, or *subcortical arteriosclerotic encephalopathy* (SAE), is another ischemia-related leukoencephalopathy. It is now considered to be a diffuse or multifocal destructive process in the central white matter that results from generalized ischemic or vascular conditions.

Pathologically, the symmetrical and diffuse white matter lesions are associated with severe arteriosclerosis of the small penetrating arteries, which are thickened, hyalinized, stenotic, or even occluded. In most patients, multiple lacunar infarcts are also present in the basal ganglia, thalami, and pons (*état lacunaire*). The lacunar state in white matter (*état criblé*) may be the same disorder or at least a variant thereof.[89]

In affected patients, CT reveals a diffuse, severe, incompletely symmetrical hypodensity of the central white matter, especially prominent in the frontal lobes and the centrum semiovale.[29, 103] MRI changes are much more striking, consisting of subcortical and periventricular lesions visible on fluid-attenuated inversion recovery (FLAIR), T2-weighted, and proton-density sequences. The areas are irregular, commonly grouped around the frontal and occipital horns, and in the centrum semiovale. Moderate, generalized cerebral atrophy is invariably present, and lacunar infarcts in the basal ganglia and thalami are common.

Although logical proof is lacking in many instances,

since the disease is nonfatal and chronic, often lasting for 10 years or more, sufficient case descriptions confirm that at autopsy some of these patients do have the typical neuropathologic features of SAE.[48, 89] The radiologic diagnosis of SAE may be suspected if diffuse or confluent hypodensity of the white matter, moderate cerebral atrophy, and lacunar infarcts are seen on CT or MRI scans of a hypertensive patient with clinical features of the disease. An interesting genetically transmitted form of the disease is known as *familial arteriopathic leukoencephalopathy,* or *CADASIL* (cerebral autosomal dominant arteriopathy with strokes, ischemia, and leukoencephalopathy) (Fig. 13–25).[28]

A milder white matter change may be noted in some elderly individuals.[32] These foci of increased MRI signal intensity are located in the immediate periventricular white matter extending from the frontal horns along the bodies of the lateral ventricles and also involving the trigones. This white matter abnormality is smooth and continuous and may be thin to more than a few millimeters thick. This entity appears to be different from ischemic leukoencephalopathy, since it is found in normal individuals, is accentuated with age, and is not necessarily associated with dementia or clinical symptomatology. Lacunar infarcts are not usually present. Rather than demyelination, the most likely explanation for this white

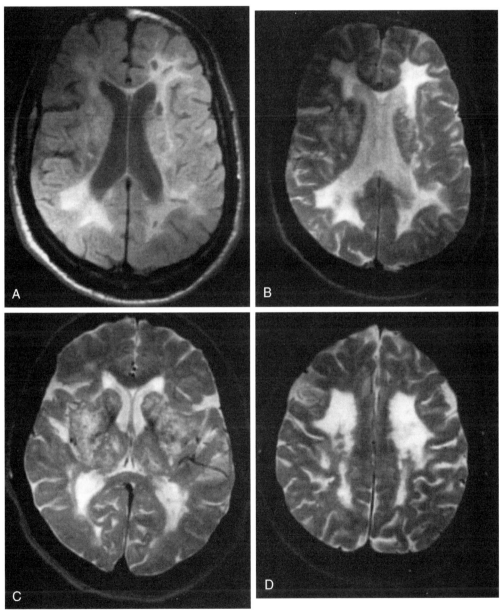

Figure 13–25. Familial arteriopathic leukoencephalopathy in two family members who were nonhypertensive with dementia. Cranial MR images are shown. Cerebral autosomal dominant arteriopathy with strokes, ischemia, and leukoencephalopathy (CADASIL) was confirmed at autopsy. *A* and *B,* Proton-density and T2-weighted axial images of diffuse symmetrical demyelination with cystic components in a 52-year-old man. *C* and *D,* T2-weighted axial MR images demonstrate extensive cribriform hyperintense signal in the basal ganglia and confluent demyelination in the centrum semiovale in a 70-year-old woman.

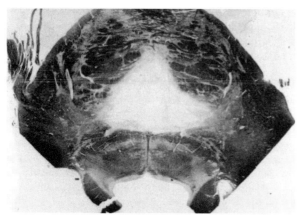

Figure 13–26. Central pontine myelinolysis (CPM), pathologic specimen. The patient is middle-aged, with chronic alcoholism and progressively impaired mental status. At autopsy, the classic triangular demyelinative lesion of CPM was found.

matter change is an aging process resulting in subependymal accumulation of fluid.

Central Pontine Myelinolysis

Central pontine myelinolysis (CPM) is a syndrome of acute pontine demyelination. Most patients with this disorder have a history of alcoholism associated with hyponatremia and exacerbated by overhydration and administration of diuretic medications. Other etiologic factors include systemic hypotension, cerebral edema, and drug-induced, inappropriate antidiuretic hormone secretion. The typical clinical presentation is a rapidly progressive, pontine-level, neurologic deficit (i.e., quadriparesis and pseudobulbar symptoms) that often progresses to a "locked-in" syn-

drome. Permanent and irreversible neurologic damage may result if appropriate treatment is not instituted early in the course. Partial or full recovery has been reported.[68]

Pathologically, the classic picture is edematous demyelination of the central ventral pons, with characteristic sparing of the tegmentum (Fig. 13–26). The demyelination may extend cephalocaudad from the superior cerebellar peduncle to the inferior olive. It is postulated that either the grid arrangement of descending and crossing tracts in the pons or perhaps its vulnerable vascularity is responsible for the peculiar focality of the lesion.

Although CT scans of patients with clinically apparent CPM may show central pontine radiolucency,[85] MRI is much more sensitive and is the imaging method of choice. Even on T1-weighted images, a low-signal-intensity lesion in the central pons may be seen (Fig. 13–27); however, T2-weighted images are much more preferable. The classic appearance is a triangle- or trident-shaped, central pontine hyperintensity seen in the axial plane (Fig. 13–28; see Fig. 13–27).

In more severe disease, almost the entire central pons may be involved with only a rim of normal signal around it (see Fig. 13–28). Peripheral contrast enhancement has been reported but is not a prominent imaging feature. The abnormality may regress with clinical treatment, leaving little or no residuum.

The differential diagnosis must include a variety of brain stem lesions, including ADEM, vasculitis, MS, Lyme disease, and, in rare cases, brain stem tumor.[37, 56] The clinical setting and the central symmetry of the lesion are usually sufficient for the imaging diagnosis of CPM.

Leukodystrophies and Dysmyelinating Disorders

The term *leukodystrophy* includes a heterogeneous group of heredofamilial diseases characterized by meta-

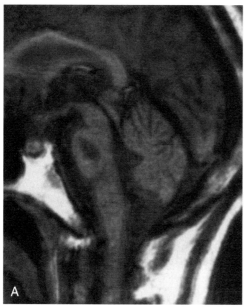

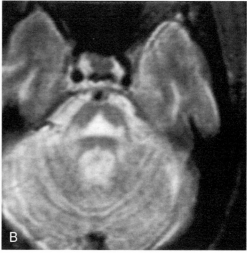

Figure 13–27. Central pontine myelinolysis (CPM) in a 56-year-old man. *A,* Midsagittal T1-weighted cranial MR image shows a triangular hypointense lesion in the midpons. *B,* Axial T2-weighted MR image at the midpontine level. Note the classic trident-shaped hyperintense lesion, characteristic of CPM.

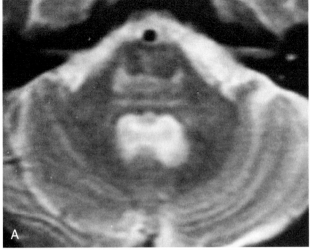
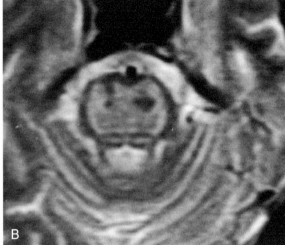
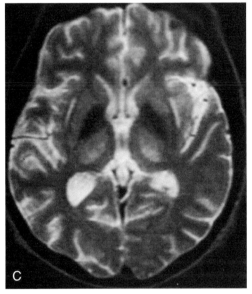

Figure 13–28. Central pontine and extrapontine myelinolysis in a 45-year-old man. *A,* T2-weighted axial MR image through the pons at the level of the brachium pontis shows a symmetric, trident-shaped hyperintense lesion of the pons. *B,* T2-weighted image through the upper pons shows that the lesion is occupying virtually the entire pons, leaving only a rim and a few islands of normal intensity. *C,* T2-weighted axial image at the level of the foramen of Monro demonstrates abnormally increased symmetric, signal intensity in the thalami and external capsules bilaterally.

bolic defects that principally affect the CNS myelin sheath. The concept of *dysmyelination* was introduced by Poser to delineate those diseases in which myelin does not form properly, is delayed or arrested in development, or is not maintained. When *demyelination* (myelinoclasis) occurs, normal myelin is destroyed, as in MS.

Included in the leukodystrophies are the following major subtypes:

• Adrenoleukodystrophy
• Metachromatic leukodystrophy
• Globoid cell leukodystrophy (Krabbe's disease)
• Neutral fat (sudanophilic and orthochromatic) leukodystrophy
• Mitochondrial disorders (Leigh's disease, MELAS syndrome, MERRF, Kearns-Sayre syndrome) (see "Mitochondrial Cytopathies" later)
• Aminoacidopathies (maple syrup urine disease, phenylketonuria, Wilson's disease)
• Mucopolysaccharidoses (Hurler's syndrome)
• Megaloencephalic leukodystrophies (Canavan's disease, Alexander's disease)

Adrenoleukodystrophy

Adrenoleukodystrophy (ALD) is a hereditary dysmyelinating disease associated with adrenocortical insufficiency and melanoderma. Its primary clinical manifestation is progressive neurologic dysfunction. The disease, caused by a deficiency of the enzyme acyl-coenzyme A synthetase, is transmitted as an X-linked recessive gene and is therefore almost exclusively confined to males, although a few sporadic cases involving females do occur.

The onset is usually in childhood, with characteristic signs of progressive behavioral aberrations, visual loss, and ataxia; there may be no clinical signs of adrenal hypofunction. The patient can live for several years, but a vegetative state leading to death is the almost inevitable outcome. Rare cases of remission, long-term survival, and response to steroid medications have been reported.[93, 102] Various subtypes involve multiple enzymatic defects, including adrenomyeloneuropathy, affecting the spinal cord and peripheral nerves, and a neonatal form.

Pathologically, the cerebral lesions are most severe in the parietal, occipital, and posterior temporal white matter, invariably sparing the overlying cortex. The lesions are confluent and often extend in continuity across the corpus callosum. The fornix, hippocampal commissure, and posterior cingulum are also usually affected. Whereas the disease is symmetrical and widespread posteriorly, frontal involvement is more asymmetrical and variable. Cerebellar white matter lesions are common.

Histopathologically, the white matter lesions of ALD are interesting for their significant inflammatory changes and for the sequential zones of involvement in a caudal-rostral distribution. The frontal advancing zone of demye-

lination is followed closely by a zone of inflammatory response, in turn followed by the largest zone of complete destruction of white matter. ALD is one of the dysmyelinating diseases with a characteristic imaging appearance.[19, 61, 88]

Lesions demonstrable by CT and MRI correlate closely with the known neuropathologic alterations (Fig. 13–29). MRI is more sensitive than CT and shows earlier changes (Fig. 13–30).[43] The typical appearance is symmetrical white matter hyperintensity on T2-weighted images in the parieto-occipital regions, adjacent to the atria of the lateral

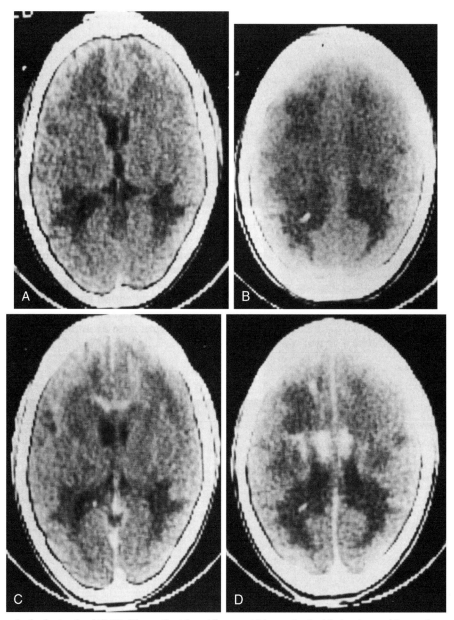

Figure 13–29. Adrenoleukodystrophy (ALD). The patient is a 13-year-old boy who had behavior problems since age 7 years and who recently experienced seizures. *A* and *B,* Precontrast CT images show white matter lucency surrounding the occipital horns and trigones of the lateral ventricles. Less severe white matter abnormalities are present bilaterally in the frontal lobes. *C* and *D,* Corresponding postcontrast sections demonstrate the peripheral serpiginous enhancement around the frontal lobe lesions and crossing the rostrum of the corpus callosum. Note the lack of contrast enhancement in the older, "burned out" posterior lesions. (Courtesy of Valley Radiologic Associates of San Jose, Calif.)

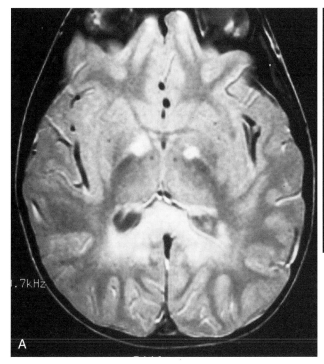

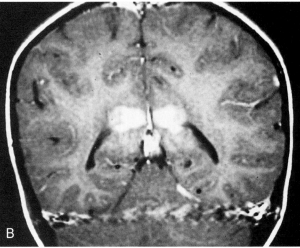

Figure 13–30. X-linked classical adrenoleukodystrophy (ALD) in a 5-year-old boy. *A,* Axial proton-density image with typical demyelination of the posterior corpus callosum and contiguous deep parietal white matter. Note also the bilateral corticospinal tract involvement. *B,* Note contrast enhancement of the splenium of the corpus callosum on the coronal T1-weighted image.

ventricles and splenium. These appear as hypointense lesions on T1-weighted images and as lucency on CT images. The overlying gray matter is entirely spared.

With contrast infusion, serpiginous, garland-shaped enhancement may be visible in the anteriormost periphery of the lesions.[55] This finding may be subtle early in the course of the disease. Mild to moderate ventricular dilatation may result from the damage caused by the disease. If the patient survives for several years, the extensive demyelinated lesions shrink, causing gross central and peripheral atrophy. Contrast enhancement is not seen at this later stage of disease.

ALD may be difficult to diagnose with confidence on MR or CT scans if imaging is performed very early or very late in the disease, and variant appearances have been described with more or less involvement of the frontal lobes. At the usual time of diagnostic workup several weeks to months after the appearance of the first neurologic symptoms, however, the combination of clinical and imaging features should be highly suggestive.

Metachromatic Leukodystrophy

Metachromatic leukodystrophy (MLD) is the most common of all the familial leukodystrophies. *Metachromatic* refers to the histologic staining characteristic caused by abnormal accumulations of sulfatides in the white matter. Sulfatide excess is caused by a deficiency of the enzyme arylsulfatase.

The disease is subclassified either clinically or biochemically. The clinical groups include (1) infantile, (2) juvenile, (3) late juvenile, and (4) adult forms. The biochemical variants are (1) arylsulfatase A deficiency (classic MLD) and (2) multiple sulfatase deficiencies. Inheritance is autosomal recessive; the diagnosis is confirmed by demon-

stration of absent or low levels of sulfatase in urine, leukocytes, or cultured fibroblasts.

In the most common form of MLD, symptoms begin in the second or third year of life and progress insidiously. Irritability, frequent crying, and anorexia herald the subsequent manifestations of hypotonicity and lack of truncal control. Further deterioration is accompanied by hypertonicity, extensor postural abnormalities, and intellectual decline. In the later stages of the disease, the patient may be blind, spastic, and unresponsive.

At autopsy the surface of the brain appears atrophic, the white matter is shrunken and sclerotic, and the ventricles are dilated. Changes in the peripheral nerve myelin explain the polyneuropathy often noted in MLD.

Although the diagnosis of MLD is usually established by enzymatic assay for arylsulfatase A deficiency or by peripheral nerve biopsy, MRI and CT have proved useful in suggesting the presence of leukodystrophy in early, undiagnosed cases and in excluding other processes, such as hydrocephalus or intracranial masses.

The typical CT appearance of MLD is a symmetrical lucency of the white matter, especially prominent in the centrum semiovale and the corpus callosum (Fig. 13–31).[94] There is no evidence of inflammation or contrast enhancement, and the cortical gray matter is spared.

MRI shows symmetrical areas of hypointensity on T1-weighted and hyperintensity on T2-weighted images (Fig. 13–32).[4, 40] Although the lesions are symmetrical, they may be patchy and there may be cerebellar white matter involvement as well. In the later stages, considerable atrophic dilatation of the lateral ventricles appears. Atrophy may be the only finding in late adult onset cases.

Although MLD has one of the more nonspecific appearances of a leukodystrophy, the diagnosis is usually considered from the combination of clinical and imaging appearances and can then be confirmed by a biochemical analysis.

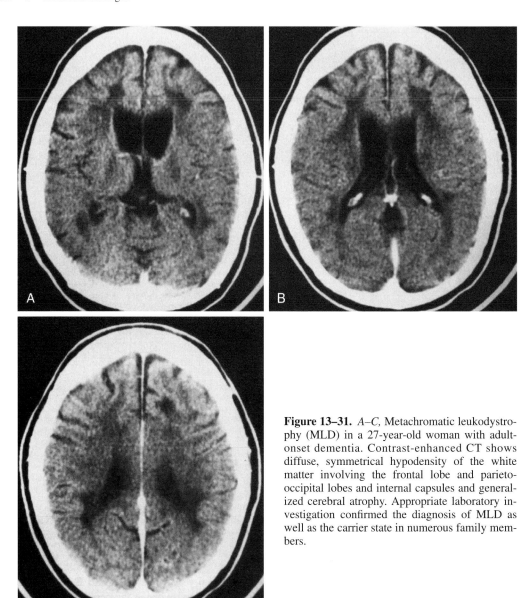

Figure 13–31. *A–C,* Metachromatic leukodystrophy (MLD) in a 27-year-old woman with adult-onset dementia. Contrast-enhanced CT shows diffuse, symmetrical hypodensity of the white matter involving the frontal lobe and parieto-occipital lobes and internal capsules and generalized cerebral atrophy. Appropriate laboratory investigation confirmed the diagnosis of MLD as well as the carrier state in numerous family members.

Globoid Cell Leukodystrophy

Globoid cell leukodystrophy (GLD), or *Krabbe's disease* (globoid body leukodystrophy), is a rare dysmyelinating disorder that is inherited as an autosomal recessive gene.

The clinical course of the disease may closely mimic that of MLD, with irritability and hypotonicity progressing to spasticity, myoclonus, and seizures. Unlike MLD, the onset of symptoms is usually earlier (<6 months of age), and the duration of the illness is shorter. Peripheral neuropathy is prominent in both diseases, a feature not present in most other cerebral lipidoses.

The deficient enzyme in GLD is β-galactocerebrosidase. This deficiency results in excessive accumulation of galactocerebrosides in myelin, found in the so-called globoid cells that are characteristic of the disease.

At autopsy, the brain of a GLD victim is shrunken because of the diffuse central myelin abnormality. The entire cerebral white matter, including the centrum semiovale, internal capsule, pons, and cerebellum, is firm, rubbery, and grayish, although areas of cystic softening may be present within. The subcortical U-shaped fibers and gray matter are unaffected. In the earlier stages of the disease, the white matter lesions would presumably be less significant. The histologic picture is dominated by the presence of globoid cells and complete myelin destruction with loss of oligodendroglia.

The CT findings in GLD range from white matter lucency to diffuse cerebral atrophy (Fig. 13–33).[3, 44] Well-defined and symmetrical decreased attenuation in the central white matter may be especially prominent in the frontal periventricular region and in the centrum semiovale.

This appearance is much more characteristic of the disease if accompanied by increased density of the thalami,

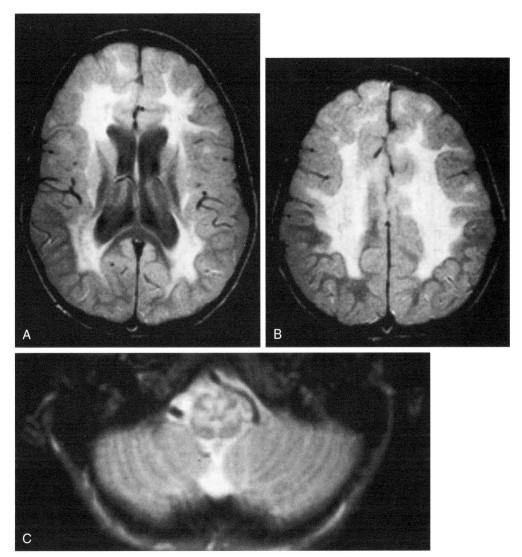

Figure 13–32. Metachromatic leukodystrophy (MLD) in a 6-year-old boy. *A* and *B,* Cranial MR axial proton-density images show severe demyelination involving the deep white matter of both hemispheres with well-defined borders at the subcortical U-fiber junction. The corpus callosum and internal capsules retain some normal hypointense myelin signal. *C,* Axial T2-weighted MR image at the level of the medulla depicts significant demyelination.

caudate nuclei, and cerebellar cortex. MRI shows prolongation of T2-weighted signal in the deep white matter and thalamic and cerebellar white matter hyperintensity (Fig. 13–34).[18] Contrast enhancement has not been demonstrated. In later stages of the disease, cerebral atrophy may be the predominant imaging feature.

Sudanophilic (Neutral Fat and Orthochromatic) Leukodystrophies

The sudanophilic (neutral fat and orthochromatic) leukodystrophies are difficult to classify. All cases show the accumulation of liberated sudanophilic myelin breakdown products. Several diseases of both sporadic and familial origin may lead to this end. The continuing advances in neurochemistry and neuropathology have served to separate and reclassify some of the entities. It is hoped that, eventually, the neutral fat leukodystrophies will be more accu-

rately characterized. Of these, *Pelizaeus-Merzbacher disease* has been studied extensively, and its imaging features are discussed here. A remaining, less homogeneous group of sudanophilic leukodystrophies is poorly understood and is considered briefly.

Pelizaeus-Merzbacher Disease

Pelizaeus-Merzbacher (PM) disease is a rare familial leukodystrophy in which the affected child or infant shows progressive signs of neurologic dysfunction similar to the signs of MLD or GLD. Ataxia, hyperreflexia, seizures, and mental deterioration eventually result in death.

The laboratory examination is only of limited value and mainly serves to exclude MLD and GLD, since enzyme assays are normal. The definitive diagnosis rests on histologic examination of the affected brain. In PM disease, there is extensive and severe demyelination, with a peculiar, unique, patchy, tigroid appearance. Sudanophilic

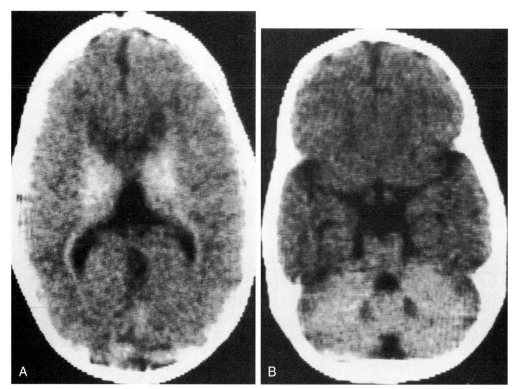

Figure 13–33. Globoid cell leukodystrophy (GLD), or Krabbe's disease, in a 3-month-old girl. Two representative CT sections disclose relative density of the cerebellum, thalami, and periventricular regions. Attenuation measurements of these regions confirm a slightly higher density than in the normal cortex. The remainder of the brain shows uniform attenuation without white matter lucency. This is a representative appearance for early GLD, with later scans usually showing minimal white matter changes but severe cortical atrophy.

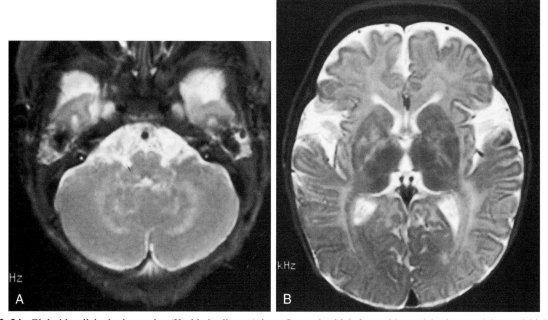

Figure 13–34. Globoid cell leukodystrophy (Krabbe's disease) in a 5-month-old infant with total body spasticity and high levels of protein in the cerebrospinal fluid. T2-weighted axial MR images. *A,* Abnormal high intensity cerebellar white matter changes. *B,* There is both white matter generalized hyperintensity as well as early T2 hyperintensity in the deep gray matter nuclei (lenticular nuclei, thalami).

breakdown products are present, but inflammation and metachromasia are absent.

The CT appearance of PM disease is nonspecific, with low density in the central white matter and with variable degrees of white matter atrophy. This pattern is diagnostic for a leukodystrophy but is not distinguishable from MLD or GLD by CT alone. On MR images, however, the predominant appearance is lack of myelination without definite evidence of white matter destruction (Fig. 13–35).[39, 64] Therefore, the brain retains the appearance of a newborn with distinct absence of myelination. Barkovich and colleagues suggest that this absence of myelination is specific for PM disease.[5] Because CT scans may be normal in early stages,[82] MRI is recommended as the imaging modality of choice whenever this or other leukodystrophies are suspected.

Cockayne's Syndrome

Cockayne's syndrome is a complex, hereditary, autosomal recessive demyelinating disorder with clinical features of dwarfism, microcephaly, retinal atrophy, deafness, and progeria (accelerated aging). Basal ganglia calcifications are a known neuropathologic feature of Cockayne's syndrome and can be detected on CT scans. The few MRI reports suggest that the changes are similar to those in PM disease, with the added feature of calcification in the basal ganglia manifesting as decreased signal intensity (Fig. 13–36). The combination of demyelination and basal ganglia calcification may therefore be helpful in the imaging of this entity.

Spongiform Encephalopathy (Canavan's Disease)

Familial spongy degeneration of the CNS (Canavan's disease) is a well-documented disease affecting infants of Ashkenazi Jewish extraction, transmitted as an autosomal recessive trait. Symptoms usually begin at 1 to 3 months of age, and the patient usually dies before the age of 4.

The infants have severe motor and mental deterioration, accompanied by hypotonia, decorticate posturing, and blindness. Progressive megalencephaly caused by enlarge-

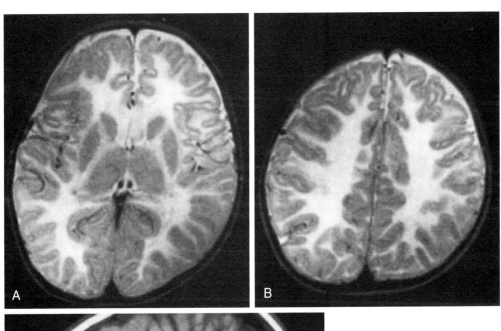

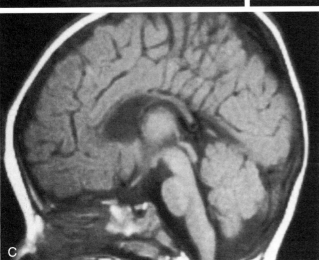

Figure 13–35. Pelizaeus-Merzbacher disease (sudanophilic leukodystrophy) in a 1-year-old with marked retardation, abnormal eye movements, and hypotonia. Cranial MR images at age 1 year. *A* and *B*, Axial T2-weighted MR images. Profound hypomyelination. Note the complete absence of myelination in the internal capsule, corpus callosum, and hemispheric white matter. *C*, Midsagittal T1-weighted image. The corpus callosum is notably underdeveloped, and a normal, hyperintense myelin signal is absent.

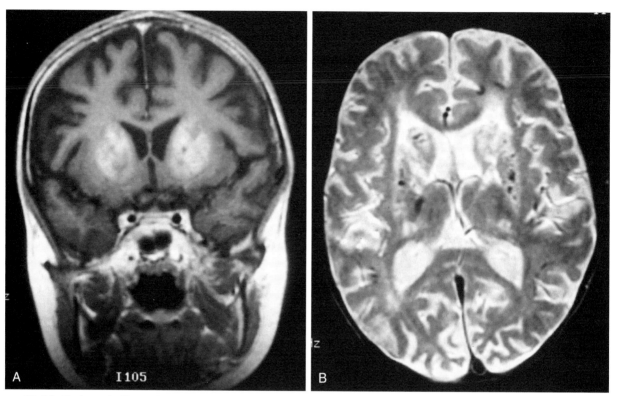

Figure 13–36. Cockayne's disease in an 11-year-old boy. *A,* T1-weighted coronal MR image demonstrates the prominent basal ganglia hyperintensity, presumably T1 shortening caused by extensive calcification. *B,* T2-weighted axial MR image, with the findings of atrophy, generalized demyelination, and signal dropout in basal ganglia from calcifications.

ment of the brain is an important differential diagnostic feature, since there are few other leukodystrophies (e.g., fibrinoid leukodystrophy, or *Alexander's disease*) in which macrocephaly is found.

The enzymatic defect in Canavan's disease is a deficiency of *N*-aspartoacylase, and the disease is classified as a metabolic disorder.

Widespread sponginess of the cerebral myelin, more pronounced in the outer zone of white matter and also affecting the subcortical U-shaped fibers and deep cortical layers, is noted pathologically. No abnormal myelin-breakdown products, globoid cells, or inflammatory changes are present.

The edematous sponginess of the white matter causes a characteristically low radiographic attenuation on CT so that it stands out in relief from the relatively unaffected gray matter (Fig. 13–37). A similar finding on MR images is extremely widespread and symmetrical low intensity on T1-weighted images, and even more prominent high signal on T2-weighted sequences.[54] Canavan's disease shows some of the most extensive white matter abnormalities, and in a child with progressive megalencephaly this can be almost pathognomonic of the disease. In very late stages, atrophic dilatation is seen, but the white matter abnormality remains. MRI also shows involvement of brain stem and cerebellum, which is difficult to identify with CT.

Fibrinoid Leukodystrophy (Alexander's Disease)

Alexander's disease, a very rare sporadic dysmyelinating disease, is a form of spongy sclerosis, similar to spongi-

form encephalopathy (Canavan's disease), in that there is megalencephaly. The distinguishing feature of fibrinoid leukodystrophy is the histologic feature of fibrinoid astroglia changes, the so-called Rosenthal fibers. The demyelination involves almost the entire cerebral white matter.

Changes on CT and MR images are widespread but have a predilection for the frontal lobes, which may help to distinguish the entity from Canavan's disease.[79] In addition, significant cystic change is a late feature in the frontal white matter. Contrast enhancement is rare but has been reported[35] (Fig. 13–38). Atrophy is notable in later stages.

Miscellaneous Neurodegenerative Disorders

Various rare hereditary and spontaneous neurodegenerative diseases may cause pathologic white matter changes that are visible on MR and CT scans.[33] A brief review of some of the more important entities follows.

Gangliosidoses

Tay-Sachs disease (GM₂ gangliosidosis) is associated with a form of dysmyelination. The loss of myelin cannot be accounted for solely on the basis of secondary wallerian degeneration. There is an abnormality of myelin sphingolipid metabolism, even though Tay-Sach's disease is classified not as leukodystrophy but as a lipidosis.

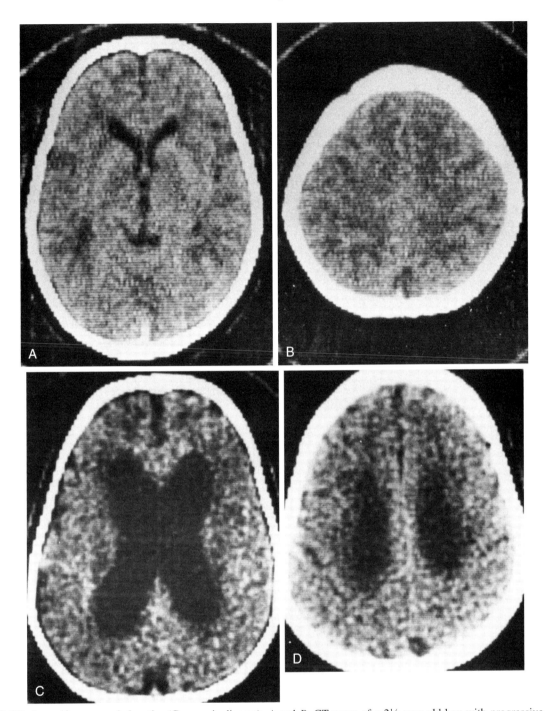

Figure 13–37. Spongiform encephalopathy (Canavan's disease). *A* and *B,* CT scans of a 2½-year-old boy with progressive neurologic deterioration and an enlarging head. There is diffuse, symmetrical, generalized lucency of the white matter. *C* and *D,* A repeated CT scan performed 2 years later, when the patient was 4½ years old and in a vegetative state. Significant ventricular dilatation has supervened. The white matter has become shrunken, resulting in central cerebral atrophy. At this final stage of the disease, the CT appearance is nonspecific. (*A–D,* From Moss AA, Goldberg I [eds]: Computed Tomography, Ultrasound, and X-ray: An Integrated Approach. San Francisco, University of California, San Francisco, Department of Radiology, 1980.)

Macrocephaly and diminished attenuation of the entire cerebral white matter have been reported on CT scans in patients with GM_1 and GM_2 gangliosidoses.[4]

With MRI, deep white matter demyelination may be prominent; thalami may show changes consistent with calcification. No abnormal contrast enhancement is described (Fig. 13–39).

Mitochondrial Cytopathies[38]

Leigh's disease (subacute necrotizing encephalomyelopathy) is a rare, inherited disorder in which multiple biochemical defects are found. The most striking neuropathologic change is symmetrical vacuolation of the basal ganglia, the brain stem, the cortex, and, to a lesser degree,

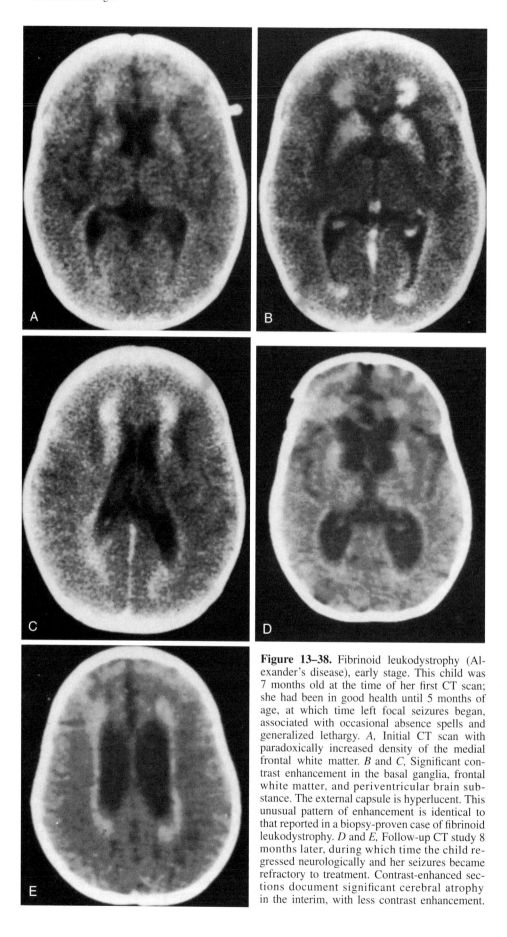

Figure 13–38. Fibrinoid leukodystrophy (Alexander's disease), early stage. This child was 7 months old at the time of her first CT scan; she had been in good health until 5 months of age, at which time left focal seizures began, associated with occasional absence spells and generalized lethargy. *A,* Initial CT scan with paradoxically increased density of the medial frontal white matter. *B* and *C,* Significant contrast enhancement in the basal ganglia, frontal white matter, and periventricular brain substance. The external capsule is hyperlucent. This unusual pattern of enhancement is identical to that reported in a biopsy-proven case of fibrinoid leukodystrophy. *D* and *E,* Follow-up CT study 8 months later, during which time the child regressed neurologically and her seizures became refractory to treatment. Contrast-enhanced sections document significant cerebral atrophy in the interim, with less contrast enhancement.

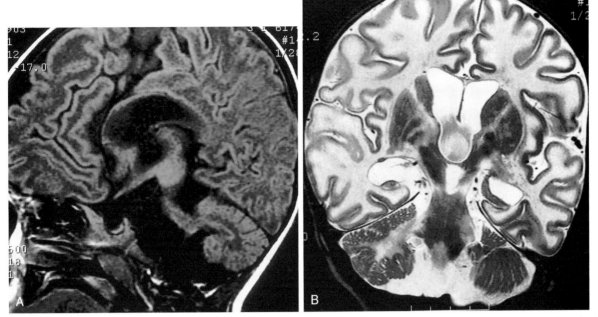

Figure 13–39. Tay-Sachs disease (hexosaminidase deficiency) in a 3-year-old girl with megalencephaly. *A,* T1-weighted sagittal MR image shows generalized white matter hypoattenuation and extreme hypogenesis of the corpus callosum (a nonspecific finding). *B,* T2-weighted axial MR shows extreme demyelination of virtually all white matter as well as characteristic T2 prolongation in thalami and lenticular nuclei.

the white matter. Low attenuation in the basal ganglia, brain stem, or central white matter may be seen on CT scans but is much better delineated on T2-weighted MR images (Fig. 13–40).[15, 17, 86] The most characteristic foci of demyelination are in the lentiform nuclei, the cerebral peduncles, the periaqueductal gray matter, the pons, and the medulla. Contrast enhancement may be seen in the acute stages.

Other mitochondrial cytopathies that have shown abnor-

malities on imaging are *MELAS syndrome* (mitochondrial myopathy, encephalopathy, lactic acidosis, and strokes), *MERRF* (myoclonic epilepsy with ragged red fibers), and *Kearns-Sayre syndrome* (Figs. 13–41 and 13–42).[73, 99]

Aminoacidopathies

Aminoacidopathies constitute another class of neurodegenerative disorders. Heritable disorders of amino acid

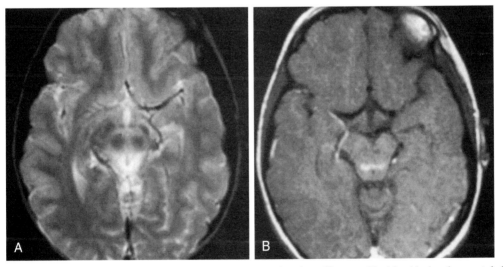

Figure 13–40. Leigh's disease (subacute necrotizing encephalomyelopathy) in a 10-year-old girl with developmental delay and slow neurologic deterioration. *A* and *B,* Initial MR scans. *C* and *D,* Follow-up scan 3 years later. *A,* T2-weighted axial MR image at the level of the midbrain. Hyperintensity of the entire mesencephalic tectum is visible, with lesser involvement of the cerebral peduncles. *B,* Postgadolinium-enhanced, T1-weighted image at the same level demonstrates symmetrical enhancement just anterior to the aqueduct.

Illustration continued on following page

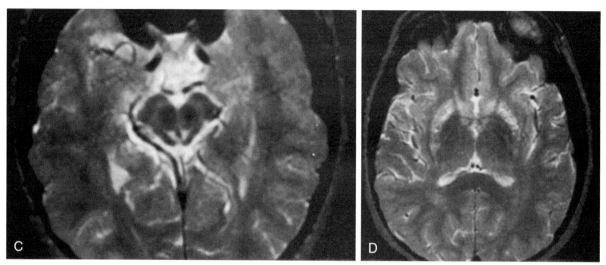

Figure 13–40. *Continued. C,* T2-weighted axial image at the midbrain level. The previously seen hyperintensities have resolved almost completely, leaving only small periaqueductal foci. *D,* There is residual persistent hyperintensity in the putamina bilaterally.

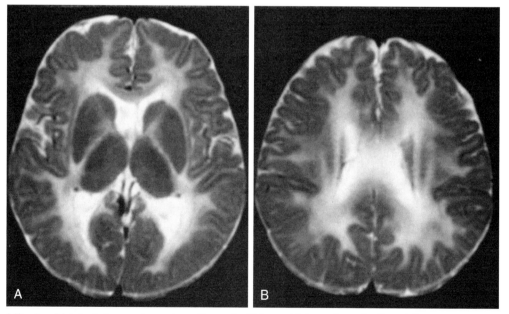

Figure 13–41. Mitochondrial depletion syndrome in an 8-month-old boy with hypoglycemia, liver failure, and pancreatic insufficiency. *A* and *B,* Cranial MR axial T2-weighted images. There is hyperintensity of virtually the entire cerebral white matter, including internal and external capsules, compatible with severe hypomyelination and demyelination.

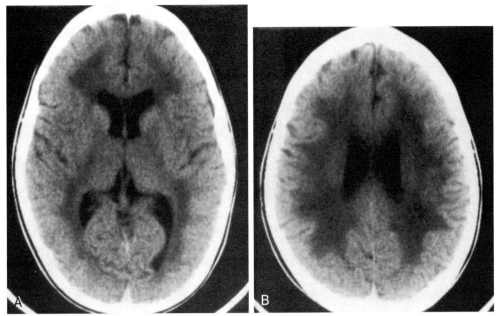

Figure 13–42. Myopathic carnitine deficiency in a 10-year-old boy with myopathy. Non–contrast-enhanced CT scans show diffuse, widespread, symmetrical lucency of the white matter, suggestive of demyelination.

metabolism may be accompanied by neurologic dysfunction, ranging from mild to severe, acute or chronic.

Some affected infants die of edema brought on by hyperammonemia or anoxia; others have been shown at autopsy to have spongy degeneration of the white matter, demyelination, or hypomyelination.

The more well-known aminoacidopathies include maple syrup urine disease (MSUD), phenylketonuria, the ketotic hyperglycinemias, urea cycle enzyme errors (ornithine transcarbamylase deficiency or citrullinemia), and nonketotic hyperglycinemias. More than 50 subtypes have been described. Depending on the time of imaging, an affected child with one of these aminoacidopathies may show cerebral edema, hypomyelination, or diffuse white matter atrophy (Fig. 13–43).[6, 51] A characteristic diagnostic feature is the demonstration of white matter edema in the neonatal period, since this excludes most classic leukodystrophies.

Wilson's Disease

Wilson's disease is a rare autosomal recessive disorder of copper metabolism. Although basal ganglia are predominantly affected, white matter tract abnormalities have been routinely characterized by MRI.[90]

Mucopolysaccharidoses

Six well-recognized syndromes are caused by enzyme defects resulting in accumulation of glycosaminoglycans in many organs. *Hurler's syndrome* is the prototype. Although demyelination is not a prominent neuropathologic feature, diffuse white matter changes simulating demyelination have been reported (Fig. 13–44).[40, 58]

Multiple Sclerosis

The most common demyelinating disease seen in adult neurologic practice is MS. Clinically, it may present in acute, chronic, or relapsing forms. The common neurologic signs are optic neuritis, paralysis, numbness, ataxia, and tremor. Repeated remissions and exacerbations are characteristic, and the average duration of disease is many years.[67, 95]

The gross pathologic features of MS have been well documented over many decades. The in vivo demonstration of demyelinated plaques was first made possible with the advent of CT, but MRI is clearly the imaging method of choice, with superior sensitivity, specificity, and characterization of the disease process.[72, 76] In many studies, MRI not only is the most accurate imaging method but also is even more sensitive than other nonimaging tests such as oligoclonal bands, somatosensory evoked potentials, and visual evoked potentials.[80]

The sensitivity of MRI has been as high as 85% in patients with clinically definite MS, and the figure is probably even higher if serial studies are performed.[59] CT, however, has probably less than half the sensitivity of MRI; nonetheless, a brief description of CT abnormalities is in order, if only for historical interest.

Three CT features are typical of MS:

1. Most characteristic is focal decreased attenuation in the periventricular white matter.
2. Another type of focal abnormality in CT scans of MS is contrast-enhancing plaque. These enhancing lesions have been shown to correspond to the acute phase of demyelination, and the blood-barrier breakdown resolves within a few weeks (Fig. 13–45).[57] The contrast enhancement may be ameliorated or abolished by the administration of corticosteroids, although the long-term

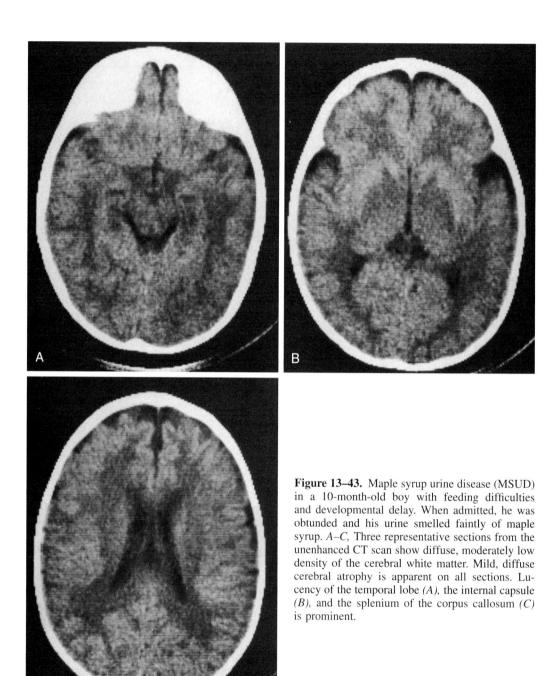

Figure 13–43. Maple syrup urine disease (MSUD) in a 10-month-old boy with feeding difficulties and developmental delay. When admitted, he was obtunded and his urine smelled faintly of maple syrup. *A–C,* Three representative sections from the unenhanced CT scan show diffuse, moderately low density of the cerebral white matter. Mild, diffuse cerebral atrophy is apparent on all sections. Lucency of the temporal lobe *(A),* the internal capsule *(B),* and the splenium of the corpus callosum *(C)* is prominent.

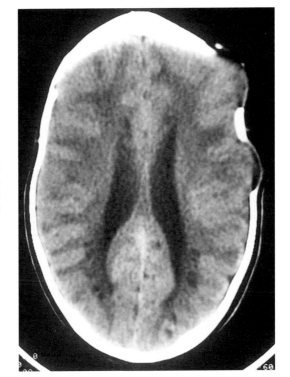

Figure 13–44. Mucopolysaccharidosis (Hurler's syndrome) in a 7-year-old girl with mild macrocephaly. CT scan demonstrates the multiple periventricular cysts, characteristic of this disease, as well as more subtle generalized white matter hypodensity. Unusual skull defects with brain herniations are also shown.

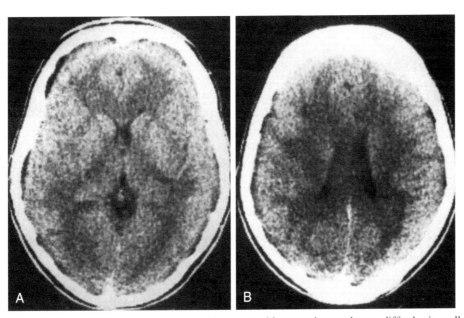

Figure 13–45. Multiple sclerosis, acute phase, in a 19-year-old woman with extremity numbness, difficulty in walking, blurred vision, and slurred speech. *A–C,* Precontrast CT sections are abnormal, with diffuse, patchy hypodensity of the white matter.

Illustration continued on following page

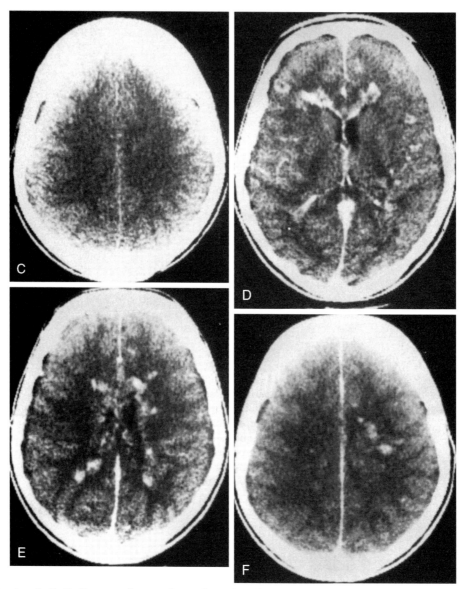

Figure 13–45. *Continued. D–F,* Corresponding sections after administration of intravenous contrast. There is prominent patchy enhancement of the periventricular white matter bilaterally. Occasionally, as in this case, a few contrast-enhancing plaques may be found in the cerebral cortex, but the periventricular lesions predominate.

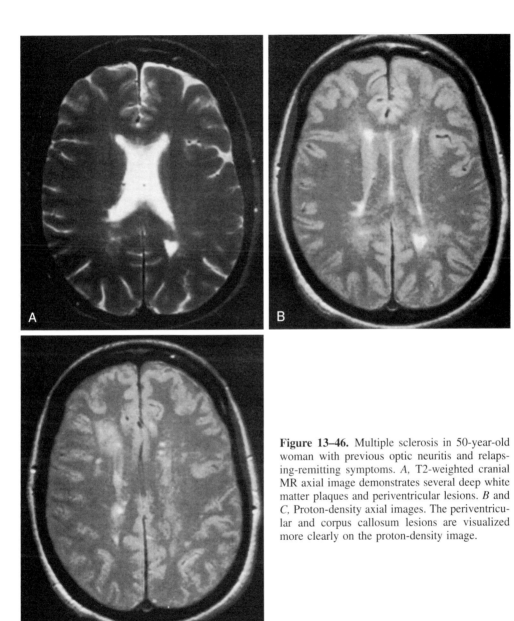

Figure 13–46. Multiple sclerosis in 50-year-old woman with previous optic neuritis and relapsing-remitting symptoms. *A,* T2-weighted cranial MR axial image demonstrates several deep white matter plaques and periventricular lesions. *B* and *C,* Proton-density axial images. The periventricular and corpus callosum lesions are visualized more clearly on the proton-density image.

course of the disease does not appear to be altered by this regimen.

3. A less common CT finding in MS is cerebral atrophy, caused by large-scale white matter shrinkage. This results in generalized ventricular and sulcal dilatation.

The foregoing discussion notwithstanding, MRI is the imaging method of choice in cases of suspected MS of the brain and spinal cord. The emphasis is not only on supporting the diagnosis of MS but on the fact that MRI is effective in differentiating MS from other processes, such as slowly growing tumors, brain stem vascular malformations, and vasculitis. The most widely used sequences for detection of MS are the T2-weighted and proton-density sequences. These are rapidly being supplemented by fast spin-echo imaging. Other techniques that may prove to be extremely useful are magnetization transfer; FLAIR; and, possibly, high-dose contrast-enhancement schemes.[21] Although magnetic resonance spectroscopy is beyond the scope of this chapter, it is evident that it is a powerful technique for the study of MS and other white matter diseases.[23]

On standard T2-weighted sequences, MS plaques appear as high-intensity lesions, usually ovoid, elongated, or round. The proton-density and FLAIR scans are very useful because high-signal plaques adjacent to ependymal surfaces may be obscured by high-signal cerebrospinal fluid on standard T2-weighted images (Figs. 13–46 to 13–49).[81]

In general, T1-weighted images are much less sensitive, but it is noteworthy that chronic plaques of MS are often

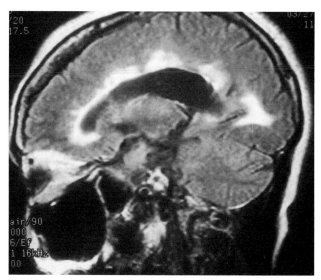

Figure 13–48. Multiple sclerosis (MS). Fluid-attenuated inversion recovery (FLAIR) parasagittal MR image depicts the extensive demyelinated plaques of progressive MS.

well shown, especially in the corpus callosum, on T1-weighted sequences, appearing as low-signal lesions surrounded by a very thin halo of mildly increased signal intensity (Fig. 13–50). Hemorrhage is not seen in MS lesions; edema and mass effect are distinctly uncommon (see later).

The most characteristic diagnostic feature of MS plaques on MR images is not their signal intensity but their anatomic distribution. There is a predilection for periventricular distribution and ependymal surfaces, especially along the occipital horns and, to a lesser degree, the frontal horns. If not pathognomonic, corpus callosum lesions are so characteristic of MS as to be almost specific.[81] Other MS sites commonly affected are the corona radiata, internal capsule, and centrum semiovale. In the posterior fossa, MS plaques are quite common, with a predilection for the surface of the pons, especially near the fifth cranial nerve entry zone, the middle cerebral peduncle (brachium pontis), the floor of the fourth ventricle, and the colliculi.

Contrast enhancement is an important part of MRI technique.[30] It is known that acute lesions of MS are accompanied by transient breakdown of the blood-brain barrier, which may be demonstrated with use of gadolinium contrast enhancement. While T1-weighted images are the standard practice, magnetization transfer may show greater detectability of these lesions because of its background suppression (Fig. 13–51; see Fig. 13–49).[21] Serial studies have demonstrated that contrast enhancement in acute lesions of MS may persist for 6 to 8 weeks after acute demyelination.[46] The enhancement may be punctate, nodular, or ringlike. In rare cases, there may be single or multiple large foci of MS with mass effect and significant contrast enhancement simulating a tumor (Fig. 13–52).[52, 101]

Although many cases of MS have these characteristic imaging features, rendering differential diagnosis relatively unimportant, MS lesions may occur anywhere in the CNS, including the cortex and other gray matter nuclei.

The lesions may be few or may be present in otherwise uncharacteristic locations. A differential diagnosis in these

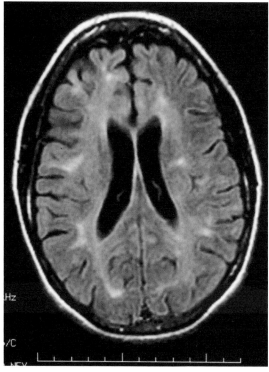

Figure 13–47. Multiple sclerosis (MS), as shown on a fluid-attenuated inversion recovery (FLAIR) MR image; the patient is a 36-year-old woman with relapsing-remitting MS. Note the conspicuity of the numerous bilateral periventricular white matter lesions.

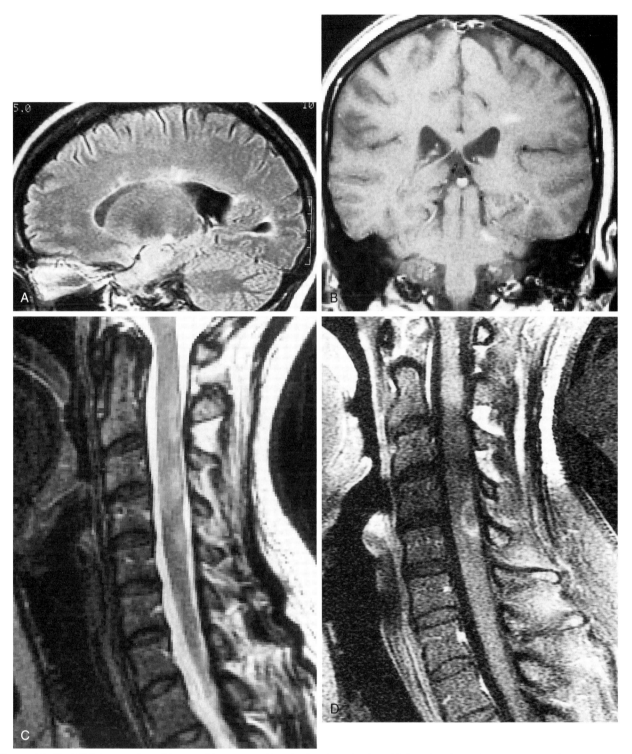

Figure 13–49. MRI features in a 32-year-old woman with spinal and cerebral multiple sclerosis (MS). *A,* Parasagittal fluid-attenuated inversion recovery (FLAIR) sequence. Numerous hyperintense plaques are clustered on the inferior surface of the corpus callosum, highly correlated with the diagnosis of MS. *B,* Contrast-enhanced, T1-weighted, magnetization-transfer coronal image; two enhancing plaques are visible, indicating active demyelination: one in the corona radiata, the other in the brachium pontis. *C,* Sagittal T2-weighted, fast spin-echo MRI of the cervical spinal cord. Numerous plaques are visible, some with evident swelling (edema). *D,* Fat-suppressed, contrast-enhanced image at the same level as in *C;* one of the lesions has ringlike enhancement.

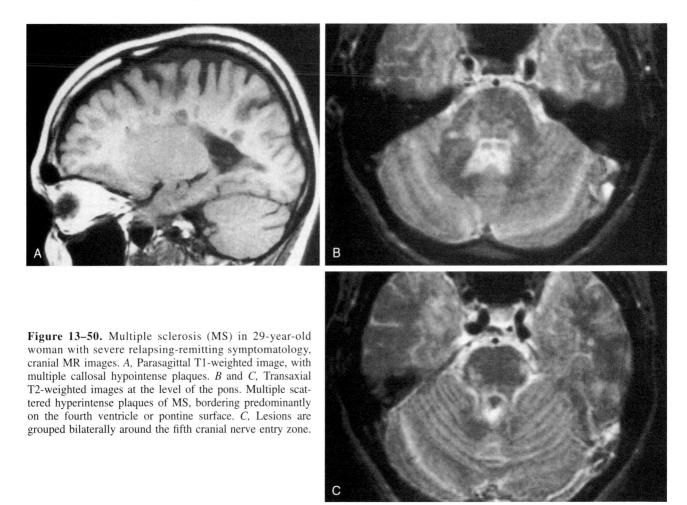

Figure 13–50. Multiple sclerosis (MS) in 29-year-old woman with severe relapsing-remitting symptomatology, cranial MR images. *A,* Parasagittal T1-weighted image, with multiple callosal hypointense plaques. *B* and *C,* Transaxial T2-weighted images at the level of the pons. Multiple scattered hyperintense plaques of MS, bordering predominantly on the fourth ventricle or pontine surface. *C,* Lesions are grouped bilaterally around the fifth cranial nerve entry zone.

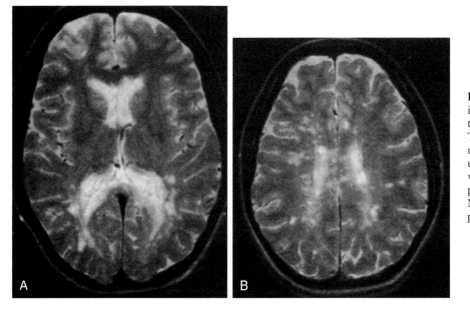

Figure 13–51. Multiple sclerosis (MS) in 37-year-old woman presenting with thoracic myelopathy. *A* and *B,* Cranial T2-weighted axial MR images show multiple, hyperintense plaques distributed bilaterally in the centrum semiovale and periventricular regions and especially grouped around the trigones. Note especially the characteristic corpus callosum lesions.

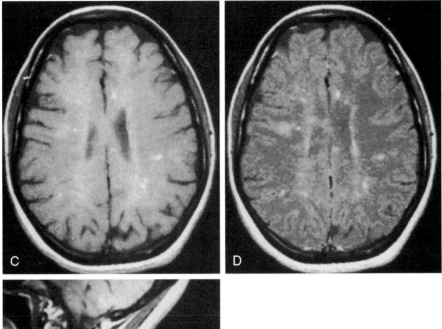

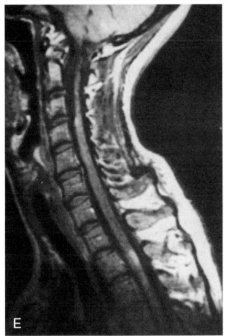

Figure 13–51. *Continued. C,* Postgadolinium-enhanced, T1-weighted axial image, with several enhancing plaques in the deep white matter. *D,* Postcontrast magnetization transfer (MT) image demonstrates more conspicuous enhancement of additional lesions than the standard T1-weighted sequence. *E,* Postcontrast midsagittal MR image of the cervicothoracic cord. There are two typical contrast-enhancing MS plaques: one in the anterior cervical cord and one in the posterior thoracic cord at the T2 level. (Incidentally visible is a moderate C5-6 disk protrusion.) Despite the multiple intracranial enhancing MS lesions, this patient had only spinal cord symptomatology.

cases must include demyelination secondary to ADEM, vasculitis, Lyme disease, sarcoidosis, ischemic disease, and, in rare cases, tumors.

As previously described, multiple ischemic white matter foci are usually seen in older patients, are associated with cardiovascular risk factors, are not located in the immediate periventricular white matter in most cases, and rarely involve the corpus callosum. Also, infratentorial ischemic lesions tend to have a different distribution than does MS in the pons and cerebellum. Despite all of these clues, some MR images are indeterminate, and the final diagnosis must await clinical confirmation or serial studies.

Spinal Cord Multiple Sclerosis

Some of the false-negative MRI diagnoses of MS are attributable to cases with only spinal cord involvement.

The spinal cord is much more of a challenge in MRI diagnosis, but newer techniques are yielding more rapid and detailed examinations of such cord lesions. These include multiarray receiver coils, fast spin-echo imaging, and the FLAIR sequence. Reports suggest that cord lesions may be detected in a majority of MS patients using such techniques. Characteristically, the cord lesions of MS appear as high signal intensity on T2-weighted sequences, with the cervical cord involved about twice as often as the thoracic cord. The lesions range from a few millimeters to extension over one or more vertebral segments (Fig. 13–53; see Figs. 13–49 and 13–51).

The most common location is lateral and posterior in the cord, but MS may involve both gray and white matter and may occupy the entire transverse diameter. Swelling of the cord is reported in a minority of cases, with diminished signal intensity on T1-weighted images sometimes

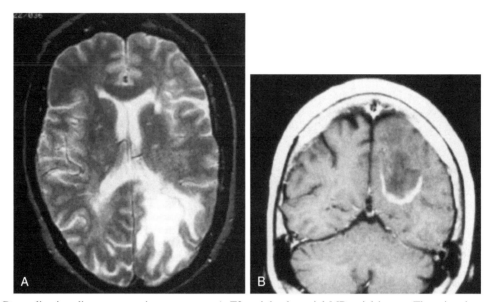

Figure 13–52. Demyelinating disease presenting as a mass. *A,* T2-weighted cranial MR axial image. There is a hyperintense masslike lesion in the left parieto-occipital lobe, surrounded by edema. A few scattered periventricular and deep white matter lesions are also visible bilaterally. *B,* Postgadolinium-enhanced, T1-weighted coronal MR image. Incomplete ringlike enhancement outlines the lesion. Biopsy showed nonspecific demyelination. Follow-up MR several months later showed almost complete spontaneous resolution of this mass. (From Jordan JE, Lane B: MRI characteristics of demyelinating disease mimicking brain tumor. Appl Radiol, December 1992, pp 36–38.)

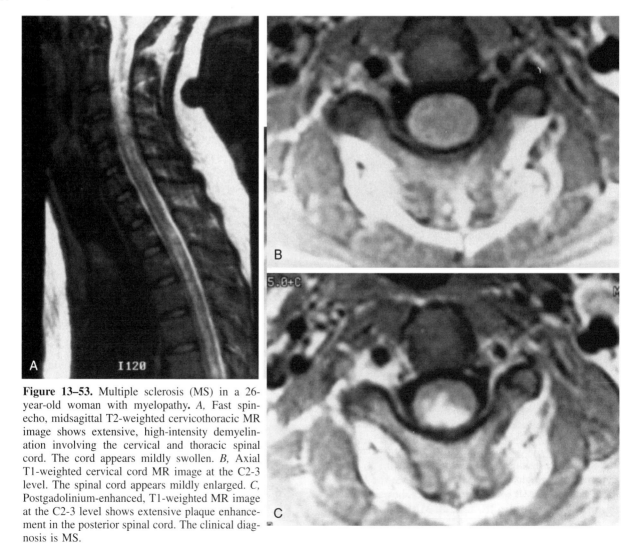

Figure 13–53. Multiple sclerosis (MS) in a 26-year-old woman with myelopathy. *A,* Fast spin-echo, midsagittal T2-weighted cervicothoracic MR image shows extensive, high-intensity demyelination involving the cervical and thoracic spinal cord. The cord appears mildly swollen. *B,* Axial T1-weighted cervical cord MR image at the C2-3 level. The spinal cord appears mildly enlarged. *C,* Postgadolinium-enhanced, T1-weighted MR image at the C2-3 level shows extensive plaque enhancement in the posterior spinal cord. The clinical diagnosis is MS.

visible. Gadolinium enhancement parallels that of MS brain lesions.

The differential diagnosis includes transverse myelitis, other inflammations, and intrinsic cord tumor. The final diagnosis is accomplished, preferably, by serial imaging studies and clinical correlation rather than by biopsy.

References

1. Arbelaez A, Castillo, M: Diffusion-weighted MR imaging of global cerebral anoxia. AJNR Am J Neuroradiol 20:999, 1999.
2. Ballesteros MC, Hansen PE, Soila K: MR imaging of the developing human brain. Part 2. Postnatal development. Radiographics 13:611, 1993.
3. Baram TZ, Goldman AM, Percy AK: Krabbe disease: Specific MRI and CT findings. Neurology 36:111, 1986.
4. Barkovich AJ: Metabolic and destructive brain disorders. In Pediatric Neuroimaging. New York, Raven Press, 1990, p 39.
5. Barkovich AJ, Lyon G, Evrard P: Formation, maturation and disorders of white matter. AJNR Am J Neuroradiol 13:447, 1992.
6. Barnes CM, Enzmann DR: The evolution of white matter disease as seen on computed tomography. Radiology 138:379, 1981.
7. Bozzo M, Capriani G, Leo L, et al: HELLP syndrome and factor V Leiden. Obstet Gynecol Reprod Biol 95:55, 2001.
8. Braffman BH, Zimmerman RA, Trojamowski JQ, et al: Brain MR: Pathologic correlation with gross and histopathology. Part 2. Hyperintense white matter foci in the elderly. AJNR Am J Neuroradiol 9:629, 1988.
9. Brant-Zawadzki M, Enzmann DR: Using computed tomography of the brain to correlate low white matter attenuation with early gestational age in neonates. Radiology 139:105, 1981.
10. Brooks RA, Di Chiro G, Keller MR: Explanation of cerebral white-gray contrast in computed tomography. J Comput Assist Tomogr 4:489, 1980.
11. Cajade-Law AG, Cohen JA, Heirer LA: Vascular causes of white matter disease. Neuroimaging Clin North Am 3:361, 1993.
12. Caldemeyer KS, Harris TM, Smith RR, et al: Gadolinium enhancement in acute disseminated encephalomyelitis. J Comput Assist Tomogr 15:673, 1991.
13. Casey SO, Sampaio RC, Michel E, Trunit CL: Posterior reversible encephalopathy syndrome. AJNR Am J Neuroradiol 21:1199, 2000.
14. Chang KH, Han MH, Kim HS, et al: Delayed encephalopathy after acute carbon intoxication: MR imaging features and distribution of cerebral white matter lesions. Radiology 184:117, 1992.
15. Chi JG, Yoo HW, Chang KH, et al: Leigh's subacute necrotizing encephalomyelopathy: Possible diagnosis by CT scan. Neuroradiology 22:141, 1981.
16. Clavier E, Thiebot J, Delangre T, et al: Marchiafava-Bignami disease: A case studied by CT and MR imaging. Neuroradiology 28:376, 1986.
17. Davis PC, Hoffman JC Jr, Braun IF, et al: MR of Leigh's disease (subacute necrotizing encephalomyelopathy). AJNR Am J Neuroradiol 8:71, 1987.
18. Demaerel P, Wilms G, Verdru P, et al: MR findings in globoid leukodystrophy. Neuroradiology 32:520, 1990.
19. Di Chiro G, Eiben RM, Manz HJ, et al: A new CT pattern in adrenoleukodystrophy. Radiology 137:687, 1980.
20. Dietrich RB, Bradley WG, Zaragoza EJ, et al: MR evaluation of early myelination patterns in normal and developmentally delayed infants. AJNR Am J Neuroradiol 9:69, 1988.
21. Dousset V, Grossman RI, Ramer KN, et al: Experimental allergic encephalomyelitis and multiple sclerosis: Lesion characterization with magnetization transfer imaging. Radiology 182:483, 1992.
22. Estrada M, El Gammal T, Dyken PR: Periventricular low attenuations: A normal finding in computerized tomographic scans of neonates. Arch Neurol 37:754, 1980.
23. Falini A, Calbrese G, Filippi M, et al: Benign versus secondary-progressive multiple sclerosis: The potential role of proton MR spectroscopy in defining the nature of disability. AJNR Am J Neuroradiol 19:223, 1998.
24. Feske SK, Speling RA, Schwartz RB: Extensive reversible brain magnetic resonance lesion in a patient with HELLP syndrome. Neuroimaging 7:247, 1997.
25. Friese SA, Bitzer M, Freudenstein D, et al: Classification of acquired lesion of the corpus callosum with MRI. Neuroradiology 42:795, 2000.
26. Gaitz JP, Bamford CR: Unusual computed tomographic scan in eclampsia. Arch Neurol 39:66, 1982.
27. Glass JP, Lee YY, Bruner J, Fields WS: Treatment-related leukoencephalopathy: A study of three cases and literature review. Medicine (Baltimore) 65:154, 1986.
28. Glusker P, Horoupian DS, Lane B: Familial arteriopathic leukoencephalopathy: Imaging and neuropathologic findings. AJNR Am J Neuroradiol 19:469, 1998.
29. Goto K, Ishii N, Fukasawa H: Diffuse white matter disease in the geriatric population. Radiology 141:687, 1981.
30. Grossman RI, Gonzalez-Scarano F, Atlas SW, et al: Multiple sclerosis: Gadolinium enhancement in MR imaging. Radiology 161:721, 1986.
31. Guo A, Petrella J, Kurtzberg J, Provenzale J: Evaluation of white matter anisotropy in Krabbe disease with diffusion tensor MR imaging: Initial experience. Radiology 218:809, 2001.
32. Hoffman E, Sedaghat-Kerdar M, Becker T, et al: Unspecific white matter lesions: Prevalence, number and distribution in cranial MRI. Eur Radiol 2:154, 1992.
33. Hokezu Y, Kuriyama M, Kubota R, et al: Cerebrotendinous xanthomatosis: Cranial CT and MRI studies in eight patients. Neuroradiology 34:308, 1992.
34. Holland BA, Haas DK, Norman D, et al: MRI of normal brain maturation. Am J Neuroradiol 7:201, 1986.
35. Holland I, Kendall BM: Computed tomography in Alexander's disease. Neuroradiology 20:103, 1980.
36. Honkaniemi J, Kahara V, Latvala M, et al: Reversible posterior leukoencephalopathy after combination chemotherapy. Neuroradiology 42:895, 2000.
37. Imiya M, Ichikawa K, Matsushima H, et al: MR of the base of the pons in Wilson disease. AJNR Am J Neuroradiol 13:1009, 1992.
38. Johns D: Mitochondrial DNA and disease. N Engl J Med 333:638, 1995.
39. Journel H, Roussey M, Gaudon Y, et al: Magnetic resonance imaging in Pelizaeus-Merzbacher disease. Neuroradiology 29:403, 1987.
40. Kendall BE: Disorders of lysosomes, peroxisomes, and mitochondria. AJNR Am J Neuroradiol 13:621, 1992.
41. Kesselring J, Miller DH, Robb SA, et al: Acute disseminated encephalomyelitis: MRI findings and the distinction from multiple sclerosis. Brain 113:291, 1990.
42. Kjos BO, Brant-Zawadzki M, Young RG: Early CT findings of global central nervous system hypoperfusion. Am J Roentgenol 141:1227, 1983.
43. Kumar AJ, Rosenbaum AE, Naidu S, et al: Adrenoleukodystrophy: Correlation MR imaging with CT. Radiology 165:497, 1987.
44. Kwan E, Drace J, Enzmann D: Specific CT findings in Krabbe disease. Am J Neuroradiol 5:453, 1984.
45. Kwong YL, Yu YL, Lam KS, et al: CT appearance in hypertensive encephalopathy. Neuroradiology 29:215, 1987.
46. Lee KH, Hashimoto SA, Hooge JP, et al: Magnetic resonance imaging of the head in the diagnosis of multiple sclerosis: A prospective 2-year follow-up with comparison of clinical evaluation, evoked potentials, oligoclonal banding, and CT. Neurology 41:657, 1991.
47. Levy RM, Rosenbloom S, Perrett LV: Neuroradiologic findings in AIDS: A review of 200 cases. Am J Neuroradiol 7:833, 1986.
48. Lotz PR, Ballinger WE, Quisling RG: Subcortical arteriosclerotic encephalopathy: CT spectrum and pathologic correlation. Am J Roentgenol 147:1209, 1986.
49. Ludwig B, Brand M, Brockerhoff P: Postpartum CT examination of the heads of full term infants. Neuroradiology 20:145, 1980.
50. Lukes SA, Norman D: Computed tomographic findings in acute disseminated encephalomyelitis. Ann Neurol 13:567, 1983.
51. Mantovani JF, Naidich TP, Prensky AL, et al: Maple syrup urine disease: Presentation with pseudotumor cerebri and CT abnormalities. J Pediatr 96:279, 1980.
52. Marano GD, Goodwin CA, Ko JP: Atypical contrast enhancement in computerized tomography of demyelinating disease. Arch Neurol 37:523, 1980.
53. Mark AS, Atlas SW: Progressive multifocal leukoencephalopathy in patients with AIDS: Appearance on MR images. Radiology 173:517, 1989.
54. McAdams H, Geyer CA, Done SL, et al: CT and MR imaging of Canavan disease. AJNR Am J Neuroradiol 11:397, 1990.

55. Melhem E, Loes D, Georgiades S, et al: X-linked adrenoleukodystrophy: The role of contrast-enhanced MR imaging in predicting disease progression. AJNR Am J Neuroradiol 21:839, 2000.

56. Miller GM, Baker HL Jr, Okazaki H, et al: Central pontine myelinolysis and its imitators. Radiology 168:795, 1988.

57. Morariu MA, Wilkins DE, Patel S: Multiple sclerosis and serial computed tomography: Delayed contrast enhancement of acute and early lesions. Arch Neurol 37:189, 1980.

58. Murata R, Nakajima S, Tanaka A, et al: MR imaging of the brain in patients with mucopolysaccharidosis. AJNR Am J Neuroradiol 10:1165, 1989.

59. Mushlin AI, Detsky AS, Phelps CE, et al: The accuracy of magnetic resonance imaging in patients with suspected multiple sclerosis. JAMA 269:3146, 1993.

60. Olsen WL, Longo FM, Mills CM, et al: White matter disease in AIDS: Findings at MR imaging. Radiology 169:445, 1988.

61. O'Neill BP, Forbes GS: Computerized tomography and adrenoleukomyeloneuropathy: Differential appearance in disease subtypes. Arch Neurol 38:293, 1981.

62. Pederson H, Clausen N: The development of cerebral CT changes during treatment of acute lymphocytic leukemia in childhood. Neuroradiology 22:79, 1981.

63. Penn RD, Trinko B, Baldwin L: Brain maturation followed by computed tomography. J Comput Assist Tomogr 4:614, 1980.

64. Penner MW, Li KC, Gebarski SS, et al: MR imaging of Pelizaeus-Merzbacher disease. J Comput Assist Tomogr 11:591, 1987.

65. Peters AC, Versteeg J, Bots GT, et al: Progressive multifocal leukoencephalopathy. Arch Neurol 37:497, 1980.

66. Picard L, Claudon M, Roland J, et al: Cerebral computed tomography in premature infants, with an attempt at staging developmental features. J Comput Assist Tomogr 4:435, 1980.

67. Poser CM: Exacerbation, activity and progression in multiple sclerosis. Arch Neurol 37:471, 1980.

68. Ragland RL, Duffis AW, Gendelmal S, et al: Central pontine myelinolysis with clinical recovery: MR documentation. J Comput Assist Tomogr 13:316, 1989.

69. Rail RL, Perkin GD: Computerized tomographic appearance of hypertensive encephalopathy. Arch Neurol 37:310, 1980.

70. Ramsey RG, Geremia GK: CNS complications of AIDS: CT and MR findings. AJR 151:449, 1988.

71. Reik L Jr: Disseminated vasculomyelinopathy: An immune complex disease. Ann Neurol 7:291, 1980.

72. Reisner T, Maida E: Computerized tomography in multiple sclerosis. Arch Neurol 37:475, 1980.

73. Rowland LP: "Ophthalmoplegia plus" or Kearns-Sayre syndrome. Arch Neurol 37:256, 1980.

74. Rowley HA, Dillon WP: Iatrogenic white matter diseases. Neuroimaging Clin North Am 3:379, 1993.

75. Ruiz-Martinez J, Martinez Perez-Basal A, Ruibal M, et al: Marchiafava-Bignami disease with widespread extracallosal lesions and favourable course. Neuroradiology 41:40, 1999.

76. Runge VM, Kirsch JE, Lee C, et al: MRI of multiple sclerosis in the brain. MRI Decisions 6(4):2, 1992.

77. Saito H, Endo M, Takase S, Itahara K: Acute disseminated encephalomyelitis after influenza vaccination. Arch Neurol 37:564, 1980.

78. Scanberger A, Tomaiuolo F, Sabatini U, et al: Demyelinating plaques in relapsing-remitting and secondary-progressive multiple sclerosis: Assessment with diffusion MR imaging. AJNR Am J Neuroradiol 21:862, 2000.

79. Shah M, Ross J: Infantile Alexander disease: MR appearance of a biopsy-proved case. AJNR Am J Neuroradiol 11:1105, 1990.

80. Sheldon JJ, Siddharthan R, Tobias J, et al: MR imaging of multiple sclerosis: Comparison with clinical and CT examination in 74 patients. Am J Neuroradiol 6:683, 1985.

81. Simon JH, Holtas SL, Schiffer RB, et al: Corpus callosum and subcallosal-periventricular lesions in multiple sclerosis: Detection with MR. Radiology 160:363, 1986.

82. Statz A, Boltshauser E, Schinzel A, Spiess H: Computed tomography in Pelizaeus-Merzbacher disease. Neuroradiology 22:103, 1981.

83. Steingart A, Hachinski VC, Lau C, et al: Cognitive and neurologic findings in demented patients with diffuse white matter lucencies on computed tomographic scan (leukoaraiosis). Arch Neurol 44:36, 1987.

84. Stovring J, Fernando LT: Wallerian degeneration of the corticospinal tract region of the brain stem: Demonstration by computed tomography. Radiology 149:717, 1983.

85. Thompson DS, Hutton JT, Stears JC, et al: Computerized tomography in the diagnosis of central and extrapontine myelinolysis. Arch Neurol 38:243, 1981.

86. Topcu M, Saatci I, Apak A, et al: Leigh syndrome in a 3-year-old boy with brain MR imaging and pathologic findings. AJNR Am J Neuroradiol 21:224, 2000.

87. Tsuruda JS, Kortman KE, Bradley WG, et al: Radiation effects on cerebral white matter: MR evaluation. AJNR Am J Neuroradiol 8:431, 1987.

88. Uchimaya M, Hata Y, Tada S: MR imaging in adrenoleukodystrophy. Neuroradiology 33:25, 1991.

89. Valentine AR, Moseley IF, Kendall BE: White matter abnormality in cerebral atrophy: Clinicoradiological correlations. J Neurol Neurosurg Psychiatry 43:139, 1980.

90. van Wassenaer–van Hall H, van den Heuvel G, Jansen G, et al: Cranial MR in Wilson disease: Abnormal white matter in extrapyramidal and pyramidal tracts. AJNR Am J Neuroradiol 16:2021, 1995.

91. Vaughn DJ, Jarvik JG, Hackney D: High-dose cytarabine neurotoxicity: MR findings during the acute phase. AJNR Am J Neuroradiol 14:1014, 1993.

92. Walker DL: Progressive multifocal leukoencephalopathy. In Vinken PJ, Bruyn GW, Klawaus HL (eds): Handbook of Clinical Neurology. New York, Elsevier, 1985, p 503.

93. Walsh PJ: Adrenoleukodystrophy: Report of two cases with relapsing and remitting courses. Arch Neurol 37:448, 1980.

94. Waltz G, Harik SI, Kaufman B: Adult metachromatic leukodystrophy. Arch Neurol 44:225, 1987.

95. Waxman S: The demyelinating diseases. In Rosenberg RN (ed): The Clinical Neurosciences, vol 1. New York, Churchill Livingstone, 1983.

96. Weingarten KL, Zimmerman RD, Pinto RS, Whelan MA: Computed tomographic changes of hypertensive encephalopathy. Am J Neuroradiol 6:395, 1985.

97. Whiteman MLH, Post MJD, Berger JL, et al: Progressive multifocal leukoencephalopathy in 47 HIV-seropositive patients: Neuroimaging with clinical and pathological correlation. Radiology 187:233, 1993.

98. Wolf R, Zimmerman R, Clancy R, Haselgrove J: Quantitative apparent diffusion coefficient measurements in term neonates for early detection of hypoxic-ischemic brain injury: Initial experience. Radiology 218:825, 2001.

99. Wray S, Provenzale J, Johns D, Thulborn K: MR of brain in mitochondrial myopathy AJNR Am J Neuroradiol 16:1167, 1995.

100. Yamamoto T, Ashikaga R, Araki Y, Nishimura Y: A case of Marchiafava-Bignami disease: MRI findings on spine-echo and fluid attenuated inversion recovery (FLAIR) images. Eur J Radiol 34:141, 2000.

101. Yetkin FZ, Haughton VM: Common and uncommon manifestations of MS on MRI. MRI Decisions 6:13, 1992.

102. Young RSK, Osbakken MD, Alger PM, et al: Magnetic resonance imaging in leukodystrophies of childhood. Pediatr Neurol 1:15, 1985.

103. Zeumer H, Schonsky B, Sturm KW: Predominant white matter involvement in subcortical arteriosclerotic encephalopathy (Binswanger disease). J Comput Assist Tomogr 4:14, 1980.

Part III

Imaging of the Head and Neck

Edited by
Charles F. Lanzieri

14

The Orbit

Jon Mark Fergenson, Neal Mandell,
James J. Abrahams

Magnetic resonance imaging (MRI) and computed tomography (CT) have revolutionized diagnostic imaging of the orbit and its contents. With its superb soft tissue contrast and ability to image in multiple planes, MRI provides excellent rendering of the orbital anatomy. CT also shows the soft tissues within the orbit very well and is best at displaying anatomy and pathology of the bony orbit.

The fine structures within the orbit require more attention to imaging protocol than many other regions of the body to ensure optimal diagnostic information.

This chapter discusses technique for the more commonly used imaging issues, presents an overview of pertinent anatomy, and touches on a cross-section of orbital pathology, including some familiar and some unusual lesions.

Anatomy

The anatomy of the orbit consists of a bony cavity within which the globe, muscle cone, optic nerve–sheath complex, lacrimal apparatus, and various vascular and nerve structures are packed into a cushion of fat.

The bony orbit is a conical structure that consists of the orbital plate of the frontal bone, the maxilla, the greater and lesser wings of the sphenoid bone, the ethmoid bone, and the lacrimal bone. The inferior and medial walls are quite thin and prone to fracture. The medial wall is named the lamina papyracea, in recognition of its paper-thin nature. Multiple foramina transmit vessels and nerves. The most prominent among these include the superior and inferior orbital fissures, the optic canal, the infraorbital and supraorbital foramina, and the lacrimal duct foramen. Other tiny foraminal spaces are not usually appreciated in imaging because of their size. The contents of the major foramina are listed in Box 14–1.

Box 14–1. Major Foramina of the Orbit

Optic Canal

    Optic nerve
    Ophthalmic artery

Superior Orbital Fissure

    III, IV, VI, V_1 cranial nerves
    Lacrimal and frontal nerves
    Superior and inferior ophthalmic veins

Inferior Orbital Fissure

    V_2 cranial nerve
    Infraorbital vessels, zygomatic nerve

The muscle cone consists of seven extraocular muscles: the superior, medial, lateral, and inferior recti as well as the superior and inferior obliques, and the levator palpebrae superioris. All but the inferior oblique muscle originate at the orbital apex at Zinn's ring and pass anteriorly to form tendinous attachments to the globe. The inferior oblique muscle originates on the inferomedial aspect of the orbit and passes in a somewhat lateral course to attach to the posterolateral aspect of the globe. The cone of the muscle has been designated a relative boundary or demarcation in addressing the position of several pathologic processes, with the orbit divided into *intraconal* and *extraconal* spaces. In general, processes involving the intraconal space require surgical attention, whereas extraconal processes are often amenable to medical management.

The globe is approximately spherical, with only a few readily visualized structures: the cornea, lens, anterior chambers, vitreous, and the retina-sclera-choroid complex. None of the conventional imaging modalities is able to visualize the retina from the choroid separately in the healthy patient. When an intervening process does occur, it causes separation of these thin membranes.

Proptosis is evaluated by axial scanning, with a line connecting the lateral orbital walls at the level of the lens and with the imaging specialist measuring from that line to the anterior aspect of the globe.[31] This measurement should not exceed 21 mm.[31]

The optic nerve–sheath complex consists of the optic nerve, its surrounding meningeal sheath, and the cerebrospinal fluid (CSF), which separates them. The sheath extends from the optic canal to the globe. The normal diameter of the nerve is up to 4 mm. The diameter of the complex may vary from 4 to 6 mm. The amount of visualized subarachnoid fluid is also variable.

Occasionally, the presence of CSF makes it possible to determine whether a tumor arises from the sheath or from the nerve itself. Tumors arising from the sheath, such as meningiomas, form a "tram track" appearance in which the outer layer is thickened but remains separated from the normal-sized nerve by a layer of fluid. Because the nerve takes a sigmoid course from apex to globe, coronal imaging is essential for assessing the optic nerve–sheath complex.

The lacrimal apparatus consists of the lacrimal gland, its secretory duct, and the ductal system, which drains these secretions into the nasal cavity. The gland lies in the superolateral aspect of the orbit. The draining ductal system lies near the medial canthus and consists of the superior and inferior puncta, their associated ducts, the lacrimal sac, lacrimal duct, and the valve of Hasner, a draining orifice inferolateral to the inferior nasal turbinate.

The anterior border of the orbit is formed by the orbital

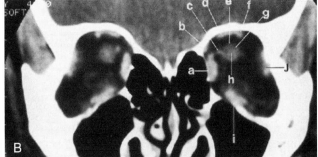

Figure 14–1. *A,* Coronal CT scan: normal anatomy. Lateral rectus (a), superior rectus (b), medial rectus (c), superior oblique (d), levator palpebrae superioris (e), lacrimal gland (f), inferior oblique (g). *B,* Medial rectus (a), superior oblique (b), ophthalmic artery (c), superior rectus/levator palpebrae superioris complex (d), dural sheath (e), superior ophthalmic vein (f), subarachnoid space (g), optic nerve (h), inferior rectus (i), lateral rectus (j).

septum, a fibrous structure adherent to the inner margin of the orbital rim with central portions that extend into the tarsus of the eyelids. Although there are a few orifices for passage of vessels, nerves, and ducts, the septum forms an effective barrier to prevent superficial processes from extending into the orbit proper. A pathologic process such as cellulitis may be designated *preseptal* or *postseptal.*

Technique
Computed Tomography

Intraorbital fat provides a natural source of contrast on CT scans. Most lesions within the orbit, whether inflammatory, infectious, or neoplastic, are relatively radiodense in comparison to the surrounding fat, and they are easily distinguished by CT. CT is rapid, and the images are obtained incrementally. Therefore, patient cooperation is less crucial than in MRI.

Commonly accepted protocols call for both axial and coronal images with the potential for multiplanar reconstruction. For most orbital studies, 3-mm sections in the axial and coronal planes are adequate. Coronal sections

should be initiated at the lateral orbital rim (to lessen exposure to the radiosensitive lens[80]) and continued to the posterior aspect of the optic canals, with the anterior clinoid or dorsum sella used as landmarks. The axial sections should include images of the entire brain, specifically to include the retro-orbital optic apparatus, with additional retrospective magnified views of the orbits.

Coronal images are especially important in that cross-sectional evaluation of all of the intraorbital structures is optimal (e.g., extraocular muscles, optic nerve–sheath–nasal complex, vessels, and globe) (Fig. 14–1). This plane is also imperative for assessing spread of processes from surrounding structures (e.g., paranasal sinuses, trauma, tumor). The prone patient position is ideal, especially with sinus-related disease,[2] but supine positioning is also acceptable.

Occasionally, a patient may be unable to tolerate positioning for direct coronal imaging. This occurs most commonly with elderly patients with severe degenerative disease of the cervical spine and in the setting of acute trauma. Recent developments in multislice CT technology allow for faster thin-slice imaging. As a result, axial thin-section images can be obtained for coronal reconstruction in these patients (Fig. 14–2).

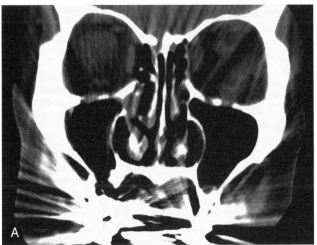

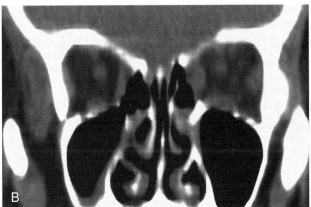

Figure 14–2. *A,* Coronal CT scan in a patient whose extensive dental hardware obscures detail in the orbits. *B,* Reformatted coronal view shows enlargement of the extraocular muscles on the left side. In view of the patient's known hyperthyroidism, this finding was thought to represent Graves' disease.

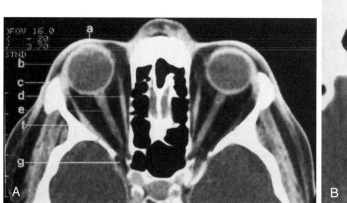
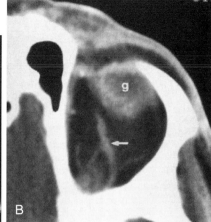

Figure 14–3. *A,* Axial CT scan: normal anatomy. Lens (a), lid (b), lacrimal gland (c), medial rectus (d), optic nerve-n-sheath complex (e), lateral rectus (f), superior orbital fissure (g). *B,* Axial CT scan: normal anatomy. Superior ophthalmic vein *(arrow)*, globe (g).

Intravenous (IV) contrast material is a necessary addition to most orbital examinations, although it is not necessary in the setting of trauma. IV contrast can increase the sensitivity and sometimes specificity of distinguishing between various entities–whether inflammatory, infectious, neoplastic, or vascular. The contrast agent can be administered by either IV drip or by mechanical injector. A single dose (e.g., 150 mL) can be used, or split doses, one for each plane or section, depending on the lesion. *Windowing* is also critical to assessing pathologic changes and should include both soft tissue and bone windows (Fig. 14–3).

Thin-section CT may be performed following the administration of contrast material into the nasolacrimal duct to evaluate patency. These CT dacrocystograms are often performed in conjunction with an ophthalmologist, who cannulates the duct and administers the contrast agent. Coronal reconstructions of the axial data can be helpful (Fig. 14–4).

Magnetic Resonance Imaging

Although MRI is relatively new, compared with CT, this modality has rapidly gained ground in the assessment of orbital disease. The capacity to produce images without ionizing radiation and in any plane of section without a change in patient position has made MRI an important tool in orbital imaging. The absence of bony artifact is an advantage over CT, especially in the orbital apex, optic canal, and parasellar regions.

MRI uses the physical properties of the proton, the hydrogen atom's nucleus, to generate imaging data. Because hydrogen is an abundant component of the water and the macromolecules in all tissues, MRI can be used to examine any body part.

The patient is placed in a strong unidirectional magnetic field, and a small population of protons become aligned with that field. The region of interest is subjected to pulsed radiofrequency (RF) energy. This serves to change the orientation of the spinning proton. The natural tendency of the perturbed proton is to realign with the overall magnetic field. This is referred to as the *T1* characteristic of the tissue. By definition, T1 is that time for which protons in a particular tissue have regained approximately 63% of the original alignment.

When the protons are "tipped" by the RF pulse, they

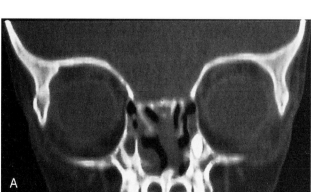
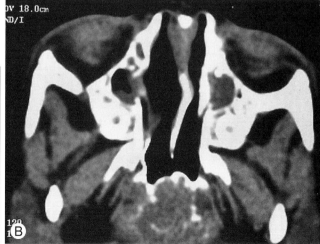

Figure 14–4. *A,* Coronal reformatted image from a CT dacrocystogram shows dilation of the lacrimal duct. The nasal septum and inferior turbinate are deviated leftward and cause obstruction at the valve of Hasner. *B,* The obstruction is only partial, as evidenced by the presence of contrast material in the posterior nasopharynx.

are initially "in phase," or are spinning together coherently in the 90-degree frame of reference. Over time, they lose cohesion and become "out of phase," called *T2 relaxation*.

T1 and T2 are inherent tissue characteristics and are not produced by the magnetic resonance itself. One uses the T1 and T2 of various tissues being imaged to enhance and accentuate contrast differences between those tissues.

Magnetic gradients are superimposed on the overall magnetic field to spatially "encode" the position of each spinning proton in space. One can obtain spatial information using the frequency of the spinning protons or their relative phase.

The most commonly used protocols today involve (1) *spin-echo* imaging and (2) *gradient-echo* imaging.

Spin-echo imaging involves an additional 180-degree pulse to "rephase" the protons to produce an "echo" at a specified time: TE, or *echo time*. The sequence is repeated as many times as needed to obtain information about the anatomic area of interest. TR, or *repetition time*, refers to those repeated intervals. For a more detailed review of MRI physics, see References 3, 15, 22, 45, 53, and 71.

Gradient-echo imaging involves the actual reversal of the image gradients used for spatial encoding in the region of interest. Acquisition imaging data can be obtained rapidly, either in a slice-by-slice format or volumetrically.

Shallow flip angles (<90 degrees) and faster techniques have been developed for even faster image acquisition (see specific articles on these techniques).

Gadolinium–diethylene-triamine-penta-acetic acid (Gd-DTPA) is an IV contrast agent that shortens the T1 relax- ation time of the tissues it penetrates. This results in higher T1 signal, or "brighter" areas on the scan images. Gadolinium contrast is analogous to the iodinated contrast material used in CT scanning and identifies tissues with greater perfusion. Within the brain, gadolinium enhancement results from breakdown of the blood-brain barrier.

As in CT scans, multiple planes are important to assess the orbit. Standard protocols usually include coronal and axial T1-weighted images as well as T2-weighted axial and coronal images (Figs. 14–5 to 14–7). The imaging specialist should include the brain posterior to the orbital area in order to evaluate the cavernous sinus, optic chiasm, optic radiations, and the nuclei of the oculomotor, abducens, and trochlear nerves in the midbrain and pons.

MRI offers the ability to suppress the normally strong T1 signal of fat. Precontrast T1 imaging should be performed without fat suppression because fat suppression diminishes the inherent contrast between the high signal of fat and the lower signal of most pathologic processes. Postcontrast imaging should be performed with fat suppression techniques to increase the difference in signal between an enhancing pathologic process and its surroundings (Fig. 14–8).

Pathology
Trauma

Traumatic lesions of the orbit can involve any or all of the orbital structures. Treatment is determined by proximity to, or disruption of, key anatomic elements.

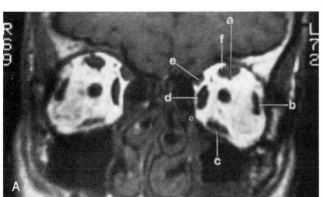
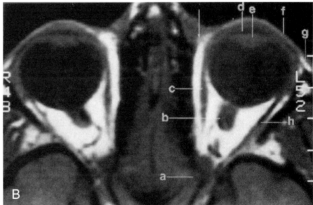
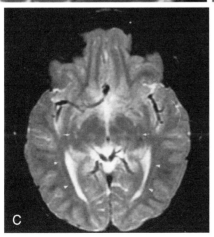

Figure 14–5. *A,* Coronal T1-weighted MRI study: normal anatomy. Superior ophthalmic vein (a), lateral rectus (b), inferior rectus (c), medial rectus (d), superior oblique (e), superior rectus–levator palpebrae superioris complex (f). *B,* Axial T1-weighted MRI study: normal anatomy. Optic nerve in the optic canal (a), optic nerve sheath complex (b), medial rectus (c), anterior chamber (d), lens (e), lid (f), medial and lateral aspects of the orbital septum *(arrows; g),* lateral rectus (h). *C,* Axial T2-weighted MRI study: posterior visual apparatus. Position of lateral geniculate body *(arrows;* a), path of optic radiations *(arrowheads).*

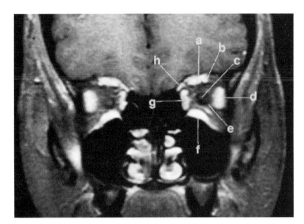

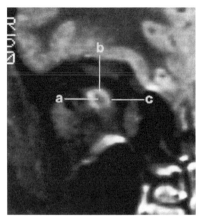

Figure 14–6. Coronal T1-weighted MRI study with fat saturation: normal anatomy. *A,* Superior rectus/levator palpebrae superioris complex. *B,* Superior ophthalmic vein. *C,* Optic nerve. *D,* Lateral rectus. *E,* Dural sheath. *F,* Inferior rectus. *G,* Medial rectus.

Figure 14–7. Coronal inversion recovery, fast spin-echo MRI study: normal anatomy. *A,* Optic nerve. *B,* Subarachnoid space with cerebrospinal fluid. *C,* Optic nerve sheath.

One of the more common entities is disruption of an orbital wall with the potential for entrapment of extraocular muscles, the so-called "blowout" fracture. The mechanism of injury is usually blunt trauma to the anterior orbit. The increased intraorbital pressure is transmitted to the walls, resulting in fracture. The inferior and medial walls, which are thinnest, are the most vulnerable. Orbital contents are often seen to herniate through the fracture. Because of its superior bone detail, CT is the study of choice in the setting of trauma. Coronal images are essential for optimal assessment of the orbital floor. The lacrimal apparatus can also be evaluated, since it is commonly affected in trauma.[73]

Because the extra-ocular muscles are tethered to the walls of the orbit by tiny fibrous strands that are too small to image on CT or MR, muscle entrapment can occur in the presence of an orbital blowout fracture, even without herniation of the muscle itself (Fig. 14–9).[34]

Foreign body evaluation usually necessitates thin-section CT scanning (1.5 mm) to rule out clinically important objects (Fig. 14–10). Wood fragments can be particularly difficult to identify because of hydrational differences of various woods or air content. Because wood can have a variety of densities, especially on CT scans, special care should be taken to evaluate both dense foci and lucent foci within the orbit if the presence of a wood fragment is suspected.[62]

Phthisis bulbi represents the end stage of traumatic or inflammatory injury to the globe. The result is a shrunken, atrophic, and usually heavily calcified globe.

Infection

Infection most commonly affects the orbit by extension from adjacent structures. Contiguous spread of sinusitis or a superficial periorbital cellulitis of the face is the most

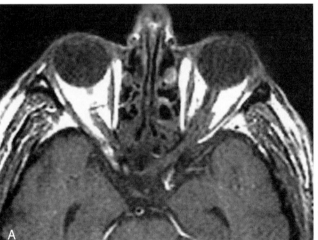

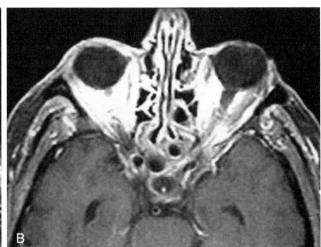

Figure 14–8. *A,* Precontrast axial T1-weighted image performed without fat suppression demonstrates a mass at the left orbital apex in a patient with known cutaneous lymphoma. *B,* Postcontrast T1-weighted image of the same patient in which the fat saturation pulse failed to suppress the orbital fat (this may be due to dental artifact). The lesion demonstrates marked contrast enhancement and is now indistinguishable from the high signal of the orbital fat. This case illustrates the importance of performing nonsuppressed precontrast images and fat-suppressed postcontrast studies.

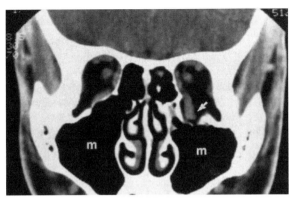

Figure 14–9. CT scan shows blowout fracture of the left orbital floor with herniation of extraconal fat and inferior rectus muscle *(arrow)*. m, maxillary sinus.

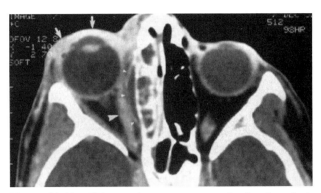

Figure 14–11. CT scan shows an extraconal subperiosteal abscess *(small arrowhead)*. This is a complication of ethmoid sinusitis. A thickened, displaced medial rectus *(large arrowhead)* and preseptal soft tissue swelling *(arrows)* are seen.

common scenario. Hematogenous infection is less common. The specific location of an orbital cellulitis is important for prognostic and therapeutic reasons. When possible, it should be determined whether a process is (1) preseptal or postseptal or (2) intraconal or extraconal.[22]

Extension of infection from the paranasal sinuses occurs most commonly from the ethmoid air cells (Fig. 14–11) in children and from the frontal sinuses (Fig. 14–12) in adults.[68] CT continues to be the examination of choice because it demonstrates not only the fluid and/or soft tissue component of the inflammatory process but also any bony changes. Findings range from mild mucoperiosteal thickening or elevation to frank intraorbital abscesses. The amount of periosteal elevation may dictate whether the patient is managed conservatively or surgically. The most common organisms in acute sinusitis are *Streptococcus pneumoniae,* beta-hemolytic streptococci, and *Haemophilus influenzae.* Staphylococci and anaerobes are less common.[68]

A mucocele is the expansion of a paranasal sinus that results from trapped mucus secretions. The expanding sinus can cause mass effect and distortion of the orbit (Fig. 14–13). MRI studies complement CT scans in this setting. In the absence of superimposed infection, the fluid is homogeneous in appearance. The fluid can have a variety of signal intensities as a result of differences in protein content from lesion to lesion. Mucoceles are seen most often

in the frontal sinuses but may be found in the other paranasal sinuses as well.[68]

Inflammation

Graves' Ophthalmopathy

Graves' disease is one entity in the spectrum of hyperthyroidism. It is thought to be caused by a circulating stimulator of thyroid function, so-called long-acting thyroid stimulator (LATS).[32] Orbital involvement demonstrates inflammatory cells that enlarge the extraocular muscles and infiltrate the retro-orbital fat. Involvement of the globe and optic nerve is rare.

The imaging findings demonstrate fusiform enlargement of the extraocular muscles, which is classically found in the belly of the muscle (Fig. 14–14; see Fig. 14–2). Typically, the tendonous attachments at the ring of Zinn are spared, which helps to differentiate Graves' disease from orbital pseudotumor. Most commonly affected is the inferior rectus muscle, both in isolation and in association with multiple muscular involvement.[54] The lack of tendonous involvement may be difficult to demonstrate in cases of massive muscle enlargement. It is important to assess for compression of the optic nerve–sheath complex, especially near the orbital apex.

In some cases, orbital involvement precedes clinically

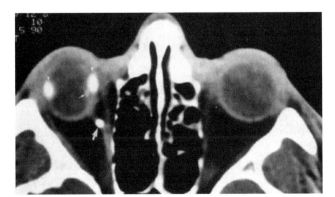

Figure 14–10. CT scan shows intraconal, metallic, foreign bodies just medial to the medial rectus *(large arrow)* and intraocular *(small arrow)*. Scleral band in place right *(arrowheads)*.

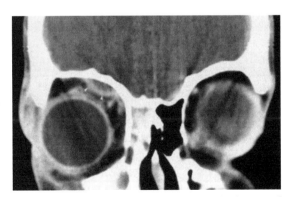

Figure 14–12. CT scan shows subperiosteal abscess of the superior orbit *(arrowheads)* from ethmoid or frontal sinus disease.

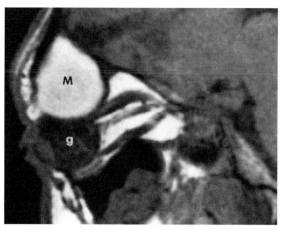

Figure 14–13. Sagittal T1-weighted MRI study shows mucocele (M) of the frontal sinus with inferior displacement of the globe (g).

apparent thyroid disease. In these circumstances, differentiation from pseudotumor can be difficult, especially when the involvement is unilateral.

Orbital Pseudotumor

Orbital pseudotumor is an idiopathic inflammatory process that may involve the extraocular muscles, orbital fat, and less commonly, other intraorbital structures.[12] The two most common appearances are a solitary intraorbital mass and diffuse muscle thickening.

The inflammation may involve any or all parts of the orbit and is usually unilateral. The diagnosis is usually based on a good clinical response to steroids[50] plus the exclusion of other inflammatory lesions of the orbit (e.g., sarcoid, Wegener's granulomatosis, multiple sclerosis). CT evaluation in the assessment of orbital pseudotumor most commonly demonstrates contrast enhancement of the involved structures, extraocular muscle enlargement, retrobulbar fat infiltration, and proptosis (Fig. 14–15A and B).

The muscular involvement in pseudotumor is classically diffuse, with extension to the tendonous attachments (Fig. 14–16). As mentioned earlier, tendonous involvement can help to differentiate pseudotumor from Graves' disease. Tumefactive or tumor-like inflammatory masses may also

occur, and differentiation from a neoplastic, infectious, or vascular process is required.

Imaging of pseudotumor and Graves' ophthalmopathy is usually accomplished with a contrast-enhanced CT scan, again with coronal and axial views essential.[17, 46] MRI studies are also useful in evaluating involvement of the optic nerve–sheath complex.

Sarcoid

Sarcoid is a noninfectious granulomatous disease that can have manifestations in almost any part of the optic pathway, from the globe to the optic radiations. The lacrimal gland and anterior layer of the globe (Fig. 14–17) and eyelids are common areas of involvement.[11] This entity shows increased signal on T1-weighted images in MRI studies.[52] Intracranial involvement by sarcoid, especially in the region of the sella turcica, is seen optimally with MRI (Fig. 14–18), although specificity and differentiation from other lesions can be difficult.

Optic Neuritis

Optic neuritis is an inflammation of the optic nerve that can have many causes, including infections (e.g., viral, bacterial, fungal, parasitic), granulomatous diseases, and demyelinating diseases such as multiple sclerosis.[68] Imaging characteristics of optic nerve inflammation are often subtle. Faint enhancement or slightly increased T2 signal may be seen. These changes are nonspecific.

Inversion recovery sequences (Fig. 14–19) are highly sensitive to increased water content, which often accompanies inflammatory processes. Increased signal on these images may be seen in optic neuritis, but this finding is also nonspecific.[18]

Neoplasms

Lymphoma

The most common neoplasm in the orbit is lymphoma, which accounts for just over half of all cases.[74] B-cell lymphomas of the non-Hodgkin's type are by far the most common. T-cell lineages are uncommon but have been described.[9] Usually, orbital lymphomas are primary to the orbit, but occasionally orbital manifestation of a systemic

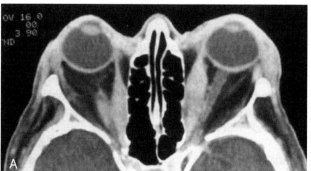

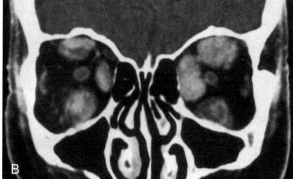

Figure 14–14. *A,* Axial contrast-enhanced CT scan shows Graves' ophthalmopathy characterized by enlarged superior, medial, and inferior recti with compromise of the orbital apex. *B,* Coronal contrast-enhanced CT scan of the same patient shown in *A.*

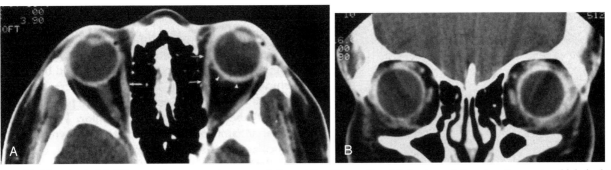

Figure 14–15. *A,* Axial CT scan shows pseudotumor of the orbit with swollen bilateral medial rectus *(arrows),* which includes tendinous insertion on the globe. Thickening and enhancement of the globe *(arrowheads)* are also shown. *B,* Coronal CT scan shows pseudotumor of the orbit (same patient as in *A*).

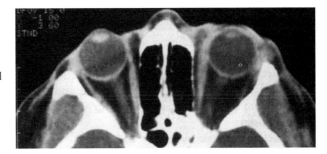

Figure 14–16. CT scan of orbital pseudotumor with bilateral medial rectus and left lacrimal involvement.

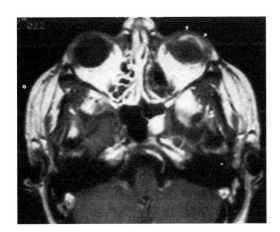

Figure 14–17. Axial T1-weighted MRI study with gadolinium shows sarcoid of the anterior left globe.

Figure 14–18. Axial T1-weighted MRI study with gadolinium shows sarcoid of the chiasm *(long arrow),* left cerebral peduncle *(large arrowhead),* lateral geniculate body *(short arrow),* and superior colliculus *(small arrowhead).*

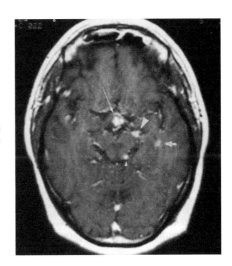

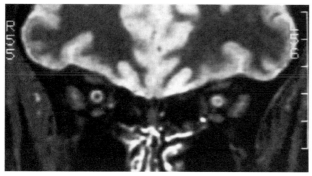

Figure 14–19. Coronal MRI study, inversion recovery fast spin echo, shows left optic neuritis with increased signal at the left optic nerve.

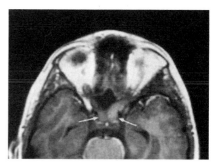

Figure 14–21. Axial T1-weighted MRI study shows optic glioma, bilateral optic nerves, with involvement of the chiasm *(arrows)* in a patient with neurofibromatosis.

lymphoproliferative process is seen. The usual appearance is a well-defined mass within the muscle cone (Fig. 14–20). Less frequently, extraconal masses or diffuse infiltration of the orbital fat can be seen.

The differential diagnosis includes pseudotumor and metastasis. Lacrimal gland involvement can be seen either in isolation or in combination with the other manifestations of lymphoma within the orbit.

Optic Glioma

Primary tumors of the optic nerve or nerve sheath are relatively uncommon. Optic gliomas most often occur in children, especially between the ages of 2 and 6 years, and are usually benign. This lesion usually involves the anterior optic apparatus (e.g., optic nerves, chiasm, and optic tracts) and causes enlargement and often tortuosity of these struc-

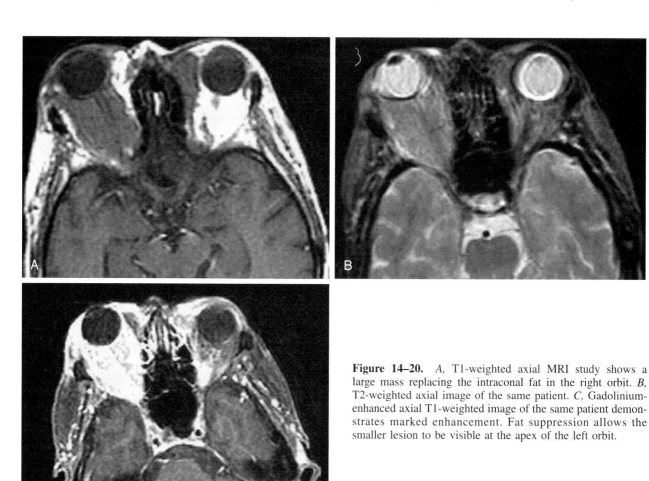

Figure 14–20. *A,* T1-weighted axial MRI study shows a large mass replacing the intraconal fat in the right orbit. *B,* T2-weighted axial image of the same patient. *C,* Gadolinium-enhanced axial T1-weighted image of the same patient demonstrates marked enhancement. Fat suppression allows the smaller lesion to be visible at the apex of the left orbit.

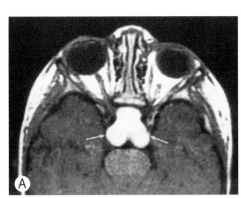
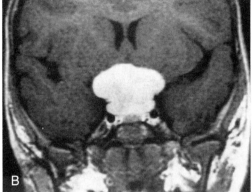

Figure 14–22. *A,* T1-weighted axial MRI study with gadolinium enhancement shows optic glioma of the optic chiasm *(arrows). B,* T1-weighted coronal MRI study with gadolinium shows same patient as in *A.*

tures. The incidence is increased in neurofibromatosis I (Fig. 14–21). These lesions do not calcify.[10]

MRI has become the modality of choice, given the necessity of evaluating the intracranial extent of the tumor (Fig. 14–22*A* and *B*). Optic gliomas are typically either nonenhancing or weakly enhancing. The lesions are generally isointense to slightly hypotense on T1-weighted images and hyperintense on T2-weighted images.[21]

CT can help in assessing bony changes and is especially valuable in detecting expansion of the optic canal. CT thus complements MRI in evaluation of these lesions.

Nerve Sheath Meningioma

The differential diagnosis of optic nerve and sheath lesions also includes meningiomas. Meningiomas tend to occur in middle-aged women rather than in children. These lesions can cause enlargement of the optic nerve sheath (Fig. 14–23*A* and *B*) or the entire complex (Fig. 14–24). Calcification is common, which helps to differentiate meningiomas from gliomas. Extension into the optic canal is rare, and extension to the chiasm is extremely rare.[25]

MRI studies are the best modality for evaluation of these lesions, but CT can be helpful for the same reasons as with gliomas, and can also show calcifications.[39] Because meningiomas tend to grow outward from the nerve sheath, they are less likely to efface the CSF layer between the nerve and sheath. This property sometimes helps to distinguish meningioma from glioma.

Melanoma

Melanoma is a malignant tumor that usually originates in the uveal layers of the globe. It can extend posteriorly to the rest of the orbit. MRI studies have been used to evaluate the intraorbital extent of melanoma and to search for metastatic disease.[57]

On MRI studies, the amount of melanin contained in the lesion determines the signal characteristics. Melanin shortens T1 and T2, thereby causing increased signal on T1-weighted images and decreased signal on T2-weighted images[19] (Fig. 14–25).

Signal is also affected by hemorrhage, which is not uncommon in patients with melanotic lesions. With hemorrhage, the differential diagnosis includes retinal and choroid detachments from other causes (Fig. 14–26). Detachments are usually distinguished clinically and radiographically.[43] Gadolinium enhancement increases the sensitivity in the detection of lesions[6] but does not increase specificity.

As previously stated, melanotic lesions have characteristic appearances, but nonpigmented melanomas cannot be reliably differentiated from other masses.[61] CT can also be used to evaluate these lesions (Fig. 14–27).

Metastatic Disease

The most common tumor to metastasize to the orbit is carcinoma of breast. Other primary sites include lung, colon, and prostate (Fig. 14–28). Metastatic lesions may

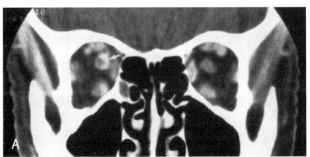
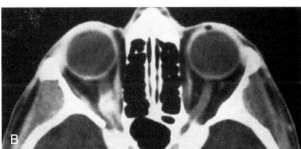

Figure 14–23. *A,* Coronal contrast-enhanced CT scan shows optic nerve sheath meningioma *(arrow). B,* Axial contrast-enhanced CT scan shows same patient as in *A.*

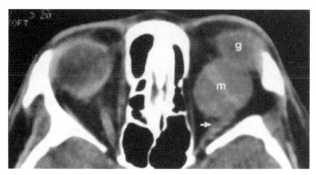

Figure 14–24. Axial contrast-enhanced CT scan shows optic nerve sheath meningioma. m, meningioma; g, globe; arrow, displaced optic nerve sheath complex emerging from mass.

affect any of the intraorbital structures as well as the bony orbit itself[30, 66] (Fig. 14–29). With a known distant primary site, a metastatic lesion should be considered. However, none of the available imaging techniques offers specificity to differentiate metastases from the many other orbital lesions. The findings may be subtle, with small areas of focal thickening of the globe, or large destructive lesions.[24] In addition, extension of tumor from an adjacent structure (e.g., the paranasal sinuses) may occur (Fig. 14–30A and B).

Cavernous Hemangioma and Lymphangioma

Cavernous hemangioma and lymphangioma are benign lesions that can be difficult to differentiate.[44]

Cavernous Hemangioma

Cavernous hemangiomas are usually discovered in young to middle-aged adults. The lesions tend to be well encapsulated with distinct margins, are usually intraconal,[55] and grow slowly. CT demonstrates a well-marginated soft tissue mass with mild or heterogeneous enhancement. MRI studies also demonstrate a well-defined intraconal lesion with isointense to slightly increased signal, when compared with the extraocular muscles on T1-weighted images. These lesions demonstrate marked signal intensity on T2-weighted images[40] (Fig. 14–31A and B).

Lymphangioma

Orbital lymphangioma presents at an earlier age, from infancy through the first decade. This lesion tends to occur either in the intraconal or extraconal compartment. Lymphangiomas are usually lobulated, with ill-defined borders, and may contain septations.[26] Multilocular or cystic blood collections are common.

These lesions are commonly hemorrhagic. CT scanning shows lobular heterogeneous masses with varying degrees of contrast enhancement. MRI characteristics include increased signal on T1-weighted images and marked signal intensity on T2-weighted images[20] (Fig. 14–32).

Retinoblastoma

Retinoblastoma is a malignant lesion with prominent tumor calcification. In its familial form, which results from loss of one copy of the Rb tumor suppressor gene,[35] it is

the most common intraocular neoplasm of children under 2 years of age. Inheritance is autosomal dominant. Metastasis may occur via direct spread along the optic nerve, hematogenously, or via lymphatics.

CT is the examination of choice because the hallmark finding is retinal calcification, for which MRI is less sensitive[58] (Fig. 14–33). MRI should be used as an additional modality, especially to detect extension into the region of the optic canal as well as to accomplish a more sensitive evaluation of parenchymal disease. Rarely, retinoblastoma may be seen in the pineal gland as well as in the eyes, the so-called "trilateral" retinoblastoma.

Indirect Involvement of the Orbit and Optic Pathways

The orbit or any part of the optic pathways may be affected by adjacent intracranial lesions. The most common lesions arise from the sella turcica and parasellar regions. The differential diagnosis includes pituitary macroadenoma (Fig. 14–34), meningioma, craniopharyngioma, metastasis, aneurysm, chordoma, and other less common entities. The posterior optic apparatus—superior colliculi, lateral geniculate bodies (see Fig. 14–18), optic radiation, and occipital lobes—may be affected by any infiltration or mass lesion (e.g., tumor, infarction, or inflammatory process).

Meningioma

One of the more common locations of an intracranial meningioma is the sphenoid wing. Visual symptoms can

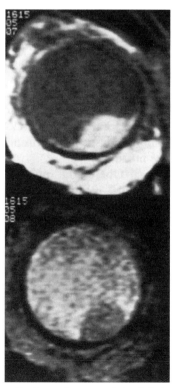

Figure 14–25. Ocular melanoma of the inferior aspect of the globe. *Top,* T1-weighted coronal MRI study. *Bottom,* T2-weighted coronal MRI study.

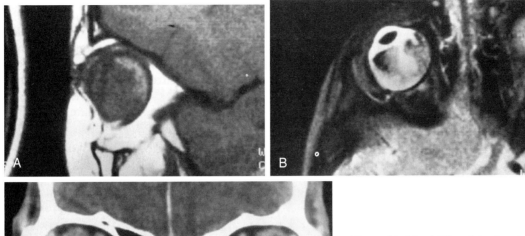

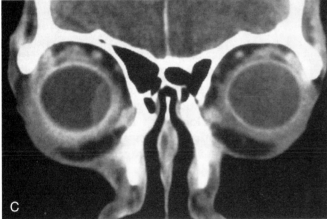

Figure 14–26. *A,* T1-weighted sagittal MRI study shows retinal detachment with hemorrhage. *B,* T2-weighted axial MRI study of the same patient as in *A. C,* Coronal CT scan shows retinal detachment (different patient). (*A* and *B,* Courtesy of Guy Wilms, M.D., Universitaire Ziekenhuizer, Leuven, Belgium.)

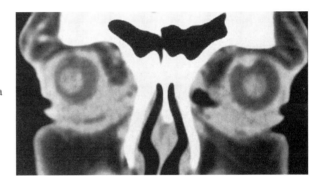

Figure 14–27. Coronal contrast-enhanced CT scan shows melanoma of the left ciliary body.

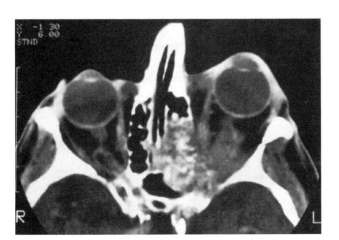

Figure 14–28. Axial contrast-enhanced CT scan shows prostate metastasis to the left orbit roof.

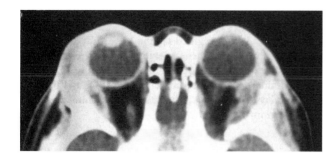

Figure 14–29. Axial contrast-enhanced CT scan shows bilateral neuroblastoma metastasis.

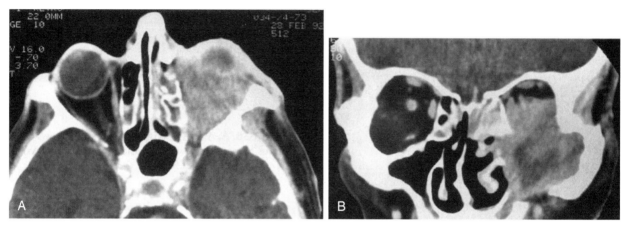

Figure 14–30. *A,* Axial contrast-enhanced CT scans shows extension of squamous cell carcinoma of the maxillary sinus to the orbit. *B,* Coronal contrast-enhanced CT scan shows the same patient as A.

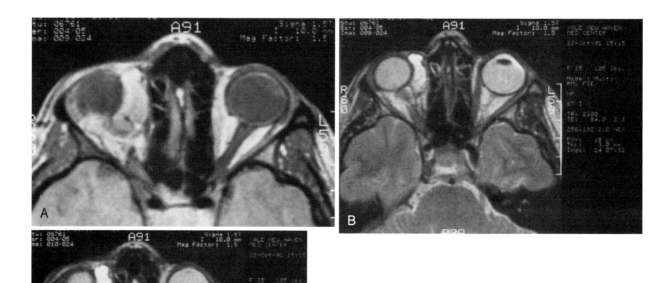

Figure 14–31. *A,* Axial T1-weighted MRI study shows cavernous hemangioma of the medial right orbit. *B,* Axial T2-weighted MRI study shows the same patient as in A.

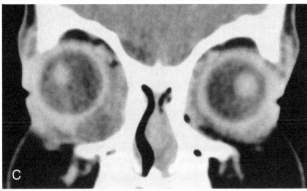

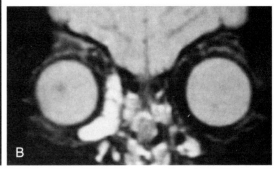

Figure 14–32. Lymphangioma. *A,* Coronal T1-weighted image. *B,* Coronal T2-weighted image. *C,* Coronal CT scan.

result from proximity to the optic canal or by mass effect on the anterior optic apparatus. Direct extension into the orbit is also possible (Fig. 14–35). On MRI studies, meningiomas are generally isointense to brain on T1-weighted and T2-weighted images with uniform, often very intense contrast enhancement.[83] However, signal and enhancement can be affected by the amount of calcification, vascularity, and heterogeneity of the lesion. The lesion can also show a variable amount of associated edema in the adjacent brain parenchyma.

Craniopharyngioma

Craniopharyngiomas are generally tumors of children, with a second peak in the middle-aged population. They most commonly present as a suprasellar mass. These tu-

mors are often well circumscribed and lobulated, often with cystic components. There may be a spectrum in signal characteristics on MRI scans, depending on whether the tumor is cystic or solid and whether the cysts contain high concentrations of cholesterol or hemorrhagic debris. Generally, the lesions are low to isointense on T1-weighted images and hyperintense on T2-weighted images.[33, 59] Gadolinium enhancement of the cyst walls and solid components have been demonstrated[78] (Fig. 14–36).

Craniopharyngiomas commonly calcify. CT and MRI are complementary studies for evaluation of these lesions.

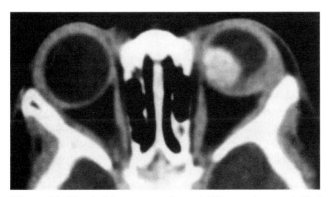

Figure 14–33. Axial contrast-enhanced CT scan shows calcified retinoblastoma of the left eye.

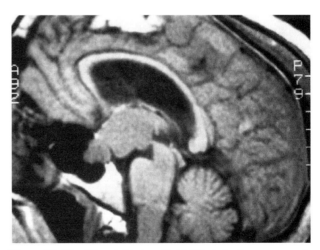

Figure 14–34. T1-weighted sagittal MRI study shows macroadenoma with suprasellar mass extension and superior displacement of the optic chiasm.

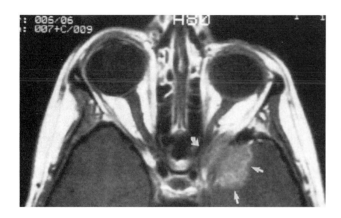

Figure 14–35. Axial T1-weighted MRI study with gadolinium shows left sphenoid wing meningioma *(arrows)*, with compromise of the optic canal *(curved arrow)*.

Lacrimal Gland and Apparatus

The most common lesions affecting the lacrimal gland are benign inflammatory processes, with tumors less common.[41]

Inflammatory, neoplastic, and traumatic processes can affect the lacrimal gland. The patient can present with deviation of the globe, proptosis, or conjunctival injection, depending on the extent of the lesion. With the possible exception of traumatic disruption, glandular enlargement is common to most lesions. Contrast enhancement does not distinguish between inflammation and neoplasia.

In the acute setting, viral adenitis accounts for most of the benign lesions and tends to affect a younger population. Chronic disease is usually secondary to granulomatous disease (e.g., sarcoid or Wegener's) or autoimmune disease (e.g., Sjögren's syndrome). Orbital pseudotumor may affect the lacrimal gland. Unilateral or bilateral glandular enlargement as well as variability of enhancement may be seen. The chronic entities tend to be more well marginated than the acute inflammatory processes.[41]

Tumors of the lacrimal gland may be either benign or malignant.[65] Approximately half of the lacrimal neoplasms are tumors of epithelial origin represented by pleomorphic adenoma (also known as *benign mixed tumor*) and adenoid cystic carcinoma (Fig. 14–37). Mucoepidermoid carcinoma and adenocarcinoma are also seen. Lymphocytic hyperplasia and lymphoma (Fig. 14–38) make up the bulk of additional tumors.[29]

CT scanning may demonstrate bone involvement in several lesions, including adenocarcinoma and mucoepidermoid carcinoma.[29] A study by Hesselink and coworkers[29] also revealed variable enhancement in both inflammatory (Fig. 14–39) and neoplastic lesions. The malignant mucoepidermoid demonstrated marked enhancement, but the adenocarcinoma showed no enhancement.

Calcified Orbital Lesions

There are many causes of orbital calcification, including such previously described entities as retinoblastoma and meningioma.[72]

Optic Drusen

One of the more common calcified lesions is optic drusen, usually seen in adults. The cause is uncertain. Drusen occur at the junction of the nerve with the globe. Drusen are composed of complex hyaline-like collections that frequently calcify.[7] Although these lesions may present with prominence of the optic disk, so-called pseudopapilledema,[63] the actual lesion is invisible funduscopically. CT scanning is used to identify drusen[60, 72] (Fig. 14–40).

Phthisis Bulbi

Phthisis bulbi is the degenerative end-stage of prior injury to the globe from trauma or infection. The globe is small, usually misshapen, and commonly densely calcified.

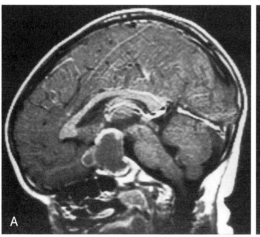
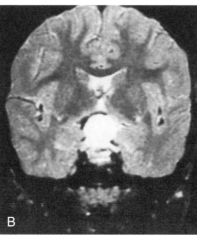

Figure 14–36. *A,* T1-weighted sagittal MRI study with gadolinium shows craniopharyngioma, mostly cystic, with sellar extension, and marked elevation of the chiasm, nerves, and tracts. *B,* Coronal T2-weighted MRI study shows the same patient as in *A.*

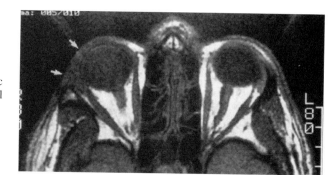

Figure 14–37. T1-weighted axial MRI study shows adenoid cystic carcinoma in the right lacrimal gland with extension to preseptal soft tissues *(arrows)*.

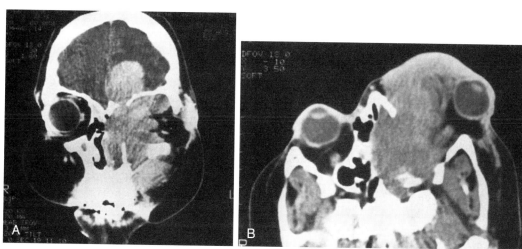

Figure 14–38. *A,* Coronal contrast-enhanced CT scan shows left lymphoma with extension into the sinuses and anterior cranial fossa. *B,* Axial contrast-enhanced CT scan shows the same patient as in *A*.

Figure 14–39. Axial contrast-enhanced CT study shows lacrimal gland pseudotumor with extension to preseptal soft tissues on the right *(arrowheads)*.

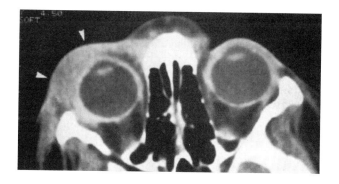

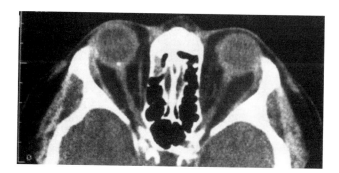

Figure 14–40. Axial CT scan shows optic disk drusen, right optic nerve head calcification, and optic nerve atrophy.

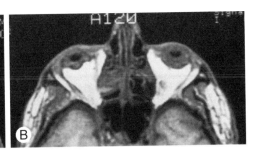

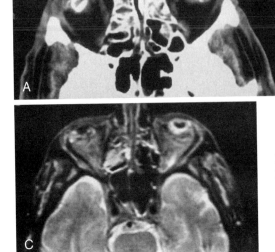

Figure 14–41. *A,* Axial CT scans shows bilateral phthisis bulbi. *B,* Axial T1-weighted MRI study, same patient as in *A. C,* Axial T2-weighted MRI study, same patient as in *A.*

This entity can be identified by either CT or MRI, but confirmation of calcification is made with CT (Fig. 14–41). Trochlear calcification has also been seen both with increasing patient age and with diabetes mellitus in younger patients.[27]

Teratoma

The teratoma is a rare benign lesion that contains mixed endodermal, mesodermal, and ectodermal elements. It usually calcifies. Because the teratoma is usually seen in neonates, knowing a patient's age can help one decide whether to include this entity on a differential diagnosis[28, 81] (Fig. 14–42).

Calcified Ciliary Muscle Insertions

Calcification of the insertions of the ciliary muscles of the pupil can be seen in elderly patients, which is often an incidental finding on CT studies of the head performed for reasons other than suspected orbital pathology.

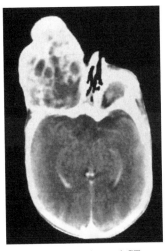

Figure 14–42. Axial contrast-enhanced CT scan shows calcified teratoma with areas of enhancement.

Vascular Lesions

A carotid cavernous fistula is an abnormal high flow communication between the arterial and venous circulations. The most common cause is post-traumatic.[53] Other causes include spontaneous fistulas, possibly related to atherosclerotic disease and rupture of an aneurysm of the intracavernous portion of the carotid artery.[14] Clinical findings include bruit, chemosis, exophthalmos (which can be pulsatile), visual loss, and swelling of the eyelid. Cranial nerve palsies are also seen, which may affect any of the nerves coursing through the cavernous sinus (III, IV, V1, V2, and VI).

Arteriography has been considered the "gold standard" for delineating the vascular anatomy and the site of fistulous communication.[13] However, CT and MRI studies also have adjunctive roles in suggesting the diagnosis and also as follow-up examinations, especially after embolization.[13] Imaging findings include proptosis, asymmetry, and distention of the affected cavernous sinus, and congestion and (usually) asymmetrical dilation of the venous structures that drain the cavernous sinus, especially the superior ophthalmic vein (Fig. 14–43*A* and *B*). Contrast enhancement, to evaluate the vascular structures, and bone windows, to evaluate fracture, are essential.[37]

The orbital varix is a venous malformation that may be represented by a large, tortuous vein or a masslike confluence of small veins, which may markedly enlarge with changes in venous pressure (e.g., Valsalva's maneuver, straining, and exertion). The changes in venous pressure and subsequent venous distention cause a painful intermittent exophthalmos.

In the past, orbital venography was the imaging procedure of choice.[36] However, contrast-enhanced CT scans are currently the ideal diagnostic test. The examination is best performed with a technique for increasing orbital pressure, such as Valsalva's maneuver[77] (Fig. 14–44*A* and *B*) or even with a gentle venous compression on the neck.[64] In addition, color flow Doppler imaging may be useful as a screening examination for a varix.[76]

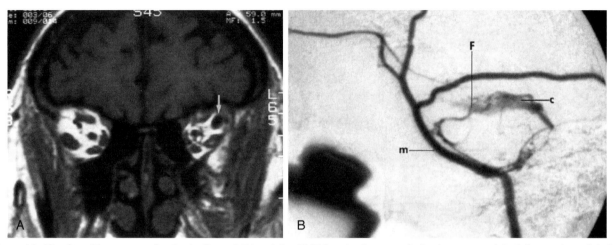

Figure 14–43. Carotid cavernous fistula. *A,* Coronal T1-weighted MRI study shows marked enlargement of the left superior ophthalmic vein *(arrow). B,* Lateral digital subtraction angiogram shows fistulous communication between branches of the external carotid and the cavernous sinus. m, middle meningeal artery; F, fistula; c, cavernous sinus.

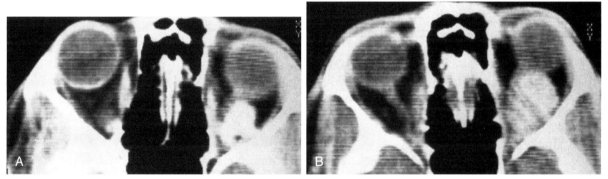

Figure 14–44. Axial contrast-enhanced CT scan. Orbital varix both before *(A)* and during *(B)* Valsalva's maneuver demonstrates the increase in size of the lesion. (Courtesy of Robert E. Peyster, M.D., Hahnemann Hospital, Philadelphia.)

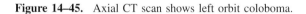

Figure 14–45. Axial CT scan shows left orbit coloboma.

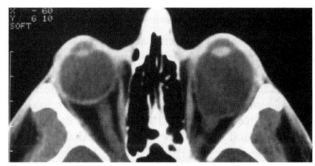

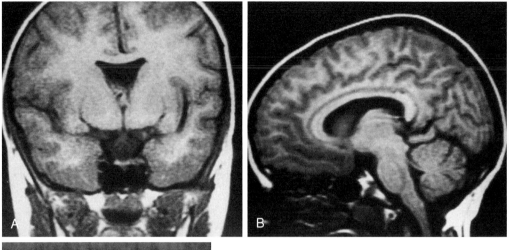

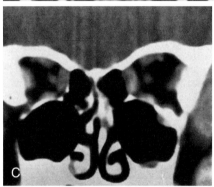

Figure 14–46. Septo-optic dysplasia MRI. *A* and *B,* Absent septum pellucidum, absent chiasm (coronal and sagittal MRI, T1-weighted). *C,* Atretic optic nerves (coronal CT scan).

Congenital Abnormalities and Anomalies

Coloboma

Optic nerve colobomas are congenital defects in the optic nerve usually near the optic disc. These lesions represent a spectrum of developmental abnormalities that result from incomplete or inadequate fusion of the optic fissure during embryogenesis and occur along the inferomedial aspect of the globe and nerve.[45] The defects can be bilateral and can be transmitted as an autosomal dominant trait.[64] They may present as a small cone-shaped defect at the optic disc or as a large retinal cyst. CT scans have been used to delineate the various elements of this lesion,[66] and thin-section axial scans through the region of the optic disc, in particular, are suggested[42] (Fig. 14–45).

Septo-optic Dysplasia

Septo-optic dysplasia is the mildest form of a spectrum of developmental abnormalities that includes holoprosencephaly. These abnormalities result from abnormal ventral induction and mesodermal differentiation. In septo-optic dysplasia, absence of the septum pellucidum and hypoplasia of the optic nerves is sometimes accompanied by pituitary or hypothalamic endocrine dysfunction.[49]

These abnormalities are often accompanied by or associated with other congenital and migrational defects.[8] MRI is therefore the modality of choice in evaluating these lesions,[5] especially because of the multiplanar capabilities and superior visualization of the sellar region, optic nerves and chiasm, and the septum pellucidum. Coronal views are especially important for evaluating the septum[78] (Fig. 14–46). Optic nerve hypoplasia may be present *without* an absent septum.

Summary

Imaging of the orbit by CT and MRI has undergone many recent technologic advances. With attention to technique, the localization and characterization of lesions can be made without difficulty. However, specificity is still an issue with many of the described lesions, and clinical correlation is essential for diagnosis.

References

1. Anzai Y, Lufkin RB, Jabour BA, Hanafee WN: Fat-suppression failure artifacts simulating pathology on frequency-selective fat-suppression MR images of the head and neck. AJNR Am J Neuroradiol 13:879–884, 1992.
2. Babbel RW, Harnsberger HR: A contemporary look at the imaging issues of sinusitis: Sinonasal anatomy physiology and computed tomography techniques. Semin Ultrasound CT MRI 12:526–540, 1991.
3. Balter S: An introduction to the physics of magnetic resonance imaging. Radiographics 7:371, 1987.
4. Barkovitch AJ: Contemporary Neuroimaging: Pediatric Neuroradiology, vol 1. New York, Raven Press, 1990, pp 106–108.
5. Barkovich AJ, Fram EK, Norman D: Septo-optic dysplasia: MR imaging. Radiology 171:189–192, 1989.
6. Bond JB, Haik BG, Mihara F: Magnetic resonance imaging of choroidal melanoma with and without gadolinium contrast enhancement. Ophthalmology 98:459–466, 1991.
7. Boyce SW, Platia EV, Green WR: Drusen of the optic nerve head. Ann Ophthalmol 10:645–704, 1978.
8. Byrd SE, Naidich TP: Common congenital brain anomalies. Radiol Clin North Am 26:755–772, 1988.

9. Coupland SE: T-cell and T/natural killer cell lymphomas involving ocular and ocular adnexal tissues: A clinicopathologic, immunohisto-chemical, and molecular study of seven cases. Ophthalmology 106: 2109–2120, 1999.

10. Chutorian AM, Schwartz JF, Evans RA, et al: Optic gliomas in children. Neurology 14:83–95, 1964.

11. Collison JMT, Miller NR, Green WR: Involvement of orbital tissues by sarcoid. Am J Ophthalmol 102:302–307, 1986.

12. Curtin HD: Pseudotumor. Radiol Clin North Am 25:583–599, 1987.

13. Debrun G: Management of traumatic carotid-cavernous fistulas. In Viñuela F, Halbach VV, Dion JE, et al (eds): Interventional Neuroradi-ology: Endovascular Therapy of the Central Nervous System. New York, Raven Press, 1992, pp 107–112.

14. Dohn DF: Carotid aneurysms and arteriovenous fistulae of the cavern-ous sinus. In Youmans JR (ed): Neurological Surgery, vol 2. Philadel-phia, WB Saunders, 1973, pp 870.

15. Flanders AE, Mafee MF, Rao VM, Choi KH: CT characteristics of orbital pseudotumor and other orbital inflammatory processes. J Com-put Assist Tomogr 13:40–47, 1989.

16. Fullerton GD: Magnetic resonance imaging signal concepts. Radio-graphics 7:579–596, 1987.

17. Gibby WA, Cohen MS, Goldberg HI, Sergott RC: Pseudotumor cerebri: CT findings and correlation with vision loss. AJR Am J Roentgenol 160:143–146, 1993.

18. Glassberg R, Abrahams JJ: Optic neuritis evaluation with inversion recovery fast spin echo (IRFSE) work in progress (personal communi-cation). New Haven, Yale Department of Radiology.

19. Gomori JM, Grossman RI, Shields JA, et al: Choroidal melanomas: Correlation of NMR spectroscopy and MR imaging. Radiology 158: 443–445, 1986.

20. Graeb DA, Rootman J, Robertson WD, et al: Orbital lymphangiomas: Clinical, radiologic, and pathologic characteristics. Radiology 175: 417–421, 1990.

21. Haik BG, Saint Louis L, Bierly J, et al: Magnetic resonance imaging in evaluation of optic nerve gliomas. Ophthalmology 94:709–717, 1987.

22. Handler LC, Davey IC, Hill JC, Lauryssen C: The acute orbit: Differentiation of orbital cellulitis from subperiosteal abscess by computed tomography. Neuroradiology 33:15–18, 1991.

23. Harms SE, Siemers PT, Hildebrand P, Plum G: Multiple spin echo magnetic resonance imaging of the brain. Radiographics 6:117–134, 1986.

24. Harnsberger HR: Head and Neck Imaging: Handbooks in Radiology. Chicago, Year Book Medical Publishers, 1990, p 358.

25. Harnsberger HR: Head and Neck Imaging: Handbooks in Radiology. Chicago, Year Book Medical Publishers, 1990, p 363.

26. Harris GJ, Sakol PJ, Bonavolonta G, et al: An analysis of thirty cases of orbital lymphangioma: Pathophysiologic considerations and management recommendations. Ophthalmology 97:1583–1592, 1990.

27. Hart BL, Spar JA, Orrison WW: Calcification of the trochlear appara-tus of the orbit: CT appearance and association with diabetes and age. AJR Am J Roentgenol 159:1291–1294, 1992.

28. Henderson JW: Orbital cysts. In Orbital Tumors, 2nd ed. New York, BC Decker, 1980, pp 75–115.

29. Hesselink JR, Davis KR, Dallow RL, et al: Computed tomography of masses in the lacrimal gland region. Radiology 131:143–147, 1979.

30. Hesselink JR, Davis KR, Weber AL, et al: Radiologic evaluation of orbital metastasis, with emphasis on computed tomography. Radiol-ogy 137:363–366, 1980.

31. Hilal SK, Trokel SL: Computerized tomography of the orbit using thin sections. Semin Roentgenol 12:137–147, 1977.

32. Ingbag SH, Woebar KA: Diseases of the thyroid. In Petersdorf RG, et al (eds): Harrison's Principles of Internal Medicine, 10th ed. New York, McGraw-Hill, 1983, pp 611–634.

33. Johnson LN, Hepler RS, Yee RD, et al: Magnetic resonance imaging of craniopharyngioma. Am J Ophthalmol 102:242–244, 1986.

34. Koornneef L, Zonneveld F: The role of direct multiplanar high resolution CT in the assessment and management of orbital trauma. Radiol Clin North Am 25:753–766, 1987.

35. Korsmeyer SJ: Genes and neoplasia. In Isselbacher KJ, et al (eds): Harrison's Principles of Internal Medicine, 13th ed. New York, McGraw-Hill, 1994, p 378.

36. Kubin DA, Amundsen P, Newton TH: Orbital venography in the diagnosis of intermittent exophthalmos. Radiology 88:930–934, 1967.

37. Lasjaunias P, Berenstein A: Surgical Neuroradiology: Endovascular

38. Lee DH, Simon JH, Szumowski J, et al: Optic neuritis and orbital lesions: Lipid-suppressed chemical shift MR imaging. Radiology 179: 543, 1991.

39. Lindblow B, Truwit C, Hoyt WF: Optic nerve sheath meningioma: Definition of intraorbital, intracanalicular, and intracranial compo-nents with magnetic resonance imaging. Ophthalmology 99:560–566, 1992.

40. Mafee MF: The orbit proper. In Som PM, Bergeron TA (eds): Head and Neck Imaging, 2nd ed. St. Louis, Mosby–Year Book, 1991, pp 800–801.

41. Mafee MF: The orbit proper. In Som PM, Bergeron TA (eds): Head and Neck Imaging, 2nd ed. St. Louis, Mosby–Year Book, 1991, pp 805–810.

42. Mafee MF, Jampol LM, Langer BG, et al: Computed tomography of optic nerve colobomas, morning glory anomaly, and colobomatous cyst. Radiol Clin North Am 25:693–699, 1987.

43. Mafee MF, Peyman GA: Retinal and choroidal detachments: Role of magnetic resonance imaging and computed tomography. Radiol Clin North Am 25:487–507, 1987.

44. Mafee MF, Putterman A, Valvassori GE, et al: Orbital space occu-pying lesions: Role of computed tomography and magnetic resonance imaging. An analysis of 145 cases. Radiol Clin North Am 25:529–559, 1987.

45. Mann I: Developmental Abnormalities of the Eye, 2nd ed. Philadel-phia, JB Lippincott, 1957, pp 68–94.

46. McNichols MMJ, Power WJ, Griffen JF: Idiopathic inflammatory pseudotumor of the orbit: CT features correlated with clinical out-come. Clin Radiol 44:3–7, 1991.

47. Merandi SF, Kudryk BT, Murtagh FR, et al: Contrast-enhanced MR imaging of optic nerve lesions in patients with acute optic neuritis. AJNR Am J Neuroradiol 12:923–926, 1991.

48. Merritt CRB: Magnetic resonance imaging: A clinical perspective—image quality, safety and risk management. Radiograph-ics 7:1001–1016, 1987.

49. Morishima A, Aronoff GS: Syndrome of septo-optic-pituitary dyspla-sia: The clinical spectrum. Brain Dev 8:233–239, 1986.

50. Motton-Lippa L, Jakobiec FA, Smith M: Idiopathic inflammatory orbital pseudotumor in childhood: II. Results of diagnostic tests and biopsies. Ophthalmology 88:565–574, 1981.

51. Munk PL, Vellet AD, Levin M, et al: Sonography of the eye. AJR Am J Roentgenol 157:1079–1086, 1991.

52. Naheedy MH, Haaga JR, Azar-Kia B, et al: MRI and CT of sellar and parasellar disorders. Radiol Clin North Am 25:819–847, 1987.

53. Newton TH, Troost BT: Arteriovenous malformations and fistulae radiology of the skull and brain: Angiography. In Newton TH, Potts DG (eds): Radiology of the Skull and Brain, vol 2. St. Louis, CV Mosby, 1971, pp 2420–2565.

54. Nugent RA, Belkin RI, Meigel JM, et al: Graves orbitopathy: Correla-tion of CT and clinical findings. Radiology 177:675–682, 1990.

55. Orcutt JC, Wulc AE, Mills RP, et al: Asymptomatic orbital cavernous hemangiomas. Ophthalmology 98:1257–1260, 1991.

56. Pavlicek W: MR instrumentation and image formation. Radiographics 7:809–814, 1987.

57. Peyman GA, Mafee MF: Uveal melanoma and similar lesions: The role of magnetic resonance imaging and computed tomography. Ra-diol Clin North Am 25:471–486, 1987.

58. Price HI, et al: The neuroradiology of retinoblastoma. Radiographics 2:7–23, 1982.

59. Pusey E, Kortman KE, Flannigan BD, et al: MR of craniopharyngi-omas: Tumor delineation and characterization. AJR Am J Roentgenol 149:383–388, 1987.

60. Ramirez H, Blatt ES, Hibri HS: Computed tomography identification of calcified optic nerve drusen. Radiology 148:137–139, 1983.

61. Raymond WR, Char DH, Norman D, et al: Magnetic resonance imaging evaluation of uveal tumors. Am J Ophthalmol 111:633–641, 1991.

62. Roberts CF, Leehey PJ III: Intraorbital wood foreign body mimicking air at CT. Radiology 185:507–508, 1992.

63. Rosenberg MA, Savino PJ, Glaser JS: A clinical analysis of pseudo-papilledema: I. Population, laterality, acuity, refractive error, ophthal-moscopic characteristics and coincident disease. Arch Ophthalmol 97: 65–70, 1979.

64. Savell J, Cook JR: Optic nerve colobomas of autosomal dominant heredity. Arch Ophthalmol 94:395–400, 1976.

65. Shnier R, Parker GD, Hallinan JM, et al: Orbital varices: A new technique for noninvasive diagnosis. AJNR Am J Neuroradiol 12: 717–718, 1991.
66. Shields JA, Bakewell B, Augsburger JJ, et al: Classification and incidence of space-occupying lesions of the orbit: A survey of 645 biopsies. Arch Ophthalmol 102:1606–1611, 1984.
67. Simmons JS, Lamasters D, Char D: Computed tomography of ocular colobomas. Am J Roentgenol 141:1223–1226, 1983.
68. Som P: Sinonasal cavity. In Som PM, Bergeron TA (eds): Head and Neck Imaging, 2nd ed. St. Louis, Mosby–Year Book, 1991, pp 150–159.
69. Spencer WM: Ophthalmologic Pathology: An Atlas and Textbook, vol 3. Philadelphia, WB Saunders, 1986, pp 2391–2409.
70. Sullivan JA, Harms SE: Characterization of orbital lesions by surface coil MR imaging. Radiographics 7:9–28, 1987.
71. Tien RD: Fat suppression MR imaging in neuroradiology: Techniques and clinical application. AJR Am J Roentgenol 158:369–379, 1992.
72. Turner RM, Gutman I, Hilal SK, et al: CT of drusen bodies and other calcified lesions of the optic nerve: Case report and differential diagnosis. Am J Neuroradiol 4:175–178, 1983.
73. Unger JM: Fractures of the nasolacrimal fossa and canal: A CT study of appearance, associated injuries, and significance in 25 patients. AJR Am J Roentgenol 158:1321–1324, 1992.
74. Valvassori GE: Imaging of orbital lymphoproliferative disorders. Radiol Clin North Am 37:135–50, 1999.
75. Wehrli FW, MacFall JR, Newton TH: The parameters determining the appearance of NMR images. In Newton TH, Potts DG (eds): Advanced Imaging Techniques. San Anselmo, Calif, Clavadel, 1984.
76. Wildenhain PM, Lehar SC, Dastur KJ, et al: Orbital varix: Color flow imaging correlated with CT and MR studies. J Comput Assist Tomogr 12:171–173, 1991.
77. Winter J, Centeno RS, Bentson JR: Maneuver to aid diagnosis of orbital varix by computed tomography. Am J Neuroradiol 3:39–40, 1982.
78. Wolpert SM, Barnes PD: MRI in Pediatric Neuroradiology. St. Louis, Mosby–Year Book, 1992, p 101.
79. Wolstencroft, SJ: Orbital metastasis due to interval lobular carcinoma of the breast: A potential mimic of lymphoma. Arch Ophthalmol 117: 14, 19–21, 1999.
80. Yeoman LJ, Howarth L, Britten A, et al: Gantry angulation in brain CT: Dosage implications, effect on posterior fossa artifacts, and current international practice. Radiology 184:113–116, 1992.
81. Youssef B: J Pediatr Ophthalmol 6:177–81, 1969.
82. Zimmerman RA: Imaging of intrasella, suprasella and parasella tumors. Semin Roentgenol 25:174–197, 1990.
83. Zimmerman RD, Fleming CA, Saint Louis LA, et al: Magnetic resonance imaging of meningiomas. AJNR Am J Neuroradiol 6: 149–157, 1985.
84. Zonneveld FW: Normal direct multiplanar CT anatomy of the orbit with correlative anatomic cryosections. Radiol Clin North Am 25: 381–407, 1987.

15

Temporal Bone

Donald W. Chakeres, Mark A. Augustyn

Many imaging modalities are available for the evaluation of the temporal bone, including plain radiographs, angiography, cerebrospinal fluid (CSF) analysis, air and non-ionic contrast cisternography, computed tomography (CT), and magnetic resonance imaging (MRI). CT and MRI are currently the most widely used techniques and have largely replaced the other modalities.[2, 3, 5, 8–10, 12, 14, 31, 57, 67] Plain films remain an inexpensive survey of large bony and air-filled structures although they often result in inaccurate diagnosis.

CT scanning excels in the evaluation of bone and air space anatomy and disorders. Because CT scans are more accurate in identifying many soft tissue abnormalities and are much less prone to artifacts,[16] they have largely replaced polytomography; there is also less radiation to the lens of the globe with CT scans than with polytomography.[14] With advances in MR technology, MRI has surpassed CT in certain areas of spatial and contrast resolution.[7]

MRI has expanded the range of pathology that can be accurately evaluated because it can image many soft tissue entities not visible by other techniques. MRI studies can also be extremely useful in the evaluation of blood vessel–related disorders of the temporal bone and is much better than CT in characterizing the CSF, brain, and cranial nerves.

Angiography is still the "gold standard" for vascular evaluation, and interventional angiography can be used in treatment of vascular lesions of the temporal bone. Each technique has its own advantages and disadvantages, and often more than one examination is necessary for a complete temporal bone evaluation.[39]

Normal Temporal Bone

Embryology and Development

The development of the *inner ear* structures (vestibule, semicircular canals, internal auditory canal [IAC], cochlea) is independent of the *middle ear* (ossicles, mastoid antrum, tympanic membrane, middle ear air spaces) and *external ear* (external auditory canal [EAC], temporomandibular joint) structures. This explains why developmental abnormalities of the inner ear are usually not seen with deformities of the external ear and middle ear, and vice versa.[23] The mechanical sound-conducting structures of the external ear and middle ear develop from the first and second branchial arches. The neural sound-perceiving apparatus of the inner ear develops from the ectodermal otocyst. Adjacent mesenchyme contributes to the development of the inner ear, middle ear, and external ear.

The first and second branchial arches mold two significant cartilaginous structures. The first arch forms Meckel's cartilage, from which the head of the malleus and short process of the incus develop. The second arch forms Reichert's cartilage, from which the remainder of the malleus and incus, styloid process, and stapes superstructure develop.[55] The stapes footplate is a bilaminar structure, with an outer portion developing from Reichert's cartilage and an inner portion developing from the ectodermal otocyst.

The middle ear cavity and mastoid antrum are fluid-filled until birth. The neonate's initial crying and breathing fill the eustachian tube system and the middle ear with air. The mastoid air cells develop as saclike extensions from the mastoid antrum, commencing at about the time of birth and continuing for several years. There is extensive variation in the degree of pneumatization. Incomplete pneumatization of the mastoid air cells may be caused by a lack of proper function of the eustachian tube during early life.[47]

Normal Anatomy (Figs. 15–1 to 15–15)

External Auditory Canal

The external auditory canal consists of a funnel-shaped, undulating, cartilaginous lateral portion and an osseous medial segment (see Figs. 15–3, 15–9, and 15–10).[11] The cartilaginous portion is continuous with the pinna. These structures are flexible and are surrounded by fat. The osseous portion constitutes two thirds of the length of the external auditory canal and is covered by skin and periosteum only.

Tympanic Cavity

The tympanic cavity is the air space between the eustachian canal and the mastoid air cells (see Figs. 15–7 and 15–8) that contains the ossicles. The *hypotympanum* is the most inferior portion of the tympanic cavity and connects anteromedially to the osseous orifice of the eustachian canal. The semicanal for the tensor tympani muscle parallels the eustachian canal. The protympanum forms the anterior triangular portion of the tympanic cavity adjacent to the carotid canal.

The *mesotympanum*, the central portion of the tympanic cavity, is bordered laterally by the scutum (or spur) and tympanic membrane and medially by the otic capsule. The scutum is a bony crest separating the external auditory canal from the epitympanic space. The tympanic membrane attaches to the scutum superiorly and to the limbus inferiorly.[22]

The *post-tympanum*, the posterior portion of the cavity, contains the facial recess laterally and the sinus tympani

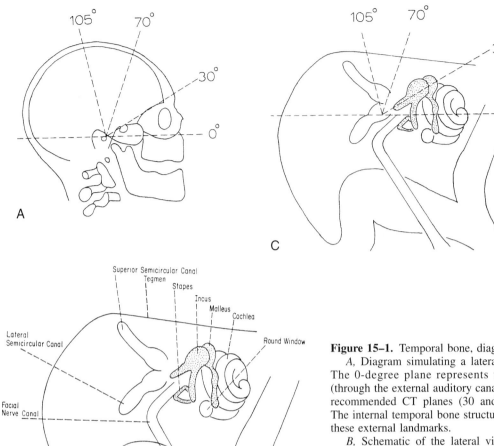

Figure 15–1. Temporal bone, diagram of normal anatomy.

A, Diagram simulating a lateral CT scout view of the skull. The 0-degree plane represents the anthropological baseline (through the external auditory canal and inferior orbital rim). The recommended CT planes (30 and 105 degrees) are illustrated. The internal temporal bone structures are consistently oriented to these external landmarks.

B, Schematic of the lateral view of the temporal bone that depicts the normal relationship of several major temporal bone structures.

C, Spatial relationship of the normal temporal bone structures to the anthropologic baseline. The four recommended tomographic planes (0, 30, 70, and 105 degrees) correspond to the scan planes through the temporal bone based on the scout positioning.

(A–C, From Chakeres DW, Spiegel RK: A systematic technique for comprehensive evaluation of the temporal bone by computed tomography. Radiology 146:97, 1983.)

medially. The triangular epitympanum forms the superior portion of the middle ear and contains the massive portions of the malleus (head) and the incus (body and short process). The epitympanic space is linked to the mastoid antrum by a narrow hourglass-shaped isthmus called the aditus ad antrum.

Mastoid Antrum

The cone-shaped antrum is interposed between the aditus ad antrum and the mastoid air cells (see Fig. 15–6). The size of the antrum varies considerably as a result of the alterations in pneumatization of the air cells that drain into it.

Ossicles

The ossicles are suspended by the tympanic membrane, the ligaments to the epitympanic walls, and the oval window (see Figs. 15–5, 15–7, and 15–13). The long process of the malleus attaches to the tympanic membrane. The neck of the malleus is connected to the tensor tympani

ligament. The circular head of the malleus articulates with the triangular body of the incus. The short process of the incus is suspended within the epitympanic space, pointing toward the aditus ad antrum. The long process of the incus articulates with the stapes.

The stapes consists of two crura and one footplate. The footplate of the stapes attaches to the oval window of the vestibule and is secured by the annular ligament.[24]

Internal Auditory Canal

The internal auditory canal is a bony conduit that transmits cranial nerves VII (facial) and VIII (vestibulocochlear) from the pontomedullary junction of the brain stem to the inner ear (see Figs. 15–5 and 15–8). Its medial orifice is the porus acusticus. The internal auditory canal is partially divided by a central anterior bony lamina called the *falciform crest* (Fig. 15–15A), which runs parallel to the long axis of the canal. The falciform crest divides the canal into a smaller superior portion containing the superior vestibular and facial nerves and a larger inferior portion containing

Text continued on page 506

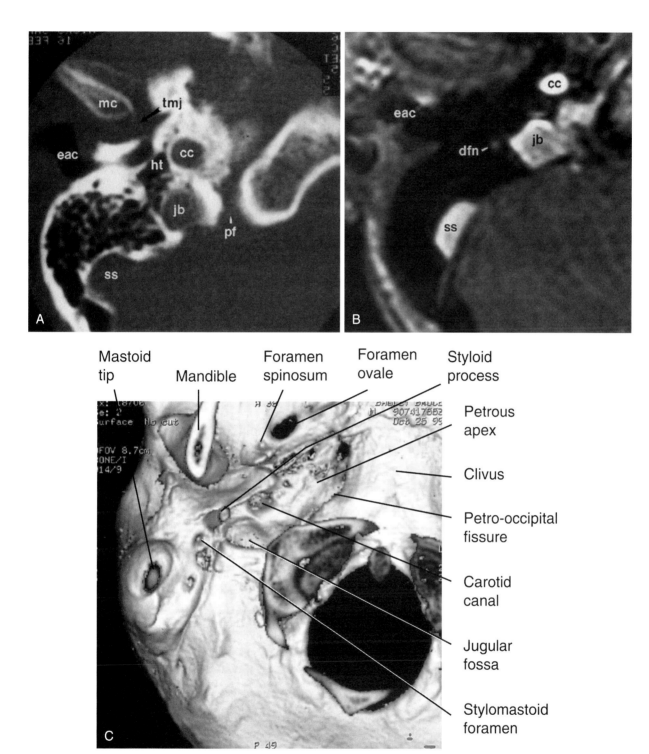

Figure 15–2. Hypotympanic jugular foramen level.

A, Axial CT section acquired through the right temporal bone.

B, High-resolution time-of-flight MRI study at a similar level where the vessels demonstrate a high signal intensity. cc, vertical carotid canal; dfn, descending facial nerve; eac, external auditory canal; ht, hypotympanum; jb, jugular bulb; mc, mandibular condyle; pf, petro-occipital fissure; ss, sigmoid sinus; tmj, temporomandibular joint.

C, Surface CT reconstruction, inferior view of temporal bone. This surface reconstruction of the inferior skull base has been processed from axial CT images. The openings for the carotid canal, jugular fossa, foramen ovale, foramen spinosum, and the stylomastoid foramen are all visible. The mandible, mastoid tip, cut end of the styloid process, external auditory canal, petrous apex, clivus, petro-occipital fissure, and stylomastoid foramen are shown.

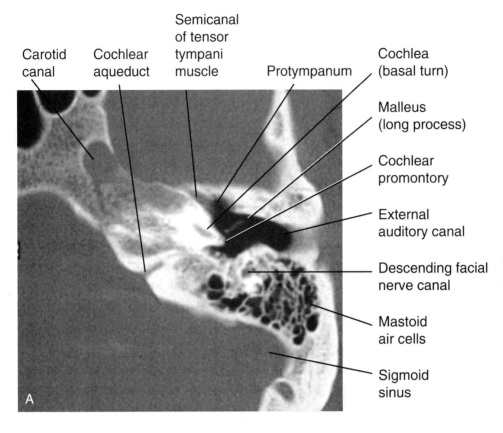

Carotid canal

Cochlear aqueduct

Semicanal of tensor tympani muscle

Protympanum

Cochlea (basal turn)

Malleus (long process)

Cochlear promontory

External auditory canal

Descending facial nerve canal

Mastoid air cells

Sigmoid sinus

A

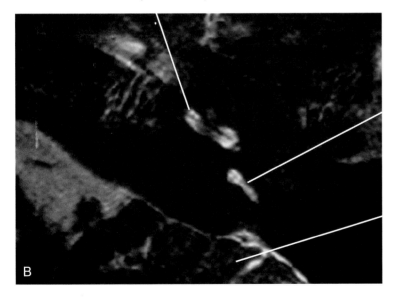

Cochlea (basal turn)

Posterior semicircular canal

Cerebellum

B

Figure 15–3. Axial views, normal anatomy.

A, Axial CT section. This is the most inferior CT axial section of the temporal bone. The external auditory canal and the long process of the malleus are seen. The tympanic membrane is too thin to be visible. The cochlear promontory and basal turn of the cochlea are visible. The thin, linear semicanal of the tensor tympani muscle is seen interposed between the protympanum and the carotid canal. The cochlear duct is seen arching from the posterior fossa toward the basal turn of the cochlea. The descending facial nerve canal, sigmoid sinus, and the mastoid air cells are shown.

B, Axial MRI section.

Carotid
canal

Cochlea
(basal turn)

Semicanal
of tensor
tympani

Round
window
niche

Middle
ear
cavity

Neck of
malleus

Long process
of incus

Stapes

Pyramidal
eminence

Facial
nerve
canal

Tympanic
sinus

Sigmoid
sinus

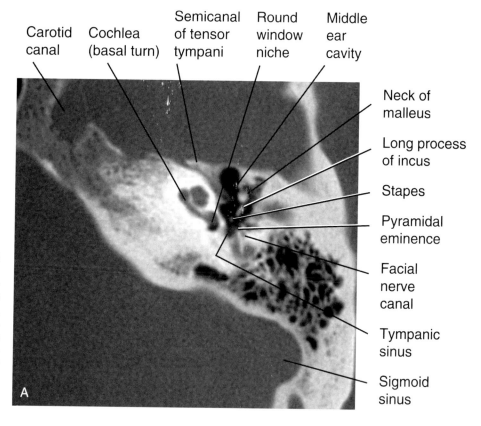

Figure 15–4. Axial views, normal anatomy.

A, Axial CT scan of the left temporal bone centered at the neck of the malleus in the epitympanic space. The adjacent long process of the malleus and the stapes are both visible posteriorly. The semicanal of the tensor tympani muscle is seen as a linear lucency just lateral to the cochlea. The ligaments are not visible. The three turns of the cochlea are all visible as well as the air space related to the round window niche. The descending facial nerve canal is seen posterior to the tympanic sinus and anterior to the mastoid air cells. Other labeled structures include the petrous apex, carotid canal, and the sigmoid sinus.

B, Axial MR image.

Anterior
inferior
cerebellar
artery

Cochlear
aqueduct

Cochlea
(basal turn)

Cochlea
(apical turn)

Posterior
semicircular
canal

Cerebellum

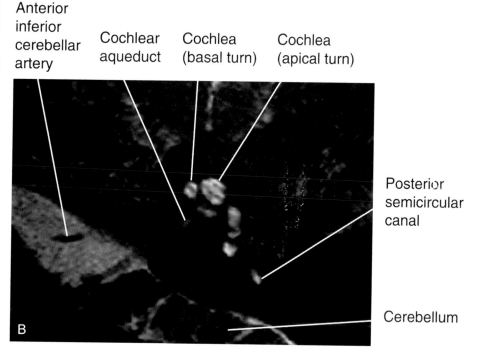

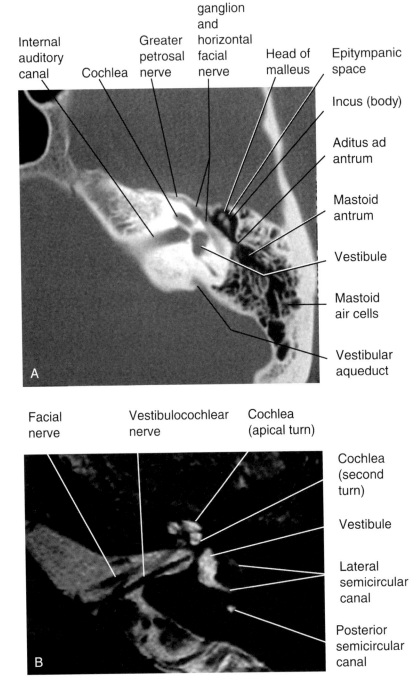

Internal auditory canal

Cochlea

Greater petrosal nerve

Geniculate ganglion and horizontal facial nerve

Head of malleus

Epitympanic space

Incus (body)

Aditus ad antrum

Mastoid antrum

Vestibule

Mastoid air cells

Vestibular aqueduct

A

Facial nerve

Vestibulocochlear nerve

Cochlea (apical turn)

Cochlea (second turn)

Vestibule

Lateral semicircular canal

Posterior semicircular canal

B

Figure 15–5. Axial views, normal anatomy.

A, Axial CT image centered over a long segment of the facial nerve canal. The geniculate ganglion and horizontal portions of the facial nerve canal are seen continuous with the internal auditory canal. The superior portion of the cochlea and the vestibule are visible. The opening of the vestibular aqueduct and endolymphatic sac is seen as a thin slit along the posterior margin of the temporal bone just medial to the mastoid air cells. The epitympanic space holds the head of the malleus and the body of the incus and is continuous posteriorly with the aditus ad antrum and the mastoid antrum.

B, Axial MR image.

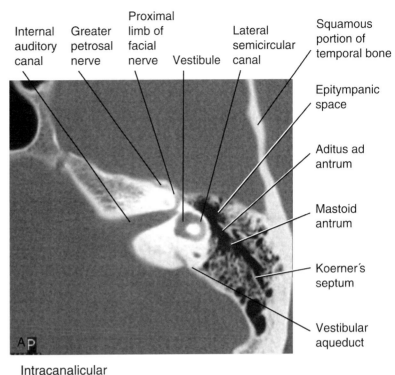

Internal auditory canal — Greater petrosal nerve — Proximal limb of facial nerve — Vestibule — Lateral semicircular canal — Squamous portion of temporal bone — Epitympanic space — Aditus ad antrum — Mastoid antrum — Koerner's septum — Vestibular aqueduct

Figure 15–6. Axial views, normal anatomy.

A, Axial CT section of the complete internal auditory canal, ending in the proximal limb of the geniculate segment of the facial nerve canal anteriorly. The vestibule and complete lateral semicircular canal are visible. The posterior semicircular canal and the vestibular aqueduct are seen posteriorly. Portions of the epitympanic space, the aditus ad antrum, and the mastoid antrum are seen in continuity. Koerner's septum is also visible. The squamous portion of the temporal bone is seen anterior to the mastoid and petrous segments.

B, Axial MR section.

C, Axial 3D reconstruction of the interior of the skull base clipped at the level of the internal auditory canal. The relationship of the temporal inner and the middle ear structures to the skull base is shown.

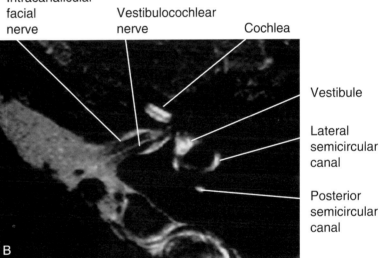

Intracanalicular facial nerve — Vestibulocochlear nerve — Cochlea — Vestibule — Lateral semicircular canal — Posterior semicircular canal

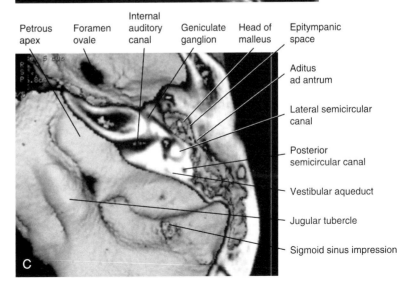

Petrous apex — Foramen ovale — Internal auditory canal — Geniculate ganglion — Head of malleus — Epitympanic space — Aditus ad antrum — Lateral semicircular canal — Posterior semicircular canal — Vestibular aqueduct — Jugular tubercle — Sigmoid sinus impression

Cochlea   Geniculate ganglion   Cochleariform process   Epitympanic space

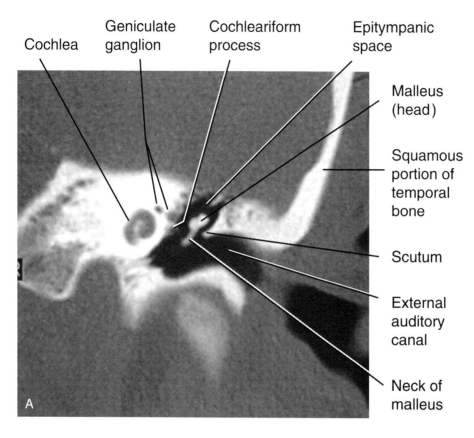

Malleus (head)

Squamous portion of temporal bone

Scutum

External auditory canal

Neck of malleus

A

Geniculate ganglion

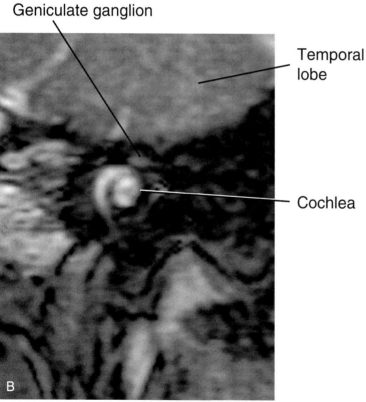

Temporal lobe

Cochlea

B

Figure 15–7. Normal anatomy.

A, Coronal CT section. This is the most anterior CT section of the left temporal bone. The scutum forming the medial margin of the external auditory canal and adjacent head of the malleus and the long process of the malleus are seen. The epitympanic space supports the ossicles. The external auditory canal appears continuous with the middle ear cavity; the tympanic membrane is frequently not visible when normal. Abnormal thick tympanic membranes are easier to image. Three small canals are just medial and superior to the anterior cochlea. These include the proximal limb of the geniculate ganglion, the distal limb of the geniculate ganglion, and the semicanal of the tensor tympani muscle.

B, Axial MR section.

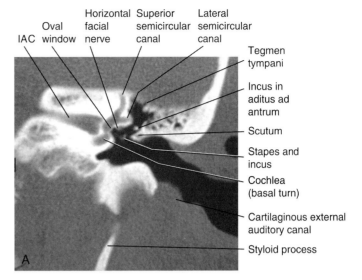

A, Oval window, IAC, Horizontal facial nerve, Superior semicircular canal, Lateral semicircular canal, Tegmen tympani, Incus in aditus ad antrum, Scutum, Stapes and incus, Cochlea (basal turn), Cartilaginous external auditory canal, Styloid process

Figure 15–8. Normal anatomy.

A, Coronal CT section made at the level of the oval window. The adjacent stapes and incudostapedial joint are visible as an L-shaped structure overlying the oval window. The horizontal portion of the facial nerve is just below the lateral semicircular canal. The short process of the incus is interposed between the scutum and the lateral semicircular canal. The internal auditory canal (IAC), middle ear, external auditory canal (EAC), stapes, and the basal turn of the cochlea are shown. Note the absence of visible soft tissues over the medial EAC, which is normal. Only the cartilaginous segment of the EAC is seen as a soft tissue component.

B, Coronal MR section.

C, Surface MRI reconstruction. This is an oblique view of the left otic capsule structures imaged by high-resolution 3D Fourier transform MRI T2-weighting and postprocessing with a surface algorithm. The three turns of the cochlea are clearly seen, with the basal turn merging with the vestibule. The superior, lateral, and posterior semicircular canals are all well visualized. The cerebrospinal fluid (CSF) in the internal auditory canal is seen as a tubular structure extending back toward the cerebellopontine angle. The anatomy appears as a "plaster cast" of the otic capsule.

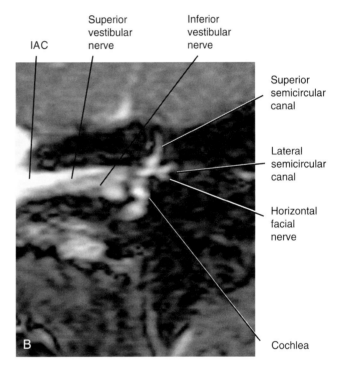

B, IAC, Superior vestibular nerve, Inferior vestibular nerve, Superior semicircular canal, Lateral semicircular canal, Horizontal facial nerve, Cochlea

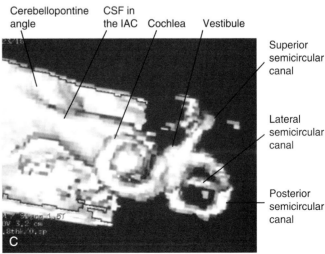

C, Cerebellopontine angle, CSF in the IAC, Cochlea, Vestibule, Superior semicircular canal, Lateral semicircular canal, Posterior semicircular canal

Internal
auditory
canal   Vestibule

Superior
semicircular
canal

Lateral
semicircular
canal

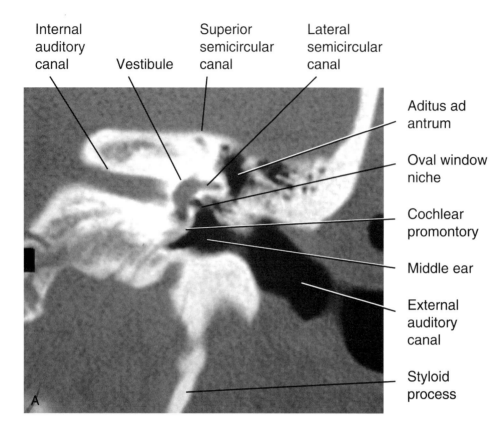

Aditus ad
antrum

Oval window
niche

Cochlear
promontory

Middle ear

External
auditory
canal

Styloid
process

A

Superior
semicircular
canal

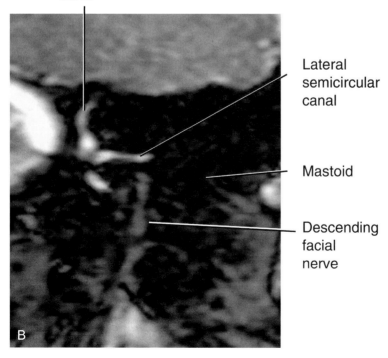

Lateral
semicircular
canal

Mastoid

Descending
facial
nerve

B

Figure 15–9. Coronal views, normal anatomy. *A,* Coronal CT section of the left temporal bone, made through the vestibule and the posterior portion of the oval window. The basal turn of the cochlea and cochlear promontory are seen. The aditus ad antrum is seen just lateral to the lateral semicircular canal. A short portion of the superior semicircular canal is visible. The internal auditory canal, middle ear, styloid process, and external auditory canal are shown. *B,* Coronal MR section.

Internal
auditory
canal

Superior
semicircular
canal

Vestibule

Lateral
semicircular
canal

Posterior
genu of
facial nerve

Tympanic
sinus

Round
window

External
auditory
canal

Styloid
process

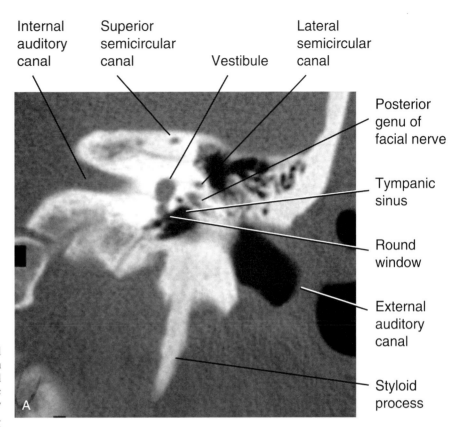

Figure 15–10. Coronal views, normal anatomy. *A,* Posterior coronal CT section of the temporal bone centered at the level of the round window and the tympanic sinus. The air spaces extend all the way to the otic capsule membrane surfaces. The adjacent posterior genu of the facial nerve and vestibule are seen. Other depicted structures include the posterior internal auditory canal, superior semicircular canal, lateral semicircular canal, styloid process, and external auditory canal. *B,* Coronal MR section.

Superior
semicircular
canal

Vestibule

Lateral
semicircular
canal

Posterior
genu
of facial
nerve

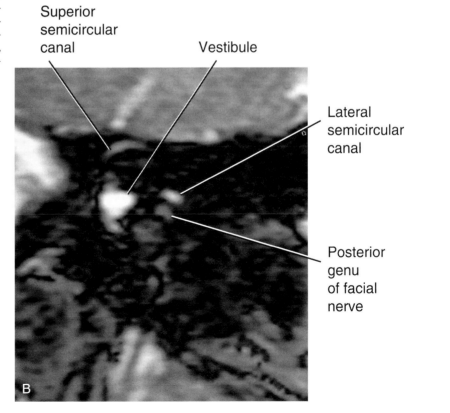

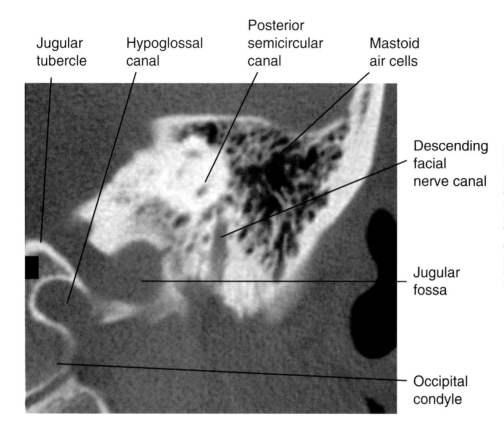

Figure 15–11. Coronal CT section. This is the most posterior section of the temporal bone. The descending facial nerve canal is seen between the mastoid air cells and the more medial jugular fossa. The jugular tubercle, hypoglossal canal, and occipital condyle all appear medial to the jugular fossa. Short segments of the posterior semicircular canal are seen.

the inferior vestibular and cochlear nerves.[23] The lateral portion of the canal is perforated by the cranial nerves where they enter the cochlea, vestibule, and facial nerve canal.

Vestibule, Vestibular Aqueduct, Endolymphatic Duct, and Sac

The vestibular cavity is the central portion of the membranous labyrinth that communicates with the semicircular canals and cochlea (see Figs. 15–6, 15–10, and 15–14). The vestibule lies immediately lateral to the fundus of the internal auditory canal, and the oval window of the middle ear forms its lateral margin. The vestibular aqueduct is a narrow bony canal that contains the small endolymphatic duct and sac (see Fig. 15–14). The endolymphatic duct originates from the posteromedial aspect of the vestibule, courses past the common crus,[5] and assumes a hockey stick shape. The endolymphatic sac, an extension of the endolymphatic duct, is a dead-end fluid space arising from the vestibule that lies beneath the dura of the posterior temporal bone.

Semicircular Canals

The semicircular canals are three orthogonally arranged circular structures of the membranous labyrinth arising from the vestibule (Figs. 15–6, 15–8, and 15–13). The lateral semicircular canal approximates the horizontal plane. The posterior and superior semicircular canals share a common crus posteriorly.

Cochlea and Cochlear Aqueduct

The spiral cochlear apparatus contains the membranous labyrinth components for hearing (see Fig. 15–4). The cochlea lies anterior to the vestibule and has 2½ to 2¾ turns around its modiolus, the central bony spiral axis. The most lateral portion of the basal turn of the cochlea projects into the tympanic cavity, forming a promontory of bone.[30]

The cochlear aqueduct, a channel that connects the cochlea near the round window with the subarachnoid space just superior to the jugular tubercle, lies inferior to the internal auditory canal.

Oval and Round Windows

The oval window of the vestibule is the interface between the mechanical and neural elements of the ear (see Fig. 15–8). It lies just inferior to the horizontal facial nerve canal and the lateral semicircular canal. It is covered by the annular ligament, which surrounds the footplate of the stapes.[23]

The round window is the bony opening of the basal turn of the cochlea and is covered by a fibrous membrane (see Fig. 15–10). It lies inferior and slightly posterior to the oval window and is adjacent to the inferior tympanic sinus.

Facial Nerve and Facial Nerve Canal (Fallopian Canal)

The facial nerve has a highly tortuous course and comes in close contact with almost every other important component of the temporal bone (Figs. 15–5, 15–8, and 15–12). The labyrinthine (cochlear) portion of the facial nerve

Text continued on page 511

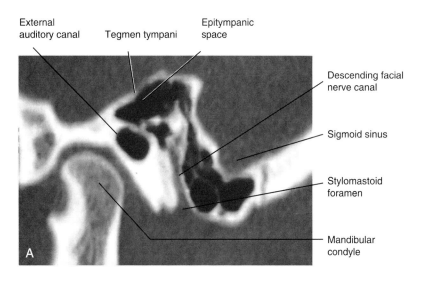

External
auditory canal · Tegmen tympani · Epitympanic space · Descending facial nerve canal · Sigmoid sinus · Stylomastoid foramen · Mandibular condyle

A

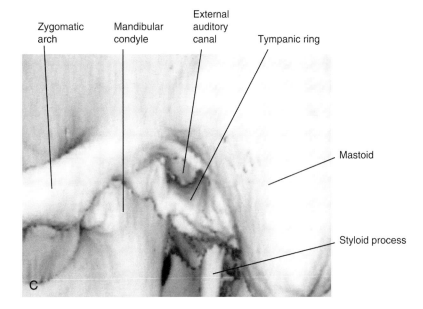

Stylomastoid foramen · Temporal lobe · Lateral semicircular canal · Cerebellum · Posterior genu facial nerve · Descending facial nerve

B

Figure 15–12. Sagittal views, normal anatomy. *A,* Sagittal CT reconstruction through the descending facial nerve canal and stylomastoid foramen. The mastoid air cells and sigmoid sinus lie just posterior to the facial nerve. The mandibular condyle, mandibular fossa, external auditory canal, and epitympanic space are visible. *B,* Sagittal MRI section. *C,* CT surface reconstruction of the lateral skull and mandible centered over the external auditory canal.

Zygomatic arch · Mandibular condyle · External auditory canal · Tympanic ring · Mastoid · Styloid process

C

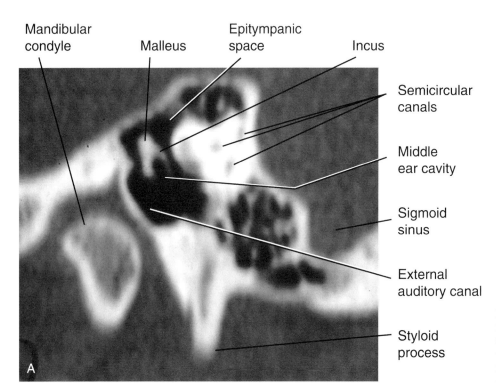

Mandibular condyle

Malleus

Epitympanic space

Incus

Semicircular canals

Middle ear cavity

Sigmoid sinus

External auditory canal

Styloid process

A

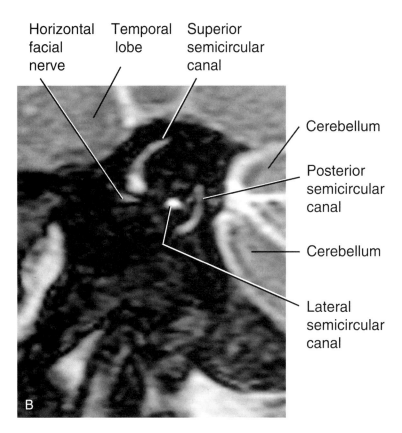

Horizontal facial nerve

Temporal lobe

Superior semicircular canal

Cerebellum

Posterior semicircular canal

Cerebellum

Lateral semicircular canal

B

Figure 15–13. Sagittal views, normal anatomy. *A,* Sagittal CT reconstruction made at the level of the epitympanic space. The most medial portion of the mandibular condyle and the mandibular fossa are seen. The styloid process and the mastoid air cells are visible. The head of the malleus and the long process of the incus are visible in the epitympanic space. The thin wall of the epitympanic space, the semicircular canals, and a portion of the facial nerve canal in the middle ear are visible. *B,* Sagittal MR section.

Oval
window
niche   Facial
nerve   Superior
semicircular
canal   Vestibule

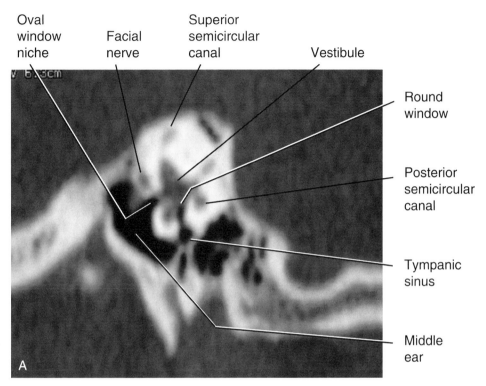

Round
window

Posterior
semicircular
canal

Tympanic
sinus

Middle
ear

Figure 15–14. Sagittal views, normal anatomy. *A,* Sagittal CT reconstruction centered at the level of the middle ear. The oval and round windows are seen with their associated niches. The vestibule and the basal turn of the cochlea are seen as well. The superior and posterior semicircular canals are visible. The tympanic sinus is continuous with the round window. *B,* Sagittal MR section.

Facial
nerve   Vestibule

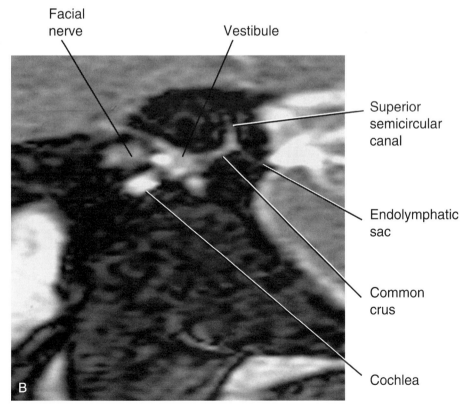

Superior
semicircular
canal

Endolymphatic
sac

Common
crus

Cochlea

Protympanum   Falciform crest

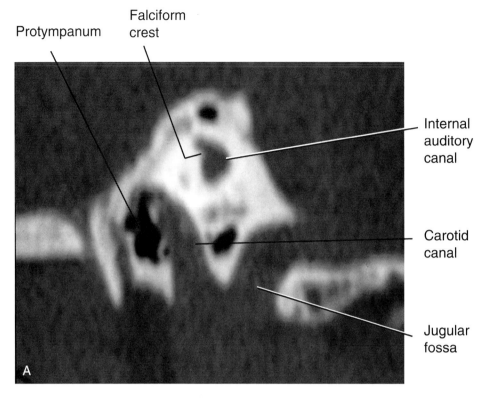

Internal auditory canal

Carotid canal

Jugular fossa

Cochlear nerve   Facial nerve

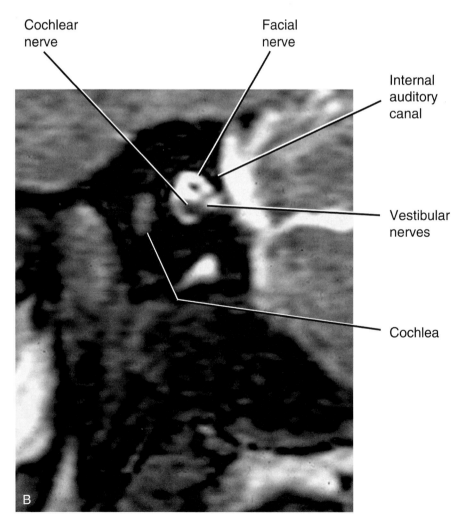

Internal auditory canal

Vestibular nerves

Cochlea

Figure 15–15. Sagittal views, normal anatomy. *A,* This sagittal CT reconstruction is the most medial section and is centered at the protympanum, carotid canal, internal auditory canal, and jugular fossa. Note the close association of the protympanum and the carotid canal. The internal auditory canal demonstrates a small anterior pointed indentation resulting from the falciform crest that separates the facial and cochlear nerves. *B* and *C,* Sagittal MR sections.

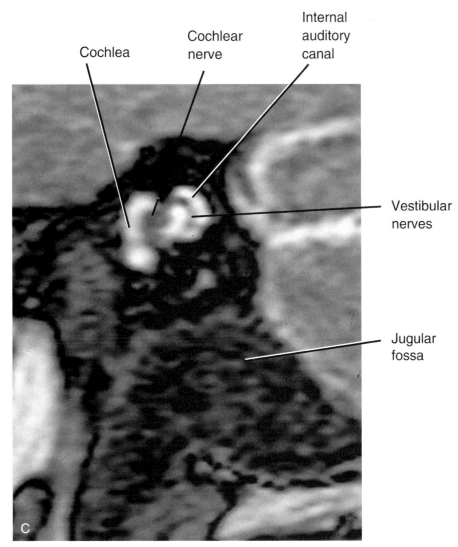

Figure 15–15 *Continued*

exits the superior anterior portion of the internal auditory canal fundus.

At the geniculate ganglion, an acute reverse (inverted V) angle of the nerve and canal is seen. The distal limb of the geniculate ganglion doubles back posteriorly to become the horizontal segment in the medial wall of the tympanic cavity. This portion of the facial nerve canal has a thin inferior bony covering that may be dehiscent.

The horizontal portion of the facial nerve runs directly inferior to the lateral semicircular canal. The facial nerve then abruptly turns inferiorly (at an angle of 95 to 125 degrees) to form the posterior genu near the tympanic sinus and the pyramidal eminence.[53]

The vertical, or descending, facial nerve in the mastoid portion of the facial nerve canal runs vertically just posterior to the external auditory canal. In this vertical portion, the nerve to the stapedius muscle and the chorda tympani (first and second branches, respectively, of the facial nerve distal to the geniculate ganglion) arise. The facial nerve then exits from the mastoid portion of the temporal bone via the funnel-shaped, fat-filled stylomastoid foramen.

Carotid Canal

The carotid canal enters the base of the skull, ascends vertically, then turns horizontally and medially toward the petrous apex (see Figs. 15–2 and 15–15). This canal lies anterior and inferior to the cochlea and is separated from the protympanum by a thin bony plate.

Jugular Foramen and Fossa

The jugular foramen is divided into a smaller anteromedial neural compartment (pars nervosa) containing cranial nerves IX, X, and XI, and a larger posterolateral vascular compartment (the pars vascularis) containing the jugular vein (see Fig. 15–11). The floor of the tympanic cavity normally forms the roof of the jugular fossa. The jugular bulbs are frequently asymmetrical, and there may be a small diverticulum from their apices.

CT and MRI Anatomy

CT scans and MRI studies are complementary. On CT scans, bony structures are demonstrated by high density and CSF by low density, and air spaces appear black. The brain and vascular structures are intermediate in density. CT is not ideal for evaluating detail of the soft tissues of the otic capsule contents, brain, and vessels. In contrast, MRI studies receive no signal from dense bone or air spaces and thus cannot be used to evaluate these components accurately in the absence of pathology. MRI, however, is superior to CT in characterizing the CSF, brain, cranial nerves, and blood vessels.

CT Techniques

The temporal bone has a high inherent radiation attenuation contrast, having both the most dense bone in the body as well as air-filled spaces. High-resolution CT images are usually acquired with thin sections (1 to 2 mm) and special bone algorithms for high detail.[14] CT scans of the temporal area can be obtained rapidly, with relatively low radiation doses, compared with many other types of CT examinations. Contrast enhancement is not essential for evaluation of pathology isolated to bone or air spaces. Intravenous (IV) contrast material is often used to assess vascular lesions, areas of breakdown in the blood-brain barrier, or soft tissue changes. CT is less expensive than MRI, although CT is limited by scan artifacts, radiation exposure, and fewer scanning planes (because of the limitations in gantry and in patient positioning).

Multiplanar CT reformations can display the complex anatomy of the temporal bone in all of the conventional polytomography projections while exposing the patient to radiation only once.[25] However, even slight motion by the patient is intolerable because the small bony structures of the temporal bone are in such close proximity that motion artifacts may obscure significant detail.[63] In addition, reformation results in slight image degradation and loss of resolution. The longitudinal oblique plane (Stenvers projection) is parallel to the long axis of the petrous bone and is ideal for the study of longitudinal temporal bone fractures.[60]

MRI Techniques

Many different techniques can be used to acquire MR images, depending on the suspected abnormality and the equipment available. T1-weighted (TR = 600 msec, TE = 20 msec) spin-echo coronal or axial images are usually acquired without contrast medium. The fat spaces have high signal intensity, and the brain has intermediate signal intensity. CSF demonstrates low signal intensity, and air and bone spaces appear as voids. This sequence also helps to differentiate fat from subacute hemorrhage.

T2-weighted (TR = 3000 or longer msec, TE = 80 or longer msec) axial spin-echo images accurately display the CSF spaces and many disease processes as high-signal-intensity regions. High-resolution, thin-section (1.5 mm or less), three-dimensional (3D) Fourier transform (3D FT) T1-weighted, gradient-echo (TR = 50 msec, TE = 7 msec; flip-angle, 30 degrees) images can be acquired with paramagnetic contrast agents. Gradient images have the advantage of high resolution, very thin sections, and blood flow information (phase or time-of-flight effects).[15, 59]

Various image contrasts are also possible, including T1, free precession, or proton-density weighting. T2-weighted,

spin-echo 3D FT imaging using multiple echo times (TE) in for each repetition time (TR) generate excellent quality images. T2-weighted or free precession at steady-state gradient-echo 3D FT imaging (SIMCAST*) with very high resolution displays the otic capsule structures as high-signal-intensity regions surrounded by signal void.[7] Three-dimensional data can also be computer-processed into maximum pixel signal intensity ray projections, planar sections, or surface reconstructions.[57]

MRI is outstanding for its ability to evaluate blood vessel–related disorders of the temporal bone.[48, 59] With many gradient-echo techniques, flowing blood can be seen as a high-intensity-signal region,[15] and phase imaging can be used to quantify velocity and flow volumes.[59] Gadolinium-diethylenetriamine-penta-acetic acid (Gd-DTPA) contrast-enhanced MRI studies using T1-weighted images are particularly sensitive for evaluating abnormalities that alter the blood-brain barrier or that are vascular, such as inflammatory disease (Bell's palsy, vestibulitis, otitis, granulation tissue, meningitis), carcinomatosis, posterior fossa infarcts, tumors,[6, 38] and demyelination.[50] Frequently, the findings of contrast enhancement are more obvious on MR images than on CT scans. MRI studies, compared with CT, also have higher resolution and are more sensitive to alteration in the fluid spaces of the inner ear and the cerebellopontine angle.

Normal Temporal Bone Images

Axial Sections

Caudad to Cephalad (see Figs. 15–1 to 15–6)

The axial or transverse plane is most suitable for a survey study of the temporal bone.[68] This suitability is based on the ease by which axial CT sections may be obtained.[63] The structures within the temporal bone are consistently oriented to the external landmarks of the skull. Axial CT sections made 30 degrees above the anthropologic baseline are parallel to the lateral semicircular canal and optimally display many structures.[14] The axial plane is of special interest for the visualization of the incudomalleolar and incudostapedial articulations, facial nerve canal, internal auditory canal, vestibular aqueduct, lateral semicircular canal, and the oval and round windows.

Axial Hypotympanic-Jugular Foramen Level (see Fig. 15–2)

The carotid canal lies just anterior to the jugular fossa, forming a "snowman"-like configuration. The carotid canal is usually smaller than the jugular fossa, and both demonstrate sharp cortical margins. Inferiorly, only a small spine separates the two as they converge to enter the carotid sheath. The hypotympanum is adjacent to these structures. The opening of the eustachian canal is triangular, with the apex extending parallel to the carotid canal.[9] The petro-occipital fissure separates the temporal bone from the occiput.

The mandibular condyle and temporomandibular joint

---

*SIMCAST, segmented interleaved motion compensated acquisition in the steady-state technique.

can also be seen on CT scans. On MRI gradient-echo studies, the descending portion of the facial nerve can be seen just lateral to the jugular bulb, and the blood vessels can be seen as high-signal-intensity regions because of flow effects.

Axial Inferior Tympanic Level
(see Fig. 15–3)

On CT scans, the anterior and posterior walls of the bony external auditory canal demonstrate dense sharp cortical margins without soft tissue covering. The anterior margin of the external auditory canal forms the posterior lip of the temporomandibular joint. The cartilaginous segment is surrounded by fat that is of low density on CT scans and of high signal intensity on T1-weighted MRI studies.

The descending facial nerve canal is easily identified on CT scans as a well-marginated circular lucency in the temporal bone posterior to the external auditory canal. On MRI studies, the facial nerve is seen as an intermediate-signal-intensity to high-signal-intensity circular structure, surrounded by a large area of signal void of the temporal bone and mastoid air spaces.

The carotid canal can be seen early in its anteromedial course through the skull base, parallel and medial to the semicanal of the tensor tympani muscle at this level. On CT scans, the medial funnel-shaped opening of the cochlear aqueduct can be seen as a triangular lucency facing the cerebellopontine angle. Its apex points toward the round window. The opening of the duct may be large and mimic the internal auditory canal. The long process of the malleus parallels the tympanic membrane.

Axial Midtympanic Level (see Fig. 15–4)

The middle ear cavity is highly complex but is constant in size and configuration among patients. The normally thin tympanic membrane is often invisible on axial CT sections. The long process of the malleus lies parallel and anterior to the long process of the incus.

The axial projection is ideally suited for demonstrating the cochlear aqueduct as a thin canal within the dense cortical bone, progressively enlarging from lateral to medial. The duct is demonstrated on CT scans but not well seen on MRI studies, possibly because of the combination of its small diameter and CSF motion artifacts.

The complex medial margin of the middle ear includes the cochlear promontory, oval and round windows, cochleariform process, tensor tympani tendon, pyramidal eminence, stapedial tendon, and lateral semicircular canal. Unless there is fluid or a mass within the middle ear, MRI cannot be used to depict these structures. On CT scans, the apical, second, and basal cochlear turns are seen at this level. On MRI studies, these fluid-filled structures are identified by their intermediate signal intensity.

Axial Epitympanic Internal Auditory Canal Level
(see Fig. 15–5)

CT images at this level display the round head of the malleus and triangular body of the incus in the characteristic "ice cream cone" configuration (incudomalleolar articulation). The stapedial superstructure is occasionally seen,

forming an arch over the oval window on high-resolution CT scans. The internal auditory canal is slightly funnel-shaped and ends in an ovoid vestibule.

These canals should be nearly symmetrical. Although there is wide variation in the exact shape and size of the canals, asymmetry of greater than 2 mm suggests pathology. Lower-resolution MRI studies can demonstrate CSF in the canal, and high-resolution MRI studies can actually demonstrate the individual nerves as filling defects within the CSF.

On CT scans, the descending facial nerve canal is seen just lateral to the sinus tympanum. On MRI studies, the cochlear fluid contents, labyrinthine and horizontal segments of the facial nerve, and the geniculate ganglion are all seen as intermediate-signal-intensity structures surrounded by the signal void resulting from their bony walls.

Axial Lateral Semicircular Canal Level (see Fig. 15–6)

The axial projection is excellent for visualizing the entire lateral semicircular canal, since both are 30 degrees above the anthropologic baseline. The vestibular aqueduct is seen as a thin, hockey stick–shaped bony lucency. On MRI studies, the endolymphatic duct and sac appear as thin, high-signal-intensity regions. The endolymphatic duct extends posteriorly from the region of the common crus. It then abruptly turns laterally between the posterior margin of the temporal bone and the posterior semicircular canal.[9]

The mastoid antrum lies posterior and lateral to the aditus ad antrum and opens into many mastoid air cells. It is bordered superiorly by the tegmen tympani, which may be extremely thin and not well visualized on CT scans. The medial margin of the antrum is the promontory formed by the otic capsule of the lateral semicircular canal. On CT scans, the posterior semicircular canal and its ampulla are demonstrated.

Coronal Sections
Anterior to Posterior (see Figs. 15–1 and 15–7 to 15–11)

Coronal CT sections are particularly useful in the evaluation of the ossicles, geniculate ganglion, oval window, stapes, jugular fossa, middle ear walls, and roof (tegmen tympani) of the tympanic cavity.[4] The internal auditory canal and vestibule as well as Koerner's septum, which separates the squamous and petrous portions of the temporal bone, may also be identified.

Coronal Anterior Tympanic Level (see Fig. 15–7)

This plane offers excellent visualization of the superior and inferior walls of the external auditory canals. The tympanic membrane often is not visible, but it may be identified as a thin, filamentous structure extending from the scutum superiorly and coursing parallel to the plane of the long process of the malleus to attach to the limbus inferiorly.[11] The head of the malleus can be seen in the epitympanic space, and the floor and roof (tegmen) of the middle ear are also well visualized on CT scans.

The basal and second turn of the cochlea, geniculate ganglion, and internal auditory canal are identified on CT scans, surrounded by the dense bone of the otic capsule.

The cochlea and geniculate ganglion can be directly viewed on MRI studies by their fluid and soft tissue signal intensity.

Coronal Midtympanic Level (see Fig. 15–8)

The CT image at this level shows the body of the incus and incudostapedial articulation as an L-shaped configuration. The stapes projects medially and superiorly from the body of the incus toward the oval window (above the cochlear promontory). The proximal limb of the geniculate ganglion is seen just superior and lateral to the cochlea.

Beneath the lateral semicircular canal, the horizontal portion of the facial nerve canal appears as a small circular structure.[53] The floor and roof (tegmen) of the middle ear are well visualized on CT scans. On MRI studies, the facial (VII) and vestibulocochlear (VIII) nerves can be seen together in the internal auditory canal, diverging laterally.

Coronal Oval Window Level (see Fig. 15–9)

The full extent of the internal auditory canal, which often includes the central crista falciformis dividing the canal into two portions, is well visualized at this level. On CT scans, the oval window is seen as a bony defect of the lateral portion of the vestibule. The stapes is oriented slightly superiorly toward the oval window, just inferior to the lateral semicircular canal and the horizontal facial nerve.

Coronal Posterior Middle Ear Level (see Fig. 15–10)

The posterior middle ear has several small niches. One of the niches is the tympanic sinus, which extends between the vestibule and the pyramidal eminence. The second niche extends toward the round window. The epitympanic space lies just lateral to the lateral semicircular canal.

Coronal Jugular Foramen Level (see Fig. 15–11)

The jugular foramen and bulb frequently have a dome-shaped outline. The descending portion of the facial nerve canal may be identified running nearly vertical, directly inferior to the lateral semicircular canal. The mastoid antrum is seen superiorly and laterally. On CT scans, this section reveals various segments of the semicircular canals as well as the articulation of the occipital bone and atlas. Just lateral to this, the descending facial nerve is seen over a long section coursing toward the stylomastoid foramen.

Sagittal Images (see Figs. 15–12 to 15–15)

Direct sagittal images or reformations[25] can show the relationship of the mandibular condyle to the glenoid fossa and external auditory canal. The external auditory canal may be seen lateral to the tympanic membrane or long process of the malleus. The aditus ad antrum, mastoid antrum, and tegmen tympani are all well demonstrated.

The third portion of the facial nerve canal, the internal and external auditory canals, and the vestibular aqueduct are also well visualized on sagittal images.[11] MRI studies can demonstrate the individual nerves in the internal auditory canal, with the facial nerve superior and anterior, the cochlear nerve inferior and anterior, and the vestibular nerves posterior.

Sagittal Descending Facial Nerve Level (see Fig. 15–12)

The circular external auditory canal lies just below the ossicles in the epitympanic space. On CT and MRI scans, the descending facial nerve and posterior genu form an upside-down hockey stick shape. On MRI studies, the soft tissue components are easily seen.

Sagittal Vestibular Level (see Fig. 15–13)

Sagittal sections through the lateral vestibule demonstrate the multiple small components of the individual semicircular canals.

Sagittal Common Crus Level (see Fig. 15–14)

The vestibule, cochlea, and semicircular canals form an "x"-like configuration on sagittal sections. The vestibule is central, and the common crus of the superior and inferior semicircular canals can be seen just posterior and superior to the vestibule on both CT scans and MRI studies. The vestibular aqueduct appears as a thin, linear structure underlying a flange of the posterior petrous bone on CT scans, and the contained endolymphatic duct and sac can be seen on MR images. On MRI studies, the endolymphatic sac can be seen as a triangular area of increased signal at the distal end of the endolymphatic duct.

Sagittal Internal Auditory Canal Level (see Fig. 15–15)

On sagittal sections, the petrous apex has a triangular configuration. On CT scans, the circular internal auditory canal may demonstrate a small ridge anteriorly, related to the falciform crest. On high-resolution MRI studies, the individual nerves can be seen as filling defects. The carotid canal and the jugular fossa are directly inferior to the other otic capsule structures.

Abnormal Temporal Bone
Congenital Malformations

Evaluation of the congenitally deaf child is very difficult. Audiologic testing, although frequently not specific, is imperative to distinguish neurosensory defects from conductive hearing problems. Neurosensory defects occur medial to the oval window and are caused by maldevelopment of the otocyst. Conductive defects occur in the external and middle ears as a result of anomalies of the branchial arch derivatives.

CT scanning is essential in evaluation of the patient with known or suspected structural deformities of the external or middle ear. If the anomaly appears to be surgically correctable, identification of associated inner malformations is essential, since the anomaly may be inoperable. MRI studies can be used to directly evaluate the fluid spaces within the otic capsule.

Middle Ear and External Ear Malformations[41]

The most common anomaly of the middle ear and the external ear is *atresia* (also called *microtia*, or absence of the external ear) (Fig. 15–16).[55] Isolated anomalies of the ossicles can occur but are less common.

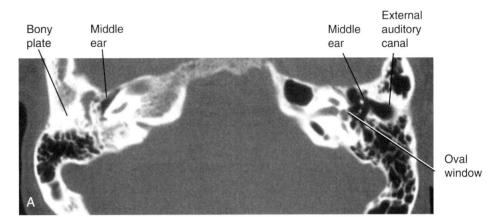

Bony plate   Middle ear   External auditory canal   Middle ear   Oval window

Figure 15–16. Atresia of the external auditory canal.

A, Axial CT scan showing a normal external auditory canal (EAC), middle ear, and oval window on the left. The right temporal bone is sectioned slightly more inferior in location and shows no external auditory canal. A thick bony plate completely covers the small middle ear cavity, centered at the cochlear promontory on the right.

B, Axial magnification view of the right ear. The deformed malleus is seen adjacent to the bony plate covering the EAC. The middle ear cavity is smaller than normal. The descending facial nerve is in a normal location. The mastoid air cells are well pneumatized.

C, Coronal CT scan showing a normal left EAC, internal auditory canal, and oval window. On the right, the otic capsule structures are intact but the EAC is completely replaced with thick bone. The descending facial nerve canal is somewhat anterior in location as it tracks toward the stylomastoid foramen.

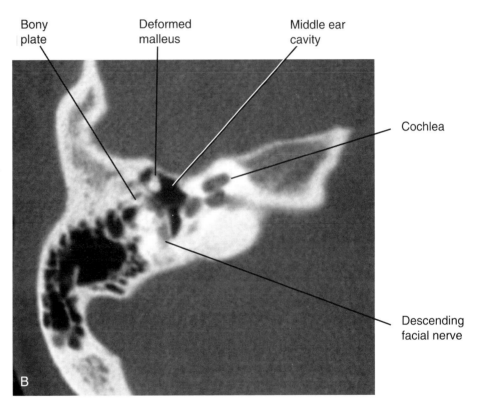

Bony plate   Deformed malleus   Middle ear cavity   Cochlea   Descending facial nerve

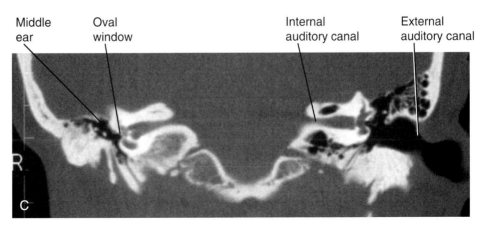

Middle ear   Oval window   Internal auditory canal   External auditory canal

Microtia may be associated with narrowing or agenesis of the bony external auditory canal. The degree of distortion can range from a web or small band of soft tissue partially covering the external auditory canal to complete absence.[11] Microtia is also associated with a number of other middle ear anomalies, including those seen in Pierre Robin and Apert's syndromes.

Numerous ossicular anomalies may be associated with atresia of the external auditory canal. The most common is fusion of the malleus and incus to the lateral epitympanic wall. Bony ankylosis of the neck of the malleus to the atresia plate is also common. Anomalies of the second branchial arch result in deformities of the long process of the incus, stapes superstructure, and a portion of the footplate of the stapes. Combined ossicular anomalies are common. The stapes is most often involved in cases of isolated deformity.

The facial nerve canal must be carefully evaluated in all cases of suspected external and middle ear anomalies, particularly if surgery is planned, because anomalous development of the middle ear may alter the course of the facial nerve. In anomalies of the second branchial arch, the facial nerve canal may be positioned within the floor of the tympanic cavity or may cross the oval window. Occasionally, the facial nerve branches into two or three portions within the temporal bone.

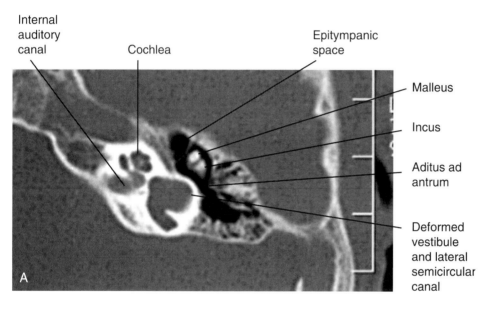

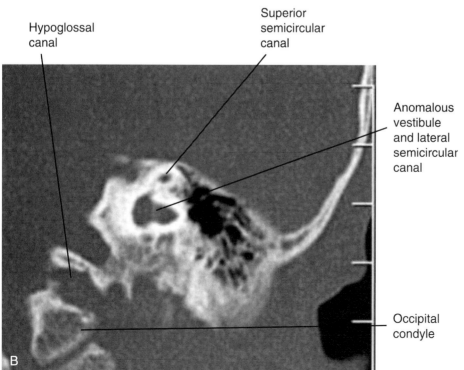

Figure 15–17. Vestibular anomaly. *A,* Axial CT image at the level of the vestibule, epitympanic space, and cochlea. The ossicles and middle ear are normal. The cochlea is dysplastic. The vestibule is deformed with a bulbous configuration. The vestibule fuses with the lateral semicircular canal. The posterior semicircular canal is also enlarged. It is important to exclude an abnormal fistulous connection between an otic capsule abnormality and the middle ear. *B,* Coronal CT slice sectioned through the anomalous bulbous vestibule. The hypoglossal canal, superior semicircular canal, and occipital condyle are normal.

Inner Ear Malformations

Severe hearing loss secondary to malformations of the membranous labyrinth may coincide with entirely normal CT findings. A subtle finding associated with hearing loss is a lateral semicircular canal diameter less than 6 mm.[44] In contrast, some patients with CT evidence of minor dysplasias of the osseous labyrinth involving the cochlea, vestibule, or semicircular canals may have no clinical evidence of deafness.

The *Mondini malformation* is associated with hypoplasia, absence, or the presence of only a rudimentary coil of the cochlea. Generally, there is a central cavity that contains the remnants of the modiolus. The defect is usually bilateral and associated with dilatation of the vestibular aqueduct. More complex anomalies of the cochlea, with dilatation of the vestibule and partial or complete absence of the semicircular canals may also occur (Fig. 15–17).[2]

A complete lack of inner ear development is the *Michel defect.* A single labyrinthine cavity with no distinct vestibule, cochlea, or semicircular canals may be seen, or petrous development may be totally absent. Occasionally, the internal auditory canal is absent.[19, 32]

CT evaluation of congenital inner ear malformations should include evaluation of the cochlear and vestibular aqueducts. In patients with large cochlear aqueducts, there is a high incidence of CSF leaks near the oval window (stapes "gusher" syndrome). There is a known association between cochlear abnormalities and dilatation of the vestibular aqueduct. Many patients with the Mondini or Michel malformation have enlarged vestibular aqueducts. This implies a deformity of the membranous labyrinth. Dilatation of the vestibular aqueduct may also occur as an isolated event, leading to fluctuating hearing loss (Fig. 15–18).

Before placement of cochlear implants, patients are often studied with CT to more fully characterize the inner ear anomaly.[67] Following inflammation, the membranous labyrinth may be fibrotic and the cochlea may not accept the implant. There may be complete obliteration of the bony cochlea. MRI studies can confirm that the space within the bony otic capsule is filled with fluid when there is a question of fibrous obliteration of the otic capsule.

Vascular Anomalies

Many of the anomalies of the vascular structures of the temporal bone that were previously visible only on angiograms are now readily recognizable on high-resolution CT scans and MR images. If the surgeon is aware of the anomalous vasculature, vessel injury may be avoided during surgery or biopsy.

The development of the intrapetrous portion of the internal carotid artery is independent of that of the remaining ear. Because a vessel must be present before its canal forms, the carotid canal does not develop in cases of agenesis of the carotid artery. Agenesis of the intrapetrous carotid artery is thus identified on CT scans by absence of the carotid canal and carotid sulcus.

An ectopic intratympanic carotid artery (Fig. 15–19) may occur when there is alteration in carotid development.[54] The carotid canal may be partially absent, resulting in dehiscence of the bony margins and ectopic placement of the vessels into the middle ear. Pulsation tinnitus or conductive hearing loss, or both, may occur.[2] An intratym-

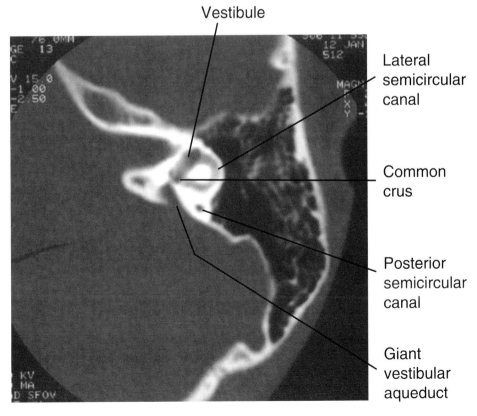

Figure 15–18. Giant vestibular aqueduct. This axial CT section is centered at the internal auditory canal and the lateral semicircular canal. The vestibular aqueduct is more than 2 mm in thickness. It is seen extending back toward the region of the vestibule and the common crus. Usually, the vestibular aqueducts are seen only as thin slits. This is a common congenital anomaly and suggests that other anomalies may be present, including those of the cochlea. The process may be bilateral as well.

Vestibule

Lateral semicircular canal

Common crus

Posterior semicircular canal

Giant vestibular aqueduct

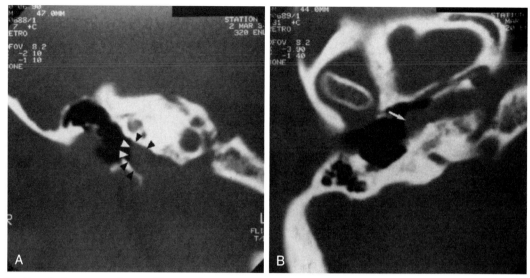

Figure 15–19. Ectopic intratympanic carotid artery in a young adult presenting with a pulsating mass behind the right eardrum. *A,* Coronal CT scan of the right ear. There is a dehiscence *(white arrowheads)* in the floor of the tympanic cavity inferior to the cochlea. The ectopic carotid artery *(black arrowheads)* bulges into the hypotympanum through this bony dehiscence. *B,* Axial CT scan through the right hypotympanum. The vessel *(arrow)* simulates a soft tissue mass in the hypotympanum. The anterior lateral portion of the bony carotid canal is absent. (Courtesy of Dr. C. Roger Bird.)

panic, ectopic carotid artery may actually represent the inferior tympanic branch of the ascending pharyngeal artery secondary to agenesis of a segment of the internal carotid artery during early development. The aberrant vessel thus takes over as a source of blood flow to the brain. In either case, high-resolution CT or MRI studies can be used to differentiate these arterial vascular anomalies from a middle ear tumor. Angiography is generally not necessary but can be useful in questionable instances. On CT or MRI studies, the first genu of the ectopic carotid artery is usually located more lateral than normal and is abnormally tortuous. With dehiscence of the carotid canal, the carotid artery fills the anterior medial middle ear. The ectopic carotid artery is commonly small and tortuous. On angiography, the genu is lateral to the vestibule.

Another type of intratympanic vascular anomaly involves substitution of the stapedial artery for the middle meningeal artery. The intratympanic course of the stapedial artery is seen with enlargement of the tympanic portion of the facial nerve canal and absence of the ipsilateral foramen spinosum. Involvement of the facial nerve canal is seen in this defect because the development of the facial nerve canal closely parallels that of the middle meningeal artery. In this substitution anomaly, the stapedial artery originates from the intrapetrous internal carotid artery, runs with the facial nerve through the tympanic cavity, and then exits into the middle cranial fossa to supply the dura of the cerebral hemisphere.

Anomalies of the jugular vein and bulb are common. A defect in the bony plate separating the jugular bulb from the hypotympanum may result in a high jugular bulb that protrudes into the middle ear (Fig. 15–20). With other jugular bulb lesions, there is loss of the normal smooth margin of the osseous bulb because of irregular bony destruction.[12, 17]

A high jugular bulb may also give rise to a jugular bulb

diverticulum (see Fig. 15–20). A diverticulum is distinct from a large jugular bulb because the diverticulum is usually posterior to the internal auditory canal and does not affect the middle ear.[3] The diverticulum is recognizable on CT scans and should not be mistaken for a tumor.[34] MRI signal from slow flow in a diverticulum may mimic a mass. Two-dimensional gradient-echo or phase-flow images are particularly sensitive to slow flow abnormalities of the venous system.[15]

Inflammatory Lesions

Both CT and MRI are important in staging the primary changes and identifying complications of temporal bone inflammatory disease. CT has proved effective in detecting bony erosions and soft tissue masses associated with middle ear inflammatory disease. Contrast-enhanced MRI studies can be used to differentiate fluid and cholesteatoma from enhancing granulation tissue or tumor.[40]

Acute and Subacute Otitis Media

Acute otitis media is associated with middle ear opacification.[56] Concomitant mastoiditis is evidenced by opacification or fluid levels in the mastoid air cells. The fluid in serous otitis media cannot be distinguished from the pus seen with purulent otitis. Subacute otitis media shows similar findings in the mastoid air cells and middle ear, with the additional finding of focal or diffuse mucosal thickening.

Chronic Otitis Media and Chronic Mastoiditis

Chronic otitis media (Fig. 15–21) results in the formation of granulation tissue that may become heaped up, obscuring the margins of the middle ear contents.[64] This

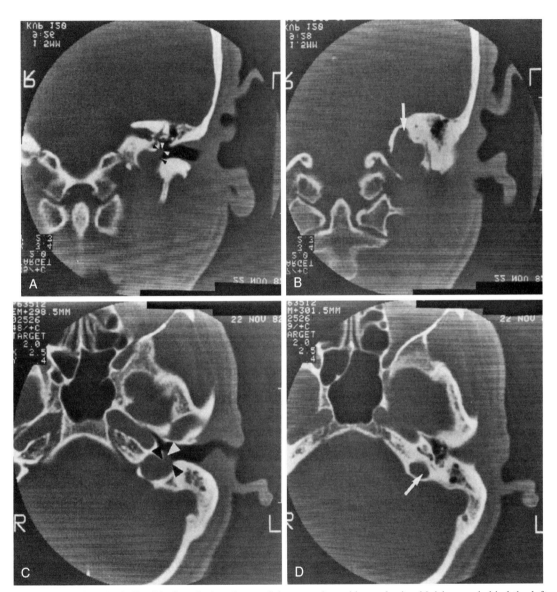

Figure 15–20. Dehiscent jugular bulb with diverticulum in an adult presenting with a pulsating bluish mass behind the left eardrum.

A and *B*, Coronal CT scans of the left ear. There is a dehiscence in the floor *(white arrowheads)* of the tympanic cavity, with extension of a portion of the jugular bulb *(black arrowheads)* into the hypotympanum *(A)*. The remaining jugular fossa is sharply defined. A small diverticulum of the jugular fossa *(white arrow)* protrudes superiorly toward the roof of the petrous temporal bone *(B)*.

C and *D*, Axial CT scans of the left ear. Note the dehiscence *(black arrowheads)* of the jugular fossa with extension of the jugular bulb simulating a mass into the hypotympanum *(white arrowhead)* *(C)*. The diverticulum *(white arrow)* extends superiorly to the level of the osseous labyrinth *(D)*. The ipsilateral sigmoid sinus impression is also large, suggesting a developmental variation rather than tumor.

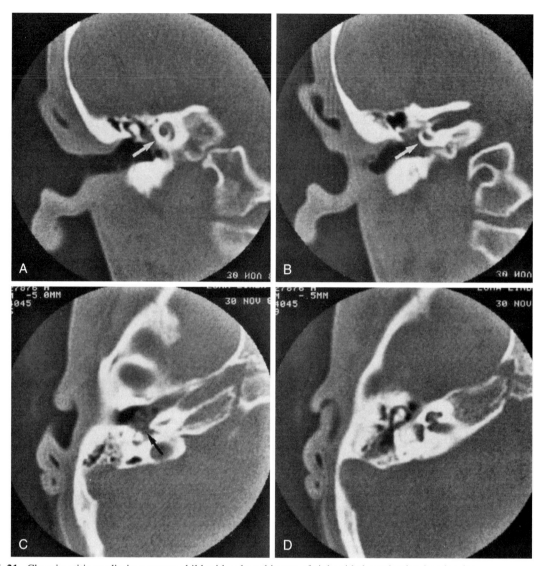

Figure 15–21. Chronic otitis media in a young child with a long history of right-sided conductive hearing loss.

A and *B*, Coronal CT scans of the right ear. There is a soft tissue density within the tympanic cavity *(arrows)*. The tympanic membrane is retracted medially. The ossicles are intact and show no evidence of bone destruction.

C and *D*, Axial CT scans of the right ear. The middle ear cavity is largely opacified. The sinus tympani is involved *(arrow)*. The mastoid air cells are poorly developed. The nasopharynx should be evaluated to rule out an obstructive lesion. In children, the nasopharyngeal process is commonly an adenoid enlargement.

process results in areas of nondependent radiodensities within the middle ear. The tympanic membrane is usually retracted inward in patients with chronic otitis media. The mastoid may be poorly developed and sclerotic, since this process begins in childhood.

Chronic mastoiditis (Fig. 15–22) follows repeated bouts of otitis media and accompanying mastoid infections. There is a gradual reduction in the number of mastoid air cells, with thickening of the mucous membrane and reactive sclerosis of the bony septa. Persistent suppuration leads to mucosal destruction and subsequent granulation tissue formation. Erosion of mastoid air cell walls rarely occurs without the presence of cholesteatoma.

Cholesteatoma

Cholesteatomas develop in patients with chronic perforations of the tympanic membrane, usually from eustachian

tube dysfunction. Most perforations occur at the pars flaccida segment of the tympanic membrane (Fig. 15–23). Perforations of the pars tensa membranae tympani are rare. In these patients, the cholesteatoma extends directly into the central portion of the middle ear (Fig. 15–24).

Histologically, cholesteatomas consist of an inner layer of desquamated, stratified squamous epithelium apposed on an outer layer of subepithelial connective tissue. The subepithelial connective tissue layer is formed by a chronic inflammatory process that deposits cholesterol crystal clusters, giant cells, and round cells. Accumulation of epithelial debris within the lumen leads to progressive enlargement of the epithelial soft tissue mass. As the lesion enlarges, it contacts the contiguous bony structures of the middle ear, mastoid air cells, and petrous pyramid, causing erosion from pressure necrosis and enzymatic lysis of bone. Cholesteatomas typically originate in the middle ear but

Figure 15–22. Cerebritis and mastoiditis in a young man who presented with a seizure and left ear drainage. This coronal T2-weighted, high-resolution, spin-echo MR image demonstrates a region of edema related to brain infection in the inferior portion of the left temporal lobe. In the adjacent left temporal bone, there is opacification of the middle ear cavity due to septic mastoiditis. Note the small fluid collection (epidural) along the superior portion of the left temporal bone related to the infection. In patients with temporal lobe pathology, a careful review of the temporal bones should always be made to exclude an extra-axial source.

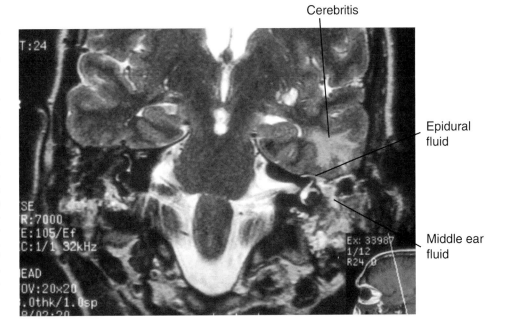

may extend into mastoid air cells and, occasionally, into the petrous pyramid.

Pus within a denuded mucosal cavity results in proteolytic erosion of the ossicles and walls of the middle ear. Chronic otitis media and cholesteatoma are thus characterized by a combination of focal or diffuse soft tissue densities in association with focal or diffuse bone destruction. This process leads to rarefying osteitis or erosive otitis media. The erosions typically involve the lateral wall of the tympanic cavity, including the scutum and the ossicles.[26] The facial nerve canal and lateral semicircular canal are rarely affected.[29] Differentiation from cholesteatoma may be impossible.

Classically, cholesteatomas expand into the antrum and mesotympanum, resulting in medial displacement of the ossicles away from Prussak's space. From the mesotympanum, the extension may be posterior into the sinus tympani or inferior into the hypotympanum. Further growth may be in several directions, most commonly into the posterolateral attic and then through the aditus into the antrum and mastoid air cells.[52]

The diagnosis of cholesteatoma is based on the identification of a sharply demarcated soft tissue mass in the middle ear and bony destruction. Most of the time, the diagnosis is clear and is based on physical examination. The purpose of imaging is to stage the lesion. Continual

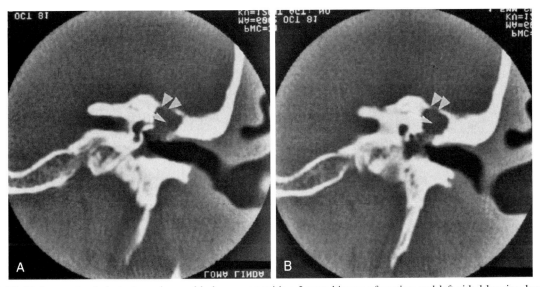

Figure 15–23. Epitympanic cholesteatoma in an elderly woman with a 2-year history of vertigo and left-sided hearing loss. *A* and *B,* Coronal CT scans of the left ear show a large, destructive soft tissue mass in the tympanic cavity, epitympanic space, attic, and antrum *(arrows).* The scutum is thinned. The walls of the middle ear cavity are expanded and amorphous. There is erosion of the cholesteatoma into the lateral semicircular canal. The tympanic membrane is retracted. The tegmen antri is thin, but there is no evidence of intracranial extension *(arrowheads).*

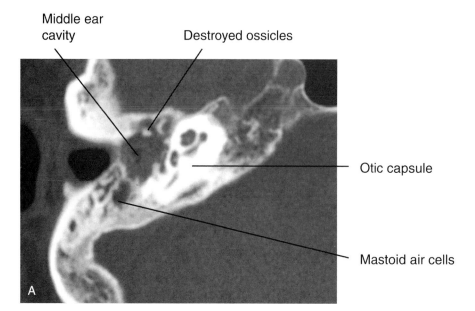

Middle ear cavity

Destroyed ossicles

Otic capsule

Mastoid air cells

A

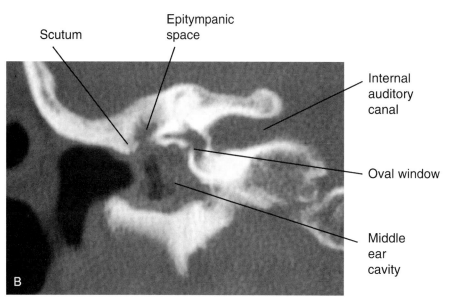

Scutum

Epitympanic space

Internal auditory canal

Oval window

Middle ear cavity

B

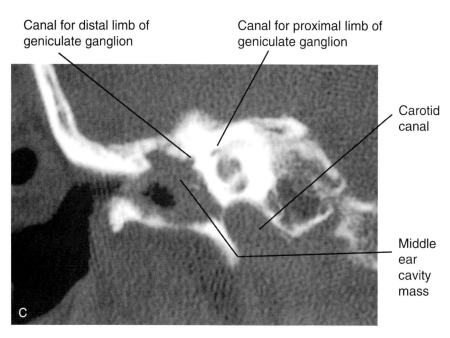

Canal for distal limb of geniculate ganglion

Canal for proximal limb of geniculate ganglion

Carotid canal

Middle ear cavity mass

C

Figure 15–24. Inflammatory cholesteatoma.

A, Axial CT through the middle ear, which is largely opacified. The ossicles are partially destroyed and pushed anteriorly. The mastoid air cells are also opacified. There is no otic capsule destruction.

B, Coronal CT image through the oval window. The middle ear is almost completely opacified. The normal ossicular structures have been eroded. The epitympanic space is opacified as well. The mass does not protrude into the external auditory canal, but the scutum is blunted.

C, Coronal CT image centered at the geniculate ganglion. The distal limb of the geniculate ganglion canal is eroded by the middle ear mass.

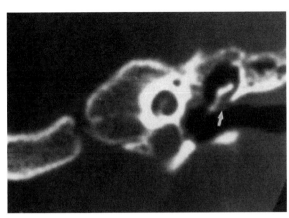

Figure 15–25. Small early cholesteatoma. Coronal CT scan of the left temporal bone shows a small soft tissue mass *(arrow)* just lateral to the malleus and medial to the scutum. There is no bone destruction. This is consistent with an early deformity of the pars flaccida and a cholesteatoma.

pressure on the ossicles may lead to necrosis or dislocation. The most common type of ossicular destruction involves the short and long processes of the incus, followed by destruction of the body of the incus and the head of the malleus.[52] Early small cholesteatomas (Fig. 15–25) may be associated with no bony change.

Patients with facial nerve palsy may have erosion of the facial nerve canal and compression of the facial nerve. Labyrinthine fistulas may form when there is erosion into the lateral or posterior semicircular canals. In rare instances, a cholesteatoma may extend into the otic capsule or the middle cranial fossa through the tegmen antri or tegmen tympani.

The cholesteatoma may be extruded spontaneously through an acquired osseous defect, usually associated with a large bony defect of the external auditory canal and mastoid (autoantrectomy) (Fig. 15–26).[28] Such an osseous defect may appear similar to a surgical defect. The residual cavity may have circumferential mural cholesteatomatous material, with an empty, air-filled central cavity.

Malignant External Otitis

Malignant external otitis (Fig. 15–27) is most often associated with a *Pseudomonas* infection in elderly, diabetic, or immunosuppressed patients. These patients complain of severe otalgia and purulent discharge from the external auditory canal.

More extensive disease causes necrosis of the adjacent soft tissues, with extensive bony destruction. The bony destruction may involve the walls of the external auditory canal and may extend into the tympanic cavity and inner ear, leading to hearing loss and facial nerve dysfunction.

The necrotizing soft tissue infection may also spread along Santorini's fissures (small clefts in the cartilaginous portion of the external auditory canal) into the soft tissues of the nasopharynx and oropharynx. Both the osseous and soft tissue spread may lead to intracranial extension. If left untreated, the disease progresses, leading to meningitis, cerebritis, and osteomyelitis of the skull base. The disease can be fatal in a short period, thus earning the term *malignant external otitis.*

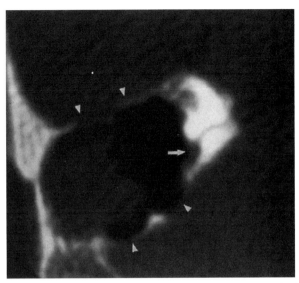

Figure 15–26. Autoantrectomy. Axial CT section through the right superior temporal bone. There is a large defect in the mastoid with thinning of the bony margins *(arrowheads).* A central soft tissue mass partially fills the space. This patient did not have surgery, but the cholesteatoma has almost completely emptied the mastoid space as a result of chronic bone destruction. There is erosion of the superior semicircular canal *(arrow).*

Early findings include soft tissue thickening of the external auditory canal with clouding of the middle ear and mastoid air cells. There are varying degrees of surrounding bone destruction involving the temporomandibular joint, petrous pyramid, tympanic cavity, or mastoid process.

CT scanning with IV contrast material is needed to define the extent of disease within the soft tissues of the head and neck. There may be widespread enhancement with multiple focal abscesses. CT and MRI studies optimally demonstrate the fat and muscle planes, illustrating the extent of the disease in the soft tissues of the pinna, parapharyngeal space, clivus, infratemporal fossa, and carotid sheath.[11] Involvement of the subtemporal fossa is evidenced by obliteration of the normal fat planes, whereas involvement of the parapharyngeal space is evident by loss of the characteristic CT low density within the space and presence of a mass lesion.[18] Marrow involvement and vessel occlusion are best seen on MR images.

CT is excellent for following the progression of the bone and soft tissue involvement after treatment. The bone erosions are usually constant. If there is no resolution after appropriate antibiotic therapy, surgery may be necessary for adequate drainage of soft tissue abscesses and removal of destroyed bone.[42]

Infection of the Endolymphatic Sac

MRI is sensitive to subtle changes of the membranes of the otic capsule structures. Transient enhancement may commonly involve the vestibule (Fig. 15–28) and is generally thought to represent a viral infection or another inflammatory process. In rare instances, enhancement of the endolymphatic duct and cochlea is seen. Suppurative infections (e.g., syphilitic, staphylococcal) produce enhancement as well, but the findings are more persistent. These infec-

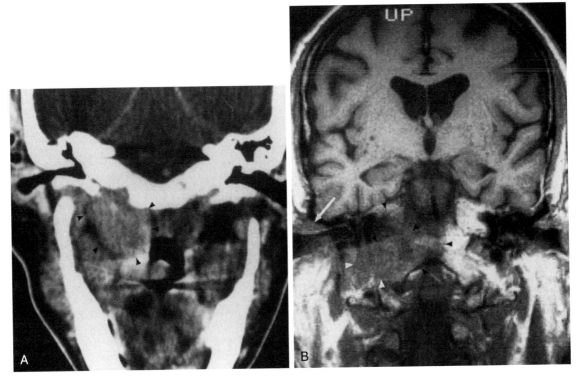

Figure 15–27. Malignant external otitis.

A, Coronal CT section through the external auditory canals. There is slight loss of the fatty interfaces surrounding the soft tissue portion of the right external auditory canal. The bulk of the pathology is centered in the parapharyngeal space and the nasopharynx. There is obliteration of the normal fat planes in the infratemporal fossa and an ill-defined soft tissue mass *(arrowheads).*

B, Coronal T1-weighted MRI study at a similar location. The fat planes directly parallel to the right external auditory canal *(white arrow)* are partially obliterated. The fatty marrow spaces of the clivus *(black arrowheads)* and the adjacent fatty soft tissue space *(white arrowheads)* have been replaced by lower-signal inflammatory tissue. The ascending internal carotid artery is enveloped by these infiltrative changes.

(A and *B,* Courtesy of Barbara Carter, M.D.)

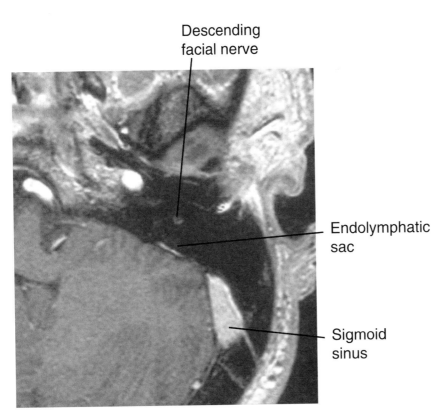

Descending facial nerve

Endolymphatic sac

Sigmoid sinus

Figure 15–28. Endolymphatic sac inflammation in a young male who presented with severe hearing loss and vertigo, probably related to a viral infection. This is an axial 3D Fourier transform T2-weighted, high-resolution MR image through the descending facial nerve and the lower endolymphatic duct. Note the abnormal enhancement of the sac. Unlike a congenital anomaly or a tumor, the sac is not enlarged. This type of finding suggests an inflammatory process and has been described in association with Meniere's disease.

tions demonstrate other more aggressive findings such as bone destruction and mass effect. Occasionally, sarcoid, metastasis, lymphoma, or eosinophilic granuloma may mimic an infection early in their course.[33, 51, 65]

Brain Abscess

Brain abscesses may develop from temporal bone inflammatory processes by several mechanisms. Petrositis of the apical air cells can extend into the epidural and skull base spaces. In these instances, CT scanning shows the bony destruction with dural enhancement adjacent to the temporal bone. This is called *Gradenigo's syndrome.* Cholesteatomas can erode through the tegmen tympani or tegmen antri into the middle cranial fossa or through the mastoid into the posterior cranial fossa. CT or MRI with contrast enhancement shows elevation and enhancement of the dura with extension of pus into the epidural space (see Fig. 15–22). Classic ring-enhancing lesions can also be seen. In patients with recurrent cholesteatomas after radical mastoidectomies, intracranial spread of the infection may develop. This occurs when the bony barriers have been surgically removed.

Meniere's disease is a poorly understood disorder of the temporal bone consisting of intermittent severe vertigo with progressive hearing loss. Some believe that it is related to inflammation of the membranes of the otic capsule leading to obliteration of the endolymphatic duct. In the active phase, enhancement of the endolymphatic sac may be seen. Later on, the endolymphatic sac may be asymmetrical or not visible. The imaging diagnosis is complicated by the fact that there are many variations in the sacs among patients and from side to side in the same patient.[66]

Neoplastic Lesions

Benign Neoplasms

Osteomas

Osteomas (Fig. 15–29) are common benign tumors of the temporal bone. Some osteomas are large enough to occlude osseous foramina such as the external auditory canal or the eustachian canal. Osteomas may also develop in the mastoid process after trauma. Bony thickening of the external auditory canal is commonly associated with prolonged exposure to cold water and is usually seen in swimmers. CT scanning demonstrates an osteoma as an area of dense thickening of compact bone.

Acoustic Schwannomas

Acoustic schwannomas are benign tumors of cranial nerve VIII, usually located within the internal auditory canal and cerebellopontine angle cistern. They classically arise at the junction of the neuroglial and Schwann cell sheaths, commonly near the porus acusticus. The vestibular nerve is the most common site of origin.

Symptoms are directly related to the size and location of the tumor. Growth of acoustic schwannomas in the internal auditory canal causes compression of the cochlear and vestibular nerves. This results in progressive neurosensory loss and tinnitus. Early vestibular dysfunction is uncommon, probably resulting from the slow growth of the

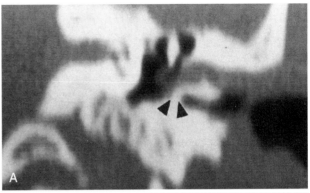

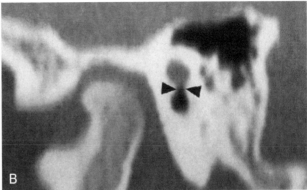

Figure 15–29. Osteoma of the left external auditory canal (EAC) in a 13-year-old boy with a history of cold-water swimming and a chronic deformity of the EAC. Coronal *(A)* and sagittal *(B)* reformatted CT images through the left EAC. The EAC is opacified, with osseous constriction of its medial portion. The osteoma *(arrowheads)* is completely incorporated into the adjacent bone *(A).* Note the keyhole constriction *(arrowheads)* of the EAC, best seen in the sagittal reformatted image *(B).* Within the stenotic EAC is a soft tissue mass that represents a secondary EAC cholesteatoma.

tumor, which allows for central compensation of the progressive peripheral dysfunction.[23] Facial nerve paresis or palsy is a rare event but may occur with large masses. Clinical symptoms from the fifth cranial nerve are actually more common than the seventh cranial nerve.

The imaging presentations of acoustic schwannomas vary widely. Some of these tumors are only a few millimeters in dimension (Fig. 15–30), and are difficult to identify, whereas others are so massive (Fig. 15–31) that they are life-threatening. They rarely occur within the vestibule or cochlea (Fig. 15–32). Some tumors cross from the internal auditory canal into the otic capsule regions, but this is uncommon.

CT scans can be used in diagnosis, as large tumors can be seen directly. Small tumors of the internal auditory canal that do not affect the bony margins necessitate either air-contrast cisternography or MRI studies. The bony changes of the internal auditory canal, porus acusticus, and otic capsule are common and help to differentiate acoustic tumors from other cerebellopontine angle masses (Fig. 15–33).[58] It is extremely uncommon for a nonacoustic tumor to expand or to erode the auditory meatus. Asymmetry of the internal auditory canals of more than 2 mm suggests the presence of a mass. IV contrast enhancement may

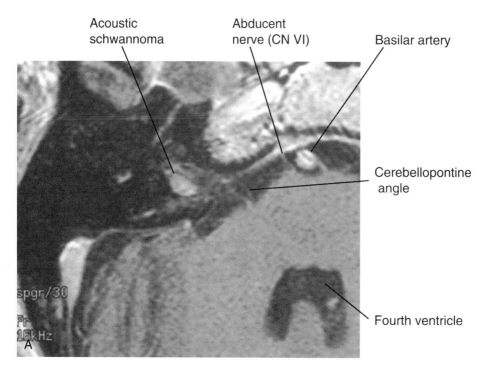

Acoustic schwannoma   Abducent nerve (CN VI)   Basilar artery

Cerebellopontine angle

Fourth ventricle

Figure 15–30. Small right acoustic schwannoma.

A, Axial T1-weighted, 3D Fourier transform, contrast-enhanced MR section through the internal auditory canal (IAC). The posterior portion of the IAC is filled with a small enhancing mass, which does not protrude into the cerebellopontine angle (CPA). There is some remodeling of the posterior margin of the IAC. Other structures depicted include the fourth ventricle, basilar artery, and sixth cranial nerve.

B, Axial T2-weighted, 3D Fourier transform, high-resolution, gradient-echo, non–contrast-enhanced image at a site similar to that in *A*. The seventh and eighth cranial nerves are seen in the CPA and the IAC. There is a small posterior filling defect related to the small tumor. The more lateral segments of the cranial nerves in the IAC are visible.

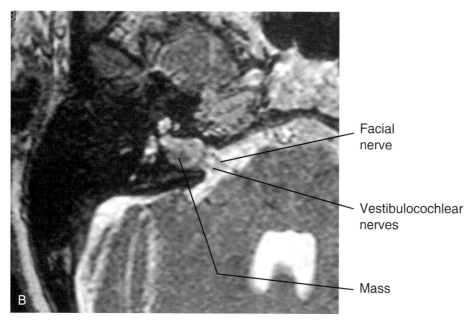

Facial nerve

Vestibulocochlear nerves

Mass

Figure 15–31. Large acoustic schwannoma. Axial T1-weighted, contrast-enhanced, spin-echo MRI study shows a large, lobulated left anterolateral posterior fossa mass *(arrowheads)*. The lesion enhances inhomogeneously. A medial cyst is adjacent to the lesion *(arrows)*. The acoustic schwannoma displaces the fourth ventricle (fv) to the right. There is massive erosion of much of the medial temporal bone, with replacement by schwannoma.

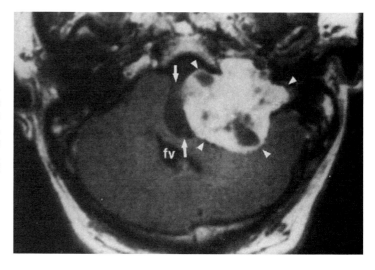

Internal
auditory
canal

Enhancing
vestibule

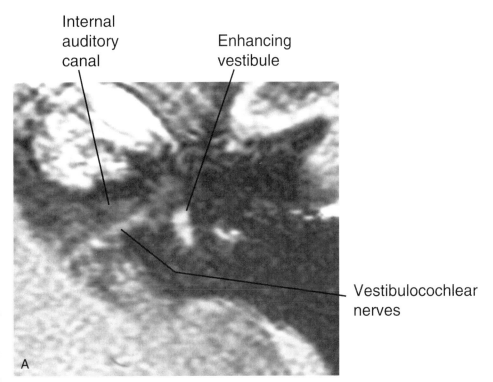

Vestibulocochlear
nerves

A

Figure 15–32. Vestibular schwannoma in a patient presenting with symptoms suggesting an acoustic schwannoma; however, no lesion was seen in the internal auditory canal (IAC).

A, Axial contrast-enhanced, high-resolution, 3D Fourier transform, T1-weighted MR image through the vestibule and the IAC. The normal eighth cranial nerve is seen in the IAC. There is abnormal enhancement of the normal-sized vestibule. This was able to be seen with vestibulitis, but this finding did not resolve in a few weeks. The imaging properties of an otic capsule schwannoma are identical to those in the IAC, but the location is different.

B, MR scan made at the same level as in *A* but with a high-resolution, 3D Fourier transform, gradient-echo, T2-weighted MR sequence. Again, the IAC and the eighth cranial nerve are normal. A filling defect is seen where the enhancing mass was centered on the contrast study. Filling defects are more likely to be tumors than inflammatory changes.

Internal
auditory
canal

Vestibulocochlear
nerves

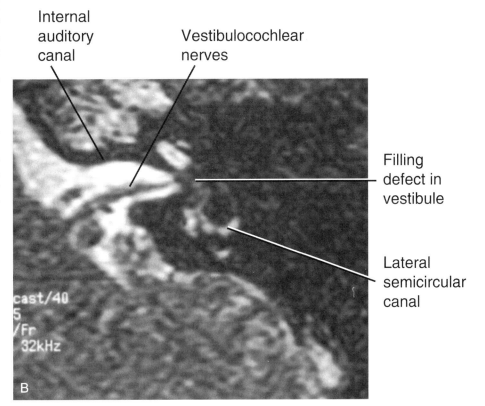

Filling
defect in
vestibule

Lateral
semicircular
canal

B

Acoustic
schwannomas

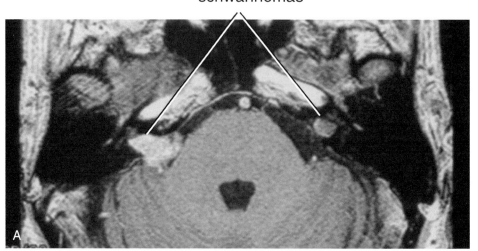

Acoustic
schwannomas

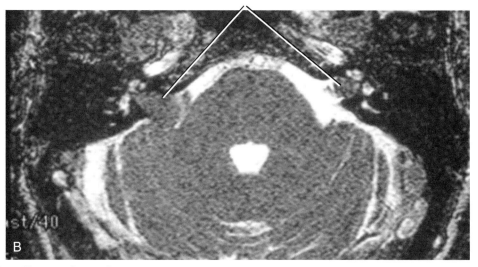

Figure 15–33. Neurofibromatosis type 2.

A, Axial T2-weighted, 3D Fourier transform, high-resolution, gradient-echo MR image acquired through the internal auditory canals. Filling defects are seen in both internal auditory canals (IACs). The mass on the right is larger and extends out into the cerebellopontine angle. Bilateral acoustic tumors suggest neurofibromatosis type 2 or carcinomatosis. No other meningiomas or neuromas are seen on this section, but they should be sought.

B, Axial T1-weighted, 3D Fourier transform, high-resolution, gradient-echo MR image acquired after contrast through the IACs. Both tumors of the IACs are seen as enhancing small masses. The mass on the right shows greater enhancement.

reveal a classic mushroom-shaped mass centered at the internal auditory canal.

Massive tumors (see Fig. 15–31) may cause severe distortion of the posterior fossa, with brain stem herniation, hydrocephalus, and displacement and compression of the fourth ventricle. Some acoustic schwannomas can be cystic. Bilateral acoustic schwannomas are associated with neurofibromatosis type 2 (Fig. 15–34; see Fig. 15–33).

In general, MRI is better than CT in the diagnosis of acoustic schwannomas. Enhancement and enlargement of the eighth cranial nerve within the internal auditory canal (or even the otic capsule) can be seen. Small lesions are visible on survey examinations without the need for cisternography. MRI can differentiate small acoustic tumors from the nerves themselves. Smaller tumors can be seen to displace the nerves in the internal auditory canal. The nerve can be seen crossing small tumors. This is important for surgical planning and usually implies a better prognosis for hearing salvage after surgery. Larger tumors totally fill the internal auditory canal and obscure the other anatomic structures. The other characteristic findings of larger tumors can also be appreciated. Careful review of other cranial nerves is important to rule out neurofibromatosis.

The rate of growth of acoustic schwannomas is variable. Accurate follow-up is important because many tumors do not grow and may not warrant therapy, particularly in the case of older patients. High-resolution imaging is essential to aid in recognition of subtle changes in tumor volume.

Better evaluation of these tumors is more important now that there are many different management possibilities, including waiting, surgery, and focused radiation.

Facial Nerve Schwannomas

Facial nerve schwannomas (Figs. 15–35 and 15–36) may be located anywhere along the course of cranial nerve VII. These tumors are gray, firm, lobulated masses that may be either schwannomas or neurilemmomas. Both originate from Schwann cell sheaths. These tumors most frequently involve the geniculate ganglion and tympanic mastoid portions of the facial nerve. Although facial schwannomas are commonly associated with facial nerve palsy, they account for only about 5% of all peripheral facial palsies. Inflammation (Bell's palsy) (Fig. 15–37), trauma, infection, and neoplasm are more common causes of cranial nerve VII dysfunction.[22]

The location of the schwannoma determines the constellation of clinical findings. Neurosensory hearing loss resulting from compression of adjacent cranial nerve VIII is seen with cerebellopontine angle and internal auditory canal tumors or erosion into the cochlea. Conductive hearing loss may be seen in tympanic cavity schwannomas associated with ossicular dysfunction.

Although the CT findings of an intracanalicular or cerebellopontine facial schwannoma are similar to those of acoustic schwannomas, erosion of the anterosuperior por-

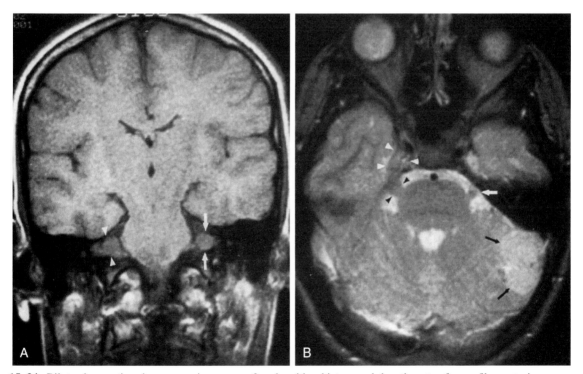

Figure 15–34. Bilateral acoustic schwannoma in a young female with a history and the stigmata of neurofibromatosis.

A, Coronal noncontrast, T1-weighted MRI study shows bilateral lobulated smoothly marginated masses in the cerebellopontine angles. The mass on the right *(arrowheads)* expands the internal auditory canal. The mass on the left is circular and isodense and is in the cerebellopontine angle *(arrows).*

B, Axial T2-weighted section superior to the internal auditory canals. There is enlargement of the right fifth cranial nerve *(black arrowheads)* and filling of Meckel's cave by a neurofibroma of the trigeminal nerve *(white arrowheads).* There is also thickening of the proximal portion of the left fifth cranial nerve *(white arrow).* A nearly isointense mass at the surface of the lateral hemisphere relating to meningioma can also be seen *(black arrows).*

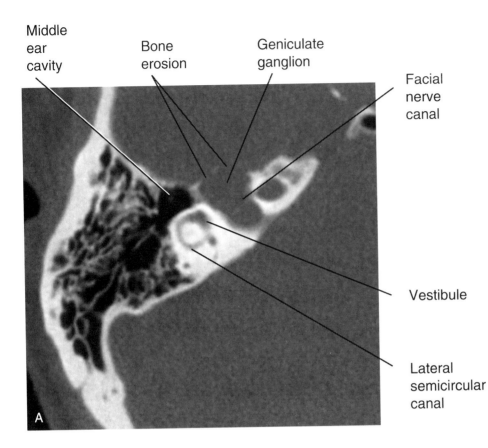

Middle ear cavity

Bone erosion

Geniculate ganglion

Facial nerve canal

Vestibule

Lateral semicircular canal

A

Geniculate ganglion erosion

Internal auditory canal

Posterior genu facial nerve canal

B

Figure 15–35. Facial schwannoma.

A, Axial CT image of the right temporal bone in a patient presenting with a long history of facial palsy that did not improve. The lateral internal auditory canal (IAC) is expanded. There is a broad opening of the IAC and the geniculate ganglion related to the schwannoma. There is erosion of the bone facing the middle cranial fossa.

B, Axial CT image, slightly inferior in relation to *A.* The geniculate ganglion is clearly expanded, with erosion of the anterior portion of the facial canal. This type of pattern can be seen with a hemangioma or with perineural spread of tumor.

Semicanal of the
tensor tympani
muscle

Geniculate
Ganglion
mass

Cochlea

Carotid
canal

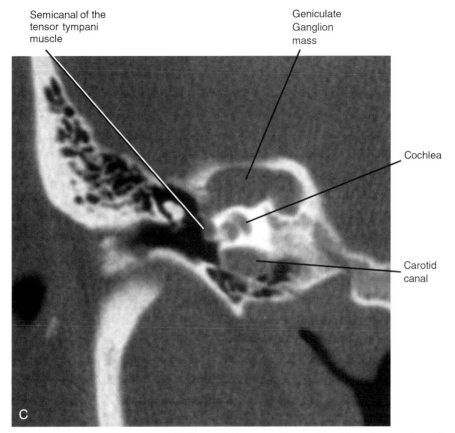

C

Figure 15–35 *Continued C,* Coronal CT image through the geniculate ganglion region. Note the massive enlargement of the canal superior and medial to the cochlea and carotid canal. The bony canal is smoothly enlarged, a common finding with facial schwannomas and acoustic schwannomas. The location of the bony expansion is centered anteriorly and superiorly in the IAC and along the facial nerve canal.

tion of the internal auditory canal and the geniculate ganglion region in particular may distinguish proximal facial schwannomas from acoustic schwannomas.[31] Tumors originating within the facial nerve canal cause enlargement and erosion of the involved segment.[61] Extracanalicular expansion of schwannomas may be evidenced by eccentric location of the tumor mass beyond the facial nerve canal, in the supralabyrinthine area, the middle ear cavity, the mastoid segment, or the parotid gland. Involvement of the geniculate ganglion is easy to detect on CT scans because of enlargement of the geniculate fossa on axial images. Most of these tumors enhance on MRI studies and have a characteristic tubular shape following the complex curves of the nerve.

Meningiomas

Most meningiomas (Fig. 15–38) arise outside the middle ear from the meninges covering the posterior petrous bone. Some meningiomas may subsequently invade the temporal bone, producing primarily otologic symptoms. Meningiomas arising within the cerebellopontine angle cause varying symptoms, including deafness, tinnitus, posterior fossa herniation, and facial paresis, although most are not symptomatic until they are large, in contrast to most acoustic

schwannomas. Meningiomas rarely originate within the internal auditory canal. When this does occur, it may simulate an acoustic tumor with vestibular and otologic symptoms. In a few instances, meningiomas may arise from ectopic arachnoid granulations within the middle ear cleft.[63] They may also be seen in neurofibromatosis.

Meningiomas of the cerebellopontine angle are classically semicircular dura-based lesions that protrude posteriorly. On CT scans, some are partially calcified and usually enhance. Hyperostosis of the posterior margin of the temporal bone is difficult to recognize because it is already highly dense, but air spaces changes are more sensitive. The internal auditory canal is usually not affected, or it is covered. Large lesions deform the adjacent brain and tract along the adjacent dural (Meckel's cave, petroclinoid ligament) structures.

On MRI studies, the lesions may be isointense with brain without contrast. The junction of the meningioma and temporal bone usually forms an obtuse angle, whereas an acoustic schwannoma usually forms an acute angle with the temporal bone.[17] In rare circumstances, the meningioma involves the mastoid and middle ear structures, either as en bloc cerebellopontine angle lesions or arising centrally without a dural surface involved. On CT scans, sclerosis

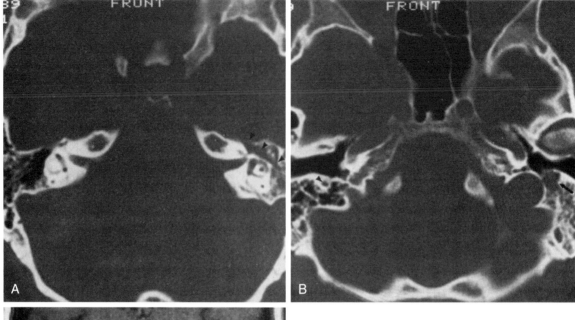

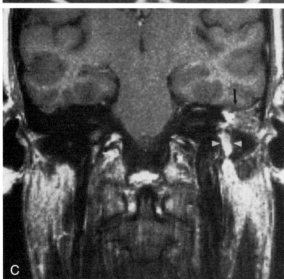

Figure 15–36. Facial schwannoma in a woman with a history of slowly progressive left facial paralysis.

A, High-resolution axial CT scan of the skull base through the internal auditory canals. The left distal limb of the geniculate ganglion and the horizontal facial nerve canals are enlarged *(black arrowheads).* There is opacification of the middle ear and mastoid.

B, Axial section, inferior in relation to *A,* at the level of the external auditory canal. The left descending facial nerve canal *(black arrow)* is much larger than the right *(black arrowhead).*

C, Coronal T1-weighted, contrast-enhanced MRI section paralleling the descending facial nerve. The nerve *(white arrowheads)* is enlarged and enhances, and there is also a component within the middle ear *(black arrow).* This pattern (tumor following the convoluted course of the facial nerve) is characteristic.

(A–C, Courtesy of Dr. Charles Lanzieri.)

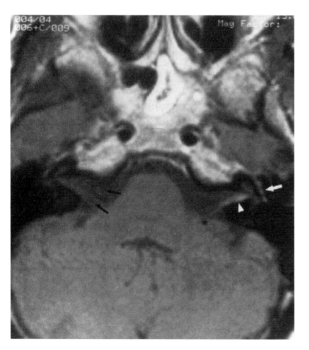

Figure 15–37. Bell's palsy in a middle-aged woman who presented with acute left facial palsy that gradually improved. This axial T1-weighted, contrast-enhanced MRI study shows linear enhancement of the seventh cranial nerve within the internal auditory canal *(white arrowhead)* and the horizontal portion of the facial nerve (fallopian) canal *(white arrow).* The seventh and eighth cranial nerves are easily seen in the cerebellopontine angle on the right *(black arrows).* There is no enlargement of the canal or bone destruction. (Courtesy of Theodore Larson, M.D.)

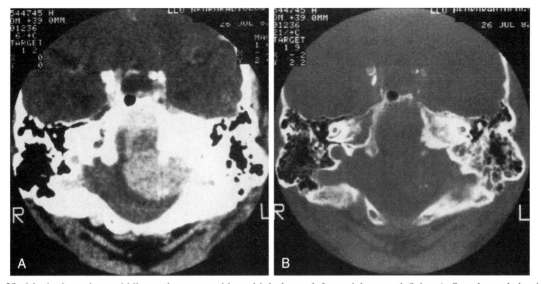

Figure 15–38. Meningioma in a middle-aged woman with multiple lower left cranial nerve deficits. *A*, Steeply angled axial CT scan of the skull base after contrast infusion. A large, enhancing, dura-based mass extends along the clivus and the left petrous bone. The tumor mass contains scattered calcifications. The adjacent brain structures are extensively deformed. *B*, High-resolution CT image at same level as in *A*. There is extensive sclerosis of the left petrous bone with partial opacification of the mastoid air cells.

and soft tissue opacification may be seen. On MRI studies, the infiltrative tumor may enhance.

Paragangliomas (Glomus Tumors)

Paragangliomas (Figs. 15–39 and 15–40), also referred to as *glomus tumors*, are slow-growing, purple-red vascular tumors that arise from chemoreceptor cells.[12, 62] They are histologically related to pheochromocytomas, are of mesenchymal or neuroectodermal origin, and secrete catecholamines in approximately 10% of instances. Arising from the ninth and tenth cranial nerves, paragangliomas are the most common tumor of the middle ear and the second most common tumor of the temporal bone after acoustic schwannoma. They occur most frequently in middle-aged women. They may be multicentric in up to 10% of patients and are commonly familial.[22] Even though most of the paragangliomas are benign and solitary, they are locally highly aggressive, simulating a malignant tumor in their local behavior. Some are malignant and metastasize.

Histologically and biologically, the lesions are similar, but historically they have unique names associated with their locations. Glomus tumors (paragangliomas) typically develop in the jugular bulb (glomus jugulare), the middle ear (glomus tympanicum), the carotid body (carotid body tumor), and the ganglion of the vagus nerve (glomus vagale).[12] Jugulotympanic glomus tumors involve both the middle ear and jugular bulb.

Symptoms are based on the location and size of the tumor. Tumors of the middle ear typically cause pulsating tinnitus, with subsequent conductive hearing loss. Paragangliomas cause permeative bone destruction; surprisingly, however, they often spare the ossicles. Erosion of the promontory or invasion into the cochlea leads to progressive neurosensory hearing loss. Vertigo may accompany the hearing loss as the tumor advances into the labyrinth. Involvement of the facial and lower cranial nerve canals may result in cranial nerve dysfunction. Extension superi-

orly into the middle cranial fossa may occur as the tumor erodes the tegmen. Because many of the tumors arise within the jugular fossa, extension intracranially or inferiorly into the upper neck with venous occlusion is common. Most posterior cranial fossa involvement is extradural. A nodular appearance of the medial intracranial border indicates intradural extension.[62]

Differentiation of these lesions is usually not possible by otoscopy alone unless the glomus tympanic mass is small enough so that its circumference is visible.[35] High-resolution cross-sectional imaging is effective in staging these tumors. Vascular anomalies as well as some other nonvascular lesions in the differential diagnosis may be accurately assessed by CT and MRI studies. Angiography is still important in their evaluation. Differentiation of paragangliomas from vascular malignant tumors (renal cell metastasis) may be difficult.

Glomus tympanicum tumors (see Fig. 15–39) are isolated to the middle ear cavity. They usually arise on the cochlear promontory and extend into the middle ear and mastoid air cells. The most common CT finding is the presence of a small soft tissue density protruding from the cochlear promontory without bony destruction.[12, 45] CT and MRI studies with IV contrast agents demonstrate a homogeneous, densely enhancing soft tissue mass within the tympanic cavity. These tumors may also fill the middle ear cavity but rarely cause ossicular destruction. The highly vascular nature of the lesions can be confirmed with angiography.

Glomus jugulare tumors (see Fig. 15–40) show bony destructive distortion at the separation of jugular fossa and hypotympanum.[12] The tumors commonly invade the hypotympanum. There may be displacement of the tympanic membrane and the long process of the malleus and erosion of the basal turn of the cochlea. On CT scans, invasion into the infralabyrinthine compartment results in a mottled appearance.[62] Infralabyrinthine involvement may

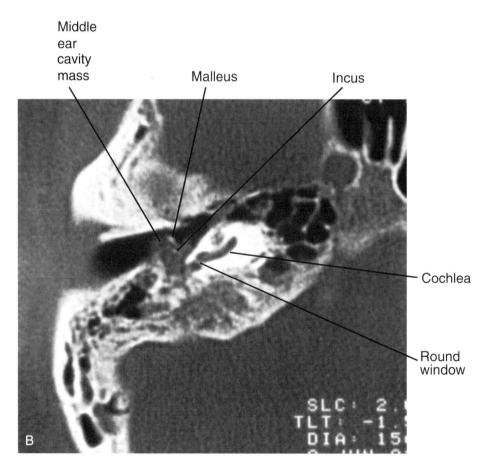

Middle
ear cavity
mass

Cochlear
promontory

Cochlea

Jugular
fossa
mass

Temporal bone
erosion

SLC: 2.0
TLT: -1.5
DIA: 156

A

Middle
ear
cavity
mass

Malleus

Incus

Cochlea

Round
window

SLC: 2.
TLT: -1.
DIA: 15

B

Figure 15–39. Glomus jugulare paraganglioma in a patient presenting with pulsatile tinnitus.

A, Axial CT image through the basal turn of the cochlea. A small, hypotympanic, soft tissue mass in the middle ear overlies the cochlear promontory. The adjacent temporal bone is eroded near the jugular fossa. The erosion is very near the descending facial nerve canal. This combination of a destructive mass arising near or in the jugular fossa and extending into the middle ear is characteristic of paragangliomas.

B, Axial CT section, slightly superior in relation to *A,* shows the mass in contact with the round window, the long process of the malleus, the long process of the incus, and the tympanic membrane. There is no destruction of the ossicles, which is typical. There is some minor opacification of the mastoid.

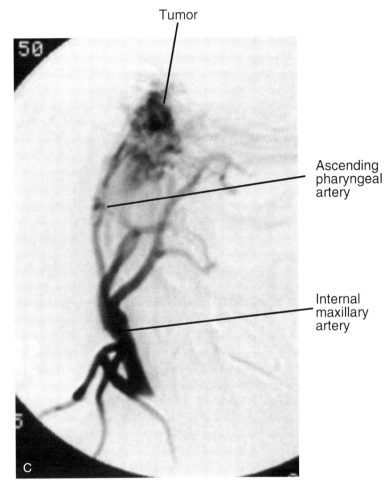

Tumor

Ascending
pharyngeal
artery

Internal
maxillary
artery

Figure 15–39 *Continued C,* Lateral angiogram of the internal maxillary artery showing enlargement of the many feeding vessels (including the ascending pharyngeal artery) extending to the jugular fossa. The highly vascular tumor is characteristic of a paraganglioma.

destroy the vertical and horizontal portions of the carotid canal. In these patients, preoperative balloon occlusion of the carotid artery may be necessary. The examination should extend inferiorly to include the upper neck, and intracranially, since these tumors commonly follow the jugular venous system from the torcular Herophili to the lower cervical jugular vein. On MRI studies, the vascular nature of the lesion is demonstrated by the presence of small tortuous signal voids.

Angiography is still important in the preembolization workup to define various vascular pedicles so that each pedicle can be individually catheterized and embolized. Catheter or magnetic resonance venography may be needed to confirm the patency of the venous structures.

Epidermoidomas (Epidermoid Cysts)[49]

Epidermoidomas *(primary congenital cholesteatomas)* consist of masses of embryonic ectodermal rests and are thus distinct from true cholesteatomas, whose formation is a reaction to inflammation and trapped squamous epithelium. These lesions may be found in several areas within the temporal bone. They can arise in the external auditory canal, leading to chronic obstruction (Fig. 15–41), termed *keratosis obturans.* Some lesions originate in the middle ear, with subsequent erosion of the ossicles, facial nerve canal, or lateral semicircular canal. Patients usually have unilateral serous otitis or unexplained unilateral conductive hearing loss. Some epidermoidomas originate in the osseous structures, typically in a supralabyrinthine location. The lesions show sharp outlines with distinct edges and appear as expansile cystic lesions along the superior portions of the temporal bone.

Typically, the lesions exhibit a "punched-out" appearance. Thy may erode into the facial nerve canal or internal auditory canal, causing facial nerve palsy or hearing loss. They may also arise in the petrous apex, forming an expansile, sharply marginated destructive lesion that can affect the clivus (Fig. 15–42).

Epidermoidomas may also originate in the cerebellopontine angle. These masses can demonstrate a wide range of imaging characteristics. On CT scans, they are frequently low density structures and may mimic a subarachnoid cyst. They can be solid or even calcified and usually do not significantly enhance. Contrast cisternography characteristically shows a frondlike pattern as the contrast enters many small channels at the irregular surface of the lesion. On MRI scans, a wide range of findings may also be seen, including expansion out of the cerebellopontine angle into Meckel's cave or the ambient cistern. These tumors do not tend to invade the brain.

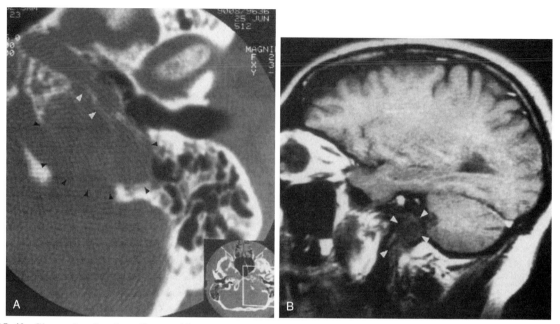

Figure 15–40. Glomus jugulare in a 40-year-old woman presenting with multiple lower cranial nerve palsies and a visible blue middle ear mass.

A, Magnified axial CT scan of the left temporal bone through the hypotympanum. The left jugular fossa is massively enlarged *(black arrowheads)* with destructive margins. A mass extends into the petrous apex. A thin margin of bone outlines the carotid canal *(white arrowheads).* The separation of the mass and the middle ear is poorly defined.

B, Sagittal non–contrast-enhanced, T1-weighted MR image through the jugular fossa. The jugular fossa is usually seen as a signal void as a result of cortical bone and blood flow. In this instance, a low-signal-intensity soft tissue mass is seen expanding the jugular fossa *(white arrowheads)* but does not extend through the dura.

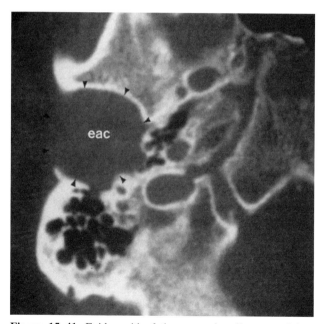

Figure 15–41. Epidermoid of the external auditory canal in a young man presenting with a chronic history of bilateral external canal obstruction. He had no history of chronic infection or tympanic membrane rupture (as would be seen with cholesteatoma). The axial CT scan through the right external auditory canal (eac) shows a smoothly marginated mass *(arrowheads)* expanding the canal. The mastoids and protympanum are intact without inflammatory changes.

Hemangiomas of the Facial Nerve

Small hemangiomas of the facial nerve are actually as common as facial schwannomas. These benign tumors most commonly affect the geniculate ganglion, but they occasionally involve the internal auditory canal. Patients usually present with progressive facial paralysis. Most of these tumors are not extremely vascular but, instead, are partially calcified. On CT scans, one sees a small lesion of mixed sclerosis with erosion of the facial nerve canal. On MRI studies, hemangiomas may display slight contrast enhancement (Fig. 15–43).

Miscellaneous Benign Lesions

A variety of neoplastic and non-neoplastic lesions occasionally involve the cerebellopontine angle and the temporal bone. Other cranial nerve tumors may occur in addition to acoustic schwannomas.

Trigeminal schwannomas typically follow the course of the nerve from the anterior pons into Meckel's cave and then into the subtemporal fossa.[3] The foramen ovale and rotundum as well as the superior orbital canal may be enlarged.

Schwannomas of lower cranial nerves IX, X, XI, and XII may mimic paragangliomas by forming a dumbbell-shaped mass that enlarges the jugular fossa (Fig. 15–44).[12] On angiograms, however, they are often less vascular.

Lipomas and some *epidermoid* or *dermoid tumors* of the cerebellopontine angle may be readily identified by CT as low-density fatty masses.[21] On MRI studies, if the masses are composed predominantly of triglyceride, they

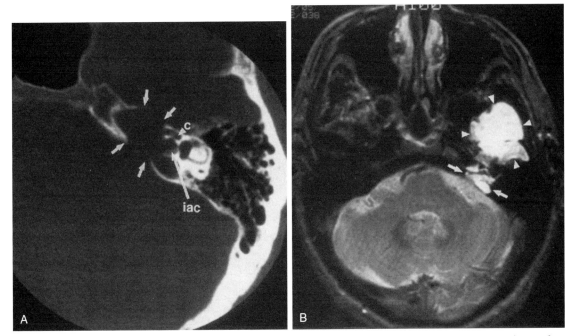

Figure 15–42. Epidermoid of the petrous apex in a 40-year-old man presenting with symptoms similar to those of an acoustic schwannoma. *A,* Axial CT image through the left internal auditory canal shows a large destructive lesion *(arrows)* involving the petrous apex, internal auditory canal (iac), and cochlea (c). The lesion is rather sharply marginated. The mastoid and middle ear are intact. *B,* Axial T2-weighted MR image demonstrates that the lesion has a very high signal (consistent with a high water content). One component is within the petrous apex *(arrows),* and a second larger area involves the anterior portion of the middle cranial cavity *(arrowheads).* There is little reaction of the adjacent brain.

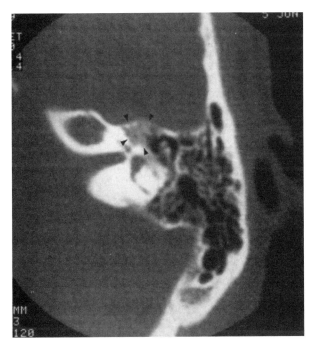

Figure 15–43. Facial nerve hemangioma in a patient with slowly progressive facial paralysis. The axial CT section through the left temporal bone shows mixed sclerosis and destruction of the geniculate ganglion region *(arrowheads).* The normal smoothly marginated canal is not visible and is replaced with an irregular cluster of calcification. There is no soft tissue component within the middle ear.

may have high signal intensity on T1-weighted images and may demonstrate chemical shift artifacts. If the fat is not triglyceride in nature, it appears as a low-density mass on CT scans but not as a high-signal-intensity mass on T1-weighted MR images.

Several non-neoplastic lesions may appear similar to their neoplastic counterparts. An *arachnoid cyst* of the posterior fossa can mimic a cystic cerebellopontine angle tumor (epidermoid). The CT appearance is that of a CSF-density mass filling the cerebellopontine angle cistern, with slight distortion of the adjacent brain structures. Scalloping of the petrous bone suggests a chronic process. It may be difficult to differentiate cystic epidermoids and dermoids from arachnoid cysts unless there is evidence of arachnoiditis. MRI is superior to CT in its capacity to help confirm the nature of cystic lesions.

Cholesterol granulomas of the petrous apex (Fig. 15–45) are slow-growing collections of blood products. These lesions are non-neoplastic. The etiology is not clear but may be related to chronic obstruction. These granulomas are common incidental findings on MRI studies that are seen as high-signal-intensity regions of subacute hemorrhage on all pulse sequences involving the petrous apex. There may be no expansion, and the CT findings are essentially normal. A minority of these lesions expand to erode the petrous apex. Most patients present with symptoms similar to those of an acoustic schwannoma. CT scanning typically shows a circular soft tissue density mass expanding the apex. There may also be involvement of the clivus and internal auditory canal. On MRI studies, the lesions are seen as expansile high-signal-intensity masses centered in the petrous apex.

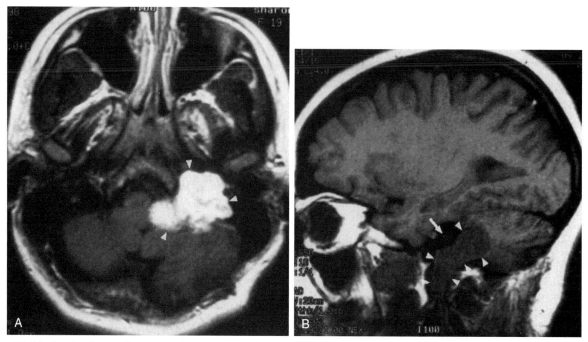

Figure 15–44. Jugular fossa schwannoma in a teenaged girl thought to have neurofibromatosis and who presented with a recurrent jugular fossa schwannoma.

A, Axial contrast-enhanced, T1-weighted, spin-echo MRI study at a level inferior to that of the internal auditory canal. A large, lobulated, enhancing mass *(arrowheads)* is centered in the left jugular fossa region. The bony margins are eroded. The mass protrudes into the posterior fossa.

B, Sagittal, non–contrast-enhanced, T1-weighted MRI study through the jugular fossa. The slightly low-signal-intensity posterior fossa mass *(arrowheads)* extends from the cerebellum through the expanded jugular fossa into the superior neck. The adjacent internal auditory canal *(arrow)* is intact.

Malignant Neoplasms

Primary malignant neoplasms of the temporal bone are relatively uncommon. When they do occur, they are most often squamous or basal cell carcinomas. These tumors usually originate from mucosal epithelium of the external auditory canal, middle ear, or mastoid air cells and are usually aggressive. Patients who have primary squamous cell carcinomas of the external auditory canal may have a history of chronic external otitis. Symptoms may also include otalgia, bleeding, otorrhea, dizziness, deafness, and facial nerve palsy. They may extend locally into the parotid gland and the temporomandibular joint. More medial invasion is associated with a worse prognosis. Lymphatic invasion and subsequent distant metastasis are rare.

The most important CT finding suggesting a diagnosis of carcinoma is erosion of the walls of the bony external auditory canal or middle ear by a soft tissue mass in a patient who does not have a history of cholesteatoma.[46] CT scanning can outline the bony erosion and can show the extension of the soft tissue mass into the adjacent normal soft tissues.[28, 64] On MRI studies, there may be edema and abnormal soft tissue with irregular enhancement after IV contrast infusion as well as distortion of the surrounding soft tissue planes (Fig. 15–46). In some patients, it is difficult to differentiate between tumor and secondary infection (malignant external otitis) because in both cases there may be soft tissue enhancement with the presence or absence of bony erosion.

Glandular neoplasms, such as adenoma and adenocarci-

noma, account for about 14% of primary temporal bone masses. The clinical and CT findings of glandular carcinoma are similar to those of squamous cell carcinomas, except that metastasis to regional lymph nodes may occur. For this reason, the lymph nodes at the skull base and upper neck should be evaluated on CT scans. Lymph node involvement is evidenced by peripheral soft tissue enhancement with central necrosis on IV contrast-enhanced CT studies.[11]

Embryonal rhabdomyosarcoma (Fig. 15–47) is the most frequently encountered malignant middle ear neoplasm in children. Involvement of the temporal bone by rhabdomyosarcoma is relatively common. The tumor is highly aggressive, and bone destruction associated with a middle ear soft tissue mass occurs quite often. The patient may also have cranial nerve deficits. Intracranial spread secondary to direct epidural extension may be seen on CT or MRI studies as an enhancing mass in continuity with the ear mass. CT scanning is the ideal examination for monitoring recurrence after surgical resection, radiation, or chemotherapy.[22] Eosinophilic granuloma may have a very similar appearance.

Malignant tumors from adjacent structures may secondarily involve the temporal bone from several avenues, including through the foramina and fissures of the skull base and from the soft tissues of the external auditory canal. The most common extensions are from nasopharyngeal cancer (Fig. 15–48) and skin and salivary gland cancers, via the eustachian canal and external auditory canal,

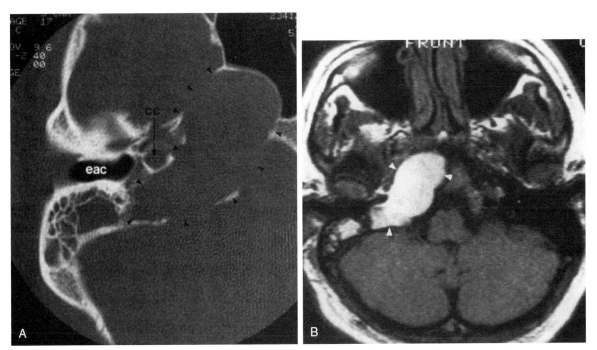

Figure 15–45. Cholesterol granuloma in a patient presenting with symptoms similar to those of an acoustic schwannoma.

A, Axial CT section through the right external auditory canal (eac) and carotid canal (cc). A large expansile mass is in the petrous apex. The margins of the surrounding bone are thinned. There is remodeling of the sphenoid sinus and the posterior margin of the temporal bone *(black arrowheads).* The mastoid is opacified. The external auditory canal is intact.

B, Axial T1-weighted, non–contrast-enhanced MRI study at the same level as in *A.* A large mass with very high signal intensity caused by subacute hemorrhage can be seen *(arrowheads).* The margins of the lesion are smooth, with displacement of adjacent structures rather than invasion. The lesion is centered at the petrous apex and involves the clivus. This lesion was of high signal intensity on all imaging sequences.

(A and B, Courtesy of William Lo, M.D.)

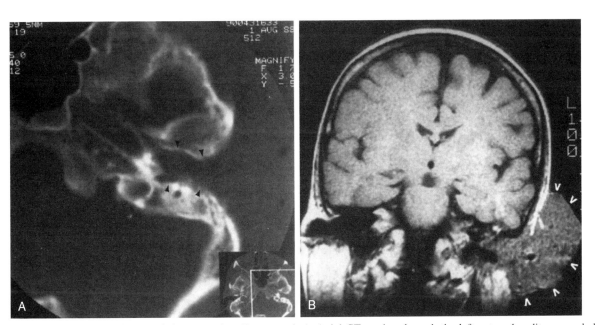

Figure 15–46. Basal cell carcinoma of the external auditory canal. *A,* Axial CT section through the left external auditory canal shows a soft tissue mass *(black arrowheads)* filling the canal and middle ear. Irregular destruction and expansion of the bony canal are shown. *B,* Coronal T1-weighted MRI study shows a large mushroom-shaped mass *(white arrowheads)* extending external from the auditory canal to involve the adjacent soft tissues. The normal fatty structures have been invaded.

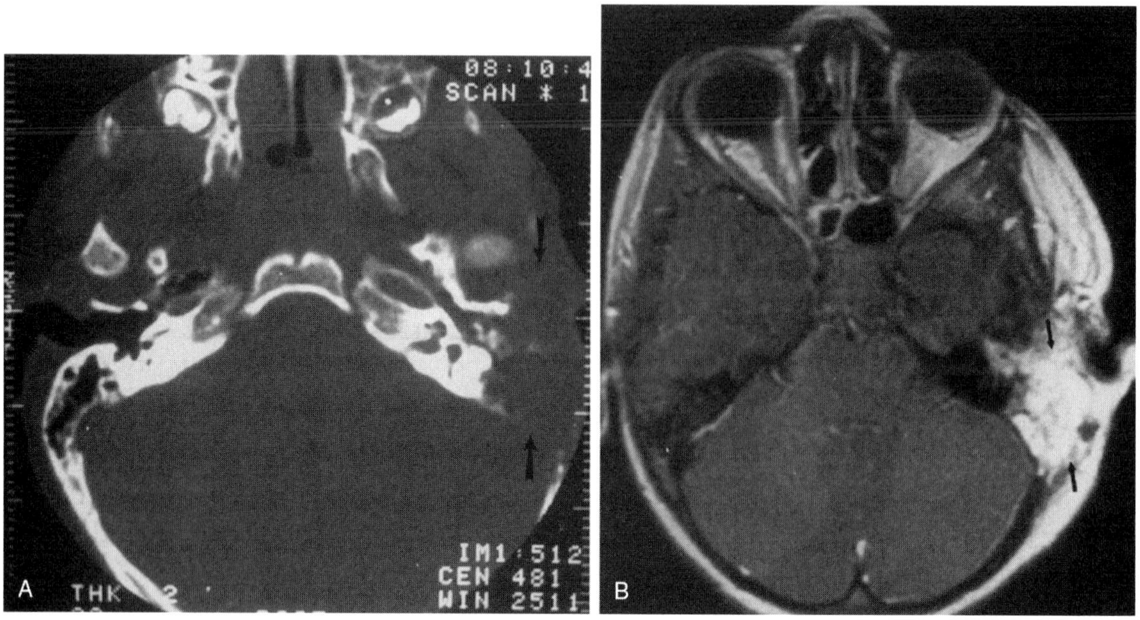

Figure 15–47. Rhabdomyosarcoma in a 5-year-old girl who presented with rapidly progressive pain and swelling of the left mastoid, mimicking an acute infection. Biopsy showed an invasive rhabdomyosarcoma.

A, Axial bone window CT scan made through the internal auditory canals. The right ear is normal. The left ear shows a large destructive lesion *(black arrows)* involving the mastoid, external auditory canal, and middle ear.

B, Axial contrast-enhanced, T1-weighted, spin-echo MRI study at approximately the same level as in *A.* A large, enhancing soft tissue mass *(black arrows)* extends laterally from the region of bone destruction. There is secondary edema and thickening of the soft tissues overlying the calvarium on the left.

respectively.[23] Perineural spread occurs when malignant tumors track along the course of normal nerves (Fig. 15–49). This is a very subtle but important finding, since the tumor may appear to spread in a discontinuous manner and to recur a long distance from the primary site. This is most frequently seen with squamous cell cancer because it is the most common head and neck malignancy. Perineural spread is especially prevalent with adenoid cystic carcinoma and lymphoma. The facial nerve is most often affected. Perineural spread through the facial nerve can arise from tumors involving the parotid region or from small interconnecting branches of the fifth cranial nerve.[20]

CSF carcinomatosis is a relatively common complication of systemic cancers (Fig. 15–50). The metastases can occur in the internal auditory canal and may mimic benign acoustic tumors transiently. When single lesions are seen, the findings are nonspecific; however, when multiple lesions are in the CSF or brain or when multiple cranial nerves are affected and dural enhancement is present, the diagnosis is clear. The prognosis for a patient with carcinomatosis is poor.

The temporal bone is susceptible to any neoplasm that typically metastasizes to bone. Hematogenous spread typically occurs from tumors of the breast, lung, stomach, prostate gland (Fig. 15–51), or kidney. These lesions cause a diffuse or focal osteolytic destructive pattern. There may be postcontrast enhancement, especially if both the epidural space and the bone are involved. Differentiation of glomus tumors from renal carcinoma metastases may be difficult, since both tumors are highly vascular. Prostatic tumors may cause osteoblastic changes that simulate a sclerosing inflammatory process, a meningioma, or Paget's disease.

Traumatic Injuries

The common local serious consequences of temporal bone trauma are hearing loss, CSF fistula, and facial nerve palsy. CT is the best diagnostic modality for identification of fractures.[27] Routine head CT examinations of trauma patients should include accurate surveys of the temporal bones. Follow-up detailed, high-resolution images can be acquired if indicated. MRI studies can be of value for vascular and brain injuries.[48, 59]

Fractures[1]

Longitudinal Fractures

Longitudinal fractures (Fig. 15–52) occur along the long axis of the petrous pyramid, which extends parallel to the external and internal auditory canal toward the petrous apex. These fractures typically extend from the temporal squamosa across the roof or posterior wall of the external auditory canal into the tympanic cavity and tegmen tympani. There may be rupture of the tympanic membrane, with hemorrhage in the external auditory canal and middle ear.[11]

Conductive hearing loss is common and may be caused by ossicular dislocation or fracture or by the presence of intratympanic hemorrhage.[47] Neurosensory hearing loss is rare with longitudinal fractures but can result from a labyrinthine injury. Facial nerve paralysis occurs in about 20% of instances. Common sites of injury include the geniculate ganglion and the posterior genu.

Axial CT sections favor the visualization of longitudinal

Temporal bone
enhancement

Nasopharynx

Dural
enhancement

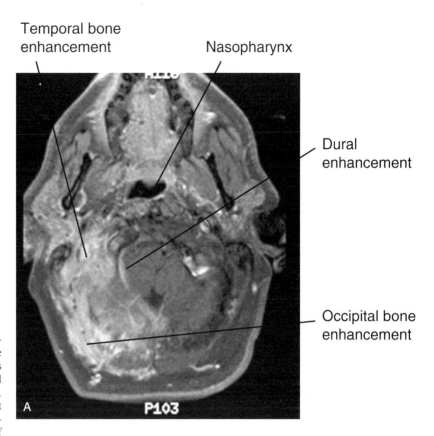

Occipital bone
enhancement

Figure 15–48. Invasive nasopharyngeal carcinoma in a young man with a very aggressive invasive carcinoma of the nasopharynx that has spread into the adjacent skull base, temporal bone, occipital bone, and posterior fossa. *A,* Axial T1-weighted, spin-echo image with fat saturation. A large arching region of tumor infiltration extends from the posterior margin of the nasopharynx all the way back to near the midline occipital bone. *B,* Axial T1-weighted spin-echo image with fat saturation centered more cephalad than in *A.* There is extensive enhancement of Meckel's caves, the right internal auditory canal, and the dural surfaces of the posterior right temporal bone.

Dural
enhancement

Meckel's
cave

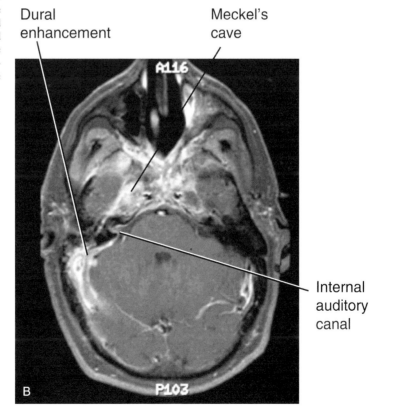

Internal
auditory
canal

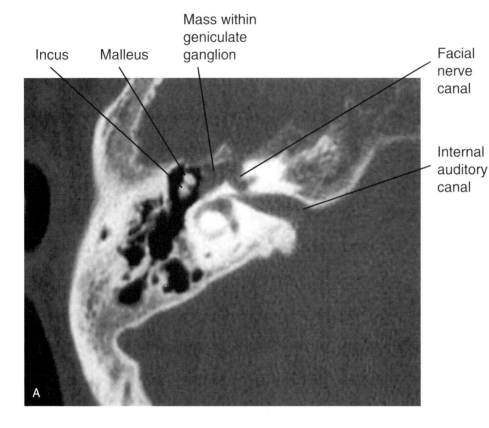

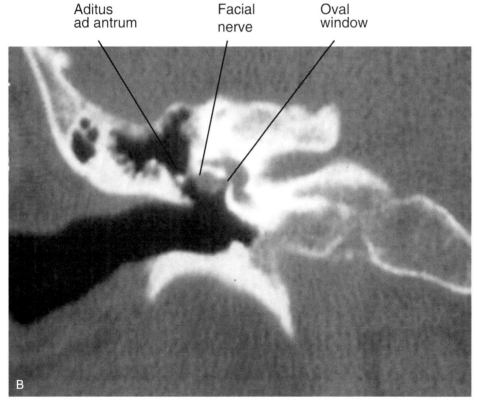

Figure 15–49. Perineural spread into geniculate ganglion in a middle-aged woman presenting with a long history of progressive right facial palsy. A CT-directed needle biopsy of the parotid showed carcinoma.

A, Axial CT image through the geniculate ganglion and internal auditory canal portions of the facial nerve canal. There is bulbous expansion of the geniculate ganglion canal. A small soft tissue component protrudes into the epitympanic space just medial to the head of the malleus and the body of the incus.

B, Coronal section through the right temporal bone at the level of the horizontal middle ear segment of the facial nerve, the oval window, and the aditus ad antrum. Note the expansion of the facial nerve that protrudes inferiorly overlying the oval window.

Meckel's
caves

Internal
auditory
canal

Cerebellopontine
angle mass

Brainstem

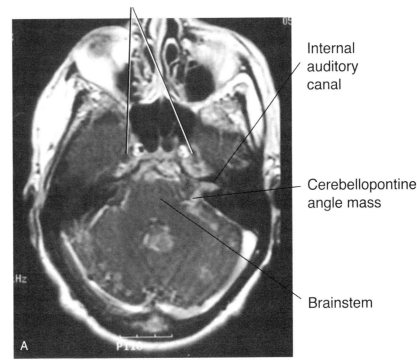

Figure 15–50. Metastatic carcinomatosis in a patient with a known primary tumor and presenting with multiple cranial nerve problems, including hearing loss.

A, Axial T1-weighted, 3D Fourier transform, high-resolution, contrast-enhanced MR image through the left internal auditory canal (IAC). The left IAC, cerebellopontine angle (CPA), and surface of the brain stem all enhance. Multiple other small lesions overlie the surface of the cerebellum. Meckel's caves are involved as well.

B, Axial T1-weighted, spin-echo MR image shows "miliary" enhancing metastases of the brain in addition to CPA disease. Isolated involvement of the IAC by carcinomatosis may mimic a small acoustic schwannoma, but frequently other lesions are imaged or multiple clinical findings may suggest a more diffuse process.

Enhancing
brain
metastases

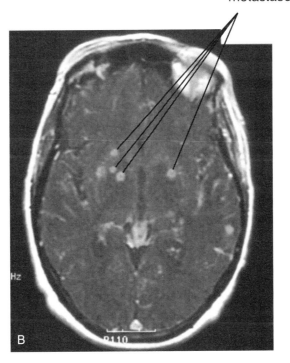

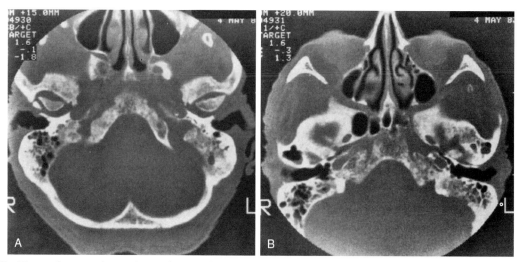

Figure 15–51. Metastatic prostatic carcinoma in an elderly man with a history of severe headaches, ear pain, and known prostate cancer. *A* and *B,* Axial CT scans of the skull base show extensive mixed lytic and blastic metastases involving the clivus and petrous apices. There is moderate destruction of the inferior portions of the petrous bones bilaterally, with patchy opacification of the mastoid air cells.

fractures. However, subtle ossicular disruptions with small bony fragments may be more readily seen on coronal images.

Transverse Fractures

Transverse fractures (Fig. 15–53) cross the temporal bone from a posterior to an anterior direction. This type of injury is less common, occurring in approximately 20% of instances. There may be associated traumatic lesions involving the temporomandibular joint, mandibular condyle, or skull base.

Transverse fractures frequently cause labyrinthine dysfunction, resulting in a totally "dead" ear whenever the fracture traverses the vestibule, semicircular canals, or cochlea. Bony fragments may impinge on the facial nerve

canal. Facial nerve palsy is commonly present and is the usual reason for radiographic investigation. CT scanning can be used to explore the facial nerve canal and to illustrate the precise site of injury.[58]

Complex Fractures

A variety of comminuted fractures (Fig. 15–54) may affect the temporal bone. Other fractures of the skull base are common, since the skull base acts as a ring. Severe trauma may be associated with the presence of CSF otorrhea or rhinorrhea. Patients with persistent otorrhea or rhinorrhea can be investigated with CT scans after injection of intrathecal water-soluble contrast material. The site of leakage through the temporal bone may thus be identified, facilitating surgical repair. Vascular injuries, such as carotid

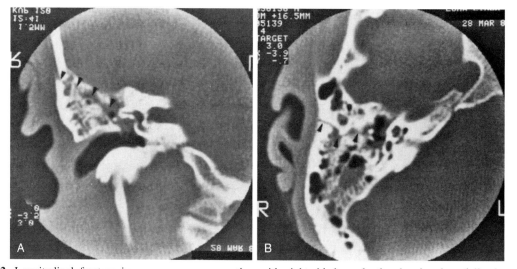

Figure 15–52. Longitudinal fracture in a young man presenting with right-sided conductive hearing loss following skull trauma. Coronal *(A)* and axial *(B)* CT scans of the right temporal bone show a fracture line *(arrowheads)* extending obliquely from the superior lateral portion of the mastoid air cells into the tympanic cavity. There is patchy air-fluid level opacification of the tympanic cavity and mastoid air cells because of hemorrhage and fluid. The ossicles are not displaced.

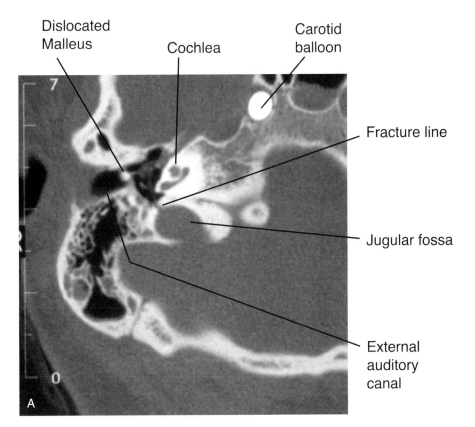

Dislocated
Malleus

Cochlea

Carotid
balloon

Fracture line

Jugular fossa

External
auditory
canal

A

Figure 15–53. Transverse fracture. *A,* Axial CT image through the cochlea demonstrates dislocation of the ossicles (head of the malleus) into the external auditory canal and tympanic membrane. The normal position of the long process of the malleus is not seen. A linear fracture crosses obliquely into the jugular fossa. *B,* CT section through the epitympanic space demonstrates an absence of the head of the malleus and the body of the incus; they have been dislocated inferiorly. An oblique transverse fracture runs posterior to the posterior semicircular canal. A fracture of the geniculate ganglion canal is too wide to be normal. The mastoid air cells are partially opacified. A balloon is present in the carotid canal as a result of a carotid-cavernous fistula.

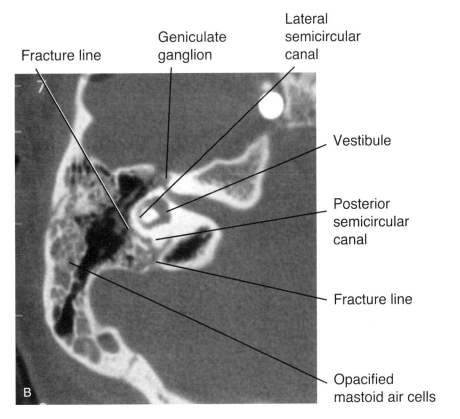

Fracture line

Geniculate
ganglion

Lateral
semicircular
canal

Vestibule

Posterior
semicircular
canal

Fracture line

Opacified
mastoid air cells

B

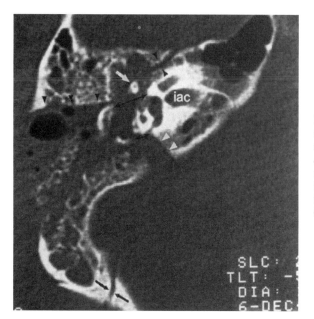

Figure 15–54. Comminuted fracture in a young man who sustained a severe traumatic skull and brain injury. Axial CT image through the right internal auditory canal (iac) shows multiple longitudinal *(black arrowheads)* and transverse *(black arrows* and *white arrowheads)* comminuted fractures. The lateral semicircular canal *(double-headed arrows)* is avulsed, and the malleus *(white arrow)* and incus are dislocated from the epitympanic space. The air spaces are opacified with fluid. Cerebrospinal fluid or otic capsule fistula could not be excluded.

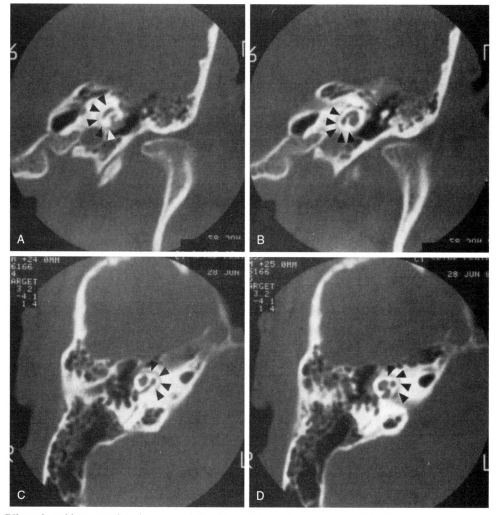

Figure 15–55. Bilateral cochlear otosclerosis an an adult with a history of progressive bilateral neurosensory hearing loss. *A* and *B*, Coronal CT scans of the left ear show a rim of hypodensity paralleling the left cochlea *(arrowheads)*. This lucency represents an area of the enchondral layer of bone formation. *C* and *D*, Axial CT scans of the right ear show similar findings *(arrowheads)*. (*A–D*, Courtesy of Dr. Galdino Valvassori.)

dissection and carotid cavernous fistulas, may also be seen. Both MRI and angiography are of value.

Facial Nerve Injury

Transient facial nerve paralysis may occur after temporal bone injury as a result of edema (see Fig. 15–53). Contusion of the facial nerve occurs at the site of greatest narrowing. Whenever there is persistent dysfunction, surgical exploration of the facial nerve may be indicated.[60] Preoperative CT examination can identify the site of injury.[27]

Metabolic and Dysplastic Lesions

The petrous temporal bone may be affected by a variety of primary bone diseases that can involve other portions of the skeleton. When they involve the temporal bone, the significance is related to disturbances of hearing, balance, or facial nerve function. Thus, these afflictions usually require detailed, high-resolution CT evaluation of the temporal bones.

Otosclerosis

Otosclerosis (Fig. 15–55) is more accurately called *otospongiosis*, which reflects the active phase of the disease.

Figure 15–56 Prostheses. *A,* Axial CT section through the round window and cochlea demonstrates a cochlear implant. The wire enters the round window and the basal turn of the cochlea and is seen as a thin, linear density. *B,* Coronal CT scan shows a metallic prosthetic stapes angled from the long process of the incus up into the oval window niche. It ends at the stapes footplate in a normal position.

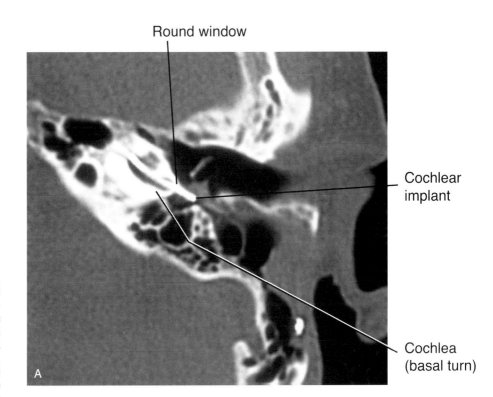

Round window

Cochlear implant

Cochlea (basal turn)

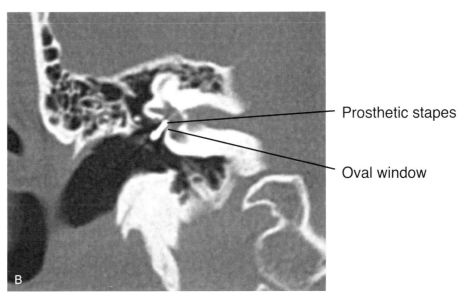

Prosthetic stapes

Oval window

Illustration continued on following page

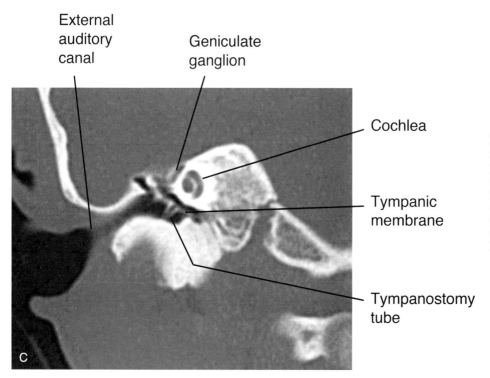

External
auditory
canal

Geniculate
ganglion

Cochlea

Tympanic
membrane

Tympanostomy
tube

C

Figure 15–56 *Continued C,* Coronal CT scan shows a small tympanostomy tube as two thin linear densities protruding from the tympanic membrane. The middle ear and the external auditory canal are clear. Other structures depicted include the cochlea and the geniculate ganglion.

This primary bone disease is fairly common; histological studies show that it occurs in up to 10% of the population, but clinical symptoms are present in only 10% of those with histologic changes. If the disease process involves the labyrinthine capsule, there may be progressive neurosensory hearing loss. Involvement of the oval window and stapes footplate causes conductive hearing loss, whereas involvement of the cochlea causes neurosensory hearing loss. Occasionally, there is a combination of both types of deafness.

The human otic capsule is unique because mature bone remains in a state of primary ossification. This enchondral capsule is never replaced by mature haversian osseous tissue. Pathologically, otosclerosis consists of replacement of the primitive and chondral bony capsule by mature haversian bone. The disease begins as scattered foci of bony resorption containing many osteoclasts, osteoblasts, and irregular, loose trabeculae. These so-called spongiotic foci are less dense than normal bone and represent the *active* disease (otospongiosis), which can cause hearing loss. In the *inactive (sclerotic)* phase, a few cells or vessels are contained within sclerotic foci. Otosclerosis usually begins before puberty, is familial, and is bilateral in about 90% of patients. Women are affected twice as often as men.

Cochlear (labyrinthine) otosclerosis (see Fig. 15–55) has a characteristic CT appearance. Crescentic low-density regions parallel the margins of the basal turn of the cochlea, the entire cochlea, or the whole otic capsule. On CT scans, the active or spongiotic phase appears as areas of demineralization involving the enchondral layer of the cochlea or the otic capsule.[37] CT scanning may be able to show a fine enchondral band of decreased density in some patients with normal hearing. Presumably, this represents histologic (incipient) otosclerosis. Other patients may have areas of inactive otosclerotic foci.

Spongiotic changes involving the oval window and stapes footplate are referred to as *fenestral otosclerosis,* a type that is more difficult to identify on CT scans. However, the otosclerotic phase may be readily appreciated.[36] Patients with early stapedial vestibular otosclerosis show small lucencies within the otic capsule with soft tissue swelling predominantly at the anterior margin of the oval window. Later on, dense otosclerotic foci may cover these structures. The round window may also be affected.

Most patients with otosclerosis are treated with stapedectomy and prosthetic implants. State-of-the-art CT scanning may be used in evaluating metallic, plastic, and ceramic prostheses after such procedures (Fig. 15–56).[13] Patients who experience recurring hearing loss after ossiculoplasties may also be examined by CT to determine whether dislocation of the prosthesis has occurred.

Osteogenesis Imperfecta

Osteogenesis imperfecta (Fig. 15–57) produces otic capsule and oval window changes identical to those seen with otosclerosis.[36, 37] Deafness is a common finding, with progressive hearing loss starting in childhood or as late as the third decade of life. When the otosclerotic process extends into the medial aspect of the cochlear capsule, the enchondral band of demineralization produces a characteristic double lucency appearance *(double-ring sign)* of the cochlea. If the process is severe and extensive, the outline of the cochlea becomes totally indistinguishable from the surrounding petrous bone.

Paget's Disease (Osteitis Deformans)

Paget's disease (osteitis deformans) (Fig. 15–58) is a chronic inflammatory disorder that results in the eventual

Cochlea   Oval window

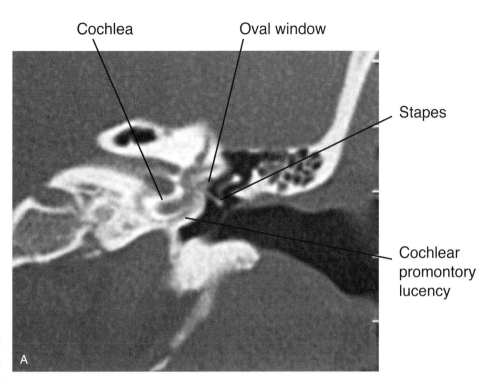

Stapes

Cochlear
promontory
lucency

Figure 15–57. Osteogenesis imperfecta in a young patient with hearing loss and facial palsy. *A,* Coronal CT image demonstrates a broad lucency adjacent to the basal turn of the cochlea. There is also thickening of the soft tissues filling the oval window niche, mimicking severe fenestral and cochlear otosclerosis. *B,* Coronal image, anterior in relationship to *A,* shows erosive changes involving the geniculate ganglion region and paralleling the cochlea.

Lucency   Cochlea   Geniculate
ganglion

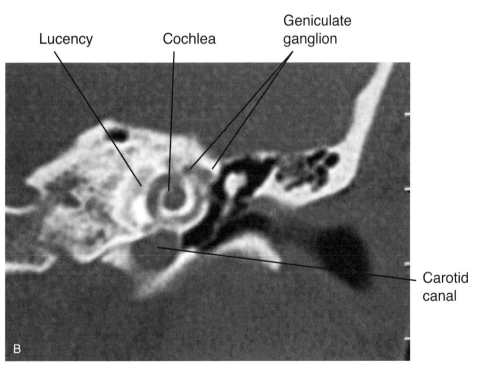

Carotid
canal

replacement of normal bone by thickened, less dense, weaker bone. The incidence of Paget's disease in patients over 40 years of age is 3%, and the skull is affected in 65% to 70% of patients. When Paget's disease involves the temporal bone, it is most often bilateral, with similar structural changes in a given pair of temporal bones.

Paget's disease can produce narrowing and tortuosity of the external auditory canal. Exostoses and chronic external otitis are fairly common and lead to the secondary development of external canal cholesteatomas. In addition to the overgrowth of bone in the external auditory canal (which may cause conductive hearing loss), there may be concentric overgrowth of the tympanic bone. This bony overgrowth leads to conductive hearing loss because the tympanic annulus and tympanic membrane become relaxed, resulting in inadequate function.

Paget's disease can affect the inner ear, with demineralization of the petrous pyramids and labyrinthine capsule. These areas of demineralization are intermixed with areas of apparent thickening in the skull base.

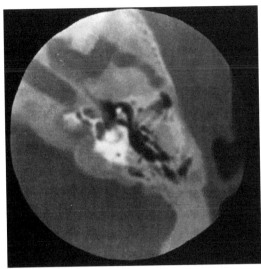

Figure 15–58. Paget's disease in an older man with bilateral neurosensory hearing loss. Axial CT scan of the left ear shows tremendous thickening of the entire temporal bone. The central portion of the otic capsule adjacent to the vestibule and semicircular canals are least affected. The internal auditory canal is not visible because of pagetoid changes in the inner ear. (Courtesy of Dr. Jacqueline Vignaud.)

Fibrous Dysplasia[43]

Fibrous dysplasia (Fig. 15–59) is a disease manifested by aberrant maturation of bone. Histologically, normal spongiotic bone is replaced and the medullary cavities of affected bones are filled by abnormal fibrous tissue. The bony structures have an increased density, in comparison with normal bone and in contrast to Paget's disease, where the thickened bone is less dense than normal bone. Solitary monostotic fibrous dysplasia of the petrous pyramid may

occur, but widespread involvement is more common. The changes in the temporal bone are usually proliferative, whereas the changes in the calvaria are usually expansile.

Patients with fibrous dysplasia can show both conductive and neurosensory hearing loss. Conductive hearing loss results from narrowing or occlusion of the external auditory canal. Such stenosis is common and may be responsible for cholesteatoma formation.[23] These external canal cholesteatomas may lead to a condition of external canal stenosis termed *keratosis obturans*. The mastoid portion may show hyperostotic thickening of cell walls, leading to obliteration of mastoid air cells.

Fibrous dysplasia may involve the petrous portion of the temporal bone. Areas of sclerosis may alternate with areas of resorption and expansion. The thickened bone is regular and typically is not fragmented.[27] Frank destruction of the petrous ridge or otic capsule is usually associated with malignant degeneration, which occurs in approximately 1 in 200 patients.

Osteopetrosis

Osteopetrosis is a heredity disorder characterized by excessive calcification of bones and spontaneous fractures. The disease process may be mild, with a benign course and normal life span (autosomal dominant). Alternatively, the disease may follow a malignant course, causing death early in life (autosomal recessive). Patients can have hydrocephalus, subarachnoid hemorrhage, extramedullary hematopoiesis, and severe headaches with progressive visual and hearing loss.

CT scans show extensive sclerosis of the petrous pyramids. There is a normal density difference between the otic capsule and the surrounding bone. Progressive neurosensory hearing loss is caused by obliteration of the labyrinth or narrowing of the internal auditory canals.

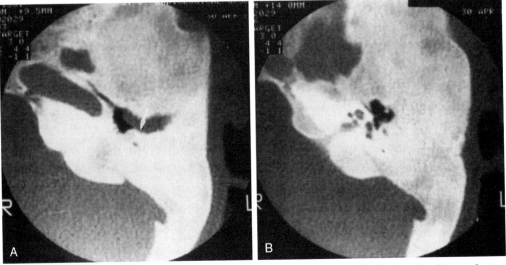

Figure 15–59. Fibrous dysplasia in a young man with a long-standing, left-sided conductive hearing loss and stenosis of the left external auditory canal (EAC). *A* and *B*, Axial CT scans of the left temporal bone show tremendous bony overgrowth, with diffuse sclerosis and thickening of the temporal bone. The labyrinthine capsule is still identifiable despite excessive new bone formation. Note the total obliteration of the mastoid air cells. The tympanic cavity is compressed, and the EAC is severely narrowed. A soft tissue mass *(arrow)* in the EAC represents a secondary cholesteatoma (keratosis obturans) caused by chronic obstruction.

Acknowledgments

We would like to acknowledge Linda Chakeres for editing the complete text and John Croyle for printing most of the images. We would also like to thank Anton Hasso, M.D., C. Roger Bird, Barbara Carter, Charles Lanzieri, Theodore Larson, William Lo, Galdino Valvassori, Jacqueline Vignaud and Jeffrey Jones, M.D., for the use of their figures.

References

1. Alvi A, Bereliani A: Acute intracranial complications of temporal bone trauma. Otolaryngol Head Neck Surg 119:609, 1998.
2. Bergeron RT, Osborn AG, Som PM: Head and Neck Imaging Excluding the Brain. St. Louis, CV Mosby, 1984.
3. Bergeron RT, et al: The temporal bone. In Som PM, Bergeron RT (eds): Head and Neck Imaging, 2nd ed. St. Louis, CV Mosby, 1991.
4. Bird CR, Hasso AN, Stewart CE: Malignant primary neoplasms of the ear and temporal bone studied by high-resolution computed tomography. Radiology 146:171, 1983.
5. Brogan M, Chakeres DW: Computed tomography and magnetic resonance imaging of the normal anatomy of the temporal bone. Semin Ultrasound CT MR 10:178, 1989.
6. Brogan M, Chakeres DW: Gd-DTPA MR imaging of cochlear schwannoma. AJNR AM J Neuroradiol 11:407, 1990.
7. Brogan M, Chakeres DW, Schmalbrock P: Comparison of high-resolution 3DFT and computed tomography in the evaluation of the otic capsule and the vestibular aqueduct. AJNR Am J Neuroradiol 12:1, 1991.
8. Chakeres DW: Clinical significance of partial volume averaging of the temporal bone. Am J Neuroradiol 5:297, 1984.
9. Chakeres DW: Computed tomography of the ear: A tailored approach. Radiol Clin North Am 22:3, 1984.
10. Chakeres DW, Kapila A: The normal CT anatomy of the brainstem and related structures using direct longitudinal scanning with metrizamide cisternography. Radiology 149:709, 1983.
11. Chakeres DW, Kapila A, LaMasters D: Soft tissue abnormalities of the external auditory canal: Subject review of CT findings. Radiology 156:105, 1985.
12. Chakeres DW, LaMasters DL: Paragangliomas of the temporal bone: High-resolution CT studies. Radiology 150:749, 1984.
13. Chakeres DW, Mattox DW: Computed tomographic evaluation of non-metallic middle ear prostheses. Invest Radiol 20:596, 1985.
14. Chakeres DW, Spiegel RK: A systematic technique for comprehensive evaluation of the temporal bone by computed tomography. Radiology 146:97, 1983.
15. Chakeres DW, Schmalbrock P, Brogan M, et al: Normal venous anatomy of the brain: demonstration with gadopentetate dimeglumine in enhanced 3-D MR angiography. AJNR 11:1107, 1990.
16. Chintapalli K, Unger JM, Shaffer K: Otosclerosis: Comparison of complex-motion tomography and computed tomography. Am J Neuroradiol 6:85, 1985.
17. Curtin HD: CT of acoustic neuroma and other tumors of the ear. Radiol Clin North Am 22:77, 1984.
18. Curtin HD, Wolfe R, May M: Malignant external otitis: CT evaluation. Radiology 145:383, 1982.
19. Dahlen RT, Harnsberger HR, Gray SD, et al: Overlapping thin-section fast spin-echo MR of the large vestibular aqueduct syndrome. AJNR Am J Neuroradiol 18:67, 1997.
20. Dailiana T, Chakeres D, Schmalbrock P, et al: High-resolution MR of the intraparotid facial nerve and parotid duct. AJNR Am J Neuroradiol 18:165, 1997.
21. Dalley RW, Robertson WD, Lapointe JS: Computed tomography of a cerebellopontine angle lipoma. J Comput Assist Tomogr 10:704, 1986.
22. Hasso AN, Vignaud J, DeSmedt E: Pathology of the temporal bone and mastoid. In Newton TH, Hasso AN, Dillon WP (eds): Modern Neuroradiology, vol 3. Computed Tomography of the Head and Neck. New York, Raven Press, 1988.
23. Hasso AN, Vignaud J, DeSmedt E: Normal anatomy of the temporal bone and mastoid. In Newton TH, Hasso AN, Dillon WP (eds): Modern Neuroradiology, vol 3, Computed Tomography of the Head and Neck. New York, Raven Press, 1988.
24. Hermans R, Feenstra L, Marchal G, Baert AL: Three-dimensional CT imaging of the ossicular chain. Clin Otolaryngol 20:475, 1995.
25. Howard JD, Elster AD, May JS: Temporal bone: Three-dimensional CT. Radiology 177:421, 1990.
26. Johnson DW: CT of the post surgical ear. Radiol Clin North Am 22:67, 1984.
27. Johnson DW, Hasso AN, Stewart CE: Temporal bone trauma: High-resolution computed tomographic evaluation. Radiology 151:411, 1984.
28. Johnson DW, Hinshaw DB, Hasso AN: Computed tomography of local complications of temporal bone cholesteatomas. J Comput Assist Tomogr 9:519, 1985.
29. Johnson DW, Voorhees RL, Lufkin RB: Cholesteatomas of the temporal bone: role of computed tomography. Radiology 148:461, 1983.
30. Koizuka I, Seo R, Kubo T, et al: High-resolution MRI of the human cochlea. Part 2. Acta Otolaryngol Suppl 520:256, 1995.
31. Latack JT, Gabrielsen TO, Knake JE: Facial nerve neuromas: Radiologic evaluation. Radiology 149:731, 1983.
32. Lemmerling MM, Mancuso AA, Antonelli PJ, Kubilis PS: Normal modiolus: CT appearance in patients with a large vestibular aqueduct. Radiology 204:213, 1997.
33. Lo WW, Daniels DL, Chakeres DW, et al: The endolymphatic duct and sac. AJNR Am J Neuroradiol 18:881, 1997.
34. Lo WWM, Solit-Bohman LG: High-resolution CT of the jugular foramen: Anatomy and vascular variants and anomalies. Radiology 150:743, 1984.
35. Lo WWM, Solit-Bohman LG, Lambert PR: High-resolution CT in the evaluation of glomus tumors of the temporal bone. Radiology 150:737, 1984.
36. Mafee MF, Henrikson GC, Deitch RL: Use of CT in the evaluation of stapedial otosclerosis. Radiology 156:709, 1985.
37. Mafee MF, Valvassori GE, Deitch RL: Use of CT in the evaluation of cochlear otosclerosis. Radiology 156:703, 1985.
38. Mafee MF, Lachenauer CS, Kumar A, et al: CT and MR imaging of intralabyrinthine schwannoma: Report of two cases and review of the literature. Radiology 174:395, 1990.
39. Mark AS, Seltzer S, Harnsberger HR: Sensorineural hearing loss: More than meets the eye? AJNR Am J Neuroradiol 14:37, 1993.
40. Martin N, Sterkers O, Nahum H: Chronic inflammatory disease of the middle ear cavities: Gd-DTPA-enhanced MR imaging. Radiology 176:399, 1990.
41. Mayer TE, Brueckmann H, Siegert R, et al: High-resolution CT of the temporal bone in dysplasia of the auricle and external auditory canal. AJNR Am J Neuroradiol 18:53, 1997.
42. Mendelson DS, Som PM, Mendelson MH: Malignant external otitis: The role of computed tomography and radionucleotides in evaluation. Radiology 149:745, 1983.
43. Palacios E, Valvassori G: Fibrous dysplasia of the temporal bone. Ear Nose Throat J 78:415, 1999.
44. Pappas DG, Simpson LC, McKenzie RA, Royal S: High-resolution computed tomography: Determination of the cause of pediatric sensorineural hearing loss. Laryngoscope 100:564, 1990.
45. Phelps PD: Glomus tumors of the ear: An imaging regime. Clin Radiol 41:301, 1990.
46. Phelps PD, Lloyd GAS: The radiology of carcinoma of the ear. Br J Radiol 54:103, 1981.
47. Phelps PD, Lloyd GAS: Radiology of the ear, Boston, Blackwell, 1983.
48. Remley KB, Coit We, Harnsberger HR, et al: Pulsatile tinnitus and the vascular tympanic membrane: CT, MR, and angiographic findings. Radiology 174:383, 1990.
49. Robert Y, Carcasset S, Rocourt N, et al: Congenital cholesteatoma of the temporal bone: MR findings and comparison with CT. AJNR Am J Neuroradiol 16:755, 1995.
50. Schmalbrock P, Chakeres DW, Monroe JW, et al: Assessment of internal auditory canal tumors: A comparison of contrast-enhanced T1-weighted and steady-state T2-weighted gradient-echo MR imaging. AJNR Am J Neuroradiol 20:1207, 1999.
51. Schmalbrock P, Dailiana T, Chakeres DW, et al: Submillimeter-resolution MR of the endolymphatic sac in healthy subjects and patients with Meniere disease. AJNR Am J Neuroradiol 17:1707, 1996.
52. Swartz JD: Cholesteatomas of the middle ear: Diagnosis, etiology and complications. Radiol Clin North Am 22:15, 1984.
53. Swartz JD: The facial nerve canal: CT analysis of the protruding tympanic segment. Radiology 153:443, 1984.
54. Swartz JD, Bazarnic ML, Naidich TP: Aberrant internal carotid artery lying within the middle ear. Neuroradiology 27:322, 1985.

55. Swartz JD, Faerber EN: Congenital malformations of the external and middle ear: High-resolution CT findings of surgical import. Am J Neuroradiol 6:71, 1985.

56. Swartz JD, Goodman RS, Russell KB: High-resolution computed tomography of the middle ear and mastoid. Radiology 148:455, 1983.

57. Tanioka H, Shirawkawa T, Michida T, Sasaki Y: Three-dimensional reconstructed MR imaging of the inner ear. Radiology 178:141, 1991.

58. Taylor S: The petrous temporal bone (including the cerebellopontine angle). Radiol Clin North Am 20:67, 1982.

59. Tsuruda JS, Shimakawa A, Pelc NJ, Saloner D: Dural sinus occlusion: Evaluation with phase-sensitive gradient-echo MR imaging. AJNR Am J Neuroradiol 12:481, 1991.

60. Valavanis A, Kubik S, Oguz M: Exploration of the facial nerve canal by high-resolution computed tomography: Anatomy and pathology. Neuroradiology 24:139, 1983.

61. Valavanis A, Kubik S, Schubiger O: High-resolution CT of the normal and abnormal fallopian canal. Am J Neuroradiol 4:748, 1983.

62. Valavanis A, Schubiger O, Oguz M: High-resolution CT investigation of nonchromaffin paragangliomas of the temporal bone. Am J Neuroradiol 4:516, 1983.

63. Virapongse C, Rothman SLG, Kier EL: Computed tomographic anatomy of the temporal bone. Am J Neuroradiol 3:379, 1982.

64. Virapongse C, Rothman SLG, Sasaki C: The role of high-resolution computed tomography in evaluating disease of the middle ear. J Comput Assist Tomogr 6:711, 1982.

65. Welling DB, Clarkson MW, Miles BA, et al: Submillimeter magnetic resonance imaging of the temporal bone in Meniere's disease. Laryngoscope 106:1359, 1996 [erratum, 107:147, 1997].

66. Welling B, Schmalbrock P, Chakeres D: Submillimeter MRI of the temporal bone in Meniere's disease. Laryngoscope 106:1359, 1996.

67. Wiet RJ, Pyle GM, O'Connor CA, et al: Computed tomography: How accurate a predictor for cochlear implantation? Laryngoscope 100:687, 1990.

68. Zonneveld FW, et al: Direct multiplanar computed tomography of the petrous bone. Radiographics 3:400, 1983.

16

The Sinonasal Cavity

Charles F. Lanzieri

Embryology[25]

The nasal sac or primitive nasal cavity begins to develop from the stomodeum as early as the 24th fetal day. The stomodeum forms on the ventral and superior aspect of the embryo between the first branchial arches. There is an eventual thinning of the cellular layers to first form a buccopharyngeal membrane. At about the 28th fetal day, the buccopharyngeal membrane disappears, and communication between the amnion and internal cavity is established.

At about the 28th fetal day, the nasal placode first forms just superior to the first branchial arch and just lateral to the stomodeum. At about the 31st day, there is an infolding in the center of the nasal placode, which forms the nasal pit. The nasal sacs grow dorsally from each nasal pit into the ventral portion of the developing brain. At first, the sacs are separated from the oral cavity by the oronasal membrane, but this membrane soon ruptures, bringing the nasal and oral cavities into communication. These regions of continuity are called the *primitive choanae*, which lie posterior to the primary palate. After the secondary palate develops, the choanae are located at the junction of the nasal cavity and the pharynx.

At about the 48th fetal day, the lateral palatine processes fuse with each other and the nasal septum; the oral and nasal cavities are again separated. This fusion also results in separation of the nasal cavities from each other.

While these changes are occurring, the superior, middle, and inferior conchae develop as elevations on the lateral wall of each nasal cavity; in addition, the ectodermal epithelium in the roof of each nasal cavity becomes specialized into the olfactory region. Some cells differentiate into olfactory cells that give origin to fibers that grow into the olfactory bulbs of the brain.

The paranasal sinuses develop during late fetal life and early infancy as small diverticula of the lateral nasal wall. During childhood, these sinuses extend into the maxilla, the ethmoid, and the frontal and sphenoid bones, reaching their maximum size at puberty.

Anatomy and Normal Variants

The nose serves to inspire and expire air and to warm, moisturize, and filter that air. It has been estimated that approximately 2 L of water is produced daily by the serous glands of the sinonasal cavity and is used to humidify the inspired air.[30] A surface film of mucus also traps larger particles, and the action of the associated cilia serves to transport the mucus and particulate matter posteriorly and inferiorly into the nasopharynx at approximately 1 cm/minute.[30]

The nasal mucosa is vascular pseudostratified columnar ciliated epithelium that contains both serous and mucous glands.[11] In the most superior portion of the nasal fossa is a less vascular and nonciliated epthelium, the olfactory mucosa.[11] It contains the efferent axon of the bipolar olfactory nerve fibers that transform the physical stimuli of odors into nerve impulses that are then transmitted through the cribiform plate into the olfactory gyri.[11] A special lipolipid is secreted by this mucosa, which is necessary for the dissolution of odors that are transmitted to the bipolar neurons.[51] Since smells can be perceived only if the substance is in solution, a dried olfactory mucosa has no perception of smell.[18] In addition, there is no ciliary action within the olfactory mucosa, so that sniffing is necessary to bring the fragrance-bearing material to the olfactory recess and to this mucosa.[45]

The medial wall of each nasal cavity is the nasal septum, which is partially bony and made up of the perpendicular plate of the ethmoid and the vomer; the more anteroinferior portion of the nasal septum is cartilaginous. The lateral wall of the nasal fossa, however, is extremely complex.[2–6, 11, 18, 30, 45, 51] The ostia for the paranasal sinuses open into the lateral wall, which is separated into either three or four fossae or meatus by either three or four nasal turbinates or chonchae (Fig. 16–1).

The tubinates are delicate projections of bone that become smaller as they ascend superiorly into the nasal cavity. Because the paranasal sinuses develop predictably from outpouchings of the lateral nasal wall, the drainage pattern is also predictable. The frontal and anterior ethmoid

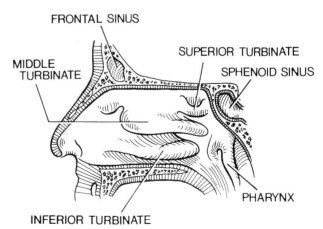

Figure 16–1. Anatomic drawing. The medial aspect of the right nasal cavity is shown. The superior, middle, and inferior turbinates divide each nasal cavity into three fossae or meatus. This anatomy and the anatomic variations are important for understanding disease processes and for surgical planning.

and maxillary sinuses nearly always drain between the middle and inferior nasal turbinates into the middle meatus. The posterior ethmoids nearly always drain between the superior and middle turbinates or middle meatus. The sphenoid sinus may drain between the superior and supreme turbinate or superior meatus or directly into the most superior and posterior recess of the nasal cavity (the *sphenoethmoidal recess*). Functionally, it is useful to think of each of these groupings of sinuses and their respective meatus as a single unit. Clinically, the most important of these is the middle meatus, also called the *ostiomeatal unit.* In the common inflammatory syndromes, the middle meatus and associated anterior ethmoid, frontal, and ipsilateral maxillary sinuses are most often involved as a unit.

The inferior turbinate is covered by a thick mucous membrane that contains a dense venous plexus with large vascular spaces and erectile tissue. In this sense, it is somewhat different from the other turbinates. The nasolacrimal duct is the only consistent opening within the inferior meatus. If one were to remove the middle turbinate and examine the middle meatus, one would find a slightly curved slit, the hiatus semilunaris, on the lateral surface of the middle meatus. Into this slit drain the ethmoid air cells and maxillary sinus. Into the anterior recess of this slit drains the frontonasal duct if this duct exists.

In approximately 50% of patients, the nasofrontal duct drains directly into the ethmoid air cells, which then drain into the frontal recess. This important drainage space is covered medially by the uncinate process of the ethmoid bone. The length and configuration of the uncinate process determine the ease of upward transportation of mucous secretions.

Just superior to the hiatus semilunaris lies the bullosa ethmoidalis, which is an inferiorly placed ethmoid air cell. The size and degree of pneumatization of this ethmoid bulla determine the size of the opening of the ostiomeatal unit into the middle meatus. The relative sizes, shapes, and configurations of these structures determine, to some ex-

tent, the frequency of obstruction and the propensity for inflammatory changes within the ostiomeatal unit.

In approximately 80% of the population, there is an alternating pattern of increased production of secretions and shunting of blood into the vascular mucosa of the inferior and middle turbinates, from side to side.[52] The nonfunctioning side retains secretions and becomes vascularly congested and engorged, while the passage of respiratory air is carried almost entirely by the open nasal side. The frequency of the cycle varies from 30 minutes to several hours. It is important to remember the existence of the nasal cycle in a fairly large portion of the human population when interpreting studies of the paranasal sinuses, because normally engorged turbinates may be mistaken for inflammatory or neoplastic processes.

The vascular and lymphatic anatomy of the nasal fossa is highly complex.[29] The arterial supply involves both branches of the internal and external carotid arteries. Of the many arteries that may supply portions of the sinonasal cavity, the sphenopalatine division of the internal maxillary artery is the most important (Fig. 16–2). This artery arises from the sphenopalatine portion of the internal maxillary artery and exits the pterygopalatine fossa. It then enters the nasal fossa posterior and superior to the middle turbinate.

The sphenopalatine artery has two major divisions: a posterolateral nasal branch and a posterior septal branch. The lateral nasal arteries ramify over the turbinates before providing collateral circulations to the paranasal sinuses. The trunk of the sphenopalatine artery extends medially along the roof of the nasal cavity, giving the posterior septal arteries as their terminal branches.

The termination of the posterior septal arteries at the anterior nasal septum continues as the nasopalatine artery, which exits the incisive canal and anastomoses with the greater palatine artery. Lymphatic drainage from the anterior portion of the sinonasal cavity is anteriorly into the face and finally into the submandibular group of lymph nodes. From the posterior half of the sinonasal cavity and

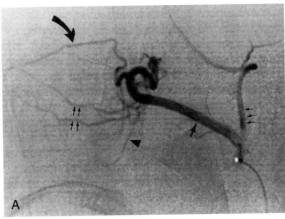 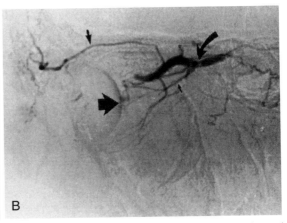

Figure 16–2. Vascular anatomy. *A,* Selective injection into the external carotid artery. The main supply to the nasal cavity and sinuses from the external carotid is via the sphenopalatine artery *(short arrow).* The terminal branches include the descending palatine artery *(arrowhead),* the inferior orbital artery *(curved arrow),* and the septal arteries *(small arrows).* The middle meningeal artery *(triple arrows)* is also shown. This vessel may be important for supply to the sinuses and orbits. *B,* Selective injection into the ophthalmic artery *(curved arrow).* The retinal blush *(large arrow)* is supplied by the central retinal artery *(small arrow).* Proximal to the origin of the central retinal artery, other branches from the ophthalmic artery may supply the soft tissue including the extraocular muscles *(mid-sized arrow).* The anterior and posterior ethmoidal arteries, which are too small to be seen in the normal patient, also arise from the ophthalmic artery.

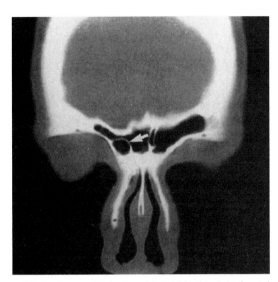

Figure 16–3. Supraorbital ethmoid. Within the right frontal sinus in this coronal CT scan is an isolated air cell *(arrow)* whose drainage pathway could be shown to be into the superior meatus. This air cell is therefore a posterior ethmoid air cell and is located within the right frontal sinus, which is important in understanding disease processes and surgical planning.

nasopharynx, lymphatic drainage is into the retropharyngeal and internal jugular lymph node chains.[45]

The venous drainage of the sinonasal cavity is into the anterior facial vein, which then anastomoses with the common facial vein and drains blood into the internal jugular vein. The anterior facial vein also anastomoses with the ophthalmic veins, which drain directly via the pterygoid venous plexus into the cavernous sinus. Therefore, infection within the sinonasal cavity may gain rapid access to the cavernous sinuses and cranial cavity.[30]

Supply from the internal carotid artery via the ophthalmic artery is through the anterior and posterior ethmoidal arteries, which send numerous small branches through the cribriform plate to anastomose with the nasal branch of the sphenopalatine artery (Fig. 16–3). An important anastomotic region is Little's or Kiesselbach's area, located anteriorly and inferiorly on the nasal septum.[29] This region is supplied by multiple branches of the facial, sphenopalatine, and greater palatine arteries and is often referred to as *Kiesselbach's plexus.* This is the site of the majority of epistaxis episodes.

Anatomic Variations
Frontal Sinuses

Embryologically, the frontal sinuses are anterior ethmoid air cells that grow into the frontal bone. They drain via the nasofrontal duct into the anterior portion of the infundibulum. The frontal sinuses are absent at birth and begin to develop after the second year of life.[8] In approximately 5% of the population, they are absent. The upward growth of the paranasal sinuses carries them to the midportion of the orbit at approximately age 4 years and to the top of the orbits at about age 8 years.[22] At approximately 10 to 12 years of age, the final adult size is reached.[49]

The size of the frontal sinuses depends on mechanical stresses from mastication and the effect of growth hormone. The intrasinus septum lies in the midline at the level of the inferior extent of the frontal sinuses but may extend far to one side, depending on the different growth rates of the two frontal sinuses.

Ethmoid Complex

The ethmoid sinuses begin to develop in the 5th month of fetal life.[8] There is wide variation in the numbers and sizes of cells. The anterior ethmoid air cells are more numerous, with more numerous septa than in the posterior ethmoid air cells. Pneumatization of the ethmoids is widely variable. Far anterior ethmoid air cells (agger nasi) cells are represented in a large portion of the population and may be situated anterior to the frontonasal duct.[45] During endoscopic nasal sinus surgery, the swelling of the agger nasi may be mistaken for the nasolacrimal duct.[16,48] The anterior ethmoid air cells may also extend superiorly into one of the frontal sinuses and into the roof of the orbit where they mimic the frontal sinus. These supraorbital ethmoid air cells should be considered distinct from the frontal sinuses themselves (see Fig. 16–3). The inferiorly located posterior ethmoid air cells may extend laterally in the infraorbital direction and bulge into the maxillary sinuses. This is the second type of "sinus within a sinus" (Fig. 16–4). The ethmoid air cells may pneumatize the middle turbinate; this condition is known as *concha bullosa* and occurs in approximately 10% of the population.[45,48] In rare instances, the superior turbinate or uncinate process may be similarly pneumatized. The concha bullosa may contribute to obstruction and inflammatory changes within the ostiomeatal unit (Fig. 16–5).

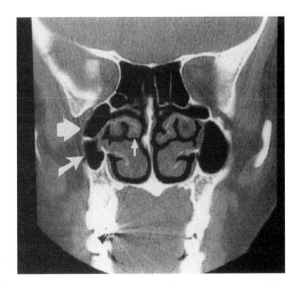

Figure 16–4. Infraorbital ethmoid. The right-sided maxillary sinus appears to have a horizontal septation within it. Closer inspection reveals that the superior portion of the right-sided maxillary sinus is actually a posterior ethmoid air cell *(large arrow)* and drains its contents superior to the middle turbinate *(small arrow).* This structure therefore represents an ectopic posterior ethmoid air cell within the expected position of the right-sided maxillary sinus, which can also be seen *(angled arrow).*

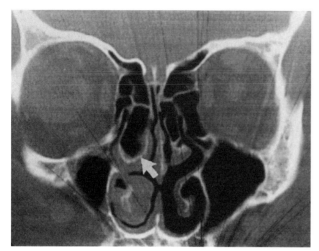

Figure 16–5. Concha bullosa. Pneumatization of the middle turbinate by anterior ethmoid air cells may cause this structure to enlarge. On this coronal CT scan, one can appreciate bilateral pneumatization of the middle turbinates, larger on the right *(arrow)*. The redundant mucosa on the surface of the right middle turbinate further narrows the middle meatus on the right side and may be the source of obstruction and secondary infection.

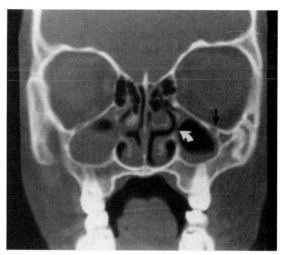

Figure 16–6. Maxillary hiatus. Coronal CT scan from a 9-year-old boy. The maxillary sinuses begin as lateral outpouchings from the lateral nasal wall and are usually present at birth, although they may not be fully pneumatized. There is progressive enlargement of the maxillary antrum in all directions. In the coronal plane, the lateral margin of the maxillary sinus usually reaches the level of the groove for the infraorbital nerve *(small arrow)* at about age 8 years. This patient has acute sinusitis with air-fluid levels present in both maxillary sinuses. Although the natural ostia of both maxillary sinuses are obstructed by a soft tissue mass, there is a small accessory opening for the left maxillary sinus called the maxillary hiatus *(curved arrow)*, which may help to drain the left maxillary sinus secretions.

Sphenoid Sinus

The sphenoid sinuses begin to develop in the 4th or 5th fetal month from a posterior outgrowth of the nasal capsule into the sphenoid bone. The sinus undergoes its major development beginning in about the 3rd year of life and reaches its adult size early in the 2nd decade of life.[49] In most people, the sphenoid sinus extends posterior to the anterior sella wall and beneath the sella floor. In less than half of the population, they extend only to the anterior wall of the sella turcica.[20]

In a small but important group of individuals (<1%), the sphenoid sinus does not reach the anterior wall of the sella turcica. This is important to the neurosurgeon considering a transsphenoidal hypophysectomy. The sphenoid sinus may extend laterally and inferiorly into the pterygoid plates of the sphenoid bone as well as superiorly and laterally into the posterior and anterior clinoid processes. The pterygoid process is described as being extensively pneumatized in nearly 10% of the population. The number of sphenoid air cells ranges from 1 to 3 with approximately one third of the population in each of these categories.

Maxillary Sinus

The maxillary sinus is the first sinus to form, beginning in approximately the 17th day of gestation. By the end of the first year of life, the lateral extent of the maxillary sinus extends into the medial portion of the floor of the orbit and reaches the infraorbital canal by the 2nd year. The adult configuration usually is attained early in the second decade of life.[24] Hypoplasia of the maxillary sinus occurs in between 1% and 7% of the population and may result from trauma, infection, surgical intervention, or irradiation. There are congenital first and second branchial arch anomalies such as Treacher Collins syndrome, in which there is congenital hypoplasia of one of the maxillary sinuses.

The maxillary sinus is unique for its relationship to the upper molar teeth and canine teeth, which may project into the maxillary antrum. Inflammatory, neoplastic, and congenital odontogenic processes uniquely affect the maxillary sinuses. In the medial wall of the maxillary sinus is a bony dehiscence known as the *maxillary hiatus* (Fig. 16–6). This is separated from the nasal cavity by the mucous membranes of both the nasal cavity and the maxillary sinus. This membranous septum is important to the surgeon seeking to irrigate the antrum and to establish a secondary pathway of drainage. It is also important for the radiologist to recognize, because it may appear to be a direct communication between the nasal cavity and maxillary sinus on imaging examinations.

Imaging Technique
Computed Tomography

Computed tomography (CT) of the paranasal sinuses is usually requested when inflammatory or neoplastic processes of the paranasal sinuses are suspected and when suspected inflammatory disease does not respond to conservative therapy.[1] An initial screening examination has been proposed as a substitute for plain film examination (Fig. 16–7).

Several types of protocols are used for this purpose. A

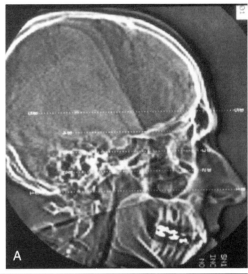

Figure 16–7. Simple CT scan. Because of the difficulty in interpreting plain radiographs of the paranasal sinuses, and because of the difficulty in reliable reproducibility for follow-up examination, a limited examination of the paranasal sinuses can be performed instead as a routine screening procedure. On the lateral topogram *(A)* five slices are chosen in equidistant intervals beginning at the hard palate and ending at the top of the frontal sinus. The images, as shown in *B*, will be identical in the same patient on all subsequent examinations. This facilitates the interpretation of follow-up studies and allows quick and easy comparison. The examination can be performed in 15 minutes at a cost similar to that for plain radiography and at a similar radiation dose.

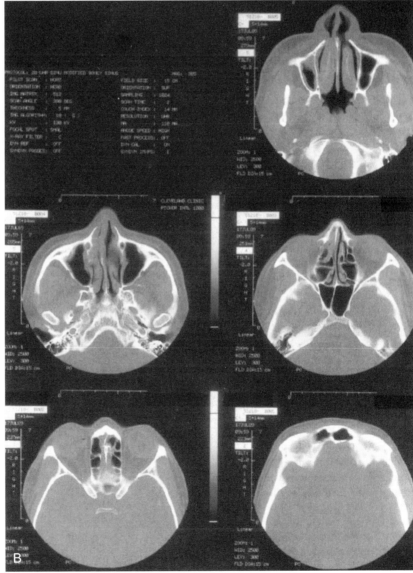

particularly effective protocol has been a limited number of axial sections through the paranasal sinuses. Approximately five or six axial images, beginning at the alveolar ridge and extending through the top of the frontal sinus, can effectively produce two images through each sinus in the axial plane in approximately 15 minutes of room time and 1 or 2 minutes of scan time. This technique has the advantage over plain film radiography in its ease of performance for both patient and technologist. It is also highly reproducible compared with plain film examinations. There is a low repeat rate of images, and the radiation dose is significantly less than the standard for plain films of the paranasal sinuses. This limited examination can be used to establish the presence of inflammatory disease on a noncontrast CT scan and for follow-up examination during medical therapy.

If surgical intervention is contemplated, especially if endoscopic nasosinus surgery is proposed, a more detailed view of the anatomy within the sinonasal cavity is re-

quired.[54] For this purpose, overlapping thin sections through the paranasal sinuses are most useful (Fig. 16–8).

The ideal examination plane is perpendicular to the hard palate; however, the nearly ubiquitous presence of dental amalgam often forces the use of a prodental or retrodental plane. This study is almost always performed without the use of intravenous (IV) contrast injection. Contrast enhancement of paranasal sinus masses has not been shown to aid in the differential diagnosis; rather, the bony architecture and anatomic configuration as well as the anatomic variations are the most important information sought in this examination.

Magnetic Resonance Imaging

Magnetic resonance imaging (MRI) studies currently offer some advantages over CT scans in imaging of the paranasal sinuses. The main purpose of the MRI study is

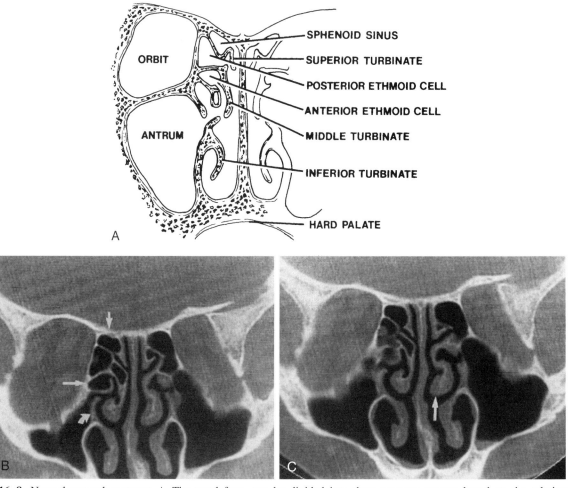

Figure 16–8. Normal coronal anatomy. *A,* The nasal fossa can be divided into three separate meatus based on the relationship of spaces within the nasal cavity to the turbinates. The nasal lacrimal duct drains into the inferior meatus below the inferior turbinate. *B,* The frontal sinuses, anterior ethmoid air cells *(long arrow),* and maxillary sinus drain into the middle meatus. The uncinate process of the ethmoid bone *(curved arrow)* is a membranous or ossified structure that forms the medial border of the infundibulum of the maxillary sinus. The posterior ethmoid air cells *(short arrow)* and sphenoid sinus drain into the superior meatus, inferior to the superior turbinate. *C,* A common anatomic variation of the middle turbinate, which on the left side curves in the lateral rather than the medial direction *(arrow).* Like the concha bullosa, this narrows the middle meatus and may lead to obstruction and inflammatory change within the ostiomeatal unit. Note the air-fluid level in the left maxillary sinus.

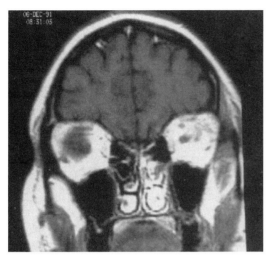

Figure 16–9. Normal MRI study. This T1-weighted image (TR500, TE32) was obtained in the coronal plane following contrast injection. The vascular nature of the turbinates is manifested as intense enhancement following contrast injection. The turbinates and nasal mucosa alternately engorge with blood and then shrink. This patient may be in the left-sided engorgement phase of the nasal cycle. Note the enlarged turbinates and thickened nasal mucosa.

to map the extent of a sinonasal mass or inflammatory process into either the orbit or cranial cavity. For this purpose, the multiplanar capabilities of MRI are unsurpassed. In addition, the signal characteristics of a sinonasal mass may help to distinguish inflammatory from neoplastic sinonasal diseases.[40, 41,44] If the mass is neoplastic, this ability allows for better surgical planning and radiation planning.

The use of gadolinium has been proposed as a method for differentiating sinonasal neoplasms from inflammatory masses.[17] The MRI protocol for examination of the paranasal sinuses should include T1- and T2-weighted images in two planes, *axial* and *coronal*. Sagittal or off-sagittal images parallel to the optic nerve may then be obtained if necessary. Gadolinium (Gd-DTPA) may then be given, and repeated scanning can be performed according to the preference of the radiologist (Fig. 16–9).

Inflammatory Processes

The "common cold" is a viral rhinitis thought to be secondary to rhinoviruses, parainfluenza, and influenza viruses.[33] Clinically, these infections last for 1 to 3 days, and the anatomic changes within the paranasal sinuses are completely reversible. There is usually mucosal thickening within the nasal fossa and turbinates as well as the mucosa of the paranasal sinuses. If a sinus ostium is obstructed, an acute bacterial sinusitis may result in superinfection. The most common bacterial pathogens in these cases are streptococci, *Haemophilus,* and staphylococci as well as *Pseudomonas.* Anaerobic infections may also occur secondary to *Bacteroides.*[10]

As previously noted, because of the unique anatomy of the maxillary sinus, the presence of the roots of the molar teeth, infections secondary to odontogenic causes account for approximately 15% of maxillary sinus infections.[45] The imaging hallmark of acute bacterial sinusitis is an air-fluid level within the affected sinus (see Fig. 16–6). This is most commonly visualized within the maxillary sinus. Repeated episodes of acute and subacute sinusitis may result in a persistent change within the paranasal sinuses (chronic sinusitis). The intrasinus mucosa may then be atrophic or hypertrophic. In any event, there is loss of the normal ciliary function and flow of secretions, resulting in a sinus that is less resistant to infection.[45] Thus, a vicious circle of infection and reinfection occurs.

Although allergic sinusitis and viral sinusitis tend to be symmetrical and involve the nasal fossa as well as the paranasal sinuses, bacterial sinusitis tends to be isolated to a single sinus or a group of contiguous sinuses. Additionally, the presence of nasal polyps is most common in allergic, rather than infected, patients (Fig. 16–10).

In the pediatric population, sinus opacification and mucosal thickening should be reported, but their significance remains in doubt especially in children under the age of 2 years.[47] Tears, normal retained secretions, and normal redundant mucosa may account for apparently abnormal findings in this population (see Fig. 16–9).

Air-fluid levels within the maxillary sinuses are usually the result of acute bacterial sinusitis. Although it has become a much less common procedure in recent years, lavage of the maxillary antrum with saline solution was previously a common cause of an air-fluid level within the maxillary sinus as well. In instances of direct trauma or barotrauma in individuals exposed to high altitude or deep immersion, hemorrhage within one of the paranasal sinuses may mimic acute sinusitis. Hemorrhage may also mimic acute sinusitis in patients with bleeding disorders such as hemophilia, or in cases of epistaxis. Intubated patients (specifically those with nasotracheal intubation) may present with air-fluid levels, especially within the sphenoid sinuses from mechanical changes within the nasopharynx. These are not necessarily acute bacterial infections (Box 16–1).

Ostiomeatal Unit

Recent advances in the understanding of mucociliary function and the pathophysiology of the nasal cavity and paranasal sinuses, along with the concomitant advances in functional endoscopic surgery directed toward restoring normal mucociliary drainage and ventilation of the sinuses, have required a more detailed evaluation of the functional anatomy of the paranasal sinuses in preoperative patients.[14,54] The ostiomeatal unit is the middle meatus of the nasal cavity and the sinuses which that meatus serves to drain: These are the frontal sinus, the anterior ethmoid sinuses, and the maxillary sinus. Radiographic evaluation is therefore directed toward assessing the patency of the maxillary sinus ostium, the ostia of the anterior ethmoid air cells, the hiatus semilunaris, and the middle meatus.

The coronal plane is best for demonstrating the anatomy of the ostiomeatal unit.[21] One should attempt to identify the natural ostium of the maxillary sinus and anterior ethmoid sinuses, establish their patency, and ascertain that

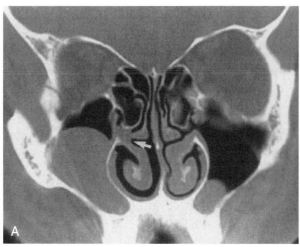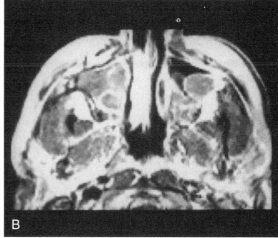

Figure 16–10. Nasal polyps. Retention cysts and nasal polyps are indistinguishable on CT scans and MRI studies. Rounded, soft tissue density structures within the maxillary sinuses on the CT scan *(A)* represent retention cysts or polyps when there is no bone destruction or expansion. These are usually asymptomatic; however, when they occur near the orifices of sinuses such as in the infundibulum *(arrow)*, postobstructive changes in the corresponding ostiomeatal unit may occur. On MRI examination following contrast injection *(B)*, there is linear enhancement on the surface of most polyps and retention cysts. This helps to distinguish them from solid masses.

these spaces are free of mucosal thickening or polypoid masses. In addition, various anatomic variations may predispose to poor mucociliary function.[14, 48,54] The most common of these is concha bullosa, which is an enlarged and pneumatized middle turbinate. This is most often small and without impairment of the function of the middle meatus, but it may become large and compress the uncinate process, obstructing the middle meatus and infundibulum. The middle turbinate may also be curved so that its convexity is directed toward the medial wall of the nasal septum. The concave portion of the middle turbinate then serves to narrow the middle meatus. This anatomic variation is known as a *paradoxical middle turbinate.*

There are several variations involving the anterior ethmoid air cells, which may narrow the middle meatus. Ethmoid air cells that extend inferior to the ethmoid bulla and within the roof of the maxillary sinus may narrow the infundibulum from above. These are called *Halle cells.* The anterior ethmoids, which form the superior contour of the middle meatus, are called the *ethmoid bullae.* These may become enlarged and extend into the hiatus semilunaris, blocking the infundibulum. The uncinate process itself may be of varying sizes, shapes, and positions.[16] For example, if it is elongated and directed laterally, obstruction of the infundibulum may result. The nasal septum is deviated to one side or another in more than 90% of people. When the deviation is significant or when a small bone spur forms at the cartilaginous junction with the bony portion of the septum, obstruction of the middle meatus may also result.

Cysts

The most common incidental finding within the maxillary sinuses is a rounded soft tissue density, which is found on routine examinations in about 10% of plain film studies and approximately 30% to 40% of CT studies.[45] Pathologically, this finding may represent a mucous retention cyst, a

---

Box 16–1. Unilateral Sinus Opacification

Congenital

Aplasia (e.g., Treacher Collins syndrome, cleidocranial dysostosis)
Normal underdeveloped sinus

Inflammatory

Sinusitis: acute, chronic
Polyp or retention cyst
Mucocele/mucopyocele

Trauma

Fracture
Intrasinus hemorrhage

Neoplastic

Benign: osteoma, antrochoanal polyp, inverted papilloma, juvenile angiofibroma, odontogenic
Malignant: squamous cell carcinoma, adenoid cystic, adenocarcinoma, lymphoma, metastases

---

Box 16–2. Expansile Sinonasal Mass

Polyp
Mucocele
Odontogenic cyst
Schwannoma
Juvenile angiofibroma
Plasmocytoma
Giant cell tumor
Lymphoma

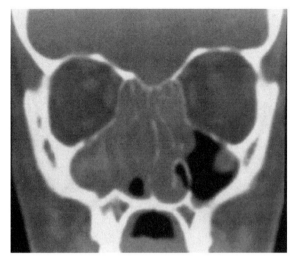

Figure 16–11. Fungal infection. Retention cysts, polyps, and fluid are usually of soft tissue density. When there is increased density within sinus cavities, as seen in this patient, one must entertain the thought of intrasinus hemorrhage, inspissated secretions, or fungal infection.

serous retention cyst, or a polyp. These three entities cannot be clearly differentiated from one another on sectional or plain film imaging modalities. This is of little consequence since all three are regarded as common benign entities (Box 16–2).

Fungal Diseases

Various fungal diseases involve the sinonasal cavities. The most common and most important of these include mucormycosis, histoplasmosis, and candidiasis and dis-

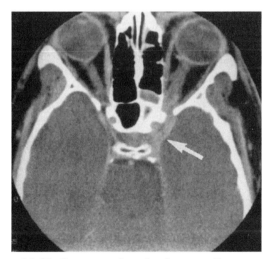

Figure 16–12. Cavernous sinus involvement. Cavernous sinus thrombosis or thrombophlebitis is most often secondary to sinus infection. Note the opacification in this patient's posterior ethmoid and sphenoid sinus on the left side. There is secondary enlargement and enhancement of the left cavernous sinus *(arrow)* and optic nerve.

Box 16–3. **Sinus with T2 Signal Void**
Air-containing: normal Hemorrhagic: tumor or trauma Chronic secretions: mucocele Fungal infection Tooth: odontogenic tumor

eases caused by *Aspergillus.*[27] The radiographic features of fungal diseases involving the paranasal sinuses are usually nonspecific and include opacification of the sinus as well as a sclerotic bony reaction (Fig. 16–11). Air-fluid levels are uncommon and, when present, suggest a bacterial infection rather than a fungal infection.[45]

Mucormycosis occurs almost exclusively in immunocompromised hosts. Fifty percent to 75% of these patients have poorly controlled or uncontrolled diabetes mellitus. The causative organisms are invasive and tend to spread rapidly from the nasal cavity to the paranasal sinuses.[27] They have a propensity for invading blood vessels. In doing so, they denude the endothelial lining and initiate thrombosis, which leads to venous cerebral infarcts. Invasion of the orbits, cavernous sinuses, and ophthalmic veins is common (Fig. 16–12). Intracranial extension, via emissary vein, may extend to the meninges and eventually lead to cerebral abscess (Fig. 16–13). Progression may be rapid, occurring within a few days. The disease also occurs in immunocompromised patients with hematologic malignancies and those with acquired immunodeficiency syndrome (AIDS). Because fungi tend to bind calcium, manganese, and other heavy metals, a large number of affected paranasal sinuses may appear hyperdense on CT scans and of low signal intensity on MRI studies[53] (Box 16–3). In the latter stages of infection, bony destruction may mimic an aggressive tumor such as squamous cell carcinoma (Box 16–4).

Box 16–4. **Opacified Sinus with Bone Destruction**	
Inflammatory	
Fungal infection:	Mucormycosis Aspergillosis
Granulomatous disease:	Wegener's granulomatosis Midline destructive granuloma
Neoplastic	
Benign:	Inverting papilloma Juvenile angiofibroma
Malignant:	Squamous cell carcinoma Adenoid cyst Adenocarcinoma Lymphoma Metastasis

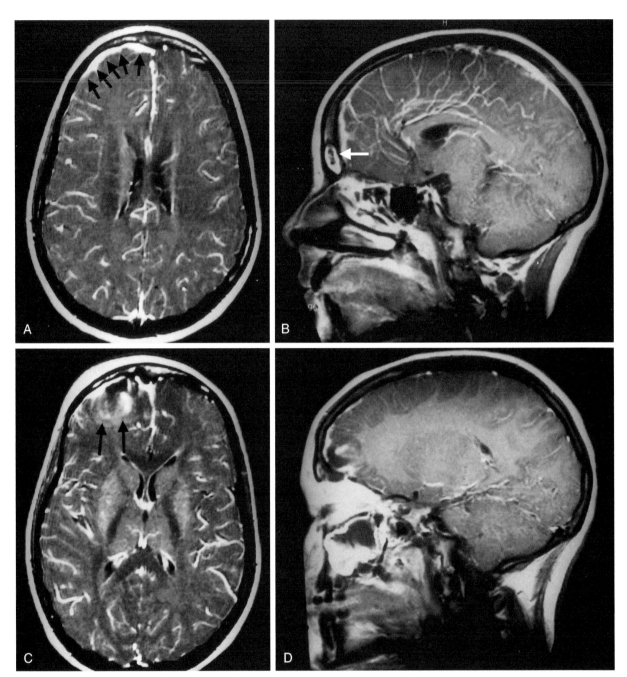

Figure 16–13. Sinusitis with intracranial extension. These contrast-enhanced T1-weighted images were obtained through the head of a patient with sinusitis and neurologic findings. *A* and *B* demonstrate meningeal enhancement *(small arrows)* in the left frontal region just posterior to the infected left frontal sinus *(large arrow)*. *C* and *D*, Adjacent slices reveal the presence of an associated cerebral abscess *(arrows)* in the left frontal lobe. Cerebral abscess has occurred by direct extension, without apparent bone involvement, probably via emissary veins.

On the other hand, *Aspergillus* infection usually occurs in otherwise healthy patients and has no relationship to pulmonary aspergillosis, which is known to occur in debilitated patients. The radiographic appearance, however, is similar to other fungal infections with opacification of a single paranasal sinus, a hyperdense paranasal sinus on CT scans, hypointense signal on T2-weighted MRI studies from heavy metal, and osseous destruction mimicking aggressive tumor in the later stages. Although less aggressive than mucormycosis, *Aspergillus* infection may cause a vasculitis that results in cerebral thrombosis as well.

Granulomatous Diseases

Various granulomas produce diseases that may involve the sinonasal cavities. These include granulomas caused by organisms such as *Nocardia* and infectious diseases such as aspergillosis,[23] actinomycoses,[34] tuberculosis, and syphilis.[5] Granulomas can be caused by autoimmune or collagen-vascular diseases such as Wegener's granulomatosis,[31] lymphoma or lymphatoid diseases such as midline granuloma, and processes such as sarcoidosis. In addition, granulomas may be the result of exposure to irritants such as beryllium and chromium.

In general, granulomatous diseases affect the paranasal sinuses first by causing a nonspecific inflammatory type of reaction with mucosal thickening and increased secretions.[45] The nasal septum may exhibit focal thickening, or septal erosions may be found. The paranasal sinuses are usually involved secondary to nasal cavity involvement. The maxillary and ethmoid sinuses, as with inflammatory diseases, are most often affected. When the sinuses are involved, a nonspecific inflammatory reaction is seen. Air-fluid levels are usually not present. Bony changes of the nasal cavity and paranasal sinuses may include thickened and sclerotic walls and septa. This is from the chronic inflammatory reaction (Fig. 16–14).

Wegener's granulomatosis is fundamentally a necrotizing granulomatous vasculitis that initially involves the respiratory tract and eventually spreads to include the kidneys as well as other organs. When the sinonasal cavity is involved, the nasal septum is affected initially with diffuse thickening followed by septal perforation. A more aggressive and idiopathic granulomatous process is so-called idiopathic midline granuloma,[13] which is characterized by a necrotizing inflammatory reaction involving the sinonasal cavities and midline of the face as well as the upper respiratory tract. This is a more localized disease with the lungs and kidneys unaffected.

Tuberculosis may involve the paranasal sinuses secondary to pulmonary infection. The sinus disease is again nonspecific. Another granulomatous disease involving the paranasal sinuses is actinomycosis, which only rarely involves the paranasal sinuses and is usually the result of direct extension from the mandible.

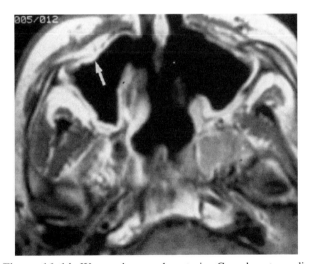

Figure 16–14. Wegener's granulomatosis. Granulomatous disease within the paranasal sinuses may be manifested as linear enhancement *(arrow)* or nodule enhancement. Destruction of osseous structures out of proportion to soft tissue thickening should lead one to think of a granulomatous process or lymphoma.

Mucoceles

Mucoceles are the most common expansile lesions of the paranasal sinuses.[45] A mucocele develops from obstruction of a sinus ostium.[50] The continued secretions of the sinus mucosa cause expansion and remodeling of the bony margins. Expansion of the sinus cavity causes erosion of internal septa and displacement of adjacent organs such as the intraorbital structures (Fig. 16–15). The frontal sinuses are most commonly affected, accounting for approximately 60% of all mucoceles.[45] The ethmoid sinuses account for approximately 25% of all mucoceles. The maxillary sinuses account for approximately 10%, and the remaining 1% or 2% are the rare sphenoid sinus mucoceles.[45] The presenting symptoms are those of mass effect with proptosis or cosmetic deformity. Pain is rare unless the mucocele is infected, in which case it is referred to as a mucopyocele.

On CT scans, a mucocele appears as an expanded sinus filled with homogeneous material of fairly low attentuation (~15 HU) (Fig. 16–16). As one would expect, on MRI studies most mucoceles are isointense to soft tissue such as adjacent brain on T1-weighted images and show increased signal on T2-weighted images because of their high water content. However, a mucocele that has been present for many months may be of low signal on T2-weighted images and may even produce a signal void. This may be because of the high concentration of proteinaceous secretions and the slow resorption of water through the mucosa.[7, 39,40]

Neoplastic Processes

Papillomas (Fig. 16–17)

The mucosa of the sinonasal cavity is ciliated columnar epithelium containing mucus-secreting glands called *Bowman's glands*. This unique mucosa is of ectodermal origin and gives rise to a distinct class of lesions with a hyperplastic zone of basement membrane enclosing epithelium that in some patients falls inward on itself, forming a polyp with an irregular or verrucose surface. These lesions are known as *papillomas* and are important to differentiate from simple cysts and polyps of the sinonasal cavity because of the possibility of malignant degeneration within the papillomas.[2,45] Fungiform papillomas make up approximately half of all papillomas. These nearly always arise from the nasal septum, are usually solitary and unilateral, and may have an irregular surface much like that of other papillomas but are not considered premalignant. Fungiform papillomas must therefore be differentiated from inverted papillomas or endophytic papillomas, which make up approximately 50% of all sinonasal papillomas. These tend to occur in middle-aged men, characteristically arise from the lateral nasal wall in the region of the root of the middle turbinate, and may extend laterally into the paranasal sinuses, especially the maxillary sinus.

The most common presenting symptoms are nonspecific, including nasal obstruction, epistaxis, and anosmia. The rate of malignancy associated with inverted papillomas is approximately 15%. Although inverted papillomas most often have degenerated into squamous cell carcinomas, other tumors such as mucoepidermoid and adenocarcinomas have been reported.

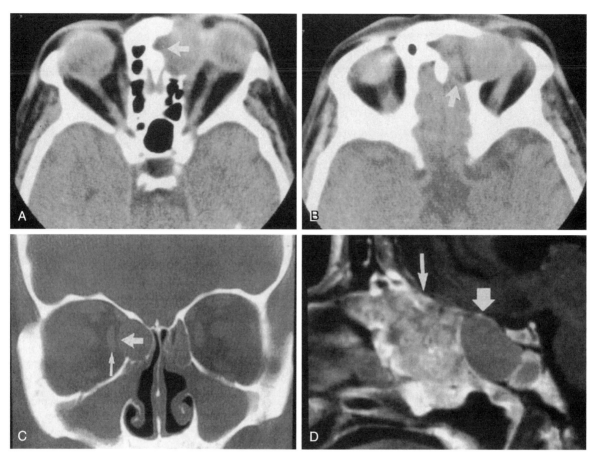

Figure 16–15. Mucocele. Sixty percent of mucoceles occur in the frontal sinus. *A,* An expansile mass is shown arising from the left frontal sinus with destruction of the lateral wall of the left frontal sinus *(arrow). B,* A slightly more superior image in the same patient depicts dehiscence of the posterior wall of the left frontal sinus *(arrow),* which is also the anterior wall of the anterior cranial fossa. *C,* An anterior ethmoid mucocele is shown with lateral expansion into the right orbit and dehiscence of the right medial orbital wall *(large arrow).* There is medial displacement of orbital contents such as the medial rectus *(small arrow),* leading to diplopia. Mucoceles may be the result of sinus obstruction from either inflammation or tumor. *D,* Postcontrast sagittal T1-weighted image (TR500, TE32) in the midline. There is solid enhancement in the region of the ethmoid air cells *(long arrow),* peripheral enhancement with central secretions within the sphenoid sinus *(short arrow),* and a mucocele with linear peripheral enhancement secondary to sinus obstruction from tumor.

Carcinoma

Squamous cell carcinoma of the sinonasal cavity arises most commonly from the maxillary sinus. This structure is involved in at least 80% of all patients with squamous cell carcinoma at some point in their course.[3] These lesions occur primarily in men in the 6th and 7th decades of life. Most are low-grade tumors that arise from the nasal septum near the mucocutaneous junction. Because of the paucity of symptoms or mild symptoms, these tumors are often misdiagnosed or go undiagnosed with such chronic complaints as sinusitis, polyposis, and lacrimal duct obstruction until a mass in the oral cavity or cheek is noticed. The 5-year survival is approximately 25% to 30%.[3] The main cause of unsuccessful response is local recurrence. When examining post-treatment patients, one may encounter radiation-induced changes. These can be differentiated from local recurrence (Fig. 16–18). The primary pathologic and therefore imaging feature of these lesions is propensity to destroy bone even in the presence of a relatively small demonstrable mass.

Because of the similarity in density of squamous cell carcinoma and other carcinomas to adjacent secretions within obstructed sinuses, a small region of bony abnormality and apparent destruction is important for the early imaging diagnosis of carcinoma, especially squamous cell carcinoma. The use of IV contrast injection for CT scanning is rarely useful for differentiating tumor from inflammatory conditions or masses within the sinuses. The tumors themselves tend to enhance very little, whereas inflammatory mucosa may sometimes enhance brightly. However, the data suggest that enhanced (gadolinium [Gd-DTPA]) MRI examinations may be most useful for differentiating neoplastic from inflammatory masses within the paranasal sinuses when this diagnosis is in doubt[17] (Fig. 16–19).

Approximately 10% of tumors of the sinonasal tract are glandular in origin. These include tumors that arise from minor salivary glands such as adenoid cystic carcinomas and mucoepidermoid carcinomas. They also include adenocarcinomas.[2, 3,45] Adenoid cystic carcinomas are unusual because of their course. Many tend to recur many years following their initial diagnosis and treatment. These lesions also tend to spread along perineural sheaths and to

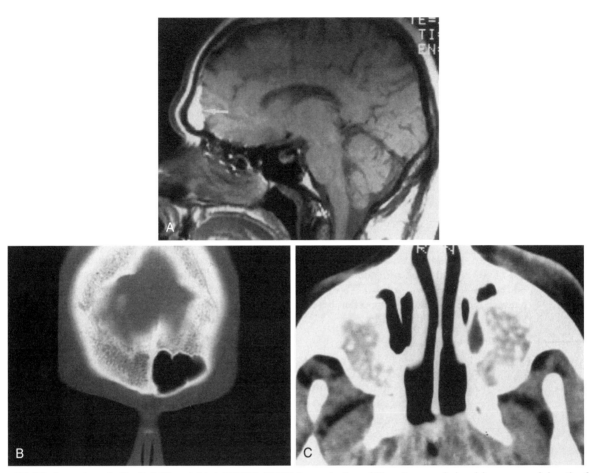

Figure 16–16. Imposters. *A*, Sagittal T1-weighted (TR500, TE32) image in the midline. Increased signal is seen overlying the frontal sinus *(arrow)*. This may represent fat, hemorrhage, or a paramagnetic substance in a metastatic tumor such as a melanoma. The accompanying coronal CT image *(B)* shows a nonpneumatized and nondeveloped right frontal sinus. The marrow signal from this right frontal sinus was thought to produce the abnormal signal on the MRI study in *A*. *C*, Non–contrast-enhanced axial CT scan through the maxillary sinuses in a patient with sickle cell disease. The speckled pattern overlying the maxillary sinuses proved to be hyperactive marrow within the maxillary sinuses.

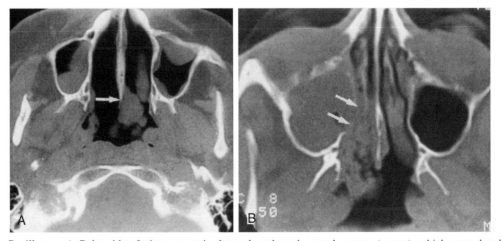

Figure 16–17. Papillomas. *A*, Polypoid soft tissue mass is shown based on the nasal septum *(arrow)*, which proved to be a fungiform papilloma on biopsy. *B*, Polypoid soft tissue mass is shown based on the lateral nasal wall *(arrows)*. This is a biopsy-proven inverted papilloma. Distinguishing between these two lesions is important because of the malignant potential of the inverted papilloma.

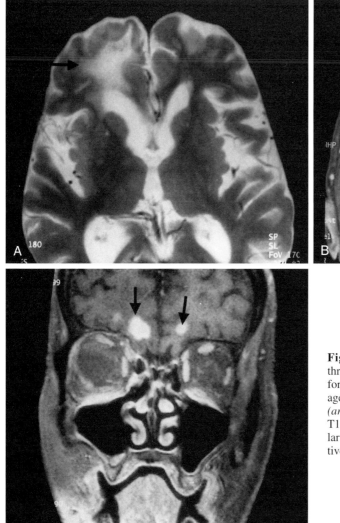

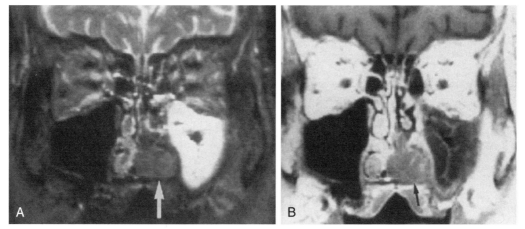

Figure 16–18. Radiation changes. These are MR images through the brain of a patient 18 months after radiation therapy for carcinoma in the paranasal sinuses. The T2-weighted image *(A)* reveals the presence of abnormal increased signal *(arrow)* in the frontal lobe white matter. The corresponding T1-weighted contrast-enhanced images *(B and C)* reveal nodular enhancement bifrontally *(arrows)*. PET scans were negative. These lesions represent radiation-induced demyelination.

Figure 16–19. Squamous cell carcinoma. *A,* On this coronal T2-weighted image (TR3000, TE60), structures containing water, such as cerebrospinal fluid and inflammatory polyps, in the left maxillary sinus are of increased signal intensity. More cellular masses such as skeletal muscle and the mass within the inferior meatus on the left *(arrow)* are of more intermediate signal intensity. Cellular masses within the nasal cavity and sinonasal tract should be suspected of being neoplasms. *B,* The accompanying post–contrast-enhanced T1-weighted image (TR500, TE32) shows the expected surface linear enhancement on the inflammatory polyps in the left maxillary sinus *(arrow)*. The turbinates and normal nasal mucosa enhance brightly inhomogeneously. The suspected nasal mass enhances somewhat less intensely than the normal turbinates. This is a biopsy-proven squamous cell carcinoma.

leave normal skip areas between the primary lesion and a local metastatic site along a nerve. This is often the case when a tumor arising in the maxillary sinus gains access to the mandibular nerve and extends toward the skull base.

At the time of radical antrectomy, the surgeon may be informed that the frozen sections showed no evidence of tumor. Some studies indicate that in many cases there has already been distant regional metastasis into the cavernous sinus at the time of surgery with an intervening normal segment of the trigeminal nerve. It has become the role of the imaging specialist, therefore, to evaluate the cavernous sinus and the more proximal portions of the trigeminal nerve in such patients to establish proper staging before radical and disfiguring surgery is undertaken.

Most adenocarcinomas arise from the ethmoid air cells and are especially common in hardwood workers and Bantu Indians.

A biopsy specimen revealing adenocarcinoma must be considered to represent a metastasis to the head and neck from kidney, lung, breast, or digestive tract until a metastatic workup is negative.

Olfactory Neuroblastoma[42]

The olfactory neuroblastoma or esthesioneuroblastoma is an uncommon tumor that originates from neural crest cells and arises from the olfactory mucosa. The incidence curve for this disease has a bimodal shape, with the first peak in the 2nd decade and the 2nd peak in the 6th decade. This polypoid tumor may be soft or firm but may be friable and bleed profusely.

A unique feature regarding olfactory neuroblastomas and the importance of these lesions to the imaging physician concerns its unique site of origin and pathway of spread. The mass may be relatively slow-growing for a malignant tumor and may cause some expansion and remodeling of bony structures. It may therefore be mistaken for benign disease. On the other hand, the tumor has a propensity for intracranial extension through the dura in the region of the cribriform plate. A change in surgical

philosophy now dictates that a craniofacial resection should be performed as the initial procedure in all patients. With this protocol, cure rates have approached the 90% survival mark. Before this approach, recurrence neared 50%, with metastasis in approximately a third of patients (Fig. 16–20).

Lymphoma

Lymphomas represent the most common sarcomas involving the sinonasal tract.[9] The majority of these are non–Hodgkin's types of lymphomas. Non–Hodgkin's lymphoma is the second most common malignancy of the head and neck following squamous cell carcinoma. It is important to try to recognize lymphoma as distinct from squamous cell carcinoma because of its different clinical course and the marked radiosensitivity of lymphomas relative to squamous cell carcinoma. Grossly, these tend to be bulky soft tissue masses that may enhance following gadolinium injection and tend to remodel bone and occasionally erode bone rather than destroy bone.[19] The nasal cavity and maxillary sinus are the most common sites of origin.

Benign Tumors

One of the most important benign tumors of the sinonasal structures—although by no means the most common benign tumor in this region—is the juvenile angiofibroma or nasopharyngeal angiofibroma (Fig. 16–21). This is a highly vascular and nonencapsulated polypoid mass that is histologically benign but highly aggressive.[4] It occurs almost exclusively in males in the second decade of life, who present with nasal obstruction and severe epistaxis as well as facial deformity and proptosis. The site of origin is thought to be the nasopharyngeal region at the pterygopalatine fossa or sphenopalatine foramen. Involvement of the pterygopalatine fossa is seen in approximately 90% of patients as asymmetry in the size or widening of this structure and an absence of the normal fat plane between

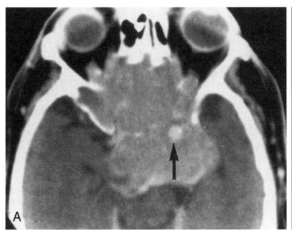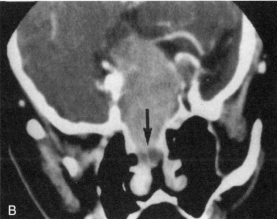

Figure 16–20. Esthesioneuroblastoma. This unique tumor arises from the olfactory mucosa in young adults. It typically spreads anteriorly into the orbital apices and posteriorly into the suprasellar region. The left carotid artery is encased *(A) (arrow)*. There is also inferior extension into the nasal cavity as seen in the post–contrast-enhanced coronal image *(B) (arrow)*.

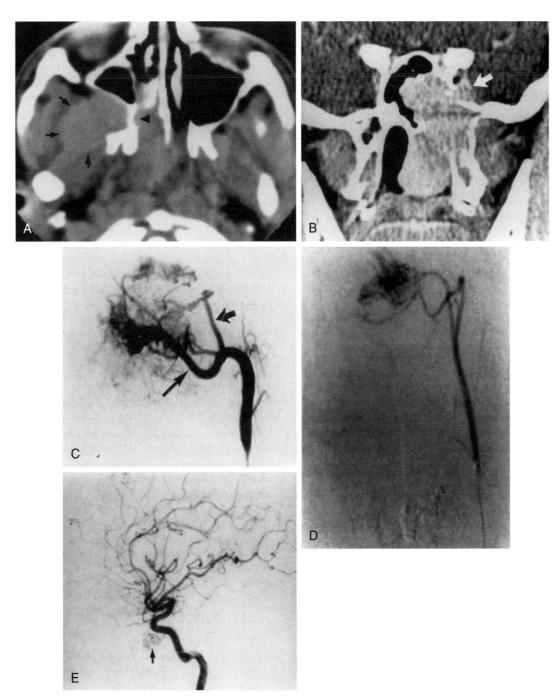

Figure 16–21. Juvenile angiofibroma. Axial post–contrast-enhanced CT scan *(A)* through the paranasal sinuses reveals an enhancing mass within the infratemporal fossa *(arrows)* that extends into and expands the pterygopalatine fissure *(arrowhead)*. In the coronal view *(B)* there is extension into the nasal cavity with destruction of the pterygoid plates and extension into the sphenoid sinus. There is also lateral extension into the region of the cavernous sinus with bone destruction *(arrow)*. These masses are usually supplied by terminal branches of the sphenopalatine artery *(C, long arrow)*. In this particular patient, because of the extension intracranially, there is supply from dural vessels such as the middle meningeal artery *(C, short arrow)*. In addition, there is also supply from other external carotid branches such as the ascending pharyngeal *(D)*. In patients with intracranial extension or with extension into the clivus, there may be supply from branches of the internal carotid artery *(E, arrow)*.

the pterygoid plates and the back of the maxillary sinus.[46] The tumor may extend anteriorly and superiorly into the maxillary and ethmoid sinuses or superiorly into the cranial fossa. There is also the possibility of extension superiorly through the inferior orbital fissure into the orbit and then through the superior orbital fissure into the brain.

Because of the extreme vascularity of the tumor and propensity for profuse hemorrhage, the imaging physician must recognize this entity when it occurs and should strongly discourage biopsy. Ultimately, an arteriogram should be performed to demonstrate the major feeding vessels, which are most often the internal maxillary artery and ascending pharyngeal artery. Preoperative embolization of these branches of the external carotid artery may greatly reduce blood loss at surgery, allowing for a more careful dissection and, therefore, complete resection in addition to minimizing the risk of multiple transfusions. Contrast-enhanced CT or MRI examination reveals a polypoid and infiltrating enhancing mass that involves the nasopharynx and pterygopalatine fissures and extends anteriorly into the nasal cavity, maxillary sinuses, and ethmoid sinuses.[45] Again, the orbits and cavernous sinuses may be involved.

The treatment of choice is surgical resection. The role of radiation therapy is not clear, although control of tumor growth has been reported. The use of estrogen therapy is also recommended.[2] Many of these tumors begin to involute toward the end of puberty, and the goal of therapy is to minimize facial deformity and bone destruction and to minimize the need for transfusions and the occurrence of fatal epistaxis, until the tumor begins to involute and fibrose as part of its natural history. There is no premalignant potential.

Neurogenic Tumor[34]

Schwannomas are benign, encapsulated, slowly growing tumors of the nerve sheath that occur in patients from the 4th to 7th decades. Few have been reported within the sinonasal cavity, although a fairly sizable proportion do occur in the head and neck. These are slow-growing expansile lesions that are important for one to recognize as differential diagnostic possibilities when faced with a similar sinonasal mass. Most importantly, they may mimic juvenile angiofibromas by bowing forward the posterior wall of the maxillary sinus. They do not, however, usually involve the pterygopalatine fissure and by that observation may be differentiated from juvenile angiofibromas in younger patients.

Neurofibromas also occur in the head and neck. These are hamartomatous lesions associated with neurofibromatosis I. Some of these may not be differentiable from schwannomas in the head and neck. When plexiform neurofibromas arise from the soft tissues or subcutaneous tissues, they may infiltrate from superficial to deep within the paranasal sinuses. At times these may be aggressive and destructive and mimic malignant tumors.

Fibro-osseous Lesions[45]

Fibro-osseous lesions are probably the most common noninflammatory benign masses of the sinonasal region. Of all the nonepithelial tumors of the paranasal sinuses, approximately 25% are thought to be fibro-osseous in origin.

One of the more common incidental findings, which is a fibro-osseous lesion, is the osteoma (Fig. 16–22). This benign proliferation commonly occurs within the frontal sinus and may cause obstruction or directly erode from the frontal or ethmoid sinus into the cranial cavity, causing a spontaneous cerebrospinal fluid (CSF) leak. These are often described as "ivory" or highly dense bone, which is obvious on both plain film and CT examinations. Osteomas

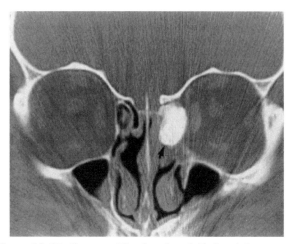

Figure 16–22. Osteoma. The densely calcified nodular structure at the base of the left frontal sinus *(arrow)* is an osteoma. This is a common benign tumor within the anterior ethmoids or inferior frontal sinuses and may cause spontaneous cerebrospinal fluid rhinorrhea.

may be small incidental findings on plain film or CT scans but may obstruct the frontal sinuses and again cause CSF rhinorrhea. When multiple osteomas are seen—especially when the skull and mandible are primarily involved—one should entertain the diagnosis of Gardner's syndrome, and investigation of the gastrointestinal tract should be undertaken in a search for intestinal polyps (Box 16–5).

Fibrous dysplasia[6] is an idiopathic disorder in which the medullary bone is replaced by a poorly organized and loosely woven bone that is also expanded compared with normal adjacent bone (Fig. 16–23). The monostotic type is the most common, involving approximately 75% of all patients. In approximately 25% of the patients, bones of the head and neck are involved, with the maxilla and mandible being the most common sites. Polyostotic fibrous dysplasia accounts for approximately one quarter of all cases of fibrous dysplasia. There is a small potential for

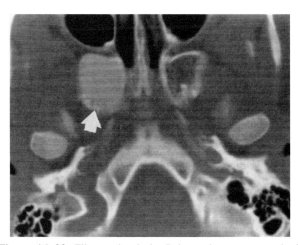

Figure 16–23. Fibrous dysplasia. Polyostotic or monostotic fibrous dysplasia frequently occurs in the facial bones. This axial CT scan through the skull base shows monostotic fibrous dysplasia affecting the pterygoid bones on the right *(arrow)*.

Box 16–5. **Syndromes Affecting the Paranasal Sinuses**

Gardner's Syndrome	**Cystic Fibrosis**
Osteoma (sinus)	Nasal polyposis
Cysts and skin tumors	Sinusitis
Intestinal polyposis	Mucoceles
Kartagener's Syndrome	**Louis-Bar Syndrome (Ataxia-Telangiectasia)**
Chronic sinusitis	Cerebellar ataxia
Bronchiectasis	Pulmonary infection
Situs inversus	Sinus infection
Basal Cell Nevus Syndrome	**Wegener's Granulomatosis**
Basal cell carcinoma	Granulomatous sinuses and respiratory tract
Dermal pits	Vasculitis
Calcification of dural structures	Glomerulonephritis
Cysts in mandible and maxilla	
Axial skeleton and rib abnormalities	

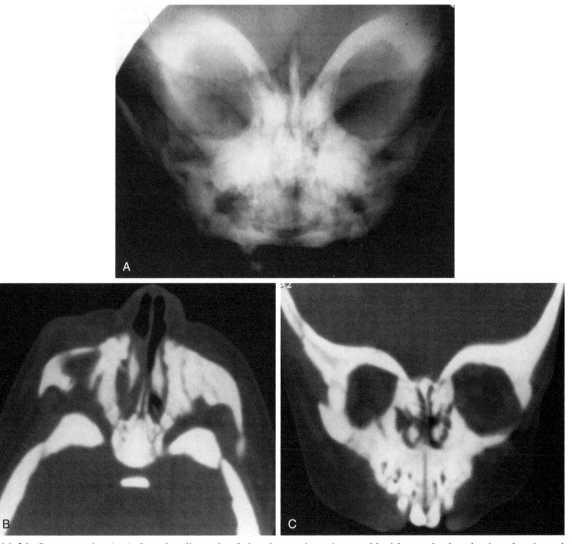

Figure 16–24. Osteopetrosis. *A,* A frontal radiograph of the sinuses in a 1-year-old girl reveals the classic sclerotic and chalky appearance of the facial bones and orbits. *B* and *C,* Axial and coronal CT scans also show the typical appearance of this rare disease with thickened sclerotic bone and secondary obstruction of the sinuses.

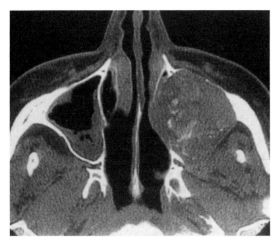

Figure 16–25. Ossifying fibroma. An expansile mass with calcified matrix forming arches or rings is indicative of a benign primary bone tumor. With expansion and destruction, a more aggressive process must always be suspected such as a chondrosarcoma or osteogenic sarcoma.

malignant transformation (~0.5% of patients). This most often occurs in the polyostotic form. Radiographically, the affected bones are noted to be abnormal because of their texture. There is a ground-glass or ivory appearance of the affected bone with expansion of the middle table blending into the inner and outer tables. Osteopetrosis rarely occurs in the paranasal sinuses (Fig. 16–24).

The ossifying fibroma, unlike fibrous dysplasia, contains a lamellar rather than woven pattern of bone and has a normal number of osteoblasts and osteoclasts (Fig. 16–25). Internal regions of disorganization with discrete zones contain either osseous issue or fibrous tissue. Pathologically, the differential diagnosis from fibrous dysplasia is difficult, whereas from an imaging standpoint the differential diagnosis is often much easier.

Giant cell tumors[43] or osteoclastomas make up approximately 5% of all primary bone lesions. Most of these are located in the epiphyseal regions of the long bones, especially around the knee. Approximately 2% of all giant cell tumors, however, occur in the head and neck. These may be located in the region of the sphenoid temporal bone or ethmoid sinuses. Approximately 10% to 15% of giant cell tumors have histologic evidence of malignancy, and these lesions should be irradiated following complete surgical excision. From an imaging point of view, these tumors are lytic lesions with narrow zones of transition. A high index of suspicion is necessary on the part of the imaging physician to raise this diagnosis early so that aggressive surgery and radiation therapy can be undertaken.[38]

Odontogenic tumors that arise from the alveolar ridge may extend to the maxillary sinus.[37] Approximately 10% to 15% of all maxillary sinus inflammatory and neoplastic diseases have an odontogenic origin. A high index of suspicion is required on the part of the imaging physician when confronted with a suspicious mass within the maxillary sinus; coronal examinations should be done to evaluate the possibility of extension of a cyst or mass from the alveolar ridge into the maxillary sinus (Fig. 16–26).

The most common odontogenic lesions involving the maxillary sinus are *odontogenic cysts*.[26] These fall into three broad categories.

Primordial cysts represent approximately 5% of odontogenic cysts and are thought to arise from a supernumerary tooth germ in a patient with an otherwise normal complement of teeth. These are cystic masses that expand from the alveolar ridge superiorly into the maxillary sinus. They are unassociated with either normal or abnormal tooth buds.

Dentigerous cysts represent approximately 95% of follicular cysts and are thought to arise from an unerupted tooth after the crown of the tooth has been developed.[45] The crown of the affected tooth projects into the cystic mass, and the roots of the unerupted tooth project centrifugally from it. These are unilocular and grow slowly, loosening and disrupting the relationship of adjacent teeth. They may also present as cystic masses within the maxillary sinus. These *periodontal* or *radicular cysts* are also known as *periapical abscesses* or *granulomas* and are the result of inflammatory changes at the tooth root associated with dental caries.

Other unusual tumors of the upper molar teeth include

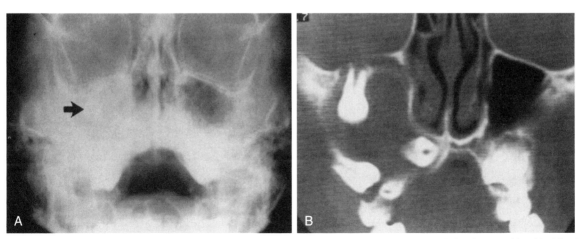

Figure 16–26. Odontogenic mass. On the Waters view of the paranasal sinuses, a teardrop-shaped density was identified in the right maxillary sinus *(A, arrow)*. The accompanying coronal CT image *(B)* revealed an expansile mass containing multiple teeth.

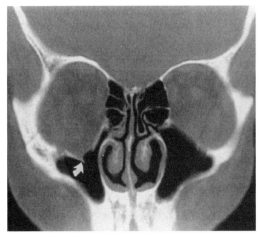

Figure 16–27. Inferior orbital wall fracture. Coronal CT scan reveals a fracture in the inferior wall of the right orbit with downward displacement of the fragment *(curved arrow)* but without herniation of the orbital contents.

multilocular ameloblastoma and the highly dense cementoma. These are beyond the scope of this chapter.

Trauma[45]

Because of extensive overlying edema, hemorrhage, and soft tissue injury, the deformity of the underlying facial skeleton is often concealed at the time of presentation to the emergency department following trauma. There may be subtle clinical signs such as palpable stepoff of the orbital rim, hypertelorism, midface elongation, or CSF rhinorrhea. Radiographic examination is key to the diagnosis of facial and orbital fractures on a timely basis so that these lesions can be treated along with other potentially life-threatening injuries.[15,32]

Before imaging evaluation of the patient with suspected facial fractures, or to rule out such fractures, one should evaluate the cervical spine for fracture and/or instability on both a clinical and imaging protocol. When it has been established that the patient can cooperate for coronal examination and is stable regarding other injuries that may have been sustained, axial and coronal noncontrast CT examination through the paranasal sinuses is recommended in all instances.

Nasal Bone

Fractures of the nasal bone are the most common fracture of the facial skeleton.[36] These may be isolated or associated with other injuries. Plain film examination with oblique cone-down views of the nasal bones is the most sensitive study for identifying and mapping these lesions. In children, when the intranasal suture is not yet ossified, dislocation of the cartilaginous portion of the nose is more common. In adults, when the nose is struck, linear fracture traversing the long axis of the nose is the expected lesion.

Orbit

A blow to the orbit most often strikes the inferior orbital rim. It is now thought that the relatively thick rim of the orbit has elastic properties that allow it to bend posteriorly and rebound anteriorly following trauma. During this posterior excursion of the inferior orbital rims, however, there may be wrinkling and then crumbling of the floor of the orbit.[12] There is a groove within the floor of the orbit (the groove for the infraorbital nerve) that acts as a fault line, allowing orbital floor fractures to occur as the most common isolated fracture of the orbit. With more extensive force, there may be fracture of both the inferior orbital rim and the orbital floor. The former lesion is known as a "pure" blowout fracture, whereas the latter lesion, involving the inferior orbital rim, is known as a "impure" blowout fracture (Fig. 16–27).

Although the medial orbital wall, the lamina papyracea, is the thinnest bone in the body, it is supported by laterally and medially running septa of the ethmoid air cells. These act as struts between free segments of the lamina papyracea to prevent medial orbital blowout. Fractures through the

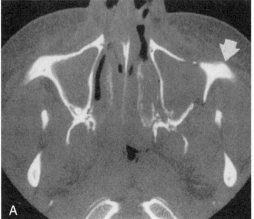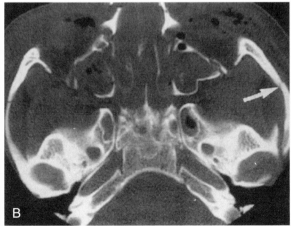

Figure 16–28. Trimalar fracture. On the axial view the trimalar fracture *(A, arrow)* is manifested as fractures of the anterior sinus wall and posterior sinus wall. *B,* Fracture of the ipsilateral zygomatic arch is shown.

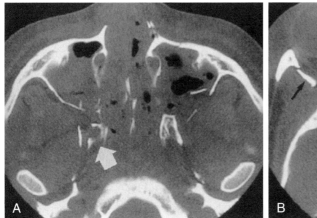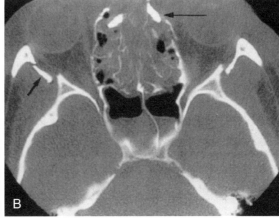

Figure 16–29. Le Fort fractures. The unifying fracture among all types of Le Fort fractures is fracture through the pterygoid plates *(A, arrow)*. Le Fort I fractures are rare. With Le Fort II types, the medial orbital wall *(B, long arrow)* is fractured, with continuation of the fracture line through the floor of the orbit and into the pterygoid plates. A Le Fort III fracture *(B, short arrow)* extends from the medial wall of the orbit to the lateral orbital wall and then inferiorly through the pterygoid plates.

medial orbital wall still occur either through transmission from direct trauma to the nose or from increased intraorbital pressure. Blowout fractures of the orbital roof also occur. Again, these may be caused by transmitted force through the superior orbital rim. More often they are the result of extension of fracture elsewhere in the skull into the superior orbital rim.

Side of the Face

Trauma to the side of the face or lateral orbital rim may result in the familiar tripod or trimalar fracture[28] (Fig. 16–28). This is a complex fracture involving the floor of the orbit, the anterior and posterior walls of the maxillary sinus, the zygomatic arch, the zygomaticofrontal suture, and the posterior wall of the orbit. Although it actually has at least four points, in any single plane it may appear as a three-pointed fracture fragment; thus, the eponyms are tripod and trimalar.

Le Fort Fractures

The unifying feature of Le Fort fractures is disruption of the pterygoid plates.[35] Because of the associated disruption of the pterygoid venous plexus, it is important to recognize these fractures as potentially life-threatening because of the relatively large nasopharyngeal hematoma that sometimes occurs.

There are three types of Le Fort fractures:

The *Le Fort I* fracture is a horizontal fracture above the hard palate with separation of the hard palate and lower portion of the pterygoid plates from the rest of the facial infrastructure.

The *Le Fort II* fracture begins at the bridge of the nose and extends laterally along the medial wall of the orbit and then inferiorly along the inferior wall of the orbit, through the anterior wall of the maxillary sinus, and then posteriorly through the alveolar recess of the maxillary sinus into the pterygoid plates.

The *Le Fort III* fracture also begins as a fracture through the base of the nose or glabella and extends along the medial wall of the orbit, much as the Le Fort II fracture does. Rather than extending into the floor of the orbit, however, there is extension of the fracture line along the lateral wall of the orbit, inferiorly through the maxillary sinus and then posteriorly through the pterygoid plates (Fig. 16–29).

References

1. Babbel R, Harnsberger HR, Nelson B, et al: Optimization of techniques in screening CT of the sinuses. AJNR Am J Neuroradiol 12: 849–854, 1991.
2. Barnes L, Verbin RS, Gnepp DR: Diseases of the nose, paranasal sinuses and nasopharynx. In Barnes L (ed): Surgical Pathology of the Head and Neck, vol 1. New York, Marcel Dekker, 1985, pp 403–451.
3. Batsakis JG: Tumors of the Head and Neck: Clinical and Pathological Considerations. In Baltihouse Z (ed): Baltimore, Williams & Wilkins, 1979, pp 177–178.
4. Bryan N, Sessions RB, Horowitz BL: Radiographic management of juvenile angiofibromas. AJNR Am J Neuroradiol 2:157–166, 1981.
5. Chapnick JS, Bach MC: Bacterial and fungal infections of the maxillary sinus. Otolaryngol Clin North Am 9:43, 1976.
6. Dehner LP: Fibro-osseous lesions of bone. In Ackerman LU, Spjut HJ, Abell MR (eds): Bones and Joints. International Academy of Pathology, Monograph No. 17. Baltimore, Williams & Wilkins, 1976, pp 209–235.
7. Dillon WP, Som PM, Fullerton GD: Hypointense MR signal in chronically inspissated sinonasal secretions. Radiology 174:73078, 1990.
8. Dodd GD, Jing BS: Radiology of the Nose, Paranasal Sinuses and Nasopharynx. Baltimore, Williams & Wilkins, 1977.
9. Duncavage JA, Campbell BH, Hanson GH: Diagnosis of malignant lymphomas of the nasal cavity, paranasal sinuses and nasopharynx. Laryngoscope 93:1276, 1983.
10. Evans FO, Sydnor JB, Moore WEC, et al: Sinusitis of the maxillary antrum. N Engl J Med 293:735, 1976.
11. Goss CM: Gray's Anatomy of the Human Body, 27th ed. Philadelphia, Lea & Febiger, 1963, pp 1167–1176.
12. Hammerschlag SB, Hughes S, O'Reilly GV, et al: Another look at blow out fractures of the orbit. AJNR Am J Neuroradiol 3: 331–335, 1982.
13. Harrison DFN: Midline destructive granuloma: Fact or fiction? Laryngoscope 97:1049, 1987.
14. Kennedy DW, Zinreich SJ, Rosenbaum AE, et al: Functional endoscopic sinus surgery. Arch Otolaryngol 111:576–582, 1985.
15. Kreipke DL, Moss JJ, Franco JM, et al: Computed tomography and

thin-section tomography in facial trauma. AJNR Am J Neuroradiol 5:423, 1984.

16. Lanzieri CF, Levin HL, Rosenbloom SA, et al: Three dimensional surface rendering of nasal anatomy for CT data. Arch Otolaryngol 115:1444–1446, 1989.

17. Lanzieri CF, Shah M, Krauss D, et al: Use of Gd-DTPA enhanced MRI for differentiating mucoceles from neoplasms in the paranasal sinuses. Radiology 178:425–428, 1991.

18. Last RJ: Anatomy Regional and Applied, 6th ed., London, Churchill Livingstone, 1978, pp 398–406.

19. Lee YY, et al: Lymphomas of the head and neck: CT findings at initial presentation. AJNR Am J Neuroradiol 8:665, 1987.

20. Levine HL: The sphenoid sinus, the neglected sinus. Arch Otolaryngol 104:585–587, 1978.

21. Maffe MF: Endoscopic sinus surgery: Role of the radiologist. AJNR Am J Neuroradiol 12:855–860, 1991.

22. Maresh MM: Paranasal sinuses from birth to late adolescence. Am J Dis Child 60:58, 1940.

23. McGill TJ, Simpson G, Healy GR: Fulminant aspergillosis of the nose and paranasal sinuses: A new clinical entity. Laryngoscope 90:748, 1980.

24. Modic MT, Weinstein MA, Berlin J, et al: Maxillary sinus hypoplasia visualized with CT. Radiology 135:383–385, 1980.

25. Moore KL: The special sense organs. In The Developing Human. Philadelphia, WB Saunders, 1973, pp 335–349.

26. Mourshed F: A roentgen study of dentigerous cysts. Oral Surg 18:47–61, 1964.

27. Myerowitz RL, Guggenheimer J, Barnes L: Infectious diseases of the head and neck. In Barnes L (ed): Surgical Pathology of the Head and Neck, vol 2. New York, Marcel Dekker, 1985, pp 1771–1822.

28. Nalcamura T, Gross CW: Arch Otolaryngol 97:288–290, 1973.

29. Osborn AG: The nasal arteries. AJNR Am J Neuroradiol 130:89, 1978.

30. Paff GH: Anatomy of the Head and Neck. Philadelphia, WB Saunders, 1973, pp 183–203.

31. Paling MR, Roberts HL, Fauci AS: Paranasal sinus obliteration in Wegener's granulomatosis. Radiology 144:539, 1982.

32. Pathria MN, Blaser SI: Diagnostic imaging of craniofacial fractures. Radiol Clin North Am 27:839–853, 1989.

33. Postic WP, Wetmore RF: Pediatric rhinology. In Goldman JL (ed): The Principles and Practice of Rhinology. New York, John Wiley & Sons, 1987, pp 801–845.

34. Richtsmeier WJ, Johns ME: Actinomycosis of the head and neck. In Batsakis J, Savory J (eds): Critical Review in Clinical Laboratory Sciences, vol II. Boca Raton, Fla, CRC Press, 1979, pp 175–202.

35. Rogers LF: Radiology of Skeletal Trauma, vol 1. New York, Churchill Livingstone, 1982.

36. Schultz RC, Oldham RJ: An overview of facial injuries. Surg Clin North Am 57:987–1010, 1977.

37. Shafer WG, Hine WK, Levy BM: A Textbook of Oral Pathology. Philadelphia, WB Saunders, 1974.

38. Smith GA, Ward PH: Giant cell lesions of the facial skeleton. Arch Otolaryngol 104:186, 1978.

39. Som PM, Dillon WP, Curtin HD, et al: Hypointense paranasal sinus foci: Differential diagnosis with MRI in relation to CT findings. Radiology 176:777–781, 1990.

40. Som PM, Dillon WP, Fullerton GD, et al: Chronically obstructed sinonasal secretions observations on T1 and T2 shortening. Radiology 172:515–520, 1989.

41. Som PM, Dillon WP, Sze G, et al: Benign and malignant sinonasal lesions with intracranial extension: Differentiation with MRI. Radiology 172:763–766, 1989.

42. Som PM, Lawson W, Biller H, et al: Ethmoid sinus disease: CT evaluation in 400 cases. Radiology 159:591–597, 1986.

43. Som PM, Lawson W, Cohen BA: Giant cell lesions of the facial bones. Radiology 147:129–183.

44. Som PM, Shapiro MD, Biller HF, et al: Sinonasal tumors and inflammatory tissues: Differentiation with MRI. Radiology 167:803–808, 1988.

45. Som PM: Sinonasal cavity. In Som PM, Burgeron RT (eds): Head and Neck Imaging, 2nd ed. St. Louis, Mosby–Year Book, 1991, pp 51–276.

46. Som PM, Cohen BA, Sacher M, et al: The angiomatous polyp and the angiofibroma: Two different lesions. Radiology 144:324, 1982.

47. Swischuk LE, Hayden CK, Dillard RA: Sinusitis in children. Radiographics 2:241–252, 1982.

48. Terrier F, Weber W, Rue fen acht D, et al: Anatomy of the ethmoid: CT endoscopic and macroscopic. AJNR Am J Neuroradiol 6:77–84, 1985.

49. Towbin R, Dunbar JJ: The paranasal sinuses in children. Radiographics 2:253–280, 1982.

50. Van Tassel P, Lee YY, Jing BS, et al: Mucoceles of the paranasal sinuses. AJNR Am J Neuroradiol 10:607–612, 1989.

51. Williams HG: Nasal physiology. In Paparella MM, Shumrick DA (eds): Otolaryngology: Basic Science and Related Disciplines, vol 1. Philadelphia, WB Saunders, 1973, pp 329–346.

52. Zinreich SJ, Kennedy DW, Kumar AJ, et al: MRI of the nasal cycle. J Comput Assist Tomogr 12:1014, 1988.

53. Zinreich SJ, Kennedy DW, Malat J, et al: Fungal sinusitis: Diagnosis with CT and MRI. Radiology 169:439–444, 1988.

54. Zinreich SJ, Kennedy DW, Rosenbaum AE, et al: Paranasal sinuses: CT imaging. Requirements for endoscopic surgery. Radiology 163:769–775, 1987.

17

Cervical Adenopathy and Neck Masses

Roy A. Holliday, Deborah L. Reede

High-resolution computed tomography (CT) and magnetic resonance imaging (MRI) have proved to be invaluable tools for evaluating the soft tissue structures of the neck. Although many imaging modalities are available for the evaluation of a neck mass, including radiography, ultrasonography, angiography, and radioisotope imaging, CT and MRI provide anatomical detail that cannot be obtained with these other modalities. CT and MRI demonstrate both the precise location of a neck mass and its relationship to adjacent vascular, muscular, and neural structures. In addition to providing this anatomical detail, CT and MRI frequently are able to characterize the vascularity and internal architecture (solid versus cystic) of a neck mass.

The combination of soft tissue characterization and anatomical localization afforded by CT and MRI allows radiologists to make a substantial contribution to the preoperative assessment of the patient with a neck mass. Although an exact tissue diagnosis is not always possible, careful analysis of the imaging features of a neck mass in combination with clinical history and physical examination produce a reasonably short differential diagnosis in nearly every case.

Imaging Technique

CT imaging of the neck is performed with the patient supine on the scanner gantry. Contiguous 5-mm-thick axial images are usually obtained from the level of the superior orbital rim to the lung apex. Care must always be taken to avoid image degradation by dental amalgam. One common solution is to acquire images from the superior orbital rim to the hard palate with the use of gantry angulation parallel to the central skull base. Images from the alveolar ridge of the mandible to the lung apex are then obtained with a gantry angulation parallel to the body of the mandible. If the patient's chin is fully extended, this latter series may be obtained with a 0-degree gantry angulation.

Intravenous contrast enhancement is essential for CT examinations of the soft tissue of the neck, to facilitate both tissue characterization of neck masses and separation of neck masses from normal vascular structures. Most investigators recommend an initial rapid bolus of approximately 50 mL of contrast material administered over 1 to 2 minutes before image acquisition, followed by a steady rapid drip infusion of the remaining 100 to 150 mL during scanning. Power injectors, commonly used for abdominal or thoracic CT scanning, can be readily adapted for neck CT examinations. Contrast administration should be interrupted during changes in gantry angulation.

Optimal MRI of the neck requires the use of surface coils. Images of the suprahyoid neck may be obtained by placement of the patient well inside many standard head surface coils. Images of the infrahyoid neck require dedicated anterior neck surface coils, because the use of posteriorly placed cervical spine surface coils results in suboptimal images owing to signal drop-off.

Current MRI techniques involve acquisition of T1-weighted images in sagittal, axial, and coronal projections with corresponding T2-weighted images obtained in the projection that best depicts the lesion. Slice thicknesses of 4 to 6 mm with 1- to 2-mm intervals between slices are commonly used. The prolonged scan times of axial T2-weighted images often result in images of diminished diagnostic quality owing to gross patient motion as well as artifacts produced by swallowing, respiratory motion, and cardiac pulsations. To overcome these problems, rapid spin-echo techniques are often used to obtain T2-weighted images in shorter scan times.[49]

Contrast administration is not essential in MRI of neck masses. The use of multiple pulse sequences and multiple projections is usually sufficient to differentiate neck masses from adjacent vascular structures. When contrast enhancement is required for tissue characterization, fat-suppressed T1-weighted images are commonly used, particularly in the assessment of cervical adenopathy.[47]

Choice of Imaging Modality

MRI and CT should be considered complementary, rather than competitive, modalities for imaging neck masses. The advantages MRI offers over CT in imaging other parts of the body (multiplanar capability, lack of ionizing radiation, safer contrast agents) also apply to imaging the soft tissues of the neck. By comparison, CT examinations offer the advantages of superior assessment of osseous integrity, shorter examination time, wider patient access, and lower cost.[12] The authors prefer to use contrast-enhanced CT as the initial study to assess neck masses in adults. In children and in adults whose clinical status precludes the use of iodinated contrast material, MRI is the study of choice, although a limited noncontrast CT study may be required for the evaluation of osseous integrity. The remainder of this chapter reflects this preference and emphasizes the normal and abnormal CT appearance of the soft tissues of the neck.

Normal Gross Anatomy

The neck is composed of the posteriorly located nucha and the anteriorly located cervix. The *nucha,* which consists primarily of the vertebral column and its associated musculature, is discussed in detail in Chapter 19. For practical purposes, the *cervix* (which also means neck) can be thought of as a cylinder of soft tissue whose superior extent is a line connecting the occiput and the tip of the chin and whose inferior extent parallels the course of the first rib at the thoracic inlet.[13]

The most important landmark to identify when one is studying the neck in any plane is the sternocleidomastoid muscle. The sternocleidomastoid muscle takes its origin from the mastoid tip and digastric notch at the skull base and extends anteriorly, inferiorly, and medially, spiraling across the anterior aspect of the neck on each side to insert as two heads on the medial third of the clavicle and the manubrium. The course of the sternocleidomastoid muscle is the basis for the division of the soft tissues of the neck into two paired spaces, the anterior and posterior triangles (Fig. 17–1). The sternocleidomastoid muscle forms the posterior border of the anterior triangle and the anterior border of the posterior triangle. All structures located anterior to the sternocleidomastoid muscle lie within the anterior triangle; those deep as well as posterior to it are in the posterior triangle.[32] It is important to remember that no septum or fascial plane physically separates the anterior from the posterior triangle.

The anterior triangles have a common side, abutting each other in the midline. Their borders are the sternocleidomastoid muscle posteriorly, the mandible superiorly, and the midline medially. The hyoid bone divides this triangle

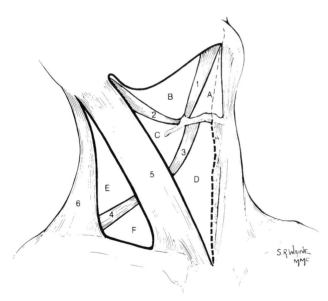

Figure 17–1. Triangles of the neck. 1, Anterior belly of the digastric muscle; 2, posterior belly of the digastric muscle; 3, superior belly of the omohyoid muscle; 4, inferior belly of the omohyoid muscle; 5, sternocleidomastoid muscle; 6, trapezius muscle. A, Submental triangle; B, submandibular triangle; C, carotid triangle; D, muscular triangle; E, occipital triangle; F, subclavian triangle. (From Reede DL, Whelan MA, Bergeron RT: CT of the soft tissue structures of the neck. Radiol Clin North Am 22:239, 1984.)

into a suprahyoid portion and an infrahyoid portion, each of which has two subdivisions.

The suprahyoid division contains the laterally located submandibular triangles and the medially located submental triangles. Superiorly these triangles are separated from the oral cavity by the mylohyoid muscle. This muscle forms a sling connecting the two inner surfaces of the mandible with the hyoid bone. By definition, structures above the mylohyoid muscle are in the oral cavity; those below are in the neck.

The base of each submandibular triangle is formed by the ramus of the mandible. The other two sides of each submandibular triangle are formed by the anterior and posterior bellies of the digastric muscle. The digastric muscle takes its origin from a depression on the skull base between the mastoid tip and the styloid process known as the *digastric notch.* The posterior belly of the digastric muscle extends anteriorly, inferiorly, and medially from the digastric notch to the greater cornu of the hyoid bone. The anterior belly of the digastric muscle extends from the greater cornu anteriorly, superiorly, and medially to insert on the anterior border of the mandible, inferior to the attachment of the mylohyoid muscle.

The major structures contained within the submandibular triangle are numerous small lymph nodes and the submandibular salivary glands. The anterior surface of the submandibular gland abuts the posterior free margin of the mylohyoid muscle, so a small portion of each submandibular gland lies within the posterior oral cavity but the majority of the gland lies within the suprahyoid neck.

The base of the submental triangle is formed by the hyoid bone. The other two sides of the submental triangle are formed by the anterior bellies of the digastric muscles. No major anatomical structures are located in this triangle except for a few small lymph nodes and branches of the facial artery and vein.

The infrahyoid division of the anterior triangle is divided by the superior belly of the omohyoid muscle into two parts, the carotid triangle superolaterally and the muscular triangle inferomedially. The infrahyoid portion of the anterior triangle contains the larynx, hypopharynx, trachea, esophagus, lymph nodes, and thyroid and parathyroid glands.

The two sides of each posterior triangle are the sternocleidomastoid muscle anteriorly and the trapezius muscle posteriorly. The base of each triangle is formed by the clavicle. The inferior belly of the omohyoid muscle crosses the inferior aspect of the posterior triangle and divides it into two unequal parts, the occipital triangle anteriorly and the subclavian triangle inferiorly.

The major structures located within the occipital triangle are the spinal accessory nerve (cranial nerve XI) and its associated chain of lymph nodes. The major structures located within the subclavian triangle are the transverse cervical vessels and their associated chain of lymph nodes. Also present within the posterior triangle are the exiting cervical nerve roots, the cervical components of the brachial plexus, and nutrient vessels.

The internal jugular vein and its associated chain of lymph nodes closely parallel the deep surface of the anterior margin of the sternocleidomastoid muscle, thereby bridging the anterior and posterior triangles. The arterial and neural components of the carotid sheath, the common carotid artery, the internal carotid artery, and the vagus nerve, also traverse the neck within the anterior triangle.[32]

Normal Sectional Anatomy

The sternocleidomastoid muscle is a constant landmark that can always be identified on axial CT scans or MR images through the neck. As one progresses from superior to inferior, the location of the sternocleidomastoid muscle moves from a far lateral position to a paramedian position. With this change in position of the sternocleidomastoid

muscle comes a change in relative sizes of the anterior and posterior triangles. Superiorly the anterior triangle occupies the majority of the cross-sectional area of the neck because there is little space between the sternocleidomastoid and trapezius muscles. Inferiorly the posterior triangle occupies the majority of the cross-sectional area of the neck because there is little space between the anterior surface of the sternocleidomastoid muscle and the midline.

The mylohyoid muscle, the major landmark separating the oral cavity from the suprahyoid neck, is readily identified on both coronal and axial images. On axial images (Fig. 17–2A and B), the muscle appears in cross-section as

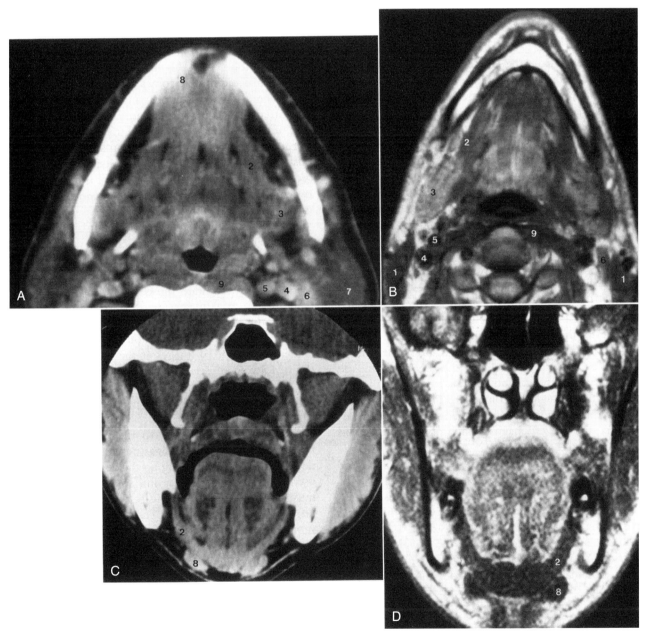

Figure 17–2. Normal sectional anatomy at the junction of the oral cavity and neck. *A,* Contrast-enhanced CT image at the level of the mandible. The sternocleidomastoid muscle is posterior to the parotid gland. *B,* T1-weighted MR image at a similar level in a different patient. Note the greater tissue contrast between the mylohyoid muscle and the submandibular gland on MRI. Coronal CT scan (*C*) and coronal T1-weighted MR image (*D*) demonstrate the anterior belly of the digastric inferior to the sling-shaped mylohyoid muscle. 1, Sternocleidomastoid muscle; 2, mylohyoid muscle; 3, submandibular gland; 4, internal jugular vein; 5, internal carotid artery; 6, posterior belly of digastric muscle; 7, parotid gland; 8, anterior belly of digastric muscle; 9, longus colli muscle.

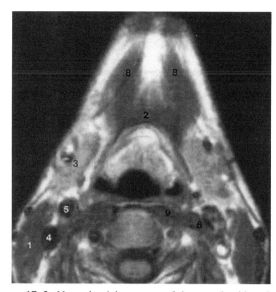

Figure 17–3. Normal axial anatomy of the suprahyoid neck. T1-weighted MR image in same patient as Figure 17–2B. The submental triangle is located between the two anterior bellies of the digastric muscle. 1, Sternocleidomastoid muscle; 2, mylohyoid muscle; 3, submandibular gland; 4, internal jugular vein; 5, internal carotid artery; 6, posterior belly of digastric muscle; 8, anterior belly of digastric muscle; 9, longus colli muscle.

two separate muscle bundles medial to the mandible. As axial images are obtained from superior to inferior, the distance between the separate bundles decreases. The superior aspect of the submandibular gland is identified on axial images at the posterior margin of the mylohyoid muscle. On coronal images, the muscle has the configuration of a hammock suspended from the medial (lingual) surface of the mandible (Fig. 17–2C and D).[12]

Immediately inferior to the mylohyoid muscle, the anterior bellies of the digastric muscle can be identified (Fig. 17–3). Depending on the degree of angulation used on axial imaging, varying amounts of mylohyoid muscle can be seen projecting between the anterior bellies of the digastric muscle. The cervical portion of the submandibular gland lies lateral to each anterior belly of the digastric muscle. The posterior belly of the digastric muscle can usually be identified medial and posterior to the parotid gland, separating the gland from the contents of the carotid sheath.[32]

The hyoid bone is the major bony landmark of the anterior neck (Fig. 17–4). The hyoid is best identified on axial CT images, where its central body and greater horns (cornua) appear in the midline as an "inverted U" approximately at the level of the C3-4 disk space. The carotid bifurcation is typically located at or near the level of the hyoid bone. The thyroid cartilage has an *inverted V* appearance on axial images. The superior third of the cartilage is not fused in the midline at the level of the thyroid notch. Immediately superficial to the two halves of

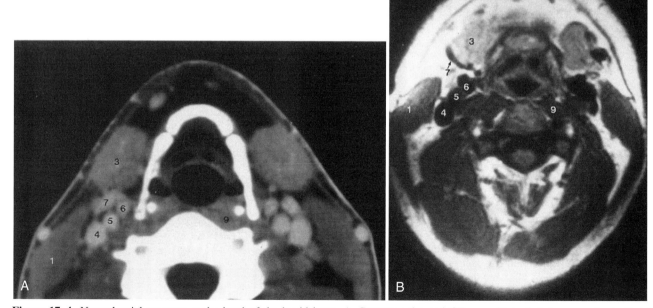

Figure 17–4. Normal axial anatomy at the level of the hyoid bone. *A,* Contrast-enhanced CT scan. Note that the normal retrofacial vein or proximal external carotid artery might be mistaken for a lymph node or other mass on a noncontrast examination. *B,* T1-weighted MR image demonstrates the same soft tissue and vascular anatomy without intravenous contrast. 1, Sternocleidomastoid muscle; 3, submandibular gland; 4, internal jugular vein; 5, internal carotid artery; 6, external carotid artery; 7, retrofacial vein; 9, longus colli muscle.

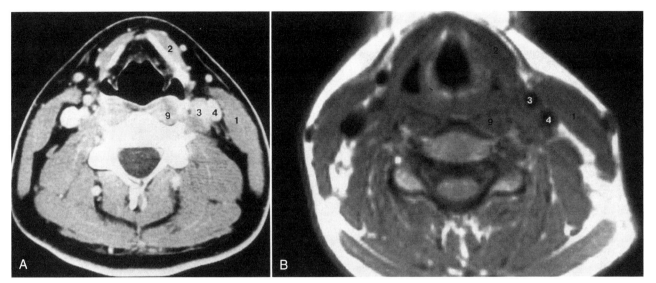

Figure 17–5. Normal axial anatomy at the level of the thyroid cartilages. *A,* CT scan. *B,* T1-weighted MR image. Note how the anterior margin of the sternocleidomastoid muscle is located anterior to the vertebral body. Compare with Figure 17–2*B*. 1, Sternocleidomastoid muscle; 2, strap muscle; 3, internal carotid artery; 4, internal jugular vein; 9, longus colli muscle.

the thyroid cartilage are the strap muscles (sternohyoid, sternothyroid, thyrohyoid, and superior belly of the omohyoid). The degree and pattern of ossification of the cartilages vary with the age and sex of the patient. Separation of nonossified cartilage from the overlying strap muscles is accomplished more easily with MRI than CT.

At the level of the thyroid cartilage (Fig. 17–5), the carotid sheath structures are situated along the anterior surface of the sternocleidomastoid muscle or slightly deep to it, posterior and lateral to the thyroid cartilage.

The superior cornua of the thyroid cartilage are easily identified as paired calcified structures located lateral to two of the extrinsic muscles of the spine, the longus colli muscles. The inferior cornua of the thyroid cartilage articulate with the posterior aspect of the cricoid cartilage.

The cricoid cartilage has a characteristic circular appearance on axial imaging. As with the thyroid cartilage, the degree of ossification of the cricoid varies with age. In adult patients, the cricoid cartilage appears on CT scans as a thin rim of calcification surrounding a lucent medullary center.[32] On T1-weighted MR images, the cricoid appears as a ring of tissue isointense to fat.

At approximately the level of the cricoid cartilage (Fig. 17–6), the superior pole of the thyroid gland appears on axial images as a triangular soft tissue structure situated between the cricoid cartilage medially and the carotid sheath structures laterally. The normal gland enhances uniformly with iodinated intravenous contrast material.[32] On noncontrast T1-weighted images, the gland is homogeneous in appearance and slightly hyperintense to skeletal muscle. The level of the cricoid cartilage also marks the point at which the omohyoid muscle crosses over the internal jugular vein.

Images at the level of the first tracheal ring (Fig. 17–7) demonstrate the lower poles of the thyroid gland and the adjacent carotid sheath structures. The sternocleidomastoid muscles have a paramedian position just superior to their insertions on the sternum and clavicle. The esophagus is

usually collapsed, lying posterior to the trachea and usually just to the left of the midline.

The posterior triangle of the normal supracricoid neck appears as a fat-filled cleft containing a few small soft tissue structures representing nutrient vessels, lymph nodes, and nerves.[32] Beginning at the level of the cricoid cartilage, the anterior scalene muscle can be identified in the medial aspect of the posterior triangle, posterior to the carotid sheath structures. The anterior scalene, which arises from the transverse processes of C3 through C6 and inserts on the superior and posterior surfaces of the medial first rib, lies directly anterior to the exiting trunks of the brachial plexus. At the level of the first tracheal ring, the brachial plexus is identified as a heterogeneous low-density or low-signal-intensity focus immedia

tely posterior to the anterior scalene muscle.

Evaluation of Cervical Adenopathy

Enlarged cervical lymph nodes are the most common cause of a neck mass in an adult. In patients older than 40 years, the enlarged nodes are most often secondary to metastatic carcinoma, usually from a primary neoplasm of the aerodigestive tract. In patients between the ages of 21 and 40, the enlarged nodes are most often secondary to lymphoma.[37] The optimal evaluation of cervical lymph nodes requires close attention to radiographic detail as well as an understanding of basic anatomical and pathologic principles of otolaryngology.

Anatomic Principles

Approximately 300 lymph nodes are located in the head and neck. The French anatomist Rouivere[34] divided these nodes into the following 10 principal groups (Fig. 17–8):[34]

1. Occipital nodes.

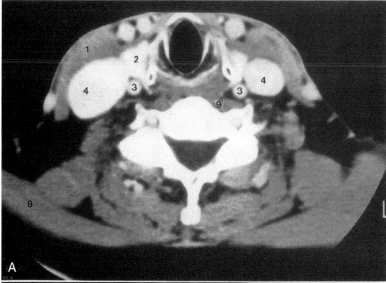
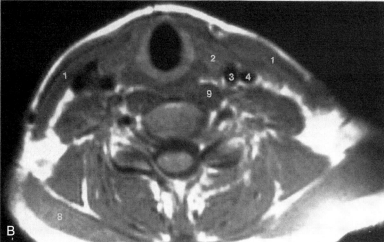

Figure 17–6. Normal axial anatomy at the level of the cricoid cartilage and inferior cornua of the thyroid cartilage. *A,* CT scan. The asymmetry in the diameters of the internal jugular veins is a normal variant. *B,* T1-weighted MR image. 1, Sternocleidomastoid muscle; 2, thyroid gland; 3, internal carotid artery; 4, internal jugular vein; 8, trapezius muscle; 9, longus colli muscle.

2. Mastoid nodes.
3. Parotid nodes.
4. Facial nodes.
5. Submandibular nodes.
6. Submental nodes.
7. Sublingual nodes.
8. Retropharyngeal nodes.
9. Anterior cervical nodes.
10. Lateral cervical nodes.

The first six groups form a *lymphoid collar* at the junction of the head and neck. Each group is responsible for the primary lymphatic drainage of a different region of the neck, as follows:

Occipital: Scalp and subcutaneous tissues of the occiput and superior neck.
Mastoid: Parietal scalp and auricle.
Parotid: Forehead, temporal scalp, lateral face, posterior cheek, lateral gingiva, buccal mucous membrane, exterior auditory canal, and parotid gland.
Facial: Lateral eyelids, anterior cheek, midface.

Submandibular: Lateral chin, lower and upper lips, lower cheek, anterior nose, medial eyelids, gingiva, anterior tongue, floor of the mouth, and submandibular and sublingual glands.
Submental: Central chin, lower lip, anterior gingiva, anterior floor of mouth, and tip of tongue.

The sublingual nodes also drain the tongue and floor of mouth but are not always identifiable as a separate group. The retropharyngeal nodes are further divided into medial and lateral groups. The medial group lies in the midline of the suprahyoid neck directly posterior to the pharynx. Enlargement of the medial group of retropharyngeal nodes is most commonly seen in neonates and young children. The lateral group is located anterior to the longus colli and longus capitus muscles, medial to the internal carotid artery, in both the suprahyoid and the infrahyoid neck. The retropharyngeal lymph nodes primarily drain the nasopharynx and posterior oropharynx as well as the paranasal sinuses, middle ear, posterior palate, and nasal cavity.

The anterior cervical nodes are toward the midline of the infrahyoid neck, located between the two carotid

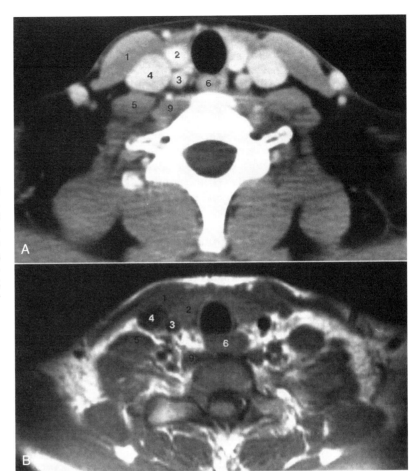

Figure 17–7. Normal axial anatomy at the level of the first tracheal ring. *A,* CT scan. *B,* T1-weighted MR image. Note the relative sizes of the fat-filled posterior triangles and the anterior triangle between the right and left sternocleidomastoid muscles. Compare with Figures 17–2*B* and 17–5*B*. 1, Sternocleidomastoid muscle; 2, thyroid gland; 3, internal carotid artery; 4, internal jugular vein; 5, anterior scalene muscle; 6, esophagus; 9, longus colli muscle.

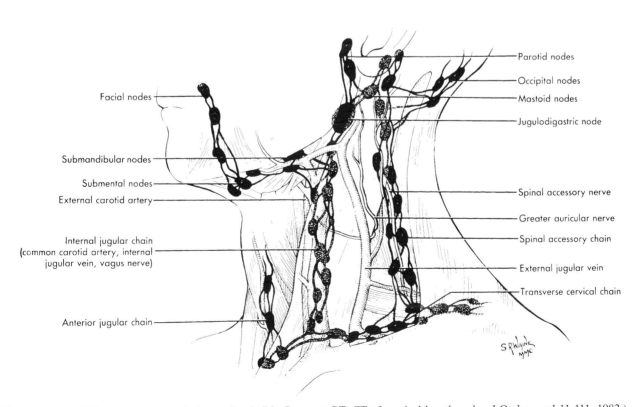

Figure 17–8. Nodal chains of the neck. (From Reede DL, Bergeron RT: CT of cervical lymph nodes. J Otolaryngol 11:411, 1982.)

sheaths. There are two divisions to this nodal group. The superficial division lies on the anterior surface of the strap muscles, following the course of the anterior jugular vein. The deep division of the anterior cervical nodes (also known as the juxtavisceral nodes or anterior compartment nodes) is located anterior to the larynx, thyroid gland, and trachea as well as in the tracheoesophageal groove. Included in the deep division is the Delphian node, located in the cricothyroid membrane of the larynx. The deep division drains the supraglottic and infraglottic larynx, piriform sinuses, thyroid gland, trachea, and esophagus.

The lateral cervical group constitutes the primary nodes of clinical interest in head and neck malignancies because it serves as a common route of drainage for all of the major regional structures. Similar to the anterior cervical nodes, the lateral cervical nodes are divided into superficial and deep divisions. The nodes in the superficial division follow the course of the external jugular vein. The deep division of lateral cervical nodes is further subdivided into the spinal accessory, internal jugular, and transverse cervical chains.

The spinal accessory chain of nodes follows the course of the spinal accessory nerve (cranial nerve XI) in the posterior triangle of the neck, deep to the sternocleidomastoid muscle. The spinal accessory chain receives drainage from the occipital and mastoid nodes as well as the lateral portions of the neck and shoulders.

The internal jugular chain of nodes follows the course of the internal jugular vein. At the superior aspect of this chain under the skull base, it is impossible to separate the internal jugular chain from the superior aspect of the spinal accessory chain. As the internal jugular vein descends in the neck, it is crossed by two muscles, the posterior belly of the digastric muscle superiorly and the omohyoid muscle inferiorly. At each junction of muscle and vein, a single lymph node, larger than adjacent nodes, is present. The jugulodigastric node (also known as the sentinel or tonsillar node) receives the lymphatic drainage from the submandibular nodes as well as the palatine tonsil and lateral oropharyngeal wall. The jugulo-omohyoid node receives all of the lymphatic drainage of the tongue.

The internal jugular nodes (also known as the deep cervical nodes) are arranged either in series or in parallel interconnecting rows adjacent to the vein. The nodes drain the parotid, submandibular, submental, retropharyngeal, and some anterior chain nodes. Nodes superior to the point where the omohyoid muscle crosses the internal jugular vein are usually located anterolateral to the vein. Nodes inferior to this point may be located anterior, medial, or posterior to the vein. This infraomohyoid node also receives lymphatic drainage from the arm and superior thorax. Among the most inferior of the internal jugular nodes are the nodes of Virchow.

The transverse cervical chain of nodes (also known as the supraclavicular nodes) follow the course of the transverse cervical vessels. The nodes in this chain connect the inferior aspects of the spinal accessory, internal jugular, and anterior jugular chains. The transverse cervical chain also receives drainage from the subclavicular nodes, the skin of the anterolateral neck, and the upper chest wall.

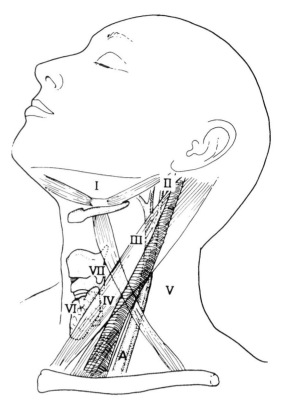

Figure 17–9. Simplified nodal classification. Diagram of the head and neck in left anterior oblique projection. Palpable nodes are indicated with use of a simplified nomenclature of Roman numerals I through VII. See text for explanation. (From Som PM: Lymph nodes of the neck. Radiology 165:596, 1987.)

In an attempt to eliminate the variations in nodal terminology, a simplified nodal classification was proposed in 1981.[36] This classification divides the clinically palpable cervical nodes into seven groups, each designated by a roman numeral (Fig. 17–9), as follows:

Level I: Submandibular and submental lymph nodes.
Level II: Internal jugular chain from the skull base to the level of the carotid bifurcation.
Level III: Internal jugular chain from the level of the carotid bifurcation to the level of the intersection of the chain with the omohyoid muscle.
Level IV: Infraomohyoid portion of the internal jugular chain.
Level V: Posterior triangle lymph nodes.
Level VI: Nodes related to the thyroid gland.
Level VII: Nodes in the tracheoesophageal groove and superior mediastinum.

It is important to remember that this system does not include all the cervical lymph nodes. Retropharyngeal nodes and transverse cervical nodes are not included. The system, however, is easily transferred to sectional imaging (Fig. 17–10). Because the carotid bifurcation is typically located at or near the level of the hyoid bone and the level of the intersection of the internal jugular chain with the omohyoid muscle is at the level of the cricoid cartilage,

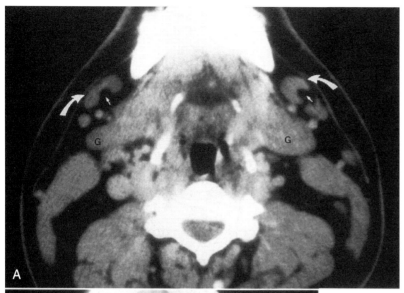

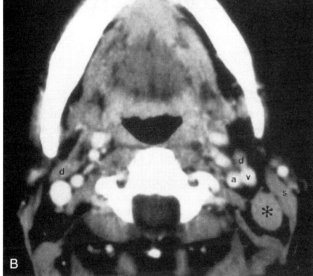

Figure 17–10. Sectional imaging using simplified nodal classification. *A,* Axial contrast-enhanced CT scan demonstrates bilateral lymph nodes (*curved white arrows*) anterior to each submandibular gland. They are level I (submandibular triangle) lymph nodes. Note the lucent zone of fat eccentrically located in each node. These zones represent prominent nodal hila. Compare with Figures 17–12 and 17–26. *B,* Axial contrast-enhanced CT scan demonstrates a homogeneous 2.5-cm diameter lymph node (*asterisk*) in the left posterior triangle deep to the sternocleidomastoid muscle (s) and separate from the internal jugular vein (v), internal carotid artery (a), and posterior belly of the digastric muscle (d). This is a level V (spinal accessory chain) lymph node. Asymmetry in the appearance of right and left digastric muscles is secondary to slight skewing of the patient's head within the scanner gantry.

the following *axial levels* may be used in staging nodal disease at imaging (Fig. 17–11)[42]:

Axial level II: Suprahyoid internal jugular chain.
Axial level III: Infrahyoid internal jugular chain above the cricoid cartilage.
Axial level IV: Infracricoid internal jugular chain.

Patients referred for imaging of cervical lymph nodes typically can be assigned to one of three categories. The first is a patient with a known malignancy of the head and neck in whom nodal staging is required. The second is a patient with a neck mass, already demonstrated by aspiration cytology to be metastatic squamous cell carcinoma, in whom no primary head and neck malignancy is identified. The third is a patient with a neck mass of uncertain origin.

Nodal Staging

CT remains the standard for assessing palpable and nonpalpable nodal metastases in patients with tumors of

the head and neck. Based on the work of Mancuso[20,21] and others, the following criteria have been adopted by most centers:

1. Normal lymph nodes are often invisible on CT. When present, these nodes have an ovoid (lima bean) shape and are of homogeneous soft tissue density. Normal lymph nodes typically measure less than 1.0 cm in diameter.
2. Any node measuring more than 1.5 cm in diameter is abnormal. Reactive as well as neoplastic nodes may produce this pattern. Reactive adenopathy is most commonly encountered in submandibular and jugulodigastric nodes.
3. Any node with a central lucency, regardless of size, is abnormal (Fig. 17–12). Nodes with this CT appearance, often referred to as *necrotic,* are focally or completely replaced with tumor (typically, metastatic squamous cell carcinoma). Actual necrosis of nodal tissue is not commonly seen on pathologic examination. Care must be

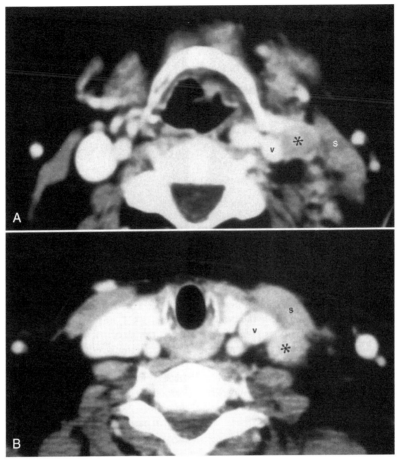

Figure 17–11. Internal jugular chain lymph nodes. *A,* Axial contrast-enhanced CT scan at the level of the hyoid bone demonstrates a 2-cm-diameter lymph node (*asterisk*) medial to the left sternocleidomastoid muscle (s) and lateral to the left internal jugular vein. This lymph node is present at the junction of axial levels II and III. *B,* Axial contrast-enhanced CT scan at the level of the cricoid cartilage demonstrates a 2-cm-diameter lymph node (*asterisk*) immediately posterior to the left internal jugular vein (v). This lymph node is present at the junction of axial levels III and IV.

taken not to mistake the fatty hilum of a normal node for the abnormal lucency. The fatty hilum is located at the periphery of the node (see Fig. 17–10A).
4. Obliteration of fascial planes surrounding a node is abnormal. The CT appearance of "dirty fat" surrounding a node may be seen in cases of extranodal spread of tumor or inflammation as well as after surgery or radiation therapy to the neck. In general, extranodal spread of tumor tends to cause a more focal obliteration of fascial planes than the other processes. Correlation with clinical history is essential (see Fig. 17–26).[31]

Many centers with active head and neck tumor services have more stringent criteria for assessing nodal size. Expounding on the pathologic studies of van den Brekel, these centers consider all lymph nodes with a short axis greater than or equal to 1.2 cm significant.[45] An alternative system is to maintain the size criterion of 1.5 cm for submandibular and jugulodigastric nodes but to consider nodes at other levels that measure 1.0 cm or larger to be significant.[42] When these criteria are used, approximately 80% of the enlarged (homogeneous) nodes are secondary to metastatic disease, and 20% are caused by reactive hyperplasia.[31]

When the extranodal changes described here obliterate fascial planes between a lymph node and adjacent structures (muscles, vessels), there may be clinical fixation of the node to these structures. The amount of fixation is subjective, depending on the individual examiner. It is difficult to predict solely on the basis of CT findings whether clinical fixation exists. The only sure sign of nodal fixation is if the structure in question is completely surrounded by a nodal mass. This point is particularly important in evaluation of the internal or common carotid artery.[24] Loss of definition of the vessel wall, with visualization of an otherwise normal lumen, is consistent with infiltration of the vessel wall (Fig. 17–13).

The utility of spin-echo MRI in evaluation of nodal disease remains limited. T1-weighted images usually provide good differentiation between intermediate signal nodes and the surrounding high-intensity fat, allowing for accurate measurement of nodal size. Assessment of central nodal necrosis is more difficult on MRI than on CT. Tumor cells within nodes tend to produce intermediate signal on T1-weighted and T2-weighted images, whereas areas of actual nodal necrosis usually appear as areas of low signal on T1-weighted images and of high signal on T2-weighted

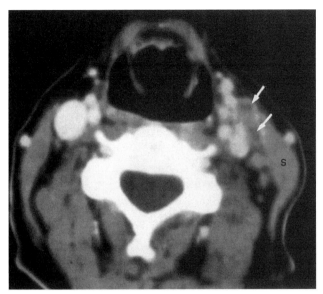

Figure 17–12. Metastases to small lymph nodes. Axial contrast-enhanced CT scan obtained at a level between the hyoid bone and the cricoid cartilage demonstrates two lymph nodes (*white arrows*) in the left internal jugular chain, each measuring 1 cm in diameter with central hypodensity not equal to that of fat. Each of these level III lymph nodes demonstrates a *necrotic center.* Multiple small nodes deep to the left sternocleidomastoid muscle (s) have a homogeneous appearance.

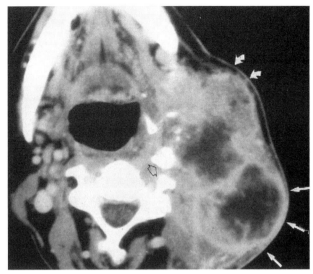

Figure 17–13. Extranodal spread of tumor. Axial contrast-enhanced CT scan demonstrates an irregular interface between the large left necrotic nodal mass and the cervical fat. Anteriorly, the overlying platysma is thickened and irregular (*curved white arrows*). Posterolaterally, there is extension through the platysma into the subcutaneous fat (*straight arrows*). This nodal mass was immobile or "fixed" on physical examination. Note how the mass engulfs the arteriosclerotic left internal carotid artery (*open black arrow*).

images.[47] One practical solution is to consider any lymph node that is heterogeneous in appearance abnormal, but even this alternative can fail if the dynamic gray scale of the images is limited or the signal-to-noise ratio low.[42]

The Unknown Primary

Approximately 5% of all patients with carcinoma and 12% of patients with head and neck carcinoma have nodal metastases as the sole presenting complaint.[40] In cases in which a head and neck malignancy is not appreciated by the otolaryngologist on initial clinical examination, knowledge of the pathways of nodal drainage, in combination with the ability of CT to detect nonpalpable pathologic lymph nodes, allows the radiologist to identify potential sites of neoplasm, particularly when the tumor is predominantly submucosal in nature.

The location of the enlarged lymph node(s) should direct suspicion of the primary site of neoplasm as follows (Fig. 17–14)[31]:

Level I: Oral cavity, submandibular gland.
Level II: Nasopharynx, oropharynx, parotid gland, supraglottic larynx.
Level III: Oropharynx, hypopharynx, supraglottic larynx.
Level IV: Subglottic larynx, hypopharynx, esophagus, thyroid.
Level V: Nasopharynx, oropharynx.
Levels VI and VII: Thyroid, larynx, lung.

Bilateral nodal disease is particularly common in tumors of the soft palate, tongue, epiglottis, and nasopharynx. Isolated nodal disease in the supraclavicular fossa is unlikely to be secondary to a malignancy of the aerodigestive tract; more likely sites are lung, breast, stomach, and thyroid.[42]

Figure 17–14. The unknown primary. Axial contrast-enhanced CT scan demonstrates a clinically palpable pathologic lymph node in level III of the right internal jugular chain (*asterisk*). Flexible nasopharyngoscopy failed to demonstrate a primary neoplasm. CT examination demonstrates asymmetrical soft tissue density in the right paralaryngeal space. Direct laryngoscopy confirmed the diagnosis of squamous cell carcinoma of the laryngeal ventricle.

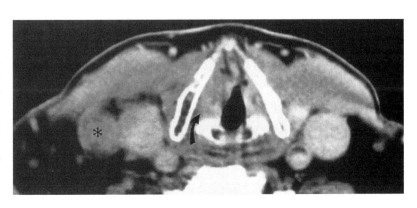

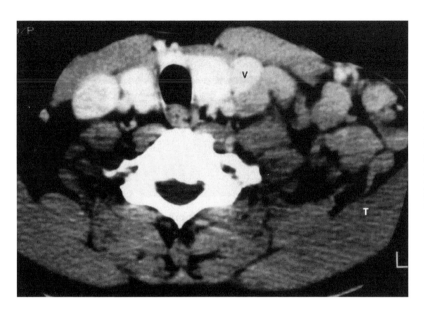

Figure 17–15. Hodgkin's disease. Axial contrast-enhanced CT scan at the level of the first tracheal ring demonstrates multiple enlarged homogeneous lymph nodes filling the left posterior triangle. Lymph nodes adjacent to the internal jugular vein (V) are level IV nodes. Lymph nodes adjacent to the trapezius muscle (T) are level V nodes.

Neck Masses

Isolated nodal masses may mimic a wide variety of lesions in the neck, including masses of congenital, neural, and infectious origins. The key to limiting differential diagnosis is correlation with clinical history. Multiple masses in the neck are most likely secondary to nodal enlargement. Although aspiration cytology or excisional biopsy is necessary to confirm the diagnosis of nodal disease, identification of certain CT patterns of nodal disease facilitates clinical evaluation, as follows:

1. Large homogeneous lymph nodes are most commonly encountered in lymphoma, sarcoid, and infectious mononucleosis. CT cannot reliably differentiate Hodgkin's from non-Hodgkin's lymphoma (Fig. 17–15).[31]
2. Total or relatively uniform enhancement of an enlarged node is usually encountered in inflammatory processes. Exceptions to this rule include nodal involvement by Kaposi's sarcoma, thyroid carcinoma, and renal cell carcinoma (Fig. 17–16).
3. Calcification within lymph nodes is unusual. Most commonly, the calcific deposits are the result of prior granulomatous disease.[28] Metastatic papillary carcinoma of the thyroid is the most common cause of neoplastic nodal calcifications.[42] In rare instances, metastatic or lymphomatous nodes may calcify after irradiation or chemotherapy.[3,5]
4. The presence of multiple nodes with a variety of CT appearances (homogeneous, necrotic, enhancing, and calcified) is most compatible with granulomatous disease of cervical lymph nodes. In urban centers, tuberculosis is the most common cause (Fig. 17–17).[28] Thyroid carcinoma may also produce this spectrum of CT appearances.[42]

Evaluation of Non-Nodal Neck Masses

The CT and MRI appearances of nodal and non-nodal neck masses often overlap. Careful attention to imaging

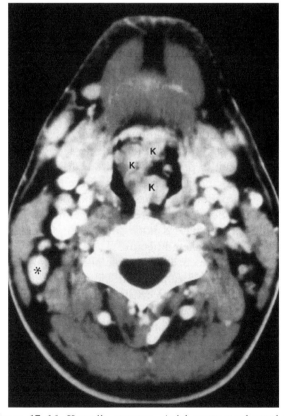

Figure 17–16. Kaposi's sarcoma. Axial contrast-enhanced CT scan at the level of the anterior bellies of the digastric muscles demonstrates multiple, uniformly enhancing masses in the anterior and posterior triangles of the neck bilaterally, the largest identified in the left spinal accessory chain (*asterisk*). Multiple oropharyngeal lesions are also present (K).

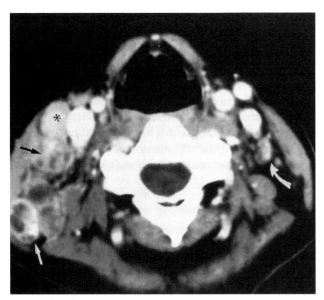

Figure 17–17. Tuberculous adenitis. Axial contrast-enhanced CT scan at the level of the thyroid cartilage demonstrates lymph nodes that are variably homogeneous (*asterisk*), necrotic (*black arrow*), enhancing (*curved white arrow*), and calcified (*straight white arrow*). The patient, who is 12 years old, has little ossification of the thyroid cartilages.

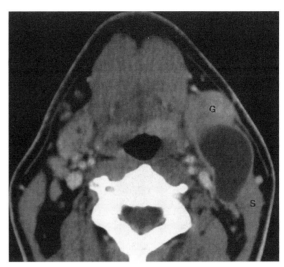

Figure 17–18. Type II second branchial cleft cyst. Axial contrast-enhanced CT scan demonstrates a unilocular cystic mass with minimal rim enhancement along the anterior margin of the left sternocleidomastoid muscle (s) displacing the left submandibular gland (G) anteriorly.

findings and correlation with clinical history are essential to correct diagnosis of a mass of developmental, inflammatory, vascular, neural, or mesenchymal origin.

Masses of Developmental Origin

The most common developmental mass identified on imaging is the branchial cleft cyst. This lesion is the result of incomplete obliteration of the first, second, third, or fourth branchial apparatus. The majority of these lesions arise from the second branchial apparatus, which forms the facial muscles, styloid process, pinna, and portions of the ossicular chain and muscles of the middle ear.[2] The second branchial cleft cyst most commonly identified at imaging is the Bailey type II cyst, which is secondary to persistence of the embryologic cervical sinus.[2] These type II second branchial cleft cysts often manifest as painless fluctuant masses along the course of the anterior margin of the sternocleidomastoid muscle. They most commonly manifest in patients between the ages of 10 and 40 years but may become clinically obvious at any age.[33]

On contrast-enhanced CT (Fig. 17–18), a type II second branchial cleft cyst characteristically appears as a well-circumscribed, unilocular, low-density mass adjacent to the anterior margin of the sternocleidomastoid muscle. CT attenuation measurements of these and other cystic masses range from 10 to 25 HU.[11] On MRI (Fig. 17–19), the contents of the cyst are usually isointense with cerebrospinal fluid on T2-weighted images. On T1-weighted images, the cyst contents are usually hyperintense to cerebrospinal fluid and may even be hyperintense to skeletal muscle.[18]

The extent of rim enhancement of branchial cleft cysts is variable. Thick rim enhancement and indistinctness of fascial margins may occur if the cyst becomes infected.

Septations are uncommon and are usually found only in cases of previous infection or needle aspiration. Infected cysts may mimic necrotic jugular chain lymph nodes or cervical abscesses on both CT and MRI.

If sufficiently large, the type II second branchial cleft cyst displaces the carotid artery and jugular vein medially or posteromedially. In contrast, the type III second branchial cleft cyst courses between the external and internal carotid arteries.[2]

Cystic hygroma is the most common form of lymphagiomatous malformation occurring in the neck. Although there are multiple theories of pathogenesis for lymphagiomas, most experts believe that cystic hygromas form because the primordial lymphatic sacs failed to drain into the veins, resulting in hugely dilated cystic lymphatic spaces.[46]

Seventy-five percent of cystic hygromas occur in the neck, and 20% in the axilla. Cystic hygromas are usually isolated malformations in patients in whom the remainder of the lymphatic system is normal. They may occasionally be associated with a more generalized failure of lymphatic system development, as seen in cases of the 45,X chromosome karyotype (Turner's syndrome).[48]

In contrast to branchial cleft cysts, cystic hygromas typically manifest at or shortly after birth. The clinical presentation is often characteristic: a painless, easily compressible mass that may transilluminate on physical examination. Patients are usually asymptomatic, unless there is significant airway obstruction.[33] Cervical cystic hygromas are most commonly found in the posterior triangle but can also occur in the floor of mouth, submental triangle, and submandibular triangles. Because up to 10% of cervical cystic hygromas may extend into the mediastinum, imaging is performed to assess the extent of the lesion and its relationship to adjacent structures before surgical resection.

On contrast-enhanced CT (Fig. 17–20), cystic hygromas are low density in appearance without peripheral rim enhancement. Larger lesions may be multiloculated and are

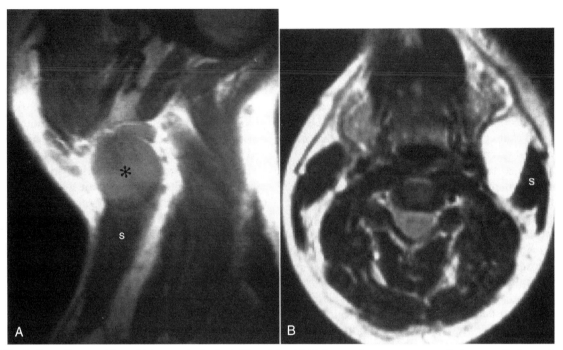

Figure 17–19. Type II second branchial cyst. *A,* Sagittal T1-weighted MR image demonstrates a well-circumscribed anterior triangle mass (*asterisk*) mildly hyperintense to muscle along the anterior margin of the sternocleidomastoid muscle (s). *B,* Axial T2-weighted MR image demonstrates a hyperintense mass along the anterior margin of the left sternocleidomastoid muscle (s). Compare with Figure 17–18.

often poorly circumscribed. In contrast to other cystic-appearing masses in the neck, cystic hygromas typically insinuate themselves between adjacent structures rather than displace vascular or muscular structures.[33]

The multiplanar capability of MRI makes it the ideal imaging modality for evaluating cystic hygromas (Fig. 17–21). On T2-weighted images, the hygromas are isointense with cerebrospinal fluid. Their appearance on T1-weighted images is more variable, either hypointense or hyperintense to skeletal muscle, depending on the relative protein concentration of the lymph fluid and prior episodes of trauma or infection.[18,38]

Thyroglossal duct cysts are the result of incomplete involution of an embryologic tract, the thyroglossal duct.

It is through the duct that the thyroid gland passes during its migration from the foramen cecum in the tongue to its final position in front of the trachea. If any portion of this epithelium-lined duct persists after birth, a cyst may develop. The hyoid bone is intimately associated with the thyroglossal duct during its development; a thyroglossal duct cyst may be located anterior to, posterior to, or within the hyoid bone.[30]

Thyroglossal duct cysts account for approximately 70% of all congenital neck masses, with the overwhelming majority occurring in the pediatric age group. Routine sectional imaging of thyroglossal duct cysts is not performed in children because the clinical presentation (a painless midline neck mass that moves on swallowing) is so typi-

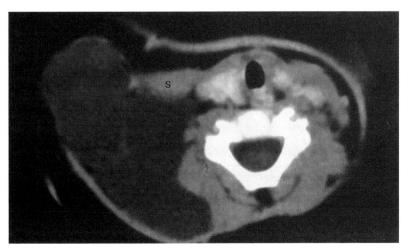

Figure 17–20. Cystic hygroma. Axial contrast-enhanced CT scan at the level of the first tracheal ring demonstrates a multilocular cystic mass without rim enhancement occupying the entire right posterior triangle extending toward the right axilla. S, Sternocleidomastoid muscle.

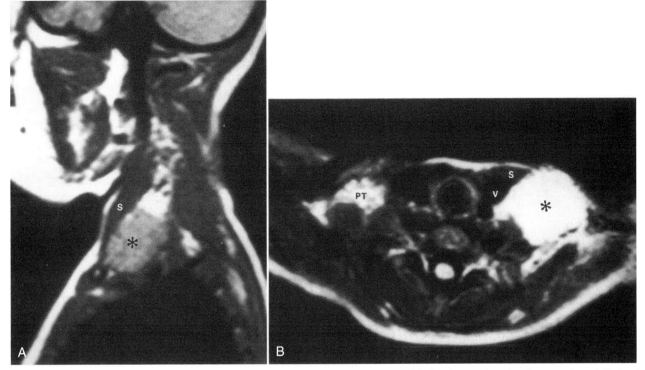

Figure 17–21. Cystic hygroma. *A,* Sagittal T1-weighted MR image demonstrates a lobulated posterior triangle mass (*asterisk*) that is moderately hyperintense to muscle and located deep to the posterior margin of the sternocleidomastoid muscle (s). Note how the hygroma tracks posterior to the internal jugular vein (V). *B,* The hygroma appears virtually isointense to fat in the right posterior triangle (PT), owing to window width and level.

cal.[33] Ultrasonography or radioisotope scanning may be performed to confirm a normal position of the thyroid before surgery.

CT or MRI is usually performed preoperatively in cases of suspected thyroglossal duct cyst in adults to confirm the diagnosis and to exclude other nodal masses. On contrast-enhanced CT, a well-circumscribed, low-density mass is present (Fig. 17–22).[30] Peripheral rim enhancement or internal septations are occasionally seen. The MRI signal characteristics of thyroglossal duct cysts are the same as those of branchial cleft cysts or small cystic hygromas.

Suprahyoid thyroglossal duct cysts are midline in location. The more common infrahyoid thyroglossal duct cysts often have both midline and off-midline components, the latter being embedded in the strap muscles. It is the location of an infrahyoid thyroglossal duct cyst in the strap muscles, not its signal or attenuation characteristics, that allows for a definitive radiographic diagnosis.[30] The presence of a solid mass along the thyroglossal duct should raise suspicion of ectopic thyroid tissue, in which occult malignancy is more likely.

Dermoid cysts are the rarest of the congenital neck

Figure 17–22. Thyroglossal duct cyst. Axial contrast-enhanced CT scan at a level immediately inferior to the hyoid bone demonstrates a cystic anterior triangle mass with peripheral rim enhancement (*asterisk*) embedded within the strap muscles to the right of midline. M, Left strap muscles; S, right sternocleidomastoid muscle.

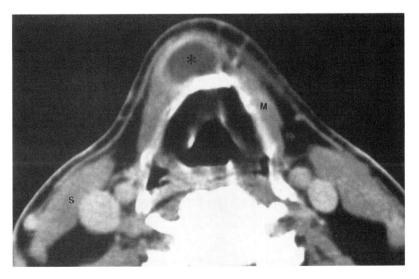

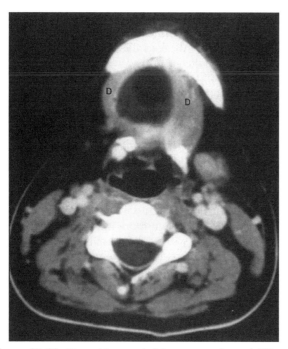

Figure 17–23. Dermoid cyst. Axial contrast-enhanced CT scan demonstrates a mass with peripheral rim enhancement in the submental triangle. The mass contains a fatty component anteriorly and a fluid component posteriorly. D, Anterior bellies of the digastric muscles. The central portion of the hyoid bone is absent because of previous surgery to remove a thyroglossal duct cyst. (From Reede DL, et al: Nonnodal pathologic conditions of the neck. In Som PM, Bergeron RT (eds): Head and Neck Imaging, 2nd ed. St. Louis, CV Mosby, 1991.)

lesions. Only 7% of all dermoid tumors occur in the head and neck. The majority of head and neck dermoids occur in the orbit, nasal cavity, or oral cavity; true cervical dermoids are rare. The term *dermoid cyst* has been used to include the following three types of cysts: (1) epidermoids or epidermal cysts, (2) dermoids, and (3) teratoid cysts.[22,33] These three types of congenital cysts can be differentiated histologically by the presence or absence of an epithelial lining and the cyst contents. Differentiation among the three types of dermoid cysts by sectional imaging is often impossible.

Most cervical dermoid cysts occur in the midline or just off-midline and are usually present at birth. In contrast to thyroglossal duct cysts, dermoid cysts typically do not move with swallowing. On CT, the presence of fat within the mass suggests a diagnosis of dermoid rather than epidermoid (Fig. 17–23. In the absence of demonstrable fat, epidermoids and dermoids cannot be distinguished by CT or MRI.

Masses of Inflammatory Origin

It is often difficult to determine clinically whether a patient with an erythematous, painful, and swollen neck has a simple cellulitis or a potentially life-threatening deep neck abscess. With sectional imaging, it is possible not only to diagnose an abscess but also to differentiate it from cellulitis.[12,33]

The CT characteristics of neck infections have been well described. Abscesses appear as single or multiloculated, low-density masses that conform to fascial spaces. When intravenous iodinated contrast agent is administered, abscesses demonstrate peripheral rim enhancement. Cutaneous and subcutaneous manifestations of infection are also seen. The manifestations include enlargement of adjacent muscles (myositis), thickening of the overlying skin, prominent linear densities within the subcutaneous fat, and enhancement of fascial planes. The presence of these cutaneous and subcutaneous manifestations without a low-density collection is consistent with cellulitis (Fig. 17–24).[12,33]

A "characteristic" appearance of cervical infections on MRI has yet to be defined. In general, abscesses appear as single or multiloculated masses that are hypointense to skeletal muscle on T1-weighted images and markedly hyperintense on T2-weighted images. The use of MRI contrast agents should demonstrate an enhancing rim in a mature abscess. Differentiation of abscesses from other noninfectious masses on MRI requires careful attention to variations in the dynamic gray scale. Particular attention must be paid to window and level settings because subtle changes in cervical fat may be obscured by the hyperintense signal of cervical fat on T1-weighted images (Fig. 17–25).

No studies have yet compared CT and MRI in the evaluation of cervical infection. Several problems have been noted by investigators using MRI to evaluate inflammatory disease: First, the cutaneous manifestations of infection are not obvious on MR images; second, subcutaneous manifestations of infection may be obscured on MR images if imaging parameters are not carefully monitored; third, after intravenous administration of contrast agent, the enhancing rim may become isointense with surrounding fat, limiting detection or delineation of the abscess unless fat-suppression techniques are used; fourth, areas of abscess formation and cellulitis both tend to be hyperintense on T2-weighted images, hampering differentiation between the two processes.[12,33]

The authors prefer the use of contrast-enhanced CT to assess suspected inflammatory disease in adults. In children and in adults whose clinical status precludes the use of iodinated contrast material, MRI is the study of initial choice, although a limited noncontrast CT study may be required for evaluation of osseous integrity. If MRI is not available, ultrasonography is an alternative modality for localizing suspected collections for surgical drainage.

Regardless of the modality used, the following important principles must be remembered:

1. Radiographic changes in the skin, fat, and fascial planes of the neck are not pathognomonic for an infectious process. Inflammatory reactions after radiotherapy or surgery can mimic cervical infections.
2. Radiographically, a necrotic tumor, nodal disease with extension into the adjacent soft tissues, and a thrombosed vessel may all mimic an abscess on sectional images (Fig. 17–26). Clinical correlation is essential.
3. Not every infectious process demonstrates the radio-

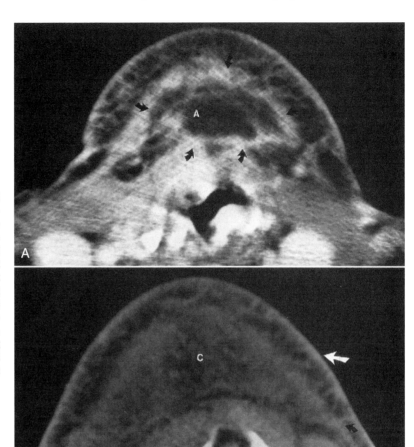

Figure 17–24. Abscess versus cellulitis. *A,* Axial contrast-enhanced CT scan demonstrates a low-density collection (A) in the anterior triangle surrounded by an irregular rim of contrast enhancement (*arrows*) consistent with abscess. *B,* Axial contrast-enhanced CT scan in a different patient demonstrates irregular linear densities in the fat of the anterior triangle (C). There is thickening of the platysma muscle (*black arrows*) and the skin (*white arrow*). No fluid collections are present. This image is compatible with cellulitis. (From Holliday RA, Prendergast NC: Imaging inflammatory processes of the oral cavity and suprahyoid neck. Oral Max Surg Clin North Am 4:215, 1992.)

graphic changes listed here. Granulomatous infections with *Mycobacterium* and occasionally *Actinomycosis* species often appear as "bland" masses, without central necrosis or peripheral cellulitic changes.

4. Inflammatory lesions are always in a state of evolution. It is possible that a patient may be studied before a cellulitis has "ripened" to a frank collection of pus. If a diagnosis of cellulitis is made and the patient shows no response to appropriate antibiotic therapy, a second examination should be performed to ensure that an abscess cavity has not formed.[12,19]

Once a diagnosis of cervical abscess is established, it is important to "map out" the sites of abscess accurately to ensure proper surgical drainage. Cervical infections frequently spread along the fascial planes within the neck. Abscesses are often located within a single compartment or "space" within the neck. The following summary of fascial anatomy is designed to facilitate mapping of cervical infections. It must be acknowledged that any classification of fascial anatomy is somewhat arbitrary because fasciae are simply the more obvious layers of the general connective tissue packing with the body. Nevertheless, the

following definitions are stressed in both the anatomical and the surgical literature (Figs. 17–27 and 17–28).

Two cervical fasciae exist, the superficial and the deep.[10, 12, 17, 23, 26,41] The superficial cervical fascia is a layer of connective tissue that surrounds the head and neck, encircling the platysma muscle. The fascia also contains blood vessels, lymphatic channels, cutaneous nerves, and hair follicles. Its primary function is to allow the skin to glide easily over the deeper structures of the neck. Infections that track along the superficial cervical fascia are often secondary to skin infections and rarely track deeper into the neck.

The deep cervical fascia consists of three layers: the superficial layer, known as the investing fascia; the middle layer, known as the visceral fascia; and the deep layer, which has two divisions separated by a potential space—the alar layer anteriorly and the prevertebral layer posteriorly.

The investing fascia surrounds all the important structures of the neck. The visceral fascia surrounds the aerodigestive tract. The deep layer surrounds the vertebral column and paravertebral muscles. All three layers are closely

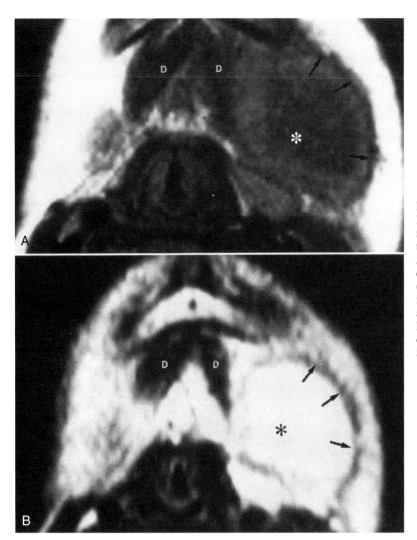

Figure 17–25. Abscess. *A,* Axial T1-weighted MR image demonstrates a mass (*asterisk*) in the right submandibular triangle that is hypointense to the anterior bellies of the digastric muscles. *B,* Corresponding axial T2-weighted MR image demonstrates hyperintense signal within the mass (*asterisk*). Note that inflammatory changes in the fat lateral to the abscess (*arrows*) are not as easily appreciated as on CT scans. (From Holliday RA, Prendergast NC: Imaging inflammatory processes of the oral cavity and suprahyoid neck. Oral Max Surg Clin North Am 4:215, 1992.)

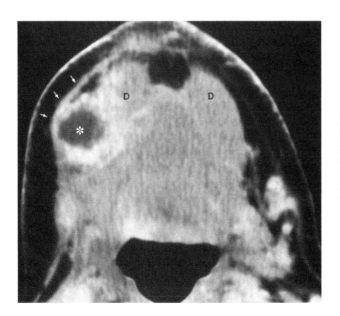

Figure 17–26. Metastatic lymph node mimicking abscess. Axial contrast-enhanced CT scan demonstrates a low-density right submandibular triangle mass (*asterisk*) surrounded by an irregular rim of contrast enhancement. The overlying platysma muscle is thickened. The patient, who was afebrile, had a history of treatment for squamous cell carcinoma of the right oropharynx 2 years before this examination. Needle aspiration of the mass yielded atypical squamous cells.

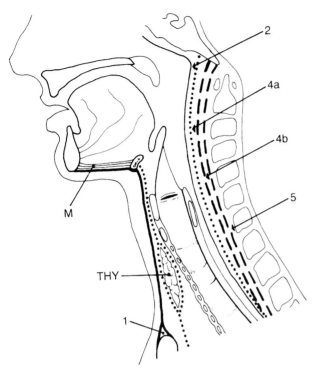

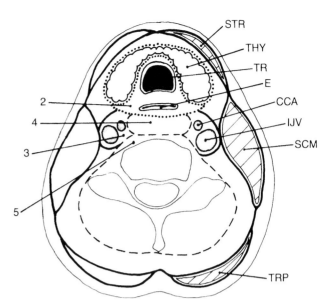

Figure 17–27. The layers of deep cervical fascia and the cervical spaces, sagittal view. *Solid line,* investing fascia; *dotted line,* visceral fascia; *broken line,* prevertebral fascia. 1, Suprasternal space of Burns; 2, visceral space; 4a, retrovisceral component of the retropharyngeal space; 4b, danger space; 5, prevertebral space. M, mylohyoid muscle; THY, thyroid gland. (Adapted from Smoker WRK, Harnsberger HR: Normal anatomy of the neck. In Som PM, Bergeron RT (eds): Head and Neck Imaging, 2nd ed. St. Louis, Mosby Year Book, 1990, pp 498–518.)

Figure 17–28. The layers of deep cervical fascia and the cervical spaces of the infrahyoid neck, axial view. *Solid line,* investing fascia; *dotted line,* visceral fascia; *broken line,* prevertebral fascia. 2, Visceral space; 3, carotid space; 4, retropharyngeal space; 5, prevertebral space. CCA, common carotid artery; E, esophagus; IJV, internal jugular vein; SCM, sternocleidomastoid muscle; STR, strap muscles; THY, thyroid gland; TR, trachea; TRP, trapezius muscle. (Adapted from Smoker WRK, Harnsberger HR: Normal anatomy of the neck. In Som PM, Bergeron RT (eds): Head and Neck Imaging, 2nd ed. St. Louis, Mosby Year Book, 1990, pp 498–518.)

associated in the anterolateral neck, where they all contribute to the formation of the carotid sheath, which surrounds the carotid artery, internal jugular vein, and vagus nerve.

The investing fascia is attached posteriorly to the ligamentum nuchae and the spinous processes of the cervical vertebral bodies. As it extends anteriorly, the fascia splits to envelope the trapezius and sternocleidomastoid muscles, forming the roof of the posterior triangle. In the suprahyoid neck, the fascia also splits to surround the parotid and submandibular glands before attaching to the body of the hyoid bone and the inferior surface of the mandible.

In the infrahyoid neck, the investing fascia splits to surround the strap muscles anterior to the larynx and trachea. The fascia also invests the omohyoid muscle, holding the muscle close to the clavicle, so contraction of the muscle results in a downward rather than a lateral pull on the hyoid bone. The investing fascia is attached superiorly to the external occipital protuberance, the mastoid process, and the skull base. It is attached inferiorly to the clavicle, the acromion, and the anterior and posterior surfaces of the sternum.

The visceral fascia extends from the central skull base to the mediastinum, encircling the pharynx, esophagus, larynx, and trachea. In the mediastinum, the visceral fascia blends with the pericardium, forming the anterior border of the retropharyngeal space. In the infrahyoid neck, the

fascia is attached anteriorly to the cricoid and thyroid cartilages and splits to form the capsule of the thyroid gland.

The deep layer of the deep cervical fascia, like the investing fascia, begins in the posterior midline. The deep layer forms the floor of the posterior triangle, covering the paraspinal and scalene muscles. The deep layer is attached laterally to the transverse processes of the vertebral bodies, where it then splits into the anterior alar and posterior prevertebral layers as they extend anterior to the vertebral body. The alar and prevertebral layers have different craniocaudad extensions; although both attach superiorly at the skull base, the alar layer blends with the visceral layer along the posterior margin of the esophagus at the level of approximately T2, whereas the prevertebral layer extends more inferiorly anterior to the anterior longitudinal ligament.

The three layers of the deep cervical fascia delineate spaces in and through which bacterial infections can spread in the infrahyoid neck. The visceral space includes all structures within the confines of the visceral fascia and is continuous with the anterior mediastinum.

The retropharyngeal space is situated in the midline directly posterior to the pharynx. The anterior boundary of the retropharyngeal space is formed by the visceral fascia, and the posterior boundary is formed by the deep layer of the deep cervical fascia.

The retropharyngeal space can be further divided by the alar layer into the *retrovisceral space* anteriorly and the *danger space* posteriorly. Depending on its location, infection in the retropharyngeal space can extend inferiorly in the retrovisceral space to the level of approximately T3 (where the alar layer and the visceral layer fuse) or in the danger space inferiorly to the level of the diaphragm. Because it is impossible to separate these two smaller spaces radiographically, the retropharyngeal space may be considered as a single radiographic space, with the recognition that all infections in the retropharyngeal space must be evaluated in full, and scans of either the superior mediastinum or entire chest may be necessary.

Infections of the retropharyngeal space in children are usually secondary to infection of the medial retropharyngeal lymph nodes. In adults, retropharyngeal space infection is most commonly the result of perforation of the posterior wall of the pharynx or esophagus. Infections of the parapharyngeal space or posterior pharyngeal wall, if unchecked, may penetrate the visceral fascia and involve the retropharyngeal space.[12] Regardless of their origin, retropharyngeal space abscesses have a characteristic "bow tie" appearance on axial images that facilitates identification.[7] Sagittal MR images are ideal for definition of the superior and inferior extension of retropharyngeal abscesses before surgical intervention (Fig. 17–29).

The prevertebral space includes those structures (vertebral bodies, paravertebral and scalene muscles, vertebral arteries) that are surrounded by the deep layer of the deep cervical fascia. Lying posterior to the retropharyngeal space, the prevertebral space may be further divided into anterior and posterior compartments by the attachment of the deep layer of deep cervical fascia to the transverse processes. Infections of the prevertebral space are usually secondary to vertebral infection (osteomyelitis) or posterior extension arising in the retropharyngeal space.

The carotid space is a potential space within the carotid sheath. Because little areolar tissue is present within the sheath, actual infection of the carotid space is rare. The carotid sheath, however, with its contributions from all three layers of the deep cervical fascia, is a conduit of infection from one space to another. Septic or reactive thrombosis of the internal jugular vein may produce swelling within the carotid space.[12]

Masses of Vascular Origin

Asymmetry in the diameter of the internal jugular veins is a normal variant and should not be confused with a mass (see Fig. 17–6). Tortuous arterial vessels may manifest as a pulsatile mass in the supraclavicular fossa or neck. Masses lying in close proximity to the internal or common carotid arteries may transmit normal arterial pulsations. Sectional imaging can differentiate between these "pulsatile" masses and aneurysms of the cervical arterial system.

Internal jugular vein thrombosis, most commonly secondary to central venous catheterization or intravenous drug abuse, is readily diagnosed on sectional imaging. On contrast-enhanced CT, the central portion of the thrombosed vessel is usually less dense than contrast-enhanced blood. Enhancement of the wall of the vein is often present and may extend into surrounding fascial planes.[1] A number of lesions may mimic a thrombosed vein on one or more sequential CT scans. Lesions that may be confused with a thrombosed vessel include necrotic lymph nodes, cervical abscesses, infected branchial cleft cysts, and thrombosed carotid arteries (Fig. 17–30). In most cases, careful analysis of sequential images and correlation with clinical history can distinguish venous thrombosis from other lesions.[33]

In the evaluation of venous patency with MRI, care must be taken not to confuse flow-related enhancement with thrombosis. The MRI diagnosis of venous thrombosis often requires partial flip angle imaging or phase imaging to confirm findings identified on spin-echo sequences.[4]

Paragangliomas, commonly known as glomus tumors, are neoplasms of neural crest cell origin that arise within the adventitial layer of blood vessels at multiple sites in the head and neck, including the middle ear (glomus tympanicum), parapharyngeal space (glomus jugulare), and larynx. The two most common paragangliomas to present as a neck mass arise at the carotid bifurcation (carotid body tumor) and along the nodose ganglion of the vagus nerve (glomus vagale). Such a mass typically manifests as a painless slow-growing mass in the anterior triangle of the suprahyoid neck. The mass is commonly pulsatile, and a bruit may be auscultated over it.[33]

The most constant feature of the glomus vagale or

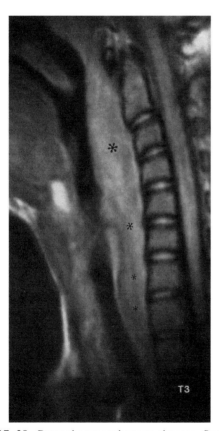

Figure 17–29. Retropharyngeal space abscess. Sagittal T2-weighted MR image demonstrates a hyperintense mass in the retropharyngeal space (*asterisks*) with anterior displacement of the airway. The abscess extends inferiorly to the level of the third thoracic vertebra (T3), implying involvement of the retrovisceral space rather than the danger space. (From Holliday RA, Prendergast NC: Imaging inflammatory processes of the oral cavity and suprahyoid neck. Oral Max Surg Clin North Am 4:215, 1992.)

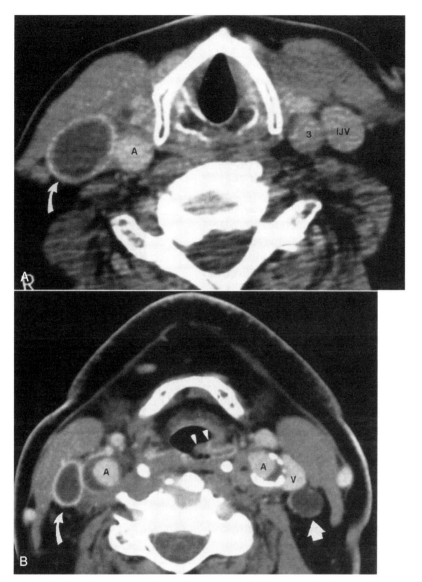

Figure 17–30. Internal jugular vein thrombosis. *A,* Axial contrast-enhanced CT scan at the level of the cricoid cartilage demonstrates hypodensity with peripheral rim enhancement (*curved white arrow*) lateral to the right common carotid artery (A). 3, Left common carotid artery; IJV, left internal jugular vein. *B,* Axial contrast-enhanced CT scan at the level of the jugular vein (*curved white arrow*) and the necrotic left internal jugular chain lymph node (*white arrow*) metastatic from the left supraglottic carcinoma (*white arrowheads*). Arteriosclerotic change is present in the common carotid arteries bilaterally (A).

carotid body tumor on CT scans is intense enhancement after intravenous contrast administration. Dynamic CT scanning after bolus contrast administration has been reported as a reliable method of differentiating paragangliomas from schwannomas, because the former have a vascular flow curve but the latter do not.[43]

MRI has all but replaced dynamic CT in the imaging evaluation of suspected glomus or carotid body tumors. Paragangliomas more than 1.5 cm in diameter should demonstrate curvilinear areas of signal void representing areas of high vascular flow (Fig. 17–31).[25] Schwannomas, which classically are avascular lesions on angiography, do not demonstrate areas of signal void.[33]

Identifying areas of signal void within a neck mass on MRI allows the confident diagnosis of paraganglioma only if the mass is present in the correct location. Carotid body tumors arise in the juxtahyoid neck and separate the internal and external carotid arteries on sectional imaging. Glomus vagale tumors arise in the suprahyoid neck and displace the internal carotid artery anteromedially and the internal jugular vein posterolaterally. Other neck masses with areas of signal void on MRI, such as nodal metastases from renal cell or thyroid carcinoma,[42] do not demonstrate these vascular displacements. This MRI appearance is not pathognomonic for paraganglioma and may be seen in a variety of high-flow lesions. An imaging diagnosis of paraganglioma should prompt a careful search for additional lesions because multiple glomus tumors occur in up to 10% of the general population and in up to 33% of patients with a family history of paraganglioma.[27]

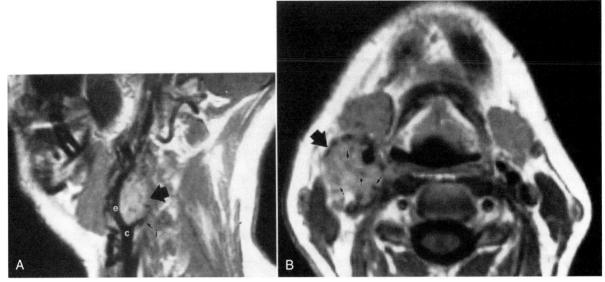

Figure 17–31. Carotid body tumor. *A,* Sagittal T1-weighted MR image demonstrates a heterogeneous mass (*arrow*) at the bifurcation of the common carotid artery (c) splaying the external (e) and internal (i) carotid arteries. *B,* Axial T1-weighted MR image at the level of the hyoid bone in the same patient demonstrates a right anterior triangle mass (*large black arrow*) with multiple internal areas of relative signal void (*small black arrows*).

Masses of Neural Origin

Schwannomas and neurofibromas are the most common types of neurogenic tumors found in the head and neck. Common sites for schwannomas and neurofibromas in the neck are the vagus nerve (cranial nerve X), the ventral and dorsal cervical nerve roots, the cervical sympathetic chain, and the brachial plexus. Associated motor dysfunction and pain in the distribution of a sensory nerve are inconstant clinical findings.[15]

Without a clinical history of neurofibromatosis, it is impossible to distinguish between these two neural masses on sectional imaging. Most neural tumors appear hypodense or isodense to skeletal muscle on noncontrast CT. These tumors tend to be hypointense or isointense to skele-tal muscle on T1-weighted MR images and variably hyperintense on T2-weighted images. Variations in the CT or MRI appearance of masses of neural origin are commonly thought to be secondary to variations in cellularity or lipid content. The enhancement pattern of neural tumors is highly variable. Intense, uniform enhancement, inhomogeneous enhancement, and lack of enhancement have all been reported. It is not unusual for an isolated schwannoma to be mistaken for a nodal mass on sectional imaging (Fig. 17–32).[11, 18, 29,42]

The correct imaging diagnosis of a neural tumor requires a thorough knowledge of the normal anatomy of the major nerves in the neck. A tumor arising from the vagus nerve manifests as a mass in the anterior triangle, displacing the internal or common carotid artery anteromedially and the

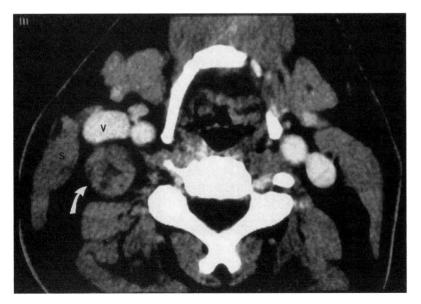

Figure 17–32. Schwannoma. Axial contrast-enhanced CT scan at the level of the hyoid bone demonstrates a heterogeneous mass (*curved white arrow*) deep to the right sternocleidomastoid muscle. An initial radiographic diagnosis of nodal metastases was offered because of the location of the mass posterior to the internal jugular vein (v) and the patient's history of prior right facial melanoma.

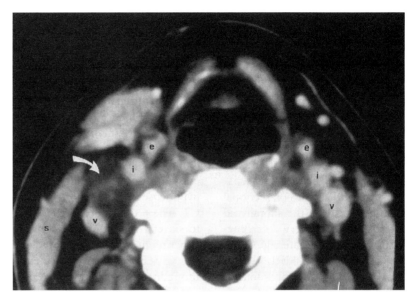

Figure 17–33. Vagal schwannoma. Axial contrast-enhanced CT scan at the level of the thyroid notch demonstrates a predominantly low-density mass (*curved white arrow*) deep to the anterior margin of the right sternocleidomastoid muscle (s) that is splaying the internal jugular vein (v) and the internal carotid artery (I). e, External carotid artery.

internal jugular vein posterolaterally (Fig. 17–33).[14] Neoplasms of the cervical nerve roots manifest a mass in the posterior triangle, which may extend into one of the neural foramina of the cervical spine (Fig. 17–34). Sympathetic chain tumors demonstrate a constant relationship with the longus colli muscles. Brachial plexus schwannomas and neurofibromas in the infrahyoid neck often displace the anterior scalene muscle anteriorly.[39]

Masses of Mesenchymal Origin

Lipomas are the most common cervical neoplasms of mesenchymal origin. They typically manifest as painless, slow-growing masses, occurring most commonly in the midline of posterior neck or the posterior triangle. Their CT appearance—a homogeneous, nonenhancing mass isodense with subcutaneous fat—is diagnostic (Fig. 17–35).[33,44] The overwhelming majority of lipomas identified on MRI are isointense to subcutaneous fat on all pulse sequences. Lipomas may or may not have a demonstrable capsule on sectional images. Liposarcomas arise from totipotential mesenchymal cells and are rarely encountered in the head and neck. Liposarcomas occur de novo and are not the result of malignant degeneration of preexisting lipomas. Liposarcomas are differentiated from lipomas on the basis of their faster growth rate and the presence of soft tissue and mucoid elements admixed with fat on sectional imaging.

None of the remaining mesenchymal tumors can be confidently diagnosed by sectional imaging alone. These rare lesions tend to appear largely isodense or isointense to skeletal muscle on noncontrast CT or T1-weighted MR images. Inhomogeneous contrast enhancement is usually observed. Rhabdomyosarcoma and other malignant mesenchymal tumors tend to destroy bone and distort soft tissue planes.[16] Desmoids and other benign mesenchymal tumors tend to have sharply circumscribed borders and typically do not infiltrate adjacent soft tissue or destroy bone.[8] The primary role of imaging is one of lesion localization, not lesion characterization.

Masses Arising from the Aerodigestive Tract

Masses may be detected on sectional images of the neck that represent cervical extensions of diseases arising within the oral cavity, larynx, or hypopharynx. A *ranula* is a mucous retention cyst that arises from an obstructed sublingual or minor salivary gland in the floor of the mouth. Simple ranulas are limited to the sublingual space and are seen as intraoral mass lesions. Diving (or plunging) ranulas herniate through or around the mylohyoid muscle and extend into the submandibular triangle. Diving ranulas have been likened to pancreatic pseudoceles because they both contain proteolytic enzymes that allow the mass to infiltrate adjacent tissues.

On CT, ranulas are thin-walled unilocular homogeneous cystic lesions. As with congenital cystic masses, prior infection or surgical intervention results in septations or irregular rim enhancement (Fig. 17–36).[8] On MRI, ranulas are typically hypointense to skeletal muscle on T1-weighted images and isointense to cerebrospinal fluid on T2-weighted images. An imaging diagnosis of diving ranula should be considered only when the lesion abuts or involves the sublingual space. The multiplanar capacity of MRI may facilitate documentation of a *tail of tissue* within the floor of mouth.[18]

A laryngocele is an abnormal dilatation of the saccule (appendix) of the laryngeal ventricle. Although a small proportion of laryngoceles are congenital, the majority are the result of chronic increases in intralaryngeal pressure. Neoplasms or localized inflammation and edema may partially obstruct the ventricle. The resulting ball-valve mechanism traps air within the saccule. Mucus produced by the respiratory epithelium of the ventricle may result in a fluid-filled laryngocele (*laryngeal mucocele*). Internal laryngoceles are limited to the paralaryngeal space. External or combined internal and external laryngoceles extend from the paralaryngeal space into the anterior triangle of the neck via fenestrations in the thyrohyoid membrane.[9] On CT or MRI, the external component of a laryngocele appears as

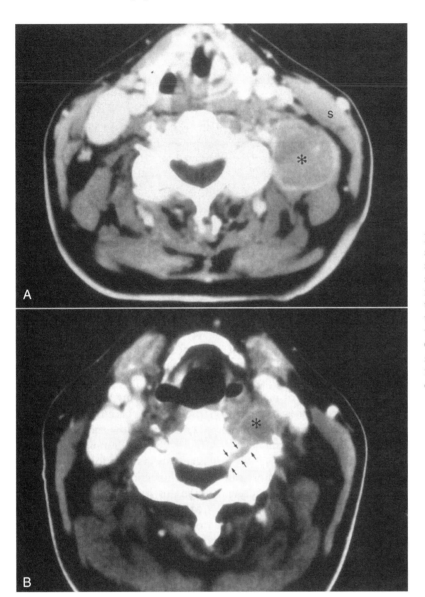

Figure 17–34. Dorsal cervical nerve root schwannoma. *A,* Axial contrast-enhanced CT scan at the level of the thyroid cartilages demonstrates a rim-enhancing solid posterior triangle mass *(asterisk)* deep to the left sternocleidomastoid muscle (S). On this single image, differentiation of neural tumor from enhancing lymph node would be impossible. *B,* Axial contrast-enhanced CT scan at the level of the hyoid bone demonstrates that the mass *(asterisk)* involves the neural foramen *(arrows),* allowing the correct radiologic diagnosis of neural tumor.

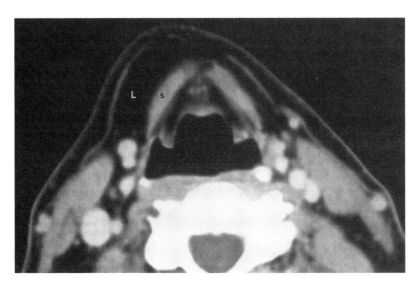

Figure 17–35. Lipoma. Axial contrast-enhanced CT image at the level of the thyroid notch in an adolescent patient demonstrates a uniform-fat-density mass in the anterior triangle (L), superficial to the right strap muscles (S). Imaging was performed to exclude the possibility of thyroglossal duct cyst. Compare with Figure 17–22.

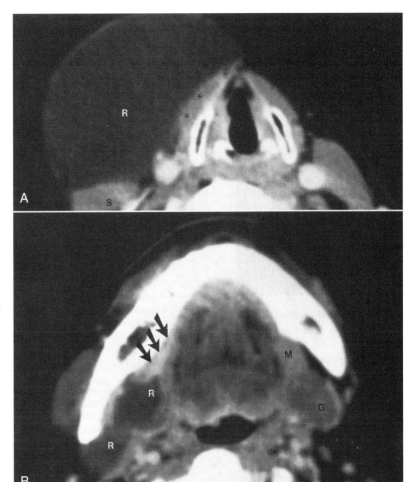

Figure 17–36. Ranula. *A,* Axial contrast-enhanced CT scan at the level of the thyroid cartilage demonstrates a unilocular cystic anterior triangle mass deforming the anterior margin of the right sternocleidomastoid muscle (S). On the basis of this single image, differential diagnosis would include second branchial cleft cyst, lymphangioma, and necrotic lymph node. Thyroglossal duct cyst should be excluded from the differential diagnosis because the mass is extrinsic to the strap muscles (*asterisks*). *B,* Axial contrast-enhanced CT image at the level of the mandible demonstrates the origin of the ranula in the posterior oral cavity, medial to the enhancing mylohyoid muscle (*arrows*). M, Right mylohyoid muscle; G, right submandibular gland.

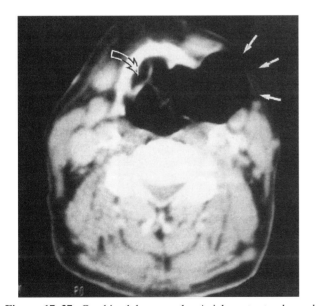

Figure 17–37. Combined laryngocele. Axial contrast-enhanced CT image at the level of the hyoid bone demonstrates a thin-walled, air-filled, right anterior triangle mass (*white arrows*) in direct continuity with the left paralaryngeal space. *Curved arrow,* right paralaryngeal space.

a thin-rimmed, fluid-filled or air-filled mass directly lateral to the thyrohyoid membrane. Continuity with the internal component can be demonstrated on axial or direct coronal images (Fig. 17–37).

A *pharyngocele* is an abnormal dilatation of the piriform sinus, which may also herniate through the thyrohyoid membrane to manifest in the anterior triangle. The less common pharyngocele is differentiated from a laryngocele by the demonstration of continuity with the piriform sinus rather than the laryngeal ventricle. Neoplasms or abscesses involving the apex of the piriform sinus may extend into the anterior triangle of the infrahyoid neck through the cricothyroid membrane.[35]

References

1. Albertyn LE, Alcock MK: Diagnosis of internal jugular vein thrombosis. Radiology 162:502, 1987.
2. Benson MT, Dalen K, Marcuso AA, et al: Congenital anomalies of the branchial apparatus: Embryology and pathologic anatomy. Radiographics 12:943, 1992.
3. Bertrand M, Chen JT, Lipshitz HL: Lymph node calcification in Hodgkin's disease after chemotherapy. AJR 129:1108, 1977.
4. Braun IF, Hoffman JC Jr, Malko JA, et al: Jugular venous thrombosis: MR imaging. Radiology 157:357, 1985.
5. Brereton ND, Johnson RE: Calcification in mediastinal lymph nodes after radiation therapy of Hodgkin's disease. Radiology 112:705, 1973.
6. Coit WE, Harnsgerger HR, Osborn AG, et al: Ranulas and their mimics: CT evaluation. Radiology 163:211, 1987.

7. Davis WL, Harnsberger HR, Smoker WR, et al: Retropharyngeal space: Evaluation of normal anatomy and diseases with CT and MR imaging. Radiology 174:59, 1990.

8. Egund N, Ekeland L, Sako M, Persson B: CT of soft tissue tumors. AJR 137:725, 1981.

9. Glazer HS, Mauro MA, Aronberg DJ, et al: Computed tomography of laryngoceles. AJR 140:549, 1983.

10. Grodinsky M, Holyoke EA: The fasciae and fascial spaces of the head, neck and adjacent regions. Am J Anat 367, 1938.

11. Harnsberger HR, Mancuso AA, Muraki AS, et al: Branchial cleft anomalies and their mimics: computed tomographic evaluation. Radiology 152:739, 1984.

12. Holliday RA, Prendergast NC: Imaging inflammatory processes of the oral cavity and suprahyoid neck. Oral Max Surg Clin North Am 4:215, 1992.

13. Hollinshead WH: Textbook of Anatomy, 3rd ed. New York, Harper & Row, 1974.

14. Jacobs JM, Harnsberger HR, Lufkin RB, et al: Vagal neuropathy: Evaluation with CT and MR imaging. Radiology 164:97, 1987.

15. Katz AD, Passy V, Kaplan L: Neurogenous neoplasms of the major nerves of face and neck. Arch Surg 102:51, 1971.

16. Latack JT, Hutchinson RJ, Heyn RM: Imaging of rhabdomyosarcomas of the head and neck. AJNR 8:353, 1985.

17. Levitt GW: Cervical fascia and deep neck infections. Otol Clin North Am 9:703, 1976.

18. Mancuso AA, Dillon WP: The neck. Radiol Clin North Am 27: 407, 1989.

19. Mancuso AA, Hanafee WN: Oral cavity and oropharynx including tongue base, floor of the mouth and mandible. In Computed Tomography and Magnetic Resonance Imaging of the Head and Neck, 2nd ed. Baltimore, Williams & Wilkins, 1985.

20. Mancuso AA, Harnsberger HR, Muraki AS, et al: Computed tomography of cervical and retropharyngeal lymph nodes: Normal anatomy, variants of normal and applications in staging head and neck cancer. I: Normal anatomy. Radiology 148:709, 1983.

21. Mancuso AA, Harnsberger HR, Muraki AS, et al: Computed tomography of cervical and retropharyngeal lymph nodes: Normal anatomy, variants of normal and applications in staging head and neck cancer. II: Pathology. Radiology 148:715, 1983.

22. New GB, Erich JB: Dermoid cyst of the head and neck. Surg Gynecol Obstet 65:38, 1937.

23. Nyberg DA, Jeffrey RB, Brant-Zawadzki M, et al: Computed tomography of cervical infections. J Comput Assist Tomogr 9:288, 1985.

24. Ogura JH, Biller HF: Head and neck—surgical management. JAMA 221:77, 1972.

25. Olsen WL, Dillon WP, Kelly WM, et al: MR imaging of paragangliomas. AJR 148:201, 1987.

26. Paonessa DF, Goldstein JC: Anatomy and physiology of head and neck infections. Otol Clin North Am 9:561, 1976.

27. Pratt LW: Familial carotid body tumors. Arch Otolaryngol 97:334, 1973.

28. Reede DL, Bergeron RT: Cervical tuberculous adenitis: CT manifestations. Radiology 154:701, 1985.

29. Reede DL, Bergeron RT: CT of cervical lymph nodes. J Otolaryngol 11:411, 1982.

30. Reede DL, Bergeron RT, Som PM: CT of thyroglossal duct cyst. Radiology 157:121, 1985.

31. Reede DL, Som PM: Lymph nodes. In Som PM, Bergeron RT (eds): Head and Neck Imaging, 2nd ed. St. Louis, 1991, CV Mosby.

32. Reede DL, Whelan MA, Bergeron RT: CT of the soft tissue structures of the neck. Radiol Clin North Am 22:239, 1984.

33. Reede DL, et al: Nonnodal pathologic conditions of the neck. In Som PM, Bergeron RT (eds): Head and Neck Imaging, 2nd ed. St. Louis, CV Mosby.

34. Rouviere H: Lymphatic system of the head and neck. In Anatomy of the Human Lymphatic System (transl. M Tobias). Ann Arbor, MI, Edwards Brothers, 1938.

35. Schwartz JM, Holliday RA, Breda SB: CT diagnosis of piriform sinus perforation. J Comput Assist Tomogr 12:869, 1988.

36. Shah JP, Strong E, Spiro RH, Vikram B: Surgical grand rounds, neck dissection: Current status and future possibilities. Clin Bull 11: 25, 1981.

37. Shumrick DA: Biopsy of head and neck lesions. In Paparella MN, Shumrick DA (eds): Otolaryngology, vol 1. Philadelphia, WB Saunders, 1973.

38. Siegel MJ, Glazer HS, St Amour TE, et al: Lymphangiomas in children: MR imaging. Radiology 170:467, 1989.

39. Silver AJ, Mawad ME, Hilal SK, et al: Computed tomography of the carotid space and related cervical spaces. Part II: Neurogenic tumors. Radiology 150:729, 1984.

40. Simpson GT: The evaluation of neck masses of unknown etiology. Otol Clin North Am 13:489, 1980.

41. Smoker WRK, Harnsberger HR: Normal anatomy of the neck. In Som PM, Bergeron RT (eds): Head and Neck Imaging, 2nd ed. St. Louis, CV Mosby, 1991.

42. Som PM: Review: Detection of metastasis in cervical lymph nodes: CT and MR criteria and differential diagnosis. AJR 158:961, 1992.

43. Som PM, Biller HF, Lawson W, et al: Parapharyngeal space masses: An updated protocol based on 104 cases. Radiology 153:149, 1984.

44. Som PM, Scherl MP, Rao VM, Biller HF, et al: Rare presentations of ordinary lipomas of the head and neck. AJNR 7:657, 1986.

45. van den Brekel MHW, Stel HV, Castelijns JA, et al: Cervical lymph node metastasis: Assessment of radiologic criteria. Radiology 177: 379, 1990.

46. Weingast BR: Congenital lymphangiectasia with fetal cystic hygroma: Report of two cases with coexistent Down's syndrome. J Clin Ultrasound 16:663, 1988.

47. Yousem DM, SOM PM, Hackney DB, et al: Central nodal necrosis and extracapsular neoplastic spread in cervical lymph nodes: MR imaging versus CT. Radiology 182:753, 1992.

48. Zadvinskis DP, Benson MT, Kerr HH, et al: Congenital malformations of the cervicothoracic lymphatic system: Embryology and pathogenesis. Radiographics 12:1175, 1992.

49. Zoarski GH, Mackey JK, Arzai Y, et al: Head and neck: Initial clinical experience with fast spin-echo MR imaging. Radiology 188: 323, 1993.

18

The Larynx

Hugh D. Curtin

Imaging of the larynx can be an extremely difficult endeavor. The anatomy is complex. The target moves with every breath and every swallow. In certain situations, however, imaging addresses questions that the clinician has difficulty in answering and can make a considerable difference in treatment planning.

Imaging must be considered in light of the capabilities of modern endoscopy.[1, 10, 18] As the technology of imaging has progressed, so too has the instrumentation available for direct visualization. The mucosa can be examined thoroughly. To be relevant, imaging must provide information that cannot be obtained by direct visualization. Thus, the usual intent of the radiologist is to evaluate the deeper tissues. In some cases, a bulky lesion of the upper larynx may block the view of the lower larynx, and imaging may assist in defining caudal extent of disease.

The radiologist seeking to assess laryngeal pathology obviously must be familiar with the anatomy. The disease processes and their behavior are important. The radiologist must also be familiar with the available therapeutic options to emphasize the information that will be important in making clinical decisions.

This chapter begins with a discussion of anatomy, including the normal appearance in the various imaging planes. A brief mention of technical considerations in applying magnetic resonance imaging (MRI) and computed tomography (CT) scans to the task of examining the larynx is followed by descriptions of imaging of various pathologic conditions. The important clinical considerations in each disease are stressed.

Anatomy

The larynx is a system of mucosal folds supported by a cartilaginous framework.[15] Tension and movement of the mucosal folds are accomplished by the actions of small muscles pulling against the cartilaginous framework.

The clinical organization of the larynx emphasizes the mucosal anatomy, making the mucosa a good starting point for the present discussion. This concept is particularly important to the radiologist because descriptions of tumors must encompass the relationship to the landmarks on the mucosal surface.

From the superior view (the view of the endoscopist), the first landmark seen is the *epiglottis*. The upper edge of the epiglottis represents the most superior limit of the larynx. The epiglottis is the anterior boundary of the entrance into the larynx. Anteriorly, two small sulci—the *valleculae*—separate the free portion of the epiglottis from the base of the tongue (Fig. 18–1). From the lateral margin of the epiglottis, the aryepiglottic (AE) folds curve around to the small interarytenoid notch. Together these structures complete the boundaries of the airway at the entrance into the larynx.

The inner mucosal surface of the larynx, or *endolarynx*, can be thought of as the working part of the organ. Two prominent parallel folds stretch from front to back along the lateral aspect of each side of the airway (Figs. 18–2 and 18–3; see also Fig. 18–1). These are the true and false vocal cords or folds, and they are in the horizontal plane. The *true cord* (the *glottis*) is the key functional component in the generation of voice and has a fine edge at the medial margin. The more superiorly placed *false vocal fold* has a more blunted medial edge.

Separating these two folds is one of the most important landmarks in the larynx. The *ventricle* is a thin cleft between the *true cord* and the *false cord*, stretching from the most anterior limit of the cord almost to the posterior limit of the larynx.

Above the false cord the mucosa sweeps upward and outward to the *aryepiglottic (AE) folds*. Inferiorly, the mucosa covering of the true cord sweeps outward into the subglottic area, eventually merging smoothly with the mucosa of the trachea.

A final important mucosal landmark is the *anterior commissure*, the point where the true vocal cords converge anteriorly to attach to the inner (posterior) surface of the anterior angle of the thyroid cartilage.

The three parallel structures—the true cord, the false cord, and the ventricle—organize the larynx into three regions: the supraglottis, the glottis, and the subglottis.

The true cord is the glottis. The glottic region of the larynx extends from the upper surface of the true cord to a line somewhat arbitrarily chosen as being 1 cm below the level of the ventricle. The subglottic region is between this arbitrary line and the inferior edge of the cricoid cartilage, the lower margin of the larynx. There is no defined mucosal structure representing the exact boundary or separation of the glottic and subglottic regions.

The supraglottic region is the part of the larynx that is above the ventricle. This region includes the false cords, the epiglottis, and the AE folds.

Laryngeal Skeleton

The laryngeal cartilages are the supporting framework of the larynx. The major cartilages include the cricoid, the thyroid, the arytenoid, and the epiglottic. The smaller cartilages, the corniculate and the cuneiform, reside in the aryepiglottic fold and are not of particular importance to the radiologist.

The *cricoid cartilage* is the foundation of the larynx and

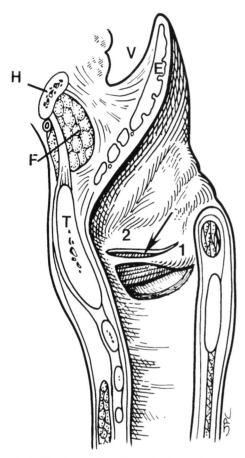

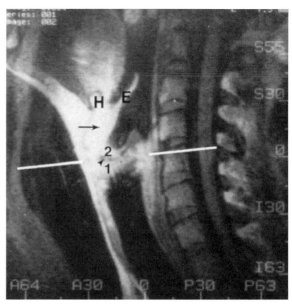

Figure 18–2. Sagittal T1-weighted MRI study. This sagittal slice is just off midline. The slice shows the anterior part of the true cord (1) and false cord (2) separated by the low signal intensity of the laryngeal ventricle *(arrowhead)*. The axial image plane should be along the ventricle, as indicated by the white line. The preepiglottic fat is shown by an *arrow*. E, epiglottis; H, hyoid. (From Curtin HD: MR and CT of the larynx. In Thrall JH [ed]: Current Practice of Radiology, 3rd ed. St. Louis, Mosby–Year Book, 1994.)

Figure 18–1. The larynx is split sagittally, with a view of the lateral wall of the airway. The mucosa over the true cord (1) has been removed to show the thyroarytenoid muscle (TAM), which extends from the arytenoid to the thyroid cartilage. The upper edge of the muscle *(arrow)* indicates the level of the ventricle. The false cord (2) is just above the ventricle. E, epiglottis; F, preepiglottic fat; H, hyoid; T, thyroid cartilage; V, vallecula. (From Curtin HD: The larynx. In Som PM, Bergeron RT [eds]: Head and Neck Imaging, 2nd ed. St. Louis, Mosby–Year Book, 1991.)

is the only complete ring. The posterior part is larger than the anterior, giving the cartilage the appearance of a signet ring facing posteriorly. The lower margin of the cricoid cartilage represents the lower margin of the larynx.

The *thyroid* and the *arytenoid cartilages* articulate with the cricoid. The thyroid cartilage is large and can be thought of as forming a shield for most of the inner larynx. The arytenoid cartilages perch on the superior edge of the posterior cricoid.

The arytenoid cartilage spans the ventricle. The upper arytenoid is at the level of the supraglottic larynx. The lower arytenoid has a pointed process anteriorly, called the vocal process. Because of its characteristic shape and position, the arytenoid cartilage can help localize the ventricle on axial scanning. This is most helpful on CT scans, where the vocal process may be directly visualized. The upper margin of the arytenoid is at the level of the lower false cord just above the ventricle. The vocal process is at the level of the true cord just below the ventricle. Indeed,

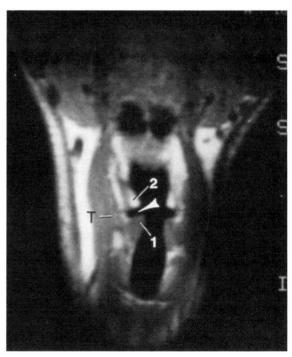

Figure 18–3. Coronal T1-weighted image. This slice would be perpendicular to the white line in Figure 18–2 at the level of 1 and 2. The thyroarytenoid muscle (1) makes up the bulk of the true cord. The paraglottic space at the level of the false cord (2) is filled predominantly with fat. The ventricle is the air-filled slit *(arrowhead)* between the two. T, thyroid cartilage. (From Curtin HD: MR and CT of the larynx. In Thrall JH [ed]: Current Practice of Radiology, 3rd ed. St. Louis, Mosby–Year Book, 1994.)

the vocal ligament, which represents the medial margin of the true cord, attaches to the vocal process.

The epiglottic cartilage, except for its superior tip, is totally contained within the external framework of the larynx. This cartilage is made up of elastic fibrocartilage and does not calcify. Grossly, this cartilage has multiple perforations resembling more a mesh than a solid plate, and the epiglottic cartilage is thus not a major barrier to tumor spread. Inferiorly, the epiglottic cartilage is connected to the inner surface of the anterior part of the thyroid cartilage by the thyroepiglottic ligament.

Muscles and Ligaments

The cartilages are connected by a system of muscles and ligaments. Several muscles are mentioned in the remainder of the chapter. One deserves special attention. The *thyroarytenoid muscle* (TAM) stretches from the arytenoid cartilage to the inner surface of the anterior thyroid cartilage (Fig. 18–4; see Fig. 18–1). This muscle parallels the true cord and makes up the bulk of the true cord.

The cricothyroid and thyrohyoid ligaments span the greater part of the intervals between the cricoid cartilage, the thyroid cartilage, and the hyoid bone and represent, along with the cartilages, the outer limits of the larynx.

Two membranes are found just deep to the mucosa. The conus elasticus (also called the *cricovocal ligament* or *lateral cricothyroid ligament*) stretches from the vocal ligament to the upper margin of the cricoid cartilage. Some descriptions indicate the membrane attaching to the inner

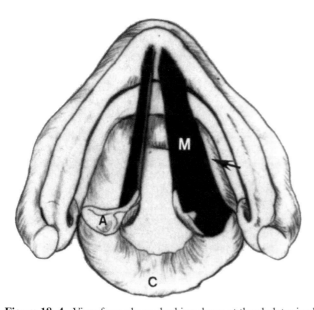

Figure 18–4. View from above, looking down at the skeletonized larynx. The thyroarytenoid muscle (M) is seen stretching from the arytenoid to the thyroid cartilage. *Arrow* indicates the point where paraglottic spread of tumor is expected to intersect the lateral cord. The opposite side shows the vocal ligament stretching from the vocal process of arytenoid to the thyroid cartilage. A, arytenoid; C, cricoid. (From Curtin HD: MR and CT of the larynx. In Thrall JH [ed]: Current Practice of Radiology, 3rd ed. St. Louis, Mosby–Year Book, 1994.)

surface of the ring as well. This membrane or fascial layer merges with the anterior cricothyroid ligament in the anterior midline.

A similar structure is seen in the supraglottic larynx. A thin ligament called the *ventricular ligament* is found in the lower margin of the false cord and the quadrangular membrane sweeps superiorly from the ventricular ligament terminating in the AE fold.

The fan-shaped hyoepiglottic ligament stretches from the epiglottis to the hyoid bone and divides the supraglottic larynx into a superior (suprahyoepiglottic) and an inferior (infrahyoepiglottic) area.[27]

Spaces

The paraglottic space and the preepiglottic space are situated between the mucosal surface and the cartilaginous outer limit of the larynx.

The paraglottic space is found laterally and represents much of the soft tissue wall of the larynx (Figs. 18–5 and 18–6). Although descriptions of the paraglottic space vary, I am using Tucker and Smith's original descriptions,[25] with the medial boundary represented by the conus elasticus and quadrangular membrane. The lateral boundary is the external skeleton of the larynx, formed predominantly by the inner cortex of the thyroid cartilage. At the level of the supraglottic larynx, the paraglottic space is filled mostly with fat. Below the ventricle, the TAM fills the paraglottic region.

A small recess of the ventricle, called the *laryngeal saccule* or *appendix*, extends upward into the paraglottic space of the supraglottic larynx. This structure is within the paraglottic fat lateral to the quadrangular membrane.

The preepiglottic space is between the epiglottis posteriorly and the thyroid cartilage and thyrohyoid membrane anteriorly.

The hyoepiglottic ligament forms the roof of the preepiglottic and paraglottic spaces.

Imaging Considerations

Although CT scanning is limited to the axial plane, it has the advantage of fast imaging speed. The advent of multidetector CT represents a significant improvement in the application to the larynx.[6] The scan is faster and thus allows the entire larynx to be covered in a single breathhold. The thinner-slice thickness allows multiplanar reformatted images comparable in quality to direct imaging.

At present, magnetic resonance imaging (MRI) is better at differentiating various soft tissues compared with CT. MRI may allow better analysis of potential cartilage invasion or improved definition of the tumor muscle interface.

Motion artifact is a significant problem in imaging of the larynx. CT scanning tries to avoid the problem by its use of fast imaging. The spiral acquisition may cover the larynx in 10 to 20 seconds. The examination can be performed during slow, shallow respiration, or the scan can be done with the breath held.

More elaborate schemes are required for MRI studies.

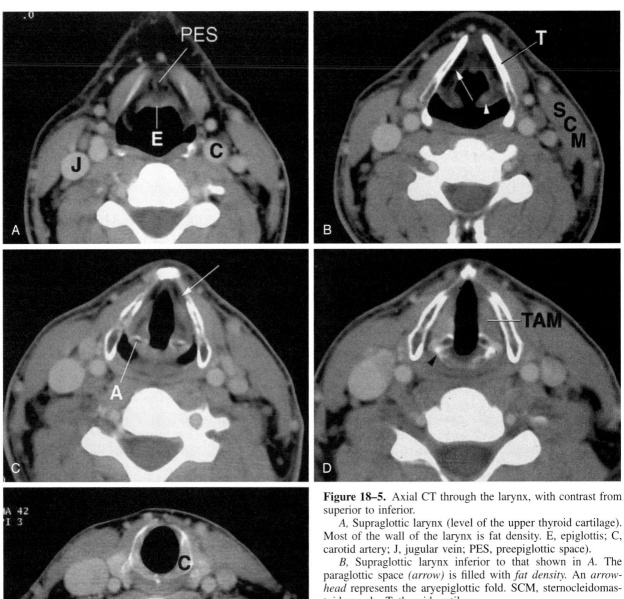

Figure 18–5. Axial CT through the larynx, with contrast from superior to inferior.

A, Supraglottic larynx (level of the upper thyroid cartilage). Most of the wall of the larynx is fat density. E, epiglottis; C, carotid artery; J, jugular vein; PES, preepiglottic space).

B, Supraglottic larynx inferior to that shown in *A.* The paraglottic space *(arrow)* is filled with *fat density.* An *arrowhead* represents the aryepiglottic fold. SCM, sternocleidomastoid muscle; T, thyroid cartilage.

C, Just above the ventricle (level of the false cord). The paraglottic space is filled with fat *(arrow).* The upper arytenoid cartilage (A) is visible.

D, True cord level. The thyroarytenoid muscle (TAM) fills the paraglottic space. The cricoarytenoid joint is shown by an *arrowhead.* The upper margin of the cricoid cartilage is visible.

E, Subglottis. The mucosa is tightly applied to the inner surface of the cricoid ring (C) without intervening soft tissue.

At our institution, before the examination begins, usually before the patient is placed on the table, the patient practices breathing with the abdominal muscles rather than with the chest muscles. Surface coils, a necessity in laryngeal MRI studies, are positioned so that any chest movement does not bump the coil. Although speed of imaging is always an advantage, some have recommended using up to multiple excitations on the T1-weighted sequence. This gives longer imaging times but averages out some of the motion. Fast spin-echo imaging also shortens imaging times.

The use of contrast agents is controversial. At our institution, contrast material is usually used for tumor imaging. Gadolinium, combined with fat suppression, has given good preliminary results.

Imaging emphasizes the importance of the ventricle, and axial images are taken along the plane of the ventricle. The position of the ventricle is estimated in axial images by the

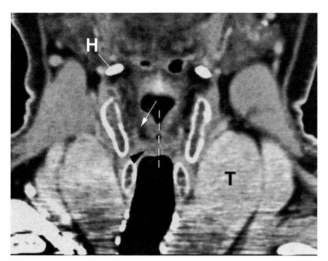

Figure 18–6. Reformatted coronal image through the larynx (multidetector CT). The patient is holding his breath. The position of the closed airway is represented by the *dashed line.* Note the density of fat in the paraglottic space at the supraglottic level *(arrow)*. The thyroarytenoid muscle *(arrowhead)* forms the bulk of the true cord (glottic level). The thyroid cartilage and cricoid cartilage are also visible. H, hyoid bone; T, thyroid gland.

appearance of the cartilages or by the transition from the fat to muscle in the paraglottic region.

In MRI studies, the coronal images are perpendicular to the ventricle. Even if the ventricle is not actually visible, its position can be predicted by the transition from fat to muscle in the paraglottic space.

Pathology

Most laryngeal imaging is performed in order to evaluate patients with tumors of or trauma to the larynx.[11–14, 21, 23, 24] The tumors can be mucosal or submucosal. In most instances, the larynx is visualized directly—if not by endoscopy, at least by mirror—and the radiologist should emphasize information that is not obtainable by direct visualization.

Mucosal Tumors

Most tumors that come to imaging are squamous cell carcinomas arising from the mucosa of the larynx.[2] With the possible exception of rare tumors arising deep within the ventricle, these tumors are detected before imaging. Indeed, imaging currently cannot rule out a small malignancy and thus is not a substitute for direct visualization.

The otolaryngologist can assess smaller lesions completely. The margins of a small tumor may be readily visible, with no further information required. Alternatively, a patient with a large tumor may obviously require a total laryngectomy, and imaging may not add significant information. Imaging is most important for the patients with moderate-sized tumors in whom some sort of voice-sparing procedure is considered. Such treatment options include partial laryngectomies and radiotherapy. The feasi-

bility of these therapies depends on the origin and the extent of the tumor. The following discussion of imaging of carcinoma of the larynx is organized according to the tumor's site of origin.

Supraglottic Tumors

The usual voice-sparing surgical option for supraglottic squamous cell carcinoma is the supraglottic laryngectomy (Fig. 18–7). The resection is made along the ventricle, and the surgeon removes the entire supraglottic larynx, leaving at least one—and usually both—arytenoid cartilages.[1, 10, 18, 26] The patient retains the true cords and can thus generate voice in the usual manner. The protective function of the supraglottic larynx, particularly the epiglottis, is lost, and the patient must learn how to swallow without aspirating.

Tumor crossing the ventricle is the primary contraindication for the supraglottic laryngectomy (Box 18–1). The incision passing along the ventricle would cut through tumor. Tumor growing along the mucosa to reach the true cord may be obvious at direct visualization. In a smaller lesion, the tumor may invade into the deeper tissues and follow the paraglottic space around the ventricle into the lateral edge of the true cord. This type of spread is unusual

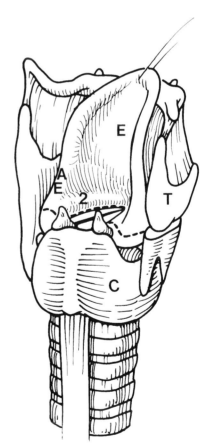

Figure 18–7. Diagram of a supraglottic laryngectomy. The *dotted line* shows the incision of a supraglottic laryngectomy and passes along the ventricle between the true cord and the false cord (2). AE, aryepiglottic fold; C, cricoid cartilage; E, epiglottis; T, thyroid cartilage. (From Curtin HD: Imaging of the larynx: Current concepts. Radiology 173:1–11, 1989.)

as an isolated phenomenon but should be checked during imaging of a supraglottic tumor.

Box 18–1. Contraindications to Supraglottic Laryngectomy

- Tumor extension onto the cricoid cartilage
- Bilateral arytenoid involvement
- Arytenoid fixation
- Extension onto the glottis or impaired vocal cord mobility
- Thyroid cartilage invasion
- Involvement of the apex of the piriform sinus or postcricoid region
- Involvement of the base of the tongue more than 1 cm posteriorly to the circumvallate papillae

---

From Lawson W, Biller HF, Suen JY: Cancer of the larynx. In Suen JY, Myers E (eds): Cancer of the Head and Neck. New York, Churchill Livingstone, 1989, pp 533–591.

Axial imaging parallels the ventricle and, therefore, is somewhat limited in its ability to identify the level of this key structure. The paraglottic space of the false cord level is predominantly fat, but at the true cord level it is predominantly muscle. The transition between the two represents the approximate level of the ventricle.

If a normal slice can be found below the tumor but still within the supraglottic larynx, the supraglottic laryngectomy is technically possible (Fig. 18–8). If the tumor can be identified at the level of the cord as well as in the supraglottis, the decision is again made and the patient cannot have the usual supraglottic resection. If surgery is chosen as the therapy, the patient must have a total laryngectomy.

On axial images, the lateral edge of the TAM should be carefully examined for the earliest evidence of transglottic spread. A narrow extension of the paraglottic fat is often seen along the outer margin of the muscle. Tumor spreading around the ventricle will grow into this fat and eventu-

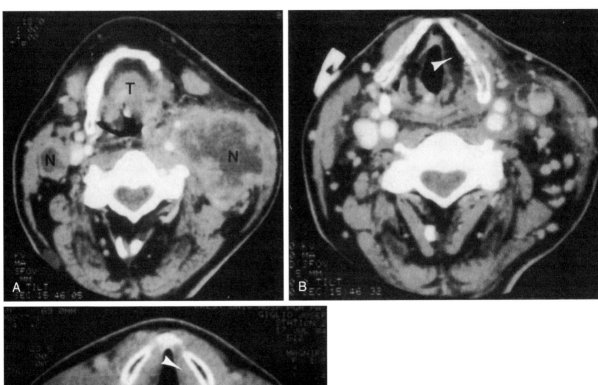

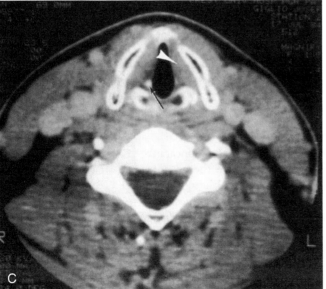

Figure 18–8. CT scan of a supraglottic tumor separated from the ventricle. *A,* Axial slice shows the tumor (T) at the level of the hyoid bone. Note the metastatic nodes (N). The left node shows considerable irregularity, indicating extracapsular tumor spread. *B,* The axial slice, slightly lower than in *A,* is normal. The normal paraglottic fat *(arrowhead)* indicates that the slice is at the supraglottic level and thus between the tumor and the ventricle. *C,* A slice through the true vocal cord would show the normal muscle density *(arrowhead).* The vocal process is represented by an *arrow.*

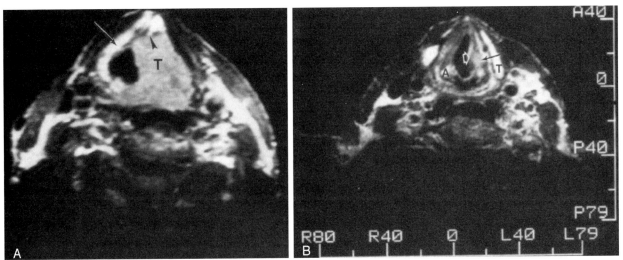

Figure 18–9. Supraglottic tumor with paraglottic spread into the lateral edge of the true cord. *A,* Axial slice through the supraglottic level shows the tumor (T). Note the interface of tumor with fat in the preepiglottic space *(arrowhead)* and the normal paraglottic fat *(arrow)* on the opposite side. *B,* Axial slice at the level of the cord shows a small amount of tumor *(arrow)* prying its way between the thyroid cartilage (T) and the thyroarytenoid muscle (TAM) *(open arrow)*. This is at the true cord level below the level of the ventricle. A, arytenoid. *(B,* From Curtin HD: MR and CT of the larynx. In Thrall JH [ed]: Current Practice of Radiology, 3rd ed. St. Louis, Mosby–Year Book, 1994.)

ally will appear to "pry" the muscle away from the thyroid cartilage.

Tumor can be distinguished readily from the fat in the supraglottic paraglottic space. The interface between tumor and muscle at the true cord level is more difficult to visualize. MRI offers the advantage of better tissue differentiation because of its various pulse sequences, but this advantage can be realized only if the patient is able to control motion (Fig. 18–9).

Coronal images are perpendicular to the ventricle and may also be helpful in showing the relationship between tumor and the lateral aspect of the true cord (Figs. 18–10 and 18–11).

Midline tumor can cross the level of the ventricle to involve the anterior commissure. This area can be difficult to evaluate either by direct visualization or by imaging. If there is deep growth from the anterior commissure into the attachment of the cord or through the cricothyroid membrane, imaging may detect tumor that is unappreciated clinically (see "True Cord").

Anterior growth from a supraglottic carcinoma brings the tumor into the preepiglottic space (see Figs. 18–8 and 18–9). The preepiglottic space as well as the paraglottic space has a rich lymphatic drainage, and tumor invasion heightens the concern regarding nodal metastases. Invasion is easily appreciated on axial imaging because the tumor is contrasted against the fat. Such involvement is not a contraindication to a supraglottic laryngectomy.

Thyroid cartilage invasion is usually considered a contraindication to the supraglottic laryngectomy. Such invasion is uncommon unless the tumor is large and has crossed the ventricle.[16] In such a case, the patient would be excluded as a candidate on the basis of ventricular involvement. Involvement of the epiglottic cartilage is not a contraindication. (Cartilage assessment is discussed in the text on true cord lesions.)

The supraglottic partial laryngectomy is the most accepted surgical therapy for tumors limited to the area above the ventricle. More extensive resections have been used for lesions extending beyond the boundaries of supraglottic laryngectomy.[19] Pearson's near-total laryngectomy is done for supraglottic cancer extending to one cord. The resection

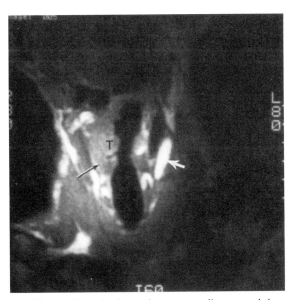

Figure 18–10. Supraglottic carcinoma extending around the ventricle into the lateral cord. The tumor (T) is readily visible to the endoscopist. A small amount of tumor *(arrow)* is seen extending around the lateral aspect of the ventricle into the superolateral margin of the thyroarytenoid muscle (TAM). The mucosa at the true cord level was normal. Thyroid cartilage is represented by a *white arrow.* (From Curtin HD: MR and CT of the larynx. In Thrall JH [ed]: Current Practice of Radiology, 3rd ed. St. Louis, Mosby–Year Book, 1994.)

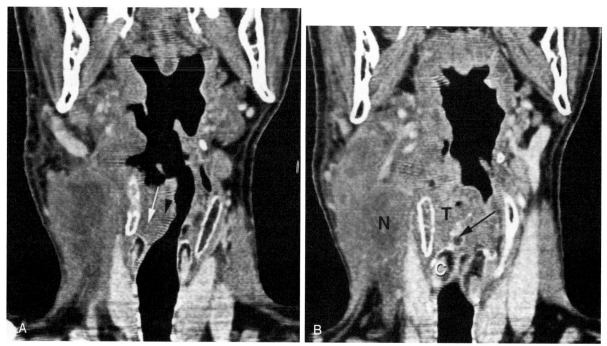

Figure 18–11. Transglottic tumor, reformatted coronal image (multidetector). *A,* The tumor follows *(arrow)* the paraglottic space around the ventricle widening the cord as the tumor infiltrates. An *arrowhead* represents the approximate level of the ventricle. *B,* Note the relationship of the tumor to the arytenoid cartilage *(arrow),* the thyroid cartilage (T) (immediately lateral), and the cricoid (C). N, metastatic node.

is continued to include the cord and to take the upper margin of the cricoid. The supracricoid partial laryngectomy with cricohyoidopexy takes the anterior cords to the level of cricoid. Minor involvement of the thyroid cartilage is not a contraindication. In either of these approaches, the inferior extent remains the most important assessment at imaging.

An alternative to the partial laryngectomies already mentioned is endoscopic laser surgery.[26] Lesions of the suprahyoid epiglottis, the AE fold, and the false cord are more appropriate for this type of surgery compared with lesions of the laryngeal surface of the epiglottis. The latter tumors are partially hidden by the epiglottis and thus are less accessible to endoscopic resection.

Radiation therapy is also performed for supraglottic cancer. The same landmarks and considerations for supraglottic laryngectomy pertain to assessment for radiation therapy. The bulk of the tumor is also a prognostic factor. Patients with larger tumors fare worse than those with smaller tumors. One study used a 6-mL volume as a separation, with larger tumors carrying a much worse prognosis than smaller ones.[20]

Nodal metastases are very common in supraglottic tumors. Metastases can be bilateral.

True Cord

There are several options for therapy of glottic carcinoma, including simple resection, laser resection, and radiotherapy. Vertical hemilaryngectomy may be considered for a lesion involving the true cord. In this procedure, the surgeon removes the true and false cord on one side of the larynx using a vertical incision through the thyroid carti-

lage. The lesion can cross the anterior commissure and involve the anterior one third of the opposite cord and still be treatable by vertical hemilaryngectomy. The incision through the thyroid cartilage is moved laterally toward the opposite side.

Contraindications for vertical hemilaryngectomy are listed in Box 18–2. The most important assessments done at imaging concern inferior extension of the tumor, deep invasion at the anterior commissure, and cartilage invasion. Submucosal superior extension crossing the ventricle into the supraglottic larynx is a problem only occasionally.

Box 18–2. Contraindications to Vertical Frontolateral Hemilaryngectomy*

- Tumor extension from the ipsilateral vocal cord across the anterior commissure to involve more than one third of the contralateral vocal cord
- Extension subglottically >10 mm anteriorly and >5 mm posterolaterally
- Extension across the ventricle to the false cord
- Thyroid cartilage invasion
- Impaired vocal cord mobility a relative contraindication

---

*This technique can still be used if the vocal process and anterior surface of the arytenoid are involved, but involvement of the cricoarytenoid joint, interarytenoid area, opposite arytenoid, or rostrum of the cricoid is a contraindication.

From Lawson W, Biller HF, Suen JY: Cancer of the larynx. In Suen JY, Myers E (eds): Cancer of the Head and Neck. New York, Churchill Livingstone, 1989, pp 533–591.

Inferior extension is quantified relative to the cricoid cartilage. The cricoid cartilage is the foundation of the

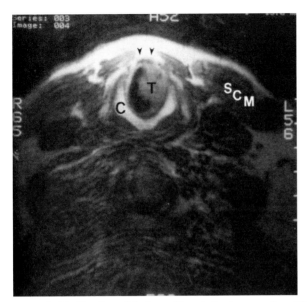

Figure 18–12. Vocal cord lesion with subglottic extension. T1-weighted MRI study. The patient presented with a lesion of the true cord (not shown). The tumor (T) is within the ring of the cricoid cartilage (C). Note the intact fat planes *(arrowheads)* just anterior to the cricothyroid membrane. SCM, sternocleidomastoid. (From Curtin HD: Imaging of the larynx: Current concepts. Radiology 173:1–11, 1989.)

larynx, and most surgeons suggest that even partial resections of this important cartilage are not possible.

At imaging, if the tumor can be identified within the ring of the cricoid cartilage, the standard vertical laryngectomy cannot be done and laryngectomy is usually recommended (Fig. 18–12).

Deep invasion at the anterior commissure may involve the thyroid cartilage or the cricothyroid membrane (Fig. 18–13; see Fig. 18–12).[17] The subtle fat plane anterior to

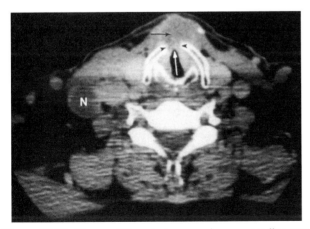

Figure 18–13. Tumor of the anterior commissure extending anteriorly. A small tumor was seen at the anterior commissure *(white arrow).* Anterior extension carried the tumor through the thyroid cartilage *(arrowheads)* with a prominent nodule in the anterior soft tissues *(black arrow).* N, metastatic node. (From Curtin HD: The larynx. In Som PM, Bergeron RT [eds]: Head and Neck Imaging, 2nd ed. St. Louis, Mosby–Year Book, 1991.)

the membrane should be examined closely on the axial image.

Cartilage invasion (discussed next) is considered a contraindication for vertical hemilaryngectomy. Minor thyroid cartilage invasion has been treated with supracricoid partial laryngectomy with cricohyoepiglottopexy.[19] In this procedure, more of the supraglottic larynx is removed and the cricoid cartilage is then suspended from the remaining supraglottic tissues and hyoid bone.

Cartilage Invasion

Cartilage invasion is considered a contraindication to both the standard supraglottic and vertical hemilaryngectomies. The subject is discussed here because such invasion is more of a concern in lesions involving the true cord.

With both CT and MRI studies, the most reliable sign of cartilage involvement is identification of tumor on the extralaryngeal or outer surface of the cartilage. Minor degrees of cartilage invasion can be difficult to detect. The variability of ossification of the major cartilages can lead to problems in detecting cartilage invasion.

The nonossified part of the cartilage can have approximately the same appearance as tumor on CT scans. MRI has the advantage of better tissue discrimination, and although there are no large series available, early results suggest that tumor can be differentiated from nonossified cartilage based on the intensity of the signal.[7, 8]

If signal is bright on the T1-weighted image, that part of the cartilage can reliably be considered normal. The high signal represents fat in ossified cartilage, and carcinoma is never that bright. On T1-weighted images, tumor and nonossified cartilage are usually dark. The nonossified cartilage may be slightly darker than tumor. Regions that are dark on T1-weighted images are examined on the long repetition time (TR) sequence. Nonossified cartilage remains relatively dark on long TR sequence images. Tumor tends to be significantly brighter than nonossified cartilage (Figs. 18–14 and 18–15). One cannot rely on the long TR image alone because fat may be fairly bright, even though the sequence is T2-weighted. Indeed, the tumor may have the same signal as the fat on T2-weighted images particularly if fast spin-echo sequences are used.

Tumor, then, is dark or intermediate on T1-weighted images and usually relatively brighter on T2-weighted images. T2-weighted images show tumor as intermediate to bright. This signal pattern does not definitely indicate tumor. Edema, fibrosis, or even red marrow have also been described with this pattern.[5]

Edema is of particular concern because squamous cell carcinoma often has a peritumoral inflammatory response. Edema may be slightly brighter than tumor on T2-weighted images, but more experience is needed before a definite statement can be made regarding separation of tumor and edema. Edema of the cartilage presumably means that tumor is at least very close. In my experience, at least the perichondrium has been invaded if edema is present in the cartilage.

At CT, irregularity of the inner cortex may suggest that tumor is eroding; however, this sign is questionable because of the variability of ossification. The cortex may be interrupted normally. Asymmetric sclerosis, particularly of

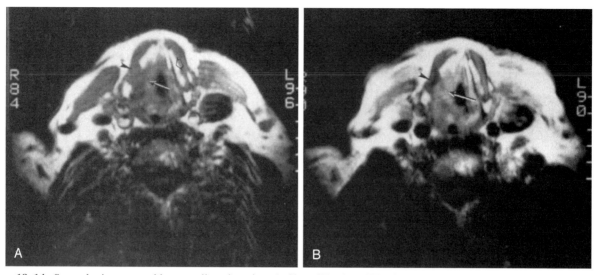

Figure 18–14. Supraglottic tumor without cartilage invasion. *A,* Short TR, short TE. The tumor *(arrow)* abuts an area of the cartilage *(arrowhead)* that has the same signal intensity. On the opposite side, a normal ossified thyroid lamina with bright signal of medullary fat *(open arrow)* is identified. *B,* Long TR, short TE. The tumor *(arrow)* is significantly brighter than the nonossified cartilage *(arrowhead).* (From Curtin HD: MR and CT of the larynx. In Thrall JH [ed]: Current Practice of Radiology, 3rd ed. St. Louis, Mosby–Year Book, 1994.)

the thyroid and cricoid cartilages, may indicate tumor.[4] Tumor may obliterate the medullary fat within the cartilage.

Further study regarding the significance of various signal patterns and CT findings is needed. For instance, the effect of the various imaging findings on prognosis of various therapies, particularly radiotherapy, may potentially change management.[9]

Subglottic Tumors

Subglottic tumors are rare. When they do occur, the only surgical option is almost always a total laryngectomy because of the proximity to the cricoid cartilage.

Hypopharynx

Although the hypopharynx is not actually part of the larynx, it is so intimately associated that discussion is warranted here. Decisions about potential surgical resection usually relate to the proximity of the tumor to landmarks within the larynx, and the assessment is thus quite similar to that of lesions within the larynx itself.

Two regions of the hypopharynx have important relationships to the larynx: the *piriform sinuses* and the *postcricoid region.*

The piriform sinuses indent the posterior wall of the

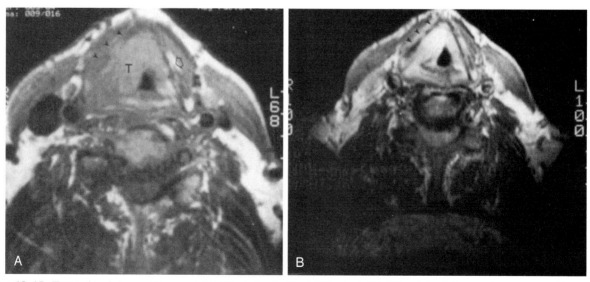

Figure 18–15. Tumor involving cartilage, axial MRI study. *A,* Short TR, short TE T1-weighted image shows tumor (T) against a suspicious area of cartilage *(small arrowheads).* The cartilage has a more intermediate signal rather than the high signal of fat. A normal thyroid lamina is seen on the opposite side *(open arrow).* *B,* Long TR, long TE T2-weighted image shows significant "brightening" compared with that in *A.* The behavior of this area is the same as that of the tumor. Nonossified cartilage remains as a dark linear structure within the higher-intensity tumor. (From Curtin HD: MR and CT of the larynx. In Thrall JH [ed]: Current Practice of Radiology, 3rd ed. St. Louis, Mosby–Year Book, 1994.)

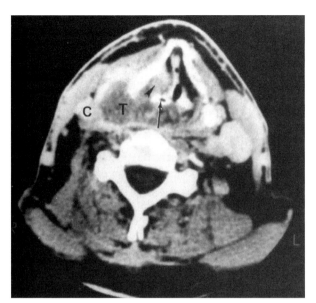

Figure 18–16. Tumor (T) of the piriform sinus. The lesion protrudes through the thyroarytenoid gap between thyroid cartilage and arytenoid *(arrow)*. The tumor thus invades the paraglottic space *(arrowhead)* of the supraglottic larynx. Compare with the fat in the paraglottic space on the normal side. C, carotid artery.

larynx. The anterior wall of the piriform sinuses represents the posterior wall of the paraglottic space. The piriform sinus makes up the lateral aspect of the AE fold.

If a tumor is localized to the upper piriform sinus, a supraglottic resection may be considered along with resection of the tumor. A tumor that invades the paraglottic region of the larynx can follow the paraglottic pathway to reach the level of the cord, and in these patients a total laryngectomy is usually required (Fig. 18–16).

The postcricoid region is that area of the lower hypopharynx that covers the posterior aspect of the cricoid cartilage. To achieve an appropriate margin, the surgeon must usually remove the cricoid and then perform a total laryngectomy. In these patients, the inferior extension within the pharynx should be estimated to help the surgeon decide the appropriate method of reconstructing the food passage.

Lymph Nodes

Metastasis to the lymph nodes is a major consideration in carcinoma of the larynx. The subject of lymph nodes is covered elsewhere in this book, but brief comments about major pathways of spread are appropriate.

Nodal metastases are a major concern with supraglottic tumors. Spread to the jugular nodes occurs very frequently because of the rich lymphatic drainage. The margin of the true cord does not have any lymphatics; therefore, tumors of the true cord do not spread to the lymph nodes unless there is deep invasion or, alternatively, unless the tumor has grown along the mucosa to involve the subglottic region.

Because the subglottic mucosa does have lymphatic drainage, a primary tumor arising in this location or a glottic tumor extending into the area secondarily can metastasize to the nodes. In these patients, the nodes along

the esophagus and in the upper mediastinum become a significant concern.

Radiation Therapy

From a surgical perspective, the evaluation of patients uses landmarks that are slightly more precise, but many of the same findings are appropriate when radiotherapy is chosen as the treatment.

The dimensions of the tumor in the axial plane are relevant, since they reflect the bulk of the tumor and relate to the depth of invasion into the soft tissues.

The vertical extent of the tumor should be estimated, although the precision relating to the ventricle is less crucial. Extension into the subglottic area is very important because the treatment portals may be changed to include the paratracheal and upper mediastinum regions.

Formerly, cartilage involvement was considered a contraindication to radiation therapy. Tumor recurrence is more frequent, as is radiation chondritis and chondronecrosis. More recently, however, some have expressed the opinion that relatively subtle involvement is not an absolute contraindication.

Other Mucosal Tumors

Many benign lesions, such as polyps and papillomas, arise from the mucosa of the larynx. These lesions are seldom evaluated by CT or MRI studies. Submucosal tumors can ulcerate through the mucosa (see "Submucosal Tumors" next).

Although almost all malignancies arising from the mucosa of the larynx are squamous cell carcinoma, occasional malignancies arise from the minor salivary glands with histologies such as adenocarcinoma, adenoid cystic carcinoma, and mucoepidermoid carcinoma.

Verrucous carcinoma is an exophytic, slow-growing variant of squamous cell carcinoma. It does not usually metastasize, but it can be locally aggressive. There are no particular imaging features, but the lesion has a typical exophytic "warty" appearance on direct inspection.

Submucosal Tumors

Lesions presenting beneath an intact mucosa usually arise from the nonepithelial elements of the larynx.[2, 3] Such tumors include chondroid lesions, hemangiomas, neurogenic tumors, and rare lesions such as leiomyoma, rhabdomyoma, and lipomas. Sarcomas arising from the same various mesenchymal elements are often submucosal, but with increasing size they can lead to mucosal ulceration.

In rare instances, a squamous cell carcinoma can appear to be entirely submucosal. Such a lesion arises in the ventricle or ventricular saccule (appendix). The tumor expands upward into the paraglottic space and downward into the true cord rather than medially toward the lumen of the larynx.

A submucosal tumor represents a different problem. Unlike the squamous cell carcinoma, in which the actual tumor can be seen and is easily accessible for biopsy, the submucosal tumor presents as a bulge beneath an intact mucosa. In these patients, imaging is used not only to show

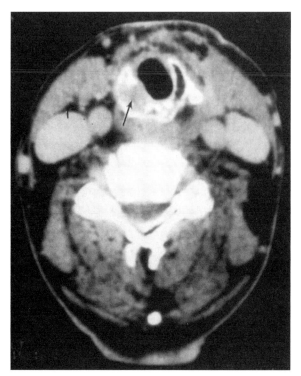

Figure 18–17. Chondroid lesion of the cricoid cartilage. The lesion *(arrow)* expands the cricoid cartilage. The apparent origin in the cartilage suggests the diagnosis. A higher slice showed calcifications.

the extent of the lesion but also to help identify the type of tumor. With certain tumors, the findings are characteristic enough that the diagnosis can be predicted accurately. When the diagnosis is not definitive after imaging, certain findings can still be helpful to the otolaryngologist.

The first question is whether the tumor is a chondroid lesion. Chondrosarcomas and chondromas arise from the cartilaginous framework of the larynx (Figs. 18–17 and 18–18); most arise from the cricoid. The thyroid cartilage is the second most common site of origin. Differentiation

between benign and malignant can be difficult even at histopathologic examination. These tumors can compromise the airway, and treatment is usually surgical. A partial laryngectomy can be curative if the entire lesion is resected. If the cricoid cartilage is extensively involved, a total laryngectomy may be considered because of the key role of this cartilage in maintaining a patent airway.

With either CT or MRI, the cricoid origin may be obvious and may give a clue as to the identity of the lesion (see Fig. 18–17). The cartilage may be expanded, indicating a lesion arising within the cricoid rather than eroding into the cartilage from a more superficial mucosal origin.

The cartilaginous matrix is the most characteristic finding at imaging (see Fig. 18–18). CT scans are better than MRI studies at demonstrating the calcifications within the matrix of the tumor. Such calcifications are extremely rare in other lesions. Relapsing polychondritis can have fairly extensive calcification; however, this is extremely rare and should not involve the larynx exclusively.

If the lesion does not have the imaging characteristics of a cartilage lesion, the radiologist tries to determine whether the lesion is vascular. Hemangiomas and paragangliomas enhance intensely on CT scans if a bolus or rapid drip of intravenous contrast material is used. The knowledge that a tumor is vascular has obvious implications if biopsy or resection is planned.

Most of the other tumors mentioned have no specific identifying characteristics. They do not have a cartilaginous matrix and do not enhance brightly. The absence of these two imaging characteristics is useful information in limiting the diagnostic possibilities.

Cysts also present as submucosal masses and are described next.

Cysts

Three types of cysts arise within or in intimate association with the larynx: The *saccular* cyst (laryngocele) and the *mucosal* cyst arise within the larynx, and the *thyroglos-*

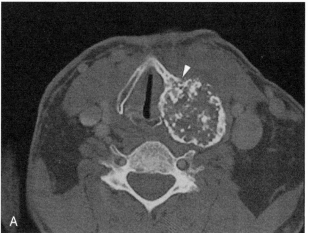
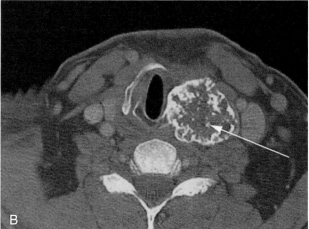

Figure 18–18. Chondrosarcoma, axial CT scan. *A,* The tumor expands *(arrowhead)* the thyroid lamina. *B,* Note the stippled density *(arrow)* within the cartilage representing cartilage formation.

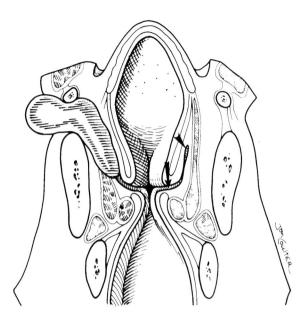

Figure 18–19. Diagram of a laryngocele. Coronal section through the larynx shows the ventricle *(arrow)* and the ventricular appendix *(arrowhead)* on the normal side. When this appendix is obstructed, it dilates (i.e., it fills with either fluid or air) to form a saccular cyst or laryngocele. In the diagram, the lateral extent of the saccular cyst protrudes through the lateral cricothyroid membrane. (From Curtin HD: The larynx. In Som PM, Bergeron RT [eds]: Head and Neck Imaging, 2nd ed. St. Louis, Mosby–Year Book, 1991.)

sal duct cyst arises just outside the larynx in close association with the strap muscles.

Saccular Cyst (Laryngocele)

The saccular cyst, or laryngocele, represents a dilatation of the ventricular saccule or appendix (Fig. 18–19). Strict terminology refers to the abnormality as a saccular cyst if it is fluid-filled and as a laryngocele if it is air-filled. Many simply refer to the lesions as air-filled or fluid-filled laryngoceles. The laryngocele is a supraglottic abnormality, and the true cord is normal.

Either presents as a submucosal mass or bulge in the supraglottic larynx (Figs. 18–20 to 18–22). The air or fluid within is readily identifiable, and the extent can be determined. A small cyst or laryngocele may be confined to the supraglottic paraglottic space and is referred to as "internal." A larger lesion may protrude laterally through the thyrohyoid membrane just anterior to the upper horn of the thyroid cartilage. Any component outside the membrane is referred to as "external" (see Fig. 18–21). A pure external laryngocele is rare. The external component is seen in combination with an internal component. This is called a *mixed laryngocele.* When the external component is large, the laryngocele can present as a neck mass.

Laryngoceles and saccular cysts are benign. However, these abnormalities can occur when tumor in the ventricle causes obstruction of the laryngeal saccule; therefore, both the radiologist and the endoscopist must carefully examine this key area (see Fig. 18–22).

Mucosal Cyst

A mucosal cyst is considered to be an obstructed mucous gland and can present anywhere mucosa is present. The benign nature of this cyst may be suggested by the smooth appearance, and this diagnosis is considered when a cystic-appearing mass is found on a mucosal surface.

Thyroglossal Duct Cyst

The thyroglossal duct cyst arises from the remnant left as the thyroid gland descends to the appropriate position in the lower neck. The cyst can arise above or below the hyoid bone. A cyst that arises below the hyoid bone is usually found just off midline in the region of the strap muscles anterior to the larynx (Fig. 18–23).

The appearance of the thyroglossal duct cyst is characteristic and should not be confused with saccular cyst arising within the larynx itself. A thyroglossal duct cyst in rare circumstances may bulge over the anterior notch of the thyroid cartilage but should not pass through the lateral aspect of the thyrohyoid membrane. The paraglottic space should not be involved.

Post-therapy Appearance of the Larynx

Both surgery and radiotherapy significantly distort the normal appearance of the larynx.

After a total laryngectomy, the food passage may dilate to mimic an airway, but the laryngeal landmarks are no longer seen. Lower CT or MRI slices show the tracheostomy site.

The appearance of the glottic and subglottic levels is unchanged by a supraglottic laryngectomy. With the supraglottic larynx removed, the characteristic landmarks of the paraglottic and preepiglottic spaces are not identified. Usually, the hyoid bone is removed. The major portion of the thyroid cartilage above the level of the cords is also removed.

The vertical hemilaryngectomy can produce a variable appearance. One cord is removed, leading to significant asymmetry at the glottic level. Part of the upper larynx is removed on the ipsilateral side. The position of the original lesion dictates the position of the cuts through the thyroid cartilage, resulting in significant variability in appearance among patients with vertical hemilaryngectomies. At times, the surgeon may attempt to reconstruct the cord using a small slip taken from the strap muscles. This can lead to significant soft tissue that cannot be readily distinguished from tumor.

Radiotherapy can cause characteristic apparent swelling of the soft tissues over the arytenoid cartilage and supraglottic region. Subtle reticulation or stranding of the supraglottic fat is seen. Initially, this represents local inflammation and edema, but small-vessel changes make the appearance more permanent.

Trauma

Direct trauma can result in fractures or dislocations of the cartilages in the larynx. Soft tissue injuries such as

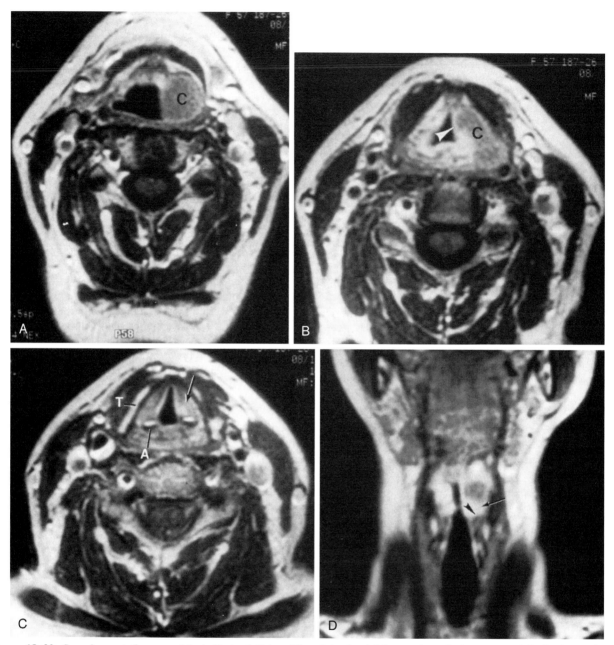

Figure 18–20. Saccular cyst (laryngocele). *A,* Postgadolinium T1-weighted axial image through the upper epiglottis shows the cyst (C). *B,* Slightly lower image shows the cyst (C) in the paraglottic space at the false cord level. The mucosa *(arrowhead)* is intact. *C,* Axial image through the true cord level shows no evidence of tumor. A, arytenoid; T, thyroid. The thyroarytenoid muscle (TAM) is shown by an *arrow. D,* Coronal image shows the lower margin of the lesion *(arrow)* above the upper edge of the TAM *(arrowhead);* thus, the cyst is above the ventricle.

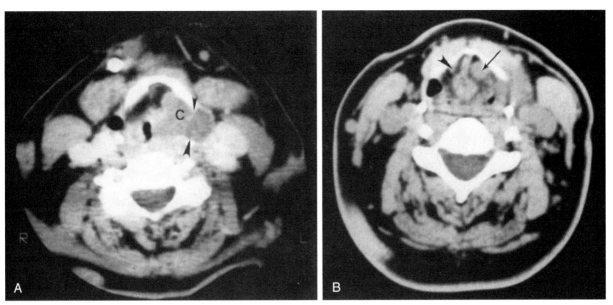

Figure 18–21. Saccular cyst (laryngocele). *A,* The cystic structure has both an internal and external component. The saccular cyst (C) protrudes through the thyrohyoid membrane, approximately at the *arrowheads.* Note the sharp margin of the cyst. *B,* Slightly lower slice shows the dilated appendix *(arrow)* just above the ventricle. Again, note the sharp margin. The fat in the paraglottic space indicates that this is still above the ventricle. A normal appendix is on the opposite side *(arrowhead).*

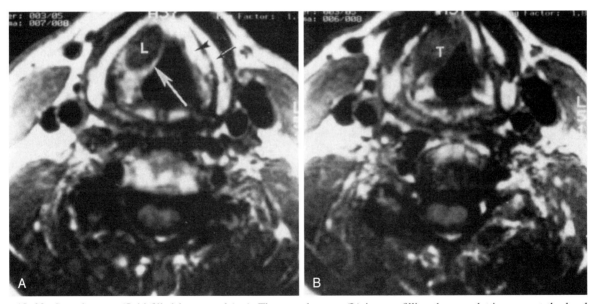

Figure 18–22. Saccular cyst (fluid-filled laryngocele). *A,* The saccular cyst (L) is seen filling the paraglottic space at the level of the false cord. Note the intact mucosa *(white arrow).* The paraglottic fat on the normal side *(arrowhead)* remains of high signal intensity. Fat is shown in the thyroid cartilage *(black arrow). B,* Slightly lower slice shows a tumor (T) filling the ventricle and causing the obstruction of the ventricular appendix, causing the saccular cyst. (From Curtin HD: MR and CT of the larynx. In Thrall JH [ed]: Current Practice of Radiology, 3rd ed. St. Louis, Mosby–Year Book, 1994.)

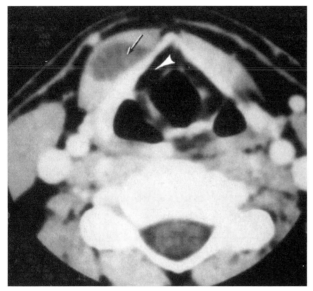

Figure 18–23. Thyroglossal duct cyst. The cystic structure *(arrow)* is seen on the outer surface of the thyroid cartilage intimately associated with the strap muscles. Note that the paraglottic fat *(arrowhead)* remains clear.

mucosal tears and hematomas can occur in isolation but are often seen in conjunction with fractures. CT scanning is usually used because of the ability to visualize the calcified cartilage and because of the speed of imaging. The fragile airway is more easily managed and monitored in the CT scan than in the more confined area of the MRI study.

In young patients, the cartilage may not be calcified but it can often be seen as slightly increased density against the contiguous soft tissues.

Fractures usually affect the thyroid or cricoid cartilage. The thyroid cartilage can have vertical or horizontal fractures (Fig. 18–24). Vertical fractures are easily detected in the axial scan plane, but horizontal fractures may be undetectable unless there is some displacement of the fracture fragments. Reformatted images may help to define horizontal fractures.

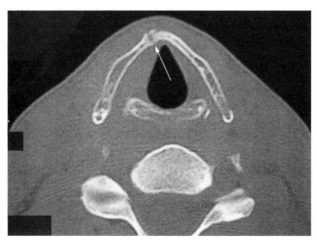

Figure 18–24. Vertical fracture of the larynx; axial CT. The *arrow* indicates a fracture.

The cricoid fracture is, characteristically, a double break (Fig. 18–25). The force of the blow pushes the anterior arch posteriorly, fracturing the ring in two or more places. The ring collapses inward. There is swelling in the subglottic soft tissues, giving apparent soft tissue against the inner surface of the cricoid cartilage, where normally the mucosa is very thin or almost invisible at imaging.

Compromise of the airway is a concern. Any inward displacement reduces the lumen of the airway. Equally of concern is the possibility of a tear of the mucosa. A fracture fragment protruding through the mucosa often results in chondritis and chondronecrosis with further airway restriction. If there is any suspicion of a fragment pushed toward the airway, direct visualization, at endoscopy or at open exploration, is indicated for a thorough assessment of the mucosa.

If there is sufficient force to fracture the thyroid cartilage, the lower epiglottis can be torn or avulsed. This situation can be seen, particularly with horizontal fractures where the fragments are pushed posteriorly, creating a shearing force across the lower epiglottis. Because the epiglottis does not calcify significantly, this abnormality is not detectable by CT scans. The only finding may be hematoma obscuring the fat in the preepiglottic space.

The arytenoid cartilage is not often fractured, but the cricoarytenoid joint can be dislocated (Fig. 18–26). This can occur with fairly minimal trauma to the lateral larynx or may result from more severe insult associated with fractures of the major cartilages. The arytenoid is normally perched just off midline. The radiologist tries to verify that the cartilage is in the normal position or grossly displaced. Currently, a subtle displacement cannot be confidently excluded.

The lower horns of the thyroid cartilage articulate with the lateral cricoid cartilage. This cricothyroid joint can theoretically be dislocated, usually in association with fractures of either the thyroid or cricoid cartilages. Because the attachment of the horn to the cricoid cartilage is fairly strong, a fracture of the lower horn is considered more common. One must be careful in making this diagnosis, since slight obliquity of the slice can cause apparent asymmetry of the space between the two cartilages. Each of the inferior horns must be followed down to the point of articulation.

Miscellaneous Problems

Although tumors and trauma account for most imaging of the larynx, imaging can be useful for several other problems.

Vocal Cord Paralysis

Vocal cord paralysis is most commonly a problem that affects the recurrent laryngeal nerve. All of the muscles in the larynx except the cricothyroid muscle are innervated by this nerve, but the most characteristic finding is the result of atrophy of the TAM. Normally, the TAM makes up the bulk of the true cord. With atrophy, the characteristic CT density or MRI intensity is no longer seen. The ventricle enlarges into the volume vacated by the atrophied muscle so that air can be seen where there should be

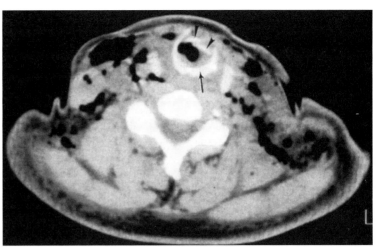

Figure 18–25. Fracture of the cricoid cartilage; the ring has been fractured. Fragments from the anterior ring *(arrowheads)* have been pushed back into the airway. These fragments would be in danger of perforating the mucosa. The lamina of the cricoid *(arrow)* is not fractured. Note the air in the soft tissues and the soft tissue within the ring of the cricoid cartilage. (From Curtin HD: MR and CT of the larynx. In Thrall JH [ed]: Current Practice of Radiology, 3rd ed. St. Louis, Mosby–Year Book, 1994.)

muscle. The vocal ligament remains, and the arytenoid cartilage may be in a fairly normal position or may be tipped slightly. The piriform sinus on the affected side often enlarges as well.

The posterior cricoarytenoid muscle is very thin, but since the axial plane provides a perfect cross-section, atrophy of this muscle may also be appreciated.[22] In this case, fat appears to be closely applied to the posterior surface of the cricoid cartilage instead of the typical muscle density.

In most instances, atrophied muscle is seen in patients with known paralysis. If the cause of the paralysis is not known, the course of the vagus nerve and the recurrent laryngeal nerve is examined. CT scanning is usually performed because of the distance that must be covered and because bone detail is important at the level of the jugular foramen in the temporal bone. The nerve is just posterior to the carotid artery and jugular vein on transit through the neck. Lower in the neck, the nerve moves forward with respect to the carotid artery. The left nerve loops around the aortic arch, and the right nerve loops around the subclavian artery. The nerve on both sides ascends along the tracheoesophageal groove to reach the larynx. A lesion at any level can involve the nerve and cause paralysis.

Superior laryngeal nerve paralysis is much less common, and characteristic radiographic findings have not been described. An extremely rare paralysis is "adductor paralysis." In this form, all muscles innervated by the recurrent laryngeal nerve are affected except the posterior cricoarytenoid. This muscle, unopposed, rotates the arytenoid and the cord laterally. This rare form of paralysis is not as well understood as the other more common paralyses but is thought to be related to an intracranial pathologic process.

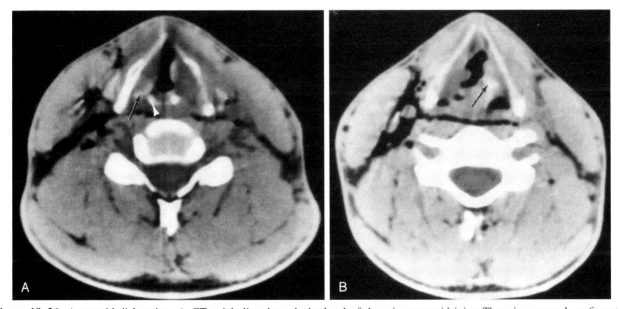

Figure 18–26. Arytenoid dislocation. *A,* CT axial slice through the level of the cricoarytenoid joint. There is a normal configuration on the right. The arytenoid cartilage *(arrow)* articulates normally with the small articular surface of the cricoid *(arrowhead)* on the superior edge of the cricoid cartilage. The arytenoid on the left is not identified in a normal position. *B,* Higher slice shows the dislocated arytenoid *(arrow)* in the supraglottic area.

Stenosis

Subglottic stenosis and tracheal stenosis can be evaluated by plain films, but imaging can give information about the cross-sectional area of the remaining airway. CT can show narrowing or stenosis of anterior and posterior commissures. The position of the cartilage relative to the airway can also be visualized. CT scans can determine whether the cartilage has collapsed into the airway or whether the cartilage remains in the normal position with the stenosis related only to soft tissue.

Such narrowing can be congenital or may be the result of trauma. Granulation tissue can develop after tracheostomy. The length of the narrowing and the relationship to the vocal cords should be estimated. Plain films can be very helpful in estimating the length of the abnormality.

Granulomatous Disease

Granulomatous disease, either of infectious or noninfectious etiology, can involve the larynx. Although rare, it can involve any of the mucosal surfaces and can be mistaken for tumor. The findings at imaging are nonspecific.

Rheumatoid Arthritis

Rheumatoid arthritis can involve the cricoarytenoid joint. This process is not usually evaluated radiologically.

Polychondritis

Relapsing polychondritis is a rare disease of unknown etiology. The cartilages of the larynx and trachea (among others) become inflamed, with edema of surrounding tissues. Calcifications of the abnormal tissue are characteristic and can be highly prominent. If calcifications are particularly prominent, the increased soft tissues and calcifications can mimic chondroid lesions.

Summary

CT or MRI can be done for tumor imaging. One approach is to do CT as a first step, reserving MRI for answering specific questions remaining after CT. MRI is then done in a small fraction of cases. At our institution we begin with MRI in those cases where supraglottic laryngectomy is contemplated. This is because of a preference for MRI when looking at the region of the ventricle and the thyroarytenoid muscle. Contrast-enhanced CT scans are preferred for imaging of submucosal masses. CT scans are done without enhancement in trauma cases.

References

1. Bailey BJ, Biller HF (eds): Surgery of the Larynx. Philadelphia, WB Saunders, 1985.
2. Barnes L, Gnepp DR: Diseases of the larynx, hypopharynx, and esophagus. In Barnes L (ed): Surgical Pathology of the Head and Neck, vol 1. New York, Marcel Dekker, 1985, pp 141–226.
3. Becker M, Moulin G, Kurt AM, et al: Non-squamous cell neoplasms of the larynx: Radiologic-pathologic correlation. Radiographics 18: 1189–1209, 1998.
4. Becker M, Zbaren P, Delavelle J, et al: Neoplastic invasion of the laryngeal cartilage: Reassessment of criteria for diagnosis at CT. Radiology 203:521–532, 1997.
5. Becker M, Abaren P, Laeng H, et al: Neoplastic invasion of the laryngeal cartilage: Comparison of MR imaging and CT with histopathologic correlation. Radiology 194:661–669, 1995.
6. Bruning R Sturm C, Hong C, et al: The diagnosis of stages T1 and T2 in laryngeal carcinoma with multislice spiral CT. Radiologie 39: 939–942, 1999.
7. Castelijns JA, Gerritsen GJ, Kaiser MC, et al: Invasion of laryngeal cartilage by cancer: Comparison of CT and MR imaging. Radiology 166:199–206, 1987.
8. Castelijns JA, Gerritsen GJ, Kaiser MC, et al: MRI of normal or cancerous laryngeal cartilages: Histopathologic correlation. Laryngoscope 97:1085–1093, 1987.
9. Castelijns JA, van den Brekel MW, Smit EM et al: Predictive value of MR imaging-dependent and non-MR imaging-dependent parameters for recurrence of laryngeal cancer after radiation therapy. Radiology 196:735–739, 1995.
10. Cummings CW, Fredrickson JM, Harker LA, et al: Otolaryngology–Head and Neck Surgery, 3rd ed, vol 3. St. Louis, Mosby–Year Book, 1998.
11. Curtin HD: Imaging of the larynx: Current concepts. Radiology 173: 1–11, 1989.
12. Curtin HD: The larynx. In Som PM, Curtin HD (eds): Head and Neck Imaging, 3rd ed, vol 1. St. Louis, Mosby–Year Book, 1996, pp 612–707.
13. Curtin HD: Imaging of the larynx. In Valvassori GE, Mafee MF, Carter BL (eds): Imaging of the Head and Neck. New York, Thieme, 1995, pp 366–389.
14. Giron J, Joffre P, Serres-Cousine O, et al: Magnetic resonance imaging of the larynx: Its contribution compared to x-ray computed tomography in the pre-therapeutic evaluation of cancers of the larynx. Apropos of 90 surgical cases. Ann Radiol (Paris) 33:170–184, 1990.
15. Gray H, Williams PL, Bannister LH: Gray's Anatomy: The Anatomical Basis of Medicine and Surgery, 38th ed. New York, Churchill Livingstone, 1995.
16. Kirchner JA: Two hundred laryngeal cancers: Patterns of growth and spread as seen in serial section. Laryngoscope 87:474–482, 1977.
17. Kolbenstvedt A, Charania B, Natvig, et al: Computed tomography in T1 carcinoma of the larynx. Acta Radiol 30:467–469, 1989.
18. Lawson W, Biller HF, Suen JR: Cancer of the larynx. In Suen JY, Myers EN (eds): Cancer of the Head and Neck. New York, Churchill Livingstone, 1989, pp 533–556.
19. Levine PA, Brasnu DF, Ruparelia A, et al: Management of advanced-stage laryngeal cancer. Otolaryngol Clin North Am 30:101–112, 1997.
20. Mancuso AA, Mukherji SK, Schmalfuss J, et al: Preradiotherapy computed tomography as a predictor of local control in supraglottic carcinoma. J Clin Oncol 17:631–637, 1999.
21. Phelps PD: Review: carcinoma of the larynx: The role of imaging in staging and pre-treatment assessments. Clin Radiol 46:77–83, 1992.
22. Romo LV, Curtin HD: Atrophy of the posterior cricoarytenoid muscle as an indicator of recurrent laryngeal nerve palsy. AJNR Am J Neuroradiol 20:467–471, 1999.
23. Sakai F, Gamsu G, Dillon WP, et al: MR imaging of the larynx at 1.5 T. J Comput Assist Tomogr 14:60–71, 1990.
24. Teresi LM, Lufkin RB, Hanafee WN: Magnetic resonance imaging of the larynx. Radiol Clin North Am 27:393–406, 1989.
25. Tucker GF, Smith HR: A histological demonstration of the development of laryngeal connective tissue compartments. Trans Am Acad Ophthal Otol 66:303–318, 1962.
26. Zeitels SM: Surgical management of early supraglottic cancer. Otolaryngol Clin 30:59–78, 1997.
27. Zeitels SM, Kirchner JA: Hyoepiglottic ligament in supraglottic cancer. Ann Otol Rhinol Laryngol 104 (10 pt 1):770–775, 1995.

19

Nasopharynx and Oropharynx

Sherif Gamal Nour, Jonathan S. Lewin

The pharynx is a fibromuscular tube that forms the upper part of the aerodigestive tract. It extends from the skull base down to the C6 vertebral level, serving as a conduit that conveys both air and food to the respiratory and alimentary tracts, respectively. The nasopharynx, oropharynx, and hypopharynx (laryngopharynx) are the three classic pharyngeal subdivisions that lie directly on the spine behind the nose, oral cavity, and larynx, respectively. The nasopharynx and oropharynx constitute the suprahyoid part of the pharynx. Formed of a thin muscle layer, the pharyngeal wall is lined by a mucous membrane and covered by loose fascia that permits pharyngeal movement during deglutition.[113, 116]

A diverse range of pathologic conditions may involve the nasopharynx and oropharynx. These may occur primarily within the layers of the pharyngeal wall or in the deep suprahyoid neck spaces adjacent to the pharynx, or they may protrude from the nose or skull base to hang in the airway as pharyngeal masses. In addition, pharyngeal disease may be a consequence of functional rather than anatomic derangement.

Prior to the modern imaging era, few tools were available for investigating pharyngeal disease. Having no more than a lateral plain x-ray, a conventional tomogram, or a contrast laryngopharyngogram, the radiologist had to depend on such signs as soft tissue fullness, intraluminal filling defects, and abnormalities in the pharyngeal margins imaged in profile[145]; all of these signs constituted indirect evidence of pathology, yet no means existed to visualize the actual disease process.

Although amenable to clinical inspection, pharyngeal mucosal lesions may be difficult to evaluate because of anatomic variations and patient compliance.[145] A mucosal lesion, as detected by endoscopy, may represent no more than the "tip of an iceberg," with the exact deep extent always remaining uncertain to the endoscopist. Moreover, associated cervical lymph nodes, unless of palpable size, may be overlooked in the clinical setting.

The advent of cross-sectional imaging exemplified in computed tomography (CT), then magnetic resonance imaging (MRI), has revolutionized the diagnosis of pharyngeal and deep neck disease. For the first time, the radiologist was able to gain true insight into the actual pathology, to define its exact site of origin, to map out its extent, and to study its effect on vital neighboring neck structures. With this wealth of information, the radiologist could interact with the clinician in a more effective manner and could make invaluable contributions to treatment decision making.

The improved understanding of the complex suprahyoid neck anatomy offered by these modern imaging modalities has led to the development of a new approach to the diagnosis of pathologic conditions involving this region that utilizes the concept of fascially defined spaces rather than the classic pharyngeal subdivisions. As CT and MRI have become the basic tools for evaluating nasopharyngeal and oropharyngeal pathology, the current classifications of nasopharyngeal and oropharyngeal carcinomas adopted by the International Union Against Cancer (UICC) and the American Joint Committee on Cancer (AJCC) are now based on cross-sectional imaging findings.

The continuing evolution of MRI has gone beyond the mere imaging of anatomic changes to approach near real-time recording of the functional status of the pharynx, and the time is not far before the radiologic focus of interest broadens to include disorders of pharyngeal function, such as obstructive sleep apnea.

Finally, interventional MRI is a rapidly growing part of current radiologic practice and has been successfully applied to the pharynx and adjoining deep neck spaces to guide biopsies and minimally invasive therapeutic procedures.

Anatomy

The topics to be discussed are summarized in Box 19–1.

Traditional Classification

Classically, the suprahyoid head and neck region is divided into the nasopharynx, oropharynx, and oral cavity (Fig. 19–1), with the exact contents of each compartment dependent on how much of the adjoining deep tissues are included.[4, 65, 128]

Nasopharynx

The *nasopharynx* is the uppermost part of the aerodigestive tract. It measures approximately 2×4 cm in anteroposterior and craniocaudal diameters, respectively. It is bounded posterosuperiorly by the basisphenoid, basiocciput, and upper two cervical vertebrae as well as by the prevertebral muscles.[65, 108, 113, 128]

Anteriorly, it communicates with the nasal cavity through the choana. Inferiorly, it is in direct continuity with the oropharynx, and the plane of division is a horizontal line drawn along the hard and soft palates and passing

Box 19–1. **Anatomy**

I. **Traditional Classification**
  A. Nasopharynx
  B. Oropharynx
II. **Spatial Approach**
  A. Superficial fascia
  B. Deep fascia
    1. Superficial layer (investing fascia)
      a. Description
      b. Spaces included
        (1) Masticator space
        (2) Parotid space
        (3) Submandibular and sublingual spaces
        (4) Muscular space
        (5) Suprasternal space (of Burns)
    2. Deep layer (prevertebral fascia)
      a. Description
      b. Spaces included
        (1) Perivertebral space
        (2) Danger space
    3. Middle layer (visceral fascia)
      a. Description
        (1) Buccopharyngeal fascia
        (2) Cloison sagittale
        (3) Fascia of tensor veli palatini
      b. Pharyngobasilar fascia (pharyngeal aponeurosis)
      c. Spaces included
        (1) Pharyngeal mucosal space
        (2) Retropharyngeal space
        (3) Parapharyngeal space
          (a) Prestyloid
          (b) Retrostyloid

posteriorly to the *Passavant's ridge* (a ridge of pharyngeal musculature that opposes the elevated soft palate).[65, 108, 113, 128, 142] The features of the lateral nasopharyngeal walls are discussed later.

Oropharynx

The oropharynx is the part of the aerodigestive tract that lies behind the oral cavity (it can be seen through the open mouth). It is separated from the oral cavity by the circumvallate papillae of the tongue, the anterior tonsillar pillars, and by the soft palate. The posterior third of the tongue and lingual tonsil are therefore considered to be within the oropharynx and not in the oral cavity.[65]

Posteriorly, the superior and middle constrictor muscles separate the oropharynx from the prevertebral muscles overlying the second and third cervical vertebrae.

Superiorly, the oropharynx communicates with the nasopharynx.

Inferiorly, it is separated from the hypopharynx by the pharyngoepiglottic fold and from the larynx by the epiglottis and glossoepiglottic fold.[65, 119, 128]

The features of the lateral oropharyngeal walls include two faucial arches:

1. The anterior (palatoglossus muscle) arch.
2. The posterior (palatopharyngeus muscle) arch.

Between them lies the tonsillar fossa, which contains the palatine tonsil on each side.[119]

Spatial Approach

Although the classic classification of nasopharynx, oropharynx, and hypopharynx is quite effective in regard to superficial mucosal lesions, such as squamous cell carcinoma, this "non-fascially based" classification is much less helpful to the radiologist attempting to accurately localize deeply seated head and neck lesions as evaluated on cross-sectional imaging.[4, 65]

The traditional classification of the suprahyoid head and neck into the nasopharynx, oropharynx, and oral cavity has thus been largely replaced by a somewhat complicated, yet more useful scheme that divides this region into multiple spaces, defined by the layers of cervical fascia. Such a "spatial approach" provides a satisfactory means of localizing the space of origin of a suprahyoid lesion and, consequently, helps to limit the differential diagnosis to a unique set of pathologic processes specific to each anatomic space.[4, 40, 65, 67, 128, 162] Moreover, it utilizes surgically and pathologically defined terminology, thereby creating a "common language" for the radiologist and the referring surgeon.[65]

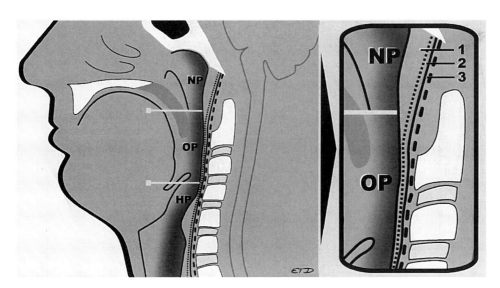

Figure 19–1. Sagittal diagram showing pharyngeal divisions and fascial lines. HP, hypopharynx; NP, nasopharynx; OP, oropharynx.

Key:

1 = Pharyngeal mucosal space (PMS)
2 = Retropharyngeal space (RPS)
3 = Danger space (DS)

- - - - - - - -   Buccopharyngeal fascia
——————— Alar fascia
— — — — — Prevertebral fascia

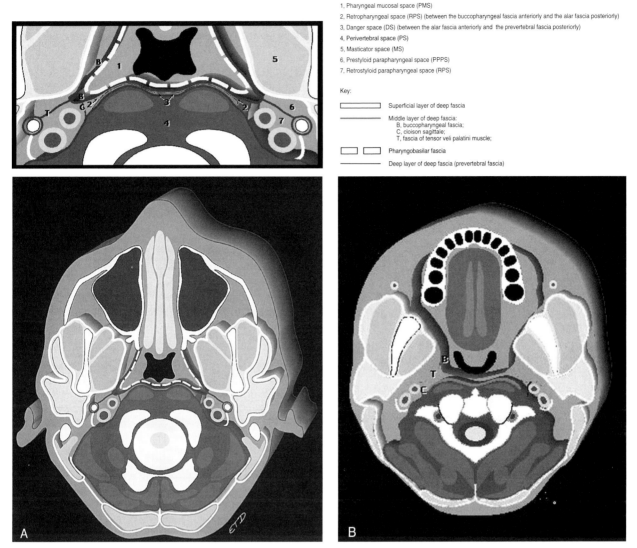

1, Pharyngeal mucosal space (PMS)
2, Retropharyngeal space (RPS) (between the buccopharyngeal fascia anteriorly and the alar fascia posteriorly)
3, Danger space (DS) (between the alar fascia anteriorly and the prevertebral fascia posteriorly)
4, Perivertebral space (PS)
5, Masticator space (MS)
6, Prestyloid parapharyngeal space (PPPS)
7, Retrostyloid parapharyngeal space (RPS)

Key:

☐ Superficial layer of deep fascia

— Middle layer of deep fascia:
  B, buccopharyngeal fascia;
  C, cloison sagittale;
  T, fascia of tensor veli palatini muscle;

☐ ☐ Pharyngobasilar fascia

— Deep layer of deep fascia (prevertebral fascia)

Figure 19–2. Diagrammatic layout of the suprahyoid neck spaces and their fascial boundaries at the level of the nasopharynx *(A)*, detail of the nasopharynx *(inset)*, and the oropharynx *(B)*.

Crucial to an appreciation of suprahyoid neck spaces is a proper understanding of the fascial framework of the head and neck (Fig. 19–2; see Figs. 19–5 and 19–6). For the sake of completeness, each of these spaces is addressed here, with particular emphasis given to those most relevant to the subject of this chapter.

Basically, two major compartments constitute the head and neck fasciae: the superficial and deep layers.

Superficial Fascia

The superficial fascia is a loose fatty layer, with the platysma muscle embedded in its deep portion.[61, 87]

Deep Fascia

The deep fascia is a complex of multiple sheets, which are generally subdivided into three layers:

- A superficial layer (investing fascia)
- A deep layer (prevertebral fascia)
- A middle layer (visceral fascia)

Superficial Layer of the Deep Fascia (Investing Fascia)

Description

The superficial layer forms a complete collar around the neck and is attached *superiorly* to the lower border of the mandibular body back to its angle and more posteriorly to the mastoid processes, the superior nuchal line, and to the external occipital protuberance.

Inferiorly, this layer attaches to the acromion and spine of the scapula, to the clavicle, and to the manubrium sterni. The two halves of the investing fascia attach *posteriorly* to the ligamentum nuchae and cervical spinal processes.

Anteriorly, they are continuous and are attached to the hyoid bone, where they converge with the middle (visceral) layer of the deep fascia, dividing the neck into suprahyoid and infrahyoid portions.[61, 113]

Spaces

The investing fascia splits to enclose number of structures within the neck, thereby forming the following fascial spaces:

Masticator Space. Above the attachment to the lower border of the mandible, a part of the investing fascia continues upward to enclose the muscles of mastication and the mandible (ramus and posterior body) by splitting into a superficial and a deep layer. The superficial layer covers the masseter muscle and then attaches to the zygomatic arch (this is continuous with the fascia covering the parotid gland forming the parotid-masseteric fascia). The deep layer runs deep to both pterygoid muscles to attach to the skull base, separating the masticator from the prestyloid compartment of the *parapharyngeal space* (PPS).[40, 61, 64, 70]

Parotid Space. The parotid space is formed as the investing fascia splits between the mastoid process and the angle of the mandible to enclose the gland, forming its capsule.[14, 16] The medial aspect of the parotid space, which contains the deep lobe of the parotid gland, extends through the stylomandibular tunnel (the gap between the styloid process and the posterior margin of the mandible) for a variable distance before it meets the prestyloid compartment of the PPS.[87]

Submandibular and Sublingual Spaces. A layer of the investing fascia splits to line the undersurface of the submandibular gland before reattaching to the mandible at the mylohyoid line, thereby forming the capsule of the gland. In the radiologic literature, the term *submandibular space* is given to the entire area superficial to the mylohyoid muscle down to the superficial layer of investing fascia as it extends from the hyoid bone to the mandible. The *sublingual space* is the area deep to the mylohyoid muscle, up to the mucosa of the mouth floor. The relevance of these spaces to this chapter is their free communication with the prestyloid compartment of the PPS.[70, 87]

Muscular Spaces. Muscular spaces are formed as the fascia splits to enclose the trapezius, the sternocleidomastoid, and the inferior belly of the omohyoid muscles.[61, 70]

Suprasternal Space (of Burns). This shallow space is formed just above the manubrium sterni as the investing fascia splits to attach to the anterior and posterior borders of the jugular notch.[61, 70]

Deep Layer of the Deep Fascia (Prevertebral Fascia)
Description

The deep layer encircles the vertebral column as well as the paraspinal and prevertebral muscles, with a firm insertion on the spinous and transverse processes of the vertebral column. The prevertebral fascia extends from the skull base down to the third thoracic vertebra, where it fuses with the anterior longitudinal ligament in the posterior mediastinum.[61, 113] Some authors have described a slip of the prevertebral fascia, the alar fascia, which is immediately anterior to it and has a similar coronal plane of orientation.[61, 87]

Spaces

Perivertebral Space. The perivertebral space (PVS) is enclosed by the circumferential prevertebral fascia and is divided by the fascial attachment to the cervical transverse processes into the anterior prevertebral and posterior paraspinal compartments.[65, 67, 128] This space extends from the

skull base to the coccyx and is tight enough to resist the superoinferior spread of infection or neoplasms.[132]

Danger Space. This thin potential space lies between the prevertebral fascia posteriorly and the alar fascia anteriorly. The space is named as such because it extends from the skull base to the level of the diaphragm and is filled with loose areolar tissue, which provides a ready conduit for the spread of infection.[132]

Middle Layer of the Deep Fascia (Visceral Fascia)
Description

There has been considerable confusion in the literature concerning the layers composing the visceral fascia, with most of the anatomic references focusing mainly on the pretracheal fascia in regard to the fascial layers between the investing and prevertebral fasciae.[61, 113] However, to give the reader a full understanding of the spatial anatomy of this region, it would be more appropriate in this context to stress the layers relevant to the suprahyoid neck. The following basic fascial planes comprise the visceral fascia above the hyoid bone.

Buccopharyngeal Fascia. This fascia is a thin layer of loose connective tissue that covers the pharyngeal constrictor muscles and permits pharyngeal movement. It attaches superiorly to the skull base, having the same attachment as the pharyngobasilar fascia (see later), and is continuous anteriorly over the buccinator muscle.[65, 70, 113, 119, 128] The buccopharyngeal fascia is not visible on CT scans or MR images.[83]

Cloison Sagittale. These bilateral, small, sagittally oriented fascial slips extend from the buccopharyngeal fascia anteriorly to the prevertebral fascia posteriorly, near its attachment to the transverse processes of the cervical vertebrae. The importance of these tiny fascial slips is that they separate the medially positioned *retropharyngeal space* (RPS) from the laterally positioned retrostyloid compartments of the PPS.[87] These slips are sometimes also called the *alar fascia*, but this term is better avoided to prevent confusion with the alar fascia described earlier.[87]

Fascia of Tensor Veli Palatini. This relatively thick fascial sheet envelops the styloid process and its musculature and extends anteromedially to merge with the fascia associated with the tensor veli palatini muscle. It then continues further anteriorly to fuse with the pterygomandibular raphe and the buccopharyngeal fascia.[40, 158] This fascial layer divides the PPS into anterolateral (prestyloid) and posteromedial (retrostyloid) compartments.[40, 158]

Pharyngobasilar Fascia (Pharyngeal Aponeurosis)

This important fourth fascial sheet lies between the superficial and the deep layers of the deep fascia, but it is usually considered to be separate from the middle layer. As a tough membrane, it forms an almost closed, very resistant chamber that determines the configuration of the nasopharynx.[83, 142] It attaches superiorly to the skull base from the medial pterygoid plates, passing posteriorly to the petrous bones just anterior to the carotid foramina, where it reflects medially on either side to be continuous over the longus capitis and rectus capitis muscles. The fascia descends from the skull base, forming an elongated ring that closes the gaps above the superior constrictor muscle of the pharynx bilaterally.

References on anatomy describe the fascia to then continue lining the inner surface of the pharyngeal musculature, thereby supporting the mucous membrane of most of the nasal portion of the pharynx, then it becomes much thinner below, at about the level of the soft palate.[70, 83, 96, 113, 119, 128] From the functional and imaging perspectives, the most relevant portion of the pharyngobasilar fascia is that above the superior constrictor muscle, hence the name the *pharyngeal aponeurosis* (see Fig. 19–5). Formed of dense fibrous tissue, the pharyngobasilar fascia shows up on MRI images as a low-intensity line extending from the medial pterygoid plate to the carotid foramen medial to the tensor palatini.[83]

Thus, the constrictor muscles of the pharynx are "sandwiched" between the pharyngobasilar fascia (inside) and the buccopharyngeal fascia (outside). Above the upper edge of the superior constrictor muscle (between it and the skull base), the two fascial layers blend to form, along with the lining mucosa, the thin wall of the lateral pharyngeal recesses (fossae of Rosenmüller).[83, 96, 113] Anterior to these recesses, a natural defect in the pharyngobasilar fascia (sinus of Morgagni) exists on each side, transmitting the eustachian tubes and levator veli palatini muscles from the skull base to the *pharyngeal mucosal space* (PMS).[83, 96, 119, 128] The torus tubarius, the most prominent anatomic landmark on the lateral nasopharyngeal walls, is a ridge lying between the orifice of the eustachian tube anteroinferiorly and the fossa of Rosenmüller posterosuperiorly on each side. It is formed by the levator veli palatini muscle together with the cartilaginous eustachian tube and the overlying mucosa.[83, 96, 119]

Spaces

The deep face and neck spaces, defined by the just-described layers of visceral fascia, are presented next.

Pharyngeal Mucosal Space. The PMS is the area of the nasopharynx and oropharynx on the inner (airway) side of the buccopharyngeal fascia. The latter separates the PMS from the PPS laterally and the RPS posteriorly. The PMS is thus composed of the five layers forming the pharyngeal wall. From internal to external, they are as follows[113]:

1. *Mucous membrane.* The upper part of the nasopharynx is lined by respiratory epithelium (pseudostratified ciliated columnar). Inferiorly, where food contact is more of an issue, the epithelium changes to a stratified squamous type.[96]
2. *Submucosa.* The submucosa contains minor salivary glands and prominent lymphoid tissue of Waldeyer's ring (adenoids, palatine tonsils, lingual tonsils, and submucosal lymphatics). Lymphoid tissue may also normally be present in the epithelium (lymphoepithelium).[65, 96, 128]
3. *Dense pharyngobasilar fascia.*
4. *Superior constrictor muscle of the pharynx.* Above this muscle, layers 3 and 5 are adherent and are pierced by the eustachian tube (cartilaginous end) and the levator palatini muscle, which are considered within the PMS.
5. *Thin buccopharyngeal fascia.* This fascia forms the outer confinement of the PMS.

Retropharyngeal Space. The RPS[87, 128] is a small, potential space that is bounded as follows:

1. *Anteriorly* by the buccopharyngeal fascia, separating it from the PMS.
2. *Posteriorly* by the prevertebral fascia, separating it from the perivertebral space.
3. *Laterally* by the cloison sagittale, separating it from the retrostyloid compartment of the PPS on each side.[87]
4. *Superiorly* by the skull base.
5. *Inferiorly* by the fusion of the buccopharyngeal and prevertebral fasciae between the T2 and T6 spinal levels.[45]

The RPS normally contains a small amount of fat and, in the suprahyoid region, the lateral (nodes of Rouviere) and medial retropharyngeal lymph nodes.[45, 65]

The medial retropharyngeal lymph nodes are located near the midline and are seldom seen unless they are pathologically enlarged.[39, 45] The lateral retropharyngeal (LRP) lymph nodes are found immediately medial to the internal carotid artery, adjacent to the longus capitis muscle, and are usually most prominent at the C1-C2 level but can occasionally be visualized down to the level of the palate.[39, 45, 101] The LRP nodes are usually identified on MR images and, to a lesser extent, on CT scans.

In adults, the nodes are usually smaller than 3 to 5 mm, but nodes of up to 1 cm can be considered normal if they are homogeneous.[45, 101] In children, the LRP nodes may be as large as 2 cm in size, particularly if the adenoids are prominent.[39] This lymph node chain provides drainage for the nasopharynx, oropharynx, middle ear, nasal cavities, and paranasal sinuses.[39, 132]

Parapharyngeal Space. The PPS is an anatomic recess, shaped like an inverted pyramid with its base at the base of the skull and its apex at the greater cornu of the hyoid bone. It occupies the space between the muscles of mastication and the deglutitional muscles.[40, 67, 131, 156, 158] It has the following boundaries and relations:

1. *Laterally*
   a. *Anterolaterally;* separated from the masticator space by the layer of investing fascia covering the medial aspect of the medial pterygoid muscle.[28, 96, 119, 158]
   b. *Posterolaterally;* separated from the parotid space by the layer of investing fascia covering the deep lobe of the parotid gland.[119, 158] However, this is a sparse fascial layer that does not present a barrier to the spread of disease.[87]
2. *Medially;* separated from the PMS by the buccopharyngeal fascia, while its extreme posterior part is separated from the RPS by the cloison sagittale.[103, 128, 158]
3. *Posteriorly;* separated from the perivertebral space by the prevertebral fascia.[103, 119, 158]
4. *Anteriorly*
   a. *Anterosuperiorly* (at the level of the pterygomandibular raphe); closed by the convergence of the buccopharyngeal fascia with the fascia covering the medial aspect of the medial pterygoid muscle.[87, 119]
   b. *Anteroinferiorly* (at the level of the mylohyoid muscle); PPS is often continuous with the sublingual and submandibular spaces, thereby allowing lesions to

pass from one space to another without crossing a fascial boundary.[36, 65, 70]

5. *Inferiorly;* PPS is generally described as extending down to the hyoid bone; however, the fusion of multiple fascial layers and muscle sheaths near the angle of the mandible limit the caudal extent of the space,[87] and the styloglossus muscle can be considered the functional inferior boundary of the PPS.[87]

The PPS, as just defined, is a larger area of the deep face than the fatty triangles seen on either side of the

pharynx. This definition, which is supported by most authors, implies the division of the PPS by the fascia of tensor veli palatini (see earlier) into the following[87, 131]:

1. *Prestyloid PPS,* anterolateral to the fascia.
2. *Retrostyloid PPS,* posteromedial to the fascia. This is the suprahyoid extension of the carotid space (carotid sheath and its contents).

The contents of the suprahyoid neck spaces along with the common disease processes involving each space are listed in Table 19–1.

Table 19–1. Anatomic Spaces of the Suprahyoid Neck: Their Contents and Common Disease Processes

	Contents	Differential Diagnosis of Lesions

Pharyngeal mucosal space (PMS)	1. Mucosa
	2. Submucosa containing
	  a. Minor salivary glands
	  b. Lymphoid tissue (adenoids, palatine, and lingual tonsils)
	3. Pharyngobasilar fascia
	4. Superior and middle constrictor muscles
	5. Buccopharyngeal fascia (enclosing layer)
	
	+ Cartilaginous eustachian tube ⎱ Originate
	+ Levator veli palatini muscle ⎰ outside PMS
		Pseudomass
		• Asymmetric fossae of Rosenmüller
		• Pharyngitis
		  • Infectious
		  • Postirradiation
		Congenital
		Thornwaldt's cyst
		Inflammatory
		• *Adenoidal and tonsillar: hypertrophy, inflammation, abscess*
		• Postinflammatory
		  • Dystrophic calcification
		  • Retention cyst
		Benign tumor
		• *Juvenile angiofibroma*
		• Pleomorphic adenoma (benign mixed tumor) of minor salivary glands
		Malignant tumor
		• *Squamous cell carcinoma*
		• *Non-Hodgkin's lymphoma*
		• Minor salivary gland malignancy
		• Rhabdomyosarcoma (pediatric)

Prestyloid parapharyngeal space (PPPS)	1. Fat
	2. Pterygoid venous plexus
	3. Internal maxillary artery
	4. Ascending pharyngeal artery
	5. Branches of the mandibular division (V3) of trigeminal nerve
		Pseudomass
		• *Asymmetrical pterygoid venous plexus*
		Congenital
		• 2nd branchial cleft cyst
		Inflammatory
		• *Spread of infection* from adjacent spaces
		  • PMS: pharyngitis, adenoiditis, tonsillitis, peritonsillar abscess, retromandibular vein thrombosis
		  • PS: parotid calculus disease, deep lobe parotid abscess
		  • MS: dental infection, 3rd upper molar extraction with violation of pterygomandibular raphe
		• Infection secondary to penetrating trauma to the lateral pharyngeal wall
		Benign tumor
		• Pleomorphic adenoma (benign mixed tumor)
		  • Extending from deep lobe of parotid gland
		  • Arising from salivary gland rests in PPS
		• Lipoma
		Malignant tumor
		• Mucoepidermoid carcinoma ⎱ of salivary
		  Adenoid cystic carcinoma ⎬ gland rest
		  Malignant mixed tumor ⎰ in PPS
		
		• *Spread of malignancy* from
		  • Adjacent spaces
		    • PMS: squamous cell carcinoma, non-Hodgkin's lymphoma, minor salivary gland malignancy
		    • PS: mucoepidermoid carcinoma, adenoid cystic carcinoma
		    • MS: sarcoma
		  • Skull base tumor

Table continued on following page

Table 19–1. Anatomic Spaces of the Suprahyoid Neck: Their Contents and Common Disease Processes
Continued

	Contents	**Differential Diagnosis of Lesions**

Retrostyloid parapharyngeal space (RPPS) Carotid space (CS)	1. Internal carotid artery
	2. Internal jugular vein
	3. Lower 4 cranial nerves (IX–XII)
	4. Sympathetic chain
	5. Lymph nodes (deep cervical chain)
		Pseudomass
		• *Ectatic internal carotid artery*
		• *Asymmetrical internal jugular veins*
		Inflammatory
		• Carotid space cellulitis or abscess
		  • Spread from adjacent spaces
		  • Breakdown of infected internal jugular lymph nodes
		Vascular
		• *Internal jugular vein thrombosis or thrombophlebitis*
		• *Internal carotid artery thrombosis, mural thrombus, aneurysm, pseudoaneurysm, or dissection*
		Benign tumor
		• *Paraganglioma*
		  • Glomus jugulare
		  • Glomus vagale
		  • Carotid body tumor
		• Nerve sheath tumor
		  • *Schwannoma*
		  • Neurofibroma
		• Meningioma (of jugular foramen)
		Malignant tumor
		• *Lymph node metastasis from squamous cell carcinoma*
		• *Direct invasion by primary squamous cell carcinoma*
		• *Non-Hodgkin's lymphoma*

Retropharyngeal space (RPS)	1. Fat
	2. Lymph nodes
	  a. Lateral retropharyngeal (of Rouviere)
	  b. Medial retropharyngeal
		Pseudomass
		• Tortuous internal carotid artery
		• Edema fluid or lymph spilling into RPS secondary to venous or lymphatic obstruction
		Congenital
		• Hemangioma
		• Lymphangioma
		Inflammatory
		• *Reactive adenopathy*
		• *Suppurative adenopathy (intranodal abscess)*
		• *Cellulitis, abscess*
		Benign tumor
		• Lipoma
		Malignant tumor
		• Nodal metastases
		  • *Squamous cell carcinoma of head and neck (most common: nasopharynx)*
		  • Melanoma
		  • Thyroid carcinoma
		• *Nodal non-Hodgkin's lymphoma*
		• *Direct invasion from primary squamous cell carcinoma (especially posterior wall primary lesions)*

Masticator space (MS)	1. Mandible (ramus + posterior body)
	2. Muscles of mastication
	  a. Lateral pterygoid
	  b. Medial pterygoid
	  c. Masseter
	  d. Temporalis
	3. Inferior alveolar and lingual nerves (branches of the mandibular division V3 of trigeminal nerve)
		Pseudomass
		• *Accessory parotid gland*
		• *Benign masseteric hypertrophy (unilateral/bilateral)*
		• Mandibular nerve (cranial nerve V3) denervation atrophy
		Congenital
		• Hemangioma
		• Lymphangioma
		Inflammatory
		• *Odontogenic abscess (especially lower 2nd and 3rd molars)*
		• Mandibular osteomyelitis
		Benign tumor
		• Osteoblastoma
		• Leiomyoma
		• Nerve sheath tumor (schwannoma-neurofibroma)
		Malignant tumor
		• *Sarcoma: chondrosarcoma, osteosarcoma, soft tissue sarcoma*
		• Malignant schwannoma
		• *Non-Hodgkin's lymphoma*
		• *Infiltrating squamous cell carcinoma from oropharynx (retromolar trigone)*
		• *Rhabdomyosarcoma (pediatric)*
		• Mandibular metastases (from cancer of lung, breast, kidney)

Table continued on following page

Table 19–1. Anatomic Spaces of the Suprahyoid Neck: Their Contents and Common Disease Processes
Continued

	Contents	Differential Diagnosis of Lesions

Parotid space (PS)	1. Parotid gland
	2. Facial nerve VII
	3. External carotid artery (ECA) (terminating in parotid gland into internal maxillary and superficial temporal arteries)
	4. Retromandibular vein
	5. Intraparotid and periparotid lymph nodes
		Congenital
		• 1st branchial cleft cyst
		• Hemangioma (pediatric)
		• Lymphangioma (pediatric)
		Inflammatory
		• Cellulitis/abscess
		• Benign lymphoepithelial lesions (AIDS)
		• Reactive adenopathy
		Benign tumor
		• *Pleomorphic adenoma (benign mixed tumor)*
		• *Warthin's tumor (papillary cystadenoma lymphomatosum)*
		• Oncocytoma
		• Lipoma
		• Facial nerve schwannoma or neurofibroma
		Malignant tumor
		• *Primary*
		  • Carcinoma
		    • *Mucoepidermoid*
		    • *Adenoid cystic*
		    • Acinous cell
		    • Squamous cell
		  • Non-Hodgkin's lymphoma
		  • Malignant mixed tumor
		• *Metastatic (within parotid nodes)*
		  • *Squamous cell carcinoma of scalp*
		  • *Melanoma of scalp*
		  • Non-Hodgkin's lymphoma

Perivertebral space (PVS)	1. Prevertebral muscles
	2. Scalene muscles
	3. Vertebral arteries and veins
	4. Brachial plexus
	5. Phrenic nerve
		Pseudomass
		• *Vertebral body osteophyte*
		• Anterior disk herniation
		Inflammatory
		• *Vertebral body osteomyelitis (pyogenic/tuberculosis)*
		• *Cellulitis, abscess*
		Vascular
		• Vertebral artery dissection, aneurysm, or pseudoaneurysm
		Benign tumor
		• Schwannoma/neurofibroma (cervical nerve roots, brachial plexus)
		• Vertebral body benign bony tumors
		Malignant tumor
		• *Primary*
		  • Chordoma
		  • Non-Hodgkin's lymphoma
		  • Vertebral body primary malignant tumor
		• *Metastatic*
		  • *Vertebral body or epidural metastases*
		  • *Direct invasion of squamous cell carcinoma*

Note: Shaded entries indicate the most common lesions.
AIDS, acquired immunodeficiency syndrome.
Data from Barakos, 1991[4]; Curtin, 1987[40]; Harnsberger, 1991[67] and 1995[65]; Lewin, 1995[87]; Norbesh, 1996[128]; and Silver et al, 1984.[156]

Normal Imaging Anatomy

The anatomy of the normal suprahyoid neck, as seen with CT and MRI, is demonstrated in Figures 19–3 to 19–6.

Imaging Rationale and Techniques

CT and MRI are currently the primary modalities for investigating the suprahyoid neck region. This region, which extends from the skull base to the hyoid bone, is surrounded, for the most part, by bones that limit external clinical examination. In addition, while the superficial extent of mucosal lesions can be readily identified by the examining physician, their deep extent as well as lesions confined to the deep spaces are almost totally inaccessible for clinical or endoscopic evaluation.

In many cases of suprahyoid neck masses, MRI offers benefits over CT because of its higher soft tissue contrast resolution, multiplanar capability, and superiority in detecting perineural tumor spread and intracranial invasion.[65]

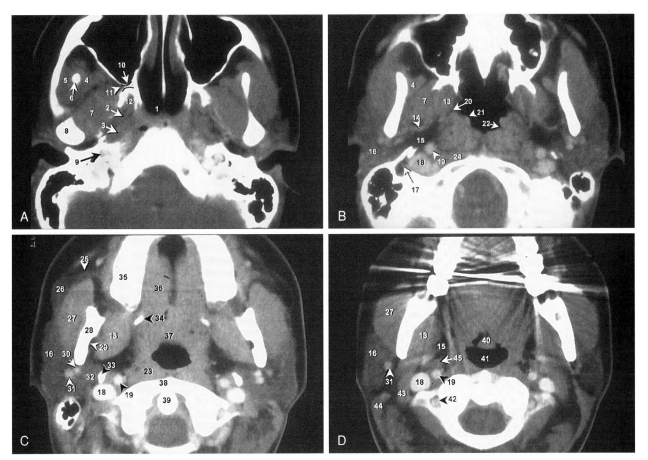

Figure 19–3. *A–G,* Normal imaging anatomy of the nasopharynx and oropharynx on a contrast-enhanced axial CT scan (5-mm slice thickness).

1 Nasopharyngeal airway
2 Tensor veli palatini muscle
3 Levator veli palatini muscle
4 Temporalis muscle (deep = medial head)
5 Temporalis muscle (superficial = lateral head)
6 Coronoid process of mandible
7 Lateral pterygoid muscle
8 Condylar process of mandible
9 Internal carotid artery in vertical segment of petrous canal
10 Pterygopalatine fossa (basal part)
11 Pterygomaxillary fissure
12 Pterygoid fossa between medial and lateral pterygoid plates
13 Medial pterygoid muscle
14 Internal maxillary vessels
15 Fat in prestyloid compartment of parapharyngeal space
16 Parotid gland (superficial lobe)
17 Facial nerve surrounded by fat in stylomastoid foramen
18 Internal jugular vein
19 Internal carotid artery
20 Eustachian tube orifice
21 Torus tubarius overlying levator veli palatini muscle
22 Lateral pharyngeal recess (fossa of Rosenmüller)
23 Longus capitis muscle

24 Rectus capitis anterior muscle
25 Parotid (Stensen's) duct
26 Accessory parotid tissue
27 Masseter muscle
28 Ramus of mandible
29 Mandibular foramen
30 External carotid artery
31 Retromandibular vein (lying superficial to external carotid artery)
32 Deep lobe of parotid gland extending through stylomandibular tunnel
33 Styloid process
34 Pterygoid hamulus (projecting inferiorly from medial pterygoid plate)
35 Alveolar process of maxilla
36 Hard palate
37 Soft palate
38 Anterior arch of atlas (C1 vertebra)
39 Odontoid process (dens)
40 Uvula
41 Oropharyngeal airway
42 Vertebral artery in foramen transversarium
43 Posterior belly of digastric muscle

Illustration continued on following page

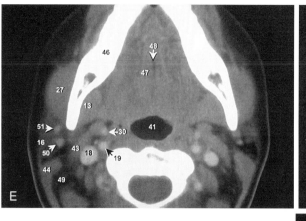

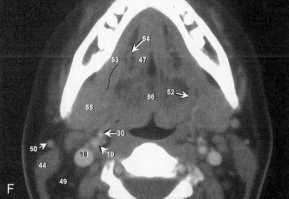

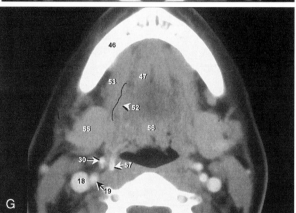

44 Sternocleidomastoid muscle
45 Styloid musculature
46 Body of mandible
47 Genioglossus/geniohyoid muscles
48 Lingual septum
49 Fat in posterior cervical space
50 External jugular vein
51 Posterior facial vein (communicating the retromandibular
    vein with the facial vein)
52 Hyoglossus muscle
53 Mylohyoid muscle
54 Lingual artery within fat in sublingual space
55 Submandibular gland
56 Tongue base
57 Superior cornu of hyoid bone

Figure 19–3 *Continued.*

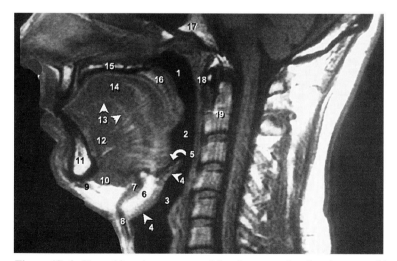

1   Nasopharyngeal airway
2   Oropharyngeal airway
3   Hypopharyngeal airway
4   Epiglottis
5   Vallecula
6   Preepiglottic fat
7   Hyoid bone
8   Thyroid cartilage
9   Mylohyoid muscle
10 Geniohyoid muscle
11 Symphysis menti
12 Genioglossus muscle
13 Lingual septum
14 Body of tongue
15 Hard palate
16 Soft palate/uvula
17 Clivus
18 Anterior arch of atlas (first cervical vertebra)
19 Odontoid process (dens)

Figure 19–4. Normal imaging anatomy of the pharynx and oral cavity on a midsagittal, non–contrast-enhanced, T1-weighted MR image.

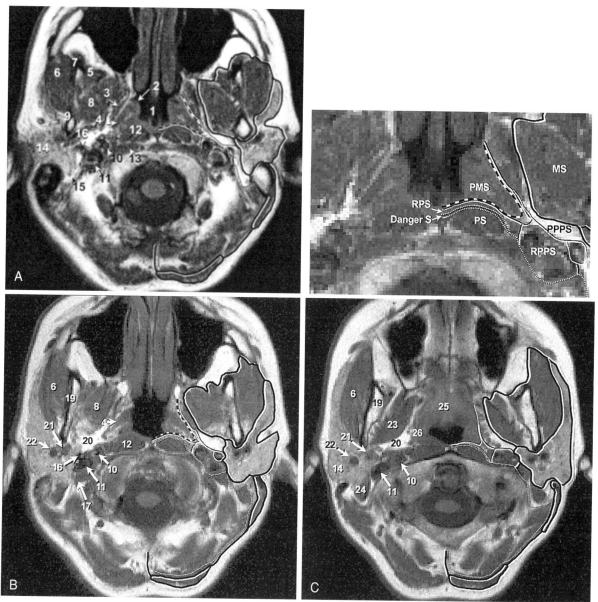

Figure 19–5. *A–I,* Normal imaging anatomy of the nasopharynx, oropharynx, and oral cavity on an axial nonenhanced, T1-weighted MR image. MS, masticator space; PMS, pharyngeal mucosal space; PPPS, prestyloid parapharyngeal space; PS, perivertebral space; RPPS, retrostyloid parapharyngeal space (carotid space); RPS, retropharyngeal space. The central region of *A* is depicted *(inset).*

1 Nasopharyngeal airway
2 Torus tubarius
3 Tensor veli palatini muscle
4 Levator veli palatini muscle
5 Temporalis muscle (deep = medial head)
6 Masseter muscle
7 Coronoid process of mandible
8 Lateral pterygoid muscle
9 Neck of the mandible
10 Internal carotid artery
11 Internal jugular vein
12 Longus capitis muscle
13 Rectus capitis anterior muscle
14 Parotid gland (superficial lobe)

15 Facial nerve emerging from stylomastoid foramen and entering parotid gland
16 Styloid process
17 Rectus capitis lateralis muscle
18 Fat in infratemporal fossa
19 Ramus of mandible
20 Fat in prestyloid compartment of parapharyngeal space
21 External carotid artery
22 Retromandibular vein
23 Medial pterygoid muscle
24 Posterior belly of digastric muscle
25 Soft palate
26 Superior constrictor muscle of pharynx

Illustration continued on following page

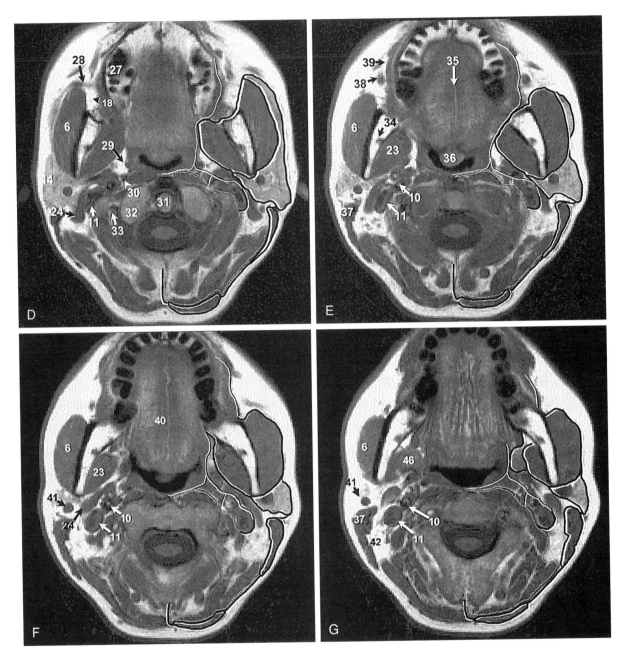

Figure 19–5. *Continued.*

27 Alveolar process of maxilla
28 Parotid (Stensen's) duct
29 Ascending pharyngeal artery overlying superior constrictor muscle of pharynx
30 Lateral retropharyngeal lymph node (of Rouviere) in retropharyngeal space
31 Odontoid process (dens)
32 Lateral mass of atlas (C1 vertebra)
33 Vertebral artery in foramen transversarium
34 Mandibular foramen transmitting inferior alveolar nerve and vessels
35 Lingual septum
36 Uvula
37 Sternocleidomastoid muscle

38 Anterior facial vein
39 Buccinator muscle
40 Genioglossus/geniohyoid muscles
41 External jugular vein
42 Fat in posterior cervical space
43 Hyoglossus muscle
44 Mylohyoid muscle
45 Fat in sublingual space
46 Submandibular gland
47 Oropharyngeal airway
48 Tongue base
49 Body of mandible

Illustration continued on following page

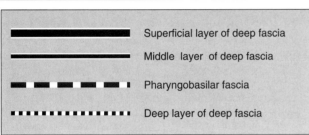

▬▬▬▬▬▬▬	Superficial layer of deep fascia
────────	Middle layer of deep fascia
▬▬▬▬▬▬	Pharyngobasilar fascia
▪▪▪▪▪▪▪▪▪▪▪	Deep layer of deep fascia

Figure 19–5. *Continued.*

Computed Tomography

Patient Positioning

Patients are examined in the supine position for axial scans and in the prone position for direct coronal scans. The prone position is recommended whenever a nasopharyngeal or palatal mass is suspected and there is a possibility of skull base erosion.[119] Scanning is done during suspended respiration and attention must always be paid to proper head position.[119]

Intravenous Contrast

A confident assessment of the possible cervical lymphadenopathy associated with nasopharyngeal and oropharyngeal pathology requires optimal vascular opacification with an iodinated contrast medium. This is achieved by delivering a loading bolus (50 mL, 2 mL/second) via a power injector, followed by continuous contrast infusion (1 mL/second).[119]

Acquisition Parameters

A preliminary lateral scout view is obtained. Axial scans are planned parallel to the infraorbital-meatal line and should cover the whole region from the external auditory canal to the upper border of the manubrium sterni. Such extended coverage ensures proper evaluation of the pharynx, skull base, and all node-bearing areas. Examination is best performed with 3- to 5-mm-thick contiguous slices and a small field of view (FOV). An additional high-resolution bone reconstruction algorithm should be used to evaluate any pathologic bone involvement.[81, 119]

Magnetic Resonance Imaging

Patient Positioning

Axial, sagittal, and coronal scans are obtainable without the need to reposition the supine patient. A head coil is convenient for scanning the nasopharynx and oropharynx. In patients with malignancies, since the entire neck must be evaluated for nodal disease, a dedicated neck coil must be used in addition in order to cover the area from the mouth floor to the supraclavicular region.[83, 96, 119] Besides head motion, pharyngeal motion (e.g., swallowing and snoring) must also be prevented to ensure optimal image quality.[119]

Intravenous Contrast

Postintravenous gadolinium-DTPA T1-weighted studies are helpful in detection of pathologic lesions. Such images improve the visualization of small lesions; provide excellent evaluation of lesion extension, subtle infiltration, and perineural spread; and aid in the assessment of tumor recurrence after radiotherapy or surgery.[108, 128, 140, 177]

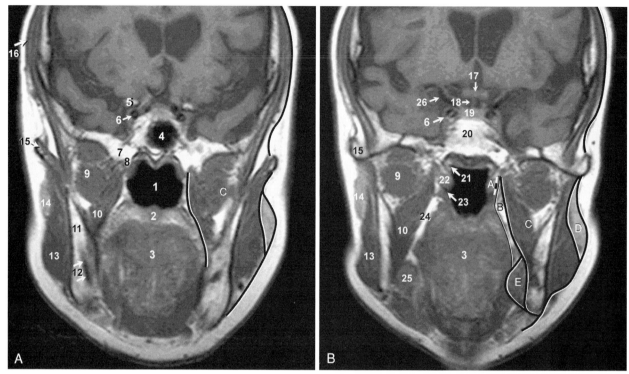

Figure 19–6. *A–D,* Normal imaging anatomy of the nasopharynx and oropharynx on a coronal non–contrast-enhanced, T1-weighted MR image. A, pharyngeal mucosal space (PMS); B, prestyloid parapharyngeal space (PPPS); C, masticator space (MS); D, parotid space (PS); E, submandibular space.

1 Nasopharyngeal airway	14 Parotid gland
2 Soft palate	15 Zygomatic arch
3 Tongue	16 Temporalis muscle
4 Sphenoid sinus	17 Optic chiasm
5 Anterior clinoid process	18 Pituitary stalk
6 Internal carotid artery	19 Pituitary gland
7 Greater wing of sphenoid bone	20 Clivus
8 Root of medial pterygoid plate of sphenoid bone	21 Fossa of Rosenmüller (lateral pharyngeal recess)
9 Lateral pterygoid muscle	22 Torus tubarius overlying levator veli palatini muscle
10 Medial pterygoid muscle	23 Eustachian tube opening
11 Ramus of mandible	24 Fat in prestyloid parapharyngeal space
12 Mandibular canal	25 Submandibular salivary gland
13 Masseter muscle	26 Middle cerebral artery

Pulse Sequences and Acquisition Parameters

In general, T1-weighted images provide the best fat-muscle and fat-tumor contrast, whereas T2-weighted images provide the best muscle–lymphoid tissue contrast.[95, 119, 171]

The axial plane is often most useful, and both axial T1-weighted and T2-weighted images, encompassing at least the region from the palate to the hyoid bone, should be performed in all cases. It is recommended that T2-weighted images, using a fast spin-echo with fat-suppression technique, be acquired because this method yields very high conspicuity of lesions.[89, 128]

Coronal T1-weighted images improve the evaluation of lesions adjacent to the skull base and within the subman-dibular or sublingual spaces, and sagittal T1-weighted images are helpful in the evaluation of midline lesions.

Contrast-enhanced T1-weighted images are also best obtained with the use of fat-suppression techniques in order to achieve better definition of the enhanced areas, particularly for blocking the marrow signal in the evaluation of the skull base or other involved bone. However, suboptimal fat-suppression techniques may create artifactual bright signals that mimic pathologic processes, particularly in the high nasopharynx and in the low orbit.[2, 128]

As stated, additional neck scanning for nodal metastases using a neck coil is required for patients with malignancies.

Slice thickness should be no more than 3 to 4 mm for T1-weighted images and 5 mm for T2-weighted images, with an interslice gap of 1 mm or less. For T1-weighted images, echo time (TE) should be kept as short as possible

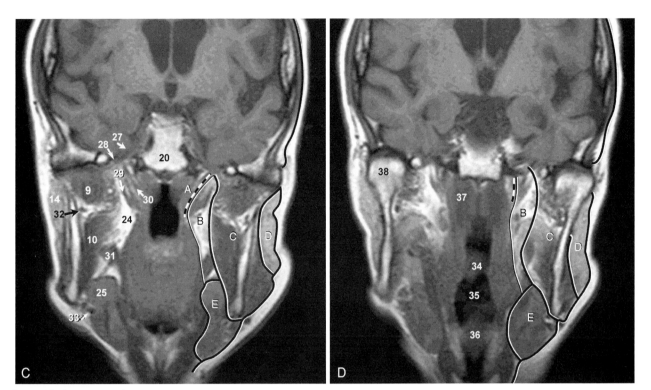

Figure 19–6. *Continued.*

27 Mandibular division of trigeminal nerve
28 Foramen ovale
29 Tensor veli palatini muscle
30 Levator veli palatini muscle
31 Styloglossus muscle
32 Internal maxillary artery
33 Facial vein
34 Uvula
35 Oropharyngeal airway
36 Epiglottis
37 Longus capitis muscle
38 Head of mandible

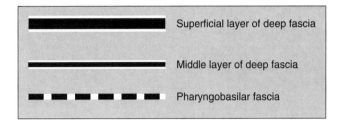

in order to reduce the magnetic susceptibility artifact. Motion compensation gradients and spatial presaturation pulses may also be helpful in reducing flow and other motion artifacts. Phase encoding should be swept in an anteroposterior direction so that the vascular "ghost artifacts" are thrown anteroposteriorly and not across the pharyngeal tissues.[65] The optimal field of view, matrix size, and number of signal averages depend upon the particular imaging system and field strength, but they should reflect a compromise between adequate signal-to-noise, spatial resolution, and total examination length.

Several newer MRI techniques have been applied to nasopharyngeal and oropharyngeal imaging, including:

1. MR angiography for evaluation of vascular occlusion or displacement by a mass.[128, 176]
2. Functional upper airway imaging to study the soft palate function in patients with sleep apnea and cleft palate.[107, 128]
3. Perfusion imaging to assess tumor vascularity and response to treatment.

4. Spectroscopy to determine the primary presentation of malignancy and possible tumor recurrence.[128]

Pathology
Lesions Arising within the Pharyngeal Wall and Adjoining Deep Neck Spaces
Lesions of the Pharyngeal Mucosal Space
Pseudomass
Asymmetric Fossae of Rosenmüller

Asymmetry of the lateral pharyngeal recesses may result from inflammatory debris or asymmetry in the amount of lymphoid tissue, thereby giving the impression of a mass in the PMS.[42, 65, 128] A true tumor is ruled out when[42, 65]:

1. The adjoining soft tissue planes in the PPS and RPS are maintained.
2. The nasopharyngeal mucosa is clinically intact.
3. The collapsed recess opens when rescanning by CT is used during the Valsalva maneuver.

Congenital Lesions

Thornwaldt's Cyst

Thornwaldt's cyst is a congenital midline posterior PMS cyst, lined by pharyngeal mucosa. It results from focal adhesion of pharyngeal mucosa to the notochord, which is then carried up as the notochord ascends to the developing skull base. A resultant nasopharyngeal diverticulum is created (a pharyngeal bursa),[28] whose orifice becomes obliterated after an attack of pharyngitis, thereby forming the cyst. Thornwaldt's cysts are present in 4% of all autopsy specimens (and MR images of the head).[42, 65, 119]

Clinical Presentation. The peak age incidence is 15 to 30 years. Thornwaldt's cyst is usually an asymptomatic, incidental finding in head MRI. The cyst is usually infected with anaerobic bacteria, and when intracystic pressure increases, the orifice opens and the patient presents with persistent or periodic nasopharyngeal drainage, halitosis, and foul taste. Dull occipital headache has also been described.[42, 65, 108, 119]

Imaging Features (Fig. 19–7). Thornwaldt's cyst appears as a well-circumscribed, thin-walled, midline (but may be slightly off-center) posterior nasopharyngeal mucosal space cyst lodged between the prevertebral muscles. It varies in diameter from a few millimeters to several centimeters. On CT scans, a small cyst may be missed whereas a larger one usually is seen as hypodense mucoid attenuation. CT attenuation of the cyst increases as does its protein content, and occasionally it may mimic a soft tissue mass. MRI readily identifies the cyst, whose T1-weighted signal intensity increases from low to high with increasing protein content.

On T2-weighted and fluid-attenuated inversion recovery (FLAIR) images, signal intensity is high.[42, 65, 77, 119] Postcontrast studies show marginal enhancement.[28] Other imaging features may include superimposed cervical adenitis secondary to cyst infection.[6, 11, 128]

Inflammatory Conditions

Adenoidal and Tonsillar Hypertrophy

Hypertrophy of these lymphoid tissues represents immunologic activity and not a disease process per se. It is most commonly seen in the adenoids,[65] which begins to be

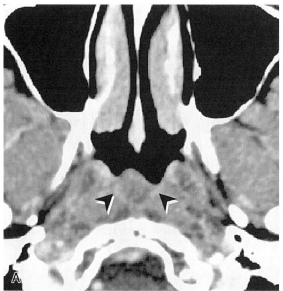
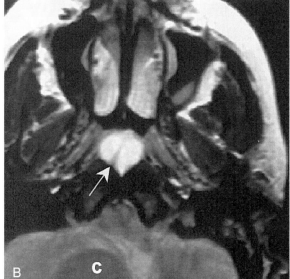
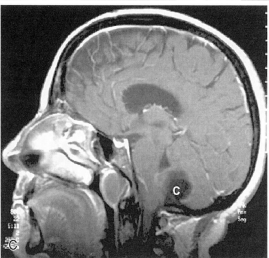

Figure 19–7. Thornwaldt's cyst. *A,* Contrast-enhanced CT scan shows a small Thornwaldt cyst occupying the typical midline posterior nasopharyngeal location. Marginal enhancement delineates the otherwise isodense cyst *(arrowheads).* Axial T2-weighted *(B)* and sagittal postgadolinium-enhanced, T1-weighted *(C)* MR image of another Thornwaldt cyst. The T2-weighted image demonstrates a sharply defined, hyperintense mass lesion resting on the posterior nasopharyngeal wall and dipping between the longus capitis muscles. An internal septum is noted *(white arrow, B).* Rim enhancement is apparent on the postgadolinium-enhanced scan. The intermediate T1-weighted signal of the cyst denotes its high protein content. Note the incidental right-sided posterior fossa arachnoid cyst (c in *B* and *C*).

prominent by the age of 2 to 3 years and to regress from adolescence onward. Failure to visualize adenoidal tissue in a young child should raise the possibility of an immune deficiency state.[119] In adults, smoking not uncommonly induces nasopharyngeal lymphoid hyperplasia.[53]

Clinical Presentation. Infants present with difficulty in feeding, whereas older children present with other symptoms of nasal obstruction, such as mouth breathing and snoring. Otitis media may result from encroachment on the orifice of the eustachian tube.[65] Dysphagia may be caused by palatine tonsillar hypertrophy.[13, 134] Adenoidectomy or tonsillectomy is indicated when hypertrophy results in nasopharyngeal airway obstruction, chronic otitis media, or serous middle ear effusion.[13, 58, 59]

Imaging Features (Fig. 19–8). Hypertrophic adenoids appears as a homogenous fullness of the nasopharyngeal mucosal space, which obliterates the fossae of Rosenmüller and encroaches upon the nasopharyngeal airway. On CT scans, the adenoid is isodense to the underlying prevertebral muscles and may contain small cysts and calcifications. On T1-weighted MRI scans, it is isointense to the muscles as well but can be identified by its bright T2-

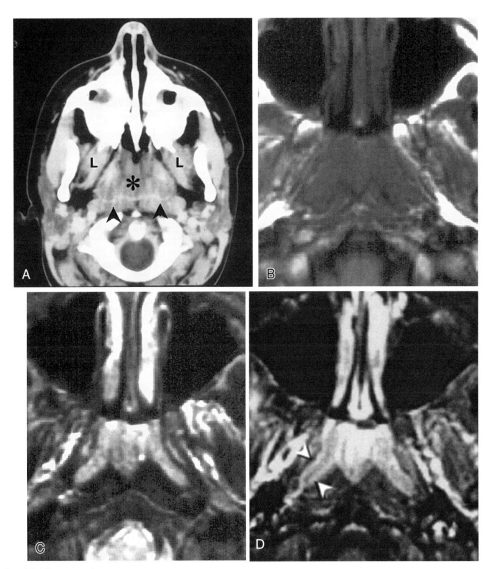

Figure 19–8. Adenoidal hypertrophy.
A, Contrast-enhanced CT scan of the nasopharynx demonstrates enlarged adenoid tissue. The thin, enhancing line separating the adenoids *(asterisk)* from the prevertebral muscles represents the intact pharyngobasilar fascia, indicating that the mass is totally within the confines of the pharyngeal mucosal space. Also note the intact fat planes separating the mass from the lateral pterygoid (L) muscles on either side.
B–D, MR images at the level of the nasopharynx in a 10-year-old girl. *B,* Axial unenhanced, T1-weighted image (TR = 570 msec, TE = 14 msec) shows a homogeneous mass filling the nasopharyngeal airway and displaying an isointense signal to the adjacent muscles. *C,* Axial T2-weighted image (TR = 2500 msec, TE = 90 msec) more accurately identifies the adenoidal tissue as a bright signal casting the shape of the airway and well contrasted against the dark prevertebral muscles. *D,* Axial gadolinium-enhanced, T1-weighted MR image (TR = 594 msec, TE = 14 msec) elegantly demonstrates the pharyngobasilar fascia as a thin, enhancing line *(arrowheads),* marginating the deep and lateral adenoid surfaces and confirming the noninvasive nature of the lesion.

weighted signal. On postcontrast scans, the pharyngobasilar fascia normally enhances as a thin, continuous line outlining the deep adenoid surface.

Identification of this line is a reliable sign of the noninvasive nature of the mass, although it does not guarantee benign pathology.[65, 119] In fact, it may be impossible to differentiate between hypertrophic adenoids and nasopharyngeal lymphoma on the basis of CT or MRI,[47] and a definitive diagnosis can be made only by biopsy. Other imaging features include reactive cervical adenopathy[119] and eustachian tube dysfunction, which is best detected as bright T2 signals of fluid in the mastoid air cells.[108]

Hypertrophic palatine tonsils are less common and present as bilateral, smooth oval, or rounded soft tissue masses encroaching upon either side of the oropharyngeal air column. Hypertrophic lingual tonsils are the least common. They occur at the tongue base and encroach posteriorly upon the valleculae. CT and MRI appearances of both are similar to those of adenoidal hypertrophy.[73]

Tonsillitis and Peritonsillar Abscess

Acute tonsillitis or adenotonsillitis may be caused by viral or bacterial infection. The disease is usually self-limited, but when severe, infection may suppurate, resulting in a peritonsillar abscess (quinsy) or, rarely, in a tonsillar abscess. A peritonsillar abscess entails accumulation of pus in the tonsillar bed (between the tonsillar capsule and the faucial arches), with medial displacement of the tonsil. The abscess may further extend deeper into the neck to involve the PPS or lateral part of the RPS.[73, 119] Peritonsillar abscesses constitute 49% of head and neck space infections in children.[173] When secondary to infectious mononucleosis, it is associated with cervical lymphadenopathy and hepatosplenomegaly.[96]

Clinical Presentation. The patient is typically a child or a young adult. Patients with simple tonsillitis present with fever and sore throat. In a patient with peritonsillar abscess, initial tonsillitis may be followed by a few days of lucidity before the development of rapidly progressive dysphagia, otalgia, and perhaps trismus if the medial pterygoid muscle is involved. Pharyngeal wall protrusion is seen on clinical examination.[65, 119]

Imaging Features. Imaging is rarely performed in the stage of acute, uncomplicated tonsillitis. When a peritonsillar abscess is clinically suspected, the radiologist's responsibilities are to[65, 73]:

1. Confirm the diagnosis.
2. Determine the degree of airway compromise.
3. Determine whether the abscess is confined to the PMS or has spread into the PPS or the RPS.
4. Comment, in the case of a deeply extending abscess, on the status of internal carotid artery and internal jugular vein.

A peritonsillar abscess confined to the PMS appears as a diffuse, ill-defined thickening of the tonsillar region that bulges medially into the oropharyngeal airway with preserved parapharyngeal fat. On noncontrast CT scans, the inflammatory process appears hypodense to isodense.[42] On MR images, it is also hypointense to isointense to the

surrounding muscles on T1-weighted images and hyperintense on T2-weighted images. Postcontrast studies are essential to delineate the enhancing rim of a mature abscess wall that requires drainage.[184]

Imaging features of a deeply extending abscess are discussed later under the appropriate topics.

Postinflammatory Dystrophic Calcification

Clumps of tonsillar calcification (tonsilloliths) may be detected incidentally on CT scans (Fig. 19–9) and indicate previous or chronic tonsillitis. Less commonly, they are seen in the adenoids or the lingual tonsil.[65, 128, 184]

Postinflammatory Retention Cyst

Postpharyngitis sequelae also include the formation of mucous retention cysts in the inflamed obstructed mucous glands. These cysts are similar to those that develop within the paranasal sinuses.[4, 184]

Clinical Presentation. These retention cysts are usually asymptomatic but may be large enough to cause a superficial pharyngeal mass or otitis media secondary to eustachian tube orifice compromise.[65]

Imaging Features. The cyst appears as a well-defined mass in the PMS. It is usually a few centimeters in diameter but can grow to a large size.[65, 128] Both CT and MRI demonstrate the appearance of a typical cyst (i.e., hypodense on CT scans, dark on T1-weighted images, and bright on T2-weighted images). However, a high protein content increases CT density and T1-weighted signal intensity.

Benign Tumors

Juvenile Nasopharyngeal Angiofibroma

This angiofibroma is a highly vascular, benign yet locally invasive, noncapsulated mesenchymal tumor.[108, 180] It

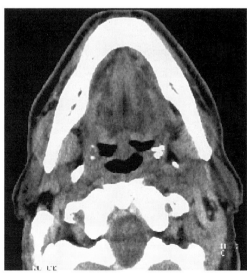

Figure 19–9. Dystrophic calcification of the faucial tonsils. CT scan at the level of the oropharynx shows bilateral clusters of tonsillar calcification (tonsilloliths), more evident on the left side.

is thought to arise near the sphenopalatine foramen[28, 184] at the junction between the nose and the nasopharynx at the root of the medial pterygoid plate. It represents 0.5% of all head and neck neoplasms,[42] and the incidence is higher in the Far East than in the United States.[184]

Clinical Presentation. Juvenile angiofibroma occurs almost exclusively in adolescent boys,[28, 184] with the mean age at presentation 15 years.[42] The most common presenting symptom is nasal speech attributed to nasal obstruction (91%), the next most common is severe recurrent epistaxis (59%), and the least common is facial deformity.[42] On examination, a dark red (probably ulcerating) mass is seen in the nasal fossa and postnasal space.[133]

Imaging Features (Figs. 19–10 and 19–11). Juvenile angiofibroma appears on CT and MRI images as a soft tissue mass varying in size from a small nodule resting on the sphenopalatine foramen and striding the choana to a quite large, locally aggressive growth extending in any or a combination of the following directions:

1. *Posteriorly.* The tumor may protrude into or may totally fill the nasopharyngeal airway.
2. *Anteriorly.* The tumor may block and expand the ipsilateral nasal fossa. Large tumors may also extend directly into the contralateral nasal fossa through the choana.
3. *Medially.* The tumor may push the nasal septum significantly to encroach upon or even to obliterate the contralateral nasal fossa.
4. *Laterally.* In 90% of cases, the tumor extends laterally through the sphenopalatine foramen into the pterygopalatine fossa.[63] The fossa is widened with classic anterior bowing of the posterior maxillary antral wall along with posterior displacement and, possibly, erosion of the pterygoid laminae. Bowing of the posterior antral wall (Holman-Miller sign)[184] is a nonspecific sign that can be produced by any slowly growing mass, whereas erosion of the pterygoid lamina is probably a pathognomonic sign.[133] From the pterygopalatine fossa, the tumor may further extend laterally through the pterygomaxillary fissure into the masticator space (infratemporal fossa).[28]
5. *Superiorly.* In 65% of cases, juvenile angiofibromas erode the floor of the sphenoid sinus to invade the sinus cavity.[180] It is important to differentiate intrasinus tumor invasion from obstructed secretions.[73] This is best done by T2-weighted MRI. The ethmoid air cells may also be invaded.[108] Intraorbital extension, with subsequent proptosis, can occur from the pterygopalatine fossa through the inferior orbital fissure, which becomes widened.[28, 42] Intracranial invasion (into the middle cranial fossa) can then occur from the orbit through the superior orbital fissure[28, 42, 180] or by direct erosion of the roof of the sphenoid sinus.[108] Coronal scans are valuable for precise detection of superior tumor extension.
6. *Inferiorly.* The tumor can grow sufficiently to push the soft palate and bulge into the oropharynx and adjoining oral cavity.

On unenhanced CT scans, the tumor appears isodense; on MR images, it displays intermediate T1-weighted and strongly bright T2-weighted signal intensities. On both T1-weighted and T2-weighted images, characteristic punctate areas of signal void indicate the highly vascular stroma. Postcontrast CT and MRI reveal intense enhancement.[42, 133, 180]

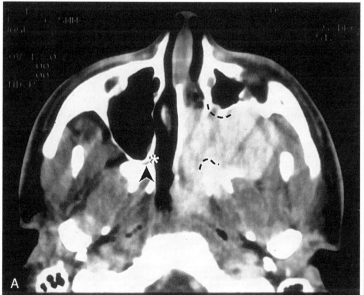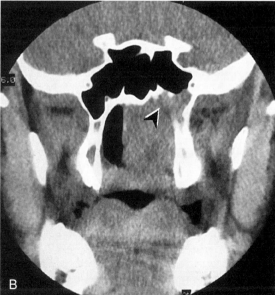

Figure 19–10. Juvenile nasopharyngeal angiofibroma. *A,* Axial contrast-enhanced CT scan demonstrates the typical features of nasopharyngeal angiofibroma (grade 2). A strongly enhancing mass lesion is centered on the markedly widened pterygopalatine fossa and is displacing the yet intact posterior maxillary antral wall forward. (Compare the distance between the *dashed lines* on the left side to the normal-sized basal part of the pterygopalatine fossa on the right side *[black arrowhead]*.) The sphenopalatine foramen, where an angiofibroma is believed to arise, is located at a higher level above the *asterisk.* *B,* Coronal nonenhanced CT scan shows a large, isodense nasopharyngeal soft tissue mass in a 14-year-old boy. The mass occupies most of the airway and is eroding the root of the medial pterygoid plate *(arrowhead)* as well as the floor of the sphenoid sinus, yet without frank intrasinus extension.

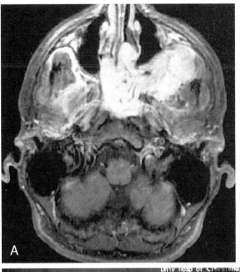
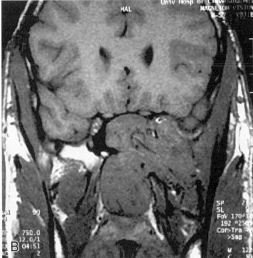
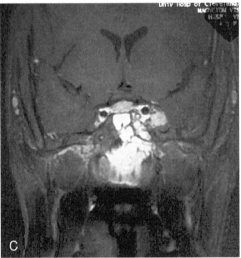

Figure 19–11. Juvenile nasopharyngeal angiofibroma. MRI scan of a grade 3 angiofibroma in a 15-year-old boy.

A, Axial postgadolinium-enhanced, T1-weighted scan (TR = 779 msec, TE = 12 msec) shows a large, intensely enhancing mass centered on the left sphenopalatine foramen region. It totally occupies the nasopharyngeal airway, plugs both choanae, and extends into the nasal fossae, more on the left side. The mass extends laterally to cause marked widening of the pterygopalatine fossa, from which it emerges through the pterygomaxillary fissure into the masticator space (infratemporal fossa). Note the remodeling and anterior displacement of the posterior wall of left maxillary sinus as a result of chronic pressure.

B, Coronal nonenhanced, T1-weighted image of the same patient shows the angiofibroma as an intermediate signal soft tissue mass with multiple linear and punctate signal voids, representing the rich tumor vascularity. The mass is eroding the floor of the sphenoid sinus to fill and expand its left-sided compartment.

C, Coronal postgadolinium-enhanced, T1-weighted image shows the same patient at a different plane. The tumor has extended into the left cavernous sinus, abutting yet incompletely encasing the cavernous segment of the internal carotid artery. Such extension has probably occurred from the pterygopalatine fossa via the foramen rotundum.

The following imaging-based grading system of juvenile angiofibromas has been proposed.[28, 136, 172, 184]

- *Grade 1,* tumor confined to nasopharynx
- *Grade 2,* tumor extending into pterygopalatine fossa or masticator space
- *Grade 3,* tumor extending into orbit or intracranially

This scheme would predict the prognosis and recurrence rate and would indicate the optimal surgical approach.

The high tumor vascularity contraindicates biopsy, and preoperative embolization is necessary. The primary supply is through the maxillary artery. Minor contributors include the ascending pharyngeal and ascending palatine branches of the external carotid artery, and sometimes the tumor may have a supply from the internal carotid artery.[42, 180, 184]

Benign Mixed Tumor of Minor Salivary Glands

Benign mixed tumor *(pleomorphic adenoma)* may arise in the minor salivary glands located in the submucosal layer of the PMS, soft palate (most common site), or tongue base. Extrapharyngeal sites include the mouth, nose, paranasal sinuses, larynx, and trachea.[119]

Clinical Presentation. The presentation varies from a small submucosal nodule to a large pedunculated mass that compromises the pharyngeal airway.[65]

Imaging Features. When the tumor is small, it is best detected by MRI as a sharply demarcated, rounded, homogeneous PMS mass of low to intermediate T1-weighted and very high T2-weighted signal intensities.[105, 184] CT and MRI show a larger tumor as a pedunculated mass encroaching upon the nasopharyngeal or oropharyngeal airway. The appearance is nonspecific, and a biopsy usually enables the diagnosis.[65, 119]

Malignant Tumors
Squamous Cell Carcinoma

Nasopharyngeal Carcinoma. Squamous cell carcinoma (SCC) constitutes 70% of adult nasopharyngeal malignancies.[108, 119, 124] These are further subdivided into[149]:

- *Type 1,* keratinized squamous cell carcinoma (25%)
- *Type 2,* nonkeratinized carcinoma (12%) (sometimes called transitional cell carcinoma)
- *Type 3,* undifferentiated carcinomas (63%)

Several etiologic factors interact to predispose to the development of nasopharyngeal squamous cell carcinoma, such as:

- Genetic susceptibility
- Environmental factors (including chemical carcinogens)
- Exposure to Epstein-Barr virus,[30] which is very highly associated with types 2 and 3 of nasopharyngeal SCC[33, 180, 184]

The highest incidence is found in southern China and southeast Asia[28] and is seven times higher in Americans of Chinese ancestry than in non-Chinese Americans.[46] A higher incidence is also found in African Americans.[49]

Other risk factors include chronic sinonasal infection, nitrosamines (in dry-salted fish), polycyclic hydrocarbons, and poor living conditions.[119, 124]

Most tumors arise in the fossa of Rosenmüller and tend toward submucosal spread to infiltrate the palatal muscles and eustachian tube orifice.[28, 30]

Clinical Presentation. Nasopharyngeal carcinoma is more common in men, and most cases in the United States are diagnosed during the sixth decade of life.[30, 119] Reports from southeast Asia, however, indicate middle age, adolescence, and even childhood presentation.[17]

Patients with early-stage disease may be asymptomatic or may present with nonspecific, commonly overlooked symptoms such as postnasal drip and nasopharyngeal irritation.[108] Middle ear effusion secondary to involvement of the eustachian tube orifice or tensor veli palatini muscle[80] is also an early sign, and older patients with otitis media should always undergo imaging to rule out nasopharyngeal tumors.[4]

Cervical lymphadenopathy prompting initial medical consultation is also a common presenting symptom.[30] Patients with advanced disease may present with nasal obstruction, epistaxis, trismus, proptosis, and various cranial nerve palsies; the trigeminal nerve is the most commonly involved.[23, 28, 108, 119, 166]

Imaging Features
Early Cancer. As stated, most tumors arise in the lateral pharyngeal recess (fossa of Rosenmüller), and their signal intensity is almost similar to that of the adjacent mucosa.[42] The earliest imaging sign is thus asymmetrical superficial nasopharyngeal mucosa. This sign, however, should be cautiously interpreted because physiologic asymmetry of the fossae of Rosenmüller does exist. In addition to the measures listed earlier in this section, careful attention must be given to the following[4, 119, 178, 184]:

1. The fat stripe between the tensor and levator veli palatini muscles. Obliteration of the normally bright T1-weighted signal of this stripe may be one of the earliest indications of nasopharyngeal carcinoma (Fig. 19–12).
2. The ipsilateral middle ear and mastoid air cells. Detection of middle ear effusion or otomastoiditis as a bright

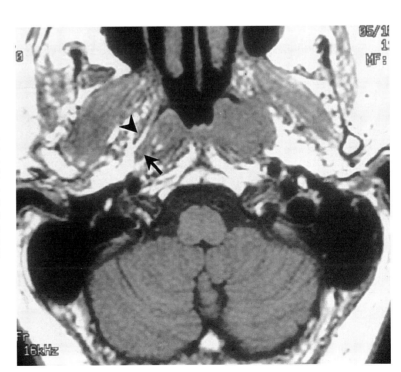

Figure 19–12. Nasopharyngeal carcinoma. Axial non–contrast-enhanced, T1-weighted MRI of the nasopharynx demonstrates a small, left-sided, isointense mass lesion in the pharyngeal mucosal space of the nasopharynx infiltrating the ipsilateral prestyloid parapharyngeal fat and barely touching the adjacent lateral pterygoid muscle. This appearance raises the possibility of masticator space invasion as well. Note the preserved fat stripe between the levator veli palatini muscle *(arrow)* and the tensor veli palatini muscle *(arrowhead)* on the normal right side.

T2-weighted signal is a warning sign of eustachian tube dysfunction.

3. Associated cervical lymphadenopathy. In particular, enlarged ipsilateral LRP lymph nodes (of Rouviere) presenting low to intermediate T1-weighted and high T2-weighted signals (Fig. 19–13).

Imaging of the entire neck with a dedicated neck coil is the essential next step, since up to 90% of these patients have cervical lymphadenopathy at presentation and about 50% have bilateral disease.[108, 110, 119] Although the LRP nodes are considered first-echelon nodes, they are first involved in only 65% of cases and skipped in the remaining 35% of patients, in whom internal jugular nodes are involved without radiographic evidence of retropharyngeal node disease.[30, 31]

Advanced Cancer. The most reliable sign of nasopharyngeal malignancy is the detection of an aggressive mass infiltrating the deep fascia and spaces around the nasopharynx (Fig. 19–14).[100, 119] On CT, it appears as an isodense mass that does not show significant enhancement in the postcontrast study even when it is large.[154]

On plain T1-weighted MR images, the tumor is isointense to the adjacent muscles.[81] This sequence is valuable for detecting replacement of the high-signal fat in the deep fascial spaces with the intermediate-signal tumor. On T2-weighted images, the tumor displays intermediate to high signal intensity.[119, 154, 178]

Considerable enhancement of the solid parts of the tumor occurs in the postgadolinium scans. Fat-saturated, postgadolinium T1-weighted images are particularly valuable for defining the extent of tumor infiltration into the marrow of the skull base or the retrobulbar fat while maintaining good contrast between the enhancing tumor and adjacent muscles.[5, 126, 154] In addition, both fat-saturated,

postcontrast T1-weighted and fat-saturated T2-weighted sequences have been shown to improve the detection of lymphadenopathy as well as the presence of nodal necrosis or extracapsular nodal spread.[5, 38, 69, 126]

Although CT is particularly helpful for detecting involvement of thin bony structures, such as the cortical bones of the skull base, paranasal sinuses, and orbits,[30, 119, 154] MRI better delineates infiltration of bone marrow.[30] It is generally agreed that MRI is the modality of choice in the diagnosis of primary as well as recurrent nasopharyngeal carcinoma.[29, 30, 76, 126, 127, 154] The imaging appearance is usually nonspecific for a particular type of malignancy, and CT and MRI images of squamous cell carcinoma may be almost identical to those of nasopharyngeal lymphoma or minor salivary gland malignancies.[65, 119]

Role of Imaging

When evaluating cases of nasopharyngeal carcinoma, the radiologist has the following primary tasks[184]:

- To provide accurate tumor staging
- To define tumor margins for the radiation oncologist
- To evaluate the response to radio/chemotherapy

The most recent (fifth) edition of the Tumor-Node-Metastasis (TNM) classification of nasopharyngeal carcinoma, published in 1997 as a collaborative project of the UICC and the AJCC, is given in Table 19–2.[1, 174]

Nasopharyngeal carcinoma has been described as spreading along well-defined routes,[30, 146] with a tendency to grow along the path of least resistance,[108, 119] as follows:

1. *Lateral spread* is the most common direction.[30, 119, 147, 165, 166, 186] The tumor creeps out of the PMS through the only dehiscence in the superolateral part of the tough pharyngobasilar fascia, the sinus of Morgagni, to reach the PPS.[119] This pattern of spread occurs quite early and

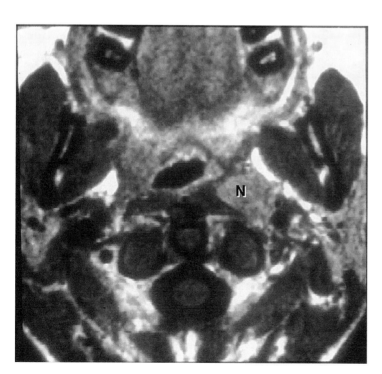

Figure 19–13. Enlarged lateral retropharyngeal lymph node (of Rouviere). Nonenhanced, axial T1-weighted MR image at the level of the oropharynx shows the typical appearance of enlarged left-sided node of Rouviere (N) in a patient with nasopharyngeal carcinoma. The enlarged node appears as a well-defined paramedian retropharyngeal small soft tissue mass of intermediate T1-weighted signal intensity. It effaces and displaces the parapharyngeal fat anterolaterally and mildly rotates the oropharyngeal airway in a counterclockwise direction.

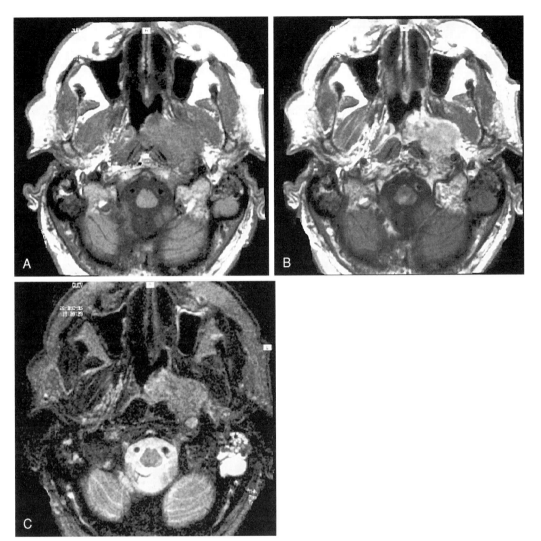

Figure 19–14. Nasopharyngeal carcinoma infiltrating the left parapharyngeal space.

A, Axial nonenhanced, T1-weighted MR image demonstrates a soft tissue mass (~4 × 2.5 cm) involving the left aspect of the pharyngeal mucosal space, bulging into the nasopharyngeal airway, and extending deeply into the ipsilateral prestyloid parapharyngeal space. (Compare the size and shape of parapharyngeal fat on both sides.) The imperceptible fat planes between the tumor and the lateral pterygoid muscle anteriorly and prevertebral muscles posteriorly suggest masticator and perivertebral space involvement.

B, Axial postgadolinium-enhanced, T1-weighted MRI scan shows considerable tumor enhancement and delineates the exact tumor boundaries except in relation to parapharyngeal fat, an issue already observed on the nonenhanced scan.

C, Axial T2-weighted MR image of the same patient shows a tumor of intermediate signal intensity. Note the associated fluid signal within the left mastoid air cells secondary to eustachian tube obstruction.

is seen in 60% of patients at presentation[29, 184] as partial or complete effacement of the parapharyngeal triangle of fat (see Figs. 19–12 and 19–14). From there, the tumor may further extend laterally to break into the masticator space, infiltrating the pterygoid muscles and giving rise to trismus.[19, 21, 30] Once the masticator space is violated, careful scrutiny should be made to detect the highly possible perineural infiltration of the mandibular nerve. The latter acts as a "cable" along which the tumor tracks upward to gain intracranial access through the foramen ovale, invade the gasserian ganglion in Meckel's cave (Fig. 19–15), and follow the preganglionic segment of the trigeminal nerve as far as the pons, often resulting in denervation atrophy of the muscles of mastication (Fig. 19–16).[30, 65] Perineural spread is often

clinically silent until the intracranial segment of the nerve has been infiltrated.[166] Such perineural infiltration is best evaluated by precontrast and postcontrast coronal T1-weighted MRI, particularly with fat-suppression techniques.[5, 166] The mandibular nerve, lying between the medial and lateral pterygoid muscles, demonstrates abnormal thickening and enhancement with effacement of the surrounding fat planes.[82, 119] Imaging signs of perineural tumor spread are detailed later (see "Oropharyngeal Carcinoma").

2. *Posterolateral spread* occurs into the retrostyloid compartment of the PPS, thereby putting cranial nerves IX through XII at risk of involvement.[30]

3. With *posterior spread*, the tumor first infiltrates the RPS, obliterating its fat stripe, then invades the periver-

Table 19–2. Tumor-Node-Metastasis (TNM) Classification of Nasopharyngeal Carcinoma

T Staging

T1	Tumor confined to nasopharynx
T2	Tumor extends to soft tissue of oropharynx and/or nasal fossa:
T2a	Without parapharyngeal extension*
T2b	With parapharyngeal extension*
T3	Tumor invades bony structures and/or paranasal sinuses
T4	Tumor with intracranial extension and/or involvement of cranial nerves, infratemporal fossa, hypopharynx, or orbit

N Staging

N0	No regional lymph node metastasis
N1	Unilateral node(s): 6 cm or less in greatest dimension above supraclavicular fossa
N2	Bilateral node(s): 6 cm or less in greatest dimension, above supraclavicular fossa
N3	Metastasis in lymph node(s):
N3a	Greater than 6 cm in dimension
N3b	In the supraclavicular fossa

M Staging

M0	No distant metastases
M1	Distant metastases are present

*Parapharyngeal extension denotes posterolateral infiltration of tumor beyond the pharyngobasilar fascia.

From Fleming I, Cooper J, Henson D, et al (eds): Manual for Staging of Cancer, 5th ed. American Joint Committee on Cancer. Philadelphia, Lippincott-Raven, 1997.

tebral space. Involvement of the prevertebral muscles is not uncommon and is best assessed by T2-weighted or enhanced MRI (see Fig. 19–14B and C). In late-stage disease, vertebral body destruction and spinal canal invasion occur at times.[30, 130]

4. *Superior spread* results in skull base erosion and/or intracranial tumor extension, most commonly into the middle cranial fossa.[29] Skull base erosion occurs in up to one third of patients,[22] whereas the frequency of detectable intracranial spread varies from 12% on CT scans up to 31% on MR images.[29, 146] The most common route of intracranial spread is through the foramen ovale,[27, 29, 30, 166] either via perineural mandibular nerve infiltration (see earlier) or by direct tumor extension into the foramen.[119] Other less common routes include:

a. Extension into the foramen lacerum, where the tumor encases the internal carotid artery, which leads it into the cavernous sinus, putting the III, IV, and VI nerves as well as the ophthalmic and maxillary divisions of the trigeminal nerves at risk of involvement.[29, 30, 119]

b. Direct destruction of the skull base (Fig. 19–17), commonly at the sites of muscular attachments, particularly the levator and tensor veli palatini.[29, 100, 119]

c. Direct invasion of the sphenoid sinus.[29]

Intracranial extension into the posterior cranial fossa may also occur through the jugular foramen along the neurovascular bundle[23, 108, 112] or through the foramen

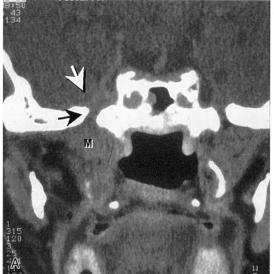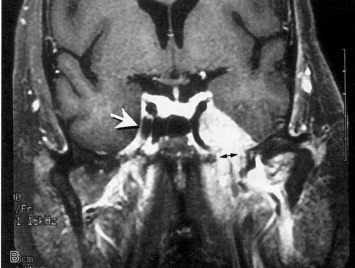

Figure 19–15. Intracranial extension of nasopharyngeal carcinoma through the foramen ovale. The following images demonstrate a common route of intracranial extension of nasopharyngeal carcinoma through the foramina ovale while the skull base is intact. Such tumor extension occurs along the mandibular division of the trigeminal nerve and indicates that the tumor has already violated the masticator space.

A, Postcontrast coronal CT scan shows a mildly enhancing, right-sided soft tissue mass lesion (M), responsible for the asymmetry of the nasopharyngeal airway and extending intracranially, as evidenced by (1) the presence of a small parasellar enhancing soft tissue component *(white arrow)* obliterating the normal cerebrospinal fluid density of Meckel's cave and (2) widening of the right-sided foramen ovale *(black arrow).*

B, Postgadolinium-enhanced, coronal fat-suppressed, T1-weighted MR image of another patient shows an intensely enhancing, left-sided parapharyngeal and masticator space mass lesion that extends intracranially through the widened ipsilateral foramen ovale *(double arrow)* to attain an extra-axial location within the middle cranial fossa, obliterating Meckel's cave and elevating the left temporal lobe of the brain. The *white arrow* indicates a normal Meckel's cave.

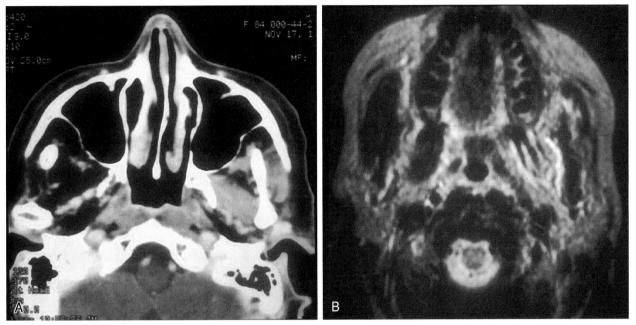

Figure 19–16. Atrophy of muscles of mastication. Enhanced axial CT scan at the level of the nasopharynx *(A)* and axial T2-weighted MRI scan at the level of the oropharynx *(B)* demonstrate atrophy of the right and left masticator spaces, respectively, with consequent abundance of intermuscular fat planes.

magnum, but it is usually associated with gross bone destruction.[27] Indirect intracranial access has also been described through the foramen rotundum[20, 24, 27, 125] and superior orbital fissure (see later).[30] A knowledge of the routes of intracranial spread of nasopharyngeal carcinoma is important in order to understand that bone erosion may not always be present. Indeed, the first sign of intracranial infiltration may be a mere dural thickening, along the floor of the middle cranial fossa,[30]

that is best appreciated on contrast-enhanced coronal MR images.
5. *Inferior spread* may occur, often submucosally, and may be clinically occult down to the oropharynx, thereby increasing the T classification from stage T1 to stage T2. The tough pharyngobasilar fascia forms a moderately resistant barrier to tumor outgrowth, and such spread may be indicated by asymmetry of the PMS below the level of the hard palate or at the level of C1-C2.[30, 108, 119]

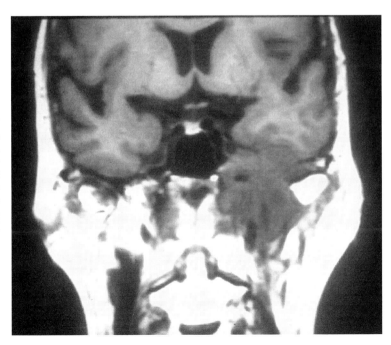

Figure 19–17. Intracranial extension of nasopharyngeal carcinoma through skull base erosion. Coronal nonenhanced, T1-weighted MRI scan demonstrates an intermediate-signal-intensity soft tissue mass infiltrating the skull base on the left side and extending into the epidural space underneath the left temporal lobe of the brain. The ipsilateral Meckel's cave is compressed yet patent (see Fig. 19–15), suggesting that intracranial extension in this case has not occurred through the foramen ovale.

6. *Anterior spread* occurs into the posterior aspect of the nasal cavity from which the tumor may extend through the sphenopalatine foramen into the pterygopalatine fossa.[30] Once within the latter, perineural infiltration of the maxillary division of the trigeminal nerve is a potential route for intracranial extension through the foramen rotundum.[20] Uncommonly, further spread from the pterygopalatine fossa may occur through the inferior orbital fissure into the orbit, then through the superior orbital fissure into the cavernous sinus and middle cranial fossa. Invasion of the maxillary antrum and posterior ethmoids is also uncommon.[30, 119] Obliteration of the normal fat within the pterygopalatine fossa on CT and MRI is a sign of its infiltration.[32, 44]

Evaluation of follow-up scans after radiotherapy is one of the most challenging parts of the radiologic work-up of nasopharyngeal carcinoma. The clinician expects the radiologist to differentiate residual or recurrent tumor from postirradiation granulation tissue, because endoscopy that is already hampered by radiation-induced mucositis is not successful in detecting deep recurrence. Furthermore, biopsy needs to be guided to areas under suspicion and is somewhat limited by the poor capacity of tissues to recover.[125]

Such evaluation is primarily the function of MRI because the CT attenuation of tumor and fibrous tissue are similar.[125] On MR images, mature scar tissue (formed of dehydrated hypocellular collagen) does not enhance with contrast and exhibits dark signal on T2-weighted images, an appearance that is readily distinguishable from tumor tissue.[30, 125, 130] Yet immature scar (formed of well-hydrated hypercellular granulation tissue) cannot be differentiated from recurrent tumor on the basis of MR signal characteristics, because both show contrast enhancement and intermediate to high T2-weighted signal.[30, 99, 125] In the latter case, the following measures may facilitate the diagnosis:

1. Ideally, a postradiotherapy baseline MRI is performed for comparison with future studies. This should be delayed for 3 to 4 months after completion of radiotherapy to allow for total resolution of slowly regressing tumors and acute postirradiation reactive changes (including thickening of the posterior pharyngeal wall and retropharyngeal edema). Progressively growing masses or tissue thickening should be deemed a recurrent tumor. Unchanging lesions do not exclude the possibility of tumor recurrence, whereas a regressive change points to a resolving postirradiation reaction or a contracting scar.[119, 125, 148]
2. When previous scans are unavailable, detection of an obviously positive lymph node is a reliable sign of recurrence.[119] Otherwise, studying the lesion's morphology may be helpful. It has been proposed that a recurrent tumor usually presents as a lobulated lump with mass effect, whereas postirradiation changes are usually a more diffuse process, giving rise to nasopharyngeal asymmetry with straight margins.[25] These criteria, however, should be considered suggestive and should not be regarded as the sole determinant of tumor recurrence.
3. When feasible, some techniques can be used to measure the metabolic activity of the mass in question, thus distinguishing a recurrent tumor by its high metabolic

rate from postirradiation scar tissue. These techniques include positron emission tomography (PET) with 18-fluorodeoxyglucose (FDG), thallium 201 scanning, and MR spectroscopy.[54, 79, 117–119]

Finally, it is worth noting that meningeal infiltration, particularly in the posterior cranial fossa, may be the only manifestation of tumor recurrence without a detectable nasopharyngeal mass (due to submucosal spread). This occurs through the jugular foramen or the foramen magnum, each an uncommon route of spread in pretreatment patients. Thus, the basal meninges, the jugular foramen, and the foramen magnum as well as the internal acoustic meatus should always be scrutinized for occult recurrence. The pattern of flow in the jugular bulb, often giving rise to an intermediate to high T1-weighted signal and postcontrast enhancement, may complicate the evaluation of tumor recurrence within the jugular foramen. T2-weighted images and MR angiography are valuable in such cases.[27]

Oropharyngeal Carcinoma. As in the nasopharynx, squamous cell carcinomas constitute the vast majority (90%) of all malignant neoplasms involving the oropharynx.[85, 108] Again, most of these are poorly differentiated carcinomas.[8] Predisposing factors for oropharyngeal squamous cell carcinoma are tobacco, alcohol, and syphilis.[108, 119] Carcinoma arises most commonly from the palatine tonsils and base of the tongue.[184] Less common sites are the faucial arches, soft palate, and the posterior pharyngeal wall. Spread pattern and lymphatic drainage vary according to the site of origin,[119] yet the overall incidence of cervical metastatic lymphadenopathy is 50% to 70%, which renders the prognosis unfavorable in most cases.[8]

Clinical Presentation. Patients often present with a sore throat, localized pain, referred ipsilateral otalgia, dysphagia, trismus, or a neck mass. Examination usually reveals a friable ulcerating mass.[55, 152]

Imaging Features

Carcinoma of the Base of the Tongue (Fig. 19–18). Base of tongue carcinoma often arises on one side behind the circumvallate papillae, and it is more aggressive and infiltrative than that involving the anterior two thirds of the tongue. As a result of the rich lymphatic network in this region, up to 75% of patients have lymph node metastases at initial diagnosis, primarily involving the internal jugular and, to a lesser extent, the spinal accessory nodes. Submandibular nodes are also involved when the tumor infiltrates the mouth floor.[119]

Unfortunately, differentiation between carcinoma and normal lymphoid tissue (lingual tonsil) at the tongue base may be difficult on the basis of tissue morphology, CT density, and MR signal characteristics. Lingual tonsils may be large, lobular, and asymmetrical. Moreover, the T2-weighted MR signal as well as the enhancement patterns on MRI and CT are similar for both carcinoma and lymphoid tissue. The usual infiltrative nature, coupled with the high incidence of metastatic lymphadenopathy associated with carcinoma, confirms the diagnosis. Otherwise, a deep endoscopic biopsy is needed.[8, 56, 62, 81]

Tongue base carcinoma may extend *anteriorly* to infiltrate the mobile portion of the tongue and the floor of

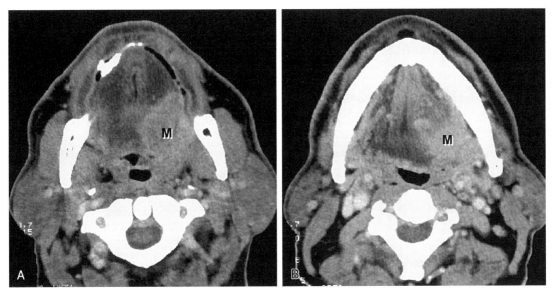

Figure 19–18. Squamous cell carcinoma of the tongue base. *A*, Contrast axial CT scan demonstrates a large, mildly enhanced mass lesion (M) involving the left root of the tongue, obliterating the normal fat plane between the pharynx and the medial pterygoid muscle, and extending posteriorly to infiltrate the anterior tonsillar pillar (palatoglossus muscle). *B*, Section at the level of floor of mouth in the same patient shows the tongue base mass to be violating the left sublingual space (harboring the left neurovascular bundle of the tongue) and infiltrating the ipsilateral genioglossus/geniohyoid muscles, yet stopping short of the midline.

the mouth; *laterally* to involve the pterygoid muscles and mandible; *superiorly* into the tonsillar fossa and soft palate; and *inferiorly* to fill the vallecula and to invade the preepiglottic space, the epiglottis, or the hypopharynx.[8]

Carcinoma of the Palatine Tonsils and Faucial Arches (Figs. 19–19 and 19–20). This carcinoma may arise from the mucosa lining the tonsillar bed, remnants of the palatine tonsils, and the anterior or, rarely, the posterior tonsillar pillar.[119] Of these patients, 76% have clinically positive lymph node metastases occurring primarily in the jugulodigastric group. Spinal accessory as well as submandibular and retropharyngeal nodes may also be involved.[8, 56, 119]

The tumor forms a bulging mass that thickens one side of the oropharynx from the soft palate to the hyoid bone.[108] Spread may occur *laterally* to invade the superior constrictor muscle into the parapharyngeal then the masticator space, with the potential risk of extension to the skull base (see "Nasopharyngeal Carcinoma"). Posterolateral extension into the retrostyloid PPS may lead to encasement of the internal carotid artery.[185] *Inferiorly*, the tumor may spread to the glossotonsillar sulcus, base of the tongue, and mouth floor, while superiorly it may infiltrate the soft palate and nasopharynx.[8] It may be difficult to differentiate oropharyngeal tumors spreading up to the nasopharynx and vice versa. However, oropharyngeal tumors extending upward tend to invade the ipsilateral nasopharynx and masticator space in contrast to nasopharyngeal tumors, which tend to infiltrate the oropharynx in a diffuse fashion.[119]

Although the tonsillar regions may normally appear asymmetrical, they should be regarded with suspicion whenever they are associated with obliteration of the PPS or cervical lymphadenopathy.[56, 123]

Carcinoma of the Soft Palate. The soft palate is associated

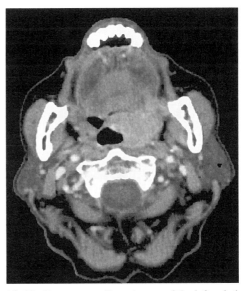

Figure 19–19. Squamous cell carcinoma of the left palatine tonsil has spared the parapharyngeal space. Axial CT scan obtained during bolus intravenous contrast administration reveals a rather ill-defined, mildly enhancing soft tissue mass centered on the left tonsillar fossa and extending along the anterior tonsillar pillar (palatoglossus muscle) into the soft palate and tongue base. Extension along the posterior pillar (palatopharyngeus muscle) into the posterior pharyngeal wall is also noted. The lost definition of prevertebral fat plane on the left side suggests perivertebral space invasion yet may be due to mere compression. The parapharyngeal space is intact.

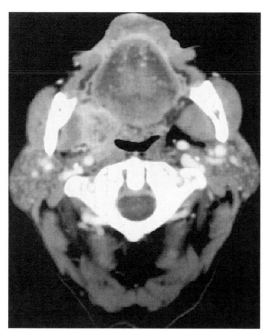

Figure 19–20. Squamous cell carcinoma of the right palatine tonsil has infiltrated the parapharyngeal space. Enhanced axial CT scan at the level of the oropharynx shows a well-defined intensely enhancing mass lesion involving the right tonsillar region, with central nonenhancing areas suggestive of tumor necrosis. The tumor infiltrates (1) the anterior tonsillar pillar into the right tongue base; (2) the posterior tonsillar pillar into the posterior pharyngeal wall, with possible involvement of the perivertebral space; (3) the prestyloid and poststyloid parapharyngeal spaces, where it abuts yet incompletely encases the internal carotid artery; and (4) the masticator space, where the tumor is seen as inseparable from the medial pterygoid muscle. Given such lateral extension, perineural spread along the mandibular nerve (V3) intracranially should be of concern.

with the best prognosis of all oropharyngeal carcinomas. The tumor usually arises on the oral side of the palate. Metastatic cervical lymphadenopathy is seen in 60% of patients at presentation; however, the incidence is far less (8%) for tumors less than 2 cm in diameter (stage T1). The high internal jugular and subdigastric nodes are first involved, followed by the lower internal jugular or retropharyngeal nodes.[119]

The tumor usually spreads first to the tonsillar pillars and hard palate. Other potential pathways include *lateral* infiltration along the tensor and levator veli palatini muscles into the PPS and up the skull base. *Superior* spread occurs to the nasopharynx or through the greater and lesser palatine foramina into the pterygopalatine fossa, then into the cavernous sinus.[119] Palatine tumors are best evaluated by sagittal and coronal T1-weighted MRI. A tumor shows up as low signal in contrast to the normal bright T1-weighted signal of the palate caused by mucous glands and fat.[119]

Carcinoma of the Posterior Oropharyngeal Wall. Fortunately, this carcinoma is rare, as it carries the worst prognosis among all oral and oropharyngeal carcinomas.[8, 56, 108] Arising in a silent area, the tumor is usually advanced at presentation. It tends to creep submucosally to infiltrate

the adjacent oropharyngeal sites, the nasopharynx, and the hypopharynx. Thus, the tumor may be relatively superficial yet extensive. Spreading *posterolaterally,* it may encase the carotid artery at an early stage. *Posteriorly,* it infiltrates the RPS, obliterating its fat stripe, but the prevertebral fascia is breached only at a later stage. Sagittal and axial postcontrast T1-weighted MRI best demonstrates this tumor, which may consist merely of subtle mucosal thickening.[56, 108, 152]

Role of Imaging

The primary roles of the radiologist in evaluating oropharyngeal carcinoma are to:

1. Provide tumor staging.
2. Relay specific information to the surgeon regarding the involvement of some key anatomic structures that are crucial to planning the treatment strategy.
3. Assess post-therapeutic tumor recurrence.

The UICC/AJCC TNM classification of oropharyngeal carcinoma is presented in Table 19–3.

A problem-oriented radiologic assessment of oropharyngeal carcinoma should include specific comments on issues having a direct effect on the type and extent of subsequent surgery. These can be detailed as follows.

Invasion of Deep Fascial Spaces, Perineural Infiltration, and Skull Base or Intracranial Extension. As described earlier, oropharyngeal carcinomas can spread to invade the various fascial spaces about the pharynx (see Figs. 19–19 and 19–20). Perineural infiltration occurs primarily along the mandibular and maxillary divisions of the trigeminal nerve up to the skull base and intracranially.

Table 19–3. UICC/AJCC Tumor-Node-Metastasis (TNM) Classification of Oropharyngeal Carcinoma

T Staging

T1	Tumor 2 cm or less in greatest dimension
T2	Tumor more than 2 cm but not greater than 4 cm in greatest dimension
T3	Tumor more than 4 cm in greatest dimension
T4	Tumor invading adjacent structures (including bone [mandible, maxilla, hard plate], soft tissues of neck, deep muscles of tongue, larynx)

N Staging

N0	No lymph node involvement
N1	Ipsilateral lymph nodes 3 cm or less
N2	
N2a	Ipsilateral lymph node greater than 3 cm, but not more than 6 cm
N2b	Multiple ipsilateral lymph nodes, but none greater than 6 cm
N2c	Bilateral or contralateral lymph nodes, but none greater than 6 cm
N3	Lymph nodes greater than 6 cm

M Staging

M0	No distant metastases
M1	Distant metastases are present

AJCC, American Joint Committee on Cancer; UICC, International Union Against Cancer.

Data from Beahrs OH, et al (eds): Manual for Staging of Cancer, 4th ed. Philadelphia, JB Lippincott, 1992[7]; and Leslie A et al: J Comput Assist Tomogr 23: 43–49, 1999.[86]

Direct imaging signs of perineural spread (see Fig. 19–15) include:

1. Thickening and enhancement of the effected nerves (with attention also paid to possible skip lesions).
2. Abnormal enhancement in Meckel's cave.
3. Lateral bulging of the cavernous sinus dural membrane.

Indirect signs include:

1. Foraminal enlargement on CT (see Fig. 19–15A).
2. Atrophy of muscles of mastication (in mandibular nerve infiltration) (see Fig. 19–16).
3. Obliteration of the normal fat plane in the pterygopalatine fossa (in maxillary nerve infiltration).[41, 82, 184]

Detection of subtle cortical skull base erosions requires coronal CT scanning, whereas MRI best assesses marrow infiltration. Intracranial extension may be first detected as abnormal meningeal thickening and enhancement. Again, this may be seen without skull base erosion.

Reporting such tumor extension changes the management of tonsillar and soft palate carcinoma from wide local excision through an intraoral approach to a more extensive surgery, depending on the structures infiltrated. At many institutions, imaging evidence of bulky tumor abutting the skull base precludes surgery.[115]

Preepiglottic Fat Infiltration. The preepiglottic space consists of the fat filling the area anterior to the epiglottis and posterior to the hyoid bone and thyrohyoid membrane. The site is best seen on sagittal T1-weighted MR images as a bright stripe (see Fig. 19–4). On axial scans, it appears as a C-shaped area of bright T1-weighted signal on MRI and low attenuation on CT.[8, 65]

The preepiglottic space may be invaded by carcinoma of the tongue base (and, less commonly, by carcinoma of the piriform sinus). Infiltration is seen as soft tissue replacement of the normal fat content on either MRI or CT.[8, 65]

A correct diagnosis is critical because preepiglottic invasion implies extension of surgery to include partial (supraglottic) or even total laryngectomy in combination with tongue base surgery. The consequent high morbidity and impairment of both swallowing and speaking adversely affect the patient's life quality.[9, 184] Peritumoral edema, adjacent inflammation, and partial-volume effect on CT may mimic preepiglottic fat infiltration and should be always excluded.[120]

Bilateral or Deep Tongue Base Invasion. Carcinoma originating primarily from the tongue base or extending to it from other oropharyngeal sites may spread across the midline or invade deeply into the floor of the mouth to involve the neurovascular bundle of the tongue (see Fig. 19–18B). The latter, consisting of the lingual artery as well as the lingual, glossopharyngeal (IX), and hypoglossal (XII) nerves, runs along the sublingual space on either side of the hyoglossus muscle to supply the tongue from posterior to anterior.[121, 184]

The precise tumor extent can be depicted on postcontrast and T2-weighted MR images. One may also assess its relationship to the neurovascular bundle on postcontrast CT by locating the enhancing lingual vessels between the hyoglossus and genioglossus muscles on each side of the floor of the mouth.[121]

Accurate detection of such tumor extension has an important impact on the subsequent surgical procedure. That is, if one lingual neurovascular bundle can be preserved, partial glossectomy would be performed and the patient would still be able to function well in regard to both swallowing and speaking. For tumors that cross the midline and violate the contralateral lingual neurovascular bundle, treatment options include either total glossectomy (with lifelong feeding gastrotomy) or radiation therapy and chemotherapy.[115, 184]

Encasement of the Internal Carotid Artery. This situation may occur from extension of oropharyngeal carcinoma into the retrostyloid PPS. Some suggest that when the tumor wraps more than 270 degrees of the arterial circumference on axial scans, it is unlikely to be resected without sacrificing the artery.[110] At many institutions, surgery is precluded when imaging studies confirm the presence of internal carotid artery encasement.[115]

Bone Invasion

Mandibular Invasion. Advanced oropharyngeal carcinoma may extend to invade the mandible. Thin-section CT best depicts subtle cortical erosion, whereas MRI is best suited for detecting marrow invasion. Infiltrated areas of bone marrow appear dark on T1-weighted images, bright on T2-weighted images, and enhanced in postcontrast studies. Before the bone marrow is classified as "infiltrated," it is important to exclude other conditions demonstrating the same MR signal behavior, such as radiation fibrosis, osteoradionecrosis, osteomyelitis, and periodontal disease.[34, 155, 184]

From a management perspective, tumors abutting the periosteum, but not fixed to it, are resected with periosteum for margin control. Tumors invading the periosteum or the cortex are removed with the cortex; for tumors infiltrating the mandibular marrow, resection of that segment of the mandible may be required.[8, 34, 184]

Maxillary Invasion. The maxilla may be invaded *directly*, by carcinoma of the soft palate, or *indirectly*, by tonsillar carcinoma invading the retromolar trigone, then the maxilla.[184] Coronal thin-section CT best demonstrates subtle maxillary erosions. When the maxilla is involved, management reverts from wide local excision to resection through a partial maxillectomy.[8]

Prevertebral Muscle Invasion. Advanced cases of pharyngeal carcinoma, particularly those arising in the posterior pharyngeal wall, may invade the prevertebral muscles. Findings such as obliteration of the retropharyngeal fat stripe, irregular muscle contour, bright T2-weighted muscle signal, or postcontrast muscle enhancement on MRI or CT (see Figs. 19–19 and 19–20) should motivate the radiologist to report possible prevertebral muscle invasion. The definite extent, however, is determined by surgical evaluation, since these imaging findings may also be due to peritumoral edema without actual muscle invasion. When the tumor is proven to be fixed, it is deemed irresectable.[8, 94, 184]

Assessment of post-therapeutic oropharyngeal tumor recurrence is often difficult because of the similar imaging appearance of recurrent tumor and post-treatment changes.[72, 167] Because oropharyngeal cancer is primarily a surgical disease, tumor resection—and sometimes the application of reconstructive procedures (e.g., myocutaneous or free flaps)—often further complicates interpretation by distorting the local anatomy.

As discussed earlier (see "Nasopharyngeal Carcinoma"), the optimal practice is to compare scans with a baseline post-treatment study. Otherwise, the detection of an obvious mass that is compressing rather than retracting the adjacent tissues or obvious lymphadenopathy will point to tumor recurrence.[119]

Non-Hodgkin's Lymphoma

Pharyngeal non-Hodgkin's lymphoma (NHL) arises from the rich extranodal lymphoid tissue of the PMS, the tongue base, or the palate.[65, 184] Generally, 60% of cases of NHL arises in extranodal lymphoid tissue; of these, 60% occur in the head and neck.[119, 182]

Clinical Presentation. Patients are usually older men presenting when having localized nasopharyngeal or oropharyngeal disease, with symptoms indistinguishable from those of squamous cell carcinoma arising at the same site.[119] However, patients may present with systemic manifestations that point to the diagnosis. These include fever, malaise, weight loss, hepatosplenomegaly, and distant lymphadenopathy.[65] Distant lymphadenopathy is present in 80% of patients with primary extranodal NHL.[119]

Imaging Features. The imaging features of NHL of the PMS may be identical to those of the more common squamous cell carcinoma on both CT and MRI. Although lymphoma tends to grow in a circumferential fashion, forming a diffuse, bulky, non-necrotic, superficial mass without early invasion of the PPS,[133] large lesions may invade the deep neck spaces, spread perineurally, and invade the skull base in a pattern similar to that of squamous cell carcinoma.[119] Superficial lymphomas primarily involving the tongue base or palatine tonsils may be also indistinguishable from benign lymphoid hyperplasia.[184]

The diagnosis of NHL is suggested when the following associations are present:

- Large non-necrotic lymph nodes in atypical drainage areas
- Extranodal, extralymphatic lesions[65]
- Clinical systemic manifestations

Malignancy of the Minor Salivary Glands

The minor salivary glands are the least common site of PMS malignancy. The tumor arises from the minor salivary glands in the submucosa of the nasopharynx and tongue base, yet its most common site is the soft palate. Generally, 50% of minor salivary gland tumors are malignant.[119] A spectrum of histologic types exists, with adenoid cystic carcinoma the most frequent, followed by mucoepidermoid carcinoma and malignant mixed tumors.[26, 28]

Clinical Presentation. Tumors usually occur in adults with no sex predilection.[119] Symptoms are nonspecific[65] and depend on the site of origin of the tumor.

Imaging Features. The tumor appears as a soft tissue mass in the PMS that is indistinguishable on both CT and

MRI from squamous cell carcinoma or NHL. Biopsy is required for the definitive diagnosis.

Among all malignant nasopharyngeal and oropharyngeal neoplasms, adenoid cystic carcinoma is associated with the highest incidence of perineural spread.[37, 41, 82, 184] Such spread is diagnosed histologically in about 50% of adenoid cystic carcinomas, and when the diagnosis is missed at initial evaluation, treatment failure may result.[119] The direct and indirect imaging signs of perineural tumor spread have been described earlier (see "Oropharyngeal Carcinoma").

Nasopharyngeal Rhabdomyosarcoma

Rhabdomyosarcoma is a malignant mesenchymal tumor that occurs primarily in children. It can arise anywhere in the body, with the head and neck the most common sites of origin (28% to 36%), followed by the urinary bladder and then the extremities.[42] Within the head and neck, the orbit and the nasopharynx are the most commonly involved areas. The tumor arises from the nasopharyngeal muscles, located within the PMS, and is associated with metastatic lymphadenopathy in 50% of cases. Distant metastases occur in the lung and bone.[42]

Clinical Presentation. The peak age of incidence is 2 to 5 years, and boys are more susceptible than girls (2:1). The usual presenting symptoms are rhinorrhea, sore throat, and serous otitis media. Skull base invasion is common, giving rise to cranial nerve palsies.[42, 119]

Imaging Features. The imaging appearance of rhabdomyosarcoma is basically that of a malignant nasopharyngeal growth in a child. The diagnosis is suggested on basis of the patient's age rather than a characteristic radiological appearance.

The tumor appears as a bulky nasopharyngeal soft tissue mass that commonly extends intracranially through both destruction of the skull base and widening of the basal foramina and fissures. CT shows an isodense mass to the brain, whereas MRI shows the tumor to be isointense on T1-weighted images and hyperintense on T2-weighted images.[42] Postcontrast studies show a variable amount of enhancement. The same imaging features may be seen in children in cases of neuroblastoma and rhabdoid tumor.[119]

Lesions of the Retropharyngeal Space

Pseudotumors

The clinical appearance of an RPS mass may result from:

1. A tortuous internal carotid artery that extends medially and results in a bulge in the posterior pharyngeal wall.
2. Retropharyngeal hematoma.
3. Edema due to jugular vein or lymphatic obstruction. Edema of the RPS most commonly involves both its suprahyoid and infrahyoid portions and demonstrates low-attenuation enlargement of the space.[45]

Congenital Lesions

Hemangioma and Lymphangioma

Hemangioma and lymphangioma are usually infiltrative lesions that do not respect the fascial boundaries (i.e., "trans-spatial" diseases) and may extend into the RPS as a part of multiple space involvement.

On CT scans, hemangiomas appear as relatively dense lesions and typically demonstrate intense enhancement.[141] On MR images, they display intermediate signal intensity on T1-weighted and intermediate-weighted images, with heterogeneous increased signal intensity on T2-weighted images.[3, 52] Following gadolinium administration, enhancement is usually intense.[3, 141] Areas of signal void from associated vascular structures may be identified but are much more common with high-flow lesions.[3]

Lymphangiomas typically appear on both CT and MRI as multiloculated, poorly circumscribed lesions.[138] They exhibit fluid attenuation and signal intensity, and they have imperceptible, nonenhancing rims.[138] Hemorrhage may occur into a lymphangioma and may manifest clinically as rapid enlargement of the lesion; this may be identified as an area of high attenuation on CT and bright signal on T1-weighted MRI.[3, 138] Hemorrhage-fluid levels may also be seen.[3]

Congenital vascular anomalies are currently classified as follows[122, 139]:

1. *True hemangiomas.* These often involute with age. Involuting hemangiomas show focal areas of bright T1-weighted signal resulting from fatty replacement.[3] Hemangiomas may look identical to venous malformations unless the venous malformation contains phleboliths.[3]
2. *Vascular malformations* (arterial, capillary, venous, lymphatic, and combined). These anomalies remain stable or slowly grow with the patient. Patients with these lesions typically require some form of therapy when cosmetic disfigurement, bleeding, or functional impairment is present.[91]

From a therapeutic perspective, the most important issue is to classify these lesions as *low-flow* vascular malformations, which are often successfully treated with percutaneous sclerotherapy,[60] and as *high-flow"* vascular malformations, which are often treated with transarterial embolization.[91, 183] T2-weighted MRI elegantly show the difference between these categories; low-flow lesions appear predominantly bright, and high-flow lesions appear predominantly signal void.[60, 91, 183]

Inflammatory Conditions
Retropharyngeal Infections

Infection of the RPS is uncommon in adults, in whom it is most often due to direct posterior pharyngeal wall trauma as may occur during endoscopy or attempted nasogastric tube insertion.[164] This decreased incidence is most likely related to atrophy of the retropharyngeal lymph node chains following puberty.[132, 164] Most commonly affected are patients 4 years of age or younger, in whom pharyngitis or infection of the adenoids or faucial tonsils (generally with streptococci or staphylococci) spreads to the retropharyngeal lymph node chains.

Typically, RPS infections progress in four successive phases and can be stopped at any stage by appropriate treatment:

1. *Reactive lymphadenopathy.* This phase represents the first response of the retropharyngeal lymph nodes to spread of infection. The nodes react by hyperplasia without disruption of their internal architecture.
2. *Suppurative lymphadenitis.* The infected nodes suppurate, with consequent development of an intranodal abscess.[145]
3. *Retropharyngeal cellulitis or abscess.* Early spread of the organism outside an affected lymph node may result in cellulitis, causing the tissues to swell without focal fluid collection.[65] When the enlarged suppurated nodes eventually rupture into the RPS, an abscess is formed. The abscess typically starts at the location of the lateral retropharyngeal lymph node chains lateral to the midline and above the level of the hyoid bone.[179] Infection then spreads to involve the entire RPS from side to side.[45]
4. *Complicated retropharyngeal abscess.* When untreated, a retropharyngeal abscess can further spread locally into adjacent neck spaces, track downward into the superior mediastinum, or penetrate the alar fascia into the danger space, where it may spread down to the level of the diaphragm.[132]

Clinical Presentation. Patients present with swelling adjacent to the soft palate, which may be displaced anteriorly; fever; sore throat; dysphagia; mild to moderate neck stiffness; and occasionally a muffled voice. Breathing may become strained or noisy if the airway becomes compromised.[179]

Imaging Features

Reactive Lymphadenopathy. At this phase, enlarged lateral retropharyngeal lymph nodes (>1 cm in diameter) can be seen, keeping the configuration of normal nodes (oval or kidney-shaped) and usually presenting a homogenous texture.[65]

Suppurative Lymphadenitis. Suppurated lymph nodes appear enlarged and demonstrate central low attenuation on CT or fluid signal intensity on MRI.[45, 179] However, these central changes can also be seen in early liquefying nodes without complete suppuration. Frankly suppurated nodes can be identified by their enhancing rims (Figs. 19–21*A*) and by the associated edema of the RPS.[65]

Retropharyngeal Cellulitis or Abscess. The most common finding in patients with infection of the RPS is that of cellulitis localized to the RPS at the level of the nasopharynx or oropharynx.[45] It is seen as diffuse thickening (>75% of anteroposterior diameter of vertebral body[42]) and as enhancement of the retropharyngeal soft tissues (see Fig. 19–21).

When an abscess forms, it appears as an area of fluid collection marginated by an enhancing rim, with possible air or air-fluid level seen within.[42] As stated, it starts at the region of lateral retropharyngeal nodes (Fig. 19–22) but may spread to involve the entire RPS (see Fig. 19–21*B*), where it may attain a characteristic "bowtie" appearance.[65] Significant mass effect is often present,[119] and the degree of pharyngeal airway compromise should always be sought.

It is also important to distinguish a true retropharyngeal abscess, which necessitates surgical drainage, from both suppurative adenitis (with surrounding edema) and cellulitis, because the latter two conditions may respond to conservative treatment without the need for intervention.[65, 119]

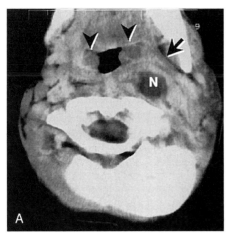
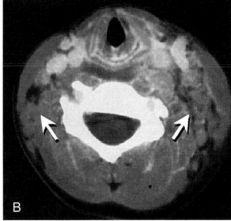

Figure 19–21. Retropharyngeal infection in a 5-year-old boy presenting with left upper neck swelling.

A, Postcontrast CT scan reveals enlarged, left-sided lateral retropharyngeal lymph node (of Rouviere) (N), displaying central low attenuation and thick, enhancing margin, a picture consistent with suppurative lymphadenitis (intranodal abscess). The associated enlargement of palatine tonsils *(arrowheads)* indicates the source of infection. Note the integrity of the ipsilateral prestyloid parapharyngeal space *(arrow).*

B, Section at a lower level in the same patient shows low fluid attenuation casting the entire retropharyngeal space. The presence of a thin, enhancing rim marginating the collection suggests a retropharyngeal abscess (caused by rupture of another suppurated lymph node), rather than a mere associated edema, and necessitates the establishment of drainage. Note the bilateral posterior cervical space lymphadenopathy *(arrows).*

Complicated Retropharyngeal Abscess. The parapharyngeal fat may appear dense as a result of associated inflammation (see Fig. 19–21). When suppuration extends into this space, however, external drainage (rather than the transoral approach used with most retropharyngeal abscesses) is indicated.[164]

Although axial CT usually demonstrates the full extent of retropharyngeal infection, sagittal MRI may occasionally

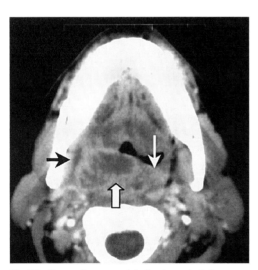

Figure 19–22. Retropharyngeal infection. Axial contrast-enhanced CT scan through the oropharynx demonstrates enhancing, thickened retropharyngeal soft tissue consistent with cellulitis *(thin white arrow)* and a low attenuation collection on the right suggesting abscess formation *(thick white arrow)* that causes significant airway compromise. Note the abscess starting at the region of the lateral retropharyngeal lymph node (of Rouviere). Associated inflammation results in increased attenuation of the prestyloid parapharyngeal fat on the right *(black arrow).*

be helpful to better define the superoinferior extent of disease and associated displacement or compression of the pharynx, larynx, trachea, or esophagus.[179]

Extension of RPS infection into the danger space cannot be differentiated from an RPS process unless abscess or cellulitis extends below the T2 to T6 vertebral level.

Benign Tumors

Retropharyngeal Lipoma

Benign tumors of the RPS are rare, although lipoma has been reported.[45] This tumor is readily identifiable on both CT and MRI as a retropharyngeal soft tissue mass with characteristic low CT density (-50 to -100 HU), bright T1 signal, and diminished signal on T2-weighted images.

Malignant Tumors

Malignant tumors of the RPS are much more common than benign tumors and are usually secondary to the following[45]:

1. Direct extension of primary squamous cell carcinoma of the nasopharynx, posterior oropharyngeal wall, or hypopharynx.
2. Metastatic involvement of retropharyngeal lymph nodes.
   a. Most commonly, from a nasopharyngeal primary squamous cell carcinoma but may also be seen with an oropharyngeal carcinoma.[45] Enlarged nodes may show central necrosis.
   b. Metastases from other areas, such as thyroid carcinoma and malignant melanoma.[45] Involved nodes may present bright T1-weighted signals, in melanotic melanoma resulting from the paramagnetic effect and in thyroid carcinoma resulting from the high protein (thyroglobulin) content.[65]

In addition, the retropharyngeal lymph node chains may

be involved by non-Hodgkin's lymphoma, either as an initial site or as a part of a multiple chain involvement. Involved nodes initially appear unilateral and homogeneous, but later extranodal progression may cause the lymphomatous tissue to fill the entire RPS.[65]

Lesions of the Prestyloid Parapharyngeal Space

Pseudotumor

Asymmetrical Pterygoid Venous Plexuses

Occasionally, the pterygoid venous plexus of one side (overlying the inner surface of the lateral pterygoid muscle) is larger than that of the other side. The vascular nature of this anatomic variant can be depicted by its racemose enhancement on postcontrast CT scans and on contrast-enhanced, fat-suppressed, axial T1-weighted MR images.[65]

Congenital Lesions

Atypical (Parapharyngeal) Second Branchial Cleft Cyst

The lower face and neck are formed from six pairs of branchial arches. Between them lay five endodermal pharyngeal pouches on the inner aspect and five ectodermal clefts on the outer aspect.[10, 16] The second pharyngeal pouch forms the tonsillar fossa and palatine tonsils, whereas the second branchial cleft (together with the third and fourth clefts) forms an ectoderm-lined tract, called the *cervical sinus*,[66] which is obliterated at a later stage of development.

Failure of the cervical sinus to become completely obliterated results in a second branchial cleft sinus, a fistula, or, more commonly, a cyst anywhere along a line from the oropharyngeal tonsillar fossa to the supraclavicular region of the neck.[66] Although the most common location for a second branchial cleft cyst is the submandibular space,[36] the cyst can atypically present in the PPS, arising from the parapharyngeal portion of the embryonal tract.[66]

Clinical Presentation. Although congenital, these cysts most commonly present in young adults and are often precipitated by respiratory tract infection or trauma.[66] Small cysts are asymptomatic. Patients with a large cyst in the parapharyngeal location may present with parotid gland bulge, dysphagia, or vague neck discomfort.[15] On examination, the posterolateral oropharyngeal wall appears to be bulging internally.[65]

Imaging Features. In its atypical (parapharyngeal) location, the cyst appears on CT and MRI as a thin, smooth-walled structure of fluid attenuation or signal intensity extending from the deep margin of the palatine tonsil into the parapharyngeal fat toward the skull base.[65] Occasionally, T1 hyperintensity may result from high protein content or intracystic hemorrhage.[15] When infected, the cyst wall may become thickened and irregular, and the surrounding fat planes may become obscured.[66]

As mentioned, the most common site of a second branchial cleft cyst is within the submandibular space, characteristically displacing the submandibular gland anteriorly, the sternocleidomastoid muscle posterolaterally, and the carotid sheath posteromedially.[36] At this location, it is important to consider cystic metastasis of papillary thyroid carcinoma in the differential diagnosis. An enhancing soft tissue nodule in cystic metastasis may provide a clue to the diagnosis.

Other cystic lesions of the submandibular space (but rarely giving the characteristic pattern of displacement of adjacent structures) include submandibular gland cysts, lymphangiomas, necrotic or cystic nerve sheath tumors, and epidermoid or dermoid cysts.[66]

Inflammatory Conditions

Parapharyngeal Space Infection

Infection of the prestyloid compartment of the PPS most commonly arises from spread of peritonsillar abscesses, retrotonsillar vein thrombophleblitis, third molar extractions with violation of the pterygomandibular raphe, penetrating injury to the lateral pharyngeal wall, or extension of deep lobe parotid abscesses or as a complication of local anesthesia for tonsillectomy or dental surgery.[164, 179] Inflammation may also spread from the submandibular glands, branchial cleft, or thyroglossal duct cysts or from temporal bone infections through petrous apex air cells.[164]

Patterns of spread of inflammatory changes within the PPS and the adjacent spaces depend on individual differences in fascial anatomy that may arise from normal variation, previous trauma, surgery, infection, or radiation therapy.[132] The virulence and antibiotic sensitivity of the invading organism, as well as the general health and immunologic status of the host, may also affect the spread of infection.[132] Once inside the prestyloid PPS, infection can readily extend into the parotid, masticator, submandibular, or retrostyloid compartment of the PPS.[164]

Clinical Presentation. Clinical presentation of the PPS and the adjacent spaces includes the sudden onset of fever and chills. Dysfunction of cranial nerves IX through XII or the sympathetic plexus may also occur with extension into the retrostyloid compartment, and trismus may occur with masticator space involvement. Painful swelling of the gingival tissues of the maxilla and of the cheek on the involved side may also be noted.[179] On clinical examination, a medial bulge of the lateral pharyngeal wall is commonly seen.[164, 179]

Complications of PPS infection include erosion of the adjacent carotid artery with fatal hemorrhage or pseudoaneurysm formation as well as extension to the RPS with possible asphyxia or dysphagia from the resulting mass effect and inflammation.[179] Paranasal sinus and orbital involvement, intracranial extension, and osteomyelitis may also result.[52]

Imaging Features. Imaging of the PPS and the adjacent spaces may be of great assistance in detecting complications of deep neck infections and determining the optimal timing and approach for surgical drainage.[164] Imaging is most useful when infection is complex, widespread, or difficult to assess clinically.[52] On CT, cellulitis may present as a soft tissue mass with obliteration of adjacent fat planes. The mass is often ill defined, enhancing, and extending along fascial planes (Fig. 19–23) and into subcutaneous tissues.[52, 179] Involved muscles may enhance and appear enlarged, and overlying subcutaneous tissues often demon-

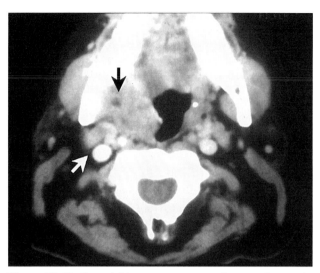

Figure 19–23. Prestyloid compartment parapharyngeal space infection from spread of tonsillitis. Axial contrast-enhanced CT scan at the level of the oropharynx demonstrates enlargement of the right faucial tonsil with obliteration of the prestyloid parapharyngeal fat on the right. One small area of decreased attenuation is noted within the inflammatory process, which may represent a small abscess cavity *(black arrow)*. Fat planes surrounding the contents of the retrostyloid compartment of the parapharyngeal space remain intact *(white arrow)*.

strate linear or mottled increased attenuation beneath thickened skin.[179]

Abscesses of the deep neck spaces, reported to represent up to 9% of masses within the PPS, often appear as unilocated or multiloculated cystic lesions with air or fluid attenuation centers. They may have somewhat irregular, enhancing walls or surrounding tissue edema and may conform to the surrounding fascial boundaries.[103, 164, 179] Occasionally, pus formation is incomplete or may be delayed by antibiotic therapy, and an area of low attenuation on CT, suggesting an abscess cavity, may not yield pus on aspiration or exploration.[179]

Although axial and coronal CT may determine the extent of disease and presence of complications, MRI often provides superior localization because of its multiplanar capabilities and better soft tissue contrast resolution. Inflammatory exudate is of low to intermediate signal intensity on T1-weighted images and is often isointense with adjacent muscle.[179] Both cellulitis and abscess cavities exhibit increased signal intensity on T2-weighted images.

Gadolinium contrast agents may help to differentiate abscess from cellulitis by demonstrating an enhancing abscess wall. Neither MRI nor CT findings can typically differentiate a bacterial from a granulomatous origin of inflammation.[179]

Benign Tumors

Most prestyloid PPS tumors are benign. Of these, the majority are of salivary gland origin, with pleomorphic adenoma representing the most common histology.[84]

Benign Mixed Salivary Gland Tumor (Pleomorphic Adenoma)

Salivary gland tumors in the prestyloid PPS commonly arise from the deep lobe of the parotid gland and extend

into the PPS through the stylomandibular tunnel.[84] However, salivary gland tumors can also arise primarily within the prestyloid compartment from congenital rests of salivary gland tissue.[84, 162]

Clinical Presentation. The patient typically presents with a painless mass, since benign salivary gland tumors seldom result in other symptoms.[68]

Imaging Features. The CT appearance of a benign salivary gland tumor is usually that of an ovoid soft tissue mass. When small, the tumor is typically homogeneous; when larger, it may show variable areas of low attenuation that represent sites of cystic degeneration or seromucinous collections. Focal areas of high attenuation representing calcification may also be present.[162]

The MR appearance of a benign salivary gland tumor is that of a well-defined mass with low to intermediate signal intensity on T1-weighted and intermediate-weighted (long TR, short TE) images and intermediate increased signal on T2-weighted images (Fig. 19–24). Smaller lesions are typically homogeneous in appearance, whereas lesions greater than 2.5 cm in diameter are often heterogeneous on all pulse sequences and may have internal foci of low signal or signal void, corresponding to areas of calcification or fibrosis (see Fig. 19–24).[162] Areas of high signal intensity on T1-weighted and intermediate-weighted MR images may also occur in larger tumors and correspond to areas of local hemorrhage.[162] With the prevalence of such findings, mass heterogeneity is not a useful predictor of a benign versus a malignant neoplasm.[162] The best predictors of a benign pleomorphic adenoma are the presence of dystrophic calcifications, best detected with CT, or a well-defined, highly lobulated tumor contour, best seen with MRI.[162]

The site of origin of prestyloid compartment salivary neoplasms is of importance in the surgical management of these patients, because a lesion arising within the deep lobe of the parotid gland is usually treated with operative control of the facial nerve in order to prevent nerve damage, whereas a lesion totally confined to the prestyloid PPS without connection to the parotid gland may be treated with little concern for facial nerve injury.[159] At some institutions, a submandibular approach without control of the facial nerve is also used for deep lobe parotid masses when the tumor does not approach the stylomandibular tunnel.

For an accurate diagnosis of an extraparotid origin of a prestyloid parapharyngeal tumor, an intact fat plane between the posterolateral margin of the tumor and the deep portion of the parotid gland must be clearly demonstrated. Careful attention is necessary because this connection may be a very thin isthmus of tissue that is best detected on high-resolution, thin-section, axial T1-weighted MR images. When lesions are greater than 4 cm in diameter, the intervening fat plane may be obliterated by mass effect alone and distinguishing between intraparotid and extraparotid origin may be impossible (see Fig. 19–24).[162] In such cases, the surgical approach for a tumor of parotid origin is often used in order to minimize the risk of facial nerve damage.[159, 162]

Parapharyngeal Lipoma

Parapharyngeal lipomas are uncommon lesions that are readily identified by their characteristic low attenuation on

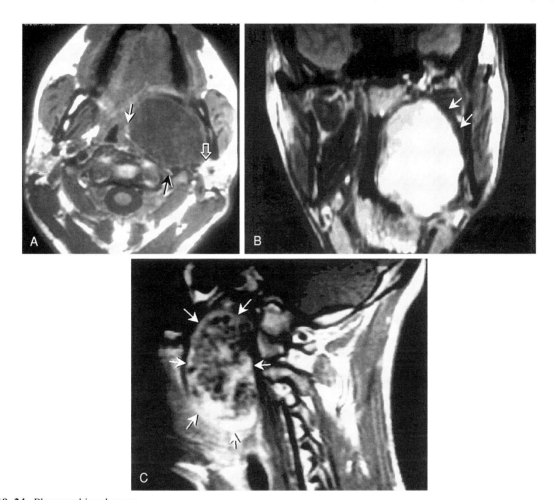

Figure 19–24. Pleomorphic adenoma.

A, Nonenhanced, T1-weighted axial image (TR = 500 msec, TE = 12 msec) demonstrates a well-defined mass of lower signal intensity than adjacent muscle, replacing the prestyloid parapharyngeal fat with minimal residual fat displaced medially *(straight white arrow)* and the internal carotid artery displaced posteriorly *(straight black arrow).* No intact fat plane can be demonstrated between the lesion and the deep lobe of the parotid gland *(open arrow).*

B, Intermediate-weighted (TR = 2500 msec, TE = 30 msec) coronal image demonstrates the mass as relatively homogeneous, of increased signal intensity relative to adjacent muscles and lymphoid tissue, and well defined. The oropharyngeal mucosa is displaced medially. The left medial pterygoid muscle is compressed and displaced superolaterally *(arrows).*

C, Contrast-enhanced, T1-weighted (TR = 500 msec, TE = 15 msec) sagittal image demonstrates marked heterogeneity of the mass, with multiple low-signal-intensity regions that may represent areas of calcification or fibrosis. Both sagittal and coronal images are useful in revealing the craniocaudal extent of the lesion, which fills most of the prestyloid parapharyngeal space *(arrows).* The mass is inseparable from the deep lobe of the parotid gland and must be considered as arising from the deep lobe for surgical planning. However, the deep lobe of the parotid gland has been compressed and displaced laterally, with no visible connection to the mass at surgery.

CT and by their characteristic signal intensity, which parallels that of fat on all MRI pulse sequences.

Malignant Tumors

Malignant tumors of the prestyloid compartment of the PPS are much less common than benign lesions. These tumors include malignancies of salivary gland origin (e.g., mucoepidermoid, adenoid cystic, and acinic cell carcinomas) along with direct invasion of malignancies of the adjacent spaces.[156, 162] Differentiation from benign tumors may be difficult because approximately two thirds of salivary gland malignant tumors have smooth, well-defined margins.[162] However, the presence of an irregular, ill-defined margin or infiltration of surrounding tissues may be

present, suggesting a more aggressive lesion. Unfortunately, an inflammatory reaction surrounding a benign tumor may occasionally result in a similar appearance.[161]

Lesions Arising Outside the Pharynx and Bulging into the Pharyngeal Airway

Antrochoanal Polyps

An antrochoanal polyp is a benign antral polyp that expands, widens the sinus ostium, and prolapses into the nasal cavity. When the polyp is large, it fills the ipsilateral nasal fossa and extends backward through the choana into

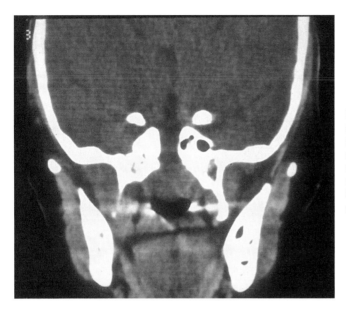

Figure 19–25. Basal cephalocele. Coronal nonenhanced CT scan shows a large midline, isodense nasopharyngeal soft tissue mass that is significantly compromising the airway in a child. The obvious associated midline skull base defect represents the persistent hypophyseal (craniopharyngeal) canal and suggests that the postnasal mass is actually a herniated pituitary gland. Note the consequent downward traction of the suprasellar cistern into the basal defect.

the nasopharynx. Occasionally, it becomes large enough to hang down into the oropharynx. Antrochoanal polyps represent 5% of all nasal polyps.[42, 119]

Clinical Presentation. The patient is typically a teenager or a young adult. A history of allergy is present in 15% to 40% of cases, with an incidence of additional nasal polyps in 8%.[42, 160]

Imaging Features. A large antrochoanal polyp appears as a smoothly outlined mass within the nasopharyngeal airway; it is continuous into the nasal cavity and maxillary antrum on one side. The maxillary ostium is widened, yet the sinus itself is not expanded. There is no bone erosion. Absence of bone erosion is a distinguishing feature from juvenile nasopharyngeal angiofibroma. An antrochoanal polyp typically presents as a homogenous, low-mucoid-attenuation (10 to 18 HU) mass on CT, but older lesions develop fibrous stroma, resulting in a higher attenuation. On MR images, these polyps display low to intermediate T1-weighted and T2-weighted signal intensity. Postcontrast studies show mucosal enhancement on the surface.[42, 97, 133, 160]

Sphenochoanal Polyps

Sphenochoanal polyps are rare, with an etiology similar to that of antrochoanal polyps. They arise in the sphenoid sinus and extend through the sphenoid ostium and sphenoethmoidal recess into the nose, then backward through the choana into the nasopharynx. Identification of the sinus of origin (sphenoid and not maxillary) is important in order to determine the surgical approach.[181]

Persistent Hypophyseal (Craniopharyngeal) Canal

Persistent hypophyseal canal is a rare congenital defect of the skull base that is worthy of mention. The canal connects the pituitary fossa to the nasopharynx, allowing the pituitary gland to herniate downward into the nasopha-

ryngeal airway and to present as a midline nasal polyp that might cause significant airway obstruction in neonates.[74]

Because acquired polyps are almost unknown in children younger than 2 years of age, it is necessary to interpret, with a high index of suspicion, midline nasal polyps in young children, particularly when the polyp is coupled with hypertelorism. In these cases, it is always best to ascertain that the sellar floor is completely intact and that the pituitary gland is normally located within its fossa. Coronal CT or MRI is best suited for such evaluation.[74] Picking up these rare cases is crucial in order to prevent inadvertent hypophysectomy and consequent panhypopituitarism.

Occasionally, a persistent hypophyseal canal may be wide enough to allow a large basal cephalocele to form in the postnasal space (Fig. 19–25).[74]

Nasopharyngeal and Oropharyngeal Trauma

The suprahyoid portions of the pharynx (i.e., nasopharynx and oropharynx) are less vulnerable to trauma than the infrahyoid pharynx (hypopharynx) or the larynx[119]; most radiologically documented nasopharyngeal or oropharyngeal injuries are described in the literature as case reports.*

The clinicopathologic outcome and the imaging findings expected after trauma to this part of the pharynx, to a large extent, are dictated by the mechanisms of trauma. By convention, these are classified into *blunt* (closed) and *penetrating* (open) types.

Blunt Trauma

Blunt head and neck trauma, such as that caused by motor vehicle accidents, may result in the formation of retropharyngeal hematoma, a condition that may progress rapidly into a life-threatening airway obstruction.[18, 45]

---

*See references 43, 75, 104, 106, 114, 129, 135, 137, 153, 157, 169, 170, and 175.

Once post-traumatic, prevertebral soft tissue fullness is seen on the emergency radiographs, the primary concern should be directed toward securing and maintaining the patient's airway,[43] followed by a CT scan to evaluate for potential cervical spine fractures. CT sections should start as high as the skull base to detect possible occipital condyle fractures[104] and should cover as low as the inferior extent of the hematoma, which may reach down to the mediastinum.

Retropharyngeal hematomas have also been reported following minor blunt trauma,[43] minor hyperextension injuries,[129] and airbag deployment in minor motor vehicle accidents.[170]

Nontraumatic causes of retropharyngeal hematoma include anticoagulant therapy and complications of aneurysms, tumors, and infections.[129]

Penetrating Trauma

Trauma leading to pharyngeal perforation may be accidental or iatrogenic. Accidental perforations usually involve the oropharynx and may be caused by foreign bodies,[45] fish bones,[169] gunshots,[162] and direct injury by intraoral sharp objects, as when, for example, a child falls with a toothbrush in the mouth.[137] Iatrogenic perforations more commonly involve the nasopharynx and may complicate upper gastrointestinal endoscopy,[175] assisted ventilation,[45] neonatal pharyngeal suction catheters, and nasogastric or tracheal intubation during resuscitation of newborns.[135]

Pharyngeal perforation may result in any or a combination of the following problems:

1. *Surgical emphysema.* Emphysema may be caused by air dissecting its way through the torn pharyngeal wall. Retropharyngeal free air is the most common sequela of perforation and is readily identified on CT. Occasionally, large amounts of interstitial air may cast multiple deep fascial spaces and may extend downward, giving rise to pneumomediastinum.[45, 143, 157, 175]
2. *Retropharyngeal abscess.* Abscess occurs less often and is due to the spread of organisms from the oral bacterial flora. Uncontrolled infection may spread into the deep fascial planes, resulting in fascitis or parapharyngeal abscess[119]; may extend downward along the RPS to cause mediastinitis; and may even enter the danger space to reach down to the diaphragm.[157] The imaging features of retropharyngeal abscess have been described earlier.
3. *Vascular injury.* Internal carotid artery thrombosis and cerebral ischemia may complicate posterolateral oropharyngeal injury, particularly when a child falls with a sharp object in the mouth. Typically, the internal carotid artery is injured 1 to 3 cm above the common carotid bifurcation, where it is separated from the oropharyngeal airway only by the tonsil and the superior constrictor muscle. The patient classically presents after a lucid interval of occasionally more than 24 hours, with disturbed consciousness, hemiplegia, and possibly expressive aphasia if ischemia involves the dominant cerebral hemisphere.[137]

Carotid artery thrombosis has also been reported following blunt intraoral[114] and minor pharyngeal injuries.[153]

Obstructive Sleep Apnea Syndrome

Obstructive sleep apnea syndrome is an episodic upper airway obstruction during sleep, most commonly occurring at the pharyngeal level.[102] The condition may be considered, in part, a neuromuscular disorder. Normally, the neural output to the pharyngeal muscles decreases with the onset of sleep, thus reducing their tone. With inspiration, the negative pressure created in the upper airway has the potential to collapse the hypotonic pharyngeal wall if the pharyngeal airway is originally smaller or more compliant than normal.[57]

Clinical Presentation. Obstructive sleep apnea is most common among obese males. The incidence also increases with age, snoring, tobacco and alcohol use, and the use of sedatives as well as with genetic and familial risk factors.[102]

The repetitive episodes of apnea during sleep, lasting from 10 to more than 60 seconds,[102] result in arterial oxygen desaturation and recurrent awakening, leading to the syndrome, which is characterized by daytime somnolence, morning headache, and poor concentration.[57, 78] Other conditions that have been linked to the syndrome include gastroesophageal reflux, impotence, cardiac arrhythmias, hypertension, and increased risk of stroke and myocardial infarction.[78, 102]

Role of Imaging. The diagnosis of obstructive sleep apnea is a clinical one that is supported by (1) overnight *polysomnography* (continuous recording of relevant physiologic changes during sleep) to determine the physiologic severity, and by (2) *transnasal fiberoptic endoscopy* to estimate the actual grade of airway narrowing.[102]

With the emergence of new imaging technology, dynamic imaging of the pharynx in near real-time has become a reality, permitting the noninvasive assessment of functional pharyngeal abnormalities. Many reports have described the use of *ultrafast CT* (electron beam CT)[12, 50, 51, 57, 163] and *MR fluoroscopy*[78, 144 150, 151, 168] for the dynamic evaluation of upper airways in these patients.

Ultrafast CT scanning utilizes an electron gun to produce a fast-moving electron beam that hits multiple detector rings in the gantry, permitting the simultaneous acquisition of multiple image sections. This results in a superior temporal resolution, and images can be obtained in as little as 50 to 100 msec.[71] Other than its use of ionizing radiation, the disadvantage of selecting ultrafast CT in evaluating patients with obstructive sleep apnea is the inability to obtain primary images in the midsagittal plane.[78]

The term *MR fluoroscopy* has been introduced with the development of numerous rapid gradient-echo sequences capable of acquiring MR images as fast as 0.3 to 7 seconds per frame.[88, 93] Fluoroscopic MR imaging has been used for functional imaging of the upper airways utilizing GRASS (gradient-recalled acquisition in the steady state[78, 150, 151] and FLASH (fast low-angle shot) sequences.[78, 168] Images are obtained in the sagittal and axial planes during quiet nasal respiration, simulation of snoring, and performance of the Müller maneuver (inspiratory effort with the mouth and nose closed).[78] Axial scans are obtained at the levels of the oropharynx and velopharynx (the lowest part of nasopharynx opposite the soft palate, which is one of the narrowest sites in patients experiencing obstructive sleep apnea).[14]

Two fundamental imaging abnormalities are sought in evaluation of these patients[57, 78]:

1. Narrowing of the luminal cross-sectional area of the pharynx, as seen on axial images. The length of narrowing is determined on sagittal images.
2. Increased compliance of pharyngeal walls. The mobility of the uvula, tongue base, and posterior pharyngeal wall is assessed on sagittal images, whereas the mobility of the lateral pharyngeal walls is assessed on axial images.

Suprahyoid Neck Biopsy and Interventional MRI

Interventional MRI is the use of MR techniques to guide radiologic interventions, including both diagnostic and minimally invasive therapeutic procedures.

In areas of complex anatomy, the tissue contrast, spatial resolution, and multiplanar capabilities peculiar to MRI provide the obvious advantages for its use to guide interventional procedures. This is particularly true for sampling suprahyoid neck lesions,[88, 92, 109] an endeavor in which CT guidance is limited by several factors, including the following:

1. The inability to maintain a confident localization of the vascular anatomy throughout the procedure.
2. The inability to go beyond a single imaging plane (usually axial).
3. The frequent improper definition of pharyngeal submucosal lesions on CT.

4. The beam-hardening artifacts inherent in CT at the skull base.

On the contrary, the major benefits of using MRI for procedure guidance in this region (Fig. 19–26) are as follows[88, 92, 109]:

1. The ability to continuously visualize the internal carotid, vertebral, and major branches of the external carotid arteries during the entire needle insertion procedure. The high vascular conspicuity is due to flow-related enhancement effects inherent in the gradient-echo sequences used for procedure guidance.
2. The multiplanar imaging capabilities that ensure precise needle centralization along the axial as well as the craniocaudal dimensions of the lesion. In addition, imaging in any arbitrary plane allows the needle trajectory to be tailored according to the individual case.
3. The ability to guide needle insertion with continuous, near real-time imaging so that the needle can be redirected in order to avoid critical structures in a time-efficient manner.
4. The ability to shift between T1-weighted and T2-weighted contrast during the procedure to maximize lesion conspicuity. T2-weighted techniques also allow sampling of the non-necrotic regions of complex masses, thus increasing the diagnostic tissue yield.

An additional use of the interventional MRI techniques that form the basis for biopsy guidance is application of these methods for the monitoring of direct intralesional drug injection, including injection for sclerotherapy of vascular malformations. The same rapid image updates used

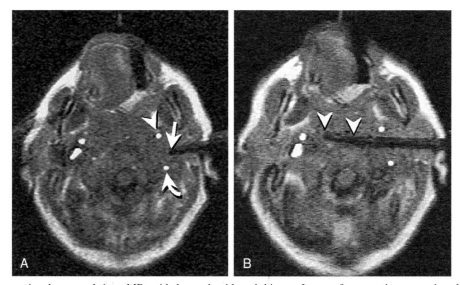

Figure 19–26. Interventional near-real-time, MR-guided suprahyoid neck biopsy. Images from continuous series obtained at 7 seconds per image with fast imaging with steady-state precession (FISP) sequence (TR = 18 msec, TE = 7 msec, 4 signal averages, flip angle = 90 degrees) obtained during guidance of needle insertion in a 68-year-old man with a C1-2 vertebral and prevertebral mass. A previous attempt at surgical transoral biopsy had been unsuccessful.

A, Image obtained early, during needle insertion, demonstrates the needle tip passing through the left parotid space. An ill-defined mass can be seen in the prevertebral space. High vascular conspicuity resulting from 2D Fourier transform technique allows ready visualization of flow-related enhancement within the internal carotid *(arrowhead)* and vertebral *(curved arrow)* arteries. The needle tip *(straight arrow)* can be interactively directed to avoid these major vascular structures.

B, The needle is redirected more anteriorly once it is safely beyond the internal carotid artery (ICA). The location of the needle's side notch is shown as an area of thinning of the distal needle tip (between *arrowheads*). Histologic examination revealed chronic osteomyelitis and cellulitis, and the offending organism was successfully isolated.

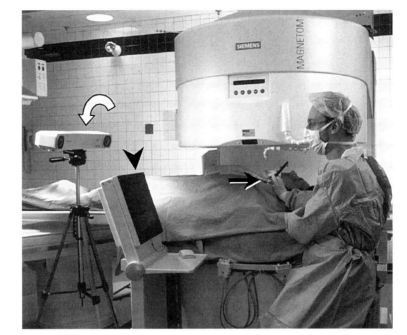

Figure 19–27. Interventional MRI suite setup for radiologic intervention has an open magnet design to provide easy patient access and a video camera sensor array *(curved arrow)* to detect the location and orientation of a hand-held probe *(black arrow).* The system automatically acquires continuous MR images based on the probe position and automatically updates display of four images on shielded liquid crystal diode monitor adjacent to the scanner *(arrowhead).* A computer mouse on the LCD console and foot pedals (not shown) allow the scanner to be operated by the radiologist throughout the procedure.

for interactive needle placement can be used to monitor the injection of sclerosing agents for the treatment of low-flow vascular malformations.[91] The multiplanar images obtained with MRI allow the injection of alcohol or other sclerosing agents to be monitored during administration to ensure filling of the entire targeted portion of the malformation and to exclude extravasation or dissipation of the agent through venous egress.[91]

The accuracy and safety of MRI-guided procedures depend on proper needle visualization. Achieving this task requires a sound understanding of a number of user-defined imaging parameters as well as needle trajectory decisions, which are beyond the scope of this chapter.[88, 90, 93, 109]

Three basic components combine to form the foundation of the modern interventional MRI suite:

1. The availability of an "open" magnet imaging system to facilitate the patient access necessary for performing the procedures (Fig. 19–27).
2. The application of new, fast gradient-echo pulse sequences that allow a wide range of tissue contrast in a time frame sufficient for device tracking (between 0.3 and 7 seconds per image), even at the low field strengths of open magnets and with the suboptimal coil position sometimes required to access the puncture site.[35, 48, 93, 98, 109]
3. The ability to view images in near real-time at the scanner side through an in-room high resolution radiofrequency-shielded monitor (see Fig. 19–27).[88, 93, 186]

With these three components, the entire procedure can be performed with the operator sitting next to the patient and without the need to remove the operator's hand from the interventional device at any time. This manner of intervention, analogous to an angiographic or sonographically guided procedure, is well suited to the skill set developed by radiologists during more conventional types of image-guided intervention.

References

1. American Joint Committee on Cancer: In Fleming I, Cooper J, Henson D, et al (eds): Manual for Staging of Cancer, 5th ed. Philadelphia, Lippincott-Raven, 1997.
1a. American Joint Committee on Cancer: In Beahrs OH, Henson DE, Hutter RVP, Kennedy BJ (eds): Manual for Staging of Cancer, 4th ed. Philadelphia, JB Lippincott, 1992.
2. Anzai Y, Lufkin RB, Jabour BA, Hanafee WN: Fat-suppression failure artifacts simulating pathology on frequency-selective fat-suppression MR images of the head and neck. AJNR Am J Neuroradiol 13:879–884, 1992.
3. Baker LL, Dillon WP, Hieshima GB, et al: Hemangiomas and vascular malformations of the head and neck: MR characterization. AJNR Am J Neuroradiol 14:307–314, 1993.
4. Barakos JA, Dillon WP, Chew WM: Orbit, skull base, and pharynx: Contrast-enhanced fat suppression MR imaging. Radiology 179: 191–198, 1991.
5. Barakos JA: Head and neck imaging. In Brant WE, Helms CA (eds): Fundamentals of Diagnostic Radiology, 2nd ed. Philadelphia, Lippincott Williams & Wilkins, 1999, pp 211–232.
6. Battino RA, Khangure MS: Is that another Thornwaldt's cyst on M.R.I.? Australas Radiol 34:19–23, 1990.
7. Beahrs OH, Henson DE, Hutter RVP, Kennedy BJ (eds): Manual for Staging of Cancer, 4th ed. American Joint Committee on Cancer. Philadelphia, JB Lippincott, 1992.
8. Becker M, Hasso AN: Imaging of malignant neoplasms of the pharynx and larynx. In Taveras JM, Ferruci JT (eds): Radiology: Diagnosis, Imaging, Intervention. Philadelphia, JB Lippincott, 1996, pp 1–16.
9. Becker M: Oral cavity, oropharynx, and hypopharynx. Semin Roentgenol 35:21–30, 2000.
10. Benson MT, Dalen K, Mancuso AA, et al: Congenital anomalies of the branchial apparatus: Embryology and pathologic anatomy. Radiographics 12:943–960, 1992.
11. Boucher RM, Hendrix RA, Guttenplan MD: The diagnosis of Thornwaldt's cyst. Trans Pa Acad Ophthalmol Otolaryngol 42:1026–1030, 1990.
12. Brasch RC, Gould RG, Gooding CA, et al: Upper airway obstruction in infants and children: Evaluation with ultrafast CT. Radiology 165: 459–466, 1987.
13. Brodsky L, Koch RJ: Anatomic correlates of normal and diseased adenoids in children. Laryngoscope 102:1268–1274, 1992.
14. Caballero P, Alvarez-Sala R, Garcia-Rio F, et al: CT in the evaluation of the upper airway in healthy subjects and in patients with obstructive sleep apnea syndrome. Chest 113:111–116, 1998.

15. Cerezal L, Morales C, Abascal F, et al: Pharyngeal branchial cyst: Magnetic resonance findings. Eur J Radiol 29:1–3, 1998.
16. Chandler JR, Mitchell B: Branchial cleft cysts, sinuses, and fistulas. Otolaryngol Clin North Am 14:175–186, 1981.
17. Chia KS, Lee HP, Seow A, et al: Trends in Cancer Incidence in Singapore, 1968–1992. Singapore, Singapore Cancer Registry, 1996.
18. Chin KW, Sercarz JA, Wang MB, Andrews R: Spontaneous cervical hemorrhage with near-complete airway obstruction. Head Neck 20: 350–353, 1998.
19. Chong VF: Masticator space in nasopharyngeal carcinoma. Ann Otol Rhinol Laryngol 106:979–982, 1997.
20. Chong VF, Fan YF: Maxillary nerve involvement in nasopharyngeal carcinoma. AJR Am J Roentgenol 167:1309–1312, 1996.
21. Chong VF, Fan YF: Radiology of the masticator space. Clin Radiol 51:457–465, 1996.
22. Chong VF, Fan YF: Skull base erosion in nasopharyngeal carcinoma: Detection by CT and MRI. Clin Radiol 51:625–631, 1996.
23. Chong VF, Fan YF: Jugular foramen involvement in nasopharyngeal carcinoma. J Laryngol Otol 110:987–990, 1996.
24. Chong VF, Fan YF: Pterygopalatine fossa and maxillary nerve infiltration in nasopharyngeal carcinoma. Head Neck 19:121–125, 1997.
25. Chong VF, Fan YF: Detection of recurrent nasopharyngeal carcinoma: MR imaging versus CT. Radiology 202:463–470, 1997.
26. Chong VF, Fan YF: The retropharyngeal space: Route of tumour spread. Clin Radiol 53:64–67, 1998.
27. Chong VF, Fan YF: Meningeal infiltration in recurrent nasopharyngeal carcinoma. Australas Radiol 44:23–27, 2000.
28. Chong VF, Fan YF: Radiology of the nasopharynx: Pictorial essay. Australas Radiol 44:5–13, 2000.
29. Chong VF, Fan YF, Khoo JB: Nasopharyngeal carcinoma with intracranial spread: CT and MR characteristics. J Comput Assist Tomogr 20: 563–569, 1996.
30. Chong VF, Fan YF, Mukherji SK: Carcinoma of the nasopharynx. Semin Ultrasound CT MR 19: 449–462, 1998.
31. Chong VF, Fan YF, Khoo JB: Retropharyngeal lymphadenopathy in nasopharyngeal carcinoma. Eur J Radiol 21:100–105, 1995.
32. Chong VF, Fan YF, Khoo JB, Lim TA: Comparing computed tomographic and magnetic resonance imaging visualisation of the pterygopalatine fossa in nasopharyngeal carcinoma. Ann Acad Med Singapore 24:436–441, 1995.
33. Chong VF, Fan YF, Toh KH, et al: Magnetic resonance imaging and computed tomography features of nasopharyngeal carcinoma with maxillary sinus involvement. Australas Radiol 39:2–9, 1995.
34. Chung TS, Yousem DM, Seigerman HM, et al: MR of mandibular invasion in patients with oral and oropharyngeal malignant neoplasms. AJNR Am J Neuroradiol 15:1949–1955, 1994.
35. Chung YC, Merkle EM, Lewin JS, et al: Fast T(2)-weighted imaging by PSIF at 0.2 T for interventional MRI. Magn Reson Med 42: 335–344, 1999.
36. Coit WE, Harnsberger HR, Osborn AG, et al: Ranulas and their mimics: CT evaluation. Radiology 163:211–216, 1987.
37. Conley J, Dingman DL: Adenoid cystic carcinoma in the head and neck (cylindroma). Arch Otolaryngol 100:81–90, 1974.
38. Crawford SC, Harnsberger HR, Lufkin RB: The role of gadolinium-DTPA in the evaluation of extracranial head and neck lesions. Radiol Clin North Am 27:219–242, 1989.
39. Cross RR, Shapiro MD, Som PM: MRI of the parapharyngeal space. Radiol Clin North Am 27:353–378, 1989.
40. Curtin HD: Separation of the masticator space from the parapharyngeal space. Radiology 16:195–204, 1987.
41. Curtin HD, Williams R, Johnson J: CT of perineural tumor extension: Pterygopalatine fossa. AJR Am J Roentgenol 144:163–169, 1985.
42. Dähnert W. Ear, nose, and throat disorders. In Radiology Review Manual, 4th ed. Baltimore, Williams & Wilkins, 1999, pp 314–35.
43. Daniello NJ, Goldstein SI: Retropharyngeal hematoma secondary to minor blunt head and neck trauma. Ear Nose Throat J 73: 41–43, 1994.
44. Daniels DL, Rauschning W, Lovas J, et al: Pterygopalatine fossa: Computed tomographic studies. Radiology 149:511–516, 1983.
45. Davis WL, Harnsberger HR, Smoker WR, Watanabe AS: Retropharyngeal space: Evaluation of normal anatomy and diseases with CT and MR imaging. Radiology 174:59–64, 1990.
46. Dickson RI: Nasopharyngeal carcinoma: An evaluation of 209 patients. Laryngoscope 91:333–354, 1981.

47. Dillon WP, Mills CM, Kjos B, et al: Magnetic resonance imaging of the nasopharynx. Radiology 152:731–738, 1984.
48. Duerk JL, Lewin JS, Wendt M, Petersilge C: Remember true FISP? A high SNR, near 1-second imaging method for T2-like contrast in interventional MRI at .2 T. J Magn Reson Imaging 8:203–208, 1998.
49. Easton JM, Levine PH, Hyams VJ: Nasopharyngeal carcinoma in the United States: A pathologic study of 177 U.S. and 30 foreign cases. Arch Otolaryngol 106:88–91, 1980.
50. Ell SR, Jolles H, Galvin JR: Cine CT demonstration of nonfixed upper airway obstruction. AJR Am J Roentgenol 146:669–677, 1986.
51. Ergun GA, Kahrilas PJ, Lin S, et al: Shape, volume, and content of the deglutitive pharyngeal chamber imaged by ultrafast computerized tomography. Gastroenterology 105:1396–1403, 1993.
52. Faerber EN, Swartz JD: Imaging of neck masses in infants and children. Crit Rev Diagn Imaging 31:283–314, 1991.
53. Finkelstein Y, Malik Z, Kopolovic J, et al: Characterization of smoking-induced nasopharyngeal lymphoid hyperplasia. Laryngoscope 107:1635–1642, 1997.
54. Fischbein NJ, AAssar OS, Caputo GR, et al: Clinical utility of positron emission tomography with ^{18}F-fluorodeoxyglucose in detecting residual/recurrent squamous cell carcinoma of the head and neck. AJNR Am J Neuroradiol 19:1189–1196, 1998.
54a. Fleming I, Cooper J, Henson D, et al (eds): Manual for Staging of Cancer, 5th ed. American Joint Committee on Cancer. Philadelphia, Lippincott-Raven, 1997.
55. Franco RA, Har-El G: Cancer of the head and neck. In Lucente FE, Har-EL G (eds): Essentials of Otolaryngology, 4th ed. Philadelphia, Lippincott Williams & Wilkins, 1999, pp 326–335.
56. Gale DR: CT and MRI of the oral cavity and oropharynx. In Valvassori GE, Mafee MF, Carter BL (eds): Imaging of the Head and Neck. Stuttgart, Thieme, 1995, pp 445–474.
57. Galvin JR, Rooholamini SA, Stanford W: Obstructive sleep apnea: Diagnosis with ultrafast CT. Radiology 171:775–778, 1989.
58. Gates GA, Avery CA, Prihoda TJ: Effect of adenoidectomy upon children with chronic otitis media with effusion. Laryngoscope 98: 58–63, 1988.
59. Gates GA, Avery CA, Prihoda TJ, Cooper JC Jr: Effectiveness of adenoidectomy and tympanostomy tubes in the treatment of chronic otitis media with effusion. N Engl J Med 317:1444–1451, 1987.
60. Govrin-Yehudain J, Moscona AR, Calderon N, Hirshowitz B: Treatment of hemangiomas by sclerosing agents: An experimental and clinical study. Ann Plast Surg 18:465–469, 1987.
61. Gray H: Muscles and fasciae. In Clemente CD (ed): Gray's Anatomy, 30th American Edition. Philadelphia, Lea & Febiger, 1985, pp 429–605.
62. Gromet M, Homer MJ, Carter BL: Lymphoid hyperplasia at the base of the tongue: Spectrum of a benign entity. Radiology 144: 825–828, 1982.
63. Gullane PJ, Davidson J, O'Dwyer T, Forte V: Juvenile angiofibroma: A review of the literature and a case series report. Laryngoscope 102:928–933, 1992.
64. Hardin CW, Harnsberger HR, Osborn AG, et al: Infection and tumor of the masticator space: CT evaluation. Radiology 157:413–417, 1985.
65. Harnsberger HR: Head and neck imaging. In Osborne AG, Bragg DC (eds): Handbooks in Radiology (series), 2nd ed. St. Louis, Mosby–Year Book, 1995.
66. Harnsberger HR, Mancuso AA, Muraki AS, et al: Branchial cleft anomalies and their mimics: Computed tomographic evaluation. Radiology 152:739–748, 1984.
67. Harnsberger HR, Osborn AG: Differential diagnosis of head and neck lesions based on their space of origin: Part 1. The suprahyoid part of the neck. AJR Am J Roentgenol 157:147–154, 1991.
68. Heeneman H, Maran AG: Parapharyngeal space tumours. Clin Otolaryngol 4:57–66, 1979.
69. Hillsamer PJ, Schuller DE, McGhee RB Jr, et al: Improving diagnostic accuracy of cervical metastases with computed tomography and magnetic resonance imaging. Arch Otolaryngol Head Neck Surg 116:1297–301, 1990.
70. Hollinshead WH, Rosse Cornelius. Pharynx and larynx. In Textbook of Anatomy, 4th ed. Philadelphia, JB Lippincott, 1985, pp 987–1006.
71. Huda W, Slone RM: Computers and computed tomography. In Review of radiologic physics. Philadelphia, JB Lippincott, 1995, pp 93–109.

72. Hudgins PA, Burson JG, Gussack GS, Grist WJ: CT and MR appearance of recurrent malignant head and neck neoplasms after resection and flap reconstruction. AJNR Am J Neuroradiol 15: 1689–1694, 1994.

73. Hudgins PA, Jacobs IN, Castillo M: Pediatric airway disease. In Som PM, Curtin HD (eds): Head and Neck Imaging, 3rd ed. St. Louis, Mosby–Year Book, 1996, pp 545–611.

74. Hughes ML, Carty AT, White FE: Persistent hypophyseal (craniopharyngeal) canal. Br J Radiol 72:204–206, 1999.

75. Hung T, Huchzermeyer P, Hinton AE: Air rifle injury to the oropharynx: The essential role of computed tomography in deciding on surgical exploration. J Accid Emerg Med 17:147–148, 2000.

76. Hunink MG, de Slegte RG, Gerritsen GJ, Speelman H: CT and MR assessment of tumors of the nose and paranasal sinuses, the nasopharynx and the parapharyngeal space using ROC methodology. Neuroradiology 32:220–225, 1990.

77. Ikushima I, Korogi Y, Makita O, et al: MR imaging of Thornwaldt's cysts. AJR Am J Roentgenol 172:1663–1665, 1999.

78. Jager L, Gunther E, Gauger J, Reiser M: Fluoroscopic MR of the pharynx in patients with obstructive sleep apnea. AJNR Am J Neuroradiol 19:1205–1214, 1998.

79. Kao CH, ChangLai SP, Chieng PU, et al: Detection of recurrent or persistent nasopharyngeal carcinomas after radiotherapy with 18-fluoro-2-deoxyglucose positron emission tomography and comparison with computed tomography. J Clin Oncol 16:3550–3555, 1998.

80. King AD, Kew J, Tong M, et al: Magnetic resonance imaging of the eustachian tube in nasopharyngeal carcinoma: Correlation of patterns of spread with middle ear effusion. Am J Otol 20:69–73, 1999.

81. King AD, Lam WW, Leung SF, et al: MRI of local disease in nasopharyngeal carcinoma: Tumour extent vs tumour stage. Br J Radiol 72:734–741, 1999.

82. Laine FJ, Braun IF, Jensen ME, et al: Perineural tumor extension through the foramen ovale: Evaluation with MR imaging. Radiology 174:65–71, 1990.

83. Lanzieri CF, Lewin JS: Oropharynx and nasopharynx. In Stark DD, Bradley WG (eds): Magnetic Resonance Imaging, 3rd ed. St. Louis, Mosby, 1999.

84. Lawson VG, LeLiever WC, Makerewich LA, et al: Unusual parapharyngeal lesions. J Otolaryngol 8:241–249, 1979.

85. Lenz M, Greess H, Baum U, et al: Oropharynx, oral cavity, floor of the mouth: CT and MRI. Eur J Radiol 33:203–215, 2000.

86. Leslie A, Fyfe E, Guest P, et al: Staging of squamous cell carcinoma of the oral cavity and oropharynx: A comparison of MRI and CT in T- and N-staging. J Comput Assist Tomogr 23:43–49, 1999.

87. Lewin JS: Imaging of the suprahyoid neck. In Valvassori GE, Mafee MF, Carter BL (eds): Imaging of the Head and Neck. Stuttgart, Thieme, 1995, pp 390–423.

88. Lewin JS: Interventional MR imaging: Concepts, systems, and applications in neuroradiology. AJNR Am J Neuroradiol 20:735–748, 1999.

89. Lewin JS, Curtin HD, Ross JS, et al: Fast spin-echo imaging of the neck: Comparison with conventional spin-echo, utility of fat suppression, and evaluation of tissue contrast characteristics. AJNR Am J Neuroradiol 15:1351–1357, 1994.

90. Lewin JS, Duerk JL, Jain VR, et al: Needle localization in MR-guided biopsy and aspiration: Effects of field strength, sequence design, and magnetic field orientation. AJR Am J Roentgenol 166: 1337–1345, 1996.

91. Lewin JS, Merkle EM, Duerk JL, Tarr RW: Low-flow vascular malformations in the head and neck: Safety and feasibility of MR imaging-guided percutaneous sclerotherapy—preliminary experience with 14 procedures in three patients. Radiology 211:566–570, 1999.

92. Lewin JS, Nour SG, Duerk JL: Magnetic resonance image-guided biopsy and aspiration. Top Magn Reson Imaging 11:173–183, 2000.

93. Lewin JS, Petersilge CA, Hatem SF, et al: Interactive MR imaging-guided biopsy and aspiration with a modified clinical C-arm system. AJR Am J Roentgenol 170:1593–1601, 1998.

94. Loevner LA, Ott IL, Yousem DM, et al: Neoplastic fixation to the prevertebral compartment by squamous cell carcinoma of the head and neck. AJR Am J Roentgenol 170:1389–1394, 1998.

95. Lufkin RB, Wortham DG, Dietrich RB, et al: Tongue and oropharynx: Findings on MR imaging. Radiology 161:69–75, 1986.

96. Mafee MF: Nasopharynx, parapharyngeal space, and skull base. In Valvassori GE, Mafee MF, Carter BL (eds): Imaging of the Head and Neck. Stuttgart, Thieme, 1995, pp 332–363.

97. Mafee MF, Carter BL: Nasal cavity and paranasal sinuses. In Valvassori GE, Mafee MF, Carter BL (eds): Imaging of the Head and Neck. Stuttgart, Thieme, 1995, pp 248–331.

98. Mahfouz AE, Rahmouni A, Zylbersztejn C, Mathieu D: MR-guided biopsy using ultrafast T1- and T2-weighted reordered turbo fast low-angle shot sequences: Feasibility and preliminary clinical applications. AJR Am J Roentgenol 167:167–169, 1996.

99. Mancuso AA: Imaging in patients with head and neck cancer. In Million RR, Cassisi NJ (eds): Management of Head and Neck Cancer: A Multidisciplinary Approach. Philadelphia, JB Lippincott, 1994; 43–59.

100. Mancuso AA, Hanafee WN: Nasopharynx and parapharyngeal space. In Computed Tomography and Magnetic Resonance Imaging of the Head and Neck, 2nd ed. Baltimore, Williams & Wilkins, 1985, pp 428–498.

101. Mancuso AA, Harnsberger HR, Muraki AS, Stevens MH: Computed tomography of cervical and retropharyngeal lymph nodes: Normal anatomy, variants of normal, and applications in staging head and neck cancer: Part I. Normal anatomy. Radiology 148:709–714, 1983.

102. Maniglia AJ, Davis JA, Maniglia JV: Obstructive sleep apnea syndrome. In Lee KJ (ed): Essential Otolaryngology: Head and Neck Surgery, 7th Edition. Stamford, Conn, Appleton & Lange, 1999, pp 859–874.

103. Maran AG, Mackenzie IJ, Murray JA: The parapharyngeal space. J Laryngol Otol 98:371–380, 1984.

104. Mariani PJ: Occipital condyle fracture presenting as retropharyngeal hematoma. Ann Emerg Med 19:1447–1449, 1990.

105. Maroldi R, Battaglia G, Farina D, et al: Tumours of the oropharynx and oral cavity: Perineural spread and bone invasion. JBR-BTR 82: 294–300, 1999.

106. Mazzon D, Zanatta P, Curtolo S, et al: Upper airway obstruction by retropharyngeal hematoma after cervical spine trauma: Report of a case treated with percutaneous dilational tracheostomy. J Neurosurg Anesthesiol 10:237–240, 1998.

107. McGowan JC 3d, Hatabu H, Yousem DM, et al: Evaluation of soft palate function with MRI: Application to the cleft palate patient. J Comput Assist Tomogr 16:877–882, 1992.

108. Mendenhall WM, Million RR, Mancuso AA, et al: Nasopharynx. In Million RR, Cassisi NJ (eds): Management of Head and Neck Cancer: A Multidisciplinary Approach. Philadelphia, JB Lippincott, 1994, pp 599–626.

109. Merkle EM, Lewin JS, Aschoff AJ, et al: Percutaneous magnetic resonance image-guided biopsy and aspiration in the head and neck. Laryngoscope 110:382–385, 2000.

110. Mesic JB, Fletcher GH, Goepfert H: Megavoltage irradiation of epithelial tumors of the nasopharynx. Int J Radiat Oncol Biol Phys 7:447–453, 1981.

111. Meyer JS, Hoffer FA, Barnes PD, Mulliken JB: Biological classification of soft-tissue vascular anomalies: MR correlation. AJR Am J Roentgenol 157:559–564, 1991.

112. Mineura K, Kowada M, Tomura N: Perineural extension of nasopharyngeal carcinoma into the posterior cranial fossa detected by magnetic resonance imaging. Clin Imaging 15:172–175, 1991.

113. Moore KL: The neck. In Clinically Oriented Anatomy, 3rd ed. Baltimore, Williams & Wilkins, 1992, pp 783–852.

114. Moriarty KP, Harris BH, Benitez-Marchand K: Carotid artery thrombosis and stroke after blunt pharyngeal injury. J Trauma 42:541–543, 1997.

115. Mukherji SK, Castelijns J, Castillo M: Squamous cell carcinoma of the oropharynx and oral cavity: How imaging makes a difference. Semin Ultrasound CT MR 19:463–475, 1998.

116. Mukherji SK, Castillo M: Normal cross-sectional anatomy of the nasopharynx, oropharynx, and oral cavity. Neuroimaging Clin North Am 8:211–218, 1998.

117. Mukherji SK, Drane WE, Tart RP, et al: Comparison of thallium-201 and F-18 FDG SPECT uptake in squamous cell carcinoma of the head and neck. AJNR Am J Neuroradiol 15:1837–1842, 1994.

118. Mukherji SK, Gapany M, Phillips D, et al: Thallium-201 single-photon emission CT versus CT for the detection of recurrent squamous cell carcinoma of the head and neck. AJNR Am J Neuroradiol 20:1215–1220, 1999.

119. Head and Neck Imaging, 3rd ed. St. Louis, Mosby–Year Book, 1996, pp 437–487.

120. Mukherji SK, Mancuso AA, Mendenhall W, et al: Can pretreatment CT predict local control of T2 glottic carcinomas treated with

radiation therapy alone? AJNR Am J Neuroradiol 16: 655–662, 1995.

121. Mukherji SK, Weeks SM, Castillo M, et al: Squamous cell carcinomas that arise in the oral cavity and tongue base: Can CT help predict perineural or vascular invasion? Radiology 198:157–162, 1996.

122. Mulliken JB, Glowacki J: Hemangiomas and vascular malformations in infants and children: A classification based on endothelial characteristics. Plast Reconstr Surg 69:412–422, 1982.

123. Muraki AS, Mancuso AA, Harnsberger HR, et al: CT of the oropharynx, tongue base, and floor of the mouth: Normal anatomy and range of variations, and applications in staging carcinoma. Radiology 148: 725–731, 1983.

124. Neel HB, Slavitt DH: Nasopharyngeal cancer. In Baily BJ (ed): Head and Neck Surgery: Otolaryngology. Philadelphia, JB Lippincott, 1993, pp 1257–1260.

125. Ng SH, Chang JT, Ko SF, et al: MRI in recurrent nasopharyngeal carcinoma. Neuroradiology 41:855–862, 1999.

126. Ng SH, Chang TC, Ko SF, et al: Nasopharyngeal carcinoma: MRI and CT assessment. Neuroradiology 39:741–746, 1997.

127. Ng SH, Chong VF, Ko SF, Mukherji SK: Magnetic resonance imaging of nasopharyngeal carcinoma. Top Magn Reson Imaging 10:290–303, 1999.

128. Norbash AM: Nasopharynx and deep facial spaces. In Eldman RR, Hesselink JR, Zlatkin MB (eds): Clinical Magnetic Resonance Imaging, 2nd ed. Philadelphia: WB Saunders, 1996, pp 1079–1109.

129. O'Donnell JJ, Birkinshaw R, Harte B: Mechanical airway obstruction secondary to retropharyngeal haematoma. Eur J Emerg Med 4: 166–168, 1997.

130. Olmi P, Fallai C, Colagrande S, Giannardi G: Staging and follow-up of nasopharyngeal carcinoma: Magnetic resonance imaging versus computerized tomography. Int J Radiat Oncol Biol Phys 32:795–800, 1995.

131. Olsen KD: Tumors and surgery of the parapharyngeal space. Laryngoscope 104:1–28, 1994.

132. Paonessa DF, Goldstein JC: Anatomy and physiology of head and neck infections (with emphasis on the fascia of the face and neck). Otolaryngol Clin North Am 9:561–580, 1976.

133. Phelps PD: The pharynx and larynx: The neck. In Sutton D (ed): Textbook of Radiology and Imaging, 6th ed. New York, Churchill Livingstone, 1998, pp 1273–1295.

134. Potsic WP: Assessment and treatment of adenotonsillar hypertrophy in children. Am J Otolaryngol 13:259–264, 1992.

135. Pumberger W, Bader T, Golej J, et al: Traumatic pharyngo-oesophageal perforation in the newborn: A condition mimicking oesophageal atresia. Paediatr Anaesth 10:201–205, 2000.

136. Radkowski D, McGill T, Healy GB, et al: Angiofibroma: Changes in staging and treatment. Arch Otolaryngol Head Neck Surg 122: 122–129, 1996.

137. Rayatt SS, Magennis P, Hamlyn PJ: Carotoid artery thrombosis following a penetrating oro-pharyngeal injury of unusual aetiology. Injury 29:320–322, 1998.

138. Reede DL, Holliday RA, Som PM, Bergeron RT: Non-nodal pathologic conditions of the neck. In Som PM, Bergeron RT (eds): Head and Neck Imaging. St. Louis, Mosby–Year Book, 1991.

139. Robertson RL, Robson CD, Barnes PD, Burrows PE: Head and neck vascular anomalies of childhood. Neuroimaging Clin North Am 9: 115–132, 1999.

140. Robinson JD, Crawford SC, Teresi LM, et al: Extracranial lesions of the head and neck: Preliminary experience with Gd-DTPA–enhanced MR imaging. Radiology 172:165–170, 1989.

141. Rossiter JL, Hendrix RA, Tom LW, Potsic WP: Intramuscular hemangioma of the head and neck. Otolaryngol Head Neck Surg 108: 18–26, 1993.

142. Ryan SP, McNicholas MMJ (eds): Head and neck. In Anatomy for Diagnostic Imaging. London, WB Saunders Company, Ltd, 1994, pp 1–44.

143. Schoem SR, Choi SS, Zalzal GH, Grundfast KM: Management of oropharyngeal trauma in children. Arch Otolaryngol Head Neck Surg 123:1267–1270, 1997.

144. Schoenberg SO, Floemer F, Kroeger H, et al: Combined assessment of obstructive sleep apnea syndrome with dynamic MRI and parallel EEG registration: Initial results. Invest Radiol 35:267–276, 2000.

145. Seaman WB: Pharynx: Radiology. In Margulis AR, Burhenne HJ (eds): Alimentary Tract Radiology, 3rd ed. St Louis, CV Mosby, 1983; pp 491–518.

146. Sham JS, Cheung YK, Choy D, et al: Nasopharyngeal carcinoma: CT evaluation of patterns of tumor spread. AJNR Am J Neuroradiol 12:265–270, 1991.

147. Sham JS, Choy D: Prognostic value of paranasopharyngeal extension of nasopharyngeal carcinoma on local control and short-term survival. Head Neck 13:298–310, 1991.

148. Sham JS, Wei WI, Kwan WH, et al: Nasopharyngeal carcinoma: Pattern of tumor regression after radiotherapy. Cancer 65:216–220, 1990.

149. Shanmugaratnam K, Sobin LH: Histologic typing of upper respiratory tract tumors. In International Histologic Classification of Tumors. No. 19. Geneva, World Health Organization, 1978.

150. Shellock FG, Schatz CJ, Julien PM, et al: Dynamic study of the upper airway with ultrafast spoiled GRASS MR imaging. J Magn Reson Imaging 2:103–107, 1992.

151. Shellock FG, Schatz CJ, Julien P, et al: Occlusion and narrowing of the pharyngeal airway in obstructive sleep apnea: Evaluation by ultrafast spoiled GRASS MR imaging. AJR Am J Roentgenol 158: 1019–1024, 1992.

152. Sheman LJ: Diseases of the oropharynx. In Lee KJ (ed): Textbook of Otolaryngology and Head and Neck Surgery. New York, Elsevier, 1989, pp 407–414.

153. Sidhu MK, Shaw DW, Roberts TS: Carotid artery injury and delayed cerebral infarction after minor pharyngeal trauma. AJR Am J Roentgenol 167:1056, 1996.

154. Sievers KW, Greess H, Baum U, et al: Paranasal sinuses and nasopharynx CT and MRI. Eur J Radiol 33:185–202, 2000.

155. Sigal R, Zagdanski AM, Schwaab G, et al: CT and MR imaging of squamous cell carcinoma of the tongue and floor of the mouth. Radiographics 16:787–810, 1996.

156. Silver AJ, Mawad ME, Hilal SK, et al: Computed tomography of the carotid space and related cervical spaces: Part I. Anatomy. Radiology 150:723–728, 1984.

157. Siou G, Yates P: Retropharyngeal abscess as a complication of oropharyngeal trauma in an 18-month-old child. J Laryngol Otol 114:227–228, 2000.

158. Som PM, Biller HF, Lawson W: Tumors of the parapharyngeal space: Preoperative evaluation, diagnosis and surgical approaches. Ann Otol Rhinol Laryngol Suppl 90:3–15, 1981.

159. Som PM, Biller HF, Lawson W, et al: Parapharyngeal space masses: An updated protocol based upon 104 cases. Radiology 153:149–156, 1984.

160. Som PM, Brandwein M: Sinonasal cavities: Inflammatory diseases, tumors, fractures, and postoperative findings. In Som PM, Curtin HD (eds): Head and Neck Imaging, 3rd ed. St. Louis, Mosby–Year Book, 1996, pp 126–315.

161. Som PM, Braun IF, Shapiro MD, et al: Tumors of the parapharyngeal space and upper neck: MR imaging characteristics. Radiology 164:823–829, 1987.

162. Som PM, Sacher M, Stollman AL, et al: Common tumors of the parapharyngeal space: Refined imaging diagnosis. Radiology 169: 81–85, 1988.

163. Stein MG, Gamsu G, de Geer G, et al: Cine CT in obstructive sleep apnea. AJR Am J Roentgenol 148:1069–1074, 1987.

164. Stiernberg CM: Deep-neck space infections: Diagnosis and management. Arch Otolaryngol Head Neck Surg 112:1274–1279, 1986.

165. Su CY, Hsu SP, Chee CY: Electromyographic study of tensor and levator veli palatini muscles in patients with nasopharyngeal carcinoma: Implications for eustachian tube dysfunction. Cancer 71: 1193–1200, 1993.

166. Su CY, Lui CC: Perineural invasion of the trigeminal nerve in patients with nasopharyngeal carcinoma: Imaging and clinical correlations. Cancer 78:2063–2069, 1996.

167. Sugimura K, Kuroda S, Furukawa T, et al: Tongue cancer treated with irradiation: Assessment with MR imaging. Clin Radiol 46: 243–247, 1992.

168. Suto Y, Matsuo T, Kato T, et al: Evaluation of the pharyngeal airway in patients with sleep apnea: Value of ultrafast MR imaging. AJR Am J Roentgenol 160:311–314, 1993.

169. Tenofsky PL, Porter SW, Shaw JW: Fatal airway compromise due to retropharyngeal hematoma after airbag deployment. Am Surg 66: 692–694, 2000.

170. Tsai YS, Lui CC: Retropharyngeal and epidural abscess from a swallowed fish bone. Am J Emerg Med 15:381–382, 1997.

171. Unger JM: The oral cavity and tongue: Magnetic resonance imaging. Radiology 155:151–153, 1985.

172. Ungkanont K, Byers RM, Weber RS, et al: Juvenile nasopharyngeal angiofibroma: An update of therapeutic management. Head Neck 18:60–66, 1996.

173. Ungkanont K, Yellon RF, Weissman JL, et al: Head and neck space infections in infants and children. Otolaryngol Head Neck Surg 112: 375–382, 1995.

174. Union Internationale Contre le Cancer: In Sobin L, Wittekind C (eds): TNM Classification of Malignant Tumors, 5th ed. New York, Wiley-Liss, 1997.

175. Verron P, Grandpierre G, Vergeau B, et al: Nasopharyngeal perforation: An exceptional accident during digestive endoscopy. Ann Otolaryngol Chir Cervicofac 115:27–28, 1998.

176. Vogl TJ, Dresel SH: New developments in magnetic resonance imaging of the nasopharynx and face. Curr Opin Radiol 3:61–66, 1991.

177. Vogl T, Dresel S, Bilaniuk LT, et al: Tumors of the nasopharynx and adjacent areas: MR imaging with Gd-DTPA. AJR Am J Roentgenol 154:585–592, 1990.

178. Wakisaka M, Mori H, Fuwa N, Matsumoto A: MR analysis of nasopharyngeal carcinoma: Correlation of the pattern of tumor extent at the primary site with the distribution of metastasized cervical lymph nodes—preliminary results. Eur Radiol 10:970–977, 2000.

179. Weber AL, Baker AS, Montgomery WW: Inflammatory lesions of the neck, including fascial spaces: Evaluation by computed tomography and magnetic resonance imaging. Isr J Med Sci 28:241–249, 1992.

180. Weissleder R, Rieumont MJ, Wittenberg J (eds): Head and neck imaging. In Primer of Diagnostic Imaging, 2nd ed. St. Louis, Mosby–Year Book, 1997, pp 547–94.

181. Weissman JL, Tabor EK, Curtin HD: Sphenochoanal polyps: Evaluation with CT and MR imaging. Radiology 178:145–148, 1991.

182. Wong DS, Fuller LM, Butler JJ, Shullenberger CC: Extranodal non-Hodgkin's lymphomas of the head and neck. Am J Roentgenol Radium Ther Nucl Med 123:471–481, 1975.

183. Yakes WF, Haas DK, Parker SH, et al: Symptomatic vascular malformations: Ethanol embolotherapy. Radiology 170:1059–1066, 1989.

184. Yousem DM, Chalian AA: Oral cavity and pharynx. Radiol Clin North Am 36:967–981, 1998.

185. Yousem DM, Hatabu H, Hurst RW, et al: Carotid artery invasion by head and neck masses: Prediction with MR imaging. Radiology 195: 715–720, 1995.

186. Yu ZH, Xu GZ, Huang YR, et al: Value of computed tomography in staging the primary lesion (T-staging) of nasopharyngeal carcinoma (NPC): An analysis of 54 patients with special reference to the parapharyngeal space. Int J Radiat Oncol Biol Phys 11:2143–2147, 1985.

20

Thyroid and Parathyroid Glands

Theodore C. Larson III, Michelle M. Smith, Wui K. Chong, William H. Martin

Thyroid Gland

The shield-shaped thyroid gland is normally positioned anterior and lateral to the cricoid cartilage, although its position may be located more superiorly, anterior to the thyroid cartilage, or more inferiorly, anterior to the trachea. The thyroid contains two lobes, each with a superior and inferior pole; an isthmus; and, in 50% to 80% of patients, a pyramidal lobe that originates from the isthmus or the medial aspect of either lobe. The pyramidal lobe develops along the distal embryonic thyroglossal duct, which explains its location. Similarly, thyroid tissue may be ectopically located anywhere along its developmental migration track (i.e., as a lingual thyroid at the base of the tongue, within a vestigial thyroglossal duct cyst, or further caudally within the mediastinum) (Fig. 20–1).

The superficial location of a normally positioned thyroid gland makes imaging easily accomplished with ultrasonography. Using a 7.5- to 10-MHz linear-array transducer provides 2-mm spatial resolution, although penetration depth and range of view are somewhat curtailed. The normal thyroid gland is homogeneous and more echogenic than muscle but less echogenic than fat. The standard examination provides transverse and longitudinal planar images with evaluation of regional cervical lymph nodes.

Ultrasonography is often the first modality used to image the thyroid gland because it is convenient, inexpensive, quick, and easy to perform. Ultrasonography readily identifies and distinguishes between cystic and solid lesions without using ionizing radiation, although thyroid disorders and diseases that are purely cystic are uncommon. Ultrasonography typically detects more thyroid masses than does computed tomography (CT), magnetic resonance imaging (MRI), or scintigraphy because of its greater spatial resolution. Limitations of ultrasonography include difficulties in evaluating ectopically located thyroid tissue, predicting the functional status of thyroid nodules, and surveying the neck for metastatic lymphadenopathy.

Radiopharmaceuticals used in evaluating the thyroid include technetium 99m–pertechnetate ([99mTc]), iodine 123 ([123I]), iodine 131 ([131I]), thallium 201 ([201Tl]), [99mTc]-sestamibi (MIBI [methyl-isobutyl-isonitrile]), fluoro-18-deoxyglucose ([18FDG]), gallium 67 ([67Ga]), indium 111 ([111In])–octreotide, and [131I]-metaiodobenzylguanidine (mIBG). [123I] is the preferred agent for imaging substernal thyroid glands, and [131I] is preferred for detecting metastases after thyroid ablation.

CT evaluation of the thyroid is performed in the axial plane, usually after the intravenous (IV) administration of iodinated contrast material. The performance of CT and scintigraphic examinations must be coordinated because the administration of IV contrast material for a CT examination interferes with thyroidal uptake of radioiodine and [99Tc] for 4 to 6 weeks. An advantage of CT is that the entire neck as well as the mediastinum can be surveyed for metastatic lymphadenopathy and ectopic thyroid tissue; CT also permits the detection of any unassociated concomitant conditions (Fig. 20–2). CT is excellent at characterizing the density of a thyroid lesion, thus defining the presence of calcification, cysts, or hemorrhage. The borders of a thyroid mass are usually well delineated by CT; thus, invasion of adjacent structures such as the trachea, larynx, and vascular structures of the carotid sheath can be identified.

MRI of the thyroid, like CT, can be used to evaluate the contents of the entire neck. Advantages of MRI over CT include improved soft tissue discrimination and lack of beam-hardening artifacts; however, MRI is not superior in the identification of malignant lymphadenopathy.[160] Differentiation between hemorrhagic lesions and lesions of increased protein content such as colloid-containing masses can be difficult, both being of either bright or dark signal

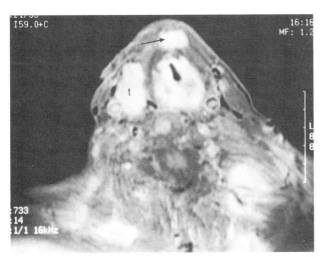

Figure 20–1. Axial T1-weighted MR postgadolinium image with fat suppression shows ovoid enhancing tissue *(arrow)* anterior to the larynx. The tissue, which shows the same signal intensity and enhancement as the enlarged right thyroid lobe (t), represents pyramidal lobe tissue involved by goiter (same patient as in Figure 20–27).

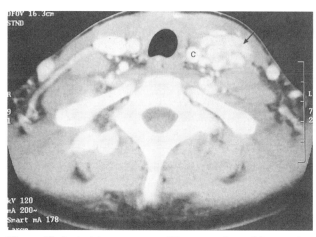

Figure 20–2. Axial postcontrast CT scan performed in a patient after thyroidectomy for papillary carcinoma. The heterogeneously enhancing mass *(arrow)* in the left neck lateral to the left common carotid artery (c) is consistent with a diagnosis of nodal metastasis.

intensity on T1-weighted and T2-weighted images. MRI also demonstrates well the relationship of thyroid lesions to adjacent structures, which assists in determining whether local invasion is present.

In most instances, fine-needle aspiration of palpable suspected thyroid masses can be accomplished freehand without imaging assistance; biopsy of small or nonpalpable lesions can be accomplished with the aid of ultrasonographic, CT, or MRI guidance.[139, 157] Solid, hypoechoic thyroid nodules 8 mm or larger are typically selected for needle aspiration. Smaller nodules can be difficult to aspirate in a precise manner and are more often followed with serial ultrasonographic examinations. A 20- or 22-gauge needle is employed for sampling the solid portion of the mass, with imaging used to guide needle placement and avoid the common carotid artery and internal jugular vein (Fig. 20–3).

Sensitivity and specificity for fine-needle aspirations are reported to be greater than 94%, but results are highly dependent on the expertise of the cytopathologist, and nondiagnostic material may be present in as many as 20% of cases.[7, 28, 31, 40, 43, 66, 139, 157] Fine-needle aspiration, with or without imaging guidance, is the most cost-effective method of diagnosis of primary and recurrent thyroid malignancy.

Pathologic Thyroid Conditions

Thyroid Malignancies

Malignant thyroid neoplasms constitute the most common endocrine cancer. These include the well-differentiated papillary and follicular carcinomas as well as a mixed papillary-follicular variety. Less common but more aggressive malignancies include medullary carcinoma, anaplastic carcinoma, lymphoma, metastatic disease, and other rare neoplasms, such as sarcoma. The most common of these is papillary carcinoma, which accounts for approximately 70% of all thyroid malignancies.[67, 106, 139] Follicular carcinoma comprises about 10%; medullary carcinoma, 5%;

anaplastic carcinoma, about 5%, and the remaining malignancies together, about 1%.[17, 67]

Imaging of thyroid neoplasms using any of a number of modalities is typically not specific for malignancy, since benign processes often simulate malignant tumors. Nodules with irregular margins or masses that invade normal local structures revealed on any imaging examination suggest a malignant process. Irregular borders are visualized in approximately 60% of thyroid malignancies, yet are also seen in approximately 45% of benign thyroid tumors.[130]

Multiple small, highly echogenic foci (with or without shadowing) on sonography strongly suggest the presence of microcalcifications within malignancies.[109] Coarse or peripheral (eggshell) calcification, visualized on CT or with sonography, suggests a benign nodule (Fig. 20–4).[109] Overall, calcification is found in 13% of thyroid masses, including 17% of malignancies and 11% of benign lesions.[130]

Thyroid masses with hemorrhage; cysts; diminished density, isodensity, or increased density (or signal intensity); contrast enhancement; and well-circumscribed margins examined on ultrasonography, CT, or MRI may be benign or malignant.[90, 159] Cystic elements are found in 38% of thyroid malignancies but also in 62% of benign thyroid entities.[130]

Although most thyroid carcinomas are hypoechoic at sonography, most hypoechoic nodules are benign because benign thyroid nodules are much more common than malignant thyroid nodules. Sonographically, 75% of thyroid

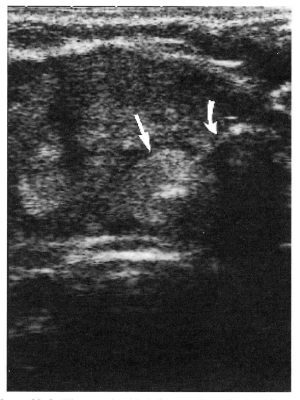

Figure 20–3. Ultrasound-guided, fine-needle aspiration of a thyroid mass. A 22-gauge needle *(curved arrow)* is being inserted into a left thyroid lobe mass *(straight arrow)* under real-time sonographic guidance. Cytologic examination revealed a follicular adenoma.

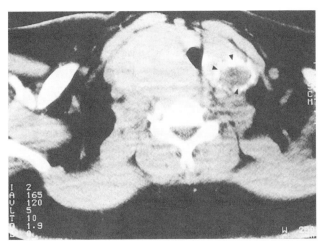

Figure 20–4. Axial CT scan through the lower neck shows peripheral coarse calcifications *(arrowheads)* in an adenoma within an enlarged, goitrous thyroid gland. This peripheral calcification may also be thin and eggshell-like.

carcinomas are hypoechoic, 23% are isoechoic, and only 2% are hyperechoic.[130] Purely cystic or completely hyperechoic nodules are very rarely malignant. Benign nodules may coexist with malignant nodules, however. For instance, 33% of thyroidectomy specimens containing papillary carcinoma also harbor benign nodules.[46]

Color Doppler imaging demonstrates the vascularity of malignant and benign thyroid nodules, with malignant nodules typically showing central intranodular vascularity and benign lesions being characterized by peripheral perinodular vascularity.[124] There is considerable overlap, however, and the distribution of vessels on color Doppler imaging is not a reliable means of differentiating benign from malignant nodules.[124]

More than 99% of "hot" thyroid masses on scintigraphy are benign, typically representing hyperplastic or adenomatous nodules.[28, 50] A "cold" nodule is associated with a 15% to 25% incidence of malignancy, which increases to as great as 50% if the patient has had earlier neck irradiation.[116]

The role of imaging includes the following:

1. Evaluation of thyroid capsule transgression.
2. Detection of neoplastic infiltration into adjacent structures, including prevertebral and local musculature, the carotid sheath, and the aerodigestive tract (Fig. 20–5).
3. Identification of malignant lymphadenopathy.

Enlarged lymph nodes, nodes demonstrating extracapsular spread, and clustered nodes suggest pathologic involvement but are not specific findings of malignant lymphadenopathy.[131, 139] None of the imaging modalities can reliably predict malignant thyroid histology.

Papillary Carcinoma

Papillary carcinoma is characterized histologically by psammoma bodies, "ground-glass" nuclear material, and a fibrovascular papillary stroma.[67] When cyst formation is present, the carcinoma is termed a *cystadenocarcinoma*. Papillary carcinomas are often encapsulated, and they are bilateral or multifocal in 10% to 15% of cases.[152] The incidence of malignant lymphadenopathy is approximately 50%,[67] and 22% of cases of malignant lymphadenopathy arise from occult thyroid tumors.[4] Malignant nodes may be cystic, necrotic, hemorrhagic, or calcified, and they may contain colloid (Fig. 20–6).[131, 132] In approximately 5% of patients, distant metastases occur to lungs, skeleton, or central nervous system.[67] With adequate resection, ^{131}I therapy, and chronic suppressive therapy with thyroxine (T₄), the 20-year survival rate is reported to be 94%.[78] Tumors with both papillary and follicular components behave like purely papillary carcinomas.

Imaging of papillary carcinoma typically demonstrates a solid, hypoechoic (77%) or isoechoic (14%) thyroid mass, often with associated microcalcifications (Fig. 20–7).[130] The lesions most commonly appear to be hypofunctioning (cold) using ^{99m}Tc-pertechnetate and radioiodine (Fig. 20–8) but may demonstrate increased uptake of ^{201}Tl, ^{99m}Tc-MIBI, or ^{18}FDG.

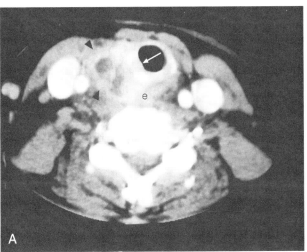
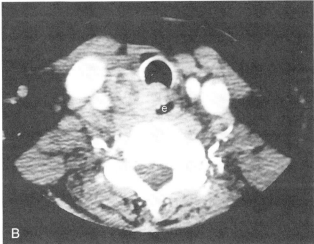

Figure 20–5. *A,* Axial postcontrast CT shows a heterogeneously enhancing mass *(arrowheads)* within the right thyroid lobe, with invasion of the cricoid ring and submucosal extension of tumor *(arrow)*. e, esophagus. *B,* CT image in the same patient at a lower level shows the mass invading the trachea and esophagus (e). Papillary carcinoma was found at surgery.

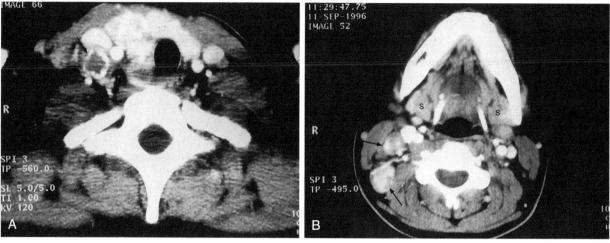

Figure 20–6. Papillary carcinoma with nodal metastases. *A,* Axial postcontrast CT shows a heterogeneous, multilobular mass involving the right thyroid lobe without tracheal invasion. A peripherally calcified lymph node *(arrow)* is seen in the right tracheoesophageal groove. *B,* CT in the same patient at the level of the mandible shows two enlarged, enhancing lymph nodes *(arrows)* within the right posterior triangle and one along the left jugular chain. Normal submandibular glands (s).

Radioiodine uptake by functioning thyroid carcinomas and their metastases is usually less than 10% that of normal thyroid tissue. Therefore, distant and nodal metastases may not be visualized by radioiodine scanning prior to the ablation of any postoperative thyroid remnant.[17] Optimal ^{131}I uptake by neoplastic tissue is also dependent on thyroid-stimulating hormone (TSH). Adequate endogenous TSH levels of greater than 40 μU/mL can be attained 2 weeks after the discontinuance of exogenous liothyronine (T_3) therapy or 4 to 6 weeks after the discontinuance of levothyroxine (T_4) therapy.[33] Preliminary experience indicates that the use of recombinant human TSH as a method of stimulating radioiodine uptake in patients taking exogenous thyroid hormone (TH) replacement yields a detection rate for metastases nearly equal to that seen following thyroid hormone withdrawal.[59]

Thyroglobulin is an iodinated glycoprotein synthesized by both benign and malignant thyroid tissue. Approximately 90% of patients with metastases demonstrate an elevated serum thyroglobulin level.[72] Following surgery and ^{131}I ablation, it should be undetectable (<5 ng/mL) if no functioning thyroid metastases remain. Serum thyroglobulin is a highly sensitive and specific indicator of

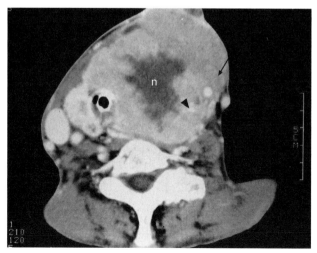

Figure 20–7. Axial postcontrast CT scan shows papillary carcinoma arising from the left thyroid lobe with calcification *(arrowhead),* central necrosis (n), and deviation of the intubated trachea. The mass encases the left common carotid artery *(arrow).*

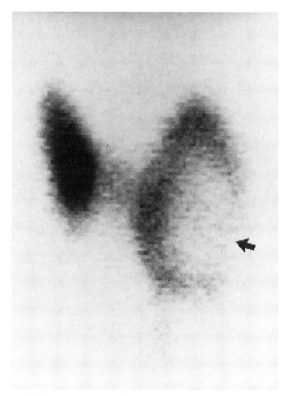

Figure 20–8. An anterior view obtained during technetium 99m–pertechnetate scintigraphy shows a large solitary hypofunctioning nodule *(arrow)* in the lower pole of the left thyroid lobe. The nodule was subsequently resected and found to represent a papillary carcinoma. The right thyroid lobe is normal.

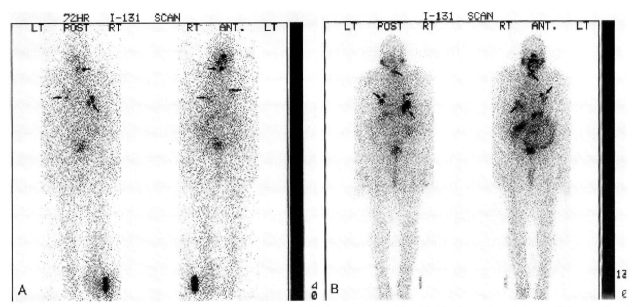

Figure 20–9. *A,* Several definite and a few equivocal metastatic foci *(arrows)* are identified in the neck and thorax 72 hours after the administration of a 3-mCi diagnostic dose of iodine 131. *B,* One week after administration of a 200-mCi therapeutic dose of iodine 131, whole body images more clearly define two metastatic foci in the neck *(arrows)* and at least five lung lesions *(arrows).*

residual or metastatic thyroid carcinoma in patients after ablation.

After surgery and ^{131}I ablation, patients with well-differentiated thyroid carcinoma (papillary and follicular) are assessed for recurrence annually (or less frequently) using whole body radioiodine scintigraphy and serum thyroglobulin monitoring. The sensitivity of ^{131}I scintigraphy for the detection of persistent or metastatic thyroid carcinoma is 50% to 70% with a diagnostic dose of 2 to 5 mCi.[115] Additional lesions are often detected or more easily defined with scintigraphy following a therapeutic dose of 100 to 200 mCi (Fig. 20–9).[8] The combination of ^{131}I scanning and serum thyroglobulin determination improves the detection of metastatic disease to 85% to 100%.[8]

Although the specificity of ^{131}I scintigraphy is high, false-positive findings related to renal, gastrointestinal (GI), other excretory pathways may be confusing. Because it is not necessary to withdraw thyroid hormone therapy prior to scanning, ^{201}Tl or ^{99m}Tc-MIBI imaging is more convenient for the patient. The sensitivity for either of these two agents is 60% to 90%.[8] It is not uncommon to see a positive ^{201}Tl or ^{99m}Tc-MIBI scan in a thyroglobulin-positive patient with a negative ^{131}I scan (Fig. 20–10). Thyroid carcinoma metastases that are poorly visualized with ^{131}I and ^{201}Tl have been successfully imaged with [18]FDG positron emission tomography (PET) while patients remained on a thyroid hormone–suppressive regimen.[13, 126]

Ultrasonography, CT, and MRI are also effective adjunctive imaging modalities in defining the extent of metastatic disease. Compared with ^{131}I scintigraphy, diphosphonate bone scanning is insensitive in detecting the skeletal metastases of differentiated thyroid carcinoma.

Follicular Carcinoma

Follicular carcinoma is usually well marginated and encapsulated, but it may be locally invasive.[158] Associated lymphadenopathy is seen in approximately 5% of patients,

but there is a greater propensity for hematogenous metastasis (Fig. 20–11).[67] Prognosis for follicular carcinoma is poorer than that for papillary carcinoma. Papillary elements may be present in follicular carcinomas, giving a mixed papillary-follicular variety with behavior similar to that of papillary carcinoma. Hürthle cell carcinoma is an unusual variant of follicular carcinoma that frequently demonstrates ^{201}Tl and ^{99m}Tc-MIBI uptake.[1] It is a nonfunctional malignancy with no radioiodine uptake.

Ultrasonography of follicular carcinomas demonstrates a hypoechoic mass in approximately 45% of cases and an isoechoic mass in the remainder (Fig. 20–12).[34, 130] Follicular carcinoma uncommonly develops cystic regions, but compared with papillary carcinoma, it more frequently invades local vasculature, including the carotid sheath.[67] CT and MRI typically demonstrate a solid mass not dissimilar to papillary carcinoma (Fig. 20–13) and are useful for demonstrating local invasion of normal anatomy, extension into the mediastinum, and cervical lymphadenopathy. Nuclear medicine imaging characteristics are similar to those of papillary carcinomas.

Medullary Carcinoma

Medullary carcinoma of the thyroid (MCT) is derived from the parafollicular C cells, which are of neural crest origin. Approximately 80% to 90% of MCTs secrete calcitonin, which is used as a sensitive indicator of tumor presence and volume.[151] MCTs that do not produce calcitonin have a poorer prognosis.[15] Most MCTs also express carcinoembryonic antigen (CEA)[151]; early studies using radiolabeled monoclonal antibodies to CEA indicate a high sensitivity and specificity for the detection of MCT and determination of its extent (Fig. 20–14).[5, 103] This is particularly useful for identifying MCT recurrence.

Although most MCTs express somatostatin receptors, only 40% to 60% are detected using somatostatin receptor scintigraphy (^{111}In-octreotide) (see Fig. 20–14).[21, 58] The

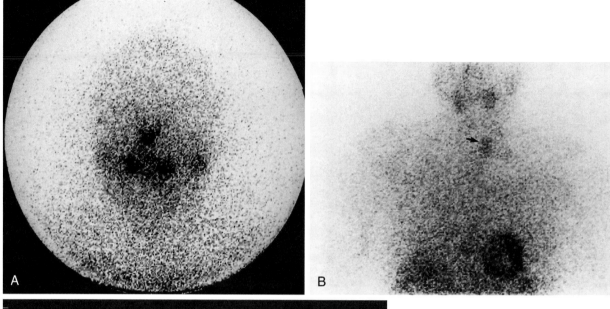

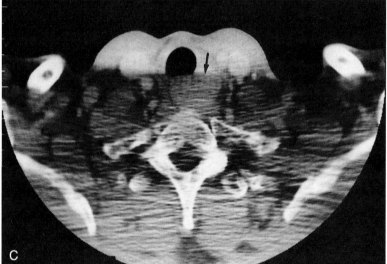

Figure 20–10. Recurrence of papillary carcinoma of the thyroid. After total thyroidectomy and three treatments with iodine 131, this patient was found to have a rising serum thyroglobulin level but a negative iodine 131 whole body scan. *A,* A spot view of the anterior neck reveals no evidence of recurrence. *B,* Subsequent whole body thallium 201 scintigraphy reveals a focus of increased activity in the left neck *(arrow). C,* CT shows a mass *(arrow)* that was congruent with the focus seen in *B.* At exploration, recurrent carcinoma was resected.

higher the serum calcitonin level, the more likely the tumor can be detected using ^{111}In-octreotide imaging. MCT is not radioiodine-avid and cannot be treated effectively with [131]I. [201]Tl, ^{99m}Tc-dimercaptosuccinic acid (DMSA), and ^{131}I-mIBG have been reported to be highly sensitive and specific for MCT, especially when basal calcitonin levels are greater than 1000 pg/mL.[6, 127] MCT may also take up [67]Ga. Evidence is emerging that FDG PET may represent the most effective imaging modality for detection of metastatic MCT.[89]

On ultrasonographic examinations, MCTs are typically hypoechoic, although focal calcium may cause echogenic foci, both at the primary site and within metastatic lymph nodes.[8, 34, 130] CT and MRI demonstrate a solid mass, are helpful for displaying surgical anatomy, and best reveal adjacent lymphadenopathy; malignant lymph nodes are seen in approximately 50% of cases.[158] CT and MRI are often inadequate for identifying MCT recurrences.[21] Selective venous sampling for calcitonin levels using transfemoral catheter techniques is a sensitive and specific method of localizing MCT, but it is invasive, time consuming, and expensive.[88]

MCT is most often sporadic, but a familial link is seen in approximately 15% of adult patients.[158] MCT is a component of multiple endocrine neoplasia type 2A (MEN-2A) and type 2B (MEN-2B) syndromes. MEN-2A is called Sipple's syndrome and MEN-2B (or MEN-3) is termed the *mucosal neuroma syndrome.* In MEN-2A, virtually all patients have MCT, one third have parathyroid hyperplasia, and roughly one third harbor pheochromocytomas. Patients with the MEN-2B syndrome, in addition to having MCT, demonstrate mucocutaneous and alimentary tract ganglioneuromas, café-au-lait spots, and marfanoid facies; in addition, pheochromocytomas develop. A missense mutation of the *ret* oncogene has been identified on chromosome 10 in families with either the MEN-2A or the MEN-2B syndrome.[88]

Anaplastic Carcinoma

Anaplastic carcinoma, typically seen in older patients, is a very aggressive head and neck malignancy that carries

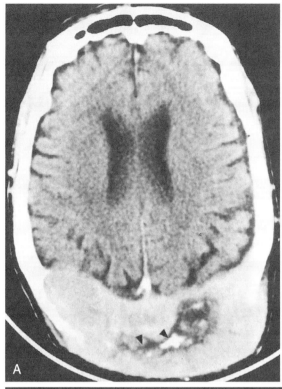

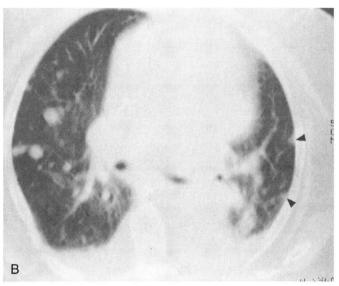

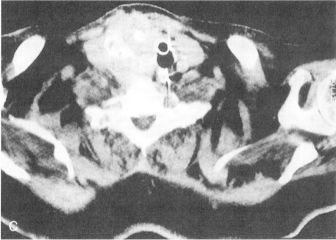

Figure 20–11. *A,* Axial postcontrast CT scan of the head shows a large destructive mass within the posterior calvaria. The lesion has a thick enhancing peripheral rim of soft tissue with central low attenuation and calcification *(arrowheads).* The brain parenchyma does not appear to be invaded. *B,* Axial CT scan through the upper thorax using lung window technique shows multiple parenchymal metastases *(arrowheads)* in both lungs. *C,* Axial CT scan through the lower neck shows papillary carcinoma of the right thyroid lobe with multiple calcifications. This lesion had metastasized to the calvaria and lungs.

a poor prognosis.[158] Patients typically survive only a few months after the pathologic diagnosis is confirmed. Metastases are often widespread. This type of thyroid malignancy can be present within goiter or may be associated with other thyroid malignancies.[67, 122]

Conventional nuclear medicine techniques using [99mTc]-pertechnetate or radioiodine demonstrate only a nonspecific hypofunctioning mass. [201Tl],[99mTc-MIBI], and [18FDG] reveal increased activity within the primary mass as well as within metastases.[122] Although these tumors are [67Ga]-avid, this radionuclide cannot be used to differentiate anaplastic carcinoma from other malignancies, thyroiditis, or thyroid granulomatous infections.

On ultrasonography, anaplastic thyroid carcinoma typically appears as a large hypoechoic mass.[34, 116] CT demonstrates calcification in approximately 60% of cases and necrosis in 75%.[142] Metastatic lymphadenopathy develops in approximately 75% of patients, and in 50% of these the

lymph nodes are necrotic.[142] Local invasion of vasculature or the aerodigestive tract is seen in approximately 40% of patients (Figs. 20–15 and 20–16),[15] and in 25% the malignancy extends into the mediastinum (Fig. 20–17).[142] CT, MRI, and ultrasonography can be used to evaluate the extent of local disease, although ultrasonography does not allow visualization of caudal advancement into the mediastinum.[142]

Lymphoma

Primary lymphoma of the thyroid gland is usually a B-cell neoplasm and is most commonly seen in older women with current or prior Hashimoto's thyroiditis.[41, 67] Virtually all patients with primary lymphoma of the thyroid have coexistent autoimmune thyroiditis.[41]

Lymphomas typically appear as solitary (80%) or multifocal hypoechoic nodules (20%) on ultrasonographic

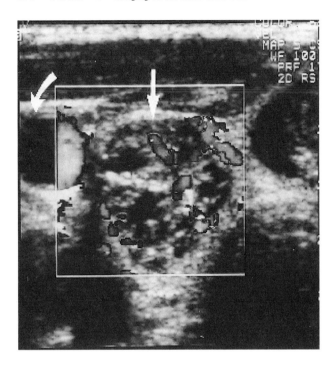

Figure 20–12. Follicular carcinoma of the thyroid. A predominantly hypoechoic heterogeneous mass *(arrow)* with central vascularity (indicated by Doppler enhancement) is seen within the right lobe of the thyroid. *Curved arrow* indicates common carotid artery.

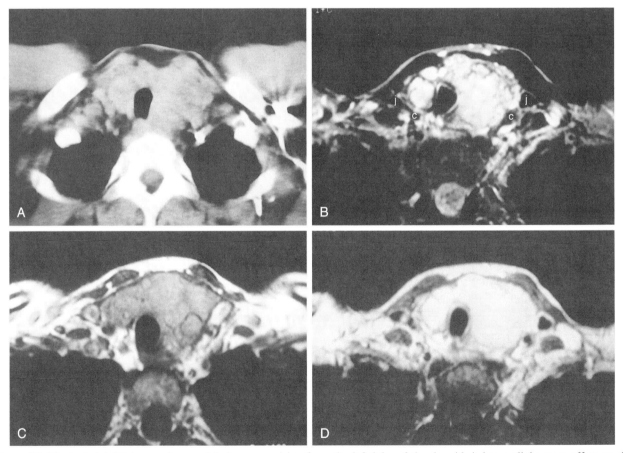

Figure 20–13. *A,* Axial CT image shows a lobular mass arising from the left lobe of the thyroid; it has a slight mass effect on the trachea. *B,* Axial T2-weighted MR image demonstrates a predominantly hyperintense mass splaying the bilateral common carotid arteries (c) and internal jugular veins (j). There is no evidence of tracheal invasion. *C,* Axial T1-weighted MR image demonstrates that the mass is of intermediate signal intensity. *D,* Axial T1-weighted MR image after contrast administration shows diffuse enhancement throughout the mass. Follicular carcinoma without tracheal invasion was seen at surgery.

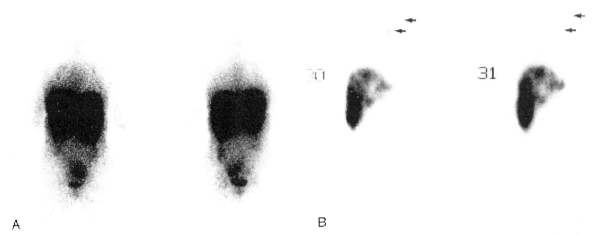

Figure 20–14. *A,* Following total thyroidectomy, a patient with medullary carcinoma of the thyroid and persistent elevation of serum calcitonin and carcinoembryonic antigen (CEA) was found to have a negative indium 111–octreotide scan. *B,* Whole body and SPECT imaging with iodine 131–labeled anti-CEA monoclonal antibody (performed at Garden State Cancer Center, Newark, N.J.) revealed two metastatic foci in the mediastinum *(arrows).* CT scan (not shown) did not demonstrate liver metastases. (From Martin WH, Delbeke D, Habibian MR: Oncologic imaging. In Habibian MR, Delbeke D. Martin WH, Sandler MP [eds]: Nuclear Medicine Imaging: A Teaching File. Philadelphia, Lippincott Williams & Wilkins, 1999, p 700).

studies,[34, 130, 141] and they are photopenic on ^{99m}Tc-pertechnetate or radioiodine scintigraphy. Although lymphomas accumulate both ^{67}Ga and [18]FDG, so may the adjacent areas involved by autoimmune thyroiditis. Gallium 67 and [18]FDG, however, may demonstrate distant metastases.[52] Most lymphomas accumulate ^{201}Tl and ^{99m}Tc-MIBI, both of which may be used to assess response to therapy.[120] These tumors are isodense or hypodense on CT, without or with IV contrast material, and typically cause homogeneous enlargement of a lobe or of the entire thyroid (Fig. 20–18).[141] Necrosis or calcification is seen in a minority of

cases.[141] Local invasion (19% to 51%) or metastasis to regional lymph nodes (14% to 44%)[141] can be demonstrated by ultrasonography, CT, and MRI, each modality having its own advantages and limitations.[143] On MRI, lymphoma often shows increased signal intensity on T2-weighted images[123] and enhances less compared with other thyroid tumors.[90]

Metastases

Approximately 3% of individuals with a primary malignancy outside the thyroid gland have metastatic disease to

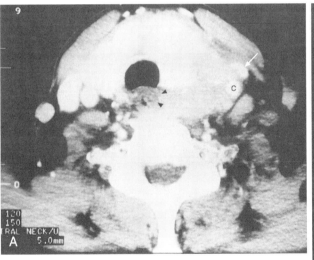
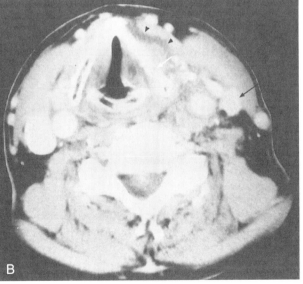

Figure 20–15. Anaplastic carcinoma. *A,* Axial postcontrast CT image shows an enhancing mass arising from the left thyroid lobe with invasion of the esophagus *(arrowheads)* and left carotid sheath. c, left common carotid artery; *arrow* indicates left internal jugular vein. *B,* CT scan of the same patient at the level of the true vocal cords shows the superior extent of the invasive tumor as it insinuates itself between the thyroid cartilage and the strap musculature *(arrowheads).* Invasion of the left thyroid ala has occurred *(white arrow).* An enhancing pathologic lymph node *(black arrow)* can be seen on the left, with spiculated margins indicative of extracapsular spread of tumor.

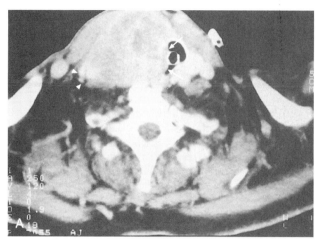
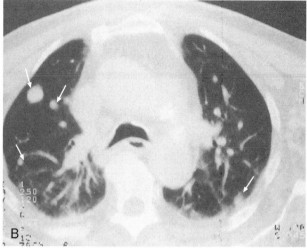

Figure 20–16. Anaplastic thyroid carcinoma. *A,* Axial postcontrast CT scan shows a large right thyroid lobe mass with tracheal invasion *(arrows).* The lesion marginates but does not surround the right common carotid artery *(arrowheads).* An endotracheal tube is in place. *B,* Axial CT scan through the thorax in the same patient shows multiple pulmonary metastases *(arrows).*

the thyroid at autopsy.[119] The two most common malignancies to metastasize to the thyroid are bronchogenic carcinoma and renal cell carcinoma. The appearance of metastatic lesions is nonspecific and may be multifocal. These lesions usually occur in the context of widespread metastases.

Other Malignant Neoplasms and Teratomas

Leukemic infiltration of the thyroid may mimic the imaging appearance of lymphoma. Squamous cell carcinoma, mucoepidermoid carcinoma, and columnar cell carcinoma of the thyroid gland have been reported sporadically. Other rare tumors of the thyroid, such as teratomas and sarcomas, typically present as solid masses. Teratomas are typically midline masses, usually contain fatty as well

as soft tissue elements and fluid, frequently calcify, and may have well-developed teeth and osseous elements.[158, 159] As with other neoplasms, ultrasonography, CT, or MRI is helpful for identifying regional lymphadenopathy and local invasion in malignant varieties.

Benign Thyroid Neoplasms

More than 95% of thyroid nodules are benign.[87] Most of these are hyperplastic (colloid) nodules (Fig. 20–19), and the remainder are adenomas. Solitary hyperplastic nodules are common incidental findings at sonography. It is estimated that 40% or more of the general population have thyroid nodules that are detectable with modern high-resolution sonography.[112]

The number of nodules increases with age. Thyroid nodules can be solid, cystic, or mixed, appearing isoechoic

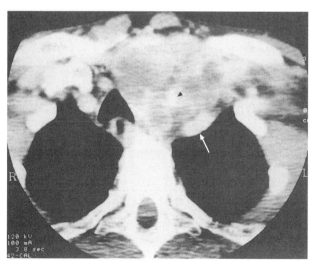
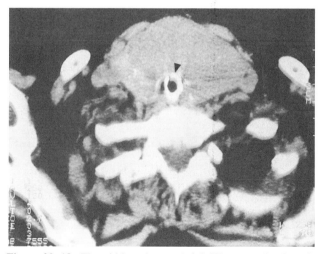

Figure 20–17. Anaplastic carcinoma. Axial postcontrast CT image demonstrates a lobulated, heterogeneously enhancing left thyroid lobe mass surrounding the left common carotid artery *(arrowhead)* and displacing the left subclavian artery *(arrow)* posteriorly. The mass extends into the upper mediastinum.

Figure 20–18. Thyroid lymphoma. Axial CT scan at the thoracic inlet shows marked thyroid enlargement involving both lobes and the isthmus. The gland is homogeneous in density, and no calcifications are present. The tracheal airway is compromised and an endotracheal tube *(arrowhead)* is in place.

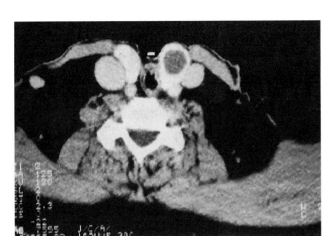

Figure 20–19. Axial postcontrast CT image shows a well-circumscribed, homogeneous, low-density mass within the left thyroid lobe. Despite its low density, the lesion is not cystic. The diagnosis was a hyperplastic thyroid nodule.

with a hypoechoic margin (or halo), hypoechoic, or hyperechoic. The presence of a hypoechoic halo makes the lesion 4 to 12 times more likely to be benign.[130] Cystic, degenerating nodules tend to have thicker walls than simple cysts and often contain solid components.

Thyroid Adenomas

Thyroid adenomas are seen more commonly in women. They are usually less than 3 cm in diameter, have well-delineated margins, and may become cystic, may involute, or may develop internal hemorrhage, necrosis, calcification, or fibrosis.[158] Most thyroid adenomas are hyperechoic or isoechoic at ultrasonography (see Fig. 20–3), whereas most carcinomas are hypoechoic, sometimes with poorly defined borders. Echogenicity alone cannot differentiate between benign and malignant nodules, however (see preceding discussion). Thyroid adenomas are typically of increased signal intensity on T2-weighted MR images but are often heterogeneous (Fig. 20–20).[30] They enhance on both CT and MR images and on CT scans appear solid or cystic when the adenoma has degenerated (see Fig. 20–4).

Thyroid adenomas may be *functioning* or *nonfunctioning*. Functioning thyroid adenomas may be autonomous or hypertrophic, and both types may result in hyperthyroidism with suppressed TSH levels but usually not until the adenoma is larger than 2.5 cm in diameter.[28] Plummer's disease defines a solitary or several autonomous hyperfunctioning (hot) nodules within an enlarged thyroid gland that are unresponsive to administration of exogenous thyroid hormone.

Both hypertrophic and autonomous functioning thyroid adenomas avidly take up ^{99m}Tc-pertechnetate and radioiodine (Fig. 20–21). A hypertrophic functioning adenoma appears cold after the administration of exogenous thyroid hormone, whereas an autonomous functioning nodule remains hot.[116] Other thyroid conditions that demonstrate avid uptake of ^{99m}Tc-pertechnetate include rare malignancies, ectopic thyroid tissue, some normal thyroid variants, and thyroiditis.[106] Radioiodine is more specific than ^{99m}Tc-pertechnetate in identifying a functioning thyroid adenoma.

When ^{99m}Tc-pertechnetate or ^{123}I is used, nonfunctioning

thyroid adenomas appear photopenic compared with adjacent uninvolved thyroid tissue, which is identical to findings with papillary carcinoma (see Fig. 20–8). Numerous other benign entities may appear similarly cold, including degenerated follicular adenomas, adenomatous hemorrhage, cysts, nodular goiters, amyloid deposition, and inflammatory disorders.[116] Although most thyroid malignancies are cold, 75% to 85% of solitary cold nodules are benign.[133] Fine-needle aspiration biopsy may be used to characterize solitary cold thyroid nodules with high sensitivity and specificity.[40]

Thyroid Cysts

Thyroid cysts are also nonfunctioning cold thyroid masses. True thyroid cysts are rare, representing fewer than 1% of all thyroid masses. Most cystic masses are degenerating adenomatous nodules.[158] These are anechoic with thin walls and through-transmission on ultrasonography (Fig. 20–22), of low density on CT (Fig. 20–23) and of increased signal intensity on T2-weighted MR images, and they may show decreased or increased signal intensity on T1-weighted MR images. The increased signal intensity on T1-weighted images is related to the presence of hemorrhage, colloid, or increased protein content. Colloid cysts typically demonstrate such increased signal intensity on T1-weighted MR images.[116] CT density also increases with infection or spontaneous or traumatic internal hemorrhage. Any cystic thyroid mass with a solid component must be approached with suspicion for malignancy (especially papillary carcinoma), although a completely cystic nodule with uniformly thin walls is almost always benign.

Goiter and Multinodular Goiter

The enlarged thyroid, termed a *goiter*, may be hypofunctioning, hyperfunctioning, or normally functioning. The enlarged thyroid may present as a neck mass with or without tracheal or esophageal compression. Thyroid enlargement is best determined by measuring the diameter of the isthmus or the anterior-posterior diameter of the thyroid lobes. The normal isthmus is less than 6 mm in thickness, and each thyroid lobe measures less than 20 to 25 mm in the anterior-posterior dimension. The association of thyroid carcinoma with goiter is less than 3%.[83]

With scintigraphy, multinodular goiter most often demonstrates heterogeneous distribution of the radiopharmaceutical, with foci of increased and decreased activity (Fig. 20–24). Ultrasonography well demonstrates individual nodules within a goiter (Fig. 20–25). These nodules may be palpable or nonpalpable, regardless of whether the patient has clinically evident thyroid disease. Doppler imaging often reveals hypervascularity throughout the goiter. Pathologic characterization of each nodule within a goiter by imaging is unreliable unless typical malignant characteristics are demonstrated (see preceding discussion) or unless the nodule is hot and thus benign on nuclear medicine scintigraphy. The rare occurrence of papillary carcinoma representing one or more of the thyroid nodules is a consideration, although it is unlikely. Multiple cold nodules within a goiter may obviate the need for biopsy; however, an enlarging or dominant mass should prompt histologic evaluation.[116, 125]

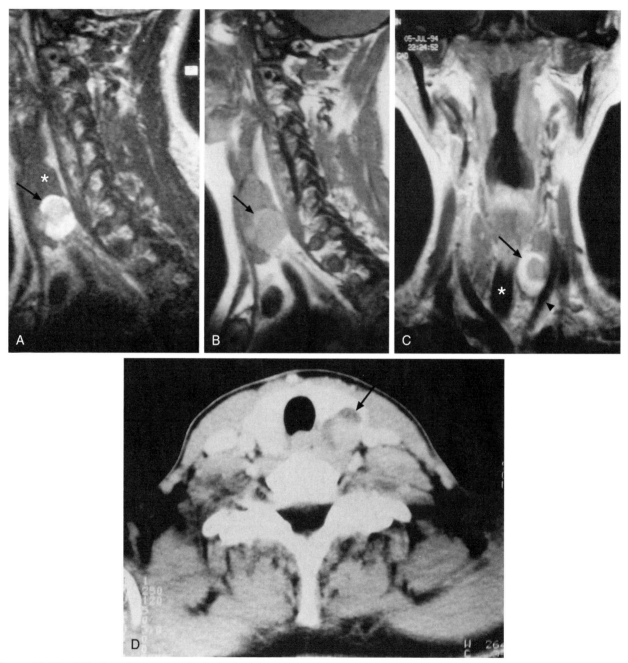

Figure 20–20. Follicular adenoma. *A,* Sagittal T2-weighted MR image demonstrates a mixed-signal-intensity ovoid mass *(arrow)* within the lower pole of the left thyroid gland. The lesion is peripherally hyperintense with a central nodule of intermediate signal. The normal thyroid parenchyma *(asterisk)* is homogeneously hypointense. *B,* Sagittal T1-weighted MR image shows the mass *(arrow)* to be of intermediate signal intensity but distinguishable from normal parenchyma. *C,* Coronal T1-weighted postgadolinium MR image shows enhancement of the peripheral component of the mass *(arrow)* with no appreciable enhancement of the central nodule. Note the relationship of the mass to the trachea *(asterisk)* and left common carotid artery *(arrowhead). D,* Axial postcontrast CT scan shows the well-circumscribed mass *(arrow)* in the posterior left thyroid lobe, with mixed attenuation. The imaging features of the nodule are nonspecific.

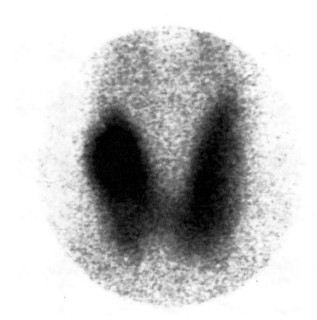

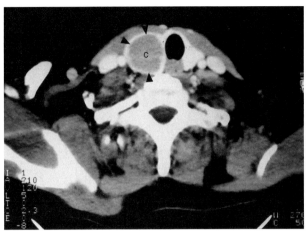

Figure 20–23. Axial postcontrast CT image demonstrates a well-circumscribed, low-density colloid cyst (C) within the right lobe of the thyroid. The nongoitrous thyroid parenchyma at the periphery of the lesion enhances normally *(arrowheads)*.

Figure 20–21. With technetium 99m–pertechnetate scintigraphy, an anterior view identifies a solitary hyperfunctioning nodule in the upper pole of the right thyroid lobe. Extranodular thyroid activity is not suppressed, consistent with a diagnosis of euthyroidism.

Ultrasonographic and CT imaging typically demonstrate the goitrous thyroid as heterogeneous and display nodular enlargement of one or both lobes with cysts and often calcification (Fig. 20–26). Hemorrhage may be seen in 60% of cases.[95] On an MR image, multinodular goiter is typically heterogeneous; signal intensity is isointense to normal thyroid or increased on T1-weighted images and mixed on T2-weighted images.[30, 95] Contrast enhancement is typically diffuse and mottled on CT and MRI scans (Fig. 20–27). In some instances, all imaging modalities demonstrate a uniform parenchymal appearance in an enlarged thyroid gland.

Ultrasonography is not an imaging option for evaluating the possibility of a substernal goiter because the sternum prevents mediastinal interrogation. CT and MRI, however, demonstrate a substernal goiter well, and both may reveal cervical thyroid tissue contiguous with the mediastinal mass (Fig. 20–28). If a radionuclide scan is contemplated, iodinated contrast media should be withheld during CT scanning because these agents may precipitate thyroid storm in some thyrotoxic patients. Because of the presence of interfering mediastinal blood pool activity with ^{99m}Tc-pertechnetate, ^{123}I should be used to assess mediastinal masses.

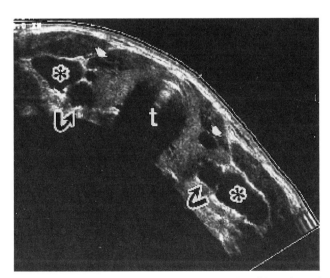

Figure 20–22. Transverse sonogram of the thyroid performed with an extended field of view (Siescape [Siemens]) shows the entire thyroid and adjacent structures. The right and left lobes are separated by the trachea (t). The isthmus lies superficial to the trachea. Simple cysts *(arrows)* are seen in the right and left lobes, which are otherwise normal. *Curved arrows* indicate common carotid arteries; *asterisks* show internal jugular veins.

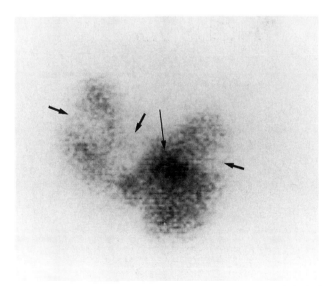

Figure 20–24. An asymmetrical thyroid gland with multiple foci of increased *(long-stemmed arrow)* and decreased *(arrows)* uptake of technetium 99m–pertechnetate is typical of multinodular goiter, but it may also be seen in Hashimoto's thyroiditis.

Hyperthyroidism

Hyperthyroidism may be caused by Graves' disease (diffuse toxic goiter), toxic nodular goiter (Plummer's disease), autonomous toxic adenomas, and, rarely, ectopic thyroid tissue, thyroid inflammation, or bulky differentiated carcinoma. At scintigraphy, uptake of the radiopharmaceutical within the gland or each functioning nodule is increased, and background and salivary gland activity are diminished. In the case of a toxic nodule, activity within the remainder of the gland is suppressed (Fig. 20–29).

Women are 10 times more likely than men to have hyperthyroidism. The diagnosis is made by the detection of elevated circulating levels of thyroid hormones, accompanied by suppressed TSH levels in all cases other than those caused by a TSH-producing pituitary adenoma. Elevated or high-normal radioiodine uptake confirms that the thyroid is hyperfunctional. Suppressed thyroid uptake generally indicates that the hyperthyroidism is caused by exogenous administration of thyroid hormone or that it is the result of thyroid parenchymal destruction due to subacute thyroiditis or postpartum thyroiditis; a rare alternative is struma ovarii (a thyroxine-producing ovarian teratoma).[155]

Patients with elevated serum thyroid hormone levels and increased thyroidal radioactive iodine uptake at 24 hours typically have Graves' disease or toxic nodular goiter. Patients with elevated thyroid function test findings and normal radioactive iodine uptake typically have Plummer's disease or a Graves' disease variant with rapid iodine turnover.

Percutaneous ethanol ablation of autonomous thyroid nodules has been successful in treating hyperthyroidism.[19, 69, 101]

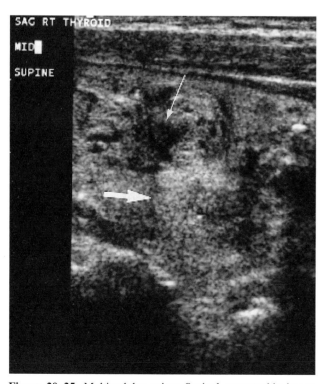

Figure 20–25. Multinodular goiter. Sagittal sonographic image of the right lobe of the thyroid reveals a heterogeneous, enlarged thyroid with predominantly hyperechoic *(large arrow)* but also hypoechoic *(small arrow)* nodules.

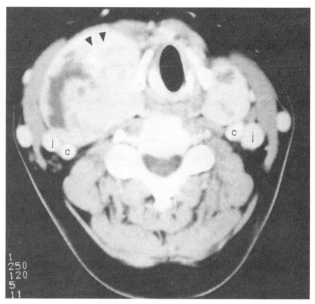

Figure 20–26. Multinodular goiter. CT scan at the level of the cricoid cartilage shows bilaterally enlarged, heterogeneous thyroid lobes. Several foci of calcification *(arrowheads)* are seen within the larger right lobe. The common carotid arteries (c) and internal jugular veins (j) are displaced posterolaterally.

Graves' Disease

Graves' disease is the most common cause of hyperthyroidism. It occurs most often in young women, is related to abnormal production of a thyroid stimulating immunoglobulin, and may be familial.

On CT or MR images, patients with Graves' disease demonstrate a diffusely enlarged, contrast-enhancing thyroid gland.[158] A hypertrophied pyramidal lobe is a common accompaniment.[158] Sonographically, the gland appears diffusely hypoechoic and markedly hypervascular by Doppler flow imaging ("thyroid inferno").[107] Nuclear medicine scintigraphy reveals markedly elevated iodine uptake by a diffusely enlarged thyroid gland (Fig. 20–30). Occasionally, a patient with Graves' disease has an enlarged thyroid gland with one or more nodules. Although a solitary cold solid nodule in a patient with Graves' disease may represent an area of nonfunctioning, TSH-dependent, hyperplastic tissue (Marine-Lenhart disease),[116] the possibility of coexistent malignancy must be entertained. Fine-needle aspiration biopsy is usually recommended and is safe despite the hypervascularity of the gland. Malignant thyroid tumors are seen only rarely in patients with Graves' disease (~0.5% of reported cases).[15, 25]

Orbital findings in patients with Graves' disease include exophthalmos, increased extraocular muscle thickness, and excessive retrobulbar fat.

Hypothyroidism

Hypothyroidism is diagnosed more often in women than in men, and the condition is found in as many as 3% to 5% of people older than age 65.[159] In the Western world, autoimmune Hashimoto's thyroiditis is the most common cause of hypothyroidism; worldwide, however, iodine deficiency is the leading cause of endemic goiter. Other

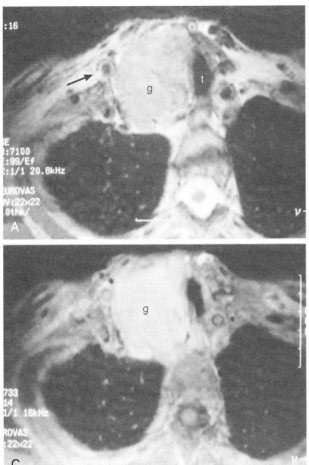

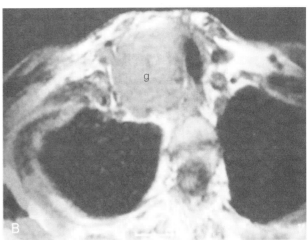

Figure 20–27. *A,* Axial T2-weighted MR image demonstrates a large goiter (g) involving the right thyroid lobe. It displaces the right common carotid artery *(arrow)* laterally and displaces and compresses the trachea (t). The goiter is relatively homogeneous and shows slightly increased signal. *B,* Axial T1-weighted image shows that the goiter (g) is of intermediate signal intensity. *C,* After gadolinium administration, the goiter (g) shows diffuse enhancement on this T1-weighted sequence.

causes include previous thyroidectomy, previous radiation (^{131}I or external beam), congenital organification defects, subacute or chronic thyroiditis, dietary or environmental goitrogens, antithyroid medications such as propylthiouracil (PTU) and methimazole, hypothalamic or pituitary disease, and exogenous iodine (medications, foods, contrast agents). Radioiodine uptake is low or low-normal in patients with hypothyroidism except when caused by iodine deficiency.

Congenital hypothyroidism may be secondary to thyroid aplasia, hypoplasia or hemiaplasia, thyroid ectopia, abnormal thyroxine production, pituitary or hypothalamic disorders, or autoimmune disease. In the infant with congenital hypothyroidism, a ^{99m}Tc-pertechnetate scan is often used to detect the amount of normally located thyroid gland and any ectopic functioning tissue. Scintigraphy and other imaging modalities are usually not necessary in the remainder of patients with hypothyroidism.

Figure 20–28. Substernal goiter. CT scan through the upper thorax shows an enlarged thyroid gland posterior to the sternum (S). Both lobes are symmetrically enlarged, with slight heterogeneity of the parenchyma. The trachea *(asterisk)* is slightly compressed in the midline, and the great vessels are displaced laterally. Neither tracheal nor esophageal *(arrows)* invasion has occurred.

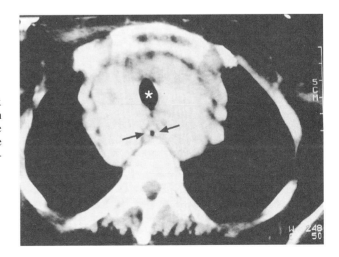

Thyroid Inflammatory Disorders

Bacterial Thyroiditis

Bacterial thyroiditis may be spontaneous, may arise from hematologic seeding, may occur in an immune-compromised host, may result from a cervical puncture wound, may develop because of an infected third or fourth branchial cleft cyst (usually left-sided),[2, 44] or may arise from an aerodigestive tract or thyroglossal duct fistula.[53] It typically follows a fulminant course. MRI or CT scans of acute bacterial thyroiditis are sometimes used to evaluate airway compromise, associated lymphadenopathy, carotid sheath inflammation (including jugular vein thrombosis), and associated congenital cysts) and to identify fistulous tracts and abscesses.[16]

De Quervain's Thyroiditis

De Quervain's thyroiditis (or subacute granulomatous thyroiditis) is a subacute condition that usually presents with a diffusely tender thyroid in middle-aged women following a viral respiratory tract infection. Coxsackievirus, adenovirus, echovirus (enteric cytopathogenic human orphan virus), influenza virus, and mumps virus have been implicated as causative agents.[67, 149] Approximately 50% of patients present with mild, transient, destruction-induced hyperthyroidism followed by mild hypothyroidism, eventually returning to euthyroidism over a period of 6 to 9 months.[106, 119]

Sonographically, the thyroid gland appears hypo-

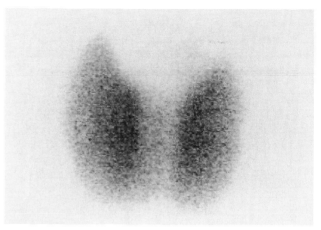

Figure 20–30. Diffusely increased radionuclide uptake in an enlarged gland is typical of Graves' disease. Background activity is absent and the isthmus is thickened.

echoic.[34] Uptake of radioiodine (or ^{99m}Tc-pertechnetate) is heterogeneous and initially low (0% to 5%); it later becomes elevated before returning to normal. On ultrasonography, MRI, CT, or nuclear scintigraphy, the end-stage thyroid gland may be atrophic, although this is rare. More than 90% of patients with subacute thyroiditis have a normal thyroid gland with normal function and normal appearance on any imaging test at long-term follow-up.

Hashimoto's Thyroiditis

Hashimoto's thyroiditis is a chronic lymphocytic infiltration of the thyroid. It is the most common of the thyroiditides, it primarily occurs in women between ages 40 and 60 years, and it is the most common thyroiditis in children.[158] The disease is caused by an autoimmune response to thyroglobulin, colloid, or other thyroid antigens. Other autoimmune diseases may be associated, such as adrenal insufficiency, pernicious anemia, and systemic lupus erythematosus. More than 50% of patients with Hashimoto's thyroiditis are hypothyroid.[158] There is also a predisposition for development of non-Hodgkin's lymphoma.[141]

The radionuclide scan may be normal, may reveal a homogeneously enlarged gland, or may demonstrate diffuse heterogeneous activity; in some patients, a solitary region of photopenia may be seen. Radioiodine uptake may be normal, low, or high.[25] The affected gland frequently accumulates [18]FDG or [67]Ga.[154]

At ultrasonography, the thyroid gland is enlarged and diffusely hypoechoic or multinodular (Fig. 20–31).[156] Calcification may be seen on CT or ultrasonography (Fig. 20–32). On T2-weighted MR images, Hashimoto's thyroiditis typically demonstrates increased signal intensity, sometimes with linear, low-signal-intensity strands, possibly representing fibrosis.[30, 104]

Riedel's Thyroiditis

Riedel's thyroiditis, also termed struma thyroiditis, is a rare chronic inflammatory condition of the thyroid gland. The gland enlarges and may demonstrate regional mass effect with hoarseness and dysphagia caused by the extensive associated neck fibrosis. The condition is more com-

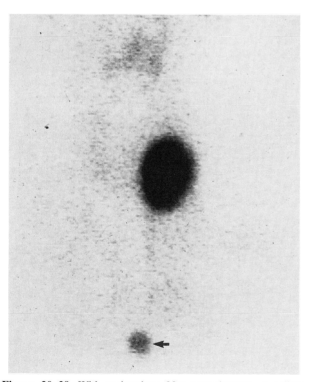

Figure 20–29. With technetium 99m–pertechnetate, a solitary large focus of increased activity is identified in the left neck. The lack of contralateral thyroid activity and the virtual absence of background activity are consistent with a diagnosis of solitary toxic adenoma. The suprasternal notch is identified with a cobalt marker *(arrow).*

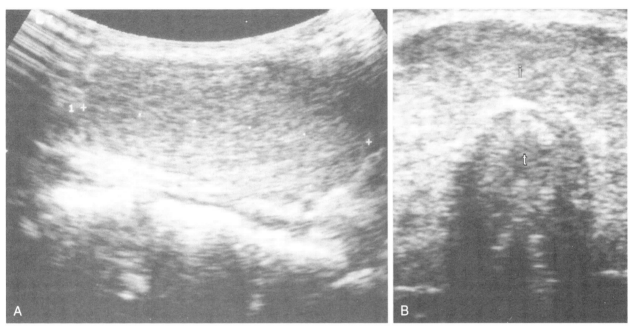

Figure 20–31. *A,* Sagittal ultrasound image of the right thyroid lobe shows an enlarged lobe with homogeneous, slightly hypoechoic echotexture. No focal nodules, cysts, or calcifications are noted in this patient with Hashimoto's thyroiditis. *B,* Transverse ultrasound image shows homogeneous, hypoechoic parenchyma with enlargement of the thyroid isthmus (i) as well as both lobes. The centrally located trachea (t) demonstrates artifact posterior to it generated by internal air.

mon in women. It may affect one or both thyroid lobes and typically causes hypothyroidism.

At imaging, the thyroid appears enlarged and homogeneously hypoechoic on ultrasonography and hypodense to isodense on CT.[34, 104] Riedel's thyroiditis may mimic malignancy with local infiltration, and it often calls for surgery for definitive diagnosis and relief of compressive symptoms.

Diminished signal intensity on T1-weighted and T2-weighted MR images is thought to be caused by chronic fibrosis.[104] Riedel's thyroiditis may be associated with other fibrotic conditions such as retroperitoneal fibrosis, mediastinal fibrosis, sclerosing cholangitis, and orbital pseudotumor.[70]

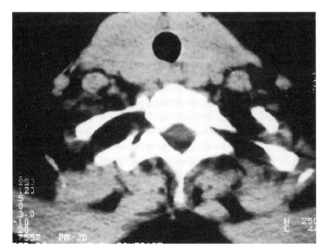

Figure 20–32. Unenhanced CT scan shows a diffusely enlarged, homogeneous thyroid gland in a patient with Hashimoto's thyroiditis. No focal masses or calcifications are noted.

Miscellaneous Thyroid Conditions

Other inflammatory but rare thyroid conditions include tuberculosis, sarcoidosis, fungal diseases, and opportunistic organisms, especially in patients with acquired immunodeficiency syndrome (AIDS). Amyloidosis and hemochromatosis may replace thyroid parenchyma and may cause decreased signal intensity on T2-weighted MR images.[158] Radiation received from external beam or radioactive iodine therapy may lead to fibrosis and atrophy of the thyroid gland.

Developmental Thyroid Anomalies

Lingual Thyroid

Lingual thyroid results from arrest of migration of the thyroid anlage at the foramen cecum in the base of the tongue to its normal location in the anterior neck. The condition occurs in one in 3000 patients with thyroid disease, and it is the most common form of functioning ectopic thyroid tissue (90% of cases).[119] Arrest of migration may be complete or incomplete, typically occurring in the midline of the tongue base between the circumvallate papillae and the epiglottis. Rare cases may involve the entire tongue. Thyroid tissue in its normal location in the neck is absent in 70% to 80% of cases,[38, 119] and most of these patients are hypothyroid.

Ectopic thyroid tissue is more common in women than men (7:1) and may present as an enlarging mass at puberty or during pregnancy secondary to hormonal changes.[158] Malignancy in lingual thyroid tissue occurs in 2.8% of cases.[85]

Radionuclide ^{99m}Tc-pertechnetate, ^{123}I, or ^{131}I scintigraphy demonstrates avid tracer uptake within the midline of

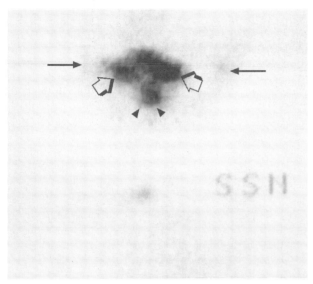

Figure 20–33. Lingual thyroid. Frontal projection of a technetium 99m–pertechnetate thyroid scan shows prominent uptake of radiotracer in the base of the tongue *(arrowheads)*. Tracer uptake is absent where it would be expected in the thyroid tissue in the lower neck. Normal uptake is noted in the parotid *(arrows)* and submandibular *(open arrows)* glands.

the tongue base if a lingual thyroid is present (Fig. 20–33). If surgery is contemplated, radionuclide evaluation with ^{123}I or ^{99m}Tc-pertechnetate is recommended to detect additional functioning thyroid tissue in the neck. Unenhanced CT

shows a hyperdense mass in the base of the tongue. With iodinated contrast material, the lingual thyroid densely and homogeneously enhances (Fig. 20–34).

MRI shows lingual thyroid tissue to be isointense to normal thyroid tissue on T1-weighted images and hyperintense on T2-weighted images.[38] The mass enhances strongly after administration of gadolinium-based contrast material. Additional thyroid tissue lower in the neck may be identified with either CT or MRI.

Thyroglossal Duct Cyst

The thyroglossal duct cyst (TDC) is the most common congenital cystic neck mass, accounting for 70% of nonodontogenic congenital neck abnormalities. The thyroglossal duct is the embryologic tract along which the thyroid anlage courses as it descends from the foramen cecum in the tongue base to its normal location in the low anterior neck. TDCs may occur anywhere along the course of the duct but typically occur about the hyoid bone. The majority of cysts (65%) are located within the thyrohyoid membrane and are infrahyoid in location.[3] Fifteen percent of TDCs are at the level of the hyoid, and 20% are suprahyoid.[3] Suprahyoid TDCs are more likely to be at the midline, imbedded between the anterior bellies of the digastric muscles. Infrahyoid lesions are paramedian and tend to be located within the strap musculature. Two percent are completely intralingual.

Most TDCs present in young adulthood, with 50% occurring before age 10 years and 70% before age 30. Rarely, they may present in older adults. There is no known sex

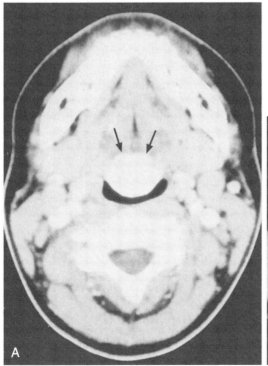

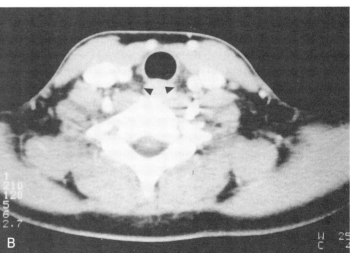

Figure 20–34. *A,* Enhanced CT image at the level of the oropharynx shows a well-circumscribed, homogeneously enhancing mass *(arrows)* in the tongue base, consistent with a diagnosis of ectopic lingual thyroid tissue. *B,* CT scan in the same patient at the expected level of the thyroid gland demonstrates no paratracheal thyroid tissue *(arrowheads)*.

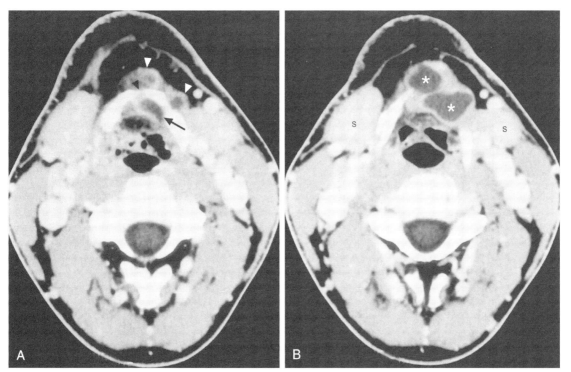

Figure 20–35. Thyroglossal duct cyst. *A,* Axial postcontrast CT scan at the level of the hyoid bone shows a multilobulated low-density mass traversing the hyoid bone. A component of the lesion is deep to the hyoid within the pre-epiglottic fat *(arrow),* and the remainder is seen anterior to the hyoid *(white arrowheads).* The bone defect can be seen within the central aspect of the hyoid bone *(black arrowhead).* Note also the submandibular glands (s). *B,* Axial CT scan in the same patient 5 mm caudal to *A* shows two low-attenuation components of the mass *(asterisks)* and their relationship to the hyoid bone. Submandibular glands are normal.

predilection. Coexisting carcinoma, usually of the papillary type, occurs in 1% of patients with TDC.[3, 45, 47] Follicular carcinoma, adenocarcinoma, and squamous cell carcinoma have been reported. Ectopic thyroid tissue is present within the wall of TDC in fewer than 5% of cases.[3, 97]

CT demonstrates a unilocular or multilocular low-density mass, usually 2 to 4 cm in diameter, present anywhere from the tongue base to the superior margin of the thyroid gland. When located within the hyoid bone, a defect in the bone itself may be apparent on CT (Fig. 20–35). TDC contents may be isodense to hyperdense because of increased protein content or hemorrhage. The capsule of the lesion may uncommonly enhance unless the patient has a history of trauma or current or previous infection. Prior or active superinfection is seen in approximately 60% of patients. Enhancement of the surrounding musculature and obscuration of fascial planes indicate TDC superinfection and overlying cellulitis (Fig. 20–36). Nodules of enhancing tissue within the cyst raise the possibility of concurrent malignancy but may represent only ectopic thyroid tissue.

MRI signal characteristics vary, depending on the protein content of the fluid within the cyst. TDCs most commonly show low to intermediate signal intensity on T1-weighted images, increased signal intensity when proteinaceous, and high signal on T2-weighted images (Fig. 20–37).

With both CT and MRI, enhancing ectopic thyroid tissue may be seen along the course of the thyroglossal duct. Scintigraphy is more sensitive in the detection of these ectopic thyroid rests. Ultrasonography of a TDC displays an anechoic, cystic mass with through-transmission. Inter-

nal echoes within the cyst may be caused by increased protein content or hemorrhage. Both ultrasonographic and nuclear medicine imaging can confirm the presence of a normal thyroid gland before TDC resection.[65]

Parathyroid Glands

Typically, four parathyroid glands are present (two superiorly and two inferiorly) along the posterior margins of

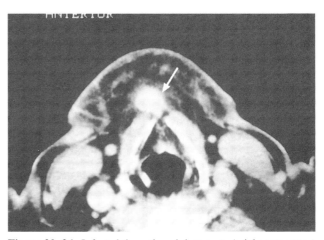

Figure 20–36. Infected thyroglossal duct cyst. Axial postcontrast CT scan at the level of the upper thyroid cartilage demonstrates an enhancing, slightly heterogeneous soft tissue mass *(arrow)* within the anterior cervical space. Stranding within the fat surrounding the lesion suggests infection.

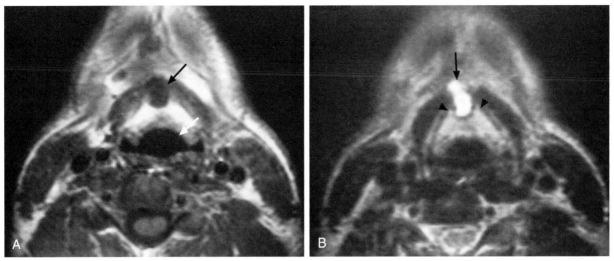

Figure 20–37. Thyroglossal duct cyst. *A,* Axial T1-weighted MR image just inferior to the hyoid bone shows a rounded, low-signal-intensity mass *(black arrow)* in the anterior pre-epiglottic fat at the superior margin of the thyroid cartilage. The normal epiglottis *(white arrow)* is demonstrated. *B,* Axial T2-weighted image slightly inferior to *A* shows the lesion *(arrow)* extending anterior to the thyroid cartilage *(arrowheads)* between the strap muscles. The lesion shows increased signal intensity on the T2-weighted sequence.

both lobes of the thyroid; however, the location of the inferior parathyroid glands may vary. In approximately 20% of patients, they are located anywhere from the carotid bifurcations to the upper mediastinum as well as within the thyroid or behind the trachea or esophagus.[28, 35, 92, 106] Ten percent to 25% of patients have more than four parathyroid glands, with the supernumerary glands most often found in the upper mediastinum.[67, 68]

Parathyroid pathology may be detected by radionuclide scintigraphy, ultrasonography, CT, MRI, angiography, and venous sampling. The success of all of these techniques, except venous sampling, depends, to a varying degree, on the size of the abnormal gland.

The radiopharmaceutical of choice for imaging parathyroid enlargement is ^{99m}Tc-MIBI, employing a double-phase protocol.[36, 62, 77, 84] ^{99m}Tc-MIBI accumulates in both parathyroid and thyroid glands but is retained longer in pathologic parathyroid tissue. Imaging 2 to 3 hours after ^{99m}Tc-MIBI injection allows physiologic washout of thyroid radioactivity but persistent accumulation within the abnormal parathyroid tissue (Fig. 20–38).[140] Increased mitochondrial content in parathyroid adenomas is believed to be responsible for the observed MIBI concentration.[99] Because of the high sensitivity of MIBI scintigraphy (80% to 90%) in detecting parathyroid adenomas,[99, 100, 140] ^{99m}Tc/^{201}Tl subtraction imaging is used only rarely in current clinical practice.[76] Oblique planar views and single photon emission computed tomography (SPECT) have been reported to improve sensitivity and localization of abnormal parathyroid glands.[86, 93, 105, 118] Subtraction of thyroid activity with ^{123}I may be used with MIBI and can be useful when concomitant thyroid disease is suspected.[9]

Ultrasonographic evaluation of the parathyroid gland employs a 7- to 10-MHz transducer and adequately delineates parathyroid gland enlargement when the glands are located in characteristic parathyroid locations. Normal parathyroid glands are not detected. When parathyroid gland enlargement is not found in the region of the thyroid, the entire anterior neck from mandible to suprasternal notch

is examined sonographically, including the retrotracheal region via a lateral approach; however, ectopic parathyroid gland location in the neck may escape ultrasonographic detection. Ultrasonography cannot be used to identify mediastinal parathyroid adenomas. Parathyroid masses within a goitrous thyroid or surgical bed are difficult to discern. Thyroid nodules (particularly when posteriorly located) and cervical lymph nodes (especially within the tracheoesophageal groove) may mimic parathyroid pathology.[60]

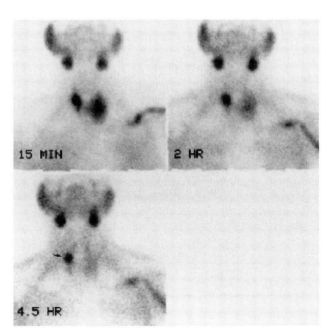

Figure 20–38. With dual-phase technetium 99m–MIBI imaging, an immediate anterior view of the neck reveals a focus of increased activity in the upper pole of the right thyroid lobe. On the 2-hour delayed image, the thyroid activity has washed out to a large degree; the persistent focus of increased activity in the upper right neck *(arrow)* was further confirmed on a 4.5-hour delayed scan, at which point there was additional thyroid washout. At surgery, a solitary parathyroid adenoma was resected.

Lymph nodes can sometimes be distinguished from parathyroid adenomas by a hyperechoic central fatty hilum and absence of the vascularity commonly seen with color Doppler imaging within parathyroid adenomas.[76] Thyroid nodules appear less vascular than parathyroid adenomas and more often demonstrate calcification, cystic changes, and heterogeneous echogenicity. A hyperechoic capsule favors a parathyroid adenoma. These sonographic features are inconsistent, however, and differentiating abnormal parathyroid glands from lymphadenopathy and thyroid masses is not always possible.

An advantage of CT is its ability to evaluate the entire neck and the mediastinum from the skull base to the aortic arch. Distinguishing lymphadenopathy from parathyroid adenomas with CT is problematic, as it is with ultrasonography. The use of CT requires the administration of IV contrast material, but only 25% of parathyroid adenomas enhance (Fig. 20–39).[135]

CT evaluation of parathyroid adenomas may produce false-negative or false-positive results as a result of artifactual obscuration of parathyroid adenomas that may be caused by patient or respiratory motion, shoulder underpenetration or beam-hardening artifact, suboptimal technical factors, or inherently poor soft tissue differentiation. Identifying parathyroid adenomas may be especially challenging in the postoperative neck, where normal tissue planes are distorted and metallic clips generate streak artifact.

MRI evaluation of the neck employs standard T1-weighted, T2-weighted, and postcontrast T1-weighted imaging. Normal parathyroid glands are not visualized by MRI.[60] Parathyroid adenomas and parathyroid hyperplasia are typically bright on T2-weighted images, show soft tissue signal intensity on T1-weighted images, and enhance with contrast material; however, approximately 40% of abnormal glands have atypical MRI signal characteristics.[42, 51, 56, 60, 61, 90, 102, 121, 134]

Pathologic parathyroid glands may contain fat, hemorrhage, sclerosis, or fibrosis, which may alter the expected MRI signal intensity.[60, 61] Contrast-enhanced T1-weighted images should be performed with fat suppression to allow the enhancing adenoma to be differentiated from dark neck

fat.[32, 48] MRI features are not specific for parathyroid adenomas, however, and cannot differentiate adenomas from other neck masses and lymphadenopathy.[60, 79, 90, 137]

High-resolution MRI scanning is currently performed with surface coils, which may have a limited region of coverage. Multiple surface coils may be necessary to evaluate the neck together with the upper mediastinum. MRI is also susceptible to artifact degradation, particularly from patient and respiratory motion, flowing blood, or cerebrospinal fluid pulsation.

Several different imaging modalities may be combined to improve the sensitivity and specificity of parathyroid adenoma and hyperplastic gland identification in the virgin neck, the previously operated neck, and in ectopic locations.[61] MRI is particularly useful for identifying abnormal ectopic parathyroid glands.[51, 60, 61, 79, 137]

Fine-needle biopsy employing ultrasonographic, CT, or MRI guidance may be used to sample parathyroid gland enlargement.[114, 128, 129] Cytology, immunocytochemistry, and radioimmunoassay for parathyroid hormone (PTH) may be conducted to evaluate the aspirated material.

Pathologic Parathyroid Conditions

Hyperparathyroidism

Hyperparathyroidism is a common endocrinopathy manifested by hypercalcemia and elevated circulating levels of PTH, with or without associated urinary, cardiovascular, GI, skeletal, or psychiatric abnormalities.[54] The solitary parathyroid adenoma is most often found along the inferior pole of a thyroid lobe[158] and is responsible for primary hyperparathyroidism in 80% of patients.[34, 35, 106, 144, 145] Hyperplastic parathyroid glands (10%), multiple parathyroid adenomas (2% to 5%), and parathyroid carcinoma (1%) make up the remainder.[34, 35, 106, 144, 145, 147] In 10% to 20% of patients, parathyroid adenomas are ectopic in location.[27, 35, 92, 106]

Therapy for primary hyperparathyroidism is usually surgical resection of the abnormal gland or glands, especially in view of growing evidence of adverse cardiac and skeletal effects of chronic hyperparathyroidism.[39, 74, 136] The use of routine preoperative imaging for patients with uncomplicated primary hyperparathyroidism is controversial.[10, 80, 111, 146] Some surgeons recommend no preoperative imaging of patients with hyperparathyroidism, reporting a 90% to 95% cure rate in previously unoperated patients.[22, 109, 111, 117, 144] The success rate of finding a hyperplastic parathyroid gland or adenoma at surgery, however, is less than 70% if the pathologic parathyroid gland is in an ectopic location.[81, 144, 158]

Some authors have justified routine preoperative imaging with claims of improving operative success rates, decreasing the risk of recurrent laryngeal nerve and normal parathyroid gland injury, and lowering cost, operating time, and blood loss.[11, 18, 36, 64, 75, 113, 117] With the emergence of minimally invasive parathyroidectomy performed using local anesthesia and a hand-held gamma probe intraoperatively, preoperative radionuclide localization is becoming standard practice.[96] In addition, preoperative imaging can identify concomitant thyroid pathology in up to 50% of patients.[29, 63, 108, 153]

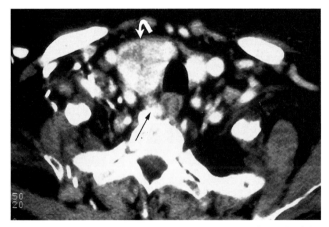

Figure 20–39. Axial postcontrast CT at the level of the clavicles shows an enhancing parathyroid adenoma *(arrow)* in the right tracheoesophageal groove. Goitrous enlargement of the right lobe of the thyroid can be visualized *(curved arrow)*.

Parathyroid Adenomas

The identification of parathyroid adenomas has been evaluated using multiple imaging modalities with a range of specificities and sensitivities. Ultrasonographic identification of parathyroid adenomas is reported to have a sensitivity of 64% and a specificity of 94%.[76, 108] The detection rate significantly improves when the parathyroid adenomas are large.[108] At sonography, parathyroid adenomas are typically homogeneously hypoechoic, sometimes with a hyperechoic capsule (Fig. 20–40).[36, 108, 135] Adenomas may be partially cystic or inhomogeneous with foci of hypoechogenicity or hyperechogenicity.

Color Doppler imaging reveals parathyroid adenomas to be uniformly hypervascular, which may help distinguish them from other neck masses.[76]

CT is reported to have a sensitivity of 70% and a specificity of 90% for parathyroid adenoma detection.[135] MRI has accuracy and sensitivity rates of 74% to 92% for identifying parathyroid adenomas (Fig. 20–41).[61, 79, 134, 137] 99mTc-MIBI imaging has a reported sensitivity rate of 82% to 100% and is generally considered the standard initial imaging modality to identify a parathyroid adenoma.[18, 36, 61, 77, 84, 99, 100, 140] It can detect not only the typical cervical single adenoma or rare dual adenomas but also ectopic and mediastinal adenomas (Fig. 20–42).

The fusion of metabolic sestamibi SPECT images with CT images offers optimized localization of a mediastinal adenoma for surgical planning and guidance, with or without the use of an intraoperative handheld gamma probe. Concomitant benign or malignant thyroid abnormalities (e.g., thyroid adenomas) may cause increased uptake of

99mTc-MIBI and lead to a false-positive scan.[81, 87, 99, 100, 140] Many of these false-positive results can be reduced by the use of subtraction techniques with 123I.[49]

Patients who are not candidates for surgical resection of parathyroid adenomas may be treated with percutaneous alcohol injection using ultrasonographic, CT, or MRI guidance.[148] This is a minimally invasive procedure with few risks if care is taken to avoid vascular structures during needle puncture. With a 22-gauge needle, 0.5 to 1 mL of 98% dehydrated alcohol is injected in multiple locations in the adenoma. Monitoring of serum calcium levels indicates success of the technique, and repeated percutaneous alcohol injections may be performed if necessary.

Parathyroid Hyperplasia

Parathyroid hyperplasia may be primary, secondary, or tertiary. Secondary and tertiary hyperparathyroidism are caused by chronic renal failure and are complicated by a variable degree of associated renal osteodystrophy. 99mTc-MIBI scanning is the imaging examination of choice to evaluate secondary and tertiary hyperparathyroidism, although only a minority of these patients require preoperative imaging. It is also the preferred imaging study for parathyroid hyperplasia evaluation, with a reported detection rate as high as 75% (Fig. 20–43).[34, 36, 61, 77, 92, 99, 100, 106, 140] False-negative MIBI results therefore occur in at least 25% of cases. Ultrasonography has been reported to have a sensitivity rate of 30% to 69%, CT 45% to 88%, and MRI 40% to 74%.[34, 35, 61, 79, 102, 106, 135, 137] Some hyperplastic parathyroid glands may calcify.[128] Imaging cannot differentiate parathyroid hyperplasia from parathyroid adenomas, and no modality typically identifies all four parathyroid glands.

Patients who are not surgical candidates may be treated by percutaneous alcohol ablation of hyperplastic parathyroid glands with the use of image guidance techniques similar to those used for adenoma reduction.[128, 129]

In approximately 30% of patients, primary parathyroid hyperplasia is familial rather than sporadic, a component of MEN syndrome. MEN-1, also termed *Wermer's syndrome*, is an autosomal dominant disorder with high penetrance. The locus for this genetic syndrome is on chromosome 11. In addition to primary parathyroid hyperplasia, patients with MEN-1 have pancreatic islet cell tumors such as insulinomas, gastrinomas (Zollinger-Ellison syndrome), pancreatic polypeptide-producing tumors, glucagonomas, or vasoactive intestinal peptide tumors (VIPomas), and pituitary adenomas. Thyroid disorders, including goiter, adenomas, or thyroiditis; adrenal adenomas or carcinomas; and carcinoid tumors have also been reported. Parathyroid hyperplasia is also a component of MEN-2A and, occasionally, MEN-2B (or MEN-3) syndrome (see earlier discussion of medullary thyroid carcinoma).

Persistent or Recurrent Hyperparathyroidism

Persistent or recurrent hyperparathyroidism after attempted surgical cure presents a serious challenge. In approximately 50% of cases, reoperation reveals abnormal parathyroid glands in a perithyroidal location that were missed at the initial surgery.[22, 80, 110] Other parathyroid ade-

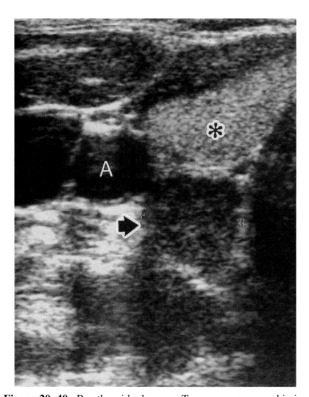

Figure 20–40. Parathyroid adenoma. Transverse sonographic image shows a hypoechoic mass *(arrow)* inferior to the right lobe of the thyroid *(asterisk)*. A, right common carotid artery.

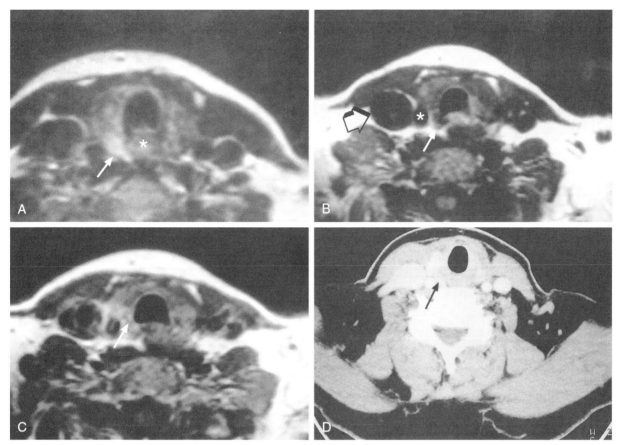

Figure 20–41. Surgically proven parathyroid adenoma. *A,* Axial T2-weighted MR image shows an ovoid mass *(arrow)* of increased T2-weighted signal posterior to the right lobe of the thyroid and adjacent to the esophagus *(asterisk). B,* Axial T1-weighted MR image demonstrates that the mass *(arrow)* is isointense to thyroid parenchyma. Flow voids can be seen in the right common carotid artery *(asterisk)* and right internal jugular vein *(open arrow). C,* Axial T1-weighted MR image after gadolinium contrast administration demonstrates enhancement within the lesion *(arrow). D,* Axial postcontrast CT image shows a homogeneously enhancing ovoid mass *(arrow)* in the right tracheoesophageal groove.

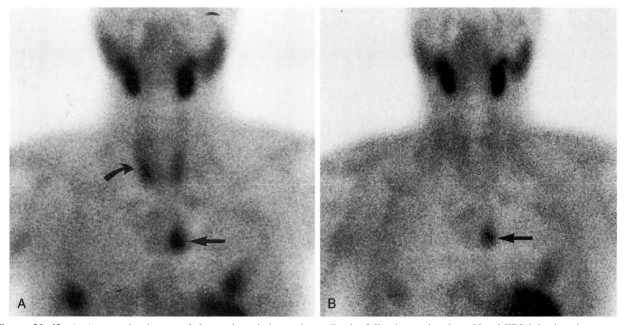

Figure 20–42. *A,* An anterior image of the neck and thorax immediately following technetium 99m–MIBI injection demonstrates physiologic thyroid activity *(curved arrow)* with a single focus of increased activity in the chest to the left of midline *(arrow). B,* Most of the thyroid activity has faded by 2 hours on the delayed images, thus accentuating the persistent mediastinal abnormality *(arrow).* At surgery, a mediastinal parathyroid adenoma was resected, resulting in postoperative eucalcemia.

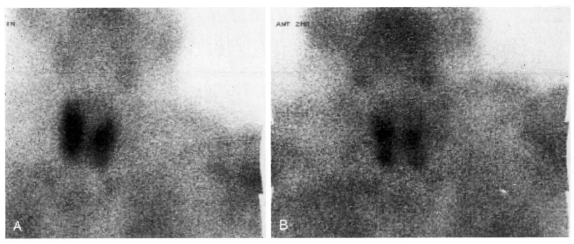

Figure 20–43. Dual-phase technetium-99m–MIBI imaging—immediate *(A)* and 2-hour-delayed *(B)* acquisitions—of a patient with chronic renal failure. Imaging reveals four persistent foci of increased activity on the delayed images *(B)*, consistent with parathyroid hyperplasia.

noma locations, however, include the anterior mediastinum, deep in the tracheoesophageal groove, and deep cervical, intrathyroidal, and parathymic locations.[60, 80, 82, 110] Imaging can assist the surgeon in preoperatively identifying a persistent or ectopic parathyroid adenoma or parathyroid hyperplasia, increasing surgical success from 60% to 90%.[61, 79, 106]

99mTc-MIBI imaging is the mainstay for identifying the source of persistent hyperparathyroidism; it has a sensitivity of 80% to 90% (Fig. 20–44).[61, 62, 73, 77, 150] Persistent postoperative thyroid MIBI uptake due to suspected thyroiditis may obscure residual parathyroid adenoma or hyperplasia.[36] Ultrasonography, CT, and MRI have variable sensitivities of between 25% and 90% for the detection of residual parathyroid tissue.[42, 51, 57, 61, 79, 81, 102, 135] Some au-

thors recommend MRI as a complementary imaging modality to 99mTc-MIBI scintigraphy.[24, 98]

Although the success of 18FDG PET imaging of parathyroid adenomas has been variable, carbon 11 (11C) methionine PET imaging is reported to be more successful than CT or ultrasonography in patients requiring either primary or reoperative resection.[94, 138] In the patient with persistent or recurrent hyperparathyroidism, most investigators recommend initial functional imaging with 99mTc-MIBI, complemented by anatomic imaging with MRI or CT; ultrasonography plays a limited role in these patients.[98] 18FDG or 11C-methionine PET may be attempted in patients without localization after 99mTc-MIBI scintigraphy.

Other approaches include parathyroid venous sampling

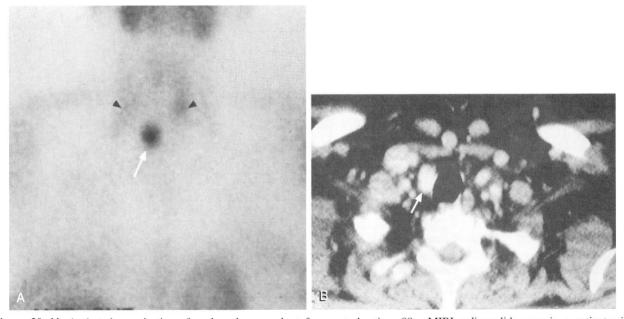

Figure 20–44. *A,* Anterior projection of neck and upper chest from a technetium 99m–MIBI radionuclide scan in a patient with persistent hyperparathyroidism after thyroidectomy demonstrates a prominent focus of tracer uptake within the low right neck *(arrow)*. Uptake within the thyroid parenchyma *(arrowheads)* is mild. *B,* Axial postcontrast CT scan through the lower neck in the same patient demonstrates an enhancing right paratracheal soft tissue mass *(arrow)*, found to be a parathyroid adenoma at reoperation.

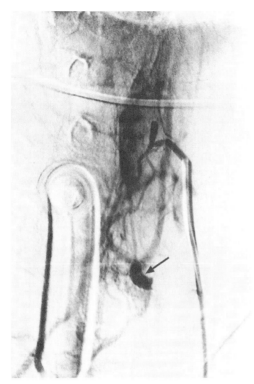

Figure 20–45. Digital subtraction angiographic image in AP projection. Left superior thyroidal artery injection shows a homogeneously enhancing mass consistent with a parathyroid adenoma *(arrow)* within the low left neck. (Courtesy of M. Mazer, M. D.)

and arteriography (Fig. 20–45).[20] These invasive procedures have sensitivities of 50% to 80%[24, 82] but may be valuable in selective cases, particularly in previously operated patients who have fibrotic scar tissue, abnormal tissue planes, postoperative inflammation, or enlarged reactive lymph nodes, which may lead to false-negative or false-positive results with other imaging studies.

Other Parathyroid Masses

Parathyroid Cysts

Parathyroid cysts are rare, comprising only 0.6% of all thyroid and parathyroid lesions,[159] but they may be large at presentation. Most present in middle-aged women.[68] Parathyroid cysts may develop from pharyngeal pouch remnants or may represent degenerated parathyroid adenomas.[158] Almost all are found caudal to the inferior margin of the thyroid, and most are associated with the inferior parathyroid glands.[159] Mimics include thyroid or thymic cysts and necrotic lymph nodes.[71]

Symptoms may be secondary to tracheal, esophageal, or laryngeal nerve compression or from cyst hemorrhage and subsequent pain.[159] Ultrasonography demonstrates an anechoic mass in a typical parathyroid gland location. CT demonstrates a well-circumscribed, low-density parathyroidal mass. MRI may demonstrate bright signal intensity on T1-weighted images if the contents of the cyst have an increased protein content or hemorrhage. ^{99m}Tc-MIBI may demonstrate a photopenic focus. Fine-needle aspiration

yields a characteristic clear watery fluid with high PTH and low thyroglobulin content and may be curative if combined with a sclerosing agent.[14]

Parathyroid Carcinoma

Parathyroid carcinoma is a rare cause of hyperparathyroidism, with an incidence of 1% to 2% and no sex preference.[159] Thirty percent of patients present with metastatic lymphadenopathy; distant metastases are seen in approximately 25%.[159] Approximately 90% of parathyroid carcinomas cause hyperparathyroidism.[67, 68] Parathyroid carcinomas are indistinguishable from parathyroid adenomas in all imaging studies except when local invasion of neighboring structures is present.[23] ^{99m}Tc-MIBI and [18]FDG PET may be used to detect local and distant metastases.[55, 73, 94]

References

1. Balon HR, Fink-Bennett TD, Stoffer SS: Technetium 99m–sestamibi uptake by recurrent Hürthle cell carcinoma of the thyroid. J Nucl Med 33:1393, 1992.
2. Bar-Ziv J, Slasky BS, Sichel TY, et al: Branchial pouch sinus tract from the piriform fossa causing acute suppurative thyroiditis, neck abscess, or both: CT appearance and the use of air as a contrast agent. AJR Am J Roentgenol 167:1569, 1996.
3. Batsakis JG: Tumors of the Head and Neck: Clinical and Pathological Considerations. Baltimore, Williams & Wilkins, 1979.
4. Beahrs OH, Kiernan PD, Hubert JP Jr: Cancer of the thyroid gland. In Suen JY, Myers E (eds): Cancer of the Head and Neck. New York, Churchill Livingstone, 1981, pp 599–632.
5. Behr TM, Gratz S, Markus PM, et al: Anti-carcinoembryonic antigen antibodies versus somatostatin analogs in the detection of metastatic medullary thyroid carcinoma: Are carcinoembryonic antigen and somatostatin receptor expression prognostic factors? Cancer 80: 2436, 1997.
6. Bigsby RJ, Lepp EK, Litwin DEM, et al: Technetium-99m pentavalent dimercaptosuccinic acid and thallium-201 in detecting recurrent medullary carcinoma of the thyroid. Can J Surg 35:388, 1992.
7. Boland GW, Lee MJ, Mueller PR, et al: Efficacy of sonographically guided biopsy of thyroid masses and cervical lymph nodes. AJR Am J Roentgenol 161:1053, 1993.
8. Briele B, Hotze AL, Kropp J, et al: Comparison of ^{99m}Tc-MIBI and Tl-201–chloride in the follow-up of patients with differentiated thyroid carcinoma. J Nucl Med 33:844, 1992.
9. Burke GJ, Wei JP, Binet EF: Parathyroid scintigraphy with iodine-123 and ^{99m}Tc-sestamibi: Imaging findings. AJR Am J Roentgenol 161:1265–1268, 1993.
10. Carlson GL, Faradon JR, Clayton B, et al: Thallium isotope scintigraphy and ultrasonography: Comparative studies of localization techniques in primary hyperparathyroidism. Am Surg 60:12, 1990.
11. Casas AT, Burke GJ, Mansberger AR Jr, et al: Impact of technetium-99m–sestamibi localization on operative time and success of operations for primary hyperparathyroidism. Am Surg 60:12–16, 1994.
12. Charkes ND: Graves' disease with functioning nodules (Marine-Lenhart syndrome). J Nucl Med 13:885, 1972.
13. Chung JK, So Y, Lee JS, et al: Value of FDG PET in papillary thyroid carcinoma with negative ^{131}I whole-body scan. J Nucl Med 40:984, 1999.
14. Clark OH: Parathyroid cysts. Am J Surg 135:385–402, 1978.
15. Compagno J: Diseases of the thyroid. In Barnes L (ed): Surgical Pathology of the Head and Neck. New York, Marcel Dekker, 1985, pp 1435–1486.
16. Coret A, Heyman Z, Bendet E, et al: Thyroid abscess resulting from transesophageal migration of a fish bone: Ultrasound appearance. J Clin Ultrasound 21:152, 1993.
17. DeGroot LJ, Sridama V: Thyroid neoplasm. In: DeGroot LJ (ed): Endocrinology. Philadelphia, WB Saunders, 1989, pp 758–776.
18. Denham DW, Norman J: Cost-effectiveness of preoperative sestamibi scan for primary hyperparathyroidism is dependent solely upon the surgeon's choice of operative procedure. J Am Coll Surg 186: 293, 1998.
19. DiLelio A, Rivolta M, Casati M, et al: Treatment of autonomous

thyroid nodules: Value of percutaneous ethanol injection. AJR Am J Roentgenol 164:207, 1995.

20. Doppmann JL: Parathyroid localization: Arteriography and venous sampling. Radiol Clin North Am 14:163, 1976.

21. Dorr U, Wurstlin S, Frank-Raue K, et al: Somatostatin receptor scintigraphy and magnetic resonance imaging in recurrent medullary thyroid carcinoma: A comparative study. Horm Metab Res 27(suppl):48, 1993.

22. Edis AJ, Sheedy PF, Beahrs OH, et al: Results of reoperation for hyperparathyroidism, with evaluation of preoperative localization studies. Surgery 84:384, 1978.

23. Edmonson GR, Charbonneau JW, James EM, et al: Parathyroid carcinoma: High-frequency sonographic features. Radiology 161:65–67, 1986.

24. Fayet P, Hoeffel C, Fulla Y, et al: Technetium-99m sestamibi scintigraphy, magnetic resonance imaging and venous blood sampling in persistent and recurrent hyperparathyroidism. Br J Radiol 70:459–464, 1997.

25. Fisher DA, Oddie TH, Johnson DE, Nelson JC: The diagnosis of Hashimoto's thyroiditis. J Clin Endocrinol Metab 40:785, 1975.

26. Frank-Raue K, Raue F, Buh HJ, et al: Localization of occult persisting medullary thyroid carcinoma before microsurgical reoperation: High sensitivity of selective venous catheterization. Thyroid 2:113, 1992.

27. Freitas JE, Freitas AE: Thyroid and parathyroid imaging [review]. Semin Nucl Med 24:234, 1994.

28. Freitas JE, Gross MD, Ripley S, et al: Radionuclide diagnosis and therapy of thyroid cancer: Current status report. Semin Nucl Med 15:106–131, 1985.

29. Funari M, Campos Z, Gooding GA, et al: MRI and ultrasound detection of asymptomatic thyroid nodules in hyperparathyroidism. J Comput Assist Tomogr 16:615–619, 1992.

30. Gefter WB, Spritzer CE, Livolsi VA, et al: Thyroid imaging with high-field strength surface-coil MR. Radiology 164:483, 1987.

31. Gharib H, Goellner JR, Johnson DA: Fine-needle aspiration cytology of the thyroid: An appraisal. Ann Intern Med 118:282–289, 1993.

32. Goddard PR: Localization of abnormal parathyroid gland: Value of fat suppression. Radiology 190:903, 1994.

33. Goldman JM, Lini BR, Aamodt RL, Robbins J: Influence of triiodothyronine withdrawal time on I-131 uptake post-thyroidectomy for thyroid cancer. J Clin Endocrinol Metab 50:734, 1980.

34. Gooding GA: Sonography of the thyroid and parathyroid. Radiol Clin North Am 31:967–989, 1993.

35. Gooding GAW, Okerlund MD, Stark DD, et al: Parathyroid imaging: Comparison of double-tracer (Tl-201, Tc-99m) scintigraphy and high-resolution ultrasound. Radiology 84:57–64, 1986.

36. Gordon BM, Gordon L, Hoang K, Spicer KM: Parathyroid imaging with 99mTc-sestamibi. AJR Am J Roentgenol 167:1563–1568, 1996.

37. Gorman B, Charbonneau JW, James EM, et al: Ultrasonic evaluation of benign and malignant nodules in echographically multinodualr thyroids. J Clin Ultrasound 22:71, 1994.

38. Guneri A, Ceryan K, Igci E, et al: Lingual thyroid: The diagnostic value of magnetic resonance imaging. J Laryngol Otol 105:493–495, 1991.

39. Guo C-Y, Thomas WEG, Al-Dehaimi AW, et al: Longitudinal changes in bone mineral density and bone turnover in postmenopausal women with primary hyperparathyroidism. J Clin Endocrinol 81:3487, 1996.

40. Hamburger JI, Hamburger SI: Fine-needle biopsy of thyroid nodules: Avoiding the pitfalls. N Y State J Med 86:241–249, 1986.

41. Hamburger JI, Miller JM, Kini SR: Lymphoma of the thyroid. Ann Intern Med 99:685–693, 1983.

42. Hamilton R, Greenburg BM, Gefter W, et al: Successful localization of parathyroid adenomas by magnetic resonance imaging. Am J Surg 155:370–373, 1988.

43. Hanbridge AE, Arenson AM, Shaw PA, et al: Needle size and sample adequacy in ultrasound-guided biopsy of thyroid nodules. Can Assoc Radiol J 46:199, 1995.

44. Hatabu H, Kasagi K, Yamamoto K, et al: Acute suppurative thyroiditis associated with pyriform sinus fistula: Sonographic findings. AJR Am J Roentgenol 155:845–847, 1990.

45. Hawkins DB, Jacobsen BE, Klatt EC: Cysts of the thyroglossal duct. Laryngoscope 92:1254–1258, 1982.

46. Hay ID: Papillary thyroid carcinoma. Endocrinol Metab Clin North Am 19:545, 1990.

47. Hays LL, Marlow SF Jr: Papillary carcinoma arising in a thyroglossal duct cyst. Laryngoscope 78:2189–2193, 1968.

48. Higgins CB: Role of magnetic resonance imaging in hyperparathyroidism. Radiol Clin North Am 31:1017, 1993.

49. Hindie E, Melliere D, Simon D, et al: Primary hyperparathyroidism: Is technetium-99m–sestamibi/iodine-123 subtraction scanning the best procedure to locate enlarged glands before surgery? J Clin Endocrinol Metab 80:302–307, 1995.

50. Hopkins CR, Reading CC: Thyroid and parathyroid imaging. Semin Ultrasound CT MR 16:279, 1995.

51. Kang YS, Rosen K, Clark OH, et al: Localization of abnormal parathyroid glands of the mediastinum with MR imaging. Radiology 189:137–141, 1993.

52. Kasagi K, Hatabu H, Tokuda Y, et al: Lymphoproliferative disorders of the thyroid gland: Radiological appearances. Br J Radiol 64:569–575, 1991.

53. Kawanaka M, Sugimoto Y, Suehiro M, et al: Thyroid imaging in a typical case of acute suppurative thyroiditis with abscess formation due to infection from a persistent thyroglossal duct. Ann Nucl Med 8:159–162, 1994.

54. Khan A, Samtani S, Varma VM, et al: Preoperative parathyroid localization: Prospective evaluation of technetium 99m sestamibi. Otolaryngol Head Neck Surg 11:467, 1994.

55. Kitapci MT, Tastekin G, Turgut M, et al: Preoperative localization of parathyroid carcinoma using Tc-99m MIBI. Clin Nucl Med 18:217–219, 1993.

56. Kneeland JB, Kruback AJ, Lawson TL, et al: Enlarged parathyroid glands: High-resolution local coil MR imaging. Radiology 162:143–146, 1987.

57. Kohri K, Tshikawa Y, Kodama M: Comparison of imaging methods for localization of parathyroid tumors. Am J Surg 164:140, 1992.

58. Kwekkeboom DJ, Reubi JC, Lamberts SW, et al: The potential value of somatostatin receptor scintigraphy in medullary thyroid carcinoma. J Clin Endocrinol Metab 76:1413, 1993.

59. Ladenson PW, Braverman LE, Mazzaferri EL, et al: Comparison of administration of recombinant human thyrotropin with withdrawal of thyroid hormone for radioactive iodine scanning in patients with thyroid carcinoma. N Engl J Med 337:88, 1997.

60. Lee VS, Spritzer CE: MR imaging of abnormal parathyroid glands. AJR Am J Roentgenol 170:1097–1103, 1998.

61. Lee VS, Spritzer CE, Coleman RE, et al: The complementary roles of fast spin-echo MR imaging and double-phase 99mTc-sestamibi scintigraphy for localization for hyperfunctioning parathyroid glands. AJR Am J Roentgenol 167:1555–1562, 1996.

62. Lee VS, Wilkinson RH Jr, Leight GS, et al: Hyperparathyroidism in high-risk surgical patients: Evaluation with double-phase technetium-99m-sestamibi imaging. Radiology 197:627–633, 1995.

63. Lever EG, Refetoffs S, Strauss FH II, et al: Coexisting thyroid and parathyroid disease: Are they related? Surgery 94:893–900, 1983.

64. Levin KE, Clark AH, Duh QY, et al: Reoperative thyroid surgery. Surgery 111:604, 1992.

65. Lim-Dunham JE, Feinstein KA, Yousefzadeh DK, Ben-Ami T: Sonographic demonstration of a normal thyroid gland excludes ectopic thyroid in patients with thyroglossal duct cyst. AJR Am J Roentgenol 164:1489, 1995.

66. Lin JD, Huang BY, Weng HF, et al: Thyroid ultrasonography with fine-needle aspiration cytology for the diagnosis of thyroid cancers. J Clin Ultrasound 25:111, 1997.

67. Livolsi V: The thyroid and parathyroid. In Sternberg SS (ed): Diagnostic Surgical Pathology, 2nd ed. New York, Raven Press, 1994, pp 523–560.

68. Livolsi VA: Pathology of the parathyroid glands. In Barnes L (ed): Surgical Pathology of the Head and Neck. New York, Marcel Dekker, 1985, pp 1487–1563.

69. Livraghi T, Paracchi A, Ferrari C, et al: Treatment of autonomous thyroid nodules with percutaneous ethanol injection: 4-year experience. Radiology 190:529, 1994.

70. Loevner LA: Imaging of the thyroid gland. Semin Ultrasound CT MR 17:539, 1996.

71. Loevner LA: Imaging of the parathyroid glands. Semin Ultrasound CT MR 17:563, 1996.

72. Lubin E, Mechlis-Frish S, Zatz S, et al: Serum thyroglobulin and iodine-131 whole-body scan in the diagnosis and assessment of treatment for metastatic differentiated thyroid carcinoma. J Nucl Med 35:257, 1994.

73. Majors JD, Burke GJ, Mansberger AR Jr, et al: Technetium Tc-99m sestamibi scan for localizing abnormal parathyroid glands after previous neck operations: Preliminary experience in reoperative cases. South Med J 88:327–330, 1995.

74. Massry SG, Goldstein DA: The search for uremic toxin(s) "X" ("X" = PTH). Clin Nephrol 11:181, 1979.

75. Mattar AG, Wright ES, Chittal SM, et al: Impact on surgery of preoperative localization of parathyroid lesions with dual radionuclide subtraction scanning. Can J Surg 29:57, 1986.

76. Mazzeo S, Caramella D, Lencioni R, et al: Usefulness of echo-color Doppler in differentiating parathyroid lesions from other cervical masses. Eur Radiol 7:90–95, 1997.

77. McBiles M, Lambert AT, Cote MG, et al: Sestamibi parathyroid imaging. Semin Nucl Med 25:221–234, 1995.

78. McConahey WM, Hay ID, Woolner LB, et al: Papillary thyroid cancer treated at the Mayo Clinic 1946 through 1970: Initial manifestations, pathologic findings, therapy, and outcome. Mayo Clin Proc 61:978–996, 1986.

79. McDermott VG, Fernandez RJM, Meakem TJ III, et al: Preoperative MR imaging in hyperparathyroidism: Results and factors affecting parathyroid detection. AJR Am J Roentgenol 166:705–710, 1996.

80. Miller DL: Pre-operative localization and international treatment of parathyroid tumors: When and how? World J Surg 15:706, 1991.

81. Miller DL, Doppman JL, Krudy AG, et al: Localization of parathyroid adenomas in patients who have undergone surgery: Part 1. Noninvasive imaging methods. Radiology 162:133, 1987.

82. Miller DL, Doppman JL, Shawker TH, et al: Localization of parathyroid adenomas in patients who have undergone surgery: Part II. Invasive procedure. Radiology 162:138, 1987.

83. Miller JM: Carcinoma and thyroid nodules: The problem in an endemic goiter area. N Engl J Med 252:247, 1955.

84. Mitchell BK, Kinder BK, Cornelius E, Stewart AF: Primary hyperparathyroidism: Preoperative localization using technetium-sestamibi scanning. J Clin Endocrinol Metab 80:7–10, 1995.

85. Montgomery ML: Lingual thyroid: Comprehensive review. West J Surg 43:661–671, 1935.

86. Morka ET, Kwan WP, Clark OH: Technetium-99m–sestamibi for parathyroid imaging. West J Med 161:413, 1994.

87. Mortensen JD, Woolner LB, Bennett WA: Gross and microscopic findings in clinically normal thyroid glands. J Clin Endocrinol Metab 15:1270, 1955.

88. Mulligan LM, Eng C, Healey CS, et al: Specific mutations of the RET proto-oncogene are related to disease phenotype in MEN 2A and FMTC. Nat Genet 6:70, 1994.

89. Musholt TJ, Musholt PB, Dehdashti F, Moley JF: Evaluation of fluorodeoxyglucose-positron emission tomographic scanning and its association with glucose transporter expression in medullary thyroid carcinoma and pheochromocytoma: A clinical and molecular study. Surgery 122:1049–1061, 1997.

90. Nakahara H, Noguchi S, Murakami N, et al: Gadolinium-enhanced MR imaging of thyroid and parathyroid masses. Radiology 202:765–772, 1997.

91. Nel CJC, van Heerden JA, Goellner JR, et al: Anaplastic carcinoma of the thyroid: A clinicopathologic study of 82 cases. Mayo Clin Proc 60:51, 1985.

92. Neumann DR, Esselstyn CB, Eastwood J, et al: Localization of mediastinal parathyroid adenoma in recurrent postoperative hyperparathyroidism with Tc-99m sestamibi SPECT. Clin Nucl Med 20:175, 1995.

93. Neumann DR, Esselstyn CB, Go RT, et al: Comparison of double-phase Tc-99m-sestamibi subtraction SPECT in hyperparathyroidism. AJR Am J Roentgenol 169:1671, 1997.

94. Neumann DR, Esselstyn CB, MacIntyre WJ, et al: Comparison of FDG-PET and sestamibi-SPECT in primary hyperparathyroidism. J Nucl Med 37:1809–1815, 1996.

95. Noma S, Kanaoka M, Minami S, et al: Thyroid masses: MR imaging and pathologic correlation. Radiology 168:759–764, 1988.

96. Norman J, Chheda H, Farrell C: Minimally invasive parathyroidectomy for primary hyperparathyroidism: Decreasing operative time and potential complications while improving cosmetic results. Ann Surg 64:391–396, 1998.

97. Noyek AM, Friedberg J: Thyroglossal duct and ectopic thyroid disorders. Otolaryngol Clin North Am 14:187, 1981.

98. Numerow LM, Morita ET, Clark OH, Higgens CB: Persistent/recurrent hyperparathyroidism: A comparison of sestamibi scintigraphy, MRI and ultrasonography. J Magn Reson Imaging 5:702–708, 1995.

99. Oates E: Improved parathyroid scintigraphy with Tc-99m MIBI, a superior radiotracer. Appl Radiol 37–42, 1994.

100. O'Doherty MJ, Kettle AG, Wells P, et al: Parathyroid imaging with technetium-99m–sestamibi: Preoperative localization and tissue uptake studies. J Nucl Med 33:313–318, 1992.

101. Özdemir H, Ilgit ET, Yucal C, et al: Treatment of autonomous thyroid nodules: Safety and efficacy of sonographically guided percutaneous injection of ethanol. AJR Am J Roentgenol 163:929, 1994.

102. Peck WW, Higgins CB, Fisher MR, et al: Hyperparathyroidism: Comparison of MR imaging with radionuclide scanning. Radiology 163:415–420, 1987.

103. Peltier P, Curtet C, Chatal JF, et al: Radioimmunodetection of medullary thyroid cancer using a bispecific anti-CEA/anti-indium-DTPA antibody and an indium-111–labeled DTPA dimer. J Nucl Med 34:1267–1273, 1993.

104. Perez Fontan FJ, Cordido Carballido F, Pombo Felipe F, et al: Riedel thyroiditis: US, CT, and MR evaluation. J Comput Assist Tomogr 17:324–325, 1993.

105. Perez-Monte JF, Brown ML, Shah AN, et al: Parathyroid adenomas: Accurate detection and localization of abnormal parathyroid glands of the mediastinum with MR imaging. Radiology 189:137–141, 1993.

106. Price DC: Radioisotopic evaluation of the thyroid and the parathyroids. Radiol Clin North Am 31:991–1015, 1993.

107. Ralls PW, Mayekawa DS, Lee KP, et al: Color-flow Doppler sonography in Graves' disease: "Thyroid inferno." AJR Am J Roentgenol 150:781–784, 1988.

108. Reading CC, Charboneau JW, James EM, et al: High-resolution parathyroid sonography. Am J Roentgenol 139:539–546, 1982.

109. Reading CC, Gorman CA: Thyroid imaging techniques. Clin Lab Med 13:711–724, 1993.

110. Rodriguez JM, Tezelman S, Siperstein AE, et al: Localization procedures in patients with persistent or recurrent hyperparathyroidism. Arch Surg 129:870–875, 1994.

111. Roe SM, Burns RP, Graham LD, et al: Cost-effectiveness of preoperative localization studies in primary hyperparathyroidism disease. Ann Surg 219:582, 1994.

112. Rojeski MT, Gharib H: Nodular thyroid disease: Evaluation and management. N Engl J Med 313:428, 1985.

113. Russell CF, Laird JD, Ferguson WR: Scan-directed unilateral cervical exploration for parathyroid adenoma: A legitimate approach? World J Surg 14:406, 1990.

114. Sacks BA, Pallotta JA, Cole A, et al: Diagnosis of parathyroid adenomas: Efficacy of measuring parathormone levels in needle aspirates of cervical masses. AJR Am J Roentgenol 163:1223, 1994.

115. Sandler MP, Martin WH, Powers TA: Thyroid imaging. In Sandler MP, et al (eds): Diagnostic Nuclear Medicine, 3rd ed. Baltimore, Williams & Wilkins, 1996, pp 911–942.

116. Sandler MP, Patton JA, Ossoff RH: Recent advances in thyroid imaging. Otolaryngol Clin North Am 23:251–270, 1990.

117. Satava RM, Beahrs OH, Scholz DA: Success rate of cervical exploration for hyperparathyroidism. Arch Surg 110:625, 1975.

118. Schurrer ME, Seabold JE, Gurll NJ, Simonson TM: Sestamibi SPECT scintigraphy for detection of postoperative hyperfunctional parathyroid glands. AJR Am J Roentgenol 166:1465–1470, 1996.

119. Schwartz SI, Shires GT, Spencer FC, et al: Principles of Surgery, 3rd ed. New York, McGraw Hill, 1979, p 1547.

120. Scott AM, Kostakoglu L, O'Brien JP, et al: Comparison of technetium-99m-MIBI and thallium-201–chloride uptake in primary thyroid lymphoma. J Nucl Med 32:1396–1398, 1991.

121. Seelos KC, DeMarco R, Clark OH, et al: Persistent and recurrent hyperparathyroidism: Assessment with gadopentetate dimeglumine-enhanced MR imaging. Radiology 177:373–378, 1990.

122. Senga O, Miyakawa M, Shirota H, et al: Comparison of Tl-201 and Ga-67-citrate scintigraphy in the diagnosis of thyroid tumors [concise communication]. J Nucl Med 23:225, 1982.

123. Shibata T, Noma S, Nakano Y, Konishi J: Primary thyroid lymphoma: MR appearance. J Comput Assist Tomogr 15:629–633, 1991.

124. Shimamoto K, Endo T, Ishigaki T, et al: Thyroid nodules: Evaluation with color Doppler ultrasonography. J Ultrasound Med 12:673, 1993.

125. Shulkin BL, Shapiro B: The role of imaging tests in the diagnosis of thyroid carcinoma. Endocrinol Metab Clin North Am 19:523–543, 1990.

126. Sisson JC, Ackerman RJ, Meyer MA, Wahl RL: Uptake of 18-fluoro-2-deoxy-D-glucose by thyroid cancer: Implications for diagnosis and therapy. J Clin Endocrinol Metab 77:1090, 1993.

127. Skowsky WR, Wilf LH: Iodine-131 metaiodobenzylguanidine scintigraphy of medullary carcinoma of the thyroid. South Med J 84: 636, 1991.

128. Solbiati L, Giangrande A, De Pra L, et al: Percutaneous ethanol injection of parathyroid tumors under ultrasound guidance: Treatment for secondary hyperparathyroidism. Radiology 155:607–610, 1985.

129. Solbiati L, Montali G, Croce F, et al: Parathyroid tumors detected by fine-needle aspiration biopsy under ultrasonic guidance. Radiology 148:793, 1983.

130. Solbiati L, Volterrani L, Rizzatto G, et al: The thyroid gland with low uptake lesions: Evaluation by ultrasound. Radiology 155:187–191, 1985.

131. Som PM: Lymph nodes of the neck. Radiology 165:593–600, 1987.

132. Som PM, Brandwein M, Lidov M, et al: The varied appearance of papillary carcinoma cervical nodal disease: CT and MR findings. AJNR Am J Neuroradiol 15:1129–1138, 1994.

133. Spies WG, Wojtowizc CH, Spies SM, et al: Value of post-therapy whole-body I-131 imaging in the evaluation of patients with thyroid carcinoma having undergone high-dose I-131 therapy. Clin Nucl Med 14:793, 1989.

134. Spritzer CE, Gefter WB, Hamilton R, et al: Abnormal parathyroid glands: High-resolution MR imaging. Radiology 162:487–491, 1987.

135. Stark DD, Gooding GAW, Moss AA: Parathyroid imaging: Comparison of high-resolution CT and high-resolution sonography. Am J Roentgenol 141:633–638, 1983.

136. Stefenelli T, Abela C, Frank H, et al: Cardiac abnormalities in patients with primary hyperparathyroidism: Implications for follow-up. J Clin Endocrinol Metab 82:106, 1997.

137. Stevens SK, Chang JM, Clark OH, et al: Detection of abnormal parathyroid glands in postoperative patients with recurrent hyperparathyroidism: Sensitivity of MR imaging. AJR Am J Roentgenol 160:607, 1993.

138. Sundin A, Johansson C, Hellman P, et al: PET and parathyroid L-[carbon-11] methionine accumulation in hyperparathyroidism. J Nucl Med 37:1766–1770, 1996.

139. Sutton RT, Reading CC, Charboneau JW, et al: US-guided biopsy of neck masses in postoperative management of patients with thyroid cancer. Radiology 168:769, 1988.

140. Taillefer R, Boucher Y, Potvin C, et al: Detection and localization of parathyroid adenomas in patients with hyperparathyroidism using a single radionuclide imaging procedure with technetium-99m–sestamibi (double phase study). J Nucl Med 33:1801–1807, 1992.

141. Takashima S, Morimoto S, Ikezoe J, et al: Primary thyroid lymphoma: Evaluation with CT. Radiology 171:439–443, 1988.

142. Takashima S, Morimoto S, Ikezoe J, et al: CT evaluation of anaplastic thyroid carcinoma. AJR Am J Roentgenol 154:1079, 1990.

143. Takashima S, Nomura N, Noguchi Y, et al: Primary thyroid lymphoma: Evaluation with US, CT, and MRI. J Comput Assist Tomogr 19:282, 1995.

144. Thompson CT: Localization studies in patients with hyperparathyroidism. Br J Surg 75:97, 1988.

145. Thompson NW, Eckhauser FE, Harness JK: The anatomy of primary hyperparathyroidism. Surgery 92:814, 1982.

146. Uden P, Aspelin P, Berglund J, et al: Preoperative localization in unilateral parathyroid surgery. A cost-benefit study on ultrasound, computed tomography and scintigraphy. Acta Chir Scand 150:29, 1990.

147. van Heerden JA, Weiland LH, ReMine WH, et al: Cancer of the parathyroid gland. Arch Surg 114:475, 1979.

148. Verges BL, Cercueil JP, Vaillant G, et al: Results of ultrasonically guided percutaneous ethanol injection into parathyroid adenomas in primary hyperparathyroidism. Acta Endocrinol 129:381–387, 1993.

149. Volpé JR: Subacute (de Quervain's) thyroiditis. J Clin Endocrinol Metab 8:81–95, 1979.

150. Weber CJ, Vansant J, Alazraki N, et al: Value of technetium 99m sestamibi iodine 123 imaging in reoperative parathyroid surgery. Surgery 114:1011–1018, 1993.

151. Williams ED: Medullary carcinoma of the thyroid. In DeGroot LJ (ed): Endocrinology. Philadelphia, WB Saunders, 1989, pp 1132–1150.

152. Woolner LB, Beahrs OH, Black BM, et al: Classification and prognosis of thyroid cancer. Am J Surg 102:354–387, 1961.

153. Yao M, Jamieson C, Blend R: Magnetic resonance imaging in preoperative localization of diseased parathyroid glands: A comparison with isotope scanning and ultrasonography. Can J Surg 36:241–244, 1993.

154. Yasuda S, Shohsu A, Ide M, et al: Diffuse F-18 FDG uptake in chronic thyroiditis. Clin Nucl Med 22:341, 1997.

155. Yeh EL, Meade RC, Reutz PP: Radionuclide study of struma ovarii. J Nucl Med 14:118–121, 1973.

156. Yeh HC, Futterweit W, Gilbert P: Micronodulation: Ultrasonographic sign of Hashimoto thyroiditis. J Ultrasound Med 15:813, 1996.

157. Yokozawa T, Fukata S, Kuma K, et al: Thyroid cancer detected by ultrasound-guided fine-needle aspiration biopsy. World J Surg 20: 848, 1996.

158. Yousem DM: Parathyroid and thyroid imaging. Neuroimaging Clin N Am 6:435, 1996.

159. Yousem DM, Scheff AM: Thyroid and parathyroid. In Som PM, Curtin HD (eds): Head and Neck Imaging, 3rd ed. St. Louis, Mosby–Year Book, 1996, p 952.

160. Yousem DM, Som PM, Hackney DB, et al: Central nodal necrosis and extracapsular neoplastic spread in cervical lymph nodes: MR imaging versus CT. Radiology 182:753, 1992.

21

Pediatric Head and Neck Imaging

John C. Egelhoff

Head and neck pathology in children encompasses diseases that are both unique to the pediatric age group as well as processes that occur in adults. The diseases that cross age barriers may have a different biologic behavior pattern or clinical presentation when they occur in children. Fortunately, most pediatric head and neck pathology is composed of benign tumors, congenital masses, and inflammatory lesions. In contrast to the situation with adults, primary malignancies are a less frequent occurrence in children. To approach the imaging algorithms and differential diagnoses in a logical method, imaging specialists should have a basic knowledge and understanding of the pathology that occurs in the head and neck in children.

The topic of the head and neck pathology in children represents a vast spectrum of diseases. This chapter focuses on extracranial disease processes of the head and neck, specifically the most common congenital masses, benign and malignant tumors, neurogenic masses, vasoformative lesions, and masslike conditions, including inflammatory processes related to adenitis. Additional topics in head and neck pathology are presented in other chapters.

Imaging

The imaging modality of choice in children with head and neck pathology depends on the clinical findings, the patient's age, and the location of the mass. Generally, the initial imaging study in the young child is sonography. The ability to perform this examination without giving sedation and the lack of ionizing radiation are primary advantages. Sonography is excellent in differentiating solid from cystic masses and is useful in defining the location and extent of these masses. Ultrasound may be helpful in the differentiation of phlegmon from abscess in cases of suppurative adenitis. Color-flow Doppler imaging can be used to assess vascular patency when masses involve the vascular bundle and to demonstrate the appearance of intralesional and perilesional vascularity.

Computed tomography (CT) enables an accurate diagnosis in most cases of extracranial head and neck pathology in children. In addition to the obvious advantage of evaluating bony involvement, CT can assess the location and extent of masses, the internal attenuation values and enhancement characteristics, and the relationship of masses to critical adjacent structures. The full extent of masses and inflammatory processes is better delineated by CT compared with sonography. With newer scanners, multiplanar reconstruction (MPR) is helpful in further defining

pathology. The speed of the new multidetector scanners should significantly decrease the need for sedation in the pediatric patient. In our experience, CT is the mainstay of imaging of pediatric head and neck pathology because of the speed and ease of the study as well as the useful diagnostic information obtained for the clinician.

Magnetic resonance imaging (MRI), with its multiplanar capabilities, is very helpful in the evaluation of skull base masses for the detection of intracranial extension. Flow-sensitive techniques and magnetic resonance angiography (MRA) are useful in assessing involvement of the vascular bundle by tumor, vascular patency, and, in rare cases, intralesional vascularity. In some cases, soft tissue signal characteristics of tumors on MRI give a more definitive diagnosis. In our experience, MRI is usually reserved as a secondary study because of the longer imaging time, necessitating the need for additional sedation; this liability also dictates the need for dedicated nursing support and monitoring equipment, which may not be available at all facilities.

Conventional angiography is used primarily in the evaluation of vascular masses that are potentially amenable to embolization. Embolization can be used as a primary means of therapy in lesions such as vasoformative masses or as an adjunctive treatment before surgery in lesions such as juvenile nasopharyngeal angiofibroma.

Congenital Masses of the Neck

The most common benign congenital masses of the neck in children include thyroglossal duct cysts (72%) and anomalies of the branchial apparatus (24%). Thymic cysts, dermoid and epidermoid cysts, and teratomas are less common congenital masses of the head and neck in the pediatric age group.[191]

Thyroglossal Duct Cyst

Thyroglossal duct cysts (TDCs) are the second most common benign cervical mass in children after reactive lymphadenopathy,[177,242] comprising approximately 70% of congenital neck masses in children.[244] At approximately 3 weeks of gestation, the thyroid gland begins to develop as a midline endodermal diverticulum from the floor of the pharynx, between the tuberculum impar and copula. Over the following 4 weeks of embryonic development, the primitive thyroid gland enlarges to form a bilobed diverticulum that will descend caudally along the epithelial-lined thyroglossal duct. This duct extends from the foramen cecum at the tongue base (at the junction of the anterior two thirds and posterior one third of the tongue) to the lower neck (at the future location of the pyramidal lobe of the thyroid gland).

As the diverticulum descends, it remains ventral to all arch derivatives caudal to the first arch. Thus, the path of the primitive thyroid gland courses over the anterior and inferior aspects of the hyoid bone (with a small posterior loop behind the hyoid), thyroid cartilage, and cricoid cartilage. Caudal migration leaves a connecting tract (thyroglossal duct) between the foramen cecum and pyramidal lobe of the thyroid gland. In the usual course of events, the duct involutes between 8 and 10 weeks of gestation. Thyroglossal duct cysts or fistula form when any part of the duct fails to involute, thus leaving functioning secretory epithelium behind.[97, 191, 244]

Thyroglossal duct cysts usually present in the first 5 years of life, with approximately 66% noted before age 7 years. Males and females are equally affected. The cysts are more commonly found in Caucasians.[5] Unless infection is a complicating factor, patients with thyroglossal duct cysts typically present with a nontender, mobile, 2- to 4-cm, subcutaneous midline neck mass of variable firmness. Occasionally, there is a history of fluctuating size; more commonly, however, the cyst demonstrates an abrupt or gradual increase in size with time. Complications of infection, fistula formation, or rupture of the mass can also lead to clinical presentation.[97, 229] Fistulous openings are almost always secondary to infection associated with spontaneous or surgical drainage.[5] Coexisting carcinoma in the wall of the cyst is reported in fewer than 1% of patients with TDC. This typically occurs in adults and is thyroid in origin.[5, 19, 34, 45]

Microscopically, TDC is lined by simple columnar or squamous epithelium. Infrequently, inflammatory changes can distort the usual mucosal findings with variable amounts of fibrous tissue in the cyst wall. This usually

forces the pathologist to make a presumptive diagnosis based on clinical and surgical evidence. Thyroid tissue is uncommonly found in the wall of the cyst, accounting for the rare occurrence of thyroid carcinoma.[97, 177, 242]

Thyroglossal duct cysts are classified by location as follows: infrahyoid (65%), suprahyoid (20%), and at the level of the hyoid (15%).[20, 164, 193, 244] Initial imaging evaluation is often performed with ultrasound, which demonstrates a well-defined, thin-walled, midline, or paramedian mass with increased through transmission and variable internal echogenicity. Infected cysts typically have a thicker wall with variable increased internal echogenicity. Thus, the pattern of internal echogenicity in these cysts may not be helpful in distinguishing infected from noninfected lesions.[141, 253] TDC appears as a mass of relatively decreased attenutation to muscle with variable rim enhancement on CT (Fig. 21–1). Cysts below the level of the hyoid are almost always embedded in the strap muscle.[193] Infection or hemorrhage alters these imaging characteristics[193] (Fig. 21–1). The primary differential considerations by imaging include: dermoid and epidermoid cysts, branchial cleft cysts (if TDC is paramedian in location), or rarely, sebaceous cysts.[177]

Historically, preoperative nuclear medicine imaging of the thyroid was performed to document normal functioning thyroid tissue, because the only functioning tissue was occasionally located within the thyroglossal duct cyst.[186] More recently, reports indicate that preoperative identification of a normal thyroid gland by ultrasound confirms the presence of a source of thyroid hormone separate from the thyroglossal duct cyst, precluding additional imaging studies.[141]

The treatment (the Sistrunk procedure) is surgical, with removal of all tissue along the course of the duct as far as the foramen cecum. Removal of the central portion of the hyoid bone as well as the tract coursing behind the hyoid has led to a decreased rate of recurrence (~3% to 5%).[177, 229]

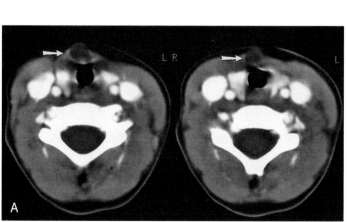
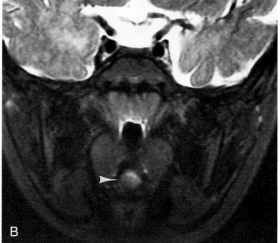

Figure 21–1. Thyroglossal duct cyst. *A,* Axial postcontrast CT scan demonstrates a midline mass of decreased attenuation *(arrows)* at the level of the thyroid gland. Minimal rim enhancement is present. *B,* Coronal fast spin-echo (FSE) MRI scan shows an oval-shaped mass of slightly hyperintense signal at the base of the tongue, in the area of the foramen cecum *(arrowhead)* in this infected cyst.

Anomalies of the Branchial Apparatus

A basic knowledge of the normal embryogenesis of the branchial apparatus and the derivatives is helpful in the understanding the imaging appearance of these anomalies.[142, 148, 191, 223] The branchial apparatus is a complex structure derived from neural crest cells. It develops between the 2nd and 7th weeks of gestation. This embryonic structure can be subdivided into five pairs of mesodermal arches that lie between five paired ectodermal branchial clefts (grooves) externally and four endodermal pharyngeal pouches internally.[148] The fifth arch lies buried near the site of the laryngotracheal outgrowth and by convention is called the sixth arch. These are the primitive structures that give rise to the muscles, bones, and ligaments of the face and neck as well as their nerve and blood supply.[191]

After 4 weeks of gestation, at which time the branchial arches are well defined, the first and second arches begin to thicken and enlarge. This thickening and enlargement of the first and second arches joins with the third and fourth arches and their intervening closing membranes to form a shallow ectodermal pit called the cervical sinus of His. The second and fifth clefts then merge with each other, obliterating the cervical sinus. The first and second pouches merge to form the tubotympanic recess that further develops into the middle ear and eustachian tube. The ventral portion of the second branchial pouch gives rise to the tonsillar fossa. The inferior parathyroid, thymus, and piriform sinus are formed by the third pouch and the superior parathyroid gland and apex of the piriform sinus by the fourth pouch. The first branchial cleft is the only cleft to give rise to an adult structure, the epithelium of the external auditory canal.[165]

Although the cause of branchial anomalies is controversial, current theories include (1) an origin as *vestigial remnants* secondary to incomplete obliteration of the branchial apparatus and (2) structures that arise from "buried" epithelial *cell rests*. In the vestigial remnant theory, incomplete obliteration of any portion of a branchial cleft, pouch, or the cervical sinus of His can lead to formation of a sinus, fistula, or cyst. In the cell rest theory, trapped cells located anywhere in the branchial apparatus are thought to be capable of forming branchial cysts later in life.[24, 148]

Anomalies of the branchial apparatus are classified as fistula, sinus, or cyst. If there is persistence of both a branchial cleft and a corresponding pharyngeal pouch, a communication in the form of a fistula can develop. In this case, an epithelium-lined tract connects the skin to the lumen of the foregut (pharyngeal mucosa). A branchial sinus is an incomplete tract that usually opens externally to the lateral skin surface of the neck. Communication with an associated cyst is variable. Both fistulas and sinuses can be lined by squamous, ciliated, or columnar epithelium. Congenital cysts of branchial origin have no internal or external communication with the skin or pharynx. The cysts are thin-walled and lined with squamous or columnar epithelium.[24, 148]

First Branchial Anomalies

First branchial apparatus anomalies account for 5% to 8% of all branchial anomalies, and are usually in the form of a cyst or sinus.[95] Although both Arnot[9a] and Work[260] attempted to classify first branchial anomalies into two distinct subtypes, Olsen found this scheme difficult in the categorization of all first branchial anomalies.[77, 180] An understanding of these anomalies is not intuitive; thus, a grasp of the regional embryology appears to be more helpful rather than an attempt to subclassify them.

The first branchial apparatus gives rise to portions of the middle ear, external auditory canal, eustachian tube, mandible, and maxilla. The formation of these structures is completed by 6 and 7 weeks of gestation. The parotid gland and facial nerve form and migrate between 6 and 8 weeks of gestation. First branchial apparatus anomalies present in a variable relationship to the parotid gland and facial nerve. They can arise anywhere along the nasopharynx, middle ear cavity, external auditory canal, superficial or deep lobes of the parotid gland, superficial to the parotid gland, angle of the mandible, or anterior or posterior to the pinna.[24]

Although this anomaly occurs in childhood, it is more commonly encountered in middle-aged women who present with recurrent abscesses or inflammatory processes at the angle of the mandible or ear. If the anomaly is related to the parotid gland, the patient often presents with recurrent parotid abscesses, which are unresponsive to therapy. Refractory cases, associated with facial nerve palsy, can mimic a parotid neoplasm clinically.[242] If the cyst drains into the external auditory canal, the initial presentation may be otorrhea.

On ultrasound, CT, and MRI, a first branchial cyst appears as a typical cystic mass that may be located within, superficial, or deep to the parotid gland and near the external canal of the ear or angle of the mandible (Fig. 21–2). Infected cysts have variable wall thickness and enhancement characteristics. When the anomaly is located in the parotid gland, imaging findings are nonspecific and do not allow this mass to be differentiated from other cystic masses of the parotid gland.[127]

Second Branchial Anomalies

Approximately 95% of all branchial anomalies are related to the second branchial apparatus. The most common

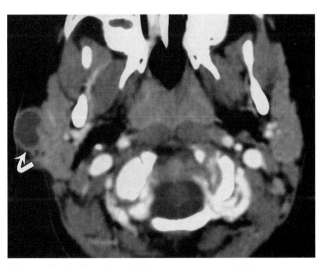

Figure 21–2. First branchial apparatus cyst. Axial postcontrast CT scan. A nonenhancing, kidney-shaped mass is seen superficial to, but contiguous with, the parotid gland (*curved arrow*).

location of this anomaly is the submandibular space; however, occurrence may be anywhere from the oropharyngeal fossa to the supraclavicular region of the neck.[127] Three fourths of these anomalies are cysts.[127] Fistulas or sinuses usually present before age 10 years, whereas cysts are more common between ages 10 and 40 years.[158, 231] There is no gender predilection.[67]

Bailey classified second branchial cysts into four subtypes based on location[12, 162, 175, 215]:

Type I cysts lie deep to the platysma muscle and the overlying cervical fascia, and anterior to the sternocleidomastoid muscle. These cysts are thought to represent a remnant of the tract between the sinus of His and skin.

Type II cysts, thought to be the result of persistence of the sinus of His, are the most common. They are located posterior to the submandibular gland, anterior and medial to the sternocleidomastoid muscle and anterior and lateral to the carotid space.

Type III cysts course medially, between the internal and external carotid arteries, and may extend to the lateral wall of the pharynx or skull base. These cysts are thought to arise from a dilated pharyngeal pouch.

Type IV cysts arise from a remnant of the pharyngeal pouch and lie in the mucosal space of the pharynx, adjacent to the pharyngeal wall.

Second branchial cleft cysts most commonly present as a fluctuant, nontender mass at the lateral aspect of the mandibular angle.[162, 230, 231] If the cyst becomes infected, patients seek medical attention with a clinical history of a slowly enlarging, painful mass.[231] If a fistula is present, an ostium is usually noted at birth at the anterior border of the junction of the middle and inferior third of the sternocleidomastoid muscle. The associated tract courses deep to the platysma muscle, ascends laterally along the carotid sheath, and continues above and lateral to the hypoglossal and glossopharyngeal nerves. It then passes between the internal and external carotid arteries before terminating in the region of the palatine tonsillar fossa.[12, 24]

Because these cysts usually present as a neck mass in the young child, sonography is often the initial imaging study. The cysts range in size from 1 to 10 cm.[58, 243] If the anomaly is uncomplicated, the sonographic appearance is typical for a cyst (i.e., a sharply marginated, anechoic, compressable mass with increased through transmission).[127] A well-circumscribed, thin-walled mass of decreased attenuation is present on CT[230] (Fig. 21–3). On MRI, the fluid within the cyst varies from hypointense to slightly hyperintense to muscle on T1-weighted images and is usually hyperintense to muscle on T2-weighted images.[95] When the cyst is infected, it can demonstrate increased echogenicity on a sonogram, relatively increased attenuation on a CT scan, and relatively hyperintense MRI signal, with variable contrast enhancement and edema of surrounding tissue.[24, 95, 162, 168, 242] Occasionally, the "beak sign," pathognomonic of a Bailey type III second branchial cyst, is present. In this case, the medial aspect of the cyst is compressed and forms a beak as it extends between the internal and external carotid arteries on axial CT or MRI.[93]

Third and Fourth Branchial Anomalies

Both third and fourth branchial anomalies are rare.[49] In spite of the rarity of third branchial cysts, they are the

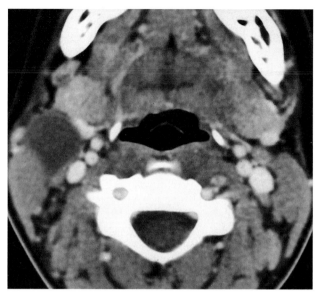

Figure 21–3. Second branchial apparatus cyst. Axial postcontrast CT scan. A rounded, nonenhancing mass is present in the typical position of a Bailey type II cyst. The cyst lies posterior and lateral to the submandibular gland, anterior and medial to the sternocleidomastoid muscle, and lateral to the carotid space.

second most common congenital lesion of the posterior cervical space after lymphatic malformation.[183] Anomalies of the fourth branchial apparatus usually appear as a sinus rather than a cyst or fistula. The majority of third and fourth anomalies are found on the left.[49]

Because the dorsal aorta between the third and fourth arches involutes, a third branchial apparatus anomaly originates in the posterior cervical space.[24] Third branchial cleft cysts must be located posterior to the common or internal carotid artery, and between the hypoglossal nerve (below) and glossopharyngeal nerve (above). If the anomaly is in the form of a fistula, it will have a cutaneous opening similar to a second branchial fistula (i.e., anterior to the lower sternocleidomastoid muscle). It then courses posterior to the common or internal carotid artery, anterior to the vagus nerve, and between the hypoglossal and glossopharyngeal nerves. The fistula pierces the thyrohyoid membrane and enters the piriform sinus anterior to the internal pharyngeal nerve.

A third branchial cleft cyst often presents as a painless, fluctuant mass in the posterior triangle of the neck after a viral upper respiratory infection. On imaging, the cyst most commonly appears as a unilocular mass with variable wall thickness and enhancement characteristics.[127]

Fistulas of the fourth branchial apparatus have not been reported.[49] Anomalies related to the fourth branchial cleft are in the form of a sinus tract. The tract arises from the piriform sinus and pierces the thyrohyoid membrane. It then descends along the tracheoesophageal groove and continues into the mediastinum, following a course under the aortic arch on the left and ascending into the neck, anterior to the common or internal carotid artery. This is in contrast to third branchial remnants, which course posterior to the carotid artery (Fig. 21–4). Rarely, the tract may descend on the right coursing under the subclavian artery.[24]

Differentiating third from fourth branchial anomalies on

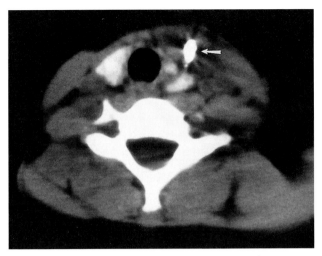

Figure 21–4. Fourth branchial apparatus sinus. Axial noncontrast CT after the patient had ingested oral contrast medium. Barium is present in a sinus tract *(arrow)* that lies anterior to the thyroid gland on the left. The tract arose from the piriform sinus and continued into the mediastinum.

imaging is problematic. Key relationships include the carotid artery and the superior laryngeal nerve. Third branchial anomalies lie posterior to the carotid artery, whereas fourth branchial anomalies are anterior to it. Those anomalies above the superior laryngeal nerve are third branchial origin, whereas those below the nerve are related to the fourth branchial apparatus.[49] On imaging, both third and fourth branchial anomalies related to the piriform sinus may appear similar to external laryngoceles.[24]

Cervical Thymic Remnants

Cervical thymic remnants are rare lesions derived from the third and fourth pharyngeal pouches. During the 6th week of gestation, thymic primordia (endoderm) develops from lateral and ventral diverticula of the third pharyngeal pouch, with a small contribution from the fourth pharyngeal pouch. These hollow outgrowths, which are connected to the pharynx by the thymopharyngeal ducts, begin to elongate in a caudal plane. At the end of the 6th week, the diverticula are obliterated secondary to epithelial proliferation. These two solid masses join in the midline before their final descent into the anterior mediastinum at the 9th week of gestation. In the 10th week of gestation, lymphocytes invade the endodermal structure to form lymphoid tissue in the thymus. The superior thymic primordia usually regresses.[17, 256]

Currently, two main theories have been reported to explain the etiology of thymic remnants. The *congenital theory*, favored by the most authorities, states that these cysts arise secondary to persistence of thymopharyngeal duct remnants. Progressive, cystic degeneration of thymic (Hassall's) corpuscles, primitive endodermal cells, lymphocytes, and the epithelial reticulum of the thymus have been proposed as the origin in the *acquired theory*.[15, 65, 266] As related to the embryologic development, these cysts may be located beneath or medial to the sternocleidomastoid

and anywhere from the level of the hyoid to the superior mediastinum.[17]

Because the thymus reaches its greatest relative size at 2 to 4 years of age and its greatest absolute size at puberty, most thymic cysts are detected in childhood.[82] Two thirds of thymic cysts are detected in the first decade of life (most commonly, at 3–8 years of age), with the remaining one third detected in the second and third decades.[33, 93, 231, 256] Seventy-three percent of thymic cysts are found in males.[33, 68, 160]

Most patients are asymptomatic, with 80% to 90% presenting with a slowly enlarging, painless neck mass near the thoracic inlet, anterior or deep to the sternocleidomastoid muscle.[57, 65, 67, 68, 88, 160, 174, 254] Hoarseness, dysphasia, stridor, and dyspnea in the newborn may occasionally be seen as the initial complaint secondary to the mass effect. Infection, hemorrhage, or Valsalva maneuvers can cause rapid enlargement of the cyst.[15, 174, 198, 231, 254] Seventy percent of thymic cysts are left-sided, 23% are right-sided, and the remaining 7% are midline or pharyngeal in location.[15, 51]

Cervical thymic remnants may be found anywhere along the path of the thymopharyngeal duct, which courses along the carotid sheath, from the level of the angle of the mandible to the superior mediastinum. The lesions vary in size (1 to 17 cm) and shape (round to elongated).[15, 26, 33] Most cysts are unilocular and have a smooth lining.[33, 65, 160, 191] A connection between the cervical thymic anomaly and the mediastinal thymic gland may persist in the form of direct extension or a remnant of the thymopharyngeal duct in 50% of cases.[38, 52, 88, 247] A fibrous strand may also remain between the cervical thymic cyst and the thyroid gland.[65] Cervical thymic cysts are often associated with thyroid and parathyroid inclusion cysts.[15]

Grossly, thymic cysts are well defined, thin-walled, uniloculated, or multiloculated masses. They are lined by stratified or pseudostratified, cuboidal, or columnar epithelium with pathognomonic Hassall's corpuscles within the wall.[15, 160] The wall may also contain lymphoid tissue or giant cells with cholesterol clefts and granulomas.[38, 65, 68, 160]

Thymic tissue must be present within the lesion for the pathologic diagnosis. Occasionally, thyroid or parathyroid tissue is also found within the cyst or cyst wall.[48, 247] As derivatives of the third and fourth branchial clefts, thymic cysts can extend through the thyrohyoid membrane and into the piriform sinus.[68] There have been no reports of malignant degeneration of thymic cysts in children or the development of myasthenia gravis or immunologic deficiencies following excision of a thymic cyst. However, malignant degeneration has been documented in ectopic solid thymic tissue.[124, 174]

Because most ectopically located thymic masses are primarily cystic, sonography usually shows a large, well-defined unilocular or multilocular cyst parallel to the sternocleidomastoid muscle with hypoechogenicity and increased through-transmission. A homogeneous, near-water attenuation, uniloculated or multiloculated, nonenhancing mass is seen located along the course of the carotid sheath on CT[26, 33, 114, 140, 161] (Fig. 21–5). MRI of thymic cysts demonstrates a fluid-filled mass with signal characteristics isointense to hyperintense to water.[149] If hemorrhage or infection is present, imaging characteristics vary accordingly.[33, 231]

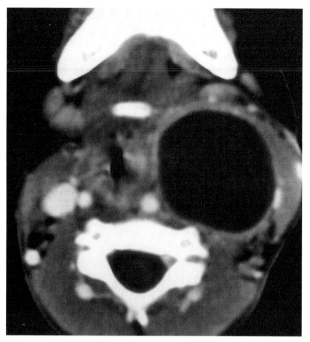

Figure 21–5. Thymic cyst. Axial postcontrast CT scan. A large, round, nonenhancing mass is present in a position similar to a second branchial apparatus cyst; however, the sternocleidomastoid muscle lies in a more lateral position.

The main differential consideration of thymic remnants is a second branchial cleft cyst. A true thymic cyst passes posterior to the carotid bifurcation and terminates in the piriform sinus, whereas a second branchial cleft cyst passes between the internal and external carotid arteries and ends in the superior tonsillar pillar. Fifty percent of cervical thymic cysts extend into the superior mediastinum, whereas mediastinal extension with branchial cleft anomalies does not occur.[15,174] If a mass is located in the area of the inferior pole of the thyroid gland, a thymic origin should be considered.[125] Other differential considerations would include thyroglossal duct cyst, lymphatic malformation, cystic neuroblastoma, lympadenopathy, external laryngocele, and vallecular cysts.[33,114]

Dermoid and Epidermoid Cysts

The terminology and classification of dermoid, epidermoid, and teratoids cysts of the head and neck can lead to confusion because of overlapping features. All of these cysts can be considered in the spectrum of teratomas. The masses share a common feature of containing tissue that is foreign to the body part from which it originates. Dermoids and epidermoids are ectoderm-lined inclusion cysts, with dermoids containing skin appendages, and epidermoids lacking these elements. Teratoid cysts may be composed of tissues of other organ systems.[108]

Dermoid cysts of the neck commonly occur near midline, along lines of embryonic fusion.[119] In the neck, the most common location is the floor of the mouth, accounting for 11.5% of all dermoids.[173] Other locations in the head and neck include the anterior neck, tongue, and palate.[172,173]

Epidermoid cysts are rarely found in the head and neck. When they occur, they are usually present in infancy.[230] There is no gender predilection with dermoid or epidermoid cysts.[104,231]

Dermoid cysts typically become clinically apparent in the second or third decades of life.[104,231] They most commonly present as a soft, slowly growing, suprahyoid, midline neck mass. Size is variable, from a few millimeters to 12 cm. A rapid increase in size can be seen secondary to association with a sinus tract, pregnancy, or increasing desquamation of skin appendage products.[182,230] Lesions lying in the floor of the mouth, in the sublingual space, are often clinically inapparent or exhibit minimal mass effect. If located in the submandibular space, the lesion usually presents with a more obvious swelling or mass effect.[104,252] In contrast to thyroglossal duct cysts, which move with protrusion of the tongue because of their association with the hyoid bone, dermoid cysts are nonmobile with this maneuver.[182]

On pathologic examination, dermoid cysts are well-defined, encapsulated masses lined with squamous epithelium. They may contain skin appendages in the form of sweat or sebaceous glands or hair follicles. Inclusion of skin appendages can lead to the formation of keratin and sebaceous material and, occasionally, hair.[225] The incidence of malignant degeneration into squamous cell carcinoma is approximately 5%. Epidermoid cysts lack skin appendages but otherwise are similar in histologic appearance to dermoids.[230]

Because dermoid cysts typically present in older children, CT is often performed as the initial imaging study. Dermoid cysts appear as a thin-walled, unilocular mass with homogeneously decreased attenuation, with CT measurements in the negative numbers (0 to −18 HU)[108] (Fig. 21–6). Occasionally, a "sac of marbles" appearance, representing multiple, small fatty nodules within the fluid, is seen within the cyst. This appearance is virtually pathognomonic of a dermoid cyst. A more heterogeneous appearance can be present secondary to a difference in composition of the various skin appendage components. Fluid-fluid levels are a rare finding. After administration of contrast medium, thin, peripheral enhancement is often present.[230] On MRI, signal changes are variable and dependent on the composition of the cyst. T1-weighted signal can be hyperintense secondary to lipid concentration or isointense to muscle; T2 signal is usually hyperintense to muscle.[104,252]

When dermoids are located in the floor of the mouth, accurate localization by imaging is important for surgical planning. Most commonly, dermoids in the floor of the mouth lie above the mylohyoid muscle, which places them in the sublingual space. These cysts are amenable to an intraoral surgical approach. Cysts that lie below the mylohyoid muscle are localized to the submandibular space, necessitating an external, submandibular approach. Coronal CT or MRI is the optimal imaging plane for localization of these masses into the appropriate space.[230]

Epidermoid cysts most commonly have homogeneously decreased attenuation on CT, with hypointense T1-weighted and hyperintense T2-weighted signal to muscle on MRI closely following water signal. With this imaging appearance, it is difficult to distinguish epidermoid cyst

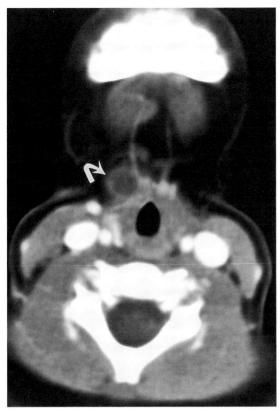

Figure 21–6. Dermoid cyst. Axial postcontrast CT scan. A well-defined mass of decreased attenuation lies in the anterior neck, slightly off midline *(curved arrow)*. Attenuation values were 0 to −5 Hounsfield units (HU).

from uncomplicated cystic lesions in the floor of the mouth, such as a lymphatic malformation or ranula.[48]

Teratoma

Teratomas constitute approximately 9% of all pediatric head and neck neoplasms, with fewer than 5% of all teratomas occurring in the head and neck.[9, 47, 115] In the pediatric population, most teratomas are extragonadal in location, with 82% found in the sacrococcygeal area.[14, 240] Locations in the head and neck include the neck, orbit, nasal cavity, paranasal sinus, oral cavity, oropharynx, nasopharynx, temporal bone, and ear.[1, 60, 97, 132, 239] Teratomas are thought to arise from misplaced, pleuripotential, primordial germ cells. They are classified as "true neoplasms" because of their biologic behavior of progressive and invasive growth patterns.[200]

Teratomas have been subclassified by Ewing and Arnold into four types[66a, 203]:

1. *Dermoids*—masses of ectodermal and mesodermal elements, composed mostly of adipose tissue with fragments of muscle, cartilage, or bone.
2. *Teratoids*—masses containing elements of all three germ layers, differing from true teratomas because of their poor histologic differentiation.
3. *True teratomas*—masses containing elements of all

three germ layers, with differentiation to enable recognizable organs by histologic examination.
4. *Epignathi*—masses containing elements of all three germ layers, with differentiation greater than true teratoma, usually incompatible with life.

Cervical Teratoma

Grossly, cervical teratomas are encapsulated, partially cystic masses with a variegated appearance on cut section. These tumors contain diverse histopathologic findings with variable degrees of maturation. Mature elements are derived from ectoderm, mesoderm, and endoderm; immature tissue arises mostly from neuroectoderm. Neuroectodermal elements (both mature and immature) tend to predominate in cervical teratomas. Although cells in this tumor can be found in any stage of differentiation, the degree of histologic maturity should not be equated with malignant potential.[9, 66a]

Clinically, teratomas are divided into (1) those present at birth or in early childhood and (2) those presenting in the first decade of life. The clinical presentation is variable and depends on the size and location of the tumor. Congenital tumors (presenting in the first 60 days of life) tend to have a benign clinical behavior, but they exhibit a high mortality rate secondary to airway compression with pulmonary compromise. Tumors that present later are usually smaller but carry a higher incidence of malignancy.[200] True cervical teratomas are large and can lead to obstetric complications, such as difficult labor with malpresentation, premature labor, stillbirth, and acute respiratory distress.[35] Extensive unilateral or more diffuse cervical swelling is often present.[222, 228] Maternal polyhydramnios has been reported in 18% of patients with cervical teratomas.[99, 197, 201]

Because of the frequent use of ultrasonography in obstetrics, the diagnosis is often made antenatally. On sonograms, teratomas demonstrate heterogeneous echogenicity with multiloculated areas of cystic and solid regions, angulated cyst walls, and acoustic shadowing from calcifications. The mass may appear well defined or, less commonly, infiltrative.[200] After birth, the patients are usually referred for CT.

Imaging characteristics directly reflect the pathologic makeup of the tumor, often demonstrating a heterogeneous attenuation pattern and appearing primarily cystic, solid, or multicystic. Most cervical teratomas are large, measuring up to 12 cm in size, with approximately 50% containing calcification[200, 258] (Fig. 21–7). Both CT and MRI are helpful in delineating the extent of the tumor and the degree of airway compromise.[105] The MRI appearance is a mass of heterogeneous signal on all pulse sequences with the fatty component, hyperintense on T1-weighted sequences, and areas of calcification, hypointense or hyperintense on T1-weighted images. Attenuation values and signal characteristics of fat and bone, in a mass of the head and neck in a young child, is nearly pathognomic of teratoma. Variable enhancement is present on both CT and MRI after contrast administration. Intubation is commonly required in these patients before scanning.[200]

The primary differential consideration of a cervical teratoma is lymphatic malformation, which more closely follows water signal on all pulse sequences on MRI. Other

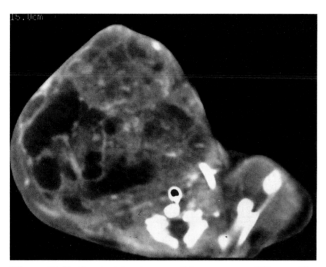

Figure 21–7. Cervical teratoma. Axial postcontrast CT scan. The majority of the anterior neck is involved with an extremely large, heterogeneous mass with mild enhancement. The vascular bundle on the right is not visualized secondary to tumor involvement. The infant required intubation because of mass effect on the airway.

differential considerations include thyroglossal duct cyst, branchial cleft cyst, goiter, hemangioma, and external laryngocele.[57]

Despite the appearance of teratomas on CT and MR, cervical teratomas do not typically infiltrate surrounding tissue; thus, complete surgical resection is usually possible.[200] Surgery is mandatory for congenital cervical teratomas, as the mortality rate is 80% to 100% secondary to airway complications, if the tumor is left untreated. Thus, differentiating this tumor from other congenital space-occupying masses of the neck is crucial. The incidence of true malignancy of congenital teratoma is low (<5%), associated anomalies are uncommon, and the prognosis with surgery is excellent.[90, 187]

Congenital Nasal Masses
Nasopharyngeal Teratoma

Greater than 50% of nasopharyngeal teratomas are seen in the first year of life, with nearly all true tridermal tumors present at birth.[255] They usually arise from the superior or lateral wall of the nasopharynx. For teratomas in the nasal cavity, there is a predilection for girls.[87] The typical clinical presentation involves a neonate with severe respiratory distress, stridor, and dysphagia. These tumors can attain a large size and protrude from the mouth or nostrils.[21, 222, 228]

The imaging appearance is similar to that of the cervical teratoma (Fig. 21–8). In addition to airway evaluation and evidence of vascular involvement, MRI is helpful in excluding intracranial extension.[258] Differential considerations for nasopharyngeal teratoma include dermoid, encephalocele, nasal glioma, rhabdomyosarcoma, hemangioma, lipoma, neurofibroma, and lymphoma.[226]

Nasal Dermoid

Nasal dermoids are thought to result from a lack of regression of a diverticulum of dura that extends through the foramen cecum between the developing nasal cartilage and nasal bone.[16, 184,209] Depending on the patency of the diverticulum and its contents, the resultant lesion can be a dermal sinus, dermoid cyst, nasal glioma, or encephalocele.[184] Nasal dermoid cysts and dermal sinuses make up 3.7 to 12.6% of all dermoids of the head and neck.[179, 209]

Most nasal dermoids are sporadic in nature; however, several familial cases have been reported.[27, 167] Nasal dermoid cysts and dermoid sinuses can present at any age but are most commonly found in younger children, with a mean age of presentation of 3 years.[184] There is no sexual predilection.[86, 184, 209] These lesions may be found at any location between the glabella and the base of the columela.[184] Approximately 56% present as midline cysts, and 44% present as midline sinus ostia.[184] Rarely, multiple sinus ostia or the simultaneous occurrence of a sinus and a cyst at the glabella and nasal bridge can be seen.[209]

The most common clinical presentation is a painless, cystic enlargement of any part of the nose, associated with one or more dimples.[179] Externally, midline pits, fenestra, or discrete masses are present. Associated hair may protrude from the defect (pit or fenestra).[3, 20, 27, 30, 167, 209] Intermittent episodes of inflammation or discharge of sebaceous or inflammatory material can cause a variation in the size of the mass. Signs and symptoms of meningitis or behavioral changes related to life-threatening frontal lobe abscess can be seen when intracranial extension is present.[179, 209]

Extension of both nasal dermoid cysts and dermal sinuses varies. These lesions can end blindly in the superficial tissues, or they may extend both intracranially and extracranially.[209] Reported incidence of intracranial extension varies between 0 and 57%.[155, 179] Intracranial extension of dermoids typically occurs into the epidural space in the region of the crista galli. There may be further extension, between the leaves in the falx; however, it is rare for the lesion to extend beyond the interdural space.[37, 184]

Both CT and MRI are useful in the evaluation of these lesions. The course of a dermal sinus is seen on CT as a well-defined gap between the nasal bones, in the midline or in the frontal bone.[179] The findings of an enlarged foramen cecum and bifid or distorted crista galli are suggestive of, but not pathognomonic of, intracranial extension (Fig. 21–9). These findings can be present with or without intracranial extension or with intracranial extension of a fibrous cord without dermoid elements.[184] The fibrous tract and ostium usually appear as an isodense or hypodense to soft tissue channel with variable extension. Bony canals are well seen on CT and can extend through the nasal bones, nasal septum, and skull base. Noninfected dermoid cysts appear on CT as nonenhancing masses of fat attenuation with an isodense rim to soft tissue. Stranding of the surrounding soft tissues and change in the attenuation value of the cyst suggests secondary infection of the mass. The appearance of an infected dermoid cyst is similar to an abscess with a peripheral rim of enhancement.[113]

MRI is extremely valuable in assessing these lesions. Thin-slice (3-mm), sagittal, coronal, and axial T1-weighted sequences should be obtained. Enlargement of the foramen cecum with intracranial extension is best demonstrated on sagittal T1-weighted images. Dermoid cysts most commonly have isointense to hyperintense T1-weighted signal as compared with brain, with associated chemical shift

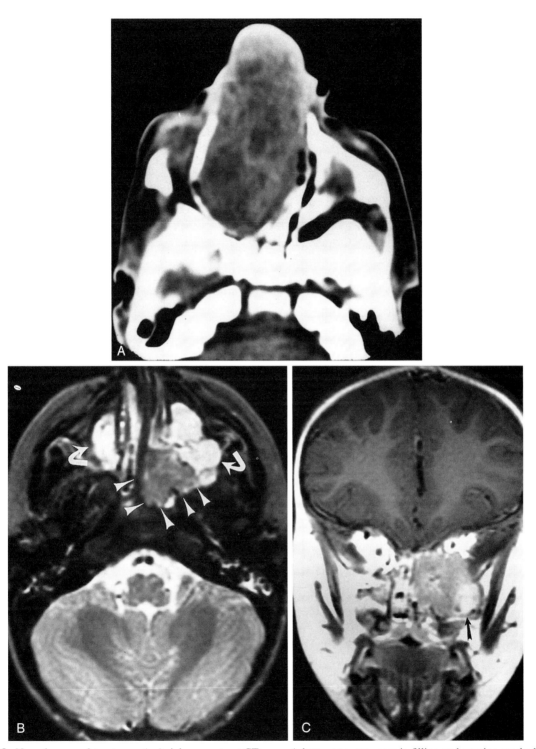

Figure 21–8. Nasopharyngeal teratoma. *A,* Axial noncontrast CT scan. A heterogeneous mass is filling and causing marked expansion of the nasal cavity in an infant. *B,* Axial T2-weighted MRI scan. A mass of the posterior nasal cavity *(arrowheads)* extends into the left maxillary sinus in another patient. The mass shows slightly heterogeneous signal, whereas maxillary sinus disease shows hyperintense signal *(curved arrow). C,* Coronal T1-weighted postcontrast MRI scan. Moderate enhancement of the mass is seen after contrast administration, with the obstructive maxillary sinus disease showing a greater degree of enhancement *(arrow).*

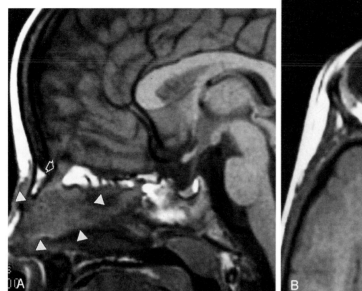
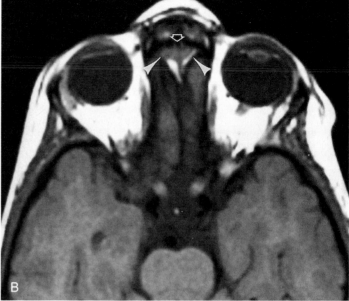

Figure 21–9. Nasal dermoid. *A,* Sagittal T1-weighted MRI scan. A mass of relative isointensity to gray matter is present in the anterior nasal cavity *(arrowheads).* It extends through an enlarged foramen cecum *(open arrow)* to the intracranial cavity. *B,* Axial T1-weighted MRI scan shows a bifid appearing crista galli *(arrowheads),* with the intracranial portion of the nasal dermoid appearing isointense to gray matter in the area of the foramen cecum *(open arrow).*

artifact. Fibrous tracts are isointense to gray matter on T1-weighted sequences.

The surgical approach with these lesions is dissection of the extracranial portion of the tract to the area of the foramen cecum. If dermal elements are found in the cephalic most portion of the specimen, intracranial dissection is performed.[184, 209]

Nasal Glioma

Nasal gliomas are congenital masses of heterotopic glial tissue with extranasal (60%), intranasal (30%), and mixed (10%) forms. These masses occur sporadically with no familial tendency or sexual predilection. They are rarely associated with other congenital malformations.[234] Extranasal gliomas lie external to the nasal bones and nasal cavity and most commonly occur slightly off midline at the bridge of the nose. The intranasal form is found within the nasal or nasopharyngeal cavity, the oral cavity, or, rarely, the pterygopalatine fossa. A communication between with the extranasal and intranasal components of the mixed form occurs via a defect in the nasal bones or around lateral edges of the nasal bones.[234]

Extranasal gliomas clinically present as a firm, reddish to bluish, skin-covered mass that is found in early infancy or childhood. These masses do not exhibit pulsations or increase in size with a Valsalva maneuver or compression of the ipsilateral jugular vein (Furstenburg sign).[233] They are typically slow-growing; however, they may grow more or less rapidly than the adjacent soft tissue.[234] Intranasal gliomas present as large, firm submucosal masses that extend inferiorly, toward or near the nostril.[234] They may cause obstruction of the nasal passage and respiratory compromise in infants or obstruction of the nasolacrimal duct

with resultant epiphora. Cerebrospinal rhinorrhea, meningitis, or epistaxis can also be seen at initial clinical presentation.

On pathologic examination, nasal gliomas resemble reactive gliosis rather than a neoplasm.[146] Metastasis or invasion of surrounding tissue has not been reported.[231] Tiny bits of fibrous or gemistocytic astrocytes, without evidence of mitotic activity, are evident on histologic examination. Fibrous septations and prominent zones of granulation tissue are also found.[231]

Distinguishing a nasal glioma from an encephalocele is difficult on imaging unless a communication between the mass and the intracranial subarachnoid space is documented. If a communication is present, the mass is classified as an encephalocele rather than a nasal glioma. Evaluation is best accomplished with MRI in the sagittal plane. Otherwise, encephaloceles and nasal gliomas appear as masses of soft tissue signal, isointense to gray matter, without a clear distinction between the two on imaging (Fig. 21–10).

Anterior Basal Encephalocele

The reported incidence of encephalocele varies geographically. The incidence of occipital encephaloceles is greater in the United States and Western Europe, whereas anterior basal cephaloceles are more common in the Far East and parts of Asia.[192] Overall, cephaloceles account for 10% to 20% of all craniospinal malformations. Anterior basal cephaloceles make up approximately 10% of cephaloceles, with the occipital form accounting for 75% and the nasal and orbital forms 15%.[133] The incidence of basal cephaloceles is between 1 and every 35,000 to 40,000 live births.[262]

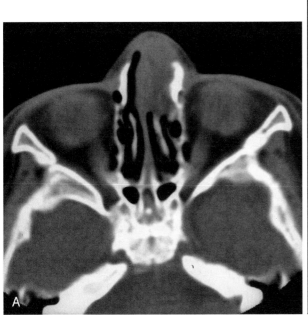
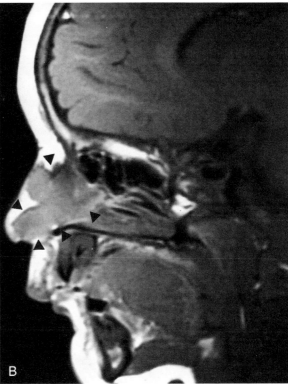

Figure 21–10. Nasal glioma. *A*, Axial noncontrast CT scan. The anterior nasal cavity on the left is filled with a mass of slightly less than soft tissue attenuation. There is bony remodeling of the nasal bone on the left. *B*, Sagittal T1-weighted MRI scan. The anterior nasal mass is isointense to gray matter *(arrowheads)* and shows no evidence of intracranial communication.

The term *cephalocele* refers to an extracranial herniation of intracranial contents through a midline defect in the skull base and dura mater. Anomalies that contain neural elements are termed *encephaloceles*; those that contain meninges and subarachnoid space are termed *meningoceles*.[133]

There is no universal agreement on the etiology of anterior cephalocele; however, the anomaly is thought to be secondary to imperfect closure of the anterior neuropore of the neural tube at approximately the 25th day of gestation. Cephaloceles related to the sphenoid bone may be secondary to persistence of the craniopharyngeal canal or failure of normal union of basilar ossification centers.[189]

On histologic examination, the herniated neural tissue in an encephalocele contains neurons with prominent astrogliosis. The cyst wall is composed of glia and fibrous connective tissue without neurons.[192] Basal cephaloceles are categorized according to location into the following:

- Sphenopharyngeal (through the sphenoid body and into the pharynx)
- Spheno-orbital (through the superior orbital fissure)
- Sphenoethmoidal (through sphenoid and ethmoid bones resulting in a posterior nasal mass)
- Trans(fronto)ethmoidal (through the cribriform plate resulting in an anterior nasal mass);
- Sphenomaxillary (a theoretical type that extends into the maxillary sinus)

A transsphenoidal cephalocele is a subtype of the sphenopharyngeal form, in which the herniated contents extend into the sphenoid sinus.[189]

The most common type of basal cephalocele, the sphenopharyngeal, usually presents as a pharyngeal mass with signs and symptoms related to airway obstruction (snoring, mouth breathing, nasal obstruction) or cerebrospinal fluid leak (runny nose).[170,262]

Frontoethmoidal encephaloceles commonly present in the neonatal or infantile period with a nasal mass or nasal stuffiness; nasopharyngeal cephaloceles present toward the end of the first decade with mouth breathing or nasal stuffiness. Craniofacial anomalies are not uncommon with frontoethmoidal cephaloceles. Pituitary and hypothalamic dysfunction and a decrease in visual acuity can be seen with sphenoethmoidal and sphenopharyngeal cephaloceles secondary to herniation of the pituitary gland, hypothalamus, and optic apparatus into the sac. Agenesis of the corpus callosum is found in approximately 80% of these patients.[16]

Coronal CT of the skull base is useful in evaluating the typically smooth and well-defined bony margins of the defect as well as the soft tissue component of the lesion. CT with intrathecal contrast material may be useful in determining the continuity of the subarachnoid space with this anomaly; however, this is rarely needed with the availability of MRI evaluation. MRI is superior in evaluating the contents of the cephalocele to include (1) the exact position of the pituitary stalk and gland; (2) the position and state of the optic nerves, chiasm, and optic tracts; (3) the state of the limbic system and cingulate gyrus; (4) the degree of bony dehiscence of the skull base; and (5) the presence of other anomalies[190] (Fig. 21–11).

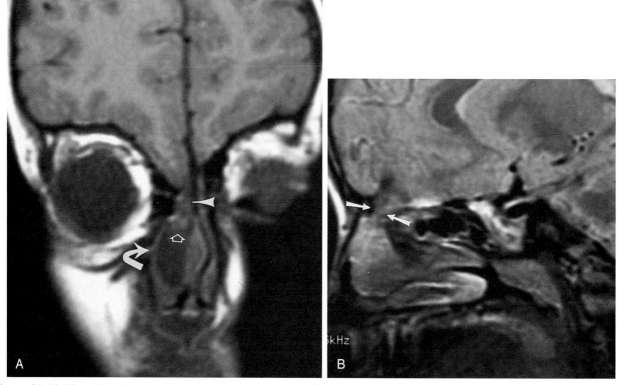

Figure 21–11. Trans(fronto)ethmoidal encephalocele. *A,* Coronal T1-weighted MR image shows inferior displacement of the right gyrus rectus, with continuity of neural tissue extending through the foramen cecum *(arrowhead)* and into the right anterior nasal cavity *(curved arrow).* The mass contains a small amount of neural tissue *(arrowhead)* in addition to cerebrospinal fluid. *B,* Sagittal intermediate-weighted image demonstrates extension of the neural tissue through the foramen cecum *(arrows).*

Malignant Neoplasms

Primary malignancies of the head and neck comprise approximately 5% of all malignant neoplasms in the pediatric age group.[111] Lymphoma and rhabdomyosarcoma are the most common tumors in this category; however, primary neuroblastoma, nasopharyngeal carcinoma, thyroid carcinoma, and synovial sarcoma also occur in children.[111]

Lymphoma

Malignant lymphoma represents a heterogeneous group of solid lymphoreticular neoplasms.[139, 217] It is the second most common solid malignant tumor in children and the most common malignancy in the head and neck in this age group.[111] This tumor accounts for approximately 50% of pediatric head and neck malignancies and is equally divided between non-Hodgkin's lymphoma and Hodgkin's lymphoma.[98, 111]

Hodgkin's Disease

Hodgkin's disease has a bimodal age distribution, with the first peak occurring in teenagers and young adults (with a fairly good prognosis) and the second peak in adults over 40 years of age (with a less optimistic prognosis). The disease is rarely encountered in children younger than 5 years of age. There is a male predominance of 3:1 in the preteen years, with the female incidence increasing with age.[146]

Most patients present with painless adenopathy, with 80% to 90% involving cervical lymph nodes. Fever, night sweats, and weight loss are seen as associated systemic symptoms.[248]

Histologically, the tumor consists of polymorphous infiltration of malignant cells (Reed-Sternberg and their mononuclear variants) with morphologically normal reactive cells (lymphocytes, plasma cells, and eosinophils). The diagnostic Reed-Sternberg cell contains multiple nuclei with eosinophilic nucleolus and moderately abundant, slightly eosinophilic cystoplasm. The Rye histologic classification is based on the proportion of lymphocytes and histiocytes in the lymph nodes.[40, 120, 145] Hodgkin's disease has been subclassified into the following forms: (1) lymphocyte predominance, (2) nodular sclerosing (rare in children), (3) mixed cellularity, and (4) lymphocyte depletion.[145]

Non-Hodgkin's Lymphoma

Non-Hodgkin's lymphoma tends to occur in children between the ages of 7 and 11 years, with a male predominance of 3:1. Approximately 15% of cases arise in the head and neck. This disease may involve virtually any structure in the head and neck; however, the majority of children with this form of lymphoma have widespread disease with bone marrow involvement at diagnosis.[92]

The clinical presentation is a neck mass or masses that can cause pressure on vital structures, leading to symptoms related to tracheal compression or superior vena cava syndrome. Primary involvement of Waldeyer's ring may lead to middle ear effusion or nasal obstruction, whereas Burkitt's lymphoma can present as a large mass of the jaw, thyroid, or parotid gland.

The most common histologic types of non-Hodgkin's lymphoma are[36, 53, 126]:

- Malignant lymphoma, lymphoblastic (30% to 35%)
- Malignant lymphoma, undifferentiated (Burkitt's and non-Burkitt's) (40% to 50%)
- Large-cell (15% to 20%)

Histologically, cytologically, and immunologically, the tumor cells in lymphoma and acute lymphoblastic leukemia share some common properties. These two disease processes are better conceptualized as a spectrum of disease rather than separate processes. Leukemia is associated with primary bone marrow involvement; non-Hodgkin's lymphoma, primary lymph node involvement. Arbitrarily, if greater than 25% of bone marrow cells are lymphoblasts, the diagnosis is leukemia.

Imaging is usually not helpful in differentiating Hodgkin's from non-Hodgkin's disease or metastatic lymphadenopathy. The sites of tumor deposition are subdivided as follows[94]:

- Nodal (most common)
- Extranodal, lymphatic (Waldeyer's ring)
- Extranodal, extralymphatic (orbit, paranasal sinuses deep fascial spaces, mandible, salivary glands, skin, and larynx)

Hodgkin's disease shows more predictable biologic behavior. The disease typically spreads from one nodal group to the next contiguous nodal group. Extranodal disease is rare in Hodgkin's disease.[40, 94, 139] In contrast, extranodal disease, with or without associated nodal involvement, occurs frequently in non-Hodgkin's disease. Waldeyer's ring, paranasal sinuses, and nasal cavity are the most common extranodal sites of disease in non-Hodgkin's lymphoma.[139] Widespread disease at presentation is also more common in patients with non-Hodgkin's lymphoma, with cervical adenopathy only part of the clinical picture rather than the major finding.[40, 94, 139] However, both Hodgkin's and non-Hodgkin's lymphomas can present as painless neck masses with unilateral or bilateral cervical adenopathy, involving the mid and lower jugular nodal chains, with relative sparing of the upper jugular chains.[94, 139]

CT demonstrates nodal and extranodal masses of intermediate attenuation (Fig. 21–12); MRI shows homogeneous, intermediate-signal-intensity masses on all pulse sequences.[92] Mild peripheral enhancement can be seen after administration of contrast medium. Calcification of lymph nodes is rare in untreated lymphoma and necrosis of lymph nodes is uncommon.[94] Sonography of cervical adenopathy in patients with lymphoma demonstrates multiple areas of decreased echogenicity, simulating cystic masses. When lymphoma involves the nasopharynx, it usually displays less aggressive imaging characteristics and lacks bone destruction; however, this is not a constant finding. When bony destruction is present, it is typically a permeative pattern rather than the aggressive, lytic pattern found in rhabdomyosarcoma and squamous cell carcinoma.[92, 139]

In addition to imaging the neck, evaluation of patients with head and neck lymphoma should include CT of the chest and abdomen. Gallium 67 scanning is also recommended in the initial staging of the tumor, evaluation of response to treatment, and detection of recurrent and metastatic disease as well as a predictor of clinical outcome in both Hodgkin's and non-Hodgkin's disease.[75]

Infectious causes, such as infectious mononucleosis syndrome and human immunodeficiency virus, as well as phenytoin (Dilantin) hypersensitivity, rheumatoid arthritis, and systemic lupus erythematosis, can produce a pattern of adenopathy similar to lymphoma on imaging.[62]

Rhabdomyosarcoma

Soft tissue sarcomas account for 7% of all malignancies in children younger than 15 years of age in the United States. More than 50% of these tumors are rhabdomyosarcomas, with approximately 38% found in the head and neck.[150] Rhadomyosarcoma is a malignant tumor that arises from primitive pleuripotential mesenchymal cells that are capable of differentiating into skeletal muscle. Thus, these tumors may develop anywhere in the body.[137]

The most common site of primary head and neck rhabdomyosarcoma in children is the orbit and nasopharynx, followed by the paranasal sinuses and middle ear. Other locations in the head and neck include the parapharyngeal soft tissues and nasal cavity.[41, 137, 207] There is a bimodal age distribution occurring at 2 to 5 years of age and in the late teenage years. Most patients are younger than 10 years of age at presentation.[150, 151]

The clinical presentation varies with the anatomic site of the tumor. Those tumors found in the neck present as a painless, enlarging mass. Parameningeal rhabdomyosarcomas usually present with a bloody discharge from the nose or ear, chronic otitis media with or without a facial nerve palsy, or symptoms attributed to an upper respiratory infection. Orbital rhabdomyosarcomas typically present with rapid development of proptosis, decreased vision secondary to optic nerve compression, or a palpable mass leading to an early diagnosis.[137, 207]

Histologically, there are four distinct subtypes of rhabdomyosarcoma:

- Embryonal
- Botryoid (a variant of embryonal)
- Pleomorphic
- Alveolar

The embryonal form is the most common subtype found in the head and neck in children. These densely cellular tumors are composed of lymphocyte-sized cells with hyperchromatic, round to oval nuclei and stellate or bipolar cell processes. Rhabdomyosarcomas tend to have a loose stromal network with a high overall water content. The pleomorphic type is seen only in adults, and the alveolar type occurs the extremities of older children and young adults.[41, 264]

The Intergroup Rhabomyosarcoma Study divided head and neck rhabdomyosarcomas into three categories based

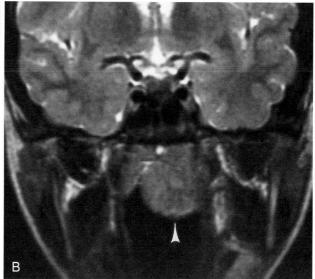

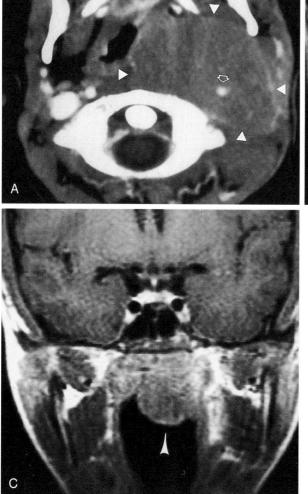

Figure 21–12. Lymphoma. *A*, Hodgkin's disease. Axial postcontrast CT scan. A large nodal mass *(arrowheads)* is present in the left neck with involvement of multiple spaces (retropharyngeal, mucosal, parapharyngeal, carotid, and posterior triangle). Mild enhancement of the mass and encasement of the internal carotid artery *(open arrow)* are present. The internal jugular vein is compressed and not visualized. *B* and *C*, Non-Hodgkin's disease. *B*, Coronal fast spin-echo (FSE) MRI scan. A rounded, intermediate signal mass is protruding into the nasopharynx from the pharyngeal tonsils. *C*, There is mild peripheral enhancement *(arrowhead)* after administration of contrast medium on this coronal T1-weighted image.

on site of origin: (1) orbit, (2) parameningeal (middle ear, paranasal sinuses, nasopharynx), and (3) all other head and neck sites. Those tumors that are paramedian in location (nasopharynx, paranasal sinuses, nasal cavity) have a tendency to extend through the skull base and to invade the meninges. Bony erosion has been reported in 18% of the tumors in this subgroup and 67% of middle ear tumors.[41, 264] The tumor spreads to the lymph nodes of the neck in 12% to 50% of cases. Hematogeneous spread also occurs to lung, bone, brain, bone marrow, and breast.[41, 257, 264]

The usual CT appearance of rhabdomyosarcoma is a poorly-defined, inhomogeneous mass that distorts soft tissue planes and causes bony destruction. After contrast administration, rhabdomyosarcomas usually enhance to the same degree as subjacent muscle on CT.[41, 137] Although MRI findings are not specific, most rhabdomyosarcomas are isointense to minimally hyperintense to muscle on T1-weighted sequences and hyperintense to muscle and fat on T2-weighted sequences. The signal intensity can be homogeneous (most common) or heterogeneous, and there

is marked enhancement after contrast administration (Fig. 21–13). Intratumoral hemorrhage can be present.[264]

Because meningeal involvement is the worst prognostic indicator in head and neck rhabdomyosarcoma, sagittal and coronal postcontrast MRI with fat saturation is crucial in evaluating potential dural and meningeal disease and intracranial extension.[25] Coronal CT is the imaging modality of choice for evaluation of bone destruction of the skull base.[41] Thus, all patients with suspected rhabdomyosarcoma should undergo both CT and MRI.

The MRI characteristics of this tumor are similar to those of lymphoma and nasopharyngeal carcinoma. AIDS-related Kaposi's sarcoma may also have similar imaging characteristics; however, generalized adenopathy in the neck is typically present with rhabdomyosarcoma.[265]

Those tumors that are not amenable to a good surgical outcome (middle ear, nasopharynx, paranasal sinuses) are treated with chemotherapy and irradiation. If intracranial extension is detected, additional radiotherapy is given to the base of the brain with whole brain irradiation as well

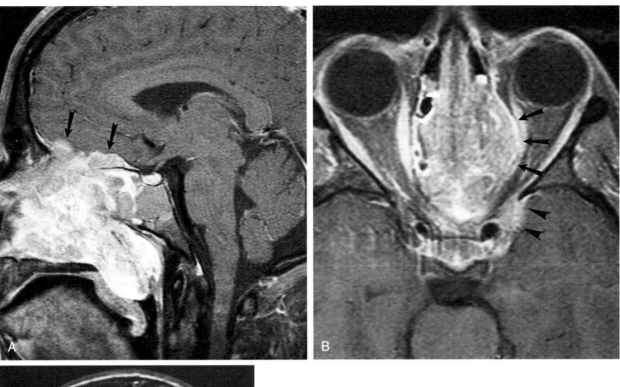

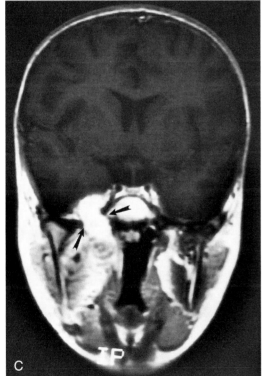

Figure 21–13. Rhabdomyosarcoma. Sagittal *(A)* and axial *(B)* postcontrast T1-weighted MRI scans. There is marked enhancement of the mass filling the nasal cavity and nasopharynx. Extension can be seen intracranially along the floor of the anterior cranial fossa *(A)* *(arrows)* and the medial aspect of the middle cranial fossa *(B)* *(arrowheads)* as well as into the left orbit *(B)* *(arrows)*. *C*, Coronal T1-weighted MRI scan in a second patient demonstrates intracranial extension of an enhancing infratemporal fossa mass through the foramen ovale on the right *(arrows)*.

as intrathecal chemotherapy. With the remainder of the tumors, it is assumed that all patients have systemic disease at presentation; consequently, they are treated locally and regionally with surgery and irradiation, or both, as well as systemically with chemotherapy.[152]

The prognosis is closely related to initial extent of disease.[238] The tumors with associated parameningeal disease commonly present with advanced disease (grade III or IV) and carry a 35% to 64% 2-year disease-free survival rate. This poor survival rate is secondary to the tendency for invasion of the skull base with associated meningeal and intracranial disease. Orbital rhabdomyosarcoma carries the best prognosis, with an 80% to 90% 2-year disease-free survival rate. All other head and neck primary tumors carry an intermediate prognosis, approximately a 78% 2-year disease-free survival rate.[79,137]

Neuroblastoma

Neuroblastoma is a neural crest tumor arising from the sympathetic nervous system. Overall, it represents the most common malignant tumor in children younger than 1 year of age, with the most frequent primary sites the adrenal gland and retroperitoneum.[129] The occurrence of this tumor in infants in a primary cervical location is rare, accounting for less than 5% of all neuroblastomas. Most neuroblastomas located in the neck represent metastatic disease from an abdominal or thoracic primary tumor.[39,224]

Patients present with a painless, smooth, rubbery mass with symptoms of dysphasia, hoarseness, stridor, and respiratory difficulty.[2,224] Horner's syndrome, with accompanying hematochromia of the iris, has also been reported.[2]

Histologic examination reveals a densely cellular tumor composed of small cells, sometimes arranged in whirls or rosette-like structures with intermingled larger primitive ganglion-like cells and intercellular neuronal tissue. A spectrum of maturational changes is seen from the most immature, malignant neuroblastoma to benign ganglioneuroma. Bone marrow involvement is common.[216]

Because patients are young infants presenting with a neck mass, ultrasound is often the initial imaging modality. Sonographic findings are nonspecific, showing a hypoechoic or complex mass with evidence of cervical adenopathy. Small echogenic foci, consistent with calcifications, are sometimes present.[2] CT scans reveal a sharply circumscribed mass in the poststyloid parapharyngeal space. Calcifications may be present on noncontrast images. Because the mass usually originates posterior to the vascular sheath, the carotid artery and jugular vein are displaced anteriorly.

After contrast administration, the tumor enhances to the same degree or slightly greater than muscle (Fig. 21–14).

Increased signal intensity to muscle is seen on T1-weighted and T2-weighted MRI. MRI is superior to CT in the evaluation of these tumors. MRI better delineates the mass and demonstrates the interfaces between the mass and surrounding soft tissue structures as well as the exact relationship of the tumor to the surrounding vessels.[61,72]

With cervical neuroblastoma, intracranial extension is rare, and only one case of intraspinal extension has been reported in this location.[54,188] Because cervical neuroblastoma is more commonly a metastatic lesion, chest and abdominal CT, as well as nuclear MIBG whole body imaging, should be performed in the initial evaluation to rule out other sites of involvement.

Differential considerations are limited to those processes that involve the poststyloid parapharyngeal and carotid spaces, including nodal tumors (metastases, lymphoma) and neurogenic tumors (schwannoma, neurofibroma, paraganglioma).

Treatment is based on stage of the disease, age of the patient at diagnosis, and other biologically determined factors.[29] The treatment is complex and may include surgery, radiotherapy, chemotherapy, and bone marrow transplant. Cervical neuroblastoma is frequently localized, at stage I or II. Infants younger than 1 year of age have the best overall survival rate (74% to 82%) with neuroblastoma. This possibly reflects both early presentation as well as spontaneous regression and maturation of the tumor to a benign ganglioneuroma in young infants. Papillary carcinoma of the thyroid has been reported in these patients years after radiotherapy treatment.[54]

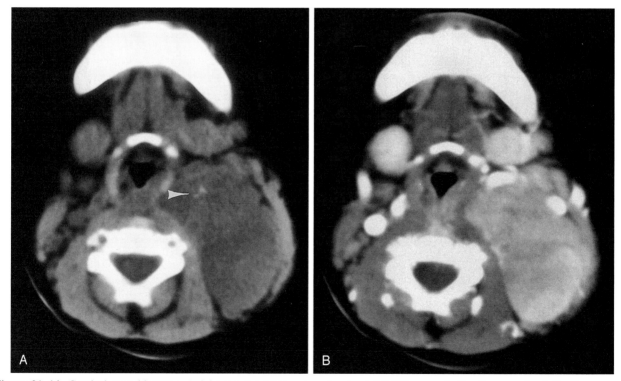

Figure 21–14. Cervical neuroblastoma. Axial precontrast *(A)* and postcontrast *(B)* CT scans. *A,* Small areas of calcification are seen *(arrowhead)* in a large mass of slightly decreased attenuation in the posterior triangle. *B,* There is moderate, homogeneous enhancement after contrast administration.

Nasopharyngeal Carcinoma

Nasopharyngeal carcinoma is rare in children, accounting for fewer than 1% of pediatric malignancies.[4, 18, 43] An increased incidence of this tumor has been noted in certain geographic locations and populations, specifically in southern China and Alaska. In Taiwan, nasopharyngeal carcinoma represents the most common cancer among Chinese males.[106] There also appears to be an increased incidence in the African American population in the United States.[63, 263]

The most common clinical presentation of childhood nasopharyngeal carcinoma is tender cervical adenopathy. This reflects the regional spread of the tumor at initial presentation. Serous otitis media can be seen from eustachian tube obstruction by the tumor or interference of muscular action of the tensor veli palatini muscle. Nasal obstruction; epistaxis; referred pain to the ear, neck, or throat; or cranial nerve paresis can be noted at presentation. Distant metastases are uncommon at initial diagnosis.[213, 237]

Nasopharyngeal carcinoma is an undifferentiated epidermoid-type tumor rather than an adenocarcinoma or a sarcoma. Multiple cell patterns (e.g., squamous cell, transitional cell, spindle cell, clear cell, polyhedral cell) can be seen with these tumors. On the basis of these cell types, a simplified approach to the classification of these tumors has been adopted by the World Health Organization, in which three types are proposed[214]:

- Type I, keratinizing squamous cell carcinoma
- Type II, nonkeratizining squamous cell carcinoma
- Type III, undifferentiated carcinoma

Types I and II have been associated with Epstein-Barr virus, whereas type III has been associated with childhood nasopharyngeal carcinoma. In the pediatric age group, nasopharyngeal carcinoma is usually an undifferentiated, epidermoid carcinoma or lymphoepithelioma (transitional cell).[70, 112, 144]

MRI or CT should be used to evaluate the nasopharyngeal area and skull base. Nasopharyngeal carcinoma usually arises in the posterior lateral wall of the nasopharynx in the region of the fossa of Rosenmueller. It may obstruct the lateral recess and cause asymmetry of the airway secondary to mass effect. The tumor can also originate from the posterior-superior wall, the posterior wall, or the anterior wall of the nasopharynx.[21]

CT is ideal for evaluation of bony erosion of the skull base, which is not uncommon with nasopharyngeal carcinoma.[220] However, MRI has been found superior to CT in the evaluation of primary lesions of the nasopharynx in both adults and children.[261] Undifferentiated carcinomas are invasive tumors with poorly defined margins and associated bony destruction. On CT scans, these tumors tend to be noncalcified with a variable enhancement pattern (Fig. 21–15). The magnetic resonance (MR) signal intensity of the masses is isointense to muscle on T1-weighted images and isointense to hyperintense to muscle on T2-weighted images.[185] Homogeneous, hypointense T1-weighted signal intensity and inhomogeneous, hyperintense T2-weighted signal intensity with inhomogeneous enhancement after contrast administration has been reported with squamous cell carcinoma of the oral cavity. Necrotic cervical adenopathy is common, particularly in the retropharyngeal and high jugular chains.[261]

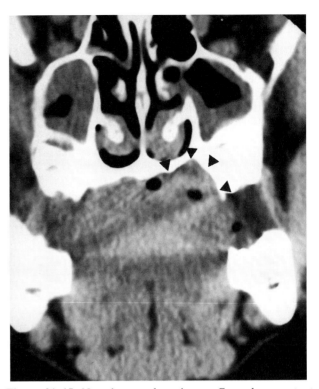

Figure 21–15. Nasopharyngeal carcinoma. Coronal noncontrast CT scan. A soft tissue mass is present in the roof of the oral cavity, causing erosion of the hard palate and maxilla *(arrowheads)*.

In children, differential considerations by imaging primarily include lymphoma, rhabdomyosarcoma, neuroblastoma, and, occasionally, juvenile nasopharyngeal angiofibroma or inflammatory processes that destroy bone.[97] The most common sites of metastatic disease are the cervical lymph nodes, lungs, and bone; as a result, survey CT of the chest and nuclear bone scanning should be included in the imaging workup of these tumors.[220]

Treatment is focused on local control of disease with radiotherapy, with or without chemotherapy, before metastatic spread occurs.[112] The 5-year relapse-free survival rate is 36%, with an overall 5-year survival rate of 51%.[111]

Thyroid Carcinoma

Thyroid carcinoma is uncommon in the pediatric age group, representing 1% to 1.5% of all malignancies in children. This neoplasm primarily occurs in older children and adolescents, particularly females. In contrast to thyroid carcinoma in adults, the tumor in children tends to be more aggressive at diagnosis; however, the prognosis is generally good.[23, 73, 78, 250, 267]

In the past, the relationship between radiotherapy and thyroid carcinoma was well known, with 20% to 50% of children with this neoplasm having a history of radiation exposure.[208, 268] The use of radiotherapy for benign conditions such as thymic enlargement, tonsillar and adenoidal hypertrophy, hemangioma, and lymphatic malformation peaked in the 1940s, with a resultant increase in thyroid carcinoma in the 1960s and 1970s.[69, 251] Although the use of radiotherapy for such benign conditions in children has declined, a greater number of children are surviving cancer with adjuvant radiotherapy. Thus, delayed thyroid carcinoma may become more of a concern in the future. The period between exposure to radiation and the occurrence of thyroid carcinoma may be as long as 25 years.[268]

The differentiated carcinomas (papillary and follicular) most commonly present with cervical lymphadenopathy or a thyroid nodule. There is a high incidence of cervical metastases (43 to 87%) and pulmonary metastases (up to 15%) at presentation in children with this type of thyroid carcinoma.[78, 202, 250] The clinical course in these children appears to be similar to sporadic thyroid carcinoma.[69, 251]

Thyroid carcinoma is subdivided into the following types:

- Differentiated (papillary or follicular)
- Medullary
- Anaplastic or nondifferentiated

The *papillary* form is the most common type found in children, accounting for approximately 90% of cases.[73, 96, 259] This tumor is well differentiated, with cuboidal epithelium on fibrovascular stalks projecting into cystic spaces. Squamous metaplasia, psammoma bodies, oxyphilic change, and lymphatic invasion are common.[156] Pure *follicular* adenocarcinoma is the second most common type of thyroid carcinoma occurring in children, accounting for 5% to 10% of cases.[73, 96]

Medullary carcinoma accounts for approximately 5% of thyroid neoplasms in children. These tumors originate from parafollicular cells (C cells), which are derived from neural crest tissue that migrate to the thyroid during embryogenesis.

Anaplastic carcinoma rarely occurs in children.[123]

Microscopically, these tumors have a variable pattern of solid and follicular growth with malignant change, demonstrated by evidence of angioinvasion or invasion of the capsule. Pulmonary and osseous metastases and blood vessel invasion are more common with follicular adenocarcinoma than with papillary carcinoma.[6, 259]

On radionuclide scanning, thyroid carcinoma is usually "cold" (nonfunctioning) but rarely may be "hot" (functioning).[78] After a mass has been localized to the thyroid gland by radionuclide scanning or palpation, sonography can determine whether the mass is cystic or solid. Cystic masses in the thyroid gland are almost always benign, representing an adenoma or colloid cyst; however, they may be complicated by hemorrhage and/or debris, simulating a solid or mixed tumor. Occasionally, malignant thyroid lesions are purely cystic.[11, 78] Most thyroid carcinomas have ill-defined margins and variable echogenicity, as compared with the normal thyroid gland.[78, 205, 221] Microcalcifications, irregular margins, and detectable flow in the mass by Doppler imaging raises the suspicion of malignancy.

Ultrasound is also useful in detecting nonpalpable metastatic lymph nodes. Echogenic foci within the mass or lymph nodes, representing calcifications, are characteristic of primary or metastatic medullary carcinoma.[78, 85] In the presence of a known thyroid carcinoma, a survey CT of the neck should be performed to evaluate for metastatic lymphadenopathy (Fig. 21–16).[76, 85, 227]

MRI has been reported to be helpful in differentiating

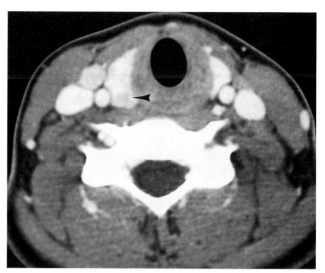

Figure 21–16. Thyroid carcinoma. Axial postcontrast CT scan. A subtle area of relatively decreased attenuation is noted in the posterior aspect of the right lobe of the thyroid gland.

recurrent thyroid carcinoma from fibrosis. On MRI, recurrent carcinoma appears as low to medium T1 signal intensity and medium to high T2 signal intensity, whereas low signal intensity on both T1-weighted and T2-weighted sequences is noted with fibrosis. In this setting, "low" signal is defined as less than muscle; "medium" signal, greater than muscle but less than fat; and "high" signal, greater than or equal to fat.[10] Thyroid masses with partial destruction of the pseudocapsule on MRI may suggest papillary carcinoma.[176]

Surgery is the mainstay of treatment for primary thyroid carcinoma.[134, 267] The best survival rates are with papillary carcinoma (86.3%) followed by follicular (85.3%), medullary (44%), and anaplastic (19%) types.[73, 96, 202] The overall mortality rate for children with thyroid carcinoma is 17%, with 75% of patients dying of complications of the tumor rather than the disease.[23, 73, 78, 250, 259, 267]

Synovial Sarcoma

Synovial sarcoma accounts for approximately 8% to 10% of all soft tissue malignancies, with 85% occurring in the extremities.[166, 218] Despite the name, these neoplasms do not arise from synovial tissue but are so named because of their similarity to synovium.[219] Synovial sarcomas usually arise in or near tendon or tendon sheaths rather than joints or bursal surfaces. Synovial tissue is not usually found in head and neck; synovial sarcomas are thought to arise from pleuripotential mesenchymal tissue that can differentiate into synovioblastic cells.[22, 91, 131] The most common sites of synovial sarcoma in the head and neck are the cervical soft tissues and parapharyngeal tissues, with an orofacial location less common.[199, 218]

Patients typically present between 15 and 35 years of age, with a slight male predominance.[165] The most common clinical presentation is a painless mass with symptoms of dysphagia, hoarseness, and headache.[7]

Histologically, synovial sarcomas may be *biphasic* and

monophasic. The biphasic type contains epithelial and spindle cell components; the monophasic type contains only spindle cells.[100] These well-circumscribed tumors contain gland-like spaces or clefts, surrounded by fibrosarcoma-like areas.[66]

CT is useful in demonstrating calcification and evaluating erosive changes of bone associated with synovial sarcomas. Calcification, in the form of round concretions, is present in approximately 30% of soft tissue sarcomas and may be a helpful finding in distinguishing this mass from other head and neck primary tumors in children.[195] MRI, however, is considered the imaging modality of choice for detection and staging of this tumor because of its inherent better soft tissue resolution. Tumor extent, vascular invasion, and intratumoral hemorrhage are better assessed by MRI.[219] Synovial sarcomas of the head and neck have variable, heterogeneous MRI signal on both T1-weighted and T2-weighted sequences, with variable heterogeneous enhancement after contrast administration.[219]

In our experience, we have found the imaging appearance to most commonly be a well-defined mass with an irregular wall, necrotic center, and minimal wall enhancement on CT; however, this tumor may be solid, cystic, or mixed in composition[195,219] (Fig. 21–17). Because 12.5% of patients have metastases to cervical lymph nodes at presentation, CT or MRI of the neck should be included in the initial evaluation. CT of the chest should also be performed, since pulmonary metastases are not uncommon.[9,199]

Treatment is surgical with wide local excision. Radiation and chemotherapy may be used as adjunctive treatment if excision is not complete.[163] The rate of local recurrence is high, with metastases to the lungs usually occurring within 2 years.[91] The survival rate is 40% at 5 years and 25% at 10 years, primarily because of pulmonary metastases.[91,165,199,218]

Benign Masses
Juvenile Nasopharyngeal Angiofibroma

Juvenile nasopharyngeal angiofibroma (JNA) comprises 0.5% of head and neck tumors in children.[56] This benign but locally invasive tumor of the nasopharynx is the most commonly encountered vascular mass of the nasal cavity in children.[22] The name of the tumor arises from the fact that it is almost exclusively found in adolescent males.[56] Patients with JNA usually present between 7 and 21 years of age, with a peak incidence between 14 and 18 years.[22] Although the etiologic mechanism of this tumor has not been defined, it arises from the fibrovascular stroma normally found in the nasopharynx. Most JNAs arise in the area of the sphenopalatine foramen and pterygopalatine fossa.[22]

Patients most commonly present with complaints of nasal obstruction (91%) or severe, spontaneous epistaxis (59%). Other signs and symptoms include purulent nasal rhinorrhea from associated sinus infection, hyponasal speech, anosmia, facial deformity secondary to the locally invasive nature of the tumor, exophthalmos, hearing loss, or rarely signs of intracranial mass effect from extension of the tumor. Episodes of recurrent epistaxis have been related to the vascular fragility of the tumor, which is thought to be secondary to increased levels of circulating estrogens.[22,136]

Histologically, JNAs are composed of spindle or stellate fibrocytes in a connective tissue stroma with many wide, thin-walled vessels. The myofibroblast represents the principal cell of the tumor. Myofibroblasts interfere with the synthesis of collagen and elastin and are capable of transforming into smooth muscle.[136] Fine vessels invade the fibrovascular stroma, producing pseudolymphatic endothelialized spaces. The final appearance of the tumor represents a spectrum from a cellular or purely fibrous mass, to a cavern-like mass with a fibrovascular stroma. If the fibrous component of the tumor predominates, the incidence of local invasion and the frequency of epistaxis are decreased.[56]

Imaging gives important information for both the diagnosis and management of these tumors. JNAs are slow-growing masses that extend along and through fissures and foramina. They usually remodel bone rather than destroy it.[102] JNAs can extend in multiple planes, including medially into the nasopharynx, laterally through the pterygopalatine fossa and pterygomaxillary fissure and into the infratemporal fossa, and superiorly via foramina at the skull base or the sphenoid sinus into the middle cranial fossa and cavernous sinus. They tend to slowly enlarge over time and may involve the paranasal sinuses (ethmoid, maxillary, and sphenoid), and orbits.[210]

Anterior bowing of the posterior wall of the maxillary sinus on plain film (Holman-Miller sign) was the earliest reported radiographic finding with JNA,[102] although this finding is not specific.[235] This tumor should be evaluated

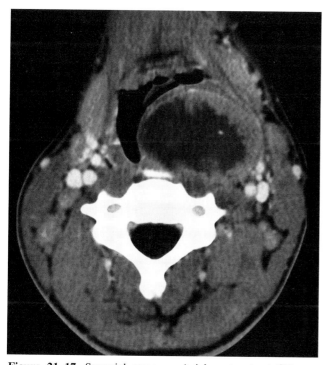

Figure 21–17. Synovial sarcoma. Axial postcontrast CT scan demonstrates a large, well-defined parapharyngeal mass with extension into the hypopharynx. The mass has an irregular wall, a necrotic center, and no evidence of significant enhancement.

with CT, MRI, and angiography. CT is useful for the evaluation of bony involvement, whereas MRI is better for determining intracranial extension of tumor and differentiating tumor extension into sinuses from postobstructive sinus disease. CT and MRI should be performed without and with contrast in axial and coronal planes. Fat saturation should be employed with postcontrast MR images.

Findings can include a nasopharyngeal mass, widening of the pterygopalatine fossa, anterior displacement of the posterior maxillary sinus wall with associated widening of the pterygomaxillary fissure, opacification of one or more paranasal sinuses, erosion of the sphenoid bone with a mass in the sphenoid sinus, erosion of the hard palate or medial wall of the maxillary sinus, deviation of the nasal septum, and intracranial extension. On MRI, JNA is isointense to hypointense to muscle on T1-weighted images and isointense to hyperintense to muscle on T2-weighted images.[80, 143] Flow voids are often present on MRI, and homogeneous, intense enhancement is typically seen on both CT and MRI scans after contrast administration (Fig. 21–18).[56, 210, 211]

Angiography is useful to define the vascular supply of the tumor for preoperative embolization. Typically, JNAs are supplied by branches of the external carotid artery, most commonly the internal maxillary or ascending pharyngeal artery. Numerous hypertrophied and tortuous vessels are seen without segmental narrowing, beading, or aneurysm formation. A persistent, dense blush is present throughout the capillary and venous phases. Early draining veins and arteriovenous shunting are usually absent.[135, 196] To fully define the potential vascular supply of the tumor, bilateral internal and external carotid artery injections as well as selective injections of the ipsilateral internal maxillary, ascending pharyngeal, and ascending palatine arteries should be performed.[135, 136]

From an imaging standpoint, the primary differential consideration is an angiomatous polyp. Patients may have similar symptoms; however, angiomatous polyps tend to occur at a slightly older age (in the 3rd decade). Angiomatous polyps are located primarily in the nasal cavity and do not invade the pterygopalatine fossa or intracranial cavity. Only rarely is there extension of angiomatous polyps into the sphenoid sinus, and the mass is hypovascular or avascular on MRA with only a few feeding vessels present. The enhancement pattern is less intense than with JNA, and flow voids are not present on MRI scans.[232] Other considerations of a nasopharyngeal mass in children include lymphoma, rhabdomyosarcoma, nasopharyngeal carcinoma, and esthesioneuroblastoma.[20]

To assist in selecting the best surgical approach, Sessions and colleagues developed a staging calcification based on extent of the lesion.[210] The most common approach to therapy is total resection (as feasible) within 24 hours of embolization. Radiotherapy is reserved for inoperative disease or residual disease, when reoperation is not practical. Intracranial extension of tumor does not always preclude surgery; however, parasellar disease may make en bloc resection impossible. In such a case, patients usually undergo debulking with extensive beam radiotherapy.[28, 89, 121] In addition to embolization, hormonal therapy and cryotherapy are reported to be adjunctive treatments to surgery. The efficacy of testosterone agonist and estrogen

therapy (to cause involution of blood vessels) and cryotherapy (to control bleeding from small tumors) have not been widely accepted.[8, 71]

The long-term prognosis of this benign tumor is good. Surgery alone carries a 25%–60% recurrence rate; radiotherapy alone carries a 25% recurrence rate.[117, 136] Recurrence usually occurs within the first 12 months of therapy and is unusual after 24 months. Factors predisposing to recurrence include the multilobulated nature of the tumor, leading to invasion of adjacent sinuses and fascial planes. The natural irregularity of the nasopharynx also makes complete extirpation difficult in some cases.[117, 136]

Neurogenic Tumors

Tumors of neurogenic origin constitute a small but significant group of head and neck masses in children.[46] Neurofibromas and schwannomas represent the most common nerve sheath tumors of the peripheral nerves in the head and neck.[21] Solitary neurofibromas and schwannomas can be seen as sporadic lesions, whereas plexiform and multiple neurofibromas occur in association with neurofibromatosis type 1.[20, 122] Approximately 25% of solitary neurogenic tumors originate along the course of a cervical or cranial nerve, with the exception of the olfactory nerve, which lacks schwann cells, and the optic nerve.[194] Twenty-five percent to 45% of schwannomas occur in the head and neck. The most common locations include the face, scalp, orbit, oral cavity, parapharyngeal space, middle ear, larynx, and neck.[55, 83, 84, 122, 233, 236]

The normal nerve fiber is ensheathed by schwann cells (the neurolemma) which in turn, is surrounded by the endoneurial fibroblasts (the neurilemma). The schwann cell is thought of as the precursor of the neurofibroma, the schwannoma, and, probably, the neurogenic sarcoma.[246]

Neurofibromas are unencapsulated nerve sheath tumors that are composed of schwann cells, with collagen in a mucous matrix. Solitary neurofibromas are typically subcutaneous and well defined, whereas plexiform neurofibromas are more commonly infiltrative with ill-defined margins. Multiple and plexiform neurofibromas are associated with neurofibromatosis type 1. Five percent to 13% of plexiform neurofibromas undergo malignant degeneration.[20]

Schwannomas are encapsulated tumors, usually attached to or surrounded by a nerve. Microscopically, they are composed of two types of tissues: cellular Antoni type A and less cellular Antoni type B. Compact spindle cells in parallel orientation with palisading nuclei oriented around bundles of fiber form Verocay bodies. Schwannomas are almost never associated with neurofibromatosis type 1 and rarely undergo malignant change.[20]

Neurofibromas can arise at any age. Schwannomas most commonly present between 20 and 50 years of age, with occasional occurrences in childhood. Neurofibromas are characteristically asymptomatic, whereas schwannomas are often painful and tender. The pain may be localized or radicular in nature with associated paraesthesias.[20]

On imaging, solitary neurofibromas and schwannomas present as well-defined lobulated masses with a tendency to cross fascial planes. Neurofibromas appear as isointense masses to muscle with rare calcification and variable en-

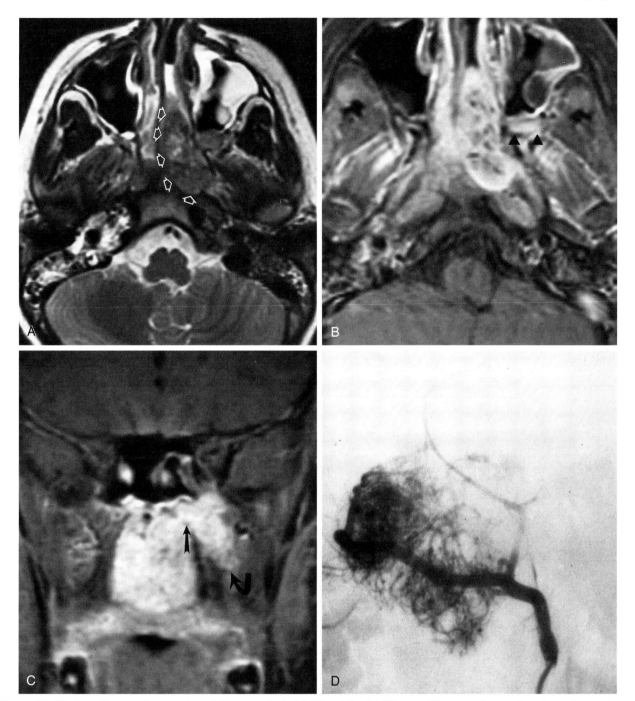

Figure 21–18. Juvenile nasopharyngeal angiofibroma. *A,* Axial T2-weighted MRI scan. The posterior nasal cavity and nasopharynx are expanded by a large mass of mixed-signal intensity *(open arrows). B* and *C,* Postcontrast axial *(B)* and coronal *(C)* MRI scans show flow voids within the mass *(B),* with extension through the sphenopalatine foramen *(C) (arrow),* the pterygopalatine fossa, and the pterygomaxillary fissure *(B) (arrowheads)* and into the infratemporal fossa *(C) (curved arrow). D,* Selective internal maxillary artery angiogram demonstrates multiple, tortuous, and hypertrophied branches supplying this nasal mass.

hancement on CT. Schwannomas typically enhance more homogeneously, with either iodinated contrast or gadolinium. On MRI, neurofibromas are hypointense to isointense to muscle on T1-weighted images and hyperintense to muscle on T2-weighted images. Variable enhancement is seen after contrast administration (Fig. 21–19). Schwannomas have intermediate T1-weighted signal and hyperintense T2-weighted signal to muscle, with more uniform enhancement after contrast administration. Heterogeneous

signal intensity can be seen centrally in these tumors secondary to cystic degeneration and hemorrhage. This event is more common with schwannomas.[233]

Plexiform neurofibromas are poorly defined, infiltrative masses that can erode bone and expand neural foramina of the cervical spine. They have a more complex appearance on MRI, with wavy cords of signal hypointensity surrounded by areas of mixed isointensity and hyperintensity on T2-weighted images.[233]

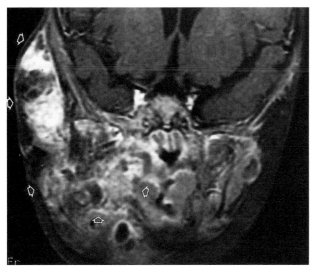

Figure 21–19. Plexiform neurofibroma. Coronal T1-weighted, postcontrast MRI scan with fat saturation. The majority of the right masticator space is involved with an ill-defined, heterogeneously enhancing mass *(open arrowheads)* in this patient with neurofibromatosis.

Esthesioneuroblastoma

Esthesioneuroblastoma, or olfactory neuroblastoma, is a neurogenic tumor related to the primordia of the olfactory apparatus. This uncommon neural crest tumor originates from olfactory epithelium of the superior nasal cavity or cribriform plate region.[159, 171, 212] Olfactory epithelium can also be found in the middle turbinates and adjacent paranasal sinuses, which may explain the occasional unusual location of these tumors.[212] Spread of tumor to the paranasal sinuses, anterior cranial fossa, olfactory bulbs, orbits, and cavernous sinus is common.[64, 118]

Esthesioneuroblastoma occurs in all age groups; however, a bimodal age peak has been noted in the 2nd and 6th decades.[110] There is a slight male predominance. The most common clinical presentations are epistaxis, reflecting the vascular nature of the tumor, and unilateral nasal obstruction.[59, 206] Other less common presenting symptoms include anosmia, sinus pain, and diplopia.[59]

The diagnosis is dependent on the demonstration of neural elements by histochemical or biochemical techniques, with electromicroscopy the most reliable method. Appearance of either an intercellar fibrillary background or Homer-Wright rosettes is diagnostic for esthesioneuroblastoma.[44, 159, 241] This tumor is often considered "the great imposter" by pathologists, as it can be confused with other small cell malignancies, such as undifferentiated squamous cell carcinoma and lymphoma.[249]

Esthesioneuroblastomas are typically superior nasal cavity lesions with both bony remodeling and destructive bony growth properties.[206] These tumors appear on CT as homogeneous, moderately enhancing, soft tissue masses centered in the superior nasal cavity, with frequent extension into the ethmoid and maxillary sinuses.[109, 249] MRI signal characteristics and enhancement patterns of esthesioneuroblastomas are nonspecific. Isointense to hypointense T1-weighted and isointense to hyperintense T2-weighted signals relative to gray matter have been reported. Enhancement patterns on MRI are variable, from mild to marked and homogeneous or heterogeneous (Fig. 21–20).[59, 206] Cysts along the intracranial margin of the sinonasal mass on MRI have been reported as highly suggestive of esthesioneuroblastoma.[234]

Destructive bony changes are usually best evaluated with coronal CT; however, the changes are typically not subtle and MRI can easily detect this finding.[206] Calcification, a finding reported as suggestive of esthesioneuroblastoma, can best be seen on CT; however, it is often difficult to distinguish true calcification from residual bony destruction with this tumor.[59, 234] Coronal, postcontrast MRI images are best for the evaluation of intracranial extension of disease (25% to 30% of cases) and extension of disease into the orbits or paranasal sinuses (40% of cases).[59, 234, 249] Coronal postcontrast, T1-weighted MRI is useful in the differentiation of nonenhancing obstructive sinus disease from enhancing tumor or recurrent disease.[59, 206]

Hematogeneous metastasis to the cervical lymph node occurs in 17% of patients at presentation. Thus, if cervical lymphadenopathy is present clinically, CT or MRI of the neck should be performed for evaluation of metastatic disease.

More widespread disease to lungs, bone, and liver occur in 14 to 20% of patients. This is unusual at presentation and more commonly occurs with relapse of disease.[64, 118, 206, 249]

Treatment is determined by stage of disease at presentation, with most patients undergoing surgical resection and adjuvant radiotherapy.[206] The 2-year survival rate is 88%.[140]

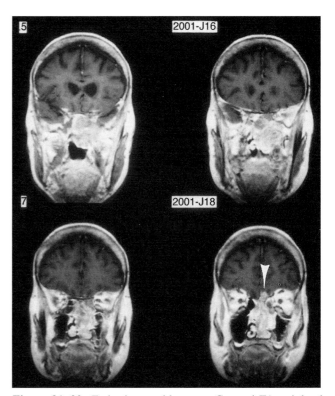

Figure 21–20. Esthesioneuroblastoma. Coronal T1-weighted postcontrast MRI scan. Marked enhancement of the mass is filling most of the nasal cavity. Intracranial extension is noted within the mass as it extends into the floor of the anterior cranial fossa on the left *(arrowhead).*

Vascular Malformations (Vasoformative Lesions)

In the past, there had been widespread use of different terminology regarding vascular and lymphatic malformations of the head and neck in children. In 1982, Mulliken and Glowacki proposed a classification of hemangiomas and vascular malformations based on cellular turnover, histology, natural history, and physical findings. The two major categories in this classification system are (1) hemangioma of infancy and (2) vascular malformation.[169]

Hemangioma of infancy behaves predictably. These masses appear in infancy, increase in size secondary to endothelial cell proliferation, and spontaneously involute by adolescence.[13] Vascular malformations are the result of abnormal development of blood or lymphatic vessels. These lesions increase in size as a child grows, have normal endothelial mitotic activity, and fail to involute.[169] In contrast to hemangiomas of infancy, which are clinically obvious at birth, vascular malformations may not become apparent until late infancy or childhood, even though the lesions are present at birth.[13] Vascular malformations can also be more complex in composition, with multiple vascular elements present. A rapid increase in size may be seen with infection, trauma, or endocrine changes (pregnancy, puberty).[169]

Vascular malformations are categorized according to the dominant component of the malformation: (1) capillary, (2) venous, (3) lymphatic, (4) arterial (with or without fistulas), and (5) combined (capillary venous, lymphaticovenous, arteriovenous [AVM]).[169]

Both hemangioma of infancy and vascular malformation can be further classified according to flow characteristics as follows[13,116]:

• Hemangioma of infancy, venous, and lymphatic malformations—low-flow lesions

• AVMs—high-flow lesions
• Combined malformations—low-flow or high-flow lesions

One report has suggested classifying capillary hemangioma of infancy as a high-flow lesion because of the presence of flow voids within the mass on MRI.[157]

On CT, hemangioma of infancy is a well-defined mass of isodense attenuation to muscle, with isointense T1-weighted and hyperintense T2-weighted signal to muscle on MRI.[13] Flow voids within the lesion on MRI are a helpful secondary to finding to distinguish this mass from other soft tissue lesions in infancy.[157] Postcontrast CT and MRI scans show a diffuse, homogeneous enhancement pattern (Fig. 21–21). These masses progressively enlarge over a period of several months before spontaneously involuting. Areas of hyperintense T1-weighted signal on MRI scans may be seen during the period of involution secondary to fatty replacement.[13,157]

Venous malformations (cavernous hemangiomas) are well-defined, predominantly solid soft tissue masses that can have associated bony remodeling or deformity. These masses tend to cross fascial planes and do not spontaneously involute. On MRI, venous malformations have characteristics of low-flow lesions; thus, they lack intralesional flow voids.[13,157] They demonstrate intermediate T1-weighted signal and heterogeneous, hyperintense T2-weighted signal to muscle with homogeneous or mildly heterogeneous enhancement after contrast administration (Fig. 21–22).[13] Heterogeneous signal secondary to intralesional phleboliths (usually hypointense T1-weighted and T2-weighted signal) and venous lakes (hyperintense T2-weighted signal) may be found within the lesion.[13,157]

AVMs do not typically cause mass effect because of a lack of an underlying supporting stroma within the lesion (Fig. 21–23). Serpiginous flow voids on T1-weighted and T2-weighted sequences and decreased T1-weighted signal secondary to intraosseous extension with marrow involve-

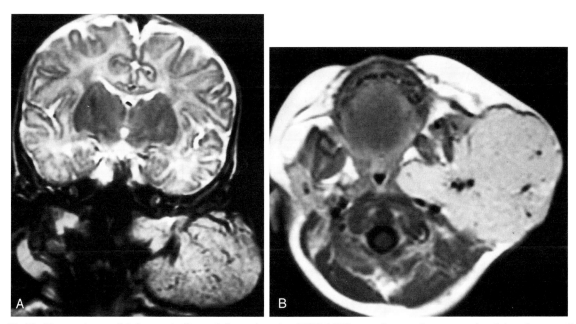

Figure 21–21. Hemangioma of infancy. *A,* Coronal fast spin-echo (FSE) MRI scan shows a large mass involving the superficial and deep components of the parotid space. The mass has multiple intralesional flow voids and diffusely hyperintense signal. *B,* Marked enhancement of the mass with intralesional flow voids is noted on this axial T1-weighted postcontrast MRI scan.

ment may be seen. The signal voids correlate with AV shunting present on angiography. Invasive, combined vascular malformations are seen as infiltrative, solid masses with serpiginous flow voids. Intermediate T1-weighted and hyperintense T2-weighted signals are seen with mixed lesions (see Fig. 21–3).[13]

Lymphatic malformations are classified according to the size of the embryonic lymphatic sacs into three types[22]:

- Lymphangioma simplex
- Cavernous lymphangioma
- Cystic hygroma

Imaging findings are variable and depend on the degree of vascularity of the lesion, the size of the intralesional cystic spaces, and the presence or absence of hemorrhage within the lesion.

Lymphangioma simplex is composed of very small cystic spaces. This subtype thus can appear as a solid mass on ultrasound, CT, or MRI.

Cavernous lymphangioma has moderate-sized cystic spaces; consequently it has a more typical cystic appearance on imaging with anechoic collections and intervening septations on ultrasound and fluid attenuation spaces on CT.[74,128] On MRI, these masses follow water signal with hypointense T1-weighted and hyperintense T2-weighted signal to muscle. Enhancement of the septations can occur after contrast administration, however, most of the lesion does not enhance.[147]

Cystic hygroma is composed of large, nonenhancing fluid-filled spaces with attenuation values and signal characteristics following water in uncomplicated lesions (Fig. 21–24). Secondary infection or hemorrhage into the mass alters the imaging characteristics, with changes dependent

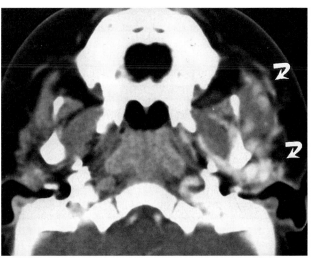

Figure 21–23. Arteriovenous malformation. Axial postcontrast CT scan. Multiple areas of vascular enhancement are present in the left masticator space *(curved arrows)* and retromandibular space, with an absence of mass effect.

on the stage of breakdown of the blood products. With infection or hemorrhage into the mass, echogenicity on ultrasound, attenuation on CT, and signal intensity on MRI typically increase, with variable enhancement of the mass and surrounding soft tissues.[147]

Angiographically, hemangiomas of infancy are distinguished from vascular malformations by the presence of a well-defined mass demonstrating intense tissue staining in an organized lobular pattern. Angiographic findings of vascular malformations are variable and depend on the predominant vascular channel type. These masses are typically diffuse lesions composed of vessels without intervening tissue stain.[32]

There are two primary options in the management of low-flow lesions of the head and neck. Hemangiomas of infancy spontaneously involute, so that conservative therapy with observation is indicated. Low-flow vascular malformations and rapidly growing hemangiomas associated with hemorrhage or ulceration and lesions posing a threat to the airway or vision, may warrant more aggressive therapy. In this case, additional therapeutic options include steroid administration, laser photocoagulation therapy, sclerotherapy, embolization, and surgical resection.[13]

Selective arteriography is indicated for complicated AVMs of the head and neck, because these patients may be candidates for embolization with or without surgical intervention. They should also be evaluated for coagulopathy if hemorrhage is noted in the lesion.[116,169] Some of the combined vascular malformations, with features of both low and high flow, may be highly invasive and resistant to all forms of therapy.[116]

Mass-Like Conditions

Fibromatosis Colli

Fibromatosis colli, also referred to as muscular or congenital torticollis, is a benign condition in infants related

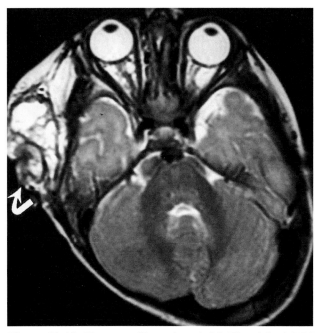

Figure 21–22. Venous malformation. Axial T2-weighted MRI scan. An irregular mass with heterogeneous hyperintense signal is noted *(curved arrow)*, involving the superior compartment of the right masticator space and associated superficial, subcutaneous soft tissues.

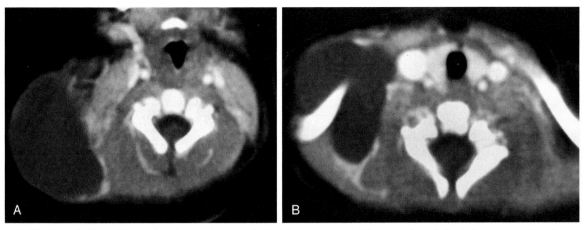

Figure 21–24. Lymphatic malformation (cystic hygroma). Axial postcontrast CT scan. *A* and *B*, A large, nonenhancing mass of decreased attenuation is present off the lateral aspect of the right neck with extension to the area of the thoracic inlet. Minimal peripheral enhancement is present.

to the sternocleidomastoid muscle (SCM). There are two main theories regarding the etiologic mechanism. These infants often have a history of breech presentation with forceps delivery. The first theory postulates birth trauma with subsequent intramuscular hematoma and fibrosis as the cause.[107] The second theory attributes the condition to fetal intrauterine malpositioning, with torticollis causing the pseudotumor. Histologic findings of fibrosis without hemorrhage in this condition favor the second theory.[154,245]

Infants typically present at 2 to 4 weeks of age with torticollis and a firm, nontender palpable neck mass. Parents are often concerned initially, because the mass may increase in size for a few weeks. However, the natural history is regression of the process by 4 to 8 months of age in 80% of infants. There is a right-sided predominance (75%).[154,245]

The goal of imaging is exclusion of other causes of a mass in the muscle, such as a primary tumor. If the patient is referred for imaging, ultrasound is the imaging modality of choice. Sonographic findings include focal or diffuse enlargement of the SCM, with variable internal echogenicity in contrast to normal muscle.[50,128] A peripheral rim of decreased echogenicity may also be present. This is thought to represent compressed subjacent normal muscle.[42] In the appropriate clinical setting, this pattern should allow the imager to make the correct diagnosis. CT and MRI are reserved for cases in which the diagnosis is not confirmed by ultrasound.[42,81] CT findings include a focally or diffusely enlarged SCM with the area of the "mass" isodense to muscle. If contrast material is administered, the mass demonstrates a variable enhancement pattern. On MRI, the enlarged muscle is isointense on T1-weighted and isointense to slightly hyperintense to muscle on T2-weighted images (Fig. 21–25).

Treatment is directed primarily toward physical therapy. In rare cases, when this treatment is unsuccessful, a muscle release may be performed.

Adenopathy or Adenitis of the Neck

Cervical adenopathy is a very common finding in children, usually related to a developing immune system that is responding to exposure to multiple new antigens. In most pediatric patients, imaging is not required, since cervical adenopathy is reactive in nature. When a case is atypical in clinical presentation or is refractory to medical treatment or when suppuration is suspected, imaging may be requested. In the case of an inflammatory process, the child typically presents with a painful and tender neck mass with associated cervical nodal masses. In this scenario, the imager specialist should address these primary questions:

- Is the process cellulitis or a drainable fluid collection?
- Is there evidence of complication in the form of vascular compromise, airway compression, or osteomyelitis?

The distinction between cellulitis and a drainable abscess is important; the former is usually treated medically, but the latter typically necessitates surgical intervention.

Sonography is a quick, noninvasive method of evaluating the presence of an abscess, with a reported sensitivity of 90% to 95%.[130,153] The usual appearance of an abscess is a mass of relatively decreased central echogenicity with variable internal echoes. Peripheral flow around an area of liquefaction on Doppler imaging is present in up to 89% of soft tissue abscesses.[138] Cellulitis has a more homogeneous or striated appearance on sonography.[31] The sonographic appearance of nonsuppurative adenitis is multiple, oval-shaped masses, with decreased or variable echogenicity. Scattered Doppler flow can be seen in the hila of nodes.[128] Although sonography is sensitive in detecting adenopathy and inflammatory masses, it lacks specificity in distinguishing infected congenital cystic masses from suppurative masses.[138]

CT has been used most often in an attempt to make this differentiation. On CT scans, cellulitis appears as an ill-defined area of decreased attenuation with mild, diffuse enhancement and "strandlike" infiltration of surrounding soft tissue. A drainable abscess is seen as a single or multiloculated area of decreased attenuation that conforms to fascial spaces and has surrounding peripheral rim enhancement (Fig. 21–26). Secondary findings of adjacent myositis, infiltration with stranding of surrounding fat, skin thickening, engorgement of veins and lymphatics, and enhancement of fascial planes can also be seen.[103,178]

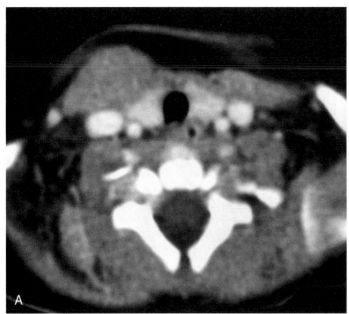

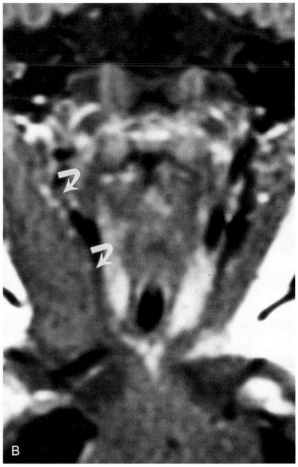

Figure 21–25. Fibromatosis colli. *A,* Axial postcontrast CT scan. There is marked asymmetry of the sternocleidomastoid muscles, with the larger muscle on the right. No abnormal enhancement is seen. *B,* Coronal T1-weighted MRI scan. The right sternocleidomastoid muscle is diffusely enlarged, with signal isointense to normal muscle *(curved arrows).*

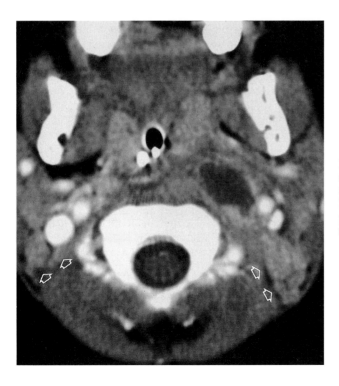

Figure 21–26. Retropharyngeal abscess. Axial postcontrast CT scan. An oval-shaped area of decreased attenuation is noted in the left retropharyngeal space with faint peripheral enhancement. Displacement of the carotid space laterally and effacement of the parapharyngeal fat are present. Bilateral spinal accessory chain adenopathy *(open arrows)* is noted.

Our experience in a CT study of 32 pediatric patients with deep-neck inflammatory processes found a specificity of approximately 75% in distinguishing abscess from cellulitis. A complete, circumferential ring of enhancement was the most sensitive imaging finding. However, this imaging appearance can also be seen with necrotic nodal disease, infected branchial cleft cysts, necrotic neoplasms, and thrombosed vessels. Thus, pertinent clinical history and findings and laboratory data are crucial elements to assist in sorting the imaging findings.

Inflammatory processes in the neck rarely cross into the mediastinum, secondary to constraints of fascial planes. If an infection is present in the visceral space anteriorly or prevertebral space posteriorly, however, the potential exists for extension into the mediastinum. The pretracheal component of the visceral space extends from the hyoid bone to the level of the aortic arch in the anterior mediastinum. The retrovisceral component of the visceral space and prevertebral space extend from the skull base superiorly to the posterior mediastinum inferiorly.[101,181] With antibiotic therapy, this complication is rarely encountered today.

References

1. Abemayor E, Newman A, Bergstrom L, et al: Teratomas of the head and neck in childhood. Laryngoscope 94:1489–1492, 1984.
2. Abramson SJ, Berdon WE, Ruzal-Shapiro C, et al: Cervical neuroblastoma in eleven infants: A tumor with favorable prognosis. Pediatr Radiol 23:253–257, 1993.
3. Ackerman WE, Phero JC: An aid to nasal tracheal intubation. J Oral Maxillofac Surg 47:1341, 1989.
4. Ahern V, Jenkin D, Banerjee D, et al: Nasopharyngeal carcinoma in the young. Clin Oncol (R Coll Radiol) 6:24–30, 1994.
5. Allard RHB: The thyroglossal cyst. Head Neck Surg 5:134–146, 1982.
6. Altman AJ, Schwartz AD: Malignant Diseases of Infancy, Childhood, and Adolescence. Philadelphia, WB Saunders, 1983.
7. Amble FR, Olsen KD, Nascimento AG, Foote RL: Head and neck synovial cell sarcoma. Otolaryngol Head Neck Surg 107:631–637, 1992.
8. Antonelli AR, Cappiello J, DiLorenzo D, et al: Diagnosis, staging and treatment of juvenile nasopharyngeal angiofibroma (JNA). Laryngoscope 97:1319–1325, 1987.
9. Arnold J: Ein fall von congenital em zusammdengesetzen lipom der zungl und des pharynx mit perforation in die schaedelhoehle. Virchows Arch 50:782, 1870.
9a. Arnot RS: Defects of the first branchial cleft. S Afr J Surg 9: 93–98, 1971.
10. Auffermann W, Clark OH, Thurnher S, et al: Recurrent thyroid carcinoma: Characteristics on MR images. Radiology 168:753–757, 1988.
11. Bachrach LK, Daneman D, Daneman A, Martin DJ: Use of ultrasound in childhood thyroid disorders. J Pediatr 103:547–551, 1983.
12. Bailey H: Branchial cysts and other essays on surgical subjects in the faciocervical region. London, Lewis, 1929.
13. Baker LL, Dillon WP, Hieshima GB: Hemangiomas and vascular malformations of the head and neck: MR characterization. AJNR Am J Neuroradiol 14:307–314, 1993.
14. Bale PM, Painter DM, Cohen D: Teratomas in childhood. Pathology 7:209–218, 1975.
15. Barat M, Sciubba JJ, Abramson AL: Cervical thymic cyst: Case report and review of literature. Laryngoscope 95:89–91, 1985.
16. Barkovich AJ, Vandermarck P, Edwards MB, Cogen PH: Congenital nasal masses: CT and MR imaging features in 16 cases. AJNR Am J Neuroradiol 12:105–116, 1991.
17. Barrick B, O'Kell RT: Thymic cysts and remnant cervical thymus. J Pediatr Surg 4:355–357, 1969.
18. Barrios NJ: Childhood nasopharyngeal carcinoma. J La State Med Soc 145:151–155, 1993.
19. Batsakis JG: Teratomas of the head and neck. In Batsakis JG

(ed): Tumors of the Head and Neck: Clinical and Pathological Considerations. Baltimore, Williams & Wilkins, 1979.
20. Batsakis JG: Tumors of the Head and Neck: Clinical and Pathological Considerations. Baltimore, Williams & Wilkins, 1979.
21. Batsakis JG, Solomon AR, Rice DH: The pathology of head and neck tumors: Carcinoma of the nasopharynx: Part II. Head Neck Surg 3:511, 1981.
22. Batsakis JG: Vasoformative tumors. In Tumors of the Head and Neck: Clinical and Pathological Considerations. Baltimore, Williams & Wilkins, 1979.
23. Becher SP, Skolnik EM, O'Neill IV: The nodular thyroid. Otolaryngol Clin North Am 13:53–58, 1980.
24. Benson MT, Dalen K, Mancuso AA, et al: Congenital anomalies of the branchial apparatus: Embryology and pathologic anatomy. Radiographics 12:942–960, 1992.
25. Berry MP, Jenkin RDT: Parameningeal rhabdomyosarcomas in the young. Cancer 48:281–288, 1981.
26. Boyd J, Templer J, Harvey J, Decker J: Persistent thymopharyngeal duct cyst. Otolaryngol Head Neck Surg 109:135–139, 1993.
27. Bradley PJ: Nasal dermoids in children. Int J Pediatr Otorhinolaryngol 3:63–70, 1981.
28. Bremer JW, Neel III HB, DeSanto LW, Jones GC: Angiofibroma: Treatment trends in 150 patients during 40 years. Laryngoscope 96: 1321–1329, 1986.
29. Breslow N, McCann B: Statistical estimation of prognosis for children with neuroblastoma. Cancer Res 31:2098, 1971.
30. Brownstein MH, Shapiro L, Slevin R: Fistula of the dorsum of the nose. Arch Dermatol 109:227–229, 1974.
31. Buckley AR, Moss EH, Blokmanis A: Diagnosis of peritonsillar abscess: Value of intraoral sonography. AJR Am J Roentgenol 162: 961–964, 1994.
32. Burrows PE, Mulliken JB, Fellows KE, Strand RD: Childhood hemangiomas and vascular malformations: angiographic differentiation. AJR Am J Roentgenol 141:483–488, 1983.
33. Burton EM, Mercado-Deane MG, Howell CG, et al: Cervical thymic cysts: CT appearance of two cases including a persistent thymopharyngeal duct cyst. Pediatr Radiol 25:363–365, 1995.
34. Butler EC, Dickey JR, Shill OS Jr, Shalak E: Carcinoma of the thyroglossal duct remnant. Laryngoscope 79:264–271, 1969.
35. Byard R, Jimenez C, Carpenter B, Smith C: Congenital teratomas of the neck and nasopharynx: A clinical and pathological study of 18 cases. J Paediatr Child Health 26:12–16, 1989.
36. Callihan TR, Berard CW: Childhood non-Hodgkin's lymphomas in current histologic perspective. In Rosenberg HS, Berstein J (eds): Perspectives in Pediatric Pathology, vol 7. New York, Raven Press, 1982.
37. Card CG: Pathologic quiz. Arch Otolaryngol 104:301, 1978.
38. Carpenter RI: Thymic cyst of the neck with prolongation to the thymus gland. Otolaryngol Head Neck Surg 90:494–496, 1982.
39. Casselman JW, Smet MH, Van Damme B, Lemahieu SF: Primary cervical neuroblastoma: CT and MR findings. J Comput Assist Tomogr 12:684–686, 1988.
40. Castellino RA: Hodgkin's disease: Practical concepts for the diagnostic radiologist. Radiology 159:305, 1986.
41. Castillo M, Pillsbury H: Rhabdomyosarcoma of the middle ear: Imaging features in two children. AJNR Am J Neuroradiol 14: 730–733, 1993.
42. Chan YL, Cheng JC, Metreweli C: Ultrasonography of congenital muscular torticollis. Pediatr Radiol 22:356, 1992.
43. Chang AY, Su SW, Zen SH, Wang WC: Nasopharyngeal carcinoma in young patients. Am J Clin Oncol 14:1–4, 1991.
44. Chaudhry AP, Haar LG, Koul A, Nickerson PA: Olfactory neuroblastoma (esthesioneuroblatoma): A light and ultrastructural study of two cases. Cancer 44:564–579, 1979.
45. Choy FJ, Ward R, Richardson R: Carcinoma of the thyroglossal duct. Am J Surg 108:361–369, 1964.
46. Coffin CM, Dehner LP: Peripheral neurogenic tumors of the soft tissues in children and adolescents: A clinicopathologic study of 139 cases. Pediatr Pathol 9:387–407, 1989.
47. Cohen AF, Mitsudo S, Ruben RJ: Nasopharyngeal teratoma in the neonate. Int J Pediatr Otorhinolaryngol 14:187–195, 1987.
48. Coit W, Harnsberger H, Osborn A, et al: Ranulas and their mimics: CT evaluation. Radiology 163:211–216, 1987.
49. Cote D, Gianoli G: Fourth branchial cleft cysts. Otolaryngol Head Neck Surg 114:95–97, 1996.

50. Crawford SC, Harnsberger HR, Johnson L: Fibromatosis colli of infancy. AJR Am J Roentgenol 151:1183, 1988.
51. Cressman W, Myer C: Clinical and pathologic diagnosis: Pathologic quiz case 1. Arch Otolaryngol Head Neck Surg 118:772–774, 1992.
52. Cressman WR, Myer III CM: Pathologic quiz case 1. Arch Otolaryngol Head Neck Surg 118:772–774, 1992.
53. Crist WM, Kelly DR, Ragab AJ, et al: Predictive ability of Lukes-Collins classification for immunologic phenotypes of childhood non-Hodgkin's lymphoma: An institutional series and literature review. Cancer 48:2070–2075, 1981.
54. Cushing BA, Slovis TL, Philippart AI, et al: A rational approach to cervical neuroblastoma. Cancer 50:785–787, 1982.
55. Das Gupta TK, Brasfield RD, Strong EW, Hajdu SI. Benign solitary schwannomas (neurilemomas). Cancer 24:355, 1969.
56. Davis KR: Embolization of epistaxis and juvenile nasopharyngeal angiofibromas. AJNR Am J Neuroradiol 7:953, 1986.
57. Day LH, Arnold GE: Rare tumors of the ear, nose and throat: Second series: Uncommon benign tumors of the head and neck. Laryngoscope 81:138, 1971.
58. Deane S, Telander R: Surgery for thyroglossal duct and branchial cleft anomalies. Am J Surg 136:348–353, 1978.
59. Derdyn CP, Moran CJ, Wippold FJ II, et al: MRI of ethesioneuroblastoma. J Comput Assist Tomogr 18:16–21, 1994.
60. DeVries SM, Decker TN: Frequency dependence of interear asymmetries and binaural interaction in the human ABR. Ear Hear 9:275–282, 1988.
61. Dietrich RB, Kangarloo H: Retroperitoneal mass with intradural extension: Value of magnetic resonance imaging in neuroblastoma. AJR Am J Roentgenol 146:251–4, 1986.
62. Dorfman RF, Warnke R: Lymphadenopathy simulating the malignant lymphomas. Hum Pathol 5:519, 1974.
63. Easton JM, Levine PH, Hyams VJ: Nasopharyngeal carcinoma in the United States: A pathologic study of 177 U.S. and 30 foreign cases. Arch Otolaryngol 106:88, 1980.
64. Elkon D, Hightower SI, Lim ML, et al: Esthesioneuroblastoma. Cancer 44:1087–1094, 1979.
65. Ellis H: Cervical thymic cysts. Br J Surg 54:17–20, 1967.
66. Enzinger FM, Weiss SW: Soft Tissue Tumors. St. Louis, CV Mosby, 1983.
66a. Ewing J: Neoplastic Diseases. Philadelphia, WB Saunders, 1942, pp 1057–1060.
67. Faerber E, Swartz J: Imaging of neck masses in infants and children. Crit Rev Diagn Imaging 31:283–314, 1991.
68. Fahmy S: Cervical thymic cysts: Their pathogenesis and relationship to branchial cysts. J Laryngol Otol 86:47–60, 1974.
69. Favus MJ, Schneider AB, Stachura ME, et al: Thyroid cancer occurring as a late consequence of head-and-neck irradiation: Evaluation of 1056 patients. N Engl J Med 294, 1976.
70. Fedder M, Gonzales MF: Nasopharyngeal carcinoma: A brief review. Am J Med 79:365–369, 1985.
71. Fitzpatrick PJ, Briant TD, Berman JM: The nasopharyngeal angiofibroma. Arch Otolaryngol 106:234, 1980.
72. Fletcher BD, Kopiwoda SY, Strandjord SE, et al: Abdominal neuroblastoma: Magnetic resonance imaging and tissue characterization. Radiology 155:699–703, 1985.
73. Frankenthaler RA, Seilin RV, Cangir A, Goepfert H: Lymph node metastases from papillary-follicular thyroid carcinoma in young patients. Am J Surg 160:341–343, 1990.
74. Friedman AP, Haller JO, Goodman JD, Nagar H: Sonographic evaluation of noninflammatory neck masses in children. Radiology 147:693, 1983.
75. Front D, Ben-Haim S, Israel O, et al: Lymphoma: Predictive value of Ga-67 scintigraphy after treatment. Radiology 182:359–362, 1992.
76. Fuji Y, Wakasugi M, Yamada K, et al: A study of ultrasonic diagnostic criteria for thyroid nodules. Paper presented at Proceedings of the Japanese Society of Ultrasound in Medicine, Tahamatsu, Japan, 1990.
77. Gainsford JC, Anderson US: First branchial cleft cysts and sinuses. Plast Reconstruct Surg 55:299–304, 1975.
78. Garcia CJ, Daneman A, McHugh K, et al: Sonography in thyroid carcinoma in children. Br J Radiol 65:977–982, 1992.
79. Gehan EA, Glover FN, Maurer HM, et al: Prognostic factors in children with rhabdomyosarcoma. Natl Cancer Inst Monogr 83–92, 1981.
80. Ginsberg LE: Neoplastic diseases affecting the central skull base: CT and MR imaging. AJR Am J Roentgenol 159:581–589, 1992.

81. Glasier CM, Seibert JJ, Williamson SI, et al: High resolution ultrasound characterization of soft tissue masses in children. Pediatr Radiol 17:233–237, 1987.
82. Goldstein G, Mackey IR: The Human Thymus. St. Louis, Warren H. Green, 1969.
83. Gooder P, Farrington T: Extracranial neurilemmoma of the head and neck. J Laryngol Otol 94:243, 1980.
84. Gore DO, Rankow R, Hanford JM: Parapharyngeal neurilemmoma. Surg Gynecol Obstet 103:193, 1956.
85. Gorman B, Charboneau JW, James EM, et al: Medullary thyroid carcinoma: Role of high-resolution US. Radiology 162:147–150, 1987.
86. Griffith BH: Frontonasal tumors: Their diagnosis and management. Plast Reconstr Surg 57:692, 1976.
87. Grosfeld JL, Ballantine TVN, Lowe D, Baehner RL: Benign and malignant teratomas in children: Analysis of 160 cases. World J Surg 4:29, 1976.
88. Guba AM Jr, Adam AE, Jaques DA, Chambers RG: Cervical presentation of thymic cysts. Am J Surg 136:430–436, 1978.
89. Guillane PJ, Davidson J, O'Dwyer T, Forte V: Juvenile angiofibroma: A review of the literature and case series report. Laryngoscope 102:928–933, 1992.
90. Gundry SR, Wesley JR, Klein MD, et al: Cervical teratomas in the newborn. J Pediatr Surg 18:382–386, 1983.
91. Hajdu SI, Shiu MH, Fortner JG: Tendosynovial sarcoma: A clinicopathological study of 136 cases. Cancer 39:1201, 1977.
92. Han MH, Chang KH, Kim IO, et al: Non-Hodgkin lymphoma of the central skull base: MR manifestations. J Comput Assist Tomogr 17:567–571, 1993.
93. Harnsberger H: Handbook of Head and Neck Imaging. St. Louis, Mosby–Year Book, 1995.
94. Harnsberger H, Bragg D, Osborn A, et al: Non-Hodgkin's lymphoma of the head and neck: CT evaluation of nodal and extranodal sites. AJNR Am J Neuroradiol 8:673–678, 1987.
95. Harnsberger H, Mancuso A, Muraki A, et al: Branchial cleft anomalies and their mimics: Computed tomographic evaluation. Radiology 152:739–748, 1984.
96. Harness JK, Thompson NW, McLeod MK, Pasieka JL, Fukuuchi A: Differentiated thyroid carcinoma in children and adolescents. World J Surg 16:547–554, 1992.
97. Hawkins DB, Park R: Teratomas of the pharynx and neck. Ann Otol 81:848–853, 1972.
98. Healy GB: Malignant tumors of the head and neck in children: Diagnosis and treatment. Otolaryngol Clin North Am 13:483–488, 1980.
99. Heroman WH, Golden SM, Yudt WM: Nasopharyngeal teratoma in the newborn. Ear Nose Throat J 59:19–27, 1980.
100. Hirsch RJ, Yousem DM, Loevner L, et al: Synovial sarcomas of the head and neck. MR findings. AJR Am J Roentgenol 169:1185–1188, 1997.
101. Hollinshead WH: Anatomy for Surgeons: The Head and Neck, vol 1. New York, Harper and Row, 1968.
102. Holman CB, Miller WE: Juvenile nasopharyngeal fibroma. Am J Roentgenol 94:292, 1965.
103. Holt GR, McManus K, Newman RK, et al: Computed tomography in the diagnosis of deep-neck infections. Arch Otolaryngol 108:693–696, 1982.
104. Howell C: The sublingual dermoid cyst. Oral Surg Oral Med Oral Pathol 59:578–580, 1985.
105. Howell CG, Van Tassel P, EL Gammal T: High resolution computed tomography in neonatal nasopharyngeal teratoma. J Comput Assist Tomogr 8:1179, 1984.
106. Hsu MM, Huang SC, Lynn TC, et al: The survival of patients with nasopharyngeal carcinoma. Otolaryngol Head Neck Surg 90:289–295, 1982.
107. Hulbert KF: Congenital torticollis. J Bone Joint Surg 32B:50, 1950.
108. Hunter T, Paplanus S, Chernin M, Coulthard S: Dermoid cyst of the floor of the mouth: CT appearance. AJR Am J Roentgenol 141:1239–1240, 1983.
109. Hurst RW, Erickson S, Cail WS, et al: Computed tomographic features of esthesioneuroblastoma. Neuroradiology 31:253–257, 1989.
110. Hyams VJ, Batsakis JG, Michaels L: Tumors of the upper respiratory tract and ear. Fascicle 25, 2nd Series. Atlas of Tumor Pathology. Washington, DC, Armed Forces Institute of Pathology, 1988, pp 180–181.

111. Jaffe BF, Jaffe N: Head and neck tumors in children. Pediatrics 51:731–740, 1973.
112. Jenkins RD, Anderson JR, Jereb B, et al: Nasopharyngeal carcinoma—a retrospective review of patients less than thirty years of age: A report from Children's Cancer Study Group. Cancer 47:360–366, 1981.
113. Johnson GF, Weisman PA: Radiological features of dermoid cysts of the nose. Radiology 82:1016, 1964.
114. Jones JE, Hession B: Cervical thymic cysts. Ear Nose Throat J 75:678–680, 1996.
115. Jordan RB, Gauderer MW. Cervical teratomas: An analysis. Literature review and proposed classification. J Pediatr Surg 23:583–591, 1988.
116. Kaban L, Mulliken JB: Vascular anomalies of the maxillofacial regions. J Oral Maxillofac Surg 44:203, 1986.
117. Kadin MR, Thompson RW, Bentson JR, et al: Angiographic evaluation of the regression of an extensive juvenile nasopharyngeal angiofibroma after radiation therapy: A case report with therapeutic implications. Br J Radiol 47:902–905, 1974.
118. Kadish S, Goodman M, Wang CC: Olfactory neuroblastoma: A clinical analysis of 17 cases. Cancer 37:1571–1576, 1976.
119. Kapadia SB, Popek EJ, Barnes L: Pediatric otorhinolaryngic pathology: Diagnosis of selected lesions. Pathol Annu 29:159–209, 1994.
120. Kaplan HS: Hodgkin's disease: Unfolding concepts concerning its nature, management and prognosis. Cancer 45:2439–2474, 1980.
121. Kasper ME, Parsons JT, Mancuso AA, et al: Radiation therapy for juvenile angiofibroma: Evaluation by CT and MRI, analysis of tumor regression, and selection of patients. Int J Radiat Oncol Biol Phys 25:689–694, 1993.
122. Katz AG, Passy V, Kaplan L: Neurogenous neoplasma of major nerves of the face and neck. Arch Surg 103:51–56, 1971.
123. Kaufman FR, Roe TF, Isaacs H Jr, Weitzman JJ: Metastatic medullary thyroid carcinoma in young children with mucosal neuroma syndrome. Pediatrics 70:263–267, 1982.
124. Kelley DJ, Gerber ME, Willging JP: Cervicomediastinal thymic cysts. Int J Pediatr Otorhinolaryngol 39:139–146, 1997.
125. Kiyosue H, Miyake H, Komatsu E, Mori H: MRI of cervical masses of thymic origin. J Comput Assist Tomogr 18:206–208, 1994.
126. Kjeldsberg CR, Wilson JF, Berard CW: Non-Hodgkin's lymphoma in children. Hum Pathol 14:612, 1983.
127. Koeller KK, Alamo L, Adair CF, Smirniotopoulos JG: Congenital cystic masses of the neck: Radiologic-pathologic correlation. Radiographics 19:121–146, 152–153, 1999.
128. Kraus R, Han BK, Babcock DS, Oestreich AE: Sonography of neck masses in children. AJR Am J Roentgenol 146:609, 1986.
129. Kretschmar CS, Colbach C, Bhan I, Crombleholme TM: Desmoplastic small cell tumor: A report of three cases and a review of the literature. J Pediatr Hematol Oncol 18:293–298, 1996.
130. Kreutzer EW, Jafek BW, Johnson ML, Zunkel DE: Ultrasonography in the preoperative evaluation of neck abscesses. Head Neck Surg 4:290–295, 1982.
131. Krugman ME, Rosin HD, Toker C: Synovial sarcoma of the head and neck. Arch Otolaryngol 98:53, 1973.
132. Lack EE: Extragonadal germ cell tumors of the head and neck region: Review of 16 cases. Hum Pathol 16:56–64, 1985.
133. Laine FJ, Nadel L, Braun IF: CT and MR imaging of the central skull base: Part 2. Pathologic spectrum. Radiographics 10:797–821, 1990.
134. LaQuaglia MP, Corbally MT, Heller G, et al: Recurrence and morbidity in differentiated thyroid cancer in children. Surgery 104:1149, 1988.
135. Lasjaunias PL: The radioanatomical basis of arterial embolization for epistaxis. J Neuroradiol 6:45–53, 1979.
136. Lasjaunias P, Picard L, Manelfe C, et al: Angiofibroma of the nasopharynx. J Neuroradiol 7:73–79, 1980.
137. Latack J, Hutchinson R, Heyn R: Imaging of rhabdomyosarcomas of the head and neck. AJNR Am J Neuroradiol 8:353–359, 1987.
138. Latifi HR, Siegel MJ: Color Doppler flow imaging of pediatric soft tissue masses. J Ultrasound Med 13:165–169, 1994.
139. Lee Y-Y, Van Tassel P, Nauert C, et al: Lymphomas of the head and neck: CT findings at initial presentation. AJNR Am J Neuroradiol 6:665–671, 1987.
140. Levine PA, McClean WC, Cantrell RW: Esthesioneuroblastoma: The University of Virginia Experience 1960–1985. Laryngoscope 96:742–746, 1986.
141. Lim-Dunham JE, Feinstein KA, Yousefzadeh DK, Ben-Ami T: Sonographic demonstration of a normal thyroid gland excludes ectopic thyroid in patients with thyroglossal duct cyst. AJR Am J Roentgenol 164:1489–1494, 1995.
142. Liston SL, Siegel LG: Branchial cysts, sinuses, and fistulae. Ear Nose Throat J 58:9–17, 1979.
143. Lloyd GA, Phelps PD: Juvenile angiofibroma: Imaging by magnetic resonance, CT and conventional techniques. Clin Otolaryngol 11:247–259, 1986.
144. Lombardi F, Gasparini M, Gianni C, et al: Nasopharyngeal carcinoma in childhood. Med Pediatr Oncol 10:243–250, 1982.
145. Lukes RJ, Butler J, Hicks EB: The prognosis of Hodgkin's disease according to the histologic type and the clinical stage: Role of the reactions of the host. Nouv Rev Fr Hematol 6:15–22, 1966.
146. MacMahon B: Epidemiology of Hodgkin's disease. Cancer Res 26:1189–201, 1966.
147. Mancuso AA, Dillon WP: The neck. Radiol Clin North Am 27:407, 1989.
148. Maran ADG, Buchanan DR: Branchial cysts, sinuses, and fistulae. Clin Otolaryngol 3:77–92, 1978.
149. Marra S, Hotaling AJ, Raslan W: Cervical thymic cyst. Otolaryngol Head Neck Surg 112:338–340, 1995.
150. Maurer HM: The intergroup rhabdomyosarcoma study: Update, November 1978. Natl Cancer Inst Monogr 56:61–68, 1981.
151. Maurer HM, Beltangady M, Gehan EA, et al: The intergroup rhabdomyosarcoma study: I. A final report. Cancer 61:209–220, 1988.
152. Maurer HM, Moon T, Donaldson M, et al: The intergroup rhabdomyosarcoma study: A preliminary report. Cancer 40:2015–2026, 1977.
153. McCurdy JA Jr, Nadalo LA, Yim DW: Evaluation of extrathyroid masses of the head and neck with gray scale ultrasound. Arch Otolaryngol 106:83–87, 1980.
154. McDonald D: Sternomastoid tumour and muscular torticollis. J Bone Joint Surg 51:432–443, 1969.
155. McQuown SA, Smith JD, Gallo AE Jr: Intracranial extension of nasal dermoids. Neurosurgery 12:531, 1983.
156. Meissner WA, Warren S: Tumors of the thyroid gland. Atlas of Tumor Pathology. Washington, DC, Armed Forces Institute of Pathology, 1969.
157. Meyer JS, Hoffer FA, Barnes PD, Mulliken JB: Biological classification of soft-tissue vascular anomalies: MR correlation. AJR Am J Roentgenol 157:559, 1991.
158. Michael A, Mafee M, Valvassori G, Tan W. Dynamic computed tomography of the head and neck: differential diagnosis value. Radiology 1985:413–419, 1985.
159. Micheau C: A new histochemical approach to olfactory esthesioneuroma: A nasal tumor of neural crest origin. Cancer 40:314–318, 1977.
160. Mikal S: Cervical thymic cyst: Case report and review of the literature. Arch Surg 109:558–562, 1974.
161. Miller M, DeVito M: Cervical thymic cyst. Otolaryngol Head Neck Surg 112:586–588, 1995.
162. Miller M, Rao V, Tom B: Cystic masses of the head and neck: Pitfalls in CT and MR interpretation. AJR Am J Roentgenol 159:601–607, 1992.
163. Miser AW, Miser JS: The treatment of cancer pain in children. Pediatr Clin North Am 36:979–999, 1989.
164. Montgomery WW: Surgery of the Upper Respiratory System. Philadelphia, Lea & Febiger, 1973.
165. Moore DM: Synovial sarcoma of the head and neck. Arch Otolaryngol Head Neck Surg 113:311–313, 1987.
166. Morton MJ, Berquist TH, McLeod RA, et al: MR imaging of synovial sarcoma. AJR Am J Roentgenol 156:337–340, 1991.
167. Muhlbauer WD, Dittmar W: Hereditary median dermoid cysts of the nose. Br J Plast Surg 29:334–340, 1976.
168. Mukherji SM, Tart RP, Slattery WH: Evaluation of first branchial anomalies by CT and MR. J Comput Assist Tomogr 17:576, 1993.
169. Mulliken JB, Glowacki J: Hemangiomas and vascular malformations in infants and children: A classification based on endothelial characteristics. Plast Reconstr Surg 69:412–420, 1982.
170. Nager GT: Cephaloceles. Laryngoscope 97:77–84, 1987.
171. Nakashima T, Kimmelman CP, Snow JB Jr: Structure of human fetal and adult olfactory neuroepithelium. Arch Otolaryngol 110:641–646, 1984.
172. New G: Congenital cysts of the tongue, the floor of the mouth, the pharynx, and the larynx. Arch Otolaryngol 45:145–158, 1947.

173. New G, Erich J: Dermoid cysts of the head and neck. Surg Gynecol Obstet 65:48–55, 1937.
174. Nguyen Q, deTar M, Wells W, Crockett D: Cervical thymic cyst: Case reports and review of the literature. Laryngoscope 106:247–252, 1996.
175. Nicolai P, Luzzago F, Maroldi R: Nasopharyngeal cysts. Arch Otolaryngol Head Neck Surg 115:860, 1989.
176. Noma S, Kanaoka M, Minami S, et al: Thyroid masses: MR imaging and pathologic correlation. Radiology 168:759–764, 1988.
177. Noyek AM, Friedberg J: Thyroglossal duct and ectopic thyroid disorders. Otolaryngol Clin North Am 14:187–201, 1981.
178. Nyberg DA, Jeffrey RB, Brant-Zawadzki M, et al: Computed tomography of cervical infections. J Comput Assist Tomogr 9:288–296, 1985.
179. Okuda Y, Oi S: Nasal dermal sinus and dermoid cyst with intrafacial extension. Childs Nerv Syst 3:40–43, 1987.
180. Olsen KD, Maragos NE, Weiland LH: First branchial cleft anomalies. Laryngoscope 90:423, 1980.
181. Paonessa DF, Goldstein JC: Anatomy and physiology of head and neck infections (with emphasis on the fascia of the face and neck). Otolaryngol Clin North Am 9:561, 1976.
182. Park Y: Evaluation of neck masses in children. Am Fam Physician 51:1904–1912, 1995.
183. Parker G, Harnsberger H, Smoker W: The anterior and posterior cervical spaces. Semin US CT MR 12:257–273, 1991.
184. Pensler JM, Bauer BS, Naidich TP: Craniofacial dermoids. Plast Reconstr Surg 82:953–958, 1988.
185. Phillips CD, Futterer SF, Lipper MH, Levine PA: Sinonasal undifferentiated carcinoma: CT and MR imaging of an uncommon neoplasm of the nasal cavity. Radiology 202:477–480, 1997.
186. Pinczower E, Crockett DM, Atkinson JB, Kun S: Preoperative thyroid scanning in presumed thyroglossal duct cysts. Arch Otolaryngol Head Neck Surg 118:985, 1992.
187. Pinelli V, Pierro V, Bottero S, et al: Dysontogenetic neoplasms of the thyroid gland in infancy: Two case reports. Int J Pediatr Otorhinolaryngol 10:101–10, 1985.
188. Plantaz D, Hartmann O, Kalifa C, et al: Dumbbell neuroblastoma. Experience at the Gustave Roussy Institute in 38 cases treated from 1982 to 1987. Arch Fr Pediatr 48:529–533, 1991 (erratum, 48:742, 1991).
189. Pollock JA, Newton TH, Hoyt WF: Transsphenoidal and transethmoidal encephaloceles: A review of clinical and roentgen features in 8 cases. Radiology 90:442–453, 1968.
190. Poncelet V, Dooms G, Mathurin P, Cornelius G: Contributory aspects of MRI in the evaluation of basal encephaloceles. J Neuroradiol 16:214–220, 1989.
191. Pounds LA: Neck masses of congenital origin. Pediatr Clin North Am 28:841–844, 1981.
192. Rapport RL II, Dunn RC Jr, Alhady F: Anterior encephalocele. J Neurosurg 54:213–219, 1981.
193. Reede DL, Bergeron RT, Som PM: CT of thyroglossal duct cysts. Radiology 157:121–125, 1985.
194. Rice DH, Coulthard SW: Neurogenic tumors of the head and neck in children. Ann Plast Surg 2:441, 1978.
195. Robinson DL, Destian S, Hinton DR: Synovial sarcoma of the neck: Radiographic findings with a review of the literature. Am J Otolaryngol 15:46–53, 1994.
196. Rosen L, Hanafee W, Nahum A: Nasopharyngeal angiofibroma: An angiographic evaluation. Radiology 86:103–107, 1966.
197. Rosenfeld CR, Coln CD, Duenhoelter JH: Fetal cervical teratoma as a cause of polyhydramnios. Pediatrics 64:176–179, 1979.
198. Rosevear W, Singer M: Symptomatic cervical thymic duct cyst in a neonate. Otolaryngol Head Neck Surg 89:738–741, 1981.
199. Roth JA, Enzinger FM, Tannenbaum M: Synovial sarcoma of the neck: A follow-up study of 24 cases. Cancer 35:1243–1253, 1975.
200. Rothschild MA, Urken ML, Catalano P: Evaluation and management of congenital cervical teratoma: A case report and review. Arch Otolaryngol Head Neck Surg 120:444, 1994.
201. Rowe LD: Neonatal airway obstruction secondary to nasopharyngeal teratoma. Otolaryngol Head Neck Surg 88:221–226, 1980.
202. Samuel AM, Sharma SM: Differentiated thyroid cancer in children and adolescents. Cancer 67:2186–2190, 1991.
203. Saphir O: Teratoma of the neck. Am J Pathol 5:313–323, 1929.
204. Reference deleted.
205. Scheible W, Leopold GR, Woo VL, Gosink BB: High-resolution real-time ultrasonography of thyroid nodules. Radiology 133:413–417, 1979.
206. Schuster JJ, Phillips CD, Levine PA: MR of esthesioneuroblastoma (olfactory neuroblastoma) and appearance after craniofacial resection. AJNR Am Neuroradiol 15:1169–1177, 1994.
207. Schwartz R, Movassaghi N, Marion E: Rhabdomyosarcoma of the middle ear: A wolf in sheep's clothing. Pediatrics 65:1131–1132, 1980.
208. Segal K, Sidi J, Levy R, Abraham A: Thyroid carcinoma in children and adolescents. Ann Otol Rhinol Laryngol 94:346–349, 1985.
209. Sessions RB: Nasal dermal sinuses—new concepts and explanations: II. Laryngoscope 92(suppl 29), 1982.
210. Sessions RB, Bryan RN, Naclerio, et al: RM. Radiographic staging of juvenile angiofibroma. Head Neck Surg 3:279–283, 1981.
211. Sessions RB, Wills PI, Alford BR, et al: Juvenile nasopharyngeal angiofibroma: Radiographic aspects. Laryngoscope 86:2–18, 1976.
212. Shah JP, Fighali J: Esthesioneuroblastoma. Am J Surg 142:456–458, 1981.
213. Sham JS, Wei WI, Lau SK, et al: Serous otitis media: An opportunity for early recognition of nasopharyngeal carcinoma. Arch Otolaryngol Head Neck Surg 118:794–797, 1992.
214. Shanmugaratnam K, Chan SH, de-The G, et al: Histopathology of nasopharyngeal carcinoma correlations with epidemiology, survival rates, and other biological characteristics. Cancer 44:1029, 1991.
215. Shidara K, Uruma T, Yasuoka Y, Kamei T: Two cases of nasopharyngeal branchial cyst. J Laryngol Otol 107:453, 1993.
216. Shimada H, Chatten J, Newton WA: Histopathologic prognostic factors in neuroblastic tumors: Definition of subtypes of ganglioneuroblastoma and age-linked classification of neuroblastoma. J Natl Cancer Inst 73:405, 1984.
217. Shlansky-Goldberg RD, Rao VM, Choi HY, et al: Hodgkin disease of the maxillary sinus. J Comput Assist Tomogr 12:507–509, 1988.
218. Shmookler BM, Enzinger FM, Brannon RB: Orofacial synovial sarcoma: A clinicopathologic study of 11 new cases and review of the literature. Cancer 50:269, 1982.
219. Sigal R, Chancelier MD, Luboinski B: Synovial sarcomas of the head and neck: CT and MR findings. AJNR Am J Neuroradiol 13:1459, 1992.
220. Silver AJ, Mawad ME, Hilal SK, et al: Computed tomography of the nasopharynx and related spaces. Radiology 147:725–731, 1983.
221. Simeone JF, Daniels GH, Mueller PR: High-resolution real-time sonography of the thyroid. Radiology 145:431, 1982.
222. Singh RK, Hasan SA, Srivastava RW: Teratoma of the nasopharynx. Ear Nose Throat J 67:692–695, 1988.
223. Smith JF, Kielmovitch I: Branchial cysts anomaly in a newborn. Laryngoscope 100:163–165, 1989.
224. Smith MCF, Smith RJH, Bailey CM: Primary cervical neuroblastoma in infants. J Laryngol Otol 99:209–214, 1985.
225. Smirniotopoulos J, Chiechi M: Teratomas, dermoids, and epidermoids of the head and neck. Radiographics 15:1437–1455, 1995.
226. Snow JB Jr: Neoplasms of the nasopharynx in children. Otolaryngol Clin North Am 10:11–24, 1977.
227. Solbiati L, Cioffi V, Ballarati E: Ultrasonography of the neck. Radiol Clin North Am 30:941–954, 1992.
228. Soller AN: Nasopharyngeal teratoma. Arch Otolaryngol 82:49–52, 1965.
229. Solomon JR, Rangecroft L: Thyroglossal-duct lesions in childhood. J Pediatr Surg 19:555–560, 1984.
230. Som P: Cystic lesions of the neck. Postgrad Radiol 7:211–236, 1987.
231. Som P, Sacher M, Lanzieri C, et al: Parenchymal cysts of the lower neck. Radiology 157:399–406, 1985.
232. Som PM, Cohen FA, Sacher M: The angiomatous polyp and the angiofibroma: Two different lesions. Radiology 144:329–334, 1982.
233. Som PM, Curtin HD: Head and Neck Imaging. St. Louis, Mosby–Year Book, 1996.
234. Som PM, Lidov M, Brandwein M, et al: Sinonasal esthesioneuroblastoma with intracranial extension: Marginal tumor cysts as a diagnostic MR finding. AJNR Am J Neuroradiol 15:1259–1262, 1994.
235. Som PM, Shugal JMA, Cohen BA, Biller HF: The nonspecificity of the antral bowing sign in maxillary sinus pathology. J Comput Assist Tomogr 5:350, 1981.
236. Stout AP: The peripheral manifestations of the specific nerve sheath tumor (neurilemomas). Cancer 24:751, 1935.
237. Su C-Y, Hsu S-P, Lui C-C: Computed tomography, magnetic reso-

nance imaging, and electromyographic studies of tensor veli palatini muscles in patient with nasopharyngeal carcinoma. Laryngoscope 103:673–678, 1993.

238. Sutow WW: Cancer of the head and neck in children. JAMA 190: 414, 1964.

239. Tanimura F, Tachibana M, Dejima K, et al: Teratoma of the soft palate with multifocal cyst formation in the tongue and the brain. Arch Otorhinolaryngol 243:320–323, 1986.

240. Tapper D, Lack EE: Teratomas in infancy and childhood. Ann Surg 198:398–409, 1984.

241. Taxy J, Hidvegi DF: Olfactory neuroblastoma: An ultrastructural study. Cancer 39:131–138, 1977.

242. Telander R, Deane S: Thyroglossal and branchial cleft cysts and sinuses. Surg Clin North Am 57:779–791, 1977.

243. Telander R, Filston H: Review of head and neck lesions in infancy and childhood. Surg Clin North Am 72:1429–1447, 1992.

244. Thomas JR: Thyroglossal-duct cysts. Ear Nose Throat J 58:21–29, 1979.

245. Tom LW, Rossiter JL, Sutton LN, Davidson RS: Torticollis in children. Otolaryngol Head Neck Surg 105:1, 1991.

246. Toriumi DM, Atihal RA, Murad T, Sisson GA Sr: Extracranial neurogenic tumors of the head and neck. Otolaryngol Clin North Am 19:609–617, 1986.

247. Tovi F, Mares A: The aberrant cervical thymus: Embryology, pathology and clinical implications. Am J Surg 136:631–637, 1978.

248. Ultmann JE, Cunningham JK, Gelhorn A: The clinical picture of Hodgkin's disease. Cancer Res 26:1047, 1966.

249. Vanhoenacker P, Hermans R, Sneyers W, et al: Atypical aesthesio-neuroblastoma: CT and MRI findings. Neuroradiology 35:466–467, 1993.

250. Vassilopoulou-Sellin R, Klein MJ, Smith TH, et al: Pulmonary metastases in children and young adults with differentiated thyroid cancer. Cancer 71:1348–1352, 1992.

251. Viswanathan K, Gierlowski TC, Schneider AB: Childhood thyroid cancer: Characteristics and long-term outcome in children irradiated for benign conditions of the head and neck. Arch Pediatr Adolesc Med 148:260–265, 1994.

252. Vogl T, Steger W, Ihrier S, et al: Cystic masses in the floor of the mouth: Value of MR imaging in planning surgery. AJR Am J Roentgenol 161:183–186, 1993.

253. Wadsworth DT, Siegel MJ: Thyroglossal duct cysts: Variability of sonographic findings. AJR Am J Roentgenol 163:1475–1477, 1994.

254. Wagner CW, Vinocur CD, Weintraub WH, Golladay ES: Respiratory complications in cervical thymic cysts. J Pediatr Surg 23:657–660, 1988.

255. Walker EA: Teratomas of the pharynx. Am Surg 29:219–226, 1963.

256. Weber PC, Rueger RG, Pickeral J: Thymic cysts. Am J Otolaryngol 17:64–66, 1996.

257. Wexler LH, Lee JH. Pediatric soft tissue sarcomas. Cancer 44: 221, 1994.

258. Wiatrak B, Myer C, Bratcher G: Report of a nasopharyngeal teratoma evaluated with magnetic resonance imaging. Otolaryngology 102:186–190, 1990.

259. Winship T, Rosvoll RF: Thyroid carcinoma in childhood: Final report on a 20-year study. Clin Proc Children's Hosp Wash 26: 327, 1970.

260. Work WP: Newer concepts of first branchial cleft defects. Laryngoscope 82:1581–1593, 1972.

261. Yasumoto M, Shibuya H, Takeda M, Korenaga T: Squamous cell carcinoma of the oral cavity: MR findings and value of T1- versus T2-weighted fast spin-echo images. AJR Am J Roentgenol 164: 981–987, 1994.

262. Yokota A, Matsukado Y, Fuwa I, et al: Anterior basal encephalocele of the neonatal and infantile period. Neurosurgery 19:468–478, 1986.

263. Young JL Jr, Miller RW: Incidence of malignant tumors in the U.S. in children. J Pediatr 86:254, 1975.

264. Yousem D, Lexa F, Bilaniuk L, Simmerman R: Rhabdomyosarcomas in the Head Neck: MR imaging evaluation. Radiology 177:683–686, 1990.

265. Yousem SA, Colby TV, Urich H: Malignant epitheliod schwannomas arising in a benign schwannoma. Cancer 55:2799, 1985.

266. Zarbo R, McClatchey K, Areen R, Baker S: Thymopharyngeal duct cyst: A form of cervical thymus. Ann Otol Rhinol Laryngol 92: 284–289, 1983.

267. Zimmerman D, Hay ID, Gough IR, et al: Papillary thyroid carcinoma in children and adults: Long-term follow up of 1039 patients conservatively treated at one institution during three decades. Surgery 104: 1157–1166, 1988.

268. Zohar Y, Strauss M, Laurian N: Adolescent versus adult thyroid carcinoma. Laryngoscope 96:555, 1986.

Part
IV

Imaging of the Spine

Edited by
Jeffrey L. Sunshine

22

Degenerative Diseases of the Spine

David S. Jacobs

Back pain resulting from degenerative disease of the spine is one of the most common causes of disability in adults of working age. Between 60% and 80% of adults suffer from low back pain at some time in their lives. Medical costs resulting from back pain exceed $50 billion per year and may be as high as $100 billion.[23, 24, 38, 83]

Back pain results from many causes, including degenerative and congenital spinal stenosis, neoplasm, infection, trauma, and inflammatory or arthritic processes. Acquired spinal stenosis due to degenerative joint and disk disease accounts for the vast majority of cases.[57]

The following structures may be responsible for the origin of degenerative spinal stenosis:

1. Bone (spondylolisthesis, spondylolysis, osteophytosis).
2. Ligament (hypertrophy of the spinal ligaments, particularly the ligamentum flavum).
3. Facet joint (facet hypertrophy, synovial cyst).
4. Disk (bulging and herniation).

Most often, acquired narrowing of the spinal canal is due to a combination of bone, ligament, joint, and disk disease. The most common location of these changes is the lumbar spine, followed by the cervical spine. Thoracic disk herniation, formerly thought to be rare, is now being recognized with increased frequency with the advent of magnetic resonance imaging (MRI).[75]

Before the emergence of computed tomography (CT), plain films of the spine, spinal tomography, myelography, and diskography were the primary imaging modalities for the diagnosis of spinal stenosis and disk herniation. CT scans provided a noninvasive, nonoperator-dependent method of direct imaging of the spinal canal without injection of intrathecal contrast. CT was superior to myelography in visualizing lateral foraminal stenoses, disk protrusions, and lateral recess stenosis. In addition, it overcame the myelographic limitation of visualizing lower lumbar narrowing. In the latter case, abundant epidural fat in the lower lumbar spine, particularly at L5, may prevent displacement of the myelographic column by a protruding disk.

Finally, and most important, myelography does not delineate the cause of the narrowing (i.e., disk versus ligamentous versus bony hypertrophy). CT scans can reveal the cause of the pathology directly. Postmyelography CT scans offer even more sensitivity because of the increased the contrast between thecal sac, nerve roots, and soft tissues of the spinal column.[19]

With the development of MRI, the debate over CT scanning versus myelography became moot. MRI has become the modality of choice in the evaluation of spinal degenerative disease. MRI is superior even to contrast-enhanced CT scans in distinguishing bone, disk, ligament, nerve, thecal sac, and spinal cord. MRI provides multiplanar imaging capability. Pulse sequences can be adjusted to evaluate specific areas of interest or to more accurately define the disease process.

CT does retain some advantage over MRI with regard to bone detail, such as in the evaluation of osteophytes. CT and myelography will remain important in patients who, for technical reasons, cannot enter the MRI scanner (e.g., those with pacemakers or claustrophobia) or in patients whose MRI findings do not correlate with clinical symptoms. Many surgeons are still more comfortable with the bone detail of CT scans as a superior "road map" for the operating room. Additionally, recent technology allows the construction of a "virtual" spine from high-resolution CT images. Superb three-dimensional (3D) images of the spine can be obtained from high-resolution axial data acquired from helical CT scanners. This provides surgeons with a preoperative and intraoperative road map of the surgical site, thus improving accuracy and safety (Fig. 22–1). CT, therefore, still has a major role in the evaluation and management of degenerative spine disease.

Lumbar Spine
Anatomic Considerations

A more extensive discussion of the anatomy of the spine is presented in Chapter 24; however, a brief review of the lumbar diskovertebral complex as it relates to degenerative disease is warranted here.

The spinal canal is formed by the vertebral body anteriorly, the pedicles laterally, the laminae posterolaterally, and the base of the spinous process posteriorly (Fig. 22–2). This arrangement forms a protective ring for the neural tube. At the inferolateral aspect of each vertebra, a bony tunnel, the neural foramen, is appreciated bilaterally. The walls of the foramina are formed by the vertebral pedicle superiorly, the pedicle of the next vertebral body inferiorly, the facets posteriorly, and the diskovertebral junction anteriorly. When viewed sagittally, the foramina have a keyhole appearance and are 5 to 10 mm deep (Fig. 22–3). All of these relationships are important to understand when evaluating spinal stenosis.

Inferior to the termination of the spinal cord at approximately T12-L1, the lumbosacral nerve roots travel in a bundle within the dural sac. As this bundle travels inferi-

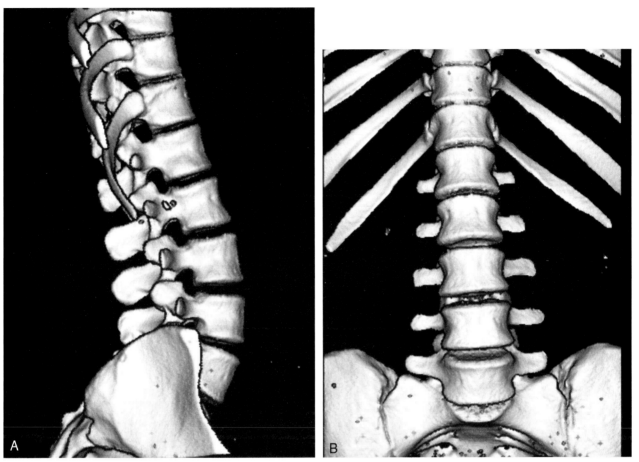

Figure 22–1. Lateral *(A)* and frontal *(B)* 3D images of the lumbar spine reconstructed from 1.5-mm-thick axial data on a helical CT scanner. Images can be rotated in any direction, thus providing a "virtual" surgical field.

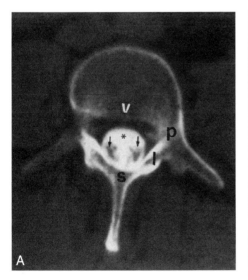

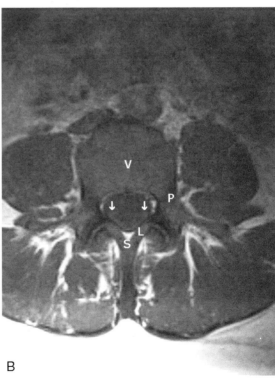

Figure 22–2. Axial postmyelogram CT scan *(A)* and T1-weighted MR image *(B)* show the borders of the bony canal. L, lamina; P, pedicle; S, spinous process base; V, vertebral body. *Arrows* indicate nerve roots in the spinal canal, which is filled with iodinated contrast in *A (asterisk).*

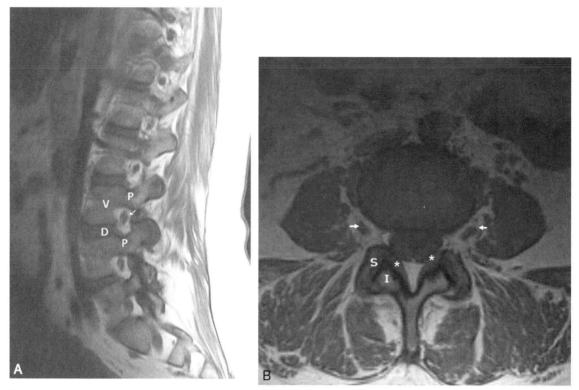

Figure 22–3. Parasagittal *(A)* and axial *(B)* T1-weighted MR images illustrate the neural foramina and its borders. D, disk forming the anterior border; I, inferior facet of the superior vertebra; P, superior and inferior pedicles forming the roof and floor; S, superior facet of lower vertebra; V, vertebra forming the anterior border. *Arrows* indicate exiting roots surrounded by bright epidural fat; on the parasagittal view *(A)*, the roots exit at the top of the "keyhole," behind the vertebral portion of the diskovertebral junction. The ligamentum flavum is indicated by *asterisks*.

orly, the most laterally positioned roots leave the group in a wide arc to exit through their respective neural foramina. The roots exit under the pedicle of the vertebra for which they are named. For instance, the L5 root exits under the L5 pedicle. Note that the roots exit through the top of the foraminal "keyhole," just posterior to the diskovertebral junction (see Fig. 22–3). Several small arteries, veins, and nerves accompany the roots through the foramina. The bottom of the keyhole, which is just posterior to the disk itself, contains primarily fat. The exiting roots are surrounded by a sleeve of cerebrospinal fluid (CSF)–containing dura for a very short distance. This sleeve terminates by fusing with the epineurium of the proximal spinal nerve.

After sending off the exiting nerve roots, the cauda equina continues inferiorly within the dural tube. A new set of roots is now positioned laterally. Before reaching the next set of neural foramina, these roots travel separately from the group within the *lateral recesses*. These are small anterolateral niches medial to the vertebral pedicles. As the roots reach the next diskovertebral junction, the process is repeated (Fig. 22–4).

On axial images of the diskovertebral junction, epidural fat lies concentrically around the thecal sac, surrounds exiting nerve roots, and continues into the neural foramina. The vertebral body and disk are seen anteriorly. Posterolateral to the thecal sac are the *facets*. The superior facet of the lower vertebral body lies anterior to the interior facet of the body above. The facets are continuous with the

laminae that fuse in the midline to form the base of the spinous process (see Figs. 22–2 to 22–4).

The synovial-lined diarthrodial facet joints lie in an oblique parasagittal plane. This plane is relatively coronally oriented in the upper lumbar spine but more sagittally oriented at lower levels. Flush against the laminae and facets is the V-shaped ligamentum flavum, which can occasionally hypertrophy enough to cause canal narrowing.

Imaging Techniques

Although MRI has largely replaced CT as the imaging modality of choice for evaluation of the degenerative lumbar spine, CT is still used as the initial imaging modality in many institutions. In disk disease and canal stenosis, for example, studies have shown greater than 80% correlation between MRI and surgical findings in type and location of pathology. Correlation between CT and surgical findings were similar.[4, 20, 53, 77] Other studies, however, dispute the validity of many of these analyses.[39] If the patient cannot enter the MRI equipment for technical reasons or if cost is a factor, high-resolution CT, especially with sagittal reconstruction, provides satisfactory images of the disk, thecal sac, and neural foramina (Fig. 22–5).

When CT is performed after injection of intrathecal contrast material, the contrast between the thecal sac and surrounding structures is improved (Fig. 22–2A), thus increasing the sensitivity of the examination.[26] This is an

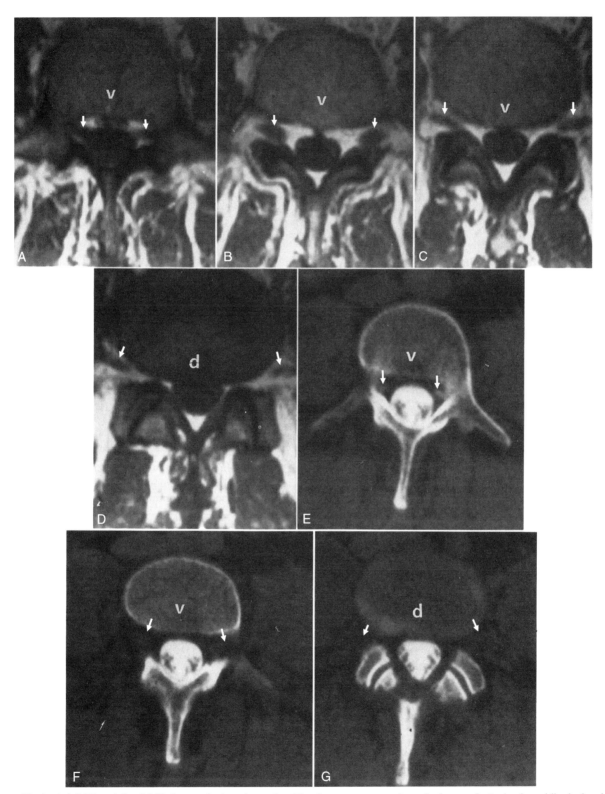

Figure 22–4. Axial T1-weighted MR image depicts the path of lumbar nerve roots through the canal. *A,* At the midbody level, the preexiting roots *(arrows)* are positioned in the lateral recesses. *B* and *C,* Just inferior to *A* at the superior aspect of the diskovertebral junction, the roots lie within the foramina. *D,* At the inferior aspect of the diskovertebral junction, the roots have already exited the foramina. *E–G,* Postmyelogram CT scan showing the same sequence of events. d, disk; v, vertebral body. Note epidural fat, bright on T1-weighted MRI and dark on CT scan, surrounding the sac and roots.

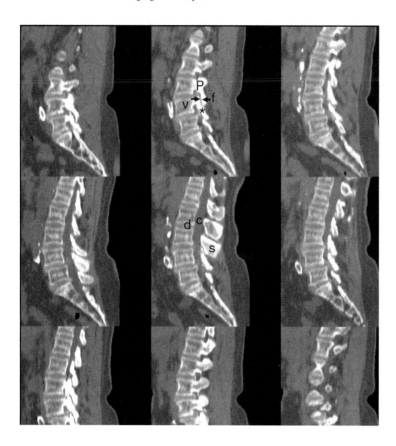

Figure 22–5. Sagittally reconstructed CT scan. Same patient as in Figure 22–1. The spinal canal (c) as well as the disk (d) is appreciated. Note excellent bone detail, particularly of the pedicle (P), pars interarticularis *(asterisk)*, and facets (f). s, spinous process.

invasive procedure, however, with the associated risks of iodinated contrast, bleeding, and infection. The multiplanar capability and high soft tissue contrast resolution of MRI provides superior delineation of disk, fat, nerves, ligaments, CSF, and bone without thecal puncture, intravenous (IV) contrast, or radiation exposure. Furthermore, routine CT imaging covers only a limited number of levels and may miss unexpected disease slightly higher or lower than the area of suspected pathology.

If CT is to be the initial imaging modality for evaluation of low back pain, slices 4 to 5 mm thick with 1 mm overlap is a typical protocol (Box 22–1). These slices should be angled parallel to the disk, compensating for the normal lumbar lordosis.

Because approximately 90% of disk herniations occur at L4-5 and L5-S1, with most of the remainder at L3-4, imaging of these levels is usually sufficient.[25, 32, 33] The slices are preferably contiguous (i.e., not only through the disk but also through the vertebral body). Selective imaging

through the disk and end plate may miss lateral recess stenosis and migrated disk fragments. Both soft tissue and bone windows should be photographed. Additional images can be obtained, depending on the clinical circumstances. Sagittal or coronal reconstruction may help in evaluation of suspected spondylolysis or spondylolisthesis (see Fig. 22–5). For useful reconstructions, however, usually thin-section images are required. If CT scans are performed after myelography, the same techniques are used. However, my preference is to image the entire lumbar spine from L1 through S1 after myelography. Although degenerative disease of the upper lumbar spine is less common, there is only "one chance" to image the spine while the contrast material is in the thecal sac. Therefore, after myelography, I am unwilling to risk missing lesions in the upper lumbar region.

The osseous anatomy of the lumbar spine is best seen with wide ("bone") window settings. This is helpful for evaluation of osteophytes, fractures, spondylolysis, and facets. Narrower (soft tissue) window settings help to differentiate disk (80 to 120 Hounsfield units [HU]) from dural sac/nerve roots (0 to 60 HU). Epidural fat (-50 to -100 HU) is also well seen on these settings. The *ligamentum flavum* is seen as a soft-tissue-density structure flush against the anterior rims of the laminae and facets (Fig. 22–6).

MRI provides an abundance of choices for spine imaging. Pulse sequences can vary considerably from institution to institution, depending on the type of scanner, MRI vendor, imaging time available, and the individual preferences of the radiologist. There is no one best way to image the spine.

At our institution, MRI of the lumbar spine is performed

Box 22–1. Routine CT Scans of Lumbar Degenerative Disease

- Axial contiguous images from L3 to S1 (begin more superiorly if higher levels are of concern)
- Slice thickness = 4 mm, intersection gap = 3–4 mm
- Intrathecal contrast optional but preferable
- Both wide and narrow window settings
- Sagittal reconstructions if spondylolysis or spondylolisthesis is suspected

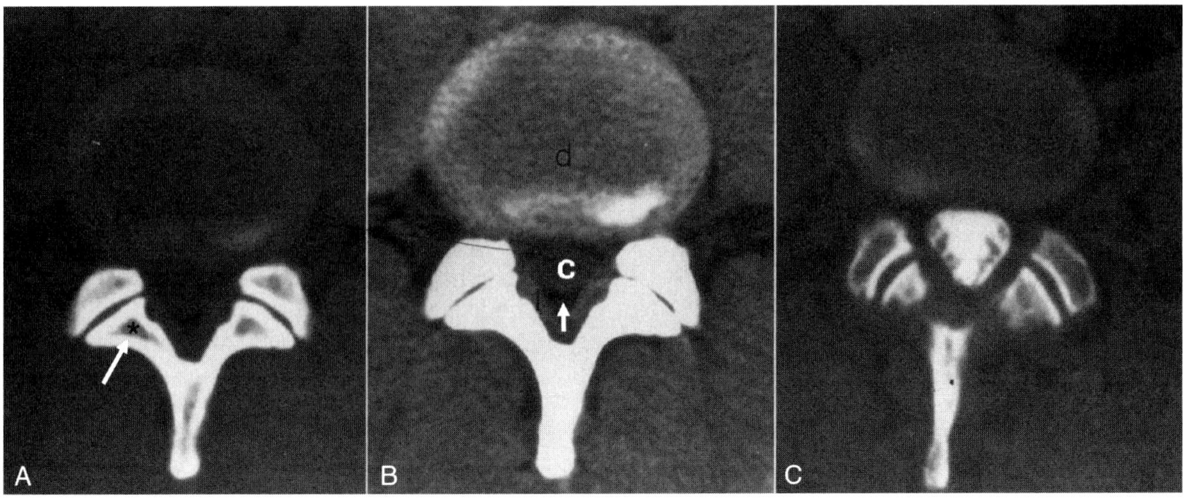

Figure 22–6. Axial CT scan using wide (bone) windows (W, 1450, L, 100) *(A)* and narrow (soft tissue) windows (W, 400; L, 40) *(B)*. Bone detail is better on the wide window settings. The cortex *(black arrow)* and marrow *(asterisk)* can best be distinguished with wide windows. However, contrast between the disk (d), epidural fat *(white arrow)*, ligamentum flavum (l), and canal (c) are best seen with narrow windows. *C,* Iohexol accentuates the contrast between the sac and the surrounding structures.

in both the sagittal and axial planes. The sagittal examination provides information on vertebral alignment and integrity of the vertebral bodies and pars and a general overview of the thecal sac, cauda equina, and nerve roots. The nerve roots within the neural foramina are well visualized on sagittal images. The overall marrow signal is also best evaluated in this plane. Any abnormality on sagittal views should be confirmed on axial views and vice versa. The sagittal plane should include the conus down to at least the level of S1.

At our institution, we obtain all scans by using *fast spin-echo* (FSE) sequences. FSE is a variant of the *rapid acquisition relaxation–enhanced* (RARE) pulse sequence.[79] This method minimizes imaging time in spine patients, who are often quite uncomfortable lying in one position for any length of time. Additionally, because the FSE sequences take less time, they allow for higher-resolution scans with higher matrices.

Our protocol consists of a set of sagittal and axial FSE T1-weighted images as well as sagittal and axial FSE T2-weighted images (Box 22–2). Sagittal views should cover the entire width of the spine from foramen to foramen. Axial views should be obtained parallel to the plane of the disk space. It is preferable that the axials cover not only the disk space but also as much of the adjacent vertebral body as possible. This is because disk herniations may extend or migrate well beyond the confines of the interspace and may be missed if they are not covered on axial views.

T1-weighted images provide the best anatomic information because the bright epidural fat outlines the normal, darker structures of the spine and spinal canal. T1-weighted images provide optimal contrast between these structures. Moreover, because vertebral marrow has a significant amount of fat, the osseous anatomy is well visualized on T1 sequences (Fig. 22–7A; see Fig. 22–4). Any infiltrative pathology of the marrow (e.g., a neoplasm) can be seen as abnormal low signal within the bright vertebral fat. Marrow is also bright on FSE T2-weighted sequences (less so on

standard T2-weighted, spin-echo sequences). Most pathologic processes, such as neoplasms, are also bright on these sequences and thus may "blend in" with the normal fat and may be missed on these images.

On T1-weighted images, bone is of intermediate to high signal intensity, depending on the degree of fatty marrow. Low signal intensity in bone suggests pathologic infiltration. Disks reflect intermediate signal intensity. The nerve roots, which also reflect intermediate signal intensity, are surrounded by low-signal-intensity CSF, which in turn is enveloped by high-signal fat. On T1-weighted images, ligamentum flavum reflects intermediate to low-signal intensity (see Figs. 22–2 to 22–4).

Box 22–2. Example of Routine MRI for Lumbar Degenerative Disease

1. Sagittal fast spin-echo, T1-weighted image to include conus to S1
   a. Field of view = 28 cm, slice thickness = 4–5 mm, intersection gap = 1 mm, matrix = 256 × 512
2. Sagittal fast spin-echo, T2-weighted image
   a. Field of view = 28 cm, thickness = 4–5 mm, intersection gap = 1 mm, matrix = 320 × 512
3. Axial fast spin-echo, T1-weighted image to include L2 through S1
   a. Field of view = 20 cm, slice thickness = 4 mm, intersection gap = 1 mm, matrix = 256 × 256
   b. Axial views obtained parallel to the plane of the disk space
   c. Extra-axial views performed through any abnormality seen at any level
4. Axial fast spin-echo, T2-weighted image
   a. Field of view = 20 cm, thickness = 4–5 mm, intersection gap = 1 mm, matrix = 256 × 256
5. If postoperative spine, repeat sagittal and axial fast spin-echo, T1-weighted images after gadolinium administration

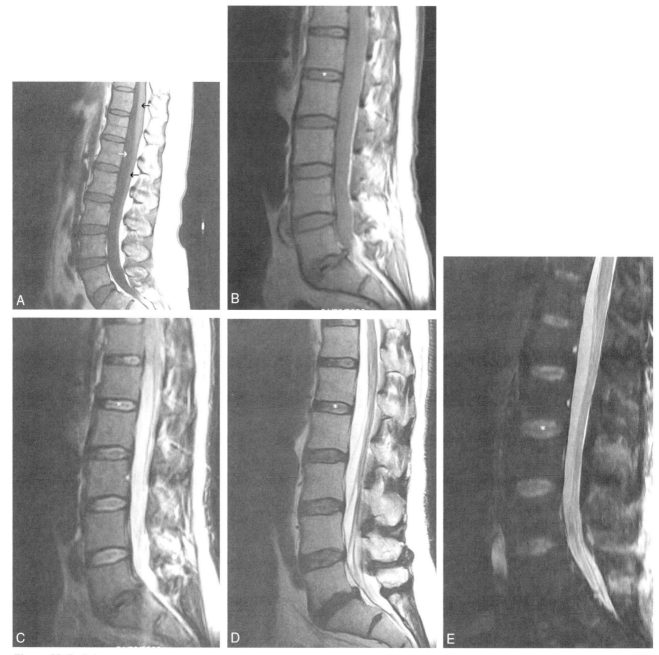

Figure 22–7. Spinous anatomy.

A, Sagittal T1-weighted (TR = 700 msec, TE_{eff} = 12 msec, ETL = 4) MR image. Marrow fat is brighter than the water-filled disk. Nerve roots *(black arrows)* are slightly hyperintense to the dark cerebrospinal fluid *(white arrows).*

B–D, Various T2-like MRI sequences. *B,* Standard proton-density (TR = 2700 msec, TE = 20 msec). *C,* Standard T2 (TR = 2000 msec, TE = 80 msec). *D,* Fast spin-echo, T2-weighted (TR = 4000, TE_{eff} = 108 msec, ETL = 16) MR image.

E, Short tau inversion recovery (STIR) sequence, used for fat suppression.

In general, the water-filled disk is brighter than bone on T2-weighted sequences. However, the contrast between various structures varies, depending on the sequence used. The "internuclear cleft" *(asterisk),* a normal structure within the disk, is best seen on the T2-like images. Note the darkened fat of the vertebral marrow on the STIR sequence relative to all the other sequences. ETL, echo train length; TE_{eff}, effective echo time; TR, repetition time.

T2-weighted images optimize contrast between disk, bone, and CSF. T2-weighted images and many of the gradient-echo sequences make the CSF "myelographically" bright and the bone darker, which helps reveal the effects of osteophytes and bony hypertrophy on the thecal sac, as noted previously. Unlike standard spin-echo images,

fat remains bright on FSE sequences. FSE sequences can therefore decrease contrast. This can sometimes decrease contrast between the bright spinal fluid and epidural fat. If necessary, fat-suppressed images can be used to ameliorate this problem. We do not find this routinely necessary unless bony neoplasm is suspected. The differentiation between disk and bone is poorer on T2-weighted images and on gradient-echo sequences. Therefore, the imaging specialist should pay careful attention to both T1-weighted and T2-weighted sequences when analyzing the images.

Nondiskogenic Spinal Stenosis

Pathogenesis

Even in the absence of disk herniation, a combination of facet overgrowth and osteophyte formation at the vertebral end plates can lead to spinal stenosis. These changes are generally referred to as *spondylosis*.

The pathogenesis of spondylosis is believed to be due to recurrent rotational forces on the diskovertebral junction during cyclic axial loading. This results in thinning of the cartilaginous end plate, disk resorption, and consequent disk thinning. Stresses are then redistributed to the bone, leading to facet hypertrophy and end-plate osteophyte formation. Facet changes are exacerbated by repeated synovial

irritation.[56] As the inferior and superior facets grind one upon another, the vertebral body becomes predisposed to either anterior (anterolisthesis) or posterior (retrolisthesis) slippage on the vertebra inferior to it.

The final result of these degenerative osteoarthritic changes is stenosis of the spinal canal, neural foramina, or lateral recesses or a combination of these.[9, 18, 22, 36, 40, 42] This causes nerve root compression as well as other pathophysiologic events, leading to the pain commonly known as *sciatica*.[60] The specific focus of narrowing depends on the structure involved.

Facet Hypertrophy

With repeated strains on the apophyseal joints, the articular cartilage is gradually stripped away and the underlying bone hypertrophies. Because the facets make up part of the wall of the neural foramen, foraminal narrowing can result, impinging on the exiting nerve roots (Fig. 22–8). These changes predominate in the lower lumbar spine.[64]

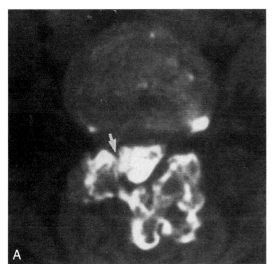

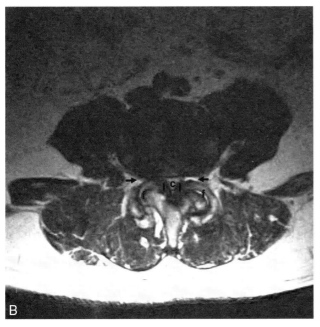

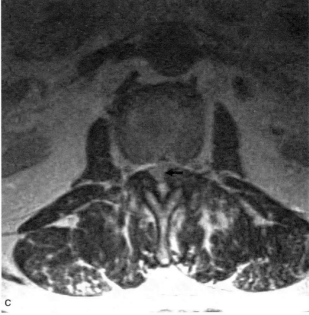

Figure 22–8. *A,* Facet hypertrophy. Postmyelogram CT scans shows massive facet hypertrophy bilaterally. *Arrow* indicates facet encroachment on the thecal sac. Compare with normal facets in Figure 22–4*G. B,* T2-weighted MR image shows hypertrophied facets (f) and ligamentum flavum (l) encroaching on the foramina, *(arrows),* obliterating the foraminal fat and severely narrowing the canal (c). *C,* T2-weighted MR image shows asymmetrical facet hypertrophy. The left facet exerts mass effect on the canal *(black arrow).* Compare with normal facets in Figures 22–3*B* and 22–4*C* and *D.*

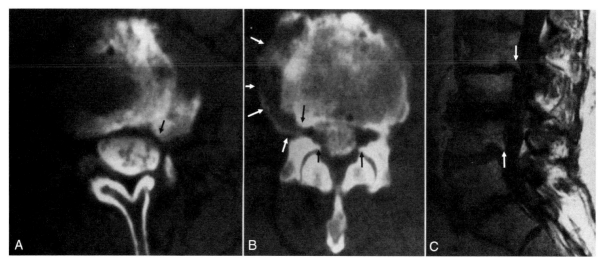

Figure 22–9. Osteophytes. *A* and *B,* Postmyelogram CT scans show osteophytes *(arrows)* encroaching on the canal and foramina. *C,* Sagittal T1-weighted MR image shows osteophytes *(arrows)* encroaching on the canal.

Osteophytes

With advancing age, osteophytosis of the lumbar vertebral end plates becomes increasingly common. The prevalence of osteophytes in patients aged 50 years and older is approximately 60% to 80%. The exact mechanism of osteophyte formation is debated, but it, too, probably results from complex stresses on the spine. Osteophytes are more common in men[64] and in individuals who are engaged in heavy physical labor. Depending on size, shape, and location, osteophytes can narrow or focally impinge on any part of the neural canal (Fig. 22–9).

Spondylolisthesis

As facets constantly grind upon one another they become smooth and "slippery." Thus, the ability of the superior (anterior) facet of a vertebral body to hold in check the inferior (posterior) facet of the vertebral body above becomes deficient. The upper vertebral body gradually slips forward over the lower one (Fig. 22–10). This is most common at L4-5, where the facets are oriented more sagittally than at any other level and are therefore most predisposed to slippage.[64]

Spondylolisthesis is divided into four grades of severity

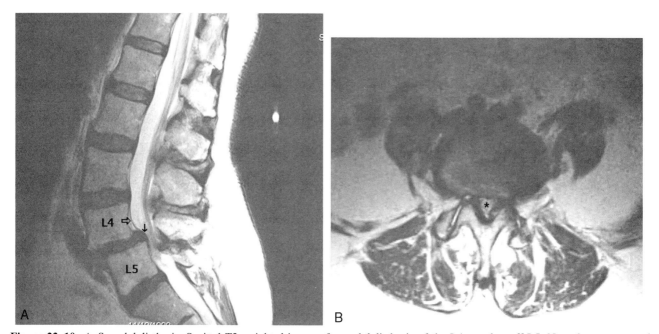

Figure 22–10. *A,* Spondylolisthesis. Sagittal T2-weighted image of spondylolisthesis of the L4 vertebra off L5. Note the severe canal stenosis caused by the slippage. The disk *(closed arrow)* is exposed by the slippage of L4, giving the false impression of herniation ("pseudoherniation"). The posterior longitudinal ligament *(open arrow)* is displaced by the spondylolisthesis. *B,* Axial scan at the L4-5 level of the same patient as in *A.* Note severe stenosis of the canal *(asterisk).*

according to whether 25%, 50%, 75%, or 100% of a vertebral body has slipped forward upon its neighbor. As slippage becomes more severe, the spinal canal and/or the neural foramina can progressively narrow at that level, producing symptoms.

Fractures of the pars interarticularis (spondylolysis) are not prerequisites for degenerative spondylolisthesis.

Ligamentum Flavum Hypertrophy

The reasons for ligamentum flavum thickening are not completely understood, but they are probably related to mechanical instability and asymmetrical stresses on the facets. Because this structure lies flush against the posterior wall of the bony canal, ligamentum flavum hypertrophy contributes to canal narrowing (Figs. 22–11 and 22–12).[64]

Lateral Recess Stenosis

Bony overgrowth of the lateral recesses can occur as part of the degenerative process, resulting in entrapment of the lateral *(preexiting)* roots. Alternatively, when herniated disk material extrudes up or down into the lateral recesses, the preexiting roots can become compromised. Facet and ligamentum flavum hypertrophy can also contribute to lateral recess stenosis (see Fig. 22–12).

Synovial Cysts

With chronic irritation, tears can develop in the capsule of the facet joint and fluid can migrate through the capsule into the epidural space and form a cyst (Fig. 22–13). The cysts are usually of simple fluid intensity (dark on T1-weighted and bright on T2-weighted images); however,

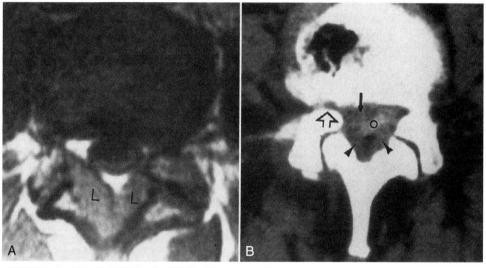

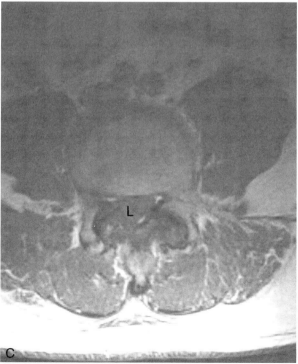

Figure 22–11. Ligamentum flavum hypertrophy. *A,* Axial T1-weighted MR image. The ligament (L) is markedly enlarged, but the capacious canal is not compromised in this case. *B,* Postmyelogram CT scan in another patient. The contrast column *(circle)* is compressed by hypertrophied ligamentum flavum *(arrowheads)* as well as by herniated disk *(arrow).* Note also lateral recess stenosis, caused by a hypertrophied facet *(open arrow). C,* T1-weighted axial MR image shows unilateral ligamentum flavum hypertrophy in the same patient as in Figure 22–8B but at a different level. The hypertrophied right ligamentum flavum (L) impinges on the canal. See also Figures 22–8B and 22–12B.

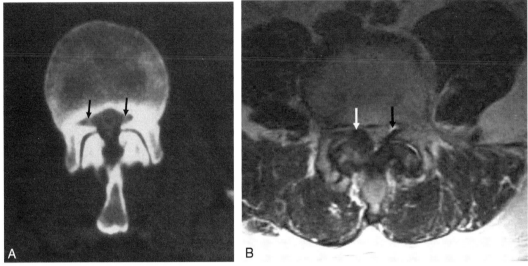

Figure 22–12. *A,* Lateral recess stenosis. CT scan shows preexiting nerve roots *(arrows)* within tiny lateral recesses. This patient with achondroplasia had nondegenerative congenital spinal stenosis. Compare with normal lateral recesses in Figure 22–4*E. B,* T2-weighted scan, same patient as in Figure 22–11*C.* The hypertrophied ligamentum flavum has obliterated the right lateral recess *(white arrow).* The left lateral recess *(black arrow)* is also narrowed by the hypertrophied facet, but some epidural fat can still be seen.

they may be brighter on T1-weighted and darker on T2-weighted images if the fluid contains proteins. These cysts can exert mass effect on or can narrow the canal, resulting in nerve-root symptoms. Synovial cysts can be resected surgically or may be aspirated under CT guidance.[46]

Other Causes of Stenosis

Disk bulges or *herniations* (see later, "Bulging and Herniated Disks") can narrow any part of the canal or foramina. Stenosis can be unilateral, bilateral, or diffuse.

Although lumbar degenerative disease typically begins at L4-L5 and L5-S1, the entire lumbar spine can become involved as mechanical stresses gradually shift cephalad.

Accurate assessment of the normal dimensions of the spinal canal can be difficult because of wide variations caused by body habitus and age. On lumbar CT scans, an anteroposterior dimension of less than 11.5 mm (measured from disk-vertebral body edge to the base of spinous process), an interpediculate distance of less than 16 mm, and a

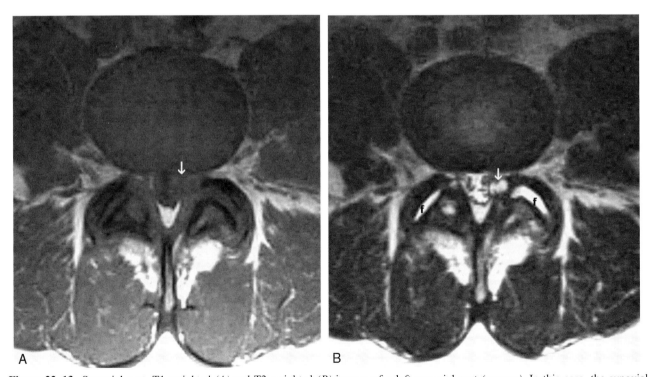

Figure 22–13. Synovial cyst. T1-weighted *(A)* and T2-weighted *(B)* images of a left synovial cyst *(arrows).* In this case, the synovial fluid is isointense to cerebrospinal fluid on both sequences. The cyst emanates from fluid (f) in the joint capsules.

cross-sectional area smaller than 1.45 mm^2 are considered small.[82]

Clinical Considerations

The clinical presentation of lumbar spinal stenosis usually begins with a history of chronic low back, bilateral-buttock, and thigh pain. If nerve-root compression is a feature, the pain may radiate down an extremity. Numbness and weakness, as well as coldness, tingling, and burning, may also occur. Many patients describe transient motor deficits.

The pain is more vague and poorly localized than that associated with a herniated disk. In fact, degenerative spinal stenosis may mimic peripheral vascular disease, simulating the symptoms of vascular claudication. In contrast to vascular claudication, however, the patient with spinal stenosis assumes a chronic stooped, flexed position (simian posture) in order to alleviate the pain. In patients with vascular claudication, pain is alleviated by standing and resting. In patients with spinal stenosis, the pain takes longer to subside, and walking distance before the onset of pain is more variable.

Physical changes resulting from peripheral vascular disease, such as decreased pulses and skin breakdown, are not present.[18, 27, 29, 41, 57, 62] On physical examination, the lumbar lordotic curve becomes straightened or reversed and pain may be reproduced on extension. Decreased lumbosacral motion is noted. It is not common to elicit motor or sensory deficits. In most cases, abnormal reflexes corresponding to L4 and L5 nerve roots are noted. Positive straight leg raising may be found. Objective weakness of the muscles may be supplied by the L5 and S1 nerves.[18, 27, 29, 41, 44, 62]

The pathophysiology of clinical symptoms related to spinal stenosis is complex, controversial, and not well understood. Most investigators believe that direct compression of nerve roots plays a major role in pain production, although arterial and venous obstruction may also be important. Some suggest that pseudoclaudication may be related to true vascular insufficiency of nerve roots.[57] Release of irritating chemicals by surrounding structures, nerve edema, chronic impairment of axonal transport, and intraneural microcirculation insufficiency may also be factors.[60]

Diskogenic Spinal Stenosis

The three major components of the intervertebral disk are the nucleus pulposus, the annulus fibrosus, and the end plate. The nucleus pulposus is the jelly-like core of the disk, containing 90% water mixed with delicate fibrous strands. The nucleus merges with the surrounding capsule, the collaginous annulus fibrosus. The cartilaginous end plate fuses the inferior and superior surfaces of the vertebral body to the disk (Fig. 22–14). The components of the disk complex optimize shock absorption from mechanical stresses on the vertebral column.

The normal intervertebral disk on CT scans are approximately 50 to 100 HU, which is somewhat denser than the surrounding ligaments and much denser than epidural fat and the fluid-filled thecal sac. This makes the disk easily distinguishable from neighboring structures, particularly in the case of disk herniation.

On T1-weighted MR images, the disk is a fairly homogeneous structure, isointense to muscle. On images with a long repetition time (TR), the disk becomes brighter because of its water content. On T2-weighted images, the nucleus pulposus, which is more hydrated than the annulus fibrosus, becomes even brighter than the annulus.

Pathogenesis

The pathogenesis of disk degeneration is complex and not well understood. End-plate and disk degeneration is probably a normal consequence of the aging process. By age 50 years, 85% to 95% of adults show evidence of degenerative disk disease at autopsy.[63] The cartilaginous end plate becomes thinner. The nucleus pulposus and, to a lesser degree, the annulus fibrosus lose up to 70% of their water content. The disk tissue also undergoes biochemical changes with respect to its collagen and proteoglycan content. The entire volume of the disk decreases with aging.[1, 11, 16] Annular fibers become stretched, leading to disk bulging (which is usually not significant unless the canal is already small). These changes occur most frequently in the parts of the lumbar spine most subjected to mechanical stresses (i.e., L4-5 and L5-S1).

Whether normal disk aging plays a predisposing role is unclear, but the sequence of events in disk herniation appears to be as follows. The annulus becomes frayed during repeated flexional and rotational forces, resulting in radial and concentrically oriented fissures in the annulus. This then predisposes the nucleus to further degeneration and subsequent herniation into and then through the annular fibers.[51] Although central disk herniations are by no means rare, disks tend to herniate posterolaterally because the posterior longitudinal ligament and annular fibers are thickest and strongest in the midline and thinner laterally.

Figure 22–14. Disk anatomy. The jelly-like nucleus pulposus is encircled by the fibers of the annulus fibrosus. The cartilaginous end plate, which fuses with the vertebral body, covers the superior and inferior disk surfaces. (Modified from Modic MT: Magnetic Resonance Imaging of the Spine. St. Louis, Mosby–Year Book, 1989.)

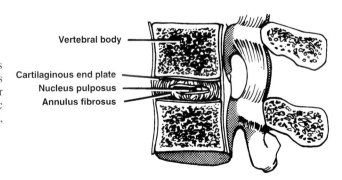

Vertebral body

Cartilaginous end plate
Nucleus pulposus
Annulus fibrosus

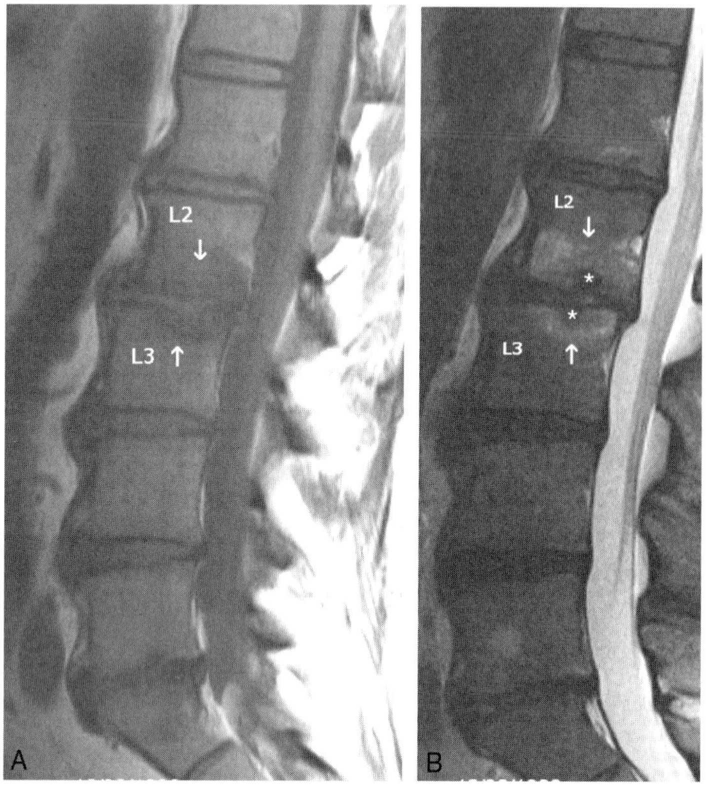

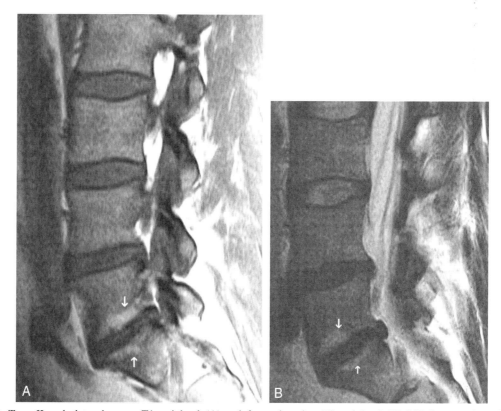

Figure 22–15. Type I end-plate changes. *A,* T1-weighted MR image shows hypointensity of the inferior L2 and superior L3 end plates *(arrows)*. *B,* T2-weighted MR image shows that the end plates have become hyperintense. This is the earliest stage of disk degeneration. The lower lumbar disks are dark on the T2-weighted scan because they have become dehydrated from degeneration. Note small Schmorl's nodes *(asterisks)*.

Figure 22–16. Type II end-plate changes. T1-weighted *(A)* and fast spin-echo, T2-weighted *(B)* MR images show fatty end plates *(arrows)*, which are hyperintense on T1-weighted and fast spin-echo, T2-weighted images.

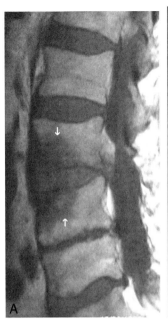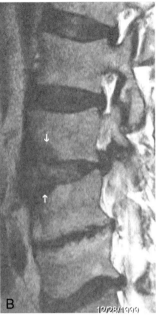

Figure 22–17. Type III end-plate changes. T1-weighted *(A)* and T2-weighted *(B)* MR images show hypointensity of the inferior L3 and superior L4 end plates on both sequences *(arrows).*

Radiographic Changes

The earliest radiographically visible changes of intervertebral disk degeneration are those that occur at the end plate. These are best seen on MRI. Three types of end-plate changes have been described[17, 56]:

Type I changes demonstrate low signal intensity on T1-weighted images and high signal intensity on T2-weighted images (Fig. 22–15). This stage is believed to reflect replacement of the end-plate marrow with vascular fibrous tissue in response to chronic "injury."

Type II changes, the next stage, show high signal intensity on T1-weighted and on FSE T2-weighted images (Fig. 22–16). This stage represents replacement of the end-plate marrow with fatty tissue. (On standard spin-echo,

T2-weighted images, the fatty end plates thus become slightly darker.) Type II changes tend to remain stable with time.

Type III changes, or the final stage if it occurs, are represented by low signal intensity on both T1-weighted and T2-weighted images (Fig. 22–17). This stage correlates with bony sclerosis seen on CT scans and plain films of severely degenerated end plates. This is the only end-plate change visible on CT scans or radiographs. Whether these end-plate changes have any prognostic significance has not been established; however, they are part of the normal aging process and must not be confused with other pathologic processes, such as tumor and infection (Fig. 22–18).

Bulging and Herniated Disks
Classification

The most important step in the analysis of the degenerative lumbar spine—after the vertebrae, end plates, ligaments, and joints—is the disk itself. As mentioned, the intervertebral disk is made up of a jelly-like nucleus pulposus, surrounded by a tough, fibrous annulus fibrosus. Unfortunately, no universally accepted classification of disk herniation exists. The one presented here[51] may differ from those offered by other texts and institutions.[47, 49]

Abnormal disks can be classified as *bulging* or *herniated*. A *herniated disk* can be subclassified as (1) protruded, (2) extruded, or (3) sequestered.

Bulging Disk

An *annular bulge* represents an extension of the disk margin beyond the confines of the adjacent vertebral end plate. The annular fibers are stretched but intact. The disk bulges diffusely around the posterior (and sometimes lateral) aspects of the end plate (Figs. 22–19 and 22–20). This does not usually lead to clinical symptoms unless the spinal canal is already congenitally small or narrow owing to spondylosis.

Protruded Disk

When some of the inner fibers of the annulus tear but the outer layers remain intact, the nucleus can focally

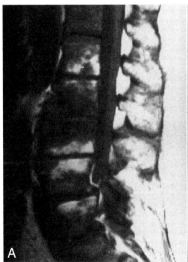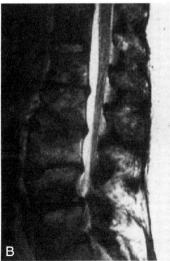

Figure 22–18. T1-weighted *(A)* and T2-weighted *(B)* MR images show end-plate changes of varying stages. The resulting marrow heterogeneity is easily confused with bone metastases.

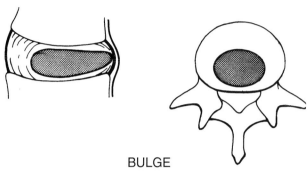

BULGE

Figure 22–19. Illustration of a bulging disk. The disk bulges diffusely beyond the vertebral body margin. The annular fibers are stretched but completely intact. (Modified from Modic MT: Magnetic Resonance Imaging of the Spine. St. Louis, Mosby–Year Book, 1989.)

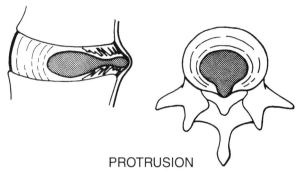

PROTRUSION

Figure 22–21. Illustration of disk protrusion. A portion of nucleus pulposus herniates focally through a rent in the inner annular fibers. The outer annular fibers are intact. (Modified from Modic MT: Magnetic Resonance Imaging of the Spine. St. Louis, Mosby–Year Book, 1989.)

herniate through the inner tear. This is the simplest (and probably earliest) type of disk herniation and is called a *disk protrusion* (Fig. 22–21).

Disk herniation is distinguished from annular bulge by its focality. Whereas a disk usually bulges fairly uniformly along its margins, a disk herniates through one particular spot—the annular tear. The signal intensity (on MRI) and density (on CT scans) of the protruded segment are generally, but not invariably, the same as those of the nonherniated portion.

Extruded Disk

A *disk extrusion* occurs when the nucleus pulposus herniates through a complete tear of the annulus fibrosus and is contained only by the posterior longitudinal ligament (Fig. 22–22). The herniated segment, however, remains attached to the parent disk but may extend cephalad or caudad. It can be difficult to differentiate between a disk

protrusion and extrusion when the amount of herniated disk is small. This distinction, however, is not clinically significant; it is more important to recognize that these are simply different degrees of herniation and that the significance of a herniated disk is its effect on the spinal canal and nerve roots (Figs. 22–23 and 22–24).

Sequestered Disk

Finally, when an extruded nucleus breaks free of the parent disk, it is termed a *sequestered disk* or *free fragment* (Fig. 22–25). The sequestered portion may or may not be confined by the posterior longitudinal ligament. In fact, it may migrate inferiorly or superiorly to a different interspace or, in rare cases, may even penetrate the dura. Free fragments also tend to resemble the parent disk on both CT scans and on short TR MR images (Fig. 22–26).

On long TR or gradient-echo MR images, sequestered disks may be of higher signal intensity than the disk of

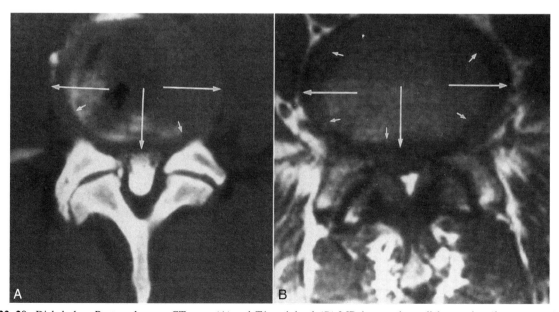

Figure 22–20. Disk bulge. Postmyelogram CT scan *(A)* and T1-weighted *(B)* MR image show disk margins *(long arrows)* diffusely bulging beyond the bone margins *(short arrows)*.

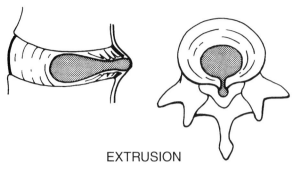

EXTRUSION

Figure 22–22. Illustration of disk extrusion. The nucleus has herniated through a complete annular tear but remains connected to the parent disk. (Modified from Modic MT: Magnetic Resonance Imaging of the Spine. St. Louis, Mosby–Year Book, 1989.)

origin. The most important distinction, however, is the lack of a connection between the extruded component and the parent disk. This is better appreciated on MR sagittal views than on axial views. On CT scans, sagittal reconstructions are often necessary to confirm the presence of a free fragment. Because there is no connection to the parent disk, free fragments can be confused with neoplasm, abscess, or postoperative epidural fibrosis.

Clinical Considerations

The clinical presentation of disk herniation is different than that of nondiskogenic spinal stenosis, in that it tends to be acute and occurs in younger individuals between ages 30 and 45. The inciting event is usually a fall, sudden lifting, or rotation. Sometimes it occurs spontaneously.

The pain usually begins in the lower back, and the patient flexes anteriorly or laterally to reduce the pain. Pain is exacerbated by standing, sitting, or by increased CSF pressure induced by coughing, sneezing, or bowel movements. Because the most commonly compressed roots are

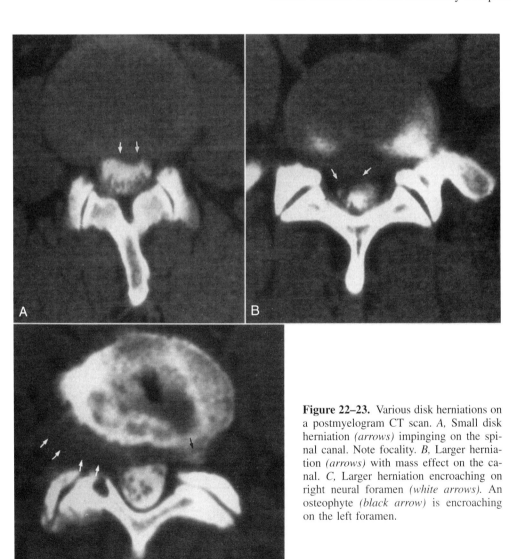

Figure 22–23. Various disk herniations on a postmyelogram CT scan. *A,* Small disk herniation *(arrows)* impinging on the spinal canal. Note focality. *B,* Larger herniation *(arrows)* with mass effect on the canal. *C,* Larger herniation encroaching on right neural foramen *(white arrows).* An osteophyte *(black arrow)* is encroaching on the left foramen.

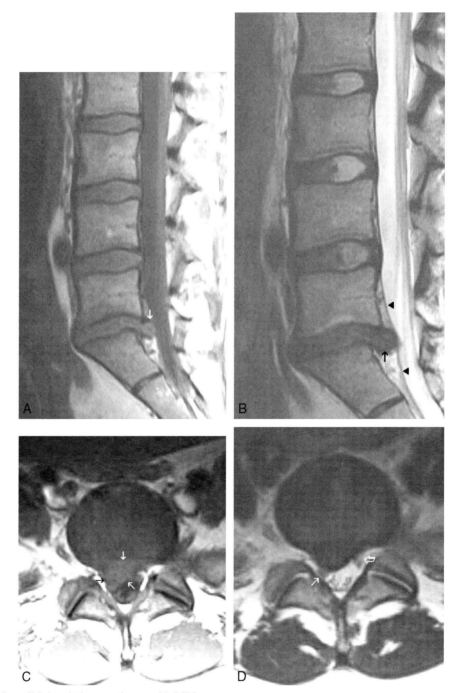

Figure 22–24. Various disk herniations as shown with MRI.

A, Sagittal T1-weighted MRI in a patient with a right paramedian disk herniation *(arrows).*

B, Sagittal T2-weighted MRI of the same patient. Disk herniation *(arrow)* and displacement of the posterior longitudinal ligament *(arrowheads)* by the disk.

C, Axial T1-weighted scan of the same patient. *Arrows* indicate the herniated disk.

D, Axial T2-weighted scan in the same patient. Note displacement of the right S1 nerve root *(closed arrow)* by the disk. The *open arrow* indicates the normal left S1 nerve root.

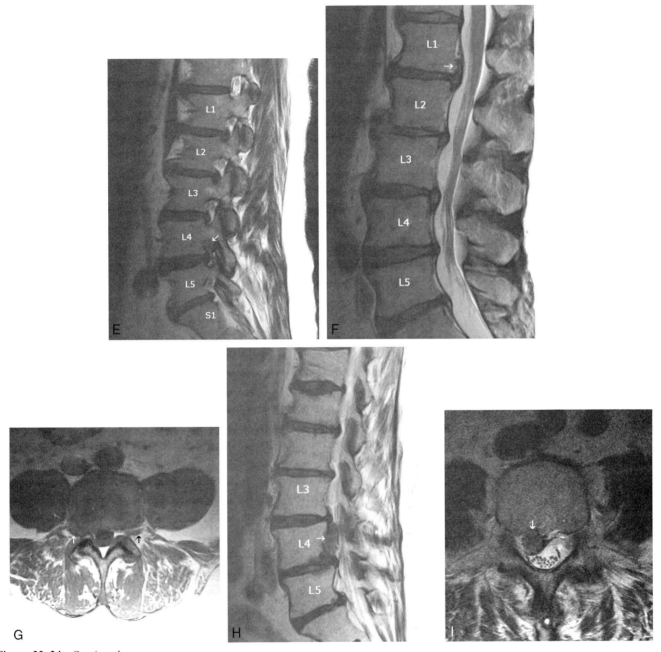

Figure 22–24 *Continued*

E–G, Multiple disk herniations in a different patient. T2-weighted right parasagittal *(E)* and midline sagittal *(F)* images. The right L4-5 foramen and nerve root *(arrow in E)* are crowded by an L4-5 disk herniation. Note how the L1-2 herniation extends superiorly behind the posterior longitudinal ligament *(arrow in F)*. *G*, Axial T1-weighted view of L4-5 herniation. The disk presses on and displaces the intraforaminal right L4 root. The herniated disk and *G*, displaced root form a large soft tissue mass *(white arrow)*. Note the normal left L4 root *(black arrow)* with surrounding fat.

H and *I*, Sagittal *(H)* and axial *(I)* T2-weighted MR images of a huge herniated disk lying behind the L4 vertebral body. The disk is so large that one cannot tell if it emanates from the L3-4 or the L4-5 interspace. The disk is probably *sequestered*, or broken off from the native disk.

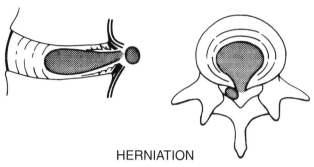

HERNIATION

Figure 22–25. Illustration of a sequestered disk. Disk material has herniated through a complete annular tear and has broken off from the parent disk. The disk fragment can migrate freely. (Modified from Modic MT: Magnetic Resonance Imaging of the Spine. St. Louis, Mosby–Year Book, 1989.)

L5 and S1, pain radiates down the lower extremity in these radicular distributions (Fig. 22–27). Paresthesias may also be a feature. The radiculopathy has both a mechanical component, owing to compression by the herniated disk, and an inflammatory component, owing to nerve root edema.

Medical treatment, usually with steroids, anti-inflammatory agents, and a regimen of physical therapy, can reverse the inflammatory component and alleviate symptoms. If pain persists as a result of the mechanical component, surgery may be necessary.[47]

Postoperative Lumbar Spine

Imaging of Complications

Scarring and Recurrent Disk Herniation

A variety of surgical techniques are available for treatment of spinal stenosis and disk disease. The surgeon may remove a variable amount of bone from the posterior elements to expose an area for *diskectomy*, spinal canal *decompression*, or both. In a *laminectomy*, much of the

vertebral body lamina is removed (Fig. 22–28). Sometimes the exposure is widened by removal of a variable amount of facet joint for better visualization and decompression. In a *laminotomy*, only a small amount of lamina is removed near a herniated disk for adequate exposure.

On CT and MRI, laminectomy sites are fairly obvious because of the bone removal involved. In a *microdiskectomy*, however, only a tiny bit of lamina is removed and sometimes the operative site is difficult to locate on CT scans or MR images. Before the advent of MRI, contrast-enhanced CT scans were the preferred method of evaluating the postoperative spine.[80] This method has essentially been replaced by MRI because of its superior ability to differentiate postoperative soft tissue changes (e.g., *scarring* versus *recurrent disk herniation*),[67] its multiplanar capability, and the use of relatively safe contrast agents. MRI changes in the postoperative spine are now well described[13, 67, 70, 71] and are summarized here.

In the immediate postlaminectomy period, the signal from normal bone and ligament is replaced by edema at the resection site. This is heterogeneously isointense to muscle on T1-weighted images and increased on T2-weighted images. In a purely decompressive laminectomy without diskectomy, significant mass effect on the thecal sac is unusual unless a hematoma is present. Between 6 weeks and 6 months after surgery, the postoperative edema is replaced by scar tissue posterior to the thecal sac. The scar appearance can range from low to high signal intensity on T2-weighted images (Fig. 22–29).

If a diskectomy is performed with the laminectomy, additional changes related to the diskectomy are appreciated. In the early postoperative period, there is edema in the anterior epidural space in addition to disruption of the posterior annular margin due to disk curettage. On T1-weighted images, this is reflected by anterior epidural intermediate signal intensity that may blend with the remaining native disk. On T2-weighted images, this area may be variably hyperintense. This probably results from edema[67] and possibly even blood.[6]

The imaging specialist must therefore exercise care in

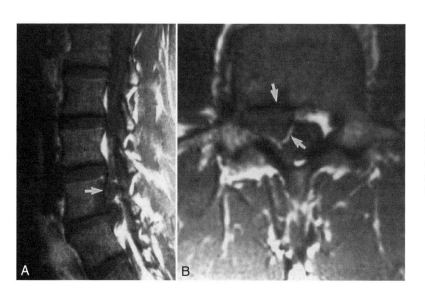

Figure 22–26. Sequestered disk. *A,* Sagittal MR image shows an L4-5 disk fragment *(arrow)* lying posterior to the L4 body. *B,* Axial MR image shows the fragment *(arrows)* obliterating the L4 root in the right lateral recess and pressing on the thecal sac. See also Figure 22–24*H* and *I.*

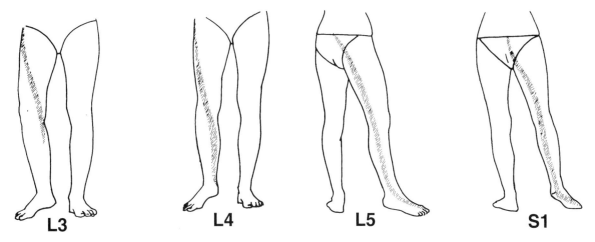

Figure 22–27. Illustration of lower extremity radiculopathies resulting from common disk herniations.

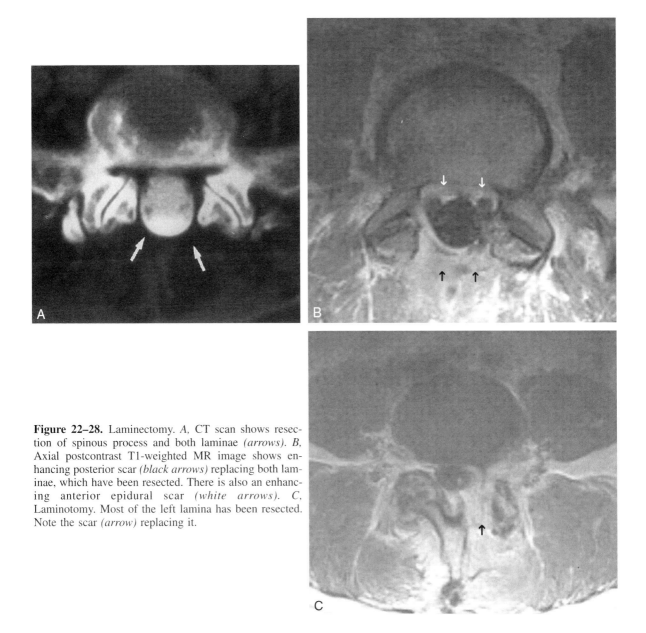

Figure 22–28. Laminectomy. *A,* CT scan shows resection of spinous process and both laminae *(arrows). B,* Axial postcontrast T1-weighted MR image shows enhancing posterior scar *(black arrows)* replacing both laminae, which have been resected. There is also an enhancing anterior epidural scar *(white arrows). C,* Laminotomy. Most of the left lamina has been resected. Note the scar *(arrow)* replacing it.

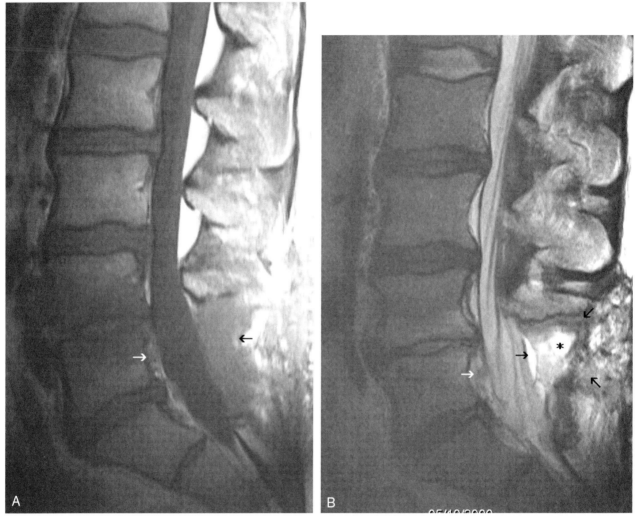

Figure 22–29. Laminectomy. *A,* Sagittal unenhanced, T1-weighted MR image shows an isointense, posterior epidural scar *(black arrow).* The anterior epidural scar from this L4-5 diskectomy is also seen *(white arrow).* Note resection of L5 spinous process. *B,* T2-weighted MR image shows the scar *(arrows)* as hyperintense but heterogeneous. A small, focal fluid collection *(asterisk)* is also visible. This is a normal postoperative finding.

interpreting early postoperative changes because this normal mass effect on the thecal sac may mimic recurrent or residual disk herniation (Fig. 22–30). Furthermore, confusing areas of gadolinium enhancement may be seen in the normal early postoperative spine, including the paraspinal muscles, facet joints, and nerve roots.[6] Therefore, gadolinium cannot be used for the evaluation of scar versus recurrent disk herniation in the early postoperative period.

The reasons for all of these normal early postoperative changes have not been completely worked out. Therefore, MRI should probably not be used in the early postoperative period unless other complications, such as hematoma, pseudomeningocele, and infection, are suspected. By 6 weeks after surgery, the edema and mass effect subside and the thecal sac margin returns to normal.

In a patient with late postsurgical recurrent back pain, the distinction between recurrent disk herniation and scarring must be made because reoperation on a scar may lead to a poor result with the formation of more scar tissue. Noncontrast MRI is at least equivalent to contrast CT

scanning in distinguishing scar from disk,[13] with a 79% accuracy rate for noncontrast MRI and a 71% accuracy rate for contrast CT scans in one study.[78]

Scar tissue tends to conform to the shape of, and often to enwrap, the dural sac and exiting nerve roots, and it does not have a definable margin (Fig. 22–31). Mass effect on the thecal sac may or may not be present; however, the dura may actually retract toward the scar.

On non–contrast-enhanced MR images, anterior epidural scar tissue is generally hypointense to isointense to disk on T1-weighted sequences and hyperintense on T2-weighted sequences. Lateral and posterior scar tissue may be somewhat more variable. Herniated disks tend to be contiguous with the native disk space (unless sequestered) and have a definable margin (see Fig. 22–24). Mass effect on the thecal sac is present. Herniated disks tend to be of low signal intensity on all pulse sequences but large, extruded, and sequestered disks can be hyperintense on T2-weighted sequences, making distinction between a disk, a scar, and CSF difficult.[48] Morphology, rather than signal characteris-

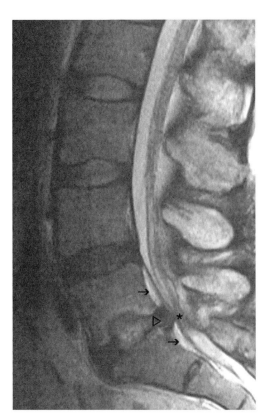

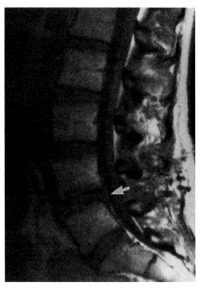

Figure 22–32. Sagittal T1-weighted postoperative MR image shows an apparent recurrent disk herniation *(arrow)* at L4-5. With contrast enhancement, this proved to be scar tissue.

Figure 22–30. Early view of the postoperative spine. T2-weighted image shows apparent severe canal stenosis *(asterisk)* from a soft tissue structure *(arrowhead),* which probably represents soft tissue swelling and blood, but mimics the appearance of disk herniation. Note subligamentous edema *(arrows),* also a normal postoperative finding. The patient was asymptomatic at this particular level.

tics, is therefore probably a more useful method of distinguishing a scar from a disk on the noncontrast MRI.[30, 67] Even so, well-defined scar tissue can mimic a disk herniation on unenhanced MR images (Fig. 22–32).

Gadolinium-enhanced MRI has met with considerable success in differentiating postoperative scarring from recurrent disk herniation. Accuracy of contrast-enhanced MRI has been reported to be as high as 96%.[31, 74] Scar tissue consistently enhances postoperatively (Fig. 22–33) and continues to enhance months to years after surgery.[31] A herniated disk should not enhance (Fig. 22–34).

One caveat: Even though anterior epidural scar invariably shows this pattern of consistent enhancement, posterior epidural scar may not. In fact, posterior epidural scar may show a rapid decline in enhancement over a period of months,[31, 68] although the reason for this is not known.

As noted previously, a herniated disk does not enhance in the immediate postinjection period. If delayed images are obtained, contrast medium may diffuse into the herniated disk from adjacent scar tissue, causing disk enhancement as well. Therefore, care must be taken to complete the enhanced portion of the examination no more than 30 minutes after injection. Gadolinium is particularly useful when a mixture of scar and recurrent disk herniation is found; the enhancing scar can be separated from the nonenhancing, low-signal recurrent disk herniation (Fig. 22–35). However, an enhancing, inflammatory reaction around a herniated disk is a common occurrence, even in the absence of prior surgery. This peridiskal reaction may actually be prominent enough to obscure a small herniation that it surrounds, thus masking it and mimicking pure scar tissue.

These enhancement characteristics generally apply to patients in the late postoperative period (>6 weeks after surgery). Scar tissue has been shown to enhance in the early postoperative period.[6] As mentioned, however, differentiation of this enhancement from the myriad normal immediate postoperative changes may be difficult. The enhancement of epidural scar is probably related to "leaky

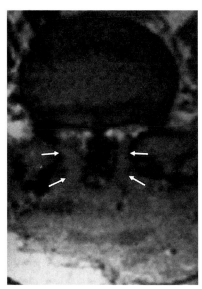

Figure 22–31. Axial T1-weighted MR image shows an epidural scar *(arrows)* partially encircling and compressing the thecal sac. The posterior margins of the scar are ill defined.

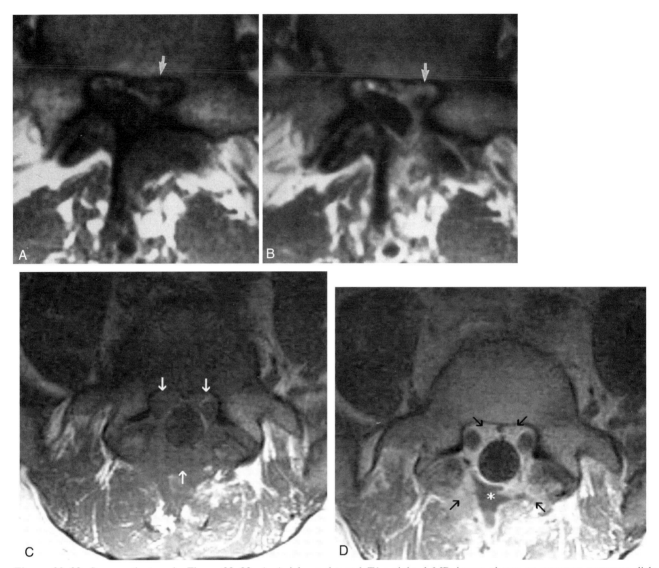

Figure 22–33. Same patient as in Figure 22–32. *A,* Axial unenhanced T1-weighted MR image shows an apparent recurrent disk herniation *(arrow). B,* After gadolinium administration, the scar tissue *(arrow)* enhances intensely, enwraps the left L5 root, and compresses the thecal sac. No evidence of disk herniation is seen. Axial unenhanced *(C)* and enhanced *(D)* T1-weighted MR images demonstrate postoperative scar *(arrows)* in another patient. Note small, nonenhancing postoperative fluid collection *(asterisk),* which can be seen only after contrast administration. This is a common postoperative finding.

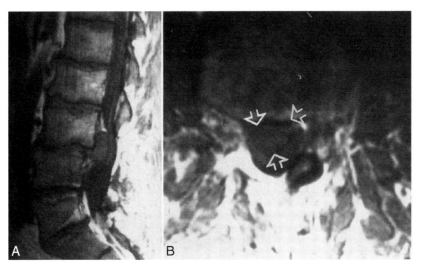

Figure 22–34. Postoperative disk herniation. *A,* Sagittal unenhanced MR image shows major disk herniation. *B,* Axial MR image after gadolinium administration shows no disk enhancement *(arrows).*

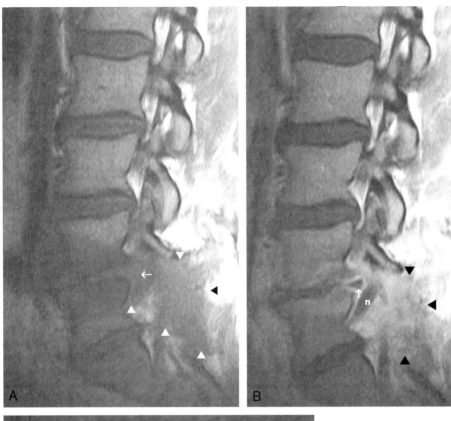

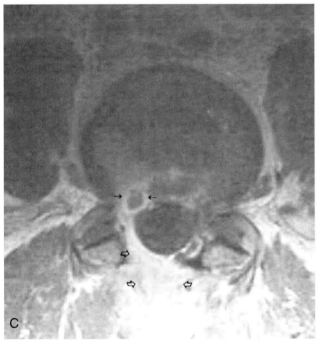

Figure 22–35. Disk herniation. *A,* Postoperative sagittal unenhanced, T1-weighted MR image. Recurrent disk herniation *(arrow)* is indistinguishable from scarring *(arrowheads).* *B,* Nonenhancing recurrent disk herniation *(arrow)* now stands out from the surrounding postoperative scar *(arrowheads).* The intensely enhancing bright rim around the disk is not a postoperative scar but, instead, peridiskal inflammation, which can be seen even on nonoperated disk herniations. n, nerve root. *C,* Axial enhanced T1-weighted MR image in the same patient shows recurrent disk herniation with surrounding peridiskal inflammation *(closed arrows). Open arrows* indicate a postoperative scar.

vascularity,"[69] which can persist years after surgery; in contrast, the herniated disk is avascular.

In summary, a recurrent herniated disk is an avascular, well-defined, low-intensity mass that does not enhance on early postinjection images. It has a well-defined margin and is usually located in the anterior epidural space contiguous with or near the native disk space. An epidural scar is a vascular structure with ill-defined margins that tends to encircle the thecal sac and roots. Anteriorly, it consistently enhances even years after surgery. Posterior epidural enhancement may decline over time. Whereas morphology and enhancement are quite reliable in differentiating a disk from a scar, signal characteristics and mass effect may overlap and should be used only as secondary signs.

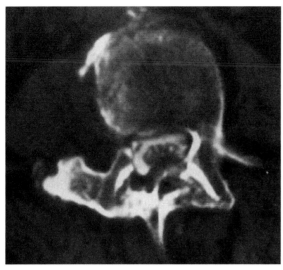

Figure 22–36. Postoperative bone overgrowth. Postmyelogram CT scan shows severe hypertrophy of posterior elements compressing the spinal canal.

Other Complications

Aside from recurrent disk herniation, several postoperative complications may occur, including:

- Bony stenosis
- Pseudomeningocele
- Arachnoiditis

- Disk space infection
- Epidural abscess

Bony Stenosis

Bony stenosis may account for up to 60% of failed back surgery cases.[80] Osteophytes and hypertrophic bone vary in MRI signal appearance, depending on degree of marrow content. CT, particularly with intrathecal contrast material, is especially helpful in evaluating canal narrowing resulting from postoperative bone overgrowth (Fig. 22–36).

Pseudomeningocele

A pseudomeningocele is a localized collection of fluid communicating with the thecal sac. This results from an iatrogenic dural tear during surgery.[81] Whereas small postoperative fluid collections along the soft tissues of the incision site may be a normal finding, a pseudomeningocele is not. MRI and CT scans show a saclike area of fluid intensity adjacent to the dura (Fig. 22–37). Blood or debris may be present within the fluid. Differentiation between abscess, postoperative fluid collection, and pseudomeningocele may be difficult. However, pseudomeningocele is likely if a communication between the thecal sac and the collection can be demonstrated, or if, on CT myelography, contrast medium enters the fluid collection.[67]

Arachnoiditis

Arachnoiditis represents an inflammatory reaction in which nerve roots adhere to the thecal sac and to each

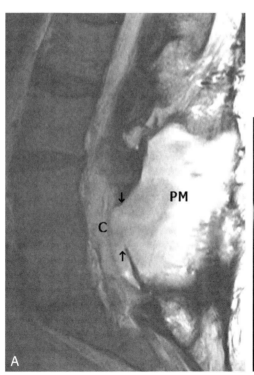

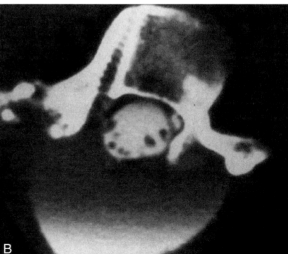

Figure 22–37. Pseudomeningocele. *A,* Postsurgical sagittal T2-weighted MRI shows large pseudomeningocele (PM). The communication (between the *arrows*) between the pseudomeningocele and the canal (C) is quite large. Compare with small, normal postoperative fluid collection shown in Figure 22–27. *B,* Axial postoperative CT scan in a different patient shows a large amount of intrathecally injected contrast pooling in a pseudomeningocele. Demonstrating the actual connection between the pseudomeningocele and the thecal sac can be difficult at times and could not be shown in this figure.

other. This can occur after laminectomy and is one of the causes of failed back surgery.[14] Normally, the nerve roots are symmetrically distributed within the dependent portion of the CSF (see Fig. 22–4G). In arachnoiditis, nerve roots clump together centrally or adhere to the dura peripherally. In advanced stages, the lumbar spinal canal is filled with inflammatory soft tissue. These changes are obvious on both MRI[72] and on CT myelography (Fig. 22–38). Interestingly, enhancement is not a prominent feature.

Disk Space Infection

Postoperative disk space infection and epidural abscess are uncommon but serious postlaminectomy complications. Although diskitis in adults is usually characterized by he-

matogeneous spread, bacterial contamination from disk manipulation can occur.

Disk space infection typically presents as hypointensity on T1-weighted images and as hyperintensity on T2-weighted images in the disk and adjacent end plates, with poor definition of the end plates themselves. These signal changes reflect reactive edema. On T2-weighted images, the internuclear cleft (the normal horizontal band of low signal intensity in the center of the nucleus pulposus) is lost. In disk space infection, the disk and adjacent end plates usually enhance with gadolinium administration (Fig. 22–39).[7] Despite the myriad early normal postoperative changes in the epidural space, generally no signal intensity or morphologic changes are found in the disk space itself or in the adjacent end plates after uncompli-

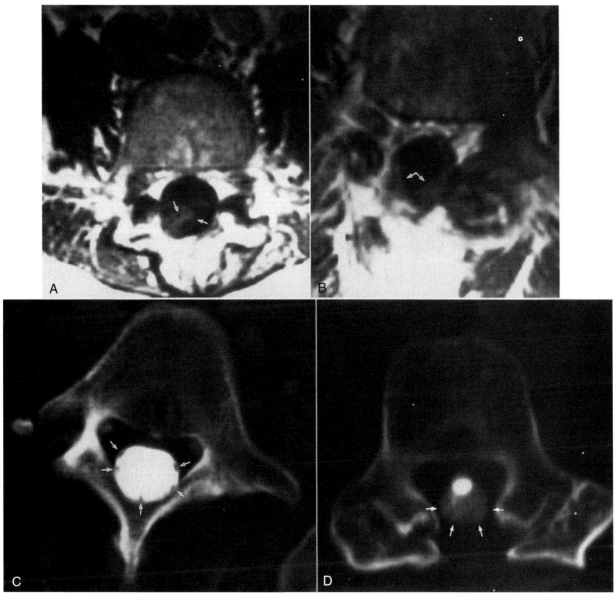

Figure 22–38. Arachnoiditis. *A,* Axial postoperative unenhanced T1-weighted MR image shows clumping of nerve roots *(arrows)* within the spinal canal. *B,* Enhanced scan in another postoperative patient shows the nerve roots adhering peripherally to the dura *(arrows).* Note that root enhancement is not a feature. *C,* Postmyelogram CT scan shows nerve roots adhering peripherally to the dura *(arrows).* This gives the appearance of an "empty" thecal sac. *D,* Postmyelogram CT scan shows advanced arachnoiditis. Most of the spinal canal is filled with inflammatory tissue *(arrows),* with only a small amount of contrast noted anteriorly.

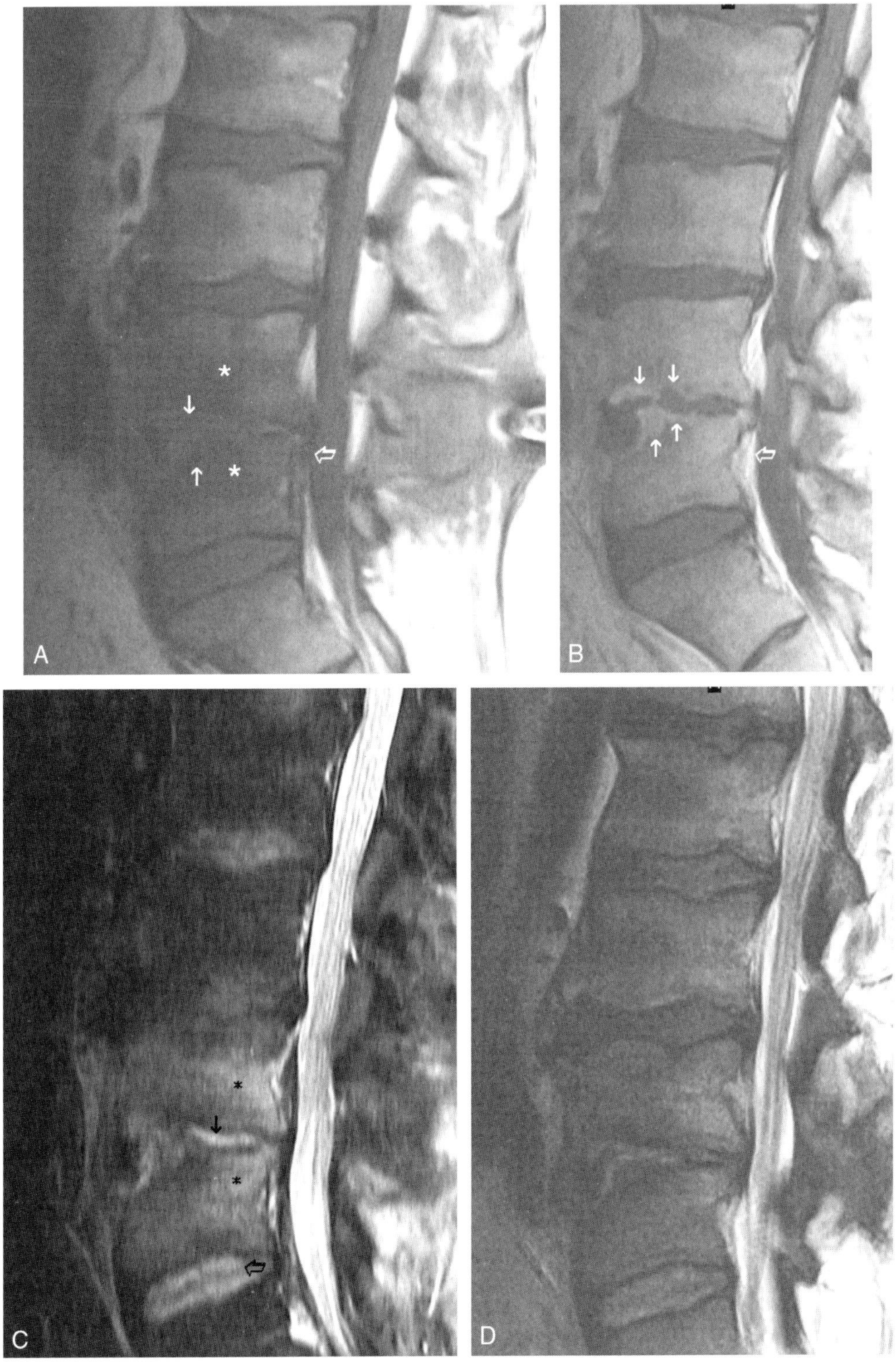

Figure 22–39. Postoperative infection.

A, T1-weighted unenhanced MR image of L4-5 diskitis/osteomyelitis. Dark signal *(asterisks)* denotes edema in the vertebral end plates and marrow. The infected disk is conforming to the shape of eroded end plates *(closed arrows)*. Abnormal soft tissue is seen in the anterior epidural space *(open arrow)*.

B, T1-weighted enhanced MR image in the same patient. The margins of the disk enhance *(closed arrows)* as does the infected anterior epidural soft tissue *(open arrow)*.

C, Short tau inversion recovery (STIR) sequence shows the bone edema *(asterisks)* markedly well. Note loss of the internuclear cleft in the infected disk *(closed arrow)* compared with a normal nondegenerated, noninfected disk *(open arrow)*.

D, Fast spin-echo, T2-weighted MR image does not show the edema nearly as well as the STIR sequence, which is indispensable for evaluation of osteomyelitis.

cated diskectomy.[7] Therefore, any disk space or end-plate abnormality in the postoperative period should be viewed with suspicion.

Several problems occur, however, in differentiating both degenerated disks and normal postoperative disks from disk infection:

1. *Type I* degenerated end plates are also hypointense on T1-weighted images and hyperintense on T2-weighted images and may enhance with gadolinium. However, no change should occur in the appearance of the unenhanced disk after uncomplicated diskectomy. Comparison of preoperative and postoperative scans is thus important. Furthermore, the cortical margins should remain sharp after uncomplicated diskectomy, whereas the margins are indistinct in infection.

2. *Type II* degenerated end plates have high signal intensity on T1-weighted images and high to slightly lower signal intensity on T2-weighted images. This high T1 signal may mask the low T1 signal found in disk space infection. In this case, too, it is important to look for abnormal disk signal, to compare preoperative and postoperative scans, and to evaluate cortical margins.

3. Infected disks and end plates usually enhance with gadolinium; uncommonly, however, the normal postoperative disk can enhance. Boden and colleagues[7] observed that it is unlikely for normal postoperative patients to have all three abnormal findings (i.e., low disk/end-plate signal on T1-weighted images, high disk/end-plate signal on T2-weighted images, and disk/end-plate enhancement with gadolinium). This "triad" suggests disk infection in the symptomatic patient.

MRI using fat suppression has made the diagnosis of postoperative diskitis/osteomyelitis easier. Short tau inversion recovery (STIR) imaging shows disk and bone edema that may be difficult to visualize on T1-weighted and T2-weighted images because of bright, fatty marrow obscuring the edema (Fig. 22–39C).

Epidural Abscess

Epidural abscess is also hypointense on T1-weighted images and hyperintense on T2-weighted images and shows mass effect on the thecal sac. Because these changes may be masked by the similar signal of CSF, gadolinium should be given when epidural abscess is suspected (Fig. 22–39).[76]

Cervical Spine

After the lumbar spine, the cervical spine is next most commonly affected by spondylosis and disk herniation.[57] The most frequently involved interspaces are C4-5, C5-6, and C6-7. This may be due to the greater degree of motion at these levels.[21] Although many concepts of nondiskogenic and diskogenic degeneration (osteophyte formation, foraminal stenosis, spondylolisthesis, and disk herniation) are much the same as in the lumbar canal, a couple of important anatomic and clinical differences should be emphasized:

1. Because the cervical spinal cord carries neurons from both the upper and lower extremities, symptoms referable to arms, legs, or both may occur.

2. Because the dimensions of even the normal cervical spinal canal are small relative to the lumbar, small spondylitic or disk changes may cause significant symptoms.

Anatomic Considerations

Although the basic anatomy of the cervical and lumbar vertebrae and diskovertebral junctions are similar, several important differences as they may relate to spondylosis warrant brief review.

Unlike the more rounded configuration of the lumbar sac, the cervical spinal canal is triangular. The cervical spinal cord is oval (Fig. 22–40). The canal decreases in size from C1 to C3 and is uniform from C3 to C7. The normal lower limit anteroposterior diameter of the canal is 16 mm at C1, 15 mm at C2, and 12 mm in the lower cervical spine.[52]

The exiting cervical nerve roots travel in an inferior direction through the foramina at about 45 degrees with respect to the coronal plane (Fig. 22–41). This differs from the lumbar roots, which travel inferiorly but nearly parallel with the coronal plane. This makes sagittal imaging of the cervical nerve roots less optimal than in the lumbar spine.

The cervical nerve roots exit above (not below, as in the lumbar spine) the pedicle of its corresponding vertebral body. Because there are eight cervical roots but only seven vertebrae, the relationship changes at the C8 root, which passes above the T1 pedicle. The T1 root then passes under the T1 pedicle and the pattern is the same as in the lumbar spine the rest of the way down.

In addition to the body, laminae, pedicles, spinous, and transverse processes, the cervical vertebrae have uncinate processes, or joints of Luschka, paired bony ridges projecting superiorly from the posterolateral margins of the vertebral bodies. They fit into notches on the posterolateral surfaces of the inferior end plates of the vertebral bodies above. On axial images, they can be seen indenting the posterolateral disk margin as they bridge the vertebral bodies (Fig. 22–42; see Fig. 22–41). The uncinate processes contribute to the anterior walls of the neural foramina; if hypertrophied, they can cause foraminal stenosis. Whereas the lumbar facet joints are fairly sagittally oriented, the cervical facets are obliquely positioned, their surfaces lying halfway between a coronal and axial plane (see Figs. 22–41 and 22–42).

The vertebral arteries pass through the bony transverse foramina, located on the lateral aspects of vertebrae C1 to C6 (see Fig. 22–40). The arteries can rarely be compressed by foraminal spurs.

Imaging Techniques

At our institution, CT scans of the cervical spine for degenerative disease are usually done following myelography (see Figs. 22–40 and 22–42). Investigators have found that the increased sensitivity of CT myelography over standard CT in the cervical spine is even greater than in the

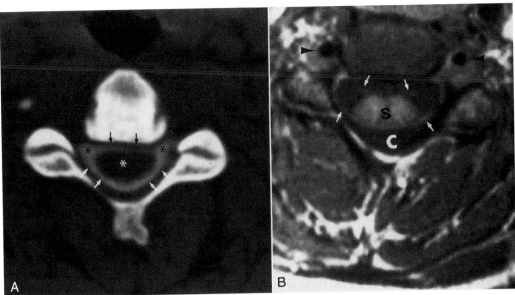

Figure 22–40. Cervical images. *A,* Cervical postmyelogram CT scan. Note the triangular configuration of the spinal canal *(arrows)* and oval shape of the spinal cord *(white asterisk).* The nerve root sheaths *(black asterisk)* can be seen exiting through the neural foramina. *B,* Axial cervical T1-weighted MR image. c, spinal canal; s, spinal cord. *Arrows* indicate nerve roots; *arrowheads* indicate vertebral arteries in the transverse foramina.

lumbar spine.[12] After myelography, 2-mm contiguous axial images through the levels of concern are obtained. Both bone and soft tissue windows are photographed. Unlike lumbar CT myelography, cervical CT myelography is done soon after the intrathecal injection because contrast mate-

rial in the cervical canal tends to flow away from the cervical canal more quickly and the injection volume is generally smaller than in the lumbar canal (Box 22–3).

As in the lumbar spine, numerous choices are available for MRI of the cervical spine. We obtain a set of fast spin-echo, T1-weighted and T2-weighted sagittal images of the entire cervical region (Fig. 22–43). These images should include the cerebellar tonsils down to the first thoracic level.

With the development of stronger x-y-z gradient coils,

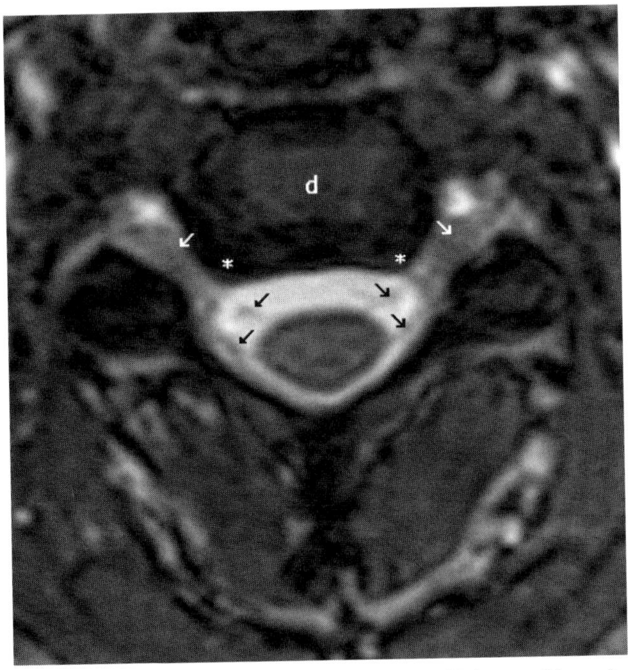

Figure 22–41. Axial cervical gradient-echo MR image. The exiting nerve roots approach the neural foramina at a 45-degree angle. Both the anterior and posterior divisions can be seen *(black arrows)*; they then join to form the dorsal root ganglia in the foramina *(white arrows).* Note hypointense uncovertebral joints of Luschka *(asterisks)* indenting the posterolateral disk (d) margins.

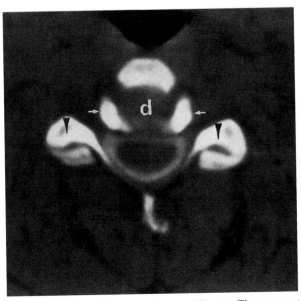

Figure 22–42. Cervical postmyelogram CT scan. The uncovertebral joints of Luschka are indenting the posterolateral disk (d) margins *(arrows)* (see Fig. 22–41). Note also the near-horizontal orientation of the facet joints *(arrowheads)* (see also Fig. 22–41).

Box 22–3. **Routine CT of Cervical Degenerative Disease**

- Axial contiguous images from C2 to T1
- Slice thickness = 2–3 mm, intersection gap = 2 mm
- Both wide and narrow window settings
- Intrathecal contrast preferable

Box 22–4. **Example of Routine MRI of Cervical Degenerative Disease**

1. Sagittal fast spin-echo, T1-weighted image to include cerebellar tonsils to T1 level
   a. Field of view = 26–28 cm, thickness = 3–4 mm, intersection gap = 1 mm, matrix = 256 × 512
2. Sagittal fast spin-echo, T2-weighted image to include cerebellar tonsils to T1 level
   a. Field of view = 26–28 cm, thickness = 3–4 mm, intersection gap = 1 mm, matrix = 384 × 512
3. Axial 2D gradient-echo sequence to cover at least C2-3 through C6-7 interspaces
   a. Field of view = 20 cm, thickness = 3 mm, intersection gap = 1 mm, matrix = 384 × 512
4. Axial 3D gradient-echo sequence contiguous to cover at least C2-3 through C6-7
   a. Field of view = 20 cm, reconstructed thickness = 2 mm, matrix = 512 × 512
   b. Apply magnetization transfer pulse
5. If postoperative spine, substitute noncontrast T1-weighted, fast spin-echo axial views for one of the gradient-echo sequences
   a. Field of view = 20 cm, thickness = 3 mm, intersection gap = 1 mm, matrix = 256 × 256

matrices in the range of 300 to 600 can be obtained, greatly increasing image resolution. The stronger gradients also allow for shorter imaging times and larger fields of view (allowing inclusion of the upper thoracic spine in the cervical images—a request often made by referring physicians) with little or no decrease in image resolution. We also obtain a set of 2D gradient-echo as well as 3D (volume) gradient-echo axial images from the C3-4 interspace down to at least the C6-7 interspace. The T1-weighted images are used for evaluation of overall anatomy and marrow abnormalities. The gradient-echo images bring out the "myelographic effect," enhancing contrast between bone-root-cord and CSF (see Fig. 22–41). We use both 2D and 3D gradient-echo axial views because we find that overall image quality tends to be better with 2D sequences, but the thinner slices obtained with 3D sequences often help to detect small lesions. We apply a magnetization transfer pulse to the 3D images to help darken the cord and roots, thus increasing the myelographic contrast effect.

Again, imaging sequences may vary widely among institutions. For instance, some centers routinely obtain T1-weighted axial views, whereas we do not, except in the postoperative cervical spine. All 2D images are 3 to 4 mm

thick with a 1- to 1.5-mm gap (Box 22–4). Given the 45-degree angle of the exiting nerve roots, some authors advocate using sagittal oblique images (perpendicular to the foramina) rather than direct sagittal views for optimal foraminal imaging.[55] This, however, requires two separate sets of oblique images, one for each side, and is therefore more time-consuming. We occasionally make use of the

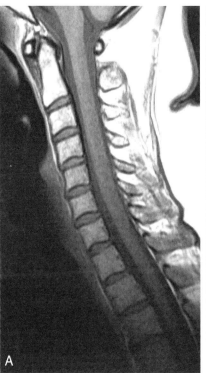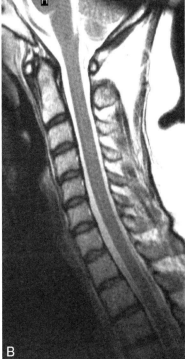

Figure 22–43. Sagittal fast spin-echo, T1-weighted *(A)* and T2-weighted *(B)* cervical MR images. The field of view should include cerebellar tonsils to at least the first thoracic level. A large field of view helps to include the upper thoracic spine.

sagittal oblique when there is obvious clinical radiculopathy without obvious MRI findings. The oblique images occasionally reveal small, but strategically located intraforaminal disk herniations.

Because the cervical spine is small and "crowded," volume averaging, patient motion, flow and pulsation artifacts, and small-structure (e.g., foraminal stenosis) evaluation are more problematic in the cervical than in the lumbar spine. More refined imaging techniques (e.g., volume imaging, fast spin-echo imaging, magnetization transfer, motion compensation) to alleviate these problems are evolving rapidly, and numerous new sequences and techniques emerge constantly.

Nondiskogenic Spinal Stenosis

Degenerative disease of the cervical spine is very common after age 40 and may, in fact, affect 70% of people older than age 70.[37, 43] In older individuals, *facet hypertrophy* and *osteophytosis* become more problematic than disk herniation; whereas osteophytes and facet disease worsen with age, disk material becomes harder, more immobile, and less likely to protrude.[8] As in the lumbar spine, osteophytes can compress any portion of the neural canal and foramina (Fig. 22–44). Ligamentum flavum hypertrophy can contribute to spinal and foraminal stenosis (see Fig. 22–44). Unique to the cervical spine are the uncinate processes, or joints of Luschka, which contribute to the anterior wall of the neural foramina. Uncinate hypertrophy or osteophytosis, therefore, may lead to foraminal stenosis (Fig. 22–45).[45, 58] Facet hypertrophy generally narrows the foramina (see Fig. 22–45).

CT is well suited for visualization of bone and facet disease. On MRI, osteophytes can be of high, intermediate, or low signal intensity on T1-weighted images, depending on their yellow marrow content.[54] Intermediate-signal and low-signal osteophytes may blend in with adjacent liga-

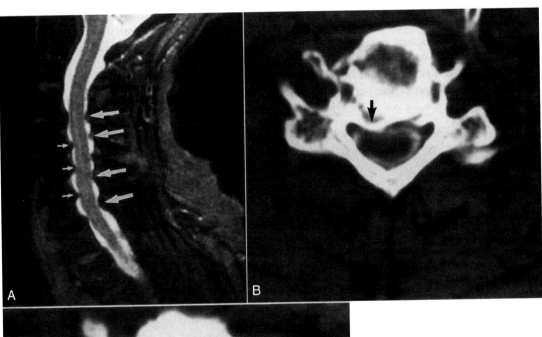

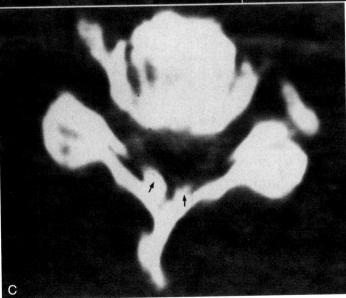

Figure 22–44. *A,* Sagittal gradient-echo MR image shows multiple osteophytes *(small arrows)* encroaching on the thecal sac. Ligamentous hypertrophy *(large arrows)* is also present posteriorly. *B,* Postmyelogram CT scan shows an osteophyte *(arrow)* flattening the right aspect of the canal and cord. *C,* Postmyelogram CT scan shows posterior element osteophytes *(arrows).*

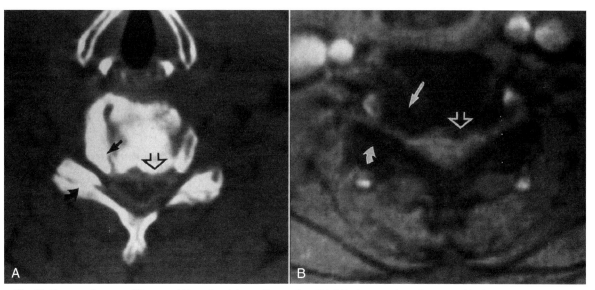

Figure 22–45. Postmyelogram CT scan *(A)* and axial gradient-echo *(B)* MR image show hypertrophied uncovertebral joint *(closed arrows)* narrowing the right neural foramen. Right-sided facet hypertrophy *(curved arrows)* contributes to this narrowing. Note also osteophytes *(open arrows).*

ments and CSF in the cervical region, where volume averaging is already a problem.

As mentioned, we obtain gradient-echo images in the cervical region, which makes bone very dark regardless of marrow content. This stands out nicely against the myelographically bright CSF. One must beware, however, of the "blooming" effect, in which osteophyte size may be exaggerated on gradient-echo sequences owing to magnetic susceptibility. Thus, spinal stenosis secondary to osteophytes seen on gradient-echo sequences should be confirmed on T1-weighted images, whose magnetic susceptibility effects are not as prominent.

Posterolateral bone, ligament, and facet disease, which impinge on the nerve roots, can lead to upper extremity radiculopathy. Central disease that compresses the cervical cord can produce myelopathy as well,[10, 28, 59] resulting in lower extremity symptoms, including spasticity, weakness, and gait disturbance.[8, 28] Clinically, this syndrome must be differentiated from other forms of myelopathy, such as multiple sclerosis, spinal neoplasm, and various intrinsic spinal cord diseases. In addition, if large spurs compress the vertebral arteries, symptoms of vertebrobasilar insufficiency may occur.[8]

Although common in Japan, *ossification of the posterior longitudinal ligament* (OPLL) is a fairly rare cause of spinal stenosis in the United States. There is no known etiologic mechanism. The ossified posterior longitudinal ligament can impinge on the spinal canal, resulting in nerve root or spinal cord compression. This entity is well visualized on plain films as a vertical band of ossified tissue along the posterior margin of the vertebral bodies. On CT scans, the involved portion of the ligament is replaced by the high density of calcium. On MR images, the ossification is represented by low signal on short TR, long TR, and gradient-echo sequences (Fig. 22–46). However, fatty marrow within the ossification can yield areas of high signal intensity on T1.[61]

Diskogenic Spinal Stenosis

Early in the course of cervical spinal osteoarthritis, the most common cause of pain is direct nerve-root compression by a laterally herniated cervical disk, which ordinarily occurs without prior trauma. This results in neck and arm pain with paresthesias in a dermatomal distribution. Both sensory and motor abnormalities occur. Cervical disk herniations are most common in the second through fourth decades of life.[8]

These herniations are well seen on both CT myelography (Fig. 22–47) and MRI (Fig. 22–48) as extradural soft tissue masses contiguous with the parent disk and focally protruding posterolaterally into the canal and/or neural foramina. Central disk herniations are less common and can cause spinal cord compression, resulting in myelopathy as well as radiculopathy (Fig. 22–48*E*).[8]

Postoperative Cervical Spine

Postoperative Changes

Most decompressive procedures on the cervical spine are now performed via an anterior approach.[15, 34, 65] With the *Smith-Robinson* technique, the disk and end-plate material are removed and are replaced with an osseous wedge from the iliac bone.[65] During the *Cloward* technique, the surgeon removes posterior and posterolateral osteophytes, drills a hole into the disk space and end plates, and reinserts a prefitted piece of bone.[15] Strut grafts are used for cervical stabilization after multilevel decompressive surgery is performed. The grafted bone bridges the involved vertebral bodies.

Although these techniques are commonly used, many other approaches, both anterior and posterior, are available (Fig. 22–49). In the immediate diskectomy-fusion postoperative period, the signal intensity of the intervertebral bone

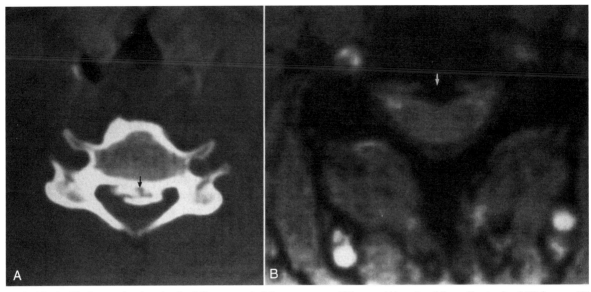

Figure 22–46. Ossified posterior longitudinal ligament. Axial noncontrast CT scan *(A)* and axial gradient-echo MR image *(B)* show the ossified ligament *(arrows)* impinging on the spinal canal.

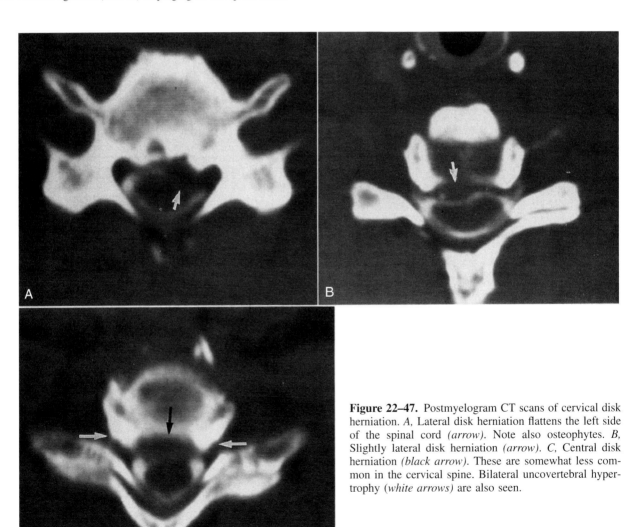

Figure 22–47. Postmyelogram CT scans of cervical disk herniation. *A,* Lateral disk herniation flattens the left side of the spinal cord *(arrow)*. Note also osteophytes. *B,* Slightly lateral disk herniation *(arrow)*. *C,* Central disk herniation *(black arrow)*. These are somewhat less common in the cervical spine. Bilateral uncovertebral hypertrophy *(white arrows)* are also seen.

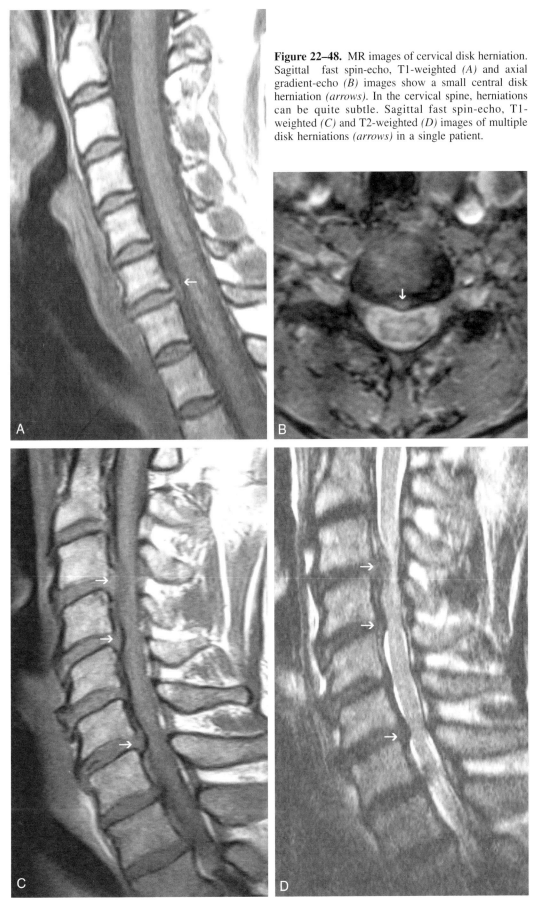

Figure 22–48. MR images of cervical disk herniation. Sagittal fast spin-echo, T1-weighted *(A)* and axial gradient-echo *(B)* images show a small central disk herniation *(arrows)*. In the cervical spine, herniations can be quite subtle. Sagittal fast spin-echo, T1-weighted *(C)* and T2-weighted *(D)* images of multiple disk herniations *(arrows)* in a single patient.

Illustration continued on following page

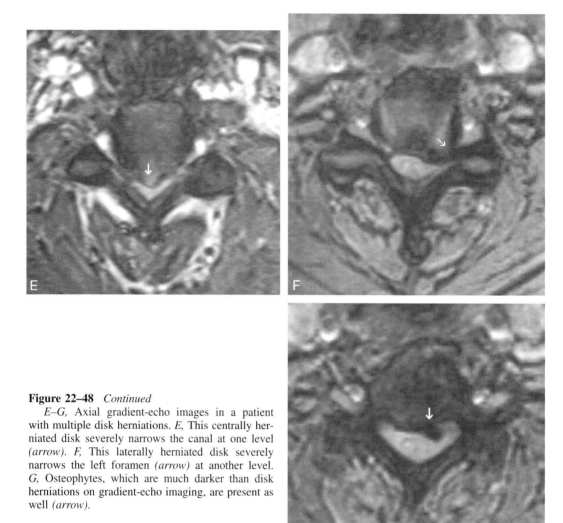

Figure 22–48 *Continued*
E–G, Axial gradient-echo images in a patient
with multiple disk herniations. *E,* This centrally herniated disk severely narrows the canal at one level
(arrow). F, This laterally herniated disk severely
narrows the left foramen *(arrow)* at another level.
G, Osteophytes, which are much darker than disk
herniations on gradient-echo imaging, are present as
well *(arrow).*

grafts on MRI may be quite variable, according to whether
the marrow is cellular or fatty and whether the bone is
cancellous or compact. Adjacent end plates can have normal signal or signal that reflects postoperative edema. Disk
and end-plate changes in the late postoperative period are
even more variable, reflecting not only the composition of
the bone graft but also, possibly, the amount of revascularization, postoperative stresses, and intraoperative trauma
received by the end plate and graft.[70, 73]

Strut grafts are easily seen as long wedges of bone
bridging the anterior aspects of the vertebral bodies. On
MR images, the signal of the bulk of the graft may be
variable but low-signal cortex outlines the graft margins
(see Fig. 22–49). Solid bony fusions without replacement
of disk by graft are seen as continuous marrow signal with
no definable interspace (Fig. 22–49C). One of the most
common types of procedures seen today involves anterior
diskectomy, followed by interbody fusion with a piece of
bone and placement of an anterior plate-screw device for
maximum stability (Fig. 22–49D–G).

Complications

Complications of cervical spine decompression are similar to those in the lumbar region, including (1) bony stenosis, (2) disk herniation, (3) pseudomeningocele, and (4)
infection. There are, however, some differences.

1. Bony stenosis may be caused not only by osteophyte
   formation but also by uncovertebral hypertrophy or by
   overgrowth of the fusion mass itself. These can produce
   spinal as well as foraminal stenosis. When one is looking at gradient-echo images of the cervical spine, the
   surgical material used may cause magnetic susceptibility
   "blooming" artifact and may mimic severe spinal stenosis when in fact no stenosis exists (see Fig. 22–49D–G).
   It is important, therefore to examine all images carefully, especially the T1-weighted and T2-weighted sequences. These sequences (especially FSE) tend not to
   exaggerate the degree of spinal stenosis. We substitute
   a set of T1-weighted axial images for one of the gradient-echo axial views to mitigate these artifacts in the
   postoperative cervical spine (see Fig. 22–49G).

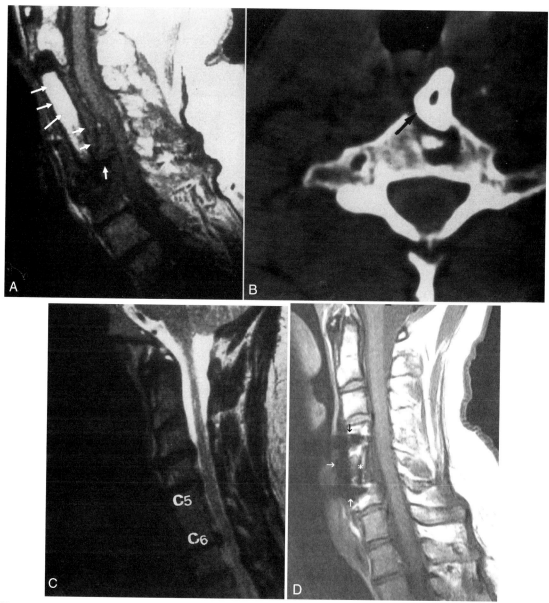

Figure 22–49. Various types of cervical fusions.

A, Large fibular strut graft *(black arrows)* for multilevel fusion. Note early postoperative edema *(white arrows)* causing cord compression.

B, Axial CT scan in a different patient shows a fibular strut graft *(arrow)* fusing C4-5.

C, Solid C5-6 fusion.

D–G, C4-6 fusion by means of plate-screw combination and interbody bone graft. *D*, T1-weighted image. *Arrows* indicate a plate-screw device. *Asterisk* indicates interbody bone graft. No significant spinal stenosis post-grafting.

Illustration continued on following page

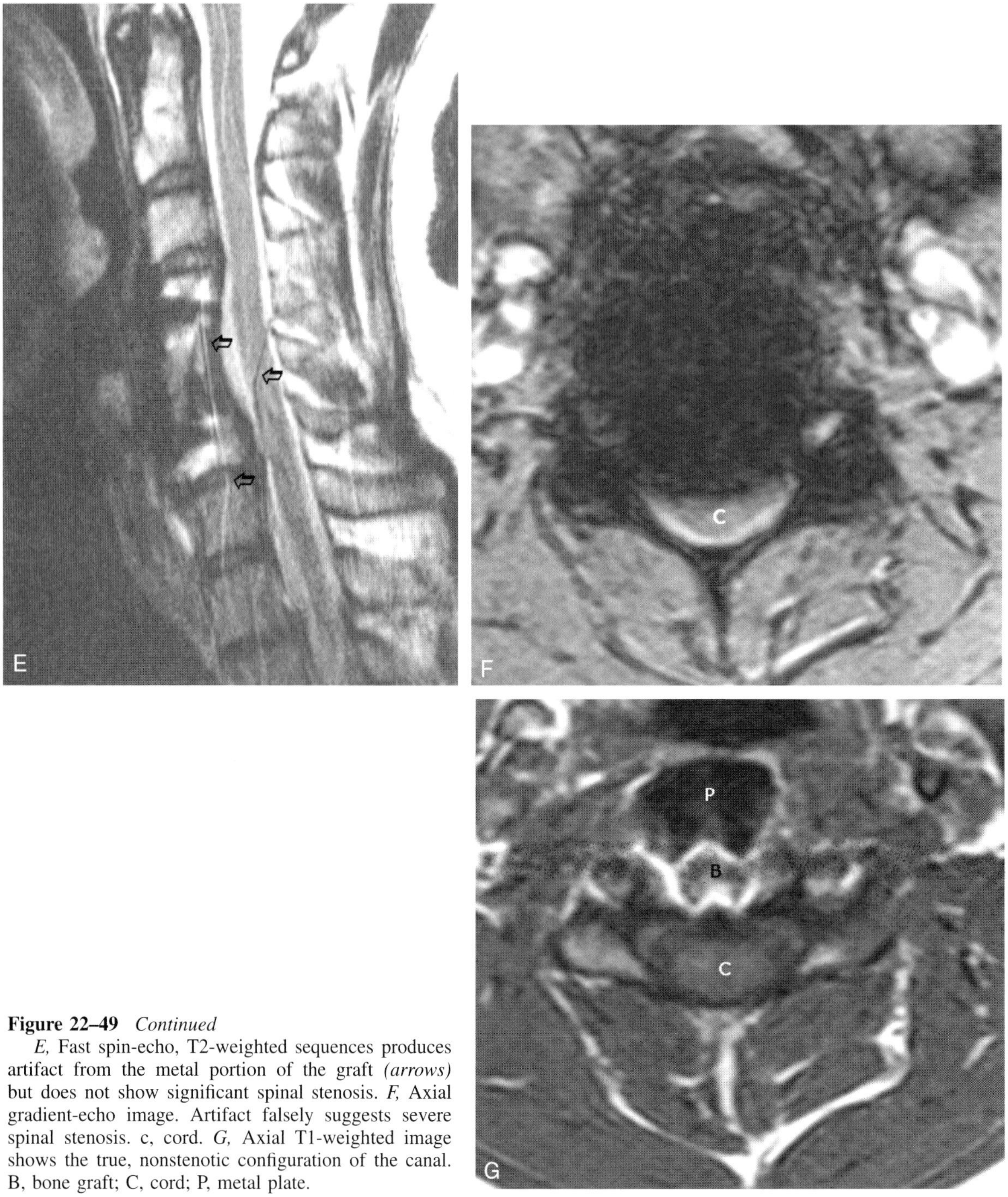

Figure 22–49 *Continued*

E, Fast spin-echo, T2-weighted sequences produces artifact from the metal portion of the graft *(arrows)* but does not show significant spinal stenosis. *F,* Axial gradient-echo image. Artifact falsely suggests severe spinal stenosis. c, cord. *G,* Axial T1-weighted image shows the true, nonstenotic configuration of the canal. B, bone graft; C, cord; P, metal plate.

2. Because most or all of a disk is removed and replaced in a cervical diskectomy and fusion, postoperative recurrent disk herniations tend not to occur unless residual disk material is inadvertently left behind. Graft extrusion, however, is an uncommon complication that can mimic a herniated disk at the operative level. Cervical disk herniations at nearby levels can occur from the altered stresses within the spine.[70]

3. Cervical spine instability can be a significant problem in a patient's status after cervical laminectomy.[67] Both MRI and CT scans with sagittal or coronal reconstructions can demonstrate postoperative scoliotic, kyphotic, and rotational deformities as well as malalignment. These scans can also be performed in flexion and extension to demonstrate abnormal motion. Unfortunately, no effective way of evaluating graft integrity by CT or MRI exists to date.

Thoracic Spine

Both disk herniation and spinal stenosis of the thoracic spine are less common than in the lumbar and cervical spine. The infrequency of thoracic spinal stenosis is proba-

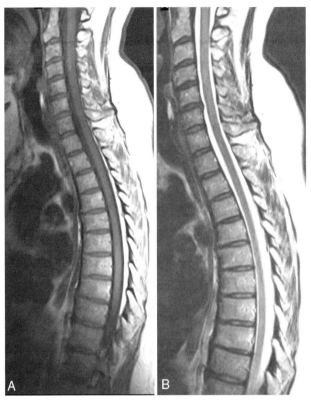

Figure 22–50. Sagittal fast spin-echo, T1-weighted *(A)* and T2-weighted *(B)* thoracic MR images. The entire thoracic spine as well as the cervical spine is easily included in the field of view.

bly due to the large size of the thoracic canal relative to the cord.[51] To produce compressive symptomatology, bony or ligamentous hypertrophy must be fairly large. The incidence of thoracic disk herniation is also less than in the remainder of the spine. This is presumably due to the limited mobility of the thoracic spine and because the weight-bearing axis does not intersect the posterior margins of the vertebral bodies.[5, 66] Most patients with operated thoracic disks report an incidence of less than 2%, although autopsy series report an incidence of between 7% and 15%.[2] With the emergence of MRI, these herniations are being recognized with increased frequency.[74]

Imaging Techniques

MRI demonstrates both thoracic canal stenosis and thoracic disk herniations quite well. MRI is also useful for

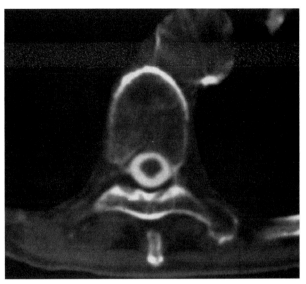

Figure 22–51. Normal postmyelogram thoracic CT scan. Note the round shape of the normal thoracic cord and canal.

excluding other causes of thoracic disease, such as tumor or infection. At our institution, we obtain T1-weighted sagittal sequences, followed by FSE T2-weighted sagittal sequences (Fig. 22–50). These images are then inspected, and axial images are obtained through the level of concern as needed (Box 22–5).

CT myelography complements MRI in evaluation of spinal stenosis caused by bony hypertrophy or ligamentous ossification owing to its superior ability to image calcium. Because of its length, covering the entire thoracic spine with CT using a reasonable number of slices is difficult. Therefore, if CT scanning is to be performed, it is probably best done after myelography or MRI to define the level of pathology (Fig. 22–51). CT images can then be obtained through the level of concern (Box 22–6). With modern, large field-of-view coils, MRI can be used to depict the entire thoracic spine in one shot (see Fig. 22–50), thus making MRI the preferred imaging modality for thoracic degenerative disease.

Nondiskogenic Spinal Stenosis

Acquired thoracic spinal stenosis can result from hypertrophy of the bony posterior elements.[84] Since the advent of CT scanning, hypertrophy or calcification of the posterior longitudinal ligament (Fig. 22–52) and degenerative ligamentum flavum hypertrophy are also being recognized with increased frequency in the thoracic spine.[3, 50]

Box 22–5. Example of Routine MRI of Thoracic Degenerative Disease

1. Sagittal T1 to include entire thoracic spine
   a. Field of view = 40 cm, slice thickness = 3–4 mm, intersection gap = 1 mm, matrix = 512 × 512
2. Sagittal fast spin-echo, T2-weighted image to include entire thoracic spine
   a. Field of view = 40 cm, slice thickness = 3–4 mm, intersection gap = 1 mm, matrix = 512 × 512
3. Axial fast spin-echo, T1-weighted and T2-weighted images through areas of concern as needed

---

Box 22–6. Routine CT of Thoracic Degenerative Disease

- Axial contiguous images through areas of concern
- Slice thickness = 4 mm, intersection gap = 4 mm
- Intrathecal contrast medium preferable
- Both wide and narrow window settings

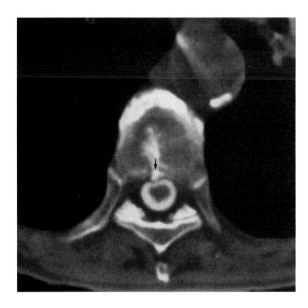

Figure 22–52. An ossified posterior longitudinal ligament *(arrow)* impinges on the thoracic spinal canal.

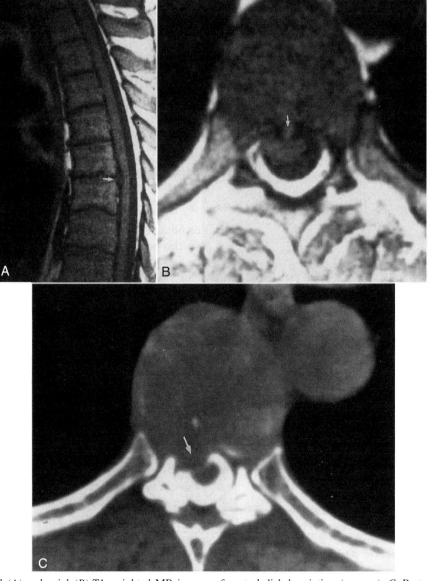

Figure 22–53. Sagittal *(A)* and axial *(B)* T1-weighted MR images of central disk herniation *(arrows)*. *C,* Postmyelogram CT scan of slightly lateral disk herniation *(arrow)*.

Diskogenic Spinal Stenosis

Most thoracic disk herniations occur in the lower thoracic spine. T11 and T12 are the most common locations. Unlike the case with the rest of the spine, most thoracic herniations are centrally, rather than laterally, located (Fig. 22–53). Multilevel thoracic herniation is rare. Most patients with thoracic disk herniations are between 30 and 50 years of age.[66]

Nondegenerative Spinal Stenosis

Nondegenerative spinal stenosis has numerous causes, the most common of which is idiopathic congenital or developmental narrowing of the spinal canal. This is probably due to inadequate development of the canal and foramina. Symptoms usually arise when degenerative changes of disks, facets, and ligaments are superimposed on an already small canal.[25]

Box 22–7 summarizes the nondegenerative causes of spinal stenosis.

Box 22–7. Nondegenerative Causes of Spinal Stenosis

A. Congenital-developmental stenosis
 1. Idiopathic
 2. Achondroplasia/hypochondroplasia
 3. Hypophosphatemic vitamin D–resistant rickets
 4. Morquio's disease
 5. Congenital dysplasias associated with lax atlantoaxial joints
 6. Down's syndrome
 7. Spondylolisthesis
 8. Scoliosis
 9. Spinal dysraphism
B. Acquired stenosis
 1. Degenerative
  a. Spondylosis
  b. Spondylolisthesis
  c. Scoliosis
  d. Ossification of the posterior longitudinal ligament
  e. Ligamentum flavum hypertrophy or ossification
  f. Intraspinal synovial cysts
 2. Postoperative
  a. Postlaminectomy
  b. Postfusion
  c. Postdiskectomy
 3. Post-traumatic
 4. Metabolic
  a. Epidural lipomatosis
  b. Osteoporosis leading to vertebral fractures
  c. Acromegaly
  d. Calcium pyrophosphate deposition disease
  e. Renal osteodystrophy
  f. Hypoparathyroidism
  g. Oxalosis
 5. Miscellaneous
  a. Paget's disease
  b. Ankylosing spondylitis
  c. Diffuse idiopathic skeletal hyperostosis
  d. Rheumatoid arthritis
  e. Fluorosis
  f. Scheurmann's disease
  g. Osteopoikilosis
 6. Combined
  a. Combined lumbar and cervical stenosis
  b. Combined developmental/congenital and degenerative stenosis

Modified from Moreland LW, Lopez-Mendez A, Alarcon GS: Spinal stenosis: A comprehensive review of the literature. Semin Arthritis Rheum 19:127–149,1989.

References

1. Adams P, Eyre DR, Muir H: Biochemical aspects of development and aging of human lumbar intervertebral disks. Rheumatol Rehabil 16:22–29, 1977.
2. Arseni C, Nash F: Protrusion of thoracic intervertebral discs. Acta Neurochir 11:3–33, 1963.
3. Barnett GH, et al: Thoracic spinal canal stenosis. J Neurosurg 66:338–344, 1987.
4. Bates DB, Rugierri P: Imaging modalities for evaluation of the spine. Radiol Clin North Am 29:675–690, 1991.
5. Blumenkopf B: Thoracic intervertebral disk herniations: Diagnostic value of magnetic resonance imaging. Neurosurgery 23:36–40, 1988.
6. Boden SD, Davis DO, Dina TS, et al: Contrast-enhanced MR imaging performed after successful lumbar disk surgery: Prospective study. Radiology 182:59–64, 1992.
7. Boden SD, Davis DO, Dina TS, et al: Postoperative diskitis: Distinguishing early MR imaging findings from normal postoperative disk space changes. Radiology 184:765–771, 1992.
8. Bohlman HH: Osteoarthritis of the cervical spine. In Osteoarthritis Diagnosis and Management. Philadelphia, WB Saunders, 1984, pp 443–459.
9. Bowen V, Shannon R, Kirkaldy-Willis WH: Lumbar spinal stenosis: A review article. Child's Brain 4:257–277, 1978.
10. Brain WR, Northfield DW, Wilkinson M: The neurological manifestations of cervical spondylosis. Brain 75:187–225, 1952.
11. Brown MD: The pathophysiology of disc disease: Symposium on disease of the intervertebral disc. Orthop Clin North Am 2:359–370, 1971.
12. Brown BM, Schwartz RH, Frank E, Blank NK: Preoperative evaluation of cervical radiculopathy and myelopathy by surface-coil MR imaging. AJR Am J Roentgenol 151:1205–1212, 1988.
13. Bundschuh CV, et al: Epidural fibrosis and recurrent disk herniation in the lumbar spine: Assessment with magnetic resonance. AJNR Am J Neuroradiol 9:169–178, 1988.
14. Burton CV, Kirkaldy-Willis WH, Yong-Hing K, Heithoff KB: Causes of failure of surgery on the lumbar spine. Clin Orthop 157:191–199, 1981.
15. Cloward RB: The anterior approach for removal of ruptured cervical discs. J Neurosurg 15:602–614, 1958.
16. Coventry MB: Anatomy of the intervertebral disk. Clin Orthop 67:9–15, 1969.
17. de Roos A, Krossel H, Spritzer C, Dalinka M: MR imaging of marrow changes adjacent to end plates in degenerative lumbar disk disease. Am J Roentgenol 149:531–534, 1987.
18. Dorwart RH, Volger JB III, Helms CA: Spinal stenosis. Radiol Clin North Am 21:301–325, 1983.
19. Dublin AB, McGahan JP, Reid MH: The value of computed tomographic metrizamide myelography in the neuroradiologic evaluation of the spine. Radiology 146:79–86, 1983.
20. Epstein NE, Epstein JA, Carras R, Hyman RA: Far lateral lumbar disc herniations and associated structural abnormalities: An evaluation in 60 patients of the comparative value of CT, MRI, and myelo-CT in diagnosis and management. Spine 15:534–539, 1990.
21. Epstein BS, Epstein JA, Jones MD: Cervical spine stenosis. Radiol Clin North Am 15:215, 1977.
22. Epstein BS, Epstein JA, Jones MD: Lumbar spinal stenosis. Radiol Clin North Am 15:227–239, 1977.
23. Frymoyer JW, Cats-Baril WL: An overview of the incidences and costs of low back pain. Orthop Clin North Am 22, 1991.
24. Frymoyer JW, Pope MH, Ciements JH, et al: Ricks factors in low back pain: An epidemiological survey. J Bone Joint Surg Am 65:213–218, 1983.
25. Gaskill MF, Lukin R, Wiot JG: Lumbar disc disease and stenosis. Radiol Clin North Am 29:753–764, 1991.
26. Goldberg AL, Soo MS, Deeb ZL, Rothfus WE: Degenerative disease

of the lumbar spine: Role of CT-myelography in the MR era. Clin Imaging 15:47–55, 1991.

27. Hall S, Bartleson JD, Onofrio BM, et al: Lumbar spinal stenosis: Clinical features, diagnostic procedures, and results of surgical treatment in 68 patients. Ann Intern Med 103:271–275, 1985.
28. Harris P: Cervical spine stenosis. Paraplegia 15:25–132, 1977–1978.
29. Hawkes CH, Roberts GM: Neurogenic and vascular claudication. J Neurol Sci 38:337, 1978.
30. Hochhauser L, Kieffer SA, Cacayorin ED, et al: Recurrent postdiskectomy low back pain: MR-surgical correlation. AJR Am J Roentgenol 151:755–760, 1988.
31. Hueftle MG, Modic MT, Ross JS, et al: Lumbar spine: Postoperative MR imaging with Gd-DTPA. Radiology 167:817–824, 1988.
32. Jackson RP, Becker GJ, Jacobs RR, et al: The neuroradiographic diagnosis of lumbar herniated nucleus pulposus: I. A comparison of computed tomography, myelography, CT-myelography, discography and CT-discography. Spine 14:1356–1361, 1989.
33. Jackson RP, Cain JE Jr, Jacobs RR, et al: The neuroradiographic diagnosis of lumbar herniated nucleus pulposus: II. A comparison of computed tomography, myelography, CT-myelography and magnetic resonance imaging. Spine 14:1362–1367, 1989.
34. Jacobs B: Anterior cervical spine fusion. Surg Ann 8:413–446, 1976.
35. Reference deleted.
36. Kallina C: Degenerative lumbar stenosis. Clin Geriatr Med 1:391–400, 1985.
37. Kellgren JH, Lawrence JS: Osteoarthritis and disk degeneration in an urban population. Ann Rheum Dis 17:388–397, 1958.
38. Kelsey JL, White AA 3rd, Pastides H, et al: The impact of musculoskeletal disorders on the population of the United States. J Bone Joint Surg [Am] 61:959–964, 1979.
39. Kent DL, Haynor DR, Larson EB, Deyo RA: Diagnosis of lumbar spinal stenosis in adults: A meta-analysis of the accuracy of CT, MR and myelography. AJR Am J Roentgenol 158:1135–1144, 1992.
40. Kirkaldy-Willis WH: The relationship of structural pathology to the nerve root. Spine 9:49–52, 1984.
41. Kirkaldy-Willis WH, Paine KW, Cauchoix J, McIvor G: Lumbar spinal stenosis. Clin Orthop Relat Res 99:30–50, 1974.
42. Kirkaldy-Willis WH, Wedge JH, Yong-Hing K, Reilly J: Pathology and pathogenesis of lumbar spondylosis and stenosis. Spine 3:319–328, 1978.
43. Lawrence JS, Bremner JM, Bier F: Osteoarthrosis: Prevalence in the population and relationship between symptoms and x-ray changes. Ann Rheum Dis 25:1–24, 1966.
44. Lipson SJ: Spinal stenosis. Rheum Dis Clin North Am 14:613–618, 1988.
45. Lipson SJ, Muir H: Vertebral osteophyte formation in experimental disk degeneration: Morphologic and proteoglycan changes over time. Arthritis Rheum 23:319–324, 1980.
46. Liu SS, Williams KD, Drayer BP, et al: Synovial cysts of the lumbosacral spine: Diagnosis by MR imaging. AJNR Am J Neuroradiology 10:1239–1242, 1989.
47. Manelfe C (ed): Imaging of the Spine and Spinal Cord. New York, Raven Press, 1992, pp 269–331.
48. Masaryk TJ, Ross JS, Modic MT, et al: High-resolution imaging of sequestered lumbar intervertebral disks. AJR Am J Roentgenol 150:1155–1162, 1988.
49. McNab I: Backache. Baltimore, Williams & Wilkins, 1977.
50. Miyasaka K, Kaneda K, Ito T, et al: Ossification of spinal ligaments causing thoracic radiculomyelopathy. Radiology 143:463–468, 1982.
51. Modic MT: Degenerative disorders of the spine. In Magnetic Resonance Imaging of the Spine. St. Louis, Mosby–Year Book, 1989, pp 75–119.
52. Modic MT: Normal anatomy. In Magnetic Resonance Imaging of the Spine. St. Louis, Mosby–Year Book, 1989, pp 35–74.
53. Modic MT, Masaryk T, Boumphrey F, et al: Lumbar herniated disk disease and canal stenosis: Prospective evaluation by surface coil MR, CT, and myelography, Am J Roentgenol 147:757–765, 1986.
54. Modic MT, Masaryk T, Malopulos GP, et al: Cervical radiculopathy: Prospective evaluations with surface coil MR imaging, CT with metrizamide, and metrizamide myelography. Radiology 161:753–759, 1986.
55. Modic MT, Masaryk T, Ross JS, et al: Cervical radiculopathy: Value of oblique MR imaging. Radiology 163:227–231, 1987.
56. Modic MT, Steinberg PM, Ross JS, et al: Degenerative disk disease: Assessment of changes in vertebral body marrow with MR imaging. Radiology 166:193–199, 1988.
57. Moreland LW, Lopez-Mendez A, Alarcon GS: Spinal stenosis: A comprehensive review of the literature. Semin Arthritis Rheum 19:127–149, 1989.
58. Munrone I: The importance of the sagittal diameters of the cervical spinal canal in relation to spondylosis and myelopathy. J Bone Joint Surg 56B:30–36, 1974.
59. Nurick S: The pathogenesis of the spinal cord disorder associated with cervical spondylosis. Brain 95L87–95L100, 1972.
60. Olmarker K, Rydevik B: Pathophysiology of sciatica. Orthop Clin North Am 22:223–234, 1991.
61. Otake S, Matsuo M, Nishizawa S, et al: Ossification of the posterior longitudinal ligament: MR evaluation, AJNR AM J Neuroradiol 13:1059–1067, 1992.
62. Paine KWE: Clinical features of lumbar spinal stenosis. Clin Orthop Relat Res 115:77–82, 1976.
63. Quinet RJ, Hadler NM: Diagnosis and treatment of backache. Semin Arthritis and Rheum 8:261–287, 1979.
64. Resnick D: Degenerative diseases of the vertebral column. Radiology 156:3–14, 1985.
65. Robinson RA, Smith GW: Anterolateral cervical disc removal and interbody fusion for cervical disk syndrome. Bull Johns Hopkins Hosp 96:223, 1955.
66. Rosenbloom S: Thoracic disc disease and stenosis. Radiol Clin North Am 29:765–775, 1991.
67. Ross JS: Magnetic resonance assessment of the postoperative spine. Radiol Clin North Am 29:793–808, 1991.
68. Ross JS, Blaser S, Masaryk T, et al: Gd-DTPA enhancement of posterior epidural scar: An experimental model. AJNR Am J Neuroradiol 10:1083–1088, 1989.
69. Ross JS, Delamarter R, Hueftle MG, et al: Gadolinium-DTPA enhanced MR imaging of the postoperative lumbar spine: Time course and mechanism of enhancement. AJR Am J Roentgenol 152:825–834, 1989.
70. Ross JS, Hueftle MG: Postoperative spine. In Magnetic Resonance Imaging of the Spine. St. Louis, Mosby–Year Book, 1989, pp 120–148.
71. Ross JS, Masaryk T, Modic MT, et al: Lumbar spine: Postoperative assessment with surface coil MR imaging. Radiology 164:851–860, 1987.
72. Ross JS, Masaryk T, Modic MT, et al: MR imaging of lumbar arachnoiditis. AJR Am J Roentgenol 149:1025–1032, 1987.
73. Ross JS, Masaryk TJ, Modic MT: Postoperative cervical spine: MR assessment. J Comput Assist Tomogr 11:955–962, 1987.
74. Ross JS, Masaryk T, Schrader M, et al: MR imaging of the postoperative lumbosacral spine: Assessment with gadopentetate dimeglumine. AJR Am J Roentgenol 155:867–872, 1990.
75. Ross JS, Perez-Reges N, Masaryk T, et al: Thoracic disk herniation: MR imaging, Radiology 165:511–515, 1987.
76. Sandhu FS and Dillon WP: Spinal epidural abscess: Evaluation with contrast-enhanced MR imaging. AJNR Am J Neuroradiol 12:1087–1093, 1991.
77. Schnebel B, Kingston S, Watkins R, Dillin W: Comparison of MRI to contrast CT in the diagnosis of spinal stenosis. Spine 14:332–337, 1989.
78. Sotiropoulos S, Chafetz NI, Lang P, et al: Differentiation between postoperative scar and recurrent disk herniation: Prospective comparison of MR, CT, and contrast enhanced CT. AJNR AM J Neuroradiol 10:639–643, 1989.
79. Sze G: Fast spin echo imaging in the evaluation of the spine. Paper presented at 30th Annual Meeting of American Society of Neuroradiology, June 1992, St. Louis.
80. Teplick JG, Haskin ME: Computed tomography of the postoperative lumbar spine. Am J Roentgenol 141:865–884, 1983.
81. Teplick JG, Peyster RG, Teplick SK, et al: CT identification of post laminectomy pseudomeningocele. Am J Roentgenol 140:1203–1206, 1983.
82. Ulrich CG, et al: Quantitative assessment of the lumbar spinal canal by computed tomography. Radiology 134:137–143, 1980.
83. Valkenburg HA, Haanen HCM: The epidemiology of low back pain. In White AA, Gordon SL (eds): American Academy of Orthopedic Surgeons: Symposium on Idiopathic Low Back Pain. St. Louis, CV Mosby, 1982, pp 9–22.
84. Yamamoto I, Matsumae M, Ikeda A, et al: Thoracic spinal stenosis: Experience with seven cases. J Neurosurg 68:37–40, 1988.

23

Extramedullary Spinal Tumors

Donna M. Plecha

Progress continues to be made in the evaluation of extramedullary spinal tumors. Magnetic resonance imaging (MRI) is usually the imaging modality of choice for evaluating the spine if there is clinical concern for tumor. Although MRI is not usually helpful in determining the specific diagnosis or for grading neoplasms, it is excellent for determining the extent of involvement as well as anatomic detail such as spinal cord compression, and it may help to limit the diagnostic possibilities. It has also facilitated the determination of whether a tumor is extradural, intradural/extramedullary, or intramedullary.

Extradural Tumors of the Spine

Extradural tumors of the spine are the most common of all spinal tumors. Most extradural tumors of the spine are metastatic lesions because the vertebral bodies are highly vascularized. The thoracic spine is most commonly involved. Spinal cord compression is seen in 5% of cancer patients with bone metastasis.[4] Metastatic lesions in the epidural space usually result from direct extension of vertebral body metastasis. Otherwise, there can be epidural involvement from hematogenous spread through the epidural and paravertebral venous plexus.[13]

Most metastatic lesions of the spine originate from breast, lung, or prostate cancer.[24] The most common initial symptoms include local pain and radicular pain. With more advanced disease, motor dysfunction and/or sphincter dysfunction may occur. Therapies include surgery and radiation, or both,[3, 4, 41] and preoperative transarterial embolization of the spinal metastasis. The latter is safe and effective; it can limit blood loss during surgery and aid in more complete tumor resection.[39] Outcome is related to the patient's condition at diagnosis, radiosensitivity of the tumor, and tumor biology.[31] Early initiation of therapy is important to preserve motor function.[41] Bach and colleagues[4] found that 79% of patients who could walk at diagnosis were still ambulatory after treatment, but only 18% of nonambulatory patients were able to walk after therapy. Therefore, timely initiation of therapy is critical.

Spin-echo (SE) T1-weighted sequences are excellent for determining the extent of metastatic disease because of their high signal-to-noise ratio. Also, the high fat content of the bone marrow contributes to excellent contrast (Fig. 23–1). The metastatic lesions alter the usual fat content within the vertebral bodies, thereby causing a decrease in signal intensity on T1-weighted SE images. T2-weighted SE sequences are also helpful as abnormal bone marrow usually demonstrates increased signal intensity on T2-weighted images. In addition, fat saturation techniques offer potential advantages for increasing the conspicuousness of bone marrow lesions. T2-weighted fat-saturated fast spin-echo (FSE) and short TI inversion recovery (STIR) sequences have also been used to increase lesion conspicuity.[26, 32]

Abnormal bone marrow signal intensity on any imaging sequence is nonspecific and does not always mean that a patient has metastatic disease. Kim and colleagues attempted to differentiate between hematopoietic malignancies and metastasis.[16] They assessed lymphoma, leukemia, and multiple myeloma lesions in an attempt to distinguish them from metastasis using the following criteria: pattern of involvement, signal change of the vertebral body, location of the paraspinal mass, cortical destruction, contour change, and compression fracture. Although the two categories overlapped, diffuse involvement was more commonly seen in hematopoietic malignancies than in metastasis, and cortical destruction was more commonly seen in metastasis that in hematopoietic malignancies. The other parameters examined failed to show any statistically significant difference between the two groups.[16] The authors found that it was difficult to evaluate young patients because of persistent red marrow.

Patients with metastatic disease often present with compression fractures. When a patient does not have widespread metastatic disease, it is sometimes difficult to differentiate between pathologic and benign compression fractures of the spine, and various MRI sequences have been used in an attempt to differentiate between them. Baker and colleagues[5] examined 53 patients with a total of 34 benign compression fractures and 27 pathologic fractures. The authors used a presaturation technique, suppressing either fat or water signal with a presaturation pulse, to obtain "fat" and "water" images. STIR and SE images were also used.

Most compression fractures more than 1 month old showed marrow signal isointense to that of the surrounding normal vertebral bodies. When the fracture was acute, however, the edema caused signal intensity changes similar to vertebral bodies involved with tumor. Only seven patients had acute benign fractures less than 1 month old. All showed high signal intensity on T2-weighted images and low signal intensity on T1-weighted SE images. In five of the patients, the water images and the T2-weighted images of the problematic vertebral bodies showed heterogeneous patterns. In the other two patients, the involved vertebral bodies showed diffusely homogeneous increased signal intensity throughout.

Another seven patients had pathologic compression fractures, all of which showed homogeneous diffuse decreased

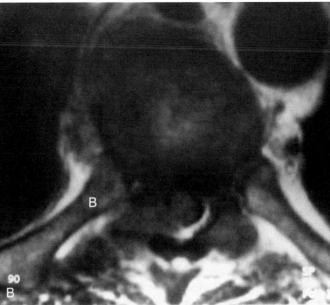

Figure 23–1. *A,* Sagittal T1-weighted image of the thoracic spine demonstrating multiple areas of abnormal bone marrow signal intensity. This patient has diffuse metastatic disease. *B,* T1-weighted axial image shows a right-sided metastatic mass causing mass effect on the spinal cord and thecal sac.

signal intensity on the T1-weighted images and increased signal intensity on the T2-weighted, STIR, and water images. The fat images showed a complete absence of fatty marrow signal intensity. Therefore, the patterns of signal intensity changes between the two groups did overlap.

Because each group was composed of only seven patients, it is difficult to determine whether the findings are statistically significant. Another difference between the benign and malignant acute fractures was that the pathologic fractures tended to have convex outward anterior and posterior margins compared to the more sharply angulated borders of the acute benign fractures.

Baur and colleagues[7] assessed MR diffusion-weighted imaging (DWI) for its ability to distinguish between malignant and benign causes of spinal compression fractures. When they studied DWI of bone marrow, they found that acute benign compression fractures either showed lower signal intensity than normal bone marrow or were isointense with normal bone marrow. They thought that this difference was caused by free extracellular water in the bone marrow edema and/or hemorrhage. When DWI is used, increased signal intensity is seen where diffusion of water is decreased or restricted, such as in vertebral bodies invaded by tumor cells. Baur and coworkers[7] demonstrated that the pathologic fractures showed increased signal intensity within the bone marrow; this corresponded to a decrease in the apparent diffusion coefficient.

MR DWI does have drawbacks, however. For example, it has low spatial resolution and a low signal-to-noise ratio. In an editorial, Le Bihan[20] argued that it is more difficult to separate the effects of T1 and T2 from diffusion effects with the steady-state free precession (SSFP) diffusion sequence than with an SE-based diffusion sequence. SSFP diffusion-weighted imaging needs to be studied further to establish its usefulness in distinguishing pathologic from benign vertebral fractures.

Percutaneous vertebroplasty has been used in patients with compression fractures (Fig. 23–2). This procedure, developed in France, involves injection of polymethylmethacrylate cement into the collapsed vertebra. The stabilization and reinforcement provided by the cement can alleviate pain. Barr and colleagues[6] performed percutaneous vertebroplasty in 47 patients (eight of whom had tumor involvement in the spine) for stabilization of the spine. Only 50% of the patients experienced significant pain relief. Possible complications of this procedure include cement extravasation and asymptomatic epidural venous filling.

Multiple Myeloma

As stated, multiple myeloma can appear similar to metastatic disease on spine images. Usually, compressive lesions involve the spine. When the disease is isolated to a single vertebral body, it is called a plasmacytoma. When multiple bones are involved, the term *multiple myeloma* is used. Multiple myeloma is more common in men and is usually seen in the sixth decade of life.

The tumor is composed of monoclonal B cells within the bone marrow. The lesions show decreased signal intensity on T1-weighted images and increased signal intensity on T2-weighted images (Fig. 23–3). A study examining

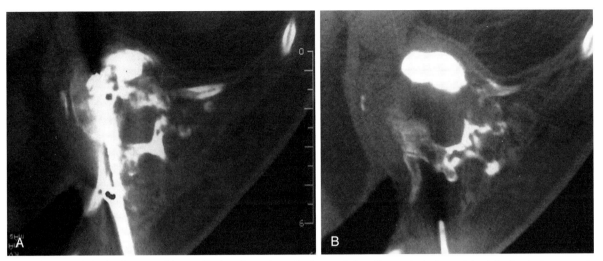

Figure 23–2. *A,* Axial CT image with needle in place through the pedicle of a metastatic vertebral body during percutaneous vertebroplasty. *B,* Axial CT image after injection of polymethylmethacrylate cement.

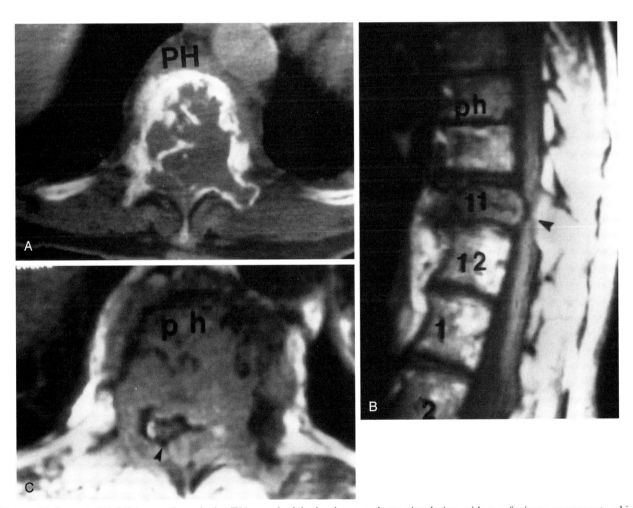

Figure 23–3. *A,* Axial CT image through the T11 vertebral body shows a destructive lesion with a soft tissue component, which proved to be multiple myeloma. *B,* Sagittal T1-weighted image through the lumbar spine shows compression and bone marrow replacement of the T11 vertebral body with associated spinal cord compression. There is also abnormal signal intensity in the surrounding vertebral bodies. *C,* T1-weighted axial image demonstrating significant spinal cord compression secondary to multiple myeloma mass involving T11. The abnormal signal intensity of the mass is isointense to muscle.

the MRI characteristics of multiple myeloma found that these lesions were better identified with T2-weighted images than with T1-weighted images in 65% of patients.[22] Another study found that STIR and T2-weighted images were better than T1-weighted images for detecting lesions and that contrast enhancement did not increase lesion detection.[34]

Various patterns of involvement of spinal multiple myeloma have been described. Focal lesions, diffuse involvement, and a heterogeneous pattern of tiny lesions on a normal marrow background were described in a study of 29 patients.[27] It was noted that diffuse and focal marrow patterns of involvement were associated with more abnormal serum hemoglobin levels and a higher percentage of marrow plasmacytosis. A similar study showed similar results: the diffuse pattern corresponded to patients with higher marrow plasmacytosis, higher cellularity, higher serum calcium, higher β_2-microglobin levels, and lower hemoglobin levels.[21]

Another classification scheme was presented in a study of 61 patients.[19] The MRI patterns noted were described as diffuse, nodular, diffuse and nodular, and normal. More patients showing the normal and nodular MRI patterns of bone marrow signal intensity survived than patients showing the diffuse and the diffuse and nodular patterns.[19]

Even though contrast-enhanced MRI was not found to be helpful in the initial detection of lesions in patients with multiple myeloma, it may be helpful for following their responses to therapy. Patterns of complete response to treatment included resolution of the marrow abnormalities seen before treatment and of persistent abnormality with peripheral rim enhancement. Signs of partial response included conversion of a diffuse pattern of involvement to a variegated or focal pattern, and a decrease of the marrow involvement seen on MRI with persistent enhancement.[28] A similar study of 18 patients demonstrated patterns of response that included rim enhancement, no enhancement, and early enhancement.[35]

Lymphoma

Lymphoma within the spine can present in several different ways. There can be extension from primary involvement in adjacent paravertebral lymph nodes into the neuroforamen and spinal canal. Primary involvement can also occur within the highly vascular vertebral body, and it commonly extends into the epidural space, causing mass effect on the spinal cord and exiting nerve roots. Lymphoma can also arise in the epidural space along the leptomeninges and, rarely, in the intramedullary space, as is seen in 0.1% to 6.5% of patients with non-Hodgkin's lymphoma (Figs. 23–4 and 23–5).[37]

Marrow involvement occurs in 4% to 14% of patients with Hodgkin's lymphoma, and the percentage is much higher in patients with non-Hodgkin's lymphoma.[29] MRI is the imaging modality of choice because it is sensitive in picking up marrow involvement and in detecting mass effect on the spinal cord and spread into the epidural space and paraspinal soft tissue. Moulopoulos and colleagues describe a "wrap-around sign": tumor envelops the cortex

of vertebral bodies without altering the shape of these vertebral bodies. This sign was found in patients with lymphoma but not in those with metastatic disease or with multiple myeloma.[29]

Primary Tumors of the Spine

Other extradural tumors include primary tumors of the spine, which occur much less frequently than does metastatic spinal disease. However, when a patient presents with a solitary lesion, a primary tumor of the spine should be considered. Both benign and malignant tumors can be seen in the spine. Patients usually present with nonspecific back pain.

Osteoid Osteoma

The lumbar spine is the most common site of osteoid osteomas, followed by the cervical, thoracic, and sacral spine.[30] Patients present with the classic symptoms of painful scoliosis, focal or radicular pain, gait disturbance, and muscle atrophy. The pain is worse at night, and salicylates usually help.[30] Vertebral posterior elements are usually involved.

Plain films reveal a round to oval area of lucency with surrounding sclerosis. Associated scoliosis may be found, with the lesion located at the concave apex of the curve. CT, the study of choice for evaluating osteoid osteoma,[11] reveals an area of low attenuation with surrounding sclerosis (Fig. 23–6) and sometimes a central calcification. MRI usually shows a nidus reflecting low to intermediate signal intensity on T1-weighted images and intermediate to high signal intensity on T2-weighted images. Any associated sclerosis or calcification shows low signal intensity on all pulse sequences.[30]

Osteoblastoma

Osteoblastoma is another benign tumor of the spine; it has no predilection for any particular location in the spine.[17] Patients usually present with dull pain, paresthesias, paraparesis, and paraplegia. Scoliosis can be associated with osteoblastoma, although less frequently than with osteoid osteomas, and it may be convex toward the side of the lesion.[30] Most commonly, osteoblastomas are expansile with small calcifications and a sclerotic rim.[18]

The second most frequent radiographic appearance of osteoblastoma is that of a central radiolucent area with surrounding sclerosis that can have central calcification. This is similar in appearance to osteoid osteoma, yet the clinical presentation and curve of the scoliosis may help to differentiate between the two. Also, osteoblastomas are usually bigger and they more commonly extend into the vertebral body.

A third possible radiographic appearance of osteoblastoma is that of more aggressive bone destruction, with expansion and extension into adjacent soft tissues.[30] CT commonly shows expansile lesions with associated sclerosis; these lesions may also have a chondroid matrix. MR imaging is usually nonspecific yet it is helpful in determining mass effect on the adjacent spinal cord and thecal sac.

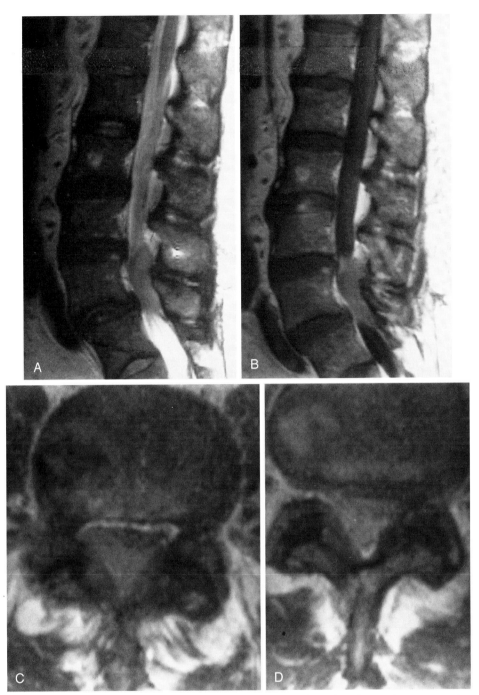

Figure 23–4. *A,* Sagittal MRI fast spin-echo T2-weighted image through the lumbar spine. A mass is seen posterior to the L4 vertebral body. The mass was biopsied and proved to be lymphoma. *B,* MRI sagittal spin-echo T1-weighted image through the lumbar spine following the intravenous administration of Gadoteridol. The mass enhances within the spinal canal. *C,* Axial T1-weighted image through the mass, which is extradural in location, causing mass effect on the adjacent thecal sac. *D,* Axial T1-weighted image through the mass, after the intravenous administration of Gadoteridol.

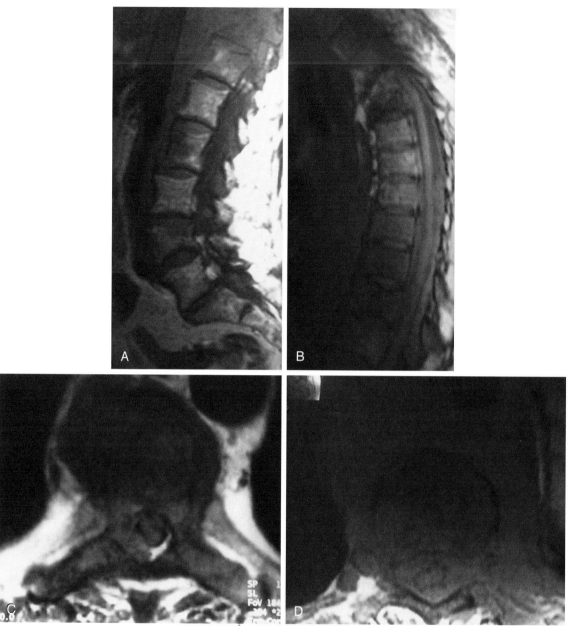

Figure 23–5. *A,* T1-weighted sagittal MRI image through the lumbar spine showing a large mass anterior to the spine from T11 to L4. There is destruction and replacement of the T11 vertebral body. *B,* T1-weighted sagittal image through the thoracic spine showing a large mass anterior to the mid and lower thoracic vertebral bodies, which turned out to be lymphoma. *C,* T1-weighted axial image demonstrating an extradural mass that is causing mass effect on the thecal sac on the right. *D,* T1-weighted axial image showing lymphoma surrounding the vertebral body and extending into the epidural space that surrounds the thecal sac.

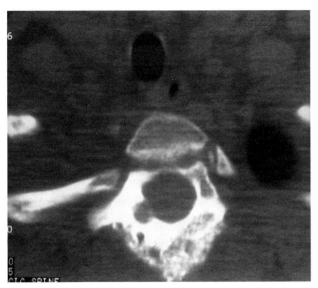

Figure 23–6. Axial CT image showing a lucency of the lamina of T1 with surrounding sclerosis, which proved to be an osteoid osteoma.

Signal intensity is usually low to intermediate on T1-weighted and intermediate to high on T2-weighted images (Figs. 23–7 and 23–8).[8, 17]

Giant Cell Tumors

Giant cell tumors (GCT) in the spine usually involve the sacrum, followed by the thoracic, cervical, and lumbar areas.[30] Pain is the most common presenting symptom; however, pain can be accompanied by neurologic deficits.[38] GCT usually presents as a large mass with bone destruction and bony expansion. When the sacrum is involved, the sacroiliac joint can be crossed. Within the spine, vertebral bodies are most commonly involved, although giant cell tumors can cross disk spaces and extend into the posterior elements, and they can be associated with vertebral collapse.[30]

CT reveals a soft tissue attenuation mass, which may have a rim of sclerosis (Fig. 23–9). If hemorrhage is involved, however, a mixed attenuation mass, or possibly fluid-fluid levels, may be seen.

MRI usually shows a mass with mixed signal intensity.[25, 30] Fluid-fluid levels of various signal intensities may be seen if hemorrhage is present. The signal intensity depends on the age and state of the blood: it may be high on both T1-weighted and T2-weighted images if blood is present. In the absence of hemorrhage, GCTs may have low to intermediate signal intensity on both T1-weighted and T2-weighted images; this may help to differentiate them from other tumors, which usually have increased signal intensity on T2-weighted images.[30]

Complete resection is the treatment of choice for GCT, yet it is not always possible. Adjuvant radiotherapy is also used. It has been argued that radiation therapy should be used for patients with incomplete excision or for those with local recurrence.[15, 38]

Aneurysmal Bone Cysts

Aneurysmal bone cysts are seen most commonly in the thoracic spine, followed by the lumbar and cervical spine. Symptoms, including pain and neurologic deficits, are usually associated with mass effect on the spinal cord.

Radiographs, CT, and MRI demonstrate an expansile lesion centered in the posterior elements that commonly extends into the vertebral bodies. This lesion is usually lytic as well as expansive, with eggshell-like peripheral calcification (Fig. 23–10). ABCs can cross disk spaces and extend into adjacent structures. Both CT and MRI can evaluate for fluid-fluid levels. MRI is, however, better at showing both the extent of the mass and the mass effect on the spinal cord and nerve roots. A soft tissue rim is often seen on CT. It appears as a rim of decreased signal intensity on all MRI sequences. This rim is a thickened periosteal membrane, which, together with septations, can enhance with gadolinium.

Complete resection is the treatment of choice, but it is not always possible because of tumor location and size. Radiation and embolotherapy have also been used as treatment.[30]

Osteochondromas

Osteochondromas of the spine are uncommon. They usually occur within the cervical spine, especially at C2, and like most benign spinal lesions they usually occur in the posterior elements. CT imaging with thin slices is the modality of choice to evaluate osteochondromas. Continuity of the cortex and the marrow between the lesion and the vertebra is visible on CT (Fig. 23–11).[30] MRI can also be helpful in identifying mass effect on the spinal canal. Central yellow bone marrow shows high signal intensity on T1-weighted images because of its fat content, and the corresponding signal intensity on T2-weighted images is intermediate (Fig. 23–12).[30] Surgical resection is the treatment of choice.

Chordoma

Chordoma is an uncommon malignant tumor of the spine arising from a remnant of the notochord. It usually occurs at the sacrococcygeal region or at the skull base. Because it is a slow-growing tumor, chordoma usually presents as a large destructive lesion with an associated large soft tissue mass. Calcifications are commonly seen within the mass on radiographs and CT, and they usually occur peripherally. Attenuation in the center of the mass is low, and it may be higher peripherally.[30, 36]

Coronal CT images are optimal for evaluating foramen and sacroiliac joint involvement. Advances in multidetector CT and in three-dimensional reconstructive capabilities may be helpful in evaluating the extent of disease. For determining the extent of disease in surrounding soft tissue, however, MRI is superior.[35] On T1-weighted images, chordoma usually shows low to intermediate signal intensity, and it shows high signal intensity on T2-weighted images because of its high water content (Fig. 23–13).[30]

Complete excision of the chordoma is necessary because of its poor sensitivity to radiotherapy and chemotherapy, but complete resection is not always possible. Preoperative MRI may help to determine the amount of involvement in the adjacent gluteal muscles; this may be important when

Text continued on page 778

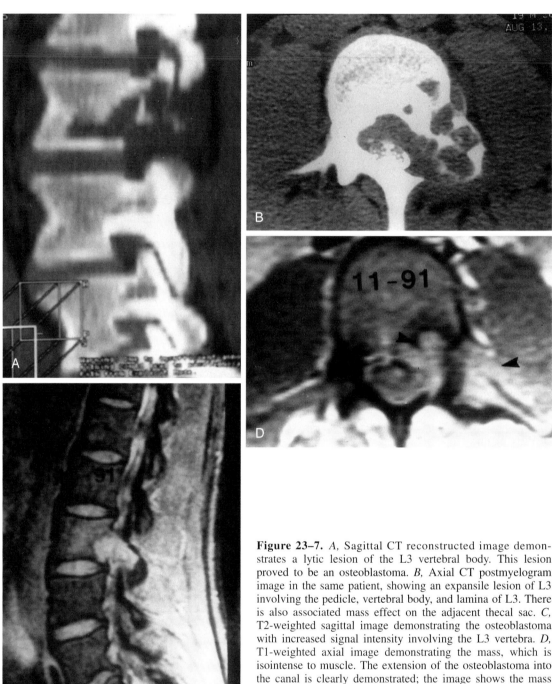

Figure 23–7. *A,* Sagittal CT reconstructed image demonstrates a lytic lesion of the L3 vertebral body. This lesion proved to be an osteoblastoma. *B,* Axial CT postmyelogram image in the same patient, showing an expansile lesion of L3 involving the pedicle, vertebral body, and lamina of L3. There is also associated mass effect on the adjacent thecal sac. *C,* T2-weighted sagittal image demonstrating the osteoblastoma with increased signal intensity involving the L3 vertebra. *D,* T1-weighted axial image demonstrating the mass, which is isointense to muscle. The extension of the osteoblastoma into the canal is clearly demonstrated; the image shows the mass effect on the thecal sac.

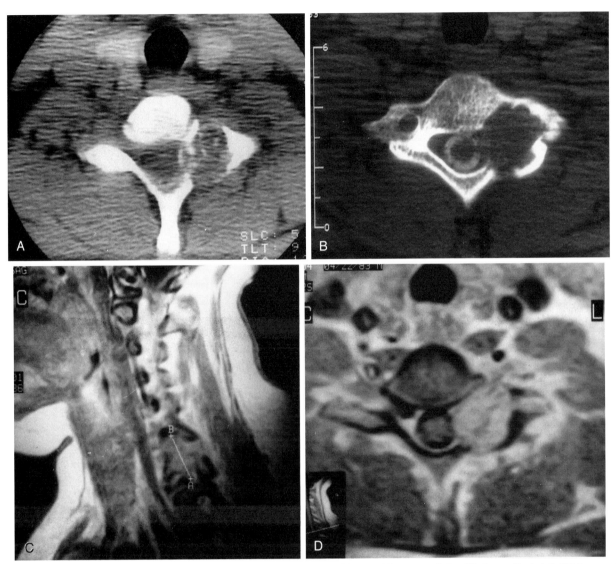

Figure 23–8. *A,* Axial CT image through C7 demonstrating an expansile osteoblastoma of the C7 facet. *B,* Axial CT image after myelogram through C7 showing the mass involving the vertebral artery foramen on the left. *C,* T1-weighted sagittal image after injection of contrast material with the enhancing mass involving the left C7 facet. *D,* T1-weighted axial image through the osteoblastoma involving the C7 facet and lamina.

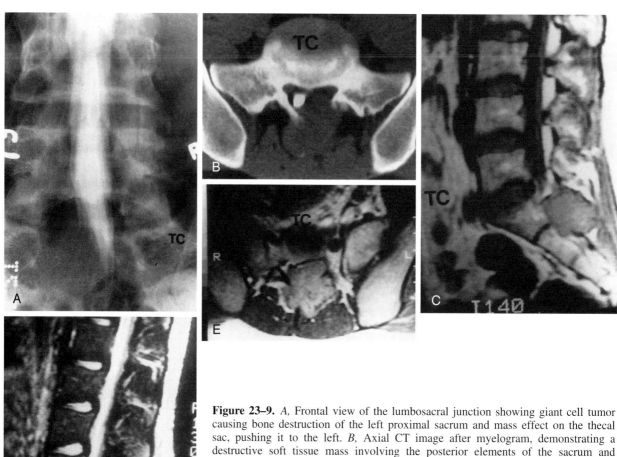

Figure 23–9. *A,* Frontal view of the lumbosacral junction showing giant cell tumor causing bone destruction of the left proximal sacrum and mass effect on the thecal sac, pushing it to the left. *B,* Axial CT image after myelogram, demonstrating a destructive soft tissue mass involving the posterior elements of the sacrum and causing mass effect on the thecal sac. *C,* T1-weighted sagittal image of the lumbar spine clearly demonstrates the giant cell tumor involving the posterior aspect of the sacrum. The mass has mixed signal intensity. Evidence of hemorrhage or fluid-fluid levels is not seen. *D,* T2-weighted sagittal image of the same giant cell tumor, demonstrating mixed signal intensity. Again, evidence of fluid-fluid levels is not seen. *E,* T1-weighted axial image of giant cell tumor of the sacrum demonstrating signal intensity that is mixed but higher than that of muscle.

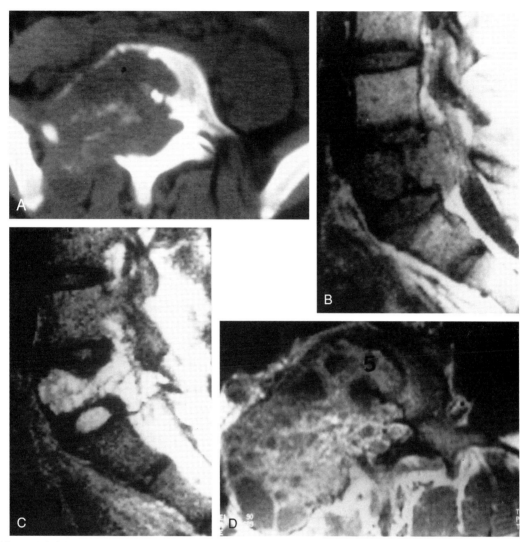

Figure 23–10. *A,* Axial CT image demonstrating an expansile aneurysmal bone cyst (ABC) of the L5 vertebral body with some rimlike calcification. The extension of the mass into the spinal canal is not well delineated. *B,* T1-weighted sagittal image through the lumbar spine, demonstrating the ABC that involves the L5 vertebral body. The mass is mixed in signal intensity and extends into the spinal canal. *C,* T2-weighted sagittal image of the lumbar spine. The ABC has increased signal intensity, with areas of lower signal intensity within it. *D,* T1-weighted axial image through the L5 vertebral body after administration of contrast material. An enhancing, expansile ABC with pockets of nonenhancing fluid signal intensity extends into the spinal canal and posterior lateral soft tissues. The septations are enhanced, as stated in the text.

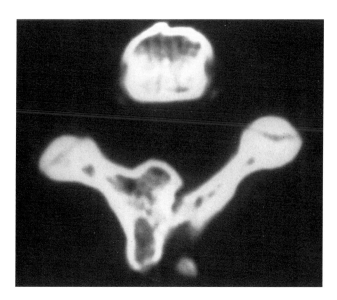

Figure 23–11. Axial CT image through an osteochondroma involving the spinous process and lamina of a vertebral body. This image demonstrates continuity of the cortex and marrow between the lesion and the vertebra.

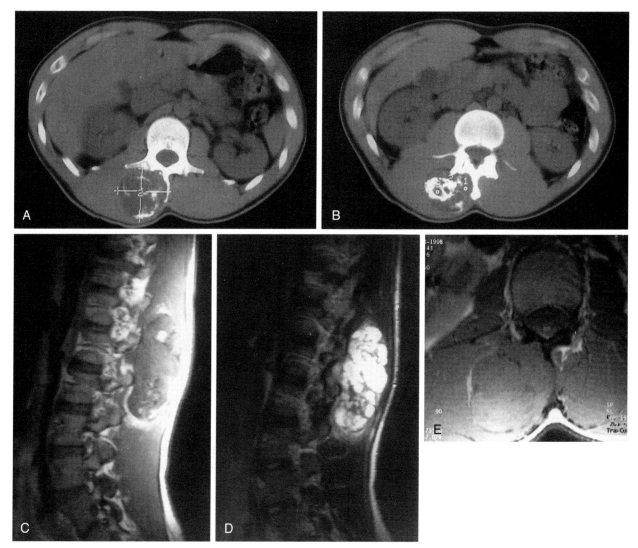

Figure 23–12. *A,* Axial CT image demonstrating an osteochondroma that involves the posterior elements of the L1 vertebral body. This mass is not in the typical C2 location, and it is larger than usually seen. There is no definite continuity of cortex and marrow between the mass and L1. *B,* Axial CT image of L1, showing the same mass with scalloping of the right aspect of the spinous process and calcification within the mass. *C,* T1-weighted sagittal image to the right of midline. The osteochondroma is mixed in signal intensity. *D,* T2-weighted image of the lumbar spine shows the same mass having mixed signal intensity. This is a nonspecific appearance. *E,* T1-weighted axial image of the lumbar spine showing that the mass has mixed signal intensity and does not involve the spinal canal.

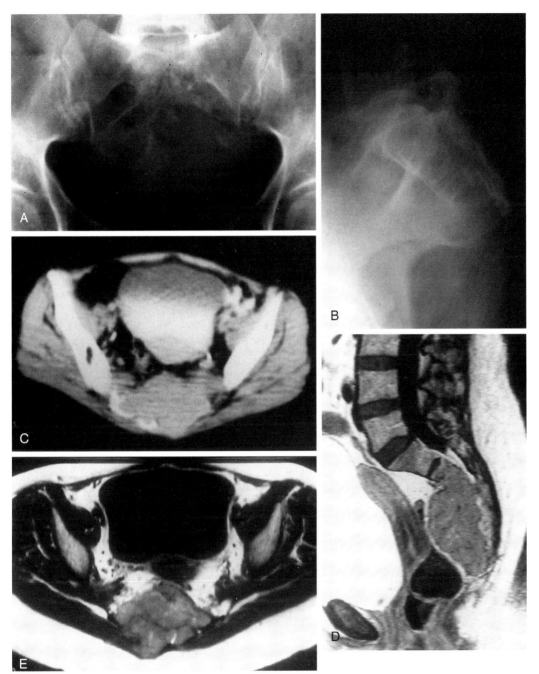

Figure 23–13. *A,* Plain film AP view of the sacrum. There is destruction of the inferior and left aspect of the sacrum. *B,* Lateral plain film of the sacrum demonstrating destruction of the inferior sacrum. *C,* Axial CT image of the sacrum. The soft tissue mass that is destroying the sacrum has proved to be a chordoma. This mass is in the usual sacrococcygeal region of the spine. *D,* T1-weighted sagittal image (with contrast enhancement) of the sacrum nicely demonstrating the extent of the soft tissue tumor, which exhibits mild enhancement. The mass is causing anterior displacement of the rectum. *E,* T1-weighted axial image of the sacrum demonstrating the chordoma and its effects on the surrounding tissues.

chordoma infiltrating the gluteal muscles may account for local recurrences.[46]

Chondrosarcoma

Chondrosarcoma is most commonly seen in the thoracic spine, but it is also found within the posterior elements or the vertebral body. Patients usually have a good prognosis, because spinal chondrosarcoma is usually low grade.[30]

CT is a sensitive modality for revealing the chondroid matrix characteristic of chondrosarcomas, the bone destruction, and the soft tissue component.[40] On CT, the soft tissue component can have decreased attenuation because its water content is higher than that of muscle.

MRI is helpful for evaluating any associated mass effect on the spinal cord and/or extension across disk spaces, which is seen in 35% of cases.[30, 40] Because of the water content of this tumor, signal intensity within the soft tissue component is usually decreased on T1-weighted images and increased on T2-weighted images. The matrix shows decreased signal intensity on all imaging sequences.[30]

Osteosarcoma

Osteosarcoma in the spine is rare; it is most commonly seen in the lumbosacral region and usually involves the vertebral body eccentrically. On plain films, osteosarcoma presents with a dense matrix; an ivory vertebral body can be seen. MRI is helpful in determining the extent of the soft tissue component and its effect on surrounding structures. If the matrix exhibits dense mineralization, it may appear to have decreased signal intensity on all MRI sequences. Patients with primary osteosarcoma of the spine have a very poor prognosis, with death usually ensuing within 2 years of the diagnosis.[30]

Ewing's Sarcoma and Permeative Neuroectodermal Tumor

Ewing's sarcoma and permeative neuroectodermal tumor (PNET) are radiographically very similar and are usually seen within the sacrococcygeal region. Presenting symptoms include pain and often bowel and bladder dysfunction. Metastatic foci are more common, yet primary lesions are also seen. These tumors usually occur in patients between 10 and 30 years of age.[30] The lesion is usually centered in the vertebral body, and a soft tissue component is commonly present.

MRI is the modality of choice to determine both tumor extent and involvement of surrounding tissue. The appearance of the tumor on MRI, however, is nonspecific. Signal intensity is intermediate on T1-weighted images and intermediate to high on T2-weighted images.[2, 14] Immunohistochemical studies are used to distinguish between PNET and Ewing's sarcoma.

Chemotherapy and radiation are the treatments of choice for both entities.[30]

Intradural Extramedullary Tumors
Nerve Sheath Tumors

Nerve sheath tumors make up the majority of extramedullary tumors within the dural space. Patients commonly present with radicular pain, possible gait disturbance, and sphincter dysfunction. The pain experienced results from the fact that the tumors usually arise on the dorsal sensory nerve root. Neurofibromas and schwannomas are both derived from Schwann cells; however, neurofibromas also have collagen and fibroblasts.[9]

Patients with neurofibromatosis type 1 (NF-1) usually have intraforaminal nerve sheath tumors extending into the spinal canal in a dumbbell-shaped configuration. Only about 1.6% of patients with NF-1 have symptomatic spinal tumors.[44] Patients with NF-2 usually have intraspinal intradural tumors, and 30% to 40% of these patients have neurologic deficits and symptoms.[23]

Plain films, which are nonspecific, may show enlargement of the neuroforamen (Fig. 23–14). MRI is the study of choice for evaluation of these tumors associated with the spine. On T1-weighted images, nerve sheath tumors are typically isointense to muscle. Increased signal intensity on T2-weighted images is typical for nerve sheath tumors whether using conventional SE or FSE imaging.[43] Postgadolinium imaging is commonly used to increase conspicuity of lesions. Nerve sheath tumors commonly enhance brightly, thereby increasing detection (Figs. 23–15 and 23–16). Fat-saturation techniques following administration of contrast material are also helpful for lesion detection.[12]

Total resection of nerve sheath tumors is needed to prevent recurrence. Neurofibromas have nerve fibers passing through them and are therefore difficult to remove completely. Schwannomas are usually eccentric in location, making total resection easier.

Paragangliomas

Extra-adrenal paragangliomas are rare, originating from cells of neural crest origin. Usually these tumors are located at the glomus jugulare or near or within the carotid body. Spinal paragangliomas are rare and can be seen in the intradural, extramedullary compartment, usually in the lumbar spine in the area of the cauda equina.[1] Rarely, they are also seen in the cervical and thoracic spine.

Paragangliomas of the spine are predominantly of the sympathetic type. Patients usually present with symptoms related to spinal cord or nerve root compression. MRI findings, which are nonspecific, reveal an enhancing lobulated or ellipsoid mass that is encapsulated and usually found in the intradural extramedullary space. Paragangliomas are usually isointense to the spinal cord on T1-weighted imaging and nonhomogeneous on T2-weighted imaging. Generally, paragangliomas are slow growing and benign.[42]

Intradural Extramedullary Metastases

Various types of intradural extramedullary metastases occur. Drop metastases originate from central nervous system primary neoplasms, such as cerebral glioblastoma, posterior fossa medulloblastoma, anaplastic astrocytoma, and ependymoma. These are seeded through the cerebrospinal fluid (CSF) from the head. They are most commonly seen in the lumbar location in the area of the conus medullaris or the cauda equina.

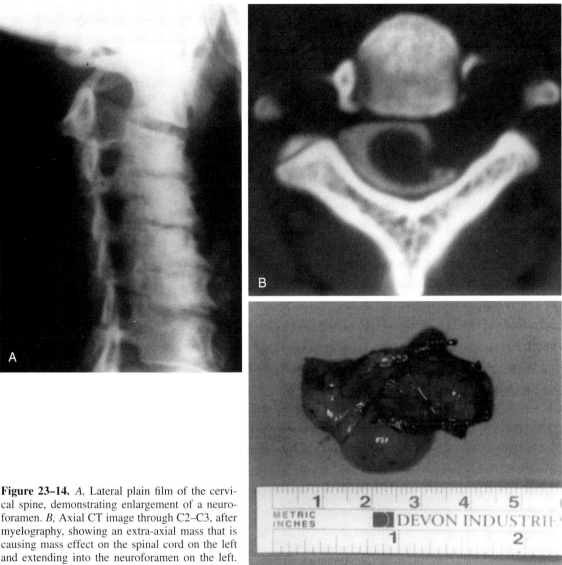

Figure 23–14. *A,* Lateral plain film of the cervical spine, demonstrating enlargement of a neuroforamen. *B,* Axial CT image through C2–C3, after myelography, showing an extra-axial mass that is causing mass effect on the spinal cord on the left and extending into the neuroforamen on the left. *C,* Gross specimen photograph of a smooth, bilobed schwannoma.

Nonvisceral neoplasms with CSF seeding include melanoma, lymphoma, and leukemia.[47] Systemic malignancies, such as breast and lung cancer, metastasize to the subarachnoid space. When these patients are diagnosed with intradural extramedullary spinal canal metastases, they usually have widespread disease and a very poor prognosis.[10] Most of the metastatic lesions are found on the conus medullaris and the cauda equina.

Whatever their source, the intradural extramedullary metastatic lesions are usually best seen on postcontrast, T1-weighted MR images of the spine. The lesions are not as well seen on either precontrast T1-weighted images or T2-weighted images; however, these sequences are helpful in evaluating for spinal bone metastasis and spinal cord compression. Therefore, a combination of precontrast and postcontrast images is used to evaluate the spine in patients with suspected intradural extramedullary metastatic dis-

ease. The metastatic lesions are usually seen as nodular enhancing lesions on the conus medullaris and the cauda equina, yet they can occur anywhere along the intradural space of the spinal canal. Abnormally thin extramedullary areas of enhancement may also indicate metastatic disease.[10]

An intraspinal meningioma can present as an intradural extramedullary mass. As in the head, this mass is isointense to the cord on MRI T1-weighted and T2-weighted images, and it homogeneously enhances after the administration of contrast medium. Enhancement of the adjacent meninges is known as the dural tail sign. Quekel and Versteege[33] argue that to evaluate spinal meningiomas for the dural tail sign, sagittal, axial, and coronal planes should all be obtained following the administration of gadolinium. The dural tail sign is very suggestive of meningioma.

Weil and coworkers[45] reported on a patient who had

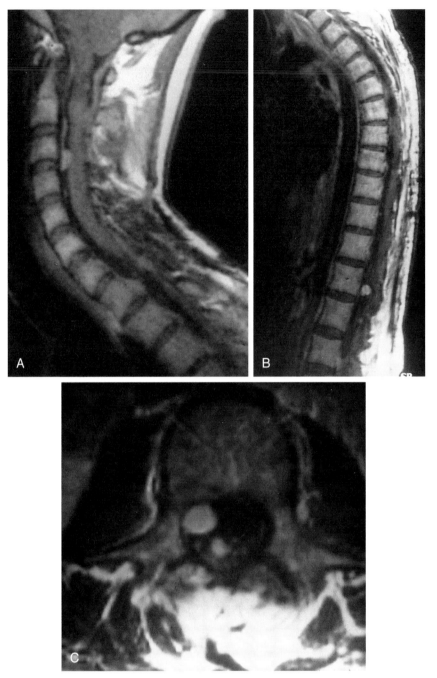

Figure 23–15. *A,* T1-weighted post–contrast-enhanced sagittal image of the cervical spine, demonstrating an enhancing extra-axial mass posterior to C2–C3 in a patient with known neurofibromatosis type 1. *B,* T1-weighted sagittal post–contrast-enhanced image through the thoracic spine, with enhancing neurofibromas in the lower thoracic spine. *C,* T1-weighted axial image showing extra-axial enhancing neurofibromas.

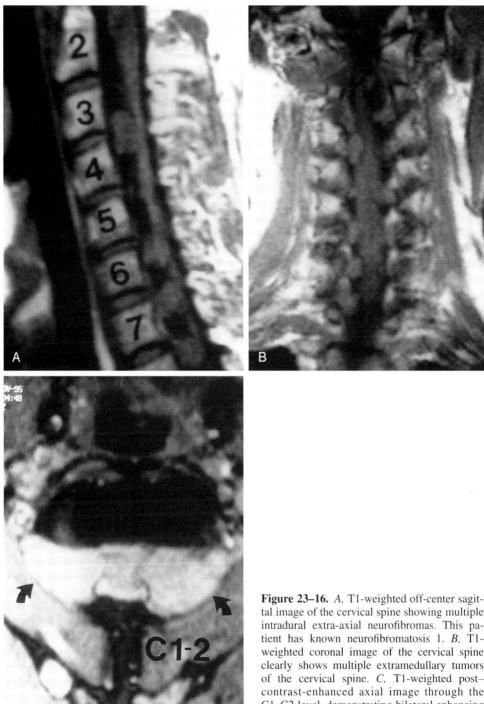

Figure 23–16. *A,* T1-weighted off-center sagittal image of the cervical spine showing multiple intradural extra-axial neurofibromas. This patient has known neurofibromatosis 1. *B,* T1-weighted coronal image of the cervical spine clearly shows multiple extramedullary tumors of the cervical spine. *C,* T1-weighted post–contrast-enhanced axial image through the C1–C2 level, demonstrating bilateral enhancing extramedullary neurofibromas in a patient with known neurofibromatosis type 1.

concurrent intradural and extradural meningiomas in the cervical spine. They recommend that when an epidural meningioma is found on MRI, special attention should be paid to the intradural space to find the high incidence of a concurrent meningioma.

Summary

Extramedullary tumors of the spine are usually best imaged with MRI, although CT can sometimes be helpful.

Although the diagnosis is not always apparent, the radiologist can provide vital pretreatment information about the extent of disease and its effects on the spinal cord and nerve roots.

References

1. Aggarwal S, Deck JHN, Kucharczyk W: Neuroendocrine tumor (paraganglioma) of the cauda equina: MR and pathologic findings. AJNR Am J Neuroradiol 14:1003–1007, 1993.

2. Baba Y, Ohkubo K, Seino N, et al: Osseous primitive neuroectodermal tumor: A case report. Radiat Med 16:297–300, 1998.
3. Bach F, Agerlin N, Sorenson JB, et al: Metastatic spinal cord compression secondary to lung cancer. J Clin Oncol 10:1781, 1992.
4. Bach F, Larsen BH, Rhode K, et al: Metastatic spinal cord compression: Occurrence, symptoms, clinical presentations and prognosis in 398 patients with spinal cord compression. Acta Neurochir (Wien) 107:37, 1990.
5. Baker L, Goodman S, Perkash I, et al: Benign versus pathologic compression fractures of vertebral bodies: Assessment with conventional spin-echo, chemical-shift, and STIR MR imaging. Radiology 174:495–502, 1990.
6. Barr J, Barr M, Lemley T, McCann R: Percutaneous vertebroplasty for pain relief and spinal stabilization. Spine 25:923–928, 2000.
7. Baur A, Stabler A, Bruning R, et al: Diffusion-weighted MR imaging of bone marrow: Differentiation of benign versus pathologic compression fractures. Radiology 207:349–356, 1998.
8. Crim JR, Mirra JM, Eckardt JJ, Seeger LL: Widespread inflammatory response to osteoblastoma: The flare phenomenon. Radiology 177:835–836, 1990.
9. Francel PC: Extrinsic spinal cord mass lesions. Pediatr Rev 19:389–395, 1998.
10. Frey I, Le Breton C, Lefkopoulos A, et al: Intradural extramedullary spinal canal secondary neoplasms: MR findings in 30 patients. Eur Radiol 8:1187–1192, 1998.
11. Gamba JL, Martinez S, Apple J, et al: Computed tomography of axial skeletal osteoid osteomas. Am J Roentgenol 142:769–772, 1984.
12. Georgy BA, Hesselink JR: MR imaging of the spine: Recent advances in pulse sequences and special techniques. AJR Am J Roentgenol 162:923, 1994.
13. Gilbert RW, Kim JH, Posner JB: Epidural spinal cord compression from metastatic tumor: Diagnosis and treatment. Ann Neurol 3:40, 1978.
14. Hashimoto M, Akabane Y, Tete E: Ewing's sarcoma of the sacrum. Radiat Med 17:451–453, 1999.
15. Khan DC, Malhotra S, Stevens RE, Steinfeld AD: Radiotherapy for the treatment of giant cell tumor of the spine: A report of six cases and review of the literature. Cancer Invest 17:110–113, 1999.
16. Kim J, Ryu K, Choi W, et al: Spinal involvement of hematopoietic malignancies and metastasis: Differentiation using MR imaging. Clin Imaging 23:125–133, 1999.
17. Kroon HM, Schurmans J: Osteoblastoma: Clinical and radiologic findings in 98 new cases. Radiology 175:783–790, 1990.
18. Kumar R, Guinto FC, Madewell JE, et al: Expansile bone lesions of the vertebra. Radiographics 8:749–769, 1988.
19. Kusumoto S, Jinnai I, Itoh K, et al: Magnetic resonance imaging patterns in patients with multiple myeloma. Br J Haematol 99:649–655, 1997.
20. Le Bihan D: Differentiation of benign versus pathologic compression fractures with diffusion-weighted MR imaging: A closer step toward the "Holy Grail" of tissue characterization? Radiology 207:305–307, 1998.
21. Lecouvet FE, Vande Berg BC, Michaux L, et al: Stage III multiple myeloma: Clinical and prognostic value of spinal bone marrow MR imaging. Radiology 209:653–660, 1998.
22. Libshitz HI, Malthouse SR, Cunningham D, et al: Multiple myeloma: Appearance at MR imaging. Radiology 182:833–837, 1992.
23. Mautner VF, Lindenau M, Hazim W, et al: The neuroimaging and clinical spectrum of NF2. Neurosurgery 38:880–886, 1996.
24. McLain RF, Weinstein JN: Tumors of the spine. Semin Spine Surg 2:157, 1990.
25. Meyers SP, Yaw K, Devaney K: Giant cell tumor of the thoracic spine: MR appearance. AJNR Am J Neuroradiol 15:962–964, 1994.
26. Mirowitz S, Apicella P, Reinus W, Hammerman A: MR imaging of bone marrow lesions: Relative conspicuousness on T1-weighted, fat-suppressed T2-weighted, and STIR images. AJR Am J Roentgenol 162:215–221, 1994.
27. Moulopoulos LA, Varma DG, Dimopoulos MA, et al: Multiple myeloma: Spinal MR imaging in patients with untreated newly diagnosed disease. Radiology 185:833–840, 1992.
28. Moulopoulos LA, Dimopoulos MA, Alexanian R, et al: Multiple myeloma: MR patterns of response to treatment. Radiology 193:441–446, 1994.
29. Moulopoulos LA, Dimopoulos MA, Vourtsi A, et al: Bone lesions with soft-tissue mass: Magnetic resonance imaging diagnosis of lymphomatous involvement of the bone marrow versus multiple myeloma and bone metastases. Leuk Lymphoma 34:179–184, 1999.
30. Murphey M, Andrews C, Flemming D, et al: From the Archives of the AFIP. Primary tumors of the spine: Radiologic-pathologic correlation. Radiographics 16:1131–1158, 1996.
31. O'Connor MI, Currier BL: Metastatic disease of the spine. Orthopedics 15:611, 1992.
32. Pui M, Chang S: Comparison of inversion recovery fast spin-echo (FSE) with T2-weighted fat-saturated FSE and T1-weighted MR imaging in bone marrow lesion detection. Skeletal Radiol 25:149–152, 1996.
33. Quekel LG, Versteege CW: The "dural tail sign" in MRI of spinal meningiomas. J Comput Assist Tomogr 19:890–892, 1995.
34. Rahmouni A, Divine M, Mathieu D, et al: Detection of multiple myeloma involving the spine: Efficacy of fat-suppression and contrast-enhanced MR imaging. AJR Am J Roentgenol 160:1049–1052, 1993.
35. Rahmouni A, Divine M, Mathieu D, et al: MR appearance of multiple myeloma of the spine before and after treatment. AJR Am J Roentgenol 160:1053–1057, 1993.
36. Rosenthal DI, Scott JA, Mankin HJ, et al: Sacrococcygeal chordoma: Magnetic resonance imaging and computed tomography. Am J Roentgenol 145:143–147, 1985.
37. Salvati M, Cervoni L, Artico M, et al: Primary spinal epidural non-Hodgkin's lymphoma: A clinical study. Surg Neurol 46:339–343, 1996.
38. Sanjay BK, Sim FH, Unni KK, et al: Giant-cell tumours of the spine. J Bone Joint Surg Br 75:148–154, 1993.
39. Shi HB, Suh DC, Lee HK, et al: Preoperative transarterial embolization of spinal tumor: Embolization techniques and results. AJNR Am J Neuroradiol 20:2009–2015, 1999.
40. Shives TC, McLeod RA, Unni KK, Schray MF: Chondrosarcoma of the spine. J Bone Joint Surg Am 71:1158–1165, 1989.
41. Simeone FA: Spinal cord tumors in adults. In Youmans JR (ed): Neurological Surgery, 3rd ed, vol 5. Philadelphia, WB Saunders, 1990, p 3531.
42. Sundgren P, Annertz M, Englund E, et al: Paragangliomas of the spinal canal. Neuroradiology 41:788–794, 1999.
43. Sze G, Merriam M, Oshio K, et al: Fast spin echo imaging in the evaluation of intradural disease of the spine. AJNR Am J Neuroradiol 13:1383, 1992.
44. Thakkar SD, Feigen U, Mautner VF: Spinal tumours in neurofibromatosis type 1: An MRI study of frequency, multiplicity and variety. Neuroradiology 41:625–629, 1999.
45. Weil SM, Gewirtz RJ, Tew JM Jr: Concurrent intradural and extradural meningiomas of the cervical spine. Neurosurgery 27:629–631, 1990.
46. Yonemoto T, Tatezaki S, Takenouchi T, et al: The surgical management of sacrococcygeal chordoma. Cancer 85:878–883, 1999.
47. Yousem DM, Patrone PM, Grossman RI: Leptomeningeal metastases: MR evaluation. J Comput Assist Tomogr 14:255–261, 1990.

24

The Spinal Cord

Jeffrey L. Sunshine, Scott Kolodny

Classically, evaluation of lesions within the spinal neural axis has been made on the basis of anatomic location. Lesions can be divided into *extradural, intradural-extramedullary,* and *intramedullary.* Intramedullary lesions of the spinal cord, in turn, can be subdivided according to their etiology into (1) ischemic disease; (2) vascular malformations; (3) neoplastic processes; and (4) infectious, inflammatory, and demyelinating diseases. After a brief review of spinal cord anatomy, this chapter focuses on the intramedullary lesions of the spinal cord and their appearances on magnetic resonance imaging (MRI) and, to a lesser extent, on computed tomography (CT) scans.

Anatomy

The spinal cord represents a caudal extension of the medulla oblongata; it terminates in the conus medullaris, typically at or just below the thoracolumbar junction in adults. The cord is slightly flattened along its anterior and posterior surfaces and is enlarged in two regions. The cord widens first for the brachial plexus at C3 to T2, then for the lumbar plexus at T9 to T12. The filum terminale represents extension from the conus to the coccyx, and the cauda equina refers to the extension of spinal nerve roots caudally from the conus within the lumbar subarachnoid space.

The three-layered meningeal covering of the central nervous system (CNS) is contiguous with the spinal cord, and all lie within the bony spinal canal. The innermost layer, the pia mater, is adherent to the surface of the cord and extends from the lateral surface of the cord to a dural arachnoid membrane, forming the dentate ligaments. The arachnoid membrane remains closely adherent to the outer layer, the dura mater, allowing for a potential subdural space between the two layers. The subarachnoid space remains filled with cerebrospinal fluid (CSF) and is contiguous with the intracranial subarachnoid space. The dura extends to the S2 level, forming the dural (thecal) sac, which is surrounded externally by epidural fat to fill the remainder of the volume of the spinal canal.

The gray matter of the spinal cord is located internally, in contradistinction to the gray matter of the brain, and is surrounded by white matter tracts; the proportion of gray matter increases in the cervical and lumbar regions. Both dorsal (sensory) and ventral (motor) roots arise along the entire length of the cord and these unite to form a total of 31 paired spinal nerves. There are 8 cervical, 12 thoracic, 5 lumbar, and 5 sacral roots.

The arterial supply to the spinal cord, although variable, can be divided into three major regions.[74] Branches of the intracranial vertebral artery, cervical vertebral arteries, and cervical trunks produce radicular arteries that form the predominant blood supply to the cervicothoracic region, generally ending after the first several thoracic vertebral segments.

A single radicular artery, usually located at approximately the T7 level, supplies the midthoracic cord. This represents the smallest territorial division and typically extends from T4 through T8.

The artery of Adamkiewicz, which arises from a low thoracic or upper lumbar artery, supplies the final thoracolumbar region. This important artery usually arises from an intercostal branch in the region of T9 to T12. In a few people, it may arise from a branch at a higher level but then the conus medullaris can be additionally supplied from a lower and smaller radicular artery. Least often, the artery of Adamkiewicz arises from the upper lumbar arteries.

At the levels of the spinal cord, radicular branches enter the spinal canal through the neural foramina and lead to the anterior as well as to the paired posterior spinal arteries on the cord surface. These spinal arteries in turn generate a rich anastomotic arcade, with the anterior artery supplying the central gray matter and the posterior arteries feeding the dorsal columns and posterior peripheral white matter. Modern MRI machines and the newer gradient sequences allow excellent anatomic depiction of the arteries and veins of the spinal cord without the need to rely solely on catheter-based conventional angiograms.[11]

Ischemia

Spinal cord ischemia can arise and lead to infarction for a variety of reasons, including trauma to or dissection of the arterial supply, atherosclerotic and embolic disease, hypotension (e.g., cardiac arrest), complications of thoracoabdominal surgery or spinal angiography, vasculitis, hypercoagulation diseases, and spontaneous idiopathic incidence. More rarely, cord ischemia and infarcts arise secondary to vascular malformations[102,108] or to hypercoagulation diseases as in patients harboring antiphospholipid antibodies.[47] Spinal cord infarction can be iatrogenic, resulting from neurosurgical procedures performed with the patient in a sitting position[90] or as a result of wayward migration of embolic materials during endovascular interventions.[73] In addition to dissection of direct arterial supply to the cord, dissection or high-grade stenoses involving larger proximal vessels, such as the vertebral artery, have also caused cord infarction.[4,115] In patients who have undergone trauma, the presence of intramedullary hemorrhage (Fig. 24–1) portends less chance of recovering motor activation and a good functional outcome.[35,36]

Spinal cord ischemia has been described in four progres-

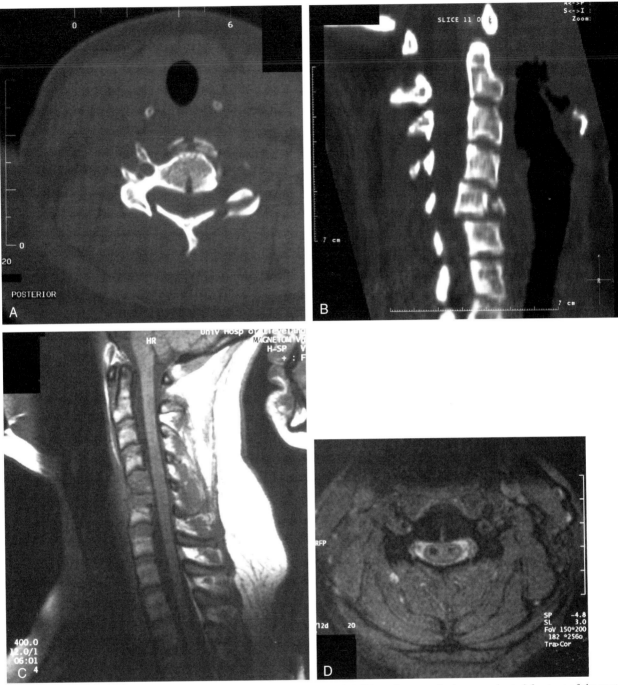

Figure 24–1. Spinal cord trauma with intramedullary hemorrhage. *A,* Axial CT section reveals the comminuted fracture of the vertebra and posterior elements with compression of the spinal canal. *B,* Sagittal CT reconstruction shows the anterior fracture of C5 and the posterior displacement of bone into the spinal canal. *C,* T1-weighted sagittal MR demonstrates the abnormal hypointense marrow signal in C5 from edema as well as the mild loss of height and again the posterior extension. No definite cord abnormality is seen. *D,* This axial FLASH (fast low-angle shot) T2-weighted section reveals two foci of abnormal hypointense regions within the cord from acute blood products.

sive patterns, best seen on T2-weighted axial MR images. The most descriptive and smallest insult produces hyperintensity limited to the paired anterior horns of the central gray matter in a pattern that has been descriptively labeled "owl's eyes."[74] Next, the paired posterior horns of the gray matter are involved in a pattern reminiscent of a butterfly (Fig. 24–2). When the insult becomes more severe, the damage extends laterally to involve the corticospinal tracts. Finally, in the worst situations, the entire area of the cord can be homogeneously affected (Fig. 24–3). Insults that cause a change of signal intensity limited to the anterior horns most often have a better functional outcome, and

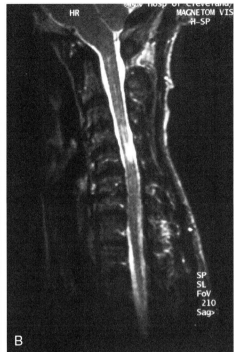

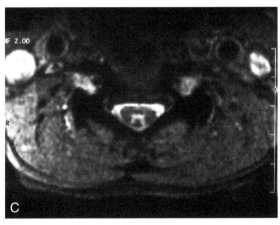

Figure 24–2. Cord infarction. *A,* T1-weighted sagittal MR image shows no definite intramedullary abnormality. *B,* T2-weighted sagittal MR image reveals marked focal hyperintensity along the central and posterior cord centered at C5. *C,* A gradient-echo, FLASH (fast low-angle shot), T2-weighted axial section demonstrates the butterfly pattern of cord infarction involving the bilateral anterior and posterior horns of the gray matter.

indeed embolic events to spinal arteries arising during catheter angiography have been reported to resolve spontaneously.[37]

T1-weighted images best demonstrate associated swelling, particularly the associated enlargement of the cord.[47] Gadolinium-enhanced T1-weighted images show disruption of the blood-brain barrier in the late acute and subacute phases of infarction. This disruption tends to involve the peripheral margins of the central gray matter, whereas in anterior cord syndrome the ventral margins tend to be involved more than the peripheral, probably as a result of the posterior collateral supply.[31,39] MRI, especially T2-weighted images, demonstrates associated abnormalities of the aorta and of adjacent vertebral bodies.[34,131]

Vascular Malformations

Vascular malformations of and around the spinal cord have been variously classified as (1) dural arteriovenous fistulas (AVFs), (2) perimedullary intradural or cord AVFs, (3) cavernous angiomas, and (4) spinal cord arteriovenous malformations (AVMs). Diagnosis of these malformations has been improved tremendously with the application of MRI techniques that enable the reliable demonstration of the primary vascular lesion and the secondary cord edema and myelopathy. Until very recently, diagnosis required confirmation by demonstration of the primary vasculopathy with conventional spinal angiograms, but the advent of contrast-enhanced MR angiography has allowed direct noninvasive demonstration of the lesions.[5, 9, 10, 71, 72]

Spinal Cord Arteriovenous Malformations

Cord AVMs are congenital in origin and are composed of the typical nidus of abnormal vessels arising from arterial feeders that then lead directly to hypertensive "arterialized" venous drainage. Those with a typically compact, wholly intramedullary nidus have been termed *glomus*

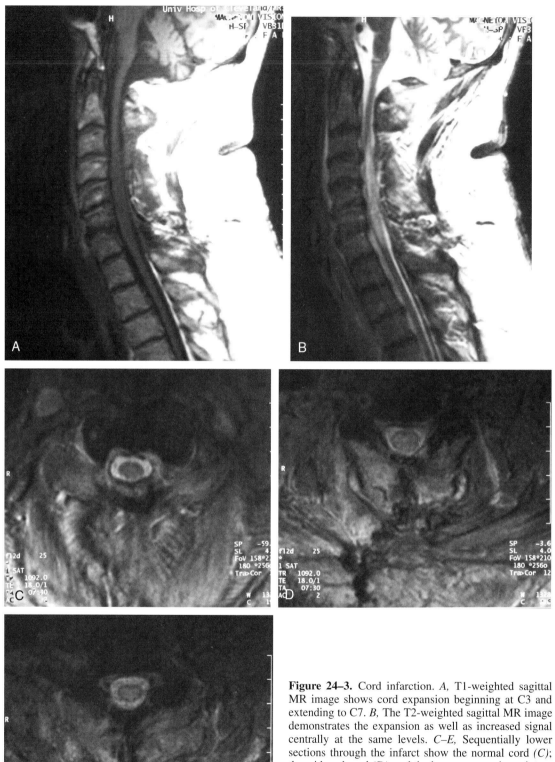

Figure 24–3. Cord infarction. *A,* T1-weighted sagittal MR image shows cord expansion beginning at C3 and extending to C7. *B,* The T2-weighted sagittal MR image demonstrates the expansion as well as increased signal centrally at the same levels. *C–E,* Sequentially lower sections through the infarct show the normal cord *(C);* the widened cord *(D),* and the homogeneous hyperintensity of the central gray matter *(E)* on these FLASH, T2-weighted axial slices.

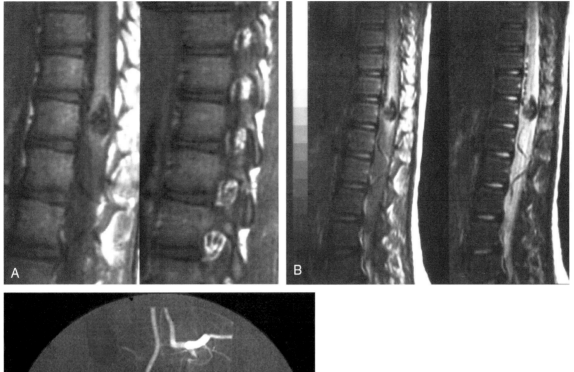

Figure 24–4. Intramedullary glomus arteriovenous malformation. *A,* T1-weighted sagittal MR image shows conus expansion around a central hypointensity that demonstrates heterogeneous signal. *B,* T2-weighted sagittal MR image demonstrates a greater heterogeneity and the more inferior extension of an enlarged curvilinear flow void probably representing a dilated draining vein. *C,* Angiographic image reveals the serpentine arterial input that enters the nidus from above and the dilated curvilinear draining vein below.

AVMs (Fig. 24–4), and those with a looser configuration that often extends into the extramedullary spaces have been labeled *juvenile-type AVMs.*[2] In rare instances, these malformations occur in conjunction with vertebral angiomas and skin nevi, all at the same metameric level; this is called the *Cobb syndrome.*[80]

AVMs present a risk of hemorrhage and ensuing complications as well as effects of venous hypertension, which may include spinal cord edema, ischemia, or infarct. Indeed, this is the only subset of vascular malformations that show associated spinal artery aneurysm formation, most likely the result of long-standing high flow. When such aneurysms occur, they frequently hemorrhage.[6]

MRI can often be used to detect spinal AVMs when the effects of high flow, signal changes about the nidus, hemorrhage, and edema are readily apparent.[61] In addition, the telltale curvilinear filling defects can be seen on CT myelography.[60] Spinal AVMs that occur within the cord substance can be complicated by associated infarct that appears bright on T2-weighted images and enhances with gadolinium.[108] If spinal AVMs spontaneously thrombose (*Foix-Alajouanine syndrome*), an associated cord ischemia can occur, leading to cord infarct.[102] Even greater sensitivity for the lesions, and in particular for the shunt, is gained through application of dynamic MRI using a T2-weighted sequence and tracking of a gadolinium bolus.[123]

Spinal AVFs are the more common spinal cord vascular malformations; they are subdivided into malformations involving only the dural branches of a radicular artery (*dural AVFs*) and those arising directly from the spinal arteries (*intradural AVFs*). Dural AVFs are probably acquired, whereas intradural AVFs are thought to be congenital. The larger congenital lesions often present in childhood with hemorrhage of focal neurologic deficits.[104]

Dural Arteriovenous Fistulas

Dural AVFs, whose point of shunt is within the dural surface, comprise the majority of all spinal vascular malformations.[93] The resultant venous engorgement can produce venous hypertensive changes in the spinal cord, often in the midthoracic to upper lumbar region, that in turn induce cord myelopathy. The myelopathic changes, both clinically and on MR images, can occur distal to the level of the fistula; this can become particularly disorienting near the cervicomedullary junction, where the fistula can be intracranial but the myelopathy cervical to thoracic or vice versa.[8, 18, 33, 92] Disruption of such a fistula can produce subarachnoid hemorrhage at a distance from the lesion.[49]

MRI typically shows hyperintensity on T2-weighted images, possible cord enlargement, and, at times, cord enhancement secondary to infarct.[65] The high vascular flow usually produces the expected flow voids in the vicinity of the fistula on MR images or dilated vessels on myelography.[41] Of interest, a surrounding peripheral rim of hypointensity on T2-weighted images has been reported with these fistulas, which may be specific in the absence of associated hemorrhage.[53] CT can be used to evaluate these fistulas immediately after endovascular embolization to confirm occlusion of the entire shunt.[20]

Intradural Arteriovenous Fistulas

Intradural AVFs lie on the cord surface, where they are further subdivided by size: type I, small; type II, larger, with dilatation of the artery and vein; and type III, largest, with multiple feeders and marked venous dilatation.[2] A variant on this classification defines type I as those draining only to meningeal veins, type II to meningeal veins and then retrograde to subarachnoid veins, and type III to subarachnoid veins only.[7] On MRI examinations, these lesions often appear with cord enlargement, edema, hyperintense signal on T2-weighted images, areas of enhancement, and abnormal flow voids.[65, 122] Spiral or multislice CT scanners enable precise localization of the fistula, which allows a greater degree of treatment planning, particularly demonstrating the relationship to surrounding bone.[48]

Cavernous Angiomas

Cavernous angiomas are most often intramedullary, and the risk to the patient is of hemorrhage into functioning tissues. Cavernous angiomas can be found at any cord level, and they are multiple in a significant minority of cases.[22, 127] These angiomas show a typical reticulated pattern of heterogeneous signal intensity on all MR sequences, producing the classic "popcorn" appearance best demonstrated on T2-weighted sequences.[15] This pattern, in association with a family history, other lesions in the neural axis, and a tendency toward diminished signal intensity over time, can confirm the diagnosis.[125]

Neoplasms

Intramedullary neoplasms consist of (1) primary cord neoplasms (e.g., ependymomas and astrocytomas) and, to a lesser extent, (2) hemangioblastomas, (3) intramedullary metastases, and (4) other even less common entities (e.g., intramedullary lipomas). In adults, intramedullary neoplasms comprise 7% to 22% of all spinal neoplasms and include, in decreasing order of frequency, ependymomas (65%); astrocytomas (25%); glioblastoma (7.5%); and rare hemangioblastomas, oligodendrogliomas, and metastases.[91, 105, 109, 113] Intramedullary metastases are usually not neural in origin; lung cancer is the most common primary tumor to metastasize to the cord, followed by breast cancer. Lymphoma, colon and renal tumors, head and neck carcinoma, and melanoma also metastasize to the cord but less commonly.[12, 23, 43] In children, intramedullary lesions account for one third of spinal neoplasms and include astrocytomas (58%), ependymomas (28.5%), teratomas, and dermoid or epidermoid tumors (5.8%).

Hemangioblastomas and intramedullary metastases, such as glioblastoma, primitive neuroectodermal tumor, and Wilms' tumor, occur infrequently in the spinal cords of children.[17, 26, 32, 81]

Diffuse fusiform or focal expansion of the cord with loss of the normal cord contour and resultant distortion of the surrounding subarachnoid space is the hallmark of intramedullary tumors on MR images as they are on CT myelograms. Differentiation between the white matter tracts and the butterfly or H-shaped central gray matter may often be obtained with high-resolution MRI.[112] MRI can also be used to demonstrate the longitudinal extent of abnormal signal and enhancement as well as the internal derangement of spinal parenchymal architecture. These abilities have established the superiority of MRI over other neuroimaging techniques in the evaluation of intramedullary processes.

Traditionally, CT myelography demonstrated intramedullary masses as expansile lesions of the spinal cord, displacing the intrathecal contrast material within the subarachnoid space peripherally; occasionally, however, intramedullary lesions are not shown to expand the cord. One series noted a normal myelographic appearance in 42% of patients with intramedullary neoplasms.[43] Abnormal signal on standard or fast spin-echo T2-weighted images and abnormal contrast enhancement confirm the presence of intramedullary neoplasms on MRI despite lack of cord expansion.[118] Exophytic growth of intramedullary lesions, most commonly in the region of the conus medullaris, may result in both focal cord expansion and cord displacement by the exophytic process. Exophytic growth of intramedullary lesions has been described in astrocytomas, mixed gliomas, ependymomas, and hemangioblastomas.

With early imaging and contrast enhancement, it is possible to locate intramedullary parenchymal lesions within specific quadrants of the spinal cord or within the central canal of the cord. Intramedullary neoplasms, however, are usually relatively large when initially imaged, and they distort the parenchyma of the cord over the length of several segments. Signal intensity changes of most intramedullary processes are nonspecific, and it is often impossible on unenhanced MRI to differentiate neoplasm from associated edema or postoperative gliosis because of similar nonspecific T1 and T2 lengthening.[27, 94, 110, 129] Tumor and edema have similar MRI characteristics, whereas associated cysts may become more hyperintense on T2-weighted sequences than the adjacent abnormal cord. Features that help distinguish tumor-related cysts from syringes include abrupt changes in diameter and position of the cyst, uneven thickness of the surrounding cord, increased T2-weighted signal of tumor cysts, and pathologic enhancement.[106, 126] Cystic lesions associated with tumor, however, may not be well defined without contrast administration.[16, 42]

After administration of contrast, there is striking and immediate enhancement of most intramedullary neoplasms on both CT scans and MR images. The focus of enhancement is usually smaller than the region of abnormal signal and spinal cord enlargement defined on the unenhanced views, helping to localize the actual neoplastic focus.[64, 79, 117] Occasionally, lesions fail to enhance and may be identified by abnormal signal intensity only.

Unfortunately, enhancement patterns are nonspecific, although astrocytomas tend to enhance in a more irregular manner compared with ependymomas or hemangioblastomas and are often eccentrically located. Cystic degeneration tends to indicate astrocytoma, whereas signal changes consistent with pigment or fat/calcium tend to indicate melanoma or teratoma, respectively.[69] Ependymomas and hemangioblastomas both enhance homogeneously and are more likely to be associated with cysts and syringes. Up to 75% of hemangioblastomas are cystic, and draining veins and cord edema, probably secondary to vascular shunt-related congestion, may also be seen in hemangioblastomas.[21, 44, 89, 111] Heterogeneous signal on T1-weighted and T2-weighted images, hypointensity at the tumor margins resulting from firm pseudocapsule formation, and intratumoral hypointensity from hemorrhage suggest ependymoma.[69, 86]

Ependymomas

Ependymomas represent 65% of spinal cord neoplasms. They are found more commonly in men and usually present between 20 and 60 years of age. They represent the most common glial tumor of the lower cord. Three quarters are myxopapillary subtypes and arise within the conus or filum terminale, and the remainder are found in the cervical and thoracic cords. Ependymomas within the cervical and thoracic cords are generally indistinguishable from astrocytomas; however, astrocytomas are far more common in the cervical cord and slightly more common in the thoracic cord than ependymomas.[78]

Ependymomas are usually histologically benign and slowly growing, which generally allows them to reach a large size by the time they manifest clinically. They may span one to five vertebral body segments and are highly vascular, often resulting in intratumoral hemorrhage that can be visualized on imaging.[132] They may be large enough to produce marked expansion of the spinal canal, and the vertebral bodies on either side of the disk may be excavated, with the pedicles and neural arches eroded. Smaller ependymomas tend to displace nerve roots, whereas larger tumors tend to engulf adjacent nerve roots and may become indistinguishable from them.

Ependymomas appear isodense to hypodense on nonenhanced spinal CT and enhance after the intravenous (IV) administration of contrast material. Although calcification has been reported to be common in posterior fossa and supratentorial ependymomas, it has not been commonly observed in spinal cord ependymomas. Ependymomas of the cauda equina are reasonably characteristic, usually appearing as a spherical mass centrally within the spinal canal. After administration of a water-soluble contrast agent, myelographic and postmyelographic CT scans demonstrate the nerve roots of the cauda equina above and below the tumor mass, thus delineating the conus as separate from the mass.

The MRI appearance of spinal ependymomas is variable, depending on the location within the spinal cord. In the cervical and thoracic regions, they appear as expansile lesions of the cord in the sagittal and axial planes and are slightly hypointense on T1-weighted images and hyperintense on T2-weighted images. In addition, intratumoral cyst cavities have occasionally been reported in these locations.[132] In the cauda equina region, the tumors are typically spherical masses with signal intensities similar to those found elsewhere (Fig. 24–5). Because of possible episodes of rebleeding from the fibrovascular stroma, however, repeated episodes of subarachnoid hemorrhage may lead to hemosiderin deposition within the subarachnoid space. This appears as areas of marked hypointensity on T2-weighted images.[132] Gadolinium enhancement is generally in a homogeneous, well-circumscribed pattern, rendering the lesion more conspicuous.

Astrocytomas

Astrocytomas represent one third of intramedullary gliomas and may occur at any location along the cord. They are most common between 20 and 50 years of age and are slightly more common in men. Seventy-five percent of these tumors are low-grade (grade I or II). Astrocytomas tend to occur in the cervical and thoracic segments, where they have an incidence equal to or greater than that of ependymomas. In children, the proportional incidence of astrocytomas to ependymomas is higher than that in adults.[132]

Intratumoral cysts within astrocytomas, as well as syringomyelia at one or both ends of the cord associated with astrocytomas, occur with variable incidences. Most astrocytomas are solitary tumors, but they can be multiple in the case of neurofibromatosis. Histologically, the low-grade tumors are fibrillary astrocytomas with pilocytic features. On noncontrast CT scans, astrocytomas of the spinal cord appear as hypointense to isointense lesions.[85] After administration of IV contrast material, these lesions often enhance heterogeneously, with nonenhancing portions of tumor representing intratumoral cyst cavities.[45] Water-soluble myelographic scans demonstrate fusiform enlargement of the spinal cord, with focal nodules or abrupt changes in size indicating the likelihood that the cord mass represents a tumor and not a syrinx. Syringes at either end of the tumor generally have a sausage-like appearance, being uniformly expanded and lacking any focal nodules. Calcification within astrocytic tumors of the spinal cord is not common.[132]

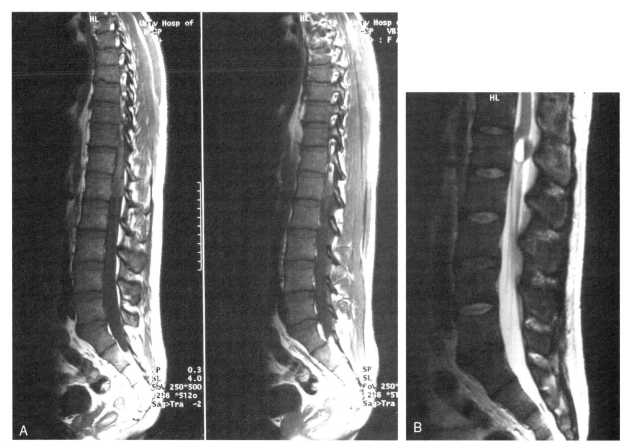

Figure 24–5. Conus myxopapillary ependymoma. *A*, T1-weighted sagittal MR image shows a hypointense expansion of the conus. *B*, T2-weighted sagittal MR image demonstrates an exophytic cystic lesion of the conus that contains a fluid-fluid level.

MRI is the best way to demonstrate enlargement of the spinal cord by an astrocytoma (Fig. 24–6). Sagittal and axial plane images demonstrate expansion of the cord. T1-weighted images demonstrate astrocytomas to be low in signal intensity whereas proton-density–weighted and T2-weighted images show them to be high in signal intensity.[107,129] Intratumoral cysts are irregular areas; their contents reflect a signal intensity similar to that of CSF. Syrinxes at either end of the tumor demonstrate parallel walls, and their contents also demonstrate signal intensity similar to that of CSF. Axial images demonstrate the asymmetrical expansion of the cord by tumor tissue. Astrocytomas tend to enhance more heterogeneously than ependymomas, partly because of the high incidence of intratumoral cysts, and IV gadolinium administration aids in the detection and characterization of astrocytomas.[94]

Hemangioblastomas

Hemangioblastomas are uncommon tumors of the spinal cord, representing 1.6% to 3.6% of spinal cord tumors; they are most often found in association with von Hippel–Lindau disease.[132] They are usually found in middle-aged adults, demonstrate no sexual predilection, and are solitary in 80% of cases. Although they are usually solitary, hemangioblastomas may be multiple in von Hippel–Lindau dis-

ease. Approximately 50% of hemangioblastomas are cystic with a mural tumor nodule. The cysts are often high in protein content and are suggestive of prior episodes of hemorrhage.[132] The tumors may arise in the cervical or thoracic cord, usually causing diffuse focal widening of the cord.

On nonenhanced CT scans, the tumor nidus appears isodense to slightly hyperdense in attenuation, and after administration of IV contrast material, the tumor markedly enhances; the enhancing tumor nodule appears distinct from the associated cyst. On contrast myelographic scans, the spinal cord appears enlarged with multiple serpentine filling defects from arteries and veins that result from this relatively vascular tumor.[132]

MR images demonstrate an enlarged, infiltrated spinal cord, and in half the cases a cyst containing a mural nodule can be identified. A large syrinx may also accompany the tumor, helping to support the diagnosis.[94] Gadolinium enhancement (Fig. 24–7) is the most useful technique to differentiate the mural tumor nidus from the associated reactive, cystic changes.[94, 116, 117]

Intramedullary Metastases

Hematogenous metastases to the spinal cord from a primary site outside the CNS (lung, breast, melanoma) are

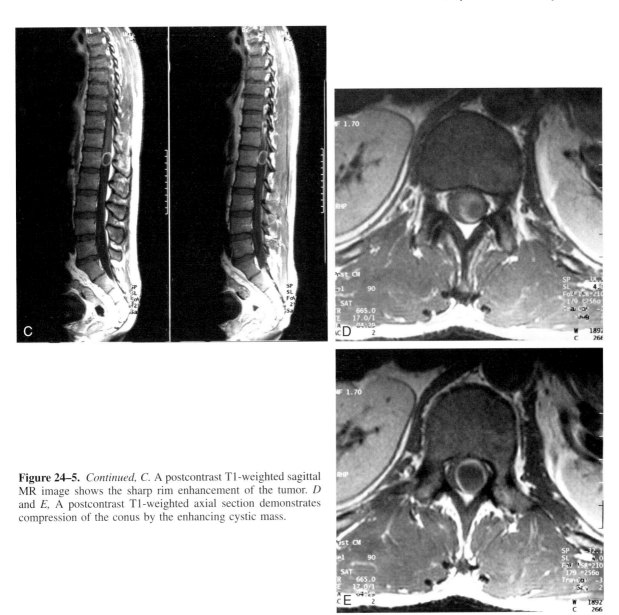

Figure 24–5. *Continued, C.* A postcontrast T1-weighted sagittal MR image shows the sharp rim enhancement of the tumor. *D* and *E,* A postcontrast T1-weighted axial section demonstrates compression of the conus by the enhancing cystic mass.

rare, even when there are metastatic lesions to other spinal structures, such as the vertebral bodies and the epidural space.[30] Of the tumors of non-neurogenic origin metastasizing to the cord, lung carcinoma is the most common (Fig. 24–8), and breast carcinoma is the second most common. Other reported primary tumors are much less common; they include lymphoma, melanoma, colorectal carcinoma, Hodgkin's disease, head and neck carcinoma, and leukemia.[99]

Drop metastases from primary brain tumors can seed down the central canal of the spinal cord and produce an appearance similar to that of an intramedullary metastasis. These metastases are usually from malignant gliomas, ependymomas, medulloblastomas, and pineal tumors. Although apparent on CT myelograms, these, like other lesions, are best detected by MRI with contrast enhancement.[50]

In most instances, the intramedullary metastatic lesion

is small and does not produce significant mass effect. Therefore, a discernible change in the size of the spinal cord cannot be noticed on either contrast-enhanced myelographic or postmyelogram CT scans.[130] In a few instances, focal enlargement of the cord may be sufficient to be seen by either modality.

MRI is the best technique for evaluating intramedullary spinal cord metastatic lesions. Enlargement of the spinal cord, even when subtle, is best seen on T1-weighted images in the sagittal plane and is the first indication of an intramedullary lesion. Lesions are hyperintense on T2-weighted images and generally enhance heterogeneously after IV gadolinium administration (Fig. 24–9). T2-weighted signal intensity changes and abnormal enhancement can be seen in the absence of cord enlargement.[99] Subsequent to the intramedullary metastasis, a blockage and then dilatation of the central canal can occur, producing a typical syrinx in association with the mass.[56,97]

Text continued on page 796

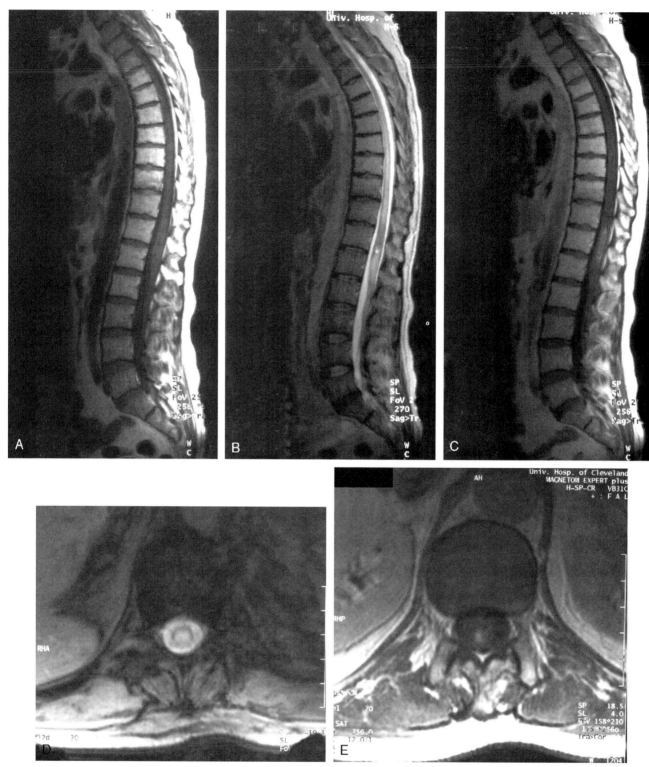

Figure 24–6. Cord astrocytoma. *A,* T1-weighted sagittal MR image shows marked expansion of the cervical cord by a large cystic lesion. *B,* T2-weighted, fast spin-echo, sagittal MR image confirms the cystic nature of the mass and better demonstrates the long inferior extent of the associated cystic syrinx. *C,* Postcontrast T1-weighted sagittal MR image reveals the heterogeneous nodular enhancement within the larger cervical cyst. *D,* Postcontrast T1-weighted axial section demonstrates the homogeneous enhancement of the solid component. *E,* T1-weighted axial section lower in the cord confirms the central syrinx.

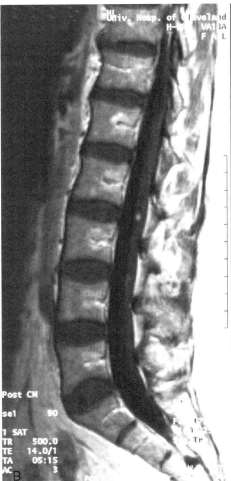

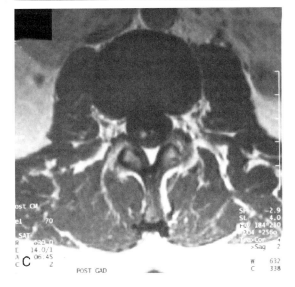

Figure 24–7. Multiple hemangioblastomas in a patient with von Hippel–Lindau syndrome. *A,* Postcontrast T1-weighted sagittal MR image of the cervical spine shows a posterior peripheral enhancing nodule at the C6–7 level. *B,* Postcontrast T1-weighted sagittal MR image of the lumbar spine demonstrates an enhancing nodule at the tip of the conus. *C,* Postcontrast T1-weighted axial section reveals the solid enhancing nodule within the peripheral substance of the conus medullaris.

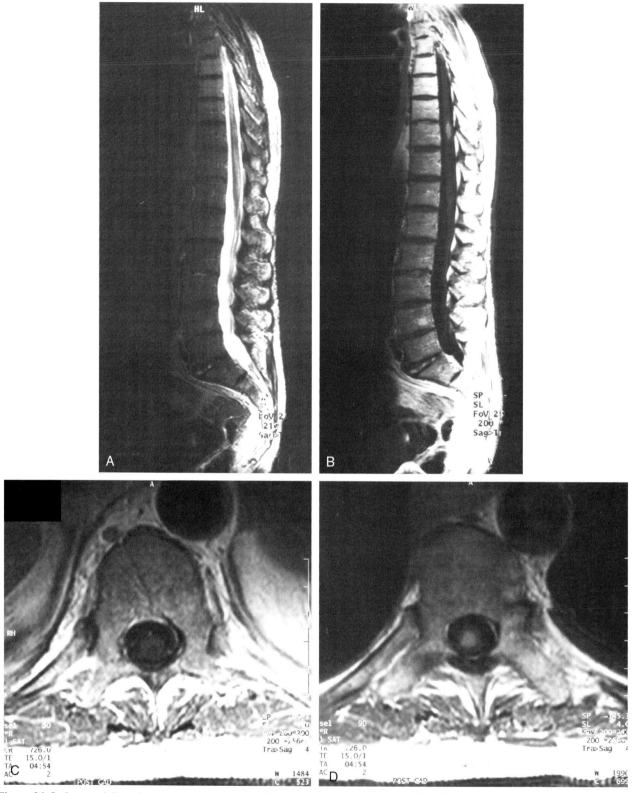

Figure 24–8. Intramedullary drop metastases to the cord from lung brain metastasis. *A,* T2-weighted, fast spin-echo, sagittal MR image shows a band of hyperintensity along the posterior cord. *B,* Postcontrast T1-weighted sagittal MR image demonstrates a heterogeneously enhancing ovoid mass in the lower thoracic cord. *C,* This T1-weighted axial section shows an eccentric hypointensity without definite distortion of the cord surface. *D,* This T1-weighted postcontrast axial section confirms the homogeneous enhancement of the mass.

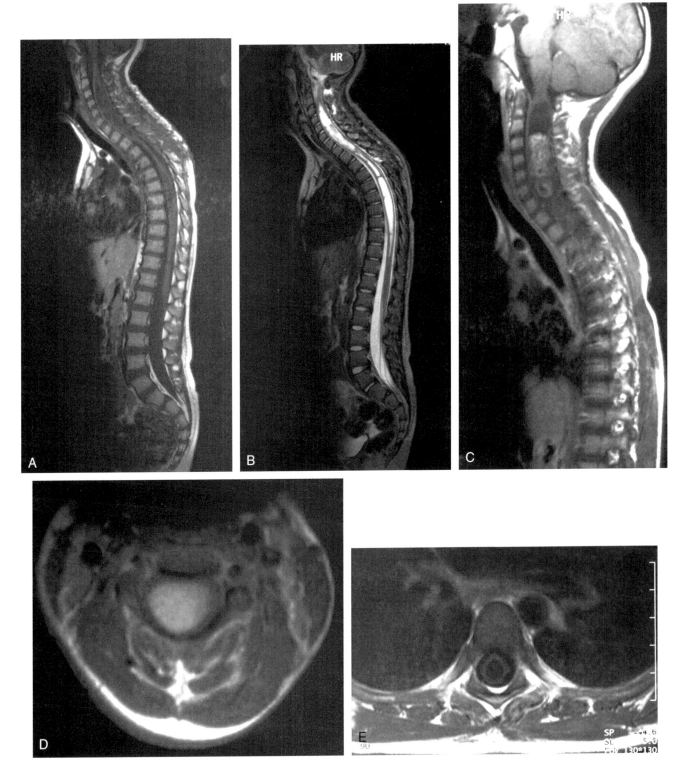

Figure 24–9. Hematogenous metastasis to the conus medullaris from lung carcinoma. *A,* T1-weighted sagittal MR image shows expansion of the inferior cord. *B,* T2-weighted sagittal MR image demonstrates abnormal hyperintense signal in the conus and a more focal area of greater signal intensity. *C,* Postcontrast T1-weighted sagittal MR image shows heterogeneous enhancement extending over the length of more than one vertebral body of the lower cord. *D,* A gradient-echo, FLASH (fast low-angle shot), T2-weighted axial section confirms cord expansion and the central signal intensity abnormality. *E,* Postcontrast T1-weighted axial section highlights a focal area of greater enhancement.

Infection, Inflammation, and Demyelination

Infectious diseases typically occur around the spinal cord, as in osteomyelitis, diskitis, and epidural abscesses, but more rarely they can involve the intramedullary substance. Cord infection can be expected to produce decreased signal with T1 weighting, increased intensity on T2-weighted images, and early variable enhancement with gadolinium, representing myelitis or abscess.[83] These lesions occur as a result of hematogenous dissemination and can arise, for example, from typical pyogenic bacteria, in syphilis or in tuberculosis.[40, 84] The myelitis can have associated enhancement that may resolve after successful antimicrobial therapy, whereas frank abscesses can show typical rim enhancement.[57, 84] A congenital lesion, such as a dermal sinus, can allow formation of an unusually high number of intramedullary abscesses.[25]

Intramedullary involvement in the prototypical granulomatous diseases, tuberculosis and sarcoidosis, is rare. When the cord is involved in tuberculosis, an enhancing intramedullary tuberculoma is expected, but fewer than 150 examples have been reported among patients with normal immune systems.[101] In patients with acquired immunodeficiency syndrome (AIDS), this entity may arise slightly more often, but the tuberculoma has a nonspecific appearance, its signal intensity is decreased on T1-weighted images and increased on T2-weighted images, and peripheral or nodular enhancement is seen.[76] Very rarely, a frank abscess within the cord arises, at times in association with meningitis of tuberculosis.[119]

CNS involvement in systemic sarcoidosis occurs in about 5% of patients, but direct primary cord lesions have been reported in fewer than 100 cases. In the cord, this disease also has a nonspecific appearance, with cord enlargement and multifocal patchy areas of enhancement, again frequently in association with meningitis.[87] These lesions should resolve, however, after appropriate steroid therapy, perhaps with the exception of infrequently reported central calcifications.[95, 128]

Parasitic myelitis can produce a similar appearance in association with a CSF eosinophilia.[63] Although rare, typical parasitic diseases have been reported to involve the spinal cord: schistosomiasis,[29] toxoplasmosis in patients with AIDS,[98, 103] and cysticercosis. When schistosomiasis invades the cord, it can cause a nonspecific myelitis, or the ova can induce formation of granulomas that can be identified on CT myelograms.[46] In patients with cysticercosis, syringomyelia or cystic intramedullary lesions can be present and are associated with brain parenchymal lesions.[68]

Involvement of the spinal cord as a direct result of fungal disease occurs only rarely and typically only in those with significant immune compromise. Aspergillosis is the most common fungal disease of the cord, typically presenting as a myelopathy but also reported as occluding principally the anterior spinal artery.[59, 96] Cord abscesses caused by *Candida, Coccidioides,* and *Nocardia* have been reported.[1, 70, 82] Similarly, cord granulomas caused by *Cryptococcus* and *Histoplasma* have been described in isolated reports.[55, 114]

Viral infections of the spinal cord are encountered most often among patients with immune compromise. In patients with AIDS, intramedullary infection with human immunodeficiency virus type I (HIV-1) causes a vacuolar myelopathy that shows nonspecific hyperintensity on T2-weighted images.[3, 124] Herpes zoster typically affects the skin but can produce a myelitis that shows cord enlargement, hyperin-

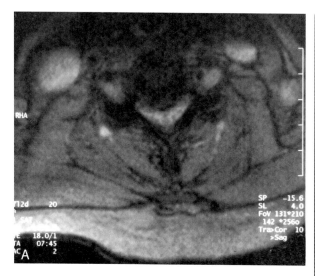
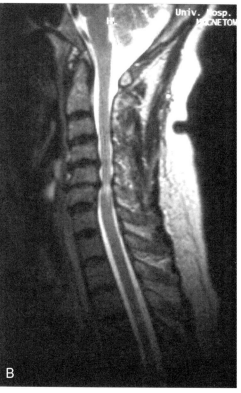

Figure 24–10. Degenerative changes of the spine with cord effect. *A,* T2-weighted FLASH (fast low-angle shot) axial section demonstrates a posterior disk-osteophyte complex impressing upon the thecal sac and the central cord. *B,* T2-weighted fast spin-echo sagittal MR image confirms the degenerative changes along the posterior vertebral line and demonstrates nonspecific abnormal hyperintensity within the substance of the cord at the C6 level.

tensity on T2-weighted images, and variable enhancement.[38,51] Cord involvement by the Epstein-Barr virus has been reported as either encephalomyelitis or isolated myelitis, demonstrating the same nonspecific findings as the preceding viral disorders.[13,28]

Degenerative and demyelinating disorders can cause an acute transverse myelitis, or myelopathy. When the spinal canal narrows because of degenerative changes in the bones, joints, and disks, pressure to the cord can occur that will cause myelopathic changes visible on MR images (Fig. 24–10). The causes are uncertain and may include edema, inflammation, ischemia, or gliosis.[75]

The lesions of multiple sclerosis, the prototypical demyelinating disease, tend to be located at the cervical level, although they can be found throughout the medullary substance, whereas the lesions of idiopathic myelitis tend to appear at the thoracic levels.[19,66] The lesions of multiple sclerosis often demonstrate multiplicity within the CNS, underscoring the need for separation in time and space to diagnose this multiphasic disease.

In contrast, acute disseminated encephalomyelitis arises as a monophasic illness after exposure to a viral vaccine; multifocal plaques may appear, but they do not recur after improvement, which is slow.[24] In the rare instances when these plaques do recur in the absence of a diagnosis of multiple sclerosis, other autoimmune disorders, perhaps

involving the presence of anti-cardiolipin antibodies, may be considered.[14] A delayed postradiation myelopathy can occur, but the diagnosis remains one of exclusion, with nonspecificity of the signal changes and enhancement on MR images.[58] Collagen vascular diseases, in particular in 1% to 2% of patients with systemic lupus erythematosus, can also cause a transverse myelitis that rarely affects the entire cord.[62,88]

Unfortunately, the lesions of all these disorders have a similar appearance: hyperintense plaques within the cord substance on T2-weighted images, possible cord enlargement, and possible enhancement. Only the spinal cord enlargement can be well seen on CT scans; thus, the modality of choice is MRI, in which the absence of cord expansion has become the best predictor of a non-neoplastic cause to an unknown cord lesion.[67,77] These lesions are best depicted with fast STIR (short tau inversion recovery) sequences, and in contrast to similar lesions in the brain, they are not well demonstrated by FLAIR (fluid-attenuated inversion recovery) sequences (Fig. 24–11).[52,54]

In multiple sclerosis, the most common source of myelitis seen in the United States, lesions tend to occur in multiples (Fig. 24–12), to be eccentrically located (Fig. 24–13), to involve less than half the cross-sectional area of the cord, and to extend less than two vertebral bodies in length.[120]

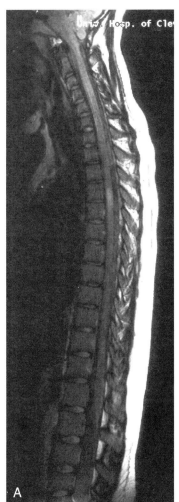
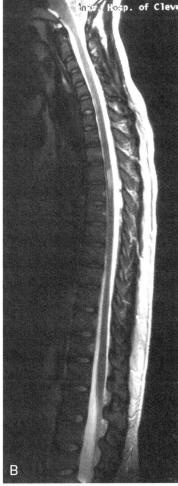

Figure 24–11. Multiple sclerosis plaque. *A,* A FLAIR (fluid-attenuated inversion recovery) sagittal MR image shows the lesion within the anterior cord centered at the third thoracic vertebra. *B,* The same lesion is even better demonstrated by the fast spin-echo T2-weighted sequence, and its appearance is not significantly diminished because of the high signal from the surrounding cerebrospinal fluid.

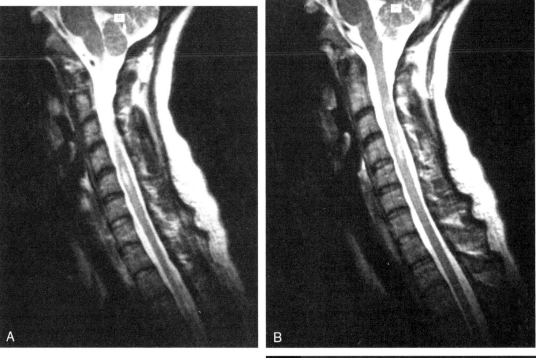

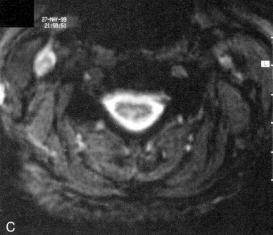

Figure 24–12. Multiplicity of multiple sclerosis plaques. *A* and *B,* These fast spin-echo, T2-weighted MR images reveal a larger ovoid area of hyperintensity centered at C5 *(A)*, and a second smaller, rounded lesion more superiorly at the level of C2–C3. *C,* An axial FLASH (fast low-angle shot) gradient-echo sequence produced this axial image showing two side-by-side lesions, the larger to the patient's right.

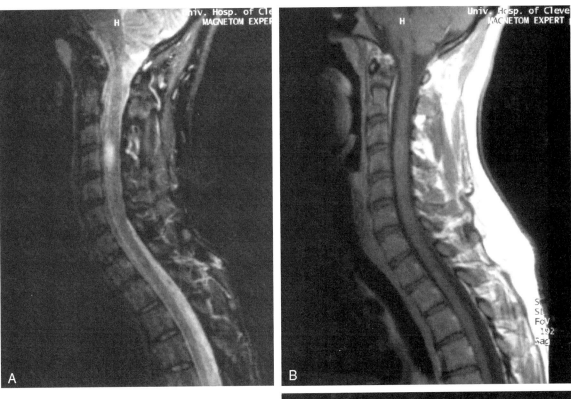

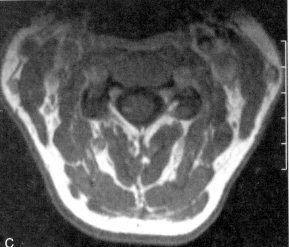

Figure 24–13. Eccentricity of multiple sclerosis plaques. *A,* A STIR (short tau inversion recovery) sagittal MR image shows a broad ovoid hyperintensity along the anterior cord at C4. *B,* The postcontrast T1-weighted sagittal MR image reveals eccentric anterior rim enhancement. *C,* The postcontrast T1-weighted axial section demonstrates a low level of rim enhancement eccentrically positioned in the right anterior quarter of the cord.

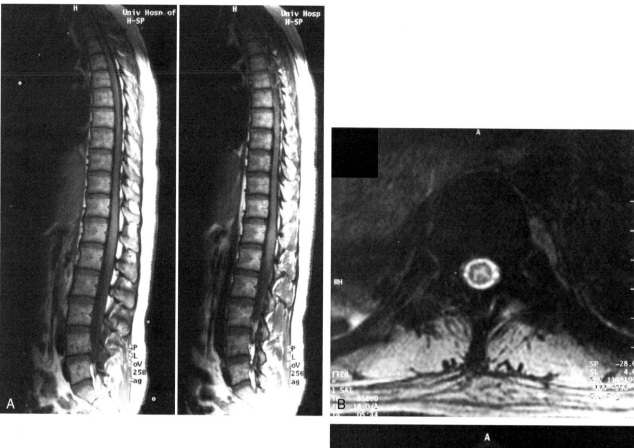

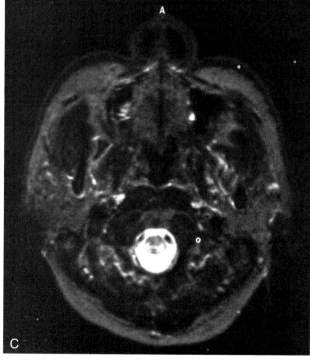

Figure 24–14. Systemic lupus erythematosus. *A,* T1-weighted sagittal MR images demonstrate cord enlargement at the conus. *B,* FLASH (fast low-angle shot) gradient-echo axial section shows abnormal hyperintense signal of the central gray matter consistent with cord ischemia secondary to a lupus vasculitis. *C,* A high T2-weighted axial section from the cervicomedullary junction shows similar abnormal signal in the bilateral posterior substance.

The relevance of enhancement depends on the underlying cause. In infection, it represents a more mature myelitis moving toward abscess; in demyelination, it represents acuity of the process with concurrent active destruction of myelin.[66] Some have reported an increased specificity when diagnosing lesions after gadolinium enhancement in multiple sclerosis.[121] Yet, any or all of these findings, including abnormal signal, cord thickening, and enhancement, can be seen in each of these disorders, even the more rare manifestations such as lupus[100]; indeed, some, as in lupus, may even appear indistinct from other causes of spinal cord infarct on MR images (Fig. 24–14).

References

1. Banuelos AF, Williams PL, Johnson RH, et al: Central nervous system abscesses due to *Coccidioides* species. Clin Infect Dis 22: 240–250, 1996.
2. Bao YH, Ling F: Classification and therapeutic modalities of spinal vascular malformations in 80 patients. Neurosurgery 40:75–81, 1997.
3. Barakos JA, Mark AS, Dillon WP, Norman D: MR imaging of acute transverse myelitis and AIDS myelopathy. J Comput Assist Tomogr 14:45–50, 1990.
4. Bergqvist CA, Goldberg HI, Thorarensen O, Bird SJ: Posterior cervical spinal cord infarction following vertebral artery dissection. Neurology 48:1112–1115, 1997.
5. Binkert CA, Kollias SS, Valavanis A: Spinal cord vascular disease: Characterization with fast three-dimensional contrast-enhanced MR angiography. AJNR Am J Neuroradiol 20:1785–1793, 1999.
6. Biondi A, Merland JJ, Hodes JE, et al: Aneurysms of spinal arteries associated with intramedullary arteriovenous malformations: I. Angiographic and clinical aspects. AJNR Am J Neuroradiol 13:913–922, 1992.
7. Borden JA, Wu JK, Shucart WA: A proposed classification for spinal and cranial dural arteriovenous fistulous malformations and implications for treatment [published erratum appears in J Neurosurg 82:705–706, 1995]. J Neurosurg 82:166–179, 1995.
8. Bousson V: Intracranial dural fistula as a cause of diffuse MR enhancement of the cervical spinal cord. J Neurol Neurosurg Psychiatry 67:227–230, 1999.
9. Bowen BC: Spinal dural arteriovenous fistulas: Evaluation with MR angiography. AJNR Am J Neuroradiol 16:2029–2043, 1995.
10. Bowen BC: MR angiography of the spine. Magn Reson Imaging Clin North Am 6:165–178, 1998.
11. Bowen BC: Vascular anatomy and disorders of the lumbar spine and spinal cord. Magn Reson Imaging Clin North Am 7:555–571, 1999.
12. Brunberg JA, DiPietro MA, Venes JL, et al: Intramedullary lesions of the pediatric spinal cord: Correlation of findings from MR imaging, intraoperative sonography, surgery, and histologic study. Radiology 181:573–579, 1991.
13. Caldas C: Case report: Transverse myelitis associated with Epstein-Barr virus infection. Am J Med Sci 307:45–48, 1994.
14. Campi A, Filippi M, Comi G, Scotti G: Recurrent acute transverse myelopathy associated with anticardiolipin antibodies. AJNR Am J Neuroradiol 19:781–786, 1998.
15. Chabert E: Intramedullary cavernous malformations. J Neuroradiol 26:262–268, 1999.
16. Chamberlain MC, Sandy AD, Press GA: Spinal cord tumors: Gadolinium-DTPA–enhanced MR imaging. Neuroradiology 33:469–474, 1991.
17. Chang WT, Chen HC, Peng HC: Solitary spinal cord metastasis of Wilms' tumor. J Pediatr Surg 25:550–552, 1990.
18. Chen CJ, Chen CM, Lin TK: Enhanced cervical MRI in identifying intracranial dural arteriovenous fistulae with spinal perimedullary venous drainage. Neuroradiology 40:393–397, 1998.
19. Choi KH, Lee KS, Chung SO, et al: Idiopathic transverse myelitis: MR characteristics [see comments]. AJNR Am J Neuroradiol 17:1151–1160, 1996.
20. Cognard C: The role of CT in evaluation of the effectiveness of embolisation of spinal dural arteriovenous fistulae with *N*-butyl cyanoacrylate. Neuroradiology 38:603–608, 1996.
21. Colombo N, Kucharczyk W, Brant-Zawadzki M, et al: Magnetic resonance imaging of spinal cord hemangioblastoma. Acta Radiol Suppl 369:734–737, 1986.
22. Cosgrove GR, Bertrand G, Fontaine S, et al: Cavernous angiomas of the spinal cord. J Neurosurg 68:31–36, 1988.
23. Costigan DA, Winkelman MD: Intramedullary spinal cord metastasis: A clinicopathological study of 13 cases. J Neurosurg 62:227–233, 1985.
24. David P: MRI of acute disseminated encephalomyelitis after coxsackie B infection. J Neuroradiol 20:258–265, 1993.
25. Dev R, Husain M, Gupta A, Gupta RK: MR of multiple intraspinal abscesses associated with congenital dermal sinus. AJNR Am J Neuroradiol 18:742–743, 1997.
26. Di Lorenzo N: Primary spinal neoplasms in childhood: Analysis of 1234 published cases (including 56 personal cases) by pathology, sex, age and site—differences from the situation in adults. Neurochirurgia (Stuttg) 25:153–164, 1982.
27. Dillon WP, Norman D, Newton TH, et al: Intradural spinal cord lesions: Gd-DTPA-enhanced MR imaging. Radiology 170:229–237, 1989.
28. Donovan WD: Case report: MRI findings of severe Epstein-Barr virus encephalomyelitis. J Comput Assist Tomogr 20:1027–1029, 1996.
29. Dupuis MJ, Atrouni S, Dooms GC, Gonsette RE: MR imaging of schistosomal myelitis. AJNR Am J Neuroradiol 11:782–783, 1990.
30. Edelson RN, Deck MD, Posner JB: Intramedullary spinal cord metastases: Clinical and radiographic findings in nine cases. Neurology 22:1222–1231, 1972.
31. Elksnis SM, Hogg JP, Cunningham ME: MR imaging of spontaneous spinal cord infarction. J Comput Assist Tomogr 15:228–232, 1991.
32. Epstein F, et al: Intramedullary tumors of the spinal cord. In McLaurin RL (ed): Pediatric Neurosurgery: Surgery of the Developing Nervous System, 2nd ed. Philadelphia, Grune & Stratton, 1989, pp 428–442.
33. Ernst RJ: Cervical myelopathy associated with intracranial dural arteriovenous fistula: MR findings before and after treatment. AJNR Am J Neuroradiol 18:1330–1334, 1997.
34. Faig J: Vertebral body infarction as a confirmatory sign of spinal cord ischemic stroke: Report of three cases and review of the literature. Stroke 29:239–243, 1998.
35. Flanders AE, Spettell CM, Friedman DP, et al: The relationship between the functional abilities of patients with cervical spinal cord injury and the severity of damage revealed by MR imaging. AJNR Am J Neuroradiol 20:926–934, 1999.
36. Flanders AE, Spettell CM, Tartaglino LM, et al: Forecasting motor recovery after cervical spinal cord injury: Value of MR imaging. Radiology 201:649–655, 1996.
37. Forbes G, Nichols DA, Jack CR Jr, et al: Complications of spinal cord arteriography: Prospective assessment of risk for diagnostic procedures. Radiology 169:479–484, 1988.
38. Friedman DP: Herpes zoster myelitis: MR appearance. AJNR Am J Neuroradiol 13:1404–1406, 1992.
39. Friedman DP, Flanders AE: Enhancement of gray matter in anterior spinal infarction. AJNR Am J Neuroradiol 13:983–985, 1992.
40. Friess HM, Wasenko JJ: MR of staphylococcal myelitis of the cervical spinal cord. AJNR Am J Neuroradiol 18:455–458, 1997.
41. Gilbertson JR, Miller GM, Goldman MS, Marsh WR: Spinal dural arteriovenous fistulas: MR and myelographic findings. AJNR Am J Neuroradiol 16:2049–2057, 1995.
42. Goy AM, Pinto RS, Raghavendra BN, et al: Intramedullary spinal cord tumors: MR imaging, with emphasis on associated cysts. Radiology 161:381–386, 1986.
43. Grem JL, Burgess J, Trump DL: Clinical features and natural history of intramedullary spinal cord metastasis. Cancer 56:2305–2314, 1985.
44. Hackney DB: Neoplasms and related disorders. Top Magn Reson Imaging 4:37–61, 1992.
45. Handel S, Grossman R, Sarwar M: Case report: Computed tomography in the diagnosis of spinal cord astrocytoma. J Comput Assist Tomogr 2:226–228, 1978.
46. Haribhai HC, Bhigjee AI, Bill PL, et al: Spinal cord schistosomiasis: A clinical, laboratory and radiological study, with a note on therapeutic aspects. Brain 114:709–726, 1991.
47. Hasegawa M: Spinal cord infarction associated with primary antiphospholipid syndrome in a young child: Case report. J Neurosurg 79:446–450, 1993.
48. Hasegawa M: The efficacy of CT arteriography for spinal arteriovenous fistula surgery: Technical note. Neuroradiology 41:915–919, 1999.
49. Hashimoto H: Spinal dural arteriovenous fistula with perimesencephalic subarachnoid haemorrhage. J Clin Neurosci 7:64–66, 2000.
50. Heinz R: Detection of cerebrospinal fluid metastasis: CT myelography or MR? AJNR Am J Neuroradiol 16:1147–1151, 1995.
51. Hirai T: Case report: Varicella-zoster virus myelitis—serial MR findings. Br J Radiol 69:1187–1190, 1996.
52. Hittmair K: Spinal cord lesions in patients with multiple sclerosis: Comparison of MR pulse sequences. AJNR Am J Neuroradiol 17:1555–1565, 1996.
53. Hurst RW: Peripheral spinal cord hypointensity on T2-weighted MR images: A reliable imaging sign of venous hypertensive myelopathy. AJNR Am J Neuroradiol 21:781–786, 2000.

54. Keiper MD, Grossman RI, Brunson JC, Schnall MD: The low sensitivity of fluid-attenuated inversion-recovery MR in the detection of multiple sclerosis of the spinal cord. AJNR Am J Neuroradiol 18:1035–1039, 1997.

55. Kelly DR, Smith CD, McQuillen MP: Successful medical treatment of a spinal histoplasmoma. J Neuroimaging 4:237–239, 1994.

56. Keung YK: Secondary syringomyelia due to intramedullary spinal cord metastasis: Case report and review of literature. Am J Clin Oncol 20:577–579, 1997.

57. King SJ, Jeffree MA: MRI of an abscess of the cervical spinal cord in a case of *Listeria* meningoencephalomyelitis. Neuroradiology 35:495–496, 1993.

58. Koehler PJ: Delayed radiation myelopathy: Serial MR-imaging and pathology. Clin Neurol Neurosurg 98:197–201, 1996.

59. Koh S: Myelopathy resulting from invasive aspergillosis. Pediatr Neurol 19:135–138, 1998.

60. Kohno M: Postmyelographic computerized tomographic scan in the differential diagnosis of radiculomeningeal arteriovenous malformation: Technical note. Surg Neurol 47:68–71, 1997.

61. Kohno M: Preoperative and postoperative magnetic resonance imaging (MRI) findings of radiculomeningeal arteriovenous malformations: Important role of gravity in the symptoms and MRI. Surg Neurol 48:352–356, 1997.

62. Kovacs B: Transverse myelopathy in systemic lupus erythematosus: An analysis of 14 cases and review of the literature. Ann Rheum Dis 59:120–124, 2000.

63. Kumar J, Kimm J: MR in *Toxocara canis* myelopathy. AJNR Am J Neuroradiol 15:1918–1920, 1994.

64. Lapointe JS, Graeb DA, Nugent RA, Robertson WD: Value of intravenous contrast enhancement in the CT evaluation of intraspinal tumors. AJR Am J Roentgenol 146:103–107, 1986.

65. Larsson EM, Desai P, Hardin CW, et al: Venous infarction of the spinal cord resulting from dural arteriovenous fistula: MR imaging findings. AJNR Am J Neuroradiol 12:739–743, 1991.

66. Larsson EM, Holtas S, Nilsson O: Gd-DTPA–enhanced MR of suspected spinal multiple sclerosis. AJNR Am J Neuroradiol 10:1071–1076, 1989.

67. Lee M: Nonneoplastic intramedullary spinal cord lesions mimicking tumors. Neurosurgery 43:788–794, 1998.

68. Leite CC, Jinkins JR, Escobar BE, et al: MR imaging of intramedullary and intradural-extramedullary spinal cysticercosis. AJR Am J Roentgenol 169:1713–1717, 1997.

69. Li MH, Holtas S: MR imaging of spinal intramedullary tumors. Acta Radiol 32:505–513, 1991.

70. Lindner A: Magnetic resonance image findings of spinal intramedullary abscess caused by *Candida albicans:* Case report. Neurosurgery 36:411–412, 1995.

71. Mascalchi M: MR angiography of spinal vascular malformations. AJNR Am J Neuroradiol 16:289–297, 1995.

72. Mascalchi M: Identification of the feeding arteries of spinal vascular lesions via phase-contrast MR angiography with three-dimensional acquisition and phase display. AJNR Am J Neuroradiol 18:351–358, 1997.

73. Mascalchi M: Posterior spinal artery infarct. AJNR Am J Neuroradiol 19:361–363, 1998.

74. Mawad ME, Rivera V, Crawford S, et al: Spinal cord ischemia after resection of thoracoabdominal aortic aneurysms: MR findings in 24 patients. AJNR Am J Neuroradiol 11:987–991, 1990.

75. Mehalic TF, Pezzuti RT, Applebaum BI: Magnetic resonance imaging and cervical spondylotic myelopathy. Neurosurgery 26:217–226, 1990.

76. Melhem ER, Wang H: Intramedullary spinal cord tuberculoma in a patient with AIDS. AJNR Am J Neuroradiol 13:986–988, 1992.

77. Merine D, Wang H, Kumar AJ, et al: CT myelography and MR imaging of acute transverse myelitis. J Comput Assist Tomogr 11:606–608, 1987.

78. Miller GM, Forbes GS, Onofrio BM: Magnetic resonance imaging of the spine. Mayo Clin Proc 64:986–1004, 1989.

79. Miyasaka K: Computed tomography and magnetic resonance imaging of intramedullary spinal cord tumors. Acta Radiol Suppl 369:738–740, 1986.

80. Miyatake S, Kikuchi H, Koide T, et al: Cobb's syndrome and its treatment with embolization: Case report. J Neurosurg 72:497–499, 1990.

81. Mock A, Levi A, Drake JM: Spinal hemangioblastoma, syrinx, and hydrocephalus in a two-year-old child. Neurosurgery 27:799–802, 1990.

82. Mukunda BN: Solitary spinal intramedullary abscess caused by *Nocardia asteroides.* South Med J 92:1223–1224, 1999.

83. Murphy KJ, Brunberg JA, Quint DJ, Kazanjian PH: Spinal cord infection: Myelitis and abscess formation [see comments]. AJNR Am J Neuroradiol 19:341–348, 1998.

84. Nabatame H, Nakamura K, Matuda M, et al: MRI of syphilitic myelitis. Neuroradiology 34:105–106, 1992.

85. Nagakawa H, et al: Computed tomography of soft tissue masses related to the spinal column. In Post MJ (ed): Radiographic Evaluation of the Spine: Current Advances with Emphasis on Computed Tomography. New York, Masson, 1980, pp 320–352.

86. Nemoto Y, Inoue Y, Tashiro T, et al: Intramedullary spinal cord tumors: Significance of associated hemorrhage at MR imaging. Radiology 182:793–796, 1992.

87. Nesbit GM, Miller GM, Baker HL Jr, et al: Spinal cord sarcoidosis: A new finding at MR imaging with Gd-DTPA enhancement. Radiology 173:839–843, 1989.

88. Neumann-Andersen G: Involvement of the entire spinal cord and medulla oblongata in acute catastrophic-onset transverse myelitis in SLE. Clin Rheumatol 19:156–160, 2000.

89. Neumann HP, Eggert HR, Scheremet R, et al: Central nervous system lesions in von Hippel-Lindau syndrome. J Neurol Neurosurg Psychiatry 55:898–901, 1992.

90. Nitta H: Cervical spinal cord infarction after surgery for a pineal region choriocarcinoma in the sitting position: Case report. Neurosurgery 40:1082–1085, 1997.

91. Nittner K: Spinal meningiomas, neurinomas, and neurofibromas, and hourglass tumors. In Vinken PJ, Bruyn GW (eds): Handbook of Clinical Neurology. New York, Elsevier North-Holland, 1976, pp 177–322.

92. Oishi H: Successful surgical treatment of a dural arteriovenous fistula at the craniocervical junction with reference to pre- and postoperative MRI. Neuroradiology 41:463–467, 1999.

93. Oldfield EH, Di Chiro G, Quindlen EA, et al: Successful treatment of a group of spinal cord arteriovenous malformations by interruption of dural fistula. J Neurosurg 59:1019–1030, 1983.

94. Parizel PM: Gd-DTPA-enhanced MR imaging of spinal tumors. AJR Am J Roentgenol 152:1087–1096, 1989.

95. Pascuzzi RM, Shapiro SA, Rau AN, et al: Sarcoid myelopathy. J Neuroimaging 6:61–62, 1996.

96. Pfausler B: Syndrome of the anterior spinal artery as the primary manifestation of aspergillosis. Infection 23:240–242, 1995.

97. Phuphanich S: Magnetic resonance imaging of syrinx associated with intramedullary metastases and leptomeningeal disease. J Neuroimaging 6:115–117, 1996.

98. Poon TP, Tchertkoff V, Pares GF, et al: Spinal cord *Toxoplasma* lesion in AIDS: MR findings. J Comput Assist Tomogr 16:817–819, 1992.

99. Post MJ, Quencer RM, Green BA, et al: Intramedullary spinal cord metastases, mainly of nonneurogenic origin. AJR Am J Roentgenol 148:1015–1022, 1987.

100. Provenzale JM, Barboriak DP, Gaensler EH, et al: Lupus-related myelitis: Serial MR findings. AJNR Am J Neuroradiol 15:1911–1917, 1994.

101. Ratliff JK: Intramedullary tuberculoma of the spinal cord: Case report and review of the literature. J Neurosurg 90:125–128, 1999.

102. Renowden SA: Case report: Spontaneous thrombosis of a spinal dural AVM (Foix-Alajouanine syndrome)—magnetic resonance appearance. Clin Radiol 47:134–136, 1993.

103. Resnick DK, Comey CH, Welch WC, et al: Isolated toxoplasmosis of the thoracic spinal cord in a patient with acquired immunodeficiency syndrome: Case report. J Neurosurg 82:493–496, 1995.

104. Ricolfi F: Giant perimedullary arteriovenous fistulas of the spine: Clinical and radiologic features and endovascular treatment. AJNR Am J Neuroradiol 18:677–687, 1997.

105. Russell DS, Rubenstein LJ: Pathology of Tumors of the Nervous System. Baltimore, Williams & Wilkins, 1989.

106. Schubeus P, Schorner W, Hosten N, Felix R: Spinal cord cavities: Differential-diagnostic criteria in magnetic resonance imaging. Eur J Radiol 12:219–225, 1991.

107. Scotti G, Scialfa G, Colombo N, Landoni L: Magnetic resonance diagnosis of intramedullary tumors of the spinal cord. Neuroradiology 29:130–135, 1987.

108. Sener RN, Larsson EM, Backer R, Jinkins JR: MRI of intradural spinal arteriovenous fistula associated with ischemia and infarction of the cord. Clin Imaging 17:73–76, 1993.

109. Shapiro R (ed): Tumors. In Myelography. Chicago, Year Book Medical Publishers, 1984, pp 345–421.

110. Slasky BS, Bydder GM, Niendorf HP, Young IR: MR imaging with gadolinium-DTPA in the differentiation of tumor, syrinx, and cyst of the spinal cord. J Comput Assist Tomogr 11:845–850, 1987.

111. Solomon RA, Stein BM: Unusual spinal cord enlargement related to intramedullary hemangioblastoma. J Neurosurg 68:550–553, 1988.

112. Solsberg MD, Lemaire C, Resch L, Potts DG: High-resolution MR imaging of the cadaveric human spinal cord: Normal anatomy. AJNR Am J Neuroradiol 11:3–7, 1990.

113. Steinbok P: Intramedullary spinal cord tumors in children. Neurosurg Clin North Am 3:931–945, 1992.

114. Su MC, Ho WL, Chen JH. Intramedullary cryptococcal granuloma of spinal cord: A case report. Chung Hua I Hsueh Tsa Chih (Taipei) 53:58–61, 1994.

115. Suzuki K: Anterior spinal artery syndrome associated with severe stenosis of the vertebral artery. AJNR Am J Neuroradiol 19:1353–1355, 1998.

116. Sze G: Gadolinium-DTPA in spinal disease. Radiol Clin North Am 26:1009–1024, 1988.

117. Sze G: Intramedullary disease of the spine: Diagnosis using gadolinium-DTPA–enhanced MR imaging. AJR Am J Roentgenol 151:1193–1204, 1988.

118. Sze G, Merriam M, Oshio K, Jolesz FA: Fast spin-echo imaging in the evaluation of intradural disease of the spine. AJNR Am J Neuroradiol 13:1383–1392, 1992.

119. Tacconi L: Intramedullary spinal cord abscess: Case report. Neurosurgery 37:817–819, 1995.

120. Tartaglino LM, Friedman DP, Flanders AE, et al: Multiple sclerosis in the spinal cord: MR appearance and correlation with clinical parameters. Radiology 195:725–732, 1995.

121. Tas MW, Barkhol F, van Walderveen MA, et al. The effect of gadolinium on the sensitivity and specificity of MR in the initial diagnosis of multiple sclerosis. AJNR Am J Neuroradiol 16:259–264, 1995.

122. Terwey B, Becker H, Thron AK, Vahldiek G: Gadolinium-DTPA enhanced MR imaging of spinal dural arteriovenous fistulas. J Comput Assist Tomogr 13:30–37, 1989.

123. Thorpe JW, Kendall BE, MacManus DG, et al: Dynamic gadolinium-enhanced MRI in the detection of spinal arteriovenous malformations. Neuroradiology 36:522–529, 1994.

124. Thurnher MM, Post MJ, Jinkins JR: MRI of infections and neoplasms of the spine and spinal cord in 55 patients with AIDS. Neuroradiology 42:551–563, 2000.

125. Turjman F, Joly D, Monnet O, et al: MRI of intramedullary cavernous haemangiomas. Neuroradiology 37:297–302, 1995.

126. Valk J: Magnetic resonance imaging in the differentiation of spinal cord tumours and hydromyelia. Acta Radiol Suppl 369:242–244, 1986.

127. Vishteh AG, Zabramski JM, Spetzler RF: Patients with spinal cord cavernous malformations are at an increased risk for multiple neuraxis cavernous malformations. Neurosurgery 45:30–32, 1999.

128. Waubant E: MRI of intramedullary sarcoidosis: Follow-up of a case. Neuroradiology 39:357–360, 1997.

129. Williams AL, Haughton VM, Pojunas KW, et al: Differentiation of intramedullary neoplasms and cysts by MR. AJR Am J Roentgenol 149:159–164, 1987.

130. Winkelman MD, Adelstein DJ, Karlins NL: Intramedullary spinal cord metastasis: Diagnostic and therapeutic considerations. Arch Neurol 44:526–531, 1987.

131. Yuh WT, Marsh EE, Wang AK, et al: MR imaging of spinal cord and vertebral body infarction [see comments]. AJNR Am J Neuroradiol 13:145–154, 1992.

132. Zimmerman RA: Imaging of tumors of the spinal canal and cord. Radiol Clin North Am 26:965–1007, 1988.

25

Magnetic Resonance Imaging of Infections of the Spine

Charles F. Lanzieri

Because infections of the spine present with subtle and nonspecific symptoms, they represent a diagnostic problem, and imaging plays a key role in the initial diagnosis and subsequent management. Clinical symptoms, which commonly include fever, malaise, back pain, and focal tenderness, are often insidious in onset and can be attributed to a variety of common conditions. By the time focal neurologic findings such as extremity weakness or meningismus appear, the stage is set for rapid progression to permanent neurologic deficits at worst and a chronic state of osteomyelitis at best. The infection can rapidly spread to the epidural space with concomitant paraplegia. Delayed diagnosis increases the morbidity and mortality of spinal infections; diagnostic imaging is therefore critical.

Infection of the spine initially involves either the disk space or the vertebral body, and spread occurs via the arterial or venous system or by direct inoculation during diagnostic procedures. Pyogenic infections evolve more rapidly than nonpyogenic infections, which have a more indolent course. Pyogenic infections are commonly caused by *Staphylococcus aureus*, which accounts for about 60% of this category of infection.[2, 5, 12] The most common cause of the nonpyogenic infections is *Mycobacterium tuberculosis*. Specific pathogens are more common in patients with predisposing conditions. For example, *Salmonella* is a common cause of osteomyelitis in patients with sickle cell disease, and *Serratia* and *Candida* are commonly seen in patients using intravenous drugs. The course of nonpyogenic infections is even more insidious and has a slower evolution than that of pyogenic infections. Infections caused by the tubercle bacillus or fungus are very difficult to diagnose.

Before cross-sectional imaging in the 1980s, radiologic diagnosis of disk space infections and vertebral osteomyelitis depended on interpretation of plain radiographs and radionuclide studies. Radiographs are usually unrevealing for the first 2 to 8 weeks of the disease process. Radionuclide studies have demonstrated incorporation of technetium 99m in 80% of infected bone sites by the 10th day of the infection.[15] These examinations, however, have significant limitations, most notably false-positive results. Radionuclide bone scans cannot reliably differentiate cellulitis from osteomyelitis. False negatives also occur when the blood supply to the infected bone or disk space is impaired.

The use of high-resolution computed tomography (CT) was found to be very useful because of its ability to demonstrate bone destruction or focal osteopenia early in the course of the infection. Its ability to demonstrate prevertebral soft tissue swelling and cellulitis, however, was disappointing.

Magnetic resonance imaging (MRI) quickly became the study of choice for evaluating patients with spinal complaints. Its advantages include multiplanar capability, superior soft tissue contrast resolution, and a unique ability to detect end-plate, disk space, and marrow changes. In addition, MRI can demonstrate subtle changes far earlier in the course of the disease than previously employed techniques. Finally, MRI is extremely useful for following patients with proven spinal infection and for planning aspirations or other interventions. This has a direct impact on patient management. MRI has dramatically changed the outcome of patients with spinal infections over the last 10 years.

Pathophysiology

Infectious processes can extend to the spine by several mechanisms. Direct extension occurs secondary to trauma or surgical intervention for reasons other than infection. Diagnostic lumbar punctures or epidural injections as well as surgery for herniated disks are common causes. Contiguous spread can occur from adjacent infected structures. Hematogenous spread can come from distant sites. A source of hematogenous dissemination can be found in up to half of the patients with spinal osteomyelitis.[4] The most common sources are the genitourinary tract, the skin, and the respiratory tract.[18] The arterial system is thought to be a much more common route of spread to the spine, although extension via the epidural venous plexus occurs via the pelvic plexus of veins.[19]

A number of events occur during the first few weeks of infectious spondylitis. The organism commonly settles in the anterior portion of the subchondral bone marrow. The infection then spreads within the marrow space or into the adjacent intervertebral disk, causing osteomyelitis and/or diskitis. Nonpyogenic infection may spread into the subligamentous space, and from there it may penetrate the ligament and the adjacent soft tissues. Disk-sparing infections of adjacent vertebral bodies are a common sign of tubercle bacillus infection.[5] Both pyogenic and nonpyogenic infections tend to remain within the vertebral body and disk spaces and do not usually involve the posterior elements and adjacent ligaments and soft tissues. This type of involvement is more typical of metastatic disease.

Although pyogenic infections rarely involve the posterior elements, tuberculosis (TB) sometimes does. The level most often involved in TB spondylitis is L1, but the thoracolumbar junction is most affected in general. The cervical and lumbar levels are less frequently involved.

Following successful therapy for infection, the reparative process can include partial or complete bony ankylosis of the disk space. Without adequate or proper therapy, bony lysis occurs, with subsequent collapse of the vertebral body. In nonpyogenic infections such as TB, anterior wedging with secondary kyphotic deformity occurs.

Pyogenic Disk Space Infections

Pyogenic infections, which have a peak incidence in the sixth and seventh decades of life, are caused by both gram-positive and gram-negative bacteria. The dominant inflammatory cell is the polymorphonuclear leukocyte. Both the vertebral body and the adjacent disk space become involved. The cancellous bone adjacent to the cartilaginous end plate is richly vascular throughout adulthood, which makes it a common site for visitation from hematogenously borne pathogens. The infection then spreads across the disk to involve the adjacent vertebral body. Most of the time, the infection is limited to the disk space and the two adjacent vertebral bodies. In about 25% of cases, multiple levels are involved.[8] Infectious agents settle in the most vascular spaces in the spine.

In children, who have a rich vascular supply in and around the disk spaces, infections can spread directly to the disk.[5] In adults, the disk space is nearly avascular; therefore, infections begin in the subchondral bone adjacent to the end plate, which is very vascular throughout adulthood. Pyogenic infections are often self-limited in children and may be cured with bed rest and antibiotics.

The population most commonly affected by vertebral osteomyelitis consists of adults in the sixth to seventh decade of life. The lumbar spine is the site most commonly affected, followed by the thoracic and cervical spine. Men are affected more often than women, at a ratio of two to one. Treatment with parenteral antibiotics for about 6 weeks is usually required for cure. Surgical intervention is necessary when there are neurologic findings and an epidural mass is identified, or when there is secondary instability and fusion needs to be performed.

Radiographic findings are usually subtle and may not appear until relatively late in the process (Fig. 25–1). The hallmark of disk space infection on plain radiographic examination is disk space narrowing. This is followed by erosion of the adjacent end plates. It may be several days or weeks before these findings are evident. The characteristic findings of disk space narrowing and end-plate irregularity may not be seen until the fourth week of the infection. Prominence of the retropharyngeal soft tissues is a variable finding. Plain films cannot demonstrate the important intraspinal complications of infection that are ultimately responsible for neurologic symptoms. CT is very useful in

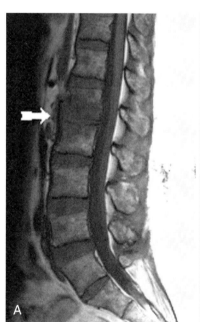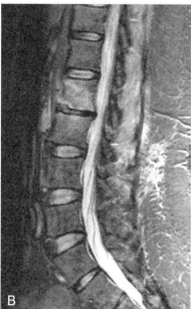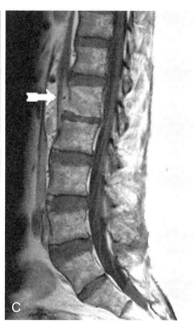

Figure 25–1. Lumbar disk space infection with osteomyelitis.
 A, T1-weighted sagittal MR image through the lumbar spine. The *arrow* indicates a disk space infection at the L1-2 level. The normal cortical dark line along both articular surfaces, especially along the inferior surface of L1, is not visible. A decrease in the signal coming from the marrow fat in both vertebrae indicates the presence of marrow edema.
 B, T2-weighted image in the same location shows edema in the marrow and slightly increased signal in the interspace. Although the disk space at L1-2 is not brighter than the adjacent disk spaces, the normal internuclear cleft is lost. In addition, a much lower signal would be expected in a partially collapsed and degenerated disk.
 C, Post–contrast-enhanced image in the same location. Although the disk space itself does not show enhancement, the vertebral bodies do. The *arrow* indicates loss of the anterior cortical margin of L1, a sign of upward spread of infection.

these patients because it is more sensitive than plain film. In addition, the soft tissue changes begin to become evident.

MRI offers the best opportunity to image and confirm vertebral infections early in their course. The first MR findings reflect the replacement of normal bone marrow by inflammatory tissue and edema in association with structural changes such as disk space narrowing.[10] The sensitivity of MRI for disk space infections is the same as that of radionuclide studies and the specificity is much higher. Even early studies using nonenhanced MRI showed a sensitivity of 96%, a specificity of 92%, and an accuracy of 92%.[10] Evidence of vertebral osteomyelitis appears at about the same time on MRI as it does on gallium or technetium 99m radionuclide studies.[10]

Marrow replacement first appears as decreased signal on T1-weighted images because of edema or infiltration of fat in the bone marrow. On T2-weighted images, marrow edema is reflected as increased signal because of the additional water content in the marrow. A band of increased signal in the subchondral bone marrow is highly suggestive of pathologic change in the adjacent disk space. Unfortunately, this change is somewhat nonspecific and can be seen in a variety of conditions including recent trauma and early degenerative disease. Changes in the disk space are seen on both T1-weighted and T2-weighted images. On the T1-weighted images, narrowing of the interspace with slight loss of signal can usually be visualized.

The most dramatic, recognizable, and reliable sign of disk space infection on MRI is the increased signal seen on T2-weighted images. In adults, this is accompanied by loss of the normal band of decreased signal that represents what is referred to as the intranuclear cleft. These findings may be supported by the observation of swelling and edema in the adjacent soft tissues (Fig. 25–2). When the

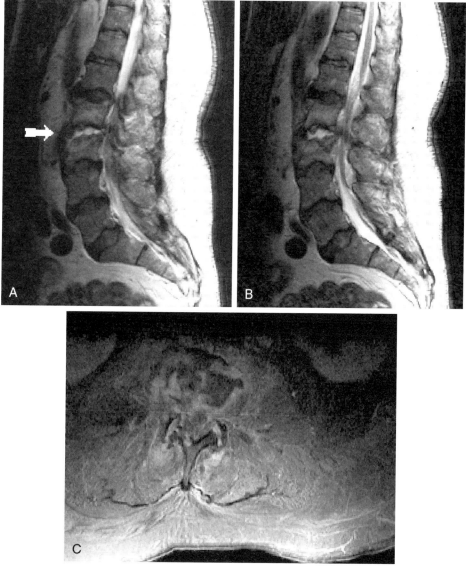

Figure 25–2. Lumbar disk space infection with osteomyelitis and paraspinal cellulitides. *A* and *B,* Sagittal T2-weighted images through the lumbar spine. Bright signal is associated with the L2-3 intervertebral disk. This is the hallmark of diskitis on an MRI scan *(arrow).* *C,* Post–contrast-enhanced axial T1-weighted image. Enhancement can be visualized in and around the L2-3 interspace, as well as in the paraspinal soft tissues and within the spinal canal. These represent paraspinal and epidural cellulitides. If left untreated, they could progress to abscess formation.

bony cortex of the vertebral body becomes involved, the normally dark cortical margin on all MRI sequences can no longer be visualized. This implies osteomyelitis. If intravenous contrast material is given, enhancement within the disk space and in the adjacent vertebral bodies usually increases diagnostic confidence.[13]

Some pitfalls exist in diagnosing disk space infections using MRI. The intermediate changes seen in degenerative disk disease may mask the early changes of a disk space infection. Both processes produce low signal on T1-weighted images. In the case of degenerative disease, the infiltration of fat into the subchondral portion of the vertebra is an intermediate change that increases the T1 signal intensity. Since infection lowers the degree of T1 signal, a canceling effect occurs that potentially masks the edema. The T2-weighted images should be reviewed carefully to search for edema in suspected infections. Occasionally, a degenerated disk transiently contains cystic areas. This causes increased signal on T2-weighted images and mimics one of the hallmarks of diskitis, a bright interspace.

Although many disk space infections represent hematogenous seeding, a significant number are secondary to surgery involving the disk space. Disk space infections follow up to 3% of surgical procedures on the spine.[5] Clinical

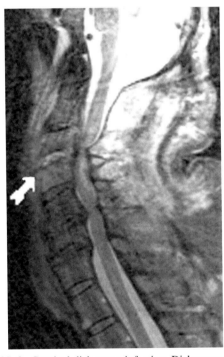

Figure 25–3. Cervical disk space infection. Disk space infections and diskitis are unusual occurrences in the cervical spine. T2-weighted sagittal image shows increased signal in the C3-4 intervertebral disk space and edema in the adjacent bone marrow fat *(arrow)*. The cortical margins remain intact and there is no evidence of a paraspinal abscess. Increased signal in the adjacent spinal cord represents the presence of myelomalacia from chronic cord compression. Although this patient had not had previous surgery, the same appearance is seen following cervical diskectomy.

suspicion is raised when, in the first few postoperative weeks, patients present with back pain radiating to the extremities and signs of infection such as elevated white blood cell count, an elevated sedimentation rate, and fever. Because signal changes in the vertebral bodies, disk spaces, and adjacent soft tissues occur following surgery, the diagnosis of postoperative infection is difficult.

Cervical vertebral osteomyelitis and diskitis are usually diseases of older people, but they occur frequently in younger patients who are intravenous drug abusers (Fig. 25–3).[16]

Epidural Abscesses

Epidural abscesses can occur either spontaneously or secondary to disk space infection and osteomyelitis. Imaging greatly improves patient outcome because a specific diagnosis based only on clinical signs and symptoms is impossible and early treatment is important. MRI is the study of choice when an epidural abscess is suspected and results are positive before radionuclide scanning.[1] Clinical signs and symptoms include back and radicular pain, stiffness, and cramping. Rapid expansion can result in permanent neurologic deficits, the result of direct cord or root compression in most cases, with secondary white matter injury. Vascular thrombosis and direct infiltration of the cord or roots are less common.

Although MRI and myelographic CT are similar in sensitivity for identifying epidural abscesses,[10] MRI offers the ability to distinguish between causes of epidural masses. Thus MRI can differentiate epidural abscess from hematoma, tumor, or disk fragment (Fig. 25–4). Because it is noninvasive, it is the obvious first choice for imaging. Epidural abscesses appear as isointense masses on T1-weighted images, and the intensity is frequently increased on T2-weighted images.[12] Patients with epidural abscess almost always have accompanying meningeal thickening and enhancement.

Without contrast injection, any fluid collection in, or necrotic portion of, the subarachnoid or epidural space can be overlooked. Although not necessary for the diagnosis of disk space infections, contrast-enhanced MRI is essential for the accurate diagnosis of abscess collections in the epidural space (Fig. 25–5). With contrast injection, epidural abscesses are easily demonstrated. Homogeneous enhancement of the mass is seen, with central necrosis indicating a focal fluid collection. Most abscesses occur adjacent to an infected interspace and generally spread to between two and four vertebral levels. Rarely, extension may involve the entire length of the spine.[14]

Tuberculosis

Tubercle bacillus infections are more insidious than pyogenic infections of the spine. As in pyogenic infections, the initial symptoms are nonspecific and early diagnosis is

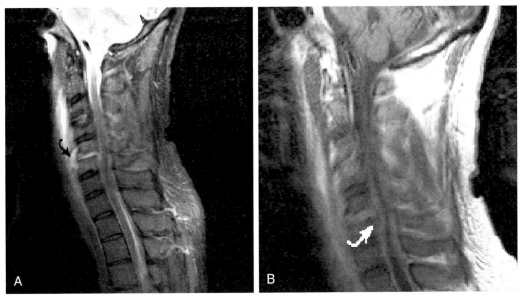

Figure 25–4. Cervical disk space infection with epidural abscess. *A,* T2-weighted sagittal image through the cervical spine. The C5-5 intervertebral disk space has increased signal, indicating the presence of diskitis. Although there is no evidence of adjacent marrow edema and the cortical margins are intact, a region of increased signal in the paraspinal soft tissues anterior to the interspace *(arrow)* indicates the presence of paraspinal cellulitis. *B,* T1-weighted sagittal image reveals contrast enhancement of the interspace, which confirms disk space infection. Thickening and enhancement of the meninges in the cervical spine and a small epidural fluid collection in the epidural space *(arrow)* indicate the presence of an epidural abscess.

difficult. In the case of TB, the symptoms may last for months or years prior to diagnosis. Tuberculous vertebral osteomyelitis remains a significant medical problem in developing countries.

The skeleton is the most common extrapulmonary site of involvement, and spinal TB occurs in 50% of the cases of skeletal TB. Vertebral osteomyelitis is estimated to occur in 0.03% of all TB cases.[7] The TB bacillus spreads to the vertebral body hematogenously and, like pyogenic organisms, lodges in the anterior and subchondral portion of the vertebral body. The granulomatous inflammatory response to the bacillus results in a tubercle, which then invades the surrounding soft tissues and forms a tuberculous abscess. As the abscess grows, the periosteum and the longitudinal ligaments of the spine are elevated and the abscess extends up and down the spine to involve adjacent vertebra. The thoracolumbar junction is most frequently involved; involvement of the cervical and thoracic spine is unusual. Classically, spinal tuberculosis initially involves the anterior and inferior portion of the vertebral body (Fig. 25–6). Extension to other vertebral bodies occurs beneath the anterior and posterior longitudinal ligaments and is referred to as subligamentous spread. The disk spaces usually remain relatively spared.

Involvement of the posterior elements of vertebral bodies is more common in TB than in other forms of infection. Infection of multiple vertebral bodies and posterior elements is involved, with sparing of the disk spaces. This makes differentiation of TB from metastatic neoplasm difficult.[17]

Nontuberculous Granulomatous Spondylitis

The granulomatous response is a nonspecific response to an antigenic stimulus, and it is observed in a variety of pathologic conditions, including infections, neoplasms, and autoimmune diseases. The pathologic hallmark is the presence of mononuclear phagocytic cells and multinucleated giant cells. Organisms that infect the spine and cause a granulomatous reaction include the tubercle bacillus, *Brucella,* and fungi. In endemic areas of the Middle East and Asia, granulomatous spondylitis is still quite common.

Brucella is a small gram-negative coccobacillus common in cattle and swine. In the United States, the most common species are *B. abortus* and *B. suis.* When infecting humans, the organism often affects the lumbar spine. The disk space is usually spared and vertebral osteomyelitis may be accompanied by soft tissue fibrosis. The morphology of the vertebral body is preserved despite evidence of infection. The posterior elements are typically spared and the disk space is slightly reduced despite being involved with infection.

Fungal infections of the spine include coccidioidomycosis (most frequently encountered in the southwestern United States), blastomycosis (found in the central and southeastern states), and actinomycosis. The findings in fungal infections are not specific to the infecting agent. Multiple vertebral bodies are involved but the disk spaces are spared. On plain radiographs, lytic lesions with sclerotic margins are seen. Lytic bony lesions with sclerotic margins are frequently seen with sparing of the interspace. Epidural

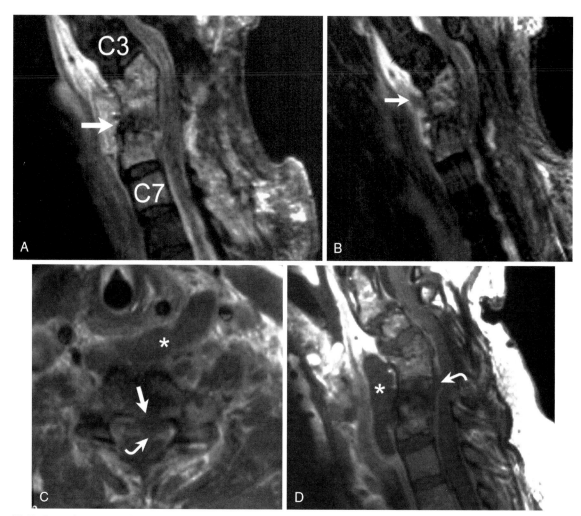

Figure 25–5. Retropharyngeal abscess with extension to the spine. Although retropharyngeal abscesses can progress to involve the adjacent spine, the opposite can also happen.

A, T2-weighted sagittal image reveals the presence of multilevel diskitis and osteomyelitis. Vertebral bodies C4 through T1 have increased signal, and the cortical margins are lost. There has been collapse of C4 and C6 and the C4-5 and C6-7 interspaces are obliterated from previous surgery and ongoing infection. A multilevel laminectomy has been performed as part of this patient's cervical decompression.

B, Post–contrast-enhanced and fat-suppressed T1-weighted image shows enhancement within the vertebral bodies and paraspinal soft tissues anterior to the spine. A focal region of nonenhancement just anterior to C5 *(arrow)* represents the presence of a small abscess in the paraspinal soft tissues. Images *C* and *D* were obtained several days later when the patient had failed to improve on antibiotic therapy.

C, Post–contrast-enhanced T1-weighted image through C6. The *asterisk* lies within a large retropharyngeal abscess that is contiguous with the C6 vertebral body. The *curved arrow* points to the thickened and enhancing meninges. The *straight arrow* indicates the presence of a fluid collection within the epidural space. This is an epidural abscess.

D, Sagittal image also shows the retropharyngeal and paraspinal abscess *(asterisk)* and the epidural abscess *(curved arrow).*

and meningeal involvement is seen with all of these types of infections, but the *degree* of involvement is usually somewhat less than that seen with TB abscess of a similar size.

Sarcoidosis

Sarcoidosis is a noncaseating granulomatous condition that affects multiple organs in adults in the third through fifth decades. About 5% of patients have central nervous system involvement. Involvement of the vertebral bodies

is rare.[6] In the spine, where it is most often seen in the thoracolumbar region, it usually manifests as leptomeningeal thickening, and enhancement is seen after injection of contrast material. Mixed lytic and sclerotic changes have been seen in single or adjacent vertebrae. The intervertebral disks are spared.

Intramedullary Cord Infections

The human immunodeficiency virus (HIV) causes a vacuolar degeneration of the central nervous system. In

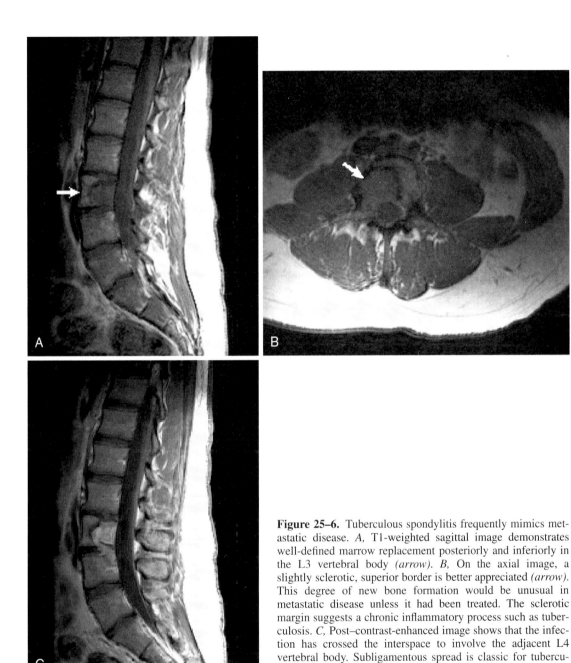

Figure 25–6. Tuberculous spondylitis frequently mimics metastatic disease. *A,* T1-weighted sagittal image demonstrates well-defined marrow replacement posteriorly and inferiorly in the L3 vertebral body *(arrow). B,* On the axial image, a slightly sclerotic, superior border is better appreciated *(arrow).* This degree of new bone formation would be unusual in metastatic disease unless it had been treated. The sclerotic margin suggests a chronic inflammatory process such as tuberculosis. *C,* Post–contrast-enhanced image shows that the infection has crossed the interspace to involve the adjacent L4 vertebral body. Subligamentous spread is classic for tuberculous spondylitis.

the brain, this feature of the acquired immunodeficiency syndrome (AIDS) is recognized as focal frontal lobe atrophy or volume loss. In the spinal cord, increased signal can be seen within a short segment of the cord. This carries the general name of transverse myelitis (Fig. 25–7), and it is caused by other infectious agents as well.

In patients who have transverse myelitis but are negative for HIV, other viral infections such as herpes zoster should be considered. A variety of noninfectious causes also exist, including nutritional deficiencies, toxins, and drugs.[3, 9] Common autoimmune and demyelinating diseases, such as multiple sclerosis and lupus erythematosus, also cause transverse myelitis.

The spinal cord itself can sometimes become infected,

and a cord abscess may form.[11] The symptoms of cord infection are indistinguishable from those of an epidural abscess. Sources of cord infection include hematogenous spread, which is known to be a complication of congenital dermal sinuses, and bacterial endocarditis.

It has been suggested that the pathophysiology of cord infection is similar to that of cerebral infection. In the initial myelitis phase, cord edema and enlargement are observed. At approximately 1 week, a poorly defined ring of enhancement begins to appear. This results in the formation of an abscess cavity, which is relatively isointense on T1-weighted images and hyperintense on T2-weighted images. Cord abscesses are less well defined and less intensely enhancing than brain abscesses. This may be

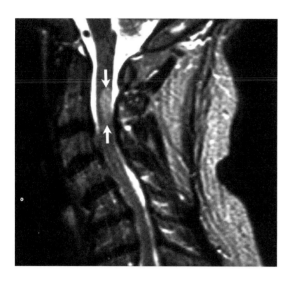

Figure 25–7. Transverse myelitis. T2-weighted sagittal image through the cervical spine demonstrates the presence of increased signal in the dorsal columns of the spinal cord. This appearance is nonspecific and can be caused by a demyelinating process or infarction. In this instance, it was associated with a transient myelitis.

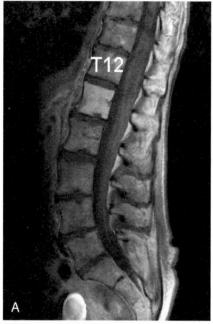

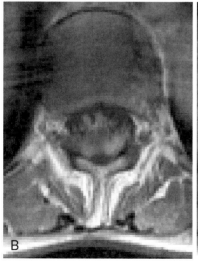
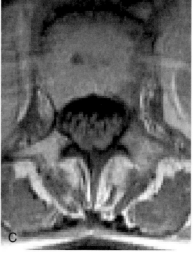

Figure 25–8. Meningeal infection, with subtle enhancement of the meninges covering the lumbar nerve roots. *A,* Post–contrast-enhanced T1-weighted image. The end of the conus medullaris at T12 is a flame-shaped structure that is slightly hypointense relative to the enhancing meninges and nerve roots. *B* and *C,* Axial contrast-enhanced images below the conus show that the nerve roots are thickened and enhancing. This nonspecific finding is compatible with meningitis and other disease processes.

because the cord is relatively hypovascular compared with the brain.

Bacterial abscess of the spinal cord has been thought to occur as a result of bacteremia.[2] Recently, cord abscesses have been reported in patients in whom the source of infection was not found.[11]

Meningeal Infection

Many infectious agents gain access to the central nervous system by first infecting the meninges. When encountered on MR images, meningeal infections produce a vague and subtle enhancement of both the dura and the leptomeninges (Fig. 25–8). Like transverse myelitis, this is a nonspecific finding; it can be caused by trauma, recent lumbar puncture, and various vascular malformations. For detecting meningeal infection, analysis of the cerebrospinal fluid is much more sensitive and specific, and much cheaper to perform, than any imaging procedure.

References

1. Angtuaco EJ, McConnell JR, Chadduck WM, Flanigan S: MR imaging of spinal epidural sepsis. AJR AM J Roentgenol 149:1249–1253, 1987.
2. Baby R, Jafer JJ, Hray PP, et al: Intramedullary abscess associated with spinal cord ependymoma. Neurosurgery 30:121–124, 1992.
3. Barakos JA, Mark AS, Dillon WP, et al: MR imaging of acute transverse myelitis and AIDS myelopathy. J Comput Assist Tomogr Comput 14:45, 1990.
4. Brant-Zawadole M: Infection. In Newton TH, Potts DG (eds): Computed Tomography of the Spine and Spinal Cord. San Anselmo, Calif, Clavadel Press, 1983, p 205.
5. Enzmann DR: Infection/inflammation. In Enzmann DR, De La Paz RL, Rubin J (eds): Magnetic Resonance of the Spine. St. Louis, Mosby–Year Book, 1990, p 260.
6. Kenney CM 3rd, Goldstein SJ: MRI of sarcoid spondylodiskitis. J Comput Assist Tomogr 16:660–662, 1992.
7. Lin-Greenberg A, Cholankeril J: Vertebral arch destruction in tuberculosis: CT features. J Comput Assist Tomogr 14:300–302, 1990.
8. Malawski SK: Pyogenic infection of the spine. Int Orthop 1:125, 1977.
9. Merine D, Way H, Kumer AJ, et al: CT myelography and MRI of acute transverse myelitis. J Comput Assist Tomogr 11:606, 1987.
10. Modic MT, Feiglin DH, Piraino DW, et al: Vertebral osteomyelitis: Assessment using MR. Radiology 157:157–166, 1985.
11. Murphy KJ, Brunberg JA, Quint DJ, et al: Spinal cord infection: Myelitis and abscess formation. AJNR Am J Neuroradiol 19:341–348, 1998.
12. Post MJD, Quencer RM, Montalvo BM, et al: Spinal infection: Evaluations with MR imaging and intraoperative ultrasound. Radiology 169:765, 1988.
13. Post MJD, Sze G, Quencer RM, et al: Gadolinium-enhanced MR in spinal infection. J Comput Assist Tomogr 14:721, 1990.
14. Post MJD, Bowen BC, Sze G: Magnetic resonance imaging of spinal infection. Rheum Dis Clin North Am 17:773–794, 1991.
15. Rinsley L, Gonis ML, Shurman DJ, et al: Technetium bone scanning in experimental osteomyelitis. Clin Orthop 128:361, 1977.
16. Ross PM, Fleming JL: Vertebral body osteomyelitis: Spectrum and natural history: A retrospective analysis of 37 cases. Clin Orthop 118:190–198, 1976.
17. Smith AS, Weinstein MA, Lanzieri CF, et al: Tuberculous spondylitis: A contradiction of the MR characteristics of vertebral osteomyelitis. AJNR Am J Neuroradiol 10:619–625, 1989.
18. Waldvogel FA, Papageorgiou PS: Osteomyelitis: The past decade. N Engl J Med 303:360, 1980.
19. Wiley AM, Trueter J: The vascular anatomy of the spine and its relationship to pyogenic vertebral osteomyelitis. J Bone Joint Surg 413:796, 1959.

26

Image-Guided Spinal Interventions

Wade H. Wong, Huy M. Do, Barton Lane

Spine Biopsies

Biopsies of the spine can play an important role in determining the correct diagnosis because imaging, although sensitive, is often nonspecific. When the patient may have an infection, a prompt biopsy can help the clinician define the organism and determine the optimal antibiotic sensitivity for early treatment. A spinal biopsy can provide a pathologic diagnosis that is critical to staging and treatment planning of neoplasms.

Image guidance for biopsies of the spine is commonly provided with fluoroscopy or computed tomography (CT) scanning. In unique situations, image guidance with magnetic resonance imaging (MRI) might be provided.

Fluoroscopy

Biopsies of the lumbar spine are readily and efficiently performed with fluoroscopic guidance. C-arm fluoroscopy is preferable to single-plane fluoroscopy because it allows the patient to remain in a stationary position while multiplanar relationships of the biopsy needle relative to the target are rapidly determined. The technique of fluoroscopic needle biopsy of the lower lumbar spine begins as follows. The patient is positioned *isocentrically* within the C-arm fluoroscope in such a way that the target area within the patient is centered in the rotational axis of the C-arm fluoroscope. This can be rapidly accomplished by first positioning the target in the lateral view and then adjusting its location so that it is centered on the anteroposterior view.

Most biopsies of the spine can be performed with local anesthesia, although conscious sedation is sometimes helpful. After the patient is prepared and draped, an anesthetic needle is used to anesthetize the skin with a rather generous wheal, so that if the point of entry must be moved, it can be done so without having to reanesthetize the skin. Leaving the anesthetic needle in the skin by detaching the syringe from the needle with the needle along the intended trajectory course saves time in subsequent needle placements. With the initial anesthetic needle serving as a relative directional marker both on images and on the skin, longer needles can subsequently be placed with positional readjustments as necessary, so that the final needle can be placed in tandem (or coaxial) fashion relative to the target zone.

Most biopsies of the lumbar spine (from about L2 to L5) can be performed from a posterior-lateral starting point, usually about 10 cm lateral to the spinous processes on an average-sized adult. The view taken from this *posterior-lateral approach* is similar to that for a facet injection or for a diskogram (Fig. 26–1). Use of this approach permits a favorable trajectory to the center of the spine while avoiding the thecal sac if the operator should direct the needle too far posteriorly or avoiding the bowel or other internal abdominal viscera if the operator should direct the needle too far laterally.

Final needle placement is confirmed through visualization of the needle position on the anterior-posterior plane as well as on the lateral plane. This helps to confirm the needle position and depth.

An alternative to the posterior-lateral approach is the

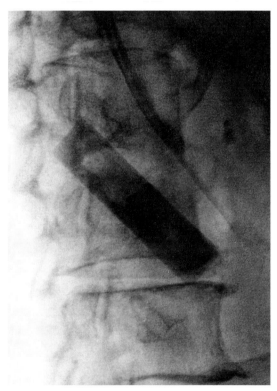

Figure 26–1. Fluoroscopically guided biopsy of L3 vertebra from a posterior-lateral approach starting about 10 cm lateral to the spinous processes in an average-size patient. This approach provides a clear view of the articular facet joints and would be the same for a facet injection or for a lumbar diskogram. When the bone is entered, anterior and lateral views should be obtained to determine the correct depth of placement in the vertebra. An 11-gauge core biopsy needle was used, and the diagnosis was staphylococcal osteomyelitis.

814

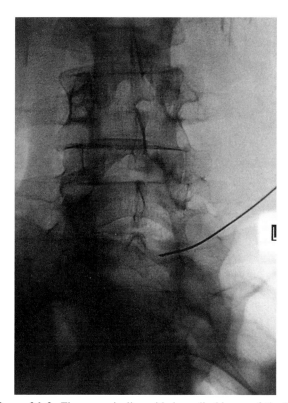

Figure 26–2. Fluoroscopically guided needle biopsy of the L5-S1 disk using a curved needle from a posterior-lateral starting point. The needle was passed over the iliac crest and then down to the level of the L5-S1 disk, at which point the needle was rotated medially to enter the disk. This is the same technique that would be used for a diskogram at the L5-S1 level. The diagnosis was diskitis due to *Streptococcus viridans*.

transpedicular approach, in which the needle is passed through the pedicle. With this approach, the needle can be angled slightly superiorly or inferiorly but movement medially or laterally is somewhat limited. For the transpedicular approach, the operator should avoid entering too far medially or inferiorly on the pedicle as this runs the risk of injury to the nerve root either in the lateral recess or at the neural foramen.

Fluoroscopically guided biopsies of the inferior margin of L5, the L5-S1 intervertebral disk, and the superior margin of S1 may be difficult from a posterior-lateral approach unless a curved needle is used to pass the needle over the intervening iliac crest and then down into the target area (Fig. 26–2). This technique is similar to performing an L5-S1 diskogram from the posterior-lateral approach.[59]

In all other areas of the spine, CT may be the preferred method of biopsy unless a transpedicular approach is taken with fluoroscopy.[4, 44] In the upper lumbar and thoracic regions, CT provides a means of visualizing the adjacent lung and other posteriorly located visceral organs, such as the kidneys, in the case of a high lumbar target.

In the cervical region, CT may also be the preferred method of image guidance for biopsies because it can be used to define the positions of the jugular vein, carotid artery, vertebral artery, and pharyngeal and esophageal structures more accurately than fluoroscopy can (Fig. 26–

3). Furthermore, to perform cervical biopsies with fluoroscopy, the operator may have to place his or her fingers in such a way as to deviate the carotid sheath laterally and the pharyngeal structures medially. This still poses the risk of inadvertent perforation of the esophagus, pharynx, or one of the major blood vessels that have been fixed in position. In addition, fluoroscopically guided needle biopsies of the cervical spine may subject the operator's hands to radiation while the fingers are pressing between the carotid sheath and the pharynx/esophagus.

For paraspinous soft tissue biopsies, fluoroscopy is at a great disadvantage, compared with CT, in that it is difficult to visualize a paraspinous soft tissue target under fluoroscopy, whereas these areas become apparent under CT (Fig. 26–4).

If CT is chosen for image guidance for spine biopsy, the area of concern should first be localized with a scout film. We often place a V-shaped reference marker over the area of concern (see Fig. 26–3A). This marker consists of a polyethylene catheter that is bent at an acute angle and taped over the target zone. The marker helps to localize the level at which the optimal target will be found by providing a measurement of the distance between the limbs of the V, and we can confirm the location through localization with the laser light. From one of the limbs of the V marker on the patient, a starting point can be measured on the CT scanner and duplicated on the patient's skin surface.

We then prepare the patient. We use progressively longer anesthetic needles and deliver local anesthetic agent with a very large skin wheal. We leave the anesthetic needles in place, after they are disconnected from the syringe, along the anticipated trajectory for the biopsy needles. We scan and then readjust the trajectory of the anesthetic needles accordingly and place progressively longer anesthetic needles to the target, correcting the course trajectory as necessary. When we finally reach the periosteum along the optimal trajectory, we direct a bone biopsy needle into the bone and into the target zone, usually from a tandem technique. If a smaller bone biopsy needle is used (e.g., a 17-gauge needle), a larger coaxial guiding needle can be used for multiple passes.

The advantage of using a coaxial system is that the operator can easily perform multiple biopsies along an intended trajectory. The disadvantage is that most bone biopsy needles are quite large, often 13 and 11 gauge, and a considerably larger guiding needle is necessary for coaxial passage.

The advances of slip ring technology with a continuously rotating x-ray tube, x-ray tubes with improved heat capacity, more sensitive semiconductor detectors, new imaging reconstruction algorithms, and high-speed parallel-array processor systems for real-time raw data reconstruction and display allowed the eventual development of real-time CT fluoroscopy.[11] Helical CT scanners with CT fluoroscopy are widely available. Depending on the vendor, frame rates vary from two to eight frames per second, and the continuous CT fluoroscopy time varies from 40 to 100 seconds.

The main advantage of CT fluoroscopy guidance, compared with conventional CT guidance, is the decreased time needed for the procedure; the operator can see in real

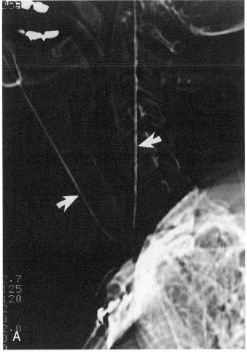

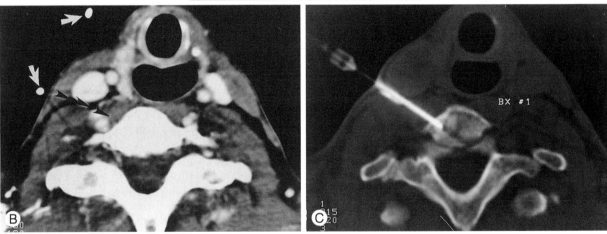

Figure 26–3. CT-guided biopsy of the cervical spine.

A, Lateral scout view of the cervical spine with an overlying V-shaped polyethylene marker for reference *(white arrows).* Measurement of the distance between the V can help to confirm the location from which biopsy samples are to be taken and can provide a reference mark for measurement to the starting point.

B, The V-shaped catheter on this patient's skin surface is outlined *(white arrows),* and the level to be targeted is confirmed by matching the distance between the V-shaped catheter at this level with what is seen on the scout view. *Black arrowheads* denote the needle course taken posterior to the jugular vein and anterior to the vertebral artery.

C, Biopsy is performed with a lightweight 17-gauge EZEM bone biopsy needle under CT guidance along the intended trajectory course. This needle has no heavy handles to throw it off course if it is unsupported when directed under CT guidance.

time the movements of the biopsy needle (Figs. 26–5 and 26–6). The disadvantage is increased radiation exposure to the operator,[11, 32, 33, 36] which should improve with the developments of special needle holders and even more sensitive semiconductor detectors, permitting improved image quality with lower milliampere doses.[11, 32, 33]

For CT needle guidance in the thoracic region, the usual trajectory is between the rib head and vertebral body *(costovertebral approach).* This approach avoids placement of the needle through the lung or through the exiting nerve root at the neural foramen. This technique usually allows

good angulation when other various zones of the vertebral body are targeted. The alternative approach to thoracic biopsies is a transpedicular approach, which provides limited medial or lateral angulation for targets throughout the vertebral body. A transpedicular approach can be used under either CT or fluoroscopic guidance (Fig. 26–7).

For cervical biopsies, most patients tolerate being on a side (lateral) position for longer periods of time than they would in a prone position, which often results in claustrophobia. The trajectory chosen should avoid the carotid sheath, pharynx, esophagus, vertebral artery, and spinal

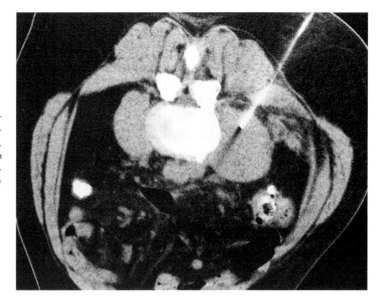

Figure 26–4. CT-guided needle biopsy of a painful paraspinous muscle mass. This lesion could not be seen fluoroscopically, and CT guidance was therefore necessary. A 25-gauge needle easily yielded cytologic samples to make the diagnosis of a metastatic transitional cell carcinoma to the psoas muscle before the primary malignancy site was discovered.

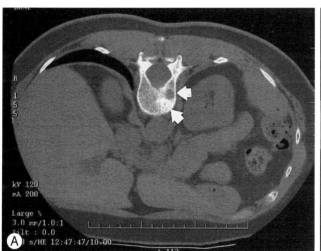

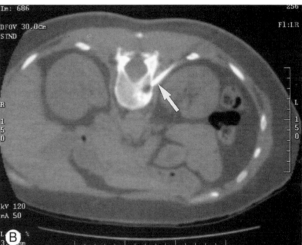

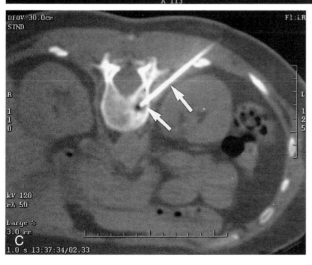

Figure 26–5. Multiple images from noncontrast CT *(A)* and CT fluoroscopy *(B* and *C)* sequences during a biopsy of a mixed lytic and sclerotic lesion in T12 vertebra. These images demonstrate the successful biopsy of this small lesion *(A)* *(arrows)*. Note that the needle angle trajectory avoids the left kidney, rib, and pedicle *(arrows)*. The cytologic diagnosis was metastatic adenocarcinoma consistent with a breast origin.

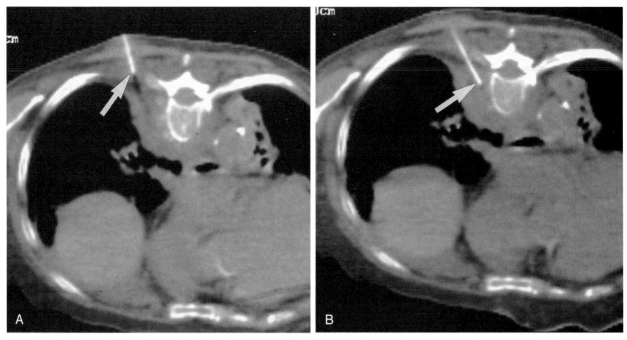

Figure 26–6. Biopsy of a left paraspinal soft tissue mass. CT fluoroscopy images demonstrate advancement of biopsy needle with changes in needle orientation and depth from *A* to *B* *(arrows)*. CT fluoroscopy allows the changes to be made in real time. The pathologic process was bacterial osteomyelitis.

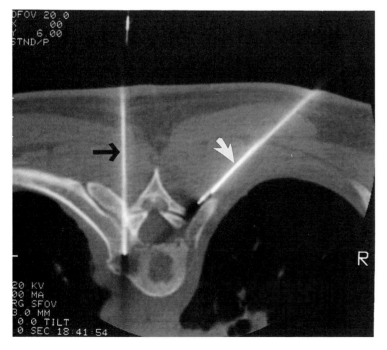

Figure 26–7. CT-guided thoracic spine biopsy; two approaches are shown. One follows the posterior aspect of the rib down to the costovertebral junction *(white arrow)*. If this approach cannot be easily made, an alternative approach is transpedicular *(black arrow)*. The diagnosis was metastatic mucinous carcinoma of the colon.

contents. Sometimes it is very difficult to select a trajectory to avoid any of these structures. In some cases, a transpedicular trajectory may have to be taken. At other times, a stiff, large-bore needle can be placed behind the carotid sheath to shove the carotid sheath anteriorly, with the needle then redirected more posteriorly toward the target. From that point, coaxial biopsy needles can be passed through the larger guiding needle into the spinal target area.

Aspiration may be necessary for biopsy of soft tissue masses or abnormal fluid accumulations, whether present in soft tissues or bone. Aspiration techniques are often best performed with two operators using two sets of hands. One set of hands directs the needle into the target and performs the biopsy with forward and back rotary motions in the area of abnormality, usually with excursions of about 1 cm or less; the other set of hands provides suction via extension tubing from the needle to a large syringe (30 to 50 mL) with about 10 to 15 mL of suction pressure. The operator should be careful not to withdraw excessive amounts of blood because this action may interfere with the pathologist's diagnosis.

Biopsy of fluid-filled necrotic masses should also include the rim of the necrotic zone because the actual abnormal histology may be around the periphery, whereas the center may contain only necrotic debris. If the operator encounters a large paraspinous abscess, percutaneous drainage of the abscess at the time of biopsy by additionally placing a large-bore (10 French) catheter either with the Seldinger technique or with a single-pass trocar system (e.g., Cope). This can provide a large-volume specimen as well as a way to initiate therapy by draining the abscess.

Before performing a biopsy on lesions that are suspected to be caused by infection, the operator should ask the referring physician whether the patient has been taking antibiotics, which can interfere with organ growth and yield false-negative results. Ideally, any lesion that is thought to be due to infection should immediately undergo biopsy well before antibiotics are started. If antibiotics have already been started, they may have to be discontinued for 1 week to 10 days before the biopsy to ensure adequate growth of the organisms for positive results.

We generally request that a pathologist be available at the time of the biopsy to confirm whether an adequate sample has been taken. If the pathologist cannot make an initial diagnosis, further specimens may be necessary. Sometimes excessive blood in the specimen interferes with the pathologist's ability to make a clear diagnosis. If a specimen of paraspinous soft tissue lesions is obtained for biopsy and considerable blood is found in the specimen, sometimes a very thin (e.g., 25-gauge) needle without aspiration (instead of a larger-bore needle) may yield positive cytology. On the other hand, a spring-loaded cutting core biopsy needle (e.g., Cook, Temno) might be considered to slice free a portion of the target without the aspiration of a great deal of blood.

If the operator suspects that the lesion is an extremely vascular mass, such as a renal cell carcinoma with metastasis to the spine, a spinal angiogram may have to be obtained. If the angiogram confirms the vascular nature of the lesion, spinal embolization, via either arterial access or direct puncture of the lesion with the injection of either absorbable gelatin powder (Gelfoam, Gel-O-Foam) or polyvinyl alcohol particles, may be necessary before sampling of the lesion are taken. This measure may help to prevent serious hemorrhage.

Needles

A variety of needles can be used for biopsy of the spine and paraspinous soft tissues.

Thin-Walled Needles

20- and 22-Gauge Needles

Straight, thin-walled needles (e.g., 20- and 22-gauge Chiba-type) can be used to aspirate abscesses, disks, soft tissues, or abnormally lytic bone lesions. Because 20-gauge needles are somewhat stouter than 22-gauge needles, directional control is more easily accomplished with 20-gauge needles, particularly if a complex curved trajectory must be used. The 20-gauge needle does not produce quite as much trauma as that from the 18-gauge needle and is usually sufficiently stout to penetrate a thin shell of bone in the presence of a lytic bone lesion.

25-Gauge Needles

The 25-gauge needle is often used in biopsies of very vascular soft tissue masses in the paraspinous areas and have the advantage of limiting the blood loss.

Core Biopsy Needles

Spring-loaded core biopsy needles (e.g., Temno or Cook) may be necessary for paraspinous soft tissue masses that are quite fibrous or reluctant to give up cells during fine-needle aspiration. Because lymphomas, schwannomas, and certain other fibrous tumors are often resistant to fine-needle aspiration, the use of a cutting type of needle (e.g., a spring-loaded core biopsy needle) may be necessary to obtain an adequate sample. With core biopsy needles, it can be difficult to maintain direction because of the weight of the handle when they are used under CT guidance. It may be best to direct the cutting needle through a coaxial guiding needle, which can be placed precisely under CT guidance, and avoid the problem of handle weight of the core biopsy needle.

Bone Biopsy Needles

A variety of bone biopsy needles are available, ranging from sharp-threaded, drilling-type 17-gauge needles (e.g., EZEM) to large-bore 11-gauge needles (e.g., Mannon, Cook). For sclerotic or blastic bone lesions of the spine, the more specimen that is collected, usually the better it is for the pathologist, because these lesions are often difficult to adequately decalcify for diagnosis. Therefore, for sclerotic bone lesions, bone biopsy needles of 11 gauge or larger are usually best.

When a spinal lesion is in a place that is difficult to access (e.g., a tight passage between the carotid sheath and vertebral artery in the upper cervical spine), lightweight short drilling needles, such as the 17-gauge EZEM, may be advantageous in setting and keeping trajectories in shallow soft tissues, in contrast to larger 11-gauge needles with heavy handles, which often throw the trajectory of the needle off course when used under CT guidance. Because the small 17-gauge EZEM needles are short and very lightweight, they can be set in shallow soft tissues during targeting and still hold their trajectory without hand support. Because they are also very sharp and are threaded, they can thus be drilled deeply into the bone to obtain core samples very effectively in most cases.

General Precautions

Before biopsy, the operator should check for coagulopathies (bleeding time, prothrombin time, partial thromboplastin time, platelets). For coagulopathic patients or patients receiving anticoagulants, the procedure may have to be postponed.

When biopsies are performed on thoracic lesions, the operator should always be cautious of a possible pneumothorax; at termination of the procedure, either a follow-up set of CT scans through the lungs with lung windows or an expiratory chest x-ray film should be obtained to rule out a pneumothorax. A chest tube kit should be obtained or arrangements for the placement of a chest tube made before biopsy of the thoracic spine.

When pushing or drilling a needle through very dense bone, and when vital structures such as the aorta, the carotid artery, or the vertebral artery are located just beyond the target zone along the trajectory path, the operator may want to use a détente technique with one hand pushing the needle toward the target and the other hand grasping the needle shaft to provide a counteraction force, if necessary, to prevent piercing beyond the target area into vital structures if resistance to the needle should suddenly give way.

The operator should also be cautious when delivering the sample to the pathologist. It is wise to have a pathology team available to accept the specimens to avoid embarrassing misplacement. When delivering a bone core that may be impacted within the bone biopsy needle, it is prudent to avoid pushing the core out of the needle with such force that it suddenly flies off the slide and becomes lost. To remove a bone core from the biopsy needle, the operator should use the appropriate trocar design that is intended for such removal.

MRI-Guided Spinal Biopsies

Increasingly, MRI is being used for guidance and control of minimally invasive percutaneous and surgical procedures. Technologic advances such as the introduction of open and short-bore magnet designs, the proliferation of fast imaging sequences, and the availability of MRI-compatible instruments have aided the growth of this field.[36] We discuss the role of interventional MRI as it pertains to percutaneous spinal biopsies. For readers interested in MRI guidance related to neurosurgical procedures, potential percutaneous vascular applications, laser therapy, radiofrequency ablation, and biopsy of other parts of the body, more detailed works are recommended.*

The best design of an MRI system with regard to high-quality images and low field inhomogeneity would be a spherical magnet.[23] However, this design presents a subop-

timal environment for MRI-guided intervention, which requires free access to the patient. Early reports of MRI-guided biopsies and aspirations were made with conventional cylindric superconducting systems.[42] This technique is similar to CT-guided procedures, in which access to the patient is limited and the patient must be withdrawn from the magnet for the manipulation of biopsy equipment, resulting in relatively long procedure times.

Three types of magnets are used clinically for MRI-guided therapy:

1. Closed, short-bore cylindrical superconducting systems operating at between 1.0 and 1.5 tesla (T).
2. Open, midfield ("double-donut") systems operating at 0.5 T.
3. Open, low-field (biplanar) systems operating at between 0.064 and 0.3 T.

The improvement in access to the patient that is afforded by the open magnets is traded for decreased field strength and image quality.[36, 54]

The main advantage of closed magnets, operating at high field strengths, is superior image quality relative to static magnetic field strengths and homogeneity. Also, the excellent signal-to-noise ratio achieved with these systems is well suited for temperature monitoring and mapping during ablative therapy with laser or radiofrequency.[1, 2, 23, 24, 36, 42] The disadvantages of this type of magnet design are the limited access to the patient and the relatively longer procedure times.

MRI-compatible accessories are available from several manufacturers. As with other cross-sectional imaging–guided modalities, such as CT and ultrasonography, the correct needle choice depends on whether tissue is required for cytologic or histologic analysis. Fine-aspiration, side-cutting, and bone biopsy needles are available in sizes ranging from 14 to 24 gauge. To achieve minimal artifact and no torque in the magnetic field, needles are composed of nonferromagnetic metals such as titanium, tantalum, and tungsten with aluminum or vanadium alloy.[43]

The main disadvantage of these needles is their relative bluntness and softness compared with stainless steel needles. Thus, in the case of intact cortical bone or sclerotic bony lesions, the biopsy procedure may be technically difficult and time-consuming and the patient may experience some discomfort. MRI-compatible bone drill systems are being developed to overcome this somewhat vexing problem.[43]

Factors such as lesion conspicuousness, needle passive image artifacts, and image contrast between the lesion and the instruments must be considered in an MRI-guided procedure. The instrumentation-based image artifacts depend mainly on the following[1, 37, 57]:

- Needle size
- Orientation of the needle to B_0
- The field strength B_0
- The imaging sequence parameters used for the procedure

The greater the angle of the needle to B_0, the more conspicuous is the artifact size, with maximum visibility at 90 degrees. The artifact becomes larger with increasing MRI field strength. Put simply, gradient-echo sequences are more sensitive to local field inhomogeneities and intravoxel

---

*See references 1, 2, 7, 24, 30, 31, 34, 39, 48, and 51 to 54.

dephasing than spin-echo sequences are. Therefore, techniques such as T2-weighted fast spin-echo sequences produce smaller artifacts than those noted with gradient-echo scans. The physical basis of these phenomena is beyond the scope of this discussion and has been well described in the literature.[1, 16, 36–38] Effective clinical application of MRI-guided procedures requires consideration of these different factors and appropriate adaptation.

Indications for percutaneous biopsy of the spine include cytologic or histologic analysis and diagnosis of soft tissue or bone lesions of unknown etiology. MRI is an alternative to CT and ultrasound in imaging guidance; MRI's multipla-

nar imaging capability probably is the most advantageous feature of this modality when compared with the other two modalities. This feature is important in planning needle trajectories in which the operator would want to avoid vascular structures (e.g., in head and neck biopsies) or in other important tissue planes (e.g., interposed bowel or the diaphragm). Occasionally, MRI can be used to visualize lesions that are either invisible or poorly seen on CT scans or sonograms. The superior soft tissue contrast and spatial resolution that MRI affords are most dramatic in the setting of bone marrow changes of unknown etiology, which are often invisible with CT (Fig. 26–8). An MRI-guided proce-

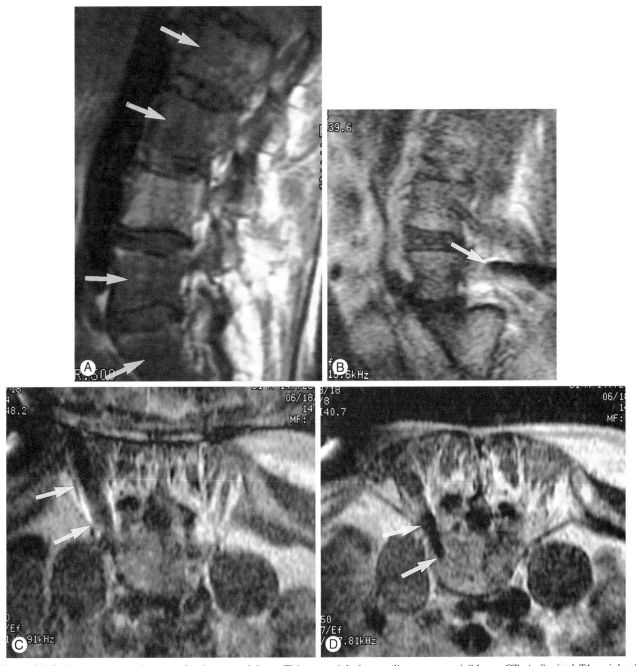

Figure 26–8. Bone marrow changes of unknown etiology. This potential abnormality was not visible on CT. *A,* Sagittal T1-weighted localizer image demonstrates patchy infiltration of the bone marrow in multiple lumbar vertebral bodies *(arrows). B–D,* Real-time axial images during left L5 transpediculate biopsy. Note susceptibility artifacts from needle. Cytologic diagnosis was negative for malignancy.

dure is also advantageous when radiation exposure is a consideration, as in younger patients, or when a patient has a history of allergy to an iodinated contrast agent.

MRI-guided biopsies of soft tissue and bony lesions of the spine appear to be safe and effective. There are obvious limitations to this technique, such as smaller lesions, which may be obscured by needle artifacts. Patient size and weight may also be limiting factors. Early results of MRI-guided biopsies seem to be as accurate as those of CT-guided techniques.[28, 43] MRI-guided techniques (not only biopsy and aspiration but also intraoperative monitoring and therapeutic procedures) are under constant evaluation and evolution and will probably become important tools in the armamentarium of radiology.

Diagnostic and Therapeutic Spine Interventions

Diskography

Indications

Diskography is commonly performed when imaging results are confusing or inconclusive. Sometimes the images may reveal more levels of abnormality than would be suspected on the basis of the clinical examination. At other times, images may fail to reveal any apparent abnormalities when the clinical examination strongly suggests a diskogenic etiology.[50] Shellhas and colleagues[49] reported that diskography could be extremely beneficial when MRI findings were negative. Colhoun and associates[8] noted that of 137 patients with positive diskographic findings, 89% derived significant sustained clinical benefit from subsequent surgery.

Diskography may also be used in the evaluation of postsurgical diskogenic pain and of presurgical fusion when disk disease is suspected in relation to underlying spinal instability.[22] Diskography is also indicated for the diagnosis of disk disease before percutaneous diskectomy or intradiskal electrolytic therapy.

Technique

The diskogram is a provocative test that is based on reproduction of the patient's original pain as a result of an increase in intradiskal pressure caused by the injection of fluid into the disk. This fluid is usually intrathecally compatible iodine contrast medium (e.g., Omnipaque 180), and the pressure increase is usually accomplished by injecting 1 to 1.5 mL into a lumbar disk or about 0.5 mL into a cervical disk. Because of the risk of infection, many operators add a broad-spectrum antibiotic to the iodine contrast mixture (e.g., cefazolin at about 50 mg per 1 mL of iodinated contrast medium).[49]

For lumbar diskography, a posterior-lateral approach is usually taken under fluoroscopic guidance. The most common disks to be injected in the lumbar region are L3-4, L4-5, and L5-S1.

Straight needle trajectories can usually be taken for the L3-4 and L4-5 disks (Fig. 26–9); however, because the iliac crest blocks a direct trajectory to the L5-S1 disk, a curved trajectory of the needle must be taken for the L5-

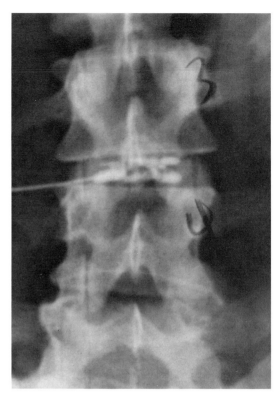

Figure 26–9. Anteroposterior view of contrast medium injected into the L3-4 disk following a posterior-lateral approach for needle placement under fluoroscopic guidance. Injection of contrast medium demonstrates a bifid configuration of medium in a normal-appearing disk. However, the patient complained of marked pain reproduction on injection into this disk.

S1 disk. The operator passes a curved needle superiorly over the iliac crest from a posterior-lateral starting point, then inferiorly to the level of the disk, and then medially into the disk (see Fig. 26–2). A C-arm fluoroscope is definitely advantageous for this complex trajectory. Some operators use CT scanning, which may be appropriate for L3-4 and L4-5 diskography, but the orientation of the L5-S1 disk makes access with CT guidance difficult unless a transthecal approach is used. For thoracic and cervical diskography, CT guidance may be preferred to fluoroscopic guidance, similar to image-guided biopsies (Fig. 26–10). Some operators prefer to perform cervical diskography with fluoroscopic guidance, in which case they deviate the carotid sheath laterally and then deviate the pharynx/esophagus medially with the fingers of one hand and then with the other hand pass a very thin (25-gauge) needle into the disk.

After diskography, a CT scan of the disk containing injected contrast medium can be performed to obtain additional information. Sometimes this secondary information reveals other corroborative evidence of disk disease, such as an annular tear (Fig. 26–11).

Complications

The frequency of complications following diskography has been reported to be as high as 3% by Fraser and associates,[17] but the general overall rate is less than

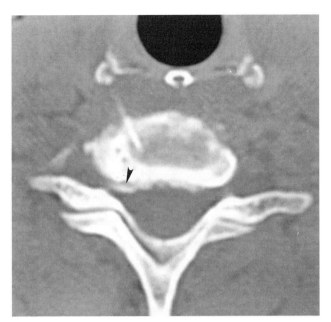

Figure 26–10. Cervical diskography at the C5-6 level performed with CT guidance using a 25-gauge needle via an anterior-lateral approach. The patient's right arm pain was reproduced exactly on injection of 0.5 mL of iodine contrast medium. After injection, the CT scan also demonstrates a small amount of contrast medium filling a right posterior-lateral disk protrusion *(arrowhead)*.

0.15%.[22] Complications can include infection, bleeding, nerve injury, chemical diskitis,[50] hypotension (vagal), pneumothorax, and cerebrospinal fluid leak leading to spinal headaches.

Initial Spine Interventions: Epidural Steroid Injections versus Joint Injections

The most common spinal interventional procedures that may be both diagnostic and therapeutic include epidural steroid injections and joint injections (facet and sacroiliac joint injections). Often, these injections represent the initial diagnostic spine interventions that lead to more definitive therapy.

The evaluation of back pain starts with a history and physical examination, and findings are correlated with the imaging study. If the pain is *radicular* in nature, the operator may start with an epidural steroid injection. If the patient benefits from this injection, a subsequent epidural steroid injection can be administered about 4 weeks later, leading to another epidural steroid injection in about 4 weeks if there is continued positive benefit. At that point, maintenance epidural steroid injections at about 2- to 3-month intervals can be administered for continued pain relief.

If at any time the patient does not experience a positive benefit, he or she should be reevaluated. If the pain instead seems to be more focal, a joint injection may be considered.

If relief does not result after the epidural steroid injections, the patient should be considered for a surgical evaluation or referred for treatment with oral medications (narcotics, nonsteroidal anti-inflammatory drugs).

If on initial evaluation the patient's pain seems to be more *focal* (i.e., over a facet or sacroiliac joint), a joint injection might be given first. If there is positive benefit, another joint injection can be administered in 4 weeks; again, if there is positive benefit, a subsequent joint injection can be administered in 4 weeks.

If there continues to be positive benefit, maintenance joint injections can be considered for long-term therapy at 2- to 3-month intervals. If the patient does not receive positive benefit from the initial three joint injections, he or she should be reevaluated.

If the pain pattern seems to be more *radicular* than *focal*, epidural steroid injections should be considered. Otherwise, the patient may be a candidate for either surgical or medical referral.

Epidural Steroid Injections

Epidural steroid injections are commonly administered when the patient is experiencing radicular symptoms, often

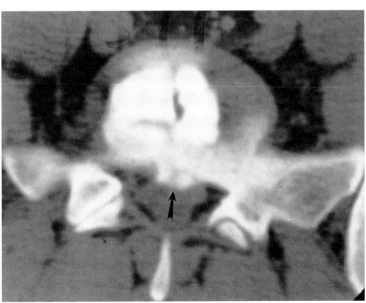

Figure 26–11. Postdiskography CT scan reveals contrast medium in the L5-S1 disk filling a small central disk protrusion. Although the CT scan appears to be abnormal, indicating an annular tear, the patient was totally asymptomatic. Thus, disk protrusion would be considered only an incidental finding at diskography.

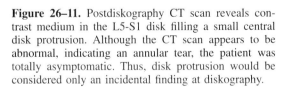

due to spinal stenosis, which may be a result of generalized degenerative changes, disk disease, or facet arthrosis. Postsurgical scarring may also be an indication for epidural steroid injections. If an exact cause of pain is not clearly discerned, an epidural steroid injection may sometimes be the first injection procedure attempted to alleviate pain.[5, 14]

Injection at Lumbar Sites

For low lumbar disease, the operator can administer a caudal injection.[45] The operator palpates an indentation along the lowest portion of the sacrum and, under fluoroscopic guidance, inserts a needle into the sacral hiatus. Caution is needed to prevent inadvertent placement of the needle anterior to the sacrum (into the rectum) or posterior to the sacrum (into the posterior sacral soft tissues). The needle should not be directed superiorly to S3 because a low-lying thecal sac might be encountered.

Iodine contrast medium is injected (~2 mL iohexol [46.36% iodine; Omnipaque 180]) to confirm optimal placement in the sacral epidural space and not into the thecal sac. A long-acting steroid (18 mg betamethasone [Celestone]) is then usually injected.

For other sites of the lumbar spine, from about L3 superior into the cervical region, the operator places an epidural needle such as a Tuohy, which has a somewhat curved blunted tip, into the epidural space, as with a myelographic approach (either midline between the spinous processes or paramedian). C-arm fluoroscopy is usually the preferred imaging modality.

Needle Placement

Two techniques are commonly deployed for placing the epidural needle in the correct location.

1. *Direct saline pressure method.* A glass syringe with saline is connected to the end of the epidural needle, and intermittent pressure is applied as the needle is directed to the epidural space under fluoroscopic guidance. On reaching the epidural space, there typically is a remarkable loss of resistance such that the plunger is easily pushed forward with very little resistance.

2. *Hanging drop method.* A drop of saline is placed over the posterior hole of the Tuohy needle, which is then guided by fluoroscopy down to the epidural space. The blunt tip of the Tuohy needle tends to depress the rather tough dura, creating a vacuum effect, and this sucks the drop of saline inward to signify that the needle has reached the epidural space. The operator confirms needle tip location by performing an epidurogram. This is easily accomplished with an injection of about 2 mL of intrathecally compatible iodine contrast (Omnipaque 180).

At fluoroscopic examination, the anteroposterior view should reveal a streaky contrast medium collection that may extend out through the nerve root sleeves; the lateral view may show a linear collection of contrast medium adjacent to the expected location of the thecal sac (Figs. 26–12 and 26–13). If the needle penetrates the thecal sac, the injection of steroids, and especially a local anesthetic agent, should be avoided. The injection procedure can be postponed for 1 week to allow the hole in the thecal sac to

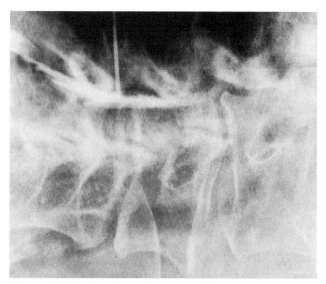

Figure 26–12. Lumbar epidural steroid injection. The lateral view demonstrating the linear accumulation of contrast medium along the posterior aspect of the lumbar epidural space. There is no intrathecal contrast filling. This epidurogram confirms optimal needle placement.

heal, or the epidural steroid injection can be administered at a different but adjacent level.

A study by Johnson and colleagues[27] that involved 5334 patients showed that the efficacy of epidural steroid injections with fluoroscopically guided needle placement and confirmatory epidurography was extremely high (97%) and the complication rate was very low (0.07%). This is in contrast to *blind* epidural steroid injections, as commonly performed by anesthesiologists, who experience up to a 30% rate of inaccurate needle placement.

Facet Injections

Facet disease can cause focal pain or referred local pain.[3, 18, 41] Median branch nerves from the nerve roots above and below the facet joints supply the innervation to the facet joints.[6] The injection into a facet joint under fluoroscopic guidance is not usually difficult unless there is considerable hypertrophic degenerative spurring, which may alter the choice of entry point into the facet joint. In those cases, targeting by CT guidance may be preferred.

On the needle's entry into a facet joint, the operator injects a very small amount of iodinated contrast agent (0.1 to 0.2 mL of Omnipaque 180) to confirm needle tip location within the facet joint. The operator should visualize a linear contrast medium accumulation in the facet joint or filling of the recesses (or both) that appears as bulbous collections of contrast medium along the superior and inferior margins of the facet joint (Fig. 26–14). A local anesthetic agent (lidocaine) can be injected for diagnostic purposes, whereas an injection of a long-acting anesthetic agent and a long-acting steroid (0.5 mL of a 50:50 mixture of 0.25% bupivacaine [0.25% Marcaine] and 6 mg/mL betamethasone) is administered. In the cervical region, a fluoroscopically guided lateral approach is usually taken (Fig. 26–15) except for the C1-2 facet joint, which is composed of the lateral masses of C1 and C2. CT guidance

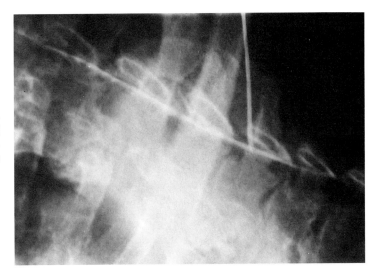

Figure 26–13. Cervical epidural steroid injection showing a linear contrast accumulation in the posterior cervical epidural space. No intrathecal contrast medium accumulation is seen. This epidurogram confirms optimal needle placement.

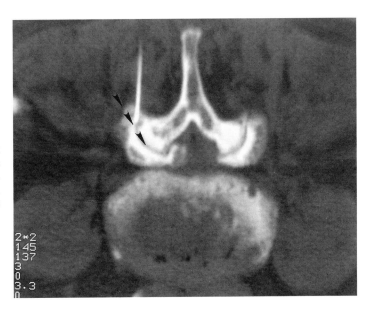

Figure 26–14. Lumbar facet injection under CT guidance. Initial attempts were performed under fluoroscopic guidance, but the visualized trajectory to the facet joint (arrowheads) was blocked by the posterior-superior articular facet osteophyte. Therefore, CT guidance was used to reveal the true posterior entry point into the joint. Most facet injections can be performed rapidly with fluoroscopic guidance, but the more difficult ones, such as this one, should be reserved for CT guidance.

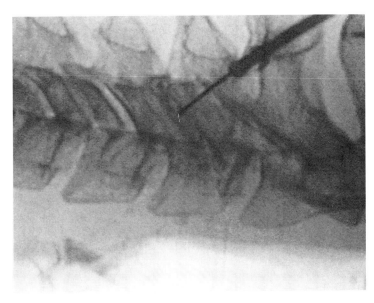

Figure 26–15. Lateral view of the cervical spine showing correct needle placement for C3-4 articular facet joint injection. The operator should not approach the joint too far anteriorly to avoid puncture of the vertebral artery. Contrast medium in the joint shows a normal linear accumulation along the joint margins, which confirms correct needle placement.

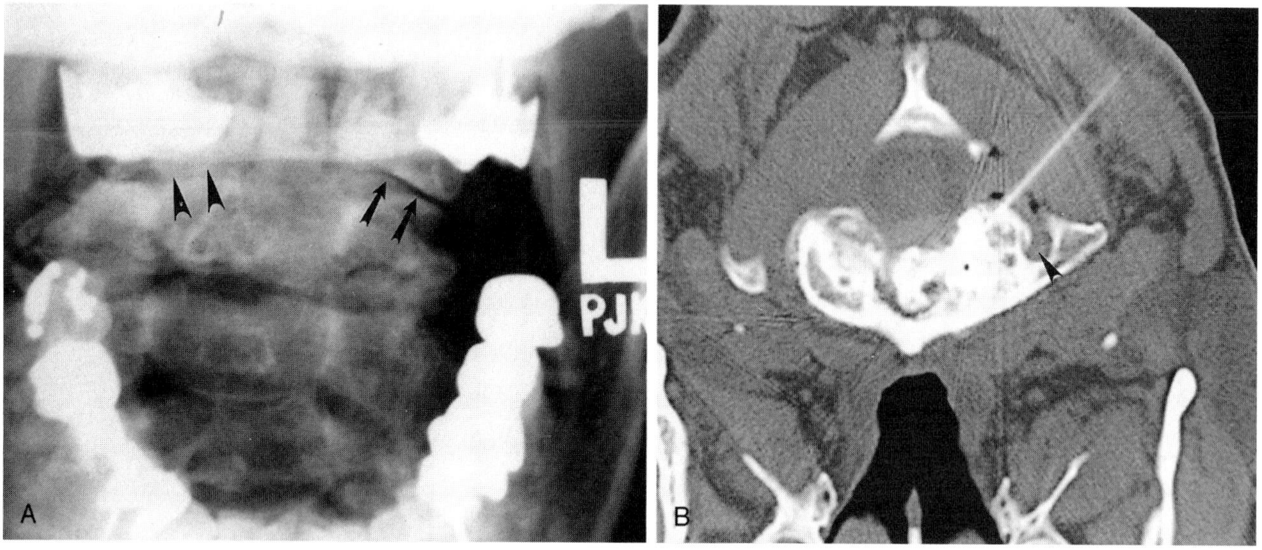

Figure 26–16. C1-2 articular facet joint injection. *A*, Anteroposterior view. Plain film of the C1-2 facet joints demonstrates that the normal facet joint *(arrows)* is made up of the lateral masses, whereas the abnormal right-sided facet joint *(arrowheads)* is extremely sclerosed. *B*, Injection of the right C1-2 facet joint with CT guidance from a posterior-lateral approach that avoids the vertebral artery *(arrowhead)*, with the needle well positioned in the C1-2 facet joint.

may be preferred to fluoroscopic guidance to avoid injury to the vertebral artery or the C1 and C2 nerve roots during injection into the C1-2 facet joint (Fig. 26–16).

An alternative to injection into the facet joints may be achieved by blocking the median branch nerves, which pass over the superior medial boundaries of the transverse processes arising above and below the level of the facet joint. This is known as a *median branch block*. If this procedure is effective in relieving pain, radiofrequency ablation of the median branch nerves may be considered for longer pain relief.[13]

As in the facet joints, pain emanating from the sacroiliac joints is typically focal, locally referred, or both. The sacroiliac joint injection is commonly made under fluoroscopic guidance. Placing the fluoroscope or the patient at an oblique angle until the joint margins are optimally seen may reveal the correct trajectory for the needle. However, overlap of the ilium and sacrum often presents problems for straight needle passage into the joint. Therefore, in some cases injection with CT guidance may be preferred (Fig. 26–17).

The sacroiliac joint is a diarthrodial joint in which the lower half is the synovial portion and thus the target area. When fluoroscopy is chosen, the optimal site for placement of a needle into the synovial portion of the sacroiliac joint is usually along the most inferior margin, which tends to have less bony overlap of the ilium on the sacrum (Fig. 26–18). Injection of iodinated contrast medium (~1 mL of Omnipaque 180) confirms correct needle placement, as defined by a linear streak of contrast medium in the joint. The operator can then inject about 3 mL of 1% lidocaine for diagnostic purposes or the same amount of a 50:50 mixture of a long-acting anesthetic agent (0.25% bupivacaine) and steroid (6 mg/mL betamethasone) for therapeutic purposes.

The complication rate following joint injection (facet and sacroiliac joints) with the use of thin 22- or 25-gauge

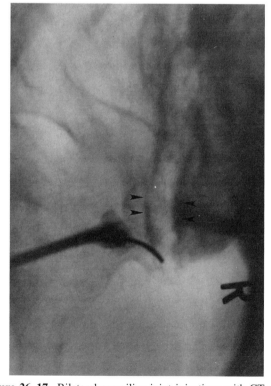

Figure 26–17. Bilateral sacroiliac joint injections with CT guidance. The left side of the sacroiliac joint was difficult to approach fluoroscopically. *Arrowheads* indicate the apparent approach to the left sacroiliac joint under fluoroscopy, but the iliac bone blocks access to this joint, which is somewhat curved. The right joint has a straighter trajectory and was able to be accessed with fluoroscopy. Nevertheless, CT provides the most accurate way of defining the opening to the sacroiliac joints. In this case, the true opening to the right side of joint was situated much more medially than was apparent under fluoroscopy.

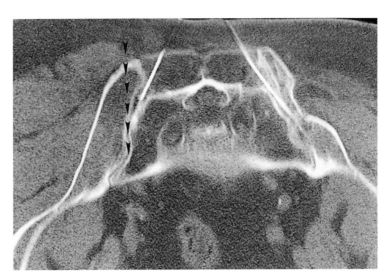

Figure 26–18. Fluoroscopically guided sacroiliac joint injection. A 25-gauge needle was placed along the most inferior margin of the right sacroiliac joint. This inferior position tends to have less bony overlap of the ilium on the sacrum than when the joint is approached from a more superior position. Iodine contrast medium has been injected and is collecting along the joint margins *(arrowheads)*, confirming correct needle placement.

needles is extremely low. Nevertheless, general precautions regarding coagulopathies, infections, allergic reactions, and hypotensive (vagal) events should always be considered.

Nerve Root Blocks

Nerve root blocks can be helpful diagnostically when the imaging findings are rather confusing. When multiple abnormalities are seen on an image, the blockade of pain related to a specific nerve root may specify the clinically relevant abnormality. Nerve root blocks may also be helpful therapeutically when there is irritation of a nerve root or when a patient is having radicular pain but is not a reasonable surgical candidate. Nerve root blocks can be achieved through injection into the ganglion at the neuroforamen,[61] but the operator must be cautious to avoid communication with the subarachnoid space if a particularly long nerve root sleeve is present.

Careful scrutiny during injection of iodine contrast medium is necessary to rule out intrathecal communication. Alternatively, the operator can inject into the nerve roots along the postganglionic segment.

Lumbar Nerve Root Injections

In the lumbar region, the operator would insert a needle just over the superior margin of the midsection of the subjacent (lower) transverse process and probe gently with a 25-gauge needle until there is a paresthesia to the lower extremity. The operator then backs the needle off very slightly and injects iodine contrast medium, which should outline the nerve root sheath, with the nerve root being seen as a linear filling defect (Fig. 26–19). At that point, the operator can inject 1 to 2 mL of 1% lidocaine for diagnostic purposes or, for more permanent therapeutic pain relief, 1 to 2 mL of a 50:50 mixture of 0.25% bupivacaine and a long-acting steroid (6 mg/mL betamethasone).

Thoracic Nerve Root Injections

In the thoracic region, the postganglionic nerve roots can be located just under the inferior margin of the rib. For

thoracic nerve root blocks, the operator should be extremely cautious of needle depth to avoid a pneumothorax. Nerve root blocks can readily be accomplished under fluoroscopy.

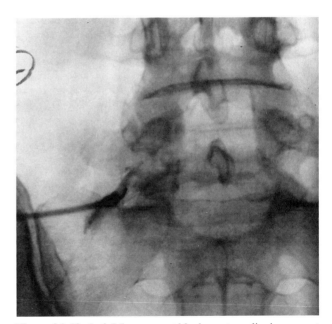

Figure 26–19. Left L5 nerve root block, postganglionic segment. A needle is directed into the ganglionic portion of the nerve root at the neural foramen or along the postganglionic portion of the nerve root. To find the postganglionic portion of a lumbar nerve root, the operator passes a needle deeply from approximately the midsection of the lower transverse process or, in this case, the equivalent midsection of the sacral wing. Gentle probing is performed until the patient acknowledges an electric shock down the lower extremity. The needle is withdrawn just slightly, and iodine contrast medium is injected along the nerve sheath. Contrast medium can be seen tracking along the nerve sheath back toward the neural foramen. Injection of lidocaine can be administered for diagnostic purposes, and injection of bupivacaine and long-acting steroid can be administered for more therapeutic measures.

Cervical Nerve Root Injections

In the cervical region, the operator may prefer CT guidance to avoid the pharynx/esophagus and carotid sheath or vertebral artery, although some operators prefer to use fluoroscopic guidance for cervical nerve root blocks, similar to the technique of cervical diskography. To avoid the vertebral artery, the operator should place the needle in the posterior neuroforamen.

Trigger-Point Injections

Local soft tissue injections of an anesthetic agent, steroids, or both may be helpful when the patient has myofascial pain, perhaps due to scarring, myofascial strain, or strain related to ununited bone fusion. Targeted areas to be injected are based on subjective responses of the patient to soft tissue tenderness. These injections may help bring about relief and allow time for healing to occur (Fig. 26–20). For diagnostic pain relief in the soft tissues, 1 to 4 mL of 1% lidocaine may be injected, whereas a similar amount of long-acting anesthetic agent and steroid can be injected for longer therapeutic relief (e.g., bupivacaine, 0.25%, and betamethasone, 6 mg/mL).

Sympathetic Ganglion Blockade

Deep visceral pain may cause considerable referred pain from visceral somatic reflex arcs, which may worsen pain cycles. Sympathetic nerve blocks may help to decrease pain by breaking up reflex arcs. The common sympathetic ganglion blocks include:

1. *Stellate ganglion block* for upper extremity and lower facial and neck pain.
2. *Celiac ganglion block* for pain of the upper abdomen.
3. *Lumbar sympathetic block* for pain related to the lower extremities.

4. *Impar ganglion block* for pain in the lower pelvis and perineal regions.

Stellate Ganglion Block

Indications for blockade of the stellate ganglion include pain in the upper arm due to arterial insufficiency, Raynaud's phenomenon, reflex sympathetic dystrophy, post-traumatic syndrome with swelling, hyperhidrosis, and cyanosis, Pancoast tumors of the upper thorax, and herpes zoster of the neck and head.

Stellate ganglion blockade is accomplished under either fluoroscopic or CT guidance by directing a thin (25-gauge) needle to the stellate ganglion located at the anterior-lateral aspect of the C7 vertebral body and the junction with its transverse process (Fig. 26–21).[15] The syringe attached to the end of the needle should be aspirated to be sure that the tip of the needle is not in a blood vessel—especially the vertebral artery. Injection of iodinated contrast medium further substantiates the location of the stellate ganglion and the absence of any intravascular filling.

For temporary pain relief, 0.25% bupivacaine (8 mL) can be injected on a weekly basis (usually up to 8 weeks). For pain ablation, 8 mL of absolute alcohol or 6% phenol can be used for neurolysis, preferably with the patient under general anesthesia, because the injection of absolute alcohol can be extremely painful. When effective stellate ganglion blockade is achieved, Horner syndrome develops and there may be venous engorgement and paresis of the ipsilateral face and arm.

The risks and complications of stellate ganglion blockade include the following:

- Intraspinal extension of the medication (particularly if a long nerve root sleeve is encountered, which may lead to paralysis or even seizures)
- Intravascular injection

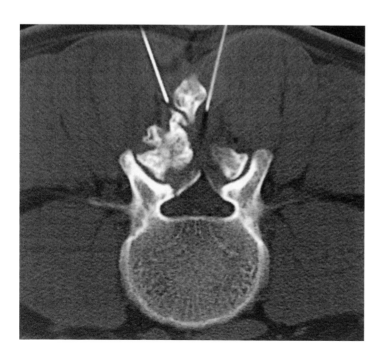

Figure 26–20. Trigger-point local soft tissue injections. The patient complained of considerable soft tissue tenderness in an area that was related to soft tissue strain adjacent to an ununited bone fusion. Weekly injections of 0.25% bupivacaine (6 mL) provided enormous pain relief for the patient until soft tissue healing was adequate.

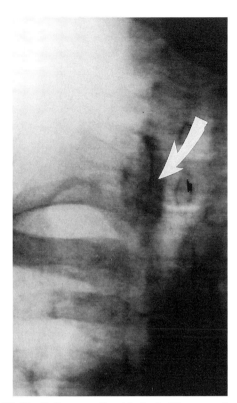

Figure 26–21. Stellate ganglion blockade. Fluoroscopic guidance was used to place a 25-gauge needle along the lateral margin of the C7 vertebra and junction with the transverse process. Iodine contrast medium was injected *(arrow)* and revealed no evidence of intravascular contrast accumulation. Next, 8 mL of 0.25% bupivacaine was injected slowly.

- Paralysis of an adjacent phrenic nerve or a recurrent laryngeal nerve (which may lead to hoarseness or even diaphragmatic paralysis)
- Pneumothorax
- Hypotension with brachycardia (accelerator nerves through the heart also pass through the stellate ganglion)

Relative contraindications include:

- Recent myocardial infarction, because the patient may not be able to elevate the heart rate in cases of stress due to blockage of the accelerator nerves to the heart
- Coagulopathy
- Contralateral pneumothorax
- Glaucoma

Celiac Ganglion Block

Celiac sympathetic plexus blockades can be extremely helpful when the patient has deep visceral pain, as commonly occurs from terminal pancreatic cancer, chronic pancreatitis, or visceral arterial insufficiency. The operator places a thin needle from either a posterior or an anterior approach into the celiac, which is located just anterior to the aorta and surrounding the celiac artery.[55] CT guidance is often preferred, although ultrasound guidance with an anterior approach through the liver has been favored by some operators.[26]

For a posterior approach with CT guidance, the operator starts by locating the celiac artery by scanning it at approximately the T12 level. A needle is directed from a posterior paraspinous location through the crura of the diaphragms in order to pass the needle anterior to the aorta at the level of the celiac artery (Fig. 26–22). The operator may need to pass a needle directly through the aorta to reach the target zone. Iodine contrast medium is injected to confirm location and the absence of intravascular communication. Temporary blockade is achieved when the operator injects bupivacaine; for permanent ablation, neurolysis can be obtained by an injection of absolute alcohol or 6% phenol.

Successful celiac blockade is usually accompanied by hypotension because blood tends to pool in the visceral circulation. This is usually treated effectively with additional intravenous fluids.

Relative contraindications to celiac ganglion blockade include bowel obstruction (because there may be an increase in motility resulting from obliteration of sympathetic input) and coagulopathy.

Figure 26–22. Celiac sympathetic plexus blockade from a posterior approach with CT guidance. Needles have been placed just posterior to the crura of the diaphragms at the T12 level. The needles are placed very close to the T12 vertebra and are directed in such a manner that the tips of the needles pass just anterior to the aorta. The celiac plexus is located at either side of the celiac artery. Iodine contrast medium confirms needle tip locations before the injection of absolute alcohol for celiac plexus ablation in a patient with severe upper abdominal pain from terminal pancreatic malignancy.

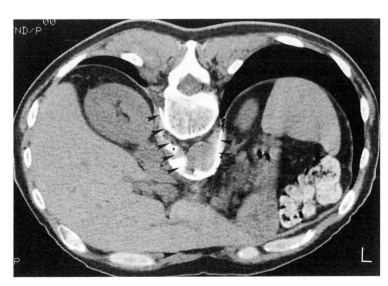

Lumbar Sympathetic Block

Blockade of the lumbar sympathetic plexus may be helpful in cases of lower extremity reflex sympathetic dystrophy, ischemia from chronic arterial emboli or Raynaud's phenomenon, phantom limb pain resulting from amputation, frostbite of the lower extremities, and hyperhidrosis of the lower extremities. The lumbar sympathetic plexus extends from approximately L5 to L2. Blockade is most effectively achieved when the operator directs a needle under either fluoroscopic or CT guidance to the anterior-lateral aspect of the L2 vertebra.[20] A posterior-anterior approach slightly off midline is usually taken.

Injection of iodine contrast medium confirms the absence of intravascular communication in either the aorta or inferior vena cava and that the needle is positioned retroperitoneally (Fig. 26–23). Temporary relief can be obtained by injection of about 10 mL of 0.5% bupivacaine on a weekly basis during a period of up to 6 to 8 weeks to break visceral somatic reflex pain cycles.

Complications may include inadvertent injections, neuralgia to the genital femoral nerve, urethral injury, hypotension, impotence, and bleeding.

Impar Ganglion Block

Blockade of the impar ganglion may be helpful when the patient has deep lower pelvic pain, pain from the perineum, or presacral pain. The operator places a thin, 22-gauge needle from a starting point between the sacrum and coccyx through the sacral coccygeal ligament and then directs it superiorly and posteriorly to the anterior surface

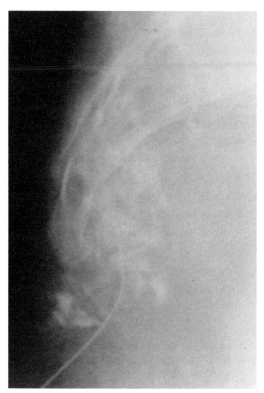

Figure 26–24. Fluoroscopic guidance of a double-curved needle in which the tip is placed just anterior to the sacrum. Iodine contrast medium reveals good dispersion without filling of the rectum. Absolute alcohol was injected for ablation of the impar ganglion in a patient with severe perineal pain from a malignancy.

of the sacrum. Iodine contrast medium is injected to ensure that the rectum has not been violated (Fig. 26–24).

For temporary pain relief, a long-acting anesthetic agent such as bupivacaine can be injected. For more permanent pain relief, absolute alcohol or 6% phenol can be injected, preferably with the patient under local anesthesia.

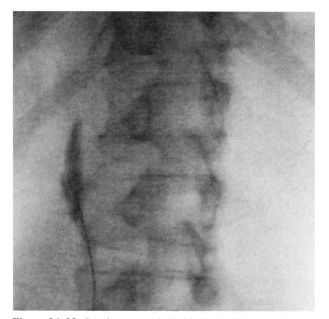

Figure 26–23. Lumbar sympathetic blockade. Fluoroscopic guidance of a 22-gauge needle from a slightly posterior-lateral approach to the anterior-lateral aspect of the L2 vertebra. Contrast medium is injected, showing retroperitoneal dispersion and the lack of intravascular communication. Then 10 mL of 0.25% bupivacaine was injected at weekly intervals for 6 weeks to ameliorate the patient's pain from reflex sympathetic dystrophy.

Vertebroplasty and Balloon Kyphoplasty: Novel Treatments of Painful Osteoporotic and Other Vertebral Compression Fractures

In the United States, there are more than 35 million cases of osteoporosis, of which 1.5 million result in fragility fractures. Seven hundred thousand of these fragility fractures affect the spine, and 200,000 of these fragility fractures of the spine are refractory to nonoperative care, resulting in frustratingly continued debilitating pain.[46, 56]

The primary cause of osteoporosis is related to aging, and this is becoming more problematic as people continue to live longer. However, secondary causes of osteoporosis may also lead to fragility fractures of the spine and include steroids, alcoholism, low calcium intake, hormonal imbalances, and metabolic problems, including malabsorption of calcium through the gastrointestinal tract and renal disease.

Conventional medical management consists primarily of bed rest, narcotics, and braces. Pain from a vertebral compression fracture may take more than 1 year to resolve with this treatment. Surgical management may involve anterior and posterior approaches with instrumentation, for which outcomes are typically poor because the bone is inherently weak. This may lead to collapse and even neurologic deficits.

Vertebroplasty

Background

The technique of vertebroplasty was begun in the mid-1980s by a French neuroradiologist, Dr. Herve Deramond, who performed this procedure to treat a painful hemangioma of the cervical spine in a desperate patient.[19] This procedure was based on the principle of treating benign tumors of bone in other parts of the body by injection of polymethylmethacrylate (bone cement). For this painful hemangioma, Deramond injected bone cement and completely ameliorated the patient's pain. He subsequently used the vertebroplasty technique to treat painful metastatic vertebral compression fractures with excellent results.

Vertebroplasty has been used to treat painful osteoporotic compression fractures with excellent results. The first vertebroplasties performed in the United States occurred in the mid-1990s.[21, 25] In 1998, a modification of the vertebroplasty technique *(balloon kyphoplasty)* was designed to reestablish vertebral body height with the use of an inflatable balloon before fixation of the vertebra through the injection of bone cement.

In a review of the literature from France and the United States, more than 336 patients have received this treatment, and 90% of these patients experienced a dramatic reduction in or disappearance of pain, usually within 48 hours.[10, 12, 21, 25, 35, 40] Average follow-ups were 1 to 3 years, but some have been for as long as 10 years. These patients continue to be free of their original fracture pain.

Complications rates have ranged from 1% to 6% and have included radiculopathies, rib fractures, bleeding, pulmonary embolus, and canal compromise.

Indications

In the United States, most vertebroplasties and balloon kyphoplasties are performed for osteoporotic vertebral compression fractures. However, vertebroplasty can also be performed for destructive osteolytic metastases, particularly when the patient is not a candidate for chemotherapy and radiation therapy (Box 26–1). Most vertebral hemangiomas

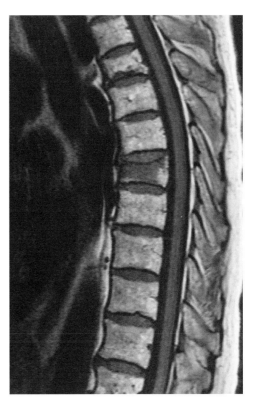

Figure 26–25. T1-weighted MR image demonstrating edema of a painful compression fracture of T7.

are asymptomatic, but for the few that cause considerable pain, vertebroplasty may be an effective treatment.

Technique

The selection of patients for vertebroplasty or balloon kyphoplasty should be based on correlation of findings on careful physical history and physical examination, plain films, MRI, and/or bone scanning (Fig. 26–25). We perform our physical examinations with fluoroscopy in an effort to correlate the focus of pain found on percussion directly over the spinous processes (Fig. 26–26). Vertebroplasty involves the placement of a large-bore (11- or 13-gauge) needle, with the tip positioned in the anterior third of the vertebral body. Percutaneous entry is used under multidirectional fluoroscopy or combined portable fluoroscopy and CT guidance.[38] A transpedicular approach is usually taken (Fig. 26–27), but a single posterior-lateral approach can be taken on the lower lumbar vertebrae.

For the smaller upper thoracic vertebrae, a costovertebral approach can be used if the pedicles are too small. Conscious sedation and a local anesthetic agent are appropriate for most patients.

Injection of the vertebra with iodine contrast medium (see Fig. 26–27C) can provide a vertebral venogram and a means of predicting unwanted runoff of the bone cement into the epidural veins or into the inferior vena cava. If exuberant filling of either epidural veins or the inferior vena cava is seen during contrast injection, unwanted embolization of bone cement to the lungs or the epidural veins can be avoided by injecting bone cement after it reaches a very doughy, viscous state.

Box 26–1. Indications for Vertebroplasty

- Osteoporotic painful vertebral compression fractures
- Compression fractures of the vertebra due to metastatic disease
- Multiple myeloma
- Painful vertebral hemangioma

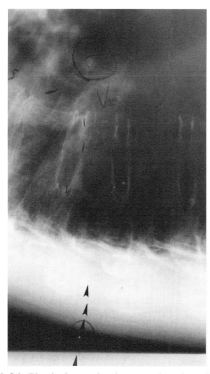

Figure 26–26. Physical examination reveals point of tenderness by percussion, which was demarcated by a lead shot marker *(arrowheads)*. This confirms that the patient's tenderness is emanating from the T7 compression fracture and correlates well with the MRI findings of marrow edema (see Fig. 26–25).

Because of the risk of infection, most operators administer prophylactic antibiotics either in the form of a broad-spectrum antibiotic such as cefazolin (Ancef) administered (2 g) intravenously or by mixing tobramycin powder (1.2 g) into the bone cement.[10, 25]

To avoid unwanted embolization of the bone cement to either the epidural veins or the inferior vena cava and lungs, optimal visualization of the bone cement during the time of injection is extremely important. Therefore, maximum opacification of the bone cement is desired and is usually obtained by mixing in 6 g of sterile USP barium.

For vertebroplasty, filling of at least the anterior two thirds of the vertebra is desired. This is done under high pressure via 1-mL Luer-Lok syringes or a high-pressure injection device (Parallax Technology). The patient should not be moved until the remaining sample of bone cement in the mixing bowl has adequately hardened (usually 20 to 30 minutes).

Generally, most patients can be treated on an outpatient basis if they are carefully observed in a recovery area for 4 to 6 hours after the procedure.

Technique Notes

The patient should be left in the prone position until the sample methacrylate in the mixing bowl is completely hardened (20 to 30 minutes). The patient is then taken to the recovery area for 4 to 6 hours, after which discharge occurs. Follow-up patient visits are made within 24 hours, at 1 week, at 4 weeks, and then at 4-month intervals or as necessary (Box 26–2).

Box 26–2. Vertebroplasty Procedure

- *Informed consent*
- *Sterile set-up*
- *Needle placement*

For placement of large-bore needles under multidirectional fluoroscopic or combined CT portable fluoroscopic technique, the choice of entry depends upon size and configuration of the vertebra. Transpedicular approaches are most common. In the lumbar region, the orientation of the pedicle in relation to the vertebra is relatively horizontal; in the thoracic region, there is a posterior-anterior downward orientation of the pedicles relative to the vertebra. This means that in the thoracic area the operator should begin somewhat higher than normally anticipated. If the pedicles are too small in the upper thoracic region, a costovertebral approach can be used.

- *Vertebral venography*

Nonionic, intrathecally compatible iodine contrast medium is used. (If the patient is allergic to iodine contrast medium, gadolinium can be used.) Usually, the injection of 3 to 4 mL of contrast medium is adequate. If the contrast medium does not wash out of the vertebra before bone cement injection, injection of a small amount of saline into the vertebra usually eliminates any residual opacity.

- If there is overly exuberant flow of contrast medium into the inferior vena cava or into the epidural veins, the bone cement should be allowed to reach a highly viscous, doughy state before it is injected.
- *Mixing the bone cement*

There are various brands. Some provide more of a doughy consistency (Zimmer). Refrigeration of the bone cement overnight increases the working time. For opacification, 6 g of USP sterile barium per level is excellent.

We usually mix the bone cement and barium for about 1 minute and load the methacrylate into 1-mL syringes. We do not inject the bone cement until it becomes somewhat doughy in consistency (~3 to 4 minutes). The 1-mL syringes provide a high-pressure injection.

- *Injection of bone cement into the vertebra*

Injection is administered under direct fluoroscopic visualization, with the needles placed in the anterior third of the vertebra. The needle is initially filled, and the methacrylate is then injected slowly and progressively in a retrograde manner to fill the more posterior portions of the vertebra. Usually, injection of approximately 2 to 3 mL of bone cement on a side is adequate. If the methacrylate clogs in the needle, the stylet of the needle can be reinserted to push the methacrylate out from the needle tip and to clear the needle for further injection of bone cement.

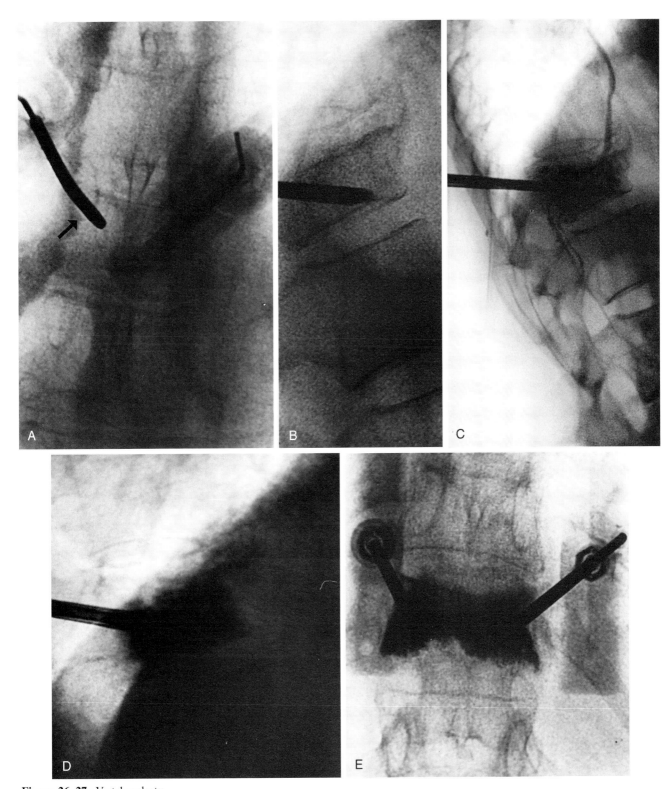

Figure 26–27. Vertebroplasty.

A, At the T7 vertebra, 11-gauge needles have been directed through the T7 pedicles *(arrow).* In the thoracic region, the pedicles run posterior-anterior in a slightly superior-inferior direction, and thus the needle passage should be made to accommodate this configuration.

B, Lateral view demonstrating needle placement via a transpedicular approach. The needles have been extended to the anterior margins of the vertebra.

C, Vertebral venography showing runoff to the inferior vena cava. Caution should be exercised during injection of bone cement (polymethylmethacrylate). If the cement is too "runny," it may embolize to the lungs.

D and *E,* Final distribution of bone cement throughout the T7 vertebra. The patient's back pain disappeared within 1 hour of the procedure.

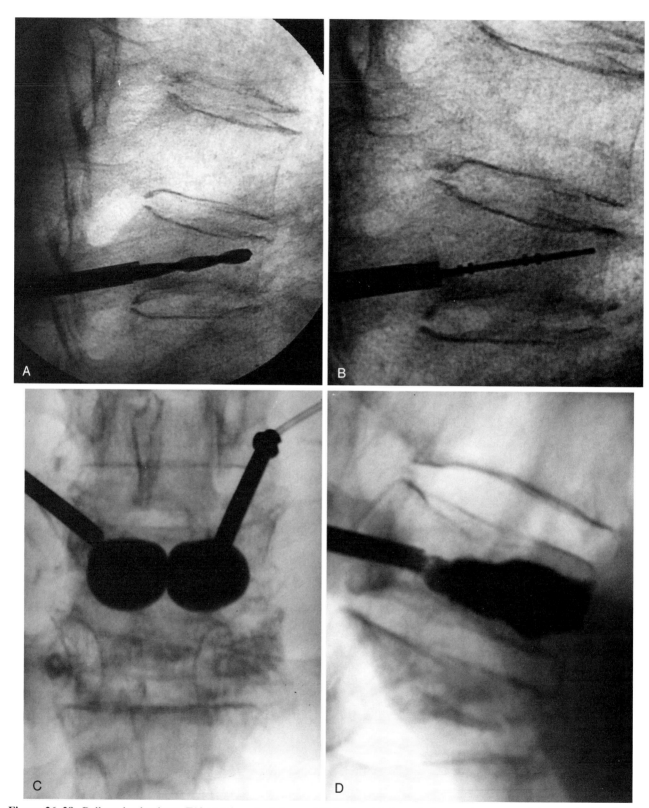

Figure 26–28. Balloon kyphoplasty, T12 vertebra. *A,* A 3-mm drill is directed through the anterior extent of the vertebral body after initial placement of 11-gauge needles and subsequent placement of a working cannula. *B,* Insertion of the inflatable balloon tamp before inflation. *C,* Inflation of the inflatable balloon tamp, anteroposterior view. *D,* Application of bone cement after height restoration. Note the rectangular, rather than previously wedge-shaped, configuration of the vertebral body.

Balloon Kyphoplasty

Although vertebroplasty is effective in ameliorating the pain of a vertebral compression fracture, it usually leaves a deformity of the vertebra (*kyphosis*). Prospective and retrospective studies have demonstrated decreased longevity of people with kyphotic vertebral compression fractures versus those without the fractures.[29] In addition, people with kyphosis who have underlying chronic obstructive lung disease continue to have exacerbating problems with their breathing as a result of decreased lung capacity.[47]

Patients with severe kyphotic curvatures often complain of gastrointestinal problems of bloating and the feeling of partial bowel obstruction along with diminished appetite because the ribs and sternum press on the lower abdomen. Patients who have a severe kyphosis have a center of gravity that has shifted anteriorly, and they may move about in an unbalanced manner.[9, 58] This may result in an increased risk of falls because of their incorrect balance position.

Balloon kyphoplasty is an attempt to reduce the unwanted effects of a kyphosis before the stability of the fracture is restored and the pain is removed. It is performed in a manner similar to that of vertebroplasty, but it also incorporates the addition of an inflatable bone tamp, which can help to reestablish vertebral body height before fixation with bone cement (Fig. 26–28). An added advantage of the use of the inflatable bone tamp may be that it creates a cavity within the fractured vertebra for which the injection of bone cement can be performed under low pressure, reducing the chances of unwanted leakage of methacrylate into adjacent venous or other structures (Box 26–3).

Box 26–3. Balloon Kyphoplasty Procedure

- *Informed consent*
- *Sterile set-up*
- *Percutaneous access to the vertebra similar to vertebroplasty with large-bore needles*
- *Insertion of guide pin through the large-bore needle*

   Remove the large-bore needle. Insert the stiffening obturator over the guide pin. Place the working cannula over the guide pin and obturator with the tip of the cannula along the posterior margin of the vertebral body.

   Remove the guide pin and obturator. Place a 3-mL drill through the working cannula, and through hand rotation advance the drill to the anterior third of the vertebra (see Fig. 26–28A). This creates a cavity for insertion of the inflatable bone tamp.

   Remove the drill. Insert the bone tamp, and inflate under direct visualization with specified pressures. Maximum expansion of the bone tamp occurs when pressure dropoffs cease, the edge of the bone tamp reaches one of the end plates, or the bone tamp reaches its maximum volume.

- *Deflation and removal of bone tamp*

   Mix the cement, as for vertebroplasty, with opacifying agents. Place bone cement in filler tube, and inject the same amount of bone cement to match the volume of the maximum balloon inflation of the bone tamp.

Results

Analysis of the first 24 kyphoplasties performed at the University of California, San Diego, revealed average vertebral body height restorations of 52% at the anterior vertebral body, 66% at the midvertebral body, and 53% at the posterior vertebral body. All patients in this group experienced dramatic pain relief, usually within hours of the procedure. There were no complications in this group.

At the time of the writing of this chapter, there are about a dozen centers at which kyphoplasties are performed. According to the Kyphon Corporation, 462 fractures have been treated in 291 procedures in 261 patients throughout these centers. Pain relief has been obtained in 90% of the cases, as confirmed by return to active daily living questionnaires. There have been no failures. The longest follow-up is 18 months. The procedure is well tolerated, and patients who require subsequent procedures look forward to undergoing the kyphoplasty.

The complication rate has been less than 2% (similar to that of vertebroplasty). No complication has been balloon-related.

Clinical trials for kyphoplasty are starting, with one randomized study comparing kyphoplasty with medical therapy. Other studies to evaluate height restoration, improved respiratory function, and improved quality of life are expected to follow.

Summary

Vertebroplasty is a procedure that can help stabilize a painful vertebral compression fracture and eradicate the pain. The balloon kyphoplasty is a modification of the vertebroplasty that provides an opportunity to restore vertebral body height before stabilization and pain ablation.

The vertebroplasty, kyphoplasty, and a variety of other image-guided spine interventions provide the radiologist with an opportunity to do much more than simply image. Using the knowledge of imaging anatomy, a radiologist can effectively intervene as both a diagnosing and a treating physician. To do so, however, requires that the radiologist also be willing to examine the patient, counsel the patient, and monitor the patient over time.

References

1. Adam G, Bucker A, Nolte-Ernsting C, et al: Interventional MR imaging: Percutaneous abdominal and skeletal biopsies and drainages of the abdomen. Eur Radiol 9:1471–1478, 1999.
2. Anzai Y, Lufkin R, DeSalles A, et al: Preliminary experience with MR-guided thermal ablation of brain tumors. AJNR Am J Neuroradiol 16:39–48; discussion, 49–52, 1995.
3. Aprill C, Dwyer A, Bogduk N: Cervical zygoapophyseal joint pain patterns: II. A clinical evaluation. Spine 15:458–461, 1990.
4. Babu NV, Titus VT, Chittaranjan S, et al: Computed tomographically guided biopsy of the spine. Spine 19:2436–2442, 1994.
5. Benzon H: Epidural steroid injections. Pain Digest 1:271–280, 1992.
6. Bogduk N, Narsland A: The cervical zygoapophyseal joint as a source of neck pain. Spine 13:610–617, 1988.
7. Castro DJ, Lufkin RB, Saxton RE, et al: Metastatic head and neck malignancy treated using MRI guided interstitial laser phototherapy: An initial case report. Laryngoscope 102:26–32, 1992.
8. Colhoun E, McCall IW, Williams L, et al: Provocation discography as a guide to planning operations of the spine. J Bone Joint Surg Br 70:267–271, 1988.
9. Cortet B, Houvenagel E, Puisisux F, et al: Spinal curvatures and quality of life in women with vertebral fractures secondary to osteoporosis. Spine 24:1921–1925, 1999.

10. Cotton A, Boutry N, Cortet B, et al: Vertebroplasty: State of the art. Radiographics 18:311–320, 1998.
11. Daly B, Templeton PA: Real-time CT fluoroscopy: Evolution of an interventional tool. Radiology 211:309–315, 1999.
12. Do H, Jensen M, Mathis J: Percutaneous vertebroplasty in treatment of patients with vertebral osteonecrosis (Kummel's disease). Article 2. Neurosurg Forum 7:1999.
13. Dreyfus P: Low back pain and the zygoapophyseal joints. Arch Phys Med Rehabil 77:290–300, 1996.
14. El-Khoury G, Renfrew D: Percutaneous procedures for the diagnosis and treatment of lower back pain: Diskography, facet joint injection, and epidural injection. AJR Am J Radiol 157:685–691, 1991.
15. Erickson SJ, Hogan QH: CT-guided injection of stellate ganglion: Description of technique and efficacy of sympathetic blockage. Radiology 188:707–709, 1993.
16. Frahm C, Gehl HB, Melchert UH, et al: Visualization of magnetic resonance-compatible needles at 1.5 and 0.2 Tesla. Cardiovasc Intervent Radiol 19:335–340, 1996.
17. Fraser RD, Osti OL, Vernon-Roberts B: Discitis after discography. J Bone Joint Surg Br 69:31–35, 1987.
18. Fukui S, Ohseto K, Shiotani M, et al: Referred pain distribution of the cervical zygoapophyseal joints and cervical dorsal rami. Pain 68: 79–83, 1996.
19. Gaibert P, Deramond H, Rosat P, Le Gars D: Preliminary note on the treatment of vertebral hemangioma by percutaneous acrylic vertebroplasty. Neurochirurgie 33:166–168, 1987.
20. Gangi A, Dietemann J, Schultz A, et al: Interventional radiologic procedures with CT guidance for cancer pain management. Radiographics 16:1289–1304, 1996.
21. Ganj A, Kastler BA, Dietemann JL: Percutaneous vertebroplasty guided by a combination of CT and fluoroscopy. AJNR Am J Neuroradiol 15:83–86, 1994.
22. Guyer RD, Ohnmeiss DD: Contemporary concepts in spine care lumbar discography. Spine 20:2048–2059, 1995.
23. Hinks RS, Bronskill MJ, Kucharczyk W, et al: MR systems for image-guided therapy. J Magn Reson Imaging 8:19–25, 1998.
24. Jager L, Muller-Lisse GU, Gutmann R, et al: Initial results with MRI-controlled laser-induced interstitial thermotherapy of head and neck tumors. Radiologe 36:236–244, 1996.
25. Jensen M, Evans A, Mathis JM, et al: Percutaneous polymethyl methacrylate vertebroplasty in the treatment of osteoporotic vertebral body compression fractures: Technical aspects. AJNR Am J Neuroradiol 18:1897–1904, 1997.
26. Jimenez A, Martinez-Nogura A, et al: Percutaneous neurolysis of celiac plexus via anterior approach with sonographic guidance. AJR Am J Radiol 161:1061–1063, 1993.
27. Johnson B, Schellhas K, Pollei SR: Epidurography and therapeutic epidural injections: Technical considerations and experience with 5334 cases. AJNR Am J Neuroradiol 20:697–705, 1999.
28. Jolesz FA, Blumenfeld SM: Interventional use of magnetic resonance imaging. Magn Reson Q 10:85, 1994.
29. Kado D, Browner W, Palerno L, et al: Vertebral fractures and mortality in older women: A prospective study. Arch Intern Med 159: 1215–1220, 1999.
30. Kahn T, Bettag M, Ulrich F, et al: MRI-guided laser-induced interstitial thermotherapy of cerebral neoplasms. J Comput Assist Tomogr 18:519–532, 1994.
31. Kahn T, Harth T, Bettag M, et al: Preliminary experience with the application of gadolinium-DTPA before MR imaging-guided laser-induced interstitial thermotherapy of brain tumors. J Magn Reson Imaging 7:226–229, 1997.
32. Katada K, Kato R, Anno H, et al: Guidance with real-time CT fluoroscopy. Nippon Acta Radiol 200:851–856, 1994.
33. Kato R, Katada K, Anno H, et al: Radiation dosimetry at CT fluoroscopy: Physicians hand dose and development of needle holders. Radiology 201:576–578, 1996.
34. Knauth M, Wirtz CR, Tronnier VM, et al: Intraoperative MR imaging increases the extent of tumor resection in patients with high-grade gliomas. AJNR Am J Neuroradiol 20:1642–1646, 1999.
35. Lemley T, Barr M, et al: Percutaneous vertebroplasty: A new technique for treatment of benign and malignant vertebral body compression fractures. Surg Physician Assist 3:24–27, 1997.
36. Lewin JS: Interventional MR imaging: Concepts, systems, and application in neuroradiology. AJNR Am J Neuroradiol 20:735–748, 1999.
37. Lewin JS, Duerck JL, Jain JR, et al: Needle localization in MR-guided biopsy and aspiration: Effect of field strength, sequence design, and magnetic field orientation. AJR Am J Radiol 166:1337–1345, 1996.
38. Lewin JS, Petersilge CA, Hatem SF, et al: Interactive MR imaging-guided biopsy and aspiration with a modified clinical C-arm system. AJR Am J Radiol 170:1593–1601, 1998.
39. Martin AJ, Hall WA, Liu H, et al: Brain tumor resection: Intraoperative monitoring with high-field-strength MR imaging: Initial results. Radiology 215:221–228, 2000.
40. Mathis J, Petric M, Naff N: Percutaneous vertebroplasty treatment of steroid induced osteoporotic compression fractures. Arthritis Rheum 4:171–175, 1998.
41. Mooney V, Robertson J: Facet joint syndrome. Clin Orthop 115: 149–156, 1976.
42. Mueller PR, Stark DD, Simeone JF, et al: MR-guided aspiration biopsy: Needle design and clinical trials. Radiology 161:605–609, 1986.
43. Neuerburg JM: MR-guided bone biopsy. In Lufkin RB (ed): Interventional MRI. St. Louis, Mosby, 1999, pp 381–386.
44. Parker SH, Stavros AT, Dennis MA: Needle biopsy techniques. Radiol Clin North Am 33:1171, 1995.
45. Renfrew DL, Moore TE, Kathol MH, et al: Correct placement of epidural steroid injections: Fluoroscopic guidance and contrast administration. AJNR Am J Neuroradiol 12:1003–1007, 1991.
46. Riggs BL, Melton LJ: The worldwide problem of osteoporosis: Insights afforded by epidemiology. Bone 17:5055–5115, 1995.
47. Schlaich C, Minnie H, et al: Reduced pulmonary function in patients with spinal osteoporotic fractures. Osteoporosis Int 8:261–267, 1998.
48. Schwartz RB, Hsu L, Wong TZ, et al: Intraoperative MR imaging guidance for intracranial surgery: Experience with the first 200 cases. Radiology 211:477–488, 1999.
49. Schellhas KP, Garvey TA, Johnson BA, et al: Cervical diskography: Analysis of provoked responses at C2-C3, C3-C4, and C4-C5. AJNR Am J Neuroradiol 21:269–275, 2000.
50. Schellhas KP, Smith MD, Gundry CR, et al: Cervical discogenic pain prospective correlation of magnetic resonance imaging and discography in asymptomatic subjects and pain sufferers. Spine 21:300–312, 1996.
51. Smits HFM, Bos C, van der Weide R, et al: Interventional MR: Vascular applications. Eur Radiol 9:1488–1495, 1999.
52. Strother CM, Unal O, Frayne R, et al: Endovascular treatment of experimental canine aneurysms: Feasibility with MR imaging guidance. Radiology 215:516–519, 2000.
53. Vogl TJ, Mack MG, Muller PK, et al: Interventional MR: Interstitial therapy. Eur Radiol 9:1479–1487, 1999.
54. Vogl TJ, Mack MG, Muller P, et al: Recurrent nasopharyngeal tumors: Preliminary clinical results with interventional MR imaging–controlled laser-induced thermotherapy. Radiology 196:725–33, 1995.
55. Waldman SD, Winnie AP: Interventional Pain Management. Philadelphia, WB Saunders, 1996, pp 269–271.
56. Wasnich U: Vertebral fracture epidemiology. Bone 18:1795–1835, 1996.
57. Wesbey G, Edelman RR, Harris R: Artifacts in MR-imaging: Description, causes, and solutions. In Edelman RR, Hesselink JR (eds): Clinical Magnetic Resonance Imaging. Philadelphia, WB Saunders, 1990, pp 74–80.
58. White A, Panjabi M: Clinical Biomechanics of the Spine, 2nd ed. Philadelphia, JB Lippincott, 1990, pp 155–163.
59. Wong W. Common spine interventions: Percutaneous biopsies. Proc Am Soc Neuroradiol 36:107–109, 1998.
60. Wong W, Kerber C, et al: Unusual nonpyogenic disk inflammation following discography: A report of 3 cases. Paper presented at 28th Annual Meeting of Western Neuroradiological Society, Syllabus 84, 1996.
61. Zenaro H, Douset V, Viaud B, et al: Periganglionic foraminal injections performed under CT control. AJNR Am J Neuroradiol 19: 349–352, 1998.

Part
V

Imaging of the Chest

Edited by
John R. Haaga

27

Non-neoplastic Parenchymal Lung Disease

Janet E. Kuhlman

Evaluation of non-neoplastic parenchymal lung disease begins with careful examination of the posteroanterior (PA) and lateral chest films, together an invaluable source of information about the nature and extent of pulmonary diseases. Increasingly, however, conventional computed tomography (CT) and more advanced imaging techniques, such as high-resolution CT (HRCT, or thin-section CT), spiral and multidetector CT, ultrafast electron beam CT, and magnetic resonance imaging (MRI), have become integral parts of the evaluation process, serving as important adjuncts to the plain film for the purposes of detection, diagnosis, and characterization of parenchymal lung disease.

CT as an imaging modality has distinct advantages over conventional radiography in displaying the anatomy and pathology of the lung. The cross-sectional format of CT permits visual examination of the lung that is unencumbered by superimposed structures, such as the chest wall, heart, and pulmonary vessels. With the advent of HRCT, delineation of the lung parenchyma down to the level of the secondary pulmonary lobule, the basic building block of the lung, is possible. This additional information provided by HRCT allows a more detailed analysis of pathologic processes affecting the lung. Increasingly, HRCT is being used as the technique of choice to evaluate diffuse and focal lung diseases.[142, 146, 168, 229, 230]

Spiral (or helical) CT takes advantage of new slip-ring technology and has revolutionized the way we look at the lung.[40, 84, 112, 171, 200, 223] A continuously rotating detector combined with continuous table feed allows rapid data acquisition through the chest during a single breath-hold.[84] Spiral CT results in a gapless, volumetric acquisition that eliminates problems of slice misregistration caused by variations in the depth of inspiration.[40, 84, 112, 171, 200, 223] The resulting data set is more accurate, more reproducible from one study to the next, and more quickly acquired. In the lung, spiral CT facilitates the process of evaluating small pulmonary nodules and allows the generation of three-dimensional (3D) images of the lung that are not degraded by respiratory motion (Fig. 27–1).[40, 84, 112, 171, 200, 223] The faster acquisition times ensure evaluation of the lung during maximum vascular enhancement and may decrease the total volume of intravenous (IV) contrast material required for adequate enhancement.

Multidetector CT takes the advantages of spiral CT several steps further by combining rows of detectors and by interleaving or interspacing multiple helical data sets that are simultaneously acquired. Multidetector scanners can cover greater distances, at faster speeds, with thinner slice thicknesses.

Ultrafast electron beam CT replaces the rotating detector gantry of conventional CT scanners with a deflectable electron beam and generates CT images in 0.1 to 0.05 second. Electron beam CT adds another dimension of speed to the data acquisition process and is fast enough to stop cardiac motion on displayed images, allowing detailed depiction of coronary artery calcifications. It has also been used to capture dynamic processes, such as air trapping resulting from small airway disease or changes in the caliber of the trachea and bronchi during various phases of the respiratory cycle.[213]

Although MRI has a clear advantage over other imaging modalities in evaluating cardiac and vascular disorders of the chest, its role in the evaluation of parenchymal lung disease has been limited. Obstacles to lung imaging include respiratory motion and magnetic susceptibility effects caused by air-tissue interfaces. Rapid evolution of MRI technology suggests that some of these problems may be overcome in the near future. Promising areas under current investigation include MRI evaluation of the pulmonary circulation, arteriovenous malformations (AVMs), and other vessel-related disorders of the lung. Assessment of chest wall disease and peridiaphragmatic processes, which do not suffer as much from respiratory or magnetic susceptibility artifacts, already benefits from the multiplanar capabilities of MRI and its improved soft tissue contrast.

Techniques

Several approaches to examining parenchymal lung disease with CT exist, and no one method is optimal for all indications.[142] Many authors advocate the use of standard conventional CT as the initial screening test, followed by a few select HRCT slices through areas of interest. In cases of occult pulmonary disease or a lung process that may affect the lung diffusely, surveying the entire chest at 1-cm intervals using HRCT techniques may be preferable. This multilevel HRCT examination is more likely to detect early or subtle manifestations of lung disease and is more accurate in determining the full extent of lung damage.

Multidetector and spiral CT are ideal for detecting and evaluating small pulmonary nodules and pulmonary emboli and for 3D imaging of the lung.[40, 112, 200] Spiral CT can

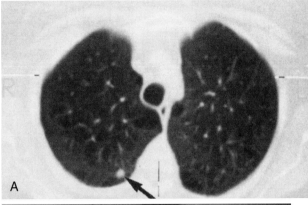

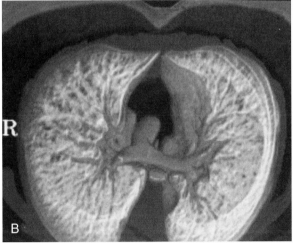

Figure 27–1. Spiral CT facilitates the detection and evaluation of small pulmonary nodules *(arrows)*. A, Axial view. Because the data are acquired in a continuous fashion during a single breath-hold, problems caused by slice misregistration are eliminated. Spiral CT data sets are ideal for generating multiplanar reconstructions, as in *B*, a sagittal reconstruction, and three-dimensional (3D) images of the lung, as in *C*. Nodule and surrounding emphysema are present in the posterior segment of the right upper lobe. *C*, A 3D image of the lung was created by applying volumetric rendering techniques to the spiral CT data set. The lung parenchyma, bronchovascular structures, major airways, and small nodule are displayed three-dimensionally without significant respiratory artifacts or image distortion. (From Kuhlman JE, Ney DR, Fishman EK: Two-dimensional and three-dimensional imaging of the in vivo lung: Combining spiral computed tomography with multiplanar and volumetric rendering techniques. J Digit Imaging 7:42–47, 1994.)

also be combined with high-resolution algorithms and thin-section techniques. Ultrafast CT, or cine-CT, is a prerequisite for evaluating airway physiology in real time, for example, capturing differences in lung attenuation and airway caliber that result from reversible or irreversible airway disease.[213]

High-Resolution CT (Thin-Section CT)

HRCT combines the use of thinly collimated CT slices that are 1 to 1.5 to 2 mm in thickness, with a high-spatial-frequency algorithm that enhances edge detection.[142] On many older CT models, the high-resolution algorithm is a bone reconstruction algorithm. On many newer CT models, a special high-resolution lung algorithm is available. Thin collimation decreases partial volume averaging and improves the ability of CT to demonstrate small pulmonary lesions. High-spatial-frequency algorithms, by decreasing the amount of smoothing of the image data, enhance edge detection and make lung structures look sharper. HRCT technical features increase spatial resolution but also increase the amount of noise visible in the image.

Although not essential, increases in kilovolt peak (kVp) and milliampere (mA) settings may be used to improve signal-to-noise ratio in HRCT images.[142] Field of view should be reduced to cover the lung parenchyma only, thus maximizing the fine detail of the lungs (Fig. 27–2). IV

contrast is not used for high-resolution CT examinations that are limited to evaluating the lung parenchyma.

To optimize an HRCT examination, additional considerations are important.[141, 142, 227, 228] Retrospective targeting of the reconstructed image to a particular area of interest can further enhance depiction of abnormal lung parenchyma (see Fig. 27–2). Confusion caused by crowded pulmonary vessels and dependent lung edema or microatelectasis is minimized if HRCT scans are obtained at suspended end-inspiratory volume. If necessary, prone views can be taken to differentiate focal dependent edema or microatelectasis, commonly seen in the lung bases of normal patients, from early pulmonary fibrosis.

Although the best HRCT results are obtained with breath-holding techniques, this is not always possible in an acutely ill patient with respiratory compromise or in a pediatric patient.[126] Faster scan times, on the order of 1 second or less, are now available on many state-of-the-art scanners and greatly reduce respiratory motion artifacts, allowing for good-quality, high-resolution examinations to be performed even in these patients.

Image processing is also important. HRCT images are viewed at lung window settings. Exact settings vary depending on the scanner make and model, but typical window settings are in the range of 1650 (window width) and −600 (window center). Images of the mediastinum can be reconstructed using a standard soft tissue algorithm and viewed using mediastinal window settings of 410 (window

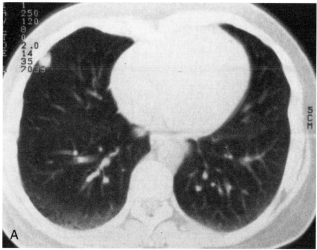
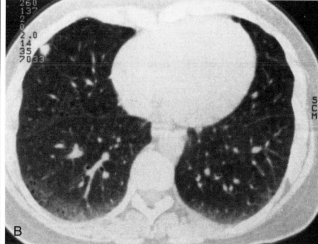
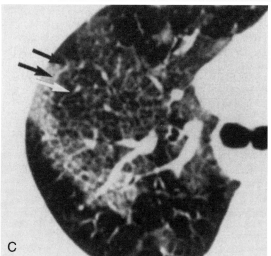

Figure 27–2. Advantages of high-resolution CT. *A* and *B*, Comparison of conventional CT and high-resolution CT techniques in a patient with a right middle lobe nodule. Conventional CT *(A)* with 8-mm slice thickness, 250 mA, 120 kVp. High-resolution CT *(B)* with 2-mm slice thickness, 260 mA, 137 kVp, and edge-enhancing algorithm. Note the increased detail and sharpness of the major fissures, the bronchi, and the tiny cysts within the lungs. The zone of dependent microatelectasis, a normal finding in many patients, is also more prominently visualized on the high-resolution CT scan. *C,* Targeted reconstruction, employing a smaller field of view, can be used with high-resolution CT techniques to optimize the display of fine lung detail, such as thickened interlobular septa *(arrows)* and "ground-glass" infiltrates.

width) and 3 (window center). Additional window settings are adjusted manually at the time of imaging to enhance depiction of subtle "ground-glass" opacities that are best appreciated on wider window settings.

Although HRCT algorithms are excellent for delineating diseases of the lung parenchyma, they are less appropriate for examining abnormalities of the mediastinum or the abdomen. The reconstruction algorithm used in HRCT makes detection of mediastinal adenopathy and focal liver lesions more difficult. High-resolution algorithms also tend to accentuate pleural thickness, an important factor to keep in mind during evaluation of patients with asbestos exposure for pleural disease. For assessment of a small pulmonary nodule for the presence of calcification, a standard lung algorithm should be used because the edge-enhancement properties of many HRCT algorithms make small nodules appear denser than they really are and can falsely simulate calcification.

Spiral or Helical CT

Spiral CT techniques can be easily adapted for evaluation of the lung.[40, 84, 112, 171, 200, 223] Most helical scanners are capable of generating a series of consecutive scans lasting

1 second or less, obtained in a continuous fashion during a single breath-hold maneuver. The operator chooses the thickness of the slice collimation with a range of 1 to 10 mm. Table speed is set to between 1 and 10 mm/second. Pitch (table speed divided by slice thickness) is usually best kept between 1 and 2. The reconstruction algorithm and interval between reconstructed images (the degree of slice overlap) are chosen to suit the clinical problems at hand.

Numerous protocol variations exist. Two examples for lung evaluation are as follows:

1. A survey examination of the chest might use a slice acquisition thickness of 7 mm, a pitch of 1.4, a reconstruction interval of 5 mm, and a lung algorithm for lung images and a standard algorithm for soft tissue images.
2. A focused study with greater detail that will cover a shorter distance might use a slice acquisition thickness of 3 mm, a pitch of 1 to 1.7, and a reconstruction interval of 1 mm employing a high-resolution lung algorithm.

Total acquisition times and recommended mA and kVp vary by manufacturer. Once axial images are reconstructed, the spiral CT data set can be transferred to a free-standing workstation where multiplanar reconstructions and 3D image analysis can be performed (see Fig. 27–1).[112]

Whether or not IV contrast is required for the chest spiral CT examination depends on the clinical question to be answered and the type of disease process anticipated.

Multidetector CT

The possible protocol variations multiply rapidly with the additional capabilities of multidetector scanners. One example of a protocol in use for evaluating pulmonary emboli uses the following multidetector CT parameters:

- Slice thickness, 1.25 mm
- Reconstruction interval, 0.6 mm
- Table speed, 7.5 mm/rotation
- Time per rotation, 0.8 second

IV contrast (150 mL) is injected at 4 mL/second, with a scan delay time of 25 seconds. Scanning begins at the diaphragm and proceeds to the top of the chest. All images are reviewed on an independent workstation using a paging mode, and selected images are also viewed from hard-copy film.

CT Patterns and Signs of Non-neoplastic Lung Disease

As experience with CT accumulates, patterns and signs of non-neoplastic lung disease have emerged. Many of the HRCT patterns and signs are refinements of those first recognized on conventional CT of the lung. In an attempt to arrive at a differential diagnosis for focal or diffuse lung disease, it is helpful first to characterize the parenchymal CT abnormalities into one of three categories[98]:

- Air space disease
- Interstitial disease
- Cystic lung disease

Once the predominant category has been established, the lung disease can be further characterized on the basis of patterns of distribution and by recognizing a few specific CT signs.

Categories of Lung Disease

Air Space Disease

One of the earliest manifestations of focal air space disease on CT scans is the presence of small 4- to 10-mm opacities called *acinar nodules*.[146] These are not true nodules when examined pathologically but, rather, represent clusters of alveoli that are filled with fluid, inflammatory cells, or blood, depending on the disease process. As air space disease becomes more severe and extensive, acinar densities coalesce to form larger opacities and eventually progress to lobular, subsegmental, segmental, lobar, and multilobar involvement (Fig. 27–3). Air-bronchograms on CT scans are hallmarks of air space consolidation, just as they are on conventional chest radiographs (Fig. 27–4).

Interstitial Disease

Features of interstitial disease on conventional CT and HRCT include nodules, reticulation, and thickening of the pulmonary septa (Fig. 27–5).[20, 177, 197, 240] Interfaces that exist between the lung and the pleural surfaces, or between the lung and the bronchovascular bundles, become irregular and shaggy (see Fig. 27–5).[240] HRCT supplements and enhances conventional CT in the detection of early interstitial lung disease by providing greater detail of the smaller, more peripheral lung elements and interlobular septa.

Cystic Lung Disease and Abnormal Air Spaces

Cystic disease of the lung encompasses a wide variety of pathologic processes that are characterized by "holes" or abnormal air-containing spaces within the lung parenchyma.[114] Cystic structures identified on CT scans include blebs, bullae, cavities, pneumatoceles, "honeycombing," (see "Subpleural Distributions" later), dilated bronchi, and dilated terminal airways and alveolar sacs. Lung diseases that produce abnormal air spaces in the lung include cavitating pulmonary infections, vascular-embolic disorders, bronchiectasis, emphysema, pulmonary fibrosis, adult respiratory distress syndrome (ARDS), and unusual disorders such as Langerhans' histiocytosis, lymphangiomyomatosis, and tracheolaryngeal papillomatosis. The mechanisms by which abnormal air spaces are produced include focal ischemic necrosis of the lung, as seen with septic emboli; disruption of elastic-fiber networks, as found in emphysema; and retractile fibrosis with remodeling of the lung architecture, as seen in the honeycomb lung (Fig. 27–6).

Characterization of Lung Disease

Once lung disease has been characterized as air space, interstitial, or cystic in nature, it can be further analyzed as to its pattern and distribution. *Focal* lung disease may demonstrate specific CT signs that aid in narrowing the differential diagnosis. *Diffuse* lung disease may be evenly or unevenly distributed throughout the lung. It may affect primarily the central regions, the subpleural zones, or the tissues surrounding the bronchovascular structures. Different lung diseases tend to exhibit different patterns of distribution, and recognizing the patterns increases diagnostic accuracy and confidence.

CT Signs of Focal Lung Disease

Non-neoplastic Pulmonary Nodules

Etiology

CT evaluation of a known or suspected solitary pulmonary nodule makes up a significant part of any chest CT schedule. According to CT criteria,[80, 90, 204, 205, 216, 217, 217a, 241] at least three benign causes of a solitary pulmonary nodule can be reliably identified:

- Calcified granulomas
- Hamartomas
- Pulmonary AVMs

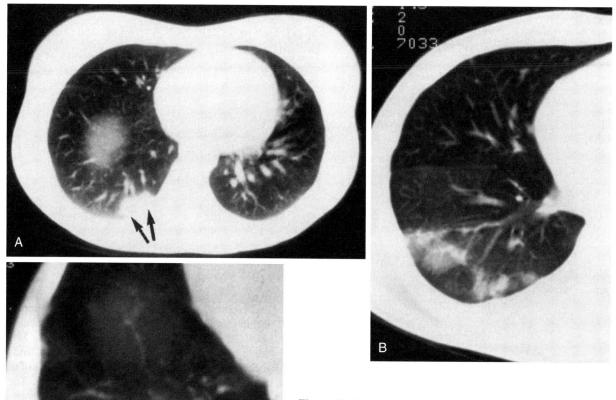

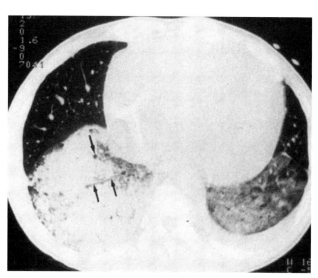

Figure 27–3. CT features of focal air space disease. *A,* A small pulmonary infarct fills the air spaces of one or two secondary pulmonary lobules with hemorrhage, producing a small air space opacity on CT *(arrows). B* and *C,* As the air space disease resulting from the infarction becomes more extensive, smaller lobular opacities coalesce to form larger subsegmental and segmental areas of involvement *(arrowheads). (A* and *C,* From Kuhlman JE: CT of diffuse lung disease. Appl Radiol 20:17–21, 1991.)

Figure 27–4. Multilobar pneumonia. Air-bronchograms are a hallmark of air space disease on CT scans, as they are on plain films. (From Kuhlman JE: CT of diffuse lung disease. Appl Radiol 20:17–21, 1991.)

Granulomas. A well-circumscribed pulmonary nodule measuring 2 cm or less in diameter that demonstrates CT attenuation in the range of calcium on a phantom-calibrated, unenhanced CT scan of the chest is usually a *benign calcified granuloma* (Fig. 27–7).[80, 90, 204, 205, 216, 217, 241] The absolute threshold value in Hounsfield units (HU) for designating calcification varies from one CT scanner and manufacturer to another, but it can be calibrated for any individual scanner using a phantom. When a solitary pulmonary nodule is not obviously calcified on CT scans but appears to be of higher CT density than soft tissue, the nodule's CT attenuation can be compared with a CT reference phantom for more accurate assessment.[80, 90, 216, 217, 240] Nodules demonstrating CT attenuations greater than the CT reference phantom were benign in 90% of cases reported in one series.[216]

In addition to the density of the nodule, the pattern of calcification is also important and must be either homogeneous throughout the nodule, in a pattern of concentric rings, or in a "popcorn" distribution to fit the CT criteria for benign calcification. The one exception is in the setting of metastatic osteogenic sarcoma. Lung metastases from osteogenic sarcoma are typically calcified in a homogeneous pattern. Although lung cancers and other malignan-

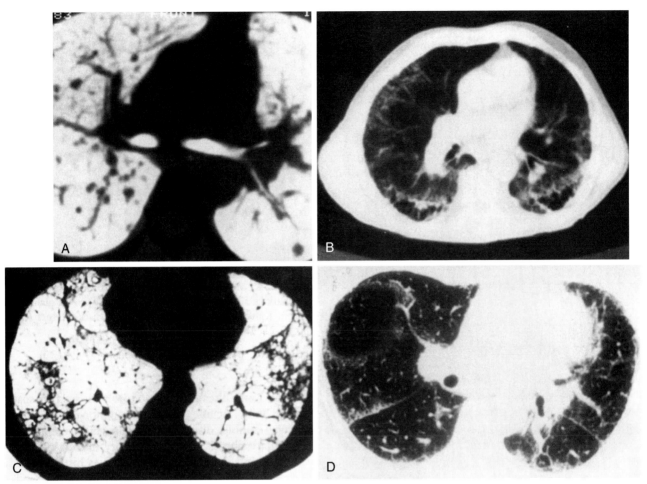

Figure 27–5. CT features of interstitial disease. *A,* Small interstitial nodules in a patient with sarcoidosis. Reticulation *(B)* and thickening of the pulmonary septa *(C)* in two patients with idiopathic pulmonary fibrosis. *D,* Irregular and shaggy interfaces between the lung and the fissures, pleural surfaces, and mediastinum are CT features characteristic of interstitial disease. Idiopathic pulmonary fibrosis. *(A, B,* and *D,* From Kuhlman JE: CT of diffuse lung disease. Appl Radiol 20:17–21, 1991.)

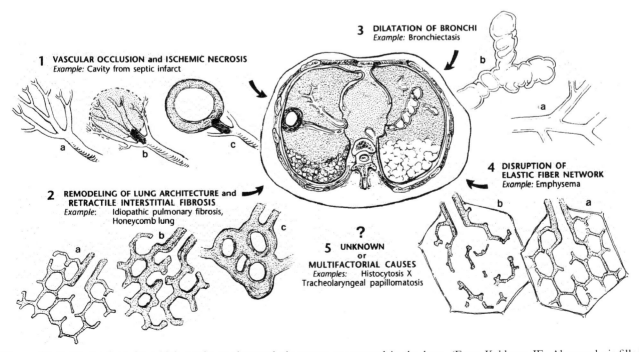

Figure 27–6. Mechanisms by which cystic or abnormal air spaces are created in the lung. (From Kuhlman JE: Abnormal air-filled spaces in the lung. Radiographics 13:47–75, 1993.)

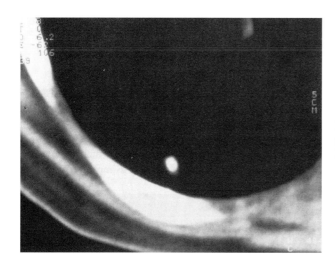

Figure 27–7. Benign calcified granuloma. Nodule is as dense as the ribs on soft tissue window settings and measures greater than 160 Hounsfield units on a calibrated, noncontrast CT scan.

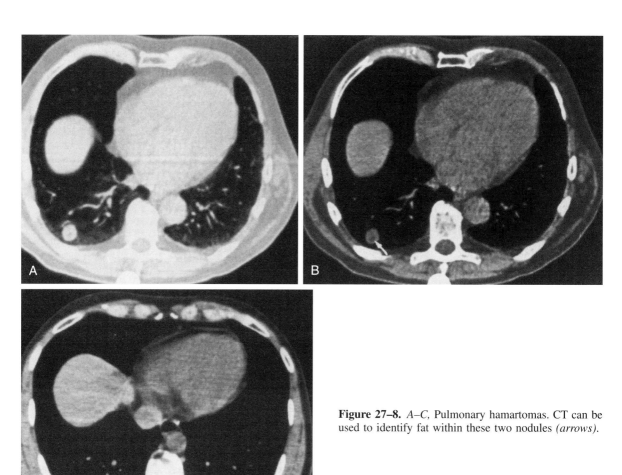

Figure 27–8. *A–C,* Pulmonary hamartomas. CT can be used to identify fat within these two nodules *(arrows).*

cies may contain small areas of calcification, they rarely demonstrate calcification in one of the benign patterns described previously.

Finally, the morphology and edge of the nodule must also be considered. The presence of spiculation or irregularity of the margins of a nodule should greatly raise a concern for malignancy, even in the presence of calcification, because many such lesions are cancerous.[241]

Hamartomas. The pulmonary hamartoma, a benign growth of multiple tissue components, may also be identified on the basis of CT attenuation properties.[205] Hamartomas are composed of a number of tissues, including soft tissue, muscle elements, and fat. About 30% of hamartomas contain enough fat to be detected by CT, and CT identification of fat within a solitary pulmonary nodule is diagnostic of hamartoma (Fig. 27–8). The CT attenuation of fat is in the range of -20 to -160 HU or less and can be reliably measured by a region-of-interest (ROI) cursor.

Hamartomas are typically well-circumscribed, smooth, round, or lobulated nodules; 20% contain calcification, often in a popcorn distribution. When fat is identified within an area of air space consolidation rather than in a nodule on CT scans, this should suggest the diagnosis of *lipoid pneumonia*. Lipoid pneumonia is usually caused by the chronic use of mineral oil nasal drops.

Pulmonary Arteriovenous Malformations. The third cause of a benign solitary pulmonary nodule that can be recognized on CT scans is a pulmonary AVM. An enlarged feeding artery leading to a pulmonary nodule and an enlarged draining vein are characteristic features of a pulmonary AVM (Fig. 27–9). Dynamic CT scanning, performed after a bolus injection of contrast material, can be used to confirm the vascular nature of the lesion by following the enhancement pattern and time-density curves of the lesion, which parallel those of the heart and pulmonary arteries.

Enhancement of Benign and Neoplastic Nodules

After administration of IV contrast material, nodules that are not calcified on CT scans may show some enhance-ment but do not show the degree and rapidity of enhancement seen with AVMs. Malignant nodules tend to enhance more than benign, inactive granulomas, which show very little or no enhancement. Studies by Swenson and others suggest that noncalcified nodules that show contrast enhancement above a certain threshold during the first 3 to 5 minutes after IV contrast injection are more likely to be neoplastic.[217, 217a, 217b, 239a, 242] However, nodules caused by active inflammatory disease, such as active granulomas resulting from fungal infection or tuberculosis (TB), may also show significant contrast enhancement.[242] Additionally, false-negative results have been reported, including a few lung cancers that did not show enhancement above the target threshold value.[242]

By preprogramming a series of short helical or dynamic scans sequentially through a nodule under investigation, one can monitor nodule enhancement during a bolus IV injection of contrast material. The characteristics of malignant nodules are discussed further elsewhere in this text.

Vessel-Related Disorders

A number of vessel-related disorders of the lung produce focal lung disease, including *pulmonary infarcts, septic emboli, hematogenous metastases,* and *pulmonary vasculitis.*[11, 33, 65, 78, 106, 109, 152, 186, 207] All of these disorders may show similar CT features, such as multiple peripheral nodules or wedged-shaped opacities that abut the pleura, that cavitate, or that demonstrate a feeding vessel.

The *feeding vessel sign* consists of a nodule or focal opacity that demonstrates a pulmonary vessel leading to it. The presence of a feeding vessel indicates either that the lesion has a hematogenous origin or that the disease process occurs in close proximity to small pulmonary vessels. The feeding vessel sign can be used to characterize lung disease that results from a disseminated neoplastic or infectious process that seeds the lung via the bloodstream, such as hematogenous metastases, septic emboli, and multiple pulmonary infarcts (Figs. 27–10 and 27–11).[33, 65, 78, 106, 142, 150, 186, 207] This sign is also visible when vasculitis affects

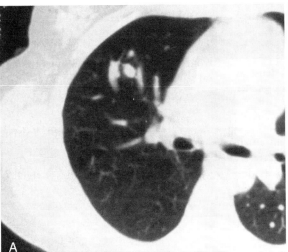
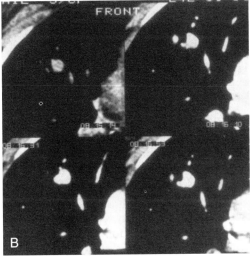

Figure 27–9. Pulmonary arteriovenous malformations. *A,* CT shows a nodule with a feeding artery and draining vein. *B,* The vascular nature of the lesion can be confirmed by dynamic CT scanning after a bolus injection of contrast material and by noting that the nodule enhances and fades as rapidly as the heart and pulmonary arteries.

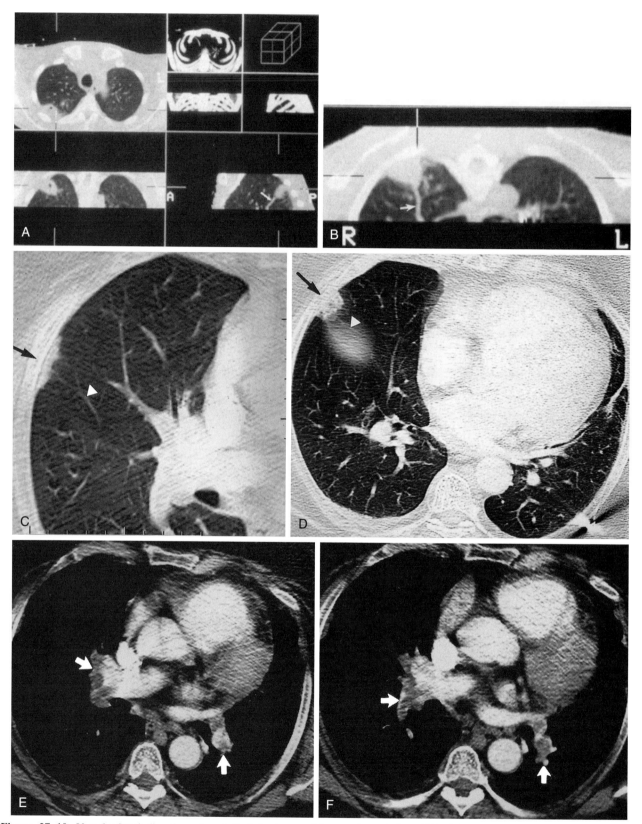

Figure 27–10. Vessel-related disorders. *A* and *B,* Infarct caused by septic embolus. CT with multiplanar reconstruction shows a peripheral, cavitating lesion abutting the pleura. Reconstructed sagittal and oblique coronal images demonstrate a feeding vessel *(arrow).* (From Kuhlman JE: AIDS-related diseases of the chest. In Kuhlman JE [ed]: CT of the Immunocompromised Host. New York, Churchill Livingstone, 1991.) *C–F,* Acute pulmonary infarcts due to thromboembolic disease. *C* and *D,* Lung windows show two peripheral, wedged-shaped opacities that abut the pleura *(arrows),* compatible with a diagnosis of pulmonary infarcts. Feeding vessels lead toward the infarcts *(arrowhead).* *E* and *F,* In the same patient, spiral CT with IV contrast enhancement demonstrates filling defects *(arrows)* within the right and left pulmonary arteries caused by multiple pulmonary emboli.

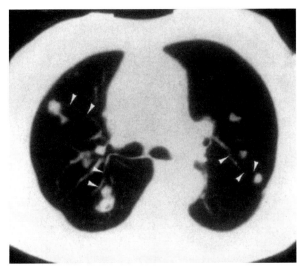

Figure 27–11. Hematogenous metastases. CT shows multiple pulmonary nodules, each with a discrete feeding vessel leading to it *(arrowheads)*. (From Kuhlman JE: CT of diffuse lung disease. Appl Radiol 20:17–21, 1991.)

the pulmonary vessels, as in Wegener's granulomatosis and lymphomatoid granulomatosis.[109]

Wegener's Granulomatosis

Wegener's granulomatosis is a necrotizing granulomatous vasculitis that affects pulmonary vessels, most commonly the small and medium-sized arteries and veins.[24, 34, 52, 236] Nodules and cavities are typical chest film findings.[2, 117, 130] On CT scans, these cavities and nodules are often peripheral and pleura-based and demonstrate a prominent adjacent vessel to the lesions (Figs. 27–12 and 27–13).[109]

In tissue studies, Wegener's lesions show central necrosis surrounded by a granulomatous reaction.[74, 135, 136, 143, 198, 225] Frequently, a thrombosed vessel demonstrating active vasculitis is identified in close proximity to the necrotic lesion, and the resulting ischemia is believed to contribute to cavity formation within the granulomatous nodule (see Fig. 27–12).[74, 135, 136, 143, 198, 225]

Wegener's granulomatosis may also present as patchy or diffuse pulmonary hemorrhage on a CT scan. This occurs when pulmonary capillaries are primarily involved by the vasculitic process (Fig. 27–14).[136]

Thromboembolism

The role of multidetector and spiral CT in the evaluation of suspected *pulmonary thromboembolic disease* is evolving rapidly but remains controversial.[14a, 183a] Large, prospective, properly designed accuracy trials are needed to provide reliable estimates of the sensitivity and specificity of spiral and multidetector CT in diagnosis of pulmonary emboli.[14a, 183a, 239b] Remy-Jardin and colleagues demonstrated that spiral CT achieved a high degree of accuracy in identifying central pulmonary emboli down to the second-order to fourth-order pulmonary arteries.[184a, 184b] In other studies, reported sensitivities of spiral CT vary from 53% to 100%, and specificities vary from 81% to 100%.[14a, 67a, 183a, 184a, 184b, 239b]

An important limitation of spiral CT is the lower sensitivity for detecting smaller peripheral emboli in subsegmental arteries, the importance of which remains uncertain.[67a] Detecting clots in obliquely oriented segmental vessels in the right middle lobe and lingula may be particularly difficult as well.[184a] False-positive results also occur when hilar and intersegmental lymph nodes, unopacified pulmonary veins, or mucous plugs are misinterpreted on spiral CT as emboli.[15a, 68a, 184a, 184b] Remy-Jardin and coworkers have shown that multiplanar images may provide additional, complementary information in difficult cases.[184b]

Findings of acute pulmonary emboli include filling defects that wholly or partially occlude the contrast-opacified pulmonary arteries, or a "tail" of clot within an opacified vessel.[116a, 184a, 184b, 239b] Chronic thrombi often appear as crescentic or laminar filling defects adherent to the walls of the pulmonary artery.[90a, 184a, 239b] Calcification may be identified in chronic clots in patients with long-standing pulmonary hypertension.[90a] Associated parenchymal lung findings in thromboembolic disease include the CT findings of acute or chronic pulmonary infarcts, and wedged-shaped, focal air space opacities that abut the pleura.[34a] Other nonspecific findings in acute pulmonary embolus include pleural effusions. In chronic thromboembolic disease, the lung parenchyma may demonstrate mosaic attenuation, with areas of decreased attenuation associated with "pruned" or attenuated vessels.[90a]

Bronchiolitis Obliterans Organizing Pneumonia

The clinical diagnosis of bronchiolitis obliterans organizing pneumonia (BOOP) is often a difficult and elusive one.[14, 18, 32, 37, 49–51, 68, 145] Patients present with a subacute onset of nonspecific symptoms, including cough, dyspnea, fever, and flulike illness. BOOP may be associated with autoimmune disorders, such as Sjögren's syndrome and polymyalgia rheumatica, or with collagen vascular and rheumatologic diseases; frequently, however, it is idiopathic. Although a definitive diagnosis of BOOP is usually made only by open lung biopsy, in the appropriate clinical setting certain CT features should suggest BOOP as a diagnostic possibility.

BOOP may have many CT appearances, but most cases demonstrate one of four patterns on CT scans: (1) a focal nodular form, (2) a form resembling pneumonia, (3) a pattern characterized by subpleural opacities, or (4) a pattern of ground-glass infiltrates (Figs. 27–15 to 27–19).[22, 32, 147, 158, 173, 228]

When BOOP is more focal in nature, it appears on CT scans as multiple nodular or masslike areas of focal consolidation that occur primarily in the periphery of the lung (see Figs. 27–15 and 27–16).[22, 147, 158, 173, 228] The opacities frequently conform in size and configuration to one or more secondary pulmonary lobules.[173] Often a small pulmonary artery or a small bronchiole can be traced into the center of the nodular area of consolidation, and a small air-bronchogram can be seen surrounded by the focal area of air space consolidation.[22] This is a common pattern of BOOP identified on CT scans, and the pathologic features of the disease help to explain the CT appearance.

In BOOP, fibrovascular plugs of granulation tissue form

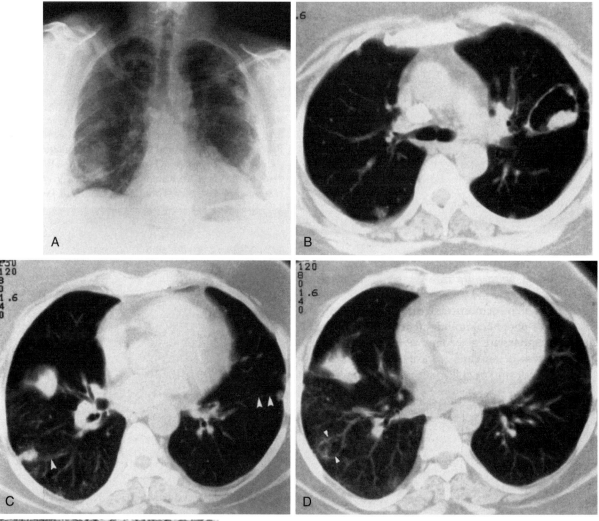

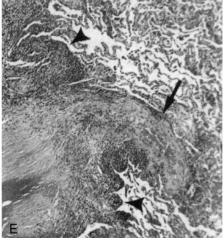

Figure 27–12. Wegener's granulomatosis. *A,* Chest film shows multiple ill-defined opacities and probable cavities. *B,* On this CT scan, a cavitating mass abutting the fissure and several tiny nodules abutting the pleura are identified. *C* and *D,* Several of the smaller lesions demonstrate a feeding vessel *(arrowheads). E,* Lung biopsy specimen shows one necrotic nodule with a surrounding granulomatous reaction *(arrowheads)* and an adjacent thrombosed arterial vessel resulting from vasculitis *(arrow). (B, C,* and *E,* From Kuhlman JE, Hruban RH, Fishman EK: Wegener granulomatosis: CT features of parenchymal lung disease. J Comput Assist Tomogr 15: 948–952, 1991.)

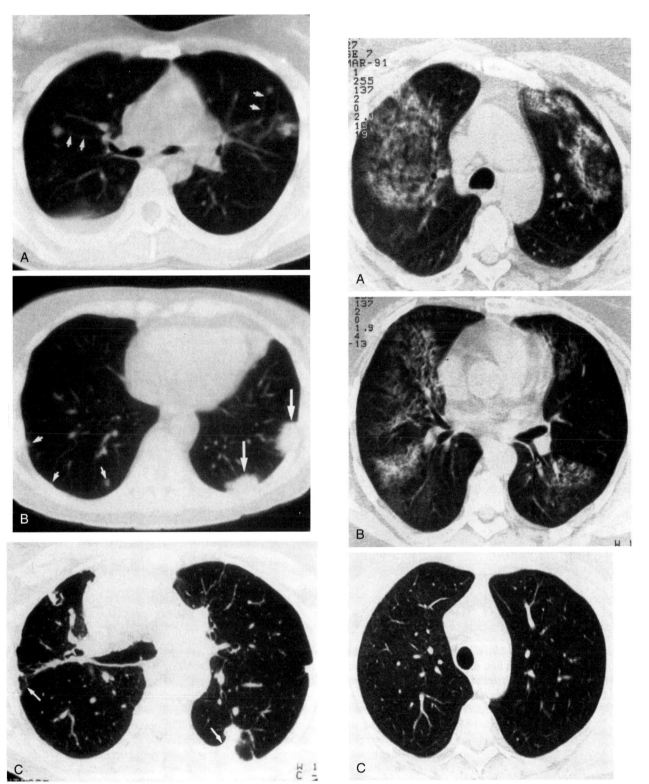

Figure 27–13. CT findings of Wegener's granulomatosis. *A,* Multiple nodules with feeding vessels *(arrows).* (From Kuhlman JE, Hruban RH, Fishman EK: Wegener granulomatosis: CT features of parenchymal lung disease. J Comput Assist Tomog 15:948–952, 1991.) *B,* Two pleura-based lesions *(large arrows)* resembling infarcts, and several smaller peripheral nodules *(small arrows). C,* Patient with long-standing Wegener's granulomatosis under treatment. Scarring, spiculation, and pleural reaction can be seen around peripheral pulmonary nodules *(arrows).*

Figure 27–14. This patient presented with hemoptysis caused by Wegener's vasculitis affecting primarily the capillaries of the lung. *A* and *B,* On CT scans, patchy air space filling is seen as a result of pulmonary hemorrhage. *C,* A few weeks later, a CT scan shows nearly complete clearing of the air space disease.

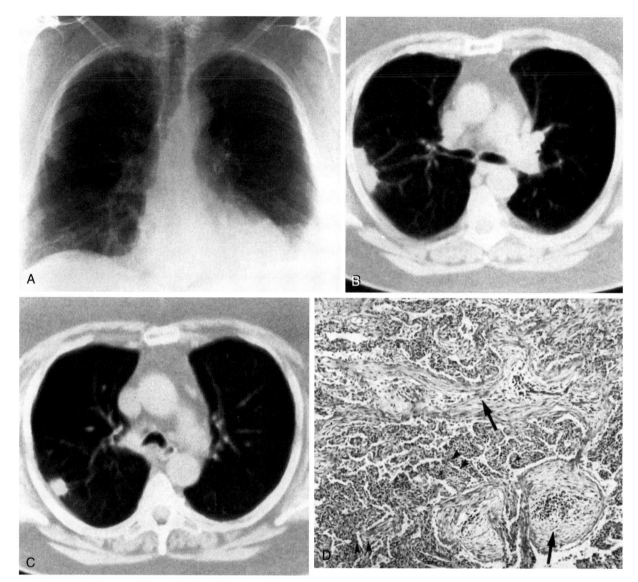

Figure 27–15. CT features of bronchiolitis obliterans with organizing pneumonia (BOOP).

A, Chest film shows ill-defined peripheral opacities.

B and *C,* On CT scans, nodular areas of focal consolidation are identified in the periphery of the lung, abutting the pleura. The opacities conform in size and configuration to one or more secondary pulmonary lobules. Small pulmonary vessels can be traced into the lesions.

D, Open lung biopsy demonstrates the classic histopathology of BOOP. The distal small airways are obliterated with fibrovascular plugs *(arrows),* and the inflammatory process has extended out from the obliterated bronchioles in a centrifugal fashion, filling the surrounding air spaces with organizing pneumonia *(arrowheads).*

(B–D, From Bouchardy LM, Kuhlman JE, Ball WC, et al: CT findings in bronchiolitis obliterans organizing pneumonia (BOOP) with x-ray, clinical, and histologic correlations. J Comput Assist Tomogr 17:352–357, 1993.)

in distal bronchioles and alveolar ducts.[35, 88, 91, 239] The inflammatory or fibrotic process then extends out from the obliterated small airway in a centripetal or radial fashion into the surrounding alveolar spaces, producing organizing pneumonia (see Fig. 27–15). Nishimura and Itoh[173] have stressed the panlobular nature of BOOP and that its distribution on CT scans and pathologic examination frequently conforms to the margins of the secondary pulmonary lobule. Review of the anatomy of the secondary pulmonary lobule is illustrative.

The secondary pulmonary lobule is a polyhedral struc-

ture that can be thought of as the basic building block of the lung. Interlobular septa containing connective tissue, pulmonary veins, and lymphatics define the margins of the secondary pulmonary lobule, whose sides measure approximately 1 to 2.5 cm in length.[73, 230] The secondary pulmonary lobule is made up of 3 to 12 acini and is supplied by several terminal bronchioles. A lobular core supplies the central portion of the secondary lobule and consists of a pulmonary artery and its accompanying bronchiolar branches. This lobular core or centrilobular complex can often be seen on HRCT as a small dot or centrilobular

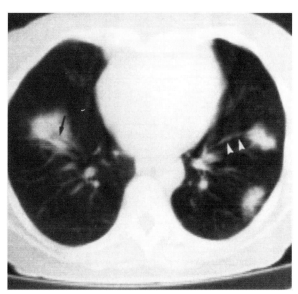

Figure 27–16. CT features of bronchiolitis obliterans organizing pneumonia (BOOP), nodular form. CT shows multiple nodular opacities with air-bronchogram *(arrow)* and associated vessel *(arrowheads)*. (From Bouchardy LM, Kuhlman JE, Ball WC, et al: CT findings in bronchiolitis obliterans organizing pneumonia (BOOP) with x-ray, clinical, and histologic correlations. J Comput Assist Tomogr 17:352–357, 1993.)

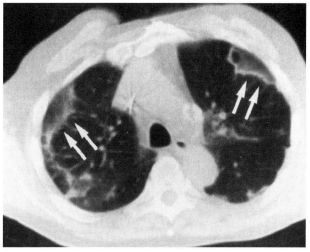

Figure 27–18. CT features of bronchiolitis obliterans organizing pneumonia (BOOP), subpleural form. Irregular peripheral bands of increased CT attenuation parallel the pleural surfaces *(arrows)*. An intervening zone of relatively spared lung can be seen between the pleural surface and the band. (From Bouchardy LM, Kuhlman JE, Ball WC, et al: CT findings in bronchiolitis obliterans organizing pneumonia (BOOP) with x-ray, clinical, and histologic correlations. J Comput Assist Tomogr 17:352–357, 1993.)

density within the center of the secondary pulmonary lobule.[73, 230] Primarily, the pulmonary artery of the lobular core is seen on HRCT because visualization of the accompanying bronchiole depends on its wall thickness, not its diameter, which is below the resolution of HRCT. Normal intralobular bronchioles and interlobular septa usually are not detected on HRCT.[230] Their presence usually indicates abnormal thickening of the bronchiolar walls or septal interstitium.

Because BOOP begins as an inflammatory process that obliterates small distal bronchiolar airways and secondarily spreads into the surrounding air spaces to fill secondary pulmonary lobules, it is easy to understand why areas of consolidation secondary to BOOP appear to be centered on small pulmonary arteries and small bronchi on CT examination.

As the organizing pneumonia of BOOP becomes more extensive, larger areas of consolidation are seen on the CT scan, and the CT appearance becomes indistinguishable from that of a bacterial pneumonia (see Fig. 27–17).

BOOP may also show other patterns on CT scans. Irregular bandlike areas of variable attenuation in the periphery of the lung are typical of some cases of BOOP (see Fig. 27–18), and subpleural reticulations can be seen in up to 23% of patients.[14, 22] Patchy ground-glass infiltrates have also been reported in this disease (see Fig. 27–19).[22, 173]

Figure 27–17. CT features of bronchiolitis obliterans organizing pneumonia (BOOP), pneumonic form. A large area of consolidation caused by BOOP is demonstrated on CT and is indistinguishable by appearance from a bacterial pneumonia. Air-bronchograms can be visualized. (From Bouchardy LM, Kuhlman JE, Ball WC, et al: CT findings in bronchiolitis obliterans organizing pneumonia (BOOP) with x-ray, clinical, and histologic correlations. J Comput Assist Tomogr 17:352–357, 1993.)

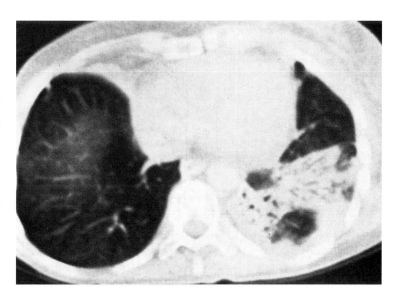

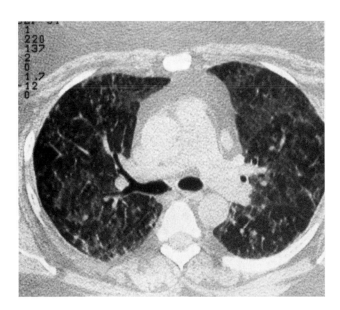

Figure 27–19. CT features of bronchiolitis obliterans organizing pneumonia (BOOP). Another CT presentation of BOOP is as diffuse, but patchy, "ground-glass" infiltrates. (From Bouchardy LM, Kuhlman JE, Ball WC, et al: CT findings in bronchiolitis obliterans organizing pneumonia (BOOP) with x-ray, clinical, and histologic correlations. J Comput Assist Tomogr 17:352–357, 1993.)

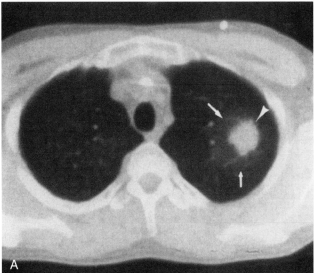

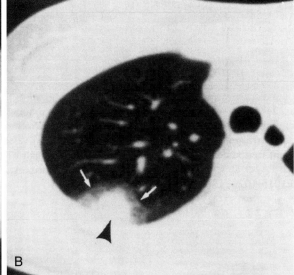

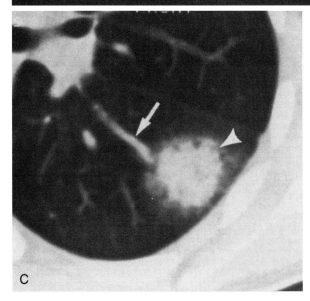

Figure 27–20. CT halo sign of invasive pulmonary aspergillosis. Three patients had acute myelogenous leukemia, prolonged aplasia owing to chemotherapy, and new-onset fever. In each case, an early focus of invasive pulmonary aspergillosis was identified with CT.

A and *B,* CT scans show a nodule *(arrowhead)* surrounded by a CT halo of intermediate attenuation *(arrows)* due to hemorrhagic infarction caused by the angioinvasive fungus. (From Kuhlman JE, Fishman EK, Siegelman SS: Invasive pulmonary aspergillosis in acute leukemia: Characteristic findings on CT, the CT halo sign, and the role of CT in early diagnosis. Radiology 157:611–614, 1985.)

C, The invaded thrombosed vessel is seen *(arrow).* (From Kuhlman JE: Opportunistic fungal infection: The neutropenic patient with leukemia, lymphoma, or bone marrow transplantation. In Kuhlman JE [ed]: CT of the Immunocompromised Host. New York, Churchill Livingstone, 1991.)

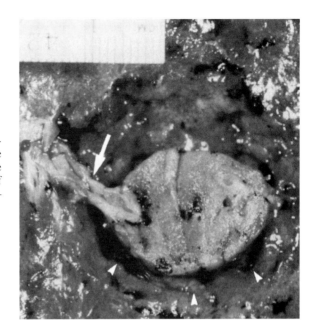

Figure 27–21. Gross pathologic specimen of invasive pulmonary aspergillosis shows an early focus of infection with surrounding hemorrhage *(arrowheads)* and invaded thrombosed vessel adjacent to nodule *(arrow).* (From Kuhlman JE, Fishman EK, Burch PA, et al: CT of invasive pulmonary aspergillosis. AJR Am J Roentgenol 150:1015–1020, 1988.)

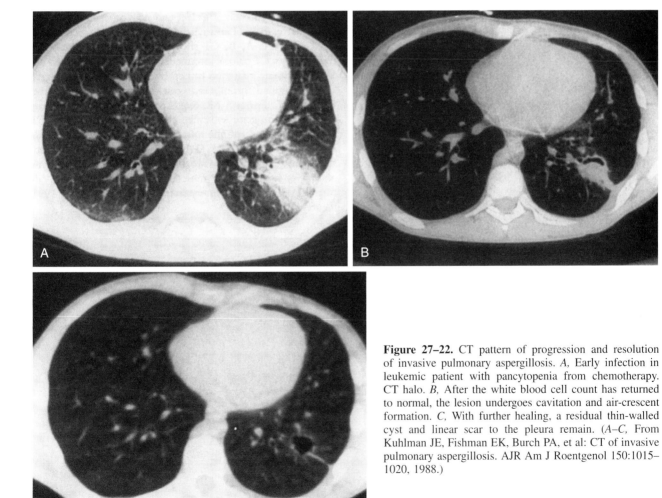

Figure 27–22. CT pattern of progression and resolution of invasive pulmonary aspergillosis. *A,* Early infection in leukemic patient with pancytopenia from chemotherapy. CT halo. *B,* After the white blood cell count has returned to normal, the lesion undergoes cavitation and air-crescent formation. *C,* With further healing, a residual thin-walled cyst and linear scar to the pleura remain. (*A–C,* From Kuhlman JE, Fishman EK, Burch PA, et al: CT of invasive pulmonary aspergillosis. AJR Am J Roentgenol 150:1015–1020, 1988.)

Invasive Pulmonary Aspergillosis

The CT *halo sign* can be used to identify invasive pulmonary aspergillosis in the patient with acute leukemia who is undergoing aplasia-producing chemotherapy.[27, 61, 97, 100, 103, 104, 107] This sign consists of a round pulmonary mass or nodule with a surrounding halo of intermediate CT attenuation (Fig. 27–20). The halo represents hemorrhage around a focal area of lung infarction caused by the *Aspergillus* organism that invades pulmonary vessels (Fig. 27–21).[76, 176] Other angioinvasive infections (mucormycosis, *Candida*, *Torulopsis*, and angioinvasive *Pseudomonas*) may produce similar CT findings, but *Aspergillus* is by far the most common organism to produce this CT finding in the specific clinical setting of a leukemic patient with prolonged bone marrow aplasia following chemotherapy.

In patients with acute leukemia undergoing chemotherapy, lung infection by invasive pulmonary aspergillosis follows a typical pattern of progression and resolution (Fig. 27–22).[27, 61, 97, 100, 103, 104, 107] As the bone marrow recovers from aplasia and the white blood cell count returns to normal, the pulmonary lesions begin to cavitate, producing the familiar air crescent sign. With further healing, the lesions tend to shrink and fade from the periphery, leaving behind thin-walled cysts or linear scars to the pleura.

In the nonleukemic, non-neutropenic patient, the CT halo sign is less specific. It may represent something other than invasive pulmonary aspergillosis, such as other types of angioinvasive infections, hemorrhagic metastases, or any process that produces a nodule with surrounding hemorrhage or edema.

Rounded Atelectasis

Rounded atelectasis is another cause of benign focal lung disease that can be differentiated from malignancy using CT criteria (Fig. 27–23).[48, 127, 128, 144] CT features of rounded atelectasis include a pleura-based mass found adjacent to an area of pleural thickening and associated with volume loss of the involved lobe. Sweeping or curling into the mass are adjacent vessels and small bronchi forming a *comet's tail* or *vacuum cleaner sign* that course down to the mass from the pulmonary hilum.[48, 127, 128, 144]

On pathologic examination, rounded atelectasis represents a focal area of atelectatic lung that rolls or curls up on itself, taking the nearby bronchi and blood vessels along with the infolding lung in the process. Rounded atelectasis is always found adjacent to an area of pleural thickening, and the process is thought to begin with an adhesive pleural effusion or pleural reaction, which entraps the adjacent atelectatic lung. Although many cases of rounded atelectasis are the result of asbestos-related pleural disease, other causes of pleural reaction may produce similar findings.

Bronchiectasis

Dilatation of one or more bronchi results in bronchiectasis.[179] Most causes of bronchiectasis are irreversible and include such diverse categories of disease as immunologic defects (X-linked agammaglobulinemia), ciliary dysmotility syndromes (Kartagener's syndrome), genetic disorders (cystic fibrosis), childhood or repeated infections (pertussis, TB), and congenital abnormalities of the bronchial

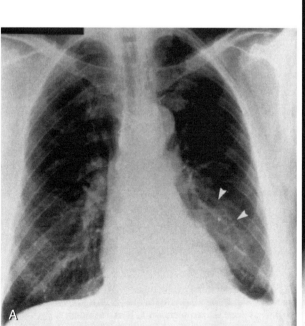

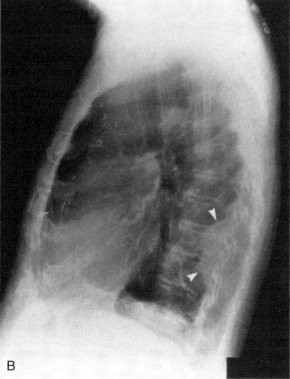

Figure 27–23. CT features of rounded atelectasis. *A* and *B*, Chest film shows ill-defined mass in the posterior left lower lobe *(arrowheads).* The patient underwent coronary bypass surgery, and now evidence of pleural thickening with blunting of the left costophrenic angle can be seen.

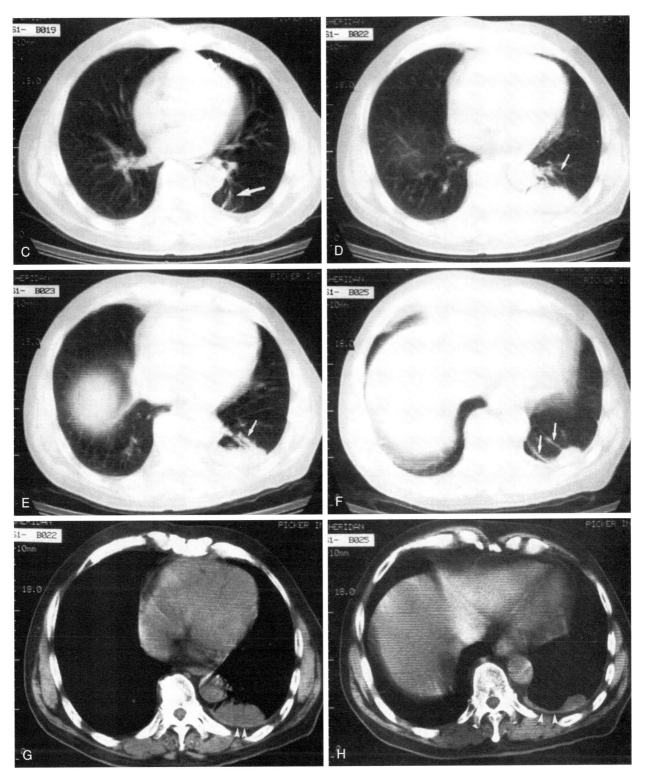

Figure 27–23. *Continued. C–H,* Typical features of round atelectasis are visualized by CT. A rounded pleura-based mass is present, with adjacent pleural thickening *(arrowheads).* Vessels and lung markings curl into the lesion, producing the comet's tail or vacuum cleaner sign *(arrows).* The predisposing cause in this patient was not asbestos exposure but previous thoracic surgery.

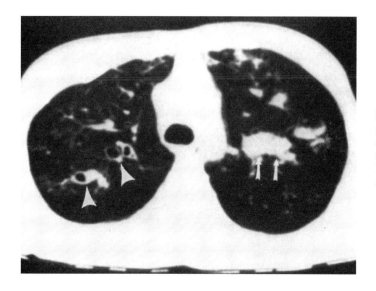

Figure 27–24. CT signs of bronchiectasis. The signet ring sign *(arrowheads)* consists of the dilated bronchus (the ring) and its accompanying pulmonary artery (the signet). A large mucous plug fills one of the dilated bronchi *(arrows)*. (From Kuhlman JE, Reyes BL, Hruban RH, et al: Abnormal air spaces in the lung. Radiographics 13:47–75, 1993.)

wall (Williams-Campbell syndrome).[214] In each case, the protective airway mechanisms that maintain airway sterility and airway clearance are disrupted. This leads to repeated bacterial infections, colonization, and mucous plugging, followed by a destructive inflammatory response and resultant bronchiectasis.

CT has replaced bronchography as the noninvasive method for diagnosis and evaluation of bronchiectasis.[45, 82, 166, 169, 202, 210, 226] Dilated bronchi demonstrate a number of characteristic features on CT scans, and when bronchiectasis affects primarily the larger proximal airways, it is not difficult to recognize. Because each bronchus is accompanied by a pulmonary artery, bronchiectasis commonly produces a *signet ring sign* (Fig. 27–24). The dilated bronchus seen in cross-section forms the ring; the accompanying pulmonary artery forms the signet of the ring.

In cylindrical bronchiectasis, when the dilated bronchus is sectioned longitudinally by the CT scanning plane, the parallel thickened airway walls resemble a *railroad track* or *tram track*. If the bronchiectasis is varicose in nature,

the structure seen on the CT scan resembles a *string of pearls* with areas of dilatation alternating with areas of constriction (Fig. 27–25). In cystic bronchiectasis, when dilated bronchi are grouped together and cut in cross-section, an appearance resembling a *cluster of grapes* is seen (Fig. 27–26).

Air-fluid levels resulting from retained secretions or superimposed infection are commonly identified in dependent portions of cystically dilated bronchi. When dilated bronchi are filled with inspissated material, mucoid impaction results. On a CT scan, *mucous plugs* are identified by recognizing the branching tubular nature of the opacity on multiple CT sections (Fig. 27–27 and see Fig. 27–24).

Bronchiectatic cysts are larger air spaces that develop in severe forms of bronchiectasis, such as cystic fibrosis. Such cysts are recognized by their connection to a dilated proximal bronchus. In contrast to blebs or bullae, bronchiectatic cysts demonstrate discrete, often thickened walls and may be multiloculated (Fig. 27–28).[70, 221]

In *central bronchiectasis,* there is marked dilatation of

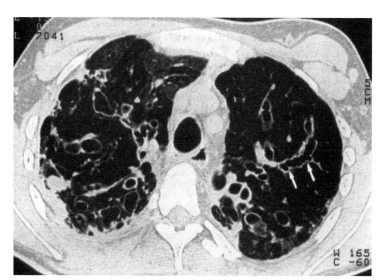

Figure 27–25. CT signs of bronchiectasis in a patient with advanced cystic fibrosis. When a dilated bronchus is sectioned longitudinally by the CT scanning plane, it often demonstrates a *string of pearls* configuration with alternating areas of dilatation and constriction *(arrows)*. (From Kuhlman JE, Reyes BL, Hruban RH, et al: Abnormal air spaces in the lung. Radiographics 13:47–75, 1993.)

Figure 27–26. CT signs of bronchiectasis. Cystically dilated bronchi when grouped closely together may demonstrate a cluster-of-grapes appearance on CT *(arrowheads)*. The relative oligemia *(large arrow)* of some of the pulmonary segments can be compared with more normal lung *(curved arrow)* in this patient with advanced bronchiectasis. This is an example of mosaic attenuation. The subtle differences in CT attenuation of the lung parenchyma reflect both the degree of vascular perfusion and the air space inflation of each segment. Relative underperfusion, resulting from reflex shunting of blood away from hypoxic segments, and hyperinflation of affected segments caused by air trapping contribute to decreased lung density on CT. (From Kuhlman JE, Reyes BL, Hruban RH, et al: Abnormal air spaces in the lung. Radiographics 13:47–75, 1993.)

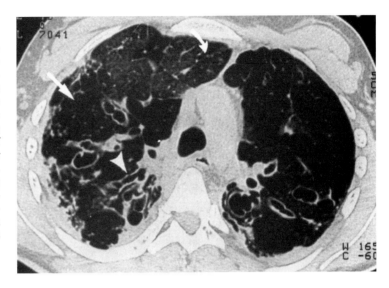

the proximal bronchi with relative sparing of more distal segments. Central bronchiectasis is a hallmark of *allergic bronchopulmonary aspergillosis* (Fig. 27–29).[42]

Allergic bronchopulmonary aspergillosis is characterized on plain films and CT by central bronchiectasis and abundant mucous plugging. This disease typically produces fleeting opacities, which come and go on plain films, and some of the more dramatic examples of the finger-in-glove sign of mucous plugging. A history of refractory asthma is the clue to the diagnosis, which can be confirmed by a set of clinical and laboratory criteria that include elevated IgE levels, precipitating antibodies against *Aspergillus*, peripheral blood eosinophilia, immediate and late skin reactions to *Aspergillus* antigen, and *Aspergillus* mycelia in sputum or mucous plugs.[225a]

Recognizing *bronchiolectases*, or disease affecting the smaller peripheral airways, is more difficult (Fig. 27–30). This is particularly true in cases of *panbronchiolitis* caused

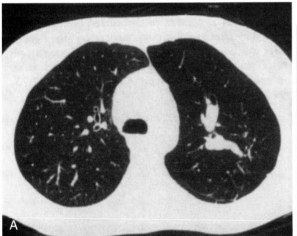

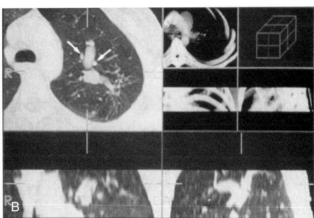

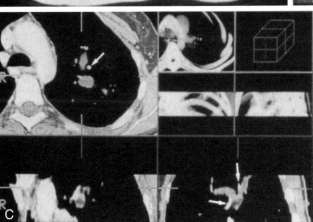

Figure 27–27. *A–C,* A new focal lung opacity was seen on chest films after fever developed in a patient with cancer who was receiving chemotherapy. With a spiral CT data set, multiplanar reconstructions of the lung identify the opacity as a branching, tubular structure compatible with a diagnosis of mucous plug. Distinct small pulmonary arteries *(arrows)* accompany the dilated, mucus-filled bronchi.

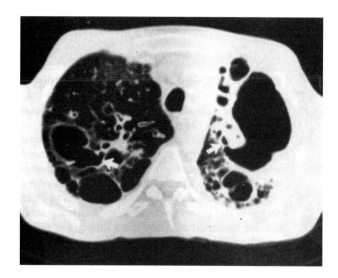

Figure 27–28. Bronchiectatic cysts are recognized on CT by identifying their connection to a dilated bronchus *(arrows)*. Histologically, the walls of bronchiectatic cysts are lined with collagenous fibrous tissue.

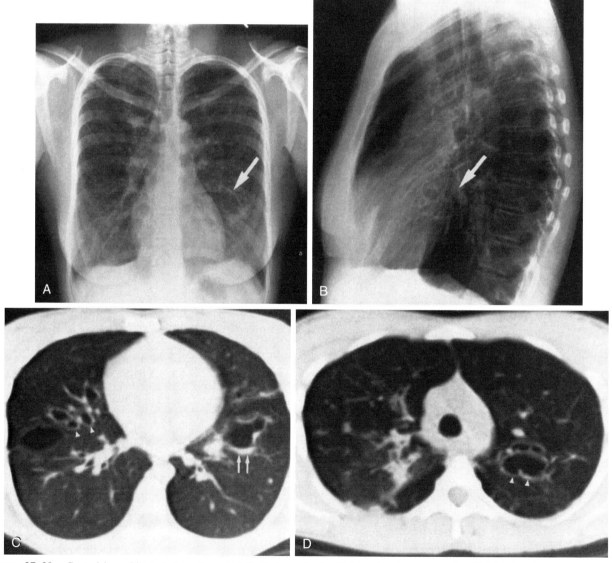

Figure 27–29. Central bronchiectasis is a characteristic feature of allergic bronchopulmonary aspergillosis. *A* and *B*, Posteroanterior and lateral chest films show central thin-walled cystic lesions *(arrows)*. *C* and *D*, CT more clearly identifies the abnormalities as dilated, tubular bronchi *(arrowheads)* and areas of cystic bronchiectasis. An air-fluid level can be visualized *(arrows)*. (From Kuhlman JE, Reyes BL, Hruban RH, et al: Abnormal air spaces in the lung. Radiographics 13:47–75, 1993.)

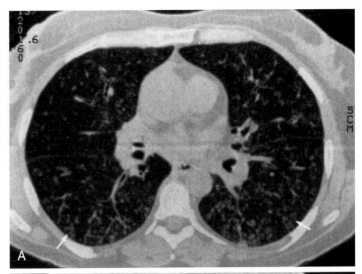

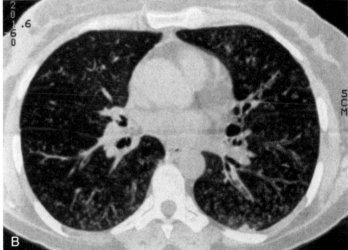

Figure 27–30. *A–C,* Panbronchiolitis. Bronchiolectases or bronchiectatic disease of the smaller peripheral airways may have an appearance on CT that mimics multiple tiny nodules. CT shows peribronchial thickening and mild dilatation of the proximal bronchi. In addition, multiple tiny dots in a centrilobular location are noted; they result from bronchiolectases of the smaller, peripheral airways. The CT appearance has been described as "tree-in-bud" opacities *(arrows).*

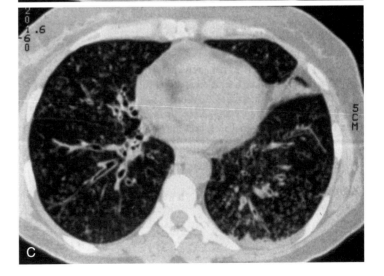

by viral or bacterial infections or other inflammations. Thickened peripheral bronchioles, because of their small size and short length, do not demonstrate the same longitudinal features seen in larger airways and may be mistaken for small nodules. If dilated, these distal small airways may mimic small cavitating nodules. The appearance of inflamed distal bronchioles often resembles small buds on a tree branch and has been described with the phrase *tree-in-bud opacities.*[80a]

CT Features of Diffuse Lung Disease

Diffuse lung disease demonstrates many patterns of distribution on CT scans. These patterns are often helpful in characterizing the nature of the lung disease and arriving at a limited differential diagnosis for the pulmonary process.[155]

Diffuse air space disease may be distributed primarily centrally or peripherally, or it may affect both the central and the peripheral zones of the lung. A few diffuse diseases of the lung produce an abnormality of the lung parenchyma referred to as ground-glass opacities (Fig. 27–31).[146, 157] These opacities may be distributed homogeneously or in a patchy or mosaic pattern, or they may be limited to the centrilobular region of the secondary pulmonary lobule.[4a]

Diffuse interstitial disease and diffuse cystic lung disease may also have several patterns of distribution, including peribronchial and subpleural locations. Examples of cystic lung disease that produce diffuse patterns of distribution include panlobular emphysema and lymphangiomyomatosis.

Ground-Glass Opacities

The ground-glass opacity is characterized by a subtle increase in CT attenuation of the lung parenchyma that does not obliterate the outlines of the bronchi or pulmonary vessels (see Fig. 27–31).[4a, 155, 157] It may be homogeneous and diffuse or more uneven in its distribution, producing a patchwork pattern often described by the term *mosaic attenuation.* Diseases that typically produce ground-glass opacities on CT scans include *Pneumocystis carinii* pneumonia (PCP), cytomegalovirus (CMV) pneumonia, alveolar proteinosis, acute pulmonary edema, extrinsic allergic alveolitis, and the acute alveolitis stage of desquamative interstitial pneumonitis (DIP) and usual interstitial pneumonitis (UIP) (see Fig. 27–31).[64, 110, 206] HRCT enhances detection of subtle ground-glass opacities, particularly in cases in which the chest film or the conventional CT scan are normal or show equivocal findings (Fig. 27–32).

Patchwork or Mosaic Attenuation Patterns

Sometimes the parenchymal abnormality is less uniform and distinctly patchy in its distribution, with areas of normal lung interspersed with abnormal zones. This pattern may be thought of as a "patchwork" pattern because of the striking, sometimes bizarre and mosaic appearance of the lung on CT scans (see Figs. 27–31 and 27–32). Patchy differences in lung CT attenuation are seen in a number of diffuse pulmonary processes, such as *obliterative bronchiolitis (bronchiolitis obliterans), bronchopulmonary dysplasia, asthma, hypersensitivity pneumonitis, PCP, DIP, pul-*

monary hemorrhage, and chronic thromboembolic disease.[98, 110, 126, 213a]

Diseases that produce mosaic attenuation on CT scans fall into three basic categories:

- Airway disease
- Vascular disease
- Infiltrative disease

The causes of the underlying differences in CT attenuation vary, depending on the disease category.[213a, 238b]

In some lung diseases, abnormal areas of lung are those that demonstrate increased CT attenuation either because the alveolar spaces are filled with edema fluid or cells (see Figs. 27–14 and 27–32) or because the relative amount of air in the alveolar space is decreased as a result of encroaching, thickened interstitium. In other diseases, such as advanced cystic fibrosis (see Fig. 27–26), obliterative bronchiolitis, and bronchopulmonary dysplasia (Fig. 27–33), the abnormal areas of lung are those that demonstrate decreased CT attenuation relative to the surrounding normal lung, as a result of focal air-trapping and reflex oligemia caused by vasoconstriction. In chronic thromboembolic disease, the lung pattern has been described by some authors as "mosaic perfusion" to reflect the belief that differences in pulmonary vascular perfusion contribute in large part to the differences in lung attenuation visualized on CT scans.[114, 126, 138]

Obliterative Bronchiolitis (Bronchiolitis Obliterans)

Also known as *constrictive bronchiolitis*, obliterative bronchiolitis has many causes: past infection, Swyer-James syndrome, inhalational injury, and drug use. It is also seen in association with collagen vascular diseases (rheumatoid arthritis, lupus, and scleroderma); in bone marrow transplant recipients with chronic graft-versus-host disease; and as the primary manifestation of chronic rejection in lung and heart-and-lung transplant recipients.[119a]

Swyer-James Syndrome

Swyer-James syndrome is a form of obliterative bronchiolitis that results from a childhood viral infection that goes on to produce postinfectious bronchiolitis obliterans (see Fig. 27–33B–D).[137a, 152a] Typical findings include a small, hyperlucent lung that demonstrates air-trapping on expiratory films or CT. A small pulmonary artery on the affected side is characteristic. On CT scans, one can better appreciate not only the small main pulmonary artery but also diminution and pruning of all the pulmonary artery branches on the affected side.

Bronchiectasis is a CT feature of Swyer-James syndrome that is not widely recognized but is often present.[137a, 152a] CT studies have shown that lung changes in Swyer-James syndrome are not exclusively unilateral.[152a]

Centrilobular and Peribronchiolar Patterns

A few lung diseases produce CT abnormalities that are confined, at least initially, to the region immediately surrounding the central core bronchioles of the secondary pulmonary lobule. On first examination, these CT abnormalities may be mistaken for tiny nodules, but closer in-

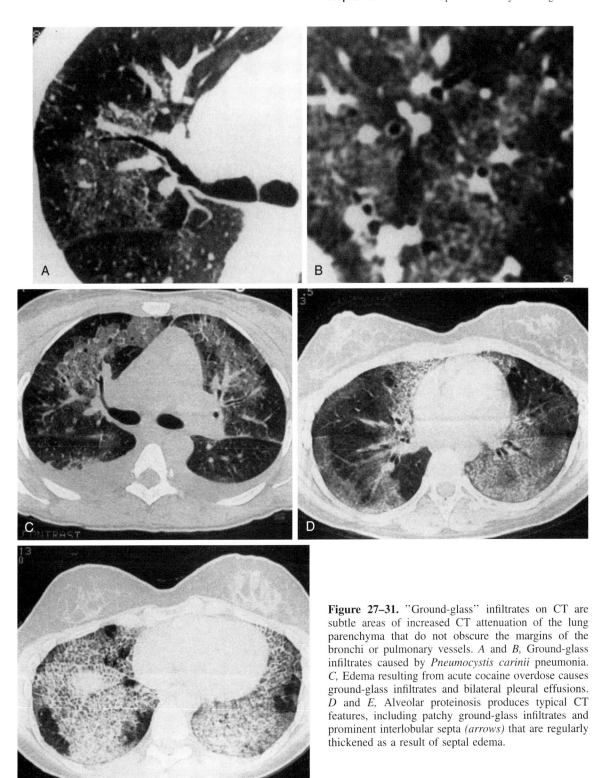

Figure 27–31. "Ground-glass" infiltrates on CT are subtle areas of increased CT attenuation of the lung parenchyma that do not obscure the margins of the bronchi or pulmonary vessels. *A* and *B,* Ground-glass infiltrates caused by *Pneumocystis carinii* pneumonia. *C,* Edema resulting from acute cocaine overdose causes ground-glass infiltrates and bilateral pleural effusions. *D* and *E,* Alveolar proteinosis produces typical CT features, including patchy ground-glass infiltrates and prominent interlobular septa *(arrows)* that are regularly thickened as a result of septal edema.

spection reveals that each represents a nodular opacity centered around the centrilobular complex of the secondary pulmonary lobule and its small bronchiolar branches.

Diseases that cause this type of CT abnormality are often characterized histologically by peribronchiolar infiltration with inflammatory cells or lymphocytes or with granulomatous reaction. Early graft-versus-host disease affecting the lung in the bone marrow transplant recipient produces such a CT appearance because of infiltration of lymphocytes around the small bronchioles. Panbronchiolitis, whether caused by infection or exposure to an irritant, may produce a similar CT appearance.[4, 4a]

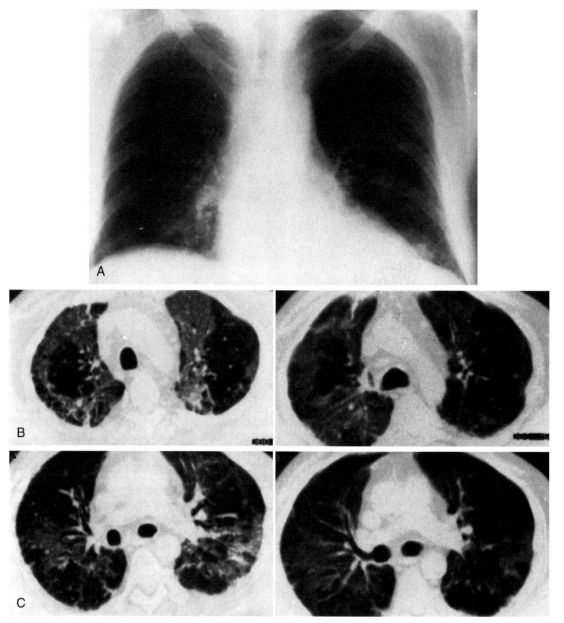

Figure 27–32. The patient is an immunocompromised heart transplant recipient with fever. *A,* The chest film was interpreted as unchanged from a baseline chest film following surgery. *B* and *C,* CT scan shows dramatic "ground-glass" infiltrates in a patchy distribution, a pattern suggestive of *Pneumocystis carinii* pneumonia, which was subsequently confirmed at bronchoscopy. (*A–C,* From Kuhlman JE, Kavaru M, Fishman EK, Siegelman SS: *Pneumocystis carinii* pneumonia: Spectrum of parenchymal CT findings. Radiology 175:711–714, 1990; and Kuhlman JE: CT of the immunocompromised and acutely ill patient. In Zerhouni EA [ed]: CT and MRI of the Thorax. New York, Churchill Livingstone, 1990.)

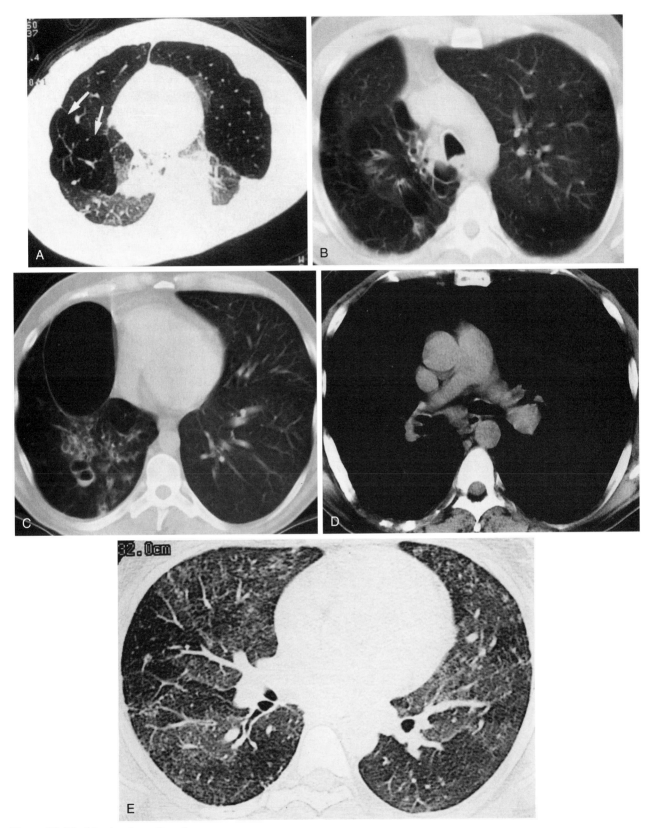

Figure 27–33. Mosaic attenuation, three cases.

A, Case 1. CT scan of bronchopulmonary dysplasia and bronchiolitis obliterans in a child demonstrates a pattern of mosaic attenuation. Segments of the lung *(arrows)* show decreased CT attenuation. Within these segments, the pulmonary vessels are small and attenuated as well. A combination of reflex vasoconstriction and hyperinflation due to air trapping probably accounts for the lower CT attenuation in these areas. (From Kuhlman JE: CT of diffuse lung disease. Appl Radiol 20:17–21, 1991.)

B–D, Case 2. Swyer-James syndrome. CT shows a small, hyperlucent right hemithorax with bronchiectasis and mosaic attenuation on the right side. Perfusion is decreased, and the caliber of the pulmonary artery branches is markedly decreased on the right. *D,* The main pulmonary artery on the right is also small, compared to the artery on the left.

E, Case 3. Mosaic attenuation accentuated on expiratory high-resolution CT views indicates air trapping. The patient is a 32-year-old woman with a history of asthma who uses an inhaler.

Bronchogenic spread of TB may also produce a focal form of this pattern when expectorated caseous material from a TB cavity is spread through the airways, becomes inspissated in small bronchioles, and secondarily causes bronchiolar dilatation, thickening, and peribronchiolar infection and inflammation (Fig. 27–34).[161] This produces the tree-in-bud appearance on CT scans. TB and other mycobacterial infections often produce some of the most dramatic examples of tree-in-bud opacities,[80a] but this finding is not necessarily specific for mycobacterial infections and can be seen in other causes of bronchiolitis, both infectious and inflammatory.

Diffuse Panbronchiolitis

Diffuse panbronchiolitis, the disease entity, is a chronic inflammatory disease of unknown cause found most commonly in Asians but occasionally in Americans and Europeans.[4, 4a] Clinically, patients present with chronic cough, dyspnea, wheezing, and sputum production. Associated chronic paranasal sinusitis is common.

CT findings include bronchiolectasis and milder bronchiectasis, peribronchiolar thickening, tree-in-bud opacities, and peripheral areas of mosaic attenuation. Bronchiolar changes are the dominant finding on CT scans and these changes are strikingly diffuse, involving all lobes.[4, 4a] Tissue studies show infiltration of the walls and tissues, centering on the respiratory bronchioles, with lymphocytes, plasma cells, and histiocytes. This inflammatory process causes secondary dilatation of the more proximal airways, beginning with the terminal bronchioles.[4, 4a]

Progression to respiratory failure is often rapid and the prognosis is poor. Treatment with long-term, low-dose erythromycin has produced some success; disease regression or progression can be monitored with CT.[4, 4a]

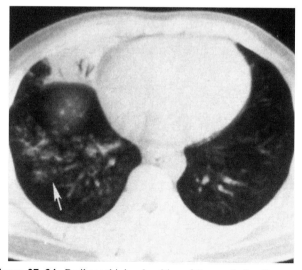

Figure 27–34. Peribronchiolar densities of "ground-glass" opacity and consolidation, resulting from spread of tuberculosis, look like tiny, "fuzzy" nodules on CT scans (called "tree-in-bud" opacities). The apparent nodules actually represent inspissated caseous material in small bronchioles, with surrounding peribronchiolar inflammation and infection.

Bronchovascular Distributions

A number of lung diseases are distributed primarily along the bronchovascular bundles and within their surrounding lymphatic interstitial tissues. Lung diseases with a distinct bronchovascular distribution include *sarcoidosis* and *Kaposi's sarcoma* (KS).[105, 108, 165, 208, 235]

Sarcoid

In addition to septal thickening, reticulation, and fibrosis, pulmonary sarcoid is characterized on CT scans by the presence of small nodules adjacent to the bronchovascular structures (see Fig. 27–5A).[108, 208] These nodules represent aggregates of granulomas that have a predilection for the peribronchovascular lymphatics.

Kaposi's Sarcoma

Kaposi's sarcoma, when it involves the lung, is another example of peribronchovascular disease.[165] The sarcoma infiltrates along and around the bronchovascular bundles and the surrounding lymphatics. On CT scans, pulmonary lesions resulting from Kaposi's sarcoma radiate from the pulmonary hila in a distinctive pattern, often appearing to encase and coat the bronchi (Fig. 27–35).[105, 165, 235]

Beaded Septum Sign

Thickening of the interlobular septa and bronchovascular interstitium is a CT feature of many diffuse interstitial lung diseases and may be smooth, irregular, or nodular. Smooth thickening of the interlobular septa is seen in diseases such as *interstitial pulmonary edema* and *alveolar proteinosis*. Irregular septal thickening, often accompanied by distortion of lung architecture, is characteristic of diseases causing interstitial pulmonary fibrosis. Prominent nodular thickening of the interlobular septa, reminiscent of beads on a string, is an appearance seen in cases of lymphangitic carcinomatosis, some granulomatous diseases, and occasionally silicosis (Fig. 27–36).[20, 146, 160, 240] Lymphangitic carcinomatosis produces the most dramatic cases of nodular septal thickening (see Fig. 27–36).

Pathologic correlation has shown that the beaded appearance is caused by endolymphatic deposits of metastatic tumor.[146, 160, 185] Sarcoidosis is an example of a granulomatous disease that may produce a similar appearance on CT scans (see Fig. 27–36).

Subpleural Distributions

A few lung diseases produce CT abnormalities that are initially most severe in the periphery of the lung, the so-called "subpleural zone." Such diseases include idiopathic pulmonary fibrosis (fibrosing alveolitis), asbestosis, BOOP, eosinophilic pneumonia, and certain types of drug-induced lung disease (Fig. 27–37). The subpleural CT abnormalities may consist of ground-glass opacities, arcades of reticulation, or a meshwork of small cystic spaces known as *honeycombing* (see Fig. 27–37).[240]

Honeycombing is a distinct form of pulmonary damage and lung remodeling that consists of multiple small cystic air spaces ranging in size from 1 to 10 mm. Histologically, the walls of the cystic spaces are composed of granulomatous or fibrous tissue, and the process has a distinct predi-

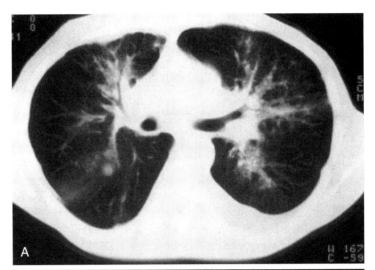

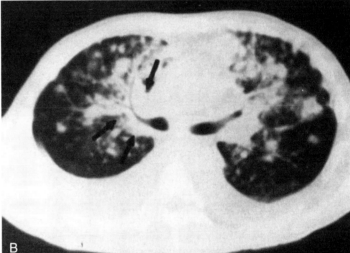

Figure 27–35. *A–C,* Bronchovascular distributions. In three patients with Kaposi's sarcoma (KS) involving the lung, the distinct tendency of KS to spread along the peribronchovascular interstitium is shown. On CT, pulmonary lesions caused by KS radiate out from the pulmonary hila and often appear to encase or coat the bronchi *(arrows).* (*A,* From Kuhlman JE: AIDS-related diseases of the chest. In Kuhlman JE [ed]: CT of the Immunocompromised Host. New York, Churchill Livingstone, 1991. *B,* From Kuhlman JE, Fishman EK, Burch PA, et al: Diseases of the chest in AIDS: CT diagnosis. Radiographics 9:827–857, 1989. *C,* From Kuhlman JE: CT of diffuse lung disease. Appl Radiol 20:17–21, 1991.)

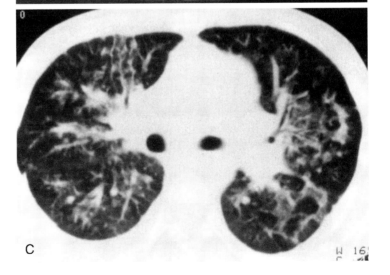

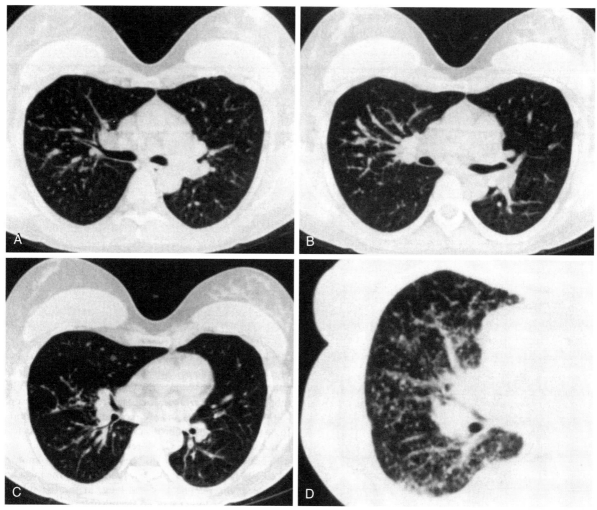

Figure 27–36. The beaded-septum sign. *A–C,* Prominent nodular thickening of the interlobular septa and the peribronchovascular interstitium due to sarcoidosis results in a CT appearance reminiscent of beads on a string. *D,* The most dramatic examples of the beaded septum sign are the result of lymphangitic spread of tumor, in this case lung cancer. (*D,* From Kuhlman JE: CT of diffuse lung disease. Appl Radiol 20:17–21, 1991.)

lection for the subpleural zones.[181] Honeycombing is the common final pathway for many diffuse lung diseases that produce interstitial fibrosis, including fibrosing alveolitis, DIP, pneumoconiosis, sarcoidosis, rheumatoid lung, scleroderma, and others.[120, 181, 211, 215, 232]

The presence of ground-glass opacities in the subpleural zone is often indicative of reversible lung injury. Treatment with corticosteroids or removal of the offending agent, such as a toxic drug, may reverse the pulmonary damage. The presence of honeycombing, however, is usually indicative of permanent, irreversible lung injury.[211]

Application of CT in Evaluation of Non-neoplastic Lung Disease

CT features are used to characterize diffuse and focal lung diseases for diagnosis, and HRCT improves both diagnostic accuracy and specificity.[19, 20] In addition to its diagnostic role, however, CT has other important clinical applications, including early detection of lung disease,

quantification of lung damage, monitoring lung response to therapy, and detection of complications.

Early Detection and Diagnosis

Early detection of pulmonary disease is crucial in a number of clinical settings. Detection of occult lung infection in the immunocompromised patient may improve survival.[27] Early documentation of lung damage caused by pneumoconiosis has important environmental health and medicolegal implications. Early identification of pulmonary drug toxicity may lead to interventions that prevent irreversible lung injury.[101]

Opportunistic Lung Infection

An immunocompromised patient with unexplained fever or respiratory symptoms presents a common and difficult clinical problem. CT has been used successfully to detect and characterize opportunistic infections in patients with leukemia, acquired immunodeficiency syndrome (AIDS),

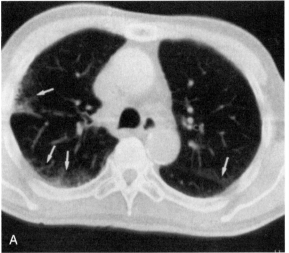

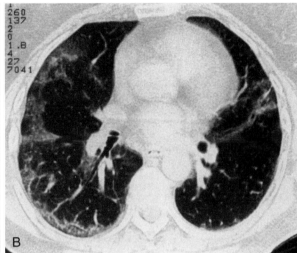

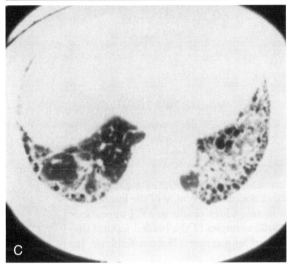

Figure 27–37. Subpleural distributions.

A, Early CT evidence of pulmonary damage resulting from bleomycin toxicity is seen in the subpleural zones *(arrows).* Increased reticular markings parallel the pleural surfaces and are most prominent posteriorly. (From Kuhlman JE: The role of chest computed tomography in the diagnosis of drug-related reactions. J Thorac Imaging 6:52–61, 1991.)

B, Idiopathic pulmonary fibrosis causing arcades and reticulation in the subpleural zone.

C, More advanced pulmonary fibrosis with honeycombing. Lung diseases that produce pulmonary fibrosis and honeycombing usually demonstrate the most severe damage in the periphery of the lung, in the subpleural zone, and at the lung bases. (From Kuhlman JE: CT of diffuse lung disease. Appl Radiol 20:17–21, 1991.)

and disorders treated with bone marrow transplantation (Fig. 27–38) (see Figs. 27–20, 27–22, 27–32).[27, 97, 100, 103, 104, 107, 110] HRCT aids in the early detection of lung infection in these patients. CT patterns and signs help to characterize the nature of the infection and direct invasive biopsy procedures to areas of the lung most affected. CT is also helpful in monitoring response of lung infection to appropriate therapy and in detecting relapse of infection.

Acquired Immunodeficiency Syndrome

When routine chest films fail to reveal a cause of unexplained fever or respiratory symptoms in a patient with AIDS, CT plays an important diagnostic and management role (see Fig. 27–38). CT can detect early or subtle lung infection when chest films remain negative or equivocal. In the patient with AIDS who may have many reasons to have fever or symptoms, the ability of CT to confirm the presence or absence of significant lung infection is critical in expediting the diagnostic workup. CT patterns of parenchymal lung involvement may suggest the most likely diagnosis, and CT can be used to select the diagnostic approach most likely to yield a positive culture specimen.

P. carinii *Pneumoniae Infection*

PCP is still one of the most common life-threatening lung infections to occur in patients with AIDS in industrialized countries.[1, 30, 31, 46, 93, 99, 105, 164] PCP can have a variety of presentations, from acute fulminant respiratory failure to a more insidious onset with nonspecific symptoms of nonproductive cough, malaise, and low-grade fever.[93] In a patient with AIDS, this more insidious presentation is more common.

The classic chest film findings of PCP are well known and include bilateral ground-glass infiltrates in a perihilar or sometimes upper lobe distribution.[1, 31, 46] The diagnosis is straightforward in patients who demonstrate these findings. Early in the course of infection, however, the chest film may appear normal or show only minimal increased lung markings, and a reported 10% of patients with documented PCP have normal or equivocal chest films.[46] In this setting, CT can be used to confirm or exclude the presence of parenchymal lung infiltrates.

CT patterns of PCP are varied, but the most common pattern is of diffuse or patchy, ground-glass infiltrates that do not obscure bronchovascular margins (Fig. 27–39).[110] Increased interstitial markings can also be seen, particularly

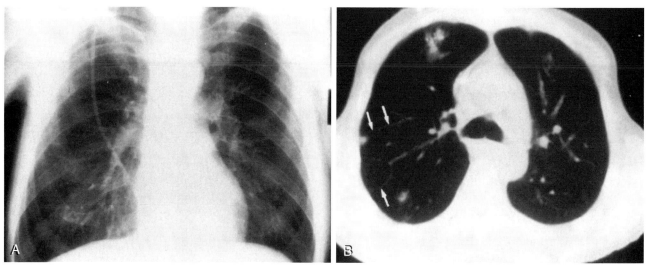

Figure 27–38. Unexplained fever in a patient with acquired immunodeficiency syndrome (AIDS). *A,* Chest film shows central venous line but no obvious infiltrates. *B,* CT identifies multiple inflammatory nodules with feeding vessels *(arrows),* compatible with a diagnosis of septic emboli. The source of the septic emboli was found to be the central venous catheter that had become infected. *(B,* From Kuhlman JE, Fishman EK, Burch PA, et al: Diseases of the chest in AIDS: CT diagnosis. Radiographics 9:827–857, 1989.)

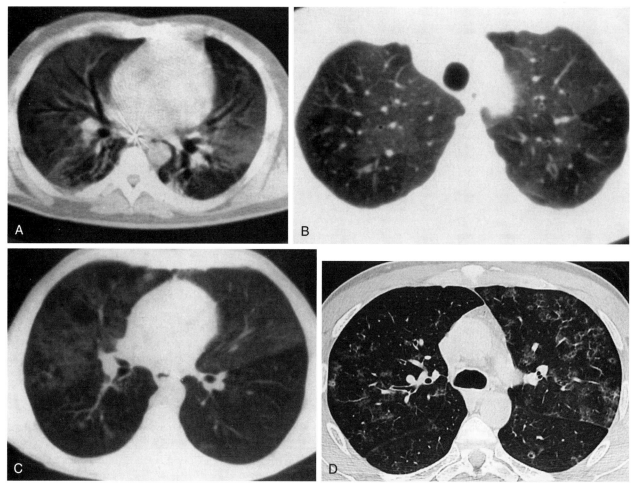

Figure 27–39. *Pneumocystis carinii* pneumonia (PCP): CT patterns of involvement.
   A, Diffuse "ground-glass" infiltrates. (From Kuhlman JE, Kavuru M, Fishman EK, Siegelman SS: *Pneumocystis carinii* pneumonia: Spectrum of parenchymal CT findings. Radiology 175:711–714, 1990.)
   B–D, Patchy ground-glass infiltrates.

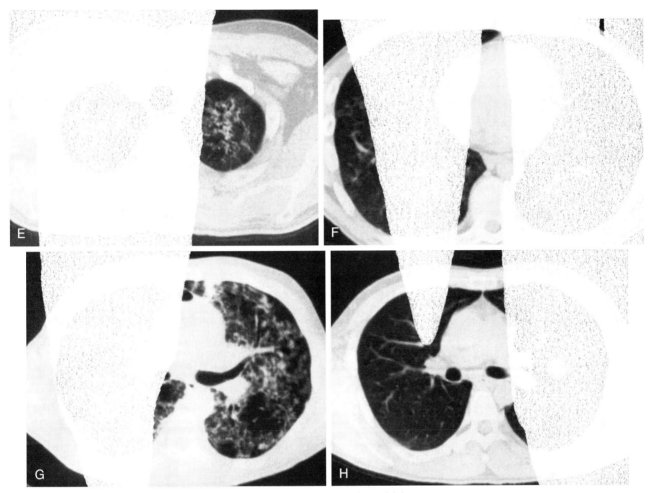

Figure 27–39. *Continued. E–G,* Mixed infiltrates with ground-glass and interstitial components.

E, From Kuhlman JE. CT of the immunocompromised and acutely ill patient. In Zerhouni EA [ed]: CT and MRI of the Thorax. New York, Churchill Livingstone, 1990; *F,* From Kuhlman JE, Fishman EK, Burch PA, et al: Diseases of the chest in AIDS: CT diagnosis. Radiographics 9:827–857, 1989; *G,* From Kuhlman JE: AIDS-related diseases of the chest. In Kuhlman JE [ed]: CT of the Immunocompromised Host. New York, Churchill Livingstone, 1991.)

H, Solitary pulmonary nodule, an unusual manifestation of PCP seen in a few patients with AIDS.

in patients who have had repeated *Pneumocystis* infections (20% to 40% of patients), because of the interstitial fibrosis that develops as the infection heals.

Another CT pattern of PCP, which is quite different in appearance, occurs with the cystic form (Fig. 27–40).* On CT scans, the cystic form of PCP is characterized by one or more thin-walled cysts or cavities that are somewhat irregular in shape and may be coarse or delicate in appearance. Surrounding ground-glass infiltrates are often present. This form of PCP may also be associated with CT manifestations of disseminated infection, including enlarged lymph nodes with calcifications found in the mediastinum and abdomen, and other calcifications in the liver, spleen, and kidneys (Fig. 27–41).[99, 183]

Many patients with cystic PCP or lymph node and visceral calcifications caused by *Pneumocystis* infection were reported to be receiving aerosolized pentamidine for prophylaxis against PCP. The aerosolized drug may par-

tially clear or partially suppress the pulmonary infection, but it may not attain high-enough concentrations in the blood to prevent dissemination of the *Pneumocystis* organism. The chronic infection that remains in the lung may predispose to cystic cavity formation. More recently, aerosolized pentamidine has been less often used as a prophylactic agent, having been replaced by other, more effective drugs. Despite this change, the cystic form of PCP continues to be seen and some report an increasing frequency of this pattern of presentation.[20a]

A rare CT presentation of PCP is the *solitary pulmonary nodule*.[13, 110] A nodule may form in those individuals positive for the human immunodeficiency virus (HIV) who have less severe immunosuppression and can still mount a granulomatous response to the infection (see Fig. 27–39D). Pleural effusions are an uncommon finding in uncomplicated PCP. Rare cases of pleural effusions caused by disseminated *Pneumocystis* infection have been reported, and pleural calcifications may be demonstrated.[20a] More often in the patient with AIDS, the cause of a pleural effusion is a bacterial, fungal, or mycobacterial infection; lymphoma;

*See References 13, 30, 41, 53, 83, 92, 105, 125, 149, 193, 203, and 222.

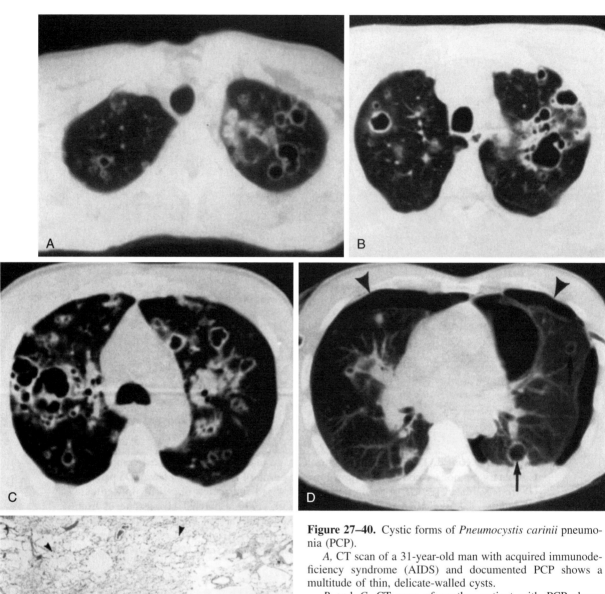

Figure 27–40. Cystic forms of *Pneumocystis carinii* pneumonia (PCP).

A, CT scan of a 31-year-old man with acquired immunodeficiency syndrome (AIDS) and documented PCP shows a multitude of thin, delicate-walled cysts.

B and *C*, CT scan of another patient with PCP shows irregular cystic lesions with coarse walls and surrounding infiltrates.

D and *E*, PCP has resulted in multiple thin-walled cysts *(arrows)*, complicated by bilateral pneumothoraces *(arrowheads)*.

E, At autopsy, cystic lung lesions in this patient corresponded to discrete foci of necrotic debris surrounded by a thin wall of fibrous tissue *(arrows)*. The surrounding lung showed organizing intra-alveolar and interstitial pneumonitis with marked inflammatory changes of nearby vessels, compatible with a diagnosis of vasculitis.

(*A* and *C*, From Kuhlman JE, Reyes BL, Hruban RH, et al: Abnormal air spaces in the lung. Radiographics 13: 47–75, 1993.)

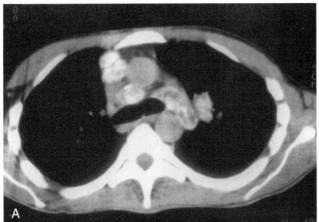

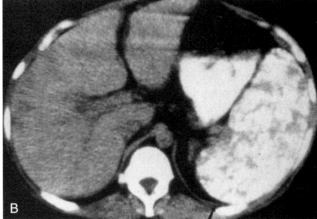

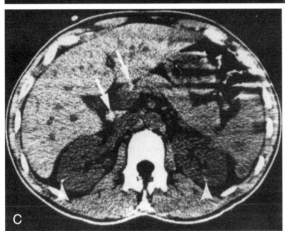

Figure 27–41. Disseminated *Pneumocystis carinii* pneumonia (PCP) infection.

A, CT shows characteristic enlarged lymph nodes with calcifications. (From Kuhlman JE: CT evaluation of the chest in AIDS. In Thrall J [ed]: Current Practice in Radiology. St. Louis, Mosby–Year Book, 1993.)

B and C, Calcifications caused by disseminated PCP can also be seen in the spleen (*arrow* in *B*), abdominal lymph nodes (*arrows* in *C*), liver, and kidneys (*arrowheads* in *C*) in patients with disseminated PCP infection. Low-attenuation splenic lesions in *C* are the result of PCP splenic abscesses. (*B,* From Kuhlman JE: AIDS-related diseases of the chest. In Kuhlman JE [ed]: CT of the Immunocompromised Host. New York, Churchill Livingstone, 1991.)

or Kaposi's sarcoma. Although less well recognized, PCP infection can also cause airway abnormalities, including bronchiolitis and bronchiolitis obliterans.[20a]

Several ancillary CT findings may be identified in patients with PCP or HIV disease. Apical and paraseptal bullae and spontaneous pneumothoraces are often noted in these relatively young patients (Fig. 27–42 and see Fig. 27–40).[15, 111, 139, 170, 195] In a patient with AIDS, pneumothoraces are often difficult to resolve because of persistent air leaks. They may require more invasive procedures than simple chest tube placement, including pleurodesis, lung stapling, or pleurectomy to reexpand the lung.

Fungal Infection

In patients with AIDS, fungal infections involving the lungs usually present as multiple nodules or cavities (Fig. 27–43).[96, 99, 105, 164] When present, fungal lung infection usually suggests disseminated disease. Other nonpulmonary manifestations of fungal disease, such as CT findings of esophagitis with esophageal wall thickening or focal lesions in the liver, may be the first indication of a disseminated fungal infection both in patients with AIDS and in other immunocompromised hosts (Figs. 27–44 and 27–45).

Any number of fungal species may cause pulmonary infection in the AIDS patient, including *Candida albicans*, *Coccidioides immitis*, *Histoplasma capsulatum*, and *Cryptococcus neoformans*. Infections caused by *Aspergillus* oc-

cur in patients with AIDS but much less frequently than they occur in other immunocompromised patients such as those with leukemia and prolonged neutropenia. This is because the body's immune response to *Aspergillus* infection requires only intact neutrophils and macrophages rather than healthy T cells or antibodies.

Neutrophil function is relatively preserved in AIDS patients until end stages of the disease. *Aspergillus* infections are seen, however, in AIDS patients who are taking corticosteroids or multidrug regimens that suppress neutrophil counts. *Cryptococcus* is the most common fungal pathogen to affect the lungs in patients with AIDS, almost always (>90% of cases) in conjunction with infection of the central nervous system.

Nocardial Infection

Nocardia is yet another opportunistic organism that is increasingly being recognized in the patient with AIDS.[96, 99, 105] On CT scans, *Nocardia* infection may start out as a small inflammatory nodule but eventually develops into a cavitary mass or more extensive cavitary pneumonia involving one or more segments or lobes of the lung (Fig. 27–46).

Although the unusual opportunistic infections are usually emphasized in regard to pulmonary infections in AIDS, it is important to keep in mind that bacterial infections, often severe, aggressive, and recurrent ones, occur fre-

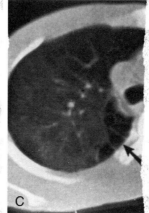

Figure 27–42. *A–C,* Apical and paratracheal bullae (arrows) in a patient with acquired immunodeficiency syndrome (AIDS) and repeated *Pneumocystis* infections. (From Kuhlman JE, Kavuru M, Fishman EK, Siegelman SS: *Pneumocystis carinii* pneumonia: Spectrum of parenchymal CT findings. Radiology 175:711–714, 1990.)

quently in patients with AIDS, including those caused by *Streptococcus pneumoniae, Staphylococcus pneumoniae,* and *Haemophilus influenzae.*

Tuberculosis

Of increasing concern is the resurgence of TB as a significant communicable pulmonary infection in the United States, resulting in part from the AIDS epidemic.[224] Emergence of multiresistant strains poses an ever-growing threat to public health on a global scale.

CT manifestations of pulmonary TB depend to a large extent on the health of the individual's immune system (Figs. 27–47 to 27–53). In the immunocompetent host, cavitation is one of the hallmarks of reactivation TB.[56, 167] Cavities develop when centers of granulomatous reaction to the TB bacillus undergo caseation necrosis. On CT scans, cavities owing to TB can be thick-walled or thin-walled and are indistinguishable from those caused by other atypical mycobacterial species.[6, 36, 114, 167, 218]

Often with the development of tuberculous cavitation, the necrotizing process erodes into the tracheobronchial tree and the expected tuberculous material spread by the endobronchial route to other parts of the lung.

Typical CT features of bronchogenic spread include patchy areas of air space disease consisting of poorly defined nodular opacities measuring from 5 to 10 mm in diameter.[36, 56, 167] Compared with the smaller discrete nodules found in miliary TB,[218] the nodular opacities seen in bronchogenic spread are uniform in size and unevenly distributed.

Various terms have been used to describe these nodular opacities, including acinar nodules, acinar lesions, acinar shadows, and tree-in-bud opacities.[56] Pathologically, the lesions seen on CT scans correspond to peribronchiolar foci of infection and granulomatous reaction that are centered around the terminal respiratory bronchioles and their surrounding alveoli.[10, 56, 80, 167, 218] In cases of suspected TB, CT can be used to identify a small or occult cavity that is the source of the bronchogenic spread and to demonstrate the full extent of the infection, which is often widely scattered in both lungs.

If the host's immune system lacks the ability to mount a granulomatous response and wall off the activated infection is often contained and healing begins with the deposition of collagen and scar tissue around areas of caseous necrosis.[8] Eventually, dystrophic calcifications form within granulomatous nodules, lymph nodes, and fibrotic strands, and the lung assumes the characteristic appearance of chronic fibrocalcific TB. Further scarring leads to lung distortion, bronchiectasis, volume loss, and cicatrizing atelectasis and compensatory emphysema. Fibrotic masslike lesions may form in the lung apices and may be difficult to distinguish from apical lung cancer, or scar carcinomas on the basis of CT appearances alone.[8]

Text continued on page 878

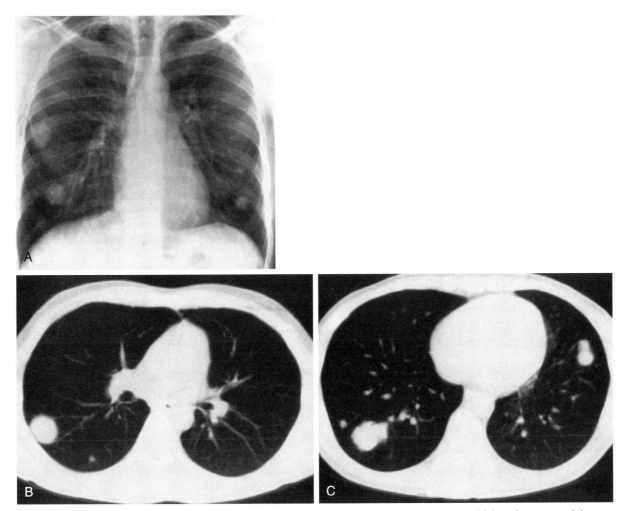

Figure 27–43. Disseminated cryptococcal infection. Chest film (*A*) and CT (*B, C*) show multiple pulmonary nodules.

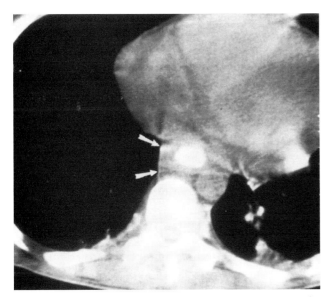

Figure 27–44. Cytomegaloviral esophagitis. Marked thickening of the esophageal wall is evident on the CT scan. Oral contrast material is retained within the dilated, inflamed esophagus. (From Kuhlman JE: AIDS-related diseases of the chest. In Kuhlman JE [ed]: CT of the Immunocompromised Host. New York, Churchill Livingstone, 1991.)

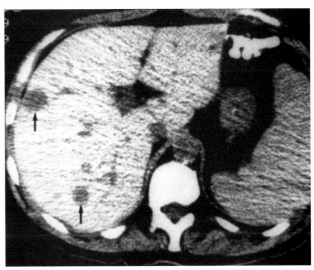

Figure 27–45. Disseminated candidiasis. CT shows multiple filling defects in the liver caused by fungal abscesses *(arrows)*. (From Kuhlman JE: CT of the immunocompromised and acutely ill patient. In Zerhouni EA [ed]: CT and MRI of the Thorax. New York, Churchill Livingstone, 1990.)

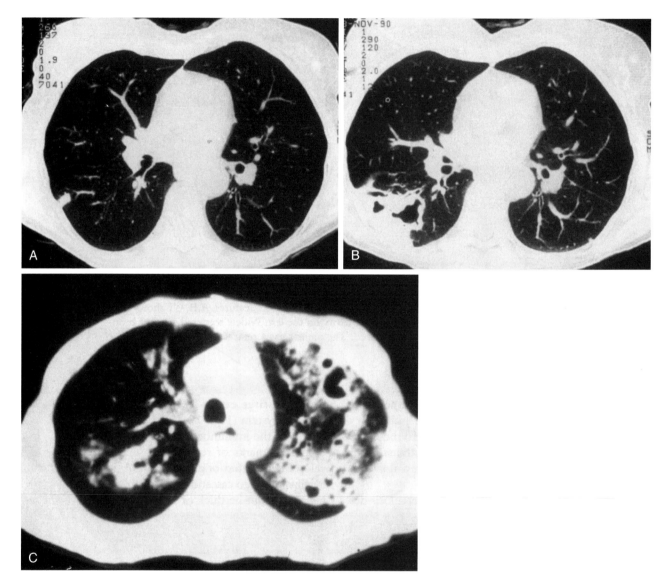

Figure 27–46. Nocardiosis in a patient with acquired immunodeficiency syndrome (AIDS). *A,* Initial CT scan on a patient with positive status for human immunodeficiency virus (HIV) infection shows a small inflammatory nodule in the right lower lobe. *B, Nocardia* infection has progressed to a large necrotic cavity. *C, Nocardia* infection in another patient with AIDS presented as a multilobar cavitary pneumonia. (*C,* From Kuhlman JE: AIDS-related diseases of the chest. In Kuhlman JE [ed]: CT of the Immunocompromised Host. New York, Churchill Livingstone, 1991.)

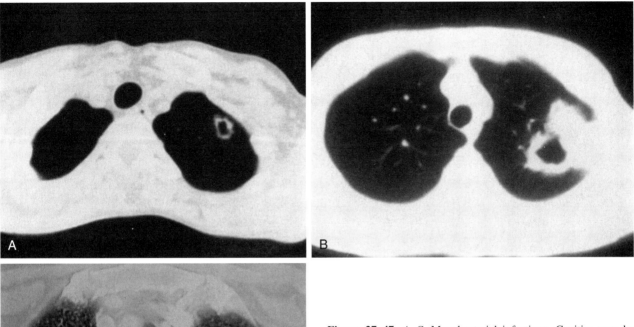

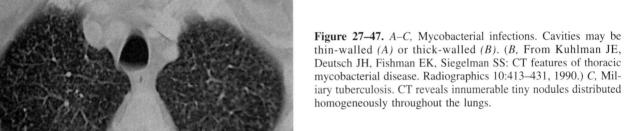

Figure 27–47. *A–C,* Mycobacterial infections. Cavities may be thin-walled *(A)* or thick-walled *(B)*. *(B,* From Kuhlman JE, Deutsch JH, Fishman EK, Siegelman SS: CT features of thoracic mycobacterial disease. Radiographics 10:413–431, 1990.) *C,* Miliary tuberculosis. CT reveals innumerable tiny nodules distributed homogeneously throughout the lungs.

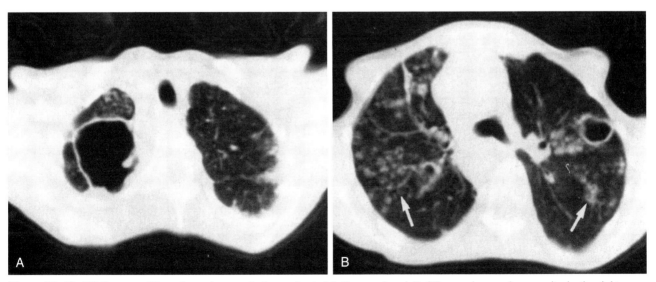

Figure 27–48. CT features of bronchogenic spread of mycobacterial disease. *A* and *B,* CT scan shows a large cavity in the right upper lobe and a smaller cavity on the left. Widely scattered areas of bronchogenic spread *(arrows)* are identified, demonstrating a "tree-in-bud" pattern. The patient has a right-sided aortic arch.

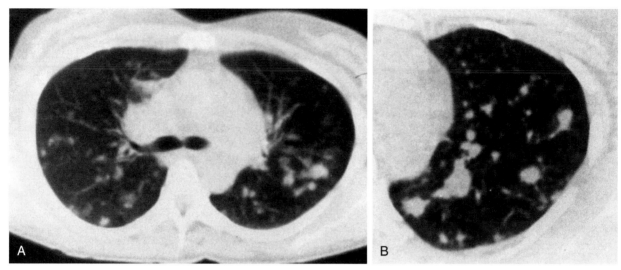

Figure 27–49. *A* and *B,* On these CT scans, areas of bronchogenic spread of tuberculosis appear as poorly marginated, "fluffy" nodular densities of variable size.

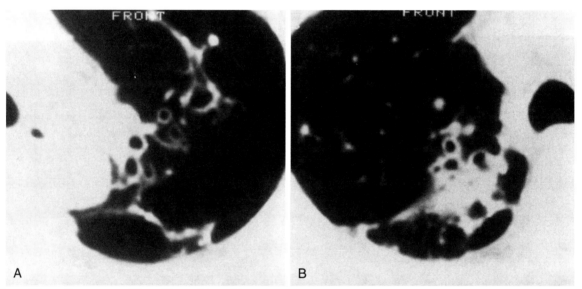

Figure 27–50. *A* and *B,* CT features of chronic fibrocalcific tuberculosis (TB) include scarring, calcified granulomata, bronchiectasis, architectural distortion, and fibrotic masses.

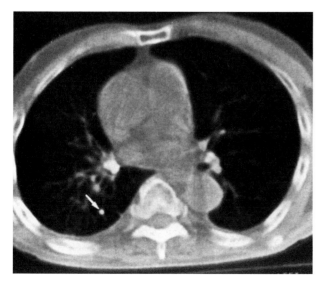

Figure 27–51. Ranke's complex. CT image shows the calcified parenchymal scar (Ghon's lesion) *(arrow)* and the calcified hilar nodes representing healed regional lymphatic involvement from the initial tuberculosis infection.

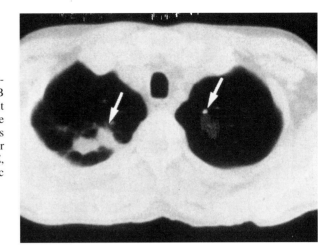

Figure 27–52. Simon's foci, an example of healed sites of tuberculosis (TB) seeded to the lung apices at the time of the primary TB infection. The masslike opacity seen in the right apex was the result of healed TB in this case, but on the basis of the CT appearance alone, it is indistinguishable from that of lung cancer. Such opacities require close, serial follow-up to ensure stability in size over time or biopsy, in some cases, to exclude neoplasm. (From Kuhlman JE, Deutsch JH, Fishman EK, Siegelman SS: CT features of thoracic mycobacterial disease. Radiographics 10:413–431, 1990.)

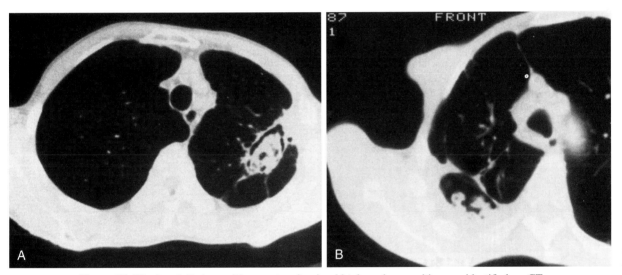

Figure 27–53. *A* and *B,* Aspergillomas, growing in old tuberculous cavities, are identified on CT.

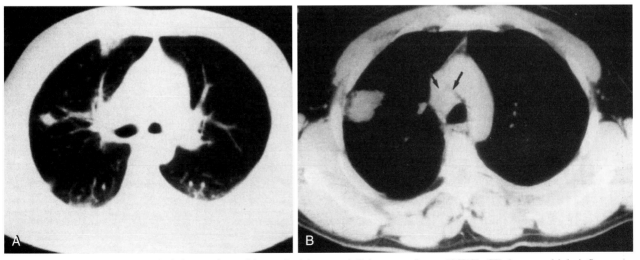

Figure 27–54. *A* and *B,* Tuberculosis in a patient with acquired immunodeficiency syndrome (AIDS). CT shows multiple inflammatory lung masses and bulky mediastinal nodes *(arrows)* resulting from tuberculosis (TB). Lymphadenopathy is the rule rather than the exception in patients with AIDS and TB. (From Kuhlman JE: CT evaluation of the chest in AIDS. In Thrall J [ed]: Current Practice in Radiology. St. Louis, Mosby–Year Book, 1993.)

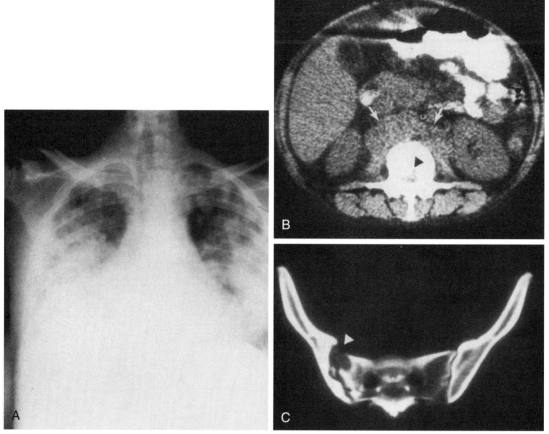

Figure 27–55. Tuberculosis in a patient with advanced acquired immunodeficiency syndrome (AIDS). A woman with status positive for human immunodeficiency virus (HIV) infection was shown at autopsy to have bilateral pulmonary infiltrates (*A*), extensive lymphadenopathy (*B, arrows*), and multiple lytic bone lesions (*B and C, arrowheads*) caused by widely disseminated tuberculosis. (From Kuhlman JE: AIDS-related diseases of the chest. In Kuhlman JE [ed]: CT of the Immunocompromised Host. New York, Churchill Livingstone, 1991.)

Frequently on CT scans, evidence of earlier TB infection can be found in the form of old healed cavities or sequelae, such as[56, 102]:

1. *Ghon's lesion,* the parenchymal scar or granuloma that occurs at the site of initial TB infection. This lesion is often calcified.
2. *Ranke's complex,* consisting of a parenchymal scar and the associated calcified lymph nodes in the pulmonary hilum or mediastinum. The presence of this complex suggests regional lymphatic spread.
3. *Simon's foci,* or healed residua of TB seeded to the lung apices at the time of primary infection.

Chronic TB cavities may permanently scar the lung and remain open even after sterilization. These chronic cavities may become complicated by superimposed infection or colonization with *Aspergillus* fungi that form mycetomas.[190]

Although TB produces many chronic lung changes, disease activity cannot be determined on the basis of CT appearances alone. Fibrotic areas of lung and cavities that look inactive on chest radiographs or CT may in fact harbor viable organisms.[56, 238] The radiologic stability of TB-induced lung changes, however, can be assessed with

serial chest films or serial CT scans. Follow-up CT examinations have become an important adjunct to sputum cultures in assessing response to treatment in infected patients.

In part because of the declining exposure rate of children to TB, a larger number of first-time exposures are occurring in adulthood, making cases of primary rather than reactivation TB in the adult more common than before. Mediastinal and hilar adenopathy is often an indication of primary TB infection.[81, 123]

Tuberculosis in Special Patient Populations

A number of individuals are at increased risk for development of active TB, including older, debilitated, and malnourished patients and patients with AIDS.[56, 81, 154, 167, 194] Special considerations also apply to patients with sarcoidosis and silicosis, in whom the prevalence of TB is increased.[56, 81, 154, 167, 194, 238]

Patients with AIDS are particularly susceptible to mycobacterial infections both from *Mycobacterium tuberculosis* and from other atypical organisms, such as *M. avium–intracellulare* (MAI), *M. avium complex* (MAC), and *M. kansasii*.[56, 134] In 10% to 20% of patients with AIDS, *M.*

avium–intracellulare infections are detected sometime during their life from blood, sputum, or bone marrow cultures. At autopsy, more than 50% of these patients are found to be infected. Despite these statistics, pulmonary infiltrates caused by *M. avium–intracellulare* are considerably less common than those caused by TB.[134]

The most common CT manifestation of *M. avium–intracellulare* infection is diffuse adenopathy. Regardless of mycobacterial species, however, the normal granulomatous response to mycobacterial infection is poor or absent in the patient with AIDS, and disseminated disease is more common than in the immunologically competent host.[6, 56, 134]

The AIDS population is particularly vulnerable to the spread of TB. In some parts of Africa, the combination of AIDS and TB has become epidemic. Manifestations of TB in the patient with AIDS depend on the degree of immunosuppression. In a patient with early HIV infection and milder immunosuppression, TB presents in a more classic fashion with cavitary disease and bronchogenic spread. TB that occurs in the setting of more severe immunosuppression or full-blown AIDS is more often atypical and aggressive in its manifestations, presenting in a manner more reminiscent of primary TB, primary progressive TB, or miliary TB.[96, 102]

In the patient with advanced AIDS, widely disseminated and extrapulmonary disease and multiple pulmonary masses with significant adenopathy are not uncommon presentations of TB. Mediastinal and hilar adenopathy as a manifestation of TB in an AIDS patient is the rule rather than the exception. After administration of contrast material, tuberculous lymph nodes demonstrate characteristic low-attenuation necrotic centers and rim enhancement on CT scans.[12, 81, 123, 154] In addition, traditional tests for TB exposure (e.g., the tuberculin skin test) are unreliable in patients with AIDS because most patients are anergic.

M. avium–intracellulare *in Older Women*

M. avium–intracellulare infection can also strike otherwise healthy, immunocompetent hosts. A distinct subtype has been reported in women between ages 50 and 90 years who have no underlying illness but present with a chronic, persistent cough. This subtype has a fairly characteristic CT appearance, with scattered areas of mild tubular bronchiectasis associated with nodular opacities and tree-in-bud forms. Cavitation is less common than in TB.[70a, 153a]

Pulmonary Drug Toxicity

Early detection of drug-induced lung toxicity is another application of HRCT that is under current investigation.* Patients with respiratory symptoms who are receiving bleomycin, methotrexate, amiodarone, or other potentially toxic agents to the lung benefit from CT evaluation (Figs. 27–56 to 27–61). Early detection of drug-induced pulmonary damage increases the likelihood that lung damage will be reversible when the drug is withdrawn.

_____

*See References 16, 17, 26, 28, 115, 116, 163, 172, 187, 188, and 209.

Bleomycin

In cases of *bleomycin lung,* HRCT has been more sensitive than chest radiographs in detecting early pulmonary toxicity, more accurate in quantifying the extent of pulmonary damage, and more helpful in monitoring disease progression or resolution.[16, 17] The extent of pulmonary damage, as seen on CT scans, correlates well with measurements of impaired gas transfer and pulmonary function.[16, 17]

CT features of bleomycin lung toxicity include linear reticulations, fibrotic bands, and nodular opacities that may mimic pulmonary metastases or recurrent tumor (see Fig. 27–58).[16, 163, 188] These changes often appear first in the periphery of the lung and at the lung bases, paralleling the pleural surfaces (see Fig. 27–37).[16, 163, 188] As the pulmonary toxicity becomes more severe, the reticular and nodular opacities coalesce to form large confluent opacities. Diffuse air space disease can also be seen with acute bleomycin toxicity.[188]

Regardless of the offending agent, early CT findings of drug-induced pulmonary toxicity are often confined to the subpleural zone. The apparent susceptibility of this region to lung toxicity may be related to the limited collateral airflow within the region or to the increased pressure and friction the zone experiences from the overlying pleura.[54]

Amiodarone

Amiodarone is an antiarrhythmic agent that can cause significant and potentially irreversible pulmonary toxicity.[62, 132, 175, 237] The drug is used primarily to treat refractory life-threatening arrhythmias. Early recognition of pulmonary toxicity is important because prompt discontinuation of the drug often results in resolution of toxicity.[62, 175]

Unfortunately, few radiographic or laboratory findings are specific for amiodarone toxicity. Symptoms are also nonspecific, making early diagnosis of pulmonary toxicity on the basis of clinical evidence difficult. Onset of symptoms may be insidious, and symptoms caused by amiodarone toxicity, such as pleuritic chest pain, shortness of breath, malaise, and low-grade fever, may be similarly produced by cardiac decompensation, pneumonia, or pulmonary infarction, all common concurrent problems in heart disease patients.[62, 175] Fortunately, because of its unique chemical composition (which contains three iodine moieties), amiodarone—when deposited in sufficient quantities within the lung—can be recognized by its high CT attenuation, which aids in diagnosis (see Figs. 27–59 to 27–61).[28, 115, 116, 172, 187, 209]

On unenhanced scans, CT features of amiodarone lung toxicity include areas of consolidation or focal atelectasis showing high CT attenuation in the range of 80 to 110 HU.[28, 115, 116, 172, 187, 209] The high-attenuation areas frequently abut the pleura, show adjacent pleural reaction, and may be wedge-shaped. Increased attenuation is also frequently demonstrated in the liver, spleen, thyroid gland, and occasionally in the heart muscle. Nonspecific pulmonary infiltrates, interstitial infiltrates, mixed alveolar and interstitial disease, and conglomerate masses may also be seen.[28, 115, 116, 172, 187, 209]

Nonenhanced CT findings of high-attenuation parenchymal abnormalities are thought to be related to the iodinated

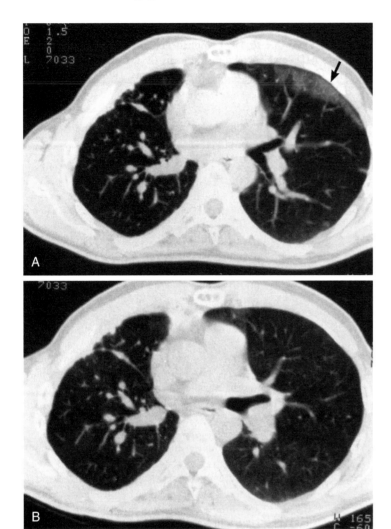

Figure 27–56. CT detection of drug-induced lung toxicity. Patient with recurrent lung cancer receiving ipomeanol, an investigational chemotherapeutic agent known to cause potential lung toxicity. *A,* CT shows development of a band of increased attenuation in the subpleural region, not detected on plain films *(arrow). B,* After discontinuation of the drug, the abnormality resolved.

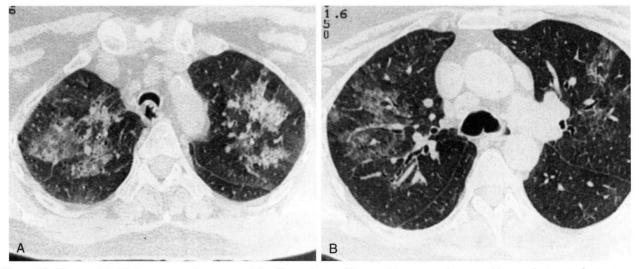

Figure 27–57. *A* and *B,* Methotrexate pulmonary toxicity. The patient, a 59-year-old woman who was taking methotrexate for treatment of severe psoriasis, experienced subacute onset of fatigue, shortness of breath, and a nonproductive cough. CT shows patchy "ground-glass" infiltrates that were difficult to appreciate on chest radiographs. Cultures were negative for infection, and a lung biopsy specimen showed changes consistent with a diagnosis of methotrexate lung toxicity.

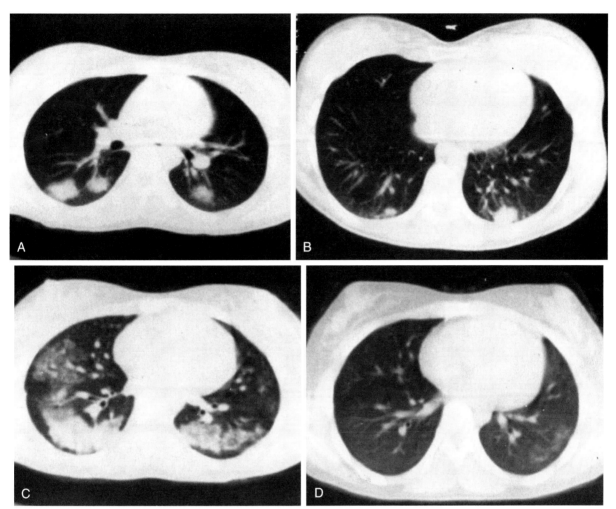

Figure 27–58. Bleomycin lung toxicity, CT features. *A* and *B,* CT shows nodular opacities, which may be mistaken for tumor recurrence or metastases but are actually caused by bleomycin toxicity, proven by biopsy. *C,* CT can be used to follow the progression or resolution of pulmonary toxicity. In this case, the nodular opacities progressed to larger areas of confluence. *D,* After discontinuation of the drug, a follow-up CT scan shows nearly complete resolution of the pulmonary lesions.

chemistry of the drug and its prolonged half-life within the lung.* Amiodarone is known to accumulate in high concentrations within the lung and the liver, where its half-life is 15 to 60 days.[137, 201] Trapped by foamy macrophages, the drug becomes incorporated within lysosomes, where the cationic, amphophilic drug interacts with phospholipids to form a drug-lipid complex that resists biodegradation.† Characteristic lamellar inclusion bodies form within the lysosomes and interfere with lipid degradation and surfactant turnover, ultimately inducing a fibrotic reaction within the lung. These unique properties of amiodarone and the use of CT to discriminate attenuation levels provide a means of identifying those patients with significant pulmonary accumulation of the drug.

Recognizing amiodarone-induced lung changes in nonenhanced CT scans is particularly important in those patients who present with pleuritic chest pain. At least three cases of acute pulmonary decompensation have been re-

ported that occurred after pulmonary arteriography was attempted in patients who presented with pleuritic chest pain caused by amiodarone lung toxicity. Performing pulmonary arteriography in these patients to exclude pulmonary infarction should be avoided if possible.[237]

High-Attenuation Parenchymal Abnormalities

A few other disease processes can produce high-attenuation parenchymal abnormalities on CT scans, as follows:

1. *Metastatic pulmonary calcifications* occurring as the result of hyperparathyroidism from renal failure or from the infusion of large amounts of calcium salts in children with congenital heart disease can cause high-attenuation consolidations on CT scans.[113, 131]
2. Focal and multifocal, high-density lung opacities have been reported in cases of *amyloid,* probably resulting from dystrophic calcification within areas of amyloid accumulation.
3. *Pulmonary ossification* in patients with long-standing

---

*See References 9, 29, 39, 44, 67, 77, 85, 115, 116, 124, 137, 162, 187, 189, and 201.

†See references 9, 29, 39, 44, 62, 67, 77, 85, 124, 137, 162, and 189.

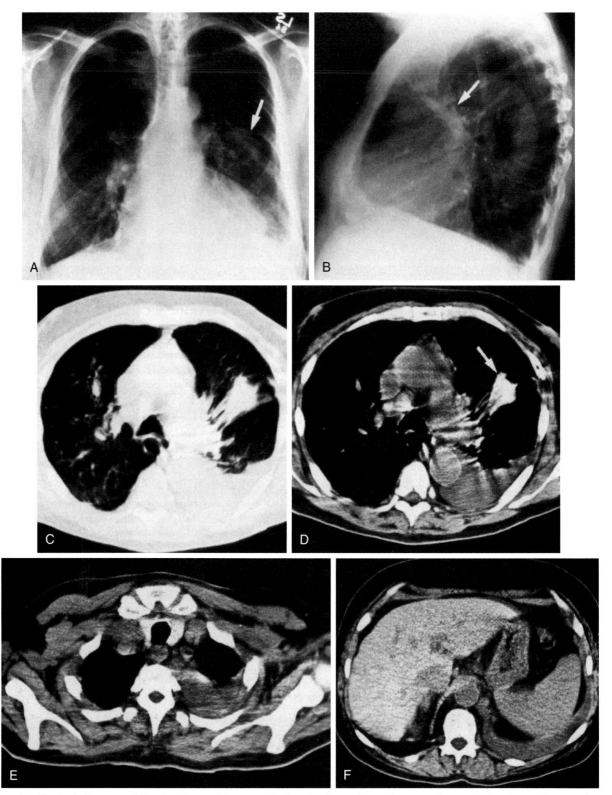

Figure 27–59. Amiodarone toxicity. A 69-year-old man with chronic obstructive pulmonary disease, ischemic cardiomyopathy, and ventricular arrhythmias required antiarrhythmic medication. He presented with a 2-week history of increasing shortness of breath and pleuritic chest pain.

A and *B,* Chest film shows ill-defined opacity or area of focal atelectasis *(arrows)* and left pleural effusion.

C and *D,* Nonenhanced CT scan shows the focal lung opacity demonstrating high attenuation on soft tissue window settings *(arrow)* compatible with a diagnosis of amiodarone toxicity. Bronchoscopy was negative for tumor and for infection and yielded abundant foamy macrophages.

E and *F,* Other CT evidence of amiodarone exposure includes dense thyroid and dense liver resulting from the iodine content of the drug, which accumulates in these organs.

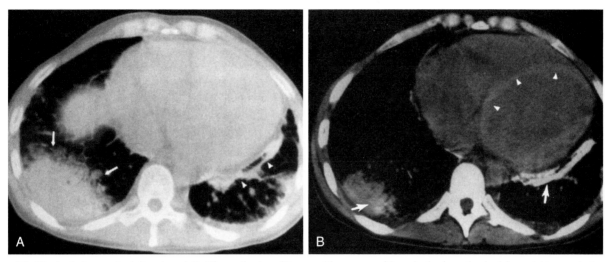

Figure 27–60. Amiodarone toxicity. *A* and *B,* The patient, a 40-year-old-woman with arrhythmias who had been taking amiodarone for 32 months, presented with pleuritic chest pain and shortness of breath. *A,* Noncontrast CT shows a large, wedge-shaped area of consolidation in the right lung base *(arrows).* A band of atelectasis is noted adjacent to the left heart border *(arrowheads).* *B,* Both areas demonstrate high attenuation on soft tissue window settings *(arrows).* The increased attenuation of the heart muscle is a result of amiodarone deposition *(arrowheads).* (From Kuhlman JE, Tergen C, Ren H, et al: Amiodarone pulmonary toxicity: CT findings in symptomatic patients. Radiology 177:121–125, 1990.)

mitral stenosis can produce high-density air space opacities in the lung parenchyma.[238a]

Occupational Lung Disease

The use of CT, especially HRCT, in the evaluation of occupational lung diseases is rapidly expanding.[3, 5, 86, 184] A number of reports suggest that HRCT is superior to conventional radiographs and standard CT in the detection of pulmonary damage resulting from asbestosis and pneumoconiosis. HRCT is being used to detect evidence of occupational lung disease, to determine the extent of the damage, and to follow the disease progression.

CT features of different types of pneumoconiosis are beginning to be recognized and characterized. HRCT findings that have been described in *silicosis* include micronodules, subpleural nodules, conglomerate masses, and focal emphysema (Fig. 27–62).[184]

CT has become an important adjunct to conventional radiographs in the evaluation of *asbestos-related diseases.*[3, 5, 86] CT is more sensitive and specific than plain films for identifying and documenting the presence of *pleural*

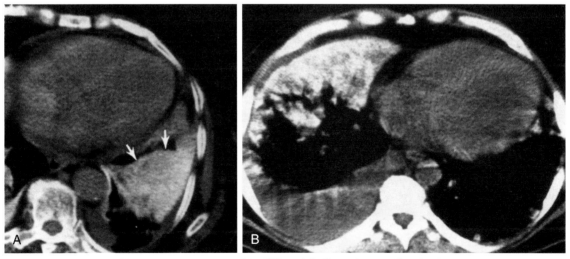

Figure 27–61. High-density infiltrates on noncontrast CT, differential diagnosis. *A,* High-density atelectatic lung measuring 105 Hounsfield units because of amiodarone toxicity. (From Kuhlman JE, Teigen C, Ken H, et al: Amiodarone pulmonary toxicity: CT findings in symptomatic patients. Radiology 177:121–125, 1990.) *B,* High-density consolidation in the right middle lobe in this patient was the result of metastatic pulmonary calcification of chronic renal failure in an area of pneumonia. (From Kuhlman JE, Ren H, Hutchins GM, Fishman EK: Fulminant pulmonary calcification complicating renal transplantation: CT demonstration. Radiology 173: 459–460, 1989.)

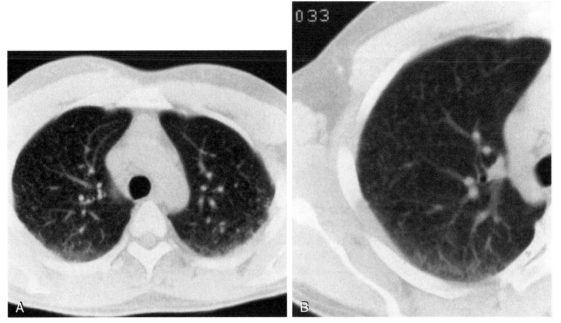

Figure 27–62. *A* and *B,* CT findings in a patient with silicosis. The diffuse profusion of micronodules is caused by silicosis. (From Kuhlman JE: CT of diffuse lung disease. Appl Radiol 20:17–21, 1991.)

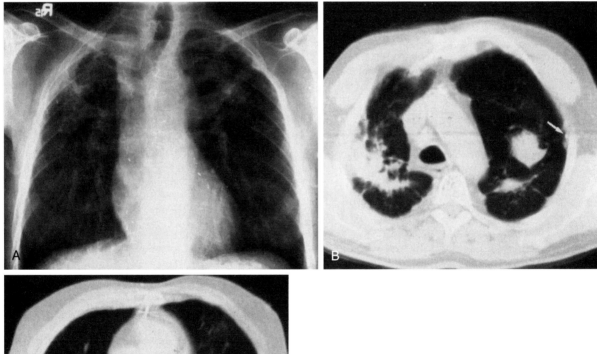

Figure 27–63. *A–C,* CT evaluation of pneumoconiosis. Chest film and CT scan in another patient with silicosis show conglomerate masses with surrounding emphysema, scarring, and upper lobe distribution of disease. CT also reveals many small subpleural micronodules and calcifications *(arrows)* and calcified mediastinal and hilar nodes.

plaques, *pleural thickening*, and *pleural calcifications*, all of which are important markers of asbestos exposure (Fig. 27–63). Mimics of pleural plaques on plain films, such as rib companion shadows, extrapleural fat, and prominent intercostal muscles, are readily distinguished from pleural plaques by CT examination.

CT is also helpful in evaluating other asbestos-related pleural changes, such as *rounded atelectasis*. Rounded atelectasis has a typical CT appearance that distinguishes it from an asbestos-related malignancy, such as *lung cancer* or *mesothelioma* (see "CT Signs of Focal Lung Disease" earlier and Fig. 27–23). HRCT is also used to search for evidence of interstitial fibrosis, which may indicate the presence of *asbestosis*. Findings such as thickened interlobular septa, honeycombing, and subpleural septal lines, although not specific for asbestosis, do indicate the presence of interstitial fibrosis and, when found in association with pleural plaques, are compatible with asbestos-induced parenchymal lung damage.[3, 5, 86]

Quantification of Lung Damage
Emphysema

Quantification of lung damage is another potential application for HRCT in the management of diffuse lung dis-ease. One such application is the assessment of the severity and extent of pulmonary emphysema.[43, 63, 148]

In emphysema, destruction of the alveolar walls and the underlying elastic fiber network of the lung results in permanent enlargement of the air spaces distal to the terminal bronchiole.[7] Involvement of the proximal portions of the acinus (the respiratory bronchioles) results in centrilobular emphysema (CLE) (Fig. 27–64), whereas enlargement of all elements, from the respiratory bronchioles to the terminal blind alveoli, results in panlobular emphysema (Fig. 27–65).[75]

Emphysema is thought to result from an imbalance in the elastase/antielastase activities within the lung. Alveolar wall destruction results from proteolytic destruction by elastin whenever there is a relative increase in elastase activity in comparison to antielastase forces, such as alpha$_1$-antitrypsin activity.[58, 75, 79, 119, 121, 196, 199, 233, 234]

CT features of emphysema include intraparenchymal low-attenuation areas, pulmonary vascular pruning, pulmonary vascular distortion, and abnormal lung density gradients (see Figs. 27–64 and 27–65).[55] Visual grading systems as well as more sophisticated computer-generated attenuation maps of the lung can be used to grade pulmonary emphysema in both a qualitative and a quantitative fash-

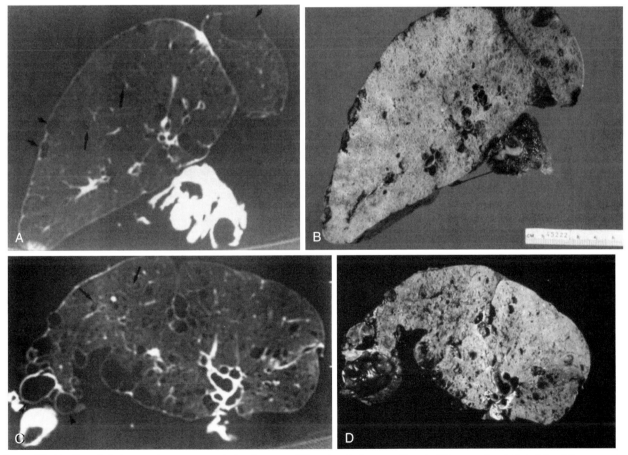

Figure 27–64. Centrilobular emphysema: correlation between CT and pathology studies. *A,* CT scan of an inflated-fixed lung specimen demonstrates focal areas of nonperipheral low attenuation *(long arrows)* and small peripheral bullae *(short arrows). B,* Corresponding gross pathologic specimen. *C,* More severe centrilobular emphysema. CT of lung specimen shows more marked dilatation of the centrilobular air spaces *(arrows)* and large peripheral bullae *(arrowheads). D,* Matching gross specimen. (*A–D,* From Hruban RH, Meziane MA, Zerhouni EA, et al: High-resolution computed tomography of fixed-inflated lungs: Pathologic-radiologic correlation of centrilobular emphysema. Am Rev Respir Dis 136:935–940, 1987.)

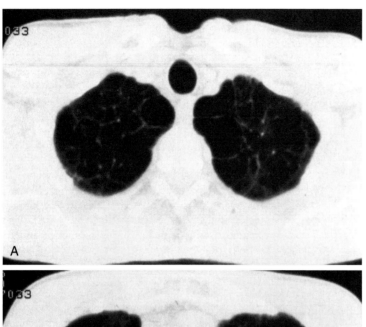

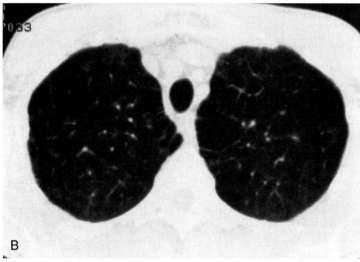

Figure 27–65. *A* and *B,* Panacinar emphysema. High-resolution CT findings of panacinar bullous emphysema include intraparenchymal low-attenuation areas (lung dropout), pulmonary vascular pruning and distortion, abnormally low CT attenuation of the lung, and enlarged air spaces.

ion.[11a] These attempts to assess the extent and severity of emphysema using HRCT criteria have achieved a high degree of success, with emphysema scores correlating well with pulmonary function tests and measurements of impaired diffusing capacity.[43, 63]

CT provides more accurate assessments of emphysema than conventional radiographs, and CT scores of centrilobular emphysema correlate well with the severity of disease demonstrated on pathologic examinations of inflated-fixed lung specimens.[43, 75, 148, 168] HRCT has also been found to be accurate in evaluating experimentally induced emphysema in pig lungs exposed to elastase.[174] Increasingly, HRCT is being used to assess the extent and severity of emphysema in clinical practice as well.[11a, 55]

Lymphangiomyomatosis

Another pulmonary disease whose severity is more accurately depicted with HRCT than with conventional radiography is lymphangiomyomatosis (LAM).[118, 156] Patients with LAM present with symptoms of shortness of breath and dyspnea on exertion that resemble those of emphysema, but the disease occurs exclusively in women of child-bearing age. The symptoms are typically out of pro-

portion to the abnormalities seen on conventional chest films, which may be remarkably normal. In more severe cases, chest radiographs may demonstrate hyperinflation, honeycombing, irregular opacities, coarse reticulations, chylous pleural effusions, and pneumothoraces.[38, 57, 95, 118, 156]

The HRCT appearance of LAM is usually dramatic and characterized by bilateral, diffuse involvement of the lung with thin-walled, cystic air spaces (Fig. 27–66).[118, 156] The cystic spaces generally measure less than 0.5 cm in mild disease but can be greater than 1 cm in diameter when more than 80% of the parenchyma is involved.[156] Most of the spaces have identifiable walls ranging from faintly perceptible to 2 mm thick. Typically, the lung is involved uniformly, with no predilection for upper or lower lobes.

Pathologically, LAM is characterized by widespread proliferation of atypical smooth muscle cells in the bronchial tree, alveolar septa, and pulmonary and lymphatic vessels (Fig. 27–67).[38, 57, 95] The pathogenesis of the cystic spaces seen on HRCT is not known. One theory suggests that obstruction of small airways by the proliferating smooth muscle cells causes distal air trapping and air cyst formation. Other evidence has shown there is an increased number of disrupted elastic fibers within the lungs of patients affected by LAM. Fukuda and colleagues[57] postulate

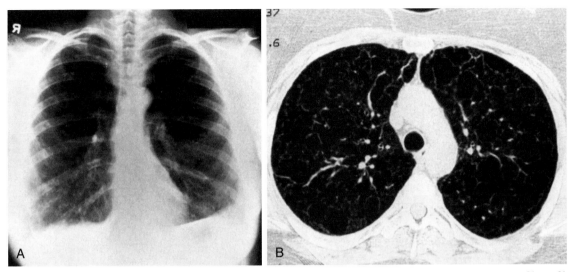

Figure 27–66. The patient is a 43-year-old woman with shortness of breath and recurrent pneumothoraces. *A,* Chest film shows hyperinflation and coarse reticulations. The severity of the symptoms was out of proportion to the chest film abnormalities. (From Kuhlman JE, Reyes BL, Hruban RH, et al: Abnormal air-filled spaces in the lung. Radiographics 13:47–75, 1993.) *B,* High-resolution CT shows extensive replacement of normal lung architecture with innumerable thin-walled, dilated, cystic air spaces that resemble severe panacinar emphysema. In fact, this patient has diffuse lymphangiomyomatosis.

Figure 27–67. Pathology of lymphangiomyomatosis. *A,* Histologic specimen shows proliferation of smooth muscle fibers in the interstitium, and alveolar septa of the lung with remodeling of normal lung architecture. *B,* Low-power view of the lung shows replacement of the lung by cystic, dilated air spaces. (From Kuhlman JE, Reyes BL, Hruban RH, et al: Abnormal air-filled spaces in the lung. Radiographics 13:47–75, 1993.)

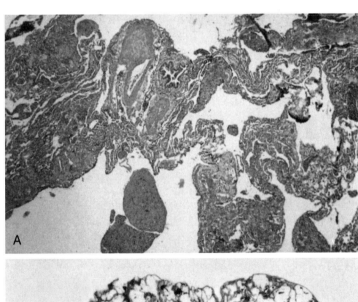

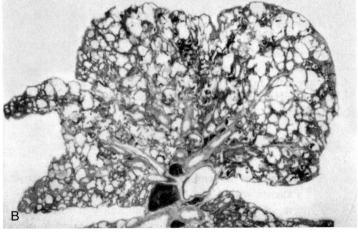

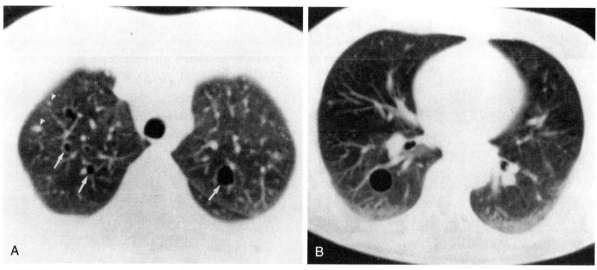

Figure 27–68. *A* and *B*, Early Langerhans' cell histiocytosis involving the lung. CT shows multiple, thin-walled regular cysts *(arrows)* and tiny nodules *(arrowheads)*. (From Kuhlman JE, Reyes BL, Hruban RH, et al: Abnormal air-filled spaces in the lung. Radiographics 13:47–75, 1993.)

that the emphysema-like lesions seen in LAM on pathologic examination result from increased elastic fiber degradation caused by an upset of the elastase/antielastase balance within the lung.

Pulmonary Langerhans' Cell Histiocytosis (Histiocytosis X, Eosinophilic Granuloma)

A lung disease whose radiographic and CT appearance resembles lymphangiomyomatosis is pulmonary Langerhans' cell histiocytosis (formerly, histiocytosis X and eosinophilic granuloma) (Figs. 27–68 to 27–71).[70b] Langerhans' cell histiocytosis is a granulomatous disease of unknown origin that may affect the lung exclusively or may affect multiple organ systems.[133] It is in the spectrum of disseminated disorders, including Letterer-Siwe disease, Hand-Schüller-Christian syndrome, and eosinophilic granuloma.[133] Granulomas, in each case, are formed by eosinophils and cells of the monocyte-macrophage system, which are Langerhans' cells. Langerhans' cell histiocytosis

affects mostly young and middle-aged adults, who present with complaints of cough, dyspnea on exertion, and sometimes chest pain from pneumothorax (20%) or bone involvement.[70b, 133] These patients are almost invariably (>90%) smokers.[70b]

Findings on plain chest films include any combination of reticulation, nodules (2 to 5 mm), cysts (<1 cm), honeycombing, and emphysematous changes.[133, 153] The upper lung zones tend to be more involved and the costophrenic angles spared. Lung volumes are usually normal but sometimes increased. This has been attributed to the opposing effects of emphysema and the cicatricial fibrosis that occurs in this disease.

HRCT demonstrates the extent and distribution of parenchymal lung damage in Langerhans' cell histiocytosis more accurately than conventional radiography.[25, 153] HRCT findings of pulmonary Langerhans' histiocytosis include small nodules (2 to 5 mm or less), cystic air spaces (usually <1 cm), honeycombing, and changes compatible with emphysema (see Figs. 27–68 and 27–70).[25, 153] Much of what

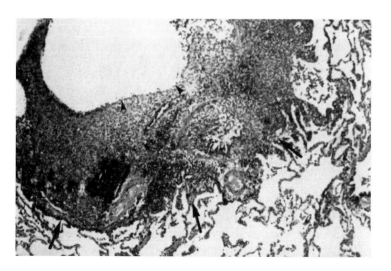

Figure 27–69. Histologic specimen of lung tissue affected by Langerhans' cell histiocytosis. A focus of granulomatous reaction *(arrows)* has created a cystic space *(arrowheads)* through retraction and remodeling of the lung architecture. (From Kuhlman JE, Reyes BL, Hruban KH, et al: Abnormal air-filled spaces in the lung. Radiographics 13:47–75, 1993.)

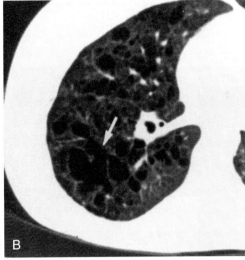

Figure 27–70. Advanced Langerhans' cell histiocytosis. *A,* Chest film in a 19-year-old woman with diabetes insipidus and dyspnea. A right pneumothorax and increased reticulations are present. *B,* High-resolution CT more clearly shows that the lung has been replaced by cystic spaces of varying sizes, some of which have coalesced into bizarre shapes *(arrow).* (From Kuhlman JE, Reyes BL, Hruban RH, et al: Abnormal air-filled spaces in the lung. Radiographics 13:47–75, 1993.)

appears to be reticulation and emphysema on plain films can be shown to be discrete cystic air spaces with definable walls on HRCT.[25] Sometimes several cystic spaces coalesce to form bizarrely shaped air spaces on CT scans. CT also demonstrates more of the smaller (<2 mm) nodules that are frequently not visible on plain radiographs (see Fig. 27–68).[25] These small nodules are more common in the early stages of the disease and tend to spare the lung bases and predominate in the upper lung zones.[70b] With progression, cystic changes take over the lung. Bullae, cavitating nodules, and traction bronchiectasis are also features of Langerhans' cell histiocytosis that can be appreciated on CT examination.[25, 153]

The mechanism by which cystic spaces form in pulmonary Langerhans' cell histiocytosis is uncertain.[87] Central necrosis of granulomatous nodules may produce the thin-walled cavities seen in early pulmonary Langerhans' histiocytosis (see Fig. 27–69). Others have postulated a check-valve obstruction of bronchioles leading to dilatation of

distal airspaces. Another theory suggests that progressive fibrosis occurs around areas of bronchiolar inflammation and granuloma formation. This leads to retractile, paracicatricial emphysema in these peribronchiolar areas with disruption and remodeling of the elastic fiber network that eventually produces a honeycomb lung (see Fig. 27–71).[70b, 87]

Tracheolaryngeal Papillomatosis

Tracheolaryngeal papillomatosis is another rare disease whose lung dissemination is best documented and assessed with CT evaluation. Laryngeal papillomatosis results from an infection by the human papillomavirus that is transmitted from mother to child during birth. Papillomas grow in the upper airways of the child and consist of cauliflower-like lesions with fibrovascular cores or stalks covered by a stratified squamous epithelium.[47]

In the juvenile tracheolaryngeal form of papillomatosis,

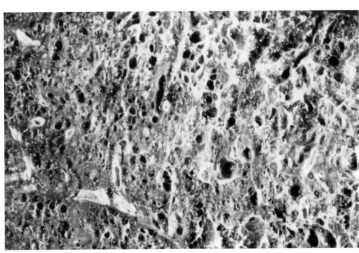

Figure 27–71. Advanced Langerhans' cell histiocytosis. Gross lung specimen shows diffuse replacement of the lung by cystic spaces.

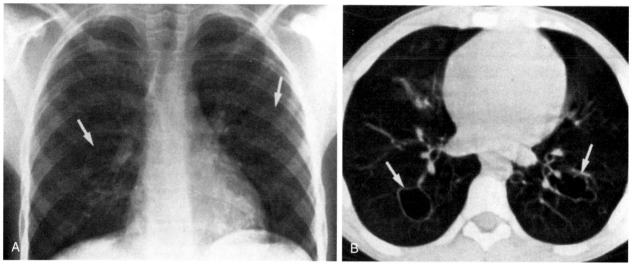

Figure 27–72. CT features of juvenile tracheolaryngeal papillomatosis. Several thin, delicate-walled cystic air spaces are seen *(arrows)* on the chest film *(A)* and the CT scan *(B)* in this 12-year-old boy with upper airway papillomas. (From Kuhlman JE, Reyes BL, Hruban RH, et al: Abnormal air-filled spaces in the lung. Radiographics 13:47–75, 1993.)

the disease extends inferiorly into the tracheobronchial tree (5% of cases) and into the lung parenchyma (1% of cases) (Figs. 27–72 to 27–74).[94] When the lung parenchyma is involved, round nodules, either solid or cystic, may be seen on chest radiographs or CT (see Fig. 27–72). The small cystic lesions eventually enlarge to several centimeters in diameter, with varying wall thickness (see Fig. 27–73).[89, 94] On CT scans, the lesions are widely distributed but with a predilection for the lower lobe and the posterior.

The pathogenesis of lung involvement in tracheolaryngeal papillomatosis is believed to be via aerial dissemination. Small fragments of papillomatous tissue break off

from the upper airways (secondary to bronchoscopy, surgery, tracheostomy) and travel through the major bronchi, where they lodge in the distal small airways causing obstruction and distal air trapping. There, the papilloma fragments enlarge centrifugally and grow along the expanded air spaces. Eventually the papillomatous masses undergo cavitation to form larger cavitary air spaces that are lined by stratified squamous epithelium (see Fig. 27–74).[89, 94]

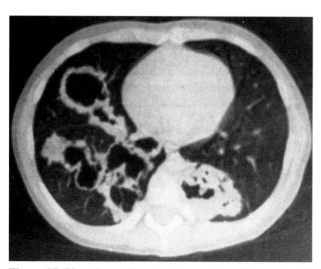

Figure 27–73. Advanced tracheolaryngeal papillomatosis. CT shows extensive cavitary spaces that have a branching and clustered appearance reminiscent of cystic bronchiectasis. The walls are thick and irregular. (From Kuhlman JE, Reyes BL, Hruban RH, et al: Abnormal air-filled spaces in the lung. Radiographics 13:47–75, 1993.)

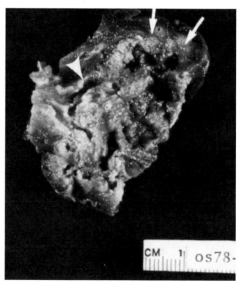

Figure 27–74. Pathology of tracheolaryngeal papillomatosis. A large cavitary space *(arrows)* is lined with verrucous papillomatous tissue. The adjacent bronchus is also involved *(arrowhead)*. Papilloma fragments lodge in distal airways, where they grow along the terminal air spaces. Cavitary spaces form when papillomatous tissues cause bronchiolar obstruction or when papillomatous tumor masses necrose. (From Kuhlman JE, Reyes BL, Hruban RH, et al: Abnormal air-filled spaces in the lung. Radiographics 13:47–75, 1993.)

Monitoring Disease Activity, Complications, and Response to Therapy

Interstitial Pulmonary Fibrosis

Interstitial pulmonary fibrosis may be idiopathic (idiopathic pulmonary fibrosis [IPF], fibrosing alveolitis, and UIP) or may be associated with a number of other disease entities, including collagen vascular disorders (rheumatoid arthritis, polymyositis, lupus, scleroderma, and mixed connective tissue–overlap syndromes), asbestosis, drug toxicity, sarcoidosis, end-stage Farmer's lung, and Langerhans' cell histiocytosis, among others.

CT is useful in diagnosis of IPF in symptomatic patients with nonspecific abnormalities on chest radiographs and in monitoring the disease status in these patients.[155, 159, 211, 215, 227–230] CT visual scoring systems of IPF correlate better than plain film findings with clinical and functional assessments of disease severity.[155, 159, 211, 215, 227–230]

In the early stages of IPF, subpleural ground-glass infiltrates and crescentic densities are identified in the peripheral aspects of the lungs and posterior segments of the lower lobes bilaterally. Later, these subpleural crescentic densities evolve into reticulation and subpleural honeycombing (Figs. 27–75 and 27–76). As honeycombing and fibrosis progress, traction bronchiectasis develops.[155, 159, 211, 215, 227–230] Some honeycomb cysts enlarge to great size as the lung parenchyma is gradually replaced and remodeled by progressive fibrosis.

CT can be used quite effectively to monitor the progression of IPF and its response to treatments such as corticosteroids. The significance of ground-glass opacities in IPF remains controversial. Some authors believe that the presence of such opacities on CT scans in cases of IPF indicates the presence of active alveolitis that may respond to treatment. Other authors have challenged this notion with pathologic correlation studies showing that ground-glass opacities can correspond to areas of alveolitis or to areas of fine fibrosis. The presence of honeycombing on CT scans, however, is a fairly reliable indication of irreversible lung damage.[155, 159]

Adult Respiratory Distress Syndrome

The patient with ARDS generally requires high positive-pressure mechanical ventilation and is at high risk for development of barotrauma in the form of interstitial emphysema, subpleural air cyst formation, pneumothorax, and pneumomediastinum (see Figs. 27–23 and 27–24).[231] Although CT has not been used extensively in patients with ARDS, it may play a role in the evaluation of acute and long-term complications in this setting.[45a, 148a] CT assessments of disease severity and their prognostic implications are currently under investigation by several authors (Fig. 27–77).[21, 45a, 66, 140, 151, 180, 212, 220]

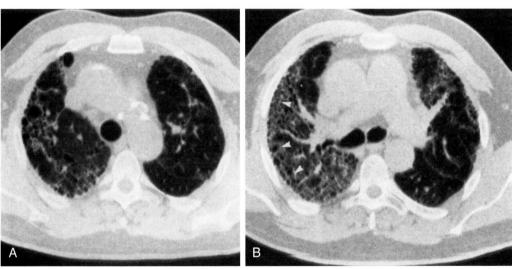

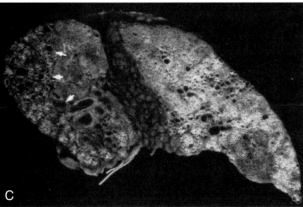

Figure 27–75. Idiopathic pulmonary fibrosis. *A* and *B*, High-resolution CT shows subpleural reticulations and small air cysts *(arrowheads)* ranging in size from 2 to 10 mm. Honeycombing is more severe in the periphery of the lung. *C*, Autopsy specimen shows many subpleural air cysts *(arrows)* in a subpleural distribution with extensive fibrosis and lung remodeling. The transition is abrupt between central normal-appearing lung and the peripheral honeycombing. (*B* and *C*, From Kuhlman JE, Reyes BL, Hruban RH, et al: Abnormal air-filled spaces in the lung. Radiographics 13:47–75, 1993.)

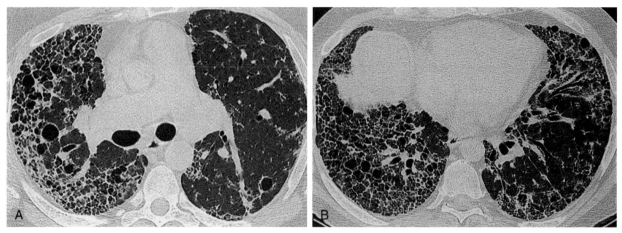

Figure 27–76. *A* and *B,* Interstitial pulmonary fibrosis associated with polymyositis. High-resolution CT shows reticulation and honeycombing in the periphery of the lung and in the lung bases, more severe on the right than on the left. Note "traction" bronchiectasis due to interstitial fibrosis.

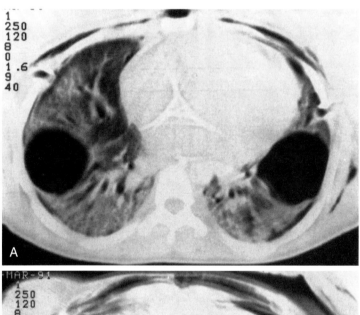

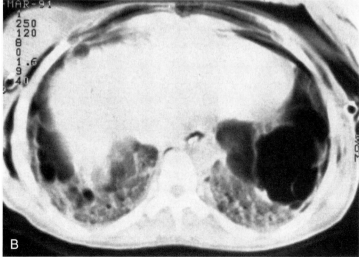

Figure 27–77. *A* and *B,* High-resolution CT of adult respiratory distress syndrome (ARDS) and its complications. Postpartum pneumonia and ARDS developed in a 17-year-old girl. Bilateral "ground-glass" infiltrates compatible with a diagnosis of ARDS are evident on CT scanning. Large extra-alveolar air cysts have developed. CT shows that these air cysts have no discernible walls and are located in the subpleural and basal regions of the lung. Bilateral chest tubes are in place for complicating pneumothoraces. Subcutaneous emphysema is present.

The pathophysiology of barotrauma-related complications in ARDS was first examined by Macklin and Macklin[129] and then further elucidated by Westcott and Cole.[231] The process begins with rupture of weaker alveoli along the margins of the interlobular septa and bronchovascular structures as a result of increased airway pressures. Air then dissects along the interlobular septa and along the perivascular spaces, producing interstitial emphysema. Interstitial air may then rupture into the pleural space causing pneumothorax or into the mediastinum causing pneumomediastinum. Or air may collect in extra-alveolar spaces within the interstitium, forming large air cysts. These air cysts typically are found in the lung bases and subpleural zones adjacent to the diaphragm or mediastinum. They may enlarge to great size, causing respiratory and circulatory compromise, and they may be mistaken for loculated pneumothoraces.[129, 231]

On CT scans, subpleural air cysts associated with ARDS appear as air spaces with no definable walls (see Fig. 27–77).[212] They typically expand into the fissures or subpulmonic zones and compress adjacent lung parenchyma as they enlarge. Although a CT scan is not as easy to obtain as a portable chest film in critically ill, ventilator-dependent patients, CT is more accurate in identifying and localizing complications of barotrauma, such as pneumothoraces, pneumomediastinum, and subpleural air cysts. This may become important in those select patients who are not responding to treatment or who deteriorate suddenly for unclear reasons. For example, what may appear to be an appropriately placed chest tube on a portable supine chest radiograph may be found to be inadequate in location on CT scans.

In addition, a few investigators have begun to correlate patient outcome in ARDS with the extent and severity of pulmonary infiltrates and complications as graded by CT.[21, 66, 140, 151, 180, 212, 220] Further study is necessary to determine whether CT findings of ARDS are reliable prognostic indicators.

Sarcoidosis

CT is used extensively to identify, stage, and monitor patients with pulmonary sarcoidosis, a disease of unknown origin that is characterized pathologically by the presence of noncaseating granuloma.[219] The lung and the intrathoracic lymph nodes are the most commonly affected organs of the body, and thoracic complications account for most of the morbidity and mortality caused by this disease.[178] Although only 60% of patients with sarcoidosis demonstrate chest film abnormalities, histologic evidence of granulomatous disease is almost always present on biopsy specimens taken from the lung.[178]

CT is more accurate than conventional radiography in detecting subtle areas of parenchymal involvement and in delineating the full extent of lung disease caused by sarcoidosis.[69, 108, 191, 208] CT features of pulmonary sarcoidosis include thickening of the interlobular septa, reticulonodular disease, multinodular disease, mixed infiltrates, and masslike consolidations. In pulmonary sarcoidosis, the noncaseating granulomas have a propensity for forming in association with the lymphatics of the interstitial tissues in the peribronchial, perivascular, and subpleural spaces as well as in the interlobular septa. These granulomas produce the reticulonodular infiltrates seen on CT scans, which may appear predominantly linear or nodular depending on the size of the granulomas and the amount of fibrosis that is present (Fig. 27–78). Granulomas that form along the interlobular septa can produce an appearance resembling the beaded septum sign seen in lymphangitic carcinomatosis.[108, 178]

Pulmonary involvement in sarcoidosis is usually bilateral, although it may be asymmetrical. Multinodular disease may have several distributions; for example, tiny nodules, 1 to 3 mm in size, distributed evenly throughout the lung in a miliary pattern, or large, coarser nodules that are more varied in size and more unevenly scattered. Subpleural nodules, septal nodules, and perihilar peribronchovascular nodules are typical of sarcoidosis. Mixed patterns with reticulation, thickening of the interlobular markings, fibrosis, and pleural thickening may also be seen.[69, 108, 191, 208]

Occasionally, sarcoidosis presents as multiple, round, masslike consolidations on chest films and CT. The masses often demonstrate air-bronchograms, and this form of sarcoidosis has been called *alveolar* or *acinar* sarcoid (Fig. 27–79).[60, 108, 122, 191, 218] These masses, however, do not represent true air space filling in the sense that a pneumonia would; rather, the masses represent numerous granulomas that have coalesced within the interstitium, forming massive conglomerates that compress the surrounding air spaces.

Pathologically, pulmonary sarcoidosis begins as an acute alveolitis followed by a phase of granuloma formation within the lung interstitium.[219] In most cases, the disease stabilizes at this stage, leaving the patient with persistent granulomas in the lung, or the lung disease resolves completely. In 20% of patients, however, the disease progresses.[178] With more advanced disease, findings of pulmonary fibrosis dominate the CT picture. Progressive fibrosis and architectural distortion lead to honeycombing, fibrocystic changes, bullae, traction bronchiectasis, and retraction of the pulmonary hila (Fig. 27–80). The upper lung zones are more severely affected, and evidence of secondary pulmonary hypertension and cor pulmonale is frequently seen. Fibrotic conglomerate masses reminiscent of those seen in silicosis may also develop in advanced disease.[69, 108]

True cavities lined by noncaseating granulomas are extremely rare (<0.6%) in sarcoidosis.[178, 191] Most apparent cavities are the result of fibrocystic disease and bullae that develop in advanced disease, and they are lined by fibrous tissue, not granulomas. Superimposed infection of fibrocystic spaces, particularly with *Aspergillus*, is a frequent complication of sarcoidosis and accounts for significant morbidity and mortality.

In the patient with advanced sarcoidosis and hemoptysis, CT is useful in detecting or confirming the presence of complicating aspergillomas, particularly when the chest radiograph is difficult to interpret because of extensive disease and fibrosis (Fig. 27–81).[69, 108, 208] CT scans obtained in the supine and prone positions usually demonstrate movement of mycetomas within cystic spaces. Superimposed bacterial infections may also complicate fibrocystic spaces in sarcoidosis, and there is a higher incidence of TB in sarcoid patients than in the population as a whole.[178]

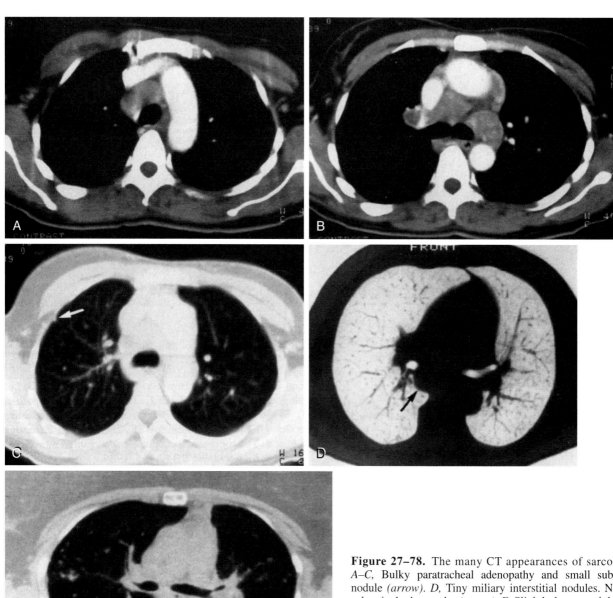

Figure 27–78. The many CT appearances of sarcoidosis. *A–C,* Bulky paratracheal adenopathy and small subpleural nodule *(arrow). D,* Tiny miliary interstitial nodules. Note the subcarinal adenopathy *(arrow). E,* Slightly larger nodules scattered throughout lung.

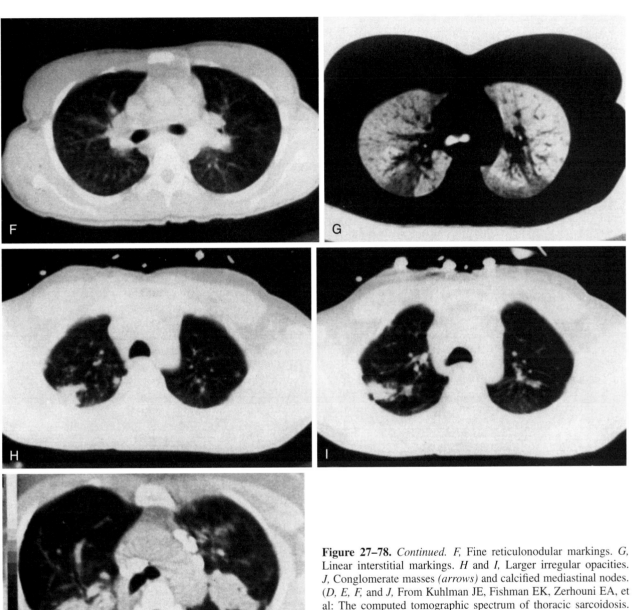

Figure 27–78. *Continued. F,* Fine reticulonodular markings. *G,* Linear interstitial markings. *H* and *I,* Larger irregular opacities. *J,* Conglomerate masses *(arrows)* and calcified mediastinal nodes. (*D, E, F,* and *J,* From Kuhlman JE, Fishman EK, Zerhouni EA, et al: The computed tomographic spectrum of thoracic sarcoidosis. Radiographics 9:449–466, 1989.)

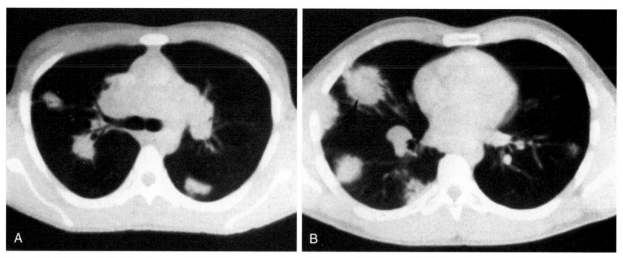

Figure 27–79. *A* and *B,* Alveolar sarcoid. CT shows round masslike consolidations with air-bronchograms. Note hilar adenopathy.

Other thoracic complications of sarcoidosis include extension of the inflammatory, fibrotic process into the mediastinum, resulting in fibrosing mediastinitis. On CT scans, abnormal fibrotic tissue can be seen to narrow and obstruct the mainstem bronchi, mediastinal vessels, and pulmonary vessels (Fig. 27–82).[69, 108]

Lymphadenopathy is even more common than parenchymal lung disease in patients with sarcoidosis, and CT is superior to chest radiography for delineating the full extent of lymphadenopathy (Fig. 27–83).[69, 178, 191] Paratracheal and hilar adenopathy are typical of sarcoidosis, but CT also may demonstrate adenopathy in the anterior mediastinum, axilla, internal mammary chain, and below the diaphragm.[69, 191, 192]

The major differential diagnosis to consider when adenopathy is seen in these locations is lymphoma, and definitive diagnosis usually requires tissue confirmation. Certain CT patterns of nodal involvement, however, favor a diagnosis of sarcoidosis. Symmetrical paratracheal and hilar adenopathy, especially when accompanied by reticulonodular infiltrates, is suggestive of sarcoidosis in the non–HIV-positive patient.[69]

In contrast to adenopathy caused by neoplastic disorders, enlarged lymph nodes resulting from sarcoidosis tend to remain discrete and maintain their rounded nodal shape, rather than coalescing into amorphous nodal masses.[69, 108] Calcifications within hilar and mediastinal nodes are common in sarcoid, which is one of the diseases that can produce eggshell calcifications in lymph nodes along with TB, fungal infections, and silicosis.

In clinical practice, CT examination of the patient with sarcoidosis is an integral part of the evaluation process at all stages of the disease. Indications for CT evaluation include establishing and confirming the diagnosis, staging the disease, monitoring disease activity and progression, assessing treatment response, and detecting and evaluating complications.[108]

Patients with chest film abnormalities and possible sarcoidosis may benefit from further characterization of their pulmonary disease by CT. CT also serves as a road map

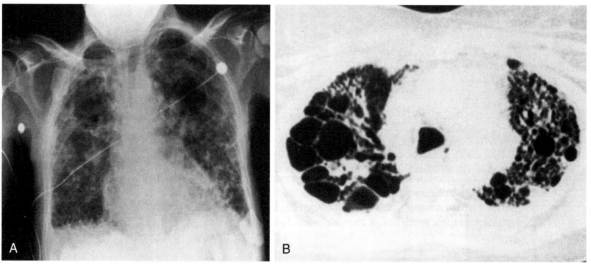

Figure 27–80. *A* and *B,* Advanced sarcoid with lung fibrosis, honeycombing, and extensive fibrocystic changes.

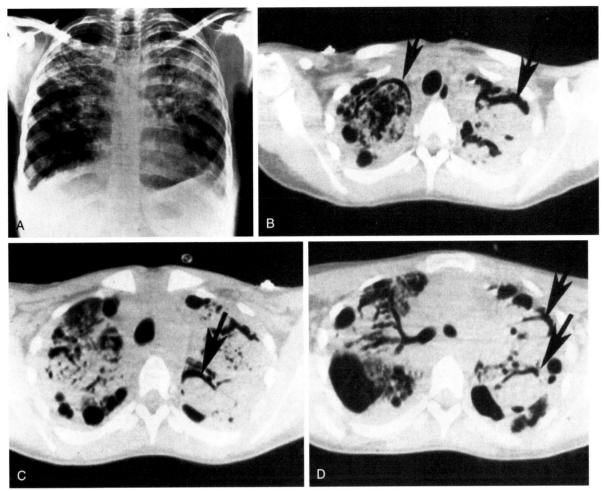

Figure 27–81. Complication of sarcoidosis—mycetoma formation. *A,* Chest film shows extensive upper lobe disease and fibrosis resulting from sarcoidosis. *B–D,* CT reveals that at least five mycetomas are present *(arrows). (A* and *B,* From Kuhlman JE, Fishman EK, Zerhouni EA, et al: The computed tomographic spectrum of thoracic sarcoidosis. Radiographics 9:449–466, 1989.)

Figure 27–82. Fibrosing mediastinitis resulting from sarcoidosis. *A,* CT shows abnormal soft tissue infiltration of the mediastinal fat with amputation of the left pulmonary artery *(arrow).* Enlarged internal mammary nodes as well as lung disease and a left pleural effusion are present. *B,* A ventilation-perfusion scan shows ventilation but no perfusion to the left lung. (From Kuhlman JE, Fishman EK, Zerhouni EA, et al: The computed tomographic spectrum of thoracic sarcoidosis. Radiographics 9:449–466, 1989.)

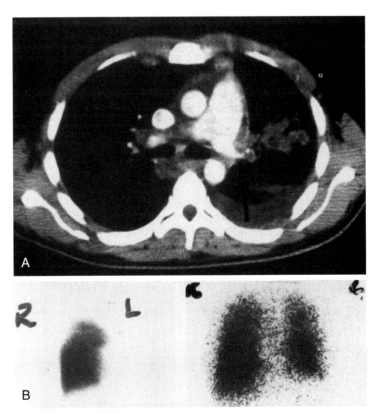

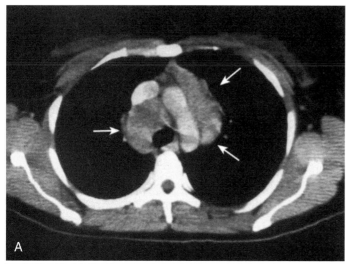

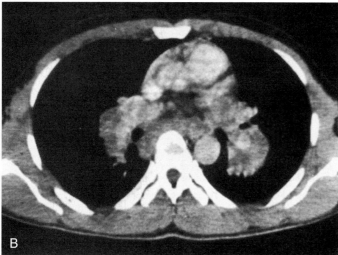

Figure 27–83. CT evaluation of sarcoidosis to determine the extent of adenopathy. *A,* Bulky anterior mediastinal and right paratracheal adenopathy *(arrows). B,* Bilateral hilar and subcarinal adenopathy. (From Kuhlman JE, Fishman EK, Zerhouni EA, et al: The computed tomographic spectrum of thoracic sarcoidosis. Radiographics 9:449–466, 1989.)

for planning biopsy procedures, localizing the best sites for transbronchial lung biopsy, percutaneous biopsy, and nodal sampling. Patients with known sarcoidosis also benefit from CT evaluation when atypical radiographic findings require further explanation or when complications are suspected but have not been detected by conventional radiography.[69, 108]

Summary

CT remains an adjunct to the conventional chest radiograph in the evaluation of non-neoplastic lung diseases. As an adjunct, however, CT is an important, indispensable asset. When combined with HRCT techniques and the emerging fast scanning capabilities of spiral, multidetector, and ultrafast electron beam CT, CT has become a powerful tool for detecting, characterizing, and quantifying non-neoplastic diseases of the lung.

References

1. Abd AG, Nierman DM, Ilowite JS, et al: Bilateral upper lobe PCP in a patient receiving inhaled pentamidine prophylaxis. Chest 94: 329–331, 1988.
2. Aberle DR, Gamsu G, Lynch D: Thoracic manifestations of Wegener granulomatosis: Diagnosis and course. Radiology 174:703–709, 1990.
3. Aberle DR, Gamsu G, Ray CS, Feuerstein IM: Asbestos-related pleural and parenchymal fibrosis: Detection with high-resolution CT. Radiology 166:729–734, 1988.
4. Akira M, Higashihara T, Sakatani M, Hara H: Diffuse panbronchiolitis: Follow-up CT examination. Radiology 189:559–562, 1993.
4a. Akira M, Kitatani F, Yong-Sik L, et al: Diffuse panbronchiolitis: Evaluation with high-resolution CT. Radiology 168:433–438, 1988.
5. Akira M, Yamamoto S, Yokoyama K, et al: Asbestosis: High-resolution CT: Pathologic correlation. Radiology 176:389–394, 1990.
6. Albelda SM, Kern JA, Marinelli DL, Miller WT: Expanding spectrum of pulmonary disease caused by nontuberculous mycobacteria. Radiology 157:289–296, 1985.
7. American Thoracic Society: Chronic bronchitis, asthma, and pulmonary emphysema. Statement by the Committee on Standards for Nontuberculous Respiratory Diseases. Am Rev Respir Dis 85:762–768, 1962.
8. Amos A, Denning D, Katz D, Smith H: Computed tomography of chest in diagnosis of miliary tuberculosis. Lancet 1:1269–1270, 1987.
9. Andreason F, Agerbaek H, Bjerregaard P, Gotzsche H: Pharmacokinetics of amiodarone after intravenous and oral administration. Eur J Clin Pharmacol 19:293–299, 1981.
10. Auerbach O, Dail DH: Mycobacterial infections. In Dail DH, Hammar SP (eds): Pulmonary Pathology. New York, Springer-Verlag, 1988, pp 173–188.
11. Balakrishnan J, Meziane MA, Siegelman SS, Fishman EK: Pulmo-

nary infarction: CT appearance with pathologic correlation. J Comput Assist Tomogr 13:941–945, 1989.

11a. Bankier AA, De Maertelaer V, Keyzer C, Gevenois PA: Pulmonary emphysema subjective visual grading versus objective quantification with macroscopic morphometry and thin-section CT densitometry. Radiology 211:851–858, 1999.

12. Barnett SM: CT findings in tuberculous mediastinitis. J Comput Assist Tomogr 10:165–166, 1986.

13. Barrio JL, Suarez M, Rodriguez JL, et al: PCP presenting as cavitating and noncavitating solitary pulmonary nodules in patients with AIDS. Am Rev Respir Dis 134:1094–1096, 1986.

14. Bartter T, Irwin RS, Nash G, et al: Idiopathic bronchiolitis obliterans organizing pneumonia with peripheral infiltrates on chest roentgenogram. Arch Intern Med 149:273–279, 1989.

14a. Bates SM, Ginsberg JS: Helical computed tomography and the diagnosis of pulmonary embolism. Ann Intern Med 132:240–242, 2000.

15. Beers MF, Sohn M, Swartz M: Recurrent pneumothorax in AIDS patients with PCP: A clinicopathologic report of three cases and review of the literature. Chest 98:266–270, 1990.

15a. Beigelman C, Chartrand-Lefebvre C, Howarth N, Grenier P: Pitfalls in diagnosis of pulmonary embolism with helical CT angiography. AJR Am J Roentgenol 171:579–585, 1998.

16. Bellamy EA, Husband JE, Blaquiere RM, Law MR: Bleomycin-related lung damage: CT evidence. Radiology 156:155–158, 1985.

17. Bellamy EA, Nicholas D, Husband JE: Quantitative assessment of lung damage due to bleomycin using computed tomography. Br J Radiol 60:1205–1209, 1987.

18. Bellomo R, Finlay M, McLaughlin P, Tai E: Clinical spectrum of cryptogenic organizing pneumonitis. Thorax 46:554–558, 1991.

19. Bergin CJ, Muller NL: CT in the diagnosis of interstitial lung disease. Am J Roentgenol 145:505–510, 1985.

20. Bergin CJ, Muller NL: CT of interstitial lung disease: A diagnostic approach. AJR Am J Roentgenol 148:8–15, 1987.

20a. Boiselle PM, Crans CA, Kaplan MA: The changing face of *Pneumocystis carinii* pneumonia in AIDS patients. AJR Am J Roentgenol 172:1301–1309, 1999.

21. Bombino M, Gattinoni L, Pesenti A, et al: The value of portable chest roentgenography in adult respiratory distress syndrome: Comparison with computed tomography. Chest 100:762–769, 1991.

22. Bouchardy LM, Kuhlman JE, Ball WC, et al: CT findings in bronchiolitis obliterans organizing pneumonia (BOOP) with x-ray, clinical, and histologic correlations. J Comput Assist Tomogr 17:352–357, 1993.

23. Reference deleted.

24. Boudes P: Purely granulomatous Wegener's granulomatosis: A new concept for an old disease. Semin Arthritis Rheum 19:365–370, 1990.

25. Brauner MW, Grenier P, Mouelhi MM, et al: Pulmonary histiocytosis X: Evaluation with high-resolution CT. Radiology 172:255–258, 1989.

26. Brown WG, Hasa FM, Barbee RA: Reversibility of severe bleomycin induced pulmonary pneumonitis. JAMA 239:2012–2014, 1978.

27. Burch PA, Karp JE, Merz WG, et al: Favorable outcome of invasive aspergillosis in patients with adult acute leukemia. J Clin Oncol 5:1985–1993, 1987.

28. Butler S, Smathers RL: Case report. Computed tomography of amiodarone pulmonary toxicity. J Comput Assist Tomogr 9:375–376, 1985.

29. Camus P, Jeannin LRE: Speculation on the mechanism for amiodarone-induced pneumonitis (Letter). Radiology 150:279–280, 1984.

30. Case Records of the Massachusetts General Hospital. Case 9–1989. N Engl J Med 320:582–587, 1989.

31. Chaffey MH, Klein JS, Gamsu G, et al: Radiographic distribution of PCP in patients with AIDS treated with prophylactic inhaled pentamidine. Radiology 175:715–719, 1990.

32. Chandler PW, Myung SS, Friedman SE, et al: Radiographic manifestations of bronchiolitis obliterans with organizing pneumonia vs usual interstitial pneumonia. Am J Roentgenol 157:899–906, 1986.

33. Chintapalli D, Thorsen MK, Olson DL, et al: Computed tomography of pulmonary thromboembolism and infarction. J Comput Assist Tomogr 12:553–559, 1988.

34. Churg A: Pulmonary angiitis and granulomatosis revisited. Hum Pathol 14:868–883, 1983.

34a. Coche EE, Muller NL, Kim K, et al: Acute pulmonary embolism: Ancillary findings at spiral CT. Radiology 207:753–758, 1998.

35. Colby TV: Pathologic aspects of bronchiolitis obliterans organizing pneumonia. Chest 102:38s–43s, 1992.

36. Contreras MA, Cheung OT, Sanders DE, Goldstein RS: Pulmonary infection with nontuberculous mycobacteria. Am Rev Respir Dis 137:149–152, 1988.

37. Cordier JF, Loire R, Brune J: Idiopathic bronchiolitis obliterans organizing pneumonia: Definition of characteristic clinical profiles in a series of 16 patients. Chest 96:999–1004, 1989.

38. Corrin B, Liebow AA, Friedman PJ: Pulmonary lymphangiomyomatosis: A review. Am J Pathol 79:348–367, 1975.

39. Costa-Jussa FR, Corrin B, Jacobs JM: Amiodarone lung toxicity: A human and experimental study. J Pathol 143:73–79, 1984.

40. Costello P, Anderson W, Blume D: Pulmonary nodule: Evaluation with spiral volumetric CT. Radiology 179:875–876, 1991.

41. Cupples JB, Blackie SP, Road JD: Granulomatous PCP mimicking tuberculosis. Arch Pathol Lab Med 113:1281–1284, 1989.

42. Currie DC, Goldman JM, Cole PJ, Strickland B: Comparison of narrow section CT and plain chest radiography in chronic ABPA. Clin Radiol 38:593–596, 1987.

43. Dakai F, Gamsu G, Im JG, Ray CS: Pulmonary function abnormalities in patients with CT-determined emphysema. J Comput Assist Tomogr 11:936–938, 1987.

44. Dake MD, Madison JM, Montgomery CK, et al: Electron microscopic demonstration of lysosomal inclusion bodies in lung, liver, lymph nodes, and blood leukocytes of patients with amiodarone pulmonary toxicity. Am J Med 78:506–512, 1985.

45. Davis SD, Berkmen YM, King T: Peripheral bronchial involvement in relapsing polychondritis: Demonstration by thin-section CT. AJR Am J Roentgenol 153:953–954, 1989.

45a. Desai SR, Wells AU, Rubens MB, et al: Acute respiratory distress syndrome: CT abnormalities at long-term follow-up. Radiology 210:29–35, 1999.

46. DeLorenzo LJ, Huang C, Maguire G, Stone G: Roentgenographic patterns of PCP in 104 patients with AIDS. Chest 91:323–327, 1987.

47. DiMarco AF, Montenegro H, Payne CB, Kwon KH: Papillomas of the tracheobronchial tree with malignant degeneration. Chest 74:4–5, 1978.

48. Doyle TC, Lawler GA: CT features of rounded atelectasis of the lung. Am J Roentgenol 143:225–228, 1984.

49. Epler GR: Bronchiolitis obliterans organizing pneumonia: Definition and clinical features. Chest 102:2s–6s, 1992.

50. Epler GR, Colby TV: The spectrum of bronchiolitis obliterans. Chest 83:161–162, 1983.

51. Epler GR, Colby TV, McLoud TC, et al: Bronchiolitis obliterans organizing pneumonia. N Engl J Med 312:152–158, 1985.

52. Fauci AS, Haynes BF, Katz P, Wolffe SM: Wegener's granulomatosis: Prospective clinical and therapeutic experience with 85 patients for 21 years. Ann Intern Med 98:76–85, 1983.

53. Feuerstein IM, Archer A, Pluda JM, et al: Thin-walled cavities, cysts, and pneumothorax in PCP: Further observation with histopathologic correlation. Radiology 174:697–702, 1990.

54. Fleischman RW, Baker JR, Thompson GR, et al: Bleomycin induced interstitial pneumonia in dogs. Thorax 26:675–681, 1971.

55. Foster WI, Pratt PC, Roggli VL, et al: Centrilobular emphysema: CT-pathologic correlation. Radiology 159:27–32, 1986.

56. Fraser RG, Pare JAP: Diagnosis of Diseases of the Chest, vol 2, 3rd ed. Philadelphia, WB Saunders, 1989.

57. Fukuda Y, Kawamoto M, Yamamoto A, et al: Role of elastic fiber degradation in emphysema-like lesions of pulmonary lymphangiomyomatosis. Hum Pathol 21:1252–1261, 1990.

58. Fukuda Y, Masuda Y, Ishizaki M, et al: Morphogenesis of abnormal elastic fibers in lungs of patients with panacinar and centriacinar emphysema. Hum Pathol 20:652–659, 1989.

59. Gale ME, Karlinsky JB: Computed Tomography of the Chest: A Teaching File. Chicago, Year Book Medical, 1988.

60. Galzer HS, Levitt RG, Shackelford GD: Peripheral pulmonary infiltrates in sarcoidosis. Chest 86:741–744, 1984.

61. Gefter WB, Albelda SM, Talbot GH, et al: Invasive pulmonary aspergillosis and acute leukemia. Radiology 157:605, 1985.

62. Gefter WB, Epstein DM, Pietra GG, Miller WT: Lung disease caused by amiodarone: A new antiarrhythmic agent. Radiology 147:339–344, 1983.

63. Goddard PR, Nicholson EM, Laszlo G, Watt I: Computed tomography in pulmonary emphysema. Clin Radiol 33:379–387, 1982.

64. Godwin JD, Muller NL, Takasugi JE: Pulmonary alveolar proteinosis: CT findings. Radiology 169:609–613, 1988.

65. Godwin JD, Webb WR, Gamsu G, Ovenfors C: Computed tomography of pulmonary embolism. Am J Roentgenol 135:691–695, 1980.

66. Golding RP, Knape P, Strack Van Schinjndel RJM, et al: Computed tomography as an adjunct to chest x-rays of intensive care unit patients. Crit Care Med 16:211–216, 1988.

67. Goldman IS, Winkler HL, Raper SE, et al: Increased hepatic density and phospholipidosis due to amiodarone. Am J Roentgenol 144:541–546, 1985.

67a. Goodman LR, Curtin JJ, Mewissen MW, et al. Detection of pulmonary embolism in patients with unresolved clinical and scintigraphic diagnosis: Helical CT versus angiography. AJR Am J Roentgenol 164:1369–1374, 1995.

68. Gosink BB, Friedman PJ, Liebow AA: Bronchiolitis: Roentgenologic-pathologic correlation. Am J Roentgenol 117:816–832, 1973.

68a. Greaves SM, Hart EM, Brown K, et al: Pulmonary thromboembolism. Spectrum of findings on CT. AJR Am J Roentgenol 165:1359–1363, 1995.

69. Hamper UM, Fishman EK, Khouri NF, et al: Typical and atypical CT manifestations of pulmonary sarcoidosis. J Comput Assist Tomogr 10:928–936, 1986.

70. Hansell D, Strickland B: HRCT in pulmonary cystic fibrosis. Br J Radiol 62:1–5, 1989.

70a. Hartman TE, Swenson SJ, Williams DE: *Mycobacterium avium–intracellulare* complex: Evaluation with CT. Radiology 187:23–26, 1993.

70b. Hartman TE, Tazelaar HD, Swensen SJ, Muller NL: Cigarette smoking: CT and pathologic findings of associated pulmonary diseases. Radiographics 17:377–390, 1997.

71. Hauser H, Gurret JP: Miliary tuberculosis associated with adrenal enlargement: CT appearance. J Comput Assist Tomogr 10:254–256, 1986.

72. Heger JJ, Prystowshky EN, Jackman WM, et al: Clinical efficacy and electrophysiology during long-term therapy for recurrent ventricular tachycardia or ventricular fibrillation. N Engl J Med 305:539–545, 1981.

73. Heitzman ER, Markarian B, Berger I, Dailey E: The secondary pulmonary lobule: A practical concept for interpretation of radiographs. I. Roentgen anatomy of the normal secondary pulmonary lobule. Radiology 93:508–513, 1969.

74. Hensley MJ, Feldman NT, Lazarus JM, Galvanek EG: Diffuse pulmonary hemorrhage and rapidly progressive renal failure. Am J Med 66:894–898, 1979.

75. Hruban RH, Meziane MA, Zerhouni EA, et al: High-resolution computed tomography of fixed-inflated lungs: Pathologic-radiologic correlation of centrilobular emphysema. Am Rev Respir Dis 136:935–940, 1987.

76. Hruban RH, Ren H, Kuhlman JE, et al: Inflation-fixed lungs: Pathologic-radiologic (CT) correlation of lung transplantation. J Comput Assist Tomogr 14:329–335, 1990.

77. Hruban Z: Pulmonary and generalized lysosomal storage induced by amphophilic drugs. Environ Health Perspect 55:53–76, 1984.

78. Huang RM, Naidich DP, Lubat E, et al: Septic pulmonary emboli: CT-radiologic correlation. AJR Am J Roentgenol 153:41–45, 1989.

79. Hunninghake GW, Gadek JE, Fales HM, Crystal RG: Human alveolar macrophage derived chemotactic factors for neutrophils. J Clin Invest 66:473–483, 1980.

80. Huston J III, Muhm JR: Solitary pulmonary nodules: Evaluation with a CT reference phantom. Radiology 170:653–656, 1989.

80a. Im JG, Itoh H, Shim YS, et al: Pulmonary tuberculosis: CT Findings—early active disease and sequential change with antituberculous therapy. Radiology 186:653–660, 1993.

81. Im JG, Song KS, Kang HS, et al: Mediastinal tuberculous lymphadenitis: CT manifestations. Radiology 164:115–119, 1987.

82. Joharjy I, Bashi SA, Adbullah AK: Value of medium-thickness CT in the diagnosis of bronchiectasis. AJR Am J Roentgenol 149:1133–1137, 1987.

83. Judson MA, Postic B, Weiman DS: PCP manifested as a hilar mass and cavitary lesion: Presentation in a patient receiving aerosolized pentamidine prophylaxis. South Med J 83:1309–1312, 1990.

84. Kalender WA, Seissler W, Klotz E, Vock P: Spiral volumetric CT with single-breath-hold technique, continuous transport, and continuous scanner rotation. Radiology 176:181–183, 1990.

85. Kannan R, Nademanee K, Hendrickson JA, et al: Amiodarone kinetics after oral doses. Clin Pharmacol Ther 31:438–444, 1982.

86. Katz D, Dreel L: Computed tomography in pulmonary asbestosis. Clin Radiol 30:207–213, 1979.

87. Katzenstein ALA, Askin FB: Surgical Pathology of Non-neoplastic Lung Disease, 2nd ed. Philadelphia, WB Saunders, 1990, pp 511–520.

88. Katzenstein ALA, Myers JL, Prophet WD, et al: Bronchiolitis obliterans and usual interstitial pneumonia. A comparative clinicopathologic study. Am J Surg Pathol 10:373–381, 1986.

89. Kawanami T, Bowen A: Juvenile laryngeal papillomatosis with pulmonary parenchymal spread. Pediatr Radiol 15:102–104, 1985.

90. Khan A, Herman PG, Vorwerk P, et al: Solitary pulmonary nodules: Comparison of classification with standard, thin-section, and reference phantom CT. Radiology 179:477–481, 1991.

90a. King MA, Ysrael M, Bergin CJ: Chronic thromboembolic pulmonary hypertension: CT findings. AJR Am J Roentgenol 170;955–960, 1998.

91. King TE: Bronchiolitis obliterans. Lung 167:69–93, 1989.

92. Klein JS, Warnock M, Webb RW, Gamsu G: Cavitating and noncavitating granulomas in AIDS patients with PCP. AJR Am J Roentgenol 152:753–754, 1989.

93. Kovacs JA, Heimenz JW, Macher AM, et al: *Pneumocystis carinii* pneumonia: A comparison between patients with acquired immunodeficiency syndrome and patients with other immunodeficiencies. Ann Intern Med 100:633–671, 1984.

94. Kramer SS, Wehunt WD, Stocker JT, Kashima H: Pulmonary manifestations of juvenile laryngotracheal papillomatosis. Am J Roentgenol 144:687–694, 1985.

95. Kruglik GD, Reed JC, Daroca PJ: RPC from the AFIP. Diagn Radiol 120:583–587, 1976.

96. Kuhlman JE: AIDS-related diseases of the chest. In Kuhlman JE (ed): CT of the Immunocompromised Host: Contemporary Issues in Computed Tomography, vol 14. New York, Churchill Livingstone, 1991, pp 27–69.

97. Kuhlman JE: CT of the immunocompromised and acutely ill patient. In Zerhouni EA (ed): CT and MRI of the Thorax: Contemporary Issues in Computed Tomography. New York, Churchill Livingstone, 1990, pp 1–22.

98. Kuhlman JE: CT of diffuse lung disease. Appl Radiol 20:17–22, 1991.

99. Kuhlman JE: CT evaluation of the chest in AIDS. In Thrall JH (ed): Current Practice in Radiology, 3rd ed. St. Louis, Mosby–Year Book, 1993.

100. Kuhlman JE: Opportunistic fungal infection: The neutropenic patient with leukemia, lymphoma, or bone marrow transplantation. In Kuhlman JE (ed): CT of the Immunocompromised Host: Contemporary Issues in Computed Tomography. New York, Churchill Livingston, 1991, pp 5–25.

101. Kuhlman JE: The role of chest computed tomography in the diagnosis of drug-related reactions. J Thorac Imaging 6:52–61, 1991.

102. Kuhlman JE, Deutsch JH, Fishman EK, Siegelman SS: CT features of thoracic mycobacterial disease. Radiographics 10:413–431, 1990.

103. Kuhlman JE, Fishman EK, Burch PA, et al: Invasive pulmonary aspergillosis in acute leukemia: The contribution of CT to early diagnosis and aggressive management. Chest 92:95–99, 1987.

104. Kuhlman JE, Fishman EK, Burch PA, et al: CT of invasive pulmonary aspergillosis. AJR Am J Roentgenol 150:1015–1020, 1988.

105. Kuhlman JE, Fishman EK, Knowles MG, et al: Diseases in the chest in AIDS: CT diagnosis. Radiographics 9:827–857, 1989.

106. Kuhlman JE, Fishman EK, Siegelman SS: CT diagnosis of pulmonary septic emboli. Radiology 174:211–213, 1990.

107. Kuhlman JE, Fishman EK, Siegelman SS: Invasive pulmonary aspergillosis in acute leukemia: Characteristic findings on CT, the CT halo sign, and the role of CT in early diagnosis. Radiology 157:611–614, 1985.

108. Kuhlman JE, Fishman EK, Zerhouni EA, et al: The CT spectrum of thoracic sarcoidosis. Radiographics 9:449–466, 1989.

109. Kuhlman JE, Hruban RH, Fishman EK: Wegener granulomatosis: CT features of parenchymal lung disease. J Comput Assist Tomogr 15:948–952, 1991.

110. Kuhlman JE, Kavuru M, Fishman EK, Siegelman SS: *Pneumocystis carinii* pneumonia: Spectrum of parenchymal CT findings. Radiology 175:711–714, 1990.

111. Kuhlman JE, Knowles MC, Fishman EK, Siegelman SS: Premature bullous pulmonary damage in AIDS: CT diagnosis. Radiology 173:23–26, 1989.

112. Kuhlman JE, Ney DR, Fishman EK: 2D and 3D imaging of the in vivo lung: Combining spiral CT with multiplanar and volumetric rendering techniques. Radiology 181(suppl):274, 1991.

113. Kuhlman JE, Ren H, Hutchins GM, Fishman EK: Fulminant pulmonary calcification complicating renal transplantation: CT demonstration. Radiology 173:459–460, 1989.

114. Kuhlman JE, Reyes BL, Hruban RH, et al: Abnormal air-filled spaces in the lung. Radiographics 13:47–75, 1993.

115. Kuhlman JE, Scatarige JC, Fishman EK, et al: CT demonstration of high attenuation pleural-parenchymal lesions due to amiodarone therapy. J Comput Assist Tomogr 11:160–162, 1987.

116. Kuhlman JE, Teigen C, Ren H, et al: Amiodarone lung: CT findings in symptomatic patients. Radiology 177:121–125, 1990.

116a. Kuzo RS, Goodman LR: CT evaluation of pulmonary embolism: Techniques and interpretation. AJR Am J Roentgenol 169:959–965, 1997.

117. Landman S, Burgener F: Pulmonary manifestations in Wegener's granulomatosis. Am J Roentgenol 122:750–757, 1974.

118. Lenoir S, Grenier P, Brauner MW, et al: Pulmonary lymphangiomyomatosis and tuberous sclerosis: Comparison of radiographic and thin-section CT findings. Radiology 175:329–334, 1990.

119. Leopold TG, Gough J: The centrilobular form of emphysema and its relation to chronic bronchitis. Thorax 12:219–235, 1957.

119a. Leung AN, Fisher K, Valentine V, et al: Bronchiolitis obliterans after lung transplantation: Detection using expiratory HRCT. Chest 113:365–370, 1998.

120. Lillington GA, Siefkin AM: Fibrosing alveolitis: Causes, characteristics and consequences. Postgrad Med 71:128–137, 1982.

121. Linhartova A: Lesions in resected lung parenchyma with regard to possible initial phase of pulmonary emphysema. Pathol Res Pract 181:71–76, 1986.

122. Littner MR, Schachter EN, Putman CE, et al: The clinical assessment of roentgenographically atypical pulmonary sarcoidosis. Am J Med 62:361–368, 1977.

123. Liu CI, Fields WR, Chung IS: Tuberculous mediastinal lymphadenopathy in adults. Diagn Radiol 126:369–371, 1978.

124. Liu FL, Cohen RD, Downar E, et al: Amiodarone pulmonary toxicity: Functional and ultrastructural evaluation. Thorax 41:100–105, 1986.

125. Liu YC, Tomashefski JF, Tomford W, Green H: Necrotizing PCP vasculitis associated with lung necrosis and cavitation in a patient with AIDS. Arch Pathol Lab Med 113:494–497, 1989.

126. Lynch DA, Brasch RC, Hardy KA, Webb WR: Pediatric pulmonary disease: Assessment with high-resolution ultrafast CT. Radiology 176:243–248, 1990.

127. Lynch DA, Gamsu G, Aberle DR: Conventional and high resolution computed tomography in the diagnosis of asbestos-related diseases. Radiographics 9:523–551, 1989.

128. Lynch DA, Gamsu G, Ray CS, Aberle DR: Asbestos-related focal lung masses: Manifestations on conventional and high-resolution CT scans. Radiology 169:603–607, 1988.

129. Macklin MT, Macklin CC: Malignant interstitial emphysema of the lungs and mediastinum as an important occult complication in many respiratory diseases and other conditions. Medicine 23:281–358, 1944.

130. Maguire R, Fauci AS, Doppman JL, Wolff SM: Unusual radiographic features of Wegener's granulomatosis. AJR Am J Roentgenol 130:233–238, 1987.

131. Mani TM, Lalleland D, Corone S, Mauriat D: Metastatic pulmonary calcifications after cardiac surgery in children. Radiology 174:463–467, 1990.

132. Marchlinski FE, Gansler TS, Waxman HL, Josephson ME: Amiodarone pulmonary toxicity. Ann Intern Med 97:839–845, 1982.

133. Marcy TW, Reynolds HY: Pulmonary histiocytosis X. Lung 163:129–150, 1985.

134. Marinelli DL, Albelda SM, Williams TM, et al: Nontuberculous mycobacterial infection in AIDS: Clinical, pathologic, and radiographic features. Radiology 160:77–82, 1986.

135. Mark EJ, Matsubara O, Tan-Liu NS, Fienberg R: The pulmonary biopsy in the early diagnosis of Wegener's (pathergic) granulomatosis: A study based on 35 open lung biopsies. Hum Pathol 19:1065–1071, 1988.

136. Mark EJ, Ramirez JF: Pulmonary capillaritis and hemorrhage in patients with systemic vasculitis. Arch Pathol Lab Med 109:413–418, 1985.

137. Markos J, Veronese ME, Nicholson MR, et al: Value of hepatic computerized tomographic scanning during amiodarone therapy. Am J Cardiol 56:89–92, 1985.

137a. Marti-Bonmati L, Perales FR, Catala F, et al: CT findings of Swyer-James Syndrome. Radiology 172:477–480, 1989.

138. Martin KW, Sagel SS, Siegel BA: Mosaic oligemia simulating pulmonary infiltrates on CT. Am J Roentgenol 147:670–673, 1986.

139. Martinez C, Romanelli A, Mullen MP, Lee M: Spontaneous pneumothoraces in AIDS patients receiving aerosolized pentamidine (Letter). Chest 94:1317–1318, 1988.

140. Maunder RJ, Shuman WP, McHugh JW, et al: Preservation of normal lung regions in the adult respiratory distress syndrome: Analysis by computed tomography. JAMA 255:2463–2465, 1986.

141. Mayo JR: High-resolution computed tomography: Technical aspects. Radiol Clin North Am 29:1043–1049, 1991.

142. Mayo JR, Webb WR, Gould R, et al: High-resolution CT of the lungs: An optimal approach. Radiology 163:507–510, 1987.

143. McDonald TJ, DeRemee RA: Wegener's granulomatosis. Laryngoscope 93:220–231, 1983.

144. McHugh K, Blaquiere RM: CT features of rounded atelectasis. AJR Am J Roentgenol 153:257–260, 1989.

145. McLoud TC, Epler GR, Colby TV, et al: Bronchiolitis obliterans. Radiology 159:1–8, 1986.

146. Meziane MA, Hruban RH, Zerhouni EA, et al: High-resolution CT of the lung parenchyma with pathologic correlation. Radiographics 8:27–54, 1988.

147. Miki Y, Hatabu H, Takahashi M, et al: Computed tomography of bronchiolitis obliterans. J Comput Assist Tomogr 12:512–514, 1988.

148. Miller RR, Muller NL, Vedal S, et al: Limitations of computed tomography in the assessment of emphysema. Am Rev Respir Dis 139:980–983, 1989.

148a. Miller WT, Tino G, Friedberg JS: Thoracic CT in the intensive care unit: Assessment of clinical usefulness. Radiology 209:491–498, 1998.

149. Milligan SA, Stulbarg MS, Gamsu G, Golden JA: PCP radiographically simulating tuberculosis. Am Rev Respir Dis 132:1124–1126, 1985.

150. Milne EN, Zerhouni EA: Blood supply of pulmonary metastases. J Thorac Imaging 2:15–23, 1987.

151. Mirvis SE, Tobin K, Kostrubiak I, Belzberg H: Thoracic CT in detecting occult disease in critically ill patients. AJR Am J Roentgenol 148:685–689, 1987.

152. Miyagawa Y, Nagata N, Shigematsu N: Clinicopathological study of migratory lung infiltrates. Thorax 46:233–238, 1991.

152a. Moore ADA, Godwin JD, Dietrich PA, et al: Swyer-James syndrome: CT findings in eight patients. AJR Am J Roentgenol 158:1211–1215, 1992.

153. Moore ADA, Godwin JD, Muller NL, et al: Pulmonary histiocytosis X: Comparison of radiographic and CT findings. Radiology 172:249–254, 1989.

153a. Moore EH: Atypical mycobacterial infection in the lung: CT appearance. Radiology 187:777–782, 1993.

154. Morgan EJ: Silicosis and tuberculosis. Chest 75:202–203, 1979.

155. Muller NL: Clinical value of high-resolution CT in chronic diffuse lung disease. AJR Am J Roentgenol 157:1163–1170, 1991.

156. Muller NL, Chiles C, Kullnig P: Pulmonary lymphangiomyomatosis: Correlation of CT and radiographic and functional findings. Radiology 175:335–339, 1990.

157. Muller NL, Guerry-Force ML, Staples CA, et al: Differential diagnosis of bronchiolitis obliterans with organizing pneumonia: Clinical, functional and radiologic findings. Radiology 162:151–156, 1987.

158. Muller NL, Staples CA, Miller RR: Bronchiolitis obliterans organizing pneumonia: CT features in 14 patients. AJR Am J Roentgenol 154:983–987, 1990.

159. Muller NL, Staples CA, Miller RR, et al: Idiopathic pulmonary fibrosis: CT and pathologic correlation. Radiology 165:731–734, 1987.

160. Munk PI, Muller NL, Miller RR, Ostrow DN: Pulmonary lymphangitic carcinomatosis: CT and pathologic findings. Radiology 166:705–709, 1988.

161. Murata K, Itoh H, Todo G, et al: Centrilobular lesions of the lung: Demonstration by high-resolution CT and pathologic correlation. Radiology 161:641–645, 1986.

162. Myers JL, Kennedy JI, Plumb VJ: Amiodarone lung: Pathologic findings in clinically toxic patients. Hum Pathol 18:349–354, 1987.

163. Nachman JB, Baum ES, White H, Cruissi FG: Bleomycin-induced pulmonary fibrosis mimicking recurrent metastatic disease in a patient with testicular carcinoma: Case report of the CT scan appearance. Cancer 47:236–239, 1981.

164. Naidich DP, Garay SM, Goodman PC: Pulmonary manifestations of AIDS. In Federle MD, Megibow AJ, Naidich DP (eds): Radiology of AIDS. New York, Raven Press, 1988, pp 47–76.

165. Naidich DP, Garay S, Rybak BJ: Kaposi's sarcoma CT: Radiographic correlation. Chest 96:723–728, 1989.

166. Naidich D, McCauley DI, Khouri NF, et al: Computed tomography of bronchiectasis. J Comput Assist Tomogr 6:437–444, 1982.

167. Naidich DP, McCauley DI, Leitman BS, et al: CT of pulmonary tuberculosis. In Siegelman SS (ed): Computed Tomography of the Chest. New York, Churchill Livingstone, 1984, pp 175–217.

168. Nakata H, Kimoto T, Nakayama T, et al: Diffuse peripheral lung disease: Evaluation by high-resolution computed tomography. Radiology 157:181–185, 1985.

169. Newmark H, Willis G, Ablemayor E, Chakmakian V: Kartagener's syndrome seen on CT. Comput Radiol 9:279–281, 1985.

170. Newsome GS, Ward DJ, Pierce PF: Spontaneous pneumothorax in patients with AIDS treated with prophylactic aerosolized pentamidine. Arch Intern Med 150:2167–2168, 1990.

171. Ney DR, Kuhlman JE, Hruban RH, et al: Three-dimensional CT: Volumetric reconstruction and display of the bronchial tree. Invest Radiol 25:736–742, 1990.

172. Nicholson AA, Hayward C: The value of computed tomography in the diagnosis of amiodarone-induced pulmonary toxicity. Clin Radiol 40:564–567, 1989.

173. Nishimura K, Itoh H: High-resolution computed tomographic features of bronchiolitis obliterans organizing pneumonia. Chest 102: 26s–31s, 1992.

174. Noma S, Herman PG, Kan A, et al: Sequential morphologic changes of elastase-induced pulmonary emphysema in pig lungs. Invest Radiol 26:446–453, 1991.

175. Olson LK, Forrest JV, Friedman PJ, et al: Pneumonitis after amiodarone therapy. Radiology 150:327–330, 1984.

176. Orr DP, Myerowitz RL, Dubois PJ: Pathoradiologic correlation of invasive pulmonary aspergillosis in the compromised host. Cancer 41:2028–2039, 1978.

177. Paltiel HJ, Azouz EM, Ellettine DW, Bernstein M: Computed tomography in interstitial lung disease. J Comput Tomogr 10:349–355, 1986.

178. Pare JAP, Fraser RG: Diseases of the chest of unknown origin. In Pare JAP, Fraser R (eds): Synopsis of Diseases of the Chest. Philadelphia, WB Saunders, 1983, pp 604–651.

179. Pare JAP, Fraser RG: In Pare JAP, Fraser RG (eds): Synopsis of Diseases of the Chest. Diseases of the Airways. Philadelphia, WB Saunders, 1983, p 558.

180. Peruzzi W, Garner W, Bools J, et al: Portable chest roentgenography and computed tomography in critically ill patients. Chest 93:728–726, 1988.

181. Pimentel JC: Tridimensional photographic reconstruction in a study of the pathogenesis of honeycomb lung. Thorax 22:444–452, 1967.

182. Pratt PC: Pathology of tuberculosis. Semin Roentgenol 14:196–203, 1979.

183. Radin DR, Baker EL, Klatt EC, et al: Visceral and nodal calcification in patients with AIDS-related *Pneumocystis carinii* infection. AJR Am J Roentgenol 154:27, 1990.

183a. Rathbun SW, Raskob GE, Whitsett TL: Sensitivity and specificity of helical computed tomography in the diagnosis of pulmonary embolism: A systematic review. Ann Intern Med 132:227–232, 2000.

184. Remy-Jardin M, Beuscart R, Sault MC, et al: Subpleural micronodules in diffuse infiltrative lung disease: Evaluation with thin-section CT scans. Radiology 177:133–139, 1990.

184a. Remy-Jardin M, Remy J, Wattinne L, Giraud F: Central pulmonary thromboembolism: Diagnosis with spiral volumetric CT with the single breath-hold technique—comparison with pulmonary angiography. Radiology 1992; 185:381–387.

184b. Remy-Jardin M, Remy J, Cauvain O, et al: Diagnosis of central pulmonary embolism with helical CT: Role of two-dimensional multiplanar reformations. AJR Am J Roentgenol 165:1131–1138, 1995.

185. Ren H, Hruban RH, Kuhlman JE, et al: High resolution computed tomography of inflation-fixed lungs: The beaded-septum sign of pulmonary metastases. J Comput Assist Tomogr 13:411–416, 1989.

186. Ren H, Kuhlman JE, Hurban RH, et al: High resolution computed tomography of inflation-fixed lungs: A wedge-shaped density and associated vascular sign in the diagnosis of pulmonary infarction. J Comput Assist Tomogr 14:82–86, 1990.

187. Ren H, Kuhlman JE, Hruban RH, et al: Computed tomography–pathology correlation of amiodarone lung. J Comput Assist Tomogr 14:760–765, 1990.

188. Rimmer MJ, Dixon AK, Flower CDR, Sikora K: Bleomycin lung: Computed tomographic observations. Br J Radiol 58:1041–1045, 1985.

189. Riva E, Gerna M, Neyroz P, et al: Pharmacokinetics of amiodarone in rats. J Cardiovasc Pharmacol 4:270–275, 1982.

190. Roberts CMR, Citron KM, Strickland B: Intrathoracic aspergilloma: Role of CT in diagnosis and treatment. Radiology 165:123–128, 1987.

191. Rockoff SD, Rohatgi PK: Unusual manifestations of thoracic sarcoidosis. Am J Roentgenol 144:513–528, 1985.

192. Saksouk FA, Haddad MC: Detection of mesenteric involvement in sarcoidosis using computed tomography. Br J Radiol 60:1135–1136, 1987.

193. Sandhu J, Goodman PC: Pulmonary cysts associated with PCP in patients with AIDS. Radiology 173:33–35, 1989.

194. Scadding JG: *Mycobacterium* tuberculosis in the aetiology of sarcoidosis. Br Med J 2:1617, 1960.

195. Scannell DA: Pneumothoraces and PCP in two AIDS patients receiving aerosolized pentamidine. Chest 97:479–480, 1990.

196. Schmidt RA, Glenny RW, Godwin JD, et al: Panlobular emphysema in young intravenous Ritalin abusers. Am Rev Respir Dis 143: 649–656, 1991.

197. Schurwitzki H, Stiglbauer R, Graninger W, et al: Interstitial lung disease in progressive systemic sclerosis: High-resolution CT versus radiography. Radiology 176:755–759, 1990.

198. Scully RE, Mark EJ, McNeely BU: Case records of the Massachusetts General Hospital. Weekly clinicopathological exercises. Case 12–1986. N Engl J Med 314:834–844, 1986.

199. Senior R, Connolly NL, Cury JD, et al: Elastin degradation by human alveolar macrophages. Am Rev Respir Dis 139:1251–1256, 1989.

200. Shaffer K, Pugatch RD: Small pulmonary nodules: Dynamic CT with a single-breath technique. Radiology 173:567–568, 1989.

201. Shenasa M, Vaisman U, Wojciechowski M, et al: Abnormal abdominal computerized tomography with amiodarone therapy and clinical significance. Am Heart J 107:929–933, 1984.

202. Shin MS, Ho K-J: CT of bronchiectasis in association with tuberculosis. Clin Imaging 13:36–43, 1989.

203. Shin MS, Liendo C, Ho KJ: *Pneumocystis carinii* pneumonia in an AIDS patient: Unusual manifestation as multiple cavitary and noncavitary peripheral nodules and spontaneous pneumothorax. Clin Imaging 13:225–227, 1989.

204. Siegelman SS, Khouri NF, Leo FP, et al: Solitary pulmonary nodules: CT assessment. Radiology 160:307–312, 1986.

205. Siegelman SS, Khouri NF, Scott WW Jr, et al: Pulmonary hamartoma: CT findings. Radiology 160:313–317, 1986.

206. Silver SF, Muller NL, Miller RR, Lefcoe MS: Hypersensitivity pneumonitis: Evaluation with CT. Radiology 173:441–445, 1989.

207. Sinner WN: Computed tomographic patterns of pulmonary thromboembolism and infarction. J Comput Assist Tomogr 2:395–399, 1978.

208. Solomon A, Kreel L, McNicol M, Johnson N: Computed tomography in pulmonary sarcoidosis. J Comput Assist Tomogr 3:754–758, 1979.

209. Standertskjold-Nordenstam CG, Wandtke JC, Hood WB Jr, et al: Amiodarone pulmonary toxicity: Chest radiography and CT in asymptomatic patients. Chest 88:143–145, 1985.

210. Stanford DW, Galvin J: The diagnosis of bronchiectasis. Clin Chest Med 9:691–699, 1988.

211. Staples CA, Muller NL, Vedal S, et al: Usual interstitial pneumonia: Correlation of CT with clinical, functional and radiologic findings. Radiology 162:377–381, 1987.

212. Stark P, Greene R, Kott MM, et al: CT findings in ARDS. Radiologie 27:367–369, 1987.

213. Stern EJ, Webb WR, Golden JA, Gamsu G: Cystic lung disease associated with eosinophilic granuloma and tuberous sclerosis: Air trapping at dynamic ultrafast high-resolution CT. Radiology 182: 325–329, 1992.

213a. Stern EJ, Swensen SJ, Hartman TE, Frank MS. CT mosaic pattern of lung attenuation: Distinguishing different causes. AJR Am J Roentgenol 165:813–816, 1995.

214. Stockley RA: Bronchiectasis: New therapeutic approaches based on pathogenesis. Clin Chest Med 8:481–494, 1987.

215. Strickland B, Strickland NH: The value of high definition, narrow section computed tomography in fibrosing alveolitis. Clin Radiol 39:589–594, 1988.

216. Swensen SJ, Harms GF, Morin RL, Myers JL: CT evaluation of solitary pulmonary nodules: Value of 185-H reference phantom. AJR Am J Roentgenol 156:925–929, 1991.

217. Swensen SJ, Morin RL, Schueler BA, et al: Solitary pulmonary nodule: CT evaluation of enhancement with iodinated contrast material—a preliminary report. Radiology 182:343–347, 1991.

217a. Swenson SJ, Brown LR, Colby TV, Weaver AL: Pulmonary nodules: CT evaluation of enhancement with iodinated contrast material. Radiology 1995; 194:393–398.

217b. Swenson SJ, Brown LR, Colby TV, et al: Lung nodule enhancement at CT: Prospective findings. Radiology 201:447–455, 1996.

218. Tellis CJ, Putnam JS: Cavitation in large multinodular pulmonary disease: A rare manifestation of sarcoidosis. Chest 71:792–793, 1977.

219. Thomas PD, Hunninghake GW: Current concepts of the pathogenesis of sarcoidosis. Am Rev Respir Dis 135:747–760, 1987.

220. Tocino IM, Miller MH, Fairfax WR: Distribution of pneumothorax in the supine and semirecumbent critically ill adult. Am J Roentgenol 144:901–905, 1985.

221. Tomashefski U, Bruce M, Stern RC, et al: Pulmonary air cysts in cystic fibrosis. Hum Pathol 16:253–261, 1985.

222. Travis WD, Lipschik GY, Suffredini AF, et al: Atypical pathologic manifestations of PCP in AIDS. Am J Surg Pathol 14:615–625, 1990.

223. Vock P, Soucek M, Daepp M, Kalender WA: Lung: Spiral volumetric CT with single-breath-hold technique. Radiology 176:864–867, 1990.

224. Wally OR: Centers for Disease Control. Tuberculosis, final data—United States, 1986. MMWR Morb Mortal Wkly Rep 36:817–820, 1988.

225. Walton EW: Giant-cell granuloma of the respiratory tract (Wegener's granulomatosis). Br Med J pp 265–270, 1958.

225a. Ward S, Heyneman L, Lee MJ, et al: Accuracy of CT in the diagnosis of allergic bronchopulmonary aspergillosis in asthmatic patients. AJR Am J Roentgenol 173:937–942, 1999.

226. Watanabe Y, Nishiyama Y, Kanayama H, et al: Congenital bronchiectasis due to cartilage deficiency: CT demonstration. J Comput Assist Tomogr 11:701–703, 1987.

227. Webb WR: High-resolution CT of the lung parenchyma. Radiol Clin North Am 27:1085–1097, 1989.

228. Webb WR, Muller NL, Naidich DP (eds): High-Resolution CT of the Lung. New York, Raven Press, 1992.

229. Webb WR, Muller NL, Zerhouni EA: High-resolution CT of the lung: Current clinical uses. Perspect Radiol 2:61–69, 1989.

230. Webb WR, Stein MG, Finkbeiner WE, et al: Normal and diseased isolated lungs: High-resolution CT. Radiology 166:81–87, 1988.

231. Westcott JL, Cole S: Barotrauma. In Herman PG (ed): Radiology of Iatrogenic Disorders: Iatrogenic Thoracic Complications. New York, Springer-Verlag, 1983, pp 79–109.

232. Westcott JL, Cole SR: Traction bronchiectasis in end-stage pulmonary fibrosis. Radiology 161:665–669, 1986.

233. Werb Z, Gordon S: Elastase secretion by stimulated macrophages. J Exp Med 142:361–377, 1975.

234. White R, Kuhn C: Effects of phagocytosis of mineral dusts on elastase secretion by alveolar and peritoneal exudative macrophages. Arch Environ Health 35:106–109, 1980.

235. Wolff SD, Kuhlman JE, Fishman EK: Thoracic Kaposi's sarcoma in AIDS: CT findings. J Comput Assist Tomogr 17:60–62, 1993.

236. Wolff SM, Fauci AS, Horn RG, Dale DC: Wegener's granulomatosis. Ann Intern Med 81:513–525, 1974.

237. Wood DW, Osborn MJ, Rooke J, Holmes DR: Amiodarone pulmonary toxicity: Report of two cases associated with rapidly progressive fatal adult respiratory distress syndrome after pulmonary angiography. Mayo Clin Proc 60:601–603, 1985.

238. Woodring JH, Vandiviere HM, Fried AM, et al: Update: The radiographic features of pulmonary tuberculosis. Am J Roentgenol 146:497–506, 1986.

238a. Woolley K, Stark P: Pulmonary parenchymal manifestations of mitral valve disease. Radiographics 19:965–972, 1999.

238b. Worthy SA, Muller NL, Hartman TE, et al: Mosaic attenuation pattern on thin-section CT scans of the lung: Differentiation among infiltrative lung, airway, and vascular diseases as a cause. Radiology 205:465–470, 1997.

239. Wright JL, Cagle P, Churg A, et al: Diseases of the small airways. Am Rev Respir Dis 146:240–262, 1992.

239a. Yamashita K, Matsunobe S, Tsuda T, et al: Solitary pulmonary nodules: Preliminary study of evaluation with incremental dynamic CT. Radiology 194:399–405, 1995.

239b. Zeman RK, Silverman PM, Vieco PT, Costello P: CT angiography. AJR Am J Roentgenol 165:1079–1088, 1995.

240. Zerhouni EA, Naidich DP, Stitik FP, et al: CT of the pulmonary parenchyma: Interstitial disease. J Thorac Imaging 1:54–64, 1985.

241. Zerhouni EA, Stitik EP, Siegelman SS, et al: CT of the pulmonary nodule: A cooperative study. Radiology 160:319–327, 1986.

242. Zhang M, Kono M: Solitary pulmonary nodules: Evaluation of blood flow patterns with dynamic CT. Radiology 205:471–478. 1997.

28

Primary Pulmonary Neoplasms

Jeremy J. Erasmus, H. Page McAdams,
Santiago E. Rossi

Although most primary pulmonary tumors are carcinomas, a large histologic spectrum of benign and malignant tumors of the lung exists. This chapter reviews the more common neoplasms according to the classification proposed by the World Health Organization (WHO) (Table 28–1) and emphasizes the radiologic manifestations of these neoplasms and the use of imaging in diagnosis and management.

Malignant Neoplasms of the Lung

Epithelial Tumors

Lung Cancer

Epidemiology

Lung cancer is a common malignancy. The American Cancer Society (ACS) estimated that 169,500 new cases would be diagnosed in the United States in the year 2001.[4, 4a] The number of new cases in men, however, decreased from a high of 86.5 per 100,000 in 1984 to 69.1 in 1997.[257] The incidence of lung cancer in women has continued to increase since the 1960s, and in 1997 although the rate of increase slowed in the 1990s, 43.1 per 100,000 new cases occurred in 1997. The annual mortality rate in men decreased during the 1990s, whereas the rate in women continues to increase.[257] Lung cancer remains the leading cause of cancer-related deaths in both men and women in the United States, and the ACS estimated that it would account for 28% of all cancer deaths in the year 2001.[4a]

Etiology

The strongest risk factor for the development of lung cancer is cigarette smoking; an estimated 85% to 90% of lung cancers in men and 80% in women have been attributable to smoking.[4, 9, 58, 234, 237] The length of time and the number and type of cigarettes smoked are directly related to the risk of lung cancer.[61, 196, 235] Squamous cell and small-cell carcinomas have the highest association with smoking, whereas adenocarcinomas are the predominant cell type in nonsmokers.[61] The change in smoking habits (use of filter tips, decrease in tar yield), however, has been postulated to account for the recent increase in incidence of adenocarcinomas in cigarette smokers.[61, 228, 262] Involuntary smoke exposure (passive smoking) is generally considered to be associated with an increased risk of lung cancer, although the numerous variables in the epidemiologic data make this difficult to conclude with certainty.[4, 185, 196, 230, 237] Spousal smoking has, however, been estimated to increase the lung cancer risk by 20% in women who have never smoked.[23]

Environmental and occupational exposures to particulate and chemical substances are additional risk factors.[212, 243] Exposure to the naturally occurring radioactive gas radon, both in homes and in mines, is the most important risk factor after cigarette smoking.[152, 196, 212, 245] It is estimated that 7000 to 30,000 lung cancer deaths occur annually in the United States as a result of residential exposure to radon.[245]

Asbestos is a carcinogen, and although there is an unequivocal association between lung cancer and asbestos exposure, the magnitude of the risk is frequently overestimated (most cohort studies show less than a twofold increase in risk).[74] Although the risk of lung cancer in workers exposed to asbestos may depend on individual occupational exposure characteristics (i.e., duration, concentration, and fiber type), the increased risk may be largely limited to those with radiologic evidence of asbestosis or to cigarette smokers.[74, 188, 236, 252] It has been estimated that as many as 33% of lung cancers that occur in smokers exposed to asbestos are the result of the synergistic effect of the two carcinogens.[53]

Additional risk factors for development of lung cancer include exposure to arsenic, chloromethyl ethers, chromium, isopropyl oil, mustard gas, nickel, beryllium, chloroprene, vinyl chloride, and various smelting by-products such as lead and copper.[212] Other factors, such as focal or diffuse pulmonary fibrosis and ionizing radiation, have been reported to increase the risk of lung cancer. Epidemiologic data, however, do not clearly establish a cause-and-effect relationship, except in some patients with Hodgkin's disease treated with radiation.[120] Finally, although not clearly understood, genetic susceptibility to lung cancer may be involved in a small number of cases.[10, 54, 177, 196]

Histologic Classification

Lung cancer is divided by the WHO Classification into two major histologic categories: *non–small-cell* lung carcinoma (NSCLC) and *small-cell* lung carcinoma (SCLC) (see Table 28–1).[227] NSCLC is further subdivided into histologic variants such as squamous cell carcinoma, adenocarcinoma, and large-cell carcinoma, according to the most differentiated portion of the tumor. Many tumors,

Table 28–1. Histologic Classification of Lung Tumors

I. **Epithelial Tumors**
A. Benign
   Papillomas
   Adenomas
B. Malignant
   Squamous cell carcinoma
      Variants: papillary, clear cell, small-cell, basaloid
   Adenocarcinoma
      Acinar adenocarcinoma
      Papillary adenocarcinoma
      Bronchioloalveolar carcinoma
      Solid adenocarcinoma with mucin
      Adenocarcinoma with mixed subtypes
      Variants: fetal, clear cell, signet-ring, colloid
   Large cell carcinoma
      Variants: clear cell, large-cell neuroendocrine, combined large-cell neuroendocrine, basaloid, lymphoepithelioma-like carcinomas
   Adenosquamous carcinoma
   Small-cell carcinoma
      Variant: combined small-cell carcinoma
   Carcinomas with pleomorphic sarcomatoid or sarcomatous elements
      Carcinomas with spindle and/or giant cells (pleomorphic carcinoma, spindle cell carcinoma, giant cell carcinoma)
      Carcinosarcomas
      Pulmonary blastoma
   Carcinoid tumor
      Typical carcinoid
      Atypical carcinoid
   Carcinomas of salivary-gland type
      Mucoepidermoid carcinoma
      Adenoid cystic carcinoma
II. **Mesenchymal Tumors**
   Primary pulmonary sarcomas
      Vascular sarcomas (angiosarcoma, epithelioid, emangioendothelioma)
      Spindle cell sarcomas (malignant fibrous histiocytoma, hemangiopericytoma, fibrosarcoma, leiomyosarcoma, synovial sarcoma)
III. **Lymphoproliferative Disorders**
   Lymphoid interstitial pneumonia
   Nodular lymphoid hyperplasia
   Low-grade marginal-zone B-cell lymphoma of the mucosa-associated lymphoid tissue (MALT)
   Lymphomatoid granulomatosis
IV. **Miscellaneous Tumors**
   Hamartoma
   Granular cell tumors
   Sclerosing hemangioma
   Clear cell tumor
V. **Tumor-like Lesions**
   Hyalinizing granuloma
   Amyloid tumor

Modified from Travis WD, Colby TV, Corrin B, et al: Histological Typing of Lung and Pleural Tumors, 3rd ed. Berlin, Springer-Verlag, 1999.

however, are composed of more than one histologic type and are classified as *combined tumors*. Additionally, NSCLC are graded as *well-differentiated, moderately differentiated*, or *poorly differentiated* according to the least differentiated feature.[227] Exceptions to this grading classification are pleomorphic carcinoma, carcinosarcoma, and SCLC, all of which are poorly differentiated tumors.[227]

Squamous Cell Carcinoma. Squamous cell carcinomas have been decreasing in relative incidence and now constitute 25% of all lung cancers. They typically occur in central bronchi and frequently manifest as postobstructive pneumonia or atelectasis (Fig. 28–1).[189, 202, 225] Mucoid impaction, bronchiectasis, and hyperinflation are uncommon radiologic manifestations (Fig. 28–2).[202, 225, 258]

Approximately one third of squamous cell carcinomas occur beyond the segmental bronchi and usually range in size from 1 to 10 cm (Fig. 28–3).[202, 225] Squamous cell carcinomas are more likely to cavitate than the other histologic cell types of lung cancer.[202] Cavitation occurs in 10% to 30% and is more common in large peripheral masses and poorly differentiated tumors.[225] Cavitation is typically eccentric with thick, irregular walls, although thin walls may occur in rare circumstances.[202] Most squamous cell carcinomas grow slowly, and extrathoracic metastases tend to occur late.[202]

Adenocarcinoma. Adenocarcinomas have increased in incidence and are now the most common cell type, compos-

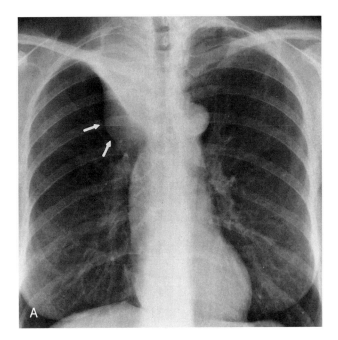
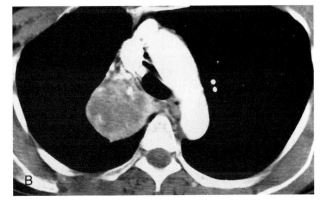

Figure 28–1. Squamous cell lung cancer seen as a central endobronchial mass. *A,* Posteroanterior chest radiograph shows complete atelectasis of the right upper lobe. Convexity in the lower portion of the atelectatic lung *(arrows)* is the result of a large central mass. *B,* CT confirms the large central mass in the region of the right upper lobe bronchus.

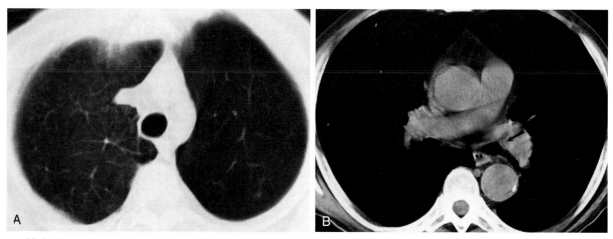

Figure 28–2. Squamous cell lung cancer with obstructive hyperinflation of the left upper lobe. *A* and *B*, CT scan shows hyperlucency of the left upper lobe and an endobronchial mass that completely occludes the left upper lobe bronchus (*arrow* in *B*).

ing 25% to 30% of all lung cancers.[189] Adenocarcinomas typically manifest as peripheral, solitary pulmonary nodules. Nodules can have an irregular or spiculated margin as a result of parenchymal invasion and an associated fibrotic response (Fig. 28–4).[202, 225] Lymphangitic carcinomatosis, although uncommon at presentation, occurs more frequently with adenocarcinomas and typically manifests radiologically as thickening of interlobular septa or multiple small pulmonary nodules (Fig. 28–5).[125] Intrathoracic metastases to hilar and mediastinal nodes are present in 18% to 40% and in 2% to 27% of patients, respectively, and tend to occur more often with more centrally located adenocarcinomas.[189, 225, 261]

Bronchioloalveolar cell carcinoma (BAC), a subset of adenocarcinoma, constitutes 0.5% to 10% of all lung can-

cers.[49] BAC can be either solitary or multifocal at the time of initial presentation. To explain this difference, it has been proposed that the origin of BAC is either *monoclonal* (with multifocality due to dissemination by aerosolization, intrapulmonary lymphatics, and intra-alveolar growth) or *polyclonal* (with multifocality due to de novo tumor growth at multiple sites).[11, 88, 128, 138, 202]

The most common radiologic manifestation is a peripheral, solitary nodule that can remain stable in size for many years (Fig. 28–6).[42, 87, 108, 225] Although cavitation in these nodules is uncommon, the occurrence of multiple small, focal, low-attenuation regions (pseudocavitation) or airbronchograms within the nodule can occasionally be useful in suggesting the diagnosis.[108, 162, 251, 273] The diffuse form may present as multiple nodules (usually small, occasion-

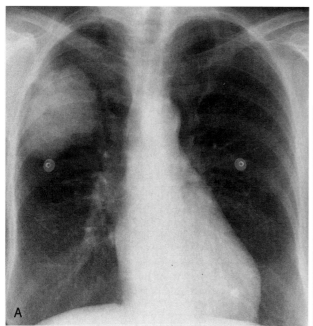

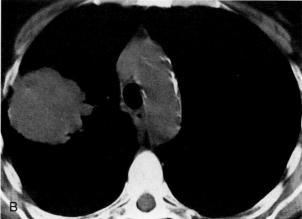

Figure 28–3. Squamous cell lung cancer manifesting as a peripheral mass. *A*, Posteroanterior chest radiograph shows a large lobular mass in the right upper lobe. Note the absence of hilar or mediastinal adenopathy. *B*, CT confirms the large lobular mass in the right upper lobe.

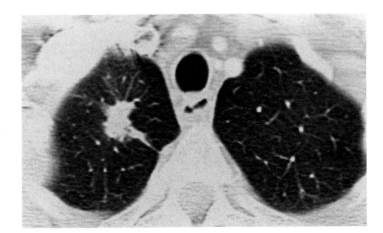

Figure 28–4. Adenocarcinoma manifesting as a pulmonary nodule. CT scan shows a nodule in the apical segment of the right upper lobe. The spiculated margin is typical of lung cancer.

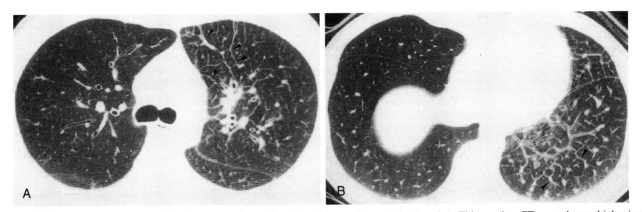

Figure 28–5. Adenocarcinoma of the lung appearing as lymphangitic carcinomatosis. *A* and *B,* Thin-section CT scan shows thickening of bronchial walls and interlobular septa *(arrowheads)* in the left lung. Nodularity of the septa is suggestive of malignancy.

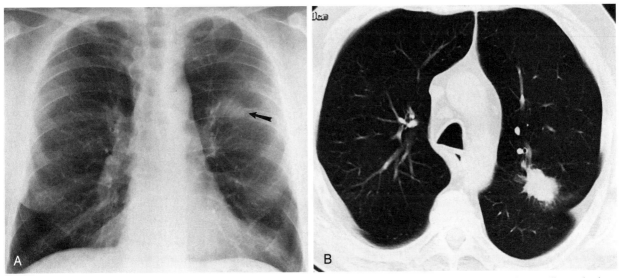

Figure 28–6. Bronchioloalveolar cell carcinoma seen as a solitary pulmonary nodule. *A,* Posteroanterior chest radiograph shows a nodule *(arrow)* in left upper lobe. *B,* CT scan reveals a spiculated margin suggestive of malignancy.

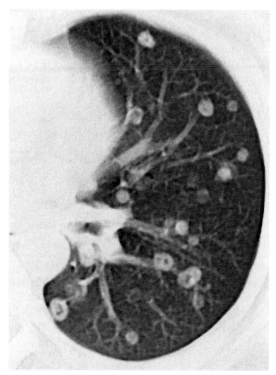

Figure 28–7. Bronchioloalveolar cell carcinoma (BAC) manifesting as multiple pulmonary nodules. CT shows small, well-marginated pulmonary nodules with central areas of cavitation (the "Cheerio" sign of BAC).

ally cavitary), "ground-glass" opacities, and opacities resembling pneumonia (Figs. 28–7 and 28–8).[2, 11, 42, 50, 87, 138, 202] Most patients with the diffuse form of BAC have a combination of these findings (Fig. 28–9).[2] Hilar and mediastinal adenopathy and pleural effusions are uncommon.[42, 87, 162, 202]

Large-Cell Carcinoma. These lesions make up 10% to 20% of all lung cancers.[58, 202] Most are peripheral, poorly marginated masses greater than 7 cm in diameter (Fig. 28–10).[21, 58, 189, 201, 202, 225] Although growth is typically rapid, cavitation is uncommon.[201] Hilar and mediastinal adenopathy occurs in up to one third of patients at presentation, and early extrathoracic metastases are common.[58, 201, 202, 225]

Small-Cell Lung Cancer. SCLCs compose 20% to 25% of all lung cancers.[58] The primary tumor is typically small, is central in location, and is associated with marked hilar and mediastinal adenopathy and distant metastases to liver, bone marrow, adrenals, and brain (Figs. 28–11 and 28–12).[58, 189, 225, 233] Pleural effusions occur in 5% to 40% of patients.[176, 202, 253] Approximately 5% of SCLCs manifest as small, peripheral, solitary pulmonary nodules without intrathoracic adenopathy, disseminated extrathoracic disease, or pleural effusions.[75, 233]

Clinical Manifestations

Most patients are in their fifth and sixth decades of life and are symptomatic at presentation.[5, 58, 196] Symptoms are variable and depend on the local effects of the primary mass, the presence of regional or distant metastases, and the coexistence of paraneoplastic syndromes.

Central endobronchial carcinomas can manifest as fever, dyspnea, hemoptysis, and cough.[5] Cough productive of copious amounts of watery sputum (bronchorrhea) typically also occurs in patients with BAC and extensive parenchymal disease, but this is rarely seen.[50] Symptoms that can occur as a result of local growth and invasion of adjacent nerves, vessels, and mediastinal structures include:

1. Chest pain (peribronchial nerve involvement); vocal cord paralysis and hoarseness (recurrent laryngeal nerve involvement) (Fig. 28–13); dyspnea due to diaphragmatic paralysis (phrenic nerve involvement) (Fig. 28–14); Horner's syndrome—ptosis, mycosis, anhidrosis (sympathetic chain and stellate ganglion involvement by superior sulcus tumors) (Fig. 28–15).[172]
2. Facial swelling, headaches, enlarged collateral chest wall vessels (superior vena cava obstruction).[172]
3. Dysphagia (esophageal invasion).

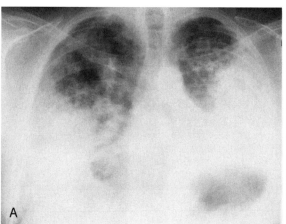
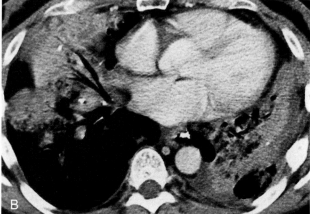

Figure 28–8. Bronchioloalveolar cell carcinoma appearing as homogeneous opacities mimicking pneumonia. *A,* Posteroanterior chest radiograph shows diffuse, bilateral, homogeneous pulmonary opacities. Surgical clips are present in the medial aspect of the left hemithorax because of prior partial pulmonary resection. *B,* CT confirms the diffuse bilateral pulmonary consolidation and reveals a small left pleural effusion.

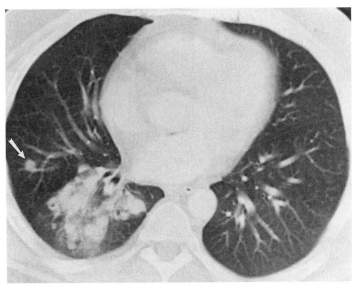

Figure 28–9. Bronchioloalveolar cell carcinoma seen as nodules and consolidation. CT scan shows an opacity in the right lower lobe resembling pneumonia and a small nodule *(arrow)*. Numerous small, well-circumscribed nodules were scattered throughout both lungs (not shown).

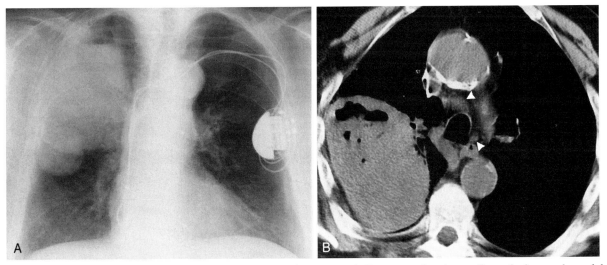

Figure 28–10. Large-cell lung cancer manifesting as a large cavitary mass. *A,* Posteroanterior chest radiograph shows a large, lobular mass in the right upper lobe. Cavitation is present with an air-fluid level in the upper aspect of mass. *B,* CT shows a well-circumscribed mass with eccentric cavitation and thick walls. Note the nonenlarged, paratracheal and low left paratracheal lymph nodes *(arrowheads)*.

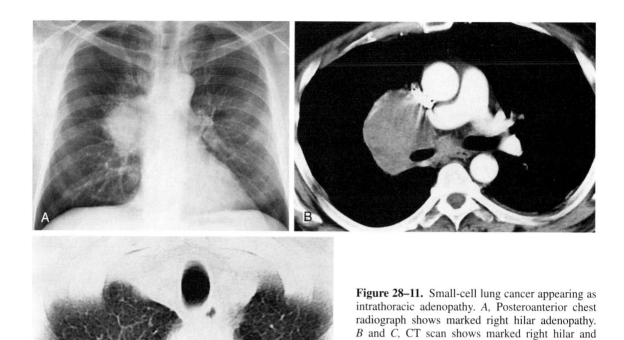

Figure 28–11. Small-cell lung cancer appearing as intrathoracic adenopathy. *A,* Posteroanterior chest radiograph shows marked right hilar adenopathy. *B* and *C,* CT scan shows marked right hilar and subcarinal adenopathy and reveals a small primary malignancy in the right upper lobe (in *C*).

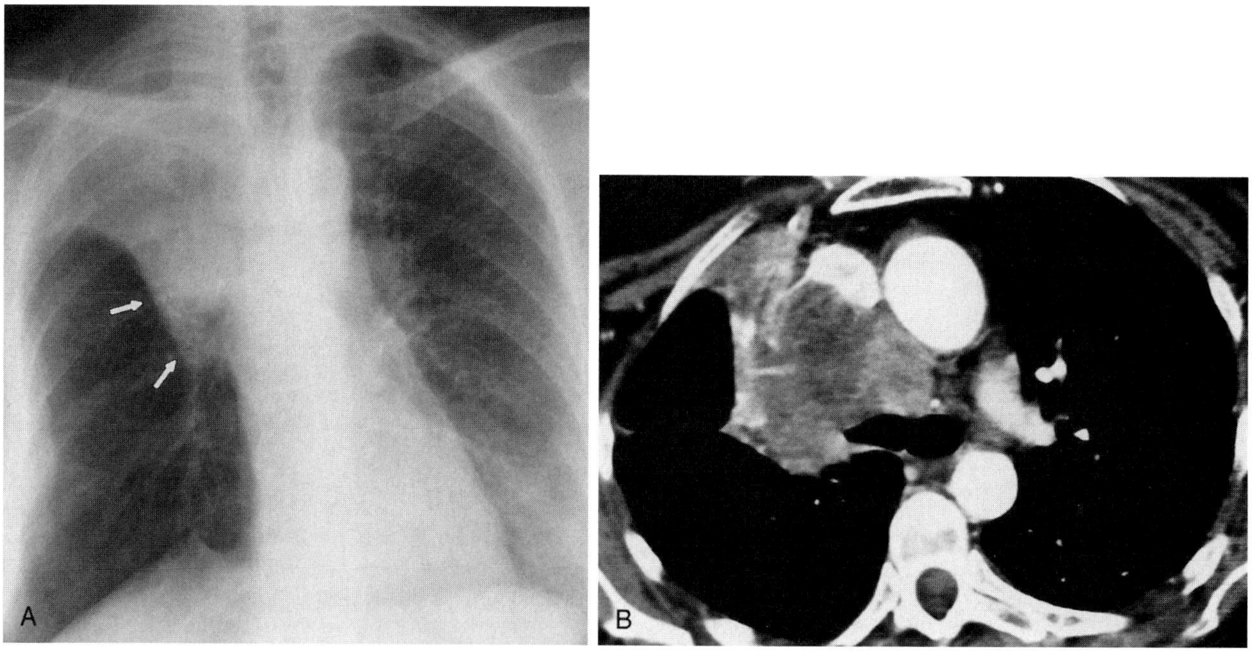

Figure 28–12. Small-cell lung cancer seen as intrathoracic adenopathy and atelectasis. *A,* Posteroanterior chest radiograph shows complete atelectasis of the right upper lobe with mild convexity of the distal aspect of the minor fissure *(arrows)* caused by an underlying right hilar mass. *B,* CT scan confirms marked hilar and mediastinal adenopathy and reveals occlusion of the right upper lobe bronchus.

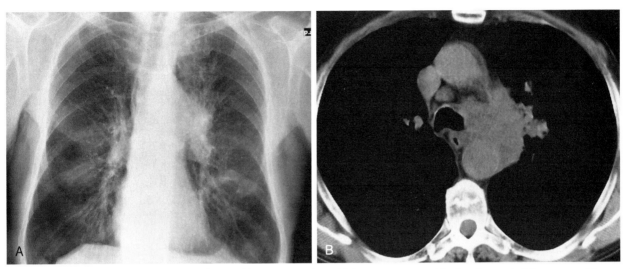

Figure 28–13. Small-cell lung cancer in a 76-year-old man presenting with hoarseness caused by involvement of the recurrent laryngeal nerve. *A,* Posteroanterior chest radiograph shows an aortopulmonary window mass. *B,* CT reveals mediastinal invasion with an extension of the mass into the aortopulmonary window (the anatomic location of recurrent laryngeal nerve).

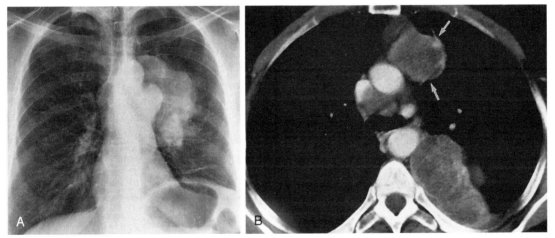

Figure 28–14. Small-cell lung cancer in a 50-year-old woman with diaphragmatic paralysis resulting from phrenic nerve involvement. *A,* Posteroanterior chest radiograph shows a large lobular mass in the left lower lobe and elevation of the left hemidiaphragm. *B,* CT reveals a necrotic mass in the left lower lobe and mediastinum *(arrows)* in the anatomic location of the phrenic nerve.

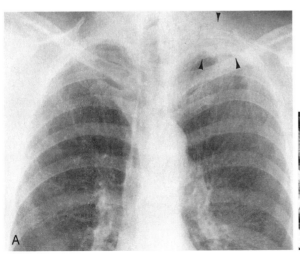

Figure 28–15. Non–small-cell lung cancer in a 54-year-old man with Pancoast's tumor and with a 2-month history of neck pain. *A,* Posteroanterior chest radiograph shows a left apical mass with destruction of the first rib *(arrowheads).* *B,* CT confirms the left superior sulcus tumor and destruction of the left first rib.

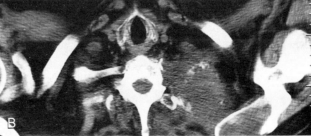

Many patients present with symptoms related to extra-thoracic metastases, most commonly bone pain or central nervous system (CNS) abnormalities.[5, 100] Clinical signs and symptoms can also be caused by tumor excretion of a bioactive substance, or hormone, or as a result of an auto-immune phenomenon.[5, 171] These paraneoplastic syndromes occur in 10% to 20% of lung cancer patients and are usually associated with SCLC.[5, 22, 124, 220] Antidiuretic and adrenocorticotropin hormones are the more frequently ex-creted hormones and can result in hyponatremia and serum hypo-osmolarity and in Cushing's syndrome (central obe-sity, hypertension, glucose intolerance, plethora, hirsutism), respectively.[27, 40, 121, 157, 199, 202] Other hormones that can be elevated are calcitonin; growth hormone; human chorionic gonadotropin; and, rarely, prolactin and serotonin.[124]

Neurologic paraneoplastic syndromes (Lambert-Eaton myasthenic syndrome, paraneoplastic cerebellar degenera-tion, paraneoplastic encephalomyelitis, paraneoplastic sen-sory neuropathy) are rare and are usually associated with SCLC.[25, 26, 28, 33, 113, 179] The neurologic symptoms typically precede the diagnosis of lung cancer by up to 2 years, are incapacitating, and progress rapidly, although improvement can occur after treatment of the lung cancer.[33, 113]

Miscellaneous paraneoplastic syndromes associated with lung cancer include acanthosis nigricans, dermatomyositis, disseminated intravascular coagulation, and hypertrophic pulmonary osteoarthropathy (HPO). Of these, HPO is the most common, occurring in up to 17% of patients with adenocarcinoma (Fig. 28–16).[143]

Radiologic Evaluation

Although imaging has an important role in the diagnosis, staging, and monitoring of patients with lung cancer, the role of imaging in screening for malignancy is not clearly defined.

Screening

Because diagnosis of lung cancer at an early stage is associated with an improved prognosis, screening has been

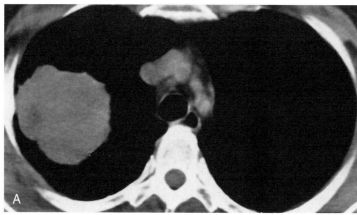

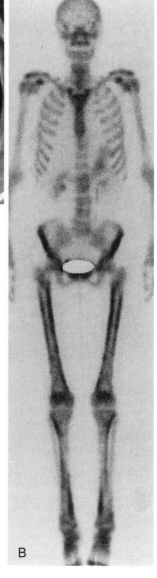

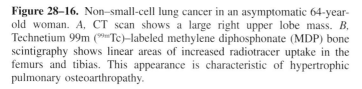

Figure 28–16. Non–small-cell lung cancer in an asymptomatic 64-year-old woman. *A,* CT scan shows a large right upper lobe mass. *B,* Technetium 99m (⁹⁹ᵐTc)–labeled methylene diphosphonate (MDP) bone scintigraphy shows linear areas of increased radiotracer uptake in the femurs and tibias. This appearance is characteristic of hypertrophic pulmonary osteoarthropathy.

advocated to detect lung cancer before clinical presentation. The ACS does not, however, recommend routine radiologic evaluation for the detection of lung cancer but instead advocates primary prevention.[59] This recommendation is based on the results of four large randomized trials undertaken in the 1970s, which evaluated the utility of chest radiographs and sputum cytology in lung cancer screening. These trials showed that screening improved long-term survival rates without reducing mortality (considered the best evidence that screening is effective, as it is not affected by lead-time bias, length bias, and overdiagnosis bias).[12, 60, 105, 151, 218]

A reanalysis of the data from these trials has suggested some justification for the use of chest radiography in lung cancer screening.[216, 217] Additionally, because of the concerns about design and methodology of the previous trials, together with improved detection of small lung cancers using computed tomography (CT), there has been a renewed interest in reevaluating screening. Consequently, new multi-institutional screening studies in the United States, supported by the National Cancer Institute as well as by other smaller trials in Japan and Germany, are being performed to reexamine the role of screening in lung cancer management.[83, 93, 161, 207]

Diagnosis

Because most patients with lung cancer have advanced disease at presentation, diagnosis is usually not difficult. Nevertheless, 20% to 30% of patients with lung cancer present with a solitary pulmonary nodule, which may be difficult to differentiate from a benign nodule.[242] Certain morphologic and physiologic features, however, may suggest a diagnosis of lung cancer:

1. *Size.* The larger the nodule, the more likely it is to be malignant.[76, 86, 273] Small size, however, cannot be used to reliably exclude lung cancer, since up to 42% of resected lung cancers are less than 2 cm in diameter.[203, 242, 269]
2. *Margins.* Lung cancers typically have irregular or spiculated margins.[76, 202, 225, 269, 273] Although suggestive of lung cancer, these findings can occasionally be seen with benign nodules.[76, 273] Furthermore, a smooth margin, a feature typical of benign nodules, cannot be used to exclude lung cancer, because 20% of malignant nodules have this appearance.[205]
3. *Internal morphology.* Except for fat (attenuation, −40 to −120 Hounsfield units [HU]) and calcification within a nodule, internal morphology is unreliable in distinguishing lung cancer from a benign nodule.[76, 160, 204, 273] Calcification occurs histologically in up to 14% of lung cancers and may be detected by CT.[123, 159] The calcification is typically amorphous in appearance (Fig. 28–17), unlike the diffuse solid, central punctate, laminated, or popcorn-like calcifications that are diagnostic of benign nodules. Amorphous calcification, however, is not diagnostic of lung cancer, because similar calcifications are occasionally detected in benign lesions. Cavitation occurs in benign nodules and lung cancer. Malignant nodules typically have thick, irregular walls, whereas benign nodules have smooth, thin walls.[259, 260, 273] These findings, however, are not specific, and wall thickness cannot be used to confidently differentiate benign nodules from lung cancer.

4. *Growth.* Lung cancers typically double in volume (an increase of 26% in diameter) between 30 and 400 days (average, 240 days).[119] Although absence of growth over a 2-year period is usually reliable for confirming that a nodule is benign,[72, 73, 118] it is difficult to reliably detect growth in small nodules because the small change in diameter associated with a doubling of volume may not be visible on radiographs. The use of CT can improve the accuracy of growth assessment. It has been reported that growth can be detected in lung cancers as small as 5 mm when CT imaging is repeated within 30 days.[264] Furthermore, the measurement of serial volumes of small nodules (which increase proportionally faster than diameters), may be an accurate and potentially useful method for assessing the rate of growth.[265] At present, the determination of when and how to observe and image small nodules in the assessment of tumor growth rate has not been resolved.
5. *Blood supply.* Blood supply to malignant pulmonary nodules is qualitatively and quantitatively different from the blood supply to benign nodules. Contrast-enhanced CT can be used to image this difference by determining nodule enhancement. Typically, malignant nodules enhance more than 20 HU, whereas benign nodules enhance less than 15 HU (Fig. 28–18).[223]
6. *Metabolism.* Metabolism of glucose is typically increased in lung cancer cells. Positron emission tomography (PET), using a D-glucose analog, ^{18}F-2-deoxy-D-glucose (FDG), can be used in imaging this increase and in differentiating malignant from benign nodules.[197]

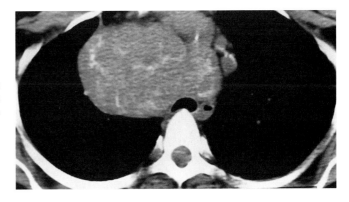

Figure 28–17. Non–small-cell lung cancer manifesting as a calcified mass. CT shows a large, right upper lobe mass with mediastinal invasion. Scattered areas of amorphous calcification in the mass are typical of, but not diagnostic for, malignancy.

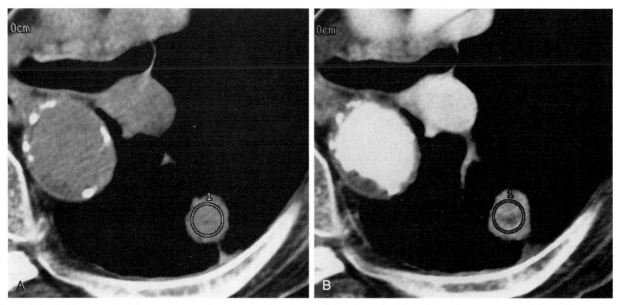

Figure 28–18. Non–small-cell cancer appearing as an enhancing nodule after administration of contrast material. *A,* Non–contrast-enhanced CT scan shows a left lung nodule with an attenuation value of 24 Hounsfield units (HU). *B,* Contrast-enhanced CT scan shows nodule enhancement of 70 HU and central necrosis. Enhancement of more than 20 HU suggests malignancy. Resection revealed non–small-cell cancer. (Courtesy of Tom Hartman, M.D., Mayo Clinic, Rochester, Minn.)

Nodules as small as 1 cm can be imaged; if FDG uptake is low, the nodules are almost certainly benign.[41, 101, 114, 173, 174] Nodules with increased FDG uptake are generally considered malignant (Fig. 28–19), although inflammatory and infectious processes (e.g., rheumatoid nodules, tuberculosis, histoplasmosis) may result in increased FDG uptake.[101, 173, 174, 238]

Staging

Non–Small-Cell Lung Cancer. Because treatment and prognosis depend on the anatomic extent of NSCLC at initial presentation, accurate assessment is important.[145, 150] The International Staging System for Lung Cancer is used to describe the extent of NSCLC in terms of the primary tumor (T status), lymph nodes (N status), and metastases (M status) (Table 28–2).[145] The TNM descriptors can be determined clinically (history, physical examination, radiologic imaging) or by pathologic analysis of samples obtained by biopsy or surgery. In general, the clinical stage underestimates the extent of disease when compared with the pathologic stage.[145]

Primary Tumor (T Status). The T status defines the size, location, and extent of the primary tumor. Because the extent of the primary tumor determines therapeutic management (surgical resection or palliative radiotherapy or chemotherapy), imaging is often performed to assess the degree of pleural, chest wall, and mediastinal invasion.

CT is useful in confirming gross chest wall invasion

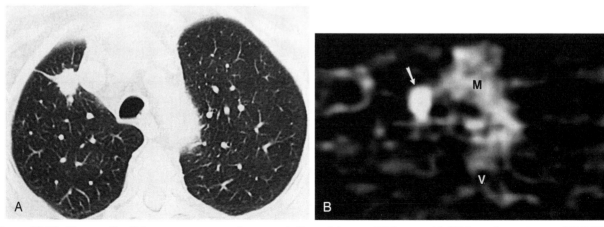

Figure 28–19. Non–small-cell lung cancer seen as hypermetabolic nodule on a PET scan with ^{18}F-fluorodeoxyglucose (FDG-PET). *A,* CT scan shows a nodule in the right upper lobe. The irregular margin suggests malignancy. *B,* Axial PET image with FDG shows increased uptake within the nodule *(arrow)* when compared to adjacent mediastinum. Findings suggest malignancy. Resection revealed squamous cell cancer. M, mediastinum; V, vertebral body.

Table 28–2. International Staging System for Lung Cancer

Primary Tumor (T)

TX	Primary tumor cannot be assessed, or tumor proven by the presence of malignant cells in sputum or bronchial washings but not visualized by imaging or bronchoscopy
T0	No evidence of primary tumor
Tis	Carcinoma *in situ*
T1	Tumor ≤3 cm in greatest dimension, surrounded by lung or visceral pleura, without bronchoscopic evidence of invasion more proximal than the lobar bronchus* (i.e., not in the main bronchus)
T2	Tumor with any of the following features of size or extent: >3 cm in greatest dimension Involves main bronchus, ≥2 cm distal to the carina Invades the visceral pleura Associated with atelectasis or obstructive pneumonitis that extends to the hilar region but does not involve the entire lung
T3	Tumor of any size that directly invades any of the following: chest wall (including superior sulcus tumors), diaphragm, mediastinal pleura, parietal pericardium; or tumor in the main bronchus <2 cm distal to the carina, but without involvement of the carina; or associated atelectasis or obstructive pneumonitis of the entire lung
T4	Tumor of any size that invades any of the following: mediastinum, heart, great vessels, trachea, esophagus, vertebral body, carina; or tumor with a malignant pleural or pericardial effusion,† or with satellite tumor nodule(s) within the ipsilateral primary-tumor lobe of the lung

Regional Lymph Nodes (N)

NX	Regional lymph nodes cannot be assessed
N0	No regional lymph node metastasis
N1	Metastasis to ipsilateral peribronchial and/or ipsilateral hilar lymph nodes, and intrapulmonary nodes involved by direct extension of the primary tumor
N2	Metastasis to ipsilateral mediastinal and/or subcarinal lymph node(s)
N3	Metastasis to contralateral mediastinal, contralateral hilar, ipsilateral or contralateral scalene, or supraclavicular lymph node(s)

Distant Metastasis (M)

MX	Presence of distant metastasis cannot be assessed
M0	No distant metastasis
M1	Distant metastasis present‡

*The uncommon superficial tumor of any size with its invasive component limited to the bronchial wall, which may extend proximal to the main bronchus, is also classified T1.

†Most pleural effusions associated with lung cancer are due to tumor. However, there are a few patients in whom multiple cytopathologic examinations of pleural fluid show no tumor. In these cases, the fluid is nonbloody and is not an exudate. When these elements and clinical judgment dictate that the effusion is not related to the tumor, the effusion should be excluded as a staging element and the patient's disease should be staged T1, T2, or T3. Pericardial effusion is classified according to the same rules.

‡Separate metastatic tumor nodule(s) in the ipsilateral nonprimary-tumor lobe(s) of the lung also are classified M1.

From Mountain CF: Revisions in the international system for staging lung cancer. Chest 111:1710–1717, 1997.

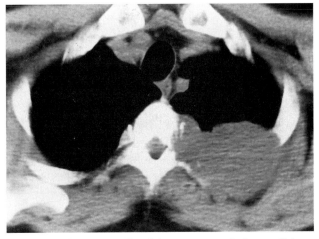

Figure 28–20. Non–small-cell lung cancer and chest wall invasion. CT scan shows a left upper lobe lung mass with destruction of the adjacent rib and the vertebral body.

perior soft tissue contrast resolution, the sensitivity (63% to 90%) and specificity (84% to 86%) of MRI in identifying chest wall invasion is similar to that of CT (Fig. 28–21).[100, 166, 182, 247] MRI is, however, particularly useful in the evaluation of superior sulcus tumors and can be used to assess invasion of the brachial plexus, subclavian vessels, and vertebral bodies (Fig. 28–22).[100, 247, 248]

Imaging with CT or MR is useful in confirming gross invasion of the mediastinum (Figs. 28–23 and 28–24), but these modalities are inaccurate in determining subtle invasion (56% to 89% and 50% to 93%, respectively).[100, 126, 134, 148, 247] CT and MRI findings that can be useful in suggesting subtle mediastinal invasion include[71, 84, 100, 134]:

- Tumor-mediastinal contact extending over more than 3 cm
- Obliteration of the fat plane between the mediastinum and tumor
- Tumor contacting more than 90 degrees of the aortic circumference

Primary lesions associated with malignant pleural effusions or pleural metastases are classified as T4 lesions. Up to 33% of patients with NSCLC have pleural metastases at presentation.[5, 145] The diagnosis of pleural metastases or malignant effusion, however, can be difficult to confirm. Pleural thickening and nodularity on CT scans suggests metastatic pleural disease (Fig. 28–25), but these abnormalities may not be present in association with a malignant effusion.[182] Furthermore, cytologic evaluation is positive in only approximately 66% of patients with a malignant pleural effusion at presentation.[5] In the absence of fluid with positive findings in cytologic studies, a T4 classification is still assigned if the effusion appears to be from the underlying malignancy.[144, 145]

Regional Lymph Nodes (N Status). The presence and location of nodal metastasis are of major importance in determining management and prognosis in patients with NSCLC.[146] To enable a consistent and standardized description of N status, nodal stations are defined by the American Thoracic Society in relation to anatomic structures or

(Fig. 28–20) but is inaccurate in differentiating between anatomic contiguity and subtle invasion.[100, 182, 184, 266] Findings suggestive of chest wall invasion include[100, 184]:

- Tumor-pleura contact extending over more than 3 cm
- An obtuse angle at the tumor-pleura interface
- Thickening of the pleura or increased attenuation of the extrapleural fat adjacent to the tumor

Although magnetic resonance imaging (MRI) offers su-

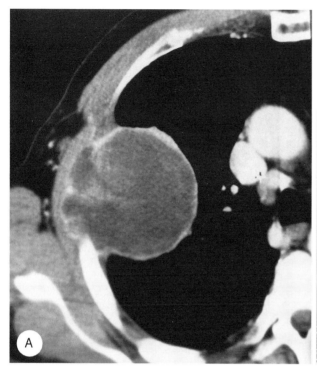

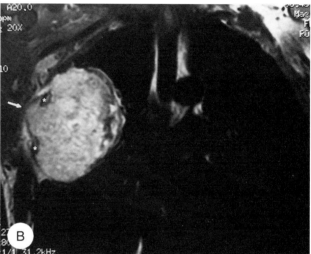

Figure 28–21. Small-cell lung cancer and chest wall invasion. *A,* CT shows a large, well-circumscribed peripheral lung mass with invasion of the chest wall. *B,* Coronal fast spin-echo MRI shows mass abutting the chest wall and the surrounding ribs *(asterisks)* and extending through the intercostal space into the soft tissues of the chest wall *(arrow).*

Figure 28–22. Pancoast's tumor with local chest wall invasion. *A* and *B,* Coronal T1-weighted MR images show a mass (M) in the apex of the left hemithorax, with loss of the adjacent soft tissue plane consistent with local invasion *(arrowheads).* Asterisks in *A* indicate rib.

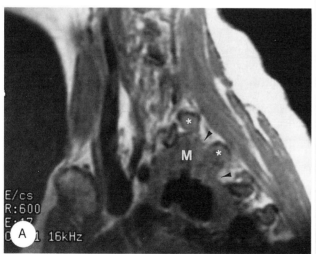

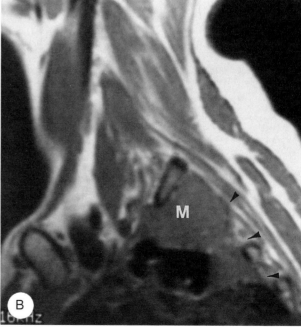

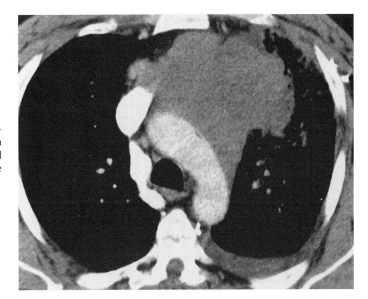

Figure 28–23. Non–small-cell cancer with mediastinal invasion. CT scan shows a large, left upper lobe mass with invasion of the anterior mediastinum. Broad abutment and loss of soft tissue plane between the mass and the transverse aorta suggest vascular invasion.

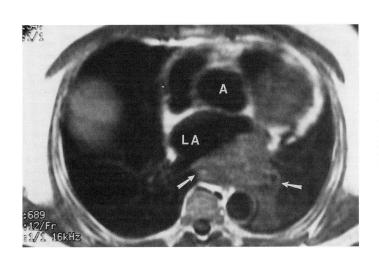

Figure 28–24. Non–small-cell lung cancer invading the left atrium. Axial T1-weighted MR image shows a left lower lobe mass that has an intermediate signal intensity extending into the left atrium *(arrows)*. A, aorta; LA, left atrium. (From Erasmus JJ, McAdams HP, Donnelly LF, Spritzer CE: MR imaging of mediastinal masses. MRI Clin North Am 8: 59–89, 2000.)

Figure 28–25. Non–small-cell lung cancer and pleural metastases. Contrast-enhanced CT shows a large right pleural effusion and enhancing nodular pleural metastases *(arrowheads)*. *Arrow* indicates compressive atelectasis of the right lower lobe and a metastatic left rib lesion.

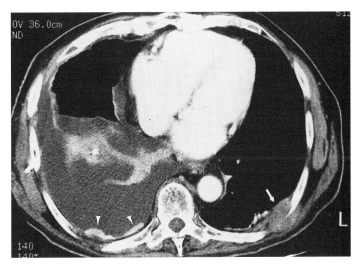

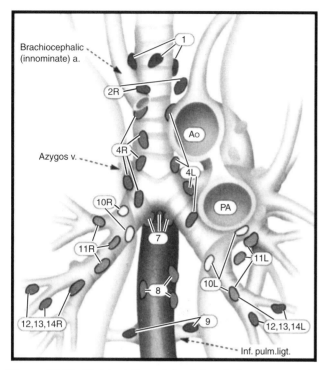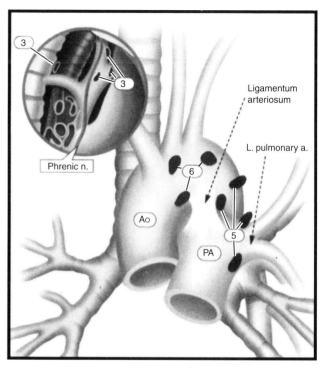

Figure 28–26. Nodal stations defined in relation to anatomic structures or boundaries. Superior mediastinal nodes: 1, highest mediastinal; 2, upper paratracheal; 3, prevascular and retrotracheal; 4, lower paratracheal (including azygos nodes); Aortic nodes: 5, subaortic (anteroposterior window); 6, para-aortic (ascending aorta or phrenic). Inferior mediastinal nodes: 7, subcarinal; 8, paraesophageal (below carina); 9, pulmonary ligament. N₁ nodes: 10, hilar; 11, interlobar; 12, lobar; 13, segmental; 14, subsegmental. (From Mountain CF: Revisions in the international system for staging lung cancer. Chest 111:1710–1717, 1997.)

boundaries that can be identified before and during thoracotomy (Fig. 28–26 and Table 28–3).[145, 146]

Size is the only criterion used to diagnose nodal metastases, with nodes greater than 10 mm in short-axis diameter considered abnormal.[69, 70] Because enlarged nodes can be hyperplastic or reactive and small nodes can harbor metastases, the accuracies of CT and MRI in detecting ipsilateral metastases to hilar nodes (N1 disease) are only 62% to 88% and 68% to 74%, respectively.[68, 126, 135, 200, 246] Fortunately, accuracy in determining N1 disease is usually not essential, because in most cases this does not prevent surgical resection.[135, 182] The accuracies of CT (56% to 82%) and MRI (50% to 82%) in detecting mediastinal nodal metastases (N2, N3 disease) are also not optimal.[7, 100, 126, 148, 211, 246, 247]

FDG-PET is more accurate (range, 81% to 96%) than CT and MRI in determining N status.[44, 175, 213, 244] FDG-PET is particularly useful in detecting metastatic disease in normal-sized nodes and in differentiating hyperplastic nodes from enlarged nodal metastases (Fig. 28–27).[213, 241, 244] It has been advocated that a normal FDG-PET scan and normal-sized nodes on CT can obviate the need for mediastinoscopy in some patients with potentially resectable lung cancer.[213, 241, 244]

Metastatic Disease (M status). Patients with NSCLC commonly have extrathoracic metastases to the adrenal glands, liver, brain, bones, and lymph nodes at presentation.[100, 145, 181] The role of imaging in detecting these metastases, however, is not clearly defined. Because a normal

clinical examination result, combined with normal routine laboratory tests, such as hematocrit, alkaline phosphatase, gamma-glutamyl transferase (GGT), and serum glutamic-oxaloacetic transaminase (SGOT), has a negative predictive value greater than 95%, radiologic evaluation for occult metastases may not be required.[206, 224] In fact, considering the high cost and low incidence (0.5% to 0.9%) of detecting metastases in patients with T1 N0 to T2 N0 disease and no clinical findings of metastases, it has been suggested that extrathoracic imaging should not be performed in the staging evaluation of these patients.[224] Routine imaging of the abdomen is still performed by many clinicians, however, because of the poor reliability of clinical and laboratory findings in the detection of intra-abdominal metastases.

Metastases to the adrenal glands are common and are detected in up to 20% of patients at presentation (Fig. 28–28).[100, 155, 164, 167, 168] A small (<3 cm) adrenal mass, however, is more likely to be benign in the absence of other extrathoracic metastases.[100] CT and MRI can be useful in the evaluation of adrenal masses.

CT and MRI features favoring malignancy include[43, 136, 140]:

- Size greater than 3 cm
- Poorly defined margins
- Irregularly enhancing rim
- Invasion of adjacent structures
- High signal intensity on T2-weighted sequences

A confident diagnosis of benignity can be made if an

Table 28–3. Classification of Regional Lymph Nodes in Lung Cancer

Nodal Station	Anatomic Landmarks
N2 nodes—All N2 nodes lie within the mediastinal pleural envelope	
1 Highest mediastinal nodes	Nodes lying above a horizontal line at the upper rim of the bracheocephalic (left innominate) vein where it ascends to the left, crossing in front of the trachea at its midline
2 Upper paratracheal nodes	Nodes lying above a horizontal line drawn tangential to the upper margin of the aortic arch and below the inferior boundary of No. 1 nodes
3 Prevascular and retrotracheal nodes	Prevascular and retrotracheal nodes may be designated 3A and 3P; midline nodes are considered to be ipsilateral
4 Lower paratracheal nodes	The lower paratracheal nodes on the right lie to the right of the midline of the trachea between a horizontal line drawn tangential to the upper margin of the aortic arch and a line extending across the right main bronchus at the upper margin of the upper lobe bronchus, and contained within the mediastinal pleural envelope; the lower paratracheal nodes on the left lie to the left of the midline of the trachea between a horizontal line drawn tangenital to the upper margin of the aortic arch and a line extending across the left main bronchus at the level of the upper margin of the left upper lobe bronchus, medial to the ligamentum arteriosum and contained within the mediastinal pleural envelope
	Researchers may wish to designate the lower paratracheal nodes as No. 4s (superior) and No. 4i (inferior) subsets for study purposes; the No. 4s nodes may be defined by a horizontal line extending across the trachea and drawn tangential to the cephalic border of the azygos vein; the No. 4i nodes may be defined by the lower boundary of No. 4s and the lower boundary of No. 4, as described above
5 Subaortic (aortopulmonary window)	Subaortic nodes are lateral to the ligamentum arteriosum or the aorta or left pulmonary artery and proximal to the first branch of the left pulmonary artery and lie within the mediastinal pleural envelope
6 Para-aortic nodes (ascending aorta or phrenic)	Nodes lying anterior and lateral to the ascending aorta and the aortic arch or the innominate artery, beneath a line tangential to the upper margin of the aortic arch
7 Subcarinal nodes	Nodes lying caudal to the carina of the trachea, but not associated with the lower lobe bronchi or arteries within the lung
8 Paraesophageal nodes (below carina)	Nodes lying adjacent to the wall of the esophagus and to the right or left of the midline, excluding subcarinal nodes
9 Pulmonary ligament nodes	Nodes lying within the pulmonary ligament, including those in the posterior wall and lower part of the inferior pulmonary vein
N1 nodes—All N1 nodes lie distal to the mediastinal pleural reflection and within the visceral pleura	
10 Hilar nodes	The proximal lobar nodes, distal to the mediastinal pleural reflection and the nodes adjacent to the bronchus intermedius on the right; radiographically, the hilar shadow may be created by enlargement of both hilar and interlobar nodes
11 Interlobar nodes	Nodes lying between the lobar bronchi
12 Lobar nodes	Nodes adjacent to the distal lobar bronchi
13 Segmental nodes	Nodes adjacent to the segmental bronchi
14 Subsegmental nodes	Nodes around the subsegmental bronchi

From Mountain CF, Dresler CM: Regional lymph node classification for lung cancer staging. Chest 111:1718–1723, 1997.

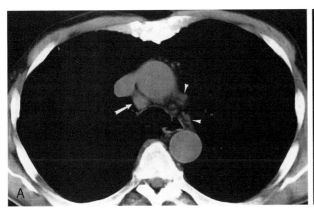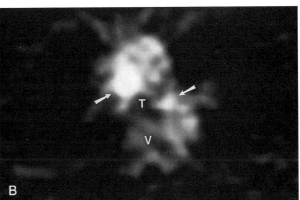

Figure 28–27. Non–small-cell lung cancer and intrathoracic nodal metastasis. *A,* CT shows an 11-mm right paratracheal node *(arrow)* and smaller, normal-sized aortopulmonary window lymph nodes *(arrowheads). B,* Axial PET image with ^{18}F-fluorodeoxyglucose (FDG-PET) shows markedly increased uptake in mediastinal nodes. Mediastinoscopy confirmed metastatic disease *(arrows).* T, trachea; V, vertebral body.

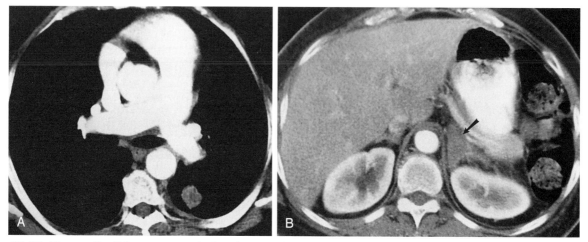

Figure 28–28. Non–small-cell lung cancer and adrenal metastasis. *A,* CT shows a nodule in the left lower lobe. There is no hilar or mediastinal adenopathy. *B,* CT of the abdomen reveals a left adrenal mass *(arrow).* Biopsy confirmed metastasis.

adrenal mass has an attenuation value less than 10 HU on a non–contrast-enhanced CT scan.[14] MRI, using chemical shift analysis and dynamic gadolinium enhancement, can also be used to determine whether an adrenal mass is benign (Fig. 28–29).[13, 165, 198] Unfortunately, the status of some adrenal lesions remains indeterminate after radiologic evaluation, and biopsy is required.[178]

CNS metastases are common and are detected in up to 18% of patients at presentation (Fig. 28–30).[89, 139] Up to 10% of these patients (usually with large-cell carcinomas and adenocarcinomas) are asymptomatic.[89, 139, 154, 195] Consequently, it has been suggested that routine CT of the brain should be performed in the initial staging evaluation of all patients with NSCLC.[56] Because CNS metastases are usually associated with neurologic signs and symptoms, however, imaging for CNS metastases in asymptomatic patients with NSCLC is not considered cost-effective and is not generally recommended.[30, 206]

Patients with skeletal metastases are usually symptomatic or have laboratory abnormalities indicating bone metastases.[195] Because occult skeletal metastases are only occasionally detected in asymptomatic patients by imaging, it is recommended that bone radiographs, technetium 99m-methylene diphosphonate (^{99m}Tc-MDP) bone scintigraphy, and MRI be performed only to evaluate a history of focal bone pain or elevated alkaline phosphatase.[122, 137, 195, 206, 214]

Because staging performed on the basis of symptomatology, abnormal laboratory indices, and conventional radiologic imaging incorrectly assigns some patients with NSCLC, FDG-PET is being used as an additional imaging modality to improve staging accuracy. FDG-PET has a higher sensitivity and specificity than CT in detecting metastases to the adrenals, bones, and extrathoracic lymph nodes.[20, 52, 114, 129, 195, 238, 249] Whole body PET imaging allows the physician to stage intrathoracic and extrathoracic disease in a single study, to detect occult extrathoracic metas-

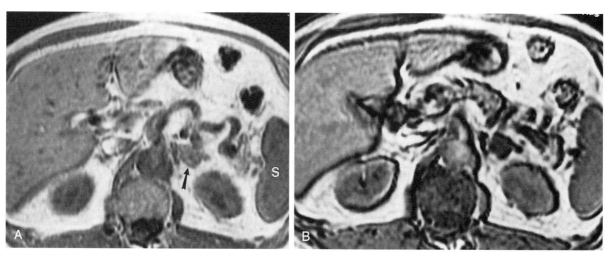

Figure 28–29. Non–small-cell lung cancer and incidental adrenal adenoma evaluated by chemical shift MRI. *A,* In-phase (TR = 200 msec, TE = 4.2 msec) spoiled gradient-recalled echo MR image shows a left adrenal mass *(arrow)* that is slightly hyperintense compared with the spleen (S). *B,* Opposed-phase (TR = 200 msec, TE = 1.8 msec) spoiled gradient-recalled echo MR image shows that the left adrenal mass is now markedly hypointense. The findings are typical of those for adenoma. The patient underwent resection of primary lung malignancy.

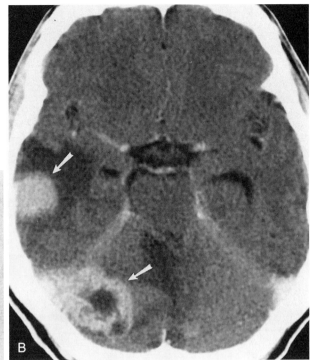

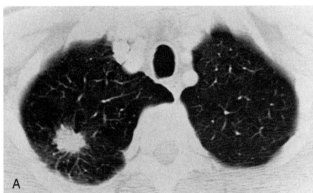

Figure 28–30. Non–small-cell lung cancer and brain metastases at presentation manifesting as ataxia. *A,* CT shows a spiculated right upper lobe nodule. *B,* Axial contrast-enhanced cranial CT scan shows enhancing metastases in the temporal lobe and the cerebellum *(arrows).*

tases in 11% to 14% of patients selected for curative resection, and to alter management in up to 40% of cases (Fig. 28–31).[114, 238, 249]

Staging Classification. The International Staging System for Lung Cancer combines the TNM subsets into categories, or stages, that have similar treatment options and prognosis (Table 28–4).[17, 145]

Stages I and II. Patients with *stage I* disease are typically optimal candidates for surgical resection with survival rates of 57% to 85%.[145] The prognostic implications of larger tumor size and location and the involvement of intrapulmonary and hilar lymph nodes are reflected in the decreased 5-year survival rates of 34% and 22% to 24% in patients with stage IIA (T1 N1 M0) and *stage IIB* (T2 N1 M0, T3 N0 M0) disease, respectively.[145]

Table 28–4. Stage Grouping: Tumor-Node-Metastases (TNM) Subsets

Stage	TNM Subset		
IA	T1	N0	M0
IB	T2	N0	M0
IIA	T1–2	N1	M0
IIB	T3	N0	M0
IIIA	T1–2	N2	M0
	T3	N1–2	M0
IIIB	T4	N0–2	M0
	T1–4	N3	M0
IV	Any T	Any N	M1

Stage III. Stage IIIA (T3 N1 M0, T1–T3 N2 M0) identifies patients with locally advanced disease (extrapulmonary extension of the primary tumor) and ipsilateral hilar or mediastinal nodes. These patients are potential surgical candidates, although extracapsular extension of metastasis or involvement of high paratracheal nodes is a contraindication to curative resection.[144] Increasing tumor size and extent of local invasion appear to be directly related to the extent of lymph node involvement and the decrease in survival rates.[145] The 5-year survival rate is 9% to 13% in clinically staged patients and 23% to 25% in surgical-pathologic staged patients.[145]

Stage IIIB (T4 N0–2 M0, T1–T4 N3 M0) identifies patients with nonresectable NSCLC (i.e., satellite nodules in the lobe with the primary tumor, malignant effusion, invasion of nonresectable structures, contralateral hila, or mediastinal nodal disease).[145] Most stage IIIB patients receive radiation therapy and adjuvant chemotherapy, and the 5-year survival is 3% to 8%.[145] The classification of satellite nodules as T4 disease, however, may imply a worse prognosis than is warranted. It has been advocated that these patients undergo definitive resection if there are no other contraindications to surgery (Fig. 28–32).[19, 112]

Stage IV. Stage IV patients have distant metastatic disease, including metastatic nodules in the ipsilateral nonprimary tumor lobes.[145] With the uncommon exception of a resectable intrathoracic NSCLC and a resectable solitary brain metastasis, stage IV carries the worst prognosis, with only 1% of patients alive at 5 years.[145, 194]

Small-Cell Lung Cancer. SCLC is generally staged according to the Veteran's Administration Lung Cancer

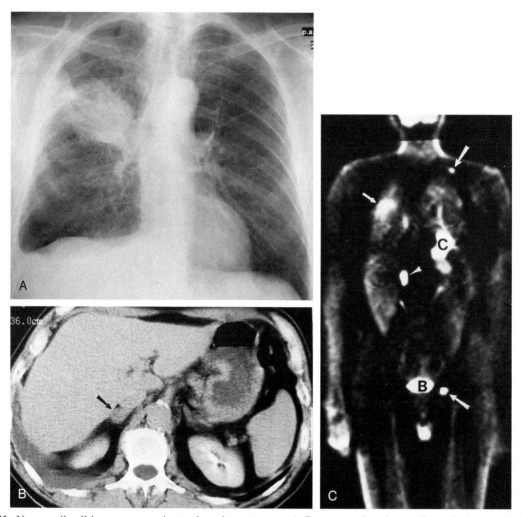

Figure 28–31. Non–small-cell lung cancer and extrathoracic metastases. *A,* Posteroanterior chest radiograph shows a right upper lobe mass. A small, right pleural effusion can be seen. *B,* CT reveals a small, right adrenal mass *(arrow)* and confirms a small right pleural effusion. *C,* Whole body PET image with ^{18}F-fluorodeoxyglucose (FDG-PET) shows increased uptake in the primary lung mass *(small arrow)* and in the adrenal metastasis *(arrowhead).* Focal areas of increased uptake in the upper aspect of the left hemithorax and pelvis *(large arrows)* were unsuspected bone metastases. B, bladder activity; C, cardiac activity.

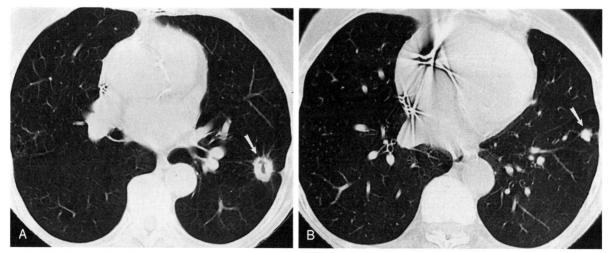

Figure 28–32. Non–small-cell lung cancer appearing as two lung nodules. *A* and *B,* CT scan shows two nodules in the left lower lobe, one of which is cavitary *(arrow in A and in B).* A satellite nodule in the ipsilateral lobe is classified as T4, not M1, disease.

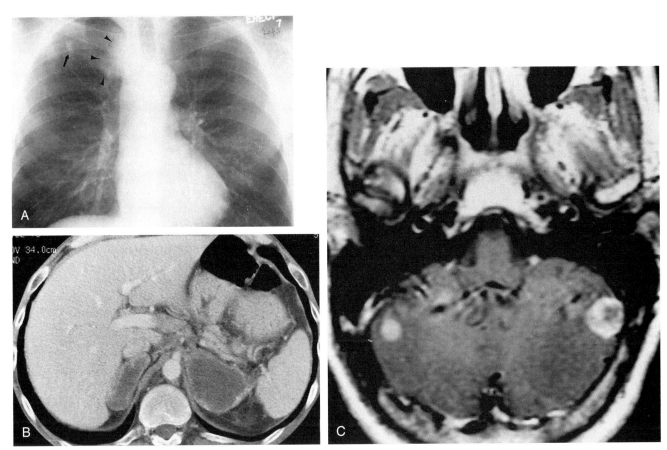

Figure 28–33. Small-cell lung cancer with disseminated metastases at presentation. *A,* Posteroanterior chest radiograph shows a poorly marginated mass in the right upper lobe *(arrowheads)* and a smaller right upper lobe nodule *(arrow). B,* CT shows large, bilateral necrotic adrenal metastases. *C,* Axial contrast-enhanced cranial MR image shows enhancing cerebellar metastases.

Study Group (VALG) recommendations as *limited disease* (LD) or *extensive disease* (ED).[37] LD defines tumor confined to a hemithorax and the regional lymph nodes. Unlike the TNM classification for NSCLC, metastases to the ipsilateral supraclavicular, contralateral supraclavicular, and mediastinal lymph nodes are considered local disease. Additionally, an ipsilateral malignant pleural effusion is often treated as limited disease.[37] ED includes tumor with noncontiguous metastases to the contralateral lung and distant metastases.[37, 215]

Most patients with SCLC have ED at presentation (Fig. 28–33).[92, 100] Common sites of metastatic disease include the liver, bone, bone marrow, brain, and retroperitoneal lymph nodes.[92] Although there is no consensus regarding the imaging and invasive procedures that should be performed in the staging evaluation of patients with SCLC, MRI has been advocated to assess the liver, adrenals, brain, and axial skeleton in a single study.[92] Evaluation of extrathoracic metastatic disease usually includes the following:

1. *Bone marrow aspiration, ^{99m}Tc-MDP bone scintigraphy, and MRI.* Patients with bone (30%) and bone marrow (17% to 34%) metastases are often asymptomatic, and blood alkaline phosphatase levels are frequently normal.[1, 37, 209, 210] Because isolated bone and bone marrow metastases are uncommon, however, routine bone mar-

row aspiration and radiologic imaging for occult metastases are usually performed only if there are other findings of ED.
2. *Brain MRI.* CNS metastases are common (10% to 27%) at presentation, and approximately 5% of patients are asymptomatic.[1, 18, 37] Because therapeutic CNS radiation and chemotherapy can decrease morbidity and improve prognosis, routine MRI of the brain is recommended in patients with SCLC.[37, 46, 240]
3. *CT or MRI of the abdomen.* Metastases to the liver (30%) and retroperitoneal nodes (11%) are common at presentation.[1, 37] Because patients are often asymptomatic and liver function tests can be normal, staging evaluation routinely includes CT or MRI of the abdomen.

Carcinomas with Pleomorphic Sarcomatoid or Sarcomatous Elements

Sarcomatoid carcinomas are lung malignancies containing carcinomatous and sarcomatous components.[149, 254] They represent a clinicopathologic continuum that includes pulmonary blastoma, carcinosarcoma, and carcinomas with spindle or giant cells.[149, 254]

Carcinomas with Spindle or Giant Cells

Sarcomatoid carcinomas (pleomorphic carcinoma, spindle cell carcinoma, giant cell carcinoma, carcinosarcoma) are rare, composing 0.3% to 1% of malignant lung neoplasms.[48, 149] Most patients are men, and mean age at presentation is 65 years (range, 44 to 78 years).[90, 149] Most patients present with cough, dyspnea, hemoptysis, chest pain, or weight loss.[48, 90, 149] Although sarcomatoid carcinomas are usually localized at presentation, distant metastases occur frequently and the prognosis is poor.[90, 149, 254]

Radiologically, these neoplasms can manifest either as large peripheral masses or as polypoid endobronchial lesions with atelectasis or postobstructive pneumonia.[90, 98, 149, 254] Calcification and cavitation are uncommon, but necrosis and hemorrhage can manifest as heterogeneous attenuation on CT.[98, 149, 254] Hilar or mediastinal adenopathy is uncommon.[149] Pleural effusion can occur as a result of local invasion.[98] Metastases involve sites similar to those of lung cancer (lung, liver, bones, adrenals, brain).[254]

Pulmonary Blastoma

Pulmonary blastoma is a rare malignancy that makes up an estimated 0.25% to 0.5% of primary lung tumors.[62, 104, 106, 111] The tumor derives its name from its histologic resemblance to fetal lung tissue. Pulmonary blastomas, however, are thought to arise from primitive pluripotential stem cells and may represent a variant of carcinosarcoma.[255] Although the age range at presentation is wide (0 to 80 years), these tumors typically occur in adults, with a peak incidence between 40 and 60 years of age.[62, 104, 106, 111] Patients are often symptomatic at presentation; cough, hemoptysis, and chest pain are frequent manifestations.[104] Pulmonary blastoma is an aggressive malignancy and the overall 5-year survival rate is poor.[34, 62]

Radiologically, pulmonary blastomas typically manifest as large (range, 2.5 to 26 cm), well-marginated masses located peripherally in the lung (Fig. 28–34).[62, 250] Multiple masses, cavitation, and calcification are rare.[250] Local invasion of the mediastinum and pleura occurs in 8% and 25%

of cases, respectively.[62] Metastases to hilar and mediastinal lymph nodes are present in 30% of resected cases.[62] Extrathoracic metastases are common and have a distribution similar to that of lung cancer.[62, 111]

Carcinoid Tumor

Primary pulmonary carcinoid tumors are low-grade malignancies that constitute 1% to 2% of primary lung tumors.[133] They are classified histologically as typical (80% to 90%) or atypical (10% to 20%) tumors, depending on the degree of cellular atypia.[38, 96, 219]

Typical carcinoid tumors occur with equal frequency in men and women; the mean age at diagnosis is 35 to 50 years.[38, 219] Tumors usually arise in lobar, segmental, or proximal subsegmental bronchi (80% to 85%) and are generally 1 to 4 cm in size. They rarely metastasize to regional nodes or beyond the thorax.[38]

Atypical carcinoid tumors are usually discovered at a slightly older age (mean, 55 to 60 years), are often larger, and have equal central and peripheral distributions.[96, 219] They behave more aggressively than do typical carcinoid tumors and frequently metastasize to regional nodes, lung, liver, and bone.[29, 96]

Clinical manifestations depend on the histologic type and the location of the carcinoid tumor.[219] Peripheral tumors are usually asymptomatic, whereas central neoplasms can manifest as cough, hemoptysis, or recurrent infection (Fig. 28–35).[38] Paraneoplastic manifestations, such as carcinoid syndrome (cutaneous flushing, bronchospasm, chronic diarrhea, and valvular heart disease) and Cushing's syndrome, are rare and more common with atypical carcinoid tumors.[38, 133]

Radiologically, carcinoid tumors manifest most commonly as central endobronchial masses, with or without atelectasis or consolidation (Fig. 28–36).[272] A peripheral, well-marginated pulmonary nodule is a less common manifestation (Fig. 28–37). The tumors are usually less than 3 cm in size, although occasionally they may be as large as

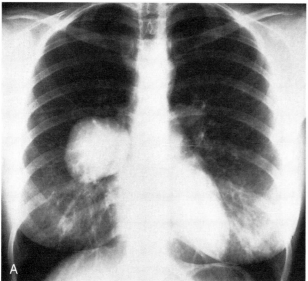

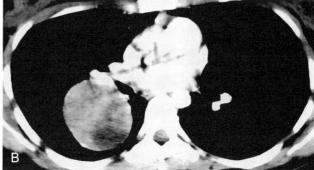

Figure 28–34. Pulmonary blastoma seen as a lobular pulmonary mass. *A,* Posteroanterior chest radiograph shows a sharply marginated, lobular mass in the right upper lobe. *B,* CT confirms the lung mass and shows heterogeneous attenuation consistent with necrosis.

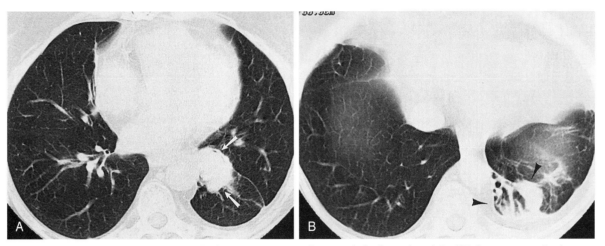

Figure 28–35. Typical carcinoid tumor manifesting as recurrent pulmonary infections. *A* and *B,* CT shows a mass in the segmental bronchus of the left lower lobe *(arrows in A),* left lower lobe volume loss, and distal bronchiectasis in the atelectatic lung *(arrowheads in B).*

10 cm in diameter.[133, 147, 239] Calcification is detected by CT in approximately 25% of carcinoid tumors (Fig. 28–38).[272] Hilar and mediastinal adenopathy and extrathoracic metastases are uncommon at presentation and occur more frequently in patients with atypical carcinoid tumors.[127, 147, 153]

Carcinomas of the Salivary Gland Type

Mucoepidermoid Carcinoma

Mucoepidermoid carcinoma (formerly categorized as a bronchial adenoma) is a rare tracheobronchial tumor composed of distinct areas of epidermoid cells and mucus-secreting cells. Although patients vary widely in age at presentation, the tumors are more common in adults, with a peak incidence between 35 and 45 years.[267] They typically occur in the main or lobar bronchi but, in rare instances, may be located in the trachea and periphery of the lung.[229, 232, 267] They are usually slow-growing, low-grade neoplasms with a benign clinical course. Although occasionally they exhibit aggressive local behavior, metastases are uncommon.[82, 267]

Radiologically, the tumor usually manifests as a central endobronchial mass and less commonly as a polypoid intraluminal tracheal or peripheral lung nodule or a mass.

Adenoid Cystic Carcinoma (Cylindroma)

Adenoid cystic carcinoma (formerly categorized as a bronchial adenoma) is an uncommon primary tumor of the lung. It occurs most often in the trachea (Fig. 28–39) and

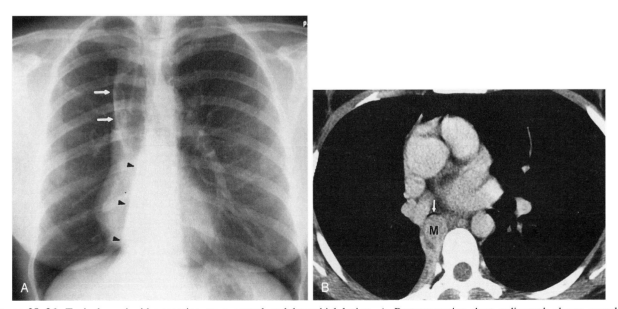

Figure 28–36. Typical carcinoid appearing as a central endobronchial lesion. *A,* Posteroanterior chest radiograph shows complete atelectasis of right lower lobe *(arrowheads)* with compensatory hyperinflation of the left lung. Note the displacement of the anterior junction line *(arrows). B,* CT confirms atelectasis of the right lower lobe and reveals an endobronchial mass (M) with marked narrowing of the bronchus intermedius *(arrow).*

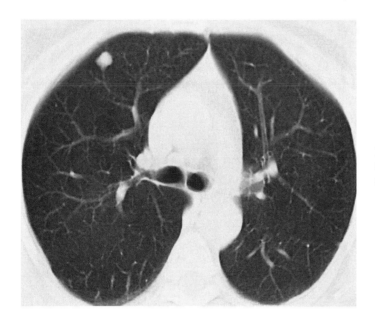

Figure 28–37. Typical carcinoid seen as a solitary peripheral nodule. CT shows a well-circumscribed small nodule in the right upper lobe.

main bronchi, although 10% to 15% are located peripherally in the lung.[3, 31, 36, 66] Adenoid cystic carcinomas occur with equal frequency in men and women; the mean age at diagnosis is 45 to 51 years.[130, 142] They typically exhibit slow, progressive growth.[31] Metastases to regional lymph nodes, lung, bone, liver, and brain are common but tend to occur late in the disease.[66]

Radiologically, the tumor usually manifests as an endotracheal or endobronchial mass that is typically lobulated or polypoid and encroaches on the airway lumen. Masses can be circumferential and may manifest as diffuse stenosis.[132] A less common manifestation is a peripheral lung nodule or mass.[31, 66]

Mesenchymal Tumors

Primary Pulmonary Sarcomas

Primary lung sarcomas with a vascular origin (angiosarcomas, epithelioid hemangioendotheliomas) are rare primary tumors of lung.[222, 256] Most angiosarcomas are lung metastases, and the existence of primary pulmonary angiosarcoma has been questioned.[208] The tumor usually occurs in young adults, and the most frequent radiologic finding is multiple, bilateral nodules.[222]

Epithelioid hemangioendothelioma is typically seen in women younger than 40 years of age (range, 7 to 76 years).[24, 187, 190, 256] Most patients are asymptomatic at presentation; complaints include weight loss, dyspnea, chest pain, cough, and hemoptysis.[24, 35, 256] Behavior is typically indolent, with survival reported up to 24 years following resection.[35]

Pulmonary epithelioid hemangioendothelioma usually manifests radiologically as multiple, 1- to 2-cm pulmonary nodules (Fig. 28–40).[35, 190, 256] Calcification is rarely detected but is common histologically.[35, 190] Hilar adenopathy and pleural effusions occur in 9% of patients.[190] Multiorgan involvement, most commonly the liver, occurs occasionally and may represent metastatic disease or multicentric origin of the tumor.[15, 45, 47, 191]

Primary lung sarcomas with a spindle origin are rare, accounting for fewer than 0.5% of primary lung malignan-

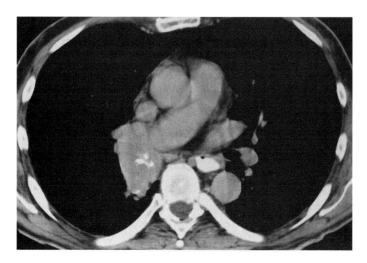

Figure 28–38. Atypical carcinoid tumor with rib and hepatic metastases at presentation. CT shows a large endobronchial mass with dense punctate calcification.

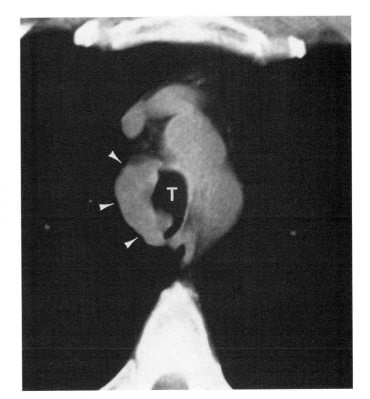

Figure 28–39. Adenoid cystic carcinoma manifesting as a tracheal mass. CT shows a soft tissue mass *(arrowheads)* arising from the lateral wall of the trachea (T). A polypoid endoluminal component can be seen.

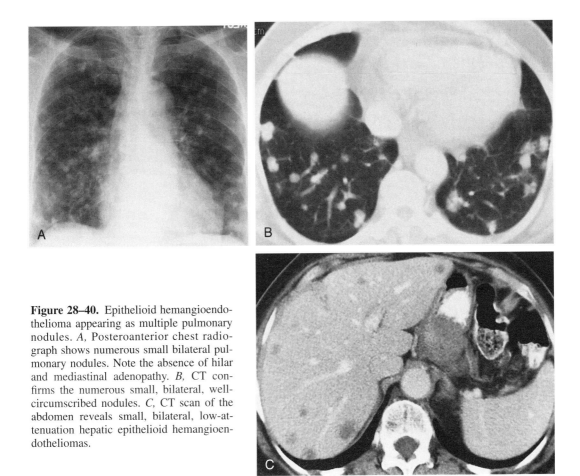

Figure 28–40. Epithelioid hemangioendothelioma appearing as multiple pulmonary nodules. *A,* Posteroanterior chest radiograph shows numerous small bilateral pulmonary nodules. Note the absence of hilar and mediastinal adenopathy. *B,* CT confirms the numerous small, bilateral, well-circumscribed nodules. *C,* CT scan of the abdomen reveals small, bilateral, low-attenuation hepatic epithelioid hemangioendotheliomas.

cies.[8, 222] Spindle cell sarcomas (malignant fibrous histiocytoma, hemangiopericytoma, fibrosarcoma, leiomyosarcoma, synovial sarcoma) are the most common primary pulmonary sarcomas.[94, 141, 222, 270] They are a heterogeneous group of tumors with morphologic similarities to their extrathoracic counterparts.[8] The diagnosis is established only after metastatic disease and sarcoma-like primary lung malignancies (sarcomatoid carcinomas) have been excluded.[8, 62, 90, 149] Pulmonary sarcomas have a peak incidence in the fifth and sixth decades.[91, 141, 222, 268, 270] The tumors are usually slowly growing with late metastases, and the prognosis is generally better than that with lung cancer.[222]

Radiologically, pulmonary sarcomas are more commonly located peripherally, although central and endobronchial masses are reported.[8, 91, 141, 222, 268] Lesions range in size from 0.6 to 25 cm; they are typically sharply marginated and occasionally calcified (Figs. 28–41 and 28–42).[8, 78, 94, 141, 222] Cavitation is uncommon, although CT can show heterogeneous attenuation resulting from necrosis within the mass.[78, 94] Diagnostic angiographic features have been reported for hemangiopericytomas in the soft tissues and bone.[78, 263] The pathognomonic hypervascularity that occurs as a result of the numerous vascular spaces within the tumor, however, are seldom seen on CT scans or MR images of primary pulmonary hemangiopericytomas (Fig. 28–43).

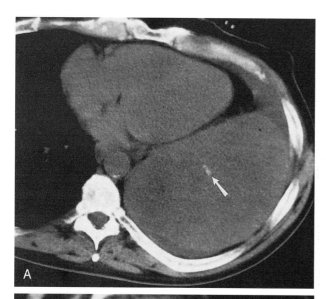

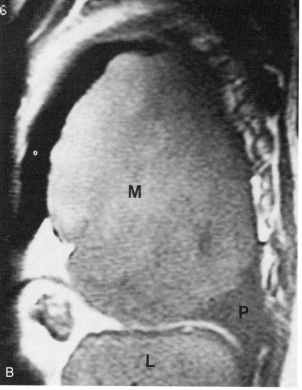

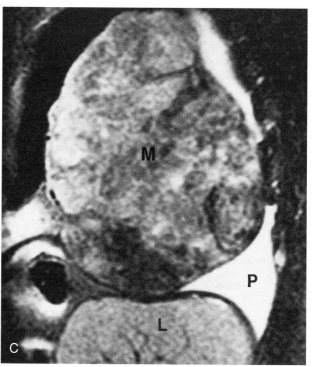

Figure 28–41. Synovial carcinoma of left lung seen as a large mass. *A,* CT shows a large mass in the left lower lobe with a small focal calcification *(arrow).* A small pleural effusion can be seen. *B* and *C,* Coronal T1-weighted *(B)* and fast spin-echo *(C)* MR images show a large heterogeneous mass abutting the diaphragm without signs of invasion. A small pleural effusion (P) can be seen. L, liver; M, mass.

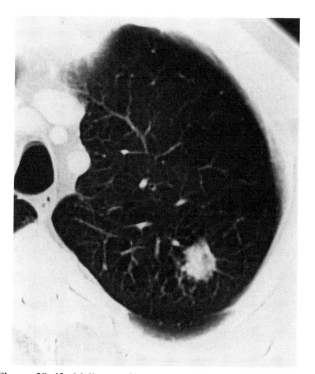

Figure 28–42. Malignant fibrous histiocytoma manifesting as a solitary pulmonary nodule. CT shows a left upper lobe nodule with irregular margins.

Lymphoproliferative Disorders

Primary Lymphomas

Primary pulmonary lymphomas account for fewer than 1% of all lymphomas.[32, 57, 103, 226] The diagnosis is generally considered if (1) the lymphoid proliferation is monoclonal and (2) there are no sites of extrathoracic lymphoma at presentation or for at least 3 months after diagnosis.[16, 32, 57, 183, 226] Criteria used to define primary pulmonary lymphomas are variable, however; some authors restrict the diagnosis to pulmonary parenchymal disease only, but others include hilar adenopathy with or without mediastinal adenopathy.

Primary pulmonary lymphomas encompass a histologic spectrum of malignant lymphomas including non-Hodgkin's lymphoma, Hodgkin's lymphoma, and lymphoproliferative disorders associated with immunodeficiency states (e.g., post-transplant lymphoproliferative disorders, acquired immunodeficiency syndrome).[77] Most primary extranodal lymphomas arise from mucosa-associated lymphoid tissue (MALT) and are sometimes referred to as *maltomas*.[32, 55, 77, 80, 103] In the lung, primary lymphomas are thought to arise from bronchus-associated lymphoid tissue (BALT) that occurs in the airway as a response to chronic stimulation.[231] These tumors are typically non-Hodgkin's lymphomas of B-cell immunophenotype composed of monoclonal lymphocytic cells with low histologic grade, and they have now been classified as extranodal marginal zone lymphomas.[57, 80, 103, 115]

Primary pulmonary lymphomas tend to remain localized

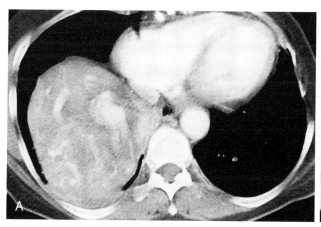

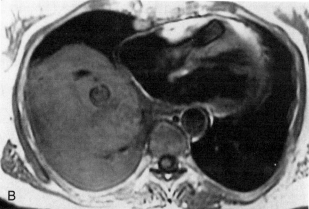

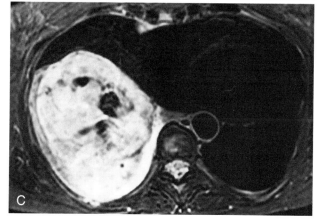

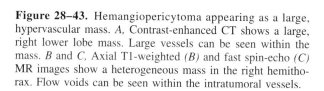

Figure 28–43. Hemangiopericytoma appearing as a large, hypervascular mass. *A,* Contrast-enhanced CT shows a large, right lower lobe mass. Large vessels can be seen within the mass. *B* and *C,* Axial T1-weighted *(B)* and fast spin-echo *(C)* MR images show a heterogeneous mass in the right hemithorax. Flow voids can be seen within the intratumoral vessels.

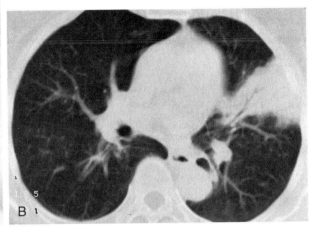

Figure 28–44. Primary pulmonary lymphoma seen as chronic consolidation. *A,* Posteroanterior chest radiograph shows a poorly marginated opacity in the left lung. Note the absence of hilar and mediastinal adenopathy. *B,* CT shows a homogeneous opacity containing air-bronchograms in the left upper lobe.

to the lung, although recurrence after treatment, often at extrapulmonary sites, occurs in up to 50%.[32, 57, 103, 115] High-grade non-Hodgkin's lymphomas, which constitute approximately 13% of primary pulmonary lymphomas, are usually B-cell tumors with aggressive behavior and a poor 5-year survival rate.[32, 57, 103, 115]

Most patients are 55 to 60 years old, although the age range is wide.[97, 115] Patients with low-grade lymphomas are usually asymptomatic at presentation, whereas patients with high-grade tumors usually present with cough, fever, or weight loss.[32]

The most common radiologic manifestations are a solitary nodule or mass and focal consolidation (Fig. 28–44).[32, 57, 109, 115, 158] Less common manifestations include multiple nodules or masses, multifocal consolidation, reticulonodular opacities, and atelectasis (Fig. 28–45).[32, 57, 115, 158] Hilar adenopathy is rare, and pleural effusions occur in 7% to 25% of patients.[32, 97, 103]

Benign Neoplasms of the Lung
Hamartoma

Hamartomas constitute 0.25% of all primary lung tumors and, although uncommon, are the most common benign tumor of lung.[193] The term *hamartoma* was initially used to describe lesions with an abnormal composition or disorganized arrangement of normal lung tissue. Now, however, hamartomas are considered true neoplasms containing a mixture of epithelial and mesenchymal tissues.[204]

Pulmonary hamartomas typically occur in patients older than 30 years, with a peak incidence in the sixth decade (range, 0 to 76 years).[79, 163, 180, 193] Most patients are asymptomatic; symptoms are typically present with central endobronchial lesions and include hemoptysis, recurrent pneumonia, and dyspnea.[63, 67, 193]

Hamartomas are typically solitary, well-marginated, slightly lobular nodules or masses that are less than 4 cm

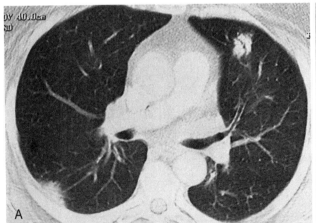
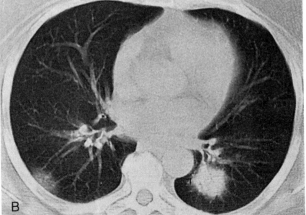

Figure 28–45. Primary pulmonary lymphoma manifesting as bilateral pulmonary opacities. *A* and *B,* CT shows focal, poorly marginated nodular opacities in both lungs. Air-bronchograms within opacities are suggestive of the diagnosis.

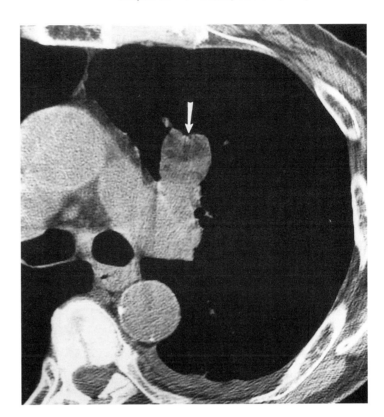

Figure 28–46. Hamartoma appearing as a solitary pulmonary nodule. CT shows a left upper lobe nodule *(arrow)* anterior to the left pulmonary artery. The diagnosis is suggested by small areas of fat (attenuation, −41 Hounsfield units) within the nodule.

in size (range, 1 to 30 cm).[63, 67, 180, 193] Most are located peripherally within the lung. Endobronchial hamartomas are less common (up to 20% of cases).[63, 79, 193] Calcification has been reported in up to 50% but is probably present in fewer than 5% of hamartomas.[107, 204] The presence of "popcorn" calcification, however, is almost pathognomonic of hamartomas. Fat (CT attenuation, −40 to −120 HU) occurs in up to 50% of cases and is a diagnostic feature (Fig. 28–46).[204] Rare radiographic manifestations include cavitation and multiple pulmonary hamartomas.[99]

Granular Cell Tumor

Granular cell tumors (formerly, *granular cell myeloblastomas*) are rare pulmonary neoplasms that are thought to arise from Schwann cells.[39, 131] Patients are usually adults (peak incidence, 30 to 50 years of age; range, 0 to 59 years), and there is a higher incidence in African Americans.[39, 102, 169, 170, 186]

Most pulmonary granular cell tumors manifest as small, central endobronchial masses (range, 0.3 to 6.5 cm in diameter).[39, 85] Multiple lesions, typically in the larger bronchi, are found in up to 25% of cases.[39, 85] Common radiologic findings include atelectasis and obstructive pneumonia, although slow-growing, solitary pulmonary nodules or masses occur in 12% of cases.[39, 85]

Sclerosing Hemangioma

Primary pulmonary sclerosing hemangioma is a benign tumor consisting of thin-walled vessels and connective tissue.[117, 156] Originally thought to represent a vascular tu-

mor, it is now considered to arise from alveolar or bronchiolar epithelium.[81] Most patients are asymptomatic women between 30 and 50 years of age (range, 15 to 77 years).[95, 221]

Radiologically, pulmonary hemangiomas usually manifest as peripheral, well-marginated solitary pulmonary nodules or masses 0.4 to 8.0 cm in diameter (average, 3.0 cm). Multiple pulmonary nodules and calcification are rare.[95, 110]

Clear Cell Tumor

Clear cell tumor is a rare neoplasm of the lung.[65, 116] Most patients are asymptomatic and between 50 and 60 years of age (range, 8 to 70 years).[64, 65] Almost all the tumors behave in a benign nature, although extrathoracic metastases have been reported.[192] Clear cell tumors typically manifest radiologically as well-marginated solitary pulmonary nodules usually less than 3 cm in diameter (range, 0.7 to 6.5 cm).[6, 64, 65, 192, 271]

References

1. Abrams J, Doyle LA, Aisner J: Staging prognostic factors, and special considerations in small cell lung cancer. Semin Oncol 15: 261–277, 1988.
2. Akira M, Atagi S, Kawahra M, et al: High-resolution CT findings of diffuse bronchioloalveolar carcinoma in 38 patients. AJR Am J Roentgenol 173:1623–1629, 1999.
3. Allen MS: Malignant tracheal tumors. Mayo Clin Proc 68:680–684, 1993.
4. American Cancer Society: Cancer Facts and Figures—1997. Racial and Ethnic Patterns. Atlanta, American Cancer Society, 1997.
4a. American Cancer Society on line: Available at *http://www.cancer. org*
5. American Thoracic Society/European Respiratory Society: Pretreatment evaluation of non–small-cell lung cancer. Am J Respir Crit Care Med 156:320–332, 1997.

6. Andrion A, Mazzucco G, Gugliotta P, Monga G: Benign clear cell (sugar tumor) of the lung: A light microscopic, histochemical, and ultrastructural study with review of the literature. Cancer 56:2657–2663, 1985.

7. Arita T, Kuramitsu T, Kawamura M, et al: Bronchogenic carcinoma: Incidence of metastases to normal sized lymph nodes. Thorax 50:1267–1269, 1995.

8. Attanoos RL, Appleton MAC, Gibbs AR: Primary sarcomas of the lung: A clinicopathological and immunohistochemical study of 14 cases. Histopathology 29:29–36, 1996.

9. Barbone F, Bovenzi M, Cavallieri F, Stanta G: Cigarette smoking and histologic type of lung cancer in men. Chest 112:1474–1479, 1997.

10. Bepler G: Lung cancer epidemiology and genetics. J Thorac Imaging 14:228–234, 1999.

11. Berkmen YM: The many faces of bronchiolo-alveolar carcinoma. Semin Roentgenol 12:207–214, 1977.

12. Berlin NI, Buncher CR, Fontana RS, et al: Early lung detection. Am Rev Respir Dis 103:545–549, 1984.

13. Boland GW, Lee MJ: Magnetic resonance imaging of the adrenal gland. Crit Rev Diagn Imaging 36:115–174, 1995.

14. Boland GW, Lee MJ, Gazelle GS, et al: Characterization of adrenal masses using unenhanced CT: An analysis of the CT literature. AJR Am J Roentgenol 171:201–204, 1998.

15. Bollinger BK, Laskin WB, Knight CB: Epithelioid hemangioendothelioma with multiple site involvement: Literature review and observations. Cancer 73:610–615, 1994.

16. Bragg DG, Chor PJ, Murray KA, Kjeldsberg CR: Lymphoproliferative disorders of the lung: Histopathology, clinical manifestations, and imaging features. AJR Am J Roentgenol 163:273–281, 1994.

17. Buccheri G, Ferrigno D: Prognostic value of stage grouping and TNM descriptors in lung cancer. Chest 117:1247–1255, 2000.

18. Bunn Jr PA, Rosen ST: Central nervous system manifestations of small cell lung cancer. In Aisner J (ed): Contemporary Issues in Clinical Oncology: Lung Cancer. New York, Churchill Livingstone, 1985, pp 287–305.

19. Burnett RJ, Wood DE: The new lung cancer staging system: What does it mean? Surg Oncol Clin North Am 8:231–244, 1999.

20. Bury T, Barreto A, Daenen F, et al: Fluorine-18 deoxyglucose positron emission tomography for the detection of bone metastases in patients with non-small cell lung cancer. Eur J Nucl Med 25:1244–1247, 1998.

21. Byrd RB, Carr DT, Miller WE, et al: Radiographic abnormalities in carcinoma of the lung as related to histological cell. Thorax 24:573–575, 1969.

22. Campanella N, Moraca A, Pergolini M, et al: Paraneoplastic syndromes in 68 cases of resectable non-small cell lung carcinoma: Can they help in early detection? Med Oncol 16:129–133, 1999.

23. Cardenas VM, Thun MJ, Austin H, et al: Environmental tobacco smoke and lung cancer mortality in the American Cancer Society's Cancer Prevention Study: II. Cancer Causes Control 8:57–64, 1997.

24. Carter EJ, Bradburne RM, Jhung JW, et al: Alveolar hemorrhage with epithelioid hemangioendothelioma: A previously unreported manifestation of a rare tumor. Am Rev Respir Dis 142:700–701, 1990.

25. Chalk CH, Windebank AJ, Kimmel DW: The distinctive clinical features of paraneoplastic sensory neuronopathy. Can J Neurol Sci 19:346, 1992.

26. Chartrand-Lefebvre C, Howarth N, Grenier P, et al: Association of small cell lung cancer and the anti-Hu paraneoplastic syndrome: Radiographic and CT findings. AJR Am J Roentgenol 170:1513–1517, 1998.

27. Chartrand-Lefebvre D, Howarth N, Grenier P, et al: Association of small cell lung cancer and the anti-Hu paraneoplastic syndrome: Radiographic and CT findings. AJR Am J Roentgenol 170:1513–1517, 1998.

28. Clouston PD, Saper CB, Arbizu T, et al: Paraneoplastic cerebellar degeneration: III. Cerebellar degeneration, cancer and the Lambert-Eaton myasthenic syndrome. Neurology 42:1944, 1992.

29. Colby TV, Koss MN, Travis WD: Tumors of the lower respiratory tract. In Atlas of Tumor Pathology. Washington, DC, Armed Forces Institute of Pathology, 1995.

30. Colice GL, Birkmeyer JD, Black WC, Littenberg B, Silvestri G: Cost-effectiveness of head CT in patients with lung cancer without clinical evidence of metastases. Chest 108:1264–1271, 1995.

31. Conlan AA, Payne WS, Woolner LB, Sanderson DR: Adenoid cystic carcinoma (cylindroma) and mucoepidermoid carcinoma of the bronchus. J Thorac Cardiovasc Surg 76:369–377, 1978.

32. Cordier JF, Chailleux E, Lauque D, et al: Primary pulmonary lymphomas: A clinical study of 70 cases of nonimmunocompromised patients. Chest 103:201–208, 1994.

33. Croft PB, Wilkinson M: The course and prognosis in some types of carcinomatous neuromyopathy. Brain 1:1969, 1992.

34. Cutler CS, Michel RP, Yassa M, Langleben A: Pulmonary blastoma. Cancer 82:462–467, 1998.

35. Dail DH, Liebow AA, Gmelich JT, et al: Intravascular, bronchiolar, and alveolar tumor of the lung (IVBAT): An analysis of twenty cases of a peculiar sclerosing endothelial tumor. Cancer 51:452–464, 1983.

36. Dalton ML, Gatling RR: Peripheral adenoid cystic carcinoma of the lung. South Med J 83:577–579, 1990.

37. Darling GE: Staging of the patient with small cell lung cancer. Chest Surg Clin North Am 7:81–94, 1997.

38. Davila DG, Dunn WF, Tazelaar HD, Pairolero PC: Bronchial carcinoid tumors. Mayo Clin Proc 68:795–803, 1993.

39. Deavers M, Guinee D, Koss MN, Travis WD: Granular cell tumors of the lung. Am J Surg Pathol 19:627–635, 1995.

40. Delisle L, Boyer MJ, Warr D, et al: Ectopic corticotropin syndrome and small cell carcinoma of the lung: Clinical features, outcome, and complications. Arch Intern Med 153:746–752, 1993.

41. Dewan NA, Gupta NC, Redepenning LS, et al: Diagnostic efficacy of PET-FDG imaging in solitary pulmonary nodules. Chest 104:997–1002, 1993.

42. Dumont P, Gasser B, Rouge C, et al: Bronchoalveolar carcinoma: Histopathologic study of evolution in a series of 105 surgically treated patients. Chest 113:391–395, 1998.

43. Dunnick NR: Adrenal imaging: Current status. AJR Am J Roentgenol 154:927–936, 1990.

44. Dwamena BA, Sonnad SS, Angobaldo JO, Wahl RL: Metastases from non-small cell lung cancer: Mediastinal staging in the 1990s: Meta-analytic comparison of PET and CT. Radiology 213:530–536, 1999.

45. Echevarria RA: Angiogenic nature of "intravascular bronchioloalveolar tumor." Arch Pathol Lab Med 105:627–628, 1981.

46. Elias AD: Small cell lung cancer. State-of-the-art therapy in 1996. Chest 112:251S–258S, 1997.

47. Emery RW, Fox AL, Raab DE: Intravascular bronchioloalveolar tumor. Thorax 37:472–473, 1982.

48. Engle AF, Groot G, Bellot S: Carcinosarcoma of the lung: A case-history of disseminated disease and review of the literature. Eur J Surg Oncol 17:94–96, 1991.

49. Epstein DM: Bronchioloalveolar carcinoma. Semin Roentgenol 25:105–111, 1990.

50. Epstein DM, Gefter WB, Miller WT: Lobar bronchioloalveolar cell carcinoma. Am J Roentgenol 139:463–468, 1982.

51. Erasmus JJ, McAdams HP, Donnelly LF, Spritzer CE: MR imaging of mediastinal masses. MRI Clin North Am 8:59–89, 2000.

52. Erasmus JJ, Patz EF, McAdams HP, et al: Evaluation of adrenal masses in patients with bronchogenic carcinoma by using ^{18}F-fluorodeoxyglucose positron emission tomography. AJR Am J Roentgenol 168:1357–1360, 1997.

53. Erren TC: Synergy between asbestos and smoking on lung cancer risks. Epidemiology 10:405–411, 1999.

54. Fearon ER: Human cancer syndromes: Clues to the origin and nature of cancer. Science 278:1043–1050, 1997.

55. Ferraro P, Trastek VF, Adlakha H, et al: Primary non-Hodgkin's lymphoma of the lung. Ann Thorac Surg 69:993–997, 2000.

56. Ferrigno D, Buccheri G: Cranial computed tomography as a part of the initial staging procedures for patients with non–small-cell lung cancer. Chest 106:1025–1029, 1994.

57. Fiche M, Caprons F, Berger F, et al: Primary pulmonary non-Hodgkin's lymphomas. Histopathology 26:529–537, 1995.

58. Filderman AE, Shaw C, Matthay RA: Lung cancer: Part I. Etiology, pathology, natural history, manifestations, and diagnostic techniques. Invest Radiol 21:80–90, 1986.

59. Fink D: Guidelines for the cancer related checkup: Recommendations and rationale. In Textbook of Clinical Oncology. Atlanta, American Cancer Society, 1991, pp 153–176.

60. Flehinger BJ, Kimmel M, Melamed MR: National history of adenocarcinoma—large cell carcinoma of the lung: Conclusions from screening programs in New York and Baltimore. J Natl Cancer Inst 80:337–344, 1988.

61. Franceschi S, Bidoli E: The epidemiology of lung cancer. Ann Oncol 10(Suppl 5):S3–S6, 1999.

62. Francis D, Jacobsen M: Pulmonary blastoma. Curr Top Pathol 73: 165–294, 1998.

63. Fudge TL, Ochsner JL, Mills NL: Clinical spectrum of pulmonary hamartomas. Ann Thorac Surg 30:36–39, 1980.

64. Gaffey MJ, Mills SE, Askin FB, et al: Clear cell tumor of the lung: A clinicopathologic, immunohistochemical, and ultrastructural study of eight cases. Am J Surg Pathol 14:248–259, 1990.

65. Gaffey MJ, Mills SE, Ritter JH: Clear cell tumors of the lower respiratory tract. Semin Diagn Pathol 14:222–232, 1997.

66. Gallagher CG, Teskey SR, Kryger M: Atypical manifestations of pulmonary adenoid cystic carcinoma. Br J Dis Chest 80:396–399, 1986.

67. Gjevre JA, Myers JL, Prakash UB: Pulmonary hamartomas. Mayo Clin Proc 71:14–20, 1996.

68. Glazer GM, Gross BH, Aisen AM, et al: Imaging of the pulmonary hilum: A prospective comparative study in patients with lung cancer. Am J Roentgenol 145:245–248, 1985.

69. Glazer GM, Gross BH, Quint LE, et al: Normal mediastinal lymph nodes: Number and size according to American Thoracic Society Mapping. Am J Roentgenol 144:261–265, 1985.

70. Glazer GM, Orringer MB, Chenevert TL, et al: Mediastinal lymph nodes: Relaxation time/pathologic correlation and implications in staging of lung cancer with MR imaging. Radiology 168:429–431, 1988.

71. Glazer HS, Kaiser LR, Anderson DJ, et al: Indeterminate mediastinal invasion in bronchogenic carcinoma: CT evaluation. Radiology 173: 37–42, 1989.

72. Good CA: Management of patient with solitary mass in lung. Chic Med Soc Bull 55:893–896, 1953.

73. Good CA, Wilson TW: The solitary circumscribed pulmonary nodule. JAMA 166:210–215, 1958.

74. Goodman M, Morgan RW, Ray R, et al: Cancer in asbestos-exposed occupational cohorts: A meta-analysis. Cancer Causes Control 10: 453–465, 1999.

75. Govindan R, Ihde DC: Practical issues in the management of the patient with small cell lung cancer. Chest Surg Clin North Am 7: 167–181, 1997.

76. Gurney JW: Determining the likelihood of malignancy in solitary pulmonary nodules with Bayesian analysis. Radiology 186:405–413, 1993.

77. Habermann TM, Ryu JH, Inwards DJ, Kurtin PJ: Primary pulmonary lymphoma. Semin Oncol 26:307–315, 1999.

78. Halle M, Blum U, Dinkel E, Brugger W: CT and MR features of primary pulmonary hemangiopericytomas. J Comput Assist Tomogr 17:51–55, 1993.

79. Hansen CP, Holtveg H, Francis D, et al: Pulmonary hamartoma. J Thorac Cardiovasc Surg 104:674–678, 1992.

80. Harris L, Jaffe ES, Stein H, et al: A revised European-American classification of lymphoid neoplasms: A proposal from the International Lymphoma Study Group. Blood 84:1361–1392, 1994.

81. Heikkila P, Salminen US: Papillary pneumocytoma of the lung: An immunohistochemical and electron microscopic study. Pathol Res Pract 190:194, 1993.

82. Heitmiller RF, Mathisen DJ, Ferry JA, et al: Mucoepidermoid lung tumors. Ann Thorac Surg 47:394–399, 1989.

83. Henschke CI, McCauley DI, Yankelevitz DF, et al: Early lung cancer action project: Overall design and findings from baseline screening. Lancet 354:99–105, 1999.

84. Herman SJ, Winton TL, Weisbrod GL, et al: Mediastinal invasion by bronchogenic carcinoma: CT signs. Radiology 190:841–846, 1994.

85. Hernandez OGT, Haponik EF, Summer WR: Granular cell tumour of the bronchus: Bronchoscopic and clinical features. Thorax 41: 927–931, 1986.

86. Higgins GA, Shields TW, Keehn RJ: The solitary pulmonary nodule. Arch Surg 110:570–575, 1975.

87. Hill CA: Bronchioloalveolar carcinoma: A review. Radiology 150: 15–20, 1984.

88. Holst VA, Finkelstein S, Yousem SA: Bronchioloalveolar adenocarcinoma of lung: Monoclonal origin for multifocal disease. Am J Surg Pathol 22:1343–1350, 1998.

89. Hooper RG, Tenholder MF, Underwood GH, et al: Computed tomographic scanning of the brain in initial staging of bronchogenic carcinoma. Chest 85:774–776, 1984.

90. Ishida T, Tateishi M, Kaneko S, et al: Carcinosarcoma and spindle cell carcinoma of the lung. J Thorac Cardiovasc Surg 100:844–852, 1990.

91. Janssen JP, Mulder JJS, Wagenaar SS, et al: Primary sarcoma of the lung: A clinical study with long-term follow-up. Ann Thorac Surg 58:1151–1155, 1994.

92. Jelinek JS, Redmond J, Perry JJ, et al: Small cell lung cancer: Staging with MR imaging. Radiology 177:837–842, 1990.

93. Kaneko M, Eguchi K, Ohmatsu H, et al: Peripheral lung cancer: Screening and detection with low-dose spiral CT versus radiography. Radiology 201:798–802, 1996.

94. Katz DS, Lane M, Leung AN, et al: Primary malignant pulmonary hemangiopericytoma. Clin Imaging 22:192–195, 1998.

95. Katzenstein AA, Gmelich JT, Carrington CB: Sclerosing hemangioma of the lung: A clinicopathologic study of 51 cases. Am J Surg Pathol 4:343–356, 1980.

96. Kayser K, Kayser C, Rahn W, et al: Carcinoid tumors of the lung: Immuno- and ligandohistochemistry, analysis of integrated optical density, syntactic structure analysis, clinical data, and prognosis of patients treated surgically. J Surg Oncol 63:99–106, 1996.

97. Kennedy JL, Nathwani BN, Berke J, et al: Pulmonary lymphomas and lymphoid lesions. Cancer 56:539–552, 1985.

98. Kim K, Flint JDA, Müller NL: Pulmonary carcinosarcoma: Radiologic and pathologic findings in three patients. AJR Am J Roentgenol 169:691–694, 1997.

99. King TE, Christopher KL, Schwarz MI: Multiple pulmonary chondromatous hamartomas. Hum Pathol 13:496, 1982.

100. Klein JS, Webb WR: The radiologic staging of lung cancer. J Thorac Imaging 7:29–47, 1991.

101. Knight SB, Delbeke D, Stewart JR, Sandler MP: Evaluation of pulmonary lesions with FDG-PET. Chest 109:982–988, 1996.

102. Korompai FL, Awe RJ, Beall AC, Greenberg SD: Granular cell myoblastoma of the bronchus: A new case, 12-year follow-up report, and review of the literature. Chest 66:578–580, 1974.

103. Koss MN: Pulmonary lymphoid disorders. Semin Diagn Pathol 12: 158–171, 1995.

104. Koss MN, Hochholzer L, O'Leary T: Pulmonary blastomas. Cancer 67:2368–2381, 1991.

105. Kubik A, Parkin DM, Khlat M, et al: Lack of benefit from semi-annual screening for cancer of the lung: Follow-up report of a randomized controlled trial on population of high-risk males in Czechoslovakia. Int J Cancer 45:26–33, 1990.

106. Larsen H, Sorensen JB: Pulmonary blastoma: A review with special emphasis on prognosis and treatment. Cancer Treat Rev 22:145–160, 1996.

107. Ledor K, Fish B, Chaise L, Ledor S: CT diagnosis of pulmonary hamartomas. J Comput Assist Tomogr 5:343–344, 1981.

108. Lee KS, Kim Y, Han J, et al: Bronchioloalveolar carcinoma: Clinical, histopathologic, and radiologic findings. Radiographics 17: 1345–1357, 1997.

109. Lee KS, Kim Y, Primack SL: Imaging of pulmonary lymphomas. AJR Am J Roentgenol 168:339–345, 1997.

110. Lee S, Lee Y, Hsu C, Lin C: Bilateral multiple sclerosing hemangiomas of the lung. Chest 101:572–573, 1992.

111. LeMense GP, Reed CE, Silvestri GA: Pulmonary blastoma: A rare lung malignancy. Lung Cancer 15:233–237, 1996.

112. Leong SS, Lima CMR, Sherman CA, Green MR: The 1997 international staging system for non-small cell lung cancer. Have all the issues been addressed? Chest 115:242–248, 1999.

113. Levin KH: Paraneoplastic neuromuscular syndromes. Neurol Clin 15:597–614, 1997.

114. Lewis P, Griffin S, Marsden P, et al: Whole-body ^{18}F-fluorodeoxyglucose positron emission tomography in preoperative evaluation of lung cancer. Lancet 344:1265–1266, 1994.

115. Li G, Hansmann M-L, Zwingers T, et al: Primary lymphoma of the lung: Morphological, immunohistochemical and clinical features. Histopathology 16:519–531, 1990.

116. Liebow AA, Castleman B: Benign clear cell (sugar) tumors of the lung. Yale J Biol Med 43:213–222, 1971.

117. Liebow AA, Hubbell DF: Sclerosing hemangioma (histiocytoma, xanthoma) of the lung. Cancer 9:53, 1956.

118. Lillington GA: Disease-a-Month, 37th ed. St. Louis, Mosby–Year Book, 1991.

119. Lillington GA, Caskey CI: Evaluation and management of solitary multiple pulmonary nodules. Clin Chest Med 14:111–119, 1993.

120. List AF, Doll DC, Greco FA: Lung cancer in Hodgkin's disease: Association with previous radiotherapy. J Clin Oncol 3:215–221, 1985.

121. List AF, Hainsworth JD, Davis BW, et al: The syndrome of inappropriate secretion of antidiuretic hormone (SIADH) in small cell lung cancer. J Clin Oncol 4:1191–1198, 1986.

122. Little AG, Stitik FP: Clinical staging of patients with non-small cell lung cancer. Chest 97:1431–1438, 1990.

123. Mahoney MC, Shipley RT, Corcoran HL, Dickson BA: CT demonstration of calcification in carcinoma of the lung. AJR Am J Roentgenol 154:255–258, 1990.

124. Marchioli CC, Graziano SL: Paraneoplastic syndromes associated with small cell lung cancer. Chest Surg Clin North Am 7:65–79, 1997.

125. Marom EM, Patz EF Jr, Swensen SJ: Radiologic findings of bronchogenic carcinoma with pulmonary metastases at presentation. Clin Radiol 54:665–668, 1999.

126. Martini N, Heelan R, Westcott J, et al: Comparative merits of conventional, computed tomographic, and magnetic resonance imaging in assessing mediastinal involvement in surgically confirmed lung carcinoma. J Thorac Cardiovasc Surg 90:639–648, 1985.

127. Marty-Ané C, Costes V, Pujol J, et al: Carcinoid tumors of the lung: Do atypical features require aggressive management? Ann Thorac Surg 59:78–83, 1995.

128. Matthews MJ: Morphology of lung cancer. Semin Oncol 1:175–182, 1974.

129. Maurea S, Mainolfi C, Bazzicalupo L, et al: Imaging of adrenal tumors using FDG PET: Comparison of benign and malignant lesions. AJR Am J Roentgenol 173:25–29, 1999.

130. Maziak DE, Todd TR, Keshavjee SH, et al: Adenoid cystic carcinoma of the airway: Thirty-two-year experience. J Thorac Cardiovasc Surg 112:1522, 1996.

131. Mazur MT, Shultz JJ, Myers JL: Granular cell tumor: Immunohistochemical analysis of 21 benign tumors and one malignant tumor. Arch Pathol Lab Med 114:692–696, 1990.

132. McCarthy MJ, Rosado-de-Christenson ML: Tumors of the trachea. J Thorac Imaging 10:180, 1995.

133. McCaughan BC, Martini N, Bains MS: Bronchial carcinoids. J Thorac Cardiovasc Surg 89:8–17, 1985.

134. McLoud TC: CT of bronchogenic carcinoma: Indeterminate mediastinal mass. Radiology 173:15–16, 1989.

135. McLoud TC, Bourgouin PM, Greenberg RW, et al: Bronchogenic carcinoma: Analysis of staging in the mediastinum with CT by correlative lymph node mapping and sampling. Radiology 182:319–323, 1992.

136. McNicholas MM, Lee MJ, Mayo-Smith WW, et al: An imaging algorithm for the differential diagnosis of adrenal adenomas and metastases. AJR Am J Roentgenol 165:1453–1459, 1995.

137. Michel F, Soler M, Imhof E, Perruchoud AP: Initial staging of non-small cell lung cancer: Value of routine radioisotope bone scanning. Thorax 46:469–473, 1991.

138. Miller WT, Husted J, Frieman D, et al: Bronchioloalveolar carcinoma: Two clinical entities with one pathologic diagnosis. Am J Roentgenol 130:905–912, 1978.

139. Mintz BJ, Tuhrim S, Alexander S, et al: Intracranial metastases in the initial staging of bronchogenic carcinoma. Chest 86:850–853, 1984.

140. Mitchell DG, Crovello M, Matteucci T, et al: Benign adrenocortical masses: Diagnosis with chemical shift MR imaging. Radiology 185:345–351, 1992.

141. Moran CA, Suster S, Abbondanzo SL, Koss MN: Primary leiomyosarcomas of the lung: A clinicopathologic and immunohistochemical study of 18 cases. Mod Pathol 10:121–128, 1997.

142. Moran CA, Suster S, Koss MN: Primary adenoid cystic carcinoma of the lung: A clinicopathologic and immunohistochemical study of 16 cases. Cancer 73:1390, 1994.

143. Morgan B, Coaldey F, Finlay DB, Belton I: Hypertrophic osteoarthropathy in staging skeletal scintigraphy for lung cancer. Clin Radiol 51:494–497, 1996.

144. Mountain CF: Prognostic implications of international staging system for lung cancer. Semin Oncol 15:236–245, 1988.

145. Mountain CF: Revisions in the international system for staging lung cancer. Chest 111:1710–1717, 1997.

146. Mountain CF, Dresler CM: Regional lymph node classification for lung cancer staging. Chest 111:1718–1723, 1997.

147. Müller NL, Miller RR: Neuroendocrine carcinomas of the lung. Semin Roentgenol 25:96–104, 1990.

148. Musset D, Grenier P, Carette MF, et al: Primary lung cancer staging: Prospective comparative study of MR imaging with CT. Radiology 160:607–611, 1986.

149. Nappi O, Glasner SD, Swanson PE, Wick MR: Biphasic and monophasic sarcomatoid carcinomas of the lung. Am J Clin Pathol 102:331–340, 1994.

150. Naruke T, Tsuchiya R, Kondo H, et al: Implications of staging in lung cancer. Chest 112:242S–248S, 1997.

151. National Cancer Institute Cooperative Early Lung Cancer Group: Manual of Procedures (NIH Pub No. 79-1972). Bethesda, Md, National Institutes of Health, 1979.

152. National Research Council, Committee on the Biological Effects of Ionizing Radiation: Health Risks of Radon and Other Internally Deposited Alpha-Emitters: BEIR IV. Washington, DC, National Academy Press, 1988.

153. Nessi R, Ricci PB, Ricci SB, et al: Bronchial carcinoid tumors: Radiologic observations in 49 cases. J Thorac Imaging 6:47–53, 1991.

154. Newman SJ, Hansen HH: Frequency, diagnosis, and treatment of brain metastases in 247 consecutive patients with bronchogenic carcinoma. Cancer 33:492–496, 1974.

155. Nielsen ME Jr, Heaston DK, Dunnick NR, Korobkin M: Preoperative CT evaluation of adrenal glands in non-small cell bronchogenic carcinoma. Am J Roentgenol 139:317–320, 1982.

156. Niho S, Suzuki K, Yokose T, et al: Monoclonality of both pale cells and cuboidal cells of sclerosing hemangioma of the lung. Am J Pathol 152:1065–1069, 1998.

157. North WG: Neuropeptide production by small cell carcinoma: Vasopressin and oxytocin as plasma markers of disease. J Clin Endocrinol Metab 73:1316–1320, 1991.

158. O'Donnell PG, Jackson SA, Tung KT, et al: Radiological appearances of lymphomas arising from mucosa-associated lymphoid tissue (MALT) in the lung. Clin Radiol 53:258–263, 1998.

159. O'Keefe ME, Good CA, McDonald JR: Calcification in solitary nodules of the lung. Am J Roentgenol 77:1023–1033, 1957.

160. O'Keefe ME Jr, Good CA, McDonald JR: Calcification in solitary nodules of the lungs. Am J Roentgenol 77:1023–1033, 1957.

161. Ohmatsu H, Kakinuma R, Nishiwaki Y, et al: Lung cancer screening with low-dose spiral CT: Proc Am Soc Clin Oncol 18:463a, 1999.

162. Okubo K, Mark EJ, Flieder D, et al: Bronchoalveolar carcinoma: Clinical, radiologic, and pathologic factors and survival. J Thorac Cardiovasc Surg 118:702–709, 1999.

163. Oldham HN Jr, Young WG Jr, Sealy WC: Hamartoma of the lung. J Thorac Cardiovasc Surg 53:735–742, 1967.

164. Oliver TW Jr, Bernardino ME, Miller JI, et al: Isolated adrenal masses in nonsmall-cell bronchogenic carcinoma. Radiology 153:217–218, 1984.

165. Outwater EK, Siegelman ES, Huang AB, Birnbaum BA: Adrenal masses: Correlation between CT attenuation value and chemical shift ratio at MR imaging with in-phase and opposed-phase sequences. Radiology 200:749–752, 1996.

166. Padovani B, Mouroux J, Seksik L, et al: Chest wall invasion by bronchogenic carcinoma: Evaluation with MR imaging. Radiology 187:33–38, 1993.

167. Pagani JJ: Normal adrenal glands in small cell lung carcinoma: CT-guided biopsy. Am J Roentgenol 140:949–951, 1983.

168. Pagani JJ: Non-small cell lung carcinoma adrenal metastases. Cancer 53:1058–1060, 1984.

169. Park SH, Kim TJ, Chi JG: Congenital granular cell tumor with systemic involvement: Immunohistochemical and ultrastructural study. Arch Pathol Lab Med 115:934–938, 1991.

170. Paskin DL, Hull JD, Cookson PJ: Granular cell myoblastoma: A comprehensive review of 15 years' experience. Ann Surg 175:501–503, 1972.

171. Patel AM, Davila DG, Peters SG: Paraneoplastic syndromes associated with lung cancer. Mayo Clin Proc 68:278–287, 1993.

172. Patel AM, Peters SG: Clinical manifestations of lung cancer. Mayo Clin Proc 68:273–277, 1993.

173. Patz EF, Lowe VJ, Hoffman JM, et al: Focal pulmonary abnormalities: Evaluation with F-18 fluorodeoxyglucose PET scanning. Radiology 188:487–490, 1993.

174. Patz EF Jr, Goodman PC: Positron emission tomography imaging of the thorax. Radiol Clin North Am 32:811–823, 1994.

175. Patz EF Jr, Lowe VJ, Goodman PC, Herndon J: Thoracic nodal staging with positron emission tomography (PET) and ^{18}F-2-fluoro-2-deoxy-D-glucose in patients with bronchogenic carcinoma. Chest 108:1617–1621, 1995.
176. Pearlberg JL, Sandler MA, Lewis JW Jr, et al: Small-cell bronchogenic carcinoma: CT evaluation. AJR Am J Roentgenol 150:265–268, 1988.
177. Ponder B: Genetic testing for cancer risk. Science 278:1050–1054, 1997.
178. Porte HL, Ernst OJ, Delebecq T, et al: Is computed tomography guided biopsy still necessary for the diagnosis of adrenal masses in patients with resectable non–small-cell lung cancer? Eur J Cardiothorac Surg 15:597–601, 1999.
179. Posner JB: Paraneoplastic syndromes. Neurol Clin 9:919, 1991.
180. Prohm P, Winter J, Schmücker P: Pulmonary hamartoma. Thorac Cardiovasc Surg 30:302–305, 1982.
181. Quint LE, Francis IR: Radiologic staging of lung cancer. J Thorac Imaging 14:235–246, 1999.
182. Quint LE, Francis IR, Wahl RL, et al: Preoperative staging of non–small-cell carcinoma of the lung: Imaging methods. AJR Am J Roentgenol 164:1349–1359, 1995.
183. Ramani S, Karnad AB: Primary pulmonary non-Hodgkin's lymphoma. N Engl J Med 88:243–245, 1995.
184. Ratto GB, Piacenza G, Frola C, et al: Chest wall involvement by lung cancer: Computed tomographic detection and results of operation. Ann Thorac Surg 51:182–188, 1991.
185. Repace JL, Lowrey AH: Risk assessment methodologies for passive smoking-induced lung cancer. Risk Anal 10:27–37, 1990.
186. Robinson JM, Knoll R, Henry DA: Intrathoracic granular cell myoblastoma. South Med J 81:1453–1457, 1988.
187. Rock MJ, Kaufman RA, Lobe TE, et al: Epithelioid hemangioendothelioma of the lung (intravascular bronchioloalveolar tumor) in a young girl. Pediatr Pulmonol 11:181–186, 1991.
188. Roggli VL, Hammar SP, Pratt PC, et al: Does asbestos or asbestosis cause carcinoma of the lung? Am J Ind Med 26:835–838, 1994.
189. Rosado-de-Christenson ML, Templeton PA, Moran CA: Bronchogenic carcinoma: Radiologic-pathologic correlation. Radiographics 14:429–446, 1994.
190. Ross GJ, Violi L, Friedman AC, et al: Intravascular bronchioloalveolar tumors: CT and pathologic correlation. J Comput Assist Tomogr 13:240–243, 1989.
191. Ruebner BH, Eggleston JC: What is new in epithelioid haemangioendothelioma of the liver? Pathol Res Pract 182:110–112, 1987.
192. Sale GE, Kulander BG: Benign clear-cell tumor (sugar tumor) of the lung with hepatic metastases ten years after resection of pulmonary primary tumor. Arch Pathol Lab Med 112:1177–1178, 1988.
193. Salminen U-S: Pulmonary hamartoma: A clinical study of 77 cases in a 21-year period and review of literature. Eur J Cardiothorac Surg 4:15–18, 1990.
194. Salvati M, Cervoni L, Delfini R: Solitary brain metastases from non-oat cell lung cancer: Clinical and prognostic features. Neurosurg Rev 19:221–225, 1996.
195. Salvatierra A, Baamonde C, Llamas JM, et al: Extrathoracic staging of bronchogenic carcinoma. Chest 97:1052–1058, 1990.
196. Samet JM: The epidemiology of lung cancer. Chest 103:20S–29S, 1993.
197. Schiepers C: Role of positron emission tomography in the staging of lung cancer. Lung Cancer 17:S29–S35, 1997.
198. Schwartz LH, Ginsberg MS, Burt ME, et al: MRI as an alternative to CT-guided biopsy of adrenal masses in patients with lung cancer. Ann Thorac Surg 65:193–197, 1998.
199. Shepherd FA, Laskey J, Evans WK, et al: Cushing's syndrome associated with ectopic corticotropin production and small-cell lung cancer. J Clin Oncol 10:21–27, 1992.
200. Shimoyama K, Murata K, Takahashi M, Morita R: Pulmonary hilar lymph node metastases from lung cancer: Evaluation based on morphology at thin-section, incremental, dynamic CT. Radiology 203:187–195, 1997.
201. Shin MS, Jackson LK, Shelton RW, Greene RE: Giant cell carcinoma of the lung. Chest 89:366–369, 1986.
202. Sider L: Radiographic manifestations of primary bronchogenic carcinoma. Radiol Clin North Am 28:583–597, 1990.
203. Siegelman SS, Khouri MF, Leo FP, et al: Solitary pulmonary nodules: CT assessment. Radiology 160:307–312, 1986.
204. Siegelman SS, Khouri NF, Scott WW Jr, et al: Pulmonary hamartoma: CT findings. Radiology 160:313–317, 1986.
205. Siegelman SS, Zerhouni EA, Leo FP, et al: CT of the solitary pulmonary nodule. Am J Roentgenol 135:1–13, 1980.
206. Silvestri GA, Littenberg B, Colice GL: The clinical evaluation for detecting metastatic lung cancer: A meta-analysis. Am J Respir Crit Care Med 152:225–230, 1995.
207. Sone S, Takashima S, Li F, et al: Mass screening for lung cancer with mobile spiral computed tomography scanning. Lancet 351:1242–1245, 1998.
208. Spencer H: Pathology of the Lung, 4th ed. Oxford, Pergamon Press, 1985.
209. Stahel RA, Babry M, Skarin AT, et al: Detection of bone marrow metastases in small cell lung cancer by monoclonal antibody. J Clin Oncol 3:455–461, 1985.
210. Stahel RA, Ginsberg R, Havemann K, et al: Staging and prognostic factors in small cell lung cancer: A consensus report. Lung Cancer 5:119–126, 1989.
211. Staples CA, Müller NL, Miller RR, et al: Mediastinal nodes in bronchogenic carcinoma: Comparison between CT and mediastinoscopy. Radiology 167:367–372, 1988.
212. Steenland K, Loomis D, Shy C, Simonsen N: Review of occupational lung carcinogens. Am J Ind Med 29:474–490, 1996.
213. Steinert H, Hauser M, Allenman F, et al: Non-small cell lung cancer: Nodal staging with FDG PET versus CT with correlative lymph node mapping and sampling. Radiology 202:441–446, 1997.
214. Stitik FP: Staging of lung cancer. Radiol Clin North Am 28:619–630, 1990.
215. Stitik FP: The new staging of lung cancer. Radiol Clin North Am 32:635–647, 1994.
216. Strauss GM: Screening for lung cancer: An evidence-based synthesis. Surg Oncol Clin North Am 8:747–774, 1999.
217. Strauss GM, Dominioni L: Lung cancer screening and the surgical oncologist: The controversy. Surg Oncol Clin North Am 8:371–387, 1999.
218. Strauss GM, Gleason RE, Sugarbaker DJ: Screening for lung cancer: Another look, a different view. Chest 111:754–768, 1997.
219. Struyf NJA, Van Meerbeeck JPA, Ramael MRL, et al: Atypical bronchial carcinoid tumours. Respir Med 89:133–138, 1995.
220. Stuart-Harris R, Ahern V, Danks JA, et al: Hypercalcemia in small cell lung cancer: Report of a case associated with parathyroid hormone-related protein (PTHrP). Eur J Cancer 29A:1601–1604, 1993.
221. Sugio K, Yokoyama H, Kaneko S, et al: Sclerosing hemangioma of the lung: Radiographic and pathological study. Ann Thorac Surg 53:295–300, 1992.
222. Suster S: Primary sarcomas of the lung. Semin Diagn Pathol 12:140–157, 1995.
223. Swensen SJ, Viggiano RW, Midthun DE, et al: Lung nodule enhancement at CT: Multicenter study. Radiology 214:73–80, 2000.
224. Tanaka K, Kubota K, Kodama T, et al: Extrathoracic staging is not necessary for non–small-cell lung cancer with clinical stage T1–2 N0. Ann Thorac Surg 68:1039–1042, 1999.
225. Theros EG: Varying manifestations of peripheral pulmonary neoplasms: A radiologic-pathologic correlative study. Am J Roentgenol 128:893–914, 1977.
226. Toh HC, Ang PT: Primary pulmonary lymphoma: Clinical review from a single institution in Singapore. Leuk Lymphoma 27:153–163, 1997.
227. Travis WD, Colby TV, Corrin B, et al: Histological Typing of Lung and Pleural Tumours, 3rd ed. Berlin, Springer-Verlag, 1999.
228. Travis WD, Lubin J, Ries L, Devesa SS: United States lung carcinoma incidence trends: Declining for most histologic types among males, increasing among females. Cancer 77:2464–2470, 1996.
229. Trentini GP, Palmieri B: Mucoepidermoid tumor of the trachea. Chest 62:336, 1972.
230. Trichopoulos D, Mollo F, Tomatis L, et al: Active and passive smoking and pathological indicators of lung cancer risk in an autopsy study. JAMA 268:1697–1701, 1992.
231. Tschernig T, Pabst R: Bronchus-associated lymphoid tissue (BALT) is not present in the normal adult lung but in different diseases. Pathobiology 68:1–8, 2000.
232. Turnbull AD, Huvos AG, Goodner JT, et al: Mucoepidermoid tumors of bronchial glands. Cancer 28:539, 1971.
233. Urschel JD: Surgical treatment of peripheral small cell lung cancer. Chest Surg Clin North Am 7:95–103, 1997.
234. U.S. Department of Health and Human Services: Reducing the Health Consequences of Smoking—25 Years of Progress: A Report

of the Surgeon General. Washington, DC, U.S. Government Printing Office, 1989.

235. U.S. Department of Health and Human Services: The Health Benefits of Smoking Cessation: A Report of the Surgeon General. Washington, DC, U.S. Government Printing Office, 1990.

236. Vainio H, Boffetta P: Mechanisms of the combined effect of asbestos and smoking in the etiology of lung cancer. Scand J Work Environ Health 20:235–242, 1994.

237. Valanis BG: Epidemiology of lung cancer: A worldwide epidemic. Semin Oncol Nurs 12:251–259, 1996.

238. Valk PE, Pounds TR, Hopkins DM, et al: Staging non-small cell lung cancer by whole-body positron emission tomographic imaging. Ann Thorac Surg 60:1573–1582, 1995.

239. Valli M, Fabris GA, Dewar AHD, Sheppard MN: Atypical carcinoid tumour of the lung: A study of 33 cases with prognostic features. Histopathology 24:363–369, 1994.

240. van de Pol M, van Oosterhout AGM, Wilmink JT, et al: MRI in detection of brain metastases at initial staging of small-cell lung cancer. Neuroradiology 38:207–210, 1996.

241. Vansteenkiste JF, Stroobants SG, De Leyn PR, et al: Lymph node staging in non–small-cell lung cancer with FDG-PET scan: A prospective study on 690 lymph node stations from 68 patients. J Clin Oncol 16:2142–2149, 1998.

242. Viggiano RW, Swensen SJ, Rosenow EC III: Evaluation and management of solitary and multiple pulmonary nodules. Clin Chest Med 13:83–95, 1992.

243. Vineis P, Thomas T, Hayes R, et al: Proportion of lung cancers in males due to occupation in different areas of the U.S. Int J Cancer 42:851–856, 1988.

244. Wahl RL, Quint LE, Greenough RL, et al: Staging of mediastinal non-small cell lung cancer with FDG PET, CT, and fusion images: Preliminary prospective evaluation. Radiology 191:371–377, 1994.

245. Wang Y, Ju C, Stark AD, Teresi N: Radon mitigation survey among New York State residents living in high radon homes. Health Phys 77:403–409, 1999.

246. Webb WR: MR imaging in the evaluation and staging of lung cancer. Semin Ultrasound CT MR 9:53–66, 1988.

247. Webb WR, Gatsonis C, Zerhouni EA, et al: CT and MR imaging in staging non-small cell bronchogenic carcinoma: Report of the Radiologic Diagnostic Oncology Group. Radiology 178:705–713, 1991.

248. Webb WR, Sostman HD: MR imaging of thoracic disease: Clinical uses. Radiology 182:621–630, 1992.

249. Weder W, Schmid RA, Bruchhaus H, et al: Detection of extrathoracic metastases by positron emission tomography in lung cancer. Ann Thorac Surg 66:886–893, 1998.

250. Weisbrod GL, Chamberlain DW, Tao LC: Pulmonary blastoma: Report of three cases and a review of the literature. J Can Assoc Radiol 39:130, 1988.

251. Weisbrod GL, Towers MJ, Chamberlain DW, et al: Thin-walled cystic lesions in bronchioalveolar carcinoma. Radiology 185:401–405, 1992.

252. Weiss W: Asbestosis: A marker for the increased risk of lung cancer among workers exposed to asbestos. Chest 115:536–549, 1999.

253. Whitley NO, Fuks JZ, McCrea ES, et al: Computed tomography of the chest in small cell lung cancer: Potential new prognostic signs. Am J Roentgenol 141:885–892, 1984.

254. Wick MR, Ritter JH, Humphrey PA: Sarcomatoid carcinomas of the lung. Am J Clin Pathol 108:40–53, 1997.

255. Wick MR, Ritter JH, Humphrey PA: Sarcomatoid carcinomas of the lung: A clinicopathologic review. Am J Clin Pathol 108:40, 1997.

256. Wiess SW, Ishak KG, Dailo DH, et al: Epithelioid hemangioendothelioma and related lesions. Semin Diagn Pathol 3:259–287, 1986.

257. Wingo PA, Ries LA, Giovino GA, et al: Annual report to the nation on the status of cancer, 1973–1996, with a special section on lung cancer and tobacco smoking. J Natl Cancer Inst 91:675–690, 1999.

258. Woodring JH: Unusual radiographic manifestations of lung cancer. Radiol Clin North Am 28:599–618, 1990.

259. Woodring JH, Fried AM: Significance of wall thickness in solitary cavities of the lung: A follow-up study. Am J Roentgenol 140: 473–474, 1983.

260. Woodring JH, Fried AM, Chuang VP: Solitary cavities of the lung: Diagnostic implications of cavity wall thickness. Am J Roentgenol 135:1269–1271, 1980.

261. Woodring JH, Stelling CB: Adenocarcinoma of the lung: A tumor with a changing pleomorphic character. Am J Roentgenol 140: 657–664, 1983.

262. Wynder EL, Hoffmann D: Smoking and lung cancer: Scientific challenges and opportunities. Cancer Res 54:5284–5295, 1994.

263. Yahmai I: Angiographic manifestations of soft-tissue and osseous hemangiopericytomas. Radiology 126:653–659, 1978.

264. Yankelevitz DF, Gupta R, Zhao B, Henschke CI: Small pulmonary nodules: Evaluation with repeat CT: Preliminary experience. Radiology 212:561–566, 1999.

265. Yankelevitz DF, Reeves AP, Kostis WJ, et al: Determination of malignancy in small pulmonary nodules based on volumetrically determined growth rates. Radiology 209(Suppl):375, 1998.

266. Yokoi K, Mori K, Miyazawa N, et al: Tumor invasion of the chest wall and mediastinum in lung cancer: Evaluation with pneumothorax. Radiology 181:147–152, 1991.

267. Yousem SA, Hochholzer L: Mucoepidermoid tumors of the lung. Cancer 60:1346–1352, 1987.

268. Yousem SA, Hochholzer L: Primary pulmonary hemangiopericytoma. Cancer 59:549–555, 1987.

269. Zerhouni EA, Stitik FP, Siegelman SS, et al: CT of the pulmonary nodule: A cooperative study. Radiology 160:319–327, 1986.

270. Zern H, Moran CA, Suster S, et al: Primary pulmonary sarcomas with features of monophasic synovial sarcoma: A clinicopathological, immunohistochemical, and ultrastructural study of 25 cases. Hum Pathol 26:474–480, 1995.

271. Zolliker A, Jacques J, Goldstein AS: Benign clear cell tumor of the lung. Arch Pathol Lab Med 103:526–530, 1979.

272. Zwiebel BR, Austin JHM, Grimes MM: Bronchial carcinoid tumors: Assessment with CT of location and intratumoral calcification in 31 patients. Radiology 179:483–486, 1991.

273. Zwirewich CV, Vedal S, Miller RR, Müller NL: Solitary pulmonary nodule: High-resolution CT and radiologic-pathologic correlation. Radiology 179:469–476, 1991.

29

Mediastinum

H. Page McAdams, Jeremy J. Erasmus,
Robert D. Tarver, Charles E. Spritzer

Many excellent textbooks and articles have been written about the mediastinum.[61, 65, 71, 101, 103, 181] This chapter refers to these articles and reviews the recent literature in regard to the anatomy, pathology, and radiologic manifestations of mediastinal diseases.

Imaging the Mediastinum

Although the chest radiograph is usually the initial study that detects a mediastinal abnormality, computed tomography (CT) is primarily used to assess the location and extent of mediastinal disease; because of its superior contrast resolution, it is also used to characterize the tissue components of masses (Fig. 29–1). CT is also useful for distinguishing vascular variants or benign processes of the mediastinum, such as lipomatosis, from true pathologic conditions.

Although CT is usually used to further evaluate an abnormality detected on the chest radiograph, it may be performed in certain clinical situations when the chest radiograph is normal. For example, because of the strong association between myasthenia gravis and thymoma, CT is often performed in patients with myasthenia gravis even when chest radiographic findings are normal (Fig. 29–2). Also, certain malignancies, such as lung cancer, have a marked predilection for metastasis to mediastinal lymph nodes. These lymph node metastases may not be visible on chest radiographs; consequently, CT is used by most thoracic surgeons and oncologists to assess the mediastinal nodes in patients with lung cancer.

Recent advances in CT imaging (i.e., spiral CT and multidetector-row spiral CT) have further improved the ability of CT to image the mediastinum. By significantly shortening scan time, respiratory motion artifacts are limited and, in some instances, the total dose of iodinated contrast medium can be reduced. Spiral CT data sets can also be effectively reconstructed in a variety of nonaxial planes, often facilitating interpretation of mediastinal abnormalities. The application of nonaxial two-dimensional (2D) and three-dimensional (3D) reconstruction techniques has proved most useful for imaging abnormalities of the central airways and great vessels (Figs. 29–3 and 29–4). For example, in the evaluation of stenoses in obliquely oriented bronchi, these reconstruction techniques can improve diagnostic accuracy and confidence of interpretation, although axial CT images usually provide all the information required for diagnosis. Nevertheless, 2D and 3D images, by presenting anatomic information in a context more familiar to referring clinicians, may demonstrate the loca-

tion and extent of an abnormality in a way that radiologic reports and axial CT images often do not.

Although CT imaging usually provides the requisite information in most patients with mediastinal abnormalities, magnetic resonance imaging (MRI), because of its multiplanar capability and high contrast resolution, is occasionally used to further evaluate the location and extent of disease. MRI is the modality of choice for imaging neurogenic tumors because not only does it demonstrate the number and nature of the lesions but also it optimally depicts intraspinal extension.

Additionally, MRI is useful (1) in confirming the cystic nature of mediastinal lesions that appear solid on CT (Fig. 29–5) and (2) in demonstrating vascular structures in patients in whom iodinated intravenous (IV) contrast medium is contraindicated (Fig. 29–6). Compared with CT, MRI has two potential disadvantages for imaging mediastinal abnormalities: its ability to demonstrate calcification and its spatial resolution are relatively poor.

CT Scanning Techniques

Techniques for CT scanning of the chest vary from institution to institution. Although standard protocols are frequently used without modification, they are occasionally altered to address specific clinical concerns.

Patient Considerations

Most patients are scanned in the supine position with their arms above their head. The prone position can be useful for patients who are claustrophobic or who find the supine position uncomfortable. Occasionally, the prone or decubitus position can be used to more accurately define pathology. CT images obtained from the decubitus position are often useful for evaluating air-fluid or fluid collections. The prone position can be used to evaluate or facilitate biopsy of abnormalities in the retrocardiac area, such as esophageal masses and azygoesophageal lymphadenopathy (Fig. 29–7).

CT scans are performed, if possible, during a single breath-hold. When scanning is performed using narrow collimation on a single-detector-row spiral CT scanner, however, it may not be possible to complete the scan in a single breath-hold. Hyperventilation prior to scanning can improve breath-holding and thus image quality. The mediastinum, however, can be scanned in less than 10 seconds when multidetector-row spiral CT scanners are used. If the patient cannot accomplish a breath-hold for this short length of time, the scan can be performed during quiet breathing, often with good results.

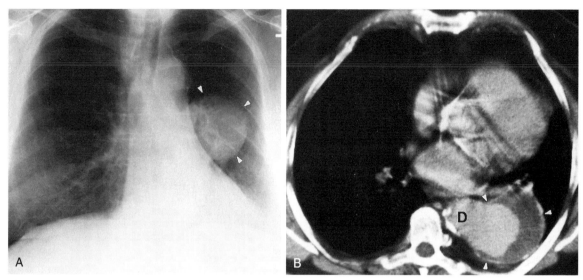

Figure 29–1. Saccular aneurysm of descending aorta. *A,* Posteroanterior chest radiograph shows homogeneous soft tissue mass *(arrowheads)* in the left hemithorax. Acute margins at interface with mediastinum suggest intrapulmonary mass. *B,* Contrast-enhanced CT shows saccular aneurysm *(arrowheads)* of descending aorta (D) with peripheral thrombus.

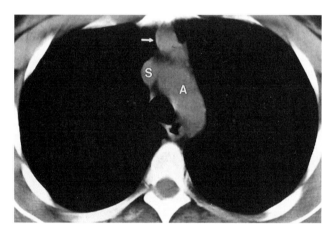

Figure 29–2. Thymoma in woman with myasthenia gravis. Chest radiograph (not shown) was normal. Because of association between myasthenia gravis and thymoma, chest CT was performed and revealed small soft tissue mass in anterior mediastinum *(arrow).* Resection confirmed thymoma. A, aorta; S, superior vena cava.

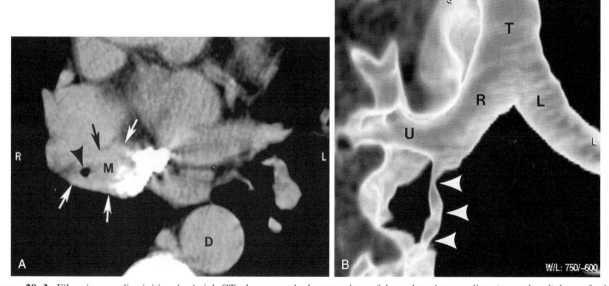

Figure 29–3. Fibrosing mediastinitis. *A,* Axial CT shows marked narrowing of bronchus intermedius *(arrowhead)* by soft tissue attenuation mass (M) *(arrows).* Note extensive subcarinal calcification. D, descending aorta. *B,* Volume-rendered shaded-surface display shows long-segment irregular narrowing of bronchus intermedius *(arrowheads).* Three-dimensional reconstructions can facilitate assessment and treatment of airway stenoses. L, left main bronchus; R, right main bronchus; T, trachea; U, right upper lobe bronchus.

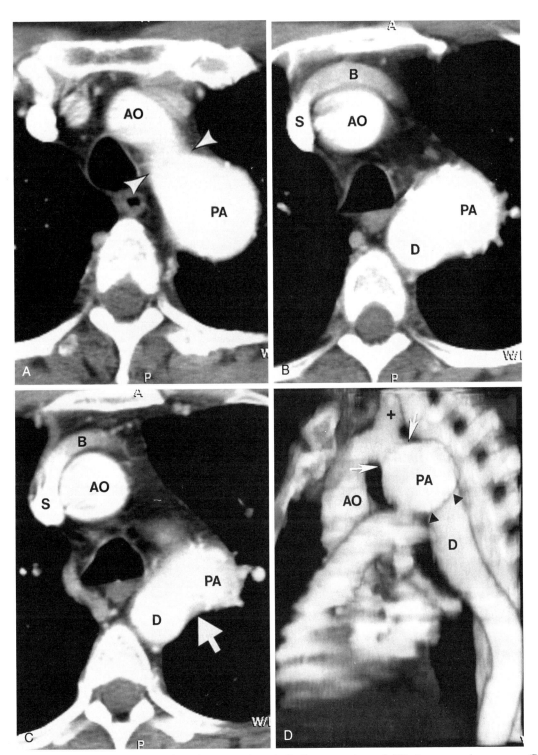

Figure 29–4. Pseudoaneurysm after repair of aortic coarctation. *A–C,* Contrast-enhanced CT shows pseudoaneurysm (P) at site of coarctation repair. A narrow isthmus *(arrowheads in A)* can be seen between the pseudoaneurysm and the transverse aorta, and a wide connection *(arrow in C)* can be seen between the pseudoaneurysm and the descending aorta. *D,* Oblique volume-rendered maximal intensity projection image clearly shows relationship of pseudoaneurysm to proximal *(arrows)* and distal *(arrowheads)* aorta as well as the brachiocephalic artery *(+)*. Three-dimensional reconstructions of CT angiograms display anatomy in a more familiar perspective to clinicians than axial CT images. A, ascending aorta; B, brachiocephalic vein; D, descending aorta; S, superior vena cava.

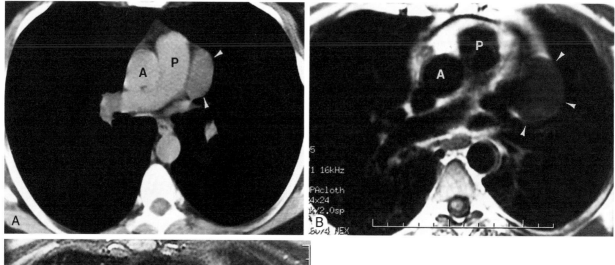

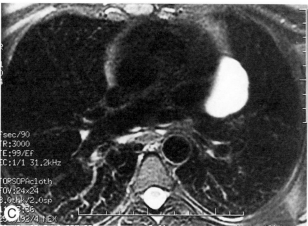

Figure 29–5. Mediastinal cyst. *A,* CT shows well-circum-scribed homogeneous mass in anterior mediastinum *(arrow-heads).* Although the mass shows lower attenuation than the vascular structures, its appearance is not diagnostic for mediastinal cyst. A, ascending aorta; P, main pulmonary artery. *B* and *C,* Axial T1-weighted and T2-weighted MR images show mass to be of homogeneous low signal intensity on T1-weighted image *(arrowheads* in *B)* and high signal intensity on T2-weighted image *(C),* which is consistent with a cyst. A, ascending aorta; P, main pulmonary artery.

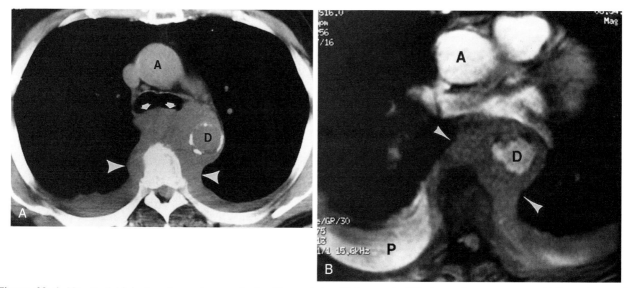

Figure 29–6. Non-Hodgkin's lymphoma in a patient with renal insufficiency. *A,* CT shows homogeneous middle and posterior mediastinal mass encasing descending aorta, anteriorly displacing the tracheal carina *(arrows)* and extending into the paravertebral region bilaterally *(arrowheads).* Small bilateral pleural effusions can be visualized. *B,* Cine gradient-recalled echo MR image performed to evaluate possible vascular invasion confirms flow within descending aorta. A low-signal-intensity mass *(arrowheads)* and a high-signal-intensity pleural effusion (P) can be seen. A, ascending aorta; D, descending aorta.

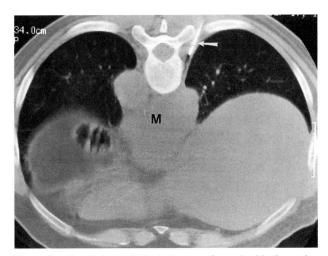

Figure 29–7. CT (extended window) performed with the patient in the prone position to improve access for biopsy of middle mediastinal mass (M). Diagnostic specimen was obtained and confirmed non-Hodgkin's lymphoma. *Arrow* indicates the biopsy needle.

CT Acquisition Parameters

The choice of CT acquisition parameters depends on the clinical situation and the CT scanner. Typically, CT of the mediastinum is performed at 120 to 130 kV and 200 to 300 mA. Most single-detector-row spiral CT machines use a 180-degree linear interpolation algorithm to reconstruct the individual axial slices. Any of a number of possible postprocessing reconstruction algorithms can then be applied to generate the final images. A smoothing or "soft tissue" reconstruction algorithm is used to decrease artifacts caused by abrupt changes between tissues of different density.

The field of view is usually between 34 and 50 cm and, combined with an image matrix of 512 × 512, yields a pixel size of about 1 mm. Smaller fields of view (15 cm) can be used to decrease the pixel size to 0.3 mm. These techniques are usually unnecessary for routine mediastinal imaging but can be useful for imaging the central airways.

With single-detector-row spiral CT, the user must choose three parameters: (1) slice collimation, (2) pitch ratio, and (3) reconstruction interval. For routine mediastinal CT, *slice collimation* is usually set between 7 and 10 mm. For evaluation of small lesions, suspected hilar pathology, or central airway lesions, slice collimation may be decreased to 3 or 5 mm.

Pitch is defined as the ratio between table speed and slice collimation. On a single-detector-row scanner using a 180-degree linear interpolation algorithm, pitch can be increased to 2.0 without significant loss of image quality. Increasing pitch is desirable whenever possible, because increasing pitch decreases scan time proportionately. Increasing pitch beyond 2.0, however, results in unacceptable loss of longitudinal resolution. For routine mediastinal CT, the pitch selected is usually between 1.3 and 2.0.

The image *reconstruction interval* is usually chosen to be the same as, or slightly less than, slice collimation for routine axial imaging. Thus, for a routine 7-mm slice collimation scan, the reconstruction interval is usually ei-

ther 5 or 7 mm. If nonaxial 2D or 3D reconstructions are to be generated from the axial images, a minimum of 20% to 30% reconstruction overlap is needed to minimize stair-step artifacts between slices. Thus, for a 5-mm slice collimation scan, axial reconstructions should be performed at least every 2 or 3 mm.

With multidetector-row scanners, the user typically has much less flexibility in protocol selection because of the complex physics involved in the reconstruction of individual axial slices from multiple overlapping helices. User-specified parameters are typically slice collimation, table speed, and operation mode. The user does not usually specify pitch per se. Most manufacturers supply information regarding acceptable choices of slice collimation and table speed to optimize image resolution. The General Electric QXi scanner, for example, allows the user to choose one of two modes of operation: *high quality* (HQ—effective pitch = 3.0) or *high speed* (HS—effective pitch = 6.0).

When an imaging protocol is prescribed for a multidetector-row CT scanner, it is best to initially select the slice collimation. The operation mode and maximum allowable table speed are then selected. For routine mediastinal imaging, 7.5-mm collimation in HQ mode with a table speed of 11.75 mm per rotation allows evaluation of most mediastinal abnormalities. Imaging of vascular structures or airways requires narrower collimation (2.5 or 5 mm) and more rapid table speed (15 to 30 mm per rotation table speed) in high-speed mode.

Use of Contrast Medium

Most routine CT scans of the mediastinum can be performed without IV contrast enhancement unless the primary indication is a suspected vascular abnormality (Fig. 29–8). Interpretation of non–contrast-enhanced CT scans, however, can be more difficult and time-consuming than interpretation of contrast-enhanced scans and requires thorough knowledge of mediastinal anatomy and normal variants. There are, however, several advantages to non–contrast-enhanced CT scanning:

1. Scan time is decreased because there is no need to establish IV access, set up the contrast-medium injector, or delay the scan as the bolus is administered.
2. There is no risk of a reaction to contrast medium.
3. The cost is lower.

When needed, IV contrast material is given through a large forearm or antecubital vein by a power injector. Contrast injection rate and total injection volume depends on the indication. For routine purposes, a rate of 2 mL/second for a total volume of 150 mL is sufficient. For vascular imaging (aorta and pulmonary artery), higher injection rates (3 to 4 mL/second) are often necessary. In such cases, it is mandatory that injection be through a relatively large-bore IV catheter (18 or 20 gauge) into a large antecubital vein. The timing of the bolus in relationship to the scan also varies and depends on both the indication (routine versus arterial imaging) and the time required to complete the scan.

Thoracic CT is usually performed without esophageal contrast medium. Oral contrast medium can, however, be helpful in identifying the relationship between the espha-

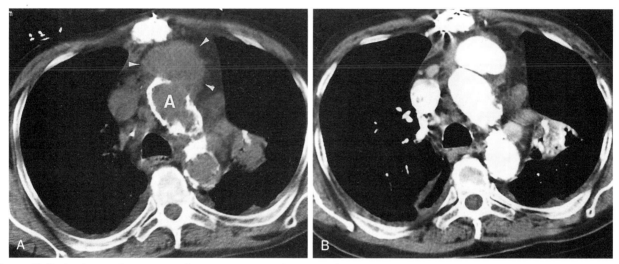

Figure 29–8. Aortic pseudoaneurysm after coronary artery bypass graft surgery. *A,* Non–contrast-enhanced CT performed 4 weeks after surgery to exclude mediastinitis shows heterogeneous low-attenuation mass in anterior mediastinum *(arrowheads),* suggestive of abscess. A, aorta. *B,* Because of the proximity of the mass to the aorta, the patient was rescanned using intravenous contrast, and the mass was shown to be a pseudoaneurysm arising from the aortic cannulation site.

gus and other mediastinal structures and occasionally, in depicting intrinsic esophageal abnormalities (Fig. 29–9). Commercial preparations of esophageal paste, made of a dilute barium mixture, are available for use. The patient must swallow several teaspoons of the paste and refrain from further swallowing during the examination.

CT Reconstruction and Image Display

CT scans of the mediastinum are usually reconstructed, filmed, and interpreted in axial format. Until recently, sagittal, coronal, and off-axis reconstructions of the thorax were not used because of slice misregistration and respiratory motion artifacts. With the advent of spiral scanning, however, continuous volume data sets can be acquired during a single breath-hold and excellent nonaxial 2D and 3D reconstructed images of mediastinal vascular structures and airways can be generated (see Figs. 29–3 and 29–4). Different reconstruction methods, such as multiplanar reformat

imaging, multiplanar volume reformat imaging, and external and internal 3D renderings, vary significantly in computational complexity and time required to generate the images.

Mediastinal CT images may be interpreted in either hard-copy (film) or soft-copy (workstation/display) format. Most axial scans are still printed and interpreted on film. When CT studies of the chest are being filmed, two different window settings are needed because of the wide range in the CT attenuation numbers of the tissues to be displayed: −800 Hounsfield units (HU) for lung and 600 HU for bone. Lung settings should have a wide width to encompass air-filled lung and soft tissue and are usually viewed at a level of −600 and a width of 1200. Because of the smaller density range between fat, soft tissue, bone, and contrast-enhanced vessels, mediastinal settings are usually viewed at a level of 50 and a width of 350.

These levels and widths can be varied to aid in the

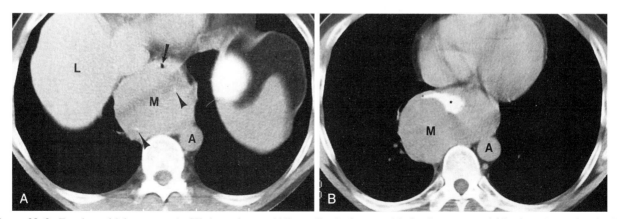

Figure 29–9. Esophageal leiomyoma. *A,* CT shows large middle-mediastinal mass with focal punctate calcifications *(arrowheads).* The esophagus is displaced anteriorly *(arrow).* The CT appearance is nonspecific and the origin of mass is uncertain. A, aorta; L, liver; M, mass. *B,* CT following ingestion of oral barium reveals distortion of esophageal lumen *(asterisk),* consistent with a mass arising within the wall of the esophagus. Resection confirmed leiomyoma. A, aorta; M, mass.

evaluation of any lesion that is not adequately differentiated on the standard settings. For example, during evaluation of a mediastinal mass for subtle calcification, setting the window width on 1 and moving the level between 50 and 300 HU while one views the monitor can often aid detection. Bone windows with a wide width and a level of near 400 HU are often needed to evaluate for possible bone metastases.

Soft-copy interpretation of mediastinal CT is increasing because of the increasing use of (1) picture archiving and communications systems and (2) cine or nonaxial modes for interpretation of complex CT data sets.

MRI Techniques

Spin-Echo Imaging

In the thorax, both T1-weighted and T2-weighted spin-echo images are usually desirable when assessing soft tissue abnormalities.* Although such simple techniques are efficacious for imaging the superior aspect of the mediastinum, cardiac pulsation and respiratory motion degrade images of the lower mediastinum. Many techniques have been developed to correct or eliminate image degradation caused by motion, including:

1. Reducing apparent motion by averaging.
2. Utilizing motion correction techniques.
3. Rapidly acquiring data such that breath-holding is possible.

The simplest method for motion correction is to average the MR signal with many acquisitions. The advantage of multiple acquisitions, however, is offset by an increase in data collection times. Furthermore, for echo times of more than 10 msec, motion artifacts persist in the hilum and adjacent to the heart. Alternatively, breath-held T1-weighted spin-echo imaging using one excitation (NEX), conjugation (half NEX imaging), and short repetition times (TRs), can be used. This technique has a poor signal-to-noise ratio and, although rapid, is still too long to prevent artifacts due to cardiac contraction.

Images can be acquired in fractions of a second using echo-planar sequences. This enables motion to be "frozen" during data acquisition. Such sequences, however, require special hardware and software. More important, because of the large chemical shift between fat and water, echo-planar imaging requires suppression or excitation of either fat or water, reducing the overall contrast available.

Between these extremes of data acquisition resides cardiosynchronous spin-echo imaging using either plethysmography or electrocardiographic (ECG) gating. Image acquisition timed to the cardiac cycle improves delineation of abnormalities within the lower mediastinum and around the heart compared with noncardiosynchronous imaging. For complete assessment of cardiac function, ECG gating is preferred because the precise temporal relationship between each image and the QRS complex is known. If only anatomic information is required, however, plethysmography is generally used because of the simplicity of patient preparation.

*See References 3, 13, 58, 61, 64, 92, 100, 102, 106, 139, and 152.

One consequence of cardiosynchronous acquisitions is that the TR is dependent on the patient's heart rate. Consequently, the acquired images may not be as T1-weighted or T2-weighted as those obtained elsewhere in the body. For example, in a patient with a heart rate of 60 beats/minute, the effective TR is 1000 msec, resulting in images that are neither T1-weighted nor T2-weighted. With a selected echo time (TE) of 20 msec, the image is somewhat proton-density–weighted. Even if the TE is lengthened to 70, images obtained are not truly T2-weighted. To obtain such an image, the TR must be lengthened by multiples of the patient's heart rate. For example, acquiring data over every two heartbeats would increase the TR to 2000 msec. One positive consequence of lengthening the TR is the capability of acquiring images at more anatomic locations. A disadvantage, however, is the doubling of acquisition time and the potentially increased image blur.

Cardiosynchronous acquisitions reduce the effect of cardiac motion but do not compensate for respiratory motion. Respiratory gating, in which MR data are acquired only during periods of apnea, when combined with cardiosynchronous data acquisitions, can be used to improve image quality. This technique, however, is more time-consuming. Using respiratory motion correction algorithms, such as respiratory compensation, can improve image quality by displacing ghost artifacts either outside the imaged field of view or by returning them to their site of origin. These techniques are easily combined with cardiosynchronous data collection and do not significantly increase data acquisition time.

Gated RARE (fast spin-echo, turbo spin-echo) techniques can be used to provide T2-weighted contrast in a fraction of the time when compared with conventional spin-echo acquisitions.

Gradient-Recalled Echo Acquisitions

White blood techniques can be used to assess mediastinal vessels. These gradient-recalled echo (GRE) techniques, such as FLASH (fast low-angle shot) and GRASS (gradient-recalled acquisition in the steady state), render fluid as high signal because of the inflow of unsaturated protons. The stationary tissues appear dark because of their repeated excitation by multiple RF pulses. Within the soft tissues, the contrast available is dependent on the particulars of the acquisition. Either a T1-weighted acquisition (e.g., FLASH) or a more T2-weighted acquisition (e.g., GRASS) can be obtained.[7, 28, 68, 91, 192, 253]

As with spin-echo imaging, the pulsatility of aortic flow and the respiratory motion of most patients results in unsatisfactory images in the lower mediastinum and adjacent to the heart. *Gradient moment nulling* (flow compensation) is routinely employed with such techniques but is generally insufficient to correct all motion artifacts. For complete motion correction, a cardiosynchronous GRE acquisition with respiratory compensation is usually obtained. These sequences have been dubbed *cine MRI*.

With a short TR, GRE data are acquired in 20- to 40-msec segments during the cardiac cycle. The temporal relationship of the data acquisition to the cardiac cycle is recorded and after sufficient data are obtained, a series of images with a frame rate of 10 to 40 frames per minute is produced and may be viewed as a continuous loop of images through the cardiac cycle. As typically performed, two to four anatomic locations are imaged in a 3- to 5-minute acquisition, depending on the patient's heart rate. The true temporal resolution of the sequence depends on the number of anatomic locations imaged per acquisition and the patient's heart rate. The slower the patient's heart rate and the smaller the number of anatomic locations imaged per acquisition, the higher the temporal resolution. Although high temporal resolution is required for cardiac analysis, a lower frame rate is sufficient to visualize mediastinal structures, allowing more anatomic locations to be acquired per acquisition. As such, 16 anatomic locations can be acquired in 12 to 15 minutes, allowing the entire mediastinum to be covered.

The main limitation of these retrospective cine techniques is their relatively long acquisition times and their sensitivity to arrhythmias. More recently, cardiac-gated, segmented k-space acquisitions have become available. These acquisitions acquire data in a single breath-hold using prospective cardiac gating. The pulse sequence consists of a fast GRE acquisition, such as turbo-FLASH or fast GRASS. TRs are on the order of 5 to 10 msec with echo times of 1 to 3 msec. Flip angles are small, typically 15 to 30 degrees.

As with retrospective techniques, the R-to-R interval in each cardiac cycle is divided into multiple frames of 20 to 80 msec in duration. During each frame, in a fashion analogous to fast spin-echo data acquisition, a number of lines of k-space are acquired. This is referred to as the number of views per segment or the number of views per phase, and it is equivalent to *echo train length* (ETL) or TURBO factor in fast spin-echo or turbo spin-echo imaging. The more views sampled per segment, the smaller the number of R-to-R intervals required and the faster the acquisition.

For example, using eight views per segment, 128 lines of k-space can be acquired over 16 R-to-R intervals, which for most patients is a 15- to 25-second breath-hold. Assuming a TR of 10 msec, view sharing of eight frames, and a heart rate of 60 beats/minute, approximately 12 frames per cardiac cycle can be produced. If the number of frames per segment is increased, the total acquisition time is reduced; however, the number of frames per cardiac cycle is also decreased. In addition, since the data acquisition time for each frame of the cardiac cycle is increased, the amount of image blur is increased.

Although much faster than retrospective cine imaging, these segmented k-space techniques have a shorter acquisition time that is associated with a reduced signal-to-noise ratio. In our experience, a dedicated surface coil is necessary to compensate for this lower signal-to-noise ratio. A final disadvantage of these techniques is the reduced intraluminal signal that results from the slow flow seen during diastole.

Contrast-Enhanced Magnetic Resonance Angiography and Venography

Both arterial and venous anatomy can be visualized with the administration of gadolinium during the acquisition of a fast GRE volume data set. Such techniques have been well described for visualizing the aorta, renal arteries, carotids, and portal vein. These techniques have a rapid acquisition time (10 to 30 seconds) and, as such, a complete MR angiography or MR venography can be acquired in a single breath-hold.

The clear disadvantages of such techniques are the expense of the contrast agent and the small risk of a contrast reaction. In addition, timing arrival of the contrast bolus to the structure of interest is required for optimal visualization.

Summary

Spin-echo imaging, although superb for visualizing the soft tissues, is less specific for assessing vascular patency. White blood or contrast-dependent techniques optimize the signal intensity of flowing blood. A consequence of this, however, is a reduced conspicuity of soft tissue abnormalities within the mediastinum. Consequently, it may be necessary to acquire sequences with both techniques for accurate interpretation of the study.

Normal Mediastinal Anatomy

Comprehensive knowledge of cross-sectional anatomy is required to accurately evaluate mediastinal abnormalities. Interpretation of mediastinal anatomy, however, can be assisted by analyzing CT images at specific levels within the chest that are easily identifiable because of their characteristic anatomic landmarks and appearance.

Thoracic Inlet Level

At the junction of the neck and the thorax, most of the mediastinal structures are vascular (Fig. 29–10). The two brachiocephalic veins are formed as the internal jugular veins join the subclavian veins and are located posterior to

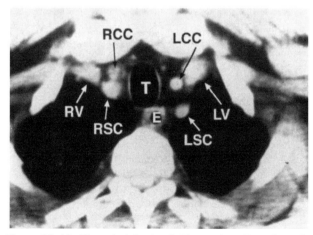

Figure 29–10. Thoracic inlet level. The trachea (T) and esophagus (E) are midline, and they separate the right and left vascular structures. LCC, left common carotid artery; LSC, left subclavian artery; LV, left brachiocephalic vein; RCC, right common carotid artery; RSC, right subclavian artery; RV, right brachiocephalic vein.

the clavicular heads. These veins are the most anterior and lateral of the six vessels. More medially are the two common carotid arteries, and just posterior to these are the subclavian arteries. The subclavian arteries and veins exit the mediastinum to enter the axilla after crossing over the first rib. The esophagus is posterior or posterolateral to the trachea. There are six major vessels at this level.

Left Brachiocephalic Vein Level

The left brachiocephalic vein crosses the midline anterior to the arterial branches of the aorta and joins the more vertically orientated right brachiocephalic vein to form the superior vena cava (SVC). (Fig. 29–11). The internal mammary veins can often be identified coursing posteriorly from a parasternal location to join the brachiocephalic veins.

The right brachiocephalic, left common carotid, and left subclavian arteries are located posterior to the left brachiocephalic vein and anterior to the trachea. The right brachiocephalic artery is the more centrally located artery, whereas the left common carotid artery (the smallest of the three arteries) and the left subclavian artery are located to the left of the midline in a more lateral and posterior position.

The esophagus is posterior or posterolateral to the trachea and anterior to the spine.

Aortic Arch Level

The transverse arch crosses the mediastinum anterior to the trachea coursing obliquely from right to left and from anterior to posterior (Fig. 29–12). The SVC is located adjacent to the anterior aspect of the transverse aorta to the right of the trachea. The fat-filled region posterior to the SVC, anterior to the trachea, and lateral to the aorta is the pretracheal space. Anterior to the transverse aorta is the fat-filled prevascular space, a compartment of the ante-

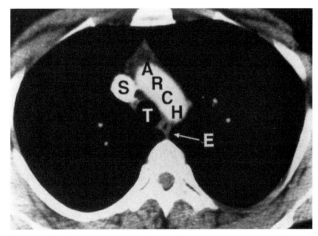

Figure 29–12. Aortic arch level. Superior vena cava (S) and aortic arch (ARCH) lie anterior to the trachea (T) and esophagus (E). The thymus, which has undergone fatty infiltration, is anterior to the arch.

rior mediastinum that extends cephalad anterior to the great vessels of the aorta and the brachiocephalic veins. If present, the thymus gland is located in this space. Both of these spaces often contain a few small lymph nodes.

The esophagus is posterior or posterolateral to the trachea and anterior to the spine.

Azygos Arch and Aortopulmonary Window Level

The azygos vein, located anterior and slightly to the right of the spine, arches anteriorly and joins the SVC at this level (Figs. 29–13 and 29–14). The azygos arch may not be seen in its entirety on one slice and may be confused with lymphadenopathy. The ascending and descending aorta are visible as separate structures at this level. The

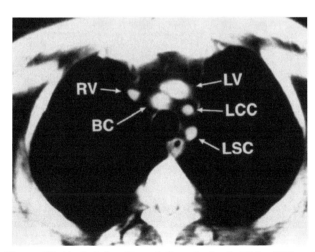

Figure 29–11. Left brachiocephalic vein level. Right (RV) and left (LV) brachiocephalic veins are anterior to right brachiocephalic artery (BC), left common carotid artery (LCC), and left subclavian artery (LSC).

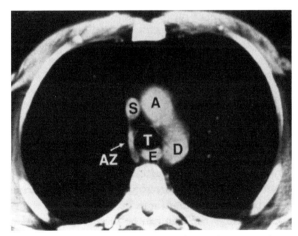

Figure 29–13. Arch of the azygos vein or the aortopulmonary (AP) window level. Azygos vein (AZ) arches from a posterior position along the midesophagus to join the superior vena cava (S), crossing over the right upper lobe bronchus. Between the ascending (A) and descending (D) aorta is the AP window region. E, esophagus; T, trachea.

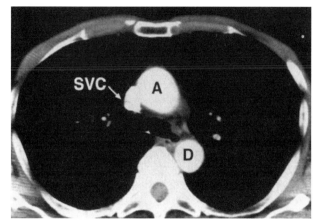

Figure 29–14. Aortopulmonary (AP) window level. AP window is between ascending (A) and descending (D) aorta. SVC, superior vena cava.

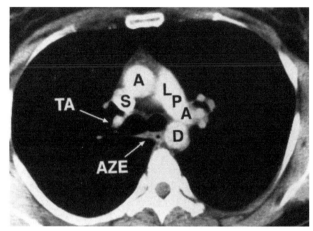

Figure 29–15. Left pulmonary artery level. To the left of the left pulmonary artery (LPA) lie the left superior pulmonary veins. The ascending (A) and descending (D) aorta and superior vena cava (S) maintain their relative positions from the level above. The truncus anterior (TA), or right upper lobe pulmonary artery, is anterior to the right upper lobe bronchus. The azygoesophageal recess (AZE) is a concavity anterior to the spine.

ascending aorta is anterior to the trachea, and the descending aorta is posterolateral to the trachea on the left. Typically, the ascending aorta (mean diameter, 3.5 cm) is larger than the descending aorta (mean diameter, 2.5 cm).

The aortopulmonary window is a space located between the inferior aspect of the aortic arch and the superior aspect of the left main pulmonary artery. In some patients, the close anatomic contiguity of these two structures prevents visualization of this space. The space is otherwise fat-filled and contains a few small lymph nodes, the left recurrent laryngeal nerve, and the ligamentum arteriosum.

The esophagus is posterior to the trachea, anterior to the spine, and medial to the descending aorta.

Left Pulmonary Artery Level

The main pulmonary artery is anterior and to the left of the ascending aorta. The left pulmonary artery curves posteriorly from its origin from the main pulmonary artery and is located anterolateral to the left main bronchus at the level of the carina (Figs. 29–15 and 29–16). The left superior pulmonary veins are located lateral to the posterior portion of the left pulmonary artery.

On the right, at the level of the carina, is the origin of the right upper lobe bronchus. Anterior to the right upper lobe bronchus lies the right upper lobe pulmonary artery or the truncus anterior. The right superior pulmonary veins are located anterior and lateral to the truncus anterior. The azygos vein is located posterior and to the right of the esophagus. The hemiazygos vein parallels the course of the azygos but is to the left of the spine.

The superior pericardial recess, a crescent-shaped extension of the pericardial space, is contiguous with the posterior aspect of the ascending aorta. The space often contains a small amount of fluid and can occasionally be confused with a lymph node. Its characteristic location, shape, and low attenuation, however, allow confident identification.

The concave extension of right lung into the mediastinum anterior to the spine is the azygoesophageal recess, which extends inferiorly from the subcarinal region to the level of the diaphragm.

Right Pulmonary Artery Level

The main pulmonary artery is anterior and to the left of the ascending aorta (Figs. 29–17 and 29–18). The right pulmonary artery extends posteriorly and to the right from the main pulmonary artery, passing anterior to the bronchus intermedius and posterior to the SVC. The right superior pulmonary vein is to the right and lateral to the intrapulmonary portion of the right pulmonary artery. Anterior to the left main and upper lobe bronchi is the left superior pulmonary vein, and posterior to the left upper lobe bronchus is the left lower lobe pulmonary artery.

Left Atrial Level

The anatomy of the mediastinum is complex at this level (Figs. 29–19 and 29–20). Anterior to the SVC is the

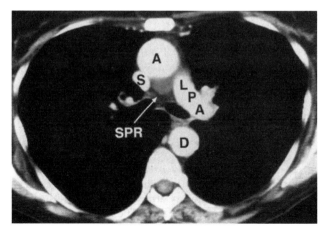

Figure 29–16. Left pulmonary artery level. The superior pericardial recess (SPR) is an extension of the pericardium. A, ascending aorta; D, descending aorta; LPA, left pulmonary artery; S, superior vena cava.

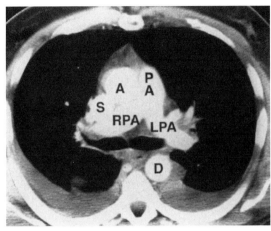

Figure 29–17. Right pulmonary artery level. The main pulmonary artery (PA) divides into the left (LPA) and right (RPA) pulmonary arteries. The right pulmonary artery passes anterior to the right main bronchus, and the left pulmonary artery passes over the left main bronchus. A, ascending aorta; D, descending aorta; S, superior vena cava.

right atrial appendage curving around the ascending aorta. The aorta is located centrally within the mediastinum, and anterior and to the left of the aorta is the pulmonary outflow tract. Posterolateral and to the left of the pulmonary outflow tract is the left atrial appendage. Within the fat, between the left atrial appendage and the aortic root, is the left main coronary artery. The left superior pulmonary vein enters the left atrium immediately posterior to the left atrial appendage. The right superior pulmonary veins enter the left atrium just posterior to the SVC.

Four-Chamber Level

All four chambers of the heart are identified at this level (Figs. 29–21 and 29–22). The posteriorly located left

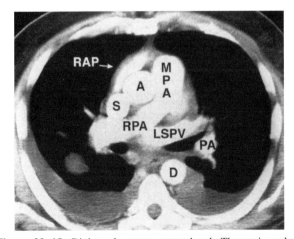

Figure 29–18. Right pulmonary artery level. The main pulmonary artery (MPA) divides into the right pulmonary artery (RPA) and the left pulmonary artery, which is more superior and not visible. The left superior pulmonary vein (LSPV) is anterior to the left main bronchus, and the left pulmonary artery (PA) is posterior. The superior aspect of the right atrial appendage (RAP) is anterior to the superior vena cava (S). A, ascending aorta; D, descending aorta.

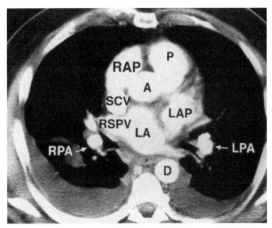

Figure 29–19. Left atrial level. The left atrium (LA) is the most superior and posterior chamber of the heart. Superior pulmonary veins enter the anterosuperior portion of the left atrium. The left atrial appendage (LAP) is situated anterior and to left of the left atrium, adjacent to main pulmonary artery (P). The right atrial appendage (RAP) is anterior to superior vena cava (SVC) and adjacent to ascending aorta (A). D, descending aorta; LPA, left pulmonary artery; RPA, right pulmonary artery; RSPV, right superior pulmonary vein.

atrium is the most cranial of all the chambers. The right and left inferior pulmonary veins enter the posterolateral aspect of the left atrium. Anterior and to the right is the right atrium. To the left and anterior to the right atrium is the right ventricle located behind the sternum. The left ventricle is to the left and posterior to the right ventricle.

The coronary arteries can be detected if they are calcified or if fat surrounds the heart. The right coronary artery lies in the right atrioventricular groove. The circumflex coronary artery lies in the left atrioventricular groove, and the left anterior descending coronary artery lies in the intraventricular groove between the left and right ventricles.

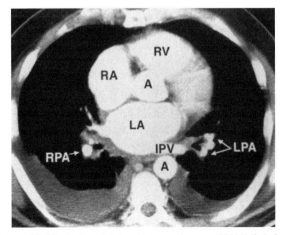

Figure 29–20. Left atrial level. A, aortic root; IPV, left inferior pulmonary vein; LA, left atrium; LPA, left lower lobe pulmonary arteries; RA, right atrium; RPA, right lower lobe pulmonary artery; RV, right ventricle.

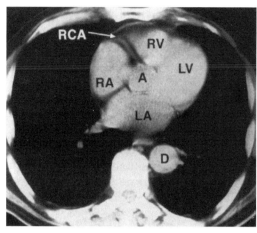

Figure 29–21. Four-chamber level. The right coronary artery (RCA) is visible in the right atrioventricular groove. A, aortic root; D, descending aorta; LA, left atrium; LV, left ventricle; RA, right atrium; RV, right ventricle.

Three-Chamber Level

The ventricles and the right atrium are identified at this level (the left atrium, because of its more cranial position, is not visible) (Figs. 29–23 and 29–24). The right atrium is located to the right. To the left and anteriorly, the right ventricle with its thin wall is located just beneath the sternum. The thick-walled left ventricle makes up the posterolateral left portion of the mediastinum. Between the left ventricle and the inferior vena cava's opening into the right atrium is the coronary sinus.

MR Images of the Mediastinum

The standard spin-echo, T1-weighted axial images of the mediastinum are similar in appearance to CT images (Figs. 29–25 to 29–29). However, signal void of the airways can occasionally be confused with the lack of signal in vessels. Coronal and sagittal MR images are helpful in depicting the anatomic relationships of normal mediastinal

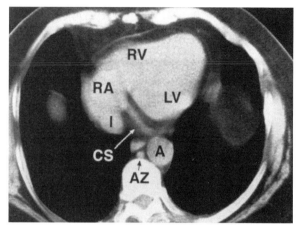

Figure 29–23. Three-chamber level. The left atrium is more cranial to this level and is not visible. The three visualized chambers are right atrium (RA), the right ventricle (RV), and the left ventricle (LV). The coronary sinus (CS) is between the inferior vena cava (I) and the left ventricle. A, descending aorta; AZ, azygos vein.

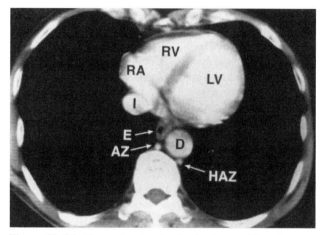

Figure 29–24. Three-chamber level. Esophagus (E) and azygos vein (AZ) form the medial border of the azygoesophageal recess. D, descending aorta; HAZ, hemiazygos vein; I, inferior vena cava; LV, left ventricle; RA, right atrium; RV, right ventricle.

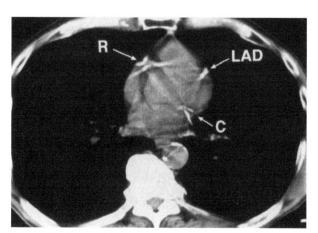

Figure 29–22. Calcified coronary arteries at the four-chamber level. C, circumflex coronary artery; LAD, left anterior descending coronary artery; R, right coronary artery.

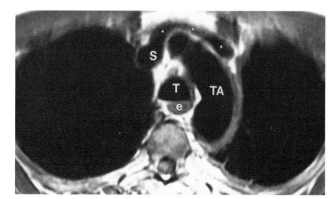

Figure 29–25. Axial MR image of the aortic arch in a patient with mesothelioma of the left hemithorax. e, esophagus; S, superior vena cava; T, trachea; TA, transverse aortic arch. The *asterisks* indicate the left brachiocephalic vein.

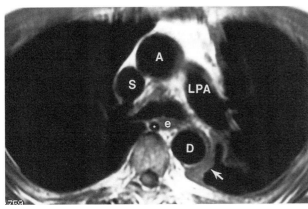

Figure 29–26. Axial MR image of the left pulmonary artery in a patient with mesothelioma of the left hemithorax. Note soft tissue mass *(arrow)* encasing the descending aorta. A, ascending aorta; D, descending aorta; e, esophagus; LPA, left pulmonary artery; S, superior vena cava. The *asterisk* indicates the azygos vein.

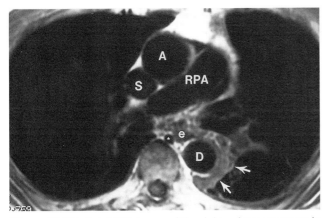

Figure 29–27. Axial MR image of the right pulmonary artery in a patient with mesothelioma of the left hemithorax. A soft tissue mass *(arrows)* encases the descending aorta. A, ascending aorta; D, descending aorta; e, esophagus; RPA, right pulmonary artery; S, superior vena cava. The *asterisk* indicates the azygos vein.

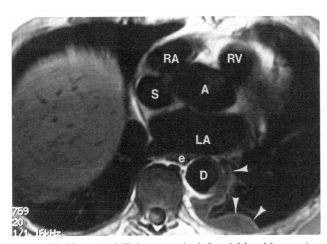

Figure 29–28. Axial MR image at the left atrial level in a patient with mesothelioma of the left hemithorax. Loculated pleural fluid *(arrowheads)* can be seen in the left posterior hemithorax. A, ascending aorta; D, descending aorta; e, esophagus; LA, left atrium; RA, right atrium; RV, right ventricle; S, superior vena cava.

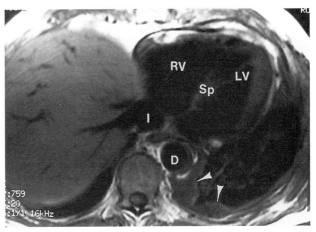

Figure 29–29. Axial MR image at the three-chamber level in a patient with mesothelioma of the left hemithorax. Loculated pleural fluid *(arrowheads)* can be seen in the left posterior hemithorax. D, descending aorta; I, inferior vena cava; LV, left ventricle; RV, right ventricle; Sp, intraventricular septum.

structures as well as in identifying and locating pathology (Figs. 29–30 to 29–34).

Mediastinal Divisions

The mediastinum extends craniocaudally from the thoracic inlet to the diaphragm and, historically, has been divided into compartments (on the chest radiograph) to facilitate lesion localization and aid in diagnosis. This division of the mediastinum into anatomic regions or compartments is still important but not essential because CT and MRI can accurately localize and, in many instances, characterize masses. Despite these advances, however, mediastinal masses are still discussed, classified, and grouped by their position on chest radiographs.

In this chapter, we use the widely accepted division of the mediastinum into superior, anterior, middle, and posterior compartments.

The *superior mediastinum* is the space between the

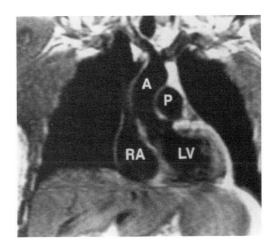

Figure 29–30. Anterior coronal MR image. A, ascending aorta; LV, left ventricle; P, main pulmonary artery; RA, right atrium.

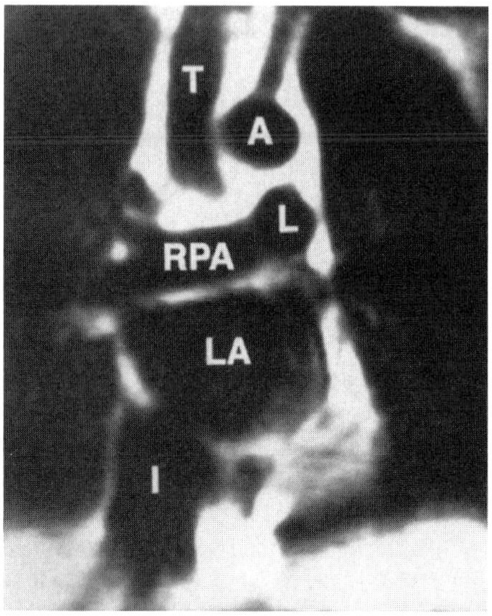

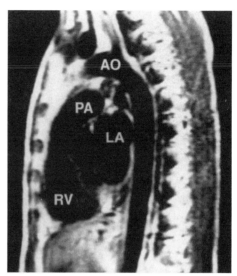

Figure 29–31. Coronal MR image at the right pulmonary artery level. A, aorta; I, inferior vena cava–right atrial junction; L, left pulmonary artery; LA, left atrium; RPA, right pulmonary artery; T, trachea.

Figure 29–33. Sagittal MR image of the main pulmonary artery. AO, aorta; LA, left atrium; PA, main pulmonary artery; RV, right ventricle.

thoracic inlet and the superior aspect of the aortic arch (i.e., all mediastinal structures above an imaginary line drawn between the sternal angle and the fourth intervertebral disk on the lateral chest radiograph).

The *anterior mediastinum* is the space anterior to the heart and great vessels on the lateral chest radiograph. It is bordered anteriorly by the sternum and posteriorly by the pericardium. Using this designation, normal anterior mediastinal structures include the thymus, the branches of the internal mammary artery and vein, lymph nodes, and fat.

Controversy exists concerning the division between the middle and the posterior mediastinum. Some authors suggest that the division should be the posterior aspect of the pericardium, but others would divide the two by an imaginary line drawn 1 cm posterior to the anterior border of

the vertebral bodies. The latter method places most aortic and esophageal lesions in the middle mediastinum and reserves the posterior mediastinum for neurogenic or other paraspinal lesions. Other methods involve dividing the middle and posterior mediastinum on the basis of the azygos arch and the aorta.

For purposes of this discussion, we define the *middle mediastinum* as the space between the anterior border of the pericardium and an imaginary line drawn 1 cm posterior to the anterior border of the vertebral bodies on the lateral radiograph. As such, it contains the heart, the aorta, the superior and inferior venae cavae, the brachiocephalic arteries and veins, the pulmonary arteries and veins, the thoracic duct, the azygos and hemiazygos veins, the phrenic and vagus nerves, the trachea and proximal bronchi, mediastinal fat, and lymph nodes.

The *posterior mediastinum* is defined as the space be-

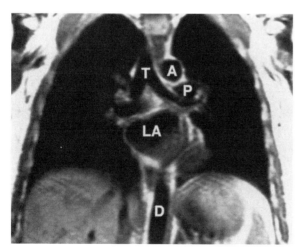

Figure 29–32. Coronal MR image at the carina. A, transverse aortic arch; D, descending aorta; LA, left atrium; P, left pulmonary artery; T, trachea.

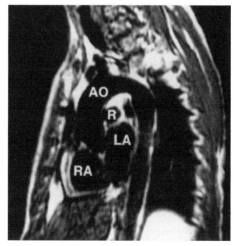

Figure 29–34. Sagittal MR image of the aorta. AO, aorta; LA, left atrium; R, right pulmonary artery; RA, right atrium.

Table 29–1. Classification of Mediastinal Abnormalities by Compartment Affected

Location	Lesion
Superior mediastinum	Thyroid goiter, tortuous great vessels
Anterior mediastinum	Thymic lesions, germ cell tumors, parathyroid adenoma, lymphatic malformations, hemangioma
Middle mediastinum	Esophageal lesions, airway lesions, foregut cysts, pericardial cysts
Posterior mediastinum	Neurogenic tumors, paraspinal abscess, extramedullary hematopoiesis
Multiple compartments	Mediastinitis, lipomatosis, lymphadenopathy (lymphoma, metastases, Castleman's disease, infection), mesenchymal tumors, vascular abnormalities and anomalies, diaphragmatic hernias

Table 29–2. Classification of Mediastinal Abnormalities Based on CT Attenuation Characteristics

CT Attenuation	Lesion
Fat	Lipoma, lipomatosis, thymolipoma, liposarcoma, teratoma, epicardial fat pad, hernia
Water	Thymic cyst, teratoma, pericardial cyst, bronchogenic cyst, esophageal duplication cyst, meningocele, neurenteric cyst
Soft tissue	Thymoma, thymic carcinoma, germ cell tumor, esophageal neoplasm, neurogenic tumor, lymphoma, lymphadenopathy
High attenuation	Calcified nodes (histoplasmosis, tuberculosis, sarcoidosis, silicosis), calcified neoplasm (thymoma, teratoma, treated lymphoma, metastases), fibrosing mediastinitis, hemorrhage, goiter, vascular
Contrast-enhancing	Vascular, goiter, Castleman's disease, hemangioma, paraganglioma

tween the imaginary line drawn 1 cm posterior to the anterior border of the vertebral bodies and the posterior paravertebral gutters. Structures in the posterior mediastinum include nerves, fat, the vertebral column, and lymph nodes.

Mediastinal Abnormalities

A useful approach for discussing mediastinal abnormalities is to divide them into those processes that predominantly affect *specific* compartments (superior, anterior, middle, and posterior mediastinum) and those processes that can affect *multiple* compartments (Table 29–1). An alternative method of classifying mediastinal masses is on the basis of their predominant attenuation characteristics on CT rather than by their location (Table 29–2).[86, 87] We will use the *former* approach in this discussion.

Superior Mediastinal Abnormalities

Common superior mediastinal abnormalities include intrathoracic extension of thyroid goiters or masses and tortuous great vessels.

Thyroid Goiter

On CT, the normal thyroid gland is typically visible at or just below the level of the cricoid cartilage (Fig. 29–35). It appears on a non–contrast-enhanced CT scan as two wedge-shaped structures of homogeneous attenuation on either side of the trachea, separated by a narrow anterior isthmus. Its attenuation is usually increased, compared with that of muscle, because of the iodine content of the gland. It typically enhances homogeneously following administration of IV contrast material. On MR images, the normal thyroid gland usually has intermediate signal intensity, slightly greater than the adjacent muscle, on T1-weighted

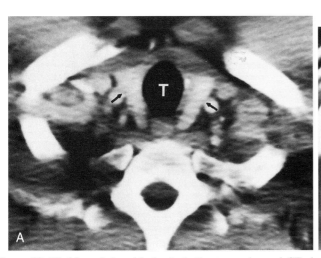
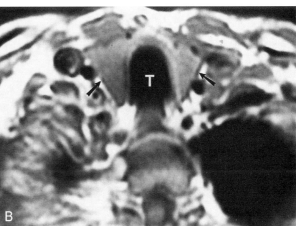

Figure 29–35. Normal thyroid gland. *A,* Contrast-enhanced CT shows typical appearance of thyroid gland *(arrows).* Enhancement is homogeneous. T, trachea. *B,* T1-weighted axial MR image shows homogeneous intermediate signal intensity typical of normal thyroid gland *(arrows).* T, trachea.

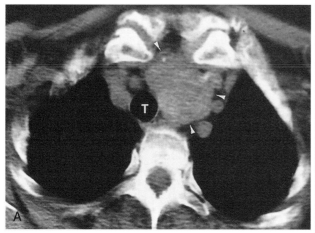

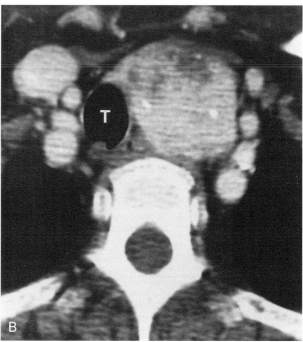

Figure 29–36. Thyroid goiter. *A,* CT shows heterogeneous superior mediastinal mass *(arrowheads)* with punctate calcification. Images at thoracic inlet (not shown) confirmed contiguity of mass with the left thyroid lobe, consistent with intrathoracic extension of goiter. *B,* Contrast-enhanced CT shows heterogeneous enhancement of mass. T, trachea.

images and higher signal intensity on T2-weighted images (see Fig. 29–35).

Most thyroid masses in the mediastinum are caused by intrathoracic extension of thyroid goiters, which can account for up to 10% of mediastinal masses resected at thoracotomy. True ectopic thyroid masses in the mediastinum are rare. Typically, a thyroid goiter extends into the thyropericardiac space anterior to the recurrent laryngeal nerve and brachiocephalic vessels, although posterior extension adjacent to the trachea occurs in 20%. Rarely, thyroid masses may extend behind the esophagus and present as a posterior mediastinal mass.

A mediastinal goiter is usually detected on chest radiographs as a thoracic inlet or superior mediastinal mass that deviates and occasionally narrows the trachea.[20, 78, 84, 105, 107, 182, 227] Although scintigraphy can detect mediastinal goiters, the uptake of technetium or iodine is variable. The CT appearance of a mediastinal goiter is variable, but the goiter can be confidently diagnosed when continuity of the mass with the thyroid gland is visible. Additional features useful in establishing the diagnosis include the following:

1. Heterogeneous attenuation with areas of both high and low attenuation on non–contrast-enhanced scans.
2. Marked enhancement following administration of IV contrast material.
3. Focal punctate or curvilinear calcifications (Figs. 29–36 and 29–37).

The cystic and adenomatoid composition of goiters results in a heterogeneous appearance on both T1-weighted and T2-weighted MR images (Fig. 29–38). On T1-weighted images, goiters may show lower signal intensity than normal thyroid, but high signal intensity can be seen in areas of subacute hemorrhage, colloid cysts, and adenomas. Goiters show high signal intensity on T2-weighted images.

Tortuous Great Vessels

Tortuosity of the great vessels is a common cause of a superior mediastinal abnormality on a chest radiograph. The most common location of the radiographic abnormality is in the right paratracheal region because the right brachiocephalic artery in older patients often has a tortuous course before giving rise to the right subclavian and common carotid arteries. CT without contrast enhancement can often determine that the tortuous vessels are the cause of the apparent mass. Calcification within the vessel walls allows confident identification of tortuous arteries. If any doubt exists as to the vascular nature of the mass, IV contrast enhancement easily identifies the vessels (Fig. 29–39).

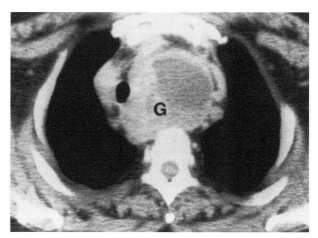

Figure 29–37. Mediastinal goiter. Contrast-enhanced CT shows large goiter *(G)* displacing the trachea to the right, and the left common carotid and subclavian arteries to the left. Enhancement is heterogeneous.

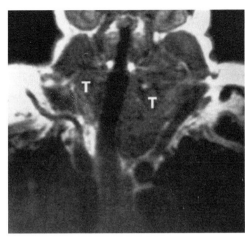

Figure 29–38. Mediastinal goiter. Coronal MR image shows mediastinal thyroid tissue (T) on both sides of trachea, which is deviated to the right at the thoracic inlet.

Anterior Mediastinal Abnormalities

Approximately half of all mediastinal masses occur in the anterior mediastinum. Lesions that occur preferentially in the anterior mediastinum include thymic lesions (cysts, thymolipoma, thymoma, thymic carcinoma), parathyroid adenoma, germ cell tumors, hemangioma, and lymphatic malformations.[34, 243] Lymphoma is another common cause of an anterior mediastinal mass, but it will be considered in the section on diffuse mediastinal disease.

Thymic Lesions

Normal Thymus

The thymus is a bilobed, triangular gland that occupies the thyropericardiac space of the anterior mediastinum and extends inferiorly to the heart.[17, 49, 70, 182, 238] The normal morphology and size of the thymus change markedly with

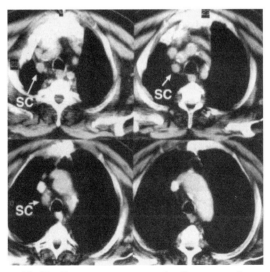

Figure 29–39. Tortuous great vessels. Contrast-enhanced CT shows tortuous right brachiocephalic and subclavian artery (SC) causing a right paratracheal "mass." Calcifications can be seen within the arterial wall.

age.[172] Wide variation exists in the normal size of the thymus, particularly in children and young adults. In the newborn, the thymus gland is often larger than the heart. Thymic size decreases with age as the gland undergoes fatty infiltration. The atrophied thymus is often visualized on CT in patients in their fourth decade of life, but it is seen in fewer than 50% of patients over 40 years of age (Fig. 29–40).

The most useful measurement is the thickness of the lobes measured perpendicular to the long axis of the gland. The normal maximal thickness is 18 mm before age 20 years and 13 mm in older patients. Although these measurements are useful indicators of thymic abnormality, thymic shape is also important; focal contour abnormality of the thymus gland is a finding suggestive of an underlying abnormality.

On CT scans, the normal thymus manifests as a homogeneous, bilobed structure of soft tissue attenuation in the anterior mediastinum (Fig. 29–41). It is usually seen at the level of the aortic arch and the origin of the great vessels. The left lobe is usually slightly larger than the right. Rarely, a lobe is congenitally absent. The normal thymus is easily demonstrated on MRI (Fig. 29–42).

Characteristically, the thymus is homogeneous with intermediate signal intensity (less than that of fat) on T1-weighted images. Because the thymus begins to involute at puberty and is replaced by fat in older patients, the T1-weighted signal intensity of the thyroid increases with age. On T2-weighted images, the thymus shows high signal intensity similar to fat in all age groups and this can make its identification difficult in patients with abundant mediastinal fat.

Thymic masses, on occasion, can be difficult to distinguish from normal thymus.[244] Two important rules should be remembered:

1. Thymic masses usually manifest on CT or MRI as round masses and do not conform to the shape of the normal thymus.
2. Thymic masses usually show heterogeneous attenuation on CT with areas of decreased attenuation and possibly calcification.

Thymic Hyperplasia

Thymic hyperplasia can occur in association with hyperthyroidism, acromegaly, Addison's disease, and stress and in patients receiving chemotherapy or radiation therapy.[22, 79, 94, 153] Differentiating between hyperplasia and other causes of thymic enlargement can be difficult as there are no specific CT attenuation or MR signal intensity characteristics associated with hyperplasia. Thymic rebound or hyperplasia occurs in patients after chemotherapy or radiation therapy and it can be difficult to distinguish this enlargement from recurrent tumor. Generally, with rebound hyperplasia, the thymus has a normal shape and shows homogeneous attenuation on CT or homogeneous signal intensity on MR images (Fig. 29–43; see Fig. 29-40B). Asymmetry of the lobes, focal contour abnormalities, and heterogeneous signal intensity on MR or CT are suggestive of tumor.

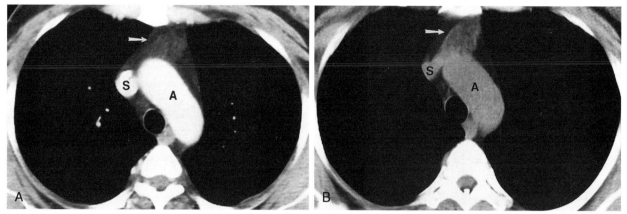

Figure 29–40. Thymus gland in a 42-year-old woman with breast carcinoma. *A,* Contrast-enhanced CT shows fatty replacement of thymus gland. Residual thymic tissue manifests as linear areas of soft tissue in anterior mediastinal fat *(arrow)*. *B,* Non–contrast-enhanced CT 6 months after bone marrow transplantation shows increased soft tissue in anterior mediastinum, consistent with thymic hyperplasia *(arrow)*. A, aorta; S, superior vena cava.

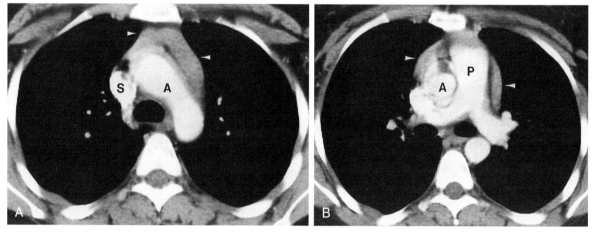

Figure 29–41. Normal thymus gland in a 17-year-old girl. *A* and *B,* Contrast-enhanced CT shows normal thymus gland in anterior mediastinum *(arrowheads)*. Homogeneous attenuation, smooth contours, and close association of lobes to vascular structures in the anterior mediastinum can be seen. A, aorta; P, main pulmonary artery; S, superior vena cava.

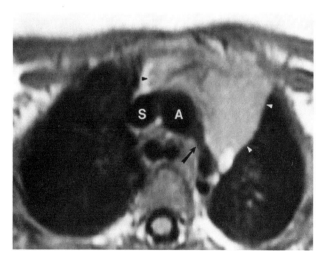

Figure 29–42. Normal thymus in 9-month-old child with coarctation of the aorta. Axial T1-weighted MR image shows thymus gland *(arrowheads)* in the mediastinum anterior to the aorta with homogeneous, intermediate signal intensity less than that of fat. The *arrow* indicates aortic coarctation. A, aorta; S, superior vena cava. (Case courtesy of Donald Frush, M.D., Duke University Medical Center, Durham, NC.)

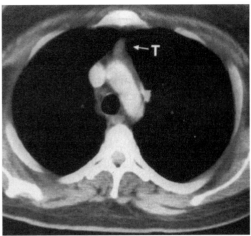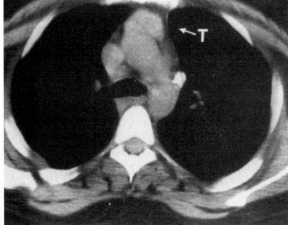

Figure 29–43. Thymic rebound. *A,* CT at the time of chemotherapy. The thymus (T) is small. *B,* CT after cessation of chemotherapy shows that the thymus (T) has increased in size.

Thymic Cysts

Thymic cysts comprise approximately 3% of all anterior mediastinal masses and are either congenital or secondary to inflammation or malignancy (Hodgkin's lymphoma, seminoma, thymic carcinoma).[18, 47, 89, 112, 118, 153, 168, 243, 246]

Congenital thymic cysts most likely arise from remnants of the thymopharyngeal duct and are usually thin-walled, unilocular lesions less than 6 cm in diameter. On CT, they are homogeneous, show the attenuation of water, and have very thin or imperceptible walls. On MRI, they manifest as well-circumscribed, anterior mediastinal masses of high signal intensity on T2-weighted images. Signal intensity usually increases with increasing TR. Occasionally, thymic cysts appear as solid masses on CT because they are filled with proteinaceous fluid. In these cases, MRI can be useful for confirming the cystic nature of the lesion (Fig. 29–44).

Acquired thymic cysts occur in the setting of inflammation or malignancy. Associated malignancies include Hodgkin's lymphoma, seminoma, thymoma, and thymic carcinoma (Fig. 29–45). These cysts usually have walls of variable thickness, are multilocular, and range in size from 3 to 17 cm in diameter. These cysts can contain hemorrhage or calcification. As such, the CT and MR features of acquired thymic cysts are more variable than those of congenital thymic cysts.

Because of their association with thymic neoplasia, care must be taken in the interpretation of cystic lesions of the anterior mediastinum (see Fig. 29–45). A thymic cyst must be evaluated further (by biopsy or resection) to exclude malignancy if it fits any of the following descriptions:

- Multilocular
- Heterogeneous
- Thick-walled
- Associated with a soft tissue component

Thymolipoma

Thymolipomas are rare, benign, slowly growing neoplasms of the anterior mediastinum.[153, 213, 232, 267] They occur with equal incidence in men and women and, although the age range of presentation is wide, most are diagnosed in young adults. On CT, these masses are typically large, show the attenuation of homogeneous fat, and conform to adjacent structures. They are not locally invasive although compression of adjacent structures occurs in approximately 50% of patients. Because they consist of fat and residual thymic tissue, thymolipomas usually show high signal intensity (similar to fat) with interspersed areas of intermediate signal intensity on both T1-weighted and T2-weighted MR images.

Thymoma

Thymomas account for approximately 20% of all mediastinal tumors and are the most common primary tumor of the anterior mediastinum.* Seventy-five percent of thymomas occur in the anterior mediastinum, 15% occur in both the anterior and superior mediastinum, and 6% occur in the superior mediastinum. Another 4% occur ectopically, with the posterior mediastinum being the least common location.

Although thymomas can occur in children, most patients are older than 40 years at presentation. Seventy percent of affected patients present in the fifth and sixth decades of life. The incidence in men and women is the same. Most affected patients are asymptomatic at presentation, and the lesion is detected on routine chest radiographs. Chest pain, cough, and symptoms related to compression of adjacent structures occur in approximately 33% of patients.

Paraneoplastic syndromes are common and include myasthenia gravis (50%), hypogammaglobulinemia (10%), and pure red blood cell aplasia (5%). Although up to 50% of patients with thymoma have myasthenia gravis, only 10% to 20% of patients with myasthenia gravis have a thymoma; however, 65% of these patients have lymphoid hyperplasia of the thymus. Because of the strong association between myasthenia gravis and thymoma, CT is commonly performed in patients with symptoms of myasthenia gravis even if the chest radiograph is normal.

Thymomas are usually 5 to 10 cm in diameter and are

---

*See References 60, 150, 153, 173, 178, 212, 217, 243, 250, 254, and 264.

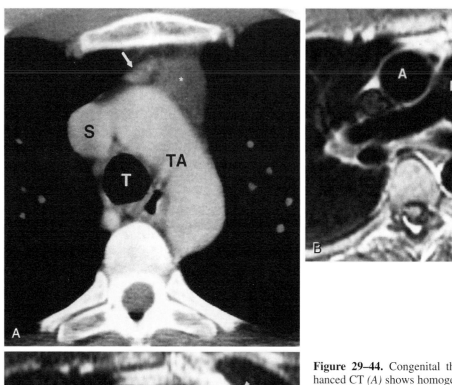

Figure 29–44. Congenital thymic cyst. Contrast-enhanced CT *(A)* shows homogeneous, water-attenuation cyst *(asterisk)* in the anterior mediastinum. Note absence of perceptible walls and residual right thymic lobe *(arrow)*. MR images obtained more caudally show that the mass *(arrowheads)* is homogeneous and of low signal intensity on the T1-weighted image *(B)* and of high signal intensity on the T2-weighted image *(C)*. The MRI appearance is typical of a cyst. A, ascending aorta; P, main pulmonary artery; S, superior vena cava; T, trachea; TA, transverse aorta.

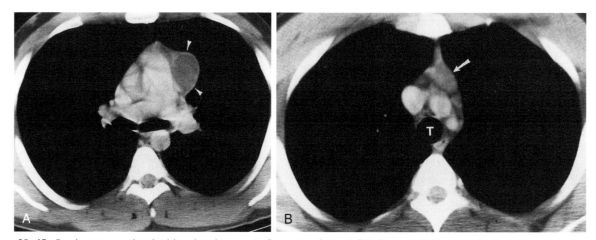

Figure 29–45. Seminoma associated with a thymic cyst. *A,* Contrast-enhanced CT shows well-circumscribed water-attenuation mass in anterior mediastinum. The wall *(arrowheads)* is thin but perceptible. *B,* A more cephalic image reveals a soft tissue component of the mass *(arrow)*. Resection revealed the seminoma. T, trachea.

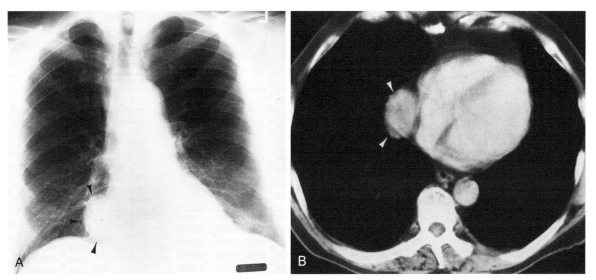

Figure 29–46. Thymoma in a patient with myasthenia gravis. *A,* Posteroanterior chest radiograph shows mass in the right cardiophrenic angle *(arrowheads). B,* Contrast-enhanced CT confirms well-circumscribed heterogeneous cardiophrenic-angle mass *(arrowheads).* Resection revealed the thymoma.

well marginated, smooth or lobulated mediastinal masses that characteristically arise from one lobe of the thymus. They are usually located anterior to the aortic arch but can occur in the cardiophrenic angle (Fig. 29–46). Most lesions are homogeneous, but necrosis and hemorrhage occur in up to one third.

On CT or MRI scans, thymomas typically manifest as smooth or lobulated masses that distort the normal contour of the thymus (Fig. 29–47). They are typically unilateral masses, although bilateral mediastinal involvement can occur. On CT they can manifest as homogeneous or heterogeneous soft tissue–attenuation masses. Intratumoral cysts or areas of necrosis may be seen. Enhancement following IV administration of contrast material is variable. Calcification, seen in up to 7% of cases, is usually thin, linear, and located in the capsule. On MR images, thymomas manifest with low to intermediate signal intensity (similar to skeletal

muscle) on T1-weighted images and high signal intensity on T2-weighted images. Because up to 33% of thymomas have focal areas of necrosis, hemorrhage, and cystic change, the masses can have heterogeneous signal intensity. MRI can occasionally reveal fibrous septa within the masses.

Up to 34% of thymomas show local invasion. Such lesions are best termed invasive thymomas rather than malignant thymomas. Histologic features and size do not seem to affect the propensity for invasive behavior. Furthermore, it can be quite difficult to predict biologic behavior of thymomas on the basis of CT or MRI findings alone. Surgical exploration is the most reliable means of determining invasion. Findings that suggest invasive thymoma on CT or MRI include the following (Figs. 29–48 to 29–50):

1. Poorly defined or infiltrative margins.
2. Definite vascular or chest wall invasion.
3. Irregular interface with adjacent lung.
4. Evidence of spread to ipsilateral pleura.

Pleural spread manifests either as isolated pleural nodules ("drop metastases") or as a contiguous pleural mass, often mimicking mesothelioma. Transdiaphragmatic spread may occur; hence, staging MR or CT studies should include the upper abdomen. Pleural effusion is uncommon despite the frequent occurrence of pleural metastases.

Thymic Carcinoma

Thymic carcinomas account for 20% of thymic tumors.[51, 60, 97, 142, 182, 201, 243, 263] They are aggressive malignancies that often exhibit marked local invasion and early dissemination to regional lymph nodes and distant sites. Distant metastases (to lung, liver, brain, and bone) are detected in 50% to 65% of patients at presentation. Tissue studies typically reveal squamous cell carcinoma and lymphoepithelioma-like carcinoma. Symptoms (chest pain, dyspnea, cough, SVC syndrome) are usually the result of

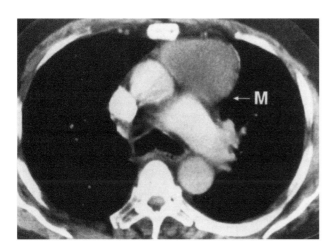

Figure 29–47. Thymoma. Contrast-enhanced CT shows large anterior mediastinal mass (M) anterior to aorta and pulmonary artery. Main pulmonary artery is displaced posteriorly.

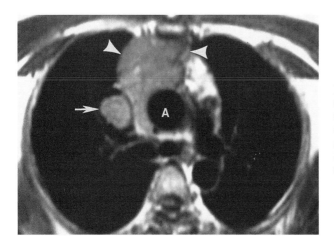

Figure 29–48. Invasive thymoma in a patient with symptoms of superior vena cava (SVC) obstruction. Axial T1-weighted MR images show infiltrative soft tissue mass *(arrowheads)* of intermediate signal intensity encasing the aorta and extending into the SVC *(arrow)*. A, aorta. (From Erasmus JJ, McAdams HP, Donnelly LF, Spritzer CE: MR imaging of mediastinal masses. Magn Reson Imaging Clin North Am 8:59–89, 2000.)

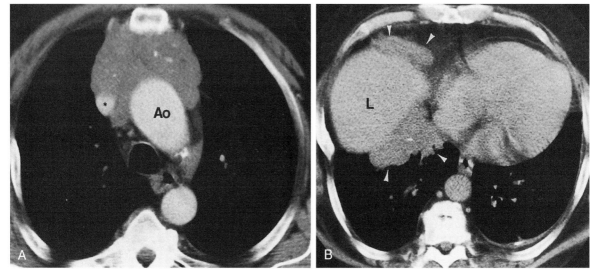

Figure 29–49. Invasive thymoma. *A* and *B*, Contrast-enhanced CT shows heterogeneous anterior mediastinal mass with focal areas of calcification. Note mass extension between superior vena cava *(asterisk)* and ascending aorta (Ao in *A*) and contiguous extension to hemidiaphragm *(arrowheads* in *B*). L, liver.

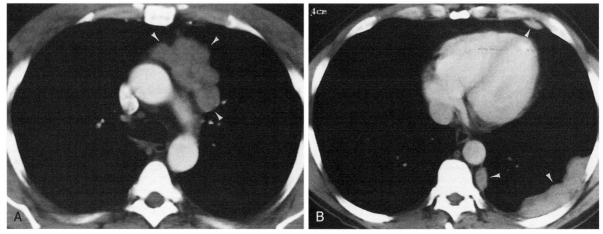

Figure 29–50. Invasive thymoma with pleural metastases. *A* and *B*, Contrast-enhanced CT shows lobular heterogeneous mass *(arrowheads* in *A*) in anterior mediastinum. Noncontiguous pleural metastases ("drop metastases") *(arrowheads* in *B*) are present in the left hemithorax.

compression or invasion of adjacent structures and, unlike thymomas, paraneoplastic syndromes are rare.

Radiologically, thymic carcinomas usually manifest as large, poorly marginated anterior mediastinal masses and are frequently associated with intrathoracic lymphadenopathy and pleural and pericardial effusions. Focal pleural implants are uncommon. On CT, they usually show heterogeneous attenuation and have poorly defined, infiltrative margins (Fig. 29–51). On MRI, they typically show intermediate signal intensity (slightly higher than skeletal muscle) on T1-weighted images and high signal intensity on T2-weighted images. Signal intensity can be heterogeneous because of hemorrhage and necrosis within the masses. MRI can be helpful for revealing local soft tissue and vascular invasion.

Neuroendocrine Tumors of the Thymus

Neuroendocrine tumors are uncommon lesions of the anterior mediastinum.[34, 35, 131, 132, 211] These tumors have varying malignant potential that ranges from relatively benign (thymic carcinoid) to highly malignant (small cell carcinoma of the thymus). Thymic carcinoid tumor is the most common of this group of tumors. Affected patients are typically in the fourth and fifth decades of life; there is a male predominance. Up to 50% of affected patients have hormonal abnormalities and up to 35% have Cushing's syndrome because of tumoral production of adrenocorticotropic hormone (ACTH). Nonfunctioning thymic carcinoids may be seen in association with the multiple endocrine neoplasia syndrome, type 1.

Radiologically, these tumors typically manifest as large masses with a propensity for local invasion. Focal areas of necrosis and punctate calcification may be present. On CT or MRI, the masses usually show heterogeneous attenuation or signal intensity, respectively (Fig. 29–52).

Germ Cell Tumors

Germ cell tumors (teratomas, seminomas, embryonal carcinomas, endodermal sinus tumors, and choriocarcino-

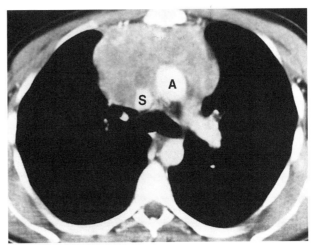

Figure 29–52. Thymic carcinoid. Contrast-enhanced CT shows large anterior mediastinal mass. The mass appears heterogeneous, and infiltration of mediastinum can be seen, with extension of the mass between vascular structures. A, aorta; S, superior vena cava.

mas) are thought to arise from mediastinal remnants of embryonal cell migration.[50, 143, 148, 149, 187, 188, 214, 243, 258] They comprise 10% to 15% of anterior mediastinal tumors. The mediastinum is the most common extragonadal primary site of these lesions, and mediastinal lesions account for 60% of all germ cell tumors in adults. Germ cell tumors usually occur in young adults (mean age, 27 years). Most malignant germ cell tumors (>90%) occur in men, whereas benign lesions (mature teratomas) occur with equal incidence in men and women.

Mediastinal Teratoma

Teratomas, the most common mediastinal germ cell tumors, are composed of elements that arise from more than one of the three primitive germ cell layers.[46, 72, 108, 149, 170, 187, 216, 220, 243] These tumors are classified as (1) mature, (2) immature, or (3) malignant.

Mature or benign teratomas are composed of different tissue types (ectoderm, endoderm, mesoderm), with ectodermal derivatives predominating. The term *dermoid cyst* is commonly applied to the tumors in which the ectodermal components predominate. Mature teratomas are common, accounting for 70% of germ cell tumors in childhood and 60% of mediastinal germ cell tumors in adults. Mature teratomas occur most frequently in children and young adults. Patients can be asymptomatic, but chest pain, dyspnea and cough, caused by compression of adjacent structures, are common symptoms. By definition, patients with mature teratoma have normal serum levels of β-human chorionic gonadotropin hormone (β-hCG) and alpha-fetoprotein (AFP); elevation of either of these markers implies a malignant component. Complete resection is the treatment for teratomas and results in a complete cure. Although they are benign, these tumors may be difficult to remove because they are adherent to local structures.

Teratomas typically occur in the anterior mediastinum, although occurrence at other sites, including the middle and posterior mediastinum, accounts for up to 20% of cases. Mature teratomas manifest on CT or MRI as smooth

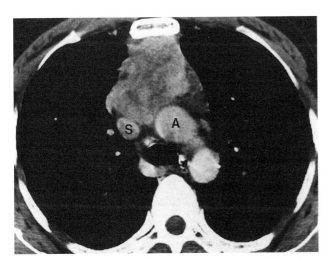

Figure 29–51. Thymic carcinoma. Contrast-enhanced CT shows heterogeneous mass in anterior mediastinum. Low-attenuation regions are consistent with necrosis. A, aorta; S, superior vena cava.

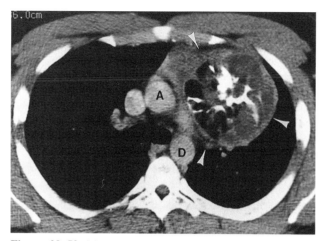

Figure 29–53. Mature teratoma. Contrast-enhanced CT shows large anterior mediastinal mass *(arrowheads)*. The mass, which is composed of fat, calcium, and fluid, is heterogeneous in attenuation. The CT appearance is typical of a mature teratoma. A, ascending aorta; D, descending aorta.

or lobulated mediastinal masses that typically have cystic and solid components, whereas malignant teratomas are usually poorly marginated masses containing areas of necrosis.

The combination of fluid, soft tissue, calcium, or fat is diagnostic of a teratoma (Fig. 29–53); the finding of a fat-fluid level within a mass on CT or MRI is also diagnostic. Fat occurs in up to 75% of mature teratomas and up to 40% of malignant teratomas; however, only 17% to 39% of mature teratomas have all the tissue components, and approximately 15% of mature teratomas manifest only a unilocular or multilocular cystic component (Fig. 29–54). Because of the varying composition of soft tissue, fat, calcium, and hemorrhage, MRI typically demonstrates heterogeneous signal intensity and this finding can be useful in differentiating teratomas from thymomas and lymphomas.

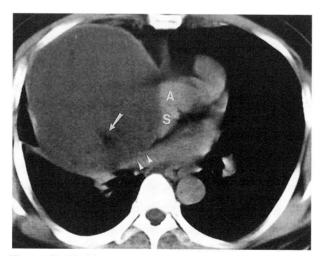

Figure 29–54. Mature teratoma. CT shows a large, predominantly water-attenuation, anterior mediastinal mass with a small focal area of fat *(arrow)*. Mass effect can be visualized on the superior vena cava (S) and the superior pulmonary vein *(arrowheads)*. A, ascending aorta.

Mature teratomas have been reported to rupture into lung, pleural space, and pericardium in up to 33% of patients, and CT or MRI can be useful in detecting fat within these regions.

Seminoma

Seminoma is the most common pure histologic type of malignant mediastinal germ cell tumor in men and accounts for 40% of such tumors.[10, 143, 175, 177, 231, 243] Affected patients are usually in the third and fourth decades of life and are symptomatic at presentation. β-hCG and AFP levels are normal; elevation of AFP indicates a nonseminomatous component of the tumor. On CT or MRI, seminomas manifest as large lobulated masses showing homogeneous attenuation or signal intensity in the anterior mediastinum (Fig. 29–55). Cysts or areas of necrosis may also be seen in association with mediastinal seminoma (see Fig. 29–45). Invasion of adjacent structures is uncommon and calcification is rare. Metastases to regional nodes may occur.

Nonseminomatous Germ Cell Malignancies

The nonseminomatous germ cell tumors of the mediastinum include embryonal cell carcinoma, endodermal sinus tumor, choriocarcinoma, and mixed germ cell tumors.[133, 148, 175] Teratoma with embryonal cell carcinoma (teratocarcinoma) is the next most common subtype, with pure endodermal sinus tumor, choriocarcinoma, and embryonal carcinoma being much less common. Most patients with malignant nonseminomatous germ cell tumors are symptomatic at presentation, with chest pain, cough, dyspnea, weight loss, and fever. Up to 80% of affected patients have elevated levels of AFP and 54% have elevated levels of β-hCG. An association exists between malignant nonseminomatous germ cell tumors of the mediastinum and hematologic malignancies. Up to 20% of affected patients have Klinefelter's syndrome.

On CT or MRI, these tumors manifest as large, poorly marginated masses showing heterogeneous attenuation or signal intensity (Figs. 29–56 and 29–57). Invasion of the adjacent mediastinal structures, chest wall, and lung, as

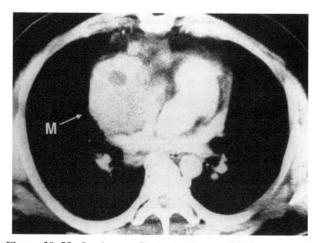

Figure 29–55. Seminoma. Contrast-enhanced CT shows anterior mediastinal mass (M) with a central area of low attenuation consistent with necrosis.

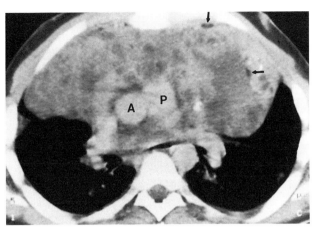

Figure 29–56. Malignant teratoma. Contrast-enhanced CT shows a large anterior mediastinal mass. The mass is heterogeneous in attenuation with components of soft tissue, fluid, calcium, and fat *(arrows)*. The mediastinal invasion is diffuse. A, aorta; P, pulmonary artery.

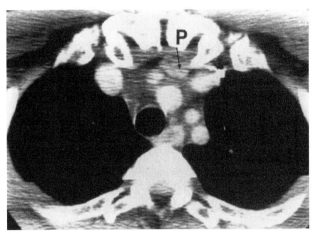

Figure 29–58. Ectopic parathyroid adenoma. CT shows a soft tissue mass in a patient who had undergone neck dissection for hyperparathyroidism with persistently elevated serum calcium. The parathyroid gland (P) is ectopic, located posterior to manubrium.

well as metastases to the regional lymph nodes and distant sites, is common.

Parathyroid Adenoma

Because neck exploration for parathyroid gland removal is curative in over 90% of patients with primary hyperparathyroidism, surgeons often do not obtain preoperative imaging studies to localize the parathyroid glands; however, 10% of parathyroid adenomas are ectopic in location and the majority of ectopic adenomas are located either in the region of the tracheoesophageal groove or in the anterior mediastinum.* Such ectopic adenomas can be missed at surgical exploration. Preoperative localization of ectopic parathyroid adenomas can reduce operative time, postoper-

---

*See References 1, 8, 114–116, 120, 127, 135, 145, 146, 189, 221, 239, and 241.

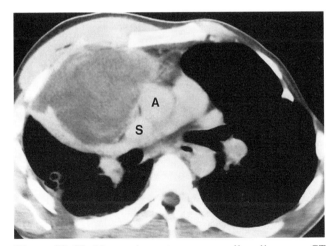

Figure 29–57. Nonseminomatous germ cell malignancy. CT shows large mixed-attenuation anterior mediastinal mass. Transthoracic needle aspiration biopsy revealed endodermal sinus tumor. The left pectoralis major muscle is absent, consistent with Poland syndrome. A, aorta; S, superior vena cava.

ative morbidity, and the need for a subsequent surgical procedure.

Imaging techniques for localizing abnormal parathyroid glands include sonography, radionuclide imaging (technetium-99m–sestamibi [^{99m}Tc-MIBI], ^{99m}Tc-tetrofosmin), CT, and MRI. On CT, ectopic mediastinal parathyroid glands manifest as 1- to 2-cm rounded masses that may resemble lymph nodes (Fig. 29–58). CT or MRI can detect these glands, but careful evaluation is required so that small lesions are not overlooked.

MRI is accurate in identifying abnormal parathyroid glands in ectopic locations. Functioning parathyroid adenomas show intermediate signal intensity on T1-weighted images and usually show marked increased signal intensity on T2-weighted images (Fig. 29–59). Similar findings are seen in cases of parathyroid hyperplasia and carcinoma. Up to 13% of abnormal glands, however, do not show high signal intensity on T2-weighted images because of fibrosis or hemorrhage. Although MR is comparable or superior to other imaging modalities for detecting parathyroid disease (sensitivity, 78%; specificity, 90%; accuracy, 90%), the most appropriate role of MRI is as an adjunct to ^{99m}Tc-MIBI radionuclide imaging. In this setting MRI provides accurate anatomic location of the adenoma and can be useful in predicting the need for mediastinotomy or lateral cervical incision.

Although the precise role of imaging in the evaluation of a virgin neck for hyperparathyroidism may be debated, imaging is useful in second-look procedures and in those patients considered to be at high risk for surgery. In this population, the success rate for surgery is reduced, ranging from 64% to 90%, and the combined use of ^{99m}Tc-MIBI and MRI has been shown to be 89% sensitive and 95% specific for preoperative localization.

Lymphatic Malformations

Lymphatic malformations (previously called lymphangiomas) are rare benign lesions that comprise 0.7% to 4.5% of all mediastinal tumors.[123, 185, 197, 225, 230, 233, 268] Approxi-

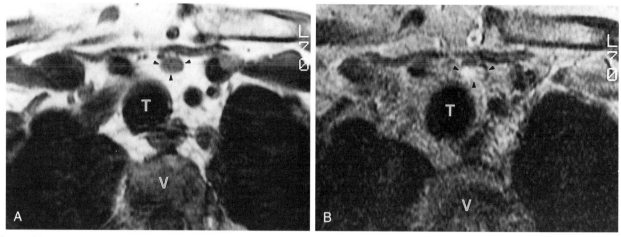

Figure 29–59. Ectopic parathyroid adenoma in a woman with persistent hyperparathyroidism after surgical neck exploration. MR images show 1-cm mass *(arrowheads)* in anterior mediastinum with intermediate signal intensity (similar to muscle) on T1-weighted image *(A)* and high signal intensity on T2-weighted image *(B)*. MR appearance is typical of parathyroid adenoma. T, trachea; V, vertebral body. (Reprinted with permission from Erasmus JJ, McAdams HP, Donnelly LF, Spritzer CE: MR imaging of mediastinal masses. Magn Reson Imaging Clin North Am 8:59–89, 2000.)

mately 75% occur in the neck, 20% in the axillary region, and 5% in the mediastinum. Primary mediastinal lymphatic malformations are rare and most mediastinal lesions are the result of tumor extension from the neck. Lymphatic malformations are usually located in the superior and anterior mediastinum, although they can occur in any mediastinal compartment. They usually occur in patients less than 2 years old and there is a male predominance. In adults, lymphatic malformations are usually located in the mediastinum and are often the result of recurrence of an incompletely resected childhood tumor.

On CT, these lesions manifest as lobular, multicystic tumors that surround and infiltrate adjacent mediastinal structures (Fig. 29–60). They can appear solid on CT because of protein or hemorrhage within the cysts. The cysts are typically 1 to 2 cm in diameter, and the septa may enhance following administration of IV contrast material.

MRI can be useful in confirming the cystic nature of these lesions; lymphatic malformations usually show markedly increased signal intensity on T2-weighted images. Their appearance on T1-weighted sequences is more variable, although most show low to intermediate signal intensity (similar to skeletal muscle) and can contain focal areas of signal intensity higher than that of muscle. Occasionally, lymphatic malformations show high signal intensity similar to that of fat on T1-weighted images.

Because surgical resection is the treatment of choice, multiplanar MRI can be useful in preoperative evaluation of local invasion and determination of anatomic extent of tumor.

Hemangiomas

Hemangiomas are rare mediastinal tumors that account for less than 0.5% of all mediastinal masses.[117, 121, 163, 223, 224]

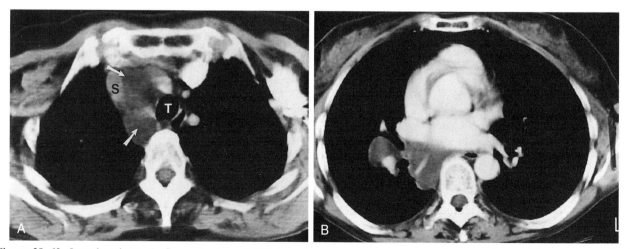

Figure 29–60. Lymphangioma. *A,* Contrast-enhanced CT shows homogeneous, water-attenuation mass *(arrows)* in superior mediastinum, which arose in the neck. S, superior vena cava; T, trachea. *B,* The mass diffusely infiltrates mediastinum and extends into the right hilum.

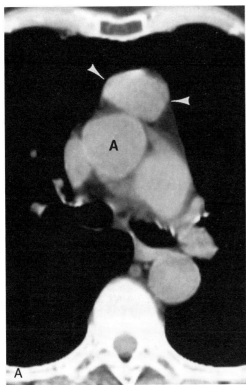

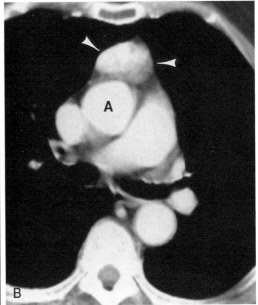

Figure 29–61. Hemangioma. *A,* Non–contrast-enhanced CT shows small homogeneous anterior mediastinal mass *(arrowheads)*. *B,* Contrast-enhanced CT shows marked enhancement, typical of hemangioma *(arrowheads)*. A, ascending aorta.

Mediastinal hemangiomas usually occur in the anterior (68%) or posterior mediastinum (22%), although multicompartment involvement occurs in up to 14% of cases. Most mediastinal lesions are cavernous hemangiomas and are composed of large interconnecting vascular spaces with varying amounts of interposed stromal elements such as fat and fibrous tissue. Focal areas of organized thrombus can calcify as phleboliths.

On radiographs, hemangiomas manifest as sharp, smoothly marginated mediastinal masses. Phleboliths are seen in less than 10% of cases. CT typically reveals a heterogeneous mass with intense central or peripheral rim-like enhancement after administration of IV contrast material (Fig. 29–61). Hemangiomas typically show heterogeneous signal intensity on T1-weighted images. In lesions with significant stromal fat, linear areas of increased signal intensity on T1-weighted images can occasionally be identified. The central vascular lakes typically become markedly hyperintense on T2-weighted images, a suggestive feature (Fig. 29–62).

Middle Mediastinal Abnormalities

Lesions that occur primarily in the middle mediastinum include esophageal lesions, airway lesions, foregut duplication cysts, and pericardial cysts.

Esophagus

Esophageal Cancer

CT is used to help stage esophageal carcinoma by demonstrating the following (Fig. 29–63):*

---

*See References 73, 93, 109, 144, 147, 153, 179, 196, 202, 207, and 248.

- Thickness of the esophageal wall
- Length of the lesion
- Involvement of adjacent structures such as airway, aorta, pericardium, and spine
- Nodal spread to regional mediastinal, celiac, and gastrohepatic ligament nodes

Endoscopy, endoscopic ultrasound, and esophagography are also helpful in staging esophageal carcinoma. Invasion of local structures is common because the esophagus lacks a serosa. CT and MRI can both overestimate or underestimate the degree of local invasion because the lack of normal fat planes between the esophagus and adjacent structures makes invasion difficult to determine.

Anterior displacement of the carina or left main bronchus suggests airway invasion; contact with the aorta that exceeds one quarter of the aortic circumference suggests the possibility of aortic invasion. All imaging findings must be interpreted in conjunction with the patient's clinical status when planning treatment. CT is also useful in planning radiation treatment ports and for imaging complications resulting from esophagectomy.

The normal esophagus is not optimally demonstrated on MRI because of peristaltic motion and relatively poor spatial resolution. Distinguishing small mucosal tumors from normal esophagus is difficult because both show intermediate signal intensity on T1-weighted images and high signal intensity on T2-weighted images. The role of MRI for intrathoracic staging of esophageal neoplasms is limited. Although some authors have reported high intrathoracic staging accuracy for MRI, most reports suggest that MRI is no better than CT in this regard. MRI can be useful as a problem-solving modality, however, when invasion of pericardium or heart is suspected on CT or if the patient is allergic to iodinated contrast material.

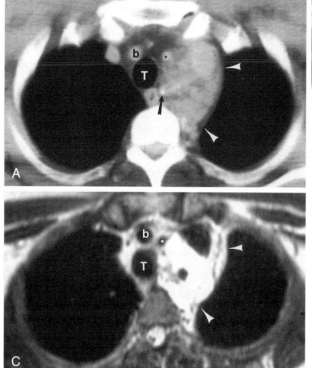

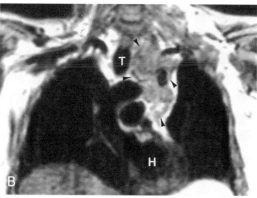

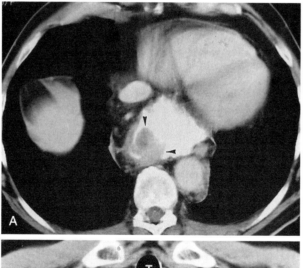

Figure 29–62. Hemangioma. *A,* CT shows hetero-geneous mass *(arrowheads)* in anterior mediastinum. Punctate calcification is consistent with phlebolith within mass *(arrow). B,* Coronal T1-weighted MR image shows mass of intermediate signal intensity *(arrowheads)* in anterior and superior mediastinum. Septa within the mass and invasion of mediastinum can be seen. *C,* Axial T2-weighted MR image shows high signal intensity within the mass *(arrowheads).* The MRI appearance is typical for hemangioma. b, brachiocephalic artery; H, heart, T, trachea. The *asterisk* indicates the carotid artery.

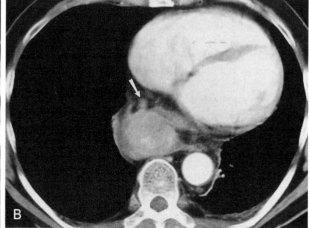

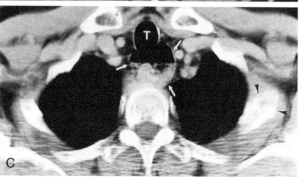

Figure 29–63. Esophageal malignancy. *A,* Contrast-enhanced CT shows a large, barium-filled hiatal hernia containing a polypoid mass *(arrowheads). B,* The more cephalic image shows a large heterogeneous esophageal mass. An adjacent lymph node is consistent with metastasis *(arrow). C,* A more cephalic image shows dilation of the esophagus and an air-fluid level *(arrows).* A metastatic left rib lesion can be seen *(arrowheads).* T, trachea.

Esophageal Dilatation

Esophageal dilatation can be easily demonstrated on CT.[52, 203] Focal dilatation occurs in Zenker's diverticulum (upper esophagus), traction diverticula resulting from granulomatous disease (middle esophagus), and epiphrenic diverticula (lower and on the right). These focal dilatations or diverticula are clearly demonstrated on CT and can be a source of confusion unless oral contrast material is administered.

Diffuse dilatation of the esophagus can occur as a result of motility disorders (achalasia, postvagotomy syndrome, Chagas' disease, scleroderma, systemic lupus erythematosus, presbyesophagus, diabetic neuropathy, esophagitis) or as a result of distal obstruction (carcinoma, stricture, extrinsic compression) (Fig. 29–64).

Airway Lesions

Tumors of the trachea or proximal bronchi can manifest as middle mediastinal masses on chest radiographs or CT.[41, 138, 164] Malignant neoplasms account for 90% of primary tracheal tumors. The most common primary malignancies of the trachea are squamous cell and adenoid cystic carcinomas.[11, 158, 159, 194] Benign neoplasms such as papilloma, adenoma, hamartoma, chondroma, leiomyoma, and granular cell myoblastoma account for less than 10% of primary tracheal tumors. The most common primary malignancy of the major bronchi is non–small cell lung cancer. Carcinoid tumors and mucoepidermoid carcinoma are less common bronchial malignancies that occur in younger patients.[129, 166, 211] These lesions are described in Chapter 28.

Foregut Cysts

Foregut cysts, which account for approximately 20% of all mediastinal masses, probably arise as a result of maldevelopment of the primitive foregut.[234, 235] Bronchogenic cysts are the most common mediastinal foregut cysts; esophageal duplication and neurenteric cysts are less common.

It is important not to confuse these cystic masses with fluid-filled structures within the mediastinum such as fluid-

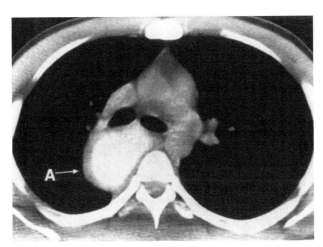

Figure 29–64. Achalasia. CT shows dilated esophagus (A) in a patient with achalasia. The esophagus displaces the azygos vein to the right.

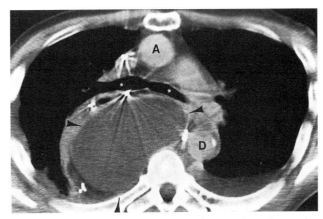

Figure 29–65. Thoracic lymphocele after esophageal resection and gastric pull-through. Contrast-enhanced CT shows large homogeneous fluid collection *(arrowheads)* in middle/posterior mediastinum displacing tracheal carina *(asterisks)* anteriorly and gastric pull-through anterolaterally. A, ascending aorta; D, descending aorta.

filled pericardial recesses, loculated pleural fluid, extension of ascites through the esophageal hiatus, mediastinal extension of pancreatic pseudocyst, or a fluid-filled and dilated esophagus (Figs. 29–65 and 29–66).

Bronchogenic Cyst

Bronchogenic cysts are thought to arise from abnormal budding of the ventral foregut.* Histopathologically, they are lined with ciliated respiratory epithelium, cartilage, smooth muscle, fibrous tissue, and mucous glands. Most bronchogenic cysts occur in the middle mediastinum, typically in the subcarinal or right paratracheal region. In up to 15% of cases, bronchogenic cysts are found in unusual locations including the pleural space, diaphragm, pericardium, lung, and abdomen.

On CT, bronchogenic cysts typically manifest as round or spherical, sharply marginated, homogeneous masses. Approximately half of bronchogenic cysts show water attenuation on CT (Fig. 29–67). The remainder show increased attenuation, most likely secondary to proteinaceous debris or hemorrhage within the lesions (Fig. 29–68). A small percentage have calcified walls or contain calcium suspended within the fluid.

On MR images, lesions typically show low to intermediate signal intensity on T1-weighted images and markedly increased signal intensity on T2-weighted images. The lesions can be heterogeneous on T1-weighted images but are typically homogeneous on T2-weighted images. These MRI characteristics can be useful for differentiating cysts that appear solid on CT from solid neoplasms or lymphadenopathy. Gadolinium administration can also be helpful for distinguishing mediastinal cysts from solid neoplasms by demonstrating a lack of central enhancement and, occasionally, rim enhancement.

Because many ECG-gated T1-weighted pulse sequences have a relatively long TR, fluid-filled lesions can show

---

*See References 14, 47, 122, 141, 153, 154, 156, 162, 180, 184, and 245.

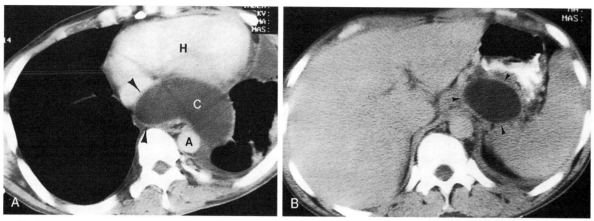

Figure 29–66. Mediastinal pseudocyst in a patient with chronic pancreatitis. *A,* Contrast-enhanced CT shows homogeneous water-attenuation mass (C) in the middle mediastinum with a thin enhancing rim *(arrowheads).* A small left pleural effusion can be seen. A, aorta; H, heart. *B,* A more caudal CT image confirms origination of mass *(arrowheads)* from the tail of the pancreas. (Case is courtesy of May Lesar, Bethesda, Md.)

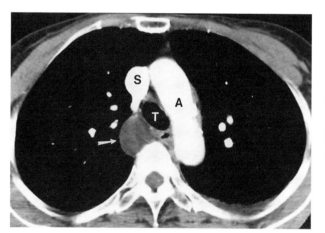

Figure 29–67. Bronchogenic cyst. Contrast-enhanced CT shows well-circumscribed, water-attenuation middle mediastinal mass *(arrow)* with imperceptible wall. The CT appearance is typical for bronchogenic cyst. A, transverse aorta; S, superior vena cava; T, trachea.

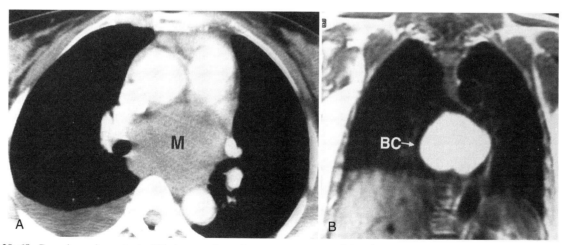

Figure 29–68. Bronchogenic cyst. *A,* CT shows a large homogeneous mass (M) of soft tissue attenuation in subcarinal region. *B,* Coronal T1-weighted MR image shows high signal intensity within the mass (BC), caused by viscous cyst fluid.

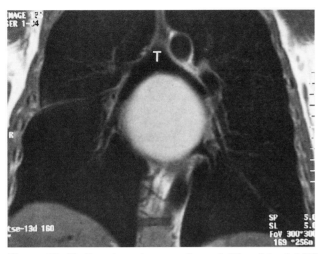

Figure 29–69. Bronchogenic cyst. Coronal T1-weighted MRI shows a subcarinal mass with high signal intensity. Both main bronchi are displaced. The subcarinal location is typical for a bronchogenic cyst. T, trachea.

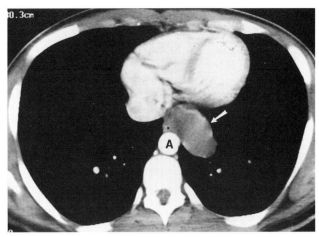

Figure 29–70. Esophageal duplication cyst. Contrast-enhanced CT shows a well-marginated, low-attenuation middle mediastinal mass *(arrow)* adjacent to the left lateral wall of the esophagus *(asterisk)*. Note the lack of enhancement. A, aorta.

intermediate signal intensity. Cysts with proteinaceous, mucinous, or hemorrhagic contents can show a further increase in signal intensity on these sequences (Fig. 29–69). These lesions usually have markedly increased signal intensity on T2-weighted images, however, suggesting their true cystic nature.

Esophageal Duplication and Neurenteric Cysts

Duplication of the esophagus[66, 130, 141, 180, 234, 245] is thought to represent a diverticulum of the primitive foregut or an aberrant recanalization of the gut in embryogenesis. These cysts are located in the middle or posterior mediastinum and may be indistinguishable from a bronchogenic cyst. They are composed of a muscular coat and mucosa that may resemble the esophagus, stomach, or small intestine, although it is usually ciliated. Esophageal duplication cysts usually occur within the wall, or are adherent to the wall, of the esophagus. They are either spherical or tubular and are usually located distally along the lateral aspect of the esophagus.

On CT, the cysts typically manifest as spherical or tubular masses in close proximity to the esophageal wall. They are usually homogeneous and demonstrate water attenuation (Fig. 29–70). Like bronchogenic cysts, however, they may be of soft tissue attenuation because of intracystic hemorrhage or proteinaceous debris. On MRI, they show signal intensity characteristics similar to those of bronchogenic cysts, with variable signal intensity on T1-weighted images, depending on intracystic content, and markedly increased signal intensity on T2-weighted images (Fig. 29–71).

Neurenteric cysts result from incomplete separation of the endoderm and notochord, resulting in a diverticulum of the endoderm. Neurenteric cysts, which are pathologically identical to esophageal duplication cysts, may have either a fibrous connection to the spine or an intraspinal component. These cysts are typically associated with vertebral body anomalies, most commonly a sagittal cleft, that occur at or above the level of the cyst. Most neurenteric cysts occur in the posterior rather than the middle mediastinum, usually above the level of the carina.

The CT and MR appearances of these lesions are similar to those of other foregut cysts. MRI is useful for optimally demonstrating extent of spinal abnormality and degree of intraspinal involvement.

Pericardial Cysts

Pericardial cysts are unilocular, mesothelium-lined cysts that arise from congenital defects related to the ventral and parietal pericardial recesses.[15, 63, 180, 219, 245] True pericardial cysts contain all layers of the pericardium and do not

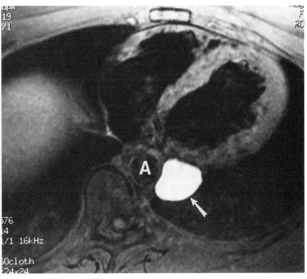

Figure 29–71. Esophageal duplication cyst. Axial T1-weighted MR image shows a well-circumscribed mass *(arrow)* with high signal intensity adjacent to the descending aorta (A). The MRI appearance, which is atypical for a simple cyst, is caused by proteinaceous fluid within the cyst.

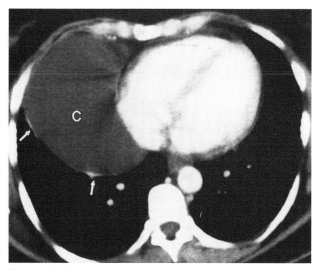

Figure 29–72. Pericardial cyst. Contrast-enhanced CT shows a large, homogeneous, water-attenuation mass (C) in the right cardiophrenic angle. The wall is imperceptible; enhancement at the periphery *(arrows)* is caused by atelectatic lung. The location and appearance are typical for pericardial cyst.

communicate with the pericardial space. They are usually found in asymptomatic adults, often as an incidental finding on chest radiographs. They are typically unilocular cystic lesions with clear fluid contents and thin walls. Pericardial cysts are variable in size and shape and most commonly occur in the right (70%) or left (22%) cardiophrenic angles.

CT shows a homogeneous, nonenhancing, water-attenuation, rounded mass adjacent to the pericardium (Fig. 29–72). The cyst wall may calcify. Pericardial cysts are usually homogeneous on MRI, showing low signal intensity on T1-weighted images and markedly increased signal intensity on T2-weighted images (Fig. 29–73).

Posterior Mediastinal Lesions

Neurogenic Tumors

Twenty percent of all adult and 35% of all pediatric mediastinal neoplasms are neurogenic tumors.[12, 47, 153, 245, 265] Neurogenic tumors account for the majority of posterior mediastinal neoplasms.[124] These lesions can be classified as tumors of peripheral nerves (neurofibromas, schwannomas, malignant tumors of nerve sheath origin), of sympathetic ganglia (ganglioneuromas, ganglioneuroblastomas, neuroblastomas), or of parasympathetic ganglia (paragangliomas, pheochromocytomas). Peripheral nerve tumors are more common in adults and sympathetic ganglia tumors are more common in children.

CT is usually performed in the initial evaluation of a suspected neurogenic tumor and is helpful for identifying intratumoral calcification and for assessing associated bone erosion or destruction. Because neurogenic tumors usually arise in a paravertebral location, intraspinal extension is common.

MRI is the preferred imaging modality for evaluating neurogenic tumors because it allows simultaneous assessment of the following:

- Intraspinal extension
- Spinal cord abnormalities
- Longitudinal extent of tumor

Although the various types of neurogenic tumor can have similar radiologic appearances, certain features aid in the diagnosis. Peripheral nerve tumors typically manifest in adults as round masses oriented along the axis of a peripheral nerve, and they may have an intraspinal component (the "dumbbell" lesion). Tumors of sympathetic ganglia typically manifest in children as oval masses that are elongated along the spine and may contain calcifications on CT.

Benign Peripheral Nerve Tumors

The benign peripheral nerve tumors (schwannomas, neurofibromas) are slow-growing neoplasms and the most common neurogenic tumors of the mediastinum.* Schwannomas are encapsulated neoplasms that arise from the nerve sheath and typically have areas of cystic degeneration and hemorrhage and small focal areas of calcification. Schwannomas grow laterally along the parent nerve and cause symptoms by compressing the nerve.

Neurofibromas differ from schwannomas in that they are unencapsulated and result from proliferation of all nerve elements, including Schwann cells, nerve fibers, and fibroblasts. They grow by diffusely expanding the parent nerve. This type of neural tumor is found in neurofibromatosis-1 (von Recklinghausen's disease). Plexiform neurofibromas are variants of neurofibromas that infiltrate along nerve trunks or plexuses.

Schwannomas and neurofibromas typically occur with equal frequency in men and women, most commonly in the third and fourth decades of life. Thirty percent to 45% of neurofibromas occur in patients with neurofibromatosis. Multiple neurogenic tumors or a single plexiform neurofibroma is pathognomonic of the disease.

On CT, schwannomas and neurofibromas manifest as sharply marginated, unilateral, spherical or lobular posterior mediastinal masses (Fig. 29–74). Pressure erosion of adjacent ribs, or vertebral body or neural foramen enlargement occurs in up to 50% of cases. Punctate intralesional calcification occurs occasionally. On non–contrast-enhanced CT, schwannomas often demonstrate lower attenuation than skeletal muscle because of their high lipid content, interstitial fluid, and areas of cystic degeneration. Neurofibromas are often more homogeneous and show higher attenuation than schwannomas because they have fewer of these histologic features. These lesions may heterogeneously enhance following administration of IV contrast material.

On MRI, schwannomas and neurofibromas show variable signal intensity on T1-weighted images but typically their signal intensity is similar to that of the spinal cord. On T2-weighted images, these neoplasms characteristically show high signal intensity peripherally and low signal intensity centrally (the target sign) as a result of collagen deposition. This feature, when present, helps distinguish neurofibromas from other mediastinal tumors. Also, areas

*See References 9, 26, 36, 74, 95, 136, 153, 155, 206, 245, 247, and 265.

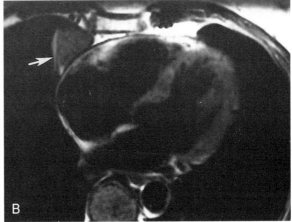

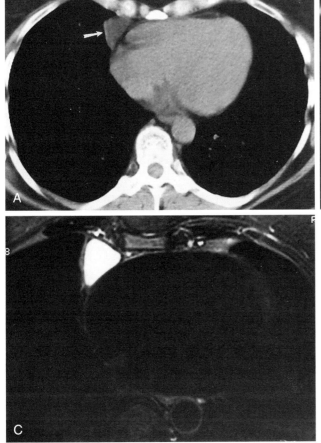

Figure 29–73. Pericardial cyst. CT *(A)* shows small, low-attenuation, well-circumscribed mass in the right cardiophrenic angle *(arrow)*. MRI shows that the mass *(arrow in B)* is homogeneous with low signal intensity on the T1-weighted image *(B)* and with high signal intensity on the T2-weighted image *(C)*. The MRI appearance is typical of a pericardial cyst.

of cystic degeneration within the lesions may result in foci of increased signal intensity on T2-weighted images.

Although the high signal intensity shown by schwannomas and neurofibromas on T2-weighted images can facilitate differentiation of tumors from spinal cord, the tumors can be obscured by the high signal intensity of cerebrospinal fluid. Schwannomas and neurofibromas, however, enhance with gadolinium and this feature can be useful in detecting and determining their intradural extension (Fig. 29–75). Ten percent of paravertebral neurofibromas and schwannomas extend into the spinal canal and appear as dumbbell-shaped masses with widening of the affected neural foramen.

CT of plexiform neurofibromas demonstrates low-attenuation infiltrative masses along the mediastinal nerves and sympathetic chains, which may occur in any mediastinal compartment. MRI of plexiform neurofibromatosis also demonstrates the infiltrative nature of the tumors, and the masses can show low signal on both T1-weighted and T2-weighted images because of the fibrous nature of the tumors (Fig. 29–76).

Malignant Tumor of Nerve Sheath Origin

Malignant tumors of nerve sheath origin (also called malignant neurofibromas, malignant schwannomas, or neurofibrosarcomas) are rare neoplasms that typically develop from solitary or plexiform neurofibromas in the third to fifth decades of life.* Up to 50% occur in patients with neurofibromatosis-1. In patients with neurofibromatosis-1, these tumors occur at an earlier age (typically in adolescence) and with a higher incidence than in the general population. Because most benign neurogenic tumors are

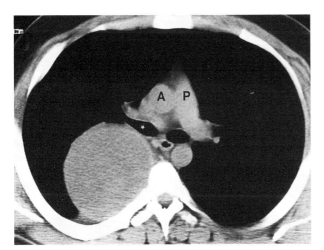

Figure 29–74. Schwannoma. CT shows a large, homogeneous, paraspinal mass. The round shape is typical of a peripheral nerve tumor. A, aorta; P, pulmonary artery. The *asterisk* indicates the right main bronchus.

*See References 9, 26, 55, 80, 110, 136, 155, 157, 245, and 247.

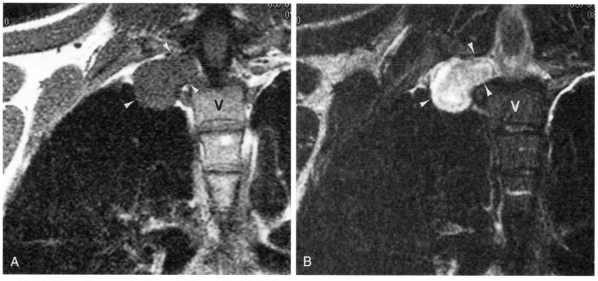

Figure 29–75. Neurofibroma. *A,* Coronal T1-weighted MR image shows a lobular mass extending into the intervertebral foramina *(arrowheads). B,* Coronal gadolinium-enhanced MR image shows heterogeneous enhancement within the mass *(arrowheads).* V, vertebral body. (From Rossi SE, Erasmus JJ, McAdams HP, Donnelly LF: Thoracic manifestations of neurofibromatosis-I. AJR Am J Roentgenol 173:1631–1638, 1999.)

asymptomatic, the development of pain often indicates malignant transformation.

On CT or MRI, malignant tumors of nerve sheath origin typically manifest as posterior mediastinal masses larger than 5 cm in diameter. Although benign and malignant neurogenic tumors cannot be differentiated with certainty, findings that suggest malignancy include a sudden change in size of a preexisting mass or development of heterogeneous signal intensity on MR images (caused by necrosis and hemorrhage). The presence of multiple target signs throughout the lesion on MRI favors the diagnosis of a plexiform neurofibroma rather than a malignant tumor of nerve sheath origin.

Sympathetic Ganglia Tumors

The sympathetic ganglia tumors (ganglioneuromas, ganglioneuroblastomas, neuroblastomas) are rare neoplasms that originate from nerve cells.* Ganglioneuromas and ganglioneuroblastomas usually arise from the sympathetic ganglia in the posterior mediastinum.

Ganglioneuromas are benign neoplasms that usually occur in children and young adults. Ganglioneuroblastomas, which exhibit varying degrees of malignancy, usually occur in patients younger than 10 years. The posterior mediasti-

---

*See References 2, 19, 40, 48, 74, 218, 229, 240, 245, 247, and 255.

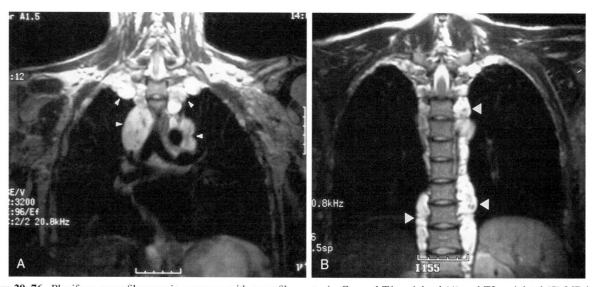

Figure 29–76. Plexiform neurofibromas in a woman with neurofibromatosis. Coronal T1-weighted *(A)* and T2-weighted *(B)* MR images show plexiform neurofibromas along the course of nerves in the superior, middle, and posterior mediastinum *(arrowheads).* Focal central hypointense regions within masses (target sign) are typical of neurofibromas. (From Rossi SE, Erasmus JJ, McAdams HP, Donnelly LF: Thoracic manifestations of neurofibromatosis-I. AJR Am J Roentgenol 173:1631–1638, 1999.)

num is also the most common extra-abdominal location of neuroblastomas: up to 30% of these tumors occur in this region. Neuroblastomas are highly malignant tumors that typically occur in children younger than 5 years. A posterior mediastinal mass in this age group should be considered a neuroblastoma until proven otherwise.

Radiologically, ganglioneuromas and ganglioneuroblastomas usually manifest as well-marginated, elliptical, posterior mediastinal masses that vertically extend over three to five vertebral bodies. They are usually located lateral to the spine and may cause pressure erosion on adjacent vertebral bodies. On CT, they are typically heterogeneous and may contain stippled or punctate calcifications (Fig. 29–77). On T1-weighted and T2-weighted MR images, they usually show homogeneous and intermediate signal intensity (Fig. 29–78). Occasionally, these lesions show heterogeneous and high signal intensity on T2-weighted images. Ganglioneuroblastomas are typically larger and more aggressive than ganglioneuromas, with evidence of local and intraspinal invasion.

On CT, neuroblastomas manifest as a paraspinal mass showing heterogeneous, predominantly soft tissue attenuation. The lesions usually contain areas of hemorrhage, necrosis, cystic degeneration, and calcium (30%). On MRI, the lesions typically demonstrate heterogeneous signal intensity on all pulse sequences and show heterogeneous enhancement following gadolinium administration. Neuroblastomas often show widespread local invasion and have irregular margins, although lesions can be well marginated on CT or MR images. Neuroblastomas also have a tendency to cross the midline.

Parasympathetic Ganglion Tumors

Paragangliomas (chemodectomas) are rare neural tumors of the extra-adrenal parasympathetic system.[71, 174] These tumors are histologically identical to pheochromocytomas and can be functional or nonfunctional. Mediastinal paragangliomas occur in one of two locations:

- In the middle mediastinum, in close association with the origins of the aorta and pulmonary artery (aorticopulmonary paraganglioma)

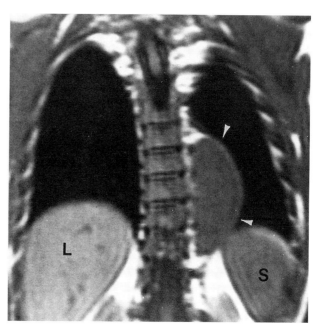

Figure 29–78. Ganglioneuroma. Coronal T1-weighted MR image shows an elliptical paraspinal mass *(arrowheads)* of intermediate signal intensity. Vertical orientation and signal characteristics are typical of a sympathetic ganglion tumor. L, liver; S, spleen.

- In the posterior mediastinum (paravertebral paraganglioma)

On non–contrast-enhanced CT, the lesions are typically heterogeneous and enhance intensely after administration of IV contrast material. On MRI, the lesions are usually hypointense on T1-weighted images and hyperintense on T2-weighted images (Fig. 29–79). Flow voids in the lesion are sometimes seen, indicating their hypervascular nature. The lesions may be well circumscribed or show invasion of surrounding mediastinal structures.

Lateral Thoracic Meningocele

Because of the pressure difference between the thorax and the subarachnoid space, pulsion diverticula, called lateral meningoceles, can develop and protrude through the adjacent neural foramina.[9, 113, 183, 205, 236] They occur most commonly in patients with neurofibromatosis-1. Lateral meningoceles manifest radiographically as well-circumscribed, paravertebral masses that usually occur on the convex side of a scoliosis. On CT, meningoceles manifest as well-circumscribed paraspinal masses that demonstrate water attenuation. The adjacent neural foramen is typically enlarged. These lesions can be confused with low-attenuation neurofibromas. Diagnosis is established by demonstration of communication with the subarachnoid space by CT myelography. MRI can also be helpful in differentiating meningoceles from neurofibromas because meningoceles typically show low signal intensity on T1-weighted images and high signal intensity on T2-weighted images, and they do not enhance after gadolinium administration. Cardiac-gated MR cine images of meningoceles can reveal pulsatile motion that results from communication with the subarachnoid space.

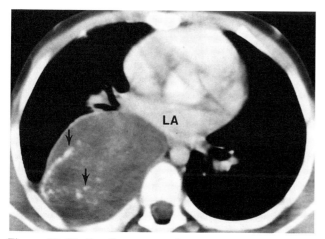

Figure 29–77. Ganglioneuroma. Contrast-enhanced CT shows well-circumscribed low-attenuation paraspinal mass containing punctate calcification *(arrows)*. LA, left atrium.

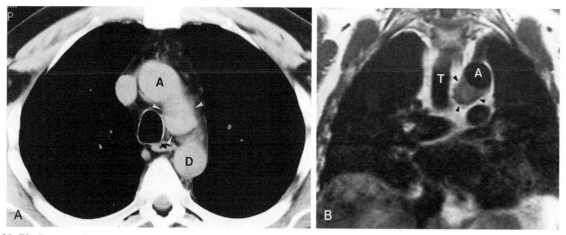

Figure 29–79. Paraganglioma. *A,* CT shows homogeneous soft tissue mass in aortopulmonary window *(arrowheads).* The mass is difficult to distinguish from the aorta. A, ascending aorta; D, descending aorta. *B,* Coronal T1-weighted MR image shows intermediate-signal-intensity aortopulmonary window mass *(arrowheads).* Biopsy revealed paraganglioma. A, aorta; T, trachea.

Extramedullary Hematopoiesis

Extramedullary hematopoiesis is a compensatory phenomenon that occurs when erythrocyte production is diminished or destruction is accelerated.[30, 81, 90, 123, 222] Extramedullary hematopoiesis is usually seen in patients with chronic hemolytic disorders such as thalassemia, hereditary spherocytosis, sickle cell disease, or extensive bone marrow replacement resulting from myelofibrosis. Extramedullary hematopoiesis usually is microscopic and commonly involves the liver, spleen, and lymph nodes. Thoracic manifestations are less common and consist of paravertebral soft tissue masses. The masses represent extrusion of the marrow through the thinned cortex of the posterior ribs. Histologically, the masses resemble splenic tissue with hematopoietic elements mixed with fat. They are usually bilateral, contain no calcification, and show no rib destruction. Additional masses can be found along the lateral margins of the ribs.

On CT, extramedullary hematopoiesis manifests as a heterogeneous mass or masses, often with focal areas of fat within the lesion (Fig. 29–80). Extramedullary hematopoiesis typically manifests on MRI as well-marginated, smooth or lobulated, unilateral or bilateral paravertebral masses. T1-weighted and T2-weighted MR images typically show bilateral heterogeneous masses with increased signal intensity on T1-weighted images because of fat within the masses.

Paraspinal Inflammation

Vertebral osteomyelitis can result in a paraspinal abscess. Causative organisms include *Mycobacterium tuberculosis*, *Staphylococcus aureus*, and anaerobic organisms. On CT, a paraspinal abscess manifests as a mass showing heterogeneous attenuation. Rim enhancement following administration of IV contrast material is characteristic (Fig. 29–81). Imaging features that suggest paraspinal abscess include (1) narrowing of adjacent intervertebral disk and (2) destruction of two or more contiguous vertebral bodies.

MRI is especially suited for identifying and demonstrating the extent of paraspinal infections. Spondylitis and

vertebral osteomyelitis are often accompanied by epidural or paraspinal inflammatory masses or abscesses. MRI is better than CT for evaluating these infections because of its ability to depict the disk space, the spinal canal and its contents, and the paraspinal regions. T1-weighted images show inflammation as low signal intensity, and T2-weighted images show high signal intensity. The addition of gadolinium diethylenetriamine-penta-acetic acid (Gd-DTPA) is helpful in demonstrating the extent of the inflammatory process.[4, 5, 45, 191]

Diffuse Mediastinal Abnormalities

Numerous lesions, including lymphadenopathy, mediastinitis, mediastinal sarcoma, and metastatic disease, can

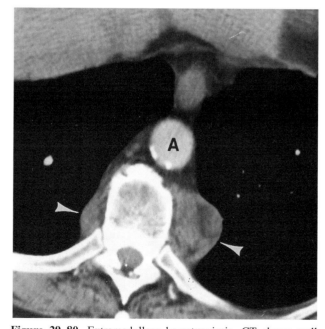

Figure 29–80. Extramedullary hematopoiesis. CT shows well-circumscribed bilateral paravertebral masses *(arrowheads).* The left mass is heterogeneous and contains focal areas of fat, typical for extramedullary hematopoiesis. A, descending aorta.

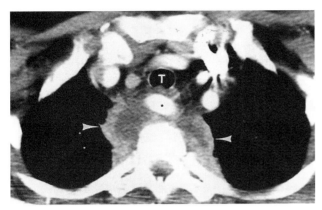

Figure 29–81. Paraspinal abscess caused by vertebral osteomyelitis. Contrast-enhanced CT shows bilateral heterogeneous low-attenuation paraspinal masses *(arrowheads). Staphylococcus aureus* was cultured from the needle aspirate. An anomalous right subclavian artery *(asterisk)* is posterior to the trachea (T).

manifest as diffuse or multicompartment mediastinal disease.

Lymphadenopathy

Lymph nodes are common in all regions of the mediastinum but they are most numerous around the tracheobronchial tree and hence in the middle mediastinum (Fig. 29–

82).* Although it is still a subject of some controversy, the generally accepted upper limit of normal for short-axis lymph node diameter is 1 cm.

Enlargement is the primary CT or MRI criterion for establishing the presence of lymph node disease, but attenuation is also important. For instance, diffuse calcification is typical of prior granulomatous infection (tuberculosis, histoplasmosis), sarcoidosis, silicosis, calcifying or ossifying metastases, and treated lymphoma (Figs. 29–83 and 29–84). Nodes with low attenuation centers and rim enhancement are often seen in patients with active infection (tuberculosis, nontuberculous mycobacterial disease) and in patients with metastatic disease to the lymph nodes (lung cancer, testicular germ cell malignancy). Diffuse, intense nodal enhancement after administration of IV contrast material is typical of Castleman's disease and some metastatic processes (renal cell carcinoma). Causes of mediastinal lymph node enlargement may be classified as follows:

- Primary neoplasms of lymph nodes (lymphoma, leukemia)
- Metastases from intrathoracic or extrathoracic primary malignancies
- Nonlymphomatous lymphoid disorders such as Castleman's disease
- Infection (e.g., tuberculosis, fungal infection)

*See References 21, 29, 53, 75, 77, 85, 153, 193, 198, and 257.

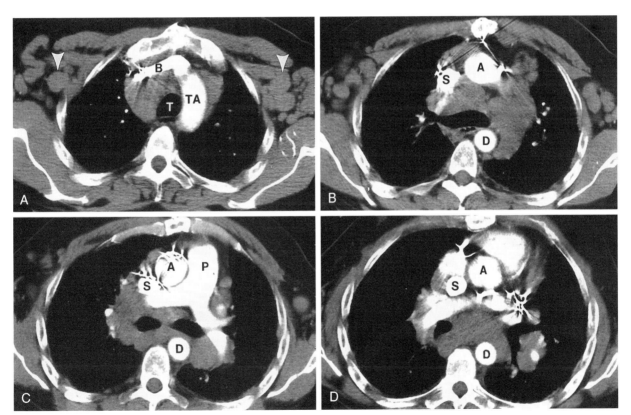

Figure 29–82. Diffuse mediastinal adenopathy in a patient with chronic lymphocytic leukemia. Contrast-enhanced CT shows marked intrathoracic adenopathy in the paratracheal and prevascular mediastinum *(A)*, precarinal region and aortopulmonary window *(B)*, left and right hilum *(C)*, and subcarinal region *(D)*. Axillary adenopathy can be seen *(arrowheads* in *A)*. A, ascending aorta; B, brachiocephalic vein; D, descending aorta; P, main pulmonary artery; S, superior vena cava; T, trachea; TA, transverse aorta.

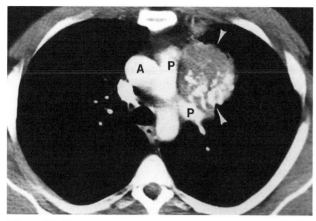

Figure 29–83. Osteosarcoma metastasis to the anterior mediastinum. Contrast-enhanced CT shows a soft-tissue-attenuation mass with extensive osteoid *(arrowheads)* in the anterior mediastinum. A, aorta; P, pulmonary artery.

CT and MRI are generally considered to be equivalent in their ability to detect mediastinal lymph node enlargement (Fig. 29–85). MRI is limited in its ability to detect calcification within nodes, a finding useful for distinguishing benign from malignant lymphadenopathy. Overlap occurs in signal intensity characteristics of benign and malignant lymphadenopathy on both T1-weighted and T2-weighted images. Thus, CT remains the primary modality for diagnosis and characterization of mediastinal lymphadenopathy. MRI can be useful, however, as a problem-solving modality in some cases and for distinguishing enlarged nodes from vascular structures when administration of iodinated contrast material is contraindicated.

Lymphoma

Lymphomas are common mediastinal neoplasms that can be either focal or diffuse.[67, 96, 125, 140, 151, 226, 242] Lymphomas are classified as *Hodgkin's disease* (HD) and *non-Hodgkin's lymphoma* (NHL). HD is the most common mediastinal lymphoma. Of the four types of HD, nodular sclerosing HD is the most common and has a unique

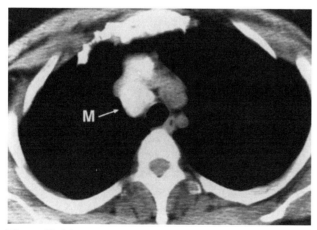

Figure 29–84. Calcified nodes. CT shows calcified right paratracheal lymph nodes (M) caused by histoplasmosis.

predilection for the anterior mediastinum. Other types of HD typically manifest with diffuse mediastinal lymphadenopathy.

NHL that involves the mediastinum usually manifests with diffuse lymphadenopathy involving anterior, middle, and occasionally posterior mediastinal nodal groups. However, large B-cell or lymphoblastic lymphoma can manifest as an isolated anterior mediastinal mass. These large tumors can obstruct the SVC, compress the airway, or invade chest wall and adjacent structures.

Hodgkin's Disease. HD accounts for 0.75% of all cancers diagnosed in the United States each year. The median age at diagnosis is 26 years, and there is a slight male predominance. The incidence of HD has a bimodal distribution, with peaks between 25 and 30 years and 75 and 80 years. The characteristic Reed-Sternberg cell is the diagnostic hallmark of HD. There are four histologic subtypes of HD:

- Lymphocyte predominance (5%), with the best prognosis
- Nodular sclerosing, the most common type (78%), with the second most favorable prognosis
- Mixed cellularity (17%), with the third most favorable prognosis
- Lymphocyte depletion (1%), with the worst prognosis

HD is staged using the Ann Arbor staging system as follows:

Stage I: Involvement of a single lymph node region
Stage II: Involvement of two or more lymph node regions on the same side of the diaphragm (II), or localized involvement of an extralymphatic organ or site and of one or more lymph node regions on the same side of the diaphragm (IIE)
Stage III: Involvement of lymph node regions on both sides of the diaphragm (III), which may also be accompanied by involvement on the spleen (IIIS) or by localized involvement of an extralymphatic organ or site (IIIE), or both (IIIES)
Stage IV: Diffuse or disseminated involvement of one or more extralymphatic organs or tissues, with or without associated lymph node involvement

The absence or presence of fever, night sweats, or unexplained weight loss of 10% or more body weight 6 months before diagnosis are denoted by the suffix letter A or B, respectively.

Stages I and II are treated with radiation alone, and stages III and IV are treated with a combination of radiation and chemotherapy or just chemotherapy alone. Survival is greater than 90% in stages I, II, and IIIA; 80% in stage IIIB; and 75% in stage IV.

Non-Hodgkin's Lymphoma. The NHLs are a heterogeneous group of diseases with differing histology, treatment, and prognosis but with enough similarities that they are considered collectively. Although NHL has no known cause, patients with impaired immune systems are at higher risk for development of this malignancy. NHL makes up 3% of all newly diagnosed cancers in the United States and is four times more common than HD. NHL is the third most common childhood cancer, although the median age

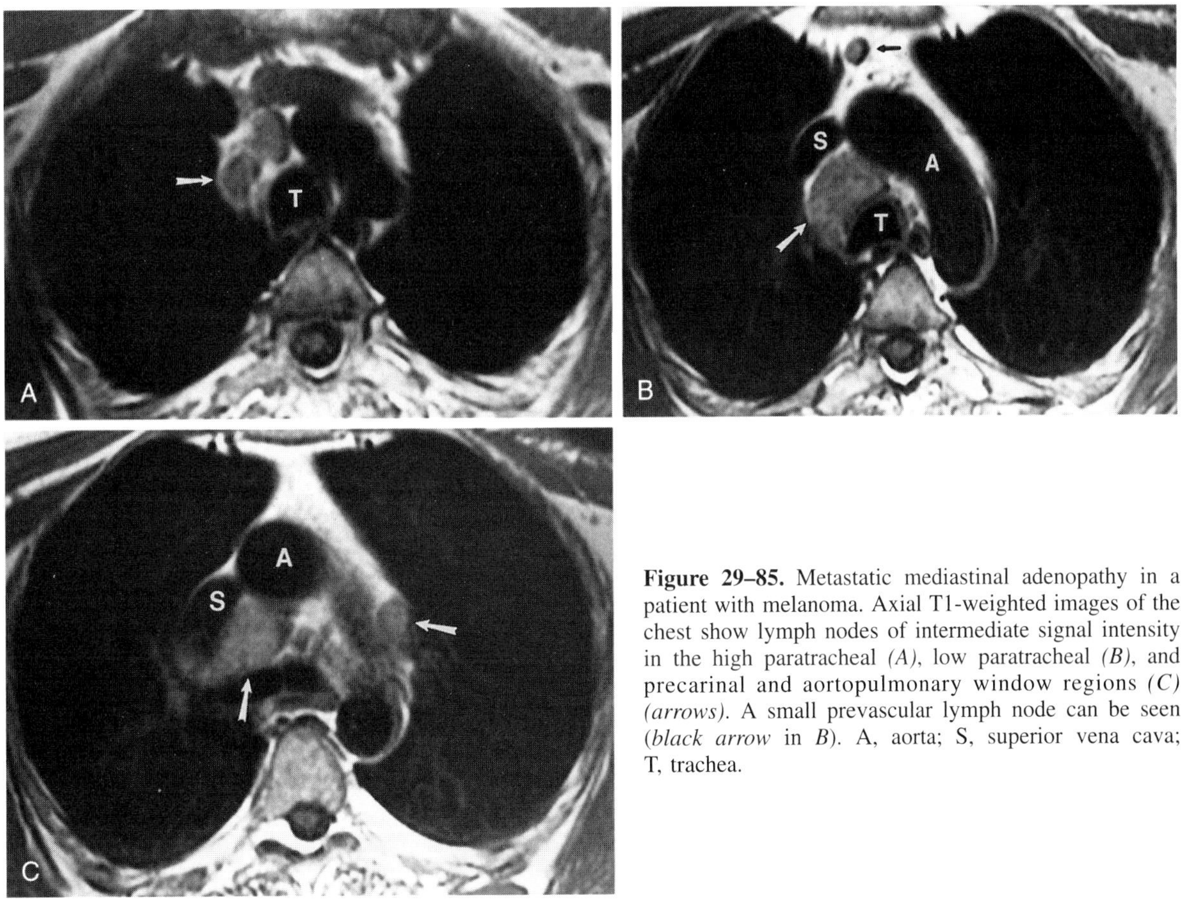

Figure 29–85. Metastatic mediastinal adenopathy in a patient with melanoma. Axial T1-weighted images of the chest show lymph nodes of intermediate signal intensity in the high paratracheal *(A)*, low paratracheal *(B)*, and precarinal and aortopulmonary window regions *(C)* *(arrows)*. A small prevascular lymph node can be seen *(black arrow* in *B)*. A, aorta; S, superior vena cava; T, trachea.

at the time of diagnosis is 55 years. There is a male predominance (1.4:1). The histologic classification of NHL is complex, with 10 different cell descriptions divided into three grades of tumors:

- *Low grade* (small lymphocytic; follicular with predominantly small cleaved cells; and follicular with mixed small and large cells)
- *Intermediate grade* (follicular with predominantly large cells; diffuse with small cleaved cells; diffuse with mixed small and large cells; and diffuse with large cells, cleaved or noncleaved)
- *High grade* (diffuse large cells; immunoblastic, small noncleaved cells; and lymphoblastic)

Treatment is complex and involves radiation for lower-grade and chemotherapy for higher-grade tumors. Survival is 50% to 70% in low-grade NHL, 35% to 45% in intermediate-grade NHL, and 20% to 30% in high-grade NHL. Several unique observations are seen in NHL. Low-grade tumors may spontaneously regress, recur, or transform into higher-grade tumors. The incidence of NHL is higher in patients with severe immunologic compromise, including congenital immune disorders, transplant immunosuppression, and human immunodeficiency virus. NHL in these patients is often more aggressive and involves extranodal sites, such as the central nervous system, lung parenchyma, and gastrointestinal tract.

Imaging of Lymphoma. CT is the method of choice for identifying and staging HD and NHL.* CT provides accurate measurement of initial tumor size and extent, and it provides a means to follow response to therapy (Figs. 29–86 to 29–93). Chest CT alters initial treatment plans in approximately 10% of patients with HD by detecting more extensive disease. The anterior mediastinal, pretracheal, and hilar nodes are the nodes most commonly involved with HD. Paracardiac, subcarinal, superior diaphragmatic, internal mammary, and axillary nodes are less frequently involved. Calcification within nodes is usually a consequence of radiation therapy but occasionally is detected before treatment. Central areas of low density represent areas of necrosis; the presence of necrosis does not appear to alter treatment response or survival.

Lymphadenopathy varies in size and extent and can manifest as a solitary large mass or as discrete nodes within masses of matted nodes. It is important to recognize bulky mediastinal lymphadenopathy, identified when the diameter of the nodal mass is greater than one third of the thoracic diameter, because its presence may alter therapy.

Intrathoracic disease is noted in only 40% to 50% of patients with NHL at presentation, compared with 85% of patients with HD. In NHL, the most common nodal sites of involvement are not those of HD (anterior, superior

---

*See References 1, 6, 24, 33, 37, 39, 76, 119, 153, 182, 186, 190, 204, 237, 252, and 269.

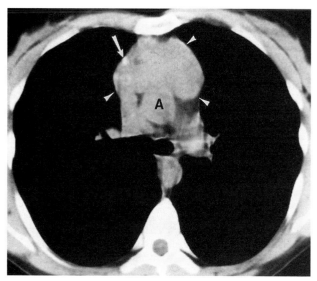

Figure 29–86. Hodgkin's lymphoma in a young woman. CT shows a homogeneous, anterior mediastinal mass *(arrowheads).* A punctate calcification *(arrow)* can be seen within the mass. A, ascending aorta.

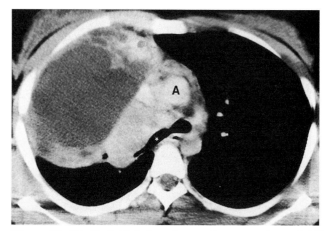

Figure 29–87. Hodgkin's lymphoma. Contrast-enhanced CT shows an anterior mediastinal mass with a large cystic component. The *asterisk* indicates posterior displacement of the right main bronchus. A, ascending aorta.

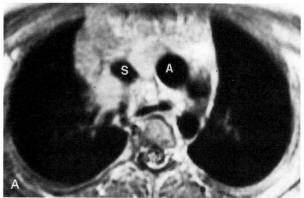

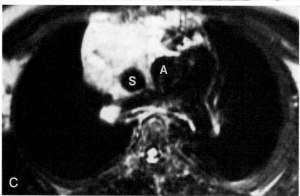

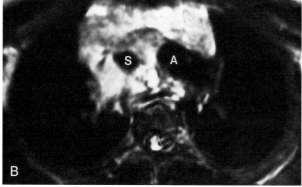

Figure 29–88. Nodular sclerosing Hodgkin's lymphoma. T1-weighted MR image *(A)* shows a lobular, heterogeneous anterior mediastinal mass with intermediate signal intensity. T2-weighted MR images *(B and C)* show the mass to have heterogeneous signal intensity. On a cephalic image *(B),* there are areas of decreased signal intensity consistent with intratumoral fibrosis. On a caudal image *(C),* the mass predominantly shows high signal intensity, similar to subcutaneous fat. A, aorta; S, superior vena cava. (Reprinted with permission from Erasmus JJ, McAdams HP, Donnelly LF, Spritzer CE: MR imaging of mediastinal masses. Magn Reson Imaging Clin North Am 8:59–89, 2000.)

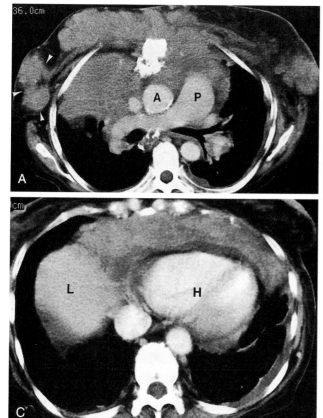

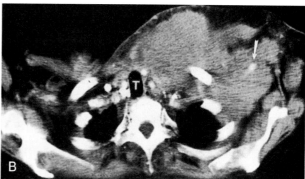

Figure 29–89. Non-Hodgkin's lymphoma manifesting as mediastinal mass with chest wall involvement. *A–C,* Contrast-enhanced CT shows a diffuse anterior mediastinal mass with chest wall invasion. The axillary nodes *(arrowheads* in *A)* are enlarged. The mass extends into neck and surrounds vessels *(arrow* in *B).* More caudally, the mass manifests as a mantle of soft tissue encasing heart *(C).* A, ascending aorta; H, heart; L, liver; P, main pulmonary artery; S, superior vena cava; T, trachea.

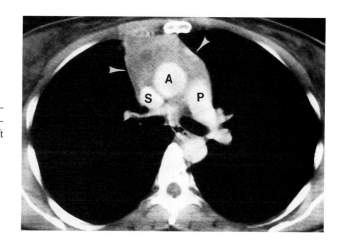

Figure 29–90. Non-Hodgkin's lymphoma manifesting as anterior mediastinal mass. CT shows a heterogeneous mass *(arrowheads)* with diffuse infiltration of the mediastinum. A, aorta; P, left main pulmonary artery; S, superior vena cava.

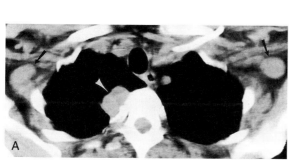

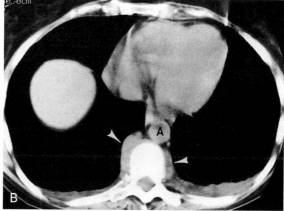

Figure 29–91. Non-Hodgkin's lymphoma manifesting as multifocal disease. *A,* CT shows right paravertebral soft tissue mass *(arrowhead).* Axillary adenopathy can be seen *(arrows). B,* CT at a more caudal level shows bilateral paravertebral masses *(arrowheads).* Small pleural effusions can be visualized bilaterally. A, aorta.

977

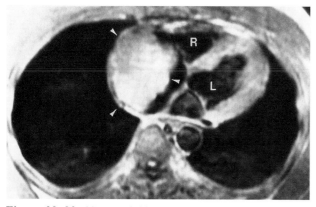

Figure 29–92. Non-Hodgkin's lymphoma with intracardiac involvement. Axial T1-weighted MR image shows a mass of heterogeneous signal intensity extending into right atrium *(arrowheads)*. MRI allows assessment of intravascular and intracardiac tumor extension without administration of intravenous contrast material. L, left ventricle; R, right ventricle. (Reprinted with permission from Erasmus JJ, McAdams HP, Donnelly LF, Spritzer CE: MR imaging of mediastinal masses. Magn Reson Imaging Clin North Am 8:59–89, 2000.)

mediastinal nodes), but rather other nodal sites, lung parenchyma, pleura, and pericardium.

CT and scintigraphy using gallium 67 (⁶⁷Ga) are usually the primary staging modalities in patients with suspected mediastinal lymphoma. Although MRI can reveal additional information in as many as 15% of cases, it is more often used for assessing suspected SVC obstruction, vascular invasion, and chest wall or mediastinal invasion. MRI has also been used to monitor and evaluate response to therapy, to differentiate fibrosis from residual tumor, and to detect recurrent lymphoma.

Residual masses are seen in the immediate follow-up period in up to 88% of patients with HD and in up to 40% of patients with NHL. These residual masses typically resolve over 12 to 18 months. The presence of residual mediastinal abnormalities is of concern because lymphoma eventually recurs in half of these patients, usually at the site of the original mass. Differentiating residual fibrotic mass from persistent or recurrent tumor can be difficult by conventional imaging. MRI can be a useful adjunct to ⁶⁷Ga scintigraphy for this assessment.

Because of its high water content, untreated lymphoma is typically homogeneous with low to intermediate signal intensity on T1-weighted images and increased signal intensity on T2-weighted images. Patients with nodular sclerosing HD occasionally have focal regions of low signal intensity within the mass on pretreatment T2-weighted images because of intralesional fibrosis.

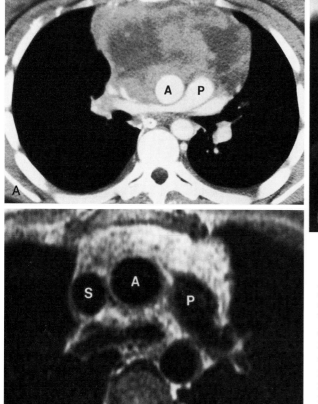

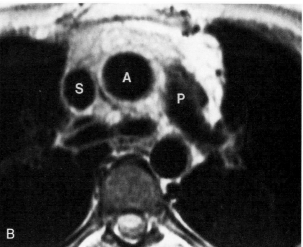

Figure 29–93. Non-Hodgkin's lymphoma. Contrast-enhanced CT *(A)* shows a large heterogeneous anterior mediastinal mass. T1-weighted image *(B)* following therapy shows an intermediate-signal-intensity mass that has decreased in size. The corresponding T2-weighted image *(C)* shows mass to have lower signal intensity than *B*. The decrease in signal intensity suggests that the residual mass is fibrotic. Biopsy confirmed fibrosis and absence of residual tumor. A, ascending aorta; P, main pulmonary artery; S, superior vena cava.

During and immediately after completion of therapy, the lesions typically become heterogeneous on MRI and signal intensity on T2-weighted images becomes more variable. Over the subsequent 4 to 6 months, the residual mass has a tendency to decrease in size and signal intensity on T2-weighted images. Six months after therapy, residual masses resulting from fibrosis should be homogeneous with low signal intensity on both T1-weighted and T2-weighted images. This homogeneous low signal intensity is typical of treated inactive lymphoma. If the mass remains heterogeneous with focal regions of high signal intensity on T2-weighted images, recurrent or residual lymphoma is suggested. Using these findings, MRI can detect persistent or recurrent tumor in treated patients as much as 8 to 12 weeks before the onset of clinical symptoms.

The presence of fat mixed with residual fibrotic tissue is, however, a pitfall on MRI. This potential misinterpretation can be avoided by realizing that regions of high signal intensity detected on T2-weighted images correlate with high signal intensity fat on T1-weighted images (rather than low signal intensity of recurrent tumor). Fat-suppression pulse sequences may also be helpful for distinguishing interspersed fat from areas of residual tumor.

Castleman's Disease

Castleman's disease is also known as angiofollicular or giant lymph node hyperplasia.[126, 134, 161, 165, 171, 195] Castleman's disease is not a distinct disease entity but rather a diverse group of rare lymphoproliferative disorders of different tissue types and biologic behaviors. It is currently classified into two major subgroups: localized and disseminated Castleman's disease. There are two major histologic variants: *hyaline vascular* (HV-CD) and *plasma cell* (PC-CD). Although Castleman's disease most often affects the mediastinum, it can occur in any location (mediastinum, 67%; neck, 14%; pelvis, 4%; axilla, 2%).

Localized Castleman's Disease. Most patients with localized thoracic Castleman's disease have HV-CD; localized PC-CD is rare. Localized HV-CD affects all age groups, with a peak incidence in the fourth decade of life. Affected patients are usually asymptomatic at presentation, although symptoms caused by compression or invasion of adjacent structures occur occasionally. Women are more commonly affected than men. Systemic signs and symptoms such as fever, weight loss, and anemia are uncommon.

Histologically, localized HV-CD manifests with massive lymph node hyperplasia, involuted germinal centers, and marked capillary proliferation with endothelial hyperplasia. These masses are typically hypervascular with large feeding vessels. Localized HV-CD can affect any thoracic compartment, but the middle mediastinum and hila are most commonly involved.

Imaging studies show one of three morphologic patterns:

- Solitary mass (50%)
- Dominant infiltrative mass with associated lymphadenopathy (40%)
- Diffuse lymphadenopathy confined to a single mediastinal compartment (10%)

Identification of the first pattern suggests that complete surgical resection is likely. Identification of the second or third pattern suggests that complete excision may be difficult or impossible.

On non–contrast-enhanced CT, localized HV-CD manifests as a homogeneous or heterogeneous mass of soft tissue attenuation. Calcification is uncommon (5% to 10%) and is typically coarse and central in location. HV-CD typically enhances intensely following IV administration of iodinated contrast material (Fig. 29–94). On MRI, the lesions are typically heterogeneous and show increased signal intensity (compared to skeletal muscle) on T1-weighted sequences. They become markedly hyperintense on T2-weighted sequences. Low signal intensity septa are occasionally visible. In larger lesions, flow voids in and around the mass may be identified and are important clues to the hypervascular nature of the lesions. Because the lesions are hypervascular, diffuse enhancement following administration of IV gadolinium is common (Fig. 29–95).

Disseminated Castleman's Disease. Disseminated Castleman's disease is currently regarded as a potentially malignant lymphoproliferative disorder that has been associated with the *POEMS syndrome* (polyneuropathy, *o*rganomegaly, *e*ndocrinopathy, *m*onoclonal proteinemia, and

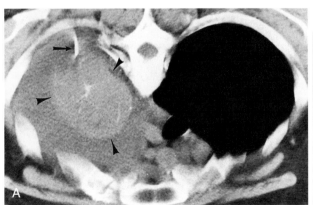
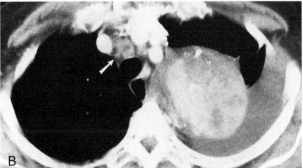

Figure 29–94. Hyaline-vascular Castleman's disease. *A,* CT performed to direct a biopsy on a patient in the prone position shows heterogeneous soft-tissue-attenuation mass in the left posterior mediastinum *(arrowheads).* The biopsy needle *(arrow),* central linear calcification, and left pleural effusion can be seen. *B,* Contrast-enhanced CT with the patient supine shows intense enhancement within the mass as well as a small associated pretracheal node *(arrow).*

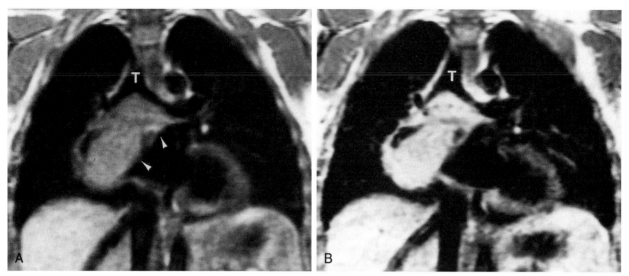

Figure 29–95. Hyaline-vascular Castleman's disease. *A,* Coronal T1-weighted MR image shows large, homogeneous mass *(arrowheads)* in subcarinal region of intermediate signal intensity. Note mass effect on the carina. *B,* Coronal T1-weighted MR image following administration of gadolinium-based contrast material demonstrates diffuse enhancement within the mass, typical of hyaline vascular Castleman's disease. T, trachea.

skin changes), osteosclerotic myeloma, Kaposi's sarcoma, and acquired immunodeficiency syndrome (AIDS). Most patients with disseminated thoracic Castleman's disease have the plasma cell form of the disease. It affects all age groups but the peak incidence is in the fifth decade of life. Women are more commonly affected than men by a ratio of 2:1. Most patients present with systemic complaints of fever, weight loss, and anemia.

Disseminated thoracic Castleman's disease usually manifests on chest radiographs as bilateral mediastinal widening. Focal mediastinal masses are rare. The anterior mediastinum is most commonly affected. On CT, diffuse lymphadenopathy involving multiple mediastinal compartments is noted (Fig. 29–96). The nodes typically range in size from 1 to 6 cm in diameter and demonstrate homogeneous attenuation on non–contrast-enhanced CT scans. As-

sociated findings such as splenomegaly or ascites are common.

Mediastinitis

Acute Mediastinitis

Acute bacterial mediastinitis is a life-threatening condition that requires prompt diagnosis and treatment. Spontaneous or iatrogenic esophageal rupture is the most common cause, accounting for up to 90% of cases. Other causes include direct spread from retropharyngeal or pleural infection and mediastinitis after cardiac surgery.[27, 32, 88, 128, 137, 169, 209, 251, 262]

Findings of esophageal perforation on CT include periesophageal fluid collections (100%), extraluminal mediastinal air (100%), esophageal wall thickening (82%), and

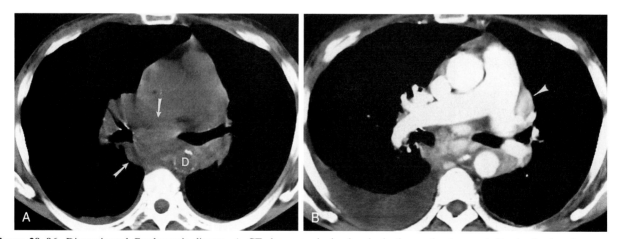

Figure 29–96. Disseminated Castleman's disease. *A,* CT shows marked subcarinal adenopathy *(arrows).* Paratracheal and prevascular adenopathy was extensive (not shown). D, descending aorta. *B,* Contrast-enhanced CT shows marked enhancement of subcarinal and aortopulmonary window *(arrowhead)* lymph nodes. A right pleural effusion can be seen.

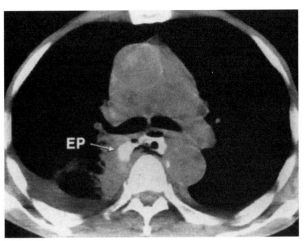

Figure 29–97. Acute mediastinitis after perforation of esophageal carcinoma. CT shows extravasation of esophageal contrast (EP) and air into mediastinum after perforation. A small right pleural effusion can be seen.

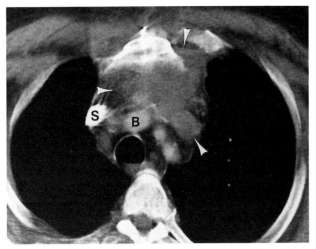

Figure 29–99. Mediastinal hematoma mimicking mediastinal abscess after coronary artery bypass procedure. Contrast-enhanced CT shows well-circumscribed soft tissue abnormality in the fat of the anterior mediastinum *(arrowheads)*. Small focal adjacent air collections *(arrow)* and surgical clips anterior to the ascending aorta can be seen. The needle aspirate confirmed hematoma and the culture was negative for organisms. A, ascending aorta; P, main pulmonary artery.

pleural effusion (82%) (Fig. 29–97). Pleural effusion tends to be right sided in patients with iatrogenic, midesophageal perforation and left sided in patients with spontaneous, distal esophageal perforation (Boerhaave's syndrome). The site of perforation is uncommonly visualized on CT (18%).

Descending cervical mediastinitis (DCM) is an uncommon but life-threatening cause of mediastinitis. Such infections begin in the head and neck region and spread via fascial planes into the mediastinum, usually in the prevertebral space; from there, the infection spreads into the middle and posterior mediastinum. Typical causes include odontogenic infection as well as suppurative tonsillitis and adenitis and retropharyngeal abscess. CT performed in patients with DCM shows fluid collections in the mediastinum that may be contiguous with fluid collections in the cervical region (Fig. 29–98). CT is essential for confirming the diagnosis; it assists in fluid aspiration to confirm infection and in monitoring the patient's response to therapy.

Mediastinitis after cardiac surgery is uncommon, occurring in only 0.5% to 1% of patients.[25, 69, 208] CT is frequently performed in patients with clinically suspected mediastinitis, but it can be difficult to interpret because fluid and air collections, hematomas, pleural effusions, and increased attenuation of anterior mediastinal fat, all potential findings of mediastinitis, are common and expected findings in the immediate postoperative period. These findings generally resolve, however, in the first days and weeks after median sternotomy.

Needle aspiration of fluid collections may be necessary to rule out infection when mediastinitis is suspected (Fig. 29–99). CT is most useful for distinguishing patients with significant retrosternal fluid collections that require open drainage from those who have only superficial wound infections (Fig. 29–100). CT, however, has limited ability for detecting early changes of sternal osteomyelitis.

Histoplasmosis and tuberculosis can cause acute pericarditis and mediastinitis. As in mediastinitis of any cause, the CT appearance is that of increased attenuation of mediastinal fat, focal fluid collections, or abscesses (Fig. 29–101). Infected lymph nodes can show low attenuation centers and peripherally enhancing rims.

Fibrosing Mediastinitis

Mediastinal fibrosis (sclerosing or fibrosing mediastinitis) is a rare benign disorder caused by proliferation of acellular collagen and fibrous tissue within the mediastinum.[62, 160, 208, 210, 228, 259] An abnormal immunologic response to antigens of *Histoplasma capsulatum* is thought to be the most common cause in the United States. Other causes include *M. tuberculosis* infection, autoimmune disease, radiation therapy, trauma, and drugs such as methysergide. A rare familial form associated with retroperitoneal fibrosis,

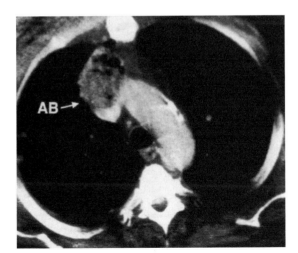

Figure 29–98. Descending cervical mediastinitis. CT shows air-containing mediastinal abscess (AB) that extended from an abscess in the neck.

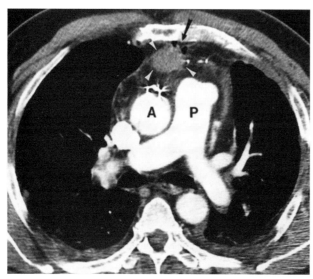

Figure 29–100. Mediastinitis manifesting as mediastinal abscess. CT shows a poorly marginated heterogeneous soft tissue mass *(arrowheads)* in the anterior mediastinum. Note the absence of air within the abscess. The needle was positive for *Staphylococcus aureus* infection. B, brachiocephalic artery; S, superior vena cava.

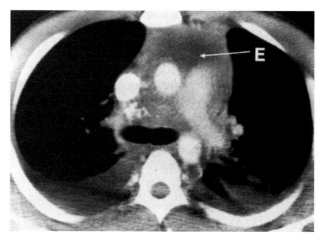

Figure 29–101. Acute mediastinitis caused by histoplasmosis. CT shows diffuse increased attenuation of mediastinal fat and pericardial effusion (E).

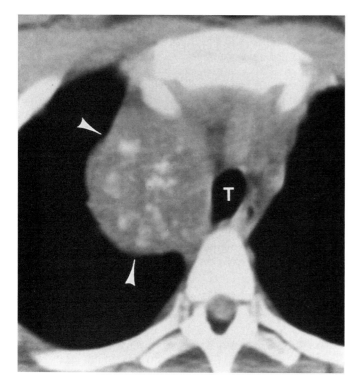

Figure 29–102. Mediastinal granuloma caused by histoplasmosis. CT shows soft-tissue-attenuation mass with punctate calcification *(arrowheads)* in the superior mediastinum. Biopsy confirmed histoplasmosis. T, trachea.

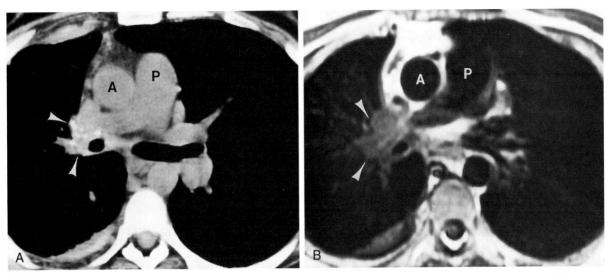

Figure 29–103. Fibrosing mediastinitis in a 45-year-old woman with chest pain. *A,* CT of the chest demonstrates an infiltrating right hilar mass *(arrowheads)* with punctate calcification and right posterior pleural thickening. *B,* Axial T1-weighted MR image shows intermediate-signal-intensity mass *(arrowheads)* and obstruction of the right pulmonary artery. The MRI appearance is nonspecific; the presence of extensive calcification on the CT scan suggests the diagnosis. A, ascending aorta; P, pulmonary artery. (Reprinted with permission from Erasmus JJ, McAdams HP, Donnelly LF, Spritzer CE: MR imaging of mediastinal masses. Magn Reson Imaging Clin North Am 8:59–89, 2000.)

sclerosing cholangitis, Riedel's thyroiditis, and pseudotumor of the orbit is also reported.

Affected patients usually present in the second through fifth decades of life with signs and symptoms caused by obstruction and compression of the SVC, pulmonary veins or arteries, central airways, or esophagus. Patients most commonly present with cough, recurrent pulmonary infection, hemoptysis, or chest pain. Pulmonary venous obstruction may result in symptoms that mimic those of mitral stenosis.

The chest radiographic findings of fibrosing mediastinitis are nonspecific and often underestimate the extent of mediastinal disease. CT and MRI are consequently useful in the evaluation of this disorder (Figs. 29–102 to 29–104). On CT, fibrosing mediastinitis typically manifests as an infiltrative, often calcified hilar or mediastinal process. CT is useful for demonstrating airway, pulmonary arterial and venous involvement.

On MRI scans, the process typically shows heterogeneous signal intensity on T1-weighted and T2-weighted images. Markedly decreased signal intensity on T2-weighted images is occasionally seen and is suggestive of the fibrotic nature of the process. MRI may be superior to CT for defining the full extent of the disease, which is of importance in preoperative planning; however, CT is better for demonstrating calcification within the lesion, a finding that is critical for differentiating fibrosing mediastinitis from other infiltrative disorders of the mediastinum such as metastatic carcinoma or lymphoma.

Hemorrhage

Bleeding can occur within the mediastinum as a result of trauma, surgery, or line placement; after endoscopy; or as a result of abnormal clotting factors. Hemorrhage may extend from the neck or retroperitoneum into the mediastinum. Hemorrhage can manifest as diffuse areas of increased density or as focal areas of increased density within the mediastinal fat.

Mediastinal Lipomatosis

Mediastinal lipomatosis is a benign accumulation of fat within the mediastinum that can manifest as widening of the mediastinum on chest radiographs.[124] Mediastinal

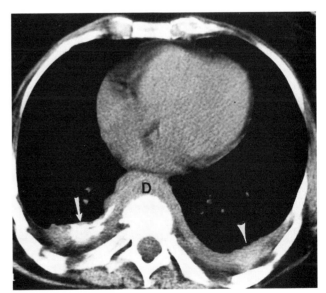

Figure 29–104. Posterior mediastinal fibrosis. CT shows diffuse soft-tissue-attenuation mass encasing the distal aorta (D) and extending into the pleural space *(arrowhead)* bilaterally. Extensive calcification *(arrow)* can be visualized in the right pleural space.

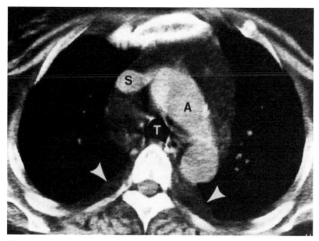

Figure 29–105. Mediastinal lipomatosis. CT shows bilateral mediastinal widening caused by mediastinal fat deposition. Fat deposition is also visible in the paraspinal and posterior pleural regions bilaterally *(arrowheads)*. The distribution is typical of mediastinal lipomatosis. A, aorta; S, superior vena cava; T, trachea.

lipomatosis may be associated with obesity, steroid use, or Cushing's syndrome, but often no predisposing factor is recognized. The accumulation of fat is more pronounced in the upper mediastinum. Mediastinal lipomatosis demonstrates a uniform fat density of −100 HU on CT (Fig. 29–105). If the fat has a higher density or strands of soft tissue density within it, other diagnoses, such as liposarcoma, hemorrhage, tumor infiltration, or mediastinitis, should be considered.

Occasionally, a prominent epicardial fat pad can result in a mediastinal mass (Fig. 29–106).

Mesenchymal Tumors

A variety of mesenchymal tumors can arise in the mediastinum and affect one or multiple compartments.[38, 54, 59, 111, 176, 249] These include malignancies such as leiomyosarcoma and liposarcoma as well as benign desmoid tumors of the mediastinum.

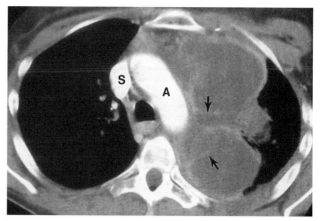

Figure 29–107. Mediastinal liposarcoma. Contrast-enhanced CT shows a large heterogeneous mediastinal mass involving multiple compartments. Note enhancing septa *(arrows)* and absence of adipose tissue within mass. A, aorta; S, superior vena cava.

Liposarcomas typically arise in the anterior mediastinum, occur in middle-aged adults, and present with symptoms of chest pain and dyspnea. Masses are typically large and diffusely infiltrate the mediastinum. Low-grade tumors can have large amounts of fat demonstrable on CT or MR images; high-grade tumors typically manifest as heterogeneous soft tissue masses on CT or MR images (Fig. 29–107).

Leiomyomas and leiomyosarcomas usually arise from the esophagus, although rarely they can arise in the mediastinum independent of the esophagus. They manifest as large middle-mediastinal masses of soft tissue attenuation or signal intensity on CT or MR images. Affected patients typically present with dysphagia.

Other less common mesenchymal sarcomas that may

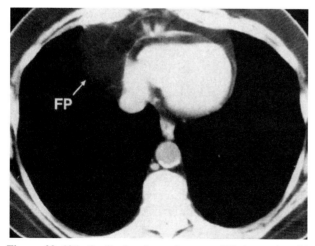

Figure 29–106. Cardiophrenic angle mass. CT shows that this mass is caused by a prominent epicardial fat pad (FP).

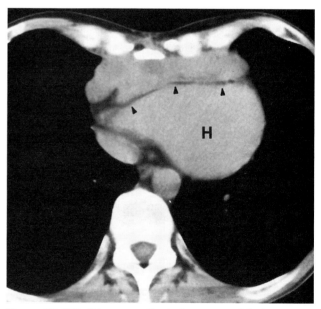

Figure 29–108. Primary mediastinal sarcoma. CT shows large, lobular, heterogeneous anterior mediastinal mass. The fat plane *(arrowheads)* between the mass and the adjacent compressed heart (H) is preserved.

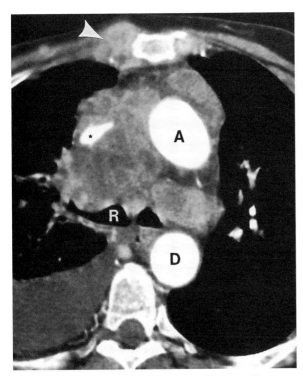

Figure 29–109. Diffuse mediastinal metastases. Contrast-enhanced CT shows diffuse infiltrating mediastinal mass caused by metastatic breast carcinoma. Narrowing of the superior vena cava *(asterisk)*, chest wall metastasis *(arrowhead)*, and large right pleural effusion can be seen. A, ascending aorta; D, descending aorta; R, right main bronchus.

arise within the mediastinum include rhabdomyosarcoma, fibrosarcoma, chondrosarcoma, and osteosarcoma (Fig. 29–108).

Desmoid tumors are uncommon proliferations of fibroblastic cells that typically arise from muscular fascia. Although histologically benign, they can exhibit aggressive behavior with a propensity for local invasion and recurrence after resection. They uncommonly arise within the

mediastinum. Most tumors that affect the mediastinum do so by extension from chest wall or head and neck lesions. On CT, desmoid tumors are usually homogeneous and show slightly increased attenuation relative to skeletal muscle. On T1-weighted MR images, they show low signal intensity; on T2-weighted images, they show variable signal intensity. Although the tumors are usually localized, extensive invasion of mediastinal structures is occasionally detected.

Metastatic Malignancy

Metastatic malignancy can occasionally result in a diffuse mediastinal abnormality. This most likely results from extranodal extension in patients with metastatic disease to the mediastinal lymph nodes. Metastatic mucinous tumors to the mediastinum (ovarian, colon) can occur in young patients, and occasionally this occurs prior to the diagnosis of the primary malignancy. Metastatic malignancy appears on CT or MR images as an infiltrating, heterogeneous mass that invades and occasionally obliterates adjacent mediastinal structures (Fig. 29–109). It can be difficult to differentiate metastatic malignancy from fibrosing mediastinitis. Features that suggest fibrosing mediastinitis rather than metastatic malignancy include the following:

• Diffuse calcification within the lesion
• Young age of patient
• No history of extrathoracic primary malignancy

Vascular Abnormalities and Anomalies

A variety of vascular anomalies can simulate a mediastinal mass.[42, 43, 98, 99, 260, 261] These include, but are not limited to, dilation of the pulmonary arteries, dilation of the vena cava, persistence of a left SVC, a persistent vertical vein, the SVC syndrome, dilation of the azygos or hemiazygos veins, mediastinal varices, aneurysms and pseudoaneurysms of the aorta, right-sided and double aortic arches, aberrant subclavian arteries, and tortuous great vessels. In all cases, CT (usually with IV contrast material) or MRI is essential for confirming the diagnosis (Fig. 29–110).

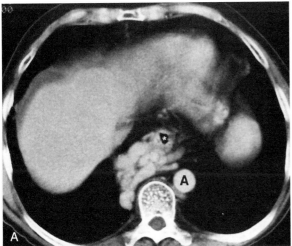
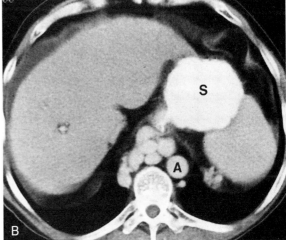

Figure 29–110. Esophageal varices. *A* and *B*, Contrast-enhanced CT shows multiple tubular contrast-enhancing structures surrounding the distal esophagus *(asterisk on A)*, compatible with esophageal varices. Note moderate ascites. A, aorta; S, stomach.

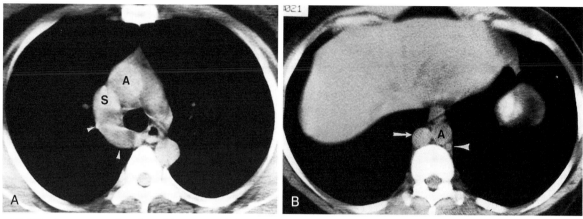

Figure 29–111. Azygous continuation of interrupted inferior vena cava. *A,* CT shows the dilated azygos vein *(arrowheads)* as it enters the posterior aspect of the superior vena cava (S). *B,* Caudal CT shows the dilated azygos vein *(arrow)* near the diaphragmatic hiatus. The hemiazygos vein *(arrowhead)* is normal. A, aorta.

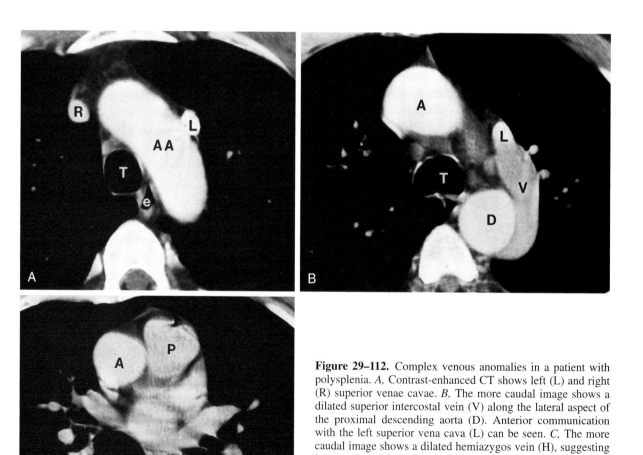

Figure 29–112. Complex venous anomalies in a patient with polysplenia. *A,* Contrast-enhanced CT shows left (L) and right (R) superior venae cavae. *B,* The more caudal image shows a dilated superior intercostal vein (V) along the lateral aspect of the proximal descending aorta (D). Anterior communication with the left superior vena cava (L) can be seen. *C,* The more caudal image shows a dilated hemiazygos vein (H), suggesting interruption of the inferior vena cava, confirmed on abdominal images. A, ascending aorta; AA, aortic arch; e, esophagus; P, main pulmonary artery; T, trachea.

Azygous Continuation of Inferior Vena Cava

Interruption of the inferior vena cava is a congenital abnormality that can be associated with polysplenia.[56, 57, 256] In this anomaly, the infrahepatic, suprarenal segment of the inferior vena cava is absent. Venous blood from the lower extremity and abdomen is diverted into the azygos, or less commonly, the hemiazygos system, resulting in dilation of these veins. Chest radiographs usually show an enlarged azygos vein and a widened paraspinal reflection, and the inferior vena cava is usually not visualized on the lateral radiograph. CT or MRI shows enlargement of the azygos or hemiazygos veins and marked dilation of the azygos arch or the left superior intercostal vein (Figs. 29–111 and 29–112).

Persistent Left Superior Vena Cava

A persistent left SVC[44] occurs in about 1 in 200 adults with normal hearts and in up to 5% of children with congenital heart disease. Most patients with this anomaly have both a right and a left SVC. Occasionally, a persistent brachiocephalic vein connects the two superior venae cavae. On CT, the left SVC is seen as a round density just to the left of the aortic arch. If contrast material is administered via the left arm, the vein enhances (see Fig. 29–112). The left SVC extends inferiorly to the region of the left superior pulmonary veins and then connects into the coronary sinus (Fig. 29–113). Rarely, the vein may connect into the left atrium, giving rise to a small right-to-left shunt.

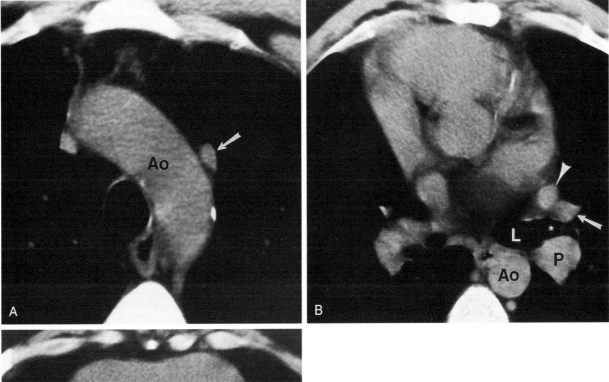

Figure 29–113. Persistent left superior vena cava (SVC). *A,* CT shows persistent left SVC *(arrow)* adjacent to the transverse aorta. *B* and *C,* The more caudal CT images show characteristic anatomic findings of the left SVC. Two vascular structures can be seen anterior to the left main bronchus (L). Left SVC *(arrowhead on B)* is anterior to the left upper lobe bronchus *(asterisk on B),* adjacent and medial to the left superior pulmonary vein *(arrow in B).* Drainage of the left SVC into coronary sinus *(arrow in C)* typically results in dilation of the sinus. Ao, transverse aorta; P, pulmonary artery; RA, right atrium.

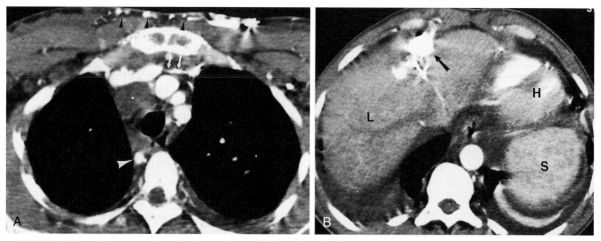

Figure 29–114. Collateral venous channels in a patient with thrombosis of the left subclavian vein caused by an indwelling catheter. *A,* Contrast-enhanced CT shows narrowing of the left subclavian vein *(arrows),* numerous enlarged veins in soft tissues of the chest *(small arrowheads)* and paravertebral region. The *large arrowhead* indicates an enlarged right superior intercostal vein, and the *asterisk* indicates paratracheal adenopathy. *B,* Contrast-enhanced CT shows collateral venous drainage in the recanalized umbilical vein *(arrow).* Bilateral pleural effusions can be seen. L, liver; H, heart; S, spleen.

The persistent left SVC should not be confused with the left superior intercostal vein. The superior intercostal vein connects the left brachiocephalic vein with the hemiazygos system. It runs parallel to the aortic arch, is often seen in the fat adjacent to the arch, and normally measures no more than 4 mm in diameter. It can become enlarged as a result of collateral flow in patients with congenital or acquired obstruction of the vena cava (see Fig. 29–112).

Superior Vena Cava or Brachiocephalic Vein Obstruction

Obstruction of the SVC or brachiocephalic veins can result from malignancy, infection, or iatrogenic causes.[23, 266] Lung carcinoma is the most common malignant cause; histoplasmosis-induced fibrosing mediastinitis is the most common infectious cause (in the Midwestern United States); and central venous catheters are the most common iatrogenic cause. In the past, upper extremity venography was the method of diagnosing SVC or brachiocephalic venous obstruction. Contrast CT is the now the most common imaging modality used (Fig. 29–114). MRI can also be useful in patients with contraindications to administration of iodinated contrast material, but it occasionally fails to differentiate complete obstruction from marked narrowing with very slow flow.

Aberrant Right Subclavian Artery

An aberrant right subclavian artery[31, 199, 200] is a common vascular abnormality that occurs in about 1 in 200 patients. In younger patients, it is usually not obvious on a chest radiograph; in older patients, however, it can manifest as a right paratracheal mass or, on the lateral radiograph, as a retrotracheal mass—like opacity. On CT, the aberrant right subclavian artery arises as the last and most posterior vessel off the aortic arch, crosses the mediastinum behind the trachea and esophagus, and continues into the neck and axilla along the right of the trachea (Figs. 29–115 and 29–116). Frequently, a diverticulum (Kommerell's) is seen

at the origin of the aberrant right subclavian artery from the aorta.

Right Aortic Arch

A right aortic arch[16, 167, 199] is commonly mistaken for a mediastinal mass on chest radiographs, and patients are often referred for CT evaluation of a right paratracheal mass. Most asymptomatic adults with a right-sided aortic arch have an aberrant left subclavian artery. Other anatomic configurations, such as mirror-image branching of the great vessels, are less common and more often associated with severe congenital heart disease. CT or MRI easily identifies

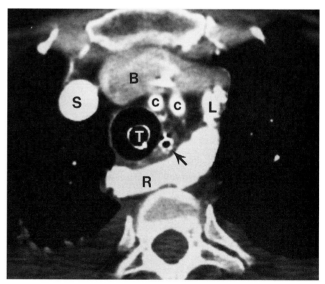

Figure 29–115. Aberrant right subclavian artery. Contrast-enhanced CT shows enhancement of retrotracheal right subclavian artery (R). A nasogastric tube can be seen in the esophagus *(arrow).* B, brachiocephalic vein; c, left and right common carotid arteries; L, left subclavian artery; S, superior vena cava; T, trachea with endotracheal tube.

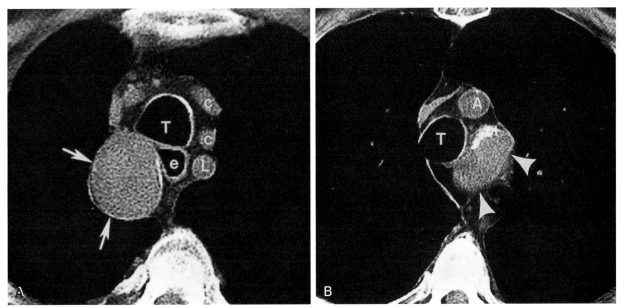

Figure 29–116. Aneurysm of aberrant right subclavian artery. *A,* CT shows homogeneous soft tissue mass *(arrows)* with rim calcification posterior to the trachea (T). *B,* A more caudal CT image confirmed that the mass is an aneurysm of the aberrant right subclavian artery, originating from the proximal descending aorta *(arrowheads).* A, common origin of carotid arteries from aorta; c, left and right common carotid arteries; e, esophagus; L, left subclavian artery.

the aortic arch to the right of the trachea. The aberrant right subclavian artery arises as the last and most posterior vessel off the right-sided aortic arch, crosses the mediastinum behind the trachea and esophagus, and continues into the neck and axilla along the left side of the trachea (Fig. 29–117). Frequently, a diverticulum is seen at the origin of the aberrant left subclavian artery from the aorta.

Double Aortic Arch

Double aortic arches typically manifest in childhood with stridor.[167, 199] Rarely, the lesion manifests in adulthood as an asymptomatic mediastinal mass. On CT or MRI, the double aortic arch is obvious as two large vascular structures encircling the trachea. Each arch gives rise to a subclavian and a carotid artery. The descending aorta is

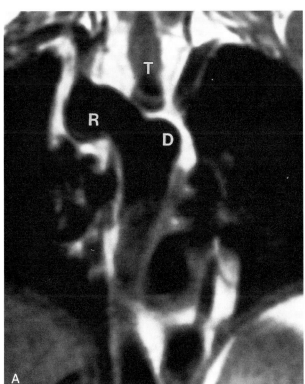

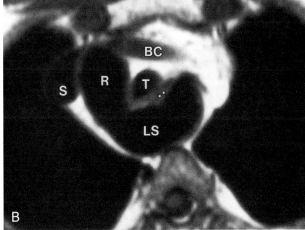

Figure 29–117. Right aortic arch with aberrant left subclavian artery. *A,* Coronal ECG-gated MR image shows right aortic arch (R) and retroesophageal aortic diverticulum (D), giving rise to aberrant left subclavian artery. *B,* Axial ECG-gated MR image shows aberrant left subclavian artery (LS) in retrotracheal location. BC, brachiocephalic vein; R, right aortic arch; S, superior vena cava; T, trachea. *Asterisks* indicate the esophagus.

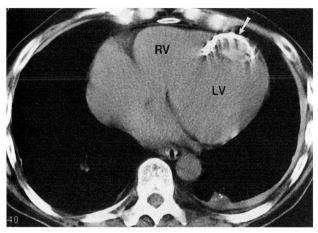

Figure 29–118. Calcified left ventricular aneurysm. CT shows a thin, curvilinear calcification *(arrow)* in the left ventricular apex, consistent with left ventricular aneurysm resulting from a prior infarction. LV, left ventricle; RV, right ventricle.

usually on the left, and the right arch is often higher and slightly larger than the left arch.

Left Ventricular Aneurysm and Pseudoaneurysm

Aneurysms and pseudoaneurysms of the left ventricle[104] often present as mediastinal masses. True left ventricular aneurysms are caused by myocardial ischemia and infarction resulting in focal thinning, dilation, and paradoxical motion of the affected portion of the ventricle. True aneurysms usually occur in the distribution of the left anterior descending coronary artery (along the anterior and apical walls of the left ventricle) and frequently calcify. On CT, they manifest as broad-based areas of thinning of the anterior or apical walls of the left ventricle, often with associated calcification (Figs. 29–118 and 29–119). Mural thrombus may be identified adjacent to the aneurysm. Cine MRI can be useful for demonstrating paradoxical wall motion in the region of the aneurysm.

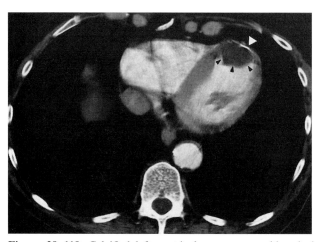

Figure 29–119. Calcified left ventricular aneurysm with apical thrombus. Contrast-enhanced CT shows a thin curvilinear calcification *(white arrowhead)* in the left ventricular apex, consistent with left ventricular aneurysm. Focal wall thinning and adjacent apical thrombus *(black arrowheads)* can be seen.

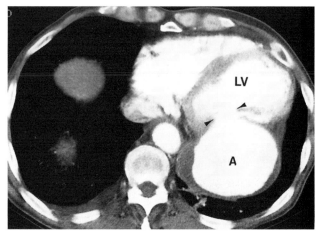

Figure 29–120. Left ventricular pseudoaneurysm. Contrast-enhanced CT shows a large pseudoaneurysm arising from the posterior wall of the left ventricle. A narrow neck *(arrowheads)* between the pseudoaneurysm (A) and the left ventricular cavity (LV) is seen.

Left ventricular pseudoaneurysms result from perforation of the ventricular wall after myocardial infarction. The perforation is contained by pericardium, resulting in pseudoaneurysm formation. Pseudoaneurysms more commonly occur along the posterior and inferior surfaces of the heart and infrequently calcify. On contrast-enhanced CT, they manifest as focal enhancing masses along the posterior or inferior surface of the ventricle, with a narrow communication with the left ventricular chamber (Fig. 29–120). It is important to differentiate pseudoaneurysms from true aneurysms, as the former are prone to delayed rupture whereas the latter are not.

Diaphragmatic Hernia

Abdominal organs or retroperitoneal fat can herniate through areas of congenital or acquired diaphragmatic weakness or tears and manifest as a mediastinal mass on chest radiographs.[71, 82, 83] Common nontraumatic sites of

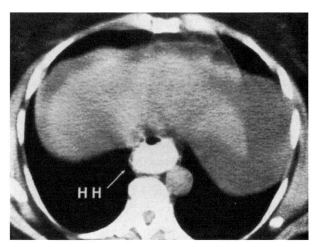

Figure 29–121. Hiatal hernia. CT shows herniation of a portion of the stomach (HH) through the esophageal hiatus.

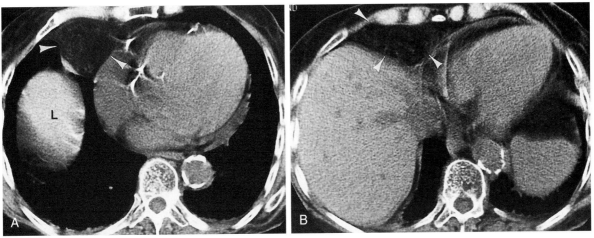

Figure 29–122. Morgagni's hernia. *A* and *B,* CT shows herniation of omental fat *(arrowheads)* into the right cardiophrenic angle. Omental vessels are seen within the fat. L, liver.

herniation include the anterior parasternal hiatus, the esophageal hiatus, and the posterior pleuroperitoneal hiatus. Hiatal hernias are a common cause of a middle mediastinal mass in the lower thorax. The diagnosis is easily made if air or contrast material is seen within the hernia (Fig. 29–121).

Herniation through the anterior parasternal hiatus (foramen of Morgagni) is uncommon and usually manifests as a right-sided mediastinal or cardiophrenic angle mass (Fig. 29–122). These defects are more commonly identified in middle-aged to older adults and are typically asymptomatic. Rarely, defects occur on the left or into the pericardium.

Herniation through the posterior pleuroperitoneal hiatus (foramen of Bochdalek) is the most common cause of congenital diaphragmatic hernia in infants. In adults, the lesions are usually small and asymptomatic and occur more commonly on the left (65%) than on the right (35%). The incidence of small, posterior, fat-containing defects increases with age and degree of emphysema (Fig. 29–123).

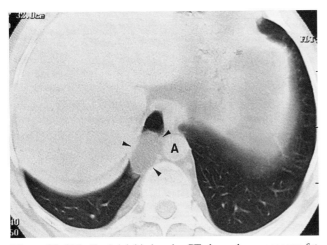

Figure 29–123. Bochdalek's hernia. CT shows homogeneous fat-attenuation mass *(arrowheads)* in the right paraspinal location. Location and CT appearance are consistent with a diagnosis of Bochdalek's hernia. A, aorta.

References

1. Abrahamsen AF, Lien HH, Aas M, et al: Magnetic resonance imaging and ⁶⁷gallium scan in mediastinal malignant lymphoma: A prospective pilot study. Ann Oncol 5:433–436, 1994.
2. Adam A, Hochholzer L: Ganglioneuroblastoma of the posterior mediastinum: A clinicopathologic review of 80 cases. Cancer 47: 373–381, 1981.
3. Alfidi RJ, Haaga JR, El-Yousef SJ, et al: Preliminary experimental results in humans and animals with a superconducting, whole-body, nuclear magnetic resonance scanner. Radiology 143:175–181, 1982.
4. al-Mulhim FA, Ibrahim EM, el-Hassan AY, Moharram HM: Magnetic resonance imaging of tuberculous spondylitis. Spine 20:2287–2292, 1995.
5. Arizono T, Oga M, Shiota E, et al: Differentiation of vertebral osteomyelitis and tuberculous spondylitis by magnetic resonance imaging. Int Orthop 19:319–322, 1995.
6. Aronberg DJ, Glazer HS, Sagel SS: MRI and CT of the mediastinum: Comparisons, controversies, and pitfalls. Radiol Clin North Am 23:439–448, 1985.
7. Atkinson DJ, Edelman RR: Cineangiography of the heart in a single breath hold with a segmented turboFLASH sequence. Radiology 178:357–360, 1991.
8. Auffermann W, Gooding GA, Okerlund MD, et al: Diagnosis of recurrent hyperparathyroidism: Comparison of MR imaging and other imaging techniques. AJR Am J Roentgenol 150:1027–1033, 1988.
9. Aughenbaugh GL: Thoracic manifestations of neurocutaneous diseases. Radiol Clin North Am 22:741–756, 1984.
10. Aygun C, Slawson RG, Bajaj K, Salazar OM: Primary mediastinal seminoma. Urology 23:109–117, 1984.
11. Azar T, Abdul-Karim FW, Tucker HM: Adenoid cystic carcinoma of the trachea. Laryngoscope 108:1297–1300, 1998.
12. Azarow KS, Pearl RH, Zurcher R, et al: Primary mediastinal masses: A comparison of adult and pediatric populations. J Thorac Cardiovasc Surg 106:67–72, 1993.
13. Bailes DR, Gilderdale DJ, Bydder GM, et al: Respiratory ordered phase encoding (ROPE): A method for reducing respiratory motion artefacts in MR imaging. J Comput Assist Tomogr 9:835–838, 1985.
14. Barakos JA, Brown JJ, Brescia RJ, Higgins CB: High signal intensity lesions of the chest in MR imaging. J Comput Assist Tomogr 13:797–802, 1989.
15. Barakos JA, Brown JJ, Higgins CB: MR imaging of secondary cardiac and paracardiac lesions. AJR Am J Roentgenol 153:47–50, 1989.
16. Baron RL, Gutierrez FR, Sagel SS, et al: CT of anomalies of the mediastinal vessels. Am J Roentgenol 137:571–576, 1981.
17. Baron RL, Lee JK, Sagel SS, Peterson RR: Computed tomography of the normal thymus. Radiology 142:121–125, 1982.

18. Baron RL, Sagel SS, Baglan RJ: Thymic cysts following radiation therapy for Hodgkin disease. Radiology 141:593–597, 1981.
19. Bar-Ziv J, Nogrady MB: Mediastinal neuroblastoma and ganglioneuroma: The differentiation between primary and secondary involvement on the chest roentgenogram. Am J Roentgenol Radium Ther Nucl Med 125:380–390, 1975.
20. Bashist B, Ellis K, Gold RP: Computed tomography of intrathoracic goiters. Am J Roentgenol 140:455–460, 1983.
21. Batra P, Brown K, Steckel RJ, et al: MR imaging of the thorax: A comparison of axial, coronal, and sagittal imaging planes. J Comput Assist Tomogr 12:75–81, 1988.
22. Batra P, Herrmann C Jr, Mulder D: Mediastinal imaging in myasthenia gravis: Correlation of chest radiography, CT, MR, and surgical findings. AJR Am J Roentgenol 148:515–519, 1987.
23. Bechtold RE, Wolfman NT, Karstaedt N, Choplin RH: Superior vena caval obstruction: Detection using CT. Radiology 157:485–487, 1985.
24. Bendini M, Zuiani C, Bazzocchi M, et al: Magnetic resonance imaging and ^{67}Ga scan versus computed tomography in the staging and in the monitoring of mediastinal malignant lymphoma: A prospective pilot study. MAGMA 4:213–224, 1996.
25. Berry DF, Buccigrossi D, Peabody J, et al: Pulmonary vascular occlusion and fibrosing mediastinitis. Chest 89:296–301, 1986.
26. Bhargava R, Parham DM, Lasater OE, et al: MR imaging differentiation of benign and malignant peripheral nerve sheath tumors: use of the target sign. Pediatr Radiol 27:124–129, 1997.
27. Bitkover CY, Cederlund K, Aberg B, Vaage J: Computed tomography of the sternum and mediastinum after median sternotomy. Ann Thorac Surg 68:858–863, 1999.
28. Bluemke DA, Boxerman JL, Atalar E, McVeigh ER: Segmented K-space cine breath-hold cardiovascular MR imaging: Part 1. Principles and technique. AJR Am J Roentgenol 169:395–400, 1997.
29. Boiselle PM, Patz EF Jr, Vining DJ, et al: Imaging of mediastinal lymph nodes: CT, MR, and FDG PET. Radiographics 18:1061–1069, 1998.
30. Boyacigil S, Ardic S, Tokoglu F, et al: Intrathoracic extramedullary haemopoiesis. Australas Radiol 40:179–181, 1996.
31. Branscom JJ, Austin JH: Aberrant right subclavian artery: Findings seen on plain chest roentgenograms. Am J Roentgenol Radium Ther Nucl Med 119:539–542, 1973.
32. Breatnach E, Nath PH, Delany DJ: The role of computed tomography in acute and subacute mediastinitis. Clin Radiol 37:139–145, 1986.
33. Brice P, Rain JD, Frija J, et al: Residual mediastinal mass in malignant lymphoma: Value of magnetic resonance imaging and gallium scan. Nouv Rev Fr Hematol 35:457–461, 1993.
34. Brown LR, Aughenbaugh GL: Masses of the anterior mediastinum: CT and MR imaging. AJR Am J Roentgenol 157:1171–1180, 1991.
35. Brown LR, Aughenbaugh GL, Wick MR, et al: Roentgenologic diagnosis of primary corticotropin-producing carcinoid tumors of the mediastinum. Radiology 142:143–148, 1982.
36. Burk DL Jr, Brunberg JA, Kanal E, et al: Spinal and paraspinal neurofibromatosis: Surface coil MR imaging at 1.5 T1. Radiology 162:797–801, 1987.
37. Canini R, Battista G, Monetti N, et al: Bulky mediastinal lymphomas: Role of magnetic resonance and SPECT-Ga-67 in the evaluation of residual masses. Radiol Med (Torino) 90:448–456, 1995.
38. Casillas J, Sais GJ, Greve JL, et al: Imaging of intra- and extraabdominal desmoid tumors. Radiographics 11:959–968, 1991.
39. Castellino RA: Diagnostic imaging studies in patients with newly diagnosed Hodgkin's disease. Ann Oncol 3(suppl 4):45–47, 1992.
40. Caty MG, Shamberger RC: Abdominal tumors in infancy and childhood. Pediatr Clin North Am 40:1253–1271, 1993.
41. Chao MW, Smith JG, Laidlaw C, et al: Results of treating primary tumors of the trachea with radiotherapy. Int J Radiat Oncol Biol Phys 41:779–785, 1998.
42. Cohen MC, Hartnell GG, Finn JP: Magnetic resonance angiography of congenital pulmonary vein anomalies. Am Heart J 127:954–955, 1994.
43. Cole TJ, Henry DA, Jolles H, Proto AV: Normal and abnormal vascular structures that simulate neoplasms on chest radiographs: Clues to the diagnosis. Radiographics 15:867–891, 1995.
44. Cormier MG, Yedlicka JW, Gray RJ, Moncada R: Congenital anomalies of the superior vena cava: A CT study. Semin Roentgenol 24:77–83, 1989.
45. Dagirmanjian A, Schils J, McHenry M, Modic MT: MR imaging of vertebral osteomyelitis revisited. AJR Am J Roentgenol 167:1539–1543, 1996.
46. Davidson AJ, Hartman DS, Goldman SM: Mature teratoma of the retroperitoneum: Radiologic, pathologic, and clinical correlation. Radiology 172:421–425, 1989.
47. Davis RD Jr, Oldham HN Jr, Sabiston DC Jr: Primary cysts and neoplasms of the mediastinum: Recent changes in clinical presentation, methods of diagnosis, management, and results. Ann Thorac Surg 44:229–237, 1987.
48. Davis S, Rogers MA, Pendergrass TW: The incidence and epidemiologic characteristics of neuroblastoma in the United States. Am J Epidemiol 126:1063–1074, 1987.
49. de Geer G, Webb WR, Gamsu G: Normal thymus: Assessment with MR and CT. Radiology 158:313–317, 1986.
50. Dexeus FH, Logothetis CJ, Chong C, et al: Genetic abnormalities in men with germ cell tumors. J Urol 140:80–84, 1988.
51. Do YS, Im JG, Lee BH, et al: CT findings in malignant tumors of thymic epithelium. J Comput Assist Tomogr 19:192–197, 1995.
52. Donner MW, Saba GP, Martinez CR: Diffuse diseases of the esophagus: A practical approach. Semin Roentgenol 16:198–213, 1981.
53. Dooms GC, Hricak H, Moseley ME, et al: Characterization of lymphadenopathy by magnetic resonance relaxation times: Preliminary results. Radiology 155:691–697, 1985.
54. Dosios TJ, Angouras DC, Floros DG: Primary desmoid tumor of the posterior mediastinum. Ann Thorac Surg 66:2098–2099, 1998.
55. Ducatman BS, Scheithauer BW, Piepgras DG, et al: Malignant peripheral nerve sheath tumors: A clinicopathologic study of 120 cases. Cancer 57:2006–2021, 1986.
56. Dudiak CM, Olson MC, Posniak HV: Abnormalities of the azygos system: CT evaluation. Semin Roentgenol 24:47–55, 1989.
57. Dudiak CM, Olson MC, Posniak HV: CT evaluation of congenital and acquired abnormalities of the azygos system. Radiographics 11:233–246, 1991.
58. Ehman RL, McNamara MT, Pallack M, et al: Magnetic resonance imaging with respiratory gating: Techniques and advantages. Am J Roentgenol 143:1175–1182, 1984.
59. Eisenstat R, Bruce D, Williams LE, Katz DS: Primary liposarcoma of the mediastinum with coexistent mediastinal lipomatosis. AJR Am J Roentgenol 174:572–573, 2000.
60. Endo M, Adachi S, Kusumoto M, et al: A study of the utility of the MR image for the diagnosis of thymic tumors—imaging and pathologic correlation. Nippon Igaku Hoshasen Gakkai Zasshi 53:1–10, 1993.
61. Erasmus JJ, McAdams HP, Donnelly LF, Spritzer CE: MR imaging of mediastinal masses. Magn Reson Imaging Clin North Am 8:59–89, 2000.
62. Farmer DW, Moore E, Amparo E, et al: Calcific fibrosing mediastinitis: Demonstration of pulmonary vascular obstruction by magnetic resonance imaging. Am J Roentgenol 143:1189–1191, 1984.
63. Feigin DS, Fenoglio JJ, McAllister HA, Madewell JE: Pericardial cysts: A radiologic-pathologic correlation and review. Radiology 125:15–20, 1977.
64. Feinberg DA, Hale JD, Watts JC, et al: Halving MR imaging time by conjugation: Demonstration at 3.5 kG. Radiology 161:527–531, 1986.
65. Felson B: Chest Roentgenology. Philadelphia, WB Saunders, 1973.
66. Fernandes ET, Custer MD, Burton EM, et al: Neurenteric cyst: Surgery and diagnostic imaging. J Pediatr Surg 26:108–110, 1991.
67. Filly R, Bland N, Castellino RA: Radiographic distribution of intrathoracic disease in previously untreated patients with Hodgkin's disease and non-Hodgkin's lymphoma. Radiology 120:277–281, 1976.
68. Foo TK, Bernstein MA, Aisen AM, et al: Improved ejection fraction and flow velocity estimates with use of view sharing and uniform repetition time excitation with fast cardiac techniques. Radiology 195:471–478, 1995.
69. Francis IR, Dorovini-Zis K, Glazer GM, et al: The fibromatoses: CT-pathologic correlation. Am J Roentgenol 147:1063–1066, 1986.
70. Francis IR, Glazer GM, Bookstein FL, Gross BH: The thymus: Reexamination of age-related changes in size and shape. Am J Roentgenol 145:249–254, 1985.
71. Fraser RS, Muller NL, Colman N, Pare PD: Fraser and Pare's Diagnosis of Diseases of the Chest. 4th ed. Philadelphia, WB Saunders, 1999.

72. Fulcher AS, Proto AV, Jolles H: Cystic teratoma of the mediastinum: Demonstration of fat/fluid level. AJR Am J Roentgenol 154:259–260, 1990.

73. Furukawa H: Magnetic resonance (MR) imaging for the detection of the invasion into neighboring structures in esophageal cancers. Nippon Geka Gakkai Zasshi 92:636–644, 1991.

74. Gale AW, Jelihovsky T, Grant AF, et al: Neurogenic tumors of the mediastinum. Ann Thorac Surg 17:434–443, 1974.

75. Gamsu G, Stark DD, Webb WR, et al: Magnetic resonance imaging of benign mediastinal masses. Radiology 151:709–713, 1984.

76. Gasparini MD, Balzarini L, Castellani MR, et al: Current role of gallium scan and magnetic resonance imaging in the management of mediastinal Hodgkin lymphoma. Cancer 72:577–582, 1993.

77. Gefter WB: Magnetic resonance imaging in the evaluation of lung cancer. Semin Roentgenol 25:73–84, 1990.

78. Gefter WB, Spritzer CE, Eisenberg B, et al: Thyroid imaging with high-field-strength surface-coil MR. Radiology 164:483–490, 1987.

79. Gelfand DW, Goldman AS, Law EJ, et al: Thymic hyperplasia in children recovering from thermal burns. J Trauma 12:813–817, 1972.

80. Ghosh BC, Ghosh L, Huvos AG, Fortner JG: Malignant schwannoma: A clinicopathologic study. Cancer 31:184–190, 1973.

81. Gilkeson RC, Basile V, Sands MJ, Hsu JT: Chest case of the day: Extramedullary hematopoiesis (EMH). AJR Am J Roentgenol 169:267, 270–263, 1997.

82. Gilkeson RC, Basile V, Sands MJ, Hsu JT: Chest case of the day: Morgagni's hernia. AJR Am J Roentgenol 169:266, 268–270, 1997.

83. Glasser DL, Shanmuganathan K, Mirvis SE: General case of the day: Acute intrapericardial diaphragmatic hernia. Radiographics 18:799–801, 1998.

84. Glazer GM, Axel L, Moss AA: CT diagnosis of mediastinal thyroid. Am J Roentgenol 138:495–498, 1982.

85. Glazer GM, Orringer MB, Chenevert TL, et al: Mediastinal lymph nodes: Relaxation time/pathologic correlation and implications in staging of lung cancer with MR imaging. Radiology 168:429–431, 1988.

86. Glazer HS, Molina PL, Siegel MJ, Sagel SS: High-attenuation mediastinal masses on unenhanced CT. AJR Am J Roentgenol 156:45–50, 1991.

87. Glazer HS, Wick MR, Anderson DJ, et al: CT of fatty thoracic masses. AJR Am J Roentgenol 159:1181–1187, 1992.

88. Goodman LR, Kay HR, Teplick SK, Mundth ED: Complications of median sternotomy: Computed tomographic evaluation. Am J Roentgenol 141:225–230, 1983.

89. Graeber GM, Thompson LD, Cohen DJ, et al: Cystic lesion of the thymus: An occasionally malignant cervical and/or anterior mediastinal mass. J Thorac Cardiovasc Surg 87:295–300, 1984.

90. Gumbs RV, Higginbotham-Ford EA, Teal JS, et al: Thoracic extramedullary hematopoiesis in sickle-cell disease. AJR Am J Roentgenol 149:889–893, 1987.

91. Haacke EM, Lenz GW: Improving MR image quality in the presence of motion by using rephasing gradients. AJR Am J Roentgenol 148:1251–1258, 1987.

92. Haacke EM, Patrick JL: Reducing motion artifacts in two-dimensional Fourier transform imaging. Magn Reson Imaging 4:359–376, 1986.

93. Halvorsen RA Jr, Thompson WM: CT of esophageal neoplasms. Radiol Clin North Am 1989 27:667–685.

94. Hara M, McAdams HP, Vredenburgh JJ, et al: Thymic hyperplasia after high-dose chemotherapy and autologous stem cell transplantation: Incidence and significance in patients with breast cancer. AJR Am J Roentgenol 173:1341–1344, 1999.

95. Harkin JC, Reed RJ: Atlas of Tumor Pathology: Tumors of the Peripheral Nervous System. Washington, D.C., Armed Forces Institute of Pathology, 1982, pp 25–150.

96. Harris NL, Jaffe ES, Stein H, et al: A revised European-American classification of lymphoid neoplasms: A proposal from the International Lymphoma Study Group. Blood 84:1361–1392, 1994.

97. Hartmann CA, Roth C, Minck C, Niedobitek G: Thymic carcinoma: Report of five cases and review of the literature. J Cancer Res Clin Oncol 116:69–82, 1990.

98. Hartnell GG: Magnetic resonance angiography of systemic thoracic and abdominal veins. Magn Reson Imaging Clin North Am 1:281–294, 1993.

99. Hartnell GG, Hughes LA, Finn JP, Longmaid HE 3rd: Magnetic resonance angiography of the central chest veins: A new gold standard? Chest 107:1053–1057, 1995.

100. Hawkes RC, Patz S: Rapid Fourier imaging using steady-state free precession. Magn Reson Med 4:9–23, 1987.

101. Heitzman ER: The Mediastinum. Berlin, Springer-Verlag, 1988.

102. Herfkens RJ, Higgins CB, Hricak H, et al: Nuclear magnetic resonance imaging of the cardiovascular system: Normal and pathologic findings. Radiology 147:749–759, 1983.

103. Herold C, Zerhouni E: The mediastinum and lungs. In Higgins CB, Hricak H, Helms CA (eds): Magnetic Resonance Imaging of the Body, 3rd ed. New York, Lippincott-Raven, 1997.

104. Higgins C, Caputo G: Acquired heart disease. In Higgins CB Hricak H, Helms CA (eds): Magnetic Resonance Imaging of the Body, 3rd ed. New York, Lippincott-Raven, 1997.

105. Higgins CB, Auffermann W: MR imaging of thyroid and parathyroid glands: A review of current status. AJR Am J Roentgenol 151:1095–1106, 1988.

106. Higgins CB, Byrd BF 2nd, McNamara MT, et al: Magnetic resonance imaging of the heart: A review of the experience in 172 subjects. Radiology 155:671–679, 1985.

107. Higgins CB, McNamara MT, Fisher MR, Clark OH: MR imaging of the thyroid. Am J Roentgenol 147:1255–1261, 1986.

108. Hoffman OA, Gillespie DJ, Aughenbaugh GL, Brown LR: Primary mediastinal neoplasms (other than thymoma). Mayo Clin Proc 68:880–891, 1993.

109. Holscher AH, Dittler HJ, Siewert JR: Staging of squamous esophageal cancer: Accuracy and value. World J Surg 18:312–320, 1994.

110. Hope DG, Mulvihill JJ: Malignancy in neurofibromatosis. Adv Neurol 29:33–56, 1981.

111. Inase N, Ichioka M, Akamatsu H, et al: Mediastinal fibromatosis presenting with superior vena cava syndrome. Respiration 66:464–466, 1999.

112. Indeglia RA, Shea MA, Grage TB: Congenital cysts of the thymus gland. Arch Surg 94:149–152, 1967.

113. Ishaque MA, Crockard HA, Stevens JM: Ossified pseudomeningocoele following laminectomy: Case reports and review of the literature. Eur Spine J 6:430–432, 1997.

114. Ishibashi M, Nishida H, Hiromatsu Y, et al: Comparison of technetium-99m–MIBI, technetium-99m–tetrofosmin, ultrasound and MRI for localization of abnormal parathyroid glands. J Nucl Med 39:320–324, 1998.

115. Ishibashi M, Nishida H, Hiromatsu Y, et al: Localization of ectopic parathyroid glands using technetium-99m sestamibi imaging: Comparison with magnetic resonance and computed tomographic imaging. Eur J Nucl Med 24:197–201, 1997.

116. Ishibashi M, Nishida H, Kumabe T, et al: Tc-99m tetrofosmin: A new diagnostic tracer for parathyroid imaging. Clin Nucl Med 20:902–905, 1995.

117. Ishii K, Maeda K, Hashihira M, et al: MRI of mediastinal cavernous hemangioma. Pediatr Radiol 20:556–557, 1990.

118. Jaramillo D, Perez-Atayde A, Griscom NT: Apparent association between thymic cysts and prior thoracotomy. Radiology 172:207–209, 1989.

119. Jochelson M, Mauch P, Balikian J, et al: The significance of the residual mediastinal mass in treated Hodgkin's disease. J Clin Oncol 3:637–640, 1985.

120. Kang YS, Rosen K, Clark OH, Higgins CB: Localization of abnormal parathyroid glands of the mediastinum with MR imaging. Radiology 189:137–141, 1993.

121. Kaplan PA, Williams SM: Mucocutaneous and peripheral soft-tissue hemangiomas: MR imaging. Radiology 163:163–166, 1987.

122. Kataoka K, Matsuura M, Seno N: Study of cystic mediastinal lesions—diagnostic usefulness of magnetic resonance imaging. Nippon Kyobu Geka Gakkai Zasshi 43:438–445, 1995.

123. Kawashima A, Fishman EK, Kuhlman JE: CT and MR evaluation of posterior mediastinal masses. Crit Rev Diagn Imaging 33:311–367, 1992.

124. Kawashima A, Fishman EK, Kuhlman JE, Nixon MS: CT of posterior mediastinal masses. Radiographics 11:1045–1067, 1991.

125. Keller AR, Castleman B: Hodgkin's disease of the thymus gland. Cancer 33:1615–1623, 1974.

126. Keller AR, Hochholzer L, Castleman B: Hyaline-vascular and plasma-cell types of giant lymph node hyperplasia of the mediastinum and other locations. Cancer 29:670–683, 1972.

127. Kelly JD, Forster AM, Higley B, et al: Technetium-99m–tetrofosmin as a new radiopharmaceutical for myocardial perfusion imaging. J Nucl Med 34:222–227, 1993.

128. Kiernan PD, Hernandez A, Byrne WD, et al: Descending cervical mediastinitis. Ann Thorac Surg 65:1483–1488, 1998.
129. Kim TS, Lee KS, Han J, et al: Mucoepidermoid carcinoma of the tracheobronchial tree: Radiographic and CT findings in 12 patients. Radiology 212:643–648, 1999.
130. Kirwan WO, Walbaum PR, McCormack RJ: Cystic intrathoracic derivatives of the foregut and their complications. Thorax 28:424–428, 1973.
131. Klemm KM, Moran CA: Primary neuroendocrine carcinomas of the thymus. Semin Diagn Pathol 16:32–41, 1999.
132. Klemm KM, Moran CA, Suster S: Pigmented thymic carcinoids: A clinicopathological and immunohistochemical study of two cases. Mod Pathol 12:946–948, 1999.
133. Knapp RH, Hurt RD, Payne WS, et al: Malignant germ cell tumors of the mediastinum. J Thorac Cardiovasc Surg 89:82–89, 1985.
134. Krishnan J, Danon AD, Frizzera G: Reactive lymphadenopathies and atypical lymphoproliferative disorders. Am J Clin Pathol 99:385–396, 1993.
135. Krubsack AJ, Wilson SD, Lawson TL, et al: Prospective comparison of radionuclide, computed tomographic, sonographic, and magnetic resonance localization of parathyroid tumors. Surgery 106:639–644 (discussion, pp 644–636), 1989.
136. Kumar AJ, Kuhajda FP, Martinez CR, et al: Computed tomography of extracranial nerve sheath tumors with pathological correlation. J Comput Assist Tomogr 7:857–865, 1983.
137. Kushihashi T, Munechika H, Motoya H, et al: CT and MR findings in tuberculous mediastinitis. J Comput Assist Tomogr 19:379–382, 1995.
138. Kwong JS, Muller NL, Miller RR: Diseases of the trachea and main-stem bronchi: Correlation of CT with pathologic findings. Radiographics 12:645–657, 1992.
139. Lanzer P, Botvinick EH, Schiller NB, et al: Cardiac imaging using gated magnetic resonance. Radiology 150:121–127, 1984.
140. Lazzarino M, Orlandi E, Paulli M, et al: Primary mediastinal B-cell lymphoma with sclerosis: An aggressive tumor with distinctive clinical and pathologic features. J Clin Oncol 11:2306–2313, 1993.
141. LeBlanc J, Guttentag AR, Shepard JA, McLoud TC: Imaging of mediastinal foregut cysts. Can Assoc Radiol J 45:381–386, 1994.
142. Lee JD, Choe KO, Kim SJ, et al: CT findings in primary thymic carcinoma. J Comput Assist Tomogr 15:429–433, 1991.
143. Lee KS, Im JG, Han CH, et al: Malignant primary germ cell tumors of the mediastinum: CT features. AJR Am J Roentgenol 153:947–951, 1989.
144. Lee T, Lee SK, Chen CL, Chen CY: Role of MR imaging of middle third esophageal carcinoma in determining resectability. Chung Hua I Hsueh Tsa Chih (Taipei) 52:363–367, 1993.
145. Lee VS, Spritzer CE: MR imaging of abnormal parathyroid glands. AJR Am J Roentgenol 170:1097–1103, 1998.
146. Lee VS, Spritzer CE, Coleman RE, et al: The complementary roles of fast spin-echo MR imaging and double-phase ^{99m}Tc-sestamibi scintigraphy for localization of hyperfunctioning parathyroid glands. AJR Am J Roentgenol 167:1555–1562, 1996.
147. Lehr L, Rupp N, Siewert JR: Assessment of resectability of esophageal cancer by computed tomography and magnetic resonance imaging. Surgery 103:344–350, 1988.
148. Levitt RG, Husband JE, Glazer HS: CT of primary germ-cell tumors of the mediastinum. Am J Roentgenol 142:73–78, 1984.
149. Lewis BD, Hurt RD, Payne WS, et al: Benign teratomas of the mediastinum. J Thorac Cardiovasc Surg 86:727–731, 1983.
150. Lewis JE, Wick MR, Scheithauer BW, et al: Thymoma. A clinicopathologic review. Cancer 60:2727–2743, 1987.
151. Lichtenstein AK, Levine L, Taylor CR, et al: Primary mediastinal lymphoma in adults. Am J Med 68:509–514, 1980.
152. Lieberman JM, Alfidi RJ, Nelson AD, et al: Gated magnetic resonance imaging of the normal and diseased heart. Radiology 152:465–470, 1984.
153. Link KM, Samuels LJ, Reed JC, et al: Magnetic resonance imaging of the mediastinum. J Thorac Imaging 8:34–53, 1993.
154. Lyon RD, McAdams HP: Mediastinal bronchogenic cyst: Demonstration of a fluid-fluid level at MR imaging. Radiology 186:427–428, 1993.
155. Marchevsky AM: Mediastinal tumors of peripheral nervous system origin. Semin Diagn Pathol 16:65–78, 1999.
156. Marin ML, Romney BM, Franco K, et al: Bronchogenic cyst: A case report emphasizing the role of magnetic resonance imaging. J Thorac Imaging 6:43–46, 1991.
157. Martin G, Kleinsasser O: Neurogenic sarcomas of the neck in neurofibromatosis. Arch Otorhinolaryngol 232:273–283, 1981.
158. Mathisen DJ: Tracheal tumors. Chest Surg Clin North Am 6:875–898, 1996.
159. Mathisen DJ: Primary tracheal tumor management. Surg Oncol Clin North Am 8:307, 1999.
160. McAdams HP: Chest case of the day: Fibrosing mediastinitis. AJR Am J Roentgenol 165:189–190, 1995.
161. McAdams HP, Rosado-de-Christenson M, Fishback NF, Templeton PA: Castleman disease of the thorax: Radiologic features with clinical and histopathologic correlation. Radiology 209:221–228, 1998.
162. McAdams HP, Kirejczyk WM, Rosado-de-Christenson ML, Matsumoto S: Bronchogenic cyst: Imaging features with histopathologic correlation. Radiology 217:441–446, 2000.
163. McAdams HP, Rosado-de-Christenson ML, Moran CA: Mediastinal hemangioma: Radiographic and CT features in 14 patients. Radiology 193:399–402, 1994.
164. McCarthy MJ, Rosado-de-Christenson ML: Tumors of the trachea. J Thorac Imaging 10:180–198, 1995.
165. McCarty MJ, Vukelja SJ, Banks PM, Weiss RB: Angiofollicular lymph node hyperplasia (Castleman's disease). Cancer Treat Rev 21:291–310, 1995.
166. McElaney B, McAdams HP: Chest case of the day: Metastatic bronchial carcinoid. AJR Am J Roentgenol 165:186–187, 1995.
167. McLoughlin MJ, Weisbrod G, Wise DJ, Yeung HP: Computed tomography in congenital anomalies of the aortic arch and great vessels. Radiology 138:399–403, 1981.
168. Merine DS, Fishman EK, Zerhouni EA: Computed tomography and magnetic resonance imaging diagnosis of thymic cyst. J Comput Tomogr 12:220–222, 1988.
169. Misawa Y, Fuse K, Hasegawa T: Infectious mediastinitis after cardiac operations: Computed tomographic findings. Ann Thorac Surg 65:622–624, 1998.
170. Moeller KH, Rosado-de-Christenson ML, Templeton PA: Mediastinal mature teratoma: Imaging features. AJR Am J Roentgenol 169:985–990, 1997.
171. Moon WK, Im JG, Han MC: Castleman's disease of the mediastinum: MR imaging features. Clin Radiol 49:466–468, 1994.
172. Moore AV, Korobkin M, Olanow W, et al: Age-related changes in the thymus gland: CT-pathologic correlation. Am J Roentgenol 141:241–246, 1983.
173. Moore AV, Korobkin M, Powers B, et al: Thymoma detection by mediastinal CT: Patient with myasthenia gravis. Am J Roentgenol 138:217–222, 1982.
174. Moran CA, Suster S, Fishback N, Koss MN: Mediastinal paragangliomas: A clinicopathologic and immunohistochemical study of 16 cases. Cancer 72:2358–2364, 1993.
175. Moran CA, Suster S, Koss MN: Primary germ cell tumors of the mediastinum: III. Yolk sac tumor, embryonal carcinoma, choriocarcinoma, and combined nonteratomatous germ cell tumors of the mediastinum—a clinicopathologic and immunohistochemical study of 64 cases. Cancer 80:699–707, 1997.
176. Moran CA, Suster S, Perino G, et al: Malignant smooth muscle tumors presenting as mediastinal soft tissue masses: A clinicopathologic study of 10 cases. Cancer 74:2251–2260, 1994.
177. Moran CA, Suster S, Przygodzki RM, Koss MN: Primary germ cell tumors of the mediastinum: II. Mediastinal seminomas—a clinicopathologic and immunohistochemical study of 120 cases. Cancer 80:691–698, 1997.
178. Morgenthaler TI, Brown LR, Colby TV, et al: Thymoma. Mayo Clin Proc 68:1110–1123, 1993.
179. Moss AA, Schnyder P, Thoeni RF, Margulis AR: Esophageal carcinoma: Pretherapy staging by computed tomography. Am J Roentgenol 136:1051–1056, 1981.
180. Murayama S, Murakami J, Watanabe H, et al: Signal intensity characteristics of mediastinal cystic masses on T1-weighted MRI. J Comput Assist Tomogr 19:188–191, 1995.
181. Naidich DP, Webb WR, Muller NL: The mediastinum. In Computed Tomography and Magnetic Resonance of the Thorax. 3rd ed. New York, Lippincott-Raven, 1999, pp 37–160.
182. Naidich DP, Webb WR, Muller NL, et al: Aorta, arch vessels, and great veins. In Computed Tomography and Magnetic Resonance of the Thorax. 3rd ed. Philadelphia, Lippincott-Raven, 1999, pp 505–602.
183. Nakasu Y, Minouchi K, Hatsuda N, et al: Thoracic meningocele in

neurofibromatosis: CT and MR findings. J Comput Assist Tomogr 15:1062–1064, 1991.

184. Nakata H, Egashira K, Watanabe H, et al: MRI of bronchogenic cysts. J Comput Assist Tomogr 17:267–270, 1993.

185. Nanson EM: Lymphangioma (cystic hygroma) of the mediastinum. J Cardiovasc Surg (Torino) 9:447–452, 1968.

186. Negendank WG, al-Katib AM, Karanes C, Smith MR: Lymphomas: MR imaging contrast characteristics with clinical-pathologic correlations. Radiology 177:209–216, 1990.

187. Nichols CR: Mediastinal germ cell tumors: Clinical features and biologic correlates. Chest 99:472–479, 1991.

188. Nichols CR: Mediastinal germ cell tumors. Semin Thorac Cardiovasc Surg 4:45–50, 1992.

189. Norris EH: The parathyroid adenoma: A study of 322 cases. Int Abst Surg 84:1–41, 1947.

190. Nyman R, Forsgren G, Glimelius B: Long-term follow-up of residual mediastinal masses in treated Hodgkin's disease using MR imaging. Acta Radiol 37:323–326, 1996.

191. O'Sullivan R, McKenzie A, Hennessy O: Value of CT scanning in assessing location and extent of epidural and paraspinal inflammatory conditions. Australas Radiol 32:203–206, 1988.

192. Pattany PM, Phillips JJ, Chiu LC, et al: Motion artifact suppression technique (MAST) for MR imaging. J Comput Assist Tomogr 11:369–377, 1987.

193. Patterson GA, Ginsberg RJ, Poon PY, et al: A prospective evaluation of magnetic resonance imaging, computed tomography, and mediastinoscopy in the preoperative assessment of mediastinal node status in bronchogenic carcinoma. J Thorac Cardiovasc Surg 94:679–684, 1987.

194. Perelman MI, Koroleva N, Birjukov J, Goudovsky L: Primary tracheal tumors. Semin Thorac Cardiovasc Surg 8:400–402, 1996.

195. Peterson BA, Frizzera G: Multicentric Castleman's disease. Semin Oncol 20:636–647, 1993.

196. Picus D, Balfe DM, Koehler RE, et al: Computed tomography in the staging of esophageal carcinoma. Radiology 146:433–438, 1983.

197. Pilla TJ, Wolverson MK, Sundaram M, et al: CT evaluation of cystic lymphangiomas of the mediastinum. Radiology 144:841–842, 1982.

198. Poon PY, Bronskill MJ, Henkelman RM, et al: Mediastinal lymph node metastases from bronchogenic carcinoma: Detection with MR imaging and CT. Radiology 162:651–656, 1987.

199. Predey TA, McDonald V, Demos TC, Moncada R: CT of congenital anomalies of the aortic arch. Semin Roentgenol 24:96–113, 1989.

200. Proto AV, Cuthbert NW, Raider L: Aberrant right subclavian artery: Further observations. AJR Am J Roentgenol 148:253–257, 1987.

201. Quagliano PV: Thymic carcinoma: Case reports and review. J Thorac Imaging 11:66–74, 1996.

202. Quint LE, Glazer GM, Orringer MB: Esophageal imaging by MR and CT: Study of normal anatomy and neoplasms. Radiology 156:727–731, 1985.

203. Rabushka LS, Fishman EK, Kuhlman JE: CT evaluation of achalasia. J Comput Assist Tomogr 15:434–439, 1991.

204. Radford JA, Cowan RA, Flanagan M, et al: The significance of residual mediastinal abnormality on the chest radiograph following treatment for Hodgkin's disease. J Clin Oncol 6:940–946, 1988.

205. Rainov NG, Heidecke V, Burkert W: Thoracic and lumbar meningocele in neurofibromatosis type 1: Report of two cases and review of the literature. Neurosurg Rev 18:127–134, 1995.

206. Reed JC, Hallet KK, Feigin DS: Neural tumors of the thorax: Subject review from the AFIP. Radiology 126:9–17, 1978.

207. Reinig JW, Stanley JH, Schabel SI: CT evaluation of thickened esophageal walls. Am J Roentgenol 140:931–934, 1983.

208. Rholl KS, Levitt RG, Glazer HS: Magnetic resonance imaging of fibrosing mediastinitis. Am J Roentgenol 145:255–259, 1985.

209. Robicsek F: Postoperative sterno-mediastinitis. Am Surg 66:184–192, 2000.

210. Rodriguez E, Soler R, Pombo F, et al: Fibrosing mediastinitis: CT and MR findings. Clin Radiol 53:907–910, 1998.

211. Rosado de Christenson ML, Abbott GF, Kirejczyk WM, et al: Thoracic carcinoids: Radiologic-pathologic correlation. Radiographics 19:707–736, 1999.

212. Rosado-de-Christenson ML, Galobardes J, Moran CA: Thymoma: Radiologic-pathologic correlation. Radiographics 12:151–168, 1992.

213. Rosado-de-Christenson ML, Pugatch RD, Moran CA, Galobardes J: Thymolipoma: Analysis of 27 cases. Radiology 193:121–126, 1994.

214. Rosado-de-Christenson ML, Templeton PA, Moran CA: From the archives of the AFIP: Mediastinal germ cell tumors—radiologic and pathologic correlation. Radiographics 12:1013–1030, 1992.

215. Rossi SE, Erasmus JJ, McAdams HP, Donnelly LF: Thoracic manifestations of neurofibromatosis-I. AJR Am J Roentgenol 173:1631–1638, 1999.

216. Ruzal-Shapiro C, Abramson SJ, Berdon WE: Posterior mediastinal cystic teratoma surrounded by fat in a 13 month old boy: Value of magnetic resonance imaging. Pediatr Radiol 20:107–109, 1989.

217. Sakai F, Sone S, Kiyono K, et al: MR imaging of thymoma: Radiologic-pathologic correlation. AJR Am J Roentgenol 158:751–756, 1992.

218. Sakai F, Sone S, Kiyono K, et al: Intrathoracic neurogenic tumors: MR-pathologic correlation. AJR Am J Roentgenol 159:279–283, 1992.

219. Salyer DC, Salyer WR, Eggleston JC: Benign developmental cysts of the mediastinum. Arch Pathol Lab Med 101:136–139, 1977.

220. Sasaka K, Kurihara Y, Nakajima Y, et al: Spontaneous rupture: A complication of benign mature teratomas of the mediastinum. AJR Am J Roentgenol 170:323–328, 1998.

221. Satava RM Jr, Beahrs OH, Scholz DA: Success rate of cervical exploration for hyperparathyroidism. Arch Surg 110:625–628, 1975.

222. Savader SJ, Otero RR, Savader BL: MR imaging of intrathoracic extramedullary hematopoiesis. J Comput Assist Tomogr 12:878–880, 1988.

223. Schurawitzki H, Stiglbauer R, Klepetko W, Eckersberger F: CT and MRI in benign mediastinal haemangioma. Clin Radiol 43:91–94, 1991.

224. Seline TH, Gross BH, Francis IR: CT and MR imaging of mediastinal hemangiomas. J Comput Assist Tomogr 14:766–768, 1990.

225. Shaffer K, Rosado-de-Christenson ML, Patz EF Jr, et al: Thoracic lymphangioma in adults: CT and MR imaging features. AJR Am J Roentgenol 162:283–289, 1994.

226. Shaffer K, Smith D, Kirn D, et al: Primary mediastinal large-B-cell lymphoma: Radiologic findings at presentation. AJR Am J Roentgenol 167:425–430, 1996.

227. Shahian DM, Rossi RL: Posterior mediastinal goiter. Chest 94:599–602, 1988.

228. Sherrick AD, Brown LR, Harms GF, Myers JL: The radiographic findings of fibrosing mediastinitis. Chest 106:484–489, 1994.

229. Shields TW, Reynolds M: Neurogenic tumors of the thorax. Surg Clin North Am 68:645–668, 1988.

230. Shin MS, Berland LL, Ho KJ: Mediastinal cystic hygromas: CT characteristics and pathogenetic consideration. J Comput Assist Tomogr 9:297–301, 1985.

231. Shin MS, Ho KJ: Computed tomography of primary mediastinal seminomas. J Comput Assist Tomogr 7:990–994, 1983.

232. Shirkhoda A, Chasen MH, Eftekhari F, et al: MR imaging of mediastinal thymolipoma. J Comput Assist Tomogr 11:364–365, 1987.

233. Silverman PM, Korobkin M, Moore AV: CT diagnosis of cystic hygroma of the neck. J Comput Assist Tomogr 7:519–520, 1983.

234. Sirivella S, Ford WB, Zikria EA, et al: Foregut cysts of the mediastinum: Results in 20 consecutive surgically treated cases. J Thorac Cardiovasc Surg 90:776–782, 1985.

235. Snyder ME, Luck SR, Hernandez R, et al: Diagnostic dilemmas of mediastinal cysts. J Pediatr Surg 20:810–815, 1985.

236. So CB, Li DK: Anterolateral cervical meningocele in association with neurofibromatosis: MR and CT studies. J Comput Assist Tomogr 13:692–695, 1989.

237. Spiers AS, Husband JE, MacVicar AD: Treated thymic lymphoma: Comparison of MR imaging with CT. Radiology 203:369–376, 1997.

238. Spritzer C, Gamsu G, Sostman HD: Magnetic resonance imaging of the thorax: Techniques, current applications, and future directions. J Thorac Imaging 4:1–18, 1989.

239. Spritzer CE, Gefter WB, Hamilton R, et al: Abnormal parathyroid glands: High-resolution MR imaging. Radiology 162:487–491, 1987.

240. Stark DD, Moss AA, Brasch RC, et al: Neuroblastoma: Diagnostic imaging and staging. Radiology 148:101–105, 1983.

241. Stevens SK, Chang JM, Clark OH, et al: Detection of abnormal parathyroid glands in postoperative patients with recurrent hyperparathyroidism: Sensitivity of MR imaging. AJR Am J Roentgenol 160:607–612, 1993.

242. Strickler JG, Kurtin PJ: Mediastinal lymphoma. Semin Diagn Pathol 8:2–13, 1991.

243. Strollo DC, Rosado de Christenson ML, Jett JR: Primary mediastinal tumors: Part 1. Tumors of the anterior mediastinum. Chest 112:511–522, 1997.

244. Strollo DC, Rosado-de-Christenson ML: Tumors of the thymus. J Thorac Imaging 14:152–171, 1999.

245. Strollo DC, Rosado-de-Christenson ML, Jett JR: Primary mediastinal tumors: Part II. Tumors of the middle and posterior mediastinum. Chest 112:1344–1357, 1997.

246. Suster S, Rosai J: Multilocular thymic cyst: An acquired reactive process—study of 18 cases. Am J Surg Pathol 15:388–398, 1991.

247. Swanson PE: Soft tissue neoplasm of the mediastinum. Semin Diagn Pathol 8:14–34, 1991.

248. Takashima S, Takeuchi N, Shiozaki H, et al: Carcinoma of the esophagus: CT vs MR imaging in determining resectability. AJR Am J Roentgenol 156:297–302, 1991.

249. Tam CG, Broome DR, Shannon RL: Desmoid tumor of the anterior mediastinum: CT and radiologic features. J Comput Assist Tomogr 18:499–501, 1994.

250. Tan A, Holdener GP, Hecht A, et al: Malignant thymoma in an ectopic thymus: CT appearance. J Comput Assist Tomogr 15:842–844, 1991.

251. Templeton PA, Fishman EK: CT evaluation of poststernotomy complications. AJR Am J Roentgenol 159:45–50, 1992.

252. Tesoro-Tess JD, Balzarini L, Ceglia E, et al: Magnetic resonance imaging in the initial staging of Hodgkin's disease and non-Hodgkin lymphoma. Eur J Radiol 12:81–90, 1991.

253. Utz JA, Herfkens RJ, Glover G, et al: Rapid Dynamic NMR Imaging of the Heart. Montreal, Canada, Society of Magnetic Resonance in Medicine, 1986.

254. Verstandig AG, Epstein DM, Miller WT Jr, et al: Thymoma—report of 71 cases and a review. Crit Rev Diagn Imaging 33:201–230, 1992.

255. Wang YM, Li YW, Sheih CP, Hsu JC: Magnetic resonance imaging of neuroblastoma, ganglioneuroblastoma, and ganglioneuroma. Chung Hua Min Kuo Hsiao Erh Ko I Hsueh Hui Tsa Chih 36:420–424, 1995.

256. Webb WR, Gamsu G, Speckman JM, et al: Computed tomographic demonstration of mediastinal venous anomalies. Am J Roentgenol 139:157–161, 1982.

257. Webb WR, Gamsu G, Stark DD, Moore EH: Magnetic resonance imaging of the normal and abnormal pulmonary hila. Radiology 152:89–94, 1984.

258. Weidner N: Germ-cell tumors of the mediastinum. Semin Diagn Pathol 16:42–50, 1999.

259. Weinstein JB, Aronberg DJ, Sagel SS: CT of fibrosing mediastinitis: Findings and their utility. Am J Roentgenol 141:247–251, 1983.

260. White CS: MR imaging of thoracic veins. Magn Reson Imaging Clin North Am 8:17–32, 2000.

261. White CS, Baffa JM, Haney PJ, et al: MR imaging of congenital anomalies of the thoracic veins. Radiographics 17:595–608, 1997.

262. White CS, Templeton PA, Attar S: Esophageal perforation: CT findings. AJR Am J Roentgenol 160:767–770, 1993.

263. Wick MR, Scheithauer BW, Weiland LH, Bernatz PE: Primary thymic carcinomas. Am J Surg Pathol 6:613–630, 1982.

264. Wilkins EW Jr, Edmunds LH Jr, Castleman B: Cases of thymoma at the Massachusetts General Hospital. J Thorac Cardiovasc Surg 52:322–330, 1966.

265. Wychulis AR, Payne WS, Clagett OT, Woolner LB: Surgical treatment of mediastinal tumors: A 40 year experience. J Thorac Cardiovasc Surg 62:379–392, 1971.

266. Yedlicka JW, Schultz K, Moncada R, Flisak M: CT findings in superior vena cava obstruction. Semin Roentgenol 24:84–90, 1989.

267. Yeh HC, Gordon A, Kirschner PA, Cohen BA: Computed tomography and sonography of thymolipoma. Am J Roentgenol 140:1131–1133, 1983.

268. Zadvinskis DP, Benson MT, Kerr HH, et al: Congenital malformations of the cervicothoracic lymphatic system: Embryology and pathogenesis. Radiographics 12:1175–1189, 1992.

269. Zinzani PL, Zompatori M, Bendandi M, et al: Monitoring bulky mediastinal disease with gallium-67, CT-scan and magnetic resonance imaging in Hodgkin's disease and high-grade non-Hodgkin's lymphoma. Leuk Lymphoma 22:131–135, 1996.

30

Pleura and Chest Wall

Barbara L. Knisely

After the initial chest radiograph, computed tomography (CT) is the standard imaging modality for the evaluation of chest wall disorders and pleural disease. CT characterizes the type of pleural disease by tissue density, evaluates the extent of pleural and chest wall disease, and differentiates between pleural and parenchymal disease.[35] Magnetic resonance imaging (MRI), with its superior soft tissue contrast, complements CT in patients with pleural disorders. The role of MRI in the chest is limited to specific problem solving, such as select cases of pleural effusions, tumors, infections, and masses.[37, 41] The ability of MRI to obtain images in the coronal and sagittal planes helps in the evaluation of chest wall and pleural abnormalities, particularly the apical regions.[15, 34, 48, 70]

This chapter discusses the CT and MRI findings of pleural and chest wall diseases.

CT Technique

Standard CT examination of the chest includes 10-mm collimation with 10-mm slices obtained from the thoracic inlet through the adrenal glands. Images are obtained with the patient supine in the scanner and with respiration suspended. Helical CT scanners can image the entire chest in a single breath-hold, diminishing respiratory artifact. Coronal and sagittal planes may be reconstructed from the helical CT data for improved evaluation of the pleura and chest wall.

The use of intravenous (IV) contrast is tailored to the individual examination. Contrast may add information in differentiating empyemas from lung abscesses, in distinguishing among solid and cystic lesions, and in identifying areas of necrosis. Images are reviewed in both lung and mediastinal window settings. High-resolution CT (HRCT) images are obtained using 1-mm slices and a high spatial algorithm to evaluate for such diseases as asbestosis in the setting of asbestos exposure.

MRI Technique

There is no standard technique used for the MRI evaluation of chest wall and pleural disease. Common sequences may be as follows:

1. T1-weighted spin-echo (SE) sequences, with a repetition time (TR) of 400 to 600 msec and an echo time (TE) of 15 to 20 msec.
2. Proton-density–weighted and T2-weighted spin-echo sequences (2200–2700/20–30, 80).

3. Fast spin-echo techniques (4000–5600/80–104; 8–12 echo train).

Fat saturation, flow compensation, and presaturation inferiorly and superiorly are added to these sequences. Sequences employed in vascular assessment are as follows:

1. Short tau inversion recovery (STIR) sequences (TR/TE/TI, 2200/43/160 msec).
2. Gradient-recalled acquisition in the steady state (GRASS) sequences (33/13, 30 degrees flip angle).

The slice thickness and intersection gap vary for each examination, depending on the region of interest. The imaging planes (sagittal, axial, coronal, and oblique) are chosen to best depict the anatomy and the abnormality.

Chest MR images are obtained with a large field-of-view scout, usually in the coronal plane, with the patient in either a torso or a body coil. Cardiac gating techniques and respiratory compensation are routinely used. Pulse sequences, imaging planes, and section thickness are designed for the individual patient.

Generally, T1-weighted images provide good anatomic resolution and superb contrast between abnormalities in the extrapleural and pleural fat.[27, 42] T2-weighted images offer good tumor-to-muscle contrast and are helpful in evaluating pleural diseases that invade the chest wall. Additional images with a smaller field of view may be obtained after the initial views with the use of specialized surface coils.

Pleura

Routine CT and MRI cannot perform imaging of the pleura. HRCT depicts the intercostal stripe as a 1- to 2-mm soft tissue line running along the inner aspect of the ribs. This stripe is composed of the visceral and parietal pleura, endothoracic fascia, and the innermost intercostal muscle.[33] The extrapleural fat is seen on HRCT internal to the ribs and is more prominent in obese patients.

Pleural Processes

The features of pleural processes often overlap with parenchymal or extrapleural processes on radiographs. Rib destruction and soft tissue involvement characterize an extrapleural process. Parenchymal lesions typically result in an acute angle with the mediastinum or chest wall.[42] In contrast, pleural processes usually result in an obtuse angle with the chest wall. Despite these general rules, differentiating pleural, extrapleural, and parenchymal processes on CT and MRI may be difficult because more than one compartment may be involved.

Pleural Effusions

A pleural effusion produces a crescent-shaped opacity in the posterior dependent thorax. Loculated pleural effusions appear as fixed lenticula-shaped opacities. Free-flowing pleural fluid in the posterior costophrenic angle may be difficult to differentiate from ascites.

A number of CT signs have been reported to help differentiate pleural from ascitic fluid, namely (1) the diaphragm,[4] (2) the interface,[75] (3) a displaced crus,[19] and (4) a "bare area" sign.[53] The interface and bare area signs are the most accurate.[29]

The interface sign describes a hazy interface with a pleural effusion and a sharp interface with ascites adjacent to the liver or spleen (Figs. 30–1 and 30–2).[75]

The bare area sign describes the restriction of ascites from contacting the posterior liver by the coronary ligaments in the right hemithorax; however, pleural effusion can freely flow in that location.[53]

The diaphragm sign describes the anatomic location of pleural effusion relative to the diaphragm. Pleural effusion is outside the diaphragm, and ascites is inside the diaphragm (see Fig. 30–2).[4]

The displaced crus sign describes the anterolateral displacement of the crus by the pleural effusion, which is located between the crus and the spine (Fig. 30–3).[19] Ascites would cause the opposite displacement of the diaphragmatic crus. On an axial image, ascites is contained within the confines of the diaphragm, whereas effusion lies outside the confines of the diaphragm.

Pleural fluid commonly is heterogeneous on MRI scans because flow artifacts are created by motion within the effusion. Simple pleural effusions show low signal intensity on T1-weighted images and high signal intensity on T2-

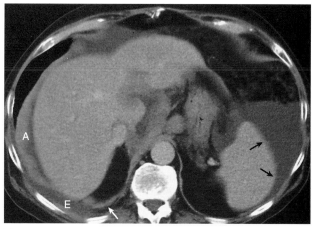

Figure 30–2. CT of "diaphragm" and "interface" signs. Ascites (A) is medial to the diaphragm *(arrow)*, and a pleural effusion (E) is identified lateral to the diaphragm. A sharp interface can be seen between the ascites and the spleen *(arrows)*.

weighted images because of their water content.[2] CT is currently the study of choice for the evaluation of pleural fluid. However, one study showed that MRI may be slightly superior to CT in the characterization of pleural fluid.[17] The MRI signal intensity of pleural effusions differentiates *transudates* from *exudates*, with exudates producing a higher signal intensity, particularly on T2-weighted images.[17]

Acutely, hemothorax shows high attenuation within the pleural fluid on a nonenhanced CT scan (Fig. 30–4). A fibrothorax may develop if a hemothorax is not drained and is allowed to organize, resulting in pleural thickening. A subacute or chronic hemothorax (Fig. 30–5) demonstrates high signal intensity on both T1-weighted and T2-weighted images.[77] The "concentric ring" sign present in a subacute or chronic hemorrhagic pleural effusion is caused by the dark outer ring (hemosiderin) and the bright

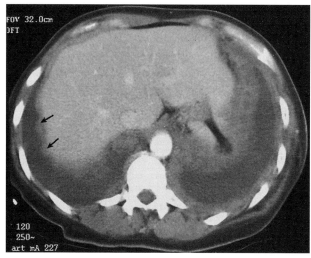

Figure 30–1. CT scan of the "interface" sign. The interface between the pleural effusion and liver laterally is hazy *(arrows)*. A sharp interface would exist between ascites and the liver.

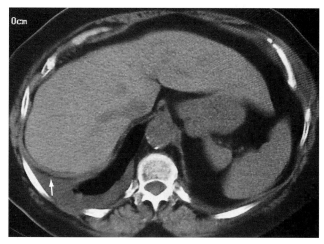

Figure 30–3. CT of "displaced crus" sign. Right pleural effusion forms a crescent-shaped opacity in the dependent portion of the thorax. Lateral displacement of the diaphragmatic crus *(arrow)* describes the displaced crus sign of a pleural effusion.

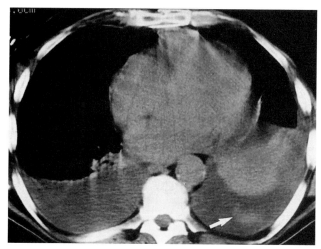

Figure 30–4. Hemothorax following endomyocardial biopsy in a 59-year-old man who developed mild shortness of breath after the biopsy. Nonenhanced CT scan shows a high-attenuation left pleural effusion consistent with hemothorax (arrow). The patient recovered without intervention. (From Knisely BL, Mastey LA, Collins J, Kuhlman JE: Imaging of cardiac transplantation and complications. Radiographics 19:321, 1999.)

central signal intensity (methemoglobin) related to the T1 shortening effects.[28, 42]

On CT scans, chylothorax usually cannot be differentiated from other types of pleural effusions, although one report did show low-attenuation fluid in a chylothorax related to its fat content.[2] Occasionally, a chylothorax may

show high signal intensity on T1-weighted and on proton-density–weighted images and lower signal intensity on T2-weighted images related to fat content.[2] On MRI, however, chylothoraces usually cannot be differentiated from simple pleural effusions.

Pleural effusions may be transudates or exudates. The visceral and parietal pleura enhance in exudative effusions, coined the *split-pleura sign*. Transudates do not usually demonstrate pleural enhancement.

Empyemas are characterized on CT by the split-pleura sign, pleural thickening, and air within the pleural space (Fig. 30–6).[72] Empyemas are often associated with parenchymal disease. It may be difficult to differentiate between the two processes. Differentiation is important; patients with empyemas require chest tube drainage, whereas patients with lung abscesses need antibiotics and postural drainage. CT findings that indicate abscess are a spherical shape, thick walls, and abrupt cut-off of vessels and bronchi in adjacent lung at the interface with the abscess.[72] Empyemas are lenticular, usually with thin walls and with compression of adjacent lung bronchi and vessels.[7, 42] Thickened and increased attenuation of the extrapleural fat can be seen in patients with empyemas and is thought to be related to edema.[80]

Malignant neoplasms that arise in the walls of chronic empyemas (most commonly tuberculous empyemas) may be detected by MRI.[44] Neoplasms associated with empyemas include non-Hodgkin's lymphoma, squamous cell carcinoma, mesothelioma, and sarcoma.[44] MRI reveals signal intensities that differ in mature fibrous tissue and in neoplastic tissue, yet the diagnostic value of this potential has not been determined.[44]

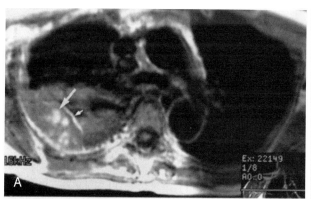

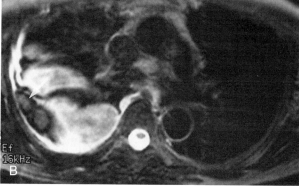

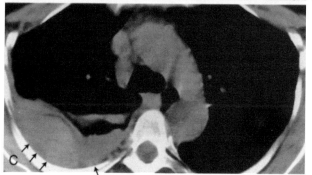

Figure 30–5. Extrapleural hematoma in a 54-year-old woman. Axial T1-weighted (TR = 810 msec, TE = 14 msec) (A) and T2-weighted (TR = 4225 msec, TE = 105 msec) (B) images show old extrapleural hematoma as a focal ovoid mass with focal areas of increased signal intensity on T1-weighted images and a low-signal-intensity rim on T2-weighted images. The extrapleural location is identified by the displaced subpleural fat line on T1-weighted images (small arrow in A). A pleural effusion, with heterogeneous signal intensity on T1-weighted and T2-weighted images, is medial to the extrapleural hematoma (large arrow in A and B). (A and B, From Knisely BL, Broderick LS, Kuhlman JE: MR imaging of the pleura and chest wall. MRI Clin North Am 8:125, 2000.) C, Noncontrast CT scan shows a high-attenuation right extrapleural hematoma (small arrows) and a medial simple pleural effusion (large arrow).

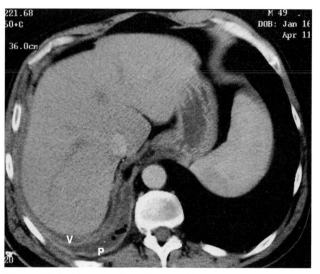

Figure 30–6. Empyema in a 49-year-old man. Contrast-enhanced CT scan shows the split-pleura sign with enhancement of the visceral (V) and parietal (P) pleura. Air bubbles are present in the empyema.

Pleural Air

Standard chest radiographs are the most commonly used radiologic examination for detection of pneumothoraces. In the supine, ventilated, or acutely traumatized patient, CT may detect pneumothoraces not visible on chest radiographs.[76]

A bronchopleural fistula is a communication between the pleura and bronchial tree that results in a persistent air leak (Fig. 30–7). Common causes include necrotizing pulmonary infections and surgical lung resections. CT, particularly thin-section CT, is the imaging modality of choice to show the communication between the airway and the pleura.[82] CT can demonstrate the location, number, size, and underlying cause of bronchopleural fistulas.[73]

Therapeutic options include surgical resection and surgical or image-guided occlusion of the bronchopleural fistula with endobronchial vascular coils or glue. Antibiotics are given to patients with an underlying infection.[56]

Pleural Masses

Benign Pleural Masses

Benign pleural processes include lipoma, asbestos-related disease, localized pleural fibroma, and rounded atelectasis.[40, 83] The most common benign chest wall neoplasms are lipoma and localized pleural fibroma.

On CT scans, lipomas have a homogeneous fat attenuation, occasionally with a few septa or calcifications in areas of fat necrosis. Lipomas are usually located in the lateral pleura, with signal intensity characteristics of subcutaneous fat on all MRI sequences. Benign fibrous tumors of the pleura (previously termed *benign mesotheliomas*) are not asbestos-related and occur in the sixth and seventh decades of life.[20] Most patients with benign pleural fibromas are asymptomatic. Large pleural fibromas may produce symp-

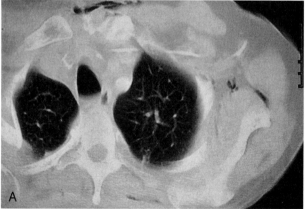

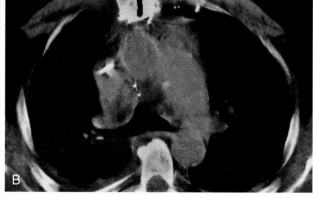

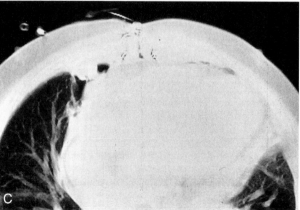

Figure 30–7. Pleuromediastinal cutaneous fistula in a 51-year-old man with coagulase-negative staphylococcal sternal wound infection 10 days after cardiac transplantation. *A,* CT scan shows subcutaneous empyema in the left chest wall. *B,* Nonenhanced CT scan obtained inferior to *A* shows air in the sternal dehiscence and in infiltrated anterior mediastinal fat, findings consistent with infection. *C,* CT scan obtained inferior to *B* shows more extensive pneumomediastinum and a right pneumothorax. (From Knisely BL, Mastey LA, Collins J, Kuhlman JE: Imaging of cardiac transplantation and complications. Radiographics 19:321, 1999.)

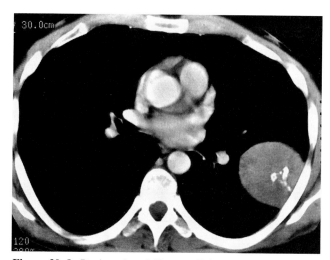

Figure 30–8. Benign pleural fibroma. Enhanced CT scan reveals a soft tissue intrafissural mass with coarse calcifications, pathologically consistent with a benign pleural fibroma. (From Knisely BL, Kuhlman JE: Radiographic and CT imaging of complex pleural disease. Crit Rev Diagn Imaging 38:1, 1997.)

toms of cough, chest pain, and dyspnea. These tumors are associated with an increased incidence of episodic hypoglycemia and hypertrophic pulmonary osteoarthropathy.[9, 20]

On microscopic examination, 60% of pleural fibromas are found to be benign with 40% malignant.[20] A malignant pleural fibroma may have an associated pleural effusion and may grow to more than 10 cm in diameter.[20] Chest wall invasion and local recurrence following surgery can occur with malignant pleural fibromas. The cure rate with surgical excision is 40% for malignant fibromas and 100% for benign fibromas.[20, 50]

The CT appearance is a homogeneous, enhancing soft tissue mass with occasional calcification and associated pleural effusion (Fig. 30–8).[63] On MR images, pleural fibromas are isointense to muscle on T1-weighted images and isointense to hyperintense to muscle on T2-weighted images, and they demonstrate enhancement with IV gadolinium.[23, 39]

Rounded atelectasis (Fig. 30–9) refers to masslike atelectasis abutting the pleura. It has most commonly been described as being related to asbestos exposure.[64, 71] Rounded atelectasis is most commonly seen in the posterior or posteromedial lower lobe, followed by the lingula and right middle lobe.[13] The "comet-tail sign" of vessels and bronchi curving into the mass is seen in both CT and MRI. Displacement of the fissures can confirm the presence of volume loss. On MRI, the signal intensity is comparable to that of liver on T1-weighted images (see Fig. 30–9).[78] The findings of rounded atelectasis on CT and MRI are vital to recognize because this condition may be similar to a pleural or parenchymal neoplasm.[45] Biopsy of rounded atelectasis may be mistaken for malignancy if findings of fibrosis are not seen on histologic examination.[18]

Asbestos-related disease includes simple pleural effusions, pleural plaques and thickening, rounded atelectasis, pleural or parenchymal neoplasms, and asbestosis (interstitial lung disease).[1] Pleural plaques, the most common and specific finding, are located along the diaphragmatic and chest wall parietal pleura.[65] Calcification of pleural plaques may occur; calcifications range in thickness from 1 to 10 mm (Fig. 30–10). Diffuse pleural thickening, which may also be seen in asbestos exposure, frequently follows an asbestos-related benign pleural effusion. On CT scans, pleural plaques are recognized as focal soft tissue masses located inferiorly along the paravertebral pleura. A fibrothorax related to previous hemorrhage or infection should be the primary differential diagnosis if unilateral, thicker, more irregular calcified pleural plaques are present in a patient without a history of asbestos exposure.

Malignant Pleural Masses

Malignant mesothelioma (Fig. 30–11) is a highly lethal tumor whose increased incidence is related to the industrial use of asbestos.[31] CT imaging of mesothelioma shows

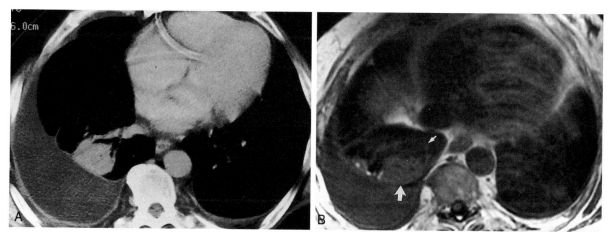

Figure 30–9. Rounded atelectasis in a 65-year-old man. *A,* Contrast-enhanced CT scan reveals right pleural effusion and right lower lobe mass of atelectatic lung with incurving bronchi and vessels. *B,* Axial T1-weighted (TR = 400msec, TE = 14 msec) image shows an ovoid mass *(large arrow)* with an inwardly curving bronchovascular structure *(small arrow)* in the right lower lobe. The mass demonstrates isointense signal intensity relative to liver. A large right pleural effusion can be seen posteriorly. (*B,* From Knisely BL, Broderick LS, Kuhlman JE: MR imaging of the pleura and chest wall. MRI Clin North Am 8:125, 2000.)

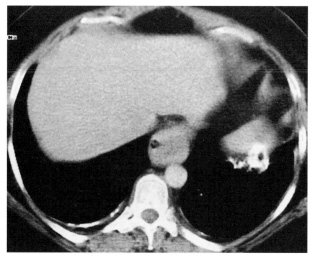

Figure 30–10. Asbestos exposure. Contrast-enhanced CT scan shows bilateral calcified pleural plaques posteriorly with involvement of the left diaphragm.

unilateral, diffuse, nodular pleural thickening, usually with associated pleural effusion. The tumor sometimes encases the lung, extends into the fissures, and causes unilateral volume loss. MRI reveals minimal increased signal intensity on T1-weighted sequences and moderate increased signal intensity on T2-weighted sequences. Mesothelioma (Fig. 30–12) occasionally presents as an effusion without soft tissue thickening or as a discrete pleural mass.[3, 36, 42]

MRI is superior to CT in demonstrating a solitary focus of invasion of the chest wall or endothoracic fascia and in showing invasion of the diaphragm.[31] MRI staging of mesothelioma does not change operative planning, and CT is the standard diagnostic examination because of its cost-effectiveness.[31] For patients who are surgical candidates,

extrapleural pneumonectomy is the procedure of choice, although the prognosis is extremely poor.

Metastatic disease is the most common neoplasm of the pleura (Fig. 30–13).[40, 42] Lung, breast, stomach, and ovarian carcinomas are the most common sources of metastatic pleural disease.[62] Lymphoma and thymoma may also involve the pleural surface.[68] Metastatic pleural adenocarcinoma can mimic the radiographic appearance of mesothelioma with diffuse nodular pleural thickening. Metastatic adenocarcinoma and mesothelioma may be differentiated by immunochemistry, histochemistry, and electron microscopy.[60]

Pleural effusion is the most common manifestation of pleural metastases. Diffuse pleural thickening and solid pleural masses or nodules may also be seen in metastatic pleural disease.

Chest Wall

Knowledge of the cross-sectional anatomy of the chest wall allows adequate evaluation of soft tissue abnormalities (Fig. 30–14). Normal chest wall musculature, vasculature, and bony structures are well visualized on CT scans. A simple method for counting ribs on CT scans is based on identification of the *sternal angle*,[38] an oval high-attenuation structure lacking bone marrow. The second costal cartilages connect to the second ribs laterally and the sternal angle medially. The third to sixth ribs are counted numerically, from anterior to posterior, on the same slice.

Benign Chest Wall Lesions

Lipoma is the most common benign soft tissue mass to involve the chest wall (Fig. 30–15).[52] On CT images, lipomas show the attenuation coefficient of fat and are well

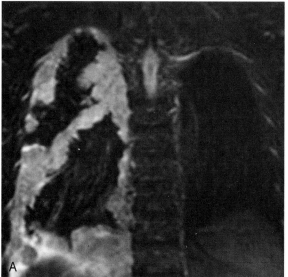

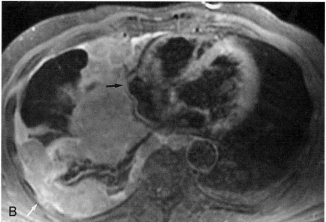

Figure 30–11. Malignant mesothelioma in a 57-year-old man. Coronal T2-weighted (TR = 4500 msec, TE = 105msec) with fat saturation *(A)* and axial T1-weighted (TR = 821 msec, TE = 14 msec) with fat saturation *(B)* gadolinium-enhanced images reveal nodular pleural tumor encasing the right lung, involving the pericardium *(black arrow)*, and extending into endothoracic fascia *(white arrow)*. (From Knisely BL, Broderick LS, Kuhlman JE: MR imaging of the pleura and chest wall. MRI Clin North Am 8:125, 2000.)

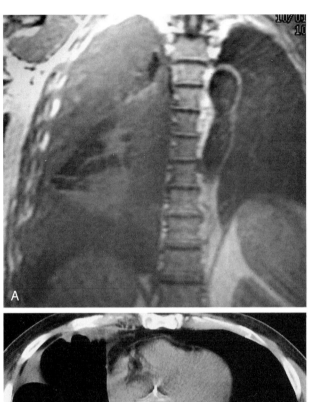

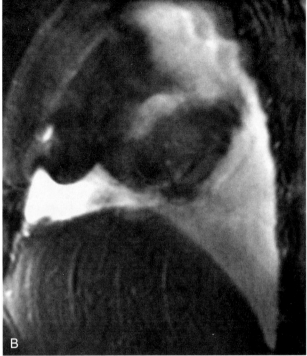

Figure 30–12. Malignant mesothelioma in a 64-year-old man. Coronal T1-weighted (TR = 821 msec, TE = 14 msec) *(A)* and sagittal T2-weighted (TR = 4054 msec, TE = 105 msec) *(B)* images show loculated, heterogeneous pleural effusion on T1-weighted and T2-weighted sequences. *(A and B,* From Knisely BL, Broderick LS, Kuhlman JE: MR imaging of the pleura and chest wall. MRI Clin North Am 8:125, 2000.) Noncontrast CT scan *(C)* shows loculated, low-attenuation right pleural effusion.

circumscribed. On MRI scans, lipomas exhibit fat signal intensities, with high signal intensity on T1-weighted and proton-density–weighted images and slightly lower signal intensity on heavily T2-weighted images. STIR and fat-saturation images depict the low signal intensity of fat. Chemical shift artifact can be seen at the interface of the lipoma with the surrounding soft tissues of higher water content. A few thin, low-signal-intensity, fibrous septations may be seen within the lipoma.[74]

A diagnosis of liposarcoma should be considered if there is heterogeneous signal intensity or if there are islands of soft tissue attenuation within the fatty tumor. MRI plays a role in surgical planning, allowing adequate evaluation of fatty masses that may infiltrate the chest wall or that lie near neurovascular structures.

Chest wall masses may result from anomalies of connective tissues and the lymphatic, vascular, and musculoskeletal systems.[32] Hemangioma (Fig. 30–16) is a broad category of lesions composed of cavernous, venous, arteriovenous, capillary, and mixed vascular malformations.[25, 43] Extraskeletal hemangiomas are uncommon benign lesions located superficially in the skin or subcutaneous tissues or deep within the synovium or musculature.[25, 43] Superficial hemangiomas have curvilinear low-signal-intensity structures on T1-weighted images and show high signal intensity on

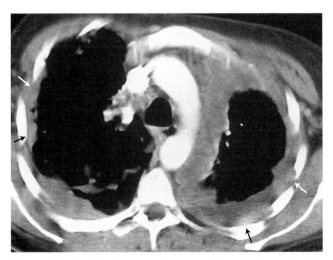

Figure 30–13. CT of metastatic pleural disease from adenoid cystic carcinoma of the parotid gland. A large loculated left pleural effusion and a smaller right effusion can be seen. Pleural soft-tissue attenuation deposits are identified bilaterally *(arrows).*

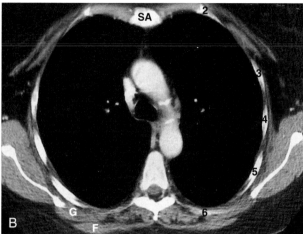

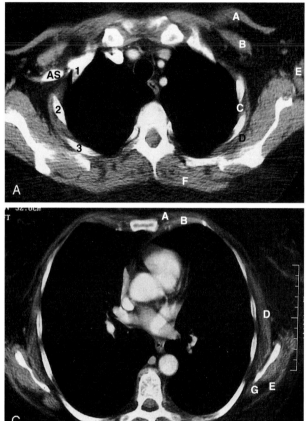

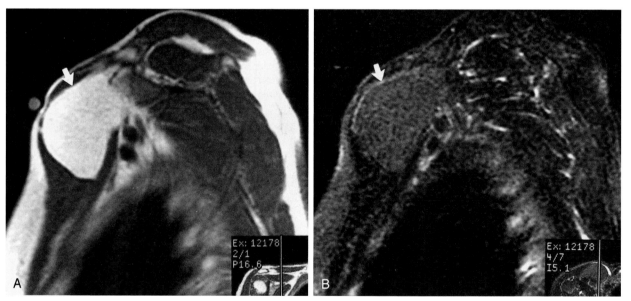

Figure 30–14. CT anatomy of the chest wall. *A,* Counting ribs one through three, the first rib is identified on the image, which shows the medial third of the clavicle. The second and third ribs are seen posteriorly along the rib cage. The axillary sheath contains the brachial plexus branches, and the axillary artery and vein. *B,* Sternal angle (SA) is shown as a high-attenuation structure connected laterally to the second costal cartilages and ribs. The third through sixth ribs are seen on the same slice counting posteriorly. *C,* Chest wall musculature is identified at an inferior level. A, pectoralis major; AS, axillary sheath; B, pectoralis minor; C, internal and external intercostal muscles; D, serratus anterior; E, latissimus dorsi; F, trapezius; G, rhomboid.

Figure 30–15. Lipoma in a 79-year-old woman. Sagittal T1-weighted (TR = 500 msec, TE = 8 msec) *(A)* and T2-weighted with fat saturation (TR = 4000 msec, TE = 105 msec) *(B)* images show a sharply defined mass *(arrow)* with signal intensity identical to that of subcutaneous fat on all pulse sequences. Fat suppression is demonstrated on T2-weighted images. (From Knisely BL, Broderick LS, Kuhlman JE: MR imaging of the pleura and chest wall. MRI Clin North Am 8:125, 2000.)

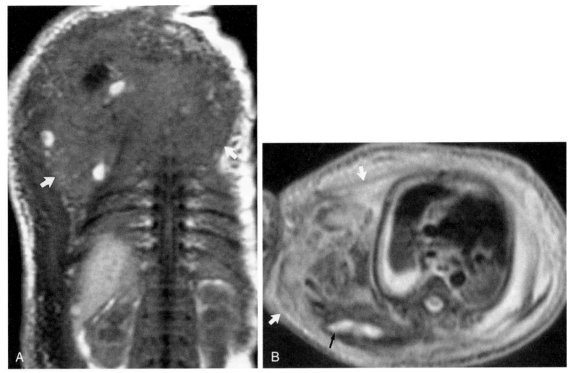

Figure 30–16. Chest wall hemangioma in a 2-day-old girl. Coronal T1-weighted (TR = 450 msec, TE = 12 msec) *(A)* and axial T2-weighted (TR = 3000 msec, TE = 102 msec) *(B)* images show heterogenous soft tissue mass *(white arrows)* involving the lateral and posterior right chest wall. High signal intensity *(black arrow)* on T2-weighted images is hemorrhage, as corresponding T1-weighted images (not shown) show high signal intensity. Multiple foci of high signal on T1-weighted image represent hemorrhage. (From Knisely BL, Broderick LS, Kuhlman JE: MR imaging of the pleura and chest wall. MRI Clin North Am 8:125, 2000.)

T2-weighted images.[25] Muscle atrophy may be a feature of the deep intramuscular hemangiomas.[25]

The MRI appearance of hemangiomas depends on the subtype and components of vascular elements (old blood, thrombus, hemosiderin), fat, and connective tissue.[25] Hemangiomas typically exhibit intermediate signal intensity on T1-weighted images and high signal intensity on T2-weighted images.[25, 32] The hyperintensity on T2-weighted images is thought to be related to stagnant or slow-flowing blood in dilated vascular beds. Arteriovenous malformations (AVMs) are characterized by tubular flow voids on T1-weighted and proton-density–weighted spin-echo sequences and by high signal intensity on gradient-recalled echo sequences.[22] The MRI finding of flowing blood allows the confident diagnosis of an AVM. MRI offers superior soft tissue contrast, which is helpful in evaluating the extension of hemangiomas into muscles, subcutaneous tissues, and the chest wall.[37]

Lymphangiomas are congenital lesions that are usually seen as a neck mass but may extend into the chest wall, axilla, extremities, and mediastinum.[69, 85] Histologically, lymphangiomas are a sequestered collection of lymphatics separated from the remainder of the lymphatic system.[85] Lymphangiomas are locally infiltrating and often recur locally, thus making surgery difficult.[69] Operative planning requires detailed identification of the lymphangioma and its relationship to adjacent neurovascular structures and muscles.

On MRI, lymphangiomas show the signal intensity of water on all pulse sequences, reflecting the fluid content of the dilated lymphatics.[37] The signal intensity of lymphangiomas is comparable to that of cerebrospinal fluid, lower than that of muscle on T1-weighted images, and higher than that of muscle or fat on T2-weighted images.[69] MRI may reveal internal septations within lymphangiomas.[69] STIR images and T2-weighted images with fat suppression show the extension and accentuate the water content of lymphangiomas.

MRI is the preferred imaging modality for evaluating lymphangiomas, especially if the administration of IV contrast medium is contraindicated.

Malignant Chest Wall Lesions

Breast carcinoma is the most common malignant soft tissue chest wall tumor.[79] Mammography is the examination of choice in the detection of breast cancer, with MRI reserved for cases of local chest wall recurrence.[79] Sarcomas (Figs. 30–17 and 30–18) are less common soft tissue tumors of the chest wall, and desmoid tumors are reported as being one of the most common chest wall sarcomas.[10, 79] Patients with soft tissue sarcomas have a 60% 5-year survival rate, a rate that is better than that of other primary chest wall malignancies.[5]

Patients with chest wall sarcomas do not typically present with pain. Pain associated with chest wall sarcoma is a poor prognostic sign.[5]

Desmoid tumors (see Fig. 30–18), previously termed *fibromatosis*, are infiltrative, poorly circumscribed, and ill

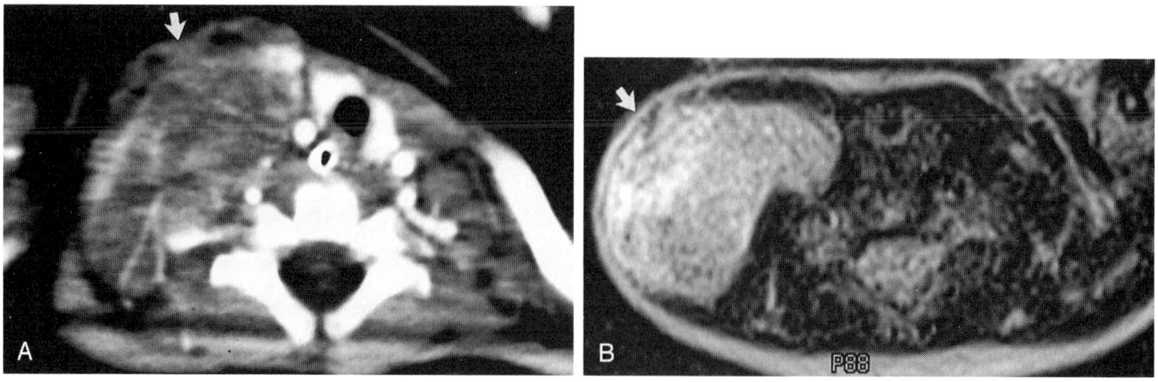

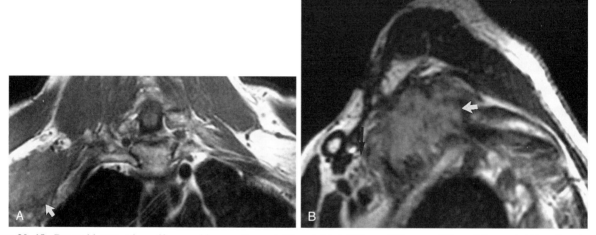

Figure 30–17. Undifferentiated sarcoma of the right neck and superior chest wall in a 4-month-old boy. *A,* Contrast-enhanced axial CT scan shows low-attenuation mass *(arrow)* in the right supraclavicular fossa, causing displacement of midline structures to the left. *B,* Axial T2-weighted (TR = 3200 msec, TE = 105 msec) image shows a tumor mass *(arrow)* demonstrating high signal intensity relative to muscle and involving the right axilla and chest wall. (From Knisely BL, Broderick LS, Kuhlman JE: MR imaging of the pleura and chest wall. MRI Clin North Am 8:125, 2000.)

Figure 30–18. Desmoid tumor in a 60-year-old man. Coronal T1-weighted (TR = 650 msec, TE = 14 msec) *(A)* and sagittal T2-weighted (TR = 2400 msec, TE = 104 msec) *(B)* images show a tumor *(white arrow)* in the right supraclavicular fossa, deviating the brachial plexus anteriorly *(black arrow).* The tumor shows slightly high signal intensity on T1-weighted and T2-weighted images relative to muscle. (From Knisely BL, Broderick LS, Kuhlman JE: MR imaging of the pleura and chest wall. MRI Clin North Am 8: 125, 2000.)

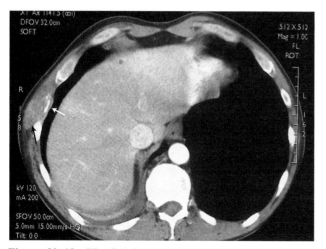

Figure 30–19. CT of right chest wall adenocarcinoma of unknown primary. Ovoid, soft tissue mass *(arrows)* has destroyed the right lateral rib and distorts the normal musculature.

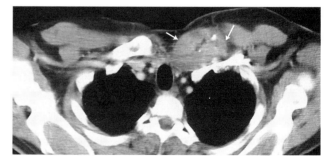

Figure 30–20. CT of metastatic melanoma to the left sternoclavicular joint. Ovoid, heterogeneous soft tissue mass *(arrows)* destroys medial left clavicle and causes posterior compression of left bronchiocephalic vein.

defined.[51] Although these tumors were once considered benign, because metastatic disease is rare, desmoids are now classified as low-grade fibrosarcomas as a result of their locally aggressive behavior.[57] The cause of desmoids is speculative; associations have been reported with estrogen therapy, pregnancy, trauma, and Gardner's syndrome.[21] Interesting to note, spontaneous cures of desmoid tumors have been reported during menopause and menarche.[59]

CT is more helpful in evaluating the extent of soft tissue chest wall tumors than in enabling a specific diagnosis.[35] MRI of desmoids shows a signal intensity isointense to muscle on T1-weighted, and variable on T2-weighted, sequences.[14] MRI of most malignant chest wall lesions shows heterogenous signal intensity, with mainly hypointensity on T1-weighted images and isointensity or hyperintensity on T2-weighted images, relative to subcutaneous fat.[22] Irregular margins and bone or vascular invasion are common findings in malignant lesions.

Current therapy includes wide local excision, with the role of adjuvant radiation therapy undefined.[10] High recurrence rates (18% to 54%) of surgically resected desmoids are seen in young patients and patients with large tumors.[10]

Chest Wall Masses with Rib Destruction

The differential diagnosis for a mass arising within a rib and causing a chest wall mass with rib destruction is limited.[58] Metastasis and multiple myeloma, respectively, are the first and second most common causes of a chest wall mass with associated rib destruction.[58] Metastases to the red marrow of ribs and sternum can occur from primary tumors of the lung, breast, kidney, and thyroid in adults (Figs. 30–19 and 30–20).[79] In children, the most common causes of lytic rib lesions are metastatic neuroblastoma and primary Ewing's sarcoma (Fig. 30–21).[58]

Ewing's Sarcoma

Ewing's sarcoma most frequently affects adolescent boys who present with a painful and rapidly enlarging chest wall mass.[5] Ewing's sarcoma is sometimes called a "medical tumor" because its prognosis is related to the extent of systemic rather than local disease. The overall 5-year survival of 48% is not affected by local recurrence after chest wall resection.[5] Five-year survival decreases to 28% with distant metastases, which occur in 75% of Ew-

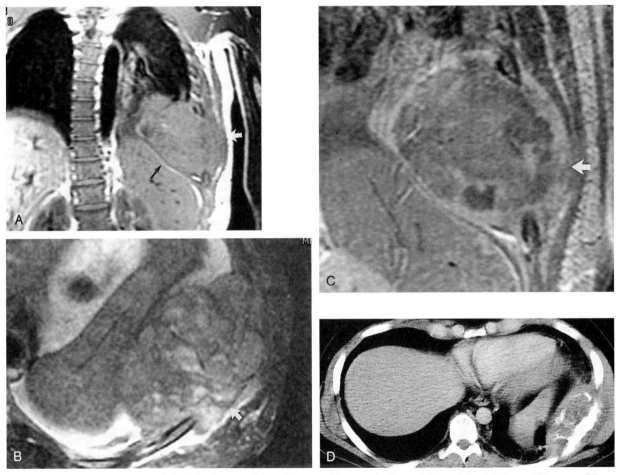

Figure 30–21. Ewing's sarcoma of the left chest wall in a 21-year-old man. *A,* Coronal T1-weighted (TR = 789 msec, TE = 14 msec) sequence shows the tumor mass as isointense to muscle. *B,* Axial T2-weighted (TR = 5217 msec, TE = 80 msec) sequence shows increased signal intensity. *C,* Coronal gadolinium-enhanced T1-weighted with fat saturation (TR = 714 msec, TE = 8 msec) sequence shows heterogeneous enhancement. A fat plane *(black arrow* in *A)* is present between the tumor and the spleen. Tumor has destroyed the left eighth rib and extends into the extrathoracic muscles *(white arrows* in *A–C).* *D,* Contrast-enhanced CT scan reveals the left chest wall mass, with low attenuation relative to muscle, destroying the rib. (*A–C,* From Knisely BL, Broderick LS, Kuhlman JE: MR imaging of the pleura and chest wall. MRI Clin North Am 8:125, 2000.)

ing's sarcoma patients.[11] Treatment includes systemic therapy and autologous bone marrow transplantation if metastatic disease is present.[46]

Askin's Tumor

Askin's tumor (Fig. 30–22) is an uncommon primitive neuroectodermal neoplasm that typically presents as a chest wall or paravertebral mass in young adults.[61] The tumor shares the histologic characteristics of rhabdomyosarcoma, neuroblastoma, Ewing's sarcoma, lymphoma, and small-cell osteosarcoma. It may be distinguished as a distinct pathologic entity on the basis of characteristic immunohistochemical and electron microscopic features.[6, 61]

CT and MRI demonstrate the mass as well as erosions of the ribs or vertebral bodies. Radionuclide technetium Tc 99m bone scans often reveal other occult bony involvement. On MRI scans, an Askin's tumor is seen as a heterogeneous soft tissue mass, representing areas of focal hemorrhage and tumor necrosis. The tumor exhibits a signal intensity greater than that of skeletal muscle on T1-weighted sequences and a high signal intensity on T2-weighted sequences.[61]

Treatment includes combinations of surgery, radiation, and chemotherapy. The overall poor prognosis is poor, however, because of the high rate of local recurrence and the development of distant metastases.[6, 47]

Primary Tumors of the Rib

Primary malignant and benign tumors of the cartilage or bone of the rib may also present as a chest wall mass

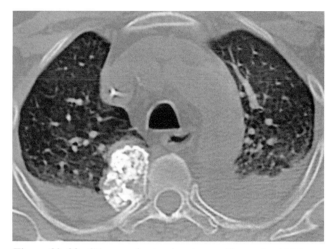

Figure 30–23. CT scan of osteochondroma. Noncontrast CT scan reveals a heterogeneous, lobulated, calcified mass with a cartilaginous cap arising from the right third rib, consistent with an osteochondroma.

with rib destruction. These chest wall tumors include osteosarcoma, fibrosarcoma, chondrosarcoma, osteochondroma (Fig. 30–23), giant cell tumor, enchondroma, round cell tumor, hemangioma, and aneurysmal bone cyst.[79]

Traumatic rib fractures (Fig. 30–24) and chest wall hematomas may have the appearance of a chest wall mass. Surgical excision of the involved rib may be necessary at

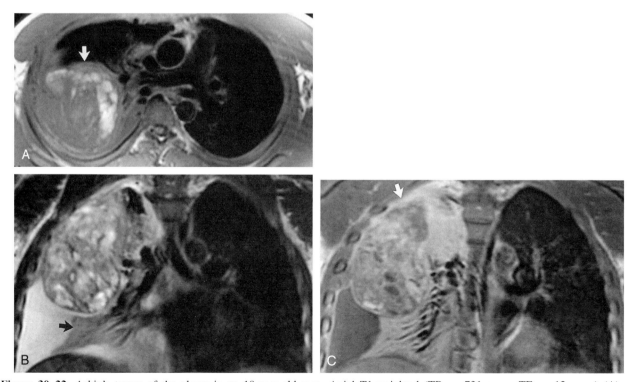

Figure 30–22. Askin's tumor of the pleura in an 18-year-old man. Axial T1-weighted (TR = 731 msec, TE = 12 msec) *(A)* and coronal T2-weighted (TR = 3500 msec, TE = 102 msec) *(B)* images show a heterogenous soft tissue mass *(white arrow)* and effusion causing compressive atelectasis of the adjacent lung *(black arrow)*. High-signal foci on T1-weighted images correspond to high-signal foci on T2-weighted axial images (not shown), consistent with hemorrhage. Coronal T1-weighted (TR = 740 msec, TE = 11 msec) contrast-enhanced image *(C)* shows enhancement of the pleural mass and lack of chest wall invasion *(white arrow)*. (From Knisely BL, Broderick LS, Kuhlman JE: MR imaging of the pleura and chest wall. MRI Clin North Am 8:125, 2000.)

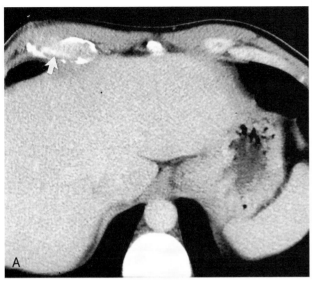

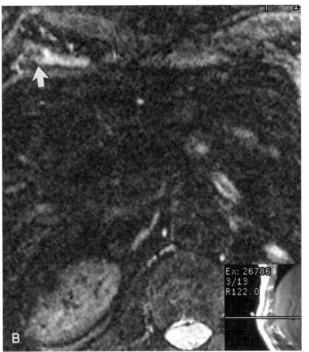

Figure 30–24. Nonunion of rib fracture. Contrast-enhanced axial CT scan *(A)* shows expansile right rib lesion with questionable chondroid matrix *(arrow)*. Axial *(B)* and sagittal *(C)* short-tau inversion recovery (STIR) sequences show ovoid peaked high-signal lesion *(arrow)* involving the anterior costochondral cartilage, consistent with granulation tissue and some fluid, which pathologically corresponded with a nonunited rib fracture. (From Knisely BL, Broderick LS, Kuhlman JE: MR imaging of the pleura and chest wall. MRI Clin North Am 8:125, 2000.)

times because differentiating the nonunion of a rib fracture from a chondroid tumor of the rib on imaging studies may be impossible. The reparative process related to a healing rib fracture may mimic an expanding neoplasm both radiologically and histologically. Rib erosion and chest wall masses may result from an expanding thoracic aneurysm, radiation osteitis, fibrous dysplasia, and eosinophilic granuloma.[66]

MRI is superior to CT in determining the extent of chest wall masses and the infiltration of the bone marrow.[37] However, CT more accurately displays the extent of cortical bone destruction. CT is helpful in evaluating post-traumatic abnormalities (Fig. 30–25) and sternal fractures not seen on standard films.

Pancoast Tumors

A Pancoast lesion (Figs. 30–26 and 30–27) is a superior sulcus mass that involves the brachial plexus and sympathetic ganglion of the lower neck and upper mediastinum.[30] Lung cancer is the most common cause of Pancoast tu-

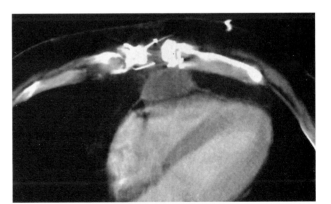

Figure 30–25. Sternal dehiscence in a 52-year-old man who sustained blunt chest trauma 17 months after cardiac transplantation. CT scan shows anterior mediastinal fluid collection consistent with resolving hematoma. (From Knisely BL, Mastey LA, Collins J, Kuhlman JE: Imaging of cardiac transplantation and complications. Radiographics 19:321, 1999.)

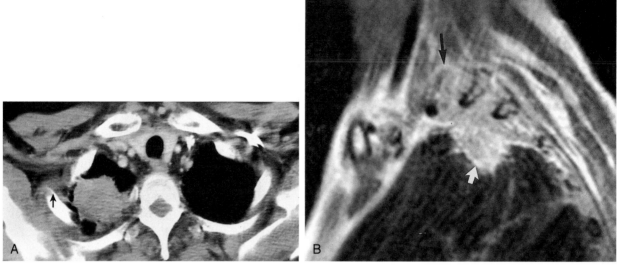

Figure 30–26. Pancoast tumor invading the brachial plexus in a 57-year-old woman. *A,* Contrast-enhanced CT scan shows large right apical mass with central low attenuation suggestive of necrosis. Abnormal soft tissue mass extends into the axilla *(arrow),* consistent with chest wall involvement. *B,* Sagittal gadolinium-enhanced T1-weighted (TR = 769 msec, TE = 14 msec) image shows enhancing bronchogenic carcinoma *(white arrow)* invading the posterior fat plane of the brachial plexus *(black arrow).* (*B,* From Knisely BL, Broderick LS, Kuhlman JE: MR imaging of the pleura and chest wall. MRI Clin North Am 8:125, 2000.)

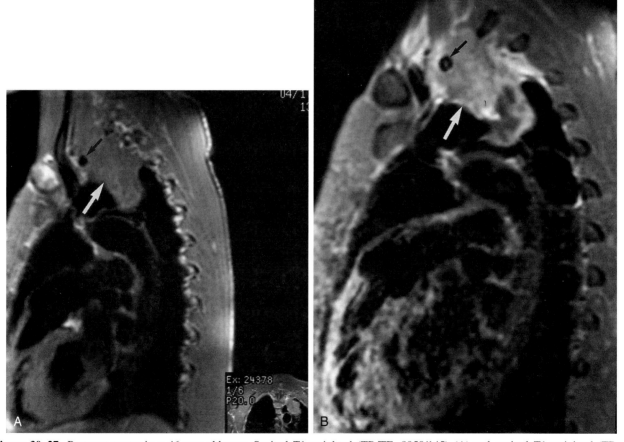

Figure 30–27. Pancoast tumor in a 46-year-old man. Sagittal T1-weighted (TR/TE, 8958/145) *(A)* and sagittal T1-weighted (TR = 869 msec, TE = 14 msec) gadolinium-enhanced with fat saturation *(B)* sequences show left apical bronchogenic carcinoma *(white arrow)* invading the supraclavicular fossa, involving the brachial plexus, and encasing the subclavian artery *(black arrow).* (From Knisely BL, Broderick LS, Kuhlman JE: MR imaging of the pleura and chest wall. MRI Clin North Am 8:125, 2000.)

mors,[32, 79] but they are also caused by metastatic disease, multiple myeloma, mesothelioma, lymphoma, and breast cancer. Pancoast syndrome is a clinical triad consisting of (1) Horner's syndrome (ptosis, miosis, anhidrosis, and enophthalmos), (2) ipsilateral arm pain, and (3) muscular wasting of the hand, which results from involvement of the nerves.[55]

The superior extension of Pancoast tumors is best depicted on the coronal and sagittal MR images. MRI has an overall accuracy rate of 94% (63% for CT) for demonstrating tumoral chest wall invasion.[30] Streak artifact from the shoulders and the axial plane limits the evaluation of superior sulcus tumors by CT. MRI can also evaluate the tumor's relationship to the supraclavicular fossa, apical fat, subclavian artery and vein, brachial plexus, and costovertebral bony structures. Lung cancer patients with tumors invading the apex on preoperative imaging studies often receive radiation therapy to shrink the tumor prior to surgical resection.[32, 79]

The survival rate in patients with Pancoast lung cancer has increased as a result of the combination of radiation therapy and surgery (with or without chemotherapy).[37]

Chest Wall Invasion by Bronchogenic Carcinoma

The treatment modality of choice for lung cancer depends on the stage and histology of the tumor. Peripheral bronchogenic carcinomas invade the chest wall in only 8% of cases.[8] Limited local invasion is resectable by either an en bloc resection of lung and chest wall or an extrapleural dissection (when tumor is limited to the parietal pleura). The soft tissue contrast resolution and multiplanar capability of MRI are superior to those of CT, making MRI slightly more accurate in the detection of tumor invasion of the chest wall.[30] MRI depicts tumor infiltration of the extrapleural fat and muscles of the chest wall better than CT does (Fig. 30–28). The sensitivity and specificity of MRI in the diagnosis of chest wall invasion range from 63% to 90% and 84% to 86%, respectively.[54, 81]

T1-weighted and T2-weighted spin-echo sequences depict direct chest wall tumor extension, with improved yield on gadolinium-contrast–enhanced sequences (Fig. 30–29).[26] MRI is the examination of choice for the local staging of superior sulcus carcinomas, providing good anatomic detail

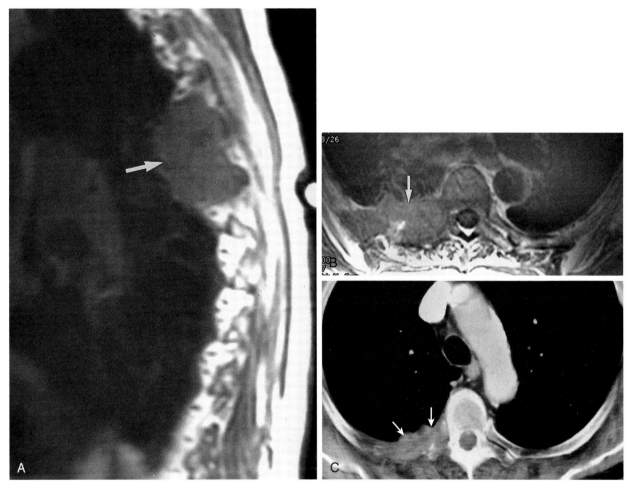

Figure 30–28. Bronchogenic carcinoma invading the posterior chest wall in a 94-year-old woman. T1-weighted sagittal (TR = 550 msec, TE = 16 msec) *(A)* and axial T1-weighted (TR = 700 msec, TE = 17 msec) *(B)* images show a mass *(arrow)* that demonstrates low signal intensity (relative to muscle) in the superior segment of the right lower lobe, invading the posterior right sixth rib and pedicle of the sixth thoracic vertebral body. *(A and B,* From Knisely BL, Broderick LS, Kuhlman JE: MR imaging of the pleura and chest wall. MRI Clin North Am 8:125, 2000.) Contrast-enhanced CT scan *(C)* reveals right posterior soft tissue pedicle mass *(arrows)* replacing posterior right rib and thoracic body.

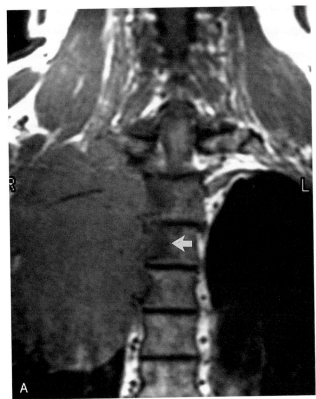

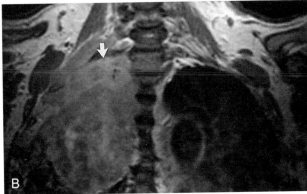

Figure 30–29. Bronchogenic carcinoma in a 60-year-old man. Coronal T1-weighted (TR = 600 msec, TE = 12 msec) *(A)* and coronal T1-weighted (TR = 800 msec, TE = 12 msec) gadolinium-enhanced *(B)* images show a large tumor. Signal intensity of abnormal bone marrow is seen within the thoracic vertebral bodies, consistent with tumor invasion *(arrow in A)* and enhancing tumor invading the apex *(arrow in B)* of the right chest wall. (From Knisely BL, Broderick LS, Kuhlman JE: MR imaging of the pleura and chest wall. MRI Clin North Am 8:125, 2000.)

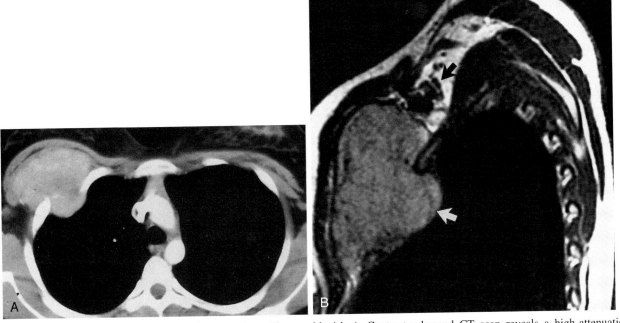

Figure 30–30. Inflammatory myofibroblastic tumor in a 15-year-old girl. *A,* Contrast-enhanced CT scan reveals a high-attenuation mass infiltrating the anterior chest, posterior to the right pectoralis major muscle. *B,* Sagittal T2-weighted (TR = 2066 msec, TE = 104 msec) image shows a mass *(white arrow)* that demonstrates high signal intensity (relative to muscle). It is beneath the pectoralis major muscle and infiltrates the anterior chest between the ribs, sparing the brachial plexus *(black arrow).* (*B,* From Knisely BL, Broderick LS, Kuhlman JE: MR imaging of the pleura and chest wall. MRI Clin North Am 8:125, 2000.)

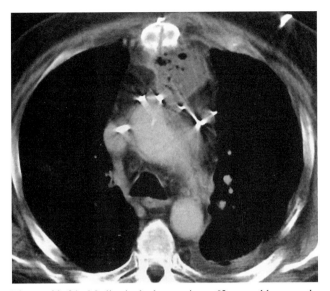

Figure 30–31. Mediastinal abscess in a 62-year-old man who developed a substernal fluid collection 6 weeks after cardiac transplantation. Contrast-enhanced CT scan shows the anterior mediastinal loculated fluid collection with air pockets. Specimen obtained from CT-guided drainage revealed gram-positive cocci, and the patient responded to antibiotic therapy and drainage. (From Knisely BL, Mastey LA, Collins J, Kuhlman JE: Imaging of cardiac transplantation and complications. Radiographics 19: 321, 1999.)

of the apices. The MRI findings of chest wall invasion include loss of the high-signal-intensity extrapleural fat on T1-weighted images and disruption of the soft tissue planes.[32] High signal intensity on T2-weighted images in the muscles suggests tumor involvement, but inflammation and edema may cause similar findings.[32]

Chest Wall Inflammatory and Infectious Diseases

Inflammatory myofibroblastic tumor (Fig. 30–30) is a rare pseudosarcomatous lesion that often involves the lungs of children and young adults.[16] It has been reported in diverse extrapulmonary locations, specifically the trunk, and is characterized by a benign, nonmetastasizing proliferation of myofibroblasts with a potential for recurrence.[16] MRI shows a lesion of intermediate signal intensity on T1-weighted sequences and increased heterogeneous signal intensity on T2-weighted sequences.[24]

Chest wall infections are rare, yet are potentially fatal.[67] Diabetes mellitus, previous surgery or trauma, and immunocompromised states are risk factors associated with infection of the thoracic wall.[67] The prognosis is variable, depending on the length of time to make the diagnosis, the organism type, the severity of immunosuppression, and the extent of infection.[67] Physical findings of fever, focal tenderness, warmth, induration, skin discoloration, redness, or necrosis often underestimate the severity and extent of the chest wall infection, particularly in the immunocompromised patient.[67]

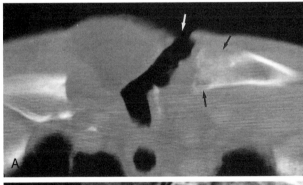

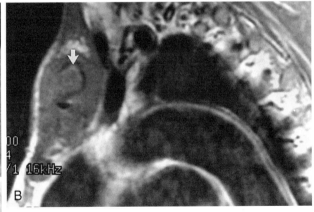

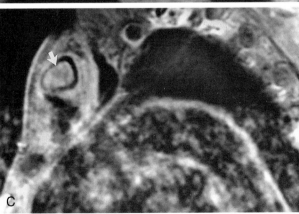

Figure 30–32. Osteomyelitis of the sternal manubrium and left clavicle in a 75-year-old man. Axial CT scan *(A)* with bony windows shows erosions *(black arrows)* of the medial left clavicle and fistulous tract *(white arrow)* between the trachea and the anterior chest wall. Sagittal T1-weighted (TR = 70 msec, TE = 14 msec) image *(B)* and gadolinium-enhanced, T1-weighted (TR = 533 msec, TE = 14 msec) image *(C)* show abnormal low signal intensity *(arrow in B)* of the clavicular bone marrow on the T1-weighted image, contrast-enhancement of the infected bone *(arrow in C)*, and surrounding soft tissue edema and inflammation. (From Knisely BL, Broderick LS, Kuhlman JE: MR imaging of the pleura and chest wall. MRI Clin North Am 8:125, 2000.)

Chest wall infections are categorized as cellulitis, pyomyositis, abscess, and the more life-threatening necrotizing fasciitis.[67] *Klebsiella* and *Staphylococcus* species are common and severe offending organisms in chest wall infections.[67] *Nocardia* and *Aspergillus* species, actinomycetes, *Blastomyces*, and *Mycobacterium tuberculosis* are less common pathogens affecting the chest wall.[67] CT may identify parasternal fluid collections in febrile postsurgical patients with air collections suggestive of mediastinitis and mediastinal abscess (Fig. 30–31). After surgery, fluid and the thickening of the presternal and poststernal soft tissues are seen for 2 to 3 weeks, with air resolving after 1 week.

MRI delineates the extent of soft tissue involvement and inflammation of the chest wall without requiring IV contrast agents.[37] Coronal and sagittal MR images are key for operative planning, identifying communications between separate, loculated abscesses and outlining the extent of the chest wall infection. On MRI, abscesses show low signal intensity on T1-weighted sequences and high signal intensity on STIR and T2-weighted sequences.[37] T1-weighted images yield superior spatial resolution; STIR and T2-weighted images, because of their superior contrast, are best for determining the degree of abscess extension and for defining the location of the abscess.[67] CT is much more sensitive than MRI for detecting gas in chest wall infections.[37]

Osteomyelitis (Fig. 30–32) of the sternum, manubrium, and clavicles is optimally imaged with MRI because of its multiplanar imaging capability and superior soft tissue contrast.[67] MR images yield a sensitivity and specificity of 88% and 93%, respectively, with focal enhancement on T1-weighted fat-suppressed enhanced images indicative of osteomyelitis.[49] Infection is identified as an area of decreased signal intensity on T1-weighted sequences, compared with the high signal intensity of fatty marrow, and high signal intensity on T2-weighted sequences.

IV drug abuse, diabetes mellitus, chronic renal failure, and immunosuppression predispose patients to sternoclavicular joint infections.[84] Subclavian venous catheter sequelae often lead to sternoclavicular joint infections (Fig. 30–33), with *Staphylococcus aureus* the most frequently isolated bacterium in this setting.[12]

Early cases of sternoclavicular joint infections are treated with conservative measures, including catheter removal and peripheral IV antibiotics, with a good response rate. En bloc resection is reserved for a sternoclavicular joint infection that extends beyond the joint on imaging studies.[12]

Summary

CT is the standard imaging modality in the evaluation of pleural and chest wall lesions. CT characterizes pleural effusions, differentiates parenchymal from pleural and chest wall lesions, and demonstrates areas of fatty attenuation or calcification. MRI plays a role in specific cases of tumors, infections, pleural effusions, and masses. MRI provides superior soft tissue contrast, which is helpful in determining the extent of infections and tumors involving the pleura and chest wall. MRI's multiplanar capability helps in the evaluation of chest wall and pleural abnormalities, particularly in the apical regions.

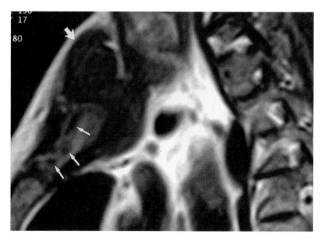

Figure 30–33. Sternoclavicular joint infection and osteomyelitis in a 48-year-old man with an infected subclavian venous catheter. Sagittal T1-weighted (TR = 400 msec, TE = 12 msec) image shows abnormal areas of low signal intensity *(arrows)* in the sternal marrow, consistent with osteomyelitis. Surrounding low signal intensity *(arrow)* in the soft tissues is consistent with abscess. (From Knisely BL, Broderick LS, Kuhlman JE: MR imaging of the pleura and chest wall. MRI Clin North Am 8: 125, 2000.)

References

1. Aberle DR, Balmes JR: Computed tomography of asbestos-related pulmonary parenchymal and pleural diseases. Clin Chest Med 12: 115, 1991.
2. Aberle DR, Gamsu G, Ray CS: High resolution CT of benign asbestos-related diseases: Clinical and radiographic correlation. AJR Am J Roentgenol 151:883, 1988.
3. Alexander E, Clark RA, Colley DP: CT of malignant pleural mesothelioma. Am J Roentgenol 137:287, 1981.
4. Alexander S, Proto AV, Clark RA: CT differentiation of subphrenic abscess and pleural effusion. Am J Roentgenol 140:47, 1983.
5. Anderson BO, Burt ME: Chest wall neoplasms and their management. Ann Thorac Surg 58:1774, 1994.
6. Askin FF, Rosai J, Sibley RK, et al: Malignant small cell tumor of the thoracopulmonary region in childhood: A distinctive clinicopathologic entity of uncertain histogenesis. Cancer 43:2438, 1979.
7. Barber CE, Hedlund LW, Oddson TA, et al: Differentiating empyemas and peripheral pulmonary abscesses: The value of computed tomography. Radiology 135:755, 1980.
8. Bone RE, Balk R: Staging of bronchogenic carcinoma. Chest 82: 473, 1982.
9. Briselli M, Mark EJ, Dickersin GR: Solitary fibrous tumors of the pleura: Eight new cases and review of 360 cases in the literature. Cancer 47:2678, 1981.
10. Brodsky JT, Gordon MS, Hajdu SI, et al: Desmoid tumors of the chest wall: Local recurrent problem. J Thorac Cardiovasc Surg 104: 900, 1992.
11. Burt M, Karpeh M, Ukoha O, et al: Medical tumors of the chest wall: Solitary plasmacytoma and Ewing's sarcoma. J Thorac Cardiovasc Surg 105:89, 1993.
12. Carlos GN, Kesler KA, Coleman JJ, et al: Aggressive surgical management of sternoclavicular joint infections. J Thorac Cardiovasc Surg 113:242, 1997.
13. Carvalho PM, Carr DH: Computed tomography of folded lung. Clin Radiol 41:86, 1990.
14. Casillas J, Sais GJ, Greve JL, et al: Imaging of intra- and extraabdominal desmoid tumors. Radiographics 11:959, 1991.
15. Castagno AA, Shuman WP: MR imaging in clinically suspected brachial plexus tumor. AJR Am J Roentgenol 149:1219, 1987.
16. Coffin CM, Watterson J, Priest JR, et al: Extrapulmonary inflamma-

tory myofibroblastic tumor (inflammatory pseudotumor): A clinico-pathologic and immunohistochemical study of 84 cases. Am J Surg Pathol 19:895, 1995.

17. Davis SD, Henschke CI, Yankelevitz DF, et al: MR imaging of pleural effusions. J Comput Assist Tomogr 14:192, 1990.

18. Doyle TC, Lawler GA: CT features of rounded atelectasis of the lung. Am J Roentgenol 143:225, 1984.

19. Dwyer RA. The displaced crus: A sign for distinguishing between pleural fluid and ascites on computed tomography. J Comput Assist Tomogr 2:598, 1978.

20. England DM, Hochholzer L, McCarthy MJ: Localized benign and malignant fibrous tumors of the pleura: A clinicopathologic review of 223 cases. Am J Surg 13:640, 1989.

21. Enzinger FM, Weiss SW: Soft Tissue Tumors, 3rd ed. St. Louis, Mosby–Year Book, 1995, p 210.

22. Fortier M, Mayo JR, Swenson SJ, et al: MR imaging of chest wall lesions. Radiographics 14:597, 1994.

23. George JC: Benign fibrous mesothelioma of the pleura: MR findings. AJR Am J Roentgenol 106:204, 1993.

24. Georgia JD, Lawrence DP, De Nobile JW: Inflammatory pseudotumor in the retrorectal space: CT and MR appearance. J Comput Assist Tomogr 20:410, 1996.

25. Greenspan A, McGahan JP, Vogelsang P, et al: Imaging strategies in the evaluation of soft-tissue hemangiomas of the extremities: Correlation of the findings of plain radiography, angiography, CT, MRI and ultrasonography in 12 histologically proven cases. Skeletal Radiol 21:11, 1992.

26. Haggar AM, Pearlberg JL, Froelich JW, et al: Chest wall invasion by carcinoma of the lung: Detection by MR imaging. AJR Am J Roentgenol 148:1075, 1987.

27. Hahn D: Mediastinum and lung. In Stark DD, Bradley WE (eds): Magnetic Resonance Imaging. St. Louis, CV Mosby, 1988.

28. Hahn PF, Stark DD, Vici GG, et al: Duodenal hematoma: The ring sign in MR imaging. Radiology 159:379, 1986.

29. Halvorsen RA, Fedyshin PJ, Korobkin M, et al: CT differentiation of pleural effusion from ascites: An evaluation of four signs using blinded analysis of 52 cases. Invest Radiol 21:391, 1986.

30. Heelan RT, Demas BE, Caravelli JF, et al: Superior sulcus tumors: CT and MR imaging. Radiology 170:637, 1989.

31. Heelan RT, Rusch VW, Begg CB, et al: Staging of malignant pleural mesothelioma: Comparison of CT and MR imaging. AJR Am J Roentgenol 172:1039, 1999.

32. Herold CJ, Zerhouni EA: The mediastinum and lungs. In Higgins CB, Hricak H, Helms CA (eds): Magnetic Resonance Imaging of the Body, 2nd ed. New York, Raven Press, 1992, p 461.

33. Im JG, Webb WR, Rosen A, et al: Costal pleura: Appearances of high resolution CT. Radiology 171:125, 1989.

34. Knisely BL, Broderick LS, Kuhlman JE. MR imaging of the pleura and chest wall. MRI Clin North Am 8:125, 2000.

35. Knisely BL, Kuhlman JE. Radiographic and CT imaging of complex pleural disease. Crit Rev Diagn Imaging 38:1, 1997.

36. Kreel L: Computed tomography in mesotheliomas. Semin Oncol 8: 302, 1981.

37. Kuhlman JE, Bouchardy L, Fishman EK, et al: CT and MR findings [letter]. AJR Am J Roentgenol 106:205, 1993.

38. Kurihara Y, Nakajima Y, Ishikawa T, Galvin JR: Counting ribs on chest CT scans: The easiest way. AJR Am J Roentgenol 165:487, 1995.

39. Lee KS, Im JG: Benign fibrous mesothelioma of the pleura: MR findings [letter]. AJR Am J Roentgenol 106:205, 1993.

40. Leung AN, Müller NL, Miller RR: CT in differential diagnosis of diffuse pleural disease. AJR Am J Roentgenol 154:487, 1990.

41. McCloud TC: CT and MR in pleural disease. Clin Chest Med 19: 261, 1998.

42. McCloud TC, Flower CDR: Imaging the pleura: Sonography, CT, and MR imaging. AJR Am J Roentgenol 156:1145, 1991.

43. Meyer JS, Hoffer FA, Barnes PD, et al: Biological classification of soft-tissue vascular anomalies: MR correlation. AJR Am J Roentgenol 157:559, 1991.

44. Minami M, Kawauchi N, Yoshikawa K, et al: Malignancy associated with chronic empyema: Radiologic assessment. Radiology 178:417, 1991.

45. Mintzer RA, Gore RM, Vogelzang RL, et al: Rounded atelectasis and its association with asbestos-induced pleural disease. Radiology 139: 567, 1981.

46. Miser JS, Kinsella TJ, Triche TJ, et al: Preliminary results of treatment of Ewing's sarcoma of bone in children and young adults: Six months of intensive continued modality therapy without maintenance. J Clin Oncol 6:484, 1988.

47. Miser JS, Kinsella TJ, Triche TJ, et al: Treatment of peripheral neuroepithelioma in children and young adults. J Clin Oncol 5: 1752, 1987.

48. Montalvo BM, Morillo G, Sridhar K, et al: MR imaging of malignant pleural mesotheliomas. Radiology 181:109, 1991.

49. Morrison WB, Schweitzer ME, Bock GW, et al: Diagnosis of osteo-myelitis: Utility of fat-suppressed contrast-enhanced MR imaging. Radiology 189:251, 1993.

50. Müller NL: Imaging the pleura. Radiology 186:297, 1993.

51. Munden RF, Kemp BL: Desmoid tumor of the chest wall. AJR Am J Roentgenol 172:1149, 1999.

52. Munk PL, Lee MJ, Janzen DL, et al: Lipoma and liposarcoma: Evaluation using CT and MR imaging. AJR Am J Roentgenol 169: 589, 1997.

53. Naidich DP, Megibow AJ, Hilton S, et al: Computed tomography of the diaphragm: Peridiaphragmatic fluid localization. J Comput Assist Tomogr 7:641, 1983.

54. Padovani B, Mouroux J, Seksik L, et al: Chest wall invasion by bronchogenic carcinoma: Evaluation with MR imaging. Radiology 187:33, 1993.

55. Pancoast HK: Superior sulcus tumor: Tumor characterized by pain, Horner's syndrome, destruction of bone and atrophy of hand muscles. JAMA 99:1391, 1932.

56. Ponn RB, D'Agostino RS, Stern H, Wescott JL: Treatment of periph-eral bronchopleural fistulas with endobronchial occlusion coils. Ann Thorac Surg 56:1343, 1993.

57. Posner MC, Shiu MH, Newsome JL, et al: The desmoid tumor: Not a benign disease. Arch Surg 124:191, 1989.

58. Reed JC: Chest wall lesions. In Reed JC (ed): Chest Radiology: Plain Film Patterns and Differential Diagnoses. St. Louis, Mosby–Year Book, 1991, p 8.

59. Reitamo JJ, Scheinin TM, Hayry R: The desmoid syndrome: New aspects in the cause, pathogenesis and treatment of the desmoid tumor. Am J Surg 151:230, 1986.

60. Roggli VL, Kolbeck J, Sanfilippo F, et al: Pathology of human mesothelioma. Pathol Annu 22:91, 1987.

61. Sabate JM, Franquet T, Parellada JA, et al: Malignant neuroectoder-mal tumour of the chest wall (Askin tumour): CT and MR findings in eight patients. Clin Radiol 49:634, 1994.

62. Sahn SA: Malignant pleural effusion. In Fishman AP (ed): Pulmonary Diseases and Disorders, 2nd ed. New York, McGraw-Hill, 1988, p 1640.

63. Schmutz GR, Fisch-Ponsot C, Regent D, et al: Computed tomography and magnetic resonance imaging of pleural masses. Crit Rev Diagn Imaging 34:309, 1993.

64. Schneider HJ, Felson B, Gonzales LL: Rounded atelectasis. Am J Roentgenol 184:225, 1980.

65. Schwartz DA: New developments in asbestos-related pleural disease. Chest 99:191, 1991.

66. Scott WW, Scott PP, Trerotola SO: Radiology of the Thoracic Skele-ton. Philadelphia, BC Decker, 1991.

67. Sharif HS, Clark DC, Aabed MY, et al: MR imaging of thoracic and abdominal wall infections: Comparison with other imaging proce-dures. AJR Am J Roentgenol 154:989, 1990.

68. Shuman LS, Libshitz HI: Solid pleural manifestations of lymphoma. Am J Roentgenol 142:269, 1984.

69. Siegel MJ, Glazer HS, St. Amour TE, et al: Lymphangiomas in children: MR imaging. Radiology 170:467, 1989.

70. Springer BI, Schiebler ML: Normal anatomy of the thoracic inlet as seen on transaxial MR images. AJR Am J Roentgenol 157:707, 1991.

71. Staples CA: Computed tomography in the evaluation of benign asbes-tos-related disorders. Radiol Clin North Am 30:1191, 1992.

72. Stark DD, Federle MP, Goodman PC, et al: Differentiating lung abscess and empyema: Radiography and computed tomography. Am J Roentgenol 141:163, 1983.

73. Stern EJ, Sun H, Haramati LB: Peripheral bronchopleural fistulas: CT imaging features. AJR Am J Roentgenol 167:117, 1996.

74. Storey TF, Narla LD: Pleural lipoma in a child: CT evaluation. Pediatr Radiol 21:141, 1991.

75. Teplick JG, Teplick SK, Goodman L, Haskin ME: The interface sign: A computed tomographic sign for distinguishing pleural and intra-abdominal fluid. Radiology 144:359, 1982.

76. Tocino I, Miller MH, Frederick PR, et al: CT detection of acute pneumothorax in head trauma. Am J Roentgenol 143:989, 1984.

77. Tscholakoff D, Sechtem U, deGeer G, et al: Evaluation of pleural and pericardial effusions by magnetic resonance imaging. Eur J Radiol 7: 169, 1987.

78. Verschakelen JA, Demaerel P, Coolen J, et al: Rounded atelectasis of the lung: MR appearance. AJR Am J Roentgenol 152:965, 1989.

79. Vock P: Magnetic resonance imaging and computed tomography of the chest wall. In Higgins C, Pettersson H (eds): Chest and Cardiac Radiology (Nycomed Intercontinental Continuing Education in Radiology Series on Diagnostic Imaging, vol 1). London, Merit Communications, 1991, p 162.

80. Waite RJ, Carbonneau RJ, Balikian JP, et al: Parietal pleural changes in empyema: Appearances at CT. Radiology 175:145, 1990.

81. Webb WR, Gatsonis C, Zerhouni EA, et al: CT and MR imaging in staging non–small cell bronchogenic carcinoma: Report of the Radiologic Diagnostic Oncology Group. Radiology 178:705, 1991.

82. Wescott JL, Volpe JP: Peripheral bronchopleural fistula: CT evaluation in 20 patients with pneumonia, empyema, or postoperative air leak. Radiology 196:175, 1995.

83. Williford ME, Hidalgo H, Putman CE, et al: Computed tomography of pleural disease. Am J Roentgenol 140:909, 1983.

84. Yood YA, Goldenberg DL: Sternoclavicular joint arthritis. Arthritis Rheum 23:232, 1980.

85. Zadvinskis DP, Benson MT, Kerr HH, et al: Congenital malformations of the cervicothoracic lymphatic system: Embryology and pathogenesis. Radiographics 12:1175, 1992.

31

Computed Tomography and Magnetic Resonance Imaging of the Thoracic Aorta

Robert C. Gilkeson, Scott Kolodny

Imaging Techniques

As in so much of radiology, advances in cross-sectional imaging have revolutionized our ability to image the thoracic aorta. Historically, aortic imaging has been performed with contrast angiography. The technique is clearly effective in the evaluation of a variety of aortic diseases. Nevertheless, because of its invasive nature, catheter angiography is not without complications, including arrhythmia, stroke, and hemorrhage. In the modern-day radiology department, delays in the performance of conventional angiography are often longer than those for magnetic resonance imaging (MRI) and computed tomography (CT) scanning, delays that can be particularly detrimental in the trauma setting. Now, with increasingly effective MRI and CT, these techniques have largely replaced conventional angiography in the evaluation of aortic disease.

Since its inception in the late 1970s, CT has become an increasingly important modality for evaluation of disease of the thoracic aorta. Early scanners were limited by their slow acquisition times, but they quickly found a role in the evaluation of mediastinal widening, aortic trauma, and aortic disease.[8, 40] CT evaluation of the thoracic aorta offered additional information about aortic wall thickness, surrounding mediastinal and parenchymal tissues, and disease that was not available from conventional aortography. The use of intravenous (IV) contrast agents and dynamic imaging at preselected sites in the thoracic aorta facilitated the diagnosis of aneurysmal disease and dissection.[39] Later in the 1980s, improvements in scanner technology and contrast delivery systems made 1- to 2-minute scanning of the thoracic aorta possible and further advanced the clinical applications of CT scanning in the thoracic aorta.[131]

The advent of spiral CT technology has represented the greatest advance in the rapid and accurate imaging of thoracic aortic disease.[59] With slip-ring CT technology, the patient moves continuously through the gantry while data are acquired. This technique has enabled more rapid acquisition of data, optimizing contrast enhancement of the aorta and its branch vessels. Equally important, spiral CT technology has allowed volumetric data acquisition.[139] Before spiral CT, the display of imaging data was largely limited to the axial plane, but the spiral CT volumetric data set enables the generation of images in a variety of planes, with the capacity for three-dimensional (3D) and endoscopic images.[56, 116] The development of spiral CT and CT angiography has been a major factor in the replacement by CT of conventional aortography for the evaluation of thoracic aortic disease.

The development of multislice CT has now allowed another quantum advance in our understanding of aortic disease. The single-detector system in traditional CT has been replaced, in multislice CT, by multidetector systems capable of acquiring multiple images in the time traditionally taken to generate one image. With most new multislice systems, imaging of the aorta can be performed four times faster than with conventional single-slice scanners. Scanning with multislice scanners that use subsecond imaging times is often eight times faster than scanning with conventional single-slice CT. The latest advances in detector technology have created eight- and 16-detector systems with rotation times of 400 to 500 msec, further decreasing imaging time and enhancing the quality of these volumetric, angiographic images of the thoracic aorta.

CT Protocols

The following three paramaters are considered important in the development of protocols for CT angiography of the thoracic aorta: (1) sensitivity to intraluminal and extraluminal aortic disease, (2) maximal contrast opacification of the thoracic aorta, and (3) optimal coverage of the pertinent anatomic structures. Maximizing sensitivity to intraluminal abnormalities like atheroembolic disease and aortic dissection requires section thicknesses of 3 to 5 mm. To optimize volumetric reconstruction, reconstruction intervals between 1.5 and 2.5 mm should be used to ensure 50% overlap and optimize spatial reconstruction algorithms. Although a significant amount of research has been aimed at optimization of pitch parameters, full width at half maximum (FWHM) profiles show little degradation of image quality with pitch values up to 2.[93] The range of the scan should be determined by the clinical problem: If there are suspicions about short segment narrowing, focal aneurysms, or branch vessel abnormalities, a range of 12 to 15 cm can be performed. A survey of the thoracic aorta, evaluating for the full extent of a dissection, aneurysm, or aortitis, generally requires coverage of 25 to 30 cm. Scan parameters, including pitch slice thickness and collimation, vary according to the range value and the ability of the patient to suspend respiration.

Optimal contrast enhancement of the thoracic aorta is crucial to the successful display of aortic disease. In most cases in which single-slice spiral CT is used, injection volumes of 125 to 150 mL are needed for optimal enhancement of the selected scan volume. Nonionic contrast media are preferable at these injection rates and volumes, because they minimize the motion[121] as well as the nausea and vomiting more common with ionic agents. Although earlier reports suggested injection rates of 1.5 to 2.0 mL/sec,[24] current literature supports injection rates of 3 to 4 mL/sec. Biphasic contrast injection protocols have been supported for consistent contrast opacification of the aortic lumen; in

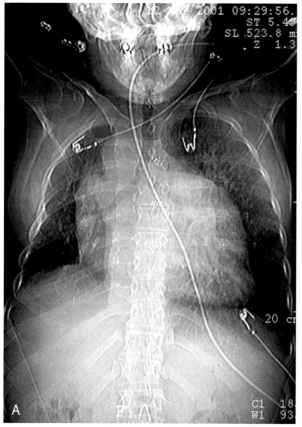

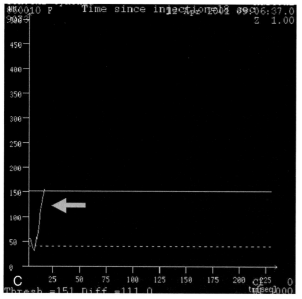

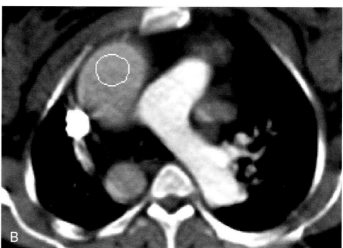

Figure 31–1. *A*, CT tomogram of a young patient with complex congenital heart disease. There is significant cardiomegaly and a right aortic arch. Using an empiric delay for contrast injection would be inappropriate in this clinical setting. *B*, Axial scan demonstrating an automated bolus tracking technique shows the region of interest drawn in the ascending aorta to optimize contrast visualization. *C*, Automated bolus tracking technique for optimizing intravenous injection of contrast material. *Arrow* denotes the time to optimal contrast enhancement of the ascending aorta.

these protocols, IV contrast is injected at 4.0 mL/sec for 50 sec, and then for 2.5 mL/sec for the remainder of the scan. Some research shows this protocol to give a more uniform delivery of contrast agent for the duration of the scan. Power injectors are therefore mandatory for CT evaluation of the aorta.

A variety of researchers have studied the effect of iodine concentration on the quality of aortic opacification.[103, 110] This work shows that there is little difference in the quality of the scans when iodine concentrations ranging from 150 to 300 mg/mL are used. Lower iodine concentrations tend to minimize venous artifacts, although the lower dilutions are often not commercially available in the United States. In our practice, we generally use an iodine concentration of 300 mg/mL; if the evaluation is being performed for suspicion of intra-aortic thrombus or atheroembolic disease, we decrease the iodine concentration to 240 mg/mL to optimize the evaluation of intraluminal disease.

There has been controversy about iodine concentration, and a variety of approaches can be used to optimize the contrast bolus. Some authors support the use of a 20- to 30-mL timing bolus to optimize contrast enhancement in the aorta. In this technique, a slice position in the aorta is preselected, and a test bolus of contrast agent is administered. Images are obtained every 2 to 3 seconds after the start of injection. A time-density curve is generated, and the time to peak opacification is determined.[105] Several commercially available techniques are now available that allow automated triggering of the scan without a test bolus (Fig. 31–1).[113] Despite these techniques, many centers still determine injection delay times empirically. In general, a scan delay of 25 to 30 seconds in patients with normal cardiac output enables optimal contrast opacification. In patients with compromised ventricular function, a scan delay of 35 to 40 seconds is used.[131]

Because of significantly faster imaging times, multislice CT techniques allow for greater flexibility in determining scanning protocols for the thoracic aorta. In general, the entire thoracic aorta can be covered in 10 to 15 seconds with the multislice scanner. At our institution, we favor a 2.5-mm slice thickness, a 1.25-mm reconstruction interval, and a pitch of 1 to 1.5 cm. With a rotation time of 500 msec and slice acquisition of 2.5 mm, the thoracic aorta is evaluated in less than 15 seconds. With standard injection rates and delays, the faster imaging time enables reduction of the volume of IV contrast agent to 100 to 125 mL. When there is a concern about specific valve abnormalities or atheroembolic disease, we often decrease slice thickness to 1.25 mm but maintain a pitch of 1 to 1.5. With the advent of prospective and retrospective electrocardiographic (ECG) gating software, we can also evaluate the thoracic aorta at specific phases of the cardiac cycle, minimizing motion and valvular artifacts.

Postprocessing Techniques

With the advent of spiral CT, volumetric data sets allowed the reformatting of axial data into a variety of imaging options. These options include multiplanar reconstruction (MPR), maximal intensity projection (MIP), volume rendering, and virtual endoscopic techniques. The clinical utility of these reconstruction techniques was initially limited because of the long computer reprocessing time. Now that computer software has become faster and more sophisticated, however, these 3D techniques have become easily accessible to the general radiologist.

Multiplanar reconstructions are one-voxel-thick sections that can be processed in any obliquity (Fig. 31–2). The use of curved MPRs allows for rapid reconstructions of the

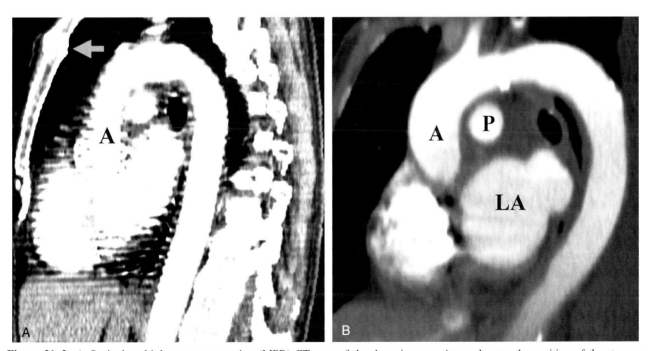

Figure 31–2. *A,* Sagittal multiplanar reconstruction (MPR) CT scan of the thoracic aorta. *Arrow* denotes the position of the sternum. Note the prominent cardiac pulsations with this conventional single-slice CT scan. *B,* Sagittal MPR CT scan of the thoracic aorta obtained with a multislice CT scanner. Note the lack of reconstruction artifacts in comparison with *A*. A = aorta; LA = left atrium; P = pulmonary artery.

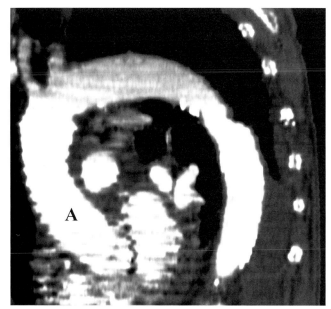

Figure 31–3. Sagittal multiplanar reconstruction CT scan of the thoracic aorta in a patient with suspected pulmonary embolism. Note the prominent cardiac pulsation artifacts. A = aorta.

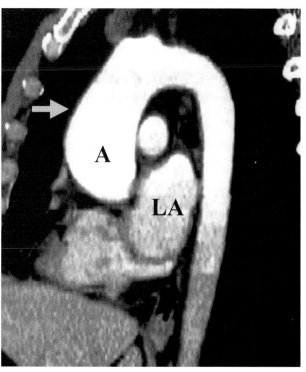

Figure 31–4. ECG-gated sagittal multiplanar reconstruction CT scan of the thoracic aorta in a patient with ascending aortic aneurysm. Note the absence of cardiac pulsation artifacts. *Arrow* denotes the ascending aorta. A = aorta; LA = left atrium.

aorta and selected branch vessels. Although MPR is the most rapid of the postprocessing algorithms, it is limited because of both partial volume effects and stair-stepping artifact due to cardiac pulsation (Fig. 31–3). This artifact can be minimized with a short reconstruction interval, and in the case of multislice scanners, retrospective cardiac gating (Fig. 31–4).

Shaded surface displays (SSDs) and MIP algorithms each have specific advantages and disadvantages in aortic

imaging. SSDs allow relatively rapid depiction of anatomic structures (Fig. 31–5), but the aortic lumen is not displayed—clearly a disadvantage in the depiction of aortic dissection and atheroembolic disease. MIP algorithms are

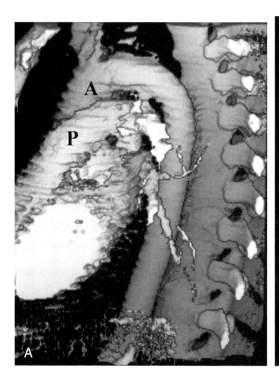

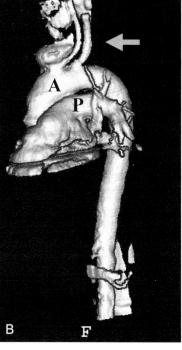

Figure 31–5. *A,* Sagittal oblique shaded surface display (SSD) shows the normal caliber of the thoracic aorta. Note the prominent cardiac pulsation artifacts in the aorta (A) and pulmonary artery (P). *B,* Sagittal oblique SSD of the normal thoracic aorta obtained with a multislice CT scanner. Note the absence of cardiac pulsation artifacts. Arrow denotes absence of pulsation artifacts in branch vessels.

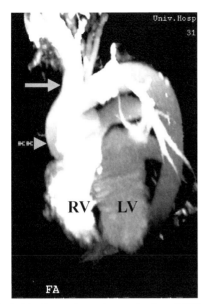

Figure 31–6. Maximum intensity projection (MIP) of the thoracic aorta with intense enhancement of the superior vena cava (*arrows*), which limits evaluation of the aorta. LV = left ventricle; RV = right ventricle.

very effective at evaluating anatomy and areas of stenoses. Their utility in the thoracic aorta is somewhat limited, however, because of the close proximity of a number of high-attenuation structures, particularly mediastinal venous structures, ribs, and spine (Fig. 31–6). Postprocessing of MIP images of the thoracic aorta requires more time and may be less useful in a busy clinical practice.

Volume-rendering techniques have proved to be of greater clinical utility than other 3D techniques.[102] These techniques allow accurate depictions of both the aortic lumen and surrounding structures (Fig. 31–7). Virtual endo-scopic techniques have proved to be of great value in our practice, particularly in the setting of atheroembolic disease and for evaluation of the postoperative aorta. The use of virtual endoscopy with SSD offers rapid visualization of the aortic lumen (Fig. 31–8), whereas volume-rendered virtual endoscopy allows closer anatomic depiction along with visualization of the aortic lumen and surrounding extraluminal structures (Fig. 31–9).[55] Although volume-rendering techniques have been historically more time-consuming than SSD techniques, improved computing time have made volume rendering more viable for clinical use.

MRI

From its earliest clinical application, MRI has been an important imaging modality in the evaluation of congenital and acquired aortic disease. MRI has traditionally been a more time intensive modality compared with CT, but improvements in software, faster gradients, new breath-hold techniques, and the use of gadolinium angiography have significantly improved the efficiency of MRI in aortic imaging.

Historically, MRI has utilized "black blood" techniques for the depiction of aortic anatomy, and "white blood" techniques for the depiction of blood flow. Black blood techniques require use of ECG-gated T1-weighted spin-echo (SE) sequences. In black blood sequences, presaturation pulses are used outside the volume of interest to saturate signal from flowing blood in the aorta.[99] Axial slices are obtained at a 7- to 8-mm slice thickness from the origin of the aortic arch vessels to the diaphragm (Fig. 31–10). Sagittal oblique images are obtained as clinically indicated. In patients in whom ECG gating and breath-holding techniques may not be possible, new half-Fourier single-shot turbo spin-echo (HASTE) imaging can be performed (Fig. 31–11).[113] HASTE images can be obtained in

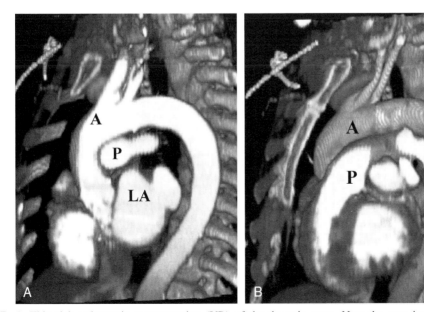

Figure 31–7. *A*, Thin-slab volumetric reconstruction (VR) of the thoracic aorta. Note the superior anatomic display of the thoracic aorta and surrounding anatomic structures. *B*, Thick-slab VR of the thoracic aorta. A = aorta; LA = left atrium; P = pulmonary artery.

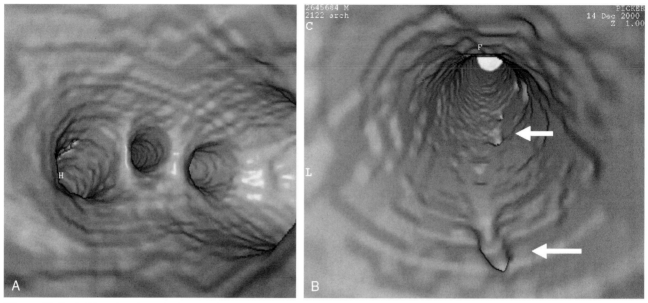

Figure 31–8. *A*, Virtual endoscopic image of the aortic arch obtained with a shaded surface display (SSD) algorithm shows the origins of the great vessels. *B*, Virtual endoscopic image of the aortic arch using an SSD algorithm demonstrates the descending thoracic aorta. Note the origins of the intercostal arteries (*arrows*).

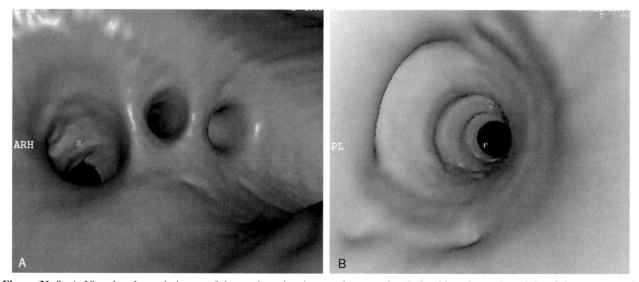

Figure 31–9. *A*, Virtual endoscopic image of the aortic arch using a volume-rendered algorithm shows the origin of the great vessels. The walls of the thoracic aorta are smoother than in the SSD algorithm images shown in Fig. 31–8. *B*, Virtual endoscopic image of the aortic arch using a volume-rendered algorithm displays the normal descending aorta.

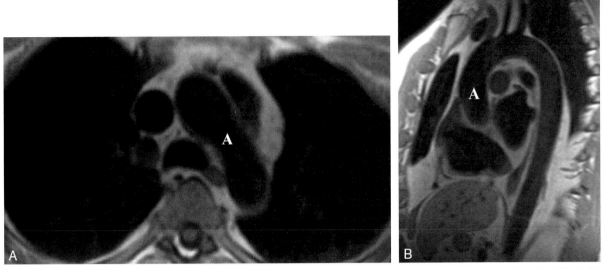

Figure 31–10. *A,* ECG-gated axial T1-weighted image of the aortic arch (A) shows the characteristic signal void ("black blood" technique) within the transverse arch. *B,* ECG-gated sagittal oblique T1-weighted image of the aorta (A) shows signal void ("black blood") within the thoracic aorta.

less than a minute with minimal loss of image quality and spatial resolution.

The standard white blood technique for evaluation of the thoracic aorta has been cine gradient-echo imaging.[6] These sequences have been used effectively in the evaluation of the thoracic aorta and have given radiologists important information about velocity, turbulent, and slow-flow states (Fig. 31–12). Further evaluation with phase-contrast angiography has allowed accurate assessment of aortic flow velocities, valvular function, and collateral blood flow[58] in cases of aortic dissection and coarctation (Fig. 31–13). However, the long imaging times needed for

these evaluations can be limiting, and a comprehensive evaluation of the entire thoracic aorta is impractical. As with black blood techniques, effective ECG gating is still important to the success of cine GRE images.

With the advent of gadolinium-enhanced aortic imaging, a new, powerful imaging technique was established.[96] Unlike cine GRE techniques, which rely on the intrinsic signal of flowing blood, gadolinium-enhanced MR angiography takes advantage of the T1-shortening effect of gadolinium within the vascular system.[69] With the introduction of stronger and faster gradients, TR and TE values can be sufficiently shortened to maximize the signal of the gado-

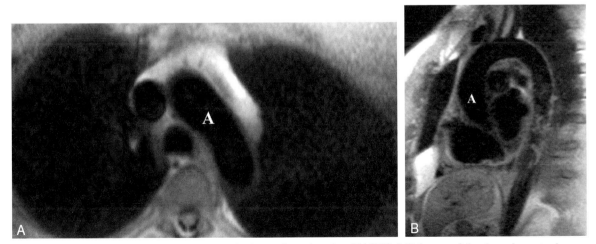

Figure 31–11. *A,* Axial half-Fourier acquisition single-shot turbo spin echo (HASTE) MR image of the thoracic aorta shows a signal void within the aortic arch, similar to that shown in Fig. 31-10*A.* Compared with standard T1-weighted MR imaging, evaluation of the surrounding anatomic structures on this HASTE image is limited. *B,* Sagittal HASTE MR image of the thoracic aorta displays anatomic information comparable to that shown in the standard T1-weighted MR images of the aorta, as shown in Fig. 31–10*B.* As in *A,* rendering of the surrounding anatomy is limited with the HASTE sequence. A = aorta.

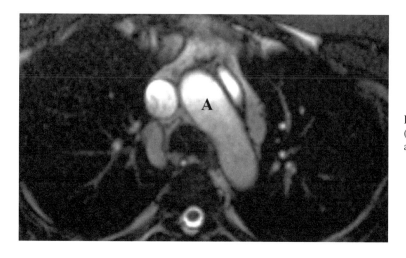

Figure 31–12. Axial cine gradient-recalled echo (GRE) MR image of the aortic arch shows the normal appearance of the transverse aorta. A = aorta.

linium-containing aorta in relation to the surrounding stationary tissues (Fig. 31–14).

The success of gadolinium-enhanced angiography depends on close attention to timing of the gadolinium bolus, because of significant variability in individual cardiac outputs and time to peak aortic enhancement. A number of techniques are available to maximize contrast enhancement in the ascending aorta. They include empiric timing based on the estimated cardiac output, use of a timing bolus, and automatic triggering.[95] Though beyond the scope of this chapter, newer techniques available in some centers include true fast imaging with steady-state precession (FISP) of the aorta (Fig. 31–15), which allows almost real-time imaging of the aorta. Such techniques promise to further enhance our accuracy and speed in the diagnosis of aortic disease.

Advanced CT and MRI techniques have similarly improved our evaluation of the aortic valve. ECG-gated multislice CT allows evaluation of the aortic valve in systole and diastole (Fig. 31–16), and virtual endoscopic imaging with multislice CT has enabled 3D imaging of the aortic valve, which is not possible with single-slice CT

scanners (Fig. 31–17). The superior time resolution made possible with cine MRI has also enhanced visualization of the normal aortic valve (Fig. 31–18).

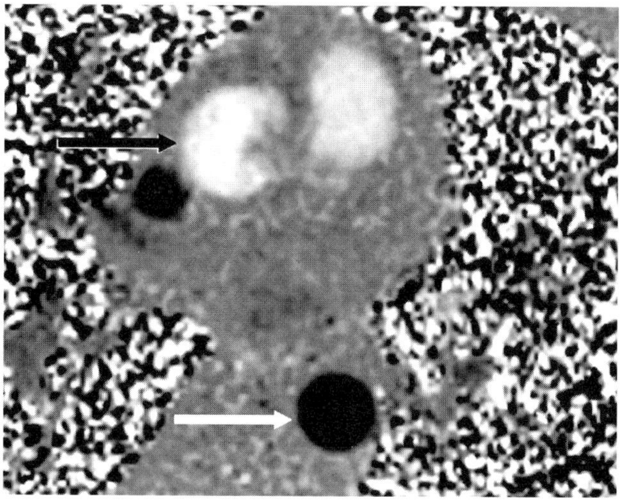

Imaging Artifacts

The accurate assessment of aortic disease is complicated by a large number of imaging artifacts that can mimic important and potentially life-threatening aortic disease. With the growing use of multislice CT scanners and ECG gating, these artifacts will be significantly reduced. However, in any discussion of the role of imaging in thoracic

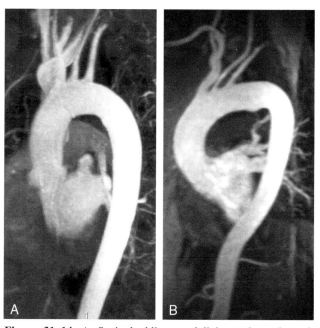

Figure 31–14. *A*, Sagittal oblique gadolinium-enhanced maximum intensity projection (MIP) of the thoracic aorta in a young adult. *B*, Sagittal oblique gadolinium-enhanced MIP of the thoracic aorta in an elderly patient shows marked unfolding of the thoracic aortic arch. Note the smooth appearance of the ductus diverticulum.

Figure 31–13. Phase-contrast MR image at the level of the mid-thoracic aorta shows cephalad blood flow displayed in white (*black arrow*), and caudad blood flow in black (*white arrow*).

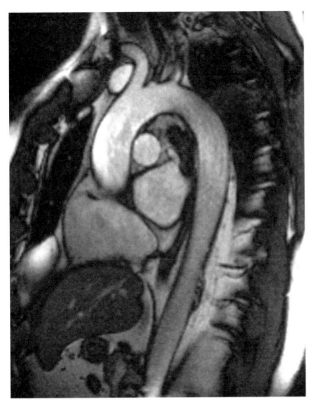

Figure 31–15. True fast imaging with steady-state precession (FISP) cine image of the thoracic aorta. Such images provide information similar to those shown by conventional cine gradient-recalled echo images but with markedly shorter imaging times.

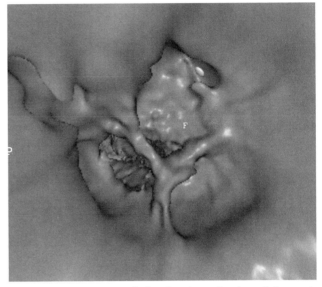

Figure 31–17. ECG-gated virtual endoscopic view of the aortic valve displays the sinuses of Valsalva captured in diastole.

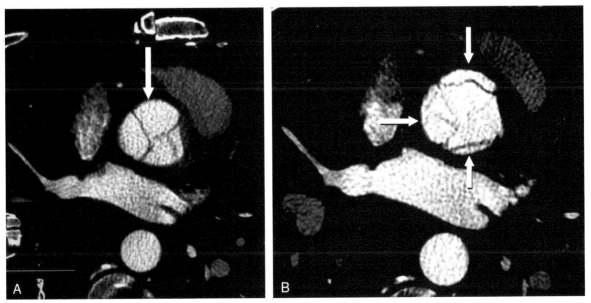

Figure 31–16. *A*, ECG-gated CT scan of the aortic root clearly delineates the three aortic cusps closed in diastole (*arrow*). *B*, ECG-gated CT image of the aortic root in systole captures the opened valve cusps (*arrows*).

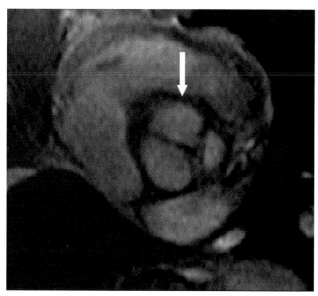

Figure 31–18. Coronal oblique image of the aortic root using a cine gradient-recalled echo (GRE) sequence delineates the three aortic cusps in diastole. Arrow denotes valve in diastole.

aortic disease, it is important to consider the wide variety of these artifacts and pitfalls.

Optimal contrast opacification is of great importance in the evaluation of aortic disease. Inadequate contrast opacification limits our evaluation of a variety of aortic diseases, particularly aortic dissection (Fig. 31–19). These limitations can be overcome with a timing bolus or the use of automated bolus-tracking techniques to optimize contrast opacification in the aorta. Even with adequate contrast opacification, there can be imaging difficulty in patients with aortic dissection, in whom there may be significant

differences in flow dynamics in the true lumen and false lumen (Fig. 31–20).[9]

Streak artifacts from adjacent vascular structures can cause artifacts that mimic aortic dissection. This appearance, most commonly seen in the ascending aorta and arch vessels, results from the high-attenuation contrast seen in the crossing brachiocephalic veins or superior vena cava (Fig. 31–21). A streak artifact can generally be distinguished from aortic dissection if one follows the artifact beyond the expected course of the aorta. Although streak artifacts can be minimized by pedal injection of the contrast agent, this route is technically more difficult and usually less acceptable to the patient. Some researchers suggest that the use of saline or diluted contrast material at the end of the contrast bolus also minimizes the streak artifacts seen from high attenuation in the brachiocephalic veins.

Adjacent anatomic structures can also mimic aortic dissections or hematoma. They include the right atrial appendage, the superior pericardial recess, and the superior intercostal vein (Figs. 31–22 and 31–23). The atelectatic lung commonly seen adjacent to the descending aorta can sometimes mimic dissection or leak (Fig. 31–24). Close examination of images superior and inferior to these images excludes dissection or hematoma.[111] Aortic pulsation artifacts (Fig. 31–25) are classic mimics of dissection flaps. Pulsation artifacts usually occur in the ascending aorta. Studies using ECG-gated electron beam computed tomography (EBCT) demonstrated significant aortic motion during the cardiac cycle and further classified their common locations. Most commonly, pulsation artifacts are seen at the 7 o'clock and 12 o'clock positions.

Aortic Arch Anomalies

It is important to recognize that the standard branching pattern of the thoracic aorta is seen in only 75% of pa-

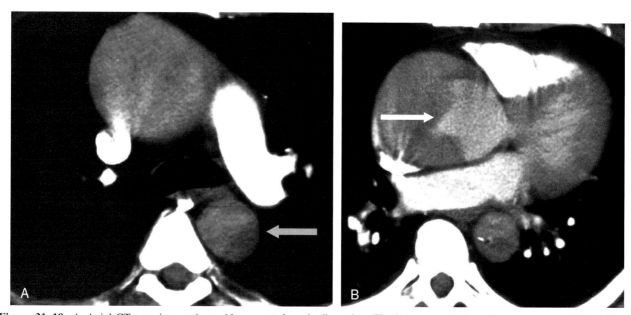

Figure 31–19. *A,* Axial CT scan in a patient with suspected aortic dissection. The intravenous bolus of contrast material is early, and visualization of the thoracic aorta is inadequate. *Arrow* shows descending aorta. *B,* Axial CT scan at the level of the aortic root shows faint opacification of the aortic root with subtle delineation of ascending aortic dissection (*arrow*).

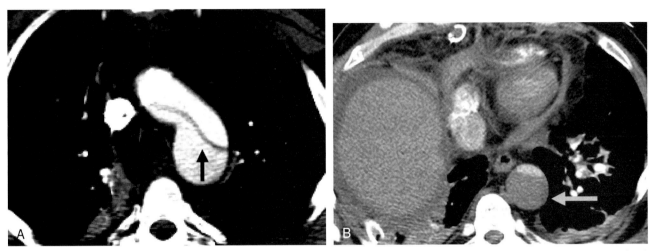

Figure 31–20. *A,* Axial multislice CT scan shows an aortic dissection flap involving the aortic arch (*arrow*). *B,* Axial scan at the level of the descending aorta shows faint opacification of the anteriorly compressed true lumen. The early injection results in inadequate visualization of the false lumen.

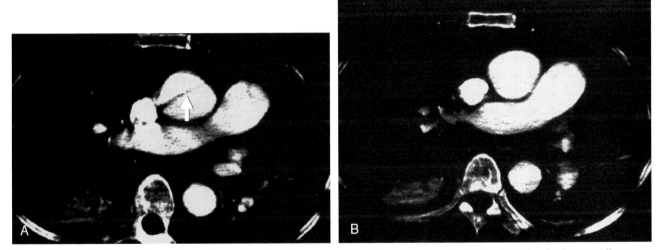

Figure 31–21. *A,* Axial CT scan above the aortic valve shows an apparent linear density mimicking dissection in the ascending aorta, secondary to a beam-hardening artifact from the presence of contrast agent in the superior vena cava (*arrow*). *B,* Axial CT scan superior to scan in *A* shows a normal ascending aorta with no evidence of dissection.

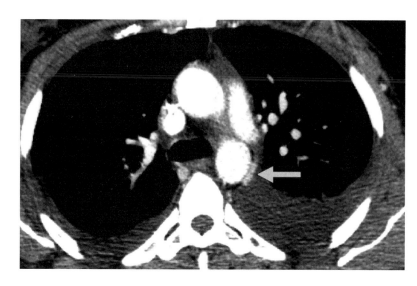

Figure 31–22. Axial CT scan demonstrates a suspicious soft tissue density (*arrow*) adjacent to the descending aorta.

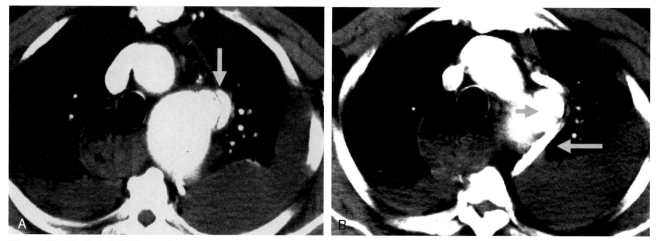

Figure 31–23. *A,* Axial CT scan in a patient with known aortic aneurysm and findings suspicious for possible dissection flap involving the descending aorta (*arrow*). *B,* Axial CT scan superior to *A* shows the full course of the superior intercostal vein (*white arrow*). Note the separate medial dissection flap (*black arrow*).

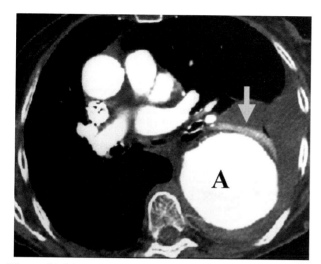

Figure 31–24. Axial CT scan in a patient with a large aortic aneurysm shows abnormal, enhancing soft tissue anterior to the aneurysm (*arrow*). This soft tissue represents atelectatic lung anterior to the aneurysm.

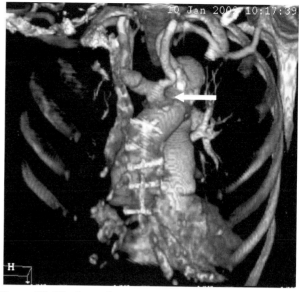

Figure 31–26. Coronal volumetric reconstruction demonstrates the common origin of the right brachiocephalic artery and the left carotid artery (*arrow*).

tients.[12] The most common aortic variant is the so-called bovine arch, in which the right brachiocephalic artery and left common carotid artery have a common origin (Fig. 31–26). Although the left vertebral artery originates from the subclavian artery in most patients, it arises directly from the aortic arch in 5% to 6% of patients (Fig. 31–27); this can be an important variant in patients undergoing cerebral angiography.[123]

Understanding congenital aortic arch anomalies requires comprehension of the embryologic double arch theory. In the standard left arch, the embryologic double arch fuses posteriorly to form the descending aorta. If the right arch is interrupted between the right subclavian artery and the descending aorta, the right subclavian and carotid arteries fuse to form the right brachiocephalic artery, resulting in the standard arch anatomy.[118]

The most common aortic arch anomaly is the left aortic arch with aberrant right subclavian artery. This anomaly occurs when the right arch is interrupted between the right common carotid artery and the right subclavian artery. The right subclavian artery arises from the diverticulum of Kommerell, a persistence of the embryologic right aortic arch. In most cases, the aberrant right subclavian artery crosses posterior to the esophagus (Fig. 31–28), but it courses between the trachea and esophagus in 18% of cases, and in front of the trachea in 4%.[60] The common left aortic arch with aberrant right subclavian artery occurs in 1 in 200 patients. On a lateral radiograph, a posterior impression on the trachea can be seen. Symptoms occur at the two extremes of life in patients with this anomaly. In children, tracheal obstruction or dysphagia can occur,[11] whereas in adults, aneurysms of the aberrant subclavian

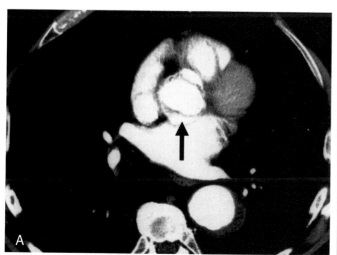

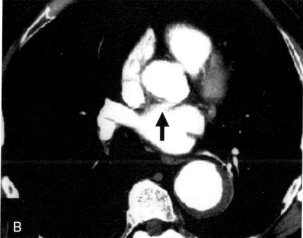

Figure 31–25. *A*, Axial CT scan shows linear pulsation artifacts in the ascending aorta that mimic aortic dissection (*arrow*). *B*, Axial ECG-gated CT scan obtained during diastole demonstrates resolution of these filling defects.

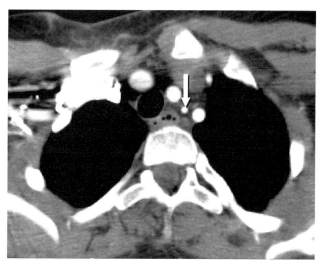

Figure 31–27. Axial CT shows direct origin of the vertebral artery (*arrow*) from the aortic arch.

artery or a prominent diverticulum of Kommerell can occur, resulting in dysphagia classically known as *dysphagia lusoria* (Figs. 31–29 through 31–31).[7] Less common descriptions of the aberrant right subclavian artery have included superior vena cava obstruction and gastrointestinal bleeding. There are isolated case reports of thrombosis with distal embolization in patients with aberrant right subclavian artery.[1]

The right aortic arch is a much less common anomaly, occurring in 0.5% of patients.[63] The three common anomalies of the right aortic arch are (1) right aortic arch with aberrant left subclavian artery, (2) right aortic arch with mirror image branching (see Fig. 31–22), and (3) right aortic arch with isolated left subclavian artery.[36] The right arch with aberrant left subclavian artery occurs in 0.6% to 0.1% (Fig. 31–32). A minority of these anomalies are associated with significant congenital heart disease, although right aortic arch is the second most common cause of vascular ring, after double aortic arch.[132] Right aortic arch with mirror image branching is commonly associated with congenital heart disease, most often seen in patients with tetralogy of Fallot, ventricular septal defects, and truncus arteriosus. We have seen a large variety of unusual

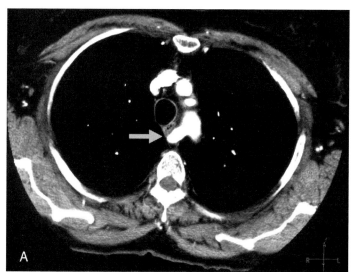

Figure 31–28. *A*, Axial CT scan shows an anomalous vessel crossing behind the esophagus, consistent with aberrant right subclavian artery (*arrow*). *B*, Axial CT scan shows the aberrant subclavian posterior to the esophagus. Note the eccentric thickening of the subclavian artery, consistent with early atherosclerotic change. *C*, Shaded surface display shows the position of the aberrant right subclavian artery (*arrow*).

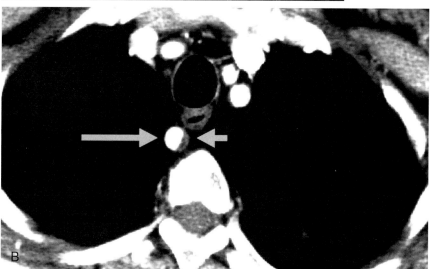

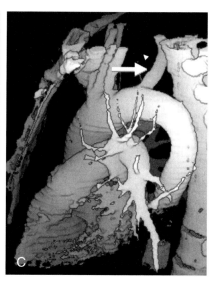

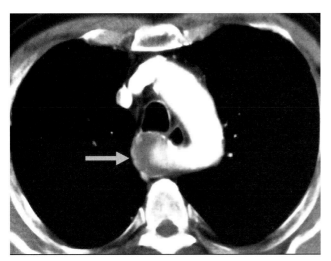

Figure 31–29. Axial CT scan shows aneurysmal dilatation of the aberrant right subclavian artery (*arrow*).

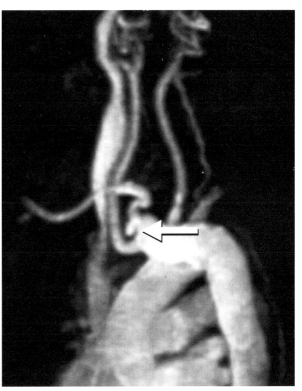

Figure 31–31. Gadolinium MR angiogram of the aortic arch demonstrates a penetrating atherosclerotic ulcer arising from the aberrant right subclavian artery (*arrow*).

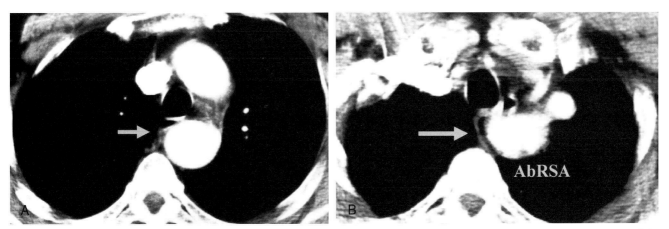

Figure 31–30. *A*, Axial CT scan shows the origin of the right subclavian artery from a diverticulum of Kommerell (*arrow*). *B*, Axial CT scan shows compression of the esophagus by the aberrant right subclavian artery (AbRSA).

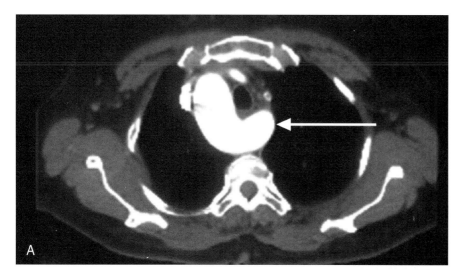

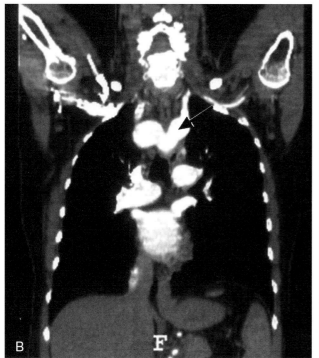

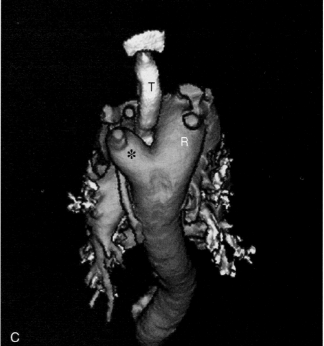

Figure 31–32. *A*, Axial CT scan demonstrates the right aortic arch with aberrant left subclavian artery (*arrow*). *B*, Coronal multiplanar reconstruction shows that the aberrant left subclavian artery (*arrow*) originates from an aortic diverticulum. *C*, Shaded surface display from a posterior perspective shows the right aortic arch (R) with the aberrant left subclavian artery (*). Note the relationship to the trachea (T).

right aortic arch anomalies not associated with congenital heart disease (Figs. 31–33 and 31–34).

Double aortic arch, the result of persistence of the embryologic double arch, is the most common cause of a symptomatic vascular ring. The anomaly is much less commonly associated with congenital heart anomalies. In double aortic arch, the right arch is generally higher and larger than the left arch (Fig. 31–35). The descending arch is on the left side in most patients. Although this anomaly is clearly seen in asymptomatic adult patients, the size of the left aortic arch is quite variable, and the effect of a relatively atretic left arch on tracheal diameter often determines the symptoms (Fig. 31–36). Multislice CT scanning has enabled enhanced visualization of the double aortic arch in infants and neonates (Fig. 31–37).

The cervical aortic arch is an uncommon anomaly of the aorta in which the aortic arch extends into the soft tissues of the neck. Patients with this anomaly are generally asymptomatic, but they can present with dysphagia, stridor, or a pulsatile neck mass (Fig. 31–38). Aneurysms involving a cervical aortic arch have been reported, with several cases of aneurysmal rupture. It is postulated that in patients with the anomaly and an aneurysm, embryologic development of the aortic arch was abnormal, and many patients exhibit cystic medial necrosis.[51]

Coarctation of the Aorta

Coarctation of the aorta is an abnormal narrowing of the descending aorta. It most commonly manifests as a focal area of narrowing distal to the left subclavian artery

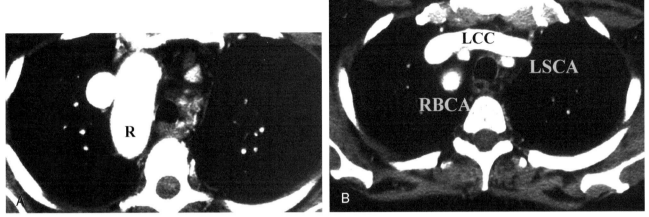

Figure 31–33. *A*, Axial CT scan shows the right aortic arch (R). There is no evidence of an aberrant subclavian artery. *B*, In the same patient, an axial CT scan superior to *A* shows the right brachiocephalic artery (RBCA), the left common carotid artery (LCC), and the left subclavian artery (LSCA), consistent with a normal left aortic arch branching pattern.

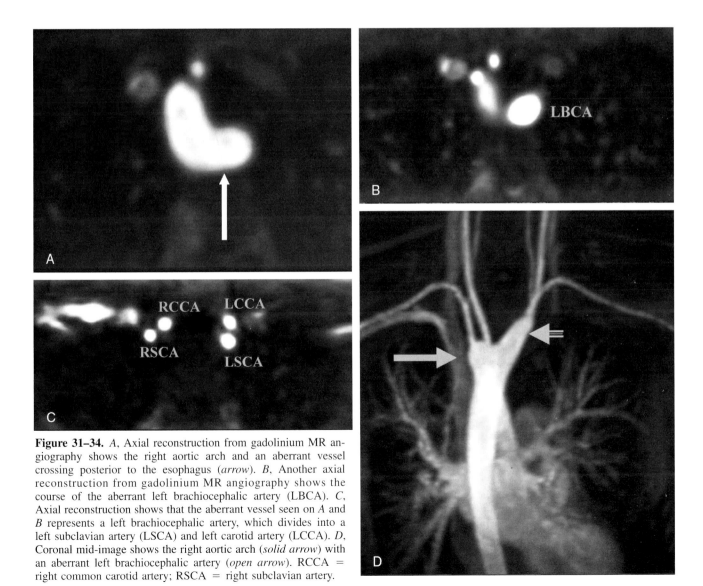

Figure 31–34. *A*, Axial reconstruction from gadolinium MR angiography shows the right aortic arch and an aberrant vessel crossing posterior to the esophagus (*arrow*). *B*, Another axial reconstruction from gadolinium MR angiography shows the course of the aberrant left brachiocephalic artery (LBCA). *C*, Axial reconstruction shows that the aberrant vessel seen on *A* and *B* represents a left brachiocephalic artery, which divides into a left subclavian artery (LSCA) and left carotid artery (LCCA). *D*, Coronal mid-image shows the right aortic arch (*solid arrow*) with an aberrant left brachiocephalic artery (*open arrow*). RCCA = right common carotid artery; RSCA = right subclavian artery.

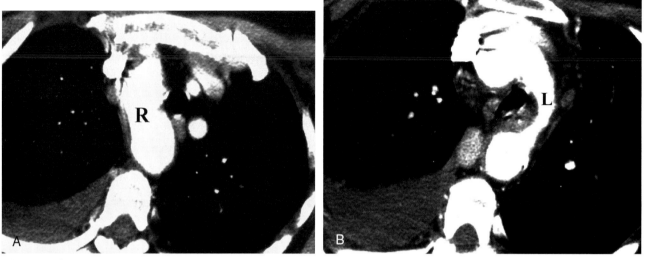

Figure 31–35. *A*, Axial CT scan shows a right-sided aortic arch (R). *B*, An axial CT scan at a level inferior to that of *A* shows a smaller left-sided aortic arch (L).

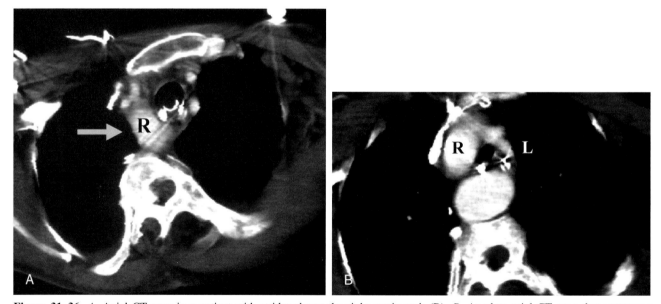

Figure 31–36. *A*, Axial CT scan in a patient with stridor shows the right aortic arch (R). *B*, Another axial CT scan demonstrates a small left aortic arch (L) and a small trachea in the same patient.

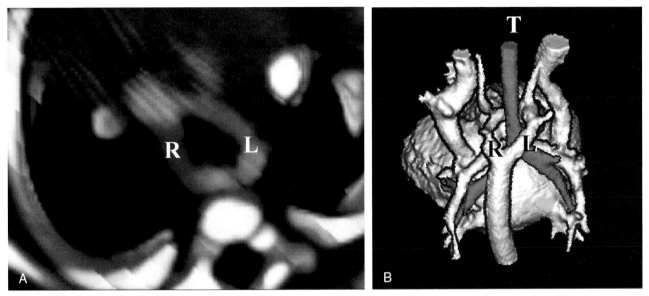

Figure 31–37. *A*, Axial volumetric reconstruction in a newborn with respiratory difficulty shows a double aortic arch. *B*, Shaded surface display in the same patient shows a double aortic arch surrounding the trachea (T). R = right aortic arch; L = left aortic arch.

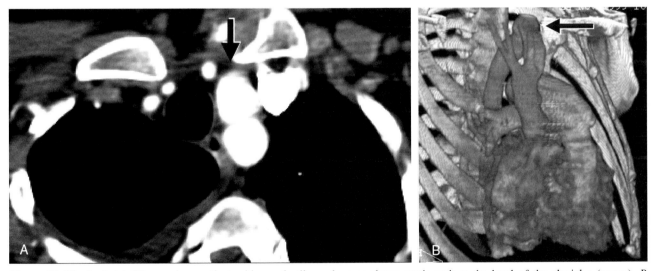

Figure 31–38. *A*, Axial CT scan in a patient with a pulsatile neck mass shows aortic arch at the level of the clavicles (*arrow*). *B*, Volumetric reconstruction demonstrates the position of the thoracic aortic arch at the level of the clavicle (*arrow*).

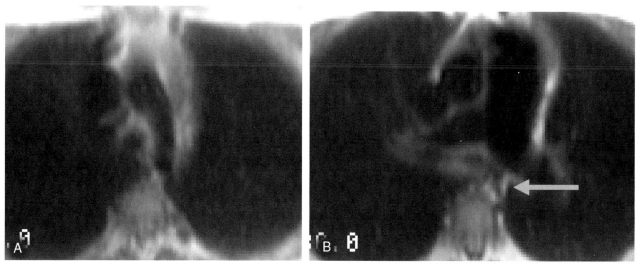

Figure 31–39. *A*, Axial ECG-gated, T1-weighted MR image of the aortic arch shows narrowing of the distal aortic arch. *B*, Axial ECG-gated, T1-weighted image of the aortic arch at a level inferior to that of *A* demonstrates absence of the proximal descending aorta (*arrow*).

(Fig. 31–39). In the infantile form, tubular hypoplasia can affect a longer segment of the descending aorta. This anomaly is associated with bicuspid aortic valve in 75% to 85% of patients (Fig. 31–40).[39, 126] Although coarctation of the aorta classically manifests in infants, 20% of patients are diagnosed in adolescence or adulthood. Presenting symptoms include a murmur, systemic hypertension, and differences in blood pressure between the upper and lower extremities. The incidence of cerebral aneurysms and accelerated atherosclerosis is higher in patients with coarctation of the aorta; these disorders are believed to represent sequelae of the systemic hypertension commonly seen in coarctation.

Imaging of aortic coarctation has been well characterized, and the disorder has been successfully imaged with echocardiography, CT, and MRI (Fig. 31–41). Echocardiography and CT have been effective in evaluation of aortic coarctation, but MRI is currently regarded as the most effective method to comprehensively assess the physiologic significance of aortic narrowing (Fig. 31–42).[115] MRI studies have shown excellent correlation with conventional angiography, whereas cine MRI and phase-contrast techniques have identified physiologically significant coarctation. Newer multislice techniques have improved the CT evaluation of aortic coarctation (Figs. 31–43 and 31–44).

Aortic Aneurysms

By definition, a true thoracic aortic aneurysm involves all components of the vessel wall. The morphologic subtypes of aneurysm are saccular (Fig. 31–45), fusiform

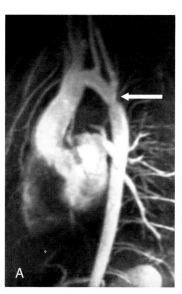
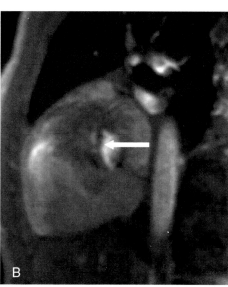

Figure 31–40. *A*, Sagittal oblique gadolinium MR angiogram of a patient with a thoracic aorta shows discrete postductal coarctation (*arrow*). *B*, Oblique cine gradient-recalled echo image demonstrates a bicuspid aortic valve (*arrow*).

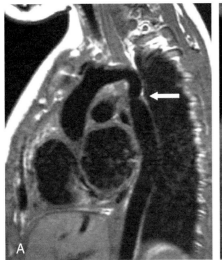
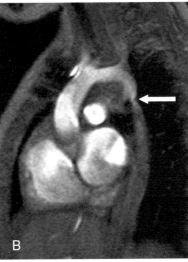

Figure 31–41. *A,* Sagittal oblique ECG-gated T1-weighted MR image (*A*) and sagittal oblique cine gradient-recalled echo image (*B*) of the thoracic aorta show discrete postductal coarctation (*arrow*).

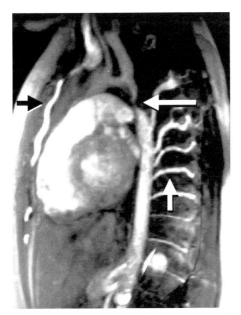

Figure 31–42. Sagittal oblique gadolinium-enhanced MR image demonstrates severe postductal coarctation (*long arrow*) with prominent intercostal aorta (*short arrow*). Note the prominent internal mammary artery (*black arrow*).

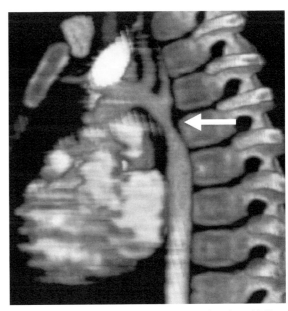

Figure 31–43. Sagittal oblique volume-rendered multislice CT scan of postductal coarctation (*arrow*).

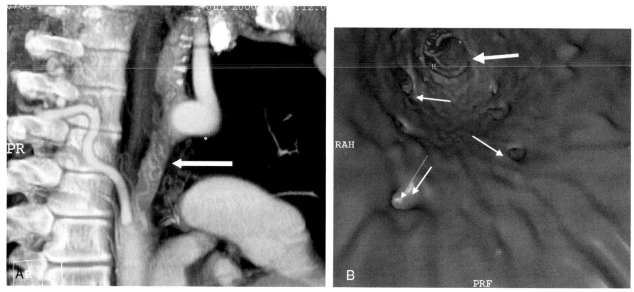

Figure 31–44. *A*, Sagittal oblique volume-rendered CT scan shows persistent coarctation (*arrow*) after surgical repair. Note the markedly enlarged third intercostal artery. *B*, *Large arrow* shows the coarctation. *Small white arrows* show prominent intercostal artery origins.

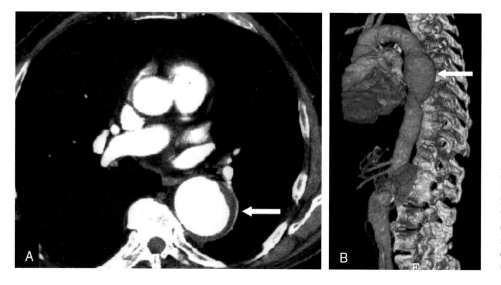

Figure 31–45. *A*, Axial CT scan shows dilatation of the descending aorta with surrounding thrombus (*arrow*). *B*, Sagittal oblique volume-rendered CT scan demonstrates fusiform aneurysm of the descending aorta (*arrow*).

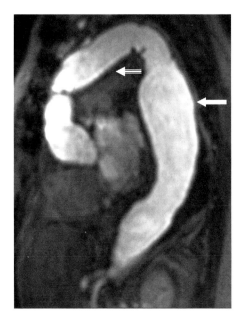

Figure 31–46. Sagittal oblique multiplanar reconstruction of gadolinium-enhanced MR angiography shows a diffuse aneurysm of descending aorta (*thick arrow*). Note the prior transverse arch repair (*thin arrow*).

(Fig. 31–46), dissecting, and false. In addition, acquired aneurysms can be atherosclerotic, mycotic, post-traumatic (Fig. 31–47), or secondary to cystic medial necrosis (Fig. 31–48). Although aneurysms are more common than dissections within the thoracic aorta, acute aneurysmal rupture is an infrequent occurrence (Figs. 31–49 and 31–50).[33, 94] Initial identification of thoracic aortic aneurysms can be suspected from chest radiographs.[50, 57] Most commonly, a mediastinal mass or enlarged segment of the aorta, often containing mural calcification, is visualized. Other findings,

such as displacement and compression of the esophagus or trachea and bronchi, may be visible on chest radiographs. Uncommon findings are erosion of the thoracic vertebrae and posterior ribs.

Contrast-enhanced CT can show that a mediastinal mass seen on chest radiographs represents an aneurysm, characterize it, and reveal its exact location. CT can also be used to ascertain whether the aneurysm affects the takeoff of the arch vessels (Fig. 31–51). In addition, CT can demonstrate the following characteristics of the aneurysm: dilatation of the aorta, calcification, intraluminal thrombi, displacement or erosion of adjacent structures, and perianeurysmal thickening and hemorrhage.[38, 39, 133, 134] Identification of mural thrombus and calcification are common with contrast-enhanced CT, because most aortic aneurysms are secondary to arteriosclerosis. Mural thrombus, reported in up to 86% of patients, is typically crescent-shaped and circular in appearance, with the residual aortic lumen appearing smooth. [48, 74, 129] Calcification within the wall of aortic aneurysm has been reported in 83% of patients and typically appears as discontinuous plaques and curvilinear segments.[39, 74] Calcification within the mural thrombus can be seen in up to 17% of aortic aneurysms and can be mistaken for the displaced intimal calcification seen in aortic dissections.[39, 47, 129]

Thoracic aortic aneurysms are most commonly located within the descending aorta at the level of the ligamentum arteriosum, just distal to the origin of the subclavian artery. They are less commonly found within the descending aorta at the level of the aortic hiatus of the diaphragm. The aortic arch is the next most common site, followed by the ascending aorta (Figs. 31–52 and 31–53).[47, 57] In a patient with an aneurysm involving the descending aorta, the esophagus is displaced to the right, and the trachea and bronchi are displaced anteriorly. Aneurysms of the aortic arch and ascending aorta produce compression rather than displacement of adjacent mediastinal structures.[57]

The presence of a thoracic aortic aneurysm should not

Figure 31–47. *A*, Axial gadolinium-enhanced MR image shows focal outpouching from proximal descending aorta. *B*, Sagittal oblique MR image with gadolinium enhancement of the aorta shows a chronic pseudoaneurysm at the level of the ductus arteriosus. A = aneurysm.

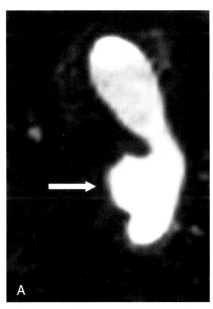
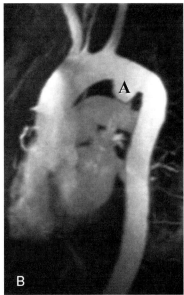

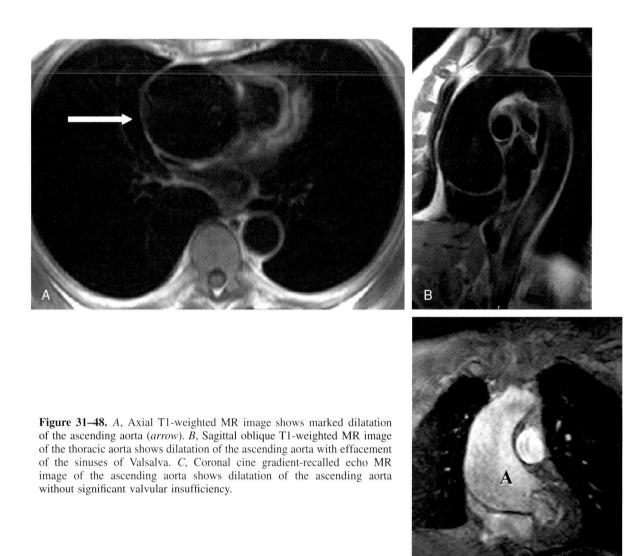

Figure 31–48. *A*, Axial T1-weighted MR image shows marked dilatation of the ascending aorta (*arrow*). *B*, Sagittal oblique T1-weighted MR image of the thoracic aorta shows dilatation of the ascending aorta with effacement of the sinuses of Valsalva. *C*, Coronal cine gradient-recalled echo MR image of the ascending aorta shows dilatation of the ascending aorta without significant valvular insufficiency.

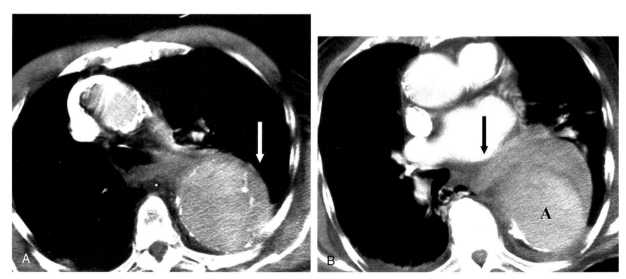

Figure 31–49. *A*, Axial CT scan shows leaking descending aortic aneurysm, with soft tissue extending beyond the mural calcification (*arrow*). *B*, Axial CT scan at a level inferior to that in *A* shows extension of the leak into the mediastinum (*arrow*).

Figure 31–50. *A*, Axial multi-slice CT scan in a patient with a leaking aortic aneurysm (A). *B*, Sagiittal oblique multislice CT scan shows a large aneurysm (A) and dependent high-density pleural fluid consistent with acute hemorrhage (*arrow*).

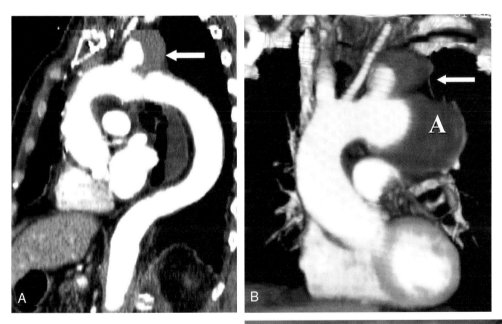

Figure 31–51. *A*, Sagittal oblique multislice CT scan shows aneurysmal dilatation of the subclavian artery with surrounding thrombus (*arrow*). *B*, Coronal volume-rendered CT scan demonstrates aneurysmal involvement of the transverse arch (A) and left subclavian artery (*arrow*). *C*, Virtual endoscopic image of the aortic arch shows relative aneurysmal dilatation of the subclavian artery (*arrow*). LCC = left common carotic artery; LSCA = left subclavian artery; RBCA = right brachiocephalic artery.

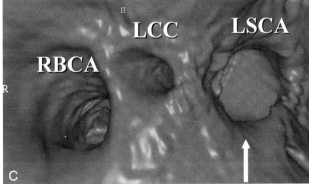

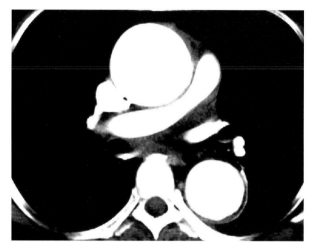

Figure 31–52. Axial CT scan demonstrates an aneurysm of the ascending aorta in a patient presenting with acute chest pain.

be concluded solely from the measurement of aortic circumference. The circumference of the aorta varies significantly according to the size, sex, and age of the patient and the width of the thoracic vertebral body.[49] For practical purposes, in the diagnosis of a thoracic aortic aneurysm, the descending aorta should never be larger than the ascending aorta at a given scan level, and the ratio of the coronal diameter of the ascending aorta to that of the descending aorta should be about 1.5:1.[49] The maximum diameter of the aneurysm correlates well with the incidence of rupture. For aneurysms less than 5 cm in diameter, the incidence of rupture is 2%; for aneurysms larger than 10 cm, the incidence of rupture is greater than 50%. Up to 50% of deaths from thoracic aortic aneurysms are caused

by rupture.[33, 94] A leaking or ruptured thoracic aortic aneurysm creates extensive tissue density from mediastinal hematoma and, occasionally, a left pleural effusion (see Fig. 31–50). Rarely, contrast material can be seen beyond the confines of the aortic wall on bolus-injected, contrast-enhanced CT scans.

The advent of helical CT scanners and the use of CT angiography have made diagnosis and characterization of aortic aneurysms easier and more accurate and have also enabled highly accurate differentiation of other diseases of the aorta.[13, 97] In contrast to conventional CT, CT angiography provides an overall picture of the aneurysm; the use of MPR, MIP, and true 3D SSD images permits very precise measurement of the maximum diameter of the aneurysm.[13] In addition, the use of thin beam collimation and maximum vascular enhancement during a single breath-hold sequence allows the extent of the aneurysm to be delineated accurately with respect to the major aortic branches.[140] CT angiography also preserves the advantages of conventional CT—demonstrating extraluminal disease and the relationship of the aneurysm to adjacent organs.

Thoracic aortic aneurysms are also easily identified with MRI.[25, 37, 72, 83, 138] MRI can identify aneurysms involving the ascending aorta, aortic arch, and the descending aorta (Fig. 31–54).[37, 138] The technique readily depicts vascular structures because of a naturally occurring contrast between the low signal intensity of flowing blood and the higher signal intensity of the vessel walls. MRI has several advantages over CT. The first is MRI's multiplanar capability, which makes characterization of the aneurysm and determination of arch vessel involvement easier. The second is that CT requires injection of iodinated contrast medium but MRI does not; this is an important consideration in patients who either have a baseline impairment in renal function or are at risk for contrast medium–induced renal

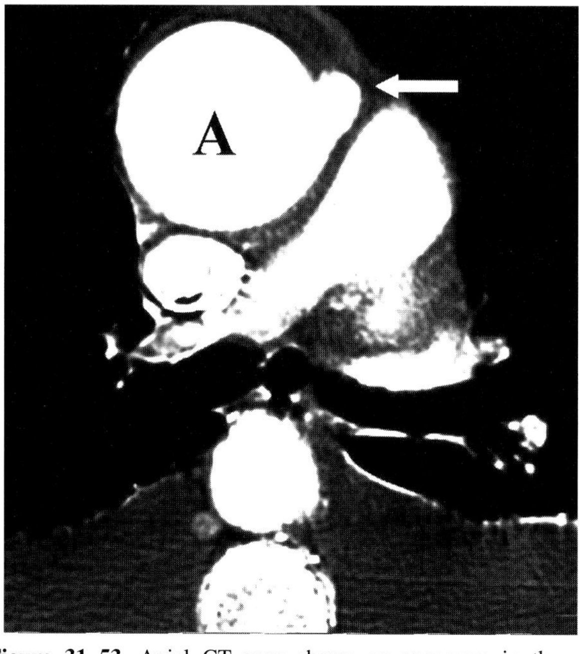

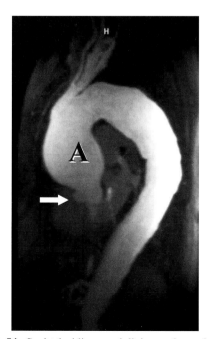

Figure 31–53. Axial CT scan shows an aneurysm in the ascending aorta with an active leak (*arrow*). The patient presented with hemorrhagic pleural effusion and died the next day. A = ascending aorta.

Figure 31–54. Sagittal oblique gadolinium-enhanced MR image shows aneurysmal dilatation of the ascending aorta (A) with sparing of the sinuses of Valsalva (*arrow*).

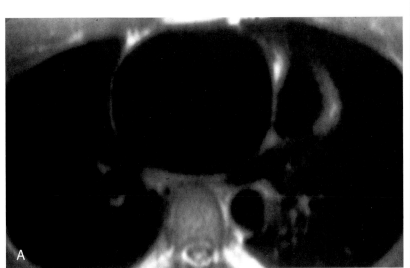

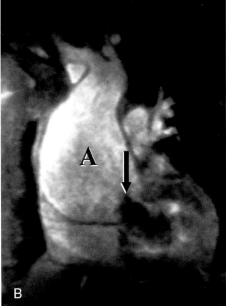

Figure 31–55. *A,* Axial ECG-gated, T1-weighted MR image of the ascending aorta shows marked dilatation of the ascending aorta in a patient with Marfan's syndrome. *B,* Coronal cine gradient-recalled echo MR image of the aorta of the same patient demonstrates a prominent ascending aorta (A) with effacement of the sinuses of Valsalva. There is significant aortic insufficiency, demonstrated by the large area of signal loss/dephasing at the level of the aortic valve (*arrow*).

failure. MRI also provides information on relative blood flow that CT cannot (Fig. 31–55).[35] The limitations of MRI compared with CT include inferior spatial resolution, the inability to ensure that the entire region of interest is imaged in one section, a failure to detect calcifications, and difficulty monitoring critically ill patients.[35] In addition, patients with cardiac pacemakers and some prosthetic cardiac valves and angiographic stents are precluded from undergoing MRI examinations because of the high field strength of the MRI magnet.

Rapidly flowing blood appears on MRI as a signal void on first-echo images, emitting little or no signal, but demonstrates a relative increase in signal intensity on second-echo images. In contradistinction, thrombus within the aortic lumen, when present, demonstrates a relative decrease in signal intensity on second-echo images.[4, 27, 133] These characteristics allow precise measurements of the diameter of thoracic aortic aneurysms and nearly exact correlation with the same measurements obtained on CT.[37] As stated previously, the ability to image in multiple planes with MRI allows accurate characterization of the extent of an aneurysm to determine whether it involves the origins of the arch vessels. Finally, MRI, like CT, is useful in providing information concerning the relationship between aneurysms and the surrounding mediastinal structures, and MRI has been reported to be ideal for detecting mediastinal hematoma, a secondary sign suggesting rupture of the aneurysm.[7]

Thoracic Aortic Dissection

Acute aortic dissection is a true medical emergency that must be recognized promptly and diagnosed accurately.

The mortality rate in untreated patients is reported to be approximately 25% during the first 24 hours, 70% during the first 2 weeks, and 90% after 2 weeks.[21, 52] Dissection occurs from a tear in the wall of the aorta with subsequent hemorrhage of blood into the media, creating a second or false lumen. This false lumen is usually located between the inner one third and outer two thirds of the media, rarely involving more than half the circumference of the aorta.[101] By far the condition most commonly predisposing to aortic dissection is systemic hypertension. Other, less common conditions are Marfan's syndrome, Ehlers-Danlos syndrome, pregnancy, syphilis and other causes of aortitis, and coarctation.[101]

The Stanford classification of aortic dissections into two types directly related to prognosis and therapy has become generally accepted.[101] Type A dissections involve the ascending aorta, account for 60% to 70% of dissections, and usually arise within a few centimeters of the aortic valve. Without treatment, type A dissections are virtually always fatal, and death usually results from extension to and involvement of the aortic valve ring and ostia of the coronary arteries, which produces aortic valvular incompetence and left heart failure.[101] Type B dissections involve the descending thoracic aorta, most commonly arising just distal to the origin of the left subclavian artery near the insertion of the ligamentum arteriosum. Classically, type B dissections do not carry the risk of proximal extension and are, therefore, best treated medically with blood pressure reduction. If the dissected segment of the aortic becomes aneurysmally dilated with time, however, surgical intervention may be needed.[101]

The 3-year mortality rates for both surgically and medically treated thoracic aortic dissections are approximately 21% for Stanford type A dissections and 29% for type B

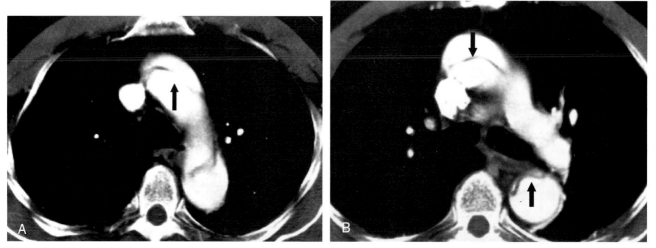

Figure 31–56. *A,* Axial CT scan shows type A aortic dissection with the dissection flap in the aortic arch (*arrow*). *B,* Axial CT scan at a level inferior to that of *A* reveals that the dissection flap involves the ascending aorta (*top arrow*). The true lumen is compressed anteriorly (*bottom arrow*).

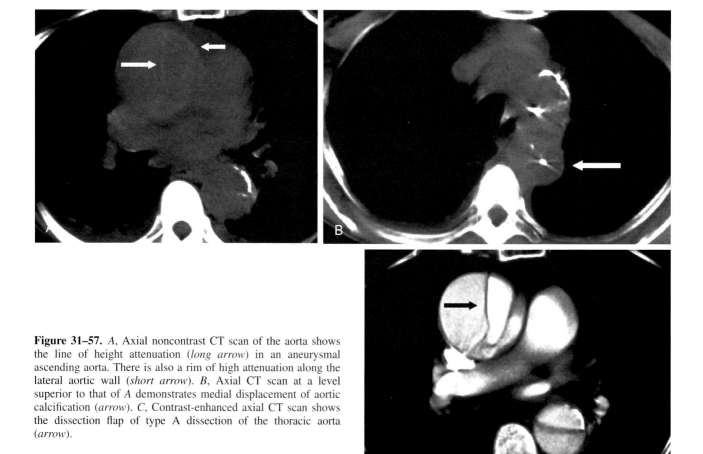

Figure 31–57. *A,* Axial noncontrast CT scan of the aorta shows the line of height attenuation (*long arrow*) in an aneurysmal ascending aorta. There is also a rim of high attenuation along the lateral aortic wall (*short arrow*). *B,* Axial CT scan at a level superior to that of *A* demonstrates medial displacement of aortic calcification (*arrow*). *C,* Contrast-enhanced axial CT scan shows the dissection flap of type A dissection of the thoracic aorta (*arrow*).

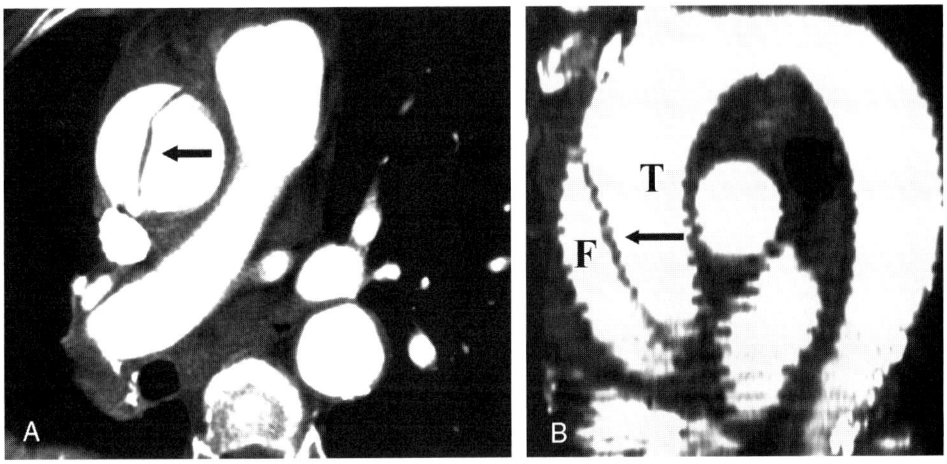

Figure 31–58. *A*, Axial CT scan shows type A dissection flap (*arrow*). *B*, Sagittal oblique multiplanar reconstruction demonstrates the dissection flap (*arrow*) demarcating the false lumen (F) from the posterior true lumen (T).

dissections.[124] Long-term prognosis depends on the development of complications, which mainly consist of new or progressive dissection and dilatation and subsequent rupture of the false lumen.[22]

Although the findings are nonspecific, chest radiographs are frequently abnormal in patients with thoracic aortic dissections.[54] Progressive widening of or progressive changes in the configuration of the aorta on sequential radiographs are highly suspicious for dissection. Unexplained differences in sizes between the ascending and descending portions of the aorta are also suspicious. As with aortic aneurysms, the trachea and esophagus may be displaced. Signs of a left pleural effusion, an apical pleural cap, and paraspinal widening may indicate leakage from a dissection. In addition, enlargement of the cardiac silhouette or plain film evidence of acute left heart failure may be secondary to aortic insufficiency from a type A thoracic aortic dissection. Although found in only a minority of patients, the most specific plain film finding in aortic dissection is displacement of intimal calcification from the outer margin of the aorta by at least 4 to 5 mm.[54]

CT has proved to be a highly reliable modality for diagnosing or excluding aortic dissection (Fig. 31–56).[48, 57, 128] Unlike for aortic aneurysms, however, diagnosis and characterization of thoracic aortic dissection requires both noncontrast and contrast-enhanced scanning.

The diagnosis of aortic dissection can be made from noncontrast scans that demonstrate a crescentic area of increased attenuation within the wall of the aorta, a sign that has been reported to be present in 44% of cases.[47, 137] This finding is believed to represent intramural hemorrhage from rupture of the vasa vasorum without an intimal tear.[137] Other findings have also been described on noncontrast scans. Displaced intimal calcifications are frequently encountered; however, this finding can create a problem if one is trying to differentiate between chronic thrombosed dissections and displaced intimal calcifications from aortic aneurysms with calcifications within thrombi (Fig. 31–57).[47, 74, 129] Rarely, in severely anemic patients, the intimal flap itself can be visualized within the aortic lumen.[23]

After administration of a contrast medium, diagnosis of aortic dissection is made on CT scans that demonstrate two opacified channels separated by an intimal flap.[39, 44, 48, 70] The two lumens are reported to be visible in at least

75% of symptomatic patients with acute aortic dissection. Within the ascending aorta, the false lumen is usually anterior (Fig. 31–58), whereas in the descending aorta, it is usually posterolateral.[70] Other, ancillary findings are less sensitive but have been reported; they include differential flow through the two lumens (Fig. 31–59), an increase in the size of the aorta, and the presence of hemopericardium.[76]

The standard for diagnosis of aortic dissections has long been angiography. However, numerous reports comparing the efficacy of CT with angiography in diagnosing aortic dissections have shown CT to be highly accurate. In most reports, the accuracy of CT compares favorably with that of angiography, including documented cases in which the diagnosis was made only with CT.[87, 104, 128] However, in a small percentage of patients with acute aortic dissection, false-negative CT findings do occur.[88, 66, 19] In addition, in a small percentage of patients with acute aortic dissection, the false channel is thrombosed and does not opacify with administration of contrast medium. This thrombosis of the false channel may represent bleeding into the wall of the aorta from rupture of the vasa vasorum without an intimal

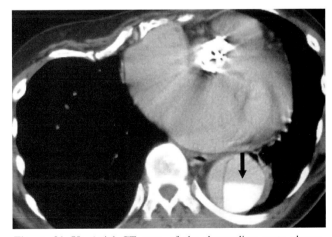

Figure 31–59. Axial CT scan of the descending aorta shows markedly delayed clearance of contrast medium in the false lumen (*arrow*) in a patient with Marfan's syndrome and type B dissection.

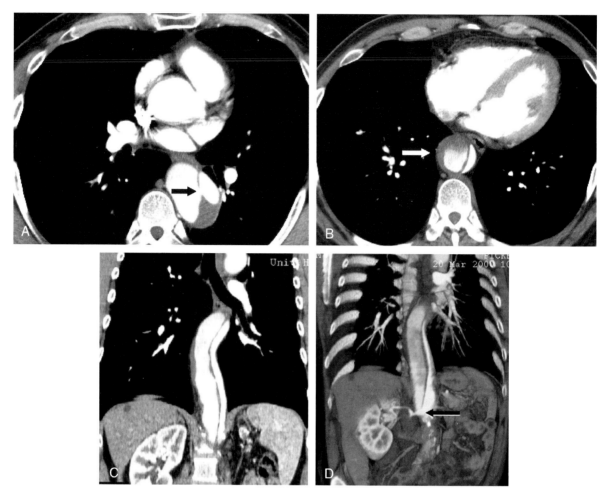

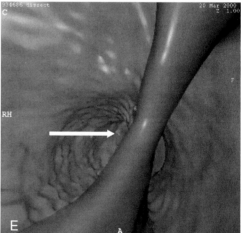

Figure 31–60. *A*, Axial multislice CT scan shows type B dissection. The entry point of the dissection is clearly delineated (*arrow*). *B*, Axial multislice CT scan at a level inferior to that of *A* shows slower flow in the larger false lumen (*arrow*). *C*, Coronal multiplanar reconstruction clearly demonstrates the extent of dissection. Note the lack of pulsation artifact in this multislice CT scan. *D*, Coronal multislice CT scan with volume rendering shows that the dissection flap extends just superior to the takeoff of the right renal artery (*arrow*). *E*, Virtual endoscopic image of the descending aorta shows the dissection flap (*arrow*) separating the true and false lumens.

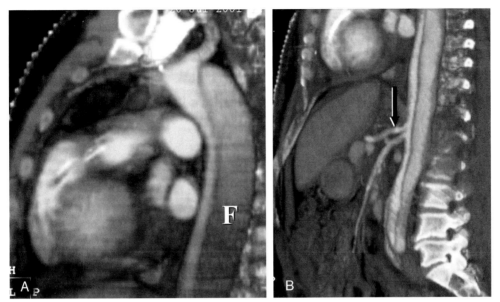

Figure 31–61. *A*, Sagittal oblique volume-rendered, multislice CT scan demonstrates a compressed true lumen with slow flow through the posterior false lumen (F). *B*, Sagittal oblique multislice CT scan shows the smaller true lumen giving rise to the celiac axis (*arrow*) and superior mesenteric artery.

tear. The false lumen is thrombosed more frequently, however, in subacute and chronic dissections. The overall accuracy of CT in diagnosing or excluding aortic dissection exceeds 90%, thereby ensuring its role as a primary modality in the assessment of thoracic aortic dissection.

The advent of helical CT scanners and CT angiography in particular further enhances the role of CT in the diagnosis or exclusion of thoracic aortic dissection. CT angiography can demonstrate the dissection flap more clearly than conventional CT, because scans are obtained during maximal arterial enhancement of the aorta and image reconstructions are thinner in section thickness. Therefore, the origin of the dissection flap as well as major aortic branch involvement can be evaluated in a larger proportion of patients by means of CT angiography (Figs. 31–60 and 31–61).[13] Also, multiplanar and 3D images allow an overall view of the dissection and clarify the anatomic relationship between the dissection flap and the adjacent great vessels, similar to the multiplanar capability of MRI. These advantages were demonstrated in a report by Chung and colleagues,[13] in which no false-positive or false-negative CT angiography findings were obtained in a series of 49 patients with suspected aortic dissection. However, unlike MRI, CT angiography has limitations in the evaluation of coronary artery involvement and aortic regurgitation.[13] Another limitation of CT angiography is that an unopacified false lumen from a short scanning delay time with slow filling of contrast medium can be confused with a thrombosed false lumen.

MRI can generally provide a definitive diagnosis of aortic dissection by demonstrating the two lumens and the intimal flap between them, similar to the criteria for CT.[3, 26, 35, 37] The intimal flap appears as a linear structure of intermediate signal intensity separating the true lumen

from the false lumen (Figs. 31–62 and 31–63). Flow characteristics within the two lumens can generally be demonstrated by MRI (Fig. 31–64). Characteristically, significant bright signal within what is presumed to be the false lumen is seen on second-echo sequences because of the presence of slow flow within the false lumen.[26, 27, 37, 133] In reality, however, accurate differentiation between the true and false lumens may not be possible, because flow within the anatomic false lumen may exceed flow within the compressed residual true lumen. In addition, identification of the site of the intimal tear is most often not possible.[37, 133] Blood within the mediastinum is readily visible on MRI, demonstrating the presence of periaortic hematoma. Also, blood within the pericardial sac can be recognized, indicating leakage from the false lumen.[3, 26]

The accuracy of MRI for the diagnosis of aortic dissection has been well established. Radiologists with experience reading MRI sequences have approximately a 95% sensitivity and 90% specificity for detecting aortic dissection.[63] In addition, CT and MRI have proved comparable in the ability to identify or exclude aortic dissection; the sensitivity of MRI has been found to range from 84% to 96%, depending on the series.[3, 35, 37, 63] Several pitfalls in interpretation of MR images of the thoracic aorta for dissection are known.[119, 136] Fluid within the superior pericardial recess can mimic aortic dissection. Less commonly, unusual origins of the arch vessels, an unusual position of the left brachiocephalic vein, motion artifacts, and aortic plaques can all mimic dissection.

MRI also has proved value in evaluating the results of aortic repair.[92, 135] After surgery for aortic dissection, MRI can detect either anastamotic leaks or aneurysmal dilatation distal to the graft site. The modality can also provide useful information about the status of the residual false lumen, which often remains patent after repair.

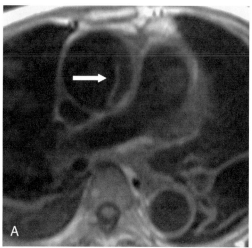

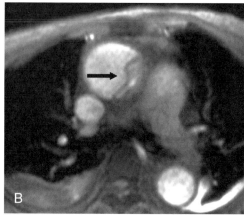

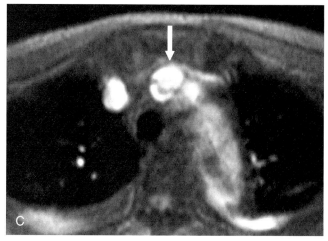

Figure 31–62. *A,* Axial ECG-gated, T1-weighted MR image of a type A aortic dissection shows an intermediate-signal dissection flap in the ascending aorta (*arrow*). *B,* Cine gradient-recalled echo (GRE) MR image demonstrates the dissection flap (*arrow*) clearly demarcated from the aortic lumen. *C,* Axial cine GRE MR image reveals extension of the dissection into the aortic arch and arch vessels (*arrow*).

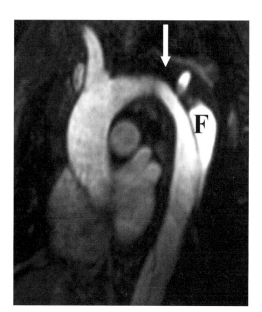

Figure 31–63. Gadolinium-enhanced sagittal oblique multiplanar reconstruction shows the dissection flap and clear demarcation of the true lumen and false lumen (F). Thrombus associated with the false lumen is well delineated (*arrow*).

Thoracic Aortic Trauma

Acute traumatic aortic injury is responsible for 10% to 20% of fatalities resulting from high-speed deceleration trauma (passengers or pedestrians involved in motor vehicle, airplane, and boat accidents and in high falls) and crush injuries to the chest.[20, 41, 65, 66, 90, 117, 122] Eighty percent to 90% of patients involved in high-speed deceleration accidents die before reaching the hospital. Of patients with untreated aortic injury, 30% die within 6 hours, 40% to 50% die within 24 hours, and 90% die within 4 months.[90] Chronic post-traumatic false aneurysms, or pseudoaneurysms, develop in 2% to 5% of patients with undiagnosed acute traumatic aortic injury (Figs. 31–65 and 31–66).[30, 90, 108] Of the patients with thoracic aortic injury who reach the hospital alive, 60% to 70% survive; therefore, prompt and accurate diagnosis and surgical management are critical.[90]

Signs and symptoms of traumatic deceleration injury of the thoracic aorta include chest and midscapular back pain, dyspnea, external signs of chest trauma, hypotension, upper extremity hypertension, bilateral femoral pulse deficits, and a systolic ejection murmur.[67] In general, the injury is a transverse laceration through the aortic intima, ranging in size from less than 1 mm to a completely circumferential tear; however, the adventitia is intact in roughly 60% of

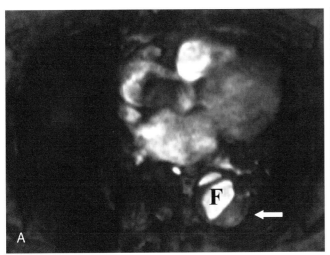

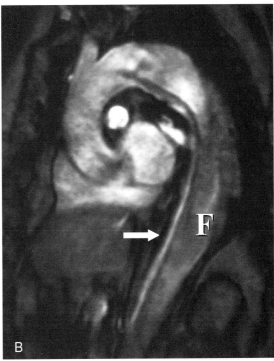

Figure 31–64. *A*, Axial cine gradient-recalled echo (GRE) MR image shows type B dissection, with a smaller, compressed true lumen and a posterior false lumen (F). *B*, Sagittal oblique cine GRE image in a patient with dissection shows bright signal in anterior true lumen, consistent with faster flow (*arrow*). F = false lumen. *Arrow* denotes thrombus surrounding the false lumen.

cases, a feature that aids the development of pseudoaneurysms that delay complete rupture.[90] No portion of the circumference of the aorta is known to be more at risk to injury than any other, but noncircumferential tears are more commonly posterior in the aorta.[90]

Ninety percent of thoracic aortic injuries occur within the proximal descending aorta at the level of the aortic isthmus, immediately distal to the origin of the left subclavian artery and just proximal to the site of attachment of the ligamentum arteriosum.[43] Thoracic aortic injury involving the ascending aorta is identified clinically in only 5%

of cases; however, at autopsy, the ascending aorta is found to be the site of injury in 20% to 25% of cases.[43]

The mechanisms of injury, as stated before, involve high-speed deceleration and crushing forces to the chest, most commonly seen in motor vehicle and boat accidents, airplane crashes, and falls from great heights. The forces involved depend on the segment of the aorta affected. Shearing and bending forces affect the aortic isthmus.

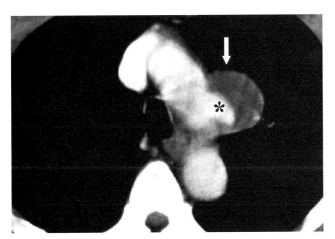

Figure 31–65. Axial CT scan in a patient with remote history of being kicked by a horse shows a large aortic pseudoaneurysm (*) and large amount of surrounding thrombus (*arrow*).

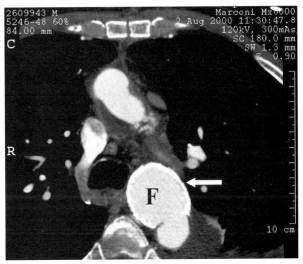

Figure 31–66. Axial CT scan shows a large calcified (*arrow*) aortic pseudoaneurysm (F) in a patient with a remote history of a high-speed motor vehicle accident.

somewhat mobile aortic arch differs from that of the relatively fixed descending aorta. Bending stress occurs as the aorta is flexed off the left pulmonary artery and mainstem bronchus.[10, 73, 112] One mechanism of injury within the ascending aorta is torsion, which occurs by displacement of the heart during impact and affects a region just above the aortic valve. The other mechanism involves the water-hammer effect, in which a sudden increase in intra-aortic pressure may lead to rupture of the ascending aorta into the pericardium and cardiac tamponade. Fractures of thoracic vertebral bodies are often associated with injuries involving the more distal descending aorta.[10, 73, 112]

Chest radiography is the front-line screening test for aortic injury, and abnormal findings on chest radiographs are the most common indication for further evaluation.[43] The anteroposterior projection with the patient in the supine position is most commonly performed and evaluated for signs of mediastinal hematoma, an indication of significant aortic injury. However, aortic trauma is the cause of mediastinal hematoma in only 12.5% of cases.[109] The most sensitive findings are widening of the mediastinum (>8 cm at the arch) and irregularity or obscuring of the aortic arch margin. However, although the sensitivity of these findings for aortic injury is high (around 80%), their specificity is no more than 50%.[91] The more specific signs (with specificities around 80%) include widening of the left paraspinal stripe and right-sided deviation of the trachea, esophagus, or both; however, the sensitivity for these signs is much lower.[91] Chest radiographs with a normal-appearing mediastinum have been documented in patients with known aortic injury.[14, 125] Therefore, chest radiographs are relatively insensitive in patients who have acute traumatic injury of the aorta but little or no mediastinal hemorrhage.

The low positive predictive value of chest radiography has dictated the performance of a large number of thoracic aortograms in the past. Aortograms have long been the reference standard in imaging the post-traumatic thoracic aorta, because of sensitivities approaching 100% and specificities of approximately 98%.[32] The positive predictive value of chest radiographs is low in the setting of aortic trauma. When chest radiography alone is used to screen for thoracic aortic injury, only 10% to 20% of thoracic aortograms are positive for aortic or aortic branch vessel injury.[78, 79] A more accurate and noninvasive screening test for thoracic aortic injury after blunt chest trauma is desirable.

Since its inception, CT has been investigated as a complementary examination for evaluation of traumatic aortic injury to reduce the number of negative aortograms.[17, 31, 34, 47, 75, 80, 81, 84, 100] Mirvis and associates[81] reported the clinical outcomes in 677 patients whose treatment was guided by findings on contrast-enhanced CT scans performed on a nonhelical, fourth-generation scanner. Aortography was performed when CT demonstrated either mediastinal hematoma or direct signs of vessel injury. This study reported a 90% sensitivity for CT, a 99% specificity, and a 90% positive predictive value, with no false-negative CT results. In addition, Gavant and colleagues[34] reported the clinical outcomes in 1518 patients who underwent CT for blunt chest trauma regardless of chest radiograph findings and whose treatment was based on the findings of contrast-enhanced helical CT scanning. Aortography was performed if CT demonstrated either mediastinal hematoma or direct vessel injury. In this study, CT had a 100% sensitivity, an 82% specificity, and a 47% positive predictive value for direct depiction of vessel injury, and no false-negative results were obtained. These findings support the inclusion of CT in the screening for traumatic aortic injury after blunt chest trauma.

Contrast-enhanced CT can be used to evaluate both indirect (mediastinal hemorrhage) and direct signs of aortic injuries. Mediastinal hemorrhage appears as either diffuse or focal soft tissue attenuation surrounding mediastinal structures, and the location of the blood has diagnostic significance. Hemorrhage in the vicinity of and surrounding the aorta and other vascular structures is more suggestive of vascular injury.[18] Direct signs of aortic injury are polypoid (clot) or linear (intimal flap) intraluminal areas of low attenuation, pseudoaneurysm, irregularity of the aortic wall, pseudocoarctation, intramural hematoma, dissection, and frank extravasation of contrast material (Fig. 31–67).[49, 80, 84]

Certain pitfalls make interpretation of CT scans difficult for thoracic aortic injury.[31, 45, 98] They include motion artifacts, partial volume averaging, and support devices. In addition, atelectatic lung (especially in the apical-posterior segment of the left upper lobe and superior segment of the left lower lobe) can mimic hemorrhage adjacent to the aorta. The thymus, pericardial recess, and unopacified vessels can also mimic blood. Knowledge of these common artifacts and mimics of mediastinal blood makes interpretation of scans more accurate.

MRI is a valuable tool for evaluation of the aorta in most trauma patients. Imaging time, incompatibility of MRI equipment with monitoring devices, and inaccessibility of the patient during the examination preclude the routine use and widespread acceptance of MRI in the evaluation of acute thoracic aortic injury.[15, 43, 77] Despite these limitations, several case reports have described MRI's ability to demonstrate acute thoracic aortic injury in awake, alert, and stable patients with no other injuries (Fig. 31–68).[15, 53] A study by Fattori and colleagues[28] concluded that MRI was accurate and reproducible for acute thoracic aortic injury compared with CT, angiography, or both in 24 patients with acute blunt chest trauma who did not undergo surgery. They also concluded that MRI provided complete anatomic data for assessing the severity of the aortic injury. It is the ideal modality for monitoring acute thoracic aortic injury prior to surgical repair.

Intramural Hematoma

The concept of the intramural hematoma was first described by Krukenberg. It describes blood within the wall of the aorta without identifiable intimal tear. Pathologically, intramural hemorrhage is defined as rupture of the vasa vasorum and propagation of subintimal hemorrhage, often secondary to a penetrating atherosclerotic ulcer. Isolated case reports have described spontaneous progression to aortic dissection.[68] Clinically, the signs and symptoms are often indistinguishable from those of dissection. Intramural hematoma progresses either by outward rupture of the aortic wall or by inward extension and formation of an intimal flap.[102]

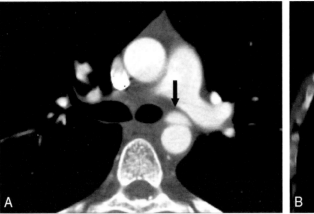
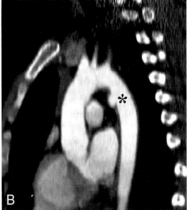
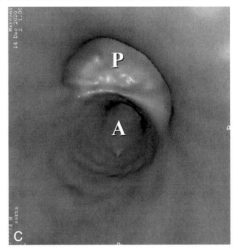

Figure 31–67. *A*, Axial CT scan in a patient who experienced a high-speed motor vehicle accident shows evidence of acute post-traumatic pseudoaneurysm (*arrow*). *B*, Sagittal multiplanar reconstruction demonstrates a focal pseudoaneurysm in the proximal descending aorta (*asterisk*). Note the acute angle of the pseudoaneurysm with the adjacent aorta, a feature that distinguishes it from a ductus diverticulum. *C*, Virtual endoscopic image demonstrates the focal nature of the post-traumatic pseudoaneurysm. P = pseudoaneurysm; A = native aortic lumen.

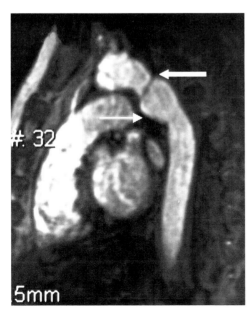

Figure 31–68. Gadolinium MR angiograph shows discrete post-traumatic pseudoaneurysm (*thin arrow*) with associated intimal flap (*thick arrow*) in a young man several months after a high-speed motor vehicle accident.

Distribution of intramural hematomas is equally divided between the ascending and descending portions of the aorta, with a small number occurring in the transverse arch. Studies have shown that the prognosis for patients with such hematomas is very similar to that for patients with aortic dissection. Intramural hematomas of the ascending aorta often progress to dissection, whereas those of the descending aorta progress less often to dissection or aneurysm formation (Fig. 31–69).[85] Our experience suggests that progression to aneurysm formation is more common in patients with descending intramural hematomas and that such patients should be followed more closely than patients with aneurysms of the descending aorta (Fig. 31–70).

The majority of intramural hematomas are the result of penetrating atherosclerotic ulcers (Fig. 31–71). First described as a distinct entity in the literature in 1986 by Stanson and associates,[120] atherosclerotic ulcers are defined by an abnormal outpouching of the contrast medium beyond the expected course of the aortic lumen.[71] Patients present clinically with chest or back pain, and the symptoms commonly mimic aortic dissection. Like dissection, intimal calcifications are displaced medially by the penetrating ulcer. There is an associated subintimal hematoma, and the spiraling flap seen in aortic dissection is absent. Penetrating atherosclerotic ulcers are generally located in the distal two thirds of the descending aorta. The penetrating ulcer can usually be distinguished from aortic dissec-

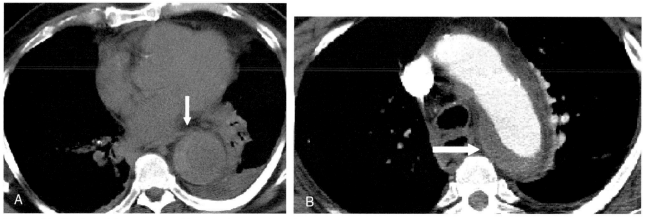

Figure 31–69. *A*, Axial noncontrast CT scan shows a rim of high attenuation of the aortic wall (*arrow*) in a patient with acute chest pain. *B*, Axial CT scan after administration of a contrast agent demonstrates diffuse periaortic soft tissue with high attenuation (*arrow*), a feature consistent with acute intramural hematoma.

tion because of the more focal, irregular nature of the defect, and the dissection flap is often smooth and well defined (Fig. 31–72).

There is controversy about the appropriate treatment of patients with penetrating ulcers. Many patients are first treated medically with antihypertensive medications. Patients for whom such treatment relieves pain and in whom the ulcer has a stable appearance on follow-up imaging can continue to be treated nonsurgically. In patients with continued pain or enlargement of the ulcerated area on follow-up imaging, surgical intervention is warranted (Fig. 31–73). Surgical treatment can be quite different; patients with atherosclerotic ulcers often require a longer interposition graft, whereas those with dissections need a shorter graft at the site of the intimal tear.[16]

Atheroembolic Disease of the Aorta

Appreciation of the importance of aortic atherosclerosis has grown with our increasingly aggressive treatment of

cerebrovascular disease. Until the 1990s, close to 40% of cerebrovascular events were classified as "cryptogenic." With the advent of transesophageal echocardiography, the importance of atheroembolic disease of the aorta has become more recognized. Retrospective studies showed that in patients with cerebrovascular accidents, the incidence of aortic atheromas was 20% to 27%,[130] compared with 5% in control subjects. Research showed that aortic plaque size determined risk, with plaques larger than 4 mm resulting in an odds ratio of 13.8 for the incidence of cerebrovascular events (Figs. 31–74 and 31–75). The absence of calcification was a poor prognostic feature, indicating those plaques most likely to embolize. Reports now suggest that CT and MRI may be complementary modalities in the detection of these atheroemboli, particularly in areas of the aortic arch where the tracheal air column limits evaluation with transesophageal echocardiography.[127] Multislice CT will continue to improve the sensitivity of CT scanning for the diagnosis of atheroembolic disease. Newer imaging techniques will prove to be of added benefit in the diagnosis and characterization of these vulnerable plaques.

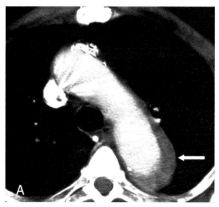
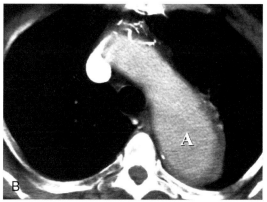

Figure 31–70. *A*, Axial CT scan in a patient with acute back pain. There is a large amount of high-attenuation periaortic soft tissue (*arrow*), a feature consistent with intramural hematoma. *B*, Axial CT scan taken 2 months later shows a rapid increase in the diameter of the descending aorta (A).

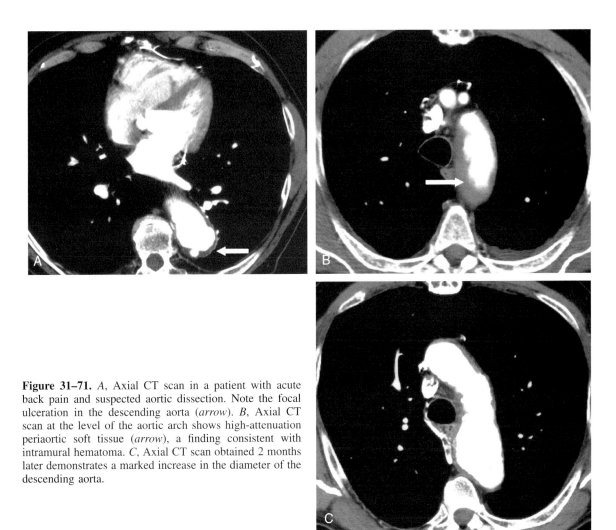

Figure 31–71. *A,* Axial CT scan in a patient with acute back pain and suspected aortic dissection. Note the focal ulceration in the descending aorta (*arrow*). *B,* Axial CT scan at the level of the aortic arch shows high-attenuation periaortic soft tissue (*arrow*), a finding consistent with intramural hematoma. *C,* Axial CT scan obtained 2 months later demonstrates a marked increase in the diameter of the descending aorta.

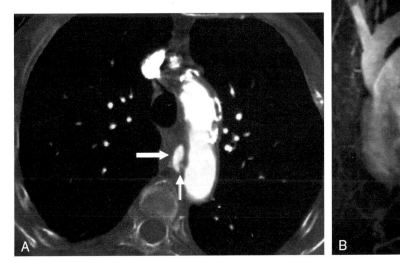

Figure 31–72. *A,* Axial CT scan in an elderly woman with acute back pain. There is a collection of contrast material medial to the descending aorta (*thick arrow*) that has a narrow but discrete communication with the aortic lumen (*thin arrow*). *B,* Sagittal oblique maximum intensity projection from gadolinium MR angiography delineates the focal atherosclerotic ulcer and its relationship with the aortic lumen (*arrow*).

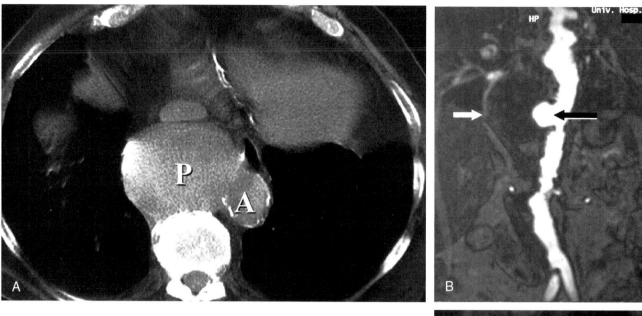

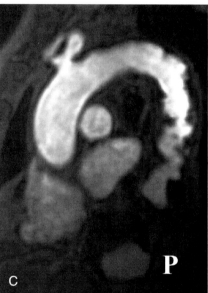

Figure 31–73. *A,* Axial noncontrast CT scan in an elderly patient who presented with a mediastinal mass contiguous with the descending aorta (P). Note the discontinuity of aortic calcification at this level. A = native aortic lumen. *B,* Sagittal maximum intensity projection from gadolinium MR angiography demonstrates an eccentric contrast collection (*black arrow*) with a large amount of surrounding thrombus (*white arrow*). *C,* Sagittal MPR image shows severe atherosclerotic ulceration of the descending aorta. P = pseudoaneurysm.

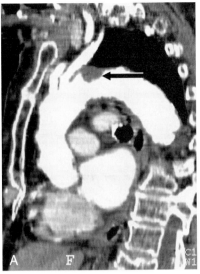

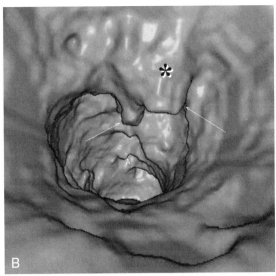

Figure 31–74. *A,* Sagittal oblique multiplanar reconstruction from multislice CT scan in an elderly woman with a history of embolic strokes. Note the large atheroma protruding into the aortic lumen (*arrow*). *B,* Virtual endoscopic image shows large protruding atheroma (*) within the transverse arch.

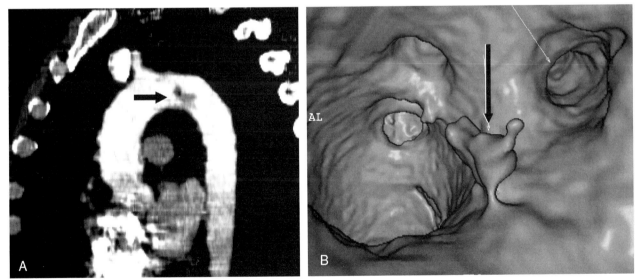

Figure 31–75. *A,* Sagittal oblique multiplanar reconstruction from multislice CT scan in a patient with a splenic infarct and arm weakness. There is a polypoid atheroma within the transverse arch (*arrow*). *B,* Virtual endoscopic image of the aortic arch shows a pedunculated atheroma (*arrow*) within the arch.

Aortitis

Inflammatory diseases of the aorta, though rare, have been well characterized in the imaging literature. Takayasu's arteritis is the best described of these disease processes. It is generally classified into four types on the basis of its anatomic location. Type 1 describes disease in the aortic arch, type 2 involves the abdominal aorta, type 3 the entire aorta, and type 4 the pulmonary arteries. In Takayasu's arteritis of the thoracic aorta, disease usually manifests as stenosis, occlusion, and aneurysm formation (Fig. 31–76). Some reports have described the superiority of CT over aortography. Although stenoses and aneurysmal changes are evaluated equivalently by the two modalities, mural changes are better evaluated with CT. In patients with suspected Takayasu's arteritis, initial noncontrast studies will show a high-attenuation aortic wall. Both aortic wall enhancement with contrast agent and delayed enhancement have been described.[89] These findings are important to define, as they may predate clinical symptoms and laboratory data. Documentation of improvement in aortic wall thickening after steroid therapy has been described.[46]

Giant cell arteritis is a vasculitis that often affects the thoracic aorta. On pathologic examination, active granulomatous inflammation with multinucleated giant cells are found in the aortic wall. Although the aortic arch vessels can be involved with stenoses, involvement of the aorta results in aneurysm formation. In a population-based study, 10% of patients with giant cell arteritis experienced aortic aneurysms (Fig. 31–77). These patients may also have aortic valve insufficiency.

Other forms of aortitis affecting the thoracic aorta are granulomatous aortitis (Fig. 31–78), lymphoplasmacytic aortitis (Fig. 31–79),[29] and aortitis associated with antineutrophil cytoplasmic antibody (ANCA).[86] These unusual forms of aortitis are often associated with aneurysm formation, but dissection has also been reported.

The Postoperative Aorta

With the increasing age of the population and the greater prevalence of atherosclerotic disease, larger numbers of aging patients are undergoing cardiothoracic surgery. Postoperative complications in the aorta are an uncommon cause of postoperative morbidity and mortality but they should be considered in patients who present with pain or in whom imaging studies show mediastinal widening. Importantly, many of these changes can occur years after the original operation. During surgery of the heart and

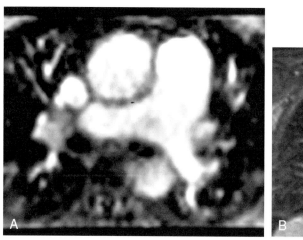
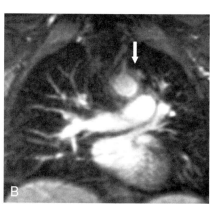
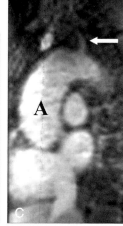
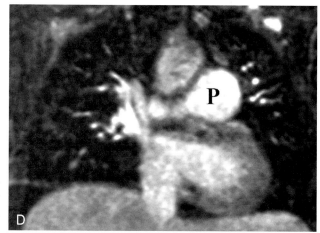

Figure 31–76. *A,* Axial multiplanar reconstruction (MPR) from gadolinium MR angiography of the thoracic aorta in a patient previously diagnosed with Takayasu's arteritis who has shown evidence of an acute stroke. The aortic root and main pulmonary artery are enlarged. *B,* Coronal MPR from gadolinium MR angiography demonstrates circumferential soft tissue thickening of the aortic arch (*arrow*). *C,* Sagittal MPR shows prominence of the ascending aorta (A) as well as occlusion of a markedly narrowed left subclavian artery (*arrow*). *D,* Coronal MPR shows dilatation of a segment of the main pulmonary artery, a finding consistent with pulmonary artery involvement in Takayasu's arteritis. P = main pulmonary artery.

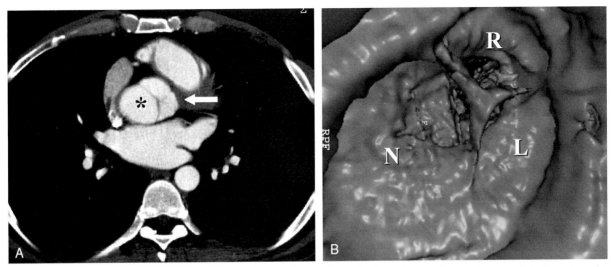

Figure 31–77. *A*, Axial CT scan in a young man in whom a chest radiograph showed an aortic prominence. Note the enlarged aortic root (*arrow*) with asymmetrical enlargement of the noncoronary cusp (*). *B*, Virtual endoscopic image shows normal appearance of the left (L) and right (R) coronary cusps and asymmetrical enlargement of the noncoronary cusp (N).

Figure 31–78. *A*, Axial half-Fourier acquisition single-shot turbo spin echo (HASTE) MR image in a young man in whom a chest radiograph showed mediastinal widening. This image reveals enlargement of the aortic root (A). *B*, Coronal cine gradient-recalled echo MR image at the level of the aortic valve during early diastole shows a linear focus of signal dephasing, a finding consistent with aortic insufficiency (*arrow*).

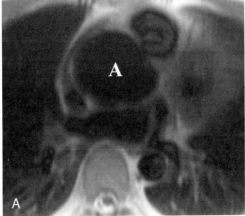
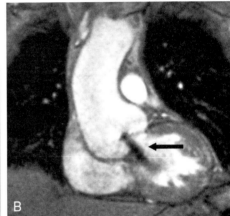

Figure 31–79. *A*, Sagittal oblique multiplanar reconstruction from CT scanning in an older woman who presented with chest pain. There is aneurysmal dilatation of the descending thoracic aorta (A) with marked irregularity or ulceration (*arrow*). *B*, Virtual endoscopic image of the descending aorta shows extensive ulceration (*arrows*).

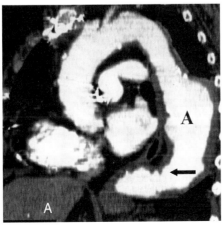
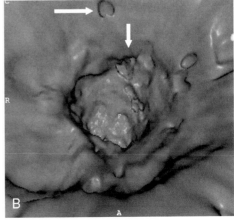

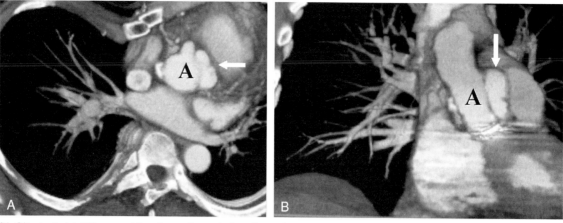

Figure 31–80. *A*, Axial CT scan with volumetric rendering shows lobulated soft tissue (*arrow*) extending from the aortic root (A). *B*, Coronal volume-rendering image shows pseudoaneurysm (A) arising from the aortic root (*arrow*).

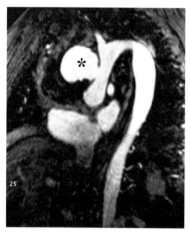

Figure 31–81. Sagittal multiplanar reconstruction from gadolinium MR angiography shows a large pseudoaneurysm (*) arising from the ascending aorta at the site of prior aortic cannulation.

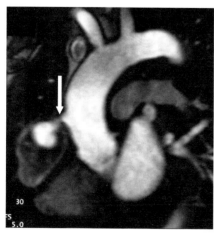

Figure 31–82. Sagittal oblique multiplanar reconstruction from gadolinium MR angiography demonstrates a lobulated aneurysm (*arrow*) arising from the ascending aorta.

great vessels, the aorta is cannulated, coronary artery grafts are placed, and, in aortic valve repair, an aortotomy is performed above the valve. These areas are all sites of potential aneurysm formation (Figs. 31–80 through 31–82).[62] Postoperative pseudoaneurysms and leaks are not uncommon after repair of aortic dissection or aneurysm and should always be considered in any postoperative patient presenting with new symptoms or a mass in the chest or mediastinum. In a large series of patients followed after aortic transposition grafts, 20% of patients required reoperation for periprosthetic pseudoaneurysms. All of the patients with pseudoaneurysms were asymptomatic. The authors of the study proposed serial evaluations in these high-risk patients to better evaluate postoperative complications.

References

1. Akers DL Jr, Fowl RJ, Plettner J, Kempczinski RF: Complications of anomalous origin of the right subclavian artery: Case report and review of the literature. Ann Vasc Surg. 5:385–388, 1991.
2. Amarenco P, Cohen A, Tzourio C, et al: Atherosclerotic disease of the aortic arch and the risk of ischemic stroke. N Engl J Med 33:1474–1479, 1994.
3. Amparo EG, Higgins CB, Hricak H, et al: Aortic dissection: Magnetic resonance imaging. Radiology 155:399–406, 1985.
4. Amparo EG, Hoddick WK, Hricak H, et al: Comparison of magnetic resonance imaging and ultrasonography in the evaluation of abdominal aortic aneurysms. Radiology 154:451–456, 1985.
5. Aronberg DJ, Glazer HS, Maden K, et al: Normal thoracic aorta diameters by computed tomography. J Comput Assist Tomogr 8:247–250, 1984.
6. Atkinson DJ, Edelman RR: Cineangiography of the heart in a single breath hold with a segmented turboFLASH sequence. Radiology 178:357–360, 1991.
7. Austin EH, Wolfe WG: Aneurysm of aberrant subclavian artery with a review of the literature. J Vasc Surg 2:571–577, 1985.
8. Axelbaum SP, Schellinger D, Gomes MN, et al: Computed tomographic evaluation of aortic aneurysms. Am J Roentgenol 127:75–78, 1976.
9. Batra P, Bigoni B, Manning J, et al: Pitfalls in the diagnosis of thoracic aortic dissection at CT angiography. Radiographics 20:309–320, 2000.
10. Beel T, Harwood AL: Traumatic rupture of the thoracic aorta. Ann Emerg Med 9:483–486, 1980.
11. Bertolini A, Pelizza A, Panizzon G, et al: Vascular rings and slings: Diagnosis and surgical treatment of 49 patients. J Cardiovasc Surg (Torino) 28:301–312, 1987.
12. Bosniak MA: An analysis of some anatomic-roentgenologic aspects

of the brachiocephalic vessels. Am J Roentgenol 91:1222–1231, 1964.

13. Chung JW, Park JH, Im J, et al: Spiral CT angiography of the thoracic aorta. Radiographics 16:811–824, 1996.

14. Cohen AM, Crass JR: Traumatic lacerations of the aorta and great vessels with a normal mediastinum at radiography. J Vasc Interv Radiol 3:541–544, 1992.

15. Cohn SM, Pollak JS, McCarthy S, et al: Detection of aortic tear in the acute trauma patient using MRI. J Magn Reson Imaging 12:963–967, 1994.

16. Cooke JP, Kazmier FJ, Orszulak TA: The penetrating aortic ulcer: Pathologic manifestations, diagnosis, and management. Mayo Clin Proc 63:718–725. 1988.

17. Costello P, Ecker CP, Tello R, et al: Assessment of the thoracic aorta by spiral CT. AJR Am J Roentgenol 158:1127–1130, 1992.

18. Creasy JD, Chiles C, Routh WD, et al: Overview of traumatic injury of the thoracic aorta. Radiographics 17:27–45, 1997.

19. Danza FM, Fusco A, Falappa P: The role of computed tomography in the evaluation of dissecting aortic aneurysms (letter). Radiology 152:827–829, 1984.

20. Dart CHJ, Braitman HE: Traumatic rupture of the thoracic aorta: Diagnosis and management. Arch Surg 111:697–702, 1976.

21. De Santis RW, Doroghaz RM, Anisten WG, et al: Aortic dissection. N Engl J Med 317:1060–1067, 1987.

22. DeBakey ME, McCollum II, Crawford ES: Dissection and dissecting aneurysms of the aorta: Twenty-year follow-up of five hundred twenty-seven patients treated surgically. Surgery 92:1118–1134, 1982.

23. Demos TC, Posniak HV, Churchill RJ: Detection of the intimal flap of aortic dissection on unenhanced CT images. Am J Roentgenol 146:601–603, 1986.

24. Dillon EH, van Leeuwen MS, Fernandez MA, et al: Spiral CT angiography. AJR Am J Roentgenol 160:1273–1278, 1993.

25. Dinsmore RE, Liberthson RR, Wismer GL, et al: Magnetic resonance imaging of thoracic aortic aneurysms: Comparison with other imaging modalities. Am J Roentgenol 146:309–314, 1986.

26. Dinsmore RE, Wedeen VJ, Miller SW, et al: MRI of dissection of the aorta: Recognition of the intimal tear and differential flow velocities. Am J Roentgenol 146:1286, 1986.

27. Dooms GC, Higgins CB: The potential of magnetic resonance imaging for the evaluation of thoracic arterial disease. J Thorac Cardiovasc Surg 92:1088–1095, 1986.

28. Fattori R, Celletti F, Bertaccini P, et al: Delayed surgery of traumatic aortic rupture: Role of magnetic resonance imaging. Circulation 94:2865–2870, 1996.

29. Faye-Petersen OM, Arnold MM, Grizzle WE, et al: Lymphoplasmacytic aortitis and acute aortic dissection: An uncommon association. Arch Pathol Lab Med 120:402–404, 1996.

30. Fishbone G, Robbins DI, Osborn DJ, et al: Trauma to the thoracic aorta and great vessels. Radiol Clin North Am 11:543–554, 1973.

31. Fisher RG, Chasen MH, Lamki N: Diagnosis of injuries of the aorta and brachiocephalic arteries caused by blunt chest trauma: CT vs aortography. AJR Am J Roentgenol 162:1047–1052, 1994.

32. Fishman JE: Imaging of blunt aortic and great vessel trauma. J Thorac Imaging 15:97–103, 2000.

33. Fomon JJ, Kurzweg FT, Broadaway RK: Aneurysms of the aorta: A review. Ann Surg 165:557–563, 1967.

34. Gavant ML, Menke PG, Fabian T, et al: Blunt traumatic aortic rupture: Detection with helical CT of the chest. Radiology 197:125–133, 1995.

35. Geisinger MA, Risius B, O'Donell JA, et al: Thoracic aorta dissections: Magnetic resonance imaging. Radiology 155:407–412, 1985.

36. Glanz S, Gordon DH: Right aortic arch with left descent. J Comput Assist Tomogr 5:256–268, 1981.

37. Glazer HS, Gutierrez FR, Levitt RG, et al: The thoracic aorta studies by MR imaging. Radiology 157:149, 1985.

38. Godwin JD: Examination of the thoracic aorta by computed tomography. Chest 85:564–567, 1984.

39. Godwin JD, Herfkens RL, Skioldebrand CG, et al: Evaluation of dissections and aneurysms of the thoracic aorta by conventional and dynamic scanning. Radiology 136:125–133, 1980.

40. Gomes ML, Macedo AM, Pena SD, et al: Genetic relationships between *Trypanosoma cruzi* strains isolated from chronic chagasic patients in southern Brazil as revealed by RAPD and SSR-PCR analysis. Acta Trop 69:99–109, 1998.

41. Greendyke RM: Traumatic rupture of the aorta: Special reference to automobile accidents. JAMA 195:527–530, 1966.

42. Groskin S, Maresca M, Heitzman ER: Thoracic trauma. In McCort JJ, Mindelzun RE (eds): Trauma Radiology. New York, Churchill Livingstone, 1990, pp 75–127.

43. Groskin SA: Selected topics in chest trauma. Radiology 183:605–617, 1992.

44. Gross SC, Barr I, Eyeler WR, et al: Computed tomography in dissection of the thoracic aorta. Radiology 136:135, 1980.

45. Harris JH Jr, Horowitz DR, Zelitt DL: Unenhanced dynamic mediastinal computed tomography in the selection of patients requiring thoracic aortography for the detection of acute traumatic aortic injury. Emerg Radiol 2:67–76, 1995.

46. Hayashi K, Fukushima T, Matsunaga N, et al: Takayasu's arteritis: Decrease in aortic wall thickening following steroid therapy, documented by CT. Br J Radiol 59:281–283, 1986.

47. Heiberg E, Wolverson MK, Sundaram M, et al: CT characteristics of aortic atherosclerotic aneurysm versus aortic dissection. J Comput Assist Tomogr 9:78–83, 1985.

48. Heiberg E, Wolverson M, Sundaram M, et al: CT findings in thoracic aortic dissection. Am J Roentgenol 136:13–17, 1981.

49. Heiberg E, Wolverson MK, Sundaram M, et al: CT in aortic trauma. Am J Roentgenol 140:1119–1124, 1983.

50. Higgins CB, Silverman NR, Harris RD, et al: Localized aneurysms of the descending thoracic aorta. Clin Radiol 26:474, 1975.

51. Hirao K, Miyazaki A, Noguchi M, et al: The cervical aortic arch with aneurysm formation. J Comput Assist Tomogr 23:959–962, 1999.

52. Hirst AE, John VJ, Kime SW: Dissection aneurysm of the aorta: A review of 505 cases. Medicine 37:217–279, 1958.

53. Hughes JP, Ruttley MS, Musumeci F: Case report: Traumatic aortic rupture—demonstration by magnetic resonance imaging. Br J Radiol 67:1264–1267, 1994.

54. Itzchak Y, Rosenthal T, Adal R, et al: Dissecting aneurysm of the thoracic aorta: Reappraisal of radiologic diagnosis. Am J Roentgenol 125:559, 1975.

55. Johnson PT, Fishman EK, Duckwall JR, et al: Interactive three-dimensional volume rendering of spiral CT data: Current applications in the thorax. Radiographics 18:165–187, 1998.

56. Johnson PT, Heath DG, Bliss DF, et al: Three-dimensional CT: Real-time interactive volume rendering. AJR Am J Roentgenol 167:581–583, 1996.

57. Joyce JW, Fairbairn JF II, Kincaid OW, et al: Aneurysms of the thoracic aorta: A clinical study with special reference to prognosis. Circulation 29:176, 1964.

58. Julsrud PR, Breen JF, Felmlee JP, et al: Coarctation of the aorta: Collateral flow assessment with phase-contrast MR angiography. AJR Am J Roentgenol 169:1735–1742, 1997.

59. Kalender WA, Seissler W, Klotz E, et al: Spiral volumetric CT with single-breath-hold technique, continuous transport, and continuous scanner rotation. Radiology 176:181–183, 1990.

60. Kalke BR, Magotra R, Doshi SM: A new surgical approach to the management of symptomatic aberrant right subclavian artery. Ann Thorac Surg 44:86–89, 1987.

61. Kastan DJ, Sharma RP, Keith F, et al: Case report: Intimo-intimal intussusception: An unusual presentation of aortic dissection. AJR Am J Roentgenol 151:603–604, 1988.

62. Katsumata T, Moorjani N, Vaccari G, et al: Mediastinal false aneurysm after thoracic aortic surgery. Ann Thorac Surg 70:547–552, 2000.

63. Kersting-Sommerhoff BA, Higgins CB, White RD, et al: Aortic dissection: Magnetic resonance imaging—sensitivity and specificity of MR imaging. Radiology 166:651, 1988.

64. Kersting-Sommerhoff BA, Seelos KC, Hardy C, et al: Evaluation of surgical procedures for cyanotic congenital heart disease by using MR imaging. AJR Am J Roentgenol 155:259–266, 1990.

65. Kirsh MM, Behrendt DM, Orringer MB, et al: The treatment of acute traumatic rupture of the aorta: a ten year experience. Ann Surg 184:308–316, 1976.

66. Kodali S, Jamieson WR, Leia SM, et al: Traumatic rupture of the thoracic aorta: A 20-year review—1969–1989. Circulation 84:140–146, 1991.

67. Kram HB, Appel PL, Wohlmuth DA, et al: Diagnosis of traumatic thoracic aortic rupture: A 10-year retrospective analysis. Ann Thorac Surg 47:282–286, 1989.

68. Krinsky GA, Ribakove GH: Spontaneous progression of ascending aortic intramural hematoma to Stanford type A dissection fortuitously witnessed during an MR examination. J Comput Assist Tomogr 23:966–968, 1999.

69. Krinsky GA, Rofsky NM, DeCorato DR, et al: Thoracic aorta: Comparison of gadolinium-enhanced three-dimensional MR angiography with conventional MR imaging. Radiology 202:183–193, 1997.

70. Larde D, Belloir C, Vasile N, et al: Computed tomography of aortic dissection. Radiology 136:147, 1980.

71. Levy JR, Heiken JP, Gutierrez FR: Imaging of penetrating atherosclerotic ulcers of the aorta. AJR Am J Roentgenol 173:151–154, 1999.

72. Lois JF, Gomes AS, Brown K, et al: Magnetic resonance imaging of the thoracic aorta. Am J Cardiol 60:358–362, 1987.

73. Lundevall J: The mechanisms of traumatic rupture of the thoracic aorta. Acta Pathol Microbiol Scand 62:34–36, 1964.

74. Machida K, Tasaka A: CT patterns of mural thrombus in aortic aneurysms. J Comput Assist Tomogr 4:840–842, 1980.

75. Mayadag MA, Kirshenbaum KJ, Nadimpalli SR, et al: Thoracic aortic trauma: Role of dynamic CT. Radiology 179:853–855, 1991.

76. Meziane MA, Fishman EK, Siegelman SS: CT diagnosis of hemopericardium in acute dissecting aneurysm of the thoracic aorta. J Comput Assist Tomogr 8:10–14, 1984.

77. Mirvis SE: Applications of magnetic resonance imaging and three-dimensional computed tomography in emergency medicine. Ann Emerg Med 18:1315–1321, 1989.

78. Mirvis SE, Bidwell JK, Buddemeyer EU, et al: Imaging diagnosis of traumatic aortic rupture: A review and experience at a major trauma center. Invest Radiol 22:187–196, 1987.

79. Mirvis SE, Bidwell JK, Buddemeyer EU, et al: Value of chest radiography in excluding traumatic aortic rupture. Radiology 163:487–493, 1987.

80. Mirvis SE, Kostrubiak I, Whitley NO, et al: Role of CT in excluding major arterial injury following blunt thoracic trauma. AJR Am J Roentgenol 149:601–605, 1987.

81. Mirvis SE, Shanmuganathan K, Miller BH, et al: Traumatic aortic injury: Diagnosis with contrast-enhanced thoracic CT. Radiology 200:413–422, 1996.

82. Moncada R, Churchill R, Reynes C, et al: Diagnosis of dissecting aortic aneurysm by CT. Lancet 1:238–241, 1981.

83. Moore EH, Webb WR, Verrier ED, et al: MRI of chronic post-traumatic false aneurysm of the thoracic aorta. Am Roentgenol 143:1195–1196, 1984.

84. Morgan PW, Goodman LR, Aprahamian C, et al: Evaluation of traumatic aortic injury: Does dynamic contrast-enhanced CT play a role? Radiology 182:661–666, 1992.

85. Murray JG, Manisali M, Flamm SD, et al: Intramural hematoma of the thoracic aorta: MR image findings and their prognostic implications. Radiology 204:349–355, 1997.

86. Nakabayashi K, Kamiya Y, Nagasawa T: Aortitis syndrome associated with positive perinuclear antineutrophil cytoplasmic antibody: Report of three cases. Int J Cardiol 75(Suppl 1):S89–S94, 2000.

87. Oudkerk M, Overbosch E, Dee P: CT recognition of acute aortic dissection. Am J Roentgenol 141:671, 1983.

88. Paiery RA, Couffinhal JC, Wellers M, et al: Computed tomography versus aortography in diagnosis of aortic dissection. Cardiovasc Intervent Radiol 5:285–291, 1982.

89. Park JH, Chung JW, Im JG, et al: Takayasu arteritis: Evaluation of mural changes in the aorta and pulmonary artery with CT angiography. Radiology 196:89–93, 1995.

90. Parmley LF, Mattingly TW, Manion WC, et al: Nonpenetrating traumatic injury of the aorta. Circulation 17:1086–1101, 1958.

91. Patel N, Stevens KJ Jr, Mirvis S, et al: Imaging in acute thoracic aortic injury due to blunt trauma: A review. Radiology 209:335–338, 1998.

92. Pernes JM, Grenier P, Desbleds MT, et al: MR evaluation of chronic aortic dissection. J Comput Assist Tomogr 975–981, 1987.

93. Polacin A, Kalender WA, Marchal G: Evaluation of section sensitivity profiles and image noise in spiral CT. Radiology 185:29–35, 1992.

94. Pressler V, McNamara J: Thoracic aortic aneurysm: Natural history and treatment. J Thorac Cardiovasc Surg 79:489–498, 1980.

95. Prince MR, Chenevert TL, Foo TK, et al: Contrast-enhanced abdominal MR angiography: Optimization of imaging delay time by auto-

mating the detection of contrast material arrival in the aorta. Radiology 203:109–114, 1997.

96. Prince MR, Narasimham DL, Jacoby WT, et al: Three-dimensional gadolinium-enhanced MR angiography of the thoracic aorta. AJR Am J Roentgenol 166:1387–1397, 1996.

97. Quint LE, Francis IR, Williams DM, et al: Evaluation of thoracic aortic disease with the use of helical CT and multiplanar reconstructions: Comparison with surgical findings. Radiology 201:37–41, 1996.

98. Raptopoulos V: Chest CT for aortic injury: Maybe not for everyone (commentary). AJR Am J Roentgenol 162:1053–1055, 1994.

99. Reddy GP, Higgins CB: MR imaging of the thoracic aorta. Magn Reson Imaging Clin North Am 8:1–15, 2000.

100. Rigants H, Marchal G, Baert AL, et al: Initial experience with volume CT scanning. J Comput Assist Tomogr 14:675–682, 1990.

101. Roberts WC: Aortic dissection: anatomy, consequences, and causes. Am Heart J 101:195–214, 1981.

102. Rubin GD: Helical CT angiography of the thoracic aorta. J Thorac Imaging 12:128–149, 1997.

103. Rubin GD, Beaulieu CF, Argiro V, et al: Perspective volume rendering of CT and MR images: Applications for endoscopic imaging. Radiology 199:321–330, 1996.

104. Rubin GD, Dake MD, Napel SA, et al: Abdominal spiral CT angiography: Initial clinical experience. Radiology 186:147–152, 1993.

105. Rubin GD, Dake MD, Semba CP: Current status of three-dimensional spiral CT scanning for imaging the vasculature. Radiol Clin North Am 33:51–70, 1995.

106. Rubin GD, Lane MJ, Bloch DA, et al: Optimization of thoracic spiral CT: Effects of iodinated contrast medium concentration. Radiology 201:785–791, 1996.

107. St. Amour TE, Gutierrez FR, Levitt RG, McKnight RC: CT diagnosis of type A aortic dissections not demonstrated by aortography. J Comput Assist Tomogr 12:963–967, 1988.

108. Sanborn JC, Heitzman ER, Markarian B: Traumatic rupture of the thoracic aorta: Roentgen-pathological correlations. Radiology 95:293–298, 1970.

109. Sandor F: Incidence and significance of traumatic mediastinal hematoma. Thorax 22:43–62, 1967.

110. Schnyder P, Meuli R, Wicky S: Injection techniques. In Remy Jardin M, Remy J (eds): Spiral CT of the Chest. Berlin, Springer, 1996, pp 41–44.

111. Sebastia C, Pallisa E, Quiroga S, et al: Aortic dissection: Diagnosis and follow-up with helical CT. Radiographics 19:45–60, 1999.

112. Sevitt S: The mechanisms of traumatic rupture of the thoracic aorta. Br J Surg 64:166–173, 1977.

113. Silverman PM, Roberts S, Tefft MC, et al: Helical CT of the liver: Clinical application of an automated computer technique, SmartPrep, for obtaining images with optimal contrast enhancement. AJR Am J Roentgenol 165:73–78, 1995.

114. Simonetti OP, Finn JP, White RD, et al: "Black blood" T2-weighted inversion-recovery MR imaging of the heart. Radiology 199:49–57, 1996.

115. Simpson IA, Chung KJ, Glass RF, et al: Cine magnetic resonance imaging for evaluation of anatomy and flow relations in infants and children with coarctation of the aorta. Circulation 78:142–148, 1988.

116. Smith PA: Virtual angioscopy using spiral CT and real-time interactive volume-rendering techniques. J Comput Assist Tomogr 22:212–214, 1998.

117. Smith RS, Chang FC: Traumatic rupture of the aorta: Still a lethal injury. Am J Surg 152:660–663, 1986.

118. Soler R, Rodriguez E, Requejo I, et al: Magnetic resonance imaging of congenital abnormalities of the thoracic aorta. Eur Radiol 8:540–546, 1998.

119. Solomon SL, Brown JJ, Glazer HS, et al: Thoracic aortic dissection: Pitfalls and artifacts in MR imaging. Radiology 177:223, 1990.

120. Stanson AW, Kazmier FJ, Hollier LH, et al: Penetrating atherosclerotic ulcers of the thoracic aorta: Natural history and clinicopathologic correlations. Ann Vasc Surg 1:15–23, 1986.

121. Stockberger SM Jr, Liang Y, Hicklin JA, et al: Objective measurement of motion in patients undergoing spiral CT examinations. Radiology 206:625–629, 1998.

122. Sutorius DJ, Schreiber JT, Helmsworth JA: Traumatic disruption of the thoracic aorta. J Trauma 13:583–590, 1973.

123. Sutton D, Davies ER: Arch aortography and cerebrovascular insufficiency. Clin Radiol 17:330–345, 1966.

124. Svenson LG, Crawford ES, Hess KR, et al: Dissection of the aorta and dissecting aortic aneurysm. Circulation 82(Suppl 4):24–38, 1990.

125. Symbas RJ, Horsley WS, Symbas PN: Rupture of the ascending aorta caused by blunt trauma. Ann Thorac Surg 66:113–117, 1998.

126. Tawes RL Jr, Berry CL, Aberdeen E: Congenital bicuspid aortic valves associated with coarctation of the aorta in children. Br Heart J 31:127–128, 1969.

127. Tenenbaum A, Garniek A, Shemesh J, et al: Dual-helical CT for detecting aortic atheromas as a source of stroke: Comparison with transesophageal echocardiography. Radiology 208:153–158, 1998.

128. Thorsen MK, San Dretto MA, Lawson TL, et al: Dissecting aortic aneurysms: Accuracy of computed tomographic diagnosis. Radiology 148:773–777, 1983.

129. Torres WE, Maurer DE, Steinberg HV, et al: CT of aortic aneurysms: The distinction between mural and thrombus calcification. AJR Am J Roentgenol 150:1317–1319, 1988.

130. Tunick PA, Perez JL, Kronzon I: Protruding atheromas in the thoracic aorta and systemic embolization. Ann Intern Med 115:423–427, 1991.

131. Urban BA, Bluemke DA, Johnson KM, Fishman EK: Imaging of thoracic aortic disease. Cardiol Clin 17:659–682, 1999.

132. VanDyke CW, White RD: Congenital abnormalities of the thoracic aorta presenting in the adult. J Thorac Imaging 9:230–245, 1994.

133. White RD, Dooms GC, Higgins CB: Advances in imaging thoracic aorta disease. Invest Radiol 21:761–778, 1986.

134. White RD, Lipton MJ, Higgins CB, et al: Noninvasive evaluation of suspected thoracic aorta disease by contrast-enhanced CT. Am J Cardiol 57:282–290, 1986.

135. White RD, Ullyot DJ, Higgins CB: MR imaging of the aorta after surgery for aortic dissection. AJR Am J Roentgenol 150:87–92, 1988.

136. Winer-Muram HT, Gold RE: Effusion in the superior pericardial recess simulating a mediastinal mass. AJR Am J Roentgenol 154: 69, 1990.

137. Yamada T, Tada S, Harada J: Aortic dissection without intimal rupture: Diagnosis with MR imaging and CT. Radiology 168:347–352, 1988.

138. Zeitler E, Kaiser W, Schuierer G, et al: Magnetic resonance imaging of clots in the heart and vascular system. Ann Radiol (Paris) 28: 105, 1985.

139. Zeman RK, Berman PM, Silverman PM, et al: Diagnosis of aortic dissection: Value of helical CT with multiplanar reformation and three-dimensional rendering. AJR Am J Roentgenol 164:1375–1380, 1995.

140. Zeman RK, Silverman PM, Berman PM, et al: Abdominal aortic aneurysms: Evaluation with variable collimation helical CT and overlapping reconstruction. Radiology 193:555–560, 1994.

32

Computed Tomography of the Heart and Pericardium

Lynn S. Broderick

Echocardiography is usually the first choice for imaging the heart, although computed tomography (CT) scanning is a preferred method of evaluating the pericardium. In the past, CT was not routinely used for evaluation of the heart. This is primarily because, with the exception of electron beam CT scanners, the scan times were not fast enough to image the heart without cardiac motion. The development of multidetector scanners, coupled with the ability to scan with prospective or retrospective electrocardiography (ECG) gating, will very likely result in increased interest in cardiac imaging by CT.

Mochizuki and associates have reported the use of ECG-gated spiral CT to create two-dimensional (2D) and three-dimensional (3D) CT ventriculography, allowing assessment of left ventricular volumes.[68] Studies are currently under way to determine the usefulness of CT angiography in evaluating the coronary arteries.[52] Even when CT scanning is performed to evaluate other structures, much information can be obtained by careful assessment of the heart and pericardium.

Anatomy

The anatomy of the heart is often well displayed on CT scans of the chest, even in the presence of motion artifact. The most important motion artifact affecting the heart is one that can simulate aortic dissection.[22, 36, 69] Cardiac motion is responsible for the movement of the aortic root, resulting in curvilinear artifacts that may mimic an intimal flap. The curvilinear artifacts are typically located in a left anterior and right posterior location (Fig. 32–1).[36, 92] Multiplanar reformatted images may show a serrated appearance of the aortic wall, confirming that the curvilinear density is artifactual.[92] Knowledge of the typical appearance and location prevents misdiagnosis.

Basic cardiac anatomy can be displayed even with conventional CT scanners. The cardiac chambers, great vessels, and veins are readily identified. With faster scanning times, other finer structures, such as papillary muscles, chordae tendineae, and valve leaflets, can also be identified (Fig. 32–2).

The coronary arteries are easily visualized. The main coronary artery arises from the left aortic cusp and courses

approximately 1 cm before giving off the left anterior descending and circumflex arteries. The right coronary artery arises from the right aortic cusp and is more caudally located than the left main coronary artery. Some structures, such as the pericardiacophrenic vein, are not routinely visualized. However, knowledge of their location is useful when they enlarge as a route of collateral circulation (Figs. 32–3 and 32–4).

Evaluation of the Cardiac Chambers

Knowledge of chest radiographic findings of valvular heart disease can be extrapolated to use in interpreting

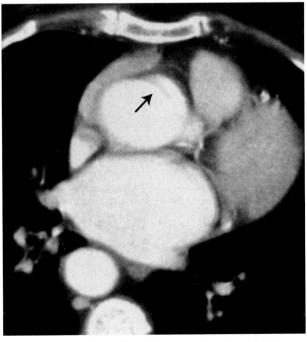

Figure 32–1. Motion artifact. Contrast-enhanced axial CT image shows apparent intimal flap *(arrow)* at the level of the aortic root. This appearance is caused by cardiac motion during scan acquisition. It can be recognized by its characteristic location at the aortic root. It is usually found in a left anterior or right posterior location.

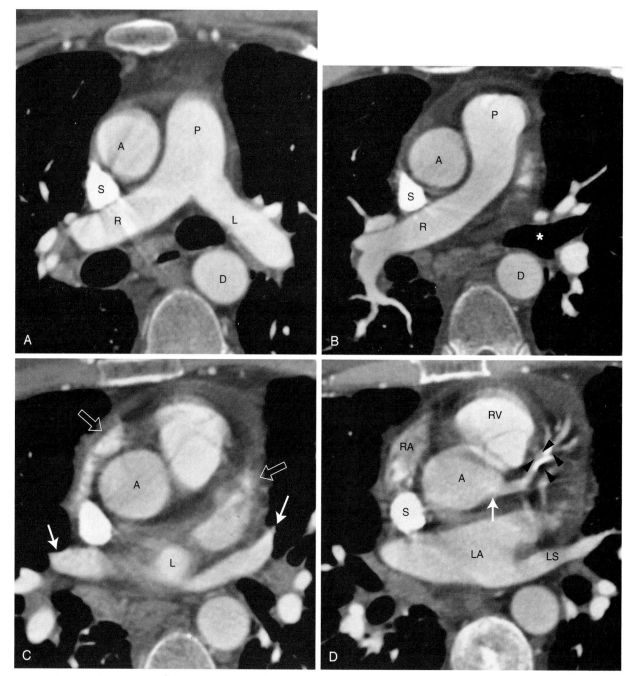

Figure 32–2. Normal anatomy. Axial contrast-enhanced *CT images* from the level of the pulmonary arteries (*A*) to the level of the inferior aspect of the heart (*J*) display normal cardiac anatomy.

A, CT image obtained at the level of the pulmonary arteries. A, ascending aorta; D, descending aorta; L, left pulmonary artery; P, main pulmonary artery; S, superior vena cava.

B, More inferior CT image demonstrates the hyparterial left mainstem bronchus *(asterisk).* A, ascending aorta; D, descending aorta; P, main pulmonary artery; R, right pulmonary artery; S, superior vena cava.

C, CT image at level of the right and left superior pulmonary veins *(arrows)* and right and left atrial appendages *(open arrows).* Linear densities within the right ventricular/pulmonary artery outflow tract probably represent the valve leaflets *(arrowheads).* L, superior aspect of left atrium; A, ascending aorta.

D, CT image at level of origin of left main coronary artery *(arrow).* Calcification is present within the left anterior descending artery *(arrowheads).* A, ascending aorta; LA, left atrium; LS, left superior pulmonary vein; RA, right atrium; RV, right ventricular outflow tract, also known as the infundibulum; S, superior vena cava.

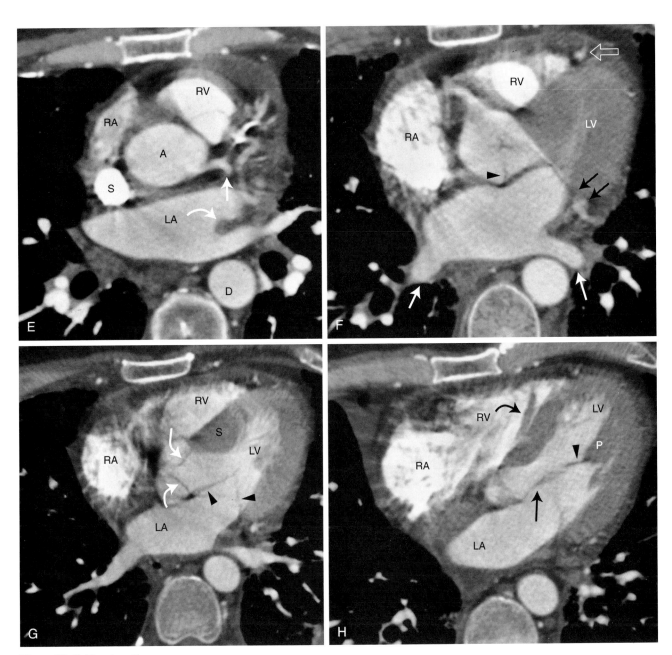

Figure 32–2 *(Continued)*.

E, CT image at level of origin of circumflex artery *(arrow)* arising from the left main coronary artery. The normal prominence of the muscle can be visualized between the left superior pulmonary vein posteriorly and the left atrial appendage anteriorly *(curved arrow)*. A, ascending aorta; D, descending aorta; LA, left atrium; RA, right atrium; RV, right ventricular outflow tract; S, superior vena cava.

F, CT image at the level of the right and left inferior pulmonary veins *(arrows)* and origin of the right coronary artery *(curved arrow)*. The left anterior descending *(open arrow)* and circumflex *(double arrow)* arteries are also visible. LV, left ventricular myocardium; RA, right atrium; RV, right ventricular outflow tract. Portions of the aortic valve are visible *(arrowhead)*.

G, CT image at the level of the mitral valve *(arrowheads)*. The aortic valve leaflets are also visible *(curved arrows)*. The mitral and aortic valves are not separated by myocardium, an indicator that this is the morphologic left ventricle. LA, left atrium; LV, left ventricle; RA, right atrium; RV, right ventricle; S, interventricular septum.

H, More inferior CT image shows the moderator band extending from the interventricular septum to the anterior free wall of the right ventricle *(curved arrow)*. In the left ventricle, the chordae tendineae *(arrowhead)* can be seen extending from the papillary muscle (P) to the mitral valve leaflet *(arrow)*. LA, left atrium; LV, left ventricle; RA, right atrium; RV, right ventricle.

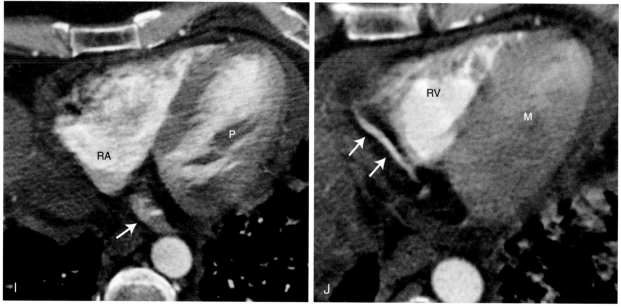

Figure 32–2. *(Continued).*

I, CT image at level of the coronary sinus *(arrow),* just before it enters the right atrium (RA). Note the papillary muscle (P) within the left ventricle.

J, CT image showing the posterior course of the right coronary artery *(arrows)* in the atrioventricular groove. M, inferior myocardium of the left ventricle; RV, right ventricle.

chest CT scans. The actual valvular structures are often not visualized. This is particularly true for the tricuspid and pulmonic valves. However, portions of the mitral and aortic valves can be identified on routine contrast-enhanced CT scans (see Fig. 32–2). Evidence of chamber enlargement and hypertrophy can also be identified on CT images. The diseased valve can be stenotic or regurgitant, or there may be combined stenosis and regurgitation.

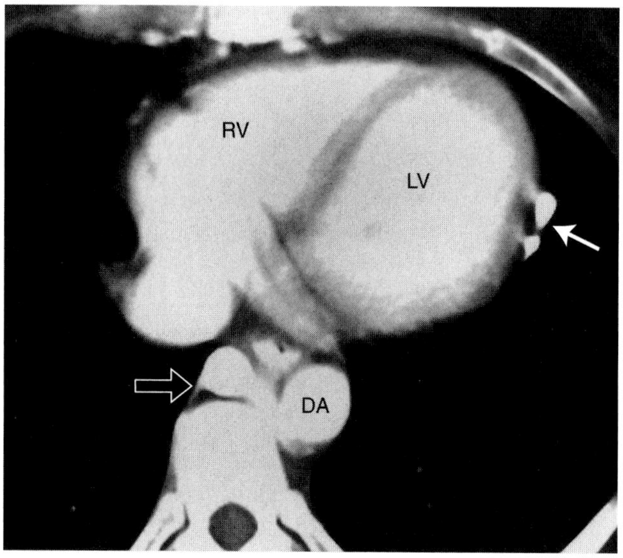

The cardiac chamber, which is proximal to a stenotic valve, must work against an increased pressure load. This results in hypertrophy and dilatation of the chamber. The chamber distal to the stenotic valve is unaffected. When the valve is regurgitant, the proximal chamber experiences an increased volume load because it receives additional blood through the regurgitant valve. This results in dilatation of the chamber. Because this increased blood volume is then pumped through the valve, the receiving chamber also experiences an increased volume load, resulting in dilatation.

Figure 32–3. Enlarged pericardiacophrenic vein. Axial CT with intravenous contrast medium shows marked distention of the pericardiacophrenic vein *(arrow),* which is acting as a collateral in this patient with SVC obstruction secondary to fibrosing mediastinitis. The distended azygos vein *(open arrow)* is also providing collateral circulation. DA, descending aorta; LV, left ventricle; RV, right ventricle.

Aortic Valve Disease

Aortic stenosis can occur secondary to the presence of a congenital bicuspid aortic valve, rheumatic heart disease, or age-related degeneration of the aortic valve. The bicuspid valve is the most common congenital heart defect and has a prevalence of 4 in 1000 live births. There is a 4:1 male-to-female ratio.[58] Patients with bicuspid aortic valve are at risk for development of aortic stenosis, bacterial endocarditis, and aortic regurgitation.

In the adult form of aortic stenosis secondary to a bicuspid aortic valve, the valve initially functions normally. The valve leaflets are continually traumatized by turbulent blood flow through the bicuspid valve and eventually become fibrotic and calcified, leading to stenosis.[86] Patients with bicuspid aortic valve tend to present with symptoms of aortic stenosis at an earlier age than do patients with degenerative aortic stenosis.

Degenerative aortic stenosis is a slowly progressive dis-

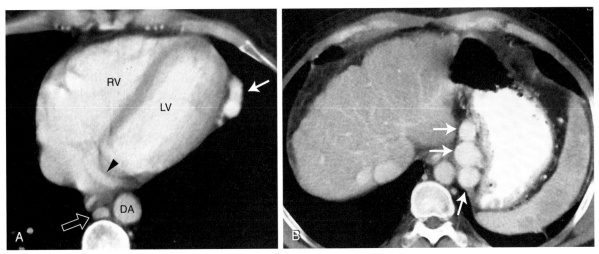

Figure 32–4. Enlarged pericardiacophrenic vein. *A,* Axial CT with intravenous contrast medium shows marked distention of the pericardiacophrenic vein *(arrow).* DA, descending aorta; LV, left ventricle; RV, right ventricle. The *open arrow* points to the azygos vein, and the *arrowhead* to the coronary sinus. *B,* More caudal image demonstrates gastric varices *(arrows)* as the cause of the distention of the pericardiacophrenic vein.

order that affects patients 65 years of age or older. It is more common in women, and it is the most common cause of aortic stenosis in older adults. Aortic stenosis may also occur as a manifestation of rheumatic heart disease. However, patients with rheumatic aortic valvular disease usually have a combination of aortic stenosis and regurgitation and the mitral valve is also usually involved. Aortic stenosis secondary to rheumatic heart disease is more common in men than in women.

Calcification of the aortic valve can be detected on CT images. In younger patients, calcification of the aortic valve should raise the question of aortic stenosis.[114] Calcification of the aortic valve in patients older than 65 years of age may be degenerative, and the patient may have no detectable aortic stenosis or may have only mild or moderate aortic stenosis.[57] In this older patient group, the greater the amount of calcification within the valve, the more likely the patient has aortic stenosis (Fig. 32–5).

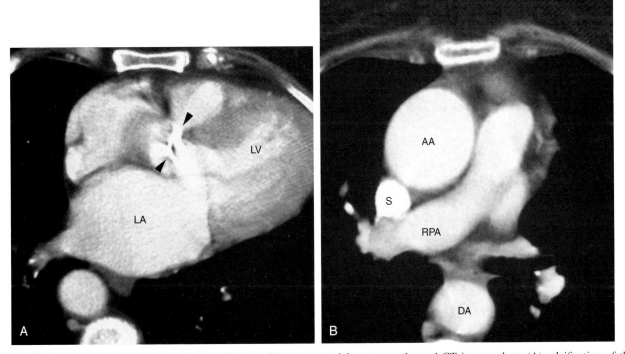

Figure 32–5. Degenerative aortic stenosis in a 73-year-old woman. Axial contrast-enhanced CT images show *(A)* calcification of the aortic valve *(arrowheads)* and *(B)* dilatation of the ascending aorta. Note the thickened myocardium of the left ventricle. AA, ascending aorta; DA, descending aorta; LA, left atrium; LV, left ventricle; RPA, right pulmonary artery; S, superior vena cava.

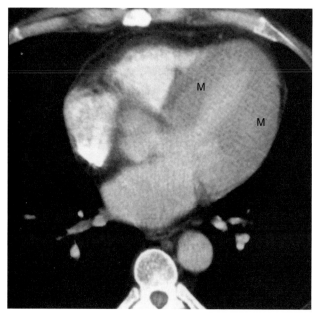

Figure 32–6. Left ventricular hypertrophy in a patient with systemic hypertension, aortic stenosis, and aortic regurgitation. Axial contrast-enhanced CT image shows the markedly thickened left ventricular myocardium (M). The aortic valve is not calcified.

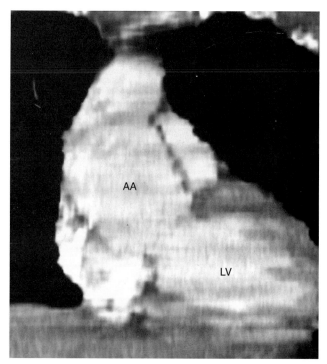

Figure 32–7. Aortic regurgitation. Coronal multiplanar reformatted image from spiral CT following intravenous contrast medium. There is dilatation of the left ventricle (LV) and aneurysmal dilatation of the ascending aorta (AA), typical findings in patients with aortic regurgitation.

CT is also useful in depicting sequelae of aortic stenosis. Hypertrophy of the left ventricular myocardium can be detected (Fig. 32–6).[86] Poststenotic dilatation of the ascending aorta is thought to result from the increased turbulence caused by the jet of blood coursing through the stenotic valve. Cystic medial degeneration has been described as occurring in 11% of patients with aortic stenosis secondary to bicuspid aortic valve, which may also play a role in aortic dilatation.[88] Other conditions associated with bicuspid aortic valve include mitral valve prolapse, aortic coarctation, and aortic dissection.[85, 88]

Aortic regurgitation results in volume overload of the left ventricle, which responds by dilating. Because the ascending aorta also receives an increased volume of blood with each left ventricular contraction, it also dilates.[86] In patients with aortic regurgitation, this combination of left ventricular dilatation and enlargement of the ascending aorta can be recognized on CT images (Fig. 32–7).

Mitral Valve Disease

Rheumatic heart disease, which causes the mitral valve leaflets to become thickened and calcified, is the most common cause of mitral stenosis.[58, 86] Because involvement of the chordae tendineae causes tethering, the mitral valve is often regurgitant as well as stenotic. Pure mitral stenosis results in left atrial enlargement (Fig. 32–8).[86] The left ventricle is not enlarged unless there is also mitral regurgitation. Calcification of the mitral valve can be seen in patients with rheumatic mitral valve disease; however, it may also be seen in elderly patients in conjunction with mitral annulus calcification.[114]

Rheumatic heart disease is also the most common cause of mitral regurgitation. Other causes include abnormal pap-

illary muscle function and endocarditis.[58] Mitral regurgitation causes volume overload of the left atrium and ventricle. When chronic, the regurgitation results in dilatation of both the left atrium and the ventricle.[86] The left atrium is usually more dilated in patients with mitral regurgitation than in patients with pure mitral stenosis.

The mitral annulus may calcify with age. It is easily recognized on chest radiographs as a C-shaped calcific density at the expected location of the mitral valve. Although it has been thought to be a clinically insignificant finding, some believe it to be related to atherosclerotic disease.[103] CT readily depicts calcification of the mitral annulus (Fig. 32–9). It may be difficult to distinguish between calcification of the valve itself and calcification of the mitral annulus. Calcification of the mitral annulus may also hamper detection of calcification within the circumflex artery.

Tricuspid Valve Disease

Tricuspid stenosis may result as a manifestation of rheumatic heart disease, in which case the mitral valve is usually affected as well.[58] Less common causes of tricuspid stenosis include lupus erythematosus and carcinoid syndrome. Tricuspid stenosis results in dilatation of the right atrium with a normal-sized right ventricle.

Tricuspid regurgitation may occur as a result of right ventricular enlargement stretching the tricuspid annulus. Carcinoid syndrome, papillary muscle dysfunction, and bacterial endocarditis may also cause tricuspid regurgita-

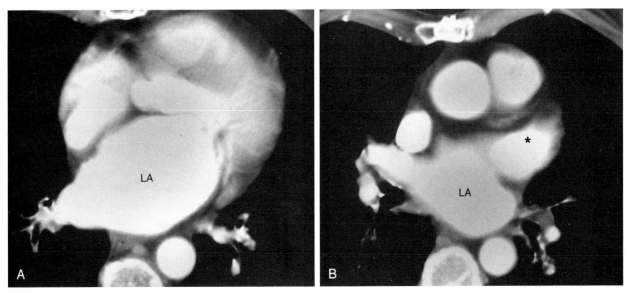

Figure 32–8. Mitral stenosis secondary to rheumatic heart disease. Axial CT with intravenous contrast medium shows *(A)* enlargement of the left atrium (LA) with *(B)* enlargement of the left atrial appendage *(asterisk).*

tion. The increased volume of blood through the regurgitant valve results in dilatation of both the right atrium and the right ventricle (Fig. 32–10). When intravenous (IV) contrast medium is used, the more densely contrasted blood within the right atrium may reflux into the hepatic veins. Reflux of contrast material into the hepatic veins may also be seen in patients with right heart failure.

Pulmonary Valve Disease

Pulmonary valve stenosis can be recognized on CT scans when there is dilatation of the main and left pulmonary arteries, which results from the poststenotic turbulent jet of blood.

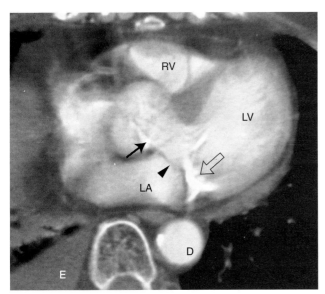

Figure 32–9. Mitral annulus calcification. Axial contrast-enhanced CT image shows calcification of the mitral annulus *(open arrow),* which was also identified on chest radiograph. Calcification within the mitral annulus may be difficult to differentiate from calcium in the circumflex coronary artery. A small amount of calcification can be visualized within the aortic valve *(arrow).* The patient did not have evidence of aortic stenosis. D, descending aorta; E, right pleural effusion; LA, left atrium; LV, left ventricle; RV, right ventricle. The *arrowhead* points to the mitral valve leaflet.

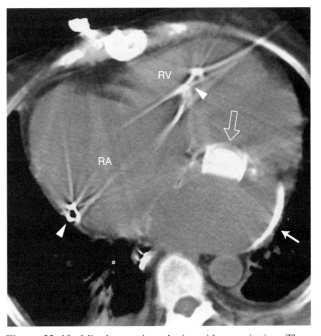

Figure 32–10. Mitral stenosis and tricuspid regurgitation. There is dystrophic calcification of the wall of the left atrium *(arrow)* in this patient with long-standing mitral stenosis who has undergone mitral valve replacement *(open arrow).* The patient also had tricuspid regurgitation resulting in marked enlargement of the right atrium (RA) and right ventricle (RV). A pacemaker is also present *(arrowheads)*

Other Causes of Hypertrophy and Chamber Enlargement

The left ventricle may be dilated as a result of ischemic heart disease or cardiomyopathy. Dilatation of cardiac chambers can also be seen in patients with cardiac shunts (Fig. 32–11).

Left ventricular hypertrophy may be seen in patients with aortic stenosis, systemic hypertension (see Figs. 32–5 and 32–6), or hypertrophic cardiomyopathy. Right ventricular hypertrophy may be seen in patients with pulmonary arterial hypertension or outflow obstruction (Fig. 32–12).

Coronary Artery Disease

Postmortem examinations have demonstrated the presence of atheroma whenever coronary artery calcification is present.[14, 83] Accordingly, several methods have been used to screen patients for calcified coronary arteries. Although calcified arteries can be detected on chest radiographs and on fluoroscopy, these methods are limited in their sensitivity because of the superimposition of overlying structures. Guthaner and coworkers reported the detection of coronary artery calcification by CT in 1979, but it was not until the last decade that CT has been evaluated as a possible screening test.[44]

Several studies have compared the calcification of coronary arteries detected by conventional CT with angiographically detected atheromatous disease.[62, 83] Masuda and coauthors[62] performed conventional CT scans (10-mm slice thickness) on 161 patients and identified coronary artery calcification in 108 patients, 90% of whom showed significant vessel narrowing on an angiogram. In addition, 80% of patients with significant lesions on angiography demonstrated calcification on CT scan.

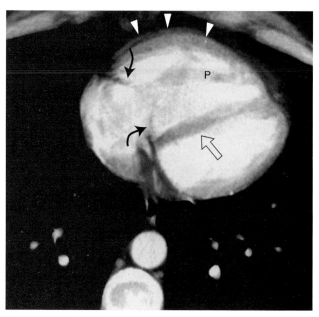

Figure 32–12. Right ventricular hypertrophy in a patient with pulmonary arterial hypertension secondary to chronic obstructive pulmonary disease. Axial contrast-enhanced CT image shows marked thickening of the free wall of the right ventricle (*arrowheads*), which is as thick as the interventricular septum (*open arrow*). P, right ventricular papillary muscle. *Curved arrows* point to the tricuspid valve.

Tamiya and coworkers studied 143 patients with 10-mm-thick conventional CT scans and correlated them with angiography. They found that a positive CT scan detecting coronary artery calcification had a 79% sensitivity and an 80% specificity when compared with significant coronary artery stenosis on angiograms.[102]

Agatson and associates[3] evaluated 584 patients with electron beam CT scans for detecting and quantifying coronary artery calcifications using a 3-mm-slice thickness. They defined calcification as densities in the anatomic location of the coronary arteries greater than or equal to 130 Hounsfield units (HU) and with an area of greater than or equal to 1 square millimeter. They scored each lesion based on the maximum density, as follows:

1 = 130–199 HU
2 = 200–299 HU
3 = 300–399 HU
4 = >400 HU

A total score was obtained by adding the scores from all of the slices. Of the 584 patients, 109 had coronary artery disease documented either by angiogram or by a positive history of myocardial infarction. For the other patients, exercise tests or angiographic findings were negative, or these patients were clinically asymptomatic. In the groups with documented coronary artery disease, 96% had coronary artery calcification scores greater than 0. The majority of patients with positive CT scans had calcifications involving the proximal arteries.

Breen's group[15] studied 100 patients undergoing elective angiography with electron beam CT scanning. A scoring system identical to that used in Agatson's study[3] was used,

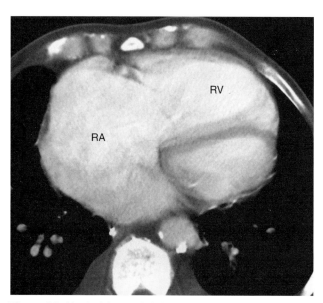

Figure 32–11. Atrial septal defect. Axial CT with intravenous contrast medium shows marked enlargement of both the right atrium (RA) and the right ventricle (RV) in this patient with atrial septal defect documented by echocardiography.

and calcification was identified as two or more adjacent pixels measuring 130 HU or more. The area and peak CT numbers were also measured. Individual scores were summed for each major vessel. Angiographically depicted stenoses were visually assessed and considered to be "mild" if the narrowing was less than 50% and "significant" if it was greater than or equal to 50% in one or more major branches. Seventy-one patients had positive angiograms, and 75 patients demonstrated calcifications. Of the 47 patients with significant stenoses, all had coronary artery calcifications. The sensitivity of the electron beam CT for detecting patients with a positive angiogram was 95%, and the specificity was 72%. No patients with negative CT scans had significant disease on angiography.

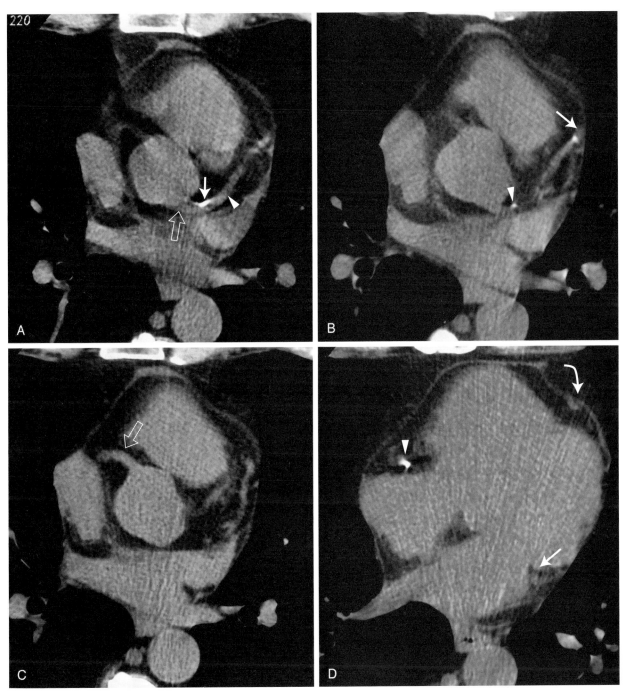

Figure 32–13. Axial CT images using retrospective electrocardiographic gating for calcium scoring. *A,* Calcification *(arrow)* is noted at the junction of the left main *(open arrow)* and left anterior descending (LAD) *(arrowhead)* coronary arteries. *B,* More caudal image shows further calcification of the LAD *(arrow)* and calcification in the inferior aspect of the left main artery *(arrowhead). C,* More caudal image shows the origin of the right coronary artery *(open arrow)* without calcification. *D,* More caudal image shows calcification *(arrowhead)* of the right coronary artery as it courses through the atrioventricular groove. The LAD *(curved arrow)* and circumflex artery *(arrow)* are not calcified at this level.

Helical CT can depict coronary artery calcification. Because of the longer acquisition time, some motion degradation of the images occurs, particularly if cardiac gating is not used. This may result in "blurring" of the calcification. Two studies were performed to quantify coronary artery calcification, with dual-slice spiral CT comparing the results with angiography. The sensitivity and specificity of these two studies were 88% to 92% and 52% to 72%, respectively.[16, 94] Note that ECG gating was not used in either study.

Since the publication of these two studies, retrospective cardiac gating has been applied to spiral CT and found to reduce cardiac motion artifact.[113] The major manufacturers of CT equipment have now added cardiac gating to their scanners. Carr and colleagues found that calcium scores obtained with retrospective cardiac gating and a subsecond helical CT scanner correlate well with calcium scores obtained from electron beam CT scanners.[26] Becker and co-workers found that calcium scores using a single-slice CT with prospective ECG gating also correlated well with electron beam CT calcium scores.[11]

Most studies evaluating coronary artery calcium have used the Agatston method of scoring, although other methods of scoring exist. Several authors have found improved reproducibility with alternate scoring methods, including volume-based and mass-based methods as well as use of the Agatston method with average instead of peak density values.[24, 95, 117]

Detection of coronary artery calcium indicates that atherosclerotic disease is present, and the more calcium found, the greater the amount of atherosclerosis (Fig. 32–13). However, the amount of calcium underestimates the true extent of atherosclerotic disease and it does not predict the site of areas of stenosis. Rumberger and colleagues published their criteria for patient selection and guidelines for intervention based on calcium scores.[87] Controversy still exists over which patients should undergo the test. Further studies evaluating clinical outcomes with calcium scores need to be performed.

CT may also detect the sequelae of coronary atherosclerotic disease. Evidence of previous myocardial infarction can be visualized on CT images of the heart, either as an area of thinned myocardium (Fig. 32–14) or as an area of dystrophic calcification (Fig. 32–15) in the infarcted area.

True ventricular aneurysms occur in approximately 10% of patients with a history of myocardial infarction.[1] Bulging of the thinned or calcified myocardium may be seen, consistent with a true aneurysm (see Fig. 32–14). The wall of a true aneurysm is made up of the myocardial scar and the overlying epicardium. It typically has a broad neck, since it is a continuation of the left ventricular cavity. A true aneurysm can gradually expand over time; however, rupture is rare.[100] Rupture of the myocardium usually results in hemopericardium and cardiac tamponade. When the rupture is contained by the pericardium, a pseudoaneurysm results.

Ventricular pseudoaneurysms are thought to occur in the presence of pericardial adhesions,[48] due either to a previous myocardial infarction with associated pericardial inflammation[104, 111] or to pericarditis.[99] Although a rare entity, left ventricular pseudoaneurysm most commonly occurs as a sequela of myocardial infarction or following cardiac sur-

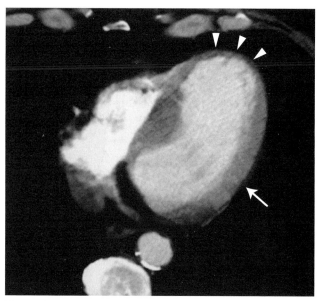

Figure 32–14. True ventricular aneurysm in a patient with history of myocardial infarction. Axial CT image of the heart after administration of intravenous contrast medium shows marked thinning of the cardiac apex (*arrowheads*) compared with the thickness of the lateral wall (*arrow*). There is slight bulging of the apex. Dyskinesis was present on the echocardiogram.

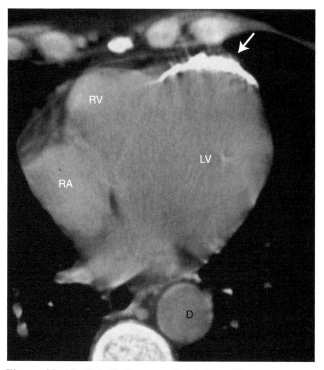

Figure 32–15. Calcified myocardial infarct. Noncontrast-enhanced CT shows dense calcification of the left ventricular apex (*arrow*) in this patient known to have a history of myocardial infarction. D, descending aorta; LV, left ventricle; RA, right atrium; RV, right ventricle.

gery.[60, 74, 84, 89] Less common causes include trauma, myocardial abscess,[60] and endocarditis.[42, 77] Pseudoaneurysms resulting from myocardial infarction occur most commonly in the inferior or posterolateral wall and typically have a narrow neck (Fig. 32–16).[51, 70, 100] The location of postsurgi-

cal pseudoaneurysms depends on the type of surgery. Unlike the more common true aneurysms of the left ventricle, pseudoaneurysms of the left ventricle are more prone to rupture, resulting in death.[39, 51, 100, 109, 116]

Coronary artery bypass grafts can be identified on CT

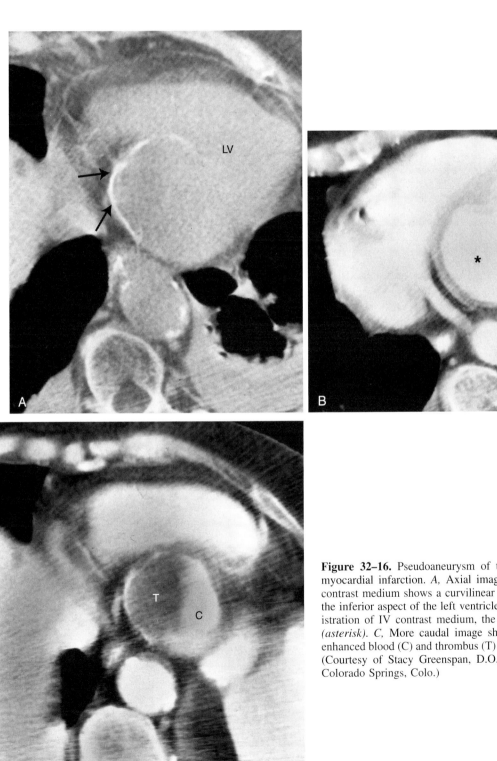

Figure 32–16. Pseudoaneurysm of the left ventricle following myocardial infarction. *A,* Axial image without intravenous (IV) contrast medium shows a curvilinear calcification *(arrows)* along the inferior aspect of the left ventricle (LV). *B,* Following administration of IV contrast medium, the abnormal area is enhanced *(asterisk). C,* More caudal image shows a mixture of contrast-enhanced blood (C) and thrombus (T) within the pseudoaneurysm. (Courtesy of Stacy Greenspan, D.O., and Chris Peeters, M.D., Colorado Springs, Colo.)

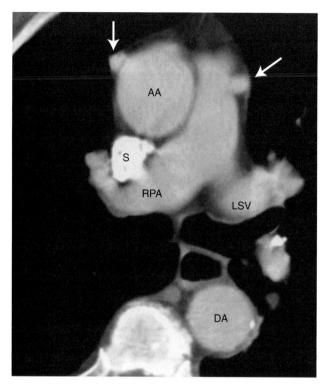

Figure 32–17. Coronary artery bypass grafts. Contrast-enhanced axial CT image shows enhancement of right and left coronary artery bypass grafts *(arrows)*. AA, ascending aorta; DA, descending aorta; LSV, left superior pulmonary vein; RPA, right pulmonary artery; S, superior vena cava.

scans (Fig. 32–17). With faster scanning times, their patency can often be determined. Although it happens rarely, a pseudoaneurysm may develop at the site of the anastomosis, usually the proximal anastomosis. These pseudoaneurysms tend to be identified within weeks to months following bypass surgery and can be associated with mediastinal infection.

True aneurysms are less common and occur in the body of the saphenous graft. They are thought to be related to graft atherosclerosis and are usually identified years after bypass surgery.[79] They are less likely to rupture than pseudoaneurysms of saphenous vein grafts.[105] Saphenous vein graft aneurysms can be detected on a chest radiograph, where it may have the appearance of a mass.[35] CT or magnetic resonance imaging (MRI) demonstrates that the mass is related to a vascular structure, and each modality can depict the amount of associated thrombus within the lumen (Fig. 32–18).

Systemic Disease

The diagnosis of anemia can be suggested on CT scans if an IV contrast agent is not used. In the anemic patient, the blood in the chambers of the heart is less dense than the myocardium because of the reduced protein content in the blood. This difference in density is best appreciated at the level of the interventricular septum (Fig. 32–19). In general, the lower the hemoglobin, the more likely that the myocardium appears denser than the blood. An increase in

density of the myocardium may also be seen in patients with hemochromatosis, because of increased iron deposition within the myocardium. In hemochromatosis, the liver is also increased in density.[34, 112] Amiodarone is known to concentrate in the heart,[61] and in patients with amiodarone pulmonary toxicity, it has been described as causing increased density of the myocardium on unenhanced CT scans.[54]

Cardiac Tumors

Metastatic involvement of the heart is more common than primary cardiac tumors, which are very rare. Patients with cardiac tumors may be asymptomatic, or they may present with arrhythmias or hemodynamic, embolic, or constitutional symptoms. The reported incidence of cardiac tumors ranges from 0.001% to 0.03%.[19, 63] Most cardiac tumors have benign histologic features (75%). Although primary cardiac tumors are often evaluated by echocardiography, CT, MRI, or both can be useful in their assessment.

Benign Cardiac Tumors

Myxoma

The most common cardiac tumor, the myxoma, accounts for about 50% of all benign cardiac tumors and 25% of all cardiac tumors. The incidence of cardiac myxoma is 0.5 per million population per year,[12] with a female predominance.[12, 81] The most common anatomic location is the left atrium (75% to 80%), followed by the right atrium (10% to 20%).[7, 12, 19, 55, 63] Less common are myxomas involving either ventricle or involving both atria (5% to 10%), and the mitral valve is rarely involved.[12, 19, 27, 81] Left atrial myxomas are typically pedunculated and arise from the interatrial septum, near the fossa ovalis. Right atrial myxomas tend to be sessile and may arise from areas of the atrium other than the septum.

Patients with myxoma may present with hemodynamic symptoms, embolic disease, or constitutional symptoms.[12, 55, 81] Hemodynamic symptoms are related to outflow obstruction by the tumor. The symptoms may be related to posture and include dyspnea, syncope, and sudden death. Myxomas are known to embolize, and patients may present with stroke or with symptoms related to peripheral or pulmonary emoblization.[12, 55, 81] Embolization of the myxomatous tissue may result in myxomatous pseudoaneurysm.[32] Myxoma may also cause constitutional symptoms, including fever, weight loss, myalgia, and arthralgia.[55] Patients may also have an elevated erythrocyte sedimentation rate, anemia, and leukocytosis.

Myxomas tend to be solitary and to occur sporadically in middle-aged individuals, although they have been reported in all age groups.[19, 63, 81] These tumors carry a low risk of recurrence after resections. Familial myxomas tend to occur at an earlier age, can be multiple (a third of cases), and have a 10% risk of recurrence following resection.[63, 64, 81] Patients tend to present at a younger age than patients with sporadic myxoma. The left atrium is the most common location of familial myxomas (61%).[107]

A third subset of myxomas was described by Carney.[25]

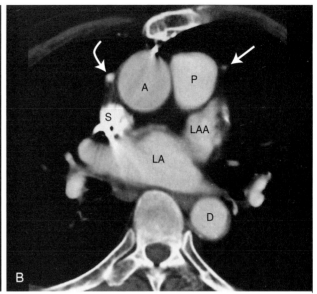

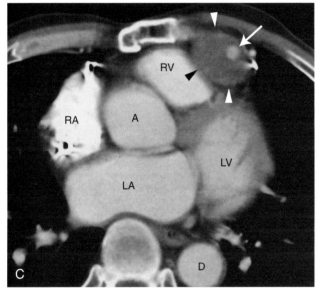

Figure 32–18. Pseudoaneurysm of saphenous vein graft. *A,* Contrast-enhanced axial CT image shows right *(curved arrow)* and left *(arrow)* coronary artery saphenous vein bypass grafts. *B,* More caudal image shows enhancement of the right graft *(curved arrow).* Enhancement of the left graft *(arrow)* is less certain. *C,* More caudal image shows contrast-enhanced blood within the left graft *(arrow).* However, the lumen is surrounded by thrombus *(arrowheads)* within the markedly dilated graft. A, ascending aorta; D, descending aorta; LA, left atrium; LAA, left atrial appendage; LV, left ventricle; P, main pulmonary artery; RA, right atrium; RV, right ventricle; S, superior vena cava.

These myxomas occur in association with pigmented skin lesions and endocrine lesions. Patients tend to present in the third decade of life and tend to have multiple, multicentric, and metachronous myxomas. Only 50% of myxomas involve the left atrium in patients with the Carney complex. Patients with the Carney complex have an increased risk of recurrence of myxoma following resection.[64] Because the Carney complex is inherited as an autosomal dominant trait, family members should be screened for the disease.[25, 78]

On CT, a myxoma has the appearance of a filling defect in the chamber of origin (Fig. 32–20). The mass is usually heterogeneous and may have areas of calcification.[7, 78]

Rhabdomyoma

Rhabdomyomas are the most common pediatric cardiac tumor, typically occurring in children younger than 1 year of age.[63] They are usually multiple and occur most commonly in either ventricle, although the atria may also be involved. They do not occur in association with the heart valves.

Patients are usually asymptomatic. However, the tumors may cause arrhythmias or obstruction, resulting in acute heart failure and sudden death. The incidence of cardiac rhabdomyoma in patients with tuberous sclerosis is 30% to 50%.[97, 110]

Rhabdomyomas are thought to be hamartomatous lesions. They do not show a significant increase in size and may regress over time[2, 37, 110]; thus, they may be monitored in asymptomatic individuals. Echocardiography is usually used for evaluation of these tumors.

Other Benign Cardiac Tumors

Cardiac lipomas are usually solitary and may occur in the myocardial tissue or in a subendocardial or subepicardial location. Because affected patients are usually asymptomatic, the lesions are usually found incidentally. Cardiac lipomas can be associated with rhabdomyomas or tuberous

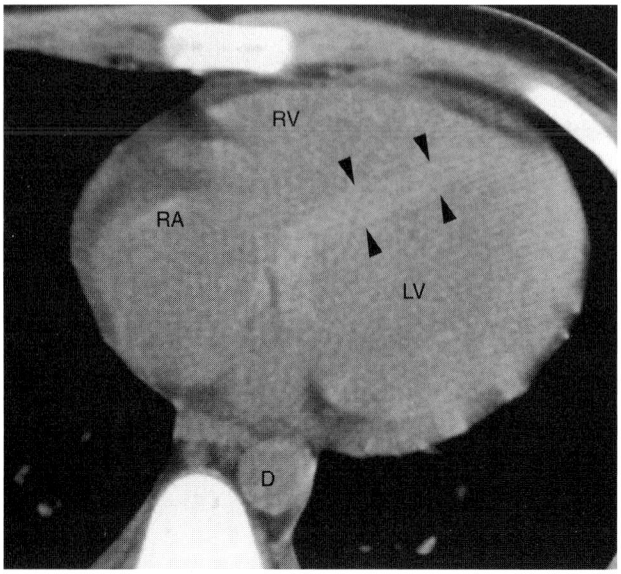

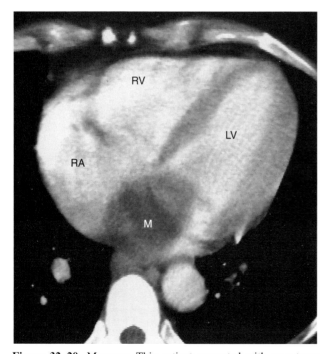

Figure 32–19. Anemia. Axial CT scan without contrast medium in an 18-year-old patient with a hematocrit of 23 mL/dL (normal range, 36 to 47 mL/dL). The interventricular septum *(arrowheads)* is visible because of the reduced density of the blood in the ventricles. D, descending aorta; LV, left ventricle; RA, right atrium; RV, right ventricle.

Figure 32–20. Myxoma. This patient presented with symptoms thought to be secondary to mitral stenosis. Axial CT with intravenous contrast medium shows a large mass (M) nearly filling the left atrium. At surgery, the tumor was found to arise from the interatrial septum. LV, left ventricle; RA, right atrium; RV, right ventricle. (Courtesy of Robert D. Tarver, M.D., Indiana University Medical Center.)

sclerosis. These lesions may be first detected by echocardiography. CT or MRI can document their fatty nature, establishing the diagnosis.[106, 118]

Papillary fibroelastoma is a rare lesion, usually affecting older adults (range, 25 to 86 years of age). The tumor occurs most frequently on the valves, but it can occur anywhere in the heart.[19, 63] The tumor is composed of multiple papillary fronds, which predispose it to form thrombi. Because of the risk of lethal embolization of the coronary or cerebral circulation, surgical resection is the treatment of choice.[19, 63] These tumors are usually evaluated with echocardiography. They are not usually seen on CT because of their small size and relation to moving valves.[7]

Cardiac fibromas are the second most common benign pediatric cardiac tumor, although they may also occur in adults. They tend to be solitary lesions that arise in the ventricular myocardium. They may cause lethal arrhythmias and heart failure. On CT, these tumors appear as soft tissue homogeneous masses, often with areas of calcification.[7] They are often fairly large when detected, and surgical resection may require chamber reconstruction.[63]

Malignant Cardiac Tumors

Angiosarcoma

Angiosarcoma is the most common primary malignant cardiac tumor.[19] These tumors usually occur in adults, although they have been reported in a wide age range.[6, 19, 23, 63] Men are affected more often than women.[19, 47, 63] Angiosarcomas usually arise from the free wall of the right atrium (Fig. 32–21) or from the pericardium.[8, 19, 23, 47, 63] Thus, patients tend to present with symptoms of right heart failure, vena cava obstruction, or pericardial disease. Most patients have metastatic disease at the time of diagnosis, most commonly involving the lung.[23] The prognosis is generally poor, although some patients survive longer than 1 year.[6, 19, 23, 47, 63, 98]

Other Malignant Cardiac Tumors

Rhabdomyosarcomas have a slight male predominance and tend to occur in adults. They can arise anywhere within the heart, including the valves, and are frequently multiple. Patients may present with symptoms of pericardial disease, chest pain, dyspnea, or embolic events. Rhabdomyosarcomas are also associated with hypertrophic pulmonary osteoarthropathy, polyarthritis, neurofibromatosis, and eosinophilia.

Fibrosarcomas are rare lesions. They occur in the right and left sides of the heart with equal frequency and are often multiple. Approximately 50% of these tumors involve a cardiac valve.

Primary cardiac osteosarcomas usually arise from the posterior wall of the left atrium near the pulmonary veins.[6, 19, 21, 63] This is in contradistinction to metastatic osteosarcomas, which usually involve the right atrium. These lesions may calcify and may be confused with calcified myxoma. They can be distinguished from calcified myxomas by their location in the posterior wall of the left atrium instead of the usual septal location of myxomas.

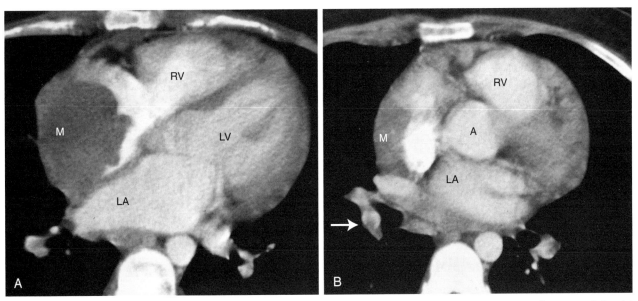

Figure 32–21. Angiosarcoma in a 23-year-old man. Contrast-enhanced axial CT images. *A,* A large mass occupying most of the right atrium. LA, left atrium; LV, left ventricle; M, mass; RV, right ventricle. *B,* Image more cephalad shows a filling defect in the right lower lobe pulmonary artery, consistent with tumor thrombus *(arrow).* The patient had pulmonary and bony metastases as well (not shown). A, ascending aorta; M, mass.

Leiomyosarcomas tend to arise from the posterior wall of the left atrium, typically in the fourth decade of life. They frequently involve the pulmonary veins or the mitral valve, causing symptoms of heart failure.

Liposarcomas are extremely rare lesions, with only 18 reported cases in the literature. Despite their name, histologically little or no fat is detectable. They can occur in the atria, ventricles, or pericardium.

Although up to 25% of patients with *lymphoma* have cardiac involvement at autopsy, primary cardiac lymphoma (lymphoma limited to the heart and/or pericardium) is very rare.[19] Primary cardiac lymphoma is usually a B-cell lymphoma. The most common location is a right-sided lesion, usually arising from the right atrium. Associated pericardial effusion is common (Fig. 32–22).

Secondary Cardiac Tumors

Metastatic cardiac involvement is much more common than primary cardiac neoplasms, but it may be undetected before death. Autopsy studies have found cardiac metastases to be present in up to 20% of patients with neoplasm. They occur most frequently in patients with lymphoma, leukemia, or melanoma (40% to 50%) and in patients with lung or breast cancer (10% to 33%). Direct extension of tumor is the most common route and typically occurs in lung and breast cancers. Symptoms tend to be related to associated pericardial involvement.

Renal cell carcinoma, adrenal carcinoma, hepatocellular carcinoma, and uterine leiomyosarcoma may involve the heart through extension into the inferior vena cava. Thyroid carcinoma may extend through the superior vena cava. Lung cancer may also spread along the pulmonary veins to involve the left atrium.

Finally, lymphangitic metastases may occur as well as hematogenous metastases. Leukemia and lymphoma are the most common tumors to cause cardiac metastases by the lymphangitic route, in which case mediastinal nodes are invariably involved.

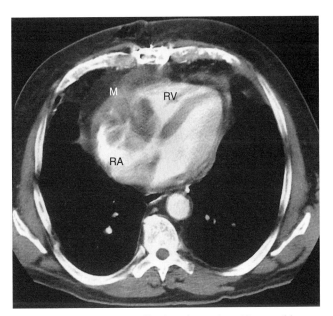

Figure 32–22. Primary cardiac lymphoma in a 42-year-old man. Contrast-enhanced CT following open biopsy shows a lobulated mass (M) within the right heart at the level of the tricuspid valve. The mass extends into the right atrial and right ventricular cavities. Open surgical biopsy confirmed the tumor involvement of the tricuspid valve, right atrium, and right ventricle. RA, right atrium; RV, right ventricle.

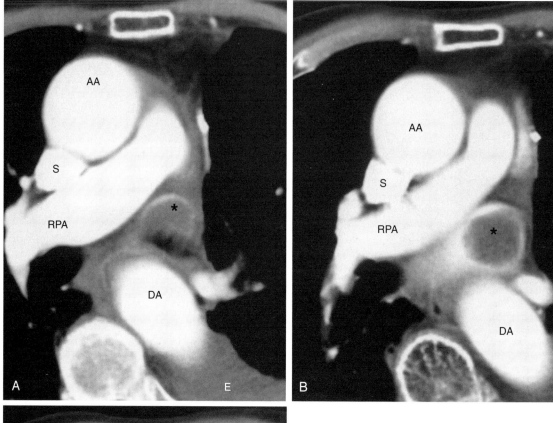

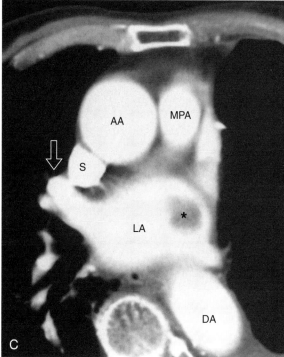

Figure 32–23. Clot in left atrial appendage in a patient with atrial fibrillation. Axial contrast-enhanced CT images at the level of the left atrial appendage *(A* and *B)* and at the level of the left atrium *(C)* show a low-density filling defect *(asterisk)* in the left atrial appendage extending into the left atrium. This is a typical location for left atrial thrombus. AA, ascending aorta; DA, descending aorta; E, pleural effusion; LA, left atrium; MPA, main pulmonary artery; RPA, right pulmonary artery; S, superior vena cava. The *open arrow* points to the right superior pulmonary vein.

Lesions That Mimic Cardiac Tumors

Thrombus

Thrombus within the heart may mimic a cardiac mass. In the atria, thrombus usually involves the appendages (Figs. 32–23 and 32–24).[90] Laminated thrombus may also occur in the left atrium between the pulmonary veins.[90] In the ventricle, thrombus usually occurs over an area of hypokinesis such as a myocardial infarction.[5, 90] If the diagnosis of clot is uncertain on CT images, MRI can be used for further evaluation.[93]

Lipomatous Hypertrophy of the Interatrial Septum

Fat may be detected in the atrioventricular grooves and the interatrial septum. Normally, fat in the interatrial septum measures less than 1 cm anterior and posterior to the fossa ovalis.[17] Lipomatous hypertrophy of the interatrial septum (LHIS), first described by Prior in 1964, results in increased fat deposition in the interatrial septum.[75] This may mimic an atrial tumor on an echocardiogram (Fig. 32–25).[5, 20] Typically, the lesion 34is dumbbell-shaped because of the sparing of the region of the fossa ovalis (Fig. 32–26).[65, 80] Both CT and MRI are able to accurately depict the fatty nature of the lesion and establish the diagnosis.[33]

Pathologically, the lesion is not a true encapsulated lipoma. The fatty tissue resembles fetal or brown fat and is intermixed with myocardial cells. This lesion is most often found incidentally, but it can be associated with atrial arrhythmias.[49, 72, 80] Treatment is directed at controlling the arrhythmia if present.

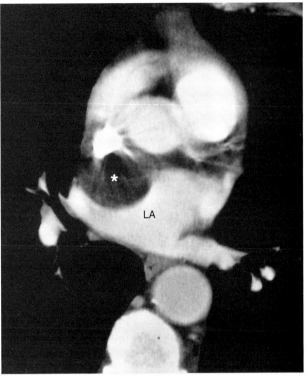

Figure 32–25. Lipomatous hypertrophy of the interatrial septum. Contrast-enhanced axial image shows fatty enlargement of the interatrial septum *(asterisk)*. The fat bulges into the left atrium (LA).

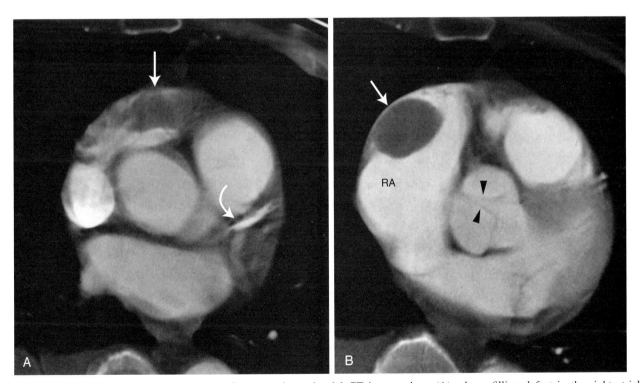

Figure 32–24. Clot in right atrial appendage. Contrast-enhanced axial CT images show *(A)* a large filling defect in the right atrial appendage *(arrow)* and *(B)* extension into the right atrium. The right atrium is enlarged. Thrombus was also found in the pulmonary arterial tree (not shown). There is calcification of the left anterior descending artery *(curved arrow)*. RA, right atrium. The *arrowheads* point to cusps of aortic valve.

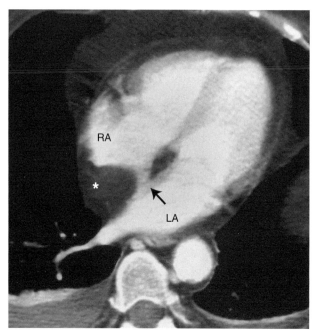

Figure 32–26. Lipomatous hypertrophy of the interatrial septum. Axial CT with intravenous contrast medium shows increased fat deposition within the interatrial septum *(asterisk).* A characteristic bilobed shape is caused by sparing of the fossa ovale *(arrow).* LA, left atrium; RA, right atrium.

Normal Anatomic Structures

Normal anatomic structures that may be mistaken for a mass include a prominent moderator band in the right ventricle, prominence of the muscle between the left superior pulmonary vein and the left atrial appendage in the left atrium (see Fig. 32–2E), prominent papillary muscles, and a prominent eustachian valve in the right atrium (Fig. 32–27).[5]

Pericardium

The pericardium has two layers: (1) a serous visceral layer (the epicardium), that is adherent to the heart, and (2) a fibrous parietal layer that is attached to the great vessels and the central tendon of the diaphragm. The pericardial space normally contains 20 to 25 mL of pericardial fluid. On CT, the pericardium can be identified when outlined by mediastinal and subepicardial fat. It normally measures only 1 to 2 mm thick.[18, 31] It is best visualized in the caudal and ventral areas. A focal area of increased thickness can usually be seen just anterior to the right ventricle and near the insertion onto the diaphragm.

Pericardial Defect

Congenital pericardial defects are thought to occur when there is premature atrophy of the left duct of Cuvier, resulting in decreased circulation to the left pleuropericardial membrane. Congenital pericardial defect is reported to occur in 1 in 7000 to 1 in 13,000 in autopsy studies. There is a 3:1 male-to-female ratio.

The defect is usually left-sided and may be partial or complete. Patients are usually asymptomatic; however, herniation of the heart or its appendage into a partial defect may result in chest pain or syncope. Also, sudden death due to herniation of the heart through the defect has been reported.[108] Associated congenital anomalies occur in 20% to 50% of patients with pericardial defect, most commonly atrial septal defect, patent ductus arteriosus, tetralogy of Fallot, bronchogenic cyst, or pulmonary sequestration.[66, 108] Most patients with pericardial defects have partial left-sided absence.[66] Much less common are right-sided absence and complete absence of the pericardium.

With a partial left pericardial defect, the typical finding is lack of pericardium covering the main pulmonary artery and the left atrial appendage.[66] In 75% of patients, there is also a large defect in the adjacent parietal pleura.[108] Chest radiographs of patients with a partial left pericardial defect show a discrete bulge in the cardiomediastinal silhouette at the level of the main pulmonary artery and left atrial appendage. Patients with complete absence of the pericardium show a shift of the heart to the left, a long prominent pulmonary artery, a flattened left heart border, and separation of the cardiac apex and diaphragm by lung. CT may demonstrate absence of the pericardium or an abrupt termination of the pericardium if the defect is partial.[50] When the left pericardium is absent, lung is interposed between the main pulmonary artery and the ascending aorta. When placed in the left lateral decubitus position, the heart migrates against the left chest wall. Absence of the sternopericardial ligaments may cause the heart to lie in a more posterior position when the patient is supine.[101]

Acquired pericardial defects also occur and usually follow surgery, although they may be secondary to trauma or to erosion of peptic ulcer disease.[101] Coronary artery bypass

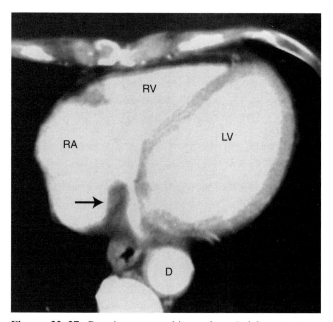

Figure 32–27. Prominent eustachian valve. Axial contrast-enhanced CT image shows a finger-like soft tissue projection within the right atrium *(arrow).* A prominent eustachian vein was detected by echocardiography. D, descending aorta; LV, left ventricle; RA, right atrium; RV, right ventricle.

graft surgery is the most common cause of a surgical pericardial defect. When a linear midline incision is made, however, it heals readily and herniation does not usually occur.[101] Large or small defects in the pericardium may result from creation of a pericardial window, treatment of pericardial constriction, and surgery for lung cancer and mesothelioma. Radiographic detection of a pericardial defect is possible if there is herniation of the heart or demonstration of continuity of gas or fluid within the pleural and pericardial spaces. As with congenital pericardial defects, CT can demonstrate the discontinuity of surgical pericardial defects.[101] Acute cardiac herniation through a surgical pericardial defect usually occurs within the first 24 hours of surgery and is often triggered by a change in body position, suctioning, or coughing.[101]

Pneumopericardium most commonly occurs secondary to trauma, either barotrauma or blunt or penetrating trauma. It may also occur secondary to erosion of the pericardium by tumor, infection, or a stomach or duodenal ulcer.

Pericardial Cyst

Most pericardial cysts are actually pleuropericardial cysts. True pericardial cysts are rare. Pericardial cysts occur in a 3:2 male-to-female ratio. Most patients are asymptomatic. The cysts are most commonly located in the right cardiophrenic angle but can occur at the left cardiophrenic angle or higher in the mediastinum, and they often have a peripherally pointed contour.[71, 115]

On chest radiographs, the appearance is that of an area of increased soft tissue density at the cardiophrenic angle. CT can demonstrate a sharply demarcated mass whose density is that of water, with very thin or imperceptible walls (Fig. 32–28). Occasionally, the attenuation in a pericardial cyst may be higher than that of water. CT can also document whether there is increased mediastinal fat, which can have a similar appearance on a chest radiograph[73] (Fig. 32–29).

Pericardial Effusion

There are many causes of pericardial effusion[4, 30, 59] (Table 32–1). On CT scans, pericardial effusion is easily detected as an increase in fluid density within the pericardial space. Fluid commonly collects in a location anterior to the right ventricle or lateral to the left ventricle.[40] Pericardial fluid may collect in one of the pericardial sinuses and may be mistaken for other pathologic processes.

Knowledge of the anatomy of the pericardial sinuses helps one to make the correct diagnosis (Fig. 32–30).[29, 43, 56, 66] The superior pericardial recess is located anteriorly and extends anterior to the aortic root to the level of the innominate artery.[29, 43, 56, 66] The superior pericardial recess also extends between the ascending aorta and the main pulmonary artery in a triangular shape. It is continuous with the transverse sinus, which lies posterior to the ascending aorta and the main pulmonary artery.[29, 43, 56, 66]

Pericardial fluid in the superior pericardial recess may mimic aortic dissection, adenopathy, or an anterior mediastinal mass.[28, 71, 91, 96] The transverse sinus often has a lenticu-

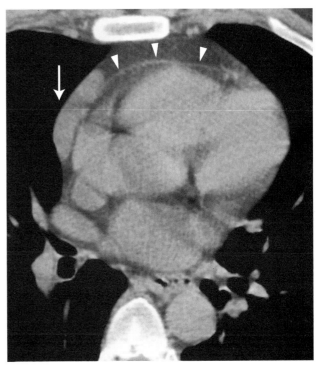

Figure 32–28. Pericardial cyst. Axial CT scan without contrast medium shows an elongated mass *(arrow)* arising from the pericardium *(arrowheads)*. The mass, whose density was similar to that of water, was resected and found to be a pericardial cyst.

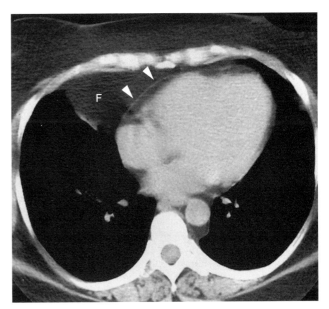

Figure 32–29. Prominent paracardiac mediastinal fat. This patient was evaluated by CT for a masslike density at the right cardiophrenic angle. Axial CT scan without contrast medium shows a collection of fat (F) at the right cardiophrenic angle, consistent with a prominent fat pad. The thin pericardium is outlined by subepicardial and mediastinal fat *(arrowheads)*.

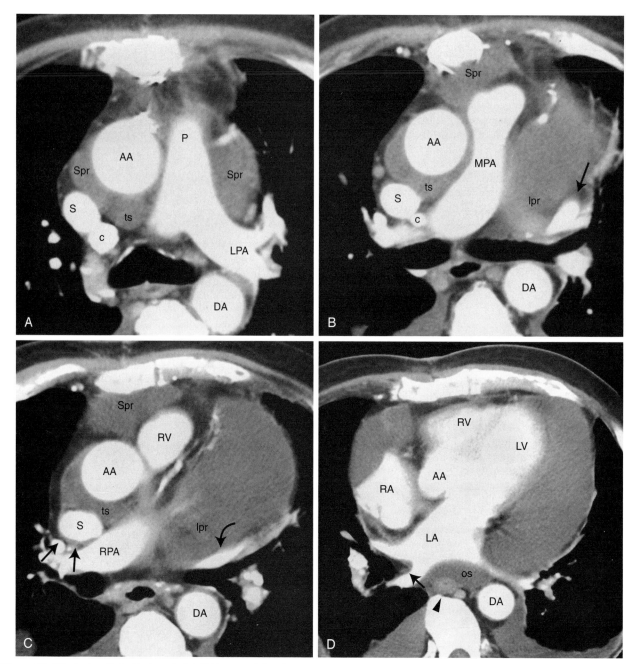

Figure 32–30. Pericardial effusion. Axial CT images following administration of intravenous contrast medium demonstrate the location of the pericardial recesses.

A, CT image at the level of the ascending aorta and main pulmonary artery. Note fluid collecting in the superior pericardial recess (spr) and the continuity of the superior pericardial recess with the transverse sinus (ts). Although fluid is not detectable in this patient, the superior pericardial recess continues along the anterior aspect of the aorta and the main pulmonary artery superiorly to the level of the aortic arch. AA, ascending aorta; C, calcified lymph node; DA, descending aorta; LPA, left pulmonary artery; P, main pulmonary artery; S, superior vena cava.

B, More caudal CT image shows fluid within the superior pericardial recess (spr), anterior to the ascending aorta (AA) and the main pulmonary artery (MPA). Fluid is also present in the transverse sinus (ts) posterior to the ascending aorta and within the left pulmonic recess (lpr). The left pulmonic recess lies anterior to the left superior pulmonary vein *(arrow)* and the left mainstem bronchus. C, calcified lymph node; DA, descending aorta; S, superior vena cava.

C, More caudal CT image shows fluid in the superior pericardial recess (spr), the left pulmonic recess (lpr) anterior to the left superior pulmonary vein *(curved arrow),* and the transverse sinus (ts). There is a tiny amount of fluid posterior to the superior vena cava (S) within the postcaval recess *(arrows).* AA, ascending aorta; DA, descending aorta; RPA, right pulmonary artery; RV, right ventricular outflow tract.

D, More caudal CT image shows a small amount of fluid within the right pulmonic vein recess *(arrow).* The right and left pulmonic vein recesses lie between the superior and inferior pulmonic veins on their respective sides. Fluid also lies within the oblique sinus (os) posterior to the left atrium (LA) and anterior to the esophagus *(arrowhead).* AA, aortic root; DA, descending aorta; LV, left ventricle; RA, right atrium; RV, right ventricle.

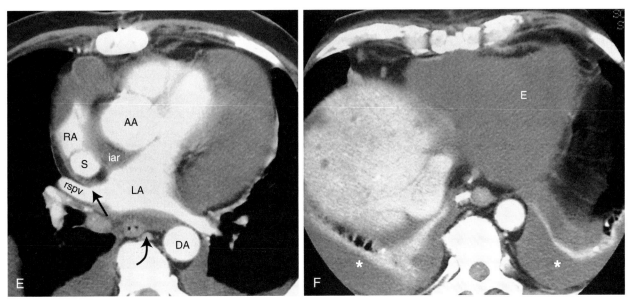

Figure 32–30. *Continued.*
E, More caudal CT image shows fluid within the inferior aortic recess (iar). This recess is located between the ascending aorta (AA) and the inferior aspect of the superior vena cava (S) or the superior aspect of the right atrium (RA). Fluid is also present in the oblique sinus *(curved arrow)* and the postcaval recess *(arrow),* which is posterolateral to the superior vena cava between the right pulmonary artery and the right superior pulmonary vein (rspv).
F, More caudal CT image shows a significant amount of fluid (E) within the inferior aspect of the pericardium. Bilateral pleural effusions are also present *(asterisks).*

lar shape, which is helpful in distinguishing it from adenopathy.[9, 10, 13] The oblique pericardial sinus lies behind the left atrium, between the pulmonary veins.[43, 56] Less commonly identified recesses include the left pulmonic recess located between the left pulmonary artery and the left superior pulmonary vein, the postcaval recess located between the superior vena cava and the right pulmonary artery and right superior pulmonary vein, and the pulmonary venous recess located between the superior and inferior pulmonary veins.[43, 56, 76]

Thickening of the pericardium, which may show enhancement following administration of IV contrast medium, may be seen in patients with pericarditis.[71] CT can document hemopericardium by showing the increased attenuation of blood within the pericardial space (Fig. 32–31).[71]

Table 32–1. Etiology of Pericardial Effusion

1. Infection (viral, bacterial, fungal, parasitic)
2. Inflammatory (sarcoid, amyloid, inflammatory bowel disease, Whipple's disease, temporal arteritis, Behçet's syndrome)
3. Immunologic (postinfectious, postcardiac injury, postcardiotomy, postinfarction, rheumatic fever, systemic lupus erythematosus, rheumatoid arthritis, Still's disease, ankylosing spondylitis, Reiter's syndrome, scleroderma, mixed connective tissue disease, Wegener's granulomatosis, Churg-Strauss syndrome)
4. Traumatic (hemopericardium, pneumopericardium, radiation)
5. Uremic
6. Neoplastic
7. Hypothyroidism
8. Chylopericarditis
9. Congestive heart failure

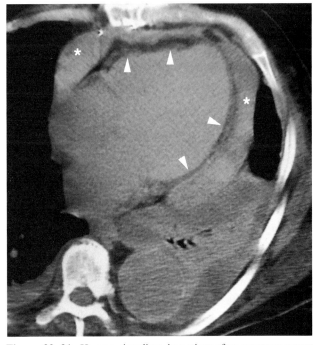

Figure 32–31. Hemopericardium in patient after coronary artery bypass graft surgery. Axial CT scan without contrast medium shows filling of the pericardial space *(asterisks),* which measured 59 HU, consistent with blood. The pericardial space is separated from the heart by a thin layer of subepicardial fat *(arrowheads).*

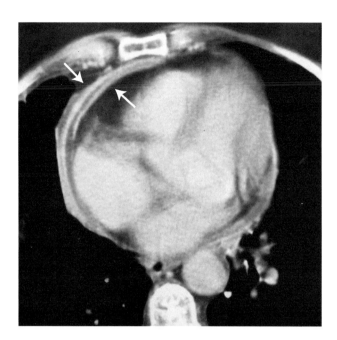

Figure 32–32. Postradiation pericardial thickening. Axial contrast-enhanced CT image shows marked thickening of the visceral and parietal pericardium *(arrows)*. The patient had received radiation for lung carcinoma.

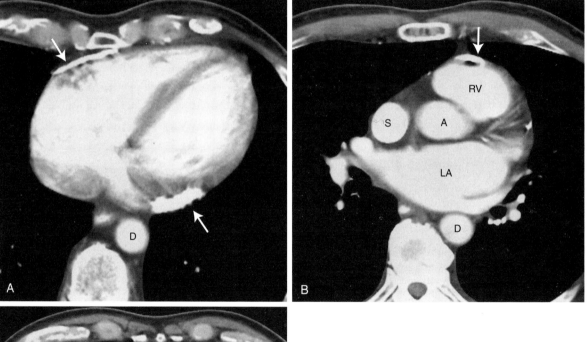

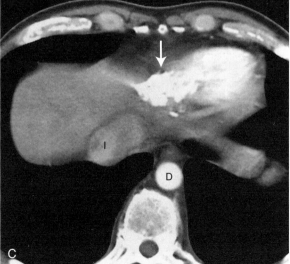

Figure 32–33. Constrictive pericarditis. *A,* Axial contrast-enhanced CT image at the level of the ventricles shows bilateral dense calcification of the pericardium at the level of the atrioventricular grooves *(arrows)*. *B,* Scan at the level of the left atrium shows an additional area of calcification anteriorly *(arrow)*. The superior vena cava is larger than the descending aorta. *C,* Scan at the level of the diaphragm shows inferior pericardial calcification *(arrow)*. The inferior vena cava is more than twice the size of the descending aorta. A, aortic root; D, descending aorta; I, inferior vena cava; LA, left atrium; RV, right ventricular outflow track; S, superior vena cava.

Constrictive Pericarditis

Constrictive pericarditis is a possible sequela in patients with previous pericardial disease, including idiopathic pericarditis, infectious pericarditis, connective tissue disease, neoplastic involvement of the pericardium, postsurgical inflammation, post-radiation therapy pericarditis (Fig. 32–32), uremic pericarditis, and drug-related pericarditis.[38] However, some patients have no known antecedent event. Patients usually present with dyspnea, peripheral edema, and ascites.

Echocardiography demonstrates elevated diastolic filling pressures because the constricting pericardium prevents normal diastolic filling of the heart. Because it is often difficult for echocardiography to distinguish between constrictive pericarditis and restrictive cardiomyopathy, patients may be further evaluated with CT or MRI to determine whether the pericardium is thickened.[38] CT has the advantage of better depicting calcium within the pericardium.

The CT signs of constrictive pericarditis include (1) diffuse, focal, or annular pericardial thickening or calcification; (2) enlargement of the atria or atrium; (3) dilatation of the superior or inferior vena cava; (4) tubelike configuration of the ventricles and narrowing of the atrioventricular groove; and (5) alteration of the normally straight interventricular septum (Fig. 32–33).[82] The constriction can be global or unilateral, or it may affect the atrioventricular groove.

Pericardial Tumors

Metastatic disease, the most common cause of neoplastic involvement of the pericardium, has been reported in up to 20% of autopsy studies. Most patients with pericardial metastases have metastatic disease elsewhere in the body.[53, 115] The most common primary tumors that involve the pericardium secondarily include lung (33%) and breast cancer (25%) and lymphoma/leukemia (15%).[46, 53, 115] Metastatic routes include hematogenous and lymphangitic spread as well as direct extension.

In many cases, the metastases are not radiographically detectable. Pericardial effusion in a patient with a known malignancy should arouse suspicion of metastatic involvement of the pericardium, although nonmalignant causes of pericardial effusion, such as radiation or drug-induced pericarditis, must also be considered. Occasionally, soft tissue nodules or masses may be demonstrated on CT (Fig. 32–34).

CT is often better than echocardiography in detecting pericardial masses. Subepicardial fat may mimic a pericardial mass on echocardiography, and in some cases a mass within the pericardium cannot be distinguished from pericardial effusion.[41, 67]

Primary tumors of the pericardium include mesothelioma, sarcoma, lymphoma, teratoma, and pheochromocytoma.[45, 53] Intrathoracic paragangliomas account for only 1% to 2% of all pheochromocytomas. The most common intrathoracic location of paragangliomas is the posterior mediastinum. Intrapericardial location is very rare.[45] Tumors tend to be large and are most commonly located adjacent to or involving the left atrium.[6, 45] Typically, pericardial mesothelioma presents with diffuse involvement of the pericardium (Fig. 32–35). Any cardiac involvement is usually superficial, and this finding is helpful in distinguishing mesothelioma from pericardial angiosarcoma, which typically has more extensive involvement of the heart.[19, 63]

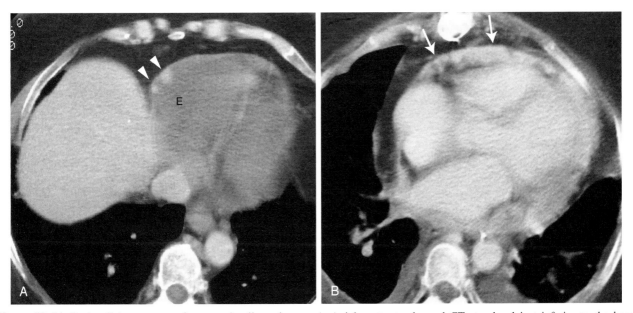

Figure 32–34. Pericardial metastases from renal cell carcinoma. *A,* Axial contrast-enhanced CT at a level just inferior to the heart shows a large pericardial effusion (E). Two soft tissue nodules are identified arising from the parietal pericardium *(arrowheads)*. *B,* Scan performed 6 months later shows filling of the pericardial space with enhancing soft tissue *(arrows)*.

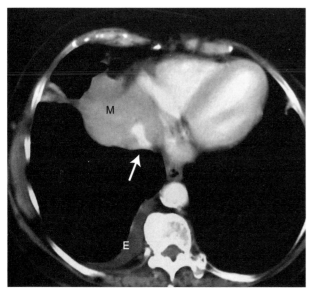

Figure 32–35. Pericardial mesothelioma. Axial contrast-enhanced CT scan shows a large mass (M) arising from the right pericardium, invading the right atrium, and encasing the inferior vena cava *(arrow)*. The patient was initially seen at an outside hospital, where the mass was thought to be arising from the lung. Bronchoscopic findings were negative. The patient was referred for biopsy. E, effusion.

References

1. Abrams DL, Edlelist A, Luria MD, Miller AJ: Ventricular aneurysm. Circulation 27:164–169, 1963.
2. Abushaban L, Denham B, Duff D: Ten-year review of cardiac tumours in childhood. Br Heart J 70:166–169, 1993.
3. Agatson AS, Janowitz WR, Hildner FJ, et al: Quantification of coronary artery calcium using ultrafast computed tomography. J Am Coll Cardiol 15:827–832, 1990.
4. Agner RC, Gallis HA: Pericarditis: Differential diagnostic considerations. Arch Intern Med 139:407–412, 1979.
5. Alam M: Pitfalls in the echocardiographic diagnosis of intracardiac and extracardiac masses. Echocardiography 10:181–191, 1993.
6. Araoz PA, Eklund HE, Welch TJ, Breen JF: CT and MR imaging of primary cardiac malignancies. Radiographics 19:1421–1434, 1999.
7. Araoz PA, Mulvagh SL, Tazelaar HD, et al: CT and MR imaging of benign primary cardiac neoplasms with echocardiographic correlation. Radiographics 20:1303–1319, 2000.
8. Aravot DJ, Banner NR, Cantor AM, et al: Location, localization and surgical treatment of cardiac pheochromocytoma. Am J Cardiol 69:283–285, 1992.
9. Aronberg DJ, Glazer HS, Sagel SS: MRI and CT of the mediastinum: Comparisons, controversies and pitfalls. Radiol Clin North Am 23:439–448, 1985.
10. Aronberg DJ, Peterson RR, Glazer HS, Sagel SS: The superior sinus of the pericardium: CT appearance. Radiology 153:489–492, 1984.
11. Becker CR, Jakobs TF, Aydemir S, et al: Helical and single-slice conventional CT versus electron beam CT for the quantification of coronary artery calcification. AJR Am J Roentgenol 174:543–547, 2000.
12. Bjessmo S, Ivert T: Cardiac myxoma: 40 years' experience in 63 patients. Ann Thorac Surg 63:697–700, 1997.
13. Black CM, Hedges LK, Javitt MC: The superior pericardial sinus: Normal appearance on gradient-echo MR images. AJR Am J Roentgenol 160:749–751, 1993.
14. Blankenhorn DH, Stern D: Calcification of the coronary arteries. Am J Roentgenol 81:772–777, 1959.
15. Breen JF, Sheedy PF, Schwartz RS, et al: Coronary artery calcification detected with ultrafast CT as an indication of coronary artery disease. Radiology 185:435–439, 1992.
16. Broderick LS, Shemesh J, Wilensky RL, et al: Measurement of coronary artery calcium with dual-slice helical CT compared with coronary angiography: Evaluation of CT scoring methods, interobserver variations, and reproducibility. AJR Am J Roentgenol 167: 439–444, 1996.
17. Broderick LS, Conces DJ Jr, Tarver RD: CT evaluation of normal interatrial fat thickness. J Comput Assist Tomogr 20:950–953, 1996.
18. Bull RK, Edwards PD, Dixon AK: CT dimensions of the normal pericardium. Br J Radiol 71:923–925, 1998.
19. Burke A, Virmani R: Tumors of the heart and great vessels. In Atlas of Tumor Pathology. Fascicle 16, Series 3. Washington, DC, Armed Forces Institute of Pathology, 1996.
20. Burke AP, Litovsky S, Virmani R: Lipomatous hypertrophy of the atrial septum presenting as a right atrial mass. Am J Surg Pathol 20:678–685, 1996.
21. Burke AP, Virmani R: Osteosarcomas of the heart. Am J Surg Pathol 15:289–295, 1991.
22. Burns MA, Molina PL, Gutiarrez FR, Sagel SS: Motion artifact simulating aortic dissection on CT. AJR Am J Roentgenol 157: 465–467, 1991.
23. Butany J, Yu W: Cardiac angiosarcoma: Two cases and a review of the literature. Can J Cardiol 16:197–205, 2000.
24. Callister TQ, Cooil B, Raya SP, et al: Coronary artery disease: Improved reproducibility of calcium scoring with an electron-beam CT volumetric method. Radiology 208:807–814, 1998.
25. Carney JA: The Carney complex (myxomas, spotty pigmentation, endocrine overactivity and schwannomas). Dermatol Clin 13:19–26, 1995.
26. Carr JJ, Crouse JR III, Goff DC Jr, et al: Evaluation of subsecond gated helical CT for quantification of coronary artery calcium and comparison with electron beam CT. AJR Am J Roentgenol 174: 915–921, 2000.
27. Chafke N, Kretz JG, Valentin P, et al: Clinical presentation and treatment options for mitral valve myxoma. Ann Thorac Surg 64: 872–877, 1997.
28. Chiles C, Baker ME, Silverman PM: Superior pericardial recess simulating aortic dissection on computed tomography. J Comput Assist Tomogr 10:421–423, 1986.
29. Choe YH, Im JG, Park JH, et al: The anatomy of the pericardial space: A study in cadavers and patients. AJR Am J Roentgenol 149: 693–697, 1987.
30. Corey GR, Campbell PT, van Trigt P, et al: Etiology of large pericardial effusions. Am J Med 95:209–213, 1993.
31. Delille JP, Hernigou A, Sene V, et al. Maximal thickness of the normal human pericardium assessed by electron-beam computed tomography. Eur Radiol 9:1183–1189, 2000.
32. Diflo T, Cantelmo NL, Haudenschild CC, Watkins MT: Atrial myxoma with remote metastasis: Case report and review of the literature. Surgery 111:352–356, 1992.
33. Dooms GC, Hricak H, Sollito RA, Higgins CB: Lipomatous tumors and tumors with fatty components: MR imaging potential and comparison of MR and CT results. Radiology 157:479–483, 1985.
34. Doppman JL, Rienmuller R, Lissner J: The visualized interventricular septum on cardiac computed tomography: A clue to the presence of severe anemia. J Comput Assist Tomogr 5:157–160, 1981.
35. Doyle MT, Spizarny DL, Baker DE: Saphenous vein graft aneurysm after coronary artery bypass surgery. AJR Am J Roentgenol 168: 747–749, 1997.
36. Duvernoy O, Coulden R, Ytterberg C: Aortic motion: A potential pitfall in CT imaging of dissection in the ascending aorta. J Comput Assist Tomogr 19:569–572, 1995.
37. Farooki ZQ, Ross RD, Paridon SM, et al: Spontaneous regression of cardiac rhabdomyoma. Am J Cardiol 67:897–899, 1991.
38. Fowler NO: Constrictive pericarditis: Its history and current status. Clin Cardiol 18:341–350, 1995.
39. Frances C, Romero, A, Grady D: Left ventricular pseudoaneurysm. J Am Coll Cardiol 32:557–561, 1998.
40. Gale ME, Kiewak MG, Hale DR: Pericardial fluid distribution: CT analysis. Radiology 162:171–174, 1987.
41. Glazer GM, Gross BH, Orringer MB, et al: Computed tomography of pericardial masses: Further observations and comparison with echocardiography. J Comput Assist Tomogr 8:895–899, 1984.
42. Grieco JG, Montoya A, Sullivan HJ, et al: Ventricular aneurysm due to blunt chest injury. Ann Thorac Surg 47:322–329, 1989.
43. Groell R, Schaffler GJ, Reinmueller R: Pericardial sinuses and recesses: Findings at elctrocardiographically triggered electron-beam CT. Radiology 212:69–73, 1999.

44. Guthaner DF, Wexler L, Harrell G: CT demonstration of cardiac structures. Am J Roentgenol 113:75, 1979.

45. Hamilton BH, Francis IR, Gross BH, et al: Intrapericardial paragangliomas (pheochromocytomas): Imaging features. AJR Am J Roentgenol 168:109–113, 1997.

46. Hancock EW, Disease of the pericardium. Cardiol Clin 8:673–682, 1990.

47. Herrmann MA, Shanderman RA, Edwards WD, et al: Primary cardiac angiosarcoma: A clinicopathologic study of six cases. J Thorac Cardiovasc Surg 103:655–664, 1992.

48. Hurst CO, Fine G, Keyes JW: Pseudoaneurysm of the heart: Report of a case and review of literature. Circulation 28:47–436, 1963.

49. Hutter AM, Page DL: Atrial arrhythmias and lipomatous hypertrophy of the cardiac interatrial septum. Am Heart J 82:16–21, 1971.

50. Jacob JLB, Souza AS Jr, Parro A: Absence of the left pericardium diagnosed by computed tomography. Int J Cardiol 47:293–296, 1995.

51. Kahn J, Risher MR: MRI of cardiac pseudoaneurysm and other complications of myocardial infarction. Magn Reson Imaging 9:159–164, 1991.

52. Klingenbeck-Regn K, Schaller S, Flohr T, et al: Subsecond multislice computed tomography: Basics and applications. Eur J Radiol 31:110–124, 1999.

53. Kralstein J, Frishman W: Malignant pericardial diseases: Diagnosis and treatment. Am Heart J 113:785–790, 1987.

54. Kuhlman JE, Teigen C, Ren H, et al: Amiodarone pulmonary toxicity: CT findings in symptomatic patients. Radiology 177:121–125, 1990.

55. Larsson S, Lepore V, Kennergren C: Atrial myxomas: Results of 25 years' experience and review of the literature. Surgery 105:695–698, 1989.

56. Levy-Ravetch M, Auh YH, Rubenstein WA, et al: CT of the pericardial recesses. Am J Roentgenol 144:707–714, 1985.

57. Lippert JA, White CS, Mason AC, Plotnick GD: Calcification of aortic valve detected incidentally on CT scans: Prevalence and clinical significance. AJR Am J Roentgenol 164:73–77, 1995.

58. Lipton MJ, Coulden R: Valvular heart disease. Radiol Clin North Am 37:319–339, 1999.

59. Maisch B: Pericardial diseases, with a focus on etiology, pathogenesis, pathophysiology, new diagnostic imaging methods, and treatment. Curr Opin Cardiol 9:379–388, 1994.

60. March KL, Sawada SG, Tarver RD, et al: Current concepts of left ventricular pseudoaneurysm: Pathophysiology, therapy and diagnostic imaging methods. Clin Cardiol 12:531–540, 1989.

61. Mason JW, Oates JA, Wood AJ: Drug therapy: Amiodarone. N Engl J Med 316:455–466, 1987.

62. Masuda Y, Naito S, Aoyagi Y, et al: Coronary artery calcification detected by CT: Clinical significance and angiographic correlates. Angiology 41:1037–1047, 1990.

63. McAllister HA, Fenoglio JJ: Tumors of the cardiovascular system. In Hartmann WH, Cowan WR (eds): Fascicles of the Armed Forces Institute of Pathology. Washington, DC, Armed Forces Institute of Pathology, 1977, pp 81–108.

64. McCarthy PM, Piehler JM, Schaff HV, et al: The significance of multiple recurrent and "complex" cardiac myxomas. J Thorac Cardiovasc Surg 91:389–396, 1986.

65. Meaney JF, Kazerooni EA, Jamadar DA, Korobkin M: CT appearance of lipomatous hypertrophy of the interatrial septum. AJR Am J Roentgenol 168:1081–1084, 1997.

66. Miller SW: Imaging pericardial disease. Radiol Clin North Am 27:1113–1125, 1989.

67. Millman A, Meller J, Motro M, et al: Pericardial tumor or fibrosis mimicking pericardial effusion by echocardiography. Ann Intern Med 86:434–436, 1977.

68. Mochizuki T, Murase K, Higashino H, et al: Two- and three-dimensional CT ventriculography: A new application of helical CT. AJR Am J Roentgenol 174:203–208, 2000.

69. Mukher JI, Varma P, Stark P: Motion artifact simulating aortic dissection on CT. AJR Am J Roentgenol 159:674, 1992.

70. Oliva PB, Hammill SC, Edwards WD: Cardiac rupture, a clinically predictable complication of acute myocardial infarction: Report of 70 cases with clinicopathologic correlations. J Am Coll Cardiol 22:720–726, 1993.

71. Olson MC, Posniak HV, McDonald V, et al: Computed tomography and magnetic resonance imaging of the pericardium. Radiographics 9:633–649, 1989.

72. Page DL: Lipomatous hypertrophy of the cardiac interatrial septum: Its development and probable clinical significance. Hum Pathol 1:151–163, 1970.

73. Paling MR, Williamson BR: Epipericardial fat pad: CT findings. Radiology 165:335–339, 1987.

74. Pappas G, Paton B, Davies H: Nonmycotic subvalvular aneurysms after aortic valve replacement. J Cardiovasc Surg 63:925–929, 1972.

75. Prior JR: Lipomatous hypertrophy of the cardiac interatrial septum. Arch Pathol 78:11–15, 1964.

76. Protopapas Z, Westcott JL: Left pulmonic recess of the pericardium: Findings at CT and MR imaging. Radiology 196:85–88, 1995.

77. Qizilbash AH, Schwartz CJ: False aneurysm of left ventricle due to perforation of mitral-aortic intervalvular fibrosa with rupture and cardiac tamponade. Am J Cardiol 32:110–113, 1973.

78. Radin R, Kempf RA: Carney complex: Report of three cases. Radiology 196:383–386, 1995.

79. Reddy GP, Steiner RM: Aneurysm of saphenous vein coronary bypass graft: Diagnosis by computed tomography. 14:147–149, 1999.

80. Reyes CV, Jablokow VR: Lipomatous hypertrophy of the cardiac interatrial septum: A report of 38 cases and review of the literature. Am J Clin Pathol 72:785–788, 1979.

81. Reynen K: Cardiac myxomas. N Engl J Med 333:1610–1617, 1995.

82. Rienmuller R, Gurgan M, Erdmann E, et al: CT and MR evaluation of pericardial constriction: A new diagnostic and therapeutic concept. J Thorac Imaging 8:108–121, 1993.

83. Rifkin RD, Parisi AF, Folland E: Coronary calcification in the diagnosis of coronary artery disease. Am J Cardiol 44:141–147, 1979.

84. Ritoo D, Sutherland GR: Posterior left ventricular pseudoaneurysm after aortic valve replacement in a patient with rheumatoid arthritis: Diagnosis by transesophageal echocardiography. J Am Soc Echocardiogr 7:429–433, 1994.

85. Roberts CS, Roberts WC: Dissection of the aorta associated with congenital malformation of the aortic valve. J Am Coll Cardiol 17:712–716, 1991.

86. Rozenshtein A, Boxt LM: Computed tomography and magnetic resonance imaging of patients with valvular heart disease. J Thorac Imaging 15:252–264, 2000.

87. Rumberger JA, Brundage BH, Rader DJ, Kondos G: Electron beam computed tomographic coronary calcium scanning: A review and guidelines for use in asymptomatic persons. Mayo Clin Proc 74:243–252, 1999.

88. Sabet HY, Edwards WD, Tazelaar HD, Daly RC: Congenitally bicuspid aortic valves: A surgical pathology study of 542 cases (1991 through 1996) and a literature review of 2,715 additional cases. Mayo Clin Proc 74:14–26, 1999.

89. Sakai K, Nakamura K, Ishizuka N, et al: Echocardiographic findings and clinical features of left ventricular pseudoaneurysm after mitral valve replacement. Am Heart J 124:975–982, 1992.

90. Salcedo EE, Cohen GI, White RD, Davison MB: Cardiac tumors: Diagnosis and management. Curr Probl Cardiol 17:73–137, 1992.

91. Schlesinger E, Fernbach SK: Pericardial effusion presenting as an anterior mediastinal mass. Pediatr Radiol 16:65–66, 1986.

92. Sebastia C, Pallisa E, Quiroga S, et al: Aortic dissection: Diagnosis and follow-up with helical CT. RadioGraphics 19:45–60, 1999.

93. Seelos KC, Caputo GR, Carrol CL, et al: Cine gradient refocused echo (GRE) imaging of intravascular masses: differentiation between tumor and nontumor thrombus. J Comput Assist Tomogr 16:169–172, 1992.

94. Shemesh J, Apter S, Rozenman J, et al: Calcification of coronary arteries: Detection and quantification with double-helix CT. Radiology 197:779–783, 1995.

95. Shemesh J, Tenenbaum A, Kopecky KK, et al: Coronary calcium measurements by double helical computed tomography: Using the average instead of peak density algorithm improves reproducibility. Invest Radiol 32:503–506, 1997.

96. Shin MS, Jolles PR, Ho KJ: CT evaluation of distended pericardial recess presenting as a mediastinal mass. J Comput Assist Tomogr 10:860–862, 1986.

97. Smith HC, Watson GH, Patel RG, Super M: Cardiac rhabdomyomata in tuberous sclerosis: Their course and diagnostic value. Arch Dis Child 64:196–200, 1989.

98. Sorlie D, Myhre ESP, Stalsberg H: Angiosarcoma of the heart: Unusual presentation and survival after treatment. Br Heart J 51:94–97, 1984.

99. Spindola-Franco H, Kronacher N: Pseudoaneurysm of the left ventricle. Radiology 127:29–34, 1978.

100. Stewart S, Huddle R, Stueard I, et al: False aneurysm and pseudofalse aneurysm of the left ventricle: Etiology, pathology, diagnosis, and operative management. Ann Thorac Surg 31:259–265, 1981.

101. Tagasuki JE, Godwin JD: Surgical defects of the pericardium: Radiographic findings. AJR Am J Roentgenol 152:951–954, 1989.

102. Tamiya E, Matsui H, Nakajima T, et al: Detection of coronary artery calcification by x-ray computed tomography and its significance: A new CT scoring technique. Angiology 43:22–31, 1992.

103. Tenebaum A, Shemesh J, Fisman EZ, Motro M: Advanced mitral annular calcification is associated with severe coronary calcification on fast dual spiral computed tomography. Invest Radiol 35:193–198, 2000.

104. Tofler GH, Muller JE, Stone PH, et al: Pericarditis in acute myocardial infarction: Characterization and clinical significance. Am Heart J 117:86–90, 1989.

105. Trop I, Samson L, Cordeau MP, et al: Anterior mediastinal mass in a patient with prior saphenous vein coronary artery bypass grafting. Chest 115:572–576, 1999.

106. Tuna IC, Julsrud PR, Click RL, et al: Tissue characterization of an unusual right atrial mass by magnetic resonance imaging. Mayo Clin Proc 66:498–501, 1991.

107. van Gelder HM, O'Brien DJ, Staples ED, Alexander JA: Familial cardiac myxoma. Ann Thorac Surg 53:419–424, 1992.

108. van Son JAM, Danielson GK, Schaff HV, et al: Congenital partial and complete absence of the pericardium. Mayo Clin Proc 68:743–747, 1993.

109. van Tassel RA, Edwards JE: Rupture of heart complicating myocardial infarction: Analysis of 40 cases including nine examples of left ventricular false aneurysm. Chest 61:104–116, 1972.

110. Webb DW, Thomas RD, Osborne JP: Cardiac rhabdomyomas and their association with tuberous sclerosis. Arch Dis Child 68:367–370, 1993.

111. Widimsky P, Gregor P: Pericardial involvement during the course of myocardial infarction. 1995 108:89–93, Chest.

112. Wojtowicz J, Rzymski K, Czarnecki R: Severe anaemia: Its CT findings in the cardiovascular system. Eur J Radiol 3:108–111, 1983.

113. Woodhouse CE, Janowitz WR, Viamonte M Jr: Coronary arteries: Retrospective cardiac gating technique to reduce cardiac motion artifact at spiral CT. Radiology 204:566–9, 1997.

114. Woodring JH, West JW: CT of aortic and mitral valve calcification. J Ky Med Assoc 87:177–180, 1989.

115. Wychulis AR, Connolly DC, McGoon DC: Pericardial cysts, tumors and fat necrosis. J Thorac Cardiovasc Surg 62:294–300, 1971.

116. Yeo TC, Malouf JF, Oh JK, Seward JB: Clinical profile and outcome in 52 patients with cardiac pseudoaneurysm. Ann Intern Med 128:299–305, 1998.

117. Yoon HC, Greaser LE, Mather R, et al: Coronary artery calcium: Alternate methods for accurate and reproducible quantitation. Acad Radiol 4:666–673, 1997.

118. Zingas AP, Carrera JD, Murray CA, Kling GA: Lipoma of the myocardium. J Comput Assist Tomogr 7:1098–1100, 1983.

33

Magnetic Resonance Imaging of the Heart

Anna Rozenshtein, Lawrence M. Boxt

Magnetic resonance imaging (MRI) provides diagnostic morphologic and functional information for the evaluation and management of patients with congenital and acquired cardiovascular disease. The usefulness of cardiac MRI lies in adaptation of motion-suppression techniques to cancel out complex cardiac contractile motion. Thus, the most important difference between cardiac and other-organ MRI is the application of electrocardiographic (ECG) gating to the acquisition pulse sequence to suppress contraction-motion artifacts. ECG gating acts by applying a timing signal coincident with cardiac motion to image acquisition.[160, 161, 168, 322] That is, by timing each phase-encoding step in an MRI acquisition to a particular point in the ECG cycle of the heart, reconstructed images are temporally coherent. By convention, the R-wave is chosen as the gating signal because it has the greatest voltage and is therefore easily identified from the ECG (Fig. 33–1). In addition, because the peak of the R-wave indicates the commencement of electromechanical ventricular contraction, images immediately following the R-wave are obtained at ventricular end-diastole, a time when the ventricles are most dilated.

For an image containing N-phase encoding steps, N cardiac cycles, or heartbeats, are needed to acquire an image at one particular phase of the cardiac cycle. Improved acquisition software provides more efficient use of the cardiac cycle. That is, by pulsing several anatomic levels, each at different delays after the R-wave, we can perform multisection spin-echo acquisition.

Short, flip-angle, gradient-echo cine *(cine) imaging*[226, 272] allows acquisition of images of the heart with greater temporal resolution, permitting evaluation of ventricular function, valvular regurgitation or stenosis, and abnormal hemodynamics in congenital heart lesions. When this pulse

sequence is used, the same anatomic section is excited with radiofrequency (RF) pulses using a short repetition time (TR) of 5 to 15 msec. The temporal resolution of the examination depends on the repetition time and heart rate. That is, a faster heart rate results in a shorter ECG RR interval (the time between R-waves) and, for any given number of discrete phases of the cardiac cycle, less time between phases. After a fixed number of excitations, the imaging system waits for the next R-wave to advance to the next phase-encoding step.

In some circumstances, an adequate ECG tracing may not be obtained before the examination is begun. This may occur in patients with low cardiac voltage, such as in pericardial effusion. In these individuals, an adequate gating signal may be obtained by application of a peripheral pulse sensor. Peripheral pulse gating (PPG) produces images of diagnostic quality, but one must take care to visually inspect imagery prior to functional analysis. That is, the peak of the peripheral pulse, the timing signal for image acquisition, is delayed in time from the ECG R-wave. Therefore, series of gradient-reversal images do not begin with the end-diastolic image and run through the cardiac cycle toward end-systole. Rather, the first image in each acquisition is obtained at a variable delay after end-diastole. Thus, the series of images acquired at each anatomic level begins somewhere in the cardiac cycle and passes through end-diastole and end-systole, out of phase with a conventionally acquired ECG-gated acquisition. The delay between the ECG R-wave and the peak of the peripheral pulse is a function of the distance between the heart and the monitored extremity artery as well as the biomechanical properties of the aorta and its branches. Series of images obtained using PPG may be of diagnostic quality for morphologic analysis, but cine examinations obtained with PPG should be analyzed with caution.

Recent advances in image-acquisition software have greatly reduced imaging time and allowed acquisition of images during a single breath-hold, thus eliminating motion artifacts and the need for respiratory gating. This is true for the gradient-echo cine acquisitions, as well as the relatively new sequences ideally adapted for morphologic imaging, such as double-inversion recovery techniques.

The high-contrast resolution of spin-echo acquisition (see appendices at the end of this chapter) allows confident differentiation between intraventricular blood and myocardium, necessary for detailed analysis of the epicardial and endocardial borders.[137] Acquisition of gradient-echo cine imagery in the axial plane displays the character of ventricular contraction, including the orientation of the interven-

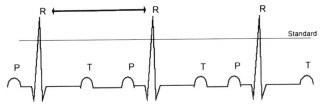

Figure 33–1. Diagram of three beats from a stereotypic electrocardiographic (ECG) strip. The P-, R-, and T-waves are labeled. The RR interval is defined as the time between cardiac cycles and is chosen for the repetition time (TR) in ECG-gated acquisitions. The standard is an arbitrary voltage used for comparison with the ECG voltage. Any signal whose voltage is greater than the standard is chosen as the R-wave for gating purposes.

tricular septum, and the status of the cardiac valves. The high temporal resolution of cine gradient-echo acquisition allows acquisition of ventricular imagery at both end-diastole and end-systole. From these acquisitions, ventricular cavitary volume[29, 86, 180, 205, 271, 292] and myocardial mass[141, 142] may be calculated.

Because MRI requires no assumptions about the shape of the ventricular chamber, end-diastolic and end-systolic ventricular chamber volume is obtained directly by calculating the sum of planimetered ventricular cavity areas times slice thickness through the entire chamber. Left and right ventricular end-diastolic and end-systolic volumes may be calculated, and from these data, stroke volume (the difference between end-diastolic and end-systolic volume),

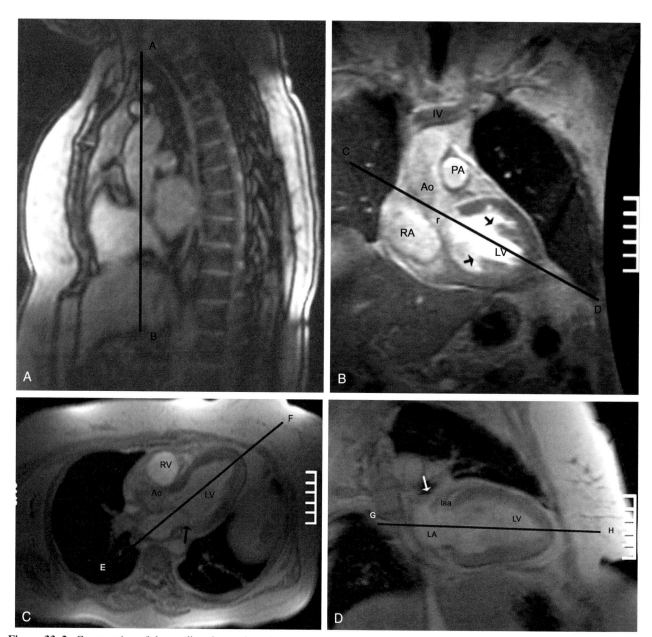

Figure 33–2. Construction of the cardiac short axis and analysis of cavity volume and myocardial mass.

A, Sagittal scout image obtained through the posterior right sinus of Valsalva. From this image, an acquisition is obtained in the coronal plane AB.

B, Coronal scout image through the posterior right sinus of Valsalva (r). The two papillary muscles *(arrows)* are well demonstrated. The innominate vein (IV), main pulmonary artery (PA), ascending aorta (Ao), and right atrium (RA) are labeled. From this image, an oblique axial image is prescribed in plane CD through the aortic valve and left ventricular (LV) apex.

C, The anteroposterior rotation of the heart is compensated for by prescribing a plane (EF) through the mitral valve *(arrow)* and the left ventricular (LV) apex. The right ventricle (RV) and the aortic root (Ao) are labeled.

D, In this section, the line (GH) drawn between the middle of the mitral valve and the apex of the left ventricle (LV) defines the long axis of the LV, its axis of rotation. Images obtained at right angles to this line are in the cardiac short axis. The left atrium (LA), the left upper lobe pulmonary artery *(long arrow),* and the ostium of the left atrial appendage (laa) are labeled.

ejection fraction (stroke volume divided by end-diastolic volume), and cardiac output (stroke volume × heart rate) may be computed (Fig. 33–2).

In a similar manner, ventricular mass is obtained by summing the volume of myocardium in each image slice over the entire heart. For each tomographic slice, the myocardial volume is the difference between the areas of the epicardial and the endocardial borders times the slice thickness. The sum of the volumes of myocardium times the specific gravity of myocardium (1.05 g/mL) is the myocardial mass.

In principle, these computations can be performed using images obtained in any anatomic section. In practice, however, images obtained in the cardiac short axis are usually used for this purpose. Thus, MRI not only reliably demonstrates morphologic ventricular abnormalities but also allows quantitation of ventricular function (Table 33–1) under pathologic conditions.

In this chapter, we review the use of ECG-gated spin-echo and cine gradient-echo MRI techniques for the diagnosis and evaluation of patients with congenital and acquired heart disease. The clinical role of MRI in the management of these patients differs from medical institution to institution. Availability of MRI scanners configured for cardiac imaging, availability of trained personnel to scan and interpret examinations, and patient referral patterns all affect the volume of clinical cardiac MRI performed at any institution. Nevertheless, the volume of

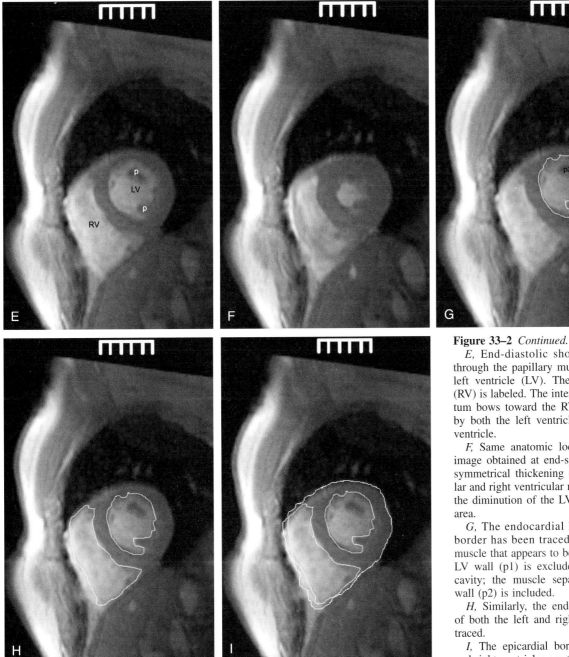

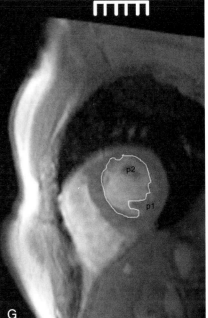

Figure 33–2 *Continued.*

E, End-diastolic short-axis section through the papillary muscles (p) of the left ventricle (LV). The right ventricle (RV) is labeled. The interventricular septum bows toward the RV and is shared by both the left ventricle and the right ventricle.

F, Same anatomic location, as in *E,* image obtained at end-systole. Note the symmetrical thickening of left ventricular and right ventricular myocardium and the diminution of the LV and RV cavity area.

G, The endocardial left ventricular border has been traced. The papillary muscle that appears to be attached to the LV wall (p1) is excluded from the LV cavity; the muscle separated from the wall (p2) is included.

H, Similarly, the endocardial borders of both the left and right ventricles are traced.

I, The epicardial borders of the left and right ventricles are traced.

TABLE 33–1. Left and Right Ventricular Cavity (Volume, Mass, and Derived Values Indexed for Body Surface Area)

Index	Value
Right Ventricle	
End diastolic volume index (RVEDVI)	67.9 ± 13.4 mL/M^2
End systolic volume index (RVESVI)	27.9 ± 7.5 mL/M^2
Stroke volume index (RVSVI)	40.1 ± 9.7 mL/M^2
Ejection fraction (RVEF)	0.59 ± 0.09
Mass index	23.3 ± 1.4 g/M^2
Left Ventricle	
End diastolic volume index (LVEDVI)	68.9 ± 13.1 mL/M^2
End systolic volume index (LVESVI)	27.1 ± 7.8 mL/M^2
Stroke volume index (LVSVI)	41.8 ± 10.9 mL/M^2
Ejection fraction (LVEF)	0.60 ± 0.11 g/M^2
Mass index	91.6 ± 3.2 g/M^2

Data from Boxt LM, Katz J, Kolb T, et al: J Am Coll Cardiol 19: 1508–1515, 1992; and Katz J, Whang J, Boxt LM, Barst RJ: J Am Coll Cardiol 21: 1475–1481, 1993.

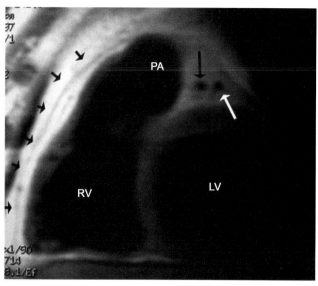

Figure 33–3. Short-axis section from a patient without cardiac disease. The right ventricle (RV), main pulmonary artery (PA), and left ventricular cavity (LV) are labeled. The signal voids of the anterior descending *(long black arrow)* and circumflex *(long white arrow)* coronary arteries are identified. The pencil-thin signal void of the anterior aspect of the pericardial space *(short black arrows)* extends to the top of the pulmonary artery.

cardiac MRI cases performed is increasing, and examinations are performed and interpreted at more and more institutions.

This chapter is best used as a handbook for planning, performing, and interpreting a cardiac MRI study. As the reader will find, although much has indeed been said, much has also been left out. We have made few comments about pulse-sequence parameters. These are set at each site during installation and applications training on the scanner. On the other hand, we pay much attention to pathophysiologic mechanisms and their effect on cardiac morphology and function as displayed in MR images. Our decided emphasis on the medical aspects of the cardiac diseases studied by MRI is intended not only to point out the usefulness of MRI in evaluating the heart but also to help radiologists in planning, performing, and interpreting cardiac MR images with a basic collection of medical data to engage in this practice.

Pericardial Diseases

The pericardium consists of the visceral pericardium (epicardium), the parietal pericardium, and the 20- to 60-mL cavity contained between them. The epicardium is a monolayer of mesothelial cells that covers the external surface of the heart. Beneath the epicardium is either myocardium or epicardial fat. This layer extends for short distances along the pulmonary veins, the superior vena cava below the azygos vein, the inferior vena cava, the ascending aorta to a point 20 to 30 mm above the root, and the main pulmonary artery as far as its bifurcation. It then reflects on itself to become the parietal pericardium, which is a 1-mm-thick outer fibrous layer composed of dense collagen lined on the inside by a monolayer of mesothelial cells.

The visceral pericardium is normally thin and is therefore not visualized separately by any imaging modality. The combination of the visceral pericardium and the small volume of physiologic pericardial fluid constitutes the normal pericardium routinely visualized on MR images as a 1- to 2-mm-thick layer[274, 290] (Fig. 33–3) that can appear focally thicker at the sites of its major attachments. On

spin-echo MRI scans, the normal pericardium appears as a pencil-thin line of low signal intensity between the epicardial and pericardial fat. The low signal intensity is attributed to the fibrous nature of the parietal pericardium, the low protein content of pericardial fluid,[317] and the nonlaminar flow patterns caused by cardiac pulsation.[309]

The reflection of pericardium around the great arteries and veins forms the two pericardial "appendages." Anterior to the aorta this contiguous pericardial space is called the *preaortic recess*; posteriorly, it is called the *retroaortic* or *superior pericardial recess* (Fig. 33–4). Posterior and lateral to the heart, the extraparenchymal pulmonary veins and the superior and inferior venae cavae are enveloped by the venous mesocardium, which has the shape of an inverted U. The intrapericardial space between the pulmonary veins is called the *oblique sinus*. It is essential to appreciate the anatomic extent and location of these pericardial sinuses because they are normally seen on MRI[134, 194] and may be confused with adenopathy[5, 165] or aortic dissection.[55, 165]

Congenital Absence of the Pericardium

Congenital absence of the pericardium is a malformation that is thought to be due to compromise of the vascular supply to the pleuropericardial membrane that surrounds the ventral cardiac tube during embryologic development. Pericardial defects may vary in size from small communications between the pleural and pericardial cavities to complete (bilateral) absence of the pericardium. The most common form is complete absence of the left pericardium, with preservation of the pericardium on the right.

Noninvasive modalities, such as contrast-enhanced CT

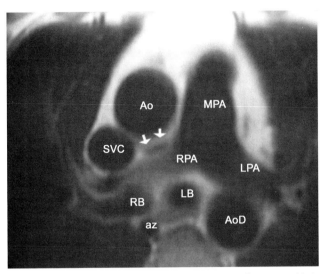

Figure 33–4. Axial spin-echo image. The ascending aorta (Ao), descending aorta (AoD), main pulmonary artery (MPA), left pulmonary artery (LPA), superior vena cava (SVC), left bronchi (LB), right bronchi (RB), and azygos vein (az) are labeled. The superior pericardial recess is seen as a signal void *(arrows)* behind the ascending aorta and anterior to the right pulmonary artery (RPA).

and MRI, have replaced diagnostic pneumothorax and cardiac angiography as the methods of choice[18, 118, 266] for definitive diagnosis of this abnormality. In particular, the multiplanar capabilities of MRI allow direct identification of the absent segment of the parietal pericardium, demonstration of contact between the heart and lung,[118] or recognition of profound leftward displacement and rotation of the heart in the chest (Fig. 33–5).

Pericardial Cysts and Diverticula

If a portion of the pericardium pinches off from pleuropericardial membrane during embryologic development, a cyst forms, containing the same mesothelial lining as the normal pericardium. Similarly, a pericardial diverticulum is a failed cyst; communication with the pleural space persists (Fig. 33–6). Both lesions appear on spin-echo MRI acquisition as fluid-filled[273] paracardiac masses whose signal intensity increases in subsequent multiecho spin-echo images.[273] Gradient-echo acquisition reveals isointensity with rapidly moving blood.

Acquired Pericardial Disease

Normal pericardium most commonly responds to insult by cellular proliferation or the production of fluid or fibrin;

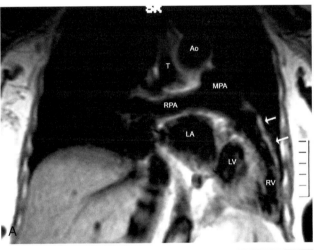

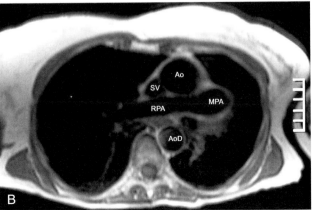

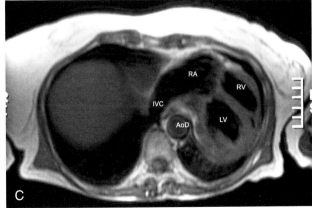

Figure 33–5. Congenital absence of the pericardium. *A,* Coronal spin-echo acquisition. The aortic arch (Ao) displaces the trachea (T) to the right. The aortic arch, the main pulmonary artery (MPA), and, in fact, the entire heart, are displaced into the left chest. Despite the apparent size of the MPA, the right ventricular (RV) cavity appears normal and the RV free wall myocardium *(arrows)* is of normal thickness. LV, left ventricle; RPA, right pulmonary artery. *B,* Axial spin-echo acquisition through the main pulmonary artery (MPA) and right pulmonary artery (RPA). The ascending aorta (Ao) and the main pulmonary artery are displaced toward the left. The MPA is smaller in caliber than the ascending aorta, indicating no increase in pulmonary blood flow. AoD, descending aorta; SV, superior vena cava. *C,* Axial spin-echo image through the cavities of the right ventricle (RV) and left ventricle (LV). Not only is the heart displaced into the left chest; it is rotated in a clockwise manner. AoD, descending aorta; IVC, inferior vena cava; RA, right atrium.

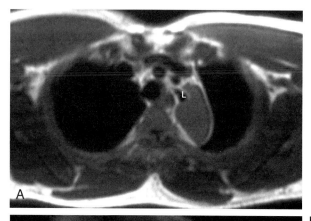

Figure 33–6. Pericardial diverticulum. Spin-echo acquisitions of a widened mediastinum in a 48-year-old man. *A,* In an axial section, an intermediate-signal-intensity mass, itself surrounded by fat, surrounds the left subclavian artery (L). TR = 485 msec, TE = 20 msec. *B* and *C,* Right anterior oblique sagittal section. TR = 485. Multi-echo acquisition; TE in *B,* 20 msec, TE in *C* = 30 msec. *B,* In this first-echo image, the intermediate-signal-intensity mass is again demonstrated. *C,* In this second-echo image, the signal intensity of all structures has decreased, whereas the signal intensity of the mass has apparently increased, indicating a fluid-filled cyst. At operation, continuity with the pericardial space was demonstrated, defining the mass as a diverticulum.

these responses can happen independently or in combination.[251] The most common manifestation of acute pericarditis is an effusion. The fluid may be serous with a clear transudate, or exudate, varying in nature with the underlying cause. Transudative pericardial effusion may develop after cardiac surgery[319] or in congestive heart failure, uremia, postpericardiectomy syndrome,[140] myxedema, and collagen vascular diseases. Hemopericardium may be found in trauma, aortic dissection, aortic rupture,[196] or neoplasm (especially primary pericardial mesothelioma).[3] Chylopericardium resulting from injury or obstruction of the thoracic duct is rare.

MRI is helpful for characterizing pericardial effusions. On spin-echo examination hemorrhagic effusion presents as areas of mixed low, intermediate, and high signal intensity, depending on the age of blood products (Fig. 33–7). Nonhemorrhagic effusions on spin-echo MRI have predominantly low signal intensity (Fig. 33–8),[273] as a result of spin

phase change[309] of the pericardial fluid. Gradient-echo MRI sequences display freely mobile pericardial fluid that has high signal intensity. Inflammatory effusion, as seen in uremia, tuberculosis, or trauma, may have medium-signal-intensity components[142, 273] on spin-echo MRI, especially in dependent areas.[142] It has been suggested[273] that the latter may be due to high-protein content of inflammatory pericardial fluid.[251] Furthermore, because adhesions are common in pericardial inflammation, inflammatory effusions may not have the normal free-flow patterns of pericardial fluid that may lead to loci of increased signal intensity on spin-echo MRI, similar in appearance to loculated pericardial effusions (Fig. 33–9). Despite these complex signal characteristics, MRI helps in distinguishing inflammatory pericardial thickening and adhesions from fluid accumulation (intermediate versus predominantly low signal intensity).[142, 273] Fibrous pericardial thickening appears as a low-signal-intensity band surrounding the heart. Pericardial inflammation, as seen in

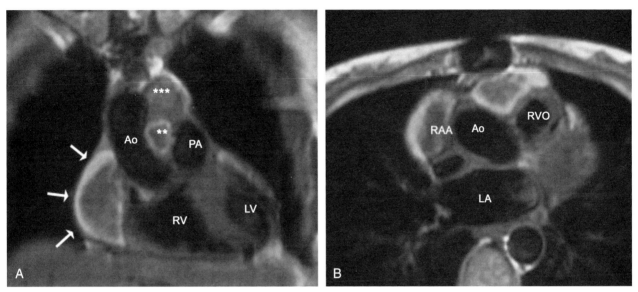

Figure 33–7. MR images obtained from a 53-year-old man who received a heart transplant 36 hours earlier, now with a widened mediastinum and cardiac silhouette. *A,* Coronal spin-echo acquisition shows a rim of increased signal intensity *(arrows)* surrounding the lateral border of the right atrium, above the top (**) of the main pulmonary artery (PA), and in the space between the ascending aorta (Ao) and pulmonary artery (***). LV, left ventricle; RV, right ventricle. *B,* Axial section through the right ventricular outflow tract (RVO). Increased signal intensity surrounds the right atrial appendage (RAA) and is insinuated between the ascending aorta (Ao) and RVO. LA, left atrium.

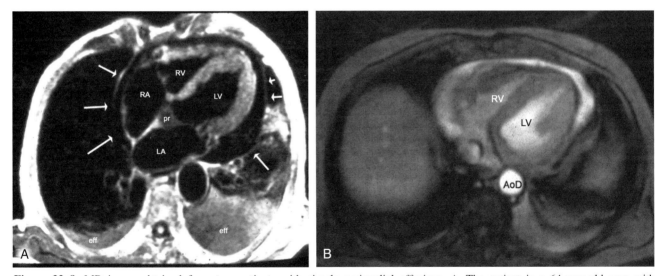

Figure 33–8. MR image obtained from two patients with simple pericardial effusions. *A,* The patient is a 64-year-old man with progressive shortness of breath. In this oblique axial section through the posterior right aortic sinus of Valsalva (pr), the parietal pericardium *(arrows)* is separated from the epicardial surfaces of the heart. The left ventricle (LV), right ventricle (RV), left atrium (LA), and right atrium (RA) are labeled. Note the bilateral pericardial effusions (eff) as well. *B,* In this axial gradient-echo acquisition (in another patient), the high-signal-intensity serous pericardial fluid surrounds the heart. AoD, descending aorta; LV, left ventricle; RV, right ventricle.

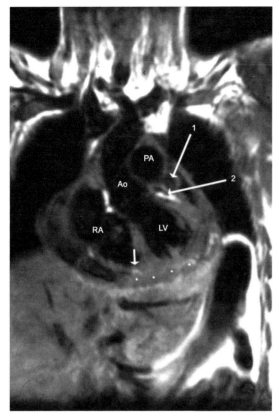

Figure 33–9. Complex pericardial thickening and loculated effusion in pericarditis. Coronal spin-echo acquisition demonstrates increased signal intensity within the pericardial space *(* * * *)* external to the epicardial fat along the inferior aspect *(arrow)* of the right atrium (RA) and left ventricle (LV). In addition, note how thick the pericardium is as it reflects on the main pulmonary artery segment (PA) and ascending aorta (Ao). The left atrial appendage *(arrow 1)* is contained within the pericardium. The proximal left anterior descending coronary artery *(arrow 2)* is identified.

ular function. In most cases, constrictive pericarditis involves the entire pericardium, compromising filling of all cardiac chambers. Occasionally, however, local chronic pericardial thickening has been reported.[54, 214] Focal pericardial thickening is more commonly seen in the postoperative patient and is frequently located anterior to the right ventricle.[184] The clinical findings of constrictive pericarditis overlap with those of restrictive cardiomyopathy, a primary disorder of the myocardium. Differentiation between these two entities is imperative because patients with pericardial constriction may benefit from pericardiectomy[231]; myocardial restriction may be rapidly progressive and necessitate cardiac transplantation.

Symptomatic pericardial constriction can be seen in the absence of conventional radiographically detectable pericardial thickening, however. Masui and associates[184] found pericardial thickening on MR images in 88% of cases of proven constrictive pericarditis. Pericardial thickening is not diagnostic of pericardial constriction[273]; demonstration of pericardial thickening greater than 4 mm (Figs. 33–11 and 33–12) in the face of characteristic hemodynamic findings distinguishes constrictive pericarditis from restrictive cardiomyopathy.[184, 273] Normal pericardium on MR[290] is less than 4 mm in thickness.

ECG-gated spin-echo MRI is an ideal method of investigating the pericardium.[134, 142, 194, 273, 290] It is exquisitely sensitive to changes in pericardial thickness as well as to morphologic and functional changes in the atria and ventricles resulting from focal or diffuse pericardial disease. In pericardial constriction, the right ventricle may appear tubular (see Fig. 33–12).[287] Gradient-echo acquisition demonstrates decreased right ventricular contractile function and limited diastolic excursion, common to both restriction and constriction. Dilatation of the right atrium, venae cavae, coronary sinus, and hepatic veins, reflecting right heart failure, may be seen in patients with constrictive pericarditis as well as in patients with restrictive cardiomyopathy.

uremic or tuberculous pericarditis or trauma following resuscitation, appears as increased signal intensity compared with myocardium on spin-echo MRI acquisition (Fig. 33–10).[273]

Pericardial Tamponade

Gradual accumulation of pericardial fluid may not produce clinical signs or symptoms. However, rapid accumulation of as little as 100 to 200 mL of fluid can impede diastolic ventricular filling. Pericardial tamponade is a condition in which reduced stroke volume limits maintenance of cardiac output. MRI is often instrumental in suggesting the cause of the effusion (i.e., hemorrhage, neoplastic involvement, inflammation due to tuberculosis or other infectious processes) in this acutely emergent situation.

Pericardial Constriction

The hallmarks of pericardial constriction are pericardial thickening and calcification and abnormal diastolic ventric-

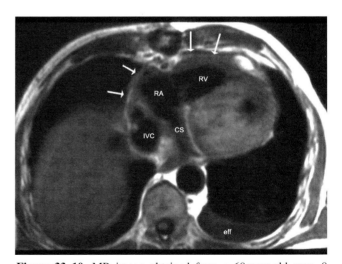

Figure 33–10. MR image obtained from a 68-year-old man, 8 years after coronary artery bypass surgery, who is now complaining of shortness of breath. There is a left pleural effusion (eff). Thickened pericardium *(arrows)* surrounds the lateral aspects of the right atrium (RA) and the anterior aspect of the tubular right ventricle (RV). The coronary sinus (CS) is mildly dilated. IVC, inferior vena cava.

Calcium does not produce an MRI signal. Therefore, on spin-echo MRI, calcification appears as loci of irregular signal voids separating the epicardial and pericardial fat. In constrictive pericarditis, the circumcardiac signal void of the pericardial space is irregular and can be identified in more images and different sections.[287]

Spin-echo and gradient-echo MRI also can accurately evaluate the thickness of the posterior left ventricular wall in patients with constrictive pericarditis. The latter has prognostic significance, because the most common cause of myocardial dysfunction after pericardiectomy is myocardial atrophy.[76] Radiographic demonstration of thinning of the free wall of the left ventricle due to myocardial atrophy was associated with markedly increased mortality after pericardiectomy.[240, 241]

Pericardial Neoplasms

The wide field of view, excellent contrast resolution, and multiplanar capability of MRI make it a method of choice for the diagnosis and evaluation of pericardial neoplasms.[2, 19, 173, 247] Primary pericardial neoplasms are rare. Malignant mesothelioma is the most common primary pericardial malignancy. Primary pericardial lymphoma has also been reported.[267] Teratomas of the pericardium may also be malignant and are most commonly seen in children.

Whether from lymphangitic or hematogenous spread or by direct invasion, pericardial metastases are uncommon[58, 318] and, when found, are usually associated with widespread malignant disease.[69] Metastatic breast carcinoma is the most common pericardial malignancy in women; metastatic lung carcinoma is the most common in men. These lesions are followed in incidence by lymphoproliferative malignancies and melanoma.[69]

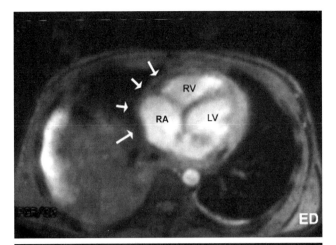

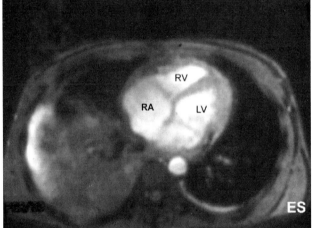

Figure 33–12. MR images obtained from a 23-year-old college student with shortness of breath. The upper gradient-echo acquisition obtained at ventricular end-diastole (ED) shows pericardial thickening increasing the distance between the cavity of the right atrium and the lateral aspect of the heart *(arrows)*. The lower figure obtained at end-systole (ES) shows little change in the volume of the ventricles and a characteristic tubular appearance of the right ventricle (RV). Bilateral pleural effusion is evident. LV, left ventricle.

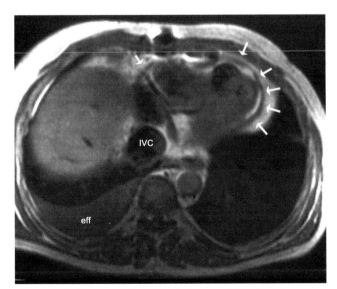

Figure 33–11. Pericardial constriction. Axial spin-echo image obtained at the dome of the right hemidiaphragm in a 59-year-old man with previous coronary artery bypass surgery reveals irregular thickening of the pericardium *(arrows)* extending from the atrioventricular ring to the posterior left ventricular wall. Note the right pericardial effusion (eff) and dilated inferior vena cava (IVC).

Pericardial effusion is the most common finding in patients with pericardial malignancy. Uncomplicated free-flowing pericardial fluid demonstrates low signal intensity on T1-weighted spin-echo MRI sequences (see Figs. 33–7 to 33–9).[273, 297] Hemorrhagic effusion, frequently associated with primary malignant mesotheliomas,[3] may present as areas of high, low, or medium signal intensity, depending on the age of hemorrhage.[273]

Focal or generalized pericardial thickening may also be found in patients with malignant pericardial involvement. Direct invasion can be inferred if the normally pencil-thin pericardium appears thickened or interrupted in close proximity to a neoplasm (Fig. 33–13). MRI is useful in suggesting the origin of the neoplasm. Intrapericardial neoplasms compress and deform the normal intrapericardial structures, whereas extrapericardial masses tend to displace the intrapericardial structures without compression or distortion.[106, 162]

Malignant pericardial neoplasms tend to be bulky, often

dium. The transmural pattern of progression is related to the greater systolic wall stress and oxygen consumption in the subendocardial zone, as well as limited subendocardial collateral flow, which is preferentially shunted to the subepicardial region. This pattern of transmural progression of myocardial infarction is otherwise known as the wavefront of myocardial necrosis.[238, 239]

The infarction is usually completed by 6 hours after occlusion. If reperfusion occurs within this period, potentially viable cells may recover. The reduction of the infarct

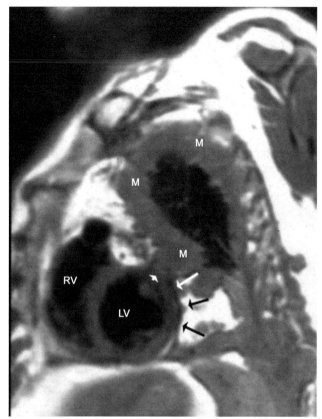

Figure 33–13. MR image of a left pleural mesothelioma in a 66-year-old man. Oblique sagittal spin-echo acquisition shows the markedly thickened pleural mass (M), with thickening of the pericardium *(arrows)* surrounding the posterior left ventricle (LV). There is a break in the pericardium *(arrowhead)* where the mass has penetrated to the left ventricular myocardium. RV, right ventricle.

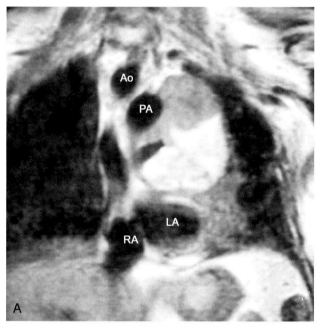

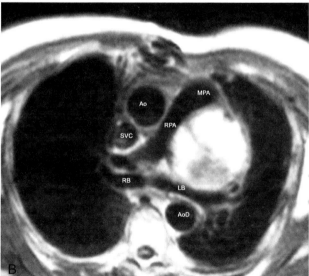

septated, inhomogeneous in signal intensity, and confined to or immediately contiguous with the pericardium and pericardial space (Fig. 33–14). MRI is excellent at providing information regarding the size, location, and extent of pericardial involvement but is not tissue specific. The fatty tumors (lipomas, fat-containing teratomas) are the exception because of their increased signal intensity on spin-echo T1-weighted MR images. Fatty tumors must be differentiated from focal deposits of subepicardial fat and non-neoplastic lesions (such as mesenteric fat in a hiatal hernia) and focal hemorrhage.

Left-Sided Heart Disease

Pathophysiology of Myocardial Infarction

Myocardial infarction is usually caused by thrombotic occlusion of an epicardial coronary artery.[32] Lack of oxygen supply to the myocardium downstream from the occlusion leads to anaerobic glycolysis with resultant accumulation of lactic acid and other by-products. Within an hour of the initial ischemic insult, subendocardial infarction ensues, subsequently progressing outward toward the subepicar-

Figure 33–14. MR images of recurrent pericardial sarcoma in a 58-year-old man. *A,* Coronal spin-echo acquisition shows this 15 × 20 cm inhomogeneous mass elevating and displacing the main pulmonary artery (PA), the right pulmonary artery (RA), and the ascending aorta (Ao). LA, left atrium. *B,* Axial section through the displaced right pulmonary artery (RPA) again shows the mass sitting on the roof of the left bronchus (LB). Ao, ascending aorta; AoD, descending aorta; MPA, main pulmonary artery; RB, right bronchus; SVC, superior vena cava.

size achieved by timely reperfusion is predominantly due to the salvage of ischemic but viable subepicardial myocardium. Viable cells also exist in the "border zone" on the lateral margins of the infarct. However, the border zone is narrow and not quantitatively significant.[83, 339]

MRI Examination of Ischemic Heart Disease

Analysis of changes in regional signal intensity after bolus injection and first-pass transit of MRI contrast medium is gaining acceptance for evaluation of myocardial perfusion. Alternative techniques include the use of endogenous tracers, such as deoxyhemoglobin (blood oxygenation level–dependent pulse sequences), spin tagging of arterial water,[6, 330] and the use of intravascular rather than extracellular contrast agents.[41, 154, 242] Intravascular contrast agents, such as ultra-small superparamagnetic iron oxide (USPIO) particles and gadolinium (Gd) chelates (Gd bound to large molecules, such as albumin) remain for a considerable time in the vascular space and thus do not require first-pass imaging.[80]

Assessment of first-pass myocardial perfusion can be obtained by means of fast gradient-echo and echo-planar imaging techniques. Perfusion studies for detection of regional ischemia are accomplished using low doses of MRI contrast media and multislice measurements in the cardiac short axis or along different axes of the heart.[320, 321] With inversion recovery and gradient-echo planar imaging, an ischemic area is identified as a zone of either *low cold-spot* or *high hot-spot signal*, respectively (Fig. 33–15).[320, 321, 341]

Signal intensity versus time curves is generally used for analysis of first-pass imaging studies. Different parameters can be calculated, including, for example[186]:

1. The rate of signal intensity increase after bolus injection of contrast agent using a linear fit.
2. The maximum signal intensity increase.
3. The time from T_{null} to the maximum signal intensity value.
4. The signal intensity decrease after the peak signal intensity using an exponential fit.

Studies comparing the ability of MRI myocardial perfusion techniques to detect hypoperfused myocardial regions with thallium 201 (^{201}Tl) and technetium 99m (^{99m}Tc) radionuclide imaging and coronary angiography have shown sensitivity rates ranging between 64% and 92% and specificity rates between 75% and 100%.[82, 120, 152, 333] Hartnell and colleagues showed an improved accuracy (similar to scintigraphy) when combining MR myocardial perfusion with cine MRI to detect associated wall motion abnormalities.[120] Wintersperger and coworkers compared myocardial perfusion with myocardial wall thickening in patients with chronic myocardial infarction.[333] Wall thickening was significantly less in hypoperfused areas than in normally perfused areas. The location of hypoperfusion and restricted myocardial wall thickening correlated well. The combination of MR perfusion and cine MRI improved the sensitivity from 72% (using only MRI perfusion) to 100%, whereas the specificity decreased slightly (98% to 93%).

Several studies have stressed the advantages of MRI myocardial perfusion compared with radionuclide imaging to obtain information concerning heterogeneous (subepicardial, midendocardial, and subendocardial) transmural enhancement, which may reflect variability in myocardial perfusion across the wall.[81, 328] Cherryman and colleagues studied 103 patients after their first acute myocardial infarction with ECG, echocardiography, ^{201}Tl single photon emission computed tomography (SPECT), and MRI perfusion.[53] They found that dynamic contrast-enhanced MRI was consistently better than Tl-SPECT for detecting anterior septal and inferior posterior infarctions.

Several groups have used the myocardial perfusion reserve or myocardial perfusion reserve index to assess patients with coronary artery disease.[1, 65, 327] The reserve index may be more reliable than determination of coronary flow reserve because the effect of (protective) myocardial collateral flow supply is taken into account. Al-Saadi and associates found a significant difference in myocardial perfusion reserve between ischemic and nonischemic myocardial segments (1.08 ± 0.23 and 2.33 ± 0.41; $P < .001$).[1] Using a cut-off value of 1.5, the diagnostic sensitivity, specificity, and accuracy for the detection of coronary artery stenosis (≥75%) were 90%, 83%, and 87%, respectively. In a similar study by Cullen and colleagues, a negative correlation was found between the myocardial perfusion reserve index and percent coronary artery stenosis ($r = -.81$; $P < .01$).[65]

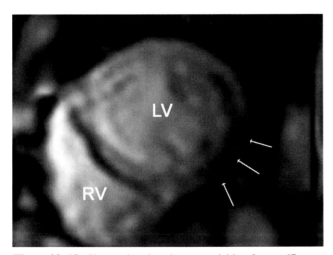

Figure 33–15. Short-axis echo-planar acquisition from a 67-year-old man with a history of acute myocardial infarction. After intravenous administration of gadolinium (Gd-DTPA), the cavity blood of the right ventricle (RV) and the left ventricle (LV) has been opacified, as has the LV myocardium. Note the region of decreased contrast agent uptake *(arrows)*, indicating previous infarction.

Functional Imaging in Ischemic Heart Disease

A major strength of MRI is its accurate assessment of ventricular function. Fast gradient-echo techniques provide high-contrast images with high temporal and spatial resolution that can be obtained within the time of a single breath-hold.[7] This allows evaluation of regional myocardial contraction, ventricular filling and ejection, valve motion, and vascular flow patterns. Excellent visualization of the endocardial and epicardial surfaces of ventricular myocardium on cine MRI displays changes in wall thickening and wall motion throughout the cardiac cycle. The accuracy of measurements and reproducibility make cine MRI appealing as the preferred imaging modality for follow-up of patients.[27] Cine MRI can be used to accomplish the following[6, 16, 128, 130, 225, 278, 324, 325]:

1. Determine regional and global sequelae of past myocardial infarction.
2. Detect ischemic myocardium in patients with coronary artery disease.
3. Differentiate between viable and nonviable myocardium in patients with chronic myocardial ischemia.
4. Measure myocardial mass.

These studies can be performed with the patient at rest or under stress.

Another unique capability of MRI is the use of myocardial tagging. A grid of tag lines is created noninvasively on the myocardium.[9, 342] These tag lines track deformation of underlying myocardium through the cardiac cycle. Myocardial tagging can be used to perform, noninvasively, a myocardial strain analysis and to decompose gross wall deformation into more fundamental units of deformation, such as principal strains or fiber strains.[26, 233] This technique has been used to depict functional recovery after thrombolytic therapy in infarcted myocardium,[25] to elucidate the mechanism of remote myocardial dysfunction,[24, 27, 156, 158] to discriminate between viable and nonviable myocardium using stress myocardial tagging,[63] and to measure the efficacy of medication on left ventricular dysfunction (Fig. 33–16).[155] As a result of the need for computer-intensive postprocessing, the clinical use of MRI tagging is still limited.

Assessment of Myocardial Ischemia, Infarction, and Viability

Demonstrating the benefit of acute reperfusion intervention (i.e., thrombolysis, transluminal angioplasty, or immediate surgical revascularization) necessitates a technique for identification and quantification of infarct size and myocardium at risk at an early stage.[227] In patients with chronic coronary artery disease and ventricular dysfunction, viable myocardium may persist in regions of chronic ischemic injury. Such myocardium may recover after revascularization and improve left ventricular function.

Proton Relaxation Times

The free water content of infarcted myocardium is related to the duration of the ischemic insult,[138, 329] prolonging T1 and T2 relaxation times.[95, 124] Regional differences in T1 and T2 relaxation times may be useful for differentiating normal myocardium from areas of necrosis.[124, 323, 329] Differences in T1 relaxation are not clinically useful for infarct detection unless paramagnetic contrast agents are administered.

Wesbey and colleagues[323] found a linear correlation between T2 relaxation time and the percentage of water content. Furthermore, infarcted tissues were visible as areas of increased signal intensity[124, 253] on T2-weighted MRI sequences (Fig. 33–17). Many groups have used this approach to detect and quantitate myocardial infarctions.[10, 46, 124, 129, 187, 195, 227, 253, 323] However, the relation between changes in relaxation times and the size and stage of myocardial infarction is complex[40, 56, 213, 228, 265, 332, 334] and not completely understood.

Stress Imaging

Pharmacologic stress MRI using the β agonist dobutamine or the vasodilator dipyridamole[17] offers an advantage in differentiating ischemic, stunned, or hibernating myocardium. Dobutamine is preferred because it offers the possibility of both low- and high-dose examinations needed for the differentiation of stunning versus ischemia.[50, 304, 305] In general, analysis of regional endocardial motion, wall thickening, or absolute increase in wall thickness as parameters of regional systolic performance provides a sensitivity and specificity of 70% to 90%.[1, 11, 14, 15, 153, 223, 224, 304, 305] These stress test results could be enhanced by the simultaneous evaluation of regional perfusion.[82, 120] High-dose dobutamine MRI has been found superior to high-dose dobutamine stress echocardiography in detecting patients with significant coronary heart disease (>50% diameter stenosis).[131, 210, 229]

Myocardial Wall Thickness and Dobutamine-Induced Wall Thickening

It is important to differentiate between left ventricular dysfunction caused by irreversible scar from that caused by viable but akinetic ventricular myocardium.[112] Chronic myocardial infarction is associated with myocardium less than 6 mm thick or the presence of focal aneurysm formation (Fig. 33–18). Moderate inotropic stimulation can transiently reverse postischemic myocardial dysfunction; these changes may be demonstrated by echocardiography or MRI. The high-contrast and spatial resolution of MRI resolves the epicardial and endocardial surfaces of the myocardium, thus allowing precise measurement of wall thickness. Baer and coworkers showed that viable myocardium is characterized by preserved end-diastolic wall thickness (>5.5 mm) and a dobutamine-inducible contractile reserve.[12, 16] Both viability parameters reliably predict improvement in regional left ventricular function and ejection fraction after revascularization.[16] Functional studies using cine MRI, performed at rest and during pharmacologic stress, can be performed during repetitive breath-holds and be completed with a contrast-enhanced study to evaluate delayed hyperenhancement in akinetic regions.[262]

Left Ventricular Failure

Left ventricular failure reflects the inability of the ventricle to pump blood and its ability to do so only from an abnormally elevated left atrial filling pressure.[33] It is frequently, but not always, caused by a systolic, contractile abnormality that results in a defect in the ejection of

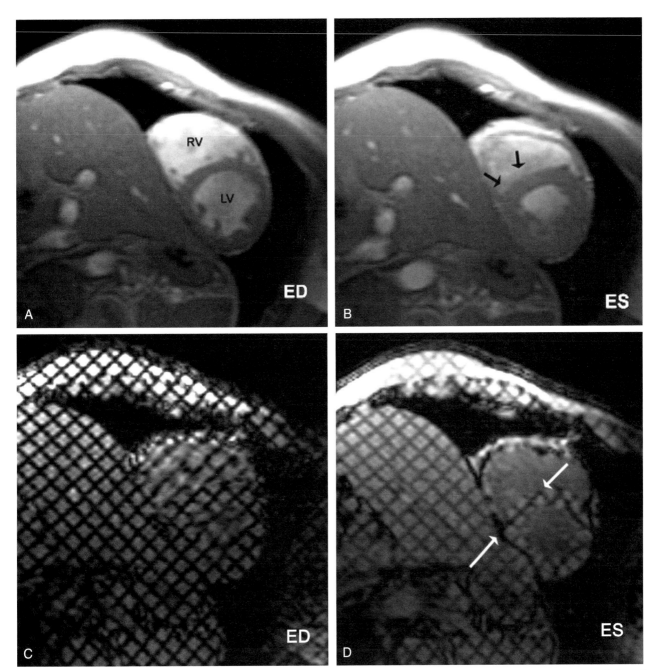

Figure 33–16. Short-axis myocardial tagging in a 62-year-old man with an old inferoseptal myocardial infarction. *A,* End-diastolic (ED) short-axis image at the midventricular level, demonstrating normal-appearing left ventricle (LV) and right ventricle (RV). *B,* End-systolic (ES) image obtained at the same anatomic level. There is thickening of both the right and the left ventricular myocardium, but there is diminished thickening of the inferior interventricular septum *(arrows). C,* End-diastolic image obtained at the same anatomic level using myocardial tagging. *D,* End-systolic tagged image. The tag line *(between arrows)* running through the inferior interventricular septum remains straight, indicating a lack of intramyocardial motion.

blood from the heart. However, an abnormality in diastolic function may lead to abnormal ventricular filling, elevated left ventricular end-diastolic pressure, and elevated left atrial pressure. Rapid-onset diastolic failure may be caused by the decrease in compliance seen in acute myocardial ischemia.[123] More insidious onset may occur if chronically ischemic myocardium has been replaced by fibrous scar tissue.

Irrespective of the etiology of the left ventricular failure,

MRI is increasingly used in clinical trials to monitor the effects of pharmaceutical therapy on ventricular mass, volume, and ejection fraction. Because MRI techniques do not depend on geometric assumptions about the shape of either ventricle and are less operator dependent than echocardiography, they may be used for accurate and reproducible quantitation of ventricular volume and myocardial mass. The goal of medical therapy in heart failure is to reverse the inexorable dilatation and hypertrophy of the diseased

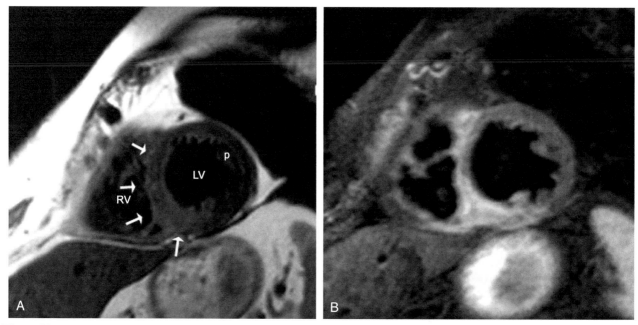

Figure 33–17. Short-axis images obtained from a 58-year-old man with an acute anterior myocardial infarction. *A,* T1-weighted image shows the normal appearance of the left ventricular (LV) and right ventricular (RV) chambers but a relative increase in signal intensity *(arrows)* of the interventricular septum and inferior LV myocardium. The papillary muscle (p) is labeled. *B,* T2-weighted image obtained at the same anatomic level exaggerates the increased signal intensity of the regional myocardial edema.

cardiac muscle. Serial calculations of the ventricular volume and myocardial mass, as well as the stroke volume and ejection fraction, provide an objective measure of the effectiveness of a medical therapeutic regimen.

Cardiomyopathy

MRI techniques allow direct demonstration of the ventricular myocardium. This provides a reproducible means of identifying the distribution of abnormal muscle and characterizing the nature of the abnormality. Cine acquisition displays the epicardial and endocardial borders of

the ventricular myocardium, providing temporally resolved imagery from which myocardial mass and ventricular chamber volumes and stroke volume can be computed. This provides a means of estimating ventricular function and allows monitoring the therapeutic response of medical or surgical intervention. Advanced tagging and phase-contrast acquisition techniques provide a means of investigating regional functional disturbance as well as myocardial blood flow.

Cine MRI is an excellent noninvasive technique used to diagnose cardiomyopathy and to distinguish between the three distinct forms of this disease. The clinical usefulness of MRI in patients with cardiomyopathy is reviewed in

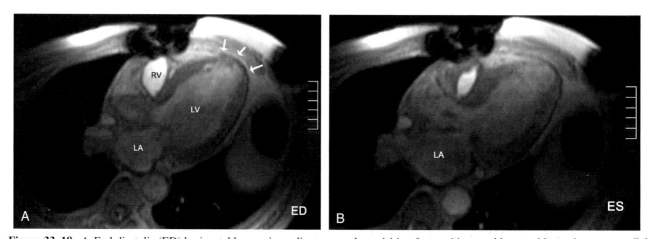

Figure 33–18. *A,* End-diastolic (ED) horizontal long-axis gradient-reversal acquisition from a 64-year-old man with previous myocardial infarction. Poor definition and probable thinning of the distal anteroapical left ventricular (LV) myocardium *(arrows)* are demonstrated. LA, left atrium; RV, right ventricle. *B,* End-systolic (ES) image reveals increased left atrial (LA) size. The anteroapical myocardium is thin and also does not thicken.

terms of information obtained in each of the major categories: dilated, hypertrophic, and restrictive cardiomyopathy.

Dilated Cardiomyopathy

Dilated cardiomyopathy is characterized by ventricular dilatation, decreased contractility, as well as alterations in ventricular diastolic function.[116] Cine MRI reliably quantifies ventricular volume and mass, ejection fraction, and wall stress in patients with dilated cardiomyopathy[99, 276, 313] and may be used to monitor the functional status of the ventricle over time. The high reproducibility of cine MRI (with the variability in volume and mass measurements of < 5%)[276] makes it an invaluable tool in the assessment of effects of medications. MRI was used to evaluate the response of patients with dilated cardiomyopathy to angiotensin-converting inhibitor therapy.[77]

Analysis of cine acquisitions has revealed regional functional abnormalities in these patients not found in normal control subjects. The normal gradient in wall thickening, with gradual increase from base to apex, is absent in dilated cardiomyopathy, as demonstrated on short-axis cine MRI[276, 277] (Fig. 33–19). Myocardial tagging techniques provide a means of quantitating regional changes in myocardial function, reflecting both regional stress-strain relationships, as well as the fibrous anatomy of the heart. Depressed strain values correlate with depressed chamber function. Both of these parameters were shown to be markedly decreased[192] in patients with dilated cardiomyopathy, with preservation of fiber orientation throughout the cardiac cycle. These findings suggest that myocardial tagging may also be a useful tool for testing therapeutic regimens[85] in these patients.

Hypertrophic Cardiomyopathy

Hypertrophic cardiomyopathy presents clinically with both diastolic and systolic dysfunction.[268] The dramatically thickened ventricular myocardium in this family of diseases has a distinctive appearance on MRI. In these patients MRI allows a significantly more comprehensive evaluation of the diseased myocardium than does echocardiography.[102, 230]

In patients with hypertrophic cardiomyopathy, MRI allows improved visualization of wall segments (97% of segments) as compared with the use of echocardiography (67% of segments).[230] Regional hypertrophy found on MRI correlated with Q-wave abnormalities demonstrated by ECG, whereas the configuration of the T-wave reflected the distribution of hypertrophy between the basal and apical segments.[264] Use of MRI allows accurate characterization of the distribution of apical hypertrophy; distribution can be described as symmetrical, asymmetrical, or only involving the cardiac apex[281] (Fig. 33–20). In a longitudinal study, MRI was used to demonstrate that the characteristic "spadelike" configuration of the left ventricular chamber may begin with a "nonspade" configuration.[293]

In patients with hypertrophic cardiomyopathy, cine MRI has been used to quantitate left ventricular mass, volumes, and ejection fraction as well as right ventricular function. Suzuki and colleagues[292] found increased right ventricular mass, reduced peak filling rate, and decreased right ventricular filling fractions in these patients. Velocity-encoded cine MRI has been used to study coronary sinus blood flow in patients with hypertrophic cardiomyopathy.[143] Resting coronary blood flow was not significantly different from that found in normal individuals. However, after dipyridamole administration, coronary sinus blood flow in patients with hypertrophic cardiomyopathy increased to a much lower level than that seen in the healthy volunteers, indicating decreased coronary flow reserve. Impaired diastolic function due to nonuniform hypertrophy with subsequent loss of myocardial contractile elements, myocardial perfusion abnormalities, and change in left ventricular geometry has been demonstrated.[338]

Using myocardial tagging, significant reduction in the wall motion of the hypertrophied interventricular septum has been shown.[174] Depressed circumferential segment shortening in the anterior and inferior regions of the interventricular septum[157] and impaired systolic wall thickening (related inversely to wall thickness)[78] have been demonstrated as well.

Restrictive Cardiomyopathy

Restrictive cardiomyopathy is a family of diseases that is characterized by primary diastolic dysfunction with com-

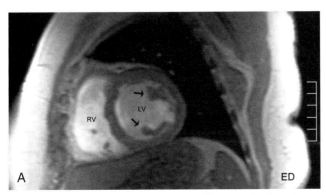
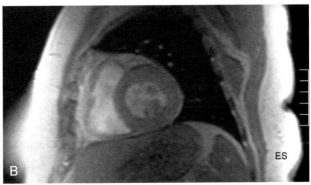

Figure 33–19. MR image of dilated cardiomyopathy in a 59-year-old woman. *A*, End-diastolic (ED) short-axis image through the papillary muscles *(arrows)* shows mild dilatation of the left ventricle (LV) with relative preservation of the right ventricle (RV). *B*, End-systolic (ES) image reveals no regional wall motion abnormality but diminished contraction and relatively increased end-systolic cavity volume.

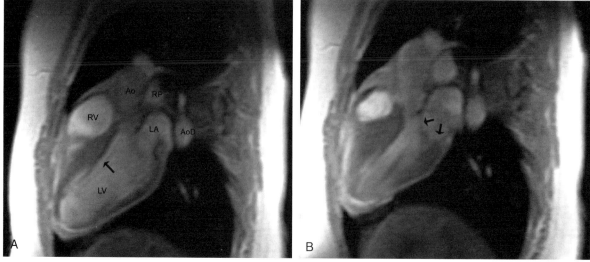

Figure 33–20. MR image obtained from a 17-year-old girl with hypertrophic obstructive cardiomyopathy. *A,* End-diastolic (ED) oblique axial-gradient reversal acquisition shows near-normal left ventricular (LV) size. The superior interventricular septum *(arrow)* is slightly asymmetrical with respect to the remainder of the LV myocardium. The right ventricle (RV), ascending (Ao) and descending (AoD) aorta, left atrium (LA), and right pulmonary artery (RP) are labeled. *B,* End-systolic (ES) image shows a dramatic difference in septal thickening, causing narrowing of the subvalvular left ventricular region. The mitral leaflets *(arrows)* are closed, and there is no mitral regurgitation.

plete or partial preservation of systolic ventricular function; it must be differentiated from pericardial constriction.[231] MRI is the study of choice in this circumstance, allowing both the characterization of the ventricular functional abnormality and demonstration of the pericardial abnormality.[184, 273] Pericardial thickening greater than 4 mm indicates pericarditis underlying the restrictive symptoms and hemodynamic measurements.[184]

Amyloidosis frequently causes restrictive cardiomyopathy. It may be recognized by widespread thickening of all chamber walls and atrioventricular valve leaflets in the face of decreased ejection fraction and abnormal segmental wall motion. When compared with patients with hypertrophic cardiomyopathy, patients with cardiac amyloidosis had enlarged right atria and increased right atrial and ventricular wall thickness.[84] Restrictive cardiomyopathy can be differentiated from hypertrophic cardiomyopathy on cine MRI, because the systolic function (ejection fraction and wall motion) is usually normal to increased in hypertrophic cardiomyopathy but reduced in amyloid heart.

Comparison of MRI findings in patients with amyloid infiltration, patients with hypertrophic cardiomyopathy, and normal volunteers demonstrated a significant decrease in myocardial signal intensity in patients with amyloid heart as opposed to the other two groups, possibly because of magnetic field heterogeneity and decreased proton concentration inherent in amyloid deposition. In addition, mitral and tricuspid regurgitation frequently associated with restrictive cardiomyopathy can be demonstrated and quantified on MRI.[75] In patients with cardiomyopathy due to cardiac sarcoidosis, loci of high myocardial signal intensity were found on T1-weighted images after administration of intravenous Gd.[51, 246]

Myocarditis

Myocarditis is an inflammation of the myocardium associated with myocyte damage or necrosis. In the United

States viral etiology accounts for most cases, although it may also be due to chemical agents, local toxin production, as well as immune-mediated diseases. The symptoms are nonspecific, because patients frequently present with palpitations, malaise, shortness of breath, and chest pain or discomfort, and they can be mistaken for cardiomyopathy or coronary artery disease. Most patients recover, but a fraction will develop cardiomyopathy.[38] Some cases of sudden death after a viral illness are thought to represent sequelae of viral myocarditis.[70, 98]

Myocarditis is often a clinical diagnosis, because the definitive diagnosis requires an endomyocardial biopsy. However, a myocardial biopsy is invasive and can be associated with severe complications. In addition, the focal nature of the disease leads to frequent nondiagnostic or false-negative results. Scintigraphy with indium 111 monoclonal antimyosin antibody[22] and gallium 67[307] used noninvasively to assess myocardial inflammation are limited by a high false-positive rate and frequent overestimation of the extent of myocardial damage.[30, 207]

The early experience with MRI for evaluation of myocarditis suggested that T2-weighted and TI-weighted, Gd-DTPA–enhanced spin-echo sequences were useful.[22, 52, 100, 188, 189] T2-weighted sequences showed increased signal in the affected muscle, probably due to myocardial edema, whereas Gd-DTPA T1-weighted sequences demonstrated enhancement of the damaged myocardial muscle. In a study of 19 patients with viral myocarditis,[97] Gd-DTPA–enhanced MRI was used to follow the course of the disease and to estimate the extent and distribution of myocardial involvement. Early in the course of the disease, myocardial enhancement tended to be localized, reflecting the focal nature of the myocardial inflammation. However, as the disease progressed, the enhancement was seen throughout the muscle, depicting an evolution of myocarditis into a diffuse process.

In a more recent study[252] a group of 20 patients was studied with Gd-DTPA–enhanced spin-echo and cine MRI; 12 had myocarditis, and 8 did not. In the group with myocarditis, wall motion abnormalities as seen on cine MRI matched exactly the regions of abnormal enhancement on Gd-DTPA spin-echo examinations. These authors concluded that in a correct clinical setting, focal myocardial enhancement strongly supports the diagnosis of myocarditis, especially when associated with regional wall motion abnormalities.

Arrhythmogenic Right Ventricular Dysplasia

Arrhythmogenic right ventricular dysplasia is a cardiomyopathy of unknown etiology that is characterized by ventricular tachycardia originating in the right ventricle, ST changes in the right-sided precordial leads of the surface ECG, regional and global right ventricular contractile abnormalities, as well as thinning and fibrofatty replacement of the right ventricular myocardium.[178] Although severe right ventricular dilatation, reduced right ventricular ejection fraction, and right ventricular failure as well as left ventricular dysfunction have been reported,[177a, 316] most individuals have localized or patchy areas of segmental right ventricular thinning and akinesia or dyskinesia and are minimally symptomatic. Differentiation between right ventricular dysplasia and pathologic fatty infiltration can be made on clinical and histologic grounds. Fatty infiltration usually does not cause clinical symptoms,[31] whereas right ventricular dysplasia does. In addition, in right ventricular dysplasia, abnormal foci of fat extend from the epicardial surface through the interstitium, displacing myocardial fibers.[169]

Right ventricular dysplasia appears to be inherited, with a strong familial tendency suggesting an autosomal dominant disorder with variable expression and penetrance.[211] It is usually diagnosed in individuals between 20 and 50 years of age,[68] but it may be diagnosed in young persons[221, 295] as well. The disease is found predominantly in men, and symptoms frequently occur with exercise. This condition must be differentiated from right ventricular outflow tract tachycardia,[37, 139] which carries a significantly lower risk of sudden death. Pathologic changes of right ventricular dysplasia are similar to those found in Uhl's anomaly.

ECG-gated cine cardiac MRI is considered a useful means of assessing right ventricular free wall myocardial thinning and fatty infiltration, as well as global and regional wall motion abnormalities.[8, 31, 243] In axial and short-axis section, the free wall of the normal right ventricle should appear as a relatively homogeneous, intermediate signal intensity extending from the fat of the anterior atrioventricular ring toward the anterior extension of the interventricular septum. There is usually a thin and tapering deposit of epicardial fat extending from the atrioventricular ring along its proximal surface, immediately subjacent to the pencil-thin line of the pericardial space.[159] The myocardium of the free wall is not always demonstrated in all sections because it is relatively thin and sometimes cannot be resolved spatially. The diaphragmatic right ventricular wall is best viewed in short-axis section and should appear slightly thicker than the free wall but thinner than the interventricular septum.

In patients with right ventricular dysplasia, the shape and volume of the right ventricular chamber may appear normal or "dilated" to the eye. The right ventricular free wall myocardium may appear diffusely thinned or have loci of "absent" myocardium, representing local areas of marked thinning (Fig. 33–21). Furthermore, on T1-weighted images, loci of increased intramyocardial signal intensity, representing fatty infiltration, are observed in both the diaphragmatic and free wall. Although these changes may be identified with conventional body coil acquisitions, use of a dedicated cardiac or general purpose chest coil provides the most reliable demonstration of free wall myocardial changes. Care must be exercised to place the coil over the anterior aspect of the heart. The center of the coil should be applied about 5 cm to the left of midline, just medial to the nipple.

Use of gradient-echo acquisition for cine examination of the right ventricle in this condition may be helpful in identifying focal areas of free wall dyskinesia. In a similar but benign syndrome, right ventricular outflow tract tachycardia, focal right ventricular myocardial wall thinning or excavation, or wall motion abnormalities may be identified. However, they are restricted to right ventricular outflow tract, differentiating them from the findings in arrhythmogenic right ventricular dysplasia.[49]

Magnetic Resonance Coronary Arteriography

All forms of MRI are exquisitely sensitive to motion and turbulent blood flow artifacts. Cardiac MRI is especially sensitive to cardiac and respiratory motion and arterial pulsation. MR coronary arteriography attempts to demonstrate vessels smaller than 5 mm in caliber running along the epicardial surface of the contracting heart. Clinical success has been mixed.

Conventional ECG-gated spin-echo (Fig. 33–22) and gradient-echo (Fig. 33–23) MRI usually demonstrate portions of the epicardial coronary arterial tree but cannot be relied on for precise morphologic diagnosis. Recent advances in fast MRI have nearly eliminated respiratory and cardiac motion artifacts; MRI may provide a noninvasive means of visualizing the epicardial coronary arteries. ECG-gated two-dimensional gradient-echo acquisition sequences depict laminar blood flow as bright signal and turbulence or absent blood flow as signal voids. Use of fat-suppression techniques increases the contrast of the epicardial coronary arteries by decreasing the relative signal produced by the epicardial fat surrounding the arteries (Fig. 33–24). In addition, rapid-acquisition sequences allow image acquisition during a single breath-hold with and without the use of k-space segmentation to provide rapid visualization of the epicardial coronary tree.[79, 167, 176, 222, 331]

In a preliminary evaluation of k-space–segmented, fat-suppressed, single–breath-hold MR arteriography[176] in 25 subjects (including 19 healthy volunteers and 6 patients undergoing diagnostic coronary arteriography), the left main coronary artery (LMCA) was identified in 24 (96%)

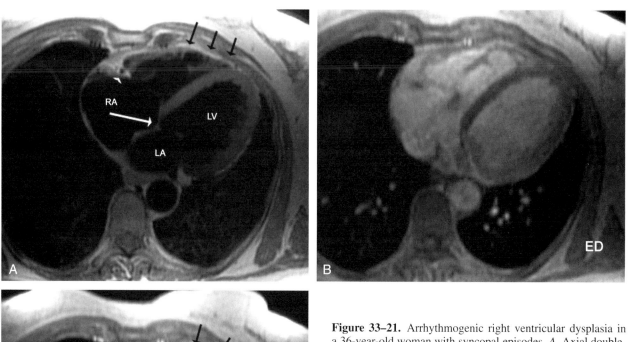

Figure 33–21. Arrhythmogenic right ventricular dysplasia in a 36-year-old woman with syncopal episodes. *A,* Axial double-inversion recovery acquisition through the atrioventricular septum *(long white arrow)* and mitral valve. The heart is rotated into the left chest secondary to right heart dilatation. The right ventricular free wall myocardium cannot be visually distinguished from epicardial fat and appears thinner *(black arrows)* than that adjacent to the atrioventricular ring (indicated by the signal void of the right coronary artery *(arrowhead)*. LA, left atrium; LV, left ventricle; RA, right atrium. *B,* End-diastolic (ED) gradient-reversal acquisition obtained at nearly the same anatomic level. *C,* End-systolic (ES) image demonstrates left and right ventricular myocardial contraction but failure of the abnormal free wall myocardium to thicken. Furthermore, the signal intensity *(arrows)* of this portion of the right ventricular myocardium is increased.

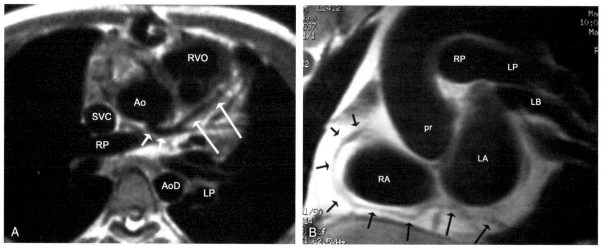

Figure 33–22. Incidental demonstration of the coronary arteries. *A,* Axial spin-echo acquisition obtained from a 52-year-old man with a history of a mediastinal mass. The origin and course of the left main coronary artery *(short arrows)* from the aortic root (Ao) as well as the proximal course of the anterior descending coronary artery *(long arrows)* are clearly seen. The right ventricular outflow tract (RVO), superior vena cava (SVC), right (RP) and descending left (LP) pulmonary arteries, and descending aorta (AoD) are marked. *B,* In this short-axis section, obtained for evaluation of pericardial thickening, almost the entire course of the right coronary artery *(arrows)* can be visualized by its contrast with surrounding fat. The left atrium (LA), the right atrium (RA), the posterior right aortic sinus of Valsalva (pr), the confluence of the right pulmonary artery (RP) and the left pulmonary artery (LP), and the left bronchus (LB) are identified.

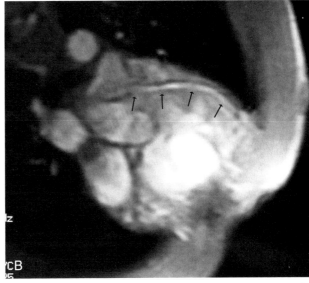

Figure 33–23. Adjacent gradient-echo four-chamber views obtained from a 39-year-old man evaluated for heart failure. *A,* The origin of the left main coronary artery from the posterior left aortic sinus of Valsalva (pl) is clearly seen. As the artery *(arrow)* dips beneath the left atrial appendage (LAA), it moves out of plane and is cut off. The right atrium (RA), the right ventricle (RV), and the posterior right aortic sinus (pr) are labeled. *B,* Gradient-echo acquisition obtained 5 mm caudad to *A.* The circumflex coronary artery *(arrows)* is seen coursing along the posterior aspect of the left ventricle.

subjects. The left anterior descending coronary artery (LAD) and right coronary artery (RCA) were visualized in all 25 individuals. The left circumflex artery (LCx) was seen in 19 (76%). Diagonal branches of the LAD were identified in 20 (80%) subjects. In the 6 patients in this series with angiographically proven coronary artery occlusion, absence of signal distal to the area of occlusion was identified by MR coronary arteriography. In a similar

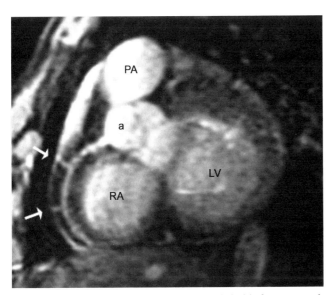

Figure 33–24. K-space–segmented, breath-hold, fat-saturated, short-axis, gradient-echo acquisition. The course of the right coronary artery from the anterior aortic sinus of Valsalva (a) is clearly visible as a result of the fat-suppressed anterior atrioventricular ring. The proximal segments of marginal branches of the right coronary artery *(arrows)* are visible. LV, left ventricle; PA, pulmonary artery; RA, right atrium.

series,[331] 39 adults referred for diagnostic coronary arteriography also underwent single–breath-hold, gradient-echo MR coronary arteriography within 1 week of their conventional arteriograms. Conventional coronary arteriography demonstrated moderate to severe proximal coronary artery narrowing in 74% of patients. Overall sensitivity and specificity of MRI for correct identification of hemodynamically significant (>50%) stenosis was 90% and 92%, respectively. Sensitivity and specificity of the technique for the LMCA were both 100%, 71% and 90% for the LCx, and 100% and 78% for the RCA, respectively.

Duerinckx and Urman[79] reported a series of 20 patients undergoing both conventional and MR coronary arteriography. They found 50% sensitivity for stenosis of the LMCA, 73% sensitivity for stenosis of the LAD, 0% for the LCx, and 62% sensitivity for significant stenosis of the RCA (overall sensitivity, 63%). Specificity in this series was 84% for the LMCA, 37% for the LAD, 82% for the LCx, and 56% for the RCA. Similarly, Pennell and coworkers[222] reviewed this technique of MR coronary arteriography in a group of 21 healthy controls and 5 patients with angiographically proved coronary artery disease. Twenty-two (85%) of the 26 subjects were successfully imaged. The LMCA was identified in 95%, the LAD in 91%, the LCx in 76%, and the RCA in 95% of studies. All five coronary occlusions in their series were identified by MR coronary arteriography. Although most missed vessels occurred early in their series, imaging the circumflex artery was problematic throughout their experience.

Preliminary experience with three-dimensional gradient-echo MRI acquisition[167] provided similar findings. The proximal coronary tree was not identified in all subjects. The LMCA was identified in 4 (57%) of 7 healthy volunteers. In this same group of volunteers, the LAD was identified in 4 (57%) of 7, the LCx in 2 (29%), and the RCA in all 7 (100%). Seven patients studied by conventional coronary arteriography and MR coronary arteriography had 17 diseased arterial segments. MR coronary arteriography demonstrated altered signal intensity in 13 (76%) of these segments.

Administration of intravenous contrast material increases contrast between blood and the surrounding arterial wall. This improves the low signal-to-noise ratios inherent to k-space–sampled breath-hold acquisitions.[108, 126, 149, 166, 237, 310, 343] In a report of the comparison of conventional x-ray angiography with intravenous contrast–enhanced breath-hold MR coronary angiography[177] in 50 patients with suspected coronary artery disease, 76.6% of arterial segments could be adequately analyzed. MR coronary angiography detected the presence of significant (>50%) stenoses and occlusions in 34 of 36 patients and excluded significant stenosis or occlusion in 8 of 14 patients. These workers found a sensitivity of 94.4%, a specificity of 57.1%, a positive predictive value of 85%, and a negative predictive value of 80% for this technique.

For MR coronary arteriography to become a useful modality in the evaluation and management planning of patients with coronary heart disease, it must first be able to reliably demonstrate the entire epicardial coronary tree. (Can one imagine the growth in use of coronary arteriography if it allowed visualization of only the proximal epicardial arteries in only 80% of cases?) MR coronary arteriography cannot as yet provide complete and reliable noninvasive demonstration of the epicardial coronary arteries and their branches. Needless to say, advances in pulse-sequence design, as well as hardware considerations (such as dedicated chest surface coils and higher RF gradients) will undoubtedly improve our ability to demonstrate the coronary arteries using MRI. We must ask whether our ability to demonstrate the coronary arteries per se improves our ability to diagnose coronary artery disease and identify patients at risk for future cardiac events. Then we must improve the sensitivity and specificity for the detection of less severe (<50%) luminal narrowing. Otherwise, the usefulness of MRI for detecting non–flow-limiting plaques, the major source of acute coronary occlusion and sudden cardiac events, will be limited. Furthermore, if MR coronary arteriography is to become a noninvasive replacement for conventional catheter coronary arteriography, then the sensitivity and specificity for detection of significant vessel stenosis must increase. Claims of MRI eventually providing combined morphologic and functional analysis of the heart do not obviate limited spatial resolution, difficulties in the sensitive and specific imaging of the posterior circulation and arterial side branches, as well as differentiation between coronary arteries and cardiac veins.

Magnetic Resonance of Valvular Heart Disease

It is unusual for MRI to be employed as the first imaging technique in the work-up of cardiac murmurs. Nevertheless, MRI yields important information concerning cardiac chamber size, myocardial mass, pulmonary blood flow, and pulmonary venous pressure in these patients. MRI may be useful for demonstration of the jets of valvular dysfunction, as well as the means of quantitating the dysfunction and

its sequelae. The response of the heart to valvular dysfunction leads to characteristic changes in chamber volume and myocardial mass to maintain myocardial wall stress and systemic cardiac output. Recognition of the morphologic changes as well as understanding the homeostatic mechanisms that lead to these changes forms the basis of cardiac diagnosis.

Mitral Stenosis

Congenital mitral stenosis is rare and is observed mainly in infants and children.[250] Rheumatic mitral stenosis results from the chronic and progressive fibrotic process instigated by the initial rheumatic inflammatory reaction. The slowly progressive process of reactive fibrosis may take 20 to 40 years before a patient with a history of acute rheumatic fever develops signs or symptoms of rheumatic mitral stenosis. Once symptoms occur, another decade may pass before symptoms become disabling.[255, 336] The mitral leaflets thicken, calcify, and fuse. The chordae tendineae become thickened, fused, and nonpliable. All of these changes cause decreased diastolic leaflet excursion and functional narrowing of the mitral orifice.[250, 336] Isolated mitral stenosis occurs in about 40% of all patients presenting with rheumatic heart disease. Nearly 60% of patients with pure mitral stenosis give a history of previous rheumatic fever.[256, 336]

In the early phases of mitral stenosis, elevated pulmonary venous pressure is transmitted across the capillary bed, resulting in "passive" pulmonary arterial hypertension. This may be identified as an increase in the caliber of the central pulmonary artery segments. However, pulmonary arteriolar resistance subsequently rises in these patients,[110, 337] causing precapillary pulmonary hypertension. On spin-echo MR images (Fig. 33–25), increased pulmonary resistance may be reflected in slowing of pulmonary blood flow, resulting in increased signal within the pulmonary arteries. Chronic elevation in pulmonary resistance results in right ventricular hypertension and myocardial hypertrophy. On gradient-echo MRI (Fig. 33–26) acquisition, thickening of the right ventricular free wall or interventricular septum is evident. Furthermore, the hypertrophic response changes the geometry of the right ventricular cavity, changing the curvature of the interventricular septum. This is first reflected as straightening and subsequently as reversal of the systolic bowing of the septum toward the right ventricle. In addition, change in the geometry of the interventricular septum affects the function of the tricuspid valve papillary muscles, inducing tricuspid regurgitation. Therefore, mitral stenosis frequently presents as a complex lesion, affecting both atria and atrioventricular valves, as well as the right ventricle. Throughout the course of mitral stenosis, until late in the disease, the left ventricular volume, mass, and function remain normal.

Mitral Regurgitation

Acute, severe mitral regurgitation imposes a sudden volume load on an unprepared left ventricle. Although this acts to increase left ventricular stroke volume, forward

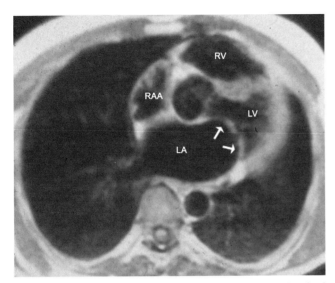

Figure 33–25. Axial spin-echo image of chronic rheumatic mitral stenosis in a 60-year-old man. Left atrial (LA) enlargement is associated with thickening and doming of the mitral leaflets *(arrows)*, increased signal in the gravity-dependent posterior lung parenchyma (indicating interstitial edema), and a normal left ventricle (LV). The right atrial appendage (RAA) and the right ventricle (RV) are both mildly dilated.

stroke volume and total cardiac output are reduced; adequate time for development of compensatory eccentric left ventricular hypertrophy does not transpire. Similarly, the left atrium cannot accommodate the rapid increase in volume, so early systolic left ventricular ejection into the left atrium results in left atrial hypertension and pulmonary vascular congestion. Patients with acute mitral regurgitation commonly present with both low cardiac output and pulmonary congestion. Acute mitral regurgitation results from sudden changes in the chordae tendineae anchoring the

valvular leaflets or damage of the leaflets themselves. A good example is infectious endocarditis, which may present with both chordae tendineae rupture and leaflet perforation. Acute papillary muscle dysfunction or rupture of the head of a papillary muscle compromises the apposition of the valve leaflets. Myocardial infarction is a frequent cause of papillary muscle rupture, commonly resulting in severe congestive heart failure and, unless treated emergently, death. Acute myocardial infarction in muscle adjacent to a papillary muscle insertion may result in papillary muscle dysfunction and mitral regurgitation. Other causes of mitral regurgitation include mitral valve prolapse syndrome, acute and/or chronic rheumatic heart disease, and collagen vascular disease. An uncommon cause of mitral regurgitation is ingestion of anorectic agents.[60]

When examined in the acute phase of mitral regurgitation, the most prominent findings are those of severe pulmonary congestion with nearly normal heart size. MRI often reveals the signal-void jet of mitral regurgitation, which appears as an early systolic fan-shaped signal void extending from the mitral annulus into the left atrium (Fig. 33–27). Left ventricular volume is not increased. Spin-echo examination may show normal left atrial size.

In cases of chronic mitral regurgitation, the initial insult may be minor and not sufficient to produce the signs and symptoms of low cardiac output and pulmonary congestion. Adequate time transpires for the ventricular myocardium to hypertrophy as well as for individual myocardial fibers to lengthen.[47, 115] This compensatory increase in left ventricular end-diastolic volume permits increased total stroke volume and restoration of forward cardiac output.[344] In an analogous manner, left atrial dilatation allows accommodation of the additional regurgitant volume at a lower left atrial pressure.

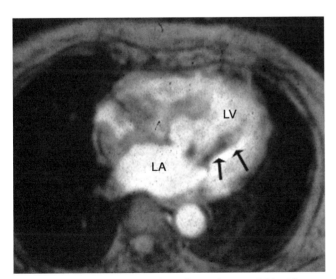

Figure 33–26. Diastolic axial gradient-echo acquisition from a 62-year-old man with chronic rheumatic mitral stenosis. Left atrial (LA) enlargement is seen in the presence of a normal left ventricle (LV). The jet of accelerating flow across the narrow valve orifice *(arrows)* is shown.

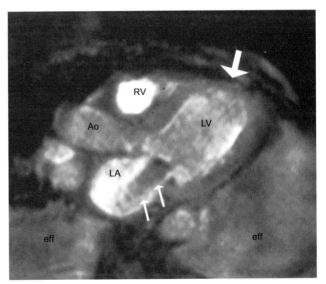

Figure 33–27. MR image demonstrating acute mitral regurgitation in a 52-year-old man suffering an acute myocardial infarction. Systolic oblique axial gradient-echo acquisition. A signal void jet *(small arrows)* extends from the mitral annulus into the normal-appearing left atrium (LA). Although left ventricular (LV) size is normal, the anteroseptal wall *(large arrow)* is akinetic. Ao, aorta; eff, pleural effusion; RV, right ventricle.

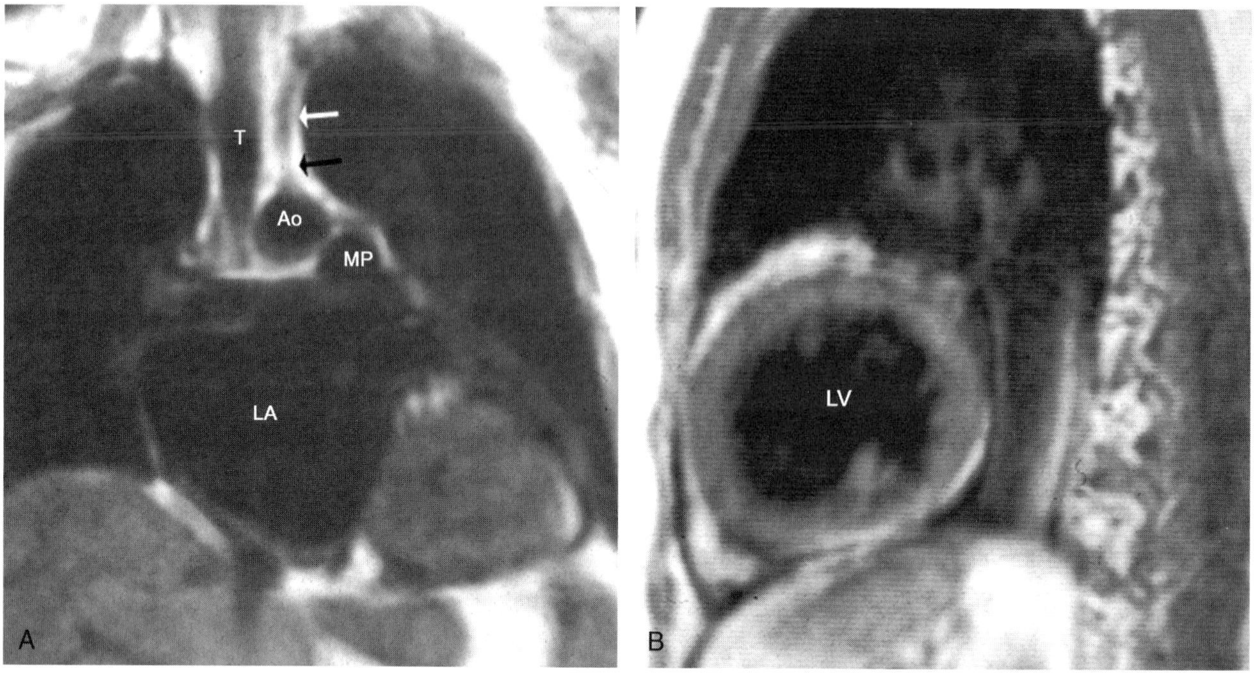

Figure 33–28. Spin-echo acquisition obtained from a 46-year-old woman with chronic mitral regurgitation. *A,* Coronal acquisition at the level of the origin of the left subclavian artery *(arrows)* from the aortic arch (Ao). The left atrium (LA) is markedly enlarged. The main pulmonary artery (MP) is no larger than the Ao, indicating normal pulmonary artery pressure. *B,* Sagittal section through the body of the dilated left ventricle (LV). T, trachea.

Chronic mitral regurgitation may result from the leaflet pathology, such as seen in myxomatous degeneration of the mitral leaflets (Fig. 33–28). In addition, secondary dilatation of the mitral orifice and loss of opposition of the mitral cusp edges due to alteration in the left ventricular geometry may also result in mitral regurgitation, as not uncommonly seen in dilated cardiomyopathy due to ischemic or hypertensive heart disease (Fig. 33–29). MRI evaluation of chronic mitral regurgitation does not demonstrate alveolar edema found in the acute phase. Rather, the dominant findings are those of left atrial and ventricular dilatation. As opposed to mitral stenosis, chronic mitral regurgitation is usually not associated with pulmonary hypertension. Right ventricular hypertrophy and right atrial and ventricular dilatation are not seen. MRI demonstrates left heart and pulmonary vein dilatation with normal or nearly normal left ventricular contractile function and the characteristic jet of mitral regurgitation (Fig. 33–30).

Aortic Stenosis

Aortic stenosis (see also the discussion on the bicuspid aortic valve in the section on congenital heart disease) can occur at, below, or above the aortic valve, that is, valvular, subvalvular, or supravalvular stenosis. Regardless of the level of left ventricular outflow obstruction, all such lesions share the physiologic common denominator of increasing left ventricular myocardial strain, with the resultant formation of myocardial hypertrophy. The most common causes of aortic stenosis are congenital, calcific degenerative, and rheumatic disease.[35, 206, 220] Subvalvular and supravalvular aortic stenoses are usually congenital in origin.[249]

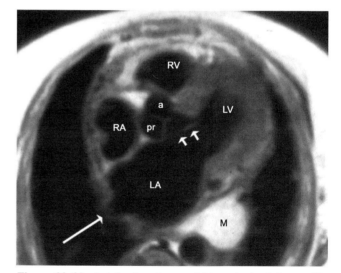

Figure 33–29. Axial spin-echo acquisition obtained from a 30-year-old man with hypertrophic obstructive cardiomyopathy being evaluated for a left atrial mass. Notice the thickened left ventricular (LV) myocardium, the dilatation of the left atrium (LA), and the entrance of the right lower lobe pulmonary vein *(long arrow).* The anterior mitral leaflet *(short arrows)* is displaced anteriorly from its posterior partner, resulting in mitral regurgitation. Incidentally, the questionable mass (M) is mesenteric fat in a sliding hiatus hernia immediately behind the left atrium. a, anterior aortic sinus of Valsalva; pr, posterior right aortic sinus of Valsalva; RA, right atrium; RV, right ventricle.

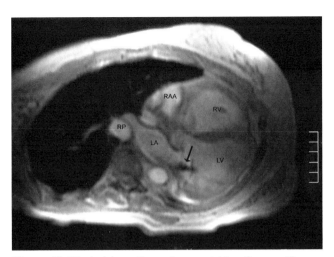

Figure 33–30. Axial gradient-echo acquisition from a 40-year-old woman with exercise intolerance and a history of previous left pneumonectomy for trauma. The heart is rotated and displaced into the left chest. The fan-shaped signal void *(arrow)* extends from the mitral valve into the left atrium (LA). The left ventricle (LV) is dilated. RAA, right atrial appendage; RP, right pulmonary artery; RV, right ventricle.

In congenital aortic stenosis, the aortic valve may be unicuspid or bicuspid. A unicuspid valve usually presents in the newborn period[206] with critical left ventricular outflow obstruction and acute heart failure. MRI is rarely indicated in these patients. If performed, the major findings would be those of interstitial and alveolar pulmonary edema secondary to left heart failure. Calcification is rarely if ever evident this early in the course of any variant of aortic stenosis.

Although a congenitally bicuspid aortic valve is malformed at birth, it rarely causes a significant pressure gradient in infancy. In the early occult stages of the disease, the distorted leaflet architecture causes turbulent blood flow across the valve that traumatizes the leaflet edges, resulting in collagenous generation, lipid deposition, fibrosis, and calcification, similar to that found much later in life in individuals with stenosis of tricuspid aortic valves. Gradually, the leaflets become more rigid and the valve orifice narrows, resulting in a pressure gradient. The congenital malformation makes the valve more susceptible to infectious endocarditis, and this may result in aortic regurgitation.

Patients who present with signs and symptoms of aortic stenosis in middle age or later life usually have tricuspid aortic valves. Their valvular disease is the result of slow, progressive degeneration, calcification of the valve annulus and leaflets, and consequent narrowing of the effective valve area. This abnormality is thought to be the result of normal wear on the valve over a period of years. Hypercholesterolemia and diabetes are important predisposing factors for degenerative aortic stenosis. Commissural fusion is not usually seen in these patients.

Rheumatic aortic stenosis results in commissural adhesion and fusion, the hallmarks of the chronic rheumatic cycle of injury and healing. These aortic valves are frequently both regurgitant and stenotic, fixed in an open configuration. In long-standing cases of rheumatic aortic

stenosis, aortic valvular calcification may be found. This further narrows the valvular orifice. Concomitant mitral valvular disease is often present but may not be recognized clinically.

Other than in cases of congenital unicuspid aortic valve, the left ventricular obstruction develops gradually, resulting in increased left ventricular mass that increases wall thickness while maintaining normal chamber volume,[263, 288] allowing the left ventricle to adapt to the systolic pressure overload. MRI reveals the thickened left ventricular myocardium in the absence of left ventricular dilatation. Furthermore, it is useful to demonstrate the abnormal architecture of a congenitally malformed valve.

In cases of valvular aortic stenosis, MRI demonstrates the poststenotic dilatation of the ascending aorta (Fig. 33–31). The aortic caliber is normal at the level of the annulus and increases to its maximum by the level of the transverse right pulmonary artery. The aorta then returns to normal diameter proximal to the arch. The aortic arch and descending aorta are usually normal in caliber. The shape and size of the signal-void jet, as well as its variable extension into the ascending aorta, depend on the shape of the orifice and the degree of its narrowing. The severity of the valvular gradient correlates with the size of the stenotic jet[71] and its extension into the aorta.

If left ventricular outflow obstruction is subvalvular, such as in hypertrophic obstructive cardiomyopathy, then there is no poststenotic dilatation of the aorta. In these patients, however, systolic anterior motion of their anterior mitral leaflet results in mitral regurgitation. Membrane-like subvalvular aortic stenosis does not result in systolic anterior motion and mitral regurgitation. The association of left atrial enlargement (volume loading) with severe left ventricular hypertrophy (pressure loading) is characteristic of subvalvular aortic stenosis. MRI examination in these patients has an additional advantage of demonstrating the

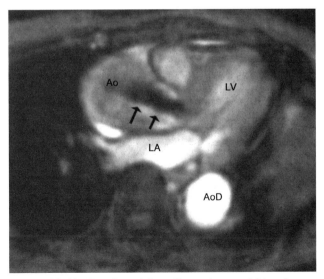

Figure 33–31. Systolic axial gradient-echo acquisition from a 67-year-old man with chronic aortic stenosis. The signal void of accelerating left ventricular (LV) flow is seen as a fan-shaped jet extending from the aortic valve into the dilated ascending aorta (Ao). AoD, descending aorta; LA, left atrium.

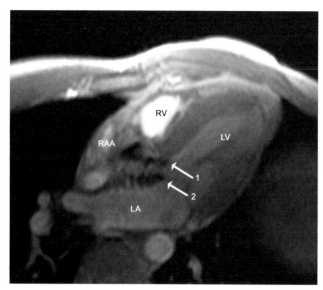

Figure 33–32. Systolic oblique axial gradient-echo acquisition from a 26-year-old man with subvalvular aortic stenosis. Fan-shaped signal voids extend from the crest of the muscular interventricular septum *(arrow 1)* and the attachment of the anterior mitral leaflet *(arrow 2)* into the ascending aorta. The left atrium (LA) is normal, and the left ventricular (LV) myocardium is hypertrophied. RAA, right atrial appendage; RV, right ventricle.

predominately septal (or other asymmetrical) variant of myocardial hypertrophy (Fig. 33–32).

Aortic Regurgitation

Aortic regurgitation may be caused by disease of the aortic valve or of the aorta, which affects the valve. Valvular etiologies include rheumatic heart disease, infectious endocarditis, congenital bicuspid aortic valve, and Marfan's syndrome. Diseases of the aorta include trauma, aortic dissection, and idiopathic dilatation of the aortic annulus. Less commonly, inflammatory and connective tissue disease involving the aorta may result in aortic regurgitation.

Infectious endocarditis, acute aortic dissection, and thoracic trauma produce acute severe aortic regurgitation. This rapidly increases left ventricular filling pressure and reduces cardiac output. These patients often present in shock. Chronic aortic regurgitation causes slow, insidious left ventricular and aortic dilatation. Although dilatation may be pronounced, the function remains normal, and these individuals experience a prolonged asymptomatic phase of their disease.

The left ventricular response to aortic insufficiency depends largely on the rate at which the volume overload develops. Acute dilatation does not allow for ventricular adaptation, resulting in decreased forward cardiac output, elevated left atrial pressure, pulmonary edema, and shock. The value of MRI in patients with acute aortic regurgitation is in noninvasive demonstration of the underlying etiology for the acute left ventricular volume load (i.e., rib fractures and periaortic hematoma in acute aortic injury or the flap of an aortic dissection extending to the aortic valve).

Chronic aortic regurgitation is characterized by in-

creased left ventricular and aortic volume without increase in left ventricular pressure. Concentric and eccentric ventricular myocardial hypertrophy compensates for the increased wall stress induced by the regurgitant volume load. MRI quantitation of left ventricular mass showed that although left ventricular wall thickness may appear normal, myocardial mass does in fact increase in these patients. Thus, left ventricular performance (as reflected in normal ejection fraction) remains normal. With time, left ventricular dilatation is progressive and may become pronounced.[48] MRI demonstrates left ventricular and aortic dilatation (Fig. 33–33). The extent of the aortic dilatation varies with the severity and chronicity of the valvular dysfunction. MRI studies of these patients have the added advantage of direct demonstration of the jet of aortic regurgitation. Typically, this appears as an early diastolic signal void, seen along the anterior mitral leaflet, extending from the aortic valve to the back wall of the left ventricle but, depending on the shape of aortic valvular orifice, may be directed elsewhere in the left ventricle.

Most patients remain asymptomatic during this compensated phase, which may last for decades. Eventually, chronic left ventricular volume loading exceeds the increased contraction of the Frank-Starling mechanism, and the left ventricle begins to fail. MR examination in these patients exhibits the dilated left ventricle and aorta, with increased signal in the lungs resulting from interstitial edema. MRI may be useful for quantifying left ventricular diastolic volume and ejection fraction and for assessing ventricular function. In addition, long-standing aortic regurgitation may cause sufficient left ventricular dilatation to stretch the mitral annulus and induce mitral regurgitation, which in turn leads to left atrial dilatation (Fig. 33–34).

Tricuspid Regurgitation

Tricuspid regurgitation may be acquired or congenital, acute or chronic. This lesion may also be seen in individu-

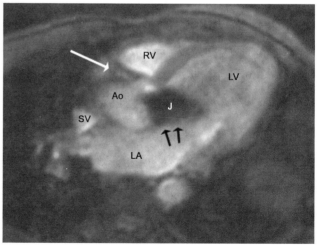

Figure 33–33. Diastolic oblique axial gradient-reversal acquisition from a 38-year-old man with congenital aortic regurgitation. A broad signal void jet (J) extends from the aortic valve into the left ventricle (LV) along the anterior leaflet of the mitral valve *(black arrows)*. The left atrium (LA) is normal. The right ventricle (RV), superior vena cava (SV), and proximal right coronary artery *(white arrow)* are identified. Ao, aorta.

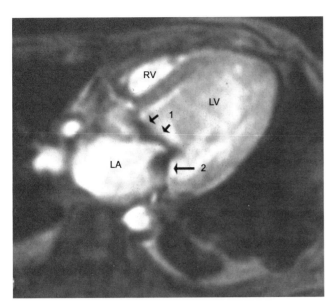

Figure 33–34. Late diastolic oblique axial gradient-echo acquisition from a 70-year-old man with mixed rheumatic aortic and mitral regurgitation. Left ventricular (LV) and left atrial (LA) dilatation in the absence of apparent LV hypertrophy is seen. The signal void jets extend from the aortic valve into the LV *(arrows 1)* and from the mitral valve into the LA *(arrow 2)*. RV, right ventricle.

als with a structurally normal valve. The most common cause of tricuspid regurgitation is pulmonary hypertension. Elevated right ventricular pressure, as seen in pulmonary hypertension of various causes, leads to right ventricular hypertrophy and alteration of shape of the interventricular septum. This distorts the function of papillary muscles originating from the septum, alters right ventricular geometry, and causes tricuspid annular dilatation,[314, 315] all of which results in valvular incompetence.

Infectious endocarditis, carcinoid disease, rheumatoid arthritis, and trauma all may cause acute valvular (including tricuspid) regurgitation. Acute pancarditis of rheumatic heart disease leads to ventricular dilatation, whereas associated valvulitis results in laxity of the mitral and tricuspid annuli. Both lead to tricuspid regurgitation. The tricuspid valve leaflets in patients with Marfan's syndrome are floppy and redundant, which results in valvular regurgitation, often involving the tricuspid valve. Ebstein's anomaly[164, 345] includes congenital malformation of the tricuspid valve, which causes varying and often severe tricuspid regurgitation.

No matter what the inciting event, initial tricuspid regurgitation volume loads the right atrium and right ventricle, resulting in their dilatation, which in turn alters right ventricular geometry, resulting in the vicious cycle of progressive valvular regurgitation.

Spin-echo and gradient-echo MRI sequences demonstrate the morphologic stigmata of tricuspid regurgitation. The right ventricle is normally found immediately behind the sternum. In patients with tricuspid regurgitation and other forms of right heart dilatation, the heart is rotated, displacing the right ventricle toward the left, and moving the right atrium to a position behind the sternum. There is

displacement of the superior vena cava medially, as well as clockwise rotation of the cardiac apex with horizontal (coronal) orientation and straightening of the interventricular septum. In severe cases, the interventricular septum bows to the left and may even extrinsically compress the left ventricle.

MRI demonstrates and accurately quantifies right ventricular myocardial hypertrophy. Furthermore, gradient-echo MRI demonstrates the signal void of the regurgitant jet (Fig. 33–35) directed toward the right atrium. Although the direction of the jet depends on the geometry of the valve and its deformity of the leaflets, it is always seen early in systole.

Differential diagnosis of tricuspid regurgitation depends on observation of coexisting findings. Tricuspid regurgitation caused by pulmonary hypertension is associated with dilatation of the right heart, the main pulmonary artery segment, and central hilar pulmonary arteries. Spin-echo MRI demonstrates increased signal in the pulmonary artery segments caused by the slow blood flow in patients with high pulmonary resistance. Left atrial enlargement and evidence of pulmonary hypertension in the face of a normal left ventricle point to mitral stenosis as a cause of the pulmonary hypertension and subsequent tricuspid dysfunction. Increased lung volumes and a normal left atrium suggest chronic obstructive pulmonary disease as the cause of the pulmonary hypertension. Patients with primary right heart failure exhibit right heart dilatation, pleural and pericardial effusion, and evidence of right atrial hypertension, including dilatation of the inferior and superior venae cavae, coronary sinus, hepatic veins, and azygos vein. Finally, right-sided heart enlargement with a small pulmonary artery indicates the decreased right ventricular output found

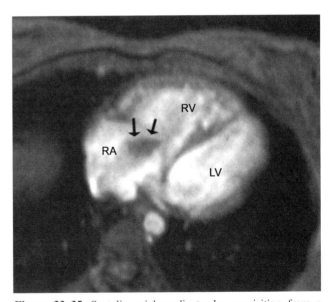

Figure 33–35. Systolic axial gradient-echo acquisition from a 24-year-old woman with primary pulmonary hypertension. The right ventricle (RV) is dilated, and the RV free wall myocardium is as thick as the interventricular septum. The signal void jet *(arrows)* of tricuspid regurgitation extends from the tricuspid valve into the dilated right atrium (RA). The right heart dilatation has rotated in a clockwise manner into the left chest. LV, left ventricle.

in patients with Ebstein's anomaly. All these findings are accurately demonstrated on MRI.

Multivalvular Heart Disease

In combined valvular heart disease, the dominant physiologic alteration, and thus, the clinical and radiologic picture, is determined by the proximal lesion. However, the radiologic appearance varies, depending on the relative severity as well as the physiologic sequelae of each particular valve lesion. The most common cause of multivalvular heart disease is rheumatic. The most common combinations are mitral stenosis with aortic regurgitation, mitral stenosis with tricuspid regurgitation, combined mitral and aortic regurgitation (see Fig. 33–34), combined mitral and aortic stenosis, and combined aortic stenosis and mitral regurgitation.

Quantitative Magnetic Resonance Imaging of Valvular Disease

Accurate estimation of the severity of a valvular lesion is crucial for timing surgical intervention. MRI provides an accurate, reproducible, noninvasive approach to quantification of valvular stenosis and regurgitation, cardiac chamber size, and myocardial mass and function. At present, valvular lesions suspected clinically or suggested on chest radiography are initially evaluated by Doppler echocardiography, followed by cardiac catheterization. Both these methods are semiquantitative and dependent on hemodynamic and technical factors.[62, 258] Valvular regurgitation can be determined by nuclear ventriculography.[144, 245] However, in addition to the drawback of radiation, this technique is influenced by multiple variables, such as the risk of superimposition of the cardiac chambers, the uncertainty of the chamber depth, and the difficulty of quantitation in the face of multiple regurgitant valvular lesions.

The pressure gradient across a valve can be indirectly quantitated using the modified Bernoulli equation.[127] In the early phase of valve disease this may be useful. However, later in the course of the disease, when cardiac output decreases, the technique becomes less accurate.[114] Valve area and cardiac output can be assessed by planimetric analysis of conventional angiocardiography and Doppler echocardiography,[182, 280] and cardiac catheterization,[111] although these techniques also have many limitations.[20, 42]

Cardiac chamber volume can be estimated from spin-echo images. However, accurate measurement of end-systolic and end-diastolic volumes is required for calculation of cardiac output and stroke volume. These values can be reliably obtained only with MRI sequences capable of high-spatial-frequency resolution, such as cine gradient-echo imaging.[119] Furthermore, breath-hold sequences allow a substantial reduction in both imaging time and motion artifacts.[133, 259]

Imaging the ventricles in short-axis section minimizes volume-averaging artifacts. Subsequently, end-diastolic and end-systolic images are selected at each anatomic level. To calculate the end-systolic volume, the areas of the ventricular cavity are measured at end-systole for each level,

summed over the entire ventricular mass and multiplied by the slice thickness. The same procedure is repeated for the end-diastolic images, giving the end-diastolic volume. Similarly, the ventricular myocardial volume (which allows estimation of the myocardial mass) is calculated as the sum of the differences between epicardial minus endocardial areas times slice thickness, summed over the entire ventricle.

The prognostically relevant parameters such as stroke volume and ejection fraction, are calculated from the end-systolic and end-diastolic volumes. Extensive research culminated in validation of MRI as an accurate and reproducible method for determining ventricular dimensions and function.[64, 141, 180, 181, 201–205, 298] At present, MRI is considered the clinical gold standard for determination of stroke volume, ejection fraction, myocardial volume (or mass), as well as ventricular volumes.

The reproducibility of ventricular volume measurements is further underscored by the small difference in the right and left ventricular volumes ($<5\%$)[170, 172, 270] in the absence of valvular regurgitation. Therefore, in patients with a solitary insufficient valve, the regurgitant volume and fraction can be calculated as a difference between and the ratio of the right and left stroke volumes.[269, 298]

Direct measurement of chamber stroke volume, regurgitant volume, and regurgitant fraction can be performed using a velocity mapping technique, based on the linear relationship between the velocity of the spins along the magnetic field gradient and their phase shift. This promising technique provides accurate results in the presence of laminar flow patterns but is detrimentally affected by the complex, turbulent flow patterns[88, 335] inherent in valvular heart disease. Recent advances have been made in reducing the influence of the complex flow patterns on the overall accuracy of this technique by decreasing the duration of the magnetic gradient field used for velocity encoding.[150, 282, 284] These pulse sequences were validated in vivo.

In patients with aortic regurgitation, velocity encoding MRI acquisitions may be used for calculating left ventricular stroke volume, as well as regurgitant volume and regurgitant fraction. In these patients, positioning of the imaging plane close to the aortic valve is crucial for accuracy, because the results are heavily influenced by the coronary blood flow and aortic compliance. When these pitfalls are kept in mind, the accuracy rate of this technique is higher than 90%.[283] Clinical relevance of these data is reflected in the usefulness of MRI evaluation of vasodilator therapy in patients with aortic regurgitation.[107] The transvalvular pressure gradient in aortic stenosis may be calculated from the peak velocity across the stenotic valve with accuracy that is higher than 85%.[283] The valve area may be demonstrated by velocity encoding with an accuracy rate that is higher than 81%. The accuracy rate of quantifying the regurgitant volume and fraction in mitral regurgitation was reported as 91% and 94%, respectively, whereas in mitral stenosis the transmural peak velocity across the valve was calculated with an accuracy rate higher than 87%.[283]

Right Ventricular Disorders

Right ventricular disease may be difficult to evaluate by conventional echocardiographic and angiographic means.

Patients with chronic pulmonary disease commonly present with hyperaerated lungs and chest wall deformities, which limit the use ultrasonographic methods. The high association of chronic heart disease, pulmonary disease, and pulmonary hypertension increases the risk of contrast right ventriculography or pulmonary arteriography in this population. MR image acquisition is not limited by pulmonary or chest wall disorders, and contrast administration for MRI evaluation of the right heart has always been interesting but may simply not be necessary.

Right ventricular function is commonly affected by disorders of the left-sided cardiac structures and the lungs. The most common cardiac causes for right ventricular dysfunction are chronic left ventricular ischemia and rheumatic mitral valve disease. Pulmonary diseases causing right ventricular dysfunction include chronic obstructive pulmonary disease and chronic interstitial diseases (i.e., idiopathic pulmonary fibrosis and cystic fibrosis). Chronic pulmonary vascular pathology, including chronic thromboembolism and primary pulmonary hypertension, also have a significant effect on right ventricular performance.

Common to all of these diseases is elevation of pulmonary vascular resistance with a commensurate increase in right ventricular pressure, resulting in right ventricular hypertrophy. Eventually right ventricular dilatation, tricuspid regurgitation, and right ventricular failure supervene. MRI provides direct, noninvasive visualization of the right ventricular chamber as well as the myocardium itself, allowing reliable demonstration of morphologic changes in the size and shape of the ventricle, thickness of the myocardium, and presence of abnormal infiltration by fat or edema. Furthermore, MRI is well suited for accurate and reproducible quantitation of right ventricular volume and myocardial mass.

Both the left and right ventricles share the interventricular septum. Thus, the septum acts as an "interface" between the left and right hearts. Right-sided heart disease impacts on left ventricular function, and vice versa, via the septum. Normally, the septum acts as if a part of the left ventricle. Viewed in short axis (see Fig. 33–19A and B), the wall segments of the left ventricle, including the interventricular septum, appear to contract radially and symmetrically during systole. The curvature of the interventricular septum is convex toward the right ventricular cavity during both ventricular diastole and systole. Changes in right ventricular shape bow the interventricular septum at the expense of left ventricular shape. That is, right ventricular dilatation may straighten, or even reverse, the contour of the interventricular septum toward the left ventricle (see Fig. 33–3). In such cases, left ventricular filling and thus end-diastolic volume may be impaired, limiting left ventricular output.

The most common cause of right-sided heart failure is chronic left-sided heart failure.[296] The common denominator of this and other left-sided heart problems causing right ventricular dysfunction is chronic left atrial hypertension. That is, the left and right hearts also "communicate" across the pulmonary vascular bed. Pulmonary hypertension and right ventricular failure in patients with mitral stenosis are caused by back-transmission of elevated left atrial pressure and pulmonary arteriolar constriction. Pulmonary arteriolar constriction leads to more severe pulmonary hypertension

and right ventricular failure.[275, 336] Chronic mitral stenosis results in severe pulmonary hypertension and right ventricular hypertrophy and, ultimately, right ventricular dilatation and failure. With time, severe pulmonary hypertension results in tricuspid as well as pulmonary insufficiency, further exacerbating the right ventricular failure. The pulmonary hypertension found in chronic mitral stenosis is more commonly found and is generally more severe than that found in chronic left ventricular ischemia. Treatment of the underlying mitral valve disease by mitral valve replacement results in a marked decline in pulmonary vascular resistance and pulmonary artery and right ventricular pressure.[34]

Other, less common causes of chronic left atrial outflow obstruction and pulmonary venous hypertension include left atrial myxoma[122] or thrombus,[294] congenital mitral stenosis,[59] and cor triatriatum.[216] In the latter condition, there is a congenital membrane interposed between the pulmonary veins and the body of the left atrium. Depending on the caliber of the membrane orifice, a pressure gradient exists between the pulmonary veins and mitral valve. Thus, one finds elevated pulmonary venous pressure in the face of normal left atrial pressure. Acquired pulmonary veno-occlusive disease is an uncommon condition that usually presents in children and young adults.[311] Pulmonary venous obstruction causes elevated pulmonary vein pressure and pulmonary resistance in the face of normal left atrial pressure, resulting in pulmonary hypertension with varying degrees of right ventricular failure.

Similar cardiac changes may be found in cor pulmonale, the syndrome of right ventricular hypertrophy, dilatation, and failure resulting from pulmonary hypertension secondary to lung disease.[57] Although this condition may be acute, as seen in sudden, massive pulmonary thromboembolism,[67, 193] it most often develops chronically, resulting from hypoxia-induced pulmonary arteriolar vasoconstriction or fibrosis of the pulmonary vascular bed.[90, 91] The basic components of cor pulmonale are increased pulmonary vascular resistance, pulmonary hypertension, and right ventricular hypertension.

Pericardial disorders, namely cardiac tamponade and pericardial constriction,[163] commonly result in acute and chronic diastolic right ventricular dysfunction, respectively. Although restrictive cardiomyopathy may initially present with right ventricular failure, it generally involves both left and right ventricles. These conditions are discussed in detail earlier in the chapter.

Not only does MR examination allow direct demonstration of the appearance and intraluminal flow characteristics of the pulmonary arteries,[43, 89, 109, 190, 232, 308] it also allows detailed visualization of the shape and internal morphology of the right ventricle.[23, 94, 180] Patients with cor pulmonale typically present with a massively dilated and hypertrophied right ventricle. Both the chamber volume and the myocardial mass are increased. Morphologic examination of the heart in these patients demonstrates thickening of the right ventricular myocardium, bowing of the interventricular septum toward the left ventricular chamber, and clockwise rotation of the cardiac apex on axial MR images (Fig. 33–36). Spin-echo images reveal morphologic changes of underlying disease, such as narrowed valve orifices, or thickened valve leaflets. Functional gradient-echo cine images may reveal the characteristic signal voids

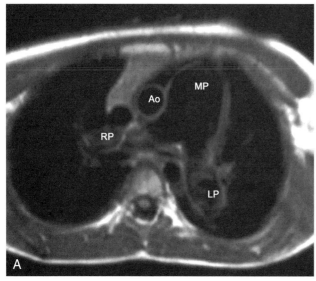

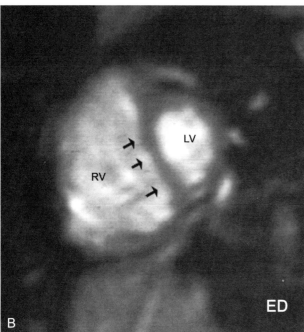

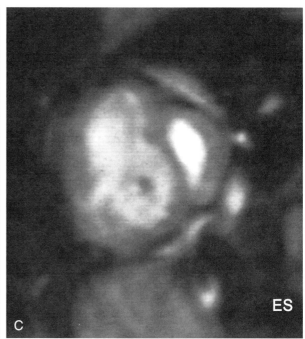

Figure 33–36. MR image obtained from a 6-year-old girl with primary pulmonary hypertension and right ventricular dysfunction.

A, Axial spin-echo acquisition through the pulmonary arteries. The main pulmonary artery (MP) and both left (LP) and right (RP) pulmonary arteries are dilated and show increased signal intensity distally. Note how these mediastinal structures have been displaced toward the left chest by right heart dilatation. Ao, aorta.

B, End-diastolic (ED) short-axis section through the midinterventricular septum. Note how the dilated right ventricle (RV) causes straightening of the interventricular septum *(arrows),* indicating diastolic RV volume loading (secondary to associated tricuspid regurgitation). LV, left ventricle.

C, In this end-systolic (ES) frame obtained at the same anatomic level as in *B,* there is reverse bowing of the interventricular septum, indicating systolic dysfunction. Although the right ventricular free wall myocardium is not clearly seen in *B,* it appears thicker than the interventricular septum and posterior left ventricular wall.

caused by mitral stenosis or tricuspid or pulmonary insufficiency.

Pulmonary Disease

Cor pulmonale results from chronic hypoxia or pulmonary vascular occlusion or both. Chronic obstructive and restrictive lung diseases lead to cor pulmonale due to chronic hypoxia. The most common parenchymal lung disease resulting in cor pulmonale is chronic obstructive airway disease.[90] Small airway obstruction results in decreased vital capacity and nonuniform distribution of inspired oxygen. Pulmonary arteriolar vasoconstriction leads to local hypoxemia, which initiates a vicious cycle of increased pulmonary arterial resistance and right ventricular failure. In patients with pure emphysema, parenchymal

destruction leads to reduction in the cross-sectional area of the vascular bed, resulting in further increase in pulmonary resistance. Typically, patients with emphysema develop cor pulmonale late in their clinical course.[39] There is a loose correlation between increased right ventricular mass[66, 200] and emphysema symptoms. In one study, all individuals with clinical evidence of cor pulmonale had depressed right ventricular ejection fraction.[21] A similar clinical picture is found in patients with asthma, chronic bronchitis, and cystic fibrosis. Right ventricular failure is a common complication of cystic fibrosis.[145] Nearly one third of patients who die with this diagnosis exhibit overt signs of right-sided heart failure within the last 2 weeks of life.[289]

Interstitial lung disease impairs oxygen diffusion. Progressive interstitial lung disease causes thrombosis and fibrous organization and a decrease in the cross-sectional area of the pulmonary vascular bed.[90, 91] Pulmonary arterial hypertension is commonly seen in patients with chronic interstitial pneumonia; advanced sarcoidosis and hemosiderosis[215]; and pulmonary fibrosis secondary to collagen vascular diseases, such as rheumatoid arthritis,[96] dermatomyositis,[132] and progressive systemic sclerosis.[257, 260, 291, 299]

Pulmonary vascular occlusive diseases result in a reduction in the cross-sectional area of the pulmonary vascular bed, which causes increased pulmonary resistance, pulmonary hypertension, and right ventricular hypertrophy. Clinical pulmonary thromboembolism is a complication of lower extremity or pelvic deep vein thrombosis.[61, 78a, 121] Silent pulmonary emboli are a relatively common phenomenon.[171] These pulmonary emboli are usually small and occlude only a small portion of the pulmonary arterial bed without eliciting symptoms. These minute thromboemboli lodge in the peripheral branches of the pulmonary arterial tree over a period of many years, resulting in increased pulmonary resistance and arterial pressure. The multiple pulmonary vascular obstructions found in chronic pulmonary thromboembolism[209] are different than the obstructing thrombi found in acute pulmonary embolism. A massive, acute pulmonary embolus must occlude more than half the pulmonary arterial bed before hemodynamic changes and clinical symptoms develop. However, in patients with recurrent thromboembolism, there frequently is underlying pulmonary hypertension. In this population, additional occlusion of a smaller portion of the pulmonary arterial tree has a hemodynamically significant effect. If pulmonary hypertension has existed for some time, the right ventricle undergoes compensatory hypertrophy to maintain adequate cardiac output in the face of the elevated pulmonary vascular resistance. Faced with sudden increase in arterial resistance due to an additional, large pulmonary embolus, the hypertrophied right ventricle cannot maintain adequate cardiac output. In chronic, recurrent pulmonary thromboembolism, emboli lodge repeatedly in the pulmonary arterial tree over a period of years. These patients experience neither pulmonary infarction nor sufficient acute occlusion of the pulmonary vascular bed to cause acute right ventricular failure. Rather, they experience a gradual occlusion of the pulmonary arterial bed accompanied by a progressive increase in pulmonary vascular resistance. Thus, time is available for right ventricular adaptation.

Primary pulmonary hypertension is a rare, progressive disease of unknown etiology[244, 312] characterized by obstructive changes at the level of the precapillary pulmonary arterioles or pulmonary veins and venules. Progression of the disease and clinical deterioration are associated with decreasing right ventricular function.

Right ventricular enlargement of any etiology causing tricuspid annular dilatation results in tricuspid regurgitation. Pulmonary hypertension is the most common cause of tricuspid regurgitation, which increases the preload as well as the afterload on the right ventricle. Tricuspid regurgitation not only results in further right ventricular and right atrial dilatation but also increased right atrial pressure. This has a deleterious effect on right ventricular function by limiting right ventricular myocardial perfusion. Elevated right atrial pressure is transmitted into the coronary sinus. Thus, the difference between aortic diastolic pressure and coronary sinus pressure (the right ventricular myocardial perfusion gradient) is decreased, causing right (and left) ventricular myocardial ischemia and systolic dysfunction.

Cardiac Tumors

Cardiac tumors are rare. They tend to grow slowly, and patients present with signs and symptoms caused by the tumor's distortion of adjacent structures or organs. Although it may be difficult to characterize a particular tissue origin from MRI, these examinations are extremely helpful for characterization of tumor morphology, evaluation of adjacent and distal structure involvement, and the effects of the tumor on cardiac function. The most common cardiac tumors are metastatic malignancies. These lesions reach the heart by direct extension from the lungs and breast. In autopsy studies, metastatic foci of melanoma is commonly found in the heart but is frequently not clinically important. MR examination is helpful for demonstrating extension of such masses through the pericardium to involve ventricular myocardium. Such information is important for evaluation of surgical resectability[173] of such masses.

Three fourths of all primary tumors of the heart are benign and of soft tissue origin,[191] including rhabdomyoma, fibroma, lipoma (Fig. 33–37), angioma, and myxoma. These tumors generally appear as infiltrating masses with signal intensity characteristic of the tissue of origin, that is, high-signal lipoma and intermediate-signal-intensity rhabdomyoma. Differentiation of these benign masses from their sarcomatous counterparts can be inferred by identification of a high-signal-intensity necrotic core, or other evidence of hemorrhage, distant metastasis, or extensive pericardial and pleural effusion. Myxoma (Fig. 33–38) is the most common benign cardiac mass found in all age groups. It can occur at any time, but more than half of the patients are in their 4th, 5th, and 6th decades. Twelve

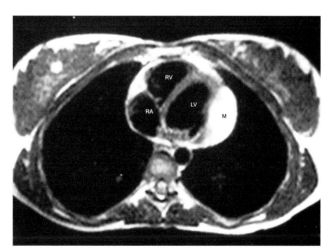

Figure 33–37. Axial spin-echo acquisition from a 35-year-old woman with a myocardial lipoma presenting as an unusual contour on the left heart border of a plain chest film. The high-signal-intensity mass (M) is isointense with subcutaneous and breast fat and infiltrates the posterior left ventricular (LV) wall. No pericardial or pleural effusion is seen. RA, right atrium; RV, right ventricle.

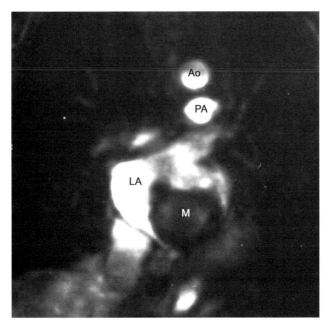

Figure 33–38. Coronal contrast-enhanced gradient-echo image obtained from a 54-year-old man admitted with a cold left lower extremity. The large filling defect of the atrial myxoma (M) is seen within the mildly dilated left atrial (LA) cavity. The normal appearance of the pulmonary artery (PA) indicates that there is no pulmonary hypertension. Ao, aorta.

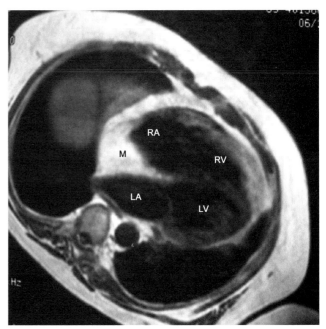

Figure 33–39. Axial spin-echo acquisition from a 59-year-old man with shortness of breath. There is marked deposition of material (M) isointense with the pericardial and subcutaneous fat. The mass extends from the interatrial septum into the right atrium (RA). LA, left atrium; LV, left ventricle; RV, right ventricle.

percent of the Armed Forces Institute of Pathology series[191] were older than 70 years of age. Three fourths of all myxomas originate in the left atrium, mostly attached to the interatrial septum in the region of the limbus of the fossa ovalis. Myxomas may be highly vascular and enhance with intravenous contrast agent administration.

Benign cardiac tumors are usually of intermediate, but homogeneous, signal intensity. Areas of increased signal intensity may represent areas of focal hemorrhage, indicating tumor necrosis, or deposits of fat, reflecting tissue inhomogeneity. Most benign tumors may be "peeled away" from the heart at operation. However, both benign and malignant lesions usually appear to infiltrate adjacent ventricular myocardium. Lipomatous hypertrophy of the interatrial septum (Fig. 33–39) is not truly a malignancy, but rather it is a collection of large fat deposits. It may be isolated to the interatrial septum or may extend along the lateral aspect of the right atrium into the right ventricle. Application of fat saturation during image acquisition may directly characterize the lesion.[4]

Malignant cardiac tumors are usually metastatic. About 10% of patients with malignant neoplasms have cardiac metastases. Clinical dysfunction is usually caused by pericardial involvement. This may be visualized as pericardial effusion, pericardial thickening, or both. Pericardial effusion may be serous or hemorrhagic. The most common metastasis in men is from lung; the most common in women is from breast (Fig. 33–40). These are followed by leukemia and lymphoma (Fig. 33–41). Cardiac involvement is often accompanied by involvement of other organs. Primary cardiac malignant tumors are mostly angiosarcoma, rhabdomyosarcoma, mesothelioma, and fibrosarcoma. Malignant tumors in children are rare. Pericardial involvement is usually found.

Magnetic Resonance Imaging of Congenital Heart Disease

Although gradient-echo (cine) technique is invaluable for evaluation of cardiac function, the increased contrast resolution of spin-echo techniques makes them the work-

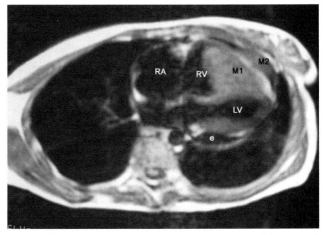

Figure 33–40. MR image obtained from a 32-year-old woman 3 years after mastectomy for adenocarcinoma of the right breast, now complaining of shortness of breath. Nearly the entire right ventricle (RV) is filled with a homogeneous intermediate-signal-intensity mass (M1). The left ventricle (LV) is extrinsically compressed by the mass. In addition, there appears to be a locus of similar material (M2) contained within the pericardial space anterior to the heart. A small posterior pericardial effusion (e) is seen as well. RA, right atrium.

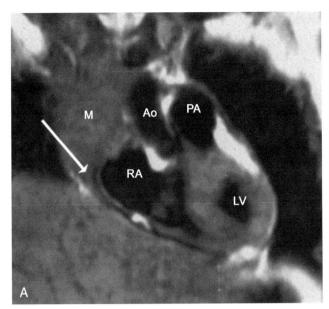 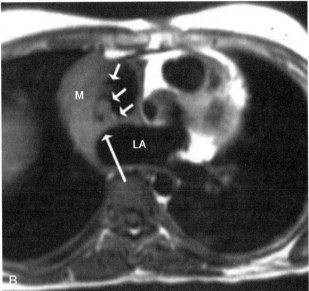

Figure 33–41. MR image obtained from a 16-year-old child with lymphoma. *A,* Coronal spin-echo image obtained through the ascending aorta (Ao) and main pulmonary artery (PA). A bulky, homogeneous, intermediate signal intensity mass is seen along the superior right cardiac border that involves the pericardial space *(arrow)* but seems to spare the right atrium. LV, left ventricle; M, mass; RA, right atrium. *B,* Axial spin-echo acquisition through the superior aspect of the right atrium and aortic valve. The paracardiac and pericardial components of the mass (M) are again seen. In this image, however, there is nodular involvement *(short arrows)* within the right atrium as well as infiltration of the interatrial septum *(long arrow).*

horse for morphologic evaluation by MR. In cases of congenital heart disease, cine acquisition supplements the anatomic and morphologic information obtained from spin-echo acquisitions. Increased spatial resolution is obtained by decreasing the field of view. Infants and small children may be examined from within a head-imaging coil; this allows thinner slice selection as well as a smaller field of view.

The difference in appearance between pediatric and adult patients with congenital heart disease reflects the hemodynamic alterations of the underlying malformation, the duration of the lesion, and the effects of superimposed acquired cardiovascular disease. Depending on the stage in the natural or "unnatural" (i.e., surgically palliated) history of the disease in which examination is performed, the sequelae and complications of the underlying disease may be different. For example, in an atrial septal defect in a child or adolescent, changes of right ventricular hypertrophy and pulmonary hypertension are usually absent. By the age of 45 years, pulmonary hypertension and right ventricular hypertrophy are to be expected. Furthermore, in the older population, altered left ventricular function and its effect on right ventricular function become issues for examination.

Atrial Morphology and Situs

The segmental approach to diagnosis[300, 302] accurately describes congenital heart lesions and is readily applied to interpretation of static and cine tomographic images obtained from cardiac MRI examination. The premise of the segmental approach is that the three cardiac segments (atria, ventricles, and great arteries) develop independently.

By localization and characterization of each of the three cardiac segments and evaluation of the atrioventricular and ventriculoarterial connections and associated anomalies (such as shunts and valve atresia), congenital heart lesions may be diagnosed in a consistent and coherent manner. The usefulness of MRI[117] lies in its ability to demonstrate characteristic morphologic findings needed to name the cardiac chambers, allowing characterization of atrial situs and atrioventricular and ventriculoarterial connections.

The morphologic right atrium (Fig. 33–42) is characterized as the atrial chamber that receives the hepatic venous drainage and the inferior vena cava. It possesses the right atrial appendage and the crista terminalis. The right atrial appendage is a broad-based, triangular-shaped extension of the atrial cavity (a trabeculated "pita pocket"). It is contained within the pericardium and lies anteriorly, medial to the right heart border. The crista terminalis is a fibrous remnant of the valve of the embryologic sinus venosus.[197] It divides the right atrial chamber into a smooth posterior portion and a moderately trabeculated anterior portion (including the appendage). The morphologic left atrium contains the left atrial appendage, which is long and narrower than the right atrial appendage (Fig. 33–43). It passes just inferior to the main pulmonary artery along the left of the heart to reach the radiographic left heart border. The walls of the left atrium are quite smooth; there is no crista terminalis. The left atrium usually receives the pulmonary veins (except in partial or total anomalous pulmonary venous return).

Atrial situs may be directly determined by analysis of the appearance (morphology) of the atria.[105] Alternatively, situs may be deduced from the situs of the lungs (Fig. 33–44). In the normal individual in situs solitus, the mor-

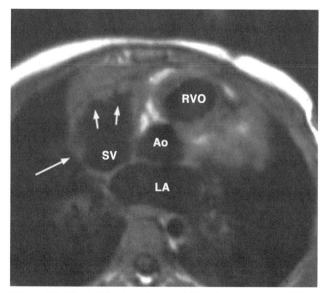

Figure 33–42. Axial spin-echo acquisition from a 6-year-old boy at the level of the aortic root (Ao) and the right ventricular outflow tract (RVO). The characteristic trabeculations of the right atrial appendage *(arrows)* and the wide orifice adjacent to the entry of the superior vena cava (SV) are shown. The high-signal-intensity crista terminalis *(long arrow)* is viewed in cross-section. LA, left atrium.

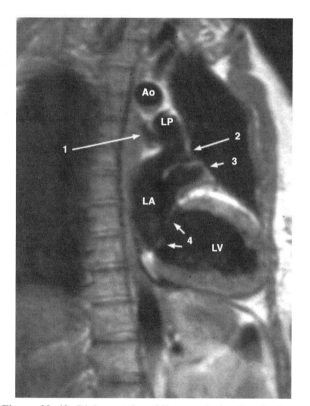

Figure 33–43. Right anterior oblique sagittal spin-echo image obtained from a 38-year-old man. The aortic arch (Ao) and the left pulmonary artery (LP), just after it crosses the left bronchus *(arrow 1)*, are seen. The left upper lobe pulmonary vein *(arrow 2)* enters the left atrium (LA) just superior and posterior to the orifice of the left atrial appendage *(arrow 3)*. The left atrium and the left ventricle (LV) are separated by the mitral valve *(arrows 4)*.

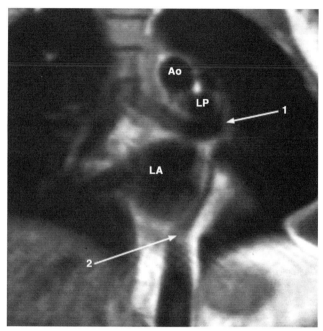

Figure 33–44. Coronal spin-echo acquisition through the tracheal bifurcation in a 40-year-old man with situs solitus. The left pulmonary artery (LP) has just crossed the left main bronchus *(arrow 1)*. The aortic arch (Ao) is superior and medial to the left pulmonary artery. The coronary sinus *(arrow 2)* courses to the right of the fat of the posterior atrioventricular ring, beneath the left atrium (LA).

phologic left bronchus is the bronchus that takes a long course from the tracheal bifurcation before giving origin to the left upper lobe bronchus; the right bronchus is the bronchus that travels for a short distance prior to the origin of the right upper lobe bronchus. The left pulmonary artery courses over the left bronchus; the right pulmonary artery runs anterior and slightly inferior to the right bronchus. Atrial situs inversus is the mirror-image analogue of situs solitus (Fig. 33–45). The morphologic right atrium lies on the left, and the morphologic left atrium is on the right.

Situs ambiguous may be indicated by the presence of symmetrical left-sided and right-sided bronchi. Two left-sided bronchi indicate left isomerism (Fig. 33–46); two right-sided bronchi indicate right isomerism. In atrial situs solitus, the upper abdominal aorta lies to the left of midline and the inferior vena cava to the right; in atrial situs inversus, the abdominal aorta lies to the right. In situs ambiguous, both the aorta and inferior vena cava lie on one side of the midline; on the left side in left isomerism, and on the right in right isomerism. Furthermore, the inferior vena cava in patients with situs ambiguous lies anterior to the aorta.

Ventricular Morphology

The right and left ventricles may be confidently differentiated by their shape, trabecular appearance, and relationship between atrioventricular and semilunar valves. The endocardial surface of the morphologic left ventricle appears smoother than that of the morphologic right ventricle.

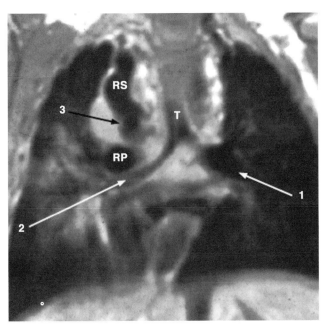

Figure 33–45. Coronal spin-echo acquisition through the tracheal (T) bifurcation in a 6-year-old boy with coarctation of the aorta in complete situs inversus. The left-sided (morphologic right) pulmonary artery *(arrow 1)* is volume-averaged with the left-sided bronchus. The right-sided (morphologic left) pulmonary artery (RP) runs over the top of the right-sided bronchus *(arrow 2)* and lies inferior and lateral to the aortic arch *(arrow 3)*. The aortic arch is diminished in caliber, and the right subclavian artery (RS) is dilated.

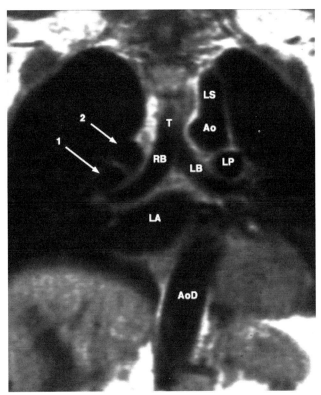

Figure 33–46. Coronal spin-echo acquisition obtained through the tracheal (T) bifurcation and left atrium (LA) from a 76-year-old woman with breast carcinoma. The left-sided bronchus (LB) and the right-sided bronchus (RB) appear symmetrical. The left-sided pulmonary artery (LP) runs over the left bronchus, and the right-sided pulmonary artery *(arrow 1)* runs over the right bronchus. Note that the inferior vena cava is not shown passing through the liver; a dilated azygos vein *(arrow 2)* indicates interruption of the IVC azygos continuation. Incidentally, note the dilated left subclavian artery (LS) originating from the distal aortic arch (Ao); the patient also had an unsuspected mild aortic coarctation. AoD, descending aorta.

The muscular trabeculations of the morphologic right ventricle are thicker and straighter than those of the relatively smooth-appearing left ventricle. These trabeculations are most apparent along the right ventricular side of the interventricular septum. The left ventricle has large papillary muscles that only originate from the free wall. Tricuspid valve papillary muscles originate from both the interventricular septum as well as the free wall of the right ventricle. These are visualized as soft tissue within the right ventricular cavity on spin-echo examination and as filling defects, which increase in size in systolic images, using gradient-echo acquisition. The most reliable means of differentiating the right ventricle from the left ventricle is by demonstration of the right ventricular infundibulum. This circumferential band of myocardium separates the tricuspid valve from the semilunar valve. MR examination is useful for demonstrating the right ventricular infundibulum (Fig. 33–47). The left ventricle has no infundibulum. There is fibrous continuity between the mitral and semilunar valves (Fig. 33–48).

Cardiac Looping

During the third week after fertilization, the ventral cardiac tube loops toward the embryonic right (D [dexter]-looping). As a result of this, the inflow to the ventricle derived from the bulbus cordis subsequently lies to the right of the inflow to the ventricle formed from the true ventricle. By the sixth week after fertilization, the D-looped

heart swings around an external axis to come to lie in the left chest, retaining the right-to-left relationship between right and left ventricular inflows. If the heart loops to the left (L [levo]-looping), the inflow to the morphologic right ventricle comes to lie to the left of that of the morphologic left ventricle. Thus, the direction of looping can be ascertained by analysis of the relationships of the inflows of the ventricular chambers.

Atrioventricular and Ventriculoarterial Connection

Atrioventricular concordance exists when blood flows from the morphologic right atrium to the morphologic right ventricle and from the morphologic left atrium to the morphologic left ventricle; this is the result of D-looping of the ventricles (Fig. 33–49). Atrioventricular concordance may exist in either situs solitus (right atrium to the right) or situs inversus (right atrium to the left). An L-looped heart exhibits atrioventricular discordance; right atrial blood flows to the morphologic left ventricle and left atrial

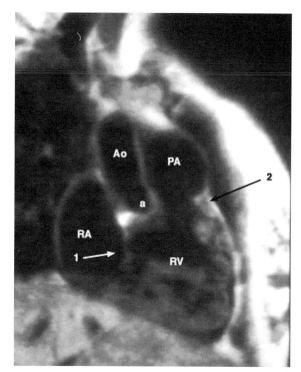

Figure 33–47. Right anterior oblique sagittal spin-echo acquisition through the anterior aortic sinus of Valsalva (a) in a 24-year-old woman with an atrial septal defect. The main pulmonary artery (PA) is dilated, as compared with the ascending aorta (Ao). The tricuspid valve *(arrow 1)* separating the right atrium (RA) from right ventricle (RV) itself is separated from the pulmonary artery by the right ventricular infundibulum *(arrow 2)*.

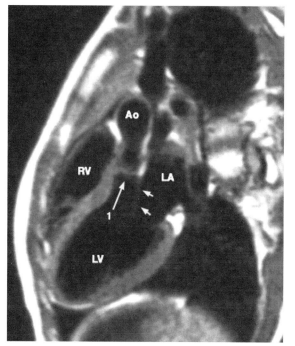

Figure 33–48. Oblique sagittal spin-echo acquisition through the aortic valve *(arrow 1)* in a 9-year-old boy with a bicuspid aortic valve. The valve is thickened, and its caliber is diminished. The anterior mitral leaflet *(short arrows)* attaches to the aortic valve. Ao, aorta; LA, left atrium; LV, left ventricle; RV, right ventricle.

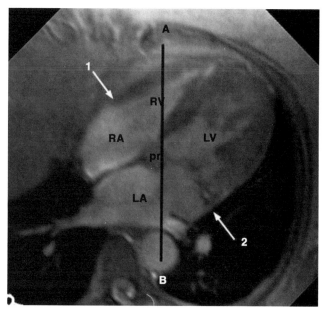

Figure 33–49. Axial early systolic gradient-echo image obtained from a 15-year-old boy with coarctation of the aorta. The line AB is drawn through the center of the heart, just to the left of the posterior right aortic sinus of Valsalva (pr). In a D-loop, the inflow *(arrow 1)* to the right ventricle (RV) lies to the right of the inflow *(arrow 2)* to the left ventricle (LV). LA, left atrium; RA, right atrium.

blood flows to the morphologic right ventricle (Fig. 33–50). Note that D-looping in atrial situs inversus results in L-loop atrioventricular relations and that L-looping in situs inversus results in D-loop relations.

Ventriculoarterial concordance exists when the morphologic right ventricle supports the pulmonary valve and pulmonary artery (see Fig. 33–47) and when the morphologic left ventricle supports the aortic valve and aorta (see Fig. 33–48). Thus, the normal great artery relationship is for the aorta to be to the right with respect to the pulmonary artery (see Fig. 33–3). Ventriculoarterial discordance therefore exists when the right ventricle supports the aorta or the left ventricle supports the pulmonary artery. Generally, ventriculoarterial discordance occurs in two important lesions: (1) D-transposition of the great arteries (D-TGA) and (2) congenitally corrected TGA (CC-TGA or L-TGA). In the former, there is ventriculoarterial discordance in the presence of atrioventricular concordance (Fig. 33–51). In CC-TGA, the association of both atrioventricular and ventriculoarterial discordance results in a double-switched circulation (Fig. 33–52). MR examination may be useful in diagnosing CC-TGA either by explicit demonstration of discordant connections or simply by demonstration of the left-sided upper heart border forming the aorta and the medially located main pulmonary artery segment.[117, 218]

Bicuspid Aortic Valve

Congenital bicuspid aortic valve is the most frequent malformation of the aortic valve, occurring in 0.9% to 2% of all individuals in autopsy series.[248] Although the valve may be stenotic with commissural fusion at birth, it is

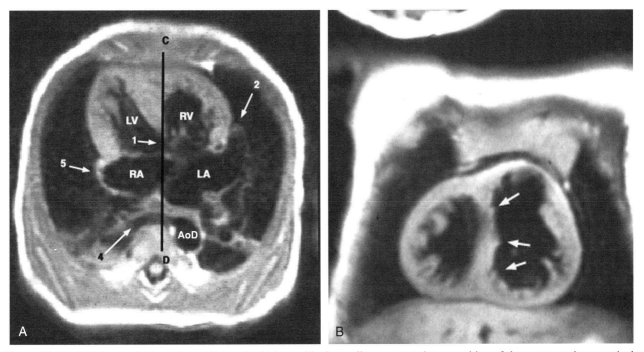

Figure 33–50. MR image obtained from a 7-month-old boy with situs solitus, corrected transposition of the great arteries, ventricular septal defect (VSD), and pulmonary atresia.

A, Axial section through the VSD *(arrow 1)*. The line CD is drawn through the center of the heart. In an L-loop, the inflow to the right ventricle (RV) is to the left of the inflow to the left ventricle (LV). The identity of the morphologic left atrium is determined by the characteristic long left atrial appendage *(arrow 2)*; the right atrial appendage *(arrow 5)* is short and broad-based. Notice the large collateral vessel *(arrow 4)* arising from the descending aorta. LA, left atrium; RA, right atrium.

B, Coronal spin-echo section through the ventricles. The right-sided ventricle gives papillary muscles only from the free wall; this is the morphologic left ventricle. The left-sided ventricle gives papillary muscles from the interventricular septum *(arrows)* as well as the free wall; this is the morphologic right ventricle.

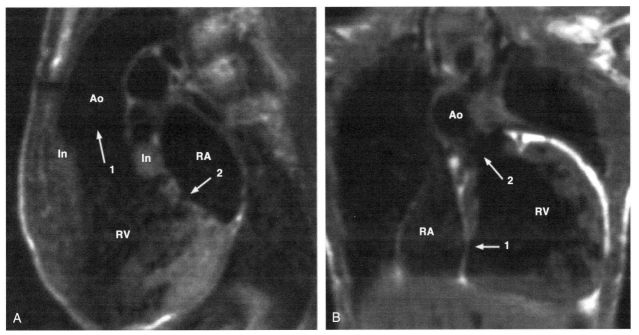

Figure 33–51. D-Transposition of the great arteries in a 4-year-old child. *A,* Sagittal section through the aortic valve. The anterior aorta (Ao) and aortic valve *(arrow 1)* are separated from the tricuspid valve *(arrow 2)* and right atrium (RA) by the circumferential muscular right ventricular (RV) infundibulum (In). *B,* Coronal section through the aortic valve *(arrow 2)*. The aorta (Ao) is toward the right. The tricuspid valve *(arrow 1)* that connects the right atrium (RA) and right ventricle (RV) is separated from the aortic valve.

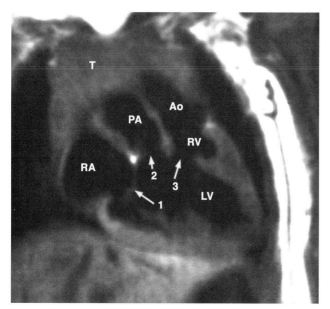

Figure 33–52. Coronal spin-echo acquisition from a 2-year-old boy with double-inlet left ventricle, congenitally corrected transposition of the great arteries, and tricuspid atresia. The thymus (T) has not yet regressed. The morphologic right atrium (RA) is connected to a ventricular chamber whose atrioventicular valve *(arrow 1)* is continuous with the pulmonary valve *(arrow 2)*; this is the morphologic left ventricle (LV) (atrioventricular discordance). The hypoplastic right ventricle (RV) is filled across a ventricular septal defect *(arrow 3)* (also known as a *bulboventricular foramen*) and supports a left-sided aorta (Ao) (ventriculoarterial discordance). PA, pulmonary artery.

more commonly not responsible for severe stenosis in childhood. However, these valves tend to present later in life, usually by late adolescence. Fibrosis, increasing rigidity and calcification of the leaflets, and subsequent narrowing of the aortic orifice[35] develop as a result of turbulence associated with the abnormal valvular architecture. Stenotic changes resemble those found in cases of degenerative calcific stenosis of a tricuspid aortic valve, but these changes occur several decades earlier in the congenitally malformed valve. About one third of patients born with congenital bicuspid aortic valve remain free of any hemodynamically significant problem. Valvular stenosis develops in about one third of patients. An additional one third of patients develop aortic regurgitation[87] on the basis of organic structural abnormality or after a bout of acute bacterial endocarditis.

The aortic annulus in these patients may be normal, but in more severe cases it is decreased in caliber. The three aortic sinuses of Valsalva may be maldistributed by the unseparated valvular commissures; the valve leaflets themselves may be thickened (Fig. 33–53). Calcium is transparent on MR examination; valvular calcification may have the appearance of thickened loci of signal void relating to the valve annulus or where one expects to find valve leaflets. Aortic valve doming may be demonstrated in off-coronal or sagittal section (Fig. 33–54). Often, dilatation of the ascending aorta and left ventricle is identified in cases of valves with mixed stenosis and regurgitation. In both instances, there is left ventricular hypertrophy; in mixed regurgitant bicuspid aortic valves, left ventricular hypertrophy is less apparent because the left ventricle is dilated as well. Gradient-echo imaging of the abnormal valve produces typical systolic signal-void jets of aortic

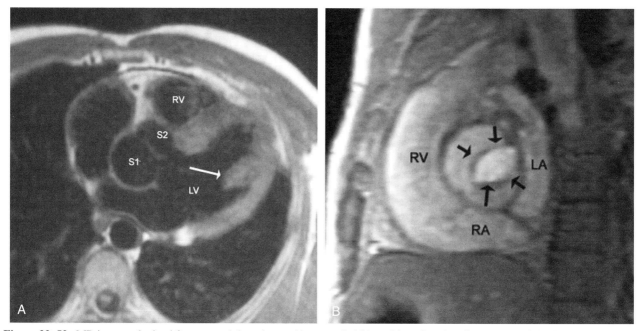

Figure 33–53. MR images obtained from two adult patients with congenital bicuspid aortic valve disease. *A,* Axial spin-echo acquisition from a 23-year-old man. Notice the asymmetry of the two aortic sinuses of Valsalva (S1 and S2). The left ventricular (LV) myocardium is thickened; note the severe hypertrophy of the papillary muscle *(arrow)*. RV, right ventricle. *B,* Systolic short-axis gradient-echo acquisition from a 27-year-old man. There is mild dilatation of the aortic root. The limited valve orifice appears as increased signal intensity sandwiched between the two aortic valve leaflets *(arrows)*. LA, left atrium; RA, right atrium; RV, right ventricle.

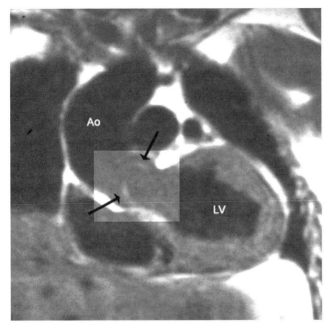

Figure 33–54. Midsystolic oblique coronal spin-echo acquisition from a 19-year-old man with congenital bicuspid aortic stenosis. The center of the image has been image-processed to bring out the appearance of the aortic leaflets *(arrows)*. Notice that the leaflets are thickened and leave a limited valvular orifice. The left ventricular (LV) myocardium is thickened, and there is mild dilatation of the ascending aorta (Ao).

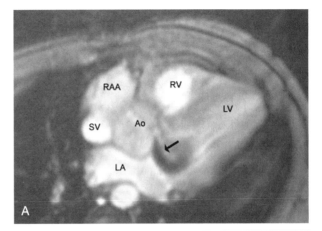

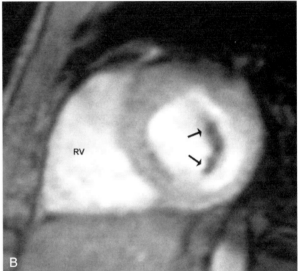

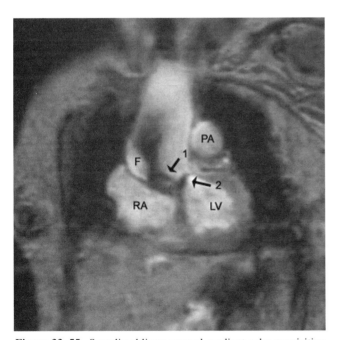

Figure 33–55. Systolic oblique coronal gradient-echo acquisition through the main pulmonary artery (PA) from a 24-year-old woman with bicuspid aortic valve stenosis and an acute aortic dissection. The left ventricular (LV) myocardium is hypertrophied. A signal void jet *(arrow 1)* originates from the signal void of the calcified aortic valve *(arrow 2)* and ricochets off the intimal flap, which separates the true aortic lumen from the false lumen (F). RA, right atrium.

Figure 33–56. MR image obtained from a 30-year-old man with bicuspid aortic valve and aortic regurgitation. *A,* Diastolic oblique axial acquisition through the aortic valve (Ao) at the entry of the superior vena cava (SV) into the right atrium and the right atrial appendage (RAA). The signal void jet of aortic regurgitation *(arrow)* passes along the anterior mitral leaflet and strikes the posterior left ventricular (LV) wall. LA, left atrium; RV, right ventricle. *B,* In this diastolic short-axis image, the signal void jet is seen in cross-section *(arrows)*. RV, right ventricle.

stenosis (Fig. 33–55) and diastolic jets of regurgitation (Fig. 33–56). Correlation between length of signal loss into the aorta and gradient across the valve[199] has been demonstrated in adult patients with aortic stenosis. Direct quantitation of valvular gradients may be obtained by use of phase-velocity mapping.[150, 151] By acquiring images with a sufficiently short echo time (<5 msec), signal loss from all but the most turbulent regions of poststenotic blood flow is eliminated. Signal intensity measurements across the face of a poststenotic jet are proportional to the flow-velocity profile across the valve. Thus, application of a modified Bernoulli equation to flow-velocity measurements provides a noninvasive estimate of valve pressure gradient.

Coarctation of the Aorta

The most common symptomatic congenital lesion of the aortic arch studied by magnetic resonance is coarctation of

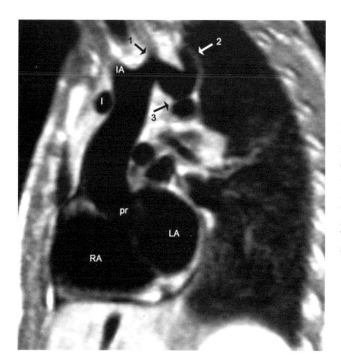

Figure 33–57. Oblique sagittal spin-echo acquisition through the posterior right aortic sinus of Valsalva (pr) from an 11-year-old boy with a 35-mm gradient between upper and lower extremities. The left atrium (LA) and the right atrium (RA) are labeled. Notice the long and undulating course of the ascending aorta and aortic arch. The dilated innominate artery (IA) origin immediately behind the innominate vein (I), the origins of the left common carotid artery *(arrow 1)* and the left subclavian artery *(arrow 2)* are seen. The left subclavian artery appears to run nearly parallel to the distal aortic arch immediately above the coarctation *(arrow 3)* itself.

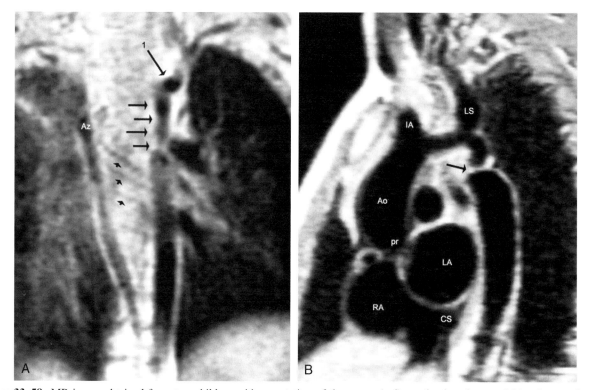

Figure 33–58. MR image obtained from two children with coarctation of the aorta. *A,* Coronal spin-echo acquisition from a 6-month-old girl with a 50-mm aortic gradient. The proximal descending aorta *(parallel long arrows)* distal to the origin of the dilated left subclavian artery *(arrow 1)* tapers to the point of maximal stenosis. Aortic collateral vessels *(arrowheads)* are seen entering the aorta distal to the coarctation. The azygos vein (Az) is labeled. *B,* The patient is a 4-year-old boy with a 60-mm gradient. Left anterior oblique sagittal spin-echo acquisition through the posterior right (pr) aortic sinus of Valsalva. The left (LA) and right (RA) atria are marked. The ascending aorta (Ao) is mildly dilated, and there is hypoplasia of the arch extending from the origin of the innominate artery (IA), beyond the origin of the left subclavian artery (LS) to the actual coarctation itself *(arrow).* Beyond the coarctation, there is mild poststenotic dilatation. CS, coronary sinus.

the aorta.[146, 306] Coarctation of the aorta is a congenital maldevelopment of the aorta (Fig. 33–57), which presents with hypoplasia of the distal aortic arch and focal narrowing of the proximal descending aorta, almost invariably at the junction of the ductus arteriosus and aorta.

Collateral circulation to the postcoarctation segment usually originates from branches of the proximal subclavian arteries (the internal mammary arteries and thyrocervical trunk). Blood flow is around the shoulder or anterior chest wall and retrograde through the intercostal arteries to the postcoarctation segment of the proximal descending aorta. Occasionally, coarctation of the aorta may be associated with an aberrant subclavian artery. In such circumstances, the aberrant artery is downstream from the coarctation (at low pressure with respect to the ascending aorta) and thus unable to provide collateral flow to the postcoarctation aorta. Plain film examination in these cases may reveal unilateral rib notching.

MR examination of patients with coarctation of the aorta is directed toward demonstration of the location and length of the coarctation segment (Fig. 33–58), the status of the aortic isthmus, and the degree of arterial collateralization present.[28, 146, 279, 306] Furthermore, the relationship of the coarctation to the origins of the left and right subclavian arteries (especially in cases with an aberrant subclavian artery) must be demonstrated. These changes are usually best appreciated in oblique sagittal or coronal sections, parallel to the axis of the ascending and descending aortas. However, in smaller children or older adults, the small caliber of the aorta or aortic tortuosity may necessitate acquisition in additional oblique sections. The origin of the left subclavian artery in many of these patients appears to be "pulled" inferiorly from the distal aortic arch toward the hourglass deformity of the coarctation itself, the so-called capture of the left subclavian artery (see Fig. 33–57). In oblique sagittal sections from the posterior chest, dilated intercostal arteries may be identified traveling along the underside of the posterior upper ribs (Fig. 33–59). The internal mammary arteries run along the inner aspect of the anterior chest wall, on either side of the lateral border of the sternum, and are best identified in axial or coronal section as dilated signal voids (Fig. 33–60). MR examination is a useful means of following the results of balloon dilatation and surgical repair of coarctation.[236, 286] Serial examination allows close follow-up and assessment of residual stenosis and early demonstration of aneurysmal dilatation.

Patent Ductus Arteriosus

The ductus arteriosus is the persistent distal left sixth aortic arch. It extends from the underside of the aortic arch just distal to the origin of the left subclavian artery to the left pulmonary artery near its origin. Usually the ductus is left sided, but, in cases of right aortic arch, it may be right sided. Bilateral patent ductus arteriosus is rarely found. This abnormality has a variable morphology. The most common shape of a patent ductus arteriosus is long and cylindrical (Fig. 33–61). An hourglass-like narrowing may be found in its midportion. Frequently, the patent duct has a funnel shape. In this variety there is a broad base on the

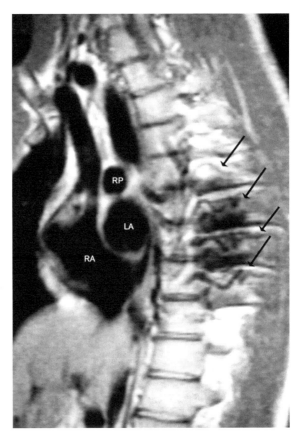

Figure 33–59. Left anterior oblique sagittal spin-echo acquisition through the interatrial septum from a 14-year-old boy with a 50-mm gradient across the coarctation. The left atrium (LA) and right atrium (RA) and the right pulmonary artery (RP) are labeled. Intercostal collateral vessels appear as serpiginous signal voids along the undersides of the ribs *(arrows)*.

aortic side and a narrow attachment to the pulmonary artery. Aneurysmal ducti are less common but may appear saccular or spindle shaped. The variable length and orientation of the duct between the aorta and pulmonary artery make its demonstration often difficult. In the coronal section, communication between the underside of the distal aortic arch or proximal aorta with the superior aspect of the left pulmonary artery may be easily demonstrated. Right anterior oblique sagittal section through the arch or proximal descending aorta may demonstrate ductal communication. MR examination for patent ductus arteriosus in infants may be limited by the size of the ductus and spatial resolution of the scanner (Fig. 33–62). There are no data concerning the sensitivity and specificity of MR examination in the diagnosis of patent ductus arteriosus.

Pulmonary Arteries

Echocardiographic examination of the pulmonary arteries may be limited.[125, 208] MRI complements echocardiographic examination for the assessment of the size, patency, confluence, and character of the extraparenchymal pulmonary arteries (Fig. 33–63).[44, 73, 103] Pulmonary arterial anomalies, including pulmonary artery sling and origin of the

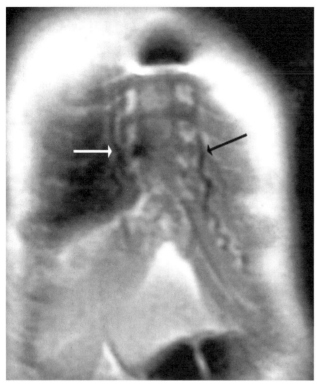

Figure 33–60. Coronal spin-echo acquisition through the posterior aspect of the sternum in a 16-year-old boy with coarctation of the aorta. Both the left and right *(arrows)* internal mammary arteries are dilated and serpiginous.

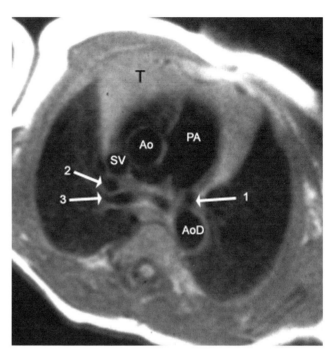

Figure 33–62. Off-axial spin-echo image obtained from a 5-week-old girl with heart failure. The thymus (T) has not regressed. The main pulmonary artery (PA) is dilated and greater in caliber than the ascending aorta (Ao). The right pulmonary artery *(arrow 2)* lies behind the superior vena cava (SV) and in front of the right bronchus *(arrow 3)*. The patent ductus is the signal void communication *(arrow 1)* between the top of the pulmonary artery and the descending aorta (AoD).

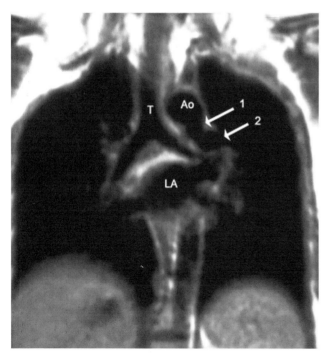

Figure 33–61. Coronal spin-echo acquisition through the trachea (T) and tracheal bifurcation and posterior left atrium (LA) from a 24-year-old woman with pulmonary hypertension. The tubular communication *(arrow 1)* between the underside of the distal aortic arch (Ao) and the top of the left pulmonary artery *(arrow 2)* is the patent ductus.

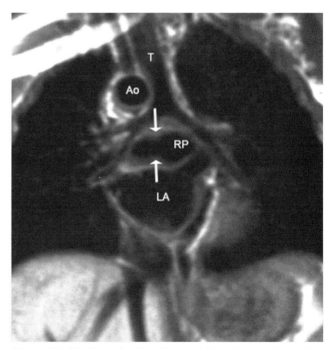

Figure 33–63. Coronal spin-echo acquisition through the trachea (T) and the tracheal bifurcation from a 16-month-old boy with tetralogy of Fallot with pulmonary atresia and right branch pulmonary artery stenosis. The aortic arch (Ao) is right-sided. There is focal narrowing of the transverse right pulmonary artery (RP) *(arrows)* as the artery crosses over the left atrium (LA).

pulmonary artery from the ductus arteriosus, may be characterized directly. Increased pulmonary blood flow, increased pulmonary artery pressure, and poststenotic dilatation of the pulmonary artery can be differentiated based on the character of flow within the dilated pulmonary artery segments. Dilated central pulmonary artery segments without increased signal indicates increased flow (see Figs. 33–36A, 33–45, and 33–62); if increased signal is present, pulmonary artery pressure is elevated. Dilatation of the main pulmonary artery, with or without associated left or right pulmonary arterial enlargement, may be seen in patients with valvular pulmonic stenosis. Aneurysmal dilatation of the pulmonary arterial tree may be found in patients with chronic, mild valvular pulmonic stenosis or pulmonary insufficiency. In patients with pulmonary hypertension and long-standing left-to-right shunts, the pulmonary arterial wall is thickened and increased in signal intensity. The central pulmonary arteries in cases of right ventricular outflow obstruction (including pulmonary atresia or tetralogy of Fallot with pulmonary atresia) may be diminutive or, if atretic, not identifiable. Focal branch stenosis proximal to the pulmonary hila may be identified directly. The main and central pulmonary arteries in cases of supravalvular pulmonic stenosis (as an isolated lesion, or in association with Williams or Noonan's syndromes), reveal diffuse or focal wall thickening (Fig. 33–64). Similarly, pulmonary arterial banding results in focal pulmonary artery narrowing.

Congenital Pulmonary Stenosis

The most common form of congenital pulmonic stenosis is valvular. So-called supravalvular pulmonic stenosis is actually pulmonary arteritis with segmental stenosis and is commonly a component of Noonan's syndrome, Williams

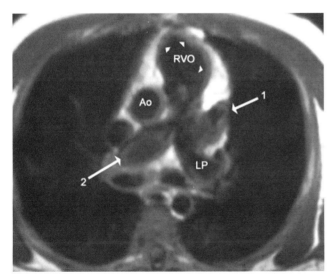

Figure 33–64. Axial spin-echo acquisition through the right ventricular outflow tract (RVO) and left atrial appendage *(arrow 1)* from a 37-year-old man with Williams syndrome. Note the infundibular right ventricular hypertrophy *(arrowheads)*. Turbulence in the right pulmonary artery *(arrow 2)* extends from beyond stenosis at its origin. Ao, aorta; LP, left pulmonary artery.

syndrome, and congenital rubella syndrome. Subvalvular stenosis is the result of local right ventricular infundibular hypertrophy; the valve is usually normal in these individuals.

In patients with noncritical pulmonic stenosis, the pulmonary valve leaflets thicken and fibrose with age, but calcification is rarely found. Right ventricular hypertrophy reflects the severity and duration of the valvular obstruction. Right-sided heart failure is uncommon in infancy and before the 5th decade. Prolonged right ventricular hypertension distorts chamber geometry, causing right ventricular papillary muscle dysfunction and tricuspid regurgitation. Some patients with moderate stenosis progress to more severe obstruction owing to late fibrosis and deformity of the valve leaflets, or superimposed infundibular hypertrophy. Survival into the 7th decade in patients with valvular pulmonary stenosis has been reported.[104, 113]

MR examination in these patients is directed toward differentiating valvular disease from diseases resulting in dilatation of the main pulmonary artery. In patients with valvular pulmonic stenosis, the main and either left or both left and right proximal pulmonary arteries are dilated. Pulmonary blood flow in these patients is normal, so a signal void is expected when examined using spin-echo technique. Gradient-echo acquisition through the right ventricular outflow and proximal main pulmonary artery shows a systolic jet of signal void owing to turbulence extending into the main or left pulmonary artery. Right ventricular hypertrophy is the rule in these individuals but, depending on the severity of the myocardial hypertrophy, the amount of tricuspid regurgitation is variable. Therefore, right ventricular dilatation is unusual, and clockwise cardiac rotation is not usually seen (Fig. 33–65).

Intracardiac Shunts

MR examination is useful for the diagnosis of intracardiac shunt by explicit demonstration of the defect. Alternatively, it may be used to define the constellation of specific chamber dilatation and hypertrophy that may be used to characterize a particular lesion, confirming questionable cases and excluding false-positive cases.

Atrial Septal Defect

Atrial septal defects (ASDs) may be classified on the basis of the location of the defect. *Primum defects*, whether or not they are associated with other atrioventricular septal defects, are medially located, immediately superior to the atrioventricular valves (Fig. 33–66). *Secundum defects* are centrally located in the septum and are usually large. These may be differentiated from a patent foramen ovale by their size (Fig. 33–67). *Sinus venosus defects* are laterally located, appearing as defects between the posteroinferior border of the inferior vena cava and the left atrium, immediately inferior and posterior to the entry of the right upper lobe pulmonary vein (Fig. 33–68).

The interatrial septum is best visualized in axial and left anterior oblique sagittal or short-axis section (Fig. 33–69; see also Fig. 33–67A). It is often infiltrated with fat, in-

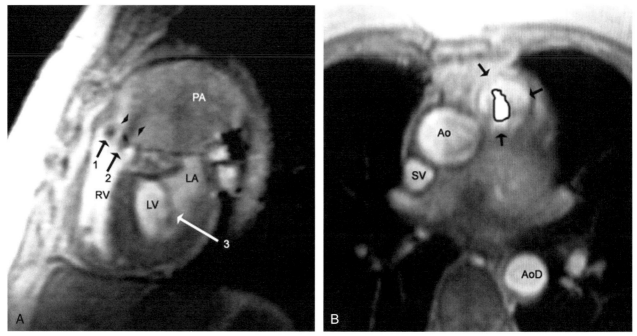

Figure 33–65. MR image obtained from a 74-year-old woman with congenital valvular pulmonic stenosis. *A,* Systolic sagittal gradient-echo acquisition obtained through the pulmonary valve. Two signal voids on the cusps of the pulmonary valve *(arrows 1 and 2)* represent calcific leaflet deposits. A fan-shaped jet of pulmonic stenosis *(arrowheads)* into the dilated main pulmonary artery (PA) can be seen. In this anatomic section, the anterior mitral leaflet *(arrow 3)* can be seen separating the left atrium (LA) from left ventricle (LV). RV, right ventricle. *B,* Systolic oblique axial section through the stenotic pulmonary valve *(arrows)*. The valve orifice has been outlined in black. One can see how valve area can be directly quantitated by this technique. Ao, aorta; AoD, descending aorta; SV, superior vena cava.

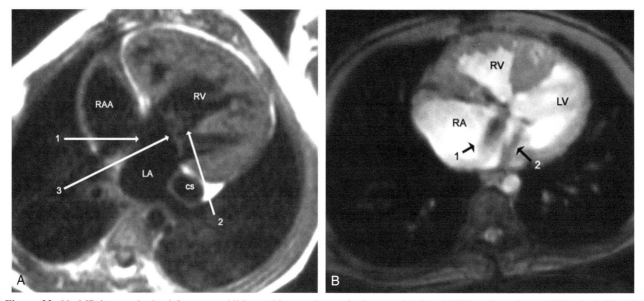

Figure 33–66. MR image obtained from two children with an atrioventricular septal defect (ASD) and a primum ASD. *A,* Axial spin-echo acquisition from a 21-month-old girl. Both the right atrial appendage (RAA) and the left atrium (LA) are dilated. There is a break in the medial aspect of the interatrial septum *(arrow 1)*, indicating a primum ASD. In addition, there is a break in the posterior interventricular septum *(arrow 2)* and a solitary bridging atrioventricular valve *(arrow 3)*. The right ventricular (RV) myocardium is severely hypertrophied. Incidentally, in this child with duplication of the superior vena cava, the left vena cava drains to the dilated coronary sinus (cs).

B, Systolic axial gradient-echo acquisition from a 15-month-old boy with ASD. Note the severe hypertrophy of the right ventricular (RV) and the septal myocardium. The signal void jet *(arrow 1)* extending from just beneath the posterior right aortic sinus of Valsalva into the right atrium (RA) is the shunt through the atrioventricular septal defect. In addition, the signal void jet *(arrow 2)* extending from the mitral valve into the left atrium represents mitral regurgitation through a cleft mitral leaflet. LV, left ventricle.

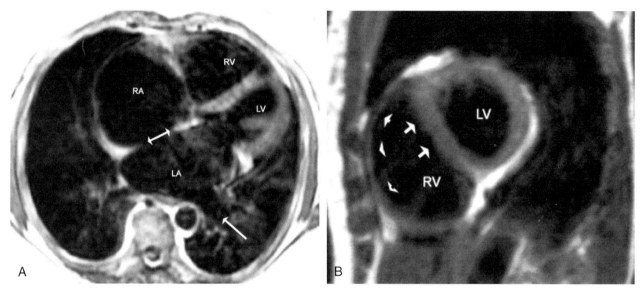

Figure 33–67. MR image obtained from two adult patients with secundum atrial septal defects. *A,* Axial spin-echo acquisition from an asymptomatic 57-year-old woman. The heart has rotated in a clockwise manner into the left chest; the right atrium (RA), the right ventricle (RV), and the left lower-lobe pulmonary vein *(single-headed arrow)* are dilated. The interventricular septum is flat. However, the left atrium (LA) and left ventricle (LV) are normal. The atrial septal defect *(double-headed arrow)* is in the center in the interatrial septum. *B,* Short-axis section from a 43-year-old asymptomatic woman. The dilated right ventricle (RV) has extended below the normal-appearing left ventricle (LV). Despite the RV dilatation, the right ventricular free wall myocardium *(arrowheads)* is not hypertrophied, but the interventricular septum *(short arrows)* is flattened.

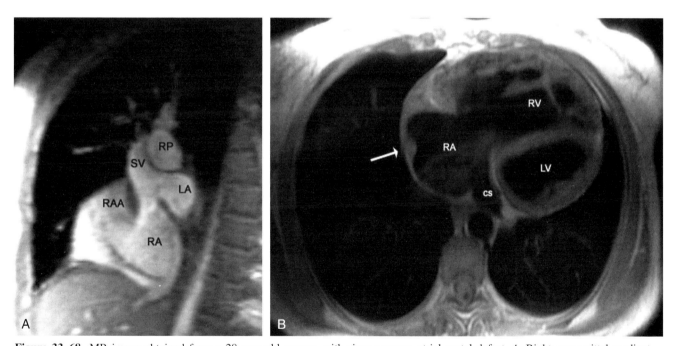

Figure 33–68. MR image obtained from a 28-year-old woman with sinus venosus atrial septal defect. *A,* Right parasagittal gradient-echo acquisition through the entrance of the superior vena cava (SV) into the right atrium (RA). The defect results in continuity among the lower SV, the left atrium (LA), and the right atrium. RAA, right atrial appendage; RP, right pulmonary artery. *B,* Axial spin-echo acquisition through the right atrium (RA) and right ventricle (RV). The right atrium, right ventricle, and coronary sinus (cs) are each dilated, and the heart is rotated into the left chest. The interventricular septum is flat, and RV myocardial trabeculae in this patient are more prominent than in the patient in Figure 33–67*B.* Note the high-signal-intensity crista terminalis *(arrow)* along the lateral aspect of the RA wall. LV, left ventricle.

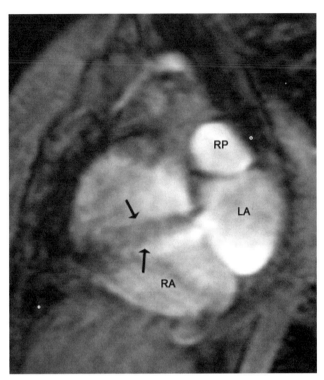

Figure 33–69. Diastolic short-axis acquisition through the interatrial septum in a 30-year-old woman with a secundum atrial septal defect. The interatrial septum is bowed toward the right atrium (RA). The signal void jet of the shunt *(arrows)* extends from the septum into the dilated RA. The left atrium (LA) is smaller than the RA, and the right pulmonary artery (RP) is dilated.

creasing its conspicuity against the signal void of the two atria, and normally bows toward the right atrium. The septum is thinner in the region of the foramen ovale. Care must be taken to avoid making the misdiagnosis of an atrial septal defect based solely on the isolated observation of a break in the septal contour. The diagnosis of a shunt is ensured if the associated morphologic and anatomic changes resulting from the altered flow of blood are identified. In particular, in an atrial septal defect, blood shunts across the atrial septum to volume-load the right atrium and ventricle and pulmonary arteries. Volume loading the right heart results in clockwise (looking from below) cardiac rotation. The plane of the interventricular septum is nearly parallel to the coronal plane. In patients with atrial septal defect, the left atrium decompresses during diastole and is therefore not enlarged. Right ventricular myocardium in simple atrial septal defect is not hypertrophied. The direction of the shunt (left-to-right or right-to-left) can be assessed using gradient-echo technique. Of course, such characterization is dependent on finding the anatomic level of the shunt itself and imaging the defect in a plane orthogonal to the flow of blood. Administration of intravenous Gd-DTPA may help characterize smaller or less apparent shunts.[175] Atrial-level shunts may be quantitated by means of analysis of velocity-encoded cine MR images.[36] Imaging in the axial plane, MR has an overall 97% sensitivity and 90% specificity for the detection of atrial septal defects.[72]

Ventricular Septal Defect

MRI is a valuable means of diagnosing the presence and size of ventricular septal defects.[74, 135, 340] Large subaortic ventricular septal defects are readily demonstrated on axial spin-echo images as signal voids to the left of the atrioventricular rings and to the right of the crest of the muscular interventricular septum (Fig. 33–70). Separation of the actual defect from the caudal extension of an aortic sinus of Valsalva is best appreciated by obtaining images in oblique sagittal section through the base of the heart. Smaller, and more distal, defects are more difficult to demonstrate directly using spin-echo technique and often necessitate construction of compound angulated sections. GRE cine acquisition portrays the turbulent blood flowing across the defect as a signal-void jet within the cavity of the right ventricle (Fig. 33–71). Membranous ventricular septal defects are identified by the absence of signal in the posterior, superiormost aspect of the interventricular septum, immediately below the aortic valve, and adjacent to the septal leaflet of the tricuspid valve. Supracristal defects may be identified in right anterior oblique sagittal section, or in axial section, immediately below the semilunar valves. Anterior extension into the muscular septum can be identified in axial or right anterior oblique sagittal sections through the interventricular septum. Muscular ventricular septal defects are more difficult to identify directly by spin-echo technique but may be identified by detection of the signal-void jet of the shunted blood using gradient-echo methods (Fig. 33–72). Careful evaluation of cine imagery allows differentiation among left-to-right, right-to-left, and bidirectional shunts.

Other Shunts

Atrioventricular septal defects (endocardial cushion defects) may involve the anterior mitral and septal tricuspid valve leaflets, the membranous interventricular septum, as

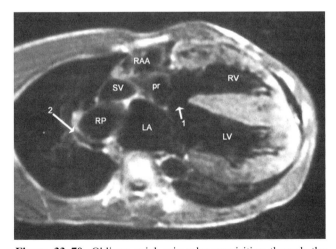

Figure 33–70. Oblique axial spin-echo acquisition through the posterior right aortic sinus of Valsalva (pr). The large membranous ventricular septal defect *(arrow 1)* communicates between the dilated and hypertrophied right ventricle (RV) and the left (LV) ventricle. The visualized right pulmonary artery (RP) lies anterior to the right bronchus *(arrow 2)*. Notice how the unsupported aortic sinus overrides the septum toward the right ventricle. LA, left atrium; RAA, right atrial appendage; SV, superior vena cava.

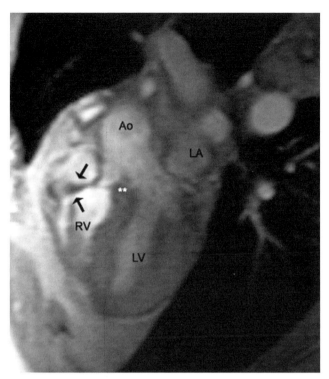

Figure 33–71. Systolic horizontal long-axis section through the posterior interventricular septum in a 50-year-old man with a pinhole ventricular septal defect. At the apex *(arrows)* of a ventricular septal aneurysm that extends between the crest of the muscular interventricular septum *(**)* and the annulus of the aortic valve is the fan-shaped signal void shunt jet into the right ventricle (RV). Ao, aorta; LA, left atrium; LV, left ventricle.

well as the atrioventricular septum and primum portion of the interatrial septum (see Fig. 33–66). Precise classification based on the morphology of the common atrioventricular valve is difficult with MR, but such defects may be characterized by the extent of endocardial cushion abnormality.[135, 219] MRI is useful in determining the size of the ventricular component of the defect as well as the presence of ventricular hypoplasia. Gradient-echo acquisition may be helpful in confirming primum atrial septal defects and demonstrating atrioventricular shunting.

Anomalous pulmonary veins may return to systemic veins above the level of the heart, including the innominate and subclavian veins, or superior vena cava. Veins may drain directly to the right atrium or coronary sinus or below the level of the heart, to the inferior vena cava or portal vein. Axial spin-echo acquisition almost always demonstrates the four pulmonary veins. In a series of 56 patients with various types of congenital heart disease but normal pulmonary venous connection, axial spin-echo MRI showed the sites of connection of all four pulmonary veins in 88% of cases; in a parallel series of 22 patients with partial or total anomalous pulmonary venous return, pulmonary venous anomalies were identified in 95% of cases[185] (Fig. 33–73).

Anomalies of individual pulmonary veins are rare but may be identified using MRI. Pulmonary vein stenosis may be identified by the increased intraluminal signal intensity of obstructed venous inflow to the heart.[254] Pulmonary venous varix may be identified as a dilated tubular structure confluent with the left atrium.[326]

Tetralogy of Fallot

The underlying malformation in patients with tetralogy of Fallot is the malalignment of the ventricular septal

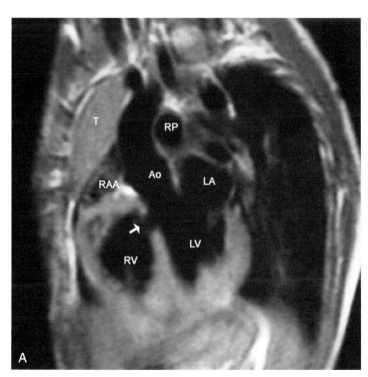

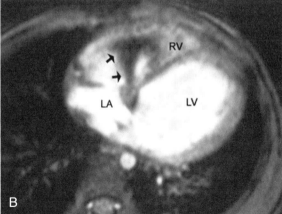

Figure 33–72. MR images obtained from a 5-year-old boy with a muscular ventricular septal defect. *A,* Oblique sagittal spin-echo acquisition through the aortic root (Ao). The defect *(arrow)* is well away from the membranous interventricular septum and the aortic annulus. LA, left atrium; RAA, right atrial appendage; RP, right pulmonary artery; RV, right ventricle; T, thymus. *B,* Systolic axial gradient-reversal acquisition through the defect shows the fan-shaped signal void jet *(arrows)* extending from the dilated left ventricle (LV), through the septum, and into the right ventricle (RV). LA, left atrium.

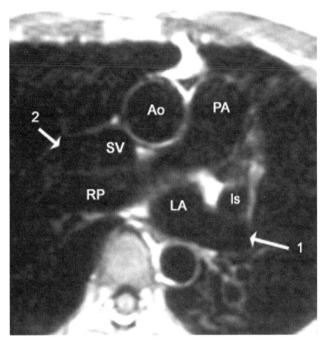

Figure 33–73. Axial spin-echo acquisition from a 23-year-old woman with a sinus venosus atrial septal defect, partial anomalous pulmonary venous return, and bilateral superior venae cavae. The main pulmonary artery (PA) and the right pulmonary artery (RP) are dilated, as is the left lower lobe pulmonary vein *(arrow 1)*. The lateral aspect of the right-sided superior vena cava (SV) is incomplete at the site of entry of the anomalous right upper lobe pulmonary vein *(arrow 2)*. Note the signal void of the left-sided superior vena cava (ls) as it enters the lateral horn of the coronary sinus. Ao, aorta; LA, left atrium.

defect. The degree to which the crista supraventricularis is malaligned determines the severity of right ventricular outflow obstruction as well as the size of the aortic root and the incidence of aortic regurgitation.[179] Aortic regurgitation is found in more than three fourths of adult patients with tetralogy of Fallot with pulmonary atresia.[45] This volume-loads both left and right ventricles but has a more significant effect on the already pressure-loaded right ventricle.

Evaluation of a patient with tetralogy of Fallot requires a series of acquisitions in different planes to characterize the severity of right ventricular outflow obstruction, the ventricular septal defect, and pulmonary morphology. Furthermore, one must assess the status of systemic-to–pulmonary artery collateral vessels and palliative surgical shunts, if present. The typically large perimembranous ventricular septal defect is usually well demonstrated in axial[198] or sagittal section (Fig. 33–74A). Aortic caliber and position of the aortic valve with respect to the interventricular septum are explicitly demonstrated in sagittal section (see Fig. 33–33). Slightly cephalad to the ventricular septal defect, the narrowed right ventricular outflow tract and hypertrophied infundibulum may be evaluated (Fig. 33–74B). Off-coronal section aids in demonstrating confluence of the pulmonary arteries as well as focal pulmonary artery stenosis (see Fig. 33–63). Addition of coronal imaging is helpful in demonstrating the presence and extent of systemic to pulmonary artery collaterals. Use of either spin-echo or gradient-echo images allows measurement of the size of the main pulmonary artery and each major branch, as well as the adequacy of the central pulmonary confluence. The most commonly used surgical shunt in these patients is a modified Blalock-Taussig shunt. MRI is effective in demonstrating the potency and defining the severity of stenosis within the shunt. Velocity-encoded cine MRI

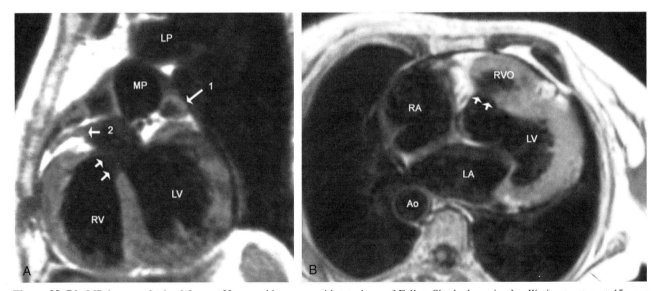

Figure 33–74. MR images obtained from a 53-year-old woman with tetralogy of Fallot. She had received palliative treatment 45 years earlier with a Blalock-Taussig shunt. *A,* Left anterior oblique sagittal spin-echo acquisition through the aortic root shows how the large subaortic ventricular septal defect (VSD) *(paired arrows)* affords communication between the hypertrophied right ventricle (RV) and the mildly dilated left ventricle (LV). The aortic root overrides the VSD. The origin of the right coronary artery *(arrow 2)* is seen. Arrow 1, left atrial appendage. *B,* Axial spin-echo acquisition obtained through the aortic valve. The anteriorly malaligned crista supraventricularis *(arrows)* causes posterior impingement on the hypertrophied right ventricular outflow (RVO) and leaves the VSD behind. Notice the right-sided descending aorta (Ao) in this patient with a mirror-image right aortic arch. LA, left atrium; LV, left ventricle; RA, right atrium.

can be used to measure flow and estimate gradients in these structures. Imaging palliative Blalock-Taussig shunts is best performed in plane with the long axis of the grafts, that is, in oblique sagittal or coronal section.

In cases of pulmonary atresia, there is increased fat deposition in the region of the atretic valve ring.[147] The main pulmonary artery may be identified (and even enlarged) if a surgical shunt procedure was performed prior to examination. More commonly, however, the pulmonary arteries are hypoplastic (Fig. 33–75). Determination of pulmonary artery continuity and exclusion of focal pulmonary artery stenosis are goals of MR examination. The right ventricular myocardium in pulmonary atresia with intact septum is markedly hypertrophied, more so than found in tetralogy of Fallot. The right ventricular cavity is small, the actual size being dependent on the size and competence of the tricuspid valve. The aorta in pulmonary atresia with ventricular septal defect as well as in tetralogy of Fallot is dilated. MR examination provides detailed anatomic information concerning the morphology of the right ventricular outflow tract, the size and course of the central pulmonary arteries, and the sources of collateral blood flow to the lungs[93, 147, 235] in these patients. Systemic-to-pulmonary artery collaterals are usually found posterior to the trachea and main bronchi. MR examination tends to underestimate their number[235] but is useful in demonstrating their origin. The site of connection with the pulmonary arterial tree is often not seen. Patency of palliative shunts may be assumed when no intraluminal signal is identified on spin-echo examination.[147, 235]

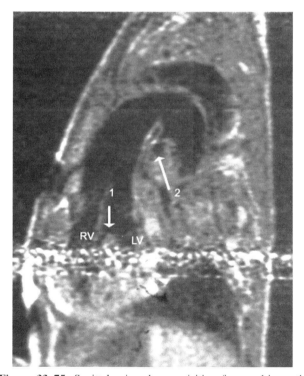

Figure 33–75. Sagittal spin-echo acquisition from a 14-month-old girl with pulmonary atresia and a ventricular septal defect (VSD). The dilated ascending aorta overrides the VSD *(arrow 1)* between the left ventricle (LV) and the hypertrophied right (RV) ventricle. The transverse right pulmonary artery *(arrow 2)* is severely hypoplastic.

In patients with tricuspid atresia, the anterior atrioventricular ring is replaced by fat,[92] and no continuity between the right atrium and right ventricle is found (Fig. 33–76). The right atrium is usually enlarged, and the right ventricle is usually smaller than normal. A large interatrial communication can usually be demonstrated. The shunt itself can be characterized using gradient-echo technique. Axial and sagittal acquisition demonstrates commonly associated lesions, including ventricular septal defect, pulmonary atresia, the relationship between the great arteries, as well as complications of elevated systemic venous pressure, such as mediastinal and pericardial venous collaterals. The results of surgical palliation by the Fontan operation may be demonstrated directly.[136, 148, 212, 217, 261, 285] In addition, application of velocity mapping techniques allows accurate assessment of conduit obstruction.[183, 234]

Univentricular Hearts

Univentricular heart is a compromise term, adopted to avoid the controversy concerning naming hearts with rudimentary ventricular chambers and unusual atrioventricular connections.[301] Generally, a double-inlet ventricle is a ventricle that fills from flow across two atrioventricular valves, or through a single ("common") atrioventricular valve.[303]

When the main chamber is morphologically left ventricular in character, the heart is labeled *double-inlet left ventricle* (the most common type); when the morphology is right ventricular in character, then the heart is named *double-inlet right ventricle*. If the main ventricular chamber cannot be characterized as either left or right ventricular, the chamber is referred to as a *common ventricle* or *ventricular chamber*.

MRI is helpful in the evaluation of patients with univentricular hearts and other complex congenital heart lesions. Direct demonstration of right or left ventricular morphology, the relationship between atrioventricular and semilunar valves, and the origins of papillary muscles all are helpful for characterizing the nature of such a ventricle. In these patients, the axial section provides the greatest amount and most reliable information about systemic and pulmonary venous return and great artery relationships. Axial and off-sagittal section provides image data for determination of atrioventricular and ventriculoarterial connections. The interventricular septum in these patients frequently takes an unusual orientation. This and the common association of atrioventricular valvular atresia often necessitate acquisition of coronal as well as off-sagittal sections.

In patients with double-inlet ventricle, both left and right atrioventricular valves empty into a dominant ventricle (Fig. 33–77). Although a rudimentary opposite chamber is usually present, it may appear only as a slit within the posterior or anterior ventricular myocardium. Isolation of the rudimentary (outflow) chamber from atrial inflow is helpful for full characterization of these lesions. In these cases, communication between dominant ventricle and rudimentary ventricular chamber is via a bulboventricular foramen, generally demonstrated in coronal or even axial section (see Fig. 33–52).

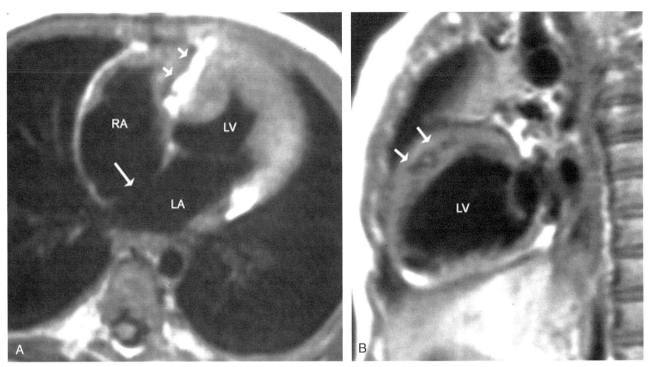

Figure 33–76. MR image obtained from a 4-year-old boy with tricuspid atresia. *A,* Axial spin-echo acquisition through the anterior atrioventricular ring *(short arrows)* shows fatty replacement in the atretic valve ring. The interatrial communication *(long arrow)* between right atrium (RA) and the left atrium (LA) is broad. Note the severe hypertrophy of the left ventricle (LV). *B,* Sagittal spin-echo acquisition through the interventricular septum. The severely hypoplastic right ventricle *(arrows)* is no more than a slit in the septum. LV, left ventricle.

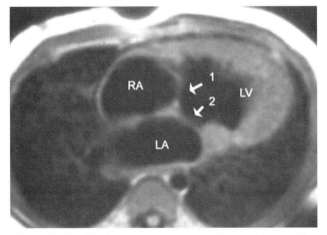

Figure 33–77. MR image obtained from a 2-year-old boy with a double-inlet left ventricle (see Fig. 33–52). Blood drains from the right atrium (RA) through the anterior atrioventricular valve *(arrow 1)* and from the left atrium (LA) through the posterior atrioventricular valve *(arrow 2)* into a dominant left ventricle (LV).

References

1. Al-Saadi N, Nagel E, Gross M, et al: Noninvasive detection of myocardial ischemia from perfusion reserve based on cardiovascular magnetic resonance. Circulation 101:1379–1383, 2000.
2. Amparo EG, Higgins CB, Farmer D, et al: Gated MRI of cardiac and paracardiac lesions. Am J Roentgenol 143:1151–1156, 1984.
3. Anderson JA, Hansen BF: Primary pericardial mesothelioma. Danish Med Bull 21:195, 1974.
4. Applegate PM, Tajik AJ, Ehman RL, et al: Two-dimensional echocardiographic and MRI observations in massive lipomatous hypertrophy of the atrial septum. Am J Cardiol 59:1151–1156, 1987.
5. Aronberg DJ, Peterson RR, Glazer HS, et al: The superior sinus of the pericardium: CT appearance. Radiology 153:489–492, 1984.
6. Atalay MK, Forder JR, Chacko VP, et al: Oxygenation in the rabbit myocardium: Assessment with susceptibility-dependent MR imaging. Radiology 189:759–764, 1993.
7. Atkinson DJ, Edelman RR: Cineangiography of the heart in a single breath hold with a segmented turboflash sequence. Radiology 178: 357–360, 1991.
8. Aufferman W, Wichter T, Breithardt G, et al: Arrhythmogenic right ventricular disease: MR imaging versus angiography. AJR Am J Roentgenol 161:549–555, 1993.
9. Axel L, Dougherty L: Heart wall motion: Improved method for spatial modulation of magnetization for MR imaging. Radiology 172:349–350, 1989.
10. Azhari H, Sideman S, Weiss JL, et al: Three-dimensional mapping of acute ischemic regions using MRI: Wall thickening versus motion analysis. Am J Physiol Heart Circ Physiol 259:28–25, 1990.
11. Baer FM, Smolarz R, Jungehulsing M, et al: Feasibility of high-dose dipyridamole MRI for detection of coronary artery disease and comparison with coronary angiography. Am J Cardiol 69:51–56, 1992.
12. Baer FM, Voth E, Schneider CA, et al: Comparison of low-dose dobutamine-gradient-echo magnetic resonance imaging and positron emission tomography with [18F]fluorodeoxyglucose in patients with chronic coronary artery disease: A functional and morphological approach to the detection of residual myocardial viability. Circulation 91:1006–1015, 1995.
13. Baer FM, Voth E, Schneider CA, et al: Comparison of low-dose dobutamine-gradient-echo magnetic resonance imaging and positron emission tomography with [18F]fluorodeoxyglucose in patients with chronic coronary artery disease: A functional and morphological approach to the detection of residual myocardial viability. Circulation 91:1006–1015, 1995.
14. Baer FM, Voth E, Theissen P, et al: Gradient-echo magnetic reso-

nance imaging during incremental dobutamine infusion for the localization of coronary artery stenoses. Eur Heart J 15:218–225, 1994.

15. Baer FM, Voth E, Theissen P, et al: Coronary artery disease: Findings with GRE MR imaging and Tc-99m-methoxyisobutyl-isonitrile SPECT during simultaneous dobutamine stress. Radiology 193:203–209, 1994.

16. Baer FM, Theissen P, Schneider CA, et al: Dobutamine magnetic resonance imaging predicts contractile recovery of chronically dysfunctional myocardium after successful revascularization. J Am Coll Cardiol 31:1040–1048, 1998.

17. Baer FM, Theissen P, Smolarz K, et al: Dobutamine versus dipyridamole-magnetic resonance imaging: Safety and sensitivity for the diagnosis of coronary artery stenosis. Z Kardiol 82:494–503, 1993.

18. Baim RS, MacDonald IL, Wise DJ, et al: Computed tomography of the absent left pericardium. Radiology 135:127–128, 1980.

19. Barakos JA, Brown JJ, Higgins CB: MR imaging of secondary cardiac and paracardiac lesions. AJR Am J Roentgenol 153:47–50, 1989.

20. Baumgartner H, Kratzer H, Helmreich G, et al: Determination of aortic valve area by Doppler echocardiography using the continuity equation: A critical evaluation. Cardiology 77:101–111, 1990.

21. Berger H, Matthay R, Loke J, et al: Assessment of cardiac performance with quantitative radionuclide angiocardiography right ventricular ejection fraction with reference to finding in chronic obstructive pulmonary disease. Am J Cardiol 41:897–905, 1978.

22. Berger-Klein J, Sochor H, Stanek G, et al: Indium-111 monoclonal antimyosin antibody and magnetic resonance imaging in the diagnosis of acute Lyme myopericarditis. Arch Intern Med 153:2692–2700, 1993.

23. Bouchard A, Higgins CB, Byrd BF III, et al: Magnetic resonance imaging in pulmonary arterial hypertension. Am J Cardiol 56:938–942, 1985.

24. Bogaert J, Bosmans H, Maes A, et al: Remote myocardial dysfunction after acute anterior myocardial infarction: Impact of left ventricular shape on regional function—a magnetic resonance myocardial tagging study. J Am Coll Cardiol 35:1525–1534, 2000.

25. Bogaert J, Maes A, Van de Werf F, et al: Functional recovery of subepicardial myocardial tissue in transmural myocardial infarction after successful reperfusion. Circulation 99:36–43, 1999.

26. Bogaert J, Rademakers FE: Regional nonuniformity of normal adult human left ventricle. Am J Physiol Heart Circ Physiol 280:H610–H620, 2001.

27. Bogaert JG, Bosmans H, Rademakers F, et al: Left ventricular quantification with breath-hold MR imaging: Comparison with echocardiography. MAGMA 3:5–12, 1995.

28. Boxer RA, Singh S, LaCorta MA, et al: Cardiac magnetic resonance imaging in children with congenital heart disease. J Pediatr 109:460–464, 1988.

29. Boxt LM, Katz J, Kolb T, et al: Direct quantitation of right and left ventricular volumes using nuclear magnetic resonance imaging in patients with primary pulmonary hypertension. J Am Coll Cardiol 19:1508–1515, 1992.

30. Bhattacharya S, Lahir A: Clinical role of indium-111 antimyosin imaging. Eur J Nucl Med 18:889–895, 1991.

31. Blake LM, Scheinman MM, Higgins CB: MR features of arrhythmogenic right ventricular dysplasia. AJR Am J Roentgenol 162:809–812, 1994.

32. Braunwald E: Myocardial reperfusion, limitation of the infarct size, reduction of left ventricular dysfunction, and improved survival: Should the paradigm be expanded? Circulation 79:441–444, 1989.

33. Braunwald E: Pathophysiology of heart failure. In Heart Disease, 4th ed. Philadelphia, WB Saunders, 1992, p 393.

34. Braunwald E, Braunwald NS, Ross J Jr, Morrow AG: Effects of mitral-valve replacement on the pulmonary vascular dynamics of patients with pulmonary hypertension. N Engl J Med 273:509–514, 1965.

35. Braunwald E, Goldblatt A, Aygen MM, et al: Congenital aortic stenosis: I. Clinical and hemodynamic findings in 100 patients. II. Surgical treatment and results of operation. Circulation 27:426–462, 1963.

36. Brenner LD, Caputo GR, Mostbeck G, et al: Quantification of left to right atrial shunts with velocity-encoded cine nuclear magnetic resonance imaging. J Am Coll Cardiol 20:1246–1250, 1992.

37. Brooks R, Burgess JH: Idiopathic ventricular tachycardia: A review. Medicine 67:271–294, 1988.

38. Brown CA, O'Connel JB: Myocarditis and idiopathic dilated cardiomyopathy. Am J Med 99:309–314, 1995.

39. Burrows B, Kettel LJ, Niden AH, et al: Patterns of cardiovascular dysfunction in chronic obstructive lung disease. N Engl J Med 286:912–918, 1972.

40. Canby RC, Reeves RC, Evanochko WT, et al: Proton nuclear magnetic resonance relaxation times in severe myocardial ischemia. J Am Coll Cardiol 10:412–420, 1987.

41. Canet E, Revel D, Forrat R, et al: Superparamagnetic iron oxide particles and positive enhancement for myocardial perfusion studies assessed by subsecond T1-weighted MRI. Magn Reson Imaging 11:1139–1145, 1993.

42. Cannon SJ, Richards KL, Crawford M: Hydraulic estimation of the stenotic orifice area: A correction of the Gorlin formula. Circulation 71:1170–1178, 1985.

43. Canter CE, Gutierrez FR, Mirowitz SA, et al: Evaluation of pulmonary arterial morphology in cyanotic congenital heart disease by magnetic resonance imaging. Am Heart J 118:347–354, 1989.

44. Canter CE, Gutierrez FR, Molina P, et al: Noninvasive diagnosis of right-sided extracardiac conduit obstruction by combined magnetic resonance imaging and continuous-wave Doppler echocardiography. J Thorac Cardiovasc Surg 101:724–731, 1991.

45. Capelli H, Ross D, Somerville J: Aortic regurgitation in tetralogy of Fallot and pulmonary atresia. Am J Cardiol 49:1979–1983, 1982.

46. Caputo GR, Sechtem U, Tscholakoff D, Higgins CB: Measurement of myocardial infarct size at early and late time intervals using MR imaging: An experimental study in dogs. AJR Am J Roentgenol 149:237–243, 1987.

47. Carabello BA: Mitral regurgitation: Basic pathophysiologic principles: I. Mod Concepts Cardiovasc Dis 57:53–58, 1988.

48. Carlsson E, Gross R, Hold RG: The radiologic diagnosis of cardiac valvular insufficiencies. Circulation 55:921–933, 1977.

49. Carlson MD, White RD, Trohman RG, et al: Right ventricular outflow tract tachycardia: Detection of previously unrecognized anatomic abnormalities using cine magnetic resonance imaging. J Am Coll Cardiol 24:720–727, 1994.

50. Cigarroa CG, de Filippi C, Brickner ME, et al: Dobutamine stress echocardiography identifies hibernating myocardium and predicts recovery of left ventricular function after coronary revascularization. Circulation 88:430–436, 1993.

51. Chandra M, Silverman ME, Oshinski J, Pettigrew R: Diagnosis of cardiac sarcoid aided by MRI. Chest 110:524–526, 1996.

52. Chandrarama PA, Bradley WG, Kortman KE, et al: Detection of acute myocarditis using nuclear magnetic resonance imaging. Am J Med 83:1144–1146, 1987.

53. Cherryman GR, Tranter J, Keal R, et al: Prospective comparison of contrast-enhanced MRI with thallium 201 SPECT and 2D echocardiography in the localization of acute myocardial infarction. In: Proceedings of International Society for Magnetic Resonance in Medicine, Sixth Scientific Meeting and Exhibition. Sydney, Australia, April 18–24, 1998, p 923.

54. Chesler E, Matha AS, Matisonn RE, Rogers MNA: Subpulmonic stenosis as a result of noncalcific pericarditis. Chest 69:425–427, 1976.

55. Chiles C, Baker ME, Silverman PM: Superior pericardial recess simulating aortic dissection on computed tomography. J Comput Assisr Tomogr 10:421–423, 1986.

56. Choi SII, Choi SH, Kim ST, et al: Irreversibly damaged myocardium at MR imaging with a necrotic tissue–specific contrast agent in a cat model. Radiology 215:863–868, 2000.

57. Chronic cor pulmonale: Report of an expert committee. World Health Organiz Tech Rep Serv 213:1, 1961.

58. Cohen JL: Neoplastic pericarditis. Cardiovasc Clin North Am 7:257–269, 1976.

59. Collins-Nakai RL, Rosenthal A, Casteneda AR, et al: Congenital mitral stenosis: A review of twenty years' experience. Circulation 56:1039–1047, 1977.

60. Connolly HM, Crary JL, McGoon MD, et al: Valvular heart disease associated with fenfluramine-phentermine. N Engl J Med 337:581–588, 1997.

61. Corrigan TP, Fossard DP, Spindler P, et al: Phlebography in the management of pulmonary embolism. Br J Surg 61:484–488, 1974.

62. Croft CH, Lipscomb K, Mathis K, et al: Limitations of qualitative angiographic grading in aortic or mitral regurgitation. Am J Cardiol 53:1593–1598, 1984.

63. Croisille P, Moore CC, Judd RM, et al: Differentiation of viable and nonviable myocardium by the use of three-dimensional tagged MRI in 2-day-old reperfused canine infarcts. Circulation 99:284–291, 1999.

64. Culham JAG, Vince DJ: Cardiac output by MR imaging: An experimental study comparing right ventricle and left ventricle with thermodilution. Can Assoc Radiol J 39:247–249, 1988.

65. Cullen JH, Horsfield MA, Reek CR, et al: A myocardial perfusion reserve index in humans using first-pass contrast-enhanced magnetic resonance imaging. J Am Coll Cardiol 33:1386–1394, 1999.

66. Cullen JH, Kaemmerlen JT, Daoud A, Katz HL: A prospective clinical pathologic study of the lungs and heart in chronic obstructive lung disease. Am Rev Respir Dis 102:190–204, 1970.

67. Dalen JE, Banas JS Jr, Brooks HL, et al: Resolution rate of acute pulmonary embolism in man. N Engl J Med 280:1194–1199, 1969.

68. Daliento L, Turrini P, Nava A, et al: Arrhythmogenic right ventricular cardiomyopathy in young versus adult patients: Similarities and differences. J Am Coll Cardiol 25:655–664, 1995.

69. Deloran L, Thurber MD, Jesse E, et al: Secondary malignant tumors of the pericardium. Circulation 26:228–241, 1962.

70. Denfield SW, Garson A Jr: Sudden death in children and young adults. Pediatr Clin North Am 37:215–231, 1990.

71. deRoos A, Reichek N, Axel L, Kressel HW: Cine MR imaging in aortic stenosis. J Comp Asst Tomog 13:421–425, 1989.

72. Diethelm L, Dery R, Lipton MJ, Higgins CB: Atrial level shunts: Sensitivity and specificity of MR in diagnosis. Radiology 162:181–186, 1987.

73. Didier D, Higgins CB: Estimation of pulmonary vascular resistance by MRI in patients with congenital cardiovascular shunt lesions. Am J Roentgenol 147:1127–1131, 1986.

74. Didier D, Higgins CB: Identification and localization of ventricular septal defect by gated magnetic resonance imaging. Am J Cardiol 57:1363–1368, 1986.

75. Didier D, Ratib O, Lerch R, Friedli B: Detection and quantification of valvular heart disease with dynamic cardiac MR imaging. Radiographics 20:1279–1299, 2000.

76. Dines DE, Edwards JE, Burchell WB: Myocardial atrophy in constrictive pericarditis. Mayo Clinic Proc 33:93–99, 1958.

77. Doherty NE, Seelos KC, Suzuki JI, et al: Application of cine NMR imaging for sequential evaluation of response to angiotensin-converting enzyme inhibitor therapy in dilated cardiomyopathy. J Am Coll Cardiol 19:1294–1302, 1992.

78. Dong SJ, MacGregor JH, Crawley AP, et al: Left ventricular wall thickness and regional function in patients with hypertrophic cardiomyopathy: A three-dimensional tagged magnetic resonance imaging study. Circulation 90:1200–1209, 1994.

78a. Dorfman DF, Cronan JJ, Tupper TB, et al: Occult pulmonary embolism: A common occurrence in deep venous thrombosis. Am J Roentgenol 148:263–266, 1987.

79. Duerinckx AJ, Urman MK: Two-dimensional coronary MR angiography: Analysis of initial clinical results. Radiology 193:731–738, 1994.

80. Dulce MC, Duerinckx AJ, Hartiala J, et al: MR imaging of the myocardium using nonionic contrast medium: Signal-intensity changes in patients with subacute myocardial infarction. AJR Am J Roentgenol 160:963–970, 1993.

81. Edelman RR, Li W: Contrast-enhanced echo-planar MR imaging of myocardial perfusion: Preliminary study in humans. Radiology 190:771–777, 1994.

82. Eichenberger AC, Schuiki E, Kochli VD, et al: Ischemic heart disease: Assessment with gadolinium-enhanced ultrafast MR imaging and dipyridamole stress [see comments]. J Magn Reson Imaging 4:425–431, 1994.

83. Factor SM, Okun EM, Kirk ES: The histological lateral border of the acute canine myocardial infarction. Circ Res 46:640–649, 1981.

84. Fattori R, Rocchi G, Celetti F, et al: Contribution of magnetic resonance imaging in the differential diagnosis of cardiac amyloidosis and symmetric hypertrophic cardiomyopathy. Am Heart J 136:824–830, 1998.

85. Fazio S, Sabatini D, Capaldo B, et al: A preliminary study of growth hormone in the treatment of dilated cardiomyopathy. N Engl J Med 334:809–814, 1996.

86. Feiglin DH, George CR, MacIntyre WJ, et al: Gated cardiac magnetic resonance structural imaging: Optimization by electronic axial rotation. Radiology 154:129–132, 1985.

87. Fenoglio JJ, McAlister HA Jr, DeCastro CM, et al: Congenital bicuspid aortic valve after age 20. Am J Cardiol 39:164–169, 1977.

88. Firmin DN, Nayler GL, Kilner PJ, et al: The application of phase shifts in NMR for flow measurements. Magn Reson Med 14:230–241, 1990.

89. Fisher MR, Higgins CB: Central thrombi in pulmonary arterial hypertension detected by MR imaging. Radiology 158:223–226, 1986.

90. Fishman A: Chronic cor pulmonale. Am Rev Respir Dis 114:775–794, 1976.

91. Fishman A: Pulmonary hypertension and cor pulmonale. In Fishman A (ed): Pulmonary Diseases and Disorders, 2nd ed. New York, McGraw-Hill, 1988, pp 999–1048.

92. Fletcher BD, Jacobstein MD, Abramowsky CR, Anderson RH: Right atrioventricular valve atresia: Anatomic evaluation with MR imaging. AJR Am J Roentgenol 148:671–674, 1987.

93. Formanek AG, Witcofski RL, D'Souza VJ, et al: MR imaging of the central pulmonary arterial tree in conotruncal malformation. Am J Roentgenol 147:1127–1131, 1986.

94. Frank H, Globits S, Glogar D, et al: Detection and quantification of pulmonary hypertension with MR imaging: Results in 23 patients. AJR Am J Roentgenol 161:27–31, 1993.

95. Frank JA, Feller MA, House WV, et al: Measurement of proton nuclear magnetic longitudinal relaxation times and water content in infarcted canine myocardium and induced pulmonary injury. Clin Res 24:217A–223A, 1976.

96. Frank S, Weg J, Harkleroad L, et al: Pulmonary dysfunction in rheumatoid disease. Chest 63:27–33, 1973.

97. Freidrich MG, Strom O, Schultz-Menger J, et al: Contrast media–enhanced magnetic resonance imaging of viral myocarditis. Circulation 97:1802–1809, 1998.

98. Frustaci A, Bellocci F, Olsen EG: Results of biventricular endomyocardial biopsy in survivors of cardiac arrest with apparently normal hearts. Am J Cardiol 74:890–895, 1994.

99. Fudjita N, Hartiala J, O'Sullivan M, et al: Assessment of left ventricular diastolic function in dilated cardiomyopathy with cine MRI: Effect on an angiotensin-converting enzyme inhibitor, benazepril. Am Heart J 125:171–177, 1993.

100. Gagliardi MG, Bevilaqua M, DiRienzi P, et al: Usefulness of magnetic resonance imaging for the diagnosis of acute myocarditis in infants and children and in comparison with endomyocardial biopsy. Am J Cardiol 68:1089–1091, 1991.

101. Manyari D, Klein G, Gulamhusein S: Arrhythmogenic right ventricular dysplasia: A generalized cardiomyopathy? Circulation 68:251–257, 1983.

102. Gaudio C, Pellicula F, Tanzilli G, et al: Magnetic resonance imaging for assessment of apical hypertrophy in hypertrophic cardiomyopathy. Clin Cardiol 15:164–168, 1992.

103. Gefter WB, Hatabu H, Dinsmore BJ, et al: Pulmonary vascular cine MR imaging: A noninvasive approach to dynamic imaging of the pulmonary circulation. Radiology 176:761–770, 1990.

104. Genovese PD, Rosenbaum D: Pulmonary stenosis with survival to the age of 78 years. Am Heart J 41:755–761, 1951.

105. Geva T, Vick GW III, Wendt RE, Rokey R: Role of spin-echo and cine magnetic resonance imaging in the presurgical planning of heterotaxy syndrome. Circulation 90:348–356, 1994.

106. Glazer GM, Gross BH, Orringer MB, et al: Computed tomography on pericardial masses: Further observations and comparison with echocardiography. J Comput Assist Tomogr 8:895–899, 1984.

107. Globits S, Blake L, Bourne M, et al: Assessment of hemodynamic effects on angiotensin-converting enzyme inhibitor therapy in chronic aortic regurgitation by using velocity-encoded cine magnetic resonance imaging. Am Heart J 131:289–293, 1996.

108. Goldfarb JW, Edelman RR: Coronary arteries: Breath-hold, gadolinium-enhanced, three-dimensional MR angiography. Radiology 206:830–834, 1998.

109. Gomes AS, Lois JF Jr, Williams RG: Pulmonary arteries: MR imaging in patients with congenital obstruction of the right ventricular outflow tract. Radiology 174:51–57, 1990.

110. Gorlin R: The mechanism of the signs and symptoms of mitral valve disease. Br Heart J 16:375–380, 1954.

111. Gorlin R, Gorlin SG: Hydraulic formula for calculation of the area of the stenotic mitral valve, other cardiac valves, and the central circulatory shunts. Am Heart J 41:1–29, 1951.

112. Gould KL: Myocardial viability: What does it mean and how to measure it? Circulation 83:333–335, 1991.

113. Greene DG, Baldwin ED, Baldwin JS, et al: Pure congenital pulmonary stenosis and idiopathic dilation of the pulmonary artery. Am J Med 6:24–40, 1949.

114. Griffith MJ, Carey C, Coltard DJ, et al: Inaccuracies in using aortic valve gradients alone to grade severity of aortic stenosis. Br Heart J 62:372–378, 1989.

115. Grossman W, Jones D, McLaurin LP: Wall stress and patterns of hypertrophy in the human left ventricle. J Clin Invest 56:56–64, 1975.

116. Grossman W, McLaurin LP, Rolett EL: Alterations in left ventricular relaxation and diastolic compliance in dilated cardiomyopathy. Cardiovasc Res 13:514–522, 1979.

117. Guit GL, Bluemm R, Rohmer J, et al: Levotransposition of the aorta: Identification of segmental cardiac anatomy using MR imaging. Radiology 161:673–679, 1986.

118. Guttierez RF, Shackelford GD, McKnight RC, et al: Diagnosis of congenital absence of left pericardium by MR imaging. J Comput Assist Tomogr 9:551–553, 1985.

119. Haase A, Frahm J, Matthaei D, et al: FLASH imaging: Rapid NMR imaging using low flip-angle pulses. J Magn Reson 67:258–266, 1986.

120. Hartnell G, Cerel A, Kamalesh M, et al: Detection of myocardial ischemia: Value of combined myocardial perfusion and cineangiographic MR imaging. AJR Am J Roentgenol 163:1061–1067, 1994.

121. Havig O: Source of pulmonary emboli. Acta Chir Scand 478(suppl):42–47, 1977.

122. Heath D: Pathology of cardiac tumors. Am J Cardiol 21:315–327, 1968.

123. Hess OM, Osakada G, Lavelle JF, et al: Diastolic myocardial wall stiffness and ventricular relaxation during partial and complete coronary occlusions in the conscious dog. Circ Res 52:387–400, 1983.

124. Higgins CB, Herfkens R, Lipton MJ, et al: Nuclear magnetic resonance imaging of acute myocardial infarction in dogs: Alterations in magnetic relaxation times. Am J Cardiol 52:184–190, 1983.

125. Hirschfel SS, Fleming DG, Doershuk C, et al: Echocardiographic abnormalities in patients with cystic fibrosis. Chest 75:351–355, 1979.

126. Hofman MBM, Henson RE, Kovacs SJ, et al: Blood pool agent strongly improves magnetic resonance coronary angiography using an inversion pre-pulse. Magn Res Med 41:360–367, 1999.

127. Holen J, Aaslid R, Ladmark K, et al: Determination of pressure gradient in mitral stenosis with a noninvasive ultrasound Doppler technique. Acta Med Scand 199:455–460, 1976.

128. Holman ER, Buller VGM, de Roos A, et al: Detection and quantification of dysfunctional myocardium by magnetic resonance imaging: A new three-dimensional method for quantitative wall-thickening analysis. Circulation 95:924–931, 1997.

129. Holman ER, van Rossum AC, Doesburg T, et al: Assessment of acute myocardial infarction in man with magnetic resonance imaging and the use of new paramagnetic contrast-agent gadolinium-BOPTA. Mag Reson Imaging 14:21–29, 1996.

130. Holman ER, Vliegen HW, van der Geest RJ, et al: Quantitative analysis of regional left ventricular function after myocardial infarction in the pig assessed with cine magnetic resonance imaging. Magn Reson Med 34:161–169, 1995.

131. Hundley WG, Hamilton CA, Thomas MS, et al: Utility of fast cine magnetic resonance imaging and display for the detection of myocardial ischemia in patients not well suited for second harmonic stress echocardiography. Circulation 100:1697–1702, 1999.

132. Hunninghake G, Fauci A: Pulmonary involvement in the collagen vascular diseases. Am Rev Respir Dis 119:471–503, 1979.

133. Hunter GJ, Hamberg LM, Weisskoff RM, et al: Measurement of stroke volume and cardiac output with a single breath-hold with echo-planar MR imaging. J Magn Reson Imaging 4:51–58, 1994.

134. Im J-G, Rosen A, Webb WR, Gamsu G: MR imaging of the transverse sinus of the pericardium. AJR Am J Roentgenol 150:79–84, 1988.

135. Jacobstein MD, Fletcher BD, Goldstein S, Riemender TA: Evaluation of atrioventricular septal defect by magnetic resonance imaging Am J Cardiol 55:1158–1161, 1985.

136. Jacobstein MD, Fletcher BD, Nelson AD, et al: Magnetic resonance imaging: Evaluation of palliative systemic-pulmonary artery shunts. Circulation 70:650–656, 1984.

137. Johnson DE, Vacek J, Gollub SB, et al: Comparison of gated cardiac magnetic resonance imaging and two-dimensional echocardiography for the evaluation of right ventricular thrombi: A case report with autopsy correlation. Cathet Cardiovasc Diagn 14:266–268, 1988.

138. Johnston DL, Brady TJ, Ratner AV, et al: Assessment of myocardial ischemia with magnetic resonance: Effects of a three-hour coronary occlusion with and without reperfusion. Circulation 71:595–560, 1985.

139. Josephson ME, Horowitz LN, Waxman HL, et al: Sustained ventricular tachycardia: Role of the 1-lead electrocardiogram in localizing site of origin. Circulation 64:257–272, 1981.

140. Kaminsky MF, Rodan BA, Osborne DR, et al: Post-pericardiectomy syndrome. Am J Roentgenol 138:503–508, 1982.

141. Katz J, Milliken MC, Stray-Grundersen J, et al: Estimation of human myocardial mass with MR imaging. Radiology 169:495–498, 1988.

142. Katz J, Whang J, Boxt LM, Barst RJ: Estimation of right ventricular mass in normal subjects and patients with primary pulmonary hypertension by nuclear magnetic resonance imaging. J Am Coll Cardiol 21:1475–1481, 1993.

143. Kawada N, Sakuma H, Yamakado T, et al: Hypertrophic cardiomyopathy: MR measurement of coronary blood flow and vasodilator flow reserve in patients and healthy subjects. Radiology 211:129–135, 1999.

144. Kelbaek H, Aldershvile J, Svendsen JH, et al: Combined first-pass and equilibrium radionuclide cardiographic determination of stroke volume for quantification of valvular regurgitation. J Am Coll Cardiol 11:769–773, 1988.

145. Kelminson LL, Cotton EK, Vogel JHK: The reversibility of pulmonary hypertension in patients with cystic fibrosis. Pediatrics 39:24–35, 1967.

146. Kersting-Sommerhoff BA, Sechtem U, Fisher MR, et al: MR imaging of congenital anomalies of the aortic arch. Am J Roentgenol 143:1192–1194, 1984.

147. Kersting-Sommerhoff BA, Sechtem UP, Higgins CB: Evaluation of pulmonary blood supply by nuclear magnetic resonance imaging in patients with pulmonary atresia. J Am Coll Cardiol 11:166–171, 1988.

148. Kersting-Sommerhoff BA, Seelos KC, Hardy C, et al: Evaluation of surgical procedures for cyanotic congenital heart disease by using MR imaging. AJR Am J Roentgenol 155:259–266, 1990.

149. Kessler W, Laub G, Achenbach S, et al: Coronary arteries: MR angiography with fast contrast-enhanced three-dimensional breath-hold imaging: Initial experience. Radiology 210:566–572, 1999.

150. Kilner PJ, Firmin DN, Reese RSO, et al: Valve and great vessel stenosis: Assessment with MR jet velocity mapping. Radiology 178:229–235, 1991.

151. Kilner PJ, Manzara CC, Mohiaddin RH, et al: Magnetic resonance jet velocity mapping in mitral and aortic valve stenosis. Circulation 87:1239–1248, 1993.

152. Klein MA, Collier BD, Hellman RS, Bamrah VS: Detection of chronic coronary artery disease: Value of pharmacologically stressed, dynamically enhanced turbo-fast low-angle shot MR images. AJR Am J Roentgenol 161:257–263, 1993.

153. Kleinhans E, Altehoefer C, Arnold C, et al: MRI measurements of left ventricular systolic wall thickening compared to regional myocardial perfusion as determined by 201Tl SPECT in patients with coronary artery disease. Nuklearmedizin 30:61–66, 1991.

154. Kraitchman DL, Wilke N, Hexeberg E, et al: Myocardial perfusion and function in dogs with moderate coronary stenosis. Magn Reson Med 35:771–780, 1996.

155. Kramer CM, Ferrari VA, Rogers WJ, et al: Angiotensin-converting enzyme inhibition limits dysfunction in adjacent noninfarcted regions during left ventricular remodeling. J Am Coll Cardiol 27:211–217, 1996.

156. Kramer CM, Lima JA, Reichek N, et al: Regional differences in function within noninfarcted myocardium during left ventricular remodeling. Circulation 88:1279–1288, 1993.

157. Kramer CM, Reichek N, Ferrari VA, et al: Regional heterogeneity of function in hypertrophic cardiomyopathy. Circulation 90:186–194, 1994.

158. Kramer CM, Rogers WJ, Theobald TM, et al: Remote noninfarcted region dysfunction soon after first anterior myocardial infarction: A magnetic resonance tagging study. Circulation 94:660–666, 1996.

159. Kriegshauser JS, Julsrud PR, Lund JT: MR imaging of fat in and around the heart. AJR Am J Roentgenol 155:271–274, 1990.

160. Lanzer P, Barta C, Botvinick EH, et al: ECG-synchronized cardiac MR imaging: Method and evaluation. Radiology 155:681–686, 1985.

161. Lanzer P, Botvinick EH, Schiller NB, et al: Cardiac imaging using gated magnetic resonance. Radiology 150:121–127, 1984.

162. Leagus CS, Gregorski RF, Grittenden JJ, et al: Giant intrapericardial bronchogenic cyst: A case report. J Thorac Cardiovas Surg 52: 581–587, 1966.

163. Lee WH, Fisher J: Right ventricular diastolic disorders. Arch Intern Med 143:332–337, 1983.

164. Lev M, Liberthson RR, Joseph RH, et al: The pathologic anatomy of Ebstein's disease. Arch Pathol 90:334–343, 1970.

165. Levy-Ravetch M, Auh YH, Rubenstein WA, et al: CT of the pericardial recesses. Am J Roentgenol 144:707–714, 1985.

166. Li D, Dolan RP, Walovitch RC, Lauffer RB: Three-dimensional MRI of coronary arteries using an intravascular contrast agent. Magn Res Med 39:1014–1018, 1998.

167. Li D, Paschal CB, Haacke EM, Adler LP: Coronary arteries: Three-dimensional MR imaging with fat saturation and magnetization transfer contrast. Radiology 187:401–406, 1993.

168. Lieberman JM, Alfidi RJ, Nelson AD, et al: Gated magnetic resonance imaging of the normal and diseased heart. Radiology 152: 465–470, 1984.

169. Lobo FV, Heggtveit HA, Butany J, et al: Right ventricular dysplasia: Morphological findings in 13 cases. Can J Cardiol 8:261–268, 1992.

170. Longmore DB, Klipstein RH, Underwood SR, et al: Dimensional accuracy of magnetic resonance in studies of the heart. Lancet 1: 1360–1362, 1985.

171. Lopez-Beret P, Pinto JM, Romero A, et al: Systematic study of occult pulmonary thromboembolism in patients with deep venous thrombosis. J Vasc Surg 33:515–521, 2001.

172. Lorenz CH, Walker ES, Morgan VL, et al: Normal human right and left ventricular mass, systolic function, and gender differences by cine magnetic resonance imaging. J Cardiovasc Magn Reson 1: 7–21, 1999.

173. Lund JT, Ehman RL, Julsrud PR, et al: Cardiac masses: Assessment by MR imaging. AJR Am J Roentgenol 152:469–473, 1989.

174. Maier SE, Fischer SE, McKinnon GC, et al: Evaluation of left ventricular segmental wall motion in hypertrophic cardiomyopathy with myocardial tagging. Circulation 86:1918–1926, 1992.

175. Manning WJ, Atkinson DJ, Parker JA, Edelman RR: Assessment of intracardiac shunts with gadolinium-enhanced ultrafast MR imaging. Radiology 184:357–361, 1992.

176. Manning WJ, Li W, Boyle NG, Edelman RR: Fat-suppressed breath-hold magnetic resonance coronary arteriography. Circulation 87: 94–104, 1993.

177. Manning WJ, Li W, Edelman RR: A preliminary report comparing magnetic resonance coronary angiography with conventional angiography. N Engl J Med 328:828–832, 1993.

177a. Manyari D, Klein G, Gulamhusein S: Arrhythmogenic right ventricular dysplasia: A generalized cardiomyopathy? Circulation 68: 251–275, 1983.

178. Marcus FI, Fontaine GH, Guiraudon G, et al: Right ventricular dysplasia: A report of 24 adult cases. Circulation 65:384–398, 1982.

179. Marelli AJ, Perloff JK, Child JS, Laks H: Pulmonary atresia with ventricular septal defect in adults. Circulation 89:243–251, 1994.

180. Markiewicz W, Sechtem U, Higgins CB: Evaluation of the right ventricle by magnetic resonance imaging. Am Heart J 113:8–15, 1987.

181. Markiewicz W, Sechtem U, Kirby R, et al: Measurement of ventricular volumes in the dog by nuclear magnetic resonance imaging. J Am Coll Cardiol 10:170–177, 1987.

182. Martin RP, Rakowski H, Kleiman JH, et al: Reliability and reproducibility of two-dimensional echocardiographic measurement of the stenotic mitral valve orifice area. Am J Cardiol 43:560–568, 1979.

183. Martinez JE, Mohiaddin RH, Kilner PJ, et al: Obstruction in extracardiac ventriculopulmonary conduits: Value of nuclear magnetic resonance imaging with velocity mapping and Doppler echocardiography. J Am Coll Cardiol 20:338–344, 1992.

184. Masui T, Finck S, Higgins CB: Constrictive pericarditis and restrictive cardiomyopathy: Evaluation with MR imaging. Radiology 182: 369–373, 1992.

185. Masui T, Seelos KC, Kersting-Sommerhoff BA, Higgins CB: Abnormalities of the pulmonary veins: Evaluation with MR imaging and comparison with cardiac angiography and echocardiography. Radiology 181:645–649, 1991.

186. Matheijssen NA, Louwerenburg HW, van Rugge FP, et al: Comparison of ultrafast dipyridamole magnetic resonance imaging with

dipyridamole SestaMIBI SPECT for detection of perfusion abnormalities in patients with one-vessel coronary artery disease: Assessment by quantitative model fitting. Magn Reson Med 35:221–228, 1996.

187. Matheijssen NAA, De Roos A, Van der Wall EE, et al: Acute myocardial infarction: Comparison of T2-weighted and T1-weighted gadolinium-DTPA–enhanced MR imaging. Magn Reson Med 17: 460–469, 1991.

188. Matsouka H, Hamada M, Honda T, et al: Precise assessment of myocardial damage associated with secondary cardiomyopathies by use of Gd-DTPA enhanced magnetic resonance imaging. Angiology 44:945–950, 1993.

189. Matsouka H, Hamada M, Honda T, et al: Evaluation of acute myocarditis and pericarditis by Gd-DTPA enhanced magnetic resonance imaging. Eur Heart J 15:283–284, 1994.

190. Mazer MJ, Carroll FE, Falke THM: Practical aspects of gated magnetic resonance imaging of the pulmonary artery. J Thorac Imaging 3:73–84, 1988.

191. McAllister A, Fenoglio JJ: Tumors of the cardiovascular system. In Atlas of Tumor Pathology, fascicle 15, series 2. Washington, DC, Armed Forces Institute of Pathology, 1978.

192. McGowan GA, Sapiro EP, Azhari H, et al: Noninvasive measurement of shortening in the fiber and cross-fiber direction in the normal human left ventricle and idiopathic dilated cardiomyopathy. Circulation 96:535–541, 1997.

193. McIntyre KM, Sasahara AA: The hemodynamic response to pulmonary embolism in patients without prior cardiopulmonary disease. Am J Cardiol 28:288–294, 1971.

194. McMurdo KK, Webb WR, von Schulthess GK, Gamsu G: Magnetic resonance imaging of the superior pericardial recesses. Am J Roentgenol 145:985–988, 1985.

195. McNamara MT, Higgins CB, Schechtmann N, et al: Detection and characterization of acute myocardial infarction in man with use of gated magnetic resonance. Circulation 71:717–724, 1985.

196. Meziane MA, Fishman EK, Siegelman SS: CT diagnosis of hemopericardium in acute dissecting aneurysm of the thoracic aorta. J Comput Assist Tomogr 8:10–14, 1984.

197. Mirowitz SA, Gutierrez FR: Fibromuscular elements of the right atrium: Pseudomass at MR imaging. Radiology 182:231–233, 1992.

198. Mirowitz SA, Gutierrez FR, Canter CE, Vannier MW: Tetralogy of Fallot: MR findings. Radiology 171:207–212, 1989.

199. Mitchell L, Jenkins JPR, Watson Y, et al: Diagnosis and assessment of mitral and aortic valve disease by cine-flow magnetic resonance imaging. Magn Reson Med 12:181–197, 1989.

200. Mitchell RS, Stanford RE, Silvers GW, Dart G: The right ventricle in chronic airway obstruction: A clinicopathologic study. Am Rev Respir Dis 114:147–154, 1976.

201. Modelvang J, Stockholm KH, Saunamaki K, et al: Assessment of left ventricular volumes by magnetic resonance in comparison with radionuclide angiography, contrast angiography, and echocardiography. Eur Heart J 13:1677–1683, 1992.

202. Mogelvang J, Stubgaard M, Thomsen C, et al: Evaluation of right ventricular volumes measured by magnetic resonance imaging. Eur Heart J 9:529–533, 1988.

203. Mogelvang J, Thomsen C, Horn T, et al: Determination of left ventricular myocardial volume (mass) by magnetic resonance imaging. Am J Noninvas Cardiol 1:231–236, 1987.

204. Mogelvang J, Thomsen C, Mehlsen J, et al: Evaluation of left ventricular volumes measured by magnetic resonance imaging. Eur Hear J 7:1016–1021, 1986.

205. Mogelvang J, Thomsen C, Mehlsen J, et al: Left ventricular ejection fraction determined by magnetic resonance imaging and gated radionuclide ventriculography. Am J Noninvas Cardiol 1:278–283, 1987.

206. Moller JH, Nakib A, Elliot RS, Edwards JE: Symptomatic congenital aortic stenosis in the first year of life. J Pediatr 69:728–734, 1966.

207. Morguet AJ, Munz DL, Kreuzer H, et al: Scintigraphic detection of inflammatory heart disease. Eur J Nucl Med 21:666–674, 1994.

208. Morin DP, Cottrill CM, Johnson GL, et al: Effect of respiration on the echocardiogram in children with cystic fibrosis. Pediatrics 65: 44–49, 1980.

209. Moser KM, Spragg RG, Utley J, et al: Chronic thrombotic obstruction of major pulmonary arteries: results of thromboendarterectomy in 15 patients. Ann Intern Med 99:299–305, 1983.

210. Nagel E, Lehmkuhl HB, Bocksch W, et al: Noninvasive diagnosis of ischemia-induced wall motion abnormalities with the use of high-

dose dobutamine stress MRI: Comparison with dobutamine stress echocardiography Circulation 99: 763–770, 1999.

211. Nava A, Thiene G, Canciani B, et al: Familial occurrence of right ventricular dysplasia: A study involving nine families. J Am Coll Cardiol 12:1222–1228, 1988.

212. Nawa S, Yamada M, Irie H, Teramoto S: Magnetic resonance evaluation of patency of stented polytetrafluoroethylene graft connecting right atrium to pulmonary artery. Chest 94:1105–1110, 1988.

213. Ni Y, Pislaru C, Bosmans H, et al: Validation of intracoronary delivery of metalloporphyrin as an in vivo "histochemical staining" for myocardial infarction with MR imaging. Acad Radiol 5:S37–S41, 1998.

214. Nishimura RA, Kazmier FJ, Smith HC, Danielson GK: Right ventricular outflow obstruction caused by constrictive pericardial disease. Am J Cardiol 55:1447–1448, 1985.

215. Noonan JA: Pulmonary heart disease. Pediatr Clin North Am 18: 1255–1272, 1971.

216. Ostman-Smith I, Silverman NH, Oldershaw P, et al: Cor triatriatum sinistrum: Diagnostic features on cross-sectional echocardiography. Br Heart J 51:211–219, 1984.

217. Park JH, Han MC, Kim C-W: MR imaging of congenitally corrected transposition of the great vessels in adults. AJR Am J Roentgenol 153:491–494, 1989.

218. Park JH, Han MC, Kim C-W: MR imaging of congenitally corrected transposition in adults. AJR Am J Roentgenol 153:491–494, 1989.

219. Parsons JM, Baker EJ, Anderson RH, et al: Morphological evaluation of atrioventricular septal defects by magnetic resonance imaging. Br Heart J 64:138–145, 1990.

220. Passik CS, Ackerman DM, Piuth JR, Edwards WD: Temporal changes in the causes of aortic stenosis: A surgical pathological study of 646 cases. Mayo Clin Proc 62:119–123, 1987.

221. Pawel BR, de Chadarevian J-P, Wolk JH, et al: Sudden death in childhood due to right ventricular dysplasia. Pediatr Pathol 14: 987–995, 1994.

222. Pennell DJ, Keegan J, Firmin DN, et al: Magnetic resonance imaging of coronary arteries: Technique and preliminary results. Br Heart J 70:315–326, 1993.

223. Pennell DJ, Underwood SR, Longmore DB: Detection of coronary artery disease using MR imaging with dipyridamole infusion. J Comput Assisted Tomography 14:167–170, 1990.

224. Pennell DJ, Underwood SR, Manzara CC, et al: Magnetic resonance imaging during dobutamine stress in coronary artery disease. Am J Cardiol 70:34–40, 1992.

225. Peshock RM, Rokey R, Malloy CM, et al: Assessment of myocardial systolic wall thickening using nuclear magnetic resonance imaging. J Am Coll Cardiol 14:653–659, 1989.

226. Pflugfelder PW, Sechtem U, White RD, Higgins CB: Quantification of regional myocardial function by rapid cine MR imaging. AJR Am J Roentgenol 150:523–529, 1988.

227. Pflugfelder PW, Wisenberg G, Prato FS, et al: Early detection of canine myocardial infarction by magnetic resonance imaging in vivo. Circulation 71:587–594, 1985.

228. Pislaru SV, Ni Y, Pislaru C, et al: Noninvasive measurements of infarct size after thrombolysis with a necrosis-avid MRI contrast agent. Circulation 99:690–696, 1999.

229. Pohost GM, Biederman RWW: The role of cardiac MRI stress testing. Circulation 100:1676–1679, 1999.

230. Pons-Ladio G, Carreras F, Borras X: Comparison of morphologic assessment of hypertrophic cardiomyopathy by magnetic resonance versus echocardiographic imaging. Am J Cardiol 79:1651–1656, 1997.

231. Portal RW, Besterman EMM, Chambers RJ, et al: Prognosis after operation for constrictive pericarditis. Br Med J 1:593–597, 1966.

232. Posteraro RH, Sostman HD, Spritzer CE, Herfkens RJ: Cine-gradient-refocused MR imaging of central pulmonary emboli. AJR Am J Roentgenol 152:465–468, 1989.

233. Rademakers FE, Rogers WJ, Guier WH, et al: Relation of regional cross-fiber shortening to wall thickening in the intact heart: Three-dimensional strain analysis by NMR tagging. Circulation 89:1174–1182, 1994.

234. Rebergen SA, Ottenkamp J, Doornbos J, et al: Postoperative pulmonary flow dynamics after Fontan surgery: Assessment with nuclear magnetic resonance velocity mapping. J Am Coll Cardiol 21:123–131, 1993.

235. Rees RSO, Somerville J, Underwood SR, et al: Magnetic resonance imaging of the pulmonary arteries and their systemic connections in pulmonary atresia: Comparison with angiographic and surgical findings. Br Heart J 58:621–626, 1987.

236. Rees S, Somerville J, Ward C, et al: Coarctation of the aorta: MR imaging in late postoperative assessment. Radiology 173:499–502, 1989.

237. Regenfus M, Ropers D, Achenbach S, et al: Noninvasive detection of coronary artery stenosis using contrast-enhanced three-dimensional breath-hold magnetic resonance coronary angiography. J Am Coll Cardiol 36:44–50, 2000.

238. Reimer KA, Jennings RB: The "wavefront phenomenon" of myocardial ischemic cell death: II. Transmural progression of necrosis within the framework of ischemic bed size (myocardium at risk) and collateral flow. Lab Invest 40:634–644, 1979.

239. Reimer KA, Lowe JE, Rasmussen MM, et al: The "wavefront phenomenon" of ischemic cell death: I. Myocardial infarct size versus duration of coronary blood occlusion in dogs. Circulation 56: 786–794, 1977.

240. Reinmuller R, Doppman JL, Lissner J, et al: Constrictive pericardial disease: Prognostic significance of a nonvisualized left ventricular wall. Radiology 156:753–755, 1985.

241. Reinmuller R, Mahmut G, Erdmann E, et al: CT and MR evaluation of pericardial constriction: A new diagnostic and therapeutic concept. J Thorac Imaging 8:108–121, 1993.

242. Revel D, Canet E, Sebbag L, et al: First-pass and delayed magnetic resonance imaging studies of reperfused myocardial infarction with iron oxide particles. Acad Radiol 3:S398–S401, 1996.

243. Ricci C, Longo R, Pagnan L, et al: Magnetic resonance imaging in right ventricular dysplasia. Am J Cardiol 70:1589–1595, 1992.

244. Rich S: Primary pulmonary hypertension. Prog Cardiovasc Dis 31: 205–238, 1988.

245. Rigo P, Alderson PO, Robertson RM, et al: Measurement of aortic and mitral regurgitation by gated cardiac blood pool scans. Circulation 60:306–312, 1979.

246. Riedy K, Fisher MS, Belic N, Koenigsberg DI: MR imaging of myocardial sarcoidosis. AJR Am J Roentgenol 15:915–916, 1988.

247. Rienmuller R, Lloret JL, Tiling R: MR imaging of pediatric cardiac tumors previously diagnosed by echocardiography. J Comput Assist Tomogr 13:621–626, 1989.

248. Roberts WC: The congenitally bicuspid aortic valve: A study of 85 autopsy cases. Am J Cardiol 26:72–83, 1970.

249. Roberts WC: Valvular, subvalvular, and supravalvular aortic stenosis: Morphologic features. Cardiovasc Clin North Am 5:97–124, 1973.

250. Roberts WC, Perloff JK: Mitral valvular disease: A clinicopathologic survey of the conditions causing the mitral valve to function abnormally. Ann Intern Med 77:939–975, 1972.

251. Roberts WC, Spray TL: Pericardial heart disease: A study of its causes, consequences, and morphologic features. Cardiovasc Clin North Am 7:11–65, 1976.

252. Roditi GH, Hartnell GG, Conhen MC: MRI changes in myocarditis—evaluation with spin-echo cine MR angiography and contrast-enhanced spin-echo imaging. Clin Radiol 55:752–758, 2000.

253. Rokey R, Verani MS, Bolli R, et al: Myocardial infarct size quantification by MR imaging early after coronary artery occlusion in dogs. Radiology 158:771–774, 1986.

254. Ross RD, Bisset GS III, Meyer RA, et al: Magnetic resonance imaging for diagnosis of pulmonary vein stenosis after correction of total anomalous pulmonary venous connection. Am J Cardiol 60: 1199–1201, 1987.

255. Rowe JC, Bland EF, Sprague HB: The course of mitral stenosis without surgery: Ten- and twenty-year perspectives. Ann Intern Med 62:741–749, 1960.

256. Rusted IE, Schiefley CH, Edwards JE: Studies of the mitral valve: II. Certain anatomic features of the mitral valve and associated structures in mitral stenosis. Circulation 14:398–406, 1956.

257. Sackner M, Akgun N, Kimbel P, et al: The pathophysiology of scleroderma involving the heart and respiratory system. Ann Intern Med 60:611–627, 1964.

258. Sahn DJ: Instrumentation and physical factors related to visualization of stenotic and regurgitant jets by Doppler color flow mapping. J Am Coll Cardiol 12:1354–1356, 1988.

259. Sakuma H, Fujita N, Foo TK, et al: Evaluation of left ventricular volume and mass with breath-hold cine MR imaging. Radiology 188:377–380, 1993.

260. Salerni R, Rodnan G, Leon D: Pulmonary hypertension in the CREST variant of progressive systemic sclerosis (scleroderma). Ann Intern Med 86:394–399, 1977.

261. Sampson C, Martinez J, Rees S, et al: Evaluation of Fontan's operation by magnetic resonance imaging. Am J Cardiol 65:819–821, 1990.

262. Sandstede JJW, Lipke C, Beer M, et al: Analysis of first-pass and delayed contrast-enhancement patterns of dysfunctional myocardium on MR imaging: Use in the prediction of myocardial viability. AJR Am J Roentgenol 174:1737–1740, 2000.

263. Sasayama S, Ross J Jr, Franklin D, et al: Adaptations of the left ventricle to chronic pressure overload. Circ Res 38:172–178, 1976.

264. Sato T, Nakamura K, Yamanari H, et al: Relationship between the electrocardiographic features and distribution of hypertrophy in patients with hypertrophic cardiomyopathy. Jpn Circ J 62:483–488, 1998.

265. Schaefer S, Malloy CR, Katz J, et al: Gadolinium-DTPA–enhanced nuclear magnetic resonance imaging of reperfused myocardium: Identification of the myocardial bed at risk. J Am Coll Cardiol 12:1064–1072, 1988.

266. Schiavone WA, O'Donnell JK: Congenital absence of the left portion of parietal pericardium demonstrated by nuclear magnetic resonance imaging. Am J Cardiol 55:1439–1440, 1985.

267. Scully RE, et al: Case records of the Massachusetts General Hospital: Malignant lymphoma, B-cell immunoblastic type, arising in the pericardium. N Engl J Med 316:1394–1404, 1987.

268. Sechtem U, Higgins CB, Sommerhoff BA, et al: Magnetic resonance imaging of restrictive cardiomyopathy. Am J Cardiol 59:480–482, 1985.

269. Sechtem U, Pflugfelder PW, Cassidy MM, et al: Mitral and aortic regurgitation: Quantification of regurgitant volumes with cine MR imaging. Radiology 167:425–430, 1988.

270. Sechtem U, Pflugfelder PW, Gould RG: Measurement of right and ventricular volumes in healthy individuals with cine MR imaging. Radiology 163:697–702, 1987.

271. Sechtem U, Pflugfelder PW, Gould RG, et al: Measurement of right and left ventricular volumes in healthy individuals with cine MR imaging. Radiology 163:697–702, 1987.

272. Sechtem U, Pflugfelder PW, White RD, et al: Cine MR imaging: Potential for the evaluation of cardiovascular function. AJR Am J Roentgenol 148:239–246, 1987.

273. Sechtem U, Tscholakoff D, Higgins CB: MRI of the abnormal pericardium. Am J Roentgenol 147:245–252, 1986.

274. Sechtem U, Tscholakoff D, Higgins CB: MRI of the normal pericardium. Am J Roentgenol 147:239–244, 1986.

275. Selzer A, Malmborg RO: Some factors influencing changes in pulmonary vascular resistance in mitral valve disease. Am J Med 32:532–544, 1962.

276. Semelka RC, Tomei E, Wagner S, et al: Interstudy reproducibility of dimensional and functional measurements between cine magnetic resonance studies in the morphologically abnormal left ventricle. Am Heart J 119:1367–1373, 1990.

277. Semelka RC, Tomei E, Wagner S, et al: Normal left ventricular dimensions and function: Interstudy reproducibility of measurement with cine MR imaging. Radiology 174:763–768, 1990.

278. Shapiro EP, Rogers WJ, Beyar R, et al: Determination of LV mass by magnetic resonance in hearts deformed by acute infarction. Circulation 79:706–711, 1989.

279. Simpson IA, Chung KJ, Glass RF, et al: Cine magnetic resonance imaging for evaluation of anatomy and flow relations in infants and children with coarctation of the aorta. Circulation 78:142–148, 1988.

280. Skjaerpe T, Hegrenaes L, Hatle L: Noninvasive estimation of valve area in patients with aortic stenosis by Doppler ultrasound and two-dimensional echocardiography. Circulation 72:810–818, 1985.

281. Soler R, Rodriguez E, Rodriguez JA, et al: Magnetic resonance imaging of apical hypertrophic cardiomyopathy. Thorac Imaging 12:221–225, 1997.

282. Sondergaard L, Thomsen C, Stalhlber F, et al: Mitral and aortic valvular flow: Quantification with MR phase mapping. J Magn reson Imaging 2:295–302, 1992.

283. Sondergaard L, Stalberg F, Thomsen C: Magnetic resonance imaging valvular heart disease: Review. J Magn Reson Imaging 10:627–638, 1999.

284. Sondergaard L, Stahlberg F, Thomsen C, et al: Accuracy and precision of MR velocity mapping in measurement of stenotic cross-

285. Soulen RL, Donner RM, Capitanio M: Postoperative evaluation of complex congenital heart disease by magnetic resonance imaging. Radiographics 7:975–1000, 1987.

286. Soulen RL, Kan J, Mitchell S, White RI Jr: Evaluation of balloon angioplasty of coarctation restenosis by magnetic resonance imaging. Am J Cardiol 60:343–345, 1987.

287. Soulen RL, Stark DD, Higgins CB: Magnetic resonance imaging of constrictive pericardial disease. Am J Cardiol 55:480–484, 1985.

288. Spann JF, Bove AA, Natarajan G, Kreulen T: Ventricular performance, pump function, and compensatory mechanisms in patients with aortic stenosis. Circulation 62:576–582, 1980.

289. Stern RC, Borkat G, Hirschfeld SS, et al: Heart failure in cystic fibrosis. Am J Dis Child 134:267–272, 1980.

290. Stark DD, Higgins CB, Lanzer P, et al: Magnetic resonance imaging of the pericardium: Normal and pathologic findings. Radiology 150:469–474, 1984.

291. Stupi A, Steen V, Owens G, et al: Pulmonary hypertension in the CREST syndrome variant of systemic sclerosis. Arthritis Rheum 29:515–523, 1986.

292. Suzuki JI, Chang JM, Caputo GR, Higgins CB: Evaluation of right ventricular early diastolic filling by cine nuclear magnetic resonance imaging in patients with hypertrophic cardiomyopathy. J Am Coll Cardiol 18:120–126, 1991.

293. Suzuki J, Shimaomoto R, Nishikawa J, et al: Morphologic onset and early diagnosis in apical hypertrophic cardiomyopathy: A long-term analysis with nuclear magnetic resonance imaging. J Am Coll Cardiol 33:146–151, 1999.

294. Tabak SW, Maurer G: Echocardiographic detection of free-floating left atrial thrombus. Am J Cardiol 53:374–375, 1984.

295. Thiene G, Nava A, Corrado D, et al: Right ventricular cardiomyopathy and sudden death in young people. N Engl J Med 318:129–133, 1988.

296. Thompson WP, White PD: The commonest cause of hypertrophy of the right ventricle: Left ventricular strain and failure. Am Heart J 12:641–649, 1936.

297. Tomoda H, Hoshiai M, Furuya H, et al: Evaluation of pericardial effusion with computed tomography. Am Heart J 99:701–706, 1980.

298. Underwood SR, Klipstein RH, Firmin DM, et al: Magnetic resonance assessment of aortic and mitral regurgitation. Br Heart J 56:455–462, 1986.

299. Ungerer R, Tashkin D, Furst D, et al: Prevalence and clinical correlates of pulmonary arterial hypertension in progressive systemic sclerosis. Am J Med 75:65–73, 1983.

300. Van Praagh R: The segmental approach to diagnosis in congenital heart disease: The cardiovascular system. Birth Defects 8:4–23, 1972.

301. Van Praagh R, David H, Van Praagh S: What is a ventricle? The single ventricle trap. Pediatr Cardiol 2:74–79, 1982.

302. Van Praagh R: The importance of segmental situs in the diagnosis of congenital heart disease. Semin Roentgenol 20:254–271, 1985.

303. Van Praagh R, Ongley PA, Swan HJC: Anatomic types of single or common ventricle in man. Am J Cardiol 13:367–386, 1964.

304. van Rugge FP, van der Wall EE, Spanjersberg SJ, et al: Magnetic resonance imaging during dobutamine stress for detection and localization of coronary artery disease: Quantitative wall motion analysis using a modification of the centerline method. Circulation 90:127–138, 1994.

305. van Rugge FP, van der Wall EE, de Roos A, Bruschke AV: Dobutamine stress magnetic resonance imaging for detection of coronary artery disease. J Am Coll Cardiol 22:431–439, 1993.

306. von Schulthess GK, Higashino SM, Higgins SS, et al: Coarctation of the aorta: MR imaging. Radiology 158:469–474, 1986.

307. Veluvolu P, Balian AA, Goldsmith R, et al: Lyme carditis: Evaluation by Ga-67 and MRI. Clin Nucl Med 17:823–827, 1992.

308. Vick GW III, Rokey R, Huhta JC, et al: Nuclear magnetic resonance imaging of the pulmonary arteries, subpulmonary region, and aorticopulmonary shunts: A comparative study with two-dimensional echocardiography and angiography. Am Heart J 119:1103–1110, 1990.

309. von Schulthess GK, Higgins CB: Blood flow imaging with MR: Spin-phase phenomena. Radiology 157:687–699, 1985.

310. Vrachliotis TG, Bis KG, Aliabadi D, et al: Contrast-enhanced breath-hold MR angiography for evaluating patency of coronary artery bypass grafts. AJR Am J Roentgenol 168:1073–1080, 1997.

311. Wagenvoort CA: Pulmonary veno-occlusive disease: Entity or syndrome? Chest 69:82–86, 1976.

312. Wagenvoort CA, Wagenvoort N: Primary pulmonary hypertension: A pathologic study of the lung vessels in 156 clinically diagnosed cases. Circulation 42:1163–1184, 1970.

313. Wagner S, Aufferman W, Buser P, et al: Functional description of the left ventricle in patients with volume overload, pressure overload, and myocardial disease using cine nuclear magnetic resonance imaging (NMR). Am J Cardiol Imaging 5:87–97, 1991.

314. Waller BF, Howard J, Fess S: Pathology of tricuspid valve stenosis and pure tricuspid regurgitation: III. Clin Cardiol 18:225–230, 1995.

315. Waller BF, Moriarty AT, Eble JN, et al: Etiology of pure tricuspid regurgitation based on annular circumference and leaflet area: Analysis of 45 necropsy patients with clinical and morphologic evidence of pure tricuspid regurgitation. J Am Coll Cardiol 18:97–102, 1986.

316. Webb J, Kerr C, Huckell V, et al: Left ventricular abnormalities in arrhythmogenic right ventricular dysplasia. Am Heart J 58:568–570, 1986.

317. Webb WR: MR of hila and mediastinum. Cardiovasc Intervent Radiol 6:793–832, 1986.

318. Weinberg BA, Conces DJ Jr, Waller BF: Cardiac manifestations of noncardiac tumors: I. Direct effects. Clin Cardiol 12:289–296, 1989.

319. Weitzman LB, Tinker WP, Kronzon T, et al: The incidence and natural history of pericardial effusion after cardiac surgery—an echocardiographic study. Circulation 69:506–511, 1984.

320. Wendland MF, Saeed M, Masui T, et al: First pass of an MR susceptibility contrast agent through normal and ischemic heart: Gradient-recalled echo-planar imaging. J Magn Reson Imaging 3:755–760, 1993.

321. Wendland MF, Saeed M, Masui T, et al: Echo-planar MR imaging of normal and ischemic myocardium with gadodiamide injection. Radiology 186:535–542, 1993.

322. Wendt RE III, Rokey R, Vick GW III, Johnston DL: Electrocardiographic gating and monitoring in NMR imaging. Magn Reson Imaging 6:89–95, 1988.

323. Wesbey G, Higgins CB, Lanzer P, et al: Imaging and characterization of acute myocardial infarction in vivo by gated nuclear magnetic resonance. Circulation 69:125–130, 1984.

324. White RD, Cassidy MM, Cheitlin MD, et al: Segmental evaluation of left ventricular wall motion after myocardial infarction: Magnetic resonance imaging versus echocardiography. Am Heart J 115:166–175, 1988.

325. White RD, Holt WW, Cheitlin MD, et al: Estimation of the functional and anatomic extent of myocardial infarction using magnetic resonance imaging. Am Heart J 115:740–748, 1988.

326. Wildenhain PM, Bourekas EC: Pulmonary varix: Magnetic resonance findings. Cathet Cardiovasc Diagn 24:268–270, 1991.

327. Wilke N, Jerosch-Herold M, Wang Y, et al: Quantitative first-pass MR imaging: Assessment of myocardial perfusion reserve. Radiology 204:373–384, 1997.

328. Wilke N, Simm C, Zhang J, et al: Contrast-enhanced first-pass myocardial perfusion imaging: Correlation between myocardial blood flow in dogs at rest and during hyperemia. Magn Reson Med 29:485–497, 1993.

329. Williams ES, Kaplan JI, Thatcher F, et al: Prolongation of proton spin lattice relaxation times in regionally ischemic tissue from dog hearts. J Nucl Med 21:449–453, 1980.

330. Williams DS, Grandis DJ, Zhang W, Koretsky AP: Magnetic resonance imaging of perfusion in the isolated rat heart using spin inversion of arterial water. Magn Reson Med 30:361–365, 1993.

331. Wintersberger BJ, Engelmann MG, von Smekal A, et al: Patency of coronary artery bypass grafts: Assessment with breath-hold contrast-enhanced MR angiography—value of a non-electrocardiographically triggered technique. Radiology 208:345–351, 1998.

332. Wisenberg G, Pflugfelder PW, Kostuk WJ, et al: Diagnostic applicability of magnetic resonance imaging in assessing human cardiac allograft rejection. Am J Cardiol 60:130–136, 1987.

333. Wintersperger BJ, Penzkofer HV, Knez A, et al: Multislice MR perfusion imaging and regional myocardial function analysis: Complimentary findings in chronic myocardial ischemia. Int J Card Imaging 15:425–434, 1999.

334. Wisenberg G, Prato FS, Carroll SE, et al: Serial nuclear magnetic resonance imaging of acute myocardial infarction with and without reperfusion. Am Heart J 115:510–518, 1988.

335. Wolf RL, Ehman RL, Riederer SJ, et al: Analysis of systemic and random error in MR volumetric flow measurements. Magn Reson Med 30:82–91, 1993.

336. Wood P: An appreciation of mitral stenosis: I. Br Med J 1:1051–1063, 1954.

337. Wood P: An appreciation of mitral stenosis: II. Br Med J 1:1113–1124, 1954.

338. Yamanari H, Kakishita M, Fujimoto Y, et al: Regional myocardial perfusion abnormalities and regional myocardial early diastolic function in patients with hypertrophic cardiomyopathy. Heart Vessels 12:192–198, 1997.

339. Yellon DM, Hearse DJ, Crone R, et al: Characterization of the lateral interface between normal and ischemic tissue in the canine heart during evolving myocardial infarction. Am J Cardiol 47:1233–1239, 1981.

340. Yoo S-J, Lim T-H, Park I-S, et al: Defects of the interventricular septum of the heart: En face MR imaging in the oblique coronal plane. AJR Am J Roentgenol 157:943–946, 1991.

341. Yu K, Saeed M, Wendland M, et al: Real-time dynamics of an extravascular magnetic resonance contrast medium in acutely infarcted myocardium using inversion recovery and gradient-recalled echo-planar imaging. Invest Radiol 27:927–934, 1992.

342. Zerhouni EA, Parish DM, Rogers WJ, et al: Human heart: Tagging with MR imaging—a new method for noninvasive assessment of myocardial motion. Radiology 169:59–63, 1988.

343. Zheng J, Li D, Kyongtae T, et al: Three-dimensional gadolinium-enhanced coronary magnetic resonance angiography: Initial experience. J Cardiovasc Magn Res 1:33–41, 1999.

344. Zile MR, Gaasch WH, Carroll JD, Levine HJ: Chronic mitral regurgitation: Predictive value of preoperative echocardiographic indexes of left ventricular function and wall stress. J Am Coll Cardiol 3:235–242, 1984.

345. Zuberbuhler JR, Allwork SP, Anderson RH: The spectrum of Ebstein's anomaly of the tricuspid valve. J Thorac Cardiovasc Surg 77:202–211, 1979.

Appendices

Normal Spin-Echo Images
of the Heart

Abbreviations

a	Anterior aortic sinus of Valsalva	LLLPV	Left lower lobe pulmonary vein
AAVR	Anterior atrioventricular ring	LMCA	Left main coronary artery
AbAo	Abdominal aorta	LP	Left pulmonary artery
Ao	Aortic arch	LSA	Left subclavian artery
AoA	Ascending aorta	LULPV	Left upper lobe pulmonary vein
AoD	Descending aorta	LV	Left ventricle
AoR	Aortic root	MP	Main pulmonary artery
APR	Anterior pericardial reflection	MV	Mitral valve
AS1	Primum interatrial septum	PAVR	Posterior atrioventricular ring
AS2	Secundum interatrial septum	pl	Posterior left aortic sinus of Valsalva
AS3	Sinus venosus interatrial septum	PM1	Superior papillary muscle
Az	Azygos vein	PM2	inferior papillary muscle
CrS	Crista supraventricularis	pr	Posterior right aortic sinus of Valsalva
CS, cs	Coronary sinus	RA	Right atrium
E	Esophagus	RAA	Right atrial appendage
HV	Hepatic vein	RB	Right bronchus
IA	Innominate artery	RCA	Right coronary artery
IV	Innominate vein	RP	Right pulmonary artery
IVC	Inferior vena cava	RULPA	Right upper lobe pulmonary artery
IVS	Interventricular septum	RULPV	Right upper lobe pulmonary vein
LA	Left atrium	RV	Right ventricle
LAA	Left atrial appendage	RVO	Right ventricular outflow tract
LADCA	Left anterior descending coronary artery	SV	Superior vena cava
LB	Left bronchus	T	Trachea
LCC	Left common carotid artery		

Appendix A Axial Sections (Figs. A1 to A10)

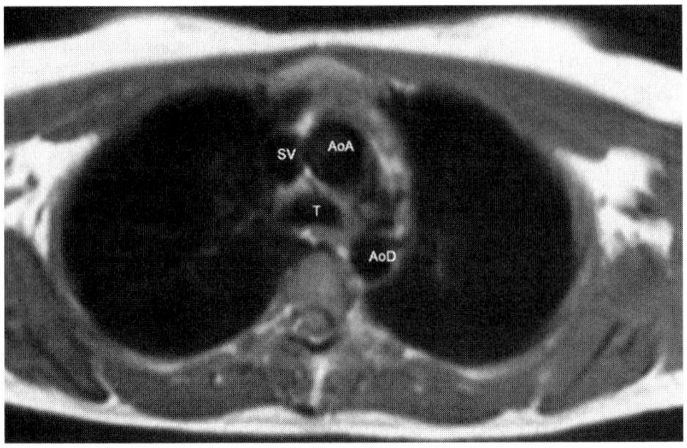

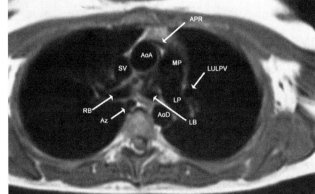

Figure A1

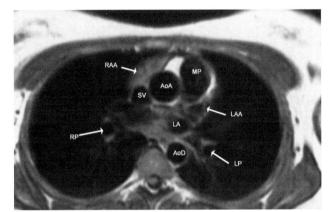

Figure A2

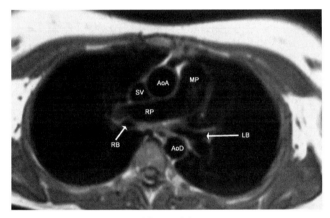

Figure A3

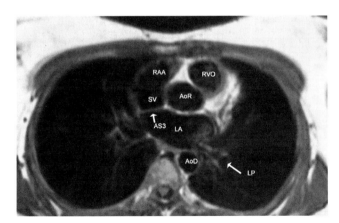

Figure A4

Figure A5

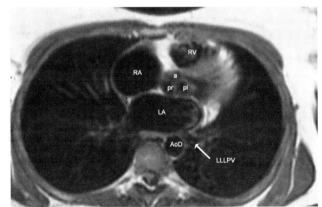

Figure A6

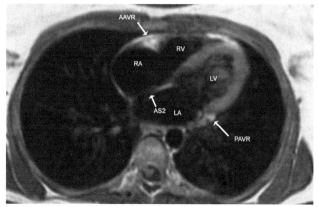

Figure A7

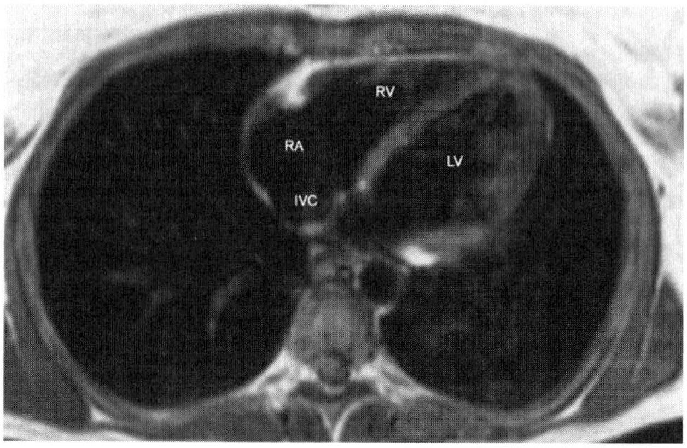

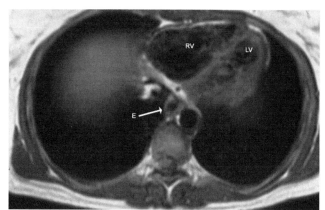

Figure A8

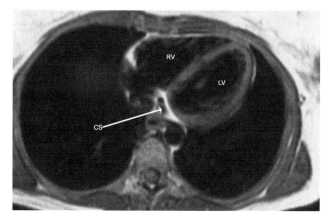

Figure A9

Figure A10

Appendix B Left Anterior Oblique Sagittal Sections (Figs. B1 to B6)

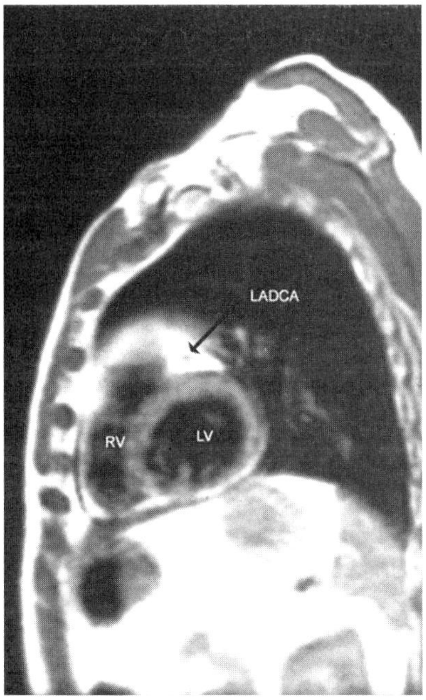

Figure B1

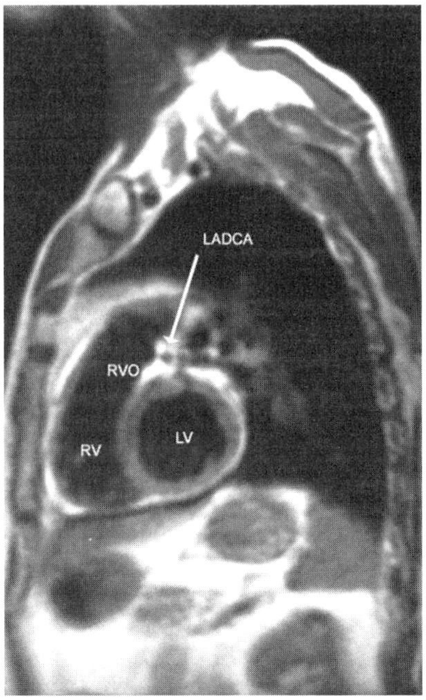

Figure B2

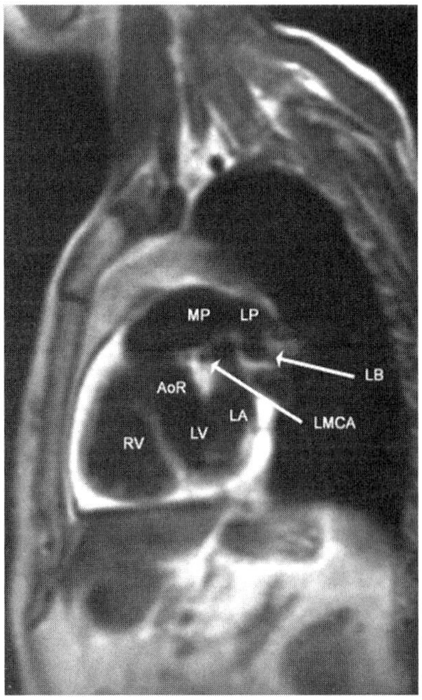

Figure B3

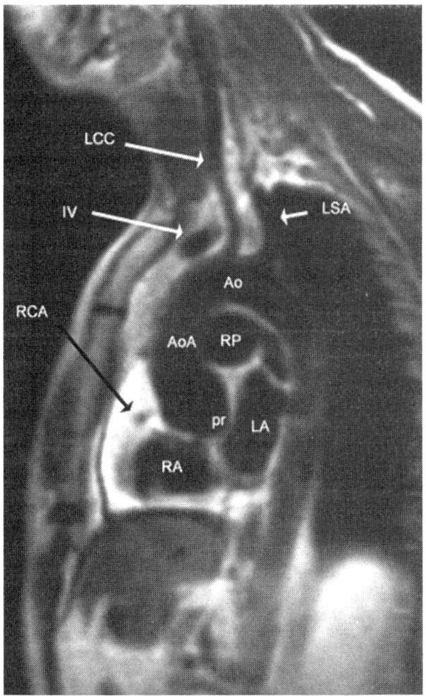

Figure B4

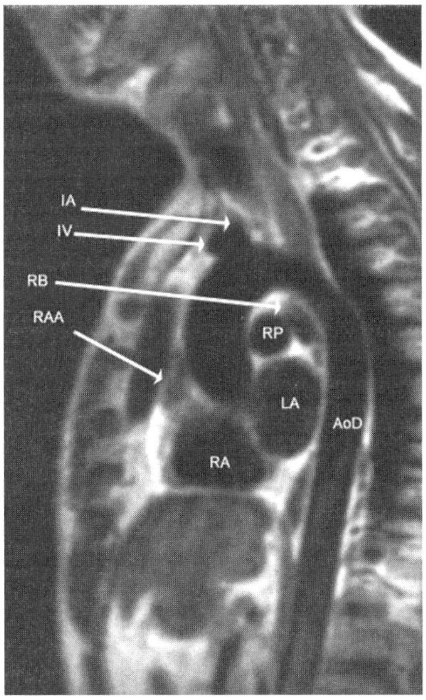

Figure B5

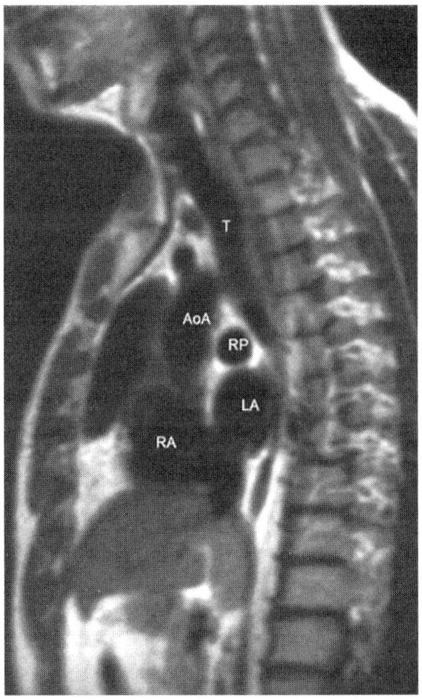

Figure B6

Appendix C Right Anterior Oblique Sections (Figs. C1 to C11)

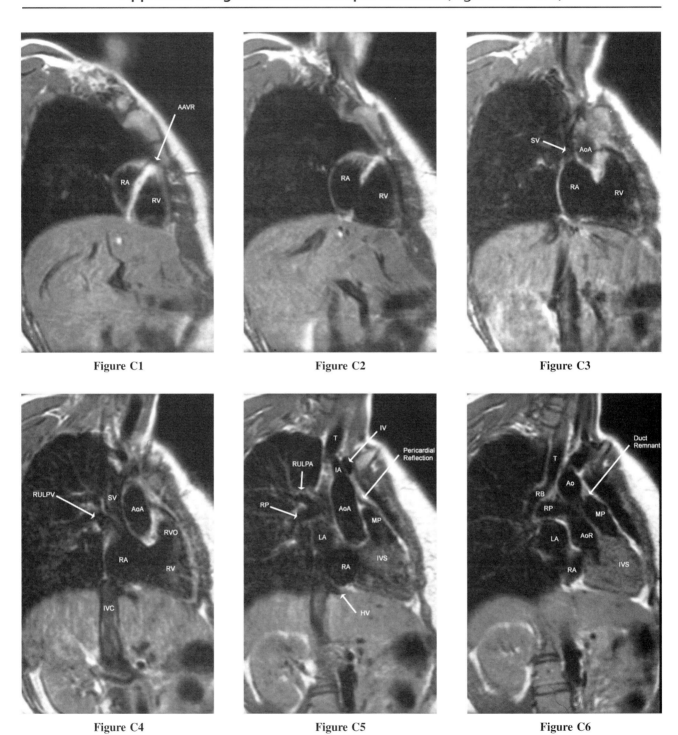

Figure C1

Figure C2

Figure C3

Figure C4

Figure C5

Figure C6

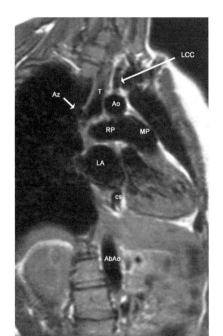

Figure C7

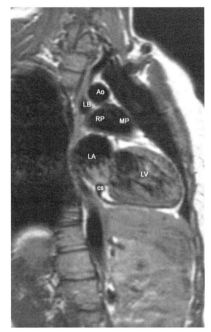

Figure C8

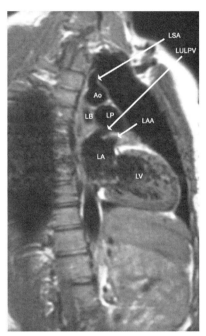

Figure C9

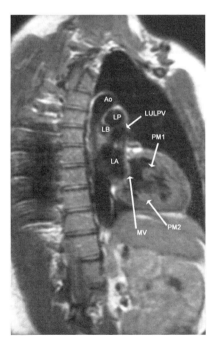

Figure C10

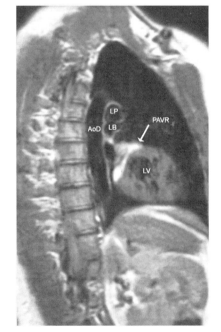

Figure C11

Appendix D Short-Axis Sections (Figs. D1 to D13)

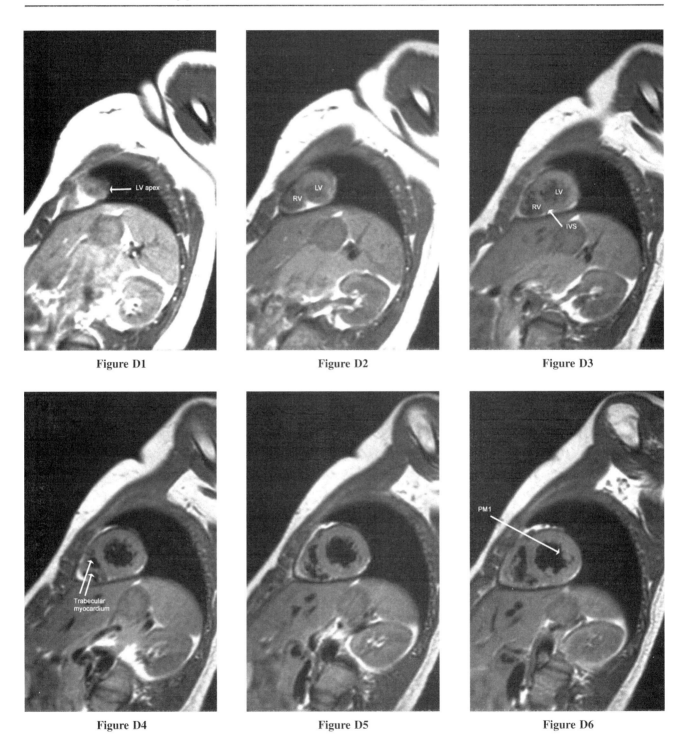

Figure D1

Figure D2

Figure D3

Figure D4

Figure D5

Figure D6

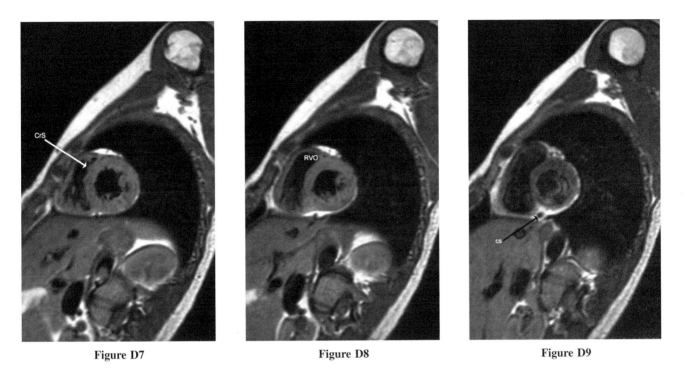

Figure D7   **Figure D8**   **Figure D9**

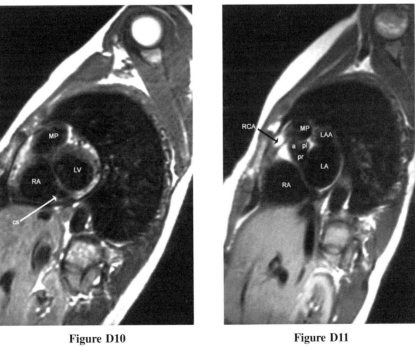

Figure D10   **Figure D11**

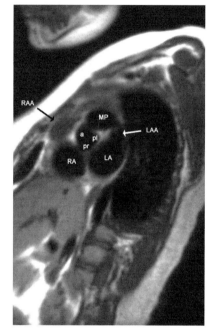

Figure D12

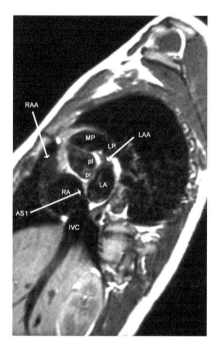

Figure D13

Index

Note: Page numbers followed by f indicate figures; those followed by t, tables; and those by b, boxes.